Ritchie Peterson

Volumes in the

GRAY AND ADAMS BIBLE COMMENTARY

VOLUME I — *Genesis - II Kings*

VOLUME II — *Chronicles - Proverbs*

VOLUME III — *Ecclesiastes - Malachi*

VOLUME IV — *Matthew - Acts*

VOLUME V — *Romans - Revelation*

BIBLE COMMENTARY

by

JAMES COMPER GRAY
and **GEORGE M. ADAMS**

(Formerly published as
"Biblical Encyclopedia" and "Biblical Museum")

VOLUME THREE

Ecclesiastes - Malachi

Zondervan Publishing House
GRAND RAPIDS, MICHIGAN

Introduction.

Title. Heb. Koheleth; Gk. Ecclesiastes, which in English is equivalent to "The Preacher." The Hebrew title is from the initial word of the book. **Author.** Unknown. The author indeed assumes the character of Solomon, but this is evidently a matter of literary form. At the close of the book (xii. 9-12), he seems to lift the mask from his face and shows us who he really is. "Although he has written in a feigned name, and, without asserting it, has so moulded his phrases, at least in the earlier chapters of his work, as to suggest to his readers that he is, if not Solomon himself, at least Solomon's mouthpiece, attributing the garnered results of his experience to one greater than himself, that they may carry the more weight—just as Browning speaks in the name of Rabbi Ben Ezra, for instance, or Fra Lippo Lippi, or Abt Vogler, borrowing what he can of outward circumstance from the age and class to which they belong, and yet really uttering his own thought and emotion through their lips—he now confesses that he is no king of an age long past, but a rabbi, a sage, a teacher, a master, who has both made some proverbs of his own and collected the wise sayings of others who had gone before him, in order that he might carry some little light and comfort to the sorely bested men of his own generation and blood. In short, he has exercised his right as a poet, or 'maker,' to embody the results of his wide and varied experience of life in a dramatic form, but is careful to let us know, before he takes leave of us, that it is a fictitious or dramatic Solomon, and not Solomon himself, to whom we have been listening throughout."—Expos. Bible. This was a very common method at that day and was well understood. The idioms and style of the Hebrew, and the public and social conditions revealed in the book are convincing evidence that the work belongs to a period long after the time of Solomon. Biblical scholars now almost universally agree in this conclusion. Perhaps the most probable date to which the book can be assigned is during the Persian period in the fourth century B. C. **Scope and design.** "Be godly, and concerning everything else be tranquil."—Luther. "The great design of this book is evidently to show the utter insufficiency of all earthly pursuits and objects, as the chief end of life, to confer solid happiness, and then to draw men off from apparent good to the only real and permanent good—the fear of God and communion with Him. 'Vanity of vanities, all is vanity,' is its first lesson; 'Fear God and keep His commandments,' is its last."—Angus. "As for the design of the book, no one now doubts that it sets before us the search for the summum bonum, the quest of the Chief Good. Its main immediate intention was to deliver the exiled Jews from the misleading ethical theories and habits into which they had fallen, from the sensualism and the scepticism occasioned by their imperfect conception of the Divine ways, by showing them that the true good of life is not to be secured by philosophy, by the pursuit of pleasure, by devotion to traffic or public affairs, by amassing wealth; but that it results from a temperate and thankful enjoyment of the gifts of the Divine bounty, and a cheerful endurance of toil and calamity, combined with a sincere service of God and a steadfast faith in that future life in which all wrongs will be righted and all the problems which now task and afflict us will receive a triumphant solution."—Expos. Bible. "Its subject is the vanity of all that is human and earthly, and by contrast and implication the steadfastness and importance of the unseen. The writer desires, in the first place (virtually, though not expressly), to comfort his countrymen under their present depressed circumstances, to teach them not to set their hopes on earthly success, or to fancy that their own efforts could secure happiness, but to make the best of the present, and to receive with thankfulness the good that God sends or permits. He also urges the avoidance of externalism in religion, and shows wherein true devotion consists. And, in the second place, he warns against despair or reckless license, as though it mattered not what one did, as if there were no higher Power that regarded; he solemnly asserts his faith in an overruling providence, though we cannot trace the reason or course of its working; his conviction that all is ordered for the best; his unswerving faith in the life everlasting and in a future judgment, which shall remedy the seeming anomalies of this present existence. In all the problems of life, in all the disappointments and difficulties that meet our best and noblest efforts, there is nothing to cling to, no anchor on which to rest, but the fear of God and obedience to His commands. Whatever happens, or however things may seem to go contrary to one's wishes and aspirations, amid the outward prosperity of the wicked and the humiliation of the good, he triumphs in the assurance that he knows certainly that it shall be well with them that fear God (ch. viii. 12)."—Pulpit Com.

Synopsis.

(According to Mr. Holden. Adopted by Horne.)

PART I.

THE VANITY OF EARTHLY CONDITIONS, OCCUPATIONS, AND PLEASURES.

Sect. 1. Vanity of earthly things.......i. 2.
Sect. 2. Labor unprofitable, life transitory i. 3—11.
Sect. 3. Vanity of laborious study..i. 12—18.
Sect. 4. Luxury and pleasure vanity.ii. 1—11.
Sect. 5. Human learning but vanity ii. 12—17.
Sect. 6. Human labor vanity......ii. 18—23.
Sect. 7. Sensual enjoyments empty ii. 24—26.
Sect. 8. A time for all things.....iii. 1—14.
Sect. 9. Vanity of human pursuits iii. 15—17.
Sect. 10. Life and death..........iii. 18—22.
Sect. 11. Vanity increased by oppression iv. 1—3.
Sect. 12. Vanity of prosperity..........iv. 4.
Sect. 13. Vanity of folly............iv. 5, 6.
Sect. 14. Vanity of covetousness.....iv. 7, 8.
Sect. 15. Dominion and empire vanity iv. 9—16.
Sect. 16. Divine worship may be vain v. 1—7.
Sect. 17. Murmuring at injustice vain v. 8, 9.
Sect. 18. Vanity of riches........v. 10—20.
Sect. 19. Vanity of avarice.........vi. 1—9.

PART II.

THE NATURE, EXCELLENCE, AND BENEFICIAL EFFECTS OF WISDOM OR RELIGION.

Sect. 20. What is the chief good..vi. 10—12.
Sect. 21. The praise of character.....vii. 1.
Sect. 22. Benefits of affliction....vii. 2—10.
Sect. 23. The excellence of wisdom vii. 11—14.
Sect. 24. An objection and the answer vii. 15—viii. 7.
Sect. 25. Wickedness and wisdom.viii. 8—13.
Sect. 26. An objection and the answer viii. 14—ix. 1.
Sect. 27. An objection and the answer ix. 2—x. 17.
Sect. 28. Banefulness of sloth.........x. 18.
Sect. 29. The power of wealth........x. 19.
Sect. 30. Speaking evil of dignities....x. 20.
Sect. 31. Charity and benevolence.xi. 1—10.
Sect. 32. Early piety...........,...xii. 1—7.
Sect. 33. The conclusion ....xii. 8—14.

CHAPTER THE FIRST.

1—3. (1) **Preacher,** Heb. koheleth, better, Debater. The Hebrew writer apparently coined the word, because he wanted a substantive which exactly expressed the idea of one who desired to present himself in that character and not as a teacher. He claimed only to be a member one of many, of the great Ecclesia of those who think.—Cam. Bib. **in Jerusalem,** the description "king in Jerusalem" is in apposition with "the Preacher" not with "David." It is noticeable that the name of Solomon is not mentioned as it is in the titles of the other two books ascribed to him (Prov. i. 1; Song of Sol. i. 1). (2) **Vanity,** Heb. hebel, found thirty-nine times in this book. That wh. fails to satisfy. **vanity of vanities,**[a] Heb. idiom for the very highest degree of vanity. Comp. "holy of holies," "song of songs." **all,** all sorts, every earthly thing. (3) **profit,**[b] The word for "profit," not meeting us elsewhere in the Hebrew of the O. T., occurs ten times in Ecclesiastes. Its strict meaning is "that which remains,"—the surplus, if any, of the balance-sheet of life. It was, probably, one of the words which the commerce of the Jews, after the Captivity, had brought into common use. **under the sun,**[c] just as we speak of this "sublunary world," so "under the sun" is the characteristic designation of the earth throughout this Book.

Vanity (vs. 2).—I. This estimate was made by a competent judge. II. Given in unqualified terms. III. Abundantly endorsed by the historical Scripture. IV. Assented to by all who have finished their course.—Stems and Twigs.

Worldly pleasure unsatisfying.—Lord Chesterfield, at the close of his life, confessed that his life had been as joyless as it had been selfish and hollow. "I have recently read Solomon with a kind of sympathetic feeling. I have been as wicked and as vain, though not as wise as he; but now I am old enough to feel the truth of his reflection, 'All is vanity and vexation of spirit.'" Repartees sparkled on his dying lips, but all was dreary within, all was darkness ahead. The fame for which he lived expired before himself: and now truth declines to write his epitaph, and virtue has no garlands for his grave.—J. Hamilton. Goethe, the greatest of German poets, whose long life was one success, said: "They have called me a child of fortune, nor have I any wish to complain of the course of my life. Yet it has been nothing but labor and sorrow; and I may truly say, that in seventy-five years I have not had four weeks of true comfort. It was the constant rolling of a stone that was always to be lifted anew." One cannot read the posthumous memoirs of Chateaubriand, without being struck with the illusive nature of worldly honors and pleasures. Contemporary applause was not wanting to cheer the craving spirit of this scholar and statesman. The author of the "Genius of Christianity" and the ambassador of France at the Court of London could not complain that honor was denied him. He says, "I know not in history a reputation that would tempt me: and were it necessary to stoop to pick up from my feet and for my own advantage the greatest glory the world could offer, I would not give myself the trouble."—Anec. Illus. of O. T.

4—7. (4) **generation,** lit. a generation goeth, and a generation cometh: Man is only a pilgrim on earth; he soon passes away, and his place is occupied by others. **earth . . ever,**[a] it is not absolutely permanent, but its continuance contrasts with the changing races on it. (5) **sun,** etc., the sun to the Hebrew seemed to be constantly changing and to labor without any results. Abraham in the Rabbinic legend is represented as looking upon the setting sun and saying, "The God whom I worship must be a God that does not set." **hasteth,** Heb. panteth.[b] The author evidently had no idea of the circular form and movement of the earth. (6) **whirleth,**[c] etc., the whole verse gains in poetic emphasis by a more literal rendering, "It goeth to the south, and it circleth to the north, circling, circling goeth the wind, and on its circlings returneth the wind." The iteration and order of the words seem to breathe the languor of one who was weary with watching the endless and yet monotonous changes.—Cam. Bib. **circuits,** or veerings. The word is not used in the modern

[a] "The theme of Ecclesiastes is the vanity of all earthly things apart from God." — Wordsworth.

[b] From a word signifying to hang over, overflow, remain over and above.

[c] "He writes with this design, that we may not dote upon this life, wh. is under the sun, but may earnestly desire that life wh. is not blighted by that vanity wh. is under the sun, but is enlightened by that truth wh. came from Him who made the sun"—St. Augustine.

Ps. xxxix. 5, 6, 11, lxii. 9, cxliv. 4; Ro. viii. 20, 21.

"The men who place spiritual principles deep in the heart of humanity have attained the greatest sovereignty beneath the Supreme Majesty. To gain a soul is to enhance the glory of our royal diadem."—Hom. Com.

"This speech of Solomon's is the speech of every soul, when being spoiled of those things which are here, she goeth to that life which is hoped for." — Gregory Nyssenus.

[a] Ps. civ. 5, cxix. 90.

[b] Comp. Ps. xix. 5.

"The metaphor applies rather to the rising sun, which seems laboriously to mount up to the meridian, than to the setting sun."—Fausset.

[c] The N. and S. winds are the

scientific sense. (7) **not full,** bec. the waters are drawn up as clouds, and sent back to refresh the earth.[d]

The stability of nature.—I. As it appears to our senses. II. As it appeals to our reason. The stability of all things about and above us: 1. Gives us time to study the nature and the causes of things, and enables one generation to hand down the results of its researches to another, so that we are constantly accumulating knowledge. 2. Gives us proof of unity of God. 3. Assures us of the mighty power of the great Author of nature, who is seen to be strong to sustain and preserve and renew. III. As it affects our life. IV. As it dwarfs our individual career. V. In the light of the spiritual and the eternal. 1. The worth of spiritual life is not determined by its duration. 2. Moreover, holy human life upon the earth leads on and up to the life which is eternal.—Clarkson.

Verse 7.—In this verse the streams are described as returning on their sources; but there is no allusion here, as we might suppose, to the tides,—and indeed tidal rivers are comparatively rare,—or to the rain which brings back the water evaporated from the surface of the streams and of the sea. The reference is, rather, to an ancient conception of the physical order of nature held by the Hebrew as by other races, according to which the ocean, fed by the streams, sent back a constant supply through subterranean passages and channels, in which the salt was filtered out of it; through these they supposed the rivers to return to the place whence they came. The ruling sentiment of these verses is that, while all the natural elements and forces, even the most variable and inconstant, renew their strength and return upon their course, for frail man there is no return; permanence and uniformity characterize them, while transitoriness and instability mark him for their own. They seem to vanish and disappear; the sun sinks, the winds lull, the streams run dry; but they all come back again: for him there is no coming back; once gone, he is gone for ever.—Exp. Bib.

8—11. (8) **full of labour,** Stuart, "All words grow weary, no man can utter them;" i. e., language would fail to tell the whole.[e] **eye.. hearing,** i. e. for man there is no present satisfaction.[f] (9) **no new thing,** no new source of pleasure. Life is a round of the same duties, cares, and pleasures. Things may seem new to individuals, they are not new in themselves.[g] (10) **old time,** Heb. ages. (11) **no remembrance,** and therefore things may be thought new wh. really have been before, a new element in the pessimism into which the writer has fallen. "Our considering old things as new is bec. of the continual extinction of the remembrance of former things."

All things new.—If it is impossible that the Book of Ecclesiastes should be written over again in the Christian ages, the reason is that the fuller and sublime revelations made by the Son of God incarnate have enriched human thought and life beyond all calculation. There is no comparison between the comparative poverty of knowledge and of life, even under the Mosaic economy in ancient times, and "the unsearchable riches of Christ." None can exhaust the treasures of knowledge and wisdom, the possibilities of consecrated service and spiritual progress, distinctive of the Christian dispensation. Christianity is emphatically a religion of newness. It is itself the new covenant; its choicest gift to man is the new heart; it summons the disciples of the Redeemer to newness of life; it puts in their mouth a new song; whilst it opens up in the future the glorious prospect of new heavens and a new earth. God comes in the Person of His Son to this sin-stricken humanity, and His assurance and promise is this: "Behold, I make all things new."—Thomson.

12, 13. (12) **Preacher,** as vs. 1. oppressed by his profound sense of the vanity of the life which man lives amid the play of permanent natural forces, Coheleth sets out on the search for that true and supreme Good which it will be well for the sons of men to pursue through their brief day.—Exp. Bib. (13) **gave my heart,** the phrase, so expressive of the spirit of an earnest seeker, is eminently characteristic of this book and meets us again in ver. 17, chaps. vii. 25, viii. 9, 16. **wisdom,** as was natural in so wise a man, he turns first to wisdom. He gives himself diligently to inquire into all the actions and toils of men. He will ascertain

two prevailing winds in Palestine and Egypt.

[d] "Not only what is most stable in creation, as the earth, and what is most glorious, as the sun, but also what seems to be most free, viz., the wind and the rivers, are bound by the same chain of lifeless continuity." — Wordsworth.

"Our eye cannot trace or follow the wandering courses of the wind,—nor can we trace the ways of God through human history."— Hom. Com.

Wild "as winds that sweep the deserts." — Dryden. "As the winds, raging and impetuous." —Durfey. "As winds and fighting seas." — Thomson.

[e] "Man cannot express all the things in the world which undergo this ceaseless, changeless cycle of vicissitudes." — Fausset.

[f] "The abundance of phenomena, wh. presses on eye, ear, and the remaining senses, is endless."—Hitzig. Pr. xxvii. 20.

[g] "All things under the sun are only reproductions or modifications of things which already exist, and were created at the beginning." —Wordsworth.

[h] Elohim is the God of nature, Jehovah the God of the covenant.

"Do you feel that you have lost your way in life? Then God himself will show you your way. Are you utterly helpless, worn out, body and soul? Then God's eternal

whether a larger acquaintance with their conditions, a deeper insight into the facts, a more just and complete estimate of their lot, will remove the depression which weighs upon his heart.—Exp. Bib. **travail,** work regarded as causing care, and anxiety, and effort. **God,** Heb. Elohim[b]. The name Jehovah does not occur in this book. **exercised,** or disciplined.

The mark of a true preacher (vs. 13).—I. He is a man of study—seeking and searching in order to know. II. He is a man of varied knowledge—"all things." III. He studies heartily, not perfunctorily. IV. He discerns the truth that travail is for the discipline of the sons of men.

Talent without principle.—An affecting illustration of the truth of Solomon's remark is furnished in the history of Combe, the unhappy author of Dr. Syntax in Search of the Picturesque. "We find," says a reviewer, "this improvident man, and all within a few years, figuring as a boy at Eton, a scholar at Oxford, a student in the Temple, with a very handsome independent fortune; a barrister pleading with success; a man of fashion intimately associating with lords and ladies, and calling himself (from his courtly dress and splendid liveries) 'The Duke;' and then an outcast spendthrift; a private soldier; a novice in a French monastery, playing the monk to get his bread for the time being; a strolling player; a gentleman's servant; and a waiter at an inn at Swansea. It was after all these metamorphoses that he turned himself into an author. His last scene of all was the King's Bench, where he wrote Syntax and some other works; and there he died, after an imprisonment (for debt) of twenty years.

love is ready and willing to help you up, and revive you. Are you wearied with doubts and terrors? Then God's eternal light is ready to show you your way, God's eternal peace ready to give you peace. Do you feel yourself full of sins and faults? Then take heart; for God's unchangeable will is, to take away those sins, and purge you from those faults."—Charles Kingsley.

a Ho. xii. 1.

b "Man cannot alter what is (apparently) unjust in God's arrangement of the world, nor make or regard its failures perfect; hemmed in within the narrow limits of the world as it is constituted, he is not able to perform the most important thing that he above all things should be able to do."—Hitzig.
Ec. vii. 13.

14, 15. (14) **works..sun,** the actions and lives of men, not the occurrences of nature. **vexation of spirit,** lit. windy effort. A feeding on wind.[a] It expresses, with a bold vividness, the sense of emptiness which accompanies unsatisfied desire. (15) **crooked,** etc., prob. a proverbial sentence. Man has no power to alter conditions fixed by God, however unsuitable he may regard them.[b] "Human labor and human knowledge cannot regenerate mankind."

Crooked things straightened (vs. 15).—I. We are all born with crooked hearts. This may be proved from the Bible, and without the Bible. II. Like the tree or the clay, our hearts are having something done with them. III. The importance of keeping straight while we are being educated. IV. How are we to get straight? Get Jesus to help us. Help ourselves.—R. Newton.

Vanity of worldly greatness.—The great Wolsey, after he had climbed the highest round of ambition's ladder, in the evening of life bitterly exclaimed, "Would that I had served my God as faithfully as I have served my king! He would not have abandoned me in my old age." The illustrious statesman, William Pitt, the favorite of king and people, "died," says Wilberforce, his friend, "of a broken heart." On his dying bed he is stated to have said, "I fear I have neglected prayer too much to make it available on a death-bed." Still more distressing was the closing scene of Sheridan's career. He who had stood on the pinnacle of glory, and gained the most flattering distinctions, writes in old age to one of his friends, "I am absolutely undone and broken-hearted." Misfortunes crowded on him, and his last moments were haunted by fears of a prison. Forsaken by his gay associates, dispirited, and world-weary, he closed his eyes in gloom and sorrow. Sir Walter Scott thus gives his dirge of life. Referring to his departure from Abbotsford, he writes:—"When I think what this place now is, and what it has been not long ago, I think my heart will break. . . . Some new object of complaint comes every moment; sicknesses come thicker and thicker; friends are fewer and fewer. The recollection of youth, health, and powers of activity, neither improved nor enjoyed, is a poor strain of comfort. The best is, the long halt will arrive at length and close all." "Save me from the horrors of a gaol," were almost the dying words of the poet Burns. Campbell, who wrote The Pleasures of Hope, speaks in this melancholy strain:—"I am alone in the world. My wife and the child of my hopes are dead. My only surviving child is consigned to a living tomb,—a lunatic asylum. My last hopes are blighted. As for fame, it is a bubble that must soon burst. Earned by others, shared with others, it was sweet; but at my

"Worldly things do not feed our souls, but rather the hunger of our souls."—St. Bernard.

Look at the convolvulus. The delicate-looking flower, with a slender stalk that loves to climb up very high, should suggest to us how weak and feeble man should forget those things that are beneath, and aspire after a crown of glory.

"We are not responsible for results. What is success in our estimation may be failure from God's standpoint. Peter was filled with the Holy Ghost and lifted three thousand people into the kingdom. Stephen was filled with the Holy

Ghost and was stoned to death. One was as great a triumph as the other, in the thought of God." —J. Wilbur Chapman.

age, to my own solitary experience, it is bitter. Left in my chamber alone with myself, is it wonderful my philosophy at times takes flight; that I rush into company; resort to that which blunts but heals no pang; and then, sick of the world and dissatisfied with myself, shrink back into solitude?" Poor Campbell! What a change would have passed over him if he had exchanged his philosophy for Christianity,—if he had known the pleasures of Christian hope,—if, in the realised presence of the invisible Jesus, and His unutterable sympathy, he had found "the balm of Gilead," to heal, not to blunt, the pangs of his wounded spirit!—Bullock.

16—18. (16) **communed,** entered into counsel with myself. **Lo, I am come to great estate,** the verb in the Hebrew is connected closely with what follows and speaks not of outward majesty, but of "becoming great" in wisdom. So taken we may read, "I became great and increased in wisdom more than all." **experience,** the knowledge was not merely theoretic. (17) **madness[a] and folly,** things in wh. many men appear to find satisfaction. He wanted his experiences to include all sides of human life. (18) **much grief,[b]** German prov., "Much wisdom causeth headache." So Cicero, "Sickness seems to me to be the lot of the wise of heart."

a Lit. vaunting extravagance.

b "We become more sensible of our ignorance and impotence, and, therefore, sorrowful, in proportion as we discover more of the scheme of providence in the government of the world; every discovery serving to convince us that more remains concealed of wh. we had no suspicion before."—Bp. Butler.

The bliss of ignorance and folly of wisdom (vs. 18).—I. The more one knows of himself, the more sad he will be at his sinfulness. II. Or of God, the more sad that he began to serve Him so late, and has served Him so poorly. III. Or of the world, the more sad that its conquest by science should be so slow. IV. But the opposite is also true, that with increase of knowledge comes increase of joy. V. And the joy outweighs the grief. VI. The greatest joy of all is to know God, and Jesus whom He has sent.

Melancolia.—In his celebrated engraving of "Melancolia," Albert Dürer has with wonderful skill depicted this mood of intellectual depression. He represents a winged figure, that of a woman seated by the seashore and looking intently into the distance, with bent brows and proud, pensive demeanor. Her thoughts are absorbed in sombre meditation, and her wings are folded. A closed book is in her lap. Near her stands a dial-plate, and above it a bell, that strikes the hours as they pass. The sun is rapidly nearing the horizon-line, and darkness will soon enshroud the earth. In her right hand she holds a compass and a circle, emblematic of that infinity of time and space upon which she is meditating. Around her are scattered the various implements of art, and the numerous appliances of science. They have served her purpose, and she now casts them aside, and listlessly ponders on the vanity of all human calculations. Above her is an hour-glass, in which the sands are running low, emblematic of the shortness of the time yet left for fresh schemes and efforts. In like manner the Preacher found that on the moral side increase of knowledge meant increase of sorrow. Knowledge of the true ideal only made him the more conscious of the distance we are from it, and of the hopelessness of our efforts to reach it. The further the research is carried, the more abundant is the evidence discoverable of our moral nature being in a condition of disorder. We find that conscience too often reigns without governing, that natural appetites and desires refuse to submit to her rule, that often motives and feelings which she distinctly condemns, such as pride, envy, selfishness, and cruelty, direct and animate our conduct. All schools of philosophy have recognized the fact of moral disorder in our nature. It is, indeed, unfortunately too evident to be denied or explained away.—J. Willcock.

Ec. xii. 12; 1 Co. iii. 18—20.

"The deeper our vision the more clearly we perceive the imperfections among the children of men, and that usually produces unrest in the mind."—Hansen.

Aristotle says, "We are more naturally disposed towards those things which are wrong, and more easily carried away to excess than to propriety of conduct." And Hume, "We naturally desire what is forbidden, and often take a pleasure in performing actions merely because they are unlawful."

CHAPTER THE SECOND.

1—3. (1) **I will prove thee with mirth,** the self-communing of the man talking to his soul, like the rich man in Luke xii. 18, 19, in search of happiness, leads him to yet another experiment. He will lay aside philosophy and try what pleasure will do, and live as others live. The choice of Faust in Goethe's great drama, presents a striking parallel in the world of creative Art. The fall of Abelard is hardly a less striking parallel in the history of an actual life. Consciously or unconsciously (probably the former) the Debater has passed from the Hebrew and the Stoic ideals of wisdom to that of the school of Epicurus.[a]—Cam. Bib. (2) **laughter,** the unrestrained cheerfulness attending sensual enjoyment. **mad,** it puts men beside themselves, out of their own self-control. (3) **unto wine,** or the pleasures of the table, rich feasting and abundant drinking. **acquainting, etc.,**[b] not abandoning himself to indulgence, but carefully observing its influence upon him. But he became the victim of his dangerous experiments.

The vanity of pleasure—an experiment in three stages.—I. The way of sensuous enjoyment (vss. 1, 2). 1. The investigation was vigorously conducted. 2. The result has been clearly recorded. II. The way of banqueting and revelry (vs. 3). This path had been and still is: 1. Much traveled. 2. Appallingly fatal. 3. Perfectly avoidable. III. The way of culture and refinement (vss. 4-11).—Whitelaw.

The drunkard's conversion.—An aged Christian gave a visitor of the poor the following account of his conversion. He said that previous to the Lord's meeting with him he was a notoriously wicked character, and among many other vices he was much addicted to drinking to excess. On a certain occasion he had what he termed "broken out," and had been in a state of intoxication for, I think he said, a fortnight. When the effects of the liquor left him, and he began to come to himself, his spirits sank unusually low, and guilt and remorse preyed on his mind so much that he was driven to despair, and felt himself so miserable that he determined on the rash act of putting an end to his existence. He accordingly procured a rope to hang himself. At that time his wife, who was a truly pious woman, was at chapel. A thought came into his mind that he should like his wife to know his fate soon after he was dead. This induced him to go round the back of the chapel to seek for a convenient place to commit the fatal deed, expecting that when the congregation came out he should be found dead, and that his wife would be informed. When passing the back of the chapel, with the rope in his pocket, the sound of the minister's voice caught his ear, and induced him to go and look in at the door. At the instant the minister was preaching in a very animated manner on the efficacy of the blood of Christ to cleanse the guilty conscience, stated that the Saviour was able and willing to save the vilest rebels, and then gave a most pressing invitation to the chief of sinners. These sentences so penetrated his heart that they produced feelings which are easier conceived than described. When the service was over he went home, fell on his knees, and cried for mercy. His wife was astonished at first at the wonderful change; but, on inquiry, she found the Lord had answered her prayer in behalf of her husband.

The disappointment of sensuality.—

My days are in the yellow leaf;
  The flowers and fruits of love are gone;
The worm, the canker, and the grief
    Are mine alone!

The fire that on my bosom preys
  Is lone as some volcanic isle;
No torch is kindled at its blaze—
    A funeral pile.

The hope, the fear, the jealous care,
  The exalted portion of the pain
And power of love I cannot share,
    But wear the chain. —Byron.

4—6. (5) **gardens,** etc., paradises, parks, or pleasure-gardens.[c] (6) **pools,** "the so-called Solomon's pools lie S. of Bethlehem, upon the usual route from Hebron to Jerusalem, and about six miles from the Holy City." An adjoining hill still bears the name of the "Little Paradise."

Pools of Solomon.—"If," says Dean Stanley, "Hebron and Bethlehem are special memorials of David, there is one spot between the two which calls to mind in a lively form the works of the peaceful reign which succeeded. In the long green vale of Urtâs, unusually green amongst

[a] I will try whether thou wilt feel contented and happy in this new object of thy experience, viz., in cheerful sensual enjoyment.

"Mirth is the entertainment of the fancy, and though it comes short of the solid delights of the rational powers, yet it is to be preferred before those that are merely carnal and sensual. Some distinguish man from the brutes, not only as animal rationale, a rational animal, but as animal risibile, a laughing animal." — Mat. Henry.

[b] "He acted not as a sensual voluptuary, but rather as a philosophical experimentalist." — Wordsworth.

"In the world, feasting comes first and fasting afterwards; men first glut themselves, and then loathe their excesses; they take their fill of good, and then suffer; they are rich that they may be poor; they laugh that they may weep; the poor shall be rich, the lowly shall be exalted, those that sow in tears shall reap in joy, those that mourn shall be comforted, those that suffer with Christ shall reign with Him." — J. H. Newman.

[c] "There was, about 50 stadia from Jerusalem, a certain place called Ethan, very pleasant in fine gardens, and abounding in rivulets of water, whither he (Solomon) was wont to go every morning, sitting on high in his chariot." — Josephus.

the rocky knolls of Judæa, Solomon 'planted him vineyards and made him gardens and a "paradise," and planted trees in them of all kinds of fruits, and made him reservoirs of water, to water therewith the wood that bringeth forth trees.' From these gardens probably came, in part at least, the imagery of the Canticles; and in these, probably more than anywhere else, the wise king cultivated his knowledge of trees, from the transplanted cedar to the native hyssop. The great reservoirs still remain; and the huge square hill in its neighborhood, by Europeans called 'the Frank Mountain,' is known to the Arabs only as the 'Jebel el Fureidis,' the 'Mountain of the Little Paradise,' evidently from its vicinity to the gardens of the Wâdy Urtâs."

7—9. (7) **got,** or bought: distinguished fr. those born in the house.[a] Those born in the house, the sons of the handmaids rose into more confidential service. **great and small cattle,** i. e. oxen and sheep. **all..before me,** comp. David's flocks and herds (1 Chro. xxvii. 29, 31). (8) **peculiar treasure,** that for wh. each district or kingdom was specially famous. **singers,** the common luxury of Eastern courts.[b] They sang and played whilst the guests were at the table. The mention of women shows that the singers meant are those that figured at state banquets. (9) **my wisdom,** "the thought expressed seems to be, as in verse 3, that the seeker, though he plunged into the pleasures of a sensual life, was never altogether their slave. They were for him experiments which he watched as with an intellectual impartiality. Like Goethe, he analysed his voluptuousness, and studied his own faculties of enjoyment."

Earth's treasures unsatisfying.—A ship, bearing a hundred emigrants, has been driven from her course and wrecked on a desert island, far from the tracks of man. There is no way of escape; but there are means of subsistence. An ocean unvisited by ordinary voyagers circles round their prison; but they have seed, with a rich soil to receive, and a genial climate to ripen it. Ere any plan has been laid, or any operations begun, an exploring party returns to head-quarters, reporting the discovery of a gold mine. Thither instantly the whole party resort to dig. They labor successfully, day by day, and month after month. They acquire and accumulate large heaps of gold. But spring is past, and not a field has been cleared, nor a grain of seed committed to the ground. The summer comes, and their wealth increases; but the store of food is small. In harvest they begin to discover that their heaps of gold are worthless. When famine stares them in the face, a suspicion shoots across their fainting hearts that the gold has cheated them. They rush to the woods, fell the trees, dig the roots, till the ground, sow the seed. It is too late! Winter has come; and their seed rots in the ground. They die of want in the midst of their treasures. This earth is the little isle, eternity the ocean round it; on this shore we have been cast. There is a living seed, but gold mines attract us; we spend spring and summer there, winter overtakes us toiling there, destitute of the bread of life, forgetting that we ought to "seek first the kingdom of God, and His righteousness; and all these things shall be added unto us."—Arnot.

10, 11. (10) **whatsoever,** etc., from such a life the idea of self-denial, even of self-control, was absolutely excluded. **my portion,**[a] this temporary joy and rejoicing was all the portion he gained, and he felt that it was not worth the labor. (11) **Then I looked,** the pursuit of pleasure was as unsatisfying as the pursuit of knowledge. Like others who have trodden the same path he had to confess that all was vanity and feeding on wind. **no profit,** no permanent satisfying profit.[b].

Pleasure.—1. The way of pleasure, however inviting, is not the way of safety or the way of peace. 2. While it cannot impart happiness to any, it may lead to everlasting misery and shame. 3. The pursuit of pleasure is not only incompatible with religion, but even at the best its sweets are not to be compared with religion's joys.—Whitelaw.

Worldly things unsatisfying.—The worm at the core.—There was a rich man at the court of King Herod; he was his high chamberlain, and was clothed in costly apparel, and lived in the greatest state and magnificence. And there came to him from distant lands a friend of his youth, whom he had not seen for many years. Anxious to do him honor, the high chamberlain made a great feast, and invited all his friends. The

"Every great man is always being helped by everybody, for his gift is to get good out of all things and all persons." —Ruskin.

[a] "On account of their natural fidelity, slaves born in the house were regarded as a very valuable possession." —O. Zockler.

[b] 2 Sa. xix. 35.

"Like flakes of snow that fall unperceived upon the earth, the seemingly unimportant events of life succeed one other. As the snow gathers together, so are our habits formed. No single flake that is added to the pile produces a sensible change; no single action creates, however it may exhibit, a man's character." —Jeremy Taylor.

"Life, like a dome of many-colored glass, stains the white radiance of eternity."—Shelley.

"Thriftless ambition, that will ravin up thine own life's means."—Shakespeare.

[a] My profit, my advantage.

[b] 1 Ti. vi. 6—11; 1 Jno. ii. 15—17.

"The Fortunate Islands, which anyone may talk of, are but mere dreams, not lying anywhere under the sun's light." —Jermin.

"When Garrick showed Dr. Johnson his fine house, gardens, statues, pictures, etc., at Hampton Court, what ideas did they awaken in the mind of that great man? Instead of a flattering compliment that was expected, 'Ah! David! David!' said the Doctor, 'these are the

tables were laden with the most delicate viands on dishes of gold and silver, and many costly vessels filled with wines of all kinds. The rich man sat at the head of his table; on his right hand sat the friend who had come from distant lands; and they ate, and drank, and were satisfied. Then said the stranger to the king's high chamberlain, "I have never seen such magnificence as this in my native land." And he praised all he saw, and esteemed his friend the happiest of men. But the rich man, the king's high chamberlain, took an apple from off a golden dish; the apple was large and smooth, and rosy as the cheek of a sleeping infant; and as he handed it to his friend he said, "Behold this apple, it lay upon a golden dish, and it is lovely to look upon." And the stranger, the friend of his youth, took the apple and cut it through; but, alas! at its core was a worm! Then the stranger gave a glance towards his host. But the high chamberlain looked down and sighed.—Krummacher.

12—14. (12) **after the king,**[c] the verse is obscure, and has been very variously rendered. So (1) the LXX., following another text, gives "What man will follow after counsel in whatsoever things they wrought it;" (2) the Vulgate, "What is man, said I, that he can follow the King, his Maker;" and (3) many modern interpreters, "What can the man do that comes after the king, whom they made long ago?" i. e. Who can equal the time-honored fame of Solomon?—Cam. B. (13) **wisdom .. folly,**[d] this is his conclusion, Even wisdom that brings sorrow is better than the mirth of fools. (14) **in his head,** In Prov. xvii. 24 we have the opposite of the same thought: "The eyes of a fool are in the ends of the earth." **darkness,** the dimness brought on by self-indulgences. **one event,** death.

> "One dark black night awaits us all;
> One path of death we all must tread."
> —Horace, Od. 1, 28, 15.

Eyes and no eyes.—The Russian proverb says of the non-observant man, "He goes through the forest and sees no firewood." Dr. Johnson once said, "Some men will learn more in the Hampstead stage than others in the tour of Europe." Sir Isambard Brunel took his first lessons in forming the Thames Tunnel from the tiny ship-worm. He saw how the little creature perforated the wood with its well-armed head, first in one direction and then in another, till the archway was complete, and then daubing over the roof and sides with a kind of varnish; and by copying this work exactly, on a large scale, Brunel was at length enabled to accomplish the work.—S. Smiles.

15—17. (15) **why..wise?** "he puts the question—To what end, with what design, has he been so excessively wise, or, as it may be, wise overmuch (ch. vii. 16)? His wisdom has, as it were, recoiled upon himself—it taught him much, but not content; it made him keen sighted in seeing the emptiness of human things, but it satisfied not his cravings."—Pul-Com. **vanity,** the arrangement that the wise is no better off in relation to death than the fool. (16) **no remembrance,** no perpetual memorial of those who have lived their lives prudently. He here speaks in a very sad and melancholy frame. The scribes and doctors, the artists and the poets of one age are forgotten in the next, and only here or there can any man be bold to say with Bacon that he commits his memory "to the care of future ages." **as the fool,** R. V., "And how doth the wise man die even as the fool!" How is it that there is no difference? see 2 Sa. iii. 33; Ps. xlix. 10. (17) **hated life,** he felt weary of life wh. had so little real result and fruitage. The term used indicates disgust, weariness, antipathy.

Disgust with life (vs. 17).—I. Rid the text of several false meanings which it may seem at first sight to countenance. We may be disgusted with life—1. Through melancholy; 2. Misanthropy; 3. Discontent; 4. Ennui. II. Proceed to justify the sense given.—W. Stevens.

18—20. (18) **man..after me,** he could not retain what he might gain. The fruit of his labors another would reap. But we need not regard this fact in so melancholy a way.[a] (19) **wise,** to make good use of it. **a fool,**[b] to squander it all away. So often the sons of the rich scatter, in frivolities, all that the parents have laboriously gathered. (20) **Therefore I went about,** in the phrase "I went about," literally, "I turned," we have,

things which make a death-bed terrible!" —J. Whitecross.

"A man's life is an appendix to his heart."—South.

c "What is any man that in this study of wisdom and folly shall come after me, who from my position have had such peculiar advantages for carrying it on?"—Spk. Com.

d "The real strength of life is in wisdom alone, whilst folly is vain, empty, and unsubstantial."— Elster.

"The baffled trial needs not be repeated." — Mat. Henry.

"The thing that seems
Mere misery, under human schemes,
Becomes, regarded by the light
Of love, as very near or quite
As good a gift as joy before."
—Robert Browning.

"In the morning we carry the world like Atlas; at noon we stoop and bend beneath it; and at night it crushes us flat to the ground." —Beecher.

"Learn of me," says the philosopher, "and ye shall find restlessness." "Learn of me," says Christ, "and ye shall find rest."—Anon.

a "One hope alone was left to the disappointed worldling, the perpetuation of his name and riches, laboriously gathered, through his 'successor." — Fausset.

b Ps. xxxix. 6.

"Worldly riches are like nuts; many clothes are torn in getting them, many a tooth broke in cracking them, but never a belly filled with eating them." — Venning.

"It is one of the vanities of wealth that a man knows not to what use it will be put by his successor."

as it were, the attitude of one who looks behind him on the road on which so far he has traveled. The retrospect was so dreary that it made the prospect drearier still.

Folly of amassing wealth for children (vss. 18, 19).—I. It takes from children the expectation and the purpose to succeed in life by their own efforts. II. It deprives children of the education and discipline of self-reliance. III. It educates children in the radical error that they are not to do service in the world, but are to be served. IV. It brings evil to parents as well as children. V. Society suffers from this evil, as, in consequence of it, it is deprived, in a great measure, of the active services of the children of the rich. VI. This evil prevents united effort among the rich for the industrial welfare of the community in which they live.—W. Clift.

Life.—

Our life is scarce the twinkle of a star
In God's eternal day. Obscure and dim
With mortal clouds, it yet may beam from him,
And darkened here, shine fair to spheres afar.
I will be patient, lest my sorrow bar
His grace and blessing, and I fall supine;
In my own hands my want and weakness are;
My strength, O God, is thine!

—Bayard Taylor.

[a] There is a common saying in the North of England to this effect, "The first generation buys the carriage, the second rides in the carriage, and the third pawns the carriage."

"The God-stayed imagination has no space for the trials and perplexities of this world. It meets them with a victorious indifference that is the wonder of the tempest-tossed worldling. Yet when the believer bears witness to the source of his marvelous peacefulness, his words find too often only deaf ears and stony hearts; and those whom he would help to the same source of comfort keep struggling along until they go down." — Anon.

"To eat and drink, and let one's soul be merry, is the triad of sensual life, wh. is sometimes used, in a bad sense, of vicious excess and indulgence, and again in a good or morally unprejudicial sense." — O. Zockler.

21—23. (21) **in equity,** R. V., "skilfulness." **not laboured therein,** it seems to be a rule of life that some are to gain, and others are to spend.[a] (22) **hath man,** i. e. the man himself, whose life is so brief after the fruits of his life-labors are won. **vexation,** worry of his business and his struggle. Here perhaps, "corroding care" would best convey the meaning. (23) **his travail,** or toil. The penalty of sin is not toil, but anxious toil, toil in the "sweat of the face." **not rest..night,** the planning and scheming even preventing sleep.

In much wisdom is much sadness.—Père Lacordaire has a fine passage on this theme. "Weak and little minds find here below a nourishment which suffices for their intellect and satisfies their love. They do not discover the emptiness of visible things because they are incapable of sounding them to the bottom. But a soul which God has drawn nearer to the Infinite very soon feels the narrow limits within which it is pent; it experiences moments of inexpressible sadness, the cause of which for a long time remains a mystery; it even seems as though some strange concurrence of events must have chanced in order thus to disturb its life: and all the while the trouble comes from a higher source. In reading the lives of the Saints, we find that nearly all of them have felt that sweet melancholy of which the ancients said that there was no genius without it. In fact, melancholy is inseparable from every mind that looks below the surface and every heart that feels profoundly. Not that we should take complacency in it, for it is a malady that enervates when we do not shake it off; and it has but two remedies—Death or God."

24—26. (24) **nothing better,** etc., the point of the verse seems to be in the last clause. Let a man live in comfort and peace, but remember that for this he is dependent on God. (25) **more than I,** R. V., margin, "For who can eat or who can have enjoyment apart from him," i. e. without the divine blessing. (26) **travail,** "the words point to a further perception of a moral order in the midst of the seeming disorders of the world. The fruitless labor of the sinner in heaping up his often ill-gotten gains is not altogether wasted. His treasure passes into hands that make a better use of it than he has done."

The use of appetite (vs. 24).—I. Man must labor in order to eat. II. He must eat in order to live. III. What is thus a necessity, is also a pleasure. IV. The pleasure of the palate a God-ordained incentive to toil, and reward of it. V. All this is also true of soul-nourishment. "Blessed are they who hunger," etc.

CHAPTER THE THIRD.

1—4. (1) **season,**[b] "The sentiment is, that the when and where of all actions and occurrences are ordained of God. They are not within the power of man to control."—Stuart. (2) **be born,** he thus impressively sets forth the fickleness and mutability of everything on earth. (3) **to kill,** judicially, or in defensive war. (4) **dance,** the expression of gladness and rejoicing. The author does not here assert that everything is predetermined, and so teach fatalism. He is but weary with the ceaseless and orderly change fr. one thing to its opposite, wh. he observes all around him.

A time to die (vs. 2).—I. It is the time of parting—of finally parting with our dear brother. II. This is a season of weeping. III. This weeping, parting season is also replete with instruction. 1. It is here we feel that our nature is social; 2. It is here that we learn that our nature is mortal; 3. It is here, too, that we learn that our nature is sinful; 4. It also confirms our faith in the validity and value of our common Christianity.—Studies for the Pulpit.

Order.—We are to understand, then, that there is a spirit of Order in creation, and that God wishes our life to be rhythmic and musical, not tumultuous and self-disappointing: a place for everything and everything in its place; a time for everything and everything done in its time. This is not mere machinery, it is not stiffness or pedantry; it is the very perfection of ease and enjoyment: it entails the least possible waste, it divides all burdens equally, it makes the wheels of life go steadily and correctly. We have lost the spirit of Order. The human race has lost its marching step, and we now go each at his own pace, wildly, confusedly, blindly. Our march is no longer a piece of music: it is an ungainly waddle; it is a jerk and rush, as if the spirit of panic had displaced the spirit of peace.—J. Parker.

5—8. (5) **stones,** it seems most simple to see herein intimated the operation of clearing a vineyard of stones, as mentioned in Isa. v. 2; and of collecting materials for making fences, wine-press, tower, etc.[a] **refrain,** or be far from. (6) **get,** the getting or the losing refer primarily, we can scarcely doubt, to what we call property. There are times when it is better and wiser to risk the loss of all we have rather than to set our minds on acquiring more. (7)**rend,** as in seasons of mourning.[b] (8) **hate,** in the usual Bible sense, wh, we can only express by "loving less," or "being indifferent to."

The time for speech (vs. 7).—I. When one has something to say suited to the hearer and the occasion. II. When one is unruffled in temper and calm in mind. III. When the occasion and the audience minister the opportunity. IV. No time but is fit for the speech of prayer.

Time for all things.—Time is the gift of God, a boon of inestimable value. What pity it should be abused or trifled with! I say not that it is to be wholly employed in meditation and devotion. That man mistakes religion who, under a notion of exalted piety, turns his back on the world, and retires into obscurity. There is a time for everything under the sun. A time for prudent consideration about our temporal interests; a time for honest labor, to procure a subsistence, and to acquire a competence; a time for food and sleep; a time for recreation and amusement. We may enjoy what God has given us, as well as labor for it.—S. Stennett.

A time for everything.—

There's a time to get, and a time to give, and a time to throw away;
There's a time to do a kindly deed, and that time is to-day.

There's a time to sing and a time to mourn, a time for joy and sorrow;
There's a time to love; but the time to hate might better be to-morrow.

There's a time to sleep and a time to wake, a time for work and play;
But the time to speak an evil thought passed by us yesterday.
—Frank A. Waugh.

[b] "He shows that all things on earth ebb and flow in a restless vicissitude, and are succeeded by their contraries, and that nothing under the heaven 'continueth in one stay,' and that it is only things spiritual and Divine wh. are not affected by the mutations of time."—St. Jerome.

"There is no music in the life that sounds with idiot laughter solely; there's not a string attuned to mirth but has its chord in melancholy."—Thos. Hood.

"Mortality is a huge time-piece wound up by the Almighty Maker; and after he has set it a-going nothing can stop it till the Angel swears that time shall be no longer."—J. Hamilton.

[a] Isa. v. 2, lxii. 10.

[b] 2 Sa. i. 2, 11, etc.

The worldling is like the hinder wheel of a carriage, ever following after the front wheel of happiness, but never overtaking it.

"O the strong buckler of a circumspect defence, silence! O the most faithful foundation of stability! For many being well settled with a stable heart, yet unawares have fallen by the error of a wandering tongue.—St. Ambrose.

"Each lawless thought will mar the plan, Each wasted day will stint the man. Wouldst thou excel? Let purpose run A thread of gold from sun to sun!" —James Buckham.

c "After reviewing the works of man in a new light, viz., as works ordained by God, and parts of His great design, he repeats his question as in ch. i. 3."—Spk. Com.

9—11. (9) **profit,**[c] "the long induction is completed, and yet is followed by the same despairing question as that of ch. i. 3, asked as from a standpoint that commands a wider horizon."—Cam. B. But Stuart thinks this question is asked in order to bring in the answer in vss. 10, 11.. (10) **sons of men,** Stuart, "I have considered the task wh. God hath given to the sons of men," etc. All these things proceed from divine arrangements. (11) **in his time,** R. V. "in its time." **world .. heart,** Stuart, "he hath put intelligence in their heart, without which no man," etc. In their proper season all his arrangements are fitting and he enables men to find this out by the intelligence bestowed upon them. **find out,** fully, or perfectly. We are always studying to know more of God; never exhausting the mysteries of creation or Providence.

The beautiful.—If we look long and far, we shall see that, though many things have an ugly aspect at first sight, God "has made everything beautiful in its time." The light and warmth of summer are good to see and feel; but is not the cold of winter invigorating? and what is more beautiful to the sight than the untrodden snow? The returning life of spring is welcome to all hearts; but are not the brilliant hues of autumn fascinating to every eye? Youth is full of ardor, and manhood of strength; but declining years possess much richness of gathered wisdom, and there is a dignity, a calm, a reverence, in age which is all its own. There is a joy in battle as well as a pleasantness in peace. Wealth has its treasures; but poverty has little to lose, and therefore little cause for anxiety and trouble. Luxury brings many comforts, but hardness gives health and strength. Each climate upon the earth, every condition in life, the various dispositions and temperaments of the human soul,—these have their own particular advantage and compensation. Look on the other side, and you will see something that will please, if it does not satisfy.—Clarkson.

"Eternity casts upon the whole course of time the shadow of mystery. We have enough light to work by, but not enough for complete revelation."

"God is continually punishing men by that which is the natural result of their own misconduct in violating the natural laws which he has established." — Am. Com.

12—15. (12) **good,** profit, vs. 9. Lasting, satisfying good. **rejoice,** with the measure of present joy that is attainable. **do good,** Ps. xxxiv. 15, xxxvii. 3. "Doing good is a principal condition of human happiness." (13) **eat,** etc., as ch. ii. 24. (14) **I know that whatsoever God doeth.** We ask whether we are brought face to face with the thought of an iron destiny immutably fixing even the seeming accidents of life, and excluding man's volition from any share in them, or whether the writer speaks of an order which men may, in the exercise of their freedom, transgress. And the answer is that the Debater, while he recognises man's freedom, has come to see a purpose and an order even in those accidents.—Cam. Bib. **fear,** with the reverence that is kin with dependence. (15) **that .. been,** as ch. i. 9. **requireth .. past,** "seeketh again that wh. is driven away." Past things are not lost. In the Divine order they are sure to turn up again.[a]

The way to front our destiny.—I. By a cheerful acceptance of our Providential lot. 1. To fret and worry ourselves is useless. 2. A rebellious temper hinders the course of true happiness. 3. The power to enjoy the good of this life is the gift of God. II. By a practical recognition of the high claims of duty. 1. Doing good brings a man into sympathy with the Supreme Disposer of all things. 2. Whatever else may be mysterious our present duty is always clear. 3. The faithful discharge of duty is the only foundation for solid joy. III. By an acknowledgment of the inflexible rule of the Divine Government. 1. God's counsels are for ever. 2. God's counsels are so certain that they are not complicated with our human distinctions of time. IV. By recognizing the righteous ends contemplated by the Divine Government. 1. To tame and subdue the heart of man. 2. To vindicate the wrongs of His people.—Hom. Com.

a "The meaning of the vs. is that there is a connection between events past, present and future; and this connection exists in the justice of God who controls all."—Spk. Com.

16—18. (16) **place of judgment,** seat of the authorized judge. **wickedness,** the special wickedness of corrupt decisions determined by bribes. **righteousness,** innocence or virtue, as applied to the individual man. (17) **God shall judge,** in view of the injustice that prevails in earthly tribunals, Koheleth takes comfort in the thought that there is retribution in store for every man, when God shall award sentence according to deserts. God is a righteous Judge, strong and patient, and his decisions are infallible. Future judgment is here plainly stated, as it is at the final conclusion (ch.

"It is an unspeakable comfort to the oppressed that their cause will be heard over again." — Mat. Henry.

xi. 14).—Pul. Com. **time there,** i. e. with God, comp. Gen. xlix, 24. (18) **concerning the estate,** etc., R. V., "It is because of the sons of men, that God may prove them, and that . . . themselves are but as beasts." **beasts,** no better than the beasts without the grace of God.[b]

Fragments of time.—As in money, so in time, we are to look chiefly to the smallest portions. Take care of the pence, and the pounds will take care of themselves. Take care of the minutes, and the hours and years will take care of themselves. Gold is not found in California for the most in great masses, but in little grains. It is sifted out of the sand in minute particles, which, melted together, produce the rich ingots that excite the world's cupidity. So the spare pieces of time, the shreds, the odds and ends of time put together, may form a very great and beautiful work. Oh, the preciousness of moments! no gold or gems can be compared to them. Yet all have them; while some are thereby enriched and others leave themselves in poverty. The wealth of time is like gold in the mine—like the gem in the pebble—like the diamond in the deep. The mine must be worked—the pebble ground and polished—the deep fathomed and searched.—Stoughton.

19, 20. (19) **that,** more accurately, "chance are the sons of men; chance is the beast; one chance is to both of them." **one breath,** the word is the same as the "spirit" of verse 23, and seems deliberately chosen with reference to the record of Gen. ii. 7. The writer asks, What after all was that "breath of life?" Was there not a like "breath of life" in every beast of the field?—Camb. Bib. **no preeminence,** in respect of the uncertainty and the peril of death. The expression must be strictly limited to its connection. (20) **one place,** the "place" thus spoken of is not the Sheol of the Hebrews or the Hades of the Greeks, which implied, however vaguely, some notion of a shadowy disembodied existence, for the souls of men as distinct from those of brutes, but simply the earth as at once the mother, the nourisher, and the sepulchre of every form of life.—Cam. Bib. The doubt suggested here about the spirit of man is not answered for the present, but is fully answered in xii. 7. **dust,** Ge. iii. 19.

Death.—Where are they who founded this goodly city? who possessed these fair houses, and walked these pleasant fields, who created these stately temples, who kneeled in these seats, who preached out of this place, but thirty years agone? Our fathers have summoned us, and we must summon our children to the grave.—H. Smith.

21, 22. (21)**that goeth,** better, "whether it goeth." It is evidently the question of the bitterly sceptical man. Of the future of the spirit of beasts nothing whatever has been revealed to us. (22) **rejoice, he** returns from consideration of moral mysteries to the simple conclusion he has already twice reached.[a] **who shall bring,** etc., make the best of what is now at your command, for your (earthly) future is uncertain.

Cheerful piety.—You often hear of the Puritans, and this has formed our adjective, Puritanical. I imagine there is a good deal of mistake about the Puritans in this matter of recreations. I can scarcely think that they would have done the noble work they accomplished had they been the kind of men this term includes. We are certainly told of John Owen, the prince of the Puritans, and the vice-chancellor of Oxford University, that "he delighted in manly exercises, in leaping, throwing the bar, bell-ringing, playing the flute, and similar amusements." These Puritans, you may rely upon it, were far more genial men than their enemies represented. It is the little nature that can only be grave; it is the little nature that can only be funny. A great nature has room in his soul for both the serious and the pleasant.—W. Guest.

CHAPTER THE FOURTH.

1—3. (1) **oppressions,** violence; refusals of justice; governmental and social tyrannies. He sees the tears of the oppressed and sighs at their hopelessness: "Oh, the pity of it! the pity of it!" We can see in this new element of despair, that which was the beginning of a better life.

b "Every man that minds his body only, and not his soul, makes himself no better than a brute, and must wish, at least, to die like one."—M. Henry.

"As there is a time for every purpose and work, so there will be a time when all things shall be ripe for Divine judgment." — Hom. Com.

"That is said to be vain which vanisheth." — Arrowsmith.

"Uncurb'd ambition, unresisting sloth, and base dependence, are the fiends accurst."— Mason.

"The lowly origin and destiny of the material part of our nature should be—a motive for humility—a rebuke to arrogance—a reason for seeking the imperishable."—Hom. Com.

a Ec. ii. 24, iii. 13.

This life is like an inn, in which the soul spends a few moments on its journey.

"Only the moment that we live in life is our possession. Every hour lived sinks irrevocably into the sea of the past; the future is uncertain. Therefore is he a fool who lets the present slip by unused, wastes it in vain amusement, or grieves with useless lamentations." —Wohlfarth.

The man was passing to use modern terms, from egoism to altruism, thinking more of the misery of others than of his own enjoyment.—Cam. B. **no comforter,** on the supposition that this present life was all to them. God is the comforter of the oppressed; but apart from Him, their life-condition seems hopeless.[b] (2) **praised the dead,**[c] as Job iii. 13—21. (3) **better is he,** etc., R. V., "better than them both did I esteem him which hath not," etc.[d]

Comfort (vs. 1).—I. Men have need of sympathy, especially under certain circumstances. II. Here is a sad case supposed; the oppressed and sad, without human comfort. III. We are reminded of the Divine Father,—the God of all consolation. IV. And of the words of Jesus,—"I will not leave you comfortless." V. And of the work of the Holy Spirit,—the Comforter.

Xerxes and Artabanus.—Xerxes, in his invasion of Greece, conceived the wish "to look upon all his host." A throne was erected for him on a hill near Abydos, sitting on which he looked down and saw the Hellespont covered with his ships, and the vast plain swarming with his troops. As he looked, he wept; and when his uncle Artabanus asked him the cause of his tears, he replied: "There came upon me a sudden pity when I thought of the shortness of man's life, and considered that of all this host, so numerous as it is, not one will be alive when a hundred years are gone by." This is one of the most striking and best known incidents in the life of the Persian despot; but the rejoinder of Artabanus, though in a far higher strain, is less generally known. I quote it here as an illustration of the Preacher's mood. Said Artabanus: "And yet there are sadder things in life than that. Short as our time is, there is no man, whether it be here among this multitude or elsewhere, who is so happy as not to have felt the wish—I will not say once, but full many a time—that he were dead rather than alive. Calamities fall on us, sicknesses vex and harass us, and make life, short though it be, to appear long. So death, through the wretchedness of our life, is a most sweet refuge to our race."—Herodotus in Exp. Bib.

4—6. (4) **every right work,** i. e. every work wh. seems right bec. it proves successful. Success is man's imperfect and unworthy test of right. **for this,** i. e. for his success.[a] So even men's successes are not all blessing to them. (5) **fool,** etc., as Pr. vi. 10, xxiv. 33. The man who, without aim or insight, leads a half brutish life and folds his hands in the attitude of indolence. **eateth . . flesh,** i. e. "he is a self-tormentor, never satisfied, his spirit preying on itself."[b] (6) **handful,** lit. what fills the hollow of a hand. **quietness,** the restfulness of honest labor. **both hands,** or fists grasping tightly. Better take this vs. as an answer to the feverish jealousy and indulgent idleness of prev. vss.

The golden mean.—1. The comparison made by the wise man in this passage is a rebuke to envy. Who can tell what, if his two hands were filled with earthly good, he might, in consequence of his wealth, be called upon to endure of sorrow and of care? 2. On the other hand, this comparison is an encouragement to contentment. A handful is sufficient; and a quiet heart, grateful to God and at peace with men, can make what others might deem poverty not only endurable but welcome. It is God's blessing which maketh rich; and with it he addeth no sorrow.—Thomson.

Envy insatiable.—Mr. Badman's envy was so rank and strong, that if it at any time turned its head against a man, it would hardly ever be pulled in again. He would watch ever that man to do him mischief, as the cat watches over the mouse to destroy it; yea, he would wait seven years, but he would have an opportunity to hurt him; and when he had it, he would make him feel the weight of his envy. This envy is the very father and mother of a great many hideous and prodigious wickednesses. It both begets them, and also nourishes them up till they come to their cursed maturity in the bosom of him that entertains them.—Bunyan.

7, 8. (7) **vanity,** in one of its particular forms. (8) **second,** the gaze of the seeker now falls on another picture. That which strikes him as another example of the vanity of human efforts is the frequent loneliness of the worshiper of wealth. He is one, and he has no companion, often none bound to him by ties of blood, yet he labors on, as though he meant

b "If religion were not taken into account, to die as soon as possible would be desirable, so as not to suffer, or witness, oppressions." —Fausset.

c "For dreadful is that gloomy vale; and then the dark descent so deep, that none can re-ascend the steeps." — Anacreon.

d Comp. Job iii. 10, x. 18; Ec. vi. 3; Je. xx. 14; Mat. xxvi. 24.

"All religion and all ethics are summed up in justice." — Conway.

"If we would add richest luxury to our own banquet, we must send a portion to the poor, and if we would know how rich and free, and mighty we are, we should go and exchange places for a time with the oppressed and the sore in heart." — J. Parker.

a Horace complains that every ancient hero found by bitter personal experience, that envy of heroism is only quenched by the hero's death.

b Is. ix. 20, xlix. 26.

"A good man and a wise man may at times be angry with the world, at times grieved for it; but be sure no man was ever discontented with the world who did his duty in it." —Southey.

"What so foolish as the chase of fame! How vain the prize! how impotent our aim! For what are men who grasp at praise

to be the founder of a dynasty. "He heapeth up riches and knoweth not who shall gather them," Ps. xxxix. 6.—Cam. Bib.

Vanity universal.—Wherefore bethink thyself at length, O deluded world! and write over all thy school-doors, "Let not the wise man glory in his wisdom;" over all thy court-gates, "Let not the mighty man glory in his might;" over all thy exchanges and banks, "Let not the rich man glory in his riches." Write upon thy looking-glasses Bathsheba's motto, "Favour is deceitful, and beauty is vain;" upon thy mews and artillery-yards, that of the Psalmist, "God delighteth not in the strength of a horse; He taketh not pleasure in the legs of a man;" upon thy taverns, inns, and ale-houses, that of Solomon, "Wine is a mocker, strong drink is raging, and whosoever is deceived thereby is not wise;" upon thy magazines and wardrobes, that of our Saviour, "Lay not up for yourselves treasures on earth, where moth and rust doth corrupt, and where thieves break through and steal." Write upon thy counting-houses that of Habakkuk, "Woe to him that increaseth that which is not his! how long? and to him that loadeth himself with thick clay!" thy playhouses, that of Paul, "Lovers of pleasure more than lovers of God;" thy banqueting houses, that of the same holy Apostle, "Meats for the belly, and the belly for meats; but God shall destroy both them and it;" yea, upon all thine accommodations, that of the Preacher, "Vanity of vanities: all is vanity and vexation of spirit."—Arrowsmith.

9—12. (9) **good reward,** in their common joy while sharing the fruits of their labor. "A man without a companion is like a left hand without a right." (10) **fall,** he turns from the isolation of the avaricious to the blessings of companionship. The special illustration appears to be drawn from the experience of two travelers. If one slips on a steep path the other is at hand to raise him. (11) **warm alone?** here again the experience of travel comes before us. Sleeping on a cold and stormy night, under the same coverlet, or in Eastern houses, with their unglazed windows and many draughts, two friends kept each other warm, while one resting by himself would have shivered in discomfort. (12) **threefold cord,** it differs from the previous illustration in suggesting the thought of a friendship in which more than two persons are joined. Three was the typical number for completeness, because the rope of three strands was the strongest cord in use.

Christian union.—Rev. T. L. Cuyler sketches this scene at a Christian Convention in Brooklyn: "The Convention closed by joining hands, and singing, 'Say, brother, will you meet us?' I saw one of Dr. Storrs' deacons and a Quaker and a Methodist standing with clasped hands, and flanked by a Baptist and a Presbyterian clergyman. It reminded me of the time when we college students, standing thus in the chemical lecture-hall, the electric current leaped from the charged battery through the whole circle in an instant."

13, 14. (13) **Better,** in the sense of happier. **child,** R. V., "youth." **who .. admonished,** who is so stiff and settled in his ways and opinions that he cannot be advised. (14) **For out of prison,** etc.,[a] R. V., "For out of prison he came forth to be king; yea, even in his kingdom he was born poor." These verses are prob. suggested by some instance known to the writer, of a foolish king repelling the affections of his subjects, who turn to his successor. Stuart thinks Jeroboam is the youth ("child").

Youth and age.—Age does not always bring wisdom, which is the gift of God, sometimes—as in the case of Solomon—conferred in early life. True excellence and honor are not attached to age and station. Wisdom, modesty, and trustworthiness may be found in lowly abodes and in youthful years. Character is the supreme test of what is admirable and good.—Thomson.

15, 16. (15) **I considered,** etc., R. V., "I saw all .. sun that they were with the youth; the second, that stood," etc. **second child,** if we take the word "second" in its natural meaning, the clause may point to the wise young ruler of the previous verse, as succeeding (i. e. coming second to) the old and foolish king.[a]—Cam. B. (16) **come after,** i. e. the

sublime, but bubbles on the rapid stream of time, that rise and fall, that swell, and are no more? born and forgot, ten thousand in an hour." — Young.

"Even diligence must be restrained by rules. It should not degenerate into an unreasonable passion."

"Crates threw his gold into the sea, saying, 'I will destroy thee, lest thou destroy me!' If men do not put the love of the world to death, the love of the world will put them to death." —Venning.

"Strong alone, but stronger with others." — Ger. Proverb.

"A single drop of water is insignificant, but united with the rest, in the ocean, it becomes an immense power. Society makes man sublime." — Hom. Com.

"We were made for one another, and to break up society into mere individualities is to commit a species of homicide. Every life waits for some other life." —Parker.

"Christianity calls upon us to make our old age into an aspect of youth. There is to be no old age in the sense of spiritual exhaustion, or moral decrepitude, or misanthropic isolation; old age is to be equivalent to increase of kingliness and bounty and holy influence." — Parker.

[a] Comp. Yakoob Khan brought out of prison to succeed Shere Ali in the rule of Afghanistan, and again a prisoner.

[b] The popularity of kings is notoriously short-lived.

"There is no kind of sinners more inconvincible and incurable than the worldly-minded. It is a rule without exception,—those sins which have the greatest appearance of reason, and the least of sensuality, are the most plausible and prevailing."—Bates.

"While men in power and authority have the people flocking about them, honoring and acknowledging them, they should be taken up with the thought of a change, and consider the people as walking with the man that shall come up in their stead, courting him; and themselves as shortly to fall one way or other."—Nisbet.

next generation after that which sets up the youthful king.[b] This is added as the crowning stroke of the irony of history. The reign which begins so brightly shares the inevitable doom, and ends in darkness, and murmuring and failure. The popular hero of the hour finds himself slighted even in life, and is forgotten by the next generation. The glory of the most popular and successful king shares the common doom and is but as a **feeding upon wind.**—Cam. Bib.

The neglected king.—The scene depicted of the ignominy into which the worthless old king falls, and the enthusiasm with which the new one is greeted, reminds one of Carlyle's vivid description of the death of Louis XV. and the accession of his grandson. The courtiers wait with impatience for the passing away of the king whose life had been so corrupt and vile; he dies unpitied upon his loathsome sick-bed. "In the remote apartments, dauphin and dauphiness stand road-ready; . . . . . . waiting for some signal to escape the house of pestilence. And, hark! across the Œil-de-Bœuf, what sound is that—sound 'terrible and absolutely like thunder'? It is the rush of the whole court, rushing as in wager, to salute the new sovereigns: 'Hail to your Majesties!'" The body of the dead king is unceremoniously committed to the grave. "Him they crush down and huddle underground; him and his era of sin and tyranny and shame; for behold! a New Era is come; the future all the brighter that the past was base" ('French Revolution,' vol. i. ch. iv.) The same kind of picture has been drawn by Shakespeare, in 'Richard II.,' act. v. sc. 2, where he describes the popularity of Bolingbroke, and the contempt into which the king he displaced had sunk. Yet, according to the Preacher, the breeze of popular favor soon dies away, and the hero is soon forgotten. "They also that come after him shall not rejoice in him." The dark cloud of oblivion comes down and envelops in its shade both those who deserve to be remembered, and those who have been unworthy of even the brief popularity they enjoyed in their lifetime. "Who knows," says Sir Thos. Browne, "whether the best of men be known, or whether there be not more remarkable persons forgot than any that stand remembered on the known account of time?"—J. Willcock.

CHAPTER THE FIFTH.

"Give thy mind to what thou art going to do."—Spk. Com.

[a] 1 Sa. xv. 22.

"The habit of an excess of words causes the speech to degenerate into vain and senseless twaddle."—O. Zockler.

Pr. x. 19.

"Remember at whose throne you are kneeling; and be not verbose, but let your words be few and emphatic, as of one who is favored with an audience from Heaven's King." — J. Hamilton.

[b] De. xxiii. 22—24.

1—3. (1) **Keep .. God,** to "keep the foot" is to be careful of the conduct, to remember what you are about, whither you are going. The precept implies that he who gives it had seen the need of it. Men went to the place where they worshiped with little thought that it was indeed a Bethel, or "house of God." **hear,**[a] another translation is "for it is better to obey than to offer the sacrifice of fools." (2) **rash,** the rule follows the worshiper from the threshold into the Temple-court and tells him how he is to act there. We are reminded of our Lord's warning against "vain repetitions," after the manner of the heathen (Matt. vi. 7). **few,** so, careful, studied, and becoming. (3) **multitude of business,** wh. oppressing the mind keeps it active all the night. **multitude of words,** often the saying is true, "The more words the less sense."

Reverence for the sanctuary (vs. 1).—I. State the duty. 1. Our duty as we enter public worship; 2. As we are engaged in it. II. Enforce the duty. 1. Impropriety of conduct in public worship is foolish; 2. Is sinful; 3. Is dangerous.—G. Brooks.

Unprofitable speech.—Madame Antoinette Sterling, when asked to go on the operatic stage, replied, "I cannot. I stand by every word I utter when I sing, and I feel I must to the death. It is not alone song with me—melodious sounds; it is the lesson inculcated: hope in the future, bright joys to come, the mercy of an all-wise God. I would not sing a wicked or a frivolous word before an audience for anything on earth." —Francis Hay.

4—7. (4) **vowest,**[b] even if thou didst it hastily, show thy manliness in paying it, whatsoever it may cost thee. **pay,** Ps. lxvi. 13, 14, cxvi. 14. (5) **not vow,** the point which the Teacher seeks to press is obviously the optional character of vows. They form no part of the essentials of religion; but to make them, and then delay or evade their fulfilment, is to tamper with veracity and play fast and loose with conscience, and so is fatally injurious.—Camb. Bib. (6) **mouth .. sin,** prob. refers to the thoughtless utterance of the rash vow. comp. James's Ep. for snares of the tongue. **the angel,** R. V., marg. "the messenger" either the priest to whom the man comes, excusing his failure to bring the promised offering, or poss. the angel who is supposed to record all our actions. **error,**[c] our relig. acts should be so serious and so thoughtful, that this should be felt as an unreasonable and wicked excuse. (7) **dreams,** vs. 3. The superstitious man who puts his faith in dreams is unpractical and unreal; the garrulous man who is rash in his vows, and in prayer thinks to be heard for his much speaking, displeases God and never secures his object.

Religious vows (vs. 4).—I. Men are apt to make vows to God—1. When in trouble; 2. When conscience-smitten under the Gospel; 3. When alarmed by the near prospect of death. II. Men are apt to forget the vows they have made. 1. They yield to temptation; 2. Passing events obliterate the impression; 3. Forgotten vows were probably made in self-reliance; 4. Men should imitate the Psalmist. Ps. lxvi. 13, 14.

Promising and performing.—The broken bowl.—Sir William Napier, when taking a long country walk in the neighborhood of Bath, met a little peasant girl, who was crying bitterly, with a broken bowl in her hand. Sir William inquired the cause of her tears, and encouraged by his kind face and voice, she told her tale; how she had broken the bowl which had held her father's dinner, and was afraid now to go home, for she knew her mother would be very angry, and would punish her. But a sudden idea seemed to strike her, and looking up in Sir William's face, she exclaimed, "But 'ee can mend it, cannot 'ee?" "No, but he could give her sixpence to buy another." He pulled out his purse, and was dismayed to find it quite empty. He told the child, however, that if she came to the same place at the same hour next day, he would be sure to meet her and to bring a sixpence with him, and that she must tell her mother this. On reaching his home, however, Sir William found a note from a friend at Bath, inviting him to dinner next day, to meet a gentleman whom he particularly wished to see. He recollected with regret his promise to the little girl, and considered whether it might not be possible to combine the two. But he soon saw this could not be done, and refused the tempting dinner invitation, saying he had "a pre-engagement." "I could not disappoint the child," he said to his daughters; "she trusted in me so implicitly."

8—11. (8) **oppression of the poor,** from the follies of the religious life we pass to the disorders of the political. As in ch. iv. 16, the thinker looks on those disorders of the world, "the poor man's wrong, the proud man's contumely," and teaches others how he has learnt to think of them. **matter,** marg. will or purpose: i. e. at what seems a strange permission of God. Be sure that those in higher office will sooner or later take notice, and be quite sure that God will overrule it all.[a] **higher,** etc., or trans. "superior watcheth superior, and superiors again watch over them." (9) **profit of the earth,** Stuart, "Moreover, an advantage of a land in all this, is a king to a cultivated field;" the writer contrasts the misery of the Oriental government of his time with the condition of Judah under the model kings who gave themselves chiefly to the development of the resources of the country by agriculture. (10) **loveth silver,** has the lust of acquisition, wh. nothing can satisfy.[b] (11) **eat them,** the fact is one which has met the gaze of the moralists of all countries. A large household, numerous retainers, these are but so many elements of trouble.

Verse 9.—A very striking illustration of the teaching here given is afforded in an incident which took place at Heidelberg in the reign of Frederic I. (1152—1190). This prince invited to a banquet all the factious barons whom he had vanquished at Seckingen, and who had previously ravaged and laid waste great part of the palatinate. Among them were the Bishop of Mentz and the Margrave of Baden. The repast was plentiful and luxurious, but there was no bread. The warrior-guests looked around with surprise and inquiry. "Do you ask for bread?" said Frederic, sternly; "you who have wasted the fruits of the earth, and destroyed those whose industry cultivates it? There is no bread. Eat, and

c "It was a thoughtlessness that I made the vow at all." Such an excuse is not weak only, but wicked. Yet this is a characteristic evasion of superficiality and levity in religious matters.

"The worth of prayer is not gauged by its dimensions. A mere cry, if prompted by earnest desire, is more to God than the most elaborate petition. What quantity of electric fluid is requisite in order to send a telegraphic message from England to the United States? Very little." — Stevenson.

"Do not fear the power of the world. When a blind man runs against you in the street, you are not angry with him. You say, 'He is blind, poor man, or he would not have hurt me.' So you may say of the world, when they speak evil of Christ, 'They are blind.'" — McCheyne.

a "There is coming a capital judgment at last, and an earnest of it in partial punishment of sinners meanwhile." — Fausset.

b 1 Ti. vi. 9, 10.

"We lose what on ourselves we spend;
We have as treasure without end
Whatever, Lord, to Thee we lend
Who givest all."

"It's no in titles nor in rank,
It's no in wealth like Lon'on Bank,
To purchase peace and rest."
—Burns.

be satisfied; and learn henceforth mercy to those who put the bread into your mouths."—Mrs. Jameson.

12—17. (12) **labouring man,** one who toils, with his hands, in the fields. He has no cares, and is weary enough to thoroughly enjoy his slumbers.[a] (13) **kept,** not distributed, so as to become a blessing to others. Hoarded up. (14) **evil travail,** unsuccessful speculations. **a son,** late in life perhaps. (15) **naked,** "the words so closely resemble those of Job i. 21 that it is natural to infer that the writer had the history in his mind as an example of a sudden reverse of fortune. In both, earth, as the mother of all living, is thought of as the womb out of which each man comes (Ps. cxxxix. 15) and to which he must return at last, carrying none of his earthly possessions with him."[b] (16) **sore evil,** he tries all his life to keep, and then at death must lose. (17) **he eateth in darkness,** the words are a natural figure of a cheerless life with no "sweetness and light" in it (comp. Mic. vii. 8).

[a] "Fears for his wealth, and an overloaded stomach, without laboring, will not suffer the rich oppressor to sleep." — Fausset.

[b] Ps. xlix. 17; 1 Ti. vi. 7.

"If thou art rich, thou art poor,
For, like an ass whose back with ingots bows,
Thou bear'st thy riches but a journey,
And death unloads thee."
—Shakespeare.

Anxieties of the rich.—In many parts of the East there are not any banks for money, or public offices, in which the affluent can deposit their riches; consequently the property must be kept in the house, or concealed in some secret place. Under these circumstances, it is no wonder that a man having great wealth should live in constant dread of its being stolen. There are those who have large treasures concealed in their houses, gardens, or fields; and, the fact being known, they are closely watched, whenever they pay special attention to any particular place or object. The late king of Kandy, after he was taken prisoner, and on his voyage to Madras, was much concerned about some of his concealed treasures, and yet he would not tell where they were. So great is the anxiety of some, arising from the jewels and gold which they keep in their frail houses, that they literally watch a great part of the night, and sleep in the day, that their golden deity may not be taken from them. I knew a man who had nearly all his wealth in gold pagodas, which he kept in a large chest in his bedroom. Neither in body nor in mind did he ever wander far from the precious treasure; his abundance hindered him from sleeping; and for a time it seemed as if it would hinder him from dying; for when that fatal moment came, he several times, when apparently gone, again opened his eyes, and again gave another look at the chest; and one of the last offices of his hands was to make an attempt to feel for the key under his pillow!—Roberts.

"Riches oftentimes make to themselves wings and fly away; and truly, many a time the undue sparing of them is but letting their wings grow, wh. makes them ready to fly away, and the contributing a part of them to do good only clips their wings a little, and makes them stay the longer with their owner." — Abp. Leighton.

18—20. (18) **good,** etc., if a man has little, let him be content with that little. If he has much, let him enjoy it without excess, and without seeking more. (19) **this is the gift of God,** the words indicate a return to the sense of dependence on Divine bounty, which we have seen in ii. 24, iii. 13. (20) **much remember,** or think on; anxiously ponder over. Thankful to God for present good, he enjoys it, and leaves in God's hands the rest. **God answereth him,** approving of his acts, and giving him the joy of a quiet conscience.[c]

[c] "In order to enjoy the good that there is in the riches of this world, it is necessary that one have a perfect rule over them, i. e. that in the use of them he may at all times act in accordance with the Divine purpose." — Hansen.

The nobleman's jewels.—A rich nobleman was once showing a friend a great collection of precious stones, whose value was almost beyond counting. There were diamonds, and pearls, and rubies, and gems from almost every country on the globe, which had been gathered by their possessor by the greatest labor and expense. "And yet," he remarked, "they yield me no income." His friend replied that he had two stones, which cost him but five pounds each, yet they yielded him a very considerable annual income. And he led him down to the mill, and pointed to the two toiling grey millstones. They were laboriously crushing the grain into snowy flour, for the use of hundreds who depended on this work for their daily bread. Those two dull homely stones did more good in the world and raised a larger income than all the nobleman's jewels. So it is with idle treasure everywhere. It is doing nobody any good. While poor souls are dying of thirst, the money is hoarded and hid away which might take the water of life to them.

"A cheerful spirit is a great blessing; it makes the yoke of our employments easy, and the burden of our afflictions light." — Mat. Henry.

Ec. xi. 9.

CHAPTER THE SIXTH.

1, 2. (1) **common,** better, "it lies heavy on men." (2) **for his soul,** here the picture is that of a man who has all outward goods in abundance, but he just lacks that capacity for enjoyment which is (as in ch. v. 20) the "gift of God," and he dies childless and a stranger becomes the heir. We are reminded of the aged patriarch's exclamation, "I go childless, and the steward of my house is this Eliezer of Damascus" (Gen. xv. 2). **a stranger,** an alien, in whom he has no interest.

Ill-health, ill-ease (vs. 2).—I. We have here an illustration of a not uncommon lot in life—great wealth, etc., with little power for enjoyment. II. We are reminded that enjoyment is often marred by the misuse of what seems to provide the opportunity. III. It is suggested that this is in accordance with laws of health, and of moral government, which none can break with impunity. IV. We infer that life should be ordered by the will of God.

The poor rich.—You pass a stately mansion, and as the powdered menials are closing the shutters of the brilliant room, and you see the sumptuous table spread and the fire-light flashing on vessels of gold and silver, perhaps no pang of envy pricks your bosom, but a glow of gratulation for a moment fills it. Happy people who tread carpets so soft, and who swim through halls so splendid! But, some future day, when the candles are lighted and the curtains drawn in that self-same apartment, it is your lot to be within; and as the invalid owner is wheeled to his place at the table, and as dainties are handed round of which he dares not taste, and as the guests interchange cold courtesy, and all is stiff magnificence and conventional inanity—your fancy cannot help flying off to some humbler spot with which you are more familiar, and "where quiet with contentment makes her home."—J. Hamilton.

"When shall we learn that he who multiplieth possessions multiplieth troubles, and that the one single use of things which we call our own, is that they may be his who hath need of them?"—Thos. Hughes.

"There is a burden of care in getting riches, fear in keeping them, temptation in using them, guilt in abusing them, sorrow in losing them, and a burden of account at last to be given up concerning them." — Matthew Henry.

"There is no self-denial deserving the name that is not willing to give up any privilege of the palate or the passions rather than endanger the least or lowest of God's children." — Bishop Huntington.

3—5. (3) **beget an hundred children,** a case is put, the very opposite of that described in the preceding verse. Instead of being childless the rich man may have children, and children's children; may live out all his days. What then? Unless his "soul be filled with good," unless there is the capacity for enjoyment, life is not worth living. Still, as before, "it were good never to have been born." **days .. be many,** Knobel trans. "and be a great man all his years." **no burial,**[a] i. e. no honorable burial,[b] through the absence of all filial esteem for the mean and miserly man. **untimely birth,** wh. involves never experiencing life at all. (4) **he,** R. V., "it," i. e. the untimely birth of vs.3.[c] (5) **this .. other,** i. e. than the avaricious man, who neither knows rest in life or in death.

Daniel Dancer.—This man was remarkable for a miserly disposition. Lady Tempest, the only person who had the least influence over him, one day prevailed on him to purchase a hat (having worn his own for thirteen years) from a Jew for a shilling; but to her great surprise, when she called the next day, she saw that the old chapeau still covered his head. On inquiry, it was found that, after much solicitation, he had prevailed on old Griffiths, his servant, to purchase the hat for eighteenpence, which Mr. Dancer bought the day before for a shilling. He generally, in severe weather, lay in bed to keep himself warm; to light a fire he thought expensive, though he had £3,000 per annum, besides immense riches. He never took snuff, for that was extravagant, but he always carried a snuff-box. This probably he would fill in the course of a month by pinches obtained from others. When the box was full, he would barter the contents for a farthing candle at a neighboring greengrocer's; this candle was made to last until the box was again full, as he never suffered any light in his house except while he was going to bed. He seldom washed his face and hands but when the sun shone forth, then he would betake himself to a neighboring pool, and use sand instead of soap; when he was washed he would lie on his back and dry himself in the sun, as he never used a towel, for that would wear, and, when soiled, the washing was expensive. Fine gold.—I remember once seeing an old merchant, at whose house I was visiting, sitting by himself against the wall. The

[a] "For a corpse to lie unburied was a circumstance in itself of peculiar ignominy and shame." — Spk. Com.

[b] Isa. liii. 9; Je. xxii. 19.

[c] He is a type of the driftless existence of him who makes riches the chief good.

"The wealth of the Cretans consists in health, vigor and courage, domestic quiet, concord, public liberty, plenty of all that is necessary, and contempt of all that is superfluous; a habit of industry, an abhorrence of idleness, an emulation in virtue, submission to the laws, and a reverence of the gods." — Fenelon.

"Worldly wealth is the devil's bait; and those whose minds feed upon riches, recede, in general, from real happiness, in proportion as their stores increase; as the moon when she is fullest of light is farthest from the sun." —Burton.

"Till the soul of man close with, and rest upon, that infinite soul - satisfying good, God reconciled to them in Christ, give it never so much of other things, the appetite will still cry, give, give; the consideration whereof should convince men that they are miserable who seek satisfaction in those things wherein it is impossible to find it." —Nisbet.

[a] "A man cannot with the greatest riches make his part good against the arrests of sickness or death, but must yield to his fate."—Mat. Henry.

[a] "One would only be justified in esteeming wealth in case he knew the future, and had it in his power. The merest chance can suddenly rob one of all that has been gathered with pain and toil. A great catastrophe may come, and sweep everything away as a flood. The practical result, therefore, is that one should strive after the true riches." — Hengstenberg.

room was filled with guests; music and dancing and merry laughter were all around; but there sat the old man, taking no heed, with his head against the wall. Fearing he was ill, I asked his son about him, and he answered—"He is only thinking about money; he is always like that."—Buxton.

6—8. (6) **thousand years,** etc., the weariness of life carries the thinker yet further. Carry it to the furthest point conceivable, and still the result is the same. The longer it is, the fuller of misery and woe. The man goes to the same place,—to the dark, dreary world of Sheol,—as the abortive birth, with nothing but an accumulated experience of wretchedness.—Cam. Bib. (7) **for his mouth,** for self-preservation and enjoyment, eating and drinking being taken as a type of the proper use of earthly blessings. (8) **knoweth .. living,** in a modest and contented style.

The Marred Image.—I saw once, lying side by side in a great workshop, two heads made of metal. The one was perfect; all the features of a noble, manly face came out clear and distinct in their lines of strength and beauty; in the other, scarcely a single feature could be recognized; it was all marred and spoiled. "The metal had been let grow a little too cool, sir," said the man who was showing it to me. I could not help thinking how true that was of many a form more precious than metal. Many a young soul that might be stamped with the image and superscription of the King, while it is warm with the love and glow of earthly youth, is allowed to grow too cold, and the writing is blurred, and the image is marred.—Canon Teignmouth Shore.

9, 10. (9) **Better,** something like the proverb, "a bird in the hand is worth two in the bush." **sight .. eyes,** to enjoy what we actually see, i. e. present opportunities, is better than the cravings of a limitless desire. (10) **That which hath been,**[a] etc. Stuart, "Th. wh. is, was long ago called by name, and it was known, because he is man, th. he is unable to contend with him who is stronger than he." The folly of striving ag. the arrangements of Providence.

The insatiableness of desire.—I. It consumes the labor of all. II. It affects the characters of all. 1. Intellectual gifts do not argue the absence of desire. 2. Material poverty does not guarantee the absence of desire. III. It disappoints the hopes of all. Lessons. 1. The danger of self-indulgence. 2. The difficulty of keeping the lower nature in subjection. 3. The propriety of preferring present and possible to future and perhaps impossible enjoyments.—Pul. Com.

11, 12. (11) **things,** those detailed in the previous ch. **better,** for all the things he seeks so earnestly, and calls so good. (12) **good,** "Who knows?" was the sceptic's question, then as at all times. After all discussions on the supreme good, some pointing to pleasure, and some to virtue, and some to apathy, who can give a definite and decisive answer? Life remained after all vain, and not worth living. **vain life,** or life of his vanity.[a]

Life.—O life, I have enjoyed thee! Not every draught from thy fountain has had a bitter taste; truly, not all upon earth is vanity, if we enjoy not the creature alone, but, in the creature, enjoy also the Creator. But that which sweetens thee do I indeed take with me; and that is, the friendship of my God, which has flowed to me through all created things, as through so many channels. Earthly channels may fail, but He knows how to provide new ones. Gone, gone, is life's enjoyment and sweetness, when we seek them in the creature only; while, on the other hand, they are ever present to those who, in the good things of this life, recognize the hand that bestows them. Thus, every day becomes a treasury and the poorest life may become a rich one. No, I do not look back upon it as mere vanity; but now, when in the silence of my chamber I survey all the past, my heart is filled with a joy which is too great for it to contain.—Tholuck.

CHAPTER THE SEVENTH.

1. **good name,** or good reputation; as Pr. xxii 1. "There are three crowns: of the law, the priesthood, and the kingship; but the crown of a good name is greater than them all."—Talmud. In the Heb. there is a play upon the similar words shem, a name, shemen, ointment.[b] **better,** more to be desired.[c] **ointment,** scent, or oil, which is in general use and highly valued in hot climates. **day of death,** etc., comp. Phil. i. 23. The author by this sentence commends a serious disposition; one that takes into consideration the ending of life.[d] "To the man with a good name death is the entrance on a better life."

A good name better than precious ointment.—I. More difficult of acquisition. II. More honorable in possession. 1. An article of greater value in itself. 2. An index of true wealth. 3. A mark of higher dignity. III. More satisfying in enjoyment. IV. More diffusive in influence. V. More enduring in continuance. VI. More blessed in its issue. Lessons.—1. Seek this good name. 2. Cherish it above all earthly distinctions. 3. Guard it from getting tarnished. 4. Walk worthy of it.—Pul. Com. The day of death and the day of birth.—1. The latter begins a life at the longest brief (Ps. xc. 10); the former a life which shall never end (Luke xx. 36). II. The latter ushers into a field of toil (Ps. civ. 23); the former into a home of rest (Rev. xiv. 13). III. The latter admits into a scene of suffering (Job v. 7; xiv. 1); the former in a realm of felicity (Rev. vii. 16). IV. The latter introduces a life of sin (Gen. viii. 21; Job xiv. 4; Ps. li. 5; lviii. 3; Rom. v. 12); the former an existence of holiness (Jude 24; Rev. xxi. 27). V. The latter opens a state of condemnation (Rom. v. 18); the former a state of glory (2 Cor. iv. 17). Lessons.—1. The secret of living well—keeping an eye on the day of one's death (Deut. xxxii. 29; Ps. xc. 12). 2. The secret of dying happily—living in the fear of God (Acts xiii. 36; Phil. i. 21).—Whitelaw.

2, 3. (2) **house of mourning,** a house where there is mourning for the dead.[a] The words manifestly record a personal experience, and lead us to think of the writer as having learnt to "visit the fatherless and widows in their affliction" (Jas. i. 27), and having found that there was some "profit" at least in this. **that .. men,** viz., the death wh. they are taking into consideration in the house of mourning.[b] **lay .. heart,** seriously ponder it and try to learn wise lessons from the brevity of life. (3) **Sorrow,** not here grief, but rather seriousness.[c] **laughter,** regarded as the expression of thoughtless and boisterous merry-making. **sadness,** etc., comp. Ps. xc. 12; 2 Cor. vi. 10. "In sadness of countenance there may be a good (cheerful) heart." "There is a moral improvement rising out of sorrow which is not gained from enjoyment however blameless."

Thanks—

How can I count thy mercies up?
  What boisterous seas hast thou made calm
  What sad sighs changed to joyous psalm;
And what rich wine has filled my cup!
  My day and night, my work and rest,
  Even my sorrows, thou hast blessed.

Thou gavest, and I took my share
  Of pain and trouble, grief and tears,
  But ever through the stormiest years
My peace was greater than my care.
  Unworthy I! And yet I pray,
  O Lord, accept my thanks to-day.
—Marianne Farningham.

4—6. (4) **wise,** like goes to like. The impulse of the fool takes him to that which promises enjoyment; that of the wise leads him to that which has the promise of a higher wisdom and therefore of a more lasting **gain. fools,** inconsiderate men, but always in Scripture with the idea of

[b] The Heb. words of the sentence are Tob shem mishemen tob.

[c] "The honor of virtue is really more valuable and desirable than all the wealth and pleasure in this world." — Mat. Henry.

"The awe and veneration which a good name inspires is the homage which society pays to virtue."— Hom. Com.

[d] "A good and reputable name, wh. secures an ideal existence with posterity, is more valuable than all sensual pleasure." — Elster.

[a] "In the cemeteries in the neighborhood of Cairo are many private burying grounds, each one belonging to one family; and if the owners be of sufficient wealth, they have erected within them a house of mourning. To this the females of the family repair twice a year, and remain there for three or more days and nights." — Gadsby.

[b] The Lord Jesus taught us that times of feasting may be sanctified by giving His presence at the marriage feast in Cana.

[c] Comp. godly sorrow, 2 Cor. vii. 10.

wilfulness, leading to wickedness. (5) **rebuke,** etc.,[d] comp. Pr. xiii. 18, xv. 31, 32. (6)**crackling,** etc., noisy for a very brief time.[e] There is a play of words in the Hebrew, which Wright expresses by translating "Like the noise of the nettles under the kettles." "Quickly blazing up, and quickly consumed."

The disguised blessing.—To have a chastened spirit, to have the heart which has been taught of God great spiritual realities, to have had an enlarging and elevating vision of the things which are unseen and eternal, to have been impressed with the transiency of earthly good and with the excellency of "the consolations which are in Christ Jesus," to be lifted up, if but one degree, toward the spirit and character of the self-sacrificing Lord we serve, to have had some fellowship with the sufferings of Christ,—surely this is incomparably preferable to the most delicious feast or the most hilarious laughter. To go down to the home that is darkened by bereavement or saddened by some crushing disappointment, and to pour upon the troubled hearts there the oil of true and genuine sympathy, to bring such spirits up from the depths of utter hopelessness or overwhelming grief into the light of Divine truth and heavenly promise,—thus "to do good and to communicate" is not only to offer acceptable sacrifice unto God, but it is also to be truly enriched in our own soul.—Pul. Com.

d Illus. fr. case of Rehoboam, 1 Ki. xii. 6—15.

e "Our boatman's boy always had to go on shore, and gather sticks, thorns, doura straw, rubbish—anything he could lay his hands upon, for boiling the men's pot. But these dried thorns, etc., though they make a great noise for a time, soon burn out, and are then quiet enough."—Gadsby.

7. **oppression,** Ps. lxii. 10. Perhaps here the pressure that is put on a wise man, as, for instance, with bribes. By this pressure he may be made mad or foolish enough to turn aside from the right. Some think the reference is to the exercise of tyrannical power by the wise. **gift,** or bribe. De. xvi. 19.[a] **heart,** i. e. the right intentions of the heart.

The mischief of oppression and bribery.—I. Justice is the only solid foundation for society. II. Oppression, extortion and venality on the part of rulers are incompatible with justice and the public good. III. The special result of corruption and oppression is the furtherance and prevalence of folly and unreason. IV. The duty of all upright men to set their faces against such evil practices.—Thomson.

a "Sometimes in Egypt bribes are taken from both plaintiff and defendant; and the decision is given in favor of him who pays the highest."—Lane.

8—10. (8) **Better** is the end, bec. the painful uncertainties and toils are over.[b] Of course, if a thing is evil in itself, the gnome is not true; we must limit our meaning to good things, or assume that the end must be a good one. **patient in spirit,** comp. N. T. Greek word, makrothumia, long suffering.[c] **proud,** impatient, hasty, self-confident. (9) **angry,** better, sensitive, easily offended. **resteth,** comp. Eph. iv. 26. "A fretful, irritable disposition is mainly found in fools." (10) **former .. better,** this question is still often asked, esp. as men grow old. Such complaints are in fact (and this is the link which connects this maxim with the preceding) but another form of the spirit which is hasty to be angry, as with indivdual men that thwart its wishes, so with the drift and tendency of the times in which it lives. The wise man will rather accept that tendency and make the best of it.

Patience and pride (vs. 8).—I. A patient spirit is more noble than a proud spirit. 1. It sees farther; 2. Is more generous; 3. Suffers less humiliation. II. A patient spirit is more advantageous than a proud spirit. 1. It produces wise counsel; 2. It maintains strong and lasting friendships; 3. It ensures constant co-operation in any good work; 4. It brings about influence and honor for its possessor. III. The patient spirit is more Christlike than the proud. See Jesus—1. Before the proud; 2. With the proud.—Stems and Twigs.

A hasty temper.—La Fontaine, chaplain of the Prussian Army, once preached a very earnest and eloquent sermon on the sin and folly of yielding to a hasty temper. The next day he was accosted by a major of the regiment with the words: "Well, sir! I think you made use of the prerogatives of your office to give me some very sharp hits yesterday." "I certainly thought of you while I was preparing the sermon," was the answer; "but I had no intention of being personal or sharp." "Well, it is of no use," said the major; "I have a hasty temper, and I cannot help it, and I cannot control it; it is impossible." And still adhering to this opinion, after some further conversation he went his way. The next Sabbath La Fontaine preached upon self-deception, and the vain excuses which men are wont to make. "Why," said he, "a man will declare that

b "Fair beginnings (like Solomon's) are often belied by what comes after."—Wordsworth.

"In a subordinate sense this prov. is one of practical and political prudence, and recommends quickness of despatch, and is a warning against tedious prolixity and desultory speaking." —Lord Bacon.

"It is better quietly to wait the course of an affair until its issue, and not to judge and act until then, than to proceed rashly, and with passionate haste, and bring upon oneself its bad consequences."—O. Zockler.

c Col. i. 11; He. vi. 12, 15; Jas. v. 7, 8.

"Self-mastery is the basis of sanity. To rule our own spirits, to

it is impossible to control his temper, when he very well knows that were the provocation to happen in the presence of his sovereign, he not only could, but would, control himself entirely. And yet he dares to say that the continual presence of the King of kings and Lord of lords impose upon him neither restraint nor fear!"—Anec. illus. of O. T. Texts. J. Bradford and J. Wesley.—Joseph Bradford was for some years the traveling companion of Mr. Wesley, for whom he would have sacrificed health and even life, but to whom his will would never bend, except in meekness. "Joseph," said Mr. Wesley, one day, "take these letters to the post." B. "I will take them after the preaching, sir." W. "Take them now, Joseph." B. "I wish to hear you preach, sir; and there will be sufficient time for the post after service." W. "I insist upon your going now, Joseph." B. "I will not go at present." W. "You won't?" B. "No, sir." W. "Then you and I must part." B. "Very good, sir." The good men slept over it. Both were early risers. At four o'clock the next morning the refractory helper was accosted with, "Joseph, have you considered what I said—that we must part?" B. "Yes, sir." W. "And must we part?" B. "Please yourself, sir." W. "Will you ask my pardon, Joseph?" B. "No, sir." W. "You won't?" B. "No, sir." W. "Then I will ask yours, Joseph." Poor Joseph was instantly melted: smitten as by the word of Moses, when forth gushed the tears, like the water from the rock. He had a tender soul; and it was soon observed when the appeal was made to the heart instead of the head.

hold every thought, desire and passion in us to its responsibility before reason and conscience, is the only way to maintain that mental and spiritual soundness which gives us the right to be at large as free and responsible beings." — Sunday-School Times.

"The gate is low through which we pass into the distinctions and honors of the kingdom of God."

"That will break a proud man's heart which will not break a humble man's sleep." — Mat. Henry.

11, 12. (11) **with an inheritance,** R. V., "Wisdom is as good as an inheritance; yea, more excellent is it for them that see the sun;" i. e. the living. (12) **defence,** lit. "shadow." Those who have wisdom are as well defended as those that have money; and, beyond this, wisdom has its own special advantages. **giveth life,** animates him. Money may be a blessing on a man's circumstances: wisdom is an additional blessing to the man himself.[a]

Wisdom and wealth. I. The great power of wealth. 1. What it cannot do. (1) Purchase salvation for the soul (Ps. xlix. 6, 7). (2) Impart happiness to the mind (Luke xii. 15). (3) Secure health for the body (2 Kings v. 1; Luke xvi. 22). 2. What it can do. (1) Defend the body against want and disease, at least partially. (2) Protect the mind against ignorance and error, also again to a limited extent. (3) Shield the heart, once more in a measure, from such anxieties as spring from material causes. II. The greater power of wisdom. 1. It can do things that wealth can. Nay, without it wealth can effect little. (1) It can often do much without wealth to avert want and disease from the body. (2) It can effectually dispel from the mind the clouds of ignorance and error. (3) It can help to keep anxiety altogether from the heart, to sustain the heart in bearing it when it does come, and to direct the heart how most speedily and effectually to get rid of it. 2. It can do things that wealth cannot. It—in its highest form, the fear of the Lord (ch. xii. 13), the wisdom of God (1 Cor. ii. 7), the wisdom which is from above (Jas. iii. 17),—can "preserve the life of him that hath it:" (1) the soul's life, by imparting to it the gift of God, which is eternal life; (2) the mind's life, by flooding it with the light of truth; and (3) the body's life, by communicating to it here on earth length of days and by restoring it at the resurrection to a condition of immortality.

[a] "Rosenmuller and others understand this to mean that wisdom preserves life in safety, or renders life calm and happy; but a deeper meaning is elicited by comparing these words with those of our Lord, 'The words that I speak unto you they are spirit and they are life' (Jno. vi. 63, and see Mat. iv. 4)."—Spk. Com.

Pr. viii. 11, xvi. 16; 2 Ti. iii. 15.

"Wisdom can do without wealth better than wealth can do without wisdom."

13, 14. (13) **work of God,** orderings of Divine Providence.[b] To "consider the work of God" intelligently is one application of the wisdom which has been praised in verses 11, 12. In so considering, the mind of the Debater goes back to verse 10, and he bids men accept the outward facts of life as they come. If they are "crooked," i. e. crossing and thwarting our inclinations, we cannot alter them.—Cam. B. **straight,** etc., for the mystery of Providence is that some things appear to us to be made crooked. (14) **joyful,** prosperous times are sent for our gladdening, and it is proper to rejoice in them. **consider,** bec. adverse times are just as truly sent to lead to seriousness and review. **one .. other** i. e. wisely proportioned them, and fitted them together in every life.[c]

[b] "Consider that every work of God is wise, just and good, and there is an admirable beauty and harmony in His works, and all will appear at last to have been for the best." — Mat. Henry.

De. viii. 2, 5; Ro. viii. 28.

Themes for the day of adversity (vs. 14).—I. Some themes for saints in the day of adversity. 1. Consider who sends the adversity; 2. Why it is sent; 3. What you have in the day of adversity; 4. What you shall

[c] "This mixture of good and evil days is by the

Div. prov. so proportioned, that it sufficiently justifies the dealings of God towards the sons of men, and obviates all our discontent and murmuring against Him."—Bp. Bull.

"When we are at home with God, in the 'secret place of the Most High,' our painful perplexity subsides in the presence of His love and comfort. The darkness of our sojourn here is but the shadow of His wings."—Leale.

be after the day of adversity; 5. What you need now to glorify God. II. Some themes for sinners in the day of adversity. Consider—1. The joys you have had; 2. What you deserve; 3. Whence your adversity comes; 4. The infinitely greater adversity of lost souls; 5. That Jesus is willing to save in this day of adversity.—Stems and Twigs.

The religion of humanity.—The so-called religion of humanity is simply an international Confucianism, and the theosophy which promises greater things than Christianity itself, if we will only drop the dogma of a personal God, is a religious philosophy already discredited amongst nine-tenths of the populations which have tried it. This attempt to vivify and popularize in our midst an ethic of the East which has a name to live, but has been dead for more than a thousand years, is like an attempt to resuscitate the mummy of Thotmes the Second by hot blankets, smelling salts, and artificial respiration. We do not get our Messiahs in that way. Social duties shorn of their spiritual sanctions, obligation with its central mystery eliminated, hero worship without any sense of the mystic qualities which are the life breath of the purest forms of heroism, will give us a wizened, unprogressive, ideal-proof mandarindom rather than a sublime kingdom of God in which tears are dried, the curse unknown, and knowledge flowing in tides overpassing those of the mighty sea.—British Weekly.

15, 16. (15) **All things,** i. e. all sorts of things. **days .. vanity,** such as he gives account of in previous chapters, when he was trying all possible experiences. **just,** etc., this mysterious association of righteousness and misfortune can be seen in every age. It was the bewilderment of Asaph and of Job. (16) **righteous over much,** "a warning against the strictly exact but hypocritical and external righteousness of the predecessors of the Pharisees in those days. Do not think thou canst grasp and apprehend these mysteries.[a] **destroy thyself,** the primary meaning of the verb in the form used here is that of "being amazed, stunned, astonished," and may have been chosen to express the besotted and bedazed spiritual pride which St. Paul paints by the participle "puffed up" in 1 Tim. iii. 5, and which was but too commonly the accompaniment of fancied excellence in knowledge or in conduct.—Cam. B.

[a] "The suggestion that these vss. are intended to advocate a middle course between sin and virtue is at variance with the whole tenor of the book."—Spk. Com.

"Poss. the author is delivering a precept against straining any one virtue to extremes." — Wordsworth.

Righteous over much (vs. 16).—I. What is the real import of this passage? The thing condemned here is evidently not having too much righteousness, but estimating our righteousness more highly than we ought, and priding ourselves in, and boasting of that which we really do not possess. II. What all of us should learn from the subject before us. 1. The importance of obtaining proper views of our own righteousness; 2. Rightly to appreciate the righteousness of Christ.—W. Snell.

Temptations.—The moral life is beset by visible concrete foes. They are not hobgoblins and will-o'-the-wisps. They are neither creatures of our own fancy nor intangible entities of the air about us. They are realities lying athwart the daily path. The poison of obscene literature creeps into the remotest hamlet. The next man you meet and with whom you establish a fellowship may prove a dangerous companion leading you on to recklessness and ruin. The college banquet with its good cheer and comradeship may offer one youth the temptations which another, differently bred, finds in the brilliantly lighted saloon. It is not the submerged tenth, alone, to whom the earliest steps in righteousness are steps up and away from the tangible things that pollute and enslave. Every one who chooses the moral life must count on the presence of such foes, not only at the outset, but all along his Christian pilgrimage.—Howard A. Bridgman.

"We shape ourselves the joy or fear
Of which the coming life is made,
And fill our future's atmosphere
With sunshine or with shade.

"The tissue of the life to be
We weave with colors all our own,
And in the field of destiny
We reap as we have sown."
—Whittier.

17, 18. (17) **over much wicked,** maliciously wicked. All are wicked from frailty, some are wicked in willfulness. Such cannot escape the due penalties. **die .. time,** sinful indulgence surely shortening life.[a] (18) **take .. this,** i. e. this counsel. And the "fear of God" is the only sufficient security from both extremes, of self-righteousness and self-indulgence.

[a] Pr. x. 27; Ps. lv. 23; Job xv. 32, xxii. 16.

The warning despised.—A minister in the neighborhood of Birmingham recently stated, in one of his discourses, the following fact. A deacon of a Christian church was walking, one Sabbath day, to the house of God, when he saw a young man, with whom he had some slight

"A hare and tortoise engaged to run a race;

acquaintance, come out of an inn and mount his horse. "Can you tell me, deacon," said he, jocosely, "how far it is to hell?" The deacon paused, reflected for a moment, then replied, "It is not far off. You may come to it sooner than you expect." The young man laughed, put spurs to his horse, and was soon out of sight. The deacon walked gently on, and as the road made a turn saw a crowd before him. Coming up to the spot, he saw the young man to whom he had just before spoken the words of warning, lying a corpse upon the ground. His horse had become restive and unmanageable, and thrown his rider, who, falling on his head, was killed upon the spot.—Bib. Treas.

19, 20. (19) **strengtheneth,** etc., Pr. xxi. 22, xxiv. 5; Eccl. ix. 13—16. Wise statesmen may do more than generals. (20) **For,** R. V. "surely." **just,** a perfectly righteous, or perfectly wise, see vs. 16. **sinneth not,** comp. Ro. iii. 9—18; 1 Jno. i. 8. Even the just man sinneth and therefore needs wisdom. A Greek proverb runs thus, "Erreth at times the very wisest man."

Dying like a Christian.—Anne de Montmorency, constable of France, having been mortally wounded at an engagement, was exhorted by those who stood around him to die like a good Christian, and with the same courage which he had shown in his lifetime. To this he most nobly replied in the following manner: "Gentlemen and fellow soldiers! I thank you all very kindly for your anxious care and concern about me; but the man who has been enabled to endeavor to live well for fourscore years past can never need to seek now how to die well for a quarter of an hour. But observe, my having been enabled to endeavor to live well, is not the ground of my dependence; no, my sole dependence is on Jesus Christ. It is by the grace of God, through Him, that I now am what I am."—Whitecross.

Conqueror—

Bright and glorious shines the crown
  Of the monarch of the field
Who has conquered every foe
  And was never known to yield.
Brighter glows the nobler crown
  Of the man who in the strife
Bravely fights and conquers self
  On the battle-field of life. J. E. D.

21, 22. (21) **take,** etc., counsel based on the consideration that all are sinners. Many things will be said by imperfect folk which you will be wiser not to hear or heed.[b] Do not be curious to hear how people judge thee. "A warning against idle curiosity, and latent desire of praise." (22)**cursed others,**[a] spoken evil of. The sense of our own frailty should ever make us considerate toward others.

Verse 21.—The wise man who remembers his own mistakes and offences will judge leniently of others, and not punish them as offenders for their occasional hasty words. Indifference to idle praise or idle blame becomes the possessor of true wisdom. For him, to use St. Paul's words, "It is a very small thing to be judged of man's judgment" (1 Cor. iv. 3). An idle curiosity to know what others think of us or say of us is the source of constant mortification. We expect praise, and forget that others are as frivolous and hasty in their criticism of us as we have been of our criticism of them. The servant who waits on us, and from whom we expect special reverence, would probably, if we could hear him without his knowledge, say much about us that would surprise and mortify us. Let us therefore not be too eager to hear our character analyzed and discussed. Some excuse may be found for the motto of the old Scottish family which expresses this indifference to the opinion of others in the most pointed form: "They say. What say they? Let them say."

23, 24. (23) **proved,** or found out. This is some of the fruit of his dearly-bought experience. **wise,** he wanted to be perfectly, absolutely wise. "Practical rules of life he might gain, and had mastered, but essential, absolute wisdom was beyond mortal grasp. Man's knowledge

but the hare, depending on the swiftness of his foot, delayed in starting off upon the proposed race so long that the tortoise reached the goal, and won the prize through its perseverance, though slow in its motion."—John Bate.

"The true heroes of our race are spiritual men, who have felt and dared to utter great truths. Other heroes have conquered enemies, yet have themselves been vanquished by deadlier foes! Spiritual men alone have conquered all. 'The good fight of faith,' is the only one that leads to any satisfactory and permanent result." — Hom. Com.

"The man of one book is always formidable; but when that one book is the Bible, he is irresistible." — W. M. Taylor.

"Christ's mastery of you will give you self-mastery." — T. L. Cuyler.

b "As therefore thou, being far from perfectly 'just' thyself, hast much to be forgiven by God, do not take too strict account, as the self-righteous do, of words spoken against thee by others."— Fausset.

"Pompey showed his wisdom and magnanimity when the papers of his enemy Sertorious were brought to him, by ordering them all to be burnt." —Ld. Bacon.

a 1 Ki. ii. 44.

and capacity are limited." 24) **That .. far off,** R. V., "That which is is far off," viz., the very innermost essence of wisdom.[b]

We know in part.—Our study of the mysteries of God, man, and nature, is not altogether barren of results. We are able to "know in part." We gather a few facts, and by a kind of prophetic insight, frame those portable and convenient statements of them called hypotheses and laws. But even the wisest must confess that the ultimate mystery is as far off as ever. There are some fixed stars whose distance is so great, that when observed from the extremes of the diameter of the earth's orbit, they show no change of direction; thus affording no data for the calculation of their distances. If we could get nearer to them, then we should discover how far off they are. He who has approached the nearest to the great secrets of God and this universe, is most of all conscious how distant he is from absolute wisdom.—Hom. Com.

[b] Ro. xi. 33.

"The books wh. once we valued more than the apple of the eye we have quite exhausted. What is that but saying that we have come up with the point of view which the universal mind took through the eyes of one scribe; we have been that man, and have passed on."—Emerson.

25, 26. (25) **the reason,** to get an insight into the inner meaning and purpose of things good and bad. "The right estimation of things." **know the wickedness,** R. V. "know that wickedness is folly, and that foolishness is madness." (26) **I find,** etc., Pr. xxii. 14.[c] It might, perhaps, be pleaded in reference to this verse that the writer speaks of one class of women only, probably that represented in the pictures of Prov. ii. or vii., but the next verses make the condemnation yet more sweeping. **pleaseth God,** the God-fearing and just man.

Wickedness of folly.—To know the wickedness of folly, the wickedness and foolishness of madness, seems equivalent to knowing the worst species of it. In his own wild career he had come in contact with folly, and he had himself wrought folly of many sorts. And now, comparing all these one with another, so as to ascertain to which of them the pre-eminence of evil should be assigned, this was the conclusion at which he had arrived. These terribly significant words point plainly to the same seducer of whose base and destructive arts so startling a picture is given in Chap. vii. of the Book of Proverbs.—Buchanan. Good and evil.—That which is truly good is more clearly seen when we consider the evil that is contrary to it. The beauty of holiness, and excellency of saving knowledge, is illustrated, and best seen, when the deformity of sin, the madness and unreasonableness of those courses which natural men take to come at their imaginary happiness, are compared therewith.

[c] "Thevenot says there is a custom amongst the Arabs, in some parts, of sending out, in a way where travelers are expected, a handsome woman, in tears, and with her hair dishevelled. The passing traveler pities her, takes her behind him on his beast; then she throws a cord about his neck and strangles him, or holds him until the robbers come."—Gadsby.

27—29. (27) **one by one,** "the words remind us, on the one hand, of Diogenes the Cynic, with his lantern, looking for an honest man at Athens, and answering, when asked where such men might be found, that good men were to be found nowhere, and good boys only in Sparta; and on the other, of Jeremiah's search to see 'if there were any in Jerusalem that sought after God.' (Jer. v. 1—5)." (28) **one man,** "whose good qualities satisfy expectations." **woman,** etc., it appears that, at the present day, the immodesty, ignorance, and degradation of the women in Eastern harems is painful to contemplate.[a] (29) **upright,** Ge. i. 27. **inventions,**[b] tricks, conceits, evil artifices. No reference is intended to scientific inventions and discoveries.

Comp. 1 Ki. xi. 1—8; Pr. ii. 16—19, v. 3, etc.

None good.—The Preacher's finding was incorrect if designed as a universal negative, in the sense that, while in a thousand men, taken at random, one might be found good, in a thousand women similarly taken not one could be found entitled to be so characterized. The best refutation of such woman-hating utterances is to point to "the numerous examples of noble women mentioned in Old Testament Writ, and of the devoted heroines of New Testament days, "whose names stand forth conspicuously side by side with those of men, in the muster-roll of the 'noble army of martyrs.'"—Whitelaw.

Back, then, complainer, loathe thy life no more,
Nor deem thyself upon a desert shore,
Because the rocks the nearer prospect close.
Yet in fallen Israel are there hearts and eyes,
That day by day in prayer like thine arise;
Thou knowest them not, but their Creator knows.
Go, to the world return, nor fear to cast
Thy bread upon the waters, sure at last
In joy to find it after many days.—Keble.

[a] Both Burckhardt and Lane give the women of Cairo a sad character for immorality; and no wonder, considering the surroundings in which they are educated, and the evil influence of the system of polygamy.

[b] "Man has visibly lost his way, and feels in himself some relics of a happy state fr. wh. he is fallen, and wh. he cannot recover. He seeks it everywhere with restlessness, and unsuccessfully in impenetrable darkness."—Pascal.

CHAPTER THE EIGHTH.

1—3. (1) **Who .. man?** whatever be the outward circumstances, the Preacher intimates that the wise man has the best of it. **interpretation,** has some insight into the meaning of things.[a] **face to shine,** lit. "illuminates his face." The word paints with a wonderful vividness the almost transfiguring effect of the "sweetness and light" of a serene wisdom, or of the joy that brightens a man's countenance when he utters his Eureka over the solution of a long-pondered problem. **boldness,** R. V., "hardness of his face is changed." Stuart, "but haughtiness disfigureth his face." (2) **oath of God,** oath of allegiance taken at the king's accession. Kings were regarded as God's anointed. "An oath of God is an oath made with an appeal to God as witness." (3) **hasty .. sight,** do not in sudden anger break away from allegiance. **stand not,** i. e. do not persist in.[b] **whatsoever,** etc., the Eastern king is independent and uncontrolled.

A wise man's superiority.—In what does it consist? I. In penetration of intellect. In particular he has insight into: 1. The secrets of nature. 2. The events of history. 3. The wonders of revelation. 4. The mysteries of grace. II. In elevation of character. "A man's wisdom maketh his face to shine." The wise man's face shines because of three things: 1. The light of truth in his understanding. 2. The light of purity in his heart. 3. The light of life in his conscience.—Whitelaw.

Transformation.—We must all of us have known cases in which true piety and wisdom, such as is learned from Christ, have had this refining and transforming influence; persons of little ordinary education or culture, to whom religion has given really new intellectual power, and whose tranquillity and peace of spirit has given an air of heavenly serenity to their whole bearing and manner. And, indeed, in every case a holy disposition of mind has a refining effect upon those who cherish it. The face is an index to the character, and if the emotions that are expressed upon it are pure and worthy, they cannot fail in time to transform it in some measure—to tone down what may have been its natural harshness, and to banish from it all traces of coarse and sensual passions. An example of religion giving intellectual power, or rather of drawing out the faculties which but for it would have remained unexercised, we may see in the life of John Bunyan. The genius which is so marvellously displayed in his works, and which gives him a high place in the literature of his country, would never have shown itself but for the wonderful change in his life, when, from being a profane, careless, godless fellow, he became a true-hearted servant of Christ.—J. Willcock.

Face medicine.—A Hindoo trader in Kherwara market once asked Pema, "What medicine do you put on your face to make it shine so?" Pema answered, "I don't put anything on." "No; but what do you put on?" Nothing. I don't put anything on." "Yes, you do. All you Christians do; I have seen it in Agra, and I've seen it in Ahmedabad and Surat, and I've seen it in Bombay." Pema laughed, and his happy face shone the more as he said, "Yes, I'll tell you the medicine; it is happiness of heart."—Ch. Miss. Gleaner.

4, 5. (4) **What doest thou?** the despot stands, or thinks he stands, as much above the questionings and complaints of his subjects, as the Supreme Ruler of the Universe does above those of men in general. (5) **feel .. thing,** be influenced by no seditious or rebellious schemes. **time and judgment,** for influencing the king, and securing the due modification of his schemes. There is no intended reference here to the doctrine of a general judgment.

Divine Right.—As is well known, both the words of the Preacher, and the teaching of St. Paul in the thirteenth chapter of Romans, have been taken as laying down the rule of passive obedience for all subjects in all circumstances. However cruel the despot, the duty of subjects to

[a] "Can solve the problem of God's dispensations with a nation."—Wordsworth.

[b] "In presence of a king it is proper to appear modest and yet firm, to show ourselves neither over timid nor obstinate towards him."—Ewald.

"Many a poet, and seer, and martyr, and reformer, and woman of the finest fibre has at times had a face that has looked like porcelain with a light behind it."—Joseph Cook.

"The beauty of the 'human face divine' lies in its expression. The light of wisdom within beams in the countenance, imparting to it the attractive aspect of intelligence and sensibility. It is a mild and lovely light. It does not dazzle and overpower by the studied brilliance of self-display, but with soft and gentle radiance inspires delight, and wins affection; for of genuine wisdom, self-diffident humility is the invariable associate. Such wisdom gives to the countenance the expression both of dignity and grace." — Wardlaw.

"As for my death, I bless God I feel and find so much inward joy and comfort to my soul, that if I were put to my choice whether I would die or live, I would a thousand times rather choose death than life, if it may stand with the holy will of God."—Edward Deering.

a "A heavy misfortune visits him as a well-deserved punishment, and he falls a victim of his foolish effort to struggle against the Divinely-sanctioned ordinances of this world." — O. Zockler.

"The trivial round, the common task,
Will furnish all we ought to ask,
Room to deny ourselves, a road
To bring us daily nearer God."
—John Keble.

a This entire clause from vs. 2 prob. concerns disobedience and disloyalty towards authority.

If the Church of Christ on earth were but what its name professes, soon would the weary world see where all its wants would find supply, and turn to him for whose love it is that it faints, and is so wretched and woebegone. — Pul. Com.

a "Their being at last overtaken by death and oblivion, shows their lot also to be vanity." — Spk. Com.

Wordsworth refers in illustration to the death of Jeroboam.

b "They see not the smoke of the pit, therefore they dread not the fire." — South.

"Because a vicious man escapes at present, he is apt to draw false conclusions from it, and from the delay of God's punishments in this life, either to conceive them at so remote a

obey him implicitly, and to make no attempt to deprive him of his power, has been held by many to be clearly laid down by the Word of God. And great stress has been laid upon the fact that the ruler of the civilized world, when St. Paul wrote the Epistle to the Romans, was Nero, one of the most infamous and cruel tyrants who ever wore the purple. In England during the seventeenth century, when the question of the prerogative of the sovereign and the rights and duties of subjects engaged the attention of all, these portions of Scripture were often interpreted to teach that the king's will was by right, and by the authority of God's Word, above all charters and statutes and acts of parliament, and that no misuse of his power could justify rebellion against him. But those who took up this ground forgot or ignored the fact that kings have duties towards their subjects, that coronation oaths bind them to keep the laws; and that St. Paul, in the very same place in which he commands subjects to obey, describes the kind of rule which has an absolute claim upon their allegiance.—Pul. Com.

6, 7. (6) **misery of man,** i. e. of the man who, neglecting to take the right time and the right way, opposes the king's will, and so rouses the king's anger.[a] (7) **when,** better, "how." He does not wisely estimate the consequences of his rebellious action.

Life and death.—Death was to the Romans the end of sensation and pleasure; yet, instead of regarding the emblems of it with aversion, they rather sought in them a higher relish for present enjoyment. A skeleton was not unfrequently introduced among the guests at festive parties, with the exhortation,—"Vivamus dum licet esse bene"—"Let us enjoy life while we may." It is related of the Egyptians, by Herodotus and others, that in order to prevent irregularities at their convivial meetings, and to give some check to excessive mirth, they were used to bring into the room after supper, when they began their wine, the image of a dead man carved in wood, or a coffin, probably containing the embalmed remains of some ancestor of the family. This spectacle was presented to each of the company by a person whose office it was to pronounce distinctly the following words: "Look upon this, and be merry; for such as this, when dead, shalt thou be."—J. Watts.

8, 9. (8) **to retain the spirit,** the word for "spirit" may mean either "the wind" or the "breath of life" in man. Taking the former, man is powerless to control the course of the wind, so is he powerless to control the drift of things that is bearing him on to his inevitable doom. **no discharge,** seldom any for the soldier when called to the battle; none for the man when called to die. So man is wholly dependent on God. His life is wholly in God's hands. There may, however, still be reference to the anger of the king, wh. commands the execution of the over-bold servant and will by no means change his purpose.[a] (9) **to his own hurt,** should be, "to his hurt"; i. e. to the injury of the subject.

The contemplation of human life (vs. 9).—I. This contemplation of human life should be with reference to God. II. With reference to the object of forming a true estimate of human nature. III. With reference to the illustration and confirmation of religious belief. IV. With reference to the faithful correction of ourselves. V. Think of what men are doing under the sun, and what they will be doing, ere long, somewhere else.—J. Foster.

10, 11. (10) **and so I saw the wicked,** etc., a very difficult passage. Stuart translates: "And then I saw the wicked buried, for they had departed, even from a holy place [Jerusalem] did they go away [were borne out to burial]; and then they were forgotten," etc. The sentiment is: The triumphing of the wicked is short. They die and are forgotten.[a] (11) **speedily,** immediately upon the sentence being pronounced. Long-suffering patience is presumed on by those whose hearts are **evil.**[b] "A very common reason for the increase of crime and wickedness." **Ro. ii.** 4, 5; 2 Pe. iii. 8, 9.

The abuse of Divine forbearance (vs. 11).—I. Sin is deservedly called an evil work; it degrades and defiles the soul; there is a sentence recorded against it. II. Sentence against an evil work is not executed speedily: if it were, this would cease to be a state of probation—God would be the destroyer rather than the governor of the world. III. The depravity of man turns Divine clemency into presumption. 1. Nothing can be more vile or base than this abuse; 2. Be assured nothing will be more fatal.—W. Jay.

Judgment of God.—We may see a rough image of this suspension of the Divine vengeance against sin, and of the real terrors of that suspension, which only a timely repentance can avert, in the mountain torrent swollen by the melting of the winter's snow. At first a sudden fuller flow announces to the inhabitants of the valley that the thaw has commenced. But the increasing of the waters suddenly ceases, not to the contentment, but to the alarm of the inhabitants of the valley below. It inspires their fears and arouses their energies. Instantly they sally out with axe and hook and cord. Mark how eagerly they climb the rugged slippery hill. They know that the present quietude of the torrent tells of future disaster. It is a plain indication to them that some tree has floated down the current, and by the whirling of the waters in the narrow channel has been forced athwart the stream; that there is being rapidly constructed a natural dam, behind which the flood will gather, and seethe, and swell, and rage, with ever-increasing fury, until it carries all before it, and bursts with devastating volume and force on the farms and fields, below, and the purpose of those men who are hastening upwards is to let out the flood before it has assumed these dangerous proportions. In like manner the guilty and impenitent have as little reason to be at ease, "because sentence against an evil work is not executed speedily."—R. A. Bertram.

12, 13. (12) **prolonged,** with a Divine patience and long-suffering that may seem to be inexplicable. **which fear before him,**[a] not mere repetition but as it were, "when I say 'God-fearing' I mean those that do fear God in reality as well as name." (13) **a shadow,**[b] where there is but a brief sunsetting, the shadows pass very swiftly. **feareth .. God,** the underlying teaching of this book is that it is every way better, for this life, to fear and serve God. "Honorable age is not that which standeth in length of time nor that which is measured by the number of years." See ch. xii. 13.

Five fears (vs. 12).—There is—I. The fear caused by an awakening conscience. II. The fear of anxiety. III. A fear which works caution. IV. The fear of jealousy. V. The fear which is felt when we have had Divine manifestations.—Spurgeon.

Thy loving kindness.—

Not always the path is easy;
 There are thickets hung with gloom,
There are rough and stony places,
 Where never the roses bloom.
But oft when the way is hardest,
 I am conscious of One at my side,
Whose hands and whose feet are wounded,
 And I'm happy and safe with my Guide.

Beter than friends and kindred,
 Better than love and rest,
Dearer than hope and triumph,
 Is the name I wear on my breast.
I feel my way through the shadows,
 With a confident heart and brave,
I shall live in the light beyond them,
 I shall conquer death and the grave.

Often when tried and tempted,
 Often, ashamed of sin,
That, strong as an armed invader,
 Has made wreck of the peace within,
That wonderful loving kindness,
 Patient and full and free,
Has stooped for my consolation,
 Has brought a blessing to me.

distance, or perhaps so uncertain, that, though he has some doubtful misgivings of the future, yet he hopes, in the main, that his fears are greater than his danger." — Sterne.

[a] Ps. xxxvii. 11, 18—20; Is. iii. 10, 11.

[b] Job xiv. 2; Ps. cii. 11, cix. 23.

"When the Orientals wish to pay you a very high compliment, they say, 'May your shadow never decline,' or incline rather, it should be. That is—'May you live for ever;' for if the shadow does not incline, life must continue." — Gadsby.

"Bear up, bear on, the end shall tell
The dear Lord ordereth all things well!"
—J. G. Whittier.

"In vain do they talk of happiness who never subdued an impulse in obedience to a principle. He who never sacrificed a present to a future good, or a personal to a general one, can speak of happiness only as the blind do of colors." — Horace Mann.

"The mind naturally makes progress, and the will naturally clings to objects; so that for want of right objects it will attach itself to wrong ones." — Pascal.

Therefore my lips shall praise thee,
  Therefore, let come what may,
To the height of a solemn gladness
  My song shall arise to-day.
Not on the drooping willow,
  Shall I hang my harp in the land,
When the Lord himself has cheered me,
  By the touch of his piercèd hand.
—Margaret E. Sangster.

c Ps. lxxiii. 14.

"Since the unequal distribution of human destiny points to the future character of all earthly occurrences and conditions, we must so much the more enjoy present happiness, and profit by it with a contented mind."—O. Zockler.

"The equality of result for the evil and just is only an external and partial one. To those whom God loves everything must be for the best, and the final issue separates the evil from the good." — Hengstenberg.

I believe:—
Because my brother said
That since the fowls are fed,
Who sow not, neither reap;
And since when lilies sleep
And toil not, neither spin,
They wake apparelled in
Far finer robes than kings:
It must be each day brings
From God, who takes such heed,
All which his children need."
—Helen Hunt Jackson.

14, 15. (14)[c] **just .. wicked,**[c] a modern writer, we feel, would have pruned, condensed, and avoided such a repetition of himself. We are dealing, however, with "Thoughts" like Pascal's Pensées, rather than with a treatise, jotted down, it may be, day by day, as has been said before, on his tablets or his papyrus, and there is, as has been said before, something significant in the fact that, wherever the thinker turns, the same anomalies stare him in the face.—Cam. Bib. (15) **mirth,** or a bright and cheerful enjoyment of present things. "He would have us cheerfully to enjoy what God has given us in the world, to be content with it, and to make the best of it." **abide with him,** a man may keep a cheerful disposition under all changes of outward circumstances.

A misunderstood providence and a mistaken judgment.—I. The misunderstood providence. 1. The providence is undeniable. 2. It is inevitable. 3. It is mysterious. 4. It is symbolic. 5. It is misunderstood. II. The mistaken judgment. 1. The judgment is wrong. 2. The reason is doubtful. Learn: 1. To trust God even in the darkest and most mysterious providence. 2. To rejoice in God rather than in any of his creatures.—Whitelaw.

Facetiousness.—Such facetiousness is not absolutely unreasonable or unlawful which ministereth harmless divertisement and delight to conversation (harmless, I say,—that is, not intrenching upon piety, not infringing charity or justice, not disturbing peace). For Christianity is not so tetrical, so harsh, so envious, as to bar us continually from innocent, much less from wholesome and useful pleasure, such as human life doth need or require. And if jocular discourse may serve to good purposes of this kind; if it may be apt to raise our drooping spirits, to allay our irksome cares, to whet our blunted industry, to recreate our minds, being tired and cloyed with graver occupations; if it may breed alacrity, or maintain good-humor among us; if it may conduce to sweeten conversation and endear society, then it is not inconvenient or unprofitable. If for those ends we may use other recreations, employing on them our ears and eyes, our hands and feet, our other instruments of sense and motion; why may we not as well to them accommodate our organs of speech and interior sense? Why should those games which excite our wits and fancies be less reasonable than those whereby our grosser parts and faculties are exercised? Yea, why are not those more reasonable, since they are performed in a manly way, and have in them a smack of reason; seeing also they may be so managed, as not only to divert and please, but to improve and profit the mind, rousing and quickening it, yea, sometimes enlightening and instructing it, by good sense conveyed in jocular expression?—J. Barrows.

All's well.—

The year's at the spring
And day's at the morn;
Morning's at seven;
The hillside's dew-pearled;
The lark's on the wing;
The snail's on the thorn;
God's in his heaven—
All's right with the world!
—Browning.

a Ps. cxlvii. 5; Ro. xi. 33.

"There is no fuller statement in Ecc. of the incapacity of every man with his finite understanding to comprehend the plans and operations of the Infinite and Eternal God."—Spk. Com.

16, 17. (16) **business,** with special reference to the anxious search of men after happiness, and after the perfect knowledge. **seeth sleep,** or enjoyeth sleep. Extreme anxiety and care will prevent sleep. The preacher prob. gives his own personal experience. (17) **cannot find out,**[a] so as to explain all the irregularities and mysteries. "From it [the knowledge of our ignorance] we may learn with what temper of mind a man ought to inquire into the subject of religion, namely, with what expectation of finding difficulties, and with a disposition to take up and rest satisfied with any evidence whatever which is real. A man should beforehand expect things mysterious, and such as he will not be able thoroughly to comprehend or go to the bottom of."—Bp. Butler. "Our ignorance is the proper answer to many things wh. are called objections against religion."

"Wait, nor against the half-learned lesson fret, Nor chide at old belief as if it erred, Because thou canst not reconcile as yet The worker and the word."—Jean Ingelow.

Lessons from verses 16, 17.—I. The fact that the thoughtful man is baffled in his endeavor to comprehend God's ways, and to comprehend human life and destiny. II. This is just what is to be expected from a consideration of (1) man's finite nature, and (2) God's infinite wisdom. III. The profitableness of this arrangement. 1. It tends to raise our thought of God to a juster elevation. 2. It calls forth (1) humility, (2) submission, and (3) faith. 3. It makes the future infinitely interesting and attractive. What we know not here we shall know hereafter. Now we know as in a mirror, dimly; then, face to face.

God is good.—

Thou who sendest sun and rain,
Thou who sendest bliss and pain,
Good with bounteous hand bestowing,
Evil, for thy will allowing,—
Though thy ways we cannot see,
All is just that comes from thee.—Bayard Taylor.

CHAPTER THE NINTH.

1—3. (1) **in the hand of God, i.** e. they are wholly dependent on Him, they are not able to control, and shape as they please, their own life. **no man knoweth,** etc., R. V., "whether it be love or hatred, man knoweth it not; all is before them." **love or hatred,**[a] i. e. as things are, no man knows by the outward events of his life whether he is the object of God's favor or displeasure. **all .. before them,** i. e. all that shall happen, all that shall shape their destiny in the future, is obscure and unknown, and beyond their control. (2) **All .. alike to all,** this is only superficially true. It is only true of the common earthly conditions. (3) **heart .. evil,**[b] the pessimism of the thinker returns once more upon him, and he falls into the strain which we have heard before in chs. ii. 14—16, iii. 19, v. 15, vi. 12. The great leveller comes and sweeps away all distinctions, and there is no assured hope of immortality. Life is "evil" even while it lasts, and death is the same for all, when the curtain drops on the great drama.—Cam. B.

a "Hatred in Scrip. is not always to be understood rigorously. It frequently signifies no more than a lesser degree of love."— Cruden.

b "Men incline to say, 'If it must be a short life, then let it be a merry one.' So they say when no light of the life to come shines upon the life that now is."—R. Tuck. Ecc. viii. 11.

A prayer.—

Dear Lord, if mine shall be a hidden way,
  To toil unseen, unknown, my lot,
For grace to crave not men's applause I pray;
  To work, to watch, to trust, to doubt thee not.
    Thy promise, Lord, fulfil to me;
    "My grace shall still suffice for thee."

Dear Lord, if mine shall be an honored place,
  If I shall stand in public view,
Still greater, then, my need of thy free grace
  To keep me humble, Lord, and ever true.
    Fulfil thy promise, then, to me;
    "My grace shall still suffice for thee."

Dear Lord, wherever thou shalt lead the way,
  To service far, or service near,

"A characteristic of the first disciples was that they promptly obeyed the Master's call. It will be a good year for any one who, hearing Christ's invitation to yet nobler, richer, and more beautiful life, will rise at once and go after him."—Anon.

I pray for grace to follow day by day,—
To follow trusting, and forgetting fear.
Thy promise, Lord, fulfil to me;
"My grace shall still suffice for thee."
—E. C. Anderson.

c Is. xxxviii. 18, 19; Comp. Ps. vi. 5, xxx. 9, lxxxviii 11, cxv. 17; Ecc. ix. 10.

d 1 Sa. xxiv. 14.

e Pr. xxx. 30.

"The meanest beggar alive has that comfort of this world, and does that service to it which the greatest prince, when he is dead, is utterly incapable of."—Mat. Henry.

f Job xiv. 10—14.

g Wordsworth thinks that Sol. here adopts the language of the worldly libertine. "If this is thy estimate of human destiny, and if thou wilt confine thy view to the perishable things of this life, then take up with the language of those who say, 'Let us eat and drink, for to-morrow we die.'"

a Ge. xxvii. 25; Ps. civ. 15.

b The constant fellowship of one kindred spirit is an important element in the enjoyment of the earthly life.

c Wordsworth, following Hengstenberg and Ewald, gives a singular turn to this passage, "Let might be right with thee. Care nothing for God or man, but use thy strength according to thy will." He regards the counsel as addressed to worldly politicians.

d "Harvest days are busy days. And we must make hay while the sun shines."—Mat. Henry.

4—6. (4) **joined .. living,** i. e. who still lives on the earth. Dread of death as the ending of the earthly life is expressed even by O. T. saints.[c] **dog,** in O. T. a metaphor of the vilest persons.[d] **lion,** regarded as the noblest of the animals.[e] The vilest and meanest creature possessed of life is better than the highest and mightiest which has succumbed to death. (5) **know .. die,** and while this may distress, it also gives opportunity for amendment, and impulse to goodness. **a reward,** of even living long in the memories of those who knew them. The dead are soon forgotten. (6) **perished,** ended and done. It was all earthly, and from earth they have passed. **under the sun,** the writer confines his attention to the connections of the dead with this world, he tells nothing of their future state.[f] The thought of the state of the dead stands on nearly the same level as that of the elegy of Hezekiah (Is. xxxviii. 9-20).

Life is everything.—I. An earnest student is better than a dead weight of learning. II. An awakened conscience is better than unconsecrated genius. III. One living soul is better than a stagnant Church. IV. One living Church is better than a large community that has lost its spiritual energy.—Clarkson.

7, 8. (7) **Go,** etc.,[g] in this passage the writer renews the advice of ch. viii. 15. Cheerfully and contentedly accept your present lot and get as much good as you can out of it. **wine,** used as a symbol and producer of joy.[a] **accepteth thy works,** the works are the eating and drinking just mentioned. By the constitution of man's nature, and by the ordering of Providence, such capacity of enjoyment is allowable, and there need be no scruple in using it.—Pul. Com. (8) **always white,** the kind of garments suitable to joyousness and festivity. **no ointment,** oil and perfumes were used on festive occasions not only among Eastern nations, but by Greeks and Romans; in time of distress or grief the anointing of the body was neglected.

Customs of modern Arabs.—The customs of the Arabs in almost every detail have remained unchanged. Thus in dress, nomadic habits, goods, the anointing with oil, they retain the habits and formalities of the distant past, and the present is but the exact picture of those periods which are historically recorded in the Old Testament. "Let thy garments be always white, and let thy head lack no ointment."—Sir S. Baker.

9, 10. (9) **the wife,** thy one wife.[b] A possible commendation of the advantages of monogamy over polygamy. **for that,** etc., reverting to his idea that the enjoyment of life is all that is now possible to man. (10) **with thy might,**[c] i. e. earnestly: put all your heart into it.[d] "In accordance with what has been already said, and to combat the idea that, as man cannot control his fate, he should take no pains to work his work, but fold his hands in resigned inaction, Koheleth urges him not to despair, but to do his part manfully as long as life is given, and with all the energies of his soul carry out the purpose of his being." **no work,** comp. Jno. ix. 4. **device,** or plan. Comp. the Christian view of the grave, now that "life and immortality have been brought to light."

Words to a worker.—I. The worker described: man. 1. Furnished with capacities for work. 2. Located in a sphere of work. 3. Appointed to the destiny of work. 4. Impelled by a desire of work. II. The worker counselled: 1. To do the duty that lies nearest. 2. To do every duty with energy. 3. To do each duty from an impulse of individual responsibility. 4. To do all duties under a sense of the value of time.—Whitelaw.

Christian workers of the past.—Adam Clarke.—Dr. Adam Clarke said that "the old proverb about having too many irons in the fire is an abominable lie. Have all in it—shovel, tongs, and poker!" It is not so much the multiplicity of employments as the want of system in them that distracts and injures both the work and the workman.—Wesley.—Wesley said, "I am always in haste, but never in a hurry; leisure and I have long taken leave of each other." He traveled about 5,000 miles in a year;

preached about three times a day, commencing at five o'clock in the morning, and his published works amounted to about 200 volumes.—Asbury and Coke.—Asbury traveled 6,000 miles a year, and preached incessantly. Coke crossed the Atlantic eighteen times, preached, wrote, traveled, established missions, begged from door to door for them, and labored in all respects as if, like the Apostles, he would "turn the world upside down." At near seventy years of age he started to Christianize India!—Luther.—It is said that Luther preached almost daily; he lectured constantly as a professor; he was burdened with the care of all the churches; his correspondence, even as now extant, fills many volumes; he was perpetually harassed with controversies, and was one of the most voluminous writers of his day.—Calvin.—The same, and even more, may be said of Calvin. While in Strasburg he preached or lectured every day. In Geneva he was pastor, professor, and almost magistrate. He lectured every other day; on alternate weeks he preached daily; he was overwhelmed with letters from all parts of Europe, and was the author of works numerous and bulky, that any man of our day would think more than enough to occupy his whole undivided time. And all this, too, in the midst of perpetual infirmity of the flesh.

Help that comes too late.—

Ah! woe for the word that is never said
  Till the ear is deaf to hear,
And woe for the lack to the fainting head
  Of the ringing shout of cheer.
Ah! woe for the laggard feet that tread
  In the mournful wake of the bier.

For baffling most in this dreary world,
  With its tangles great and small,
Its lonesome nights and its weary days,
  And its struggles forlorn with fate,
Is that bitterest grief, too deep for tears,
  Of the help that comes too late.
—Margaret E. Sangster.

11, 12. (11) **race,** etc.,[a] he is still looking gloomily at life. Now he suggests that there is no certain advantage to the diligent and the earnest. Even when working "with our might" we must cherish the feeling that the results of our work are uncertain. **chance,** all human purposes are liable to be changed or controlled by circumstances beyond man's power, and incapable of explanation. A hand higher than man's disposes events, and success is conditioned by superior laws which work unexpected results. (12) **snared,** etc., men are suddenly overtaken by calamity, which they are totally unable to foresee or provide against.

Death inevitable and often sudden (vs. 12).—I. The time of every man's death is uncertain to him. II. Death often approaches men in a secret, unsuspected manner. III. When the snares of death fall on the sons of men there is no way of escape. IV. Death is often sudden. 1. Without previous warning; 2. No time for preparation; 3. Little reliance to be placed on death-bed repentance. V. The snares of death fall on some in an evil time. 1. To such as are immersed in the snares of the world; 2. To those who are engaged in the pleasures of the world; 3. To all who are unprepared.—Lathrop.

One thing to all.—If one thing happens to all in the journey of life, what advantage have the good? Much every way, and specifically thus:—The hardness which disciples experience in following the Lord is righteousness rubbing on the remaining lusts, and so wasting their deformities away; whereas the hardness of a transgressor's way is the carnal mind, in its impotent enmity, dashing itself against the bosses of the Almighty's buckler. The one is a strainer, made strait to purge the impurities away, through which the purified emerges into peace; the other is the vengeance which belongeth unto God, beginning even here to repay."—Arnot.

13—15. (13) **This wisdom,** or this illustration of wisdom. Wisdom

"A man is relieved and gay when he has put his heart into his work, and done his best; but what he has said or done otherwise, shall give him no peace."—R. W. Emerson.

"It is our best work that He wants, not the dregs of our exhaustion."—Geo. MacDonald.

"The soul's play-day is Satan's work-day: the idler the man the busier the tempter."—South.

"Jesus, Master,
  whom I serve,
Though so feebly
  and so ill,
Strengthen hand,
  and heart, and
  nerve,
All thy bidding
  to fulfil;
Open thou mine
  eyes to see
All the work
  thou hast for
  me."
—Frances R. Havergal.

a "Human actions are regarded as in this world dependent entirely on Div. fate, and their success, therefore, is too often in no comparison with the real ability and strength of the actor."—O. Zockler.

"He that by a constant holiness secures the present, and makes it useful to his noblest purposes, turns his condition into his best advantage by making his unavoidable fate become his necessary religion."—Jeremy Taylor.

"Not because I raise myself above something, but because I raise myself to something, do I approve myself."—Jacobi.

of this kind. (14) **little city,** etc., comp. 2 Sa. xx. 16—22. This account is a parable rather than a historical incident.[b] **bulwarks,** military works, mounds, etc., such as besiegers raise. (15) **he .. delivered,** etc., so it seems that wisdom can, in part, avail against evil destiny. **remembered,** "as soon as the exigency which brought him forward was past, the poor man fell back into his insignificance, and was thought of no more; he gained no personal advantage by his wisdom; his ungrateful countrymen forgot his very existence."

The saviour of the city (vs. 14).—I. I shall make some observations on this ideal poor wise man. 1. Although he had known he had been unhonored, it was still his duty to save the city; 2. The same wisdom which enabled him to save a city would enable him to bear ingratitude; 3. No doubt this neglect was the best thing for the poor wise man—very often the load of honor turns men's brains. Am I addressing any poor wise man who has saved a city? Do I address any poor man who thinks he could save a city as well as anybody, if he were in his proper place? II. I shall adduce a case in point,—the great example of the unappreciated poor wise man—Jesus of Nazareth. 1. Like the poor man in the text, He was a public benefactor; 2. He was wise; 3. The one barrier to His popularity was His poverty; 4. His poverty was no barrier to usefulness—nay, it contributed to His usefulness.—Stems and Twigs.

Men who saved cities.—It is not unlikely that in these words Solomon referred to some real historical fact, for such a fact is recorded in more than one instance. Archimedes, by his extraordinary wisdom, saved the city of Syracuse, when besieged by the Romans. He did this, not by fighting, nor by teaching others to fight; he acted not as a soldier, but as a philosopher—constructing machines and burning lenses, which destroyed the Roman ships as they approached the walls of the city. It is true the city was taken, yet not by the Roman forces, but by the treachery of one who betrayed it. Nor was Archimedes either rewarded or even spared on account of his skill, but was cruelly murdered while in the act of working out a new problem for the further safety of the city. There is also a story of Anaximenes, who met Alexander when he was marching to destroy Lampsacus. Alexander, suspecting that Anaximenes was coming to intercede for the safety of the city, immediately resolved to frustrate his purpose by taking an oath that he would not grant him anything that he should ask. Then said Anaximenes, "I request that you will destroy this city." Alexander was thus outwitted, but he respected his oath, and the city was spared. Thus it was the wisdom of one man which, by suddenly taking advantage of Alexander's oath, saved a noble city from destruction. In like manner, when Alexander was marching against Jerusalem, he was met by Jaddua, the high-priest, whose wise policy subdued the vengeful determination of Alexander, won his favor, and caused the city to be saved from destruction. Solomon could not, of course, have one of these instances in view, because he lived long before they occurred; but he might have others in view equally true. His design was to show that in this life virtue and wisdom may perform the most important services, and yet often be unrewarded.—W. Cooke.

16—18. (16) **Wisdom,** or mental energy, and skill. **strength,** or mere material, brute force. **despised,** and this he puts among the strange things that perplex him in the affairs of this world.[a] The power of the purse too often prevails against the wisdom of the poor. (17) **in quiet,** the thought is like that of the "great cry and little wool" of the English proverb. That which tells on men, in the long run, is the wisdom whose words are wary, and calm, and few, not the declamation of the wind-bags of popular oratory. (18) **one .. good,** the sinner here is "one of those coarse miscreants or fools, who can command physical strength, but are destitute of wisdom."—Zöckler.

Power of evil example.—We may estimate the serious and lamentable mischief of an evil life if we think that a godless man may be injuring his neighbors: 1. By weakening or undermining their faith; causing them to lose their hold on Divine truth, and thus sinking into the miseries of doubt or into the darkness and despair of utter unbelief. 2. By undoing the integrity of the upright; leading them into the fatal

[b] "The Chaldee Targum explains this passage as an allegory: 'The city is the human body, the great king is an evil desire, the poor man a good disposition.' But this is wholly unnecessary." —Spk. Com.

"I would advise all in general, that they would take into serious consideration the true and genuine ends of knowledge; that they seek it not either for pleasure, or contention, or contempt of others, or for profit, or fame, or for honor and promotion, or such-like adulterate or inferior ends; but for merit and emolument of life, that they may regulate and perfect the same in charity."—Bacon.

[a] Knowledge is that information which the mind receives either by its own experience or by the testimony of others. The beneficial use of knowledge is wisdom. That portion of knowledge, the truth of which can be demonstrated, is science." —Maunder.

[a] "Wisdom, however splendid, if in lowly state, is so obscured by the cloud of poverty that in a brief time it has all eyes averted, and utterly fails from the memory." —Cartwright.

"The ambition of one man may plunge nations into deadly warfare. The heresies of one man may divide the Church, weaken her influence, and provoke the rage of an irritating controversy." —Hom. Com.

morass of an immoral life. 3. By cooling, or even killing, the consecration of the zealous; causing them to slacken their speed or even to leave the field of noble service. One man, by his own evil example, by his words of folly and falsity, by his deeds of wrong, may enfeeble many minds, may despoil many hearts, may misguide many souls, may blight and darken many lives.—Clarkson.

[b] "The thought wh. underlies the whole ch. is the advantage of that wisdom wh. includes piety and patience, as practical guidance through all the perplexities of life." — Spk. Com.

CHAPTER THE TENTH.

1. "This ch. consists entirely of rhythmical sentences, giving advice, more or less, as to conduct."[b] **Dead flies,**[c] Heb. flies of death. Deadly poisonous insects, which, finding their way into a vase of precious ointment, would turn its fragrance into a fœtid odor. **ointment,** the word intimates valuable and delicate perfume. **apothecary,** perfumer. Dealer in spices. **little folly,** R. V., "so doth a little folly outweigh wisdom and honor." "It is a painful fact that a little folly, one foolish act, one silly peculiarity of manner or disposition, will suffice to impair the real value of a man's wisdom and the estimation in which he was held. The little element of foolishness, like the little insect in the ointment, obscures the real excellence of the man, and deprives him of the honor that is really his due. And in religion we know that one fault unchecked, one secret sin cherished, poisons the whole character, makes a man lose the grace of God."—Pul. Com.

A little evil spoils much good (vs. 1).—I. We will take two or three illustrations of the passage before us. It is true, as a general principle and rule, that a little evil will counterbalance much good. History shows this. The distinguishing sins and follies of individual nations and men: Benvenuto Cellini—passion; Bacon—avarice. II. Account for what we have thus illustrated. 1. The presence of folly in the midst of wisdom and honor—traceable to a sinful nature, to onesidedness of culture, to overlooking of little things, to malice of the enemy, to worldly opposition; 2. The power of a little folly in marring reputation for wisdom. Because there is so much folly in the world. Men are apt to point at the folly of others. Men form their judgment of others by little things.

[c] "The swarms of flies in the E. very soon corrupt and destroy any moist unguent or mixture wh. is not carefully covered fr. them, and pollute a dish of food in a few minutes."—Tristram.

"A certain grace and attractiveness of behavior is necessary to give full effect and influence to the finest assemblage of virtues. In addition to the greatest excellencies, we must have 'whatsoever things are lovely.'" — Leale.

A white garment appears worse with slight soiling than do colored garments much soiled; so a little fault in a good man attracts more attention than great offences in bad men.

"A single worm killed that tree."—During the summer of 1853 (writes a gentleman) I was an invalid, and was induced, on the recommendation of my physician, to go to the Hydropathic Establishment at Sudbrook Park, near Richmond, in Surrey. During my sojourn there, I was one day walking through the romantic grounds and park with some friends and the proprietor, Dr. Ellis, when the doctor drew our attention to a large sycamore tree, decayed to the core. "That fine tree," said he, "was killed by a single worm." In answer to our inquiries, we found that about two years previously the tree was as healthy as any in the park, when a wood-worm, about three inches long, was observed to be forcing its way under the bark of the trunk. It caught the eye of a naturalist who was staying at the establishment, and he remarked, "Let that worm alone, doctor, and it will kill the tree." This seemed very improbable, but it was agreed that the black-headed worm should not be disturbed. After a time it was found that the worm had tunnelled its way a considerable distance under the bark. The next summer the leaves of the tree dropped off very early, and in the succeeding year it was a dead, rotten thing, and the hole made by the worm might be seen in the very heart of the once noble trunk. "Ah," said one who was present, "let us learn a lesson from that dead tree. How many, who once promised fair for usefulness in the world and the church, have been ruined by a single sin!"

2—4. (2) **right hand,** this gnome is based on the fact that the right hand is more expert than the left.[a] **at his left,** not having right self-control, he goes about things as awkwardly as a left-handed man.[b] (3) **walketh .. way,** comes out into public view and relations. In all his

[a] "The wise man goes about his business with dexterity, turns his hand readily to it, and goes through it with despatch." —Mat. Henry.

[b] "A wise man's sense is in its place ready to help and protect him; but a fool's is missing when it is wanted, and so is useless."—Rosenmuller.

intercourse. **saith .. fool,** exposing his folly in his speech and acts. (4) **against thee,** in anger. **leave .. place,** in thine anger against him. **yielding,** the spirit of patience often wins the victory, calming down anger.

"He is arrogant as well as ignorant; he despises the wise, and thinks them fools; and is not conscious that he is a fool, but thinks himself wise." —Wordsworth.

The pacifying power of patient submission.—"Yielding pacifieth [allayeth] great offences." It is not required that the injured party should approve the action of his injurer; or affirmed that no opportunity may occur of just and dignified rebuke. But silence, quietness of spirit, and control of natural impulse, will in many cases produce a good result. He who bears wrong patiently is the stronger and better for the discipline; and his demeanor may melt the wrong-doer to contrition, and will at all events lead him to reflection. Thus the threatened conflict may be avoided; a lesson may be administered to the hasty and arrogant, and the best interests of society may be promoted. Thus the Word of God is honored, and witness is given to the power which Christ possesses to subdue and govern the unruly nature of man.—Thomson.

5—7. (5) **error .. from the ruler,** the last word serves as a link connecting this verse with the preceding. It might be wise to bow to the temper of a despotic ruler, but the ruler was not always right. What the Debater had seen was to him a blot upon the government of him who allowed it.—Cam. B. (6) **Folly .. dignity,** through the favoritism of the ruler, wh. blinds him to the unfitness of the persons he raises to high places.[a] **rich,** in wisdom rather than in wealth. The noble and distinguished. (7) **upon horses,** so put out of their proper place by the caprice of the king.[b] **princes walking as servants,** eminent and virtuous men degraded.

[a] One of the most frequent weaknesses of kings is the injudicious selection of high officials.

[b] Pr. xxx. 21, 22.

"When a fool is set in dignity, it is as when a handful of hay is set up to give light, which with smoke and smell offendeth all that are near it."—Jermin.

Favorites.—In Oriental courts, where "the eunuch and the barber held the reins of power," men of no reputation or character had a chance of promotion. And even in Western courts and more modern times the same kind of evil has been only too common, as the history of the reigns of Edward II. and James I. of England, and of Louis XI. and Henry III. of France, abundantly proves. The reason for making favorites of low-born and unprincipled adventurers is not far to seek; they have ever been ready tools for accomplishing the designs of unscrupulous princes, for doing services from which men who valued their station and reputation in society would shrink.—J. Willcock.

8—10. (8) **diggeth,** etc.,[c] he digs a pit that his enemy may fall into it, and he falls into it himself. Plots and conspiracies are as often fatal to the conspirators as to the intended victims. The literature of all nations is full of like sayings, among which that of the engineer "hoist with his own petard" is perhaps the most familiar. **shall fall,** not absolutely shall, but it is likely that he will. **breaketh,** etc., the hedge is rather the wall of stones and plaster usually built round a vineyard: in the crevices serpents are wont to nestle.[d] Pulling down a wall may refer metaphorically to the removal of evil institutions in a state, wh. involves the reformer in many perils. (9) **hurt,** is in danger of being hurt by their falling on him. (10) **whet,** or sharpen. If we apply the whole verse to the case of disaffection with the government or open rebellion, the caution given would signify—See that your means are adequate to the end, that your resources are sufficient to conduct your enterprise to success.

[c] Esth. vii. 10: Ps. vii. 15; Pr. xxvi. 27.

[d] Isa. xxxiv. 13; Am. v. 19.

"The breaking of this hedge appears clearly as an action by which one seeks to injure his neighbor." — O. Zockler.

The workman and his tools.—Consider—I. The work we have to do. Trees to fell. Ignorance, bad habits, social drawbacks, natural disqualifications to overcome. These are trees of hard wood. II. The tools we have to use. We have axes to use: mind, memory, resolution, heart, conscience. These we have about us. There are others also, as books, schools, etc. III. How to use them. Three ways:—1. When the axe gets blunt, whet it. Exercise thought, memory, feeling, etc.; study books, obey teachers, etc. 2. Otherwise put on more strength. If we have not wherewith to whet the iron, we must be more diligent with such means as we have. 3. The best way. Whet the iron, and put on strength as well. To do this, seek wisdom profitable to direct: God gives it; we all need it; all may have it. Hint:—(1) Seek wisdom; (2) Use wisdom.—Hive.

"The man who sets himself to pull down or to alter the fabric of the constitution of a country, undertakes a work of no light or trifling difficulty, and a work always of hazard to himself, and very often of fearfully doubtful benefit to others. It is a vast deal easier to find fault than to mend; to complain of what is wrong, than to substitute what is right." — Wardlaw.

Verses 8—11.—Various proverbs expressing the benefit of prudence and caution, and the danger of folly. The connection with what has preceded is not closely marked, but is probably to be found in the bearing of the maxims on the conduct of the wise man who has incurred the resentment of a ruler, and might be inclined to disaffection and revolt. They are intentionally obscure and capable of a double sense—a necessary precaution if the writer lived under Persian despots.—Pul. Com.

11—13. (11) **without enchantment,** R. V., "If the serpent bite before it be charmed, then is there no advantage in the charmer." "As one may escape the serpent by charms, so one may escape the sting of a calumniator by discretion." **babbler,** lit. "Master of the tongue."[a] (12) **gracious,** full of kindliness and grace: doing good to those who hear him. **swallow up,**[b] this is a stronger expression than "ruin" or "destroy." Speaking without due forethought, he compromises himself, says what he has shamefully to withdraw, and brings punishment on his own head. (13) **beginning,** etc., his foolish talk tends to become worse than foolish.

Serpent charmers.—In the East there have always been persons who, by means of music and legerdemain, exert great influence over some species of serpents, so that whilst under their spell the deadly cobra may be handled, as if he were utterly harmless. But if the charmer tread on the snake unawares, or be bitten when off his guard, he will be poisoned like another man. And to certain minds there has been given an ascendancy over other minds, like the influence of the serpent charmer. Sagacious and eloquent, they are able to soothe the fury of fierce tempers, and mould rancorous natures to their will. Like David's transforming harp, as the strain advances, it looks as if a new possession had entered the exorcised frame, and a seraph smiled out at those windows where a demon was frowning before. But alas for the harper, if Saul should snatch the javelin before David has time to touch the strings; Alas for the wise charmer, and also for the good cause, if the tyrant's passion towers up, or the decree of the despot goes forth before a friendly counsellor has time to interfere.—J. Hamilton.

14, 15. (14) **full of words,**[c] R. V., "multiplieth words." He talks very freely about things of which he knows nothing. (15) **wearieth,** bec. he does not conduct his business with wisdom and skill. Intelligence lightens labor. **knoweth .. city,** i. e. they have not the capacity to apprehend the plainest thing, such as the entrance into a great city. The words probably imply a reminiscence of a childhood not far from Jerusalem as the city of which the proverb spoke. Isaiah's description of the road to the restored Jerusalem as being such that "the wayfaring men, though fools, shall not err therein" (Isai. xxxv. 8) supplies an interesting parallel.

Full of words.—Dr. Oliver Wendell Holmes, in the course of an interesting article on the photographic art, delivers himself of the following astounding paragraph: "Then we replace the slide in the shield, draw this out of the camera, and carry it back into the shadowy realm where Cocytus flows in black nitrate of silver, and Acheron stagnates in the pool of hyposulphite, and invisible ghosts, trooping down from the world of day, cross a Styx of dissolved sulphate of iron, and appear before the Rhadamanthus of that lurid Hades!"—Some years ago, a physician, while in his patient's room, thus addressed a surgeon: "You must not fail to phlebotomise the old gentleman to-morrow!" "I will never suffer it," cried the sick man, in a fright. "Sir, don't be alarmed," replied the surgeon, "the doctor only orders you to be bled." "O, as for the bleeding," replied the venerable patient, "it matters little; but as for the other, I would sooner die than endure it." Who will dare blame our aged friend for such a determination? What sane man would submit to the barbarous and excruciating operation of being phlebotomised?—Andrew Jackson was once making a stump speech in a country village out West. Just as he was concluding, Amos Kendall, who sat behind him, whispered, "Tip 'em a little Latin, General; they won't be satisfied without it." The "Hero of New Orleans" instantly thought of a few phrases he knew, and in a voice of thunder, wound up his speech by exclaiming, "E pluribus unum—sine quâ non;—ne plus ultra!—multum in parvo!" The effect was tremendous, and the shouts could be heard for miles.—Jeffers.

16, 17. (16) **a child,** young in years: but especially young in intelligence. **princes .. morning,** the kind of life condemned is the profligate

---

a "One of ready tongue, not making timely use of his gift; a hero with his tongue, but without energy and promptness in action." — O. Zockler.

"Instances are not wanting where the serpents have been deaf to the voice and music of the charmers, and fastened upon them; when death has taken place in a few minutes."—Gadsby.

b Pr. x. 32, xii. 13; Matt. xii. 36.

"There is a ridiculous disproportion between the passionate language of a fool and the insignificant causes which excite it."

c Jas. iv. 13.

"There is nothing that makes a man suspect much, more than to know little; and therefore men should remedy suspicion by procuring to know more, and not to keep their suspicions in smother."—Lord Bacon.

"The end of man is an action, and not a thought, though it were the noblest." — Thomas Carlyle.

"St. Augustine! well hast thou said
That of our vices we can frame
A ladder, if we will but tread
Beneath our feet each deed of shame!"
—Longfellow.

[a] "The peasants build very ephemeral habitations with small stones and mud, which, if deserted, soon fall and melt away like summer snow on the mountains. The roof of any of these huts, forsaken or neglected through idleness, will 'drop through' in a single winter, and then the unprotected walls wash down by the rain, and speedily become mere shapeless heaps." — Thomson.

"He who would do some great thing in this short life must apply himself to the work with such a concentration of his forces, as, to idle spectators, who live only to amuse themselves, looks like insanity." — Francis Parkman.

"He who does no good, gets none. He who cares not for others, will soon find that others will not care for him."

"Do good, cast thy bread into the water; it shall one day be repaid thee."—Arab. Proverb.

"When you give a loaf or a coin to a poor man, you do not lose it, but you sow it; for, as from one grain of seed many grains grow, so it is likewise with loaves and money." — Lapide.

luxury which begins the day with revels, instead of giving the morning hours to "sitting in the gate" and doing justice and judgment. Morning revelling was looked upon naturally as the extreme of profligacy. (17) **son of nobles,** Heb. fig. for "one of noble disposition. **in due season,** after duty is properly performed. In E. much public duty is done in the early morning.

Eating in the morning.—It is considered unmanly in Samoa to eat early in the morning. It is even the language of abuse to hint that a person does so. It is like comparing him to a pig, which is fed the first thing in the morning.—Turner.

18—20. (18) **building decayeth,** the subject is still the state. Under the image of a house which falls into ruin for lack of needful repairs, is signified the decay that surely overtakes a kingdom whose rulers are given up to indolence and debauchery, and neglect to attend to the affairs which require prompt care.—Pul. Com. **droppeth through,** the rain coming through, and breaking down, the flat roof.[a] (19) **money .. things,** Cam. B. translates: "For revelry they prepare food and wine that rejoices life, and money answereth all things," i. e. meets all they want. The words obviously point to the conduct of the luxurious and slothful princes condemned in verses 16, 18. Regardless of their duty as rulers and of the sufferings of their people, they aim only at self-indulgence and they look to money, however gained, as the means of satisfying their desires. (20) **thy thought,** bec. there is danger of even seditious thought gaining some expression, in look or attitude if not in word. **bird,** etc., a proverbial saying common to all languages.

Laziness.—Who can tell the pains which lazy people take? the muddles into which they bring themselves? They are driven to falsehood to excuse their sloth, and one lie leads on to more. Then they scheme and plot, and become dishonest. I knew one who fell out with hard work, and soon he fell in with drink and lost his position. Since then, to earn a scanty livelihood he has had to work ten times as much as was required of him in his better days, and he has hardly had a shoe to his foot. Meanwhile, a simple, plodding man has gone onward and upward, favored, as he confesses, by Providence; but, best of all, upheld by his integrity and industry; to him there has been success and happiness. He works hard, but his lot is ease itself compared with the portion of the sluggard.—Spurgeon.

CHAPTER THE ELEVENTH.

1. **Cast .. waters,** the bread in the East is made in the form of thin cakes, which would float for a time if thrown into a stream; and if it be objected that no one would be guilty of such an irrational action as flinging bread into the water, it may be answered that this is just the point aimed at. Do your kindnesses, exert yourself, in the most unlikely quarters, not thinking of gratitude or return, but only of duty. And yet surely a recompense will be made in some form or other.—Pul. Com.

Sowing.—The world seems to be a great field in which every man drops his seed, and which gives back to every man, not just the same thing which he dropped there, any more than the brown earth holds up to you in the autumn the same black berry which you hid under its bosom in the spring, but something which has its true correspondence and proportion to the seed to which it is the legitimate and natural reply. Every gift has its return, every act has its consequence, every call has its answer in this great live, alert world, where man stands central, and all things have their eyes on him and their ears open to his voice.—Phillips Brooks. Whitefield and the lantern-boy.—Whitefield often stood on the outside of the Court-house in Philadelphia, and preached to the thousands who crowded the streets below. On one of these occasions a youth pressed as near to his favorite preacher as possible, and, to testify his respect, held a lantern for his accommodation. Soon after the sermon began he became so absorbed in the subject, that the lantern fell from his hand and was dashed to pieces, and that part of the audience in the immediate vicinity of the speaker's stand was not a little discomposed by the occurrence. Some years after, Mr. Whitefield, in the course of his fifth visit to America, about the year 1754, on a journey from the southward, called at St. George's, via Delaware, where Mr. Rodgers was then settled in the ministry, and spent some time with him. In the course of the visit, Mr. Rodgers, riding one day with his visitor in a close carriage, asked him whether he recollected the occurrence of the little boy who was so much affected with his preaching as to let the lantern fall? Whitefield answered, "Oh! yes, I remember it well, and have often thought I would give anything in my power to know who that little boy was, and what had become of him." Mr. Rodgers replied with a smile, "I am that little boy." Mr. Whitefield, with tears of joy, started from his seat, clasped him in his arms, and with strong emotion remarked that he was the fourteenth person then in the ministry whom he had discovered in the course of that visit to America, of whose conversion he had been the instrument.

2, 3. (2) **Give,** etc., i. e. do not stint your generosities, for at best you can do but little toward relieving human sorrows.[a] (3) **empty,** etc., the thought is linked to that which precedes it by the mention of the "evil coming upon the earth." In regard to that evil, the sweeping calamities that lie beyond man's control, he is as powerless as he is when the black clouds gather and the winds rush wildly. He knows only that the clouds will pour down their rain, that the tree will lie as the tempest has blown it down. **tree fall,**[b] etc., wherever the misfortune comes, if you are in the way, you will have to bear it.

Law and life (vs. 3.).—I. The key to the passage, the broad idea which underlies the whole, is in the first verse. The main point here then is, that in all husbandry there are two elements—the intelligence and energy of the man, and the co-operation of a secret force, the springs of which and the methods escape him, but on which absolutely depend all his fruits. II. The writer of this book asks us to consider how much that has the most important bearing on the results of our activity is hopelessly beyond the control of our hand. 1. The awful force and inevitable certainty of the processes of nature; 2. There is the absolutely certain sequence of physical causes and effects, or antecedents and consequents, which we call laws of nature, which vary not one hair's breadth from their ordained order in obedience to the mandates of our will, but which, by observing and mastering the principle of that order, we can use for the accomplishing of our ends; 3. The writer, while he sees this constant order, had a dark sad vision of the uncertainties which cross it. III. There being this law of calamity at work, defying all calculation and all defence, what is the true policy of life? 1. Do not be afraid of giving with a bountiful hand, lest your charity should be wasted; 2. Do not be afraid of working, lest your toil should be fruitless; 3. Do not be afraid of loving, because every love is a sure germ of pain. —J. B. Brown.

"The Dairyman's Daughter" in Turkey.—"That well-known tract The Dairyman's Daughter, written in the Isle of Wight, by the Rev. Legh Richmond, found its way to Constantinople. There it was translated into the Armenian tongue by the Rev. Dr. Goodell, an American missionary to Turkey. A copy of this version was carried to Nicomedia (or Ismid), and fell into the hands of a Vartabed, or preaching priest of the Armenian Church. He, upon perusing it, was deeply affected by the picture it presented of simple and genuine Christianity, the result of faith in Jesus and the operation of the Holy Ghost, such as he supposed to have existed only amongst the primitive Christians. Comparing the spirit and principles of this sweet story with the condition of the Armenian Church, he was led to the study of the New Testament; and the result was his own conversion by the Divine grace. He then communicated the knowledge of this wondrous tract, and his own blessed experience, to another Vartabed, with the same results in his case also. These two converted priests, expelled from their own communion, were the chief beginnings of the evangelical church now in Nicomedia.—Blackwood.

[a] "Or, you know not what reverses may befall either that person who by your liberality will be strengthened to meet them, or yourself, who may come to need grateful friends. Comp. Lu. xvi. 9."—Spk. Com.

[b] This image is not in any way connected with the state of departed souls.

"Our life is like that wax melting in the flame. Death puts his stamp on it, and then it cools, and the impress never can be changed. Or like the burning metal, running forth from the cauldron into the mold, Death cools us in that mold, and we are cast into that shape throughout eternity."—C. H. Spurgeon.

"Follow with reverent steps the great example
Of Him whose holy work was 'doing good;'
So shall the wide earth seem our Father's temple,
Each loving life a psalm of gratitude."
—Whittier.

[a] "The farmer would get on badly, who, instead of sowing and reaping, spent his time in watching the wind and clouds."—Fausset.

"If we stand thus, magnifying every little difficulty, and making the worst of it, starting objections and fancying hardship and danger where there is none, we shall never go on, much less go through with our work, nor make anything of it."—Mat. Henry.

"He whom the weather does not suit, and who is ever waiting for a more favorable season, misses finally the proper period for action." — O. Zockler.

[b] Also Job xxxi. 15; Ps. cxxxix. 13—16; Jer. i. 5.

"Work is the holiest thing in earth or heaven,
To lift from souls the sorrow and the curse;
This dear employment must to us be given
While there is want in God's great universe."
—Lucy Larcom.

4—6. (4) **observeth .. sow,** such watching the clouds would be a sign of a timid hesitancy that would ensure failure.[a] The very watching for opportunities may end in missing them. There are times when it is our wisdom to "be instant out of season" (2 Tim. iv. 2). (5) **spirit,** or wind, comp. Jno. iii. 8. **bones,** etc., Job x. 8—12.[b] **works of God,** the issues of God's will: His ways in the future. (6) **whether shall prosper,** the ignorance of men as to the results of their labor, still more the apparent or the actual failure of their earlier efforts, tempts them too often to despondency and indolence. The maxim, like that of verse 6, bids them take comfort from that very ignorance. The seed sown in the morning of life may bear its harvest at once, or not till the evening of age. The man may reap at one and the same time the fruits of his earlier and his later sowing, and may find that "both are alike good."—Cam. Bib.

I. Every day has its evening.—1. With its quiet hour for meditation—as with Isaac; 2. With its vacant hour to be filled up with some work for Jesus. II. Every life has also its evening. 1. It is clouded or bright, for the most part, as the day has been; 2. Sometimes the evening is unlike the day,—a contrast to it. III. The evening does not always commence at the same hour—short and long days,—with some the sun goes down while it is yet noon. Learn:—In secular things men live for the evening of life; let it be so in things spiritual.

Timid hesitancy.—If you stand at the door and look at the clouds you will not get your sowing done in the field. A man says he will not go to church because he may slip down on the road and hurt his foot; he will not take a railway journey because the boiler may burst or a wheel may take fire; he will not open his window in summer because an insect may crawl in. There are people in the world exactly so foolish, though at first this may appear to be simply incredible. Make any proposition to them you please, and they will tell you what difficulties surround it, and what awful possibilities are ahead of it. Such people live in circumstances, events, occurrences, and their imagination is quick on the side of perceiving dangers and losses. These are not the people who should set themselves to lead the world. This will be admitted as a philosophy, and yet, strange to say, these are the people who hinder the progress of society more than any others.—J. Parker.

Man's Life—

Man's life is but a working day
  Whose tasks are set aright:
A time to work, a time to pray,
  And then a quiet night.
And then, praise God, a quiet night,
  Where palms are green and robes are white,
A long-drawn breath, a balm for sorrow,—
  And all things lovely on the morrow.
—Christina G. Rosetti.

[a] The "light" here stands for "life," of which it is the symbol. Comp. Job iii. 20; Ps. xxxvi. 9, xlix. 19, lvi. 13.

[b] Regarded as the dark prison beneath the earth.

"While the sun of earthly prospects shines, we are apt to feel the day of evil at a distance from our minds; we are reluctant to admit the possibility of a

7, 8. (7) **the light,**[a] of life; wh. the young are especially able to enjoy. **behold the sun,** Ps. lviii. 8; Jno. xi. 9. (8) **days of darkness,** these are clearly not the days of sorrow or adversity (though the phase as such might admit that meaning), but those of the darkness which is contrasted with the light of the sun, with the light of life, the land that lies behind the veil, in the unseen world of Hades or of Sheol,[b] the darkness of the valley of the shadow of death.—Cam. Bib. **All that cometh is vanity,** all that comes after this life is ended, the great future, is nothingness; shadow, not substance; a state from which is absent all that made life, and over which we have no control.

The Christian aspect of the subject.—We know that this life will soon be over, may reach its terminus any day, and must come to its conclusion before many years have gone. What shall we be concerned about in this? 1. Not the hour or act of dying. Common human fortitude will carry us through that experience, as it has done in countless millions of cases already; much more will Christian faith and hope. 2. Not the silence and darkness of the grave. What does it signify to us that our mortal body will lie long in the grave, when we are hoping to be "clothed upon with our house which is from heaven?" 3. The long future of heavenly life. Not the many days of darkness, but the long, the everlasting day of glory is before us who believe in Christ, and who hope to dwell with him for ever. For that endless day of blessedness the life we are now living is not only the preliminary but the preparation. Therefore let every day, every hour, be sacred; be so spent in faith, in love, in holy labor, in ennobling joy, that the future will be but the continuance of the present—the continuance, but also the enlargement, the glorification. Thus shall there not fall upon the life that now is the shadow of the tomb; there shall shine upon it some beams from the glory that is beyond.—Clarkson.

A cloudless sky.—When in Madeira, I rose early one morning, hoping to reach the summit of a certain mountain, to gaze upon a magnificent scene, and enjoy the balmy air. I had a servant with me, and we had got up some two thousand feet, when a thick mist was seen descending upon us, quite obscuring the whole face of the heavens, and I thought we had no chance left but at once to retrace our steps. But as the cloud came nearer, my guide ran on, penetrating the mist, and calling to me ever and anon, and saying, "Press on, master, press on! There is light beyond." I did press on; in a few minutes the mist was passed, and I gazed upon a scene of transcendent beauty. All was bright and cloudless above; and below was the almost level mist, concealing the world below, and glistening in the rays of the sun like a field of untrodden snow;—there was nothing between us and heaven. I have often thought since there was nothing like "pressing on" in every trial of life, assured that, although the mists of earth may hang around us at certain stages of our journey, there is light beyond. You, the friends of Sunday schools, have present difficulties, but I would ask you to listen to the voice which on that occasion came from the untutored Madeiranese—"Press on! there is light beyond"—in this world; and, by-and-by, there shall be the light, all unclouded, of heaven; and, rejoicing in that light, we shall be constrained to exclaim, "Hallelujah, for the Lord God Omnipotent reigneth: the kingdoms of this world have become the kingdoms of our God and of His Christ."—Corderoy.

9, 10. (9) **Rejoice,** "the Debater falls back on the fact that life is after all worth living, that it is wise to cultivate the faculty of enjoyment in the season when that faculty is, in most cases, as by a law of nature, strong and capable of being fashioned into a habit." **God .. judgment,** in good faith he tells the young man to "rejoice in his youth," to study the bent of his character, what we should call his æsthetic tastes, but all this is not to be the reckless indulgence of each sensuous impulse, but to be subject to the thought "God will bring thee into judgment." (10) **sorrow,** or that wh. will surely work out at last into sorrow. **thy flesh,** the body being the organ of sensual and sinful indulgences; 2 Ti. ii. 22.

An antidote to dissipation (vs. 10).—Our text teaches us—I. That there will be a future judgment. 1. The time of it is appointed; 2. The precursors are described; 3. The judge is named. II. That God will bring us into judgment. 1. All will be judged: some will be glad, others will shrink; 2. God will bring all into judgment. III. God will bring us into judgment for all these things. The heart prompts to many evil ways.—Omega in 100 Sks.

"And then":—"Oh, if I were lucky enough to call this estate mine, I should be a happy fellow," said a young man. "And then?" said a friend. "Why, then I'd pull down the old house, and build a palace, have lots of prime fellows round me, keep the best wines, and the finest horses and dogs in the country." "And then?" "Then I'd hunt, and ride, and smoke, and drink, and dance, and keep open house, and enjoy life gloriously." "And then?" "Why, then, I suppose, like other people, I should grow old, and not care so much for these things." "And then?" "Why, then, I suppose, in the course of nature I should leave all these pleasant things—and—well, yes—die!" "And then?" "Oh, bother your 'thens!' I must be off." Many years after, the friend was accosted with, "God bless you! I owe my happiness to you!" "How?"

change of scene; we shut out the thought of calamity and distress as an unwelcome intruder. Experience, in most cases, soon alters the sentiments, and events arise which impress an indelible conviction of the short duration of earthly good."—Robert Hall.

"We are big with the hopes of that part of life which is coming on, and live day after day upon the fancy of what to-morrow will produce, like the spectators of a play still in expectation of the next scene; but yet, when to-morrow comes, we find it just like yesterday, vain and without content; and so will every to-morrow be when it comes to be to-day." — Norris.

"These sentences mark the gradual progress in self-indulgence, to which the young especially are prone; they see the roses, but do not discover the thorns, until pierced by them." — Fausset.

"Thoughtless and sensual young man, ... gratify thy appetites, indulge all thy passions, deny thyself nothing, eat, drink, and be merry; disregard the admonitions of conscience, trample under foot the authority of revelation, but think not that thou shalt always prosper in the ways of sin, or carry for ever that air of jollity and triumph." —J. A. James.

Ro. ii. 6—9.

"Enthusiasm means 'in God;'

"By two words spoken in season long ago—'And then?'"—Bib. Ill.—A thoughtless soldier.—Dr. John Evans, the author of some excellent sermons on the Christian temper, introduced, on one occasion, a sermon to young people in the following manner:—"Shall I be allowed to preface this discourse with relating a passage concerning an acquaintance of mine, who has been many years dead, but which I remember to have received, when young, from himself? When he was an apprentice in this city, the civil war began; his inclination led him into the army, where he had a captain's commission. It was fashionable for all the men of that army to carry a Bible along with them; which, therefore, he and many others did, who yet made little use of it, and hardly had any sense of serious religion. At length he was commanded, with his company, to storm a fort, wherein they were, for a short time, exposed to the thickest of the enemy's fire. When he had accomplished this enterprise, and the heat of the action was over, he found that a musket ball had lodged in his Bible, which was in his pocket, upon such a part of his body, that it must necessarily have proved mortal to him, had it not been for this seasonable and well-placed piece of armor. Upon a nearer observation he found the ball had made its way so far in his Bible as to rest directly upon that part of the first unbroken leaf where the words of my text are found. It was Ec. xi. 9; 'Rejoice, O young man, in thy youth; and let thy heart cheer thee in the days of thy youth, and walk in the ways of thine heart, and in the sight of thine eyes; but know thou, that for all these things God will bring thee into judgment.' As the surprising deliverance, you may apprehend, much affected him, so a passage which his conscience told him was very apposite to his case, and which Providence in so remarkable a way pointed to his observation, made the deepest and best impression on his mind; and, by the grace of God, he, from that time, attended to religion in earnest, and continued in the practice of it to a good old age; frequently making the remark, with pleasure, that his Bible had been the salvation both of his body and his soul."—R. T. S.

and I can't understand how any man can realize his standing before God and not be on fire three hundred and sixty-five days in the year. Any man who goes into business and doesn't throw his heart into it doesn't succeed. Now, why not go into the Lord's work as earnestly as into athletics?" —D. L. Moody.

"Knowledge, when wisdom is too weak to guide her, is like a headstrong horse that throws the rider."—Quarles.

Childhood does sometimes pay a second visit to man — youth never. How responsible are we for the use of a period so precious in itself, which will soon pass away and never return.

'You are old: nature in you stands on the very verge of her confine." — Shakespeare.

"Years steal fire from the mind as vigor from from the limb." —Byron.

"Men will invest millions to get gold out of the heart of a mountain, if you can only convince them it is there. Surely, when we can see a tithe of the possibilities that Christ saw in the heart of the most of sinful men, we shall be more eager to redeem it than to rescue the richest treasures of gold." —J. F. Cowan.

CHAPTER THE TWELFTH.

1. **Remember,** think on: keep ever before thee the law of thy Creator. He who makes has right of rule over the thing made. **evil days,** the evil days are those which are painted in the verses which follow; not necessarily the special forms of evil that come as the punishment of sensual sins, but the inevitable accompaniment of declining years, or of disease. **no pleasure,** etc., i. e. the time of old age, when the senses are dulled.

The period here recommended for the religious life.—Religion is indeed adapted to the whole of our existence; and what applies to every age of life, applies with especial force to childhood and youth. 1. Youth has peculiar susceptibilities of feeling, and religion appeals to them. 2. Youth has especially oportunities of acquiring knowledge and undergoing discipline, and religion helps us to use them. 3. Youth has abounding energy, and religion assists us to employ this energy aright. 4. Youth is the time of great and varied temptations, and religion will enable us to overcome them. 5. Youth is introductory to manhood and to age; religion helps us so to live when young that we may be the better fitted for the subsequent stages of life's journey. 6. Youth may be all of life appointed for us; in that case, religion can hallow those few years which constitute the earthly training and probation.—Pul. Com.

To-day—

Whatever length of life God may
Hold for us in His store
Nothing is certain but to-day;
We own no more.

Use well the little narrow span
Between the dawn and dark,
Nor waste your time to think and plan
Beyond its mark.

To-morrow promises to pay,
But when the note comes due
Full apt the culprit runs away,
And none pursue.

The rascal runs from place to place
And flees from land to land.
Give me To-day with honest face
And gold in hand!—Ella Wheeler Wilcox.

2—4. (2) **not darkened,**[a] by reason of weakness or disease, which prevents their enjoyment. The approach of old age is likened to the rainy season in Palestine. **clouds .. rain,** fig. for trouble coming again and again.[b] The body is represented as a house with its various occupants. (3) **keepers,**[c] etc., the arms with the hands, wh. become tremulous in the aged. **strong men,** the legs, wh. in age lose their muscular power. **grinders,** or teeth. Fem. gender, bec. work of hand-mill was done by women.[d] **look .. windows,** the eyes, sight of the aged is dim. (4) **doors,** etc., the lips in allusion to the silent mumbling of their food by those who have lost their teeth. **rise .. bird,** Stuart, "for it rises to the voice of a sparrow," i. e. the old man's voice becomes a "piping treble" like the note of a bird. **daughters .. low,** he can no longer sing, or enjoy singing.

Description of old age.—We have here an elegant description of old age. "Then the sun, and the light, and the moon, and the stars, will be darkened." That is, all outward comfort and prosperity, whether by day or by night, will be eclipsed and withdrawn. "And the clouds will return after the rain." That is, one bodily distemper and trouble will follow another in quick succession. Then will "the keepers of the house tremble." That is, the arms and hands, which defend the body, will by reason of their cold and dry temper shake and quiver. "And the strong men will bow themselves." That is, the thighs and legs, which have strongly borne up the structure of the body, will be weak, and need the support of a staff to assist them. "And the grinders will cease because they are few." That is, the teeth, which chew and grind our food, will break, decay, and fall out; so that, being reduced to a few, they will be unable to do their office. "And those who look out at the windows will be darkened." That is, the sight will fail; the eye, through which, as through a window, the soul looks out, being dim and weakened. "And the doors shall be shut in the streets." That is, the lips and mouth will be disabled from speaking and eating. . . . . "And all the daughters of music shall be brought low." That is, our ears will grow dull, so that the sweetest music will have lost all its charms. "And they shall be afraid of that which is high." That is, we shall, by reason of weariness, dizziness, and want of breath, be afraid of ascending high places, and of attempting such high things as in youth we adventured upon without hesitation. "And fears shall be in the way." That is, we shall be afraid in our journeying, lest we dash our weak and weary foot against a stone. "And the almond tree shall flourish." That is, our head will grow white, like the almond tree, which soon ripens. "And the grasshopper shall be a burden." That is, the least weight will be too heavy for our infirm body; yea, we, being then like enough to grasshoppers, shall be a burden both to ourselves and others. "And desire shall fail." That is, all our bodily appetites will cool and cease. —R. Smith.

The darkness—
The dark comes down ere it be late;
I stand amid the shades and wait,

[a] The darkening of the lights of heaven denotes a time of affliction and sadness.

Comp. Job iii. 9; Is. v. 30; Eze. xxxii. 7, 8. Contrast 2 Sa. xxiii. 4, 5.

[b] "The season of weakness and decrepitude when no sooner has one cloud of sorrow discharged its dark contents and disappeared, but another black cloud, swollen with showers of sorrows, returns in its place."—Wordsworth.

[c] Some e.g., Umbreit, Elster, Cox, think this and foll. vss. a poetic description of the day of death, represented under fig. of a fearful tempest.

[d] Ex. xi. 5; Mat. xxiv. 41.

"Even in the downfall of his mellow'd years, when nature brought him to the door of death."—Shakespeare.

"Time's chariot-wheels make their carriage-road in the fairest face." — La Rochefoucauld.

Home is more near,
O Lord, by every passing day;
Home is more dear
By every prayer I pray.
—Henry N. Cobb.

"I am old now, and these same crosses spoil me."—Shakespeare.

"Every man desires to live long; but no man would be old."—Swift.

Not knowing whether left or right
  Will bring me to the open gate
Where I can pass to home and light.
  O God, with whom is endless day,
  Guide thou my steps; teach me thy way.

The distant lights like beacons shine;
  The city they illume is mine;
The friends I love are gathered there.
  Give me thy help, O Guide divine,
For hope and faith are in my prayer;
  And morn will break and I shall stand
  At daybreak in my fatherland.—Marianne Farningham.

5, 6. (5) **high,** prob. high ground. The aged cannot ascend hills.[a] **fears,** nervously dreads any journeying; wants to be left quietly at home. **almond,** wh. bears white flowers.[b] **flourish,** R. V. "blossom." **grasshopper,** or locust. Even an insect is felt a burden to the weak old man. **desire,** lit. the caper berry, wh. was eaten before meals to provoke appetite; even it would no longer have its effect. **long home,** literally, "to the house of his eternity," so the grave is conceived.[c] (6) **silver cord,** by wh. the house-lamp was hung from the ceiling.[d] **bowl,** the lamp itself. **pitcher,** the body compared to an earthen vessel.[e] **wheel,** the cistern wheel by wh. the bucket is lowered and raised; illus. the vital processes of the body. In the sixth verse the figurative character of the whole section reaches its highest point. The figures are symbolic of nothing less than death. We come to the actual dissolution of soul and body.

Old age.—Will ye give the bounding pulse, and the soaring thought, and the eager glance, and the rushing purpose, to the slavery of time and created things, and think of bringing the jaded energies, the thin grey hairs, the emaciated limbs, and consecrating them to the service of God? We know that even in old age the kingdom may be sought, the kingdom may be found; we dare not, therefore, and we thank God that we dare not, regard any individual, be he ever so old, be he ever so hardened, as having outlived the opportunity of being saved. We preach to the man of four-score years; and though, in the expressive language of Solomon—"the daughters of music are brought low, and the grasshopper is a burden, and the silver cord is almost loosed, and the golden bowl broken," we still say to him, "Now is the accepted time; now is the day of salvation." And yet it is impossible not to feel, that where there has been, for forty, or sixty, or seventy years, a determined resistance to all the proffers of the gospel, the case is growing comparatively hopeless. We may go on with our work; but it is impossible to go on with a very light heart. And never does the minister of Christ seem charged with a commission in which success is so doubtful, as when sent to the infirm and worn-out sinner, who, having given the strength of life to Satan and the world, has at last only the dregs with which to make an offering to his God.—H. Melville.

7. **dust,** Ge. iii. 19. The body formed of dust. **spirit,**[a] rightly has the Targum paraphrased the words "The Spirit will return to stand in judgment before God, who gave it thee." The long wandering to and fro in many paths of thoughts ends not in the denial, but the affirmation, of a personal God and therefore a personal immortality.

Our dead—

Yet love will dream and faith will trust
(Since He who knows our need is just)
That somehow, somewhere, meet we must.
Alas for him who never sees
The stars shine through his cypress trees!
Who, hopeless, lays his dead away,
Nor looks to see the breaking day
Across the mournful marbles play!

a "Of ascending an eminence wh. would be difficult on account of their sunken chests and short breath." — O. Zockler.

b "It is the type of old age whose hair is white;... the white blossoms completely cover the whole tree; the green leaves do not appear till some time after."—Thomson.

c "The ancient Egyptians called their tombs their 'long home,' or 'everlasting habitations.'"—Gadsby.

d The thread of life.

e 2 Cor. iv. 7.

"Each step but
  takes me nearer home.
Life's journey,
  long or short,
  is blest,
If it but end in
  Heaven's
  rest!"
—Kate Cameron.

a "The spirit of every man after death, good or bad, in some sense goes to God either as a Father or as a Judge, to be kept somewhere under the custody of His Almighty power, in order to the receiving of His final sentence at the last judgment, either of happiness or misery." — Bp. Bull.

"Do thy part with industry, and leave the event with God. I have seen matters fall out so unexpectedly that they have taught me in all affairs neither to

Who hath not learned, in hours of faith,
The truth to flesh and sense unknown,
That life is ever lord of death,
And love can never lose its own! —Whittier.

8—10. (8) **all is vanity,** "the Preacher does not follow the destiny of the immortal spirit; it is not his purpose to do so; his theme is the fragility of mortal things, their unsatisfying nature, the impossibility of their securing man's happiness; so his voyage lands him at the point whence he set forth, though he has learned and taught faith in the interval. If all is vanity, there is behind and above all a God of inflexible justice, who must do right, and to whom we may safely trust our cares and perplexities."—Pul. Com. (9) **knowledge,** gave practical counsel for the ordering of life while we have it. "What the writer here asserts is that Koheleth did not merely possess wisdom, but had made good use of it for the instruction of others. The author throws aside his disguise, and speaks of his object in composing the book, with a glance at the historical Solomon whom he had personated. That he uses the third person in relation to himself is nothing uncommon in historical memoirs, etc." (10)**acceptable words,** Heb. words of delight: pleasant, agreeable. **and that which,** etc., R. V., "acceptable words, and that which was written uprightly, even words of truth." The meaning is that what he wrote had two characteristics—it was sincere, that which he really thought and believed, and it was true objectively.

"despair nor presume; not to despair, for God can help me; not to presume, for God can cross me; I will never despair, because I have a God; I will never presume, because I am but a man."— Feltham.

A model preacher.—I. A wise man. 1. Possessed of secular knowledge. 2. Endowed with heavenly wisdom. II. A diligent student. 1. Of the sacred Scriptures. 2. Of human nature. 3. Of the material creation. III. A skillful teacher.—Pul. Com.

11, 12. (11) **goads,** used by herdsmen to drive cattle, so the words of the wise are stimulating, they arouse to exertion. **nails,** or tent-pegs. The allusion is to their being driven into, and fixed in, the memory. **masters of assemblies,**[a] it seems best to take the word translated "assemblies" as denoting collections, not of people, but of proverbs; and the phrase "masters of assemblies" or "chiefs of collections" would thus mean proverbs of an excellent character, the best of their sort gathered together in writing. **one shepherd,** God, the one source of wisdom for all teachers. (12)**many books,** "the words, which would have been singularly inappropriate as applied to the scanty literature of the reign of the historical Solomon, manifestly point to a time when the teachers of Israel had come in contact with the literature of other countries, which overwhelmed them with its variety and copiousness, and the scholar is warned against trusting to that literature as a guide to wisdom." **study,**[b] "you may weary your brain, exhaust your strength, by protracted study or meditation on many books, but you will not necessarily thereby gain any insight into the problems of the universe or guidance for daily life."

[a] "The master of assemblies is the sheikh, who orders the gathering together of the tent dwellers, and the pitching of the encampment."—Van Lennep.

Preaching.—Well did John Ruskin say that the issues of life and death for modern society are in the pulpit: "Precious indeed those thirty minutes by which the teacher tries to get at the separate hearts of a thousand men to convince them of all their weaknesses, to shame them for all their sin, to warn them of all their dangers, to try by this way and that to stir the hard fastenings of the doors where the Master himself has stood and knocked yet none opened, and to call at the openings of those dark streets where Wisdom herself hath stretched forth her hands and no man regarded. Thirty minutes to raise the dead in." And he who hath known the joy of encouraging some noble youth who is discouraged, the rapture that comes when at least one who hath become long snared and held in the cruel trap hath been freed, the joy of feeling that blind eyes have come to see things unseen and deaf ears to hear notes that once were unheard, or hath swung wide some dungeon door to lead forth some prisoner of conscience, will know that no profession conceals such hidden springs, receives such hidden messages, is fed with such buoyancy and happiness as the ministry—the Christian teacher, who brings divine truth to men for God's sake and for man's sake.—Bib. Sacra, July, 1898.

[b] "This is only the discouragement of the prurient and roving curiosity which is always craving something new, however pernicious and poisonous, and has no appetite for what is old, however wholesome it may be."—Wordsworth.

"It is right to be contented with what we have, but never with what we are." — James Makintosh.

"Knowledge always desires increase: it is like fire, which must be first kindled by some external agent, but which will afterwards propagate itself." —Johnson.

13, 14. (13) **Fear God,** etc., "this injunction is the practical result of the whole discussion. Amid the difficulties of the moral government of the world, amid the complications of society, varying and opposing interests, one duty remained plain and unchanging—the duty of piety and obedience."—Pul. Com. **this is .. of man,** lit, this is for every man: i. e. a law of universal obligation. The duty is expressed in the most general terms as applicable to the whole human family; for God is not the God of the Jews only, but of Gentiles also (Rom. iii. 29). (14) **into judgment,** Ro. ii. 16, xiv. 10; 2 Cor. v. 10.[c]

The whole duty of man (vs. 13).—This is real religion. I. It is the design of man's creation. II. The object of God's providential dispensation. III. The chief excellency of man's character. IV. The sole foundation of his happiness. V. It harmonizes with all his circumstances.

Photographs on the wall.—The infinite galleries of the past await but one brief process, and all their pictures will be called out and fixed for ever. I had a curious illustration of this great fact on a humble scale. When a bookcase, long standing in one place, was removed, there was the exact image left on the wall of the whole, and of many of its portions. But in the midst of this picture was another, the precise outline of a map which had hung on the wall before the bookcase was placed there. We had all forgotten everything about the map until we saw its photograph on the wall. Thus, some day or another, we may remember a sin which has been covered up, when this lower universe is pulled away from before the wall of infinity, where the wrong-doing stands self-recorded.—O. W. Holmes. Fear of God.—A proper fear of God originates in faith; a wrong fear, in doubt. A right fear bends towards hope, because it springs from faith, and we hope in the God whom we believe; an improper fear leads to despair, because we dread Him in whom we have not faith. This fears to lose God, and that to find Him.—Blaise Pascal. The root of character.—What is deepest in every man, and most influential, however little at times it may seem so, is, after all, his relation to God and the Unseen. The genuine root of character is here, as trial soon proves. How a man believes concerning God and the higher world—how his soul is—will show itself in his whole life. From this inner source, its essential and determining qualities will run. On this foundation its structure rests. The religious belief of young men, therefore, is a subject of the most vital moment for themselves and for all. Whatever tends to affect it is pregnant with incalcuable consequences. To weaken or lose it, is to impair the very life of society. To deepen and expand it, is to add strength to character and durability to virtue.—Tullock. So long as life is full of strife and conflict, so long as men are the children of misfortune, adversity, and defeat; so long as troubles roll over the earth like sheeted storms; so long as dark minds need light and inspiration, and the pilgrim band. floundering through the wilderness, needs a leader, and a pillar of cloud by day and a pillar of fire by night, will religion remain the guide, the hope, the friend, and support of the people.—N. D. Hillis.

c "Because God is infinitely just, He will neither let hidden evil be unpunished, nor hidden good be unrewarded." —Wolle.

"We shall see of what vast consequence it is to us that we be religious, if we consider the account we must every one of us shortly give of himself to God." —Mat. Henry.

"The kingdom of God is not going to religious meetings and hearing strange religious experiences; the kingdom of God is doing what is right—living at peace with all men, being filled with joy in the Holy Ghost." Drummond.

"The one secret of life and development is not to devise and plan, but to fall in with the forces at work; to do every moment's duty aright, that being the part in the process allotted to us; and let come — not what will, for there is no such thing—but what the eternal Thought wills for each of us, has intended in each of us from the first."—Geo. Macdonald.

Introduction.

I. **Author.** The author is unknown. The heading which ascribes the book to Solomon, "is not the work of the author and has no more authority than other similar headings." "Assuredly, Solomon could not have been the author of this lovely poem in praise of the love and fidelity of a country maiden and her swain, and the simplicity of their rustic life. It would be difficult to find a man in all history who more conspicuously illustrated the exact opposites of these ideas." II. **Time.** The reference to Tirzah, associating it with Jerusalem as though of similar importance (vi. 4), is a strong reason for assigning the book to the half century after the death of Solomon, when Tirzah was the northern capitol. But some modern writers prefer a much later date, even as late as 300 B. C. III. **Structure** and **Interpretation.** Two leading views on these points have divided the multitude of commentators, viz: the allegorical view and the literal view. Down to a comparatively recent date the allegorical view in some form commanded the approval of most Biblical scholars and of the Christian church at large. This view is, that, either with or without some historical basis, the aim of the book is to represent the relation between Christ and the church.

The literal view is set forth by Dr. Kitto as follows: "The design of this charming poem is to teach us a lesson of practical righteousness by the record of an extraordinary example of virtue in a young maiden in humble life, who encountered and conquered the greatest temptations from the most exalted personage in the land. The simple story, divested of its poetic form, is as follows: A village girl, the daughter of a widowed mother of Shulam, is betrothed to a young shepherd, whom she met whilst tending the flock. The brothers of the Shulamite employ her in the vineyard on their farm. Whilst on the way to this vineyard she one day falls in with the cortège of King Solomon, who is on a spring visit to the country. Struck with her great beauty the king captures her, conveys her to his royal pavilion, then conducts her to Jerusalem in great pomp, in the hope of dazzling and overcoming her with his splendor, and eventually lodges her in his harem. But all is in vain. True to her virtuous love, she resists all the allurements of the exalted sovereign, spurns all his promises to elevate her to the highest rank, and in the midst of the gay scenes assures her humble shepherd that her affections are sacredly and inviolably pledged to him. Solomon, convinced at last that all his advances are in vain, allows her to quit the royal residence. Hand in hand the two faithful lovers return to her native place."

Synopsis.

Bossuet, Bishop of Meaux, was of opinion that this Song is a regular drama, explained by the Jews celebrating their nuptials for seven days together. He accordingly divides it in the following manner:

Day	1,	Chapter	1—2:6.
"	2,	"	2—7—17.
"	3,	"	3—5:1.
"	4,	"	5:2—6:9.
"	5,	"	6:10—7:11.
"	6,	"	7:12—8:3.
"	7,	"	8:4—14.

With Bossuet agree essentially some Biblical scholars of the present day.

Dr. Good, after others, considered it as forming not one continued and individual poem, but a series of sacred idyls, 12 in number, thus:

Idyl	1,	Chapter	1:1—8.
"	2,	"	1:9—2:7.
"	3,	"	2:8—17.
"	4,	"	3:1—5.
"	5,	"	3:6—4:7.
"	6,	"	4:8—5:1.
"	7,	"	5:2—6:10.
"	8,	"	6:11—13.
"	9,	"	7:1—9.
"	10,	"	7:10—8:4.
"	11,	"	8:5—7.
"	12,	"	8:8—14.

CHAPTER THE FIRST.

1—3. (1) **song of songs,** i. e. the chief of songs. Its theme is "a faithful love." A Shulamite maiden captured by the king's forces has been brought to the palace at Jerusalem where the king tries in vain to win her affections. She is already pledged to a young shepherd to whom she remains faithful. **which is Solomon's,** lit. to, or for, Solomon. Usually regarded as ascribing the authorship to Sol.[a] (2) **kiss me,**[b] in vss. 2, 3, 4a the women of the harem sing of Solomon. **better than wine,** which was regarded as "making glad the heart." (3) **savour .. ointments,** R. V. "Thine ointments have a goodly fragrance; Thy name," etc. these were freely used in dressing for entertainments.[c] **poured forth,** the fame of the king has gone abroad like a spicy odor. **virgins,** all the court ladies are admirers of the brilliant and lovely king.

The Song of Songs.—In this poem pure love and simple living are exalted in opposition to the luxury and vices of the royal seraglio. A poem that sets forth the beauty of a simple country life as the scene of the true love of husband and wife in contrast to the degradation of a corrupt court is distinctly elevating in tone and influence, and the more so for the fact that it is not didactic in form. It is not only in kings' palaces and amid scenes of oriental voluptuousness that the influence of such ideas as are here presented is needed. Christian civilization has not progressed beyond the condition in which the consideration of them may be resorted to as a wholesome corrective. But another idea of highest importance emerges. It is not love, now, but fidelity, that claims our attention. The simple girl, protected only by her virtue, who is proof against all the fascinations of the most splendid court, and who prefers to be the wife of the poor man whom she loves, and to whom she has plighted troth, to accepting a queen's crown at the cost of deserting her humble lover, is the type and example of a loyalty which is the more admirable because it appears where we should little expect to find it.—Expos. Bible. The Bridegroom and the bride.—Love's native language is poetry. When strong and happy feeling dominates the soul, it soon bursts into a song. As young life in a fruit tree breaks into leaf and blossom, so the spiritual force of love unfolds in metaphor and music. Among the lyrics composed by King David, those which celebrate the Messiah-Prince have the richest glory of fervor, blossom most into Oriental imagery. The deep and inseparable union between Christ and his saints is by no one set forth so clearly as by Jesus the Christ; hence love is strong and tender, because love's Object is noble, winsome, kingly, Divine.—Pul. Com. Altogether lovely.—Jesus Christ is comprehensive of all things that are lovely. He seals up the sum of all loveliness: things that shine as single stars with a particular glory, all meet in Christ, as a glorious constellation. Cast your eyes among all created beings; survey the universe; observe strength in one, beauty in a second, faithfulness in a third, wisdom in a fourth; but you shall find none excelling in them all, as Christ doth. Bread hath one quality, water another, physic another; but none hath all in itself, as Christ hath. He is bread to the hungry, water to the thirsty, a garment to the naked, healing to the wounded, and whatsoever a soul can desire is found in Him.—J. Flavel.

4—6. (4) **Draw me,** by some look of love that will give me encouragement. **run,** immediately responding to such a love-sign. **king .. chambers,** here for the first time the Shulamite speaks realizing her surroundings. **We will be glad,** etc., the women welcome her and extol the king. **remember,** R. V. "make mention of." **upright,** R. V. "Rightly do they love thee." (5) From 5-7 the Shulamite speaks. **black,** swart, or dark-hued. **tents of Kedar,**[a] Ge. xxv. 13. **curtains,** i. e. comely as the curtains of Sol.'s tent. (6) **black,** etc., R. V. "swarthy, because the sun hath scorched me." **angry,** the cause of this anger is not given but its result only. For other reference to these brothers comp. viii. 8, 9. They

Luther calls this "The High Song."

a "In many Ps. the same Heb. particle occurs in the title as a sign of authorship." — Spk. Com.

b "For a king to permit his hands, or even garment, to be kissed, was counted a great honor, but that he should himself kiss another with his mouth is the greatest honor." — Fausset.

c Jno. xii. 3.

"To become like Christ is the only thing in the world worth caring for, the thing before which every ambition of man is folly, and all lower achievement vain. Those only who make this quest the supreme desire and passion of their lives can even begin to hope to reach it."—Drummond.

"Hawthorne compares Christianity to a grand cathedral with divinely pictured windows. Viewed from without, it is impossible to gain the slightest conception of the beautiful forms and radiant colors manifest to those who look at them from within. So it is with Christ. There is a glory in him not visible to those without, but revealed to those who dwell in his heart of hearts."—Peloubet's Notes.

a "The Arab tent is made of goat's hair cloth, always black, or of a dark brown, manufactured by

were her natural protectors. **keeper,** etc., thinking to keep me safe by finding work for me. **mine own vineyard,** i. e. I have been careless of my personal attractiveness; Comp. viii. 12.

The cry of the bride (vs. 4).—I. The request. It is—1. Earnest; 2. Constant; 3. Believing; 4. Personal; 5. Unconditional. II. The promise—"We will run," etc. Notice this promise in its—1. Boldness; 2. Greatness; 3. Humility; 4. Object. III. How the request is answered. Jesus draws by—1. Silence; 2. A look; 3. A word; 4. By former promises brought to mind; 5. By afflictions; 6. By the ordinances.—Stems and Twigs.

Internal beauty procured through unselfish service.—The bride was really comely, though she had been compelled to work, like a slave, in the vineyards; yea, she was comely in character, as the result of this toil. Very true is it that no persecution can injure us; it brings, sooner or later, real advantage. The noblest characters have been fashioned and burnished in the furnace of suffering. Even of the Son of God we are told that "he learned obedience by the things which he suffered." The statue is not perfected until it has felt ten thousand strokes of the chisel. The diamond does not sparkle at its best until it has been well cut on the wheel of the lapidary. The pearl of great price is the fruit of pain. The verdict of experience records, "It was good for me that I was afflicted." Suffering is God's lancet, whereby he produces health. A vital lesson is here taught. Without personal piety there can be no permanent usefulness. A man's character is the mightiest instrument for recovering and elevating others. If we long to see the vineyards of others fair and fruitful, our own vineyard must be a pattern of good culture. Our first duty is respecting ourselves. If we are full of light, we can lead others along the path to heaven. Personal holiness is the great desideratum.—Pul. Com.

7, 8. (7) **thou feedest,** R. V. "Where thou feedest thy flock, where thou makest it to rest at noon," her heart goes out to her shepherd lover.[b] **turneth aside,** R. V., marg. "wandereth beside the flocks." (8) **If,** etc., answer taken up by the chorus of women, with a tone of irony.[c] **footsteps,** if you prefer your rustic lover to the king, go and find him.

The saint and the Saviour (vss. 7, 8).—I. The address of the saint to the Saviour. 1. An acknowledgment of His love; 2. A longing for communion; 3. A dread of declension. II. The reply of the Saviour to the saint. 1. A slight reproof; 2. A warm expression of admiration; 3. A plain direction.—J. Brooks.

Verse 8.—These pampered beauties of the Harem deem her a foolish virgin indeed to keep thinking of a plain country lad, when King Solomon offers her a place in his royal, albeit rather miscellaneous, affections. In their reference to kids instead of lambs in the shepherd's flock, there may be an allusion to the worship of the Phœnician goddess Astarte, or Ashtaroth, as the Hebrews called her. In the rites of this moon-goddess a kid was the emblem of love. The pure virgin of Shunem was a devout servant of Jehovah, while many of the women in Solomon's harem were idolaters to this Phœnician Venus. For that very reason they were as unable to understand or sympathize with the strict principles of the chaste Shulamite, as is the heathen woman of to-day in polygamy to enter into the mind of the Christian maiden. To one familiar with the literature, customs, speech, and ideas of the women who live where idolatry prevails, and the rulers and chief men of the country keep harems, the amazing purity and modesty of maidens reared in Christian homes is like a revelation from Heaven.—Griffis, The Lily among Thorns.

9—11. (9) **compared,** etc., this is the address of the king. **my love,** R. V. margin "my friend," so throughout, comp. Judg. xi. 37. **company,** R. V., "to a steed[a] in," etc. (10) **rows of jewels,** R. V. "plaits of hair," simple and unadorned. **chains,** R. V. "strings of jewels," or beads, not of great value, comp. Eze. xvi. 11—13. (11) **borders,** R. V. "plaits." The meaning of this passage is clear as Griffis translates: "Thy cheeks are comely in their fringes of coins, thy neck in its necklace of beads. We will make thee headbands of gold and a necklace of knobs of silver." He would win the girl by an offer of ornaments.

the women of the household, and cut in long strips, wh. are stitched together at the edges until the desired width is obtained. This tent cloth possesses the double advantage of being waterproof, and of absorbing the sun's rays, and it is thus actually cooler than the white tent of the more civilized traveler."—Van Lennep.

"There are negroes in central Africa who never dreamed that they were black until they saw the face of a white man; and there are people who never knew they were sinful until they saw the face of Jesus Christ in all its whiteness and purity." —A. J. Gordon.

b "The sheep are led to pasture only towards sunset during the greater part of the year, and return home in the morning, or spend the day, sometimes the noon-day hours only, in the breezy shade of a friendly grove, or under booths prepared for the purpose." —Van Lennep.

c "It was jeeringly intended, and if it did not exactly wound her deeply, it was certainly adapted to increase her longing for her lover."—O. Zockler.

a "The simile is peculiarly appropriate on the lips, or from the pen, of Sol., who first brought horses and chariots from Egypt. 1 Ki. x. 28, 29." —Spk. Com.

The enticement of worldly glitter.—And thus Solomon appealed to the natural love of adornment in a young maiden all unused to such rich presents. How many a woman's heart has been won by them! how the love of them has made many a home miserable by the extravagance to which they have been the temptation! how many a fair character has been blasted and lives ruined by their deceitful glitter! And are not such facts parables of one of the chief temptations of the soul, whereby it is sought to seduce it from God? Jewels and pearls and gold, how they flash and sparkle! how they dazzle and delight poor human nature! Types are they of more terrible things still—the pomps and vanities of this wicked world, for the sake of which all too many men are only too ready to sell their souls. How Moses was tempted by them! How brilliant was the career offered him! he, the cast-out child of a slave, to be adopted into the house and family, the possessions and honors, of the imperial dynasty, the Pharaohs of Egypt! How our Lord was tempted in like manner! "All these things"—all the kingdoms of the world and the glory of them—"will I give thee if," etc.—Pul. Com. Sympathy of Christ.—But if my dear husband, Christ, do for my trial leave me alone unto myself, alas! I know in what case I shall be then; but if for my proof He do so, yet I am sure He will not be long or far from me. Though he stand behind the wall and hide Himself, as Solomon says in his mystical ballad (Cant. ii.), yet will He peep in by a cleft to see how I do. He is so tender-hearted a Joseph, that though He speak roughly to His brethren, and handle them hardly, yea, and threatens grievous bondage to his best-beloved brother, Benjamin, yet He cannot contain Himself from weeping with us, and upon us, with falling on our necks and sweetly kissing us. Such, such a brother, is our Christ unto us all; wherefore hasten to go unto Him, as Jacob did, with his sons and family, leaving their own country and acquaintance. Yea, this our Joseph hath obtained for us His brethren, that Pharaoh the infidel shall minister unto us chariots wherein at ease we may be carried to come unto Him; as we have had experience how our very adversaries do help us unto our everlasting bliss by their speedy dispatch; yea, and how all things have been helping unto us, blessed be our God!—Saunders.

"On account of her youthful bloom, and her unaffected demeanor, whose lovely charms are still further heightened by the simple ornaments worn upon her head and neck." — Delitzsch.

"Persian ladies wear two or three rows of pearls round the head, beginning on the forehead, and descending down the cheeks, and under the chin, so that their faces seem to be set in pearls."—Olearius.

"The only greatness is unselfish love. There is a great difference between trying to please and giving pleasure." — Drummond.

Divine love makes the soul better at obeying than disputing.

12—14. The Shulamite speaks. (12) R. V. "While the king sat at his table, my spikenard[a] sent forth its fragrance," i. e. "while the king was away from me, at table with his guests, my love (for another) was active, and filled me with delicious memories."—Driver. (13) **myrrh,**[b] a costly myrrh-gum wh. the ladies of the East are in the habit of carrying in their bosom, perhaps in a little bag. **he . . breasts,** R. V. "that lieth betwixt," she parries the compliments of the king by reminiscences of her absent lover. (14) **camphire,** R. V. "henna-flowers," this she prefers to the jewels the king offers; the Orientals are extravagantly fond of the odor of the henna-flowers.—Thomson. **En-gedi,** famed for its aromatic shrubs.[c]

A bundle of myrrh (vs. 13).—Jesus is like a bundle of myrrh. I. Precious—a very valuable drug. II. Pleasant. III. Perfuming. IV. Preserving. V. A disinfectant. VI. A cure. VII. A beautifier. VIII. It was connected with sacrifice.—C. H. Spurgeon.

Verse 13.—Note here how differently the words in verse thirteenth sound as we re-read them naturally. In the proper rendering of the Hebrew, the unrevised and offensive phrase "he shall lie all night," etc., disappears, and with it the last suggestion of anything inconsistent with propriety. Grammar and parallelism show that the reference of place is to the myrrh and not to the lover. The young girl is simply comparing her betrothed to spikenard, myrrh, and cypress flower, or what is sentimentally equal to our buttonhole, belt, or corsage bouquet, which she wears for ornament, instead of the jewelry promised by Solomon. The maidens of Israel, as we learn from the Hebrew of Isaiah, called the pretty vials of perfume, made of snow-white onyx or alabaster, which they wore suspended round their necks between their heart and their garments, "soul-dwellings," or "the houses of the soul," the perfume inclosed being the soul of their favorite friend or lover. While virgin modesty bows her head under the royal flatteries, the sweet odor

[a] Obtained from an Indian plant now called jatamansi.

Jno. xii. 1—3.

[b] Ps. xlv. 8.

[c] Jos. xv. 62; 1 Sa. xxiii. 29, xxiv. 1; 2 Chr. xx. 2; Eze. xlvii. 10.

"Love is the highest word; it is the synonyme of God."— Lamartine.

"Love is the road to God; for love, endless love is Himself." Sonnenberg.

"The blossoms of the henna are white, and grow in clusters. Their sweet perfume makes them special favorites with the women, who are fond of placing bunches of them in their bosoms." — Van Lennep.

"Her eyes are homes of silent prayer." — Tennyson.

"True eyes
Too pure and too honest in aught to disguise
The sweet soul shining through them."
—Meredith.

"Your eye discourses with more rhetoric than all the gilded tongues of orators." — Marmion.

"What needs a tongue to such a speaking eye? that more persuades than winning oratory."—Old Play, "Edward the Third."

on her own bosom ascends gratefully to the sense of smell, reminding her of him whom she always calls "the beloved," now far away.—Griffis.

15—17. (15) **doves' eyes,** R. V. "Thine eyes are as doves," the likeness of the bride's eyes is to doves, to the lustrous and shimmering plumage of the dove. (16) **Behold,** etc., taking up the king's words the Shulamite speaks (i. 16—ii. 1) of her shepherd lover, thinking of his manly beauty, the green bank where she fancies him, the trees above them, and herself a wild flower fit for such rustic life only. **bed,** R. V., "Couch;" Griffis, "arbor." (17) **house,** fancifully referring to the trees that hung over and shaded them, as if they were pillars and beams of a palace.

Most fair (vs. 16).—I. Jesus is fair from every point of view. 1. How amiable in our trials; 2. In our afflictions; 3. In our persecutions. II. He is fair in all His offices. III. In every act of His life. IV. In every trait of His character. Learn to be constantly looking unto Jesus.

God's house.—The picture drawn in these verses (16, 17) is one of rural delight—the soft and verdant turf, the o'erarching and umbrageous trees, the noble cedar, the stately fir, beneath which those spoken of have cast themselves down. The ideas suggested are those of happy rest. Ps. xxiii., "Thou makest me to lie down in green pastures," etc., tells substantially of the same spiritual rest. And the house of the Lord is the place of such blessed rest of heart and soul and mind. Because of this, we find those many impassioned expressions in the Psalms as to the psalmist's delight in the house of the Lord; how he had rather be a doorkeeper there than hold any place of worldly honor or pleasure, however exalted (Ps. lxxxiv.). The agitations and cares of the mind hush themselves to rest there.—Pul. Com.

CHAPTER THE SECOND.

1, 2. (1) **rose,** (comp. Is. xxxv. 1) the autumn crocus.[a] Evidently some wild flower is meant. **Sharon,** the most beautiful meadow land of Palestine. **lily,** not the white lily with wh. we are familiar, but the red lily,[b] or a red anemone, as if she said "I am only a wild flower of the plain, a humble lily of the valley." (2) **among thorns,** the king speaks. Using her figure of a lily he says she is as incomparable as a lily among thorns. All other women are as thorns.

The lily among thorns (vs. 2).—I. This illustrates the lavish bestowment of the love of God. II. It illustrates the power possessed by the love of Christ of rendering beautiful objects morally unsightly. III. It illustrates also the tenacity of Divine love. IV. It suggests also the jealousy and power of the love of Christ of and over all other and opposite plans and principles.

The Rose of Sharon.—The extreme fragrance and beauty of the rose in some parts of Western Asia have attracted the notice of many travelers. It is also cultivated, not merely as a garden plant for pleasure, but in extensive fields, from the produce of which is prepared that valued and delicious perfume called rose-water. The size of the rose-trees, and the number of the flowers on each, far exceed in the rose districts of Persia anything we are here accustomed to witness.—Pictorial Bible. The Rose of Sharon.—The plain of Sharon is still renowned for its fertility and beauty, though roses, properly speaking, do not grow there. The flower referred to may be the cistus, which is found there in abundance, and is well known in our English gardens. It is supposed that the myrrh (ladanum) referred to in verse 13 of last chapter, as well as in Gen. xxxvii. 25, was the product of this plant. In the East this flower is extremely fragrant, and has always been much admired. In no country of the world does the rose grow in such perfection as in Persia; in no country is it so cultivated and prized by the natives. Their gardens and courts are crowded with its plants, their rooms ornamented with vases filled with its gathered bunches, and every path strewn

[a] Thomson identifies with the malva, or marsh mallow. Fausset says meadow-saffron, with flower of white or violet color.

[b] "There is a wild flower extremely common in all Western Asia, which presents the appearance of a small tulip, while it is superior to it in beauty, and it is mistaken easily for it. This delicate and graceful flower is remarkable for the great variety of colors it assumes; it is often seen of a bright scarlet, and of every shade of purple and pink, as well as straw color and white." — Van Lennep.

with the full-blown flowers, plucked from the ever-replenished stems. Even the humblest individual, who pays a piece of copper money for a few whiffs of a kelioun, feels a double enjoyment when he finds it stuck with a bud from his dear native tree.—R. K. Porter.

3, 4. The Shulamite speaks, vss. 3-7, "applying to her shepherd lover the comparison suggested by the king in vs. 2. (3) **apple tree.** In Heb. poetry the word comes from a root meaning "to breathe," referring to the fragrant breath of the tree. (Griffis.) After referring to herself as a modest field flower this figure for her lover is doubly beautiful. It better fits the conception of country life than of a royal lover. (4) **banqueting house,** lit. house of wine. "O that he would bring me into his vineyard, his very shadow over me being love."—Griffis. **banner,** etc., "love waves as a protecting and comforting banner over my head when I am near him."—Delitzsch.

The hieroglyphic of love (vs. 3).—The apple tree was the emblem of love. This emblem teaches us—I. The great superiority of Divine love. Consider—1. The majesty of Divine love; 2. The compass of Divine love; 3. The expressions of Divine love. II. The abundant provisions of Divine love. 1. Shelter; 2. Refreshment; 3. Enjoyment. III. The blessed freeness of Divine love, "I sat down," etc.—Stems and Twigs.

The apple-tree.—As the apple tree with its sweet fruit and its fragrant smell excels the barren trees of the wood, so the bridegroom excels all other men in the eyes of the bride. It is uncertain what the tappauch,[a] called in our version "apple tree," really is; it has been identified by different writers with the quince, the citron, or the orange. It is enough for our purpose to know that it excels the trees of the wood, that its foliage gives a pleasant shade, that its fruit is sweet and fragrant and possesses certain restorative properties.—Pul. Com. The citron is a large and beautiful tree, always green, perfuming the air with its exquisite odor, and extending a deep and refreshing shade over the panting inhabitants of the torrid regions. Well, then, might the spouse exclaim: "As the citron tree among the trees of the wood; so is my beloved among the sons. I sat down under his shadow with great delight, and his fruit was sweet to my taste." A more beautiful object can hardly be conceived than a large and spreading citron, loaded with gold-colored apples, and clothed with leaves of the richest green. Maundrell preferred the orange garden, or citron grove, at Beyroot, the palace of the Emir Facardine, on the coast of Syria, to everything else he met with there, although it was only a large quadrangular plot of ground, divided into sixteen smaller squares; but the walks were so shaded with orange trees, of a large spreading size, and so richly adorned with fruit, that he thought nothing could be more perfect in its kind, or, had it been duly cultivated, could have been more delightful.—Paxton. Shade, according to Mr. Wood, in his description of the ruins of Balbec, is an essential article in Oriental luxury. The greatest people seek these refreshments, as well as the meaner. So Dr. Pococke found the patriarch of the Maronites (who was one of their greatest families) and a bishop sitting under a tree. Any tree that is thick and spreading doth for them; but it must certainly be an addition to their enjoying of themselves, when the tree is of a frangrant nature, as well as shady, which the citron tree is.—Harmer. The pre-eminence of Immanuel.—In Eastern lands, far more than in Western, men are dependent on ripe fruit to allay their hunger. A man may walk all day among the oaks of Bashan or among the cedars of Lebanon, and find no food. To discover an apple tree or a citron tree among the trees of the forest would come as a surprise—as a meal direct from Heaven. Equally true is it that men wander from teacher to teacher, from one religious system to another, in quest of saving knowledge, and find it nowhere, until they find Jesus, the Christ. For Jesus, the Son of God, is the only Saviour, and, apart from him, the soul is starved, diseased, undone. "As the citron tree among the trees of the wood, so is my Beloved among the sons."—Pul. Com.

[a] Pr. xxv. 11; Joel i. 12.

"It is a generic word (like malum in Latin), and may include the citron and lemon."—Wordsworth.

"As the planets by gravitation are held in their courses by the sun, so are souls led to feel the attraction of our Saviour-God. But whilst material things obey unwittingly, it is for spiritual natures consciously and voluntarily to yield to the spiritual attraction of him who is the Centre, the Law, the Life of all."—Pul. Com.

"That you may be beloved, be amiable."—Ovid.

"No cord or cable can draw so forcibly, or bind so fast, as love can do with only a single thread." — Burton.

"The pleasure of love is in loving."—La Rochefoucauld. "They do not love that do not show their love." — Shakespeare.

"We love only partially till we know thoroughly. Grant that a closer acquaintance reveals weakness; — it will also disclose strength." — Bovee.

"Love keeps the cold out better than a cloak. It serves for food and raiment."—Longfellow.

"Love reflects the thing beloved."—Tennyson.

[a] "The original term means grapes compressed into cakes, which were an article of food." —Ayre.

Hos. iii. 1. See also 1 Sa. xxx. 12.

"The agreeable and healthful qualities of the apples of Syria are celebrated by travelers and physiologists."—Wordsworth.

"The district of Askelon is especially celebrated for its apples, wh. are the largest and best I have ever seen in this country." —Thomson.

"O Love Divine, how sweet thou art!
When shall I find my willing heart
All taken up by thee?
I thirst, I faint, I die to prove
The greatness of redeeming love,
The love of Christ to me."

[c] "What elegant creatures those gazelles are, and how gracefully they bound! These lovely harts are very timid, and descend at night to the plains to feed among the lilies until the day-break, and the shadows flee away."— Thomson.

[a] "Windows of female members of the household are screened with lattice-work made of narrow slats of wood, arranged diagonally at right angles with each other, and so close together that persons within can see without being seen." — Van Lennep.

5—7. (5) **flagons,**[a] R. V. "raisins," thinking of the vineyard and the apple tree she longs for their fruits. **comfort,** or refresh me. **sick,** faint and exhausted, so as to need reviving food. (6) **left,** "oh that he would put his arms about her and support her as in the old days before she was carried away."—Adeney. (7) **charge you,** R. V. "adjure you." **roes,**[c] or gazelles; figures of country love, pure and free and simple. **awake,** etc., R. V., "nor awaken love, until it please," this formula occurs four times, at the end of decisive scenes, dividing the composition into five parts. It is an appeal not to stir up wantonly the God-born gift of love, not to interfere with the course of true love or endeavor to deflect its course. Emphasizes one theme of the whole poem.

Verse 7.—Next follows a verse which is repeated later, and so serves as a sort of refrain. The Shulamite adjures the daughters of Jerusalem not to awaken love. This verse is misrendered in the Authorized Version, which inserts the pronoun "my" before "love" without any warrant in the Hebrew text. The poor girl has spoken of apples. But the court ladies must not misunderstand her. She wants none of their love apples, no philtre, no charm to turn her affections away from her shepherd lover and pervert them to the importunate royal suitor. The opening words of the poem which celebrated the charms of Solomon had been aimed in that direction. The motive of the work seems to be the Shulamite's resistance to various attempts to move her from loyalty to her true love. It is natural, therefore, that an appeal to desist from all such attempts should come out emphatically.—Expos. Bib.

The antelope.—The antelope, like the hind, with which it is so frequently associated in Scripture, is a timid creature, extremely jealous and watchful, sleeps little, is easily disturbed, takes alarm on the slightest occasion; and the moment its fears are awakened, it flies, or seems rather to disappear, from the sight of the intruder. Soft and cautious is the step which interrupts not the light slumbers of this gentle and suspicious creature. It is probable, from some hints in the sacred volume, that the shepherd in the Eastern desert sometimes wished to beguile the tedious moments by contemplating the beautiful form of the sleeping antelope. But this was a gratification he could not hope to enjoy, unless he approached it with the utmost care, and maintained a profound silence. When, therefore, an Oriental charged his companion, by the antelope, not to disturb the repose of another, he intimated, by a most expressive and beautiful allusion, the necessity of using the greatest circumspection. This statement imparts a great degree of clearness and energy to the solemn adjuration which the spouse twice addresses to the daughters of Jerusalem.

8, 9. Here begins the second great division of the poem, extending to iii. 5. In vss. 8-15 the Shulamite recounts a scene from her past life, a visit from her shepherd lover. (8) **voice,** Oettli considers this a real interview, the lover finding her and conversing through a window. Notice that the descriptions of the lover are fit for a shepherd lover, hardly for the king. (9) **wall,** "the clay-built wall of the house or vineyard of the bride's family." A different word from that meaning the strong wall of a city or fortress. **looketh forth,** R. V. "looketh in." **windows .. lattice,**[a] the beloved was looking in from the outside.

The voice of the beloved (vs. 8.)—I. The beloved. Christ is—1. The beloved of the Father; 2. Of the angels; 3. Of His people. II. The revelation of the beloved—the voice. He reveals Himself—1. By His Word; 2. By His Spirit dwelling in the heart. Note—This voice is pleasant, instructive, influential. III. The coming of Christ. 1. This was the language of primitive and expectant saints; 2. He came by His incarnation; 3. He comes to the penitent sinner; 4. To the afflicted saint; 5. He comes at death to receive the soul to glory; 6. He will come in judgment to complete the salvation of His people.—Pulpit Themes.

Christ's coming makes a new epoch in our history.—Nature is a mirror in which God is seen, and all the processes of nature are samples of God's works in us. Such analogies we ought to expect, because all the forces in nature are the projections of God's thoughts and purposes. The same God who works so mightily in the material world works with mighty grace in us. If, in the visible creation, he gives life to dead matter, so does he likewise give life to dead souls. The sun which rides in royal majesty across the heavens is a picture of the great Sun of Righteousness, who arises on the soul "with healing in his beams." As the coming of spring makes a new epoch in the material world, so the coming of Immanuel is the opening of a new era to the soul. It is nothing short of a spiritual evolution. We pass out of winter into spring; out of death into life.

Windows in the East.—In Eastern countries the windows are made of lattice-work, so closely set together, that a person outside cannot see what is taking place within; while any one within can see all that goes on outside. In the centre of this lattice work, however, there is a small door, opening on hinges, about the size of a face, through which a person can hold communication with any one outside. When one does not wish to be seen at the opening, or to communicate with the outside, he has only to step a little aside, where he is unobserved, though he can observe. "The mother of Sisera looked out at the window, and cried through the lattice," Judg. v. 28. Windows, in Eastern countries, from their peculiar construction, have thus suggested the images, so expressive and beautiful, used in many passages of Scripture.

10—13. (10) **Rise up,** vss. 10—14, a serenade of the shepherd lover. Comp. with i:9—11 and note how different the language. (11) **rain,** "for the six summer months rain rarely falls in Palestine." (12) **singing,** not merely of birds, though spring is the special time for their songs. **turtle,**[b] the turtle-dove, a bird of passage in Palestine; its return indicated spring. (13) R. V., "The fig tree ripeneth her green figs, And the vines are in blossom, They give forth their fragrance." **fig,** etc., lit. "the fig tree spices its fruit." **vines,**[c] when just in blossom.

A song of three eras (vss. 12, 13).—We may regard these words—I. As a prophetic song of the first advent, when the winter of exclusiveness and moral darkness was past. II. As an experimental song of Christ's advent to the soul. III. As a prophetic song of the final glory. 1. Be patient, the winter will soon be past; 2. Be diligent; 3. Be appreciative; 4. Be earnest, think of the winter of the ungodly.—Stems and Twigs.

Verses 11, 12.—This is one of the sweetest songs of spring that ever was sung. In our colder climate we acknowledge that this is the most beautiful season of all the round year; but in Palestine it stands out in more strongly pronounced contrast to the three other seasons, and it is in itself exceedingly lovely. While summer and autumn are there parched with drought, barren and desolate, and while winter is often dreary with snow-storms and floods of rain, in spring the whole land is one lovely garden, ablaze with richest hues, hill and dale, wilderness and farmland vying in the luxuriance of their wild flowers, from the red anemone that fires the steep sides of the mountains to the purple and white cyclamen that nestles among the rocks at their feet. Much of the beauty of this poem is found in the fact that it is pervaded by the spirit of an eastern spring. This makes it possible to introduce a wealth of beautiful imagery which would not have been appropriate if any other season had been chosen.—Exp. Bib. Singing of birds.—But the nightingale, another of my airy creatures, breathes such loud music out of her little instrumental throat, that it might make mankind to think miracles are not ceased. He that at midnight, when the very laborer sleeps securely, should hear, as I have very often, the clear airs, the sweet descants, the natural rising and falling, the doubling and redoubling of her voice, might well be lifted above earth, and say, "Lord, what music hast Thou provided for the saints in heaven, when Thou affordest bad men such music on earth?"—I. Walton.

"Put ye on the new man."—All Nature does this at spring-tide. We in our dwellings and in our dress try to imitate her and do the like. They who can, get new garments; they who cannot, try to make the old look new. Let us learn the lesson in things higher still. Is there not much room for it? In too many even Christian people the remains of what Paul calls "the old man" are too plentifully visible—in homes, in habits, in speech, in thought, in temper. How much we need yet to be created anew in Christ Jesus, to "put on the new man!" And he who

b "The more common species of turtle-doves come up from the south in the early spring, and gradually fill the whole land, not only of Palestine and Syria, but the whole Peninsula of Asia Minor."—Van Lennep.

c Figs in the Holy Land ripen about the end of June.

"This description of spring has not perhaps its equal in any of our poets (Greek or Latin)."—Mercier.

"Ah, how wonderful is the advent of the spring, — the great annual miracle of the blossoming of Aaron's rod, repeated on myriads and myriads of branches!"—Longfellow.

"Fair Spring! whose simplest promise more delights
Than all their largest wealth, and through the heart
Each joy and new-born hope
With softest influence breathes."
—Anna L. Barbauld.

"Airs, vernal airs, breathing the smell of fields and grove, attune the trembling leaves."—Milton.

maketh "all things new" is ready to help us herein if we will have his help.—Pul. Com.

14, 15. (14) **clefts,** etc.,[a] with reference to the dove, wh. hides in holes of the rocks. This was his song once, and now she hears him calling her to come forth from her present hiding place behind the bars in the king's harem. **in the secret places,** etc., R. V., "in the covert of the steep place." **let me hear thy voice,** an invitation to sing. (15) **foxes,** better, jackals, shy animals, wh. come forth only at night, and then do great mischief in the vineyards, as they are excessively fond of grapes. **tender grapes,** R. V., "For our vineyards are in blossom." This had been the song which she sang in answer to his invitation. It is undoubtedly part of a well-known folk song. Perhaps it was a laughing jibe at him as wishing to rob the vineyard even of its keeper. See prev. reference to the bride being busy in the vineyards, ch. i. 6.

The dove and the rock (vs. 14).—I. The title given by Christ to the converted soul. Dove—1. Beautiful; 2. Cleanly; 3. Harmless; 4. Loving; 5. Fruitful; 6. Sociable; 7. Defenceless; 8. Swift in flight; 9. Homely; 10. Quick-sighted; 11. Used in sacrifice; 12. Lures wild doves to the dove-cote. II. Place of residence. 1. Clefts of rock, Christ the spiritual Rock; 2. Secret place of the stairs, ordinances, prayer, etc. III. The request. 1. Let me see Thy countenance; 2. Let me hear Thy voice. IV. The motives. Apply—1. To those who are not in the clefts of rock; 2. To those who are; 3. To all.—W. Stevens. The little foxes (vs. 15).—I. Some of the little foxes that spoil the vine. The little foxes of—1. Unsanctified tempers; 2. Of the tongue; 3. Of the habits of the life; 4. Of irregularity and neglect; 5. Of pernicious thoughts and judgings; 6. Of selfishness. II. How they spoil the vine. 1. They deprive of spiritual strength; 2. They prevent growth and fruitfulness; 3. They endanger spiritual life. III. What we are to do with them. 1. Vigilance is necessary; 2. They must be entrapped; 3. They must be destroyed. Learn:—Let the subject lead to—(1) Self-examination; (2) Fidelity; (3) Resolution.—J. Burns.

The "little foxes."—In the gardens of Hampton Court you will see many trees entirely vanquished and well nigh strangled by huge coils of ivy, which are wound about them like the snakes around the unhappy Laocöon; there is no untwisting the folds, they are too giantlike, and fast fixed, and every hour the rootlets of the climber are sucking the life out of the unhappy tree. Yet there was a day when the ivy was a tiny aspirant, only asking a little aid in climbing; had it been denied then the tree had never become its victim, but by degrees the humble weakling grew in strength and arrogance, and at last it assumed the mastery, and the tall tree became the prey of the creeping, insinuating destroyer. The moral is too obvious. Sorrowfully do we remember many noble characters which have been ruined little and little by insinuating habits. Drink has been the ivy in many cases. Reader, see to it, lest some slowly advancing sin overpower you: men who are murdered by slow poisoning die just as surely as those who take arsenic.—Old Test. Anec.

16, 17. (16) She affirms to the women of Jerusalem her loyalty to the absent lover. **feedeth,** R. V. "feedeth his flock," repeated in **v.** 3. Notice how she describes her lover. "Never as king or courtier or dweller in cities." (17) **day break,** "day be cool," Griffis translates, "When the day cools, and the shadows flee away, return, haste, O my beloved, and be thou like a gazelle over the separating mountains." **Bether,**[a] this may mean "mountains of separation."

The mountain of myrrh.—

Up to the fair myrrh-mountain,
The fresh frankincense hill,
I'll get me in this midnight,
And drink of love my fill.
O hills of fragrance, smiling
With every flower of love;
O slopes of sweetness, breathing
Your odors from above,—
Ye send me silent welcome,

[a] Tame pigeons are fond of building their nests in the secret places underneath the stairs leading to the roofs of houses.

"Foxes are observed by many authors to be fond of grapes, and to make great havoc in vineyards. Aristophanes (in his Equites) compares soldiers to foxes, who spoil whole countries, as the others do vineyards. Galen (in his Book of Aliments) tells us that hunters did not scruple to eat the flesh of foxes in autumn, when they were grown fat with feeding on grapes." — Burder.

"Not miracles of battle nor one great heroic act of mighty martyrdom, make up the true Christian life. The avoidance of little evils . . . . . these go far to make up at least the negative beauty of a holy life." — Andrew A. Bonar.

[a] Mr. Williams believes that he has found the ancient Bether in Wady Beitir, which comes down from the south, and unites with Wady el Werd.

Eusebius says Bether was an impregnable fortress not far from Jerusalem.

"The Christian man is the man

I waft you mine again;
Give me the wings of morning,
Burst this still-binding chain.
For soon shall break the day.
And shadows flee away.

There my Beloved dwelleth,
He calls me up to Him;
He bids me quit these valleys,
These moorlands brown and dim.
There my long-parted wait me,
The missed and mourned below;
Now, eager to rejoin them,
I fain would rise and go.
Not long we here shall linger,
Not long we here shall sigh;
The hour of dew and dawning
Is hastening from on high.
For soon shall break the day,
And shadows flee away.

O streaks of happy dayspring,
Salute us from above;
O never-setting sunlight,
Earth longeth for thy love.
O hymns of unknown gladness,
That hail us from these skies,
Swell till you gently silence
Earth's meaner melodies.
O hope, all hope surpassing,
For evermore to be;
O Christ, the Church's Bridegroom,
In Paradise with Thee!
For soon shall break the day,
And shadows flee away.

CHAPTER THE THIRD.

1—5. (1) **By night,** the Shulamite relates a dream, to show that even in her sleep her heart and mind are with the shepherd lover. She thinks she has lost him. She hunts for him and finds him and brings him to her home. (2) **rise now,** R. V. "I said I will rise now," etc. **city,** Jerusalem, or perhaps Shunem. (3) **watchmen,** night-guards, or sentinels. (4) **mother's house,** proof of the simplicity and purity of the maiden's love. The artlessness of all this dream, its very impossibility as a reality, is in keeping with the idea that we have a picture of true and simple-hearted love of lad and lassie. (5) **charge,** R. V., "adjure," this refrain occurs four times (comp. ii. 7, v. 8 and viii. 4). See note on ii. 7. **awake,** R. V., "nor awaken love, until it please."

The strength of love.—Mercer's Hall stands upon a most interesting site. Here was the house of Gilbert Becket, a yeoman, who, whilst following his lord to the Holy Land during the crusades, was taken prisoner by a Saracen emir, and confined in a dungeon. The emir had a daughter, who saw and pitied the captive. Pity in this instance proved akin to love, and under the influence of these feelings she contrived to set him free. Gilbert returned to England, leaving his benefactress behind, pining in sorrow for his loss, which at last grew so insupportable that she determined to seek him through the world. She went to the nearest port, and embarked on the sea, the words "London" and "Gilbert" being all the directions she had to guide her. The first sufficed to guide her to the English capital; but when there, she could only wander from street to street, repeating with touching pathos the other,—"Gilbert! Gilbert!" How the fond and single-hearted girl succeeded in finding Gilbert the

who has found to whom he belongs. The world wants men who know where they belong and to whom they belong. — W. W. Moore.

"Love one human being purely and warmly, and you will love all. The heart in this heaven, like the wandering sun, sees nothing, from the dewdrop to the ocean, but a mirror which it warms and fills."—Richter.

"Love is not love which alters when it alteration finds, or bends with the remover to remove; O no! it is an ever fixed mark, that looks on tempests, and is never shaken; it is the star to every wandering bark whose worth's unknown, although his height be taken."—Shakespeare.

"A man may be a miser of his wealth; he may tie up his talent in a napkin; he may hug himself in his reputation; but he is always generous in his love. Love cannot stay at home; a man cannot keep it to himself. Like light, it is constantly traveling. A man must spend it, must give it away." — Macleod.

"No one can perfectly love God who does not perfectly love some of His creatures.— Marguerite de Valois.

"Solomon tried all that the world can give, and under the most favorable circumstances, yet found all to be vanity and vexation of spirit. Byron, with rank and wealth, and all manner of pleasure, failed of content and happiness. Alexander conquered the world, but it did not satisfy his soul; and, if he could have conquered all the worlds that stud the heavens, he would still have wept for more. For God has not created a single human soul so small and poor that all the material universe can fill it. All literature is full of expressions of the failure of worldly things to satisfy the soul." — Peloubet's Notes.

story sayeth not; but she did find him, and was rewarded for all her troubles, obtained the fruition of all her hopes. The yeoman welcomed her with tears of joy, had her immediately baptised, and was then united to her in marriage. The son of the fair pagan and the yeoman was the far-famed Thomas à Becket.—Old England.

6—8. Here begins the third general division of the poem, extending from iii. 6-v. 8. The rest of the chapter gives conversation between several citizens. (6) **wilderness,** or the country. The maiden is brought to a place where she can see Solomon riding into the city with his splendid equipage. It is hoped to impress her favorably with the spectacle. The **smoke,** is from the incense burned in the royal procession. The air is full of its perfumes. (7) R. V., "Behold, it is the litter of Solomon;" a second citizen speaks. **valiant men,** to form a body-guard. (8) **upon his thigh,** ready for instant use. **fear,** of robbers attacking the procession.[a]

Perfumes.—The use of perfumes at Eastern marriages is common; and upon great occasions very profuse. Not only are the garments scented till, in the Psalmist's language, they smell of myrrh, aloes, and cassia; it is also customary for virgins to meet, and lead the procession, with silver gilt pots of perfumes; and sometimes aromatics are burned in the windows of all the houses in the streets through which the procession is to pass, till the air becomes loaded with fragrant odors. In allusion to this practice it is demanded, "Who is this that cometh out of the wilderness like pillars of smoke, perfumed with myrrh and frankincense?" So liberally were these rich perfumes burned on this occasion, that a pillar of smoke ascended from the censers, so high, that it could be seen at a considerable distance; and the perfume was so rich, as to equal in value and fragrance all the powders of the merchant. The custom of burning perfumes on these occasions still continues in the East; for Lady Mary Wortley Montagu, describing the reception of a young Turkish bride at the bath, says, "Two virgins met her at the door; two others filled silver gilt pots with perfumes, and began the procession, the rest following in pairs, to the number of thirty." And Maillet informs us that when the ambassadors of an Eastern monarch, sent to propose marriage to an Egyptian queen, made their entrance into the capital of that kingdom, the streets through which they passed were strewed with flowers, and precious odors, burning in the windows from very early in the morning, embalmed the air.—Paxton.

"Talk not of wasted affection, affection never was wasted;
If it enrich not the heart of another, its waters returning
Back to their springs, like the rain, shall fill them full of refreshment;
That which the fountain sends forth returns again to the fountain."
—Longfellow.

A great lack.—There is nothing in all this glory of pomp and wealth which marks the presence of those Godward riches which alone are real; nothing to satisfy the soul of man or to help it in its life. The soul might starve, as Solomon's did, in spite of all this glory; and, on the other hand, the soul can prosper well though it can call none of this glory its own. We cannot help desiring earthly riches—they are designed in due measure to attract and stimulate us; and they will do us no harm if we are careful, all the while we seek them, to be rich towards God; to possess, as we may, "the unsearchable riches of Christ." But poor and miserable is that soul, though he have all Solomon's glory, if he have not these.—Pul. Com.

"'Tis love combined with guilt alone, that melts the soften'd soul to cowardice and sloth; but virtuous passions prompt the great resolve, and fan the slumbering spark of heavenly fire."— Johnson.

9—11. (9) **chariot,** R. V., "palanquin," margin, "car of state." Another speaker describes this conveyance in which the king is borne. **wood of Lebanon,** very costly, and fragrant. (10) **pillars,** to support the canopy. **covering,** R. V., "seat." **paved,** R. V., marg., "inlaid," etc., reference is probably to mosaic work or tapestry. **for,** R. V., "from," i. e. as a gift of love from the women of Jerusalem. (11) **Go forth,** to meet the procession. **mother,** i. e. Bathsheba. The crown referred to is the festive coronet of gold and silver wh. bridegrooms wore at Israelitish weddings. It is a significant fact that he now has it on. Is it in honor of the Shulamite? Let her realize the greatness of the honor.

"Loveliness
Needs not the foreign aid of ornament,
But is, when unadorned, adorn'd the most."
—Thomson.

The King coming to his capital.—In Asiatic lands wheeled carriages were rare, and are rare still. This is accounted for by the absence of roads. To construct and maintain roads through a hilly country like Palestine required more engineering skill than the people possessed; and further, there was a general belief that to make good roads would pave the way to military invasion. Hence all over Palestine the pathways from town to town were simply tracks marked out by the feet of men and beasts. Over the level plain of Esdraelon Ahab might ride in a chariot;

but if Solomon brought up wheeled chariots from Egypt he had a prior undertaking, viz. to make a road from Beersheba to the capital. Therefore traveling princes rode in a covered palanquin, which served to screen from the hot sun by day, and became a bed at night. Owing to the scorching heat, much of the journey would be taken during the cool hours of night, and hence the need for a strong body-guard. Before the rapt imagination of the sacred poet such a scene passed. The stately procession arrested his attention, and he asks, "Who is this?" What great king is this? Such is the poetic imagery. Now, what is the religious instruction? It is the march of Christ through the ages—a march beginning with the wilderness and terminating with his coronation in the new Jerusalem. Though he has been long hidden, the day is coming when the King of Zion shall be revealed to the eyes of men, and he shall "be admired by all who love his appearing."—Pul. Com. Work of women.—All through the East, women are despised, down-trodden, treated as an inferior race. If in Western lands women are ennobled and honored, it is wholly due to the grace of our King. So from the very beginning Jesus intimated that the service of women would be acceptable. He was dependent on an earthly mother's care. Once and again, women ministered to him "of their substance." The deed which he predicted should be known throughout the world was the deed of a woman. Women gathered round his cross in sweetest sympathy, while others laughed and jeered. Women performed the last acts of care for his dead body. Women were the first to greet him on the resurrection-morn. "In Christ Jesus there is neither male nor female."—Pul. Com.

CHAPTER THE FOURTH.

The scene evidently changes here. vss. 1—5, Solomon tries to win the maiden's love, comp. i. 9—11; i. 15; ii. 2. **1—3.** (1) **doves' eyes,** ch. i. 15, R. V., "Thine eyes are as doves behind thy veil." **hair .. goats,** i. e. "her locks were jet, glossy black, like the Syrian goats." **appear,** R. V., "that lie along the side of." **teeth .. sheep,** R. V., "a flock of ewes that are newly shorn," "one of the pleasantest sights to be witnessed under the clear and brilliant sky of Western Asia is a flock of snow-white sheep, scattered over the surface of a fine green meadow."—Van Lennep. **bear twins,** better, "are equal pairs and none is lost," referring to the regularity and completeness of the teeth. (3) **scarlet,** contrasting beautifully with the white of the teeth. **speech,** R. V., "mouth." **temples,** likened to a sliced pomegranate blushing with its fruitful seeds. "The fruit is of a flesh color, with tints of a deeper rose." **within,** etc., R. V., "behind thy veil."

Charm of true beauty.—The Church of Christ may well be encouraged and cheered by the assurance that the Divine Spouse appreciates those spiritual excellences which are due to the operation of his own Spirit. "Behold, thou art fair, my love," is the language of the Bridegroom as he looks upon his beloved. And our Saviour is not insensible to those signs of grace, those revelations of spiritual beauty, which he daily discerns in his own. Those who would please Christ may well be animated by the knowledge that he never looks with indifference upon the proofs of sincere affection, upon the evidences of spiritual assimilation to himself. Well may the Christian adopt the language of St. Augustine, "Take from me, Lord, all that injures me and displeases thee, and give me all that is requisite to please thee; give me words, affections, desires, and works which may draw upon me thine eyes, thy delight, and thy love!"

4—7. (4) **tower,** etc., see Ne. iii. 25—27; Mi. iv. 8. **hang,** "Thy neck is like the town of David built for trophies," Griffis, i. e. to hang trophies of love upon it, as the shields of the mighty men were hung on the walls of David's town. (5) **young roes,** R. V. "two fawns that are twins of a

"A beautiful eye makes silence eloquent; a kind eye makes contradiction an assent; an enraged eye makes beauty deformed."—Addison.

"For when with beauty we can virtue join,
We paint the semblance of a point divine."
—Prior.

"Whatever we make sacrifices for we count beautiful. Our love pierces through the outer husk of circumstance and evil habit, and sees the beauty within; and it is for that we will make sacrifice if need be. And so with our most blessed Lord—his eye of love pierced through the often hideous husk of men's vile habits and ways to the soul on which his heart was set, that he might redeem and save it, and make it beautiful, like his own."—Pul. Com.

"Love is like the spirit in Ezekiel's wheels, that made them move so swiftly; so that dulness, sluggishness, and wearisomeness is quickly dispelled by heavenly love, as the ice is presently dissolved by the sunbeams."—Anthony Burgess.

"All dark thoughts of God and of God's dealings shall by-and-by disappear. All his mysterious ways will be illuminated in the blaze of noon. Whereas now we feel some of our earthly conditions hard to bear, then shall we discover that these were ordered by the ripest wisdom, combined with tenderest love. Every puzzling doc trine shall be made plain. Gracious reasons will appear for every disappointment, every sorrow, every conflict, we endured on earth. The mysteries of pain and sin and death will all be solved, and God's great plan for training men will be pronounced the best."—D.

"Solid love, whose root is virtue, can no more die than virtue itself."—Erasmus.

roe," beautiful and delicate, and exactly matching. (6) **break,** R. V., "**be** cool," comp. ii. 17. Here as then the maiden speaks. Unmoved by the flattery of the king she remains loyal to her lover. "In thought she returns to her mountain home, where rise the fragrant mountains rich in odorous forests."—Griffis. (7) **all fair,** The king speaks again. It is possible that vs. 6 is also his speech, meaning that he will bathe himself in perfume to be worthy of her presence.

The Hûleh lily.—This flower is very large, and the three inner petals meet above, and form a gorgeous canopy, such as art never approached, and king never sat under, even in his utmost glory. And when I met this incomparable flower in all its loveliness, among the oak-woods around the northern base of Tabor and on the hills of Nazareth, where our Lord spent his youth, I felt assured that it was to this he referred. We call it Hûleh lily because it was here that it was first discovered. Its botanical name, if it has one, I am unacquainted with, and am not anxious to have any other than that which connects it with its neighborhood. I suppose, also, that it is this identical flower to which Solomon refers in the Song of Songs, "I am the rose of Sharon, and the lily of the valleys. As the lily among thorns, so is my love among the daughters." The bride, comparing her beloved to a roe or a young hart, sees him feeding among the lilies. Our flower delights most in the valleys, but is also found on the mountains. It grows among thorns, and I have sadly lacerated my hands in extricating it from them. Nothing can be in higher contrast than the luxuriant, velvety softness of this lily, and the crabbed, tangled hedge of thorns about it. Gazelles still delight to feed among them, and you can scarcely ride through the woods north of Tabor, where these lilies abound, without frightening them from their pasture.—Thomas.

8, 9. Oettli thinks the shepherd lover here again obtains a stolen interview with his bride. Ewald, Griffis and others that the Shulamite describes an imaginary meeting giving iv. 8—15, the lover's invitation, and her reply iv. 16 and v. 1 his final response. (8) **Lebanon,** the district fr. whence the bride was brought. **spouse,** R. V., "bride," notice the entire change of character in this address from that of Solomon (iv. 1—7). "He does not waste his breath in formal compliments."—Adeney. The reference to the mountains may mean, "come down from your lofty heights to me, your shepherd lover of the plains." **Amana,** the part of the Antilibanus that looks over Damascus. **Shenir,** another peak of the same range. **lions' dens,** referring to the throne-room, with its lions crouching on either side, comp. I. Ki. x. 18—20. Or perhaps the king is the lion. (9) **ravished,** taken away. **one .. eyes,** or "one look of thine."—Gesenius.

One of thine eyes.—There is a singularity in this imagery, which has much perplexed the critics; and perhaps it is not possible to ascertain the meaning of the poet beyond a doubt. Tertullian mentions a custom in the East, of women unveiling only one eye in conversation, while they keep the other covered: and Niebuhr mentions a like custom in some parts of Arabia.—Williams.

Value of Words.—Mr. Hervey, in a letter, says: "I have lately seen that most excellent minister of the ever-blessed Jesus, Mr. ———. I dined, supped and spent the evening with him at Northampton, in company with Dr. Doddridge, and two pious, ingenious clergymen of the Church of England, both of them known to the learned world by their valuable writings; and surely I never spent a more delightful evening, or saw one that seemed to make nearer approach to the felicity of heaven. A gentleman of great worth and rank in the town invited us to his house, and gave us an elegant treat; but how mean was his provision, how coarse his delicacies, compared with the fruit of my friend's lips!—they dropped as the honey-comb, and were a well of life."—Whitecross.

10, 11. (10) **spouse,** R. V., "bride," in all cases; in the other passages, attributed to Solomon, "my friend" or "my love" is employed. (11) **drop,** honey, as the honeycomb does. **under thy tongue,** so as to sweeten thy words. **smell,** etc., comp. Ge. xxvii. 27.[a]

[a] Comp. Ps. xlv. 8.

Proverbs. — "Nobody's sweetheart is ugly."—Dutch. "People in love think other people's eyes are out."—Spanish. "Love is blind."—English. — "Faults are thick where love is thin."—Welsh. "To love and to be wise is impossible."—Spanish. "True love never grows heavy." "Who would be loved must love."—Italian.

The heavenly Bridegroom.—Thrice happy souls that have Christ for their Commander, and are led, governed, and conducted by Him as their King and Captain of their salvation. His very "banner" over them is love; all His commands are commands of love; all the service He requireth of them is imposed in love; He never enjoineth them anything but what is for their good. They are never losers by obeying His pleasure; all their losses come by their disobedience: He never putteth them upon any suffering, but it is done in love. He chooseth the sweet attribute of love, showing that it is a special act of His love that He leadeth on His followers to conflict, intending to make them happy gainers, "more than conquerors."—J. Maynard (1646).

12—15. (12) **inclosed,** marg. barred (ch. viii. 9). **fountain sealed,**[b] i. e. barred and sealed against the flatteries and seductions of the king and his court. A statement of confidence in the absolute purity of the maiden. (13) **plants,** R. V. "shoots." **pomegranates,**[c] regarded as a sacred fruit. **camphire,** R. V. "henna"[d] (ch. i. 14). (14) **Spikenard,** etc., different kinds of spices that were highly esteemed. **Saffron,** or crocus. **calamus,** a sweet cane, brought from Arabia Felix. **cinnamon,** if the well-known article of commerce it came fr. Ceylon. (15) R. V. "Thou art a fountain," etc. "In free unstudied diction, which lacks the perfect rhetorical finish of the king's addresses, and drawing his metaphors from wild nature within the view of the life of the toiler, his words burn with passion."—Griffis.

The sealed fountain.—This morning we went to see some remarkable places in the neighborhood of Bethlehem. The first place that we directed our course to was those famous fountains, pools, and gardens, about an hour and a quarter distant from Bethlehem, southward, said to have been the contrivance and delight of King Solomon. Close by the pools is a pleasant castle of a modern structure; and at about the distance of one hundred and forty paces from them is a fountain, from which, principally, they derive their waters. This the friars will have to be that "sealed fountain" to which the holy spouse is compared, Cant. iv. 12, and, in confirmation of this opinion, they pretend a tradition, that King Solomon shut up these springs, and kept the door of them sealed with his signet, to the end that he might preserve the waters for his own drinking, in their natural freshness and purity. Nor was it difficult thus to secure them, they rising under ground, and having no avenue to them but by a little hole, like to the mouth of a narrow well. Through this hole you descend directly down, but not without some difficulty, for about four yards, and then arrive in a vaulted room, fifteen paces long, and eight broad. Joining to this is another room, of the same fashion, but somewhat less. Both these rooms are covered with handsome stone arches, very ancient, and perhaps the work of Solomon himself. Below the pools here runs down a narrow rocky valley, enclosed on both sides with high mountains. This the friars will have to be the "enclosed garden" alluded to in the same place of the Canticles before cited. What truth there may be in this conjecture, I cannot absolutely pronounce. As to the pools, it is probable enough they may be the same with Solomon's; there not being the like store of excellent spring-water to be met with anywhere else throughout all Palestine.—Maundrell.

"Thy vineyards and thine orchards are
  Most beautiful and fair,
Full furnished with trees and fruits
  Exceeding rich and rare.
Thy gardens and thy gallant walks
  Continually are green;
There grow such sweet and pleasant flowers
  As nowhere else are seen."

16. . north . . south, "the north wind is cool and refreshing, the south wind heals and ripens." She who gave no direct answer to the king thus replies to her lover. She accepts his arrival, and calls upon the winds to increase her gifts that she may bestow them all upon him. **his garden,** hers, but she willingly acknowledges it as his.

The union between the bridegroom and the bride.—Marriage is further ennobled in our thought since God has chosen this most intimate and sacred union to illustrate the union between Christ and His Church. On the plains of Northern Italy there stands an ancient and beautiful city. Near its center rises a building of pure white marble, wonderful for its grandeur and beauty, seeming more like a dream from heaven

[b] "The garden and the spring being locked up and sealed, naturally indicates that the access is open only to the owner and possessor himself."—O. Zockler.

Comp. Ge. xxix. 3; Da. vi. 17.

[c] "One species of pomegranate has kernels of a deep crimson color, preferred by some on account of their strong acidity, their juice being sometimes used instead of vinegar. The other variety is nearly white, of a pleasant sweet flavor, very refreshing. These trees are often seen in gardens by running water, but they are also grown in extensive orchards."—Van Lennep.

[d] The henna is a shrub rising five or six feet high, with fragrant whitish flowers growing in clusters (Lawsonia alba).

"Love is poesie—it doth create; from fading features, dim soul, doubtful heart, and this world's wretched happiness, a life which is as near to heaven as are the stars."—Bailey.

"When hearts are join'd in virtuous union, love's impartial beams gild the low cottage of the faithful swain with equal warmth, as when he darts his fires on canopies of state."—Fenton.

"Love must be attracted by beauty of mind and body."—Ovid.

"He who is a friend must love; but he who loves is not therefore

than a creation of the earth. As one stands upon the roof of this cathedral of Milan, surrounded by the multitude of its dazzling pinnacles and spires, he may look far off to the north, over the plains and hills, until his eye rests upon the snowclad summit of the Alps, those other pinnacles and spires which God Himself created, and clothed with the ever pure white garments of the skies. So, from this purest of earth's relationships, we lift our thoughts to the mystical union of life and love, between the heaven and the earth, the marriage of the Church to her Divine Lord. Who shall speak of the love and faithfulness of this Divine Bridegroom, the love which knows no changing, which led Him to lay down His life for His Church? How steadily and warmly should her love go out to Him!

a friend. Friendship, consequently, always profits; love sometimes does harm."—Seneca.

"Draw my soul to Thyself by the secret power of Thy love, as the sunshine in the spring draws forth the creatures from their winter cells; meet it half-way, and entice it to Thee, as the loadstone doth the iron, and as the greater flame attracts the less." —Baxter.

"Love looks not with the eyes, but with the mind;
And therefore is winged Cupid painted blind."
—Shakespeare.

CHAPTER THE FIFTH.

1. These words, repeated here by the Shulamite, are either her fancy of what the shepherd lover would say in response; or, better, her repetition of what he did say—(perhaps at their betrothal)—just before she was borne away by the officers of Solomon. **spouse,** better, bride. **eat .. abundantly,** an invitation addressed to the guests. If this is the marriage of Solomon, as some suppose, and the maiden, "then the second half of the poem is left without a motive. It may better be taken as a reminiscence of an earlier passage in the lives of the Shulamite and the shepherd lover, and it is a maiden betrothed who has been carried away to the harem of the king.—Adeney.

Open-air customs in the East.—The inhabitants of the great towns of Syria, during the pleasant weather in winter, frequently leave their homes and give entertainments to their friends under tents pitched in the country for that purpose. In April and part of May they retire to the gardens, and in the heat of the summer receive their guests in the summer-houses, or under the shade of the trees. The same custom seems, from the invitation of the bridegroom, to have prevailed in the land of Canaan in the time of Solomon. When the poet says the flowers appear on the earth, he does not mean the time when the earliest flowers disclose their bloom, but when the verdant turf is thickly studded with all the rich, the gay, and the diversified profusion of an Oriental spring. This delightful season is ushered in at Aleppo about the middle of February by the appearance of a small crane's bill on the bank of the river which meanders through its extensive gardens; and a few days after, so rapid is the progress of vegetation, all the beauty of spring is displayed: about the same time, the birds renew their songs. When Thevenot visited Jordan on the sixteenth of April, he found the little woods on the margin of the river filled with nightingales in full chorus. This is rather earlier than at Aleppo, where they do not appear till nearly the end of the month. These facts illustrate the strict propriety of the poet's description, every circumstance of which is accurately copied from nature. —Paxton. The flesh and the spirit.—There are many people of whom one would have much more hope if they were a little better or a little worse than they are. They are generally decent people outwardly; they never offend against the conventionalities; they are to be found in all Churches, more's the pity; for they are but caricatures of the Christian character. They are dull, cold, selfish, hard, and spiritually dead. What is to be done with such? They are the despair of the earnest Christian, who would almost be willing that they should fall—were it possible—into some miserable sin if so only their present self-conceit could be shattered and they made to wake up.—Pul. Com.

2—4. The Shulamite's second dream (vss. 2—7), in which she imagines that she hears her shepherd lover at the door, but on arising to open finds him vanished, and seeks him in vain through the city.—Driver-Ewald. (2) **sleep .. waketh,** R. V. "I was asleep, but my heart waked;" i. e. in a dream her heart went out to her beloved. All that follows is in keeping with the idea that the Shulamite was a bride when borne away to the harem. **knocketh,** as at the door of the house.[a] **un-**

[a] "The sleep of Orientals is proverbially heavy, and loud and repeated knockings at doors are sometimes heard at the dead of night, accompanied by the reiterated shouts of some belated traveler, reechoed by the narrow streets, and arousing all the barking curs of the neighborhood; then a parley ensues, the gate opens to admit the stranger, and the street is again hushed and silent." — Van Lennep.

defiled, or perfect one. **filled with dew,** through waiting so long in the night air. (3) **feet,** which were bare during the day, so needed washing at night. (4) **hole .. door,** Zockler translates "through the window." **my bowels,** R. V. "my heart."

Eastern locks.—In the capital of Egypt, also, all their locks and keys are of wood; they have none of iron, not even for their city gates, which may with ease be opened without a key. The keys, or bits of timber with little pieces of wire, lift up other pieces of wire that are in the lock, and enter into certain little holes out of which the ends of the wires that are in the key have just expelled the corresponding wires, upon which the gate is opened. But to accomplish this a key is not necessary; the Egyptian lock is so imperfectly made that one may without difficulty open it with his finger, armed with a little soft paste. The locks in Canaan at one time do not seem to have been made with greater art, if the poet here alludes to the ease with which they were frequently opened without a key.—Paxton.

5, 6. (5) **dropped with myrrh,**[b] the lover had left upon the handle which he had touched the fragrance of myrrh. "It was a custom among Greek and Roman youth to anoint with perfumes the door-handles of the residences of their beloved."—Houghton. (6) **withdrawn himself,** characteristic of the dream. **my soul failed,** R. V. margin, "my soul went forth to him," explains her sorrow at failing to find him.

Hands dropping myrrh.—When the spouse rose from her bed to open to her beloved, her hand dropped myrrh (balsam), and her fingers sweet-smelling myrrh, on the handles of the lock. In this remark she seems to allude rather to a liquid than a powder; for the word rendered dropped, signifies to distil as the heavens or the clouds do rain, or as the mountains are said to distil new wine from the vines planted there, or as the inverted cups of lilies shed their roscid or honey drops. The same term is figuratively applied to words or discourse, which are said to distil as the dew, and drop as the rain; but still the allusion is to some liquid. As a noun, it is the name of stacte, or myrrh, distilling from the tree of its own accord, without incision. Again, the word rendered sweet-smelling signifies passing off, distilling, or trickling down; and therefore, in its present connection, more naturally refers to a fluid than to a dry powder. If these observations be just, it will not be difficult to ascertain the real sense of the passage. When the spouse rose from her bed to open the door of her apartment, she hastily prepared to receive her beloved, by washing herself with myrrh and water, or, according to an established custom in the East, by anointing her head with liquid essence of balsam, a part of which, in either case, might remain on her hands and fingers, and from them trickle down on the handles of the lock.—Paxton.

O Love unspeakable! that thou shouldst be
Patient amidst the night's chill falling dews
While I thy proffered fellowship refuse,
Slothful to rise and ope the door to thee!
Long have I tarried, dreading yet to bear
The emblems of thy suffering, thorns and cross,
Lost in idolatry of Mammon's dross,
And lured by pleasure's transitory glare.—W. R. Weale.

7, 8. (7) **watchmen,** night police. **veil,** the greatest insult to an Oriental woman. The veil was her mark of betrothal or marriage. (8) **charge,** R. V. "adjure," a very earnest form of request. **sick of love,** "the memory of the dream still haunts her and impels her to make a fresh avowal of her love." (Comp. ii. 5). The dream of her lover visiting her and of her failing to secure him, coming when the king's importunities are threatening to separate them forever, is very true to nature.—Driver.

The charge.—The bride cannot find her beloved. She seeks the help of the chorus of maidens, the daughters of Jerusalem. She adjures them in her eager anxiety, "If ye find my beloved, what will ye tell him? That I am sick of love." She had used the last words once before (ch. ii. 5),

[b] "Pure, or perhaps liquid myrrh, that wh. weeps or drops from the tree, the most esteemed but most expensive of this class of perfumes." — Good.

"Oh! there is nothing holier in this life of ours than the first consciousness of love—the first fluttering of its silken wings—the first rising sound and breath of that wind which is so soon to sweep through the soul, to purify or to destroy!" — Longfellow.

"Love, only Love can guide the creature
Up to the Father-fount of Nature;
What were my soul did Love forsake her:
Love guides the mortal to the Maker."
—Schiller.

"They plucked off her veil, in order to discover who she was. It is well known that the eunuchs, in the Eastern countries, are at present authorized to treat the females under their charge in this manner."—Burder.

"Even He that died for us upon the cross, in the last hour, in the unutterable agony of death, was mindful of His mother, as if to teach us that this holy love should be our last worldly thought —the last point of earth from which the soul should take its flight for heaven." — Longfellow.

"To me there is but one place in the world, and that where thou art; for where'er I be, thy love doth seek its way into my heart, as will a bird into her secret nest; then sit and sing; sweet wing of beauty, sing."—Bailey.

but in a different connection. Then his banner over her was love; then the joy of his love was almost too great for her; she was sick of love. Now it is her longing for the absent bridegroom which produces the heart-sickness which she describes. She fondly thinks that if he only knew her yearning for him he would return; he would forgive all that was past, and bring her again under the banner of his love. So the Christian soul, awakened out of sleep, longs for the Saviour's presence. She feels that she is sick. She needs the great Physician. Without Him all is dark; without Him there is no spiritual health, no joy, no hope. She seeks him in earnest prayer. She asks for the intercession of Christian friends; she would have them bring her distress and longing before the throne. "My God, my soul is cast down within me;" "My soul thirsteth for God, for the living God;" "Why art thou cast down, O my soul? and why art thou disquieted within me? hope in God: for I shall yet praise Him, who is the health of my countenance, and my God."—Pul. Com.

9. **What .. beloved,** the ladies of the court speak. If the only lover is Solomon the question is obviously absurd. It proves that she has been speaking of some other lover, of whom the women now speak in irony.

The Divine Bridegroom (vs. 9).—I. The transcendent excellencies of the Redeemer. 1. As they are in themselves; 2. As they are compared with those of others. II. The regard we owe Him. 1. We should prefer Him to every person and to every object that can become His rival; 2. We should beware of provoking Him to withdraw from us His gracious presence; 3. If on any occasion we have lost a sense of His presence, we should employ diligently the appointed means of regaining it; 4. If He condescends to return, we should find our chief happiness in His communion, and surrender ourselves completely to His will.—G. Brooks.

Seeing no beauty in Christ.—Corregio has a picture of St. Catherine of Sienna's mystical marriage. This mediaeval saint had a vision, in which she saw the Saviour approach and place on her hand a ring, in which blazoned a diamond of unearthly purity and beauty, with which He espoused her to Himself. The jewel ever burned with a splendid radiance to her eye, though invisible to all others.—Old Test. Anec.

10—13. The Shulamite eulogizes her lover vss. 10—16. (10) **white,** "the complexion most admired in youth." Lit. dazzling white. **ruddy,** with reference to his rosy, tinted cheeks. His body is white, cheeks red, face and hands bronzed or golden, Comp. vs. 14. **the chiefest,** or a standard-bearer.[a] (11) **head,** etc., i. e. "it is noble and precious as the finest gold." **bushy,** curled, lit. hill upon hill. **black,** sign of youth and strength. (12) **eyes,** R. V. "His eyes are like doves beside the water brooks."[b] comp. ch. i. 15. **fitly set,** R. V. margin, "sitting by full streams," referring to the moisture of the sympathetic and loving eye. (13) **sweet flowers,** R. V. "as banks of sweet herbs;" marg., towers of perfume; with possble reference to the beard and its fragrant ointment.

Verses 10—16.—The mocking question of the harem women rouses the Shulamite, and affords an opportunity for descanting on the beauty of her love. He is both fair and ruddy, the chiefest among ten thousand. For this is what he is like: a head splendid as finest gold; massive, curling, raven locks; eyes like doves by water brooks, and looking as though they had been washed in milk—an elaborate image in which the soft iris and the sparkling light on the pupils suggest the picture of the gentle birds brooding on the bank of a flashing stream, and the pure, healthy eyeballs a thought of the whiteness of milk; cheeks fragrant as spices; lips red as lilies (the blood-red anemones); a body like ivory, with blue veins as of sapphire; legs like marble columns on golden bases. The aspect of him is like great Lebanon, splendid as the far-famed cedars; and when he opens his lips his voice is ravishingly sweet. Yes, he is altogether lovely.—Expos. B. Christ's personal qualities incomparable.—Every virtue, human and Divine, blossoms in His soul. There's not an excellence ever seen in men or in angels that is not found, the perfect type, in Jesus Christ. For nearly nineteen centuries shrewd men have turned their microscopes on the Person of Jesus, if haply they could find the shadow of a spot. The acutest eye has failed, and Jesus stands before

[a] "Conspicuous as a standard amidst a host of other men."—O. Zockler.

[b] "Doves delight in clear water brooks, and often bathe in them, and then their liquid loving eyes, 'fitly set' within a border of softest skyey blue, do look as though just washed in transparent milk." —Thomson.

"These doves start up from every spring and water-course."—Van Lennep.

"As certain silkworms have their silk colored by the leaves on which they feed, so if we were to feed on Christ, and nothing else but Christ, we should become pure, holy, lowly, meek, gentle, humble. What wonderful meat this must be!"—Spurgeon.

the world to-day a paragon of moral perfection. His character is better known and better appreciated to-day than in any previous age. Modern criticism confesses at the bar of the universe, "I find no fault in Him." As all the colors of the prism meet and blend in the pure rays of light, so all noble qualities blend in our beloved Friend. As in a royal garden or in the fields of nature there is unspeakable wealth of flowery bloom, all forms and colors composing a very paradise of beauty, so is it in the character of Jesus. Other men were noted for some special excellence—Moses for meekness, Job for patience, Daniel for constancy; but Jesus has every quality of goodness, and has each quality full-orbed and resplendent.—Pul. Com.

14—16. (14) **rings,**[a] R. V. marg., "His hands are as cylinders of gold set with topaz." Hands and head are golden, i. e. bronzed by the sun. "Topaz" refers to yellowish color of finger nails. **bright ivory,** R. V. "his body is as ivory work," etc. (15) **pillars,** fig. of strength and steadfastness. **sockets of gold,** fig. for the sandals. **as Lebanon,** taking fig. fr. the majestic mountain form. **excellent,** etc., the cedar being regarded as a peculiarly handsome tree. (16)**mouth,** Heb. palate, regarded as the organ of speech. His words are full of affection. **altogether, i. e.** all of him is precious.[c]

The believer's boast (vs. 16).—This is my Friend. I. Let me tell you how I made His acquaintance. II. Let me tell you how He treats me. 1. He never speaks of my past ingratitude; 2. He never fails to supply my wants; 3. He never shuns to rebuke me for my follies; 4. He never seems to grow weary of me; 5. He never treats me as a mere dependent; He calls me His friend. III. Let me tell, further, what I think of Him. 1. He is as condescending as He is rich; 2. His love is as ardent as it is constant; 3. He is as jealous of my affection as He is deserving of it; 4. He is as lavish of His promises as He is faithful in their performance. IV. Let me ask, Do you know Him? He is gracious—1. To be the friend of such a miserable being as I; 2. To let it be known to all the world; 3. To tell me freely to invite all my friends to His house and home, to be His friends as I am.—Stems and Twigs.

[a] "Rings are worn on all the fingers—even on the thumbs—and are often set with precious stones." — Van Lennep.

"The hands bent in are compared to beautiful rings, in which beryl is set, as the nails are in the fingers."—Fausset.

[c] "Why should I thus endeavor to express His beauty piecemeal, when He is in Himself and altogether the One longed for?" —Theodoret.

"A learned man once accounted for his eminent acquisitions by the fact that he had never hesitated to ask questions respecting the unknown. To find Christ is eternal life, therefore let us use every wise measure in order to gain so great a boon."—Pul. Com.

CHAPTER THE SIXTH.

1—3. (1) The ladies of the court again speak ironically. **Whither,** how explain this question if Solomon has been the theme of v. 10—16?[a] (2) The Shulamite answers (vs. 2, 3). **beds of spices, or balm.** To the maiden her old home, and the place of her beloved, is a garden. (3) **I .. beloved's,** a reiteration of the unwavering love by which she solaces herself while in captivity and peril. **feedeth,** R. V. "feedeth his flock," ch. ii. 16.

The lily in the East.—"Our camels were scattered on the numerous slopes in search of food. On these heights the lilies abounded, with grass and low shrubs between. I noticed that the camels did not touch the lilies at all, but cropped what lay between. It reminded me of the words 'He feedeth among the lilies,'—among, but not on the lilies; for while the lily furnishes no acceptable food for flocks and herds, it seems, by the shade of its high broad leaves, to retain the moisture, and so to nourish herbage, wherever it grows. The place of lilies would thus be the place of the richest pasture, as the poet evidently indicates when, using the figure, he speaks of the 'young roes which feed among the lilies.'"

4—6. Solomon (vss. 4—9) endeavors anew to win the affection of the Shulamite by praise of her beauty and description of the honors in store for her. (4) **Thou,** etc., Renewed declaration of love. **Tirzah,** an old Canaanitish royal city;[a] a remarkably beautiful and charming town in northern Palestine. The exact site is not now known. **Jerusalem,** Ps. xlviii. 2. **terrible,**[b] etc., or awe-inspiring. This dread of the heroine's eyes is incredible if she were his exultant bride, but intelligible if she is resisting his devotion. (5) **overcome** me, or taken me by storm. **hair,** etc., ch. iv. 1. **appear,** etc., R. V. "lie along the side of." (6) **teeth,** etc., ch. iv. 2., where see R. V.

[a] Jos. xii. 24. The name Tirzah signifies pleasantness; Tirzah was the first capital of the kingdom of Israel, where Jeroboam lived, and where the other earlier kings of Israel lived before Omri removed the capital to Samaria. 1 Ki. xvi. 15—18, 24."—Wordsworth.

[b] "The artillery of the eyes is an idea common to poets of every nation."—Good.

"Have you a glimpse of Christ now that you are dying?" was the question asked of an old Scottish saint, who,

Tirzah.—The mention of Tirzah as the equal of Jerusalem is also an evidence of the northern origin of the poem; for it is not at all probable that a subject of the mutilated nation of the south would describe the beauty of the rebel headquarters by the side of that of his own idolized city, as something typical and perfect. But the poem throughout gives indications of its origin in the country parts of the north. Shunem, famous as the scene of Elisha's great miracle, seems to be the home of the heroine. The poet turns to all points of the compass for images with which to enrich his pictures—Sharon on the western coast, Gilead across the Jordan to the east, Engedi by the wilderness of the Dead Sea, as well as the northern districts. But the north is most frequently mentioned. Lebanon is named over and over again, and Hermon is referred to as in the neighborhood of the shepherd's home. In fact, the poem is saturated with the fragrant atmosphere of the northern mountains.—Exp. B.

raising himself, made the emphatic reply, "I'll hae none o' your glimpses now that I am dying, since that I have had a full look at Christ these forty years gane." —Annals of the Early Friends.

"Turn away thine eyes."—Who has not felt the power of the eye? The beggar looked so imploringly that we gave him alms; the child's eye so darkened with disappointment that we indulged his desire; the sick man gazed so sadly at our departure that we turned back and lengthened our visit. But the eyes of those we love master us. Does a tear begin to form? We yield at once. We cannot endure that the beloved eyes should weep. Our Lord uses this figure to most encouraging purpose. The weeping eyes of prayer move the loving heart of Jesus. Matthew Henry says, "Christ is pleased to borrow these expressions of a passionate lover to express the tenderness of a compassionate Redeemer, and the delight he takes in his redeemed, and in the workings of his own grace in them."—Spurgeon.

7—9. (7) **piece .. locks,** ch. iv. 3. (8) **queens,** etc., Sol. had a large harem,[c] but he intimates here his preference for her above all others. (9) **but one,** the one to whom he speaks. "If this is a continuation of Solomon's speech, as the flow of the verses would suggest, it must mean that the king would set his newest acquisition quite apart from all the ladies of his harem, as his choice and treasured bride."—Griffis.

[c] 1 Ki. xi. 3.

"Love is the purification of the heart from self; it strengthens and ennobles the character, gives higher motives and a nobler aim to every action of life, and makes both man and woman strong, noble and courageous." —Miss Jewsbury.

"Where woman is held in honor, there the gods are well pleased; where she receives no honor, all holy acts are void and fruitless.'"—Mann.

"Love is the golden ladder upon which the heart mounts to heaven." — Geibel.

Spiritual beauty.—God has given to the human soul a faculty that discerns and appreciates what is beautiful. We detect what is beautiful in material nature, viz., symmetry of form and harmony of color. We discern also what is beautiful in human character and in human conduct. All beauty springs from God, the Fount. He is perfect Beauty, as much as perfect Righteousness. The constituent elements of spiritual beauty are humility, holiness, and love. These, wisely blended, form a comely character. It is always unsafe, because an inducement to pride, to praise the bodily beauty of a maiden within her hearing. But one of the elements in spiritual beauty is lowliness; hence public praise is an advantage rather than a peril. For commendation is a spur to fresh effort, and whatever quickens our exertion in the culture of humility and holiness is a boon to be prized. Nor is this spiritual beauty evanescent. It is a permanent acquisition. It will develop and mature towards perfection, as the ages roll on. The sun will be quenched in darkness, the stars will disappear or else assume new forms; but the ransomed saints will be rising in excellence, and adding to their spiritual adornments, world without end. This high estate of beauty is not yet an actual possession. But it is in course of development, from the bud to the open flower. It is clearly seen in its perfectness by the prescient eye of our Immanuel.—Pul. Com.

10, 11. (10) **Who,** question now asked by the women, aroused by this language of the king, and quoting his words. **as the morning,** the dawn being regarded as beautiful. **moon,** or the White One.[a] **sun,** or burning heat, comp. Ps. xix. 9. **terrible,** etc., perhaps with special reference to the starry host. The fig. is differently used in vs. 4. (11) **nuts,** Heb. egôz, the walnut; still common in northern Palestine:[b] The Shulamite tells what she was doing when the king and his followers found her; vss. 11, 12. **fruits,** R. V. "green plants."

[a] Job xxv. 5, xxxi. 26.

[b] "The nuts mentioned here were probably the almond, walnut, filbert, and pistachio." — Van Lennep.

The moon, refulgent lamp of night,
O'er heaven's clear azure spreads her sacred light.
When not a breath disturbs the deep serene,
And not a cloud o'ercasts the solemn scene.
The conscious swains, rejoicing in the sight,
Eye the blue vaults and bless the useful light.
—Homer.

The rose of Sharon.—A gentleman being with Mr. Hervey, in his garden, he plucked a rose, and desired the gentleman to present it to his wife, to put her in mind of the Redeemer, the Rose of Sharon. She put such a respect upon the giver and the gift, as to put it into a frame with a glass: upon hearing of this, he wrote the gentleman:—"Your lady has shown the most welcome complaisance to me, and to the rose, in putting it to such a use; and could that poor vegetable be sensible, it would rejoice to be a remembrancer of its amiable Creator. I heartily wish she may every day become more and more acquainted with the Rose of Sharon; that His loveliness, riches, and glory may be revealed in her heart by the Holy Ghost."—Whitecross.

12, 13. (12) **Or ever,** Heb. I knew not. **soul,** etc., R. V. "my soul set me among the chariots of my princely people." Ewald, "I knew not that my soul (i. e. my desire—to roam about—) had set me," etc., i. e. brought me into the neighborhood of the king's retinue. (13) **What will ye see,** etc., R. V. "why will ye look upon the Shulamite, as upon the dance of Mahanaim?" The question is asked by the Shulamite, and perhaps means "why do you look upon me, a simple country girl, betrothed to another, as if I were a public dancer?"

Conquest as the result of conflict.—"Terrible as an army with banners." The metaphor imports a majesty of active power that moves onward with confident step to overthrow its foes. "Terrible as a bannered host." The Church on earth is a Church militant. Many regiments of believers make up one army. This consecrated host of God's elect is commissioned to fight against error, ignorance, superstition, vice, and all immorality. Until the day of complete triumph dawns, she must station her sentinels, discipline her recruits, boldly contend with sin, and lead men captives to the feet of Christ. In proportion to her internal holiness and utility and zeal she will be "terrible" to ungodly men. The main secret of her terribleness is the fact that Jehovah dwells in her midst. As the Canaanites of old feared the host of Israel because the rumor of their power had spread on every side, and the mystic presence of Jehovah was with them, so is it still. The more that evil men discern the tokens of God's presence in the Church, the more they tremble. On the banner of the Church, men see the pattern of the cross. This inspires courage in the army, but terror among opponents. And the old battle-cry of the Crusaders is still the battle-cry of the Church, "By this we conquer!"—Hom. Com. The Church's mission.—We have learned to see in the bride of the Song of Songs a figure of the Church, which is the bride of Christ. The mission of the Church is to "make disciples of all nations, baptizing them into the name of the Father, and of the Son, and of the Holy Ghost; teaching them to observe all things whatsoever the Lord commanded" (Matt. xxviii. 19). The heavenly Bridegroom is with the bride while she obeys his precept; for he adds, "Lo, I am with you all the days, even unto the end of the ages." Therefore "the Spirit and the bride say, Come" (Rev. xx. 17). The Church, taught and strengthened by the Holy Spirit, calls men to the knowledge of Christ. Her feet are beautiful as, "shod with the preparation of the gospel of peace" (Eph. vi. 15), she moves ever onward, bringing the light of truth into the regions that were lying in darkness and the shadow of death. Missionary work is a most important part of the duty of the Church; when carried on in faith and love and forgetfulness of self, it is beautiful in the sight of God.—Pul. Com.

"Love is the bond and the sanction which connects not only man with man, but with everything which exists. We are born into the world; and there is something within us which, from the first instant that we live, more and more thirsts after its likeness." —Shelley.

"Love is of all stimulants the most powerful. It sharpens the wits like danger, and the memory like hatred; it spurs the will like ambition; it intoxicates like wine." — A. B. Edwards.

CHAPTER THE SEVENTH.

1—3. Solomon speaks (vss. 1—9) almost without restraint, voicing his admiration and the nature of his passion. Many commentators suppose it to be a description of the Shulamite dancing. But that is not necessary. Another view of the passage is that the Shulamite dances before only the ladies of the harem, and that vss. 1—7 are the words of the women. (1) **shoes,** R. V. "in sandals."[a] **joints,** etc., "Thy rounded thighs" (marg. R. V.), referring to perfection of form. (2) **which wanteth not,** etc., "wherein no mingled wine is wanting," the wine giving color to the goblet. Griffis translates: "Thy round dances are perfect circles; let not variations be wanting. Thy body is like a sheaf of wheat garlanded with lilies." **heap .. lilies,** the Jews were in the habit of strewing

[a] "The richer class wear either socks or stockings, of cotton or wool, or a morocco "mest," wh. is a boot or sock of soft leather, with a sole of the same, and is worn inside the shoe." —Van Lennep.

flowers round their heaps of wheat when threshed in the open air. (3) **two breasts,** as ch. iv. 5.

The Heavenly Foot Society.—The Chinese women are beginning to rebel seriously against the fashion of compressing their feet, which has so long limited their energies. It appears that a missionary has been preaching to them on the subject, and they have taken the matter so much to heart that they have started a "Heavenly Foot Society." "How beautiful are the feet of them that preach the gospel of peace, and bring glad tidings of good things."—Peloubet's Notes.

"He who determines to love only those who are faultless will soon find himself alone." — Vihischti.

4, 5. (4) **neck,** ch. iv 4. **fishpools,** etc., Heshbon was a royal city of the Amorites. A large pool is still found in the neighborhood.[b] **Bath-rabbim,** better trans. the populous city; or the daughter of multitudes. **tower of Lebanon,** a straight nose was regarded as forming a handsome profile. The tower referred to is not known. (5) **Carmel,** wh. has a soft and rounded top. **purple,** of the deepest shade, with special reference to its lustre. **held .. galleries,** R. V. "held captive in the tresses thereof."

b "The simile well sets forth the appearance of a large clear liquid eye."—Spk. Com.

Note on vs. 4.—Whatever is majestic and comely in the human countenance, whatever commands the reverence and excites the love of the beholder—Lebanon, and its towering cedars, are employed by the sacred writers to express. In the commendation of the Church, the countenance of her Lord is as Lebanon, excellent as the cedars: while in the eulogium which he pronounces on His beloved, one feature of her countenance is compared to the highest peak of that mountain, to the Sannin, which rises, with majestic grandeur, above the tallest cedars that adorn its summits: "Thy nose is as the tower of Lebanon, which looketh towards Damascus." Calmet imagines that the sacred writer alludes to an elegant tower of white marble, which, in his days, crowned the summit of a lofty precipice, at the foot of which the river Barrady foams, about the distance of two miles from Damascus. When Maundrell visited the place he found a small structure, like a sheikh's sepulchre, erected on the highest point of the precipice, where it had probably stood. From this elevated station, which forms a part of Lebanon, the traveler enjoyed the most perfect view of the city. So charming was the landscape, so rich and diversified the scenery, that he confessedly found it no easy matter to tear himself away from the paradise of delights which bloomed at his feet.—Paxton.

"O how beautiful it is to love! Even thou that sneerest and laughest in cold indifference or scorn if others are near thee,—thou, too, must acknowledge its truth when thou art alone, and confess that a foolish world is prone to laugh in public at what in private it reveres as one of the highest impulses of our nature; namely, love." — Longfellow.

6, 7. (6) **for delights,** or among delightsome things. (7) **palm tree,** wh. grows straight and tall.[a] **grapes,** or dates growing on the palm tree.

The righteous like a palm.—"Well is the life of the righteous likened to a palm, in that the palm below is rough to the touch, and in a manner enveloped in dry bark, but above it is adorned with fruit fair even to the eye; below, it is compressed by the enfoldings of its bark; above, it is spread out in amplitude of beautiful greenness. For so is the life of the elect, despised below, beautiful above. Down below it is, as it were, enfolded in many barks, in that it is straitened by innumerable afflictions; but on high it is expanded into a foliage, as it were, of beautiful greenness by the amplitude of the rewarding."—St. Gregory the Great.

a "The stem, tall, slender, and erect as rectitude herself, suggests to the Arab poets many a symbol for their lady-love." — Thomson.

8—10. (8) **go up to,** R. V. "climb up into." **nose,** R. V. "breath." (9) **roof,** R. V. "And thy mouth like the best wine, that goeth down smoothly for my beloved, gliding through the lips of those that are asleep." The Shulamite vii. 10—viii. 4, "heedless of the king's admiration, declares her devotion to her shepherd-lover and her longing to be with him in the open fields.—Driver. (10) **my beloved's,** as vi. 3.

"Love's voice doth sing as sweetly in a beggar as a king." —Decker.

Sweetness of speech.—Christian speech is sweet when it testifies to the love and faithfulness of the Lord. There is no exercise more congenial to Christ's people, more acceptable to Christ himself, than this. The powers of speech cannot be more holily and honorably employed than in uttering forth the high praises of God, in lauding and magnifying the redeeming love of Christ. The hymn which is lisped by the little child, the anthem which rings through the cathedral aisles, the quiet word of witness in which the friend commends the Saviour to him who is dear to his heart,—these are but some of the forms in which language may show forth the greatness, the goodness, the wisdom, of the Eternal. What theme so worthy of the tongue, "the glory of the

"The fibre of the palm is so elastic that no imposed weights can hinder its upward growth. Hence probably its branches are used as tokens of victory and triumph. Nothing is able to separate the believer from Christ, who is his life, or to prevent his spiritual growth and final perfection." —Hom. Com.

frame," as this? The voice of praise and thanksgiving is dear to the heart alike of God and man.—Pul. Com.

11—13. (11) **Come,** etc., this is what she will say to her lover when she meets him safe at home once again."—Griffis. **field,** or country: where in quietness mutual society may be enjoyed. (12) **let us see,** etc., ch. vi. 11. (13) **mandrakes,** Ge. xxx. 14. Heb. dudaim, love-apples.[a]

Note on vs. 11.—In the gardens around Aleppo, commodious villas are built for the use of the inhabitants, to which they retire during the oppressive heats of summer. Here, amid the wild and almost impervious thickets of pomegranate, and other fruit-bearing trees, the languid native and exhausted traveller find a delightful retreat from the scorching beams of the sun. A similar custom of retiring into the country, and taking shelter in the gardens at that season, appears to have been followed in Palestine, in ages very remote. The exquisite pleasure which an Oriental feels, while he reclines under the deep shade of the pomegranate, the apple, and other fruitful trees in the Syrian gardens, which, uniting their branches over his head, defend him from the glowing firmament, is well described by Russel. "Revived by the freshening breeze, the purling of the brooks, and the verdure of the groves, his ear will catch the melody of the nightingale, delightful beyond what is heard in England; with conscious gratitude to heaven, he will recline on the simple mat, and bless the hospitable shelter. Beyond the limits of the gardens, hardly a vestige of verdure remains, the fields are turned into a parched and naked waste." —Paxton.

CHAPTER THE EIGHTH.

1—4. (1) **as my brother,** then follows the joyful, innocent outburst of a guileless child, to whom, though she be a maiden grown, a lover is but a good brother.—Griffis. This, however, contradicts the idea that she was already the bride of the shepherd. (2) **my mother's,** the references to the mother are beautiful and significant, comp. iii. 4. **spiced .. pomegranate,** "the juice of the pomegranate forms a very agreeable sherbet." (3) **left,** etc., see ii. 6. (4) **charge you,** again the refrain R. V. "I adjure you .. that ye stir not up, nor awaken love until it please." (comp. ii. 7; iii. 5.) This marks the end of the fourth section.

Note on vs. 2.—The fragrant odor of the wines produced in the vineyards of Lebanon seems chiefly to have attracted the notice of our translators. This quality is either factitious or natural. The Orientals, not satisfied with the fragrance emitted by the essential oil of the grape, frequently put spices into their wines to increase their flavor.—Paxton.

What men despise is altogether reasonable and right.—That men might see this is what is so desired here. But men are as a child playing on a railway line in front of an advancing train. Some kind bystander rushes forward and clutches the child and puts it out of danger before the train is upon it. The child probably only stares displeasedly at him who has roughly interrupted its play; no spark of gratitude is there. So men now do not see what Christ has done for them and is willing to do, and so their hearts are cold to him. The truth, therefore, that "God so loved the world" must be held up, insisted on, and shown by lives consecrated to him under the sense of that love.—S. C.

Old and new in the formation of character.—That which is old in our experience is that part of our life which has become habitual. That ought to be the largest part of our moral and religious life. The formation of good habits—habits of devotion—such as church-going, Bible study, private meditation, secret prayer; habits of just and considerate and kindly speech; habits of careful and discriminating thought; habits of activity in all good work, and of fidelity in the discharge of every obligation we assume; habits of benevolence in giving and in serving; habits of courtesy and temperance, and manly dignity and womanly grace—this is a most important element in moral and religious culture .. Yet the character thus formed needs to be continually reformed. New light, new truths, new relations, new powers, call for new adjustments of our thoughts and new departures in our conduct.—Washington Gladden.

[a] Mandragora vernalis, or Atropa mandragora. A wild plant common in Pal., of the same genus with the belladonna, bearing small yellow apples, about the size of a nutmeg.

"Every garden is a lesson-book for humanity; every well-kept garden is a portrait of a saint; every fruitful vineyard is an emblem of Christ's Church."

"Lovers say, the heart hath treble wrong, when it is barr'd the aidance of the tongue."—Shakespeare.

"The ancients sought to increase the strength of their potations by a mixture of spices with their wine; and so likewise do modern Orientals."—Van Lennep.

"More loved by me than by the eye the light."—T. Cooke.

"Not without hope e'er loved the brightest fair;
But Love can hope, where Reason would despair."
—Lord Lyttleton.

"It is not safe to despise what Love commands. He reigns supreme, and rules the mighty gods."—Ovid.

"Make haste to live, and consider each day a life."—Seneca.

"Love is old, old as eternity, but not outworn; with each new being born, or to be born."—Byron.

"That love alone, which virtue's laws control, deserves reception in the human soul." — Euripides.

"O artless love, where the soul moves the tongue, and only nature speaks what nature thinks." —Dryden.

"Love stops not to think how much must be given and what may be kept; it gives all."—H. W. Webb-Peploe.

"There is a comfort in the strength of love; 'twill make a thing endurable, which else would break the heart." —Wordsworth.

"It is like the sun in the sky, that throws his comfortable beams upon all and forbears not to warm even that earth that beareth weeds. Love extends to earth and heaven. In heaven it affecteth God, the Maker and the Mover; the angels, as our guardians; the triumphant saints, for their pious sanctity. On earth, it embraceth those that fear the Lord especially; it wisheth conversion to those that do not; it counsels the rich; it comforts the poor; it reverenceth superiors, respecteth inferiors; doth good to friends, no evil to foes; wisheth well to all. This is the latitude of love." —T. Adams.

"Nothing is sweeter than love, nothing more courageous, nothing higher, nothing wider, nothing more pleasant, nothing fuller nor better in heaven or earth; because love is born of God, and cannot rest but in God, above all created things."—Thomas a Kempis.

5. **Who,** etc., "shepherds of Shulem, perceiving the Shulamite's return, leaning on her lover's arm."—Ewald and Driver. Solomon has permitted her to depart. **I raised thee,** R. V. "I awakened thee." The shepherd lover speaks.

Leaning on Christ (vs. 5).—Observe what this attitude denotes. I. Weariness. II. Dependence. III. Communion. IV. Tenderness. V. Activity.—Stems and Twigs. Dependence on the Saviour (vs. 5).—I. Resting on His promises. II. Relying on His power. III. Realizing His love. IV. Rejoicing in His salvation.—J. T. Nollidge. Coming from the wilderness (vs. 5).—I. This world may be compared to a wilderness. 1. It is unfruitful; 2. Changeful; 3. Dangerous. II. The Christian coming up from it. 1. He has ceased to regard it as his home; 2. He is detaching his affections from it; 3. He is soon to be removed to another scene. III. As he comes up from it he leans on his Beloved. 1. Resting on His promises; 2. Trusting in His grace; 3. Enjoying His sympathy; 4. Realizing His presence. IV. His movements in it excite attention. 1. Inquiry; 2. Admiration; 3. Congratulation.—G. Brooks.

Shelter only in Christ.—A Chinese convert is spoken of by Dr. Medhurst as having used the following language to illustrate the futility of human merits, and the necessity of relying on Jesus Christ alone for salvation:—"How can a man trust in his own righteousness? It is like seeking shelter under one's own shadow; he may stoop to the very ground, and, the lower we bend, we still find that our shadow is beneath us. But if a man flee to the shadow of a great rock, or of a wide spreading tree, he will find abundant shelter from the rays of the noonday sun. So human merits are unavailing, and Christ alone is able to save to the uttermost those who come unto God by Him."—Nollidge.

6, 7. This is "the richest gem of the poem, the Shulamite's impassioned eulogy of love."—Adeney. (6) **Set .. heart,** i. e. let me be united to thee for ever. The Shulamite, after her terrible experience, passionately declares the irresistible power of true love. **cruel,** or hard. **the coals,** etc., R. V. "the flashes thereof are flashes of fire, a very flame of the Lord." This explains the place of a love-poem in the canon. Love is from God, "the very flame of the Lord," and pure and faithful love is a sacred thing. (7) **it would,** R. V. "he would."

The love that passeth knowledge (vs. 7)—The text singles out two things about this love. I. It is unquenchable by the waters of—1. Shame and suffering; 2. Of death; 3. Of our unworthiness; 4. Of our long rejection; 5. Of our daily inconsistency. II. It is unpurchasable. 1. As a gift to persuade Him to love; 2. As a payment for having been loved; 3. As a bribe to tempt Him not to love; 4. As a substitute for love.—Bonar.

"Love is strong as death."—Who can resist grim death? who escape its iron clutches? Who can resist mighty love, or evade its power? The illustration is startling in the apparent incompatibility of the two things drawn together for comparison. But it is a stern and terrible aspect of love to which our attention is now directed. This is apparent as the Shulamite proceeds to speak of jealousy which is "hard as the grave." If love is treated falsely, it can flash out in a flame of wrath ten times more furious than the raging of hatred—"a most vehement flame of the Lord." This is the only place in which the name of God appears throughout the whole poem. It may be said that even here it only comes in according to a familiar Hebrew idiom, as metaphor for what is very great. But the Shulamite has good reason for claiming God to be on her side in the protection of her love from cruel wrong and outrage. Love as she knows it is both unquenchable and unpurchasable. She has tested and proved these two attributes in her own experience. At the court of Solomon every effort was made to destroy her love for the shepherd, and all possible means were employed for buying her love for the king. Both utterly failed. All the floods of scorn which the harem ladies poured over her love for the country lad could not quench it; all the wealth of a kingdom could not buy it for Solomon. Where true love exists, no opposition can destroy it; where it is not, no money can purchase it. As for the second idea—the purchasing of love—the Shulamite flings it away with the utmost contempt.—Exp. Bib. A seal on the heart.—This alludes to jewels having the name or portrait of the beloved person engraved on them, and worn next the heart or on the arm. In the pictures of the Eastern princesses and heroines there is sometimes a large square jewel on the forepart of the arm, a little below the shoulder. "When all the persons had assembled in the divan every one remained sitting or standing in his place without moving, till in about half an hour came two kapudschis, one of whom carried the imperial signet-ring, and presented it to the grand vizier, who arose from his sofa and received the signet-ring with a kind of bow, kissed it, put it on his hand, took it off again, and put it in the bag in which it had been before, and placed both in a pocket at the left side of his kaftan, as it were upon his heart.—Rosenmüller.

The Lord's love is free as the air; full as the ocean; boundless as eternity; immutable as His throne; and unchangeable as His nature.

8—10. (8) **little sister,** she repeats the words that her brothers had once uttered about her, in order to show how well she has fulfilled their desire for her. (9) **wall,** i. e. steadfast in virtue. **palace of silver,** R. V. "turret of silver, i. e. marry her to one of high estate. **door,** light-minded, easily moved fr. virtue. **inclose her,** defending her from temptation. (10) R. V. margin, "I was a wall." **like towers,** R. V. "like the towers thereof," "means that in her resistance to Solomon's entreaties she had been as an impregnable fortress and had secured from her assailant terms of peace." —Driver.

An Eastern palace.—The eye is lost in contemplating the rich assemblage of ornaments which appear in every part of this noble hall. From the pavement to the beginning of the arches, the walls are decorated with elegant mosaic; the panels between the arches are filled with a very delicate ornament, which, at a little distance, has the appearance of a plain mass, and the ceiling is composed of stalactites in stucco, and is finished in a style of equal elegance. The distribution of the various parts of this noble apartment is truly enchanting. The balconies above were occupied by musicians; below sat the women; while a jet d'eau in the centre diffused a refreshing coolness through the hall. The windows in the background are finished in a similar manner, and look into a little myrtle garden.—Murphy.

11—14. (11) **Baal-hamon,** a tower so named is mentioned as being in Samaria. **keepers,** tenants.[a] (12) **My vineyard, must have,** etc., R. V. "shall have the thousand." "Let Solomon and his vineyard-keepers receive the proceeds of the king's actual vineyard" her own vineyard—i. e. her own person and charms (comp. i. 6)—is at her own disposal still. (13) **cause .. hear,** as ch. ii. 14. The lover asks for a song. (14) **Make haste,** she sings as before (ii. 17) inviting him to come to her.

[a] "Vineyards are often let out to husbandmen. The price or hire is always paid in kind, and amounts to one-half the produce of the vineyard. We have, however, personally known many cases in which the hire was paid in money."—Van Lennep.

Mountains of Israel.—The only remarkable mountain on the western border of Canaan is Carmel, which lies on the sea-coast, at the south end of the tribe of Asher, and is frequently mentioned in the sacred writings. On this mountain, which is very rocky, and about two thousand feet in height, the prophet Elijah fixed his residence; and the monks of the Greek Church, who have a convent upon it, show the inquisitive stranger the grotto, neatly cut out in the solid rock, where, at a distance from the tumult of the world, the venerable seer reposed. At the distance of a league are two fountains, which they pretend the prophet, by his miraculous powers, made to spring out of the earth; and lower down, towards the foot of the mountain, is the cave where he instructed the people. It is an excavation in the rock, cut very smooth both above and below, of about twenty paces in length, fifteen in breadth, and very high; and Thevenot, who paid a visit to the monks of Mount Carmel, pronounces it one of the finest grottos that can be seen. The beautiful shape and towering height of Carmel furnish Solomon with a striking simile, expressive of the loneliness and majesty of the Church in the eyes of her Redeemer: "Thy head upon thee is like Carmel, and the hair of thy head like purple; the King is held in the galleries." The fields around have been celebrated in all ages for the extent of their pastures and the richness of their verdure. So great was the fertility of this region, that, in the language of the sacred writers, the name Carmel is often equivalent to a fruitful field. This was undoubtedly the reason that the covetous and churlish Nabal chose it for the range of his numerous flocks and herds.—Paxton. A trust faithfully fulfilled.—In the parable the keepers or tenants are represented as having cultivated the vineyards entrusted to them with skill and

"When we come to know Christ, we know ourselves as members of a universal family, and all men children with us of the same God. It is Jesus Christ who has given the thought of universal brotherhood its hold on the hearts of men."—Barrows.

"There are depths of love in Christ beyond what we have seen; therefore, dig deep, and labor and take pains for Him, and set by so much time in the day for Him as you can. He will be won with labor." — Rutherford.

success, so that they were able to pay the king the rent which was agreed upon or the tribute which he required. In this they are representatives of all those who, having received privileges and enjoyed opportunities, turn them to good account. The scholar who cultivates his mind, enlarges his knowledge, and fits himself to influence aright the opinion and convictions of his less-favored fellow-men; the man of wealth who employs his riches in a spirit of wise and expansive knowledge; the Christian minister who cultivates the corner of the spiritual vineyard committed to his care; every faithful child of God who diligently and prayerfully endeavors to do the will of the heavenly Husbandman, may be said to be faithful in his discharge of the obligations of his trust.—Pul. Com. Love.—"Love is the root of creation; God's essence. Worlds without number lie in His bosom like children; He made them for His purpose only,—only to love and to be loved again. He breathed forth His spirit into the slumbering dust, and upright standing, it laid its hand on its heart, and felt it was warm with a flame out of heaven; quench, O quench not that flame! it is the breath of your being."—Longfellow.

Introduction.

Historical conditions. "When Isaiah began his public work Judah had attained a degree of wealth, power and civilization which must have placed it, along with Israel, in the front rank of the petty principalities that now separated Egypt from Assyria. The great political fact of the time was the westward extension of the Assyrian Empire. This commenced in earnest, after a pause of 40 years, with the accession of Tiglath-pileser III. in 745; and was thenceforward prosecuted by a succession of vigorous monarchs, till it reached its goal in the conquest of Egypt by Esarhaddon (672). It must have been evident to thoughtful observers, even before Isaiah's entrance on public life, that the independent existence of all the smaller nations of Western Asia was endangered by the steady advance of this new and formidable power. Singly, they were helpless against the solid and disciplined might of Assyria; while at the same time they possessed too little stability of purpose to present a united front to the common enemy." (Cambridge Bible.) We owe it in large part to the influence Isaiah was able to exert in the long period of his prophetic career, that the southern kingdom was not overwhelmed, as the northern kingdom was, by the Assyrian power. "The Israelites, who were carried away into Assyrian captivity in B. C. 722, are untraceably lost. They were absorbed by their conquerors. Had the same fate befallen Judah and Jerusalem, they too would have disappeared. That their ruin was delayed a century and time gained in which religion could firmly establish itself and strike deep roots, so as to survive the overthrow of Judah and Jerusalem, was Isaiah's work and merit." (Cornill, the Prophets of Israel.) "The spiritual religion which lay in germ in the teaching of Isaiah was not as yet capable of existing apart from the nationality in which it had been born, and hence the preservation of the Hebrew state was of paramount importance for the conservation of the true knowledge of God." The success of Isaiah in persuading the weak king, Hezekiah, and the wavering people to put their trust in the Lord and to withstand the enemies who sought their ruin, was an event which has had "more influence on the life of subsequent generations than all the conquests of Assyrian kings; for it assured the permanent vitality of that religion which was the cradle of Christianity." (Robertson Smith.)

Synopsis.

(According to Delitzsch.)

First Half of the Collection i.—xxxix.

Second Half of the Collection xl.—lxvi.

CHAPTER THE FIRST.

1. **vision,**[a] something seen by the spiritual intuition, cf. ch. ii. 1). The prophet is a "seer" (hozeh), and his perception of divine truth a "vision" (hazon). The word here refers to the collection of prophetic utterances.—Cam. Bib. **Isaiah,** lit. The salvation of Jehovah. A name very significant of the subject of his prohecies. **Amoz,** not elsewhere mentioned. The name in Heb. is not the same with Amos the prophet. **Judah,** the kingdom of the two tribes. **Jerusalem,** its capital and central city. All Is.'s prophecies bear directly on the interests of God's covenant people. **Uzziah,** etc., kings of Judah from B. C. 782 to 686.

God's charges against His people (vss. 1—9).—I. The striking preamble with which these charges are introduced (vs. 2). 1. We are shown the importance of what is going to be uttered; 2. Its publicity; 3. Its veracity. II. The several particulars which these charges embody. 1. Ingratitude; 2. Ignorance and inconsideration; 3. Abounding transgressions; 4. Incorrigibleness; 5. Spiritual loathsomeness. III. The retribution with which these evils were visited. 1. The severity of God; 2. The goodness of God.

The seer.—A preacher who is not in some way a seer is not a preacher at all. You can never make people see religious realities by correct definitions. They will not believe in the reality of God on the word of a man who merely demonstrates it to them. You must see such things yourself if you are going to help others to see them. This is the secret of all the preaching that ever was good since preaching began.—Beecher. Prophecy.—The sweet stream of the prophet's doctrine did, as the rivers, make its own banks fertile and pleasant, as it ran by and flowed still forward to after ages, and by the confluence of more such prophecies grew greater as it went, till it fell in with the main current of the Gospel in the New Testament, both acted and preached by the Great Prophet Himself, whom they foretold to come, and recorded by His apostles and evangelists, and thus united into one river, clear as crystal. This doctrine of salvation in the Scriptures hath still refreshed the city of God, His Church, under the Gospel, and still shall do so, till it empty itself into the ocean of eternity.—Abp. Leighton.

2—4. (2) **Hear, O heavens,**[b] comp. Deut. xxxii. 1, i. e. since His children will not hear, I call on the heavens to listen. **hath spoken,** comp. He. i. 1. **children,**[c] Cheyne translates, "sons I have made great and high and they have broken away from me." **rebelled,** apostatized, with ref. to the national idolatry.[d] (3) **The ox,** etc., for appeal to the habits of animals, see Je. viii. 7. The instinctive regard of animals for the owner who finds them shelter and food, is contrasted with Israel's wilful neglect of God the Father. "The ox and the ass are mentioned as the only thoroughly domesticated animals of the Hebrews." (4) **laden with iniquity,** bec. sin surely becomes a burden and brings a burden.[e] **corrupters,** that corrupt themselves and one another. Sinners easily become tempters. **they have provoked,** etc., R. V., "They have despised the Holy One of Israel, they are estranged and gone backward." **Holy .. Israel,**[f] a phrase apparently coined by the writer and emphasizing that attribute, holiness, which was fundamental in his conception of God in relation to Israel. (Cam. Bib.).

Inconsiderateness (vs. 3).—Why do not men consider? 1. Not for want of opportunity; 2. Not for want of encouragement. I. The reasons of inconsiderateness. 1. It saves intellectual trouble; 2. It saves moral compunction; 3. It escapes social obligation. II. Its results. 1. Practical atheism; 2. Spiritual feebleness; 3. Needless alarm; 4. Self-deprivation. Learn.—There is hope of any man who is thoughtful.—Parker.

Ingratitude.—It is an excellent representation of St. Austin: **if a sculptor, after his fashioning a piece of marble in a human figure, could inspire it with life and sense, and give it motion and understanding and speech, can it be imagined but the first act of it would be to prostrate itself at the feet of the maker in subjection and thankfulness, and to offer**

[a] "Isaiah was enabled to see the moral corruption which was lurking beneath the fair surface of external forms and specious shows of religion." — Wordsworth.

"Isaiah says he will first of all accuse the times of degeneracy. This is not a grateful task. More loudly would he be welcomed who came to pronounce a eulogy upon the age. He will be an iconoclast; nothing will be spared by the iron rod of his vengeance: yea, though they be gods, they shall go down; though they be idols well cared for they shall be smitten as if they were common clay.—Peop. Bib.

[b] De iv. 25, 26, xxx. 18, 19, xxxi. 28, 29.

[c] Ex. iv. 22; De. xxxii. 5, 6; Ho. xi. 1; Mal. i. 2, 6; Ro. ix. 4.

[d] "Especially by violating that peculiar covenant which bound God to His people."— J. A. Alexander. De. xxxii. 5, 6, 15.

[e] "The fig. of a burden most naturally conveys the notion of the oppressive property of guilt, and the unsupportable punishment which it entails." — E. Henderson.

[f] 2 Ki. xix. 22; Ps. lxxi. 22, lxxviii. 41, lxxxix. 18; Eze. xxxix. 7.

whatever it is, and can do, as homage to him? The almighty hand of God formed our bodies, He breathed into us the spirit of life, and should not the power of love constrain us to live wholly to His will?—Bates. Heedlessness.—No man is in so much danger as he who thinks there is no danger. Why, when the bell rings, when the watchmen rend the air with cries of "Fire! Fire! Fire!" when in every direction there is the pattering of feet on the sidewalk, and when the engines come rattling up to the burning house, one after another the inmates are awakened, and they rush out; and they are safest that are most terrified, and that suffer most from a sense of danger. One only remains behind. He hears the tumult, but it weaves itself into the shape of dreams, and he seems to be listening to some parade, and soon the sounds begin to be indistinct in his ear, and at length they cease to make any impression upon him. During all this time he is inhaling the deadly gas with which his apartment has become filled, gradually his senses are benumbed, and finally he is rendered unconscious by suffocation. And in the midst of peril, and the thunder of excitement, that man who is the least awake, and the least frightened, is the very man that is the most likely to be burned up.—Beecher.

5, 6. (5) **Why..more?** R. V., "Why will ye be still stricken, that ye revolt more and more?" Why bring on new punishments by continued rebellion? Cf. Ezek, xviii. 31. Or, "To what purpose shall one smite you more?" seeing you will learn nothing under the most gracious chastisement.[a] **head .. heart,**[b] their sins have been both intellectual and moral, reason and affections are diseased. (6) "The whole nation is one miserably diseased body; not a sound spot to be found. And yet no one has sought a remedy. **bound up,** a common figure for spiritual healing. Hos. vi. 1; Ps. cxlvii. 3; Luke iv. 18, etc. **mollified,** "the art of medicine in the E. consists chiefly in external applications."[c] **ointment,** or olive-oil.

The sinfulness and incorrigibleness of the nation (vss. 4, 5).—These words lead us to set before you—I. Our sinfulness. 1. The general description of the Jews is equally suitable to us; 2. So also is the particular charge. II. Our incorrigibleness. 1. What improvement have we made of our chastisements? 2. What reason have we to hope that our troubles will be sanctified to our good? Apply:—1. Adore God for His long patience; 2. Tremble at His judgments; 3. Take encouragement from His present dealings with us.—C. Simeon.

Results of Sorrow.—Sorrow is in itself a thing neither good nor bad; its value depends on the spirit of the person on whom it falls. Fire will inflame straw, soften iron, or harden clay; its effects are determined by the object with which it comes in contact. Warmth develops the energies of life, or helps the progress of decay. It is a great power in the hothouse, a great power also in the coffin; it expands the leaf, matures the fruit, adds precocious vigor to vegetable life; and warmth, too, develops with tenfold rapidity the weltering process of dissolution. So, too, with sorrow. There are spirits in which it develops the seminal principle of life; there are others in which it prematurely hastens the consummation of irreparable decay.—F. W. Robertson. The physician and his patient.—As long as the physician hath any hope of the recovery of his patient, he assayeth all manner of means and medicines with him, as well sour and sharp as sweet and pleasant; but as soon as ever he beginneth to doubt of his recovery, he suffereth him to have whatsoever himself desireth. Even so the heavenly Physician, as long as He hath any hope to recover us, will not always suffer us to have what we most desire; but as soon as He hath no more hope of us, then He suffereth us for a time to enjoy all our own pleasure.—Wermullerus.

7—9. (7) **Your country,** the condition of the land was as bad as that of the people. In this description "nearly every word corresponds to the curses threatened in Lev. xxvi. and Deut. xxviii. The prophet intentionally employs the words of the law to describe his own times."—Delitzsch. **desolate,** etc., could not have been written in times of Uzziah or Jotham, but was true during Hezekiah's reign, and points therefore to the time of the writing of this prophecy, as do vss. 10—18. **Overthrown by strangers,**[a] the word for "overthrow" never occurs elsewhere except in connection with Sodom (xiii. 19; Deut. xxix. 23, etc.). Hence Ewald, Cheyne and others read **"like the overthrow of Sodom."** **(8) daughter of**

[a] "They had found that the stroke of God's rod had always, in severe mercy, followed sin. Why then did they continue to revolt, and provoke this ever-advancing series of Divine punishments, when already the body was one mass of festering stripe-wounds?" —Spk. Com.

Jer. ii. 30, v. 3.

[b] "The two noblest parts of the human body are here selected to represent the body politic." —E. Henderson.

[c] "Among all nations, in the early stage of medical practice, attention was in a great degree confined to outward applications, and what we should now call surgical practice."—Kitto.

[a] Comp. De. xxviii. 48, 50, 51.

Zion, poetic name for Jerusalem.[b] **cottage.**[c] **cucumbers,** or melons.[d] Jerusalem is spared. But it stands in the midst of desolation, like a booth in a field of cucumbers, as the watch-man looks forth from it. (9) **the Lord of Hosts,** "title first appears in the times of Eli," (1 Sam. i. 3, 11, etc.) It refers not simply to the armies of Israel, but to all the hosts of God, by which He executes His almighty power. **as Sodom,**[e] i. e. we should have been completely destroyed.

Cottage in a vineyard.—This allusion is illustrated by the following passage from Sir William Hamilton's account of Mount Vesuvius:—"In the vineyards there were several straw huts, which had been erected for the watchmen of the grapes. They remind us of those alluded to by Isaiah. The daughter of Zion plainly means Jerusalem, and the comparison is designed to convey an idea of loneliness and desolation, such as resulted from invading armies, destroying all before them with fire and sword (vs. 7), till Jerusalem itself was left alone to withstand the foe. Extensive fields of ripe melons and cucumbers adorn the sides of the river (Nile); they grow in such abundance, that the sailors freely helped themselves. Some guard, however, is placed upon them. Occasionally, but at long and desolate intervals, we may observe a little hut, made of reeds, just capable of containing one man, being, in fact, little more than a fence against a north wind. In these I have observed, sometimes, a poor old man, perhaps lame, feebly protecting the property. It exactly illustrates the above passage. The abundance of these most necessary vegetables brings to mind the murmurs of the Israelites (Numb. xi. 5, 6), "We remember .. the cucumbers, and the melons, and the leeks, and the onions, and the garlic; but now our soul is dried away."—Jewett.

b "The city grouped around the fortress of Zion, and nestling in its shade."—Wordsworth.

c "A rude hut, standing on piles, in which a man was stationed by night to scare away jackals and other wild animals." — Tristram.

d "Longer than the common cucumber, of a deeper green, a softer and smoother skin, sweeter, and more easy of digestion; being very cooling, they are greatly in request."—E. Henderson.

e Eze. xvi. 49; see Ge. xix. 24, 25; 2 Pe. ii. 6.

For them that fear and sin not God's mercy is a holy mercy; where it pardons, it heals.—Watson, 1696.

10, 11. (10) **rulers of Sodom,**[a] in wickedness, indeed, Jerusalem is like Sodom, so its rulers are called "rulers of Sodom," "a striking apostrophe said to be unequalled."—Cheyne. The word "rulers" refers to the cadi, or judges,[b] regarded as leaders of the people's wickedness. **the law,** "not the Mosaic Law, but the prophetic revelation which followed."—Cam. Bib. (11) **multitude .. me?** i. e. sacrifices as merely outward acts now worthless. "The observance of the ceremonial law had no value except as the expression of a godly disposition."—Oehler (cf. 1 Sam. xv. 22; Hos. vi. 6; Isa. lviii. 3; Jer. vii. 21—23; xiv. 12).[c] **full of,** sated with. Figurative, but suggested by the idea that the sacrifices were the food of the gods.

The service which alone is pleasing to God (vss. 10—17).—From the text we see—I. The inadequacy of ritual observances. Hence—This address may be applied to self-righteous formalists; 2. To many who make a profession of vital godliness. II. The necessity of moral attainments. In relation to these two things are required—1. A renunciation of accustomed sins; 2. A performance of neglected duties. Hence see—(1) The nature of true religion; (2) The danger of self-conceit; (3) The excellency of the Gospel.—C. Simeon.

Sincerity in worship.—Fruit-trees that bring forth the fairest and most beautiful blossoms, leaves, and shoots, usually bring forth the fewest and least fruits; because where nature is intent and vigorously pressing to do one work, spending its strength there, it is at the same time weak about other works; but distinct and several works of nature, in moderate and remiss degree, are all promoted at the same time. Generally those persons who are excessive and most curious about the forms of duties, have least of the power of godliness. The Pharisees were excessively careful about the outside of God's worship. So it was among us of late years; bowing at the name of Jesus, the communion-table, surplice, common prayer, etc., and suchlike were pressed with all eagerness and strictness. The body of religion was large and monstrous, but without a soul; or, if any, it was lean and feeble. These persons are like the Indian fig-tree that Pliny speaks of, which had leaves as broad as targets, but fruits no bigger than a bean. This is a foul fault among us at this day: men stand more about the forms of worship than about the power of it: they look so much after the way, manner, and circumstances that they almost lose the substance; things which are but as husks or shells to the kernels, or as leaves in respect of fruits.—Austen.

a Re. xi. 8.

b Arab proverb—"More unjust than a judge of Sodom." —Gesenius.

c Pr. xv. 8, xxi. 27; Is. lxvi. 3; Je. vi. 20; Am. v. 21; Mic. vi. 6—12.

"The people of Jerus. pleaded their displays of religious zeal and devotion in the services and sacrifices of the temple, as a bar to the Prophet's severe verdict upon them. He says, they are mere empty shows, hypocritical masques and disguises." — Wordsworth.

" 'Examine yourselves:' a metaphor from metal, that is pierced through to see if it be gold within. A man must search his heart for sin as one would search a

12, 13. (12) **tread,** R. V. "trample," like heedless animals.[a] (13) **vain oblations,**[b] i. e. offerings with no heart in them. Lit. lying meat-offerings, **incense,** wh. is the symbol of prayer, ascending to God; but lacking the spirit of prayer it was hateful. **new moons,** etc., your specially holy seasons and gatherings. **I cannot away,** R. V. "I cannot away with iniquity and the solemn meeting." The combination is unbearable, laxity of morals and strictness in liturgy! **solemn meeting,** the eighth day of Feast of Tabernacles, and the seventh day of the Passover.[c]

Irreverence.—I have sometimes had the misfortune to sit in concerts where persons would chatter and giggle and laugh during the performance of the profoundest passages of the symphonies of the great artists; and I never fail to think, at such times, "I ask to know neither you, nor your father and mother, nor your name: I know what you are, by the way you conduct yourself here—by the want of sympathy and appreciation which you evince respecting what is passing around you." We could hardly help striking a man who should stand looking upon Niagara Falls without exhibiting emotions of awe and admiration. If we were to see a man walk through galleries of genius, totally unimpressed by what he saw, we should say to ourselves, "Let us be rid of such an unsusceptible creature as that." Now I ask you to pass upon yourselves the same judgment. What do you suppose angels, that have trembled and quivered with ecstatic joy in the presence of God, think when they see how indifferent you are to the Divine love and goodness in which you are perpetually bathed, and by which you are blessed and sustained every moment of your lives? How can they do otherwise than accuse you of monstrous ingratitude and moral insensibility, which betoken guilt as well as danger!—Beecher.

14, 15. (14) **appointed feasts,** the stated festivals dependent on the season of the year. These were ordained by God Himself. **My soul hateth,** (cf. xlii. 1, "my soul delighteth"), a rare and very emphatic expression. **a trouble,** lit. "a burden." (15) **spread . . hands,** a very usual and appropriate gesture of prayer.[a] The lifting up of the hands in prayer was a presentation of ones-self. To have "clean hands" was a well understood ceremonial requirement, signifying a clean life. **full of blood,** the traces of violence and crime,[b] not necessarily murder, but also, as context shows, injustice, oppression, causing anguish and even death.

God oppressed (vs. 11).—God, being the holiest, feels sin the most. The language indicates—1. The exquisite sensibility of God; 2. The amazing patience of God; 3. The remedial agency of God.—Thomas.

God's hatred of sin.—God hates sin, because it destroys what He loves. He could live high and lifted up above all noise of man's groaning, all smoke of his torment; but His nature is to come down after man—to grope for him amid all the dark pollutions of sin, and, if possible, to rescue and cleanse him. God hates sin very much, as mothers hate wild beasts. One day a woman stood washing beside a stream. She was in a wild frontier country, and the woods were all around. Her little, only child was playing about near her. By and by she missed the infant's prattle, and, looking about, she called its name. There was no answer. Alarmed, the mother ran to the house, but her babe was not there. In wild distress the poor woman now fled to search the woods, and there she found her child. But it was only its little body that she clasped to her heart. A wolf had seized her treasure, and when, at last, she rescued it from those bloody fangs, its spirit had gone. Oh, how that mother hated wolves! And do you know that this is the very figure Christ uses to show what feeling He has towards the sin that is seeking to devour His children?—Beecher.

16, 17. (16) **Wash you,** comp. the duty of priests before sacrificing.[c] **put away . . eyes,** "to remove their ill-doings from before the All-seeing Eyes, was, in fact, altogether to cease from it." (17) **judgment,** the expression of righteousness in our actions and relations. **relieve,** Heb. "set right the oppressor," restrain him within **the bounds of justice. Ill-**

---

house for a traitor: or as Israel sought for leaven to burn it."—Watson.

[a] "A term of contempt purposely borrowed from the action of the cattle brought into the outer court for sacrifice." —E. Henderson.

[b] Le. ii. 1—3; Nu. xxviii. 12, etc.

Comp. Mat. xxi. 12, 13.

[c] Le.. xxiii. 36; Nu. xxix. 35; De. xvi. 6.

"A remembrance of God's omnipresence will quell distractions in worship. Oppose to every intruding thought the idea of the Divine omnipresence, and put it to silence by the awe of His majesty." —Charnock.

[a] 1 Ki. viii. 38, 54; 1 Ti. ii. 8.

[b] "Nothing could be more incongruous than to spread open to the view of Holy Omniscience hands which had been stained by acts of atrocious wickedness." —E. Henderson.

"Under the term blood all sins of violence and gross injustice are to be comprehended." —Calvin.

"Will men's prayers be answered? Not if they pray as boys whittle sticks—absently, hardly knowing or caring what they are about." —Beecher.

[c] Ex. xxx. 19—21.

"Heart - cleansing, turning away from evil, proper fruits of repentance: such is the Divine service that the Lord requires." —Nagelsbach.

treatment of the orphan and widow[a] are sure signs of a low state of public morality. The righteous are merciful and tender.

Repentance necessary (vs. 16).—I. God doth primarily desire the good of all His creatures. II. He doth not desire man's salvation without his return. III. He doth not desire man's return without his own consent.—B. Whichcot.

Elements of a noble character.—It is not great, or special, or extraordinary experiences which constitute in the best sense the religious character. It is the uniform daily walk with God, serving Him in little things as well as great—in the ordinary duties and everyday avocations, as well as in the midst of grave and eventful contingencies. As the sublimest symphony is made up of separate single notes;—as the wealth of the cornfield is made up of separate stalks, or rather of separate grains;—as the magnificent texture, with its gorgeous combinations of color, is made up of individual threads;—as the mightiest avalanche that ever came thundering down from its Alpine throne, uprooting villages and forests, is made up of tiny snowflakes;—so it is with the spiritual life. That life is itself the grandest illustration of the power of littles. Character is the product of daily, hourly actions, words, thoughts; daily forgivenesses, unselfishnesses, kindnesses, sympathies, charities, sacrifices for the good of others, struggles against temptations, submissiveness under trial. Oh it is these, like the blending colors in a picture, or the blending notes of music, which constitute the man.—Macduff.

a "Orphans and widows are continually spoken of in Scripture as special objects of Divine compassion, and as representing the whole class of helpless innocents."— J. A. Alexander.

"Rooting up the large weeds of a garden loosens the earth, and renders the extraction of the lesser ones comparatively easy." Eliza Cook.

18. reason, G. A. Smith and others translate "Come now and let us bring our reasoning to a close." "God reasons with man, that is the first article of religion according to Isaiah. Revelation is not magical but rational and moral. Religion is reasonable intercourse between one intelligent Being and another."—Smith. **as scarlet . . red like crimson,**[b] the promises in this verse are conditional on obedience to vss. 16—17. **white as snow,** the sense is best rendered in the Polychr. Bib., "If your sins be scarlet they may become white as snow: Be they red as crimson they may become as wool."

Forgiveness (vs. 18).—I. There is assumed the existence of enormous guilt. 1. "Scarlet" and "crimson" indicate sins of peculiar flagrancy; 2. Sin extends to the whole human race; 3. These principles extend to ourselves; 4. The great sin is the neglect of the great salvation. II. There is the promised bestowment of pardoning mercy. 1. This promise is consistent with the holiness and justice of God; 2. Note the manner in which the promised blessing is bestowed; 3. The sufficiency by which this promised blessing of forgiveness is characterized. III. There is desired the exercise of wise consideration. Procrastinate not a moment longer. Believe the saving testimony now. Wash in the fountain now. Seek for glory, honor, and immortality now.—J. Parsons.

Double-dyed.—Certain scarlet cloth is first dyed in the grain, and then dyed in the piece; it is thus double-dyed. And so are we with regard to the guilt of sin; we are double-dyed, for we are all sinners by birth, and sinners by practice. Our sins are like scarlet, yet by faith in Christ they shall be as white as snow: by an interest in Christ's atonement, though our offences be red like crimson, they shall be as wool; that is, they shall be as white as the undyed wool.—"Friendly Greetings."

Sin and Grace.—Like some black rock that heaves itself above the surface of a sunlit sea, and the wave runs dashing over it, and the spray, as it falls down its sides, is all rainbowed and lightened, and there comes beauty into the mighty grimness of the black thing; so a man's transgressions rear themselves up, and God's great love comes sweeping itself against them and over them, makes out of the sin an occasion for the flashing more brightly of the beauty of His mercy, and turns the life of the pardoned penitent into a life of which even the sin is not pain to remember.—Maclaren. Divine alchemy.—In nature there is hardly a stone that is not capable of crystallizing into something purer and brighter than its normal state. Coal, by a slightly different arrangement of its particles, is capable of becoming the radiant diamond. The slag cast out from the furnace as useless waste forms into globular masses of radiating crystals. From tar and pitch the loveliest colors are now manufactured. The very mud of the road, trampled under foot as the type of all impurity, can be

b "Scarlet was regarded as the most fast or fixed of colors. Neither dew, nor rain, nor washing, nor long use could remove it."—Kitto.

With the Jews, white was the symbol of purity, red of crime, especially of cruelty and murder.

Mi. vii. 18, 19; Is. xliii. 25, 26; Ps. li. 7; 1 Jno. i. 7.

"There is an antipathy between sinning and praying. The child that hath misspent the whole day in playing abroad, steals to bed at night for fear of a chiding from his father. Sin and prayer are such contraries, that it is impossible at a stride to step from one to another. Prayer will either make you leave off sinning, or sinning will make you leave off prayer." — Gurnall.

"He is rich in mercy, abundant in goodness and

truth. Thy sins are like a spark of fire that falls into the ocean, it is quenched presently; so are all thy sins in the ocean of God's mercy. There is not more water in the sea than there is mercy in God."—Manton.

"Princes very often pardon traitors to please others more than themselves, or else it would never be done; but God doth it chiefly to delight and gladden His own merciful heart." — Gurnall.

changed by chemical art into metals and gems of surpassing beauty; and so the most unpromising materials, the most worthless moral rubbish that men cast out and despise, may be converted by the Divine alchemy into the gold of the sanctuary, and made jewels fit for the mediatorial crown of the Redeemer. Let the case of Mary Magdalene, of John Newton, of John Bunyan, of thousands more, encourage those who are still in the gall of bitterness and in the bond of inquity. Seek to be subjected to the same purifying influences; yield yourselves up into the hands of the Spirit to become His finished and exquisite workmanship; seek diligently a saving and sanctifying union with Christ by faith, and He will perfect that which concerneth you, and lay your stones with fair colors (Ps. lxviii. 13).—Macmillan. God's pity and warning.—God indeed tells us of hell, but it is to persuade us to flee to heaven; and as a skilful painter fills the background of his picture with his darker colors, God introduces the smoke of torment, and the black thunder-clouds of Sinai, to give brighter prominence to Jesus, the Cross of Calvary, and His love to the chief of sinners. His voice of terror is like the scream of the mother-bird when the hawk is in the sky. She alarms her brood, that they may run and hide beneath her feathers; and as I believe that God had left that mother dumb unless He had given her wings to cover them, I am sure that He, who is very "pitiful," and has no pleasure in any creature's pain, had never turned our eyes to the horrible gulf unless for the voice that cries, "Deliver from going down to the pit, for I have found a ransom." We had never heard of sin had there been no Saviour. We had never heard of hell had there been no heaven. "Sufficient for the day is the evil thereof." And never had Bible light flashed before the eyes of the sleeping felon, to wake him from his happy dream, but that he might see the smiling form of Mercy, and hear her as she says, with finger pointing the way, "Behold I have set before thee an open door."—Guthrie.

[a] "Temporal blessings, 'in the land of their possession,' were prominent in the O. T. promises, as suited to the childhood of the Church. Ex. iii. 17."—Fausset.

[b] Is. xxi. 17, xxii. 25, xxiv. 3, xxv. 8, xl. 5, lviii. 14.

"The wages that sin bargains with the sinner, are life, pleasure, and profit; but the wages it pays him with are death, torment, and destruction; he that would understand the falsehood and deceit of sin, must compare its promises and payments together."—South.

"'Tis greatly wise to talk with our past hours, and ask them what report they bore to heaven, and how they might have borne more welcome news." —Young.

19, 20. (19) **willing,**[a] notice that the demands here (vss. 16-17) **are** external, not spiritual, and the reward "the good of the land" was equally external. This is not the deepest message of the prophet. (20) **refuse,** i. e. to be just and relieve the oppressed, etc., then ye shall suffer by the sword. Note the antithesis "ye shall eat"—"ye shall be devoured." **mouth,** this is not human judgment but the direct verdict of God from His lips.[b]

The magnitude of Divine pity.—God's pity is not as some sweet cordial poured in dainty drops from some golden phial. It is not like the musical water-drops of some slender rill, murmuring down the dark sides of Mount Sinai. It is wide as the whole scope of heaven. It is abundant as all the air. If one had art to gather up all the golden sunlight that to-day falls wide over all this continent, falling through every silent hour; and all that is dispersed over the whole ocean, flashing from every wave; and all that is poured refulgent over the northern wastes of ice, and along the whole continent of Europe, and the vast outlying Asia, and torrid Africa; if one could in any wise gather up this immense and incalculable outflow and treasure of sunlight that falls down through the bright hours, and runs in liquid ether about the mountains, and fills all the plains, and sends innumerable rays through every secret place, pouring over and filling every flower, shining down the sides of every blade of grass, resting in glorious humility upon the humblest things—on stick and stone and pebble, on the spider's web, the sparrow's nest, the threshold of the young fox's hole, where they play and warm themselves; that rests on the prisoner's window, that strikes radiant beams through the slave's tear, that puts gold upon the widow's weeds, that plates and roofs the city with burnished gold, and goes on in its wild abundance up and down the earth, shining everywhere and always since the day of primal creation, without faltering, without stint, without waste or diminution, as full, as fresh, as overflowing, to-day, as if it were the first day of its outplay;—if one might gather up this boundless, endless, infinite treasure, to measure it, then might he tell the height and depth, and unending glory of the pity of God. In light,—in the sun its source,—you have God's own figure of the immensity and copiousness of His mercy and compassion—Beecher.

21—23. (21) **"Ah! how,"** This is a peculiar word used in the beginning of Elegiac utterances (e. g. Lamentations). It is preceded by a rhetorical pause, as if awaiting a reply. None comes, and the prophet **breaks** out in lamentation. **faithful city,** that once was faithful. He remembers the days of David and the glory of Israel. **harlot,** by being faithless to her covenant with Jehovah. Not only idolatry but every kind of sin brings this condemnation. Notice the introduction here of the symbol of the bridal relation betw. Israel and Jehovah, far more commonly used in O. T. than that of filial relationship, employed in vs. 2. **murderers,** the worst class of violent wrong-doers put to include all others.[a] (22) **silver .. wine,** the nobles and leaders of the land,[b] cf. Jer. vi. 28—30; Ezek. xxii. 18. The best metal of your citizenship is worthless. The best blood has run thin. (23) **princes,** your civil and military leaders take bribes and connive at extortion and robbery. **companions,** better, accomplices. **judge,** etc., because these are weak and poor and cannot bribe.

Liberality.—If we so love our riches that we would eternally possess them, let us not hoard them up in the earth, where we are sure to leave them, carrying nothing with us but the canker of our coin, which shall bear witness against us at the Day of Judgment; but let us send them before us into heaven, delivering them unto the poor, who are God's factors and receivers; and so having conveyed and made over our goods, as it were by bills of exchange, we shall find the Lord a sure and all-sufficient paymaster, who will give us more than double usance, and yet pay us at the first sight. If we would have our coin continue sweet and good for a great space, let us know that there are for this purpose no garners comparable to poor men's stomachs, which will preserve our grain for our use unto life eternal. If we would have our clothes preserved from moths, and to last long, the backs of the naked are our safest wardrobes.—Downame. Silver becomes dross thro' little failings.—You need not break the glasses of a telescope, or coat them over with paint, in order to prevent you from seeing through them. Just breathe upon them, and the dew of your breath will shut out all the stars. So it does not require great crimes to hide the light of God's countenance. Little faults can do it just as well. Take a shield, and cast a spear upon it, and it will leave in it one great dent. Prick it all over with a million little needle shafts, and they will take the polish from it far more than the piercing of the spear. So it is not so much the great sins which take the freshness from our consciences, as the numberless petty faults which we are all the while committing.—Beecher.

[a] Comp. condition of city in Manasseh's reign. 2 Ki. xxi. 16, xxiv. 4.

Spk. Com. comp. the condition of Jerusalem in the siege that followed on the rejection of the Lord Jesus Christ.

[b] "The silver is said to be turned into dross, and the pure wine to be mixed with water, when judges and senators turn from purity and grave manners, from integrity, sincerity, and candor, and prostitute their own dignity." — Vitringa.

24—27. (24) **the Lord,** Heb. Adonai. **Lord of hosts,**[c] three names heaped together to emphasize the absoluteness of the verdict and the omnipotence of the Judge. **the mighty One,** a title rarely used (cf. xlix. 26; lx. 16; Gen. xlix. 24; Ps. cxxxii. 2). **ease me,** by getting rid of them. **enemies,** the unfaithful among the Jews themselves. (25) **turn,** "bring back," in judgment. **purely,** R. V. "thoroughly," marg. "Heb. as with lye,"—cf. Job ix. 30.[a] **tin,** or lead, as when coin or silver vessels are melted the lead alloy is separated from the pure silver. (26) **at the first,** cf. Jer. ii. 2. "The regeneration of Israel will be as wonderful as its first foundation under Moses, and Joshua and Samuel."—Cheyne. (27) **with judgment,** or Divine severities. **converts,** returning penitent ones.

The influence of holiness.—There is an energy of moral suasion in a good man's life, passing the highest efforts of the orator's genius. The seen but silent beauty of holiness speaks more eloquently of God and duty than the tongues of men and angels. Let parents remember this. The best inheritance a parent can bequeath to a child is a virtuous example, a legacy of hallowed remembrances and associations. The beauty of holiness beaming through the life of a loved relative or friend is more effectual to strengthen such as do stand in virtue's ways, and raise up those that are bowed down, than precept, command, entreaty, or warning. Christianity itself, I believe, owes by far the greater part of its moral power, not to the precepts of parables of Christ, but to His own character. The beauty of that holiness which is enshrined in the four brief biographies of the Man of Nazareth has done more and will do more to regenerate the world, and bring in everlasting righteousness, than all the other agencies put together. It has done more to spread His religion in the world than all that has ever been preached or written on the evidences of Christianity.—Chalmers.

[c] Is. iii. 1, x. 16, 33, xix. 4.

[a] "The totality of the nation shall be subjected to a purifying process wh. the Prophet compares to the process by which silver ore is freed from the mixture of ignoble metal, and rendered solid silver. The separation of the lead ore is promoted by applying alkali." — Nagelsbach.

Ro. xi. 26, Re iii. 19.

"Christianity ends not in negatives. The soul may be cleansed from all blots, and yet still be left but a blank." —South.

28—31. (28) **And,** R. V., "But," by contrast with vs. 27. **destruction,** lit. breaking into shivers.[b] **transgressors,** Cheyne, "renegades," who have inwardly and outwardly broken away from Jehovah; same word as in vs. 2, "rebelled." **together,** in a mass, at once, and utterly. **consumed,** Ps. xxxvi. 20.[c] (29) Polychr. Bib. calls vss. 29—31 "a fragment against Tree-worship." **oaks,** R. V. margin, "terebinths," a sacred tree in Canaan and Cyprus, an object of worship. **gardens,** or idol-groves.[d] Peculiarly favorable for the sensual rites connected with idol-worship. (30) **leaf fadeth,** "the falling leaf and the failing spring would mean, to nature worshipers, the decay of divine life that was within the terebinth and the sacred garden."—Cam. Bib.[e] **maker of it,** R. V. "and his work," i. e. his work shall be the cause of his destruction, as the spark fires the tow. His sin shall find him out. **spark,**[f] a man's sin lighting up his judgment.

Gardens.—In the language of the Hebrews, every place where plants and trees were cultivated with greater care than in the open field was called a garden. The idea of such an enclosure was certainly borrowed from the garden of Eden, which the bountiful Creator planted for the reception of His favorite creature. The gardens of primitive nations were commonly, if not in every instance, devoted to religious purposes. In these shady retreats were celebrated, for a long succession of ages, the rites of pagan superstition. Thus, Jehovah calls the apostate Jews "a people that provoked Me continually to anger to My face, that sacrificeth in gardens."—Paxton. Moral beauty of shame.—A young girl was one day censured by her mother for some fault, upon which she deeply blushed, burst into tears, and retired into a corner. Gotthold was present, and observed to the mother: "How beautiful your reproof has made your daughter! That crimson hue, and silver tears, become her better than any ornament of gold and pearls. A full-blown rose, besprinkled with the purest dew, is not so beautiful as this child blushing beneath her parent's displeasure, and shedding tears of sorrow for her fault. A blush is the sign which nature hangs out to show where chastity and honor dwell."—Gotthold.

b "The crushing, utter ruin. The terms of this vs. are appropriate to all kinds of sin, but seem to be peculiarly descriptive of idolatry, as defection or desertion from the true God to idols."—J. A. Alexander.

c Ps. civ. 35; Pr. xxix. 1; Re. xxi. 8.

d Is. lxv. 3, lxvi. 17; Eze. vi. 13; Ho. iv. 13.

e Comp. Je. ii. 13, xvii. 13.

f "Sin is the match which ignites the sinner with the fire of the punishment that will consume him." —Wordsworth.

CHAPTER THE SECOND.

There is no connection between chaps. i. and ii. But chaps. ii—iv. are a continuous prophecy of a future vindication of God's holiness.

1, 2. (1) **word,** or message Divinely entrusted to Is. **saw,** by spiritual intuition. "The original meaning of the Hebrew word saw, which is used in the title to this series, is to cleave, or split; then to see into, to see through, to get down beneath the surface of things and discover their real nature."—G. A. Smith. (2) **last days,**[a] lit. "in the sequel of the days"—that is in the day of results, when the conclusion of present conditions comes, comp. Mi. iv. 1, 2, vss. 2—4 are not originally Isaiah's own words, but those of another prophet, taken out of their connection. Perhaps Isaiah and Micah quoted from some common source. (Delitzsch). **mountain .. mountains,** a fig. expression, meaning that Jerusalem should be given the highest place in religious and political supremacy. Possibly also a physical elevation was thought of (Ezek. xl. 2). **top of,** R. V. "at the head."[c] **flow,** in a procession that may be likened to a river.

The Gospel conspicuous (vs. 2).—I. The coming glory of the Church. 1. A universal brotherhood; 2. A reign of love; 3. An age of progress. II. Signs of its approach. 1. The accomplishment of prophecy; 2. Dissemination of useful knowledge; 3. The connection of minds by scientific discovery; 4. The extension of evangelical truth.—W. Whythe.

The spiritual magnet.—There is an Eastern fable about a great mountain of loadstone out in the middle of the sea, that attracted all the ships which came near it, by the iron nails and bolts which fastened their timbers together, and then, drawing these out, left the vessel to strew the waves, a mass of beams and boards and spars. This mountain of the Lord's house is a grand spiritual magnet, and it draws souls, not to destruction, but everlasting life.—Edmond.

3. people, R. V. "peoples." **of his ways,** "the preposition has a posi-

a Je. xxiii. 20, xxx. 24; Da. x. 14; Ho. iii. 5.

b "Instead of saying, in modern phraseology, that the Church, as a society, shall become conspicuous and attract all nations, he represents the mountain upon which the temple stood as being raised and fixed above the other mountains, so as to be visible in all directions." —J. A. Alexander.

c "Its crest the summit of the whole range."—Spk. Com.

"The Church which was first founded at Jerusalem was the **seminary** or seedplot of all Churches of Christendom.

tive sense, 'somewhat of his ways' (cf. Ps. xciv. 12), each people receiving such direction as is adapted to its peculiar circumstances."—Cam. Bib. **out of Zion . . from Jerusalem,**[a] these are the emphatic words of this verse, declaring Zion and Jerusalem to be the source of all wisdom and righteousness. "Salvation is of the Jews," John iv. 22.

The mountain of the Lord's house (vss. 2—4).—I. The period referred to. The Christian dispensation. II. The cheering truth declared. 1. Elevated position; 2. Permanent duration. III. The general interest awakened. 1. The invitation given; 2. The considerations by which it is enforced. IV. The happy results secured. 1. A consummation devoutly to be wished; 2. Absolutely certain is its realization; 3. The means whereby it shall be accomplished.

Origin and glory of the Gospel.—As to its origin and glory, the Gospel may be compared to an angel "standing in the sun;" as to the territorial range of its commission, it may be compared to "an angel flying in the midst of heaven;" as to the gracious mysteries of salvation to which it points, it may be compared to the angels looking into the ark of the covenant; as to the pure and holy worship which it enjoins, and over which it presides, it may be compared to the angel standing beside the altar of incense; as to the hopes and inspirations which it warrants and sustains, it may be compared to an angel at heaven's gate, saying to us, poor dusty wayfarers, "Come up hither." But looking at the relations of the Gospel to men in the business of everyday life, we may regard it still as an angel (losing nothing of its ethereal beauty and celestial brightness); but then, it is an angel full of condescension and brotherly companionship; an angel mingling with us, and talking to us—helping, and guiding, and comforting us; an angel, recognizing our earthly wants, and sympathizing with us in our earthly trials, like the angel who came to Abraham under the trees of Mamre, and to Lot in his house at Sodom; like the angel who appeared to Ornan while he was threshing wheat; like the angel who appeared to Zechariah in the shop of the four carpenters; like the angel who touched Elijah asleep, and showed him a "cake baken on the coals, and a cruse of water at his head;" and like the angel who came to Peter in prison, and took off his chains and set him free! Thus does the religion of the Bible come home to us, and put itself on a level with us, entering fully into our temporal circumstances, temporal necessities, temporal duties, and temporal trials.—Stoughton.

4. he shall judge, the coming Messiah shall administer justice as a king. **rebuke,** R. V., "reprove," better still, "arbitrate for," i. e. the influence of the coming kingdom will be to put arbitration in the place of force. **pruning hooks,** such will be the influence of the reign of justice that men will neither desire nor need to make war any more. Therefore instruments of war become useless. **learn war,** the arts of war. Among the prophetic anticipations is a time when war shall cease. "All weapons are to be destroyed (Micah v. 4—10; Zech. ix. 10; Hosea ii. 18; Ps. xlvi. 9; Ezek. xxxix. 9—10, etc.), the new Church is unapproachable in its protected retirement (Micah vii. 14). The new city of God is no more to be desecrated by enemies (Joel iii. 7)."—Oehler.

Weapons of war.—I have been laboring among a people who once delighted in war; but, since Christianity has prevailed there, war has ceased altogether, and they are astonished how they ever engaged in all those deeds of savage cruelty, which, according to their usual practice, threatened the extermination of their race; but now the Prince of Peace reigns there. I have seen the musket-barrel taken from the stock, and carried to the anvil, and beaten into a spade or a hoe, though not into a ploughshare, for the plough does not yet turn up their fruitful soil, and the warrior who has used it in battle now employs it in cultivating the land. They have even gone further in illustration of this beautiful description of the Prophet; for they have devoted the implements of war to the service of the sanctuary. The last Sabbath I was there, I went into one of their chapels, and ministered to a large congregation of about fifteen hundred persons. A rude sort of pulpit was erected, and stairs led up to it, the railings of which, smooth and polished, were literally composed of the handles of warriors' spears, who had thus transferred their weapons, with themselves, to a nobler and better purpose—the service of

And well might the Prophet say that the law shall go forth from Zion; for the Gospel streamed forth with its living waters from that fountain and well-spring, and irrigated the world."— S. Jerome.

a Je. l. 5; Zec. viii. 21—23; Lu. xxiv. 47.

"All who profess the Gospel and have not sincerity, are as clouds without water, trees without fruit, or lamps without oil; but those who love God with undivided hearts, participate a constant succession of pleasures in His approbation and in their own minds." —Beaumont.

"So much does the Syrian ploughshare resemble the short sword used by the ancient warriors, that it may with very little trouble be converted into that deadly weapon, and when the work of destruction is over, reduced again to its former shape."—Barnes.

Ps. lxxii. 7; Je. xxiii. 6; Zec. ix. 10.

"People are always expecting to get peace in Heaven; but you know whatever peace they get there will be ready-made. Whatever of making peace they can be blest for, must be on the earth here."— Ruskin.

"A weary and discouraged woman said: "Everything looks dark, dark.' 'Why don't you turn your face to the light, aunty dear?' said a little niece.

The words were a message from on high, and the weary eyes were turned toward Him in whose light alone we see light."

Ps. lxxxix. 15; Is. lxi. 19; Jno. xii. 35, 36; 1 Jno. i. 7; Re. xxi. 23, 24.

"'Where the sun does not enter, the physician must;' so say the Italians, and their witness is true. Sunlight has not only a cheering but a health-giving influence. Along the Riviera, invalids owe everything to the sun; and when it is gone, they shrink into their own rooms."

the sanctuary of God.—W. Ellis. The promise of peace.—What words are these! What ideas! What radiances of glory and hope for the long-afflicted Church! Nations abolishing war and crimes, to cultivate righteousness and peace! nations emerging from ignorance and idolatry, to join themselves to the Church, and to walk in the light of the Lord! How marvelous that words like these should proceed from the Hebrew prophets! that men of the most confined education with regard to the Gentiles should thus lose the glory of Israel in the overflowing glory of the converted world! Can we ask for clearer proof that those holy men were purely the organs of the Holy Ghost, and transported in the spirit to publish the righteousness of God to every nation and language of the earth?—Sutcliffe.

5. **house of Jacob,** comp. Ex. xix. 3: here is an abrupt transition as of one returning from a vision to every-day realities. **light of the Lord,** to walk in the light of the Lord is to walk in the way he has revealed, i. e. according to His instructions, Ps. cxix. 105.

Exhortation to a holy walk (vs. 5).—Let us walk in—I. The light of His truth. It now shines with meridian splendor. II. Of His countenance. This is the privilege of the true believer; let us enjoy our privilege. III. Of His commandments. These are given as a light to our feet: let us make them the rule of our conduct. Addressing the house of Jacob—1. Speak to those who are so nominally; 2. Those who are really so.—C. Simeon.

The satisfaction of holiness.—The knowledge of God and conformity to Him are in their own nature apt to satisfy the desires of the soul, and even now actually do so in the measure wherein they are attained. Some things are not of a satisfying nature; there is nothing tending to satisfaction in them. And then the continual heaping together of such things doth no more towards satisfaction than the accumulating of mathematical points would towards the compacting of a solid body, or the multiplication of cyphers only, to the making of a sum. But the hungry, craving soul, that would fain be happy, but knows not how, needs not spend its days in making uncertain guesses and fruitless attempts and trials; it may fix its hovering thoughts, and upon assurance here given, say, "I have now found at last where satisfaction may be had; and have only this to do, to bend all my powers hither and intend this one thing, the possessing myself of this blessed rest. Happy discovery! welcome tidings! I now know to which way to turn my eye and direct my pursuit. I shall no longer spend myself in dubious toilsome wanderings, in anxious vain inquiry. I have found it! I have found it! blessedness is here." —J. Howe.

a "The word 'replenished' suggests a reference to the pythons, and other diviners, who were filled with an afflatus from an evil spirit." —Vitringa.

b "As if that could be a god to them wh. was not only a creature, but their own creature." —Matt. Henry.

6—9. (6) **Therefore,** R. V. "for." Turning to God, the Prophet says, "I thus exhort Thy people, because Thou hast forsaken them," etc. **replenished from,** R. V., "filled with customs from." **the east,** the cradle of the occult arts and sciences. Filled with Oriental luxuries and idolatries.[a] **soothsayers,** sorcerers, practicing hidden arts. Cheyne translates "diviners of the clouds." **Philistines,** 1Sa. vi. 2; 2 Ki. i. 2. **please themselves,** R. V. "strike hands with"; make covenant with. (7) **horses,** the wealth of the land has enormously increased, and they have standing armies, sources of peril to any nation, comp. De. xvii. 16, 17. (8) **own hands .. made,** the usual prophetic satire of idols.[b] (9) **boweth .. humbleth,** R. V., "is bowed down," and "is brought low," i. e. (ch. v. 15) as a judgment upon them. **forgive,** etc., "and forgive them—no, that thou wilt not," Delitsch. The prophet's conviction is that God cannot forgive this sin.

National apostasy (vss. 6—8).—We have here—I. A catalogue of Israel's sins. 1. Unhallowed intercourse with God's enemies; 2. Divination; 3. Worldliness; 4. Idolatry. II. A denunciation of Israel's punishment. 1. God forsakes them; 2. Withholds forgiveness.—Lyth.

"In the library of the world, men have hitherto been ranged according to the form, the size, and the binding. The time is coming when they will take rank and order according to their

The sinner's plea.—"A man called at my house some time ago for charity—an arrant beggar, I have no doubt. Thinking that the man's rags and poverty were real, I gave him a little money, some of my clothes, and a pair of shoes. After he had put them on and gone out, I thought, 'Well, after all, I have done you a bad turn very likely, for you will not get so much money now as before, because you will not look so wretched an object.' Happening to go out a quarter of an hour afterwards, I saw my friend; but he was not wearing the clothes I had given him, not he! Why, I should have ruined his business if I could have compelled him to look respectable. He had been wise enough to slip down an archway, take all the good clothes off, and put his rags on again. Did I blame him? Yes, for being a rogue; but not for carrying on his business in a business-like manner. He only wore his proper livery, for rags are the livery of a beggar. The more ragged he looked, the more he would get. Just so it is with you. If you are to go to Christ, do not put on your good doings and feelings, or you will get nothing; go in your sins, they are your livery. Your ruin is your argument for mercy, your povert is your plea for heavenly alms, and your need is the motive for heavenly goodness."—Spurgeon.

contents and intrinsic merits." —E. Cook.

"This is a true and literal description of India: the traveler cannot proceed a mile through an inhabited country without seeing idols and vestiges of idolatry in every direction." —Roberts.

10, 11. (10) **Enter,** etc.,[c] because God cannot forgive (vs. 9) it only remains for you to flee to the cares from His wrath. **dust,** "as travelers endeavoring to escape the sweeping simoon of the desert." **for fear,** or fr. before the terror of the Lord. **glory .. majesty,** some great manifestation of His power in judgment.[d] (11) **lofty looks,** lit. eyes of loftiness. **exalted,** as judge and sovereign. **that day,** i. e. the one about to be described in vss. 12—16.

[c] Of old Is. fled before an invading army into caves and rocks. Ju. vi. 2; 1 Sa. xiii. 6.
See Re. vi. 15.

[d] "The terror shall be like that which spreads before an overpowering invasion of the enemy."—Lange.

A great day (vss 10—12).—I. A description of the day of the Lord. 1. It is the day of the revelation of the Divine glory; 2. Of the exaltation of the Divine majesty; 3. Of the utter overthrow of human pride; 4. Of the abolition of idolatry and superstition; 5. Of the confusion and destruction of God's foes. II. An exhortation to prepare for it. 1. Enter into the rock; 2. Hide thee in the dust; 3. Cease from man. III. Grounds for the exhortation. 1. This day will be very terrible and glorious; 2. A place of shelter is provided—a rock, a cleft in the rock; 3. We have the means of securing this shelter—humble thyself in the dust, enter by faith.—Lyth.

12, 13. (12) **day of the Lord,**[a] the usual phrase for a time to come when God will insure the triumph of His kingdom by overwhelming His enemies, called "the day of Jehovah," "the day of Jehovah's anger" (Zeph. ii. 3). "The great and terrible day of Jehovah" (Mal. iv. 5), etc. Comp. N. T. term, "day of judgment." (13) **cedars,**[b] "the totality of nature is bound up with man in one common history." This is the constant Biblical teaching, and it is a striking figure here used which shows the wrath of the Creator, beginning by mowing down the great cedars and oaks and mountains, and then towns and ships, and then men themselves.

[a] Joel i. 15.

"More exactly—'For the Lord hath a day.' He hasit in reserve, ready to be brought out when the time of forbearance is over." — Spk. Com.

[b] "The most distinguished objects of nature and art are used metaphorically to represent the different persons whom the judgments of God would hurl into ruin."—E. Henderson.

Humility in God's presence.—A minister named Winstanley was the means of comforting and edifying the great Dr. Johnson on his deathbed. In a letter to a friend, Hannah More, alluding to this, says: "I cannot conclude without remarking what honor God has hereby put upon the doctrine of faith in a crucified Saviour. The man whose intellectual powers had awed all around him, was in his turn, made to tremble when the period arrived at which all knowledge appears useless, and vanishes away, except the knowledge of the true God and Jesus Christ whom He has sent. Effectually to attain this knowledge, this giant in literature must become a little child. The man looked up to as a prodigy of wisdom must become a fool that he might be wise."—Old Test. Anec.

14—16. (14) **mountains .. hills,** first the forests, then the mountains themselves shall be overwhelmed. (15) **high tower,** then the things that men have builded, towns, walls, ships. (16) **ships of Tarshish,** the great merchant ships,[c] put as the type of the commerce in wh. men placed so great confidence. **pictures,** R. V., "imagery," an obscure word, found only here.

[c] "Richly-laden and far-going vessels, like our term East Indiamen."—Fausset.

"Ships delightful to look upon." — E. Henderson.

"Such as were built for the Ophir trade at the ports of the Aelanitic gulf." —Spk. Com.

"All the noble vessels and instruments of commercial prosperity."—Wordsworth.

A corrective of pride.—Libussa, princess of Bohemia, first ennobled, and then married Primaslaus, who before was a plain husbandman. In remembrance of his former condition, he preserved a pair of wooden shoes. Being asked the cause of his doing so, he made the following answer: "I have brought these shoes with me for the purpose of setting them up as a monument in the castle of Visegrade, and of exhibiting them to my successors, that all may know that the first prince of Bohemia was called to his high dignity from the cart and the plough; and that I myself, who am elevated to a crown, may bear constantly in mind that I have nothing whereof to be proud."

17—19. (17) **loftiness,** etc., and when man has witnessed all this, then his pride shall be humbled. (18) **the idols,** as for his idols, in which he has trusted, they shall vanish. **abolish,** R. V., "shall utterly pass away:" a use of these words in the Hebrew, "the idols—vanished," suggestive of swift and complete destruction.[d] (19) **holes,** etc., comp. vs. 10. Then shall the stricken mortals, deprived of all in which they had trusted, creep into caves and cellars, to escape the terrible majesty of Jehovah, cf. Rev. vi. 15—17.[a]

The triumphs of the Gospel (vs. 18).—I. The condition implied. Idolatry: define this—carved objects of worship, supreme affections set on other than God, the idols of the heart. II. The glorious change predicted. 1. The conversion of their adherents to a purer faith; 2. The extent to which this change shall be affected. III. The means appointed for its accomplishment. 1. Earnest prayer for the outpouring of the Holy Spirit; 2. The preaching of the Gospel. IV. The encouragement. 1. The faithfulness of God's word; 2. The success already granted; 3. The condescension of God in owning and blessing the feeble efforts made for His glory.

An unfortunate idol.—There are few positions more melancholy than that of an Indian god who has seen better days, and it is difficult to read the accounts in the Indian papers of the present condition of Jagarnath without a deep feeling of commiseration for that unfortunate deity. Jagarnath, according to the Pioneer, has been in a bad way since his hereditary protector, the Rajah of Puri, has gone to live in the Andamans. The affairs of the temple have been found to be in a pitiable state, the Rajah having greatly mismanaged the revenue. His mother, the Rani, has done all that her ingenuity could suggest to mend matters, but there are serious arrears in the pay and perquisites of the servants of the temple and family dependents, to pay up which would take a large revenue. Since the conviction of the Dibya Singh Deb the pension to the family has been stopped, and the local feeling is that the Rani is harshly treated by having the sins of her son visited on her own head. A further calamity in the shape of a famine has long been hanging over Puri, and the car festival was a miserable affair. At first no timber for the great car could be got, as the usual agent blankly refused to send an inch of wood, and it seemed as if Jagarnath would have to dispense with his customary airing. The Rani, however, was indefatigable, and in spite of difficulties managed to do the work of her worthless son.—Pall Mall Gazette.

20, 21. (20) **cast his idols,** He seems to forget the former figure of utter destruction and now emphasizes man's own disgust at the uselessness of the idols when a time of testing comes. Perhaps vs. 18 is incomplete as Polychr. Bib. suggests. **which they made,** notice repetition of idea, upon which the prophet dwells elsewhere. **to the moles,** etc., creatures of the darkness; the one burrowing in the dark ground, the other flying in the dark sky.[b] The expression is a proverbial one for "contemptuous rejection." (21) **To go,** unencumbered, seeking a safety for themselves wh. their idols fail to give. **tops,** crevices; fissures of the cliffs.

The long reign of idols.—Trace human history back as far as all extant records will enable you to do so, and you will find idols enthroned in the affections of men. That they should ever have been set up there must be regarded as one of Satan's subtlest and greatest triumphs. The instincts that lead men to worship are so strong, that his only hope of preventing fallen men from returning to their allegiance to God lay in persuading them to worship some other thing or being. His difficulty and his device were those of Jeroboam (1 Kings xii. 26—28). He seems to have led men down step by step: stars, images as their representatives, then the images themselves: first, natural principles, then living creatures in which these principles were supposed to be embodied, then the living creatures themselves. To have begun at the end would have been too great a shock; the absurdity as well as the wickedness of such worship would have been too obvious. Thus was the empire of the idols founded, and it continues to this day.—Hom. Com.

22. **Cease .. man,** i. e. cease to trust in him, see Ps. cxlvi. 3, 4. The prophet is overcome with a sense of the folly and weakness of man, who

d "In a verse consisting of three words, their destiny is declared as with a flash of lightning." — Delitzsch.

a Am. i. 1. Comp. He. xii. 26.

"Even in heathen countries, men are becoming ashamed of their idols, and are representing them as merely the media of worship. The victory of Christianity over idolatry is already assured."—Hom. Com.

"None but the true God can discover [make known] what the true worship of God is. As that glorious eye of heaven is not to be seen but by its own proper light,—a million of torches cannot show us the sun: so it is not all the natural reason in the world that can either discover what God is, or what worship He expects, without Divine and supernatural revelation from Himself." — Arrowsmith.

b "A confession that they had buried themselves away in the darkness of earthly desires, and of foul, grovelling superstition." — Spk. Com.

"A religion that does not take hold of the life that now is, is like a cloud that does not rain. A religion that consists in the observance of magnificent ceremonies, but that does not touch the duties of daily life, is a religion of show and of sham."—Beecher.

is so high in his own esteem, and is to be so completely humiliated. **breath .. nostrils,** the quick passing breath being a symbol of his fleeting life. Man regarded as helper, saviour, defender, is of little worth. **accounted of,** or valued. "In what way can he be reckoned as having intrinsic worth?"[a]

[a] Job vii. 17, 18; Ps. viii. 4, cxviii. 8, 9, cxliv. 3, 4, cxlvi. 3, 4.

"Here, like a shepherd gazing from his hut,
Touching his reed, or leaning on his staff,
Eager Ambition's fiery chase I see;
I see the circling hunt of noisy men
Burst law's enclosure, leap the mounds of right,
Pursuing and pursued, each other's prey;
As wolves for rapine; as the fox for wiles;
Till Death, that mighty hunter, earths them all.
Why all this toil for triumphs of an hour?
What though we wade in wealth, or soar in fame?
Earth's highest station ends in 'Here he lies'—
And 'Dust to dust' concludes her noblest song."
—Young.

"Applause is the spur of noble minds, the end and aim of weak ones."— Colton.

"God will not give ammunition to any soldier who is not willing to go into battle." —Anon.

Trust not in man (vs. 22).—I. Man may be endowed with rich and varied talents and distinctions. Illustrations. II. All men are fragile and mortal. 1. This agrees with the account of his creation; 2. Is philosophically true; 3. It exhibits the uncertainty of life; 4. In old age breathing is weak; 5. At death it ceases; 6. This is the condition of all men. III. The wise and reasonable conclusion of the text. 1. We ought to recognize talent and greatness, should honor it, greatly value it, when removed mourn its loss; 2. But should not trust in man, for the wisest man may err, the best may do wrong, all men will die; 3. If we cease from man we shall make God our hope, adhere to principles which are immortal; Jesus stands in contrast to all others.—Burns.

The certainty of death—

The glories of our birth and state
Are shadows, not substantial things;
There is no armor against fate:
Death lays his icy hand on kings;
Sceptre and crown
Must tumble down,
And in the dust be equal made
With the poor crooked scythe and spade.

Some men with swords may reap the field,
And plant fresh laurels where they kill;
But their strong nerves at last must yield;
They tame but one another still;
Early or late
They stoop to fate,
And must give up their murmuring breath,
When they, pale captives, creep to death.

The garlands wither on your brow;
Then boast no more your mighty deeds;
Upon death's purple altar, now,
See where the Victor Victim bleeds!
All heads must come
To the cold tomb!
Only the actions of the just
Smell sweet and blossom in the dust!

—Shirley.

CHAPTER THE THIRD.

1—3. (1) **Lord .. hosts,** "the divine name given here, with which Isaiah everywhere introduces the judicial acts of God (cf. i. 24; x. 16, 33; xix. 4), is a proof that the proclamation of judgment commences here afresh."—Delitzsch. **stay .. staff,** every kind of support.[a] **bread .. water,** the natural and necessary means of subsistence. "This clause seems out of place in view of what follows and is probably a marginal gloss which has crept into the text."—Cam. Bib. (2) **the mighty man,** the prophet, accepting the popular position, names first among the props of the state, the soldier. **prudent,** R. V. "the diviner." **ancient,** or elder. (3) **honourable man,** or man of high rank. **eloquent orator,**[b] R. V. "the skillful enchanter."

National calamity (vss. 1—8).—Here are—I. Some forms of national calamity. 1. Famine; 2. Removal of men prominent in influence; 3. An upstart and inefficient Government; 4. Mutual oppression; 5. General in-

[a] Le. xxvi. 26.

[b] "The entire apparatus of State machinery of that day is mentioned." — Nagelsbach.

"A sublime idea remains the same, from whatever brain, or in whatever region, it had its birth."—Menzek

subordination; 6. No healer of the sick State; 7. Utter ruin. II. The causes which occasion them. 1. Ungodliness in speech; 2. In act; 3. In spite of light and knowledge.—Lyth.

"The great cause of our neglecting the Scriptures is not want of time, but want of heart, some idol taking the place of Christ." —From "Words and Weapons."

Preparation for death—

So live, that, when thy summons comes to join
The innumerable caravan, that moves
To that mysterious realm where each shall take
His chamber in the silent halls of death,
Thou go not like the quarry slave at night
Scourged to his dungeon; but, sustained and soothed
By an unfaltering trust, approach thy grave
Like one that wraps the drapery of his couch
About him, and lies down to pleasant dreams.

—Bryant.

"Some apply this in a strict sense to the weak and wicked reign of Ahaz; others, in a wider sense, to the series of weak kings after Isaiah. But the most probable opinion is that the incompetent rulers are called boys or children not in respect to age, but character." — J. A. Alexander.

4, 5. (4) **children,** as in cases of Ahaz and Manasseh (King at 12). Delitzsch suggests that by "princes" reference is made to the councillors of the king. It being a greater evil than that the king himself should be a youth. **babes, etc.,** this is really an abstract noun and means outrage. The better translation is "and Outrage shall rule over them." (5) **be oppressed,**[c] etc., the marks of these evil days will be, class hatred and injustice, irreverence, and the supremacy of the baser elements of society.

c "When weak hands hold the reins of government a condition of lawlessness ensues, and of defencelessness for the weak. The strong then do as they wish. They exercise club law."—Nagelsbach.

The relation of classes.—Whilst all that is purely mechanical and arbitrary is to be viewed with suspicion, yet there is a natural sequence in things, there is indeed what is called a fitness or harmony of things; and when society is rightly inspired the base man knows that he is base, and his baseness is his weakness, and his weakness defines his position; and the child knows himself to be but a child, and therefore he behaves himself with discretion, and is limited by circumstances which he cannot control. Once let the moral centre be lost, and then you have lost all arithmetical counting, all geometrical relationship, all figure and form and mechanism and security, and the foursquare is thrown out of its parallel, and that which was right is numbered with that which is forbidden. How is society held together but by moral and political considerations? Some of the strongest men physically are amongst the weakest mentally and morally. When society is properly ordered and organized wisdom goes for everything; wisdom rules the city; wisdom directs the war; wisdom is consulted in the day of perplexity and in the night of desperation. Once let moral security give way, and you have this picture repeated: "The people shall be oppressed, every one by another, and every one by his neighbor": complete chaos shall reign; the child shall spit in the face of the ancient, and the base man shall claim the throne of the honorable. We are more dependent upon righteousness than we sometimes suppose. A sense of honesty keeps men right; a sense of moral inferiority determines the right classification of society. Aristocracy is mental, not hereditary. There is a genealogy of blood; there is also a genealogy of mind. When moral considerations are supreme all these questions are settled easily and finally.—Peop. Bib. "Our country—whether bounded by the St. John's and the Sabine, or however otherwise bounded or described and be the measurements more or less;—still our country, to be cherished in all our hearts, to be defended by all our hands."—Winthrop.

" There is no slight danger from general ignorance; and the only choice which Providence has graciously left to a vicious Government, is either to fall by the people, if they are suffered to become enlightened, or with them, if they are kept enslaved and ignorant." — Coleridge.

"Heaven forming each on other to depend,
A master, or a servant, or a friend,
Bids each on other for assistance call,
Till one man's weakness grows the strength of all."

—Pope.

6—8. (6) **a man,**[a] etc., "the choice of the people falls on a landed proprietor who has been fortunate enough to retain his ancestral estate (his "father's house,") and whose outer garment is a sufficient badge of respectability."—Camb. Bib. **ruin .. hand,** an offer of absolute control, to

a They would make a ruler or a judge any man with a decent coat on his back.

remedy this ruinous condition. (7) **not to be a healer,** or binder up. Even he will decline the responsibility.[b] **neither,** etc., this respectable show is all even this man has. Beneath it he is as poor and helpless as the rest. Or else he is one of those who having sufficiency refuse responsibility on the plea of poverty. **provoke,** etc., or defy Him to His face. **the eyes of his glory,** God is the glorious One, and abhors all this uncleanness and evil. It is the all-searching eyes of such an One whom these rebels provoke to wrath.

Reason for ruin.—A man cannot lay up a character and fall back upon it if his present conduct is out of keeping with it; he himself takes the juice and sap out of the character which he once lived. "Jerusalem is ruined." Why? There is a moral reason. There is always a moral reason for divine judgment. That reason reads thus: "Because their tongue and their doings are against the Lord, to provoke the eyes of his glory." In their fancy they give him eyes of omniscience, and in their action they defy those eyes to see the rottenness of their conduct. Men do not come to ruin because they are good; it is nowhere recorded that because a man prayed he was blasted by the lightning of heaven. Ruin has a moral explanation behind it, an explanation we may be ashamed to give, or to confess, or to recognize even within the secrecy of our own consciousness; but there is the eternal law—wherever there is death there has been sin: the wages of sin is death. We are not speaking now of the mere death of the body, of the death which dogs die, but of that second death, that inner decease, that decessus or exodus of the character, when the soul goes out of a man, and abandons him, because it has been ill-used, dethroned, discrowned.—Peop. Bib.

b "The state of affairs was so ruinous and calamitous that he would not attempt to restore them—as if in the body disease should have so far progressed that he would not undertake to restore the person, and have him die under his hands, so as to expose himself to the reproach of being an unsuccessful and unskilful physician." —Barnes.

9—11. (9) **shew,** etc., brazen daring; bold, staring effrontery; impudence.[a] **as Sodom,** their wickedness is stamped upon their faces; but they do not care to conceal it, they proclaim it aloud; see Ge. xiii. 13, xviii. 20, 21, xix. 13. **unto themselves,** the destruction that shall come upon them they have invited. Sin is suicidal. (10, 11) **the fruit .. the reward,** an exposition of the statement in vs. 9.—Each class is preparing its own reward..

Conscience.—Many sinners who seem so jocund in our eyes have not such merry lives as you think. A book may be fairly bound and gilded, yet have but sad stories writ within it. Sinners will not tell us all the secret rebukes that conscience gives them. If you will judge of Herod by the jollity of his feast, you may think he wanted no joy; but at another time we see that John's ghost walked in his conscience. And so doth the Word haunt many, who appear to us to lay nothing to heart. In the midst of their laughter, their heart is sad: you see the lightning in their face, but hear not the thunder that rumbles in their conscience.—Gurnall.

a "An unblushing recklessness of character is indicated."— E. Henderson.

Is. lix. 12; Ho. v. 5, vii. 10.

"Conscience, as an expression of the will and mind of God, is not now to be implicitly depended on. It has been deranged and shattered by the fall. So far as doctrines and duties are concerned, not conscience, but the revealed Word of God, is our one, only sure and safe directory." — Guthrie.

12, 13. (12) **my people,** notice the affection of the prophet even while he condemns. **children,** "this language points to a time when the vigorous administration of Uzziah and Jotham had been succeeded by the weak and inefficient government of Ahaz."—Driver. **women,** either their rulers are as unfit as women; or these rulers are under the government of their seraglios. **they which lead,** i. e. the prophets, who should correct and guide the people, lead them astray. "Thy leaders are misleaders." —Delitzsch. cf. Micah iii. 5; Is. ix. 15—16; Jer. xxiii. 25—26. **destroy,** swallow up, i. e. "the landmarks of national righteousness have been effaced from the minds of the people by the conduct of their leaders." (13) **standeth up,** the sign of earnestness. The beginning of the end has come: the verdict is now to be declared.

Following principle.—Men know where they are going when they follow a principle; because principles are rays of light. If you trace a ray of light in all its reflections, you will find that it runs back to the central sun; and every great line of honesty, every great line of honor, runs back towards the centre—God. And the man that follows these things knows that he is steering right Godward. But the man that follows policies, and worldly maxims, does not know where he is steering, except that in general he is steering toward the devil.—Beecher.

"Reason is God's candle in man. But, as a candle must first be lighted, ere it will enlighten, so reason must be illuminated by Divine grace, ere it can savingly discern spiritual things." — Toplady.

14, 15. (14) **ancients,** or elders. **for ye,** R. V. "It is ye that." **eaten up,** as devouring beasts; not tended and watched, as faithful husbandmen.[b] (15) **beat,** or crush, as in a mortar. Notice the ground of the condemnation; the leaders have misled the people, devoured their possessions, and overwhelmed the poor with violence and oppression. These are all social evils.

Servilia.—Among the numerous victims of the tyranny of Nero, was one Bareas Soranus, a man, as Tacitus informs us, of singular vigilance and justice in the discharge of his duty. During his confinment his daughter Servilia was apprehended, and brought into the senate to be arraigned. The crime laid to her charge was, that she had turned into money all her ornaments and jewels, and the most valuable part of her dress, to defray the expense of consulting magicians. To this the young Servilia, with a flood of tears, replied, "That she had indeed consulted magicians, but the whole of her inquiry was to know whether the emperor and senate would afford protection and safety to her dear and indulgent parent against his accusers. "With this view," continued she, "I presented the diviners, men till now utterly unknown to me, with my jewels, my apparel, and other ornaments peculiar to my quality, as I would have presented my blood and life, could they have procured my father's liberty. But whatever this my proceeding was, my unfortunate father was an utter stranger to it; and if it is a crime, I alone am guilty." This pathetic appeal was lost on the sanguinary monster; and Servilia and her father were condemned to die.—Percy Ames.

16—18. (16) **daughters of Zion,**[a] with this description cf. Prov. xxxi. 10 ff. where industry, benevolence, liberality and skill in handiwork mark the excellent woman; also Pr. xi. 16, 22; xii. 4. **haughty,** Isaiah sees in the women of Jerusalem as unfavorable signs as Amos (iv. 1) saw in Samaria a generation earlier. The character of a people is well revealed by the character of its women. **necks,** stretched out with the proud uplifting of the head.[b] **mincing,** or tripping, "though well versed in sin and old in years they tried to maintain a youthful appearance."—Delitzsch. **tinkling,** with their ankle-rings.[c] (17) **scab,** bring disgrace in form of offensive diseases. **discover,** lay bare, giving them over to the hands of barbarous enemies, so that they who have lived in lust shall suffer the lust of others. (18) **tinkling ornaments,** R. V. "anklets." **cauls,** or headbands: braided tresses of hair, with little bells attached. **round tires,** ornaments for the neck.[d]

Differences in society.—To us there seems a wide difference between the judge, with the robes of office on his back, mind in his eye, and dignity in his mien, and that poor, pale, haggard wretch at the bar, who throws stealthy glances around, and hangs his head with shame. Yet the difference that looks so great to man may be very small in the eyes of God; and would look small in ours if we knew the different upbringing and history of both. The judge never knew what it was to want a meal; the felon often went cold and hungry to bed. The one, sprung of wise, kind, reputable, and perhaps pious parents, was early trained to good, and launched, with all the advantages of school and college, on an honorable and high career; while the other, bred up a stranger to the amenities of cultivated and Christian society, had no such advantages. Born to misery, his struggles with misfortune and evil began at the cradle. None ever took him by the hand to lead him to church or school. A child of poverty, and the offspring of abandoned parents, he was taught no lessons but how to swear, and lie, and drink, and cheat, and steal. The fact is, it is just as difficult for some to be honest as it is easy for others. What merit has that judge in his honesty? None. He had no temptation to be else than honest. And so, I suspect, much of the morality of that unblemished character and decent life in which many trust, saying to some poor guilty thing, "Stand aside, I am holier than thou," and pluming themselves on this, that they have not sinned as others have done—is due, less to their superior virtue, than to their more favorable circumstances. And so the difference between many honest men and decent women on the one hand, and those on the other hand on whom a brand of infamy has been burned, and the key of a prison turned, may be just the difference between the green branch on the tree and the white ashes on the hearth. This is bathed in the dews of night and fanned by

---

b "The most natural interpretation is that which applies it to the act of grinding the face upon the ground by trampling on the body." — J. A. Alexander.

Ps. xii. 5; Is. v. 7. "Ah! my lord, do not thus crush my face. Alas! alas! my nose and other features will soon be rubbed away. Is my face to be made quite flat with grinding? My heart is squeezed; my heart is squeezed. That head man has been grinding the faces of all his people." —Roberts.

a "The worldliness of the people was reflected in the luxury of the females, and the costly variety of their robes and ornaments." Spk. Com.

"The following eight vss. contain the most complete description of Oriental female attire to be met with in any ancient writing."— E. Henderson.

Comp. 1 Pet. iii. 3, 4.

b Ps. lxxv. 5.

c "Metallic rings or bands worn round the ankles. Still used in Syria, Egypt, and India."

d "The women of Samaria wear now a head-dress which perfectly illustrates the Proph. description. It is a sort of bonnet with a horseshoe shape in front, and in the front are some silver coins lapping over one another, and making a crescent-shaped tire (resembling the crescent moon) round the forehead and down to the ears."—Bib. Things.

the breath of heaven, while that, once as green, has been thrust into the burning fire—the one has been tried in a way that the other has not.—Guthrie.

19—23. (19) **chains,** prob. ear-drops, or pendants from the neck. **mufflers,** or veils ornamented with spangles.[a] (20) **bonnets,** ornamental head-dresses. **of the legs,** or stepping-chains, arranged to make the lady take short and mincing steps. **headbands,** R. V. "sashes." **tablets,** R. V. "perfume-boxes." **earrings,** R. V. "amulets," or charms.[b]. **rings,** i. e. finger-rings. **nose jewels,** or rings.[c] (22) **suits,** R. V. "festival robes." **mantles,** or sleeve-frocks, worn over the inner tunic. **wimples,** R. V. "shawls." **crisping pins,** R. V. "satchels." (2 Ki. v. 23). (23) **glasses,** R. V. "hand-mirrors;" polished metal plates, cf Job xxxvii, 18; I Cor. xiii. 12. Glass was made for other purposes, but seems not to have been used for mirrors. **linen,** of the inner tunics. **hoods,** or turbans. Stockings and handkerchiefs are not mentioned in this list. The former were introduced from Media long after Isaiah's time.—Delitzsch.

Anklets.—Besides ornamental rings in the nose and the ears, they wore others round the legs, which made a tinkling as they went. This custom has also descended to the present times; for Rauwolf met with a number of Arabian women on the Euphrates, whose ankles and wrists were adorned with rings, sometimes a good many together, which, moving up and down as they walked, made a great noise. Chardin attests the existence of the same custom in Persia, in Arabia, and in very hot countries, where they commonly go without stockings, but ascribes the tinkling sound to little bells fastened to those rings. In the East Indies, golden bells adorned the feet and ankles of the ladies from the earliest times; they placed them in the flowing tresses of their hair; they suspended them round their necks; and to the golden rings which they wore on their fingers, to announce their superior rank, and exact the homage which they had a right to expect from the lower orders; and from the banks of the Indus, it is probable the custom was introduced into the other countries of Asia. The Arabian females in Palestine and Syria delight in the same ornaments.—Paxton.

24—26. (24) **instead of sweet smell,** etc., R. V. "instead of sweet spices there shall be rottenness; and instead of a girdle a rope." The prophet foresees the doom that will fall upon these women in coming days of beggary and slavery. "Not merely would the articles of finery be removed, but everything that was coarse, vulgar, and disgusting was to supply their place." **baldness,** through skin disease fostered by dirt. **stomacher,** or full flowing mantle. **sackcloth,**[a] covering of the very poor, and of mourners. **burning,** R. V. "branding," as of slaves.[b] (25) **thy mighty,** lit. thy might,[c] this explains how the reverses just declared are to come about. The protectors of Jerusalem are to be destroyed in battle, and the women will be the prey of the enemy. (26) **lament,** etc., as those who wail for the dead.[d] **she .. shall sit,** Jerusalem shall mourn the loss of her sons.

Perfumes for the person.—"Sweet smell." No one ever enters a company without being well perfumed; and in addition to various scents and oils, they are adorned with numerous garlands, made of the most odoriferous flowers. "A girdle." Probably that which goes round the waist, which serves to keep the garments from falling, while the girls are dancing. It is sometimes made of silver. "Well-set hair." No ladies pay more attention to the dressing of the hair than do these; for as they never wear caps, they take great delight in this their natural ornament. "Baldness" in a woman makes her most contemptible; and formerly, to shave their head was a most degrading punishment. "Stomacher." I once saw a dress beautifully plaited and stiffened for the front, but I do not think it common. Here, then, we have a strong proof of the accurate observations of Isaiah in reference to the Jewish ladies; he had seen their motions, and enumerated their ornaments; and here we have a most melancholy picture of the fallen state of "the daughters of Zion."—Roberts.

Two forms of temptation.—Sometimes temptation comes to us like an army with open attack, but more often like a malaria. We breathe in the poisoned air from neighboring marshes; we bring the deadly sewer

[a] "Fluttering veils." — Gesenius.

[b] "Gems or metal plates with an inscription on them, wh. were worn as a protection as well as an ornament."—Delitzsch.

[c] "It is the custom in almost all the East for the women to wear rings in their noses, in the left nostril, which is bored low down in the middle. These rings are of gold, and have commonly two pearls and one ruby between, placed in the ring."—Chardin.

Ge. xxiv. 22.

"Fell Luxury! more perilous to youth
Than storms or quicksands, poverty and chains."
—Hannah More.

[a] 2 Sa. iii. 31.

[b] "Or perhaps a sunburnt countenance, owing to their hoods and veils being stripped off whilst they had to work as captives under a scorching sun."—Fausset.

[c] Military force, used collectively for mighty warriors.

[d] "On Roman medals, struck by order of Titus, in commemoration of his conquest of Jerusalem, Judaea actually appears in the posture of a female, sitting on the ground, under a palm tree, and giving way to inconsolable grief."—E. Henderson.

"Vanity is as ill at ease under indifference as tenderness is under the love which it cannot return." —George Eliot.

"Those who live on vanity must not unreasonably expect to die of mortification."—Mrs. Ellis.

gas into our houses by the very triumph of modern conveniences; cesspools in hundreds of yards send up their malaria to enter every open window in summer, and then in winter we shut up every crack and crevice lest God's pure air enter our rooms, to save coal; till our whole systems are poisoned, and in some hour of weakness or overwork suddenly we are consumed with a burning fever. If the fever had come like a deadly serpent, we would have avoided it; if it had come like the north wind, we would have sheltered ourselves from it; if in battle array, we could fight it. But it has come with our daily breath, its footsteps unheard, without knocking at the door, and has insidiously poisoned our whole system before we were aware of our danger.—Peloubet, Sugges. Illus.

CHAPTER THE FOURTH.

1. This verse belongs with the third chapter. "A companion picture to iii. 6. The male population are in search of a ruler, the women in search of a husband."—Cheyne. **one man,**[a] "the image which the prophet has in mind is that of a disaster in the field: the warriors of Judah defeated and slain; their wives and daughters in the hands of the conquerors. The women that remain crowd around the few warriors, not to obtain support, but that the reproach of childlessness may not rest upon them forever."—Driver. **called .. name,** it was customary for the wife to be named after the husband.[b] **reproach,** i. e. the disgrace of being unmarried. cf. Jud. xi. 37f.

[a] "The paucity of males in the community, resulting from this general slaughter, is now expressed by a lively figure representing seven women as earnestly soliciting one man in marriage and that on the most disadvantageous terms, renouncing the support to which they were by law entitled." — J. A. Alexander.

[b] Ge. xii. 17, xlvi. 19; 2 Sa. xi. 3.

"All true penitence must take account of God's willingness and readiness to forgive." — G. F. Pentecost.

Rage of battle—
Still pressing forward to the fight, they broke
Through flames of sulphur and a night of smoke,
Till slaughter'd legions fill'd the trench below,
And bore their fierce avengers to the foe.
High on the works the mingling hosts engage,
The battle kindled into tenfold rage.
With showers of bullets, and with storms of fire,
Bombs in full fury, heaps on heaps expire;
Nations, with nations mix'd, confus'dly die,
And lost in one promiscuous carnage lie.
The western sun now shot a feeble ray,
And faintly scatter'd the remains of day,
Ev'ning approach'd; but oh! what hosts of foes
Were never to behold that ev'ning close!
Thick'ning their ranks, and wedged in firm array,
The close-compacted Britons win their way;
In vain the cannon their throng'd war defaced,
With tracks of death, and laid the battle waste.
—Addison.

2—4. "Beyond the great judgment there is revealed to the prophet a vision of the ideal religious community, blessed with an exuberant super-natural fertility imparted to the soil (vs. 2), purified from sin (vss. 3, 4), and overshadowed by the protecting presence of Jehovah (vss. 5, 6). It is a picture of the glorious Messianic age which immediately follows the day of the Lord."—Cam. B. (2) **branch,** etc.[a] this is not the same word rendered "branch" in xi. 1, and this is best rendered "the growth of Jehovah," that which Jehovah causes to grow. That is, as the destruction of the earth was first mentioned in judgment (ii. 13) so here the fruitage of the earth is the first token of Divine pleasure. Polych. Bib. translates "the self-springing plants" and refers it to wild growth dependent on God's care. **escaped of Israel,** the remnant, the faithful few. (3) **left,** the same as the "escaped." Those whom God would acknowledge as His people. **holy,**[b] that is, "consecrated and inviolate" as well as pure.—Camb. Bib. These whom the Lord has preserved will be looked upon by Him as His chosen. In fact they will be the pure ore that sur-

[a] Je. xxiii. 5, xxxiii. 15; Zec. iii. 8, vi. 12.

[b] Ex. xix. 6; De. xxviii. 9.

vives the smelting. **written,**[c] etc., i. e. inscribed in the register of its living citizens. By "the living" the prophet means on earth, in the redeemed city, under new conditions. It is a vision of the kingdom when it has come on earth.—Driver. (4) **washed away,** by His judgments and captivities. **spirit of burning,** regarded as having both a destroying and purifying influence.[d]

The branch of the Lord (vss. 1—6).—We have—I. A special period implied. II. An attractive object presented. III. An encouraging fact announced. IV. An important process declared. V. A state of blessedness promised. God is set forth in connection with His people—1. As their guide; 2. As their guard.

The use of affliction.—As God makes use of all the seasons of the year for the harvest, the frost of winter as well as the heat of summer, so doth He of fair and foul, pleasing and unpleasing providences for promoting holiness. Winter providences kill the weeds of lusts, and summer providences ripen and mellow the fruits of righteousness. When He afflicts it is for our profit, to make us partakers of His holiness (Heb. xii. 10). Bernard compares afflictions to the teasel, which though it be sharp and scratching, is to make the cloth more pure and fine. God would not rub so hard if it were not to fetch out the dirt that is ingrained in our natures. God loves purity so well that He would rather see a hole than a spot in His child's garments. When He deals more gently in His providences and lets his people sit under the sunny bank of comforts and enjoyments, fencing them from the cold blasts of affliction, it is to draw forth the sap of grace, and hasten their growth in holiness.—Gurnall.

5, 6. (5) **cloud and smoke,** recalling the pillar of cloud and fire over Israel, and assuring of the Divine protection and guidance. **defence,** R. V. "over all the glory shall be spread a canopy;" of Div. protection. (6) **tabernacle,**[e] all this is a vision of the New Jerusalem described in Rev. xxi, which is the vision of the kingdom of God when it has come in its completeness.

Divine shelter.—Somewhere in the East there is a tree which is a non-conductor of electricity. The people know it, and when a storm comes, they flee towards it for safety. Beautiful picture of the Saviour! Beautiful emblem of the tree of Calvary! It is a non-conductor of wrath. Get underneath it, and you are safe—safe for ever.

CHAPTER THE FIFTH.

This chapter records another prophecy—later than that of Chs. ii—iv., but similar in cause and tone. "The difference between the two sets of prophecies is that in the former we have the obscure and tortuous path of a conviction struggling to light in the prophet's own experience; here, we have its careful array in the light and before the people."—G. A. Smith. **1, 2.** (1) **a song,** the prophet appears as a minstrel and proceeds to recite in verse the story of the experience of a beloved friend, within his vineyard. **vineyard,** Ps. lxxx. 8—16. **fruitful hill,** lit. on a horn, a son of fatness. [a] (2) **fenced it,** R. V. "made a trench about it." **stones,** wh. tended to make it barren. **choicest vine,**[b] "a technical word for the finest sort of grapes grown in Syria."—Cam. Bib. Lit. vine of Sorek, the name of a valley bet. Askelon and Gaza. **tower,** for the watchman. **winepress,** R. V. "hewed out a winepress" in the rock. It was the proof that the owner fully expected good fruitage in answer to his labor. **wild grapes,** such as would grow on a poor vine that received no care.

Fruit required.—I. Fruitfulness is, first and before all things else, in character, in holiness, in what we are rather than in what we do, and only in what we do so far as that is the genuine outcome and spontaneous revelation of what we are. Usefulness is the result of character, and must never be lost sight of; but character is first, and in that the fruit of our position in God's vineyard is chiefly to appear. II. God expects fruit from a tree on which he has bestowed such exceptional advantages, and that is the second point to which I would here give prom-

[c] Phil. iv. 3; Re. iii. 5, xvii. 8.

[d] "In the burning fire of God's judgments there is a Spirit of love, which, while it scorches, purifies." —Wordsworth.

"God has never yet left the world without a nucleus of heaven. There is always a remnant, the one left, the true heart, the faithful among the faithless found." —Peop. Bib.

"All other books will perish in the flame; only the writing of God will survive. In that register the humblest man may have a place. Pitiable is the life of him whose name is written everywhere but in the life-book!" —Peop. Bib.

[e] "The 'Branch of the Lord' is Himself the restored 'Tabernacle of David.'" —Spk. Com.

"Though God may seem to frown in His providences, yet He always smiles in His promises."

[a] In the Hebrew idiom a thing is said to be the son of whatever quality it possesses.

[b] Je. ii. 21.

The grapes of this vine are small in size, reddish in color, with small or scarcely any stones, and they have a very sweet taste. The present Arab name is Serki, or Sherki, or Zerka.

"How bitter must have been the disappointment of the father of the Prodigal when he went away into a far country! Such disappointments break the hearts of tens of thousands of fathers and mothers; and precisely such disappointment it is, only vaster, deeper, sadder, that fills the heart of our Heavenly Father when His children go astray." —Hom. Com.

a "God has done all that could be done for the salvation of sinners, consistently with His justice and goodness. The God of nature is, as it were, amazed at the unnatural fruit of so well cared for a vineyard." —Fausset.

Matt. xxiii. 37.

"Who seeks and will not take when once 'tis offer'd
Shall never find it more."
—Shakespeare.

"There is a tide in the affairs of men,
Which, taken at their flood, leads on to fortune.
Omitted, all the voyage of their life
Is bound in shallows and in miseries."
—Shakespeare.

"The promises of eternal blessedness are not given to the strength of faith, but to the truth of faith; not to the degrees of faith, but to its reality."

"True blessedness consisteth in a good life and a happy death." —Solon.

"The more a man denies himself, the more he shall obtain from God." —Horace

inence. If we have so much more than other nations, we ought to be just so much better than they. For the fruit in this case is that of character. III. Now observe, in the third place, that God pronounces sentence of destruction on all who, having had such privileges, bring forth no fruit.—W. M. Taylor.

Opportunities neglected.—A prisoner is under sentence of death. The fatal hour of execution is concealed from him, but he is told that if before it strikes he petitions the governor, his life wlll be spared. He says, "I'll send to-morrow," and when to-morrow comes he says again, "Oh, there's time enough yet; I'll wait a little longer." Suddenly his dungeon doors open, and behold the sheriffs and the executioners! "Oh, wait, and I'll sign the petition." "No," they say, "the clock has struck; it's too late—you must die."

3, 4. (3) **judge,** act as umpires. He intended to make them convict themselves. **me and my vineyard,** here he reveals partially his meaning. The prophet speaks in this manner only when speaking for Jehovah. (4) **what .. done more,** to the awakening consciences he puts the question, "Was the failure due to lack on the part of the owner?"[a] **wherefore,** the whole situation reminds of Nathan's parable to David, 2 Sam. xii. 1—13.

A sad canticle (vss. 4—6).—The similitude under which the Church is represented. The vineyard—1. Represented prosperity; 2. Was associated with rejoicing; 3. As a scene of labor; 4. Was specially noticed by God. This vineyard was in a very favorable locality, planted with the choicest vine, carefully fenced, diligently cultivated, having husbandmen living in its midst. II. The just complaint of the Lord,—founded not on the poverty, but on the nature of the crop. III. The terrible condemnation He pronounces. Observe—its mercy; its severity.

The wine-press.—The wine-press, constructed for expressing the juice of the grapes, does not seem to be a movable implement in the East; and our Lord, in the parable of the vineyard, says expressly that it was formed by digging. Chardin found the wine-press in Persia was made after the same manner; as it was a hollow place dug in the ground, and lined with mason-work. Besides this, they had what the Romans called lacus, the lake, a large open place or vessel, which, by a conduit or spout, received the must from the wine-press. In very hot countries it was perhaps necessary, or at least convenient, to have the lake under ground, or in a cave hewed out of the rock, for coolness, that the heat might not cause too great a fermentation, and sour the must.—Paxton. Self-interrogation.—Let me judge myself! Could anything more have been done for me than has been done? I am constrained to answer, There has been nothing lacking on the part of God. It is not for me to compare myself with other men, and to say their advantages have been greater than mine; possibly that may be so; yet I have had advantages enough to have brought forth an abundance of grateful fruit. How much have I produced? Are mine lifeless branches? Are my grapes wild grapes? These are the questions that tear the life, these the songs the music of which we forget in the terribleness of their judgment. But this is healthy investigation; this is the kind of heart-searching which, if properly received, ends in edification. We cannot repent sooner than to-day; behold, now is the accepted time for repentance; now is the chosen hour for the real improvement of our innermost life.—Peop. Bib. Harmony with God.—To be godly is to be godlike. The full accord of all the soul with His character, in whom, as their native home, dwell "whatsoever things are pure, whatsoever things are lovely," and the full conformity of the will to His sovereign will, who is the life of our lives—this, and nothing shallower, nothing narrower, is religion in its perfection, and the measure in which we have attained to this harmony with God is the measure in which we are Christians. As two stringed instruments may be so tuned to one keynote that if you strike the one, a faint ethereal echo is heard from the other, which blends undistinguishably with its parent sound; so drawing near to God, and brought into unison with His mind and will, our responsive spirits vibrate in accord with His, and give forth tones, low and thin indeed, but still repeating the mighty music of heaven.—Maclaren.

5, 6. (5) **go to,** no corresponding Heb. word. Translate "Now I will tell you," etc. The minstrel prophet pauses at end of verse 4, but the hearers are silent. He therefore passes on to give sentence. **wall,** wh. was sometimes put up outside the hedge. New suggestions here of the thoroughness with which he had protected and cared for his vineyard. Since now the vine has brought forth wild grapes it shall be treated as wild vines are. (6) **waste,** i. e. "put an end to it." **briers and thorns,** a phrase peculiar to Isaiah (vii. 23; ix. 18; x. 17; xxvii. 4; lv. 15), one of his many references to sympathy of nature with man. **clouds,** the first clear hint that it is God who is speaking through His prophet.

Sinking in the quicksand.—It sometimes happens that a man walking on the beach at low tide suddenly notices that for several minutes he has been walking with some difficulty. The strand beneath his feet is like pitch; his soles stick to it; it is sand no longer—it is glue. The eye, however, has noticed no change. The man pursues his way, goes forward, inclines to the land. He is not anxious. Only he feels somehow as if the weight of his feet increases with every step he takes. Suddenly he sinks in two or three inches. Decidedly he is not on the right road; he stops to take his bearings. All at once he looks at his feet. His feet have disappeared. He draws his feet out of the sand; he turns back; he sinks in deeper. The sand comes up to his ankles; he pulls himself out and throws himself to the left; the sand is half-leg deep. He throws himself to the right; the sand comes up to his shins. Then he recognizes with unspeakable terror that he is caught in the quicksand. He throws off his load, if he has one, lightens himself like a ship in distress. It is already too late, the sand is above his knees. If there is no help in sight, it is all over.—Abridged from Victor Hugo.

Proverbs. — "What may be done at any time will be done at no time. Strike while the iron is hot. Take time while time is, for time will away." —English. "God keep you from 'It is too late.' When the fool has made up his mind, the market has gone by." — Spanish. "A little too late, much too late." — Dutch. "Some refuse roast meat, and afterwards long for the smoke of it."—Italian.

"If importunity can prevail with an unjust judge, what must it do with a just one?"

7. For, etc., now appears clearly who the Beloved is and what the vineyard.[a] **house of Israel,** the whole people, and especially Judah which had been most signally blessed. God's prophecies and messages do not often recognize the division of the Israelites into two kingdoms. He addresses the entire covenant people. **judgment,** etc.,[b] the play upon words is striking in the Heb. "He looked for mishpat, but behold mispat (bloodshed); for tsedaqua, but behold tscaqua (the cry of the oppressed).

[a] 2 Sa. xii. 5.

[b] Lu. xiii. 7.

The dying soldier.—A soldier, who had enlisted as a Christian, but had for three years, though a man of uprightness and integrity done nothing to make known the name of Christ, said when dying, "I die as a Christian, and I die contented; but oh, if I could have died as a Christian worker!" "I am peaceful and assured in view of death," he said again, "but I am not joyful and glad; those three lost years keep coming back upon me." Then lying a moment quiet with closed eyes, he added, "Chaplain, do you suppose we shall be able to forget anything in heaven? I would like to forget those three years." Sword and Trowel. —The lost opportunity.—A passenger comes bustling into a railway station. He is just too late, for the engine has sounded its whistle, and the train is gliding rapidly out of sight. He looks after it in despair. He had important business to transact. Ruinous may be the consequences of delay. He sits down on his trunk, leaning his head upon his hand, and, absorbed in vain regrets, gazes vacantly forward. But see! another train is at the platform, just about to start for the same destination. Other passengers have arrived, and are eagerly crowding in. The bell rings, again the whistle sounds, again the engine bears away its living freight, and, starting up, our friend again bewails an opportunity lost! Oh! sit not down again despondingly. There is yet another chance; throw not this away too, but at once take your seat in this third train which now is preparing to follow the other two.—Newman Hall.

"The shortest and surest way to live with honor in the world is to be in reality what we would appear to be."—Socrates.

"Opportunity is like a string of stepping - stones across a ford. The traveler, coming up to them, may find the river so swollen with the rains that the stones are all but covered. If he delay, though his home be on the opposite bank, and full in sight, it may be too late to cross, and he may have a journey of several miles to reach his home." —Union Magazine.

8—10. The second section of this chapter vvs. 8—24 describes the "wild grapes" of this vineyard—in six "woes." (8) **Woe,** comp. our Lord's denunciations, Mat. xxiii. 13—29. **house to house,**[a] "by violently expelling the poorer proprietors."—Cheyne. cf. Job xx. 19; Mic. ii. 1—5; **Ezek xlvi. 18.** The evil of cruel landlordism has cursed many lands.

[a] "The monopoly of houses and landed property was diametrically opposed to the spirit of the Mosaic law, and a virtual infraction of the enactment

relative to the year of jubilee." —Henderson.

Le. xxv. 10, 13, 25, etc.; Lu. xii. 15—21.

[b]Still, one of the gravest of national and social evils, is the gathering of the landed property into a very few hands.

The homer was a dry measure equal to ten baths; the ephah perhaps equalled six pecks.

"Gather the rosebuds while ye may, old Time is still a-flying; and that same flower that blooms to-day, to-morrow shall be dying."—Herrick.

[a] "Early drinking was considered by the Jews, as it was by the Romans, a mark of the most depraved sensuality." — Henderson.

[b] Eccl. x. 16, 17; comp. Is. xxii. 13, lvi. 12; Am. vi. 6.

[c] "Sensual indulgences steel the heart against religious impressions, and cause their victims to sport on the very brink of ruin." —Henderson.

"What good does physic poured down a dead man's throat? If he cannot be chafed to some sense of his condition, all applications are hopeless; and if sharp affliction, which is the strongest physic, leaves the sinner senseless, there is little prospect that anything else will do him good." — Gurnall.

See Pr. xxiii. 29, 30; Eph. v. 18, 19; Col. iii. 16, Ja. v. 13.

that they may be placed alone, R. V., "and ye be made to dwell alone,"[b] i. e. so that only the few are land-owners and householders, while he who seeks a bit of land can find "no place." (9) **In mine ears** (cf. xxii. 14.) the ears of the prophet, i. e. this I heard distinctly, as if the Lord had spoken in mine ear. Of a truth, an emphatic introduction in the nature of a solemn oath. **shall be,** better, are becoming; the Prophet sees the penalty actually beginning. (10) **one bath,** about 8 gallons. instead of the 500 which it ought to produce. **homer,** eight bushels of seed would yield only three pecks of produce. The picture is of the complete failure of harvest and vintage. "Barrenness, Jehovah's remedy for land-grabbing."—Cam. Bib.

Covetousness (vss. 8—10).—I. The sin here denounced. Covetousness defined. It is—1. Desiring more than is necessary for the purposes of life; 2. Worldliness; 3. Trusting and delighting in it; 4. Selfish monopoly. II. Its punishment. 1. Here—disappointment, loss, ruin, death; 2. Hereafter—misery, destitution. III. The certainty of this punishment. 1. God announces it to His servants; 2. Few believe it.—Lyth.

Oppression.—What shall become of the oppressor? No creature in heaven or earth shall testify his innocency. But the sighs, cries, and groans of undone parents, of beggared widows and orphans, shall witness the contrary. All his money, like hempseed, is sowed with curses.—Adams. Avarice.—I doubt not many covetous men take a great deal of pleasure in ruminating upon their wealth, and in recounting what they have; but they have a great deal of tormenting care and fear about it; and if they had not, it is very hard to understand where the reasonable pleasure and happiness lies of having things to no end. It is, at the best, like that of some foolish birds, which, they say, take pleasure in stealing money, that they may hide it; as if it were worth the while for men to take pains to dig silver out of the earth, for no other purpose but to melt it down and stamp it, and bury it there again.—Tillotson.

11, 12. (11) **rise early,** the second sin is drunkenness. Men plunge into debauchery as soon as the sun rises. This vice must describe a wide-spread condition, for the nation is denounced on account of it. Of course it refers mainly to the wealthy classes. **continue until night,**[b] R. V. "tarry late into the night." The land question and liquor question appear here as the marks of a corrupt national life on the verge of overthrow. (12) **harp,** etc., joining riotous mirth to sensual indulgence. **tabret,** or tambourine. **pipe,** or flute.[c] **work .. Lord,** i. e.. God is not in their thoughts. Though His work is all about them, in nature and history they do not heed it, nor see their impending punishment.

The degradation and ruin of intemperance (vss. 11, 12).—I. The sin, with its concomitants and connections, described in the text. 1. The Prophet refers to intemperance and its associate habits of festivity and dissipation—it is both bad in principle and degrading to character, it has a greater tendency than almost any other to destroy the feeling of shame and to harden conscience, it leads to other great sins, it is dangerous to the peace of society, and puts to hazard the lives of men; 2. The Prophet points out the connection between intemperance and unhallowed festivity and an infidel disregard of the works and ways of God. II. The woe denounced by the Prophet upon the sons and daughters of intemperance. Learn:—1. Habits of intemperance are progressively formed; 2. Beware of the first step, of the first temptation, of the first indulgence. —E. A. Cox.

Drinking habits in the East.—Such practices as these condemned by the Prophet are, unhappily, still common in the East. Mr. Morier, in his narrative of travels, describes the following scene:—"Returning from a morning ride about seven o'clock, I saw, at about forty yards from the roadside, a party of well-dressed Persians seated on a carpet close to a rising ground in the plain, with a small stream of water, near a field of rising corn, flowing before them, and surrounded by their servants and horses. As I passed, they sent a lad to me with a message to the following purpose: 'The Khan sends his compliments, says be happy, and join his party.' At the same time the whole company hallooed out to me as loud as they could, 'Be happy! be happy!' I afterwards learnt that this party was given by a Yuzbashee, or colonel of the king's troops, and that they were in the height of enjoyment when I passed, for they were all apparently much intoxicated. We one day met a party in one of the king's pleasure-houses nearly under similar circumstances; and we found that the Persians, when they commit a debauch, arise betimes, and esteem the morning as the best time for beginning to drink wine, by which means they carry on their excess until night."—They consider not.—This awful picture has already received a verification in the past history of Israel, and will yet again be verified even more markedly. But though primarily belonging to them, is it not equally true of ourselves? Does this chapter admit of no application to favored Protestant England? In our case, indeed, the judgments may for a time be chiefly moral—blindness of heart, famine of truth, moral perversion; but these things are judgments. When men, after having been brought into near proximity to light, suddenly renounce the things which they have professed to receive, and rush eagerly into darkness, is it not an evidence that delusion, causing them to believe lies, has fallen upon them; and is that no judgment? There is no infliction more terrible than that of judicial blindness. Is not society in England dividing itself between sacerdotal idolatry and philosophic scepticism? Can the anointed eye of faith look upon our stately temples, our "broad-ways," our marts, our cities, and not see them crowded by "men of hunger,"—men famished as to the bread of life, and yet they know it not?—J. Newton.

Knowledge—

Oh, for the coming of that glorious time
When, prizing knowledge as her noblest wealth
And best protection, this imperial realm,
While she exacts allegiance, shall admit
An obligation, on her part, to teach
Them who are born to serve her and obey;
Binding herself by statute to secure
For all the children whom her soil maintains
The rudiments of letters, and inform
The mind with moral and religious truth,
Both understood and practised,—so that none,
However destitute, be left to droop
By culture unsustained; or run
Into a wild disorder; or be forced
To drudge through a weary life without the help
Of intellectual implements and tools;
A savage horde among the civilised;
A servile band among the lordly free.

—Wordsworth.

13, 14 (13) **are gone into captivity,** better "goeth into." This is "the only explicit mention of exile in Isaiah."—Cam. Bib. **no knowledge,** the expression may mean "without knowing it," "unawares." G. A. Smith refers this to the "captivity" of drunkenness, in keeping with following verses. My people have become captives to strong drink, without knowing it. **honourable men .. multitude,** the aristocracy and the common people, drunkards alike, reach the point where neither hunger nor thirst can be satisfied. (14) **hell,**[a] Sheol: "the appetite of hell itself has to be enlarged to suffice for the consumption of the spoils of strong drink."—G. A. Smith. Even the place of the dead is not large enough, but must extend its limits to receive those who are about to enter it because of this evil. **herself** R. V., "her desire." **and their glory,** etc., Camb. Bib. translates, "And down goes her (Jerusalem's) pomp, and her tumult and her uproar and all that it so jubilant in her."

Ignorance.—As blindness is the deformity of the face, so is ignorance the deformity of the soul. As the want of fleshly eyes spoils the beauty of the face, so the want of spiritual eyes spoils the beauty of the soul. A man without knowledge is as a workman without his hands, as a painter without his eyes, as a traveler without his legs, or as a ship without sails, or a bird without wings, or like a body without a soul.—Brooks. Preparation for eternity.—Why should a man defer that which ought to

" The Persians, when they commit a debauch, arise betimes, and esteem the morning as the best time for beginning to drink wine, by which means they carry on their excess till night."—Morier.

"No man oppresses thee, O free and independent franchiser! but does not this stupid porter-pot oppress thee? No son of Adam can bid thee come or go; but this absurd pot of heavy wet, this can and does! Thou art the thrall, not of Cedric the Saxon, but of thy own brutal appetites, and this scoured dish of liquor. And thou pratest of thy 'liberty,' thou entire blockhead"—Carlyle.

"All their glory has faded away; it has vanished into a poor and pitiful handful of starvelings."—Wordsworth.

a "Poetically it is represented as enlarging itself immensely, in order to receive the countless hosts of Jews wh. should perish."—Fausset.

Sheol was figured as a vast and profound subterranean region, the entrance to wh. was furnished with gates and bars, into which men went down, and from which there was no return to the present world.

Comp. Is. xiv. 9—15.

"Ignorance opens the door for Satan to enter in with his troops of lusts; where the watch is blind, the city is soon taken."—Gurnall.

be the occupation of a life, which ought to command all his powers in all their vigor—why should a man defer that to the last few abrupt moments, to his departure from time to eternity? When a man is going to any distant part of the globe—say to America—what preparation there is! How much it is talked about! It is a long, a distant, an eventful journey. The man talks about it; his friends prepare in every conceivable way. Oh, what infatuation and stupidity, what folly it is for a man to make no preparation for this distant voyage—the voyage to eternity!—Beaumont. He that knew not his Lord's will, because he wilfully rejected the means of coming to the knowledge of it, deserves to be beaten with as many stripes as if he had known it and would not. He that will not take notice of the king's proclamation, or will stop his ears when it is read, and afterwards offends against it, does equally deserve punishment with those who have read it, and heard it, and disobey it; because he was as grossly faulty in not knowing it; and there is no reason that any man's gross fault should be his excuse.—Tillotson. Absence of misery a mercy.—And that our present happiness may appear to be the greater, and we the more thankful for it, I will beg you to consider with me how many do, even at this very time, lie under the torment of the stone, the gout, and toothache; and this we are free from. And every misery that I miss is a new mercy; and therefore let us be thankful. There have been, since we met, others that have met disasters of broken limbs; some have been blasted, others thunder-strucken; and we have been freed from these and all those many other miseries that threaten human nature: let us therefore rejoice and be thankful. Nay, which is a far greater mercy, we are free from the insupportable burden of an accusing, tormenting conscience—a misery that none can bear: and therefore let us praise Him for His preventing grace, and say, Every misery that I miss is a new mercy. Nay, let me tell you, there be many that have forty times our estates, that would give the greatest part of it to be healthful and cheerful like us, who, with the expense of a little money, have ate; and drunk, and laughed, and angled, and sung, and slept securely; and rose next day, and cast away care, and sung, and laughed, and angled again, which are blessings rich men cannot purchase with all their money.—I. Walton.

"Misery and ignorance are always the cause of great evils. Misery is easily excited to anger, and ignorance soon yields to perfidious counsels."—Addison.

15—17. (15) **mean man,** comp. ch. ii. 9. the reference is to those in lowly circumstances. **eyes .. lofty,** all classes are included in the coming doom. The common crowd and the military hero and the "first families," all shall be humbled. (16) **exalted,** or honored in men's view. **sanctified,** by the display of the holiness of His character, seen in the just punishment of the wicked.[b] (17) **After their manner,** R. V., "as in their pasture," where the city was, flocks shall graze among the ruins. **strangers,** nomads, wandering tribes. Judæa should become a vast pasturage. Le. xxvi. 43.

The lambs of the fold (vs. 17).—There are two ways of regarding this text. I. Taken literally, we have—1. An accomplished prophecy—the waste condition of the Holy Land—overrun with Bedouins and strangers; 2. A certain proof of the faithfulness of God's word—there may be delay, but all shall be fulfilled. II. Taken figuratively, we have—1. God's care of His lambs—He feeds them with sufficiency, in peace; 2. His judgments upon the proud—He takes them away, gives their substance to others.—Lyth.

Sin.—The evil spirit called sin may be trained up to politeness, and made to be genteel sin; it may be elegant, cultivated sin; it may be very exclusive and fashionable sin; it may be industrious, thrifty sin; it may be a great political manager, a great commercial operator, a great inventor; it may be learned, scientific, eloquent, highly-poetic sin! Still it is sin, and, being that, has in fact the same radical and fundamental quality that, in its ranker and less restrained conditions, produces all the most hideous and revolting crimes of the world.—Bushnell.

[b] "The judicial act is a realization of the idea of righteousness." —Nagelsbach.

"In that hour of righteous retribution His absolute supremacy and holiness shall stand out clearly to view." —Spk. Com.

Eze. xxviii. 22; Ro. ii. 5; Re. xv. 3. 4.

"The hearer sometimes complains that there is no food for his soul; when the truth is that there is no soul for the food."—Joseph Parker.

18, 19. The third woe. (18) **draw .. vanity,** they, as it were, yoke themselves in the harness of iniquity, and put forth all their strength to drag the burden along.[a] Or if we read "draw punishment near with cords," etc., then we have the antithesis in verse 19. of "the drunkards mocking Isaiah, 'Let Jehovah make speed', while they are dragging his

[a] Other explanations are, "Woe to them who draw calamity

judgment near as with cart ropes." The figure is of "sinners jeering at the approach of calamity, while they actually wear the harness of its carriage."—G. A. Smith. (19) **Let him,** etc., the spirit at once of unbelief and defiance. Whatever Isaiah may say, they do not believe in a day of Divine retribution.[b] **counsel,** or warning of punishment, of wh. the Prophet made so much. "This defiant unbelief seems to have been the reigning spirit in the political circles of Isaiah's time; xxviii. 14 f. 22; cf. Jer. v. 12; xvii. 15."—Camb. Bib.

with cords of iniquity, and punishment with ropes of wickedness."—Sugg. by Henderson.

[b] Comp. Ge. iv. 23, 24.

Power of sin over the unregenerate.—So long as a man is dead in trespasses and sin, there is no iniquity which may not get the mastery of him. Where the body is, thither will the vultures of hell be gathered together. The devil finding him dead, calls up his hosts of temptations and his bands of evils to feed on him. Nothing but the new life can secure a man from the worst fiends in the Pandemonium of vice, for they gather like a scattered pack to a feast. Vices seldom come alone; where there is room for one devil, seven other spirts more wicked than himself will find a lodging. We may say of sins as Longfellow of birds of prey, in his song of Hiawatha:—

"Never stoops the soaring vulture
On his quarry in the desert,
On the sick or wounded bison,
But another vulture watching,
From his high aërial look-out
Sees the downward plunge and follows;
And a third pursues the second,
Coming from the invisible ether,
First a speck, and then a vulture,
Till the air is dark with pinions."

"Woe to them that harness themselves as brute beasts to iniquity, with cords of falsehood, and drag on the weight of sin, as a waggon, with the ropes of vicious habits."—Wordsworth.

"Not content with the ordinary progress of iniquity, they spin ungodly theories, by which to make their massive loads of sin move more readily through the land."—Spk. Com.

"Like the beasts lay themselves to the traces with all their might, in order to start the load, so these lay themselves out to sin with all their might."—Nagelsbach.

Retribution is sure.—Many a man has gone on in sin, practising secret fraud and villanies, yet trusted and honored, till at length, in some unsuspected hour, he is detected, and, denounced by the world, he falls from his high estate as if a cannon-ball had struck him—for there is no cannon that can strike more fatally than outraged public sentiment—and flies over the mountains, or across the sea, to escape the odium of his life. He believed that his evil course was building him up in fame and fortune; but financiering is the devil's forge, and his every act was a blow upon the anvil, shaping the dagger that should one day strike home to his heart and make him a suicide. The pea contains the vine, and the flower, and the pod, in embryo, and, I am sure, when I plant it, that it will produce them and nothing else. Now, every action of our lives is embryonic, and, according as it is right or wrong, it will surely bring forth sweet flowers of joy, or the poison fruits of sorrow. Such is the constitution of this world, and the Bible assures us that the next world only carries it forward. Here and hereafter, "whatsoever a man soweth, that shall he also reap."—Beecher.

20. call evil good, "the fourth woe, against those who confuse moral distinctions. Amongst the "wise men" of the time (Prov. xxv. 1) there may have been a class of teachers who employed their subtlety in making out a case for abuses condemned by the unsophisticated moral sense."[a]—Camb. Bib.

Confounding right and wrong (vs. 20).—Our subject is the guilt of confounding right and wrong, by changing their names. I. It confounds moral distinctions, and perplexes one in regard to his duty. II. But it not only perplexes men—it deceives and misleads them. Now how is this confounding of right and wrong done? 1. When we slander one another by giving false names to each other's acts; 2. When we deceive ourselves in respect to our own character and conduct; 3. When we relieve our consciences by giving to our actions false names; 4. When by giving decent names to gross sins the standard of public morality is lowered. Learn:—(1) Be not deceived by false names; (2) Do not practise such impositions upon others; 3. Call things by their right names.—S. G. Buckingham.

[a] "Those do a great deal of wrong to God and religion, and conscience — to their own souls, and to the souls of others, who misrepresent these, and put false colors upon them; who call drunkenness good fellowship and covetousness good husbandry, and, when they persecute the people of God, think they do Him good service: and, on the other hand, who call seriousness ill-nature, and sober singularity ill-breeding, and say all manner of evil falsely concerning the ways of godliness."—Matthew Henry.

The deceptive influence of words.—The world is generally governed by

a "Drunkenness not merely incapacitates judges for the discharge of their official functions, but tempts them to make a trade of justice, with a view to the indulgence of this appetite."—J. A. Alexander.

"By ignorance is pride increased;
Those most assume who know the least;
Their own self-balance gives them weight,
But every other finds them light."
—Gay.

"O that men should put an enemy in their mouths, to steal away their brains!" —Shakespeare.

"In the bottle, discontent seeks for comfort, cowardice for courage, and bashfulness for confidence." —Johnson.

words and shows: for men can swallow the same thing under one name, which they would abominate and detest under another. The name of king was to the old Romans odious and insufferable; but in Sylla and Julius Cæsar they could endure the power and absoluteness of a king, disguised under the name of dictator.—South. Honest words.—I think that one of the master incantations, one of the most signal deceits, which we practice upon ourselves, comes from the use of language. There are words that we learn in childhood which we abandon when we come to manhood. Generally speaking, our fireside words are old Saxon words—short, knotty, tough, and imbued with moral and affectional meanings; but as we grow older these words are too rude and plain for our use, and so we get Latin terms and periphrases by which to express many of our thoughts. When we talk about ourselves we almost invariably use Latin words, and when we talk about our neighbors we use Saxon words. And one of the best things a man can do, I think, is to examine himself in the Saxon tongue. If a man tells that which is contrary to truth, let him not say, "I equivocate;" let him say "I lie." Lie! why, it brings the judgment-day right home to a man's thought. Men do not like it, but it is exactly the thing that will most effectually touch the moral sense; and the more the moral sense is touched the better. If a man has departed from rectitude in his dealings with another, let him not say "I took advantage," which is a roundabout, long sentence: let him say, "I cheated." That is a very direct word. It springs straight to the conscience, as the arrow flies from the bow to the centre of the mark. Does it grate harshly on your ear? Nevertheless, it is better that you should employ it; and you should come to this determination: "I will call things that I detect in my conduct by those clear-faced, rough-tongued words that my enemies use if they wanted to sting me to the quick."—Beecher.

21—23. (21) **wise .. eyes,** fifth woe, directed against those who confident of their own superior wisdom "interfered in the conduct of the State, and prepared arrogant policies of alliance and war that were the distress of the prophet all his days."—G. A. Smith. (xxviii. 9 f, xxix. 14 f, xxx. 1, 10 f.) (22) **mighty,** sixth woe, returns again to the drunken leaders of the people, who are mighty at drinking and mixing drinks, but nothing else. (23) **for reward,** or on receiving bribes. Still one of the common forms of Eastern iniquity. **righteousness,**[a] rob him of his character by declaring him guilty of crimes of which he is innocent.

Intellectual pride (vs. 21).—Woe to the intellectually proud. I. To the self-conceited sceptic, who sits in judgment upon the Word of God and condemns it. II. To the self-conceited enthusiast, who substitutes his own fancies in the face of Divine truth. III. To the self-conceited Pharisee, who trusts in his own works. IV. To the self-conceited sinner, who despises instruction.—Lyth.

Drunkenness.—It is a perfect shipwreck of a man; the pilot is drunk, and the helm dashed in pieces, and the ship first reels, and by swallowing too much, is itself swallowed up at last. And therefore the Navis Agrigentina, the madness of the young fellows of Agrigentum, who, being drunk, fancied themselves in a storm, and the house the ship, was more than the wild fancy of their cups; it was really so, they were all cast away, they were broken in pieces by the foul disorder of the storm. "The senses languish, the spark of divinity that dwells within is quenched; and the mind snorts, dead with sleep and fulness in the fouler regions of the belly." So have I seen the eye of the world looking upon a fenny bottom, and, drinking up too free draughts of moisture, he gathered them into a cloud, and that cloud crept about his face, and made him first look red, and then covered him with darkness and an artificial night; so is our reason at a feast....The clouds gather about the head, and according to the method and period of the children and productions of darkness, it first grows red, and that redness turns into an obscurity and a thick mist, and reason is lost to all use and profitableness of wise and sober discourses; "a cloud of folly and distraction darkens the soul," and makes it crass and material, polluted and heavy, clogged and loaden like the body; and, there cannot be anything said worse, reason turns into folly, wine and flesh into a knot of clouds, the soul itself into a body, and the spirit into corrupted meat: here is nothing left but the rewards and portions of a fool, to be reaped and enjoyed there, where flesh and corruption shall dwell to eternal ages.—Jer. Taylor,

24, 25. (24) **devoureth,** nothing could provide a more impressive figure of hopeless sinking into destruction than that of chaff and dried grass sinking in the flames. **root .. blossom,**[b] by which life is perpetuated. The root shall have no life in it, and the blossom shall be as sterile as dust. This burning up, as with fire, is a fitting description of the end of drunkenness. **cast away,** or rejected. (25) **against them,** that very hand which had been so tenderly and graciously for them. **hills .. tremble,**[c] with the tread of the foe. **carcases,** of the slain. **torn,** R. V. "were as refuse." **all this,** a refrain which occurs again in ch. ix. 12, 17, 21; x:4, indicating that probably that section is out of place and belongs here, betw. vss. 25 and 26.

Discontent at restraints of God's law.—The spring of the law is love. With its "Thou shalt not do this," and "Thou shalt not do that," the law presents rather an ungracious aspect. We like ill to be bidden, but worse to be forbidden. But does love never forbid? A mother, does she never forbid her child; but, on the contrary, indulge every caprice and grant all its wishes? How disastrous the fate, and brief the life, of a child denied nothing, indulged in everything, allowed to play with fire, or fire-arms; to devour the painted but poisonous fruit—to bathe where the tide runs like a racehorse or the river rushes roaring into the black, swirling pool. And he who frets against the restraints of God's holy law because it forbids this and the other thing, is no wiser than the infant who weeps, and screams, and struggles, and perhaps beats the kind bosom that nurses it, because its mother has snatched a knife from its foolish hands.—Guthrie.

b "Those roots and blossoms that ought properly to be fresh and full of sap, shall fly away, dissolved as they are in dust and decay, as easily as hay and stubble are devoured by the flames." — Nagelsbach.

Mat. iii. 12.

c Explained by Hendework as the earthquake of Am. i. 1; Zec. xiv. 5.

26—28. (26) **ensign,** God himself will summon a nation (the better reading) and give the signal for its rendezvous.[a] No nation is named. But the Assyrians are referred to. **hiss,** a fig. from drawing bees out of a hive by hissing or whistling. **they shall come,** He is the governor of all the earth and all nations serve Him. **swiftly,** this word will characterize the movement in the description following. The language rushes on, figure following figure, most graphically representing the mighty and onrushing invasion of the Assyrians. (27) **none .. weary,** etc., strong poetical figures of the greatest activity and readiness for conflict. **girdle**[b] **loosed,** for resting times. They would move forward without any intermission. (28) **horses' hoofs .. flint,** as the horses were not shod, the hardness of the hoof was a prime quality of a good horse, especially if used for war in the rocky land of Palestine. **whirlwind,** revolving so fast—in their onward rush.

National judgments (vss. 26—30).—I. God uses one nation to punish another. II. Summons them at His pleasure. III. Disposes them to do His will,—promptly, efficiently. IV. Fits them for His service. V. Ensures their success. VI. The transgressor has no hope of escape.—Lyth.

Conscience.—There is a warning conscience and a gnawing conscience. The warning comes before sin; the gnawing conscience follows after sin. The warning conscience is often lulled asleep, but the gnawing conscience wakes her again. If there be any hell in this world, they who feel the worm of conscience gnawing on their hearts may truly say that they have felt the torments of hell. Who can express that man's horror but himself? Nay, what horrors are those which he cannot express himself! Sorrows are met in his soul as at a feast; and fear, thought, and anguish divide the soul between them. All the furies of hell leap upon his heart like a stage. Thought calls to Fear; Fear whistles to Horror; Horror beckons to Despair, and says, Come, and help me to torment this sinner. One says that she comes from this sin, and another says that she comes from that sin. So he goes through a thousand deaths, and cannot die. Irons are laid upon his body like a prisoner. Thus he lives as it were upon the rack, and says that he bears the world upon his shoulders, and that no man suffers that which he suffers. So let him lie, says God, without ease, until he confess and repent and call for mercy.—Henry Smith.

a "Reference is to the military custom of planting a pole with a flag on a high mountain, either to serve as a signal of rendezvous or to point out the direction in which an army is to proceed. The latter is here intended." — Henderson.

b The military girdle is meant, which had attached to it the sheath with the sword.

"Afflictions are but the shadows of God's wing." —George Macdonald.

"Many do with opportunities as children do at the sea-shore: they fill their little hands with sand, and then let the grains fall through, one by one, till all are gone." —T. Jones.

29, 30. (29) **roaring,**[c] translate, "He has a roar like that of a lioness,

c Hab. i. 6—10; Je. xxxii. 5—28, xxxvii. 8—10.

d "Let the distressed look wh. way they will everything appears dismal; for, if God frown upon us, how can any creature smile?" — Mat. Henry.

he roars like young lions and growls seizing the prey."—Camb. Bib. A figure suggested by the hoarse war-cry and the cruel fury of the coming invader. (30) **roaring . . sea,** the nation is like a storm-wracked ship. The ocean roars over it, ready to engulf it. They look toward the land for help but there is no land—only darkness and despair. The very light of the heavens dims, and is swallowed up in blackness.[d]

Sin conceals the favor of God.—Sin is as a thick cloud, stopping the sunshine of God's mercy; but if we turn from sin, this will melt the cloud, and cause the Sun of Righteousness to shine upon us. Sin is a wall of separation between God and us. To turn from sin will break down this wall. To turn from sin is a key to unlock all the chests of God's mercies. Oh, the Divine rhetoric and omnipotent efficacy of repentance! This is that rainbow, which, if God seeth shining in our hearts, He will never drown our souls. That star which will bring us to Christ. A repenting faith ties God's hands, and charms His wrath. There is no thunderbolt so great, no wrath so furious in God, but repentance will abolish it.—E. Calamy.

CHAPTER THE SIXTH.

1, 2. (1) **Uzziah died,** disgraced, of leprosy, a type of weak human power; in that year (740 B. C.) Isaiah had a vision of the King of kings. Uzziah had been great but his glory faded away. Here is true and unfading glory. **saw,** pictured in vision. **the Lord,** Adonai, the supreme Ruler and Judge. **throne,** "the Prophet sees the earthly temple transfigured until it seemed a miniature of the Universal Temple."[a] **train,** "the skirts of the royal mantle falling in ample folds conceal from the prophet the Form seated upon the throne."—Driver. (2) **seraphims,**[b] not to be likened to the cherubim who seem to be only symbolic figures. But these, according to vs. 6, are angelic beings of the highest order. They are represented in human form, with wings. The name probably comes from an arabic root meaning "noble." **covered his face,** for even the highest angels cannot bear to look upon the full glory of God. **covered his feet,** an Eastern token of reverence. **did fly,** the wings were set ready at once to fly in obedience to Div. command.

a "Isaiah is outside, near the altar in front of the temple. The doors are supposed to be open, and the veil hiding the holy of holies to be withdrawn, unfolding to his view a vision of God, represented as an Eastern monarch, attended by seraphim as His ministers of state, and with a robe and flowing train (a badge of dignity in the E.), which filled the temple."—Fausset.

b Comp. Rev. iv.

The vision of Isaiah (vss. 1—8).—I. We have to observe the vision which the Prophet beheld. It was—1. A vision of the Divine supremacy; 2. Of the Divine attendants; 3. It connects holiness with the Divine greatness; 4. By this connection, a remarkable effect is stated to have been produced. II. The effect which this vision produced upon the Prophet's mind—1. As a man; 2. As an intended messenger of God. III. The sustaining visitation which was made, in connection with the effect produced. 1. The agent sent: note his celerity; 2. The assurance communicated; 3. The manner in which the assurance is testified. IV. The commission which, in connection with this visitation, was proposed and accepted. 1. The messenger who goes out, God sends by His own power; 2. Such messengers are fully devoted to God; 3. They must proceed without debate to the object of their mission.—J. Parsons.

"No rebellions shake the throne of God; though "the heathen rage, and the people imagine a vain thing," yet "He that sitteth in the heavens shall laugh; the Lord shall have them in derision." The throne of God is a rock in the midst of the ever-rolling ocean of created existence, that heaves and swells with ceaseless change; but, in compari-

Isaiah's inaugural vision.—It is now universally acknowledged that this chapter records Isaiah's initiation into the office of a prophet. The opinion of many older commentators that it represents a renewal or recovery of the prophetic consciousness after several years of public activity, was based on the erroneous assumption that the order of the book is in the main chronological and that the previous chapters contain prophecies from the reign of Uzziah. Everything in the narrative itself suggests that it is an inaugural vision, a record of the experience by which Isaiah was made a prophet. The consciousness of standing in a peculiar relation to God, of personal reconciliation to Him, of being in His council, and bearing a definite commission straight from Himself, dates from the moment when in an ecstasy he "saw the Lord." The vision is undoubtedly an actual experience, not the mere embodiment of an idea; it occurred in the death-year of Uzziah, as the prophet, looking back after some lapse of time, distinctly recalls. Then Isaiah saw God, not indeed with his bodily eyes, but in a prophetic trance, in which the ordinary operations of the mind were suspended and spiritual realities assumed concrete and visible forms.—Camb. Bib. The prophet's call.—Once for all must he who was to be a prophet have become absolutely certain of the true relation of the world and Jehovah,—must have beheld, as in a distinct form, the sublime and holy character of Jehovah, and felt that he was directed by Him alone; once for all must he have recognized the divine power of truth against the whole world, and himself as living and moving in it alone; once for all must he have entered, with the effectual energy and act of his whole inner being, into the counsels of God, and found himself for ever bound by them, and endowed by these bonds with true power and freedom:—this was the first condition and the true beginning of all the work of the prophet, the holy consecration and the inner call, without which none can become a true prophet. —Ewald.

son of Him, its mightiest billows have but their moment of existence, and sink into the mass at the base of the immovable throne of the Everlasting One." —Watson.

One of the mottoes on the walls of the temple at Delphos was, "Know thy opportunity."

3, 4. (3) **one .. another,** responding the one to the other. **Holy,**[a] this is not a scholastic definition of the Deity, nor is intended to convey the idea of the Trinity, but is an emphatic declaration of the nature of God. He is Holy, holy, holy. This is His great characteristic which the formalists, liturgists, sensualists of the day needed to realize. The death of Uzziah stricken with leprosy for his irreverence made the teaching timely for Isaiah and the nation. Holiness is the keynote of Is.'s prophecies. **whole .. glory,** "the fulness of the whole earth is His glory," is the proper rendering. The wealth and beauty of all the world is His glory.[b] (4) **posts,** R. V. "foundations of the thresholds." **filled with smoke,** comp. Ex. xix. 18, xl. 34; 1 Ki. viii. 10. Intended to produce a solemn awe in the beholder; perhaps also to moderate for Isaiah the vision of the Divine glory.

a "Holy, though His work in redeeming Israel seems to have come to naught, and His pretermission of human sin appears to militate against justice." —Spk. Com.

b "The Jews thought the glory of God should be confined to their land; but it is here intimated that in Gospel times the glory of God should fill all the earth, the glory of His holiness, which is indeed the glory of all His other attributes." — Mat. Henry.

The vast and the minute.—

"There's nothing great
Or small," hath said a poet of our day;
And truly I reiterate, "There's nothing small,
No pebble at my feet but proves a sphere;
No chaffinch but implies a cherubim;
No hum of lily-muffled bee but finds
Some coupling music with the whirling stars.
"Earth's crammed with heaven;
And every common bush afire with God;
But only those who see take off their shoes;
The rest sit round it, and eat blackberries."
—E. B. Browning.

5. **Woe is me,** the awe produced by the sense of God's presence passed into a deep humiliation and fear, in the feeling of his own sinfulness.[c] **unclean lips,**[d] unworthy to speak to the unclean people until his own lips, and life, had been cleansed. The sense of the uncleanness of the nation, himself included, came from the vision of the Holiness of God. **seen the King,**[e] I am undone, because, being full of sin I have come into the presence of the Holy God.

God's calls.—We are apt to think that if calls came to us with the distinctness with which they came to men of the olden time we should readily and gladly respond. If anything as dramatic as the vision Isaiah had could be duplicated in our experience we, too, would be overwhelmed with a sense of God's presence and of our own unworthiness to be commissioned by him. If, again, as we were pursuing our commonplace avocations, a majestic and gracious person should appear beside our boats, our counters, close to our office desks, we, too, would be quite willing to drop our numerous interests and rise up and follow him. But are we right in thinking that the heavenly word does not press in upon our lives today, that the Son of Man is not walking through our streets as he went up and down the highway of Galilee? There is a celebrated picture in the National Gallery in London which represents St. Augustine sitting with his hand in that of his mother, Monica. The rapt expres-

c "The Prophet, appalled by the display which he saw of the Divine glory, the theme and loud peals of the seraphim, the concussions of the earthquake, and a sense of his own sinfulness, and that of his nation, apprehended instant destruction." —Henderson.

d "That he emphasizes the unclean lips comes from the fact that he had just heard the seraphim bring an offer of praise with clean lips." —Nagelsbach.

e Comp. Jno. i. 18; 1 Ti. vi. 16.

sion on both faces shows that they have risen above earthly things. The tradition is that at this moment St. Augustine said: "O, that God would speak to us!" His noble mother replied: "My son, perhaps he is speaking to us." If, instead of looking for such extraordinary tokens of God's presence, we should keep quiet long enough and our spirits humble enough, perhaps we should learn that God is speaking to us all the time.

6—8. (6) **live coal,** to this cry of penitence God sends a messenger to purify. Notice that it is not an act of sacrifice on the part of Isaiah, but of the angel. The man confesses and God cleanses and consecrates his lips. **the altar,** either that of burnt-offering, or that of incense. (7) **my mouth,** comp. Je. i. 9.[a] **iniquity,** etc., i. e. his conscious unworthiness to act as God's messenger. (8) **voice of the Lord,** not until then did he hear the Lord speaking to him. **for us,** the Lord does not think of Himself alone nor of His work as His own alone,—but as that of His Kingdom.—Cam. B. refers to the "council of the holy ones," Ps. lxxxix. 7, R. V. **send me,** the call implies that even he may serve God, and his loyal spirit responds at once.

A missionary spirit described (vs. 8).—I. The proposal made referred to a mission which God intended to send to His people. II. The answer given. We should offer ourselves to serve Him—1. Instantly; 2. Without reserve. III. The peculiar obligation which lies on us to follow the Prophet's example. We may be considered as having—1. More glorious discoveries of Christ; 2. More abundant communications of the Spirit; 3. More certain assurances of the forgiveness of our sins.—C. Simeon.

Preparation for service.—If thou, then, wouldst have thy soul surcharged with the fire of God, so that those who come nigh to thee shall feel some mysterious influence proceeding out from thee, thou must draw nigh to the source of that fire, to the throne of God and of the Lamb, and shut thyself out from the world—that cold world which so swiftly steals our fire away. Enter into thy closet, and shut to thy door; and there, isolated, "before the throne," await the baptism; then the fire shall fill thee, and when thou comest forth, holy power will attend thee, and thou shalt labor, not in thine own strength, but "with the demonstration of the Spirit, and with power."—W. Arthur. Promoters of missions.—There was a race of parents that could raise a race of missionaries. Let me give you an instance of an old Moravian woman. A friend called upon her with sadness in his looks. "Your son," said he to the mother, "is gone." "Is Thomas gone to heaven through the missionary life? Would to God that He would call my son John!" Well, John did become a missionary; and he fell. And this time the committee were very sad; but, before opening their lips, the old woman anticipated the story, and exclaimed, "Thank God! Would that He would call my last son, William!" And William, too, went, and fell; when the noble woman exclaimed, "Would that I had a thousand sons to give to God!" Oh! would that I had a thousand such mothers! Then would our ranks be full.—Durbin.

9, 10. (9) **Hear,**[b] etc., "the most decisive judgment to which men are subjected lies in the abundance of the revelations of God to them."—Camb. Bib. (Mat. xiii. 14; Acts xvi. 26; Ro. xi. 8; John iii. 19). "Spiritual blindness is the punishment of the Jews for refusng to see, obduracy is their chastisement for hardening their heart." Je. vii. 26. (10) **Make,** etc.,[c] this would be the result of his preaching, not the object he was to seek.[d] "The O. T. calls the highest degree of sin obduracy, or hardening of the heart. (Ex. iv. 21; Ps. xcv. 8; Prov. xxviii. 14, etc.) This is the condition in which a man, by continually cherishing sin, has [in a sense] lost the ability to withstand it."—Oehler. **convert,** R. V. "turn again." Notice that the O. T. always speaks of this hardening of the heart only in connection with a divine revelation offered to the sinner but rejected by Him. This divine revelation results in the rebellious act, so that both God and the man are spoken of as causing the hardened heart. To "turn again" will be to accept and act upon the revelation.

Pitying the heathen.—In the whole history of the human family there is nothing that is better fitted to draw from our eyes tears of compassion, even yet, than those things that men are wont to laugh at. Is it but a poor and childish superstition that leads the Indian of the forest

[a] "The fire is applied to the lips for a twofold reason: 1. To show that the particular impediment of which the Prophet had complained was done away; and 2. To show that the gift of inspiration is included."—J. A. Alexander.

Oh, dull of heart! Enclosed doth lie,
In each "Come, Lord," a "Here am I."
Thy very prayer to thee was given,
Itself a messenger of heaven.
—Trench.

"If ever a man ought to be all there, it is when he is called to the service of God. He should marshal all his faculties, and every faculty should reply, "Here am I." The whole of a living man is something worth having, but a fragment is only fit to be buried."—Spurgeon.

[b] "The language is proverbial in its character, and savors strongly of sacred irony, of wh. we have a decided instance in Mat. xxiii. 32." — Henderson.

[c] "Render them the more hardened by your warnings." — Maurer.

[d] "Forasmuch as they would not be made better by his ministry, they should be made worse by it; those that were wilfully

to go through his incantation? The incantation is poor enough, and childish enough; but the heart-ache which there is in the Indian's bosom is just as sublime as it was in Socrates. Is it a sad and pitiful thing to see the heathen go down to the river, to the jungle, to the idol temple, and pass through fires, or floods, or expiations? and are these things foolish, and utterly without power either to change the character or to appease an intelligent God? The thing may be imbecile, if you please; but the soul-want, the shadow of a great fear that rests upon these untaught children that have felt the power of moral government, but that do not know what that government is, nor the way to it—that is full of heroism even. None more than we can afford to throw away the superstitions; but none so much as we should pity those poor, thralled hearts, that are bound by superstition, and that know not where to find a Redeemer.—H. W. Beecher.

blind should be judicially blinded."—Mat. Henry.

"There is light enough for those whose sincere desire is to see; and darkness enough for those of a contrary disposition." — Pascal.

11—13. (11) **how long?** bec. Is. knew that God's times of judgment were but steps to times of salvation. **Until,** etc., i. e. until it has utterly ruined the people, and driven them from their country. (12) **far away,** to Babylon; there was to be no permanent recovery until after the great captivity. (13) **But yet in it,** etc., Cam. Bib., "And should there still be in it a tenth, it must again pass through the fire, like the terebinth and like the oak, to which a stump (remains) when they are felled; a holy seed is the stump thereof." i. e. As the terebinth and oak when cut down retain the principle of vitality in their roots, which will again spring up into a great tree (cf. Job xiv. 7 ff.), so the ruined Israel contains the indestructible germ of the future kingdom of God, the "holy seed" is wrapped up in it. Here is the important prophetic doctrine of "the remnant." Though the present nation shall be destroyed, there shall remain a vestige of life from which a new nation shall arise. Is. lxv. 8 ff. Zeph. iii. 12, 13; Mic. ii. 12; v. 6. Jer. xxiii. 3.[a]

The leafless tree (vs. 13).—Having explained the meaning of the passage, I shall make the application—I. To the Jews. II. To the Church of Christ. III. To each believer. 1. Men lose their leaves when they lose their comforts; 2. Some Christians lose their leaves, not by doubts, but by sin.—C. H. Spurgeon.

Fulfilment of prophecy.—Heathens, Christians and Mohammedans have alternately possessed Judæa. It has been the prey of the Saracens; the descendants of Ishmael have often overrun it; the children of Israel have alone been denied the possession of it, though thither they ever wish to return; and though it forms the only spot on earth where the ordinances of their religion can be observed. And, amid all the revolutions of states, and the extinction of many nations, in so long a period the Jews alone have not only ever been aliens in the land of their fathers, but whenever any of them have been permitted, at any period since the time of their dispersion, to sojourn there, they have experienced even more contumelious treatment than elsewhere. Benjamin of Tudela, who travelled in the twelfth century through great part of Europe and of Asia, found the Jews everywhere oppressed, particularly in the Holy Land. And to this day (while the Jews who reside in Palestine, or who resort thither in old age, that their bones may not be laid in a foreign land, are alike ill-treated and abused by Greeks, Armenians, and Europeans) the haughty deportment of the despotic Turkish soldier, and the abject state of the poor and helpless Jews, are painted to the life by the Prophet.—Keith. Possibilities of excellence.—As the eye of the cunning lapidary detects in the rugged pebble, just digged from the mine, the polished diadem that shall sparkle in the diadem of a king; or as the sculptor in the rough block of marble, newly hewn from the quarry, beholds the statue of perfect grace and beauty which is latent there, and waiting but the touch of his hand,—so He who sees all, and the end from the beginning, sees oftentimes greater wonders than these. He sees the saint in the sinner, the saint that shall be in the sinner that is; the wheat in the tare; the shepherd feeding the sheep in the wolf tearing the sheep; Paul the preacher of the faith in Saul the persecutor of the faith; Israel a prince with God in Jacob the trickster and the supplanter; Matthew the Apostle in Levi the publican; a woman that should love much in a woman sinning much; and in some vine of the earth bring-

[a] "However frequently the people may seem to be destroyed, there shall still be a surviving remnant, and however frequently that very remnant may appear to perish, there shall still be a remnant of the remnant left, and this indestructible residuum shall be the holy seed, the true Church."—J. A. Alexander. Job xiv. 7; Eze. xi. 16.

"The historical matters of Scripture, both narrative and prophecy, constitute as it were the bones of its system; whereas the spiritual matters are as its muscles, blood-vessels and nerves. As the bones are necessary to the human system, so Scripture must have its historical matters. The expositor who nullifies the historical groundwork of Scripture for the sake of finding only

ing forth wild grapes and grapes of gall a tree which shall yet bring forth good fruit, and wine to make glad the heart; so that when some, like those over-zealous servants in the parable, would have Him pluck it up, and to cast it without more ado into the wine-press of the wrath of Almighty God, He exclaims rather, "Destroy it not, for a blessing is in it," and is well content to await the end.—Trench.

spiritual truths everywhere, brings death on all correct interpretation." —J. A. Bengel.

"As for our opportunities, we can make a heroic life out of whatever is set before us to work with or upon."—Anna Robertson Brown.

CHAPTER THE SEVENTH.

Chaps. vii. 1—ix. 7 contain a collection of prophecies belonging to the reign of Ahaz. Chap. vii. is divided into two sections, vss. 1—17 and 18—25. Date 735 B. C. **1, 2.** (1) **Ahaz,** 2 Ki. xvi. 5. **Rezin,** this name is found in the Assyrian inscriptions as that of a king of Damascus, and tributary of Tiglath-Pileser. **went up toward,** for the earlier part of this war, comp. 2 Ki xv. 37; 2 Chr. xxviii. **could not prevail,**[a] for what reason does not appear. This verse gives a summary of the whole adventure and issue of the war, by way of introduction. The narrative proper begins with verse 2.—(G.·A. Smith.) (2) **house of David,** the expedition was really directed against the family of David: its expressed object (vs.6) is not conquest—but a change of dynasty. **confederate**[b] with, Camb. Bib. trans. "Syria hath alighted upon Ephraim." That is, the Syrian armies, moving against Jerusalem have already settled, like a great swarm of locusts, on the land of Israel. **moved, i. e.** trembled—as trees tremble in the wind.

The purpose of Isaiah in his interview with Ahab.—In order to understand Isaiah's words and actions at this period it is necessary to realise as clearly as possible the salient features of the political situation created in Judah by the Syro-Ephraimitish invasion. It is generally supposed that the ultimate motive of the attack was to coerce Judah into a coalition to oppose the westward progress of the Assyrian arms. To allay what he perceived to be a groundless alarm on the part of the king and court was one purpose of Isaiah's memorable interview with Ahaz. But this of itself does not explain the extraordinary vehemence and urgency of the prophet's appeal. It becomes fully intelligible only when we understand that he wished to warn the king against the fatal step, which he afterwards took, of calling in the aid of Assyria against his two petty foes. It is only reasonable to suppose that this obvious and tempting expedient had already been discussed in the royal council and was favourably entertained by Ahaz. Isaiah was no doubt alive to the grave political dangers which would result from placing the country in a position of servitude to the Assyrian Empire. He also perceived how unnecessary it was for Judah to make any advances in that direction at this time, since it was quite certain that the ambitious schemes of Rezin and Pekah would speedily be crushed by Tiglath-pileser, whether Ahaz applied to him or not. All this must have been evident to any sagacious observer who kept his head amidst the general panic caused by the approach of the allied armies. But the prophet perceived that higher interests than the political future of the nation were at stake. He was opposed, on religious grounds, to all compacts with heathen powers as involving disloyalty to Jehovah and distrust of His power. The crisis presented itself to him as a test of the religious mind of the people, of its capacity for exercising that fearless trust in Jehovah's word which alone could guide it safely through the complications of the immediate future to the felicity that lay beyond. Hence the great object of this encounter with Ahaz is to bring round the king to Isaiah's own attitude of calm reliance on the help of God, and above all things to dissuade him from compromising his position by entering into direct relations with Assyria. Cam. Bib. —Obstacles in the path of sin. Augustine, in his Confessions, makes thankful note of the maner in which, in the years of his ungodliness, God had raised up obstacles in his path of sin. When sinful desires raged within him, he says, the means for gratifying them were absent; or when the desires and the means of gratifying them came together, some witness was present to deter him; and when the means were present, and no

a "Ahaz had applied to the king of Assyria, and the news that the latter was in motion in response to the request of Ahaz, moved the allied kings to hasten home into their countries."—Nagelsbach.

b "Hitherto the northern kingdom had for the most part acted as a barrier between Syria and Judah. Now Syria had gained Israel over, and could use Samaria as a base of operations against Judah." —Spk. Com.

If you wish to be miserable, you must think about yourself,— about what you want, what you like, what respect people ought to pay to you, what people think of you; and then to you nothing will be pure. You will spoil everything you touch; you will make sin and misery for yourself out of everything which God sends you; you will be as wretched as you choose. —Charles Kingsley.

witnesses stood by to hinder him, the desire to transgress was wanting. He rightly judged that these were no mere accidents or coincidences.

3, 4. (3) **Shear-jashub,** meaning, a remnant shall return. Isa.'s sons were used as signs. The presence of this son was a call to penitence. **end .. pool,** the prob. ref. is to a pool 700 yards from the Jaffa gate, from wh. an aqueduct led the water into the city.[a] "In the historic sieges of Jerusalem the assailants always suffered more for want of water than did the defenders."—Cambridge Bible. **highway,** or causeway beside the aqueduct. **fuller's field,** or bleaching ground for clothes washed in the pool. (4) **be quiet,** i. e. do not be alarmed. Keep cool, and trust in God. Do not be afraid of these enemies. Who are they? Mere burned out stumps of fire-brands. Their threats are smoke. **two tails,**[b] etc., this enterprise is but the last flicker of two expiring torches.

Fear not.—Fear not—I. For thyself. I will wash thee thoroughly from thine iniquities. I will console thee in trouble. I will be with thee in the dark valley. II. For any among thy kindred and acquaintance of the same family of God. There is a shield over the head of each. III. Amid changes however startling; circumstances however unexpected. I am the perfect Ruler of a perfect providence.

God's message.—"Then said the Lord unto Isaiah——" There is always some man to send, some man of purged lips, some man fire-touched, who will face the occasion under the inspiration and comfort of the Paraclete. Here, as ever, human ministry is employed to carry out divine purposes. Then here is a man sent of God so confident that he becomes contemptuous of the opposition. Isaiah said unto the king: "Be quiet; fear not, neither be fainthearted for the two tails of these smoking firebrands." The figure is that of two torches that have been burned down to the root, and nothing is left of them but smoke; the fire is nearly out, and a little wreath of smoke expresses the strength of these two firebrands. The contempt which Righteousness can assume is a terrible sarcasm. When Judgmet laughs, the laugh is spectral and heart-shaking; it sends a sense of dismay into the innermost parts of the spirit: when God laughs at our calamity, our calamity is multiplied by infinity.—Peop. Bib. Groundless fear.—It was wise advice of Sydney Smith, when he said that those who desire to go hopefully and cheerfully through their work in this life, should "take short views:" not plan too far ahead; take the present blessing, and be thankful for it. It was indeed the best of all possible advice; for it was but a repetition, in another form, of the counsel of the kindest and wisest: "Take therefore no thought for the morrow: for the morrow shall take thought for the things of itself: sufficient unto the day is the evil thereof." Whenever I see man or woman, early old with anxiety, and with a face deeply lined with care, I think of certain words which deserve infinitely better than to be printed in letters of gold; and I wish that such a one, and that all I care for, were numbered among the people who have a right to take these words for their own: "Be careful for nothing; but in everything, by prayer and supplication with thanksgiving, let your requests be made known to God. And the peace of God, which passeth all understanding, shall keep your hearts and mind through Christ Jesus."

5, 6. (5) **son of Remaliah,** i. e. Pekah, a usurper whom Isaiah never calls by name, but "son of Remaliah," to recall his low birth, and in contrast with the House of David, the absence of Divine promise. **evil counsel,** planning a mischievous design. Their secret scheme, Isaiah, by prophetic power, discloses to Ahaz.[c] (6) **vex it,** strike horror into it: harass it. **make a breach,** or take by storm. **set a king,** a creature of their own, whose policy they might control. **son of Tabeal,** this person is unknown, but the name is a Syriac one, and not a Hebrew, indicating that the man was a foreigner.

Faith in God makes men fearless.—The difference, which is made in the character and habits of men if the country they live in has a powerful government or not, is well known. If there be no such central authority, it is a case of every man's hand against his neighbor. Men walk armed to the teeth. A constant attitude of fear and sus-

[a] Robinson and Smith identify with a large tank at the head of the valley of Hinnom. It is full in the rainy season, and its waters are then conducted by a small rude aqueduct, which is the conduit mentioned.

"Ahaz was superintending the works for defence, and the cutting off of the water supply from the enemy and securing it to the city."—Fausset.

[b] "The hot fire of their anger was now turned to smoke and almost quenched." —J. A. Alexander.

"God hath three hands wherewith he distributes earthly things: A hand of common providence; with this he feeds the ravens when they cry. A hand of special love; with this he feeds his children who commit their way to him and trust in him. A hand of anger and wrath; with this he gives to those who are impatient." — Philip Henry.

[c] "The objects at which the confederates aimed were the entire destruction of the house of David, and the placing of a foreigner upon the throne." — Henderson.

'We do far too much for ourselves; we suppose we are more

picion warps the whole nature. The passions are excited and magnified; the intelligence and judgment are dwarfed. Just the same after its kind is life to the man or tribe, who believe, that the world in which they dwell and the life they share with others have no central authority. They walk armed with prejudices, superstitions and selfishnesses. They create, like Ahaz, their own providences, and still, like him, feel insecure. Everything is exaggerated by them; in each evil there lurks to their imagination unlimited hostility. They are without breadth of view or length of patience. But let men believe that life has a central authority, that God is supreme, and they will fling their prejudices and superstitions to the winds, now no more needed than the antiquated fortresses and weapons by which our forefathers, in days when the government was weak, were forced to defend their private interests. When we know that God reigns, how quiet and free it makes us! When things and men are part of His scheme and working out His ends, when we understand that they are not monsters but ministers, how reasonably we can look at them! Were we afraid of Syria and Ephraim? Why, the head of Syria is this fellow Rezin, the head of Ephraim this son of Remaliah! They cannot last long; God's engine stands behind to smite them. By the reasonable government of God, let us be reasonable! Let us take heed and be quiet. Have faith in God, and to faith will come her proper consequent of commonsense.—Expositors' Bible.

than a match for the enemy, and therefore we play off our resources against his: better to pray than to plan; better to forgive than to circumvent; better to think of God than to think of man—or to think of God and thus think more truly and profoundly of man. Sometimes we do everything by doing nothing. Sometimes we win the battle by simply standing still and watching the wondrous ways of Providence."—Parker.

7—9. (7) **Lord God, or** Lord Jehovah, who will keep His covenant. **not stand,** this plot has no foundation. It will not succeed. Notice the positive tone of the prophet. He is sure of what he promises. He displays that calmness and certainty which he advises to the king. (8) **head of,** or the capitol of.[a] "We may even suppose (with Ewald) that Isaiah intended to add "But the head of Judah is Jerusalem, and the head of Jerusalem is Jehovah of hosts."—Cam. Bib. **broken,** so as to be no longer a distinct nation.[b] (9) **head,** etc., What are these heathen kingdoms and kings against Jehovah and His people! **If .. established,**[c] Oehler calls this "the thesis of prophetism"; If you do not trust in God you have no sure foundation." 2 Chron. xx. 20. Jer. xvii. 5. Ps. cxii. 7. Is. xxx. 15.

The sin of unbelief (vs. 9).—The sin of unbelief may be called the white devil. It is that sin, above all others—1. That hath some show of reason in its attempts; for it keeps the soul from Christ by pretending its present unfitness and unpreparedness; 2. It most suiteth with the conscience, which tells the sinner that he hath nothing good; 3. It most suiteth with the wisdom of the flesh, which thinks it prudent not to be too rash and presuming upon Jesus Christ; 4. It is continually whispering in the soul's ear mistrusts of the faithfulness of God, and of the willingness of Christ to save: 5. It is always at hand to enter an objection to the promises, which by the Spirit of God are brought to the heart to comfort us.—J. Bunyan.

10—12. (10) **spake again,** so absolutely does Isaiah act as the mouthpiece of God that the prophet's further exhortation is referred to as "the Lord spake again." (11) **a sign,**[d] He offers to give proof of his authority by some sign of divine help—such as the king might choose. Comp. Judg. vi. 17, 36 ff. 1 Ki. xiii. 1 ff. Li. vii. 8 ff. etc. **depth .. height,** either on the earth, or in the heavens. (12) **tempt,** in the sense of put to the test.[e] Ahaz is afraid of being committed to a policy he does not like, and therefore, under a pretence of reverence, he declines the ordeal.[f]

Hypocrisy.—Satan, we are told, appears sometimes in the guise of an angel of light, and in this respect his children are wonderfully like him; they are marvellously ingenious in using holy principles to cover unholy purposes. But what does all this ingenuity amount to? Whom do they succeed in deceiving? Not men for any length of time. The wolf never succeeds in long completely covering itself with the sheep's clothing. The mask of the hypocrite will slip aside. And when it does so, men despise him for wearing it. Did he show himself as he is, men might, would, condemn him; but they would not despise him so much. And God—He is never deceived. He loathes the false pretenders to righteousness; and ere long He will strip them bare, and expose them to the execration of the universe.—De La Bruyere.

13, 14 (13) **house of Dav.,** represented by this their wilful king. Isa.

a "They should neither of them (Syria nor Israel) enlarge their dominions, nor push their conquests any farther. They shall be made to know their own; their bounds are fixed, and they shall not pass them."—Mat. Henry.

b 2 Ki. xvii. 1—6.

c "God's faithfulness is as the strong mountains; if ye would be strong, ye must plant your feet on His promise."—Spk. Com.

d A present visible pledge of the certainty of something invisible or future.

e De. vi. 16.

f "As if it would be a tempting of God to do that wh. God Himself invited and directed him to do."—Mat. Henry.

"Who seeks, and will not take when once 'tis offered, shall never find it more."—Shakespeare.

turns from him to the people of the covenant. **weary men,** such as the Prophet. **my God,** Isaiah seems to regard the action of Ahaz as practically a denial of Jehovah as his God? comp. "thy God" in vs. 11. (14) **virgin,** Heb. almah, i. e., "a young woman of marriageable age." Immanuel,[a] i. e. "God with us." Many commentators find in this vs. a prophecy of the Messiah. Others suppose the name Immanuel was given to a child born soon after the words of the prophet were spoken and that the fulfilment within a few years, of vs. 16 would be a sign and proof to Ahaz of the later fulfilment of the prophecy in vs. 17.

True righteousness.—It is possible to enrich dead things from the outside. Soft wood may be veneered with mahogany, nickel may be coated with silver, and silver plated with gold, but living things must be developed from the inside. Would the husbandman have a rich flush upon the rose? Let him feed the roots. Would the mother have the bloom of beauty upon the cheek of the child? Let her feed the babe with good food, and the pure blood on the inside will lend the rosy tint to the cheek on the outside. Men cannot be made wise or strong or moral by exterior laws or agencies. There are two ways to help a thriftless man. One is to build him a house and place him therein. The other is to inspire in him the sense of industry, economy, and ambition, and then he will build his own house. All tools, books, pictures, laws, on the outside, begin with ideas on the inside. Inspire the reason, and man will fill the library with books. Wake up the taste and imagination in young men, and they will fill the galleries with pictures. Stir the springs of justice, and men will go forth to cleanse iniquities and right wrongs. Quicken the inventive faculty, and men will create tools and machines. It is as useless to seek to make men good or wise by law as to adorn leafless trees by tying wax flowers to bare branches. The time was when men talked about being clothed with righteousness and character, as if God was a wholesale goods merchant, and kept great bales of integrity, and cut off a new suit for each poor sinner. But righteousness and character are not made for man on the outside. Love, joy, justice represent something done with man on the inside.—N. D. Hillis.

15, 16. (15) **Butter and honey,** "this has to be explained by vs. 22, where the eating of butter (lit. "thick milk") and (wild) honey is a symptom of the primitive simplicity to which human life is reduced by the cessation of agriculture. The meaning is that the youth of Immanuel will be spent amidst the privations of a land laid waste by foreign invaders."—Camb. Bib. **that .. know,** R. V., "when he knoweth" i. e. when he "is capable of exercising intelligent choice between the pleasant and the painful." (comp. 2 Sam xix. 35) or in two or three years. (16) **before,** etc., i. e. within three years. **forsaken,** R. V., "the land whose two kings thou abhorrest shall be forsaken," The land of the two kings, Syria and Israel, was first of all laid waste by the Assyrians, and their inhabitants carried into captivity.

Butter and honey.—D'Arvieux, visiting the camp of the Grand Emir, was treated with great consideration. The Arab prince lived in splendor, and on the first morning treated his guest with little loaves, honey, new-churned butter, and loaves of cream, more delicate than any he ever saw, together with coffee. In another passage the same writer assures us that one of the principal things with which the Arabs regale themselves at breakfast is cream, or new butter mingled with honey; a mixture, he observes, which seems odd, but which experience proves not to be bad.

17—19. (17) **Ephraim departed,**the revolt of the ten tribes under Jeroboam was the heaviest disaster that had ever befallen the house of David. **king of Assyria,**[a] but not only the two kings—Judah also shall be overwhelmed; and that by the ally whom Ahaz had chosen rather than Jehovah, namely,the king of Assyria. (18) **the fly .. and the bee,** i. e., Egyptians, whose land swarms with flies, and the Assyrians who are still famous for their bees and honey.[b] Sometimes Judah inclined to lean on Egypt. and sometimes on Assyria; both at last helped to accomplish her destruction. (19) **thorns,** prickly lotus.[c] **bushes,** R. V. pastures.

Note on vs. 18.—The allusion which this text involves, is the practice of calling out the bees from their hives, by a hissing or whistling sound, to

[a] "The Prophet renews the promise of deliverance, and connects it with the birth of a child, whose significant name is made a symbol of the Div. interposition, and his progress a measure of subsequent events."—J. A. Alexander.

"Let your light shine. A light under cover is a light beginning to go out." —Anon.

"How often we look upon God as our last and feeblest resource! We go to Him because we have nowhere else to go. And then we learn that the storms of life have driven us, not upon the rocks, but into the desired haven." — George Macdonald.

2 Ki. xv. 30, xvi. 9.

"Patience and struggle; an earnest use of what we have now, and all the time an earnest discontent until we come to what we ought to be —are not those what we need?" —PhillipsBrooks.

[a] "The kings of Babylon are reckoned among the kings of Assyria, and are designated as such, as being their successors and representatives."— Wordsworth.

[b] "Bee-keeping is an established trade in Assyria to the present day." — Spk. Com.

[c] "Palestine, fr. the combined heat and dryness of its climate, and the rockiness

of its surface, has a peculiar tendency to form thorns even in groups where we should least expect them." — Tristram.

"Man, as the minister and interpreter of nature, does and understands as much as his observations on the order of nature, either with regard to things or the mind, permit him, and neither knows nor is capable of more. . . Nature is only subdued by submission." —Bacon.

their labor in the fields, and summoning them again to return, when the heavens begin to lower, or the shadows of evening to fall. In this manner, Jehovah threatens to rouse the enemies of Judah, and lead them to the prey. However widely scattered, or far remote from the scene of action, they should hear His voice, and with as much promptitude as the bee, that has been taught to recognise the signal of its owner, and obey his call, they should assemble their forces; and although weak and insignificant as a swarm of bees in the estimation of a proud and infatuated people, they should come with irresistible might, and take possession of the rich and beautiful region which had been abandoned by its terrified inhabitants. This insect is called Zimb. It is, in size, very little larger than a bee, of a thicker proportion, and its wings, which are broader than those of a bee, placed separate, like those of a fly. As soon as this plague appears, and their buzzing is heard, all the cattle forsake their food, and run wildly about the plain till they die, worn out with fatigue, fright, and hunger. No remedy remains but to leave the black earth and hasten down to the sands of Atbara; and there they remain while the rains last, this cruel enemy never daring to pursue them farther. All the inhabitants of the sea-coast of Melinda, down to Cape Gardefan, to Saba, and the south coast of the Red Sea, are obliged to put themselves in motion and remove to the next sand, in the beginning of the rainy season, to prevent all their stock of cattle from being destroyed. This is not a partial emigration; the inhabitants of all the countries, from the mountains of Abyssinia northward to the confluence of the Nile and Astaboras, are once a year obliged to change their abode, and seek protection on the sands of Beja.

20—22. (20) **A razor,** the people of Judah will be utterly despoiled. Even the hair on head and feet will be shaved off. Nay more, worst of all indignities, the beard will go with the rest. And the razor with which this utter despoiling will be accomplished will be this King of Assyria, to whom Ahaz looks for help, instead of looking to Jehovah. **beyond the river,** the Euphrates. **head . . beard,** a strong figure for the manner in which Assyria would desolate the country and sweep away all its treasure. The Orientals consider the removal of the hair as ignominious. (21) **nourish . . sheep,** the former prosperity would be reduced to the most miserable housekeeping. One man would keep alive, with the greatest care, a milch cow and two head of sheep. But this would be quite enough, for there would be only a few men left in the land; and as all the land would be pasture the small number of animals would yield milk in abundance. Whoever escaped the Assyrian razor, would eat curds and honey, that and nothing but that, without variation."—Delitzsch. The fig. indicates that agriculture would cease, and the land become one great pasture-ground. (22) **abundance,** through having such a wide range for feeding in.[a],

[a] "Instead of living on the fruits of the soil, they shall subsist upon spontaneous products, such as milk and honey, wh. shall be abundant only because the people will be few, and the uncultivated grounds extensive." — J. A. Alexander.

"Verse 25 continues and completes the description of the general desolation, as manifested first by the people's living upon milk and honey, then by the growth of thorns and briers in the choicest vineyards and the terraced hills, and by the conversion of these carefully-tilled spots into dangerous solitudes, hunting grounds, and pastures." — J. A. Alexander.

Shaving.—To tell a man that you will shave him is as much as to say you will ruin him—entirely overthrow him. "Our king has shaved all his enemies," means, he has punished them; reduced them to the most abject condition, so that they have not a single vestige of power in their possession. "What, fellow! didst thou say thou wouldst shave me?" "I will give thy bones to the crows and the jackals. Begone, hald-head, get out of my way."—Roberts.

23—25. (23) **silverlings,** i. e. "silver shekels." (24) **With arrows,** etc., i. e. seeking wild animals in these once cultured gardens. (25) **And on all hills,** etc. R. V. "And all the hills that were digged with the mattock, thou shalt not come thither for fear of briers and thorns, but it shall be for the sending forth of oxen and for the treading of sheep." That is, the places that once were cultivated gardens shall become thorny pastures. "The hills of Judæa were anciently cultivated to the very top:" they were to become mere ranges for the cattle.

Verse 25.—These words embody the opinion that the slopes and brows of the hills, which had, by the industry of man, been reduced to a state of cultivation, should again relapse into their natural wildness, the thorns and briers should be allowed to resume their ancient empire, the beasts of the chase should again lodge in the thickets, and the sheep and the ox feed in the grassy labyrinths between them, as in times of old.

CHAPTER THE EIGHTH.

This chapter furnishes a series of detached oracles and may be analyzed as follows—1—4; 5—8; 9—10; 11—15; 16—18; 19—22. **1, 2.** (1) **roll** R. V. "tablet,"[a] "The prophet is to take a tablet, large enough for him to engrave upon it in lasting characters the prophecy which he was to deliver."—Lowth. **man's pen,**[b] "i. e." with large characters easily read by the common and unlearned classes." **Maher-shalal-hash-baz,** these words to be the writing on the tablet, and they mean,[c] "Swift spoil, speedy prey," implying the certainty of the fall of Damascus and Samaria.—Driver. This writing kept the Divine message before the people until the child was born and named. (2) **witnesses,** who should see this tablet put up, understand its meaning, and afterward, when the event had occurred, should tell the people of the warning and its fulfilment.

[a] The laws of Solon were inscribed on tablets of wood.

"Among the ancients stone, brass, lead, wood, and the like, were employed when the design was to promulgate public decrees, or record memorable events for posterity."—Henderson.

[b] Heb. enosh, wh. means a common man as contrasted with the upper ranks.

[c] "The spoil (i.e. the spoiler) hastens, the rapine speeds forward."—Maurer. "They (the Assyrians) hasten to the spoil (i.e. to spoil Syria and Samaria), they speed to the prey." — Gesenius.

Christianity and the future.—Sometimes the Lord's judgments are "abroad" in the earth, and sometimes they work with subtlety that cannot be valued by human criticism. What does Maher-shalal-hash-baz mean? Speed-plunder, haste-spoil: the man shall arise who will do God's judgments, and do them with earnestness, alacrity, precision, completeness. How the prophet lives in the future! There is always a Child to be born who will advance the kingdom of God. Do not believe that the ages have seen their greatest birth. Even Jesus Christ when he went away said: If I go away, I will send a Comforter, even the Paraclete, who shall abide with you for ever. The greatest births will be found by-and-by to be spiritual births—new conceptions of God; new in the sense of being larger, juster, more pregnant with joy and promise. Christianity has to deal with the future. The Lord Jesus Christ made but few references to the past, but he did make some, and they were distinct and solid; but his eyes were set towards the coming Sun, the coming Kingdom, his own return, not as a man that could be seen, but as an inspiration and a sovereignty felt in every mind and heart, and owned by all who should come under its gracious and redeeming and sanctifying touch.—Peop. Bib.

Writing materials.—Amongst the materials upon which the ancient Scriptures were written, were skins—tanned, or dyed red or yellow. These were not bound by the edge, but so fastened together as to form one continuous roll: hence the word volume, from Lat. volumen—a roll.[a] Some were written on prepared skins called parchments, so called from Pergamos, the place where parchment was first made. "Sometimes tables of wood[b] or stone, called caudices, or codices, were employed: hence the term codex (Lat.—tablet) came to be applied to a manuscript on any material;" and hence also a system of laws was called a code, because the use of such tables was once frequent for legal purposes, where durability was important. "These tables were written on in their natural state (or, when used for temporary purposes, covered with wax) with an iron needle (Job xix. 24) called a stylus:" hence we have the term style, now applied to the character of the composition.

[a] Jer. xxxvi. 2; Zech. v. 1.

[b] Exod. xxxii. 15; Deut. vi. 9; Isa. xxx. 8; Hab. ii. 2; Luke i 63; 2 Cor. iii. 3.

"The body sins not; 'tis the will That makes the action good or ill."—Herrick.

3, 4. (3)**prophetess,** only called such as being Isaiah's wife. **A son** This is the second son. (comp. vii. 3.) (4) **to cry, my father,** i. e. before he should be able to talk; within some two years.[c] **spoil . . Assyria,** "an allusion to the ancient custom of carrying in triumph before the victor the spoils taken from the enemy."

[c] "Pekah was assassinated in the fourth year of Ahaz, and Tiglath-Pileser's invasion of Damascus belongs prob. to the early part of the fourth of Ahaz." — Spk. Com.

2 Ki. xvi. 9, xvii. 5, 6.

A great Name.—What a thought it is, that One Name should cover all names; that One Name should signify more than all names! As all things which are named came from one God, there must be a far greater fulness of meaning in His sigle name than in all the names put together of all the creatures and things in heaven and earth. The earth, and all that is in it; the firmament, with all the stars; the heavens, with all the angels,—are contained in God; but they do not contain God. Nothing is easier than to say the word "universe;" and yet it would take us millions and millions of years to bestow one hasty glance upon the surface of that small portion of it which lies within the range of our glasses.

"One day is the same as another.

But what are all suns, comets, earths, moons, atmospheres, seas, rivers, mountains, valleys, plains, woods, cattle, with beasts, fish, fowl, grasses, plants, shrubs, trees, minerals, and metals, compared with the meaning of the one name God! We are learning here under these heavens, from the heavens and from the earth, what that Name is, from whom all things, named and unnamed, came. After death,—our emancipated souls, our new eyes, our new friends, and the new scenery, helping us,—we shall commence anew the study of that Name. And to all eternity, all that we shall ever see and hear will only help us to a more humbling, worshipful appreciation of the incomprehensibility of that Name.—Pulsford.

Prayer, worldly business, calls to be devout, charitable, and faithful,—these are the duties that each hour brings in its turn; and if I am faithful in their fulfilment, God will be always ready to help me, and then what signifies a little ennui, pain, or misfortune?" —Gold Dust.

5—8. (5) **spake.** (6) **waters of Shiloah,**[d] flowing past Zion and Moriah, were a familiar type of the temple and its Lord. comp. Jer. xvii. 13. "They have rejected the fountains of living waters, even Jehovah." **go softly,** quietly, making no noise in their beneficent flowing. **rejoice .. son,** this evidently refers to a party in Jerusalem that traitorously favored the Syrian schemes, and the pretensions of the "Son of Tabeal." (7) **the river,** the Euphrates, symbol of the Assyrian power.[e] "From the Euphrates shall mighty floods of water overflow first Ephraim and then Judah. (8) **pass through,** R. V., "sweep onward into," in contrast with the quiet waters of Shiloah is this torrent of the Euphrates which shall completely submerge Israel, and Judah shall hardly keep head above water. Comp. xxx. 28. **the neck,** not going right over the head. Jerusalem was not at first to be destroyed. **wings,** by a hasty change of figure the Assyrian is represented as a huge bird of prey hovering over its victim. **of the land, O Immanuel,** this may with equal exactness be translated, "of the land. For with us is God." Cam. B.

d "The fountain of Siloam, in its name, and in its mysterious subterranean derivations and flowings forth, was a remarkable figure of Christ, the Incarnate Word, the fountain of living waters."—Wordsworth.

"The only perennial fountian of Jerus. here used as a symbol of the Divine protection."—J. A. Alexander.

e "The Euphrates overflows its banks in spring and summer, after the snows of Armenia begin to melt. The armies of Assyria should now in like manner overflow their usual boundaries."—Spk. Com.

2 Ki. xviii. 9—16.

Mercy and judgment (vss. 6—8).—We deduce the following truths. I. That the mercies of our present life flow softly, as by a gentle stream. They flow—1. Vivifyingly; 2. Constantly; 3. Softly. II. That the abuse of the stream of mercies is an immense crime. Here is—1. Rejection; 2. Presumption. III. That this crime will bring on the tumultuous river of retribution. 1. The abuse of mercy leads to retributive misery; 2. The streams of retributive misery stand in awful contrast with those of mercy.—Thomas.

The village of Siloam.—The valley is the southern entrance to the valley of Jehoshaphat, and derives its name from having the village and fountain on its opposite sides, and from its receiving the waters of the latter. The village is situated at the base of the Mount of Olives, and consists of about sixty poor dwellings, scarcely distinguishable from the surrounding tombs. "So rich and full of interest," says a traveler, "is the walk round Mount Zion, down to the brook of Kidron, the village of Siloam, to the garden of Gethsemane, and from thence up the Mount of Olives, that we cannot look upon it without delight and heartfelt admiration." The gentle waters of Shiloah, a small fountain and brook just without Jerusalem, which supplied a pool within the city for the use of the inhabitants, are an apt emblem of the state of the kingdom and house of David, much reduced in its apparent strength, yet supported by the blessing of God; and are finely contrasted with the waters of the Euphrates, great, rapid, and impetuous; the image of the Babylonian empire, which God threatens to bring down like a mighty flood upon all these apostates of both kingdoms, as a punishment for their manifold iniquities.—Burder.

"God's help, though it may seem inconsiderable as Shiloah's stream, is yet, like that stream, constant. Our reliance upon it will never issue in disappointment." — Hom. Com.

"Our opportunities to do good are our talents." —C. Mather.

9, 10. (9) **Associate yourselves,** R. V., "make an uproar," he flings out a challenge to the nations:—raise the war-cry, do your worst. **broken,** etc., your schemes miserably failing. **gird yourselves,** i. e. arm and equip yourselves. (10) **take counsel, etc.,** i. e. make what plans you may, none can avail; utter threats or declare your resolutions it matters not, for with us is God.[a]

a "The world power must shiver on the rock Israel, for it is thereby the strong rock in that God is with it." — Nagelsbach.

The slave-mother crossing the Ohio.—We remember, says a writer in The True American, the story of a cruel master, who, without cause, had determined to separate a slave mother and her only child. She had been faithful under the very worst usage, and she determined to remain so, until he told her that on the morrow her child must be borne to New Orleans to be sold there in the slave mart. It was mid-winter. The earth was frosted with a hard crust, yet at midnight she started for the

Ohio, determined, if she could, to live and die with her child. She reached its banks as the pursuers rose on the hill behind; no boat was near—masses of broken ice were sluggishly drifting along—what was she to do? Trusting to heaven, she put her feet on the treacherous element, and with it bending and breaking beneath her (spectators on either side expecting to see her and her child sink at every moment), she boldly pushed on from cake to cake, until she landed safely on the Ohio shore. Five minutes sooner and she must have perished—two minutes later and she would have met with a watery grave, for before she had proceeded twenty steps, the ice behind her, close on the Kentucky side, had broken and was scattered ere she reached the mid-river. "Thank God you and your child are safe," exclaimed the hard-hearted master, as he saw her land, rejoiced that he had escaped the responsibility of their death. "Brave woman," said a Kentuckian who had witnessed her escape and met her at the landing, "you have won your freedom and shall have it." The mother and the child were kept together, and liberty and love is now their lot in their humble but happy home. Was there not true heroism here, and is not the scene worthy the sweetest song of poetry, or the holiest praise of man?

Let all the ends thou aim'st at be thy country's,
Thy God's, and truth's.
—Shakespeare.

"Ask God to give thee skill
In comfort's art,
That thou may'st consecrated be
And set apart
Unto a life of sympathy.
For heavy is the weight of ill
In every heart;
And comforters are needed much
Of Christ-like touch."

11, 12. (11) strong hand,[a] this was not an ordinary communication, but he was completely grasped, as it were, by God, who impressed upon his consciousness the following line of conduct and speech. **not .. people,** i. e. not be carried away by the spirit of the hour. (12) **confederacy,** R. V., "conspiracy." **to all them,** etc., R. V., "concerning all whereof this people;" the conspiracy is the Syro-Ephraimitish alliance which Isaiah is warned not to treat as a serious danger.[b]

a Eze. i. 3, iii. 22, xxxiii. 22, xxxvii. 1; comp. Eze. iii. 14.

b "Do not join with those that, for the securing of themselves, are for making a league with the Assyrians, thro' unbelief and distrust of God and their cause." — Mat. Henry.

Je. i. 17—19.

The panic.—There was a general panic among the people: "their heart was moved as the trees of the wood are moved by the wind," when they heard that Syria was confederate with Ephraim; their cry was everywhere, "A confederacy has been made against us, and we must meet it by a counter-alliance with Assyria;" and the prophet says that he too should have fallen under the influence of this panic, if Jehovah had not laid hold of him with a strong hand, to keep him in the way of dependence on Himself, and if He had not taught him to escape the fear which possessed his fellow-countrymen, by making the Lord of hosts his fear and his dread, by sanctifying Him himself, as he now in His Name calls on them to do. To sanctify Jehovah is in mind and practice to recognize Him as the holy God, the Lord who is absolute, free from the limitations which hinder all other beings from carrying their wills into full operation, and to believe with the whole heart that God does and can govern all things according to the counsel of His own will. To the nation which thus sanctifies Jehovah, He (says Isaiah) will be their sanctuary—their protection against all their enemies. Such was His original covenant with both the houses of Israel, and it still holds good. If, therefore, they will break and renounce it, it becomes a stumbling-block to them. When their statesmen endeavor to remedy present mischief and secure future prosperity, by craftily playing off against one another the nations whom they cannot hope to match by force, they are attempting to go counter to the whole plan of Jehovah's government, and they will do it only to their own confusion.—Strachey. Comfort in tribulation.—There is an island in a distant sea, from whose shores the fishermen sail in tiny crafts to procure the treasures of the deep. During their absence thick mists often descend and cover highland, cliff, and beacon with so thick a veil, that these hardy mariners are left without a mark by which to steer their laden barques. But in these dull hours they are not left to wander, unguided, on the pathless sea. When the time for their return arrives, the women of the islet—mothers, wives, sisters and daughters—descend to the shores and raise the voice of song. Borne on the quiet air, their voices soon fall sweetly on the ears of the loved ones on the sea. Guided by the well-known sounds, they steer their boats in safety to the shore. And thus to thee, O Christian, comes the voice of love from the celestial shore, as thou wanderest, a bewildered child of tribulation, on the misty sea of life. Hearken! "Be of good cheer!" is the cry that greets thee. It comes from Jesus, who has overcome this world, which is the scene and source of your trials. His

"That song is sweetest, bravest, best,
Which plucks the thistle-barb of care
From a despondent brother's breast,
And plants a sprig of heart's-ease there."
—Andrew Downing.

"There is but one road to lead us to God—humility; all other ways would only lead astray, even were they fenced in with all virtues." — L'Abbe Boileau.

"A beam of comfort, like the moon through clouds, gilds the black horror, and directs my way."
—Dryden.

"Every step toward Christ kills a doubt. Every thought, word,

conquest of your adversary is the pledge of your victory. Therefore, "be of good cheer!"

13—15. (13) **Sanctify,**[e] but, on the other hand, put all your confidence in Jehovah Sabaoth, the Lord of all the hosts of heaven and earth. **him .. fear,** i. e. fear to resist Him. Dread lest He be against you. (14) **sanctuary,** or defence in the evil time. **stone, etc.,** "two figures are used to set forth the threatening side of Jehovah's relation to both the houses of Israel: the stone against which one heedlessly stumbles to one's own destruction; and the snare in which a wild animal is caught unawares. Jehovah is a secret and sudden danger to those who walk in blind unbelief. Cf. Ps. xviii. 26." Camb. Bib. (15) **many,** not all, the remnant shall be spared. **stumble,** etc., figures taken from the means used in catching wild animals.

A Double-edged Fact.—God is the one great fact of life, but what a double-edged fact—a sanctuary to all who put their trust in Him, but a rock of offence to both houses of Israel! The figure is very picturesque. An altar, a common stone on steps, one of those which covered the land in large numbers—it is easy to see what a double purpose that might serve. What a joy the sight would be to the weary wanderer or refugee who sought it, what a comfort as he leant his weariness upon it, and knew he was safe! But those who were flying over the land, not seeking Jehovah, not knowing indeed what they sought, blind and panic-stricken—for them what could that altar do but trip them up like any other common rock in their way? "In fact, Divine justice is something which is either observed, desired, or attained, and is then man's weal, or, on the other hand, is overlooked, rejected, or sought after in a wild, unintelligent spirit, and only in the hour of need, and is then their lasting ruin."—Exp. Bib. Stone of Stumbling.—The idea appears to be taken from a stone, or a block of wood, being thrown in the path of travelers, over which they fall. "Well, friend, did the king grant you your request?" "No, no; there was a Udaru-katti, a stumbling-block in the way." "Just as Valen was attaining the object of his wishes, that old stumbling-block, the Modeliar, lay down in the way, and the poor fellow stumbled, and fell." "Why are you so dejected this morning?" "Because I have had a severe fall over that stumbling-block, my profligate son."—Roberts.

16—18. "The prophet, recognizing the failure of his work as regards the nation, prepares a written record of his teaching, and deposits this as a sealed document in the custody of his disciples. By this solemn act he forms an inner circle of religious fellowship, which is the nucleus of the new people of God." Camb. Bib. (16) **Bind,** etc., may be translated "I will bind" and "I will seal;" an indication that this particular message was complete; also that some time would elapse before the fulfilment. (17) **wait upon,** R. V., "wait for," God's time for fulfilment. **hideth his face,** the time of judgment has come. Comp. Ps. xiii. 1; Job xiii. 24; Deut. xxxi. 7, etc. **look for him,** i. e. watch for signs of His working and of His coming. (18) **children,** Isaiah and his children were for figures and emblems of redemption; Isaiah—salvation of Jehovah: Shear-Jashub—a remnant shall return: Maher-shalal-hash-baz—swift spoil, speedy prey. "Living omens of a happier future."—Driver.

Verse 16.—I agree with Vitringa, Drechsler, and others in regarding verse 16 as the prophet's own prayer to Jehovah. We "bind"—tie together—what we wish to keep from getting separated and lost; we "seal" what is to be kept secret, and only opened by a person duly qualified. And so the prophet here prayed that Jehovah would take his testimony with regard to the future, and his intimation, which was designed to prepare for the future that testimony and thorah which the great mass, in their hardness did not understand, and in their self-hardening despised, and lay them up well secured and well preserved, as if by bond and seal, in the hearts of those who received the prophet's words with loving obedience. For it would be all over with Israel unless a community of believers should be preserved, and all over with the community if the word of God, which was the ground of their life, should be allowed to slip out of their hearts.—Delitzsch.

and deed for Him carries you away from dis couragement."—Cuyler.

e "To sanctify God means here to cherish and evince a due sense of His character, as worthy of entire confidence, being able to defeat all the enemies of His people, and faithful to fulfil His promises of protection and deliverance." —Henderson.

"How little have we accepted and made use the legacy of peace and joy which Christ left to us! Instead of faces telling the world what a full salvation we have, how often a long face has suggested that men had better take their fill of happiness first before they leave it behind by becoming Christians!"—J. Hudson Taylor.

"In proportion as one has a true fear of God, he will feel no fear of man. It was a saying of Col. Gardiner, 'I fear God, therefore there is none else that I need fear.'"

"Blessings may appear under the shape of pain, losses, and disappointments, but let him have patience, and he will see them in their proper figure." —Addison.

"The true reward of the prophet, the only one that really enriches him, is the growing power of seeing more deeply into the deep things of God, and the growing power of revealing these more and more clearly to men. The true reward of the righteous man is his becoming more righteous

Religious confidence—

Not seldom, clad in radiant rest
  Deceitfully goes forth the morn;
Not seldom, evening in the west
  Sinks smilingly forsworn.

The smoothest seas will sometimes prove
  To the confiding barque untrue;
And if she trust the stars above,
  They can be treacherous too.

The umbrageous oak, in pomp outspread,
  Full oft when storms the welkin rend,
Draws lightning down upon the head
  It promised to defend.

But Thou art true, incarnate Lord!
  Who did vouchsafe for man to die;
Thy smile is sure, Thy plighted word
  No change can falsify.

I bent before Thy gracious throne,
  And asked for peace with suppliant knee;
And peace was given,—nor peace alone,
  But faith, and hope, and escstasy.

—Wordsworth.

still, his finding the virtuous principles within him growing stronger, the vicious in their presence becoming weaker, his finding the path of duty before him growing clearer and clearer, and himself more able to walk in it without stumbling."—Hom. Com.

19, 20. The prophet, having now discontinued and "sealed up" his public "testimony," appears to address himself in what follows to his own immediate followers. The passage presents, in vivid contrast, two pictures; one of the darkness and despair that are settling down on the incorrigible nation, the other of the light and joy that are to break upon it with the advent of the Messianic salvation. (19) **Seek unto,** asking guidance from. **them that have,** etc., that is "consult a medium." Comp. Lev. xx. 27, etc.; 1 Sam. xxviii. 8. **familiar spirits,** Le. xix. 31. **wizards,** Le. xix. 31. **peep,** or chirp. **mutter,** speak in a low, hollow manner, as if their voices came from the ground. **living .. dead,** R. V., "on behalf of the living should they seek unto the dead?" This is the reply that the faithful ones must give to the spirit-seekers. "What madness to consult the dead in the interests of the living." (20) **law,** etc.,[a] the will of God, as authoritatively revealed in His Word, and by His Prophets. **it is because .. their,** R. V., "surely there is no morning for them." There is no light, no morning-dawn, for those who seek light from these other sources, or no morning-dawn for them.

The Duty of Prayer (vs. 19).—I. The proof that prayer is a duty. 1. From the relations in which we stand to God; 2. From the express commands of God; 3. From the practice of the saints in all ages; 4. From the example of Christ. II. The objections to the validity of this proof. 1. From the greatness of God; 2. From the knowledge of God; 3. From the goodness of God; 4. From the unchangeableness of God.—G. Brooks.

The Holy Scriptures are to be read with an high and reverent esteem of them; with a firm persuasion that they are the very Word of God, and that He only can enable us to understand them; with desire to know, believe, and obey the will of God revealed in them; with diligence and attention to the matter and scope of them; with meditation, application, self-denial, and prayer.—The Larger Catechism.

To the Law and to the Testimony.—When men look up into heaven and there is no light, and round them upon the earth and there is no dawn, when they wait for the coming of the sun in heaven, and when through all the darkness they can see no shining of the stars, then Isaiah would seem to say they will turn to the word and to the testimony, that is, to the true revelation of God. No man need be in any difficulty as to duty, as to the course of right, as to the discharge of all his highest responsibilities; the Bible, whatever else may be said about it or even

[a] Ps. xix. 7, 8, cxix. 129, 130; 2 Pe. i. 19—21.

"It is by doing our duty that we learn to do it. For God accompanies it with the influences of his blessed Spirit, and each performance opens our minds for larges influxes of His grace, and places them in communion with him." — E. B. Pusey.

"The more we work, the more we need to pray. In this day of activity there is great danger, not of doing too much, but of praying too little for so much work." — Alexander McLaren.

"Holy Scripture containeth all things necessary to salvation: so that whatsoever is not read therein, nor may be proved thereby, is not to be required of any man, that it should be believed as an article of the faith, or be thought requisite or necessary to salvation."

in disparagement of it, utters no uncertain sound as to the culture of the soul and the obedience of the whole life to the divine sovereignty. If men say they are willing to receive light if they could only get it, they are deceiving themselves so long as the Bible lies unopened, unread, or unappreciated. Everything needful for the salvation of the soul, the culture of the spirit, and the most blessed destiny of the life, is revealed in the volume which we hold to be inspired. We are to test all prophets by this book. We are not to be deceived by the glamor of their poetry, or by the passion of their rhetoric; we are to test everything by the law and by the testimony. Thus the soul is pointed in the direction of sureness and is led into the sanctuary of rational as well as pious contentment.—Peop. Bib.

21, 22. (21) **through it,** obviously, the land; but something must have fallen out before this verse, to account for the reference of the pronoun. The subject is either the whole nation or an individual Israelite. He wanders through the land, perhaps seeking an oracle (Am. viii. 12). Cam. B.; perhaps seeking pasture for cattle. Pul. Com. **and curse,** etc., R. V., "and curse by their king and by their God." **look upward,** as speaking defiance against the God who will not let him have his own wilful way.[a] (22) **unto the earth,** or around them, and there they shall see nothing to give them hope. **dimness,** etc., R. V., "the gloom of anguish." **driven to darkness,** or, "in thick darkness is he driven away, i. e. cast out of the land which he has despised and profaned." Spk. Com. "Driven onward, as by a sweeping storm."

[a] "Detailed description of the despair wh. they shall fall into who seek necromancy instead of God." —Fausset.

"Hard, honest, practical work is a panacea for many ills. Under a fresco of the 13th century, discovered at Cortona, in Italy, is inscribed the motto, 'Sum misero nisi teneam bigonem;' —I am miserable unless I hold a spade." —The Scottish Pulpit.

"The Prophet here describes in strong language the desperate condition of those who reject the Divine Word, and adhere to their own devices, or to the sinful inventions and practices of men." —Henderson.

Mi. iii. 6.

"The eternal ground of thanksgiving is to be found in the righteousness of God, in the consciousness that under all human life there is a foundation which no man can disturb, and that life is so organized that no man can be happy, restful, or prosperous in doing evil; that at every turn he is smitten with

Finding Fault with God.—General Burn, in describing the effects of a violent storm that assailed the vessel in which he was returning to England, off the coast of Whitehaven, says, "As beings imagining they had but a few moments to live, all strove with dying eagerness to reach the quarter-deck, but we had scarcely raised ourselves upright when the ship struck a second time, more violently than before, and again threw us all prostrate. The scene was enough to make the heart of the stoutest sinner tremble. I very well remember the agony of one of my poor messmates. This man had acquired considerable property in Jamaica, and during the voyage, like the rich man in the parable, was frequently devising plans of future happiness. At this awful moment, he exclaimed bitterly against the treatment of Heaven, that had made him spend so many toilsome years in a scorching and unhealthy climate to procure a little wealth; and when with pain and trouble he had heaped it together, had tantalized him with a sight of the happy shore where he expected peaceably to enjoy it; but now with one cruel, sudden stroke, had defeated all his hopes. The cutting reflections and bitter complaints that came from this man's mouth, expressed such black despair that he appeared more like a fiend of the bottomless pit than a sinner yet in the land of hope."—Whitecross. Hunger an Impulse to Labor.—Hunger is one of the beneficent and terrible instincts. It is, indeed, the very fire of life, underlying all impulses to labor, and moving man to noble activities by its imperious demands. Look where we may, we see it as the motive power which sets the vast array of human machinery in action. It is hunger which brings these stalwart navvies together in orderly gangs to cut paths through mountains, to throw bridges across rivers, to intersect the land with the great iron-ways which bring city into daily communication with city. Hunger is the overseer of those men erecting palaces, prison-houses, barracks, and villas. Hunger sits at the loom, which, with stealthy power, is weaving the wondrous fabrics of cotton and silk. Hunger labors at the furnace and the plough, coercing the native indolence of man into strenuous and incessant activity. Let food be abundant and easy of access, and civilization becomes impossible; for our higher efforts are dependent on our lower impulses in an indissoluble manner. Nothing but the necessities of food will force man to labor which he hates and will always avoid when possible. And although this seems obvious only when applied to the laboring classes, it is equally though less obviously true when applied to all other classes, for the money we all labor to gain is nothing but food, and the surplus of food, which will buy other men's labor. If in this sense hunger is seen to be a beneficent instinct, in another sense it is terrible; for when its progress is unchecked it becomes a devouring flame, destroying all that is noble in man, subjugating his humanity, and making the brute dominant in him, till finally life itself is extinguished.—Smiles.

penalties, and that real happiness and satisfaction are bound eternally to right thinking and right acting."—From The Outlook.

CHAPTER THE NINTH.

1, 2. (1) **Nevertheless,** etc., R. V., "But there shall be no gloom to her that was in anguish. In the former time he brought into contempt the land of Zebulun and the land of Naphthali, but in the latter time hath he made it glorious, by the way of the sea, beyond Jordan, Galilee of the nations." **Zebulun,** etc.,[b] these districts had borne the brunt of the invasions from the north and east; so they were to be the first favored with the new light. **way of the sea,** i. e. the tract about the sea of Galilee. **of the nations,** or Gentiles, so called bec. the people were of a mixed race, and the land bordered on Gentile territories. The people of this district were greatly despised by the strict Jews. (2) **have seen,** the perfects throughout are those of prophetic certainty. The writer is transported into the future. **great light,** Is. lx. 1—3; Lu. i. 78, 79, ii. 32; Jno. 4, 5, 9. **shadow of death,** denoting the densest gloom, the most awful darkness. "The darkness of ignorance and the darkness of distress." We reach in these verses the climax of the series of prophecies that began with vii. 1.

[b] Zebulun stretched across from the Mediterranean Sea at Mount Carmel to the Sea of Tiberias; Naphthali fr. the northern boundary of Zebulun, between that sea and Lebanon.

Mat. iv. 13, 15, 16.

Night and Morning (vs. 2).—I. Our state by nature is set forth by the idea of night, which is a word that suggests—1. Sleep; 2. Peace; 3. Darkness; 4. Sin; 5. Helplessness., II. Christ's advent to the soul typified by the sunrise. 1. There was light; 2. Life; 3. Warmth; 4. Growth; 5. A sense of security and confidence. Apply:—(1) Has this great light risen on your soul? (2) Or is it still night?—Stems and Twigs.

Jews and Tiberias.—A residence at Tiberias is highly valued by the Jews, because of the ancient renown of the place in connection with Jewish literature, and because they expect that the Messiah will make His appearance in the parts of Galilee bordering on the Lake of Tiberias—a remarkable fact when it is borne in mind that the true Messiah was rejected by them on this ground among others, that He did, as it seemed to them, come from this part of the land. It is understood that they found this expectation upon Isa. ix. 1, 2; not knowing—but may they soon know—that this very passage has found an application in the Gospel to the very neighborhood in which they dwell: for Matthew, after reciting that Jesus left Nazareth and "came and dwelt in Capernaum, which is upon the sea-coast, in the borders of Zabulon and Nephthalim," adds, "That it might be fulfilled which was spoken by Esaias the prophet, saying, The land of Zabulon, and the land of Nephthalim, by the way of the sea, beyond Jordan, Galilee of the Gentiles; the people which sat in darkness saw great light; and to them which sat in the region and shadow of death light is sprung up," Matt. iv. 12—16.—Kitto.

"The change for the better, which was promised at the close of the 8th chap., is described in the 9th as consisting in the rise of the Great Light upon the darkness.... the advent of a Divine successor to David, who should establish, restore, and enlarge his kingdom without any limitations."—J. A. Alexander.

"Blessed is he that is invited to the supper of the Lamb, who here below receives the sacrament of his love, and waits in patience until he be called to sit down to the banquet in heaven." —Thomas a Kempis.

3. **and not increased,** R. V., "thou hast increased." This verse is most naturally regarded as picturing the joy of the people in the dawning light of Messiah. **joy in harvest,**[a] the joy of realizing at last what had been long waited for. **divide the spoil,** gaining thus unexpected or surprising possessions.

Earthly Joy (vs. 3).—Four kinds are noted in Scripture as most excellent and enjoyable. I. Nuptial joy; 2. The joy of children; 3. The joy of conquest; 4. The joy of harvest.—J. Flavel.

Harvest.—They had scarcely any foreign trade—none till Solomon's time. Every family lived upon its own inheritance and upon the produce of its own land. Consequently, if harvest failed, all failed. They expressed their joy by solemn offerings to the Lord. Not a field was reaped before the wave-sheaf was placed upon the altar; and when it had been waved there, amidst the loud thanksgiving of the people, before the Lord of the whole land, the messengers from the Temple carried the proclamation to the husbandmen in the field, "Put ye in the sickle and reap."—Thodey.

4, 5. (4) **broken, etc., the yoke with wh. Israel was burdened. staff,**

a Ps. iv. 7; Is. xxv. 9; comp. Ps. cxxvi. 5, 6.

"The condition of successful work with sinners is, first of all, that we ourselves have the joy of this salvation." —B. P. Raymond.

Comp s. x. 26.

"For every boot of tramping warrior, and the garment rolled in blood, shall even be for burning, for fuel of fire." —Kimchi.

"None can love freedom heartily but good men; the rest love not freedom, but license, wh. never hath more scope or more indulgence than under tyrants. Hence it is that tyrants are not oft offended by, nor stand much in doubt of, bad men, as being all naturally servile; but in whom virtue and true worth most is eminent, them they fear in earnest, as by right their masters; against them lies all their hatred and corruption." —Milton.

a Comp. Is. xxii. 22; Re. iii. 7.

b "This hope of a Prince of Peace, who should quell the great enemy of man, was shadowed forth in mystical history by the priestly king of Salem; projected into prophecy under the title of 'Shiloh' (the tranquil one); realized humanly, in faint outlines, in the person of Solomon (Shelomoh, the peaceful one); then again limn-

or wooden part of the yoke that presses on the shoulder. **oppressor,** or "task-master." The language reminds of Egyptian bondage. But not the whole nation is to be redeemed only a remnant, "so it is compared to the **day of Midian,** when Gideon broke the seven years dominion of Midian" forever (Ju. vii. 22.[a]) in this very district of the country. (5) **For every battle,** etc., R. V., "For all the armor of the armed men in the tumult, and the garments rolled in blood, shall even be for burning, for fuel of fire," i. e. after the great victory of Jehovah every reminder of war shall be burned up as the kingdom of endless peace will have dawned. Comp. Ezek. xxxix. 9 ff.

Freedom—

Ye clouds! that far above me float and pause,
  Whose pathless march no mortal can control!
  Ye ocean waves! that whersoe'er ye roll,
Yield homage only to eternal laws!
Ye woods! that listen to the night-birds' singing,
  Midway the smooth and perilous slope reclined,
Save when your own imperious branches swinging
  Have made a solemn music of the wind!
Where, like a man beloved of God,
Through glooms which never woodman trod,
  How oft, pursuing fancies holy,
My moonlight way o'er flowering weed I wound,
  Inspired beyond the guess of folly,
By each rude shape and wild unconquering sound!
O ye loud waves! and O ye forests high!
  And O ye clouds that far above me soar'd!
Thou rising sun! thou blue rejoicing sky!
  Yea, everything that is and will be free!
  Bear witness for me, wheresoe'er ye be,
  With what deep worship I have still adored
  The spirit of divinest liberty! —Coleridge.

6. "The last and greatest cause of joy is the birth of the Messiah and his wonderful character and government. When Isaiah expected the event to take place, cannot be gathered from this prophecy. There is no reason for supposing that the reference is to a child already born; the perfect tense is used, as throughout the passage, from the ideal standpoint of the writer, which is within the Messianic age. The birth of the child is most naturally conceived as taking place in the age of miracle which succeeds the overthrow of the Assyrian; hence no part is assigned to him in effecting the national emancipation." Camb. Bib. **For,** intimates the ground on wh. such expectations rest. **unto us,** Israel and all mankind. **government .. shoulder,** "the ensign of office used to be worn on the shoulder, in token of sustaining the government."[a] **Wonderful Counsellor,** these two words should go together, "one who counsels wonderful things." **mighty God,** this coming ruler has not only supernatural wisdom but strength in like measure, so that what he plans he can execute. **everlasting Father,** His reign will be fatherly in its nature and eternal in duration. **Prince of Peace,**[b] reigning over a kingdom of established peace. Comp. Mic. v. 5; Zech. ix. 10.

The Incarnation of Christ (vs. 6).—I. The event here celebrated may be interpreted historically. II. It may be interpreted experimentally. III. The glorious character by which this gift is distinguished. 1. Its greatness; 2. Purpose; 3. Appropriateness; 4. Manner; 5. Obligations which it imposes. IV. Sentiments appropriate to the subject. 1. Personal interest; 2. Lively joy; 3. Boundless gratitude.

Deliverance.—The writer found himself, in the fortunes of war, a prisoner in the Libby, at Richmond. One evening, as the prisoners lay down to sleep, the story was whispered among them that a flag-of-truce boat had come up the river, and that some one of their number was to be released the next day. That was glad tidings for all. But the question in every prisoner's mind was, "Am I to be released?" There were many dreams of home that night on that prison floor. In the early morning, after roll-call, there was breathless expectancy for the name of the favored prisoner. It was the name of Chaplain Trumbull. Those glad tidings had a meaning for him they could not have had for any of his companions. To him there came that day the message of deliverance from bondage, and he passed out from the prison-house thanking God that the message was to him. "Unto you" is a Saviour born. Whoever you are whatever are your sins, there is salvation for you.—H. C. Trumbull. Eternal Life.—It seems to me to glorify life, it seems to me to banish the shadow of gloom from death, to feel that that majestic figure—of Brother, Teacher, Friend, Redeemer—which towers supremely over the centuries, which made the earth sublime by its advent, which seemed in ascending to unite it to the heavens, has equal place in worlds to come! that we may trust his imperative word; that we may serve His Kingly cause; that we may see the illumined Universe, for us as for Him, a house of Victory and of Peace! that we may stand, by and by, with Him, amid the light as yet unreached, and say, each one, "I believed in Thy religion; I saw its triumphs in the earth; I felt its power in my heart; I rose to God in love upon it; I foreknew by it, what now I find—Eternal Life." Mighty to Save.—Come, ye miserable sinners, laden with the insupportable burden of your sins; come, ye troubled consciences, uneasy at the remembrance of your many idle words, many criminal thoughts, many abominable actions; come, ye poor mortals, condemned first to bear the infirmities of nature, the caprices of society, the vicissitudes of age, the turns of fortune, and then the horrors of death, and the frightful night of the tomb; come, behold the Wonderful, the Counsellor, the Mighty God, the Everlasting Father, the Prince of Peace; take Him into your arms, learn to desire nothing more when you possess Him.—B. Murphy.

7. **no end,** no limit. It should go on increasing until it embraced the whole earth. **throne of David,**[a] the Messiah is to succeed to David's throne and doubtless is conceived as his lineal descendant. Camb. Bib. **to order it,** etc., R. V., "to establish it, and to uphold it with judgment and with righteousness from henceforth," etc. This Messianic rule over all the earth is to be established not by means of force, not by militarism, but by the exercise of justice and righteousness. **zeal,** or jealousy,[b] "in the idea of divine holiness is included that God is a jealous God (Ex. xxxiv. 4; Deut. vi. 5). This jealousy turns especially against idolatry (Deut. xxxii. 21), and generally against all sins by which God's holy name is desecrated. These terms are used not to indicate change in the divine nature, but to keep awake the consciousness of the living, holy God."—Oehler.

Zeal of the Lord.—The word rendered "zeal" is the root-word out of which comes the term jealousy; zeal and jealousy mean the same thing in this connection—The jealousy of the Lord of hosts will perform this. The Lord is jealous over the daughter of Zion; he is jealous over the integrity of His own oath. When He has declared that the whole earth shall be filled with a divine glory, not one iota of that promise can fail; the Lord's jealousy or zeal is involved in the fulfilment of the terms. The Lord worketh. If the conversion of the world were dependent upon our mechanical agencies, that conversion would be long delayed, it might, indeed, be expunged from any record of the possibilities; but the battle is not ours, it is God's; the banner that is to float from the heights of a conquered world is to be planted there by Him whose name is King of kings, Lord of lords. Heaven takes a long time in its working, but its work is done for ever. We should wish to see the whole world at peace to-day, and we should love to run from tower to tower and tell the metal in every belfry to ring out the old and ring in the new, for the very Christ has come; but the matter is of greater consequence to Christ than it can be to us. It is well, therefore, for us if in faith and rest and love we can say, Lord, Thy time is best: we will pray Thine own prayer, "Thy kingdom come. Thy will be done, in earth, as it is in heaven."—Peop. Bib. Prophetic Titles Given to the Messiah.—In the Talmud the idea first appears that Hezekiah was the son in whose birth the Prophet saw the advent of an era of glory for the Jewish people; but the reason of this application of the text, so unlike the manner in which generally the Jewish traditions are so true to the national conviction, that the

ed by Solomon himself with greater richness of prophetic detail; and at last fully and clearly embodied in Isa.'s predictions concerning the righteous King and the 'Servant of the Lord,' by whom our peace would be worked out."—Spk. Com.

"You cannot limit 'love' in its syntax. You can write grammars for pedants, but when the heart burns, when all love turns the heart to divinest uses, then we use redundance of words, because we require all possible multiplications of terms in order to give but a dim hint of the rapture which makes our souls ecstatic."—Peop. Bib.

[a] 2 Sa. vii. 11—16.

[b] "The two ideas of God's jealous partiality for His own people, and His jealous sensibility respecting His own honor, are promiscuously blended in the usage of the word, and are perhaps both included in the case before us. The expressions are derived from the dialect of human passion, but describe something absolutely right on God's part for the very reasons wh. demonstrate its absurdity and wickedness on man's." — J. A. Alexander.

"The remarkably emphatic repetition of the idea of His ruling in righteousness, justice, and real benevolence, suggests how fearfully the world has been misgoverned, and how little the great body of human government in even civilized nations have sought and practically secured the welfare of the millions."—Cowles. In the glass of Scripture we may catch many glimpses of the glory of Christ; the full vision will be when we are wihtin the veil, and behold the Lord in the plenitude of His glory.

"Whensoever in our search of the Scriptures we find a promise specially adapted to our needs, let us lay hold of it, saying with joyful confidence, 'The zeal of the Lord of hosts will perform this!' :"

Christ is the Pearl of great price. Pearls are not like pebbles, which are found on the sea-shore; they lie in the depths of the ocean, and require much labor to secure them.

[a] "The impenitent Ephraimites treat with contempt the results of Tiglath-Pileser's invasion, and boast that they will speedily place their affairs in a far more prosperous condition than before." —Henderson.

Pr. xvi. 18, 1 Pe. v. 5.

"A man under God's affliction is like a bird in a net; the more he strives, the more he is entangled."—Bishop Hall.

"Great gifts are beautiful as Rachel; but pride makes them also barren like her.

Prophets in all similar passages spoke of the Messiah, is to us confirmatory rather than the contrary of the belief that our Lord is the object of Isaiah's words. For their difficulty lay in the phrase, "The mighty God." They had hardened themselves into the settled belief that the Messiah was to be a national hero, their Cyrus and Alexander, who should command their armies, win for them battles, found for them an empire, and establish their supremacy over the hated heathen; he was to be a man whose sons should reign in his stead; and therefore the title "The Mighty God," contradicted their expectations, and in enmity to the Christian interpretation they sought for some other person to whom they might apply the words. It is evident, therefore, that the translation whereby modern commentators make this title signify nothing, had not suggested itself to them; for these tell us that, according to the idiom of the Hebrew language, the words may mean only "a god-like hero," whereas the Jews themselves translated it "a strong God," and were not aware in their expositions of the possibility of rendering it in any other way. To the Christian this phrase is the strongest proof that the Prophet was speaking of Christ; for in Him only has God become incarnate in the flesh: and as he reads the titles whereby the dignity of the Child is shadowed forth, he thinks with reverence upon the mystery of the Godhead united with the manhood, whereby Jesus of Nazareth was able to be the Prince of Peace, the Reconciler of lost man unto a just though merciful God.—R .P. Smith. We see here the universal extent of the Redeemer's kingdom; and, in this respect, how much does it differ from all the kingdoms of the earth! A universal empire, in the hands of a mortal, is a huge, unwieldy thing; a heap of confusion; a burden to mankind; and it has always rushed headlong from its glory, and fallen to pieces by its own weight. But Jesus is equal to the immense province of an empire strictly universal; His hand is able to hold the reins; and it is the blessing of our world to be under His administration. He will turn what appear to us scenes of confusion into perfect order, and convince all worlds that He has not taken one wrong step in the whole plan of His infinite government.—Davies.

8—10. (8) Beginning with this verse is a section (ix. 8—x. 4) which is probably out of place and should follow v. 25, which closes with the refrain repeated here in vss. 12, 17, 21; x:4. The passage prob. belongs to the earliest period of Isaiah's ministry. **sent a word,** the figure is one of personification, as if "the word" were living (comp. Ps. cxlvii. 15, 18. cvii. 20; Is. lv. 10, 11) a messenger of His will. And now it **hath lighted upon Israel,** making itself heard. (9) **know,** or feel by personal suffering. **stoutness of heart,** shown in resistance of the Divine messages. (10) **build .. stones,**[a] "calamity did not make this people thoughtful." What the earthquake has overthrown they will rebuild more durably. They did not recognize the Lord shaking the land, so He sent their enemies to steal it from them."—G. A. Smith. **sycamores,** a "light-wood, unfit for massive buildings."

Building Materials.—The houses of the lower orders in Egypt are in like manner constructed of unburnt bricks, or square pieces of clay, baked in the sun, and only one story high; but those of the higher classes, of stone, are generally two, and sometimes three stories high. These facts are at once a short and lively comment on the words of the Prophet: "All the people shall know, even Ephraim, and the inhabitants of Samaria, that say, in the pride and stoutness of heart, the bricks are fallen down, but we will build with hewn stones; the sycamores are cut down, but we will change them into cedars." Bricks dried in the sun, are poor materials for building, compared with hewn stone, which, in Egypt, is almost equal to marble, and forms a strong contrast between the splendid palace and mud-walled cabin. And if, as is probable, the houses of the higher orders in Israel were built with the same species of costly and beautiful stone, the contrast stated by the Prophet places the vaunting of his wealthier countrymen in a very strong light. The boastful extravagance of that people is still further displayed by the next figure: "The sycamores are cut down, but we will change them into cedars;" the forests of sycamore, the wood of which we have been accustomed to employ in building, are cut down by the enemy, but instead of them we will import cedars, of whose fragrant and beautiful wood we will construct and adorn our habitations. The sycamore grew in abundance in the low country of Judea, and was not much esteemed; but the cedar was highly valued; it was brought at a great expense, and with much labor, from the distant and rugged summits of Lebanon, to beautify the dwellings of the great, the palaces of kings, and the temple of Jehovah. It was therefore an extravagant boast, which betrayed the pride and vanity of their depraved hearts, that all the warnings, threatenings, and judgments of the living God were insufficient to subdue or restrain. —Paxton.

11, 12. (11) **adversaries,** etc., this is the second great calamity, loss of territory, the first being the earthquake (ch. v. 25), and three more to follow. **against him,** i. e. Israel. Assyria would first conquer Syria, and then attack Israel. **and join his,** R. V., "and shall stir up his." (12) **Syrians .. devour Israel,**[a] "guerilla warfare, armed raids, the land eaten away bit by bit."—G. A. Smith.

Verse 12.—Professor Duhm calls the latter part of this verse "one of the most effective refrain-verses that have ever been composed." The figure of Jehovah, with His arm stretched out in wrath, is kept before the mind of the reader, as the prophecy advances to its conclusion.

13—15. (13) **For the people turneth not,** R. V., "yet the people hath not turned," they do not learn from this second calamity. **smiteth,** or chastiseth, in order to humble. **seek,** the forgiveness of.[b] (14) **head and tail,** the high and the low, all ranks. The next consequent calamity passes from the land to the people themselves. A great battle is described, in which the nation is dismembered in a day.—G. A. Smith. **branch,** palm branch, growing right at the top of the tree. **rush,** sedge in the marshy ground; a type of the poor. (15) **The ancient,** etc., an explanation of verse 14, with the prophet's characteristic scorn of false teachers, who cater to the people rather than lead them; such are the worst and meanest of the people.

Calls to repentance.—Wherever we may be, there are voices which call us to repentance. Nature, as well as our whole life, is full of them, only our ears are heavy and will not hear. There is an awakening call in the rolling thunder, which is a herald of infinite majesty—in the lightning, which darts down before thee, carrying with it destruction—in the stars, which look down upon thee from such remote regions, as if they would say, "How far, O man! art thou cast out from thy home!" —in the flower of the field, which, in its transient blooming and fading, depicts thy own brief existence upon earth—in the midnight hour, when the church-bell strikes upon thy ear, like the pulse of time, which rapidly hastens away, and calls out to thee to hasten to save thy soul. Nay, where are we not surrounded by awakening voices of this nature? They sit upon the tombstones of our churchyards, and their language is, "It is appointed unto men once to die, and after that the judgment." Their warning voice resounds from every funeral-car that rolls past thee. It may be heard on every birthday which thou celebratest; in every fit of illness by which thou art attacked; in every danger that threatens thy life; as well as in that secret uneasiness which incessantly steals through thy soul.—Krummacher.

16—19. (16) **leaders,** ch. iii. 12. **destroyed,** Heb. swallowed up. (17) **fatherless,** etc., usually such objects of tenderest Divine compassion. **every one,** "the whole nation shares the ruler's guilt; as ruler so people. War brings out as nothing else does, the solidarity of a people in guilt."—G. A. Smith. **hypocrite,** R. V., "profane," or impious. Comp. x. 6; xxxii. 6; xxxiii. 13. (18) **wickedness .. burneth,** blazes forth.[a] The fourth calamity, internal anarchy. "There is a panic of wickedness, sin spreading like mania. The physical metaphors of the prophet are evident: a forest fire, and the consequent famine, whose fevered victims feed upon themselves."—G. A. Smith. **shall mount,** etc., R. V., "roll upward in thick clouds of smoke," miserable ending of their wealth and pride. (19) **darkened,** R. V., "burnt up." This conflagration of evil passions is the punishment of a nation for its falseness. **spare,** in the general woe none shall care for the other. Comp. the bloody scenes of the French Revolution.

Man's readiness to invent excuse for sin.—A traveler in Venezuela

Either we must lay self aside, or God will lay us aside." — Gurnall.

"No striving with supreme powers: we must submit ourselves unto the mighty hand of God, acknowledge our offences, call to Him for mercy. If He strike, He alone must help."—Burton.

a 2 Chr. xxviii. 18, 22, 23.

b "To seek God in the idiom of Scrip. is to pray to Him (Is. lv. 6), to consult Him (Is. viii. 19), to resort to Him for help (Is. xxxi. 1), to hold communion with Him (Am. v. 4, 5)." —J. A. Alexander.

"It is not a trivial matter to be well or ill led. How true this is politically, commercially, legally; it is not less true religiously. That community shows little wisdom that chooses its leaders carelessly. That community is insane which demands that its prophets shall prophesy unto it only smooth things (Isa. xxx. 10)." — Hom. Com.

a "God having withdrawn His Providential restraints, the pent-up passions of men have broken out like flames." — Spk. Com.

"When the heart begins once to be kindled, it is easy to smother the smoke of passion, which else will fume up into the head and gather into so thick a cloud that we shall lose the very sight of ourselves, and what is to be done." —Sibbes.

illustrates the readiness of men to lay their faults on the locality, or on anything rather than themselves, by the story of a hard drinker who came home one night in such a condition that he could not for some time find his hammock. When this feat was accomplished, he tried in vain to get off his riding-boots. After many fruitless efforts he lay down in his hammock, and soliloquized aloud, "Well, I have traveled all the world over; I lived five years in Cuba, four in Jamaica, five in Brazil, I have traveled through Spain and Portugal, and been in Africa, but I never yet was in such an abominable country as this, where a man is obliged to go to bed with his boots on." Commonly enough are we told by evil-doers in excuse for their sins that no man could do otherwise were he in their position, that there is no living at their trade honestly, that in such a street shops must be open on a Sunday, that their health required an excursion to Brighton on the Sabbath because their labors were so severe, that nobody could be religious in the house in which they were engaged, and so on, all to the same effect, and about as truthful as the soliloquy of the drunkard of Venezuela.—C. H. Spurgeon.

20, 21. (20) **snatch,** a vivid picture of the general distress: each gets food how he can, and thus cannot satisfy himself.[b] **eat .. arm,** fig. for plucking away and eating the food of his nearest and dearest relatives. Fighting with those who are dear to him as his own arm. It is "the cruelty of rival political factions" that is referred to. (21) **Manasseh, Ephraim,** the two leading tribes of the ten making up the northern kingdom.[c] "Ancient tribal jealousies would naturally be revived in a period of anarchy and civil war. Something of this kind seems to be implied in the account of the accession of the usurper Pekah, who murdered Pekahiah, at the head of a band of fifty Gileadites (2 Ki. xv. 25). The tribal names, however, need not be taken quite literally; indeed, it is hardly probable that the tribes had preserved their separate identity to so late a time." Camb. Bib.

Divine anger.—The anger which God feels and displays is always anger against sin. It is never against sinners as offenders against Himself personally, but as violators of the eternal laws of righteousness and love. It is not possible for the most daring transgressor to injure God in the slightest degree, and therefore He can never feel anything approaching to that personal vindictiveness which we feel against those who have wronged us. His anger against sin and sinners is no passion of personal vindictiveness, but is the natural revulsion of purity from impurity, of honesty from fraud, of truthfulness for falsehood; the instinctive abhorrence of generosity for meanness, of benevolence for malice, of kindness for cruelty. If God did not feel and manifest this anger against sin, it would be impossible to respect and love Him. If He could look down on the mean and dastardly things that are done every day, and yet remain cold and emotionless as an iceberg, as indifferent to the sufferings of His creatures as some Oriental despots have been to the miseries of their wretched subjects, our whole soul would rise up in righteous condemnation of Him.—R. A. B.

[b] "In times of anarchy, cruelty and self-will appear to grow more inordinate by being indulged." — Spk. Com.

"Place one spark amid combustible material in London. Let it alone. What will be the result? It will leap from point to point, house to house, street to street, until the whole city is in flames. Sin has spread in an exactly similar way. One sin, to the individual; one wrong action, to the family; one immoral look, to thousands; one crime, to a kingdom." — Hom. Com.

CHAPTER THE TENTH.

The fifth calamity is the threat of captivity, vs. 1—4. "Turning now from the past, and from the fate of Samaria, with which it would appear he has been more particularly engaged, the prophet addresses his own countrymen in Judah, and paints the future for them. It is not a future in which there is any hope."—G. A. Smith. **1, 2.** (1) **decree,** in the courts of justice. That is, they make laws which enable them to commit grievous wrongs under legal forms. **and that write . prescribed,** R. V., "and to the writers that write perverseness," referring to the professional interpreters of the law.[a] (2) **turn aside,** etc., or exclude, prevent from gaining their right. **take away,** by fraud and violence.[b] **my people,** the tone of affection toward those who are thus unrighteously oppressed. **widows .. fatherless,** the helpless. comp. Jas. i. 27.

God's hatred of injustice.—The Lord's voice is always for righteousness. What is it that is denounced? It is the very thing that is to be

[a] "Or magistrates who caused unjust decisions to be recorded." — Fausset.

"Execute written documents which exact what is unjust." —Wordsworth.

[b] There is no surer sign of the misery of a people than is found in the corrupt administration of justice.

Is. xxix. 21; Am. v. 12; Pr. xviii. 5.

"How many sentences have I seen more criminal than the crimes themselves! all which makes me remember the ancient opinions, 'that there is a necessity a man must do wrong by retail, who will do right in gross; and injustice in little things, that will come to do justice in great.' " —Montaigne.

denounced evermore. There is nothing local or temporary in this cause of divine offence. The Lord is against all unrighteous decrees, unnatural alliances, and evil compacts. This is the very glory of the majesty of omnipotence, that it is enlisted against every form of evil and wrong. Then—"Woe unto them that decree unrighteous decrees, and that write grievousness which they have prescribed"—scribes or registrars who preserve all the forms of the court, and keep their pens busy upon the court register, writing down every case, and appearing to do the business correctly and thoughtfully; and yet all the while these very registrars were themselves plotting "to take away the right from the poor, that widows may be their prey, and that they may rob the fatherless." The court of law was turned into a means of robbery, as it is in nearly every country under the sun. The scribes who wrote down the law were men who secretly or overtly bróke it; the judge used his ermine as a cloak, that under its concealment he might thrust his hand further into the property of those who had no helper. "For all this his anger is not turned away." Blessed be His name! Oh, burn thou against us all; mighty, awful, holy God, burn more and more, until we learn by fire what we can never learn by pity. The Lord speaks evermore for the poor, for the widow, for the fatherless, for the helpless. Here we pause, as we have often done before in these readings, to say, How grand is the moral tone of the Bible; how sweetly does God speak for truth and righteousness; how condescendingly does He enlist omnipotence on the side of innocent helplessness.—Peop. Bib.

"Or, 'if they do not bow down under the captives, they shall fall under the slain.' " —J. A. Alexander.

"Or, sinking, for very shame and self - reproach, lower than the captives."—Spk. Com.

"Bow down, as in the stocks, in which the head, feet, and hands were cramped together." — Wordsworth.

3, 4. (3) **day of visitation,** when God takes judgment on such iniquities. **desolation,** or storm. **from far,** i. e. distant Assyria. **leave .. glory,** i. e. your wealth and treasures. How will you secure them in the evil day? (4) **bow .. prisoners,** better, "They shall only crouch among the prisoners or fall among the slain." This is the answer to the questions of vs. 3. There is nothing left to them but captivity or death. **For all .. still,** the last time that this refrain occurs. This whole section (ix. 8—x. 4) should follow v. 25 preceding vss. 26—30, which are an appropriate conclusion.

The uses of affliction.—There is a little plant, small and stunted, growing under the shade of a broad spreading oak, and this little plant values the shade which covers it, and greatly does it esteem the quiet rest which its noble friend affords. Once upon a time there comes along the woodman, and with his sharp axe he fells the oak. The plant weeps and cries: "My shelter is gone, every rough wind will blow upon me!" "No," says the angel of the flower; "now will the sun get at thee, now will the shower fall on thee in more copious abundance than before; now thy stunted form shall spring into loveliness, and thy flower, which could never have expanded itself to perfection, shall now laugh in the sunshine, and men shall say How greatly hath this plant increased, how glorious hath become its beauty through the removal of that which was its shade and delight.—Spurgeon.

The judgment of the world power: an oracle against Assyria, vss. 5—34. **5, 6.** (5) **O Assyrian,** better, "Woe to thee also, O Assyrian." **the rod,** comp. Jer. i:20, the agent used for the punishment of My people. A great empire, but only a rod in God's hand. **indignation, i. e.** the instrument for expressing My indignation. (6) **hypocritical,** R. V., "profane," all Israel, first northern Israel in the 6th year of Hezekiah's reign and then Judah in his 14th year. **people .. wrath,** who, by their continued transgressions, have become the objects of Divine wrath.[a]

[a] Comp. Eze. xxix. 19, 20.

"Justice is as strictly due between neighbor nations, as between neighbor citizens. A highwayman is as much a robber when he plunders in a gang, as when single; and a nation that makes an unjust war is only a great gang of robbers." — Franklin.

The Assyrian (vss. 5—19).—I. His commission—subordinate, a mere rod in God's hand—defined. II. His pride: he boasts of his schemes, his achievements, his strength and wisdom, of what he will do against God. III. His rebuke: just, keen, humiliating. IV. His punishment: irresistible, sudden, signal, effected by Divine power.—Lyth.

"Justice is the idea of God, the ideal of man, the rule of conduct writ in the nature of mankind." — Theodore Parker.

Verses 5—34.—"This great prophecy is the clearest and probably the earliest exposition of that conception of the divine government of the world which was the guiding principle of the latest period of Isaiah's ministry. The leading idea of the passage is the contrast between the mission assigned to Assyria in the scheme of Jehovah's Providence, **and the ambitious policy of universal dominion cherished by the rulers**

"Where evil may be done, 'tis right to ponder; where only suffer'd, know, the shortest pause is much too long." — Hannah More.

"God beholds thee, wretch, though wrapped in prayer,
A wolf disguised, a painted sepulchre;
Regards no more thy cant, and godly whine
Than yon dumb statue on the marble shrine,
Whose hands are seen in holy rapture closed
And steadfast eyes to heaven alone disposed,
Prayer's senseless image where no soul within
Speaks through the form and animates the mien."
—J. Scott.

of that empire. Assyria was the instrument chosen by Jehovah to manifest His sole deity by the extinction of all the nationalities that put their trust in false gods." But the great world-power, intoxicated by its success and attributing this to its own wisdom and resource, recognizes no difference between Jehovah and other gods, but confidently reckons on proving His impotence by the subjugation of His land and people. Hence it becomes necessary for Jehovah to vindicate His supreme Godhead by the destruction of the power which has thus impiously transgressed the limits of its providential commission. And this judgment will take place at the very moment when Assyria seeks to crown its career of conquest by an assault on Jehovah's sanctuary on Mount Zion, the earthly seat of His government. These are the ideas which lay at the root of Isaiah's heroic faith in the crisis of Sennacherib's invasion. He did not doubt that Judah's sins required an exemplary chastisement, or that that chastisement would come by means of the Assyrians, but he had the firmest conviction that Jehovah's purpose did not include the violation of His sanctuary, which would in that age have been equivalent to the extinction of the true religion.—Cam. Bible. Assyria.—We know what the Assyrians were in the history of the world. They do not stand alone; they belong to a class of men who have appeared again and again, and are numerously represented in the world to-day—men of enormous force, of abounding energy, of vast ambition, of unscrupulous determination. Such men as Ghengis-Khan, Nebuchadnezzar, Alexander the Great, Caesar, and Napoleon, are their conspicuous representatives, but their representatives only. They are to be found elsewhere than on thrones and at the head of armies. They have been represented in the Church by ambitious and unscrupulous popes, cardinals, and bishops not a few. They are represented among our nobles by domineering landlords; in commerce by great capitalists, who brook no competition, but will crush a rival at any cost. This chapter concerns men who live in England to-day, and it has for us more than an historic interest.—Hom. Com.

7—9. (7) **meaneth not so,**[a] it is not the purpose of Assyria to act as the servant of Jehovah; in what he does he is not guided by moral but by selfish interests. **heart think,** the heart in the O. T. is the organ of knowledge, so that the Heb. word has often the meaning of intellect, insight. Prov. xxiii. 7, "as he thinketh in his heart." (8) **princes,** i. e. "officers." **kings,** many of them were subjugated kings (2 Ki. xxv. 28), and any one of them excelled in dignity the petty sovereigns of the independent states. The title "King of kings" was already assumed by Assyrian monarchs. (9) **Is not,** etc., i. e. was any one of these cities able to withstand me?[b] "Hamath was taken by Sargon in 720. Arpad by Tiglath-Pileser in 740; Samaria by Sargon in 722; Damascus by Tiglath-Pileser in 732; Carchemish by Sargon in 717. The date of capture of Calno is not known. But, thus far, the nations had been powerless before the Assyrian."—Driver..

[a] "This uprooting of conquered nations was a new thing in the world; devised by Syria as a means of carrying out that imperial policy wh. originated with it; as if it were bent on realizing the dream of the old Babel builders."—Spk. Com.

[b] Is. xxxvi. 19, 20, xxxvii. 12, 13.

Hypocrisy.—Some hypocrites and seeming mortified men, that held down their heads like bulrushes, were like the little images that they place in the very bowing of the vaults of churches that look as if they held up the church, but are but puppets.—Bacon.

Atrocity of hypocrisy—

Why, I can smile, and murder while I smile;
And cry content, to that which grieves my heart
And wet my cheeks with artificial tears,
And frame my face to all occasions.
I'll drown more sailors than the mermaid shall;
I'll slay more gazers than the basilisk;
I'll play the orator as well as Nestor,
Deceive more slyly than Ulysses could,
And, like a Sinon, take another Troy:
I can add colors to the chameleon;
Change shapes, with Proteus, for advantages,
And set the murderous Machiavel to school.
Can I do this, and cannot get a crown?
Tut, were it further off, I'll pluck it down.—Shakespeare.

"The spider weaves a web, and that is its world. It retires into its corner for observation, and has no concern for any surrounding objects, except as they may be caught upon its net, and appropriated to its use. So they who live without God reticulate life with selfishness. Nothing concerns them except as it may be drawn into the mesh of scheming for ministering to their own wants and wishes." —Bellew.

Hypocrisy—
It was withal a highly polished age,
And scrupulous in ceremonious right.
When stranger stranger met upon the way,
First each to each bowed most respectfully,
And large profession made of humble service,
And then the stronger took the other's purse;
And he that stabbed his neighbor to the heart,
Stabbed him politely and returned the blade
Reeking into its sheath with graceful air.—Pollok.

10, 11. (10) **idols,** lit. "nonentities."[a] He uses the same scornful word that the prophet employed (ii. 8); from his conception of the conquering power of Ashur the word is intelligible. **excel,** in number, and in fame or importance, such as certain shrines or idols possess. **Samaria,** from this and vs. 9 it is evident that the prophecy is written after the fall of Samaria in 721, while the preceding prophecies were written about 732. (11) **her idols,** "her nonentities, so do to Jerusalem and her images." The Jews were to blame for this conception that the gods of the Jews were images and idols like the gods of other nations.

An Indian youth.—A native gentleman of India, in relating his history to one of the missionaries, said:—My father was an officiating priest of a heathen temple, and was considered in those days a superior English scholar; and, by teaching the English language to wealthy natives, realized a very large fortune. At a very early period, when a mere boy, I was employed by my father to light the lamps in the pagoda, and attend to the various things connected with the idols. I hardly remember the time when my mind was not exercised on the folly of idolatry. These things, I thought, were made by the hand of man, can move only by man, and, whether treated well or ill, are unconscious of either. Why all this cleaning, anointing, illuminating, etc.? One evening, these considerations so powerfully wrought on my youthful mind, that instead of placing the idols according to custom, I threw them from their pedestals, and left them with their faces in the dust. My father, on witnessing what I had done, chastised me so severely, as to leave me almost dead. I reasoned with him, that if they could not get up out of the dust, they were not able to do what I could; and that instead of being worshipped as gods, they deserved to lie in the dust, where I had thrown them. He was implacable, and vowed to disinherit me, and, as the first step to it, sent me away from his house. He relented on his death-bed, and left me all his wealth. Compromise.—Ships, when the tide rises and sets strongly in any direction, sometimes turn and seem as if they would go out upon it. But they only head that way, and move from side to side, swaying and swinging without moving on at all. There seems to be nothing to hinder them from sailing and floating out to sea; but there is something. Down under the water a great anchor lies buried in the mud. The ship cannot escape. The anchor holds her. And thus are men holden by the cords of their own sins. They go about trying to discover some way to be forgiven, and yet keep good friends with the devil that is in them.—Beecher.

12—14. (12) An abrupt transition. The impious language of the Assyrian leads the prophet to declare that when Jehovah has punished Israel He will remember and punish the pride of Assyria. **performed,** lit. "cut off." The figure is taken from the cutting off of the finished web from the loom. Comp. xxxviii. 12, and Zech. iv. 9. **punish .. heart,** lit. "the fruit of the pride of his heart," which fruit is boasting against God, lust of empire and cruelty, hateful to God in any people. Notice, though God uses a man or an army as His instrument, if the instrument sins it shall suffer for its sin. (13) **strength .. hand,** again the king is quoted, as he describes his victories, and ascribes it to his own absolute strength and wisdom.[c] **I am prudent,** i. e. have insight. **removed the bounds,** it was his policy to obliterate boundaries and mingle conquered peoples by deportation and colonization. **like a valiant man,** "like a bull," the Assyrian symbol of strength. (14) **moved .. wing,**[b] "The magnificent simile represents the ease with which the Assyrians

[a] "He regarded foreign gods as impotent and worthless esp. after having with so much ease, conquered the cities and countries of wh. they were the supposed protectors."— Henderson.

A mother was describing to her little son the idols which heathen nations worship as gods. "I suppose, mamma," said the boy, "that these heathens do not look up to the same sun, and moon, and stars which we do." "Yes, my dear, they do." "Why, then, I wonder that they do not think there must be a better God than those idols."

[a] Comp. Nebuchadnezzar and Belshazzar.

[b] "The Assyrian compares his conquests not to the easy work of seeking nests, but the much easier one of gathering eggs fr. forsaken nests. The people fled before him, leaving their treasures in his hands."—Nagelsbach.

Ha. iii. 11—15; 2 Ki. xix. 20—24.

"As an eagle, though she enjoy her wings and beak, is wholly prisoner if she be held but by one talon; so are we, though we could be delivered of all habit of sin, in bondage still, if vanity hold us but by a silken thread."—Donne.

had rifled the countries of their treasures, and the panic terror which their approach everywhere produced."—Camb. Bib.

Note on vss. 13, 14.—These are the sentiments and boastings of Sennacherib, a proud Assyrian monarch, who viewed and treated cities just as we in Africa viewed and treated ostrich nests, when they fell in our way; we seized the eggs as if they had been our own, because we had found them, and because there was no power that could prevent us. So did Sennacherib seize and plunder cities with as little compunction as we seized the eggs of the absent ostrich; never thinking of the misery for life which he thereby brought on many peaceable families, who had done nothing to injure or offend him.—Campbell.

15, 16. The prophet speaks again. (15) **boast,** or vaunt. "The idea is not merely that of boastful opposition, but of preposterous inversion of the true relation bet. agent and instrument, bet. mind and matter."[c] **staff .. wood,** R. V., "staff should lift up him that is not wood," i. e. the man who uses it. (16) **Lord of hosts,** an unusual combination of Divine names.[d] **fat ones,** choice soldiers. **leanness,** prob. some withering disease.[e] **a burning,**[f] "the serried battalions of Assyria appear to the imagination of the prophet as the trees of some huge forest, irresistible in their strength and countless in their number; but the light of Israel kindles majestically into a flame; and at the end of a single day a child may count them."—Driver.

The worker and his tools (vs. 15).—These words point to one of the common temptations of strong men in every sphere of action to rely on their own skill and power. Consider—I. The real connection of human industry with God—useful and fine arts belong to the original idea of man as a working being; note the kind of world which God has made our present home, also the mode in which the Scriptures speak of the arts; learn to separate human handiwork from human sin. II. The disconnection of industrial pursuits from God in the minds of men generally: this evil may exist either in a positive or in a negative sense; the sources of it are religious ignorance and alienation from God, the forms in which it is developed are various; the duties especially incumbent upon the Christians of this land in connection with their daily labor are the unfailing recognition of the Divine Providence,—humility, justice, and kindness.—S. Martin.

17—19. (17) **light of Israel,** God is fire (Deut. ix. 3), and light (1 John i. 5). The holiness of God is light, revealing; and flame, consuming. Now it is to burn in wrath against Assyria. **thorns and briers,** "the splendid forces of Asshur were nothing but a mass of thistles and a bed of thorns," fit only to be burned.—Delitzsch. (18) **forest,** the wilder districts. **fruitful field,** the cultivated districts; intimating the desolation of the whole country. **soul and body,** a proverbial expression meaning utterly. **standard-bearer,**[a] R. V. margin, "as when a sick man pineth away," like a consumptive, hopelessly growing weaker from day to day. (19) **rest,** i. e. those surviving the destruction. **child,** who cannot count up to high numbers, a prophecy remarkably fulfilled for but a fragment of the army that marched against Jerusalem ever escaped.

Uncertainty of riches.—Riches take to themselves wings, and flee away. The wicked have been in great power, and they have departed without telling whither they have gone; they have not left even the rustle of a wing behind them to indicate the direction of their flight. We have much now; upstairs and downstairs, all full; to-morrow every chamber will be emptied, and yet not a door will have been opened by human hand. Seal up your treasures; take wax, and plenty of it; melt it down, stamp it with your crest—frailest sign of vanity—and to-morrow will find you empty-handed, and you will open your mouth in wonder, and ask who did it; and the secret-keeping air, the confidant of God, will not allow even a little bird to tell you whither the property has gone. Use it well! Blessed is the true and faithful servant who toils and prays!—Peop. Bib.

20, 21. (20) **remnant,** comp. Is. lxv. 8ff. Zeph. iii. 12, 13; Mic. v. 7, 8; Jer. xxiii. 3. **again stay,** i. e. lean for support on Assyria,[a] "an allusion to the alliance contracted by Ahaz (2 Ki. xvi. 7 ff.), a policy, however,

c "The absurdity of Assyria's vaunting is forcibly depicted by supposing the case of an inanimate tool disengaging itself from the power of the intelligent agent by whom it is used, and treating him as if they had exchanged places with each other."—Henderson.

d "Ha-Adon, the Supreme Judge, who is also Sovereign Ruler, Adonai-Sebaoth, Lord of Hosts."—Spk. Com.

e Ps. cvi. 15; Isa. xvii. 4.

f 2 Chr. xxxii. 21; Isa. xxxvii. 36.

a "Some think the ref. may be to the Assyrian king, and propose to read, 'He shall be utterly dispirited, and like the fainting away of a sick man;' i. e., he shall resemble a wretched invalid, sinking through weakness and want of sustenance." — Henderson.

"From his exhaustless store the Prophet produces another figure, and calls Assyria a weakling, who pining dies away." — Nagelsbach.

a "It is evident that this passage was composed when the Assyrian alliance was already an historical fact." — Nagelsbach.

2 Ki. xvi. 7.

"Every hour life's sands are sliding from beneath incautious feet, and with sin's fatal flower in the incautious hand the trifler goes to his doom. The requiem of each departure is an echo of the Saviour's question, What shall

whose evil consequences were not fully realized till the reign of Hezekiah. From the false situation in which the nation was then placed no escape was possible except by the intervention of Jehovah. After that deliverance the survivors shall adopt the attitude, consistently advocated by Isaiah, of steadfast reliance on Jehovah alone; they shall stay (themselves) upon Jehovah, the Holy One of Israel, in truth (in faithfulness)."—Camb. Bib. (21) **the mighty God,** comp. ix. 6, where this is given as one of the names of the coming Messiah.

A happy conversion (vs. 20).—Refer to history of the Jews, their sins, and punishment. I. Consider what is said of their former error. 1. They had exercised an improper dependence; 2. Their dependence had been disappointed; 3. Their folly was to be corrected by their sovereign. II. What is said of their renewed experience. 1. It is enlightened; 2. Extensive; 3. Blessed. III. The reality of their change. 1. They shall stay upon the Lord, in distinction from mere pretensions: 2. In distinction from imaginary confidence.—W. Jay.

A remnant.—We can hardly understand such language as this, because in our national life and personal history we have never been subject to those strange mutations which befell the kingdom of Israel. We can hardly understand what it means where a whole nation is torn up by the roots, and carried away into a foreign land; and where, by and by, in a capricious mood of some despot, a portion of them are allowed to go back again,—a mere fragment. For in the carrying away of a million people, how many perish! And when a few are gathered together, and they turn to go back, how much is this remnant to be pitied! Wandering from place to place in the promised land, crossing the Jordan, finding a heap where once there was a flourishing city, drawing near to the home of their ancestry and finding it in the hands of foreigners, themselves regarded as intruders and outcasts, what a harrowing experience theirs must be! It was under such circumstances as these that the prophets did their chief work. It was one of their principal functions to encourage a nation plunged into profound despondency. In this chapter the prophet, with words of cheer, and with an inexpressible richness of imagery, comforts the poor, despoiled band of people, and makes them feel that the hand of power shall not for ever be so strong against them.—Hom. Com.

22, 23. (22) **though thy people,**[b] etc., trans. "though thy people, O Israel, were as the sand of the sea only a remnant." The prophet emphasizes the greatness of the calamities overhanging the nation. It is a remnant, only a remnant that will survive.[c] **consumption,** "Render: extermination is decreed overflowing in righteousness. The 'extermination' is the judgment which reduces the teeming population of Israel to a mere remnant; this will be an overwhelming manifestation of Jehovah's judicial righteousness."—Camb. Bib. (23) **consumption,** R. V., "consummation," that is a final work; **determined,** i. e. irrevocably decided upon.

God's mercy.—Oh, who can read of a Manasseh, a Magdalene, a Saul, in the roll of pardoned sinners, and yet turn away from the promise, out of a fear that there is not mercy in it to serve his turn? These are landmarks that show what large boundaries mercy hath set to itself, and how far it hath gone, even to take into its arms the greatest sinners that make not themselves incapable thereof by final impenitency. It were a healthful walk, poor doubting Christian, for thy soul to go this circuit, and oft see where the utmost stone is laid and boundary set by God's pardoning mercy, beyond which He will not go. It is harder to get sin felt by the creature, than the burden, when felt, removed by the hand of a forgiving God. Never was tender-hearted surgeon more willing to take up the vein, and bind up the wound of his fainting patient, when he hath bled enough, than God is by His pardoning mercy to ease the troubled spirit of a mourning penitent.—Gurnall.

24, 25. (24) Here the prophet turns to a message of consolation to the faithful that yet look to Jehovah. **dwellest in Zion,** this is the emblem of security, since it is there that Jehovah will beat back and destroy the Assyrian, comp. vss. 32—34. **rod .. staff,** the instruments rather of chastisement than of destruction. **manner of Egypt,** recalling to mind how God overruled for His people's good even the sufferings of

a man give in exchange for his soul?"

"Live as in God's sight, mindful of thy position as a child of God, and as a servant of Jesus. Meditate on His Word; pray always. Then you will know when to close and when to open the lips: when to listen; and how to behave, if wrongfully accused."

[b] For the expression comp. Sol.'s prayer, 1 Ki. vii. 30, etc.

[c] Ge. xxii. 17.

[d] The meaning is, that the destruction of the great mass of the people would be an event involving an abundant exhibition of God's justice."—J. A. Alexander.

"God will justly bring this consumption upon a provoking people, but He will wisely and graciously set bounds to it."—M. Henry.

"In war men will venture their lives, because they think some will escape, and why not they? In traffic beyond the seas many adventure a great estate, because some grow rich by a good return, though some miscarry. The husbandman adventures his seed, though sometimes the year proves so bad that he never sees it more. And shall not we make a spiritual adventure, in casting ourselves upon God, when we have so good a warrant as His command, and so good an encouragement as His promise, that He will not fail those that rely on Him?"—Sibbes, 1577-1635.

their time in Egypt. (25) **indignation,** against Israel. **shall cease,** R. V., "shall be accomplished." **mine anger .. destruction,** i. e. and then mine anger will be turned to their (the Assyrians') destruction. Very shortly after they think to utterly demolish Israel they will themselves be overwhelmed by Jehovah.

Divine deliverance (vs. 25).—I. The deliverance of God's people is coincident with the destruction of their enemies. II. The reason of this arrangement: their enemies exist as a test, for their instruction, correction. III. The inference deducible from it: when God's people are perfected they will be delivered and their enemies destroyed. IV. The gracious assurance that this shall be speedily accomplished.—Lyth.

Mercy—
The quality of mercy is not strain'd;
It droppeth as the gentle rain from heaven
Upon the place beneath: it is twice bless'd;
It blesseth him that gives, and him that takes:
'Tis mightiest in the mightiest; it becomes
The throned monarch better than his crown:
His sceptre shows the force of temporal power,
The attribute to awe and majesty,
Wherein doth sit the dread and fear of kings;
But mercy is above this sceptred sway,
It is enthroned in the hearts of kings,
It is an attribute of God Himself;
And earthly power doth then show likest God's,
When mercy seasons justice. Therefore,
Though justice be thy plea, consider this,—
That, in the course of justice none of us
Should see salvation: we do pray for mercy;
And that same prayer doth teach us all to render
The deeds of mercy. —Shakespeare.

26, 27. (26) **for him.** R. V., "against him." The Almighty will swing the whip over Asshur and smite it as once the Midianites were smitten. —Delitzsch. **Oreb, Ju. vii. 25.**[a] **and as His rod, etc.,** R. V., "and his rod shall be over the sea, and he shall lift it up," etc., so that this sea of affliction which had threatened Israel shall overwhelm Assyria. (27) **his burden,** that of Assyria. **because of the anointing,**[b] the best translation of this passage is margin, cf. R. V., "the yoke shall be destroyed by reason of fatness." "Judah is compared to an animal which as it increases in strength and size, bursts the yoke which presses and galls its neck."—Driver.

Divine chastisements.—They are—I. Tender, "O My people." II. Merciful, "be not." III. Necessary, "he shall." IV. Of short duration. V. Without partiality. VI. End in deliverance.—Lyth.

Providence in history.—We shall see all the meaning of sword and pestilence and grim famine, of cloud and storm and angry thunder, of love, and mercy, and hope, and gospel sacred with the blood of sacrifice. By-and-by, yet a little while, no cloud is eternal; it is but vapor after all, and the wind will cleanse it away. When the vision is declared we shall know that Righteousness is the security of the universe, hell the necessity of unrepented sin, and heaven is the God-built, eternal home of men who touched the atoning Saviour with the reverent, grateful hand of faith. History is in a great tumult: nation clashes against nation in the shock of war; man eats the flesh of the arm of man, and grows the hungrier for his feast of blood; the poor are little counted of, the weak go to the wall; banners red as blood are being figured all over with lines of fire, with the motto, "Might is right." O Lord, how long? In reply to this question we are entitled to go back upon all the record of history, and trace the line of providence through the whole—a line now terrible as righteousness, now gracious as the love of Christ. The Lord reigneth.—Peop. Bib. Results of moral discipline.—The law of habit, when enlisted on the side of righteousness, not only strengthens and makes sure our resistance to vice, but facilitates the most ardu-

"Life, like a dome of many-color'd glass, stains the white radiance of eternity."— Shelley.

a Isa. ix. 4.

Comp. the fate of Oreb and of Sennacherib, 2 Chr. xxxii. 21; Isa. xxxvii. 38; and Ju. vii. 25.

b Or for the sake of the anointing, which was one seal of the Divine covenant.

The Targum reads—"And the nations shall be broken before the Messiah."

The following suggestion, by Kocher, is curious — "Whereas yokes are commonly preserved by oil, this shall be destroyed by it."

"Mercy, not justice, is the throne of princes. For what is power, though boundless and almighty? A deity of awfulness and fear; but in the whirlwind of its wrath, when flies the burning shaft, if mercy's saving hand arrests its flight, then we kneel and worship, and mix our praise with gratitude and love." — Francis.

"Men reckon the extreme penalty to be death; but in the Divine court of justice this is scarcely the beginning." —Philo.

"Why cannot we, slipping our hand into His each day, walk trustingly over that day's appointed path, thorny or flowery, crooked or straight, knowing that evening will bring us sleep, peace and home?"—Phillips Brooks.

ous performance of virtue. The man whose thoughts, with the purposes and doings to which they lead, are at the bidding of conscience, will, by frequent repetition, at length describe the same track almost spontaneously,—even as in physical education, things laboriously learnt at the first come to be done at last without the feeling of an effort. And so, in moral education, every new achievement of principle smooths the way to future achievements of the same kind; and the precious fruit or purchase of each moral virtue is to set us on higher and firmer vantage-ground for the conquests of principle in all time coming. He who resolutely bids away the suggestions of avarice, when they come into conflict with the incumbent generosity; or the suggestions of voluptuousness, when they come into conflict with the incumbent self-denial; or the suggestions of anger, when they come into conflict with the incumbent act of magnanimity and forbearance, will at length obtain, not a respite only, but a final deliverance from their intrusion. Conscience, the longer it has made way over the obstacles of selfishness and passion, the less will it give way to these adverse forces, themselves weakened by the repeated defeats which they have sustained in the warfare of moral discipline: or, in other words, the oftener that conscience makes good the supremacy which she claims, the greater would be the work of violence, and less the strength for its accomplishment, to cast her down from that station of practical guidance and command, which of right belongs to her. It is just because, in virtue of the law of suggestion, those trains of thought and feeling, which connect her first biddings with their final execution, are the less exposed at every new instance to be disturbed, and the more likely to be repeated over again, that every good principle is more strengthened by its exercise, and every good affection is more strengthened by its indulgence than before. The acts of virtue ripen into habits; and the goodly and permanent result is the formation or establishment of a virtuous character.—Chalmers.

28, 29. The section (vss. 28-32) is called by Driver "a passage of astonishing power, in which the prophet, conscious of his strength, resorts to a species of irony." Delitzsch says, "This description is one of the most magnificent that human poetry has ever produced." It describes the march of the Assyrian army, its triumphant progress and final complete failure. It was exactly fulfilled. (28) **He is come,** i. e. the Assyrian general with his army. **Aiath,** prob. Ai, 10 miles N. of Jerus. **Migron,** prob. Makrun, a little S.E. of Bethel.—Robinson. **Michmash,** some 8 miles N. of Jerus., a strategic point marking the N. frontier of Judah. Here was "a long, narrow defile where a large army might easily be checked by a handful of resolute defenders. But they pass through it triumphantly, having previously seized Migron at the southern end, by skilful strategy. **carriages,** R. V., "baggage"; the heavy baggage was left under guard at this point bec. the steep Wady Suweinit had to be passed. (29) **passage,** or defile. **Geba,** etc., see Jos. xviii. 21—28; 1 Sa. xiii. 2, 3. "Geba they have made their night-quarters."

God overruling nations.—Man may be the crown of creation, but he is only a creature, and set to do God's most delicate and particular work. So far as we can understand the history of our world, we can see that great nations have been raised up to do certain things for God, and they have done them, either with their wills or against them. Egypt was raised up to educate the childhood of God's chosen people. Assyria was raised up, as we see in this chapter, to be the rod of God wherewith he might punish his people for their sin. Babylon was commissioned to guard the years of Jewish captivity. Greece was exalted to show the world that "the beautiful" is not, of necessity, "the good." Rome proved to the world that "restraint of law" can never take the place of the "liberty of righteousness." The Gothic nations were commissioned to overthrow a debased and worn-out civilization. France shows how the passion for "glory" can lead men astray. America illustrates the principles of self-government. England tells what can be achieved under the inspiration of duty.—Pul. Com.

30—32. (30) **Lift up,** Heb. cry shrill. **Gallim, Laish,** "these places cannot be identified."—Camb. Bib. **Anathoth,** now Anata, 3 miles only fr. Jerus. (31) **Madmenah,** an unknown village. **is removed,** R. V., "is a fugitive." **gather . . flee,** hastily collect their property and fly before

"Heart - work must be God's work. Only the great heart-maker can be the great heart-breaker."—Richard Baxter.

"A patriotism that inspires us to give all to our native land and die for it ought to teach us to live those same lives in the service that will best help our native land." —Albert Bryant.

"A Christian warrior should always carry his fighting Testament in his pistol - pocket. If you cannot carry around with you a double-barreled Testament, always carry a single - barreled one." —William Ashmore.

the enemy.[a] (32) **As yet shall he remain,** etc., Polychr., "This very day he will halt in Nob: his clenched hand he shakes against," etc. The prize seems to be within his grasp, and the conqueror insolently shakes his fist at Jerusalem.

Note on vs. 32.—This is a part of the description of the march of Sennacherib against Jerusalem. When he arrives near the city, he lifts up his hand and shakes it, to denote that he will soon inflict signal punishment upon it. How often may this significant motion of the hand be seen; it is done by lifting it up to the height of the head, and then moving it backward and forward in a cutting direction. Thus, when men are at so great a distance as to be scarcely able to hear each other's voice, they have this convenient way of making known their threatenings. Sometimes, when brawlers have separated, and apparently finished their quarrel, one of them will turn round and bawl out with all his might, and then shake his hand in token of what he will still do.—Roberts.

a "Showing what imminent danger Jerusalem was in, when its enemies made so many bold advances towards it, and its friends could not make one bold stand to defend it."—M. Henry.

"Do not weaken and distress yourself by looking forward to things which you cannot see, and would not understand if you saw them." —Charles Kingsley.

33, 34. (33) **lop .. terror,** when lo, "by an unseen stroke" this boastful conqueror is stricken down as a tree is felled by a woodman,[b] the fig. of a sudden and fearful destruction. The word used signifies "beautiful branches," or "leafy boughs," with special reference to the pride of the officers, boasting of their forced and unopposed march. (34) **thickets,** referring to the soldiers. **Lebanon,** i. e. "the army of Asshur which is now standing opposite to Mt. Zion, like Mt. Lebanon with its forest of cedars, falls down."—Delitzsch. **a mighty one,** comp. xxxiii. 21; Ps. lxxvi. 5; xciii. 4. In the account of the fulfilment (xxxvii. 36) it is "the angel of the Lord," who is represented as destroying the camp.

b For fig. of Assyria as lofty tree comp. Eze. xxxi. 5, 6, 8, 12, 13.

Fall of pride.—If God seems to delay in his humblings, we may be sure it is only that the proud man may get finished the work which, all unknown to himself, God is making him do. Then we may well learn to be always thankful for grace received, talents entrusted, opportunities given, and achievements won; but never boast, never either think or say, "I have done it;" "My arm hath gotten me this victory." Boast, if you must boast, like Paul, of what God has wrought in you and by you; but never boast of what you have wrought, for it is an ever-working and necessary law that "pride must have a fall," and the "Lord alone shall be exalted in that day."—R. Tuck. True fear of God.—Senator Rhett of South Carolina in reply to a challenge said: "But my second reason for not calling the Senator from Alabama into the field was of a still higher and more controlling nature. For twenty years I have been a member of the Church of Christ. The Senator knows it; everybody knows it. I can not and will not dishonor my religious profession. I frankly admit that I fear God more than I fear man." True courage is best evinced by the firm maintenance of our principles amidst all temptations and all trials.—The Field of Honor.

"God was wroth with the angels, and drove them out of heaven. God was wroth with Adam, and thrust him out of paradise. God was wroth with Nebuchadnezzar, and turned him out of his palace. God was wroth with Cain, and though he was the first man born of a woman, yet God made him a vagabond upon his own land. God was wroth with Saul, and though he was the first king that ever was anointed, yet God made his own hand his executioner." —Henry Smith.

CHAPTER THE ELEVENTH.

The Messiah and His Kingdom vss. 1—9.—1. **rod .. stem,** R. V., "shoot out of the stock." "The imperial power of the world falls without hope, but in Israel spring is returning."—Delitzsch.[a] **stem of Jesse,** or hewn-down stock of Jesse. "The idea is that the Davidic family shall become as obscure as it was formerly, when its head was a plain Bethlehemite citizen—(comp. 1 Sam. xxv. 10 ff and Mic. v. 2) and that on a sudden, someone of its members shall be divinely chosen to be a second David."—Polychr. Bib. **Branch .. roots,** R. V., "and a branch out of his roots shall bear fruit," shall come to maturity.

The Stem from the Rod of Jesse (vv. 1—9).—That this refers to the Lord is undoubted. Note—I. His descent. 1. Meanness or obscurity; 2. Progression; 3. Secret and mysterious operation. II. His personal and official endowments. 1. Their nature; 2. Their range; 3. Their durability; 4. Their purposes, that He might discriminate the characters of men, to defend the cause of the oppressed, to punish the workers of iniquity. III. The blessed state of things which will be realised under His administration. 1. The condition described; 2. The transformations effected; 3. The means of it.—Lyth.

a "To further indicate its mean condition, the name of David, wh. would have suggested notions of dignity and splendor, is suppressed, and that of his father Jesse is employed, wh. conveys the ideas of rustic simplicity and obscurity." —Henderson.

"Nothing is of full compass in benevolence and philosophy and true wisdom that

Rooted in God.—There are trees that can be cut down, and they have no to-morrow; and there are others which, though cut down to the very surface of the earth, have sap within themselves, and have laid such hold upon the earth, and upon the whole solar system through the earth, that they will renew their youth, and be green next year. What is the symbol of our power? Is ours an influence that can be cut down and never revive? or are we so rooted in the Eternal that though persecution may impoverish us, and we may suffer great deprivation and depletion of every kind, yet we shall come up again in eternal youthfulness, and great shall be our strength and just pride?—Peop. Bib.

Immanuel.—The following phrases, as gathered from the Scriptures, may serve to illustrate this view of Christ. He is spoken of as "Jehovah; as Jehovah of glory; as Jehovah our Righteousness; as Jehovah above all; as Jehovah, the First and the Last; as Jehovah's Fellow and Equal; as Jehovah of hosts; as Jehovah of David; as Jehovah the Shepherd; as Jehovah for whose glory all things were created; as Jehovah the Messenger of the Covenant: invoked as Jehovah; as the Eternal God and Creator; as the Mighty God; as the Great God and Saviour; as God over all; as the True God; as God the Word; as God the Judge: as Immanuel; as King of kings and Lord of lords; as the Holy One; as the Lord from heaven; as the Lord of the Sabbath; as Lord of all; as Son of God; as the Only Begotten Son of the Father: as One with the Father; as sending the Spirit equally with the Father; as entitled to equal honor with the Father; as Owner of all things equally with the Father; as unrestricted by the law of the Sabbath equally with the Father; as unsearchable equally with the Father; as Creator of all things; as Supporter and Preserver of all things; as possessed of the fulness of the Godhead; as raising the dead; as raising Himself from the dead; as Eternal; as Omnipresent; as Omnipotent; as Omniscient; as discerning the thoughts of the heart; as Unchangeable; as having power to forgive sins; as Giver of pastors to the Church; as Husband of the Church; as the Object of Divine worship; as the Object of faith; as God, He redeems and purifies the Church unto Himself; as God, He presents the Church unto Himself; Saints live unto Him as God."—J. Bate.

does not begin at the lowest point, and work through all the strata to the very surface and uppermost line of things." —Peop. Bib.

"In the roots covered with earth, and only rising a little above it, there shows itself a netzer, i.e., a fresh, green shoot. In the historical account of the fulfilment, even the ring of the words of the prophecy is noticed: the netzer, at first so humble and insignificant, was a poor despised Nazarene (Matt. ii. 23). — Delitzsch.

2, 3. "The stormy scene of tumult and destruction (in ch. x) is succeeded by a marvelous picture of the just and perfect rule of the ideal Prince."—Driver. (2) **the spirit of the Lord,** "the spirits of the Lord mentioned here are prevailingly intellectual;" a predominant characteristic of the Holy Spirit in Bible teaching. **rest,** or permanently abide. In Christ dwells "the fulness of the Godhead bodily."[b] **wisdom and understanding,** wisdom the special gift of the ruler, as called to judge difficult cases: understanding, or keen, quick discernment. **counsel,** the power to form wise plans. **might,** the faculty of carrying plans into execution. **knowledge,** practical acquaintance with the will of God. **fear,** that disposition wh. keeps us ever anxious to do God's will. (3) **and shall make,** etc., R. V., "and his delight shall be in the fear of the Lord." Not only possesses this "fear" himself, but delights to recognize it in others. **after the sight,** He will not depend upon appearances. He "knows what is in man," and He will judge unerringly.[a]

Discernment.—How comes it that men who are religious are thought to be mentally inferior? They ought to be the highest minds in the world; they ought to have the candle of the Lord at their disposal—a candle which lets its revealing light fall upon all the secret corners and cunning devices. There should be no possibility of deceiving the spirit of righteousness which is in the renewed man; he will know the hypocrite by his very attitude. Yet it may be possible to deceive even the very elect. But we cannot deceive the Lord. The Lord looketh upon the heart; even though we have many qualities that are unworthy, yet he can see beneath them all, and detect the genuine seed, the real desire after His kingdom, and the real sympathy with His purpose. That is the difference between the bad man and the good man: the bad man endeavors to keep an outwardly reputable surface, and all his iniquity is within, at the very center and core of things; the good man's imperfections are many, and are broadly seen, but the more deeply you go

[b] Col. ii. 9.

"The person whose origin and descent are metaphorically described in the preceding verse, is here described by his personal qualities, as one endowed with the highest intellectual and moral gifts by the direct influences of the Holy Spirit." —J. A. Alexander.

[a] "Christ, the Judge of all, will have no respect of persons in judging..... He will examine the heart and pronounce His judicial sentence accordingly." —Wordsworth.

Christ is before God for me; I am before the world for Christ.

b "The poor, who have no means of commending themselves to the eye; the meek, in whose mouth are no eloquent self-vindications to win the ear." —Spk. Com.

into his character the more rich he is; he is honest at the core. By this God will judge us. If we say, Lord, thou knowest all things, thou knowest that I love Thee, though yesterday I denied Thee, the appeal will stand if it be the appeal of an honest man; the wound, the slight, will be forgiven, forgotten, on the sight of the first penitential tear, and the ardent desire to be better will be accepted, and answered like a prayer.—Peop. Bib.

Gifts of Christ to His Church (vs. 2).—I shall—I. Call attention to the particulars described of spiritual influence on Christ. 1. He had the spirit of wisdom and understanding; 2. Of counsel and might; 3. Of knowledge and the fear of the Lord. II. Show how the graces of spiritual influence flow from Christ to His people. 1. They first descended from the Apostles; 2. On the multitudes at the preaching of the Word; 3. These rich streams are not exhausted.—J. Ayre.

Power of Christ's Teaching.—The truths revealed in the life and teachings of Christ are of sovereign power, and are the most influential upon the motives and the conduct of human life. They go to the very root of moral consciousness. They reveal human character by applying to it a standard higher than any that was ever before applied to it. They define and mark the nature of sin in human conduct. They establish obligations upon immutable grounds, leaving them not to the shifting ingenuity of human reason, but imposing them according to Divine principles. They reveal the infinite reach of moral conduct and its eternal consequences. Thus they reveal to man the nature of himself, the nature of the government under which he lives, the nature of God, and the nature of immortality.—H. W. Beecher.

4, 5. (4) **righteousness,** the "right" irrespective of persons and conditions: absolute right. **judge,** in contrast to the corrupt princes (i. 23: x. 2) He will consider the cause of the poor and treat with equity the humble and oppressed. **reprove with equity,** etc., Polychr. B. "with equity will He give decision for the destitute in the land." **smite the earth,** Cam. B., "smite the oppressor." **rod .. mouth,** (comp. Rev. i. 6; Acts v:1—10) reveals "the spirit of might." His words have divine efficacy (Hos. vi. 5). (5) **girdle,** "the symbol of vigorous, unimpeded strength."[c] **faithfulness,** truth in keeping promises. These will be the strength of the Messianic kingdom.

c Eph. vi. 14; see Ps. xciii. 1.

"The girdle is mentioned as an essential part of Oriental dress, and that which keeps the others in proper place, and qualifies the wearer for exertion."—J. A. Alexander.

The death of Christ was a greater and more costly sacrifice than if the whole human family had perished eternally; the reason is, that it was not that of a mere man, but of God-man in one Person.

The Effects of Christianity upon Human Society (vss. 4—9).—I. How far is it the object of the Gospel to improve the social state? II. What are the social tendencies of Christianity? III. What have been its actual achievements?—J. Styles.

Christ the Power of the World.—Christ walked like a shadow in His day; and if you had asked at that time, "Where are the secrets of power in the world?" any Jew would have pointed to the old temple, and said, "There are the secrets of the world's power." If, as he said it, you had seen some Greek smiling, and you had asked him, "Where is the secret of power in the world?" he would have said, "Have you been in Athens? Have you seen her temples and statues? Have you seen the Parthenon? Have you seen her art and read her literature? Have you entered the depths of the learning of her Plato and Aristotle? The world's history is wrapped up in Athenian art and literature." And if, while he yet spoke, a disdaining Roman had passed by, and you had followed him and said, "Wherefore that smile?" he would have said, "The Jews and the Greeks are filled with superstitions, and are blinded as to the true source of the world's power. That power is centered in Rome, whose greatness is unequalled by that of any other nation on the globe." And how would Jew, and Greek, and Roman have joined in mirthful derision if you had pointed to that person, Jesus Christ, who was to be crucified, and said, "In that man is the secret of the whole world's power." But the Jews, the Greeks, the Romans, with their philosophies, their governments, and their power, have gone down, while this shadow has risen into greater and greater power, until it fills the world.—H. W. Beecher.

6, 7. "The rest of creation will sympathize with this reign of virtue and piety. Evil having been eradicated from the nature of man," it will also disappear among the lower animals. (Cheyne). The Bible throughout carries this idea of the close connection of nature with the fall and redemption of man (comp. Gen. vi. 12; Hos. ii. 20; Rom. viii. 19—22). As in the primitive state (Gen. ii. 4 ff.), so in the future kingdom there is no antagonism betw. man and beast and no slaughter of domestic animals. (6) **wolf .. lamb,** "each animal is coupled with that one wh. is its natural prey."[a] **lie down,** i. e. in the same pastures.[b] little child, they will be so meek as not to need even a strong man's restraints. (7) **lion .. straw,** denoting a total change of habit.[c]

Verses 6—9.—This remarkable prophecy of the idyllic state of the brute creation is imitated in the Sibylline Oracles (iii. 766 ff.) and more faintly echoed in the Fourth and Fifth Eclogues of Vergil. Similarly, an Arabic poet (Ibn Onein, quoted by Ges.) speaks of "a righteousness, through which the hungry wolf becomes tame."—The description is not to be interpreted allegorically, as if the wild beasts were merely symbols for cruel and rapacious men. Neither perhaps is it to be taken quite literally. It is rather a poetic presentation of the truth that the regeneration of human society is to be accompanied by a restoration of the harmony of creation (cf. Rom. viii. 19—22). The fact that tame and wild animals are regularly bracketed together shows that the main idea is the establishment of peace between man and the animals (Hos. ii. 20); the animals that are now wild shall no longer prey on those that are domesticated for the service of man. But the striking feature of the prophecy is that the predatory beasts are not conceived as extirpated (as Ezek. xxxiv. 25, 28) but as having their habits and instincts changed.—Camb. Bib.

The Influence of a Child.—A young man had been extremely profane, and thought little of the matter. After his marriage to a high-minded, lovely wife, the habit appeared to him in a different light, and he made spasmodic efforts to conquer it. But not until some years had passed did he become victor, when the glowing evil was set before him, by a little incident, in its real and shocking sinfulness. One Sunday morning, standing before the mirror shaving, the razor slipped, inflicting a slight wound. True to his fixed habit, he ejaculated the single word "God!" and was not a little amazed and chagrined to see reflected in the mirror the pretty picture of his little three-year-old daughter, as laying her dolly hastily down she sprang from her seat on the floor, exclaiming as she looked eagerly and expectantly about the room, "Is Dod here?" Pale and ashamed, and at a loss for a better answer, he simply said, "Why?" "'Cause I thought He was when I heard you speak to Him." Then noticing the sober look on his face and the tears of shame in his eyes as he gazed down into the innocent, radiant face, she patted him lovingly on the hand, exclaiming assuringly, "Call Him again, papa, and I dess He'll surely come." Oh, how every syllable of the child's trusting words cut to his heart! The still, small voice was heard at last. Catching the wondering child up in his arms, he knelt down, and for the first time in his life implored of God forgiveness for past offences and guidance for all his future life, thanking him in fervent spirit that he had not "surely come" before in answer to some of his awful blasphemies. Surely "a little child shall lead them."—Old Test. Anec. Dawn of a New Era.—The Talmud says that after Adam and Eve had sinned, never having known night before, as the light grew paler, the wretched ones clasped one another in an agony of despair; then all grew dark, and they fell on the earth, and thought that God had withdrawn his light forever. They spent the night in tears. But a beam of light began to rise over the eastern hills, and the clouds blushed crimson, and the golden sun came back and dried the tears of Adam and Eve; and they greeted it with cries of gladness.—Baring Gould's Legends of the Patriarchs. Nothing could be more unlikely in the black night of Isaiah's prophecy than the dawning of a new day, but it came.

The Two Mothers and the Babe.—A young and beautiful woman, already a wife and mother, was living with her infant in a retired village in one of the remote provinces of France. Her husband and his father were both in Paris. During the disturbances which took place previous to the execution of the king, the father, having too openly expressed his opinions, was thrown into prison, and it was expected his

a "These may be figures for men of corresponding animal-like characters." —Fausset.

"The Prophet furnishes a description of the peace and happiness to be enjoyed under the reign of Messiah, wh., for boldness and exquisite choice of imagery, far surpasses the sublimest passages in which the classical poets celebrate the renewal of the golden age." — Henderson.

b "While the wolf, as a rule, attacks sheepfolds, a leopard can follow the goat along precipices where no wolf would venture, and the lion will carry off oxen, which neither leopard nor wolf could move." — J. G. Wood.

c Col. iii. 12, 13.

"Pointing to such well might Cornelia say,
When the rich casket shone in bright array,
'These are my jewels!' Well, of such as he,
When Jesus spake, well might the language be,
'Suffer these little ones to come to me.'
—Rogers.

At a preacher's meeting the query was started as to the ages at which the different ministers present were converted. It was ascertained that of those present twenty were converted under fourteen years of age; twenty-two under eighteen; thirteen under twenty-one; and four overtwenty-one.

"Thus with something of the seer Must the moral pioneer· From the future borrow; Clothe the waste with dreams of grain, And on the midnight sky of rain Paint the golden morrow."
—Whittier.

"There is something exceedingly thrilling in the voices of children singing. Though their music be unskilful, yet it finds its way to the heart with wonderful celerity. Voices of cherubs are they, for they breathe of Paradise; clear, liquid tones, that flow from pure lips and innocent hearts, like the sweetest notes of a flute, or the falling of water from a fountain!" — Longfellow.

son would share his fate. On receiving these sad tidings the lady quitted her retreat, leaving her child to the care of a faithful friend. On reaching Paris, she sought the presence of the judges, and earnestly entreated them to pardon her father; but they were inexorable. Being at this moment deprived of the assistance of her husband, who had been obliged to fly, her perplexity was extreme, though her courage even then did not fail. Finding her efforts for the captive's deliverance of no avail, she petitioned for leave to share the prison of the venerable old man; touched by her devotion, the tribunal allowed her to spend several hours every day with the captive. She came like a sunbeam in his solitary cell, cheering his spirits with hope for the future. When the day of trial arrived, his daughter-in-law was permitted to attend him, and for three days sat at his feet,—on the third he was condemned and taken back to prison. The lady made her way through the crowd until she reached the top of a flight of stone steps leading from the hall to the street. On her arrival at this spot she became alarmed at perceiving a crowd of excited women with children in their arms, who, on seeing her about to descend, cried out, "Behold the daughter of a traitor!" Remembering that on that very spot the Princess de Lambella had been savagely murdered, she became terrified; but it was only for a moment. Observing a young woman with an infant in her arms, she met her halfway, saying, "What a fine child you have." The woman looked at her for an instant, and, presenting her babe, said, "Take it; and when you are in safety, return it to me." The lady took the child, and pressing it to her breast, walked down the steps. The crowd opened to let her pass; and, as if guarded by some invisible hand, she crossed the street in safety. As soon as the mother saw she had escaped the danger, she reclaimed her child; no words were spoken, but the women understood each other.—Paxton Hood.

I may not stay to see the day
When the great Saviour shall bear sway,
And earth shall glitter in the ray
That cometh from above;
But come it fast, or come it slow,
'Twill come at last, I surely know,
And heaven and earth shall feel the glow,
And men shall call it Love.

8, 9. (8) **sucking child,** "the most startling contrast of all, the innocent babe playing with the deadly serpent." **asp,** poss. the cobra; certainly a poisonous serpent. **cockatrice,** R. V., "basilisk's."[a] (9) **hurt nor destroy,** this scene is not to be taken as allegorical, but as meaning literally that peace and not conflict shall prevail in all of God's creation, among men and beasts alike. **holy mountain,** Zion regarded as the seat of the Church. **knowledge,** etc., of His true nature. This is the great need of mankind, for as men know Him they become like Him. And when the whole earth is full of this knowledge His spirit will rule everywhere. The word **"for"** is explanatory. The preceding ideal condition will exist for the earth shall know God. The expression indicates also submission to that rule. **the sea,** poetical for the bed of the sea.

[a] "The cerast, or horned serpent—a small viper, little more than a foot in length, so called from the feelers which are protruded fr. its head, while it lies hid in the sand. It is exceedingly venomous." — Michaels.

"A living, experimental, practical knowledge of God." — Nagelsbach.

Christ has a greater interest in you than you have in Him.

A colored Presbyterian deacon was in the habit of shutting his eyes, while he sang with great

The Millennial Glory.—

The animals, as once in Eden, lived
In peace. The wolf dwelt with the lamb, the bear
And leopard with the ox. With looks of love,
The tiger and the scaly crocodile
Together met, at Gambia's palmy wave.
Perched on the eagle's wing, the bird of song,
Singing, arose, and visited the sun;
And with the falcon sat the gentle lark.
The little child leaped from his mother's arms,
And stroked the crested snake and rolled unhurt
Among his speckled waves, and wished him home;

And sauntering schoolboys, slow returning, played
At eve about the lion's den, and wove
Into his shaggy mane fantastic flowers.
To meet the husbandman, early abroad,
Hasted the deer, and waved his woody head;
And round his dewy steps, the hare, unscared,
Sported and toyed familiar with his dog.
The flocks and herds o'er hill and valley spread,
Exulting cropped the ever-budding herb.
The desert blossomed, and the barren sung;
Justice and mercy, holiness and love,
Among the people walked; Messiah reigned,
And earth kept jubilee a thousand years.—Pollok.

unction, "Fly abroad, thou mighty gospel!" and not seeing the contribution-plate. "Oh, yes!" said the plate - bearer; "but you just give something to make it fly."

10. **ensign,** the Messiah; He shall be lifted up as a sign to all nations; of Him shall all peoples seek knowledge: around Him, as Teacher, they shall gather. Comp. our Lord's word, "I, if I be lifted up, will draw all men unto Me."[b] **Gentiles,** nations other than the Jews.[c] **rest,** R. V., "resting place." The place of Messiah's dwelling in His Church. **glorious,** where He is manifest there shall be glory (John i. 14),—the glory of God,—the shekinah,—the divine splendor in its full revelation.

The Holy War (vs. 10).—Our Lord as an ensign—1. Musters His forces for the battle; 2. Marches with His forces to the battle; 3. Mingles with His forces in the battle.—F. W. Brown.

Ancient morality was essentially national and exclusive. Its creed was that a man was born not for himself, but for his parents, his family, and the state. The state was surrounded by others with which, unless some treaty had been concluded, it was at war. To do as much good as possible to one's own state, and as much harm as possible to all other states, was therefore the whole duty of a man.—Ecce Homo. The Reconciler of Men.—Christ inaugurated the empire of universal brotherhood and love. Wars have not yet ceased even among nations professing Christianity, but they are no longer openly gloried in by those who wage them; they are apologized for as sad necessities. The apology is often insincere, but the fact that it is made at all is a marvelous tribute to the influence and authority of Christ. Wherever His true followers meet, national distinctions are forgotten, and they feel drawn to each other by a mightier and sweeter bond. As the centuries pass away, the love of Christ becomes more and more the uniting power of the world.—Hom. Com.

b Jno. xii. 32.

c Ro. xv. 12; Ac. x. 45, 46, xxviii. 28.

"The Church, though despised by the world, having upon it the beauty of holiness, is truly glorious."—Mat. Henry.

When God gave us Christ, He gave us all gifts in one.

"Christ's love to God, and his love to men were not two great passions, but one. He loved man because he saw God in him. This must ever be the pulse of a powerful philanthropy — to see God in man. In the humblest—aye, in the most sinful human being—we see one whom God loves, whom the Saviour died for, and who may be an heir of the glory of Christ."—James Stalker.

11—13. (11) **second time,** differences of opinion prevail as to the meaning of this term. "If the standpoint (actual or ideal) of the prophecy be post-exilic, the most probable reference would be to the first return from exile under Cyrus. Otherwise, we must understand 'the first time' of the exodus from Egypt, which is hardly natural, although the prophecy does abound in allusions to that great deliverance." Camb. Bib. **recover,** or purchase. **Pathros,** Upper Egypt. **Cush,** Ethiopia.[a] Elam. Elymais, in S. Media.[b] **Shinar,** land on the Euphrates and Tigris. **Hamath,** in Syria; N. foot of Lebanon. **islands,** of the Mediterranean.[c] (12) **ensign,** see vs. 10; xlix. 22, a signal to the nations to bring back the captives. **corners,** Heb. wings. (13) **envy,** wh. kept up separation bet. the kingdoms of Israel and Judah.[d] One of the constantly repeated features of the time of Redemption will be the return of Israel to Jerusalem, the restoration of the city, and the reunion of the 12 tribes (comp. Joel. iii. 20; Amos ix. 15; Judges xxi. 3—6; Hosea ii. 2; iii. 5, especially Ezek. xxxvii. 15—22; Zeph. iii. 10).

Verses 11, 12.—The gathering of the "dispersed of Israel." It is of course impossible to disprove that in Isaiah's time scattered Israelites were to be found in all the countries mentioned at the end of vs. 11. Some might have been included among the captives whom Sargon settled in Elam, Babylonia and Hamath; fugitives from the Northern Kingdom might have taken refuge in considerable numbers in Egypt at the fall of Samaria; and the slave-trade might have carried small groups of Hebrews to the remoter regions. But the language here

a i.e. Nubia and Abyssinia.

b Or Persia.

c Ps. lxxii. 10; Jer. ii. 10; Est. x. 1.

d "This was one of the happy effects of the Assyrian and Chaldaean captivities; they put an end to the rivalry between the two kingdoms of Israel and Judah."—Wordsworth.

seems to imply a Jewish dispersion on a large scale, and the only wholesale deportations that had taken place in Isaiah's time were those of Northern Israelites to the Assyrian Empire (2 Ki. xv. 29, xvii. 6). On the other hand, the references exactly fit the circumstances of the post-exilic period, when large colonies of Jews are known to have been spread over the lands here enumerated.—Camb. Bib.

The United States Seal.—The ordinary great seal of the United States is commonly seen; but the design of the reverse side I have never seen except on the outside of the postal cars and in the encyclopedia. The design is an unfinished pyramid; over it is an eye symbolizing God's providence, and the motto, "Annuit Coeptis." "He favors what has been begun;" and, underneath the motto, "Novus ardo seculorum," "A new order of the ages," and with Him not only the individual man, but the world will be completed.—Peloubet.

14—16. (14) **fly,** or swoop, as a bird of prey (Hab. i. 8), **not a** spiritual but a military conquest. "In passing from the second to the third part of this prophecy, we cannot but feel that we descend to a lower point of view and a less pure atmosphere of spiritual ambition. Isaiah, who has just declared peace between man and beast, finds that Judah must clear off certain scores against her neighbors before there can be peace between man and man. He admits, indeed, the reconciliation of Ephraim and Judah; but the first act of the reconciled brethren, he prophecies with exultation, will be to swoop down upon their cousins Edom, Moab and Ammon, and their neighbors the Philistines; he could not as yet perceive any way for the conversion of the rest of the world except through Israel's political supremacy."—G. A. Smith. **Upon the shoulders,**[a] Polychr. B., "slope." **spoil . . east,** i. e. the Arabs of the Eastern desert. (15) **utterly destroy,** "several ancient versions read 'shall dry up' (comp. l. 2). **the tongue,** etc., i. e. the gulf of Suez. **mighty wind,** R. V., scorching wind. **the river,** i. e. the Euphrates (vii. 20; viii. 7). **in . . seven,** R. V., "into seven streams."[b] (16) **highway,** or road clear of obstructions (xxxv. 8; xl. 3, 4; xlii. 16; xlix. 11, etc).

Harsh Discipline the Way to Joy.—A little child, dropped as a waif in New York, alas! made beautiful, now coming to be thirteen or fourteen years of age, without friends, and with many that have lustful eyes upon her, is met by the gracious missionary at the "Five Points." And he beholds her, and his heart yearns toward her. He finds out where she lives in her little chamber, as yet not quite fallen, not quite overborne, yet coarse and rude and already beginning to love the taste of the poison of flattery, already beginning to listen willingly, already beginning to calculate and to throb evil thoughts. He looks upon her, and is sad for her. While others would open her chamber door and endeavor to persuade her to dismiss her industry; while others say to her, "Go, flutter, and be gay: take life and enjoy it while you may," he loves her more than they do. They love as the swine loves the husk, which he chews for the juice, and spits out a rejected cud; but he loves that child with the consciousness of what her immortality is, of what is the treasure of the riches that is in her, if only it can be saved and educated. And he would shut the door. They would open it. He would rather see her weep. They would rather see her laugh. He would rather see her suffer, and go poorly clad. They would be glad if she would take temptation under the proffer of ribbons and jewelry. They would be glad to see her dressed in all these gewgaw trifles. He, gaining influence with her, seems to her, in her moments of temptation, like a hard master. And yet, tell me, if it was your child, and if, after years had passed by, you found that this wanderer from your house had been saved by this missionary, and brought up in cramped circumstances, and familiar with poverty, and that he had been a faithful teacher to her, so that at length, when she reached her majority, she was still a virtuous woman, and beginning to love virtue more than vice, would you not say that he had been the truest sympathizer? And who would sympathize most with you? Would it be that "indulgent deity" who should make the present hour pleasant to you, and leave you to the waste of an eternal undoing? or would it be One who loved you so much that He was willing to administer discipline

[a] "The Heb. for shoulder is in Nu. xxxiv. 11, used also of a maritime coast." —Fausset.

"The prophecy was fulfilled, as regards Philistia, when the returned captives under Antiochus Epiphanes and Jonathan, etc., secured the seaboard of Canaan." — Henderson.

"Truth is quite beyond the reach of satire. There is so brave a simplicity in her that she can no more be made ridiculous than an oak or a pine." —J. R. Lowell.

"How many a Christian pilgrim would never have seen anything of the spiritual manna and the spiritual stream from the rock, had God listened to him, when, with fear and trembling, he besought Him not to lead him into a desert." — Krummacher.

" 'My burden is light.' A light burden indeed, wh. carries him that bears it. I have looked through all nature for a resemblance of this, and I seem to find a shadow of it in the wings of a bird, which are indeed borne by the creature, and yet support his flight towards heaven." — Bernard.

and watching and pain, and wring tears, that through those tears He might open the fountain of future joys? Is not that the divinest and truest sympathy? Are there any of us that do not need just such a friend as this in Jesus Christ?—H. W. Beecher.

CHAPTER THE TWELFTH.

1—3. (1) **that day,** of recovery and triumph. "This chap. is the conclusion of the first great division of the book. It consists of two short hymns of praise (vss. 1, 2, and 3—6), which are put in the mouth of the ransomed people." **wast angry,**[a] a word found elsewhere in the Psalms only. Ps. ii. 12; lx. 1, etc. (2) **my salvation,** tracing the deliverance wholly to His providence and grace. **Lord Jehovah,** Heb. Yah-Yahveh, a reduplication of the sacred covenant name (ch. xxvi. 4), a verbal quotation of Ex. xv. 2. (3) **with joy,** produced by such perfect trust. **draw water,** at the feast of Tabernacles one of the ceremonies of late origin was the daily libation of water, supposed to have been suggested by this verse (Oehler), and referred to by Christ in John vii. 37:viii. 12. The water was brought in a golden pitcher, from the fountain of Siloah, through the water-gate into the Temple, and there, mixed with wine, it was poured on the sacrifice, with great rejoicing (Lowth).

Elim (vss. 1—3).—In this wilderness are wells, or fountains, from whence we may receive strength and comfort. Let us show—I. To what the privilege is traceable. 1. To the reconciliation affected by the Mediator; 2. To the penitence and faith of the recipient. II. In what the privilege consists. 1. God's unmerited yet abundant love to sinners; 2. The everlasting nature of the promises of God; 3. The finished work and constant intercession of our Lord Jesus; 4. The descriptions of the final home of the saints; 5. The presence and rich grace of the Holy Spirit. III. How the privilege should be regarded. To embrace it eagerly, we must have—1. The vessel of faith; 2. The chain of prayer. IV. In what manner the privilege should be embraced. "With joy." 1. Instance several considerations to lead to this joyous state of heart; 2. Show after what manner this joy should be expressed.—Stems and Twigs.

The Wells of Salvation.—It is said that while the French engineers were boring for water in the African desert, the Arabs looked on in silent wonder, until they saw the precious stream actually gushing forth, and then their joy knew no bounds; and sweet and precious as the cooling waters are now to the weary, laboring child of the desert, so precious were they to the people to whom the words of the Prophet were originally addressed; and the promise to them of an indefinite supply of that element would be highly appreciated by them, and well calculated to inspire their gratitude and joy.—Lessons from Jesus.

4, 5. (4) **Praise,** give thanks to; a quotation again from Ps. cv. 1. **call upon,** lit. "call by (means of) His name," i. e. use His name in solemn invocation. comp. I Ki. xviii. 24. Worship Him by the name Jehovah. (5) **excellent things,** i. e. He hath wrought triumphantly. **known,** R. V. "let this be known."

Joy of Communion with Christ.—No sooner do you pass the brow of the St. Gothard pass, on your way to Italy, than you perceive that, beyond all question, you are on the sunny side of the Alps. The snow lying there is nothing in comparison to the vast accumulation upon the Swiss side of the summit, the wind ceases to be sharp and cutting, and a very few minutes' ride brings you into a balmy air which makes you forget that you are so greatly elevated above the sea level. There is a very manifest difference between the southern side and the bleak northern aspect. He who climbs above the cares of the world, and turns his face to his God, has found the sunny side of life. The world's side of the hill is chill and freezing to a spiritual mind, but the Lord's presence gives a warmth of joy which turns winter into summer. Some pilgrims to heaven appear never to have passed the summit of religious difficulty; they are still toiling over the Devil's Bridge, or loitering at

[a] "God's people can truly thank Him even for His severe discipline, which would not let them glide on smoothly to ruin. His wrath was but 'the jealousy' of true love." — Spk. Com.

Ro. vi. 17.

"It is the water that is so precious, not the wooden cup or the golden chalice that contains it. It is not new "theories" and "views" and "opinions" that are precious, but the Word of the living God, which is the pure water of life, and of which whoso drink shall live; for the written Word all leads to the living Word — Jesus Christ, the Saviour of men."—Pul. Com.

"Take the Gospel. What is it? It brings us glad tidings of great joy. It is infinitely important, it is eternally interesting to us. It is our life. It is all our salvation, and it should be all our desire. Therefore we should receive it as a faithful and worthy of all acceptation. We should receive it as a dying man would a remedy, or as a condemned criminal would hail a reprieve. We should receive it with feelings superior to those with which we receive anything else. It is a subject which rises infinitely above all others in interest and importance, and demands all the energies of the soul."—Jay.

Andermatt, or plunging into the deep snowdrifts of their own personal unworthiness, ever learning, but never coming to a full knowledge of the truth; they have not attained to a comfortable perception of the glory, preciousness, and all-sufficiency of the Lord Jesus, and therefore abide amid the winter of their doubts and fears. If they had but faith to surmount their spiritual impediments, how changed would everything become! It is fair traveling with a sunny land smiling before your eyes, especially when you retain a grateful remembrance of the bleak and wintry road which you have traversed; but it is sorry work to be always stopping on the Swiss side of the mountain. How is it that so many do this?—C. H. Spurgeon. Excellent things.—Is it true that God hath done excellent things—say for ourselves? Do not search ancient history for the excellent things done by God, but search your own little life; and if in that life no excellent things have been wrought, say so, and be dumb so far as this sacrifice of religious praise is concerned. You have a right to be silent. If your life has had no sunshine, no blessing, no help, no sympathy, you have a right to say in the sanctuary, I will not sing, and thus to chide God by your silence. But be sure you can say it. "Life" is a large term; it covers all the days of your breathing, from earliest infancy up till the present moment: it will certainly be a phenomenon without a parallel if any man can say that the sunshine never fell upon his life, that what good he has he has by his own strength and wit, and that he owes nothing to supernatural or superhuman power.—Peop. B.

6. Cry out and shout, so that men everywhere shall hear your good tidings (Comp. xxiv. 14; liv. 1). **inhabitant,** fem. inhabitress, the Church dwelling in Zion, daughter of Zion.[a] **midst of thee,** Zech. iii. 15, 17.

The Duty of Gladness (vs. 6).—Note two things: the person addressed, the admonition given. I. The truth upon which the admonition is founded. This includes—1. The character; 2. The greatness; 3. And residence of God, who is in the midst of His people universally, socially, individually. II. The exhortation enjoined. It teaches two things. 1. That as religion has to do with the feelings, it is absurd to place it in forms, etc.; 2. That religion is not only animated but rational, a reasonable service, etc.—W. Zarg.

Zion.—Is this the city of which such glorious things are spoken—that the Highest Himself should establish her, that she should not be moved? Where are His mighty promises of perpetuity? Where is that foundation which no power should ever shake—that Zion, in which the poor of His people were to trust? Brethren, look around you, and you behold the evidences of its existence, and of the eternal faithfulness of Him who is pledged to its immortality. A greater than Zion inherits her name; a greater than Zion bore it in the far-reaching scope of the prophetic vision. That "city of the great King" was but a perishable emblem of a "city whose builder and maker is God." It is true she was honored by His symbolic presence and sanctified by His sacred worship; it is true that for ages she alone, in a world of darkness, held the precious lamp of His truth; but what are these characters of honor to hers, whose every living stone is quickened by His indwelling energy, whose worship is no more in type and shadow, but in spirit and in substance; whose preaching and teaching, no longer shrouded in obscurity and limited to a corner of the earth, spreads over all lands, embraces the whole family of mankind, and makes even the course of that sun whose "going forth is from the end of the heaven and his circuit unto the ends of it, and from whose light nothing is hid," a faint image of the power with which she diffuses through all nations "the light of the knowledge of the glory of God in the face of Jesus Christ." (See also 2 Cor. iii. 10, 11.)—Archer Butler.

CHAPTER THE THIRTEENTH.

xiii. 1 to xiv. 23 treats of the fall of Babylon. Here begins the second division of Isaiah and the first of a series of oracles dealing with foreign nations. Ch. xiii has three main divisions: vss. 2—8, the im-

---

[a] "All honor and all salvation of Zion rest in this, that it has the Lord in the midst of it as its living and personal shield and fountain of life."—Nagelsbach.

"It is the honor and happiness of Israel that the God who is in covenant with them, and in the midst of them, is infinitely great."—M. Henry.

"It is recorded by Plutarch that when the Romans delivered a certain people from the tyranny of the Macedonians and the Spartans, the cry of the delivered men was so great that it dissipated the very air, and birds flying across that plane of the hemisphere fell down amazed. Have we ever rent the air with our cries and shouts of delight and thankfulness?"

"Revelation never volunteers anything that man could discover for himself, on the principle probably that it is only when he is capable of discovering it that he is capable of appreciating it."—Drummond.

The ground, league beyond league, like one great cemetery is covered o'er with moldering monuments, and let the living wander where they will, they cannot leave the footsteps of the dead.

The Spanish mariners never touched upon new land without at once setting up the standard of Ferdinand and Isabella. Wherever the Christian goes, his first thought should be to take possession of all hearts in the name of the Lord Jesus.

pending attack; 9—16, the meaning of the judgment; 17—22, the fate of Babylon.—Camb. Bible. **1. burden,**[b] R. V. margin, "oracle concerning." The word means literally "the lifting up" (of the voice). **did see,** with prophetic insight (comp. i. 1 and ii. 1).

Typical Burdens (vs. 1).—I. The burden of Babylon, the doom of the empire of force. II. The burden of Egypt, the doom of craft and false wisdom. III. The burden of Tyre, the doom of unhallowed commerce; these burdens are illustrations of principles in themselves, they are also true of the Church.—Paxton Hood.

Babylon.—1. Name of place afterwards called Babylon was Babel =confusion (Ge. xi. 8, 9), or gate of Il, a Babylonian deity. 2. Situation: on the river Euphrates (Ge. xi. 31, cf. Jos, xxiv. 2, 3), about 300 miles from the mouth. 3. Description: if accounts of ancient writers (as Herodotus, Ctesias) are to be believed, it must have been of wonderful size and beauty. In shape, square; 120 furlongs each way. Walls 50 cubits thick, and 200 high (Jer. li. 53—58). "Upon the top of walls, and along the edges of them, they constructed buildings of a single chamber, facing one another, leaving room between for a four-horse chariot to turn. 100 brazen gates; houses three or four stories high. Taking the least of ancient measurements, Babylon must have=four or five times the size of London." 4. Present state of Babylon. Nothing remains but mounds of rubbish, and heaps of bricks covered with arrowhead characters. Already the investigations of Rawlinson, and others, have thrown much light on its ancient history, and strikingly confirmed the Scripture narrative.—Topics for Teachers.

The Need of Revelation.—It is well that there are some men who see what may be called the more majestic and overpowering aspects of God. Some of us are afraid almost to utter the great words which properly belong to the deity as descriptive of His nature and attributes and government. Herein what a wonderful difference there is between the Old Testament and the New, between the Hebrew and the Greek! Neither is sufficient alone: some men never look at the sky; they look only at the earth; others are not satisfied with looking at what is under their feet, they must with eager yet reverent eyes search the mystery of the heavens. We need all kinds of revelation in order that we may approximate to an idea concerning God's nature, so wondrous, yet so simple; so lifted up above all time and space as known to us, and yet walking by our very sides, and tabernacling within us as an invited guest.—Peop. Bib.

2, 3. "This prophecy differs from all that precede it in the remarkable circumstance that it stands unrelated to Isaiah's own age .. The Jews are represented as in exile and about to be delivered (xiv. 1, 2)." Hence it is believed to have been written by some one during the exile. —Driver. (2) **Lift .. mountain,**[a] i. e. raise the standard in a conspicuous place. **exalt .. hand,** summon them on with voice and hand, shouting to them and beckoning. **gates .. nobles,** i. e. through the gates of a city of princes, ancient dynasties which these Medes were to overthrow. (3) **sanctified ones,** or "consecrated ones," set apart to do God's work. Note that He is speaking of the Median armies. This is one of the many passages that refer to God's guidance of the history of other nations beside Judaea (comp. Amos i. and ix. 7; Is. xix. 2, 23, 25; Hab. i. 5, 6; Ezek. i. 9; Is. xlv. 22). **even them that rejoice in my highness,** R. V. "even my proudly exulting ones," "the phrase describes the exuberant spirits of the warrior."—Cheyne. (comp. Zeph. iii. 11).

Lifting Up the Banner.—Truly, in Christian warfare we might learn something from military enterprise. Have we put our banner in the right place? It is not enough to have a banner, we must be careful where we plant it; it may be mistaken for a tree, it may get entangled among the branches of great oaks or cedars: it is not enough to have a light, we must put it on the candlestick, and set it on the table, and not cover it with a bushel so that the darkness may be unrelieved by its presence: it is not enough to have intelligence, we must properly display it, use it for the benefit of those who are not so intelligent as we are: it is not enough to have schools, we must set the doors wide open, and compel the ignorant to enter that they may return from the sanc-

[a] The Medes came from mountain districts. Reference is to the gathering of warriors under Cyrus, whom God made His agent for the destruction of Babylon.

"Escape means nothing more than the gradual emergence of the higher being from the lower and nothing less. It means the gradual putting off of all that cannot enter the higher state or heaven and simultaneously the putting on of Christ. It involves the slow completing of the soul and the development of the capacity for God." — Drummond.

tuary of wisdom instructed and mentally fortified: it is not enough to have a church, we must open every door and every window, and bid all the people welcome—the more wicked, the more welcome; the more ignorant, if willing to learn, the more desired with the solicitude of sympathy and interest.—Peop. Bib.

4, 5. (4) **The noise,** etc., Polychr. Bib. translates:

"Hark! a tumult in the mountains as of a great multitude!
Hark! an uproar of kingdoms, of nations gathered together!
It is Jehovah Sabaoth mustering the warlike host."

the mountains, N. E. of Babylon, over which the Medes were to approach. **kingdoms of nations,** Medes, Persians, and Armenians, making up Cyrus's army. (5) **far country,** emphasizes the breadth of the sway of the Lord of Hosts, and His power to raise up His armies from unexpected and unknown quarters.[a]

Every Man's Life a Plan of God.—The Christian minister has the right, without special vision, to declare to every man that God has a purpose to be fulfilled in his particular life, and that he is marshalling events and mustering "forces" in order that it may be carried out. It ought to raise our estimate of the sacredness and value of the life God has given us to live on the earth when we remember that "every man's life is a plan of God," and that by it He desires and designs to accomplish some special end.—Pul. Com.

6—8. (6) **Howl,** as those on whom sudden calamity comes. **the day of the Lord,** (ii. 12 ff.) i. e. His day of battle and victory, when His righteousness shall be vindicated, whether against the sinners of Israel or, as here, against other unrighteous nations. Not the final day of judgment. Instead of howling or fearing, Babylon was found feasting in self-security. **destruction,** or like a sudden stroke. **the Almighty,** i. e. El-shaddai, a title found first in Gen. xvii. 1 and xxviii. 3; xxxv. 11, etc., peculiarly a patriarchal name for God, and refers to Him as exhibiting special deeds of power.—Oehler. (7) **faint,** R. V. "feeble," the suddenness of the attack would prevent resistance, and fill all with the spirit of hopelessness. (8) **amazed .. another,**[b] trans., "Stupefied each will look at the other." **flames,** in the flush of excitement and alarm.

God's Instruments for Punishment.—God has two sets of instruments—natural agents, such as storm, lightning, blight, pestilence, etc.; and intellectual and moral agents, or persons. It depends entirely on his own will whether he will employ agents of the one kind or of the other. In dispensing good to man he employs largely natural agents, "making his sun to rise on the evil and on the good, and sending rain on the just and on the unjust" (Matt. v. 45). But in punishing men he seems to make use, to a greater extent, of persons. Now he raises up a tyrannical and oppressive kind, like Rameses II. or Nebuchadnezzar, to carry out his sentence of suffering; now he allows a democratic assembly to establish a reign of terror in a sinful land; anon he uses the arrows of savage hordes, or the guns and bayonets of disciplined hosts, to chastise an offending people. Once only has he ever used his power to strike with sudden death on a large scale, and even there he employed a spiritual agent; it was "the angel of the Lord," who "went out and smote in the camp of the Assyrians one hundred and fourscore and five thousand" (2 Kings xix. 35).—Pul. Com.

9—11. (9) **cruel,** unrelentingly severe. (10) **stars,** lit. their Orions.[c] In this day of divine wrath even the heavens shall withhold their light[d] (Am. v. 18). The stars which Babylon has worshipped, and sun and moon, will cease to shine. (11) **the world,** which, so far as then known, seemed to be under Babylonian empire.

The Day of Jehovah.—The thought that God holds inquisition for evil and evil-doers is deeply stamped in Bible lore. There are heresies which he cannot and will not tolerate. They are not identical with what some call heresies. These are often departures from our fashions of life and thought; but it is only disagreement with him and his law of inward right that is the condemnable dissent. Again, it is his object to bring down the pride and arrogance of the haughty. How deeply marked, again, is this thought of overstepping our proper limits as the

a "Great princes and armies are but tools in God's hand, weapons that He is pleased to make use of in doing His work, and it is His wrath that arms them, and gives them success."—M. Henry.

b Da. v. 6.

"He lives long who lives well; and time misspent is not lived, but lost. Besides, God is better than His promises, if He takes from him a long lease, and gives a freehold of a better value."—Fuller.

"What man made man may destroy; what God has made, God will preserve. The grass of infidel oratory withereth, the flower of Christian interpretation often fadeth, but the Word of our God shall stand forever." — R. S. MacArthur.

c "Heb. Kesilim. Kesil, the self-confident, is the title given to the constellation Orion." — Spk. Com.

d "A fine specimen of the figurative manner in which the Heb. Prophets depict the horrors of national calamity. The metaphors of light and darkness are common; but when the effect is to be heightened, the writer represents the sources of light as being themselves affected. See Is. xxiv. 23, xxxiv. 4; Eze. xxxii. 7, 8; Joel ii. 10, iii. 15; Am. viii. 9; Mat. xxiv. 29."—Henderson.

essence of sin, from the Fall onwards! It is fixed in the word "transgression." The "lust to seem the thing we are not" is at the root of display, of ambition, of domineering over others. The prophets saw in the bloated dominion of great states like Egypt and Assyria the effects of these unbalanced lusts, which must sooner or later topple the tyrants into ruin. And thus the purpose of judgment resolves itself into that of sifting mankind—to make the people "rarer than fine gold, and men than Ophir's treasures." When ill weeds are cleared away, there is a chance for good plants to flourish; and when a mass of human evil has disappeared, room is made for something of another quality, to renew the tradition of the Divine in man.—Pul. Com.

12, 13. (12) **more precious,** indicating the completeness of the national destruction. **wedge of Ophir,** R. V. "the fine gold of Ophir," the gold country of India that lay nearest to the Phoenicians, the finest gold being brought from this district.[a] (13) **shake the heavens,** "by the outbreak of Jehovah's wrath the material universe is shaken to its foundations. Such representations are common in the descriptions of the day of the Lord, and are not to be dismissed as merely figurative." Cf. ch. ii. 12 ff.—Camb. Bib.

Dignity of Human Nature Shown from its Ruins.—Dr. Horace Bushnell has a fine sermon in 'New Life,' p. 16, entitled, "The Dignity of Human Nature shown from its Ruins." After speaking of many who "magnify the dignity of human nature, by tracing its capabilities, and the tokens it reveals of a natural affinity with God and truth. They distinguish lovely instincts, powers, and properties allied to God, aspirations reaching after God," he undertakes to "show the essential greatness and dignity of man from the ruin itself which he becomes;" and then he says, "Nor is it anything new, or a turn more ingenious than just, that we undertake to raise our conceptions of human nature in this manner, for it is in just this way that we are accustomed to get our measures and form our conceptions of many things; of the power, for example, of ancient dynasties, and the magnificence of ancient works and cities, such, for example, as Egypt, Rome, Thebes, Karnac, Luxor, or Nineveh. So it is with man. Our most veritable, though saddest, impressions of his greatness, as a creature, we shall derive from the magnificent ruin he displayed. In that ruin we shall distinguish fallen powers that lie as broken pillars on the ground; temples of beauty, whose scarred and shattered walls still indicate their ancient, original glory; summits covered with broken stones, infested by asps, where the palaces of high thought and great aspiration stood, and righteous courage went up to maintain the citadel of the mind—all a ruin now—archangel ruined."

14—16. (14) **as the chased,** or as it is with the chased roe. Comp. Jer. l. 16; li. 9, Ezek. xvii. 4: The multitude who had made Babylon their home for purposes of commerce now hurriedly flee to their native lands. (15) **found,** present in the city at the time of the siege, both the proper inhabitants, and the foreigners resident there. The ruin will be general. **joined unto them,** R. V. "taken," that is, in flight. (16) **children,** etc., "that the capture of Babylon should be marked by the atrocities here spoken of was no doubt to be expected from the character of the Medes, but no such crimes appear to have stained the actual victory of Cyrus. According to Babylonian records he took possession of the city peacefully. Cf. Ps. cxxxvii. 9; Nah. iii. 10; Hos. xiii. 16; 2 Kings viii. 12. The last half of the verse is repeated in Zech. xiv. 2."—Camb. Bib.

Hope in Misery.—When you see a surgeon performing a terrible operation on a patient, you are sure that he is confident that the patient will be restored to health. So when we look at the world as it is, we are certified that there is a better world to be. God would never have permitted the world to be, if He did not see how out of this present misery He could educe eternal and triumphant blessedness. Towards that better future God is leading on the world. The revulsion of feeling with which we read this prediction is one proof of it; there was a time when such incidents in the prosecution of a war would have been regarded as a matter of course. That it should not be so now marks an advance, and is a prophecy of further advances.—Hom. Com.

[a] 1 Chr. xxxix. 4. The locality of Ophir is still an open question.

"A banner long unused and laid away grows dusty and moth-eaten, and needs to be unrolled and shaken out, and borne high in air. So spiritual life decays in the confinement and darkness of the world; and that it may gain new vigor, our thoughts must now and then be unfolded and held high, and shaken in the air of heaven." —Sunday Teachers' Treasury.

"If we neglect the ordinary means of keeping a garden in order, how shall it escape running to weeds and waste? Or if we neglect the opportunities for cultivating the mind, how shall it escape ignorance and feebleness? So, if we neglect the soul, how shall it escape the natural retrograde movement, the inevitable relapse into barrenness and death?" —Drummond.

"Let us see that our knowledge of Christ is not a powerless, barren; unpractical knowledge. Remember, a holy calling never saved any man, without a holy heart. If our tongues only be sanctified, our whole man must be condemned." —Flavel.

17, 18. (17) **Medes,**[a] became a leading power in 606 B. C. when they joined with the Chaldæans in over-throwing Assyria. Cyrus was originally a vassal-king of the Median empire, reigning over a narrow territory to which then the name of Persia was restricted. In 549 he overthrew the Median dynasty and in 538 conquered Babylon. **regard silver,** not to be bought off. They care not for money. They are after mastery. "They come not to rob but to displace." Xenophon tells us that "disregard of riches" was a characteristic of the Medes. (18) **bows,** "for wh. the Persians were famed."[b]

Bows.—Both Herodotus and Xenophon mention that the Persians used large bows; and the latter says particularly, that their bows were three cubits long. They were celebrated for their archers (Jer. xlix. 35). Probably their neighbors and allies, the Medes, dealt much in the same sort of arms. In Psalm xviii. 34, and Job xx. 24, mention is made of a bow of brass. If the Persian bows were of metal, we may easily conceive that with a metalline bow of three cubits' length, and proportionably strong, the soldiers might dash and slay the young men, the weaker and unresisting part of the inhabitants, in the general carnage on taking the city.—Lowth.

19, 20. (19) **glory of kingdoms,** Isa. xiv. 4, xlvii. 5; Je. li. 41. The great central metropolis of many nations. **beauty,** etc., transl. "the proud boast of the Chaldæans," "it was the primitive dwelling place of the Chaldæans of the lowlands."—Delitzsch. **as .. Gomorrah,** i. e. as utterly and hopelessly destroyed. Comp. Gen. xix. 24 ff; Deut. xxix. 23; Jer. xlix. 18; Amos. iv. 11. (20) **never be,** Cyrus did not utterly destroy the city. Darius (in 518 B. C.) levelled most of its walls; other conquerors carried on the work and by the time of Strabo (60 B. C.) it was a perfect desert and has so remained.[c]

Verses 9—20.—This passage bears a close resemblance to Ezekiel's dirge over the fall of Pharaoh and his host (Ez., xxxii. 19 ff.). Many questions of great interest and importance are suggested by both. The most important is how far such representations are to be taken as expressing the fixed belief of the writers or their age with regard to the state after death. Their affinities with Babylonian speculation on that subject, taken in connection with the fact that such elaborate descriptions of the underworld do not occur before the Exile, may indicate that the imagination of the writers had been influenced by their contact with the religion of their conquerors. In that case it may be reasonable to suppose that they freely availed themselves of the material thus laid to their hand merely as poetic imagery, without meaning to attribute strict objective reality to all the conceptions. At the same time there was a common basis of belief underlying the Hebrew and Babylonian ideas regarding the future state, and all that is essential to the understanding of this passage was probably familiar to the minds of the Israelites before the Exile. In the conception as here presented the following point is to be noted. Sheol, which is figured as a vast subterranean region, is the common gathering-place of all the dead. They exist there as shades, repha'im (vs. 9), a word which is usually explained to mean "feeble ones,"—weak, pithless adumbrations of the living form. These are represented as capable of being roused to a transient interest in human affairs by the arrival amongst them of so distinguished a personage as the king of Babylon; but their ordinary condition is one of utter inactivity, a sort of conscious death rather than life. It is true that the writer speaks only of kings and potentates, and throws little light on the state of the common man after death. Still the Old Testament as a whole knows nothing of separate spheres of existence for the righteous and for the wicked, and that idea is certainly not to be imported into the present passage.—Camb. Bib.

Re-Entrance of Nature.—Beware of arrogancy, pride, worldliness, self-sufficiency; beware of the betrayal of trusts; nature will re-enter if we be unfaithful. If the gardener is too late by one day with his spade or seed or other attention, nature begins to re-enter; and if he tarry for a week he will find that nature has made great advances into the property. It is so with education, with the keeping up of intelligence, with the maintenance of healthy discipline; relax a month, and

[a] At this time the Medes were subject to Assyria.

[b] Isa. xxii. 3, 6.

"In many of those who seem utterly free from the love of money, it is only dormant. Many who appear to be utterly free from the love of money are so simply because they have never possessed more than sufficed for their bare necessities. Let them possess more, and avarice will show itself."

[c] Travelers remark that the Bedawin Arabs still have a superstitious dread of lodging on the site of Babylon." —Spk. Com.

"The region was once most fertile, but owing to the Euphrates being now no longer kept within its former channels, it has become a stagnant marsh, unfit for flocks; and on the wastes of its ruins, bricks and cement, no grass grows."—Fausset.

"Out of such scenes as those the prophet depicts, a solemn voice seems to speak, declaring that human life and glory are held cheap in comparison with those profound and, from us, half-hidden, half-revealed ends towards which the whole creation moves." —Johnson.

"As the little living seeds dropped into the crack of the huge temple become the upspringing plants which push their way through the strong masonry and at length overturn the tall

nature re-enters, and nature plays the spoiler. Nature is not a thrifty, careful husbandman. Nature has a function of desolation; she will grow weeds in your richest flower-beds if you neglect them for a day.—Peop. Bib. Fulfilment of prophecy.—Babylon also furnishes another instance. Surrounded by such scenes as the modern traveler describes, and comparing them with the pictures of history and prophecy, one may well exclaim with Brownlee:—

"Where are the cities which of old in mighty grandeur rose
Amid the desert's burning sands, or girt with frozen snows?
Is there no vestige now remains, their wondrous tale to tell,
Of how they blazed like meteor-stars, and how, like them, they fell?
Hark! hark! the voice of prophecy comes o'er the desert wide!
Come down, come down, and in the dust thy virgin beauties hide:
O 'daughter of Chaldæa,' thou no more enthroned shalt be,
For the desert and the wilderness alone shall tell of thee.
Though old Euphrates still rolls in his everlasting stream,
Thy brazen gates and golden halls, as though they ne'er had been;
Where stood thy massy tower-crowned walls, and palaces of pride,
The dragon and the wild beast now therein securely hide;
The 'besom of destruction' o'er thee hath swept its way
In wrath, because thine impious hand on God's Anointed lay."

columns and the massive walls and lay the whole structure on the ground; so the seed of Divine truth, inserted in the temple of error, of vice, of tyranny, of idolatry, of iniquity, shall spring and grow, and thrust and overturn, until the frowning walls have fallen and the structure of sin is a harmless ruin." —Pul. Com.

21, 22. (21)**doleful creatures,** howlers. **owls,** R. V., "ostriches." dwellers in ruins, **satyrs,**[a] probably demons are meant, the evil spirits whom Oriental peoples believe inhabit deserts and dangerous places. (22) **desolate houses,** R. V., "and wolves shall cry in their castles." **dragons,** R. V., "jackals." 'All these animals mentioned are really found there, on the soil of ancient Babylon." Comp. Rev. xviii. 3: Jer 1:39. Is. xxxiv. 14, 15. **time is near,** only a century and a half away. **prolonged,** by any reprieve or delay.

Babylon's Effacement.—When Babylon was first deserted of its inhabitants, the Persian kings turned it into a park for hunting, and kept their wild beasts there. When the Persian empire declined, the beasts broke loose so that, when Alexander the Great marched eastward, he found Babylon a perfect desert. He intended to restore Euphrates to its ancient channel, but the design not having been completed, the river overflowed its banks, and the greater part of that once celebrated city became a lake or pool of water. Theodorus who lived about 400 years after Christ, tells us that Babylon was the receptacle of snakes, serpents, and all sorts of noxious animals, so that it was dangerous to visit it. Benjamin of Toledo, a Jew who visited it in 1112, informs us, that few remains of it were left nor were there any inhabitants within many miles of it. Rawolffe, a German who traveled to the east in 1572 found it very difficult to discover the place on which it stood, nor could the neighboring inhabitants give him proper directions.—Whitecross.

[a] "The Moco, or Macacus Arabicus, is at present found in Babylonia." — Tristram.

"The essential idea is that Babylon should one day be inhabited exclusively by animals peculiar to the wilderness, implying that it should become a wilderness itself." — J. A. Alexander.

About B. C. 20 the site of Babylon was described by Strabo as a vast desolation.

CHAPTER THE FOURTEENTH.

1—3. This chapter contains a spirited triumphal song prepared for the hour of deliverance. vss. 1—4 are introductory and connect the song with the preceding prophecy. (1) **have mercy,** in restoring Israel after captivity, **yet choose,** yet again, "as if by a second act of electing grace." **strangers,**[a] "Proselytes," from among the heathen, will return with them, as Ruth did with Naomi, having learned from the exiles to believe in God. (2) **the people,** of Babylon. **for servants,** Ezr. ii. 65. captives,[b] the tables will be turned. (Comp. xlv. 14 and lvi. 6, 7.) This is retribution, but not necessarily revengeful. These masters will be inspired by a different spirit from their former oppressors. (3) **rest,** etc., in the gracious providence wh. brought Israel back to Canaan.

Without God:—Three ways a man may be said to be without God. 1. By profane atheism. 2. By false worship. 3. By want of spiritual worship. Great is the misery of those who are without God. God is a fountain of life; whoso is far from Him must perish.—Paul Bayne.

[a] "Tacitus, a heathen, attests the fact of numbers of Gentiles having become Jews in his time."—Fausset.

See Est. viii. 17; Ac. ii. 9—12.

[b] "There would be, a change of conditions bet. them and their oppressors."— J. A. Alexander.

"Thou hast made us for Thyself, O Lord: and our heart is restless until it rests in Thee." —St. Augustine.

"The rest of God is the rest of character and

of love; and the rest for man is the rest of character and of trust — of that character which grows up out of the root "trust." —Pul. Com.

"The law produces legal conviction and leads to despair; the gospel produces evangelical conviction and leads to hope." — A. J. Gordon.

"The law slays the sinner, grace slays the sin."— Ada R. Habershore.

Work of Christians.—You are forgiven and accepted. You owe all to Christ. You look forth from your position of safety, and behold a world lying in wickedness. You pity the sinful, as the Lord pitied you. Having been saved, you desire, as if by an instinct, to be a saviour. You begin. You grasp a fallen brother by the best band, a brother's love, and draw him to yourself that you may draw him to the Saviour. For a time you seem to have gained your brother. But after a while, at some unguarded moment, and through some unguarded opening, seven devils enter and dwell again in the partially reformed heart, and the last state of the man seems worse than the first. You are weary; but you must still work. Now is the time for toil: the rest remaineth. Two young men were disporting on the ice of a Scottish lake. One, approaching incautiously a treacherous spot, fell through. His companion came quickly to the rescue. Himself sometimes in the water and sometimes on the ice, he many times grasped the drowning man and drew him considerably above the surface; but each time the weight of the wet and paralysed body prevailed; each time it sunk again, until at last the worker's strength was exhausted, and the victim perished. Had you been there when for the last time that strong willing worker drew with all his might to save a sinking brother, and then lay down exhausted, leaving that brother to sink, you would have seen a workman wearied by his work. His hands were wearied with the greatness of his effort, and his heart was weary because the effort had failed. Such is the work to which Christians are called in the world, and such often, though not always, are the disappointments which they meet. At death the weariness of the worker will wholly cease.—Arnot.

4. proverb,[c] R. V., "parable," "The Hebrew word (mashal) is used in a variety of senses. Originally signifying a similitude, it came naturally to denote a popular proverb or gnomic saying, and finally acquired the sense of a satire or taunt-song, as here (Hab. ii. 6; Num. xxi. 27). In ancient Israel wit seems to have passed into sarcasm as readily as in more recent times."—Camb. Bib.[d] **"How hath the oppressor,"** the opening words of the Ode. It should have been translated in poetic form and must be studied as a whole. "Its perfection as a work of art, its picturesque imagery, the delicate and subtle vein of irony by which it is penetrated will not endure partial quotation or paraphrase."—Driver. **golden city ceased.**—Camb. B., How is the oppressor stilled—stilled the insolent rage!

c "The passage, vss. 4—23, moves in lengthened elegiac measure like a song of lamentation for the dead, and is full of lofty scorn."—Herder. "A son of derision about the representative of the Babylonish world-power cannot be appropriate while one is in its power. When one is out of reach of his arm, then the long pent-up resentment may find expression. —Nagelsbach.

d "The Bab. monarchy bade fair to be an absolute, universal, and perpetual one, and in these pretensions vied with the Almighty." —Mat. Henry.

"'Tis liberty, fair liberty alone,
That gives the fleeting flower of life its sweetness and perfume."

"They who live to the flesh are living crumbling lives, and are going towards dissolution all the time. It is only they who

Triumph Over Enemies.—"The song of Deborah and Barak" expresses the feelings which have usually animated the victors in national contests from the beginning of the world to the present day. The poems of Homer show us the great warriors of the heroic age giving the freest possible vent to their passions of scorn and hatred on such occasions. The heroes of Germany and Iceland indulge in the same strain. North American Indians are said to have been equally outspoken. The "natural man" would, beyond all question, on every occasion of the kind, give free and unfettered expression to his feelings of triumph and delight, nor would he see any reason for checking his feelings, or making any effort to moderate them. Insult and scorn are but indications of hate, or of hate mingled with contempt for those who have been proved weak, and so seem to be legitimately bestowed on beaten foes. But the Christian may hate no man, may despise no man, knowing that each human soul is in God's sight of priceless value. Consequently, although he may rejoice in victory, and even compose songs of triumph, he is bound to avoid anything like insultation over the defeated. They are his brethren, they are souls for whom Christ died; they may be among those with whom he will hold sweet converse in the world to come.—Pul. Com. Oppression and Its Downfall.—There is no deeper passion, nor one more just, than the hatred of tyranny, in the human breast. If we look at the question from the point of view of the tyrant himself, his lot is odious. Xenophon represents Hiero of Syracuse lamenting to the poet Simonides his unhappiness. He must surround himself with guards whom he cannot trust. Intimate friendship, such as blesses the meanest of his subjects, must be to him denied. He cannot close the sleepless eye of suspicion. Amiable he may be and sympathetic by nature, yet his heart may not expand in the chilling atmosphere which surrounds him. The cruel necessities of power may even render the lot of the oppressor less enviable than that of the oppressed. The heart of the people in every land and age cries out against tyranny as an abuse of the moral order, a violence done to the nature of things. And the true prophet, ever feeling in unison with that heart, translating its dim yearnings into articulate oracles, denounces and predicts the downfall of tyranny as inevitable, if the kingdom of Jehovah on earth is a reality. "There remaineth a rest for the people of God."—"The empire is peace." These words, once uttered vainly by a potentate in our time, and soon sternly refuted by the roar of artillery from around the walls of his fair city and from a score of battle-fields throughout his pleasant land, contain the policy of the kingdom of the Messiah. Selfishness, ambition, tyranny of individual wills,—these are the most constant causes of restlessness and war. When "all man's good" shall be "each man's rule," such evils will be impossible; the "unsuffering kingdom" of the Messiah will come, and the meek will inherit the earth.—Pul. Com.

live the life of faith that have before them 'the ages to come.' They are those who live toward happiness, singing more and more, rejoicing more and more, the circles and the waves of their experience running with wider and wider sweep."—Beecher.

5, 6. (5) **staff,** sign of imperial power. **rulers,** better, tyrants, Gesenius. (6) **continual stroke,** Heb. "stroke without removing." Oppression ever maintained, and never relieved,[a] **is persecuted .. hindereth,** R. V., "with a persecution that none restrained." Camb. Bib. prefers a rendering which preserves the balance of clauses:—

"That struck the peoples in anger,—
With incessant stroke:
That trod down the nations in wrath,—
With unrelenting tread."

Sin Makes No True Friends.—Adversity is the test of faithfulness. Until the dark hour comes we cannot be quite sure whether our acquaintances are, or are not, our friends; then we "know the proof" of them. In the hour of Babylon's discomfiture there would be found "none to hinder" (ver. 6) her destruction. Her allies would fail her then; her dependencies would make no effort to save her; she would be "alone when she fell" (Eccles. iv. 10). The "friends" whom sinners make are not "friends in deed," for they will not prove to be "friends in need." If financial ruin, the loss of his good name, overwhelming bereavement, protracted sickness, the near prospect of death, should overtake a man, it is not to his ungodly companions he would resort, for to them he would look in vain. The man of God will not be without those who will graciously and generously intervene to "hinder" the calamity which impends, to alleviate the sorrows which are wounding the spirit.—Pul. Com. The False Staff.—Wicked men often have such power over others that they can use them for their evil schemes, and bribe them so that they tell no tales that shall bring shame and dishonor. But this does not last. Some "revealing hour" comes. The man that has been "lifted up" is laid low; he can no longer use his old power. Lost character has left him discrowned. Even worldly men will not trust him now. The Josephs are honored; the Daniels are trusted. The Mordecais are doomed. No staff will support in life or death but the old staff: "Thy rod and thy staff they comfort me."

[a] Kingdoms won by violence are only maintained in subjection by continuous tyranny.

"As for him who smote the nations in wrath, his stroke shall not be removed: he that ruled the nations in anger is persecuted and cannot hinder it." —Trans. by Junius.

"There appears to exist a greater desire to live long than to live well! Measure by man's desires, he cannot live long enough; measure by his good deeds, and he has not lived long enough; measure by his evil deeds, and he has lived too long."—Zimmerman.

7, 8. (7) **The whole earth,** regarded as put in fear as long as Bab. remained in power; able to sing when Bab. was destroyed. (8) **fir trees,**[b] before conquering armies forests are razed. And great nations despoil them for their own adornment, for palaces and temples and navies. Therefore at the fall of Babylon the very trees sing for joy.[c]

"At thy fate the pine-trees rejoice
And Lebanon's cedars, saying:
No woodman comes up against us
Since thou art laid low."—Polychr. B.

Sympathy of Mind with Nature.—Socrates said that "trees did not

[b] "One of the most characteristic trees of Lower Lebanon, the Aleppo pine, which is inferior only to the cedar." — Tristram.

[c] For Assyria as a cedar, see Eze. xxxi. 3.

"I am glad to think
I am not bound to make the wrong go right,
But only to discover and to do.
With cheerful heart, the work that God appoints."
—Jean Ingelow.

teach him anything, but man." Let us adapt the saying to religious feeling. The trees will yield no oracles but those which have been first heard in the inmost conscience. And if there are times when they seem to whisper of gladness, or to smile and clap their hands for joy, it is because God has already opened a fountain of perennial trust and hope within the soul. Then "fruitful trees and all cedars" will praise the Lord, when the heart is filled with praise. "The outward face of nature is a religious communication to those who come to it with the religious element already in them, but no man can get a religion out of the beauty of nature. Those who have first made the knowledge of themselves and their own souls their care, its glory has ever turned to light and hope. They have read in nature an augury and a presage; they have found in it a language and a revelation."—Mozley.

b "Some of its tenants, once mighty monarchs, are represented by a bold personification as rising from their seats in astonishment at the descent among them of the humbled king of Babylon." —Fausset.

9. **Hell,** translate "Sheol beneath." The prophet "accompanies in thought the shade of the king of Babylon as it journeys to the Underworld, and imagines the ironical greeting which there meets it from the lips of the other kings—still, as on earth, supposed to be invested with the panoply of state."—Driver. **is moved,** with expectancy. Those inhabiting it join in the joy at thy humiliation. **stirreth up,** urges all to unite in the triumph over thee.[b] **the dead,** R. V., marg. "the shades." Heb. Rephaim. **from their thrones,** an indication of the idea that in the future life men continue their political and social relations, uninterrupted by death.

c "Who would have thought it? It is what thou thyself didst not expect it would ever come to when thou wast so hard upon us. Thou that didst rank thyself among the immortal gods, art thou come to take thy fate among us poor mortal men?"—M. Henry.

The Contemplation of Past Greatness.—From the depth of sorrow men learn to measure past blessings, from the lowest point of abject humiliation the height of previous greatness. Two things, in all history, in all legend, in the experience of daily life, impress the imagination, and through the imagination the moral conscience—the rise of the obscure into glory, and the fall of the great into ignominy. Such changes hint at a great law, the principle of which is one, the effects of whose operation are dual and diverse. The King of Babel had been as the morning star, the type of the Orient in all its splendor of intellectual light, heralding the dawn and the onward march of the sun. How true a proposition is it in reference to human culture, "Light comes from the East"! Babylonia was an early centre of such culture; and dimly through the records of the past we may there discern all those passions and energies at work in that great kingdom which lead first to external greatness, then to moral corruption, finally to external ruin.

d "His body, once so dearly cared for and couched, has now maggots for a couch, and worms for a covering." —Nagelsbach.

10, 11. (10) **Art thou,** etc.,[c] the language of wondering surprise. "There is uncommon beauty in the brevity of this address." (11) **Thy pomp,** etc., this is the continuance of the song, not the exclamation of the "shades" in Hades. Pomp is the expression and display of pride. **grave,** better, "Sheol," the place of departed spirits. **viols,** the music of the courts. **worms,**[d] "his lot is far worse than that of other potentates. No kingly throne is reserved for him in Sheol, but as one who has been denied honorable burial on earth (vs. 19) he is laid in the 'recesses of the pit' (vs. 15) and makes his bed in corruption."—Camb. Bib.

The best Christian will be the best citizen. He who is most loyal to God's law will be most obedient to the law of the land.—H. B. Grose.

Proud Monuments (vs. 11).—While some have studied monuments, others have studiously declined them, and some have been so vainly boisterous, that they durst not acknowledge their graves; wherein Alaricus seems most subtle, who had a river turned to hide his bones at the bottom. Even Sylla, that thought himself safe in his urn, could not prevent revenging tongues, and stones thrown at his monument. Happy are they whom privacy makes innocent, who deal so with men in this world, that they are not afraid to meet them in the next; who, when they die, make no commotion among the dead, and are not touched with that poetical taunt of Isaiah. Pyramids, arches, obelisks, were but the irregularities of vainglory, and wild enormities of ancient magnanimity. But the most magnanimous resolution rests in the Christan religion, which trampleth upon pride, and sits on the neck of ambition, humbly pursuing that infallible perpetuity, unto which all others must diminish their diameters, and be poorly seen in angles of contingency. To subsist in lasting monuments, to live in their productions, to exist in their names and predicament of chimeras, was large satisfaction unto old expectations, and made one part of their Elysium. But all this is nothing in the metaphysics of true belief. To live, indeed, is to be again ourselves, which

"A man goes to bed willingly and cheerfully, because he believes he shall rise again the next morning, and be renewed in his strength. Confidence in the resurrection would make us go to the grave as cheerfully as we go to our beds."

being not only a hope but an evidence in noble believers, 'tis all one to lie in St. Innocent's churchyard, as in the sands of Egypt: ready to be anything, in the ecstasy of being ever, and as content with six feet as the moles of Adrianus.—Sir T. Browne.

12. **Lucifer,** in his splendor he is likened to the morning star; which was worshipped by the Babylonians under the name of Istar. The translation "Lucifer" (light-bearer) is quite correct, and is needlessly abandoned by the R. V.—Camb. Bib. **cut down,** hewn down. The metaphor is here changed, and the fig. taken from the demolition of the Asherahs, or idols erected to Ashtoreth (i. e. Venus, or the morning star).[b] **didst weaken,** R. V., "didst lay low." Thou who didst prostrate others how prostrate art thou!

Lucifer.—There is no name we know so abused and misapplied as this truly beautiful name. Lucifer, the light-bringer, is the Latin equivalent of the Greek Phosphoros, which is used as a title of our blessed Lord in 2 Pet. i. 19, to which corresponds the phrase "bright and morning star" of the Book of Revelation (xxii. 16). Applied to Him the epithet is most expressive, for He is the true Light who enlightens every man who cometh into the world, and who has shed a flood of light upon life and immortality. But, unfortunately, the name has been given, almost appropriated, in the first place, to Satan, the "prince of darkness," who is the enemy and destroyer of light in the souls of men. The misapplication and degradation of a noble name arose, in the first instance, from a misinterpretation of Isa. xiv. 12, "How art thou fallen from heaven, O brilliant one [or bright star], son of the morning!" Our translators have used the word Lucifer here, and some expositors referred the whole passage, which is a highly poetical and beautiful description of the king of Babylon, to the devil; and so in common speech the evil one, who has no light in him, has been named Lucifer.

13—15. (13) **exalt .. stars,** fig. for supreme and universal dominion. "The Bab. thought the several constellations to be connected with particular nations, over whose destiny they dominated."—Spk. Com. **mount,** etc., "an allusion to Babylonian mythology, referred to in Assyrian inscriptions, the Mt. Aralu where the great gods assemble."—Camb. Bib. **sides .. north,** R. V., "the uttermost parts of the north."[a] (14) **like .. High,** this was the height of presumption and wickedness.[b] "In the wall-sculptures of the Assyr. palaces, the king has the symbols of deity assigned to him." (15) **hell,** "Sheol." **sides,** the most dismal parts of the land of darkness. These apparently are reserved for those who have not obtained honorable burial. Comp. vss. 18—20.

Christianity's Work of Destruction.—History enables us to look back and to measure events by the right standard. Regarded in this light, history is a continual testimony to the almightiness and the all-goodness of heaven. Where are the enemies of the faith? Mighty men have risen to put down the Cross: where are they to-day? Ponderous works have been written in order to disprove the Christian argument, or to divest it of its moral appeals: where are those works? Negation builds no churches. Destruction can point to no temple of paradise, no asylum of protection, no Bethlehem of promise. Christianity itself has a work of destruction to do; but it would be comparatively powerless if it did not connect its constructive with its destructive vocation. The Son of man is not come to destroy men's lives but to save them. When Christ kills, He kills that He may make alive. This is the difference between Christianity and its opposing theories; the theories live in opposition only, but Christianity lives in positive and helpful faith.—Peop. Bib.

16, 17. (16) The scene now changes from Sheol to the earth, and the dead body of the king is seen on the battlefield. **shall narrowly look,** scrutinizing the body, "Is this really the king?" **consider,**[c] thoughtfully, feeling its significance. (17) **opened .. prisoners,** R. V., "that let not loose his prisoners to their home?" i. e. that they might die in their own land and be honorably buried there.

Opposition to God, of No Avail.—The mightiest power is weaker than weakness itself when pitted against the throne of God. Enemies appear to be great in the distance. They are actually great when they are looked at simply within their own limits: see what learning they have; see what iron instruments the soldiers bring to the field of war;

"The appellation may have been applied to the king of Babylon, on account of the worship of the celestial bodies by the Chaldaeans, and bec. they claimed to be under their special protection." — Wordsworth.

b "These idols seem in some cases to have had horns, representing prob. rays of light." — Spk. Com.

"Ambition has but one reward for all:
A little power, a little transient fame,
A grave to rest in and a fading name."
—W. Winter.

a "The starry region round the North Pole, high above the earth, always visible and luminous, is a natural type of the heaven of glory, the special abode of the Most High." — Birks.

b Da. iii. 1, 13—15, viii. 8, 9—11.

"The Assyrian monarch was a thorough Eastern despot, ... rather adored as a god than feared as a man."— Layard.

"Be always displeased at what thou art, if thou desire to attain to what thou art not; for where thou hast pleased thyself, there thou abidest."— Quarles.

c Ps. iii. 7.

"The man who seeks one thing in life, and but one,

May hope to achieve it before life be done;
But he who seeks all things, wherever he goes,
Only reaps from the hopes which around him he sows,
A harvest of barren regrets."
—OwenMeredith.

a Diodorus says that the Egyptians paid far more attention to the dwellings of the dead than of the living.

For the disgrace of not being buried, compare 1 Ki. xiii. 22; 2 Chr. xxi. 20, xxxiv. 24.

b "He, the conqueror, was cast away into the heap, on the field of battle." —Spk. Com.

c "This prophecy was minutely fulfilled. On entering the city, the army of Cyrus marched straight to the palace, and meeting the king, who was coming out sword in hand, they slew him, and put all who followed him to the sword; and though Xenophon specially notices the permission given to bury the dead, he takes no notice whatever of the royal corpse." —Henderson.

a Strabo states that enormous hedgehogs were found in the islands of the Euphrates.

b "Babylon lay low, so that when it was deserted, and no care taken to drain the land, it soon became pools of water, standing noisome puddles, as unhealthful as they were unpleasant." —M. Henry.

see what mighty captains ride forth as if plumed already with victory before the battle begins; yet hear this voice of sarcasm, which says to them when they are stretched out upon the field of war, "Is this the man that made the earth to tremble?" How small he is, how weak, how utterly helples now! And this is the fate of all who set themselves to counterwork the purposes of Providence.—Peop. Bib.

18—20. (18) **lie in glory,** R. V., "sleep in glory," embalmed and in a grand tomb. **house,** or mausoleum.[a] (19) **cast out,** unburied. **of thy grave,** from being laid in thy grave. **branch,** or useless sucker, wh. the gardener cuts down, and flings away. **and as .. slain,** R. V., "clothed with the slain,"[b] i. e. surrounded by and covered with the slain. **stones .. pit,** i. e. those ordinarily slain in battle are covered with stones, but thou art exposed, open to all insult.[c] (20) **shalt not be joined,** etc., i. e. with the kings and nobles who have fallen in battle. **because .. land,** not a true king, therefore, but a tyrant even to your own people and hated by them. **slain thy people,** by thine ambitious wars. **seed,** or dynasty of the prostrate king. The entire dynasty was destroyed. The name of the godless race was extinguished.

The Seed of Evildoers.—As a matter of fact, we see that a wicked course of life is regarded as a shame. It is held up as a beacon to be avoided, whilst the career of the good is held up as a model to be followed. History is full of examples of men whose names are held in universal detestation, notwithstanding their connection with ingenuity, wealth and power. Each of us knows how well the fact is proved by myriads of examples in social life. A persistently wicked course is known to be a blighted one, and any attempt to invest it with glory or renown is felt to be wrong. We recoil even from the thought that it should be possible for such a course to command the homage of men. If it were possible for wrongdoing to gain for itself imperishable renown, we might tremble for the safety of those principles of righteousness and truth which have always been regarded as the main support and stay of good men. Reckless folly and wild presumption would become exalted and enthroned, and we might well shudder at the possibility that, under the attractions of successful wickedness, men would rush in masses, and bow down to Evil, declaring it to be their Good. This abandoned idolatry, this deep depravity, is now reached only in isolated cases, and such are regarded even by godless men as deplorable and hopeless. It is a hopeful fact that evildoers have to carry on much of their work in the dark, for it is a sure token that, as the light widens and deepens, the works of darkness must fall; their covering will be removed, and their shelter will be gone.—Hom. Com.

21—23. (21) **slaughter,** or a slaughter-house. This is a Divine charge to the Medes and Persians. **for his children,** the spirit which has made such tyranny possible must not be reproduced. **not rise,** to take their father's place. (22) **cut off,** etc., wholly preventing the restoration of the dynasty. **nephew,** R. V., "son's son." "After the storming of Babylon by the Medes, the new Babylonian kingdom and royal house established by Nebopolassar vanished entirely from history. The last child was slain as the child of conspirators."—Delitzsch. (23) **it,** the site of Babylon. **bittern,**[a] R. V., "porcupine." **pools of water,** by neglect of the canals, and flooding of the Euphrates.[b] **sweep it,** i. e. sweep it away.

Force of Heredity.—Though there is a hereditary law in the matter both of evil and of good, it must not be understood that a man is hopelessly condemned because his ancestors were evil, or that a man is necessarily saved because his ancestors were good. The general law may be modified by particular instances. If any man, looking over a long list of progenitors, cannot find a good name amongst them, that is no reason why he himself should not repent and pray. On the other hand, a man may look through a long family record adorned with illustrious names, yet if he himself be not faithful, if he himself be not in Christ by the power of the soul's trust, wrought by the energy of the Holy Ghost, his family record will stand him in no good stead in the day of judgment. The renown of the hypocrite is a poor reward. The blessing that rests upon the righteous is itself of the quality of heaven.—Peop. Bib. The Overthrow of Evil.—It is a blessed thing to be engaged on the side of righteousness. First and most, because it is the cause of God, of man, of truth, on which we are leagued; and also because we are sure to win at last. The wise and the good may meet with many a check, but they will gain the victory; the unholy and the evil-minded may snatch many an advantage, but the end shall be a miserable disaster, an utter overthrow, a dragon-haunted desert. Let us see to it that we are fighting on God's side, and, once sure that we are, let us strike our blow for truth and wisdom, confident that, however strong and high stand the towers of sin, its citadel will be taken, its day will descend into darkness, its million-peopled streets become a doleful desert.

24, 25. "Vss. 24—27 are an announcement of Jehovah's purpose to destroy the Assyrians on the soil of Canaan. In spite of the absence of a title these verses cannot without violence be explained as a continuation of the oracle on Babylon. They bear every evidence of being a genuine prophecy of Isaiah; and both in form and substance they shew an obvious resemblance to those of ch. x. 5 ff. and ch. xviii. Some critics, indeed, regard them as a misplaced fragment of one or other of these chapters. Without going so far as this we may at least with some confidence assign the passage to the same period of Isaiah's ministry, probably the early years of Sennacherib's reign."—Camb. Bib. (24) **purposed,** in the great providential plan. (25) **break,** etc., by a sudden calamity. **mountains,** the army was destroyed on the hills near Jerus. **his yoke,** that laid by Assyria on Judah. "From the blow inflicted on Sennacherib Assyria never rallied."

The Strong Assurances of Jehovah.—He is represented here and in other passages as taking an oath that he will fulfill his word. But in such oaths he can appeal to no mightier name, he can invoke no power more awful than his own. Homer makes Zeus swear by the Styx, the dark river of the Underworld. And Zeus is himself subject to necessity, to fate. But the God of the Hebrews comprises in himself all the associations of woeful necessity, of irresistible fate; in a word, of law, of intelligence at one with will, of will equal to the execution of all the designs of intelligence. Where men are weak it is that the brain is separated from the hand and the foot. The thoughts that rise before them, they either cannot or they dare not translate immediately into fact. A chain of means, of secondary causes, lies between them and their ends. And so we have the great thinkers who cannot act, and the great actors who fail in thought. Magnificent poets, philosophers, dreamers, on the one side; on the other, magnificent conquerors—Alexanders, Napoleons; both stupendous failures. In God are united omniscience and omnipotence—the All-Thinker, the All-Doer. His purposes are equivalent to deeds; his deeds are living and visible thoughts.—Pul. Com.

26—28. (26) **whole earth,** regarded as conquered, and put under tribute by Assyr.; all shall be delivered, as Judah will be soon. **the hand .. stretched out,** a return in thought and phrase to ch. v. 25:ix. 12, etc., suggesting the place where these prophecies belong. (27) **disannul it,** with ref. to Sennac.'s taunts, and Babylon's pride. Delitzsch explains the place of this prophecy (22—27) by saying, "At a time when the prophecy against Assyria had actually been fulfilled, the prophet attached it to the still unfulfilled prophecy against Babylon to give a pledge of the fulfillment of the latter." (28) This verse and following four are an oracle against Philistia.[a] **year .. died,** prob. B. C. 727. The Philistines were finally subdued by Hezekiah.[b]

Immutability of God's Counsels (vs. 27).—We will consider this subject—I. In a general view: the Scriptures continually represent God as having ordained everything from before the foundation of the world; His decrees to whatever they relate are unchangeable. II. In reference to the particular points specified in the context. 1. The deliverance of God's people; 2. The destruction of His enemies. Apply:—(1) On what a slender foundation are the hopes of the generality fixed; (2) On what an immovable foundation does the believer stand.—C. Simeon.

The Immutable Counsel of Jehovah.—Assyria and Babylon destroyed, heathendom must vibrate through all its extent, and totter to its fall. About a thousand years later, and we find Rome shaking beneath that outstretched hand. We may see the mementoes of that shock to-day, in the ruins of the Palatine and the Forum and the Sacred Way. Yet a

"Truth is forced
To manifest itself through falsehood; whence divorced
By the excepted eye, at the rare season, for
The happy moment, truth instructs us to abhor
The false, and prize the true, obtainable thereby."

"It is some compensation for great evils that they enforce great lessons."
—Bovee.

"Evil events from evil causes spring."
—Aristophanes.

"To the estrangement of the soul from God the best of theology traces the ultimate cause of sin. Sin is simply apostacy from God, unbelief in God."
—Drummond.

"We are ruined, not by what we really want, but by what we think we do; therefore never go abroad in search of your wants. If they be real wants, they will come home in search of you; for he that buys what he does not want, will soon want what he cannot buy."—Colton.

[a] 2 Chr. xxviii. 18—21.

[b] 2 Ki. xviii. 8.

"Consider what the hand is to man: it is the chief instrument by which he executes his purposes, — farmer, builder, artist, author, etc.; and by the hand of God is meant His executive force in all its varied forms. God has the means of doing all His will, and

He is not an unconcerned spectator of human affairs — these truths inspire God's people with hope, courage, and joy; and they ought to inspire with terror all who are in rebellion against Him."

"The perfection which the creatures possess they derive from God, and it is faintly shadowed forth after its archetype. The more of it they possess, the nearer they are to God and have the greater likeness to Him (Ro. xi. 35, 36; 1 Cor. iv. 7; Ac. xvii. 28, 29; 2 Cor. iii. 18; 2 Pe. i. 4)."—Arminius.

thousand years, and again she shakes, this time to her inmost conscience, beneath that hand, that voice of judgment. At the Reformation it might seem that the Almighty was about to make a short work in the earth. But a thousand years are in his sight but a day. "The mills of God grind slowly, yet they grind exceeding small." Let us remember that the great cycles of history are repeated in small in the round of each man's life. The great world, the macrocosmos, is mirrored in the microcosmos, the small world of each conscience. Above every one of us the hand is outstretched—shall it be to bless or to curse? "To-day if ye will hear His voice, harden not your hearts."—Pul. Com. God's purpose of restoration will one day be accomplished. There may be many obstacles in the way. Difficulties may, to the eye of human calculation, seem actually insurmountable; the estimable forces of truth may appear unequal to cope with the overwhelming agencies of error and evil. But this our great hope is not a bold enterprise of man; it is the purpose of the living God, the Lord of hosts. "His hand is stretched out, and who shall turn it back?" Let the Christian worshipper offer expectant prayer; let the Christian workman go up to his post with holy confidence; for the purpose of God, though it be long delayed, shall assuredly be fulfilled.

29, 30. (29) Each verse of this oracle forms a strophe of four lines, as in vss. 30, 31, below. **whole Palestina,**[a] R. V., "O Philistia, all of thee," alluding to the principalities into which Philistia was divided (comp. Is. ix. 8). **is broken,** rejoicing over the disaster to Israel is premature. That rod which has stricken Philistia before is to be re-established in more terrible form. **serpent,** prob. fig. for Uzziah, who put Philistia under tribute. **cockatrice,** R. V., "basilisk," fig. for Hezekiah, as a more overwhelming enemy. **his fruit,** or descendant, i. e. Uzziah's. (30) Trans.:—

> "The poor will feed on my meadows,
> And the needy will lie down securely;
> But thy seed will I kill with famine
> And thy remnant will I slay."—Polychr. B.

[a] Josephus calls the country occupied by the Philistines, Palaistine.

" Mythology is not religion. It may rather be regarded as the ancient substitute, the poetical counterpart, for dogmatical theology."—Hare.

"According to my view of the Unity of the Divine nature, God is one, as we meet Him in the Old Testament and the Oldest; in the New and the Newest. There are four Testaments: an Oldest and an Old, a New and a Newest. The Oldest Testament is the Nature of Things. The newest is Christ's continued life in the present influences of the Holy Spirit. The oldest and the newest are unwritten; the old and new are written; but the voices of the four are one."—Joseph Cook.

Note on vs. 29.—In Egypt, and other Oriental countries, a serpent was the common symbol of a powerful monarch; it was embroidered on the robes of princes, and blazoned on their diadem, to signify their absolute power and invincible might, and that as the wound inflicted by the basilisk is incurable, so the fatal effects of their displeasure were neither to be avoided nor endured. These are the allusions involved in the address of the Prophet to the irreconcilable enemies of his nation.—Paxton.

Death of an Individual.—The wicked nation, or the unprincipled party, or the unscrupulous man that indulges a feeling of security because some strong opponent is dead may, probably will, find itself (himself) miserably disappointed. The resources of a righteous providence are not exhausted, though a very pillar of justice be fallen. Or, on the other hand, the righteous may fear too much from the death of a powerful friend. Will not the good cause perish now that the tongue of its most able advocate is silent in death? Christianity did not perish with the departure of Christ or with the death of the apostles. The Father of spirits will not let righteousness expire for want of righteous men, whom he can create and endow and send forth into the world.—Pul. Com.

31, 32. (31)—

> "Howl, O gate! Cry, O city!
> Faint in all thy borders Philistia!
> For out of the North comes the smoke of the foe,
> And no straggler is found in his levies."—Polychr. B.

whole Palestina, R. V., "O Philistia, all of thee," i. e. let the cities and walls cry out and the whole country grow faint before the approaching doom. **north,** reference to the Assyrians. **smoke,** of signal fires, calling hosts together. **none .. times,** i. e. there shall be no stragglers or unwilling ones, when the call is made to muster for attack on thee. (32) "The oracle ends, in a manner characteristic of Isaiah, with a piece of practical advice to the political leaders of the state. Some words have probably dropped out of the first half of the verse." **the messengers of the nation,** "are no doubt Philistine envoys endeavoring to negotiate an alliance with Judah. They are probably to be regarded as actually waiting in Jerusalem while the court deliberates on the expediency of joining the rebellion. The prophet's answer is an unhesitating refusal."—Camb. B. **founded Zion,** the source of its strength is in God, not in its rocky fortresses nor its armies. **and the poor .. in it,** R. V., "and in her shall the afflicted of his people take refuge."

Strength and Mission of the Church (vs 32).—All around are the evidences of the existence of the Church: what destiny there may yet be in store for the Church we do not know. I. The strongest, most fundamental title of protection is creation; no one frames an object in order to destroy it. Behold how God has loved the world, but to the Church His honor is pledged, its ultimate perfection is the reward of the sorrows of the Lord. II. How does the Church fulfill the promise that she should be the guide and friend of the poor? She is one vast institute for the benefit of the poor, the truths she teaches just those the poor need.—Archer Butler.

The Church's Mission.—It is in meeting his sorrow with tidings of glory to come, in brightening the gloom of his humble home with the hallowed light of eternity, in soothing his days of hard and heavy toil with her peaceful Sabbaths, in watching over his bed of sickness with a patience as unwearied as if his poor chambers were gorgeous with gilded ceilings and silken tapestry; it is in these things that the Church carries on that loveliest attribute of Her Lord, "Thou hast been a strength to the poor, a strength to the needy in his distress."—Archer Butler.

"There are a good many real miseries in life that we cannot help smiling at, but they are the smiles that make wrinkles and not dimples." — Holmes.

CHAPTER THE FIFTEENTH.

1, 2. An oracle on Moab occupies chs. xv.—xvi., of which ch. xv. describes the distress of Moab. (1) **Moab,**[a] this country had prob. made common cause with Israel and Syria against Assyria; consequently it incurred the vengeance of Assyria. **because,** better, surely. **Ar,** or the city, i. e. the capital of Moab. **laid waste,** comp. Je. xlviii. **brought to silence,** R. V., "brought to naught." **Kir,** prob. Kir-chareseth.[b] Or the word may mean a citadel. It was, in fact, the chief fortress of Moab. There is still a fortification there. (2) The best translation is:—

"Dibon's people go up to the sanctuaries to weep,
On Nebo and on Medebah Moab wails,
On all heads baldness, every beard shorn."—Polychr. B.

Dibon, a few miles S. of the Amon would be first to hear the news. **Nebo,** a mountain, and **Medebah,** a hill on which are still the ruins of a temple. **baldness,** the greatest mark of sorrow and mortification.[c]

Idolatry.—1. "God's many," true God—one. 2. Idolatry not confined to heathens, or worship of wood or stone idols (1 Cor. x. 14; Col. iii. 5; Phil. iii. 9). 3. Whatever, other than God, is enshrined in the heart as the chief object of affection is an idol.

"We do not bend the adoring knee
To demon gods 'neath forest tree;
And when the fair round moon returns,
No heart in votive rapture burns;
But wrong desire, and cherish'd sin,
And selfish care enshrin'd within,
And angry passions, prompt to wake,—
These are the idols Christians make.
The great Lord God enthron'd on high
He sees the soul's idolatry;
He claims the first love of our heart,
Nor takes what is but His in part."
—Verses for Holy Seasons.

[a] Comp. 1 Sa. xiv. 47; 2 Sa. viii. 2; 2 Ki. i. 1, iii. 4, 5; 2 Chr. xx. 1—30.

[b] Isa. xvi. 7; 2 Ki. iii. 25.

[c] Isa. iii. 24, xxii. 12; Am. viii. 10.

"Ponder deeply upon the moral of Night; the darkness should instruct us, remind us of our exhaustion, helplessness, and dependence upon others for security and rest, and should above all things lead us to put our confidence in him to whom the darkness and the light are both alike." — Peop. Bib.

"I'll give thee misery, for here she dwells; this is her house, where the sun never dawns; the bird of night sits screaming o'er the roof: grim spectres sweep along the horrid gloom, and nought is heard but wailings and lamentings." — Rowe.

"There's nothing bright above, below, from flowers that bloom to stars that glow, but in its light my soul can see some feature of the Deity."—Anon.

"I never knew a man in all my life who could not bear another's misfortunes perfectly like a Christian." — Pope.

3, 4. (3) **tops,** flat roofs. **weeping,** "running down with tears." (4) **Heshbon,** an Amorite city, twenty miles E. of Jordan. It had been taken by Moab after the carrying away of Israel. **Elealeh,** near Heshbon. **Jahaz,** "this site where Sihon gave battle to the Israelites (Nu. xxi. 23) has not been identified."—Camb. B. **therefore,** i. e. bec. of the sudden overthrow of their cities. **his life .. unto him,** R. V., "his soul trembleth within him," i. e. the soul of Moab.

Misery and Happiness.—The misery of human life is made up of large masses, each separated from the other by certain intervals. One year the death of a child; years after, a failure in trade; after another longer or shorter interval, a daughter may have married unhappily;—in all but the singularly unfortunate, the integral parts that compose the sum total of the unhappiness of a man's life are easily counted and distinctly remembered. The happiness of life, on the contrary, is made up of minute fractions; the little soon-forgotten charities of a kiss, a smile, a kind look, a heartfelt compliment in the disguise of playful raillery, and the countless other infinitesimals of pleasurable thought and genial feeling.—Coleridge. National Distress Leads Men to God.—Like the voyager, men can easily dismiss the thought of God when, for long times together, seas are calm and heavens are clear; but when the skies are black, and the wild waves shake the frail ship, and fear whitens every face, the soul begins to cry for a sight of God and a touch of His protecting hand. We are with God as our little children are with their mothers. They run about and play, taking little heed of her, until the head aches, and the pulse is high, and pain wearies; and then there is nobody in all the world will do but their mother. National distress brings nations back to the thought and love of God. The atheist, the agnostic, and the secularist have their chance when the sun shines; nobody wants such vain helpers when the tempests rage. Then nobody will do but the God of our fathers.—Pul. Com.

5—7. (5) **My heart shall cry,** even the prophet is moved with sympathy for Moab, with whom Israel was often on friendly terms. **unto Zoar,** in the remote south. **his fugitives .. Luhith,** R. V., "her nobles flee into Zoar, to Eglath-shelishiyah; for by the ascent of Luhith," etc. **Luhith,** a mountain-ascent in Moab. **Horonaim,**[a] near Zoar. (6) **Nimrim,** the northern part of the country, which is overrun with the enemy and destroyed. (7) **brook,** etc. (Jer. xlviii. 36). "The fugitives have now reached the border of their own land, and prepare to cross into Edom. The boundary between the two countries was formed by the Wadi el-Asha ('valley of water-pits,' the scene of the miracle in 2 Ki. iii. 16 ff.). In all probability this Wadi is identical with the brook of the willows here mentioned."—Camb. Bib.

The Weeping Willow.—The Salix Babylonica, or the willow of Babylon, or our English weeping willow, is a native of the Levant, the coast of Persia, and other places in the East. The manner of its introduction into England is curious, and the story is as follows:—Pope, the celebrated poet, having received a present of Turkey figs, observed a twig of the basket, in which they were packed, putting out a shoot. This twig he planted in his garden; it soon became a fine tree; and from this stock all our willows have descended.

8, 9. (8) **Eglaim,** Eze. xlvii. 10. **Beer-elim,** the well of the princes. (9) **Dimon,** prob. another form of Dibon. **more,** i. e. additions of the blood of the slain. **lions,** "an enigmatical description of a conquering foe, either Judah (Delitzsch), comp. Gen. xlix. 9., or more probably (see xiv. 29; xxi. 16, 17; xvi. 14) the Assyrians" (Cheyne and Camb. Bib).

Despair the Desperation of the Soul.—
I can grapple
With certain ill, and bid it strike, and shrink not;
Woo danger with my sword, and dally with her
Like some pale bride, in battle won and ravish'd;
Making that pastime which is others' toil.
Give peril but a name, and I will seek it
Front join'd to front. But when the laden bosom,
With its own weight oppress'd, sees not its foe,
And struggles with it knows not what,—some phantom

[a] The word means the two poles.

"If one thing more than another is impressed on devout minds by a review of life, it is the marvelous way in which Divine wisdom has found the best, most adapted forms for judgment and chastisement to take. Chastisement sent by the Divine Father is always precisely corrective of the evil which has called for it, and always precisely corrective to the individual and to the particular nation." — Pul. Com.

"All things have their end;
Temples and cities, which have diseases like to man,
Must have like death that we have."

Like that which rides the sleeper in his dreams,
Stifling all utterance, benumbing motion,
And stagnating the life-blood at the heart,—
Then I am but a coward.
Fear, like a warder, sentinels my steps,
And haunts me in a myriad shapes—not one,
Yet all without a shape, and undefined.—Smedley.

CHAPTER THE SIXTEENTH.

1, 2. (1) **Send ye .. wilderness,** R. V., "send ye the lambs for the ruler of the land from Sela which is toward the wilderness." **lamb,** i. e. the tribute-lambs, which the prophet now exhorts Moab to pay to Judah, thus acknowledging allegiance and winning protection. **the ruler,** i. e. the king of Judah. **Sela,** or Petra. (2) **as bird .. nest,** R. V., "as wandering birds, as a scattered nest." **wandering bird,** "When the robber came to rifle their nest, they flew away. As soon as he retired, they came back, tho' timorously, to their old homes."—Spk. Com. **fords of Arnon,** their old neighborhood before they fled.

Demand of Tribute.—"Send ye the lambs of the prince of the land from Sela desert-wards to the mount of the daughter of Zion." In former days Mesha, the King of Moab, was said to be a "sheep-master," and he rendered a yearly tribute of a hundred thousand lambs, and a hundred thousand rams, with the wool, to the King of Israel till the death of Ahab (2 Kings iii. 4). What was then sent to Samaria must now be sent to Jerusalem. Under the form of this demand is signified an appeal to the people of Moab to submit to the house of David as their only hope of safety. Spiritually, the appeal may be construed as the call to nations and to men to submit to the spiritual rule of the Messiah, as anointed King and Saviour of the world.—Pul. Com.

3, 4. (3) **Take counsel .. execute judgment,** or apply counsel, arbitrate for us; Moab calls upon Judah "to adopt wise and effective measures to defend them from their enemies." **make .. shadow,** be to us as "the shadow of a great rock in a weary land." (4) **let mine outcasts,** etc. "Let the outcasts of Moab sojourn with thee" (as protected guests).—Camb. B. **extortioner,** "the rest of this verse cannot, in this form, be uttered by the Moabites. We may either suppose that a word meaning 'until' has been lost, or (better) with Hitzig take the clauses as protasis to vs. 5, 'for when the extortioner,' etc. This is perhaps preferable to regarding it as a reflection of the prophet himself."—Camb. Bible.

Promised Relief.—During the long and terrible siege of Lucknow, the garrison resolved never to surrender; and the women and children under their protection determined never to fall alive into the hands of the bloody Sepoys. They sent a messenger through the enemy's lines to Sir Henry Havelock, who was approaching for their deliverance. He returned the reply, "Hold out: I am coming and will be with you soon." With a small force he had to fight his way, and even to await re-enforcements; but the devoted Havelock kept his promise. At length the sound of his guns was heard, and he was soon hailed as the deliverer. Besieged soul, your resistless Lord sends you a similar answer. Hold out: He is coming to your relief.

5. **And in mercy,** if we follow Hitzig's view of vs. 4 this would be rendered "then in mercy." **the throne,**[a] etc., Polychr. B. translates:—

"The throne is established by kindness,
There sits upon it in faithfulness in David's tent
A judge who is both zealous for judgment and
Skilled in justice."

Infinitude of Mercy.—
Say not that any crime of man
Was e'er too great to be forgiven:
Can we within our little span,
Engrasp the viewless mind of heav'n?

"Though numberless drops be in the sea, yet, if one be taken out of it, it hath so much the less, though insensibly; but God, because He is infinite, can admit of no diminution. Therefore are men niggardly, because, the more they give, the less they have; but Thou, Lord, mayst give what Thou wilt without abatement of Thy store. Good prayers never come weeping home: I am sure I shall receive either what I ask or what I should ask."—Bp. Hall.

God presides over all things and over all men. He shapes our courses. He loves the world, and bears it in His arms as a mother carries her child in her bosom. He watches over it. He smiles at the fantasies of tyranny, and mocks the heirs of oppressors. He knows in His heart that the day is coming when every man shall sit under his own vine and fig tree, and none shall make him afraid.

"Self-trust is the essence of heroism."—Emerson.

[a] "He foresees and foretells the destruction of the Assyrian power, under Sennac., and the prosperous times of Hezekiah, to whom, after that great deliverance, many brought gifts (2 Chr. xxxii. 22, 23). Doubtless Moab was among the number, and was received into the protection of Judah."—Wordsworth.

"Mercy turns her back on the unmerciful."—Quarles.

Shall we attempt with puny force
To lash back ocean with a rod?
Arrest the planets in their course?
Or weigh the mercies of a God?

Our mercies, like ourselves, may be
Small, finite, and ungracious ever;
May spurn a brother's bended knee,—
But God forsakes the contrite, never!
Vast as Himself they shine above;
To eyes that look through sorrow's tear;
Great though the crime, great is the love,
If those who seek it are sincere.—Mackay.

6, 7. (6) **pride of Moab,** here the prophet seems to return from his vision of the future to the facts in the present. Moab, as yet, is proud, indeed, and boastful, but her lies will come to naught. Her professions will not deceive, Je. xlviii. 29.[b] **lies .. so,** R. V., "his boastings are naught," i. e. not according to fact.[c] (7) **Therefore,** on account of the refusal of the Jews to give an asylum to the Moabites. **howl for Moab,** i. e. the cry of lament from one locality meets that of the next.[d] **the foundations,** R. V., "the raisin cakes," made of compressed grapes and used at religious feasts (Hos. iii. 1 R. V.). "The word never means foundations." **Kir-hareseth,** one of the principal fortresses (ch. xv. 1; 2 Ki. iii. 25). **mourn .. stricken,** R. V., "shall ye mourn, utterly stricken," crushed and spirit-broken.

Moab (vss. 6—11).—I. The sins of Moab—pride, wrath, falsehood. II. The sorrows of Moab—destruction of its cities, desolation of the land. III. Pity for Moab—human, Divine.—Lyth.

Pride.—The trouble with us is, our proud hearts refuse to accept the position in which God's Word places us. It charges us with sin and corruption, and we would like to excuse ourselves and harp a little upon the dignity of human nature. God tells us that without Him we can do nothing. We are apt to think that by our reasoning powers and high culture, we can of ourselves do wonders. Not until we accept the position of sinfulness and weakness are we prepared to receive His blessing. —A. C. Dixon. Allow God to take His place in your heart and life. Luther often said to people when they came to him about difficulties, "Do let God be God." Let God be all in all, every day in your life, from morning to evening. No more say, "I and God;" let it be "God and I." God first and I second; God to lead, and I to follow; God to work all in me, and I to work out only what God works; God to rule, and I to obey. Even in that order there is a danger, for the flesh is so subtle, and one might begin to think, "It is God and I. Oh, what a privilege that I have such a partner!" There might be secret self-exaltation in associating God with myself. There is a more precious word still—"God and not I; not God first and I second; God is all, and I am nothing."—Andrew Murray.

8. fields .. languish, additional reason for lamentation. Not the towns only but the wheat-fields and vineyards are destroyed. Heshbon was the western part of the high table land E. of Jordan.[a] **Sibmah,** half a Roman mile from Heshbon town, and famous for its grapes. **lords .. heathen,** or the nations; a title claimed by the kings of Assyria.[b] **broken down,** R. V. margin, "Her choice plants did break down the Lords of the nations," so strong was this wine of Sibmah! (so Cheyne and Camb. Bib.). **they are come,** i. e. the choice plants of this vine "had reached to Jazer[c] on the north, strayed to the desert on the east, and passed to the (Dead) Sea on the west;" referring to the extensive cultivation of this famous vine.

Homiletic Hints.—I. Righteousness exalteth a nation. Happy is the people whose God is the Lord. II. Be thankful to Him by whom kings reign, for the civil and religious liberty of this land. III. Pray for the continued prosperity of this country. IV. Seek to increase the moral power of the nation by our individual piety. V. Fenced cities fail as places of refuge: the Lord is a strong tower, into which the righteous run and are safe. VI. Have you made Him your refuge?

---

[b] Is. xiii. 11, xxv. 9—12.

[c] "His boastful, lying, treacherous, random talk has no reality in it." — Wordsworth.

[d] "Or, the survivors for those who are lost."—Spk. Com.

"Pride lives with all; strange names our rustics give to helpless infants, that their own may live; pleased to be known, they'll some attention claim, and find some by-way to the house of fame." — G. Crabbe.

"When the weak head with strongest bias rules,
Is Pride, the never - failing vice of fools."
—Pope.

"Pride hath no other glass
To show itself, but pride; for supple knees
Feed arrogance, and are the proud man's fees."
—Shakespeare.

[a] "The traveler Legh brought so-called Heshbon wheat to England having 84 grains in the ear, wh. weighed four times as much as an English ear of wheat." — Nagelsbach.

[b] On the inscription at Khorsabau, Sargon says: "The gods Assur, Nebo, and Merodach, have given me the lordship of the nations."

[c] The ancient capital of the Ammonites, 15 miles from Heshbon.

"The call to meet some need comes in an hour that we think not. The door of

Ratification of the Prophecy.—"After the lapse of almost three thousand years," says Barnes, "every successive traveler who visits Moab, Idumaea, or Palestine, does something to confirm the accuracy of Isaiah. Towns bearing the same name, or the ruins of towns, are located in the same relative position he said they were; and the ruins of once splendid cities, broken columns, dilapidated walls, trodden-down vineyards, half-demolished temples, and fragments broken and consumed by time, proclaim to the world that those cities are what he said they would be, and that he was under the inspiration of God." And how powerfully come back to us from such scenes those "truths which wake, to perish, never!" Amidst the gloom the word of prophecy shines as a light in a dark place. Its voice prevails over time; imparts warmth to the heart amidst the rigors of Providence; calls to mind witih its persuasive strain long-slighted truths; teaches that while

> "Trade's proud empire hastes to swift decay,
> As oceans sweep the labor'd mole away,"

the state or the individual that is possessed of moral strength may be blessed in poverty; that there is a good which is not dependent on the fertility of a land, or the strength of its fortresses—which will survive the desolation of its fields, the downfall of its kings, the overthrow of its idols.

9—11. "These verses are among the most beautiful in the poem." They describe the sympathy that the prophet feels for this people even while he denounces them. This human characteristic of prophecy, often revealed, should not be overlooked. (9) **weeping of Jazer,**[a] i. e. weeping as genuine as Jazer's own. **Elealeh,** Nu. xxxii. 3, 37. In later times occupied by Moab. **for the shouting .. fallen,**[b] R. V., "for upon thy summer fruits and upon thy harvest the battle shout is fallen." The same word means the shout of the wine trader (Jer. xxv. 30) and the soldier's war-cry (Jer. li. 14). (10) **gladness,** etc., comp. Je. xlviii. **shouting,** R. V., "joyful noise." 33. **treaders,**[c] these give place to the tramplers. (11) **bowels,** used in Heb. as the seat of yearning compassion. **like an harp,** vibrating at the touch of the plectrum. The harp best expresses the wailings of grief.

The Failure of Harvest (vss. 9, 10).—It is—I. A grievous calamity. II. Not accidental. III. Generally traceable to moral causes. IV. Should call forth humiliation and repentance.—Lyth.

The Sadness of a Silent Land.—These verses bring before us the picture of a country from which, at the proper seasons, there rises no harvest and no vintage song. "Gladness is taken away, and joy out of the plentiful field; and in its vineyard there shall be no singing, neither shall there be shouting." In every age and every land the gladness of the people has found expression in the joy of harvest, and no picture of woe, want, and desolation could be so effective as this simple one of the harvest-fields from which arise no song.—Pul. Com.

12—14. (12) **when it is seen .. weary on,** R. V., "when Moab presenteth himself, when he wearieth himself upon," etc. **his sanctuary,** that of Chemosh, the god of Moab. **not prevail,** not gain any relief by thus praying to a false god.[d] Some commentators, guided by Jer. xlviii. 13—translate "When Moab presenteth himself . . . and does not prevail, then he shall be ashamed of Chemosh, and turn to Jehovah." So Ewald and Cheyne. (13) **since that time,** the time "when Moab's pride and resistance to God were first heard of."—Spk. Com. The previous prophecies had been general, now the prophet fixes a time for the Divine judgments. (14) **as .. hireling,** who will take care not to serve beyond the allotted time.[e] **contemned,** or brought into contempt.

The Vanity of Human Glory (vs. 12).—I. What does it cost! II. How easily can God destroy it! III. How soon will it terminate! IV. Is it worth the price which men set upon it?—Lyth.

Ineffectual Prayer.—What is more sad in the life of superstition than this passionate resort to any means, however irrational, to wring a favor from the deities of special shrines and sanctuaries? As if the true help were not ever near; as if, that being neglected, there could be hope elsewhere! Calvin observes, "While idolaters have their ordinary temples and

opportunity opens suddenly, unexpectedly; and unless one is ready on the instant to pass through, the door closes again."—Anon.

Ps. lxxx. 8—11.

[a] "It is not unlikely that the people's means of subsistence were chiefly derived from their vineyards." —Henderson.

[b] "The battle shout instead of the usual harvest song."—Fausset.

[c] In Wilkinson's Anc. Egyp. are repres. of persons treading out the grapes. Some six or seven, holding by as many ropes suspended from a common hook in the ceiling, stamp in the press or upper trough, and thus press out the juice, wh. flows into the trough below.

Je. xiii. 17; Lu. xix. 41.

[d] "The term expresses the fruitless fatigue and trouble to wh. idolaters must submit in worshiping a deity from which no aid can be obtained." —Henderson.

Je. xlviii. 13.

[e] No specific historical account of the destruction of Moab is given, but we know that when they marched into Canaan the Assyrians usually ravaged the trans - Jordanic districts (see 1 Chr. v. 26).

places of worship, if any uncommon calamity befalls them, they go to another temple more sacred than the rest, expecting that there they will be more abundantly favored with the presence of their god. In like manner, the Papists of the present day, when they are reduced to any uncommon danger (for this fault has existed in all ages), think that they will more readily obtain their wish by running to St. Claude, or to Mary of Loretto, or to any other celebrated idol, than if they assembled in some neighboring church. They resolve that their extraordinary prayers shall be offered up in a church at a great distance. It is in this sense that the prophet applies the term sanctuary to that most highly celebrated among the Moabites, and says they will go to it without any advantage." One cannot help thinking of those melancholy pilgrimages to Lourdes, that focus of superstition in our own times. So do men continue to hew out to themselves cisterns that hold no water; and so necessary still is the living word of prophecy, to remind the world that only in a genuine spiritual relation to the Eternal, only in a faith and worship which is independent of place, because ever fixed in the heart, can true comfort and help be found.—Pul Com. The Moabite Inscription.—The stone containing the inscription in question was a monumental altar erected by Mesa, king of Moab, at Karhah, after his revolt on the death of Ahab, to signalize his victories over Israel. Until his days, says, he, Chemosh was irritated against the land of Moab and oppressed it, but then became more favorable, and so Israel began to perish. Then a number of successes follow—his general, Omri, takes Medeba, erects several buildings in it, amongst them a temple (?) of Chemosh. Mesa himself builds Baal-Meon and Kirjathaim, fights against Israel at Jaazer (?), retires towards the land of Moab, and performs his devotions (?) to Chemosh at Kerioth, remaining with his men till the next day. Then by order of Chemosh he besieges Nebo (a great lacuna), Jahaz, and at last takes Dibon. Next he declares himself to have built Karhah, the walls of ha-Yearim and .. with its gates and towers; he orders the people to dig cisterns in the interior of Karhah, and compels the Israelite captives (?) to surround it with a trench. Mesa also mentions the construction of a fortress or ford at the Arnon, the building of Beth-Bamoth, Bezer, of the fortifications of Dibbon, and other towns which he added to his land; he built also...Beth-Diblathaim and Beth-Baal-Meon, to which last he transferred some Moabites (?). Finally, at the command of Chemosh he fought against Horonaim (a great lacuna). All these towns, the conquest of which is here related, were acquired by Mesa after the death of Ahab, during the two years of his successor Ahaziah and the first year of Jehoram; at the end of these three years, as mentioned in Isa. xvi. 14, "the glory of Moab was contemned" by the expedition of the three kings, related in 2 Kings iii., in which all the newly-made conquests were lost.—Ad. Neubauer. [See also Vol. II. of this work, p. 890].

"If we had prayed more we need not have worked so hard. We have too little praying face to face with God every day. Looking back at the end I suspect there will be great grief for our sins of omission— omission to get from God what we might have got by praying." — Andrew A. Bonar.

" Though the angels and saints have different degrees of glory, yet every one is perfectly happy and pleased. As the strings of an instrument differ in the size and sound; some are sharp and high, some grave and deep, others, a mean, so that if every string had judgment and election, it would choose to be what it is; so from the different degrees of glory in heaven, the most amiable and equal order appears that satisfies every one." — Bates.

CHAPTER THE SEVENTEETH.

Oracle for Damascus, vss. 1—11. "One of the earliest and most crisp of Isaiah's prophecies. Of the time of Syria's and Ephraim's league against Judah, somewhere between 736 and 732."—G. A. Smith. **1—3.** (1) **Damascus,** the metropolis of Syria.[a] Now one of the most opulent cities of the East, with a population of over 100,000.[b] **ruinous heap,** comp. figs. Mi. iii. 12. One one of the Assyr. inscrip. Tiglath says, "Cities of the Damascus land I desolated like a heap of rubbish." (2) **cities of Aroer,** "represent the whole land east of the Jordan; there the judgment upon Israel began."—Delitzsch. **none .. afraid,** bec. the country should be desolated even of ordinary enemies to flocks. (3) **fortress,** "perhaps: 'And the bulwark shall be removed from Ephriam,' meaning the kingdom of Damascus, which had been like a breakwater, sheltering Israel from the Assyrian onslaught. It is, however, equally possible to understand the 'fortress' collectively of the fortified cities of North Israel."—Cam. Bib. **kingdom,** or royalty. **remnant .. Israel,** translate, "and the remnant of Syria shall be as the glory," etc.

Damascus (sketch of history).—According to Josephus (J. Ant. i. 6),

[a] Ge. xiv. 15, xv. 2.

"No Eastern city has been so often overthrown and rebuilt as Damascus." — Vitringa.

Tiglath - Pileser, king of Assyria, was the agent in the fulfilment of this prophecy B.C. 740 (2 Ki. xvi. 9).

[b] Damascus is almost the only one of all the cities of Biblical antiquity that flourishes still down to the present day."— Nagelsbach.

Damascus was founded by Uz, son of Aram, grandson of Shem. First named in Scripture (Ge. xiv. 15) in connection with Abraham, whose steward, Eliezer, was a Damascene (xv. 2). Tradition asserts that Abram, on his way to Canaan, stayed some time at Damascus. Damascus reduced to subjection by David (2 Sam. viii. 5, 6; 1 Ch. xviii. 5, 6), who probably allowed a native prince, said to be Hadad (J. Ant. vii. 5, 2), to retain the throne. In time of Solomon, one Rezin took Damascus (1 Ki. xi. 23—25). Afterwards Ben-Hadad occupied the district (1 Ki. xx. 34), and his son, the foe of Ahab (xx., xxii.; 2 Ki. vi., vii.). To him succeeded Hazael (viii. 15), and then his son Ben-Hadad (xiii. 3, 24), in whose reign it may have been that Damascus was subjected by Jeroboam II., king of Israel (xiv. 28). We hear no more of Damascus till time of Ahaz, who, having asked aid of Tiglath-Pileser, the Assyrian, came, killed Rezin, and occupied Damascus, where he was met by Ahaz (xvi. 5—10). This predicted (Is. xvii.; Am. i. 3—5). Further troubles foretold (Jer. xlix. 27—32); fulfilled, according to Josephus (J. Ant. x. 9, 7), by invasion of Chaldæans. It afterwards passed into hands of Persians (Strabo. xvi. 2, 19), and for its strength was chosen by Darius as a store for his treasures. It afterwards became a possession of the Greeks, and from them passed under the Romans (J. Ant. xiv. 2, 3). In New Testament times it was the scene of St. Paul's conversion (Acts ix.), part of kingdom of Aretas, an Arabian (2 Cor. xi. 32); later it was reckoned to Decapolis. It grew in splendor under the Greeks, and when taken by Mohammedans, in A. D. 634, was one of chief cities of East. Taken by Turks 1006, and by Tamerlane 1400. It is still a great city under the Turks. Population 140,000, of whom 12,000 Christians, and as many Jews. In 1860, in consequence of a dispute between the Druses and Maronites, the Mohammedans massacred about 3,000 Christians. Many were rescued by Abd-el-Kader. Fuad Pasha executed 160 for these outrages and by conscription made 11,000 of the inhabitants soldiers.

"That valley was fruitful; it was called in the old time 'The Valley of Giants.' The Philistines kept their eyes constantly upon it, and when the chosen people held the valley, and when it was filled with corn, then the Philistines fell upon it and took it away. So shall it be with men who try contests with God, who invite the Lord to battle." —People's Bib.

"Glories, like glowworms, afar off shine bright, but look'd too near, have neither heat nor light." — Webster.

4, 5. Here follow three figures to describe the fate of Israel: wasting disease; harvesting of corn; and gathering of olives. In each case there is a remnant only left. (4) **made thin,** reduced to almost nothing. **fatness .. lean,** fig. taken fr. the growing leanness of a fat man in famine-time.[a]. (5) **gathereth the corn,** these fig. imply the clean sweeping away of the people from the land. **with his arm,** grasping them while he cuts off the ears of the grain. In the E. the straw is left in the field. **gathereth ears,** comp. Ruth ii. 2, 7, 15 ff. It is the figure of a gleaner. He will find but few ears, so thorough has been the previous harvesting. **Rephaim,**[b] a fruitful plain S. W. of Jerusalem, sloping towards Bethlehem.

Moral and Religious Suggestions.—1. Association of Abram with ancient history of Damascus may illustrate the rescue from oblivion of interesting spots by incidents and casual allusions of sacred writings. 2. Eliezer served Abraham. The world is the servant of the Church (many irreligious men aided Noah in building the ark). 3. Eliezer of Damascus a faithful servant. Upright men among the heathen. How much of his goodness may be traced to his connection with the patriarch? 4. Most beautiful spots of earth have often been the scenes of greatest crimes and disasters. 5. No earthly paradise should cause us to forget the better land. "Here we have no continuing city." 6. The famous Damascus most celebrated as the scene of a memorable conversion. St. Paul's spiritual birthplace; next to Bethlehem, the most important and influential place of nativity in the world. 7. Beautiful places not always safe for good men. Paul by night fled from Damascus, and by night also Lot fled from Sodom. 8. The story of Naaman a comment on the world's incompetence to supply spiritual needs; and formal ablutions to cleanse away moral pollution.

[a] "Or the fig. is that of a man in a consumption, that is become a mere skeleton, and reduced to skin and bones." —Gill.

[b] The name is due to the belief that it was originally occupied by a section of the race of Canaanitish giants, Jos. xv. 8.

Proverbs: "You will never make a crab walk straight forwards."—Greek. "The wolf changes his coat, but not his disposition." —Latin. "Drive away nature, and back it comes at a gallop."—French. "What's bred in the bone will never be out of the flesh."—English.

6—8. (6) **gleaning grapes,** etc., better: "Yet a gleaning remains from it." **shaking .. tree,** "the first gathering of olives is by the hand, then the branches are shaken or beaten; but there is still a gleaning left."—Spk. Com. De. xxiv. 20. The reference is to the scattered few left in the land.[a] (7) **look to,** under the pressure of exceeding calamity they would turn to Jehovah. **Holy One,** see Is. i. 4. (8) **altars,** associated with his former idolatrous confidences. **groves,** R. V. "the Asherim." "The Asherah or Sacred Pole was an emblem of divinity which seems to have stood regularly by the side of the altar in a Canaanitish sanctuary (Jud.

[a] "The gleanings here are the ignoble refuse who survived the deportation of the ten tribes by Assyria, not the pious remnant." —J. A. Alexander.

"One thorn of experience is worth a whole wilderness of warning." — Lowell.

"From the lowliest depth there is a path to the loftiest height." —Carlyle.

"What we call life is a journey to death; and what we call death is a passport to life. True wisdom thanks Death for what he takes, and, still more, for what he brings. There is nothing formidable about death but the consequences of it; and these we ourselves can regulate and control. The shortest life is long enough if it lead to a better; and the longest life is too short if it do not."— Colton.

"Infancy is the perpetual Messiah, which comes into the arms of fallen men, and pleads with them to return to Paradise." — Emerson.

vi. 13, 25; Deut. xvi. 21; 2 Ki. xviii. 4, etc.). It is regarded by some as an artificial survival of the sacred tree, under which the altar stood; by others as the symbol (or image) of a goddess of the same name. Whether a goddess Asherah was actually worshipped is a much controverted point; if so, she was probably nothing more than an impersonation of the material symbol here referred to."—Camb. Bib.. **images,** R. V. "sun-images," emblems of a Phœnician deity, Baal-Hammam, "Lord of the sun's heat."

Redemption of the Remnant.—This word, "The remnant shall return," is the standing word of promise and of hope for Israel. It contains the "law of Israel's history." The ring is gone, but the finger remains; the tree is felled, but the root-stump may yet send out suckers; from the bared harvest-field some gleanings may yet be gathered. And so Israel stands as the type of human life. All is not lost while conscience remains, while will may still exert its energy against evil, and in the reformation of the habits. But there must be this reformation, which begins with a looking up to God. The state of the soul depends on the direction of its gaze. We look where we love, and our looking may produce love.—Pulpit Com. "Yet."—That is a gospel word; that is the nature of an anthem. There is the token of hope, the signal of possible deliverance and return and enfranchisement. Something shall be left. Just one or two little ears—multiply them by God's intention, and they shall become a harvest: "two or three berries in the top of the uppermost bough"—take them down, multiply them by the purpose of the divine love, and they shall become as a field of fruitfulness. Is it not so with us? We have something left yet: the little child is left; the business is not wholly ruined; we have good health or good spirits; we have a friend or two here and there, kindly voices are not wholly dead: what is the meaning of these remnants of things? These remnants mean that God wants us home again; wants to see us in tears of penitence; wants to meet us at the cross of Christ; wants to reclaim us from the power and the captivity of the devil; wants to make us in very deed his own children; wants to recover us from our wandering, and set us like a fallen star in the brotherhood of the suns, to go out no more forever. Return, O wanderer, to thy home!—People's Bible.

9—11. (9) **forsaken bough,** etc., probably the Sept. gives the proper reading "be like the deserted places of the Amorite and the Hivite, which they forsook before the children of Israel."—Camb. Bib. (10) **rock,** familiar Scr. term for God.[a] **plant,** etc., with reference to the importation of foreign idols, and idolatrous systems, fr. Syria and Phœnicia. (11) **day .. grow,** R. V. "in the day of thy planting thou hedgest it in." **shall be a heap,** R. V. "fleeth away," i. e. In the beginning the undertaking will seem to be successful, but it will vanish in a day of great trouble. Polychr. B. translates vss. 10 b and 11 as follows: "Therefore, though thou plantest little gardens with shoots for Adonis, and stockest them with scions dedicated to a foreign god, even though as soon as thou plantest them thou fencest them in, and early bringest thy shoots to blossom, therefore the harvest shall vanish in a day of sickness and desperate pain."

[a] De. xxxii. 4, 15, 18, 30, 31; Is. xxvi. 4, marg.; 1 Co. x. 4.

O God, Thou Art my God.—Lord, I have viewed this world over in which Thou hast set me; I have tried how this and that thing will fit my spirit and the design of my creation, and can find nothing on which to rest, for nothing here doth itself rest; but such things as please me for a while in some degree, vanish and flee as shadows from before me. Lo! I come to Thee—the Eternal Being—the Spring of Life—the Centre of Rest—the Stay of the Creation—the Fullness of all Things—I join myself to Thee: with Thee I will lead my life and spend my days, with whom I am to dwell forever, expecting when my little time is over, to be taken up into Thine own eternity.—Arthur H. Hallam. "O God, who art the truth, make me one with Thee in everlasting love; I am often weary of reading and weary of working. In Thee alone is the sum of my desires. Let all teachers be silent: let the whole creation be dumb before Thee, and wilt Thou speak unto my soul?"—Thomas a Kempis.

A legend says that a powerful and rich king, troubled in heart in spite of all his possessions, went to a holy dervise, and asked him for the secret of happiness. The dervise led him forth in front of a high rock, on the top of which an eagle had built her nest. Then the dervise said, "Imitate that bird: build thy throne in heaven, and thou shalt reign there unmolested and in peace."

12—14. "A short independent oracle springing from the same historical situation as the following chapter." It describes the annihilation of the Assyrians.—Camb. Bib. (12) **Woe,** etc., R. V. "Ah, the uproar of many peoples, which roar like the roaring of seas." **many people,** i. e. the various nationalities of which the Assyrian army was composed. **rushing,** indicating the haste of forced marches. (13) **rebuke them,** with reference to the sudden and overwhelming discomfiture of Sennacherib. **rolling thing,** etc., R. V. "like the whirling dust before the storm." (14) **eveningtide,** "the destruction of the Assyrian shall be accomplished between evening and daybreak. The expression denotes a very short space of time, as in Ps. xxx. 5; Job xxvii. 19; but the destruction of Sennacherib's army took place literally in the night (ch. xxxvii. 36)."—Camb. Bib.

The Destruction of Sennacherib (vss. 12—14).—I. The foe—numerous, mighty, furious. II. The invasion—sudden, alarming, terrible. III. The defence—sufficient, available. IV. The defeat—utter, signal, ruinous. V. The interval of suspense—short, transient. VI. The triumph—complete, inspires confidence.—Lyth.

Care of God.—"Do you see this lock of hair?" said an old man to me. "Yes; but what of it? It is, I suppose, the curl from the head of a dear child long since gone to God." "It is not. It is a lock of my own hair; and it is now nearly seventy years since it was cut from this head." "But why do you prize a lock of your own hair so much?" "It has a story belonging to it, and a strange one. I keep it thus with care because it speaks to me more of God, and of His special care, than anything else I possess. I was a little child of four years old, with long curly locks, which, in sun, or rain, or wind, hung down my cheeks uncovered. One day my father went into the wood to cut up a log, and I went with him. I was standing a little way behind him, or rather at his side, watching with interest the strokes of the heavy axe, as it went up and came down upon the wood, sending off splinters with every stroke in all directions. Some of the splinters fell at my feet, and I eagerly stooped to pick them up. In doing so I stumbled forward, and in a moment my curly head lay upon the log. I had fallen just at the moment when the axe was coming down with all its force. It was too late to stop the blow. Down came the axe. I screamed, and my father fell to the ground in terror. He could not stay the stroke, and in the blindness which the sudden horror caused, he thought he had killed his boy. We soon recovered—I from my fright, and he from his terror. He caught me in his arms, and looked at me from head to foot, to find out the deadly wound which he was sure he had inflicted. Not a drop of blood nor a scar was to be seen. He knelt upon the grass, and gave thanks to a gracious God. Having done so he took up his axe, and found a few hairs upon its edge. He turned to the log he had been splitting, and there was a single curl of his boy's hair, sharply cut through and laid upon the wood. How great the escape! It was as if an angel had turned aside the edge at the moment it was descending on my head. With renewed thanks upon his lips he took up the curl, and went home with me in his arms. That lock he kept all his days, as a memorial of God's care and love. That lock he left to me on his death-bed. I keep it with care. It tells me of my father's God and mine. It rebukes unbelief and alarm. It bids me trust Him for ever. I have had many tokens of fatherly love in my threescore years and ten, but somehow this speaks most to my heart. It is the oldest and perhaps the most striking. It used to speak to my father's heart; it now speaks to mine."

Our Comrades—

Unseen they walk beside us every day,—
The three, Faith, Hope, and Love;
True comrades, cheering us along the way
That leads above.

One cries: "Be brave; endure, as in the sight
Of him who conquered death!
He is thy shield and buckler; up, and fight!
Be brave!" cries Faith.

And one: "O, hasten on; the heavenly gates
Gleam yonder, up the slope!
There to receive and crown thee Jesus waits.
Haste!" whispers Hope.

"Let nothing disturb thee: nothing affright thee: all things are passing: God never changeth."—Longfellow.

"Our times are in His hand, who saith, 'A whole I planned.' Youth shows but half; trust God, see all, nor be afraid."—Browning.

"Thousands whose experiences of the delivering hand of God are not less signal, stop short at the powers of nature, and instead of bending the knee before the All-merciful God, content themselves to express with cold hearts their admiration of the changes of the destiny of man."—Tholuck.

"Heaven helps those who help others. No man is so sure of the divine assistance as he who has remembered the divine unselfishness. God is very present with those who dwell helpfully with others. God's hand takes hold of our work, when our work is done out of love in brotherly kindness. Diligent selfishness has the reward of diligence, but the curse of selfishness; diligent unselfishness has the reward of diligence and the blessing of heaven." —S. S. Times.

"Unlike the soldier on the battle-field, who, if he eats at all, snatches a hasty meal and, wearied and but half refreshed, hurries again to the fight, the Christian warrior pauses to rest and feast."

"He who God's will has borne and done, And his own restless longings stilled; What else he's done, or has foregone, His mission he has well fulfilled."

And one: "Hast any here besides? O bring
Them with thee; for above
Is room for all, and welcome from the King.
Bring them!" pleads Love.

Marching and fighting thus we onward move,
With Faith for general,
With Hope for banner-bearer, and with Love
Watching o'er all.—R. G. Sutherland.

CHAPTER THE EIGHTEENTH.

This chapter contains a prophetic response to certain Ethiopian ambassadors who come seeking an alliance with Judah. **1, 2.** (1) **Woe .. wings,** R. V. "Ah, the land of the rustling of wings,"[a] the allusion is to Egypt with its swarms of insects that abound around the Nile. **Ethiopia,** or Cush, the land beyond the White and Blue Nile. Highland Ethiopia. At the time referred to Tirhakah was king of Ethiopia, and a monarch of great military renown. The ultimate object of Sennacherib was the conquest of Egypt, so news of his destruction was good news for Tirhakah. (2) **ambassadors,** to Israel. "In 702 when Sennacherib had taken the field to chastise Phœnicia, Philistia and Judah, Taharga sent ambassadors to Jerusalem to announce the despatch of an Egyptian army, and to encourage Hezekiah to make a manful resistance to the invaders."—Polychr. B. **sea,** i. e. the Nile, still called "the sea" in Arabic. **bulrushes,** R. V. "papyrus," i. e. paper or reed canoes, easy of transportation on land and carrying one or two passengers on the river. **saying,** this word should be omitted. With the words **"Go ye swift messengers"** the charge of Isaiah to the ambassadors begins. He sends them back with the message that follows. Notice the courtesy with which he rejects their overtures. **scattered and peeled,** R. V. "tall and smooth," reference is to the martial and handsome peoples, like the Nubians of the Soudan.[b] **a nation .. spoiled,** R. V. "a nation that meteth out and treadeth down, whose land the rivers divide."

a "The fig. of a disk with double wings is a symbol of Ethiopian royalty."---Canon Cook.

"The reference of the fig. may be to the protection wh. Egypt promised to the Jews." — Henderson.

b "Some take the reference to be to Ethiopia, and Israel is to send messengers of Sennac.'s defeat. Then the words are regarded as indicating the vigor and martial energy of Tirhakah's people."—So Wordsworth.

Lessons.—1. The providence of God over the Church. He shows that he takes care of the Church, and that, though he determines to chastise it, still he comes forward at the proper season to hinder it from perishing, and displays his power in opposition to tyrants and other enemies, that they may not overthrow it or succeed in accomplishing what they imagined to be in their powers. 2. The indestructibility of the spiritual life. This must not be confounded with the institutions in which it dwells for a time. But, understanding the "Church" in the spiritual or mystical sense, it cannot perish. 3. The self-concealment of God. The trial of faith in all ages. Oh that he would show his face, bare his arm, disclose his majesty, exert his power, appear as Judge to end once for all the strifes of the world! But we must learn to say, "God's in his heaven, all's right with the world." At the proper season he will come forth. 4. The unity of religion the prophetic ideal. "Mount Zion" was its ancient symbol; for us it is not Rome, nor any other city or mount,—it is the human heart, with all its pathos, its faith, hope, and love, its regenerate life and aspirations it is one spirit universal in mankind.—Pulpit Com.

"Like a blind spinner in the sun, I tread my days; I know that all the threads will run Appointed ways." — Helen Hunt.

"All I have seen teaches me to trust the Creator for all I have not seen." —Emerson.

Floods in Egypt.—Great injury has often been done to the lands contiguous to large and rapid rivers, especially when inundations have happened. Sonnini relates a circumstance of this kind, to which he was a witness in passing down the Nile. He says, "The reis and the sailors were asleep upon the beach; I had passed half of the night watching, and I composed myself to sleep, after giving the watch to two of my companions, but they too had sunk into slumber. The kanja, badly fastened against the shore, broke loose, and the current carried it away with the utmost rapidity. We were all asleep; not one of us, not even the boatmen stretched upon the sand, perceived our manner of sailing down at the mercy of the current. After having floated with the stream for the space of a good league, the boat hurried along with violence, struck with a terrible crash against the shore, precisely a little below the place from

" A Christian man's life is laid in the loom of time to a pattern which he does not see, but God does; and his heart is a shuttle. On one side of the loom is sorrow, and on the other is joy; and the shuttle struck

whence the greatest part of the loosened earth fell down. Awakened by this furious shock, we were not slow in perceiving the critical situation into which we were thrown. The kanja, repelled by the land, which was cut perpendicularly, and driven towards it again by the violence of the current, turned round in every direction, and dashed against the shore in such a manner as excited an apprehension that it would be broken to pieces. The darkness of the night, the frightful noise which the masses separated from the shore spread far and wide as they fell into deep water —the bubbling which they excited, the agitation of which communicated itself to the boat, rendered our awakening a very melancholy one. There was no time to be lost. I made my companions take the oars, which the darkness prevented us from finding so soon as we could have wished; I sprung to the helm, and encouraging my new and very inexperienced sailors, we succeeded in making our escape from a repetition of shocks by which we must at length all have inevitably perished; for scarcely had we gained, after several efforts, the middle of the river than a piece of hardened mud, of an enormous size, tumbled down at the very spot we had just quitted, which must, had we been but a few minutes later, have carried us to the bottom."—Trav. in Egypt.

3, 4. (3) **All ye,** etc., here begins the answer which the ambassadors are to give. See what Jehovah can do! (4) **take my rest,** "I will hōld me still, and look on in my place."—Polychr. Bib. For a time it seemed as if God did not notice the progress of the Assyr. **consider,** look on, watch, wait My time. **clear .. herbs,** R. V. "clear heat in sunshine,"[a] "the points of comparison are apparently two: (1) the motionless stillness of the noon-tide heat and the fleecy cloud are an emblem of Jehovah's quiescence. (2) As these natural phenomena hasten the ripening of the fruit, so all providential agencies appear to further and mature the schemes of Assyria. But the development is suddenly arrested just before its fruition."—Camb. Bib.

Grace of God as Dew.—The grace of God is like dew to the barren and parched hearts of men, to make them fruitful. And there are many things wherein the proportion and resemblance stand. I. None can give the dew but God. It comes from above; it is of a celestial original; the nativity thereof is from "the womb of the morning." None can give grace but God. II. Dew is the fruit of a serene, clear, and quiet heaven: for dew never falleth either in scorching or tempestuous weather, as philosophers have observed. In like manner, the grace, favor, and blessings of God are the fruits of His reconciled affection towards us. III. Dew is abundant and innumerable. Who can number the drops of dew on the ground, or the "hairs of little rain?"—for so they are called in the original, because of their smallness and number (Deut. xxxii. 2). So Hushai expresseth the multitude of all Israel: "We will light upon him as the dew falleth upon the ground." Such is the grace of God unto His people after their conversion; unsearchable, it cannot be comprehended or measured, nor brought under any number or account (Ps. lxxi. 15, cxxxix. 17, 18). IV. Dew is silent, slow, insensible in its descent. You cannot see, hear, feel, or smell its coming; you see it when it is come, but cannot observe how it comes. In this manner was God pleased to fill the world with the knowledge of His Gospel, and with the grace of His Spirit, by quiet, small, and, as it were, by insensible means. V. Dew is of a soft and benign nature, which gently insinuateth and worketh itself into the ground, and by degree moisteneth and mollifieth it. In like manner, the Spirit, the Grace, the Word of God is of a searching, insinuating, softening quality. VI. Dew is of a vegetating and quickening nature. So is the Grace, and Word, and Spirit of God. VII. Dew is of a refreshing and comforting nature—causes the face of things to flourish with beauty and delight, especially in the hot countries of the East. So God promises to be unto His people in their troubles, "as a cloud of dew in the heat of harvest." His grace gives comfort, peace, joy, strength, and the beauty of holiness to them.—Bp. Reynolds.

No drop but serves the slowly lifting tide,
No dew but has an errand to some flower,
No smallest star but sheds some helpful ray;

alternately by each, flies back and forth, carrying the thread, which is white or black as the pattern needs. And in the end, when God shall lift up the finished garment, and all its changing hues shall glance out, it will then appear that the deep and dark colors were as needful to beauty as the bright and high colors."—Beecher.

[a] "This quiet observant waiting of God's, the Prophet compares to that weather wh. is most favorable for maturing the harvest, warm days and dewy nights." — Nagelsbach.

"God would let the enemy proceed in the execution of his purposes until they were nearly accomplished."—J. A. Alexander.

"The weakest among us has a gift, however seemingly trivial, which is peculiar to him, and which, worthily used, will be a gift also to his race."—Ruskin.

"The serene, silent beauty of a holy life is the most powerful influence in the world, next to the might of the Spirit of God."—Spurgeon.

"The dews of the evening most carefully shun; those tears of the sky for the loss of the sun."—Chesterfield.

"When the end of God's working is the persuasion of His fatherly love, then we find His means marvelously adapted and effective."

And man by man, each giving to all beside,
Makes the firm bulwark of the country's power;
There is no better way.

5, 6. (5)**afore,** i. e. just before; when the invader is feeling perfectly sure of accomplishing his purpose; then, and in the most humiliating way, his desolation shall come. **bud is perfect,** etc., R. V., "when the blossom is over, and the flower becometh a ripening grape." "The ripening crops represent the maturing plans of the Assyrians: Jehovah looks on, and in appearance promotes them, as a favorable sun and sky advance the grape; but, just before maturity is reached, fruit and branch alike are violently cut away, i. e. the enemy's plans are abruptly intercepted."—Driver. **cut off,** fig. of ruinous destruction of a fruit tree. (6) **left together,** i. e. the carcasses of thousands of the Assyr. army. They shall be a prey to the ravenous mountain birds, who shall have a long feast on the slain. **summer . . winter,** i. e. for a whole year.

God Can Work.—1. God's working is well-timed. 2. God's working is full of energy. 3. God's working is always effective to its end.—Pul. Com.

Use of Nature to Man.—Every part of nature seems to pay its tribute to man, in the great variety of kinds or tribes, as well as the prodigious number of individuals of each various tribe, of all creatures. There are so many beasts, so many birds, so many insects, so many reptiles, so many trees, so many plants upon the land; so many fishes, sea-plants, and other creatures, in the waters; so many minerals, metals, and fossils, in the subterraneous regions; that there is nothing wanting to the use of man, or any other creature of this lower world. The munificence of the Creator is such, that there is enough to supply the wants and conveniences of all creatures, in all places, all ages, and upon all occasions. And this boundless variety is a most wise provision for the uses of this world in every age and in every place. God has created nothing in vain. Some things are for food, some for physic, some for habitation, some for utensils, some for tools and instruments of work, and some for recreation and pleasure, either to man, or to some of the inferior creatures themselves. It is evident that all the creatures of God (beasts, birds, insects, and plants) have, or may have, their several uses even among men. For although in one place things may lie neglected, and out of use, yet in another place they may be of great use. So what has been rejected in one age has been received in another; as the new discoveries in physic, and alterations of diet, sufficiently witness. Or if there be many things of little immediate use to man, in this or any other age, yet to other creatures they may afford food or physic, or be of some necessary use. How many trees and plants, nay, even the very carcasses of animals, the very dust of the earth, and the prodigious swarms of insects in the air and in the waters, of no apparent use to man, yet are food, or medicine, or places of retreat and habitation to birds, fishes, reptiles, and insects themselves; for whose happy and comfortable subsistence the bountiful Creator has liberally provided, as well as for that of man.—Derham.

7. In that time, when this revelation of Jehovah's power has been made. **the present,** R. V. "a present." **of a people,** read "from a people." The meaning is that then Ethiopia shall be converted and pay homage to Jehovah. Comp. Zeph. iii. 10; Ps. lxviii. 31. **scattered and peeled,** R. V., "tall and smooth," (other changes as in vs. 2.) **to the place,** etc., the simplest explanation is that some present came fr. Ethiopia to Zion in grateful acknowledgment of this deliverance.

Earthly Judgments (vs. 7).—I. Are intended not to destroy, but to benefit mankind. II. Must ultimately command attention and belief. III. Then repectful homage will be presented in Zion. IV. Even the most distant and unlikely nations shall be converted unto Him.—Lyth.

Sometime.— ,

Sometime when all life's lessons have been learned,
And sun and stars forevermore have set,
The thing which our weak judgments here have spurned,
The things o'er which we grieved with lashes wet,
Will flash before us out of life's dark night,

"A certain emperor said to the Egyptians, 'Draw from me as from your river Nilus;' but what can be drawn from a man but hopes, which swell like bubbles of water till they burst? It is from God that we must draw, for He is a fountain which perpetually distilleth, who quencheth the thirst of all the world, and hath in Himself but one want, which is that all men should still thirst for His bounty and have it."—Caussin.

"Rowland Hill once conversed with a celebrated sculptor, who had been hewing out a block of marble to represent that great patriot, Lord Chatham. 'There,' said the sculptor, 'is not that a fine form?' 'Now, sir,' said Mr. Hill, 'can you put life into it? else, with all its beauty, it is still but a block of marble.' God put life into His creation, and man became a living soul. Christ puts new life into dead men."—Bp. H. Goodwin.

"It is curious to note the fact that Abyssinia (Ethiopia) is the only great Christian power in the E. at this day."—J. A. Alexander.

"Judgment was his strange act, mercy his delight. The grandeur of his character was indeed displayed in the former scene; but it was displayed, as was needful, on its sterner side. In this there was equal moral grandeur; but it was the grand-

As stars shine most in deeper tints of blue;
And we shall see how all God's plans are right,
And how what seemed reproof was love most true.
* * * * * *
When we shall clearly see and understand,
I think that we will say, "God knew the best."—M. R. Smith.

God—the great first cause.—

Great System of perfections! mighty Cause
Of causes mighty! Cause uncaused! Sole root
Of Nature, that luxuriant growth of God!
First Father of effects! that progeny
Of endless series; where the golden chain's
Last link admits a period, who can tell?
Father of all that is or heard, or hears!
Father of all that is or seen, or sees!
Father of all that is, or shall arise!
Father of this immeasurable mass
Of matter multiform; or dense, or rare;
Opaque, or lucid; rapid, or at rest;
Minute, or passing bound! in each extreme
Of like amaze, and mystery, to man.
Father of these bright millions of the night!
Of which the least full godhead had proclaimed,
And thrown the gazer on his knee. Or, say,
Is appellation higher still Thy choice?
Father of matter's temporary lord!
Father of spirits! nobler offspring! sparks
Of high paternal glory; rich endowed
With various measures, and with various modes
Of instinct, reason, intuition; beams
More pale, or bright from day divine, to break
The darker matter organised (the ware
Of all created spirit): beams, that rise
Each over other in superior light,
Till the last ripens into lustre strong,
Of next approach to godhead. Father fond
(Far fonder than e'er bore that name on earth)
Of intellectual beings! beings blest
With powers to please Thee! not of passive ply
To laws they know not; beings lodged in seats
Of well-adapted joys, in different domes
Of this imperial palace for thy sons;
Of this proud, populous, well-policed,
Though boundless habitation, planned by Thee;
Whose several clans their several climates suit;
And transposition, doubtless, would destroy.
Or, oh! indulge, immortal King, indulge
A title less august indeed, but more
Endearing. Ah! how sweet in human ears;
Sweet in our ears and triumph in our hearts!
Father of Immortality to man!—Young.

eur of graciousness and grace."—Morison.

"That you may find success, let me tell you how to proceed. To-night begin your great plan of life. You have but one life to live; and it is most important that you do not make a mistake. To-night begin carefully. Fix your eye on the fortieth year of your age, and then say to yourself, 'At the age of forty, I will be an industrious man, a benevolent man, a well-read man, a religious man, and a useful man. I resolve; and I will stand to it.' My young friends, pray to God that this resolution may stand like the oak, which cannot be wind-shaken." — C. Brooks.

"Come, let us fashion acts that are to be, when we shall lie in darkness silently."—George Eliot.

"If a man constantly aspires, is he not elevated?"—Thoreau.

CHAPTER THE NINETEENTH.

"This chapter contains one of the most note-worthy and characteristic of Isaiah's foreign prophecies. A period of unexampled collapse and decay, affecting every grade and class of society is about to commence for Egypt, to be succeeded, ultimately, by the nation's conversion and spiritual renovation."—Driver. 1, 2. (1) **Egypt,**[a] from 1500 to 1300 B. C. Egypt was the leading nation in culture, arts, and military prowess. In 730 the Ethiopians gained the upper hand. For some time now, (720) at the date of the prophecy, her power was waning. **rideth .. cloud, the Scrip.** sign of august majesty,[b] Comp. Ps. xviii; 9-14.

[a] Egypt stretched fr. the Medit. Sea on the N. to Ethiopia on the S., with the Red Sea on the E., and the Lybian desert on the W. It was intersected by the Nile throughout the whole of its length.

[b] Da. vii. 13; Mat. xxiv. 30; Re. i. 7.

The majesty of the clouds, especially in storm, has naturally been considered a revelation of Jehovah's presence. **idols,** lit. nonentities, a striking word when the grandeur of the idol-figures of Eg. is considered.[c] **Moved,** i. e. tremble with fear. **heart .. melt,** fig. for loss of national confidence. (2) **against his brother,** i. e. one part of the country against the other. Civil war does more mischief to a nation than foreign war.

Judgment Upon Egypt (vss. 1—17).—I. Effected by the direct interposition of God, a cloud comes from cloudless Egypt, comes from heaven, moves slowly. II. Affects its social conditions, puts contempts on its idolatry, dissolves the bonds of society, destroys its superstitious hopes, subjects it to an oppressive tyranny. III. Affect its physical conditions, dries up the river, ruins vegetation, destroys the fisheries, puts an arrest upon trade and manufactures. IV. Affects its intellectual condition: the wise become fools, the brave cowards, the industrious idle, the people are filled with dread of the anger of the Lord.—Lyth.

Historical Notes on Egypt.—Egypt is supposed to be a contraction of Aia-gyptos=land of Kyptos; or, the black land. According to ancient mythology, the name is derived from Ægyptus, the son of Belus. 1. Egypt, the Mizraim of the LXX., is called Matzor (Is. xix. 6; R. V.); Eretz Hham = land of Ham (Ps. lxxviii. 51, cv. 23); Rahab (Is. xxx. 7, R. V. li. 9; Ps. lxxxvii. 4); Sihor (Is. xxiii. 3); and house of bondmen (Ex. xiii. 3, 14; Deu. vii. 8). In Scripture the name is often used in the singular Misr, and Bochart is of opinion that Mizraim, the dual form, refers to Upper and Lower Egypt. To this day the Arabs call it Misr. 2. Race: it was peopled by Mizraim's posterity (Gen. x. 6, 13, 14); idolatrous (Ex. xii. 12; Nu. xxxiii. 4; Is. xix. 1; Ez. xxx. 13); practised magic (Ex. vii. 11, 12. 22, viii. 7); were ruled by kings called Pharaohs (Gen. xii. 14, 15, xl. 1, 2; Ex. i. 8, 22); aided by a governor (Gen. xli. 41—44); and princes and counsellors (Gen. xii. 15; Is. xix. 11); people were superstitious (Is. xix. 3); hospitable (Gen. xlvii. 5, 6; 1 Ki. xi. 18); often intermarried with strangers (Gen. xxi. 21; 1 Ki. iii. 1, xi. 19; Chr. ii. 34, 35); hated shepherds (Gen. xlvi. 34); abhorred sacrifice of oxen (Ex. viii. 26); they were not to be hated by Israel (Deu. xxiii. 7); received into congregation in third generation (Deu. xxiii. 8). 3. Customs: mode of entertaining (Gen. xliii. 32, 34); diet (Nu. xi. 5); embalming (Gen. l. 3). 4. Political character: proud (Ez. xxix. 3, xxx. 6); pompous (Ez. xxxii. 12); mighty (Is. xxx. 2, 3); ambitious (Jer. xlvi. 8); treacherous (Is. xxxvi. 6; Ez. xxix. 6, 7); yet offered an asylum to strangers (Gen. xii. 10, xlvii. 4; 1 Ki. xi. 17, 40; 2 Ki. xxv. 26; Matt. ii. 12, 13). 5 Its armies: described (Ex. xiv. 7—9); captured Gezer (1 Ki. ix. 16); besieged Jerusalem (1 Ki. xiv. 25, 26); invaded Assyria and killed Josiah (2 Ki. xxiii. 29); deposed Jehoahaz, and made Judæa tributary (2 Ki. xxiii. 31—35).—Topics.

3, 4. (3) **the spirit,** "used here of intellectual power." **counsel thereof,** the sagacity of the rulers should fail.[a] **seek,** for advice. **charmers,** etc., the sign of want of confidence in the government.[b] "The power of cool and rational deliberation ceases: advice is sought by recourse to those magical arts for which in antiquity Egypt was celebrated."—Driver. (4) **give over .. cruel lord,**[c] "the words suggest a foreign ruler and are quite applicable to any Assyrian monarch likely to undertake the conquest of Egypt. Esarhaddon in 672 and again Asshurbanipal in 662 ravaged the country as far as Thebes; the Empire was broken up into twenty petty principalities, and all attempts at revolt were sternly suppressed until 645, when Psammetichus, one of the native princes, succeeded in shaking off the Assyrian yoke and uniting Egypt under his own sway."—Camb. Bib.

Temptation to Trust in Diviners.—I. The universal desire to pierce the unseen and the future. On this desire rests the success of modern spiritualism. II. Moral reasons why the future is hidden from us: 1. It is necessary for our probation. 2. It prevents procrastination by impression of the supreme value of now. 3. It keeps from self-security. 4. It makes our life a life of faith. III. Religion gives rest from the care about the future.—Pul. Com.

Geographical Notes, etc., on Egypt.—1. Situation: in Africa, at the N.E. corner. 2. Extent: about 480 miles long, by 250 at its widest. Area capable of cultivation about 16,000 square miles, or about half area of Ireland. 3. Boundaries: (Ez. xxix. 10) on north the Mediterranean; east, Red Sea and Isthmus of Suez; south, Ancient Ethiopia; west, Lybia.

[c] Of the colossal fig. of Rameses Dean Stanley says, "Nothing wh. now exists in the world can give any notion of what the effect must have been when he was erect."

Ex. xii. 12; Je. xliii. 7—13.

"The cloud that appears to be nothing but vapor, may enshrine the Deity; the bush, yesterday so common that any bird might have alighted upon it, to-day burns with unseen, infinite energy." —Parker.

"But I," cried the fresh-hearted New Year, "I shall try to leave men wiser than I find them. I will offer them freely whatever good gifts Providence permits me to distribute, and will tell them to be thankful for what they have, and humbly hopeful for more."—Hawthorne.

"Poverty is the gift of God, as well as riches." —Vavasor Powell.

[a] The land of Eg. fell into a decline; every one did as he pleased; long years there was no sovereign for them that had the supreme power over the rest of things. The land of Eg. belonged to the princes of the districts. One killed another in jealousy.— From papyrus of Rameses III., discovered by Harris, in 1855.

[b] Is. viii. 19.

"Do not think that years leave us and find us the same."—Owen Meredith.

[c] "The king here mentioned is identified by J.

4. Divisions: (1) Lower east, called also the delta. This portion borders on the Mediterranean south, and being enclosed by the two chief mouths of the Nile, takes the form of the Greek letter, "delta." This district is about 80 miles from north to south. (2) Central Egypt, or Heptanomis: extending about 150 miles further south. (3) Upper Egypt, or Thebais, reaching still further south about 250 miles. 5. Physical features: Egypt may be described as the valley of one great river—the Nile (Gen. xli. 1—3; Ex. i. 22). This river is constantly bringing down a quantity of alluvial soil, which it deposits throughout its whole course. At the delta this soil has been deposited to a thickness, in the banks, of 30 feet (Amos viii. 8). Hence Egypt is slowly undergoing a process of elevation. Little rain falls in Egypt, about four or five showers annually at Thebes (Deu. xi. 10, 11)—(Wilkinson). Absence of rain is compensated by copious night dews. 6. Productions: a great corn country; to this day its corn exportations very great. Turkey is mainly dependent on Egypt for corn, and it was anciently the granary of the Romans. It produces also large quantities of flax and cotton. The "fine linen" of Egypt was famous. Many birds, of different kinds, "the numbers numberless, of all manner of birds—vultures and cormorants, and geese, flying like constellations through the blue heavens; pelicans standing in long array on the water-side; hoopoos and ziczacs, and the (so-called) white ibis, the gentle symbol of the god Osiris, in his robes of white;—walking under one's very feet."

D. Michaelis with Sethos, by Grotius, Gesenius, and others, with Psammetichus, by the Rabbins with Sennacherib, by Hitzig and Hendewerk with Sargon, by Clericus with Nebuchadnezzar, by Vitringa with Cambyses or Ochus, and by Cocceius with Charlemagne."—J. A. Alexander.

"We rise in glory as we sink in pride."—Young.

5—7. (5) **waters shall fail,** either as result of act of Jehovah, or from lack of attention to reservoirs and dykes, owing to the chaotic civil conditions. **sea,** the Nile.[a] **wasted,** or parched up, by withholding of the usual flood.[b] (6) **And they .. dried** up, R. V., "And the rivers shall stink: the streams of Egypt shall be minished and dried up." The word translated "defence" in A. V. is a rare name for Egypt. **reeds and flags,**[c] growing on the mud banks. (7) **paper reeds,** etc., R. V., "The meadows by the Nile, by the brink of the Nile, and all that is sown by the Nile, shall become dry, be driven," etc. "The meadows will become so parched that they blow away like ashes."—Delitzsch.

From the sources and springs of the mighty Nile up to the seat of thought, passion and motion in the mightier human heart, all are in the hands of Jehovah. Alike in every occupation of the industrial and of the political and intellectual world, let us own our dependence upon Him.—Pulpit Com.

The Paper Reeds.—The tourist in Egypt, looking for Bible illustrations, is likely to be disappointed when he finds no 'bulrushes" or "reeds," answering to those spoken of in the history of the infant Moses. No sign of flag, reed, or other aquatic plant appears, either along the Nile or elsewhere. Yet there must have been such plants in former times. The monuments depict them in great variety—the lotus being a favorite. And the rolls of papyrus found in the tombs testify to the existence of such plants, the papyrus having been made from the bark of the paper reed. How interesting to the Scripture student to find that the disappearance of these plants was specifically predicted by the Scripture writers! Says the Prophet Isaiah, "The reeds and flags shall wither; the paper reeds by the brooks, by the mouth of the brooks, and everything sown by the brooks shall wither, be driven away, and be no more." But the question comes, why do not aquatic plants now grow in Egypt? Are not the physical conditions now existing in this country the same which have always prevailed? And does the Divine fiat now resist natural laws, for the fulfilment of prophecy? I answer that aquatic plants,—which, as Herodotus testifies, were extremely valuable,—were reared, in the time of Egypt's prosperity, by artificial means—involving the preparation of reservoirs and "brooks." Thus, too, by means of "ponds" and "sluices," the fish were multiplied. And the prediction of Isaiah relates to the destruction of the nice arrangements of artificial life, on which depended the country's high prosperity. And how entirely natural that the bathing place of Pharaoh's daughter should be a cultivated garden bordering the Nile, where seclusion could be had.—The Far East by Burt.

[a] Is. xviii. 2, xxvii. 1; Nah. iii. 8.

"It was called a sea, not merely bec. of its normal breadth within its own banks, but also bec. it really spreads out like a sea at the time of its overflow."—Nagelsbach.

[b] "The Nile, being the source of her plenty, was worshiped by the Eg.; and the Div. judgment on the Nile was like a smiting of her god."—Wordsworth.

[c] Ex. ii. 3.

See also under verses 11, 12.

"See that you personally know and daily live upon Christ."

"What each day needs, that shalt thou ask. Each day will set its proper task."—Goethe.

8—10. (8) **fishers,** upon whom one of the leading industries of Egypt depended. **the brooks,** R. V., "the Nile." (9) **flax,** from which linen cloth

a "Both flax and cotton abounded in Eg., and the manufacturing of linen and cotton cloths afforded support to many thousands of its inhabitants. In ancient times linen was worn by the people generally; the priests officiated in linen dresses; and we know that the cloths forming the bandages of the nunneries are linen."—Henderson.

"Little minds are tamed and subdued by misfortune, but great minds rise above it."—Washington Irving.

"Losses, disappointments, ill tongues, loss of friends, houses, or country, are God's workmen, set on work to work out good to you, out of everything that befalleth you."—Samuel Rutherford.

a Nu. xiii. 22; Ps. lxxviii. 43.

"I cannot recollect any (ruin of ancient city) that impressed me so deeply with the sense of fallen and deserted magnificence." — Macgregor.

b Comp. Is. xli. 22, 26, xliii. 9, xlv. 21, xlviii. 14.

"The wind and the waves are always on the side of the ablest navigators." — Gibbon.

"If I shoot at the sun, I may hit a star."—P. T. Barnum.

"If there be some weaker one,
Give me strength to help him on;
If a blinder soul there be,
Let me guide him nearer Thee;

was made for the priests, and for mummy wrappings. It also depends for its growth upon the irrigation of the fields by the river. **networks,** R. V., "white cloth," i. e. cotton goods, the clothing of the great mass of the people.[d] (10) **And they shall be broken,** etc., R. V., "And her pillars shall be broken in pieces, all they that work for hire shall be grieved in soul." Gesenius thinks the higher and lower classes of society are put together in this vs. as alike affected by the failure of the Nile. The higher classes being called the pillars or foundations of the state; the lower classes being mentioned as those who labor for hire.

The Wonderful Way in Which all Prosperity is Made Dependent on the First Gifts of God.—Man's riches are God's gifts. Man can never add to the wealth of the world by exchanges, which only vary the possessors. Air, rain, sunshine, water, electricity, coal, increase from field and beast, are man's riches; and these are first things that are absolutely dependent on God, and out of man's control. God withholds the rains, and a nation is in misery; God tempers the air, and plague sweeps away the multitudes; God stops the flood, and Egypt pines away in its helplessness. The source of all real good is God, in whose hands are the very springs and sources of all human happiness and prosperity.—Pul. Com.

Fish-ponds.—This may allude to the enclosures or weirs which the Orientals construct most skillfully for catching fishes. They put down across a stream a vast number of stakes, which extend some hundreds of yards, and which resemble a low hedge. When there has been a flood or influx of the tide, the water rises considerably above the tops of the stakes, and the fish go up with the flow; and whilst they are engaged in seeking food at the bottom of the stream, the water gradually and imperceptibly retires, till at length it becomes so shallow as to prevent them from escaping over the hedge. They are then easily taken. At other times the ground is so staked out as to leave a convenient opening, through which, when the fishes attempt to retire into the deep water, they are caught in nets placed there by the wily fishermen. Kings and men of high rank have large ponds, where fish are sacredly kept, none being allowed to molest them. In a few years the surface of the water exhibits a mass of living creatures.—Roberts.

11, 12. (11) **Zoan,** the ancient capital of the Pharaohs. Tanis, at the N.E. of Egypt.[a] Here if anywhere should statesmen be found. But before this catastrophe their advice is worthless. **fools,** utterly foolish. "None seemed able to foresee the impending ruin, or avert the national calamities." **how say ye,** in your boastings, "The wisdom of Egypt was the hereditary possession of the priestly caste to which the early dynasties belonged. The counsellors are here introduced boasting of the purity of their descent from these kings and sages of the olden time. Read (in both cases) a son."—Camb. Bib. (12) **Where,** etc., appeal of the Prophet[b] to Pharaoh. Where are your wise men? If there are any such let them declare what is about to happen to Egypt.

Additional Note on vs. 7.—Never had prophecy greater circumstances of improbability to overcome, and never was prediction more completely fulfilled. The indispensable papyrus in the time of Isaiah flourished through the whole of the Thebaid, Heptanomos, and the Delta, as the three divisions of ancient Egypt were named. Of its utility no European reader can form an adequate idea. Stringent laws were established for its protection and cultivation, and from its first appearance to maturity the papyrus was considered to be under the especial care of local deities; it was planted, tended, and cut with an almost religious ceremonial. Adaptable for various uses, not only paper, cloth, and brushes, but the roughest and most delicate manufactures were produced from it alike. Sails, cordage, and baskets for shipping, sandals, hats, skirts, carpets, chairs, and seats for domestic service were made of it. Men and animals fed upon the tender shoots. A syrup was obtained and medicine extracted from it. It formed the cradle of the Nubian baby; it decorated the canopy of Pharaoh's throne; it was scattered in processions through the streets; it was painted on the houses; it was wrought in granite on the temples. The Egyptian ladies twined the living blossoms in their hair, or wore it in chains around their necks as an amulet. Princes, priests, and peasants offered it on the altar in commemoration of the

dead. The papyrus was the plaything of the child and the sceptre of the god, the glory of the country, the staple of its commerce, and the hieroglyphic emblem of its name. By withholding the supply of the papyrus, Ptolemy Philadelphus was enabled to repress the formation of a rival library by the Pergamean kings; while, by opening the markets of the Delta, the poetry of Greece and the philosophy of Rome were transmitted throughout the whole of the then known world. Alas for the permanence of mundane glories! thirty centuries of oppression, superstition, and neglect have dried up the artificial lakes in which the plant was cultivated. Rush after rush has been cut down to warm an Arab's bath, or litter a pasha's horse, and no successors have been planted. The hot wind of the south, and the sands of the desert, have exterminated the lovely paper rush in the empire of the Pharaohs, and there is not a single indigenous papyrus in the whole of Egypt proper. A stream in Sicily, and the marshes of Merom in Palestine, alone contain the nearly extinct vegetable; and in the conservatories of London, Sion, and Kew, England actually possesses more living papyri than can now be found from Syene to Alexandria.

Make my mortal dreams come true
With the work I fain would do;
Clothe with life the weak intent,
Let me be the thing I meant;
Let me find in Thy employ,
Peace that dearer is than joy;
Out of self to love be led,
And to Heaven acclimated,
Until all things sweet and good
Seem my natural habitude."
—J. G. Whittier.

13, 14. (13) **Noph,** or Memphis. "The second capital, and celebrated Necropolis of Egypt."—Henderson. Psammetichus made this the capital of the kingdom. Princes of Zoan and of Memphis are the very highest officials of all Egypt; not only princes but priests, the "wise men" of the land. But they have led Egypt astray in spite of their boasted wisdom. **stay .. tribes,** R. V. "corner-stone," of her castes.[a] (14) **perverse spirit,** hostile influences as well as persons or spirits are used by God to be instruments of His wrath. (Comp. 1 Sam. xvi. 14—23; Ps. lxxv. 8; 1 Ki. xxii. 19—23.) Divine judgments on a nation may come as the confusion of its counsellors. God's judgments may as properly fall on minds as on bodies, or on estates. **as a drunken,** having lost all self-control, blundering about stupidly, this way and that, only to fall into greater shame.

[a] "The class on which the whole Egyp. body politic rests, the priestly class, leads the whole land astray." —Nagelsbach.

Noph signifies the haven of the good, in reference to their being buried there. The Heb. word is Moph in Ho. ix. 6.

Human Views of God.—One stands in Milan Cathedral, under the nave, and looks up into those mysterious depths, until it seems as though he would exhale and fly into space. There, in the brooding darkness, the feeling of reverence weighs upon his very soul. And the Milan Cathedral to him is that which it seems to be when the low-lying sun has shot through the window and kindled the whole interior. At the very same moment there stands upon the roof another man, and about him are those three thousand statues carved and standing in their several niches and pinnacles; and everything looks like the bristling frost-work in a forest of icicles; and far above and far on every side swell the lines of beauty. How different is his conception from that of the man who stands in the nave below! But, at the same time, a man stands outside looking at the cathedral's fretted front and its wondrous beauty and diversity, while a fellow-companion and traveler is on the other side looking also at the exterior. Here are four men—one before the structure, one behind it, one on the roof, and one in the interior; and each of them, as he gives his account of the Milan Cathedral, speaks of that which made the strongest impression upon his mind, and the most carried him away. But it takes the concurrent report of these four men to represent that vast work of architecture. Is it so with a man-built cathedral? and shall it not be so with the mighty God who is from eternity to eternity? Is there any man that can take the reed of his understanding and lay it along the line of God's latitude and longitude as if He were measurable as a city? Is there any man who can cast his plummet into the depths of the Infinite, and say, "I have sounded God to the bottom?" Is there any man that has an imagination by which he can fly so high that he can say, "I have reached the point above which God is not?" Is there any man who "by searching can find out God? Canst thou find out the Almighty unto perfection?" Each man learns a little, and learns that which he is most susceptible of learning. Each man has that conception of God which he is capable of receiving. Men's Minds a Sphere in Which God's Judgments May Work.—"The Lord hath mingled a perverse spirit in the midst thereof." Failure in recognizing men's minds and wills, as spheres of Divine operation, makes difficult to us such cases as that of Pharaoh, whose heart the Lord is said to have hardened; or that of the prophets in the time of Ahab,

"I have had many things in my hands, and I have lost them all; but what ever I have been able to place in God's, I still possess." —Martin Luther.

"'Hold thy peace!' says Wisdom to Folly. 'Hold thy peace!' replies Folly to Wisdom. 'Fly!' cries Light to Darkness; and Darkness echoes back, 'Fly!' The latter chase has been going on since the beginning of the world, without an inch of ground gained on either side. May we believe that the result has been different in the contest between wisdom and folly?"—Hare.

amongst whom God had sent a "lying spirit." But the apostle distinctly taught that all the sides and all the forces of man's nature are in God's control, and that he can work his purposes through them all. Writing to the Romans (i. 28), Paul says of the Gentiles, "God gave them over to a reprobate mind, to do those things which are not convenient." And the heathen have a motto which embodies the same truth, "Whom the gods would destroy they first dement"—a sentence involving a belief in the control of the gods over men's minds. A further illustration may be found in the prayer offered by David in the time of his extreme peril: "O Lord, I pray thee, turn the counsel of Ahithophel into foolishness" (2 Sam. xv. 31). This truth we can clearly see and fully accept.—Pul. Com.

"With what cracked pitchers go we to deep wells in this world." — E. B. Browning.

15—17. (15) **any work,** i. e., no successful plan to avert trouble is carried out by any one, either by the leaders, or by the mob. **branch or rush,** fig. of high class and low. (16) **unto women,** easily frightened; quite lacking manly spirit. **the shaking,** etc., i. e. "by the repeated blows with which Jehovah smites them, comp. xxx. 32; x. 32; xl. 15."—Camb. Bib. (17) **land of Judah,** wh., being directly associated with Jehovah, will recall at once to the mind of Egypt their reasons for fearing His judgments.[a] "The mere mention of the name of Judah will strike terror in Egypt into all that hear it."—Driver.

[a] This prophecy need not be fixed to any precise historical event. When in a helpless condition, Egypt would be full of fear at the least threatening of Jehovah, from whom they had already suffered so much.

Infinite Knowledge of God.—A little child sits on the verandah and watches the worm. He is a voyager for his food on the leaf of the mulberry tree, and he goes eating, eating, eating. Let us suppose that some Divine Power enables that worm to be so far intelligent as to say, "It is said that there are beings who can understand this whole tree; but it does not seem to me possible. I can comprehend how there might be beings that should understand this leaf, and the next three or four; but to take in all the million leaves on this tree is a thing that transcends my conception. I do not believe it possible for any magnified worm to understand so much." It is not possible for any worm. But there is a little Sunday-school child sitting on the verandah, who looks on the tree and sees the whole of it; and not only sees the whole of it, but can individualise the leaves at its pleasure. How easy it is for that little child to take in that whole tree! and how hard it is for that worm to take in more than three leaves! And let that child grow up, and be educated, and trained in landscape-gardening, and it will take in, not merely a tree, but a whole forest. If one leaf is colored, if one twig is broken, if there is a dry branch, it does not escape his notice. Differences of hue, light, and shadow, the infinite diversities that come in forest life—he takes them all in, and has a kind of omnipresence in his consciousness of the facts of this whole matter. What could a worm understand or imagine of a being that is competent to take in the realm of philosophy, and that makes himself the measure of creation? He says, "It does not seem reasonable to me that anybody can understand more than twenty leaves. I cannot; and I do not see how anybody else can." And yet, do not you understand how a person can take in sections, and gradations, and ranks, and degrees infinitely above what a worm could understand? And have you anything more to do than to carry on that idea to imagine a Being before whom all eternity passes, and to whom all the infinite treasures of this eternity shall be just as simple as to you the leaves on the individual tree are? It only requires magnitude of being, infinity.—H. W. Beecher.

"The good man cares not who comes up the path, he can bring no danger to him. The honest soul is not frightened by the rustling of a leaf, no footfall shakes down the cowardice of his frail security; he says, I live in God, I am the servant of the living God, I know no will but God's; come, go, who will, who may, my foundation standeth sure, and is inscribed in letters of gold with this legend, 'The Lord knoweth them that are his.'"

18—20. (18) **five cities,** there were some 20,000 cities in Egypt. Five is a small number, but marks a beginning, either through conversion or colonization. Large numbers of Jews, in later years, became resident in Egypt. **city of destruction,**[b] one of these cities is Heliopolis (îr, hachéres,) "the city of the sun"; it shall be called "the city of destruction," (îr, ha-héres), the place where sun-worship is destroyed. A play on words, comp. Jer. xliii. 13. (19) **altar,** "in lieu of the obelisks and other heathen emblems with which Egypt abounded, there will henceforward be the tokens that it is a land devoted to Jehovah."—Driver.[c] (20) **saviour,** prob. Alexander the Great, who delivered Eg. from the Persian yoke.

[b] Coverdale renders this clause, "and Heliopolis shall be one of them."

[c] "A strange conception for one who wrote at a time when the old Egyp. priesthood seemed more powerful than ever!"—Spk. Com.

"Past blessings and graces are a sort of guarantee for future ones." — F. W. Faber.

Homiletic Hints.—I. No power political, numerical, intellectual, physical, able to resist God. II. Love your enemies. III. Be assured of reformation of wicked, before you receive them into friendship. IV.

"Man's best directed efforts accomplish a kind of dream. * * * God is the sole worker of realities." — Hawthorne.

Jesus found an asylum but not a home in Egypt; the world a lodge, not a rest for the Church. V. Conversion of this land predicted; do not despair of the salvation of the worst. VI. How mighty is the grace of God. He is able to save to the uttermost—even you.—Topics.

O Pity Me.—
Immortal Love, within whose righteous will
Is always peace,
O pity me, storm-tossed on waves of ill,
Let passion cease;
Come down in power within my heart to reign,
For I am weak, and struggle has been vain.

The days are gone, when far and wide my will
Drove me astray;
And now I fain would climb the arduous hill,
That narrow way,
Which leads through mist and rocks to Thine abode,
Toiling for man and Thee, Almighty God.
—Stopford A. Brooke.

21, 22. (21) **known,** R. V. (margin) "make Himself known." This deliverer of Egypt shall be a revelation of Jehovah. And it will be successful. They shall **know the Lord,** recognize His presence, and begin to worship Him by sacrifices, etc. **sacrifice .. vow,**[a] "prophecy does not contemplate the abolition of sacrifices in the coming period of salvation, for the rites of worship in this future and enlarged kingdom of God are connected in respect to sacrifice and festival with the O. T. ritual."—Oehler. In this passage it is noteworthy that the worship in Egypt is instituted by the Egyptians themselves. (22) **smite,** in judgment. **heal,** in mercy.[b]

Love of Mercy.—It is related that during the first few days of the reign of Queen Victoria, then between nineteen and twenty years of age, some sentences of a court-martial were presented for her signature. One was death for desertion. A soldier was condemned to be shot; and his death-warrant was presented to the queen for her signature. She read it, paused, and looked up to the officer who had laid it before her, and said, "Have you nothing to say in behalf of this man?" "Nothing: he has deserted three times," said the officer. "Think again, my lord," was her reply. "And," said the gallant veteran, as he related the circumstance to his friends (for it was none other than the Duke of Wellington), "seeing her Majesty so earnest about it, I said, 'He is certainly a bad soldier; but there was somebody who spoke to his good character; and he may be a good man for ought I know to the contrary.'" "Oh, thank you a thousand times!" exclaimed the youthful queen; and, hastily writing "Pardoned" in large letters on the fatal page, she sent it across the table with a hand trembling with eagerness and emotion.

23—25. (23) **highway,**[c] leading through Palestine. The three countries shall be united in peace, under one faith and worship, for Assyria also will accept the rule of Jehovah. "Never before had the faith of prophet soared so high, or approached so near to the conception of a universal religion."—W. R. Smith. **serve,** the living God, as vs. 21. (24) **the third,** one of three, forming a triple union in the service of God. Note the position of Israel as between Egypt and Syria. **a blessing,** as promised, Ge. xxii. 18. (25) **my people,** become Mine by their union in My worship. **work .. hands,** wh. has brought about their conversion. These titles have elsewhere been confined to Israel. **inheritance,** so actual Son and Head of the entire earthly family of God.

The Conversion of Jews and Gentiles (vss. 24, 25).—Consider—I. The event in which God expresses such delight: it is the conversion of the whole world to God; in this event God will greatly rejoice. II. The effect which the prospect of it should produce on us. It should prevail—1. To enlarge our philanthropy; 2. To raise our expectations; 3. To quicken our exertions.—Simeon.

Unity in Religion Joins Together the Bitterest Foes.—As, ultimately, **the establishment of the kingdom of Christ among all the nations of the**

"Apart from Thee all gain is loss,
All labor vainly done;
The solemn shadow of thy cross
Is better than the sun."
—J. G. Whittier.

[a] "Lit. fulfilled when Ptolemy Euergetes, after his victory over Seleucus, B.C. 244, came to Jerusalem, and 'offered many sacrifices and made many presents,' so that in his person Egypt did homage to the true God."—Spk. Com.

[b] "The intention of healing is prominent all through the smiting."—Delitzsch.

For doctrine of this vs. comp. Job v. 17—19; Ho. v. 15, vi. 1, 2; Is. lvii. 15—19.

[c] A fig. for free, easy, peaceful communication.

"The Lord in going away from a people sometimes suddenly turns round and looks at them, and behold there is a smile where once there was a frown."—People's Bible.

"Adversity is like the period of the former and latter rains,—cold, comfortless, unfriendly to man and to animal; yet from thence come the flower and the fruit, the date, the rose, and the pomegranate."—Sir Walter Scott.

earth (ch. ii. 2) will produce a reign of universal peace, so that men will everywhere "beat their swords into ploughshares, and their spears into pruning-hooks" (ch. ii. 4), so, on a lesser scale, wherever true religion prevails, asperities are softened, old enmities die out and disappear, a friendly spirit springs up, and former adversaries are reconciled and become friends. Assyria, Egypt, Israel, long the bitterest foes, were drawn together by a common faith in the later days of Judaism and the earlier ones of Christianity—felt sympathy one with another, and lived in harmony.—Pul. Com.

CHAPTER THE TWENTIETH.

1, 2. (1) **Tartan,** see 2 Ki. xviii. 17. **Sargon,** king of Assyria immediately before Sennacherib, from 722 to 705. The date of this prophecy is 711. "The expedition mentioned is minutely related in two of Sargon's inscriptions." **Ashdod,**[d] prob, this town was taken in order to open the way to Egypt, and secure a defensive post on the line of the communications. (2) **loose the sackcloth,** "the prophets are frequently required to express the substance of the divine messages by symbolic actions. In many of these cases, however (especially in Ezekiel) it may be questioned whether the action really took place externally, as e. g in Isa. xx:2, or whether it belongs merely to vision."—Oehler.[e] For other examples comp. 1 Sam. xvl. 37; 1 Ki. xi. 30; Jer. xxvii. 2 ff; Ezek. xii. 1—7. "That he actually performed it cannot reasonably be questioned."[f]—Camb. Bib. **naked,** i. e. in his under garment. Comp. 1 Sam. xix. 24; John xxi. 7.

Verse 2.—The act is: 1. Expressive of strong feeling; suited to Oriental effusiveness, though not to our colder habits. The mind needs, in moments of strong feeling, to see itself reflected in some outward form. We all acknowledge this in connection with the great epochs of life—the funeral, the wedding. The great heart of the prophet throbbing in sympathy with his nation, must signify his grief at its condition by some change in his attire. And then: 2. It is a means of impressing others. We speak, not only by our words, but by our appearance, our apparel, our manners. Let us at least learn this lesson, that life should be significant. It should mean something; not be neutral, utterly without emphasis; or dubious to the eye and ear, like heathen oracles and heathen symbols. Without affectation and folly, we can find a way to make others feel that we feel and think and have a purpose in existence.

Readiness to Do God's Will.—There is no use of life, but just to find out what is fit for us to do; and doing it, it seems to be little matter whether we live or die in it. God does not want our work, but our willingness to work; at least, the last seems to answer all His purpose.—Hawthorne.

3, 4. (3) **three years,** there is an interval of three years between vss. 2 and 3. Then comes the explanation of the long humiliation of Isaiah, as a protest against the reliance upon help from Egypt and Ethiopia. (4) **lead away,** Heb. lead the captivity, i. e. the captives. **shame of Egypt,** wh. made much of being poorly clothed.[a]

Influence of Dress.—I have no intention to argue against gold chains, velvet caps, or sables, or anything of this nature; but, granting this furniture may be somewhat of a guard to authority, yet no public person has any reason to value himself upon it; for the design of this sort of state is only to comply with the weakness of the multitude. It is an innocent strategem to deceive them into their duty, and to awe them into a just sense of obedience. A great man will rather contemn this kind of finery, than think himself considerable by it. He will rather be sorry that his authority needs the support of so little an artifice, and depends, in any measure, upon the use of such trifles. To stoop to the vulgar notion of things, and establish one's reputation by counterfeit signs of worth, must be an uneasy task to a noble mind. Besides, we are not to think the magistrate cannot support his office without fine clothes; for, if he is furnished with general prudence, with abilities particular to his business, and has a competent share of power, he needs not doubt his influence over the people.—Jer. Collier.

d One of the 5 principal cities of Philistia, Jos. xiii. 3; 1 Sa. vi. 17. Psammetichus spent 29 years in its siege, the longest siege recorded in history. Now an inconsiderable village, called Esdud.

e "The Heb. Prophets wore a mantle, or cloak, of hair-cloth, as a badge of office, most prob. designed to indicate indifference to worldly refinement and indulgence." — Henderson.

f "What he did was only at variance with custom (in order to call attention to the sign), but not at all inconsistent with decency." —Wordsworth.

a "On the royal tombs at Thebes are representations of captives led away in triumph either in a state of complete nudity, or with a small scarf suspended round their loins and hanging down the front." —Henderson. "Egypt was a big - mouthed, blustering power, believed in by the mob; to expose her required public, picturesque and persistent advertisement. So Isaiah continued his walk for three years." — Exp. Bib.

5, 6. (5) **they,** i. e. God's people; who were so much disposed to trust to Egypt for help. **afraid,** R. V., "dismayed," when they see what has happened to those on whose help they relied. **their glory,** i. e. the subject of their boasting. (6) **isle,** R. V., "coast-land," i. e. Judah in particular but all Palestine also, for all were involved and all would be alarmed. **flee,** R. V., "fled." **how .. escape,**[b] Egypt being reduced, no defence remained for Israel against the overwhelming power of Assyria.

Providential Escapes.—Two brothers were walking together, when a violent storm of thunder and lightning overtook them. One was struck dead on the spot, the other was spared; else would the name of the great reformer, Martin Luther, have been unknown to mankind. By the siege of Leicester, a young soldier, about seventeen years of age, was drawn out for sentry duty. One of his comrades was very anxious to take his place. No objection was made, and this man went. He was shot dead while on guard. The young man first drawn afterwards became the author of the Pilgrim's Progress. John Wesley, when a child, was only just preserved from fire. Almost the moment after he was rescued, the roof of the house where he had been fell in. John Knox was always wont to sit at the head of the table with his back to the window. On one particular evening, without being able to account for it, he would neither himself sit in the chair, nor permit any one else to occupy his place. That very night, a bullet was shot in at the window purposely to kill him: it grazed the chair in which he usually sat, and made a hole in the foot of a candlestick on the table.

[b] "This was the cry of despair at Jerusalem. But in such despair was her only hope. The destruction of Egypt and Ethiopia by the arms of Sennacherib weaned her from looking any longer to earthly powers for help, and raised her eyes to heaven."—Wordsworth.

So nigh is grandeur to our dust,
So near to God is man,
When Duty whispers low, Thou must,
The youth replies, I can.
—Emerson.

CHAPTER THE TWENTY-FIRST.

Driver, Cheyne and others refer this prophecy to a siege of Babylon by the Assyrians in Isaiah's own time, 710 B. C. **1, 2.** (1) **desert** of the **sea,** "the country that was once a sea (Herod i. 184), and shall be so again."—Camb. Bib.[a] **whirlwinds,** lit. sweepers. **south,** "in Babylonia the S. W. wind, which comes from the Arabian desert, was specially dreaded: see the images of the demon of this wind in our museums."—Polyc. Bib. **it cometh,** the judgment of God, by hostile armies. (2) **grievous,** hard, difficult to understand, and stern in character. **treacherous,** etc., "the lawless oppressor, Asshur-Babel, continues his ravages." **Go up,** i. e. against Babylon. **sighing,** i. e. of captive Israel. The conquest of Bab. by Cyrus secures deliverance for Israel.[b]

Ch. XXI. Oracles on Babylon, Edom and Arabia.—These three short and difficult oracles form together one of the most singular passages in prophecy. Common to all three are (a) the obscure oracular utterance, in striking contrast to the terse lucidity of Isaiah's style, (b) the strongly-marked visionary element in the writer's experience, and (c) a certain readiness of sympathy with the foreign nations concerned in the predictions. These features indicate, if not identity of authorship, at least a peculiar type of prophetic inspiration, to which no complete parallel is found in the acknowledged writings of Isaiah. It is true that expressions characteristic of Isaiah occur in vss. 1—10, but they are hardly sufficient to remove the impression that the individuality of the writer is distinct from that of Isaiah. In the rest of the chapter the linguistic evidence is decidedly adverse to Isaiah's authorship.

Prophecy Must be Fulfilled.—Two rabbis approaching Jerusalem observed a fox running upon the hill Zion. And Rabbi Joshua wept; but Rabbi Eliezer laughed. "Wherefore dost thou laugh?" said he who wept. "Nay, wherefore dost thou weep?" demanded Eliezer. "I weep," replied Rabbi Joshua, "because I see what is written fulfilled. Because of Mount Zion, which is desolate, the poor walk upon it." "And therefore," said Rabbi Eliezer, "do I laugh; for I have thereby a pledge that as God has fulfilled His threatenings to the very letter, so not one of His promises shall fail; for He is ever more ready to show mercy than judgment."

3, 4. (3) **loins .. pain,** the Prophet sympathizes with the sufferings of Babylon,[c] as in the case of Moab (xv. 5). **bowed down,** etc., R. V., "**I am pained so that I cannot hear: I am dismayed so that I cannot**

[a] "Babylonia with its surging masses of people, was like a sea desert, a wilderness of peoples."— Spk. Com.

[b] The vision is given in 3 scenes: 1. Babylon in the height of its oppressions; 2. Media and Persia uniting for its overthrew; 3. Israel relieved by the Median success.

Elam, a part of Persia, is put for the whole.

"Every day is a vessel into which a great deal may be poured, if we will actually fill it up; that is, with thoughts and feelings, and their expression in deeds as elevated and amiable as we can reach to." —Goethe.

[c] "The Proph. has lived in Bab., and with its people, until his lot seems bound up with theirs, and the first hearing of their suddenly approaching ruin fills him with dismay."—Mat. Arnold.

see,"[d] so great is his mental distress at what he is told. **night,** R. V., "the twilight that I desired hath been turned into trembling unto me." The evening time, time of contemplation and visions, generally a joy, had become a time of terrible revelations.

Interpretation of Prophecy.—Prophecy was not addressed to the reason, nor to the statistical faculty, but to the imagination; and I should as soon think of measuring love by the scales of commerce, or of admiring flowers by the rule of feet and inches, or of applying arithmetic to taste and enthusiasm, as calculations and figures to these grand evanishing signals which God waves in the future only to tell the world which way it is to march.—Beecher.

Fear of God.—The pagan nations have ever stood in awe of deities, whose wrath they have deprecated, but whose love they have never dared to hope for. In the East India museum, in London, there is an elaborately-carved ivory idol, from India, with twelve hands, and in every hand a different instrument of cruelty. Papists put God far away, and trust to the intervention of priests, of saints, and of the Virgin. Prayers for a man must still go on after his death, and money be paid to buy God off from His vengeance. On the door of the Cathedral of St. Nicholas, in Fribourg, Switzerland, I saw a notice requesting the prayers of the charitable for a youth who had died a few days before, "fortified by the sacraments of the church;" and, inside, a painting of sundry persons in the flames of purgatory, with a contribution-box underneath, and this inscription, "Oh! rescue us; you, at least, who are our friends."—C. D. Foss.

Unfounded Fear.—

O, it is life indeed to live
  Within God's kingdom strangely sweet;
And yet we fear to enter in,
  And linger with unwilling feet.
We fear this wondrous rule of Thine,
  Because we have not reached Thy heart;
Not venturing our all on Thee
  We may not know how good Thou art.
—Jean Sophia Pigott.

5, 6. (5) **Prepare,** R. V., "They prepare," i. e. Babylon, not expecting a siege. This is what the Prophet sees in vision; the scenes connected with the destruction of Babylon. See the narration in Da. v., comp. Je. li. 39, 57. **arise,** the call of the Proph., who sees the danger to which the feasting princes are so heedless. **anoint the shield,** the usual custom before a fight. The shields were made of leather.[a] (6) **set a watchman,** "the Lord bade him get on his watch-tower—this is the phrase for observing the signs of the times—and speak whatever he saw."—G. A. Smith.

Anointing the Shield.—The ancient warrior did not yield to the moderns in keeping his armor in good order. The inspired writer often speaks of furbishing the spear, and making bright the arrows; and the manner in which he expresses himself in relation to this part of the soldier's duty, proves that it was generally and carefully performed. But they were particularly attentive to their shields, which they took care frequently to scour, polish, and anoint with oil. The Oriental soldier seems to have gloried in the dazzling lustre of his shield, which he so highly valued, and upon which he engraved his name and war-like exploits. To produce the desired brightness, and preserve it undiminished, he had recourse to frequent unction; which is the reason of the Prophet's invitation: "Arise, ye princes, and anoint the shield." As this was done to improve its polish and brightness, so it was covered with a case, when it was not in use, to preserve it from becoming rusty. This is the reason the Prophet says, "Kir uncovered the shield." The words of David, which we read in his lamentation over Saul and Jonathan, may refer to this practice of anointing the shield, rather than anointing the king: "The shield of the mighty is vilely cast away, the shield of Saul, as though it had not been anointed with oil;" the word he being a supplement, the version now given is perfectly agreeable to the original text.—

d "Too much confounded to hear, too much frightened to see." — Ewald.

"What can that man fear who takes care to please a Being that is able to crush all his adversaries." — Addison.

"Fear is a kind of gong which rings the mind into quick life: it is the soul's signal for rallying." —Beecher.

"As a father in a garden stoops down to kiss a child, the shadow of his body falls upon it. So, many of the dark misfortunes of our life are not God going away from us; but our heavenly Father stooping down to give us the kiss of his infinite and everlasting love." — Talmage.

"In the deepest night of sorrow God gives us so much to be thankful for that we need never cease our singing." — Coleridge.

a "Commonly of bull's hide, with the hair outwards; sometimes strengthened by one or more rims of metal, and studded with nails or metal pins. It was oiled that the enemies' weapons might glide off it."—Wilkinson.

"Religion does not make all Christians alike, nor give them the same work to do. There is an infinite variety of endowments, and great differences of capacity both in kind and degree, and a great diversity in the matter of oppor-

Paxton. Watchmen.—We need in the Church quiet, observant, contemplative men. Yet there must be a limit even to a watchman's silence. The lifting of a finger may be enough in some instances, or the holding forth of an appointed signal. In other cases there must be a loud crying out, so that men may know what danger is imminent.—People's Bible.

7, 8. (7) R. V., "And when he seeth a troop, horsemen in pairs, a troop of asses, a troop of camels,[a] he shall hearken diligently," etc. (8) R. V., "And he cried as a lion: O Lord, I stand," etc. Complaining of his long and weary watching all in vain, for he sees nothing. But even while he thus complains, the army suddenly comes in sight.[b]

Lion Hunt.—In a lion hunt at Baroda, in the East Indies, in 1816, a small party of the gentlemen of the residency, accompanied by ten sepoys, after killing a lioness, went in search of her companion. After some time, the animal was traced by his footsteps to one of the high hedges which intersected a garden within a mile of the town. The party approached within eight yards, when two gentlemen and two sepoys fired; the animal then moved off to the other side of the hedge, groaning with rage and pain. Some pieces were instantly discharged, which, exasperating him, he rushed out, and nobly charged his assailants, his tail being curled over his back. In his advance he was saluted with great coolness with several balls from all the gentlemen and a few sepoys of the party who had come up; and though within a few yards of the object of his attack, he suddenly turned off and sprung upon a sepoy detached to the right, with whom he grappled, and afterwards by the violence of the exertion fell to the ground beyond him. At this moment the party gallantly, and for the humane purpose of saving a fellow creature, rushed forward, and with bayonets and swords put an end to the monster. The sepoy was wounded in the left shoulder, but not dangerously.—Percy Anec.

What Matter I or They.—

Others shall sing the song,
Others shall right the wrong,—
Finish what I begin,
And all I fail of, win.

What matter I or they,
Mine, or another's day,
So the right word be said,
And life the sweeter made.—Whittier.

9, 10. (9) **a chariot**, etc., R. V., "a troop of men, horsemen in pairs." vanguard of a detroying host. The Prophet knows what it means, and raises the wail for Babylon fallen. **images .. broken,** Cyrus was an enemy to the Bab. idolatry.[c] (10) "The application to Israel, addressed as 'my threshing (i. e. threshed one) and my child of the threshing-floor'—forcible figurative epithets of Israel as a nation crushed and down-trodden by the brutal tyranny of Babylon (cf. ch. xli. 15; Mi. iv. 12. f.; Jer. li. 33, etc.)."[d]—Camb. Bib.

Note on vs. 9.—This is a prophecy, and yet speaks as if the event to which it relates had been already accomplished. It is common in Eastern speech, in order to show the certainty of anything which shall be done, to speak of it as having been already accomplished. Thus the Psalmist, in speaking of the iniquities of bad men as having already received their reward, evidently alludes to the certainty of future punishment. It is therefore of the first importance to know in what tense the verb is meant, as that alone will give a true view of the intention of the writer. In the Tamul language the past tense is often elegantly used for the future: thus, in the Nan-nool (the Native Grammar) this distinction is beautifully illustrated. Does a note require to be taken to another place in a very short time, the messenger, on being charged not to loiter on the way, replies, "I have already returned:" whereas he has not taken a single step of his journey. "My friend," asks the priest, "when do you intend to go to the sacred place and perform your vows?" "I have been and returned," which means he is going immediately. "Carpenter, if you are not quick in finishing that car, the gods will be

tunity for service. Each has precisely what is fitted to his ability and circumstances, — no more, no less. Every man has just as many opportunities for service as he can use with advantage."— Taylor.

a "Cyrus had a great number of camels in his army, and his successor, Darius Hystaspis, is said to have gained a great victory over the Scythians by means of the number of asses in his service."—See Herodotus.

b The suddenness of the Median approach is vividly indicated by its coming in sight just as the watchman began to complain of his bootless watching.

"Who does not in some sort live to others, does not live much to himself."— Montaigne.

"Man's rank is his power to uplift."—Geo. MacDonald.

"The war-chariots, the cavalry moving in double file, the trains of asses and camels, correspond to the appearance of the Perso-Median army."—Spk. Com.

c "The strong antipathy of the Medes and Persians to image-worship is well known. Their iconoclasm is a thing to wh. the ancient world supplies no parallel outside Israel." — Spk. Com.

" The Persians deem it unlawful to form images, or construct temples and altars, and charge those with stupidity who do so." — Herodotus.

d "Under the fig. of a threshing-ground, and the

son of a threshing-floor (i.e. the corn threshed upon it), the Prophet describes his own beaten, crushed and pounded people." — Mat. Arnold.

Am. ix. 9; Mat. iii. 12; Re. xiv. 14, 15.

"He that wrestles with us strengthens our nerves and sharpens our skill. Our antagonist is our helper." — Burke.

"Let us learn upon earth the things which can call us to heaven."—Jerome.

"If ye seek for My help, and prove yourselves to be children of My faithful servant Abraham, then light will dawn upon you. Turn to Me with your whole heart, and I will receive you."—S. Jerome.

"An ear
Quick to hear
Eternal melody;
An eye quick to see
All beauty,
Christ, in thee;
A mouth
Seasoned with charity,
Softer than soft wind of the South—
Grant these, O Lord, to me!"
—Anna E. Hamilton.

"That there is night in this world few will question. He must be a bold optimist who thinks everything as it is, is for the best possible in the best possible of worlds. Darkness still covers the earth. God's children, who have a glorious light within them, have a dark night all round about them. Night is the symbol of gloom and suffering; and it is the season of sin. It is moral night, because 'men love dark-

angry with you." "My lord, the work is already done;" when perhaps some months will have to elapse before the work can be finished. But they also use the past for the future, to denote certainty as well as speed. Do the ants begin to run about with their eggs in their mouths, it is said. "It has rained," though a single drop has not fallen upon the ground. The meaning is, the sign is so certain, that all doubt is removed. "Why does that man go to the village? Does he not know the cholera is sweeping as a besom? Alas! Alas! he is already dead;" which means, he will certainly die. Should the friends of a young man inquire whether he may go to sea, the soothsayer says (if the signs are unfavorable), "He is already drowned." But the future is also used instead of the past, as in the case of the deliverer from Bozrah: "I will stain," for "I have stained." Should a man refuse to obey an officer, and inquire, "Where is the order of the king?" the reply is, "He will command," which strongly intimates that it has been done, and that other consequences will follow (1 Sam. iii. 13). See margin, 1 Kings iii. 13, also vi. 1, and xv. 25; 2 Kings viii. 16; Dan. ii. 28, also iii. 29; for all of which see marginal readings. See Dr. A. Clarke on Matt. iii. 17, also xxvi. 28, blood is shed, for will be shed.—Roberts.

11, 12. (11) **Dumah,** "a play on the name Edom." The word means, silent land. **Seir,** the principal mountain in Idumæa: S. of the Dead Sea, in Arabia Petræa. **what .. night?** "our translation, though picturesque, is misleading. The voice does not inquire, 'What of the night?' i. e. whether it be fair or foul weather, but 'How much of the night is passed?' literally 'What from off the night?' This brings out a pathos that our English version has disguised. Edom feels that her night is lasting terribly long."—G. A. Smith. (12) " The watchman's answer is designedly obscure. It may mean either that the seer has obtained no clear vision of the destiny in store for Edom; or that he foresees a transient gleam of prosperity to be followed by a new night of distress; or that hope is dawning for some and gloom settling down upon others." **morning,** i. e. the return of joy and prosperity. **also the night,** i. e. new calamities are in the future. **return, come,** R. V. marginal, "come ye again," i. e. the answer is not final: Let them ask at another time.

The Edomites were very impatient under the Babylonish yoke, and very importunate in their inquiries after deliverance; reiterating the question, "What of the night? Watchman, what of the night?" When will this dark and long captivity be ended? And now that their hopes are repulsed by the watchman's answer, they are exceedingly unwilling to relinquish them. Loth to depart with an answer so ungrateful, they linger, and inquire again and again, in hopes that the sentence may be reversed. But they are told that all their lingering is in vain. "If ye will inquire, inquire ye, return, come" again; yet shall your answer be the same. And what was the crime of the Edomites that should draw down upon them this heavy burden, this irresistible doom? Their inveterate hatred of the people of God (Obad. 10). Perhaps there was no nation whose treatment of Israel was so invariably spiteful, and whose enmity was accompanied with such aggravating circumstances. They were descended from Abraham and Isaac, and were treated by Israel, at the time they came out of Egypt, as brethren; but as they then returned evil for good (Num. xx. 14—21), so it was ever afterwards. Their conduct, on the melancholy occasion of Jerusalem being taken by the Chaldeans, was infamous (Obad. 10—16).—Andrew Fuller. Prophetic Declaration.—"The morning cometh." Always a musical note that. To the sufferer in the chamber of affliction, longing for the first beams of day; to the dismantled ship out far away on the melancholy sea; to the oppressed people waiting for deliverance; to the idolatrous Israel in returning to the true and living God. "The morning cometh." A thought to be meditated on in all long and weary nights of disappointment, disaffection, doubt, and trial. "Weeping may endure for a night, but joy cometh in the morning." Patience, poor heart! The morning cometh to the penitent Peter and the doubtful Thomas. "The morning cometh." Not for Israel only, but for the world. The nations that sat in darkness have seen a great light.—Pul. Com. A Curious Custom.—The following used to be, and perhaps now is, the curious mode in which watchmen announce the hours of the night at Herrnhuth, in Germany:—

VIII. Past eight o'clock! O Herrnhuth do thou ponder;
Eight souls in Noah's ark were living yonder.
IX. 'Tis nine o'clock! ye brethren, hear it striking;
Keep hearts and houses clean, to our Saviour's liking.
X. Now, brethren, hear, the clock is ten and passing;
None rest but such as wait for Christ embracing.
XI. Eleven is past! still at this hour eleven,
The Lord is calling us from earth to heaven.
XII. Ye brethren, hear, the midnight clock is humming;
At midnight, our great Bridegroom will be coming.
I. Past one o'clock! The day breaks out of darkness:
Great Morning Star appear, and break our hardness!
II. 'Tis two! on Jesus wait this silent season,
Ye two so near related, will and reason.
III. The clock is three! The blessed Three doth merit
The best of praise, from body, soul, and spirit.
IV. 'Tis four o'clock! when three make supplication,
The Lord will be the fourth on that occasion.
V. Five is the clock! five virgins were discarded,
When five with wedding garments were rewarded.
VI. The clock is six! and I go off my station;
Now, brethren, watch yourselves for your salvation.

ness rather than light.' Every true-hearted, earnest Christian is a watchman: he watches for his own soul, and for the souls of others; and he longs for the advent of the world's new morning, when the shadows shall flee away."—Hom. Com.

Five verses containing the oracle on Arabia. A vision (13—15) and its interpretation (16—17). **13—15.** (13) **forest**[a] instead of the open pastoral plains. "In the time of the insecurity of the Assyrian invasion the traveling merchants have to go aside from their great trading roads in the evening to lodge in the thickets." **travelling companies,** wandering tribes. **Dedanim,** see Ge. xxv. 3; 1 Chr. i. 32. "They carried on commerce bet. Arabia and Tyre" (Eze. xxvii. 15). (14) Cam. B., "To the thirsty bring water, O ye inhabitants of the land of Tema, meet the fugitive with bread [suitable] for him."[b] Tema is the modern Teima in the northern highlands of Arabia. Je. xxv. 23; Job. vi. 19. (15) **grievousness,** etc., or press of victorious battle.

a "Region of thick underwood, rugged and inaccessible."—Fausset.

b "The inhabitants of Tema are called to perform the rites of hospitality towards the fugitives."—Henderson.

True Courage and Gentleness go Hand in Hand.—The brave man is generous and forbearant, never unforgiving and cruel. It was finely said of Sir John Franklin by his friend Parry, that "he was a man who never turned his back upon a danger, yet of that tenderness that he would not brush away a mosquito." A fine trait of character—truly gentle, and worthy of the spirit of Bayard—was displayed by a French officer in the cavalry combat of El Bodon in Spain. He had raised his sword to strike Sir Felton Harvey, but perceiving his antagonist had only one arm, he instantly stopped, brought down his sword before Sir Felton in the usual salute, and rode past.—Smiles. Fleeting Honors of Life.—"I remember," observes one, "having heard a sensible person say he could never covet the office of chief magistrate of London, because that honor continued only one year. Might not the idea be justly extended to all the honors and enjoyments of this life? None of them are permanent."—Whitecross.

"The soul, secured in her existence, smiles at the drawn dagger, and defies its point."—Addison.

"Where life is more terrible than death, it is then the truest valor to dare to live."—Sir Thos. Browne.

16, 17. (16) **hireling,** comp. similar expression, ch. xvi. 14. **Kedar,**[a] Ge. xxv. 13. They ranged from the desert of the Red Sea as far as Euphrates. "The glory of the wealthy pastoral tribe of Kedar (lx. 7)—here used to include by implication its less influential neighbors—will be past, and of its warriors only an insignificant remnant will survive."—Driver. (17) **archers,** the Ishmaelites were famed for their archery.[b].

a "All the Ishmaelites are called 'sons of Kedar' by the Hebrew rabbis."—Wordsworth.

b Ge. xxi. 20.

Uncertainty of Possession.—Our joy may be turned into sorrow; the root out of which came bud and blossom and fruit, beautiful to the eyes and to be desired to make one wise, may grow nothing but poison. We hold nothing certainly, with an assurance that cannot be broken, with guarantees that cannot be violated. When we grip any prize with our poor five fingers, the fingers themselves may fail to hold the blessing, and that which we thought secure may vanish in a moment. Make the best of the present time; realize what is written as soon as you can, turn it into positive, absolute property, into soul, into manhood, that cannot be taken away from you but by your own consent.—Peop. Bib.

"Care is no cure, but rather a corrosive, for things that are not to be remedied." — Shakespeare.

"War ought never to be accepted unless it is offered by the hand of necessity." — Sir P. Sidney.

"Our life is scarce the twinkle of a star in God's eternal day." — Bayard Taylor.

CHAPTER THE TWENTY-SECOND.

The first fourteen verses consider "The Inexpiable sin of Jerusalem." **1—3.** (1) **valley of vision,** a poetical name for Jerusalem. **what aileth,** etc., a question as of a stranger, who would know the reason of the prevailing excitement and distress. **housetops,**[c] "the flat roofs of the houses are thronged by excited citizens keeping holiday, perhaps watching some public spectacle. The prophet, wandering disconsolate through the streets, ironically inquires the reason of this unseasonable demonstration."—Camb. Bib. (2) **stirs,** R. V. "shoutings," what means this cheering and joyfulness? **not .. sword,** as in open battle, but with famine, in the siege.[d] (3) **bound by the archers,** Polyc. B., "without the shooting of a bow they were made prisoners," i. e. without having defended themselves.

c The flat roofs of Eastern houses are convenient for watchers.

d For distress of sieges see 2 Ki. vi. 24, xviii. 9, 10.

"Thus sometimes hath the brightest day a cloud, and after summer evermore succeeds barren winter with his wrathful nipping cold; so cares and joys abound as seasons fleet."—Shakespeare.

"He is the happiest, be he king or peasant, who finds peace at home."—Goethe.

Housetops (vs. 1).—The houses in the East were in ancient times as they are still, generally, built in one and the same uniform manner. The roof or top of the house is always flat, covered with broad stones, or a strong plaster of Paris, and guarded on every side with a low parapet wall. The terrace is frequented as much as any part of the house. On this, as the season favors, they walk, they eat, they sleep, they transact business, they perform their devotions. The house is built with a court within, into which chiefly the windows open; those that open to the street are so obstructed with lattice-work, that no one either without or within can see through them. Whenever, therefore, anything is to be seen or heard in the streets, every one immediately goes up to the housetop to satisfy his curiosity. In the same manner, when any one had occasion to make anything public, the readiest and most effectual way of doing it was to proclaim it from the housetops to the people in the streets.—Bp. Lowth.

4, 5. (4) **Look away,** and leave me to weep.[a] (5) Polyc. Bib. and Camb. Bib. translate. "For a day of tumult and of trampling and of confusion has in store the Lord Jehovah of hosts: In the valley of vision they break down the wall and the crying sounds to the mountain." **valley of vision** is an obscure expression, thought by some to refer to some part of Jerusalem.

a Comp. Je. ix. 1.

"Man is a child of sorrow, and this world has cares enough to plague us; but it hath means withal to soothe these cares; and he who meditates on others' woe shall in that meditation lose his own."—Cumberland.

"Men die, but sorrow never dies;
The crowding years divide in vain,
And the wide world is knit with ties
Of common brotherhood in pain."—Susan Coolidge.

Anxiety Versus Trust.—One day, while Flattich, a pious minister of Wirtemberg, was sitting and meditating in his arm-chair, one of his foster-children fell out of a second-story window, right before him, down upon the pavement below. He calmly ordered his daughter to go down and pick up the child. On doing so, she found the child not only alive, but without having sustained the least injury. The noise occasioned thereby had called out a neighbor's wife, who reproached Flattich for his want of attention to his foster-children; for she had seen him quietly reposing in his arm-chair when the boy fell out of the window. While she was thus scolding, her own child, which she had brought along, fell from a bench in the room, and broke one of its arms. "Do you see, good woman?" said Flattich; "if you imagine yourself to be the sole guardian of your child, then you must constantly carry it on your arm. I commend my children to God; and, if they then fall, they fall into the arms of an angel."

Sorrow—

Do not cheat thy Heart and tell her,
  "Grief will pass away.
Hope for fairer times in future,
  And forget to-day."
Tell her, if you will, that Sorrow
  Need not come in vain;
Tell her that the lesson taught her
  Far outweighs the pain.—A. A. Proctor.

b "Elam here is treated as subject to Babylon; afterwards it was used by God as an instrument against it (Is. xxi. 2)."—Wordsworth.

6—9. (6) **Elam**[b] .. **Kir,** "Elam in the S.E., and Kir in the N.W., represent the limits of the Assyrian empire." **uncovered the shield,** wh. when not used had a protecting covering, or bag. (7) R. V. "and it came to pass," etc., "were full," etc., "horsemen set themselves," etc. **at the gate,** close up to thy gates. (8) **discovered,** R. V. "took away," i. e. revealed the defencelessness of the state. Polyc. Bib. translates "and the enemy drew aside the screen of Judah," and explains, "the capturing of the strong cities of Judah was like removing the screen of a sanctuary." **armour .. forest,** Solomon's cedar palace had been converted into an arsenal.[c] (9) **breaches,** those occasioned by the neglect of previous governors, not those made by the enemy. **waters .. pool,** comp. Hezekiah's act.[d]

Man's Trust in His Weapons.—It may be dangerous self-confidence to trust weapons only. It may be mere listlessness to trust God only. It is the essence of piety to brace ourselves to all noble and wise endeavor, and keep through all our doings a soul full of trustings in God. This is but illustration in the war-spheres of the universal rule, "Work out your own salvation with fear and trembling; for it is God which worketh in you, both to will and to do, of his good pleasure."—R. Tuck.

10, 11. (10) **broken .. fortify,** removing exposed houses, and repairing the walls with the materials. They numbered, or examined, the houses, to see which could be best spared or used. comp. Jer. xxxiii. 4. (11) **ditch,** R. V. "a reservoir," for storing water, when the springs outside the city were cut off. **not .. maker,** the people had confidence in their own schemes, not in the help of their Divine King.[a] **long ago,** "to Isaiah, history is the evolution of a consistent, pre-determined plan of Jehovah; to the men of his day it was merely a confused struggle between opposing forces. Their failure to discern the hand of God in the events that had befallen them was the crowning proof of their spiritual insensibility; their ill-timed frivolity on this occasion seemed to the prophet to seal their fate."—Camb. Bib.

God in His Works.—While all things are of God, by God, and to God, and God is in all things, God is not all things, nor are all things God. This is Pantheism, and I wish to guard against this blunder of human philosophy. God is in His works as an author is in his book; as a builder is in his building; as a mechanic is in his mechanism, with this difference, God is the creator of the materials as well as the organizer and constructor of them in their multitudinous forms and relations. But whoever would affirm that the book was the author, or the author the book?—that the building was the builder, or the builder the building?—that the mechanism was the mechanic, or the mechanic the mechanism? Because God is said to be in nature, it does not therefore follow that God is nature, or nature, God. The Creator must have existed before His creation, as an author must have existed before his book, the builder before his building, and the mechanic before his mechanism. In the completion of His works, God was no more absorbed in and confounded with them, than at the completion of any work of man the author or workman thereof is absorbed in and confounded with it, so that an observer should regard them as inseparable and undistinguishable. No; God maintains an existence distinct from nature, though in nature, as its Conserver; and were all material things annihilated, He would still have a being, as a man may, though all his works may be utterly destroyed.—J. Bate.

12—14. (12) **call to weeping,** this was really the message that was in the calamity, to wh. the people would give no heed. **baldness,** ch. xv. 2; Mi. i. 16. (13) **joy,**[b] etc., with the defeat of Egypt comes moral chaos in Jerusalem. "What had been a city of devotees becomes in a moment a city of revellers," (G. A. Smith) as men will do in a plague stricken city. **eat .. die,** see 1 Cor. xv. 32.[c] "When the moment of danger came, it found the people so unprepared that not only was an ignominious disaster the result, but the survivors were demoralized, and abandoned themselves to despair, regardless of the future."—Driver. (14) **till ye die,** Divine response to their self-confident boastings. Reference is to the utter death, or desolation, of the city and the nation. Reference to the second death is not necessary.

Insensibility to Calamity.—In the midst of the distresses with which France was harassed in the reign of Charles VII., and whilst the English were in possession of Paris, Charles amused himself and his mistresses with balls and entertainments. The brave La Here, coming to Charles

---

c 1 Ki. vii. 2—7, x. 21.

d 2 Chr. xxxii. 4.

"Sin degrades everything, blights all the flowers, hushes all the music, turns back all the light; it hates the morning, because the morning reveals, detects, and makes stand out in ghastly clearness things that long to hide themselves in some merciful cloud." —Peop. Bib.

a "They did not depend upon God for a blessing upon their endeavors, saw no need for it, and therefore sought not to Him for it, but thought their own powers and policies sufficient for them." —Mat. Henry.

"The gospel is not opposed to the search for truth in all fields. It welcomes all the discoveries of science, and gives the right hand of fellowship to all sincere investigation, knowing well that the works of God, rightly understood, will ever help us to understand the Word of God who did the works." —Peloubet.

"The best critics are they
Who, with what they gainsay,
Offer another and better way."

b "Nothing more strikingly evinces the strength of human depravity than trifling and reckless bravery when men are on the brink of destruction." —Henderson.

c Comp. Lu. xvii. 26—30.

"It has been disputed whether these words are expressive of contemptuous incredulity, or of a desperate determination to spend the residue of life in pleasure."—J. A. Alexander.

"On the tomb of Sardanapalus is said to have been written, 'Eat drink, and love; for the rest is little worth;' and yet the tomb itself is a witness that there hovers before the mind the thought of the future, in which man would still live and still be remembered by his fellows, even though only by means of the lifeless stone."

The foreign form of the name Shebna indicates that this officer was an alien, and prob. a heathen.

"The Prophet upbraids him with making provision for himself and his posterity in a land to wh. he was an alien, and from wh. he was so soon to be expelled." —J. A. Alexander.

"Man's will sometimes is strong, and carries him over and through great difficulties; but God is ever stronger than he, and grasps him with effectual restraints." — R. Tuck.

"Think of 'living'! Thy life, wert thou the 'pitifullest of all the sons of earth,' is no idle dream, but a solemn reality. It is thy own; it is all thou hast to front eternity with. Work, then, like a star, unhasting, yet unresting." — Carlyle.

one day to talk to him on some business of importance, whilst the luxurious Prince was occupied in arranging one of his parties of pleasure, was interrupted by the Monarch, who asked him what he thought of his arrangement. "I think, Sire," said he, "it is impossible for any one to lose his kingdom more pleasantly than your Majesty."—Whitecross. Iniquity that Cannot be Purged in this Life.—There is an important sense in which the forgiving God "by no means clears the guilty." The child of the drunkard or the sensualist will not have the spirit of drink or of passion taken out of him, nor will he be renewed from his physical deterioration, because his father becomes a Christian in his later years. Consequences of wrong reach on until they get altogether beyond handgrasp. Do any wrong, and for the soul of the wrong there is forgiveness, and full restoration, in the Divine mercy, through the precious blood-shedding; but you may pursue all your life after the natural consequences, and you shall never overtake them, never master them, never remove them. On they go, carrying their burdens of woe to the third and fourth generation. And Isaiah reminds us that there are some special kinds of iniquity to which the rule must more especially apply, for whose consequences there can be no earthly purging.—Pul. Com.

15, 16. Here begins a new section telling of the removal of Shebna the prefect of Hezekiah (vss. 15—25). (15) **"this treasurer, a Heb. word** not elsewhere found," seems to mean "associate" or "adminstrator."—(Camb. Bib). Polyc. Bib. translates, "this prefect." **Shebna,** probably a partisan of the Egyptian alliance, and his office, the highest in the court, measures his influence with the king. (16) "what right hast thou here, and what kin hast thou here," etc.—Polyc. Bib. **sepulchre here,** in so conspicuous a place! The prefect, sure of his position, had made him a sepulchre among the nobles of Jerusalem.

Man's Plans for Himself Frustrated by God's Plan for Him.—The answering New Testament case to this is our Lord's account of the prosperous farmer, who had no room to bestow his fruits and his goods. He said to himself, "I will pull down my barns and build greater." But God said, "Thou fool, this night shall thy soul be required of thee." In the passage before us, Shebna, in the full assurance that he will die quietly, and be buried honorably in the neighborhood of Jerusalem, proposes to build a tomb or sepulchre for himself. It would be one of the rock-hewn sepulchres on the slopes of the hills surrounding the holy city. God's plan for him was quite different to his plan for himself. He was to be carried away into captivity, and the fair creation of his energies would fall into ruins. "Man proposes, God disposes."—Pul. Com.

17—19. (17) R. V. "Behold, the Lord will hurl thee away violently as a strong man; yea, he will wrap thee up closely." That is he shall be forcibly thrust out of his lofty position and cast out of the land as one hurls a ball. (18) "He will roll, roll thee on, thou rolling-stone, like a ball thrown out on broad level ground; there shalt thou die."—G. A. Smith. **and there .. house,** R. V. "and there shall be the chariots of thy glory, thou shame of thy lord's house;" the chariots in which he had paraded his power, driving about the city, should go with him. (19) **station,** as the highest officer of the court.

Verse 18.—The image is that of throwing a ball upon a level and smooth surface, so that it rolls to an indefinite length; without attrition or hindrance of an appreciable kind, away rolls the smooth ball over the smooth surface, far beyond the measurement of men. Let us take heed to this. We can build nothing that God cannot unroof. God may begin, and does begin, at either of two points in his work of dehabilitation. Say he will come down upon the wicked man and work out his judgment; he will take part of the roof away, and a roof is no stronger than its weakest point—even a roof yields to that general law—and through that unroofed space the storm will pour down in pitiless fury. But God has another way of working out his judicial purpose, a way very secret, and wholly beyond the control of men; in that way he touches the foundation line, takes off the cornerstone, and the whole fabric is shaken down, and none can hinder the fall. The entire volume of human history is full of illustration of this. None can tell in what way God will come; the great and blessed and all-saving truth is that he is coming, does come, must come,

and none can hinder, and that his coming means judgment to the wicked **and** recognition to the good.—Peop. Bib.

20—23. (20) **Eliakim,** "a man with a father" in contrast to Shebna whose father is not mentioned. (21) **robe,** the sign of office. **a father,**[a] **not** a tyrant, as Shebna in his egotism and pride had been. Father intimates that he would be to the people protector, counsellor, and friend. (22) **key .. shoulder,** the keys of the E. being often large, are carried hanging from a kerchief over the shoulder.—Fausset. The key was the emblem of office, as indeed it is still. "Among the Greeks the key was worn as a badge of sacerdotal dignity." **open .. shut,** Re. iii. 7. (23) "I will drive him in like a nail fastened in a firm place," (Polyc. Bib.) **i. e.** I will make his position secure that he shall not be removed. **throne .. house,** i. e. would be a great support to his family and kindred, by securing them office and honor.

A Nail in a Sure Place (vs. 23.)—I. The lesson of the nail: little things may be very important things. II. The lesson of the sure place. 1. Good words, in order that they may do good, need good memories, and the good memory is the sure place; 2. A good example in a fruitful life, is a "nail in a sure place;" 3. Faith fixed on a good object, is "a nail in a sure place." III. The lesson of the fastening. 1. In order to the fastening, a nail needs guiding; 2. Fastened: some things, once fixed, are fixed for ever; 3. In a good place fastened."—Preacher's Lantern.

The Key of the House of David.—The most ancient lock ever discovered is that described by Mr. Bonomi as having secured the gate of an apartment in one of the palaces of Khorsabad. He says, "At the end of the chamber, just behind the first halls, was formerly a strong gate of one leaf, which was fastened by a large wooden lock, like those still used in the East, of which the key is as much as a man can conveniently carry, and by a bar which moved into a square hole in the wall. It is to a key of this description that the Prophet probably alludes: 'And the key of the house of David will I lay upon his shoulder,' and it is remarkable that the word for key (muftah) in this passage of Scripture is the same in use all over the East at the present time."—Metal Trades' Advertiser. God-given Responsibility.—How one man becomes the head of the family, the strength of the nation, the leader of the people, the dependence of empires! Were that man to be taken out of his place, it would seem as though the whole nation would perish by his removal; were that character to fail, it would seem as if the whole Church would go mourning the rest of her days, sighing, sobbing, because the son of the morning had lost his centre and plunged into infinite night. That is what God does in society: he makes some men as nails and pegs, on which are hung great responsibilities; he makes some men as pillars on whom he rests all that is uppermost in the temple of his providence; he makes some men leaders, shepherds going in advance, that they may lead God's nations and flocks and households to his appointed place: let us recognize their character and their standing, and though we may not emulate their power, we can give them the joy of knowing that we never forget them in our tenderest prayers.—Peop. Bib.

24, 25. (24) **hang,** etc., a word of warning, perhaps written later, when abuses of trust in Eliakim's family shewed themselves. Upon this nail all the kith and kin of Eliakim would try to hang themselves, like kitchen utensils on a hook. **vessels of flagons,** prob. bottles or pitchers. (25) **that day,** when that happens the nail will break—or be broken down, and the family of Eliakim like that of Shebna come to disgrace. Not necessarily within the minister's life-time.

The Nail Removed.—How is it that man, once high in esteem and general confidence, came to be weighed in the balances and found wanting? Some weakness of flesh and blood, some undue leaning to one's kith and kin, some element of partiality or favoritism, is often the cause. "His family makes a wrong use of him; and he is more yielding than he ought to be, and makes a wrong use of his office to favor them! He therefore falls, and brings down all with him that hung upon the peg, and who have brought him to ruin through the rapacity with which they have grasped at prosperity."—Delitzsch. Note on vs. 25.—The Orientals, in fitting up their houses, were by no means inattentive to the comfort and satisfaction arising from order and method. Their furniture was scanty and plain;

[a] Job xxix. 16.

Is. ix. 6, 7.

Here poss. rather the peg on wh. things are hung in the house. A strong peg on wh. reliance can be placed.

"Men are to be estimated, as Johnson says, by the mass of character. A block of tin may have a grain of silver, but still it is tin; and a block of silver may have an alloy of tin, but still it is silver. The mass of Elijah's character was excellence; yet he was not without the alloy. The mass of Jehu's character was base; yet he had a portion of zeal which was directed by God to great ends." —Cecil.

"Minute events are the hinges on which magnificent results turn. In a watch, the smallest ratchet, cog or crank is as essential as the mainspring itself. If one fall out, the whole will stand still." —Cumming.

"When a man in power has given a situation to another, it is said of the favored individual, 'He is fastened as a nail.' 'Yes, his situation is fixed, he will not be moved.' 'What! has Tamban lost his glory? I thought he had been fastened as a nail.'" — Roberts.

"Whatever there is in sorrow which is not judgment is discipline. And of this latter, we must all have our share; we shall find our future will be very different from that which

but they were careful to arrange the few household utensils they needed so as to not to encumber the apartments to which they belonged. Their devices for this purpose, which, like every part of the structure, bore the character of remarkable simplicity, may not correspond with our ideas of neatness and propriety, but they accorded with their taste, and sufficiently answered their design. One of these consisted in a set of spikes, nails, or large pegs, fixed in the walls of the house, upon which they hung up the movables and utensils in common use that belonged to the room. These nails they do not drive into the walls with a hammer or mallet, but fix them there when the house is building; for if the walls are of brick they are too hard, or if they consist of clay, too soft and moldering, to admit the action of the hammer. The spikes, which are so contrived as to strengthen the walls, by binding the parts together, as well as to serve for convenience, are large, with square heads like dice, and bent at the ends so as to make them cramp-irons. They commonly place them at the windows and doors, in order to hang upon them, when they choose, veils and curtains, although they place them in other parts of the room, to hang up other things of various kinds. The care with which they fixed these nails, may be inferred as well from the important purposes they were meant to serve, as from the promise of the Lord to Eliakim: "And I will fasten him as a nail in a sure place." Pins and nails, Dr. Russel observes, in a manuscript note, are seldom used (at Aleppo) for hanging clothes or other articles, upon which are usually laid one over the other, on a chest, or particular kind of chair. This intelligent writer does not refuse that they are occasionally used in modern times; and it is evident from the words of the Prophet, that it was common in his time to suspend upon them the utensils belonging to the apartment: "Will men take a pin of it to hang any vessel thereon?" The word used in Isaiah for a nail of this sort is the same which denotes the stake, or large pin of iron, which fastened down to the ground the cords of their tents. These nails, therefore, were of necessary and common use, and of no small importance in all their apartments; and if they seem to us mean and insignificant, it is because they are unknown to us, and inconsistent with our notions of propriety, and because we have no name for them but what conveys to our ear a low and contemptible idea. It is evident from the frequent allusions in Scripture to these instruments, that they were not regarded with contempt or indifference by the natives of Palestine. "Grace has been showed from the Lord our God," said Ezra, "to leave us a remnant to escape, and to give us a nail in His holy place;" or, as explained in the margin, a constant and sure abode. The dignity and propriety of the metaphor appears from the use which the prophet Zechariah makes of it: "Out of Him cometh forth the corner, out of Him the nail, out of Him the battle bow, out of Him every oppressor together." The whole frame of government, both in Church and State, which the chosen people of God enjoyed, was the contrivance of His wisdom, and the gift of His bounty: the foundations upon which it rested; the bonds which kept the several parts together; its means of defence; its officers and executors, were all the fruits of distinguishing goodness; even the oppressors of His people were a rod of correction in the hand of Jehovah, to convince them of sin, and restore them to His service.—Paxton.

we picture it now: boyhood will not prove to be all that childhood imagines; still less will manhood be what youth supposes; friends will forsake us, schemes will be thwarted, hopes will be extinguished, props will be cut in twain, clouds will come up and rains will pour down, as we little think to-day. The hour will come when the nail that now seems so fast will be removed, and all that hangs upon it be brought to the ground." — Pul. Com.

"If a sheep stray from his fellows, the shepherd sets his dog after it, not to devour it, but to bring it again: even so our Heavenly Shepherd, if any of us, His sheep, disobey Him, sets His dog of affliction after us, not to hurt us, but to bring us home to consideration of our duty towards Him." — Cawdray.

CHAPTER THE TWENTY-THIRD.

1. **Tyre,**[a] situated partly on a rocky island close to the coast of Phœnicia, and partly in a wide and fertile plain upon the coast itself, the chief Phœnician city, "pioneer of commerce, parent of colonies, mistress of the sea." **ships,** plying between Tyre and Tarshish. These ships, homeward bound, are met on their arrival at Cyprus by the intelligence that the harbors of Phœnicia are closed to them. **Tarshish,** prob. Tartessus in Spain,[b] the farthest point of their voyages, and the chief centre of the produce they carried.

Tyre.—Few of the cities of the past were, in their way, more flourishing and wealthy than the celebrated Tyre. The Hebrew Prophets, being commanded to foretell its overthrow, on account of the wickedness

[a] "Tyre sustained 3 sieges by Asiatic powers, the first by Shalmanezer, in the reign of Hezekiah, B.C. 717; the second by Nebuchadnezzar, B.C 573; and the third by Alexander the Great, B.C. 332." —Henderson.

[b] Eze. xxvii. 12, 25.

"The practical point to keep in view is that commercial nations are always in peril of getting to merely use other nations, and so to neglect their responsibilities to them."

of the inhabitants, delivered their predictions with great minuteness and circumstantiality (see Isa. xxiii.; Jer. xxv.; Ezek. xxvi.—xxviii.; Amos i. 9, 10; Zech. ix. 1—8; Joel iii 4—8). That these predictions have been literally accomplished, let the present state of this once famous city bear witness. Concerning that state, Dr. Thomson thus writes: "It (an insignificant village) is all that remains of her. But weep not for Tyre; this very silence and repose are most eloquent and emphatic on themes of the last importance to the Christian faith. There is nothing here of that which led Joshua to call it 'the strong city,' more than three thousand years ago (Josh. xix. 29); nothing of that mighty metropolis which baffled the proud Nebuchadnezzar and all his power for thirteen years, until every head in his army was bald, and every shoulder peeled in the hard service against Tyrus (Ezek. xxix. 18); nothing in this wretched roadstead and empty markets to remind one of the times when merry mariners did sing in her markets; no visible trace of those towering ramparts which so long resisted the utmost efforts of the great Alexander; all have vanished like a troubled dream.

"Our reverence for the past is just in proportion to our ignorance of it."—T. Parker.

2, 3. (2) "Extinct are the inhabitants of the coast, the merchants of Phœnicia, who traversed the sea, whose messengers were on many waters," etc. (Pol. Bib.) **Zidon,** stands for Phœnicia as a whole, as it was the oldest of the Phœnician settlements. R. V. "And on great waters the seed of Sihor, the harvest of the Nile, was her revenue: and she was the mart of nations."[a] The harvests of the Nile were carried to all lands by Tyrian ships, and the Tyrian revenue largely came from this carrying trade. **Sihor,** prob. a name for the Nile. Jer. ii. 18. **mart of nations,** Egyptian corn being first warehoused at Tyre, and thence conveyed to ports on the Mediterranean.

[a] "The produce of the Nile, called Shihor, or the Black River."—Wordsworth.

"Though Egypt abounded in grain, yet the inhabitants left its exportation to foreigners."—Henderson.

Wealth of Tyre's Trade.—The Phœnician empire, it has often been remarked, presents a very close analogy to that of Great Britain; but even more entirely than in the case of Great Britain the glory of that empire was the wealth of its trade, and the character of the people was the result of their mercantile habits. A little strip of land, one hundred and forty miles long, and never more than fifteen broad, with the sea upon one side and the mountains upon the other, compelled its inhabitants to become miners and seamen. The hills shut off the narrow coast from the continent to which it belongs, and drove the increasing populations to seek their destiny by way of the sea. These took to it kindly, for they had the Semite's born instinct for trading. Planting their colonies all round the Mediterranean, exploiting every mine within reach of the coastland, establishing great trading depots both on the Nile and the Euphrates, with fleets that passed the Straits of Gibraltar into the Alantic and the Straits of Bab-el-Mandeb into the Indian Ocean, the Phœnicians constructed a system of trade, which was not exceeded in range or influence till, more than two thousand years later, Portugal made the discovery of America and accomplished the passage of the Cape of Good Hope. From the coasts of Britain to those of Northwest India, and probably to Madagascar, was the extent of Phœnician credit and currency. Their trade tapped river basins so far apart as those of the Indus, the Euphrates, probably the Zambesi, the Nile, the Rhone, the Guadalquivir. They built ships and harbors for the Pharaohs and for Solomon. They carried Egyptian art and Babylonian knowledge to the Grecian archipelago, and brought back the metals of Spain and Britain. No wonder the prophet breaks into enthusiasm as he surveys Phœnician enterprise! And on great waters the seed of Sihor, the harvest of the Nile, was her revenue; and she was the mart of nations.—Exp. Bib.

"'Tis Use alone that sanctifies Expense
And Splendor borrows all her rays from Sense."—Pope.

"Fell luxury; more perilous to youth
Than storms or quicksands, poverty or chains."—Hannah More.

"Peter the First, King of Portugal, to restrain luxury, and prevent the ruin of families, absolutely forbade all his subjects to buy or sell any of their commodities without immediate payment, and made the commission of that offence death!"—Percy Anec.

4, 5. (4) **the strength of the sea,** R. V. "the stronghold of the sea." The fine figure of the lonely sea denying that she ever had children is somewhat marred by the introduction of this clause, as if the poet had corrected himself by an afterthought, and changed the subject of personification from the sea to Tyre. One is tempted to remove the words as a gloss. **I travail not,** "after all her pains and care, she is left childless. The family which she had reared, and advanced to high dignity, has perished."—Spk. Com. (5) R. V. "When the report cometh to Egypt, they shall be sorely pained at the report of Tyre," not only from friendliness to Tyre but also because Assyria is the enemy of Egypt.[a]

"Tyre bewails her childlessness by reason of her captivity."—Wordsworth.

[a] See Eze. xxix. 18, 19.

"The biggest blaze is not a sign of the most heat. A straw-pile will give a brighter blaze than a ton of coal."

"Life lies before us as a huge quarry lies before the architect; he deserves not the name of an architect except when out of this fortuitous mass he can combine with the greatest economy and fitness and durability some form, the pattern of which originated in his spirit."—Goethe.

"Order is the sanity of the mind, the health of the body, the peace of the city, the security of the state. As the beams of a house, so is order to all things."—Robert Southey.

"Praise the sea, but keep on land."— G. Herbert.

"In every object here I see
Something, O Lord, that leads to Thee;
Firm as the rocks thy promise stands,
Thy mercies countless as the sands,
Thy love a sea immensely wide,
Thy grace an ever flowing tide."
—John Newton.

"It is a city remarkable to posterity, both for the antiquity of its origin and for its frequent change of fortune." —Quintus Curtius.

"The duration of time is no guarantee against the coming of judgment; Tyre was a 'joyous city, whose antiquity was of ancient days,' but judgment would fall upon her in God's chosen time."—Pul. Com.

The Voice of the Sea (vs. 4).—It speaks—I. Of the greatness and goodness of God. II. Of the vastness and grandeur of the forces of nature. III. Of the ingenuity of man. IV. Of the dangers of those who sail upon it. V. Of our duty to those who sail upon it.—G. Brooks.

Tyre and the Sea.—How proud had Tyre been! How she thrived upon her corn trade in Egypt! Egypt had no timber, and therefore could not build ships; and if she had had a whole Bashan full of oaks she never would have cut a plank, for Egypt from time immemorial detested the sea. You never caught an Egyptian on the sea if he could stow himself away anywhere else. The Tyrian liked the sea, did not care how broad it was, or deep; he had a spirit of locomotion and daring and enterprise, and wherever the corn was the man of Tyre might be seen. Tyre enriched herself with the harvests of the Nile; she thought Sihor flowed for her advantage; the harvest of the river was her revenue, and she was a mart of nations. Honor to whom honor is due. She had acquired a great position in the world, and therefore she must have had elements of character of conspicuous value.—Peop. Bib.

Dangers of the Sea.—Nathaniel, an assistant to the Moravian missionaries in Greenland, when engaged in the seal fishery, being in company with another brother, who was yet inexperienced in the management of a kayak (a Greenland boat), met a Neitsersoak, the largest kind of seal, which he killed. He then discovered his companion upon a flake of ice, endeavoring to kill another of the same species, and in danger; he therefore left his dead seal, kept buoyant by the bladder, and hastened to help his brother. They succeeded in killing the seal; but suddenly a strong north wind arose, and carried off both the kayaks to sea; nor could they discover any kayaks in the neighborhood. They cried aloud for help, but in vain. Meanwhile the wind rose in strength, and carried both the kayaks, and also the piece of ice, swiftly along with the waves. Having lost sight of the kayaks, they now saw themselves without the least hope of deliverance. Nathaniel continued praying to his Saviour, and thought with great grief of the situation of his poor family, but felt a small degree of hope arising in his breast. Unexpectedly, he saw his dead seal floating towards him, and was exceedingly surprised at its approaching against the wind, till it came so near the flake of ice that they could secure it. But how should a dead seal become the means of their deliverance? and what was now to be done? All at once, Nathaniel resolved, at a venture, to seat himself upon the dead floating seal; and by the help of his paddle, which he had happily kept in his hand when he joined his brother on the ice, to go in quest of the kayaks. Though the sea and waves continually overflowed him, yet he kept his seat, made after the kayaks, and succeeded in overtaking his own, into which he crept, and went in quest of that of his companion, which he likewise found. He also kept possession of the seal; and now hastened in search of the flake of ice, on which his companion was most anxiously looking out for him; having reached it, he brought him his kayak, and enabled him to secure the other seal, when both returned home in safety. When relating his dangerous adventure, he ascribed his preservation not to his own contrivance, but to the mercy of God alone.—Whitecross.

6, 7. (6) **to Tarshish,** see vs. 1. Flee as far away as possible. **(7) joyous city,** ch. xxii. 2. Being a prosperous city it was full of feastings and pleasure-seeking. **antiquity,** "the Tyrian priests asserted that their temple had been built 2,300 years previously."—Herodotus. **own feet,** R. V., "whose feet carried her," etc., refers not to flight but to the long journeys that her merchants had been accustomed to take.

Notes on Tarshish.—Situation: prob. Tartessus, "a city and emporium of the Phœnicians in south of Spain." Proof—1. Similarity of name. Tartessus=Tarshish in Aramaic form (Bochart). 2. The connection between Tarshish and Tyre, as once between Tartessus and Phœnicians. "Tartessus was founded by the Phœnicians (Arian). 3. The articles supplied by Tarshish are precisely those known to have been obtained from Spain (Ez. xxvii. 12). "Ships of Tarshish" is a term denoting a certain class of vessel, i. e. those fitted for long voyages, as "East Indiaman" was a name for ships, some of which might never go to the East Indies. Ships trading to Tarshish (Tartessum) sailed from Joppa (Jonah i. 3, iv. 2). But a navy of Tarshish—i.e. of large trading vessels—also sailed once in three years to other regions from the Red Sea (1 K. ix. 26, x. 22). —Topics.

8—12. (8) **crowning city,** or "the crown-giver," Tyre is rightly so-called, inasmuch as some of her colonies (Kition, Tarshish and Carthage) were ruled by kings, subject to the mother-city. **traffickers,** or traders. (9) **Lord of hosts,** the real Lord even of idolatrous Phœnicia. **stain,** or pollute. Show that no true honor can belong to any nation apart from the fear and service in righteousness of the one living God. Man's pride against God must everywhere be humbled.[a] (10) The third strophe (vss. 10—14), as usually explained, deals mainly with the emancipation of the Phœnician colonies from the somewhat stringent control of Tyre. But the passage presents many difficulties; and from the utter uncertainty as to the meaning of vs. 13 the general sense is doubtful. **as a river,** R. V., "as the Nile," in its flood goes where it will without hindrance, so you are at liberty. **strength,** R. V., "there is no girdle about thee any more," i.e. no hindrance. (11) **against,** etc., R. V., "concerning Canaan," i.e. Phœnicia. (12) **oppressed,** etc., or thou "outraged virgin-daughter." "The epithet 'virgin' is applied to Zidon as a fortress hitherto unviolated by a conqueror. It is an almost inevitable inference that the calamity here described is the first she has known, at least within living memory. This would apply to the campaign of Shalmaneser, but not to that of Sennacherib."—Camb. Bib.

Note on Chittim.—(Chittim) Cyprians, by some thought=to Hittites. Cyprians were a race descended from Javan, of family of Japheth (Gen. x. 4; 1 Ch. i. 7, Kittim). Phœnicians traded with Cyprus; one of their settlements there being Citium, on south-east coast. People of Citium= Kittæi of the Greeks. The name given to this settlement, spread over the whole island, and to the people who after occupied settlements which had been Phœnician.

13, 14. (13) **Behold,** this verse reverts to the fact that Babylon, wh. was agent of the destruction of Tyre, should presently be itself destroyed. **was not,** etc., R. V., "is no more; the Assyrian hath appointed it for the beasts of the wilderness: they set up their towns: they overthrew the palaces thereof; he made it a ruin." Polyc. B. translates: "Behold the land of Chaldea; they have appointed Tyre for desert-beasts; they have razed the palaces thereof;" etc. **dwell .. wilderness,** i.e. for the beasts of the desert. This would be the issue of all its founder's ambitious schemes.[b] **he brought,** i.e. God, discomfiting their schemes of universal empire. (14) **strength,** or stronghold.

Tyre.—
The wild and windy morning is lit with lurid fire;
The thundering surf of ocean beats on the rocks of Tyre—
Beats on the fallen columns, and round the headland roars,
And hurls its foamy volume along the hollow shores,
And calls with hungry clamor, that speaks its long desire:
"Where are the ships of Tarshish, the mighty ships of Tyre?"

Within her cunning harbor, choked with invading sand,
No galleys bring their freightage, the spoils of every land;
And like a prostrate forest, when autumn gales have blown,
Her colonnades of granite lie shattered and o'erthrown;
And from the reef the pharos no longer flings its fire,
To beckon home from Tarshish the lordly ships of Tyre.

Where is the wealth of ages that heaped thy princely mart?
The pomp of purple trappings, the gems of Syrian art?
The silken goats of Kedar, Sabaea's spicy store;
The tributes of the islands thy squadrons homeward bore,
When in thy gates triumphant they entered from the sea
With sound of horn and sackbut, of harp and psaltery?

Howl, howl, ye ships of Tarshish! the glory is laid waste:
There is no habitation; the mansions are defaced.
No mariners of Sidon unfurl your mighty sails;
No workmen fell the fir-trees that grew in Shenir's vales,

a "To show the vanity of their efforts to deify themselves." —Spk. Com.

Eze. xxvii. 3, describes their luxury even in their shipping.

See also Eze. xxviii. 2, etc.

"A beggar being once asked what he was, answered: 'I am a king!' 'Where is thy kingdom?' 'It is in my soul. I can so rule my external and internal senses that all the faculties of my soul are subject to me.' And who doubts that this kingdom is better than all the kingdoms of the world?"—Francis Taylor.

b "Some take this as indicating the rude and unlettered condition of the Chaldaeans previous to their settlement in Babylonia."—Henderson.

"If a man, sick on his bed, burning of a fever, fetching his breath with straitness and shortness, looking like earth, says he is well in health, we do not believe him: so if we see men swelling with pride, flaming with lust, looking earthy with covetousness, and yet flattering themselves with hope of salvation, we cannot credit them, all the world cannot save them." —Adams.

"God sometimes answers at once; sometimes he gives us some better thing in the place of the particular thing we ask; sometimes he answers by the very con-

And Bashan's oaks that boasted a thousand years of sun,
Or hew the masts of cedar on frosty Lebanon.

Though silent and forgotten, yet Nature still laments
The pomp and power departed, the lost magnificence.
The hills were proud to see thee, and they are sadder now;
The sea was proud to bear thee, and wears a troubled brow;
And evermore the surges chant forth their vain desire—
"Where are the ships of Tarshish, the mighty ships of Tyre?"
—Bayard Taylor.

15, 16. (15) **forgotten,** i. e. put into obscurity and comparative poverty. **one king,** better, one dynasty,[a] "during the reign of one line of kings."—Pol. Bib. **shall Tyre,** etc., R. V., "it shall be unto Tyre as in the song of the harlot," referring to a well known ballad. (16) **Take a harp,** this is the quotation from the song, a verse of six lines of two words each, in the Heb.

Insensibility to Moral Danger.—A plough is coming from the far end of a long field, and a daisy stands nodding, and full of dew-dimples. That furrow is sure to strike the daisy. It casts its shadow as gaily, and exhales its gentle breath as freely, and stands as simple and radiant and expectant as ever; and yet that crushing furrow, which is turning and turning others in its course, is drawing near, and in a moment it whirls the heedless flower with sudden reversal under the sod! And as is the daisy, with no power of thought, so are ten thousand thinking sentient flowers of life, blossoming in places of peril, and yet thinking that no furrow of disaster is running in toward them—that no iron plough of trouble is about to overturn them. Sometimes it dimly dawns upon us, when we see other men's mischiefs and wrongs, that we are in the same category with them, and that perhaps the storms which have overtaken them will overtake us also. But it is only for a moment, for we are artful to cover the ear, and not listen to the voice that warns us of danger.—Beecher.——They say of the silly ostrich that when she hides her head in the sand, and does not see her pursuers, she thinks she is safe; that is the policy of many men. They spread their sails, and get up the steam, and go with double speed straight ahead. What, not look at the chart! No, they do not want to know whether there are rocks and breakers ahead. Arrest that captain, put him in irons, and find a sane man to take charge of the vessel. Oh for grace to arrest that folly which is the captain of your bark, and put sound sense in command, or else a spiritual shipwreck is certain.—Spurgeon.

17, 18. (17) **visit Tyre,** in restoring merely,[b] **turn to her hire,** R. V., "return, etc., i. e. shall resume her former lucrative activity; her commerce is put into the figures of this vs. (18) **holiness to the Lord,**[a] i. e. dedicated to God, used by Him. No evidence here of conversion of the Tyrian merchants—but only of God's purposes for his people. **dwell before,** etc., i. e. for the Jewish people. The prophecy is of a time when the Lord will restore her commerce to Tyre,—not for her own sake, but for the sake of Israel.

Commerce of Tyre.—Of all the cities of antiquity, Tyre was the most celebrated for the extent of its commerce. The Tyrians obtained the productions of the East, of which it was the grand emporium, by sailing up the Red Sea or Arabian Gulf, and then passing across Arabia Petræa to Rhinocolura. Alexander seems to have determined on the destruction of Tyre, in order to found a city which he might dignify with his name, and enrich with the commerce of the East; for which Alexandria was placed in a better situation than Tyre. Of Tyre, "whose merchants were princes, whose traffickers were the honorable of the earth," there now exist scarcely any traces. Some miserable cabins arranged in irregular lines, dignified with the name of streets, and a few buildings of a rather better description, occupied by the offices of the government, compose nearly the whole of the town. It still, indeed, makes some languishing efforts at commerce, and continues to export annually to Alexandria cargoes of silk and tobacco, but to a very trifling extent. "The noble dust of Alexander traced by the imagination till found stopping a beer-barrel," would scarcely afford a stronger contrast of

trary of what we wished, and out of that springs the particular thing that we prayed for."

[a] "It was destroyed by Nebuchadnezzar much about the time that Jerusalem was, and lay as long as it did in its ruins."—Mat. Henry.

"Silly man is like the foolish chickens; though the kite comes and takes away many of their fellows, yet the rest continue pecking the ground, never heeding their owner, never minding their shelter. Death comes and snatches away one man here, a second there; one before them, another behind them, and they are killed by death, undone for ever; yet they who survive take no warning, but persist in their wicked, ungodly ways (Job iv. 20, 21).—Swinnock, 1673.

[b] Prob. Cyrus, who befriended the Jews; also encouraged the Tyrians to rebuild their city.

Better to be a "publican," like Zacchaeus, if one-half of the gains made be devoted to feeding the poor, than to follow the most elevated calling and appropriate all the proceeds to one's self. "Gain" becomes "godliness," when the great wealth, which is the result of high qualities wisely employed, and blessed by God in such employment is made an offering to him, in the person of his Church or of his poor.

grandeur and debasement than Tyre at the period of its siege by that conqueror, and the modern town of Soor erected on its ashes.—Percy Anec.

CHAPTER THE TWENTY-FOURTH.

1—3. (1) Behold, "the chapter is mainly an announcement of the last judgment, but partly also a gloomy survey of the actual state of the world. The writer feels that he is living in the last days, and in the universal wretchedness and confusions of the age he seems to discern the 'beginning of sorrows.' His thoughts glide almost imperceptibly from the one point of view to the other, now describing the distress and depression which exist, and now the more terrible visitation which is imminent."—Camb. Bib. "With the very first verse the prophecy leaps far beyond all particular or national conditions: 'Behold, Jehovah shall be emptying the earth and rifling it; and He shall turn it upside down[a] and scatter its inhabitants.'[b] This is expressive and thorough; the words are those which were used for cleaning a dirty dish. To the completeness of this opening verse there is really nothing in the chapter to add. All the rest of the verses only illustrate this upturning and scouring of the material universe."—G. A. Smith. (2) **priest,** or prince. "All ranks and classes shall fare alike."[c] (3) **land,** R. V., "earth." **Lord .. word,** absolute certainty of the impending judgment.

Desolation and Misrule.—"The government of the Turks in Syria is a pure military despotism, that is, the bulk of the inhabitants are subject to the caprices of a faction of armed men, who dispose of everything according to their interest and fancy. In each government the pasha is an absolute despot. In the villages, the inhabitants, limited to the mere necessaries of life, have no arts but those without which they cannot subsist. There is no safety without the towns, nor security within their precincts." Volney.—"Few men left." After estimating the number of inhabitants in Syria in general, Volney remarks, "So feeble a population in so excellent a country may well excite our astonishment; but this will be increased, if we compare the present number of inhabitants with that of ancient times. We are informed by the philosophical geographer, Strabo, that the territories of Yanmia and Yoppa, in Palestine alone, were formerly so populous as to bring forty thousand armed men into the field. At present they could scarcely furnish three thousand. From the accounts we have of Judæa, in the time of Titus, which are to be esteemed tolerably accurate, that country must have contained four millions of inhabitants. If we go still further back into antiquity, we shall find the same populousness among the Philistines, the Phœnicians, and in the kingdoms of Samaria and Damascus." Though the ancient population of the land of Israel be estimated at the lowest computation, and the existing population be rated at the highest, yet that country does not now contain a tenth part of the number of inhabitants which it plentifully supported, exclusively from their industry, and from the rich resources of its own luxuriant soil, for many successive centuries; and how could it possibly have been imagined that this identical land would ever yield so scanty a subsistence to the desolate dwellers therein, and that there would be so few men left?—Keith.

4—6. (4) **mourneth,**[a] throughout the chapter this language is more than figurative and indicates that sympathy between nature and man taught everywhere in the Scripture. **haughty people,** lit. "the height of the people," i. e. the noblest of the people. (5) **defiled,** i. e. desecrated.[b] "That the land of Israel is profaned by the sins of its people, is a prominent idea in the O. T.; the conception is here extended to the whole earth." **everlasting covenant.** "An allusion to the covenant with Noah. (Gen. ix. 1—17.)." A covenant with the race, which the world has broken. **(6) curse,** or penalty to wh. the party who breaks the covenant is subjest.[c] **desolate,** R. V., "found guilty."

Judgment.—Who does not rejoice that there is a spirit of judgment in the universe? A languishing world should give us pleasure; a fading tree, provided that tree is an upas tree, should make us shout for joy.

[a] "The fig. is that of a bottle or other vessel drained of its contents by being turned upside down."—J. A. Alexander. Comp. Eze. xxi. 27.

[b] De. iv. 27, xxviii. 64, xxx. 3.

[c] "This accumulation of antitheses strikingly marks the indiscriminate ruin in wh. the inhabitants of Judah should be involved. No distinction would be made bet. the diff. ranks and conditions of life."— Henderson.

"Let not those that are advanced in the world set their inferiors at too great a distance, because they know not how soon they may be put upon a level with them." — Matthew Henry.

"To each his sufferings; all are men
Condemned alike to groan;
The tender for another's pain,
The unfeeling for his own."
—Gray.

[a] Is. iii. 26; He. iv. 3.

[b] "Therefore they must be driven out, as Cain was driven out of Eden."—Knobel.

[c] De. xxix. 20.

"Many a man who postpones his penitence till he cannot help it, postpones his penitence till it cannot help him, and will not see the Lord turning till he turns and looks upon him in judgment. Then, indeed, he goes out to weep. But it is out into that night which knows no dawn." —Drummond.

When the bad man is brought to justice, righteous men should sing the praises of God. When the thief is caught, when the evildoer feels the cold hand of justice on his neck, they who look on should bless God for these guarantees of legitimate and useful civilization. That there is a perdition for the Iscariots of the world is a source of profoundest satisfaction to those who love righteousness. Were Iscariot to be free of heaven, there would be no heaven to long for. The curse is personified as a beast of prey—"therefore hath the curse devoured the earth."—Peop. Bib.

7—9. (7) **new wine,** must. No one is left to attend to the newly-gathered grapes. **merryhearted,** with prob. ref. to the joy usually shown at the vintage-season. (8) **tabrets,** timbrels. A kind of drum, or tamborine.[a] "Music is the common token and accompaniment of mirth." (9) **be bitter,** i. e. by reason of national calamities they should lose all appetite for that which had been associated with joy and song.

The Consequences of Sin are Meant to Wean From Sin.—The penalty annexed to it is, in the first instance, corrective, not penal. Fire burns the child, to teach it one of the truths of this universe—the property of fire to burn. The first time it cuts its hand with a sharp knife, it has gained a lesson which it will never forget. Now, in the case of pain, this experience is seldom, if ever, in vain. There is little chance of a child forgetting that fire will burn, and that sharp steel will cut; but the moral lessons contained in the penalties annexed to wrong-doing are just as truly intended to deter men from evil, though they are by no means so unerring in enforcing their application. The fever in the veins and the headache which succeed intoxication are meant to warn against excess. On the first occasion they are simply corrective; in every succeeding one they assume more and more a penal character, in proportion as the conscience carries with them the sense of ill-desert.—F. W. Robertson.

10—12. (10) **of confusion,**[b] or "of chaos," Gen. i. 2. **house .. shut up,** because every man is in fear of enemies and suspicious of his fellows. (11) **for wine,** R. V., "because of the wine," the vineyard having been destroyed. A fig. for the entire cessation of all joyousness, and all good fellowship. (12) **gate .. destruction,** or, "into ruins is the gate beaten down."[c]

Hugh Miller has told how, by an act of youthful decision, he saved himself from one of the strong temptations so peculiar to a life of toil. When employed as a mason, it was usual for his fellow-workmen to have an occasional treat of drink, and one day two glasses of whiskey fell to his share, which he swallowed. When he reached home, he found, on opening his favorite book,—"Bacon's Essays,"—that the letters danced before his eyes, and that he could no longer master the sense. "The condition," he says, "into which I had brought myself was, I felt, one of degradation. I had sunk, by my own act, for a time, to a lower level of intelligence than that on which it was my privilege to be placed; and though the state could have been no very favorable one for forming a resolution, I in that hour determined that I should never again sacrifice my capacity of intellectual enjoyment to a drinking usage; and with God's help, I was enabled to hold by the determination." It is such decisions as this that often form the turning-point in a man's life, and furnish the foundation of his future character. And this rock, on which Hugh Miller might have been wrecked, if he had not at the right moment put forth his moral strength to strike away from it, is one that youth and manhood alike need to be constantly on their guard against. It is about one of the worst and most deadly, as well as extravagant, temptations which lie in the way of youth. Sir Walter Scott used to say "That of all vices, drinking is the most incompatible with greatness."—Smiles.

13—15. (13) "Yea, thus will it be throughout the earth in the midst of the peoples, as at the shaking of the olive-trees,[d] as at the gleaning of the grapes, when the vintage is done."—Polyc. Bib. The images are borrowed from ch. xvii. 6, and are used in the same sense. (14) **from the sea,**[a] "the prophet hears songs of praise ascending from distant parts of the earth, hailing the coming day." (15) **in the fires,** R. V., " in the east;" strictly "the (regions of) lights." The idea would then be that the West calls on the East to join in the praise of Jehovah.

[a] Je. vii. 34, xvi. 9, xxv. 10; Eze. xxvi. 13; Ho. ii. 11.

"Character is consolidated habit, and habit forms itself by repeated action. Habits are like paths beaten hard and clear by the multitude of light footsteps which go to and fro. The daily restraint or indulgence of the nature, creates the character which, whether it be here or there, settles the destiny." — J. Baldwin Brown.

[b] "Which, having set at nought Divine law and order, had fallen back into a state of chaos."—Spk. Com.

"Such would be the quantity of rubbish collected before the houses that were left, that they would be quite inaccessible." — Henderson.

Comp. Is. xxiii. 1; Je. xiii. 19.

[c] "With a great tumult the gate is battered down." — Horsley.

"Christ says, 'I am the way.' Wherever you are, at whatever point of experience, at whatever stage of sin, this way begins where you are, and you have but to take it and it leads to God. From your person, as you are at this moment, there leads a way to the Father."—Marcus Dods.

[d] "Men shall be scarce as the single olives left to be shaken down, or the few grapes left to be gleaned, after the harvest is gathered. Those who remain shall glorify God and His dealings."—Mat. Arnold.

[a] "It may be noted that 'it was chiefly in

Verse 13.—Explaining the figure used in this verse, Thomson says, "Early in autumn the olive berries begin to drop of themselves, or are shaken off by the wind. They are allowed to remain under the trees for some time, guarded by the watchman of the town—a very familiar Bible character. Then a proclamation is made by the governor that all who have trees go out and pick what has fallen. Previous to this, not even the owners are allowed to gather olives in the groves. This proclamation is repeated once or twice, according to the season. In November comes the general and final summons, which sends forth all Hasbeiya. No olives are now safe unless the owner looks after them, for the watchmen are removed, and the orchards are alive with men, women, and children. Everywhere the people are in the trees, 'shaking' them with all their might, to bring down the fruit. The effort is to make a clear sweep of all the crop; but, in spite of shaking and beating, there is always a gleaning left. These are gathered by the very poor, who have no trees of their own; and by industry they collect enough to keep a lamp in their habitation during the dismal nights of winter, and to cook their mess of pottage and bitter herbs."

lands bordering on the Mediterranean that the first Christian churches rose.' " —Spk. Com.

16. uttermost part, lit. the wing. **glory to the righteous,** etc., this is the song which the writer hears from certain far away lands, but as for himself he sees only reason for lamentation. **leanness,** R. V., "I pine away, I pine away," or in Polyc. Bib. "But I say: For me, misery; alas for me!" **treacherous,** etc., trans. "The deceivers deceive, with deceit the deceivers deceive." A wailing over the sad defection and wickedness of the Prophet's own people.

"We hear promises and praise to the righteous, but our actual experience is that of misery."—J. A. Alexander. Je. v. 11.

"Sweetest the strain when in the song
The singer has been lost."
—Elizabeth Stuart Phelps.

The Glory of the Righteous.—There are divers kinds of glory. But God's glory is the glory of the cross! There is an empty glory of self-righteousness, but that is not the glory of the righteous. Far from it. The glory of strength is to help the weak. The glory of wisdom is to enlighten the ignorant. The glory of righteousness is to shape into order that which is wrong. Yes. Glory to the righteous! for they are the salt of the earth, the safety of the nation.

17, 18. (17) **Fear .. snare,** "Terror, and Pit and Snare upon thee, O inhabitant of the earth!"—G. A. Smith. The fig. in the verse is taken from the hunted animal, which is driven into the pit, or the snare.[a] (18) **windows .. open,** recalling the desolations of the Divine judgment in the time of the flood.[b]

[a] Comp. Je. xlviii. 43, 44.

" 'Fear' is the term applied to the cords with feathers of all colors which, when fluttered in the air, scare beasts into the pitfall, or birds into the snare." —Fausset.

Lu. xxi. 34, 35.

[b] Ge. vii. 11, etc.

A Hardened Conscience Alarmed.—Richard Crowninshield was a murderer. As long as he thought the evidence of his crime was concealed he was cheerful and confident even in prison. He was a very desperate, hardened, strong-minded, remorseless villain. He was the leader of a knot of infidels, who jeered at all sacred things, and taught young men in habits of abandoned wickedness. There were accessories to his crime, not one of whom, as he thought, was suspected; and he knew that so long as that was the case, not a link of condemning evidence could be obtained against him. At length a letter, intercepted in the postoffice, led to the arrest of one of his accomplices. That arrested man was carried into the gaol at midnight; but so profound was the sleep of that hardened murderer, that all the clanging of the bolts and bars of the prison, at that unusual hour, did not wake him. The next morning the sheriff came into his cell and entered into familiar conversation with him. He was standing calmly at the foot of his truckle bed. "Well," said the sheriff, "did you hear the noise last night?" "No; what noise? I slept well." "Why, did you not know that they had arrested Frank Knapp, and brought him here last night at midnight?" The strong, guilty man put his hand to the wall to steady himself, but, unable to conceal his feelings, or to recover from the shock, fell back senseless on the bed. The recoil, the scorpion sting, had reached him at last; his sin had found him out; the sword had pierced through the rocky casement around the conscience of the desperate criminal, and was grinding in his soul. What passed that night none can tell, nor how long the man endured the terrible conflict with conscience and despair. But when the sheriff entered his cell next morning, he was hanging dead, self-murdered. Such is the power of sudden overwhelming evidence, bringing the sense as well as the proof of guilt into the soul. Men would flee from it, if they could, at the last day. If there were still a third

"When earthly comforts shall be taken from us, and at the day of judgment, then an ill conscience, look where it will, it hath a matter of terror."—Sibbes.

"They who look to time and chance for deliverance are only deluding themselves with a hope which will certainly "make ashamed" those that cherish it." —Pul. Com.

"Every character has an inward spring. Let Christ be it. Every action has a keynote. Let Christ set it."—Drummond.

a "It is rent and fractured; it bursts open in fissures: its basement gives way: then it totters, sways rapidly to and fro, and falls." — Spk. Com.

b "Heb. a hanging couch, suspended from the trees by cords, such as Niebuhr describes the Arab keepers of lands as having, to enable them to keep watch, and at the same time be secure from wild beasts."— Fausset.

c Ps. xxxviii. 4.

b "What Isaiah here predicts is the subversion for a season of the entire Jewish polity, or the removal to Babylon of those who ministered in the temple, and of the royal state." —Henderson.

c "For sun, moon, etc., as symbols of governments and rulers, comp. Joel ii. 31, iii. 15; Is. xiii. 10; Mk. xiii. 24, 26; Re. xx. 11.

"Eternal Spirit of the chainless Mind,
Brightest in dungeons, Liberty thou art,
For there thy habitation is the heart—
The heart which love of thee alone can bind;
And when thy sons to fetters are consign'd—
To fetters and the damp vault's dayless gloom,
Their country conquers with their martyrdom."—Byron.

"To accept the will of some men is hard; but God touches our feelings, wakens our confidence, commands our reverence, and

world into which souls could plunge out of the eternal world by a second self-murder, they would do it.—Cheever.

19, 20. "Broken, utterly broken, is the earth; shattered, utterly shattered, the earth; staggering, very staggering, the earth; reeling, the earth reeleth like a drunken man: she swingeth to and fro like a hammock."—G. A. Smith. (19) **broken down,** the fig. of a house ruined by an earthquake.[a] (20) **like a cottage,**[b] or "hammock suspended between the branches of a tree, liable to be tossed hither and thither in a storm." **transgression .. heavy,** the material fabric of the earth is, as it were, crushed beneath the accumulated guilt of its inhabitants (comp. vs. 5, xxvi. 21.[c]—Camb. Bib.

Danger Leads to Seeking God.—As the child, fearing nothing, is so fond of his play that he strays and wanders from his mother, not so much as thinking of her; but if he be scared or frightened with the sight or apprehension of some apparent or approaching danger, presently runs to her, casts himself into her arms, and cries out to be saved and shielded by her: so we, securely enjoying the childish sports of worldly prosperity, do so fondly dote on them that we scarce think of our Heavenly Father; but when perils and dangers approach, and are ready to seize upon us, then we flee to Him, cast ourselves into the arms of His protection and providence, crying and calling to Him by earnest prayer for help and deliverance in this our extremity and distress.—Downame.

21—23. (21) **high ones,**[b] "the 'host of the height' is equivalent to the 'host of heaven' (Jer. xxxiii. 22; 1 Kings xxii. 19; Neh. ix. 6). That celestial beings of some kind are meant appears clearly from the emphatic contrast with the 'kings of the earth' in the second half of the verse."—Camb. Bib. (22) **shut .. prison,** comp. Jude 6; 2 Pet. ii. 4; and the book of Enoch xviii. 14, 16; xxi. 6. (23) **moon,** etc[c] figures of speech to indicate the glorious splendor of the restored Israel. **ancients,** R. V. margin, "before his elders shall be glory."

The Reign of Christ Glorious (vs. 23).—To give you some idea of the Messiah's advent, as it is here described, I will endeavor to set before you—I. The nature of His kingdom: differs from all others, laws are not restrictive only, but preceptive. II. The extent of His kingdom: always extending, will presently be universal. III. The happiness of His subjects: estimated by honor, wealth, enjoyment. IV. The glory of His reign: Christ will reign in every heart and soul. Apply:—1. What you should effect on earth; 2. What blessedness awaits you in the eternal world.—C. Simeon.

Kingdom of God to be Prayed and Worked for.—Wise work is cheerful, as a child's work is. Now, I want you to take one thought home with you, and let it stay with you. Almost every one has been taught to pray daily, "Thy kingdom come." Now, if we hear a man swear in the streets, we think it very wrong, and say he takes God's name in vain. But there's a twenty times worse way of taking His name in vain than that. It is, to ask God for what we don't want. He does not like that sort of prayer. If you don't want a thing, don't ask for it; such asking is the worst mockery of your King you can mock Him with; the soldiers striking Him on the head with a reed was nothing to that. If you do not wish for His kingdom, don't pray for it. But if you do, you must do more than pray for it; you must work for it. And to work for it, you must know what it is; we have all prayed for it many a day without thinking. Observe, it is a kingdom that is to come to us; we are not to go to it. Also, it is not to be a kingdom of the dead, but of the living. Also, it is not to come all at once, but quietly; nobody knows how. "The kingdom of God cometh not with observation." Also, it is not to come outside of us, but in the hearts of us: "The kingdom of God is within you." And being within us, it is not a thing to be seen, but to be felt; and though it brings all substance of good with it, it does not consist in that: "The kingdom of God is not meat and drink, but righteousness, peace, and joy in the Holy Ghost;" joy, that is to say, in the holy, healthful, and helpful spirit. Now, if we want to work for this kingdom, and to bring it and enter into it, there's just one condition to be first accepted. You must enter into it as children, or not at all: "Whosoever will not receive it as a little child, shall not enter therein." And again, "Suffer little children to come unto Me, and forbid them not, for of such is the kingdom of heaven." "Of such," observe. Not of children themselves, but of such as children. I believe most mothers who read that text, think that all heaven is to be full of babies. But that's not so. There will be children there, but the hoary head is the crown. "Length of days, and long life and peace," that is the blessing; not to die in babyhood. Children die but for their parents' sins; God means them to live, but He can't let them always; then they have their earlier place in heaven: and the little child of David, vainly prayed for; the little child of Jeroboam, killed by his mother's step on its own threshold—they will be there. But weary old David, and weary old Barzillai, having learned children's lessons at last, will be there too; and the one question for us all, young or old, is, Have we learned our child's lesson? It is the character of children we want, and must gain at our peril.—Ruskin.

so to us his will seems most beautiful, ever right, ever wise, ever gracious. And we know the spirit of his kingdom—it is the obedience which love renders."—Pul. Com.

CHAPTER THE TWENTY-FIFTH.

1. "Here the prophet transports himself to the period of deliverance, and identifying himself with the redeemed community, utters in their name a hymn of thanksgiving."—Driver. **Lord,** better, Jehovah. **my God,** comp. Ex. xv. 2, 11; Ps. cxviii. 28, cxlv. 1, etc. **wonderful things,** lit. wonders: as Ex. xv. 11.[a] **counsels of old,** R V., "even counsels of old, in faithfulness and truth." Original plans and purposes. God keeps to them, working them out in the course of long years. He, the covenant-maker, is also the covenant-keeper.[b]

The Language of Real Piety (vs. 1).—Piety has often been counterfeited, true piety knows nothing of guile. This is the language of—I. Choice. II. Assurance. III. Enjoyment. IV. Expectation. V. Gratitude.—Theta in 100 Sks.

Seeking First the Kingdom of God.—A recruiting officer in Massachusetts heard that a young man was ready to enlist, and hastened to call upon him. He was put off with the statement that he was not ready yet. The call was several times repeated, with like results. This vacillation seemed strange to those who knew the young man's straightforward character. Afterwards he confessed that he did not wish to enlist till he felt himself ready to die. He was profane and wicked, as were all his friends and associates, save one sister. He did not have confidence enough to communicate his feelings to any one, but purloined his sister's Bible, and began to read at the beginning, to learn how to become a Christian. He came to the Commandments in course, and in them thought he had found that which would prepare him to enlist. He learned them by heart, and then tried to keep them. He was conscious of breaking only one, that against profanity. Against this he struggled; but the more he struggled, the more he swore. He then thought he would try prayer. He could not put off the recruiting officer much longer. He knelt, and cried out in much abasement and excitement, "Lord, help, help!" His prayer was answered. He passed the provocations of the next day without an oath. When the recruiting officer next came, he put down his name, and said, "Now I am ready to face anything; rebels or death." He went before the Church, and told his experience, and was reminded that he had said nothing about Jesus. His explanation was, that he had not got to Him yet in his Bible. He had read to the Psalms, but thought he must begin at the other end to find Jesus. He went to the army, as every one should enter the battle of life, a happy Christian, ready to do, suffer, or die.

a Is. xi. 5, cl. 2.

b He. vi. 17, 18.

"If a person was to attend the levee of an earthly prince every court-day, and pay his obeisance punctually and respectfully, but at other times speak and act in opposition to his sovereign, the king would justly deem such a one an hypocrite and an enemy. Nor will a solemn and stated attendance on the means of grace in the house of God prove us to be God's children and friends,—if we confine our religion to the church walls, and do not devote our lips and lives to the glory of that Saviour we profess to love."—Salter.

2, 3. (2) **a city,** Babylon, the world-renowned city. **heap,** or pile of rubbish.[a] **defenced city,** or citadel. Fortified city. **of strangers,** i. e. of strangers and enemies to Israel. (3) **strong people,** "therefore (many) a strong people shall glorify Thee, (many) a city of terrible nations shall fear Thee." No special city is meant.—Camb. Bib. (Comp. Da. iv. 34. 35, vi. 25—27.)

Goodness of God.—As the sun sends forth a benign and gentle influence on the seed of plants, that it may invite forth the active and plastic power from its recess and secrecy, that, by rising into the tallness and dimensions of a tree, it may still receive a greater and more refresh-

a "'Heaps' is a graphic picture of Nineveh and Babylon, as they now are."—Fausset.

Je. li. 26, 37; Re. xix. 1—3.

"When men do anything for God, the very least thing, they never know where it will end, nor what amount of work it will do for Him. Love's secret therefore is to be always doing things for God, and not to mind because they are very little ones." —F. W. Faber.

ing influence from its foster-father, the prince of all the bodies of light, and, in all these emanations, the sun itself receives no advantage, but the honor of doing benefits: so doth the Almighty Father of all the creatures. He at first sends forth His blessings upon us, that we, by using them aright, should make ourselves capable of greater; while giving glory to God, and doing homage to Him, are nothing to His advantage but only to ours; our duties towards Him being vapors ascending from the earth, not at all to refresh the regions of the clouds, but to return back in a fruitful and refreshing shower; and God created us, not that we can increase His felicity, but that He might have a subject receptive of felicity from Him.—Bp. Taylor.

b "The Chaldea paraphrase has, a storm which overthrows a wall. And this is prob. the right sense; a storm so violent that it sweeps down walls before it." —Mat. Arnold.

4, 5. (4) **thou,** i. e. Jehovah. **strength,** or stronghold. **blast .. wall,** as a storm of rain beats upon a wall, so the Bab. persecution beat upon the captive Jews.[b] (5) **shalt bring down,** etc., better, "humblest the pride of aliens." **even the heat,** etc., R. V., "as the heat by the shadow of a cloud, the song of the terrible ones shall be brought low."[c] The meaning is that as natural heat, however intense, is abated by an intervening cloud, so Jehovah has means of bringing to an end the fiercest oppression to which His people can be exposed.—Camb. Bib. The song of the terrible ones may be their song of triumph when victorious over God's people.

c "As clouds quell heat, so God quells the tumult of the 'strange children.'" — Mat. Arnold.

"God could relieve His people as speedily as when a thick cloud floating across the sky cools the atmosphere." — Spk. Com.

The Storm and the Refuge (vs. 4).—I. Of what do storms remind us? 1. That this world is a place for storms; 2. That this life is a time for storms; 3. That every storm is raised and guided by the hand of God; 4. Every storm so raised is benevolently designed. II. What does the refuge suggest? 1. It is well that the refuge is God, and no creature; 2. God is often spoken of as a refuge; 3. The refuge must be outside the storm, or so much stronger as to resist its influence. Apply:—(1) Expect storms, and wonder that they are so few; (2) What refuge have we against the next storm? (3) How welcome we are to this refuge! (4) What can we do to aid those who are out in the storm?—S. Martin.

The Shadow of a Cloud.—About mid-day, when the heat was very oppressive, a small cloud, scarcely observable to the eye, passed over the disc of the burning sun. Immediately the intense heat abated, a gentle breeze sprang up, and we felt refreshed. The immediate relief afforded us by the interposition of a small and almost imperceptible cloud, taught us the lesson of the Prophet, with what Divine ease and speed God can relieve His suffering Church, and bring low her proudest enemies.

a "The lees, or sediment, of wine produced by the bubbles of fixed air, which during fermentation rise to the surface, and bring along with them the skins, stones, or other grosser matters of the grapes, thus forming a scum, which, after a time, breaks and falls to the bottom." —Henderson.

6, 7. The text here is connected with the concluding thought of ch. xxiv. (6) **this mountain,** i. e. Zion. **fat things,** richest meats. **wines on the lees,** i. e. matured wines: bettered by having been kept.[a] **well refined,** carefully strained. (7) **destroy,** cause to disappear. **face of the covering,** the covering of sorrow, worn over the head in time of mourning (comp. 2 Sam. xv. 30, xix. 4; Jer. xiv. 3, 4; Esther vi. 12), this will be destroyed for sorrow will be at an end.

The Feast for All People (vss. 6, 7).—I. The feast here promised and described. 1. The place where God engages to make the feast; 2. The feast itself: the Gospel; 3. The provisions carefully selected, dearly purchased, supremely excellent, highly gratifying; 4. The guests for whom the feast is provided. II. The benefits which result from attendance at the feast. 1. Removal of darkness; 2. Conquest over death; 3. Deliverance from sorrow; 4. Justification from reproach. Apply:—(1) Come; (2) When you come expect what is promised; (3) And let your deportment be answerable to the entertainment.—Alpha in 400 Sks.

"Who does not recognize, in the unrivalled excellence of the blessings the Gospel conveys, the most powerful arguments for missionary exertion? Who can think of the Gospel feast, in contrast with the famine of the heathen, without wishing that they also might be bidden to the heavenly entertainment?" —Hom. Com.

Jehovah's Feast after Reconciliation.—The picture in this text is based upon the familiar custom in Judaism of associating a sacrificial feast with a thank offering or peace offering. Such feasts were highly festive and joyous occasions. As an instance of the custom, reference may be made to the scene of the anointing of King Saul. Samuel made a feast, after sacrifice, to which some thirty persons were bidden (1 Sam. ix. 19, 22). "According to the Mosaic law, the fat pieces of the victim were to be devoted to Jehovah immediately by burning, and the next best piece, the breast, mediately by giving it to his servants the priests:" the rest was a foundation for a feast in which the offerers shared. The "wines on the lees" are those kept long, that have become old and mellowed. "Full of marrow" indicates superior quality. The first reference may be to the joy of the returned captives when God permitted a revival of Jerusalem; but the full reference must be to the spiritual provisions of Messianic times.—Pul. Com.

8. R. V., "He hath swallowed up death forever."[b] "A promise not only to the Jewish nation (as Hos. xiii. 14), as a community, but to all its believing individual members, a necessary inference from the next clause."—Cheyne. **wipe .. faces,** as Re. vii. 17, xxi. 4. "When Jehovah removes the veil he sees the tears and wipes them away.' **rebuke,** etc.,[c] the shame of their degradation in captivity.

The Universal Extent of the Blessings of Christianity.—"The Lord of hosts shall make unto all people a feast of fat things." 1. They are adapted to all people. 2. They are sufficient for all people. 3. They were designed for all people. 4. The wide world shall, sooner or later, partake of them.—Hom. Com.

Life Triumphs Over Death.—In Christ life rules, hope rules, goodness rules, eternity rules. Man may despairingly look upon his partially raised schemes, and say, "Alas! I shall die." But the Christian man builds on bravely and hopefully. He knows that beneath all the outward show he is raising a structure of character on which death has no power, and he says, "I shall never die." The difference that is made by our letting death rule our thoughts and hopes and endeavors, and letting Christ rule them, may be illustrated by the change wrought in the land of Persia, when Zoroaster proclaimed that Ormuzd, the Good, was the real ruler of humanity. When Zoroaster came, the religious instincts of the people were debased, the divinty worshipped was malevolent, the moral tone was low, the social habits were vicious, the land of Iran was overgrown with thorns and weeds; men were idle, negligent, like the surfeited inhabitants of Sodom, given up to sensuality; they thought of their divine ruler as evil, malicious, cruel; they had the crushing, despairing, disheartening sentiments which always follow the belief that death, the representative of evil, rules. Zoroaster brought back the old and lost truth that God rules—not evil, not death. Evil is subject to God. The good God is the God of life, and life is mightier than death; of light, and light triumphs over darkness. Ormuzd was the god of production, and if they would sow and plant and weed, they would be sure to win, under his benediction, a glorious triumph over waste and barrenness and death. We are not yet free as we should be from the notion that death still reigns. We have not yet opened our hearts fully to the glorious truth that Jesus, the conqueror of death, now reigns. Above everything else our age wants to yield its allegiance to Christ, ruling in morals, in education, in literature, in science, in politics, in commerce, and in society; triumphing now over all the forms of evil that death can symbolize.—Pul. Com.

9. in that day,[a] vss. 9—12 introduce a song of which the theme is the manifestation of God in the humiliation of Moab. Evidently "that day" is not the day of final judgment; and this section is not connected in thought with what immediately precedes. In Polyc. Bible it is printed separately. Others think vs. 9 alone is "a brief strain from the hymn of the redeemed" (Cheyne), and vss. 10—12 a prophecy against Moab.

Waiting on God.—"This is our God; we have waited for Him, and He will save us." 1. Waiting on God. 2. Waiting for God. 3. Waiting on when all is dark. 4. Waiting still, when commotions and troubles surround us. 5. Bidding us wait for Him, a way of the Lord's dealing with us. 6. Making it hard to wait, a sign of God's severer dealing with us. 7. And waiting sanctified to our soul-culture. These are subjects very suggestive to Christian meditation.—Pul. Com.

The Overflowing Goodness of God.—We know God by the superabundance of the festival. He never gives merely enough. Yet he never exercises his dominion in wantonness and prodigality, but always with that economy which waits upon the wisest generosity. If we sin against the light we insult the whole noontide. It is no little artificial light that flickers in the infinite darkness that we despise, but a whole firmament of glory. If we sin against Providence, it is against a full table that we rebel; and it is upon an abundant harvest that we pronounce our curse. The Lord leaves nothing half done, does nothing with a grudging hand, keeps

b 1 Co. xv. 54.

c "The reproach of failure cast on the people of righteousness." —Mat. Arnold.

"'A little while' Pursue the way of faith; Though toilsome be the path, Some day the darksome haze will vanish quite, And on thy sight Celestial morn will drop its changeless light."

"Can any duty be more obviously founded in reason and justice, humanity and piety, than that of sending the bread of life to our perishing fellow-creatures? The most hateful and inexcusable of all monopolies is the monopoly of Christian truths and consolations."-Hom. Com.

"He who fears death has already lost the life he covets." —Cato.

a "Those who have trusted God thro' the darkness will, when the returning light comes, say, 'This is the God of whom we have spoken, and for trusting in whom we have so often been derided. We have waited long, but He has come at last, to vindicate His truth and our reliance on Him." —J. A. Alexander.

"An ill conscience when it should be most comforted, then it is most terrible. At the hour of death we should have most comfort, if we had any wisdom."--R. Sibbes.

back nothing for his own enrichment. Doth not the goodness of the Lord lead thee to repentance? What a noble companion would Goodness make for any man who longed to see home again! Goodness, beginning with the spring, passing into the summer, reddening and purpling with the hospitable autumn—yes, and not scorning the field of snow and the wind all frost, for even there God keeps sanctuary and the Most High his testimony. Sinners, therefore, with an infinite turpitude are they who force their way to the lowest nature, to their original type, to the hell that awaits unrighteousness, through goodness so vast, so delicate, so infinite.—Parker.

10—12. (10) **rest,** i. e. in order that He may continue at, and complete, His work of grace. **Moab,** put here as the symbol of all Israel's remaining enemies. **trodden down,** as worthless straw is by the foot of cattle. **under him,** R. V., "in his place," i. e. where he stands. **dunghill,** better, dung-pit, cesspool. The word used is Madmenah, which seems to refer to the Moabitish town so called. (11) R. V. "And he shall spread forth his hands in the midst thereof," represents Moab as trying to swim in the dung-pit into which he has been cast. **to swim,** i. e. hand over hand.[a] **spoils,** R. V., "the craft," spells of sorcery. (12) In R. V. tenses are all past, "hath he brought down," etc.

God's Protecting Hand.—I. Of every enterprise we should ask ,"Is it right?" If wickedness be in "the mountain," God's protecting hand will not rest upon it. A just cause creates a good conscience, and hence inspires strength. It is only the just man who feels that God "teaches his hands to war and his fingers to fight, so that a bow of steel is broken by his arms." II. Material force allied with injustice will eventually become weak as straw, vile as a dung-heap. The strong places of Moab had no inherent lastingness, because built in a godless spirit (Ps. cxxvii. 1). III. Forts and castles, ironclads and armies, can never save an unrighteous nation from decay. National selfishness, oppressive enterprises, weaken the strongest defences, corrupt the richest treasures. Babylon became a marsh, Nineveh a forsaken mound, Tyre a deserted rock. The walls of Moab were levelled with the dust. By justice only can peoples be strong. If God be in the city, its walls will be lasting as the hills.—William Parkes.

[a] The people of the E. all swim "hand over hand," alternately raising each arm out of the water, and thus never presenting the whole breast, but only one side, to the stream. Among the Assyrian sculptures which represent persons in the act of swimming, there is not one which gives a different testimony.

"If you wish to be held in esteem, you must associate only with those who are estimable."—Bruyere.

CHAPTER THE TWENTY-SIXTH.

1, 2. A third poem of four stanzas to be sung in the great coming Day (1—6; 7—10; 11—15; 16—19). (1) **that day,** the day of Jehovah's kingdom. **strong city,** Jerusalem is strong, not by reason of its condition and fortifications, but because specially under the Divine protection. **walls and bulwarks,**[b] by the bulwarks we understand the trench with the ante-mural earthworks exterior to the wall. About this time another prophet writes, Zech. ix. 6. (2) **truth,** i. e. troth, faithfulness. The prophet conceives of this city as empty—just as God has builded it—and he calls that the gates be opened that the faithful ones may enter in.[c]

Prophetic Vision.—What salvation is there in the world? what sense of divine communion? what identity with God? what confidence that time and space are only stumbling-blocks, and the real city is a city of fellowship with infinite ideas and purposes, infinite love and truth? Who is there that does not leave early Sacrament to talk about the coldness of the morning? So contradictory may men be, and superbly foolish, that they can open their eyes from looking upon God to remark upon the phenomena of space! We need the spirit of transport, the spirit that lifts itself into third heavens, and asks, Are there no higher heights; are there no seventh heavens? In such rapture we see most of the spiritual universe. We are only critics, not rhapsodists. The poet is the man we want, because he speaks ultimate truths; he puts into a line a whole revelation, he wraps up in a sentence all the births of the ages, forgetting the pang and throe and misery in the holy issue. But who can be in the spirit and in the body at the same time? Who can see salvation as a temple and praises as a cathedral whilst he is victimized and laughed at by his own five senses? We need prophets, therefore, who have the seeing eyes—the eyes that see what to others is invisible; and they must

[b] "God's salvation shall be in place of walls and bulwarks to His Zion. See Is. lx. 18—22."—Mat. Arnold.

[c] As a nation they are regarded as being righteous, bec. they had given up their idolatry, and again entered into covenant with Jehovah.

Ps. cxviii. 19, 20.

"When this corruptible has put on incorruption, and this mortal has put on immortality, when standing within that city where the wicked cease from troubling and the weary are at rest, will the redeemed of the Lord shout this song as never before: "We have a strong city,' etc."—Hom. Com.

put up with our impertinence and rudeness for a time; they can bear it, for our ingratitude hardly reaches them; they have flung their music upon the world, and vanished from the world's vengeance and anger.—Peop. B.

3. "The man of steadfast mind Thou keepest in welfare, for in Thee is his trust."—Polyc. Bib. This verse "states the conditions of membership in the ideal Zion; a 'steadfast mind' may share the 'peace' which the ideal city is to enjoy."—Driver. **perfect peace,** lit. peace, peace, the quietness of perfect trust in the Almighty One. **stayed,**[a] fully reliant. **trusteth,** "implies entire repose of faith, such as leads a man to cast away human anxiety."—Spk. Com.

Perfect Peace.—I. The Author of this peace is none other than God Himself. Earthly honors, riches, friendships, leave the heart devoid of enduring peace, because they can do nothing to dispel the sense of guilt and the consequent apprehensions of the future. We cannot have peace unless we have God for our portion. II. The peace which God imparts to His people is "perfect." 1. In its source; 2. In its measure; 3. In its adaptation to our needs. It erects its brightest monuments on the ruins of earthly hopes. III. If this perfect peace is to be ours we must link ourselves on to God by a simple, earnest, childlike faith. 1. This is essential; 2. This is sufficient. IV. It is the duty, as it is the privilege, of all believers to seek for "perfect peace."—David Magee.

Christian in the World.—I remember an illustration in a black folio of the seventeenth century: As a watch, though tossed up and down by an agitation of him who carries it, does not on that account undergo any perturbation or disorder in the working of the spring and wheels within; so the true Christian's heart, however shaken by the joltings it meets with in the pressure and tumult of the world, suffers no derangement in the adjustment and action of its machinery; the hand still points to eternity.—R. A. Wilmott.

Rest.—

When winds are raging o'er the upper ocean,
  And billows wild contend with angry roar,
'Tis said, far down beneath the wild commotion,
  That peaceful stillness reigneth evermore.

Far, far beneath the noise of tempest dieth,
  And silver waves chime ever peacefully,
And no rude storm, how fierce soe'er he flieth,
  Disturbs the sabbath of that deeper sea.

So to the heart that knows Thy love, O Purest,
  There is a temple, sacred evermore,
And all the babble of life's angry voices
  Dies in hushed silence at its peaceful door.

Far, far away, the roar of passion dieth,
  And loving thoughts rise calm and peacefully,
And no rude storm, how fierce soe'er he flieth,
  Disturbs the soul that dwells, O Lord, in Thee.

Oh, rest of rest! Oh, peace serene, eternal!
  Thou ever livest; and Thou changest never,
And in the secret of Thy presence dwelleth
  Fulness of joy, forever and forever.

—Harriet Beecher Stowe.

4. **for ever,** i. e. always and altogether. **Jehovah,** or Jah: the Eternal, Immutable, and Covenant-Keeping God. **strength,** R. V., "an everlasting rock;" lit. "a Rock of Ages."[b] We may read: "for the Lord Jehovah is a Rock of Ages."

Perfect Trust, Perfect Peace (vs. 4).—Man must trust; he has no resources of his own. I. The true object of supreme trust, "the Lord Jehovah. 1. His sufficiency; 2. His graciousness; 3. His immutability. II. The character of the trust enjoined. 1. Absolute; 2. Unquestioning; 3. Comprehensive; 4. Continuous. III. The result of such trust, "perfect peace." 1. Fearlessness of present foes; 2. Calmness amid pres-

[a] Ps. cxi. 8, cxii. 8.

"Faith is not only intended to pacify the conscience and purify the heart, but also to rescue the mind from earthly troubles. Our passage through life is attended with storms; we sail upon a boisterous sea, where many tempests are felt, and many are feared, which look black, and bode mischief, but pass over. Now, faith is designed for an anchor, to keep the mind steady, and give it rest." — Hervey.

"To be the sun is to be bright; to have peace is to have perfect peace. This is the sublimity of faith. The end of discipline is not to make men critical, facetious, pedantic, pharisaic, self-sufficient; the end of all life-discipline is to make men complete, and completeness is peace. Where there is want of peace there is want of completeness." — Parker.

[b] Is: xlv. 17; De. xxxii. 15; 1 Sa. ii. 2.

"The eternity and immutability of God are here alleged as a ground of the most unlimited confidence on the part of the people." — Henderson.

"Those that trust in God shall not only find in Him, but receive from Him, everlasting strength, strength that will carry them to everlasting life, to that blessedness wh. is for ever."—Mat. Henry.

"As a garrison seizes and retains a stronghold, so 'the peace of God' takes military possession of the soul, and beats off all outside assailants. It has an active as well as a passive side, like a staff which we can draw forth for a fight as well as lean on for rest."—G. R. Miall.

"Family pride entertains many unsocial opinions." — Zimmerman.

ent peril; 3. Contentment in the midst of want; 4. Tranquility in the prospect of the future.—Stems and Twigs.

Lean Hard.—It seemed as if I could not sit without support through the service, and oh! how desirable seemed rest! God sent it in an unexpected way, for a woman came and seated herself directly behind me, so that I could lean on her, and invited me to do so. I declined, but she drew me back, saying, "If you love me, lean hard.' And then came the Master's own voice, repeating the words, "If you love me, lean hard!" and I leaned on Him too. I wondered that I was not weary that night nor the next morning; and I have rested ever since, on those sweet words, "If you love me, lean hard!"—Fidelia Fiske. Comfort of Believing.—I envy not quality of the mind or intellect in others; nor genius, power, wit, or fancy: but if I could choose what would be most delightful. and, I believe, most useful to me, I should prefer a firm religious belief to every other blessing; for it makes life a discipline of goodness; creates new hopes when all hopes vanish; and throws over the decay, the destruction of existence, the most gorgeous of all lights; awakens life even in death, and from corruption and decay calls up beauty and divinity; makes an instrument of torture and shame the ladder of ascent to Paradise; and, far above all combinations of earthly hopes, calls up the most delightful visions and plains and amaranths, the gardens of the blest, the security of everlasting joys, where the sensualist and the sceptic view only gloom, decay, annihilation, and despair.—Sir H. Davy.

5, 6. "The hostile city is humbled to the dust; and the poor may now walk unhindered over its ruins."—Driver. (5) **bringeth down,** or, hath brought down. **lofty city,** Babylon is again in the Prophet's mind. (6) **foot .. down,** a fig. for the exultation of the Jews in the final overthrow of the city of their foes. "The feet of the afflicted trample upon it, the steps of the helpless."—Polyc. Bib.

Pride Fettered.—

Prayer is the net that snareth him; prayer is the fetter that holdeth him:
Thou canst not nourish pride while waiting as an almsman on thy God,—
Waiting in sincerity and trust, or pride shall meet thee even there:
Yea, from the palaces of Heaven hath pride cast down his millions.
Root up the mandrake from thy heart, though it cost thee blood and groans,
Or the cherished garden of thy graces will fade and perish utterly.
—Tupper.

7. "The path for the righteous is good fortune; a road for the righteous Thou levelest."—Polyc. Bib. In that ideal city the way of the righteous will be free from trouble. **uprightness,** or straightness. **weigh .. just,** or make level. "Thou makest his way straight before his face."[a]

The Righteousness of God and His People.—I. Righteousness is the characteristic of God and His redeemed people. 1. God Himself, His laws, His providential government, are all signalized by perfect rectitude; 2. God's people share in the same righteousness. The grace of God produces a new nature which assimilates them to the Divine nature. II. When righteousness characterizes a person it will dictate his conduct. He is erect in his moral manhood.—J. Rawlinson.

An Upright Farmer.—A farmer called on the late Earl Fitzwilliam, to represent that his crop of wheat had been seriously injured in a field adjoining a certain wood, where his lordship's hounds had, during the winter, frequently met to hunt. He stated that the young wheat had been so cut up and destroyed, that, in some parts, he could not hope for any produce. "Well, my friend," said his lordship, "I am aware that we have frequently met in that field, and we have done considerable injury; and if you can produce an estimate of the loss you have sustained, I will repay you." The farmer replied that, anticipating his lordship's consideration and kindness, he had requested a friend to assist him in estimating the damage, and they thought that as the crop seemed quite destroyed, £50 would not more than repay him. The earl immediately gave him the money. As the harvest, however, approached, the wheat grew, and in those parts of the field which were most trampled, the corn was strongest and most luxuriant. The farmer went again to his lord-

a With special reference to the straight course prepared for them in the providence of God, by which to return to Palestine.

"Amidst the shakings of the nations and the storms of life, it is delightful to know that the sceptre of universal power is in the hand of Infinite Love. He reigneth, be the earth ever so unquiet."—Sam'l Thodey.

"Some seem to imagine that all demands of righteousness are met by the acceptance of

ship, and being introduced, said, "I am come, my lord, respecting the field of wheat adjoining such a wood." His lordship immediately recollected the circumstance. "Well, my friend, did not I allow you sufficient to remunerate you for your loss?" "Yes, my lord, I find that I have sustained no loss at all, for where the horses had most cut up the land, the crop is most promising, and I have therefore brought the £50 back again." "Ah!" exclaimed the venerable earl, "this is what I like; this is as it should be between man and man." He then entered into conversation with the farmer, asking him some questions about his family —how many children he had, etc. His lordship then went into another room, and returning, presented the farmer with a cheque for £100, saying, "Take care of this, and when your eldest son is of age, present it to him, and tell him the occasion that produced it."

8, 9. (8) **the way . . for thee,** i. e. have stood by the way along which we expected and desired Jehovah to appear—in judgment. The rest of the verse should be translated as in R. V., "to thy name and to thy memorial is the desire of [our] soul." "Name" and "memorial" are synonymous, as in Ex. iii. 15; Ps. cxxxv. 13; Jehovah's memorial is that by which He makes Himself to be remembered (see vs. 13).—Camb. Bib.[a] (9) **in the night,** of affliction. **early,** i. e. earnestly. **when,** and not till then. **thy judgments,** the manifestation of God in punishment of evil.

Seeking God in the Night.—I. We desire God in the night of our sorrows. Thick clouds come over the heart. Alone in the darkness it seeks His face. II. We desire God in the night of our doubts. These will come. Old evidences do not afford the same basis of faith. In this temporary eclipse of faith we want God Himself—the living God. III. We desire God in the night of our separations. They must come. Be the tie ever so tender, it must be cut. Then the soul cries out, "O God, be not far from me.'" IV. We desire God in the night of our own departure. Death is a dark hour. But One can lighten that.—Pul. Com.

I Will Remember Thee.—Dr. Jessup, the Syrian missionary, says that when his father, long a Vice-President of the American Board of Missions, had been twice paralyzed, his memory gone, and even his own house no longer recognized, he was at home when he got into his church, or remembered the Missionary Board, and wrote a letter to its representatives, full of the spirit of missions. He could conduct family prayers as well as ever, and was perfectly sound in mind and memory as to the Redeemer's kingdom. It was like the disintegrated quartz falling away from the pure gold.—O. T. Anec. Judgment Teaching Righteousness.—Not only the Church but the world will learn two great lessons, viz., that God is righteous, and be led into the way of righteousness. In The Hand of God in History we read that "the devastating wars of Napoleon I. produced a shock which taught all Europe that Jehovah is the God of nations." The Emperor Alexander of Russia, who from that time to his death is believed to have been an humble follower of Jesus, once observed that "the burning of Moscow lighted the flame of religion in my soul." Professor Tholuck says that "when Germany was called to contend for freedom, this memorable event awakened religious desires in hearts that had remained strangers to every Christian sentiment. The inhabitants of Prussia felt that the moment was come for the display of the eternal justice which governs the world, and from that time the heart of the king was opened to the truths of Christianity." When cholera raged in Great Britain, thousands who never thought seriously before felt that it was high time to awake out of sleep, and turned unto the Lord.

10, 11. (10) **favour,** or mercy. To the wicked mercy seems only weakness, so he despises "goodness and forbearance." **the land of uprightness** "is the Holy Land; even there, surrounded by the institutions of a pure religion, the wicked outrages the dictates of morality, having no eyes for the majesty of Jehovah."—Camb. Bib. (11) R. V., "Lord, Thy hand is lifted up, yet they see not; but they shall see Thy zeal for the people, and be ashamed; yea, fire shall devour Thine adversaries." The hand of God has been manifest to the eye of faith. But some are blind and for them only terrible judgments will suffice.[a]

Obdurateness.—All is lost upon him. Let the summer-day rain all its gathered clouds upon the sand of the desert, and it will not make

Christ and the experience of spiritual feeling, while they overlook the demands of human relationships. Others confine their view to men. They imagine all demands are met, when they are fair and honorable in their dealings with men, while God is left out of consideration. The Divine idea of righteousness is not thus partial.—Hom. Com.

[a] "God's character was connoted by His Name, and was handed down in the historical memorial of His deeds of love and power." —Spk. Com.

"Night appears to be a time peculiarly favorable to devotion. Its solemn stillness helps to free the mind from that perpetual din which the cares of the world will bring around it; and the stars looking down from heaven upon us shine as if they would attract us up to God."—C. H. Spurgeon.

Miss Frances E. Willard died Feb. 18, 1898. Her last words as she was passing into the other world were, "How beautiful to be with God!"

James II., after his defeat at La Hogue, expressed his satisfaction thereat, because what God orders is best, and nothing is well done which is not done by Him.

[a] "The wrath of God, as a sudden, rapid, irresistible and utterly destroying agent." —J. A. Alexander.

a garden of it; all the rich rain will be swallowed by the burning lips, and at eventide the desert shall thirst as with the thirst of fire: otherwise, the world would be converted to-day, and would have been converted at the very time of the revelation of the Son of man. The spirit of discontentment is in some men, and do what you will for them you find no flowers in their conduct, no fruit upon their life-tree, nothing but leaves, and the leaves half-grown, as if ashamed to be seen upon branches so unfruitful, so unblessed. Doth not the goodness of God lead thee to repentance? Think of it! health, and children, and love, and prosperity, and social honor, and all these a staircase leading thee—no where! All these marble steps should conduct thee to heaven. But as soon as the earthquake ceases men begin again to curse and swear, and as soon as the earth is felt to have recovered from her vibrations men go back to the tavern and drink themselves to death; when the heavy thunder ceases, and the vivid lightning withdraws itself, men come from the sanctuary of the cellar to repeat their brutalities in their higher chambers.—Parker.

"Shall our very next neighbor's house be on fire, and we look on as men unconcerned in the danger? It cannot be, it must not be. There is, without all doubt, the same combustible stuff—the same, if not greater sins—lodged in our hearts, and the same punishment hovering over our heads; it is, therefore, high time to look about us."—Donne.

12—14. (12) **for thou also,** etc., "for even our whole work thou hast wrought for us," i. e. all that we have achieved has been due to thy working for us. (comp. Ps. xc. 16, 17). (13) **other lords,** the reference is to foreign despotisms, an invasion of Jehovah's sovereignty. (14) **dead,**[b] "Dead men do not live; shades do not arise: wherefore Thou visitest," etc.—G. A. Smith and see margin R. V.

[b] Ps. xxx. 7; Pr. x. 7.

A Penitential Confession.—The dominion of evil in human souls is: 1. Multiform. It assumes many shapes. The gods the Jewish people served were numerous as the nations under whose influence they fell. So the form of evil most congenial to a man's own nature is sure to assail him. 2. Wrongful. The language implies that God ought to have had the dominion. Then it must be wrong to give it to others. He is the rightful sovereign on every ground. 3. Voluntary. It has been entirely with our own consent.—J. Rawlinson.

"We have all to fight the same lions, tread the same road, try the same gates, fall by the same difficulties. Such is the mystery of this disciplinary life! Blessed are they who can speak of other lordships in the past tense, in a tense that is completed, saying, Other lordships have had dominion over us, but the lordships and their rulings have vanished and ended, and now we stand in the empire of God."—Peop. B.

Peace Through the Gospel.—"Some years ago," says a Belgian pastor, "I visited a gardener, and induced him to obtain a New Testament. This displeased his wife so much that she begged me one day to leave her husband alone. My wife continued to see him, and while speaking of flowers and plants she spoke of the Gospel. Although professing unbelief, he would say, 'I respect you, for you are good and sincere, but I would not allow a priest to speak to me so.' The man fell ill, and was for a long time laid up. My wife used to read the Scriptures to him. A few days before his death I went to see him, and he answered all my questions in a most touching manner. A priest, furious at his receiving my visits, threatened him with damnation. 'Let me die in peace,' he answered, 'I now believe in the Gospel.' The priest left him, and he died in peace. His widow, his son, and the whole family now attend our chapel regularly."

15—17. (15) **art glorified,** "thou hast glorified thyself" by thus exalting Israel.[a] **hadst .. earth,** R. V. "thou hast enlarged all the borders of the land." (16) **visited thee,** sought Thee as penitents and suppliants. (17) **in thy sight,**[b] better "because of Thee," i. e. Thy chastening hand.

[a] "In doing all this Thou hast made an exhibition of Thy power, justice, truth, and goodness." — J. A. Alexander.

[b] "This verse contains an image of anguish accompanied with expectation, to be followed by joy that will cause the anguish utterly to be forgotten." —Fausset.

Encouragements to Prayer.—1. Abraham's servant prays—Rebekah appears. 2. Jacob wrestles and prays—Christ is conquered. Esau's mind is wonderfully turned from the revengeful purpose he had harbored for twenty years. 3. Moses cries to God—the sea divides. 4. Moses prays—Amalek is discomfited. 5. Joshua prays—Achan is discovered. 6. Hannah prays—Samuel is born. 7. David prays—Ahithophel hangs himself. 8. Asa prays—a victory is gained. 9. Jehoshaphat cries to God—God turns away his foes. 10. Isaiah and Hezekiah pray—185,000 Assryians are dead in twelve hours. 11. Daniel prays—the dream is revealed. 12. Daniel prays—the lions are muzzled. 13. Daniel prays—the seventy weeks are revealed. 14. Ezra prays—God answers (Ezra viii. 21—23). 15. Nehemiah darts a prayer—the king's heart is softened in a minute (Neh. ii. 6). 16. Elijah prays—a drought of three years succeeds. 17. Elijah prays—rain descends apace. 18. Elisha prays—Jordan is divided. 19. Elisha prays—a child's soul comes back. Prayer reaches eternity. 20. The Apostles pray—the Holy Ghost comes down. 21. The Church prays ardently in a prayer-meeting—Peter is delivered by an angel.—J. Campbell.

Bishop Reynolds says: "A godly heart is like those flowers which shut when the sun sets, and

Divine Help Sought by Prayer.—For help in duty or, in danger prayer is an unfailing source of strength. When King William IV. expired at Windsor Castle about midnight, the Archbishop of Canterbury immediately hastened to acquaint the Princess Victoria of her succession to the throne. On receiving the momentous intelligence the youthful Queen became much agitated, but her first words were, "I ask your prayers on my behalf." They kneeled down together, and our Queen began her reign in the spirit of Solomon of old, by imploring from the King of kings "a wise and understanding heart."—The Children's Hour.

18, 19. (18) **brought .. wind,** "the reference is to the futility of all the self-originating schemes and hopes of the Jews in Babylon, which had for their object their political regeneration. They humbly acknowledge that deliverance did not come until God delivered. **fallen,** R. V. margin "been born," i. e. the mother nation has brought forth no children to people the world."—Camb. Bib. (19) R. V. "Thy dead shall live; my dead bodies shall arise."[a] "The answer to the utterances of disappointed hopes in vs. 18 is the promise of the Resurrection. The speaker throughout is the community, and the words are addressed to God, with the exception of an apostrophe to the buried Israelites in the middle of the verse." **for thy dew,** etc., better, "for a dew of lights is thy dew" (O Lord), i. e. a heavenly supernatural dew, which falling on the dead, restores them to life.—Camb. Bib. **cast out the dead,** better, "bring forth the shades." (Rephaim).

The Doctrine of the Resurrection here presented is reached through the conviction, gradually produced by the long process of revelation, that the final redemption of Israel could not be accomplished within the limits of nature. It became clear that the hopes and aspirations engendered by the Spirit in believing minds pointed forward to the great miracle here described, and thus the belief in the resurrection was firmly bound up with the indestructible hopes of the future of Israel (cf. Rom. xi. 15). The idea is exhibited in a form which is immature in the light of New Testament teaching, but it practically represents the highest development of Old Testament revelation on this subject. The only passage which is slightly in advance of this is Dan. xii. 2, and even there a universal resurrection is not taught. Here the hope is restricted to Israelites (see vs. 14) and no doubt to those Israelites who had departed this life in the faith and fear of God. On the other hand, the teaching of this vs. is quite different from such passages as Hos. vi. 2; Ezek. xxxvii. 1—14. There, rising from the dead is but a figurative clothing of the idea of national regeneration, whereas there can be no doubt that here a literal resurrection of individuals is foretold.—Camb. Bib. Beautiful Death Scene.—When one of Martin Luther's children lay on her deathbed, the great man approached her, and said to her, "My dear little daughter, my beloved Margaret, you would willingly remain with your earthly parents; but, if God calls you, you will go with your Heavenly Father." "Yes, dear father, it is as God pleases." "Dear little girl," he exclaimed, "O how I love you! The spirit is willing, but the flesh is weak." He then took the Bible, and read to her the passage: "Thy dead men shall live; together with My dead body shall they arise. Awake and sing, ye that dwell in dust: for thy dew is as the dew of herbs, and the earth shall cast out the dead." He then said, "My daughter, enter thou into thy resting-place in peace." She turned her eyes toward him, and said, with touching simplicity, "Yes, father!"

20, 21. (20) "Resumes the connection of the prophetic discourse, interrupted since xxv. 8; and this continues to the end, broken only by the lyrical passage, xxvii. 2—6. The contents, however, are of a somewhat mixed character, and the divisions are clearly marked."—Camb. Bib. **come,** the prophet bids the people withdraw into the privacy of communion with God, whilst the judgment—that, viz., described in xxiv. 1-12, 17-20—visits those who are doomed to perish by it."—Driver. Comp. Mat. vi. 6; Job xiv. 13; Dan. xi. 36. (21) **punish .. earth,** the heathen nations that had oppressed Israel. **blood,**[a] the innocent blood shed upon it.[b]

The Duty of Retirement.—I. Make time for devout reflection. In busy, outwardly active times, when there is an imperious demand on every hand for "work," there is urgent need to enter into the solemn and sacred chamber of meditation. II. Compel each day to yield its hour of direct intercourse with God. We cannot live spiritually upon public de-

open again when the sun returns and shines upon them."

"From the mountain of prayer did the great Captain of humanity conduct all His wars and gain all His conquests."—Lange.

[a] "Sublimely recovering himself, the Prophet cries that God's saints, though they are dead, shall live, and, with the lifeless but reanimated body of the restored exiles, shall found the kingdom of righteousness, after the present distress." — Mat. Arnold.

[b] This verse is regarded as indicating a prevalent belief in the resurrection of the dead.

"As no writer could draw a figure from what was unknown to himself, so, if he sought to teach, he would not draw one from what was unknown to his readers. As Isaiah could not talk about a resurrection if he had never known the idea and the words to express it, so he would not expect to be understood unless his readers were also familiar with it."—Hom. Com.

"The whole life of a philosopher is the meditation of his death."—Cicero.

[a] Ge. iv. 11.

[b] "These words may be applied almost exclusively to the retribution which awaited the Chaldaean for the slaughter of God's people."—J. A. Alexander.

votion, the soul needs private, individual fellowship with God. III. Take up the attitude of reverent expectation. Having done all, it is our duty to wait on the Lord.—Pul. Com.

Christian Security.—Faith is the Christian's foundation, and hope is his anchor, and death is his harbor, and Christ is his pilot, and heaven is his country; and all the evils of poverty, or affronts of tribunals and evil judges, of fears and sad apprehensions, are but like the loud winds blowing from the right point,—they make a noise, but drive faster to the harbor. And if we do not leave the ship, and jump into the sea; quit the interest of religion, and run into securities of the world; cut our cables, and dissolve our hopes; grow impatient; hug a wave and die in its embraces,—we are safe at sea, safer in the storm which God sends us, than in a calm when we are befriended by the world.—Bp. Taylor.

"He has gained on behalf of his people the comforting certitude that a great exhibition of the Divine justice is on the point of taking place; and his counsel is to withdraw from the doomed into the privacy of communion with God."— Cheyne.

CHAPTER THE TWENTY-SEVENTH.

1. "In this chapter the prophet dwells upon particular aspects of the coming future—sometimes the judgments on Israel's foes being foremost, sometimes the period of felicity which is to ensue."—Driver. **sore,** i. e. hard, unrelenting. **sword,** fig. for Jehovah's judgment.[c] **leviathan,** perhaps the kingdom of Asshur Babel. **piercing serpent,** R. V. "swift." **crooked serpent,** the curved and winding river the Euphrates. **dragon,** the usual Bible symbol for Egypt.

Spiritual Wickedness in High Places Powerless to Resist God.—As Isaiah was, somehow or other, brought into contact with the dualistic doctrine of the Zoroastrians (ch. xlv. 5—7), it was important that he should bear witness to the impotency of the powers of evil when they matched themselves against Jehovah. The Zoroastrians taught that there were two great principles, one of good, and the other of evil, whom they called respectively Ahura-mazda and Angro-mainyus, who were both of them uncreated and independent one of the other, and between whom there had been from all eternity, and always would be, a bitter contest and rivalry. Both principles were real persons, possessed of will, intelligence, power, consciousness, and other personal qualities. The struggle between them was constant and well-balanced, with certainly no marked preponderance of the good over the evil. It was probably to meet this doctrine, and prevent its having weight with his disciples, that Isaiah taught so explicitly the nothingness of the highest powers of evil in any contest with the Almighty. He had already stated that, at the end of the world, God would visit and punish "the host of the high ones that were on high," as well as the kings of the earth upon the earth (ch. xxiv. 21). He now presents evil in a threefold personal form of the highest awfulness and grandeur, and declares its conquest, in this threefold form by Jehovah. God is to "punish" the two leviathans with his sword, and actually to "slay the dragon." The triumph is complete, final, unmistakable. Evil can do nothing against good, but is wholly overcome by it.—Pul. Com.

c De. xxxii. 41, 42; Is. xxxiv. 5; Eze. xxi. 3, 4, 5.

"We are assured, though there be many windows and ports and doors for temptation to enter at, there is but one key to let us out or to lock us up against it, God's assistant or preventient grace."—Archdea. King.

"We cannot refer the serpent or the dragon to the storm-cloud, or lightning, as some have done. Something much deeper seems to be meant. The dragon is symbolic, in ancient thought generally, of the power of death, of the underworld, into which humanity in its sinfulness and weakness is prone to fall. Jehovah will overcome this fiendish power: such seems to be the meaning of the prophecy."—Johnson.

2, 3. Here follows "a fourth song of thankfulness, in which the redeemed nation expresses, under the figure of a vineyard its sense of the divine protection under which it rests."—Driver. (2) **day,** of judgments. **unto her,** to the captive and afflicted Church of God. **red wine,** better "a pleasant vineyard."[a] (3) **keep it,** defend, and watch over it. **water . . moment,** or, at moments, i. e. whensoever it is needing refreshment. The sign of constant care.[b] **hurt it,** in the coming time of commotion and calamity.

The Watchfulness that Never Sleeps.—"By night and by day." In the darkness and in the night. For the darkness is no darkness to God. As Sentinel he never sleeps. Our watch-fires die out, and the beasts of the forest break into the camp in the silent hours of darkness. We cannot "keep." But the soul is too precious to be left to finite watchfulness. The Tower of London contains no jewelled crowns so rich in value as the nature that contains the pearl of great price. The temple of Jerusalem had costly vessels and sacred altars; but the temple of the soul has in it the true Shechinah. This is God's promise. This is his own testimony to himself; and it is a promise to wear as an amulet on the heart in such a world as this.—Pul. Com.

a Ps. lxxx. 8; Is. v. 1.

b Comp. Is. v. 6.

"Not the superiority of its soil to that of the surrounding country makes the vineyard, but its separation. It is not because the saints are by nature better than others that they are God's vineyard, but because they are set apart by Him. The idea

4—6. (4) **Fury .. me,** "wrath have I none." He had chastised them, but He does not "keep His anger for ever." **set .. battle,** R. V. "would that the briers and thorns were against me," etc. "I would march upon them," i. e. upon the foes who have overrun Israel. (5) **Or,** i. e. or else. If any would be saved. **hold .. strength,** i. e. escape My severity by embracing My goodness. (6) R. V. "In days to come shall Jacob take root," .. "and they shall fill," etc.[c] Verse 6 is attached to the song but forms no integral part of it.

Taking Hold of God's Strength.—I. In what God's strength consists. Almightiness, wisdom, truthfulness, justice and mercy. Christ is God's strength. II. How may man take hold of God's strength? 1. By submission. 2. By prayer. 3. By obedience. 4. By implicit trust in God's mercy. III. The results. Divine strength is infused into our minds. We partake of the Divine nature.—William Parkes.

The Father Subdued.—The Rev. R. Toller's most affecting illustrations (and the power of illustrating a subject was his distinguishing faculty) were drawn from the most familiar scenes of life; and, after he became a father, not unfrequently from the incidents which attach to that relation. An example of this will afford the reader some idea of the manner in which he availed himself of images drawn from the domestic circle. His text was, "Let him take hold of My strength, that he may make peace with Me; and he shall make peace with Me." "I think," said he, "I can convey the meaning of this passage, so that every one may understand it, by what took place in my own family within these few days. One of my little children had committed a fault, for which I thought it my duty to chastise him. I called him to me, explained to him the evil of what he had done, and told him how grieved I was that I must punish him for it. He heard me in silence, and then rushed into my arms, and burst into tears. I could sooner have cut off my arm than have then struck him for his fault: he had taken hold of my strength, and he had made peace with me."—R. Hall.

7—9. (7) "Hath Jehovah smitten Israel as He smote those that smote it? Is Israel slain as Jehovah's slain ones are slain?" i. e. Is Israel exterminated"[d]—Driver. (8) R. V. "In measure when thou sendest her away, thou dost contend with her; he hath removed her with his rough blast in the day of the east wind."[a] In measure, not in excess, has Jehovah "contended" (comp. Jer. ii. 9) with His people when He put it from Him. The "rough blast" passed over the nation but did not destroy it.—Driver. (9) **this,** the graciously ordered captivity. **stones .. sunder,** destroying all idol-symbols, as a sign of utter abandonment of idolatry. **the graves,** etc., R. V. "so that the Asherim and the sun-images shall rise no more,"[b] this was the "fruit" or purpose of the captivity.

Judgment and Chastisements.—These verses set forth two modes of apprehending the afflictions and sorrows of life, and help us in estimating the distinction between the modes. I. The distinction between judgments and chastisements. In a sense we may say that judgments are ends in themselves, and chastisements are means to a higher end. Then has God two ways of dealing with men? God's final end is always recovery. But he works over indefinitely long periods; and his immediate end may not always be remedial. II. The purpose of judgment apprehended as chastisement. Apprehended as only judgment, our mind is overborne by our calamity. Apprehended as chastisement, the mind is started with new and trustful thoughts. The trouble may at first crush, but soon we learn to accept it calmly.—R. Tuck.

Object of Divine Punishment.—The object of punishment, then, is not destruction. When God sends his rough wind he does not send it as a wind of judgment, for the purpose of destroying men, carrying them tempestuously away into abysses on which the sun never shines. Let us understand the spirit and the purpose of Providence. When God tears a man down, it is to do the man good; when the rough wind comes into a man's estate and uproots the oldest trees, it is to make way for other growths of a kind more approved and more fruitful. If we could grasp this doctrine and commit ourselves to it, then the wind might blow at noonday and at midnight and we should say, The Lord is sifting, separating, taking away the dross, taking away the wicked, taking away the mean, and he will leave behind the pure silver, the true character, the

of separation as regards the Church is made conspicuous in every age." —Rhyddieithol.

c "The metaphor is borrowed from the practice of horticulture, and was naturally suggested by the subject of the preceding verses."—Henderson.

"Israel has its voice in every land and every age, pleading for the foundation-principles of religion, which are the unity and spirituality of God. Israel is a tree whose branches overspread the earth; these are its leaves, and these leaves are for the healing of the nations that are diseased and dying of idolatries and sensuousness."

d "Assyria and Babylon were left without remnant, not so Israel." — Spk. Com.

"Exile was in God's eyes a sufficient punishment for Israel, and his putting away idolatry is a sufficient title for readmission to God's favor. Not such is Babylon's punishment and end, for Babylon is 'a people of no understanding.'"—Mat. Arnold.

a "He winnoweth, purgeth, with His rough blast of affliction in the day of the east wind."—Wordsworth.

b The Jews were wholly cured of idolatry in the time of their captivity.

"Repentance is to leave
The sins we loved before;
And show that we in earnest grieve,
By doing so no more."

"He tempers the wind to the shorn lamb."—L. Sterne.

c Is. v. 17, xvii. 2, xxxii. 17.

"The greatest test of character is to be found in what is common rather than extraordinary. It is easier for the soldier to be faithful in the rush of battle, when sustained by a catching enthusiasm, than to maintain a high tone of consistent principle under the many trials of daily drill." —Macleod.

"As one travels in Europe for the first time, he is struck with the colored uniform worn by servants. He makes inquiries and is informed that the servants of such a nobleman wear yellow; of such, green; so the servants of the various noblemen are easily recognized wherever seen. So the servant of God bears his mark, and the servant of the devil bears his mark." — G. E. Reed.

"Despondency is not a state of humility; on the contrary, it is vexation and despair of a cowardly pride." Fenelon.

a "God's threshing-floor would be a vast one, wherever Israel was scattered, from the Euphrates to the brook of Egypt." —Wordsworth.

"Under the fig. of sifting corn is announced the final collection and restoration of all the true Israel, however outcast and scattered." — Mat. Arnold.

noble soul. God will never destroy anything that has in it virtue, health, reality of value. Then let the great wind blow; let us be thankful for the sifting wind. Many of us would never sift ourselves. We are so blinded that we mistake chaff for wheat in many instances, and we think there is some value even in the dross when we cannot part with pleasures that give the palate even one moment's joy. The whole process of sifting must be done from without.—Parker.

10, 11. (10) R. V. "For the defenced city is solitary, an habitation deserted and forsaken, like the wilderness," a description of the desolation of Jerusalem, which only through such suffering would be brought to repentance. **calf feed,**[c] the sign of its abandonment to desolation. (11) **women come,** the duty of gathering fuel in the East devolves on the women. The fine fruit trees would come to this sad ending. **no understanding,** words which describe the folly of the people of Israel.

Desolation.—Josephus describes Galilee, of which he was the governor, as "full of plantations of trees of all sorts, the soil universally rich and fruitful, and all, without the exception of a single part, cultivated by the inhabitants. Moreover," he adds, "the cities lie here very thick, and there are very many villages which are so full of people, by the richness of their soil, that the very least of them contained above fifteen thousand inhabitants." Such was Galilee at the commencement of the Christian era, several centuries after the prophecy was delivered; but now "the plain of Esdraelon, and all the other parts of Galilee which afford pasture, are occupied by Arab tribes, around whose brown tents the sheep and lambs gambol to the sound of the reed, which at nightfall calls them home." The calf feeds and lies down amid the ruins of the cities, and consumes, without hindrance, the branches of the trees; and, however changed may be the condition of the inhabitants, the lambs feed after their manner, and, while the land mourns, and the merry-hearted sigh, they gambol to the sound of the reed. The precise and complete contrast between the ancient and existing state of Palestine, as separately described by Jewish and Roman historians and by modern travelers, is so strikingly exemplified in their opposite descriptions, that, in reference to whatever constituted the beauty and the glory of the country, or the happiness of the people, an entire change is manifest, even in minute circumstances. The universal richness and fruitfulness of the soil of Galilee, together with its being "full of plantations of all sorts of trees," are represented by Josephus as "inviting the most slothful to take pains in its cultivation." And the other provinces of the Holy Land are also described by him as "having abundance of trees, full of autumnal fruit, both that which grows wild, and that which is the effect of cultivation." Tacitus relates that, besides all the fruits of Italy, the palm and balsam tree flourished in the fertile soil of Judæa. And he records the great carefulness with which, when the circulation of the juices seemed to call for it, they gently made an incision in the branches of the balsam, with a shell, or pointed stone, not venturing to apply a knife. No sign of such art or care is now to be seen throughout the land. The balm tree has disappeared where long it flourished; and hardier plants have perished from other causes than the want of due care in their cultivation.—Keith.

12, 13. (12) **beat off,** rather: Jehovah shall thresh out from the corn-ears of the River (the Euphrates) unto (those of) the brook of Egypt, i. e. all that grows between those limits.[a] The term "beat out" is applied both to the beating of olives from the tree (Deut. xxiv. 20) and to the beating out of grain with a staff—a more careful process than the ordinary methods (xxviii. 27; Jud. vi. 11).—Camb. Bib. **one by one,** either that none be lost, or so that only the true Israelites be brought back. (13) **trumpet,** the proclamation of liberty to all who had been under the sway of the Babylonian and Egyptian kings. "Such proclamations were made by Cyrus, Cambyses, Darius, etc." **Egypt,** to wh. country many had fled in the time of the captivity.

The Return of God's Absent Ones.—The relation of God to all his absent children. I. The breadth of His kingdom. God's rights and claims extend to all peoples, to all classes. He looks everywhere for fruit to be beaten off, to be gathered in, at the time of harvest. II. The need of his interposition. This fruit which God is seeking is spiritual; it is the reverence, the love, the worship, the obedience, of his own children. But these his sons and daughters are: 1. Afar off. They are outcasts, a long way from home. 2. Or they are at the point of extinction. Those who have not been fascinated and won by ruinous seductions, are a mere remnant, and even their life, like Elijah's, is at stake. III. His summons to return. The "great trumpet" is being blown; its notes are sounding far and wide. "The voice of Jesus sounds o'er land and sea," saying, "Return unto thy Rest;" "Come unto me, all ye that labor." IV. His distinguishing kindness. God does not content himself with issuing a general proclamation which each man may interpret and apply. He comes to every human soul hmself. In the Person, and by the direct influence of his Holy Spirit, he makes his appeal to the individual heart and conscience. V. The gathering-place of his returned ones. All they who return unto God (1) gather at his house on earth for worship there; and (2) meet in the heavenly city, the new Jerusalem, for "nobler worship there."

The Gospel Trumpet.—As chaplain I was a little while in the army. Early every morning we were awakened by a trumpet sounding the rèveille. At that sound all the troops arose from the tents, hastened to their places in the line, and answered the roll-call. That done, they went to their morning rations. We who are the soldiers of Christ cannot always be marching and fighting. The evening will come. The shadows will gather, and we must go to the white tents of the grave. There we shall sleep soundly. But the night will pass along, and the first thing we shall hear will be the trumpet-call sounding the réveille of the resurrection; and we shall come up and fall into the long line of light, the trophies of Christian conflict gleaming in the unsetting sun. The roll shall be called, and we shall answer to our names; and then we shall go to the morning repast of heaven (1 Cor. xv. 52—55).—De Witt Talmage. Rev. Dr. Waugh.—The following pleasing occurrence was related by a zealous missionary to the heathen: On the 13th of April, 1814, the late Rev. Dr. Waugh preached at Bridport. His text was, "And it shall come to pass in that day, that the great trumpet shall be blown, and they shall come which were ready to perish, and shall worship the Lord in the holy mountain at Jerusalem" (Isa. xxvii. 13). The words "ready to perish" furnished him with solemn, awful, melting views of the miserable condition of the heathen. The "blowing of the great trumpet" drew forth every feeling of his mighty mind. He did blow it, indeed, with power and sweetness too. It was the trumpet of the Gospel. It suited him. He loved it. It was sweet melody from his lips. It proclaimed salvation! After expatiating for some time on this particular, he raised his voice with uncommon energy; his eyes flashed fire as he spake; he seemed as if he would have sprung over the pulpit to his auditors, while he exclaimed, "We want men of God to blow this great trumpet to the heathen, and we must have them! The heathen are 'ready to perish;' and they will perish, if the great trumpet does not bring them the joyful sound. I say again, we want men of God to blow this great trumpet, and we must have them!" Then, after this peal of thunder, he paused, and, is a softened melting tone, inquired, "Is there not one young disciple of the Lord Jesus Christ present who has love enough in his heart to his Divine Master to volunteer his services, and to say, 'I will go!'" This word reached my heart; it penetrated my inmost soul. I silently said, "Yes, Lord, if Thou wilt help me, I will go. There is not in this congregation a greater debtor to mercy; and perhaps there is not one present who has more ardently longed to be engaged in missionary work. If Thou wilt accept me, O Lord, I will go."

"To preach practical sermons, as they are called, that is, sermons upon virtues and vices, without inculcating those great Scripture truths of redemption, grace, etc., which alone can incite and enable us to forsake sin and follow righteousness—what is it but to put together the wheels, and set the hands of a watch, forgetting the spring, which is to make them all go?"—Bp. Horne.

"I remember one of my parishioners at Halesworth telling me that he thought 'a person should not go to church to be made uncomfortable.' I replied that I thought so too; but whether it should be the sermon or the man's life that should be altered so as to avoid the discomfort, must depend on whether the doctrine was right or wrong."—Abp. Whately.

"To show that the good of man was the will of God, to show that doing good to one another is the chief duty of man—this was at once the object of Christ's coming into the world, and the proof that he had begun a new epoch in the history of mankind." — Dean Stanley.

CHAPTER THE TWENTY-EIGHTH.

1, 2. (1) Woe to, chapters xxviii to xxxiii constitute a book in themselves, having six portions, each beginning with a Woe! This chapter contains four separate discourses: 1—6, 7—13, 14—22, 23—29. **crown of pride,** "the proud coronet." "The prophet fuses two images together—that of the revellers with their chaplets of flowers (Lam. v. 16) and of the picturesque Samaria[a] with its crown of towers and the greenery of its vines and olives."—Polyc. Bib. **drunkards,** comp. Am. iv. 1; Hos. vii. 5;

[a] For refs. to Samaria see 1 Ki. xvi. 24; Am. iii. 9, iv. 1, vi. 1.

drunkenness was a characteristic sin of Samaria. **glorious .. flower,** R. V. "and to the fading flower of his glorious beauty." (2) "The reason for the woe of vs. 1. Render: Behold Jehovah hath a mighty and strong one, like a tempest of hail, a destroying storm; like a flow of mighty overflowing waters, which casts down to the earth with violence."—Camb. Bib. Ref. is to the king of Assyria.[a]

Samaria.—The city of Sebaste, the ancient Samaria, beautifully situated on the top of a round hill, and surrounded immediately with a rich valley and a circle of other hills beyond it, suggested the idea of a chaplet, or wreath of flowers, worn upon their heads on occasions of festivity; expressed by the proud crown and the fading flower of the drunkards. That this custom of wearing chaplets in their banquets prevailed among the Jews, as well as among the Greeks and Romans, appears from Wisdom ii. 7, 8. The Beast In Us.—Sir Thomas Browne says: "We are all a composition of man and beast, wherein we must endeavor to hold the reign of man above the beast and to make sense sit at the feet of reason." That beast in us, that gross sense, is easily roused. No wise man will needlessly put himself in companionships which stir it into life. Nothing more quickly waken it than intoxicating drink.

Samaria was built on a beautiful fruitful hill, strong by nature, from its insulated situation in the middle of a deep and broad valley, and rendered still more so by the fortifications that were erected for its defence." — Henderson.

3, 4. (3) **trodden under feet,** or, with feet. The fig. of the city as a garland on the drunken at feasts is carried on. (4) **fading flower,** a withering garland. **hasty fruit,** R. V. "the first ripe fig," that ripens in June is esteemed a delicacy, but it very readily drops from the tree.[b] **eateth it,** swalloweth greedily.[c] The idea is that Samaria, when taken, would be instantly destroyed.

Life a Spring-time.—Let us look at spring as the emblem of human life. The Bible so regards it. "He cometh up like a flower," etc. First. Both in spring and human life there are vast capabilities of improvement. Spring is the season when Providence submits to the agriculturist what sort of harvest he shall have. With skill and industry he may, during the spring days, make nature yield him wonderful results. The cloud, the sky, the dew, the shower, the soil of spring, have special powers for the future. So is human life. Out of the human soul now seraphic powers, and forms, and faculties may grow. Secondly. Both in spring and human life there is remarkable changeability. No season so changeable as spring; alternate cloud and sunshine, storm and calm, cold and heat, "make up the April day." What an emblem of human life! What a scene of vicissitudes! Thirdly. Both in spring and human life there are many fallacious promises. Spring is the season of promise. The rich bud and blossom of fruit trees, the strong green stalks of the cornfields, have often created bright hopes, which in autumn have been terribly disappointed. So in life. Look at youth, etc. Fourthly. Both in spring and human life there is nothing can substitute for the present. No other season can do the work of spring. The man who neglects his field in the spring may toil on it to the utmost in summer without effect. So it is with life. There is no period that can be substituted for the present.—Thomas.

5. 6. (5) **that day,** "points to the indefinite future of the Messianic age."—Camb. Bib. **residue,** i. e. to the remnant left of Israel and Judah. (6) **sitteth in judgment,** "Jehovah is not only the beauty of the redeemed nation but the source of all civic and martial virtues."—Camb. Bib. **turn .. gate,**[d] God would be also with the armies. "The two great requisites of civil government are here described as coming from Jehovah."—J. A. Alexander.

The Glorious Crown.—Oh, that we were all invested with this crown of holiness, dignity, and beauty. How many are content with the gilded coronets and fading chaplets of the world. You remember the scene in the "Pilgrim's Progress," part ii., which has been made the subject of a painting by Sir Noel Paton—the man raking straw while one held a glittering crown over his head. Make Christ your boast. The crown of pride shall be hurled to the ground, the garlanded revellers shall sink in their own corruption, the honors which men so eagerly seek are as a fading flower, but this crown shall sparkle for ever on the believer's head (Dan. xii. 3; Ps. xc. 17).—William Guthrie.

7, 8. (7) **they,** R. V. "these." Having described Samaria the prophet goes on to say—but the people of Jerusalem are no better. **have erred,**

a Eze. xxx. 24. Samaria was taken by Shalmaneser, about B.C. 721.

b "The regular season for ingathering of figs is from Aug. to Nov., so that a ripe fig in June is regarded as a rarity, and eaten with the greater relish... The immediate eating of the fruit is only mentioned as a sign of eagerness or greediness." — J. A. Alexander.

c 'As soon as he has got it into his hand, he can't keep it there to look at, or forbear eating it, but greedily devours it and swallows it down at once."—Gill.

d "To the gate, i.e., of the enemy; not only repelling his attack in Judaea, but driving him back into his own fortifications." — Henderson.

"Turn back war at the gate; i.e. war which has advanced even up to the gate of the besieged city." — Spk. Com.

"How fearfully the vice of drunkenness had spread is seen from the fact that even priests and prophets

see Le. x. 1—9. **err in vision,** "they reel during their visions, they totter while giving judgment," i. e. even the religious leaders of the people are unfitted for their most sacred offices by drunkenness. (8) **vomit,** the revolting consequences of excess.

Erring Through Strong Drink.—Mr. J. W. Kirton, author of "Buy your own Cherries," etc., tells a painful story of a clergyman of the Church of England—a man of such power that he filled every seat and aisle with a congregation, and wherever he preached cleared out the chapels and churches for miles round. Souls were converted, and a blessed influence rested on the town. By-and-by a whisper got abroad that he was fond of drink, and ultimately it proved to be too true. He was seen staggering in the streets; the bishop instituted inquiries, and the case turned out so bad that the clergyman's gown was taken from him, and he was deprived of his living. All restraint seemed then removed. He wandered about the town, sold his library, and spent the money in drink amongst the worst characters in the town where he had preached the gospel for years. His plate followed, then his furniture, and ultimately he marched to the work-house and asked for admission. He was received, and week after week he went with the other paupers into the very church where he used to preach. His friends took compassion upon him, took him out of the work-house, put him into a cottage and started him as a schoolmaster; but he eventually "broke out" again, spent all he had in drink, had another attack of delirium tremens, and was taken, a hopeless maniac, to the county lunatic asylum.—Old Test. Anec.

Drunkenness.—It is not so much the money that drunkenness wastes as the misery it produces—the domestic, temporal, and eternal misery—which most of all appals us. As to the expense of this vice, great as it is, that we least deplore, for the loss of money, we hate it least. On the contrary, we should be content were the money and the vice to perish together. We should be content to pay that hundred million as yearly tribute, would this enemy to God and man, this foe to our peace and piety, leave these shores. We wish to keep, and were it possible to get back, something far more precious than money. Give that mother back her son, as he was on the day when he returned from his father's grave, and in all the affection of his uncorrupted boyhood, walked to the house of God with a widowed weeping woman leaning on his arm. Give that grieved man back his brother as innocent and happy as in those days when the boys, twined in each other's arms, returned from school, bent over the same Bible, slept in the same bed, and never thought that the day would come when brother should blush for brother. Give this weeping wife, who sits before us wringing her hands in agony, tears dripping through her jewelled fingers, and the lines of sorrow prematurely drawn on her beautiful brow; give her back the man she loved, such as he was when her young heart was won, when they stood side by side on the nuptial day, and receiving her from a fond father's hands, he promised his love to one whose heart he has broken, and whose once graceful form now bends with sorrow to the ground. Give me back, as a man, the friends of my youthful days, whose wrecks now lie thick on this wreck-strewn shore. Relieve us of the fears that lie heavy on our hearts for the character and the souls of some who hold parley with the devil by this forbidden tree, and are floating on the outer edge of that great gulf-stream, which sweeps its victims onwards to most woful ruin. Could this be done, we would not talk of money. The hundred millions which drink costs this land is not to be weighed or even mentioned with this. Hearts are broken which no money can heal. Rachel is "weeping for her children," refusing to be comforted.—Guthrie.

9—11. (9) **Whom,** etc. "Whom is he going to teach knowledge, and upon whom is he trying to force 'the Message' as he calls it. Them that are weaned from the milk and drawn from the breasts?" Does he take us for infants?—G. A. Smith. **doctrine,** R. V. "the message." (10) **precept,** etc.,[a] "We must conceive the abrupt, intentionally short, reiterated and almost childish words of verse 10 as spoken in mimicry, with a mocking motion of the head, and in a childish, stammering, taunting tone."—Ewald. (11) **stammering,** "but Isaiah turns upon them with their own words: 'You call me, Stammerer! I tell you that God, Who speaks through me, and Whom in me you mock, will one day speak again to

were addicted to it, and that not only in their private life, but they even performed their official functions in a state of intoxication." —Nagelsbach.

"A tree in South America, called the Judas Tree, has beautiful scarlet blossoms, but it has a deadly opiate. The insects are charmed with it. But under and all around this tree there are millions of dead carcases lying." —Old Test. Anec.

"Not only has the author of Proverbs pointed out the evils which attend those who tarry long at the wine, but all the precepts and denunciations against drunkenness, all the details of the flagitious arts perpetrated under its influence, which are recorded in the Bible, from Genesis to Revelation, are directed against the inordinate drinkers of wine. It is needless to say more respecting them, but refer them to that Sacred Volume, with the hope that it may guide them to salutary contrition and penitential sorrow."—Hodgkin.

[a] Heb. "Tsav la-tsav, tsav la-tsav; Kav la-kav, kav la-kav; zeeir sham, zeeir sham."

you in a tongue that shall indeed sound stammering to you.[b] When those far-off barbarians have reached your walls, and over them taunt you in uncouth tones, then shall you hear how God can stammer.' "—G. A. Smith.

The Precept, the Line, and the Little (vs. 10).—I. The lesson of the precept is in order that we may be right and do right. II. The lesson of the line is in order that we may be right and do right; we must try over and over again. III. The lesson of the little is that we must not be discouraged if we do not make great advances.—Preacher's Lantern.

"Here a Little, and There a Little."—A friend called on Michael Angelo, who was finishing a statue. Some time afterwards he called again; the sculptor was still at his work. His friend, looking at the figure, exclaimed, "You have been idle since I saw you last!" "By no means," replied the sculptor; "I have retouched this part, and polished that; I have softened this feature, and brought out this muscle; I have given more expression to this lip, and more energy to this limb." "Well, well," said his friend, "but all these are trifles." "It may be so," replied Angelo; "but recollect that trifles make perfection, and that perfection is no trifle." Perpora and His Pupil.—Perpora, the great Italian music master, kept one of his pupils learning the same lesson for three years. The pupil began to murmur, but the master was firm. Four, five, six years passed, and yet he was still at the same, until at last, when he began to fear he, might after all, be just at the beginning, the great teacher set him free with the words, "Go, my son, for thou hast nothing more to learn," and he found himself the first singer of Italy. So God keeps teaching us the same lesson over and over again—our utter nothingness, our complete helplessness, and our perfect sinfulness.—Old Test. Anec. The Claims of Children.—Dr. Leonard Bacon once preached a sermon on what he called the obverse side of the Fifth Commandment—the duty of parents to be worthy of honor. The child is born into the world with this right. His pure eyes look to his elders for example. His soul waits for impulse and inspiration from them. Woe unto that parent who, by unworthy character, causes one of these little ones to stumble; it were better for him that a millstone were hanged about his neck, and that he were drowned in the depths of the sea.—Christian Union.

[b] Some refer this to the Assyrians, as people of another tongue, by whom they should be punished.

"Try to gain a little for God, a little for heaven, a little more of grace every day. Do this in little things and you will accomplish great things. Here a little and there a little will carry you on from step to step, from grace to glory."—G. B. Cheever.

"As light to the sun, as the heart to the body, as weight to the hammer, as the foundation to the building, as point to the spear, as edge to the sword, as fruitfulness to the tree, so is Christ in preaching; and preaching without Christ can no more enlighten the world than the sun without light, etc., etc."—John Bate.

12, 13. (12) **This ..rest**, R. V. "This is the rest, give ye rest to them that are weary," i. e. cease your warfare. (13) **But**, etc., R. V., "Therefore shall the word of the Lord be unto them," etc., all that they had scoffingly said about Isaiah's message; a monotonous, intolerable succession of judgments."—Camb. Bib.[a]

Little Things.—A holy life is made up of a number of small things; little words, not eloquent speeches or sermons; little deeds, not miracles of battle nor one great heroic act of mighty martyrdom, make up the true Christian life. The little constant sunbeam, not the lightning; the waters of Siloam that "go softly" in the meek mission of refreshment, not the "waters of the river, great and many," rushing down in noisy torrents, are the true symbols of a holy life. The avoidance of little evils, little sins, little inconsistencies, little weaknessness, little follies, indiscretions and imprudences, little foibles, little indulgences of the flesh; the avoidance of such little things as these goes far to make up at least the negative beauty of a holy life.—A. R. Bonar.

Rest.—Ministers are said to be behind the times when they offer in Christ's own name rest to weary souls; teachers are said to have fallen astern when they speak of refreshing, and comfort, and high inspiration nerving the soul to the discharge of moral duty; and they are supposed to be contemporaneous prophets who chatter the gossip of the day, and annotate the newspaper which to-morrow will be forgotten.—Parker.

Rest is not quitting
  This busy career;
Rest is the fitting
  Of self to one's sphere.
'Tis loving and serving
  The highest and best;
'Tis onward, unswerving:
  And this is true rest.—Goethe.

[a] "They may despise the instruction given to them as puerile, but they shall have no other: and being thus left to act according to the dictates of their own supposed wisdom, they must utterly perish." —Henderson.

1 Pe. ii. 8; Mat. xxiii. 37.

14, 15. (14) **scornful,** Ps. i. 1; Pr. xxix. 8; i. e. "the politicians who rested all their hopes upon the alliance with Egypt," and treated Isaiah's warnings with scorn. (15) **said,** by your conduct, if not in actual words. **covenant with death,** we have arranged a plan by which we are no longer afraid of defeat by death.[b] **scourge,** the invasion of the Assyrian army, like a mighty flood; "the reference probably is to false grounds of confidence, such as false oracles (Ezek. xiii. 6—8; Mic. ii. 11), Isaiah putting his own language into their mouth."—Camb. Bib.

Mr. Whitefield.—An extraordinary attestation to the excellence of Mr. Whitefield as a preacher was furnished by Hume, the historian, well known for his infidelity. An intimate friend having asked him what he thought of Mr. Whitefield's preaching, "He is, sir," said Mr. Hume, "the most ingenious preacher I ever heard: it is worth while to go twenty miles to hear him." He then repeated the following passage, which occurred towards the close of the discourse he had been hearing: "After a solemn pause, Mr. Whitefield thus addressed his numerous audience: 'The attendant angel is just about to leave the threshold, and ascend to heaven. And shall he ascend, and not bear with him the news of one sinner, among all this multitude, reclaimed from the error of his ways?' To give the greater effect to this exclamation, he stamped with his foot, lifted up his eyes and hands to heaven, and with gushing tears, cried aloud, 'Stop, Gabriel! Stop, Gabriel! Stop, ere you enter the sacred portals, and yet carry with you the news of one sinner converted to God.' He then, in the most simple but energetic language, described what he called a Saviour's dying love to a sinful man, so that almost the whole assembly melted into tears. This address was accompanied with such animated yet natural action that it surpassed anything I ever saw or heard in any other preacher." Happy had it been for Mr. Hume if he had received the doctrine, as well as admired the manner, of the preacher! But the pride of a false philosophy steeled his heart against the truth, and thus prevented his yielding to its converting and sanctifying influence.

16, 17. (16) **a stone,** this stone is the one immovable and basal element in history—Jehovah's covenant with Israel. This covenant relation is established, and confirmed and strengthened by all divine guidance. "Not diplomacy but faith in God is the true insurance against disaster."—Polyc. Bib. **believeth,** relies on the covenant of Jehovah, symbolised in this Zion-foundation. **make haste,** "No need of swift couriers to Egypt, and fret and fear of poor political brains in Jerusalem."—G. A. Smith. (17) R. V. "And I will make judgment the line and righteousness the plummet," comp. 2 Ki. xxi. 13. These are the guides by which to build on this sure foundation.

The Sure Foundation (vss. 16, 17).—I. God has Himself laid the foundation for human happiness. II. He calls men to build their hopes upon that Foundation alone. III. Nevertheless men neglect that Foundation in favor of inventions and devices of the world. IV. God will critically and exactly try every man's foundation and superstructure. V. The issue will be in one case entire ruin, and in the other triumphant to every believer.—The Corner Stone.—I remark—I. That a great difference exists between a mere general dependence on Christ, and a conscious, intimate life with Him. II. That this intimate, daily life with Him is the great aim of the Gospel. III. That men, and wise men too, deem it impossible and delusive for a mortal man to live by faith in an invisible Being, and thus enjoy communion with Him. IV. That the Saviour is very precious to His followers as their hope and foundation.—H. W. Beecher.

Note on vs. 16.—Every promise is dated, but with a mysterious character; and for want of skill in God's chronology, we are prone to think God forgets us, when, indeed, we forget ourselves, in being so bold to set God a time of our own, and in being angry that He comes not just then to us. We are over-greedy of comfort, and expect the promise should keep time with our own hasty desires, which, because it doth not, we are discontented. A high piece of folly! The sun will not go faster, for setting our watch forward; nor the promise come the sooner, for our attending it. God seldom comes at our day, because we seldom reckon right, yet He never fails His own day.—Gurnall (1670).

[b] "Their foundation (and confidence) was their falsehood and deceit, by the aid of which they hoped that they would have nothing to fear from death and Hades." — Nagelsbach.

"They thought themselves as sure of their lives, even when the most destroying judgments were abroad, as if they had made a bargain with Death, upon a valuable consideration, not to come till they sent for him."—Mat. Henry.

" 'Scorners,' in the language of Scripture, are those who set at nought God's prophets, or His messages, or his Holy Word, or His Church, or His ministers."—Pul. Com.

[a] The fig. is taken fr. the foundations of Sol.'s temple, 'the remains of which have been preserved to the present day, and appear almost indestructible." Ewald.

"If you had a bridge to cross which had stood for centuries and over which thousands of people had passed every day with entire safety, you would feel no hesitation in making use of it yourself. So is Christ set before you—a tested foundation of hope."— Hawes.

18—20. (18) **covenant,** vs. 15. **disannulled,** obliterated, as the writing on a wax tablet is wiped out. (19) **From the time,** R. V. "As often as it passeth through," it will be a repeated scourge. **and it shall be a vexation,** etc., R. V. "And it shall be naught but terror to understand the message," then the prophecies you shall hear shall be only terrible. (20) **bed,**[a] etc., "a proverbial expression for the intolerable situation which the politicians are preparing for themselves and their country."—Camb. Bib.

[a] "They flattered themselves that they had prepared an easy and secure couch to slumber upon; their carnal wisdom and Pharisaic righteousness — how miserably insufficient should it prove." — Spk. Com.

"Those that do not build upon Christ as their foundation, but rest in a righteousness of their own, will prove in the end thus to have deceived themselves; they can never be easy, safe, nor warm: the bed is too short, the covering too narrow." — Mat. Henry.

God's Indisposition to Smite.—It is a strange work, a strange act, to God (ver. 21). To confer and to sustain life, to impart blessing, to multiply riches, to enlarge the mind, to strengthen and sanctify the soul, to fill with hope and joy,—this is the work which is natural, congenial, pleasant to him whose Name is love. But to visit with penalty, to smite rather than to spare, to inflict sorrow and humiliation,—this is strange, ungenial, joyless to the heavenly Father. "As I live," saith God, "I have no pleasure in the death of the wicked." He delighteth in mercy, but he is constrained to punish.—Pul. Com.

Covenanting with Liars.—You cannot make any binding covenant with a bad man, much less with all evil, symbolized and typified in the word death or hell. The bad man will serve you so long as it suits his purpose to do so. A man who will tell lies for you will tell lies to you. A man who will make you rich through robbery will make you poor through the same means when it suits his purpose to do so. You cannot enter into a binding agreement with a liar.—Peop. Bib.—Inadequate Religion.—Human nature is impure. It needs cleansing as well as pardon. Some imagine this is accomplished by sacramental grace, through baptism, which is supposed to regenerate; and the mysterious influence of the consecrated bread and wine. All this is inadequate. No outward rite can effect an inward and spiritual change. There must be a new nature. There must be a love of holiness and a living growth into holiness. There must be a new birth. There must be the conviction of sinfulness; the acceptance of Christ; the surrender to the authority of Christ. For this the Gospel provision is adequate. There is the word of God which proclaims the mercy and offers the inducement. There is the Holy Spirit which changes the heart. Be not satisfied with inadequate religion. Remember the solemn importance of possessing an adequate religion.—J. Rawlinson.

21, 22. (21) **Perazim,** see 1 Chr. xiv. 11,[a] **Gibeon,** see 1 Chr. xiv. 17. **strange,** because performed with foreigners against his own people. (22) **be ye not,** a final appeal to the scoffing ones, (vs. 14) not to resist Jehovah. **consumption,** burning up, Da. ix. 27. "A strict decree of destruction."—Polyc. Bib.

[a] See also 2 Sa. v. 18—24.

"Mercy is God's right hand, that He is most used to. Wrath is 'strange work'—He is unused to it."

"Mockery is the most annoying form of attack; it is most keenly felt; it is most difficult to answer. It serves the purpose when argument fails. One grinning Voltaire may do more execution than many reasoning Humes." —J. Rawlinson.

His Strange Work (vs. 21).—I. It was strange there should be occasion for the work. II. It was strange because foreign to His heart. III. It was strange on account of the method He adopted. IV. It was strange because unusual. V. It was strange, for it excited wonder on all hands.—Stems and Twigs.

Scorners Abased.—Armies revolt, melt away by sickness and desertion, suffer defeat, become demoralized, surrender themselves; a police fails and fraternizes with revolution; a treasury becomes exhausted; allies draw back in the hour of danger, as the Egyptians did in Israel's greatest need; and the mighty potentate who has scorned God and his laws finds himself, together with his advisers, brought to shame, defeated, ruined. So with the "scorners" whose mental pride has puffed them up. God can abase them in a moment by mental disease, brain-softening, paralysis, sense of depression, disgust with life. How the bold atheist trembles, and wishes that he could retract his daring speeches, when he is struck down by sickness, crippled, bed-ridden, palsied perhaps. God does not always launch his bolts in this life; but he can at any time do so, and he does it with sufficient frequency to leave men without excuse if they do not note, and profit, by his warnings.—Pul. Com.

23—25. "The discourse closes with a parable of comfort addressed by the prophet to his own circle of friends. It is drawn from the occupations of agriculture."—Driver.[a] (24) **all day,** "Is the ploughman never done with his ploughing, with the opening and harrowing of ground?"—Polyc. Bib. Does the preparatory process go on for ever? (25) **fitches, anise.**

[a] "The general idea of the parable is this. The whole world is the field of the Divine Husbandman. He plants it with different kinds of crops, each of which is

cummin, cultivated for its aromatic seeds. R. V. "And put in the wheat in rows, and the barley in the appointed place and the spelt in the border thereof." Each kind of seed is treated appropriately.

Physical Husbandry the Effect and Emblem of Divine Teaching (vs. 23).—I. Physical husbandry is the effect of Divine teaching—all true secular ideas, as well as spiritual, are from God. 1. This suggested by a priori reasoning; 2. Sustained by Scripture; 3. Implied in the doctrine of Providence. II. Physical husbandry is the emblem of Divine teaching. 1. Moral fruitfulness is the great end of God's dealings with man; 2. To realize this end, God employs a great variety of instrumentalities. Conclusion:—Divinity of life; man the organ of Divine thought, and the object of Divine operation.—Homilist.

Affliction Inevitable.—We must all go through some kind of threshing process. The fact that you are devoting your life to honorable and noble purposes will not win you any escape. Wilberforce, the Christian Emancipator, was in his day derisively called "Doctor Cantwell." Thomas Babington Macaulay, the advocate of all that was good long before he became the most conspicuous historian of his day, was caricatured in one of the Quarterly Reviews as "Bubble-tongue Macaulay." Norman M'Leod, the great friend of the Scotch poor, was industriously maligned in all quarters. All the small wits of London took after John Wesley, the father of Methodism. If such men could not escape the maligning of the world, neither can you expect to get rid of the sharp, keen stroke of the tribulum. All who will live godly in Christ Jesus must suffer persecution.—The Purpose of Affliction.—It is from God, and the end ever kept in view is the good of the soul and its productiveness. The ploughman does not plough for ploughing's sake. He opens the soil, turns up the furrows, breaks the clods with the harrow, and all to prepare for the sowing of the seed. And so far the tiller is an image of God and of his operations on the spirit of man. There is seeming severity of method, but ever beneficence in the end. Again, there is variety of method in God's husbandry of the soul. As the farmer adapts his plans to the soil and to the kind of grain, selects the best modes of preparing the ground, of sowing the grain, of collecting the harvest, of separating the corn from the chaff. "He does not always plough, nor always sow, nor always thresh. He does not deal with all lands and all grains in the same way. Some he threshes in one mode, some in another, but he will be careful not to break the grain or destroy it in threshing it. However severe may appear to be his blows, his object is not to crush and destroy the grain, but to remove it from the chaff and save it. In all this he acts the part of wisdom, for God has taught him what to do. So with God."—Pul. Com.—God's Chastening.—When God chastens us, it is not that He means to destroy us, but because He has set His heart on saving us, because He has appointed us to life and not to death. He works with discrimination. He employs various methods, sends sorrows of all sorts and sizes, that He may adapt Himself to every man's needs, and to all our varieties of place, time, and circumstances. Just as the husbandman varies his treatment of the soil, and allots to each kind of seed a soil and place suitable to its kind; just as, after the harvest has been gathered in, he employs only such instruments as are best adapted for separating the different kinds of grain from the straw and the chaff. With like wisdom and discretion God deals with us, assigning to each of us our proper station and lot, and, when we sin against Him, adapting His judgments to our several needs. The sorrows, losses, bereavements which befall us are but as the sharp edge of the share, or the keen teeth of the harrow, and are intended to prepare us to receive the good seed, and to bring forth much fruit.—Cox.

26, 27. (26) All this is done in obedience to an inherited, almost instructive, wisdom, which rests ultimately on Divine inspiration. See vs. 29. **discretion,** for the adaptation of treatment. (27) **fitches .. staff,** bec. the seeds are readily detached from the seed-pods. **rod,** stronger than the staff, bec. the seed-pods of cummin are harder. The method suitable for each kind of grain is employed by the husbandman.

The Necessity of the Spirit of Wisdom.—Ploughing is not an art of our discovery. We discover somewhat of the plough, but the ploughing is a far greater thing than the plough. We mistake the instrument

treated with a tillage and culture fitted to it. He does each of His works of moral and spiritual agriculture in its proper season; and all the world will be His threshing-floor, in which each kind of grain will be dealt with in a manner suited to its character."—Wordsworth.

"There are men who suppose they are the Lord's favorites, simply because their barns are full, and their bank account is flush, and there are no funerals in the house. It may be because they are fitches and cummin, while down at the end of the lane, the poor widow may be the Lord's corn. You are little pounded, because you are little worth, and she bruised and ground, because she is the best part of the harvest. By carefulness of the threshing, you may always conclude the value of the grain."—Hom. Com.

Co-worker in Christ! be content to sow little seeds for Him; be patient to wait a long time for their growing; be strong to endure much opposition; be hopeful, expecting sublime fruitage; these are the chief lessons.

for the music in many instances. We think that having fashioned a hammer we have sundered a rock; we suppose that because we have made a mechanical arrangement we have got into the very secret of creation and are working from the internal centre. Ploughing was in man at his very creation. Almost the first thought he had was about ploughing. But he had no plough. Given the inspiration of ploughing, and the plough will soon be found. Given the desire to find God, and God will soon be forthcoming. Given the passion for reading, and books will be procured if they cannot be bought or borrowed. The spirit of wisdom will find out the sanctuary of understanding. What is wanted is the spirit, the genius, the inspiration, the overwhelming spiritual impulse.—Peop. Bib.

28, 29. (28) **Bread .. bruised,** or crushed in the mill: **break it,** R. V. "and though the wheel of his cart and his horses scatter it, he doth not grind it." He does not go on threshing forever, but gathers it for grinding. (29) **This also,**[a] the application of the parable is that God follows method and reason in all that he does. Man is taught by Him and reflects the divine method.

The Wonderfulness of God's Counsel (vs. 29).—I. Its nature is wonderful—reconciliation. II. Its formation is wonderful. 1. Its gradualness; 2. Its instruments. III. Its propagation is wonderful. 1. The character of those to whom its propagation was first entrusted; 2. The class to whom it was first offered; 3. The pressing of it on those who frequently reject it.—Homilist.

Divine Providence.—Mr. John Craig, a distinguished minister, and colleague of Knox, having gone to reside in Bologna, in a convent of Dominicans, found a copy of Calvin's Institutes which God made the means of his conversion to the reformed faith. He was seized as a heretic soon after, and carried to Rome, where he was condemned to be burnt; but on the evening preceding the day of execution, the reigning pontiff died, and according to custom the doors of all the prisons were thrown open. All others were released; but heretics, after being permitted to go outside the walls, were reconducted to their cells. That night, however, a tumult was excited, and Craig and his companions escaped. They had entered a small inn at some distance from Rome, when they were overtaken by a party of soldiers sent to recapture them. On entering the house, the captain looked Craig steadfastly in the face, and asked him if he remembered having once relieved a poor wounded soldier in the neighborhood of Bologna. Craig had forgotten it. "But," said the captain, "I am the man; I shall requite your kindness; you are at liberty: your companions I must take with me, but for your sake I shall treat them with all possible lenity." He gave him all the money he had, and Craig escaped. But his money soon failed him; yet God, who feedeth the ravens, did not. Lying at the side of a wood, full of gloomy apprehensions, a dog came running up to him with a purse in its teeth. Suspecting some evil, he attempted to drive the animal away, but in vain. He at length took the purse, and found in it a sum of money, which carried him to Vienna.—Whitecross.

CHAPTER THE TWENTY-NINTH.

1, 2. (1) **Ariel,** R. V., "Ho Ariel, Ariel," a symbolic name for Jerusalem. Word prob. means altar-hearth. This best fits the reference to "sacrifices." **kill sacrifices,** R. V., "let the feasts come round," once or twice more, keeping up the yearly round of feasts; the outward sign of obedience. (2) "Then will I distress Ariel, so that there will be moaning and bemoaning, and it will become to me a true Ariel."—Polyc. Bib. **as Ariel,** a real altar-hearth, where many will be consumed.

Verses 1—8.—The impending humiliation and deliverance of Jerusalem. Jerusalem, apostrophized by the mystic name of "Ariel," is at present gay and careless and secure, the festal calendar follows its accustomed course, and this state of things may endure for a short time longer (1). But already in vision the prophet sees her beset by hosts of enemies, and reduced to the lowest depths of despair **(2—4) when suddenly**

[a] "His judgments are usually in the line of our offences; by the nature of the judgment we may usually ascertain the nature of the sin."—Barnes.

"God's government of the world comprehends the minutest attention to detail with an all-comprehending unity of design."—Spk. Com.

"The practical idea conveyed is, that God mingles mercy with His judgments."—Henderson.

"To the child of God yearning for holiness, there is something exceedingly precious and delightful in approaching a command that seems to be naturally impossible; because he realizes that the Lord gave the Word, and that it is for the Lord to make possible of fulfilment in His child that which he commands. Surely we can say with Augustine, 'Give what thou commandest, and then command what thou wilt.'"—H. W. Webb-Peploe.

"If there have been raised up in our own country men mighty in the exhibiting and establishing truth, and if in the lapse of time we grow indifferent to the truth, and perhaps even half inclined to the errors which were exposed and expelled, will it not be made a matter of accusation against us that ours is the land in which those worthies dwelt?" —Hom. Com.

the Lord Himself, arrayed in the terrors of earthquake and tempest, appears in judgment (6), and in a moment the scene is changed. In the very hour of their triumph, the enemies of Zion are disappointed of their expectation, and vanish like a vision of the night (7, 8).—Camb. Bib. Divine Corrections Through Temporal Distress.—The Mosaic system had established the idea that men would be sure to get good things by being good. This was founded in truth, but it involved men's having right ideas of what are "good things," and what is "being good." Men made it mean that they would be sure to get temporal blessings if they made large outward show of goodness. And therefore temporal distresses and anxieties were precisely the things that would awaken men to a sense of their mistake, and to a worthier apprehension of Divine claims. Temporal safety and blessing did not attend such goodness as theirs, and so they were led to suspect their goodness. So we, finding our religion fail us in the evil day, are brought to see that formal religion never can be acceptable unto him who "desires truth in the inward parts." —Pul. Com.

3, 4. (3) **a mount,** R. V., "a fort." **forts,** R. V., "siege works," comp. Ezek. iv. 1. (4) Explains the "moaning and bemoaning" of vs. 2. The verse reads: "And thou shalt be laid low, speaking from (beneath) the earth, and thy speech shall come humbly from the dust; and thy voice shall be like (that of) a ghost (coming) from the earth, and thy speech shall squeak from the dust." The allusions in the latter half of the verse are explained under ch. viii. 19. The figures signify the utter abasement and exhaustion of the "joyous city."—Camb. Bib.

Recognizing God's Hand in History.—Carlyle says in a note to Cromwell's fourth speech to Parliament, that "the Bible of every nation is its own history." This note is drawn from Carlyle by Cromwell's frequent insistence, that we must ever be turning from forms and rituals to study God's will and ways in history. And that speech of Cromwell is perhaps the best sermon ever delivered on the subject of this chapter. For he said: "What are all our histories but God manifesting Himself, that He hath shaken, and tumbled down and trampled upon everything that He hath not planted!" And again, speaking of our own history, he said to the House of Commons: "We are a people with the stamp of God upon us, . . . whose appearances and providences among us were not to be outmatched by any story." Truly this is national religion:—the reverential acknowledgment of God's hand in history; the admiration and effort of moral progress; the stirring of conscience when we see wrong; the expectation, when evil abounds, that God will bring justice and purity to us if we labor with Him for them.—Expos. Bib. Note on Verse 3.—Movable towers of wood were usually placed upon the mount, which were driven on wheels fixed within the bottom planks, to secure them from the enemy. Their size was not always the same, but proportioned to the towers of the city they besieged, the front was usually covered with tiles, and in later times the sides were likewise guarded with the same materials; their tops were covered with raw hides, and other things, to preserve them from fireballs and missive weapons; they were formed into several stories, which were able to carry both soldiers and several kinds of engines. All these modes of attack were practiced in the days of Isaiah, who threatens Jerusalem with a siege conducted according to this method: "And I will encamp against thee round about, and will lay siege against thee with a mount; and I will raise forts against thee." The Prophet Ezekiel repeats the prediction in almost the same words, adding only the name of the engine which was to be employed in battering down the walls: "Thou also, son of man, take thee a tile, and lay it before thee, and portray upon it the city, even Jerusalem; and lay siege against it, and cast a mount against it; set the camp also against it; and set battering-rams against it round about."—Paxton.

5, 6. (5) **strangers,** R. V., "foes," a prophecy that the enemies of Israel in their seeming hour of victory should be suddenly overcome, as happened in the siege by Sennacherib. (6) **Thou**, R. V., "she," i. e. Jerusalem. The last words of vs. 5 belong here. "And then suddenly—full suddenly she shall be visited," etc. God will come to her rescue. **thunder**, etc., ch. xxviii. 17.

False Security.—The saint's sleeping time is Satan's tempting time;

"All things have rest—why should we toil alone? We only toil who are the first of things, and make perpetual moan, still from one labor to another thrown; nor ever fold our wings, nor cease from wanderings." — Tennyson.

"Nothing so much offends God as pride, haughtiness of heart, presumption; and when this is manifested by his people, they may expect to be abased to the very dust, until their spirit has been renewed and they have learned humility under his correcting hand."—Pul. Com.

"My soul repairs its fault
When, sharpening sense's hebetude,
She turns on my own life! So viewed,
No mere mote's breadth but teems immense
With witnessings of providence:
And woe to me if when I look
Upon that record, the sole book
Unsealed to me, I take no heed
Of any warning that I read!"
—Browning.

"I grow weary of the perpetual spurring on of God's people to service, — as if any father ever cared so much to have his children toiling for him as loving and trusting him,—and the more so as the God-possessed Christian invariably does serve." — C. I. Scofield.

every fly dares venture to creep on a sleeping lion. No temptation so weak, but is strong enough to foil a Christian that is napping in security. Samson asleep, and Delilah cut his locks. Saul asleep, and the spear is taken away from his very side, and he never the wiser. Noah asleep, and his graceless son has a fit time to discover his father's nakedness. Eutychus asleep, nods and falls from the third loft, and is taken up dead. Thus the Christian asleep in security may soon be surprised, so as to lose much of his spiritual strength.—A 17th Century Divine.

7, 8. (7) **munition,** or fortress; the stronghold of Zion. **as a dream,** comp. the sudden destruction of Babylon. (8) **dreameth,** but gets no satisfaction.[a] The description suits the bootless attack of Sennacherib.

Note on vs. 8.—As the simile of the Prophet is drawn from nature, an extract which describes the actual occurrence of such a circumstance will be agreeable. "The scarcity of water was greater here at Bubaker than at Benown. Day and night the wells were crowded with cattle lowing, and fighting with each other to come at the trough. Excessive thirst made many of them furious: others being too weak to contend for the water, endeavored to quench their thirst by devouring the black mud from the gutters near the wells; which they did with great avidity, though it was commonly fatal to them. This great scarcity of water was felt by all the people of the camp, and by none more than myself. I begged water from the negro slaves that attended the camp, but with very indifferent success: for though I let no opportunity slip, and was very urgent in my solicitations both to the Moors and to the negroes, I was but ill supplied, and frequently passed the night in the situation of Tantalus. No sooner had I shut my eyes, than fancy would convey me to the streams and rivers of my native land; there, as I wandered along the verdant bank, I surveyed the clear stream with transport, and hastened to swallow the delightful draught; but, alas! disappointment awakened me, and I found myself a lonely captive, perishing of thirst amid the wilds of Africa.—Mungo Park.

9, 10. (9) R. V. "Tarry ye and wonder: take your pleasure and be blind;" your amazement and blindness with regard to the prospect I lay before you is no evidence against its truth (Driver). **not with wine,** not this time, but by a spirit of infatuation. (10) **Lord .. sleep,** God's judgments coming upon men's minds and feelings as truly as on men's bodies and circumstances.[a] **the prophets .. covered,** Polyc. Bib. "and covered your heads."

Priestly Terror.—The ignorance which prevailed in reference to the Scriptures, when Luther was raised up by God to reform the Church, in the beginning of the sixteenth century, was indeed surprising. Conrad, of Heresbach, a grave author of that age, relates the following saying of a monk to his companions, "They have invented a new language, which they call Greek: you must be carefully on your guard against it; it is the matter of all heresy. I observe in the hands of many persons a book written in that language, and which they call the New Testament: it is a book full of dangers and poison. As to the Hebrew, my brethren, it is certain that whoever learns it becomes immediately a Jew." Evils of Ignorance.—That sovereign and universal Truth which illuminates intellectual nature, as the sun enlightens the material world. He who has never received this pure emanation of Divinity is as blind as those who are born without sight: he passes through life in darkness like that which involves the polar regions, where the night is protracted to half the year; he believes himself to be wise, but is indeed a fool; he imagines that his eye comprehends every object, yet he lives and dies without seeing anything; or, at most, he perceives only some fleeting illusions by a glimmering and deceitful light; some unsubstantial vapors, that are every moment changing their color and shape, and at length fade into total obscurity.—Fenelon.

11, 12. "A distinction is drawn between the ignorance of the educated and that of the uneducated classes. The man of culture is like one who will not break the seal of a sealed book that he may read it; the man in the street cannot read it even if unsealed. The passage is interesting as illustrating the diffusion of literary education in Isaiah's time (cf. Jer. v. 4, 5)."—Camb. Bib. (11) **of all,** i. e. the vision throughout. (12) **not learned,** makes no profession of skill.[b]

---

[a] "Dreams, in their development, have breath, and tears and tortures, and the touch of joy; they leave a weight upon our waking thoughts; they make us what we were not—what they will, and shake us with the vision that's gone by."—Byron.

"If we can sleep without dreaming, it is well that painful dreams are avoided. If, while we sleep, we can have any pleasing dreams, it is, as the French say, tant gagne, so much added to the pleasure of life."—Franklin.

[a] Ro. xi. 7, 8.

"The wisdom of the ancients—where is it? It is wholly gone. A school-boy today knows more than Sir Isaac Newton knew. His knowledge has vanished away. You buy the old editions of the great encyclopaedias for a few pence. Their knowledge has faded away. And all the boasted science and philosophy of this day will soon be old."—Drummond.

"A true and genuine impudence is ever the effect of ignorance, without the least sense of it."—Steele.

[b] "These verses teach the moral impossibility of those understanding Divine revelation whose minds are under the dominion of sin....The point of comparison lies in the disinclination or aversion of the mind." — Henderson.

Heart Learning.—There is a learning of the heart, and herein we find the sphere of inspired genius, inspired intuition—that marvelous instinct, sagacity, soul-power, which knows without having been to school. "How knoweth this man's letters, having never learned?" There are people who never can get away from the idea that heaven is to be scaled by a ladder: they forget that there are wings. There are many ways to truth, to God, to rest, not known by those who live simply in the letter. When the Bible is fully opened, annotated from beginning to end as with light, it will be done by the meek soul, the modest spirit. He will see most who first excludes the visible: then by pureness of heart and simplicity of motive, he may see God.—Peop. Bib.

2 Co. iii. 14, 15; Ac. xiii. 27.

"The power of a petition is not in the roof of the mouth, but in the root of the heart."— Trapp.

13, 14. "This spiritual insensibility of the people is the outcome of its whole religious attitude, which is insincere, formal, and traditional. The contrast implied is that between a religion of mere ritual and one of moral fellowship with God."—Camb. Bib. **their fear,** R. V., "their fear of me is a commandment of men which hath been taught them," or "but a precept of men learned by note."—Pol. Bib. **precept of men,** as distinct from the revealed will of God. The religion in our Lord's days was almost entirely an elaborate and painful system of human precepts. (14) **proceed to do,** "Therefore, behold, I will deal with it again in a fashion so wonderful and astonishing that the wisdom of their wise men will be lost and the discernment of their discerning ones will disappear."—Pol. Bib. **wisdom .. perish,**[a] they will be as absolutely silenced before it as if they had become fools and ignorant.

[a] "Their politic contrivances for maintaining Judah's national existence, and their whole method of reasoning about Divine things." — Spk. Com.

Comp. the Divine judgment in hardening Pharaoh's heart.

1 Co. i. 19—21.

Jargon Without Knowledge.—I heard two persons on the Wengern Alp talking by the hour together of the names of ferns; not a word about their characteristics, uses or habits, but a medley of crack-jaw titles, and nothing more. They evidently felt that they were ventilating their botany, and kept each other in countenance by alternate volleys of nonsense. They were about as sensible as those doctrinalists who forever talk over the technicalities of religion, but know nothing by experience of its spirit and power. Are we not all too apt to amuse ourselves after the same fashion? He who knows mere Linnaean names but has never seen a flower, is as reliable in botany, as he is in theology who can descant upon supra-lapsarianism, but has never known the love of Christ in his heart.

"True religion's more than doctrine,
Something must be known and felt."—Spurgeon.

"The world has a right to look worshipers, as they come out of church, in the face, and ask them, What do you bring away from your altar, your psalm, your sermon, your benediction? What gifts have you to distribute in your neighborhood?" — Bp. Huntington.

Illustrative of vs. 14.—One Mr. Soper, while residing at Alfriston, in England, having been called to the knowledge of the truth, separated himself from his former gay associates. Some of these giddy youths, meeting him one day when going to the chapel, thus addressed him: "Well, Soper, you seem to be very zealous for religion; we shall soon hear that you are a preacher. Come, can't you preach us a sermon?" Soper very gravely replied, "No; I will name a text and will leave you to preach the sermon." Then, with great emphasis, he recited the above passage: "Beware, therefore, lest that come upon you which is spoken of in the Prophets: Behold, ye despisers, and wonder and perish; for I work a work in your days, a work which ye shall in nowise believe, though a man declare it unto you." The words fell with such a weight upon their minds that not one of them could make a reply, nor did they ever ridicule him any more.—Whitecross.

"We do not need to be preaching in public in order to carry Christ to others. We can always find a congregation if we wish. The workshop, the warehouse, the college, the home, will yield us hearers, if our hearts are set on winning men to Christ." —A. McLaren.

15—17. Here begins the third "Woe," against the political intrigue with Egypt. (15) **seek deep,** etc., or lay their plans in utmost secrecy, thinking thus to hide them from God.[a] (16) R. V. "Ye turn things upside down! Shall the potter be accounted as clay; that the thing made should say," etc. **turning .. down,** or attempt to subvert the divine plans. **potter's clay,**[b] "You evidently confuse things, you are the clay, not the potter." **work say,** etc., see ch. xlv. 9. **no understanding,** and therefore man, the creature, must take his affairs out of the hands of God his Creator. (17) **Lebanon,** "which now produces vines only on its slopes, will then bear them even on its highest points, while the land which already bears vines and trees shall then be like a splendid forest."—Pol. Bib. A millennial picture of the time when nature shall, with man, be redeemed and renewed.

[a] "The reference is to the secret plan which many of the Jewish nobles had of seeking Egyptian aid against Assyria, contrary to the advice of Isaiah."— Fausset.

[b] "Another rendering is, 'Ye invert the order of things, putting yourselves instead of God;'

just as if the potter should be esteemed as the clay."—Horsley.

Mi. iii. 12; Is. xxxii. 15; Mat. xxi. 43; Ro. xi. 12.

"Not only does Nature annually revive in spring from her winter's trance, but throughout the universe exhaustion is continually occurring at irregular intervals, and recoveries from exhaustion, i.e. revivals, are the only mode by which Nature is recruited and enabled to maintain herself."—Pul. Com.

"God never meant that man should scale the heavens
By strides of human wisdom. In his works,
Though wondrous, he commands us in his word
To seek him rather where his mercy shines."
—Cowper.

The Millennium Fast Approaching (vs. 17).—I. The event anticipated. 1. The event in prediction in my text relates to one great event, the conversion of the whole world to Christ. This accords best with the words of the text, with the general strain of prophecy, and is most clearly marked in the context. 2. And a most glorious event it will be. II. The evidence of its near approach. 1. The Prophet judged it near in his day; 2. Much more may we consider it near at this time. Efforts making for its accomplishment. Actual commencement of a work of grace in many places. Apply:—(1) Let us look forward with holy earnestness to this blessed time; (2) Let us pray for the hastening of this long wished for day; (3) Let us each one try to help it forward.—C. Simeon.

"The instinct of worship is so strong within the soul that men everywhere worship something. It may be the hideous fetish of the African or the artistic statue of the refined Greek, but something the Greek and the barbarian must have. When that young mother, in the days of Solomon, arose in the morning and found a dead child by her side instead of her own living one, how severe must have been the shock! Had there been no child by her side, no dead substitute, she might have thought that her own child lived somewhere and might sometime be found. But that dead substitute at first nearly killed her by despair. It is bad to withdraw a living heart from the Lord, but to substitute a dead one is first to rob God and then wickedly insult Him."—Wm. Parkes.

Note on vs. 17.—The storms and tempests which, gathering on the highest peak of Lebanon, burst on the plains and valleys below, are often severe. When De la Valle was traveling in the neighborhood of that mountain, in the end of April, a wind blew from its summits so vehement and cold, with so great a profusion of snow, that though he and his company "were in a manner buried in their quilted coverlets, yet it was sensibly felt, and proved very disagreeable." It is not therefore without reason that Lebanon, or the White Mountain, as the term signifies, is the name by which that lofty mountain is distinguished: and that the sacred writers so frequently refer to the snow and the gelid waters of Lebanon. They sometimes allude to it as a wild and desolate region; and certainly no part of the earth is more dreary and barren than the Sannin, the region of perpetual snow. On that naked summit, the seat of storm and tempest, where the principles of vegetation are extinguished, the art and industry of man can make no impression; nothing but the creating power of God Himself can produce a favorable alteration. Thus, predicting a wonderful change, such as results from the signal manifestations of the Divine favor to individuals or the Church, the Prophet demands, "Is it not yet a very little while, and Lebanon shall be turned into a fruitful field?" The contrast in this promise, between the naked, snowy, and tempestuous summits of Lebanon, and a field beautiful and enriched with the fairest and most useful productions of nature, expresses, with great force, the difference which the smiles of Heaven produce in the most wretched and hopeless circumstances of an individual or a nation.—Paxton.

[a] Ja. ii. 5.

"Acquaint thyself with God, if thou wouldst taste
His works. Admitted once to his embrace,
Thou shalt perceive that thou wast blind before;
Thine eye shall be instructed; and thine heart
Made pure shall relish, with divine delight
Till then unfelt, what hands divine have wrought."
—Cowper.

18, 19. (18) **deaf,** the spiritually obtuse. Comp. fig. of sealed book in vss. 11, 12. (19) **The meek,** comp. ch. lxi. 1; Mat. iii. 5, xi. 29, etc. The meek are they who submit themselves to the righteousness of God, as contrasted with those who "go about to establish their own righteousness." **poor,** see Mat. v. 3.[a]

Gospel to be Preached Simply.—Of the works of a famous alchymist of the thirteenth century it is said that "whoever would read his book to find out the secret would employ all his labor in vain." All the gold makers who have written upon their favorite mystery are in the like predicament; no one can comprehend what the secret is which they pretend to divulge. May we not shrewdly guess that if they had any secret to tell they would put it in intelligible language, and that their pompous and involved sentences are only a screen for their utter ignorance of the matter? When we hear preachers talking of Divine things in a style savoring more of metaphysical subtlety than of Gospel plainness; when the seeking sinner cannot find out the way of salvation because of their philosophical jargon, may we not with justice suspect that the preacher does not know the Gospel, and conceals his culpable ignorance behind the veil of rhetorical magniloquence? Surely if the man understood a matter so important to all his hearers as the way of salvation, he would feel constrained to tell it out in words which all might comprehend.—C. H. Spurgeon.

Meekness does not mean timidity (2 Tim. i. 7); not the craven spirit of the coward, but the quiet power of the strong man (Prov. xxviii. 1). It does not mean the absence of courage, but the absence of that ignorant and arrogant self-sufficiency which Peter showed when he said, "Though all men forsake Thee, yet will not I." It is that calmness of spirit which grows not out of reliance on self, but out of reliance on God. It is recorded of one whose courage at times had flashed up like a consuming fire, "Now the man Moses was very meek, above all the men which were upon the face of the earth." His meekness was not feebleness, but a calm strength; quiet endurance in the doing of duty under difficulties. He was not provoked by the wrong-headedness or irritated by the ingratitude of the nation he wished to serve, but he quietly bore their stubbornness, and persisted in doing them good against their will. Hence a quiet doing and a quiet bearing of the will of God is one constituent in this quality of the mind "meekness." It does not mean that equableness of disposition which comes from nature, so much as that calmness of spirit which comes from grace.—Hom. Com.

20, 21. (20) **terrible one,** "For tyrants will have then disappeared," Pol. Bib., oppressors of the poor, or foreign tyrants. **scorner,** or scoffer at the idea that God overruled. **watch for iniquity,** i. e. for the opportunity of doing evil. (21) R. V., "in a cause," i. e. find out occasions for condemning men.[b] Comp. the judicial treatment of our Lord, and of Stephen. **reproveth .. gate,**[c] would not allow any one publicly to denounce their wrong-doing. Comp. their treatment of Isaiah and Jeremiah. **turn aside the just,** from his right. **for a thing of naught,** on an empty pretext.

Religious Progress.—We might have expected in advance that all growth and progress would have been regular and gradual. But the fact is otherwise. In all the fields of human energy, in art, in science, in philosophy, in religion, long periods of comparative deadness and apathy occur, during which there is scarcely any perceptible advance at all, followed by shorter intervals of activity and energy, when progress is made "by leaps and bounds." The scientific energy of the last half-century is a case in point. The history of the Church, dispassionately viewed, shows a manifest progress; but the progress has been far from uniform. Many centuries have been centuries of stagnation. Religion has just kept itself alive, and that has been all. Then some stir has come from within or from without, and a rush of vitality has supervened, which has exercised an influence for good on all later times. Indifference to doctrinal truth was overspreading the world, when the dogmatic revival of the fourth century at once saved the faith, and advanced it. The expansion of the Church, which is a special mark of its life, had almost ceased, when missionary zeal broke out suddenly in the West, and the seventh and eighth centuries saw the conversion of England, Scotland, Friesland, Batavia, Switzerland, and most of Germany. A general deadness and dulness had come over Christendom between the eighth and the eleventh centuries, when the Crusades, which were a political necessity, produced the revival of the twelfth and thirteenth. The greatest revival of all was the Reformation, which recovered spiritual religion when it seemed almost lost, and exerted a purifying influence even in those parts of Christendom which most opposed it. Lesser revivals have been—in Germany Pietism, in France Jansenism, among ourselves Methodism and the Church movement still in progress. It seems scarcely too much to say that, without revivals, religion—even the Christian religion—would perish.—Pul. Com.

22—24. (22) **redeemed Abraham,** "there is no incident in the Biblical history of Abraham to which the expression "redeem" is specially appropriate; there is, however, a late Jewish legend about his being delivered from a fiery death prepared for him by his heathen relations (Book of Jubilees, ch. xii.)."—Camb. Bib.[a] **not now,** in the time the Prophet is foretelling. **wax pale,** "with shame and disappointment at the wicked degeneracy of his posterity, and fear as to their punishment."—Henderson. (23) **sanctify,** etc., the idea of the vs. is that the time would

[b] "Lead men into sin by words, i.e. supplying them with some plausible reason to excuse sin, or to tempt to sin."—Spk. Com.

[c] Am. v. 10.

"He who knows the language he speaks, speaks in all companies with perfect confidence and therefore with perfect ease. It is the uncertain grammarian that sits in silence, or picks his way daintily and inoffensively over commonplaces which nobody can remember."—Peop. Bib.

"If new-got gold is said to burn the pockets till it be cast forth into circulation, much more may new truth!"—Carlyle.

[a] "The phrase may be naturally understood, either as signifying deliverance fr. danger, and the Divine protection generally, or in a higher sense as signifying Abraham's conversion and salvation."—J. A. Alexander.

Ho. iii. 5; Zec. xii. 10; Ac. vi. 7; Ro. xi. 26.

The light of the Gospel often shines upon men as the sun upon a dead wall,—it meets with no entrance.

Mr. Baxter says: "Some holy Nonconformists I have known that would rarely mention God, but with their hats put off, or bowing down their heads, and it hath often affected me more than a sermon."—Old Test. Anec.

come when the Jews would rejoice in welcoming the Gentiles as "fellow heirs," children of God with them. (24) **erred in spirit,** i. e. the unbelieving Jews (ch. xxviii. 7). "The blinded and refractory Jews should at length embrace the doctrines of the Gospel."—Henderson.

Harmony of Gospel Truth.—Christ did not commit to the care of His Church any one class of truths and duties, or any number of classes of doctrines and obligations, but all of them. Christians are, therefore, to teach all the doctrines, and inculcate all the duties found in the Scriptures. There is no sectarianism in inspiration. The Holy Spirit is the Spirit of truth, and of the entire body of truth "as it is in Jesus." Sectarianism divides the doctrine of the Spirit into its various hues, and sects and parties are formed by good men attaching themselves to one class of colors, whereas "the true light" is made up of all colors. We would never live in an atmosphere of rainbows; it might appear more beautiful than clear daylight, but it would not be so useful for the world. In a lens, no one class of rays gathered into a focus will burn an object; this is done only by a concentration of all the rays. It was by exhibiting the whole counsel of God that Paul produced in his converts the kindlings of repentance towards God, and faith in our Lord Jesus Christ. If the churches think it proper to put forth the vivid hues of beauty and splendor, in their respective creeds and theological systems, let them also exhibit them witih all the blendings and softenings, the harmony and symmetry of the bow in the cloud, the sign of peace and good-will to the whole earth.—F. W. Jenkyn.

CHAPTER THE THIRTIETH.

A series of oracles on the Egyptian Alliance. **1—3.** (1) **rebellious children,**[b] inasmuch as they have sought alliance with Egypt, without the approval of the Lord. **not of me,** "carrying out a purpose which is not mine, and concluding a treaty contrary to my spirit, thus adding sin to sin."—Pol. Bib. **covering,** lit. "a drink offering" accompanying the conclusion of a treaty. (2) **walk,** etc., or, who are now on the way down to Egypt. (3) **your shame,** bec. Egypt will prove unable to help you.[c]

Influence of Confidence.—Mr. Pillsbury, warden of the State Prison in Connecticut, once received into the prison a man of gigantic stature, whose crimes had for seventeen years made him the terror of the country. He told the criminal, when he came, he hoped he would not repeat the attempts to escape which he had made elsewhere. "It will be best," said he, "that you and I should treat each other as well as we can. I will make you as comfortable as I possibly can, and I shall be anxious to be your friend; and I hope you will not get me into difficulty on your account. There is a cell intended for solitary confinement; but we have never used it, and I should be sorry ever to have to turn the key upon anybody in it. You may range the place as freely as I do: if you trust me, I will trust you." The man was sulky, and for six weeks showed only gradual symptoms of softening under the operation of Mr. Pillsbury's cheerful confidence. At length, information was brought of the man's intention to break the prison. The warden called him, and taxed him with it: the man preserved a gloomy silence. He was told it was now necessary for him to be locked in the solitary cell, and was desired to follow the warden, who went first, carrying a lamp in one hand and a key in the other. In the narrowest part of the passage, Mr. Pillsbury, a small, light man, turned round and looked in the face of the stout criminal. "Now," said he, "I ask whether you have treated me as I deserve. I have done everything I could to make you happy. I have trusted you; but you have never given me the least confidence in return, and have even planned to get me into difficulty. Is this kind? And yet I cannot bear to lock you up. If I had the least sign that you cared for me——" The man burst into tears. "Sir," said he, "I have been a very demon these seventeen years; but you treat me like a man." "Come, let us go back," said the warden. The convict had free range of the prison as be-

b "Jewish ambassadors were at the time on their way to Egypt to seek aid against Assyria." — Fausset.

c Is. xx. 5; comp. fig. in Is. xviii. 1.

"In time of trouble go not out of yourself to seek for aid; for the whole benefit of trial consists in silence, patience and resignation. In this condition divine strength is found for the hard warfare, because God Himself fights for the soul." — M. Molinos.

"Sacerdotalism is just the 'man-trust' which prophets denounce. In public life and association the tendency is to lean on, and worship, material strength. We seek the help of riches for the carrying out of all our religious schemes. We fly to men rather than to God."—Pul. Com.

fore; and from that hour he began to open his heart to the warden, and cheerfully fulfilled his whole term of imprisonment.

4, 5. (4) "For though [his vassals] the princes are in Zoan, and his messengers go as far as Hanes, none wins aught but disappointment from a people which can avail nothing, which brings no help, but disappointment and disgrace."—Pol. Bib. **Zoan,** or Tanis, N.E. frontier of Egypt, and the scene of the great plagues. **Hanes,** further south; the same as Tahpanes, the Anysis of Herodotus. (5) R. V. "They shall be ashamed," etc. **ashamed,** bec. they get nothing but promises, and Egypt utterly fails them in the evil day.[a]

Responsibility for Companions.—Mention is made of two travelers that walked together to the same city, whereof the one was wise, the other foolish. And when they came where two ways met, the one broad and fair, the other strait and foul, the fool would needs go the broader way; but the wise man told him, though the narrow way seemed foul, yet it was safe, and would bring them to a good lodging; and the other, seeming fair, was very dangerous, and brought them to a desperate inn. Yet because the fool would not yield to any reason, but believed what he saw with his eyes, rather than what he heard with his ears, the wise man, for company's sake, was contented to go the worse way; and being both robbed by thieves, detained in their company, and at last apprehended with the robbers, and carried before the magistrate, these two began to accuse one another, and each to excuse himself. The wise man said he told his fellow the dangers of that broad way, and therefore he only was to be blamed because he would not yield unto his counsel; but the fool had so much wit to reply, that he was a very silly creature, and knew neither the way, nor the dangers of the way, and therefore he was to be excused and the wise man to be condemned because he would follow such a fool's counsel. Whereupon the judge, having heard them both, condemned them both,—the fool because he refused to follow the counsel of the wise, and the wise man because he would not forsake the fool's company.—Spencer.

6, 7. (6) He dwells upon the dangers of the desert between Palestine and Egypt (comp. Deut. viii. 15; Jer. ii. 6) to magnify the folly of the embassadors. **the south,** i. e. the Negeb, or southern districts of Canaan. "The beasts of the south are the young asses and camels on which the present or subsidy was conveyed to Egypt."—Henderson. **into the land,** better, through a land, the wilderness district between Canaan and Egypt. **flying serpent,** a kind wh. springs from the trees on its prey. (7) **help in vain,** "to a people who can profit no one, whose help is but vapor and emptiness."—Pol. Bib. **therefore,** etc., R. V., "therefore have I called her Rahab that sitteth still." He describes Egypt "as a worthless, procrastinating power, loud in the making of promises, but sitting inactive" when the time comes for performing them.—Driver.

Trust.—One evening when Luther saw a little bird perched on a tree, to roost there for the night, he said, "This little bird has had its supper, and now is getting ready to go to sleep here, quite secure and content, never troubling itself what its food will be, or where its lodging on the morrow. Like David, it 'abides under the shadow of the Almighty.' It sits on its little twig content, and lets God take care."

8, 9. (8) **table, or tablet.**[a] "Since a 'book' is mentioned along with the tablet, it is probable that Isaiah at this time wrote down a summary of all his deliverances on the subject of the Egyptian alliance. Not improbably the 'book' so prepared was the basis of the present collection of prophecies, ch. xxviii.—xxxii. The incident is closely parallel to that referred to in ch. viii. 16, where Isaiah prepares documentary evidence of his prophetic actions after his advice had been rejected by the court and people."—Camb. Bib. (9) **lying children,** since they desire not even to know the truth. But it shall be revealed against them.

Dislike to Ministerial Fidelity (vs. 9).—I. State the truths which are usually obnoxious to such persons. Spirituality of Divine law. Depravity of human nature, etc. II. The causes of this dislike of ministerial fidelity—absolute unbelief, refinements of modern society, wounded pride, painful forebodings of future misery. III. The folly, sin and danger of a desire to suppress the faithful voice of truth, and to be flattered with the smooth language of deceit. Its folly is apparent from the

---

[a] "Egypt gives them promises, but no substantial help; while the alliance brings down on Israel the anger of Assyria."—Spk. Com.

Je. xliii. 7; also Je. ii. 36.

"All is of God that is, and is to be;
And God is good." Let this suffice us still,
Resting in childlike trust upon his will,
Who moves to his great ends, unthwarted by the ill.
—Whittier.

"Be still, my soul!—the Lord is on thy side;
Bear patiently the cross of grief and pain;
Leave to thy God to order and provide,—
In every change he faithful will remain."

"The Prophet sees the ambassadors of Israel carrying costly presents through the waste howling wilderness, for the purpose of securing the Egyptian alliance." — J. A. Alexander.

[a] "Some think that two distinct inscriptions are commanded, one on a tablet, for temporary use, and one on parchment for preservation; but the terms used are probably equivalents." — J. A. Alexander.

Zec. vii. 11, 12. vss. 9, 10. H. Marriott, 400.

"Why, friends, you needn't borrow any trouble about the old Book; it is going to stand. Some people think it is a back number; you and I will become back

consideration that no concealment of the situation of the sinner can alter his condition in the sight of God: it is sinful in its origin, its nature, its consequences. Its danger is equal to its sin and folly.—T. A. James.

A Word May Save a Soul—The Pious Baker.—A baker who traveled the country disposing of his bread, stopped at a public house, where he was waited on at table by a young girl. When opportunity offered, he asked the girl if she loved the Saviour. She answered that she did not. He then in earnestness and simplicity unfolded to her the way of salvation, and urged her to accept Christ as her Saviour. The words were but few, and he returned home. Again he found himself at the same public house, but now an older woman served the table. She recognized him, and asked him if he remembered the former visit. He did. "Do you remember the girl that served you?" "I do." "She was my daughter; and O, how can I thank you for the few words you said to her on the subject of religion. They were the means of her conversion; and O, dear sir," bursting into tears, "they prepared her for a sick and dying bed, to which she was suddenly brought. She often referred to the interview, and she passed away in triumph. She is now with that Saviour you made known to her."

10, 11. (10) **smooth,** the popular man was not he who declared the truth, but he who uttered what the people liked to hear. **deceits,** or illusions.[a] (11) **out of the way,** give us something new. We are tired of these prophecies that run forever in the same path, the same rut. **Holy One of Israel,**[b] "trouble us no more with Israel's Holy One!"—Pol. Bib. "They are weary of the monontony with which a prophet like Isaiah appeals constantly to the Divine right by which he speaks, and which he urges on his opponents."—Driver.

The Swearer Reproved.—Three gentlemen were traveling from the north to London by the mail train, and, as people generally do, sat without speaking to one another for a considerable time. At Rugby, while taking refreshments, the bell rang, and the train was off almost before one of the three had time to take what he required. Angry, he entered the carriage, uttering an oath. This led to a conversation between him and one of the passengers, who in a kind and gentlemanly way expostulated with him on swearing. The conversation continued till they reached a London junction, where the third passenger left them. Thus alone, the gentleman who had begun the conversation proposed they should engage in prayer. They did so, and when the train reached Euston-square they exchanged cards and parted. A little while after, the one who resided in London received a letter from his fellow-traveler, stating that in consequence of that conversation he had given his heart to God, and in the great city in which he lived had erected a Gospel-hall.—Christian World.

12, 13. (12) **this word,** viz., the warning against going for help to Egypt. **oppression,** better, "perverseness and crookedness" as contrasted with the straight way of truth and faith in God. **perverseness,** "and trust in wile and policy."—Pol. Bib. (13) "Disaster will follow their policy with the necessity of a natural law. The best translation seems to be: Therefore this guilt shall be to you as a rent descending (lit. 'falling') (and) bulging out in a high wall, whose crash comes, etc. The slight beginnings of transgression, its inevitable tendency to gravitate more and more from the moral perpendicular, till a critical point is reached, then the suddenness of the final catastrophe,—are vividly expressed by this magnificent simile. Comp. Ps. lxii. 3."—Camb. Bib.

A Remarkable Preservation.—A few years ago a circumstance occurred in connection with these words, which is remembered with thankful hearts by those who met with a providential escape. A carriage passed a high wall, which was precisely in the condition described in the text—indeed, no words could have better described its state; and it was remarked by those seated in it how very dangerous it was in a high road, and where so many were coming and going. The words were scarcely spoken, and the danger passed, than a terrible crash was heard. The breaking had come "suddenly at an instant," and the road behind was utterly impassable from the stones and rubbish of the fallen wall.

14. "Yea, it breaks, as one dashes an earthen pitcher to pieces, shattering it ruthlessly, so that among its shattered pieces not a sherd

---

numbers, but this Book is going to remain."—D. L. Moody.

"It is the virtue of few words to render plain that which thousands have obscured; as one glass will transmit a bright image of the sun, where hundreds produce but darkness and confusion."—Macculloch.

[a] Comp. Je. v. 31, xi. 21, xxvi. 8—24; Am. ii. 12.

[b] Isaiah here prob. translates not what the people said by word of mouth, but what they virtually said by their wilful and wayward doings.

"No man can mortgage his injustice as a pawn for his fidelity."—Edmund Burke.

"The spendthrift is getting poorer every month for many years, but bankruptcy comes on him suddenly at last. The dishonest man is getting hopelessly involved for years, but his reputation is blasted in an hour. Passion may have been winning the mastery from youth upwards, but at a certain point it blazes forth, and the life-blood is shed. Penalty generally comes at last with seeming suddenness, like the breaking wall that has long bent but comes down in a moment."—Pul. Com.

"As the Orientals most frequently construct their walls of clay or soft brick, dried in the sun, they are extremely liable to rend, and be washed down by rain."—Henderson.

is found," etc.—Pol. Bib. **break** it, i. e. the Jewish nation, which these politicians thought to preserve. **sherd,** broken piece of earthenware. **pit,** "cistern."

Potsherds.—It must be remembered that nearly all the cooking utensils in the East, all the domestic vessels, were made of earthenware; so that not to have a potsherd, a fragment, left, betokens the greatest misery. Even Job, in all his poverty and wretchedness, was not so destitute; for he had "a potsherd to scrape himself withal." "A sherd to take fire from the hearth." This allusion may be seen illustrated every morning in the East. Should the good woman's fire have been extinguished in the night, she takes a potsherd in the morning, and goes to a neighbor for a little fire to rekindle her own; and as she goes along, she may be seen, after proceeding a few steps, now and then blowing the burning embers, lest the small spark should expire. The Jews were not to have a sherd out of which they could drink a little water. Pumps not being in general use in the East, the natives are obliged to have something in which to convey water from the well or tank. Of a very poor country it is said, "In those parts there is not a sherd out of which you can drink a little water." "The wretchedness of the people is so great, they have not a sherd with which to take water from the tank."—Roberts. Sin and Death.—When we find it stated that the wages of sin is death, we are in the heart of the profoundest questions of theology. What before was merely enmity against society becomes enmity against God, and what was "vice" is "sin." The conception of a God gives an altogether new color to worldliness and vice. Worldliness it changes into heathenism, vice into blasphemy. The carnal mind, the mind which is turned away from God which will not correspond with God, this is not moral only, but spiritual death.—Drummond.

"You will find that a little sin will shake your trust and disturb your peace, more than the greatest sufferings; yea, in those sufferings, your assurance and joy in God will grow and abound most if sin be kept out. So much sin as gets in, so much peace will go out."—R. Leighton.

15—17. (15) **returning and rest,** "the first expression describes the external policy,[a] the second the attitude of mind, demanded by the occasion. On the one hand, averseness to war (Mic. ii. 8), renunciation of earthly help and a wise passivity in international affairs; on the other, calm reliance on Jehovah: in this last, the prophet says, they would have manifested the truest 'strength' or courage."—Camb. Bib. **quietness,** etc., that waiting for God, and waiting on God, which the Scriptures so often commend.[b] (16) **flee upon horses,** these being introduced from Egypt are the symbol of Egyp. help.[c] (17) **thousand .. one,** the reversal of the promise, De. xxxii. 39. **beacon,** tree bereft of branches,[d] stripped and solitary.

[a] "Retrocession from the unlawful measures and negotiations." — Grotius.

[b] La. iii. 25, 26, etc.

[c] "The riding upon horses refers to the Egyptian cavalry, which they expected would be sent for their deliverance." — Henderson.

De. xvii. 16; Ho. xiv. 3.

[d] "Solitary, like a flag-staff." — Wordsworth.

"The idea suggested by this last clause is that no two of them should be left together." — Hitzig.

Salvation (vs. 15).—Your attention is invited—I. To the blessing, salvation. II. To the manner of obtaining it. 1. By returning to God from whom we have wandered; 2. By rest, at the foot of the cross, on the Word of God.—J. Mannering.

Human Means Unavailing for Salvation.—When some one was enlarging to Coleridge on the tendency for good of some scheme which was expected to regenerate the world, the poet flung up into the air the down of a thistle which grew by the road-side, and went on to say, The tendency of that thistle is towards China; but I know, with assured certainty, that it will never get there—nay, it is more than probable that, after sundry eddyings and gyrations up and down, backwards and forwards, it will be found somewhere near the place where it grew. Such has ever been the issue of those boasted schemes of human wisdom which have professed to change the heart of man. Human nature is in this respect like the salt sea—all the rivers that run into it have not changed its saltness. The sun is daily evaporating its waters; but does not drink up one particle of that saline ingredient. If men will drink of its bitter waters, they sicken and madden, and die. It is thus with that malignant nature which we inherit and propagate; all human means have failed to purify it, and it stimulates to madness, disease, and death.—McCusp.

"As the play of the lightning is more brilliant during the darkness of the night, so God's mercy shines out most gloriously through the murky night of man's sin." — Hom. Com.

18. wait, "therefore Jehovah longs to be gracious to you,[a] therefore He lifts Himself up to show mercy to you: for Jehovah is a God of justice;[b] happy are all who long for Him!"—Pol. Bib.[c] The language is much more gracious than suggested by the R. V. **exalted,** "lifts Himself," etc., to be in readiness to show mercy if you make it possible.

Waiting upon God (vs. 18).—We consider—I. The character of God,

[a] Comp. Ho. v. 15.

[b] "Who will not let His children go uncorrected, yet will order His chastisement with never-failing equity; allowing mercy her full rights." —Spk. Com.

[c] Ps. ii. 12, xxxiv. 8; Pr. xvi. 20; Je. xvii. 7.

"Blessed be God's voice; for it is true, and falsehoods have to cease before it!"—Carlyle.

a God of judgment. Therefore—1. He is able to teach His children; 2. And how to correct them. II. God's appearances on account of His people are sometimes delayed. He does not always appear on behalf of His people—1. In answer to prayer; 2. In relieving them from their afflictions; 3. In explaining Himself with regard to their afflictions; 4. In affording the joys of salvation. III. Your duty in the meantime. Waiting includes—1. Calmness of mind; 2. Attention; 3. Patience; 4. Expectation. IV. The blessedness that will attend the exercise of waiting for Him. 1. The work itself is blessed; 2. It will prevent matter for bitter reflection; 3. His coming will amply recompense their waiting.—W. Jay.

Man Waiting for God.—"Blessed are they that wait for Him." We have seen how He waits for us to be gracious unto us, to be exalted in having mercy upon us, and we should wait in humble faith to receive these priceless blessings, bringing our empty vessels that they may be filled. The blessedness of so waiting is set forth in numerous passages of Scripture. What entire satisfaction and peace do they enjoy who take this attitude of soul described as waiting on the Lord! In waiting for man we are often disappointed and deceived, but how can we ever exhaust the Divine mercy and goodness? O happy soul that waits for God, and rejoicing in the plentitude of His goodness sings,

[d] Comp. Ho. xiv. 1—3, 4, etc.

"I must have all things and abound
Since God is God to me."

[e] "The teachers shall no more be forced to hide themselves from persecution, but shall be openly received with reverence."—Maurer.

If God had not first waited for us, we never would have waited for Him. He took the initiative. Why should any of us keep God waiting longer? Are your sins too great? Have you been proud and rebellious? It is precisely to such the promise is made. God is waiting now to be gracious, but the day of grace will soon be past.—William Guthrie.

19—21. (19) **For the people,** etc., better, "For, O people in Zion that dwellest in Jerusalem." **weep no more,** shalt lie no longer under the heavy burden of Divine chastisement. **cry,** the cry of the penitent. **when,** etc.,[d] "so that when He has heard it, He has already answered you."—Pol. Bib. (20) **removed,** etc., R. V., "hidden,"[e] the verb is in the singular. Better read "Yet will not thy Teacher any longer withdraw Himself, but thine eyes will constantly see thy Teacher," (Pol. Bib.) the reference is Messianic. (21) **hear a word,** the warning, guiding word of the great Teacher.

"The veil taken away, thou wilt behold Him, no longer dimly revealed thro' the similitudes of the law, and the enigmas of prophetic vision, but manifested in the flesh."—Spk. Com.

Ps. xxxii. 8; Is. xlii. 16, lviii. 11; Jno. xvi. 13, 14.

The Unerring Monitor (vs. 19).—I. There is a way from earth to heaven. 1. Divine; 2. Ancient; 3. Revealed; 4. Direct; 5. Circumscribed. II. From this way there are many diverging paths. 1. The right, adding to God's method of salvation; 2. The left, omissions; 3. Tendency to turn to right or left. III. The means provided for our security, the Word. 1. Infallible; 2. Living; 3. Speaking. Apply:—(1) Place ourselves under its guidance; (2) Carefully listen; (3) Follow its directions.—F. Burns.

"Look! the clay dries into iron, but the potter molds the clay: Destiny to-day is master — man was master yesterday."
—Arnold.

As the radiation of the sun's beams of yesterday will not suffice for to-day, so neither will the grace which you received a week or a month ago be sufficient for the present moment.

The Tenderness of the Gospel.—What then is the nature of this so marvelous transforming message of the Gospel? It is a story, a simple story, such as a child will feel and weep over; such as a sage of seventy winters cannot fathom. It tells of a law holy as that eternal heart from which it springs; it paints the portrait of the righteousness consummate which images that law in the life; it celebrates the triumph of the moral conquest that makes the enfranchised conscience sovereign of man. Yet this were no more than others could in their measure rival. But, oh! a tale more touching than all this solemn strain is its exclusive privilege to unfold. It speaks,—it alone can speak of One whose purity, too perfect to brook one unatoned sin in the vast universe of His creation, was accompanied by a love too tender to endure that one pang should continue to exist for which His own high wisdom could provide a remedy; of a love which drew the living Author of the law from His transcendent abode into our narrow nature, that He might quench the lightnings of His own avenging justice in streams of His own human blood. It tells of that inexpressible attachment of which all human relationships (for it names them all) are too weak to be the faintest shadows of a Creator who is father and brother, and husband of His redeemed; and by all the

"In the days of unfettered liberty and universal privilege the Christian Church

insults of His humiliated life, by His despised poverty and His accumulated wrongs, by a sight which made the angels tremble and weep, though—mystery of unfathomed ingratitude!—men, its objects, can slumber as they listen, or wake to scoff. By the groans of Gethsemane and its bloody sweat, by the nails and thorns of Calvary, by the last dark tortures of an expiring God, it prays us to love Him in return! This may fail to move, but it is certain that this appeal to the grateful affections is the legitimate path to the great object of a renovation, that it is a justifiable path, that it is a practicable path, that if it fail, no other that men have ever devised can offer a chance of success.—Butler.

Take Heed—

"How wrought I yesterday?" Small moment now,
To question with vain tears, or bitter moan,
Since every word you wrote upon the sands
Of yesterday, has hardened into stone.
"How shall I work to-day?" O soul of mine:
To-day stands on her threshold, girt to lead
Thy feet to life immortal; strive with fear;
Deep pitfalls strew the way; take heed—take heed!
—Augusta Moore.

22—24. (22)**covering of,** see vs. 1. The reference is to the gold or silver covering or plating of the idol images. **cast .. away,** R. V. "cast them away as an unclean thing."[a] (23) **rain of thy seed,** "And He will give rain for thy seed ...... and thy wheat, the produce of thy ground, will be rich and nourishing."—Pol. Bib. (24) **ear the ground,** or till the ground. **clean provender,** or salted food.

Note on vs. 24.—In these words the Prophet foretells a season of great plenty, when the cattle shall be fed with corn better in quality, separated from the chaff, and (as the term rendered clean in our version properly signifies) acidulated, in order to render it more grateful to their taste. The evangelist clearly refers to the practice, which was common in every part of Syria, of ploughing with the ass. In rice-grounds, which require to be flooded, the ass was employed to prepare them for the seed, by treading them with his feet. It is to this method of preparing the ground that Chardin supposes the Prophet to allude when he says, "Blessed are ye that sow beside all waters, that send forth thither the feet of the ox and the ass." They shall be blessed under the future reign of the promised Messiah. In times anterior to His appearing, their country was to be made a desolation; briers and thorns were to encumber their fields; their sumptuous dwellings were to be cast down; their cities and strongholds levelled with the dust. But when Messiah commences His reign times of unequalled prosperity shall begin their career. The goodness of Jehovah shall descend in fertilizing showers, to irrigate their fields, and to swell the streams which the skill and industry of the husbandman conducts among his plantations, or with which he covers his rice-grounds. Secure from the ruinous incursions of aliens, and in the sure hope of an abundant harvest, he shall scatter his rice on the face of the superincumbent water, and tread it into the miry soil with "the feet of the ox and the ass." Prosperous and happy himself, he will consider it his duty, and feel it his delight, "to do good and to communicate,"—to succor the widow and the fatherless, to open his doors to the stranger, to diffuse around him the light of truth, and to swell, by the diligent and prudent use of all the means that Providence has brought within his reach, the sum of human enjoyment.—Paxton.

25, 26. (25) **mountain .. rivers,** to a dry country like the hill country of Palestine this was the greatest of blessings. **slaughter, when the towers fall,** "poetic allusion to the day of the Lord, when all his enemies are destroyed." (26) **light,** etc., The light which now is enough for a week will then be concentrated in a single day, "night and day alike will be preternaturally bright"; this is a part of the general expectation that nature shall share the glory of the Messianic Kingdom. **breach,** vs. 14.

The Bliss of Being Reconciled to God (vs. 26).—Refer to history of context, and point out other seasons when this promise receives its fuller accomplishment. I. At the first reconciliation of the soul with God. 1. The convictions of an awakened conscience are as deep wounds;

will delight itself in God; its songs of peace and of hope will arise from every valley; its life will be touched and lighted with the sunshine of a holy gladness. The light of God's countenance will rest upon it, and it will rejoice greatly in his salvation." —Clarkson.

[a] "The Bab. captivity effected this change in the Jews thoroughly, as regards gross idol-worship. For their deliverance from subtler forms of idolatry, a higher purification was needed (Phil. iii. 8)." — Spk. Com.

"If you count the sunny and the cloudy days of the whole year, you will find that the sunshine predominates."— Ovid.

"It shows a weak mind not to bear prosperity as well as adversity with moderation." — Cicero.

"A description of the height to which agriculture would be carried, by means of artificial irrigation, after the overthrow of the Assyrians." —J. D. Michaelis.

"What shall the universality and copiousness of the 'rivers and streams of water' profit us, if we will not drink of them? In the natural world a man would be nothing benefited, though the light of the sun was augmented sevenfold, if he studiously closed and sealed every opening by which it entered his

2. Reconciliation with God heals those wounds; 3. And this is a season wherein the knowledge and joy of the soul are much enlarged. II. At any return of the soul to God after a season of darkness. 1. God finds it necessary sometimes to hide His face from His people, and then their wounds open afresh; 2. But the return of God to the soul binds up this breach; 3. And this is also another season of peculiar instruction and comfort. The full accomplishment of the text will take place—III. At the hour of the Christian's dissolution. 1. God never entirely withholds His chastening rod in this world; 2. But at death there is an end of all that is penal and painful; 3. Then will this promise be fulfilled to the utmost extent. Inference:—(1) They who have never been wounded in their souls on account of sin are yet strangers to all spiritual light and happiness; (2) They who feel a wounded spirit should labor to improve their convictions to the utmost.—Studies for the Pulpit.

The Way to be Saved.—The Hindoo's Confession.—When one of the converted Hindoos came to be baptised, he made this confession. He said he had been for years searching for a way of happiness in Poojahs (holy places in the river, etc.), but all in vain; but when he heard the word of Christ he could not rest. He sat up a whole night in distress of mind. He had great fears about his sins. When asked how he lost them, he said, "They went away in thinking of Christ." Thus we shall never get rid of our fear in any other way than by thinking on Christ, His atoning sacrifice, His finished righteousness, His great love, His free promise, His willingness to save. It was this that made another Hindoo say, when he was asked how he hoped to be saved, "I am a sinner, I have nothing to give to God, but if a rich man become a poor man's surety, he may trust in him; thus I place my trust in Christ Jesus."

27, 28. (27) **the name of the Lord** appears here to be synonymous with what is elsewhere called the "glory of Jehovah" (cf. the parallelism, ch. lix. 19; Ps. cii. 15) i. e. the visible manifestation of His presence. It may have the same sense in ch. xviii. 7, the Temple of the future being conceived as the scene of a perpetual Theophany (Ezek. xliii. 2 ff.). Amongst the later Jews the expression "the Name" was commonly used, out of reverence to avoid the use of Jehovah (cf. Lev. xxiv. 11).—Camb. Bib. **cometh from far,** "in Jud. v. 4; Deut. xxxiii. 2, the Theophany comes from Seir or Sinai; here its origin is left indefinite. Jehovah's coming is like that of the thundercloud which appears on the distant horizon, no eye having observed the mysterious process by which it was formed. In what follows the figure of the storm is inseparably blended with an anthropomorphic representation of Jehovah." **the burden.** R. V., "in thick rising smoke." (28) **reach . . neck,** R. V., "And his breath is as an overflowing stream that reacheth soon unto the neck." Is. viii. 8. **sieve of vanity,** the sieve that separates the chaff of their vanity, vain plans and schemes. **people,** R. V., "peoples," i. e. Assyrians, whom Jehovah will turn aside from their purpose thwarting their plans.

God's Name.—What is a person's name? That word or expression in which the person is called up or represented to us. When I mention or hear a name, it calls up before me the whole man, what I know of him, and also the impression he has made on me. The name of a king includes his honor, his power, his kingdom. His name is the symbol of his power. And so each name of God embodies and represents some part of the glory of the Unseen One. And the name of Christ is the expression of all He has done, and all He is and lives to do as our Mediator.—Andrew Murray. A Case of Retribution.—A gentleman, who was very ill, sending for the late Dr. Lake, told him that he found he must die, and gave him the following account of the cause of his death:—He had, about a fortnight before, been riding over Hounslow Heath, where several boys were playing at cricket. One of them striking the ball, hit him just on the toe with it, looked him in the face, and ran away. His toe pained him extremely. As soon as he came to Brentford, he sent for a surgeon, who was for cutting it off. But unwilling to suffer that, he went to London. When he arrived there, he immediately called another surgeon to examine it, who told him his foot must be cut off. But neither would he hear of this; and so, before the next day, the mortification seized his leg, and in a day or two more struck up into his body. Dr. Lake asked him whether he knew the boy that struck the ball? He answered, "About

dwelling, or if he placed an impervious bandage tightly over his eyes whenever he went abroad (John xii. 36)."—Packer.

"God can do much work in a short time. Many are the examples in the Acts of the Apostles. And, blessed be God, there are now many living proofs that He is still mighty to save." — J. Wesley.

There seems to be a mixed reference in these verses to the calamities of Judah in Hezekiah's days, and to the final destruction of Judah's enemies.

As well may you try to write upon a sheet of water, or engrave upon rotten wood, as to convert a heart without the grace of God.

"The dominion of any sinful habit will fearfully estrange us from His presence. A single consenting act of inward disobedience in thought or will is enough to let fall a cloud between Him and us, and to leave our hearts cheerless and dark."—H. E. Manning.

"Truth is the bond of union and the basis of human happiness. Without this virtue there is no reliance upon language, no confidence in friendship, no security in promises and oaths."—Jeremy Collier

"God sent his singers upon earth,
With songs of sadness and of mirth,
That they might touch the hearts of men,
And bring them back to heaven again."
—Longfellow.

ten years ago, I was riding over Hounslow Heath, where an old man ran by my horse's side, and begged me to relieve him, and said he was almost famished. I bade him begone. He kept up with me still; upon which I threatened to beat him. Finding that he took no notice of this, I drew my sword, and with one blow killed him. A boy about four years, who was with him, screamed out that his father was killed! His face I perfectly remember; that boy it was who struck the ball against me, which is the cause of my death."—Whitecross.

29, 30. Songs of rejoicing arise within the city, while the Assyrians are slaughtered under its walls. (29) **solemnity,** R. V. "feast," the passover-memorial of national deliverance, the only festival that included a nocturnal ceremony, in the O. T. times. **with a pipe,** "It is said that each band of pilgrims on its way to Jerusalem was headed by a person who played the flute."—Vitringa. **Mighty one,** R. V., "Rock." (30) **glorious voice,** lit. the majesty of His voice, in the exertion of His power. **lighting down,** in stroke of judgment.

Music at Night.—Music is considered far more enchanting at night than at any other period; "it gives cheerfulness to darkness, and pleasure to the heart." Their favorite proverb is, "the day song is like the flower of the gourd," i. e. devoid of smell. Nothing is more common than for adults to sing themselves to sleep: thus, as they recline, they beat a tabret and chant the praises of their gods, till through heaviness they can scarcely articulate a word. At other times the mother or wife gently taps the instrument, and in soft tones lulls the individual to repose. In the night, should they not be able to sleep, they have again recourse to the same charm, and not until they shall have fairly gone off in fresh slumbers will their companions have any rest. Hence, in passing through a village or town at midnight, may be heard people at their nightly song, to grace the festive scene, to beguile away their time, to charm their fears, or to procure refreshing sleep. The Jews then were to be delivered from the proud Assyrian's yoke, and again to have their pleasant song in the night.—Roberts.

31—33. (31) **smote .. rod,** "Assyria will be terror-stricken at the voice of Jehovah when He smites with the rod."—Pol. B. (32) **grounded staff,** R. V. "and every stroke of the appointed staff," **tabrets and harps,** signifying the joy of the redeemed ones. **battles of shaking,** "battles of waving"—the figure is of Jehovah waving his enemies, as the priests wave the victim that is about to be sacrificed on the altar. Comp.—G. A. Smith. (33) **Tophet,** or a place of burning[a] (2 Ki. xxiii. 10). The place in valley of Hinnom where fires constantly burned the refuse. R. V., "for a Topheth is prepared of old;" this is the close of the drama, not an ordinary battle but a solemn holocaust is already prepared by Jehovah. It is deep and wide, to receive an army of corpses, and with fire from heaven will its flames be lit.

Miracles of Providence.—On the 5th of August, 1530, an awful crisis for the Reformation, when the firmest seemed to swerve, and the boldest to tremble, Luther thus wrote to Chancellor Bench: "I have recently witnessed two miracles. This is the first: As I was at my window, I saw the stars and the sky, and that vast and glorious firmament in which the Lord has placed them. I could nowhere discover the columns on which the Master has supported His immense vault; and yet the heavens did not fall. And here is the second: I beheld thick clouds hanging above us like a vast sea. I could neither perceive the ground on which they reposed, nor cords by which they were suspended; and yet they did not fall upon us, but saluted us rapidly, and fled away."

CHAPTER THE THIRTY-FIRST.

1, 2. This chapter is remarkable for three very unusual descriptions of God. They rise in climax, enforcing three truths:—that in the government of life we must take into account God's wisdom (1-3),—we must be prepared to find many of His providences grim and savage-looking (4); but we must also believe that He is most tender and jealous for His people, (5-9).—G. A. Smith. (1) **Egypt for help,** see ch. xxx. 1—3.[b] **chariots,** "in Assyrian sculptures chariots are represented drawn by three

"Singing songs when we are well out of fears is easy work; singing songs even while struggling with our fears is the beautiful triumph of faith."—Pul. Com.

"When men seek to entice you to forego communion with God and to follow the world with them, let your face shine with the brightness that comes from your communion with the Master, and they will cease to trouble you. Christians can sometimes do more by shining for God, than by speaking for Him."—Andrew A. Bonar.

a "It is universally agreed that the destruction of the Assyrian king is here described as a burning of his body at a stake, or funeral pile."—J. A. Alexander.

"If piety be thus debarr'd access on high; and of good men, the very best be singled out to bleed, and bear the scourge,—what is reward, and what is punishment? But who shall dare to tax Eternal Justice?" —Congreve.

b "That the Egyptians were noted at a very early period for their attention to the breeding of horses, and their using them in chariots, appears fr. Gen. xlvii. 17, l. 9; Ex. ix. 3, xiv. 7, 9."—Henderson.

horses, and with three men in them." (2) **is wise,**[c] and therefore able to deal with this rebellious people. **evil,** "brings trouble," **the house,** i. e. the whole race. **the help,** i. e. the Egyptian helpers.

The Fear of Hell Peoples Heaven.—There is a legend that the devil once put on a monk's hood, and went into the pulpit and preached hell and its terrors. As he knew his subject so well, he sent all his congregation into transports of terror, ready to say they believed anything, or to confess or promise anything, so that only they might escape such horror and despair. And when he returned from his mission, his friends bitterly repreached him, and said, "What have you done? Don't you know that men say, 'The fear of hell peoples heaven'? You have ruined and undone your own kingdom." But he replied, "Never fear: I know what I am doing. The heaven which the fear of hell peoples is one of my own devising (for its roots are in selfishness), and the more men seek that, the better for me! Since thus shall they never know that love of God, which is the one thing that utterly defeats and thwarts me."—Old Test. Anec.

God's Superior Wisdom.—After Moscow Napoleon is reported to have exclaimed, "The Almighty is too strong for me." But perhaps the most striking analogy to this satire of Isaiah is to be found in the "Confessions" of that Jew, from whose living sepulchre we are so often startled with weird echoes of the laughter of the ancient prophets of his race. When Heine, Germany's greatest satirist, lay upon a bed to which his evil living had brought him before his time, and the pride of art, which had been, as he says, his god, was at last crushed, he tells us what it was that crushed him. They were singing his songs in every street of his native land, and his fame had gone out through the world, while he lay an exile and paralyzed upon his "mattress-grave." "Alas!" he cries, "the irony of Heaven weighs heavily upon me. The great Author of the universe, the celestial Aristophanes, wished to show me, the petty, earthly, German Aristophanes, how my most trenchant satires are only clumsy patchwork compared with His, and how immeasurably He excels me in humor and colossal wit." That is just a soul writing in its own heart's blood this terrible warning of Isaiah: Yet God also is wise.—Exp. Bib.

3. men, Heb. adam, made out of the ground. Only creatures. **flesh,** strikingly contrasted with spirit, or spiritual aid, such as God can give.[a] "That men could not stand against God, or flesh against spirit, Isaiah's contemporaries did not need to be taught; what separated him from his hearers was the conviction that there is but one Divine Person, and one spiritual power in the universe, viz.: Jehovah and His moral government as revealed in the consciousness of the prophet."—Camb. Bib. **he that helpeth,** i. e. the Egyptian. **fall,** R. V. "stumble." **he that is holpen,** i. e. the people of Judah. "Fulfilled when Nebuchadnezzar invaded Judæa and Egypt."—Henderson.

The Arm of Flesh.—Regiments of cavalry have a very imposing aspect to the eye which looks upon and judges by the surface of things; they seem invincible, overwhelming, an invaluable ally when the enemy is approaching. And not only the well-equipped cavalry in time of war; but, in time of peace and in the ordinary life of men, the sagacious counsellor, the wealthy merchant, the influential statesman or courtier, the eloquent and admired speaker or pleader,—these men seem to have in them a source of strength on which we may build, or to which in the time of peril we may repair. But "the Egyptians were men, and not God;" their promised word might be broken, their overtures might turn out to be selfishly made and to be unscrupulously withdrawn; their cavalry might be ridden down by troops still stronger than they. Being but men and but horses, they might prove—as they would prove—nothing better than a broken reed, which would pierce the hand that leaned on it (ch. xxxvi. 6). And the human strength on which we are all so inclined to lean will very likely prove to be nothing more or better. How often the sagacity of the prudent, the riches of the wealthy, the influence of the great, the eloquence of the orator, fail us at our hour of need, and we "go down to our house" bitterly disappointed, or perhaps stricken, stripped, ruined! "The arm of flesh will fail you."—Pul. Com.—Spiritual **Natures.—It is the law of Divine wisdom that no spirit carries with it into**

---

[c] "They had come to consider obedience to God's law a piece of old-world simplicity; which debarred them from the advantages of Eg. culture and intelligence." — Spk. Com.

"Would not infinite wisdom, engaged on their side, stand them in more stead than all the policies of Egypt?" — Mat. Henry.

[a] "The antithesis of flesh and spirit, like that of God and man, is not metaphysical, but rhetorical, and is intended simply to express extreme dissimilitude or inequality."— J. A. Alexander.

Comp. Je. xxxvii. 5—7, xlvi. 1, 2.

"The grace of Jesus, which is infinitely pure, like the fountain from whence it flows, cannot unite with the love of sensual pleasure and true enjoyment of the world. If, therefore, thou desirest the heavenly gift, thou must banish from thy heart every affection that obstructs its entrance."—Thomas a Kempis.

another state and being any habit or mental qualities except those which may be connected with its new wants and enjoyments; and knowledge relating to the earth would be no more useful to these glorified beings than their earthly system of organized dust, which would be instantly resolved into its ultimate atoms, at such a temperature: even on the earth the butterfly does not transport with it into the air the organs or the appetites of the crawling worm from which it sprung. There is, however, one sentiment or passion which the moral or spiritual essence carries with it into all its stages of being, and which in these happy and elevated creatures is continually exalted; the love of knowledge or of intellectual power, which is, in fact, in its most ultimate and perfect development, the love of infinite wisdom and unbounded power, or the love of God. Even in the imperfect life that belongs to the earth, this passion exists in a considerable degree; increases even with age; outlives the perfection of the corporeal faculties, and at the moment of death, is felt by the conscious being; and its future destinies depend upon the manner in which it has been exercised and exalted.—Sir H. Davy.

"Leaning on Him, make with reverent meekness His own thy will, And with strength from Him shall thy utter weakness Life's task fulfil." —J. G. Whittier.

4, 5. (4) "In a very striking figure the prophet represents Jerusalem as the helpless prey in the grasp of Jehovah, and shows how impossible it is that any earthly power should intervene for its deliverance."—Camb. Bib. **lion,** frequent image of the power of God.[a] **roaring,** better growling,[b] to prevent any from attempting its rescue. **multitude of shepherds,** representing the combination to deliver Judah from the Divine judgments. **fight for,** better, "against." (5) **birds flying,** "as little mother birds hovering," i. e. over their young, when they see danger threatening the nest. Strong as a lion, tender as a mother bird.[c] **passing over,** with allusion to the destroying angel passing over Israel when Egypt's firstborn were destroyed.[d]

[a] Ho. v. 14, xi. 10, xiii. 7, 8; Am. iii. 8; Re. v. 5.

[b] The word used denotes a suppressed sound.

[c] Mat. xxiii. 37.

[d] "This promise of Div. defence is conditioned on vs. 6, that God's people turn from their deep falling away from Him." —Nagelsbach.

Calmness Under Excitement.—There was a heavy swell from the westward, which, coming on in broadly heaving undulations, gave the idea of power indeed, but of power in repose, as when a lion crouches in his lair with sheathed talons and smoothed mane and half-closed eyes. But no sooner does each broad swell, dark and polished, come into contact with these walls and towers of solid rock, than its aspect is instantly changed. It rears itself in fury, dashes with hoarse roar, and apparently resistless might, against the opposition, breaks in a cloud of snowy foam, which hides the rocky eminence, and makes us for a moment think the sea has conquered. But the next, the baffled assailant is recoiling in a hundred cascades or writhing and grovelling in swirls around the feet of those strong pillars which still stand in their majesty, unmoved, immovable, ready to receive and to repel the successive assaults of wave after wave with ever the same result.—Gosse. The Albatross.—The albatross has often served poor Jack a good turn for food when his larder has run low, or when he has been cast upon some desolate sea-bird island; and many anonymous anecdotes are told in the forecastle respecting them. But the most remarkable I have heard, bordering indeed upon the marvelous and incredible, if not itself a providential miracle, is the following, contained for substance in a letter from an officer of the eighty-third regiment of the English army to his friends in Montreal. While the division to which the writer belonged was on its way to the Orient, being at the time a short distance eastward of the Cape, one of the men was severely flogged for some slight offense. Maddened at the punishment, the poor fellow was no sooner released than, in sight of all his comrades and the ship's crew, he sprang overboard. There was a high sea running at the time, and, as the man swept on astern, all hope of saving him seemed to vanish. Relief, however, came from a quarter where no one ever dreamed of looking for it before. During the delay incident on lowering a boat, and while the crowd on deck were watching the form of the soldier struggling with the boiling waves, and growing every moment less distinct, a large albatross, such as are always found in those latitudes, coming like magic, with an almost imperceptible motion, approached and made a swoop at the man, who, in the agonies of the death-struggle, seized it and held it firm in his grasp, and by this means kept afloat until assistance was rendered from the vessel. Incredible as this story seems, the name and position of the writer of the letter, who was an eye-witness of the scene,

Dr. Wolff relates that he and his companions in travel remained two nights in a village inhabited by the tribe Shiho, who are shepherds. While sleeping with them under the trees, they were constantly disturbed by the attempts of lions to enter the sheepfold, and the efforts of the shepherds to expel them. Dr. Wolff says that so great was the noise occasioned by the roar of the lions, that the force of the description in the text could be easily felt.

"Not the thunder of men's anger, but the quiet evening breeze of men's humble prayer, goes right in to the throne of God." —R. Tuck.

Truth is a strong citadel. However often besieged, it remains invulnerably secure. The arrows of falsehood may often assail it; but unharmed, and unshaken, it stands out in serene majesty, immutable as its Author, imperishable as eternity.

places its authenticity beyond a doubt. But for the assistance thus afforded, no power on earth could have saved the soldier, as, in consequence of the tremendous sea running, a long time elapsed before the boat could be manned and got down, all this time the man clinging to the bird, whose flutterings and struggles to escape bore him up. Who, after this, should despair? A raging sea—a drowning man—an albatross; what eye could see safety under such circumstances? or who will dare to call this chance? Is it not rather a lesson intended to stimulate faith and hope, and teach us never to despair, since, in the darkest moment, when the waves dash, and the winds roar, and a gulf seems closing over our heads, there may be an albatross at hand with a commission to save us from Him of whom it is said, "As birds flying, so will the Lord of Hosts defend Jerusalem; defending also He will deliver it, and passing over He will preserve it."—Cheever.

6, 7. (6) "Contains the only summons to repentance in this whole series of discourses. It must be understood as implying that the deliverance of Jerusalem is conditional upon a national repentance. The verse is connected with vs. 7; and the thought is that the approaching deliverance will be a decisive manifestation of the sole deity of Jehovah, which will put idolatry to shame; and therefore the prophet calls on his hearers to realize the magnitude of their sin in having forsaken the one true God."—Camb. Bib. **Turn ye,** see Ho. xiv. 1. **from whom,** etc., R. V., "from whom ye have deeply revolted, O children of Israel" **deeply revolted,** even with deliberate plan and purpose.[a] (7) **cast away,** as the sign that they had for ever abandoned their trust in them.

a "An argument enforcing repentance is drawn from the preceding promises of Divine interposition."—Henderson.

Is. ii. 20, xxx. 22.

A Day of Awakening.—There is to be a day of awakening, a day memorable for its religious penetration; men are to see that they have been making idols where they thought they were making deities. When men become ashamed of their religion, and pray that its very name may not be mentioned to them; when they seek out of their secret places idols of silver and idols of gold, and say, Throw them anywhere—but let it be out of sight! then has come to pass the realization of divinest prophecy. Who would have all his old ideas named to him? Though they be innocent, yet they be so imperfect, so poor, so shallow, so wanting in insight and sagacity, their own thinker would not hear of them any more, but would say with somewhat of penitence and shamefacedness, but with no sense of guilt, When I was a child, I thought as a child: I am a man now, and I have seized a wider philosophy: spare me the recollection of infantile thinking.—Peop. Bib.

Grace is the very opposite of Nature, and if we were to sum up the evidence of growth in grace in one word, we should say that it is to grow less and less like ourselves.

8, 9. (8) **not . . man,** R. V. "not of man; and the sword, not of men, shall devour him: and he shall flee from the sword, and his young men shall become tributary." Refer. may be, in the first case, to Sennacherib's overthrow, by the unseen visitation of God. (9) **pass . . stronghold,**[b] **"he** shall overpass his rock from terror." **ensign,** "the banner of Jehovah protecting the Jews."—Maurer. **whose fire,** hearth and altar fire; the sign that God regards Jerusalem as His house, and therefore will defend it.[c]

b "He shall have no confidence in his strongholds, and will not halt in his flight till he has arrived at Nineveh."—Wordsworth.

2 Ki. xix. 35, 36.

An Evil Conscience.—An ill conscience is no comfortable companion to carry with thee. An ill conscience is like a thorn in the flesh. A thorn in the hedge may scratch you as you pass by it; but a thorn in the flesh rankles with you wherever you go: and the conscience, the ill conscience, the conscience that is ill at ease, it makes you ill at ease. You cannot have peace so long as you have an evil conscience, so long as there is that continual monition flashing across your mind: "Judgment cometh, death cometh: am I ready?" Many a time, when you go to your worldly scenes of pleasure, this conscience, like the finger writing on the wall of the palace of the king of Babylon, alarms and frightens you. You tell nobody about it. Strange thoughts strike across your mind. You have no rest. Can a man rest on a pillow of thorns? Can a man rest with the heartache? Can a man rest with his soul disturbed with the horrors of guilt? I tell thee there is no rest to thee till thou comest to Christ. He alone can calm a conscience.—S. Coley.—Wrong Fleeing From Revenge.—See the vivid picture of Carker fleeing from Dombey (Dickens): "Shame, disappointment, and discomfiture gnawing at his heart, a constant apprehension of being overtaken: the same intolerable awe and dread that had come upon him in the night returned unweakened in the day: . . . rolling on and on, always postponing thought, and

c "The true explanation of the clause seems to be that which supposes an allusion both to the sacred fire on the altar, and to the consuming fire of God's presence, whose altar flames in Zion and whose wrath shall thence flame to destroy His enemies."—J. A. Alexander.

"Enthusiasm is needed; without it we have no motive force. Evil will yield to nothing else than to the heart aflame with piety, the tongue of Heaven-kindled fire."—Johnson.

always racked with thinking . . . pressing on . . . change upon change . . . long roads and dread of night . . . and still the old monotony of bells and wheels and horses' feet, and no rest."

CHAPTER THE THIRTY-SECOND.

Pol. Bib. divides, "The Messianic Age described (1—8): Warning to the fine ladies of Jerusalem, (9—14): The Regeneration of Israel, (15—20)." "or rather, royalty—putting aside the person altogether."—Cheyne.[a] **princes,** the subordinate authorities. **in judgment,** or justly; "when this crisis, described in chap. xxxi., is past, society will be regenerated, kings and nobles will be the guardians of justice and great men the protectors of the poor."—Driver.

The Ideal Reign.—When Isaiah wrote he may have had grounds for the charitable belief that his sovereign would really be equal to the demands providentially made upon him. But the prophecy is Messianic. Its anticipations are only fully realized in the kingdom of Christ. Weber says, "The picture which the prophet paints here of the Church of the last time is the picture of every true congregation of Christ. In it the will of the Lord must be the only law according to which men judge, and not any fleshly consideration of any sort. In it there must be open eyes and ears for God's work and word; and if in some things precedence is really allowed to the children of this world, still in spiritual things the understanding must be right and the speech clear. Finally, in it persons must be valued according to their true Christian, moral worth, not according to advantages that before God are rather a reproach than an honor."—Christ's Righteousness.—Salvation, through the transference of righteousness from the Saviour to the sinner, may be thus illustrated:—Before you stands a bath, as it is called—a large vessel full of acid liquor. At one end, immersed in the fluid, hangs a sheet of silver; while above, and passing from side to side, is extended a thread of metal, ready to be connected with a powerful battery, which, when I saw the process, was concealed in a room below. A vessel of common metal being produced was hung on the wire, and plunged into the bath; in which I may remark, the fluid was so clear that you could see to the bottom. The wire on which it was suspended was then connected with the electric battery; and what happened? A very remarkable result. By means of the mighty though unseen agent that was thus brought into action, the particles of silver were taken from the sheet of it, and passing invisibly through the translucent fluid, were transferred to the vessel that had been immersed in the bath. No sound accompanied the mysterious process, no violent action, no sign of motion,—the eye saw nothing but the dull metal beginning to assume a brilliant appearance, and in time, through what looked more like magic than common art, this base metal shone in a coating of the purest silver. Such a change, but far greater and more thorough, is wrought on the soul through the unseen and almighty influence of the Holy Spirit, as soon as faith has established a connection between the Saviour and the sinner. Righteousness is withdrawn from the former, and transferred to the latter. In the words of an inspired apostle, the believer puts on Christ, to stand before God covered with those merits, and justified by that righteousness which makes a sinner just. If this process of art suggested that resemblance, it presented under one aspect a mighty difference. Robbed of its precious metal, what was once a sheet of silver became in time a dull, attenuated, worthless thing. Its treasures were exhausted; Christ's never are. It could coat and cover a certain number,—no more. But in Him there is righteousness for all the world, enough of mercy in the Father, of merit in the Son, and of grace in the Spirit, for every child of guilt.—Guthrie.

2. a man, comp. Zech. vi. 12; "while, of course, the Messiah[b] was to Isaiah the ideal of human[c] character, and therefore shared whatsoever features he might foresee in its perfect development, it is evident that in this verse Isaiah is not thinking of the Messiah alone or particularly. When he says with such simplicity a man, he means any man, he means the ideal for every man."—G. A. Smith. **hiding .. wind,** shade of a rock

[a] "It is as if Isaiah had said, the day is coming when power shall be exercised and government administered, not as at present (in the reign of Ahaz), but with a view to the faithful execution of the laws." — J. A. Alexander.

Ps. xlv. 1, 6, 7; Ze. ix. 9.

"When we want nothing, we find nothing. When we want little, we find little. When we want much, we find much. But when we want everything, and get reduced to complete nakedness and beggary, we find in Christ God's complete treasure - house, out of which come gold and jewels to enrich us, and garments to clothe us in the richness and righteousness of the Lord."—Sears.

"It is not barely said that 'He,' but, as the original has it, 'He Himself shall save.' Joshua saved Israel, not by his own power, not of himself, but God by him; neither saved he his own people, but the people of God; whereas Jesus Himself, by His own power—the power of God—saves His own people, the people of God."—Bp. Pearson.

[b] "To interpret the sublime imagery of this verse in application to a mere human being, would be quite repugnant to the spirit of the sacred writers."—Henderson.

[c] "Christ's humanity is here asserted, bec. it was by suffering and perfect obe-

to a heated traveler. **rivers,** etc., or streams to desert traveler. **weary,** or wearying, by reason of its heat and its drought.[d]

The Suffering World and the Relieving Man (vs. 2).—I. The suffering world. 1. A tempest: conflicting thoughts, sinful passions, guilty memories, terrible foreboding; 2. A drought; 3. Exhaustion. II. The relieving Man. 1. He is a shelter from moral storms; 2. He is a river in moral droughts; 3. He is the recruiting, resting place in exhaustion.—D. Thomas.

Our Hiding Place.—Well do I remember being caught in the mistral at Hyeres, when it blew with unusual fury; it not only drove clouds of dust with terrible force, but boughs of trees, and all sorts of light material were propelled with tremendous force. One wondered that a tree remained upright, or a fence in its place. What a joy it was to hide behind a solid wall, and under its shelter to run along till we were safe within doors! Then we knew in some measure the value of a hiding-place from the wind. But what is that to a cyclone, which tears down houses, and lifts ships upon the dry land? Friends who have lived abroad have startled us with their descriptions of what wind can be, and they have made us cease to wonder that a hiding-place should be greatly prized by dwellers in eastern lands.—Spurgeon.—Shadow of a Rock.—The road to-day lay through St. Ann's, one of the most luxuriant parts of this luxuriant island. By eleven o'clock I had reached Roaring River, and stopped there to rest and refresh myself and horse. Here is a scene almost beyond description. Above the bridge a hundred streams are seen pouring through a thick wood, and at every yard tumbling over stumps and stones. Just as they reach the arch they all unite and rush over a high ledge, from side to side of which the bridge is thrown, sweeping away below in a foaming torrent, through a deep channel worn in the rocks, and hastening, as it were, impetuously over a succession of falls, to throw itself into the bosom of its parent ocean. Oh, how delightful such a cool spot is to rest in the midst of a long journey from the meridian sun of this burning clime! It is then we feel the truth and power of the Scripture expressions, "The shadow of a great rock in a weary land," and "streams in the desert." I remembered what a boy once answered when I asked him what kind of a place heaven is; he said, "It must be a very cool place;" and I compared it with what the Scriptures say of the same blessed regions, "The sun shall not light on them, nor any heat; for the Lamb that is in the midst of the throne shall feed them, and shall lead them unto living fountains of waters."

3, 4. (3) **eyes .. dim,** comp. threatening, ch. vi. 9, 10. "Them that see" refers to the Prophets or teachers of the people. **them that hear,** the people who are under instruction. Teachers will be willing to see the truth and the people will be ready to hear it. (4) **rash,** marg. hasty: "who from want of faith were ever for precipitating matters, instead of abiding God's time." "Superficial and precipitate judgments will be replaced by discrimination."—Driver. **stammerers,** "hesitancy and vacillation will give way before the prompt and clear assertion of principle."[a]

Spiritual Anatomy—the Eye (vs. 3).—1. There are the blinded and the open eyes; 2. There are the eyes rightly and wrongly directed; 3. There are the eyes of the proud and of the humble; 4. There are the eyes of the covetous and of the humble; 5. There are vain eyes and those that delight in truth; 6. There are the eyes of the impure and of the holy; 7. There are the eyes of the cruel and of pity and compassion; 8. There are eyes reddened with wine; 9. There are eyes dim with age, grief, and sickness; 10. There is the eye of holy joy and gladness. Apply:—(1) How important a renewed understanding; (2) A rich use of the eyes; (3) A watchful care; (4) Hopeful expectation.—F. Burns.

5, 6. (5) "No more will the fool be called noble, nor the knave any more be named gentle."—Pol. Bib. **vile person,** literally "the fool," that is "the ungodly man, sin being the highest folly."—Cheyne. **churl,** or niggard, but rather with the idea of crafty, "knave." Characteristics of the "fool." Render: For a fool speaks folly and his heart works mischief, to practice impiety (cf. ix. 17) and to speak error (xxix. 24) against Jehovah, etc. The fool here depicted is a free thinker, a practical atheist, as in Ps. xiv. 1; the baneful effect of his principles is seen in his conduct towards his fellow-men, in his pitiless and cruel selfishness."—Camb. Bib.

---

dience in His human nature that He received the kingdom here described (Phil. ii. 8, 9)." —Wordsworth.

d Is. iv. 6, xxv. 4; Ps. lxiii. 1.

"The claims of Jesus Christ upon our gratitude and devotion are such that we gladly borrow language from any that may help us to utter his praise. Thus Dr. Marsh adopted Pope's lines, altering only the last words,—

'Not bubbling waters to the thirsty swain,
Not rest to weary laborers, faint with pain,
Not showers to larks, not sunshine to the bee,
Are half so precious as thy love to me—
My Saviour.' "

a "Possibly with reference to the drunken scorners who, in stammering style, imitated Isaiah's warnings to mock them (Is. xxviii. 7—11, 13, etc.)" —Maurer.

"Enquirers should be answered. It is never well to be dumb to attentive ears. As some one has wisely said, 'we shall have to give an account of idle silence, as well as of idle speech.' "—Spurgeon.

the soul, i. e. the life, the fool is impious toward God and keeps bread and drink from his fellows.

Profanity.—The profaneness of which we speak to-day, is not only or chiefly a profaneness of speech. There is a fashion in these things. Men of a past generation habitually used expressions which would now be scouted in society as shockingly blasphemous. But not on that account is profaneness (in the Scripture sense of the word) either obsolete or unfashionable. "Profane" is the opposite, not of "reverent," but of "sacred." When we speak of things sacred and profane we mean to express, however inaccurate or even erroneous the idea, that God is in the one and not in the other. Esau was profane, because the consecrating mark was not on him; Jacob, whatever his faults, lived to realize that appropriation of life and soul to God which makes the character sacred and the man a saint. When we seek to try and examine ourselves by the test here proposed—"lest there be among you a profane person as Esau"—we may use as our criterion the suggestion of the text. Esau was profane, because "for a morsel of meat he sold his birthright." "Behold, I am at the point to die, and what profit shall this birthright do to me?" Can the remote prospect of an inheritance, ages hence, for my posterity, of this land, in which my father, like his father, is the inmate of a tent, having no possession there but of a melancholy cave for burial—can the idea, beautiful but unsubstantial, of a possible place in the march of great events, long millenniums distant—events by which spiritual evils shall be remedied, and blessings, of the very nature of which I have the dimmest, darkest vision, introduced—can this feed me or give me drink? What, in all the world, can be at this moment so real as this hunger, or so important to me as its relief? We can talk afterwards of things spiritual. God has so made us, that one clamorous bodily want necessarily precludes every thought save that of its satisfaction. "He did eat and drink, and rose up, and went his way. Thus Esau despised his birthright." And for doing so he was "profane." Whenever we allow the present to overbear the future; whenever we suffer the body, with its appetites or its passions, to drown the voice of conscience, or obscure the vision of promise; whenever we prefer indulgence to duty, ease to exertion, self-interest to self-control, things temporal to things spiritual, the world to heaven, the present to the eternal—then we are profane. Whenever we argue—and who has never done so?—"What profit shall this birthright do me?" in the face of some immediate instant gratification; what substance is there, what certainty, in the recompense of the reward, that I should give up for its sake the opening for advancement, that offer of gain, that enjoyment of which I know the sweetness, that sin which arrays itself in every charm and bids me make sure of it, if I die for it?—then we are profane. We show that the consecrating mark is not upon us, or is faded, blurred, illegible; we are looking at things seen and temporal, and have no eye for the unseen and the eternal; like Esau, we are bartering birthright for pottage; like Esau, we are profane.—C. J. Vaughan.—Honesty.—The truth of the good old maxim that honesty is the best policy is upheld by the daily experience of life; uprightness and integrity being found as successful in business as in everything else. As Hugh Miller's worthy uncle advised, "In all your dealings give your neighbor good measure heaped up and running over, and you will not lose by it in the end." Integrity of word and deed ought to be the very corner stone of all business transactions. To the tradesman, merchant and manufacturer, it should be what honor is to the soldier, and charity to the Christian. In the humblest calling there will always be found scope for the exercise of this uprightness of character.—Smiles.

7, 8. (7) **instruments,** schemes and plans for making money. **when .. right,** has right on his side. (8) "But the noble devises noble things and in noble things will he persist."—Pol. Bib.[a] **liberal,** or noble-minded. Some think the reference is to Hezekiah, and cite in illus. 2 Chr. xxx. 22—24.

Whitefield.—While the Rev. G. Whitefield was preaching on one occasion at Plymouth, he lodged with Mr. Kinsman, a minister of the town. After breakfast on Monday, he said to his friend, "Come, let us visit some of your poor people. It is not enough that we labor in the pulpit; we must endeavor to be useful out of it." On entering the dwellings of the afflicted poor, he administered to their temporal as well as their spir-

"When men's eyes are opened, they will no longer confound the essential distinctions of moral character. Things will then be called by their right names."—J. A. Alexander.

"The rulers and teachers who urged men to exchange the guidance of religious faith for that of worldly wisdom, and to prefer the license of Syrian or Egyptian rites to the holiness of God's law, left men, amidst all their joviality with hungry and parched souls."—Spk. Com.

"He that is habituated to deceptions and artificialities in trifles, will try in vain to be true in matters of importance, for truth is a thing of habit rather than of will. You cannot in any given case, by any sudden and single effort will to be true, if the habit of your life has been insincerity."—F. W. Robertson.

"As the owl is hooted and wondered at among other birds; even so the godly are often made a gazing-stock and wonderment to the ungodly, because the course of godliness is most strange and foolish in their eyes." — Cawdray.

"When thou hast thanked thy God
For every blessing sent,
What time will then remain
For murmurs or lament?"
—R. C. French.

[a] 2 Co. ix. 6.

"Men might be better if we better deemed

ritual wants. Mr. K., knowing the low state of his finances, was surprised at his liberality, and suggested that he thought he had been too bountiful. Mr. W., with some degree of smartness, replied, "It is not enough, young man, to pray, and put on a serious face; true religion and undefiled is this—to visit the widow and the fatherless in their affliction, and to supply their wants. My stock, it is true, is nearly exhausted, but God, whom I serve, and whose saints we have assisted, will, I doubt not, soon give me a supply." His hopes were not disappointed. A stranger called on him in the evening, who addressed him thus: "With great pleasure I have heard you preach; you are on a journey, as well as myself, and traveling is expensive. Do me the honor to accept this," at the same time presenting him with five guineas. Returning to the family, Mr. Whitefield, smiling, held out the money in his hand, saying, "There, young man, God has speedily repaid what I bestowed. Let this in future teach you not to withhold what it is in the power of your hand to give. The gentleman to whom I was called is a perfect stranger to me; his only business was to give me the sum you see." It is remarkable that this gentleman, though rich, was notorious for a penurious disposition: but Elijah was fed by ravens.—Cheever.

Of them. The worst way to improve the world Is to condemn it."
—Bailey.

"Scorn to trample upon a worm, or sneak to an emperor."
—Saadi.

"Teach me to feel another's woe,
To hide the fault I see;
That mercy I to other's show,
That mercy show to me."
—Pope.

9—11. (9) "The women are addressed partly as representing best certain aspects of the public mind, luxury and complacent ease (ch. iii. 16 ff.; Am. iv. 1 ff.); partly because of their function as mourners in seasons of calamity (Jer. ix. 20)."—Camb. Bib. **women .. ease,** whose luxurious habits contributed very seriously to the existing evils. Comp. ch. iii. 16—26.[b] **careless,** as not apprehensive of the threatened and swift-coming dangers. (10) **Many days,** R. V., "For days beyond a year."[c] **the gathering,** Pol. Bib., "the gathering of fruit." (11) **strip,** etc., the usual E. signs of grief, distress, and humiliation. The Prophet intimates that these troubles would come to them in the Assyrian invasion.

Woman's Besetting Sins.—The besetting sins of either sex are its virtues prostituted. A man's greatest temptations proceed from his strength; but the glory of the feminine nature is repose, and trust is the strength of the feminine character, in which very things, however, lies all the possibility of woman's degradation. Woman's faith amounts at times to real intuition; but what risks are attached to this prophetic power—of impatience, of contentment with the first glance at things, "the inclination," as a great moralist has put it, "to take too easily the knowledge of the problems of life, and to rest content with what lies nearest her, instead of penetrating to a deeper foundation." Women are full of indulgence and hope; but what possibilities lie there of deception, false optimism, and want of that anxiety which alone makes progress possible. Women are more inclined than men to believe all things; but how certain is such a temper to sacrifice the claims of truth and honor. Women are full of tact, the just favorites of success, with infinite power to plead and please; but if they are aware of this, how certain is such a self-consciousness to produce negligence and the fatal sleep of the foolish virgins.—Exp. Bib.

b "The Prophet having reproved the sceptical and worldly spirit of the men of Jerusalem, passes on to censure the voluptuousness of the women."
—Wordsworth.

c "Or, in little more than a year."—Maurer.

Retribution to the Careless.—Though retribution sleep, it must come and will not tarry. The Jews were spared forty years after the Saviour had wept over their doomed city. So with the sinner; there comes a time when he can be indifferent no longer; the realities of judgment and eternity produce a conviction which will go on deepening for ever. How it will embitter the soul then to dwell upon this carelessness of the past. Recollection itself a source of misery (Luke. xvi. 25). What words can express the anguish of a soul thus reminded of lost opportunities, etc.? Throw off this lethargy. From this moment seek the Lord with your whole heart, and call upon Him while He is near. Why run the desperate hazard of having to do all this on a dying bed?—Mark Tucker.

Wonderful alchemy of God's grace it is which transmutes tribulation into triumph, turns waters of Marah into a healthful fountain, enables one to gather grapes of thorns and figs of thistles, causes the rose to bloom through a whole winter of trials, and helps the soul to regard afflictions as promises and not threatenings.

12, 13 (12) **teats,** R. V., "They shall smite upon the breasts." **pleasant fields,** yielding abundant harvests, but soon to be made barren by advancing enemies. (13) **thorns and briers,** the signs of a desolated and neglected land.

"Ye shall knock upon your breasts." —Coverdale.

Thorns and Briers.—Thorns and briers are by no means a conspicuous feature in our English landscape. Were a prophet, therefore, to rise up, and by way of plague or judgment to foretell to England the general spread of such a vegetation, his words would not be particularly im-

"To rejoice in the prosperity of another is to partake of it."—William Austin.

pressive. It was different in Palestine. There the ononis, with its long tough cables underground, and its keen lancets above, was a constant hindrance to the plough. And in a country where the most frequent of trees is the zizyphus, a scrubby, shockheaded ruffian, with trailing flexible twigs, carrying spines an inch or two long, each "as sharp as a needle, as hard as a bone," we can not only understand the frequent allusions to "thorns in the side," "thorns in the eyes," "a thorn in the flesh," "a thorn going up into the hand of a drunkard," but we can see what a terrible judgment it was, if the day could be foretold when these Philistines of the vegetable kingdom would win the battle, and repossess the goodly land.

14, 15. (14) "for the palace shall be forsaken; the populous city shall be deserted; Ophel and the Watch-tower shall be," etc.—G. A. Smith. **palaces,** "palace," i. e. of the king at Jerusalem. **forts,** R. V., "the hill and the watch-tower," The first word is 'Ophel, the name of the southern projection of the hill on which the temple stood (Neh. iii. 26 f., xi. 21; 2 Chr. xxvii. 3, xxxiii. 14), and is doubtless mentioned as the aristocratic quarter of the city, near the royal palace. The word translated "watch tower" occurs nowhere else, and is of uncertain significance; probably, like Ophel, it denotes a particular locality in the capital. **dens,** mere shelter places for the wild beasts. (15) at last the great transformation of all things will be ushered in, by an outpouring of spirit (the Heb. has no art.) from on high; i. e. from heaven, as in ch. xxxiii. 5. The spirit, conceived as a subtle essence descending upon and then permeating the human world, is said to be "poured out" as in ch. xxix. 10; Ezek. xxxix. 29; Joel ii. 28 f. Here the word "spirit" denotes the Divine principle of life, and especially the power by which the will of God is made to prevail in human society (vss. 16 f.).[a]—Camb. B.

Doctrine of the Holy Spirit.—What is the doctrine of the Holy Spirit? It is the doctrine of the interworking of the Spirit of God upon the souls of men. I have no philosophy about it. All I say is this: that God knows what is the secret way in which mind reaches mind. I do not—you do not. I do not know why words on my tongue wake up thoughts corresponding to those words in you. I do not know why the soul of man, like a complex instrument of wondrous scope, is played upon by my words, so that there are waked up in it notes along the whole scale of being. I do not understand why these things are so, but unquestionably they are so. I do not know how the mother pours her affection on the child's heart; but she does. Two stars never shone into each other as two loving souls shine into each other. I know it is so, but I do not know why it is so. I do not know how soul touches soul, how thought touches thought, or how feeling touches feeling; but I know it does. Now that which we see in the lower departments of life—that which exists between you and your friends, and me and my friends—that I take, and by my imagination I lift it up into the Divine nature, and give it depth and scope and universality; and then I have some conception of the doctrine of God's Spirit poured upon the human soul.—H. W. Beecher.

16, 17. (16) **judgment,** or equity: justice. Justice and righteousness shall prevail, the foundations of social peace and order. **dwell,** or permanently abide. (17) **work,** or influence; same as effect, or result. **peace,** internal and external.[b]

Peace.—Faith looked at in reference to God is a spirit of quietude and repose. Nothing so full of conscious helplessness and simple trust. No little bird beneath its parent's wing, no child upon its mother's lap, so gentle and confiding. A lion in conflict with the powers of hell, faith lies down like a lamb at the feet of the Lord of heaven. It returns and rests "in quietness and in confidence." Indeed, in this way it obtains salvation and strength. The calm resting upon God makes it victorious over all beside. In truth, it is He who fights for the believer, with the believer, in the believer. Faith does nothing alone, nothing of itself, but everything under God, by God, through God. It is only in a qualified sense that faith makes war and gets victory. "The excellency of power is of God, and not of us." Its humble dependence, its meek, child-like spirit, after all constitute its proper self. These are the essence and life of faith.—J. Stoughton.

[a] "The general by a special Divine influence a meaning is, until total revolution shall take place in the character, and as a necessary consequence in the condition, of the people." —J. A. Alexander.

Is. xliv. 3, 4; Zec. xii. 10.

"Peter, when asked how the work of Pentecost was done, said: 'With the Holy Ghost.' The greatest works for God have been wrought with such power of the Holy Ghost that there has been no consciousness of forthputting of human energy." —A. J. Gordon.

"Where is the hope of the world's conversion, or of the salvation of dear loved ones, out of Christ? If the Spirit of God come not to our aid, our eyes may fail with looking for these much - valued blessings." —Lewis.

[b] Is. liv. 13, 14.

"It is rare when injustice, or slights patiently borne, do not leave the heart at the close of the day filled with marvelous joy and peace." —Gold Dust.

"Fancy the bright sun saying, 'Now I must appear bright to-day;' or the Atlantic saying, 'Well, to-day I must appear great.' Why, they are bright and great! Be, and you will appear." —Thomas Jones.

Ec. xi. 1.

"Let us not think the time wasted which is spent in introducing to Jesus those who, if they live, are to be the men and women of the coming generation, and who, if they die early, may be among the first to welcome us to our heavenly home."—Biblical Treasury.

"The common deeds of the common day
Are ringing bells in the far-away."
—Harry Burton.

Capacity for Christian Work.—To sow a field requires some knowledge of the kind of work. City men would make sorry work. So the spiritual sowing requires some capacity. Two mistakes may be made. There is the mistake of those who think any kind of work will do; and of those who estimate the requirements so highly and their own power so humbly that they never venture anything. The latter deterrent operates largely. It falls in with the love of ease. It is sometimes said that the extension of popular education demands a higher class of Sunday-school teachers, for instance, than sufficed some time ago. Many Christians think their own education inadequate. It is a mistake. If we cannot realize our ideal, let us do our best. Besides, experience does not show that boys and girls are ahead of teachers of average intelligence. And spiritual earnestness is a greater qualification than even intellectual endowment. Capacity for Christian work, like any other, perhaps more than any other, increases by exercise.—Hom. Com. Liberal Sowing.—Every period of existence is to be spent unto God. Swift and resistless the waters of life glide on. But beside them all, the Christian sows his good seed. Equally in youth, middle age, and in advancing years, whatsoever his hand finds to do, he does it heartily, as unto the Lord; and in each he reaps a harvest according to his sowing in that which preceded it. Blessed through eternity will he be who sowed wisely and liberally beside all the waters of life.—J. R. Woodford.

18—20. (18) **peaceable habitation,** free from all fear of foes. "There is something tranquilizing in the very sound of this delightful promise." (19) **hail,** an image of Divine judgments. R. V., "But it shall hail in the downfall of the forest; and the city shall utterly be laid low." "In those years 705—702 Isaiah did not forget that something must come between him and this paradise. Across the very middle of his vision there dashes a cruel storm." He beholds the Assyrian invasion.—G. A. Smith. **coming .. forest,** so as to overthrow it. (20) **sow .. waters,** "the prophet apostrophizes the happy agricultural population of the renovated land of Israel. The sentiment may be in part due to his own delight in the avocations of the husbandman, but it has to be remembered that agricultural prosperity naturally holds a prominent place in Messianic prophecy, as the antithesis to the false refinements and military pomp of the civilization that is to be swept away. The features of the description are, the happiness of the people, the abundance of water for the irrigation of the fields, and immunity from danger, so that 'the ox and the ass' can be safely driven out to pasture, without fear of their not returning (cf. ch. i. 3). The 'thither' of the A. V. is a misleading assertion."—Camb. Bib.

After Many Days.—In 1835 Dr. Meadows, in making a journey along the coast of China, called for a few hours at a small island, where he distributed some tracts and small religious books. The island remained unvisited by any European for thirty-three years, when a missionary went thither and began to preach the Gospel. To his astonishment, one of his hearers said, "We know that doctrine;" and on being asked whence they had obtained their knowledge, the man replied: "Many years ago a foreigner came here and left some little books and other writings, which contained that doctrine which you preach. He gave them to my father, who charged me when dying to read them, and keep them carefully, and, perhaps, some day, God would send some one who would teach us the doctrine more fully." The result of the seed sown by Dr. Meadows, thirty-three years before, was the formation of a church which speedily numbered sixty members, and is now in a healthy and thriving state.—E. R. Barrett.

a "The proud and false Assyrian justly reckoned with for all his fraud and violence, and laid under a woe."—Matthew Henry.

Is. xxi. 2.

CHAPTER THE THIRTY-THIRD.

There is no doubt that chapter xxxiii. refers to the sudden disappearance of the Assyrian from the walls of Jerusalem. It was written, part perhaps on the eve of that deliverance, part immediately after morning broke upon the vanished host.—G. A. Smith. 1. **thee that spoilest,** poss. Sennacherib, as representing the Assyrian power.[a] **dealest treacherously,** or wastest.[b] **shalt cease,** as if you had completed your work.

Victims of Treachery.—In the year 1784 the captain of a vessel trading on the coast of Africa went up the country, where he was introduced to a Moorish king. This prince being pleased with the polite manners of the English, entertained them with great civility, and at last reposed so much confidence in the captain as to entrust him with a son, about eighteen years of age, and another fine youth, to be brought to England for education. The captain promised to protect them; but basely sold them for slaves. Fortunately for the two princes their betrayer died on his passage home, and the officers related the circumstance when they arrived. On hearing this, Government sent to pay their ransom; and on their being brought to England, they were placed under the care of the Earl of Halifax, who caused them to be kindly treated, and well educated. They were afterwards introduced to his majesty, and proved themselves worthy of the kindness they experienced.—Percy Anec.

b Violence and treachery are the crying sins of arbitrary powers."—J. A. Aleander.

"The wings of every hour shall bear Some thankful tribute to thine ear."

2—4. (2) **waited for thee,** as ch. xxvi. 8. **arm,** on wh. they may lean during the long waiting time. (3) **the tumult,** "hardly has Isaiah uttered his petition when he is conscious that it is answered: The 'multitudes' of whom Sennacherib has boasted are in flight."—Driver. **people,** or peoples: the armies made up of confederate peoples. (4) **your spoil,** addressed to the Assyrians.[a] **running .. locusts,** R. V., "as locusts leap they shall leap upon it," wh. swiftly devour the vegetation on wh. they alight. The Jews spoiled Sennac.'s forsaken camp.

Gladness of Salvation.—Is hope sweet where despair had almost begun to reign? Is it a joy to be emancipated from a shameful slavery, or set free from a noxious dungeon? Is it gladness to be raised, as if by miracle, from a bed of feebleness and suffering to sudden health and instantaneous vigor? Then what a gladness salvation must be! For, as there is no earthly misery like sin, so is there no deliverance like that with which Jesus makes us free. Words will not tell it. Thought only can think it, and it must be thought out of an enlightened mind and a burning heart dwelt on for a long, long while.—F. W. Faber.

a "The enemy having been destroyed, or made to flee, the inhabitants of Jerusalem would eagerly run up and down thro' the deserted camp, to collect the spoils." —Henderson.

"Minutes came fast, but mercies were more fast and fleet than they."

5, 6. (5) **exalted,** in His judgment of the oppressor. **judgment and righteousness** can mean nothing else than personal and civic virtues in the inhabitants of the city. Isaiah could not have written thus of the Jerusalem he knew (cf. i. 21); if he is the author the words must express a vivid anticipation of the great change in the national character which is now on the eve of accomplishment.—Camb. Bib. (6) **wisdom,** R. V., "And there shall be stability in thy times, abundance of salvation, wisdom and knowledge." In this time to which he is looking the nation shall be rich in the fear of the Lord and strong with wisdom and knowledge.[b]

The Use and Excellency of True Wisdom (vs. 6).—I. Consider wisdom as promoting the stability of an empire. II. As advancing the prosperity of the soul. It is a mine of wealth. 1. Intellectual; 2. Moral; 3. Spiritual; 4. Eternal.—C. Simeon.

Our Wisdom Under Differing Circumstances.—It is a wise thing to exhibit prudence and hopefulness in their proper degrees and seasons. Some are so exultant at success as to become rash, and thereby secure for themselves a disaster; others are so depressed by a defeat as to be incapable of future action. The old Latin distich is worth quoting:

"Si modo victus eras, ad crastina bella parato;
Si modo victor eras, ad crastina bella paveto."
"If conquer'd, for to-morrow's fight prepare:
If conqueror, of to-morrow's fight beware."

When we are most unsuccessful in our Lord's work we should rally all our forces for new attempts, hoping that the tide will turn, and believing that to perseverance the crown is certain. On the other hand, when the Lord favors us with the largest degree of blessing we must watch with holy anxiety lest by any negligence or sin we should grieve the Holy Spirit, and so forfeit all hope of future triumph.—C. H. Spurgeon.

b "The security of those times is the effect of the treasure, the wealth in treasures of salvation." —Nagelsbach.

"Man's extremity is often God s opportunity; because not until his case is desperate, will he cast himself unreservedly upon God. So man often retards the arrival of the right moment. Meanwhile the innocent (comparatively) suffer for the guilty, the good for the bad, the just for the unjust. But there is always a 'thus far and no farther.' 'Now will I rise, saith the Lord.'" —Hom. Com.

7—9. (7) From this vision of the future the prophet returns to present conditions. "The disconsolate envoys (the 'ambassadors of peace') have just returned from Lachish: the country districts are beset by the foe, and impassable."—Driver. **valiant ones,** or messengers sent to sue for peace are rejected. **weep bitterly,** bec. of the failure of their overtures.[a] (8) **wayfaring,** or traveler. The roads were not safe for such.[b] **he .. covenant,** reference is to Sennac.'s breaking his treaty with Hezekiah. **despised the cities,** contemning the defences. (9) **hewn down,** R. V., "withereth away." **Sharon,**[c] the fruitful plain between Carmel and Joppa. **Bashan,** range of hills on N.E. These are regions famous for their beauty. In sympathy with the inhabitants they wither and become desert.

Footprints of the Creator.—A French sceptic, a man of some learning, was crossing the great Sahara, in company with an Arab guide. He noticed, with a sneer, that at certain times the guide, whatever obstacles might arise, put them all aside, and, kneeling on the burning sands, called on his God. Day after day passed, and still the Arab never failed; till at last, one evening, when he rose from his knees, the philosopher asked him, with a contemptuous smile, "How do you know there is a God?" The guide fixed his eyes on the scoffer for a moment in wonder, and then said solemnly, "How do I know that a man, and not a camel, passed my hut last night in the darkness? Was it not by the print of his feet in the sand? Even so," and he pointed to the sun, whose last rays were flashing over the lonely desert, "that footprint is not of man."

10—12. (10) **rise,** as one about to act, aroused by His people's misery. (11) **conceive chaff,** your plans shall prove worthless as chaff. **your breath,** or rage, this would lead them to act in ways wh. would secure their own destruction. (12) **people,** or nations composing Sennac.'s army. **lime,** i. e. as if burned to lime. **thorns cut up,** burning swiftly and fiercely.[d]

Thorns Cut Up.—Here, on the brow of this rocky hill, we have the lime-kilns, and men in the very act of breaking up sarcophagi to feed them. It is unpardonable sacrilege thus to destroy these venerable antiquities. It is outrageous vandalism. Instead of hurling anathemas at these barbarians, we had better drop a tear of compassion over such ignorance, and then see if we cannot draw some lesson of instruction from even these destructive kilns. You see an immense quantity of this low, matted thornbush collected around them. That is the fuel with which the lime is burned. And thus it was in the days of Isaiah. "The people," says he, "shall be as the burnings of lime: as thorns cut up they shall be burned in the fire." Those people among the rocks yonder are cutting up thorns with their mattocks and pruning-hooks, and gathering them into bundles to be burned in these burnings of lime. It is a curious fidelity to real life, that, when the thorns are merely to be destroyed, they are never cut up, but set on fire where they grow. They are only cut up for the lime-kiln.—Thomson.

13, 14. (13) **far off .. near,** "The far off hear what I have done and the near acknowledge my heroic might."—Pol. Bib. The prophet declares that the deed is so magnificent that all nations see its far-reaching significance. (14) **sinners,** those who doubted that God would deliver. **hypocrites,** or profane ones. The wicked and unbelieving portion of the Jews. **devouring fire,** common symbol of Divine judgment. **among us,** the exclamation of the sinners when they witness the supremacy of Jehovah. **everlasting,** i. e. "there is of course no allusion here to eternal punishment. The 'fire' is Jehovah's holiness, manifested in the destruction of His enemies; and this is called eternal because the Divine wrath against sin is inexhaustible."—Camb. Bib.

The Awfulness of God.—We see it reflected from the horror-struck faces of the ungodly and the profane. He is indeed seen to be a "consuming Fire," having his "furnace in Jerusalem" (ch. xxxi. 19). And all the immoral and the unprincipled, the heedless and the worldly, feel themselves as fuel for His wrath—they whom the continual returns of the Word preached do not alter, so that their old sins remain firm, entire, and unbattered, the baseness of their inclinations unchanged, the levity of their discourse and behavior; those whose former distresses and disasters have not laid low in the valleys of humility, nor circumscribed the lashings out of their luxury; they whose past miseries and restraints give only a relish instead of a check to present pride and intemperance;

a Comp. 2 Ki. xviii. 14—16, 19.

b Comp. Ju. v. 6.

c "A beautiful poetical amplification of the description. The most magnificent and fruitful scenes of nature are represented as converted into barrenness and desolation." —Henderson.

The omniscience of God is a great check to sin, and motive to virtue. A heathen philosopher advised his pupils to imagine that some distinguished character was always looking at them, as the best aid to excellence of life.

d "In Palestine the low matted thorns are cut up with mattocks and hooks to be burnt in the lime-kilns near the spot where they grow." —Thomson.

"There would seem to be a confirmation here of the view that the Assyrian army was consumed by a hot pestilential wind from the Lord, in the valley of Hinnom, on the S. of Jerusalem." —Wordsworth.

"Burnings of lime in a lime-kiln, of which the peculiarity is that all seem to be on fire together." —Matt. Henry.

"Who can dwell with His never-relaxing holiness?" — Spk. Com.

"Gentleness or lenity is a virtue by which God preserves moderation concerning anger in taking vengeance, lest it should be too vehement — lest

those whom all the caresses of Providence have not been able to win upon, so as to endear them to a virtuous strictness, or deter them from a vicious extravagance;—all such—unless the great God be trivial and without concern in his grand transactions with our immortal souls—during this condition, so far as we can judge, are fashioning for wrath.—Pul. Com.

15, 16. "In two beautiful verses Isaiah gives the answer and sketches the portrait of the man who even in that appalling time may deem himself secure."—Driver. (15) **walketh,** The God-fearing man is not troubled by the presence of Divine judgments.[a] **shaking .. bribes,** expressive gesture of indignant refusal.[b] **hearing of blood,** schemes of violence and murder. **seeing evil,** or conniving at it. (16) **on high,** safe up out of the tumult and danger. **munitions of rocks,** strongholds or sure refuges. **waters .. sure,** even in times of national calamity. Waters from a perennial fountain.[c]

Refusing a Bribe.—The borough of Hull, in the reign of Charles II., chose Andrew Marvell, a young gentleman of little or no fortune, and maintained him in London for the service of the public. His understanding, integrity, and spirit, were dreadful to the then infamous administration. Persuaded he would be theirs if properly asked, they sent his old school-fellow, the Lord Treasurer Danby, to renew acquaintance with him in his garret. At parting, the Lord Treasurer slipped into his hand £1,000, and then went to his chariot. Marvell, looking at the paper, called after the treasurer, "My Lord, I request another moment." They went up again to the garret, and the servant-boy was called, "I ask, child, what had I for dinner yesterday?" "Don't you remember, Sir, you had the little shoulder of mutton that you ordered me to bring from a woman in the market?" "Very right, child. What have I for dinner to-day?" "Don't you know, Sir, that you bid me lay the blade-bone to broil?" "It is so; very right, child, go away. My Lord, do you hear that? Andrew Marvell's dinner is provided: there is your piece of paper, I want it not; I know the sort of kindness you intended; I live here to serve my constituents, the ministry may seek men for their purpose; I am not one."—Whitecross. The Bankrupt's Entertainment.—Dr. Franklin relates the following anecdote of Mr. Denham, an American merchant, with whom he once went a passenger to England. "He had formerly," he says, "been in business at Bristol, had failed in debt to a number of people, compounded, and went to America; there, by close application to business as a merchant, he acquired a plentiful fortune in a few years. Returning to England in the ship with me, he invited his old creditors to an entertainment, at which he thanked them for the easy compensation they had favored him with; and when they expected nothing but the treat, every man, at the first remove, found under his plate an order on a banker for the full amount of the unpaid remainder, with interest."—Cheever.

17—19. (17) Again he returns to the picture of the golden age to come. **king .. beauty,**[a] The Messiah, the glorious king.[b] **far off,** R. V., "they shall behold a far stretching land," the world-wide dominion of the coming king. (18) **meditate terror,** R. V., "Thine heart shall muse on the terror: where is he that counted; where is he that weighed the tribute?" Looking back to past times of danger and oppression with wonder. (19) "The insolent people wilt thou see no more, the people of obscure, unintelligible speech, gibbering in a meaningless tongue."—Pol. Bib. **stammering,** barbarous.[d] So languages seem which we do not understand.

The Seeing and the Sight (vs. 17).—I. The eyes. 1. Eyes that have been shut to evil; 2. That have delighted in every manifestation of evil; 3. That have been well employed; 4. That were often filled with tears; 5. Glorified eyes. II. The seeing. 1. See without interruption; 2. Without weariness or weakness; 3. Without curiosity; 4. Without disappointment; 5. Without insensibility. III. The sight. Christ shall be seen—1. With beauty of countenance; 2. In His beautiful garments; 3. Surrounded by those beautified with salvation; 4. Crowned with many crowns.—Stems and Twigs.

the severity of the anger should certainly correspond with the magnitude of the wickedness perpetrated." —Arminius.

a Comp. Ps. xv., xxiv.

b "Won't receive any, but when they are put into his hands, shakes them out."—Gill.

c Ps. xxxiv. 10.

"I creep under my Lord's wings in the great shower, and the waters cannot reach me. We may sing, even in our winter's storm, in the expectation of a summer's sun at the turn of the year. No created powers in hell, or out of hell, can mar our Lord's work, or spoil our song of joy." — Rutherford.

"God hath provided a sweet and quiet life for his children, could they improve and use it; a calm and firm conviction in all the storms and troubles that are about them, however things go, to find content, and be careful for nothing." — R. Leighton.

a "Thine eyes shall see the Shechinah of the king of ages."—Targum.

b Comp. Ps. xxvii. 4, lxiii. 2; Is. xxxviii. 11.

d "The Assyrian was a foreign dialect, though of the same Semitic family with the Hebrew."—Wordsworth.

Jeremy Bentham mentions that the current of his thoughts and studies was directed for life by

Far Away.—

Upon the shore
Of Evermore
We sport like children at their play
And gather shells
Where sinks and swells
The mighty sea from far away.

Upon that beach,
Nor voice nor speech
Doth things intelligible say;
But through our souls
A whisper rolls
That comes to us from far away.

Into our ears
The voice of years
Comes deeper day by day:
We stoop to hear
As it draws near,
Its awfulness from far away.

At what it tells
We drop the shells
We were so full of yesterday,
And pick no more
Upon that shore,
But dream of brighter far away.

And o'er that tide,
Far out and wide,
The yearning of our souls doth stray:
We long to go
We do not know
Where it may be, but far away.

The mighty deep
Doth slowly creep
Upon the shore where we did play;
The very sand
Where we did stand
A moment since, swept far away.

Our playmates all,
Beyond our call,
Are passing hence, as we, too, may,
Unto that shore
Of Evermore,
Beyond the boundless far away.

We'll trust the wave
And Him to save,
Beneath whose feet as marble lay
The rolling deep,
For He can keep
Our souls in that dim far away.—Frazer's Mag.

20. Behold Zion as it will then be! Our city of festivals, safe, peaceful; secure as a tent which no storm can overthrow. **stakes,** by which the tent ropes were fastened.[a] Terms borrowed from the nomadic life.

The City of Our Solemnities (vs. 20).—I. The object of contemplation—Zion symbolical of the residence of the living God; the place of holy convocations. II. The contemplation of the object. 1. To the worldling; 2. To the awakened penitent; 3. To the believer; 4. A prayer to God Himself, to look upon Zion, etc.—W. Jay.

A Citizen Saint.—According to the legend, Omobuono was a mer-

a single phrase that caught his eye at the end of a pamphlet—"The greatest good of the greatest number."

There was an ancient custom of putting an hour-glass into the coffin of the dead to signify that their time had run out, a useless notification to them. Better put the hour-glass into the hand of every living man, and show them the grains gliding steadily out. Soon all will be gone.

"Beauty lies in symmetry and completeness; he was perfectly holy, without spot or blemish. Beauty lies in subtle harmonies; and in Christ justice, love, and wisdom were all united in one. Beauty lies in conformity with moral law; and he was 'harmless, undefiled, and separate from sinners.'" — Pul. Com.

"Soul-eyes see the King. They are quick to discern God's presence. They detect him everywhere and in everything. Life is serious, life is glorious, to them, because God is always 'walking in the garden,' always close by."—Pul. Com.

[a] "The peculiar beauty of the imagery lies in ascribing permanence to a tent, which, from its very nature, must be movable. This may either imply a previous state of agitation and instability, or that the Church, though weak in herself, should be strengthened and established by the power of God." — J. A. Alexander.

chant of Cremona, who had received from his father but little school-learning; yet, from the moment he entered upon the management of his own affairs, a wisdom more than human seemed to inspire every action of his life. Diligent and thrifty, his stores increased daily, and, with his possessions, his almost boundless charity. Nor did his charity consist merely in giving his money in alms, nor in founding hospitals, but in the devotion of his whole heart towards relieving the sorrows as well as the necessities of the poor, and in exhorting and converting to repentance those who had been led into evil courses. Neither did this good saint think it necessary to lead a life of celibacy. He was married to a prudent and virtuous wife, who was sometimes uneasy lest her husband's excessive bounty to the poor should bring her children to beggary; but it was far otherwise. Omobuono increased daily in riches and prosperity, so that the people of the city believed that his stores were miraculously multiplied. It is related of him, that being on a journey with his family, and meeting some poor pilgrims who were ready to faint by the wayside with hunger and thirst, he gave them freely all the bread and wine he had provided for his own necessities; and, going afterwards to fill his empty wine-flasks from a running stream, the water, when poured out, proved to be most excellent wine; and his wallet was found full of wheaten bread, supplied by the angels in lieu of that which he had given away. As the life of Omobuono had been in all respects most blessed, so was his death; for one morning, being at his early devotions in the Church of St. Egidio, and kneeling before a crucifix, just as the choir were singing the Gloria in Excelsis, he stretched out his arms in the form of a cross, and in this attitude expired. He was canonized by Pope Innocent III. on the earnest petition of his fellow-citizens.—Mrs. Jameson.

"As the earth's loftiest peaks rise not in their snows on some isolated hill that stands like a lonely pyramid on a level plain, but where the mountains are grouped and massed together, so the saint's most heavenly happiness is not attained in solitude, nor even amid domestic scenes, but where religious life exists in its social character."—Guthrie.

21, 22. (21) **glorious Lord,** R. V., "But there the Lord will be with us in majesty, a place of broad rivers," etc.[a] "Here Jerusalem is represented like the great cities of the Nile and Euphrates (cf. Nah. iii. 8), as surrounded by an expanse of waters, protecting it from the approach of an enemy. The idea, of course, is purely poetical."—Camb. Bib. **galley,** boat propelled by oars. **gallant ship,** vessel of burden; both used in hostile sense, as war vessels. (22) **judge,** etc.,[c] in the New Jerusalem Jehovah is Judge, Lawgiver and King, and therefore also its Deliverer from every danger.

Is. xxvi. 1—3; Ps. cxxvii. 1, 2.

a "He is our fortification, our moat, and our river. Other cities, like Nineveh and Babylon, are protected by broad dykes and streams." —Wordsworth.

c "This beautiful triplet expresses the confidence of the Church in the government and protection of Jehovah." — Henderson.

The Gospel Church (vs. 21).—I. The peace and tranquility of the Church of God, from—1. The character of its Governor; 2. The peaceful tempers of its inhabitants; 3. The security of its fortifications; 4. The destruction of its enemies. II. Its permanency and security. The tabernacle was—1. Of heavenly origin; 2. Its artificers Divinely inspired; 3. It exhibited tokens of the Divine glory. III. The nature of the supplies afforded to us. 1. They are Divine; 2. Abundant; 3. Inexhaustible; 4. Near, unmolested. Apply:—The doctrine of the text should—(1) Induce gratitude; (2) Inspire confidence; 3. Excite expectation.

Loyalty.—Three centuries ago the Spaniards were besieging the little town of St. Quentin, on the frontiers of France. Its ramparts were in ruins, fever and famine were decimating its defenders, treason was gliding among its terrified population. One day the Spaniards shot over the walls a shower of arrows, to which were attached little slips of parchment, promising the inhabitants that if they would surrender, their lives and property should be spared. Now, the governor of the town was the great leader of the Huguenots, Gaspard de Coligni. As his sole answer he took a piece of parchment, tied it to a javelin, wrote on it the two words Regem habemus—"We have a king"—and hurled it back into the camp of the enemy. There was his sole answer to all their threats and all their seductions. Now that was true loyalty—loyalty in imminent peril, loyalty ready to sacrifice all. But who was that king for whom, amidst sword and flame, amid fever and famine, Coligni was defending those breached and battered walls? It was the weak and miserable Henry II. of France, whose son, Charles IX., was afterwards guilty of the murder of Coligni and the infamies of St. Bartholomew. Hav you a king? Is Christ your King? Ah, if He be, He is not a feeble, corrupt, false, treacherous man like Coligni's master, but a King who loves you, who died for you, who pleads with you even now on the

"Let your aim be to please our dear Lord perfectly in little things and to attain a spirit of child-like simplicity and dependence. In proportion as self-love and self-confidence are weakened, and our will bowed to that of God, so will hindrance disappear, the internal troubles and contests which harassed the soul vanish, and it will be filled with peace and tranquillity." —Jean Nicolas Gron.

right hand of the Majesty on High. Are you loyal to Him as Coligni was to the wretched Henry II.? Are you loyal at all—much more, would you be loyal to Christ, even unto death? If so, what will you do for Him? That is the test.—Old Test. Anec.

23, 24. (23) **tacklings,** contrast again of the present and the future. Now "thy tacklings hang loose, they do not hold fast the foot of the mast, nor keep the sail spread out," but then "spoil in abundance will be divided, even the lame will seize on a prey."[a] In the first part of the vs. Zion is compared to an unseaworthy ship. **mast,** or cross-beam. The fittings are represented as broken by the Divine storm that discomfits them. **lame, etc.,** a fine poetical touch, indicating how utterly the spoil was left at the disposal of anybody. (24) **inhabitant,** of Jerusalem.[a] In the day of Divine deliverance and gracious rule.

Encouragement to the Weak (vs. 23).—Note the history in the context. I. How it was fulfilled on the occasion referred to. II. How it is fulfilling at this time. 1. Still are the weak triumphant through the power and grace of God. Are any weak in understanding, in grace, in faith? III. How it shall be fulfilled in the millenial age. Behold then—1. What encouragement is here given to serve the Lord; 2. What honor will be given to the Saviour at the last day.—C. Simeon.

"Some church-members have their roots on one side of the church wall and their boughs all hang over and drop the fruit on the world's side. It is not only a question of where your roots are, but where the boughs hang and the apples fall." —Theodore L. Cuyler.

a "This is the evang. Prophet's anticipation of Him who said to the sick man, 'Son, be of good cheer; thy sins are forgiven thee.' "—Sir E. Strachey.

"Comfort — 'tis for ease and quiet: it sleeps upon the down of sweet content, in the sound bed of industry and health." — Havard.

Trust not so much to the comforts of God, as to the God of comforts. The greatest temptation Satan hath for the Christian is his comforts.

CHAPTER THE THIRTY-FOURTH.

The judgment upon all nations, with special reference to Edom. Comp. Ezek. xxv. 12; xxxv.; Obad. 10—16. Mal. i. 2—5. **1—3.** (1) **nations,** all peoples are to be instructed by God's dealings with and for His people.[a] (2) **all nations .. armies,** "it is remarkable that no reason is assigned for Jehovah's anger." (3) **cast out,**[b] as was the case with Sennac.'s army before Jerusalem. **stink,** Joel ii. 20. **melted .. blood,** as they are washed down by rains.

God's Dealing with One Nation for the Sake of Many.—Illustration of this point may run along three lines. I. A man's or a nation's genius is not for self. "The earth must hear," and know about it. All gifts are trusts. II. A man's or a nation's sufferings are not for self. The most striking illustration in a man is Job; in a nation, the people of Israel. All sufferers bear their part in the moral education, the redemption, of the race. III. A man's or a nation's judgments are not for self. We are not punished for our own sakes alone. Judgments follow us for the sake of the on-lookers.—Pulpit Com.

No Man Liveth to Himself.—

> The healing of the world
> Is in its nameless saints. Each separate star
> Seems nothing, but a myriad scattered stars
> Break up the night, and make it beautiful.—E. B. Browning.

4. host .. dissolved, the rebellious spirits that have co-operated with the rebellious nations are involved in the judgment.[c] **rolled .. scroll,** fig. from the books of the period.[d] **fall down,** R. V., "fade away, as the leaf fadeth," when the vine is stricken with frost or blight.

Things That are Eternal.—We look upon "all the host of heaven" as the very symbols of security. When we would signify some idea of eternity, we think of the sun that burns from age to age, without loss of light. But there is nothing eternal but right; nothing grand but truth; nothing worth preserving but pureness and love. In vain we seek to hide ourselves behind the sun; God's judgment will strike through that wall of fire and find us if we had stood before it face to face in open defiance: in vain we think to plunge ourselves into the forests of the constellations, and lose ourselves in the mysteries of the intricacies of the heavens; when God looks all things fall away from his gaze, and the sun is left to return to an angry yet loving God.—People's Bible.

5, 6. (5) **For,** etc., now begins the specific sentence against Edom.[e] **sword .. bathed,** R. V., "hath drunk its fill," having first executed vengeance on the evil hosts of heaven it will now descend to the earth.

a Ps. xlix. 1.

b "This suggests the several ideas of contemptuous neglect, of a multitude too vast to be interred, and perhaps of survivors too few to perform the duty." —J. A. Alexander.

c Mat. xxiv. 29; 2 Pe. iii. 7—10; Re. vi. 13, 14.

d "Prob. allusion to the phenomena of storms, in wh. the sky is first overcast, and then covered with clouds, the motion of which gives it the appearance of being rolled together." —J. D. Michaelis.

e "Edom was the ancient and inveterate enemy of the Jews."—Henderson.

Nu. xx. 14—21; Ps. cxxxvii. 7; Ob. 10—15.

Idumaea, Edom.[f] (6) **fat .. rams,** the slaughter of the people of Edom is described under the fig. of a great sacrifice. **Bozrah,** the chief city of Edom. Now El Busaireh, in the mountainous region S.E. of the Dead Sea, half-way between it and Petra.[g]

Idumæa as it is, a Testimony to the Truth of Scripture.—The publication, in 1838, by Laborde and Linant, of their great work, Voyage de l'Arabie Petrêe, with its splendid engravings, has presented before the mind a bird's-eye view of the utter desolation of the country of Esau, such as would be beyond the power of mere verbal description. The topographical view of the land, taken from El Nakb, gives at a glance a most striking view of the land of Edom as it is, "most desolate," the "desolation of desolations," a once fertile region made bare, the line of confusion, and the stones of emptiness stretched over it. When He whose prerogative it is to define the bounds of our habitation gave to Esau his inheritance, it was thus described through the lips of the patriarch Isaac:—"Behold, thy dwelling shall be the fatness of the earth, and the dews of heaven from above;" and that it was such a land the allusions and descriptions of the Book of Job give abundant evidence (Job xix. 23, 24, xxxi. 35, 36,). It was a land exalted as high as wealth and art could raise it, the abode of a high state of civilization and commerce, and a country in which the arts had made considerable progress (Job. xxxiii. 1—11). But the sons of Edom transgressed, and woes were denounced against them and their territory, which have been as strikingly fulfilled as those beneath whose tremendous weight Nineveh, and Babylon, and Tyre, and Bethsaida, and Capernaum lie prostrate and forgotten. "Behold, O mount Seir, I am against thee, and I will make thee most desolate. Because thou hast had a perpetual hatred, and hast shed the blood of the children of Israel by the force of the sword in the time of their calamity" (Ezek. xxxv. 3, 5). Now "wisdom is departed from Teman, and understanding has perished out of the mount of Esau," and the wanderers in that region are sunk in the grossest folly, regarding the ruins around them as the work of evil spirits (Obadiah 8). Travelers assert that the minds of the Bedouins are as bare and uncultivated as the deserts they traverse. "Our sheikh, Hassan," says Dr. Robinson, "had never known a Bedouin who could read; he had only heard that there were some in the far east."

7, 8. (7) **unicorns,** R. V., "wild oxen," an animal now extinct, but pictured on Assyrian bas-reliefs.[a] **fatness,** i. e. enriched by the decaying bodies of the slain.[b] (8) **vengeance,** ch. lxiii. 4. **controversy of Zion,** i. e. God arises to plead for Zion.[c]

The Real Needs of Those to Whom Preaching is Addressed.—It cannot be denied that fear is a strong constraining motive. Human laws are enforced by penalties, the object of which is to "put men in fear." Punishment holds its place in every system of moral training, and punishment is an appeal to fear. Whatever may be the case with a chosen few, the bulk of mankind will always be more readily influenced by fear than by hope, by punishments than by rewards, by threats than by promises. The preacher cannot afford to lose the moral force which is thus put within his reach. It is hard enough to restrain men from evil courses, and induce them to lead a godly life, by freely using all the means of persuasion that are in our power. To refrain from using one of the most potent would be to fight Satan with one hand instead of two.—Pul. Com.

9, 10. (9) **pitch,** "This may plausibly be taken for a graphic description of an eruption of bitumen," such as was not uncommon. Sodom was in the neighborhood.[d] Edom extended from the S.E. shore of the Dead Sea, the tomb of the cities of the plain. (10) **not be quenched,** comp. **Jude 7. smoke,** etc., Re. xviii. 18, xix. 3. "The eternity of the desolation is four times asserted."

Degeneracy.—It is a sad descent, a melancholy instance of degeneracy, when the thickly peopled city is abandoned by mankind, is untrodden by the human foot, and becomes the haunt of the wild beast, of the obscene bird, and of the "night-monster." The last and worst penalty which God's indignation inflicts on the children of men is utter spiritual degeneracy—the mind losing its intellectual faculties, and becoming imbecile through vice and folly; the will broken down and become helpless, bent and swayed with every breeze; the heart hardened so that

f "Type of those who, belonging to the seed of promise, forfeited their privileges." — Spk. Com.

g Ge. xxxvi. 33.

"Give me the comforts of God, and I can well bear the taunts of men. If my God will give me ever the light of His smile, and glance of His benediction, it is enough. Yea, death, slay me, but I have another life, a life in the light of God's countenance." — Spurgeon.

"It was an ethical maxim, extensively accepted among ancient nations, that men must suffer the same pains that they inflicted on others. The later Greeks called this the Neoptolemic tisis, from the circumstance that Neoptolemus was punished in the same way in which he had sinned. He had murdered at the altar, and at the altar he was murdered."

a Job xxxix. 9.

b Virgil says that Rom. blood had twice enriched the soil of Macedonia.

c "To assert the rights of the true city of God against all that harass her." — Spk. Com.

d Is. xiii. 19; De. xxix. 23, 24.

Comp. Is. lxvi. 24.

"There are to the S. E. of the Dead Sea, within three days' journey, upwards of eighty ruined towns absolutely desolated; several with large edifices."—Volney.

all feeling of pity and affection has departed; the soul foregoing and forgetting its higher aspirations and sunk into the condition in which it craves nothing better than worldly increase or animal indulgence. Sad as is the loss of position or estate when the powerful prince becomes a menial or the wealthy merchant becomes a beggar, immeasurably sadder in the sight of Heaven is that spiritual degeneracy in which, as the inevitable wages of sin, a human spirit loses all its nobility of character and becomes an outcast in creation, mere driftwood on **the ocean, the** sport of the devouring waves.—Pul. Com.

"The punishment of degeneration is simply degeneration — the loss of functions, the decay of organs, the atrophy of the spiritual nature." — Drummond.

11—13. (11) **cormorant,** R. V., "pelican."[a] **bittern,** R. V., "porcupine," ch. xiv. 23. **owl,** better, heron or crane.[b] **line of confusion.** "Jehovah will stretch out thereon the measuring line of Chaos and the plummet of Desolation."—Pol. Bib.[c] **stones,** R. V., plummet. (12) **nobles,** fr. whom the Edomite kings were elected. (13) **dragons,** R. V. "jackals."[c] **owls, R. V.** "ostriches."

[a] Le. xi. 18; De. xiv. 17; Ps. cii. 6.

This bird frequents places remote from the habitations of man: so is a sign of desolate desert regions.

[b] Mangles, while at Petra, describes the screaming of the eagles, hawks, and owls, seemingly annoyed at any one approaching their lonely habitation.

"It should be laid waste with as much care and exactness as men usually apply in building."—Spk. Com.

Idumæa.—Dr. Robinson finding himself on the "rolling desert of Arabah," says,—"A more frightful desert it had hardly been our lot to behold. Now and then a lone shrub of the Ghudah was almost the only trace of vegetation. The mountains beyond presented a most uninviting and hideous aspect; precipices and naked conical peaks of chalky and gravelly formation rising one above another without a sign of life or vegetation." True, after stumbling over many gulleys, they met with a fountain of which he says, "The water was sweet, but, like all desert fountains, had a sickly hue, as if it could bless nothing with fertility." All modern travelers unite in the declaration that it is one broad plain of barrenness and desolation, and that its present state could not be more graphically described than it is in the words of the prophetic writers. "These portray," says Dr. Olin, "a state of desolation and ruin the most absolute and irretrievable, such as probably no portion of the globe once populous and fertile now exhibits." The fearful denunciations of the Prophets against this once rich and beautiful region and its highly civilized inhabitants, and their fulfilment, furnish an invulnerable argument in favor of the inspiration of the Holy Scriptures. In the words of a modern writer, "Read here in the word of prophecy what desolations are foretold,—look here, over the land of Edom, how all is fulfilled, and can you but confess that this book is from God?"

[c] Is. xiii. 22.

"Animals that delight in solitude are certainly meant, but the particular species is, more or less, matter of conjecture."—Pul. Com.

Desolation.—

"On rolls the stream with a perpetual sigh;
The rocks moan wildly as it passes by;
Hyssop and wormwood border all the strand,
And not a flower adorns the dreary land."—Bryant.

14, 15. (14) **wild beasts,**[d] Is. xiii. 21, 22. **Meet with the wild beasts,** R. V., "meet with the wolves," **satyr,** or shaggy he-goat; **screech owl,** R. V., "the night monster shall settle there." Heb. Lilith, from lil, night.[e] "Charms against Lilith may be bought today in East London."—Pol. Bib. Render with Cheyne: the night-hag. Lilith appears to be a creation of the Babylonian demonology. "This Lilith plays a great part in the Talmudic demonology; the cabalistic Rabbis forged a whole legend in which this spirit is said to have taken a feminine form to deceive Adam, and to have united herself to him."—Lenormant. She is mentioned in the Bible only here.—Camb. Bib. (15) **great owl,** R. V., "arrow-snake." **lay .. shadow,** quite undisturbed by any passers by.[f] **mate,** indicating settlement in the district for breeding purpose.

[d] "The wild cats shall meet the jackals." —Henderson.

[e] "Lilith corresponding to the Lamia of Greek and Roman demonology, a she-demon haunting waste places, and supposed to be especially fatal to children."—Mat. Arnold.

The Soul's Desolation and Need of Reconciliation:—Certainly a soul, sensible as to what the loss of communion with God is, counts it hath not fulfilled all its errand, when it hath bare peace given it. Should God say, "Soul I am friends with thee, I have ordered that thou shalt never go to hell, here is a discharge under My hand that thou shalt never be arrested for any debt more: but as for any fellowship with Me, thou canst expect none: I have done with thee for ever, never to be acquainted with thee more." Certainly the soul would find little joy with such peace. Were the fire out as to positive torments, yet a hell would be left in the dismal darkness which the soul would sit under for want of God's presence. A wicked heart seeks reconciliation without any longing after fellowship with God. Like the traitor, if the king will but

[f] "The general sense evidently is that a human population should be succeeded by wild and lonely animals, who should not only live, but breed there, implying total and continued desolation." —Alexander.

pardon and save him from the gallows, he is ready to promise him never to trouble him at Court; 'tis his own life, not the king's favor, he desires.—W. Gurnall.

16, 17. (16) **book** the expression "book of Jehovah" appears to point to the existence of a prophetic canon; and the opening exhortation presupposes a habit of searching for evidences of the fulfilment of prophecy. All these circumstances would indicate a late date for the composition of this oracle."—Cam. Bib.[a] **of these,** "take the book of Isaiah with you to Edom, and you will find that this reference to wild creatures is strictly accurate."—Pol. Bib. (17) **cast the lot,** i. e. arranged their lot; appointed Edom for these wild beasts. With evident allusion to God's dividing the land of Canaan among His people by lot.[b]

[a] Comp. De. xxviii. 58, xxix. 20, 27; 2 Ki. xxii. 13; Is. xxix. 11, 12, 18, xxx. 8.

[b] "He who originally allotted the land to the people (Nu. xxvi. 55; Jos. xix. 51) will now make it over by a formal act of transfer to these gloomy denizens." — Spk. Com.

"I would that every student of the Bible would take the motto which Bengel took for his guidance in study: "Apply thyself wholly to the Scriptures, and the Scriptures wholly to thyself." Learned critics are applying themselves wholly to the Scriptures with microscopic intensity of search and research, but they neglect the other half. We hear of some people who are famous at taking a sword and cutting up the Scripture, but we would like to see the Scripture, which is itself a sword, go through these men and cut some of them up, to their improvement as men.—A. J. Gordon.

CHAPTER THE THIRTY-FIFTH.

From the picture of judgment the prophet turns to that of the redemption of Israel. **1, 2.** (1) **wilderness,**[a] as contrasted with Edom—in Palestine there shall be no desert place. **rose,** probably the meadow saffron, an autumnal flower with bulbous roots.[b] "The beautiful white narcissus so common in spring in the plain of Sharon."—Pol. Bib. (2) **glory,** etc., i. e. what had lain barren and waste was now to equal the most beautiful and magnificent scenes of nature. **Lebanon,** famous for its trees. **Carmel,** famous for its flowers. **Sharon,** famous for its fertiity.[c] "The fairest parts of the Holy Land shall share their beauty with less favored districts."—Cheyne. **they shall see,** i. e. the returning people of God.

Glorious Prospects of the Gospel Church (vss. 1, 2.)—I. The state of persons and places unenlightened by the Gospel. 1. Such a place must be a dreary wilderness; 2. The same is true of souls. II. The state to which they are brought by the Gospel. 1. Beautiful description of the change; beauty of the rose; stability of the cedar; 2. Fruitfulness of the richest pastures; 3. Unutterable joy as the result of all. III. Particular view of the Gospel by which these effects are wrought. Simple exhibition of Christ crucified, and perfections of God united in the work of redemption. 1. To this it is ascribed in the Word of God; 2. To this it is traced in experience of all.—Simeon.

Prevailing Joy.—The whole strain of the passage is jubilant, and it speaks of the desert "rejoicing with joy and singing." Sin and sadness are most intimately associated; even if they are not so inseparably allied as to be always seen together, they are so essentially connected that when one appears the other is sure to follow. It is a guilty world that knows so much of disappointment, of regret, of grief, of shame. But when the truth of God has wrought its full effect on the human soul, the prevailing note, even of the earthly life, will be that of joy. The near presence of the heavenly Father, the close friendship of the Divine Redeemer, the happy service of love, the blessed work of doing good, the exulting hope of heavenly bliss,—these are sources of joy which quicken and animate the soul, which make a holy human life radiant with a blessedness which anticipates the glory of the skies.—Clarkson. Civilization Unable to Renew Heathendom.—The civilization of Greece and Rome did not affect anything in the way of changing spiritual death into spiritual life. The utmost which it succeeded in effecting was to cover the frightful corruption of death with a more beautiful funeral pall—to hide the naked hideousness of sin behind a veil spangled with silver, and gold, and precious stones. But death was there none the less, and sin of such a kind that the foulest impurities of the most degraded heathen could not exceed the impurities of Athens and of Rome. The old lesson is being taught us, if we would but learn it, in our own day. It is not civilization that can change the moral desolation of France, of Spain, of Austria. It is not civilization, as understood by men of science and doctrinaire philosophers, that can change the moral wilderness existing in our large cities, and in much of our rural population. It will only do what it did in Greece; it will merely cover the ghastliness of death with a more decent covering.—Kay.

[a] "In contrast to the ruin of Edom the Prophet now describes Israel's triumphant march home through the blossoming wilderness."—Matthew Arnold.

Comp. Is. xli. 18, 19, xliii. 20, xlviii. 21, li. 3, 11, lv. 12, 13.

[b] Song Sol. ii. 1. "Colchicum autumnale, or meadow saffron."—Gesenius.

[c] Comp. Song Sol. iii. 9, iv. 8, 11, 15, vii. 4, ii. 1.

"There is not the least flower but seems to hold up its head, and look pleasantly, in the secret sense of the goodness of its heavenly Maker. This silent rhetoric, though we cannot hear, but only see it, is so full and expressive, that David thought he spoke neither impropriety nor nonsense, in a strong line, when he said, 'even the valleys break forth into singing.'"

"It would be thought a great thing for a king to bend down and release the slave. Yet God's own Son, God Himself 'manifest' is our Deliverer." — Pul. Com.

a Heb. xii. 12.

b "The image presented is that of persons who can scarcely lift up their hands, or stand upon their legs."—Gill.

c "Impatient of delay in the execution of God's promises." — Clericus.

"Sorrow, that like an ocean, dark, deep, rough, and shoreless, roll'd its billows o'er the soul perpetually, and without hope of end."—Pollok.

d "So conspicuous and overpowering would be the interference of God on behalf of His people, that those of the most obtuse intellect could not fail to perceive it." — Henderson.

Our Lord appeals to this prophecy. See Mat. xi. 4—6; Lu. vii. 22.

e See Ex. xvii. 6; Ps. lxxiv. 15, lxxviii. 15, 16.

The word sharab, "parched ground," A. V., more exactly

3, 4. (3) **Strengthen ye,**[a] by encouraging assurances. The journey from Babylon to Jerusalem was a very long, difficult, and wearying one. especially trying to the weak and feeble ones of the company. **weak hands,** "that are relaxing their hold on God's promises."[b] (4) **fearful heart,** lit. hasty, whose heart palpitates through fear.[c] **behold your God,** etc., R. V., margin: "behold your God! vengeance cometh, the recompence of God." **vengeance,** upon His people's enemies. **he will come,** emphatically He Himself.

To the Fearful-hearted (vs. 4).—I. A counsel. Be strong—1. In the power of religious principle; 2. In the power of prayer; 3. In the power of Divine grace; 4. In the power of Christ. II. A caution. Fear not—1. On account of the greatness of your sins; 2. On account of your remaining corruptions; 3. On account of the dark dispensations of Providence.—G. Brooks.

The Believer's Weakness.—A believer finds himself weak in knowledge; a simple child in the knowledge of God and Divine things. He is weak in love; the sacred flame does not rise with a perpetual fervor. He is weak in faith; he cannot suspend his all upon God's promises with cheerful confidence, nor build a firm fabric of hope upon the rock, Jesus Christ. He is weak in hope; his hope is dashed with rising billows of fears and jealousies. He is weak in repentance; troubled with that plague of plagues, a hard heart. He is weak in resisting temptations; he is weak in prayer, a filial boldness, in approaching the mercy-seat. He is weak in courage to encounter the king of terrors. He is weak in everything in which he should be strong. These weaknesses the believer feels, and bitterly laments; and this sense of weakness keeps him dependent on Divine strength, enabling him to say: "When I am weak, then am I strong."—Pres. Davis. The Comprehensive Character of the Church of Christ.—In it are the weak as well as the strong. There is nothing whatever that is narrow about the Christian faith. It is not adapted to any particular class or character. In Jesus Christ there is neither male nor female, Greek nor Jew, cultivated nor uncultivated, bond nor free. And in him there is no favor reserved for any special disposition. It is not a gospel for those in particular who are most admired of men—for the strong, for the brave, for the wise, for the winning; it is a refuge for the weak, for the timid, for the unknown and the unbeloved. Those who are of no account at all amongst men, those whom human leaders would gladly leave out of their army as weakening rather than strengthening their forces,—these are all welcome to flock to the standard and to fight under the banner of the heavenly Prince.—Pul. Com.

5, 6. (5) **eyes . . opened,** comp. Is. vi. 9, 10.[d] (6) **lame . . leap,** for literal fulfilment in Messianic times, see Ac. iii. 18, xiv. 10. **waters break out,** to the Eastern mind this bursting forth of a plentiful stream in an arid desert is one of the most beautiful and affecting images.[e] Comp. Is. xli. 18, xliii. 19, 20, xliv. 3, 4. All of these figures declare a wonderful, blessed and miraculous change that is to occur, as if those who were blind were suddenly to receive their sight, etc.

The Way to the Better Land.—No jars and discords shall spoil the melody of our spheres; our holiness shall need no crutch, but reach the fulness of a perfect stature. This vale of tears quit for rivers of eternal pleasures, our rights can never be invaded there; nothing can stain the comforts of that world; no blots nor wounds are there contracted or endured; no troubles in that Israel. There are no pauses of astonishment through surprisals of affliction; death smites no corners there; providence makes no storms; the glory of that place knows no eclipse nor cloud; there charity knows no breach; there are no wrinkles on the brow of God, nor frowns upon the face of Majesty.—M. Sylvester.

7, 8. (7) **parched ground,** i. e. burning sand which produces the deceptive mirage. **dragons,** R. V., "jackals," or wolves, whose haunts are in dry places. **reeds and rushes,** the sure sign of moisture. (8) **highway,** see Is. xi. 16. A plain open path even through the desert regions. **way of holiness,** i. e. the way marked out by the Holy One, for the holy ones to walk over. **for those,** "better (with an emendation of the text): "but it shall be for his people." It is probable also that the next words should be joined to this clause,—"it shall be for His people when it walks in the way; fools shall not see therein."—Camb. B.[a] **fools.** unable to guide themselves: these should have Divine guidance.

The King's Highway (vs. 8).—I. The path by which they go—"a highway." II. The pilgrim's passport—"a way of holiness." III. The protection they enjoy—"He shall be with them." IV. The immunity vouchsafed—"the wayfaring men, though fools, shall not err therein."—Preacher's Portfolio.—1. Highway of salvation is a raised, or made way. Illustration from custom of levelling roads and taking out stones for a royal progress. Show how Christ in His work levelled the road to God. 2. Highway of salvation is a holy way. No unclean pass over it. Yet it is for sinners, but only penitent sinners. Show who out of Bible story have trodden it. 3. Highway of salvation is a simple way. The difficulties we put in the way. A wicket-gate lies at head of the way, and by it we must enter.

A Safe Way.—This is important in our own country, where there are no ferocious animals lying in wait to destroy; but it was peculiarly important in Judæa and the countries adjoining it. Many parts of these are said to have been infested with beasts of prey, which frequently rushed from their places of concealment upon the passing traveler, and rendered even the public roads exceedingly dangerous. Hence the prophet says of the way to heaven through Christ, that "no lion shall be there, nor any ravenous beast go up thereon; it shall not be found there." Not that we are to conclude that the redeemed have no foes to combat, and no difficulties to surmount in their course. Like the Israelites returning from Babylon, they have to pass through an enemy's country in their journey to Zion. But He who has redeemed them accompanies them in their pilgrimage; and though they are called to struggle and fight, He gives them the victory, and renders their path as safe as though there were no dangers near it, nor any to hurt and destroy.—Bradley. The Lord's Highway.—The difficulties we make; they are not really in the way. The way of salvation seems to wise people full of mystery, yet it is grasped by the wayfaring, the fool, the child. None need miss the way, for it is thoroughly well fitted with directions and guide-posts. We may blind ourselves, and refuse to see them. We may put obstacles in our own path. The one great obstacle takes many forms. What we really want is to keep our wilfulness; to make a way of our own; to get God to save us on our own terms. There is the highway open right before us, and we persist in looking this way and that, if so be we may find any way but Christ's way of penitence and faith.—R. Tuck.

9, 10. (9) **lion,** type of perils in the wilderness from savage animals. **walk,** or advance safely and securely along this way. A change has occurred in the animal world as wonderful as that in the nature of the desert. This the constant thought of prophecy. All nature is to be redeemed with man. (10) **ransomed,** Is. li. 11. **return,** to their own beloved city.[a] **obtain,** Cheyne, "overtake."

The Joy of the Ransomed (vs. 10).—I. The people here mentioned, "The Ransomed of the Lord." II. What is said of them, "They shall return," etc. III. Their future portion. "They shall obtain joy," etc. IV. Remarks in application.—R. L. Armstrong.

"Looming sand-waste," refers to the mirage, of which it is the Arabic name. The vain shadows of the world, which deceive and never satisfy, are to be replaced by the enduring joys of the kingdom of God.—Birks.

[a] "For the chosen people, who shall find the way so plain and easy, that the weakest can march in it without difficulty." — Matthew Arnold.

No one can imagine, without actual experience, the delight and eager expectation (when the vision first is seen), or the intense and bitter disappointment which the appearance of a mirage occasions to travelers, specially when their supply of water is spent.

"The Lord's highway is a well-kept way, broad, plentifully supplied with sunshine, margined with all fairest flowers and most fruitful trees; and the whole avenue, stretching heavenward, shall be filled with the ransomed of the Lord, bought, but not with money, redeemed, but not with price, and they shall come to Zion with songs. The song must always have a place in human history. The fool tries to sing his sorrow away, but there is no reason in the music, so the song is a failure. But this music is to be the last expression of a long process of discipline and chastening." — Parker.

CHAPTER THE THIRTY-SIXTH.

"Chaps. xxxvi., xxxvii. give the historical narrative of the events, the moral results of which we have seen so vivid in chap. xxxiii.—the perfidous return of the Assyrians to Jerusalem after Hezekiah had bought them off and their final disappearance from the Holy Land."—G. A. Smith. **1—3.** (1) **came to pass,** comp. with the narratives in the historical books, 2 Ki. xviii. 13—20, xix; 2 Chr. xxxii. **fourteenth year,** B. C. 701. **Sennacherib,** this name on the Assyrian inscriptions can be recognized only with some uncertainty. Sennac. was viceroy for Sargon, his father, who was king at the time.[a] **defenced cities,** outlying forts, intended to check an invader. (2) **Rabshakeh,** an official title said to mean "chief of the officers." For the other officers see 2 Ki. xviii. 17. **Lachish,** a frontier

[a] Herodotus informs us that the expedition

was made against Sethos, king of Egypt, and rebellious Judah, wh. had refused its tribute, was to be dealt with on the way.

[b] Jos. x. 3; 2 Chr. xi. 9; Jer. xxxiv. 7.

"Blessed is any weight, however overwhelming, which God has been so good as to fasten with His own hand upon our shoulders." — F. W. Faber.

"God forgive them that raise an ill report upon the sweet cross of Christ; it is but our weak and dim eyes, that look but to the black side, that make us mistake." — S. Rutherford.

"We have nothing to fear from the boastful Rabshakehs of our day. The assaults to which our faith is now subjected are nothing new. Old weapons are refurbished, old stratagems resorted to; but it has survived attacks as clever as those now made upon it." —Wm. Guthrie.

"It was a good remark made by Professor Ball to a lady who put to him some questions about comets, to each of which he replied, 'I do not know.' 'Then,' she said, 'may I ask what is the use of your science?' 'To let me know, madam,' he replied, 'that I cannot know some things.'"

[a] "Rabshakeh speaks here as if he had been instructed by some of the apostate Israelites, who pretended to worship 'the Lord' under the forms of heathen worship. To them Hezekiah

town S.W. of Jerusalem.[b] **conduit,** etc., see Is. vii. 2. (3) **scribe,** or secretary. **recorder,** or royal historian.

Sennacherib's Bismarck.—In all the Bible there is not a personage more clever than this Rabshakeh, nor more typical. He was an able deputy of the king who sent him, but he represented still more thoroughly the temper of the civilization to which he belonged. There is no word of this man which is not characteristic. A clever, fluent diplomatist, with a traveler's knowledge of men and the conqueror's contempt for them, the Rabshakeh is the product of a victorious empire like the Assyrian, or, say, like the British. Our services sometimes turn out the like of him—a creature able to speak to natives in their own language, full and ready of information, mastering the surface of affairs at a glance, but always baffled by the deeper tides which sway nations; a deft player upon party interests and the superficial human passions, but unfit to touch the deep strings of men's religion and patriotism. Let us speak, however, with respect of the Rabshakeh. From his rank (Sayce calls him the Vizier), as well as from the cleverness with which he explains what we know to have been the policy of Sennacherib towards the populations of Syria, he may well have been the inspiring mind at this time of the great Assyrian empire—Sennacherib's Bismarck.—Exp. Bib.

4, 5. (4) **to Hezekiah,** obs. that "Rabshakeh nowhere calls him king." **What confidence,** the officer assumed that, confident of Egyptian help, Hezekiah had thrown off the Assyrian yoke by refusing the tribute. (5) **I say,** R. V., "I say, thy counsel and strength for the war are but vain words;" others translate, "Thinkest thou a mere word of the lips is counsel and strength for war?" (Cheyne, Camb. Bib.)[a] Rabshakeh would not understand Hezekiah's trust in God. **rebellest,** "Eight years after the destruction of the kingdom of Israel, Hezekiah refused to pay his tribute any longer."—Mat. Arnold.

The Believer's Trust (vs. 5).—I. An important question. II. The Christian's answer. 1. In the Father, believing that He has chosen me, that He will protect me, teach, guide; 2. In His Son, my Brother, my Saviour, my Intercessor, my Advocate; 3. In the Holy Spirit, that He will drive all sin out, curb my temper, subdue my will, enlighten my understanding, comfort my despondency, help my weakness, etc. III. Application:—If we trust the triune God, we trust a power that is never exhausted, a love that never wanes, a kindness that never changes, a wisdom that is never nonplussed, a faithfulness that never fails.—C. H. Spurgeon.

The Believer.—
All joy to the believer! He can speak—
Trembling yet happy, confident yet meek—
"Since the dear hour that brought me to Thy foot,
And cut up all my follies by the root,
I never trusted in an arm but Thine,
Nor hoped but in Thy righteousness divine:
My prayers and alms, imperfect and defiled,
Were but the feeble efforts of a child;
Howe'er performed, it was their brightest part
That they proceeded from a grateful heart;
Cleansed in Thine own all-purifying blood,
Forgive their evil, and accept their good;
I cast them at Thy feet,—my only plea
Is what it was—dependence upon Thee,
While struggling in the vale of tears below,
That never failed, nor shall it fail me now."—Cowper.

6, 7. (6) **staff .. reed,** Eze. xxix. 6, 7. The reed, or cane, of the Nile was the symbol of the country. Sargon had already inflicted a heavy blow on Egypt. **so is Pharaoh,** comp. the experience of Samaria, Is. xxx. 3. (7) **Lord our God,** Rabshakeh had a very confused notion of the religion of the Jews, and fancied that Hezekiah had offended the national God, by the abolition of the local sanctuaries, and so even His protection had been removed from him.[a] **this altar,** the parallel passage of 2 Kings (xviii. 22) has "this altar in Jerusalem." **The brazen altar in the**

great court of the temple is, of course, meant. Hezekiah had cleansed it from the pollutions of the time of Ahaz (2 Chron. xxix. 18), and had insisted on sacrifice being offered nowhere else (2 Chron. xxix. 21—35; xxx. 15—24; xxxi. 1, etc.). Such a concentration of worship was unknown to any of the heathen nations, and may well have been unintelligible to them.—Pul. Com.

Modern Scepticism.—I put you on your guard against the scepticism of our time. And do you think that I am about to enlarge upon the scepticism of Rousseau, of Diderot, of Voltaire, of Bolingbroke, of Hobbes, and of Hume?—that was swept away with their ashes, and is buried. The great scepticisms of our time are market scepticism, political scepticism, and religious scepticism. Men who feel that it would be wicked to sacrifice great pecuniary interests for the sake of principle; men who think it would be a tempting of Providence to refuse profitable business speculations, to leave profitable situations, or to refuse dividends of evil; men whose consciences will not permit them, as the members of a corporation, to expose its wickedness; men who stand in the market, and feel that they have a right to do anything that wins,—these men are infidels. You need not tell me that they believe in the Bible: they believe in an empty Bible,—a Bible of the letter, and not a Bible of the spirit, which says to a man, "Sacrifice your right hand before you do your integrity."—H. W. Beecher.

was an irreverent iconoclast, a narrow - minded bigot." — Spk. Com.

"Neither scepticism nor agnosticism ever won a victory, ever slew a sin, ever healed a heartache, ever produced a ray of sunshine, ever saved an immortal soul. Unbelief is foredoomed to defeat; do not risk your eternity on that spider's web." — Theodore L. Cuyler.

8—10. (8) **pledges,** hostages, as security that payment of tribute shall be resumed. The hostages were to be two thousand soldiers fit for cavalry. Evidently Rabshakeh intended to taunt Hezekiah concerning his military inefficiency. The Jews were specially weak in cavalry, and in this branch the Assyrian army was strong.[b] (9) Pol. Bib. "How then canst thou repel the onset of one the least servants of my Lord? And yet thou puttest thy trust in Egypt," etc. (10) **the Lord said,** "that the Assyrian should represent himself as commissioned by Jehovah to avenge the desecration of his sanctuaries is not by any means incredible. A precisely similar sentiment it put into the mouth of Cyrus in his account of the conquest of Babylon. It expresses no serious religious conviction (see vs. 20)"—Camb. Bib.

[b] "Hezekiah might have furnished 2,000 men for Rabshakeh's army, but not 2,000 trained for cavalry, as the training of cavalry was forbidden by Mosaic law." —Henderson.

11, 12. (11) **Syrian language,** the Aramaic, the language of commerce, especially used in W. Asia. **Jews' language,** the Hebrew. It was the purpose of the Rabshakeh to destroy both the religious and military confidence of the common soldiers. This the Jewish officers also feared. (12) **men .. wall,** throughout Rabshakeh treats Hezekiah and his officers most contemptuously.[a] **that .. eat,** etc. Pol. Bib., "who will be driven to eat and drink filthy food with you?" **i. e.** as a result of Hezekiah's policy. Comp. vs. 16.

[a] "Isaiah, as a faithful historian, records the filthy and blasphemous language of the Assyrian, to mark aright the true character of the attack on Jerusalem." —Fausset.

Philosophical Doubt.—Although it has done harm, has also done good; good results have come with the spirit of investigation that has been developed. It was no great credit to Thomas that he did not believe the resurrection of Christ as others did, and yet what a wonderful chapter in the evidences of Christianity was opened by his scepticism! It was no great credit to men that they called in question the authenticity of the four gospels, but how their scepticism has stimulated scholarly inquiry and strengthened the defenses of the gospel narratives! When the elevated railroad was first started in New York the people were a little timid about riding on it; so the proprietors of the road took great pleasure in apprising the public of the fact that this road had been subjected to a most abnormal and enormous tonnage, and that consequently people of ordinary weight might deem themselves quite safe in traveling over that road. I feel the same way about the four gospels—that I can take my way to heaven above the din and dust of daily life because this elevated road has had all Germany upon it and that as yet it has given no sign of instability.—Francis L. Patton.

"If I once learn that there is the blessing of God in everything, what a life of blessing, and love and joy unspeakable I shall have. If I am a child of God every circumstance of my life, every comfort and every trial, comes from God in Christ. So if I give up my whole life to Jesus, nothing really harmful can touch a hair of my head." — Andrew Murray.

13—17. (13) **cried,** with evident intention of shaking the allegiance of the people, the customary policy of Sennacherib. (14) **deceive you,** by his assurances and promises. (15) **trust in the Lord,** he not only insults Hezekiah, but flings his insults directly at Jehovah, whose name and power were soon after vindicated in the awful destruction of Sennacherib's host. (16) **Make ..present,** R. V., "Make your peace with me, **and come,"** etc. **come out to me,** the ordinary phrase for surrender of a city. (17) **Until I come,** back from successful war with Egypt. **take you away,** it was regarded as politically necessary to the schemes of Assyria to remove the kingdom of Judah, which might seriously interfere with the conquest and holding of Egypt. Rabshakeh smoothes this over with fair promises.

Utility of Opposition.—A certain amount of opposition is a great help to a man. Kites rise against, and not with the wind. Even a head-wind is better than none. No man ever worked his passage anywhere in a dead calm. Let no man wax pale, therefore, because of opposition. Opposition is what he wants, and must have, to be good for anything. Hardship is the native soil of manhood and self-reliance. He that cannot abide the storm without flinching or quailing, strips himself in the sunshine, and lies down by the wayside to be overlooked and forgotten. He who but braces himself to the struggle when the winds blow, gives up when they have done, and falls asleep in the stillness that follows.—F. Neal.

18—21. (18) **any .. delivered,** Rabshakeh has the name of the Jews' God, but he classes Him with the gods of other nations. (19) **Hamath .. Arphad,** Is. x. 9. **Sepharvaim,**[a] now Sipphara, on the E. of Euphrates, above Babylon. (20) **that the Lord should,** this is a direct challenge to Jehovah to show Himself other than the gods of the nations. (21) **peace,**[b] **answer him not,** "we are not to suppose that the Jewish king was at a loss for an answer. He did not choose to bandy words with an envoy who had behaved himself so outrageously."

The Rabshakeh.—So clever were the speeches of the Rabshakeh. We see why he was appointed to this mission. He was an expert both in the language and religion of this tribe, perched on its rock in the remote Judæan highlands. For a foreigner he showed marvelous familiarity with the temper and internal jealousies of the Jewish religion. He turned these on each other almost as adroitly as Paul himself did in the disputes between Sadducees and Pharisees. How the fellow knew his cleverness, strutting there betwixt army and town! He would show his soldier friends the proper way of dealing with stubborn barbarians. He would astonish those faith-proud highlanders by exhibiting how much he was aware of the life behind their thick walls and silent faces.—G. A. Smith. God's Honor Vindicated by His Word.—Once upon a time a grand old Methodist preacher, called John Nelson—a man whose life ought to be read often on Saturday night by preachers who have got their skeletons ready, in order that they might be fired to do their work—was obliged to become a soldier, and as he was arrayed, and was being mocked by many, a woman came to him and said, "Nelson, where is now thy God? Thou didst say at Shent's door that thou hadst no more fear of all his promises failing than thou hadst of falling through the center of the earth. Where is now thy God?" You know how mocking a bad woman can be, what sharpness there is in her voice. Nelson, in whom the word of God dwelt richly, said, "You will find the answer in the seventh chapter of Micah, the eighth and tenth verses." "Rejoice not against me, O mine enemy; when I fall, I shall arise; when I sit in darkness, the Lord shall be a light unto me. Then she that is mine enemy shall see it, and shame shall cover her which said unto me, Where is the Lord thy God? mine eyes shall behold her: now shall she be trodden down as the mire of the streets." Everything is in the Bible!—Peop. Bib.

22. clothes rent, as a sign of their distress at the blasphemies to wh. they had been compelled to listen. See Is. xxxiii. 7, xxxvii. 1; Matt. xxvi. 65.

Unavailing Fear.—He that trembles at the very sight of his burden, with what courage will he be able to stand under it? Can the trembling of the lamb keep off or mitigate the rage of the wolf? He that continually torments himself with the fear of an approaching evil, does anticipate his misery, not avoid it. Every strong apprehension of an object is a certain approximation of it to the soul. Fear makes the evil that is feared present to a man, in respect of its trouble, before it can be present in its existence: wherefore it is so far from keeping off a calamity that it brings it before its time. It was not Hezekiah's fear of Sennacherib, but his confidence in God that did protect him.—Smith.

"Christ never failed to distinguish between doubt and unbelief. Doubt is 'can't believe'; unbelief is 'won't believe.' Doubt is honesty; unbelief is obstinacy. Doubt is looking for light; unbelief is content with darkness." —Drummond.

"Young gentlemen, believe your belief, and doubt your doubts; do not make the mistake of doubting your beliefs and believing your doubts." —C. F. Deems.

a Ki. xvii. 24.

b Ex. xiv. 14.

"Silence is the birthplace of the world's progress, and from the rays of truth that flash into it are born the grand visions of the prophets of God, and kingly purposes too; and from these are forged the weapons with which men shall sweep away the hindrances to all wisdom." — J. Macrae Simcock.

"Very many of the bravely uttered scepticisms of our time are only designed to draw attention to those who utter them. Leave them alone. They are nothing; we must take care not to swell them into something by directing attention to them. Those who have faith in God make grave mistakes when they too vigorously defend God against the arrows of mere children." —Pul. Com.

Van Lennep says that nowadays this tearing of garments is quite a sham. They only split a seam down a little way, so that it can easily be mended.

CHAPTER THE THIRTY-SEVENTH.

1, 2. (1) **sackcloth,** rough hair garment: a further sign of humiliation and grief.[a] (2) **unto Isaiah,** "the embassy consists of two chief ministers, and the 'elders of the priests.' The appearance of Shebna on such an errand was a striking evidence of the completeness of Isaiah's moral victory (ch. xxii. 15 ff.)."—Camb. Bib.

Believing is Trusting.—There is a boy whose father was buried yesterday. To-day he is wearing his father's gold watch. Some wicked lads are trying to take it from him. He is struggling to keep it; but they are too strong for him. He is just about to lose it, when I come up, and say, "Give it to me, my boy, and I'll keep it safe for you." For a moment he looks at me with doubtful eye; but as I say to him, "Trust me!" and he sees that I am earnest and sincere, he hands it over to me, and I prevent him from being robbed. That is just what the Apostle Paul says of himself. He had, as you have, something far more precious than a gold watch—an immortal soul; and he was afraid of losing it: he could not keep it himself. Jesus said, "Give it to Me," and he gave it to Him; and then you hear him say rejoicingly, "I know whom I have believed" (which is the same thing as whom I have trusted), "and am persuaded that He will keep that which I have committed to Him against that day." You, my dear friends, have souls too, and they are in danger of being lost; there is only one way of getting them saved—giving them into the keeping of Jesus, "trusting" Him with them. What warrant have you for trusting Him? Just what Paul had—His own word; and that is always enough.—J. H. Wilson.

[a] 1 Ki. viii. 29. Ps. lxxiii. 16, 17, lxxvii. 13.

"Of the king's prompt appeal to God in his extremity, Gill quaintly says, Hezekiah does not sit down to consider Rabshakeh's speech, to take it in pieces, and give an answer to it, but he applies unto God."—Alexander.

"In all ages the people of God have really had nothing to trust to but God Himself..... It has always been difficult to trust the purely spiritual." —Parker.

3—5. (3) **rebuke,** or reproof, for an Assyrian policy of Ahaz, the bitterness of which the people were now made to feel. **blasphemy, R. V.,** "contumely." **children .. forth,**[b] a poetical figure for disappointed expectations. When Hezekiah threw off the Assyrian yoke, the people looked for perfect security from evil consequences. But now they were humiliated and in extreme peril. (4) **lift up thy prayer,** act, that is, as national intercessor. **remnant, i. e.** the two tribes composing the kingdom of Judah.

The Greatness of Prayer that Rises to be Intercession.—Man's power of prayer is a faculty full of high possibilities. It may rise even to this—it may go beyond all self-spheres, and become intercessory. While prayer keeps in the self-sphere there is a certain narrowness and even meanness about it. It is all concerned with what we want, and what we feel, and we are greatly comforted if we have any fervor of emotion in such prayer. But we feel that a course of daily prayer from which the interceding element is removed would be most injurious to the spiritual life. It lacks the generous, sympathetic, unselfish element, and it will very soon lack fervor and faith. No one can long keep up a prayerful life, and persist in praying altogether about himself. Power comes, love grows, when prayer includes intercession. Limitations of earnestness and importunity pass away; the soul is free to urge its pleas with persevering instancy; we can ask for another what we dare not fashion into a prayer for ourselves. The prayers of Scripture are, for the most part, intercessory—Abraham's for Sodom; Moses', Joshua's, Samuel's, for the people of Israel in their distresses. Daniel prays with the window open towards desolate Jerusalem, that he may be reminded of the captive people. Our last sight of Job finds him in the attitude of the mediator, praying for God's mercy on his mistaken and cruel friends. And the Apostle Paul writes again and again of the constancy of his intercessions. We may learn the secret of the poverty and formality of much Christian praying. It has so little intercession in it. When some beloved friend is smitten down with imperiling sickness, our prayer suddenly gains strength, and becomes a thing full of fervor and pathos. All our souls then go out in strong crying and tears. But this power might be in our praying always. We might be not only prayerful men, but also prayer-leaders, carrying the burdens of others to the throne of grace, and ourselves sanctified through the carrying.—Pul. Com.

[b] Is. xxvi. 18.

"But be not long; for in the tedious minutes—exquisite interval—I'm on the rack; for sure the greatest evil man can know bears no proportion to this dread suspense."—Froude.

"Why should I start at the plough of my Lord, that maketh deep furrows in my soul? I know He is no idle husbandman, He purposeth a crop."—S. Rutherford.

"There is but one thing of which I am afraid, and that is fear."—Montaigne.

"The direst foe of courage is the fear itself, not the object of it; and the man who can overcome his own terror is a hero and more." —George MacDonald.

"Some are in the habit of shouting, 'No surrender;' but I say we should all surrender; we should surrender our passions, and our prejudices, and our uncharitableness towards others. We should seek to win as much as we can from the common humanity of our adversaries. The good and the wise will pursue this course, and they will succeed; whilst the treacherous, the arrogant, and the intolerant will dwindle far behind in the march, and will perish of self-contention, instead of coming up to win the laurels." —Bamford.

a "Tirhakah was one of the most famous conquerors of ancient times. He was at this time either in close alliance with Egypt, or more prob. in actual possession of Thebais, or Upper Egypt."—Alexander.

b Comp. Is. xxxvi. 18—21.

"It is the want of the discerning faculty, the clairvoyant power of seeing the eternal in the temporal, rather than the failure of the reason, that begets the sceptic."—Drummond.

a Is. xiv. 16.

b 2 Ki. xvii. 6, xviii. 11.

"The Gauzanitis of Ptolemy. To it a portion of the ten tribes were transferred by Shalmaneser. The modern Kaushan." —Alexander.

Tel means a hill in Arabic and Assyrian names.

c Musculus understands the dual form of Sepharvaim as denoting that it

6, 7. (6) **not afraid,** there was no reason for fear if God took up the case, and vindicated His insulted majesty. **blasphemed me,** obs. that the Me is emphatic. (7) **blast,** R. V., "I will put a spirit in him," i. e. "a spirit of craven fear, depriving him of his natural courage and resourcefulness. How the spirit will work is stated in what follows: a mere rumor will drive him back to his own land, there to meet his death (cf. 2 Ki. vii. 6). There is no allusion in this oracle to the disastrous blow recorded in vs. 36. The 'rumor' is no doubt that of the approach of Tirhakah (vs. 9)."—Camb. Bib.[a]

"We cannot at times help the entrance of evil, but we can help the entertainment of it. We must treat all the evil surmises of wicked men with the disdain that they deserve. We can, as Solomon suggests, 'turn from it and pass away.' Besides, just as there is in love what Dr. Chalmers calls 'the expulsive power of a new affection,' so there is in love to God a power to banish all that old love of the world which makes men mingle with the irreverent and undevout. The syren voice of evil whisperings will have no charm for us when we hide God's Word in our heart. The best answer is to trust in God and do the right."

8—10. (8) **Libnah,** ten miles north of Lachish, and nearer to Jerusalem. Whether he had taken Lachish does not appear. (9) **Ethiopia,** see Is. xviii. for an account of Tirhakah.[a] **sent messengers,** bec. he could not execute immediate vengeance on Hezekiah, as he required all his army to meet Tirhakah. So he gave Hezekiah a respite, but severely threatened him. (10) **God .. deceive,**[b] the action lacks the assurance of the Rabshakeh's threats. It is evident that Sennacherib now fears lest an alliance may be effected.

The God in Whom We Trust.—Do we find men leaning on God, and so leaning on Him that their hearts are full of peace, of spiritual rest, of hope, of heavenly joy? Is "the God in whom we trust" a phrase that has as large and full of meaning to our minds as it should have? Is not a living, sustaining, rejoicing trust in God a comparatively rare, rather than a constant and universal thing, even in Christian hearts? And why is it so, if so it be? Is it not because we allow ourselves to be so sadly imposed upon by the temporal and the superficial? We persist in representing to ourselves that the visible, the audible, the tangible, the material, is the real, the true, and the substantial. We, who walk by faith and not by sight, whose life is spiritual, who are citizens of heaven, ought to understand that it is this which is illusive, evanescent, unreal, and that the invisible, the intangible, the eternal, is the real and the reliable; we ought to know and to realize that he, whom not having seen we love, the invisible but ever present, the almighty and never-failing Saviour, is the One who is worthy of our confidence, and in the deepest and fullest sense it should be true that it is the Lord in whom we trust.—Pul. Com.

11—13. (11) **all lands,** the language of boastfulness.[a] **destroying them,** lit. devoting them: treating them as Divinely accursed. (12) **Gozan,** a district of Mesopotamia, on the river Chabour.[b] **Haran,** Ge. xi. 31. The Carrhae of the Romans. **Rezeph,** about a day's journey W. of Euphrates. **Eden,** a region in Mesopotamia, in wh, poss., the garden of Eden was situated. **Telassar,** now Tel-afer, W. of Mosul.—Layard. All of these names are additional to those given by Rabshakeh. (13) **Hena, and Ivah,**[c] in Babylonia (see 2 Ki. xvii. 24).

Modern Infidelity.—I understand that as the most dangerous, because the most attractive, form of modern infidelity which, pretending to exalt the beneficence of the Deity, degrades it into a reckless infinitude of mercy, and blind obliteration of the work of sin; and which does this chiefly by dwelling on the manifold appearances of God's kindness on the face of creation. Such kindness is, indeed, everywhere and always visible, but not alone. Wrath and threatening are invariably mingled with the love; and, in the utmost solitudes of nature, the existence of hell seems to me as legibly declared by a thousand spiritual utterances as of heaven. It is well for us to dwell witih thankfulness on the unfolding of the flower, and the falling of the dew, and the sleep of the green fields in the sunshine; but the blasted trunk, the barren rock, the moaning of the bleak winds, the roar of the black, perilous whirlpools of the mountain's streams, the solemn solitudes of moors and seas, the continual fading of all beauty into darkness, and all strength into dust, have these no language for us? We may seek to escape their teachings by reasonings touching the good which is wrought out of all evil; but it is vain sophistry. The good succeeds to the evil as day succeeds the night; but so also does the evil to the good. Gerizim and Ebal, birth and death, light and darkness, heaven and hell, divide the existence of man and his futurity.—Ruskin.

14. **the letter,** containing the insults and threatenings given in the preceding verses. It seems to have been a proper official document from Sennacherib, but prob. was composed and written by Rabshakeh, as it so nearly resembles his speech. **went .. Lord,** comp. vs. 1. **spread it,** it was written on a scroll which Hezekiah unfolded, that Jehovah might take notice of the arrogance displayed by it. The act is symbolic. Similarly the Jews at the beginning of the Maccabee insurrection spread out in prayer a copy of the Law, defaced with idolatrous pictures, as a witness to the outrages perpetrated against their religion (1 Macc. iii. 48).[d] —Camb. Bib.

Answers to Prayer.—The Bible is full of stories that show us what great blessings have been received through prayer. Abraham's servant prayed when he was seeking a wife for his master Isaac, and he found the right one. Jacob prayed when he was wrestling with the angel, and he got a blessing from him. Moses prayed, and his prayer opened a way of escape for the Israelites through the Red Sea. Hannah prayed, and Samuel was born. What a blessing that was. David prayed, and the blessing he received was victory over the giant. Elijah prayed, and his prayer shut up the windows of heaven, so that there was no rain for three years. He prayed again, and his prayer brought abundance of rain to refresh the parched earth. What a blessing that was! Isaiah and Hezekiah prayed, and an army of an hundred and eighty-five thousand men were killed in one night. Daniel prayed in the lion's den, and his prayer shut the mouths of the lions. Jonah prayed in the belly of the whale, and his prayer brought him up from the bottom of the sea, and set him down safely on the dry land again. Shadrach, Meshach, and Abednego prayed in the burning, fiery furnace, and their prayers kept them from being hurt by the fire. These are a few of the cases mentioned in the Bible which show us the blessings obtained by prayer.

15—17. (15) **prayed,**[a] comp. 2 Chron. xxxii. 20, where Isaiah is represented as joining the prayer. (16) **God of Israel,** comp. 2 Chr. xxx. 1, 5. **dwellest,** R. V., "sittest upon the cherubim," lit. the inhabiter of the cherubs.[b] **thou alone,** so that there is no comparison between Jehovah and the gods of the nations to whom Sennac. referred. **made .. earth,** so absolutely all power must be in Thine hand. "This prayer reveals how pure and elevated a Monotheism God's spirit had at last developed from the national faith of Israel."—G. A. Smith. (17) **thine ear,** etc., see 2 Chr. vii. 15, 16. Note the singular ear and plural eyes.[c]

18—20. (18) **Of a truth,** or, it is true, Lord, even as he boasts.[d] **laid waste,** lit. dried up. **countries,** R. V., "land." (19) **no gods,** having no claim to the dignity, or share of the power, properly belonging to God: only idols.[e] (20) **know,** the loftiest souls among the Jews felt that their nation was meant to be God's witness to the rest of the world. Comp. 1 Sam. xviii. 46, etc.—Lumby.

Work of Men's Hands.—In a letter written by a French Jesuit, about a hundred years ago, it is stated, that at a place several leagues westward of Madras, some masons, who had embraced Christianity, were employed by a Brahmin to repair the embankment of a reservoir of water. It is customary among the Hindoos to place in such situations a number of small idols made of stone. These the workmen designedly buried in the earth which they threw up to strengthen the embankment. The Brahmin coming to inspect their progress, said, "I see nothing of our gods; what have you done with them?" "What is it you mean, Sir?" replied the overseer; "I saw a heap of stones which I thought would be of use to strengthen the embankment; but as for gods, I saw nothing of the kind." "Those were the things you ought to have taken care of," said the Brahmin; "did you not know they were our gods?" "Those things," answered the overseer, "I understand as well as anybody; it is

consisted of two towns, perhaps on different sides of the Euphrates, and that Hena and Ivah were the distinctive names of these towns." —Alexander.

d "God knows our necessities before we ask Him, but He delights in our unfolding them to Him with filial confidence." —Fausset.

Is. xxxiii. 22.

a "A most appropriate and beautiful prayer, expressive of a clear faith and confident trust in Jehovah, as the only God, in opposition to the claims advanced by idolaters in behalf of their deities; and recognizing the Divine glory as the result of the supplicated deliverance." —Henderson.

b Ps. lxxx. 1, xcix. 1.

c "When we would listen to any one we naturally incline one of our ears towards him, but when we would look at anything we open both our eyes." — Gesenius.

d "Faith does not seek to evade any seemingly adverse facts urged by infidelity. The Assyrian's induction as to the vanity of the 'religions of the world' was correct; but it did not prove Hezekiah's affiance to be vain." —Spk. Com.

e "Whatever idolaters may theoretically hold as to the nature of their deities, they identify them practically with the stocks and stones to wh. they pay their adorations." — Alexander.

"Our life is a trust, not a gift; let us use it accordingly." — Robert E. Speer.

"He that saveth his time from prayer shall lose it. He that loseth his time for communion with God shall find it in blessing."— R. P. Wilder.

"This, indeed, is one of the best uses of prayer, namely, the enlargement of soul which follows it, the glow which makes the whole heart glad, and the sense of divine nearness which inspires timidity itself with invincible courage." — Parker.

my business to do so; and, take my word for it, Sir, they were nothing but stones: if they were gods, as you say they are, they could easily get up again into their old places."—Whitecross.

A Prayer.—

Thou, who dost dwell alone;
Thou, who dost know Thine own;
Thou, to whom all are known,
From the cradle to the grave—
Save, O save!

From the world's temptations, from tribulations,
From that fierce anguish wherein we languish,
From that torpor deep wherein we lie asleep,
Heavy as death, cold as the grave—
Save, O save!

When the soul, growing clearer, sees God no nearer;
When the soul, mounting higher, to God comes no nigher,
But the arch fiend Pride mounts at her side,
Foiling her high emprise, sealing her eagle eyes;
And when she fain would soar, makes idols to adore,
Changing the pure emotion of her high devotion
To a skin-deep sense
Of her own eloquence;
Strong to deceive, strong to enslave—
Save, O save!

From the ingrained fashion
Of this earthly nature that mars Thy creature;
From grief, that is but passion;
From mirth, that is but feigning; from tears that bring no healing;
From wild and weak complaining; Thine own strength revealing—
Save, O save!

From doubt, where all is double, where wise men are not strong,
Where comfort turns to trouble, where just men suffer wrong,
Where sorrow treads on joy, where sweet things soonest cloy,
Where faiths are built on dust, where love is half mistrust,
Hungry, and barren, and sharp as the sea—
O set us free!

O let the false dream fly, where our sick souls do lie
Tossing continually.
O where Thy voice doth come, let all our doubts be dumb;
Let all words be mild, all strife reconciled.
All pains beguiled.
Light brings no blindness, love no unkindness,
Knowledge no ruin, fear no undoing—
From the cradle to the grave,
Save, O save! —Mat. Arnold.

[a] Comp. Is. xxx. 19.

"Faith is the rock, while every good action is as a stone laid thereon. As the foundation without the walls is of slender value, so the building without a basis cannot stand; they are so inseparable that their conjunction makes them good."—J. Beaumont.

"Natural religion depends on the energy of the flesh. Supernatural religion depends on the energy of the Spirit of God, which comes down from above. It is quite possible to be perfectly right in the forms of our service, and yet destitute of divine power."— George F. Pentecost.

21, 22. (21) **sent,** etc.,[a] obs. that the answer of God in those days came through the prophet, not through the priest. (22) **virgin,** i. e. hitherto, since David's time, Jerusalem had never been conquered. **daughter of Zion,** Is. i. 8. **at thee,** or after thee, as if she watched Sennac.'s humiliating retreat. "To shake the head was, among the Hebrews, an expression of contempt."—Henderson.

The Boldness of the Citizen of Zion (vs. 22).—Strong faith enables the servants of God to look with calm contempt upon their most haughty foes. I. We know that our enemies are attempting impossibilities. II. We know their weakness. III. Above all, we know that the Most High is with us.—C. H. Spurgeon.

Answers to Prayers.—It would seem as if the Lord replied to Hezekiah's prayer through the instrumentality of Isaiah, for Isaiah begins his answer to Hezekiah, saying, "Thus saith the Lord God of Israel,

Whereas thou hast prayed to Me against Sennacherib king of Assyria: this is the word which the Lord hath spoken concerning him." This is remarkable as showing in how many ways we may receive answers to prayer. It could not have been thought that the Lord would answer a prayer addressed to Him by sending a message through some other man. But thus we are to look for answers to our petitions. We cannot tell how the reply will come—by man, or woman, or child, or unexpected event, or unknown correspondent, or impressions produced upon the mind apparently without any ability on our part to trace their origin or account for their suddenness or their emphasis. We should always be looking for answers to prayers, not always by lifting up our heads and directing our eyes to the far-away heavens; we should open our ears to listen to the words which are being spoken immediately around us, for in the common conversation of the day we may receive some hint as to the destiny and effect of our own prayers.—Peop. Bib.

23—25. (23) **Whom,** a solemn call to consider the glory and power of Jehovah. **Holy .. Israel,** the name for God frequently used by Isaiah, and most characteristic of him. (24) **servants,** in allusion to Rabshakeh's boastings. **Lebanon,** one of the choicest parts of Palestine and its glorious trees the pride of the country.[a] **height .. border,** R. V., "and I will enter into his farthest height, the forest of his fruitful field." (25) **digged,** getting water in waste desert places, where there seemed to be none. **dried .. places,** equally overcoming the difficulties of moats and rivers.[b] "The king of Assyria is represented as boasting of the ease with which he triumphs over all natural obstacles in the pursuance of his plans; such language is blasphemy against Jehovah, the Lord of Nature; although the king himself may be hardly conscious of the sin he is committing."—Camb. Bib.

The Intoxication of Success.—This is the common consequence of success—even of success which is not unholy, which is not obtained regardless of the power and will of God; it is sometimes the unhappy result of success in sacred ministries; how much more so must it be, and is it found to be, the result in the case of those who "fear not God, nor regard man!" Unholy success intoxicates. It makes men imagine that they have done far greater things than they have achieved, and that they have become far greater people than they are. It often rears its head so high that, as with Sennacherib, arrogance passes into blasphemy (vs. 23) or into presumptuous impiety.—Pul. Com.

26, 27. (26) R. V., "Hast thou not heard how I have done it long ago, and formed it of ancient times?" **I have done it,** i. e. in all thou hast done thou hast been but an instrument working out My purposes.[a] **ancient times,** see prophecy of De. xxviii. 49. **to lay waste,** as executor of Divine judgments. (27) **small power,** lit. short of hand, weak to resist. **as the grass,** soon cut down, and withered. **on the housetops,** with little rooting or moisture.[b] **corn blasted,** R. V., "as a field of corn before," etc.

God All in All.—It is a poor philosophy and a narrow religion which does not recognize God as all in all. Every moment of our lives, we breathe, stand, or move in the temple of the Most High; for the whole universe is that temple. Wherever we go, the testimony to His power, the impress of His hand, are there. Ask of the bright worlds around us, as they roll in the everlasting harmony of their circles, and they shall tell of Him whose power launched them on their courses. Ask of the mountains, that lift their heads among and above the clouds; and the bleak summit of one shall seem to call aloud to the snow-clad top of another, in proclaiming their testimony to the Agency which has laid their deep foundations. Ask of ocean's waters; and the roar of their boundless waves shall chant from shore to shore a hymn of ascription to that Being who hath said, "Hitherto shall ye come, and no further." Ask of the rivers; and, as they roll onward to the sea, do they not bear along their ceaseless tribute to the ever-working Energy which struck open their fountains and poured them down through the valleys? Ask of every region of the earth, from the burning equator to the icy pole, from the rock-bound coast to the plain covered with its luxuriant vegetation; and will you not find on them all the record of the Creator's presence? Ask of the countless tribes of plants and animals; and shall they

[a] "He boasts of having overcome all kinds of natural impediments. In arid regions he had digged and drunk water; in lands like Egypt, or Babylonia, he had dried up the streams of fortified places."—Spk. Com.

Is. xix. 6.

"That the kings of Assyria made havoc in the forests of Lebanon by hewing down the cedars and cypresses appears from their own records, in extant Assyrian inscriptions." —Wordsworth.

"The trouble with us is, our proud hearts refuse to accept the position in which God's Word places us." —A. C. Dixon.

[a] "Nothing could be more sublime in effect than the suddenness with which Jehovah here interrupts the boasting monarch."—Henderson.

Comp. Is. x. 5, 15.

[b] Ps. cxxix. 6—8.

"Not thus our infidels th' Eternal draw, a God all o'er consummate, absolute, full orbed, in His whole round of rays complete; they set at odds heaven's jarring attributes, and with one excellence another wound; maim heaven's perfection, break its equal beams, bid mercy triumph over God Himself, undeified by their opprobrious praise: a God all mercy is a God unjust."--Young.

not testify to the action of the great Source of Life? Yes, from every portion, from every department of nature, comes the same voice: everywhere we hear Thy name, O God; everywhere we see Thy love. Creation in all its length and breadth, in all its depth and height, is the manifestation of Thy Spirit, and without Thee the world were dark and dead. The universe is to us as the burning bush which the Hebrew leader saw: God is ever present in it, for it burns with His glory, and the ground on which we stand is always holy. How, then, can we speak of that Presence as peculiarly in the sanctuary, which is abroad through all space and time?—Francis.

28, 29. (28) **abode,** R. V., "sitting down,"[c] Assyria might think itself independent; it was, in fact, altogether in the hands of the God it despised and insulted. **going .. in,** De. vi. 7.[d] (29) **tumult,** R. V. margin, "careless ease" in contrast with "raging." **hook,** etc, as a wild beast is led by a ring through the nose.[e] "The word used implies a hook or ring such as was used for securing large marine animals, and for curbing land animals, camels, buffaloes, etc.

God's Agents are Never Beyond His Restrainings.—He used Assyria, but he holds Assyria in with bit and bridle. The horse may plunge, and rear, and trample, and seem to be beyond all restraint; but God never looses the rein, and draws it in when He pleases. The figures used are even more striking. He puts "a hook in the nose," which Michaelis explains in this way: "The Orientals make use of a contrivance for curbing their work-beasts, which is not adopted among us. They bore the nose through both sides, and put a ring through it, to which they fasten two cords. When a beast becomes unruly, they have only to draw the cord on one side, which, by stopping his breath, punishes him so effectually that, after a few repetitions, he fails not to become quite tractable, whenever he begins to feel it. To this contrivance the Arabian poets often allude."—Pul. Com.

30—32. (30) **a sign,**[a] or assurance. The time of national distress, thro' the invasion of Sennacherib, would be limited to two years, part of which had already passed. **groweth of itself,** without the ordinary processes of agriculture. **third .. sow,** bec. by that time the land would be freed of the enemy, and special Divine provision no longer needed. "Probably the sign does not fix the term of the Assyrian occupation, but refers to wider effects of the invasion, the depopulation of the country, the destruction of homesteads, etc., which rendered an immediate resumption of agricultural activity impossible."—Camb. Bib. (31) **remnant,** vs. 4.[b] **take root,** as the tree shaken and uprooted for a time. "Just as in the case of their crops so shall it be with the people. God shall preserve a remnant who shall once more grow up, in spite of their present low state."—Lumley. (32) **go forth,** to reoccupy, and till the ravaged lands. In times of siege country people take shelter within the fortified city. **zeal,**[c] or jealousy of the Divine honor.

Root and Fruit.—Assuming that we are bound to employ our powers in the direction in which our own preferences lead us, and granting that it is well for human character to partake of much variety, it remains true that we should make an earnest effort to attain to some completeness of character by attention to those elements which we are tempted to neglect. In every department of human action we recognize the duty of bestowing special care on the weakest point—the candidate for literary honors on the subject with which he is least familiar; the builder on that part of the ground where the foundation is least substantial; the general on that outpost which is least defensible.—Pul. Com.

33—35. (33) **shall not,** etc., by these figures Hezekiah is assured that the threatened siege of Jerusalem shall not even be attempted. Sennacherib never came nearer than he was when he sent the threatening messages. **bank,** for the battering-rams, and other engines. (34) **return,** humiliated and discomfited: back to Nineveh. (35) **defend,** or cover over as with a shield. **own sake,** Eze. xxxvi. 21, 22. As a witness of Himself to all the world. **David's sake,** Ps. lxxxix. 28.

True and False Conceptions of God.—If your God is made out of conceptions derived from the great and heartless round of the natural world; if you have a great crystalline God, such as philosophy deduces

[c] Ps. cxxxix. 2.

[d] De. xxviii. 6; 1 Ki. iii. 7; Ps. cxxi. 8.

[e] "There are representations of prisoners led by a hook through the nose and lip in the bas-reliefs of Holevan and Khorsabad, wh. may, however, be symbolical."—Spk. Com.

Job xli. 1, 2; Eze. xix. 4, xxix. 4, xxxviii. 4.

[a] Is. vii. 14.

"There was to be an abundant supply of provisions during these two years of suffering, although the people were unable properly to till and sow their lands. God's thus sustaining them was the sign that He would presently deliver."—Henderson.

[b] 2 Ch. xxx. 6.
[c] Is. ix. 7.

"It is supposed that the time of the address was autumn, probably near the Equinox, which was the beginning of a new year. The best historians tell us that the Assyrian invasion had stopped all tillage in the previous spring, and the people had to rely upon the spontaneous products of the fields." — Peop. Bib.

"Sometimes we have a remote promise stretching far away beyond the ages, and which the living men can never hope to see fulfilled, but in order to assure their faith and brighten their hope, something is promised to them which they can immediately re-

from the material globe, you can conceive of no such thing as His detracting from His dignity by coming down to burrow, as you call it, in this lower sphere. If you have a God whom mountains represent, or if you have a vast marble God, that sits as the central idol of the universe, it is to you contemptible to think of His bowing down and coming among men! But if you have a God fashioned from the elements revealed in the human soul, if you understand that greatness in the Divine Being does not mean muscular greatness, nor physical greatness, but purity, and depth, and scope of all the feelings of the heart, then the greater your God is, the more exquisite will be the things He will do in detail, the more possibility will there be of His descending and coming among men, and the more certainly will He be expected to be found among His family. As the mother is found where her child cries, and as the father is found where his son stumbles, so we should expect that, if God is a being whom we may know from the analogies of our own nature, He would be found living where men are tempted, and where they sin, and suffer, and die.—H. W. Beecher.

36. angel, etc., 2 Ki. xix. 35. Whether the agency used were simoon or plague, does not appear from the narrative. This did not happen before the walls of Jerusalem. Nor is the locality of the disaster certain, though there is sufficient evidence of it from other than Biblical sources. **they arose,** i. e. the few who were spared.

The Egyptian Account.—Sennacherib's objective point was Egypt. According to Herodotus, he reached Pelusium among the marshes near the Serbonian bog and the eastern mouth of the Nile, on the borders of Egypt. Here the Egyptian king met him, but was in great terror. "As the two armies lay here, opposite one another, there came in the night a multitude of field mice, which devoured all the quivers and bowstrings of the enemy, and ate the thongs by which they managed their shields, so that the following day, being deprived of their weapons, they were put to flight and many of them fell. And this king, imaged in stone, still stands in the temple of Hephoestus, holding in his hand a mouse."—Herodotus. Since the mouse was among the Egyptians a symbol of pestilence, we may infer that the basis of truth in the legend was a deadly epidemic in the Assyrian camp.—Camb. Bib.

37, 38. (37) **departed,** he prob. was not with this part of his army, but its destruction necessitated his giving up his expedition and returning home. **dwelt at Nineveh,** remained quiet, not again attempting to attack Jerusalem. History intimates that he lived for sixteen years after this event.[a] "The Biblical and Assyrian accounts of this campaign, though both imperfect, are in substantial agreement."—Driver. (38) **Nisroch,** from Nisr, eagle, and och, great.[a] The eagle was worshiped by the ancient Persians and Arabs. **Armenia, R. V., "Ararat."**[b] **Esarhaddon,** see Ezra iv. 2, reigned from 681—668.

CHAPTER THE THIRTY-EIGHTH.

1. those days, preceding the embassy of Merodach-Baladan (ch. xxxix) who ruled 721—709 in Babylon. Probably the event occurred about the 14th year of Hezekiah (714) and these two chapters are misplaced. **sick unto death,**[c] many commentators think of the plague, others of a malignant pustule,[d] or carbuncle. **set .. order,** or give charge to thy house. Perhaps "make arrangement for the succession to thy throne." At the time Hezekiah had no son.

God's Message to Hezekiah (vs. 1).—The folly of man in minding the trifles of the moment, and neglecting the claims of eternity. The admonition implies—I. Set thy temporal affairs in order. II. Attend to thy spiritual concerns. III. Thou, especially, art warned. IV. Man's great wisdom is to know how to set his house in order. Apply:—(1) When God strikes, our only method is to turn to Him; (2) Our true remedy in all cases; (3) Be encouraged by the success of Hezekiah's prayer.—R. Cecil.

2, 3. (2) **face .. wall,** so as not to be disturbed by what was passing

alize. Thus from point to point, and from day to day, we are drawn forward, by the good hand and the living Spirit of God."—Parker.

"How shocking must thy summons be, O Death!
To him that is at ease in his possessions;
Who, counting on long years of pleasure here,
Is quite unfurnished for that world to come!"
—Blair.

[a] "The eagle-headed human figure in Assyrian sculptures is no doubt Nisroch, the same as Asshur, the chief Assyrian god. The corresponding goddess was Ashera, or Astarte." — Fausset.

[b] Ge. viii. 4.

"All things that are on earth shall wholly pass away
Except the love of God, which shall live and last for aye."
—Bryant.

"Rest in the Lord; wait patiently for Him." In Hebrew, "Be silent to God and let Him mould thee." Be still, and he will mould thee to the right shape. —Martin Luther.

"He who makes war his profession cannot be otherwise than vicious. War makes thieves, and peace brings them to the gallows."—Machiavelli.

[c] 2 Ki. xx. 1; 2 Ch. xxxii. 24.

[d] See vs. 21.

"The sick are not usually so much alarmed at

in the room.[a] **prayed,** see Is. xxx. 19. (3) **in truth,** or sincerity. **perfect heart,** lit. "with a whole heart," one absolutely devoted to Jehovah.[b] Cf. 1 Ki. viii. 61, xi. 4, xv. 3, 14, where the expression occurs with the addition of the words "with Jehovah." The motive of this prayer is clearly expressed in the Song of Thanksgiving which follows (see vss. 11, 18, 19)."—Camb. Bib.

Duty Toward the Sick and Dying.—Most unreasonable is their conduct who, in the beginning of sickness, drive away all serious thoughts from the soul, through a fear of injuring the body. Even if this were necessarily the case, the risk is so far less in dying soon than in dying unprepared, that the former danger should be cheerfully encountered rather than incur the possibility of the latter. But the cases of sickness are very few in which, at the beginning of a disorder, such religious considerations can do our bodily health any harm. On the contrary, that awe and tranquility of soul which are induced by them may in many cases be of real advantage.—Heber.

4—6. (4) **Then,** "in 2 Ki. xx. 4 we read that 'afore Isaiah was gone out into the middle court,' this message came to him. So quickly was the king's prayer answered. A somewhat similar instance of the revocation of one prophetic communication by another is that of Nathan in the matter of the building of the Temple (2 Sam. vii. 3, 4 ff.)."—Camb. Bib. (5) **add,** to the length of life as at first appointed for thee.[c] **fifteen years,** the Jewish tradition is that there were fifteen steps in the ascent to the Temple area.[d] (6) **deliver,** this verse is generally believed to have been an interpolation.

Fifteen Years Added to a Life—In the autumn of 1799, the late Rev. T. Charles, of Bala, met with an afflicting dispensation. While traveling over Mount Migneint, in Carnarvonshire, on a freezing night, one of his thumbs became frost-bitten. It was so severely affected, that he was taken very ill, and his life was in danger. To prevent mortification, it was deemed necessary to have it amputated. When he was considered to be in a dangerous state, a special prayer-meeting was called by the members of the chapel at Bala. Fervent supplications were offered up in his behalf. Several prayed on the occasion; and one person, in particular, was much noticed at the time, for the very urgent and importunate manner with which he prayed. Alluding to the fifteen years added to Hezekiah's life, he, with unusual fervency, entreated the Almighty to spare Mr. C.'s life at least fifteen years. He several times repeated the following words, with such melting importunity as greatly affected all present:—"Fifteen years more, O Lord; we beseech Thee to add fifteen years more to the life of Thy servant. And wilt Thou not. O our God, give fifteen years more for the sake of Thy Church and Thy cause?" Mr. C. heard of this prayer, and it made a deep impression on his mind. He afterwards frequently mentioned it as a reason why he should make the best use of his time, saying, that his fifteen years would soon be completed. The last time that he visited South Wales. and was asked when he should come again, his answer was, at least to some, that his fifteen years was nearly up, and that he should probably never visit them again. He mentioned this to several of his friends the last year of his life, and especially to his wife. It is remarkable his death occurred just at the termination of the fifteen years. What is not less remarkable, it was during this time that he performed the most important acts of his life. It was during this time that he wrote the most valuable of his works; established Sabbath-schools; was one means of originating the Bible Society; and was instrumental in doing great good both to Scotland and Ireland.—Whitecross.

7, 8. (7) vss. 21—22 belong here. Comp. 2 Ki. xx. 7, 8. **sign,** Is. xxxvii 30. "The token that God was willing to change on this occasion the ordinary working of natural law."—Spk. Com. (8) R. V., "behold, I will cause the shadow on the steps, which is gone," etc.—Pol. Bib. "Behold I will cause the shadow to go back as many steps as the sun has gone down on the step-clock of Ahaz, so on the step-clock the sun went back the ten steps which it had gone down." Josephus thinks the degrees were steps ascending to the palace of Ahaz, the time of day being indicated by the number of steps reached by the shadow.[e]

the thought of death as is supposed. At any rate, it seems only fair to them that they should know the seriousness of their position."—Rawlinson.

a "The couches in the E. run along the walls of the houses. He turned away from the spectators to hide his emotion, and collect his thoughts for prayer."—Fausset.

Comp. 1 Ki. xxi. 4.

b 1 Ki. ix. 4, 5.

c Comp. 2 Ki. xx. 5, 6.

d Eze. xl. 26, 31.

"Prayer, says St. Jerome, is a groan. Ah, our groans are prayers as well. The very cry of distress is an involuntary appeal to that invisible power whose aid the soul invokes." —Mdm. Swetchine.

"Whatever crazy sorrow saith.
No soul that breathes with human breath
Hath ever truly longed for death.
'Tis life whereof our nerves are scant;
For life, and not for death, we pant;
More life and fuller that we want."

"Why will men always attack the wrong point as if it were a wonderful thing that a man should have fifteen years added to his life; and yet we omit the stupendous miracle that man ever began to live." —Parker.

e "It is not at all unlikely that Ahaz, who appears to have

Believing Without Understanding.—"I will not believe anything but what I understand," said a young man in an hotel one day. "Nor will I," said another. "Neither will I," chimed a third. "Gentlemen," said one who was on a journey, and who sat close by, "do I understand you correctly, that you will not believe anything that you don't understand?" "I will not," said one; and so each one of the trio said. "Well," said the stranger, "in my ride this morning I saw some geese in a field eating grass: do you believe that?" "Certainly," said the three unbelievers. "I also saw pigs, cows, and sheep eating grass: do you believe that?" "Of course," was again replied. "Well, but the grass which they had formerly eaten had, by digestion, turned to feathers on the backs of the geese, to bristles on the backs of the swine, to wool on the sheep, and on the cows it had turned to hair: do you believe that, gentlemen?" "Certainly," they replied. "Yes, you believe it," he rejoined,; "but do you understand it?" They were confounded, silent, and evidently ashamed.

9, 10. (9) **writing,** this poem, not given in the parallel passage in 2 Kings, must have been inserted here from an independent source.—Camb. B. (10) **I said,** recalling the moanings of his despondent time, when Isaiah's message came to him. **cutting off,** R. V., "the noon-tide." Hezekiah was then just at what we call "middle life." **grave,** Sheol, the abode of spirits. **deprived,** of the years I might reasonably have hoped to live. He regarded this shortening of his life as a Divine judgment.

Hezekiah's Dread of Death.—Death appears to the natural man in the light of a bondage, an imprisonment. He is going down to the gates of Sheol (Ps. ix. 13; cviii. 18; Job xxxviii. 19). In the lore of ancient nations similar ideas appear: the place of the departed is a strong fortress, a Tartaros, an Acheron, surrounded by strong walls and a moat; or an inaccessible island. In the house and folk lore of the peoples abundance of such ideas are to be found. Everywhere the like pathos and the like ideas meet us; and death remains the "standing dire discouragement of human nature."—Pul. Com.

11, 12 (11) **the Lord,** there was as yet in the Jewish conception no clear hope for the future. Death is the end of all communion both with God and men. In Sheol there would be no joy in the worship of God. **land of the living,** comp. Ps. xxxiv. 12. **of the world,** i. e. the under world, Hades. In the grave the king could take no share in the grand human events in which he was so greatly interested.[a] (12) **shepherd's tent,** lightly put up for the night, and taken down in the morning.[b] **cut off,** R. V., "rolled up." **like a weaver,** or as the web is cut off from the beam. **with pining sickness,** R. V., "from the loom."[c]

Human Life a Weaving (vs. 12).—I. It is worth while looking at the work itself, the formation of personal character. In this work there is—1. The weaver's own; 2. Increasing progress; 3. A work of growing ease. II. It is worth while looking at the materials. 1. All supplied by the Master; 2. Only materials after all. III. It is worth while looking at the end. 1. The fabric lasts for ever; 2. The work is over at death; 3. The Master inspects it; 4. The Master disposes of it according to its worth. Apply:—(1) What a mercy if we are spared and furnished for this work; (2) What a motive to begin early; (3) How soon we shall have nothing but our work left.—W. Wheeler.

Old and New Testament Ideas of Death.—We may not expect Christianity in Hezekiah as we find it in the Apostle Paul. In the whole of the New Testament we find a sense of welcome in the presence of death. Paul had "a desire to depart, and to be with Christ; which is far better:" he did not want to be unclothed, he did not care in any sense of self-will to be quit of the body, but if the Lord were to say to him, Servant of mine, come up! he would fly to him. The tone of the New Testament contrasts very instructively with the tone of the Old Testament in relation to death and the grave and the future. The New Testament is all future. Understand the sense in which that declaration is intended to be received. The Old Testament is historical, it lives in the past, it mourns the days are gone, it sees the grave like a black line lying across the disc of to-morrow. The New Testament says in effect, Men, start on, proceed: you know nothing yet as it ought to be known: God lives in

been fond of foreign objects of art (2 Ki. xvi. 10), obtained a sundial from Babylon."—Henderson.

"The stairs, or dial, may have been a large structure; so that the motion of the shadow could be seen by the king through the window, as he lay on his couch." — Spk. Com.

"The simple, constant, exclusive, absolute duty of the Christian is to believe God in Christ." — John Bate.

"Count especially the young man blessed, who has looked into the grave before he has faced the great temptations of the world, and has not entered the race of life till he has learned his stride in the race with death." — Exp. Bib.

a "I, being with the inhabitants of the grave (lit. the place of ceasing to act), shall behold man no more." — Wordsworth.

b 2 Cor. v. 1, 4; 2 Pe. i. 13, 14.

c "His web, carefully woven, and rolled up as it advanced, has been but half finished; and it is to be suddenly cut in two."—Spk. Com.

"The shepherds of the East are often obliged to remove their flocks to distant places to find pasturage; hence their habitations are exceedingly light, in order to be the more easily removed. The 'lodge in a garden of cucumbers,' and the frail resting-place of the shepherd, great-

the future, all destiny is ahead, as for earth and death and the grave, they are to be overpast and overcome: we are to set our feet upon them, and our motto is to be, Onward, ever onward!—Peop. Bib.

13, 14. (13) **I reckoned,** Camb. B. "I cried until morning: As a lion," etc. **as a lion,** whose power and purpose seem to be resistless. **day .. to night,** the pain was unremitting. (14) **chatter,** "both birds are noted for the circles and evolutions which they make in the air, and their noise when setting out on their journeys."[a] **oppressed,** or like one in the hands of an exacting creditor. **undertake,** R. V., "be thou my surety."[b] (Job. xvii. 3) "The image is that of a debtor who is being committed to prison." (Mat. xviii. 30) "But what a deep thought is involved here in the application. For He who is asked to interpose is also the creditor."—Cheyne.

The Litany of Distress (vs. 14).—We are often oppressed—1. Because we have not cried, "undertake for me;" 2. Because we have cried, "undertake for me;" 3. That we may cry, "undertake for me;" 4. We are, though "oppressed," never forsaken, for we can always cry, "undertake for me."—Stems and Twigs.

God, the Only True Burden-Bearer.—Robert Alfred Vaughan had long been ill, but one morning his wife saw signs which struck her with hopelessness. In her grief she thought of going to unbosom her trouble to her friend Mrs. George Dawson. Ere she could leave her house, that friend came in, she had come to open a new sorrow to her friend—her only girl had been seized with fits of a kind which put in peril intellect and life. Those women lifted each others' burdens by opening them in the confidences of friendship. We lose our burdens by freely telling God all about them. There is another way of rolling burdens on God, which is less easy to put into words—which is a matter of soul-feeling. We can give up the self-management of our lives. It can become a conscious ruling thought with us that we live, not for self, but for God; we can inwardly realize that God takes our life-rule into his hands; we go where he sends, we do what he bids. Come to the simplicities of life. How does a wearied child roll his burden on his mother? How does the husband lighten his life-care by rolling it upon a loving wife? Verily, the little things of man will help us to understand the great things of God.—Pul. Com.

15, 16. Two difficult verses. Probably incomplete in text. (15) "What shall I speak and say to Him—since He has done it? I toss to and fro all my sleeping time because of the bitterness of my soul."—Duhm.[a] **bitterness .. soul,** Delitsch, "after the bitterness," etc. (16) **by these,** i. e. the Divine will, voice, and mercies.[b] The thought expressed by A.V. is somewhat as follows: "By such Divine words and deeds (vs. 15) men are preserved in life; and by such things my spirit is revived." **recover me,** R. V., "Wherefore recover thou me," etc. God is the only source of life.

The Speed of Life Impressing Probation (vs. 16).—In illustration of this thought, let us notice—I. The fact that life is fast speeding away. II. That it deeply impresses our probation. 1. It rarely allows us to complete our plans; 2. It keeps us always in effort; 3. It gathers more thickly about us the changes, trials, etc., of life; 4. It soon hurries us from earthly scenes, and often in the full vigor of our power, etc. Apply:—(1) Retribution is near; (2) We should prepare; (3) No wonder this world does not satisfy; (4) Probation will soon end.—T. Edwards.

Restoration of Belief.—Many are conscious, in later life, that their earthly faith has passed away. It was unquestioning, enthusiastic. It depended much on those we loved. Religious feelings which had been without us and not within, slowly and necessarily died away. Becoming more and more liberal, we also became more and more unbelieving, and at last realized that our soul was empty. Are we to settle down into that? It is suicide, not sacrifice, which abjures immortality and prefers annihilation. Our past belief was borrowed too much from others. Resolve to accept of no direction which will free you from the invigorating pain of effort. Free yourself from the cant of infidelity. It boasts of love, it boasts of liberality. Its church is narrower than our strictest sect. Bring yourself into the relation of a child to a father. We need

ly resemble each other." — Roberts.

a "There is peculiar force and beauty in the comparison here made between the dying believer and migratory birds, about to take their departure to a distant and more genial clime." — Henderson.

De. xxviii. 29, 33; Ps. lxxii. 4.

b Ge. xliii. 9, xliv. 32; Ps. cxix. 121—123.

"Learn to be as the angel, who could descend among the miseries of Bethesda without losing his heavenly purity or his perfect happiness. Gain healing from troubled waters."—J. H. Newman.

a "Obs. the sudden transition here from sorrow to joy; his heart is so full that he cannot find words to express his emotion."—Wordsworth.

" The passage may be rendered, 'I will behave myself humbly in remembrance of my past sorrow and sickness, fr. wh. I have been delivered by God's mercy.' "—Fausset.

1 Ki. xxi. 27, 29.

b De. viii. 2.

"When all desire at last, and all regret,
Go hand in hand to death, and all is vain,
What shall assuage the unforgotten pain,
And teach the unforgetful to forget?"

to come to our second self, which is a child—to possess a childhood of feeling in the midst of manhood.—Stopford A. Brooke.

Life Crumbles Away.—
Sad is our youth, for it is ever going,
Crumbling away beneath our very feet;
Sad is our life, for onward it is flowing
In current unperceived, because so fleet;
Sad are our hopes, for they were sweet in sowing,
But tares, self-sown, have overtopp'd the wheat;
Sad are our joys, for they were sweet in blowing,
And still, oh, still, their dying breath is sweet;
And sweet is youth, although it hath bereft us
Of that which made our childhood sweeter still;
And sweet is middle life, for it hath left us
A nearer good to cure an older ill;
And sweet are all things, when we learn to prize them,
Not for their sake, but His who grants them or denies them!
—DeVere.

17, 18. (17) **for peace,** R. V., "Behold it was for my peace that I had great bitterness," that is, this trouble came to me for my good.[c] Comp. Ro. viii. 28; 2 Cor. iv. 17. **pit of corruption,** fig. for the grave. **cast .. back,** Oriental figure for oblivion.[d] (18) **cannot praise,** etc.,[e] they can take no part in the concerns of this life.

The Bitter and the Sweet.—Dr. Watts, from his early infancy to his dying day, scarcely ever knew what health was; but however surprising it may appear, he looked on the affliction as the greatest blessing of his life. The reason he assigned for it was, that, being naturally of a warm temper, and an ambitious disposition, these visitations of Divine providence weaned hs affections from the world, and brought every passion into subjection to Christ. This he often mentioned to his dear friend, Sir Thomas Abney, in whose house he lived many years.—John Whitecross.

19, 20. (19) **living,** those to whom life is prolonged, as mine has been. **father to children,** or one generation to another. **known thy truth,** so that Thy constant praise may be maintained. The truth of God is, especially, His faithfulness in keeping His promises. (20) Thought to be a liturgical addition adapting the Psalm for congregational use. **ready,** not in the Heb. The sentence should read, "Jehovah was for my salvation." **we,** i. e. Hezekiah and his people.

The Place of Devotion.—"In the house of the Lord." This will ever be sacred to the true Christian. What memories of sacred vision and of spiritual emotion are connected with the sanctuary! What fellowship we have had there with each other and with God! The best part of our nature has been developed there—the part which, like God himself, "no man hath seen at any time, or indeed can see." For, apart from the associations of place, there is the inspiration of mutual faith, mutual hope, mutual service, and mutual love. Thus we meet and mingle in the house of the Lord, till, clothed with white robes and with palms in our hands, we join the victors who utter their hallelujahs around the throne of the Lamb, in the "house not made with hands, eternal in the heavens."—W. M. S.

21, 22. These verses are out of place and belong after verse 6. (21) **boil, or** swelling. Figs are used in a similar way to soften and bring to a head gatherings nowadays. Some think the boil indicates one feature of the disease of leprosy. Others think a painful and perilous carbuncle is indicated. Others, again, think it was an inflamed ulcer, produced by the plague.[a] (22) **What .. sign,** comp. 2 Ki. xx. 8.

Life Reviewed.—Dr. Doddridge dreamed that he died, and, clad in a seraphic form, was borne by an angelic attendant to a glorious palace, in one of the rooms of which he left him, saying, "Rest here. The lord of the mansion will soon be with you: meanwhile, study the apartment." The next moment he was alone, and, upon casting his eyes round the room, he saw that the walls were adorned with a series of pictures. To his great astonishment, he found that it was his past life delineated there. From the moment when he had come into the world a helpless infant, and God had breathed into him the breath of life, unto the recent hour,

c 'Not for my hurt, but with a view to my obtaining true peace." — Knobel.

d 1 Ki. xiv. 9; Neh. ix. 26; Ps. l. 17.

e Ps. vi. 5, xxx. 9, lxxxviii. 10—12; Ecc. ix. 10.

"It is easier to win spoils from death than to keep them untarnished by life." —Exp. Bib.

"Life is not one of the homeless forces which promiscuously inhabit space, or which can be gathered like electricity from the clouds and dissipated back again into space. Life is definite and resident; and Spiritual Life is not a visit from a force, but a resident tenant in the soul." —Drummond.

a "From the ulceration on the body of Hezekiah, it has been concluded that the disease with which he was afflicted was the plague." — Henderson.

"Life is a sacred thing, a religious gift, a holy trust, and it is handed to us that we may make it an instrument of divine praise. Marvellous life! no man has seen it; it will not be looked at. It may be seen in incarnation, in temporary form, in some transient phase, but itself will never be gazed upon. Men have attempted to surprise life, but they have always failed in their endeavor." —Parker.

when he had seemed to die, his whole existence was there marked down: every event which had happened to him shone out conspicuously on its walls. Some he remembered as perfectly as though they had occurred but yesterday; others had passed from his memory into oblivion, until thus recalled. Things obscure in life, which had caused him doubt, perplexity, even uneasiness, were rendered clear now. The perils of his life were there,—the accidents which had overtaken him in his mortal state, all of which he had escaped from untouched or but slightly hurt. One in particular caught his attention,—a fall from his horse,—for he recollected the circumstance well: it had been a perilous fall, and his escape was marvelous. But scattered in every picture, all along the whole career, he saw merciful, guiding, shielding angels, who had been with him unsuspected throughout his life, never quitting him, always watchnig over him to guard him from danger. He continued to gaze on these wonderful pictures; and the more he gazed the greater grew his awe, his reverence, his admiration of the unbounded goodness of God. Not a turn did his life take, but it rested on some merciful act of interposition for him. Love, gratitude, joy, filled his heart to overflowing.

CHAPTER THE THIRTY-NINTH.

[a] Comp. 2 Ki. xx. 12—19; 2 Chr. xxxii. 31.

[b] Jer. l. 2.

1, 2. (1) **Merodach-baladan,**[a] Merodach was the name of a Babylonian god.[b] This king reigned from B. C. 721 to 709. **and a present,** in accordance with established Oriental practice. The alliance of Hezekiah might be valuable to Baladan in his revolt against Assyria. (2) **glad of them,** he did not see the wrongfulness of trusting this new power offering its alliance, and was quite flattered, and thrown off his guard by the gracious embassy.[c] **precious things,** i. e. his treasury. In this would be the spoils fr. the Assyrian camp, with, possibly, the stores of weapons, gold, etc. All of this would show how valuable he would be as an ally, he thought.

[c] "Was it not a ground for reasonable self-congratulation that he would have so powerful an ally in case of any future Assyrian attack! So he fell away from the simplicity of faith." —Spk. Com.

Hezekiah's Strength and Weakness.—If his purpose was to impress upon the Babylonians the greatness of his strength, the story of the destruction of Sennacherib would have answered his purpose much better. If Hezekiah had taken the ambassadors to the Temple, and told them how he had spread Sennacherib's letter before the invisible presence of his God in that holy house, and how he had prayed that the designs of his enemy might be brought to nought, and how that eventually the Assyrians had all either perished or fled, the men of Babylon would have been far more impressed with the power of Hezekiah, believing as they would that he was under the protection of an unseen Hand, than they possibly could be by the mere vulgar display of treasures and armor, which their own country could show in abundance, and which was the very thing calculated to excite their desire of plunder.—Goodwin.

"Wealth is a weak anchor, and glory cannot support a man. This is the law of God, that virtue only is firm, and cannot be shaken by a tempest." — Pythagoras.

3, 4. (3) **from a far country** "he answers that part of the question which involved least embarrassment. It is hardly likely that he means to hint that an alliance with so distant a country was out of the question; more probably he will excuse himself on the ground of hospitality to strangers who had come so far. It is noticeable that he does not mention the ostensible motive of the embassy."—Camb. Bib. **from Babylon,** wh. does not seem at the time to have been regarded as an aggressive, dangerous power. Nebuchadnezzar subsequently raised it to the height of its fame. (4) **all .. seen,** Hezekiah does not perceive that he has done anything more than show courtesy to strangers from a far country.

"I would not wrong virtue, so tried, by the least shade of doubt: undue suspicion is more abject baseness even than the guilt suspected." —Aaron Hill.

The Sin of Presuming.—Matthew Henry says of Hezekiah, "He was a wise and good man, but when one miracle after another was wrought in his favor, he found it hard to keep his heart from being lifted up, nay, a little thing then drew him into the snare of pride. Blessed Paul himself needed a thorn in the flesh to keep him from being lifted up with the abundance of revelations." The sin of presumption is a more common, and a more serious, sin than we are wont to consider it. It is one that finds frequent illustration in Holy Scripture. The sin that lost Eden was presumption. Jacob's grasping at the birthright was presumption. Moses' smiting the rock twice was presumption. Saul's forcing himself

"The way to wealth is as plain as the way to market. It depends chiefly on two words, 'industry and frugality;' that is, waste neither time nor money, but make the best use of both.

to sacrifice when Samuel tarried was presumption. David's numbering the people was presumption. Peter striking off the ear of Malchus was presumption. These are but specimen cases, readily recalled. A careful estimate of many sins will reveal presumption at the root of them. Still, if we read our lives aright, we shall find that we are constantly presuming on what God would have us to do, and acting without making due inquiries of him.—Pul. Com.

5—7. (5) **the word,** "Isaiah's tone is threatening, because he sees in this thing a sin against Jehovah. It was not necessary to specify wherein the offense consisted; king and prophet understood each other perfectly. The reception of an embassy from the sworn enemy of the king of Assyria was in itself an act of rebellion likely to precipitate a conflict which Isaiah strove to avert; and the childish vanity displayed by Hezekiah, his pride in earthly resources, and his readiness to enter into friendly relations with the powers of this world, were tendencies against which Isaiah's ministry had been a continuous protest. All these tendencies sprang from a single root, the lack of that absolute faith in Jehovah as the all-sufficient guide and protector of the nation which was the fundamental article of Isaiah's political programme."—Camb. Bib. (6) **carried to Babylon,** the proud display of wealth would have a very different influence to that wh. Hez. had intended. It would show the Babylonians that Judæa was worth conquering. **Nothing shall be left,** nothing worth taking was left when the city was captured. (2 Ki. xxv. 9—17.) (7) **thy sons,** comp. 2 Chron. xxxiii. 11. **eunuchs,** court officers and servants: especially occupied in attending to the seraglios of Eastern courts.[a]

8. **Good,** the language of submission, with some recognition of his mistake. **peace,** or prosperity in general. **truth,** the prevalence of true religion. "Hezekiah recognized that this was more than he deserved."[a]

The Treasure of the Christian.—In a dark and stormy night, a ship sees afar off the shining of the lighthouse, which, as it plunges beneath the wave, is lost; and as, struggling and rolling the water off from its deck, it comes trembling up again on the refluent wave, it gets a glimpse once more, only to lose it. So, in this world, men who propose bright aims to themselves in the midst of the turmoils of passion, the strivings of pride, and the biases of self-interest, in all the whirls of sympathy, and in the discordances of human example, find that they sometimes forget and sometimes violate their ideals; and the fight to maintain our ideals is almost as much as life itself is worth. You must frame your ideal; but after you have done that, you are like a man who makes a voyage. When you have marked the harbor, your work is not done. You have yet to bear hardness as good soldiers. Putting on your armor, you are to aim at things high and noble. And you must fight your way toward them through ten thousand hindrances. And only then shall you be crowned and laurelled when your victory is won, and you stand in Zion and before God. He who has in him absolute soul-qualities, and regards them as his chiefest treasures, and has them for his ideal—come weal or come woe, he has that for which he has been living. Bankrupt him you cannot. You may take his furniture, and strip his walls of pictures, and rob his library shelves of their books, and bear off his portfolios, and carry away his utensils, and leave him without any article of property whatsoever; and, passing by his hollow house, whose bare floors echo to every footstep, men may say, "He is peeled and bankrupt;" but it is not so. No, no! he is not peeled nor bankrupt whose house is a house not made with hands—whose house is the soul, whose treasures are those that neither thieves break through to steal, nor sheriffs. There is no bankruptcy with a man whose purpose and aspirations, and yearnings and longings, are in the direction of his manhood. And the blessing of an ideal is, that it stimulates men to live for those things that time and chance cannot touch nor harm.—H. W. Beecher.

CHAPTER THE FORTIETH.

1, 2. "Proclamation of forgiveness and promise of deliverance to the exiled nation."—Camb. Bib. (1) **Comfort ye,** God's command to His

Without industry and frugality, nothing will do, and with them, everything." —Franklin.

[a] Da. i. 3.

"There is always a Babylon which itself becomes a ruin. Grecian art is taken to Rome, there to be demolished in the sacking of the city. Treasures are taken in after years to Paris, there to be lost in flames. How few relics of any time or nation remain! and in due course these are lost to the possessors. If this is true on the great scale of nations, how manifestly true it is of ourselves! Let us look around on all the present possessions of earth, and remember that, so far as we are concerned, 'nothing shall be left.' 'Thou fool, this night thy soul shall be required of thee: then whose shall those things be?"—Pul. Com.

[a] 2 Chr. xxxii. 26.

"Are you not surprised to find how independent peace of conscience is, and how much happiness can be condensed in the humblest home? A cottage will not hold the bulky furniture and sumptuous accommodation of a mansion; but if God be there, a cottage will hold as much furniture as might stock a palace." —J. Hamilton.

"O preposterous and vain man, thou who couldest not make a finger-nail of thy body, thinkest thou to fashion

Prophets. **my people,** those who have gone into captivity. (2) **comfortably,** Heb. to the heart. **Jerusalem,** means the people, not the city—but Jews everywhere in their exile. **warfare,** properly, military service, and, by implication, hardship, privation, suffering. **double,**[b] Je. xvi. 18, xvii. 18; the word is used poetically, to denote abundance, "the demands not merely of justice but of wrath have been satisfied."—Pol. Bib.

The God of Consolation (vs. 1).—I. What God says to me as a minister of the Gospel. 1. That I am to comfort His people; 2. That I am to persevere in this; 3. That I am to proclaim comfort with His authority. II. What God bids me say to you as belonging to His people. 1. That your conflicts are near their end; 2. That your sins are expiated and forgiven; 3. That you will receive an abundant compensation for all sorrow on account of sin. Apply:—(1) The message is to the people of God; (2) Are you of their number?—G. Brooks.

Chapters 40—66.—The division of the Book of Isaiah into two parts at the end of ch. xxxix., although indicated by no superscription, is at once suggested by the intervention of the narrative section, chs. xxxvi.—xxxix., and is fully justified by the character of the last 27 chapters. Whether these chapters form a single continuous prophecy, or whether, as some think, the work of different hands can be distinguished, they are pervaded by a unity of spirit and aim which separates them from the undisputed prophecies of Isaiah. It is this part of the book which has gained for that prophet the name of the Evangelist of the Old Testament, and whoever the author may have been, that designation aptly characterizes the tendency of the chapters. Critical writers, as is well known, generally assign them to an anonymous prophet, living in the latter part of the Babylonian Exile. The prophecy may be conveniently divided into three nearly equal sections: chs. xl.—xlviii., xlix.—lv., and lvi.—lxvi. (A) Chs. xl.—xlviii. The Restoration of Israel through the instrumentality of Cyrus. (B) Chs. xlix.—lv. The work of Jehovah's Servant and the glorification of Zion. (C) Chs. lvi.—lxvi. The future blessedness of the true Israel contrasted with the doom of the apostates.—Camb. B. The Prologue, verses 1—11.—This first proclamation of glad tidings to Zion (see ch. xli. 27) is a passage of singular beauty, breathing the spirit of new-born hope and enthusiasm with which the prophet enters on his work. The announcement of a miraculous restoration of the exiles to their own land is the central theme of his prophecy, and the point around which all the ideas of the book crystallize. As yet the historical fact is but dimly outlined, the writer's mind being occupied with its ideal significance as a revelation of the glory and the gracious character of Jehovah (vss. 5, 10 f.). His state of mind borders on ecstasy; his ears are filled with the music of heavenly voices telling him that the night is far spent and the day is at hand; and although his home is with the exiles in Babylon, his gaze is fixed throughout on Jerusalem and the great Divine event which is the consummation of Israel's redemption.—Camb. B.

3. In vss. 3—11 we have an imaginative description of the process by which the promise is to be fulfilled. **the voice,** as of a herald.[a] **prepare,** R. V. "crieth, Prepare ye in the wilderness the way," etc. Pol. Bib., "Hark! there is a cry: Clear ye in the wilderness the way of Jehovah, make plain in the desert a highway for our God," i. e. Israel is addressed under the aspect of a desolate land. But even there the voice shall be heard and in that wilderness a way prepared for the King. **the way,** it was, and is, customary in the E. for heralds to require the public repair of the roads before the approach of a great king or general.

Note on vs. 3.—When a great prince in the East sets out on a journey, it is usual to send a party of men before him, to clear the way. The state of those countries in every age, where roads are almost unknown, and, from the want of cultivation, in many parts overgrown with brambles and other thorny plants, which renders traveling, especially with a large retinue, very incommodious, requires this precaution. The emperor of Hindostan, in his progress through his dominions, as described in the narrative of Sir Thomas Roe's embassy to the court of Delhi, was preceded by a very great company, sent before him to cut up the trees and bushes, to level and smooth the road, and prepare their place of en-

---

this wonderful, mysterious, subtle soul of thine after the ineffable Image? Wilt thou ever permit thyself to be conformed to the Image of the Son? Wilt thou, who canst not add a cubit to thy stature, submit to be raised by the Type-Life within thee to the perfect stature of Christ?" —Drummond.

"There is ever a certain languor attending the fulness of prosperity. When the heart has no more to wish, it yawns over its possessions, and the energy of the soul goes out, like a flame that has no more to devour."—Young.

[b] "They had suffered as much chastisement as amply sufficed to clear the Divine character, and correct them of the great evil of idolatry."—Henderson.

Ro. v. 20.

"There can be no doubt that this chapter was meant for the people at the close of their captivity in Babylon. But do not let us miss the pathetic fact, that Israel is addressed not in her actual shape of a captive people in a foreign land, but under the name and aspect of her far-away, desolate country. If you, poor captives as you are, begin to act upon the grace whispered in your trembling hearts, the world will show the result. All things will come round to your side." —Exp. Bib.

[a] Mat. iii. 3; Mk i. 3; Lu. iii 4; Jno. i. 23.

"The edict of Cyrus is connected with the

campment. Balin, who swayed the imperial sceptre of India, had five hundred chosen men, in rich livery, with their drawn sabres, who ran before him, proclaiming his approach, and clearing the way. Nor was this honor reserved exclusively for the reigning emperor; it was often shown to persons of royal birth. When an Indian princess made a visit to her father, the roads were directed to be repaired, and made clear for her journey; fruit trees were planted, water vessels placed in the roadside, and great illuminations prepared for the occasion.—Paxton.

4, 5. (4) **valley,** etc., beautifully figurative of the removal of all obstructions and impediments. **crooked,** or perhaps the declivities. Eastern roads are not properly made and levelled, they are mere tracks marked by the passers, so they have to be virtually made for the progress of a prince. (5) **glory .. Lord,** in His redeeming grace heading, as it were, the return of His people from captivity. **see it,** comp. Lu. ii. 30,[a] shall behold the mighty acts—and moreover shall recognize that it is Jehovah; the seeing will be spiritual as well as physical. **hath spoken,** Nu. xiv. 21.[b]

Paths of Preparation.—There are the ruins of the old military roads of the Cæsars, but the Cæsars are gone. There the Ptolemies of olden time made incursions, but their sway is past. But the highways of commerce, the freer intercourse of peoples, the more humanizing influences of equity in law, and reformation in punishment, the kindly workings of pity and charity to the neglected and forgotten—all these are preparation-paths for the great King who is to reign in righteousness. Not alone through the royal gates of olden prophecies, but through the triumphal arches of redeeming ideas and influences which he has set at work, the Messiah shall come.—Pul. Com.

6—8. "The second voice proclaims the double truth that all earthly might is transitory and the word of God is eternal." (6) **the voice,** better, "Hark! one saying, Cry."[a] **and he said,** Camb. B. "and I said." **flesh is grass,** "all human things, however goodly, are transitory."[b] (7) **spirit,**[c] R. V. "breath," i. e. "the wind (Ps. ciii. 16), especially the scorching east-wind (Hos. xiii. 15) or Sirocco, which blows chiefly in the spring, blighting the fresh vegetation."—Camb. Bib. **is grass,** or frail as the grass. (8) **stand for ever,**[d] through all the changes that may be going on around it. The expression is "a common Heb. phrase for perpetuity, security, and sure fulfilment."

Sudden Departure of Glory.—I was running over again recently the career of that hapless Queen of France, Marie Antoinette. Who that has once read it can forget the tragic history? For a brief space she was the idol of her realm. Then her enthusiastic subjects offered to take the horses from the royal carriage and draw it with their own hands down the streets of her gay capital. How terrible the transition when, a little later, along those same avenues they dragged the widowed sovereign to execution, rending the air with curses that ceased only when the bloody head was held up in sight.—Vassar.

9. O Zion, R. V. "O thou that tellest good tidings to Zion."[a] **high mountain,** "local elevation extending the diffusion of the sound."[b] **O Jerusalem,** R. V. "to Jerusalem" (as above). **be not afraid,** as to the fulfilment of what you promise.

God's Power.—No doubt it seemed to the Jews a very glorious illustration of Divine power to overcome all the obstacles that stood in the way of their return from exile—to guide them into and establish them in the land of their fathers. But it is an incalculably greater instance of Divine power to overcome all the hindrances in the way of a spiritual redemption of the race, and to secure that glorious issue. This is that which the ruling and overruling arm of the Almighty is now accomplishing. Well might such a work be published with farthest-reaching voice from the highest mountain! God is doing that with which no victories that human monarchs ever won will for one small moment compare. He is triumphing over the prejudices, the superstitions, the vices, the selfishness, the individual and the organized iniquities of the world; and on the ruins of sin and wrong he is rearing the mighty and majestic edifice of universal righteousness and peace.—Pul. Com.

10, 11. These verses contain the further proclamation of the herald.

---

preaching of John the Baptist." — Wordsworth.

"The situation of Babylon, on the river Euphrates, must have made causeways necessary to those that had occasion to go thither or come from thence, as marks set up must have been very requisite to those that had to pass through the deserts that lay between Chaldaea and Palestine."— Paxton.

[a] Lu. iii. 6.

"Men are dazzled with false glory, with meretricious ideas of empire, and they see no beauty in Christ that they should desire him. But one day—as the esthetic student realizes in time what is true art, as the musician understands the majesty of Beethoven — the moral nature of men being quickened and renewed by the Spirit, they shall see the glory of the Lord and the excellency of our God." — Pul. Com.

[b] 1 Pe. i. 24, 25; Is. li. 12; Ps. xc. 5.

[c] Ps. ciii. 16.

[d] There is a tacit antithesis between the word of God and man; what man says is uncertain and precarious, what God says cannot fail." — Alexander.

[a] " 'Thou' is the collective personification of the messengers who announce God's gracious purpose to Zion." —Fausset.

[b] "J. D. Michaelis compares the ancient practice of transmitting

news by shouting from one hill-top to another, as described by Caesar." — J. A. Alexander.

[c] Vitringa proposes to render "against the strong one," i. e. Satan.

[d] Is. lix. 16.

[e] Ge. xlviii. 15.; Ps. xxiii.; Jno. x. 1—18.

A little Chinese boy who wished to join the church gave this touching answer to those who thought him too young: "Jesus has promised to carry the lambs in His arms. I am only a little boy, it will be easier for Jesus to carry me."

[f] "The ver. sets forth the wisdom and power of God in the disposition and sustentation of the different parts of the universe. Comp. Job xxxviii." —Henderson.

There is only one great character in the world that can really draw out all that is best in men. He is so far above all others in influencing men for good that he stands alone. That man was the founder of Christianity. —Drummond.

[a] "Who assigned Him the limits of His operations; marking out when He was to brood over the formless waste with life-giving energy (Ge. i. 2), and when to breathe in displeasure over corrupt creation, so that it should wither away?"—Spk. Com.

Ro. xi. 34; 1 Co. ii. 16.

(10) **with strong hand,**[c] R. V. "as a mighty one," manifesting His strength. **arm,** the symbol of power.[d] **for him,** i. e. His own power shall suffice. **his reward,** comp. Ph. ii. 9. **his work,** R. V. "recompence," i. e. the reward which He will bestow on his followers. (11) **feed,** etc., figures borrowed from the most tender aspects of pastoral life.[e] **with young,** Ge. xxxiii. 13, R. V. "that give suck."

An Oriental Shepherd.—An Eastern traveler tells of seeing precisely what Isaiah so poetically describes. "One shepherd led his flock, by a zigzag path, up the almost perpendicular bank of the glen. Behind it two young lambs trotted gaily along at the feet of their mother. At first they frisked about, and jumped lightly from stone to stone; but soon they began to fall behind. The poor little things cried piteously when the path became steeper and the rocks higher, and the flock more and more distant. The mother cried too, running back and forth—now lingering behind, now hastening on before, as if to wile them upwards. It was in vain. The ascent was too much for their feeble limbs. They stopped trembling on the shelving cliff, and cried; the mother stopped and cried by their side. I thought they would certainly be lost; and I saw the great eagles that soared in circles round the cliffs far overhead, sweeping lower and lower, as if about to pounce upon their prey. But no! The plaintive cries of distress had already reached the ear of the good shepherd. A minute more, and he was standing by them. Then taking them up in his arms, he put them—one on each side—in his bosom, in the ample folds of his coat, which was bound round the waist by a girdle."

12. Here begins a new section extending to verse 31. Its theme is "Jehovah, the Incomparable," as viewed in His sovereignty and omnipotence. **Who,**[f] etc., "who can vie with Jehovah in power? The point of these questions lies in the smallness of the measures figured as being used by Jehovah in creating the universe,—the hollow of the hand, the span, etc." "The conception of the universe as measured out by its Creator appears to include two things. There is first the idea of order, adjustment and proportion in Nature, suggesting intelligence at work in the making of the world. But the more important thought is that of the infinite power which has carried through these vast operations as easily as man handles his smallest instruments of precision. The passage is not a demonstration of the existence of God, but assuming that He exists and is the Creator of all things, the prophet seeks to convey to his readers some impression of His Omnipotence, which is so conspicuously displayed in the accurate determination of the great masses and expanses of the material word."—Camb. Bib.

The Incomparableness of the Great God (vs. 12).—I. The greatest things in the material world are nothing in comparison with Him. II. The greatest minds in the spiritual universe are nothing in comparison with Him. 1. His universe must be regarded as the expression of Himself; 2. His laws are the revelation of Himself; 3. His conduct is absolutely irresponsible. III. The greatest institutions of human society are nothing in comparison with Him. IV. The greatest productions of human labor are nothing in comparison with Him.—Thomas.

13, 14. (13) directed, i. e. regulated it. What man has guided the will of God? **Spirit,** or Divine creative agency.[a] **taught him,** as a confidential adviser. (14) **with whom,** etc., further appeal solemnly affirming the absolute independence of God.

The Great Creator.—He who exhibited such matchless skill in the organization of material bodies, and such exquisite taste in their formation, has superadded that ethereal beauty which enhances their permanent qualities, and presents them to us in the ever-varying character of the spectrum. If the objects of the material world had been illuminated with white light, all the particles of which possess the same degree of frangibility, and were equally acted upon by the bodies on which they fall, all nature would shine with a leaden hue, and all the combinations of external objects, all the features of the human countenance would have exhibited no other variety than that which they possess in a pencil-sketch, or a China-ink drawing. The rainbow itself would have dwindled into a narrow arch of white light, the stars would have shone through a grey sky, and the mantle of a wintry twilight would have replaced the golden vesture of the rising sun.—Brewster.

15—17. (15) **nations,** the insignificance of collective humanity before Jehovah. **drop,** lit. drop hanging on a bucket,[b] "trickling down its side, and about to fall; the idea is of smallness and feebleness."—Pol. Bib. **isles,** this word, rendered elsewhere lands by the sea and far countries, occurs 12 times in this part of Isaiah always (except xlii. 15) with reference to the islands of the Mediterranean.—Pol. Bib. **little thing,** or, as a grain of fine dust. (16) **Lebanon,** famous for its forests, and multitudes of living creatures. **burn,** etc., "so infinitely great is Jehovah that the forests of Lebanon would not yield fuel enough, nor its wild animals victims enough, for a holocaust worthy of Him." (17) **nothing,** Da. iv. 35.

Jehovah Incomparable.—God's Being is simple, unique, absolutely original. In a like sense to that which we say the works of a great poet are his unassisted productions, does the prophet say the world is the work of God. "Contrast the Babylonian myth of a joint action of Bel and the gods in the creation of man; and the Iranian of co-creatorship of Ormuzd and the Amshaspands;" or the crude cosmogonic notions of the Greeks. All parts of the world, all habitable lands and nations, are dependent on him, derived from his will, subject to his power. How, then, can earth's noblest products add anything to his riches, or further illustrate the glory of One to whom they already belong?

18. **liken God,** the folly of all idolatry, comp. Acts. xvii. 29, "because God has not His like, therefore there is no creature form that is like Him, and under whose image one may represent Him visibly."—Hägelsbach. **what likeness,** "What image will you set by His side as His resemblance?"[a]

God Incomparable.—One day, when Mr. Richards, missionary in India, was conversing with the natives, a Fakeer came up, and put into his hand a small stone about the size of a sixpence, with the impression of two human likenesses sculptured on the surface; he also proffered a few grains of rice, and said, "This is Mahadeo!" Mr. Richards said, "Do you know the meaning of Mahadeo?" The Fakeer replied, "No." Mr. R. proceeded, "Mahadeo means the Great God—He who is God of gods, and besides whom there can be no other. Now, this Great God is a Spirit; no one can see a spirit, who is intangible. Whence, then, this visible impression on a senseless, hard, immoveable stone? To whom will ye liken God? or what likeness will ye compare unto Him? God is the high and lofty One that inhabiteth eternity, whose name is Holy. He hath said, 'I am Jehovah; there is no God beside me.'" The poor Fakeer was serious, respectful, and attentive; continually exclaiming, "Your words are true."—Whitecross.

19, 20. (19) **melteth,** casteth. **graven image,** so called because usually graven after it was cast. **spreadeth .. gold,** "the idol consists of a core of brass which is cast by the workman and then hauled over to the goldsmith to be covered with gold plate," comp. xxx. 22. **chains,** for the ornamentation of the figure.[b] (20) **impoverished,** or sunk in circumstances. **tree .. rot,** a piece of sound oak or cedar. **cunning,** clever, skilful. **not be moved,** "that will not totter." If an idol leant over or fell over it was the worst of omens. 1 Sam. v. 3, 4. "There is here, and for almost the first time in history, the same intellectual intolerance of images, the same burning sense of the unreasonableness of their worship, which has marked all monotheists, and turned even the meekest of their kind into fierce scorners and satirists—Elijah, Mohammed, Luther, and Knox. We hear this laughter from them all. Sometimes it may sound truculent or even brutal, but let us remember what is behind it."—G. A. Smith.

Egyptian Idol-makers.—The particulars in this description of idol-making are more minute than we elsewhere find in the Bible. In many respects it seems so strikingly to agree with the process followed by the Egyptian idol-makers that we add the following particulars, for which we are indebted principally to Mr. Wilkinson's Materia Hieroglyphica, printed at Malta, 1828—1830. When the Egyptians intended to sculpture, they began by smoothing the surface, and drawing a number of parallel lines at equal distances, at right angles to which were traced other lines forming a series of squares. The size of these squares depended upon

[b] "Whole nations count for no more before the Almighty God than the small drop of a bucket which the bearer does not notice." — Nagelsbach.

"Isaiah, speaking of the sea as held in God's hand, as one might hold a drop of water, is a better poet than Byron, who apostrophizes the sea as a living being." — Pul. Com.

"In the light of these truths, how monstrous appeared the folly of those who made an image to represent or symbolize Deity."—Spk. Com.

"How should the image-deities of idolatrous Babylon be compared to this Almighty and unsearchable God of Israel?" —Mat. Arnold.

[a] De. iv. 15, 16; Ex. xx. 4.

[b] These represent the kinds of idol-figures made for the rich.

"Egyptian relics show that idols were suspended in houses by chains."— Fausset.

"Just so truly as God and the world are at war, so the moment our lives are laid down in uncompromising obedience to him, they are laid down in utter and uncompromising contrariety with the things he has told us we are not to love. We must choose between the evil love of the world and the overflowing love of God."—Robert E. Speer.

"Are you men that have faith in God when the sun shines, and that have no faith in Him when it is cloudy? Are you men that have arms when there is no enemy at hand, but that throw them away when the enemy comes? God is a God for times of war as well as a God for times of peace." —H. W. Beecher.

the size of the figures to be formed; but whatever was their size, nineteen parts or spaces were always allowed for the height of the human figure. If smaller figures were to be introduced, intermediate lines were then ruled which formed smaller squares, and consequently a figure of smaller proportion. May not this explain the marking out with a line and with a compass mentioned in Isaiah? After the first outlines of the figure had been traced, it was inspected by a master, who wrote in various parts of it such observations and instructions as he wished to be attended to by the artists in the progress of the work, and which of course were obliterated as the sculptures were formed. These were the work of other artists, distinct from the draughtsmen; and the remainder was completed by others, who added the color, gilding, or polish, and who introduced the minute parts of dress and ornament. To this it may not be amiss to add that the sculptors were not only guided by certain artistic rules, but in the representations of their gods were bound to observe certain forms prescribed by the priests, and which it was accounted sacrilege to transgress. The more effectually to accomplish this object, and preclude the intervention of anything forbidden by the laws in subjects accounted sacred, the profession of an artist was not allowed to be exercised by any common or illiterate person. Indeed, Mr. Wilkinson has shown the probability that they were, in some sort, attached to, and formed a branch of the priesthood.—Kitto.

[a] Ro. i. 20; see Ac. xiv. 17, xvii. 24.

"Do not look forward to what may happen tomorrow; the same everlasting Father who cares for you to-day will care for you to-morrow, and every day. Either He will shield you from suffering or He will give you unfailing strength to bear it."—Francis deSales.

"Earth is but the frozen echo of the silent voice of God."—Hageman.

"Such is the world. Understand it, despise it, love it; cheerfully hold on thy way through it, with thy eye on highest lode-stars!" —Carlyle.

21, 22. (21) **known,**[a] are your hearts deaf and blind? Is the tradition of God's doings, as old as creation, unknown to you? Do you learn nothing from nature or history? (22) **It is he,** Jehovah sits exalted upon "the vault of the heavens" (Pol. Bib.) so high that men appear but as locusts before Him. **curtain,** thin transparent veil. Think of his power! The heavens he spread out as it were a piece of fine cloth, he cast them over us as a tent!

God Revealed in Nature.—"The whole system of the world is but a standing copy and representation of the Divine goodness, writing little images of itself upon every the least portion of this great body." "The night itself cannot conceal the glories of the heaven; but the moon and stars, those lesser lights, then show forth their lesser beauties. While the laborer lies down for his rest, the astronomer sits up and watches for his pleasure." When men were talking atheism around Napoleon on the passage to Africa, the great man exclaimed, pointing to the starry sky, "It is all very well for you to talk, gentlemen; but who made all that?"

Voice of God.—

God hath a voice that ever is heard
In the peal of the thunder, the chirp of the bird;
It comes in the torrent, all rapid and strong,
In the streamlet's soft gush as it ripples along;
It breathes in the zephyr, just kissing the bloom;
It lives in the rush of the sweeping simoom;
Let the hurricane whistle, or warblers rejoice,
What do they tell thee but God hath a voice?
God hath a presence, and that ye may see
In the fold of the flower, the leaf of the tree;
In the sun of the noon-day, the star of the night;
In the storm-cloud of darkness, the rainbow of light;
In the waves of the ocean, the furrows of land;
In the mountains of granite, the atom of sand;
Turn where ye may, from the sky to the sod,
Where can ye gaze that ye see not a God?—Eliza Cook.

[a] Je. iv. 23. Ps. ii. 2, 10.

[b] Ps. xxxvii. 35; Da. iv. 10.

[c] "Our thoughts are carried chiefly to Judah. Men might have supposed that David was to be the plant of renown; that Sol.'s line was to be the seed which the Lord had blessed; that Hezekiah was the rod from the stock of Jesse; but none of these proved to be so."—Spk. Com.

23, 24. (23) **Princes and judges,** i. e. the power and glory and wisdom of men he brings to nothingness.[a] (24) **shall not be,** R. V. "have not been" (Past tense throughout.) The princes and judges are often compared to tall trees.[b] **sown,** so their race becomes extinct. **blow,** etc., no sooner have these princes and judges established themselves—taken root—than He blows upon them and they wither or vanish as dust before a whirlwind.[c]

Whirlwinds (vs. 24).—Whirlwinds occasionally sweep along the country in an extremely frightful manner, carrying away in their vortex, sand, branches, and stubble, and raising them to an immense height in the air. Very striking is the allusion which the Prophet makes to this phenomenon: "He shall also blow upon them, and they shall wither, and the whirlwind shall take them away as stubble." With equal force and beauty the Psalmist refers to the rotary action of the whirlwind, which frequently impels a bit of straw over the waste, like a wheel set in rapid motion: "O my God, make them like a wheel, as the stubble before the wind." Sometimes it comes from no particular point, but moves about in every direction. Mr. Bruce, in his journey through the desert of Senaar, had the singular felicity to contemplate this wonderful phenomenon in all its terrific majesty, without injury, although with considerable danger and alarm. In that vast expanse of desert, from west and to north-west of him, he saw a number of prodigious pillars of sand at different distances, moving at times with great celerity, at others stalking on with majestic slowness; at intervals he thought they were coming in a very few minutes to overwhelm him and his companions. Again they would retreat so as to be almost out of sight, their tops reaching to the very clouds. There the tops often separated from the bodies; and these, once disjointed, dispersed in the air, and appeared no more. Sometimes they were broken near the middle, as if struck with a large cannon-shot. About noon they began to advance with considerable swiftness upon them, the wind being very strong at north. Eleven of these awful visitors ranged alongside of them about the distance of three miles. The greatest diameter of the largest appeared to him, at that distance, as if it would measure ten feet.—Paxton.

25, 26 "form the peroration of a passage of striking elevation. The writer makes a final appeal to the imagination of his audience by pointing to the nightly pageant of the starry hosts mustered at the command of Him who is Jehovah of Hosts." (25) **equal,** so as to make even comparison possible. **the Holy One,** "this is the final distinction bet. God and the creature," he is holy. (26) **host,** the multitude, and orderly array of the stars. **by names,** as soldiers summoned by a muster-roll. **in power,** etc., R. V. "and for that he is strong in power, not one is lacking."[a]

The Majesty and Infinitude of God.—A magnificent city, with the tombs of departed and the palaces of living kings, is an imposing monument of human passion and human intelligence. Nineveh and Babylon "seemed planted for eternity, firmly rooted in the soil; but to the prophets, regarding them from the point of view of the future, they seemed as though they had never been." Profound faith in the Eternal fills the mind with contempt for the gloria mundi, which seems to be withering in the very hour it most proudly flourishes. The prophet falls back upon the thought of the holy and incomparable One, who marshals the starry hosts, who is Lord of the physical universe and of the world of man's spirits. We need to rest our thought upon the infinite power of God. Weak ourselves, we need to lean upon that which is strong and enduring. And here we are liable to many illusions—the illusion of the permanence of physical systems, the illusion of the permanence of human customs and institutions. God can cause the heavens to be shrivelled like a scroll, can efface the cities of the nation as if they were so many rubbish-heaps from the face of the earth. He and the soul alone abide.—Pul. Com.

God is Love.—
How great soe'er things being or done of man,
To be, to do, is less than to believe:
For to believe God is to know Him love.
As on some hill at day-dawn we see born
Of early light the sun, head of all worlds,
Who hour by hour exalts his own place; truth
Instructing us the while it is earth beneath
Which rolls away; he, lord of time, in his
Eternal zenith throned, climbs not nor stoops;
So they, in spirit knowledge wisest, know,
As more and more the soul is purified,

"This is the state of man: to-day he puts forth
The tender leaves of hope, tomorrow blossoms,
And bears his blushing honors thick upon him;
The third day comes a frost, a killing frost,
And — when he thinks, good easy man, full surely
His greatness is a-ripening — nips his root,
And then he falls."
—Shakespeare.

"The wind, a sightless laborer, whistles at his work." —Wordsworth.

"Dost thou love life, then do not squander time, for that is the stuff life is made of." —Franklin.

a "By reason of abundance of (their inner essential) force and firmness of strength, not one of them is driven astray; referring to the sufficiency of the physical forces with which He has endowed the heavenly bodies, to prevent all disorder in their motions." —Horsley.

While many of the world's religions have some things that are good in them, only the Christian religion offers a Christ. Said a young Brahman to a missionary:—"Many things which Christianity contains I find in Hindooism: but there is one thing which Christianity has and Hindooism has not." "What is that?" the missionary asked. His reply was, "A Saviour."

It is their own fleshly ignorance from them rolled,
Which opens them to heaven and to God's light,
Unvarying and supreme, due ingress gives.
It is we who change towards Him, not He towards us;
As therefore to the sun, nor east nor west,
Nor day nor night is, but one timeless noon
So from the Lord of life unbounded beams
One everlasting effluence, which is love.
To gain this, to prepare for this, is all.—Bailey.

"The great lever by which to raise and save the world is the unbounded mercy and love of God."— Beecher.

"It is faith's work to claim and challenge loving kindness out of all the roughest strokes of God." — S. Rutherford.

27, 28. (27) **O Jacob,** reminding the disconsolate Jews of Ge. xxxii. 26. **My way,**[b] etc., the despairing language of the captives in Babylon. **judgment .. God,** or my cause is neglected by my God.[c] (28) **not known,** comp. vs. 21. **heard,** by the tradition of the fathers. **everlasting God,** Ge. xxi. 33; Do. xxxiii. 27. **no searching,** Ps. cxlvii, 5, therefore your failure to understand His purposes is no proof of his failure in loving kindness.

b "Covered by so dense a mass of misery, that even His light could not penetrate." — Spk. Com.

c "They had been so long in the power of their enemies, that they concluded they were quite overlooked by the God of their fathers."—Henderson.

Trust in the Lord Recommended (vss. 27—31).—I. The doctrine taught. 1. The existence of a Supreme Creator; 2. The doctrine of a superintending Providence; 3. The efficacy of religion. II. The reproof administered. III. The correction offered. IV. The instruction afforded. 1. To consider the Lord as the only proper object of worship and of confidence; 2. To expect confidently; 3. Even in times of trial we may mount above the world; 4. We may make rapid and delightful progress in religion; 5. That we may persevere in piety.

Strength Renewed.—When a man wants his bodily strength renewed, his purpose may be effected by eating a good meal. He has grown empty through hunger, and there is nothing in him; he must be filled up with substantial nourishment, and then the human engine will generate fresh force. Oh, ye who are weak in spirit, come and feed upon Christ! Sometimes a man may renew his strength by taking a little rest. He has grown weak through stern labor and long fatigue, and he must be quiet and repose till he recovers. Oh, ye weary, heavy-laden, where is there rest for you except in the Christ of God? We have known men's strength renewed by breathing their native air. They have risen out of a hot and fœtid atmosphere into the cool breeze of the mountain-side, and the bracing breeze has made them strong again. Oh, to have the breath of the Spirit blowing upon us once again!—Spurgeon.

29—31. (29) **faint,** Not only is He thus powerful but his power is for us, for the faint and weak. (30) **youths,** whose glory and boasting are in their strength.[a] "Even though youth faint and young men lose their strength, yet," etc. (31) **wait upon,** or wait for. **as eagles,** which are noted for the untiring strength of their wing.

a 1 Jno. ii. 14.

Waiting Upon God (vs. 31).—I. The characters described. The waiting includes earnest desire, confident expectation, patient reliance. II. The blessings promised. 1. Exemplary privileges in the exercises of the Divine life; 2. A. perpetual renewal of the powers of Divine grace; 3. Persevering endurance; 4. Ultimate success.—C. Jones.

"From God, the overflowing spring,
Our souls shall drink a fresh supply;
While those who trust their native strength
Shall melt away and droop and die."

"People of ordinary goodness walk in God's way, but the devout run in it, and at length they almost fly therein. To be truly devout, we must not only do God's will, but we must do it cheerfully."—Francis de Sales.

Sonnet.—

I think we are too ready with complaint
In this fair world of God's. Had we no hope
Indeed beyond the zenith and the slope
Of yon gray blank of sky, we might be faint
To muse upon Eternity's constraint
Round our aspirant souls. But since the scope
Must widen early, is it well to droop,
For a few days consumed in loss and taint?
O pusillanimous heart, be comforted,—
And, like a cheerful traveler, take tne road,
Singing, beside the hedge. What if the bread
Be bitter in thine inn, and thou unshod
To meet the flints? At least it may be said,
Because the way is short, I thank Thee, God!
—Elizabeth Browning.

CHAPTER THE FORTY-FIRST.

The nations are called upon to explain the rise of Cyrus, vss. 1—3. The answer in vs. 4. **1. Keep silence,** or "listen in silence to Me."[b] **islands,** a term used to include all maritime countries: all regions beyond the sea.[c] **people,** R. V., "peoples," i. e. all nations. So generally. A fact not evident in A.V. **renew their strength,** collect all their force to answer Me.[d] **come near,** so as to take a close and careful review of the evidence (comp. Is. i. 18).

Renewals (vs. 1).—I. All things on earth need to be renewed. II. Man's life cannot be sustained without renewal from God. III. We must also repair the waste of the soul. 1. By feeding on the Word of God; 2. By listening to the Word; 3. By the table of the ordinances. IV. Without constant restoration we are not ready for the perpetual assaults of hell, for the stern afflictions of heaven, or even for strifes from within.—C. H. Spurgeon.

2, 3. (2) R. V. "Who hath raised up one from the East, whom he calleth in righteousness to his foot? he giveth nations before him," etc. **the righteous,** Cyrus is undoubtedly here referred to;[e] and regarded as the minister of God's righteousness. **called.. foot,** fig. for engaging in his service, in order to follow him and perform the duties prescribed.[a] **gave .. nations,** "first the kingdom of the Medes, then Lydia, the kingdom of the rich Crœsus, and the Greek cities of Asia Minor." **gave .. bow,** Pol. Bib. "His sword makes them like dust, his bow like driven stubble." (3) **safely,** or securely. **way .. feet,** better translate "the path with his feet he does not tread," a picture of the celerity of his movements.—Camb. Bib.

Cyrus.—Cyrus was to the Gentiles a type of the Messiah, even as David or Solomon to the Jews; and accordingly we find him spoken of as the Lord's anointed (ch. xlv. 1). Comparing the things which are related of him with the history of Eastern kings and conquerors of his age or that preceding, and especially with the monstrous oppressions, butcheries, massacres, and cruelties recorded on the slabs of Nineveh, he seems like a man of another world. It is a gleam of sunshine breaking through thunder-clouds. The soberest and most truthful of the Greek philosophers (himself a statesman, general, and historian) has selected him as the pattern of a perfect prince, and made his education the theme of a most interesting and instructive book. Whence had he that education? Who raised up that one from the east? called him to His foot? At whose feet was he brought up? and from whose precepts did he receive instruction in righteousness?—W. B. Galloway.

4—7. (4) **calling .. beginning,** guiding the course of all nations and peoples since the creation. **I the Lord,** this gives the answer. **first .. last,** Jehovah existed before all things, and He will outlast them all.[b] (5) **drew near,** etc., consulting together how to defend themselves against the conquering Persians. (6) **good courage,** and set to work to make, and secure the favor of, new gods. (7) **goldsmith,** or founder; smith. **soldering,** R. V., "saying of the soldering, It is good." The irony is severe, but true to the facts as Herodotus relates them. The statesmen hoped to keep back Cyrus by sending sobbing messages to one another, Be of good courage; the priests "by making a particularly good and strong set of gods."—G. A. Smith.

God's Help in Emergency.—The God who raised up Cyrus, who constrained him to answer his own Divine ends, who empowered him to do such great things, and to triumph over such serious obstacles, is One who evidently gives heed to individual souls, and who both can and will select the very instruments which are needed to work out the redemption for which we are waiting and hoping. He who similarly raised up Luther, Zwingle, Calvin, Tyndale, Knox, etc., to take their place and do their work when such men as they were wanted, will not fail us in our emergency now.—Pul. Com.

8, 9. But Israel is bidden "Fear not" because of its peculiar relation to Jehovah. **my servant,** as worshipers of the true God. **chosen,** De. iv.

---

b "To make still clearer the contrast between the power and wisdom of the God of Israel and of the gods of the heathen, these latter are challenged to show and compare their performances beside His."—Mat. Arnold.

c Je. xxv. 22.

Ps. xlvi. 10; Ha. ii. 20; Zec. ii.13.

d "Jehovah here summons the idolators themselves to enter into controversy with Him. The challenge is a general one, directed to the whole heathen world."—J. A. Alexander.

e "The man called is Cyrus, from Persia, wh. is easterly both to Babylonia and to Palestine. Cyrus had the character of a mild and just prince. His religion, the religion of Persia, rejected and forbade idols like the religion of Israel." — Mat. Arnold.

a "To call to one's foot is a Heb. idiom for calling to one's service, or summoning to take a place among one's followers."—J. A. Alexander.

b Is. xliii. 10, xliv. 6, xlviii. 12; Re. i. 17, xxii. 13.

"From history we learn that the Cumoeans consulted the Milesian oracle, 'alarmed at the power of the Persians.' And Croesus sent round to all the principal oracles for their advice."—Spk. Com.

37, vii. 6, 7. **my friend,** 2 Chr. xx. 7;[a] Ja. ii. 23. (9) **chief men,** R. V., "corners," i. e. Haran in Mesopotamia, Abraham's fatherland, (Gen. xxiv. 4, 7.) To one in Palestine this would seem a far away land.

Servants (vs. 9).—1. It is by Divine grace that we are made servants of God; 2. Unfaithful, unprofitable, yet servants; 3. Once we were servants of sin; 4. Not only servants, but chosen ones; 5. We are, too, His servants for ever.—C. H. Spurgeon.

The Divine Choices Are Wise Selections.—Abraham and Jacob are God's chosen ones as founders, and first fathers, of the Israelite race. By this we are to understand that they were selected, in the Divine wisdom, as having just the qualities which, developed in a race, would make a people precisely fitted to carry out his purposes. We are not to understand that, in a way of accident, or in a way of mere sovereignty, these first fathers were picked out. God's choices are never arbitrary; they are always judicious selections. "The race is described as God's servant and his elect, or, combining the two characters, his chosen servant, chosen to be his servant." This special relation to Jehovah is the thing which distinguishes the people of Israel from the heathen nations around them. "What advantage then hath the Jew? . . . Much every way: chiefly, because that unto them were committed the oracles of God" (Rom. iii. 1, .. Divine choices are selections, on the ground of recognized fitness.—Pul. Com.

10. **Fear thou not,** however other nations may fear. Cyrus would prove no enemy to God's people, bec. God was using him to work out His purposes. **dismayed,** so as, like the nations. to look about anxiously for help. **will strengthen,** or perhaps have strengthened, etc. **right .. righteousness,** or "with My just right hand."[a]

Strength (vs. 10).—I. We all need to be strengthened. 1. For temptation assails us; 2. The world is around us; 3. There is sin within us; 4. There are duties before us. II. God has a great reserve of strength with which to discharge this engagement. He who is able to uphold the universe will never prove unable to fulfil His promises.

God's Help.—You know what a grand matter is God's help. A minister was one day bringing his book upstairs into another room, for he was going to have his study on the first floor instead of downstairs, and his little boy wanted to help father carry some of the books. "Now," said the father, "I knew he could not do it, but as he wanted to be doing something, to please him and to do him good by encouraging his industry, I told him he might take a book and carry it up." So away he went, and picked out one of the biggest volumes—Caryl on Job or Poli Synopsis, I should think—and when he had climbed a step or two up the stairs, down he sat and began to cry. He could not manage to carry his big book any further; he was disappointed and unhappy. How did the matter end? Why, the father had to go to the rescue, and carry both the great book and the little man. So, when the Lord gives us a work to do, we are glad to do it, but our strength is not equal to the work, and then we sit down and cry, and it comes to this, that our blessed Father carries the work and carries the little man too, and then it is all done, and done gloriously. It is a simple illustration, but may it comfort some desponding heart. "Yea, I will help thee."—Spurgeon.

Strength from Communion with God.—
"Lord, what a change within us, one short hour,
Spent in Thy presence, will avail to make?
What heavy burdens from our spirits take,
What parched grounds refresh as with a shower!
We kneel, and all around us seems to lower;
We rise, and all, the distant and the near,
Stands forth in sunny outline, brave and clear.
We kneel, how weak!—we rise, how full of power!
Why therefore should we do ourselves this wrong
Or others, that we are not always strong;
That we are ever overborne with care;
That we should ever weak or heartless be,
Anxious or troubled, when with us is prayer,
And joy and strength and courage are with Thee."—Trench.

a "'Khalil-Allah,' or, as he is more usually called, 'El Khalil,' simply, 'The Friend,' is a title which has, in Mussulman countries, superseded altogether his own proper name." — Stanley.

De. vii. 6, x. 15.

"Friendship is the nearest thing we know to what religion is. God is love. And to make religion akin to friendship is simply to give it the highest expression conceivable by man."—Drummond.

a "The right hand that does right." — Nagelsbach.

"Travelers tell us of some countries which are so full of aromatic plants and flowers that they perceive the fragrance at some distance, and are highly refreshed by the pleasing gales. Do you not think it is the same with the Christian traveler, as he bears up towards the heavenly country, of which 'the land flowing with milk and honey' was a figure, a shadow, a very inadequate resemblance?" — Lavington.

"The breath of Divine knowledge is the bellows of Divine love, and the flame of Divine love is the perfection of Divine knowledge." — Quarles.

"The words which give us the secret of the old Hebrew courage reveal the source of the courage we need as Christians. The notion, indeed, has

11, 12. (11) **ashamed,** with the shame of defeat. **strive,** or "the men of thy strife." (12) **contended,** they who made war with thee. **nothing,** etc., R. V., "They that strive with thee shall be as nothing, and shall perish."

The Effective Spread of Christianity a Growth (vs. 11).—I. It is a natural growth. There is—1. Gradualness; 2. Variety; 3. Beauty. II. It is a valuable growth. 1. It produces true morality, righteousness; 2. True religion, praise. III. It is a universal growth. IV. It is a Divine growth. For—1. He prepares the soil; 2. Deposits the seed; 3. Imparts the quickening influence. Apply:—(1) This subject corrects an error in Christian propagandism; (2) Indicates the true method of teaching the Gospel; (3) Affords a touchstone to the character.—Thomas.

13, 14. (13) **will hold,** better, do hold. **will help,** or do help thee. (14) **worm Jacob,** "creature of the dust, prostrate and helpless;"[b] comp. Ps. xxii. 6. **ye men,** or ye few men. **redeemer.** Read with R. V. and thy Redeemer is the Holy One. The word for "Redeemer" is Gó'él, the technical term for the person charged with the duty of buying back the alienated property of a kinsman, of avenging his death, and certain other obligations (see Lev. xxv. 48 f.; Num. xxxv. 19 ff.; Ruth iii. 12, etc.). It is a standing title of Jehovah in the latter part of Isaiah, occuring in 12 passages (the corresponding verb in 6 others). The verb means originally to assert a right by purchase: hence fig. to reclaim, rescue.—Camb. Bib.

Fear Not (vs. 14).—I. Before we can do anything for God there must be a sense of weakness. 1. This is learned by contemplation; 2. By suffering; 3. By labor. II. There must be trust in promised strength. III. There must be the removal of fear by this promise. 1. Fear is painful; 2. Is weakening; 3. Dishonors God.—C. H. Spurgeon.

Courage.—Omniscience watches over the chosen, and omnipotence supports them. Among other "gifts and graces" let us recognize courage and resolution. Timidity, faint-heartedness, is a universal weakness, and the higher or sacred courage one of the rarest possessions of the soul. Perhaps, next to wisdom, it is Heaven's greatest gift. It "gives and obtains kingdoms, turns swords into sceptres, crowns the valiant with victory, and the victorious often with a diadem." Presence of mind: what can impart it like the feeling that God is ever with us, that our feeble hand is enclosed in his? "It is a kind of ecstasy and inspiration, a beam of Divine light darting in upon reason, and exalting it to a pitch of operation beyond its natural and accustomed measures. Perhaps there was never any person in the world remarkably and heroically great, without some such kind of enthusiasm—a mighty principle which at certain times raised him up to strange, unaccountable heights of wisdom and courage. He who in the strength of such a spirit can look the most menacing dangers in the face, and, when the state of all things about him seems desperate, can yet bear his great heart above despair—such a one for the most part makes fortune itself bend and fall down to him, difficulties vanish, and dangers fly before him; so much is victory the claim of the valiant, and success the birthright of the bold."—Johnson.

15, 16 (15) **threshing instrument,** either a sledge armed with iron and sharp stones, or a system of rough rollers (tribulum). **mountains,**[a] allegorical for empires and kingdoms. (16) **fan them,** alluding to another agricultural operation, that of winnowing. "This weakest of nations shall become a power against which nothing can stand. Fulfilled in a slight degree in the Maccabaean wars." In the plains of Hamath grain is still threshed by revolving sledges.—Cheyne.

The Worm Jacob, Threshing the Mountains (vss. 14—16).—Addressing his people, God declares—I. Their character. II. Their labors. III. Their successes. IV. Their triumphs. Learn hence—1. The folly of unbelief; 2. The need of constant exertions.—C. Simeon.

Threshing-floors.—They are arranged all round the town, and the scene is picturesque and novel. The most common mode of threshing is with the ordinary slab, called mowrej, which is drawn over the floor by a horse or yoke of oxen, until not only the grain is shelled out, but the straw itself is ground up into chaff. To facilitate this operation, bits of rough lava are fastened into the bottom of the mowrej, and the driver sits or stands upon it. It is rare sport for the children to sit on these slabs, and even our own delight, to get out to the baidar, as the floor is called,

gone forth that the ancient fortitude has no place in the life of the Christian, but if this means that the Christian is to be only a loving, and not a righteous man, then the teaching of Christ Himself contradicts it." — Hom. Com.

b "However weak and despised and trodden under foot thou mayest be, in thy captivity and exile, yet fear not, I will help thee." — Wordsworth.

Is. xliii. 1, xliv. 1, 2.

"When the soul leaves God once, and looks downward, what is there to stay it from disquiet? Remove the needle from the polestar, and it is always stirring and trembling, never quiet till it be right again. So, displace the soul by taking it from God, and it will never be quiet. The devil cast out of heaven and out of the Church, keeps ado; so do unruly spirits led by him."—Sibbes.

a "The highest and strongest, and most stubborn of thine enemies."—Mat. Henry.

"The Church will not be filled with a perilous complacency; it will rejoice in the Lord its God—in the honor in which he is universally held; in the love with which all hearts are filled toward him; in the service which every human life is paying him. These ingredients will fill to the brim its pure cup of joy."—Clarkson.

and ride round on the mowrej. The Egyptian mowrej is a little different from this, having rollers which revolve on the grain, and the driver has a seat upon it, which is certainly more comfortable. In the plains of Hamath I saw this machine improved by having circular saws attached to these rollers. It is to this instrument, I suppose, that Isaiah refers: "Behold, I will make thee a new sharp threshing instrument having teeth: thou shalt thresh the mountains, and beat them small, and shalt make the hills as chaff. Thou shalt fan them, and the wind shall carry them away, and the whirlwind shall scatter them."—Thomson.

"We often need encouragement.. The greatness of the consolation offered proves the greatness of the impending danger." —Hom. Com.

If God does not hold us up, we shall faint, and fail utterly.

17, 18. "With great pathos the prophet recalls to mind the miserable condition of Israel in the present, and adapts his glorious promise to their sense of need. He is thus led to a glowing description of the marvels of the desert journey, in which, however, a spiritual meaning is not lost sight of."—Camb. Bib. (17) **poor .. water,** a promise that should be referred to the difficulties of the journey back from Babylon to Palestine.[a] Perhaps with special reference to those who had been conscious of the religious privations of the captivity, who had thirsted for the water of life. **faileth,** or is rigid, parched. (18) **rivers,** recalling the provisions made during the wilderness journey from Egypt.[b] **high places,** R. V., "on the bare heights."

[a] "On the march of the suffering exiles through the desert in the promised and approaching return of the Jews to their country. In these regions water is almost the first object of a man's thoughts. God promises His people to provide water in the wilderness and on the bare highlands for them, and verdure in the desert, that their return may be made easier." —Mat. Arnold.

[b] Is. xxx. 25, xxxv. 7.

Note on vs. 18.—A most important pastoral duty in the Eastern regions is to provide water for the flock. The living fountain and the flowing stream generally furnish a sure and abundant supply; but these are seldom found in the burning desert, where the Oriental shepherd is often compelled to feed his cattle. In such circumstances, happy is he who finds a pool where his flocks may quench their thirst. Often, as he pursues his journey, a broad expanse of water, clear as crystal, seems to open to his view, and, faint and weary under the fierce sunbeam, he gazes on the unexpected relief with ineffable delight, and fondly anticipates a speedy termination to his present distress. He sees the foremost camels enter the lake, and the water dashed about by their feet. He quickens his pace, and hastens to the spot; but to his utter disappointment the vision disappears, and nothing remains but the dry and thirsty wilderness. To such deceitful appearances the Prophet opposes, with admirable effect, the real pool, the o'erflowing fountain, and the running stream; the appropriate symbols of those substantial blessings of grace and mercy that were laid up in store for the Church of Christ in the last days: "And the parched ground (or the scorching heat) shall become a pool, and the thirsty land springs of water." "I will open rivers in high places, and fountains in the midst of the valleys; I will make the wilderness a pool of water."—Paxton.

"There is spiritual thirst quenched and spiritual refreshment provided. The desert becomes a lake, the wilderness a garden. God opens streams, not only in the valleys, but on the hills; 'high places.'" —Birks.

19, 20 (19) **cedar,**[a] **2 Sa. ii. 2—7. shittah,** R. V., "acacia," Ex. xxv. 5. **myrtle,** Ne. viii. 15. **oil tree,** or wild olive. **fir tree,** or cypress. **pine,** or plane (elm) **box tree,** or sherbin, a tall cedar. The prophet names here four trees at least which are "the glory of Lebanon"—he evidently means that the very desert shall become as glorious as Lebanon has been. (20) **created it,** i. e. the purpose of this miracle will be to demonstrate the creative power of Israel's God.

[a] "The main idea of this vs. is that of trees growing where they never grew before." — J. A. Alexander.

"These trees are all fragrant and durable." —Spk. Com.

The Voice of Nature.—Standing at Chamounix a poet exclaims:—

Ye ice-falls! Ye that from the mountain's brow
Adown enormous ravines slope amain,—
Torrents, methinks, that heard a mighty voice
And stopped at once, amidst their maddest plunge!
Motionless torrents! Silent cataracts!
Who made you glorious as the gates of Heaven
Beneath the keen full moon? Who bade the sun
Clothe you with rainbows? Who with living flowers
Of loveliest blue, spread garlands at your feet?—
God! let the torrents, like a shout of nations,
Answer, and let the ice-plains echo, God!
God! sing, ye meadow streams, with gladsome voice!
Ye pine groves, with your soft and soul-like sounds!
And they too have a voice, yon piles of snow,
And in their perilous fall shall thunder, God!—Coleridge.

"With earth's poor, caresome droilings tired, opprest,
What right have I to lean upon Thy breast;—
Because Thou offerest to the weary, rest."
—M. J. Preston.

God in Nature.—The Hebrews had no notion of what we denominate "secondary laws," but believed that God acted directly upon matter, and was the immediate, efficient cause of the solemn order and the varied and wonderful phenomena of nature. Dispensing thus with the whole machinery of cause and effect, as we employ those terms in philosophical language, their minds were brought into immediate contact with God in His manifold works, and this gave, both to devotion and the spirit of poetry, the liveliest inspiration and the freest scope of action. Heaven and earth were governed by His commands; the thunder was His "voice;" the lightning His "arrows." It is He who "causeth the vapor to ascend from the ends of the earth." When the famished city should call upon the corn, the wine, and the oil, and those should call upon the earth for nourishment, and the parched earth should call upon the heavens for moisture, and the heavens should call upon the Lord for permission to refresh the earth, then Jehovah would hear and supply. He gave the rain, and He sent the drought and famine. The clouds were not looked upon merely as sustained by a law of specific gravity, but God spread them out in the sky; these clouds were God's chariot, the curtains of His pavilion, the dust of His feet. Snow and hail were fearful manifestations of God, often sent as the messengers of His wrath.—Hibbard.

"With God time is not. Unto Him all is present eternity. Worlds, beings, years, with all their natures, powers, and events, — the range whereof, when making, He ordains,—unfold themselves like flowers. He foresees not, but sees all at once." —Bailey.

"The Master's work may make weary feet, but it leaves the spirit glad."—Mrs. Charles.

21, 22. The argument of vss. 1—4 is resumed, but now the idols, not the worshipers are addressed. Foreknowledge is the test of divinity. Can the idols show any sign of it? (21) **produce,** etc., evidence of their claims to divinity. **strong reasons,** forcible arguments and proofs. (22) **what shall happen,** putting their heathen oracles over against Jehovah's predictions.[a] **consider them,** so as to see if oracle and event have matched.

A True Test of Divinity.—The idols of the heathen were valueless; they could not tell "things to come hereafter;" they were utterly ignorant; they had no voice to answer the most urgent and pressing questions which men were asking. Those great and profound inquiries which we are now putting are beyond the reach of nature and of man. Nature, at the demand of science, can shed no light at all on the most sacred problems, the solution of which is everything to us. It makes no sign, it leaves us as we were. Its teaching is as consistent with one conclusion as with the opposite. Man, unaided by special illumination, can reach no certainty, can attain to nothing like assurance; he can guess, can argue, can hope, but he cannot know. God alone, the author of our being, the Lord of our life, the Arbiter of our destiny, can tell us whence we came and whose we are and whither we go. He can tell us "things to come hereafter," and much else which it is as urgent that we should know.—Pul. Com.

[a] "The proof to which they are challenged is Divine foreknowledge. It is placed at their option either to adduce prophecies uttered by them in ancient times, that they might be compared with the events to which they referred; or distinctly to announce some future contingent events." —Henderson.

Is. xliii. 9.

23—25. (23) **do good,** Pol. Bib. "Yea, do something, either good or bad, that we may at once marvel, and have somewhat to see." **dismayed,** at the signs of Divine power these heathen gods put forth. (24) **of nothing.** No answer comes and the prophet exclaims "Behold—you are naught—and he who worships you is an abomination." **abomination,** De. vii. 26. (25) Here follows a summary in evidence of Jehovah's claims. **north,**[b] North is the region of mystery and East the region of light. The terms are poetic.—Camb. Bib. **come upon,** better "trample upon," Pol. Bib. **princes,** prefects or deputies.

[b] Je 1, 3, 9.

"How did the atheist get his idea of that God whom he denies?" — Coleridge.

Omnipresence of God.—To the Hebrews, the external universe is just a black screen concealing God. All things are full of, yet all distinct from, Him. The cloud on the mountain is His covering; the muttering from the chambers of thunder is His voice; that sound on the top of the mulberry trees is His "going;" in that wind, which bends the forest or curls the clouds, He is walking; that sun is His still commanding eye. Whither can they go from His spirit? Whither can they flee from His presence? At every step and in every circumstance they feel themselves God-enclosed, God-filled, God-breathing men with a spiritual presence lowering or smiling on them from the sky, sounding in wild tempest, or creeping in panic stillness across the surface of the earth; and if they turn within, lo! it is there also—an "eye" hung in the central darkness of their own hearts. Hence the muse of the Hebrew bard is not Dame Memory, nor any of her syren daughters, but the Almighty, all-pervading Spirit Himself, who is at once the subject, the auditor, and the inspirer of the song.—Gilfillan.

"Such is the conclusion of the trial. The idols are utterly destitute of strength to aid their friends or distress their foes. Jehovah alone is worthy of confidence and regard, as the true God, Protector, and Guide. In times of deepest dis tress he can raise up a deliverer like Cyrus, and in his own way and time rescue his people from all their calamities." — Johnson.

a "This is the summary conclusion of the whole preceding controversy as to the divinity of any gods except Jehovah."—J. A. Alexander.

b The Jewish writer Abarbanel says that they who do not interpret this of Messiah are smitten with blindness.

"The law of prophetic suggestion leads Isaiah fr. Cyrus to the far greater Deliverer, behind whom the former is lost sight of." — Fausset.

Mat. xii. 18-20.

c 2 Sa. xxi. 6; Ps. cvi. 23.

"I believe that this world utterly and absolutely needs Christ and His life, and that without Christ and His life this world is, without any reference to the future, a lost and dying world."—Robert E. Speer.

a "God's servant shall bring to men's hearts the word of God's righteousness and salvation by a gentle, inward, and spiritual method." — Mat. Arnold.

b Is. lxi. 1-3; Mat. xi. 28-30.

c "The wick of a candle newly lighted, which is ready to go out again." — Mat. Henry.

d "The main idea seems to be that the end in question is to be accomplished not by clamor, not by violence, but by the truth."—J. A. Alexander.

26—29. (26) **Who,** etc., the speakers are Jehovah and His worshipers. They place themselves, in imagination, at the time of the fulfilment of this prediction, when this question will naturally be asked?—Cheyne. (27) **The first,** "I first have said unto Zion." Jehovah first announced by His Prophet the approach of the conqueror; before any other god or prophet. (28) R. V., "And when I look there is no man, even among them there is no counsellor," etc., i. e. among the idols is no one to forewarn or give advice. (29) **all,** R. V., "All of them," i. e. idols and people together. **nothing,** pure fiction and imposture. **wind,** etc., unsubstantial and fruitless. **confusion,** chaos.[a]

CHAPTER THE FORTY-SECOND.

1. my servant, this term has been applied both to Israel and to Cyrus; here it is applied to Messiah.[b] "The first traces of distinction between the real Servant and the whole nation are to be found in the Program of His Mission, Ch. xlii. 1—7."—G. A. Smith. **elect,** R. V., "my chosen,"[c] **spirit upon him,** Is. xi. 2, lxi. 1. **bring forth,** the ultimate purpose of the work of this Servant is the spread of the true religion over all the earth. **judgment** "means the religion of Jehovah regarded as a system of ordinances."—Camb. Bib.

The Character of the Messiah (vs. 1).—I. The person here designated—not Cyrus, or the Jewish people, or Isaiah, but Christ. II. For what office was He set apart? III. How He discharged this office. 1. Without violence; 2. He loved secrecy; 3. With great sympathy with men; 4. With truth and fidelity.—I. Wolfendale.

The Love of the Father.—If we have any saving acquaintance with the Gospel, we are at all times disposed to offer to the Son of God the homage of gratitude and praise for the work of redemption. But there are times when we are in danger of falling into the mistake of regarding the Saviour as offering Himself as a sacrifice to propitiate an angry God. We are prone to contemplate the Father as a stern, uncompromising, and unpitying Judge, actuated by vindictive feelings, taking pleasure in exacting punishment and inflicting pain; or a personification (so to speak) of the attributes of almighty power, unerring wisdom, and unswerving justice. But there our view of the great Creator stops, and there our apprehension of Him who is the Moral Governor of the world becomes defective. . . . Contemplating the bleeding Victim, voluntarily bleeding to atone for the guilty, and to bring back rebels to reconciliation and peace, the justice, power, and love of the Father are well-nigh forgotten in the sight of the tenderness and self-abandonment displayed by the Son. . . . But this Scripture combines with others to teach us that if we would love Him "who first loved us," we must pass on from Calvary to Him whose will is accomplished by the death and passion of His Son.—Kemble.

2, 3. (2) **cry,**[a] "the Servant's unobtrusive manner of working.[b] Not by clamorous self-assertion in the high places of the world, but by silent spiritual influences his great work shall be accomplished. Comp. the striking application in Matt. xii. 17 ff. This feature of the Servant's activity can hardly have been suggested by the demeanor of the prophets of Israel; and for that reason the prophecy is all the more wonderful as a perception of the true conditions of spiritual work. It reminds us of the 'still small voice' in which Elijah was made to recognize the power of Jehovah (1 Ki. xix. 12 f.)."—Camb. Bib. (3) **bruised reed,** a reed that is bruised is so easily broken. **smoking flax,** or a dim wick.[c] The patience of the Servant with the weak and hopeless, with those who have but little good left in them. **unto truth,** in accordance with truth.[d]

The Song of the Reed to the Bruised (vs. 3).—The Shepherd does not break His reed, for—I. He remembers its former services. II. He remembers there is a paucity of such reeds. III. He knows the possibility of the reed being rectified. IV. He prizes it because He fashioned it. 1. He chose it; 2. It cost Him very much; 3. He bruised the reed. Apply:—(1) Let us recognize the fitness of the metaphor; (2) Believe the declaration; (3) Believe much more.—Stems and Twigs.

Note on vs. 3.—Perhaps this imagery may be derived from the practice of the ancient shepherds, who were wont to amuse themselves with the music of a pipe of reed or straw; and when it was bruised they broke it, or threw it away as useless. But the bruised reed shall not be broken by this Divine Shepherd of souls. The music of broken sighs and groans is indeed all that the broken reed can afford Him; the notes are but low, melancholy, and jarring; and yet He will not break the instrument, but He will repair and tune it; till it is fit to join in the concert of angels on high; and even now its humble strains are pleasing to His ears. Surely, every broken heart must revive while contemplating this tender and moving imagery.—Pres. Davies.

4. **fail,** etc., the servant is here regarded as if he were the lamp and reed.. **set judgment,** or fully established the true religion.[e] **Shall wait,** perhaps "do wait," i. e. are looking, perhaps unconsciously, for something better than their own religion gives them.

Preaching of Christ.—Our Lord found many a topic of discourse in the scenes around Him. Even the humblest objects shine in His hands as I have seen a fragment of broken glass or earthenware, as it caught the sunbeam, light up, flashing like a diamond. With the stone of Jacob's well for a pulpit, and its water for a text, He preached salvation to the Samaritan woman. A little child, which He takes from its mother's side, and holds up blushing in His arms before the astonished audience, is the text for a sermon on humility. A husbandman on a neighboring height, between Him and the sky, who strides with long and measured steps over the field he sows, supplies a text from which He discourses on the Gospel and its effects on different classes of hearers. In a woman baking; in two women who sit by some cottage door grinding at the mill; in an old, strong fortalice, perched on a rock, whence it looks across the brawling torrent to the ruined and roofless gable of a house swept away by mountain floods—Jesus found texts. From the birds that sung above His head, and the lilies that blossomed at His feet, He discoursed on the care of God—these His text, and providence His theme.—Guthrie.

5—7. "A new revelation (followed by a solemn pledge) defining the mission of the Servant with greater precision."—Cheyne. (5) **saith God,** to His servant, Messiah. **spread .. earth,**[a] Ps. cxxxvi. 6. **people,** i. e. the whole human race. (6) **in righteousness,** "the meaning is that there is some consistency between the processes in creation and the efforts He calls on us to make."—G. A. Smith. **covenant,** or a mediator.[b] (7) **open,** etc., Is. lxi. 1; Lu. iv. 18; He. ii. 14, 15.

The Bondage of the Grammar; the Freedom of Literature.—Just as the child, after he has learned to read, through the bondage of alphabets and grammar and dictionaries, comes into the glorious liberty of literature, and roams through all its fields without thinking of the alphabet or grammar; as the musician, after his training in the laws of music, comes into the freedom where it is part of his nature to act according to those laws, and soars away beyond them in the delights and ecstacies of song or oratorio; so the Christian has entered a state far beyond the slavery of law, where it is natural and easy for him to do right; he acts from love, not law. He belongs to a higher sphere of action.—Peloubet.

8. **the Lord,** i. e. Jehovah; "God's distinguishing and incommunicable name."[c] "The self-existent and immutable." **glory .. another,** i. e. I will keep my promises and not give to the false gods any glory from my failure. **graven images,** put for idols in general.

Idolatry.—A lady, who lived some years at Serampore, in India, thus writes in a letter: "One evening, as I was walking with my husband by the river-side, we saw two respectable natives carrying a woman in their arms. We asked them what they were going to do with her. They very coldly answered, 'we are going to put her into the river, that her soul may go to heaven, for she is our mother!' I asked them if she was ill. They said, 'She is not very ill, but she is old, and has no teeth, and what is the use of her living?' I felt a great deal on hearing this, and said, 'What! have you no compassion on your mother? Will you drown her because she is old?' The woman instantly fixed her eyes on me, and said, 'What sort of a woman are you!' I told her I was an Englishwoman, and wished to prevent her children from drowning her, and, if they did, I would acquaint the governor with it, and have them both

"I will answer for it, the longer you read the Bible, the more you will like it; it will grow sweeter and sweeter; and the more you get into the spirit of it, the more you will get into the spirit of Christ." — Romaine.

[e] Je. xxiii. 5.

"Mild and gentle as he would be towards the broken - hearted and desponding, no power should depress his spirit, impede his progress, obscure his glory, or thwart his purpose." —Henderson.

Conquerors take away kingdoms; the heralds of Christ offer a kingdom.— Van Doren.

"God writes the Gospel not in the Bible only, but on the trees and flowers and clouds and stars." —Luther.

[a] "This clause is not a scientific but a poetical description. To the eye the heavens have the appearance of a canopy or curtain, and the verdant surface of the earth that of a carpet."—J. A. Alexander.

[b] Is. xlix. 8.

"It is the lack of liberty that causes so much deadness in the pulpit and deadness in the pew. Oh, for the liberty of the Spirit!"—A. J. Gordon.

[c] Ex. vi. 3; Ps. lxxxiii. 18, xcvi. 5; Ho. xii. 5.

"It was characteristic of idolatry that large promises were made to men by oracle and priest, for which there was no guarantee; and there is no more miserable chapter in the history of idols than the chapter of excuses for disappointed promise-holders. No reproach of men can be more severe and searching than this, 'They feared the Lord, and served other gods.'" — Pul. Com.

"The true measure of loving God is to love Him without measure." — St. Bernard.

[a] Comp. Jos. xxi. 45.

[b] "A botanical metaphor, aptly introduced to show that no appearances existed which gave the least indication of the things predicted. They were, as it were, hid under ground from the sight of mortals." —Henderson.

[c] "In the convulsions of war and change coming upon the earth God's arm was about to be shown in the overthrow of idolatrous Babylon, and in the restoration of His chosen people; hence this song of triumph." — Mat. Arnold.

[d] Is. xxi. 16.

[e] Is. xvi. 1.

"Make us to meet what is or is to be
With fervid welcome, knowing it is sent
To serve us in some way full excellent,
Though we discern it all belatedly."
—J. W. Riley.

The blessedness of God's house is that there men praise him. This it was that made that house so precious to the Psalmist.

hanged. They said, 'Never mind;' and proceeded towards the river. My husband then ran down the bank, and, taking hold of the woman, insisted upon their taking her home. They did so; but, sad to tell, they brought her again the next evening, and Mr. Felix Carey saw them throw her into the water, without performing the usual ceremony of giving her water in the name of their gods."—Whitecross.

9, 10. (9) **former things,** things previously prophesied, which have been fulfilled:[a] Spring forth[b] "Events shoot forth from predictions. The new things are not merely the victories of Cyrus, but much more, the glorious future of Israel, of which those victories are the condition. No mere politician could guess that Israel would be treated by Cyrus differently from other peoples, and that Jerusalem would become the religious capital of the world."—Pol. Bib. (10) **Sing,** as the sign of universal joy in the delightful expectation.[c] **down..sea,** comp. Ps. xcvi. 11.

The Praying Light-keeper.—We were fog-bound in Penobscot Bay, and made harbor at Eagle Island. Just as the sun was setting we went on shore, and walking toward the lighthouse, were attracted by the voice of someone in prayer. It was an impressive scene. Before us stretched out the broad Atlantic; the gathering shades of evening deepened the solitude. In the light above us was the keeper, where he had just lighted his lamp. His face was turned toward the sea; his long hair and beard were whitened with the snows of many winters. His arms were outstretched and his voice alone broke the silence, as he besought the Almighty, in the hollow of whose hands the seas are held, to protect the sailor, and to forgive his sins. "Them prayers will go higher than the light," said our skipper, and all of us felt that we had come into the near presence of God, on that lonely island far at sea. Who can measure the Divine Providence that shines out from the lighthouse on Eagle Island, because of that praying lighthouse-keeper?—Old Test. Anec.

11, 12. (11) **wilderness,** etc., the expanse of desert country bet. Babylonia, Palestine, and Arabia. **cities,** i. e. villages on the oases, where the Arabs live. **Kedar,** an Arabian people, Ge. xxv. 13. Prob. put here for the Arabs generally.[d] **the rock,** R. V., "of Sela," the rock city of Edom.[e] (12) **islands,** as previously, a general term for coasts and countries. The districts here referred to lay westward, as the Arab countries lay eastward.

Power of Sacred Song.—Duncan Matheson, a Bible-reader to the soldiers in the Crimea, was returning one night to his lodgings in an old stable. Sickened by the sights he had seen, and depressed with the thought that the siege of Sebastopol was likely to last for months, he trudged along in the mud, knee-deep. Happening to look up, he saw the stars shining calmly in the clear sky. Weariness gave place to the thought that in heaven is rest, and he began to sing aloud the old hymn:

How bright these glorious spirits shine!
Whence all their bright array?

The next day was wet and stormy. While going his rounds, Matheson came upon a soldier standing under the veranda of an old house. The man was in soiled and ragged clothes, and his shoes were so worn that they did not keep his feet from the mud. The Bible-reader drew him into conversation, cheered him by encouraging words, and gave him money to buy shoes. "I am not what I was yesterday," answered the man, his heart opening to Matheson's sympathy. "Last night I was tired of life and of this blundering siege. I took my musket and went down yonder, determined to blow out my brains. As I got round that hillock I heard some one singing, 'How bright these glorious spirits shine!' It recalled to me the Sabbath school where I used to sing it, and the religious truths I had heard there. I felt ashamed of being such a coward. I said to myself, 'Here is a comrade as badly off as I am, but he is not a coward—he's bearing it!' I felt that that man had something which I did not possess to make him accept with cheerfulness our hard lot. I went back to my tent, and to-day I am seeking that thing which made the singer so happy."—Youth's Companion.

13, 14. (13) "The reason for this universal exultation: Jehovah takes the field against His enemies. The gracious side of His intervention is reserved for vs. 16."—Camb. Bib. **man of war,** Ex. xv. 3; Ps. xxiv. 8. **jealousy,**[f] better "zeal." **roar,** the shout, or battle-cry, of a warrior. **prevail,** marg. behave himself mightily. (14) **cry .. woman,**[g] intimating a sudden and strong Divine determination. **destroy, etc.,** R. V., "I will gasp and pant together."

The Severe Aspect of God.—There is a power beyond man's; and nothing is held safely that is not held by consent of that power. God cannot be described in parts; He is to be studied in the unity of His character. Men are bound to be as common-sense in their theology as in the ordinary works of life; in building character they should be at least as sagacious as in building houses; they must build for tempestuous as well as for fine weather. We prepare for the severe side of Nature—why ignore the severe aspect of God? This is not preaching the mere terrors of the Lord; it is being simply faithful to facts. The so-called success of the bad man has yet to stand the strain of the Divine trial. God will examine our title-deeds. Remember, we are not stronger than our weakest point.—Hom. Com.

15, 16. "Judgment and redemption side by side." (15) **mountains,** etc., as prev., the symbols of governments, such as the Babylonian, wh. hindered His people from their return to their own land. **rivers,** the great rivers of Mesopotamia. (16) **blind,** etc., i. e. the spiritually blind, who cannot discern God's purposes; or "the perplexed and desponding" to whom life is pathless. **darkness, etc.,** figures for overcoming all kinds of difficulty. **These .. them,** "These are the things I have determined to do and not leave undone."—Camb. Bib.

The Way of the Blind (vs. 16).—God's conduct towards His people gives a striking view—1. Of the state in which they set out in life, spiritually blind; 2. Of the manner in which this blindness is removed; 3. Of the necessary steps that are taken to make this deliverance a blessing indeed; 4. This view of the conduct of Divine grace is crowned with the promise of persevering grace, and support to the end of life.—T. N. Toller.

17, 18. (17) **turned back,** then, after such evidences of the providence of Jehovah, the idolaters shall be ashamed and turned back. (18) **deaf .. blind,** the subject here addressed is Israel as it is, "At present the deaf and blind appear to predominate among the exiles."—Pol. Bib.

19, 20. (19) **Who is blind,**[a] Israel is the blind and deaf nation par excellence, because no other nation has been so tested by the opportunity of seeing and hearing.—Camb. Bib. **perfect,** R. V., "at peace with me," Heb. meshullam, he that is God's favored friend. (20) **Seeing .. not,** R. V., "Thou seest many things, but thou observest not; his ears are open, but he heareth not," i. e. Great events have occurred before Israel which they heeded not nor understood.[b] Is. liii. 1. The Jews had, through long ages, been honored with special Divine revelations.

Live Souls.—To have faculties that have fallen into disuse, to have the symbols of manhood but no virility, to look a man, and yet be but a thing, to seem to have a heart and yet have no response to human want and pain,—that is the inconceivable but possible irony. Having eyes, they see not; having ears, they hear not; having hearts, they do not understand. Yet are they counted as of the population of the earth. A man may withdraw himself from the working force of society, and from the real manhood of the world, and may occupy room of which he is not worthy. Only they should be counted whose souls are alive.—Peop. Bib.

21, 22. (21) R. V., "It pleased the Lord for his righteousness sake to magnify the law," etc., i. e. by extending the knowledge of it to all mankind.[c] **the law,** Pol. Bib. "his instruction," i. e. the true religion. Comp. xlii. 1.[d] (22) **robbed,** etc., ch. xvii. 14, descriptive of the sufferings of Israel in exile. **snared,** Babylon, to a faithful Jew was a pit, or dungeon. Comp. Zech. ix. 11. **spoil,** Heb., a treading.[e]

Origin of the Commandments.—An infidel of acute mind sought an acquaintance with the truth of the Bible, and began to read at the Book of Genesis. When he had reached the ten commandments, he said to a friend, "I will tell you what I used to think. I supposed that Moses was the leader of a horde of banditti; that, having a strong mind, he acquired great influence over superstitious people; and that on Mount Sinai he played off some sort of fireworks to the amazement of his ignorant fol-

And what Christian man can climb higher than this,—to find in the praise of God the greatest joy of his life?—J. J. S. Perowne.

[f] Better rendered zeal, because our associations with the word jealousy make it unsuitable as applied to God. If used of God it should be distinctly understood to mean, "sensitive regard for His own honor, and for the welfare of His people."

[g] Ga. iv. 19.

"No soul was ever lost because its fresh beginning broke down; but thousands of souls have been lost because they would not make fresh beginnings." — Faber.

[b] Comp. Is. xliii. 8: Mat. xv. 14.

[a] "Israel, as a whole, is fainthearted, is slow to understand God's great purposes for it, and incredulous of them, in spite of all the experience it has had of God's guidance." — Mat. Arnold.

[b] Lu. vii. 23.

[c] "The people, being thus unfaithful to their trust, had no claim to be treated any longer as an object of Jehovah's favor; and yet He continues propitious, not on their account, but out of regard to His own engagements, and for the execution of His righteous purposes." — J. A. Alexander.

[d] Mat. v. 17; Ro. x. 4.

[e] "Notwithstanding all God's favor to Israel, Israel is

lowers, who imagined, in their mingled fear and superstition, that the exhibition was supernatural. I have been looking into the nature of that law. I have been trying to see whether I can add anything to it, or take anything from it, so as to make it better. Sir, I cannot. It is perfect. I have been thinking, Where did Moses get that law? I have read history. The Egyptians and the adjacent nations were idolaters; so were the Greeks and Romans; and the wisest or best Greeks or Romans never gave a code of morals like this. Where did Moses get that law which surpasses the wisdom and philosophy of the most enlightened ages? He lived at a period comparatively barbarous; but he has given a law in which the learning and sagacity of all subsequent time can detect no flaw. Where did he get it? He could not have soared so far above his age as to have devised it himself. I am satisfied where he obtained it. It came down from heaven. I am convinced of the truth of the religion of the Bible." The infidel (infidel no longer) remained to his death a firm believer in the truth of Christianity.

spoiled, and carried captive, and why? Not because of any failure in God's love, but because of their sins; because they are willfully blind and deaf." — Wordsworth.

23—25. (23) "The question expresses the prophet's wish that now at last some of the people should begin to realize the significance of their relation to Jehovah, and prepare themselves for the great deliverance. **will give ear to this,** i. e. to the substance of the present exhortation,—the contrast between the ideal calling of Israel and its present position, its failure to realize its mission, and (especially) the reason of that failure (vss. 24 f.)."—Camb. Bib. (24) **the Lord,** the blind people thought it was Babylon that had overthrown Jerusalem. **We .. sinned,** the prophet identifies himself with the people. (25) **Knew not,** i. e. did not understand it. **burned him,** in the Divine chastening fires.[a]

[a] De. iv. 24—28.

"In the great majority of things habit is a greater plague than ever afflicted Egypt; in religious character it is a grand felicity." — John Foster.

God's Loving Care.—Christ laid hold of in faith to-day will sustain us in the overflowing of the waters to-morrow. Though now, in the full flush of youth and health and strength, every nerve instinct with intense vitality, we cannot look at death without pain and shuddering, let us not fear. Dying grace will come with dying. God, who hath so loved us, will not leave us then. A father does not caress his child through the long summer day to abandon him at nightfall. Darkness may veil him from the little one's sight, or slumber lull him to temporary forgetfulness, but his loving-kindness wraps his child about, in the still hours, and a fatherly presence is in the house for good.—Gail Hamilton.

"O Lord take my heart, for I cannot give it to Thee, and when Thou hast it, oh! Keep it, for I cannot keep it for Thee; and save me in spite of myself, for Jesus Christ's sake." — Fenelon.

CHAPTER THE FORTY-THIRD.

1. Israel shall be saved. **But now,** marks a transition of thought. "There has been a conflict between divine love and divine wrath and the former has gained the victory. Now Jehovah will deliver and restore his people."—Cheyne. **created thee,** i. e. as a nation. **redeemed thee,** better "I redeem" and "I call," i. e. as one who is dear to me.[a] **mine,** i. e. wholly separated to the carrying out of My purposes.

[a] "To call by name includes the ideas of specific designation, public announcement, and solemn consecration to a certain work." — J. A. Alexander.

Fear Not.—Shall I tell you which commandment God gives most frequently? "Fear not." He says this more than eighty times—I believe eighty-four times; this is much oftener than any other commandment.

2. water .. fire, "when Jehovah was angry the fire burned Israel (ch. xlii. 25), but now with Jehovah on its side, it is invulnerable in the severest trials. 'Water' and 'fire' are common images of extreme peril; the former in Ps. xxxii. 6, xlii. 7, cxxiv. 4 f.; the latter in ch. xlii. 25 (cf. Dan. iii. 17, 27); both together Ps. lxvi. 12."—Camb. Bib.

"God's grace never shines so brightly as when it shines through the cloud of His people's sins. Nor does it ever appear so glorious as when displayed in the depth of their unworthiness. When nature is at the lowest, grace is generally at the highest." — Jas. Smith.

Support and Protection in the Day of Trial (vs. 2).—I. The people to whom these promises were addressed. II. The condition of that people as supposed in the text. III. The promises made to God's people in that condition.—E. Edwards.

Fear Not.—There is a printed leaf preserved in the Museum of Greenwich Hospital, England. Nothing is known of its history but this: It was found in the polar regions among the few relics of Sir John Franklin's expedition. It is a leaf torn from Todd's Student's Manual, and is the only relic of a book discovered. From the way the leaf is turned down it is plain the person meant to call attention to the dialogue there printed:—"Are you not afraid to die?" I asked. "No." "No! Why does

"Images of the greatest troubles and dangers, and promises of perfect security."—Henderson.

the uncertainty of another state give you no concern?" "Because God has said, Fear not: when thou passest through the waters, I will be with thee; and through the rivers, they shall not overflow thee."

3, 4. (3) **gave Egypt,** etc., The richest powers in the world should be given up as a ransom for Israel, to compensate Cyrus for the loss of it. Cambyses, the son of Cyrus, conquered Egypt, and invaded Ethiopia.[a] **Seba,** or Saba, i. e. Meröe on the upper Nile.[a] (4) **Since,** i. e. because thou art precious, honorable, and I love thee. **men for thee,** as the price of thy recovery fr. the Babylonish captivity. **people,** R. V., peoples, i. e. nations.

The Lord's Delight in His People (vs. 4).—The Lord will adorn the soul that He loves, hence we may discover who are the chosen people of God. When the Lord takes a sinner out of the world He will adorn that soul. He casts over him the robe of righteousness.—R. Cecil.

Trust in God.—

The child leans on its parent's breast,
Leaves there its cares, and is at rest;
The bird sits singing by his nest,
And tells aloud
His trust in God, and is blest
'Neath every cloud.

He has no store, he sows no seed;
Yet sings aloud, and doth not heed;
By flowing stream, or grassy mead
He sings to shame
Men who forget, in fear of need
A Father's name.

The heart that trusts for ever sings,
And feels as light as it had wings;
A well of peace within it springs;
Come good or ill,
Whate'er to-day, to-morrow brings,
It is His will!—I. Williams.

5—7. (5) east, etc.,[b] at the destruction of Jerus., and during the captivity, God's people had become scattered into all lands, so they were to be restored not from Babylon only. (6) **my daughters,** notice "the kind and even respectful mention of the female sex in Messianic descriptions. xi. 12: lx. 4: Joel ii. 28; Gal. iii. 28."—Cheyne. **ends .. earth,** none being too far away to be beyond the Divine reach. (7) **created,** as a member of My special kingdom.

Never Fear (vs. 5).—I. The exhortation. 1. Fear not anxieties; 2. Fear not want; 3. Enemies; 4. Duties; 5. Perils; 6. Death. II. The promise. 1. I am with thee to aid thee; 2. To comfort thee; 3. To guide thee; 4. Protect thee.—W. W. Whythe.

The Calmness of Trust.—When the steamship Massachusetts was wrecked in Long Island Sound, there were two mothers, each with a child, who were noticeable for their respectful calmness during the hours of greatest peril and anxiety, when it seemed as if the vessel must shortly go to pieces. A passenger from Philadelphia says that his attention was first called to them by their voices in singing. Going towards them, he found a little boy standing there with his life-preserver on, and the little fellow was just joining with his mother in singing a hymn of trust and confidence. And when rescue came, and the passengers were safely on another vessel, those same sweet voices were again heard, this time in a ringing strain of praise for their deliverance.—Pul. Com.

8, 9. "Another imaginary judgment scene (vss. 8—13) in which Israel appears as Jehovah's witness to the truth of his prophecies."—Camb. Bib. (8) **blind .. eyes,** i. e. the Jews.[a] (9) **people,** R. V., "peoples," i. e. the various nations. "The preceding verses (1-7) show us that it is the whole people, in their bulk and scattered fragments, who are referred to. Blind though they be, yet are there eyes among them; deaf though they be, yet they have ears. And so Jehovah addresses them all, in contradistinction to the heathen peoples (vs. 9). as His Servant."—G. A. Smith,

[a] "The worship of Ammon and Osiris was here celebrated in the most sumptuous manner." —Henderson.

"Sight is not necessary to the conscious presence of even an earthly friend. The room may be dark, not a word may be spoken, not a sound heard; but we feel that he is there. God's conscious presence fills the soul with faith, hope, peace. It is the consciousness of love and sympathy. It is the invisible, secret, gentle power of His Spirit that gives calmness and strength while trouble is pressing most heavily, and while external circumstances are the most distressing. — J. Rawlinson.

[b] "This promise, which had an initial fulfillment in the return fr. Babylon, and a larger one in the gathering in of Gentile converts, looks on yet further to the final recovery of Israel." — Spk. Com.

"Every regenerate individual is formed anew for God; in his new regenerate life he is to show forth God's praise." — Pul. Com.

[a] "Set free My people Israel, who have been blind to My ways but shall see them, and deaf to My word but shall hearken to it." — Mat. Arnold.

"For truth it is ever the fitting time; who waits till circumstances completely favor his undertaking will never accomplish anything." —Luther.

who .. things, Is. xli. 21. **or let,** etc., if they cannot plead, let them quietly listen to Me.

Sinning Against Light.—Carlyle quotes out of the Koran a story of the dwellers by the Dead Sea, to whom Moses was sent. They sniffed and jeered at Moses; saw no comeliness in Moses; and so he withdrew. But Nature and her rigorous veracities did not withdraw. When next we find the dwellers by the Dead Sea, they, according to the Koran, are all changed into apes. "By not using their souls, they lost them." "And now," continues Carlyle, "their only employment is to sit there and look out into the smokiest, dreariest, most undecipherable sort of universe. Only once in seven days they do remember that they once had souls. Hast thou never, O traveler! fallen in with parties of this tribe? Methinks they have grown somewhat numerous in our day." The old Greek proverb was that the avenging deities are shod with wool, but the wool grows on the eyelids that refuse the light. "Whom the gods would destroy, they first make mad;" but the insanity arises from judicial blindness. Jeremy Taylor says that whoever sins against light kisses the lips of a blazing cannon.—Old Test. Anecdotes.

"We take with solemn thankfulness
Our burden up, nor ask it less,
And count it joy that even we
May suffer, serve, or wait for Thee,
Whose will be done."
—Whittier.

10, 11. (10) **my witnesses,** the gods are unable to meet the challenge and Jehovah turns to his servant Israel, who could abundantly testify to the Divine faithfulness and goodness.[b] **no God formed,** i. e. He was, before these other gods were formed. (11) **beside me,** "I, I am Jehovah, and beside me there is no deliverer."[c]

b "The Jews are a monument of the wonderful fulfilment of the most extraordinary prophecies they themselves preserve, and bear witness to, though they shut their eyes to the fulfilment of them." —Whately.

c Is. xlv. 21.

God's witnesses (vs. 10).—I. Some of the principal things which believers are called to witness for God. 1. To His being and glorious perfections; 2. To the equity of His holy law; 3. To the excellence of His Gospel; 4. To the power of His grace; 5. To the influence of His truth; 6. To the use of His ordinances; 7. To the attention of His providence; 8. To the fulfilment of His promises; 9. To the glorious nature of His rest. II. Describe the character and qualification of God's witnesses. They are called, chosen, impartial, experimental, practical, tried, sworn, many, continued, continual, living, dying. They are competent, credible, unanswerable, and at the last day they will be convincing or condemning witnesses.—Ryland.

The witnesses against God whose testimony is most dishonoring to him, and at the same time most injurious to mankind, are the unworthy professors of belief in him. To confess God with the lips while denying him in the life, is to do him the greatest dis-service that is possible. It is to cast a doubt upon the value of all the human testimony borne in his favor, since who shall say how much of it is insincere? The Christian religion would, it is probable, have, long ere this, overspread the world, had it not been for the vicious lives of professing Christians. The testimony of their acts takes away all its force from the testimony of their words, and changes them from witnesses for God into most persuasive witnesses against Him. —Pul. Com.

12, 13. (12) **I,** emphatic; I Myself, and I alone. "The meaning of all this is plain. Jehovah is God alone, because He is directly effective in history for the salvation of His people, and because He has published beforehand what He will do. The great instance of this, which the prophecy adduces, is the present movement towards the liberation of the people, of which movement Cyrus is the most conspicuous factor."—G. A. Smith. (13) **before the day,** R. V. margin. "Yea, from this day forth I am the same." **work,** "Jehovah is not only the Immutable, but also the Omnipotent and Irresistible." **let it,** hinder it; turn it back.

14, 15. (14) **I have sent,** Cyrus, as My messenger. **have brought,** R. V., "and I will bring down all of them as fugitives, even the Chaldaeans, in the ships of their rejoicing," i. e. the ships that formerly resounded with shouts of joy and exultation.[a] **Chaldaeans,** the proudest part of the nation. (15) **your King,** Ps. lxxiv. 12, lxxxix. 18.

a "'I make the Chaldaeans to flee upon the barks that had before served for

Greatness of God.—When the French Government took steps to adorn the Academy of Design in Paris, they gave to Delaroche the painting of that picture which has now become world-renowned, called "The Hemicycle," in which, in some seventy or eighty figures, he grouped around an imaginary art-tribunal all the great architects, sculptors, engravers, and painters both of the ancient and modern world. Now imagine a larger court than this, and that in some vast area you had gathered together all the great souls that have adorned human life, and made the world rich, from the beginning—all great thinkers, all great legislators, commencing with the greatest, Moses; all great poets, who stand next to legislators as ordainers of the people's life; all great diplomatists; all great philosophers; all men who have had a deep insight into nature; all men of great bounty, and benevolence, and liberality; all men of princely wealth; all men eminent as artists; all noted scholars; all men of every age and class who have risen so high that their names have come down to us in history,—imagine that you had gathered together such an assembly of men, that each one was full of exquisite consciousness and susceptibility as regards the speciality in which he excelled, so that Michael Angelo had a full consciousness of all those wonderful combinations which populated his mind; so that Raphael had a full consciousness of all those sweet and exquisite conceptions which presented themselves to his interior vision; so that all that Murillo saw, and all that Claude fancied, and all that every other artist who had become eminent had ever conceived, should stand forth in them with exquisite, living sensibility, and then bring down from the highest point of heaven this Christ, and let Him stand in the midst, and let one after another speak to Him, each of the thing which is most to him; and, one by one, as they speak to Him, let them find that all of thought which they possess is His thought, that all of conception which they have is His conception, that all of sensibility and taste which they are conscious belong to their being are His sensibility and taste; let them find that He is familiar with everything in which they have stood pre-eminent; let the poet find that, as compared with Christ, he is but a prattling child; let the sculptor find that, as compared with Christ, he is but an unbegun artist; let the orator find that his words, in comparison with those of Christ, fall paralysed upon his lips, and they would, every one of them, bow before Him, and say, "Never Man spake like this Man." The architect, the sculptor, the poet, the orator, the philosopher, the scientist—every man in his own speciality; he that has ransacked the world in the line of beauty; he that has explored nature in the range of colors; they who have produced works of art that have challenged the admiration of the world; they who have moved masses with their eloquence; they who have soared anywhither in the fields of knowledge, or science, or art—these would each say, instantly, "I am but a spark, and here is the great and glowing soul out of which I flew as a mere spark." They would cry, "Were all of us gathered and tempered into one great nature, melted into one living being, we should still be less than nothing in the presence of this majesty of excellence, that includes everything in heaven, and all that can be on earth, and out of whom sprang everything that is, and everything that has been." The universal acknowledgment to Him would be, "In Thee we live, and move, and have our being."—H. W. Beecher.

16—19. "The sequel to the overthrow of Babylon is the deliverance of Israel, the method of which is compared with the greatest miracle in Israel's past history, the exodus from Egypt."—Camb. Bib. (16) **way in the sea,** Ex. xiv. 16, 22; Jos. iii. 13, 16. (17) **chariot,** etc., in allusion to the destruction of Pharaoh's army. (18) **Remember not,** i. e. that which is to happen will be so much greater than former things as to almost drive them out of the memory. **former things,** see Is. xlii. 9. (19) **Know it?** i. e. do you not recognize it? **way .. desert,** for the return of Israel from Babylonia to Palestine.[a]

20, 21 (20) **dragons,** R. V., "jackals." Ps. xci. 13. **owls,** R. V., "ostriches," even the wild creatures will praise God for their share in the abundance of water. (21) **This people,** R. V., "the people which I formed for myself, that they might set forth my praise," i. e. the water was for them.

God's Workmanship.—In ancient history we read of a prince, who, from the summit of his palace beholding the metropolis of his extensive empire, exulted thus, "This is Babylon the great—Babylon, which I have built for the house of my kingdom, by the might of my power, and for the honor of my majesty." He beheld the rising domes, the solemn temples, the numberless palaces of his lords; his heart bounded at the prospect, and his soul inflated with pride. Small cause, however, to be proud, had he recollected that these buildings were inhabited by a nation of slaves, and these temples filled with superstition and idolatry. In the sentence just read you have a far more noble potentate, even the King of kings Himself, reflecting upon the work of His hands, and rejoicing in the review of it. Beholding the triumphs of His grace, the accomplishment of His sacred purposes, and the wonders of His power, He expresses His complete satisfaction. His labor is not found in vain, His exertions are crowned with the designed success, and the production exactly corresponds with the plan laid down. With pleasure He reviews His

their pleasure.' The great feature of Babylon was its river, the Euphrates, with its quays, cuts, and artificial lakes; it served alike for use and for pleasure." — Mat. Arnold.

"The secret of the failure of the Divine judgments is the great secret of failure still; it is this — when men fall into trouble they persist in looking only at the second causes, and will not recognize the true and only cause, or recognize God's hand in them. It has been so in all ages. One of the most striking instances is that of the Roman siege of Jerusalem under Titus. Distinctly foretold as a Divine judgment on the nation for its rejection of Messiah, the Jews to this day will not so regard it. To them it is still only a national calamity, and so it has been hitherto ineffective in the production of a due sense of national sin."

"We cannot tell how far is the nearest fixed star, and we know that could we approach nearer, we would, for the first time, learn how far we were! Surely it is so with our religious estimates of approximation to the light and glory of God. It is only he who struggles nearer that begins at length to perceive the true amount of the distance." — Archer Butler.

a "The circumstances connected with the return should be altogether novel in their charac-

workmanship, and already anticipates that chorus of praise which will perpetuate the honor of His name through eternal ages.—Lambert.

22—24. (22) **not called,** "yet not upon me hast thou called, O Jacob, nor about me hast thou wearied thyself O, Israel," i. e. this salvation is all the more wonderful in that it is given to the people before they had penitently sought it.—Comp. Ro. v. 8. (23) **small cattle,** or lambs, Ps. l. 8. Offering of sacrifice publicly had ceased during the captivity, but it seems that private sacrifice had ceased also. **caused . . serve,** laid no servile task on thee. (24) **sweet cane,** Calamus aromaticus, Je. vi. 20.[a] **made me to serve,** "this is the contrast which the prophet has had in view from the beginning of the section: while Jehovah has not burdened His people even with the offerings which it had been too ready to bring, it has burdened Him with its sins; and while Israel has taken its whole relation to Jehovah lightly, He has accepted the burden, and labored in its service for the removal of its guilt."—Camb. Bib.

Weary of God (vs. 22).—I. The nature of this evil. II. Its manifestations. III. Its occasion. IV. Its causes. V. Its bitter fruits. VI. Its prevention. VII. Its cure.—S. Martin.

Physical Weariness.—Sometimes our weariness is physical. Who can add up the debts of the body? Who can send in a true bill of particulars to the flesh? How it drags us down, overshadows us, mocks us, aggravates its own weight, until we cannot lift it, and then it suffocates us with heavy oppressiveness. Others are physically weak; they suffer on the other side of fleshly limitation and burdensomeness; they are not full-blooded, they inherit a thousand difficulties, perplexities, blindnesses, which they cannot explain and cannot escape; the head aches, the poor strength gives way under the increasing burden, the eyes become so dim that they cannot see whether the hand is going to the right or to the left or seizing the right instrument. God knows it all, and he will not judge the weak one harshly. He has special promises for the weak, and as for his Son it is among his glories that he has the tongue of the learned, and is able to speak a word in season to him that is weary. Let us here pluck up courage like men who have heard a message from the King, and are told that weakness is not faithlessness when it can be traced to physical causes.—Peop. Bib.

25, 26. (25) **blotteth,** etc., Ps. li. 9. Figure for erasing from public records the charge of crime. **mine own sake,** "from motives derived purely from My own nature, uninfluenced by any cause in you."[b] (26) **us plead together,**[c] i. e. Israel and God. **declare,** R. V., "set thou forth thy cause." **justified,** shown to be in the right. The desire of God is to bring home to His people the sense of their guilt.

Forgiveness of Sin (vs. 25).—I. The nature of the blessing. 1. There is remission; 2. There is reconciliation. II. The author of the blessing. 1. The only being who has a right to bestow it; 2. Or the power; 3. Or who has devised and executed a plan for bestowing it. III. The ground on which the author of the blessing bestows it. 1. Not on the ground of anything in us; 2. But of something in Himself. Apply:—(1) Seek this blessing; (2) Accept; (3) Be grateful for it.—G. Brooks.

Apprehension of Forgiveness.—Sin is but the cloud, as it were, behind which the everlasting sun lies in all its power and warmth, unaffected by the cloud; and the light will yet strike, the light of his love will yet pierce through, with its merciful shafts, bringing healing in their beams, and dispersing all the pitchy darkness of man's transgressions. And as the mists gather themselves up and roll away, dissipated by the heat of that sun in the upper sky, and reveal the fair earth below, so the love of Christ shines in, melting the mist and dissipating the fog, thinning it off in its thickest places, and at last piercing its way right through it, down to the heart of the man that has been lying beneath the oppression of this thick darkness.—Maclaren.

27, 28. (27) **first father,** perhaps with reference to Jacob: see vs. 22.[a] "Prob. a more general sense is meant to be given to the expression 'thy forefathers,' 'thy race from its first beginning.'"—Mat. Arnold. **teachers,** i. e. prophets and religious leaders. If these have sinned how much more the great body of the people. (28) **profaned,** i. e. deprived of their sacred dignity.[b] **princes,** etc., or the chief priests. **and have given,** render: and

---

ter. To indicate that every provision for comfort and security would be made, the boldest poetical images are employ e d." — Henderson.

Je. xxiii. 7.

[a] "An ingredient of the holy anointing oil (Ex.xxx.23). It is mentio n e d with cinnamon. "Dr. Boothroyd has 'sweet reed.' Tamal, 'sweet b a r k!' This probably means cinnamon, as we k n o w that 'sweet bark' was used by Moses in the service of the sanctuary: and it is in connection with the sacrifices of the Most High that it is here mentioned by the Prophet." —Roberts.

[b] Is. xxxvii. 35, xlviii. 11; Eze. xxxvi. 22, etc.

"Take this as the test of your Christian hope. If it makes you work, it is right; if it does not, there is something wrong with it." — Alexander McLaren.

[c] "The Jews are called upon to specify a single instance in wh. they had done anything really meritorious." — Henderson.

"A love of the good things of the world vitiates a Christian's w o r k; but self-denial is the unanswerable, unfathomable element in Christian character. Self- assertion the world understands, but it is nonplussed before self-denial." — E. S. Tead.

[a] Ho. xii. 2, 3.

[b] "I have left them to suffer the same treatment as the

had to deliver Jacob to the ban. R. V. changes the translation for the worse.—Camb. Bib. **curse,** a solemn anathema, or excommunication. **reproaches.** Ps. cxxiii. 3, 4.

Note on vs. 27.—It may be considered as implied, that all their fathers who had since lived, shared in the original depravity, and thus the same sense is obtained that would have been expressed by the collective explanation of "first father," while the latter is still taken in its strict and full sense as denoting the progenitor of all mankind.—Alexander.

common people, stripped of their holy office, and in captivity."—Fausset.

CHAPTER THE FORTY-FOURTH.

1, 2. (1) **now,** marking the contrast, exactly as in ch. xliii. 1. **chosen,** selected as special agents for preserving My truth in the world.[a] (2) **formed,** etc., their birth, or origin, as from Egypt, is here referred to. **Jesurun,** i. e. "the upright one, a poetical title for Israel, designating the nation under its ideal character. Comp. Deut. xxxii. 15."—Pol. Bib.[b]

Peace With Respect to the Future.—The crosses which we make for ourselves by a restless anxiety as to the future, are not crosses which come from God. We show want of faith in Him by our false wisdom, wishing to forestall His arrangements, and struggling to supplement His Providence by our own providence. The future is not yet ours: perhaps it never will be. If it comes, it may come wholly different from what we have foreseen. Let us shut our eyes, then, to that which God hides from us, and keeps in reserve in the treasures of His deep counsels. Let us worship without seeing; let us be silent; let us abide in peace.—Fenelon.

[a] Is. xli. 8.

[b] The Greek has, "My beloved Israel;" Luther, Frommer, pious one.

De. xxxii. 15, xxxiii. 5, 26.

"Of all created comforts, God is the lender; you are the borrower, not the owner."—Rutherford.

"Blessed is any weight, however overwhelming, which God has been so good as to fasten with His own hand upon our shoulders." — F. W. Faber.

3, 4. (3) **pour,** etc., ch. **xxxii.** 15.[c] Comp. xi. 2, 3; xlii. 1, 4. "To be full of the knowledge and fear of God, and to make the world-wide spread of the true religion the chief object of life."—Cheyne. **thirsty .. dry ground,** figures to represent the hopeless condition of the captive people. **my spirit,** "the 'spirit' is the agent both of physical and moral regeneration, as in ch. xxxii. 15 (cf. Ez. xxxvii. 11—14); the former idea being prominent; hence the parallelism 'spirit'—'blessing,' the former being the cause, the latter the effect."—Camb. B. (4) **Spring..courses,** better read, "So that they spring up as grass amidst waters, as willows by water-courses."—Pol. Bib. The images denote luxuriance and abundance.

The Holy Spirit (vs. 3).—I. A special province has been assigned to the Holy Spirit in the economy of redemption. II. The promise of the Holy Spirit is the great promise of the Christian dispensation. III. The influences of the Holy Spirit are manifold,—enlightening, sanctifying, comforting. IV. The indwelling and inworking of the Holy Spirit may be confidently expected of all believers. V. The bestowment of the Holy Spirit is connected with an appointed order of means, especially prayer. VI. The want of the influences of the Holy Spirit is not only a calamity but a sin.—G. Brooks.

Times of Blessing.—During Mr. Sherman's ministry in Reading, his flock was visited by remarkable "times of refreshing," which can never be forgotten. He says himself: "One Whit-Sunday morning, I was preaching from Isa. xliv. 3-5, 'For I will pour water upon him that is thirsty, and floods upon the dry ground,' and as if to illustrate it, the Spirit of the Lord came like a flood over the parched souls of the congregation, and all became sensible that there was something more than human argument convincing the judgment. The congregation was melted to tears, and one poor backslider, on whom my hopes had long rested, unable to restrain himself, when I cried out, 'Who will "subscribe with his hand to the Lord" to-day?' cried out, 'I will.' The congregation caught the infection, and hands seemed involuntarily stretched out, as if ready to sign their names. It pleased God to move eighty-one souls, most of them young, to devote themselves to His service that day."—Old Test. Anec.

[c] Is. xxxv. 7; Joel ii. 28; Jno. vii. 38; Ac. ii. 18.

"This describes the effect of the irrigation and effusion promised in the one before it....The simple meaning is, that they shall grow as willows grow among the grass, i.e. in the moist and marshy spot." — J. A. Alexander.

"See the soft green willow springing, where the waters gently pass; every way her free arms flinging o'er the moist and reedy grass. Long ere winter blasts are fled, see her tipp'd with vernal red, and her kindly flower display'd ere her leaf can cast a shade." —Keble.

5, 6. (5) **One .. Lord's,** the result of this revelation of God in Israel will be that foreigners will seek to enter the Jewish community. "Israel is to remain the mediatory nation at the head of the nations and Jerusalem the central point of the Kingdom."—Oehler. **subscribe,** "rather: inscribe his hand 'To Jehovah.' The allusion is to the practice of branding

"Servants were inscribed with the names of their masters; soldiers inscribed themselves with the names of their general; and votaries of deities with the names of their god." — Wordsworth.

Re. xiii. 16.

[b] Comp. Mat. xxvii, 40, 42.

[c] Re. i. 8, 17, xxii. 13.

Vs. 6. The thought here so sublimely expressed is one which occurs in a striking manner also in the sacred book of the Buddhists.

[a]—Comp. Is. xli. 21—24.

[d] De xxxii. 4; Is. xvii. 10, xxvi. 4.

[a] "The exposure of idolatry in this and the following vss. is inimitably forcible and beautiful. With the most exact disposition of the parts are combined an exactness and vividness of delineation, a pointedness of sarcasm, a force of argument, and a concision and elegance of expression, wh. entitle the passage to the highest place among the compositions of the seer." —Henderson.

"They themselves have the plain evidence of the nulity of their gods, but they are blind to it that they may come to shame and ruin."—Mat. Arnold.

[a] Je. x. 5; Hab. ii. 18.

"Find earth where it grows no weed, and you may find a heart wherein no error grows." — Knowles.

slaves with the name of their owner, or perhaps to the religious custom of tattooing sacred marks on the person (Lev. xix. 28). See Ezek. ix. 4; Gal. vi. 17; Rev. vii. 3, xiii. 16."—Camb. Bib. (6) Here begins a new section extending to vs. 23. The theme is "The sole divinity of the Lord proved by His prophecies. **King,** ch. xliii. 15[b] **first .. God,** ch. xli. 4, xliii. 1, 10—12.[c]

Note on vs. 5.—You have doubtless seen upon the hands or arms of seamen the name of the ship in which they have served, rendered indelible by puncture, or by staining; this, perhaps, is one of the oldest customs in the world. The slave, in former days, used thus to be marked with the name of his master; the soldier, of his commander; the idolater, with the name of his god; while one of the Christian fathers tells us that in his day, "many marked their wrists or their arms with the sign of the cross, or with the name of Christ." This, then, will give you a very distinct idea of what the Lord requires of you, and what He will enable you to perform; it is such a decided choice of the Lord for your portion, such an avowal by your daily actions, that you are not your own, but His who has bought you with the price of His precious blood, that all shall know it as certainly, and that your actions shall proclaim it as unequivocally, as if the name of Christ were inscribed on the back of your hand, and could be seen and read in all companies, and on all occasions.—Blunt.

7, 8. (7) "And who is like me? let him stand forth and cry; let him declare it and set it in order before me! Who has announced very long since the future? and things that are to come let the vain gods declare to us."—Pol. Bib. **them shew,**[a] i. e. the fictitious gods who are in rivalry with Jehovah. (8) **Fear,** or quake not. **that time,** i. e. from the very time when I chose thee, and made thee acquainted with My will and purpose. **no God,** R. V., "no Rock."[d] Comp. Deut. xxxii. 4.

God Absorbs in Himself all the Ideas Which Idolatry Seeks to Embody.—Poetically conceived, the figures of Baal or Jupiter are only representations of certain powers—of life, warmth, rule, wisdom, etc., which are living, unseen beings. Our God says there are no such beings. Every one of these powers is in himself. He is Zeus, and Baal, and Venus, and Diana, and Moloch, so far as any of these represent necessary powers belonging to Deity. We must not divide him into many beings; he is only One. So far as idols are mere creations of men, there is nothing existing that corresponds to them. So far as they represent real powers, these powers all meet in the One God—our God!—Pul. Com.

9. **Delectable things,** the things in which they delight.[a] **own witnesses,** etc., R. V., "and their own witnesses see not, nor know," i. e. the devotees of these idols are blind. The consequence of their blindness is that they are put to shame.

The Folly of Idolatry.—The Malagasy Idol-maker.—The following illustration of this text is given by Messrs. Freeman and Johns, formerly missionaries in the island of Madagascar: "A married couple went some few years since to a person of this description, living about fifteen miles from the capital, and wished to purchase an idol. He had none to sell, but desired them to come next day. They went; he was still without any, but promised to have one by the evening. They remained till evening. The man went to a neighboring forest, selected his tree, cut down a large bough, brought it home, and prepared his idol, leaving the smaller branches littered about near his fireplace. In the evening he invited our married friends to take their meal of rice with him, and they saw him put some of these selfsame branches in the fire to boil the rice. They returned home, having paid about two dollars for their new god. Shortly afterwards a young man, a Christian, called at their house, and happened to read to the wife that graphic description of idolatry in the forty-fourth chapter of Isaiah, 'With part thereof he roasteth roast, maketh a fire, warmeth himself, and the residue thereof he maketh a god,' etc. She was astonished. It reminded her of what had just occurred, helped to convince her of the truth of the sacred volume, awakened deep attention, and led to the abandonment of the idol. She continued a learner, became a true disciple, and is now well known as Rafaravavy."

10, 11. (10) **Who .. nothing?** strongly ironical question. A man making a god is a contradiction in terms.[a] (11) **fellows,** "the word denotes the members of a guild, and is understood by A.V. of the gang of craftsmen employed in the making of the idol. It should rather be interpreted as the 'adherents,' the clientèle of the false god himself, as in R. V. marg., "all that join themselves thereto." Cf. Hos. iv. 17 ('associated with idols'). and 1 Cor. x. 20."—Camb. Bib. **of men,** are mere mortal men. **gathered together,** "to see if their unanimity in error will be of any service."—Spk. Com.

Modern Idolatry.—After leaving Zurich, we traveled on to Einsiedeln, at which place is an abbey founded by Meinrad, about A. D. 861, on the occasion of his receiving from Hildegard, abbé of Zurich, a miraculous (?) image of the Virgin. We were shown an image, alleged to be "the very same,"—since "miraculously rescued from the hands of sacrilegious robbers,"—now "more than 1,000 years old,"—a great black doll, a horrid-looking thing, with a glory of brass around its head, studded with jewels, and dressed in tawdry finery. Oh! how our hearts ached as we saw the poor deluded crowd of worshipers bowing before it, uttering their prayers, and seeking the intercession of one who had no power to help. As we "beheld their devotions" we longed to tell them of Him through whose finished work alone could they find acceptance, and "who ever liveth to make intercession for us."—J. C. Harrison.

12, 13. (12) **smith,** worker in iron. **with the tongs,** R. V., "maketh an axe." **hungry,** etc., so he is but a weak, dependent creature. (13) **his rule,** R. V., "a line." **with a line,** R. V., "with a pencil."[b] **planes,** or chisels. **remain . . house,** a guardian for the family. A household deity.[c]

Heathenism.—We have a lamentable instance of heathenish superstition in the following incident, related by a missionary, resident for many years in the neighborhood of the place where the circumstance occurred. There is a practice amongst the inhabitants of the isles of the South Seas, who still retain their idolatrous worship, of revering those of their fellow-creatures who have done some wonderful or daring deed, as gods, and worshiping them as such. In Samoa there is a high, steep, and craggy mountain; a young man, a native of the isle, was very desirous of becoming a god; he thought there was something very grand in being worshiped and prayed to; so, on one occasion, being in company with a number of his friends and companions, he turned to them, and said, "I will go to the top of that great mountain, and, if you see me flying, I shall be a god." His credulous companions shouted to him, "Away, away, we will worship you; away away!" He toiled up the sides of the mountain, and arrived at the top. His friends eagerly watched him; presently he stretched out his arms. and the people cried out, "He is flying, he is flying; he is a god." Then the young man was seen to rise from the mountain, and he disappeared; his friends shouted again. "He is a god, he is a god; we will worship him." And so they did for many years; but after a long time his mangled body was found at the bottom of the other side of the mountain, from which he had thrown himself down, while the people thought he was flying.

14, 15. (14) **strengtheneth,** R. V., "and strengtheneth for himself one among the trees," etc., "must mean 'allows to grow strong' in its native forest. Nay, in some cases the future deity has been actually planted by his worshiper, and nourished by the rain from heaven!"—Camb. Bib. (15) **to burn,** various uses being found for the parts of the same tree. The incongruity of the uses is clearly set forth. The man puts his worship on a level with baking his bread.

An Idolater's Confession (vs. 14).—A convert, who, in his heathen days, had been priest of a temple, said, on being baptised at Goobee, "I have traveled, day by day, to gather flowers; I have talked, and put on temple garments; I have made offerings to the idols: yet no idol, either in dreams or when awake, has said to me, 'Thy sins are forgiven; thou receivest salvation; thy sins are washed away.' I have fasted and prayed; but it has never been said to me, 'Thou shalt escape hell, and enjoy heaven!' The idol is a lie. I forsake it, and embrace Jesus Christ as my Saviour and my God."

16, 17. (16) **He burneth part,** etc. Pol. Bib. "Half of it he has burned in the fire, and upon the coals thereof he roasts flesh; he eats the roast; he warms himself also," etc. **seen the fire,** "I feel the glow."—Pol. Bib.[a]

"Idols certainly require the care of human hands. There are still shops in the cities of India and China, with this inscription on their signboards, 'Here old gods are repaired and renovated.'" —Leonhard.

[b] "Sharp stylus." — Gesenius.

[c] Comp. Is. xl. 20, etc.

"The idol is made, then a temple is built, and the idol is put there and chained, that he might not be stolen. God too has a temple; but He is the architect of His own temple, erected it not for Himself but for us; worship is for the benefit of man. It is getting, not giving; receiving, not imparting." — Caleb Morris.

"Error is sometimes so nearly allied to truth that it blends with it as imperceptibly as the colours of the rainbow fade into each other." —W. B. Clulow.

"You can't jump away from your shadow, but if you turn to the sun, your shadow is behind you; and if you stand under the sun, your shadow is beneath you. What we should try to do, is to live under the meridian sun, with our shadow self under our feet." — F. B. Meyers.

[a] "To see, is constantly used in the generic sense, to perceive, by the senses." — Gesenius.

Je. x. 3—5.

(17) **residue,** i. e. the other half. **thou .. god,** the Heb. pronoun is emphatic, thou, and thou alone.

18—20. (18) **They,** etc., i. e. those thus foolishly thinking to make a god. **shut,** Heb. daubed,[b] "For their eyes are bedaubed, past seeing, and their minds past comprehending."—Pol. Bib. (19) **considereth,** etc., R. V., "calleth to mind." **abomination,** the Bible term for an idol.[c] (20) **ashes,** most part of his god—the tree of which it was made—having been reduced to ashes.[d] **deceived heart,** when it is wrong it easily leads the intellect astray. **lie..hand,** i. e. is not my handiwork a deception?[e]

Feeding on Ashes.—Like the "apples of Sodom," like the "little book" of the prophet's vision (Rev. x.), a guilty action (or a sinful life) is very pleasant on the outside or at the beginning; but within, afterwards, it is bitter and disappointing in the last degree. Crime begins in successful violence or enriching fraud; it ends in the prison or the garret. Vice begins in unholy pleasure, in unprincipled companionship; it ends in distracting pain, in mortal sickness, in cruel loneliness. Ungodliness begins in the delights of eager but unhallowed ambition, of happy but unsanctified affection; it ends in weariness, in heart-ache, in the discovery that earthly distinctions and human love cannot fill the heart that God made for himself, cannot gladden and ennoble the life that he fashioned for his service. A life spent without God, devoted to selfish gratification, is a life of deep disappointment; the mistaken sinner finds out that the delectable food which he plucked with such keen anticipation is only ashes between his teeth.—Pul. Com.

21, 22. (21) **remember,** or think on these things, so as to take warning from them. **be forgotten,** or as Pol. Bib. "thou wilt not renounce Me." (22) **blotted out,** or swept away.[b] **thick cloud,** fig. to denote what is transient and evanescent. **return,**[c] "the Israel of God cannot perish; the only question which remains is one for man's free will to settle; viz., the numbers of those who shall constitute it."—Cheyne.

Not a Cloud to be Seen (vs. 22).—Your attention is invited—1. To the Divineness of forgiveness; 2. Look at the completeness of pardon; 3. At the assurance which God gives the pardoned that they are forgiven; 4. The knowledge of pardon is a power to awaken love; 5. A motive to the pursuit of holiness; 6. And encourages us to bring others to God; 7. The assured are those who confess to God their sins.—S. Martin.

Our Sins a Cloud.—Sin is but the cloud, as it were, behind which the everlasting sun lies in all its power and warmth, unaffected by the cloud; and the light will yet strike—the light of His love will yet pierce through, with its merciful shafts, bringing healing in their beams, and dispersing all the pitchy darkness of man's transgressions. And as the mists gather themselves up and roll away, dissipated by the heat of that sun in the upper sky, and reveal the fair earth below—so the love of Christ shines in, melting the mist and dissipating the fog, thinning it off in its thickest places, and at last piercing its way right through it, down to the heart of the man that has been lying beneath the oppression of this thick darkness, and who thought that the fog was the sky, and that there was no sun there above.—Maclaren.

23. Sing, etc., poetical call to inanimate creation to praise God for the promised deliverance. "The prediction of glorious and joyful changes, as in many other cases, is clothed in the form of an exhortation to all nature to rejoice." **lower parts,** or "depths of the earth," i. e. Sheol; let heaven, and earth to its lowest depths, even to the abode of the departed, rejoice. **break forth,** Is. xiv. 7. **glorified himself,** R. V. "and will glorify," etc., bring honor to His name by His gracious work of redemption.

Redemption a Ground of Joy (vs. 23).—I. The Lord hath redeemed His people. 1. By price; 2. By power. II. Herein He hath also glorified Himself. 1. His grace and mercy; 2. His truth and faithfulness. III. This is a ground of most exalted joy to the whole creation. 1. All, in earth and in heaven, are required to rejoice in it; 2. The joy should be in proportion to the occasion of it.—C. Simeon.

Joy at its very fullest is uncontainable, inexpressible. He wrote well who said, "I were little happy could I say how much." There are times when we feel that we want every one and everything to be vocal with the gladness of our own soul. If the children did not shout, the very

"Deep-rooted customs, though wrong, are not easily altered; but it is the duty of all to be firm in that which they certainly know is right for them."—John Woolman.

"It is thy duty oftentimes to do what thou wouldst not; thy duty, too, to leave undone what thou wouldst do."—Thomas A'Kempis.

b Is. vi. 10.

c "Not merely abominable, but the essence of what is so, in the eyes of a jealous God (1 Ki xi. 5, 7)."—Fausset.

d Ashes often mentioned in Bible either as a symbol of human frailty (Ge xviii. 27), or of deep humiliation (Jon. iii. 6).

e Je. x. 14, xvi. 19; Ro. i. 25.

b "As speedily as the wind sweeps away the thick clouds, so do I drive away thy transgressions."—Wordsworth.

"More than once we had noticed in our early mornings dull masses of cloud in the sky. As the sun got up these all vanished. They did not drift away, or pass into a different region of the heavens, but they vanished on the spot, such was the absolute power of the desert sun."—Bonar.

c De xxx. 2, 8; Ho. xiv. 1.

"How little have we accepted and made use of the legacy of peace and joy which Christ left to us! Instead of faces telling the world what a full salvation we

stones would have to speak the joy of that glad hour (Luke xix. 40). When the great and gracious purposes of God are accomplished in the redemption of one human soul from sin and its restoration to the love and the likeness of God, there is occasion for more joy than human songs can celebrate; how much more so when a nation is redeemed! and how much more yet will there be when the whole race is transformed, and when the kingdoms of this world shall have become the kingdoms of our God and of his Christ.—Clarkson.

24—26. Here begins a new section extending to xlv. 25. Theme:—Cyrus chosen to bring about, by his victories, the universal recognition of God. (24) **maketh all,** not merely, hath created all, but doeth all; executeth whatever He designs. **the earth,** etc., R. V., "the earth; who is with me?" i. e. who helped me? No one. "Jehovah asserts the exclusiveness of His creative and providential power." (25) **liars,** Je. l. 36. "Signs of the praters," i. e. the agencies of the heathen sooth-sayers, specially thou of Babylon. xlvii. 13.—Cheyne. **diviners,** or conjurers.[a] **backward,** with shame, especially by their predictions being unfulfilled. Defeated and disappointed. (26) **word,** or prophecy: esp. that of Isaiah. Comp. xx. 3.

God's Willingness to Bestow Good.—A root set in the finest soil, in the best climate, and blessed with all that sun and air and rain can do for it, is not in so sure a way of its growth to perfection, as every man may be, whose spirit aspires after all that which God is ready and infinitely desirous to give him. For the sun meets not the springing bud that stretches towards him with half that certainty, as God, the source of all good, communicates Himself to the soul that longs to partake of Him.—Wm. Law.

27, 28 (27) **deep,** is a figure for the obstacles to the deliverance of Israel. It has been thought by some commentators (including Vitringa and Lowth) that the verse contains an allusion to the well-known stratagem by which Cyrus is said to have got possession of Babylon (Herodotus I. 185—191). The Hebrew word for "deep" might no doubt be applied to a river, as a cognate word is in Zech. x. 11. But the recently discovered Cyrus-inscriptions seem to shew that the narrative of Herodotus is legendary.—Camb. Bib. (28) **Cyrus,** the servant of God formerly introduced, but sometimes not named. **shepherd,** to collect and send home God's scattered flock. **Thou .. built,** comp. 2 Chr. xxxvi. 22; Ezr. i. 1; Is. xlv. 13. This is the verse which Josephus says stimulated Cyrus to restore the Jewish Temple and nation.

Cyrus.—One of the most remarkable characters of ancient history, and one that is particularly interesting to the Biblical student, is Cyrus, who was the subject of a prophecy that the most stubborn unbeliever cannot deny to have been fulfilled. The advent, and name, and acts of this great monarch were with a wonderful exactness predicted by the Prophet Isaiah (xliv. 28, xlv. 1—4, 13), and were most wonderfully accomplished (compare Ezra. i. 1—4). Josephus, indeed, narrates (Antiq. xi. i. 1. 2) a remarkable story. He says that the prophecies of Isaiah respecting Cyrus were shown to that king, and that, struck with the Divine record, he was induced to issue his decree.

CHAPTER THE FORTY-FIFTH.

1, 2. (1) **his anointed,** this is the only passage where the title is bestowed upon a foreign ruler. Comp. Ps. xviii. 50.[a] Cyrus was God's instrument. He was raised up and directed by Jehovah, to work out His purpose of grace concerning His own people. **loose,** ungird or disarm. **two leaved gates,** those, viz., of Babylon. "In Babylon there were a hundred gates, all of brass." (2) **crooked,** R. V., "rugged." Figure for difficulties that might be in the way of Cyrus.

Encouragement (vs. 2).—I. Every good work is sure to meet with interruption and opposition. II. In every journey there will necessarily be rough places. III. Christians are not required to go anywhere where their Captain has not gone before them. IV. We are not to wait till difficulties are removed before we advance; "go forward," and as the feet

have, how often a long face has suggested that men had better take their fill of happiness first before they leave it behind by becoming Christians! May God give us so to live winning lives that others will be allured to desire the same blessings we enjoy."—J. Hudson Taylor.

"What I can fancy, but never can express."—Juvenal.

a "Astrologers; men leading a retired, contemplative life, in order to study divination by the signs of the stars." — Vitringa.

"There will be mistakes in divinity while men preach, and errors in governments while men govern."—Sir D. Carleton.

"Heb. Koresh, which meant, in ancient Persian, the Sun. According to Strabo his original name was Agradates; so that the name Cyrus was one of honor." — Spk. Com.

"It is the greatest honor of the greatest men to be employed for God as instruments of his favor to his people. It was more the praise of Cyrus to be God's shepherd than to be Emperor of the East."

a "He, first of the ancient conquerors, appears in other than a merely despotic and destructive aspect. Both in Greek and Heb. literature he is represented as the type of a just and gentle prince." — Stanley.

touch the waters the stream will be divided. Faithful discharge of duty in everyday life is doing God's work; the promise therefore may be applied to the removal of crooked places in business, the family, etc.—Analyst.

Note on vs. 2.—These figures indicate the removal of all obstacles and hindrances out of the way of him who is called of God, entrusted with some particular work for God, and helped of God in the doing of that work. Historical illustration is found in the fact, stated on the authority of the monuments, that the city capitulated, as a consequence of the defeat of Nabonidus in the field. Professor Sayce says, "Another fact of an equally revolutionary kind, which the inscriptions teach us, is that Babylon was not besieged and taken by Cyrus. It opened its gates to his general long before he came near it, and needed neither fighting nor battle for its occupation." Grote, in his 'History of Greece,' says, "The way in which the city was treated would lead us to suppose that its acquisition cannot have cost the conqueror either much time or much loss . . . it is certain that the vast walls and gates were left untouched." The assurances of the text are even better fulfilled by moving obstacles out of the way, than by Cyrus actually mastering them. Herodotus tells us that Babylon had a hundred gates of brass, with posts and hooks of the same metal.—Pul. Com.

"Every noble life leaves the fibre of it interwoven forever in the work of the world; by so much, evermore, the strength of the human race has gained."

"Men of faith are like the mountain streams that make their way down amid the rocks; if they cannot get over the rocks they go round them, but they will not be stopped." — R. Tuck.

3, 4. (3) **treasures,** i. e. treasures hid in darkness. The treasures referred to are chiefly the loot of Sardis, which Xenophon describes as "the richest city of Asia next to Babylon" (Cyrop. vii. 2. 11), and of Babylon itself (Jer. l. 37, li. 13). If, as is probable, the capture of the former city was past before the date of the prophecy, rumors of the fabulous wealth of Crœsus, which then found its way into the coffers of Cyrus, may have reached the prophet.—Camb. Bib. **mayest know,** or gain a deep impression of the fact.[a] (4) **surnamed thee,** calling thee "My shepherd," as in ch. xliv. 28. There may be reference to his new, or second name, Cyrus.

a "This prophecy was prob. read by Cyrus, and exerted its influence on him. Such an influence Josephus tells us was exerted, and it is implied in the monarch's solemn recognition of Jehovah as the true God, and the author of his successes (Ezr. i. 2)."—J. A. Alexander.

The Divine Surnaming.—We all have some special work to do for God in the world, and so we all have some special endowments for the doing of it. Every man is called of God, guided by God, surnamed by God, and the moment when he clearly sees what his life-work is, is the moment when he becomes conscious of his call. Bushnell says, "What do the Scriptures show us but that God has a particular care for every man, a personal interest in him, and a sympathy with him and his trials, watching for the uses of his one talent as attentively and kindly, and approving him as heartily in the right employment of it, as if he had given him ten? and what is the giving out of the talents itself but an exhibition of the fact that God has a definite purpose, charge, and work, be it this or that, for every man?" "Every human soul has a complete and perfect plan cherished for it in the heart of God—a Divine biography marked out, which it enters into life to live."—Pul. Com.

"As the branch ascends, and the bud bursts, and the fruit reddens under the co-operation of influences from the outside air, so man rises to the higher stature under invisible pressures from without."—Drummond.

5, 6. (5) **beside me,** De. iv. 35, 39, xxxii. 39; Is. xliv. 8. **girded thee,**[a] R. V., "will gird thee." fig. for personally strengthening him. (6) **they may know,** i. e. all the world.[b] **sun .. west,** "the two most distant geographical points known to the ancients are fixed on, including all the regions between."—Henderson.

a Ps. xviii. 32.

b "Several important movements in the direction of monotheism (notably, the Pythagorean) had their commencement about the time of Cyrus."—Spk. Com.

The Unknown Influence of God.—A great Babylonian library, consisting of numerous clay tablets, with arrow-head inscriptions burnt into them, has recently been deciphered. The results are most astounding, confirming once questioned statements of Scripture history, throwing light upon obscure events, and correcting not a few false impressions. Among the principal corrections thus afforded is that of our views regarding the person and religion of Cyrus. Cyrus, it seems, was not a Persian, but an Elamite, and was not a Monotheist, but a worshiper of heathen divinities, adopting Merodach, the god of Babylon, when he conquered that city. The last fact adds great emphasis to our text. Cyrus, to whom the words are addressed, is now proved to be a pagan, a polytheist, an idolater. Yet even he was girded by the unknown God of heaven and earth.—Hom. Com.

Mal. i. 11.

Who is that boy sitting on the steps there? He has a hat on that was made for any head but his own; and his coat, who made it? His mother, very likely—rough spun, not too well fitting. What is he wait-

"Our programme is a short one: it is this. 'We will go into such and such a city, and abide there a year, and buy and sell and get gain.'

ing for? To get the job of sweeping the steps he sits on? Perhaps. Years pass by and a portly man comes down those steps. Broad his face, a great round shining blessing, kindness in his eye, power in the uplifting of his hand. Who is he? That is the boy, grown now fully, physically, intellectually and socially. The boy and the man are both Horace Greeley, an editorial prince, a man whose writings no one among his countrymen can afford to decline to read. "I girded thee, I brought thee to those steps, I set thee down upon them, I appointed an angel to watch thee all the time: it was my way of nursing and caring for thee, and training thee." He bringeth the blind by a way that they know not.—Parker.

7, 8. (7) **light .. darkness,** the assertion of the Divine unity as opposed to the dualistic notions of the Persians, who believed in two beings—Ormuzd, light; Ahriman, darkness.[c] **peace,** or national prosperity. **evil,** "i. e. not moral evil, but physical evil, calamity. Cf. Am. iii. 6, 'shall evil befall a city and Jehovah hath not done it?' The prophet's words are startlingly bold, but they do not go beyond the common O. T. doctrine on the subject, which is free from the speculative difficulties that readily suggest themselves to the mind of a modern reader. There is no thought in the O. T. of reducing all evil, moral and physical, to a single principle. Moral evil proceeds from the will of man, physical evil from the will of God, who sends it as the punishment of sin. The expression 'create evil' implies nothing more than that. It is true (as we see from the Book of Job, etc.) that the indiscriminateness of physical calamities had begun to cause perplexity in the age to which the prophecy belongs. But the discussion of that question never shook either of the two positions, that sin originates in man, and that God is the author of calamity."—Camb. Bib. (8) **drop down,**[d] "the heavens are represented as showering down gracious influences, which fructify the earth and cause it to bring forth the fruits of salvation." **let righteousness spring,** R. V., "and let her cause righteousness to spring up together." God's fidelity to His promise is His righteousness, and salvation or deliverance for His people that promise assures.[e] **have created it,** this righteousness which the earth is to cause to spring up.,

The Efficacy of the Gospel (vs. 28).—I. The import of this prophecy. 1. Its primary reference is to the restoration of the Jews to their own land; 2. Its ulterior reference is to the establishment of the Messiah's kingdom. II. The peculiar beauty of the image under which it is conveyed. I. Their mutual dependence as here intimated; 2. Their united operation as here described; 3. The true source and origin of all their efficacy. Apply:—(1) What a blessing the Gospel is! (2) What is to be done on our part to render it effectual? (3) To whom are we indebted if ever we are influenced by it for good?—C. Simeon.

Moral Evil.—Moral evil is certainly not "created" by God, in the same direct way as physical evil. He has not necessitated it by the arrangements of his universe. He has but allowed it to come into existence. And this he seems to have done in consequence of a necessity in the nature of things. Either he must have limited his creation to objects that moved mechanically and were incapable of moral action, or, by creating moral agents, have allowed the possibility of moral evil coming into being. A free agent must be free to do right or to do wrong; if he is not free to do wrong, he is really not free when he does right. And when millions of free agents were created, each with a power of doing wrong, that some of them would choose to do wrong was to be expected, and was of course foreseen by the Creator. From the fact that, though thus foreseeing the introduction of sin into his universe, God nevertheless determined to create moral beings, we may gather that it is better in God's sight, and therefore better absolutely, that the two classes of good and bad moral beings should coexist, than that there should be no moral beings at all. Further, moral evil is certainly, like physical evil, a great means of developing higher forms of moral goodness. The virtue that resists contact with vice, the influence of bad example, the seductions of those who make all possible efforts to corrupt it, is of a higher form than that untried virtue which has passed through no such ordeal. The religion that leads men to plunge into the haunts of vice, and give themselves to the reclaiming of the lowest outcasts among

Very well. We put a full stop there: God puts a comma; our punctuation is unskilled and unwise, God's punctuation alone measures out the languages, and metes in fair proportion the weird and solemn music of life." — Parker.

c "The great Persian reformer, Zoroaster, or Zerduscht, taught that there are two principles working in the universe—one good, the other evil. The one was termed Ormuzd, and was the presiding agent of all good; the other, Ahriman, in the same manner presided over all evil. From the opposing action of these two powers Zoroaster explained the commingling of good and evil in the universe and in every creature." — Bib. Things Not Gen. Known.

d De xxxii. 2.

e "The final aim of all God's providential acts was that the kingdom of heaven—and therein righteousness and salvation — should be planted upon earth." —Spk. Com.

"We must co-operate with God. If there is any sin in my heart that I am not willing to give up, then I need not pray. You may take a bottle and cork it up tight, and put it under Niagara, and there will not a drop of that mighty volume of water get into the bottle. If there is any sin in my heart that I am not willing to give up, I need not expect a blessing."--D. L. Moody.

the dregs of our populace, is the highest form of religion. If there were no moral evil, moral goodness would fall far short of being what it is—there would be no Howards, no Frys, no Havelocks, no Livingstones. By the moral furnace through which it passes, "the trial of men's faith, being much more precious than that of gold that perisheth, though it be tried with fire," is found and will "be found unto praise and honor and glory of the appearing of Jesus Christ" (1 Pet. i. 7).—Pul. Com.

9, 10. The four following verses are addressed to those exiles who resented the idea of deliverance through a foreign king, or murmured at the delay of the deliverance. **potsherd,** Job. ii. 8.[a] "a potsherd like other potsherds of earth!"—Pol. Bib. **clay,** etc., ch. xxix. 16, lxiv. 8. (10) **Woe .. forth,** "The writer's main design is to represent the doubt and discontent of men in reference to God's future dealings with them as no less monstrous than the supposition of a child's objection to its own birth."—Alexander.

Thwarting God.—"Woe to him that striveth with his Maker!" Pharoah did it, and was overthrown in the Red Sea; Saul did it, and was deposed; Jehoiakim did it, and he perished; Judas did it, and he hanged himself; the Pharisees did it, and their city was destroyed; Julian the Apostate did it, and, falling back upon the field of battle, said, "Thou hast conquered, O Galilean!" You can tell a man who has thwarted God if you know much about him. Many old fossils give the same experience twenty years after their conversion that they gave the month after. In a prayer-meeting many pray the same stererotyped prayer year after year. Some ministers are just where they were in their doctrine and the expression, and in their very sermons, as when they commenced their ministry—arrested, dwarfed.—F. B. Meyer.

11—13. (11) **Ask,** "Of things to come will ye question me! and concerning the work of my hands will ye lay commands upon me!"—Pol. Bib.[b] (12) **my hands,** fig. for the putting forth of Divine power. (13) **him,** Cyrus; against whose agency in their deliverance some of the Jews found objection. **will direct,** R. V., "will make straight," i. e. will carry him through. **my captives,** R. V., "my exiles." **not for price,** etc., lit. "not for hire and not for a bribe." That is he will do it not for some outward benefit but in answer to an inward guidance.

Man Cannot Comprehend God.—In our pride of heart we are very unwilling to admit the limitation or imperfection of our faculties. We can know so much; why cannot we know God? We can see so much; why cannot we see God? Men are restless, and bitterly fret, because the dark mists still fringe and hide the "mountain-peak of a God." They say, "If it be so to our vision down in the plains of common life, then we will climb the hills of science, get up above, and look down on the peak, and shatter for ever the mysteries that surround him." Some expect to return to us with a scornful smile, prepared to say, "There is no God, only a high peak, which the unclouded sun gilds with a perpetual radiance; and this, shining through the clouds, made you think there was a God."

"Then all goes wrong: the old foundations rock;
  One scorns at him of old who gazed unshod;
One, striking with a pickaxe, thinks the shock
    Shall move the seat of God.

"A little way, a very little way
  (Life is so short), they dig into the rind,
And they are very sorry—so they say—
    Sorry for what they find.

"O marvelous credulity of man!
  If God indeed kept secret, couldst thou know
Or follow up the mighty Artisan
    Unless he willed it so?"—Jean Ingelow.

14, 15. "The collapse of the heathen religions is here dramatically represented under the image of a procession of conquered nations of Africa, who pass before Israel, as tributaries and slaves, acknowledging that Israel's God is the only true divinity."—Camb. Bib. (14) **The labour**

[a] Je. xviii. 6; Ro. ix. 20.

"A Christian is just one who does what the Lord Jesus tells him. Neither more nor less than that makes one a Christian."—George Macdonald.

"Mankind at large always resembles frivolous children; they are impatient of thought, and wish to be amused."--Emerson.

"He lives long that lives well; and time misspent is not lived but lost."—Fuller.

[b] "Will ye take the disposition of things out of My hands, and direct Me how I am to deal with My own chosen people?" Mat. Arnold.

"If men would but believe that they are in process of creation, and consent to be made,—let the Maker handle them as the potter his clay, yielding them selves in respondent motion and submissive hopeful action with the turning of His wheel.—they would, ere long, find themselves able to welcome every pressure of that hand upon them, even when it was felt in pain, and sometimes not only to believe, but to recognize the divine end in view, the bringing of a son into glory."—George MacDonald.

of, comp. ch. xliii. 3. **Ethiopia,** Cush. **Sabeans,** people of Sabea, or Meröe, on the Upper Nile, center of a great caravan trade bet. Ethiopia, Egypt, and North Africa, Arabia and India. **men of stature,** Agatharchides describes the Sabeans as singularly handsome; and Herodotus speaks of the Ethiopians as the tallest of men. **over unto thee,** i. e. to acknowledge Israel's God. **fall down unto,** i. e. in prayer. "Strictly speaking they pray through Israel (as a prophetic mediator) to Jehovah, who has hidden Himself to all the world except Israel. For Judah is God made known."—Pol. Bib. (15) **hidest thyself,** Seph. paraphrases, "For thou art God and we knew it not;" God had hidden Himself in some manner even from Israel.[a]

Mystery of Nature.—We stand in the midst of a mighty temple, the whole visible frame of nature rising around us, like the walls of a gorgeous sanctuary; and we gaze on the beautiful arch of heaven, on the sun walking in his brightness, on the moon, and the stars, and the dark cloud of thunder; but what know we of this magnificent array? What account can man give of the hidden springs of such vast machinery? Who will tell us what is that light which makes all things visible? Who will explain that secret wondrous energy which retains, century after century, so many worlds, each in its separate orbit? Whose penetration is not utterly baffled by the growth of a blade of grass, by the falling of a stone, by the floating of a feather? When asked, we state reasons, and assign causes, but this is only a shifting of the difficulty. It were easy to talk of the gravity of matter, and the laws of nature: philosophy is at fault: the learned man knows little more than the savage of the amazing processes which go on daily in the laboratory of nature: while he may be sitting on the lofty pinnacle of science, a child shall propose questions which shall perplex and confound him, and bring him down from his lofty eminence, and force him to the humiliating confession that what can be discovered by man bears no proportion to what is hidden by God. There is nothing teaches us our own ignorance as knowledge when pushed to its utmost limits. In enlarging the sphere of light, you equally enlarge the surrounding sphere of darkness.—Melvill.

16, 17. (16) Here the prayer of the conquered peoples ends and the prophet speaks. **They,** i. e. idol makers, and idol worshipers[b] (17) **everlasting salvation,**[c] "as is usual in the prophets, the perfect dispensation, or what is called the Messianic age, is conceived as issuing immediately from the historical crisis which is the subject of the prophecy, in this case the deliverance from Babylon."—Camb. B. **world without end,** an expression wh. justifies our applying the promise to God's Church in all ages.

The Conversion of the Gentiles Gradual, but Ultimately Complete.—Three stages in the conversion of the Gentiles seem to be marked—one in vs. 3; another in vs. 20; a third in vs. 23. I. The first stage. The nations within a certain moderate radius of Palestine are naturally the first to come in—Egypt and Ethiopia, in Africa; and by parity of reasoning, Syria, Mesopotamia, and Asia Minor, in Asia; Greece, Italy, and Southern Gaul, in Europe. This was very much the range of Hebrew influence during the five centuries preceding Christianity, and of Christian influence during two centuries afterwards. II. The second stage. The circle gradually widens, and a time comes when the gospel may be said, roughly, to have penetrated everywhere, and "the earth" to be "full of the knowledge of the Lord, as the waters cover the sea" (ch. xi. 9). Missionaries have visited the remotest ends of the earth; and the nations generally may be challenged to "assemble themselves, and come," and make their choice between true religion and their own false and absurd systems. But conversion has not kept pace with preaching. On many nations very little, on some no, impression has been made. Prayer is still offered widely to deities "that cannot save." This is the state of things at the present day. Scarcely a nation in the world has not heard of the salvation of God; but a large number—as much as three-fourths of the population of the globe, we are told—have not yet accepted it. III. The third stage. God has "sworn by Himself, the word is gone out of His mouth in righteousness, and shall not return"—that ultimately "unto Him every knee shall bow, and every tongue shall swear" (vs. 23). In "a new heaven and a new earth" (ch. lxv. 17) the Messiah, "the Ancient

[a] "In this vs. the Church admires the mysterious character of the Divine counsels and modes of action, with special reference to the captivity and restoration."
—Henderson.

"God always gives us strength and sense enough for what He wants us to do. If we either tire ourselves, or puzzle ourselves, it is our own fault."—Ruskin.

"A Science without mystery is unknown; a Religion without mystery is absurd. The elimination of mystery from the universe is the elimination of Religion. However far the scientific method may penetrate the Spiritual World, there will always remain a region to be explored by a scientific faith."
—Drummond.

[b] "The domination of Persia conduced greatly to the overthrow of idolatry at Babylon, and in other countries, and so prepared the way for the preaching and reception of the true religion." — Wordsworth.

[c] Is. xxvi. 4.

"'Time, like a dome of many-colored glass, stains the white radiance of eternity.' What is all life and time, nature and human fashion, but a veiling of God? How can we see him except 'through a glass darkly'? What is thinking but dreaming, and dreams what but pictured screens, concealing and revealing the truth? We are in bond-

of days" (Dan. vii. 6), will rule over a kingdom which will contain "all people, nations, and languages" (Dan vii. 14). How this will be brought about, what exactly will be the scene of the kingdom, what the condition of its members, is not revealed, otherwise than in mystical words, and cannot be laid down with definiteness; but in that kingdom, beyond a doubt, "all people will fall down before Jehovah, all nations will do Him service"—the prophecies of Isaiah will have full effect: "all flesh will worship before the Lord" (ch. lxvi. 23).—Pul. Com.

18, 19. (18) For thus says Jehovah, the Creator of the heavens,—He is the true God; the Former and Maker of the earth,—He established it, etc.—Pol. Bib. **not in vain,** R. V., "not a waste,"[a] but to be inhabited by men. He will not, therefore, destroy the race. (19) **in secret,** contrast the openness of Divine revelations, with the uncertainty and secrecy of heathen oracles.[b] **dark place,** etc., R. V., "in a place of the land of darkness." Comp. Jer. ii. 31. Jehovah's revelation has not been hidden, but given in the light. Certainly not a thing of caves and pits and the under-world as with heathen oracles.

The Earth Prepared for Man.—"It is evident that there is a manifest progress in the succession of beings on the surface of the earth. This progress consists in an increasing similarity to the living fauna, and among the vertebrates, especially in their increasing resemblance to man. But this connection is not the consequence of a direct lineage between the faunas of different ages. There is nothing like parental descent connecting them. The fishes of the Palæozoic age are in no respect the ancestors of the reptiles of the Secondary age, nor does man descend from the mammals which preceded him in the Tertiary age. The link by which they are connected is of a higher and immaterial nature, and their connection is to be sought in the view of the Creator Himself, whose aim in forming the earth, in allowing it to undergo the successive changes which geology has pointed out, and in creating successively all the different types of animals which have passed away, was to introduce man upon the surface of our globe. Man is the end towards which all the animal creation has tended from the first appearance of the first Palæozoic fishes."—Agassiz. The Suppliant.—Archbishop Trench, in his poem, "The Suppliant," represents a man as praying all night. When the morning dawns without an answer, the Tempter stands by him and says:

"Oh, peace! What profit do you gain
From empty words and babblings vain!
'Come, Lord; oh, come!' you cry alway;
You pour your heart out night and day;
Yet still no murmur of reply;
No voice that answers, 'Here am I.'"

He yielded and ceased praying. Then an angel came, and, learning the reason, exclaimed:

"Oh, dull of heart! enclosed doth lie
In each 'Come, Lord!' a 'Here am I.'
Thy love, thy longing are not thine,
Reflections of a love divine:
Thy very prayer to thee was given
Itself a messenger from heaven."
—Peloubet's Suggcs. Illus.

20, 21. He now addresses the heathen who have escaped destruction after Cyrus's victories. (20) **up**[a] "bear about their wooden idols," the gods of Babylonia were carried about in sacred boats at the great festivals, especially at that of New Year."—Pol. Bib. (21) **Tell,** etc., R. V., "Declare ye and bring it forth." **declared this,** again reverting to the fulfillment of Jehovah's prophecies as proof of Jehovah's sole Divine claim. **just,** etc., Ro. iii. 26.

Jehovah a Just God and Saviour (vs. 21).—Consider—I. The character of God here stated. 1. As contrasted with that of all the heathen deities; 2. As shining forth in His own proper and harmonious perfections. II. The regard due to Him in that character. 1. Fear; 2. Trust; 3. Obedience.—Simeon.

age to sense, to belief, to fancy. But our deliverance draws near; and no confusion will await them that have believed to the end."—Johnson.

"There is in man a higher than love of happiness: he can do without happiness and instead thereof find blessedness!"—T. Carlyle.

a "There seems to be here a special reference to the deserted state of the Holy Land during the captivity." — Henderson.

b Comp. Jno. xviii. 20; De. xxix. 29, xxx. 11.

"No man saw the building of the New Jerusalem, the workmen crowded together, the unfinished walls and unpaved streets; no man heard the clink of trowel and pickaxe; it descended out of heaven from God."—Seeley.

"To recount almighty works
What words of tongue or seraph can suffice,
Or heart of man suffice to comprehend?"
—Milton.

"In studying the Word of God digest it under these two heads: either as removing some obstructions that keep God and thee asunder, or as supplying some uniting power to bring God and thee together."
—Cecil.

a Je. x. 5; Am. v. 26.

"Nature is the thrifty thing in the world; she never wastes anything; she

22, 23. (22) **ends of the earth,**[a] remnants gathered from the most distant places. (23) **sworn,** Ge. xxii. 16; He. vi. 13. **the word,** etc., "a true word has gone out of my mouth, a word that shall not be recalled."—Pol. Bib. **knee .. bow,** Phi. ii. 10[b] "This universal turning to God belongs to the final Messianic kingdom."

Looking to Christ (vs. 22).—I. The duty: looking to Jesus with the eye of faith. 1. Exclusively; 2. Earnestly; 3. Humbly; 4. Hopefully; 5. Continually. II. The blessing. Salvation—1. From sin; 2. From hell. III. The persons. 1. Men of all nations; 2. Of all circumstances; 3. Of all characters. Apply:—Look—(1) Because the blessings are great: (2) Because the terms are simple; (3) Because the Saviour is God; (4) Because if you look not to Jesus, you must look in vain elsewhere.—G. Brooks.

The Life Look.—There is an affecting story of a celebrated literary man Heinrich Heine, who was prematurely disabled by disease, and utterly heart-sick and weary. In one of the art palaces of Paris there is the famous statue called the Venus of Milo, the bewitching goddess of pleasure, which, by the rude accident of time, has lost both her arms, but still preserves much of her supreme, enchanting beauty. At the feet of this statue Heine cast himself down in remorse and despair, and, to use his own words, "There I lay a long time, and wept so passionately that a stone must have had compassion on me. The goddess looked down compassionately upon me, but she was helpless to console me. She looked as if she would say—'See you not that I have no arms, and that therefore I can give you no help?'" So, vain and useless is it to look to any for spiritual help and comfort, except to Him of whom it is declared, "Behold, the Lord's hand is not shortened, that it cannot save."—Spurgeon.

24, 25. (24) **Surely,** R. V., "Only in the Lord, shall one say unto me, is righteousness and strength." **righteousness,** or fidelity to promise. **strength,** ability to execute what is promised. (25) **the seed of Israel,** refers to the Israel of God out of all the human race.—Delitzsch. **justified,** or shown in deliverance to be the God-fearing nation.[c] **glory,** or boast themselves.

Glorying in the Lord (vss. 24, 25).—I. The believer's source of salvation. 1. The source of his righteousness; 2. Of his strength; 3. Of his justification. II. The believer's humble acknowledgment. It is the language of—1. Humble confession; 2. Of humble gratitude; 3. Of humble confidence; 4. Of humble but exulting triumph; 5. This language is rendered more striking by contrast. Apply:—(1) To Him men shall come; (2) To Him they ought to come.—Zeta in 400 Sks.

Our Surety.—O how marvelous a contrivance is there where the blessed Majesty of God finds an argument in Himself, when man had none wherewithal to plead! The Son was found in the form of a servant, and became our nearest kinsman, to redeem the inheritance, where His people's standing is ensured by another surety and strength than their own; not on their apprehending, but their being apprehended; where the Lord does oblige Himself by bond to make that good which is only of grace, and is most freely given; where he both frames the desire within the soul and satisfies it. (Isa. xlv. 24; Jer. iii. 19; Ezek. xvi. 4, 9.)—Fleming.

undergoes change, but there is no annihilation; the essence remains; matter is eternal."—Binney.

[a] Comp. Nu. xxi. 8; Jno. iii. 14, 15.

[b] Ro. xiv. 9—11.

"Be not like the man in the Interpreter's house, whose eyes were fixed on the ground where he was raking together straws and dust, and who would not look up to him who was offering him a celestial crown. Look up! Look up!"

[c] "The people of the Jews shall in the Lord be justified before men, and openly glory in their God. The oppressors reproached them, loaded them with calumny, and boasted even of a right to oppress them, as abandoned by their God; but when God shall work out their deliverance, that shall be their justification from these hard censures, and therefore they shall glory in it."—Mat. Henry.

1 Co. i. 30, 31.

CHAPTER THE FORTY-SIXTH.

Chap. xlvi. is a definite prophecy complete in itself. Here comes to a head the contrast between idols and the living God, which previous chapters have elaborated.—G. A. Smith. **1, 2.** (1) **Bel .. Nebo,** Bel was prob. the same as the Phœnician sun-god Baal; and Nebo, the planet Mercury, or Hermes.[a] Bel appears in such names as Belshazzar, and Nebo in such as Nebuchadnezzar. **upon .. cattle,** helpless things that needed to be carried.[b] **carriages,** R. V., "The things that ye carried about are made a load, a burden to," etc. "At the New Year's festival the images of Merodach and his son Nebo were carried through Babylon in solemn procession on sacred barques of great magnificence, and along

[a] "In the star-worship of Babylon, Bel was the planet Jupiter; and it has been conjectured that Nebo was the planet Mercury. The temple of Bel was one of the wonders of Babylon."—Mat. Arnold.

[b] "The Prophet describes the fall and removal of the Bab. idols in language of the keenest satire. They had formerly been carried about by the priests in solemn procession, but should now be

a promenade prepared for this purpose since Nabopolassar."—Delitzsch. (2) **They stoop,** etc., i. e. the gods. **not deliver,** the captive and dishonored images in wh. they were supposed to reside. **themselves,** Heb. their soul; prob. used sarcastically.

broken in pieces, and borne away by the enemy on the backs of beasts of burden, which, sinking down under their weight, they should not be able to relieve."—Henderson.

3, 4. (3) **borne,** etc., "the Babylonians had to carry their gods: the Israelites have been and still are carried by their God. The Israelitish people is considered as a living organism, which passes through successive stages of existence, like a human being."—Pol. Bib. (4) **I am He,** unchangeably the same.

"Your golden images, wh. were once carried by you with joy in festal processions, are now lifted up as loads to be carried away on the back of beasts of burden, panting under their weight."—Wordsworth.

Is. xxi. 9; Je. l. 2.

God's Promise to the Aged (vs. 4).—I. God's promise to His aged servants in the text. 1. He promiseth to support them under their burdens, and carry them through their difficulties; 2. He will comfort them under their afflictions and sorrows; 3. He will deliver them out of all their fears and tribulations. II. To consider the reasons suggested in the text, why they should confide in this promise. 1. He is your Maker; 2. He hath been careful of you and kind to you hitherto; 3. He is an unchangeable God. Apply:—(1) Unreasonable and unbecoming for aged saints to sink under their burdens and afflictions; (2) Aged saints are under great obligations to God, and should be faithful unto death; (3) Young persons should choose God as the guide of their youth, if they desire that He should be the support and comfort of their age.—Job Orton.

Some may wonder what guilt is because they are selfishly or dishonestly tracing the bitterness and unrest of their lives to some other source than their own wicked wills; but the thing is man's realest burden, and man's realest burden is what God stoops lowest to bear. —Exp. Bib.

The Heavenly Father's Care.—"Does my heavenly Father really care for me?" The words came from a lady sitting by an open window; her brow bore the trace of care and sadness; her eyes were suffused with tears. Within two years death had thrice entered the home circle. The husband and two children, whose smiles made home happy, were sleeping in the graveyard near by. As her bereavement, her loneliness, her blighted prospects recurred to her mind, she exclaimed, almost with a spirit that questioned her Maker's goodness, "Does my heavenly Father really care for me?" A servant girl, who perhaps scarcely knew she was doing anything for the Master, passed by the window singing:—

"Though waves and storms go o'er my head;
  Though strength and health and friends be gone;
Though joys be withered all and dead;
  Though every comfort be withdrawn—
On this my steadfast soul relies,
Father, Thy mercy never dies."

"God compares Himself to a nurse, tenderly carrying a child; contrast Moses' language, Nu. xi. 12."—Fausset.

The cadences of those beautiful words, borne on the still summer air, found an echo in that stricken soul. She rose from her reverie of sadness, wiped away the falling tears, and looking not toward the silent tomb where bodies were crumbling to dust, but to the spirit-land whither her loved ones had gone, she said, with a faith she had never before known, "Though He slay me, yet will I trust in Him."—Hom. Com.

Ex. xix. 4; De. xxxii. 11, 12, xxxiii. 27, Is. lxiii. 9.

5—7. (5) **liken me,** Is. xl. 18, 25. (6) **They,** i. e. the idol-worshipers, especially the wealthier class of them.[a] **lavish,** "better as an exclamation of contempt: They that pour gold, etc. The gold and silver are the material out of which the images (or at least their plating) are to be made by the goldsmith (xl. 19)."—Camb. Bib. (7) **bear .. shoulder,** as a heavy dead weight to his appointed place. He cannot go himself nor remove thence. **not remove,** seeing he has no life or power. **not answer,** having no hearing and no voice.

[a] "The picture given of the stupid conduct of the idol-worshipers is exceedingly striking, and quite drawn to the life.—Henderson.

Inspiration of Christ's Personality.—If in the thick of the battle a leader is able to infuse himself into his followers, so is Christ. If one man's word has lifted thousands of defeated soldiers to an assault and to a victory, even so have Christ's lifted millions: lifted them above the habit and depression of sin, above the weakness of the flesh, above the fear of man, above danger and death and temptation more dangerous and fatal still. And yet it is not the sight of a visible leader, though the Gospels have made that sight imperishable; it is not the sound of another's Voice, though that Voice shall peal to the end of time, that Christians only feel. It is something within themselves; another self—purer, happier, victorious. Not as a voice or example, futile enough to the dying, but as a new soul, is Christ in men; and whether their ex-

"Ignorance is the curse of God, Knowledge the wing wherewith we fly to heaven." — Shakespeare.

"Ignorance seldom vaults into knowledge, but passes into it thro' an inter-

haustion needs creative forces, or their vices require conquering forces, He gives both, for He is the fountain of life.—Exp. Bib.

8—11. "An appeal to history and prophecy in proof of Jehovah's divinity." (8) **shew . . men,** "Remember ye this, and own yourselves guilty: lay it to heart ye apostates."—Pol. Bib. Both R. V. and A. V. translations are incorrect. (9) **former things,** the miracles wrought by Jehovah for the fathers.[a] (10) **Declaring,** or prophecying. **My counsel,** or My purpose shall be executed. (11) **ravenous bird,** or bird of prey,[b] referring to Cyrus as coming from Persia.

The Goodness of God's "Pleasure."—What is pleasant to God must be kind. That is, it must have taken all due consideration of the well-being and the wishes of others; and it must involve a going out of God, as it were, beyond himself, to live in the feelings of others. The essence of pleasure is unselfish concern for others. And God may do all his "pleasure," because He proposes only that which secures our highest welfare. What may be spoken of as the highest pleasure God can know? We are assured that He has "no pleasure at all in the death of the wicked, but that he turn from his evil way and live." God's supreme pleasure is found in redeeming; in all that this most suggestive and comprehensive word involves. "The Lord taketh pleasure in them that fear Him, in those that hope in His mercy."—R. Tuck. You Cannot Print Me (vs. 8).—Mr. Spurgeon, in a recent sermon, said to his hearers: "Read the sermons of Wesley and Whitefield, and what is there in them? It is no severe criticism to say that they are scarcely worthy to have survived, and yet those sermons wrought marvels, and well they might. In order to understand such preaching, you need to see and hear the man; you want his tearful eye, his glowing countenance, his pleading tone, his bursting heart. I have heard of a great preacher who objected to have his sermons printed, 'Because,' said he, 'you cannot print me!' "

12, 13. (12) **stouthearted,** "ye obdurate in heart," that is, strong, sound, but too sound to adapt their preconceived notions to God's new revelation. **far from righteousness,** "in spite of their sound opinions as to how it ought to come."—G. A. Smith. But Pol. Bib. reads, "ye discouraged ones, who are far from the thought of Israel's victory." (13) **my righteousness,** in distinction from the righteousness of the Jews. "It is evident that from the idolaters Jehovah has turned again, in these last verses, to the pedants in Israel, who were opposed to Cyrus because he was a Gentile, and who cherished their own obdurate notions of how salvation and righteousness should come. Ah, their kind of righteousness would never come, they would always be far from it! Let them rather trust to Jehovah's, which He was rapidly bringing near in His own way." —G. A. Smith.

Insincerity in Religion.—A great deal is being said just now in our country of upholding the great articles of the faith. Certainly let us uphold them. But do not let us have in our churches that saddest of all sights, a mere ecclesiastical procession,—men flourishing doctrines, but themselves with their manhood remaining unseen. We know the pity of a show, sometimes seen in countries on the Continent, where they have not given over carrying images about. Idols and banners and texts will fill a street with their tawdry, tottering progress, and you will see nothing human below, but now and then jostling shoulders and a sweaty face. Even so are many of the loud parades of doctrines in our day by men, who, in the words of this chapter, show themselves stout of heart by holding up their religion, but give us no signs in their character or conduct that their religion is holding up them. Let us prize our faith, not by holding it high, but by showing how high it can hold us. Which is the more inspiring sight,—a banner carried by hands, that must sooner or later weary; or the soldier's face, mantling with the inexhaustible strength of the God who lives at his heart and bears him up?—Exp. Bib.

CHAPTER THE FORTY-SEVENTH.

Ode on the Fall of Babylon. **1—3.** (1) **virgin daughter,** used of Tyre, ch. xxiii. 12; and referring to Babylon's boast that she had **never**

mediate state of obscurity, even as night into day through twilight." — Coleridge.

"Falsehood always endeavored to copy the mien and attitudes of truth." —Johnson.

[a] Comp. Is. xlii. 14, xliii. 13, xlv. 21.

[b] Esp. the eagle. It appears that Cyrus was the first to use the eagle as a military ensign. He was also singularly rapid in his movements, and so resembled the eagle.

"Falsehood avails itself of haste and uncertainty." — Tacitus.

"Our thoughts and speeches in most things run to waste; yea, as water spilt on the ground is both lost, cannot be gathered up again, and is polluted, mingled with dust. But no word spoken to God is lost. He receives it, and returns it unto our bosom with advantage. A soul that delights to speak to him will find that he also delights to speak to it." —Abp. Leighton.

"Great minds erect their never-failing trophies on the firm base of mercy." — Massinger.

"O ceremony, show me but thy worth!
What is thy soul of adoration?
Art thou aught else but place, degree, and form,
Creating awe and fear in other men?"
—Shakespeare.

been captured. **no throne,** R. V., "sit on the ground without a throne, O daughter," etc. **daughter .. Chaldaeans,** Chaldaea being the country, and Babylon the capital. **tender and delicate,**[a] De. xxviii. 54. (2) **grind meal,** menial work.[b] **uncover,** R. V., "remove thy veil, strip off thy train," etc., descriptive of the miserable and shameful plight in wh. they would be who had once lived as princesses. Squalid and half clad. **over the rivers,** into exile. (3) **meet .. man,** R. V., "and will accept no man."[c] No translation is satisfactory. Best is Pol. Bib. "Irreversible vengeance will I take, says our Redeemer," etc.

Note on vs. 2.—To grind flour in the East is the work of servants or slaves, and to make it by pounding with a pestle and mortar is the office of female servants or slaves. There being but few bridges, those who are in a low condition are obliged to ford the rivers; hence may be seen large companies going to the opposite banks, who have been obliged to "make bare the leg" and to "uncover the thigh." Thus were the "tender and delicate" daughters of Babylon, who had been nurtured on a throne, to be reduced to the condition of menials, and to cross the rivers as people of the lowest degree.—Roberts. A medal was struck by Vespasian on the subjugation of the Jews: on the reverse is seen a palm-tree, and a woman sitting on the ground at the foot of it, with her head leaning on her arm, weeping; and at her feet different pieces of armor with this legend, "Judea capta" (taken). Thus was exactly fulfilled the saying of the same prophet, "And she, being desolate, shall sit upon the ground."—Whitecross.

4, 5. our redeemer,[d] connected with verse 3 according to Pol. Bib. (5) **silent .. darkness,** fig. for state of humiliation and captivity. **lady of kingdoms,** so called bec. of the number of tributary states over which she ruled; all of this power she is to lose forever, because of her cruelty to Israel.

Longing for a Redeemer.—As the earth in its long polar night seeks to supply the absence of the day by the generation of the northern lights, so does each people in the long night of its heathen darkness bring forth in its yearning after the life of Christ, a faint and glimmering substitute for the same. From these dreamy longings after the break of day have proceeded oracles, priests, sacrifices, lawgivers, and the like. Men have nowhere given up hoping; nor acquiesced in the world's evil as the world's law. Everywhere they have had a tradition of a time when they were nearer to God than now, a confident hope of a time when they should be brought nearer again.—Abp. French.

6, 7. (6) **polluted,** better, profaned, suffered my chosen people to be treated as a common people, and to be defeated, and led captive. **thou,** Babylon. **the ancient,**[a] who would suffer much in captivity. The Jews were reverent to old age. "Perhaps the prophet refers to cruelties of the first days of the Babylonian triumph. Comp. Lam. iv. 16; v. 12."—Cheyne. (7) **lady for ever,**[b] Pol. Bib., "And thou saidst: I shall last forever, yea, be mistress perpetually," so Camb. Bib. **latter end,** the certain ultimate consequences of such pride and cruelty.

The Boast of Babylon (vs. 7).—"I shall be a lady for ever," suggests that lengthened prosperity in the case of the ungodly leads to—1. False security; 2. Presumption, "in my own right;" 3. Boasting, "a lady superior to others;" 4. Self-satisfaction, "I am a lady now," etc.; 5. Abandonment to luxury, "I mean to be at ease;" 6. Spiritual blindness.—Stems and Twigs.

Doing God's Work Unworthily.—God had entrusted Babylon with the work of executing his Divine judgments on his people. The work was done, but God could not approve of the way in which it was done. Compare, for illustrative purposes, the cases of King Saul and of Jehu. Saul was made executioner of the Divine judgment on Amalek, but God could not approve of his work: he erred on the side of laxity. Jehu was made executioner of the Divine judgment on the house of Ahab, but God could not approve of his work: he erred on the side of severity. The complaint God makes against Babylon is that it had "shown no mercy," and one specific instance is given— there had been no considerateness shown toward the aged among the captives; even "upon the ancient hast

a "Not so much descriptive of voluptuous and vicious habits, as of a delicate and easy mode of life, such as that of a princess compared with that of a female slave."—J. A. Alexander.

b "Grinding grain with a hand-mill was chiefly the labor of female slaves, and it was even regarded as the hardest labor."—Nagelsbach.

c "The evil was far too deep-seated; had been of far too long continuance. It was full time for vengeance to step in; for in no other way could the work of redemption be accomplished."—Spk. Com.

d "These words give the impression of a joyful welcome greeting, which meets one approaching, who is recognized as a friend." — Nagelsbach.

"There are errors which no wise man will treat with rudeness while there is a probability that they may be the refraction of some great truth still below the horizon." — Coleridge.

a Comp. 2. Ki. xxv. 5, 6, 26; Je. l. 17, li. 34.

b "Through thy vain expectation of being a queen for ever, thou didst advance to such a pitch of insolence as not to believe these things, concerning thy overthrow, possible."—Fausset.

"He who begins by halving his heart between God and mammon will end by being whole-hearted for the world, and faint-

thou very heavily laid thy yoke." Even the old people were made to do the tasks of bond-slaves.—Pul. Com.

Assumptions of Pride.—

Ask for whose end the heavenly bodies shine;
Earth for whose use? Pride answers, 'tis for mine.
For me kind nature wakes her genial power,
Suckles each herb and spreads out every flower.
Annual for me, the grape, the rose, renew
The juice nectareous and the balmy dew;
For me the mine a thousand treasures brings;
For me health gushes from a thousand springs;
Seas roll to waft me, suns to light me rise;
My footstool earth, my canopy the skies.—Pope.

8, 9. (8) **carelessly**, in uttermost security; with no suspicion of danger.[c] **widow**, a figure for supreme desolation and affliction. **they shall come, etc.**, R. V., "in their full measure shall they come upon thee, despite of the multitude of thy sorceries and the great," etc. "In one thing the law of Jehovah stood by itself (in contrast with other faiths) and that was in its intolerance of all augury and divination."—G. A. Smith. **sorceries**, see Da. ii. 2.

Historical Note on Sorceries, etc.—1. At entrance of Christianity the world was overrun with magicians and conjurers of various grades (Gal. v. 20). "Impostors fr. the E., pretending to magical powers, had great influence over the Rom. mind. All the Gk. and Lat. literature of the period, fr. Horace to Lucian, abounds in proof of the prevalent credulity of this sceptical period. Unbelief, when it has become conscious of its weakness, is often glad to give its hand to superstition. The faith of the educated Roms. was entirely gone, . . . they greedily welcomed the most absurd and degrading superstitions. . . . Syrian fortune-tellers "flocked into the haunts of public amusement. . . . The more remote districts of Asia Minor sent them itinerant soothsayers. . . . Marius had in his camp a Syrian prophetess, by whose divinations he regulated the progress of his campaigns." (Conybeare and Howson's Paul, i. 177—182.) Brutus, Pompey, Crassus, Cæsar resorted to oracles at Delphi, etc. Juvenal (x. 93) desc. the Emperor Tiberius with his Chaldæans around him. 2. Christianity attacked and defeated the popular superstition at all points of contact (Acts xiii. 8, xvi. 16, xix. 3, see esp. xix. 17—20). "This scene must have been long remembered at Ephesus. It was a strong proof of honest conviction on the part of the sorceress, and a striking attestation of the triumph of Jesus Christ over the powers of darkness" (Ibid. ii. 20).—Topics.

Comparative Value of Things.—You will notice that in the placid waters of a lake everything which is highest in reality is lowest in the reflection. The higher the trees, the lower their image. That is the picture of this world; what is highest in this world is lowest in the other, and what is highest in that world is lowest in this. Gold is on top here; they pave the streets with it there. To serve is looked upon as ignoble here; there those that serve reign, and the last are first. Any girl is willing to fling away paste diamonds for the real stones; when a man understands what God can be to the soul, he loses his taste for things he used to care for most.—F. B. Meyer.

10, 11. (10) **perverted thee,** "augury and divination exerted two evil influences. They paralyzed the industry and politics of a nation and confounded the moral sense of a people. They wearied a people's intellect, stunted their enterprise, distorted their conscience."—G. A. Smith. (11) **know .. riseth**, R. V. margin, "how to charm it away." So most modern commentators. An evil shall come and your charms shall fail. **put it off,** "expiate it" with all thy sacrificial oblations to thy gods.

Worldliness.—We are living under a materializing influence that is disastrous to a more serious and devotional view of life. In the minds of a great many good people the ideal of human existence is a great deal of material comfort and a large surplus of pleasure that can be purchased in the form of desirable surroundings. These ideals rise in the scale of magnitude and grandeur every year, and men say, "When I can realize this ideal of earthly paradise, I am going to devote a great deal of time

hearted for Christ. We are so constituted that it is impossible for us to exercise a divided allegiance; we must be out-and-out for God, or we shall be in-and-in for the world and all its interests." — A. J Gordon.

c "According to Xenophon the Babylonians looked on Cyrus with contempt."—Spk. Com.

"It is the nature of man to be proud, when man by nature has nothing to be proud of. I am ashamed of their glory whose glory is their shame. If nature will have me to be proud of something, I will be proud only of this, that I am proud of nothing."—Warwick.

"This generation ought to exult in its transcendent opportunities for service. But it is possible to see these opportunities and yet feel no thrill of new life unless there is added the quickening touch of the divine Spirit."—Josiah Strong.

"The athletes of Greece and Rome were inspired to run or wrestle by the knowledge of the fact that they were surrounded by a vast assembly of spectators (Heb. xii. 1). Oh! if we but realized God's presence, our life would become brave and beautiful and holy. God is not only present everywhere, but everywhere present to inspire, and aid, and bless."

"Earthly pride is like the passing flower, that springs to fall, and blossoms but to die."—H. K. White.

"I do believe that the Divine love and compassion follow us in all words, and that the Heavenly Father will do the best that is possible for every creature He has made. What that will be must be left to His infinite wisdom and goodness." — Whittier.

to devotional preparation for the next world." The trouble is that they no sooner get their house on the sea-shore than they want a house in the mountains, and when they have that they want a house somewhere else. They say, "Wait till my cat-boat grows into a sloop, and my sloop into a schooner, and my schooner into a steam yacht; then I will devise liberal things." But the "then" never comes. Meanwhile they have become so immersed in this world, and so filled with the spirit of this world, and so absorbed in the pursuit of this world's pleasure and comfort, that they have no time to read the Bible as they ought.—Francis L. Patton. Man's Helplessness in Presence of Divine Calamities.—The point impressed is that disaster takes unexpected and overwhelming forms, against which the wisest man fails to take precautions. Man can only affect the smallest of circumstances that are put into his control, and the few persons who are under his immediate influence. But each one of us belongs to a great whole, and is affected by great forces, which God alone controls. We are carried whither we would not. We are borne down by evils which we seem to have done nothing to create. We are helpless before the hurricanes and earthquakes and pestilences with which God can smite. But we may so stand that no event arranged by the Divine wisdom can take shape for us as calamity.—Pul. Com.

12, 13. (12) **Stand now,** "pray, persist in thy spells," (Pol. Bib.), stake everything on them (Lev. xiii. 5; Jer. xlviii. 11; Ezek. xiii. 5). A scornful challenge to the multitude of Babylon's magicians. **from thy youth,** with allusion to their claim to an extraordinarily early origin.[a] **if so be,** or perchance. (13) **wearied,** bec. their efforts are fruitless of results. **astrologers,** or "dividers of heaven," alluding to the signs of the Zodiac, which are of Babylonian origin.—Pol. Bib. **stargazers,** those who prophesy upon observation of the stars. **monthly,**[b] etc., "refers to the preparation of monthly almanacs in which coming disasters were foretold, lucky and unlucky days pointed out," etc.—Camb. Bib.

Astrology, etc.—The earliest objects of idolatrous homage were prob. the sun, moon, stars (2 Ki. xxiii. 5; Acts vii. 42), and afterwards earthly creatures (Ro. i. 23, 25). The following are among the chief, as ref. to in the Bible, of the creatures worshiped. [Sun] as Osiris by Egyptians, fr. them prob. learned by Israelites. On (Bethshemesh or Heliopolis—city of the S.), so called fr. his temple (Jer. xliii. 13). Wife of Joseph was dau. of his priest (Ge. xli. 45.) Sun worshiped by Phœnicians under name of Baal-shâmayim (Lord of heaven), and Adon (Gk. Adonis), and Thammuz (Ez. viii. 14); by Ammonites as Molech or Milcom; by Moabites as Chemosh; by Syrians as Hadad (hence names Benhadad, Hadadezer, etc.). The Bel or Belus of Assyrians=Baal. As by Persians (Bochart), late kings of Judah dedicated horses to S. (2 Ki. xxiii. 11), [Moon] under name of Astarte worshiped by Phœnicians, known as Ashtaroth or Asthtoreth to Hebs. (Jud. ii. 13, x. 6; 1 S. vii. 3, xii. 10); goddess of Zidonians (1 Ki. xi. 33). [Stars] Early adored by Israelites (Am. v. 26; Ac. vii. 42, 43; hence a strict law (Deu. xvii. 3), and constant calling of God as the true Jehovah Zebaoth (Lord of Hosts) (Dan. iv. 35, 37; Deu. x. 14). S. worship was encouraged by Manasseh (2 Ch. xxxiii. 3).—Topics.

a "The Babylonians are reported by Diodorus Siculus, and other writers, to have carried back their own antiquity, as proved by recorded scientific observations, to an extravagant and foolish length."—J. A. Alexander.

b "It would appear that the astronomers of Babylon published a monthly table of the leading events that might be expected to happen."— Henderson.

"The superstition in which we were brought up never loses its power over us even after we understand it." —Lefling.

14, 15. (14) **fire,** of God's wrath, manifested in national calamities. **not a coal,** "no glowing coal to warm oneself withal; no fire to sit before!" i. e. not a hearth fire but a conflagration.—Camb. Bib. (15) **Thus,** R. V., "Thus shall the things be unto thee wherein thou hast laboured: they that have trafficked with thee," etc. There never was a truer picture of the quick ruin of a merely commercial community, or of the ultimate loneliness of a mercenary and selfish life, than the headlong rush of traders, each as he could find passage, from the city that never had other attractions even for her own citizens than those of gain or of pleasure." —G. A. Smith.

Burning the Stubble.—This is a strong description of a fire made with dried grass and stubble. While the hand of the cottager supplies fresh fuel, though but for a few moments, the flame may illumine his dwelling, and cheer himself with the blaze; but there is no fire to sit before, no coals to warm at. The embers wear but a momentary smile, and are then extinct. Thus has it fared with Babylon, against which these judgments were denounced, more than two thousand years since.

"Nothing is more depressing than to fail again and again. Yet precisely this is the ever-repeated consequence of self-trust and self-help. Blessed is it when weariness does not pass into despair, but leads to the abandonment of self-reliances, that full trust may be placed in God."—R. Tuck.

CHAPTER THE FORTY-EIGHTH.

"This chapter is largely a recapitulation of certain outstanding themes of the prophecy, several of which are here touched upon for the last time."—Camb. Bib. 1, 2. (1) **waters of Judah,** better, "loins of Judah" (comp. vs. 19). **who swear by,** i. e. avow allegiance to (Deut. vi. 13, x. 20). **not in truth,** not sincerely.[b] (2) **the holy city;**[c] first time this title is used of Jerusalem in the O. T. Used afterward lii. 1 and in Nehemiah and Daniel (comp. Matt. iv. 5).

Insincerity is Sometimes a Drift.—We get into it, and it becomes a confirmed condition we scarcely know how; we are not conscious of having exercised any will in the matter. With some there is a great idea of "keeping up appearances," and the effort to do this tends to nourish insincere habits and ways. And sometimes we are carried into expressions of religious feeling and experience that are quite beyond us, by surroundings of religious excitement; and the pleasure of the insincere fascinates us. We drift into this evil by the use of sensational hymns, and by listening to ecstatic religious experiences; and there is no graver danger besetting the Church of our day than this tendency to nourish the insincere in the expressions of religious life. God's reproaches fall on many who think themselves very holy, but whose professions are not really matched by heart and life.—Pul. Com.

3—5. (3) **former things,** such as the fall of Assyria.[a] (4) **obstinate,** hard, stubborn, stiff-necked. This "tough, defiant, natural force which lived in Israel is a genuine Semitic trait."—Oehler. **brow brass,** like the hard brow of butting animals. Shamelessly persistent in opposition to the truth. (5) **commanded them,** "many of the wonderful things of old, Jehovah predicted long before they happened, and so left His stubborn people no excuse for an idolatry to which otherwise they would have given themselves (vs. 5). Now that they see that wonderful past complete, and all the predictions fulfilled, they may well publish Jehovah's renown to the world."[b]—G. A. Smith.

A Leipsic Jew.—A poor student of the university of Leipsic, having occasion to undertake a journey to his distant friends, being destitute of the money needful for the purpose, was compelled to go to a Jew, and pawn his Hebrew Bible and Greek Testament. The latter contained the Greek and German text in opposite columns. The Jew, little as he valued this book, was prevailed on to give the student half a rix dollar for it. During the absence of the student, he determined to read it through, with a view of confirming his enmity against Jesus, and to be the better prepared to testify his zeal for the Jewish faith. He concealed it from his family, and commenced its perusal, which, as the young man was absent seven weeks, he had time to do. As he read, he was surprised and impressed, and at times was ready to exclaim, "Oh that Jesus was my Saviour!" He was compelled a third time to read the book; and now the history, the doctrines, and the promises of Jesus destroyed his opposition, and melted his soul. He was overcome to tears, and resolved on embracing the doctrines of the cross. He announced his change to a Christian minister, purchased the New Testament of the student, to whom he became a warmly attached friend, and continued to give evidence of being a consistent Christian. The Beginning of Moral Obstinacy a Loss of Spiritual Sensibility.—The proper attitude before God is one of openness, humility, and self-distrust. The renewed soul is delicately sensitive to every expression of the Divine will, and to everything that is in harmony with the Divine mind. And the maintaining of that sensitiveness is absolutely essential to the keeping of right relations with God. Piety is closely akin to meekness and gentleness. It loves to obey, to follow, to be led. We have no will but God's will for us. To lose this "sensibility" is grave danger. It is to step on a slippery slide. Therefore should we "keep our heart with all diligence," and be most jealous over those various spiritual influences that help to make our hearts more tender.—Pul. Com.

"In this ch. Israel is warned against his old hardness of heart, and bidden to receive the declaration of that wh. is God's present will,—the deliverance of Israel through Cyrus. But, for the wicked, let Israel know there is no deliverance." —Mat. Arnold.

b Je. v. 2; Jno. iv. 24.

c Is. lii. 1; Da. ix. 24; Ne. xi. 1; Mat. iv. 5. This designation, at first a mere epithet, eventually became a proper name, and Je - ha - Kodesh seems, in some cases, to have superseded the more general name of Jerusalem.

The Mohammedans call Jerusalem El Khoods or The Holy.

a Is. xli. 24.

b De. xxxi. 26—29.

"I have always found in my scientific studies that, when I could get the Bible to say anything upon the subject, it afforded me a firm platform to stand upon, and a round in the ladder by which I could safely ascend."—Lieut. Maury.

"I must confess to you that the majesty of the Scriptures astonishes me; the holiness of the Evangelists speaks to my heart, and has such strong and striking characters of truth, and is, moreover, so perfectly inimitable, that, if it

6—8. (6) **heard, see,** heard the predictions, now see the fulfilments. **declare it,** so that others may learn of the true and only God. **have showed,** Camb. B. "I show." **new things,** those named in vs. 14. **hidden things,** things kept in reserve. (7) **created now,** by immediate Divine decree. God not only arranging from the beginning, but actually presiding and working now.[a] **even before,** etc., R. V., "and before this day thou heardest them not," "therefore cannot lay claim to the knowledge as something drawn from itself."—Delitzsch. (8) **heardest not,** by reason of hardheartedness and obstinacy.[b]

Defects of Believers (vs. 8.)—I. They are too often in a measure spiritually insensible, "Yea, thou heardest not." II. They are often carelessly ignorant, "Yea, thou knewest not." III. Yet all this was foreknown of God, and yet He has been pleased to deal with us in a way of mercy. IV. Pray for the Holy Spirit, that we may henceforth have the hearing ear and the understanding heart.—C. H. Spurgeon.

Hidden Things.—The earth is full of latent forces. Take heat, for instance: how it hides in the secret places more stealthily than the panther! Take electricity: here it is quite close to us—within us; and what a masterful power it is!—how it can rend the rock and lay low the lofty palaces! These are beneficent forces, though, and do their work well, for the security, health, and comfort of man. There are hidden forces that are baneful. The latent seeds of disease lie hidden behind that pearly skin—that pure and radiant complexion. And when we have to speak of sin, what a latent force there is hidden in the breast of a child!—concealing itself under the cloak of outward respectability in manhood, and by its manifestations here and there like the volcano, telling us what depths of evil there are in the human heart, which only Christ and his cross can overcome. Men understand much, but they do not understand themselves.

9—11. (9) **defer mine anger,** Ex. xxxiv. 6.[c] **refrain,** from adequately punishing them for their stubbornness and rebellion.[d] (10) **refined thee,** by the chastising fires of captivity. **with silver,** better, as silver,[e] or as Pol. Bib. "without gain of silver," i. e. without obtaining any pure metal as a result. The sense is uncertain. (11) **name .. polluted,** or defamed, as it would be if God proved unfaithful to His chosen people. **glory .. another,** ch. xlii. 8.

The Refining Power of Affliction.—It is rough work that polishes. Look at the pebbles on the shore! Far inland, where some arm of the sea thrusts itself deep into the bosom of the land, and, expanding into a salt loch, lies girdled by the mountains, sheltered from the storms that agitate the deep, the pebbles on the beach are rough, not beautiful, angular, not rounded. It is where long white lines of breakers roar, and the rattling shingle is rolled about the strand, that its pebbles are rounded and polished. As in nature, as in the arts, so in grace; it is rough treatment that gives souls as well as stones their lustre; the more the diamond is cut, the brighter it sparkles; and in what seems hard dealing their God has no end in view but to perfect his people's graces. Our Father, and the kindest of fathers, he afflicts not willingly; he sends tribulations, but hear St. Paul tell their purpose. "Tribulation worketh patience, patience experience, experience hope."—Guthrie. The Furnace of Affliction.—The late Professor George Wilson thus quaintly expresses the various effects of affliction in a letter to his friend, Daniel Macmillan: "The furnace of affliction puffs away some men in black smoke, and hardens others into useless slags, and melts a few into clear glass. May it refine us into gold seven times purified, ready to be fashioned into vessels for the Master's use." And like the effect of affliction is that of the habitual prospect of death. In a letter to the same friend, in 1848, he says, "I have been reading lately, with great sadness, the Memorials of Charles Lamb, and the Life of Keats. There is something in the noble brotherly love of Charles to brighten, and hallow, and relieve the former; but Keats's death-bed is the blackness of midnight, unmitigated by one ray of light. God keep you and me from such a death-bed! We may have physical agonies as great to endure. It is the common lot. I feel that our heavenly Father can better choose for us than we can for ourselves, of what we should die; but I pray our blessed Lord and Master to be with us in our last fight with the last enemy, and to give us the

---

had been the invention of man, the inventors would be greater than the greatest heroes."—Rousseau.

[a] "The things wh. the Prophet prophesied concerning Babylon and Cyrus could not, by any possibility, have been anticipated by human sagacity." — Henderson.

[b] De. xxix. 4, xxxi. 27.

"Great occasions do not make heroes or cowards; they simply unveil them to the eyes of men. Silently and imperceptibly, as we wake or sleep, we grow and wax strong, we grow and wax weak, and at last some crisis shows us what we have become."—Canon Westcott.

[c] A beautiful exhibition of the forbearance of Jehovah.

[d] Ps. lxxviii. 38.

[e] "The refiner of silver may lose some grains of the good ore in the smelting, but I will not lose a single grain of thee in the spiritual process of refining thee by the furnace of affliction at Babylon." — Wordsworth.

"Till the root has firm hold of the soil, there can be neither flower nor fruit. The soul cannot safely bear much sunshine till it is rooted in God. Let me then lift up my thought constantly to the Divine realm, the summer land of the soul, for help and guidance. Let me make God my own, and then all that He possesses will be mine also." — Old Test. Anec.

victory. If He does, what shall pain be but like other bitter medicines, the preparative for the unbroken health of an endless life?"—Old Test. Anec.

12, 13. (12) **first**, etc., Listen to Me! It is the Eternal who speaks, the Creator. My words you must heed, ch. xli. 4, xliv. 6; Re. i. 17, xxii. 13. (13) **spanned,** R. V. "spread out." **I call,** etc., the universe heeds my call and stands ready to obey.

God Over All.—Nations are not cards with which politicians play at gambling: they may think they do, they may seem to do so, but the Lord reigneth, the earth is the Lord's and the fulness thereof, and he says to the nation as he says to the individual, "The very hairs of thy head are all numbered." Ralph Waldo Emerson has a beautiful little parable about this. He pictures a republican convention: he has in it several very stormy spirits who have undertaken to carry the republic at all costs—mighty little straws hardly strong enough to hold a fly. They have a meeting and storm at one another a long while, and when the meeting is broken up, kind mother Nature, all her stars alight, all her winds quieted down to a touching and pathetic minor, says to the hottest of these conventionalists, "Why art thou so hot, little sir?" The little sir thinks he has been manipulating a nation, settling the affairs of a republic—that without him the republic would be nowhere, and great quiet solemn Alma Mater, every lamp aflame, bends over him, "Why so hot, little sir?" It is the same with this great England of ours. There is a House, in which men point to one another, charge honorable gentlemen opposite—these honorable gentlemen are always opposite—shake their fists almost at the right honorable gentlemen opposite—and kind great Nature waits for them, and when they come out, she says to the fiercest and fussiest of them, "Why so hot, little sir?" The Lord reigneth, the earth is the Lord's and the fulness thereof: everything is mapped out in his providence and brought within the circle of his decree: he has a purpose to realize, and no man can thwart it. Oh that we were less hot and less fierce, that we had the repose of strength, the quietness of omnipotence! —Peop. Bib.

14, 15. (14) **All ye**, He now summons His people, and contrasts them with the heathen nations. **loved him,** i. e. Cyrus. Love so far as shown in selecting him as His agent. Delitzsch translates "He whom Jehovah loveth will accomplish his will upon Babel, and his arm upon the Chaldæans." (15) **I,** notice the emphatic repetition of this pronoun.

A Special Providence—Major-General Burn.—General Burn records, in his Life, the following interesting facts:—Last week, just as my heart was poring over the disappointment I met with in my expected promotion, and anticipating all the miseries of accumulating debt, a dear friend of mine, in the military profession, called upon me; and, taking me aside into a private room, made me promise I would ask him no questions, which when I had done, with some hesitation, he put a bank-note into my hand, saying, he was desired to give it to me, but with the strongest injunctions never to divulge from whence it came. I put it into my pocket without looking at it, repeatedly thanking him and my generous benefactor for the very acceptable present. Dinner being upon the table, we went in, sat down, and dined; my mind all the while occupied about which of my creditors I should pay off first, imagining I had perhaps a ten or twenty pound note, which I longed to look at, but was ashamed to do so before my friend. Soon after dinner, I took an opportunity to step out of the room to satisfy my anxious curiosity. But, oh! how was my heart filled with grateful emotions when I found two notes, one of five, and the other of a hundred pounds—a present of a hundred guineas! To attempt a description of my feelings at that time would be in vain: those who have experienced the overflowings of a grateful heart can only guess at them. I was so overcome with a view of the Lord's goodness, that I knew not how to express myself, and was afraid my friend would think me insensible of the favor bestowed. When he was gone, and I had communicated the purport of his visit to Mrs. B., we both wept, and in broken accents, with eyes and hearts directed to heaven, expressed our obligation to the God of all our mercies for His seasonable and ample supply, in answer to our united and repeated prayers. I have now en-

"Even legal punishments lose all appearance of justice when too strictly inflicted on men compelled by the last extremity of distress to incur them." — Junius.

"The manner in which the Creator has contrived a supply for the thirst of man, in sultry places, is worthy of admiration. He has placed amidst the burning sands of Africa a plant, whose leaf, twisted round like a cruet, is always filled with a large glassful of fresh water. He has planted, in some other districts of the same country, a great tree, the trunk of which, of a prodigious bulk, is naturally hollowed, like a cistern. In the rainy season it receives its fill of water, which continues fresh and cool in the greatest heats, by means of the tufted foliage which crowns its summit. In some of the parched rocky islands of the West Indies there is found a tree, called the Water Lianao, so full of sap that if you cut a single branch of it, as much water is immediately discharged as a man can drink at a draught, and it is perfectly pure and limpid." — St. Pierre.

"God never meant that man should scale the heavens
By strides of human wisdom. In His works,
Though wondrous, he commands us in his word
To seek him rather where his mercy shines."
—Cowper.

joyed the pleasure of paying all my debts, of contributing to the relief of others, and of purchasing many articles absolutely necessary to my family. Oh, how good the Lord has been to us, unworthy as we are of the least of all His mercies!

16, 17. (16) **now the Lord,** render, "now the Lord Jehovah hath sent me and His Spirit," i. e. hath sent both me and His Spirit.—Camb. Bib. **his Spirit,** the spirit of prophecy in Isaiah.[a] This very difficult verse has been attributed either to Jehovah in the first three clauses and to the Servant in the fourth (Delitzsch); or in the same proportion to Jehovah and the prophet (Cheyne and Bredenkamp); or to the Servant all through (Orelli); or to the prophet all through (Hitzig, Knobel, Giesebrecht). (17) **teacheth .. profit,** though it may be in the furnace of affliction.

Profitable Teaching and Right Leading (vs. 17).—The whole scope of the passage points to God—I. As a Redeemer—1. From the captivity of evil, the Babylon of sin; 2. The mercy of the Redeemer at work in the city of bondage. II. As a teacher. 1. Look at the Gospel as a teacher; 2. Learning is never easy, yet all the teaching is profitable. III. As a leader. 1. The way God would have us go is not always according to our inclination; 2. The knowledge that it is His way should be enough.—J. Parrish.

The Ways of God.—In this world we are children standing on the bank of a mighty river. Casting our eyes upward and downward along the channel, we discern various windings of its current; and perceive that it is now visible, now obscure, and now entirely hidden from our view. But being far removed from the fountain whence it springs, and from the ocean into which it is emptied, we are unable to form any conceptions of the beauty, usefulness, or grandeur of its progress. Lost in perplexity and ignorance, we gaze, wonder, and despond. In this situation, a messenger from heaven comes to our relief, with authentic information of its nature, its course, and its end; conducts us backward to the fountain, and leads us forward to the ocean. This river is the earthly system of providence: the Bible is the celestial messenger: and Heaven is the ocean in which all preceding dispensations find their end.—Dwight.

18, 19. (18) **peace,** or national prosperity. **river,** i. e. "a perennial stream, such as the Euphrates (cf. Am. v. 24). It is easy to understand the impression made on the mind of a native of Palestine, accustomed to 'deceitful brooks' that run dry in the summer, by the sight of a great river, flowing on for ever in undiminished volume. The actual history of Israel had been like the wadis of Judæa, transient gleams of prosperity being interrupted by long intervals of misfortune; the river suggests to the writer an image of the boundless and unfailing blessedness which would have followed the keeping of the Divine commandments."—Camb. Bib. **righteousness,** moral prosperity. **waves,** which roll up and flow on continually.[b] (19) **seed .. sand,** abundant offspring being regarded in the E. as a special sign of Divine favor. **the gravel,** R. V., "the grains." **name,** that of the "seed," as Jehovah's nation.

The Commandments of God (vs. 18).—I. God hath given to us commandments—1. Authoritative in their import; 2. Perspicuous in their style; 3. Universal in their application; 4. Reasonable in their claims. II. God's commandments deserve attention. 1. They should be read; 2. Remembered; 3. practised. III. Such attention produces the happiest results. 1. The nature of that tranquillity which the people of God enjoy; 2. Its perpetuity; 3. Its increase; 4. Thy righteousness as the waves of the sea. IV. The people of Israel were inattentive to God's commandments. This conduct was—1. Ungrateful; 2. Rebellious; 3. Unnatural; 4. Ruinous. Learn—(1) That attention to God's commandments is a highly important duty; (2) Where they are disregarded, peace is forfeited; (3) God most compassionately commiserates the circumstances of His creatures; (4) Man's final ruin is wholly of himself.—Beta in 400 Sks.

Human Freedom.—Jehovah laments that Israel had forfeited its heritage, had used its freedom to disobey, had cut itself off from his generous design (vs. 18). What God would gladly have bestowed, the foolish nation had resolved to refuse. Such power of choice has the Creator given to his creature, man. And what fearful use has man made of this his freedom! It is not Israel alone that has elected to forego splendid op-

"Not a flower But shows some touch, in freckle, streak, or stain, Of his unrivalled pencil."—Cowper.

"Thou great mysterious Power, who hast involved Thy wise decrees in darkness, to perplex the pride of human wisdom, to confound the daring scrutiny, and prove the faith of Thy presuming creatures!"—Hannah More.

"O Eternal Providence, whose course, amidst the various maze of life, is fix'd by boundless wisdom and by boundless love, I follow Thee, with resignation, hope, with confidence and joy; for Thou art good, and of Thy rising goodness is no end."—Thomson.

[a] "In this vs. the Prophet, charged with these messages from God, speaks in his own name, and testifies to his countrymen that he has from the beginning pointed out to them God's hand and beck in these great events now happening."—Mat. Arnold.

"God enters by a private door into every individual."—Emerson.

"To him, no high, no low, no great, no small; He fills, he bounds, connects, and equals all."—Pope.

[b] Comp. De xxxii. 29; Mat. xxiii. 37.

"The reason why we hate the law," said some idolaters to a missionary, "is because it is holy. If it

portunities. What might not Rome have been, and Egypt, and those European lands to which the knowledge of the gospel has been carried! It is not too late to ask—What may not England be? The record of her history is not yet complete; her sands are not yet run; her gate of opportunity is not yet closed. She may yet rise to the height of her privilege, as she may yet sink grievously and fatally beneath it. With the same solemn and awful freedom every individual soul is invested by its Creator. Every one of us is at liberty to thwart his gracious purpose if we choose; at liberty also to realize it, in all its glorious fulness, if we will.—Pul. Com.

The Perceiving Heart.—"Two sit together and hear the same sermon. One finds a hidden spiritual virtue in the Word, by which he lives and grows and thrives. Another finds no such virtue in it; perhaps it pleases his reason, and there is an end. This proceeds from the want of the spiritual, perceiving heart. Why is it that a man is so affected with music that all his passions are moved by it, while brutes are not at all pleased? Because there is in man a principle of reason concurring with his sense, which discovers the sweetness and harmony of the sounds that bare sense is not able to discern." And so of the things of God. Open thou mine eyes and mine ears; let my noblest faculties be ever in communion with the noblest, my spiritual nature be awakened by the Spirit, and again respond to His influence!—this should be our prayer. We will hearken unto and obey Him who hath the words of eternal life: this should be our resolve.—J.

The Lost Ideal.—

"Have we not all, amid life's petty strife,
Some ideal of a noble life,
That once seemed possible? Did we not hear
The flutter of its wings, and feel it near?
And just within our reach it was; and yet
We lost it in this daily jar and fret;
And now live idly, in a vain regret.
But still our place is kept, and it will wait
Ready for us to fill it, soon or late.
No star is ever lost we once have seen;
We always may be what we might have been."

20—22. (20) **flee ye**, as at the Exodus. **singing**, as when you reached the further shores of the Red Sea.[a] (21) **thirsted not**, "the exile has been only a temporary failure. The promises will yet be fulfilled. The exile is to be followed by restoration, and the exiles are summoned to go forth from Babylon. As in the Exodus from Egypt so will it be in this greater Exodus. Waters will burst from the rock to quench the thirst of those whose path leads through the desert to the promised land."—Briggs.[b] (22) **no peace,** as before, in the sense of national prosperity through the Divine blessing. A refrain occurring lvii. 20, 21, and the idea lxvi. 24.

Peace (vs. 22).—I. What kind of peace? "The peace of God, which passeth all understanding, shall keep your hearts and minds through Christ Jesus." II. How shall we get it? "Being justified by faith, we have peace with God through our Lord Jesus Christ." III. What will be the effect of it? "And the work of righteousness shall be peace; and the effect of righteousness, quietness and assurance for ever." IV. Where will it lead us? "Unto the city of the living God, the heavenly Jerusalem, and to an innumerable company of angels, to the general assembly and church of the firstborn, which are written in heaven, to God, the Judge of all, and to Jesus, the Mediator of the new Covenant." "Seeing that you look for such things, be diligent that ye may be found of Him in peace."

would allow us to rob freely, if it taught us to be revenged on our enemies, and give way to our passions without being exposed to their consequences, we would embrace it; but because it is holy we reject it, and command you and the catechist to depart immediately."

Equanimity, in every condition of life, is a noble attribute."—Cicero.

"Peace is the happy, natural state of man; war his corruption, his disgrace." —Thomson.

"There is an hour in each man's life appointed
To make his happiness, if then he seize it."
—Beaumont and Fletcher.

"Who seeks, and will not take when once 'tis offer'd,
Shall never find it more."
—Shakespeare.

[a] Ex. xv.

[b] "God always connects the mercies of the Anodus from Babylon with those of the Exodus from Egypt." —Wordsworth.

"Away among the Alleghanies there is a spring so small, that a single ox in a summer day could drain it dry. It steals its unobtrusive way among the hills, till it spreads out in the beautiful Ohio. Thence it stretches away a thousand miles, leaving on its banks, cities, villages, and cultivated farms, and bearing on its bosom more than half a thou-

CHAPTER THE FORTY-NINTH.

1. O isles, comp. xl. 15, word used 12 times in this part of Isaiah, probably means "far countries," referring to coastlands as well as islands. **called me,** the personal servant of God. The greater than Cyrus, whom **he, in measure, typified.**

Note on ch. xlix.—The beginning of ch. xlix. seems to mark a distinct advance in the development of the prophet's conceptions. "The controversial tone, the repeated comparisons between Jehovah and the idols, with the arguments based upon them, disappear; the prophet feels that, as regards these points, he has made his position sufficiently secure. For the same reason, allusions to Cyrus and his conquest of Babylon cease also; that, likewise, is now taken for granted" (Driver). In the remaining discourses (ch. xlix.—lv.) the author concentrates his attention almost exclusively on his central message of consolation, and the glorious future in store for Israel.—Camb. Bib.

2, 3. (2) **my mouth,** Messiah's work would be teaching. **sharp sword,** He. iv. 12. **shaft,** or arrow.[a] This section is an advance upon the conception of the previous section. There, he was endowed with the divine Spirit; here he is called from the womb and assigned His ministry prior to birth. There he was a sharp threshing instrument; here his mouth is like a sharp sword hidden in the hand of Jehovah, and an arrow concealed in His quiver.—Briggs. **hid,** R. V. "kept me close," protected by God as the arrow by the quiver. (3) **O Israel,** Pol. Bib. regards these words "O Israel" as a later addition to the text. If they were genuine it would be almost impossible to hold that the Servant is an individual. **glorified,** Jno. xii. 28.[b]

The Sword and Arrow were the chief weapons of the ancients, and were emblems of powerful and persuasive speech. The Tartars proclaim a powerful prince thus:—"His word shall be as a sword." Of Pericles it is said, "His powerful speech pierced the hearer's soul, and left deep behind in his bosom its keener point infixed." Such is the power of the Gospel.—Thodey. Glorifying God.—Light is never revealed of itself, but always when shining from, or burning in, something else. To be seen, light requires a surface that will reflect, or a substance that will consume. And so, to break into glory, God requires something outside Himself. A responsive portion of humanity is indispensable to Him,—a people who will reflect Him and spend itself for Him. Man is the mirror and the wick of the Divine. God is glorified in man's character and witness,—these are His mirror; and in man's sacrifice,—that is His wick. Carlyle said, and it was almost his last testimony, "The older I grow, and I am now on the brink of eternity, the more comes back to me the first sentence of the catechism, which I learned when a child, and the fuller does its meaning grow—'What is the chief end of man? Man's chief end is to glorify God and enjoy Him for ever.'"—Exp. Bib.

4. **laboured .. nought,** descriptive of the apparent results of Messiah's mission.[c] Christ made comparatively few disciples, and seemed to make but little impression on the Jewish nation. **judgment,** or reward, the true fruitage of My work. **work,** R. V. "recompence."

An Encouragement to Labor.—Other men do not see the full result of their labor—they know not how many lamps are kindled by their torch. Did you ever hear of Thomas Barber? Probably not. His name is written but in pale ink on the world's scroll, yet that man was the means of converting Dr. Adam Clarke, one of the world's deepest scholars and most luminous expositors of the Divine Word. Did you ever hear of Robert Burnard? Probably not; yet that good man laid hold of a drunken mason's son in Plymouth workhouse, and watched over him with ever-helpful generosity, until that deaf pauper was known throughout the world as Dr. John Kitto. These are but two names out of a long roll. They show how even obscure names may be associated with stupendous results.—Hom. Com.

5. **though .. gathered,** R. V. "and that Israel be gathered to him."[a] **yet,** etc., R. V. "(for I am honourable .. my strength)," a parenthetical clause. The quotation referred to in this verse begins vs. 6. **my strength,** or my salvation.

"Ah if we but knew the power that worketh in us and the power that worketh for us, there would be less talking and more working, and things that seem to be, from the joint of unbelief and panic-strickenness, almost too big to attempt, would be seen to be natural and obvious."—John McNeill.

Work for God.—When a young man is converted, he is almost al-

sand steamboats. Beautiful representation of a Christian's peace! Peace 'as a river.'"—H. W. Beecher.

"If there be not a religious element in the relations of men, such relations are miserable and doomed to ruin." — Carlyle.

"The measure of choosing well is whether a man likes what he has chosen."—Lamb.

a "The metaphors of a sword and an arrow, in the best state of preparation, aptly set forth the penetrating and subduing efficacy of the Gospel."—Henderson.

b Jno. xii. 31, xiv. 13, xvii. 1, 4.

"What to thee is shadow to Him is day, And the end He knoweth." — J. Whittier.

"Far away th in the sunshine are my brightest aspirations. I cannot reach them, but I can look up and see their beauty, believe in them, and try to follow where they lead." — Louise May Alcott.

c Comp. Jno. i. 11, xii. 37.

"Here it seems to point to the obstinancy of the Jews, among whom Christ went in person preaching the Gospel of the kingdom, labored and spent His strength. So very few were brought in, when one would think none should have stood out." — Mrs. Henry.

a So marg., Sept., Syr., Arab., Delitzsch. etc.

ways inclined at first to say, "I know I could do far more good if I was a preacher, so I'll leave my business and become a preacher of the gospel." But very often mistakes are made just in this way. God may have given you some work to do for Him in the position in which He has placed you which no one else could do if you were to leave it undone. We should be very careful how we wish to change from whatever position in life into which God has seen fit to put us.—Andrew A. Bonar.

6. R. V. "Yea, he saith, It is too light a thing," etc., i. e. compared with the sublime trust committed to Messiah of saving the whole world.[b] "The restoration of Israel is the least part of thy vocation as my servant."—Camb. Bib. **preserved,** the spared of so many national calamities. **light,** etc., comp. Lu. ii. 32; Ac. xiii. 47; Ro. xv. 10.[c] "So I set thee as a light of the nations, that my deliverance may be to the end of the earth," Pol. Bib. This is the greater mission of the Servant.

The Messiah's Commission (vs. 6).—I. God's gift to mankind. 1. The Person given; 2. The Saviour's appointment, office, or undertaking. II. God's intention respecting mankind. 1. To raise up the tribes of Jacob; 2. The enlightening of the Gentiles. We infer—(1) We ought very highly to value our own souls; (2) We should accept the salvation of God; (3) Love Him who has manifested such love to us; (4) Give proof of our love; (5) Confidently expect all things that are necessary to life and godliness; (6) Employ both our example and influence to open the eyes of our fellow-men.—Zeta in 400 Sks.

Lights in the World.—If you go into a dark room filled with vermin, you cannot see anything; but if you light a match you see some crawling creatures; if you light a lamp, you see more; and if you turn on an electric light, it reveals the good and the evil in sharp contrast. "That which doth make manifest, is light," and Christians are to be lights in the world. When the Christian holds up his light, men are able to see good and evil. The church establishes the moral standard for men who never go near it and for communities who reject it.—Charles A. Blanchard.

7. man despiseth,[a] the first condition of this servant will be that he will be looked upon with contempt, he will arouse the abhorrence of the people and will be the servant, i. e. under the power of tyrants. **nation abhorreth,**[b] the Jewish nation, as such, rejected Messiah. **and arise,** i. e. to do homage to the great King-Saviour.[c]

Christ's Future Reign (vs. 7).—I. The representation which is here given of the Messiah; note the description given of Him; this is the character of Christ, it is His character to this day. II. The determination of God respecting Him; He has decreed that all shall bow to His sceptre, for this He pledges the veracity of His word. Learn—1. What a glorious period is approaching; 2. What encouragement have all ministers; 3. How happy are all believers.—Simeon.

The Messiah's Humiliation and Exaltation.—This verse has been called "a prelude of chap. liii." It anticipates that minute and graphic exhibition of the Messiah's sufferings and glories, which we have so often pondered, and prize so highly. In brief compass it states the leading points presented in that chapter. This is the twig which is there expanded into a magnificent tree. Here, as there, the prophet transports himself into the time when our Lord lived and suffered on earth, and stands at the point of transition between the humiliation and the exaltation. The shame, the indignities, the rejection, the cruel sufferings are stated as present facts; the glory, the honor, the worship, the world-wide influence are viewed as future. When Jesus died upon the cross, and His body was consigned to Joseph's tomb, His degradation seemed complete, His cause hopeless. His persecutors never dreamt that He would ever be heard of again, and even the faith of His disciples was shaken (Luke xxiv. 21). Never were surmises more signally falsified; never were fears and doubts more effectually relieved than when the Redeemer rose on the third day, and, after showing Himself to His disciples, ascended to the seat of honor and power. From this time onward His career is an entire reversal of the circumstances connected with His previous earthly course. The Prophecy as a Description of our Own Spiritual History.—Once, it may be, we were indifferent to Christ and despised Him in our hearts, evading the very thought of Him. But now

"We have a supernatural work to do, and we must have supernatural power with which to do it." — A. J. Gordon.

[b] "Israel had come to look on itself as possessed of exclusive privileges; a view altogether derogatory to God's glory. Even to re-establish Israel in its entirety would have been a small thing; but —how few were the preserved of Israel who survived the successive national judgments." —Spk. Com.

[c] Is. xlii. 6, 7, lx. 3.

"When the church is afire with missionary zeal, she will light the world to Christ."—The Wellspring.

[a] "Despised by the mere animal passion of man, which judges according to the outward appearance; and is therefore carnal, and not spiritual." — Wordsworth.

[b] "The Jews contemptuously always call Jesus Tolvi, the crucified." —Fausset.

[c] "Kings being usually seated in the presence of others, are described as rising from their thrones; while princes and notables, who usually stand in the presence of their sovereigns, are described as falling prostrate."—Hitzig.

"There is majesty in the name of God; there is independent being in the name Jehovah; there is authority in the name Lord; there is unction in the name Christ; there is friendship in the name Immanuel; there is help in the name Advocate; but, in the name Jesus alone is there salvation." — G C. Needham.

"If you do not wish for God's kingdom, don't pray for it. But if you do, you must do more than pray for it; you must work for it." — Ruskin.

"Educate men without religion, and you make them but clever devils." — Duke of Wellington.

[a] 2 Cor. vi. 2.

[b] "The object of address is still Messiah and His people, whose great mission is again described." — J. A. Alexander.

[c] "Colonize the waste wilderness of heathenism with inhabitants, who will inherit it in successive generations." —Wordsworth.

"All our happiness results from the Son's interest in the Father. And this makes the gospel-time an acceptable time, welcome to us, because we are accepted of God, and reconciled and recommended to him." — Matthew Henry.

[e] "Messiah will abundantly satisfy all the wants, both of literal Israel on their way to Palestine, and of the spiritual on their way to Heaven, as their Shepherd." —Fausset.

[a] "Built up so as to form a high and clear causeway to travel on." —Mat. Arnold.

we have tasted and seen that the Lord is gracious. God has shown us the madness of despising His Son (Gal. i. 15, 16). Our experience resembles that of the Jewish converts as expressed in chap. liii. 2—6. They who hid their faces in shame at the sight of the Messiah now own Him as their Saviour. There is nothing in Him to draw the carnal eye. The sensual mind has no appreciation of His excellence; the self-deluded and impenitent can dispense with His sacrifice; the sin-loving soul is repelled by His holiness; the ignorant and indifferent disregard Him. If the unbeliever studies Christ at all, he is forced to maintain that He is not the Son of God, and that His death was the merited punishment of His claim to be the Son of God. But he whose eyes have been opened is entranced by the vision of His divine glory and self-sacrificing love (Eph. v. 8; John ix. 25; 2 Cor. v. 17). Would that all of us could see the glory of the cross, the true character and dignity of the Redeemer! As preachers we do all in our power to draw aside the veil of ignorance and prejudice, that the glories of Christ might break upon the benighted soul. What think ye of Christ, then? Do you despise Him, or do you worship Him?—W. Guthrie.

8, 9. (8) **acceptable time,**[a] a suitable time for showing grace or favor.[b] **covenant .. people,** ch. xlii. 6. **establish,** etc., R. V. "to raise up the land," metaphors borrowed from nomadic life. "To raise up the earth from its present state of ruin, and to cause to inherit the moral wastes of heathenism."[c] (9) **prisoners,** first, exiled and captive Israelites, then those in spiritual bondage. **ways,** or roads along which they are led. **pastures .. places,** comp. ch. xli. 17, 18. The fig. is taken from the shepherd leading home his flock.

The Greatness of Christ's Salvation (vss. 8—10).—I. The promised diffusion of the Gospel. 1. This was begun in the Apostolic age; 2. It is still existing; 3. It will be fully achieved in the millennium. II. The felicity of those who shall embrace it. Here is assured—1. Provision; 2. Protection; 3. Guidance; 4. Refreshment.—Simeon.

The Gospel Light.—Many thousands have looked upon "The Dream of Pilate's Wife," that great picture of that great commentator in color, Gustave Doré, and have marked as its most wonderful conception the distant Calvary with its empty cross bathed in mysterious light, and the innumerable throngs that toil upward to it with their shining faces, and the deep night-sky that seems to over-brim with angels. So the cross will shine at last above the dark continent where Moffat lived, and Livingstone died praying; over India where Carey planted his forlorn hope, and grand old Samuel Wesley would have gladly laid his dust; and the shining hosts shall be the souls of all the saved, and the wondrous light the morning of the new heaven filling the new earth; for Christ will have drawn all men unto Himself.—W. J. Dawson.

10—12. (10) **hunger,** etc., Re. vii. 16. Still keeping up the fig. of the flock as led by the shepherd, with the most tender and patient care. **heat,** "the hot wind," i. e. the sirocco. **lead..guide,** comp. Ps. xxiii.[e] "He whose compassion has been excited by their long pining misery (xli. 17—20) is leading them, and bringing them along in comfort by babbling springs of refreshing water."—Delitzsch. (11) **mountains,** fig. for obstructions in a road. **high-ways .. exalted,** depressed parts raised to proper level.[a] The word used means an artificial road made by throwing up the earth. (12) **Sinim,** Pol. Bib. "from the land of the Syenites," a little to the N. of the first cataract of the Nile. Thus the text mentions the three chief centres of Jewish dispersion. So Camb. Bib. and Pol. Bib. But others regard the promise as referring to the ingathering of the Gentiles, and suppose the land of Sinim to be China.

Christ a Physician.—As a physician, Christ differs from all others. 1. In that He never studied for the profession; 2. In that He never walked the hospital to acquire practice; 3. In that He never experimented upon individuals; 4. In that He never failed to effect a cure upon a patient; 5. In that He cured body and soul; 6. In that He never delivered any bill of charges; 7. In that He accomplished such cures as none before or since Him accomplished.—J. Bate.

Christ the Preacher's Great Theme.—The best sermon is that which is the fullest of Christ. A young man had been preaching in the presence of a venerable divine, and after he had done, he foolishly went to the old minister and inquired, "What do you think of my sermon, sir?" "A very poor sermon indeed," said he. "A poor sermon!" said the young man; "it took me a long time to study it." "Don't you know, young man, that from every town, and every village, and every little hamlet in England, wherever it may be, there is a road to London?" "Yes," said the young man. "Ah!" said the old divine, "and so from every text in Scripture there is a road to the metropolis of the Scriptures, that is Christ."—C. H. Spurgeon.

The Ideal State.—When men are all holy, then their surroundings may be all beautiful. There is no smiting heat, no chilling cold, no lack of food, no biting hunger, no raging thirst, no wearing pain, no blinding tears, no separating sea, no remorseless death, in heaven, because all who dwell there are established in goodness, and so there is no mission for disabilities to accomplish; their "occupation's gone." And just so far as we win goodness on earth we rise above all our disabilities, heaven is begun below; as with everything, so with love; "perfect love casteth out fear."—R. T.

13, 14. (13) **sing**, etc., "a joyful anticipation of the happy state of things under the Messiah, as set forth in the preceding verses."—Henderson. (14) Here begins a new section extending to ch. l. 3, which may be entitled, "Consolation of Zion and her Children." **said,** in the time of her doubting and fear. "The great body of the Jews were made despondent by their long adversity."[b]

The Divine Unreasonableness of Doubt.—Knowing what he is, and what he is purposing and doing, man's doubt must always seem unreasonable to God; and his one response to every doubter is, "Cannot you trust me?" It is the love of God, the unchangeable love of God, which puts our best-grounded doubts and fears to shame. Exactly this is pressed on the attention of despondent Israel by God's comparing himself to a mother whose child is daily feeding on her own life. Such mothers have a most sacrificing, passionate love for their children, and no intenser simile could have been found. "Thou art more than mother dear;" then how can we doubt? Why not rest in the love, and be at peace?—R. Tuck.

15. woman, etc., comp. Ps. ciii. 13; Mat. vii. 11. "A woman cannot but have compassion on a child, as both harmless and helpless. A mother, esp. cannot but be concerned for her own child. A nursing mother, most of all, cannot but be tender to her sucking child; her own breast will soon put her in mind of it if she forget it."—Mat. Henry. **yea, they may,** or "should even these forget," etc.—Pol. Bib.

God's Love Greater Than a Mother's (vs. 15).—I. A mother's love for her child is but a fraction derived from God's love for man. II. The strongest affection of a mother is subject to mutations. 1. The conduct of the mother may cool, or even quench this spark within her; 2. The conduct of the child may even cool or quench this spark within her. III. The object of the mother's love is not so near to her as the object of the Divine affection. 1. The mother is not the owner of the child; 2. The mother is not the life of the child. IV. The failure of the mother's affection towards her offspring would not be so terrible as the failure of God's affection towards the good.—Thomas.

Maternal Courage.—As we passed through the streets of Nazareth, loud screams, as of a person frantic with rage and grief, drew our attention towards a miserable hovel, whence we perceived a woman issuing hastily with a cradle containing an infant. Having placed the child upon the area before her dwelling, she as quickly ran back again; we then perceived her beating something violently, all the while filling the air with the most piercing shrieks. Running to see what was the cause of her cries, we observed an enormous serpent, which she had found near her infant, and had completely despatched before our arrival. Never were maternal feelings more strikingly portrayed than in the countenance of this woman. Not satisfied with having killed the animal, she continued her blows until she had reduced it to atoms, unheeding anything that was said to her, and only abstracting her attention from its mangled body, to cast, occasionally, a wild and momentary glance towards her child.—E. D. Clark.

"The creature is dead, but he don't know it," said an Irishman, as he looked at the moving legs of a turtle whose head he had cut off a few hours before. "The flesh is dead in me," says the modern opponent of Paul; but the lively motions of the flesh that are often seen by the onlooker makes him doubt if the flesh knows it. The remedy in all things for a believer is, to know Christ. —D. W. Whittle.

[b] Is. xl. 27.

"No language could more pathetically and tenderly describe the feelings of the Jewish Church, or the love of God towards her, than that here employed." —Henderson.

"Memory like a purse, if it be over-full that it cannot shut, all will drop out of it; take heed of a gluttonous curiosity to feed on many things, lest the greediness of the appetite of thy memory spoil the digestion thereof." — Fuller.

"There is in all this cold and hollow world, no fount of deep, strong deathless love, save that within a mother's heart."—Mrs. Hemans.

There is free love in God for me. This free love flows out and down to me in consequence of another's work and worth. To believe this is salvation!

16, 17 (16) **graven thee**, i. e. a picture, or plan, of thee (De. vi. 8). **upon the palms,** i. e. "as close to Him as He is to Himself, and facing Him unforgotten, a part of Himself amid all the emotions of His divine life."—Delitzsch. **before me,** in My sight and memory. (17) **Thy children,** many versions read, "thy builders." **make haste,** hurrying homewards, at tidings of thy restoration. **destroyers,** internal enemies. These, as anxiously, hurry away.[a]

Graven Upon the Palms.—This is an allusion to the Eastern custom of tracing out on their hands, not the names, but the sketches of certain eminent cities or places, and then rubbing them with the powder of the hennah or cypress, and thereby making the marks perpetual. This custom Maundrell thus describes: "The next morning nothing extraordinary passed, which gave many of the pilgrims leisure to have their arms marked with the usual ensigns of Jerusalem. The artists who undertake the operation do it in this manner: they have stamps in wood of any figure that you desire, which they first print off upon your arm, with powder or charcoal; then taking two very fine needles tied close together, and dipping them often, like a pen, in certain ink, compounded, as I was informed, of gunpowder and ox gall, they make with them small punctures all along the lines of the figure which they have printed, and then washing the part in wine, conclude the work. These punctures they make with great quickness and dexterity, and with scarce any smart, seldom piercing so deep as to draw blood.—Burder.—Graven on the Hands.—Faithful Jews who were about to take a distant journey employed an artist to grave or paint a picture of Jerusalem upon the palms of their hands; so that when they were far away from the beloved city of the sanctuary they had but to open their hand and behold its memorial before them. In like manner, our Lord has gone into a "land of far distances." But he too has carried inside the veil the memorial of his beloved church. Those pierced hands remind him of his cross and passion and of the victory he has achieved over sin. And they are busy hands; every day and hour they are recording as with the graving of a diamond in the register of God the names of some new souls born into the kingdom of heaven.—George C. Needham.

18, 19. (18) **Lift,** etc., the eyes that have been cast down, that she may see her children gathering in from all lands. Comp. ch. lx. 4. **come to thee,** lit. for thee; to be thy own.[b] **clothe,** etc., Lowth says, "describing the bride as binding children round her," but the point of comparison between type and antitype is not children, but decoration. **bind,** "as an embroidered sash wh. fastens the bridal attire." (19) R. V., "For as for thy waste and thy desolate places and thy land that hath been destroyed surely now shalt thou be too strait for the inhabitants."[c] **swallowed,** etc., Zion's foreign conquerors shall leave her to her own children.

Christ Hidden Away in the Church.—Not long ago, a researcher of art in Italy, who reading in some book that there was a portrait of Dante painted by Giotto, was led to suspect that he had found where it had been placed. There was an apartment used as an outhouse for the storage of wood, hay, and the like. He besought and obtained permission to examine it. Clearing out the rubbish, and experimenting upon the whitewashed wall, he soon detected the signs of the long-hidden portrait. Little by little, with loving skill, he opened up the sad, thoughtful, stern face of the old Tuscan poet. Sometimes it seems to me that thus the very sanctuary of God has been filled with wood, hay, and stubble, and the Divine lineaments of Christ have been swept over and covered by the painting hands of men; and I am seized with an invincible ardor to draw forth from its hiding place, and reveal to men, the glory of God as it shines in the face of Christ Jesus! It matters little to me what school of theology rises or what falls, so only that Christ may rise and appear in all His Father's glory, full-orbed, upon the darkness of this world! It matters little to me what Church comes forth strong, or what becomes weak, so only that the poor, the sinful, the neglected, the lost among men, may have presented to them, in the Church, a Saviour accessible, reached easily by the human understanding, and available in every hour of temptation, or of remorse, or of want.—H. W. Beecher.

a Is. ix. 10, 18.

"Trust in yourself, and you are doomed to disappointment; trust in your friends and they will die and leave you; trust in money and you have it taken from you; trust in reputation and some slanderous tongue may blast it; but trust in God and you are never to be confounded in time or eternity."—D. L. Moody.

"Moment by moment I'm kept in his love;
Moment by moment I've life from above;
Looking to Jesus till glory doth shine,
Moment by moment, O Lord, I am thine."
—D. W. Whittle.

b "They should be to her as an ornament, a gold or silver headdress; for she is now again a joyous bride. Ever since Horeb, when she violated her vows of betrothal, the Israelic Church had put off her joyous 'ornament.'" —Spk. Com.

c "This prophecy was literally fulfilled in the immense population of Judea, between the return from captivity and the time of our Lord."—Henderson.

"The Holy Spirit must have the right atmosphere to work in. You must have air to convey sound, and you must have the Spirit in order to carry home the truth to men's hearts."—D. L. Moody.

20, 21. (20) **children .. other,** R. V., "The children of thy bereavement shall yet say in thine ears," etc., i. e. the children born while in exile. **give place,** so that I may extend my borders. Reference may be to the extension of the Church among the Gentiles. (21) **Who,** etc., she had supposed herself childless, and now utters her surprise to find her people so numerous.[a] **a captive,** R. V., "an exile."

22, 23. The first of the three short oracles describes the restoration of the exiles as a spontaneous act of homage on the part of the Gentiles. The conception is intermediate between that of ch. xlv. 14 ff., where the nations acknowledge the divinity of Jehovah and the religious supremacy of Israel, and that of ch. lx. 4, 8, lxvi. 20; cf. ch. xi. 11, 12. For Gentiles read "nations."—Camb. Bib. (22) **people,** R. V., "peoples," i. e. all nations and races. This world-wide outlook of Isaiah is generally obscured by A.V. **arms,** lit. bosom, the part of the garment which opens at the bosom, in which young children are carried. **daughters .. shoulders,** so children are borne when able to sit up.[a] (23) **kings,** etc., figures of the zeal, liberality, and kind helpfulness afforded to the Jews on the return to their own land. **lick .. dust,** falling prostrate and kissing the ground on which the Church stood or walked.

A Missionary King.—When Messrs. Tyerman and Bennett, in their visit to the southern islands, held a large missionary meeting previously to their departure for the Marquesas Islands, at which several persons offered to accompany them as missionaries, to introduce the Gospel where it was at present unknown; after some offers of this kind had been accepted, Hautia, the regent of the island, who was virtually king, and held valuable hereditary possessions upon it, and received large contributions to support his royal state, both from chiefs and people, rose: his noble countenance betrayed much agitation of spirit, and he hesitated for awhile to unburden his mind in words. At length with an air of meekness and humility, which gave inexpressible grace to the dignity of the highborn highland chief, he said, "I have a little speech, because a thought has grown up in my heart, and it has grown up also in the heart of Hautia Vahine (his wife). But perhaps it is not a good thought; yet I must speak it; and this is our thought: if the missionaries, and the deputation, and the church of Huahine, think that I and my wife would be fit companions for Auna and his wife, to teach the good word of God to those idolatrous people, who are as we were, and cause them to become as we are here, and in Tahiti, and Eimeo, and Raiatea, and Borabora, we should be rejoiced to go; but perhaps we are not worthy, and others may be better suited for the blessed work; yet we should love to go." This declaration produced a most extraordinary sensation throughout the whole assembly, as the speaker had given good evidence of his true Christianity. When, however, it was represented to him that his usefulness where he was in the church, as the superintendent of the schools, and in the exertion of his influence among his subjects, was far more extensive than that of any other person could be; and that, though it was well that this thought was in his heart, yet he could not on these accounts be sent, he was deeply affected, and replied, "Since you say so, perhaps it is the Lord's will that we should not go to the Marquesas, but stay in Huahine; perhaps we may serve Him better here. Be it so; and yet I wish that it had fallen to me and my wife to go." Patient Waiting for God's Work in Ourselves.—I believe that if we could only see beforehand what it is that our heavenly Father means us to be,—the soul beauty and perfection and glory, the glorious and lovely spiritual body that this soul is to dwell in through all eternity,—if we could have a glimpse of this, we should not grudge all the trouble and pains He is taking with us now, to bring us up to that ideal, which is His thought of us. We know that it is God's way to work slowly, so we must not be surprised if he takes a great many years of discipline to turn a mortal being into an immortal, glorious angel.—Annie Keary.

24—26. (24) **prey .. mighty,** Zion, who still dreads the Babylonian power (xlix. 12, 13) asks an incredulous question. The answer is in the affirmative, verse 25, Babylon shall be made to disgorge its prey."—Pol. Bib. (25) **I will contend,** in turn bringing Divine judgments on them. (26) **feed .. flesh,** phrase for internal strifes.[a] **sweet wine,** must. The pure juice which flows from a heap of grapes before they are pressed.

[a] "The general conception, so clearly and affectingly presented, is of a childless mother finding herself suddenly surrounded by the clamor of a multitude of children, and asking in amazement whence they came, and who they are."—J. A. Alexander.

Dr. Judson, the devoted missionary to Burmah, during his visit to Boston, was asked, "Do you think the prospect bright of the speedy conversion of the heathen?" "As bright," he replied, "as the promises of God."

[a] "Among the South Sea Islanders, it is a mark of honor for females to be borne astride on men's shoulders."—Henderson.

"When your garments are white," says Jesus, "the world will count you mine."—John Bunyan.

Ps. lxxii. 11; Is. lx. 16.

"God hath provided a sweet and quiet life for his children, could they improve and use it; a calm and firm conviction in all the storms and troubles that are about them, however things go, to find content, and be careful for nothing."—R. Leighton.

"Trials must and will befall;
But with humble faith to see
Love inscribed upon them all,
This is happiness to me."
—W. Cowper.

[a] "As the antagonistic factions in Jerusalem, during the Roman siege."—Spk. Com.

The Resources of the Adversary and the Means of Their Destruction (vss. 24, 25).—I. The defences and resources of the enemy. 1. Idolatry; 2. Imposture; 3. Papal superstition; 4. Despotic government; 5. Crime; 6. An easy-going religion; 7. Corrupting the purity of revivals of religion. II. The means of their destruction. 1. The judgments of heaven; 2. The universal propagation of the Gospel; 3. General revivals of religion. Apply:—(1) There must be more faith in God; (2) A more intense love for Christ and His Church; (3) More courage; (4) More zeal; (5) Religious education; (6) More of charitable effort; (7) To **guard** against the dangers of religious prosperity.—Lyman Beecher.

One Saviour for Prince and Peasant.—His Royal Highness, the Duke of Kent, father of Queen Victoria, during his illness, asked his physician if he was accustomed to pray. "Please your Royal Highness, I hope I say my prayers; but shall I bring a prayer book?" "No," was the reply, "what I mean is, if you are accustomed to pray for yourself, you could pray for me in my present situation." The doctor then asked if he should call the duchess. "Do," said the prince. The duchess came and offered up a most affectionate prayer on behalf of her beloved husband. On another occasion, when the duke expressed some concern about the state of his soul in the prospect of death, his physician endeavored to soothe his mind by referring to his high respectability and his honorable conduct in the distinguished situation in which Providence had placed him, when he stopped him short, saying, "No; remember, if I am to be saved, it is not as a prince, but as a sinner." When his Royal Highness felt that he was approaching the termination of his earthly career, he desired the infant princess to be placed before him while he sat up in bed. In this position he offered a most affecting prayer over her, the last part of which was to this effect, if not in this very language, that "if ever this child should be Queen of England, she might rule in the fear of God." Having uttered these words, he said, "Take the child away," and this was the last time he ever beheld her.

"Before the capture of Babylon by Cyrus, Evil-Merodach had been murdered by Neriglissor; Laborosoarchodus, the son and successor of the latter, was likewise put to death." — Henderson.

Diocletian, the last and the worst of the Roman persecuting emperors, observed, that the more he sought to blot out the name of Christ, the more legible it became; and that whatever of Christ he thought to eradicate, it took the deeper root, and rose the higher in the hearts and lives of men.

CHAPTER THE FIFTIETH.

This oracle, vss. 1—3, answers the fear that the covenant relation has been severed forever. **1. bill .. divorcement,** De. xxiv. 1, 2.[a] "Zion is the mother, the Jews are the children, and God is the Husband and Father." **whom,** R. V., "wherewith I have put her away," i. e. there is none. I have not put her away. **creditors,** this question is asked on the assumption that God had sold His people into captivity for His own advantage. **sold yourselves,** comp. Le. xxv. 39, 47. R. V., "were ye sold." Comp. Judges ii. 14, etc.

The Falling Away of Christian Professors—The Brittle Branch.—In the summer of 1870 a young man, who lay under the shadow of one of the elm trees in the forest of Windsor, was killed by the falling down upon him of one of the largest branches. There was no storm of wind at the time; on the contrary, the air was calm and motionless, and not a leaf in the forest stirred; the branch was not old and rotten; on the contrary, it was fresh, full of sap, and covered with rich green foliage. This strange thing not unfrequently happens to the elm during the long continuance of dry and sultry weather, which has the effect of making its wood brittle, so that the branches part easily from the tree, and fall down by their own weight. How many professing Christians are made fickle and unsteadfast during a period of trial, so that they lose their hold of the Church, and fall away from it at once, while apparently green and flourishing!—Macmillan.

2, 3. (2) **I came,** God by His word and providence, prepared to deliver and redeem.[b] **no man,** ready to believe My message and promise. A strong way of indicating the general unbelief. **hand shortened,** common Arabic phrase for powerlessness.[c] Then follow passages to emphasize the power of God. **dry .. wilderness,** recalling scenes of Ex. xiv. 21; Jos. iii. 16. (3) **blackness,** recalling the plague of darkness in Egypt, and indicating God's power over the elements.

Note on vs. 2.—The Krooman (or Koorooman) river, in Africa,

[a] Comp. Je. iii. 8; Matt. v. 31.

"Zion complains that her children are lost, and she is divorced. God answers: Can a writing of divorcement be shown against Me as in a man's case, to prove a formal divorce? Or, have I creditors, to whom, as a human debtor, I sell My children? Zion is abandoned, and her children lost to her, but for a time, because of her sins, and while her sins last."— Mat. Arnold.

[b] Some refer this to the Prophets, others to Messiah. But the first reference is plainly to the Divine intervention for the deliverance of captive Israel.

[c] "Shortness of hand or arm is a common Oriental figure for defect of power, esp. in reference to some particular effect, which is thus represented as beyond the reach. —J. A. Alexander.

which is a considerable stream, used to run in an oblique direction across the great southern Zahara desert, till it emptied itself into the Great Orange River. Now it sinks out of sight into the sand almost immediately on entering the desert, only a few miles after the junction of the Macklareen river with its waters. As a proof that it had once run in the desert, I traveled ten or fifteen miles on its hard dry channel along which it had run after entering the desert, having a steep bank on both sides, beyond which there was nothing but deep sand. The aged natives told me that in their young days there was a considerable river in that channel, and sometimes rose so high that it could not be crossed for a long time. They first blamed the Matslaroo people for drying it up by means of witchcraft, but afterwards acknowledged it must have been done by the hand of God.—Campbell.

4. In vss. 4, 5, "the servant unfolds the most beautiful and true understanding of the secret of prophecy that ever was unfolded in literature."—G. A. Smith. **given me,** in the singular way peculiar to Isaiah; references to the Prophet himself, to the servant of Jehovah, and to the Messiah, are closely blended. In this vs. the reference is evidently to Messiah. **learned,** or fully instructed. **word in season,**[a] R. V., "to sustain with words him," etc. **weary,**[b] or dispersed ones. **morning by morning,** i. e. it was a daily experience. Every day he received this instruction, indicating touch with each day's life, duties and messages. **wakeneth mine ear,**[c] "the prophet learns his speech, as the little child does, by listening. Grace is poured upon the lips through the open ear."—G. A. Smith. **learned,** or learners.

A Word in Season to the Weary.—I. The state and character of them that are weary. 1. Those who have spent their time in fruitless searches after human knowledge; 2. Those who are oppressed with the load of sin and guilt; 3. Those who are under the weight of affliction; 4. Those who have labored in fruitless endeavors to overcome their corruptions; 5. Those who have vainly sought to work out salvation by their own righteousness; 6. Those deeply involved in the cares of this world; 7. Those who are tired of living in this world. II. The character and person of the Lord Jesus Christ constitute Him a seasonable and all-sufficient Saviour to all those who are weary. Apply the former heads in succession.—J. Matheson.

"Humble love, and not proud science, keeps the door of heaven." —Young.

a Pr. xv. 23, xxv. 11.

b Mat. xi. 28.

c "The Father did not speak in dreams or visions to the well-beloved Son; but continually every morning He spake in His opened ear, and declared what He was to say; and thus the Messiah was the wisdom of God speaking unto men face to face." — Wordsworth.

"God oftentimes delays that His people may come to Him with greater strength and importunity. He puts them off, that they may put on with more life and vigor. God seems to be cold, that He may make us the more hot; He seems to be slack, that He may make us the more earnest; He seems to be backward, that He may make us the more forward in pressing upon Him."—Thomas Brooks, 1650.

5, 6. (5) **opened mine ear,**[a] comp. 1 Sam. ix. 15. ch. xlviii. 8. **not rebellious,** contrasted with Israel's rebelliousness. (6) **spitting,** "an expression of contemptuous abhorrence."[b] "These are not national sufferings. They are no reflection of the hard usage which the captive Israel suffered from Babylon. They are the reflection of the reproach and pains, which, for the sake of God's word, individual Israelites more than once experienced from their own nation."—G. A. Smith.

Messiah's Sufferings and Supports (vss. 5—9.).—I. His sufferings. 1. They were great and various; 2. He willingly undertook to sustain them all. II. His supports. 1. Effectual succor; 2. A triumphant issue. Contemplate this holy Sufferer—(1) As the predicted Saviour of the world; (2) As the great Pattern of all holy obedience.—C. Simeon.

Scourging.—The severity and barbarity of a Roman scourging has been brought out by Dr. C. Geikie, who says, "Jesus was now seized by some of the soldiers standing near, and, after being stripped to the waist, was bound in a stooping posture, his hands behind his back to a post, or low pillar, near the tribunal. He was then beaten till the soldiers chose to stop, with knots of rope or plaited leather thongs, armed at the ends with acorn-shaped drops of lead, or small sharp-pointed bones. In many cases, not only was the back of the person scourged cut open in all directions; even the eyes, the face, and the breast were torn and cut, and the teeth not seldom knocked out. The judge stood by, to stimulate the sinewy executioners by cries of 'Give it him!' but we may trust that Pilate, though his office required his presence, spared himself this crime. Under the fury of the countless stripes, the victims sometimes sank, amidst screams, convulsive leaps, and distortions, into a senseless heap; sometimes died on the spot; sometimes were taken away, an unrecognizable mass of bleeding flesh, to find deliverance in death, from the inflammation and fever, sickness and shame." Few New Testament readers duly appreciate the sufferings which Messiah endured in the judgment-hall.

a Ps. xl. 6.

b Job xxx. 10.

Spitting in the Face.—"This instance of contempt and reproach offered to Christ was at the same time an expression of malice and a compliance with custom. The practice has descended to later generations; for in the year 1744, when a rebel prisoner was brought before Nadir Shah's general, the soldiers were ordered to spit in his face, an indignity of great antiquity in the East." — Hanway's Travels.

The cross so fills their vision that they fail to see how much he endured before the cross and its final strain and agony were reached.

7—9. (7) **will help me,** "God will bring him through and vindicate him in the eyes of the world." **like a flint,** a fig. for holy endurance and set purpose.[c] (8) **justifieth me,**[d] i. e. declares that I am right. **adversary,** Heb. master of my cause, who has sufficient ground of accusation against me. (9) **wax .. garment,** his adversaries shall vainly attempt to condemn him, and shall become, as it were, old and moth-eaten ere they succeed. Two striking parallels to the latter part of this discourse occur in the Book of Jeremiah. See ch. xvii. 17 f.; "Thou art my refuge in the day of evil. Let them be ashamed that persecute me, but let not me be ashamed . . . bring upon them the day of evil, and destroy them with double destruction"; and xx. 7, 11 ff.: "I am become a laughingstock all the day, every one mocketh me . . . " "But the Lord is with me as a mighty one and a terrible; therefore my persecutors shall stumble, and they shall not prevail; they shall be greatly ashamed," etc. Cf. also Ps. xxii. 6—21.—Camb. Bib.

c "Set Myself resolutely, not to be daunted from My work of love by shame or suffering." —Fausset. Eze. iii. 8, 9.

d "The charge was, that, in claiming to be the Son of God, He had committed blasphemy. The resurrection justified Him (Ro. i. 4)." —Spk. Com.

1 Pe. ii. 21—23.

"Watch for His way. When He ties your hands be still; when He puts tools into your hands, use them for His honor."

He is Near (vs. 8).—I. This is the assurance of Christ. II. The experience of the saints in the time of adversity. III. The conclusion of faith. 1. From His relationship; 2. From His promises. IV. And should be the song of His people.—Stems and Twigs.

Man's Arraignment Idle.—Man's arraignment of his fellow-men can have no effect at all excepting in this world. He may bring them before tribunals, obtain their condemnation, their execution, their temporal disgrace. He may gibbet them in history, misrepresent, malign, blacken their names and their reputations. But over their real selves he is powerless. God justifies them, pardons them, receives them into his kingdom, looks on them with favor, reckons them among his saints, gives them the blessing of eternal communion with him in heaven. What matters it to them that somewhere, in a paltry planet, ignorant and ephemeral mortals speak evil of them and brand their memories? "It is God that justifieth." One justifying word from him may well outweigh any amount of human dispraise, of human contumely. Their end in this world may have been "without honor;" but their entrance into the next is with words at once of promise and of high honor, "Well done, good and faithful servant; enter thou into the joy of thy Lord."—Pul Com.

John Ashworth, in his "Strange Tales," dwells on the satisfying fullness of the short and simple prayer, "Lord, help me!" It will fit in everywhere. It sums up all our need. It appropriately meets us whatever our circumstances.

10, 11. "A double message of encouragement and warning based on the preceding soliloquy of the Servant. It seems evident that the Servant here is regarded as the nucleus of the godly party who are addressed in vs. 10; in other words, as a personification of the true Israel which is in process of being separated from the unbelieving part of the nation. These last are addressed in vs. 11 as opponents and persecutors of the faithful Israelites."—Camb. Bib. (10) **Who,** God here speaks. Whosoever. **that walketh,** R. V., "he that walketh in darkness, and hath no light, let him trust," etc., even under such circumstances. **trust .. God.**[a] gaining confidence by the multiplied experiences of His faithfulness. (11) **kindle a fire,** fig. for methods of trying to relieve and help themselves, so as not to depend on God. **Compass,** etc., R. V., "that gird yourselves about with fire brands," i. e. with schemes against the true servants of Jehovah. **sparks,**[b] or torches. **in sorrow,**[c] ch. xliii. 17, lxvi. 24.

a Ps. xlvi. 1, lxii. 8, cxviii. 8, 9; Mi. vii. 8; Ha. iii. 17, 18.

b Heb. Zikoth, fiery darts.

c "This is said to the Jews, who receive with incredulity, anger, and persecution God's message and messenger. God warns these Jews that their anger and violence shall be turned against themselves, and they shall 'lie down in sorrow.'" — Mat. Arnold.

Encouragement Only to the Devoted and Obedient (vs. 10).—I. It might be applied to a case like that of Joseph while lying under the reproach of a crime which he never committed, and which he abhorred. II. The situation of David during the lifetime of Saul was such as would have justified the application of the text. III. The case of the Church at the present day when looking at the moral condition of the world in connection with the prophecies.—W. C. Walton.

Verse 11.—How strongly contrasted this with the Divine principle of recompense, according to which every forward step which a man makes in conformity to God's Image, and obedience to God's commands, is attended by an increase of joy and peace—an increase sometimes very sensibly felt at the close of a Christian's career, when, as his tempest-tossed bark nears that haven of rest where he would be, a mighty spiritual refreshing breathes in upon his heart, like perfumed gales from the shore of a land of spices. His bliss is not merely an abiding, but also

"Every consecration made in the darkness is reaching out toward the light, and in the end must come out into the light, strong in the strength which

an increasing bliss. It not only endures, but also enlarges itself with the dawn of eternity.—Goulburn.

CHAPTER THE FIFTY-FIRST.

1—3. A second series of exhortations in face of "Doubters in the Way of Return." Now they doubt their own ability. (1) **follow .. righteousness,** the address is now directed to the faithful few of Israel: those really desiring to be conformed to the will of God.[a] **seek the Lord,** Ps. xxiv. 6. **rock .. pit,** fig. for their origin in Abraham and Sarah.[b] (2) **him alone,** R. V., "for when he was but one I called him," etc.[c] Their present state is unpromising, but let them look back upon the more unpromising nature of their origin. (3) **comfort Zion,** etc., i. e. rest assured that He who abundantly blessed Abraham will abundantly bless Abraham's seed.[c]

Retrospection (vs. 1).—I. The persons addressed. 1. They that follow after righteousness in state and in character; 2. They that seek the Lord by prayer. II. The duty enjoined. 1. The thing to be done—mental survey, etc.; 2. The ends to be served by it—deepen humility, inflame love, stimulate obedience, etc.—G. Brooks.

The Rock and the Pit.—Dean Stanley, preaching in aid of the Palestine Exploration Fund, chose his text from Isaiah li. 1. He mentioned three results of the work done in Jerusalem which he thought might reasonably be hoped from the present undertaking:—1. A monument of the Old Testament of peculiar and special interest, the catacomb containing the tombs of David and the kings of Judah, the prototype of all the royal tombs of the modern world. It alone, of all tombs, was permitted to be within the walls of the city. In it, around the central cell of the founder, were grouped nearly all the kings of his line,—his wise son Solomon, his great successors Asa and Jehosaphat, with the high priest Jehoiada, the one personage of humbler rank who had been allowed a place there. Apart from anything that might be found in the tombs, its discovery would be of immense value as fixing the position of the "city of David." The last time it was seen was when Herod the Great broke into it in search of treasure; but there could be no reasonable doubt that it was still buried beneath the rubbish, and still recoverable. 2. Another monument was the "holy sepulchre." The church in which this was shown had been the centre of pilgrimage and crusade for many a century, but latterly the feeling had very much cooled towards it. Many considerations tended to throw doubt on the present position, and the question ought to be cleared up, which it could only be by excavation of the course of the walls. 3. There were the natural features of the old Jerusalem; and here the Dean spoke of the discovery which had been already made by the Palestine Exploration Fund, by which the enormous depth of those sacred walls had been for the first time revealed, and the accuracy of Josephus substantiated, and a new force given to the narrative of the temptation of Christ.

4, 5. "The universal extension of the true religion is the second ground of comfort which the prophet is commissioned to offer to his fellow believers. The language of vss. 4, 5 is obviously molded on that of ch. xlii. 1—4; the functions there assigned to the Servant of the Lord are here assumed by Jehovah Himself. At the same time the thought is implied that the restored Israel is to be the bearer of salvation to the world at large, and thus the further idea is suggested that the ideal represented by the Servant will be realized by the people of Israel when it emerges purified from the discipline of the Captivity."—Camb. Bib. (4) **my people,** i. e. the Jews.[a] **law .. judgment,** the Gospel dispensation and institutions.—Fausset. Law, as Divine revelation unfolding man's duty. **rest,** settle, establish. **light,** moral guidance. **people,** R. V., "peoples"—i. e. again a reference to all nations. (so in next verse.) (5) **righteousness,** or faithful fulfilment of promises. **near,** and therefore ready to be revealed. **arms,** common fig. of the actual arm or hand of God swaying human affairs. **the isles,**[b] "the far countries as xlii. 4.

The Absolute in Human History (vs. 4).—Rectitude and salvation are

---

it won in its life and struggle in the dark."

[a] "How are the people of God to be described? They are such as 'follow after righteousness,' such as are very desirous and solicitous both to be justified and to be sanctified; are pressing hard after this, to have the favor of God restored to them, and the image of God renewed on them."—Mat. Henry.

[b] "Whence were these living stones quarried, of wh. the house of Israel is built?" — Spk. Com.

[c] Zion is the cor-relative of Sarah, the mother of us all.

We associate with the garden the thought of tranquillity and peace. The Church should be the home of peace and joy. To it we should be glad to retire from the bustle and strife of life; in its fold we should find the purest and the sweetest satisfaction which earth can yield. There have been Churches which might justly be called the arena of conflict or the wilderness of neglect. The ideal Church—that at which we should aim, and for which we should strive and sacrifice—is one that might be appropriately designated, 'The garden of the Lord.' "
—Clarkson.

[a] "O peoples, . . nations, i.e. the Gentiles." — Gesenius.

Is. xlii. 1—4, 6.

[b] Is. xlii. 4, 10, xlix. 1, lx. 9.

the elements of God's revelation, and they are the absolute in human history. I. They are for all lands. II. They are for all times. Words suggest—1. That man is related to two distinct systems of things—material and spiritual; 2. That one of the systems to which man is related is transient, the other is permanent; 3. That the permanent should command man's chief concern. The great lesson is to beware of practical materialism.—Thomas.

Trust.—If we can put our trust in God when we are in total darkness, when may we not trust Him? Sometimes we are called upon to trust in God when he seems to go right back against all His promises. That is trusting Him in the darkness. Weak faith will judge God's promises by one's feelings, by one's evidences, when we ought to judge the feelings and the evidences by the promises. As long as I have the promises, God give me grace to trust Him, whatever befall, and bid my soul keep still, knowing that he will never fail.—Marcus Painsford.

6. heavens..smoke,[c] the ancient conception of the heavens was of a solid arch. For it to perish would be the end of all things, so contrasting the perishable nature of all earthly things with the durability of the Gospel blessings. **in like manner,** lit. like a gnat. **my salvation,** the true religion is not only universal, it is eternal.

God's Everlasting Salvation (vs. 6).—I. God's salvation is independent of, and will outlive, everything human. II. It will outlive the material earth. III. Over the whole earth broods the mighty law of change.—D. Johnson.

The Short-lived Glory of Earthly Things.—Mark the glory of collective man. United he puts on the appearance of strength. He founds empires, builds cities; he guards by his armies, he cements all by his policy. But trace the track of civilized man through the world, and you find it covered with the wreck of his hopes; and the monuments of his power have been converted into the mockery of his weakness. His eternal cities moulder in their ruins. The serpent hisses in the cabinet where he planned his empire. Echo itself is startled by the foot which breaks the silence which has reigned for ages in his hall of feast and song. Columns stand in the untrodden desert; and the hut of the shepherd or the den of the robber shelters the only residents of his palaces. And the glory which now exists is crumbling everywhere, where it has not the cement of Christianity, and where it takes not something of perpetuity from the everlasting Word. All heathen glory and Mahommedan pride creak in the blast and nod to their fall. The withering wind or the raging tempest shall pass over them in turn; and men shall sit upon the ruins of their proudest grandeur, and be reminded that all flesh is grass.—Watson.—Mutability.—In vain the laborious master painted for eternity; in vain the skilful statuary inscribed his name, or inwrought his own image, with that of some divinity which he carved into stone; the colors of the picture are long since faded, the stone is moldered or dashed into pieces. In vain the Egyptian tyrants raised a monument to their power and greatness, which might last as long as earth; the pile indeed stands, but the name of the builder is forgotten; and as for all the rest of all the boasted wonders of the world, the very ruins of them are lost and forgotten. Nay, the sure and firm-set earth itself partakes of this character of mutability. The sun shines but for a season; the earth crumbles with the foot that treads upon it.

7, 8. "He exhorts them to do that in which the servant has been set forth as an example." **Hearken,** comp. vss. 1, 4. **law,** here and elsewhere means instruction. **men,** Heb. enosh, or frail men. **revilings,** taunts on the assumed failure of God's plans. (8) **moth .. eat,** "they shall be destroyed by as insignificant instrumentality as the moth that eats a garment." "The smallest exertion of strength is quite sufficient to annihilate their sham greatness."—Delitzsch.

Christian Courage.—There is a religion called the Christian, whose founder was Jesus, named the Christ. This religion, which has lasted eighteen centuries, and which calls itself the natural development of that Judaism which ascends near to the cradle of the world, had the Apostles for its first propagators. When these men wished to establish it they had for adversaries—the national pride of the Jews; the implacable hatred of the Sanhedrim; the brutal despotism of the Roman emperors;

"If any one would tell you the shortest, surest way to all happiness and all perfection, he must tell you to make it a rule to yourself to thank and praise God for everything that happens to you. For it is certain that whatever seeming calamity happens to you, if you thank and praise God for it, you turn it into a blessing." —Wm. Law.

c Ps. cii. 26; Mat. xxiv 35; 2 Pe. iii. 10, 12.

"Those whose happiness is bound up in Christ's righteousness will have the comfort of it when time and days shall be no more." — Mat. Henry.

"As those birds that fly highest in the firmament are not so quickly snared by the fowlers' gins; so those men that have always an eye through faith unto Jesus Christ, are not so soon snared by the flesh, the world, and the devil, as others."

Is. l. 9, li. 6.

"Where life is more terrible than death, it is then the truest valor to dare to live." — Sir Thomas Browne.

"He hath borne himself beyond the promise of his age; doing in the figure of a lamb the feats of a lion." —Shakespeare.

"The name of Jesus is not only light, but also food; it is likewise oil, without which all the food of the soul is dry; it is salt, unseasoned by which whatever

the railleries and attacks of the philosophers; the libertinism and caste spirit of the Pagan priests; the savage and cruel ignorance of the masses; the fagot and bloody games of a circus. They had an enemy in—every miser; every debauched man; every drunkard; every thief; every murderer; every proud man; every slanderer; every liar. Not one of the vices, in fact, which abuse our poor humanity which did not constitute itself their adversary. To combat so many enemies, and surmount so many obstacles, they had only—their poverty; their obscurity; their weakness; their fewness; the cross. If you had been their contemporary at the moment when they began their work, and Peter had said to you, "Join with us, for we are going to the conquest of the world; before our word Pagan temples shall crumble, and their idols shall fall upon their faces; the philosophers shall be convinced of their folly; from the throne of Cæsar we shall hurl the Roman eagle, and in its place we shall plant the cross; we shall be the teachers of the world; the ignorant and the learned will declare themselves our disciples;" as you are tolerant from nature and principle, you would have defended him before the Sanhedrim, and counselled it to shut up the fisherman of Bethsaida and his companions in a madhouse. And yet, sir, what you would have thought a notable madness, is to-day a startling reality with which I leave you face to face.

is presented to us is insipid; it is honey in the mouth, melody in the ear, joy in the heart, medicine to the soul; and there are no charms in any discourse in which His name is not heard."—Bernard.

9, 10. These verses are addressed to Jehovah by the community of the Israelites. (9) **O Arm of the Lord,** "the furthest point which Hebrew personification has reached. There are various expressions for the self-revealing aspect of Deity. (xl. 10; lxiii. 12) but only here is that personified aspect addressed."—Pol. Bib.[a] **ancient days,** Ps. xliv. 1. **Rahab** is one of the names of the chief antagonists of Jehovah; (Job. ix. 13; xxvi. 12). **The dragon** was another. (Job. ii. 8, etc.).—Pol. Bib.[b] (10) **dried the sea,** ch. 1. 2.

[a] "In the animated language of poetry, Jehovah is represented as addressing His own omnipotence, and calling for its renewed exercise, for the liberation of His people."—Henderson.

"The only prob. hypothesis is that which puts the words into the mouth of the people, or of the Prophet as their representative."—J. A. Alexander.

The Intercession of Christ—Amintas and Æchylus:—"A rare illustration of the efficacious intercession of Christ in heaven we have in that famous story of Amintas, who appeared as an advocate for his brother Æchylus, who was strongly accused, and very likely to be condemned to die. Now Amintas having performed great services, and merited highly of the commonwealth, in whose service one of his hands was cut off in the field, he comes into the court, in his brother's behalf, and said nothing, but only lifted up his arm and showed them an arm without a hand, which so moved them that without speaking a word they freed his brother immediately. And thus if you look in Rev. v. 6, you shall see in what posture Christ is represented visionally there as standing between God and us: 'And I beheld, and, lo, in the midst of the throne and of the four beasts, and in the midst of the elders, stood a Lamb as it had been slain;' that is, bearing in His glorified body the marks of death and sacrifice. Those wounds He received for our sins on earth are, as it were, still fresh bleeding in heaven; a moving and prevailing argument it is with the Father to give us the mercies He pleads for."—Flavel.

[b] "As God smote Egypt of old, and delivered His people, so He wil deliver them now."—Mat. Arnold.

"There is no beautifier of complexion, or form, or behavior, like the wish to scatter joy and not pain around us."—R. W. Emerson.

11. redeemed, etc., see ch. xxxv. 10.

"The Book of Consolation."—i. e. "The Bible is the great Book of Consolation for Humanity," wrote Ernest Renan, the French sceptic. It brings peace, because it leads to the source of peace—a Person, who, as a Hebrew prophet affirmed, will keep in perfect peace the man whose mind is stayed on Him. It is in the hour of need that the pious sufferer realizes the force of the words of "the Book of Consolation." Sir John Kaye, in his book, "The Sepoy War," narrates how a transforming power came into the hearts of English men and women from a few words of the Bible, while they were fleeing from the cruel mutineers. He writes: "A young English baronet, Sir Mounstuart Jackson, with Lieutenant Burnes, Mrs. Orr, Miss Jackson and some little children, were trying to escape from Seetapore, and went through sufferings almost unspeakable, as they struggled forward, mostly by night, ragged, tattered, ill and with matted hair. Their only comfort came from the word of God. They had no Bible among them, but one day some native medicines were brought to Mrs. Orr wrapped in a piece of printed paper, which proved to be part of a leaf of the book of Isaiah [Is. li. 11—14]; and the message which came to them through Mohammedan hands was this:—'They shall obtain

"Lord, with what courage and delight
I do each thing,
When thy least breath sustains my wing.
I shine and move
Like those above,
And, with much gladness
Quitting sadness,
Make me fair days of every night." — H. Vaughan.

Lightning and light may suitably illustrate the difference between the joy of the sinner and the saint. The one is like lightning,—short, hurried, transient, scorching; the other is like light,—lasting, healthful, beautiful, and healing.

a "Prob. alluding to the custom of putting a prisoner into the five-holed wooden machine which held the body in a bent posture, the head as well as the hands being fixed in it. A more distressing posture cannot well be imagined." — Henderson.

"Love has power to give in a moment what toil can scarcely reach in an age." —Goethe.

"A religion of effortless adoration may be a religion for an angel, but never for a man. Not in the contemplative, but in the active, lies true hope; not in rapture, but in reality, lies true life; not in the realm of ideals, but among tangible things, is man's sanctification wrought." —Drummond.

a Is. lxv. 17.

"Will you follow Christ, and wil you desire to be worthy of His leadership, by slinking away from suffering? Do not seek it; but if it comes, remember that no sorrow comes but with His knowledge. If He does not draw the golden bow that sends the silver arrow to your heart, He knows it is sent, and sees it fall." —H. W. Beecher.

b Ps. lx. 3.

"That giant of Jesus Christ who drew the Gospel chariot from Jerusalem to Rome, and had the care of all the Churches on his heart,

gladness and joy; and sorrow and mourning shall flee away. I, even I, am he that comforteth you; who art thou, that thou shouldest be afraid of a man that shall die, and of the son of man which shall be made as grass; and forgettest the Lord thy maker, . . . and hast feared continually every day because of the fury of the oppressor, as if he were ready to destroy? and where is the fury of the oppressor? The captive exile hasteneth that he may be loosed, and that he should not die in the pit, nor that'—and here the bit of paper was torn off. But the words of love thus strangely and mysteriously brought to them, comforted them in the midst of their sorrow. The torn fragment of a text which came to them through heathen hands seemed like a promise of deliverance."

12—14. "Jehovah again speaks as the comforter of His people. That the passage is a direct answer to the importunate appeal of vss. 9. f., seems probable, although it cannot be confidently affirmed; it is at all events virtually an answer." (12) **thou,** fem., addressing Zion. **be afraid,** considering who thy protector is. **a man,** such as the king of Babylon. **as grass,** ch. xl. 6; 1 Pe. i. 24. (13) **as if,** etc., R. V., "when he maketh ready to destroy." (14) **captive exile,** or bending prisoner.[a] **hasteneth,** is just on the point of being. **pit,** or cistern without water, converted into a dungeon. **bread . . fail,** he shall not starve while he waits deliverance.

The Comparative Fear of God and Man (vs. 12).—I. As to the two parties, Scripture sets forth the nothingness of man and the glory of God. To celebrate this theme the Scriptures employ the grandest machinery, etc. II. In the common intercourse of the world man rather than God is the object of reverence, respect, and fear. III. Consider the question with which these words commence, "Who art thou?"—H. Woodward.

God's Care of His People.—I am fallen into the hands of publicans and sequestrators, and they have taken all from me. What now? Let me look about me! They have left me the sun and moon, fire and water, a loving wife, and many friends to pity me, and some to relieve me; and I can still discourse; and unless I list, they have not taken away my merry countenance, and my cheerful spirits, and a good conscience; they have still left me the providence of God, and all the promises of the Gospel, and my religion, and my hopes of heaven, and my charity to them too. And still I sleep and digest, and eat and drink; I read and meditate; I can walk in my neighbor's pleasant fields, and see the varieties of natural beauties, and delight in that in which God delights—that is, in virtue, and wisdom, and in the whole creation, and in God Himself. The best is left.—Jer. Taylor.

15, 16. (15) **divided the sea,** Je. xxxi. 35. R. V., "which stirreth up the sea, that the waves thereof roar," referring to the power of Jehovah. (16) **thy mouth,** addressed to the restored Israel. **plant,** fig. from fixing up a tent. **heavens,**[a] "the last verse of this reply is notable for the enormous extension which it gives to the purpose of Jehovah in endowing Israel as His prophet,—an extension to no less than the renewal of the universe."—G. A. Smith. "The verse throws an important light on the idea of the Servant of the Lord. Language which is elsewhere used of the Servant is here applied to Israel, to whom the verse is undoubtedly addressed. This would be a strong confirmation of the theory that the Servant is in some sense a personification of Israel."—Camb. Bib.

The Mediation of Christ (vs. 16).—I. The mission of Christ was reserved until the appointed time. II. It is through a Mediator that the Father has made known His mind and will to the children of men. III. Through the mediation of Christ the foundations of the earth were established. IV. And the heavens were planted. V. The mediation of Christ brings men into a new relation to God.—H. J. Bevis.

17, 18. Here begins a new section: "words of cheer to prostrate Zion;" extending to lii. 12. (17) **awake,** vs. 9. **O Jerusalem,** seen by the Prophet in its terrible desolation. **cup . . fury,** for thy sin. **trembling,** R. V., "Thou hast drunken the bowl of the cup of staggering and drained it."[b] The prophet seeks to rouse the prostrate city by a picture of her condition. (18) **none to guide,** because all were overcome with the greatness of the calamity. None had hope.

God's anger must, of course, be understood in a manner in accordance with the Divine nature; and we are not to suppose that precisely the same passions or the same feelings are referred to when this language is used of God which is implied when it is used of men. It means that His nature, His laws, His government, His feelings, are all arrayed against the wicked; that He cannot regard the conduct of the wicked with favor; that He will punish them. He is angry with the wicked continually, constantly, always. It is not excitement, it is not a temporary passion, such as we see in men. It is not sudden emotion, soon to be succeeded by a different feeling when the passion passes off. It is the steady and uniform attribute of His unchanging nature to be always opposed to the wicked,—to all forms of sin; and in Him, in this respect, there will be no change. The wicked will find Him no more favorable to their character and course of life to-morrow than He is to-day; no more beyond the grave than this side of the tomb.—Barnes. The wrath of God is like great waters that are damned for the present; they increase more and more, and rise higher and higher, till an outlet is given; and the higher the stream is stopped, the more rapid and mighty is its course when once it is let loose. If God should only withdraw His hand from the floodgate, it would immediately fly open, and the fiery floods of the fierceness and wrath of God would rush forth with inconceivable fury, and would come upon you with omnipotent power; and if your strength were ten thousand times greater than it is, yea, ten thousand times greater than the strength of the stoutest, sturdiest devil in hell, it would be nothing to withstand or endure it.—Jonathan Edwards.

19, 20. (19) **two things,** "a double woe befell thee: who can fitly condole with thee? Storming and destruction; famine and sword. Who can comfort thee."—Pol. Bib. (20) **wild bull,** R. V., "antelope,"[a] Deut. xiv. 5.

Heart-sickness.—A brave crusader on the field of battle was always conspicuous in armor richly gilt. Amidst the sombre hues in which others were arrayed, amidst the cold blue light of gleaming steel, his harness shone golden like the sun. There was a gaiety in his very armor that seemed to speak of a light heart within. But when one day he fell, pierced with a Saracen dart, they undid the fastenings of his breast-plate, and to the amazement of his comrades found that the inner surface of his armor was studded with iron points that pierced the quivering flesh. The panoply which gaily flashed back the sunbeams, was all the while an instrument of self-inflicted torture to its wearer. There are more men who wear such armor than we wot of. There are many who wear a gay countenance, but feel within the bitterness of death. For the appetite for sin has palled. The heart has grown weary and sick of sin, thinking of lost purity, and broken promises, and departed self-respect; the very life becomes a burden, and yet they dare not die. "They weary themselves to commit sin."—Cheney.

21—23. (21) **afflicted,** etc., ch. xxix. 9, dizzy and staggering. (22) **taken .. trembling,** fig. for removing the Divine punishment. (23) **But .. thee,** ch. xlix. 26.[a] **laid .. ground,** conquerors often actually trod on the necks of conquered kings.

Note on vs. 23—The Doseh.—This passage refers to the ancient practice of setting the foot upon the necks of captives and trampling them under feet, an act by which conquerors signalized triumph over their enemies. A custom which would appear to be a relic of this practice exists amongst the Durweeshes of Cairo, and is celebrated at certain periods as a religious ceremony, called the Doseh, or treading.

CHAPTER THE FIFTY-SECOND.

"In a second strophe (vss. 1—6) he addresses her in conscious contrast to his taunt-song against Babel. Babel was to sit throneless and stripped of her splendor in the dust; but Zion is to shake off the dust, rise, sit on her throne and assume her majesty. For God hath redeemed His people. He could not tolerate longer 'the exulting of their tyrants, the blasphemy of His name.'"—G. A. Smith. **1. awake,** ch. li. 9, 17. **thy strength,** ch. xlv. 24. Arouse thee from thy depression, and put on thy confidence in God. Take courage. **beautiful garments,** holiday attire, as for a day of victory and joy. **holy city,** ch. xlviii. 2. **uncircumcised,** etc.,[b] "not foreigners generally, but the destroyers and wasters who at present desecrate Zion."—Camb. Bib.

never complained of being tired. The secret was that he never chafed his powers with a moment's worry. He was doing God's work, and he left God to be responsible for the results. He knew whom he believed, and felt perfectly sure that all things worked together for good to them that loved the Lord Jesus." —Cuyler.

"The first presence of sorrow crushes out from our hearts the best wine; afterwards the constant weight of it brings forth bitterness, — the taste and stain from the lees of the vat." — Longfellow.

a "Swift, and strong, and handsome, but hunted down into the net; and now exhausted with fruitless attempts to escape." — Spk. Com.

"It is not by change of circumstance, but by fitting our spirits to the circumstances in which God has placed us, that we can be reconciled to life and duty."— Robertson.

a Je. xxv. 15—29; Ze. xii. 2.

"There is a degree in Christianity, to the which whosoever cometh they see and feel more than others can do. 'Come and see' will speak better things of Him than I can do. 'Come nearer' will say much."—Rutherford.

b Na. i. 15.

"No man ever puts on spiritual strength except on his knees. It

The Strength and Beauty of the Church (vs. 1).—I. The alarm sounded. 1. The impenitent sinner is as one asleep; 2. The lethargic Christian requires to be awakened; 3. The discouraged and despondent disciple needs reviving. II. The directions given. 1. Distinct apprehension of the atonement; 2. Reliance on the Saviour's righteousness; 3. Communion with the Holy Spirit; 4. Manifestation of the Christian graces; 5. Exercise of believing fervent prayer. III. The dwelling-place described. 1. The Church is a city; 2. Heaven is a city.

Note on vs. 1.—Jerusalem had long been afflicted by her foes, but the time of her deliverance was at hand, and in token of that she was to deck herself in her glorious attire. At the time of famine, sickness, or sorrow, the people clothe themselves in their meanest apparel, and their ornaments are laid aside: but on the return of prosperity, they array themselves in their most "beautiful garments."—Roberts.

2, 3. (2) **dust,** figuring Zion as a captive lying prostrate in the dust.[c] **sit down,**[d] as opposed to crouching, as a captive. **bands .. neck,** yoke of captivity. Animals are usually fastened by the neck.[e] (3) **for nought,** ch. l. 1. Babylon had seized Israel, but was not its purchaser, so it had no legal rights over Israel. **without money,** ch. lv. 1.

Bondage and Redemption (vs. 2).—I. Here notice man's fallen and sinful state. 1. What ye have sold; 2. To whom have ye sold yourselves? 3. For what have ye sold yourselves? 4. Who sold you? II. Man's redemption by Christ Jesus. 1. The redemption of the soul by price; 2. This redemption is also by prayer. Apply:—(1) Man's sinfulness and misery entirely of himself, his salvation entirely of Jesus; (2) All mankind the bondslaves of Satan, or the freemen of the Lord; (3) The price of our redemption should lead us to value our souls; (4) We have no evidence of our interest in redemption unless we have felt its power in our deliverance from sin.—Studies for Pulpit.

Note on vs. 2.—The other point illustrated occurs in the second verse of this chapter, where the sense of the last expression is, to an Oriental, extremely natural: "Shake thyself from the dust, arise, sit down, O Jerusalem." It is no uncommon thing to see an individual, or a group of persons, even when very well dressed, sitting with their feet drawn under them, upon the bare earth, passing whole hours in idle conversation. Europeans would require a chair; but the natives here prefer the ground. In the heat of summer and autumn, it is pleasant to them to while away their time in this manner, under the shade of a tree. Richly adorned females, as well as men, may often be seen thus amusing themselves. As may naturally be expected, with whatever care they may, at first sitting down, choose their place, yet the flowing dress by degrees gathers up the dust; as this occurs, they, from time to time, arise, adjust themselves, shake off the dust, and then sit down again. The captive daughter of Zion, therefore, brought down to the dust of suffering and oppression, is commanded to arise and shake herself from that dust; and then, with grace, and dignity, and composure, and security, to sit down; to take, as it were, again, her seat and her rank amid the company of the nations of the earth, which had before afflicted her and trampled her to the earth. It may be proper to notice that Bishop Lowth gives another rendering, "Arise, ascend thy lofty seat," and quotes Eastern customs to justify the version; but I see no necessity for the alteration, although to English ears it may sound more appropriate. A person of rank in the East often sits down upon the ground, with his attendants about him.—Jowett.

4—6. (4) **down .. Egypt,** Ge. xlvi. 6. **sojourn,** tarry during famine-time; but Egypt put her guests under bitter bondage. **the Assyrian,** the word used is Ashur, wh. includes the Assyrian bondage of Israel, and the Babylonian bondage of Judah.—Delitzsch. (5) **now therefore,** rather, but now, accentuating the gravity of the present situation. Exile and oppression were indeed no new experiences for Israel (vs. 4), but no such overwhelming disaster as this had ever befallen it hitherto.—Camb. Bib. **what .. here,** as if God were taking special notice of the misery of His people. **for nought,** the writer wishes to express the illegitimateness of the several oppressions of Israel. What advantage has accrued to Jehovah from the carrying away of Israel into exile?—Pol. Bib. **make .. howl,** R. V., "do howl," i. e. the rulers howl with blasphemous exulta-

was there that the apostles found it. Upon their knees; in those days of prayer, in the upper chamber in Jerusalem. It is upon our knees that the Church must put on its strength! Then shall our work be "mighty, through God, to the pulling down of strongholds."—W. M. Paxton.

c Comp. Job ii. 12, 13.

d "In a more dignified place; on a divan, or a throne."—Lowth.

"As a queen on a throne."—Targum.

e "Better rend. 'the bands of thy neck are unloosed;' they have fallen off at the sound of God's voice."—Spk. Com.

Charles Lamb had fame, and what did he say? "I walk up and down thinking I am happy, but knowing I am not." The great Dr. Johnson had fame, and what did he say? "I am afraid that some day I shall get crazy." Such testimonies multiply daily. Verily, "all is vanity."

"The holy city had figuratively been in the dust, but she was now to arise, to take the shackles from her neck, and to sit down in the place prepared for her."—Roberts.

"If we practice goodness, not for the sake of its own intrinsic excellence, but for the sake of gaining some advantage by it, we may be cunning, but we are not good."—Cicero.

tion.[a] (6) **know my name,**[b] "know by experience what my name imports." —Camb. Bib.

Bondage of Sin.—The bitterest experience with most believers is the presence and power of sin. They long to walk through this grimy world with pure hearts and stainless garments. But when they would do good, evil is present with them. They consent to God's law, that it is good; they endeavor to keep it; but they seem as unable to perform it as a man whose brain has been smitten with paralysis is unable to walk straight. What rivers of tears have been shed over the penitent's psalm by those who could repeat it every word from the heart! And what regiments of weary feet have trodden the Bridge of Sighs, if we may so call the Seventh of Romans, which sets forth in vivid force the experience of a man who has not learned God's secret! Surely our God must have provided for all this. It would not have been like Him to fill us with hatred of sin and longings for holiness if there were no escape from the tyranny of the one and impossibility of attaining the other. It would be a small matter to save us from sinning on the other side of the pearly gate; we want to be saved from sinning now and in this dark world. We want it for the sake of the world, that it may be attracted and convinced. We want it for our own peace which cannot be perfected while we groan under a worse than Egyptian bondage. We want it for the glory of God, which would be then reflected from us with undimming brightness, as sunshine from burnished metal. Thank God, we may have deliverance through Jesus Christ.—F. B. Meyer.

7. mountains, ch. xl. 9.[a] "but from the ruin of his city, which has so stirred and made turbulent his passion, the prophet lifts his hot eyes to the dear hills that encircle her; and peace takes the music from vengeance. Often has Jerusalem seen rising across that high margin the spears and banners of her destroyers. But now the lofty skyline is the lighting place of hope. Fit threshold for so Divine an arrival, it lifts against heaven, dilated and beautiful, the herald of the Lord's peace, the publisher of salvation."—G. A. Smith. **him,**[b] "the prophet sees the messenger come bounding over the mountains to bring the news to Jerusalem that her deliverance is come."—Spk. Com. **Thy God reigneth,** "so long as Israel was in captivity, and Jerusalem in ruins, God's earthly sovereignty (1 Sam. xii. 12) was in abeyance. The moment that the Jews were set free and allowed to return and to rebuild their city, his sovereignty was re-established."—Spk. Com.

Publishing the Gospel (vs. 7).—I. We may consider this passage as an epitome, outline, or index to the Gospel. 1. It is good tidings; 2. It is a message of peace; 3. It is a message of salvation. II. The publishing of the Gospel. 1. This is by preaching it; 2. For this certain rules are laid down. III. The publishers of the Gospel. 1. They are men; 2. The manner in which they should be estimated. Appeal to men to hear, believe, and live the Gospel.—A. Fletcher.

8. "Hark, thy watchmen! They lift up the voice, together do they sing."—Camb. Bib. **Thy watchmen,** "Persons set on towers to give the earliest notice of the approach of any messenger with tidings."—Fausset. **bring again Zion,** R. V., "returneth to Zion."[d]—Fausset.

Note on vs. 8.—In the poetical style of the East, the watchmen are represented as standing on their watch-tower, or post of observation, and stretching their vision to the utmost point of the horizon, as if in eager expectation of the appearance of a news-bearing messenger. On a sudden the wished-for object appears in sight, on the summit of the distant mountain, speeding his rapid way to the city, while the watchmen, anticipating the tenor of his tidings, burst forth in a shout of gratulation and triumph. "Thy watchmen shall lift up the voice: with the voice together shall they sing." The imagery strikingly represents the expectant attitude and heedful vigilance of the believing part of the teachers and pastors of the nation of Israel on the eve of the Messiah's manifestation. The reason of the outbreak of their holy joy is immediately given: "For they shall see eye to eye, when the Lord shall bring again Zion," i. e. they shall have a clear and unclouded discernment of the actual execution of the Divine purposes. As faithful watchmen, intent **upon their duty, and** earnestly looking out for the signs of promise, they

---

[a] "Now, says God, this is not to be suffered. I will go down to deliver them; for what honor, what rent, what tribute of praise have I from the world, when My people, who should be to Me for a name and a praise, are to Me for a reproach? For their oppressors will neither praise God themselves, nor let them do it."—Mat. Henry.

[b] Ex. iii. 14, 15, xxxiv. 5, 7.

"Sin is the only thing in the world which never had an infancy, that knew no minority." —South.

"The grand difficulty is to feel the reality of both worlds, so as to give each its due place in our thoughts and feelings, to keep our mind's eye and our heart's eye ever fixed on the land of promise, without looking away from the road we are to travel toward it."—Augustus Hare.

[a] "The Prophet beholds a messenger coming over the mountains (wh. stand around Jerusalem, Ps. cxxv. 2) with glad tidings; the watchmen of Zion discern him at a distance, and they exult at the sight, and call on her to rejoice." —Wordsworth.

[b] Ro. x. 15; Na. i. 15.

Nu. xiv. 14.

"Nothing is more natural than for one person whose feelings are elated with joy, to look to the glistening eyes of another who is equaly interested in the cause by which it is produced." —Henderson.

shall be favored with a clear, distinct, luminous perception of the objects of their gaze, in which they shall be honorably distinguished from a class of watchmen spoken of by the same Prophet, ch. lvi. 10, of whom it is said, "His watchmen are blind;" instead of seeing clearly, they see nothing. That this is the genuine force of the expression, "they shall see eye to eye," is to be inferred from the parallel usage, Num. xiv. 14, "For they have heard that thou, Lord, art among this people; that thou, Lord, art seen face to face" (Heb. eye to eye); i. e. in the most open, evident manner. Of equivalent import are the expressions, Ex. xxx. 11, "And the Lord spake unto Moses face to face, as a man speaketh unto his friend." Num. xii. 8, "With him will I speak mouth to mouth, even apparently, and not in dark speeches;" where the latter part of the verse is exegetical of the former.—Bush.

"A believer's watchfulness is like that of a soldier. A sentinel posted on the walls, when he discerns a hostile party advancing, does not attempt to make head against them himself, but informs his commanding officer of the enemy's approach, and leaves him to take the proper measures against the foe. So the Christian does not attempt to fight temptation in his own strength; his watchfulness lies in observing its approach, and in telling God of it by prayer." —W. Mason.

9, 10. (9) **waste places,** or ruins. **comforted,** with signs of His restoring grace. **redeemed,** to be taken both in a national and spiritual sense. (10) "The prophet withdraws his gaze from the future and describes Jehovah as preparing Himself for the conflict." **holy arm,** metaphor from warriors who bare their arm for battle.[a]

[a] Eze. iv. 7.

"A holy arm because His omnipotence is used in vindicating His holiness and righteousness, and in punishing those who are unholy and unrighteous." —Wordsworth.

Ps. xcviii. 3; Lu. iii. 6.

Newton and Jay.—Mr. Jay was once invited to preach before the Baptist Miss. Soc. in London. He beautifully sketched the origin of the missionary spirit, and the difficulties it had to encounter. He stated that he himself, then a comparative youth, had some doubts as to whether the time was come for the evangelization of the earth, and at length he determined to call and converse on the subject with the venerable John Newton. The aged apostolic clergyman received his younger brother with ardent affection, and requested him to detail the peculiar difficulties which oppressed his mind. Mr. Jay did this at considerable length, especially insisting on the manifold obstacles which idolatry and human depravity, in all their various forms, presented to the extension of the gospel. When he had ceased, the venerable clergyman slowly laid down his pipe, gathered up his form to an erect posture, and looking his junior brother full in the face, said, in a most emphatic tone, "My brother, I have never doubted the power of God to convert the heathen world since he converted me!"

"They that love beyond the world cannot be separated by it."—William Penn.

11, 12. (11) **from thence,** i. e. from Babylon, on the march back to the Holy Land. **no unclean thing,** this new exodus is to partake of the nature of a religious ceremonial. **bear .. vessels,** in xlv. 13 it is said that Cyrus shall rebuild Jerusalem. In xliv. 26, that the foundations of the Temple shall be laid. What more natural than that the returning exiles shall carry back with them the sacred vessels. That the writer lays so little stress on the recovery of the vessels need not surprise us. He would have desired an exceedingly simple sacrificial system." (Comp. xliii. 22—24).—Pol. Bib. (12) **with haste,** as they did from Egypt,[b] so they could have no excuse for carelessness. **Lord .. rereward,** indicating a solemn and public procession. Comp. Ex. xiv. 19.

[b] Ex. xii. 39; De. xvi. 3.

"When they came out of Egypt, they brought with them the idolatrous customs of Egypt (Eze. xxiii. 3), which were their ruin: let them take heed of doing so now that they were come out of Babylon." —Mat. Henry.

Jehovah will go Before You.—Has He not gone before His Church in act and deed? Perilous has been the journey of the Church from the day when first it left Paradise even until now. I see the Church going out from Ur of the Chaldees; afterwards going down to the land of the cruel Pharaohs. But now the Church has to come up out of Egypt, and God goes before her still. But why need I go through all the pages of the history of the Church of God in the days of the old dispensation? Hath it not been true from the days of John the Baptist until now? If you read the history of the Church, you will be compelled to confess that whenever she went forward she could discern the footsteps of Jehovah leading the way.—Spurgeon.

The Servant's Martyrdom and Reward, lii. 13—liii. 12. "The conception here given of the servant of the Lord makes the prophecy the most remarkable anticipation in the O. T. of the sufferings of Christ and the glory that should follow."—Camb. Bib. **13—15.** (13) **prudently,** R. V., margin, "prosperously," i. e. his career shall be crowned with complete success. **extolled**, or praised, Ph. ii. 6—9. (14) Delitzsch, Camb. Bib., etc. trans. "Just as many were astonished at thee,—so disfigured from that of man was his aspect and his form unlike the children of men,—so will he startle many nations. Before him kings will be awe-struck

"The ancient Jews always connected these three vss. with what follows in the liii. ch., and applied them to the same person, the Messiah."—Wordsworth.

in silence," etc., i. e. the amazement at the humiliation will be equalled by that of the exaltation. (15) **sprinkle,**[c] R. V., margin "startle." **shut .. mouths,** dumb with awe. **not .. told,** Ro. xv. 21. **consider,** R. V., "understand."

Surprise at the Appearance of God's Servant.—It is certainly singular that no trustworthy traces of the appearance of our Lord have come down to us. Everybody may imagine for himself what were the features and expression of his Divine Master; and it is better that our free imaginations should have no limitations to the representation of any artistic genius. All that Scripture asserts is that, so far as face and form were concerned, there was nothing arresting about Christ; you might have passed him by as a common man. Dean Plumptre remarks, "These words (of vs. 14) conflict strangely with the type of pure and holy beauty with which Christian art has made us familiar as its ideal of the Son of man. It has to be noted, however, that the earlier forms of that art, prior to the time of Constantine, and, in some cases, later, represented the Christ as worn, emaciated, with hardly any touch of earthly comeliness; and that it is at least possible that the beauty may have been of expression rather than of feature or complexion."—Pul. Com.

"In this prophecy Isaiah speaks so plainly of Christ, that he seems to perform the part of an evangelist, rather than a prophet." — S. Jerome.

The saints endeavor to imitate the strong resolve of their Lord to yield themselves up. For instance, a Scottish peasant, dying as a martyr on the scaffold, said, "I came here to die for Christ, and if I had as many lives in my hand as I have hairs on my head, I would lay them all down for Christ."

CHAPTER THE FIFTY-THIRD.

1, 2. (1) **our report,** "who believed that which was revealed to us," etc.—Camb. Bib., ch. lii. 7.[a] **to whom,** among the unbelieving Jews. **arm,** ch. lii. 10. (2) **tender plant,** suckling.[b] **root,** for that which springs from the root. **dry ground,** implying a feeble sickly growth.[c] **no form,** no striking features to draw men's attention. "In vss. 2 and 3 the penitent speakers give us the reasons of their disregard of the Servant in the days of his suffering. In these reasons there is nothing peculiar to Israel, and no special experience of Jewish history is reflected by the terms in which they are conveyed. They are the confession, in general language, of an universal human habit."—G. A. Smith.

Christ's Sufferings and Glory (vs. 1).—The ancient prophecies are justly included among the evidences of the Christian religion; those which relate to Christ generally refer to His sufferings and glory. I. The report here spoken of. 1. Its general contents; 2. Its great importance. II. How we are required to believe it. 1. Practically, with our hearts unto righteousness; 2. Seasonably, without delay; 3. Perseveringly, without declension. III. The effect with which this belief is attended. 1. It delivers from the burden of guilt; 2. It blesses; 3. It keeps; 4. It rewards.—Alpha in 400 Sks.

Note on vs. 1.—In the East the greater part of their clothes are long and flowing, loosely cast about the body, consisting only of a large piece of cloth, in the cutting and sewing of which very little art or industry is employed. From the simplicity of their form, and their loose adaptation to the body, the same clothes might be worn with equal ease and convenience by many different persons. The clothes of those Philistines whom Samson slew at Ashkelon required no altering to fit his companions; nor the robe of Jonathan to answer his friend. These loose dresses, when the arm is lifted up, expose its whole length. To this circumstance the Prophet Isaiah refers. "To whom is the arm of the Lord revealed?"—uncovered—who observes that He is about to exert the arm of His power?—Paxton. Pain is one of the bonds that hold the race of men together. Browning makes his Ferishtah ask:

> "What were the bond 'twixt man and man, dost judge,
> Were pain abolished? . . . . .
> Put pain from out the world, what room were left
> For thanks to God, for love to man?
> . . . . . From man take these away,
> And what is man worth?

The prophet saw this when he wove the pathos of undeserved pain into his picture of the suffering servant. (Isa. liii). All the sublimest among the imaginery or real representatives of our humanity—Prometheus, Socrates, Jeanne d'Arc, Savonarola—have been visibly sufferers. From

[a] Comp. Is. xlix. 1—8, l. 7—11; Jno. xii. 38; Ro. x. 16.

[b] "Here a sucker, or shoot sprouting up from the root of a tree that has been cut down to the ground."— Henderson.

"Not a tender plant, which implies beauty, delicacy, and fostering care, but a slender plant, thin and insignificant." Mat. Arnold.

[c] "In arid lands nearly all the plants have tuberous roots, buried far beneath the ground, beyond the scorching effects of the sun, and composed of succulent tissue, fitted with a deliciously cool and refreshing fluid. It may have been one of these that suggested to the Prophet this beautiful and expressive emblem."—Hugh Macmillan.

"Historical faith is only (as it were) a looking on the Saviour; but saving faith cleaves to Him and rests on

the same root of pain have sprung the finest utterances of our human speech, in the words of poets who "learnt in sorrow what they taught in song." We see that the best that is in a man can be got out of him only by affliction. But for the wreck and ruin of his friends, Shakespeare never would have written "Hamlet," "Macbeth," or "Lear," nor would Milton have given us "Paradise Lost."—S. S. Times. Three Links.—William Carter in a sermon to the outcasts of London, said: "Hear what Jesus declares: 'Verily, verily, I say unto you, he that heareth My word, and believeth on Him that sent me, hath everlasting life, and shall not come into condemnation, but is passed from death unto life.' Here, my friends, there are three links in the blessed chain of truth—hearing, believing, and having. The devil always tries to cut these links off, and give three links of his own forging, viz., doing, praying, feeling." This item was copied into a religious weekly newspaper in this country, and was there read by a gentleman, when after three weeks of waiting for the feeling of a change in his heart, he had given up all hope, and concluded that there was no salvation for him. God's way of salvation at once seemed plain, and the gentleman was soon a happy Christian.—Old Test. Anec.

3. **despised,** ch. xlix. 7.[a] **rejected of men, better,** "man-forsaken," i. e. one with whom men refuse to associate, or, perhaps, one who renounces the hope of human fellowship. The corresponding verb is used by Job when he complains of the estrangement of his friends: "my kinsfolk have failed")ch. xix. 14).—Camb. Bib. **man of sorrows,** i. e. of manifold and special sorrows.[b] **grief,** or sickness.[c] **hid .. faces,** R. V. "and as one from whom men hide their face he was despised, and we," etc.

The Man of Sorrows (vs. 3).—I. His sorrows arose from the felt relation of a loving being to a ruined race. II. From the crushing pressure of His mediatorial work. III. From His certain knowledge that the result of His mission would not be equal to the benevolence of His will.—Evan Lewis. The Suffering Saviour.—I. His life began with persecution and peril. II. His deep condition of earthly abasement. III. The vile suspicions and bitter misrepresentations He had to bear. IV. He was constantly exposed to personal violence. V. The fierce temptations of the devil. VI. His sufferings were associated with a perfect prescience of all the evils and agonies He had to endure. VII. He saw how they were to culminate from every quarter. 1. Man; 2. Hell; 3. Heaven. Apply:—(1) Their cause: sin; 2. Their result: redemption; 3. His claims: love, gratitude, service.—J. Burns.

Christ a Man of Sorrows.—All that Christ came for was, or was mingled with, sufferings: for all those little joys which God sent, either to recreate His person, or to illustrate His office, were abated or attended with afflictions; God being more careful to establish in Him the covenant of sufferings, than to refresh His sorrows. Presently after the angels had finished their hallelujahs, He was forced to fly to save His life, and the air became full of the shrieks of the desolate mothers of Bethlehem for their dying babes. God had no sooner made Him illustrious with a voice from heaven, and the descent of the Holy Ghost upon Him in the waters of baptism, but He was delivered over to be tempted and assaulted by the devil in the wilderness. His transfiguration was a bright ray of glory; but then also He entered into a cloud, and was told a sad story, what He was to suffer at Jerusalem. And upon Palm Sunday, when He rode triumphantly into Jerusalem, and was adorned with the acclamations of a King and a God, He wet the palms with His tears, sweeter than the drops of manna, or the little pearls of heaven that descended upon Mount Hermon, weeping, in the midst of this triumph, over obstinate, perishing, and malicious Jerusalem. For this Jesus was like the rainbow, which God set in the clouds as a sacrament to confirm a promise and establish a grace; He was half made of the glories of the light, and half of the moisture of a cloud; in His best days He was but half triumph and half sorrow: He was sent to tell of His Father's mercies, and that God intended to spare us; but appeared not but in the company or in the retinue of a shower, and of foul weather. But I need not tell that Jesus, beloved of God, was a suffering person: that which concerns this question most is, that He made for us a covenant of suffering: His doctrines were

Him. Historical faith looks on Christ, but acts not on Him, closes not with Him; and therefore such as have this only, and no more, sink and perish without getting good of Him." —Durham.

"The star of Bethlehem is still rising, and it will continue to rise until all the false lights of the world have been obscured."—W. T. Ellis.

a "Of so mean appearance that he was 'no longer reckoned with men.'" — Aben Ezra.

b "Bodily and mental, proceeding from a perfect sense of the heinousness of sin in God's sight, the depths of which no mind of man has ever fathomed." —Wordsworth.

"'One continued chain of labor, sorrow, and consuming pain.'" —Sir R. Blackmore.

c "So worn and macerated was He with continual grief that when He was but a little above 30 years of age, He was taken to be nearly 50. Jno. viii. 57."—Mat. Henry.

"What a difference between the first and second comings of our Lord. When he shall come a second time it will be to be glorified and admired, but when He came the first time He was despised and rejected of men." — Spurgeon.

Every Macedonian felt that he could endure any fatigue if Alexander could. This day, assuredly, we can

such as expressly and by consequence enjoin and suppose sufferings, and a state of affliction; His very promises were sufferings; His beatitudes were sufferings; His rewards, and His arguments to invite men to follow Him, were only taken from suffering in this life, and the reward of sufferings hereafter.—Jer. Taylor.

4. **borne .. sorrows**, Mat. viii. 17. A strong assertion of the substitutionary character of His work. Camb. B. "surely it was our sickness that he bore and our pains that he carried." **stricken**, under Divine judgment on sin.[a] "The earliest and most common moral judgment, which men pass upon pain, is that which is implied in its name—that it is penal. A man suffers because God is angry with him and has stricken him. So Job's friends judged him, and so these speakers tell us they had at first judged the Servant."—G. A. Smith.

Redemption (vs. 4).—I. The need—sheep, but astray. The way lost, i. e. he who is on the way is lost. II. The means,—the reality of the redemption seen in the fact that Christ died. III. The effect,—sin atoned for; iniquity borne away; necessity of a personal relation to Christ by faith; depth of His love the measure of our obligation, and as that cannot be fathomed, our obligation can never be fully realized.—R. V. Price.

A Suffering God the Preacher's Theme.—The Jews and the Greeks were both ready to receive a God that could shape all the powers of nature, and that could make an illustrious appearance, and address Himself to all that was highest and most admirable in human nature; but to hear preached to them a God who could humble Himself and become a man; who could be subject to those infirmities that inhere in the human condition; who could take death and disgrace upon Him; who could feel weakness, and be willing to feel it; who could feel death, and be willing to feel it—that they could not bear. And we can hardly bear it any better than they could; for we, who believe that Christ is God, dodge the declaration that He died, and change it so that it shall mean something else. We do not like to see it in a hymn, or in a sermon, that God died. And so we attempt to say that it was the human that died in Christ. In other words, there is in us just that same feeling which the ancients had, that there is something which lowers the conception of God to preach that Christ was from God; that His weakness and sufferings and death were part and parcel of a real Divine experience, and typical of the everlasting experience of God; that the Lamb was slain from the foundation of the world; and that, though we saw it clearly set forth, this had been going on before, and was to go on for ever and for ever. The conception that it is the nature of God not to sit star-crowned, not to sit gazed upon and sung to, not to sit wrapped in chanting and luxurious praise—the conception that God is a living power, projecting and supervising—yea, thinking and loving and sacrificing as much on the throne as on the cross, as much in heaven as on earth—the conception of Divinity as being perfect wisdom, perfect purity, perfect love, and as addressed to the recuperation of the weak and the wicked, working and working, suffering and suffering, laboring and laboring, for ever and for ever,—this conception is yet unwelcome. Our prejudices do not like it. And as it is now, so it was in the time of the Apostle. Therefore he declared all the way, "I preach," not Christ, but "Christ crucified." I will not preach Christ in such a way as that the cross shall be left out. It is this suffering in Christ that is the secret of the Divine power.—H. W. Beecher.

Christ's Sympathy.—

We have no tears Thou wilt not dry;
We have no wounds Thou wilt not heal;
No sorrows pierce our human hearts
That Thou, dear Saviour! dost not feel.
—Harriet McEwen Kimball.

5. **wounded**, "pierced," with special reference to the piercing of our Redeemer's hands, feet, and side. **bruised**, "crushed,"[a] **for**, because of; in fulfillment of His purpose to deliver us from our iniquities. **chastisement**, etc., i. e. by which our peace has to be won. **stripes**, or bruises, with reference to His scourgings, as part of His great sacrifice. "That the people themselves had suffered for their sins is not excluded, but is

bear poverty, slander, contempt, or bodily pain, or death itself, because Jesus Christ our Lord has borne it." —Spurgeon.

a "The Jews were taught to regard disease (and calamity) as the temporal punishment of sin." — Henderson.

"Christ's entire life was devoted to the service of man; and His death was but the giving up in one final act of surrender what had all along been consecrated to the same high and holy ministry." — Gibson.

"It is well known that the Earl of Rochester was for many years an avowed infidel, and that a large portion of his time was spent in ridiculing the Bible. One of his biographers has described him as "a great wit, a great sinner, and a great penitent." Even this man was converted by the Holy Spirit in the use of His Word. Reading Isa. liii. he was convinced of the truth and inspiration of the Scriptures, and the Deity and Atonement of Christ. On that atonement he rested, and died in humble expectation of heavenly happiness."

a "There are no stronger terms in the language than are here used to signify the extremity of the sufferer's affliction."— Delitzsch.

Mat. xxvii. 26; 1 Pe. ii. 24.

"He cures the mind of its blindness, the heart of its

hardness, the nature of its perverseness, the will of its backwardness, the memory of its slipperiness, the conscience of its benumbness, and the affections of their disorder, all according to His gracious promises: Ezek. xxxvi. 26, 27."—John Willison.

Dora Greenwell beautifully says, "Belief in that one great doctrine of the Atonement is to me like the blue flower of the German legends: long sought and hidden, but when found admitting into every guarded treasure, which without the possession of it, would have been closed up."

a Ze. xii. 10.

b "The antithesis is, in ourselves we were scattered; in Christ we are collected together; by nature we wander, driven headlong to destruction; in Christ we find the way to the gate of life."—Calvin.

2 Cor. v. 21; Ga. iii. 13; He. ix. 28.

c Jno. i. 29.

"The Vulgate, wh. throughout this ch. translates so as to heighten the identification with Christ, has here, 'He was offered because He Himself chose to be.'"—Mat. Arnold.

"He was oppressed and He Himself submitted to affliction."—J. A. Alexander.

"No man can know or conceive what that anguish must have been. To Christ alone was this agony possible, and it

apparently implied in the last words ("we are healed"), and is expressly said in other parts of the book (ch. xl. 2, xlii, 24 f. etc.). What the verse teaches is that the people could not be healed by their own suffering; it was only through the Servant's voluntary submission to the divine chastisement (vs. 7), and his bearing it in an extraordinary degree, that an atonement was effected between Jehovah and Israel (see on ch. xl. 2)."—Camb. Bib.

Christopathy.—The Balsam-tree sheds its balm to heal the wounds of those that cut it; and did not our blessed Saviour do the like? They mock him, and he prays for them; they shed his blood, and he makes it a medicine for their healing; they pierce his heart, and he opens therein a fountain for their sin and uncleanness. Was it ever heard, before or since, that a physician should bleed, and thus heal his patient; or that an offended prince should die to expiate the treasons of his rebellious subjects? Our heavenly Balsam is a cure for all diseases. If you complain that no sins are like yours, remember that there is no salvation like Christ's. If you have run the complete round of sin, remember that the blood of Jesus Christ cleanseth from all. No man ever perished for being a great sinner, unless he was also an unbelieving sinner. Never did a patient fail of a cure who accepted from the great Physician the balm of his atoning blood See how Christ, whose death was so bitter to himself, becomes sweetness itself to us. Rejection was his, but acceptance is ours; the wounding was his, but the healing is ours; the blood was his, but the balm is ours; the thorns were his, but the crown is ours; the death was his, but the life is ours; the price was his, but the purchase is ours. There is more power in Christ's blood to save than in your sin to destroy. Do but believe in the Lord Jesus, and thy cure is wrought.—Spurstow's "Spiritual Chymist."

6. All we, the Prophet speaks in the name of Israel. Penitent confession of believers and of Israel in the last days.[a] **sheep .. astray,** Ps. cxix. 176; 1 Pe. ii. 25.[b] **laid on him,** made to light on Him. This verse gives us the obverse and complement of the preceding verse. The pain was his in consequence of the sin that was ours. **iniquity,** inclusive of its guilt and consequences. Nothing could be plainer than these words. The speakers confess, that they know that the Servant's suffering was both vicarious and redemptive.—G. A. Smith.

Straying (vs. 6).—We wander—I. Like sheep, without reason—the pasture was rich, the shepherd kind, the fold secure. II. Like sheep, aimlessly. The lion prowls for food, the hart in search of water, the sheep without aim. III. Like sheep, persistently despise the coming shades of evening, the distant bleatings of the abandoned flock, loss of fleece and smarting wounds. IV. Like sheep in peril—defenceless, surrounded by dangers and foes. V. Like sheep—sought; the Good Shepherd calls to us, saying "Return."—Straws and Twigs.

7. R. V. "He was oppressed, yet he humbled himself and opened not," etc., refers now to "the outrages inflicted on the Servant by his contemporaries, in consequence of their false judgment of him."—Camb. Bib. **opened .. mouth,** Mat. xxvi. 63, xxvii. 12; Mk. xiv. 61, xv. 5. **as a lamb,**[c], comp. Ac. viii. 32.

The Sheep Before the Shearers.—He had never been slow of speech when He could bless the sons of men, but He would not say a single word for Himself. "Never man spake like this Man," and never man was silent like Him. Was this singular silence the index of His perfect self-sacrifice? Did it show that He would not utter a word to stay the slaughter of His sacred person, which he had dedicated as an offering for us? Had He so entirely surrendered Himself that He would not interfere in His own behalf, even in the minutest degree, but he bound and slain an unstruggling, uncomplaining victim. Was this silence a type of the defencelessness of sin? Nothing can be said in palliation or excuse of human guilt; and, therefore, he who bore its whole weight stood speechless before His judge. Is not patient silence the best reply to a gainsaying world? Calm endurance answers some questions infinitely more conclusively than the loftiest eloquence. The best apologists for Christianity in the early days were martyrs. The anvil breaks a host of hammers by quietly bearing their blows. Did not the silent Lamb of God furnish us with a grand example of wisdom? Where every word was occasion for new blasphemy, it was the line of duty to afford no fuel for the flame of sin. The ambiguous and the false, the unworthy and the mean, will ere long overthrow and confute themselves, and therefore the true can afford to be quiet, and finds silence to be its wisdom. Evidently our Lord, by His silence, furnished a remarkable fulfillment of prophecy. A long defence of Himself would have been contrary to Isaiah's prediction. By His quiet He conclusively proved Himself to be the true Lamb of God.—Spurgeon.

wrung from Him 'sweat wh. was as great drops of blood.' " — Martin Luther, 1530.

8, 9. (8) **taken .. judgment,** R. V. "By oppression and judgment he was taken away; and as for his generation, who among them considered that he was cut off," etc. "By violence wh. cloaked itself under the formalities of a legal process." **cut off,** i. e. who cared, or noted his death? (9) **grave .. wicked,** this animosity even followed him to his grave. He was buried as a felon.[a] **rich,** Mat. xxvii. 57. **death,** word only used in Eze. xxviii. 10, and there for a violent death. **because,** R. V. "although."

[a] "Our Saviour was destined by the Jews to have the ignoble burial of those who underwent capital punishment." — Henderson.

Christ Stooping to Save.—The mother, wan and pale with incessant vigils by the bedside of a sick child;—the fireman, maimed for life in bravely rescuing the inmates of a blazing house;—the 300 Spartans at Thermopylæ;—Howard, dying of fever caught in dungeons where he was fulfilling his noble purpose of succoring the oppressed and remembering the forgotten;—the Moravian missionaries, who voluntarily incarcerated themselves in an African leper-house in order that they might preach the glad tidings to the lepers,—all these, and many other glorious instances of self-devotion, do but faintly shadow forth the love of Him who laid aside Divine glory, and humbled Himself to the death of the cross.—Huntingdon.

Christianity alone is still young as the morning, full of an unwasted power, exuberant yet with strong expectation. — Storrs.

10, 11. "The main thought of the following verses is that the Servant is to be the instrument in establishing the true religion, by removing the burden of guilt and bringing many to righteousness. As the reward of his sufferings he will enjoy a brilliant future and have a numerous spiritual offspring. He will become a great power in the world, attaining a position like that of a mighty conqueror. The idea of a resurrection from the dead appears to be necessarily implied."—Camb. Bib. (10) **pleased,** i. e. **the Lord,** the men who persecuted and slew Him only carried out a gracious Divine purpose.[b] **thou shalt make,** better, "when His soul shall make."—Delitzsch. **see .. seed,** Ps. xxii. 30, xxiv. 6, xxv. 13. The long line of His descendants, though He was a childless man, is the Church of the Christian ages. **prolong,** etc., therefore He must rise again. **pleasure,** i. e. the purpose of the Lord, to establish his universal religion. (11) **travail,** fruits of His travail.[c] **his knowledge,** i. e. the knowledge which he possesses and imparts to others.

[b] Ac. ii. 23, iii. 18.

[c] "He shall see the fruits of His sufferings in the many whom His life and death have turned to God and saved." —Mat. Arnold.

The Sufferings of Christ (vss. 10, 11).—I. His character. 1. God's servant; 2. A righteous servant; 3. As such, a perfect example, and an acceptable Mediator. II. His sufferings. 1. Their extent; 2. Their singularity; 3. Their general nature. III. The happy effects of His sufferings. 1. He shall prolong His days; 2. He shall justify many; 3. He shall see His seed; 4. The pleasure of the Lord shall prosper in His hand; 5. He shall see of the travail of His soul and be satisfied. Apply:—God's claims on you as the subjects of redeeming grace.—Alpha in 400 Sks.

"O Cross,
Uplifted high before men's curious gaze,
My soul beholds, in wonder and amaze,
A glorious throne.
O Man,
Dying betrayed, heart - broken and alone!
Haste Thou the day when all the world shall own
Thee Lord and God."
—A. J. Janvrin.

The Humiliation of Christ.—He that came to save men, is sent for His first lodging to the beasts. The stable is become His inn; the cratch. His bed. O strange cradle of that great King, which heaven itself may envy. How easy had it been for Thee to have made place for Thyself in the throngs of the stateliest courts! Why wouldest Thou be thus homely, but that, by contemning worldly glories, Thou mightest teach us to contemn them? that Thou mightest sanctify poverty to them whom Thou callest unto want? That, since Thou, which hadst the choice of all earthly conditions, wouldest be born poor and despised, those which must want out of necessity might not think their poverty grievous.—Bp. Hall.

"Christ is the righteousness of sinners to God, and the righteousness of God to sinners." — Venning.

12. "As the reward of his unmerited sufferings and his mediatorial work, the Servant shall attain an influence equal to that of the great potentates of the world." **divide the spoil,** the rights of a great conqueror.[a] **his soul,** or life. **numbered with,** and so treated as if He were a transgressor. "He was put on the same footing with the transgressors."

[a] "Metaphors borrowed from the ancient military life, in wh. a victorious general had conferred on him, by his monarch, the spoils which he had won, and again distributed them among his soldiers."— Henderson.

Victory Achieved by Christ's Death (vs. 12).—1. Let us consider the

"Christ is the world's Cyrus." —Wordsworth. Ro. viii. 34; He. vii. 25, ix. 24; 1 Jno. ii. 1.

"Do not think that if you are despised, or ill-treated, you are out of your place. It does not follow that Livingstone or Bishop Hannington were out of their places, because one died and the other was murdered in Central Africa, any more than it follows that Jesus Christ was out of His place because He was crucified. The kingdom of God was founded and is built up in sacrifice." — G. R. Ferguson.

death of Christ as appointed of God. 2. Look at it with regard to the identity of this appointment, in God's proposal of salvation, pervading all the Divine dispensations. 3. Consider the absolute necessity of this appointment for fallen man. 4. We have the express declaration of God to this truth, made by His own mouth, by His word, and by His ministers. 5. Consider the absolute necessity of receiving this doctrine. 6. The actual seal that God hath set to His own truth concerning the way of salvation, with the certainty of the effect; because He hath poured out His soul, unto death, He shall divide the spoil with the strong.—R. Cecil.

No Satisfaction Without Travail of Soul.—We all would like that the law of Christian, and, indeed, of other life and success, were very different from this, and just as in the world people would like to get wealth without paying the price of it in labor, and would like to gain influence without rendering service by which it alone is won, and would like to get the love of their fellow-men without the life of friendliness that attracts it, so in spiritual things we would like cheaply, easily to gain the precious things on which we set our eyes—forgiveness without repentance, perfect sanctity without the gradual and laborious self-denial by which alone it can be reached; usefulness we would like to get in some cheap and easy way without any sweat of agony, and without any strain of sympathy. We would all like in this way to get various things that are good—forgiveness, usefulness, raptures, light, conviction, assurance, without any travail. Now I do not know any lesson that it is more requisite for the young to learn, and more requisite for older men to keep themselves from forgetting than this—that without travail there is no abiding satisfaction.—Glover.

b Ga. iv. 27; comp. Ge. xi. 30.

"God's people, thus purged and healed, shall be eternally established; Israel shall extend his borders and multiply his sons; his enemies shall come over to him; this is the heritage of the servants of the Lord, and their promised justification through God's righteous servant."— Mat. Arnold.

"A man is relieved and gay when he has put his heart into his work and done his best; but what he has said or done otherwise shall give him no peace."—R. W. Emerson.

"In the moral world there is nothing impossible, if we bring a thorough will to it. Man can do everything with himself; but he must not attempt to do too much with others." — Wm. von Humboldt.

CHAPTER THE FIFTY-FOURTH.

"Zion, the restored Bride of Jehovah." The chapter is divided in two sections: vss. 1—10. The bride comforted and promised a numerous offspring and lasting happiness; vss. 11—17. Zion, the city, restored and filled with a happy and invincible people. **1. O barren,** ch. xlix. 18—21.[b] **travail,** comp. Mic. iv. 10; Is. lxvi. 7, 8. **desolate .. married,** "More are the children of Jerusalem, when she seemed to be a widow, i. e. when her Temple and her city were in ruins, than when she was married, i. e. when the Temple was still standing, and God's presence was visibly revealed in it."—Wordsworth.

God's Relation to His People.—In ch. liv. the people of God are represented under the double figure, with which the Book of Revelation has made us familiar, of Bride and City. To imagine a Nation or a Land as the spouse of her God is a habit natural to the religious instinct at all times; the land deriving her fruitfulness, the nation her standing and prestige, from her connection with the Deity. But in ancient times this figure of wedlock was more natural than it is among us, in so far as the human man and wife did not then occupy that relation of equality, to which it has been the progress of civilization to approximate; but the husband was the lord of his wife.—as much her Baal as the god was the Baal of the people,—her law-giver, in part her owner, and with full authority over the origin and subsistence of the bond between them. Marriage thus conceived was a figure for religion almost universal among the Semites. . . . But the prophets of Jehovah dared the heavier task of retaining the idea of religious marriage, and won the diviner triumph of purifying and elevating it. It was, indeed, a new creation. Every physical suggestion was banished, and the relation was conceived as purely moral. Yet it was never refined to a mere form or abstraction. The prophets fearlessly expressed it in the warmest and most familiar terms of the love of man and woman. With a stern and absolute interpretation before them in the Divine law, of the relations of a husband to his wife, they borrowed from that only so far as to do justice to the Almighty's initiative and authority in His relation with mortals; and they laid far more emphasis on the instinctive and spontaneous affections, by which Jehovah and Israel had been drawn together. Thus, among a people naturally averse to think or to speak of God as loving men, this close relation to Him of marriage was expressed with a warmth, a tenderness and a delicacy, that exceeded even the two other fond forms in which the Divine grace was conveyed,—of a father's and of a mother's love.—Exp. Bib.

2, 3. (2) **Enlarge,** etc., bec. increase of people demands enlargement of accommodation.[a] **cords .. stakes,** the cords to keep the tent steady are tied to wooden pegs, or stakes. "As the family increases the tent is proportionally enlarged, and requires the cords to be longer, and the stakes to be stronger in proportion."—Henderson. (3) **break forth,** R. V. "spread abroad." **right .. left,** prob. indefinite expressions, meaning, in all directions. **Gentiles,** R. V., "possess the nations," a promise that the spiritual children of Israel will spread over all the earth, migrating and colonizing and christianizing all lands.

Carey's Sermon.—This verse has an interesting history as the text of Carey's memorable sermon, the preaching of which, at Nottingham, in June, 1792, may be affirmed, without extravagance, to have marked an epoch in the history of modern missions. After observing that the Church was, in these words, compared to some poor, desolate widow who lived alone in a small tent, that she who thus lived in a manner forlorn and childless, was told to expect such an increase in her family as would require a much larger dwelling, and this because her Maker was her husband whose name was not only the Lord of Hosts and the Holy One of Israel, but the God of the whole earth, he proceeded to bring out the spirit of the passage in two memorable exhortations—1. Expect great things from God. 2. Attempt great things for God. In private conference with his brethren immediately afterwards, Carey formally laid himself on the missionary altar, saying to Pearce and Fuller in those immortal words, "I will go down into the pit, if you will hold the ropes;" and so was formed the Baptist Missionary Society, and a mightier impulse given to missionary zeal all over the world.—W. Guthrie.

Joy at Finding Salvation.—We are told of some Turks, who have, upon the sight of Mohammed's tomb, put out their eyes, that they might not defile them, forsooth, with any common object, after they had been blessed with seeing one so sacred. I am sure many gracious souls there have been, who, by a prospect of heaven's glory set before the eye of their faith, have been so ravished by the sight, that they desired God even to seal up their eyes by death, with Simeon, who would not by his good-will have lived a day after that blessed hour in which his eyes had beheld the salvation of God.—W. Gurnall.

[a] "So large a family requires that she should rebuild her tent on a far larger scale (Is. xlix. 18, 20)."—Spk. Com.

Eze. xvi. 46.

"In Africa, when we expected an increase of hearers, the Hottentots moved the pins all round, a yard or a yard and half farther from the tent, towards which they stretched the canvas, and fastened it, which considerably increased the room inside." — Campbell.

4, 5. (4) **forget the shame,** the national apostasy which had brought on them the Divine judgments. **widowhood,** clearly refers to the period of the Exile when Zion regarded herself as cast off by Jehovah.[a] The sense of the shame of thy youth is less obvious. Since the conception has some affinities with the striking allegory in Ezek. xvi. it is probable that the reference goes back to the origin of the nation (cf. Ezek. xvi. 4—8); the reference being to the Egyptian oppression."—Camb. Bib. (5) **is thine husband,** and now has come into restored relations with His Church. **be called,** that is, the Husband of Zion is the recognized ruler of the whole earth.[b]

Meaning of a Husband—It means literally "the band of the house," the support of it, the person who keeps it together, as a band keeps together a sheaf of corn. There are many married men who are not husbands, because they are not the band of the house. Truly, in many cases, the wife is the husband; for oftentimes it is she who, by her prudence and thrift and economy, keeps the house together. The married man who by his dissolute habits strips his house of all comfort is not a husband. In a legal sense he is, but in no other: for he is not a house-band; instead of keeping them together, he scatters them among the pawnbrokers.—French.

[a] Je. iii. 5; Ea. v. 3.

"The youth of the Jewish Church was the period of her servitude in Egypt; her widowhood that of the captivity in Babylon."—Henderson.

[b] Zec. xiv. 9; Ro. iii. 29, 30, xi. 12.

"The darkness of sorrow has often been shown to be the shadow of God's wing as he drew near to bless."

6—8. (6) **called thee,** "Zion has been punished but not divorced by her husband and is now recalled to favor. Comp. Esth. ii. 14."—Pol. Bib. **a woman,** R. V. "a wife," who had been neglected but not put away. **wife of youth,** fig. for one specially beloved. **wast refused,** R. V. "when she is cast off." Better perhaps, Pol. Bib., "and one who has been wedded in youth, can she be rejected? says thy God." (7) **small moment,**[c] the 70 years of Bab captivity. **great mercies,** the greatest tenderness.—Henderson. (8) **little wrath,** R. V. "in overflowing wrath I hid," etc.[c] **everlasting,** the strong fig. for abiding, unchanging.

c "The period of alienation is not here described as short, but the anger which occasioned it."—Hitzig.

c "Breaking forth like a flood, to wh. there is a reference in what follows, and which was of short duration."—Wordsworth.

"The wrath is little, but the mercies are great. See how one is set over against the other, that we may neither despond under our afflictions, nor despair of relief.." — Mat. Henry.

Strong Consolation (vs. 7).—Three particulars in these words. I. The displeasure they intimate. II. The mercy they breathe. III. The confidence which these words encourage. 1. It is God who speaks; 2. There is the oath of God; 3. There is His covenant.

Excellencies of a husband.—
Faithful—as dog, the lonely shepherd's pride;
True—as the helm, the barque's protecting guide
Firm—as the shaft that props the towering dome
Sweet—as to shipwreck'd seaman land and home
Lovely—as child, a parent's sole delight;
Radiant—as morn, that breaks a stormy night;
Grateful—as streams, that, in some deep recess
With rills unhoped the panting traveler bless,
Is he that links with mine his chain of life,
Names himself lord, and deigns to call me wife.—*Æschylus.*

9, 10. "The permanence of the new covenant relation is illustrated first by the promise made to Noah, of which the rainbow is the perpetual token, and then by the steadfastness of the unchanging hills."—Camb. Bib. (9) **for this,** viz., this visitation of Divine judgment.[d] **sworn,** Ge. viii. 21, ix. 11. The promise then made God had faithfully kept, and as certainly He would keep the new promises made to His people. (10) "Though mountains should move, and hills should totter, yet from thee my kindness will not move, nor will my command of peace totter."—Pol. Bib. **mountains,** etc., indicating even greater changes than those caused by flood.[a] **my kindness,** Ps. lxxxix. 2, 28, 33. **covenant .. peace,**[b] the covenant whereby I have made thee at peace with Me.

d "I deal with My people respecting this their captivity in Babylon as I dealt with them respecting Noah's flood." — Mat. Arnold.

a Mat. xxiv. 35.

b Eze. xxxiv. 25. xxxvii. 26.

"There can no more be another such effusion of My wrath than there can be another deluge, here called the waters of Noah." — J. A. Alexander.

The Eternal Constancy.—We all sometimes think of Divine mercy as though its meridian had passed, and as though God's grace was setting over the plains of life. We have an ever-living Saviour, an indwelling Spirit, the blessing of spiritual sonship, the foretaste of the sweet vineyards of Canaan, and a fountain ever open for sin and uncleanness. Let us seek to make God's kindness in its constancy the image of our own. Love is the law of heaven; the angels are all ministering spirits. And we are to be ministering spirits too. A part of our nature, constituted as it is to live in others, would be shorn of its blessedness if we could not also be ministers of kindness. Onward, then, my brethren, with these words on your banner. The light which falls on the letters of gold will attract the eyes of others, as you show them what a religious faith can do in renewing the life of the world.—Pul. Com.

11—13. (11) **thou afflicted,** representing God's people by their city, wh. had been so long in ruins. There seem to be blended in the poet's mind references to the perils of the Ark in the waste of waters. **fair colours,** lit. stibium, the substance with wh. Eastern ladies anoint their eyelids. The cement of the walls is compared to it. **sapphires,** transparent blue stones. Comp. Rev. xxi. 18—21. (12) **windows,** R. V., "pinnacles of rubies." **carbuncles,** lit. sparkling gems.[c] (13) **all .. Lord,** Jno. vi. 45. "When the work of the Servant is completed (liii. 11) all the children of Zion will be, like himself (l. 4), disciples of the divine Teacher. Comp. Jer. xxxi. 34; Joel ii. 28, 29."—Pol. Bib.

c "These seem to be general images to express beauty, magnificence, purity, strength, and solidity, agreeably to the ideas of Eastern nations, and to have never been intended to be strictly scrutinised, or minutely and particularly explained, as if they had each of them some precise moral and spiritual meaning."—Lowth.

Instruction and Peace (vs. 13).—I. The instruction spoken of in the text, "All thy children shall be taught of the Lord." 1. Nothing of which men are prouder than knowledge; 2. This is the highest knowledge; 3. It has the best teacher; 4. It is extensive. II. The second blessing is peace. 1. Its kind; 2. Its degree. View it in five stages. (1) The relief it brings the conscience under a sense of pollution; (2) Under the afflictions of the righteous; (3) In the hour of death; (4) At the last day; (5) See it in heaven.—W. Jay.

Bitterness Turned to Blessing.—It is delightful to sit down beside a child of God who has in his hand a bitter cup of trial. Jesus has turned the bitterness into such a blessing that he "tastes the love" of Jesus in every drop. I love to hear old Richard Baxter exclaim, after a life of constant suffering, "O my God! I thank Thee for a bodily discipline of eight-and-fifty years." I love to sit down by Harlan Page and hear him say, "A bed of pain is a precious place, when we have the presence of Christ. God does not send one unnecessary affliction. Lord! I thank Thee for suffering. I deserve it. I deserve death eternal. Let me not complain nor dictate. I commit myself to Thee, O Saviour, and to Thy infinite love. I stop my mouth, and lie low beside Thee!" So God built up that blood-built soul faster than disease was pulling down the frail tenement in which it dwelt. And through the rents heaven's glory shone in with rapturous radiance!—Old Test. Anec. Divine Favor Reaching to the Children.—The conditions of modern civilized life put the religious education of thousands of children altogether into the hands of Christ's Church. Multitudes of parents cannot, or will not, train their children in the nurture and admonition of the Lord. But in all such cases the Church can do a noble supplemental work. We may see the special Divine favor resting on our age, and the best security for the permanence and nobility of our nation, in the wide spreading and vigorous improvement of our Sunday schools. The "peace" assured to the children is a term designed to include all sorts of good. We cannot be wrong in thinking that the better tone of society and family life in our day is the direct result of our increased concern for the moral and religious culture of the nation's children.—Pul. Com.

"This figurative way of speaking is in exact keeping with the Eastern notions of magnificence: thus the abodes of the gods, or distant kings, are described as having pillars of red coral; rooms made of crystal; r u b y doors; thrones of the nine precious stones; walls of gold, surrounded by emerald rivers. Such passages, therefore, are not to be received literally, but as being indicative of great splendor and unrivalled prosperity." — Roberts.

14, 15. (14) **righteousness,** "both the thought and action of Jerusalem will be righteousness then and it will thereby acquire strength. Through righteousness wilt thou be fortified."—Delitzsch.[a] **far .. oppression,** i. e. from suffering oppression. **not fear,** or have nothing to fear. (15) Pol. Bib. "If any should stir up strife, it will be against my will; whoso stirs up strife against thee will be brought by thee to ruin."

[a] Isa. ix. 7, xvi. 5, xxxii. 16.

Joel, iii. 11, 12; Eze. xxxviii. 18; Re. xx. 9.

An Example of Trust.—William Napier once in his walks met with a little girl of five years old, sobbing over a pitcher she had broken. She, in her innocence, asked him to mend it. He told her that he could not mend it, but that he would meet her trouble by giving her sixpence to buy a new one, if she would meet him there at the same hour the next evening, as he had no money in his purse that day. When he returned home he found that there was an invitation waiting for him, which he particularly wished to accept. But he could not then have met the little girl at the time stated, and he gave up the invitation, saying, "I could not disappoint her; she trusted in me so implicitly." That was the true Christian gentleman and soldier.—Dean Stanley.

"Whate'er God does is well,
Whether He gives or takes!
And what we from His hand receive
Suffices us to live.
He takes and gives, while yet He loves us still.
Then love His will."
—B. Schmolck.

16, 17. (16) **created the waster,** all desolating conquerors are as much in God's hands as the smith.[a] (17) **weapon .. tongue,** the two ways in which enmity may be shown, by act and by word. **servants of the Lord,** the first time this title has been used in its wide application. The ideal of the servant is to be reproduced in each citizen of this newly established kingdom. From this point on the phrase is often used. **righteousness,** or justification.[b] **of me,** I will see to it: I will undertake to secure it. If God secures and defends it, we may be sure it is safe from all attacks.

The Divine Control of Evil Forces.—The "waster" here is a comprehensive term for the great conquering kings of Assyria and Babylonia, at whose hands Israel had so grievously suffered. Isaiah declares that God raised them up; God sent them forth; God gave them their work. He assures the new Jerusalem that it is quite safe, for God does not intend to send against them any such "wasters;" and they may dismiss for ever from their thoughts that any other being exists who can send "wasters" forth.—Pul. Com.

[a] "Destroyers and destruction are God's work; they reach those only whom He means them to reach, and He does not mean them to reach Israel." — Mat. Arnold.

[b] Is. lxi. 10.

CHAPTER THE FIFTY-FIFTH.

Invitation to the Blessings of the New Covenant. Two divisions: 1—5, 6—13. **1. Ho,** a sort of loud trumpet call.[c] **every one,** comp. Mat. xi. 28; Jno. iii. 16; Re. xxii. 17. **thirsteth,** with a spiritual thirst, represented by the suffering of the desert-traveler; thirsteth for the "righteousness" spoken of in ch. liv. 17. **waters,** suggested, perhaps, by xli. 18, the

[c] Comp. Jno. vii. 37.

"Under these figures are included all things essential to the spiritual life."—Calvin.

fountain opened by Jehovah for the relief of His people. Water, wine and milk are figurative representations of spiritual revival, recreation and nourishment. Comp. 1 Pet. ii. 2.—Delitzsch. **buy .. price,** a strong way of saying that all our spiritual need is met by free and sovereign gifts.[d]

The Offer of Salvation (vs. 1).—I. The blessings offered under the figures of "water," "wine," "milk." 1. They are New Testament blessings; 2. They are spiritual things; 3. Important not to spiritualize too far. Water, the grace of the Holy Spirit—cleanses, refreshes, satisfies; one of the first principles of life. Wine strengthens; milk nourishes. II. The persons to whom these blessings are promised—the thirsty and the hungry. 1. Our natural condition is one of great destitution; 2. It is necessary to feel this. All spiritual blessings are originally both undeserved and undesired; repentance, faith and prayer bear no proportion to gifts of grace. III. Enforce the exhortation. 1. Come; 2. Some things to be done—we have to part with some, and acquire other things; 3. Experimental possession only sufficient.—Superville (pere).

2, 3. (2) **spend,** lit. weigh.[e] **satisfieth not,** this the true spiritual food of righteousness would do. **good,** pleasant, satisfying. **fatness,** or rich dainties. (3) **Incline,** etc., intimating your personal responsibilities. **soul .. live,** for it the food of righteousness is provided. **everlasting covenant,** ch. liv. 10. **sure .. David,** alluding to 2 Sam. vii. 8—16. The comparison of the everlasting covenant to these Davidic "mercies" cannot mean simply that the one is as sure as the other. It is identity rather than comparison that is implied, the idea being that the contents of the covenant are the same as the mercies promised to David, and that it will be the fulfillment of the hopes that clustered round the Davidic dynasty.[f] —Camb. Bib. Lu. i. 32, 33.

The Way in Which the Call is to be Made Sure.—1. It must be heard. "How can they believe in Him of whom they have not heard?" "O earth! earth! hear the Word of the Lord." "If any man hath ears, let him hear." "Hear, and your soul shall live." 2. It must be understood. The truth as it is in Jesus must be comprehended. 3. It must be believed. Truth only realizes the call. Matthew believed; Saul believed; the Samaritans believed. 4. It must be retained. The profession of faith must be held fast. "Abide in Me," says Christ. So we must continue Christ's disciples to the end.—Burns.

Unsatisfying Food—The nardoo plant.—A strange plant, called the nardoo, closely allied to the fern tribe, grows in the deserts of Central Australia. A peculiarly melancholy interest is connected with it, owing to the fact that its seeds formed for months together almost the sole food of the party of explorers who a few years ago crossed the Continent. The nardoo satisfied their hunger; it produced a pleasant feeling of comfort and repletion. The natives were accustomed to eat it in the absence of their usual roots and fruits, not only without injury, but actually with positive benefits to their health. And yet day after day King and his friends became weaker and more emaciated upon this diet. Their flesh wasted from their bones, their strength was reduced to an infant's feebleness, and they could only crawl painfully a mile or two a day. At last, when nearing the bourne of their hopes, they perished one by one of starvation; a solitary survivor being found in the last extremity under a tree, where he had laid him down to die, by a party sent out in search of the missing expedition. When analysed, the nardoo bread was ascertained to be destitute of certain nutritious elements indispensable to the support of a European, though an Australian savage might for a while find it beneficial as an alterative. And thus it happened that these poor unfortunate Englishmen perished of starvation even while feeding fully day by day upon food that served to satisfy their hunger. Is it not precisely so in the experience of those who are seeking and finding their portion in earthly things? They are contented with it, and yet their hunger is in reality unappeased. Their desires are crowned, and yet they are actually perishing of want. God gives them their request, but sends leanness to their souls.—H. Macmillan. Trusting the Promises.—Last winter a man crossed the Mississippi on the ice, and, fearing it was too thin, began to crawl on his hands and knees in great terror; but when he gained the opposite shore, all worn out, another man drove past him

d "They must come and procure it, though it be given away without price." — Spk. Com.

"The love of Christ is the conducting medium to the love of all mankind."— Jowett.

"Religion should be the element in which a Christian lives, rather than the sanctuary to which he retires."

e "The custom of weighing uncoined gold and silver in mercantile transactions anciently obtained among the Hebrews and other nations; and it still obtains in Turkey and other parts of the East."—Henderson.

f "The same sure unfailing mercies which I showed to David."—Mat. Arnold.

If I were in a boat on the river in the rapids, it would not be necessary, to insure my destruction, that I should enter into violent controversy with those who would urge me from the shore, to take heed and come to land: all, I should have to do would be to shut my ears to their entreaty, and leave myself alone; the current would do the rest. Neglect of the gospel is thus just as perilous as the open rejection of it. Indeed, half the evils of our daily life in temporal things are caused by neglect; and countless are the souls who are lost for this same cause.— W. M. Taylor.

gaily, sitting upon a sled loaded with pig-iron. That is just the way most Christians go up to the heavenly Canaan, trembling at every step lest the promises shall break under their feet, when really they are secure enough for us to hold our heads and sing with confidence as we march to the better land.—Old Test. Anec.

4, 5. (4) **given him,** this vs. goes back to the promise made to David, but regards it as one destined to be fulfilled in the person of his son the Messiah. **witness,** or as one who delivers a testimony.[a] Jno. xviii. 37. **people,** R. V., "peoples," i. e. all nations. (See note, ch. li. 4.) **leader,** prefect, or prince. **commander,** or supreme head. (5) **thou shalt,** etc. This is explained most easily as addressed to the regenerated people of Israel. Thou shalt call many a nation hitherto unknown to thee.[b] (5) **glorified thee,** Acts iii. 13.

The Faithful Witness (vs. 4).—Christ is a witness—I. For the declaration of Gospel mysteries. 1. The covenant of salvation; 2. The mystery of Gospel righteousness; 3. The doctrine of providence. II. For the confirmation of Scripture truth. III. For the decision of practical controversies.

The Leadership of Christ.—The devotion of his soldiers to Napoleon Bonaparte was extraordinary; but that great commander, with all his egotism, acknowledged that this was nothing compared with the devotion of Christian men to the Person of Jesus Christ. The pity with which he pitied us in our low estate, the tender interest with which he has sought and rescued us, the shame and the sorrow which he bore for us, the death he died for us, the patient love with which he has been loving us,—all this will well account for the fact that, as no king, or general, or statesman has ever done before, Jesus Christ has shown himself the Leader of men by attaching them to his Person with a passionate and unwavering devotion.—Pul. Com. Christ, Our Leader.—Christ has a right to command us, not only as one who possesses us, but also as one who has absolute, unquestionable authority over us. We sing to this day of the glory of the "Charge of the Light Brigade." They knew perfectly well that no one was justified in giving them the order to ride to needless annihilation. No one would have blamed their refusal to obey that order. But without questioning the order they rode straight into the jaws of death, into the mouth of hell. If men in war will obey commands which they know to be unreasonable simply because given by those in authority, what shall be said of us who call Jesus Christ "Lord," who know it is impossible for Him to give us anything but loving and reasonable commands, and who still allow these commands to go unheeded and disobeyed? It is not our place to raise objections or postpone obedience by excuses. The Master will take care of things if we obey Him.—Robert E. Speer.

6, 7. (6) **Seek ye,** prob. addressed specially to the Jews.[a] **while .. near,** Je. vi. 8. The intimation is that God may withdraw His favor from the Jews. (7) **wicked,** etc., comp. ch. i. 16—20. **abundantly pardon,** or multiply to pardon. "God's graciousness is felt more and more the longer one knows Him."

Exhortation to the Wicked (vs. 7).—I. The counselled. 1. The wicked; 2. The unrighteous. II. The counsel. 1. To abandon their evil habits of action and thought; 2. To return to God in the way which He has appointed. III. The promise annexed to the counsel. 1. Of mercy; 2. Of pardon; 3. Of abundant pardon. Address the impenitent and unbelieving.—G. Brooks.

God's Merciful Pardon.—Every day, from my window, I see the gulls making circuits and beating against the north wind. Now they mount high above the masts of the vessels in the stream, and then suddenly drop to the water's edge, seeking to find some eddy unobstucted by the steady-blowing blast; till at length, abandoning their efforts, they turn and fly with the wind; and then how like a gleam of light do their white wings flash down the bay, faster than the eye can follow! So, when we cease to resist God's influences, and, turning towards him, our thought and feelings are upborne by the breath of the Spirit, how do they make such swift heavenward flight as no words can overtake!—H. W. Beecher.

[a] "The term designates the prophetical office of the Messiah, in the discharge of which He communicates to mankind, and to His Church in particular, the saving knowledge of Divine things." —Henderson.

[b] "The most natural supposition concerning this vs. is, that after speaking of the Messiah, the Prophet turns to Him, and addresses Him directly."—J. A. Alexander.

Let your desires be few and simple; then if they are not gratified, you will have less to regret.

"That sin which is not too great to be forsaken, is not too great to be forgiven." —Spurgeon.

[a] Ps. xxxii. 6; Isa. lxv. 1; Mat. xxv. 1—13; Jno. vii. 34.

"Mercy in us, it is no more than a drop; but in God it is an ocean; in us it is no more than a little stream; in God it is a springing and flowing fountain. A spring continually runs, an ocean is never drawn dry. What is a little sparkle of fire, if it fall into the main sea? The same are the sins of a penitent person when dealt with by the mercy of God."— Thomas Horton.

8, 9. (8) **not your thoughts,**[b] "Jehovah's thoughts transcend those of man as much as the heaven is higher than the earth. The point of the contrast is not the moral quality of the Divine thoughts as opposed to those of the 'wicked'; the thoughts and ways of Jehovah are His purposes of redemption, which are too vast and sublime to be measured by the narrow conceptions of despairing minds (xl. 27 f.). Comp. Jer. xxix. 11. ('I know the thoughts that I entertain towards you, thoughts of peace and not of evil, to give you a future and a hope'), Mic. iv. 12. The verses, therefore, furnish a motive not merely for repentance but also for eager and expectant hope."—Camb. Bib. (9) **heavens,** etc., comp. Ps. lvii. 10, lxxxix. 2, ciii. 11. The heaven-wide difference is in the fact that men's ways are fickle, unreliable and powerless.

God's Thoughts Superior to Ours (vs. 8, 9).—I. They are superior in reference to man, his being, his essence. II. God's thoughts respecting the perils of this being are higher than ours. III. God's thoughts respecting the perfection and restoration of our being are brighter than ours. 1. Man has deep wants, and God can supply them; 2. The same thing may be said of conscience; 3. His thoughts are of mercy.—Caleb Morris.

10, 11. (10) **snow,** wh. covers plants from frost in winter, and when melted in spring, waters the earth.[a] **returneth not,** in the sense of failing to fulfill its gracious designs. (11) **my word,** of promise concerning Israel and Messiah. **void,** having achieved nothing, as 2 Sam. i. 22. **I please,** the plans of God if not the desires and plans of men will be accomplished.

Resemblance Between the Bible and the Snow and Rain (vss. 10, 11). —I. In their origin: African rain-makers, Livingstone, Bible, God's own Book, self-evidencing. II. In their importance: importance of rain, effects of drought, more important is the Bible. III. In the mode of their operation: gradually, nature does nothing at a bound, nor the Bible; influence of Bible truth on the hearts of men, according to nature of soil, need of preparation, connection with use of means, reign of law in the kingdom of grace. IV. In the certainty of their success: success of Bible seen sometimes at once, sometimes after an interval. Apply:—1. We never leave the Church as we enter it; 2. We have great encouragements to circulate the Bible.—G. Brooks.

12, 13. (12) **go out,** i. e. from Bab. captivity. **led forth,** by Jehovah himself. xl. 10, 11; lii. 12. **mountains .. singing,** representing nature as meeting the returning Jews with exulting joy. This conception of nature rejoicing in the redemption of the race is constant in O. T. and often repeated in Isaiah. **clap .. hands,** Ps. xcviii. 8. (13) **thorn,** etc., "nature is represented as undergoing a complete change to indicate the prosperous and happy condition of God's people." **fir tree,** or cypress. **brier,** perhaps nettle.[b]—Fausset.

Figurative Use of Trees.—The thorn, the brier, and the thistle are generally used in Scripture to denote any kind of useless and noxious plants that grow spontaneously. In the following instances they are used figuratively:—To denote desolation (Prov. xxiv. 31); the visitation of Providence (Num. xxxiii. 55); and difficulties, hindrances, and troubles (Prov. xv. 19, xxii. 5). The fir tree is a well-known and valuable evergreen, and once grew with rich luxuriance on the now comparatively bare slopes of Lebanon. It was used in Palestine for ship-building, musical instruments, and parts of sacred edifices. It is generally a tall, fine-looking tree, and is used in Scripture to denote power and grandeur. Storks sometimes build their nests in the upper branches. The springing up of a fir is emblematical of verdure and plenty. The myrtle is a beautiful, fragrant, and ornamental evergreen: groves of which are still found in some parts of Palestine. The seeds of one species of myrtle are gathered and dried before they are ripe; and are then called pimento, or allspice. The myrtle in ancient times formed the wreaths for heroes and victors. At the Feast of Tabernacles it was used by the Jews to cover their tents. Thus we find a happy comparison between the thorn and brier, on one hand which denote desolation and trouble; and the fir tree and myrtle, on the other, which represent plenty and prosperity. This

[b] "This and foll. vss. reply to those objections that the natural man opposes to the new way of salvation proposed by God, vss. 1—3. It may be objected as inconceivable that man can obtain salvation simply by believing, and not by his own works."—Nagelsbach.

[a] "The hearts of men, once barren of spirituality, shall be made, by the outpourings of the Spirit under Messiah, to bear fruits of righteousness."—Fausset.

Samuel Longfellow, the poet-clergyman, brother of Henry Wadsworth Longfellow, once gave so good a prescription for "the blues" that it deserves to be read every morning on setting out in the day. He said—"Whatsoever it be that disorders, annoys, grieves you, makes life look dark and your heart dumbly ache, or wets your eyes with bitter tears, look at it steadily, look at it deeply, look at it in the thought of God and His purpose of good, and already the pain and annoy of it will begin to brighten."

[b] So Vulg. "It is some prickly plant growing freely in the desert."—Wordsworth.

Dr. O. W. Holmes says, "Men, like peaches and pears, grow sweet a little while before they begin to decay." This is true; but Christian men should be sweet from the hour that they are re-

comparison is used by the Prophet to illustrate the prosperity and glory of the Church,—that Church which our Saviour proclaims His "well-beloved."

CHAPTER THE FIFTY-SIXTH.

The prophecies (xiv. 1; xliv. 5) have begun to be fulfilled. Proselytes are offering themselves. But the strict Israelites raise objections against them. Some Hebrews, while in captivity, have been made eunuchs, and are distressed. (Ps. cxxvii. 3.) Vss. 1—8 are addressed to these classes especially. **1, 2.** (1) **judgment,** or equity. **justice,** R. V., "righteousness." **near to come,** comp. Matt. iii. 2.[a] (2) **layeth hold,** R. V., "holdeth fast by it," a promise made to every son of man, i. e. not to the Jew only but to all mankind. **keepeth the sabbath,** i. e. "so as not to profane it," (so vs. 6). The same emphasis on Sabbath observance appears in ch. lviii. 13, and so in Ezek. xx. 12 ff., xxii. 8, 26 (cf. Jer. xvii. 19 ff.). Although one of the most ancient of Israel's religious institutions (Ex. xx. 8; Deut. v. 15; Am. viii. 5) the Sabbath acquired peculiar significance during the Exile, "when the ordinances of public worship were suspended and the Sabbath and circumcision became the chief external badges of fidelity to the covenant of which it was the sign."[b]—Camb. Bib.

The Lord's Day.—There are those who say that all days should be sacred,—a philosophy which we accept, if it is not followed by the immorality which neglects to keep any day. We never find that people are peculiarly observant of the Sabbath day who generalise their love over the whole week; and we never find that people are careless during the intervening time who conscientiously, intelligently, and adoringly receive the Sabbath day as a rich gift from God. There are those who say all money is God's, and therefore they never set apart a Lord's account. It is to be feared they may be deluded, and that the Lord may suffer on account of that generality which does not identify itself with peculiar and isolated sacrifice. Let every man examine himself herein. A blessing is pronounced upon those who do God's commandments—not an external blessing. There is all the difference in the world between a reward that is added to a service and a reward that comes up out of the service itself. In the case of religious devotion the blessing is in the service. To serve is to be blessed.—Peop. Bib.

Sabbath-keeping and Sabbath-breaking—The Isle of Man.—Between twenty and thirty years ago, the little Isle of Man was a bright example to the surrounding islands. The Manx people then highly reverenced the Sabbath, and their peaceful condition in those days, as contrasted with their present state, will abundantly prove the truth of the words, that in keeping of God's commandments there is great reward. At that time a gentleman from England visited the island. On the Sabbath he walked to Peel, one of the principal towns, historically celebrated for its ancient castle. On arriving he found the streets deserted. An air of complete rest and Sabbath stillness reigned, and all things seemed to say, "In six days may work be done, but in the seventh is the Sabbath of rest holy to the Lord." At last he discerned two figures seated in the bottom of one of the boats, and on going nearer discovered two sailors busily engaged in reading; the one a Manx, the other an English Bible, which they were thus comparing. They would not, for any reward, put out the boat or row the few yards needful on the Sabbath day. But tourists increased and they could not withstand their offers of money. The change was described by an old resident: "Twenty years ago," he said, "we slept in peace, none making us afraid. We thought not of locking or bolting a single door, for such things as house-breaking and robbery were unheard of." Of late years how is the case altered! Thousands of visitors arrive yearly. Shops are now open on the Sabbath, boats on the bay and cars with pleasure parties break the calm of the Sabbath day. We can no longer say that locks and bolts are unneeded, for Sabbath-breaking and other crimes have gone hand-in-hand.—Bibl. Treas.

newed in heart. Yet even then maturity brings a special mellowness.

[a] "The Prophet designedly declares in the present passage that one should not suppose moral uncleanness is compatible with participation in the promised salvation."—Nagelsbach.

"The nearer the manifestations of God's mercy, whether in time or in eternity, the louder the call to righteousness of life."—J. A. Alexander.

[b] "During the exile all the services and sacrifices of the Temple had ceased, and the one testimony of faithfulness to their religion wh. the Jews among an idolatrous people could give was the observance of their Sabbath; their Sabbath was the one outward thing wh. brought their religion to their mind. Hence its observance acquired quite a special value."—Mat. Arnold.

Ex. xxxi. 14, 16.

"O day of rest!
How beautiful, how fair,
How welcome to the weary and the old!
Day of the Lord! and truce to earthly care!
Day of the Lord, as all our days should be!"
—Longfellow.

Of twelve hundred and thirty-two convicts who had been committed to the Auburn State Prison previously to the year 1838, four hundred and forty-seven had been watermen, either boatmen or sailors —men

3—5. (3) **stranger .. ennuch,** by Mosaic law these were not to enter into the congregation of the Lord.[a] This exclusion was henceforth to cease. **dry tree,**[b] he could not become the head of a family in Israel, and therefore felt that he had no real and permanent share in the hopes of the nation. (4) **please me,** sacrificing their own pleasure for Mine. **my covenant,** ch. lv. 3.[c] (5) **a place,** or memorial, monument. **better .. daughters,** who perpetuate to succeeding generations a father's name. **everlasting name,** illus. in Eunuch of Candace, Acts. viii. 27—39.

Acceptance of All True Worshipers (vss. 4—7).—I. The characters which God approves. 1. Their obedience to His will; 2. Their affiance to His covenant. II. The approbation with which He will honor it. God will—1. Accept him in all his services; 2. He will number him amongst His most favored children. Apply:—(1) We have an antidote to despondency; (2) A stimulus to exertion in the cause of Christ.

Note on vss. 4, 5.—It is supposed by the most competent annotators that the customs of Eastern temples and of later synagogues suggest that these words may refer primarily to the memorial tablets which were put up in such places in commemoration of distinguished benefactors.—Peop. Bib.

6—8. (6) **sons .. stranger,** R. V., "the strangers." vs. 3. Such had been united with the Jewish Ch. only as proselytes of righteousness. They were to become full members of the spiritual and Messianic Church. (7) **holy mountain,** Zion. **burnt offerings,** etc., including all kinds of religious services.[d] **house of prayer,** a more spiritual title.[e] **people,** R. V., "peoples,' i. e. for all nations. (comp note, ch. li. 4.) This is the emphatic point. (8) **gather others,** comp. Jno. x. 16: the Gentiles, in addition to the scattered Jews. **beside,** etc., R. V., "beside his own that are gathered."

The House of Prayer (vs. 7).—1. Need of revelation of Divine existence. 2. Does He take an interest in the affairs of this world? 3. Is He accessible? 4. Will He pardon? 5. Is He thus accessible and gracious to all? 6. Is there reason to conclude that this result shall be realized? 7. How may this sacred place be made effectually, more effectually, to subserve this great end? 8. Here then we are to come in the spirit of prayer. 9. Here everything is to be done with a view to lead to prayer.

A new section begins here, extending to lvii. 21. "A prophecy against the evil rulers of Jerusalem and against the Samaritans."—Pol. Bib. **9, 10.** (9) **beasts,** etc., the apostrophe to the wild beasts is suggested by the following comparison of the people to an ill-guarded and therefore defenceless flock. (10) **His watchmen,** the negligent rulers and guides of Israel. **blind,** not discerning the signs of the times: **dumb,** not daring to speak against what they know to be evil. (Comp. Ezek. xxxiii. 1 ff.) **sleeping,**[a] R. V., "dreaming," or Camb. Bib. **"raving"** as one delirious in illness.

Preaching Fruit and Flowers.—At Hampton Court Palace every one regards with wonder the enormous vine loaded with so vast a multitude of huge clusters; just outside the vine-house is as fine a specimen of the Wistaria, and when it is in full bloom the cluster-like masses of bloom cause you to think it a flower-bearing vine, as the other is a fruit-bearing vine. Fit emblems these two famous trees of two ministries, both admired, but not equally to be prized; the ministry of oratory, luxuriant in metaphor and poetry, and the ministry of grace, abounding in sound teaching and soul-saving energy. Gay as are the flower-clusters of the Wistaria, no one mistakes them for the luscious bunches of the grape; yet, there are many simpletons in spiritual things who mistake sound for sense, and seem to satisfy their hunger not on solid meat, but on the jingle of a musical dinner-bell.—Spurgeon.

11, 12. (1) **greedy,** lit. strong of appetite. **shepherds .. understand,** are unable to comprehend the spiritual wants of the people. **own way,** or selfish interests. **from his quarter,** or better, one and all of them. (12) **fetch wine,** i. e. when judgment is actually at hand, they are for revelry.[b] **and much more,** etc., R. V., "a day great beyond measure."

Influence of Evil Habits.—The following will serve as a fearful illustration of the melancholy influence which drinking, gambling, and betting have in blunting and destroying the moral feelings:—Two fellows at a tavern having summoned the waiter, the poor man had scarcely entered, when he fell down in a fit of apoplexy. "He's dead!" exclaimed

---

who, to a great extent, had been kept at work on the Sabbath, and thus deprived of the rest and privileges of that day. Of those twelve hundred and thirty-two convicts, only twenty-six had conscientiously kept the Sabbath.

[a] De. xxiii. 1—8.

[b] "Phrase used still in the E. of a person of either sex who has no children." — Henderson.

[c] Je. ix. 24.

"Lovely flowers are the smiles of God's goodness." —Wilberforce.

"Where all are selfish, the sage is no better than the fool, and only rather more dangerous." — Froude.

[d] "Seven centuries had yet to elapse before the Levitical dispensation would terminate, so its language is retained." — Spk. Com.

[e] Mat. xxi. 13.

Whether in sorrow or success, he has learned the great lesson, that religious faith is the most valuable and most sacred of human possessions. — Hawthorne.

[a] "Some suppose a particular allusion to the murmuring or growling of a dog in its dreams."—J. A. Alexander.

Eze. iii. 17, 18.

[b] "The language here employed strikingly depicts the feelings of the voluptuous in every age." — Henderson.

Pr. xxiii. 32—35.

one. "He'll come to!" replied the other. "Dead for five hundred!" "Done!" retorted the second. The noise of the fall, and the confusion which followed, brought up the landlord, who called out to fetch a doctor. "No! no! we must have no interference; there's a bet depending." "But, sir, I shall lose a valuable servant." "Never mind! never mind! you can put him down in the bill."—Whitecross.

"The reason that many men want their desires is, because their desires want reason. He may do what he will that will do but what he may." —Warwick.

CHAPTER THE FIFTY-SEVENTH.

1, 2. (1) **righteous perisheth,** reference is to early and untimely deaths removing those who were the strength of the nation. **to heart,** as if it were a national loss. **merciful men,** lit. "godly men." **none considering,** the purpose of Divine providence in graciously removing the righteous, that they might not share in the calamitous times.[c] "From the writer's point of view the poor are the righteous, and the rich the wicked. Neh. v. 8 shows that even good men lent corn and money on usury and vss. 3—5 prove exorbitant charges."—Pol. Bib. (2) **enter into,** R. V., "He entereth into peace; they rest in their beds, each one that walketh in his uprightness."[d] i. e. Every man who led a straightforward life would find rest only in the grave. Comp. Job. iii. 13 ff. **beds,** refers to the bier or coffin. Comp. 2 Chron. xvi. 14; Ezek. xxxii. 25.

The Death of the Good (vs. 1).—I. Their death is the perishing of the body. 1. Why then pamper the body? 2. Why centre interests on the wants of the body? II. Their death is generally disregarded by mankind. 1. The thought of death is repugnant to the heart; 2. The concerns of life are all-absorbing. III. Their death is a deliverance from all the evils that are coming on the world. IV. Their death is a step into a higher life. 1. Their bodies sleep· 2. Their souls march on.—Thomas.

The Christian's Death.—The Christian does not terminate his thought by the grave, for he lives in the light of a larger and nobler revelation. The grave is no longer a bed, a final resting-place; it is but a point to halt at; the spirit has gone beyond the boundaries of the tomb, and is already rejoicing in the dewy morning of eternal day. Thus we are lifted up in contemplation, thus we are strengthened in faith, thus we are ennobled in all intellectual thought, by coming into contact with the spirit and revelation of Jesus Christ. The grave is no longer a boundary line; it is but a transient shadow soon to be driven away by the rising light. Beyond it lies the garden of the Lord; one inch beyond, and all heaven glows in infinite summer.—Parker.

c "His removal is a sign that the evil is near at hand." —Spk. Com.

d "Each one who has walked in the way lying straight before him, instead of turning to the right hand or to the left."—Wordsworth.

"To die is landing on some silent shore,
Where billows never break nor tempests roar.
Ere well we feel the friendly stroke, 'tis o'er."
—Garth.

"There is no Death! what seems so is transition;
This life of mortal breath
Is but a suburb of the life elysian,
Whose portal we call Death."
—Longfellow.

3—5. Invective against an idolatrous party, vss. 3—13. (3) **adulterer,** etc., "refers partly to the mixed origin of the Samaritans, partly to their impure religion. The prophet here attacks the Samaritans whose friendly relations to the Jews (Ezra ix. 1, 2: Neh. xiii. 28) were dangerous in the eyes of pious patriots."—Pol. Bib. (4) **Against whom,**[a] it seemed to be against the Prophet, it really was against Jehovah. **sport,** in derisive mirth. **wide mouth,** Ps. xxxv. 21. (5) **green tree,** reference is to the consecrated groves of the false gods. **slaying,** etc., the most famous sacrifices of this kind were those in the valley of Hinnom.[b] **valleys,** etc., probably weird and desolate places were chosen by preference for these revolting rites, although this is the only passage where such a thing is suggested.—Camb. B.

Verse 5.—The reference is, as Mr. Cheyne says, to the "orgiastic cults in the sacred groves of Palestinian heathenism." The nature of these cults is well stated by Professor Döllinger ('Jew and Gentile,' vol. i. p. 430): "At the spring festival, called by some the 'brand-feast,' by others that of torches, which was attended by streams of visitors from every country, huge trees were burnt, with the offerings suspended on them. Even children were sacrificed; they were put into a leathern bag, and thrown the whole height of the temple to the bottom, with the shocking expression that they were calves, and not children. To the exciting din of drums, flutes, and inspired songs, the Galli cut themselves on the arms; and the effect of this act, and of the music accompanying it, was so strong upon mere spectators, that all their bodily and mental powers were thrown into a tumult of excitement.

a "The righteous dies, and is at rest; but ye. what will ye make at last of your derision of the righteous, and of the follies and idolatries wherein ye trust? Nothing."—Mat. Arnold.

b Je. vii. 31; see also 2 Chr. xxviii. 3, xxxii. 6.

"Prune thou thy words, the thoughts control
That o'er thee swell and throng;
They will condense within thy soul,
And change to purpose strong".
—J. H. Newman.

c "In the earlier times, all the Greeks worshipped, in place of images of the gods, undressed stones." — Pausanias.

"There is a stone set up to the south of St. Columbus' Church, in the island of Eriska, about 8 ft. high and 2 ft. broad. It is called by the natives the bowing stone; for when the inhabitants had the first sight of the church, they set up this stone, and then bowed, and said the Lord's Prayer." —Martin.

a "Prob. small images like those of the Roman Penates, or household gods, which were in every private family, and were the objects of prayers and offerings."— Mat. Arnold.

"The weary traveler, unable to drag his tired limbs one step further through the leaden air and under the copper sky of the East, lies down to rest. When the sun fills the east with rosy light he is up and off again; freshened and cheered, he is young once more! So with grace. God has provided refreshment for us all. We need not despair of reaching the goal."— Pul. Com.

a Isa. xxxv. 8, xl. 3, 4.

"Men every day measure the Christ by themselves. How much better if we measured ourselves by the Christ!" — Lew Wallace.

"Progress —the stride of God!" —Victor Hugo.

6, 7. (6) **smooth stones,** of which the altars were builded.[c] **portion,** as Jehovah is the portion of His people these altars to Moloch are the portion and lot of the idolators. **receive comfort,** R. V., "Shall I be appeased for these things?" i. e. shall I overlook or forgive such offences? (7) **high mountain,** in allusion to worship in "high places." **thy bed,** carrying on the representation of idolatry as adultery.

Stones Used as Idols.—The stones here referred to were consecrated to the honor of certain deities, and supposed to be instinct with their presence. "I have," says Turner, in his work on Polynesia, "several 'smooth stones of the stream' from the New Hebrides, which were used as idols, and have heard of precisely similar stones being used in other parts of the Pacific. But what do they do with the stones? Very much like what the Earl of Roden says the people of Inniskea, off the coast of Mayo, do, or did, with their sacred stone. 'A stone, carefully wrapped up in flannel, is brought out at certain periods to be adored; and when a storm arises this god is supplicated to send a wreck on their coast.' Some of the Polynesian stone gods were prayed to for the removal of storms; and others were supposed to act as rain-makers and rain-stoppers. There was one of these rain-controlling stones in a district in Samoa. When there was too much rain, those who kept the stone put it to the fire to dry, and cause the rain to stop. If there was great drought, they took the stone to the water and dipped it, thinking that by wetting the stone, rain would be the consequence."

8, 9. (8) **thy remembrance,** "thy symbol," i. e. token of some deity in this false religion, set up in the home where it would be readily seen.[a] (9) **king,** "to Melek"—, the name of a deity, probably same as Molech, or Milkom, the chief God of the Ammonites, with whom the Samaritans were in alliance (Neh. ii. 10; iv. 7, etc.) **ointment,** etc., presents to propitiate him; **unto hell,** or Hades: consulting the oracles of the Under-world.

10—12. (10) **wearied ..way,** R. V., "with the length of thy way." in the effort to gain rest and satisfaction by such idolatrous wilfulness. **no hope,** unwilling to believe such idolatry could be quite in vain. **life .. hand,** R. V., "thou didst find a quickening of thy strength; therefore thou wast not faint." i. e., she stirred up her remaining strength and persisted in her course. (11) **of whom,** of which of their helpless idols. **held my peace,** in gracious forbearance, which had been interpreted as indifference. (12) **declare,** i. e. show it up, prove how empty and hollow it is. **thy works,** R. V., "and as for thy works they shall not profit thee."

Weariness Comes With Unbelief.—It was so in the old world, and so it will be in the new. The Greeks had an underlying sadness in their outwardly beautiful life, as Luthardt so well shows in his volume on the Christian evidences. It is faith which gives life and zest. Thomas Carlyle says in his essay on Diderot, "All epochs, wherein unbelief, under whatever form soever, maintains its sorry victory, should they ever for a moment glitter with a sham splendor, vanish from the eyes of posterity; because no one chooses to burden himself with study of the unfruitful." So he shows us how French philosophism vanished into non-entity. Yes, that is it; there is non-entity, no-being in unbelief. What a glorious creed is the Christian creed—meeting all deepest necessities of sin, and want, and sorrow, and immortal instinct, by its doctrines of Divine atonement, fatherhood, sympathetic brotherhood, and eternal life! Who can be weary when he believes in One who is himself the revelation of the Father? Bringing life and immortality to light, Christ has made this world more beautiful. There is a deeper life even in human love. As Esther Lyon says, in 'Felix Holt,' "One likes a beyond everywhere." Men must be weary who have lost faith.—Pul. Com.

13, 14. (13) **criest,** in the time of thy calamity. **companies,** R. V., "them which thou hast gathered," "multitudinous troops of idols and idolaters." **possess the land,** comp. ch. lx. 21; Ps. xxxvii. 9. (14) **Cast ye up,** i.e. make a smooth highway for My returning people.[a] Now the tone changes and the prophet sets forth the gracious will of Jehovah toward His repentant people.

The Ministry of Angels.—Without intruding it on the reader's attention, Isaiah is continually implying the interest which angels take in all God's dealings with his Church, and the assistance which they render,

Voices fill the heavenly sphere around him and about him, which can only be angelic utterances, and from time to time he records the sayings. Sometimes he records them openly as angelic; e. g. the seraph's words, when he took the live coal from the altar in the court of heaven, and therewith touched the prophet's lips (ch. vi. 7). But more often he names no speaker, but simply gives the words or introduces them impersonally with the phrase, "and one said" (see ch. xxi. 11; xxvi. 2; xl. 6, etc.).—Pul. Com.

15, 16. "They have been worshiping idols, creatures of their own fears and cruel passions. But He is the high and lofty one—two of the simplest adjectives in the language, yet sufficient to lift Him they describe above the distorting mists of human imagination. They thought of the Deity as sheer wrath and force, scarcely to be appeased by men even through the most bloody rites and passionate self-sacrifice.—G. A. Smith. (15) **Holy,** or Holy One. **holy place,** 1 Ti. vi. 16. **contrite .. spirit,** the new test of religion, see ch. lxvi. 2. The word contrite comes from a verb meaning to bruise, crush.[b] (16) **contend,** prolonging even chastisements unduly. **the spirit,** of man, which cannot bear an overweight of even just Divine indignation. **Souls,** Gen. ii. 7. Refers to the creation. He will not undo His own work and annihilate those to whom His own breath was imparted.

The Greatness and Condescension of God (vs. 15).—I. The greatness of God. 1. His superiority to all others in the scale of being; 2. His eternity; 3. His holiness; 4. His self-manifestation. II. The condescension of God. 1. Its objects; 2. Its expression; 3. Its purpose. Apply:—(1) Are we contrite and humble? (2) Let not God's greatness prevent our coming to Him.—G. Brooks.

Jerusalem.—

Jerusalem, Jerusalem! enthroned once on high,
Thou favored home of God on earth, thou heaven below the sky!
Now brought to bondage with thy sons, a curse and grief to see,
Jerusalem, Jerusalem! our tears shall flow for thee.

Oh! hadst thou known thy day of grace, and flocked beneath the wing
Of Him who called thee lovingly, thine own anointed King;
Then had the tribes of all the world gone up thy pomp to see,
And glory dwelt within thy gates, and all thy sons been free.

"And who art thou that mournest me?" replied the ruin grey,
"And fear'st not rather that thyself may prove a castaway?
I am a dried and abject branch, my place is given to thee;
But woe to every barren graft of thy wild olive tree!

"Our day of grace is sunk in night, our time of mercy spent,
For heavy was my children's crime, and strange their punishment;
Yet gaze not idly on our fall, but, sinner, warned be,
Who spared not His chosen seed may send His wrath on thee!

"Our day of grace is sunk in night, thy noon is in its prime;
Oh turn and seek thy Saviour's face in this accepted time!
So, Gentile, may Jerusalem a lesson prove to thee,
And in the new Jerusalem thy home for ever be!"—Heber.

17, 18. (17) **covetousness,**[a] ch. lvi. 11. The besetting sin of the time; strictly means unjust gain. **hid me,** hiding of face was a token of displeasure. **frowardly,** turning away, or backsliding. **heart,** or wilful heart. (18) **ways,** i. e. wilful ways. **heal him,** with restoring mercies. **restore comforts,** make consolations abound over his troubles. **mourners,** spiritual ones, ch. lxi. 2; lxvi. 10; Mat. v. 4.

Divine Mercy and Anger Contrasted (vs. 17).—1. A dispensation of health to those spiritually diseased; 2. A proclamation of peace to those who are far off and to those who are near; 3. A declaration of ruin to the impenitent.—R. Cecil.

19, 20. (19) **fruit of .. lips,** which is thankful praise. God makes it by giving His gracious healing and restoring mercies. "I make the lips blossom anew with speech." (Comp. Prov. x. 31; xii. 14).—Pol. Bib. **far off ..**

[b] "The most sublime description of the Divine majesty and condescension to be found in the Scrip. The words require no comment, but they have a depth of meaning wh. no finite mind can fully comprehend." — Henderson.

"Isaiah encouraged those who were trodden down to perseverance, by reminding them that real dignity is something very different from present success.." — F. W. Robertson.

"What God wants is men great enough to be small enough to be used."— H. W. Webb-Peploe.

"Lowliness is the base of every virtue, and he who goes the lowest, builds the safest."— Bailey.

"The peace of Christ is not something that He puts into your heart, and that you must keep, that it may keep you. If the peace of God is to rule in my heart it is because the God of peace Himself is there." — Andrew Murray.

[a] "The terms indicate a rapacious person, one who breaks thro' all bounds in order to acquire gain." —Henderson.

"That which is intended to draw near, sometimes drives away. Godly sorrow works repentance; but sorrow, taken ill and treated wrongly, works death. If the heat does not melt, it hardens." — Pul. Com.

near, with reference to Jerusalem (comp. Dan. ix. 7). Those "far off" are the Jews of the Dispersion. For all who are of the true Israel, (Ps. lxxiii. 1.) the day of realized ideals, of Messianic felicity has dawned. For all but the wicked there is perfect peace."—Pol. Bib. (20) **cannot rest,** better, "for it cannot rest." **mire,** etc., "Its waters work up mire and filth."—Lowth.

The Fruit of the Lips (vs. 19).—I. The nature of the blessing which is proclaimed in the Gospel. 1. There is war between God and man; 2. There is war between the higher and the lower principles of human nature. II. The persons to whom this blessing of peace is offered. 1. In respect of religious privileges; 2. Of social advantages; 3. Of moral character; 4. Local distance. III. The influence of this blessing upon its recipient. 1. Beneficial in its operation; 2. Individual in its efficiency; 3. Divine in its agency. IV. Its practical issue. 1. The fruit of the lips is thanksgiving; 2. God creates the occasion and the disposition.—G. Brooks.

21. no peace, ch. xlviii. 22. "Again this warning as to the sole condition upon which God's salvation can be had."—Mat. Arnold.

No Peace to the Wicked (vs. 21).—I. Who are the wicked? 1. Not only the openly ungodly, but those who have misconceptions of the nature of duty and of the character of God; 2. Those who reject Christ; 3. Those who reject the Spirit of God; 4. Those who live after the dictates of their own evil will. II. How it is that there is no peace to wicked men. 1. He loves that which must destroy his peace; 2. He is every moment under the wrath of his Maker; 3. He is especially without peace when he needs it most, as in the day of affliction, etc. Apply:—(1) Seek peace with God; (2) Now; (3) In the spirit of prayer; (4) Let those who have this peace rejoice in it, and make it known.—B. W. Noel.

Our Sin Finding us Out.—Audley was an old English usurer, who used to lend money to the thoughtless young men of his day, at ruinous rates of interest. He counted out the pounds for them, with many well-affected remonstrances on their extravagance, but his pity never led him away so far as to make him forget his securities. As long as he knew a debt to be safe, he was quite indifferent as to delay of payment, and many an unsuspecting victim was lulled into false security by the old usurer's apparent unconcern; and they were only awakened, on some dark and unfortunate day, by the terrible discovery that interest and principal had swallowed up all their estates. Such is the ruinous percentage which thousands will be called on to pay to the great Enemy of Souls, for what are commonly described as "the pleasures of sin." Fear of Death.—William the Conqueror, extremely alarmed on his death-bed, entreated the clergy to intercede for him. "Laden with many and grievous sins," he exclaimed, "I tremble; and being ready to be taken soon into the terrible examination of God, I am ignorant what I should do. I have been brought up in feats of arms from my childhood; I am greatly polluted with effusion of much blood; I can by no means number the evils I have done these sixty-four years, which I am now constrained, without stay, to render an account to the just Judge."

"When the intemperate heats of the spirit break out in scurrilous and abusive language, then the troubled sea casts forth mire and dirt."—Mat. Henry.

"Thou troubled sea,
Oh, troubled, fretful sea!
What can the causes be
That thy soft, silvery breast
So rarely is at rest?

"E'en when there wind is none,
And thou art let alone,
Thy heart, self-troubled, will
Keep palpitating still.

"Ah, well may thy unrest
Emblem the human breast;
Yea, the great world around,
Where troubles so abound!"

"Every lot is happy to a person who bears it with tranquility." —Boethins.

"There will be a great change in men's characters; those that were as thorns and briers, good for nothing but the fire, nay, hurtful and vexations, shall become graceful and useful as the fir tree and the myrtle tree." — Mat. Henry.

CHAPTER THE FIFTY-EIGHTH.

"How to fast aright." A prophecy against a popular religious error. Comp. Zech. vii. 8. The community is pre-occupied with the question of legal righteousness. By fasting and prayer they hope to hasten the coming of the Messianic kingdom. The prophet says moral reform is needed. —Pol. Bib. **1, 2.** (1) **aloud,** lit. with the throat. This call is made to the Prophet.[a] **spare not,** ch. liv. 2. **trumpet,** Ho. viii. 1. **sins,** esp. of hypocrisy. (2) **seek me,** reference is to the outward religious zeal shown, wh. God knew was not really the expression of inward feeling.[b] **ask .. justice,** "as if they were injured persons, whose rights God did not defend."—Spk. Com. **approaching to God,** while their hearts were far from Him.

Formalism (vs. 2).—I. Explain it. A form of religion includes—1. Some degree of religious knowledge; 2. Attendance on public ordinances; 3. Membership in the Christian Church; 4. Respectable moral character.

[a] Isa. xl. 6.

[b] "Here is a warning to all, that there may be much outward show of religion, in daily approaches to God in His house, while there is no vital piety." — Wordsworth.

"Their words fly up, their thoughts remain below;
Words without thoughts never to heaven go."

II. Expose its deficiencies. 1. It does not satisfy the great wants of human nature; 2. It does not yield the pleasure found in spiritual religion; 3. It tends to foster intolerance; 4. It is diametrically opposed to the spirit and precepts of the Gospel.—G. Brooks.

3—5. Many prophetic addresses have for their theme the fact that "the ceremonial law had no value except as the expression of a godly disposition." Comp. 1 Sam. xv. 22: Hosea vi. 6; Amos v. 21 ff.; Isa. i. 11ff.; Jer. vi. 20; vii. 21 ff. Mic. vi. 6 ff. (3) **fasted,** the religious act which seemed so suitable to their captive and humbled condition.[c] The only fast-day appointed by the Mosaic law was the Day of Atonement.[d] **thou seest not,** comp. Mal. iii. 14. **afflicted,** etc., by the fasting. **find pleasure,** rather "business," i. e. you find opportunity to do a profitable stroke of business.—Camb. Bib. **exact .. labors,** make your dependents work while you fast. (4) **smite,** etc., indicating harsh, violent treatment of dependents. **voice .. high,** R. V., "ye fast not this day so much as to make your voice to be heard on high;"[a] God does not hear it. (5) **bow .. sackcloth,** outward signs of humiliation. "One of the great surprises of the human heart is, that self-denial does not win merit or peace. But assuredly it does not, if love be not with it. Though I give my body to be burned and have not love, it profiteth me nothing. Self-denial without love is self-indulgence."—G. A. Smith.

Philanthropic Piety (vs. 5).—I. Its ritual is philanthropic service. II. Its influence is gloriously beneficient. III. Its spirit is acceptable to God.—Thomas.

Formalism.—The tendency to turn Christianity into a religion of ceremonial is running with an unusually powerful current to-day. We are all more interested in art, and think that we know more about it than our fathers did. The eye and the ear are more educated than they used to be, and a society as "æsthetic" and "musical," as much English society is becoming, will like an ornate ritual. So, apart altogether from doctrinal grounds, much in the condition of to-day works toward ritual and religion. We freely admit that the Puritan reaction was possibly too severe, and that a little more color and form might with advantage have been retained. But enlisting the senses as the allies of the spirit in worship is risky work. They are very apt to fight for their own hand when they once begin, and the history of all symbolic and ceremonial worship shows that the experiment is much more likely to end in sensualising religion than in spiritualising sense. The theory that such aids make a ladder by which the soul may ascend to God is perilously apt to be confuted by experience, which finds that the soul never gets above the steps of the ladder. The gratification of taste, and the excitation of æsthetic sensibility, which is the result of such aids to worship, is not worship, however it may be mistaken as such. All ceremonial is in danger of becoming opaque instead of becoming transparent, as it was meant to be, and of detaining mind and eye instead of letting them pass on and up to God. You are men in Christ; do not go back to the picture-book A B C of symbol and ceremony, which was fit for babes. You have been brought into the inner sanctuary of worship in spirit; do not decline to the beggarly elements of outward forms.—Maclaren.

6, 7. (6) **loose,** etc., i. e. "dissolve every tie wherewith one has unjustly bound his fellow men."—Fausset. **heavy burdens,** R. V., "the bands of the yoke." **oppressed,** lit. "broken" either with servitude or poverty. Comp. Neh. v. 1—13. (7) **deal thy bread,** fig. for charity and hospitality, wh. in the East are regarded as cardinal virtues.[b] **own flesh,** "it is claim enough that they are Jews. The tribal divisions have been so much weakened that Israel is now one great clan. Comp. Neh. v. 5.—Pol. Bib.

8. light, the emblem of prosperity. **"break forth"** is the verb used in ch. xxxv. 6; Gen. vii. 11; Ps. lxxiv. 15, of the bursting of waters through a fissure in the earth's surface; by a vivid metaphor the dawn was conceived as "splitting" the heavens and flooding the world with light. The same word occurs on the Moabite Stone (l. 15) in the phrase "from the splitting of the dawn."—Camb. Bib. **health,** R. V., "healing." **go before thee,** further fig. of a people marching, in reference to the return of Jerusalem. **rereward,** like a rearguard on the march.

Revelation of Light, a Morning.—Mornings have often come alike

c "Besides the regular fasts of the Jewish religion, there were, during the captivity in Babylon, special fasts appointed as days of repentance and prayer for Israel." —Mat. Arnold.

d Le. xvi. 29, 31.

a Matt. vi. 16—18.

Fasting, in the sense of a refusal of all food, belongs to ceremonial religion and had its origin in Eastern lands. Fasting in its most spiritual form, as personal self-restraint, will-mastery over habits and preferences, must ever be binding upon all Christians.—R. Tuck.

"In these vss. the Prophet says nothing of bodily mortification. He only names the works of righteousness towards the oppressed, and beneficence towards the poor and needy." —Nagelsbach.

b Comp. Mat. xxv. 35, 36.

"Hospitality is a virtue wh. has always held the very first rank among the Oriental nations; and any symptom of indisposition to exercise it has ever met with execration." —Henderson.

Desolate homes, starving children, patient women from whose hollow eyes the worm looks out already, men smitten from their manhood into feebleness until they have lost almost all remembrance of the bold and brave beings they were—these are our clients. "Inasmuch," etc.—that is our never-failing argument. "Ye know the grace," etc.—that is our example. "She hath done what she could"—that is our measure.—W. M. Punshon.

Ps. xcvii. 11, cxii. 4; Pr. iv. 18; Mal. iv. 2.

"As the earth, either in its beauties or deformities, can only be seen by the light of the sun; so man can only discover his true moral character before God by the light which shines upon him from the Sun of righteousness."—J. Bate.

a "The pointing of the finger is a gesture of derision."—J. A. Alexander.

"Indicative of mockery and insolence towards the pious and persisting part of the nation."—Mat. Arnold.

b "Draw it out of its narrow self-love, that it may go along with the dole wh. passes from thy hand."—Spk. Com.

a "When you go in at the gate of an Eastern house, you find a paved court, a piazza, and doors or windows opening upon it, or upon the garden in the rear. The ornament most prized in a garden is the marble tank. These tanks are often very tastefully cut and ornamented. It is the height of Oriental luxury to spread a carpet on the grass, sit cross-legged upon it, and draw the narghile, or sip a cup of coffee."—Van Lennep.

in Jewish and Christian history. Isaiah awakened the Hebrew nation to a new life. Mediævalism with its dark superstitions, the inquisition with its abhorrent cruelties, did not destroy Christianity. What has been well called the "morning of the Reformation" came. Look back now to Savonarola, and you will see what one man can do to herald a better day in darkest times. "Then"! Not by an accident in history, nor by an arbitrary decree of God; but by obedience to his Word and by the baptism of his Spirit. And beautiful as are all mornings, when the sun touches the clouds with gold, and fills the earth with splendor, and makes dancing sunshine on the sapphire sea, none are so beautiful as the mornings of new moral life for the world.—Pul. Com.

9, 10. (9) **Then**, when you have returned to righteousness. **the yoke,** the sign of their oppression. **putting .. finger,** "the finger of scorn pointed at simple-minded godly men." Sign of contempt.[a] **vanity,** R. V., "wickedly." (10) **soul .. hungry.**[b] probably error in text; should be, "bestow thy bread on the hungry."—Camb. Bib. So the Sept. and Syriac. **light .. obscurity,** fig. for prosperity suddenly succeeding calamity.

Buying Heaven.—In Herefordshire there was one very rich man in my parish who had a sudden paralytic stroke when I was away from home for a holiday. He was a common, ignorant farmer, and had come into 80,000 pounds through the death of a brother. He had told me that he did not care for his brother's money because he had as much as he wanted before, and yet he had not given more than sixpence a year for charity. As soon as I returned home, I went down to see him and he said, "The Lord has stricken me and I am afraid I may die. I have sent for you at once that I may do what I suppose is right before God; I want to go to heaven, and I want you to take a hundred pounds for the poor." I looked him straight in the face and said, "Do you think you are going to buy your soul's way to glory by a paltry hundred pounds! Give your money where you like; I will not touch it!" That was rather strong; but blessed be God, the man lived seven years, and was a very different man before he died.—H. W. Webb-Peploe.

11, 12. (11) **guide thee,** such a man (filled with the spirit of love) will enjoy without intermission the guidance of divine grace."—Delitzsch. **drought,** "parched places." **make fat,** or "strengthen thee." **watered garden,** the Oriental conception of the beautiful and happy.[a] (12) "Thy sons shall build up the ancient ruins, thou wilt rear again the long deserted foundations, and men will call thee "Repairer of Ruins, Restorer of Destroyed Places for Inhabiting.'"—Pol. Bib. The importance attached to the restoration of the ruined places shews that what the prophet has in view is chiefly the recovery of temporal and political prosperity. It may also throw some light on the date of the prophecy. The description of the ruins as "ancient" suggests a period considerably later than the Exile (which only lasted half a century), although the argument is not one that can be rigorously pressed.—Camb. Bib. **foundations,** etc., i. e. wh. for generations had lain bare and exposed.

Under Repairs (vs. 12).—I. Damage has been done—1. To the Divine image in man; 2. To the relationship of man. II. Damaged man is under repairs. 1. The method is his; 2. The materials are his; 3. The ministries are his; 4. The memorial is his. III. These repairs must be done in time. 1. How much time has been absolutely wasted! 2. How little really improved! 3. The remaining portion is little enough for the work.—H. F. Miller.

A well-watered garden indicates the presence of life. To speak of a garden without life would be unmeaning and absurd, however much may be done by art and skill to create a pleasing scene. This thought has a real application for human souls. We are too apt to confine our ideas of life to the outward and superficial aspects of mere existence. We see around us a great deal of the machinery and parade of life. But the suspicion will force itself upon us that much of this is but the fencing in of uncultivated regions—useless labor bestowed upon barren and unproductive spots which are not "rich towards God." There is the secret of the well-watered garden. Christ emphasizes the life that is in it, and a life, too, which can be deep, and full, and abiding, only as it is centered in the Divine fullness itself. This suggests the value of the promise to ancient Israel. As long as they were a scattered flock, separated from

God above all by their evil affections, they were losing life. Their spiritual strength was decaying, they were living in a wilderness where all their powers were parched and blighted, and they were doing what so many are doing now—they were losing their own souls in the mere materialism of a godless and undevout life. We may depend upon it that things are going badly, and even tragically with us, when the roots of a growth towards God are showing no signs. We are made for the achievements of faith: if that life of faith be not in us, "the world is too much with us." Only by being transformed as into "a watered garden" can our true life be secured.—W. Manning.

13, 14. (13) **sabbath,** see ch. lvi. 2.[a] **thy pleasure,** "thy business" (vs. 3). **a delight,** source of real joy.[b] **own pleasure,** i. e. business. Pol. Bib., "Not doing thy wonted things, nor minding thy business, nor speaking vain words." **(14) ride .. earth,** De. xxxii. 13; descriptive of conquest and triumphant possession.[a]

The Sabbath (vs. 13).—I. In what light we should view the Sabbath. 1. Holy; 2. Honorable; 3. Delightful. II. In what manner we should employ it. 1. What is forbidden; 2. What is commanded. III. The benefits we may expect from a due observance of it. 1. Delight in God; 2. Victory over our spiritual enemies; 3. The full possession of the heavenly Canaan. Apply:—(1) How reasonable are the requirements of God in His Gospel; (2) How just will be the condemnation of those who disobey them.—G. Brooks.

An Arctic Explorer and Sabbath Keeping.—Dr. Scoresby, of Arctic fame, was a devoted Christian, and not ashamed of the Gospel of Christ amid the pursuits and honors of science. It was in the year 1820 that he introduced on board of his ship the regulation as to no fishing on the Lord's day, to the successful working of which he long after published an emphatic testimony. He always kept up the habit of reading prayers and sermons on board ship, and one of his own prayers, offered in name of the whole ship's company, on setting out on a voyage, has been preserved in his biography, and is singularly rich, and humble, and full of unction. We may notice that, during his stay in Edinburgh, on one occasion, he made the acquaintance of Sir Walter Scott, and, being invited to meet a party at his house on the Lord's Day, wrote in reply—"I fear I cannot have the honor of waiting upon you on Sunday at dinner, agreeably to the arrangement you were so kind and polite as to propose. For some years, indeed, I have declined visiting on that day of the week; though I readily and honestly acknowledge that in this instance the privation is greater than on any occasion that ever before occurred."—Old Tes. Anec.

[a] Comp. Je. xvii. 12—27; Eze. xxii. 8, 26.

[b] "The observance of the Sabbath has, in all ages, been found essential to the maintenance and prosperity of spiritual religion."—Henderson.

[a] In early times and in the warfare of early times the high and rocky situations were also the strong and defensible situations, and therefore he who occupied them was formidable and powerful."—Mat. Arnold.

"A corruption of morals usually follows a profanation of the Sabbath."—Blackstone.

CHAPTER THE FIFTY-NINTH.

1, 2. "The whole of this chapter is simply the expansion of the first two verses."—G. A. Smith. (1) **not shortened,** the answer to the question why deliverance was so long delayed. **bear heavy,**[c] dulled with deafness. (2) **your iniquities,** etc., "instead therefore of finding fault with God, they should criminate themselves."[d] **hid his face,** caused Him to withdraw His favor (viii. 17).

God's Hand Not Shortened (vs. 1).—I. Can Christ save in every part of our fallen world? II. Can the arm of the Lord save the most polluted and despicable of the human race? III. Can the Divine hand save the masses of the fallen? IV. Can the hand of God save men for ever? V. Can the hand of God save to the highest degree of purity and glory? Apply—1. It is of the Lord's salvation of which the text speaks; 2. It is His actual salvation; 3. His ear is open, and must be addressed by prayer; 4. God's omnific hand faith must grasp; 5. The Divine, inexhaustible ability of Christ should engage our grateful attention.—Burns.

3, 4. (3) **hands .. blood,**[e] Is. i. 15. Reference is to the putting to death of the innocent, or to the violence with wh. crime was attended.[f] (4) R. V., "None sueth in righteousness and none pleadeth in truth." **calleth,** i. e. none brings a just suit into court. **they trust,** etc., Camb.

[b] "The Prophet merely pauses, as it were, for a moment, to exonerate his Master from all blame, before continuing his accusation of the people."—J. A. Alexander.

[c] Isa. vi. 10.

[d] "They stood in their own light, and put a bar in their own door."—Mat. Henry.

[e] "This, and what follows, is a picture of the sins of the unfaithful part of the Jewish nation during the captivity in Babylon, and in spite of the lessons taught by that captivity."—Mat. Arnold.

[f] Pr. i. 11, 12.

Bib., "Trusting in emptiness and speaking vanity! Conceiving mischief and bringing forth evil!"

Human Sacrifices in Burmah.—The correspondent of the Daily News at Rangoon sends the following account of the massacres at Mandalay: When the city was built, he says, human sacrifices were offered up. A new monarch usually has a new capital, and the evil spirits are irritated that there has lately been no change of capital, the virtue of the old sacrifices being gone. They have, therefore, plagued the city with small-pox, and to appease them the astrologers declared it necessary to offer up 700 lives—men, women, boys, girls, pounhas, priests, and foreigners. A hundred each of all ranks were consequently buried alive under the towers of the city walls. An attack was made on the Roman Catholic convent unsuccessfully, and a frightful panic prevails at Mandalay, whence the people are leaving by hundreds.

5, 6. (5) **cockatrice' eggs,** R. V., "basilisk's eggs," refers to the injurious nature of all they undertake, see ch. xi. 8. **spider's web,**[a] "they spin vain, foolish schemes, which can only come to nought." **eateth eggs,** fig. for adopting their principles. **crushed,** etc., or, "if one is crushed there creeps out a viper," i. e. their words are all evil and their acts are directed to the injury of their neighbors.—Delitzsch. (6) **not .. garments,** things like "spiders' webs" are useless for garments.

Sin Universal.—The existence of sin; of sin as an acknowledged fact; of sin as an acknowledged evil, which has not only tainted the nature, but has poured its corruption upon every part of man; found everywhere,—alike in the crowded city streets, and among the scantier tribes of the savanna; alike where refinement and civilization gild and soften crime, and where, in the swarthy-bearded Druse, it reigns tameless as the pennon that flutters upon the lance of his djerrid; alike in sordid man and lost woman, in generous youth and smiling babe, in all circumstances, in all countries, in all parallels of latitude, in all diversities of language,—there is no escape, and there is no exception from this disastrous uniformity of evil. The fountain has been corrupted, and the streams of necessity must flow polluted and impure. Every mouth must be stopped, for all the world is guilty before God.—Punshon.

7, 8. (7) **feet,** etc., Pr. i. 16; Ro. iii. 15. "During the captivity the true believers were persecuted even to the death by their countrymen who had forgotten God." **their paths,** the ways they wilfully mark out for themselves. (8) **way of peace,**[b] which is ever identical with the way of righteousness. **crooked paths,** as opposed to the straight road of righteousness. Comp. Prov. ii. 15; x. 9, etc.

The Importance of a Man's Thoughts.—A man is as his thoughts. This is the fact and truth on which we may dwell. Any one who would truly judge his fellow-man must know his secrets and judge his thoughts. Therefore man's judgment of his fellow-man is always imperfect and uncertain. God alone can judge perfectly, because he is the "Discerner of the thoughts and intents of the heart." There is an impression resting on the minds of many religious persons that they have no control over the suggestions that are made to their minds, and no responsibility for the contents of their thoughts, only for the cherishing of the thought and dwelling upon it, and letting it take shape in action; or, as the Apostle James puts it, only when "lust is allowed to conceive, and bring forth sin." This, however, is true only within very narrow limits, and it is altogether healthier for us to accept a large measure of responsibility, even for the contents of our minds; for only then shall we be likely to watch over what goes in as over what goes out.—Pul. Com.

9, 10. (9) **judgment,**[a] "our right," i. e. Israel's, as against its enemies (xl. 27). "Redress does not overtake us." Have the self-righteous Jews become penitent? Or are these the words of the humble-minded poor? —Pol. Bib. **justice,** R. V., "righteousness." **light,** some sign of the coming redemption-day: but the night still lingers. (10) **grope,** "along the wall," seeking an outlet. Deut. xxviii. 29.—Camb. Bib. **desolate .. dead,** R. V., "among them that are lusty we are as dead men." We wander about like ghosts while others are fat and flourishing.

Spiritual Blindness.—It is one of the saddest consequences of sin that the power of spiritual perception continually lessens; the "eyesight" of the soul becomes weaker and weaker. Great truths are less clearly

---

a Job viii. 14.

"Opposition seems only to produce evil of a worse type." —Spk. Com.

"You pity the poorly-clad amid the biting frosts and snows of winter, but more to be pitied are they who advance into the winter of declining years, the chill region of death, and the storms of judgment, with no sufficient clothing for their defenceless souls!" —William Guthrie.

"A man protesting against error is on the way towards uniting himself with all men that believe in truth." —Carlyle.

"Truth is the summit of being; justice is the application of it to affairs. —Emerson.

b "Either in relation to God, to their own conscience, or to their fellow men." —Fausset.

Isa. lvii. 21; Ro. iii. 17, 18.

"It is no proof of a man's understanding to be able to confirm whatever he pleases; but to be able to discern that what is true is true, and that what is false is false; this is the mark and character of intelligence." —Emerson.

a "Divine judgments interposed to vindicate the cause of the nation." —Henderson.

"If I do what I may in earnest, I need not mourn if I work no great work on this earth." —George Macdonald.

apprehended. Confusion takes the place of distinctness, until at length good is mistaken for evil, and evil for good: "the light that is in us becomes darkness;" the very organ of spiritual understanding misleads us. And the aggravating circumstance is that this failure of the soul's sight takes place "at noonday," when others are walking and rejoicing in the light of the Lord.—Pul. Com.

11—13. (11) **roar,** as expression of impatience.[b] **mourn,** etc., the dove is noted for its plaintive note.[c] "The language of dissatisfaction, grief, and despair." (12) **multiplied,** "the sense of guilt is so vivid, even in the case of the prophets who know themselves to be the servants of God, that they include themselves in the sinful mass of the people for whom an atonement is needed."—Oehler.[d] **with us,** i. e. known to us, we are conscious of them. (13) **transgressing,** etc., the forms of sin against God, and men, are here detailed.

14, 15. (14) **judgment .. backward,** repelled from law court, and society. Better read, is thrust back. **fallen .. street,**[a] i. e. "the market place, where justice is administered, and where she should be preserved upright."—Delitzsch. (15) **faileth,** R. V., "is lacking," not to be found anywhere. **a prey,** or would surely be plundered.[b] **and the Lord saw,** "introduces the peroration of the discourse, in which the prophet describes the manner in which salvation shall at last 'overtake' the sinful and misgoverned community. The logical development of the argument seems to be arrested by the conviction that the existing situation is hopeless, and only to be terminated through the personal intervention of Jehovah. This conviction clothes itself first of all in a prophetic vision of Jehovah as He appears to judgment; which is followed by an announcement of the consequences of His interposition for the two classes within Israel and for mankind at large."—Camb. Bib. **no judgment,** i. e. no just judgment; no prevailing principles of righteousness.

The Righteous a Prey to the Wicked (vs. 15).—It is my intention—I. To establish this fact. 1. This will be found to be true in former ages; 2. Nor is it less true at the present hour. I come now to—II. Account for it. The righteous—1. Irritates and incenses Satan; 2. He reproves and condemns the world. Address—(1) Those who through fear of man are induced to continue in evil; (2) Those who are called to suffer for righteousness' sake.—C. Simeon.

Truth.—The royal diamonds of England cost much, but they are not for sale. The merchant-man who found the pearl of great price sold all he had that he might buy it, but it was never on the market again; he would not sell it. So with truth. The Christian, especially the preacher, should be willing to pay any price for it, but it should not be for sale. No inducement should lead him to give up one jot or tittle of truth, moral, religious, or experimental. It often costs no little for a man to be honest and truthful; to contend "for the faith once for all delivered to the saints;" to get the living truth, which he can learn only in the school of trial; but he should be willing to pay the price of it. It is worth all it costs.—A. C. Dixon.

16, 17. (16) **no man,** "possessing the disposition or the power to stem this corruption."—Delitzsch. **intercessor,**[c] "because of the prophets' share in the people's sin (vs. 12) no valid intercession can proceed from them."—Oehler. **his arm,** ch. lxii. 5. In the return from the captivity God's power, not any man's plan, is exalted. **righteousness,** "zeal for the right, the steadfast purpose to establish righteousness on the earth."—Camb. Bib. (17) **breastplate,**[a] "the inexorable justice of God is compared to an impenetrable coat of mail; His joyful salvation to a helmet which glitters from afar; His vengeance to the cloak worn over the mail, and His wrathful zeal to a mantle. No weapon is mentioned, for His own arm procures Him help."—Delitzsch.

Armor.—The helmet is of continual use. We shall need it as long as our war with sin and Satan lasts. The Christian is not beneath hope, so long as above ground; nor above hope, so long as he is beneath heaven. Indeed, when once he enters the gates of that glorious city, then farewell hope, and welcome love, for ever. He may say with the holy martyr: "Armor becomes earth, but robes heaven." Hope goes into the field, and waits on the Christian till the last battle be fought and the field cleared; and then faith and hope together carry him in the chariot

"We can make no progress without the full use of all the intellectual powers that God has endowed us with." —Drummond.

[b] "We complain loudly and obstreperously, and we complain with whining and moaning; in vain, because our heart is not right with God." —Mat. Arnold.

[c] Isa. xxxviii. 14; Eze. vii. 16.

[d] "To aggravate the guilt of sin, it is frequently spoken of in the Scriptures as being committed in the presence of, or before God."—Henderson.

[a] "Or, in the forum, the place of judicature, usually at the gate of a city." —Fausset.

[b] "He as good as surrenders himself to be plundered by all." — Spk. Com.

Ps. xii. 1.

"For sin, like unto a stone that is cast into the water, multiplies itself by infinite circles." —Basil.

[c] Such as Aaron, Nu. xviii. 1, 2; of Phinehas, Nu. xxv. 7.

"In his usual anthropopathic style Isaiah represents God as filled with amazement at the discovery that no one should be found qualified to reform and save the nation." —Henderson.

[a] Eph. vi. 10—17; 1 Th. v. 8.

"When the oppressors shall come in like an overflowing of the river Euphrates, they shall be broken by the word of the Lord." —Targum.

of the promise to heaven's door, where they deliver up his soul into the hands of love and joy, which stand ready to conduct him into the blissful presence of God.—Gurnall.

18, 19. (18) **deeds,** better deserts. **islands,** here for distant countries, whereon the rebellious Jews may be. No reference here to world judgment based on Israel's sin. (19) **So,** i. e. when the delivering and redeeming power of God has been so gloriously manifested. **when the enemy,** etc., R. V., "For he shall come as a rushing stream which the breath of the Lord driveth." "he," i. e. Jehovah, shall make so wonderful a display of His power that all nations shall recognize and acknowledge it.

The Enemy (vs. 19).—I. There is an enemy. II. That enemy has tremendous influence, "like a flood." III. That enemy is unable to overcome the resources of God. Apply:—1. This promise of the Spirit must not discourage watchfulness, but must—2. Inspire hope.—Parker.

20, 21. (20) **the Redeemer,** "He comes as a Redeemer for Zion." **them .. Jacob,** moral preparation for His reception being necessary. (21) **my covenant,** the new covenant. The inward work of Divine grace, through the Messiah, should be continuous and unchanging.[b] **My spirit,** "the new Church is to be a spiritual Church (comp. xliv. 3; Ezek. xxxix. 29; Joel ii. 28), no age or station is to be excluded from the possession of the spirit."—Oehler.

God's Word in the Home.—Mr. Philip Henry, in a sermon preached in 1659, mentioned it as the practice of a worthy gentleman, that in renewing his leases, instead of making it a condition that his tenants should keep a hawk or a dog for him, he obliged them that they should keep a Bible in their houses for themselves, and should bring up their children to learn to read, and be catechised. "This," said the gentleman, "will be no charge to you, and it may oblige them to that which otherwise they would neglect."—Whitecross.

[b] "Does the Spirit of God remain, then also does His Word; does the Word remain, then preachers also remain; do preachers remain, then also hearers do; do hearers remain, then also remain believers; and therefore the Christian Church remains also."—Cramer.

He. viii. 10, x. 16.

CHAPTER THE SIXTIETH.

"Poem on Glorified Zion." "Ch. lx. is a prophecy as complete in itself as ch. liv. The City, which in liv. was hailed and comforted from afar, is in ch. lx. bidden rise and enjoy the glory that has at last reached her. Her splendors, hinted at in ch. liv., are seen in full and evident display. In chs. lxi.—lxii. her prophet, her genius and representative, rehearses to her his duties, and sets forth her place among the peoples." —G. A. Smith. **1 O arise,** comp. ch. h. 17, lii. 2. Zion is here addressed as the restored city.[a] **thy light,**[b] the promised deliverance. **glory .. Lord,** the Shechinah of the Godhead: figured as the morning sun, ushering in a new and joyous day.[c]

Light in the World.—There is a little church on a lonely hillside where they have neither gas nor lamps, and yet on darkest nights they hold Divine service. Each worshiper, coming a great distance from village or moorland home, brings with him a taper and lights it from the one supplied and carried by the minister of the little church. The building is thronged, and the scene is said to be "most brilliant!" Let each one of our lives be but a little taper—lighted from the Life of Christ, and carrying His flame—and we shall help to fill this great temple of human need and human sin with the light of the knowledge of the glory of God.—Old Test. Anec.

2, 3. (2) **people,** R. V., "peoples," i. e. all nations (comp. note on li. 4). While Zion is in the light the rest of the world is yet in darkness.[d] **Lord .. thee,** as the sun rises to quicken and gladden the day. (3) **Gentiles,** R. V., "nations," so great shall be the attractiveness of Zion.

Light of Revelation in the Thought of God.—Even in the Old Testament that thought was most inaccurate. Even in the ancient nations that loved righteousness there was no entire conception of the nature and character of God. One cannot read the "Republic" of Plato, e. g., without being struck with the accuracy of the thoughts and the beauty of the pictures he brings out, with the power of the argument and the keenness of the criticism; and yet through it and above it all with the darkness, and sadness, and despair. God not known; no real grasp of

[a] The Greek, the Vulg., and the Chaldaic insert the explanatory word Jerusalem.

[b] Isa. ii. 2—5.

[c] "The glory of Jehovah is His manifested presence, with allusion to the cloudy pillar and the Shechinah."—J. A. Alexander.

"To prayer, to prayer; — for the morning breaks,
And Earth in her Maker's smile awakes."
—H. Ware.

[d] "The kingdoms of the earth are breaking up amid gloom and misery." — Mat. Arnold.

Mat. ii. 1, 2, xii. 20—24, 32.

"God wants you to be ambitious to have good works that somebody can see; light travels faster than sound, and so, with Christians, you see the flash before you hear the report, if they are the right sort." — A. J. Gordon.

the eternal goodness; no real thought of the eternal life. Christ came and taught men not only by His stately words, but by His loving life, that God is love. Surely when we feel that no rest can be found in a passing life unless we rest upon God, then we acknowledge the truth of the prophet's saying, "Thy light is come."—Hom. Com.

4, 5. (4) **Lift,** etc., ch. xlix. 18. Describing the flocking of the nations to the restored Zion. **sons .. daughters,** those who have been scattered during the exile.[e] **nursed .. side,** "carried on the side."[f] (5) **flow together,** R. V., "be lightened." The word which the A. V. translated "shall flow together," and our R. V. "lightened," means both of these. It is liquid light,—light that ripples and sparkles and runs across the face; as it best appears in that beautiful passage of the thirty-fourth Psalm, "they looked to Him and their faces were lightened." Here it suggests the light which a face catches from sparkling water.—G. A. Smith. **fear,** "shall throb," with a joy at the great deliverance. **sea,** put for the maritime forces of the Mediterranean.[a] **forces,** R. V., "wealth."

The Church Triumphant.—With other eyes than ours the Jews must have read these glowing words. They saw in them a fascinating picture of a triumphant people; they saw the Jerusalem of their knowledge and of their love made strong and glorious in some coming time. Their patriotic hopes were kindled and must have been raised to a white heat of intensity as they dwelt on the gladdening, transporting promise. In the midst of surrounding darkness covering the whole earth (vs. 2), Zion shines forth with a light which proceeds from nothing less than the Divine Presence itself (vss. 1, 2). Attracted by its radiant beams, her exiled sons and daughters return from the strange lands whither they have gone into captivity, while from every quarter the wealth of Gentile nations flows to her feet. She trembles for very joy, her heart expands with the fullness of its emotion, as she welcomes her children to her heart, as she receives these treasures into her gates (vss. 4—6). The produce of other lands is laid on the altar of Jehovah, and brightens the lustre of that glorious house (vs. 7). Precious tribute is brought from distant coasts (vs. 9), and they who once contemptuously humiliated her, now build up the walls of her strength and find their safety in her service.—Pul. Com.

6, 7. "The next verses are simply the expansion of these two clauses, —about the sea's flood and the wealth of the nations. Vss. 6—9 look first landward and then seaward, as from Jerusalem's own wonderful position on the high ridge between Asia and the sea."—G. A. Smith. (6) **camels,** chief beasts of burden on the caravan routes. **dromedaries,**[b] "young camels." **Midian and Ephah,**[c] noted for their caravan trade. **Sheba,** or Arabia Felix; noted for its spices. (7) **Kedar,** ch. xxi. 17. **Nebaioth,** a tribe of Northern Arabia. **come up,** of their own accord. These animals are supposed to seek the altars of Israel. **glorify .. glory,** lit. "my house of beauty will I beautify."

How God glorifies the Church (vs. 7).—I. The place, the Church. 1. Planned by Divine wisdom, erected by Divine power; 2. Contains special manifestations of the Divine presence and glory. II. The promise. 1. By accepting the services and offerings which are there performed; 2. By making it a place for special communion and fellowship with Himself; 3. By protecting it permanently against all the efforts of hostile powers; 4. By extending its influence; 5. By consummating it finally in the splendor and happiness of heaven.

8, 9. "From the East the prophet turns to the West, and describes the ships of the Mediterranean 'like white doves upon the wing' converging on Jerusalem. These also bring from afar the exiled sons of Zion, as well as rich treasures from the nations."—Camb. Bib. (8) **as a cloud,** borne rapidly along by the wind. **windows,** dove-cotes. (9) **isles,** "yea, to me the ships gather, in the van of the vessels of Tarshish," etc.—Pol. Bib. **Tarshish,**[d] Tartessus, a Spanish port used by the Phœnicians. **the name,** i. e. to Jehovah, the name standing for the Person.

The Cloud of Doves.—Everybody knows that large flocks of pigeons assemble at the stroke of the great clock in the square of St. Mark, Venice. Believe me, it is not the music of the bell which attracts them, they can hear that every hour. They come, Mr. Preacher, for food, and no mere sound will long collect them. This is a hint for filling your

[e] "The nations amongst wh. the Jews are scattered shall bring them back to the Holy Land, with offerings and treasures to restore the Temple service, and rebuild Jerusalem." — Mat. Arnold.

[f] "It is the custom in the E. to carry the children astride on the hip, with the arms around the body." — Fausset.

"Hindu mothers may often be seen carrying a child seated on their hip." — Spk. Com.

[a] See ver 9.

[b] "The dromedary is not a two-humped camel but any camel wh. is used for riding purposes." — Van Lennep.

[c] Ge. xxv. 2, 4; 1 Chr. i. 33.

"The sunshine, streaming through the windows of the old cathedral, fills the whole place with wondrous and solemnizing lights and shades; and the sunshine of the Divine presence fills the heart and the sanctuary with the only true glory and beauty and joy."

[d] Isa. xxiii. 10.

"God's children love communion and fellowship one with another that they may mutually be comforted and edified in faith; they fly

like a cloud, and as doves to their windows; that is, to the house or church of God." — Benj. Keach.

"It is only fire that kindles fire. It is only life that propagates life. It is only spiritual energy that stirs spiritual energy in other accessible and responsive souls."— R. S. Storrs.

"Birds of a feather flock together."

"Here the open gates have their special reason assigned: to admit the ever in - streaming world, with its offerings and homage." —Mat. Arnold.

"Animalism is nothing; inventive spiritualism is all." — Carlyle.

"Because perseverance is so difficult, even when supported by the grace of God, thence is the value of new beginnings. For new beginnigs are the life of perseverance."—Pusey.

"I am so impressed with the importance that God attaches to sweet voluntariness that I am often tempted to resolve never to beg a cent for God again, but rather spend my energy in getting Christians spiritualized, assured that they will certainly become liberalized." — A. J. Gordon.

[a] "Thou shalt draw to thyself, and enjoy, all that is valuable of the possessions of the Gentiles." — Fausset.

"The time shall come when every evil thing from being and

meeting-house; it must be done not merely by that fine, bell-like voice of yours, but by all the neighborhood's being assured that spiritual food is to be had when you open your mouth. Barley for pigeons, good sir; and the gospel for men and women. Try it in earnest, and you cannot fail; you will soon be saying, "Who are they that fly as a cloud, and as doves to their windows?"—Spurgeon. A Lesson from the Birds.—A writer in "Nature" states that the small birds, that are unable to fly the three hundred and fifty miles across the Mediterranean Sea, are carried over on the backs of cranes. When the first cold weather comes, the cranes fly low, making a peculiar cry. Little birds of every species fly up to them, while the twittering of those already settled may be distinctly heard. But for this provision, many species of small birds would become extinct. So, many converts that are young and feeble need much assistance in seeking Christ. Let those that are strong help the weaker ones in their spiritual flight.

10—12. "The rest of the chapter is occupied with the rebuilding and adornment of Jerusalem, and with the establishment of the people in righteousness and peace. There is a very obvious mingling of the material and the moral. The Gentiles are to become subject to the Jew, but it is to be a voluntary submission before the evidence of Jeusalem's spiritual superiority. God Himself, in evident presence, is to be her light and glory."—G. A. Smith. (10) **build .. walls,** gladly rendering service to the Lord's people. (11) **gates .. open,** comp. Re. xxi. 25. The continual stream of people will compel the gates to be kept open.[a] **forces,** "wealth," vs. 5. (12) **not serve thee,** the prosperity of every nation will depend upon its service of the kingdom of God.

Character and Doom of a Corrupt Nation (vs. 12).—I. The character of a corrupt nation. Text implies two things. 1. That there is a certain course of human life which the Bible recognizes as serving the Lord; 2. That nations as well as individuals are bound to pursue that course. II. The doom of a corrupt nation. 1. It is most calamitous; 2. It is most certain. Our subject explains—(1) National convulsions; (2) The true method of promoting national stability.—Thomas.

13, 14. (13) **glory of Lebanon,** etc., "a reminiscence of the building of Solomon's temple." (14) **sons,** the children of those who were their enemies shall recognize the power and righteousness of their God.

Humility.—We have come so much to regard humility a cardinal virtue of Christianity that we may have forgotten that the Christian should be ambitious. I think he should be the most ambitious person on the earth. To whom is the promise of eternal life spoken but to those who, in patient endurance, in well-doing, seek for glory, honor, and immortality, than which there cannot be a much higher ambition? Humility is sometimes only pride turned wrong side out, just as you turn a garment, and dye it, and refit it. A person says, "If I can get into heaven at last I am willing to occupy a back seat." But Scripture very certainly indicates that you are to seek not only barely to get into heaven, but you are to seek "an abundant entrance," which "shall be given you unto the kingdom of God." The back seats are all spoken for, and God wants us to get as near the throne as possible.—A. J. Gordon.

15—17. "Instead of being shunned and hated by all nations, Zion shall become the joy of the whole earth, her wants being abundantly supplied from the best that the nations can bestow."—Camb. Bib. (15) **no .. thee,** i. e. no traveler, trader, or caravan. **eternal excellency,** "an everlasting pride, a joy for age upon age."—Pol. Bib. (16) **suck,**[a] as in a previous passage kings and queens were to be her foster-parents (Is. xlix. 23), so here she is "to suckle at the breast of nations and their monarchs sustained by their riches."—Briggs. (17) **brass .. gold,** the days of poverty, when iron and brass and stone were her only possessions are past. **thy officers,** etc., "and I will make peace thy governor, and righteousness thy magistrate."—Camb. Bib., Pol. Bib., etc.

The Golden Age (vs. 17).—Morally this will include three things. 1. That for practical atheism there will be godliness; 2. That for dominant materialism there will be spirituality; 3. That for controlling selfishness there will be benevolence.—Thomas.

18—20. (18) **wasting,** etc., the image of the most perfect security and peace. **gates Praise**, comp. ch. iii. 26.[a] "And thou wilt call thy walls Deliverance, and thy gates Renown." The Deliverance of God is its fortification, and its Fame the gateway of the nations. (19) **sun,**[b] etc., comp. Rev. xxi. 23: "And the city had no need of the sun, neither of the moon, to shine in it; for the glory of God did lighten it, and the Lamb is the light thereof;" and xxii. 5. It is not implied that the sun and moon shall cease to exist; all that is said is that the new Jerusalem shall not be dependent on these natural luminaries. But that an actual physical illumination of the city by the glory of Jehovah is contemplated by the prophet can hardly be doubted. The basis of the conception is perhaps to be found in Ezek. xliii. 2.[b]—Camb. Bib. (20) **days .. mourning,** the time of the Divine hiding, and Divine judgment.

Gone into the World of Light.—Never since the great minstrel of the border was borne from Abbotsford to Dryburgh Abbey has the valley of the Tweed been so moved as when the sage of Allerly, Sir David Brewster, was carried to his tomb in the old abbey of Melrose, amidst sorrowing crowds of friends and neighbors, and representatives from the seats of learning and science. There he rests till the resurrection morn, and the stone that marks the spot where he lies bears the simple and appropriate words—"The Lord is my Light."—Old Test. Anec. An Inscription on a Tombstone.—Of all the inscriptions in the metropolis of Glasgow, none strikes a visitor so much as the texts of Scripture inscribed on the monument of Dr. Beattie, who died in his fortieth year. One gives the mortal side: "Thy sun shall go down while it is yet day;" the other turns the medal, and we read the inscription, full of immortality: "Thy sun shall no more go down: for the Lord God shall be thine everlasting light, and the days of thy mourning shall be ended."—Old Test. Anec.

21, 22. (21) **all righteous** emphasis on "all."[a] **the branch,**[b] the righteous people planted again in the old and sacred soil. **glorified**, by the goodness and abundance of the fruit.[c] For the figure of the vs. comp. ch. v. 1, 2. (22) **strong nation,** "the smallest will become a clan; the least a large nation."—Pol. Bib. **in his time,** "as this point of time is known to Him only, the predicted glory will burst at once with startling suddenness upon the eyes of those who have waited for Him."—Delitzsch.

Benevolence of Christianity.—The erection of hospitals and infirmaries for the poor is one of the distinguishing ornaments and fruits of Christianity. You might have traversed the Roman empire in the zenith of its power, from the Euphrates to the Atlantic, without meeting with a single charitable asylum for the sick. Monuments of pride, of ambition, of vindictive wrath, were to be found in abundance; but not one legible record of commiseration for the poor. It was reserved for the religion whose basis is humility, and whose element is devotion, to proclaim with authority, "Blessed are the merciful, for they shall obtain mercy."—R. Hall.

CHAPTER THE SIXTY-FIRST.

In this passage the idea of the Servant of Jehovah reaches its climax. With its description, comp. xlii. 1—7. "Ch. lx. presented the external glory of God's people. Ch. lxi. opens with the program of their inner mission."—G. A. Smith. **1. The Spirit,** etc., used by Messiah of Himself. Lu. iv. 18. **anointed,** the term is used here, as often in a metaphorical sense. **preach,** or proclaim. **meek,** or afflicted. Comp. terms used in Mat. v. 3, 5, xi. 5, 29. **liberty,** etc., figures takes from the Jewish year of Jubilee.[d] **opening**, etc., or "to those that are bound, complete deliverance."—Henderson.

The Gospel of the Poor.—We shall more clearly see how it is that Christ's gospel is for the poor, if we contrast it with some of the many human schemes which we are assured are an excellent substitute for the gospel of Christ. 1. There is that parody of the gospel of Christ which I will call the gospel of philanthropy. This gospel says educate the poor, refine their tastes, open your museums on the Sunday. These things have softening and humanizing influence, so long as they are not

remembrance both shall die. The world is one solid temple of pure gold."—Bailey.

"An ill man is always ill; but he is then worst of all when he pretends to be a saint." — Lord Bacon.

a "The most natural explanation of the last clause is that which makes it mean that the walls shall afford safety, and the gates occasion of praise."—J. A. Alexander.

b Re. xxi. 25.

"These prophecies are already daily fulfilled in part in the Christian Church; but they wait for their perfect accomplishment in the end of the world, and in the second coming of Christ."—S. Jerome.

a Isa. liv. 13, lvii. 13.

b Or, "the shoot from My plant."

c Jno. xv. 8.

"The Dutch endeavored to monopolize the spice trade, by confining the nutmeg tree to the narrow limits of Bonda, and extirpating it from all other islands where it naturally grew; but the wild pigeons scattered the nuts over the Moluccas and adjoining islands, thus propagating the tree, and defeating the selfishness of the Dutch."

d Le. xxv. 10; Je. xxiv. 8, 9.

"A little pebble placed near the eye will intercept the light of the sun; and a little object may keep away from us the smile of God and the sweet sanction of our own conscience,"

made substitutes for religion. But there is a refined sensuousness as well as brutal. These things will not save man. 2. There is the gospel of science. This gospel says to the poor man, "Your condition is the result of inevitable laws. It is the rule of nature that in the struggle for existence the weakest shall go to the wall. If therefore you are weak you must submit to the common lot." This gospel gives no comfort. 3. There is the gospel of socialism. This says, "All men have equal rights. The rich are your oppressors; your poverty is the result of cruel laws made by the rich for their benefit." Wreck these and you will soon correct the inequality. This is a gospel of hate. But the gospel of Jesus Christ is the gospel of power, for it is the gospel of good tidings; of Him who was poor. And what makes this gospel so strong and attractive is that it is a gospel of sympathy. It is also a gospel of hope, because it is the gospel of the resurrection. It is a gospel of brotherhood.—Dean Perowne.

The True Ministry.—The great appeal which Christianity makes to the world is this:—"I come to make human life freer, grander, purer; I come to open worlds in which human life can be more perfectly developed; I come to set man towards man in the relation of brother towards brother; to break the chains of human captivity; to dispel intellectual and moral darkness, and to bring in an unending summer day." —Parker.

2. **acceptable year,** "a year of Jehovah's favor."—Camb. Bib. A year for joy—a day for vengeance. **day of vengeance,** the day of Divine vengeance upon their enemies.[a] **that mourn,** for the fall of Zion, comp. Mat. v. 4.

3. **To appoint,** settle, arrange, as a permanent thing.[b] **mourn in Zion,** lit. the mourners of Zion: ch. lvii. 18. **beauty,**[c] R. V., "a garland." **for,** i. e. "instead of." **oil of joy,** in time of suffering or grief the oil of the toilet was not used[d] **garment of praise,** the robe suited for a festive season. **spirit of heaviness,** or a despondent spirit, for which sackcloth might be suitable. **trees of righteousness,** lit. "oaks," the evergreen being a natural emblem of the righteous (Jer. xvii. 8; Ps. i. 3; xcii. 3).

4—6. (4) **build .. wastes,** ch. lviii. 12, because not room enough in the former places of habitation. (5) **strangers,** etc., ch. xiv. 1, 2. (6) **priests .. Lord,** "as standing between Jehovah and the heathen who have now to be shown how to worship the true God." (Comp. 2 Ki. xvii. 27, 28.) Pol. Bib. "a kingdom of priests," Ex. xix. 6. **eat,** etc., comp. ch. lx. 6. **glory,** etc., or "to their glory shall ye succeed."—Camb. Bib.

The True Preacher.—
He was humble, kind, forgiving, meek;
Easy to be entreated, gracious, mild;
And, with all patience and affection, taught,
Rebuked, persuaded, solaced, counsell'd, warn'd,
In fervent style and manner. All
Saw in his face contentment, in his life
The path to glory and perpetual joy.
. . . A skillful workman he
In God's great mortal vineyard: what to prune
With cautious hand he knew, what to uproot;
What were mere weeds, and what celestial plants,
Which had unfading vigor in them, knew;
Nor knew alone, but watch'd them night and day,
And rear'd and nourish'd them, till fit to be
Transplanted to the Paradise above.—Pollok.

7—9. (7) "Because their contumely was in double measure and shame and spitting was their lot, therefore in their land they shall possess double,[a] their joy will be everlasting."—Pol. Bib., ch. xl. 1, 2. (8) **love judgment,** this is given as the reason for His gracious dealings when Israel returns to righteousness. **robbery,**[b] R. V., "with iniquity." **direct their work,** R. V., "give them their recompense in truth." (9) **seed,** the Orientals valued so highly the retention of blessings through succeeding generations. **seed .. blessed,** Ge. xxii. 17, 18.

Mosque Built by Fraud.—An incident mentioned by Mrs. Poole, in her work, The Englishwoman in Egypt, shows that even a follower of

---

"If the end of one mercy were not the beginning of another, we were undone." —Philip Henry.

"We cannot serve God by accident. We must want to do it and plan to do it." —Melancthon.

"Liberty is always the child of discipline. They alone are free who are most helplessly bound, but whose chains and fetters do not chafe them." —Edward D. Rand.

a Is. lix. 18, 19.

"In the multitude of our thoughts within us the Divine comforts do delight our souls; and it is they only that can do it. Miserable are all other comforters, and vain is all the comfort that they administer." —Norris.

b "To make firm and stable arrangements for securing to them all that follows." — Spk. Com.

c "The ashes of lamentation for sin will be taken from their heads, and they will be crowned with a bridal diadem." —Wordsworth.

d Ps. xlv. 6, 7; He. i. 9.

a Double is used indefinitely to denote a large proportion." — J. A. Alexander.

b "It is a truth much to the honor of God that ritual services will never atone for the violation of moral precepts, nor will it justify any man's robbery to say, 'It was for burnt-offerings,' or 'Corban,' it is a gift." —Mat. Henry.

the false prophet can feel the impropriety of such conduct as the text (according to the Authorized Version) condemns. Speaking of the mosques at Cairo, she says, "Many of these buildings are doubtless monuments of sincere piety; but not a few have certainly originated in ways far from creditable to their founders. I passed by one, a handsome building, respecting which I was told the following anecdote. The founder, on the first occasion of opening his mosque for the ceremonials of the Friday prayers, invited the chief 'Ulama to attend the service, and each of these congratulated him before the congregation, by reciting some tradition of the prophet, or by some other words of an apposite nature, excepting one. This man the founder addressed, asking wherefore he was silent. 'Hast thou nothing to say,' he asked, 'befitting this occasion?' The man thus invited readily answered, 'Yes. If thou hast built this mosque with money lawfully acquired, and with a good intention, know that God hath built for thee a mansion in Paradise, and great will be thy felicity. But if thou raised this temple by means of wealth unlawfully obtained, by money exacted from the poor by oppression and tyranny, know that there is prepared for thee a place in hell, and evil will be the transit thither.' The latter was the case; and within a few hours after he had thus spoken, the only one among the company of 'Ulama who had dared to utter the language of truth on this occasion—to do which, indeed, required no little courage—suddenly died, a victim, as was well known, of poison."

10, 11. (10) **I .. rejoice,** Jerusalem, or perhaps the prophet in the name of righteous Israel, speaks as anticipating and even already possessing the promised blessings. For the figures comp. vs. 3.[a] **ornaments,** R. V., "with a garland." **bride,** ch. xlix. 18.[b] (11) **For,** etc., Ps. lxxii. 3, lxxxv. 11; Isa. xlv. 8, lv. 10, 11. **bud,** or springing shoots. **all the nations,** or universally.

Conversion of the World (vs. 11).—I. The comparison here instituted between the natural and the moral world—barren if not cultivated, fruitful when brought under cultivation. 1. So are those countries that are destitute of spiritual cultivation; 2. By the Gospel a great change is wrought; 3. This effected by the instrumentality of man; 4. But the power that effects it is God's alone. II. The change itself which is predicted in it. 1. The change described; 2. The excellency of it. Apply:—(1) What you should seek for yourselves; (2) What you should desire for the world at large.—C. Simeon.

Joy in the Divine Adornings.—A lady once took me into her garden, and I found there beds filled with all kinds of beautiful flowers; but at the end of the garden I came to the edge of a steep precipice, and as I stood looking down at the great black rock beneath, I thought what a dreadful place that would be to fall down. "Come with me," said the lady, "and I will show you something beautiful." She led me round to the foot of the rock and desired me to look up, and when I did I could see no rock, it was completely covered with beautiful white roses. Oh, thought I, that is just a picture of a poor sinner; he is a black, unsightly thing like that rock, but the "Rose of Sharon" comes and covers him; and when God looks, he cannot see the sinner, for between is Christ, and He covers him witih the spotless robe of His own righteousness.—Richard Weaver. Christ Covering the Sinner.—An American citizen had been condemned in a Spanish court, and was to die; but the consul interposed and declared that the Spanish authorities had no power to put him to death. Being determined to save him, he was wrapped round in the flag, the stars and stripes. "Now fire if you dare," he said. "If you do, you defy the great nation represented by this flag." There stood the man, and before him the soldiers, and yet he was invulnerable as though in a coat of mail. So is the sinner wrapped round by the blood-red robe of Christ.—Old Test. Anec.

CHAPTER THE SIXTY-SECOND.

Intercession for the Salvation of Zion, with further Predictions of Her Glory. Although the chapter is commonly treated as forming along with ch. lxi. a single discourse, it has a distinct character of its own, and

"Satan was the first that practiced falsehood under saintly show, deep malice to conceal, couch'd with revenge." —Milton.

"Oh, to drop all lying and craftiness! to lay the ear to the heart of dear old Earth, and then rise up and speak her murmured truths!" — Ferdinand Blanchard.

"It seems impossible to understand
How joy and sorrow may be hand in hand.
Yet God created when the Earth was born
The changeless paradox of night and morn."
—William H. Hayne.

a "Jerusalem may be here personified. Instead of any longer sitting in the dust, in squalid attire, and with a downcast look, she is decked in the most splendid festal garments." —Henderson.

b Re. xix. 7, 8, xxi. 2.

"The dear Lord's best interpreters
Are humble human souls."
—Whittier.

"Providence throws a veil of obscurity over its deepest designs, and the seed of glorious futures lies slumbering in the rough husk until the appointed time for its germination and growth."

"Corrupted human nature is not made to yield the fruits of holiness without toil. Every conversion represents more labor than can be made to appear to the eye."—Wm. Jackson.

is perhaps better regarded as the last member of the Trilogy commencing with ch. lx. There are three clearly marked sections: 1—5; 6—9; and 10—12.—Camb. Bib. **1, 2.** (1) **will I,** the speaker is apparently the Prophet,[c] from the work described in lxl. 1—3. **as brightness,** or light shining out of darkness.[d] (2) **new name,** symbol of a new character and a new relation to God. Rev. ii. 17, iii. 12; Isa. lxv. 15. This new name is a mystery yet to be disclosed.—Camb. Bib.

The Prevailing Inefficiency of the Church and the Remedy (vs. 1). —I. The prevailing inefficiency of the means employed for promoting the cause of religion. 1. Not doctrinal unsoundness; 2. Not strife; 3. Not lack in the system; 4. But power, earnestness. II. The means by which we may be aroused to that high earnestness which properly belongs to the Christian profession. 1. We must be impressed with the sin of apathy; 2. We must have a due sense of our mission; 3. We must individually possess an interest in the cross of Christ.

3, 4. (3) **in the hand,** not his chief crown, but yet a crown, which he has wrought and glories in. (4) **Forsaken,** Heb, Azubah,[a] wh. strikingly contrasts with Hephzibah.[b] **Beulah,** or married.[c]

The Church a Royal Diadem (vs. 3).—I. In what estimation God holds His Church and people. 1. As an emblem of His power; 2. As a monument of His love; 3. As an object of His peculiar care. II. The interest which we also, from this consideration, should take in their welfare.—Simeon.

The Music of a Promise.—When Ulysses passed by the island of the syrens, the classic story tells us that, to save himself from their snares, he bound himself with mighty thongs to the masts, and secured his sailors' safety by filling their ears with wax, that they might not be bewitched. But when the sweet singer, when Orpheus, voyaged by the same syren island, he bound himself to no mast. He started a sweeter, nobler music than the syrens could ever reach, and so sailed by in triumph. If we are to win men and keep men—men who have been charmed with the syren voices of the world all the week—our melody must be one that comes down from heaven; the music of forgiveness and mercy, of grace and help, of God's love, and God's care, and God's everlasting throne.—Pul. Com.

5. sons marry, etc., the harshness of the conception is obvious; and it is hardly relieved by pointing to the double meaning of the verb ba'al ("marry" and "possess"). Lowth and others, by a slight emendation of the text, read "so shall thy Builder (Jehovah) marry thee." (So Cheyne, who refers to Ps. cxlvii. 2: "Jehovah is the builder up of Jerusalem.")—Camb. Bib.[d]

God's Delight in His People (vs. 5).—I. God's relation to His people. 1. The words primarily relate to the Jewish Church; 2. They may also be applied to the Church of Christ. II. His delight in them. 1. No earthly joy superior to that which a bridegroom feels on his wedding day; 2. Such is God's delight in the objects of His choice. Apply:—(1) Let us all desire this high honor; (2) Let those who stand in this near relation walk worthy of it.—C. Simeon.

6, 7. (6) **watchmen,** "Jehovah gives to the restored Jerusalem faithful prophets, whom he stations upon the walls of the city, that they may see far and wide and be heard afar off."—Delitzsch. **make mention,** R. V. "Ye that are the Lord's remembrancers, take ye no rest." **not silence,** i. e. never cease from urgent intercession. (7) **no rest,** lit. silence. "Constrain Him to utter His decree for Zion's salvation."

Note on vs. 6.—The image in this place is taken from the temple service, in which there was appointed a constant watch day and night by the Levites. Now the watches in the East, even to this day, are performed by a loud cry from time to time by the watchmen, to mark the time, and that very frequently, and in order to show that they themselves are constantly attentive to their duty. "The watchmen in the camp of the caravans go their rounds, crying one after another, 'God is one, He is merciful;' and often add, 'Take heed to yourselves.'"—Tavernier.

8, 9. (8) **arm,** etc., Ps. lxxxix. 10. The instrument of accomplishing His will and purpose. **sons .. stranger,** members of foreign nations. (9) **gathered .. eat,** the indication of national security and tranquility.[a] **holi-**

c "For these blessings (of ch. lxl.) the Prophet will not cease to pray and wrestle until they arrive, and the glorious salvation of the renewed Zion shines forth."—Mat. Arnold.

d "'Until her Just One go forth as brightness, and her Saviour be lighted as a lamp.'"—Vulgate.

a Azubah was the name of Jehoshaphat's mother, 2 Chr. xx. 31.

b Hepkzibah, or "My delight in in her," was the name of Hezekiah's wife, 2 Ki. xxi. 1.

c Isa. liv. 4—6; Re. xxi. 2—4.

"Let death do what it will, there is just one thing it cannot destroy, and that is life."—George Macdonald.

d "It bodes well to a land when its own natives and inhabitants are pleased with it, prefer it before other lands, when its princes marry their country, and resolve to take their lot with it." —Mat. Henry.

"Both prosperity and adversity tend to make us forgetful of our God. Even the steady ongoing, that has no ups and downs, makes the thought of God fade in our minds. So we need the witness of our watchers, our praying men, and their muezzin, or call to prayer."—R. Tuck.

a "The enemies of Israel having all been swept away by the powerful judgments of God,

ness, R. V. "sanctuary," they will enjoy again the sacred harvest feasts. Deut. xiv. 22—27.

10, 11. (10) **Go through,** comp. ch. xl. 3. In imagination, the triumphant return seems already begun. **prepare,** etc., the few, but now thoroughly earnest inhabitants of Zion are commanded to "go out and make level the way for the return of the great mass of the people."—Pol. Bib. **a standard,** for the people to rally round.[b] (11) **daughter of Zion,** here meaning the rightful inhabitants of Jerusalem. **his work,** R. V. "his recompence."

Go Through the Gates (vs. 10).—I. There are gates which we cannot help going through,—the gate of life and the gate of death. II. There are gates through which we should escape,—the gate out of sin; out of temptation; out of bondage. III. There are gates through which we should strive to enter into the kingdom of grace,—by the gate of repentance; by the gate of faith; by the gate of obedience. IV. There are gates which shut us in for enternity,—there is the gate of hell and the gate of heaven. —J. Bolton.

Hinderers.—The point of interest here is that, so far as Jehovah was concerned, all things were arranged for the return of the exiles, and the restoration of the long-depressed nation. But some men were hindering the return by their hesitancies and doubtings and selfishnesses. Therefore Jehovah pleads with all who trust his Word, urging them to clear the way of the people, and get these hindrances moved out of their path. There are always hinderers to every good work, and there is always the Lord's call to us not to let these hinderers do their evil work. They take the heart out of all good schemes, and often do much worse mischief than the active oppoinents, because they are a foe within the city, and have deceptive ways which are seldom fully recognized. Removers of Hindrances.—Men of firmness and persistency are needed in every sphere of Christian enterprise; and it is all the better if they have some pleasantness and even humor, and can remove hindrances without offending hinderers. Men of faith are always needed, who, clearly seeing what God would have done, go steadily on towards its accomplishment, refusing to turn aside either to the right hand or to the left. If we cannot, or will not, help toward the on-coming of Christ's kingdom, at least we can get out of the way of those who will work.—Pul. Com.

12. holy people, vs. 2, ch. lxi. 6. **redeemed,** ch. xxxv. 9, 10. **sought out,** "much sought after, a city in which men will gladly settle and which never again will be without inhabitants."—Delitzsch. "Men would resort to her to see her glory and to examine into the wonders which God had wrought for her."—Spk. Com.

The Constitution of the Church.—Jerusalem was a glorious city, the pride of every pious Jew, the yearly resort of the tribes. It was the centre of the nation's religious life, the rallying-point of their religious affections. Such the Church of Christ ought to be to us. It is a society of men and women regulated by the laws of Jesus Christ, and it goes in Scripture under the figure of a city, because God is its Architect and Ruler. "The one Lawgiver in the Church is the Lord Jesus Christ, and its one statute-book is the Bible." It exists for the mutual benefit of its members and the defence and propagation of the truth (1 Tim. iii. 15). The Church, then, is a witness for Christ, wherein He displays the wonders of His redeeming grace. How distinguished the honor! how lofty the privileges! how great the obligations of those who are citizens of the spiritual Jerusalem!—Wm. Guthrie.

CHAPTER THE SIXTY-THIRD.

Oracle of vengeance on Edom, representing the final triumph of Jehovah. **1. Who is this,** a conqueror, with blood-stained garments, is supposed to appear. **Edom,** "is specially brought forward as an object of judgment (Jer. xlix. 7; Isa. xxxiv.; Ezek. xxxv.) as a type of those nations which are nearest to the kingdom of God, but only oppose that kingdom with the more deadly hatred."—Oehler. **Bozrah?** a place in Edom. **speak in righteousness,** or speak truly. "This conqueror is

---

the most perfect tranquility shall reign throughout the land, and those who may go up to worship at Jerusalem shall enjoy unmolested the fruit of their labor." — Henderson.

b Isa. lx. 3.

"I like the man who faces what he must
With step triumphant and a heart of cheer,
Who fights the daily battles without fear;
Sees his hopes fail, yet keeps unfaltering trust
That God is God; that somehow, true and just
His plans work our for mortals."

"True to thyself and others; swerving not
From what the voice within pronounces good.
Who lives well, dies well."
—R. H. Stoddard.

"When we find anything particularly well done, we may be sure that the worker is broader and taller than the work." —Julian Hawthorne.

"Hypocrites do the devil's drudgery in Christ's livery." —Matthew Henry.

"Self reverence, self knowledge, self control,
These three alone, lead life to sovereign power."
—Alfred Tennyson.

"And not by our flaws will God judge us;
His love keeps our noblest in sight."
—Lucy Larcom.

[a] Ps. xlv. 3, 4.

"Who treads the path of love and loss,
With humble steps and head bowed down,
May bear on earth the heaviest cross,
But wears in heaven the brightest crown."
—George Arnold.

"We must all rise so high into the Spirit of the eternal God that we can take men, straw and chaff and all, and gather them with the many imperfections of the vehicles in which they grow." —Beecher.

"Life is joy and love is power,
Death all fetters doth unbind;
Strength and wisdom only flower
When we toil for all our kind."
—James Russell Lowell.

"Deep, unspeakable suffering may well be called a baptism, a regeneration, an initiation into a new state."— George Elliot.

"He loved much! — that is gospel good,
Howe'er the text you handle;
From common wood the cross was hewed,
By love turned priceless sandal."
—J. R. Lowell.

"Let us only take care that, by the glance being turned inward or strained onward or lost in vacant reverie, we do not

Jehovah and Rev. xix. 13 in its representation of the triumph of the Messianic Word of God has this passage in view."—Briggs.[a]

A Mighty Saviour (vs. 1).—I. What are we to understand by the words, "to save"? II. How can we prove that Christ is mighty to save? III. Why is Christ mighty to save? 1. Because of the infinite efficacy of His atoning blood; 2. By the infinite energy of the Holy Spirit. IV. What are the inferences that are to be derived from the fact that Jesus is mighty to save? 1. That ministers should preach in faith, nothing wavering; 2. That those who pray should pray on; 3. That those who are not saved should at once hope in His mercy.—C. H. Spurgeon.

Edom on the Skirts of Palestine.—Sin hangs on the borders of goodness everywhere, as just across her southern boundary-line Edom always lay threateningly upon the skirts of Palestine. We open any page of human history and what do we see? There is a higher life in man. It is imperfect, full of mixture, just like that mottled history of Hebrewdom. But always right on its border lies the hostile Edom, watchful, indefatigable, inexorable, as the redoubtable old foe of the Jews. Always it is the higher life pressed, watched, haunted by the lower; always it is Judah with Edom at its gates. No one great battle comes to settle it for ever; it is an endless fight with an undying enemy. But "who is this that cometh from Edom?" Is it possible that this One that we see coming, this One on whose step, as he moves through history, the eyes of all the ages are fastened—is it possible that he is the Conqueror of the enemy and the Deliverer of the soul? He comes out of the enemy's direction. The whole work of the Saviour has relation to and issues from the fact of sin. If there had been no sin there would have been no Saviour. He comes from the right direction, and he has an attractive majesty of movement as he appears. He seems strong. What does he say to the anxious questioner; what account of himself does he give; what has he done to Edom; and what mean those blood-stains on his robes?—Pul. Com.

Able to Save.—
A lowly Man—He takes my sins, and bears the heavy load;
A lowly Man—He takes my hand, and leads me up the road;
And when I know this lowly Man is my Creator! God!
Oh, this hath solved me much dark speech; and loosed tongues that were dumb!
For all creation round me now a gospel has become;
And what had seemed to me before mere wild, confused Babel,
Is now a fire-tongued Pentecost proclaiming,—Christ is able!
The thunders, in the crashing skies, announce it as they roll;
The lightnings, on the black storm wall, write it in vivid scroll;
And stars repeat it, down the dark, in mystic jewelled light,
The Urim and the Thummim on the breastplate of the night;
And strong Orion shouts to me what slumbered in old fable,
And echoes from eternal night-vaults answer, Able! Able!
And comet, cresting bended heavens, waves echo to the word,
Like waving white plume in the star-mailed helmet of the Lord:
For all creation its evangel utters forth abroad,
Into mine ear, when now I know my Saviour Christ is God!
—W. B. Robertson.

2—4. (2) **red,** it was noticeable that his garments were deeply dyed or stained. (3) **alone,** "the keynote of the piece is the loneliness of the Hero. The avenging Saviour has a fierce joy in being alone. We see One great form in the strength of one great emotion."—G. A. Smith. **tread them,** R. V. "I trod them," past tense all through, to verse 7. (4) **day of vengeance,** announced in lxi. 2. The time, known beforehand to God alone, has come, a time for annihilation of foes and final deliverance of the true Israel.

The Symbol of the Blood.—This symbol of the blood—and by-and-by, when we turn from the Old Testament to the New, from the prophecy to the fulfillment, we find that it was not only the enemy's blood, but his own blood too, that stained the victorious Deliverer's robes—this symbol of the blood bears this great truth, which has been the power of salvation to millions of hearts, and which must make this Conqueror the

Saviour of your heart too, the truth that only in self-sacrifice and suffering could even God conquer sin. Sin is never so dreadful as when we see the Saviour with that blood upon his garments. And the Saviour himself, surely he is never so dear, never wins so utter and so tender a love, as when we see what it has cost him to save us. Out of that love born of his suffering comes the new impulse after a holy life; and so when we stand at last purified by the power of a grateful obedience, it shall be said of us, binding our holiness and escape from sin close to our Lord's struggle with sin for us, that we "have washed our robes and made them white in the blood of the Lamb."—Phillips Brooks.

5, 6. (5) **none to help,** against these enemies. Notice that this whole passage does not refer to the suffering of the Messiah, but to the awful victory of Jehovah over His enemies. The blood is theirs, not his own on His garment. (6) **tread,** "and I stamped upon the peoples in my wrath, and broke them to pieces in my fury, and spilled their juice on the ground."—Pol. Bib. There was a fulfillment of this vision in the days of the Maccabæans, also upon the enemies of Messiah in the destruction of Jerusalem A. D. 70.

Supernatural Assistance.—The belief of a supernatural assistance is so reasonable, so consonant to our ideas of the Divine goodness and of human frailty, that philosophers, even in the heathen world, were sensible how much it was wanted, and have expressly asserted that, without Divine assistance, no man could make progress either in wisdom or virtue. What reason suggested to them, revelation has ascertained to us, which represents us as temples and habitations of the Holy Spirit.—G. Carr.

7. **mention,** here begins a new section, extending to lxiv. 12. Israel's Prayer: "A liturgical composition of great historical and theological interest."—Pol. Bib.[a] **according to all,** "as is seemly for all," etc.

Loving-Kindness of the Lord (vs. 7).—I. What there is in the loving-kindness of the Lord that deserves particular attention. 1. Its freeness and sovereignty; 2. Its richness and variety; 3. Its constancy and continuance. II. In what manner and for what ends we should notice it. —Simeon.

8, 9. (8) **for he said,** "the retrospect goes back to the beginning of the nation's history, when Jehovah's affection for the people was unimpaired." Comp. Hos. xi. 1; Ex. xv. 2. **children .. lie,** R. V. "deal falsely,[a] and He became to them a Saviour."—Pol. Bib. (9) **he was afflicted,**[b] nearly all commentators now reject this reading and accept, "No angelic messenger, but His own presence delivered them."—Pol. Bib. **in his love,** De. vii. 7, 8.

The Love of God.—Mr. Spurgeon, a few years before he died, went to visit a friend who had built a new barn on which was a weather-vane and on that weather-vane the text, "God is love." Mr. Spurgeon said, "Do you mean that God's love is as changeable as the wind?" "No," said his friend; "I mean to say that God is love whichever way the wind blows."—D. L. Moody.

The Kingdom of God.—

I say to thee, do thou repeat
To the first man thou mayest meet,
In lane, highway, or open street,—

That he, and we, and all men move
Under a canopy of love
As broad as the blue sky above;

That doubt and trouble, fear and pain
And anguish, all are shadows vain;
That death itself shall not remain;

That weary deserts we may tread,
A dreary labyrinth may thread,
Through dark ways undergound be led,

Yet if we will one Guide obey,
The dreariest path, the darkest way,
Shall issue out in heavenly day.

And we on divers shores now cast,
Shall meet, our perilous voyage past,
All in our Father's house at last.

And e'er thou leave him, say thou this
Yet one word more; they only miss
The winning of that final bliss,

---

miss our turn of service, and pass by those to whom we might have been sent on an errand straight from God." — Elizabeth Charles.

"A loving spirit is its own reward. Its love may not be returned, but its love cannot be lost. The gain of loving and its reward is—in loving"—Sunday School Times.

"The casting down of our spirits in true humility is like throwing a ball on the ground, which makes it rebound the higher towards heaven." —John Mason.

[a] "From this vs. to the end of the foll. ch. God's people are provided with a formulary of confession and supplication, couched in the elegiac form, pathetic and elegant." —Henderson.

[a] "The expression of a reasonable expectation of what the Jewish nation would have proved, considering the peculiar relation into wh. they had been brought to Jehovah." —Henderson.

[b] "'In all their affliction He did not afflict them,' i. e., so as to abandon them to it, or leave them in it, without pity or deliverance." —So the Targums.

"If there is a right thing to be done, and we seem to pass through a wrong thing on our way to it, depend upon it there's another way to it and a better one, and it is our own fault, and not God's, that we do not find it." —Edward Gannett.

Who will not count it true that Love,
Blessing, not cursing, rules above,
And that in it we live and move.

And one thing further make him know
That to believe these things are so,—
This firm faith never to forego,

Despite of all which seems at strife
With blessing, all with curses rife,—
That this is blessing, this is life.
—R. C. French.

10, 11. (10) **rebelled:** in all their history down to and including the exile. (Comp. xlii. 24, 25). **holy Spirit,**[c] "implies that in the Spirit Jehovah acts as a person. The way is prepared in the O. T. by the doctrine of the Malakh and the Spirit for the N. T. doctrine of the Trinity." —Oehler.[d] (11) **he remembered,** i. e. Israel remembered. **where is he,** for under judgment God seems to men as if He had forsaken them. **shepherd,** here Moses.

Vexing the Spirit (vs. 10).—The Spirit of God is styled—1. The Spirit of truth; 2. Of grace; 3. Of faith; 4. Of contrition and repentance; 5. Of love; 6. Of power and life; 7. Of holiness; 8. It is a heavenly Spirit. Show how in each case a man may vex the Spirit of God.—J. Howe.

Grieving the Spirit.—Among the weapons of the spiritual warfare we read of the "sword of the Spirit," as though the activity of the Christian depended on the Spirit. The highest attainments of Christian life have been made, not by quiet folk, who set themselves only on personal culture, but by active folk, who have gone forth to witness for God, taking their lives in their hands. Wherever there is shrinking back from active service—which is virtual rebellion—the Spirit is grieved. We are grieved when we see a man with great powers abusing or neglecting to use them. The Spirit would act through our energies, and is checked if we hold our powers back from him. And we suffer ourselves. The spiritual sluggard's garden will surely be like the natural sluggard's. Thorns and thistles will spring up and riot there. If he would but toil, and sow, and weed, and train, the dews and rains and sunshine would help on his work. This is the reason of our barrenness, not that we have had no dews from heaven, no Spirit of God with us, but that we have neglected our part of the work, and, withholding our loving obedience and active service, have grieved his Holy Spirit.—Pul. Com.

12—14. (12) **that led them,** etc., R. V. "that caused his glorious arm to go at the right hand of Moses," i. e. enabled him to work miracles. **dividing,** etc., Ex. xiv. 21. (13) **deep,** of the Red Sea. **wilderness,** i. e. prairie, flat pasture land, comp. Ps. cvi. 9. (14) **as a beast,** who goes down into the sheltered and fertile valleys for food and rest.[a] **caused him to rest,** i. e. brought him (the nation) to the resting place, the promised Land.

God's Constant and Personal Supervision of His People.—The following is an incident of travel in which light is thrown upon a beautiful expression of Isaiah, "That led them as an horse in the wilderness, that they should not stumble." Two English gentlemen were conveying their horses across the wilderness to be used in Palestine. The journey lasted for more than six weeks, and during all that time these horses were only occasionally mounted; they were led by hand almost every step of the way, being watched over with particular care by special attendants, that they might take no harm from the somewhat rude ordeal to which their owners thought it well to expose them. And when I saw those two horses led thus carefully through the rocky desert, and marked how carefully the guides picked out the easiest tracks for them, and paid continual attention to their food, and to their health, and to the state of their hoofs, which were sorely tried by the hard and burning soil on which they trod, I could neither help recalling this passage in Isaiah, nor recognizing in the picture an illustration of the prophet's idea. Each master would take the bridle of his steed upon his arm, and would walk beside him, encouraging him with kindly words. Especially when the track led over one of the frightful passes of the Sinaitic region, where a sort of staircase of slippery rock leads up or down on the

"God knows forever the thoughts of His creatures; Knows their true value. Therefore before Him It were but vain that a pretense were offered for true devotion." —Tracy Robinson.

c Ex. xv. 24; Nu. xiv. 11; Ps. lxxviii. 56, xcv. 9.

d Ac. vii. 51.

"A man who is filled with the Holy Spirit will have an undoubted assurance of his sonship; moreover he will be cleansed from the power and love of indwelling sin; he will be tempted, but will find that his inner nature is like a tinder-box which has become damp. The devil will still try to strike his matches upon him, but the man will not respond. He will be so saturated with the Holy Spirit that there will be no response as in other days."—F. B. Meyer.

a "As the cattle go instinctively down to sheltered places for their rest, so Israel was led to places of rest and security."—Mat. Arnold.

"A man who would have God's guidance must be willing to make spiritual things his main business." —H. C. Mabie.

"When God beckons you forward he is always responsible for the transport." —F. B. Meyer.

"Every regenerated soul sets out on its voyage with an invisible Captain

edge of a yawning ravine, the master would be sure to give his personal aid in guiding his terrified favorite safely over so perilous a place. I can fancy I see the picturesque group at this moment; the skilful Arab groom and the affectionate English master busied in restraining the snorting, rearing creature whose reluctance taxed all their patience and gentle force. One time they would cover his eyes, that he might not see all the danger that lay in front of him; at another they would urge him forward with mingled caresses and blows; sometimes they would stoop down to plant his feet in the securest spots, and when safe ground was reached at length, they would lavish a thousand endearments upon him, as though he had verily done something worthy of reward and praise, instead of owing all his success to the wisdom and care of his anxious guides.—Old Test. Anec.

15, 16. (15) **Look down,** Ps. lxxx. 14. **zeal,** R. V., where is thy zeal and thy mighty acts? The yearning of thy bowels[a] and thy compassions are restrained toward me. (16) **Abraham,** etc., though in exile, and seeming aliens, they yet were God's people. They humbly cling to their relationship, "Thou art our Father." **our redeemer,** R. V. "our redeemer from everlasting is thy name."

God's Relation to the Good (vs. 16).—Consider this as a fact—I. Most encouraging under trial. The word Father implies—1. Spiritual causation; 2. Spiritual resemblance; 3. Spiritual education; 4. Spiritual providence. Redeemer implies—(1) Original captivity; 2. Present deliverance. II. As a fact independent of man's acknowledgment, whether by—1. Politically; 2. Scientifically; 3. Ecclesiastically great men. —Thomas.

17—19. (17) **made us to err,** "by His great anger, revealed in these calamities, Jehovah had hardened the character of the people and made it seem vain to serve God."—Pol. Bib. (18) **possessed,** held possession of the promised land and holy city. **adversaries,** Babylon, and the other heathen nations. (19) R. V. "we are become as they over whom thou never bearest rule; as they that were not," etc., so far as the manifestation of God is concerned it would be hard to distinguish between Israel and the nations round about.[b]

Origin of a Wicked Heart.—A caviller once asked Dr. Nettleton of America, "How came I by my wicked heart?" "That," he replied, "is a question that does not concern you so much as another, namely, how you shall get rid of it. You have a wicked heart, which renders you entirely unfit for the kingdom of God; and you must have a new heart, or you cannot be saved; and the question which now most deeply concerns you is, how you shall obtain it." "But," said the man, "I wish you to tell me how I came by my wicked heart." "I shall not," replied Dr. Nettleton, "do that at present; for if I could do it to your entire satisfaction, it would not in the least help you towards obtaining a new heart. The great thing for which I am solicitous is, that you should become a new creature, and be prepared for heaven." As the man manifested no wish to hear anything on that subject, but still pressed the question how he came by his wicked heart, the doctor told him that his condition resembled that of a man who is drowning, while his friends are attempting to save his life. As he rises to the surface of the water, he exclaims, "How came I here?" "That question," says one of his friends, "does not concern you now; take hold of this rope." "But how came I here?" he asks again. "I shall not stop to answer that question now," replies his friend. "Then I'll drown," says the infatuated man, and, spurning all proffered aid, sinks to the bottom.—Whitecross.

CHAPTER THE SIXTY-FOURTH.

1—3. Prayer for a manifestation of God in His might. (1) **rend the heavens,** as at Sinai.[a] "The heavens appear to be regarded as an outspread tent." **flow down,** better, tremble, quake. (2) **melting fire,** R. V. "as when fire kindleth the brushwood, and the fire," etc. (3) **terrible things,** such were the signs at Sinai, and in the Exodus. **camest down,**

on board, who knows the nature of our sealed orders from the outset, and who will shape our entire voyage accordingly if we will only let him."—A. J. Gordon.

"So much we miss
If love is weak,
so much we gain
If love is strong,
God thinks no pain
Too sharp or lasting to ordain
To teach us this."
—H. H. Jackson.

a "A powerful argument is here drawn from the tenderness of parental affection, as formerly displayed in so signal a manner in behalf of the nation." —Henderson.

"It was a hard icy winter with them, because the sun had withdrawn." —Spk. Com.

"After all, God best knows what is best for us, and will assuredly do what is best for us. We are safe in his hands. In his own good time he will give us all that we need. Let us not be impatient, or imagine ourselves wiser than he. If he delays to give us that which we desire, we may be sure there is a reason for the delay. In quietness and confidence should be our strength."—Pul. Com.

a Ps. lxviii. 7, 8; comp. Ex. xix. 18.

"By the action of fire on dry twigs or brushwood, as also on water, noise is produced, and thereby the effect of the phenomena heightened." — Henderson.

Mi. i. 4; 2 Pe. iii. 10; Na. i. 5, 6.

i. e. Thy working for us was Thy coming to us, and such coming we ask again.

Prayer for Manifestations of God.—Men do not pray for "lightning" who duly recognize what the "light" is doing. Yet the silent forces are the mighty ones. Atmosphere does more than wind; dew does more than storms; moisture does more than rains. God works his best work silently, quietly. We think big things must make a big noise. It is true of our everyday lives; the things that make our happiness and success are not prominent things that happen occasionally, but the ten thousand little things that pass almost unheeded, and that seem to us too small to hold God. It is true of our spiritual life. Living in the warmth of the smile of God does more for us than any special times of manifestation. It is true of the kingdom of God in the world. It cometh on secretly, no man knoweth how.—Pul. Com.

b 1 Co. ii. 9.

"That is, although the mercies and miracles of the Exodus and of Sinai were great, yet God has greater in store for His ancient people the Jews. The Holy Spirit, speaking by St. Paul, teaches us that these words refer to the miracles and mercies of the Gospel." — Wordsworth.

"The poets fabulously fancied that the giants scaled heaven by heaping mountain upon mountain. What was their fancy is the Gospel truth. If you would get to heaven, you must climb thither by putting Mount Zion upon Mount Sinai." — Bp. Hopkins.

4. **eye seen,** etc.,[b] R. V. "neither hath the eye seen a God beside thee, which worketh for him that waiteth for him," i. e. from the beginning no man hath heard or seen a God to be compared with Jehovah, who gives His aid to those who wait upon Him. **waiteth,** implying faith, hope, and patient acquiescence.

The Unknown Blessedness of Heaven (vs. 4).—I. The subject of this declaration. 1. What God hath prepared; 2. For whom God hath prepared this; every one who waits upon God, none who are destitute of true godliness; 3. How God has prepared this; by His ordination and appointment, by the redeeming work of Christ, and the whole process of salvation. II. The declaration itself. 1. How far are these things known? we know the moral state, and the substance of the enjoyment; 2. Wherein are they so great a secret? we cannot conceive the mode and conditions of our future being. III. There are some means by which we may conceive the grandeur of the glory. 1. The cost of preparation; 2. The character of God; 3. What He actually gives of spiritual enjoyment now.

Man's Ignorance of God's Goodness to Him.—A very old weakness of humanity it is to try and find somebody who may be preferred to God, and this comes out of the fact that God is so very imperfectly known, or else is so very strangely misunderstood. A hint is here given us of the reason why there is so much misunderstanding of God—he has to be waited for. It is quite true of him that he is always working for us; but it is also true that he is often a long time in the working out of his purposes. Then, because men cannot get what they want done, done quick, they foolishly begin to think that God cannot do it for them, or will not do it for them. They fail to see the Lord's goodness. The point of impression may be, that in all the reviews we can take of the past, God has surely wrought good things, even if he has been long at the working. We may, therefore, cherish trustful thoughts concerning him, and be quite willing to leave the unfoldings of all the future in his supreme control.—Pul. Com.

a Ps. xcvii. 12.

b "The way of God's commandments, and of His providential dispensations." —J. A. Alexander.

Isa. lviii. 2, lxiii. 17.

c "The meaning of the whole is this: though we are now punished on account of our transgressions, yet as the ways in which God manifests His goodness are everlasting, we may confidently hope for deliverance." — Henderson.

"Unbroken continuity of mercy for the penitent." — Spk. Com.

d Le. xiii. 45, 46.

5, 6. . . (5) **meetest,** as a friend.[a] **remember . . ways,**[b] instead of walking in their own ways. **behold,** etc., "behold, thou wast wroth, and we sinned: in them have we been of long time, and shall we be saved?" **in those,** i. e. in the sins. Can we, who have so long lived in sins, yet be saved?[c] (6) R. V. "for we are all become as one that is unclean," etc., in the universal sin the prophet includes himself, comp. Ps. cxxx. 3; Isa. xliii. 27; vi. 5; Dan. ix. 4 ff. 18. **unclean,** i. e. as those excluded from the congregation.[d] **fade,** Ps. xc. 5, 6.

Human Mortality (vs. 6).—I. Consider the certainty and universality of death. II. Review the various phases of death. 1. Marvellous diversity in death-bed scenes; 2. Fading leaf reminds us of beauty in death. III. Reflect on the gradual approach of death. IV. Observe the season of death. The mission of the leaf is—1. To shelter the weary; 2. Delight the eye of beauty; 3. Nourish and bless the tree of humanity; 4. Proclaim the wisdom of the Creator. V. Ponder the cause of death. Apply:—1. A word of recapitulation; 2. A word of encouragement.—Stems and Twigs. Life as a Leaf.—The leaf has been a recipient from the trunk, drinking in its vital juices, but it has been giving as well as receiving; it has been absorbing sunshine and air and moisture, and has been passing these on to the trunk, doing this in the very act of decaying, so that when the leaf has fallen its most precious part remains behind. We are large recipients from the society to which we belong, but we should be continually giving as well as taking. Before we fall, and even as we fade, we may be, and should be, imparting wisdom and truth, all wholesome and helpful principles, a reverent and holy spirit, by which the community will be the better and the richer when we are no longer seen or even remembered.—Pul. Com.

"Leaves have their time to fall,
And flowers to wither at the north wind's breath,
And stars to set; but all—
Thou hast all seasons for thine own, O Death."—Mrs. Hemans.

7, 8. (7) **stirreth,** etc., rouseth himself from spiritual drowsiness. **consumed,** Heb. "melted." "Not Thy wrath, but our sin, is the fire which has consumed us." (8) The prayer closes (8—12) with a supplication that God will cause His wrath to cease. **our father,** 1 Chr. xxix. 10; Isa. lxiii. 16. **clay,** ch. xiv. 9; Ro. ix. 20, 21.[e]

The Neglect of Prayer (vs. 7).—I. The nature of prayer. 1. It is calling upon God; 2. It is taking hold of God; 3. It is stirring up oneself to take hold of God. II. The general neglect of prayer. 1. There are some who never pray; 2. Others who only occasionally lift up their hearts in prayer; 3. Others who maintain with constancy an external regard to this duty. III. The consequences of this neglect of prayer; those who are chargeable with this neglect will be visited with the tokens of God's displeasure. 1. He will not reveal to them His glory; 2. He will not manifest to them His love; 3. He will not communicate to them His blessings.—G. Brooks.

The Averted Face.—We are made to enjoy nature and men. We are constituted for every variety of joy. But as one nerve in agony can destroy all the rest of night, so a sin that separates us from God can darken all other joy. Even in the sweet summer-time, when holiday comes, we still need him. The golden-sanded bay, the landscape full of greens and greys, the iridescence of light through the clouds above the mountains, the scent of the pines, the delicate harmonies of color in the fields, the mossy carpet of the woods, the russet roofs of cottages half hidden in the blossoms of summer,—all these, so restful and refreshing, lose their charm if the Saviour's smile be absent, if we cannot hear his voice amid the groves and hills, and at evening feel "we have walked with God to-day." It was true in the old dispensation, when the revelation was through patriarchs, and prophets, and symbols, and sacrifices; but it is intensely true now, that we have seen God in the face of Jesus Christ—that God's averted face is the soul's severest punishment. We have come very near to God. No human priesthood intervenes now. We have boldness of access by faith to the throne of God. No veil is over the holy of holies now. We draw near through the rent veil—that is to say, Christ's flesh. Consequently enjoyment deepens; consequently also the sorrow deepens when I sin. Why? Because the more clearly I have seen the face, the more I feel its averted glance.—Pul. Com.

9—12. (9) **wroth very sore,** Ps. lxxix. 8. **all thy people,** this is reminding God of the covenant. (10) **cities,** plural bec. "if the land is holy all its cities are holy." The phrase does not occur elsewhere. **wilderness,** or ruin.[a] (11) **house,** or temple. **pleasant things,** or objects of desire. "Our homes, our cities, and all our dear associations." (12) **refrain,** from redeeming and restoring them.[b]

Intercessory prayer.—

When hearts are full of yearning tenderness
For the loved absent, whom we cannot reach
By deed or token, gesture, or kind speech,
The spirit's true affection to express;
When hearts are full of innermost distress,
And we are doomed to stand inactive by,
Watching the soul's or body's agony,
Which human effort helps not to make less,—
Then, like a cup capacious to contain
The overflowings of the heart, is prayer;

"The greater and more original a character is, the less dependent is it on the peculiarities of its environment. It is fed from deep well-springs within itself." — James Stalker.

[e] "Unable to mold themselves aright, they beg the sovereign will of God to mold them unto salvation, even as He made them at the first, and is their Father." —Fausset.

Be not afraid to pray—to pray is right.
Pray if thou canst, with hope; but ever pray,
Though hope be weak, or sick with long delay:
Pray in the darkness, if there be no light.
—Hartley Coleridge.

"And we may always be sure, whatever we are doing, that we cannot be pleasing Him if we are not happy ourselves."
—John Ruskin.

[a] "The picture exhibited of the state of Palestine, in this and the following vs. is still faithfully correct, as it has been for numerous ages past." — Henderson.

[b] Ps. lxxiv. 10, 11, lxxxiii. 1.

"Humility, like darkness, reveals the heavenly lights."—Thoreau.

"Full oft the lips that never part
Hold deeper prayers within the heart."
—Holahan.

The longing of the soul is satisfied,
The keenest darts of anguish blunted are;
And though we cannot cease to yearn or grieve,
Yet we have learned in patience to abide.—French.

CHAPTER THE SIXTY-FIFTH.

Pol. Bib. thinks this chap, parallel to lxvi. 1—5, as an attack upon the Samaritans. G. A. Smith, Delitzsch and others think it God's reply to prayer in lxiv. 1. **am sought,**[c] He has been nigh to His people,[d] ready to be sought of them and to answer them, but they have not responded. Present tenses in A. V. should be past. "Render: 'I was to be enquired of by those that asked not, I was to be found by them that sought me not,' etc. The first verb in each line is of the form Niphal, which is to be understood not as a simple passive, but in its tolerative sense: 'I let myself be enquired of,' i. e. 'I was ready to answer,' exactly as Ezek. xiv. 3, xx. 3, 31, xxxvi. 37: 'I let myself be found,' as ch. lv. 6. Jehovah's readiness to hear is contrasted with the people's unwillingness to pray."—Camb. Bib. **not .. name,** "that did not call on my name."

Good Out of Evil.—Some years ago a young man, in one of the civil wars in Syria, was out on a marauding expedition, and took, for his share of the plunder in an enemy's house, a Bible, which happened to be there; and on reading it he became enlightened, and in the end found the way of life and peace, and was afterwards the means of bringing many of his neighbors to a knowledge of the truth. A church is very soon to be organized in his native village (one of the highest on the range of Lebanon), and that young man is to be ordained its pastor.—F. H. Calhoun.

2, 3. (2) **spread .. hands,**[e] the attitude of invitation; Pr. i. 24. **rebellious,** see Ro. x. 21. (3) **gardens,**[f] ch. i. 29. **altars of brick,** lit. "upon bricks," perhaps with ref. to the flat tiled roofs of the houses.

"I Have Spread Out My Hands."—It is a thought full of deep pathos and Divine beauty, that God no less seeks men than they seek him. He in a sense prays them to be reconciled to him. While, therefore, prayer is in one aspect the going forth of active desires after God, on the other hand it is the response to his action upon us. Not a day passes but the gentle mercy and love expressed in his providence offers its silent plea to heart and conscience: "Child of man! I love thee; come to me, and be at peace."

4, 5. (4) **graves,** custom of worship of ancestors. **the monuments,** R. V. "the secret places," sacred caves, where familiar spirits were thought to dwell. **swine's flesh,** in sacrificial meals, a custom of all nations except Jews. **broth,** in wh. the meat was boiled, and having fragments of the abominable meat in it. (5) **holier than thou,** should be, "else I sanctify thee." "The words express no Pharisaic sense of superior virtue: they are addressed by a Mystagogue (see on lxvi. 17), or at least a member of a special religious fellowship, to the uninitiated, warning them against the dangerous degree of holiness (taboo) which would be incurred by contact with the initiated (cf. Ezek. xliv. 19). The situation becomes perhaps still more intelligible if we suppose the description to apply to descendants of the colonists settled by Assyrian kings in Samaria."—Camb. B.

Verse 5.—A deep insight is here given us into the nature of the mysterious fascination which heathenism exercised on the Jewish people. The Law humbled them at every turn, with mementoes of their own sin, and of God's unapproachable holiness. Paganism freed them from this, and allowed them (in the midst of moral pollution) to cherish lofty pretentions to sanctity. The man who had been offering incense on the mountain-top despised the penitent who went to the temple to present a "broken and contrite heart." If Pharisaism led to a like result, it was because it, too, had emptied the Law of spiritual import, and turned its provisions into intellectual idols.—W. Kay.

6, 7. (6) **written before me,** indicating that the sentence against the wrongdoers has actually been pronounced and recorded. **their bosom,**

[c] Ro. x. 20.

[d] "He has called His people, but in vain; they have been obstinately deaf to Him, unfaithful and superstitious. The unfaithful shall be punished; but a faithful remnant shall be saved and restored to Zion, and from them the promises shall take effect." — Mat. Arnold.

[e] Mat. xxiii. 37, 38.

[f] "The gardens and sacred groves of the false gods." — Mat. Arnold.

"From the very nature of salvation it is plain that the only thing necessary to make it of no effect is neglect. Hence the Bible could not fail to lay strong emphasis on a word so vital." — Drummond.

"It is well to organize charity to relieve destitution, but it is a thousand times better to practice charity,—kindliness is the true rendering—Love thy neighbor as thyself." — Albion W. Tourgee.

"Heaven's gates are wide enough to admit of many sinners, but too narrow to admit of any sin."—Howels.

fig. taken from the E. custom of carrying things in the ample folds of the **hyke or cloak.** (7) **incense .. mountains,** this is so often mentioned as a characteristic feature of idolatry.[a] **measure,** R. V. "therefore will I first measure their work," etc., i. e. appropriate punishment to their sin.

Men's Sins Recorded in God's Book.—As far back as the time of Moses, God announced through him that men's sins were "laid up in store with him, and sealed up among his treasures" (Deut. xxxii. 34). The later prophets (Mal. iii. 16), with the Psalms (Ps. lvi. 8), and the Revelation of St. John (xx. 12—15), speak of "a book," or "books, of remembrance," which contain the record of human frailty. The heavenly registers record the acts of men, both good and bad; and in one register seem to be written the names of those whom God regards as "living ones" (ch. iv. 3). This register is called "the book of life" (Rev. iii. 5; xiii. 8; xx. 12, 15). Such are the biblical statements on the subject. The expressions used are doubtless accommodations to human modes of thought, and are not to be taken literally. The great truth, however, which they convey is to be understood in the most absolute literalness. Men's sins will not be forgotten, even when they are forgiven. They are all registered in God's memory; and perhaps it may be found that each man's sins are also registered in some secret place of his own memory, though at present he is unable to recall the greater part of them.—Pul. Com.

8—10. "In spite of the gross idolatries denounced in the preceding section, there is that in Israel which makes it precious in the sight of Jehovah, and ensures for it a brilliant future."—Camb. Bib. (8) **new .. cluster,** "The juice that shall one day be wine is in the grape-cluster, and the grape cluster is preserved for its sake;" so Israel shall be preserved for the sake of the faithful remnant. (9) **my mountains,** Palestine regarded as a hilly country. (10) **Sharon,** the western coast from Joppa to Cæsarea.[a] **valley of Achor,** on the east side, by Jericho.[b]

The Plea of Faith and Pity.—That root that looks dead is not dead, and under careful nourishment it will revive. That soul that seems dead is not dead; there is a seed of life in it still; beneath all its folly, its waywardness, its vice, its guilt, there is a possibility of true repentance; there is a sensibility which will respond to patient, human love; there is a spiritual capacity which the truth of God, made mighty by the Spirit of God, will touch with renewing power, and from which unsuspected beauties and graces will arise. Within the ugliest and most worthless souls there may lie concealed germs of real nobility. Wait long, very long, before you abandon to destruction. Over them, and of them, the Divine voice may be whispering, "There is a blessing in them for the loving, patient, prayerful workman."

11, 12. A renewed threat against the apostates. (11) **forsake the Lord,** ch. i. 4. **troop,** R. V. "that prepare a table for Fortune, and that fill up mingled wine unto Destiny;" Heb. Gad, or luck. **number,** Heb. Meni, or fate, destiny. Babylonian names of two star deities.[c] The rites described are the lectisternia, well known throughout the ancient world, in which a table was spread, furnished with meats and drinks as a meal for the gods, cf. Jer. vii. 18, xix. 13, xliv. 17, 1 Cor. x. 21. A parallel in the O. T. religion is the Shewbread in the Temple (or Tabernacle). (12) **number you,** R. V. "I will destine you unto," etc. **called,** Pr. i. 24.

Neglect.—A man who has been poisoned only need neglect the antidote and he will die. It makes no difference whether he dashes it on the ground, or pours it out of the window, or sets it down by his bedside and stares at it all the time he is dying. He will die just the same, whether he destroys it in a passion or coolly refuses to have anything to do with it. And as a matter of fact, probably most deaths, spiritually, are gradual dissolutions of the last class rather than rash suicides of the first.—Drummond.

13, 14. (13) **eat .. hungry,** forcible contrast of the two lots, based upon the two characters. (14) **vexation,** lit. breaking. Contrast the truly broken and contrite heart.

Contrasted Lots.—Trust in God brings peace and heart-rest. Those who know what soul-rest is, find it easy to sing and give thanks. "The **joy** of the Lord is their strength." There is good cheer and high hope

---

[a] Isa. lvii. 7, etc.

"The earth is our workhouse, but heaven is our storehouse. This is a place to run in, and that is a place to rest in." —Secker.

"The kingdom of heaven is large enough when you get into it, but the gate is so low that you cannot come in save on your knees." —Talmage.

"The pure in heart not only see God themselves, but they become a medium for transmitting His thoughts to others. It is at last as if God were thinking through every look and movement of the purified soul." — Lucy Larcom.

[a] Isa. xxxiii. 9.

[b] Jos. vii. 24; Ho. ii. 15.

"The vine-dresser, as he is about to cut down a degenerate vine, espies a rich cluster on one part, and gives orders that the plant shall not be wholly destroyed; so shall it be now with the vines of Jacob and Judah." — Spk. Com.

[c] "The description admirably suits worldly and infidel characters, who not only have no regard for, but laugh at religion; have no god but riches, and regard human affairs as governed by chance." —Henderson.

Jer. xliv. 17, 18.

"Noble deeds are held in honor, but the wide world sorely needs
Hearts of patience to unravel this, — the worth of common deeds."
—Edmund C. Stedman.

in their souls. "God's servants shall rejoice and sing for joy of heart; they have constant cause for joy, and there is nothing that may be an occasion of grief to them but may have an allay sufficient for it. But, on the other hand, they that forsake the Lord shut themselves out from all true joy, for they shall be ashamed of their vain confidence in themselves, and their own righteousness, and the hopes they had built thereon. When the expectations of bliss, wherewith they had flattered themselves, are frustrated, oh, what confusion will fill their faces!"—Matthew Henry. Man is so constituted that nothing short of his highest good contents him. Earthly blessings, health, wealth, success, fame, power, glory, leave a void in the heart which nothing earthly can fill up. The worldling is always dissatisfied, always desires more than he has, craves some fresh excitement, desires some "new pleasure." "Hungry and thirsty, their souls faint in them" (Ps. cvii. 5). With God's servants the case is different. A Divine contentedness fills their hearts. They have been given to drink of a water of which "whosoever drinketh shall never thirst," but it "shall be in him a well of water springing up into everlasting life" (John iv. 14). They have God for their Saviour; they are at one with him; and in this communion they rest satisfied; they neither hunger nor thirst.—Pul. Com.

15, 16. (15) **slay thee,** put generally for "bring judgments on thee." **another name** "the names of their leaders will survive only in the speech of those who curse, but Israel will receive a new name as much greater than its present name as Israel was greater than Jacob."—Pol. Bib. (comp. Jer. xxix. 22.) (16) **God of truth,** "using such expressions as, "May the God of truth bless me." By the fulfillment both of His threatenings and His promises Jehovah will have shown Himself to be the God of truth, so that a blessing uttered in His name is certainly effective."

Hindrance to Receiving Blessings.—Why is there no water in the pipes of some of our houses in winter? It is not because the city has no water supply; it is not because the streets are not threaded all through their length from the great reservoirs with a perfect system of piping; it is not that the system of piping does not go into every house. Then why do we turn the tap in vain in our houses? Because there is a block of ice in the pipes. Why is the blessing not leaping and laughing like bubbling water through humanity? It is not because the great ocean and fountain of fullness is not there; it is not because the links of communication between Divine fullness and our emptiness are not formed. Christ is there, and his church is here, and all the channels and tubes and pipes of prayer and promise and supplication are there. What is wrong? There is ice in the pipe. That is the trouble. The frost has come on our hearts—we are frozen and need to be thawed out by the fire of the Holy Spirit.—John McNeill.

17. new heavens, etc., a poetical description of a great moral and spiritual renovation.[a] "With the breaking up of the heathen kingdoms and the restoration of Israel begins a new epoch."

New Heavens and New Earth (vs. 17).—I. The glorious prospect that is here set before us. 1. The event itself will be most glorious; 2. It may be fitly called a new heaven and a new earth. II. The feelings with which it should be contemplated. We should rejoice—1. For the benefits that will accrue to God's ancient people; 2. To the whole world; 3. For the honor that will arise to God Himself. Address—(1) Those who never yet have tasted of this joy; (2) Those who have reason to hope that this new creation is already begun in them.—C. Simeon.

The Divine Exultation on the New Creation.—It was said of the Creator at the beginning that he looked with complacent joy upon his works. All was very good. It was the "joy of God to see a happy world." How much deeper the Divine complacency in moral renewal! Note the emphasis and iteration of the thought. Rejoicing, exultation, is the very key-note of the passage; weeping and the sound of crying is to be as unheard as at the gayest scene of festival. And may we not feel that beneath all the sadness, the discord, the gloom of this enigmatic world, the prophetic pulse of the Divine creation, love, is ever exultantly beating? May we not believe that there is ever before his eye the picture, rising to clearness of outline and brilliancy of color out of Erebos

"Striving to be good is a very direct road toward Goodness; and if life be so tempered by high motive as to make actions always good, Faith is unconsciously won."—Donald G. Mitchell.

"Yet blessed, though neglected and despised—
Who for the world himself hath sacrificed,
Who hears unmoved her witless mockery,
While to his spirit, slighted and misprised,
Whisper the voices of eternity."
—Coates.

"We think of heaven as something that must visit us from afar, . . . But the new heaven and the new earth will only be the unveiling to us of what already is. . . . To-day, or never—here, or nowhere—is eternity."—Lucy Larcom.

a Isa. lxvi. 22; 2 Pe. iii. 13; Re. xxi. 1.

"The creation of the new heavens and the new earth began with the Gospel, and is consummated at the Second Advent."—Vitringa.

"Consider it
(This outer world we tread on) as a harp,—
A gracious instrument on whose fair strings
We learn those airs we shall be set to play
When mortal hours are ended."
—Jean Ingelow.

"The things of earth
Are copies of the things in heaven, more close,

and Chaos, of eternal day, of the new heavens and earth wherein dwell righteousness? There should be in every heart a prophetic sympathy, which should vibrate in unison with these oracles of God.—Pul. Com. The End of the Solar System.—When all the phenomena in the heavens indicate a law of progressive creation, in which revolving matter is distributed into suns and planets, there are indications in our own system that a period has been assigned for its duration, which, sooner or later, it must reach. The medium which fills universal space, whether it be a luminiferous ether, or arise from the indefinite expansion of planetary atmospheres, must retard the bodies which move in it, even were it 360,000 millions of times more rare than atmospheric air; and, with its time of revolution gradually shortening, the satellite must return to its planet, the planet to its sun, and the sun to its primeval nebula. The fate of our system, thus deduced from mechanical laws, must be the fate of all others. Motion cannot be perpetuated in a resisting medium; and where there exist disturbing forces, there must be primarily derangement, and ultimately ruin. From the great central mass, heat may again be summoned to exhale nebulous matter; chemical forces may again produce motion, and motion may again generate systems; but, as in the recurring catastrophes which have desolated our earth, the great First Cause must preside at the dawn of each cosmical cycle; and, as in the animal races which were successively reproduced, new celestial creations of a nobler form of beauty and of a higher form of permanence may yet appear in the sidereal universe. "Behold, I create new heavens and a new earth, and the former shall not be remembered."—N. Brit. Rev.

18—20. (18) **Jerusalem,** the new, regenerate Jerusalem. (19) **rejoice,** etc., a beautiful description of the millennial happiness of the Jewish people. (20) **infant .. days,** child and man shall alike attain to a patriarchal age. **hath not filled,** i. e. has become prematurely old. **shall be accursed,** "premature death, and even death in a moderate old age, shall be unknown; he who dies a hundred years old shall be considered as dying in childhood, or as cut off by a special malediction. The whole is a highly poetical description of longevity."—Alexander.

The Aged Sinner (vs. 20).—I. See the shortness of human life; a man a hundred years old is a wonder. II. See the long-suffering of God; He sees and hates sin, and yet delays the stroke for a hundred years. III. See the malignity of sin; there is no self-restoring power in the soul as is in the body. IV. See the inexhaustibleness of the curse; it is not exhausted by a century. V. See the claims of religion on the aged; depict the dangers of aged sinners.—G. Brooks.

Old Age.—Many an aged saint can testify to the continued goodness of God. Is old age a second childhood? God is a tender parent, unwearied in His attention. Is it a time of diminished comforts? One great comfort is still left, all the more soothing when others are gone. Is the old man lonely, like the last leaf which the storm has left clinging to the tree? The life-long Friend still remains, "when other helpers fail and comforts flee." And the result is that the aged believer is often a "grand old man" still bringing forth fruit, counselling others from his ripe experience, cheered by happy memories and glowing hopes, not frowning on the happiness of others, contented, trustful, loving, kind.

"On he moves to meet his latter end,
Angels around befriending virtue's friend:
Sinks to the grave with unperceived decay,
While resignation gently slopes the way.
And all his prospects brightening to the last,
His heaven commences ere the world be past."—Goldsmith.

21—23. (21) **and inhabit them,** not be cut off by death from enjoying their dwellings which they have erected. (22) **another inhabit,** they shall live long enough to enjoy the fruits of the vineyards they have planted. **days of a tree,**[a] Ps. xcii. 12, 13. (23) "They shall not labor for nothing, or bring forth children to see them perish."—Pol. Bib.

Life a Fine Art.—We grow up at random, carrying into mature life the merely animal methods and motives which we had as little children. And it does not occur to us that all this must be changed; that much of it

More clear, more near, more intricately linked, More subtly, than men guess."
—Edwin Arnold.

"A little Swedish girl was walking with her father one night under the starry sky, intently meditating upon the glories of heaven. At last, looking up to the sky, she said, 'Father, I have been thinking if the wrong side of heaven is so beautiful, what shall the right side be!' "

"The matter is not great whether our lives on earth be long or short, but whether we live the lives of saints, or the lives of sinners." — Mat. Henry.

"To resist with success the frigidity of old age, one must combine the body, the mind, and the heart; to keep these in parallel vigor, one must exercise, study and love." — Bonstetten.

We do not count a man's years, until he has nothing else to count."—Emerson.

a "Man's life shall have, instead of its present brief term, the far longer term allotted to the life of trees."—Mat. Arnold.

"A tree may flourish undisturbed in its home in Lebanon for one thousand years."
—Spk. Com.

must be reversed; that life is the finest of the Fine Arts; that it has to be learned with life-long patience, and that the years of our pilgrimage are all too short to master it triumphantly.—Drummond.

24, 25. (24) **before .. answer,**[b] contrast ch. lxiv. 7. (25) **wolf, etc.,** ch. xi. 6, 7. "All that can harm is to be done away. (comp. Hos. ii. 18, 23 ff; Amos ix. 13; Ezek. xxxiv. 25 ff, etc.). The nature of wild beasts is to be changed, comp. Isa. xi. 6—8."—Oehler. **dust .. meat,** i.e. serpents shall become harmless, and instead of preying upon beasts, or birds, or reptiles, shall be content with the food assigned them in the primeval decree, "dust shalt thou eat all the days of thy life," Gen. iii. 14.

b Ps. xxxii. 5; Da. ix. 20, 21.

"My altars are the mountains and the ocean, Earth air, sea, all that springs from the Great Whole, Who hath produced and will receive the soul."

"God hath sworn to lift on high Who sinks himself by true humility." —Keble.

Humility, that low, sweet root, From which all heavenly virtues shoot." —Moore.

"The means that Heaven yields must be embraced, And not neglected; else, if Heaven would, And we will not, Heaven's offer we refuse, The proffered means of succor and redress." —Shakespeare.

"It is a serious thing to live to have responsibility not only for your own life, but for your conscious and unconscious influence. No act and no word can be known to be without future consequences." —Mary Lyon.

"Faith is the root of all blessings. Believe, and you shall be saved. Believe, and you must needs be satisfied. Believe, and you cannot choose but be comforted and happy." — Jeremy Taylor.

Swift Answers to Prayer.—One of the wonderful revelations of the day that is coming will be God's showing us the many answers he sent to prayers of ours that never took shape in human words, that were no more than the outlook and uplook of our souls. The point impressed by the prophet here is that, by reason of man's sinfulness, delays in answering his prayers are often necessary, delay doing a very essential disciplinary and corrective work. But if a man were holy—in full harmony with God's will—there would never be any question about his prayers, never any need for delay in answering them. God could respond at once. "In man's experience of men, often, as things are now, in his relations with God, there is an interval between prayer and answer. In the new Jerusalem the two would be simultaneous, or the answer would anticipate the prayer."—Pul. Com.

CHAPTER THE SIXTY-SIXTH.

"The eternal blessedness of the True Israel; the doom of the apostates." The Pol. Bib. regards vss. 1—5, 17, 18, as addressed to the Samaritans. **1, 2.** (1) **Thus .. Lord,** "winding up the prophetic discourse with an express prediction of the change of dispensation, and a description of the difference between them."—F. A. Alexander. **my throne,** ch. vi. 1; Ac. vii. 48—50. **my footstool,** ch. lx. 13, "place of my feet." **house .. me,** R. V. "what manner of house will ye build," etc., comp. 1 Ki. viii. 27. (2) **hand made,** R. V. "hand made, and so all these things came to be;" he created the heavens and the earth. **poor,** etc., ch. lvii. 15. **trembleth .. word,** Ezr. ix. 4, x. 3. "These two verses contain one of the most explicit declarations of the spirituality of religion to be found in the O. T., anticipating the principle enunciated by our Lord in John iv. 24."—Camb. Bib.

God's Compassion for the Poor and Contrite (vs. 2).—I. Let us look into the import of each of these characters. 1. The poor, sensible of his own insufficiency, deep humility and self-abasement, sensible of his need of the Holy Spirit, an importunate beggar at the throne of grace; 2. Contrite, broken, bruised, heartbroken with fears; 3. Trembleth at My word. II. The Divine blessing bestowed upon them: He does not look as a careless spectator, but as a Father, Friend, Benefactor; His looks are efficacious, compassionate, discriminating. Consider—1. The perfection and condescension of God as illustrated by this subject; 2. What must it be to be out of His favor!—Pres. Davies.

God Revealing Himself.—A star in the far depths attracted the attention of an observer. It seemed to be a single star, but to his educated eye it resolved itself into two stars. Those two proved to be each a star, centre of a planetary system like our own. Those two stars, which seemed but one, were really distant from each other five hundred times the distance separating our earth and the sun. Who of us can conceive such sublime spaces as are thus unfolded? What must he be who walketh among the shining lights, whose throne rises higher than these stars, whose canopy is gemmed with myriad suns! And if the telescope can put such meaning into the figure of the heavens, the microscope puts equal meaning into the figure of the earth. God needs this whole earth for a "footstool." This great earth, with its giant trees, and inaccessible mountains, and unfathomable waters, and millionfold forms of life, cannot hold God; it is but a resting-place for his foot.—Pul. Com.

3, 4. (3) **killeth an ox,** merely as a formality. **as if,** i. e. he is as offensive before God as if his act were a direct violation of law. **lamb,** or kid. **dog's neck.**[a] refers to a form of heathen sacrifice. In each couplet a legitimate form of worship is connected with some idolatrous habit, and the meaning may be that certain Jews did both. (4) **choose their delusions,**[b] these are what they have chosen (vs. 3). "And I will choose troubles that will harass them and the things which they dread will I bring on them, because," etc.—Pol. Bib.

Words to the Faithful (vs. 5).—"Men who tremble at his Word." It is another way of describing those of humble and contrite heart. They are hated by their brethren; they have suffered in the cause of true religion. They are exposed to taunts—Where is their God? Let Jehovah show himself glorious! Nevertheless, his fiat has gone forth, "They shall be ashamed." Shame and pain are the inseparable effects of sin; the "wages assigned to it by the laws of Heaven;" the rightful inheritance of the sinner. Nor is there anything which the nature of man does so abhor as these. They are destructive of all our enjoyments. They touch both soul and body—shame being the torment of the one, and pain of the other. "The mind of man can have no taste or relish of any pleasure in the world while it is oppressed and overwhelmed by shame. Nothing does so intolerably affect the soul as infamy; it drinks up and consumes the quickness, gaiety, and activity of the spirit; it dejects the countenance made by God to look upwards; so that this noble creature, the masterpiece of the creation, dares not so much as lift up either his head or his thoughts, but it is a vexation to him even to look upon others, and yet a greater to be looked upon by them."—South.

"And still there are sweet souls who tread earth's ways
With peaceful hearts and faces strangely bright;
Some secret gladness seems to fill their days,
Some wondrous vision charms their inward sight;
Heedless of aught that hinders or delays,
They seek till death this Prince of Love and Light."
—Hunter.

5. tremble .. word, vs. 2, addressed to the faithful part of the nation. **said, Let the Lord,** etc., Camb. B. "have said, Let Jehovah show Himself glorious that we may see your joy"—a sarcastic allusion to the enthusiastic hopes entertained by the pious Jews of a manifestation of Jehovah to their joy. Cf. ch. v. 19. **and they,** R. V. "but they."

6, 7. (6) **voice of noise,** the Prophet here supposes the Divine deliverance and restoration to be taking place, and notes its suddenness and rapidity.[a] (7) A new section begins here, of the sudden restoration of the city. **man child,** "the sudden repopulation of the city by her children. The figure is taken from ch. xlix. 17—21, liv. 1; the fact set forth being the instantaneous return of the exiled Israelites, by which, without effort, the poor and struggling Jewish community becomes at once a great nation."—Camb. Bib.

The Call of God.—The one lesson God has taught me, if he has taught me anything in connection with the grace of God, is that there is such a thing as a divine plan in a man's life, and that the only wisdom in this world is to find out what that plan is and to be led into it step by step, and not to mind what is the end of it. There is much said about the divine call, little said about the end of it. Why? Because no tongue, not even the divine tongue, will attempt to tell what is the outcome of a life that is led of God. Even the Bible with all its majesty and divinity does not undertake to tell how great that life is which takes its way into the life of God; it only gives a clue by which we can find the way step by step. Only two patterns are possible. The Bible does not present a third. Every man must live the life of Cain, the first rejector of the gospel, or the life of Abel, the first believer. A man must live the life of Jacob the supplanter, or of Israel, the prince of God. He must live the life of Saul, the persecutor of the church, and of the Lord Jesus Christ Himself, or the life of Paul, apostolic in its tone, and spirit, and temper, and outcome. He will live the life of the old man, or the life of the new man.—H. C. Mabie.

[a] De. xxiii. 18 "The dog was an abomination according to Jewish law, possibly bec. it was venerated in Egypt." —Fausset.

[b] "Their wayward, childish follies, which in the end would mock them with grievous disappointment." —Spk. Com.

"We know not how much we love the world till we find pain and difficulty in parting with its good things." —Wilson.

"The higher a man is in grace the lower he will be in his own esteem."—Spurgeon.

"Extremes meet, and there is no better example than the haughtiness of humility." — Emerson.

"The humble man lives according to a rule, and with compliance to public customs, without any affectation of singularity."—Jeremy Taylor.

"Humility is the Christian's greatest honor; and the higher men climb the farther they are from heaven." —Burrows.

[a] "Four years before the Roman siege of Jerusalem, one Jesus, the son of Auanus, cried out in the temple and through the streets of Jerusalem — 'A voice from the East, a voice from the West, a voice from the four winds; a voice against Jerusalem and the sanctuary; a voice against bridegrooms and brides, a voice against the whole people.' " —Josephus.

8, 9. (8) **earth .. day,** R. V. "shall a land be born in one day?" comp. Ro. viii. 22. (9) **bring to the birth.** Should I arrange all the preliminary circumstances for the restoration of my people and stop there?—Cheyne. "The God by whom every thing has been already so far prepared, will suddenly cause Zion to become a mother; a boy, viz., a whole people after Jehovah's own heart, will suddenly lie in her lap, and this new Israel will build a temple for Jehovah."—Delitzsch.

The Restoration of Israel.—With great energy the thought is put before us that Israel in these last days has sprung into new birth and life. The gift of male children was especially dear to the Israelitish heart. Now there is to be a great and sudden increase of Zion's children. Something unlike the usual course of nature and of human affairs is hinted. Slow is the growth of vegetation, slow the growth of human institutions. Here an event as startling as the breaking forth of the tree out of the seed in a single day is contemplated; "a nation born at once!" In fact, Christianity is such a wonder. A plant out of a dry ground, mysterious in its origin, despised in its professors, humble in its early associations, yet speedily, almost suddenly, overshading the lands with its branches, and yielding fruit and healing for the nations. "The expansiveness of Zion is such that nought but Omnipotence will be able to check it; and as Omnipotence has no motive for checking it, Zion has nothing to fear in heaven or earth."—Pul. Com.

The Blessedness of the Restored Church.—Though the Church is frequently, if not even continually, oppressed and downtrodden by the world, yet a glory attaches to her, whereof no persecution, no contempt, no contumely, can altogether deprive her. She is, whatever the world may think or say, "the holy Catholic Church," with Christ as her Founder, with Christ as her Lord and Master, with Christ as her King, the oldest and most venerable society in the Western world at any rate, and one in which membership cannot but ever be a high honor.—Pul. Com.

10, 11. (10) **Rejoice,** etc., "then comes a call to the children, restored, or about to be restored, to congratulate their mother and to enjoy her. The prophet rewakens the figure, that is ever nearest his heart, of motherhood,—children suckled, borne and cradled in the lap of their mother fill all his view; nay, finer still, the grown man coming back with wounds and weariness upon him to be comforted of his mother."—G. A. Smith. (11) **consolations,** those granted so abundantly to her, in the mercy of her God.

God Delights to Comfort His People (vs. 10—13).—I. A general view of the consolations which God has prepared for His people. 1. In the work and offices of His Son; 2. In the fulness and stability of His covenant; 3. In the richness and variety of His ordinances; 4. In the gifts and trials of His ministers. II. A more particular view of them as represented in the image before us. 1. His attention to our wants; 2. His sympathy with us in our troubles; 3. His forbearance towards us in our perverseness; 4. His affectionate endearments. Address—(1) Those who are strangers to our Jerusalem; (2) Those who love and mourn for her.—C. Simeon.

12—14. (12) **peace,** wh. carries with it the assurance of prosperity. The word extend means turn, and it suggests that Israel had herself hindered the flowing of the stream of peace towards her. **glory .. Gentiles,** ch. lx. 4, 5. **her sides,** and **her knees,** should be "the side," "the knees," referring to the Gentiles who are to serve Israel, comp. lx. 4, xlix. 22. (13) **mother comforteth,** i. e. with an infinite tenderness. (14) **like an herb,** R. V. "like the tender grass."

God's Love and a Mother's (vs. 13).—I. God has a mother's simplicity of instruction. II. God has more than a mother's favoritism. III. God has more than a mother's capacity for attending to little cares. IV. God has more than a mother's patience for the erring. V. God has more than a mother's way of putting a child to sleep.—Talmage.

Carrying Children in the East.—Labor in the East, as in all uncivilized countries, falls principally to the lot of the women. It is possible that from this cause they cannot so well carry their young children in their arms, and hence the custom of their sitting across their mothers'

"What was it that gave the Apostles power to come forth into the light themselves, and shed the light in such effulgence upon a benighted world? Christ the Sun of Righteousness risen in their own souls."—W. E. Boardman.

"I believe there was a legislature that made a law and forgot to attach a penalty, and it was the laughing stock of the day. Do you suppose God has made a law without a penalty? What an absurd thing it would be! If God turned Adam out of Eden for that one sin, do you think he is going to allow us into heaven with ten thousand sins?" — D. L. Moody.

"It is the great design of the Gospel to restore us to holiness as well as to happiness. Hence the law, in the commands of it, runs through all the gracious dispensations of God to fallen man. Nor will God have any regard to them in a way of grace, who have no regard to His law in a way of obedience. The Gospel is not prepared for such as knowingly and wilfully renounce the law of God, which is holy, and just, and good." — Watts.

"Friends should not only live in harmony, but in melody."—Thoreau.

"You cannot stop the rivers. Dam them up a little while, and they are sure to gather, and flood the land until they can find the stream again and flow

hips, or, as rendered in Bible words, being "borne upon her side." For example, in India the women grass-cutters are out the whole day, searching for the fine grass required for the horses of the regiments. Towards evening they may be seen returning with their bundles on their heads. One hand is generally up to keep their burden in its right position, while the vacant arm is round the waist of a young child, seating across its mother's hip. It is astonishing, the ease and comfort with which, in this manner, they are enabled to carry their little ones; and how, with their arms comparatively unemployed, they can the more easily, and with less fatigue, perform the duties allotted them.

The Love of God.—

Like a cradle, rocking, rocking,
  Silent, peaceful, to and fro,
Like a mother's sweet looks dropping
  On the little face below,—
Hangs the green earth, swinging, turning,
  Jarless, noiseless, safe, and slow;
Falls the light of God's face bending
  Down and watching us below.

And as feeble babes that suffer,
  Toss and cry, and will not rest
Are the ones the tender mother
  Holds the closest, loves the best,—
So when we are weak and wretched,
  By our sins weighed down, distressed,
Then it is that God's great patience
  Holds us closest, loves us best.

O great heart of God! whose loving
  Cannot hindered be nor crossed;
Will not weary, will not even
  In our death itself be lost—
Love divine! of such great loving
  Only mothers know the cost,—
Cost of love, which, all love passing,
  Gave a son to save the lost.—Saxe Holm.

15, 16. "In fire and tempest—the accompaniments of the theophany —Jehovah will appear to take vengeance on His enemies. There is a connection with the last clause of vs. 14; but the passage reads like a continuation of vs. 6. Comp. ch. xxix. 6, xxx. 27 ff.; Ps. l. 3."—Camb. Bib. (15) **with fire**, the symbol of avenging wrath. (16) **plead**, or enter into judgment.[a] **all flesh**, not the Jews only, but all humanity.

The Purging of the Earth by the Destruction of the Wicked.—The kingdom of Christ cannot be fully set up in all its blessedness until the earth is prepared for its reception; and the main preparation required is the elimination from it of those wicked persons who, while they remain, must always constitute a disturbing element, inimical to the earth's peace and a hindrance to the Church's happiness. The teaching of Scripture is that, before the Church is finally established in the blissful position which it is intended to occupy, the removal of this element will have taken place. Partly by wars and tumults, by their swords being turned against each other, but still more completely by some miraculous outpouring of God's wrath, typified under the figure of fire, the wicked will be cleared out from all parts of the earth's surface, and only the godly will remain. The description of the day of vengeance is given, with the greatest fullness, in the Revelation of St. John (xix. 11—21), where, however, it is difficult to determine how much is imagery, how much literal description.—Pul. Com.

17, 18. (17) **behind one tree,** etc., Camb. B. "after one in the midst," i. e. following the actions of a hierophant or mystagogue, who stands in the midst of the brotherhood and regulates the important ceremony of purification. Comp. Ezek. viii. 11, ". . . seventy men of the elders of the house of Israel, and in the midst of them stood Jaazaniah the son of

on. So the cares and sorrows of life may seem to stop the good man's peace. But it cannot be; over and under and round the Divine waters will flow, find their way back to their channel, and flow on again."—R. Tuck.

"Our Father rules! Why should we shrink in fear?
Why should we mourn because our path is drear?
Why heed the the petty ills that line life's way?
Mere wayside weeds, they flourish for a day;
Immortal life is ours! and heaven is near!" — Julia A. F. Carney.

a Lu. xix. 27; Re. xix. 21.

"If thou desire rest unto thy soul, be just; he that doth no injury fears not to suffer injury; the unjust mind is always in labor; it either practises the evil it hath projected, or projects to avoid the evil it hath deserved." —Quarles.

"What greater calamity can fall upon a nation than the loss of worship." —Emerson.

"A contented spirit is the sweetness of existence."— Dickens.

"Oh, make us Thine! Teach us who waits best sues;
Who longest waits of all most surely wins.
When Time is spent, Eternity begins." — Helen Hunt Jackson.

Shaphan, with every man his censer in his hand." **swine's flesh,** vs. 3.[b] **the abomination,** a general term for unclean things, "swarming creatures."—Poi. Bib. **mouse,** an unclean animal acc. to Lev. xi. 29. "A dainty bit with epicures; was fattened by the Romans."—Delitzsch. (18) **gather all nations,** see Joel iii. 2; Zep. iii. 7—9.

The Jews to Convert the Gentiles (vss. 18—20).—I. God's purpose respecting the Gentile world—1. Proclaimed by all the Prophets; 2. Assuredly to be fulfilled in its season. II. The instrumentality by which He will effect it. 1. By the ministry of the Jews; 2. The success that shall attend their labor. Apply:—Of what importance the conversion of the Jews is to the whole world.—C. Simeon.

19. a sign,[c] i. e. perform a miracle which shall convince them of Jehovah's divinity. **that escape,** out of this general slaughter (vs. 16) of the enemies of Israel some shall be spared, and those Jehovah will send as his heralds to the yet other nations of the world. Delitzsch. **Pul,** perhaps Libya.[d] **Lud,** Eze. xxx. 5. **Javan,** i. e. "the Ionians, the Hebrew name for the Greek race." Camb. Bib., Ge. x. 2. **isles,** western lands of the Gentile world.

The Gospel is still the power of God unto salvation. For its attestation we need not go back to the first century. It cast the devil out of Saul and transformed the persecutor into the Christian missionary; out of Augustine, and made the graceless libertine the father of Christian theology; out of Calvin the "accusative," and made of the young lawyer the thinker of the reformation; out of John B. Gough, and made of the ruined drunkard, the apostle of temperance; out of Jerry McAuley, and made of the jail-bird the bishop of the fourth ward.—Peloubet. God's Glory.—What could the world give Christ that was not already His? What could it add to the position of one of whom it was said, "By Him were all things made, and without Him was not anything made that was made"? What could the world add to the glory of Him, who had been by the Father seated at His own right hand, far above principalities and powers and thrones and dominions with a name above every other name? There was but one new glory Christ could acquire—that of service and sacrifice. All crowns were already His, save one—the crown of thorns. His whole life was a ministry of love, of instruction to the ignorant, pardon to the penitent, healing to the sick, and comfort to the suffering.—M. D. Hoge.

20, 21. (20) **brethren,** Gentiles who accept the Christian faith. **offering,** "in gratitude for their deliverance the nations which have not suffered in the recent judgment bring the Jews of the Dispersion with reverential care to the spot upon which Jehovah's glory has so brilliantly risen, viz. Jerusalem (lx. 3, 9)."—Pol. Bib. (21) **of them,** i. e. of the Gentiles. **priests,** breaking down the barrier that confined the ministerial office to the sons of Aaron, and family of Levi.

Offerings to God.—Too often man has offered his temples as an act of sacrifice. He has given them to God in the vain hope that, satisfied with them, God would cease to ask for higher and holier things. We, indeed, in these days, flood no altars with the blood of sacrifices, yet do we not think to offer God rest in the beauty of our churches and the charm of our services? Are we not, even under this spiritual dispensation, offering God things instead of persons? And yet even we men cannot be satisfied with things; then how can we expect our God to be? Our hearts cannot rest in the artistic fittings of our dwellings, the creations of genius, or the associations of culture. We want love; we must have persons. We are "the figures of the true;" shadows in our feeling of the feeling of God. He, too, puts aside all the things we offer him, be they temple, or gold, or work, and persuasively pleads thus with us, "My son, give me thy heart." We may give him our things, if we have given him ourselves. Things dead cannot please him. Things alive with holy love, quickened by the humble, contrite, thankful heart, may find for him the rest he seeks. We may give him our buildings when they are alive with the spirit of consecration, our services when they are filled with the spirit of reverential worship, our works when they are animated with gratitude and devotion.—Pul. Com.

22—24. (22) **new heavens,** ch. lxv. 17. **your seed .. name,** as the re-

---

b "Swine are always spoken of in the Old and New Testaments with horror and disgust; partly on account of their dirty habits, the supposed unwholesomeness of their flesh, their occasional carnivorous ferocity, and, above all, their association with many forms of paganism."—Bib. Things.

c "A banner on a high place, to indicate the place of meeting for the dispersed Jewish exiles preparatory to their return to their land." — Fausset.

d "Phul is the country mentioned with Lud in Exe. xxvii. 10, and by him there called Phut, where the Greek and the Vulgate translate Libyans. An African people is meant, and an African people famous for the use of the bow, wh. the Ethiopians, for example, were."—Mat. Arnold.

"The Gentiles are here represented as using their modes of conveyance in bringing the Jews back to Jerusalem."—Fausset.

"The gift to be true, must be the flowing of the giver unto me, correspondent to my flowing unto him."—Emerson.

"The gift without the giver is bare."

"The church is weighed down to earth by bags of gold, and cannot lift itself heavenward. You will have to give an account of that which God has intrusted to you to be kept for Himself and not for yourself."—David Baron.

stored ones, the holy people. (23) "Month by month and week by week all flesh shall come to Jerusalem to worship, while the dead bodies of the rebellious Israelites shall remain as a fearful spectacle and an abhorring to all flesh."—Camb. Bib. **all flesh,** the new dispensation, in Christ, being in no sense exclusive, but embracing all humanity.[b] (24) **go forth** outside of the New Jerusalem. **worm not die,** Mk. ix. 44. "The resurrection of the ungodly first appears in Dan. but the transition to it is in this verse, where "it is evidently assumed that the corpses of the wicked are still endued with sensation."—Oehler. "The idea is that 'the mutilation of the body will have a corresponding effect upon the soul,' (Tylor,) hence this passage implies spiritual suffering, and unending."

Beauty of Earth and Heaven.—

I praised the earth, in beauty seen
With garlands gay, of various green,
I praised the sea, whose ample field
Shone glorious as a silver shield;
And earth and ocean seem'd to say,
"Our beauties are but for a day."

I praised the sun whose chariot roll'd
In wheels of amber and of gold;
I praised the moon, whose softer eye
Gleamed sweetly through the summer sky,
And moon and sun in answer said,
"Our days of light are numbered."

O God! O Good beyond compare!
If thus thy meaner works are fair,
If thus thy bounties gild the span
Of ruin'd earth and sinful man,
How glorious must the mansion be,
Where thy redeemed shall dwell with Thee!

Bp. Reginald Heber.

It is a perilous thing to separate feeling from action, to have learned to feel rightly without acting rightly. Feeling is given to lead to action. If feeling be suffered to awake without passing into duty, the character becomes untrue."—F. W. Robertson.

"For our idols are made from great fundamental desires and pleasures, which, so long as they are rooted and grounded in Christ, are good trees, bringing forth good fruit. It is the axe of selfishness that cuts them down, and makes from them idols, dead and deadening."—Amos R. Wells.

[b] "Every part irradiated by the glory of the throne of grace."—Spk. Com.

Introduction.

I. Title. So called from the name of the—**II. Author.** Jeremiah, a priest of Anathoth (i. 6) in Benj. He was son of Hilkiah, perhaps the Hilkiah who was high priest in the 18th year of Isaiah and discovered the Book of the Law in the house of the Lord (2 Ki. xxii. 8). Jeremiah was called to proph. office 70 yrs. aft. d. of Isa., in 13th yr. of K. Josiah (i 1). Some yrs. later Jer. came to Jerus., visited cities of Judah, prophesying about 40 years (ii. 6). Jehoiakim spurned his predictions, cut the roll in pieces, and burned it. Jer. rewrote it with additions (xxxvi.). Falsely accused, in the reign of Zedekiah, of deserting to Chaldæans, he was imprisoned. By order of Nebuchadnezzar he had the choice of going to Babylon, but preferred to remain with his own people. They, disobeying his message, went to Egypt, taking him and Baruch with them (xliii. 6), there he still sought to turn the people (xliv.), but we have no further acc. of him. Trad. says the Jews put him to death at Tahpanhes (Jerome). Jer. was contemp. with Zeph., Hab., Eze., and Dan. "The hist. of Jer. brings before us a man forced, as it were in spite of himself, from obscurity and retirement into the publicity and peril which attended the prophetical office. Naturally mild, susceptible, and inclined rather to mourn in secret for the iniquity which surrounded him than to brave and denounce the wrong-doers, he stood forth at the call of God and proved himself a faithful, fearless champion of the truth, amidst reproaches, insults, and threats. In Eze., on the other hand, we see the power of Divine inspiration acting on a mind naturally of the finest texture, and absorbing all the powers of the soul" (Angus). **III. Time.** B. C. 629-586. "The style of Jer. corresponds with the character of his mind; it is peculiarly marked by pathos. He delights in expressions of tenderness, and gives touching descriptions of the miseries of his people" (Angus). "His style, though inferior to that of Isaiah in power and sublimity, is marked by pathos and tenderness, in accordance with what seems to have been the cast of his mind. He excels in expressing and awakening the softer emotions" (Litton, Lowth). "On many occasions he is very elegant and sublime, especially in chaps. xlvi-li. 58, which are wholly poetical, and in which the Prophet approaches very near the sublimity of Isaiah" (Horne).

The character of Jeremiah is reflected in his writings. His speech is clear and simple, incisive and pithy, and though generally speaking somewhat diffuse, yet ever rich in thought. If it lacks a lofty strain, the soaring flight of an Isaiah, yet it has beauties of its own. It is distinguished by a wealth of new imagery which is wrought out with great delicacy and deep feeling, and by a "versatility that easily adapts itself to the most various objects, and by artistic clearness" (Ewald). In the management of his thoughts Jeremiah has more recourse than other Prophets to the law and the older sacred writings; and his style is rich in repetitions and standing phrases. These peculiarities are not, however, to be regarded as signs of the progressive decline of the prophetic gift, but are to be derived from deeper foundations, from positive and fundamental causes. The continual recurrence to the law and the frequent application of the prophetic parts of Deuteronomy, were prompted by the circumstances of the time. The wider the people's apostacy from the law of God extended itself, so much the greater became need for a renewed preaching of the law, that should point to the sore judgments there threatened against hardened sinners, now about to come into fulfilment. And as against the guile of false prophets, whose influence with the infatuated people became ever greater, the true witnesses of the Lord could have no more effective means of showing and proving the Divineness of their mission and the truth of their testimony than by bringing strongly out their connection with the old Prophets and their utterances (Delitzsch).

Synopsis.

(According to Horne.)

Introduction—Title, i. 1—3. Call of Jer. 4—10.

PART I.—PROPHECIES DELIVERED IN REIGN OF JOSIAH............ii.—xii.

Discourse 1 ....ii.—iii. 5.
Discourse 2 ....iii. 6—vi.
Discourse 3 ....vii.—x.
Discourse 4 ....xi., xii.

PART II.—PROPHECIES DELIVERED IN REIGN OF JEHOIAKIM.

Discourse 1 ....xiii.
Discourse 2 ....xiv., xv.
Discourse 3 ....xvi., xvii., 1—18.
Discourse 4 ....xvii. 19—27.
Discourse 5 ....xviii.
Discourse 6 ....xix., xx.
Discourse 7 ....xxii., xxiii., 1—8.
Discourse 8 ....xxiii. 9—40.
Discourse 9 ....xxv.
Discourse 10 ....xxvi.
Discourse 11 ....xxxv.
Discourse 12 ....xxxvi.—xlv.
Discourse 13 ....xlvi.—xlix. 6.

PART III.—PROPHECIES DELIVERED IN REIGN OF ZEDEKIAH.

Discourse 1 ....xlix. 34—39.
Discourse 2 ....xxiv.
Discourse 3 ....xxix. 1—32.
Discourse 4 ....xxx.—xxxi. 38.
Discourse 5 ....xxvii.—xxviii. 16.
Discourse 6 ....l., li. 1—58.
Discourse 7 ....xxi. 1—14.
Discourse 8 ....xxxiv. 1—22.
Discourse 9 ....xxxvii. 1—21.
Discourse 10 ....xxxii.
Discourse 11 ....xxxiii.
Discourse 12..........xxxviii., xxxix. 1—18.

PART IV.—EVENTS IN JUDAH FROM TAKING OF JERUS. TO RETREAT INTO EGYPT.

Discourse 1 ....xl.—xlii.
Discourse 2 ....xliii.—xliv.
Conclusion ....lii.

APPROXIMATION TO A CHRONOLOGICAL ARRANGEMENT OF THE CONTENTS OF THE BOOK.

(Cambridge Bible.)

Chaps.	
1—12	Josiah.
14—20	Jehoiakim.
26	1st year of Jehoiakim.
25	4th " "
[1]46—49	do. " "
35, 36	do. " "
45	do. " "
13	Jehoiachin.
29	(? 1st year of) Zedekiah.
27	do. "
50, 51	4th year of Zedekiah.
28	do. " "
[2]21—24	9th " "
34	do. " "
37	9th (10th) "
30—33	10th " "
38	10th " "
52	11th " "
39—44	Period of exile.

[1] Except 46, 13—28........................Period of exile.
49, 34—39 ....1st year of Zedekiah.

[2] But originally spoken at various times. See 22, 1.

CHAPTER THE FIRST.

1—3. (1) The words, not the usual introduction ("the word of the Lord which came," etc.) Eccles. i. 1 and Amos i. 1 are the only similar passages. **Jeremiah,** variously interpreted, Gesenius says "appointed of Jehovah"; Simonis, "the Lord's exalted one." **Hilkiah,** poss. the well-known high-priest of this name. **Anathoth,** Jos. xxi. 13, 18.[a] (2) **came,** lit. was, or began to come, from this time onward. **thirteenth year,** B.C. 629, the year after Josiah began his national reformations. (3) **Jehoiakim,** etc., Jehoahaz and Jehoiachin are omitted in this reference, for they reigned only three months each.[b] **fifth month,** when the city was burned by the captain of Nebuchadnezzar, and the walls torn down.

The young Christian.—The young Christian, trembling on the threshold of life of service, is equipped and comforted by his Master. I. The young Christian's fears, arising from sense of—1. Weakness, "a child," without influence, experience, stability; 2. Ignorance: how comprehend a theme into which angels desire to look? 3. Unworthiness: might not some one better known do the work required of him better? 4. Human opposition: he saw how men hate the truth. II. The young Christian's encouragements. 1. God sends him to work: "I ordained thee:" God will aid whom He sends; 2. Disclosure of God's purpose: no less God's purpose to send him than to save Israel; God's plan to use us, as well as to save others; 3. Promise of Divine presence: "I am with thee:" Wesley's saying, "the best of all is, God is with us;" 4. The message should be supplied, vs. 9: His words are spirit and life; wisdom and power of God. Learn:—(1) Advance courageously; (2) Expect opposition: "they hated Me before they hated you;" (3) Look constantly for Divine aid.—Hive.

Anathoth.—A poor village of some twenty houses, built among white rocks and white ruins, on a bare, grey mountain side. No trees, no verdure, no richness, nor grandeur, nor beauty; here, amid mountain solitudes and rocky dells, Jeremiah mourned and wept over the foreseen calamities of his beloved country .. One can trace in nearly all the images and illustrations with which his writings abound, the influence of those wild scenes amid which he passed his boyhood. Mountains, rocks, wild beasts, shepherds, are again and again introduced.—Porter.

4—6. (4) **word .. came,**[c] the way in which Divine messages came to the Prophets is never described. Probably they heard an inward voice; or felt an impulse to utter certain things. (5) **formed thee,** the figurative assertion of God's predestination of Jeremiah to the prophetic office, in fulfilment of the Divine plan.[d] **knew thee,** in the sense of "approved of thee" as a fit agent for My purpose, comp. Ps. i. 6; Gen. xviii. 19; Nahum i. 7. **sanctified thee,** in the sense of "set thee apart," dedicated thee to God's service, Judg. xvii. 3; 1 Ki. ix. 3; Lev. xxvii. 14. **ordained thee,** R. V., "I have appointed thee." **nations,** to other beside the Jewish nation, an O. T. prophet to the Gentiles. (6) **child,** either as young in years,[e] or as inexperienced.[f] This vs. emphasizes the fact that Jeremiah did not himself choose, but shrank from the office. Comp. Ex. iii. 11; iv. 10, 13.

Fears and comforts in prospect of labor for God (vss. 5—9).—I. The fears of God's servant in prospect of labor. 1. He feels his weakness, having no influence, no experience, being unstable; 2. He feels his ignorance; 3. His unworthiness; 4. He dreads the enmity of man. II. The comforts of God's servants in the prospect of labor. 1. The assurance they are called to the work; 2. The knowledge of the purpose of God; 3. The promise of the presence of God; 4. The fact that the message is from God.—Stems and Twigs.

Jeremiah.—

I am the man sore smitten with the wrath
Of Him who fashion'd me; my heart is faint,

---

[a] Josephus says this town is 20 stadia distant fr. Jerusalem, and Jerome describes it as three Rom. miles north of that city.

"Dr. Robinson considers the present Anâta to occupy the site of this ancient town, portions of the wall of which, as also the foundations of some of the houses, still remain."—Henderson.

[b] "The first and last of the kings under whom each Prophet prophesied are often thus specified in the general title."—Fausset.

Plato, seeing a child do mischief, went and corrected the father for it.—Hom. Com.

"Joy is a prize unbought, and is freest, purest in its flow when it comes unsought."—Horace Bushnell.

[c] "This call was part of Jeremiah's first address to the people. It was no afterthought, but a public proclamation, by wh. from the first he stood forth, claiming to act by an external authority, and to speak not his own words, but those of Jehovah."—Spk. Com.

[d] Is. xlix. 1, 5.

[e] It is supposed that at his call Jeremiah was under 25 years of age.

[f] For the reluctance of men to do God's work, comp. Ex. iv. 10, vi. 12, 30; Jno. i. 3.

"We must be little children in our own sight, in order to be prophets."—Wordsworth.

And crieth out, Spare, spare, O God! Thy saint;
But yet with darkness doth He hedge my path.

My eyes with streams of fiery tears run down
To see the daughter of my people slain,
And in Jerusalem the godless reign.
Trouble on trouble are upon me thrown;

Mine adversaries clap their sinful hands
The while they hiss and wag their heads, and say,
"Where is the temple but of yesterday—
The noblest city of a hundred lands?"
We do confess our guilt; then, Lord, arise,
Avenge, avenge us of our enemies!

—G. Smith.

"Selfdistrust is the first proof we give of having obtained a knowledge of ourselves."—Zimmerman.

7—10. (7) **Say not,** etc., comp. Ex. vi. 30, vii. 1, 2. **thou shalt go,** he would need to go only where he was sent, and speak what he was commanded. (8) **of their faces,** R. V., "because of them," kings, and priests, foreigners and evil men at home, to whom, he knew, the word of prophecy must be spoken. **I am with thee,** the usual and all sufficing assurance.[a] (9) **touched my mouth,**[b] as a symbol of the gift of prophetic speech. (10) **set thee over,** lit. "made thee an over-seer," Hebrew term corresponding to "Episcopos" in N. T. a bishop of the nations, to consider their moral and spiritual life, **build .. plant,** that which God is to do, the prophet, His messenger, is said to do; to "pull down" and to "build up."

[a] Ex. iii. 12; De. xxxi. 8; Jos. i. 5.

[b] Comp. Is. vi. 7, li. 16.

"The sign-posts that point the way by the side of the road, never have a quotation of poetry upon them, or sentences from Isocrates or Sophocles. There is just the word, and that is enough."—C. H. Spurgeon.

Obedience.—We can have no idea what we should be able to do if we were completely lost in accord with God; if we sought no will but His; if not a word of our mouths, not a beat of our hearts, not a thought of our minds, not a movement of our souls or bodies but were turned to Him obediently, in the spirit of Samuel, "Speak Lord, for thy servant heareth." There have been men who have shown what a man can do, —a Luther, a Calvin, a St. Paul, a Moses—these men have shown what a man can do when he only seeks to obey the will of God.—A. Monod.

11—16. The call is enforced by two visions. (11) **seest thou,** this indicates that God guided the Prophet by visions, **rod,** or branch, **almond tree,** "the Hebrew used here (shâkêd) is not the ordinary word for an almond tree, but a poetical expression, meaning that which is awake, and referring to the blossoming of this tree as taking place while others are still in their winter sleep. Accordingly the almond tree is made the subject of this vision—an 'emblem of wakefulness and activity,' as is shewn by the interpretation given in vs. 12." Camb. Bib.[a] (12) **hasten,** R. V. "I watch over," i. e. this is my emblem. I am awake to my word, and will perform it. The day of the revelation of Jehovah is near at hand. (13) **toward,** R. V. "from," i. e. leaning to the south, and will presently spill out its contents. **north,** the district of the Chaldæans.[b] (15) **families .. north,** all the clans, or races of the kingdoms. The great empire is composed of many provinces. **his throne,** as in a judicial act, the princes of the north will place their thrones over against Jerusalem and judge her for her crimes.[c] (16) **judgments,** by this means (vss. 14, 15) I will voice my condemnation upon Judah.

[a] It is the first of trees to blossom, and hence the Romans applied to it the epithets "vigilant" and "watchful." Its blossoms, which are white and plentiful, burst forth in January, even before the leaf-buds appear.

[b] The seething pot is a figure of the Chaldæans; and the conception seems to be that it will boil over, and the contents pour down to the desolation of Jerusalem.

Lit., fromthe face of the region situated towards the north.

[c] "Or 'Each prince shall pitch his royal pavilion, with all the marks of sovereignty belonging to it, in token of having obtained a complete victory, and taken entire possession of the city.'"—Lowth.

The Almond Tree in Blossom.—A little after sunrise, went out by the Jaffa gate, and, turning to the left, took the path that winds down the slope of Zion. As I went along, the pleasant sound of bees, "the wild bees of Palestine," clustering over the pink blossoms of an almond tree on the left, greeted me. The tree itself, all flower, without a single leaf, was a gay contrast to the dark olives below. A few days ago it was brown and bare; to-day it is all brightness; and to this sudden change reference is made when Jeremiah is taken to one of the orchards of Anathoth and bidden look at the "rod of the almond tree," for it is added, "I will hasten My word to perform it."—Bonar.—Note on vs. 13.—To compensate in some measure for the scarcity of fuel, the Orientals endeavor to consume as little as possible in preparing their victuals. For this purpose they make a hole in their dwellings, about a foot and a half deep, in which they put their earthen pots, with the meat in them, closed up, about the half above the middle, three fourth parts they lay about with stones, and the fourth part is left open, through which they fling in any combustible substances they can procure, which burn immediately, and produce so great a heat, that the pot becomes as hot as if it stood over a strong fire of coals; so that they boil their meat with greater expedition and much less fuel than it can be done upon the hearth. The hole in which the pot is set has an aperture on one side, for the purpose of receiving the fuel, which seems to be what Jeremiah calls the face of the pot. "I see," said the Prophet, "a pot, and the face thereof is towards the north;" intimating that the fuel to heat it was to be brought from that quarter. This emblematical prediction was fulfilled when Nebuchadnezzar, whose dominions lay to the north of Palestine, led his armies against Jerusalem, and overturned the thrones of the house of David.—Paxton.

"In the destruction of Jerusalem the Chaldæans would but fulfil the purposes and councils of God."—Henderson.

"Even the world honors consistency and courage, and the plainest speaker will have, in general, the most hearers. The only part by which a bull can be safely taken is the horns."—Power.

"Out of the North."—The swelling waters of a flood, are a usual type of an overwhelming calamity (Ps. lxix, 1, 2), and especially of a hostile invasion (Isa. viii. 7, 8); but this is a flood of scalding waters, whose very touch is death. The caldron represents the great military empires upon the Euphrates. . . . The tide of passion and carnage is sure finally to pour itself upon Judea. The caldron looks ominously towards Jerusalem, but it has not yet overturned; and if Judah repent, God may make it exhaust its fury upon itself (Nineveh and Babylon being in conflict), or a defeat instead of victory at Charchemish may alter the whole tide of events. But if Judah remain impenitent, it must become the prey of whosoever conquers in the plains of Mesopotamia.—Speaker's Com.

17—19. (17) **gird .. loins,** the sign of earnest preparation for work.[a] **confound,** marg., "break to pieces." (18) **a defenced city,** i. e. like one, guarded well round with Divine defences.[b] **iron pillar,** symbol of his Divinely strengthened will. **the kings,** viz.: Josiah, Jehoahaz, Jehoiakim, Jehoiachin, Zedekiah. (19) **not prevail,** "they shall no more prevail against thee, than they could against an impregnable wall or fortress." Reference is made to this again, xv. 20, 21. Comp. Ps. cv. 15.

Opposition (vs. 19).—In proportion as we are faithful to God we are assailed by man. I. The vehemence of our foes, "fight against thee;" they do not fight against principle so much as against persons. II. The certainty of our security, "they shall not prevail." Saints may be weary, maimed, fearful; but not, in the end, defeated. III. The source of our confidence. 1. The abiding presence of the Lord; 2. The constant manifestation of the power of the Lord.—Stems and Twigs.

Courage before Kings.—Said the Roman emperor to Chrysostom, "I will banish thee." "Thou canst not," was his answer, "for the world is my Father's house." "Then will I kill thee." "That is not in thy power, for my life is hid with Christ in God." "I will deprive thee of all thou possessest." "Nay, for my treasure is in heaven, and my riches are within me." "But I will exile thee, that thou shalt not have a friend or companion left." "Neither canst thou do that; for my Friend is He who will never leave me, and from whom none can sever me. I defy thee, proud emperor; thou canst do me no harm at all!"

[a] Job xxxviii. 3; 1 Pet. i. 13.

"And how can man die better
than facing fearful odds,
For the ashes of his fathers, and
the temple of his gods."
—Macaulay.

"He holds no parley with unmanly fears;
Where duty bids he confidently steers,
Faces a thousand dangers at her call,
And trusting in his God, surmounts them all."
—Cowper.

[b] Comp. Eze. iii. 9. Also Je. xv. 20, xxiii. 18, etc., xxvi. 10, xxxv. 15, xxxviii. 16.

CHAPTER THE SECOND.

1—4. (1) **Moreover,** this first prophecy is recorded in chapters ii.—vi. given (iii. 6) during the reign of Josiah. (2) **ears of Jerusalem,** i. e. in the most public places where audience is to be gained. **remember thee,** or, for thee; what thou hast so strangely forgotten. **kindness,** i. e. Israel's early affection for Jehovah. "Israel is here represented as a young bride."[c] The reference is to the forty years in the wilderness of Sinai.[d] (3) **holiness,** i. e. a consecrated thing. (Lev. xxii. 10, the same word is used.) **devour him,** i. e. Israel who has just been spoken of as

[c] Eze. xvi. 9; Ho. ii. 20; Joel i. 8.

[d] "Prob. the vs. is intended to set forth the zeal and piety they had evinced at that early period, and which were as strikingly contrasted with their idolatrous practices at the time of the Prophet."—Henderson.

"consecrated," and "first fruits." Those who "devour him" are the enemies of Israel when they attacked Israel. **offend,** R. V., "be held guilty," as one, not a priest, who should eat of the sacred "first-fruits." (4) **Jacob . . Israel,** the whole nation is addressed.

The Ingratitude of Men (vss. 4—6).—Here we are called to consider—I. The complaint he makes; it may be urged against us, for there is—1. The same folly; 2. The same ingratitude. II. His challenge in relation to it. 1. Have you ever found Him a hard master? 2. Or less gracious or merciful than He professed to be? Tell me then—(1) What will ye say in justification of yourselves? 2. What line of conduct will ye henceforth pursue?—Simeon.

"I remember thy youth."—The retrospect on youth is too often like looking back on what was a fair and promising country, but is now desolated by an overwhelming torrent. Or it is like visiting the grave of a friend whom we have injured, and are precluded by his death from the possibility of making him an atonement.—J. Foster.

5—8. (5) **What iniquity,** R. V., "unrighteousness,"[e] What act of mine explains this unfaithfulness? Comp. Isa. v. 4. **vanity,** the usual description of idols, and idolatrous worship.[f] **become vain,** its worshipers acquiring its character,[g] Ps. cxv. 8. (6) **Led . . wilderness,** comp. De. viii. 15, 16, xxxii. 10.[h] **deserts,** etc., they seem to have forgotten and to be ungrateful for God's past wonderful goodness.[i] (7) **plentiful country,** lit. a Carmel-land. The fertile district of Carmel being made to represent the whole land.[k] (8) **handle the law,** i. e. Levites comp. Deut. xxiii. 10. **pastors,** R. V. "rulers," i. e. kings. **prophets, i. e. those who received** and communicated special Divine messages.

Three Shameful Possibilities of Human Life (vss. 6—8).—I. The possibility of dishonoring the great memories of life. 1. As when the vividness of their recollection fades; 2. When their moral purpose is overlooked or misunderstood; 3. When their stimulating and strengthening function is suspended. II. The possibility of under-estimating the interpositions of God. 1. Remember the Deliverer; 2. And the Giver. III. The possibility of the leading minds of the Church being darkened and perverted. 1. Such men should watch themselves with constant jealousy; 2. Such men should never be forgotten by those who pray.—J. Parker.

Note on vs. 6.—When the Prophet describes this wilderness, according to our version, as the land of the shadow of death, his meaning has been differently understood by different people. Some have supposed it to mean a place where there were no comforts or conveniences of life, but this seems too general; and to explain it as a particular and distinct member of the description, pointing out some quality different from the other circumstances mentioned by Jeremiah, seems to be a more just, as it is undoubtedly a more lively way of interpreting the Prophet. Others have accordingly understood this clause as signifying, it was the habitation of venomous serpents, or destroying beasts; some as endangering those that passed through it, as being surrounded by the hostile tribes of Arabs; some as being overshadowed by trees of a deleterious quality. They might better have introduced the whirlwinds of those southern deserts than the last particular, which winds, taking up the sand in great quantities, darken the air, and prove fatal to the traveler. This last would be giving great beauty and energy to the expression (the shadow of death), since these clouds of dust, literally speaking, overshadow those that have the misfortune to be then passing through those deserts, and must, at the same time, give men the utmost terror of being overwhelmed by them, and not unfrequently do in fact prove deadly. Another clause, a land of pits, is also a part of the Prophet's description. Irwin affords a good comment on this part of our translation: in the one place he says, "The path winded round the side of the mountain, and to our left, a horrid chasm, some hundred fathoms deep, presented itself to our view. It is surprising no accident befell the loaded camels." In another, "On each side of us were perpendicular steeps some hundred fathoms deep. On every part is such a wild confusion of hanging precipices, disjointed rocks, and hideous

[e] Mi. vi. 8.

[f] Je. x. 15, xiv. 14, 22, xvi. 19; 1 Co. viii. 4.

[g] "A people's character never rises above that of its gods, wh. are its 'better nature.'" — Bacon.

[h] Is. lxiii. 9, 11, 13; Ho. xiii. 4, 5.

[i] "A more frightful desert it had hardly been our lot to behold. The mountains beyond presented a most uninviting and hideous aspect; precipices and naked conical peaks of chalky and gravelly formation, rising one above another, without a sign of life or vegetation."—Robinson.

[k] Is. x. 18, xvi. 10, xxxvii. 24.

"Unthankfulness is a monster in nature, a solecism in manners, a paradox in divinity, a parching wind to dry up the fountain of further favor." — Trapp.

"The Dead Sea drinks in the Jordan, and is never the sweeter; and the ocean all rivers, and is never the fresher; thus, we take all God's mercies with insensibility."

"After we had passed the salt desert, we came to the Malek-el-moat-dereh, or the valley of the angel of death. This extraordinary appellation, and the peculiar nature of the whole of this tract of land, broken into deep ravines, without water, of a dreariness without example, will, perhaps, be found forcibly to illustrate Jer. ii. 6." —Morier.

"Gratitude is the fairest blossom, which springs from the soul; and the heart of man knoweth none more fragrant." —Hosea Ballou.

"A common lamp may go out, but if the light on a lighthouse goes out or is misplaced, it leads great ships on to the rocks."

chasms, that we might well cry out with the poet, 'Chaos is come again.' Omnipotent Father! to Thee we trust for our deliverance from the perils that surround us. 'It was through this wilderness that Thou didst lead Thy chosen people.' It was here Thou didst manifest thy signal protection, in snatching them from the jaws of destruction which opened upon every side." And in the next page, "At two o'clock we came suddenly upon a dreadful chasm in the road, which appears to have been the effect of an earthquake. It is about three hundred yards long, one hundred yards wide, and as many deep; and, what is a curiosity, in the middle of the gulf, a single column of stone raises its head to the surface of the earth. The rudeness of the work, and the astonishing length of the stone, announce it to be lusus naturæ, though the robbers declared to us that beneath the column there lies a prodigious sum of money; and added, with a grave face, they have a tradition, that none but a Christian's hand can remove the stone to come at it. We rounded the gulf, which was called Somah, and leaving it behind us, we entered a valley where we found a very craggy road." The first clause in this passage, through a land of deserts, is the most obscure and difficult to ascertain. Instead of traveling in the night, as he had proposed, to avoid the burning heat of the sun, he says, "At seven o'clock we halted for the night. The Arabs tell us that the roads are too rugged and dangerous to travel over in the dark." Under the next day, "we reached the foot of a prodigious high mountain, which we cannot ascend in the dark." The following day, he tells us, "by six o'clock we had accoutred our camels, and leading them in our hands, began to ascend the mountain on foot; as we mounted the steep, we frequently blessed ourselves that we were not riding, as the path was so narrow, the least false step must have sent the beast down the bordering precipice." Under another day he remarks that the greatest part of that day's journey was "over a succession of hills and dales, where the road was so intricate and broken, that nothing but a camel could get over it. The appearance of the road is so frightful in many places, that we do not wonder why our people have hitherto lain by in the night."—Harmer.

9—13. "In these five verses, the apostasy of Israel from his own God is held up as a fact unique in history—unexampled and inexplicable. Whether you look westward or eastward, across the sea to Cyprus, or beyond Gilead to the barbarous tribes of the Cedrei (Ps. cxx. 5), nowhere will you find a heathen people that has changed its native worship for another." Exp. Bib. (9) **plead,** as in a court of law.[a] **children's children,**[b] who will further develop the idolatry and rebellion. (10) **isles of Chittim,**[c] coast lands of the Mediterranean. **Kedar,** fig. for the Eastern lands.[d] (11) **changed their gods,** the tenacity with which men keep hold of national religions has always been very marked. **their glory,** Him who, because the only true God, was their chief glory. (12) **very desolate,** or dry. The heavens are called on to shrivel up in horror at such conduct. (13) **broken cisterns,**[e] such as have cracks or rents, through which the water wastes away.

The Fountain and the Cistern (vs. 13).—In these two evils we have all the sins of the people summed up,—apostasy and self-sufficiency. I. The fountain forsaken. 1. Its nature; 2. Its contents,—God, a Fountain of cleansing influence—of cheering influence—of reviving power—of fertilising results. This fountain is forsaken when men cease to think of God as the chief end of their life—when they overlook the law of God—when they do not cleave to the word of God—when they are beginning to look back to old times of bondage—when they look away from the cleansing fountain to their own works. II. The cistern preferred. 1. Domestic happiness; 2. Professional life; 3. Intellectuality; 4. Social life. III. The disappointment involved. 1. That of one who has spent his best time and strength to no purpose; 2. Of one who must after all go to the rejected fountain; 3. Who finds that his past life has been a grievous sin.

Idolatry.—We perceive, as much from the words of the prophet as from the history, that this idolatry has now become deep and radical. The state of mind latent in them is the utter incapacity for ac-

[a] "The expression is taken from the pleas of plaintiff and defendant, used in a court of justice."—Lowth.

[b] "This expression is designedly used, to intimate that the final judgment on the nation would be suspended for many generations." —Horsley.

[c] See Kittim, Ge. x. 4.

[d] Ge. xxv. 13; Ps. cxx. 5; Cant. i. 5.

[e] "The usual plan is to dig a tank in the ground, build round with stonework, sometimes raising this several feet above the ground, and putting on it a roof. These cisterns are very liable to crack and leak, esp. those near the surface of the ground and unscientifically constructed; and no more expressive fig. of un-

knowledging a God not appealing to the senses, which Jeremiah discovers in his contemporaries. He boldly sets up the faith of the heathen as a lesson to the Israelites.—"Kings and Prophets;" Maurice.

"A long course of sin was needed so to deaden and blind the heart of man as to make idolatry possible. Age after age gave in its contribution, so that, besides the original sin of each man, there was a sinful tradition of mankind. Every generation bequeathed to the next a further measure of declension from God."—Manning.

14—19. (14) **slave?** God called him to be son, not slave, Ex. iv. 22. **why .. spoiled?** R. V., "become a prey." The answer must be on account of his sins, so he must not charge God with his calamities. (15) **young lions,** when the land was depopulated it actually became the haunt of lions. (2 Ki. xvii. 25.) (16) **Noph, Tahapanes,**[a] places in Egypt. **broken .. crown,** marg. "feed on thy crown," or devour the best part of thy country; refers to the tax which Egypt levied on Judah during the alliance with Jehoiakim. (17) **unto thyself,** by thy own doings. (18) **way of Egypt,** in vss. 18—28 the people are reproached with seeking help alternately of Assyria and Egypt and of devotion to gods which cannot aid them. (Driver.)[b] (19) **correct,** i. e. chastise, the natural consequences of wrong-doing prove to be Divine judgments.

Sin its Own Punishment.—Look for the man who has practised a vice so long that he curses it and clings to it; that he pursues it because he feels a great law of his nature driving him on towards it, but, reaching it, knows it will gnaw his heart and tear his vitals, and make him roll himself in the dust with anguish.—Sidney Smith. When Nicephorus Phocas had built a strong wall about his palace for his own security in the night-time, he heard a voice crying to him, "O Emperor! though thou build thy walls as high as the clouds, yet, if sin be within, it will overthrow all!"

20—22. (20) "For long ago didst thou break thy yoke [i. e. cast off allegiance to Jehovah], didst thou burst thy bonds, and saidst, I will not serve: for upon every high hill and under each evergreen tree thou wast crouching," etc. Exp. Bib.[c] (21) **noble vine,** see Is. v. 1, etc. **right seed,** fructified and of good quality. **unto me,** or to my grief. (22) **nitre,** R. V., "lye," the natron of Egypt, a mineral alkali.[d] **sope,** Heb. borith, a plant which was burned and from the ashes lye was made. **marked,** as a stain that cannot be got out.

"Thine iniquity is marked."—Let a blot lie a while on a pure sheet of white satin paper; try to remove it erasure may ultimately rid the sheet of that "one dark spot," but the paper is injured, the satin gloss is gone, and if you try to write on the place again, the lines smear. Sin effects permanent injury, cannot be removed by most careful efforts; the "mark" remains when all is done. Holiness is not mere cleanness; it has no mark of injury. It is pure light; the concentration of all the prismatic colors into unity.

23—25. (23) **say,** in self-defence.[e] **valley,** of Hinnom, ch. vii. 32.[f] **swift dromedary,** a "young female wh. has never had a foal." **traversing,** running this way and that. (24) **wild ass,** "symbol of an untamed and reckless nature." **her occasion,** the pairing season. (25) **thirst,** refers "to the shameless doings and insatiable cravings of lust." Exp. Bib. **no hope,** "Thou saidst, It is vain," (so i. e. to urge me.) ' No! for I love the strangers and after them I will go." Exp. Bib.

"Swift dromedary."—The camels of the Bible are of two kinds, the difference being the result simply of breeding and training. The first kind, used as a beast of burden, will carry from 500 to 1,000 pounds twenty-four miles a day. The second, used to convey intelligence, will travel upwards of 100 miles in twenty-four hours; this kind is called the dromedary.—Gray.

26—30. (26) **house of Israel,** the whole Heb. people, "The Shame" is the title of opprobrium which the prophets apply to Baal. Accordingly, the point of vs. 26 sqq. is, that as Israel has served the Shame, the idol-gods, instead of Iahvah, shame has been and will be her reward: in the hour of bitter need, when she implores help from the One true God, she is put to shame by being referred back to her senseless

trustworthiness could be found than a leaky tank." — Thomson.

[a] "Noph, or Memphis, capital of Lower Egypt, on the W. bank of the Nile. Tahapanes, or Daphne, on the Tanitic branch of the Nile. These two cities stand for the whole of Egypt." —Fausset.

[b] "The two rivers are the two empires, and to drink their waters is to adopt their principles and religion."—Spk. Com.

[c] Ex. xix. 8; Jos. xxiv. 18; Ju. x. 16; 1 Sa. xii. 10.

[d] "It was an incrustation at the bottom of the lakes, after the summer heat has evaporated the water. It was used for washing. (Job. ix. 30; Pr. xxv. 20.)—Fausset.

[e] "The people prob. appealed to the maintenance of the daily sacrifice, and the Mosaic ritual. All such pleas availed little as long as the rites of Molech were still privately practised." —Spk. Com.

[f] 2 Ki. xxiii. 10.

idols.—Expos. Bib. (27) **back unto me,** a token of contempt. (28) **where .. gods,** why do not they comfort and help you? Comp. Judges x. 10—14. **cities .. gods,** not because your gods were few. For you had one in every city. (29) **plead with me,** remonstrate at the reproaches and warnings of Jehovah. (30) **sword .. prophets,** with prob. allusion to the violent persecutions of Manasseh.[a]

The folly of neglecting God (vss. 27, 28).—I. The conduct of sinners towards their God. 1. It is a state of ease; 2. Of trouble. II. The folly and danger of it. 1. The disappointment it will occasion; 2. The reflections to which it will give rise. Address—(1) Those that are at ease in their sins; (2) Those who are brought into any kind of trouble; (3) Those that have already begun to seek the Lord.—C. Simeon.

Folly of idolatry shown.—The following incident occurs in the life of the Anglo-Saxon missionary, Winfrid, afterwards called Boniface. On his recommencing his missionary work in Hessia, he found that, during his absence (at Rome), many of the converts had relapsed into their old superstitions, and therefore he resolved to destroy one of the chief objects of veneration in the neighborhood in which he was laboring; this was an eminent oak near Giesmar, in Upper Hesse, which for ages had been sacred to Thor, the god of thunder. Many times had the zealous missionary declaimed against this idolatry, but without effect. He determined, therefore, to strike a blow at the object itself, and remove, if possible, the stumbling-block from their midst. Mr. Maclear (Missions of the Middle Ages) thus describes the scene:—"One day, accompanied by all his clergy, he advanced, axe in hand, to cut down the offending monarch of the forest. The people assembled in thousands to witness the great controversy between the new and the old belief, many enraged at the interference of the stranger preacher, many more confident that an instant judgment would strike down so daring an offender. But scarcely had the missionary begun to ply his axe than it was apparent that Thor could not defend his own. If he was a god. he was certainly either 'gone on a journey,' or was 'asleep and needed awaking;' for in vain his votaries supplicated his vengeance. After a few blows of the axe, a crashing was heard in the topmost boughs; a mighty rushing wind, says the chronicler, seemed to shake every branch, and then the leafy idol came down to the ground, and split into four quarters. 'The Lord, He is the God!' the people shouted, thus acknowledging the superior might of the new faith."—Hassell.

31—34. (31) "Have I been to you like a land without food—like a way without light?"[a] **are lords,** R. V., "We are broken loose," going where we will, unbridled. (32) **ornaments,** Oriental females pride themselves on their ornaments. **attire,** the marriage girdle, in the E. taking the place of the marriage ring with us. (33) **trimmest,** etc., guiding your course to seek idolatry. **wicked .. ways,** R. V., "therefore even the wicked women hast thou taught thy ways." (34) **souls,** used simply in the sense of persons. **poor innocents,** R. V. "innocent poor," (comp. 2 Ki. xxi. 16, xxiv. 4.) not able to defend themselves from tyrannical rapacity. **not .. secret,** "not at house-breaking didst thou catch them." The allusion, which is completely obscured in the English Version, is to the law (Ex. xxii. 2) by which it was permitted to slay a thief caught in the act of breaking into a house. The persons whom Israel had thus treated were in no such position, but such was nevertheless their fate. Camb. Bib. **but upon all these,** better, "but because of all these things;" i. e. not for any crime, but bec. of thy zeal for the false gods.

Judah's corrupt condition.—Not only had the nation refused warning and despised instruction, and defeated the purposes of the Divine discipline. They had slain their spiritual monitors, the prophets, with the sword; the prophets who had founded upon the national disasters their rebukes of national sin, and their earnest calls to penitence and reform (1 Kings xix. 10; Neh. ix. 26; St. Matt. xxiii. 37). And so when at last the long deferred judgment arrived, it found a political system ready to go to pieces through the feebleness and corruption of the ruling classes; a religious system, of which the spirit had long since evaporated, and which simply survived in the interests of a venal priesthood,

[a] Josephus tells us that both the prophets, and religious men generally, were put to death in large numbers by this relentless king.

"As there is a foolish wisdom, so there is a wise ignorance, in not prying into God's ark, not inquiring into things not revealed. I would fain know all that I need, and all that I may: I leave God's secrets to Himself. It is happy for me that God makes me of His court, though not of His council."—Bp. Hall.

"A man is never astonished or ashamed that he doesn't know what another does, but he is surprised at the gross ignorance of the other in not knowing what he does."—Haliburton.

"One of the ancient fathers replied to a clamorous disputant who shouted, 'Hear me, hear me,' 'I will neither hear thee, nor do thou hear me, but let us both hear Christ.'" — Dict. of Illus.

[a] "So far was Jehovah from proving a niggardly and austere sovereign to the Jews, that He had evinced Himself to be their most liberal benefactor. Nothing but wantonness could have induced them to renounce their subjection to Him."—Henderson.

"A hypocrite is in himself both the archer and the mark, in all actions shooting at his own praise or profit."—Fuller.

"Sincerity! thou first of virtues, let no mortal

and its intimate allies, who made a trade of prophecy; and a kingdom and people ripe for destruction.—Exp. Bib.

35—37. (35) **innocent,** "thou saidst, I am innocent; surely his anger hath turned from me." The people "were generally prosperous and went on with their medley of religious rites trusting that Jehovah, at any rate, had no longer any complaint against them."—Cheyne. **plead,** as a judge. (36) **gaddest,** turning now to Egypt and now to Assyria. (37) **from him,** i. e. from Egypt. **hands . . head,** the sign of failure and despair.

The Egyptian alliance, like the former one with Assyria, was destined to bring nothing but shame and confusion to the Jewish people. The prophet urges past experience of similar undertakings, in the hope of deterring the politicians of the day from their foolish enterprise. But all that they had learnt from the failure and loss entailed by their intrigues with one foreign power was, that it was expedient to try another. So they made haste to "change their way," to alter the direction of their policy from Assyria to Egypt. King Hezekiah had renounced his vassalage to Assyria, in reliance, as it would seem, on the support of Taharka, king of Egypt and Ethiopia (2 Kings xviii. 7; cf. Isa. xxx. 1-5); and now again the nation was coquetting with the same power. An Egyptian force lay at this time on the confines of Judah, and the prophet may be referring to friendly advances of the Jewish princes toward its leaders.—Exp. Bib.

leave thy onward path, although the earth should gape, and from the gulf of hell destruction cry, to take dissimulation's winding way.—Home.

Be truly religious, and do not care to seem to be so.

CHAPTER THE THIRD.

1—3. (1) **They say,** connect with ii. 37, "hath rejected," . . . "saying. If a man," etc. **shall . . again,**[c] see the law, De. xxiv. 4. **that land,** in wh. such people dwelt as could take back an adulteress. **yet return,** better, "and thinkest thou to return unto Me?"—Spk. Com. (2) **high places,** R. V., "the bare heights," the scenes of idolatries, which are regarded as spiritual adulteries. **in the ways,** illus. by Ge. xxxviii. 14. **Arabian,** or desert robber, watching for prey.[a] (3) **showers,** etc., see De. xxviii. 24, as a token of divine displeasure. But you paid no heed.

"No latter rain."—Because we obstruct God's access to us, His beneficence does not reach us. We throw heaven and earth into confusion by our sins. For were we in right order as to our obedience to God, doubtless all the elements would be conformable. But as our lusts tumulate against God, as we provoke Him by our pride, perverseness, and obstinacy, it must needs be that all things above and below should be in disorder. This is to be ascribed to our sins.—Calvin.

4, 5. (4) **from this time,** i. e. the time of Josiah's reformation. 2 Chron. xxxiv. 3; xxxv. 19. Will you not now repent and cry out Jehovah "My Father," etc. **the guide,**[b] "husband." Prov. ii. 17. (5) **spoken,** etc., "thou hast spoken thus, but hast done evil things." **as thou couldest,** R. V. "and hast had thy way." "Her words were fair, but her deeds were false."

The proper prayer of youth.—Relate some story to illustrate the usefulness of guides to travelers in foreign lands, as among the mountains of Switzerland, etc. I. The journey of life. 1. Things unknown—length, trials, enemies, temptations, etc.; 2. Things desired—prosperity, length of days, friends, happiness, to "rejoice and be glad all our days," etc. 3. Things certain—a journey to be only once made, will certainly end; the end will answer to the way. "What will ye do in the end?" II. The pilgrim of life. A youthful traveler is supposed. 1. Such are inexperienced; 2. Think they know more than they really do; 3. Often wilful and wayward; 4. Traveling through unknown land; 5. Need help and provision of a spiritual kind for the journey. III. The guide of life. Many false guides—custom, fashion, human reasons, etc. Only one safe Guide—God. He has all that a good guide should have. 1. Knowledge of way; 2. Sympathy with the traveler; 3. Strength and vigilance to meet

c "Contrary to all precedent in the case of adultery, Jehovah offers a return to Judah, the spiritual adulteress." — Fausset.

a "The Arabs of the desert to the east and south of Palestine were notorious for their habit of robbing travelers, as they still are at the present day."—Henderson.

b "As having espoused them in the days of their youth, before their manners were corrupted by idolatry. Je. ii. 2; Ho. ii. 15." —Lowth.

"As the firstfruits of the ground were offered up to the Lord in the olden time, so offer up to Him your youthful affections and your youthful service." —Mogridge.

"Youth what man's age is like to be, doth show: We may our ends by our beginnings know." — Denham.

and defeat danger; 4. Constant presence. If we say "yes" to the text, then—(1) The start will be in the right direction; (2) The way will be in the safe path; (3) The end will be in the best place.—Hive.

"It is a truth but too well known, that rashness attends youth, as prudence does old age."—Cicero.

Lady Huntingdon.—It is recorded of the late Countess of Huntingdon, who afterwards so warmly espoused the cause of God and His truth, that in her early youth, when about nine years old, the sight of a corpse about her own age carried to the grave induced her to attend the funeral, when the first impressions of deep seriousness respecting an eternal world were made on her conscience.

6—11. (6) **said also,** on another occasion. **backsliding,** not an adjective, but a substantive, "Hast thou seen Backsliding, even Israel?" (7) **turn thou,** R. V. "She will return unto me." **treacherous sister,** Judah was as bad as Israel, but Judah made a good outward show.[a] (8) R. V., "And I saw, when, for this very cause that backsliding Israel had committed," etc. **bill of divorce,** a fig. for God's putting away the ten tribes. (9) **stones,** etc., ch. ii. 27. (10) **feignedly,** Heb. "in falsehood."[b] (11) **justified herself,** R. V., "shewn herself more righteous." **more . . Judah,** bec. Judah had the additional warning of the fate of Israel, and disregarded even that.[c]

[a] Comp. Eze. xxiii. 4, etc.

[b] Comp. Je. vii. 18, xix. 4; and also 2 Chr. xxxiv. 33.

[c] Eze. xvi. 51.

The one determining question is not: "Have you a label outside?" but, "Have you the grace of God in your heart?" —Joseph Parker.

External reform.—We make beautiful churches more often than we do beautiful Christians. We carve marbles, and rear fine proportions in stone; we decorate walls and altars; but these are only physical representations, material symbols, while the quality of beauty is in holiness. The beauty of love in all its infinite inflections, the beauty of justice and of truth, these languish.—H. W. Beecher.

12—15. (12) **toward the north,** the region to wh. the "ten tribes" had been carried by Shalmaneser. **anger to fall,**[d] R. V., "I will not look in anger upon you." **merciful,** this is the highest and most moving of all incentives to repentance.[e] (13) **acknowledge thine iniquity,** penitence being the essential condition of restoration. (14) **married unto you,** R. V. "I am a husband unto you." **one . . family,** prob. a prophetic fig. of the fact that only a few will ever return, but for even the few God will care.[f] (15) **pastors,** as before, temporal rulers.

[d] Not receive you with averted looks. So LXX., Syr., and Vulg.

[e] Ps. lxxxvi. 15, ciii. 8, 9.

[f] "However few the converts might be, Jehovah would not despise them, but would restore them to their own land. Or that, should there only be one found in a foreign city, or two in any of the nations, they should not be forgotten."—Henderson.

Pardon—conditional.—Pardon can only be secured by the consent of both parties. I may have offended you. You may come to me and say, "You have deeply grieved me; but I forgive." I can snap my fingers in your face and say, "Take your forgiveness away; I don't want to be forgiven by you." Observe, therefore, that you have not the power to forgive me. You can forgive the crime, but you cannot forgive the sinner. But if I come to you and say, "I have injured you; I see I must have given you pain; I did you wrong; I am sorry in my heart," and you then say, "With my heart I forgive you;" then the transaction is based on moral principles. It is so with God. God cannot pass an act of universal amnesty: He cannot open all the prison-doors of the universe and say to the criminals, "Come forth; I forgive you all." But if they in their condemned cells would but heave one sigh of penitence, and utter one cry for God's forgiving mercy, every bolt would fall off, every lock fly back, and there would be no prison in all the universe of God.—Parker.

16—19. (16) **in those days,** the recognized formula for the times of Messiah. **The ark,** etc., regarded as the centre of the Mosaic system. It appears that the ark was finally lost in the Babylonish captivity. **visit it,** better, "neither shall it be missed." **that be done,** or, "neither shall it be made, or repaired."[g] (17) **Jerusalem,** the whole city, not specially the temple. **nations,** i. e. the Gentiles.[h] **imagination,** R. V. "stubbornness." (18) **with . . Israel,** clearly intimating that the return was to be a united one.[i] (19) **How,** i. e. how gloriously!

[g] "Because the tabernacle of God will be one 'made without hands' (Heb. ix. 11), even the heart of His believing people."—Spk. Com.

[h] Ro. ix. 25, 26.

[i] "Most of the prophecies which mention the restoration of the Jews join Judah and Israel together, as equal sharers in that blessing. (See Je. xxx. 3, xxxi. 1; Is. xi. 13; Eze. xxxvii. 16, 22; Ho. i. 11; Zec. x. 6)."—Lowth.

God's relations to His people (vs. 19).—I. The honors which God desires to confer upon us. 1. To make us members of His family; 2. To make us heirs of heaven. II. The difficulties that beset the conferring these honors upon us. 1. Arising from God's character; 2. From our own character; 3. From the greatness of the blessings. III. The effect which uniformly follows the conferring of these honors—a filial spirit towards God. 1. Reverence; 2. Love; 3. Obedience.

Apply:—Encourage those who doubt the possibility of their salvation; (2) Warn those who see no difficulties in the way of their salvation; (3) Exhort those who profess to be in the way of salvation.—G. Brooks.

20—23. (20) **Israel,** the whole nation. (21) **weeping,** etc., the signs of real penitence on the part of the people. High places the customary places of lamentation, also the places where idolatry had been practiced. (22) **Return,** etc.,[a] comp. the similar passage, Ho. xiv. 1. (23) **hills,** R. V., "Truly in vain is the help that is looked for from the hills,[b] the tumult on the mountains."

Backsliders reclaimed (vs. 22).—I. God inviting backsliders to return to Him. 1. The characters addressed; 2. The sin and consequence of backsliding; 3. God's message to such characters. II. Backsliders complying with God's invitations. 1. The ready compliance they manifest; 2. The way they return to God.

Man's Restoration.—I have read of one who was for ever reclaimed from the deadly sin of drunkenness by the deep anguish of heart which he experienced when he found that one day, when brutalized by drink, he had smitten to the ground his own dear child, and wounded her with a wound the scar of which she would never lose; and that he had done this whilst she was lovingly seeking to lead him away from the place and the people who were tempting him to his ruin. When he came to himself and knew what he had done, his horror and remorse had no bounds. "The drink! ay, it was all the drink!" he exclaimed when, years after, telling the story. "Could I ever touch it again? I kept my finger lightly on the little maid's forehead, and lifted my face to heaven, and vowed that I would never touch the murderous thing again as long as I lived, and with a broken heart I prayed the Lord to help me." That well-known story serves to illustrate how, in this great matter of man's restoration to God, he who once was a godless rebel becomes filled with another heart, and God can, as he desires to, place him amongst the children. For when I clearly see the wounds which I in my mad sin have inflicted on him who sought to save me, and who tenderly loves me still notwithstanding all I have done, the sight of his cross and of those wounds will fill my soul with such a hatred of sin and love of God that I am no longer what I was; I am born again, I have passed from death unto life.—Pulp. Com.

a "The whole description is most graphically conceived. The people weeping upon the hills; God's gracious voice bidding them return; the glad cry of the penitents proclaiming that they come; the profession of faith won from them by the Divine love; these form altogether a most touching picture of a national repentance." — Spk. Com.

b "The altars wh. were erected on high places to the heathen gods abounded to such a degree, that they were seen in every direction."— Henderson.

24, 25. (24) **shame,** etc., R. V. "But the shameful thing hath devoured," i. e. Baal, hath devoured us. (25) **We lie down,** R. V., "Let us lie down in our shame and let our confusion cover us." The miseries of the captivity were recognized as Divine judgments on the national sins[c]. The expressions are taken from those who cast themselves down upon the ground, and cover themselves with dust or ashes out of grief and anguish of mind.

God the salvation of Israel (vs. 23).—Let me ask if this be not—1. A mighty salvation? 2. A merciful salvation? 3. A free salvation? 4. An unchangeable salvation? 5. A soul-satisfying salvation?—W. Wilkinson.

Shame is a great restraint upon sinners at first; but that soon falls off; and when men have once lost their innocence, their modesty is not like to be long troublesome to them. For impudence comes on with vice, and grows up with it. When men have the heart to do a very bad thing, they seldom want the face to bear it out.—Tillotson. The legend says, that a sinner being at confession, the devil appeared, saying that he came to make restitution. Being asked what he came to restore, he said. "Shame; for it is shame that I have stolen from this sinner, to make him shameless in sinning; and now I have come to restore it to him, to make him ashamed to confess his sins."—Dict. of Illus.

c **Ezr. ix. 7.**

"Though Satan be endeavoring to bind his chains fast about thee, though thy heart quake and be ready to fail for the many sins that encompass it, though destruction and death be in thy way, yet fear not; "behold thy King cometh," trust Him; He will restrain, He will defend." — Bogatsky.

CHAPTER THE FOURTH.

"This chapter should begin with vs. 3. Verses 1, 2, belong to the preceding prophecy."—Cheyne. **1, 2.** (1) **put away,** this would be the outward sign of the necessary repentance, **then . . remove,** "and not stray," these words do not complete the sentence which runs on in vs. 2. (2) **swear,** "then thou shalt swear," etc., i. e., you will be able to because you will realize it.[a] **The Lord liveth,** better, "as the Lord liveth."

From the Eng. Version we might suppose that this is itself the subject, and not simply the form, of the oath. The Living God is "not the thing sworn to, but the thing sworn by." Oaths by other gods are to be dismissed from their mouths.

Sin banished, or no heaven. The first physic to recover our souls is not cordials, but corrosives; not an immediate stepping into heaven by a present assurance, but mourning, lamentation, and a bitter bewailing of our former transgressions. With Mary Magdalene, we must wash Christ's feet with our tears of sorrow before we may anoint His head with the 'oil of gladness.'—Browning. When Ben's master died, they told him he had gone to heaven. Ben shook his head. "I 'fraid massa no gone there." "But why, Ben?" "'Cos when massa go North, or go journey to the Springs, he talk about it long time, and get ready. I never hear him talk about going to heaven, never see him get ready to go there."

3—6. (3) **Break . . ground,** "it is a condensed parable, borrowed from his favorite Hosea (x.12), with which he begins the prophecy of the northern invasion."—Cheyne. "Repent of your idolatry."[b]. **thorns,** as they were doing now. (4) **Circumcise,**[c] i. e., put away all impurity, your idolatries, etc. **fury,** or vengeance. **fire,** with a consuming power. (5) The verse pictures the fright of the people at the presence of a hostile army. (6) **standard,** or signal round which to rally the people.

The plough for the fallows (vs. 3).—I. The hearts of unregenerate men are like fallow ground. II. It is their duty to break up their fallow ground.—S. Tomlyns. The life of the sinner a foolish agriculture (vs. 3).—Notice here two things. I. A grand evil. 1. Loss of seed; 2. Loss of labor; 3. Loss of hope. II. An urgent duty, evangelical repentance for sin. 1. Hard work; 2. Indispensable work.—Thomas.

Verse 5.—With this verse begins a group of addresses here given in substance, and reaching to the end of chap. x. The general subject is the same throughout, a declaration of the coming evil. The words as we have them, in all probability, formed a part of the roll as read in the ears of Jehoiakim, or afterwards enlarged, and represent the gist of Jeremiah's preaching during the latter part of Josiah's reign, that of Jehoahaz, and the beginning of that of Jehoiakim. During the greater part of this time it was still possible for the people to avert calamity by repentance and amendment of life. After Jehoiakim's reign had fairly begun and he had shewn that even the check which Josiah's personal character and influence had put upon idolatry was now removed, the condition of the nation became desperate. The near approach or actual arrival of that condition therefore was present to Jeremiah's mind throughout this section and colored all his utterances. He speaks of the hostile army and of the destruction which it is about to deal. Judgment comes from the north, like the hot blast of the tempest not to be warded off by any human devices. At the beginning of chap. vii. there is a break caused by a new heading, and that with the three chapters that follow probably give us the exact words spoken by Jeremiah on a special occasion during this period. This and the subsequent verses are connected with the preceding as being an expanded description of the punishment there threatened. They give us a graphic picture of the excitement and dismay caused throughout the defenseless portions of the land by the approach of the enemy, and the hasty retreat to walled towns on the part of the country people.—Camb. Bib.

7—10. (7) **lion,** "not certain who is meant. Herodotus speaks of an invasion of Scythians at this time."—Driver. **destroyer,** "a destroyer of nations," not an ordinary conqueror. **on his way,,** lit. has broken up his encampment. (8) **gird,** etc., ch. vi. 26. **is not turned back from us,** the wickedness of the days of Manasseh has not been repented of. Any reformation has been merely on the surface, and those who imagine that it has been sufficient to recover God's favor towards His people will

a "Swearing by the name of God is mentioned elsewhere as a solemn part of religious worship, and opposed to the custom of swearing by false gods, which was practised among idolaters."—Lowth.

b "The unhumbled heart is like ground wh. may be improved, being let out to us for that purpose, but wh. is as yet fallow, overgrown with weeds, its natural product."—Fausset.

c De. x. 16.

"Happy those who are able in truth to say, 'My Lord and my God!' Here is the noblest inspiration for life, strength for work, comfort in trouble, hope in death." — William Forsythe.

A poor man told Rowland Hill that the way to heaven comprised three steps: "Out of self, unto Christ, into heaven."

"As it is never too soon to be good, so it is never too late to amend: I will, therefore, neither neglect the time present, nor despair of the time past. If I had been sooner good, I might perhaps, have been better; if I am longer bad, I shall, I am sure, be worse." —Warwick.

find their mistake. (9) **heart of the king,** i. e. his courage. "Great calamities often deprive men of their presence of mind." **astonished .. wonder,** bec. both these had joined in persuading the people that no such troubles should come upon them. (10) God is represented as having done the evil which in point of fact He only permitted to occur. A mode of thought and speech familiar to the Jew. (Comp. 1 Ki. xxii, 21-23.)—Camb. Bib.[a]

Helplessness of Israel's leaders. The lion out of the thicket is manageable enough if the man against whom he advances happens to have a loaded rifle in his hand, and the power of using it with unerring aim; but what if he has nothing more than a cudgel? Kings and princes, priests and prophets, might successfully join in counsel to mislead and keep down their own people; but a strong and proud army, that has come forth like a mighty wild beast intent on prey, is not to be turned back by mere counsels. In the last resort strength must be opposed to strength. The sole virtue of skill lies in this, that it can make the most of strength. But where the strength is lacking, skill can do nothing. No amount of skill can make a walking-stick do the work of a rifle, and the great peril of most human lives lies just in this, that they go on in the contented use of ordinary resources for ordinary needs. Practically speaking, extraordinary needs are not thought of till they come. There are voices to us, even as to these kings, princes, priests, and prophets of old; but we do not heed them, and meanwhile the lion out of the thicket, all unsuspected, is coming nearer and nearer to us.—Pul. Com.

11—14. (11) **At that time,** the time of the Babylonian invasion. **dry wind,** or hot pestilential wind: the simoom.[b] **fan,** for such purposes the husbandman uses the wind; but he would not use the simoom. (12) **full wind .. places,** R. V. marg. "a wind too strong for this shall come for me," stronger, than winds that fan or cleanse. **unto me,** i. e. to perform my will. (13) **he,** the enemy. **as clouds,** gathering for a storm. **whirlwind,** swiftly moving, and overwhelming, comp. Isa. v. 28; lxvi. 15. **eagles,** De. xxviii. 49. (14) **thine heart,** for this after all was the source of the evil.

Vain thoughts (vs. 14).—I. The characteristics of vain thoughts. 1. Cannot reap any good from them; 2. They cannot associate with good and useful thoughts; 3. Must be driven out to attend to serious matters; 4. They dwell largely and habitually on trifles; 5. They trifle with important things; 6. They are fickle; 7. Those pertinaciously fixed upon an unworthy object; 8. Will again and again return to it; 9. Such as are on speculative fancies; 10. Those bent on schemes of worldly felicity. II. The correctives of vain thoughts. 1. The substantial state of the mind must be cured of vanity; 2. We should have specific subjects of serious interest to employ thought; 3. Self-detection in the act of sin; 4. Recourse to acts of devotion; 5. Practical employment; 6. Communion with thoughts of wise and good.—J. Foster.

15—18. (15) **Dan,** the border-town of Palestine on the north. **mount Ephraim,** within ten miles of Jerusalem. "The language intimates the rapid approach of the enemy. But now they were at Dan. Already they are on the mountains at Ephraim."—Camb. Bib. (16) **Make mention,** "the nations are summoned to witness the vengeance about to fall." **watchers,**[a] or besiegers. (17) **keepers of a field,** who watch to frighten away the wild beasts. 18) **this .. wickedness,** this final siege is the issue of thy wickedness.

Bitterness of sin (vs. 18).—I. Sin is bitter. 1. It is so comparatively; 2. Absolutely. II. It reaches to thine heart. 1. It defiles it; 2. It disquiets it; 3. It ruins it. Apply:—(1) Since sin is bitter, bitter remedies must be taken; (2) It is a mercy that grace reaches to the heart as well as sin.—Beddome.

Note on vs. 17.—In Arabia, and probably in other parts of the East, instead of a solitary watchman in the middle of the plantation, they place guards at certain distances round the whole field, increasing or diminishing their numbers according to the supposed danger.—Saxton.

[a] "Deeply affected by this state of things, the Prophet cannot restrain his feelings, but gives them utterance in what, at first sight, appears to be a blasphemous charge against Jehovah. It is, however, but a strong Orientalism."— Henderson.

"Nazianzen compares the soul to a pair of writing-tables, out of which must be washed whatsoever was written with sin, and instead thereof must be entered the writing of grace; both these are necessary in true repentance."

[b] It generally blows from the southeast across the dry sandy deserts to the east of Palestine. "This simoom extends its ravages all the way fr. the extreme end of the Gulf of Cambaya up to Mosul; it carries along with it flakes of fire like threads of silk; instantly strikes dead those that breathe it, and consumes them inwardly to ashes."—Col. Campbell.

[c] Joel ii. 2.

"'Tis not in things o'er thought to domineer. Guard well thy thought: our thoughts are heard in heaven."—Young.

[a] "Scouts to warn men of the approach of an enemy. Here the Prophet, by way of irony, calls the Chaldæan army, by that name."—Lowth.

"'Tis very true, my grief lies all within; And these external manners of lament

Bitter at heart.—

Through many a clime 'tis mine to go,
With many a retrospection curst;
And all my solace is to know
Whate'er betides, I've known the worst.
What is that worst? Nay, do not ask.
In pity from the search forbear;
Smile on, nor venture to unmask
Man's heart, and view the hell that's there.
—Byron.

19—22. (19) **bowels,** regarded as the seat of emotion. Most deeply is the Prophet moved by his vision of the coming woes of the land. **maketh a noise,** R. V., "is disquieted." (20) **Destruction,** etc., or complete, utter destruction. **tents .. curtains,** poetical for the dwellings. (21) **standard,** vss. 5, 6. (22) **wise .. evil,** vs. 21 was an appeal to God. This is His answer, "they have studied all the arts of sin and wickedness, but are strangers to the obligations of religion and virtue."—Spurgeon.

"Sottish children."—This was the sad thought that, even while Jerusalem was going down, lower, lower, towards the hour of its capture and desolation, there were yet in it many men who had the power, if only their hearts had been right, to do much towards saving and blessing their country. But all their thoughts, their utmost acuteness of mind, were given to build and enrich self.—Pul. Com.

23—26. (23) **I beheld,** "in this, and the following vss., the Prophet sees in vision the desolate condition of Judæa during the Babylonish captivity."—Spk. Com. The imagery is highly poetical. **without form,** R. V., "waste," Gen. i. 2. This is a return to primitive chaos. (24) **moved lightly,** R. V., "to and fro." (25) **birds .. fled,** bec. in the desolate land they could not find their food. (26) **fruitful place,** "the garden land," i. e. all this fertile country.

Sin, its wide consequences.—Sages of old contended that no sin was ever committed whose consequences rested on the head of the sinner alone; that no man could do ill and his fellows not suffer. They illustrated it thus: "A vessel sailing from Joppa carried a passenger who, beneath his berth, cut a hole through the ship's side. When the men of the watch expostulated with him, "What doest thou, O miserable man?" the offender calmly replied, "What matters it to you? The hole I have made lies under my own berth." This ancient parable is worthy of the utmost consideration. No man perishes alone in his iniquity; no man can guess the full consequences of his transgressions.—Spurgeon.

27—31. (27) **thus,** Jeremiah now puts the message into plainer language. **full end,** "the overthrow shall not be such as that which sooner or later befalls all other kingdoms. The contrast between the chosen people and the rest of the nations is thus very remarkable, as is also the frequency and consistency with which the promise of final deliverance appears even in the midst of the severest threatenings. This feature of prophecy is found as early as Lev. xxvi. 44. Compare chap. v. 10; also Is. vi. 13, xi. 11, 16; Ezek. xx. 34; Amos ix. 8; Mic. ii. 12."—Camb Bib. (28) **not repent,** bec. the iniquity of Judah could now only be met by judgments. (29) **horsemen,** etc., the cavalry and archers of Chaldæa. (30) **rentest thy face,** R. V., "enlargest thine eyes,"[a] trying to make yourself attractive, seeking alliances. (31) **bewaileth,** R. V., "gaspeth for breath." **Woe is me,** for the hopelessness of the calamity. **is wearied,** etc., R. V., "fainteth before the murderers."

Woe-stricken.—The world affords not a sadder sight than a poor Christless soul shivering upon the brink of eternity. To see the poor soul that now begins to wake out of its long dream, at its entrance into the world of realities, shrinking back into the body and crying, "O I cannot, I dare not die!"—Flavel. Come home, wandering, tired, grieved soul! Love where thy love shall not be lost. Love Him that will not reject thee, nor deceive thee, nor requite thee with injuries as the world doth. God will receive thee when the world doth cast thee off, if thou cast off the world for Him!—Baxter.

Are merely shadows of the unseen grief
That swells with silence in the tortured soul:
There lies the Substance."
—Shakespeare.

"God's ministers must have their hearts fired, not with passion but with love. The thunderbolt may crash, but the sun melts. It is better to love as a pastor than speak as an angel." — Watson (1649).

"The efforts of men to explain the origin of sin, this throws no more light upon it than a candle upon a widely extended landscape veiled in mists, and wrapped in midnight darkness."
—Guthrie.

"Ah! when the means are gone that buy this praise,
The breath is gone whereof this praise is made.
Feast-won, fast-lost; one cloud of winter showers,
These flies are couch'd."
—Shakespeare.

[a] "The use of their paint was to contract the eyelids, and make their eyes appear more large and full, which they thought a great beauty."—Lowth

"What is needed is that, even in the days of youth and strength, of unimpaired faculties of sense and intellect, one should remember that far other days are coming. What sadder sight can there be than an old man, clinging to the worn, torn, weather-beaten, age-marked sides of his earthly tabernacle, and

Painting the eyes.—Almost all writers and travelers in the East afford us proof of the unchanging character of Oriental fashions. A gentleman, describing his visit to a Jewish family in Damascus, says: "They were rich, stylish people, consequently we may conclude that their dress and ornaments were consistent with all that was thought proper or fashionable. The gentlemen of the family being from home, the ladies received me in a handsome apartment, with the utmost courtesy and kindness. The ceiling and walls of the room were highly ornamented with painting and gilding; the walls similarly decorated and hung with looking-glasses. The dress of the ladies was splendid: they wore loose Eastern robes of silk, stomachers covered with gold, and jewelled ornaments on their heads. But one decoration attracted my attention from all the others, and seemed to my unaccustomed eyes to mar their beauty in a high degree. From the outer corner of each eye a black line was painted upon the cheek, which gave exactly the appearance of two slits or rents. Now you will no longer be at a loss to understand what was the singular custom alluded to by Jeremiah, of which there can be little doubt that this fact affords an interesting illustration."

doing his best to resist every incursion from the forerunners of death; simply because he knows of no better mansion, because he is utterly ignorant of the "house of God not made with hands, eternal in the heavens!"—Pul.Com.

CHAPTER THE FIFTH.

1, 2. (1) **Run,** etc., "one of those exaggerations to which from his temperament this prophet was peculiarly liable."—Cheyne. Jeremiah refers to the mass of the people, or more particularly to the leaders of the people. **executeth,** R. V., "doeth justly," who is just in his dealings toward his fellows. **truth,** good faith; not simply truthfulness. **it,** i. e. Jerusalem. Comp. Ge. xviii. 32. (2) **the Lord liveth,** the most solemn form of oath. **swear falsely,** though not by false gods, they swear in a false spirit. They were hypocrites when not idolaters, see vs. 7.

"The true sense of this passage is that Josiah's reforms were frustrated by the immorality prevalent among all classes; which, though checked for a time, yet was too deeply ingrained to be really eradicated by all that good king could do."—Spk. Com.

Right kind of men (vs. 1).—I. In the estimation of God the true excellence of man is moral and religious. 1. A strict obedience to the Divine will as far as it is known; 2. An earnest endeavor to attain an accurate acquaintance with the Divine word. II. There are states of society in which men of this description are exceedingly rare. 1. They may be removed by death; 2. They may be withdrawn into concealment; 3. They may be reduced in numbers by the progress of degeneracy. III. In the worst states of society such men are very valuable. 1. They avert Divine judgments; 2. Draw down Divine blessings; 3. Promote the work of reformation.—G. Brooks.

"Ghislerus reminds us of a story which Pliny relates of King Demetrius who retired from the city of Rhodium because he could not take it on its accessible side without destroying some celebrated paintings of Protogenes. This one man's merits saved the city."—Lange.

"Seek, if ye can find a man." Diogenes, the cynic, having lighted a lamp, ranged the streets peering about as if searching for something. Being asked what he looked for, he answered, "A man;" or, as is usually recorded, "An honest man!" But the words in Laertius are, "I seek a man." He sought not alone a man with honesty and truth in his character, but a man in whom all right and noble qualities were combined. He constantly reviled the society of Greece with its lack of manhood.

"There are some men who, like pictures, would be perfect in their moral characters were it not for some blemish which you discover on the eye, or the ear, or the mouth, or some other part of the exposed person." — John Bate.

The host of Nola being bid to summon the good men of the town to appear before the Roman censor, gat him to the church yard, and there called at the graves of the dead; for he knew not where to call for a good man alive.—Trapp.

Actions, looks, words, steps, form the alphabet by which you may spell character."—Lavater.

Streets in Jerusalem.—In ancient times the streets of Jerusalem seem to have had their names; and it is worth our while to notice how many of these are mentioned in Scripture. There was the Bakers' Street, from which King Zedekiah ordered Jeremiah's food to be sent to him (Jer. xxxvii. 21). There was "East Street," into which Hezekiah gathered the priests and Levites, when exhorting them to cleanse the house, and to carry forth the filthiness that had been allowed to lie there in heaps in the reign of Ahaz (2 Chron. xxix. 4). There was the "Street of the House of God," into which the men of Judah and Benjamin came together in the days of Ezra (Ezra x. 9). There was the "Water-gate Street," where the people came together in the days of Nehemiah (Neh. viii. 1, 3, 16). There was "Ephraim-gate Street," where they met to celebrate the feast of tabernacles (Neh. viii. 16). Nor were these streets few, for Jeremiah, when warning Israel against the increase of her false gods, says, "According to the number of the streets of Jerusalem have ye set up altars to that shameful thing," Jer. xi. 13. In the days of that Prophet the idolatry seems to have been more open than before, and the public streets were the place where altars and idols were set up. Hence there are more allusions to the "streets of Jerusalem" in his prophecies than in all the other Prophets together (Jer. v. 1, vii. 17, 34, ix. 21, xi. 6, 13, xiv. 16, xxxiii. 10, xliv. 6, 9, 21). He was specially the prophet of the street, the "out-door" preacher; and he was thus brought more keenly and frequently into collision with the inhabitants than any of his "fellow-servants the Prophets."—Christian Treas.

3—6. (3) **eyes .. truth,** i. e. thou lookest for and knowest the truth. God is the God of truth;[a] and desireth truth in the inward parts. **stricken,** with chastisements that were designed for correction.[b] **faces .. rock,** fig. for an obstinate unwillingness to receive Divine instruction. (4) **poor,** etc.,[c] they must belong to those classes which, in all ages, are found least susceptible of religious impressions. (5) **great men,** men of education and position. **altogether,** R. V., "with one accord," these were even worse. The rich were more wicked than the poor.[d]. (6) "The beasts here mentioned are literally meant, and are not figurative of the enemy. This is shewn by the different sorts which are enumerated. Compare for this form of punishment Lev. xxvi. 22; 2 Kings xvii. 25; and so Ezek. xiv. 15."—Camb. Bib. But many commentators take the beasts to be figurative of the Babylonians. **evenings,** better, "deserts."

Comparison of the rich and the poor.—When I compare different classes as existing at this moment in the civilized world, I cannot think the difference between the rich and the poor in regard to mere physical suffering so great as is sometimes imagined. That some of the indigent among us die of scanty food is undoubtedly true, but vastly more in this community die from eating too much than from eating too little, vastly more from excess than starvation. So as to clothing: many shiver from want of defences against the cold; but there is vastly more suffering among the rich from absurd and criminal modes of dress, which fashion has sanctioned, than among the poor from deficiency of raiment. So the poor are often overworked; but they suffer less than many among the rich, who have no work to do, no interesting object to fill up life, to satisfy the infinite cravings of man for action. According to our present modes of education, how many of our daughters are victims of ennui—a misery unknown to the poor, and more intolerable than the weariness of excessive toil! The idle young man, spending the day in exhibiting his person in the street, ought not to excite the envy of the overtasked poor; and this cumberer of the ground is found exclusively among the rich.—Channing. Chastening.—Suppose that away in South Africa, there is a woman whose husband has gone on a long journey into the interior. He is to be away for months, cut off from all postal coummunication. The wife is very anxious to receive news. In months she has had no letter or tidings from him. One day, as she stands in her door, there comes a great savage Kafir, carrying his shields and spears, and with a terrible face. The woman is frightened, and she rushes into the house, closing the door. He knocks at the door; she is in terror. She sends her servant, who comes back and says, "The man says he must see you." She goes all affrighted. He takes out an old newspaper, which he has brought from her husband, and inside the dirty newspaper, she finds a letter from her husband, telling her of his welfare. How that wife delights in that letter! She forgets the face that has terrified her. Weeks pass away again, and she begins to long for that ugly Kafir messenger. After a long waiting, he comes again and this time she rushes out to meet him, because he is the messenger from the beloved husband, and she knows that with all his repelling exterior, he is the bearer of a message of love. Beloved, have you learned to look at tribulation and vexation and disappointment as the dark, savage-looking messenger, with a spear in his hand that comes straight from Jesus?—Andrew Murray.

[a] De. xxxii. 4.

[b] Is. ix. 13; Je. ii. 30.

[c] "The Prophet supposes that such evil could only exist among the mass of the uninstructed vulgar, and then he goes on to express his hope that he would find things in a very different state among those constituting the higher ranks of society, who had enjoyed superior advantages." — Henderson.

[d] "They bid open defiance to God's laws, and cast off all obligations of duty and conscience; like headstrong oxen that will not be brought under the yoke, but break through any bonds whereby you would restrain them, or bring them under discipline." —Lowth.

Ignorance of the price of pearls makes the idiot slight them. Ignorance of the worth of diamonds makes the fool choose a pebble before them. Ignorance of the satisfaction learning affords makes the peasant despise it. So with religion. — Anthony Horneck.

"No man has a right to do as he pleases except when he pleases to do right."

7—9. (7) **How,** or why. What reason can be offered for any expectation of pardon? **sworn .. gods,** again and again the "swearing" is noticed as a solemn act of religion. **fed .. full,** should read, "though I made them to swear (allegiance to me), yet they committed adultery;" comp. Ps. lxxiii. 27, which favors reference to a relapse into heathenish worship. —Cheyne. **harlots' houses,** idol temples, with allusion to the unclean rites of idol worship. (8) **fed,** etc., Eze. xxii. 11. (9) **visit,**[a] in severe judgments.

Blessings changed to curses.—The noblest physical gifts may be shattered, wrecked, by sins against the body. The mind—capable of such high service and a channel of such vast blessing—men may, do, pollute, corrupt, and pervert and so curse their blessings. The moral nature—this a great gift of God, the power to judge, choose, resolve; but see how soon man cursed that and turned his blessing into a curse. The gifts of providence are also abused in the same way. The home. Oh, what joy comes to men through the blessings that were designed to be forever associated with that word! But how often men, by self-indulgence, neglect, evil example, utter failure in parental duty, turn the blessing of home into a curse! And even the gospel of Christ itself—God's unspeakable gift—men may make the knowledge of it to be "a savor of death unto death" for themselves. "This Child is set for the fall of many in Israel," said Simeon of our Lord.—Pul. Com. Sin a hindrance to our receiving blessings.—When our spiritual supplies fail, the channel is sometimes at fault, and not the stream; the hindrance to their coming lies with us and not wtih our heavenly Father. The supply of fuel to our city in midwinter sometimes fails, not because the coal-fields are exhausted, but because the weather has frozen our rivers, detained our colliers in the channel, and blocked up our railways. The supply of water or of gas to our houses is sometimes insufficient, not because the reservoirs are low, but because the pipes which connect our dwellings with the main service are choked up or broken. News fails to reach us, not because our correspondent has neglected to write, but because the means of transmission have been imperfect.—S. Martin.

[a] Je. v. 29, ix. 9, xliv. 22.

vs. 8. "The same term is used in the East to denote a similar thing. It is said, 'Listen to that evil man, he is always neighing.' 'O that wicked one, he is like the horse in his frenzy.' 'The men of that family are all neighers.' Heathenism is ever true to itself; impurity is its inseparable companion."—Roberts.

"What is remote and difficult of access we are apt to overestimate; what is really best for us lies always within our reach, though often overlooked."—Longfellow.

10—13. (10) **Go ye,** an apostrophe addressed to the Babylonians. They were to execute the Divine judgment. **full end,** final and complete destruction, vs. 18. **battlements,** R. V., "branches," it is not the vine that is to be destroyed. **not the Lord's,** He having withdrawn from their defence, by reason of their iniquities. (12) **belied,** R. V., "denied."[a] **not he,** i. e. "he is not the true lord of the world, a denial of God's moral government."—Cheyne. (13) a continuation of the speech of the unbelieving Jews. **word,** i. e. any word or message from God.[b] **thus .. them** "may the evil which the Prophets threaten fall upon their own head."

Vain defences (vs. 10).—I. The sinner's consciousness of danger. 1. His danger is real; 2. He has a deep-seated apprehension of it. II. His inadequate means of defence. 1. Sometimes in an absolute denial of the moral government of God; 2. In mistaken views of the Divine character; 3. In a false estimate of personal merit or excellence.—G. Brooks.

[a] "They denied the Divine government over human affairs; ascribing His judgments to chance or fortune, and disbelieving all threatenings of sword or famine which the Prophets have denounced in His name, wh. is, in effect, to give Him the lie."—Lowth.

14—18. (14) **words .. mouth,** ch. i. 9. Because ye (the people) deny that the word is from me, I will make thy (Jeremiah's) words to come to pass and their fulfilment to devour the people as fire devours wood."—Camb. Bib. (15) **from far,** Is. xxxix. 3. **language . . not,**[c] as threatened, De. xxviii. 49, a people to whom it would be useless to appeal for mercy in a tongue not understood. (16) **quiver,** see ch. iv. 29. (17) **bread,** here put for bread-corn. **impoverish,** R. V., "beat down," with the battering-ram. **sword,** here in a general sense for the instruments of siege. (18) R. V., "But even in those days." **full end,** as vs. 10, ch. iv. 27.

God's word a thorn to unbelievers.—An infidel said, "There is one thing that mars all the pleasure of my life." "Indeed!" replied his friend, "what is that?" He answered, "I am afraid the Bible is true. If I could know for certain that death is an eternal sleep, my joy would be complete. But here is the thorn that stings me, the sword that pierces to my very soul: if the Bible is true, I am lost forever."

[b] Ho. i. 2.

[c] "This would render them more pitiless, as they would not understand their cries for mercy."—Spk. Com.

"Our actions are our own; their consequences belong to heaven."—Francis.

19—24. (19) **Like as,** etc., retribution in kind.[d] They had given themselves up to worship foreign idols, they should now be given up to

[d] "All God's promises were made upon condition of your obedience, and if you forsake God, you

are not to expect that the promise of dwelling in this land should be made good to you any longer."—Lowth.

[e] De. xxi. 18, 20.

serve foreign masters. (21) "The prophet speaks to all bystanders who will share in his sorrow and zeal for reformation."—Camb. Bib. (22) **sand .. decree,** Job xxxviii, 10, 11; Ps. civ. 9. (23) **heart,** or disposition, will.[e] (24) **fear,** in the religious sense of "worship." **giveth rain,** etc., comp. Ps. cxlvii. 8; Mat. v. 45; Ac. xiv. 17. Early rain between Oct. and Dec.: the latter rain in March and April. **reserveth,** etc., lit. "He keepeth for us the weeks—the statutes of harvest," i. e. the weeks which are the appointed conditions of harvest. **weeks .. harvest,** the seven weeks intervening bet. the Passover and Pentecost, dating fr. the 16th day of Nisan.

Indifference (vs. 21).—I. What God has done to produce pious consideration. 1. He has given powers of mind adapted to it; 2. He has given us the means to answer to these powers; 3. His Holy Spirit to strive, convince, etc. II. The indifference men often exhibit. 1. Of some it is total, without any concern; 2. Of others considerate only of the externals of religion; 3. Of some only to the intellectual parts of truth; 4. Of others only occasional. III. The consequences of this difference. 1. It is extremely foolish; 2. Detrimental to the soul; 3. Specially offensive to God; 4. Must end in the soul's ruin.—Burns.

[a] "In metaphors taken fr. bird-catchers, the Prophet describes the cunning of the more abandoned part of the nation, and the great wealth wh. they had unjustly acquired."—Henderson.

25—28. (25) **these things,** i. e. the benefits already mentioned in preceding verse, comp. ch. iii. 3, xii, 4.—Pul. Com. 26) **lay wait,** or "pry as fowlers lie in wait."[a] (27) **cage,** or basket coop full of birds that have been caught. **full of deceit,** i. e. of treasures acquired by fraud. (28) **fat,** De. xxxii. 15. **overpass,** surpass in wickedness even the wicked. **yet they prosper,** R. V., "that they may prosper," i. e. the orphans.

National delinquency (vs. 25).—Notice the chief of our national sins. 1. Ungodliness; 2. Immorality; 3. General indifference to the truth. Apply:—(1) Lay it to heart personally; (2) Pray for your country.—J. J. Cart.

[b] "Both priests and prophets agree to speak pleasing things to the people, thereby to keep up their interest and authority with them; and what can this end in but a total corruption of manners? the consequence of wh. must be utter ruin and destruction."—Lowth.

29—31. (29) **not visit,** vs. 9. (30) **wonderful,** better, "terrible," (31) **by their means,** according to the guidance and directions of these false prophets. **love to have it so,** prefer the license wh. such false teachings give.[b] Mi. ii. 11.

"What will ye do in the end?" (vs. 31.)—I. There is an end to every evil course—a termination, and a result which God fore-knows as a certain termination, and as an inevitable result, if an evil course be persisted in and persevered in. II. The end is not far distant; it draws nigh. III. The proximate end of some things is already realized, and the end of other things is beginnng to appear. IV. Some of our fellows are, under our eye, realizing the proximate end of many of their evil ways; while others, by looking to the end, have forsaken their evil ways. Appeal to different characters, as the hypocrite, the neglecter of salvation, to the criminal, etc.—S. Martin.

CHAPTER THE SIXTH.

[c] "Every one knows that Jerusalem is situated in the tribe of Benjamin. As for Tekoa, we see every day with our own eyes that it is a little town upon a hill about twelve (Roman) miles from Jerusalem. Between these is another village, called in the Heb. and Syr. tongues, Beth-acharma, which also is placed upon a hill."—S. Jerome.

1—5. (1) **of Benjamin,** a name for Jerusalem, as being situated within the limits of this tribe. Jeremiah was himself a Benjamite. **Tekoa,** 11 m. S. of Jerusalem. The south was the only road open to those who would escape. **Beth-haccerem,** Ne. iii. 14.[c] (2) **comely,** R. V., "The comely and delicate one, the daughter of Zion, will I cut off." (3) **shepherds,** etc., the consuming Babylonians, who should feed upon this pasture. (4) **Prepare,** literally "sanctify," i. e. make the necessary sacrifices that preface war. **at noon,** the usual resting time; but, in their eagerness, the Chaldæans would advance even at noon. **Woe,** etc. evening however finds them still on the march. (5) **go by night,** i. e. the soldiers clamor for a night assault.

Note on vs. 1—Fire signals.—Fire signs are used as a telegraph in some parts of the South Seas. A native of Tanna, in giving me the news one morning, said, "There will be a party over from the island of Aneiteum today or tomorrow." "How do you know?" "Because we saw a great bonfire rising there last night." The natives of heathen islands are also in the habit of kindling fires, as a smoke signal, to attract the notice of a vessel which may be off their shore. Sometimes when we are wondering whether there are any natives among the dense bush which we see from the ship, up goes a column of smoke, and removes all doubt.—Turner. Note on vs. 2.—A passage of D'Arvieux shows the attention usually paid by the great men of the East to the complexion of their wives, as well as the great tanning power of the sun in Palestine. "The princesses, and the other Arab ladies, whom they showed me from a private place of the tent, appeared to me beautiful and well shaped; one may judge by these, and by what they told me of them, that the rest are no less so; they are very fair, because they are always kept from the sun." It is on this account, without doubt, that the Prophet Jeremiah, when he would describe a comely woman, describes her by the character of one that dwelleth at home. The delicate, and those that are solicitous to preserve their beauty, go very little abroad: it seems it was so anciently, and therefore the Prophet uses a term to express a woman of beauty, which would not be very applicable to many modern fine ladies.—Harmer.

6—8. (6) **cast a mount,** lit. "pours a mount" or bank. The fig. of pouring has reference to the emptying of the baskets of earth wh. were brought to make the mound.[a] (7) **grief,** etc., of those suffering by reason of the wickedness wh. calls for these judgments. (8) **instructed,** or learn the lessons of thy chastisement. **my soul,** or I Myself: "lest My mind and affection be utterly alienated from thee."

A solemn admonition (vs. 8).—I. The benefits of instruction in national danger. II. The destructive consequences of this instruction being sent in vain. Apply—1. To the man who rests in the mere external observances of a public fast; 2. To those who are desirous of instruction. —R. Cecil.

God's withdrawment from man.—Think of God sending a famine upon the soul, of minds pining and dying because Divine messages have been withdrawn! We know what the effect would be if God were to withdraw the dew, or to trouble the air with a plague, or to avert the beams of the Sun; the garden would be a desert, the fruitful field a sandy plain, the wind a bearer of death, summer a stormy night, and life itself a cruel variation of death: so penetrating, so boundless is the influence of God in nature. Is it conceivable that the withdrawment of God's influence would be less disastrous upon the spirit of man?—Joseph Parker.

9—12. Here begins a second section, extending to vs. 15. (9) **turn back,** or go over the vineyard again to be quite sure no stray grapes are left.[a] Addressed to the leader of the attack upon the land. **into the basket,** R. V. margin. "Upon the shoots." (10) **ear is uncircumcised,** not dedicated to God, ch. vii. 26; Ac. vii. 51. "Closed against the precepts of God by carnality." **reproach,** they turn it into ridicule. (11) **weary with holding in,** and must utter my denunciations, wh. shall reach all classes, young, middle-aged, and old. **I will pour it out,** "pour it out" (imperative). This command is addressed by the prophet to himself, rather than by God to the prophet. The declaration is made without distinction of age, because the approaching punishment includes all alike.—Camb. Bib. **full of days, i. e.** who have lived to the full term and period of human life. (12) **houses . . others,** De. xxviii. 30.

13—17. (13) **to covetousness,** or gaining gains,[a] the acquisition of exorbitant or unjust gains. **falsely,** or fraudulently. (14) **daughter . . people,** omit "daughter of." **slightly,** only making a surface-healing, without reaching the deep cause. **saying, Peace,** this would be the hope based on Josiah's reforms.[b] (15) **Were they ashamed,** the passage means that the people were too hardened to feel ashamed of their acts. (16) A fourth section begins here extending to vs. 21. **old paths,** the neglected and despised ways of allegiance to Jehovah, and obedience to His will.[c] (17) **watchmen,** the Prophets. **the sound of the trumpet,** the mode of announcing the approach of danger. (Compare ver. 1; Amos iii. 6.) As sentinels are posted on the walls of a city to warn the inhabitants of the enemy's approach, so have the true prophets of the nation warned them of the consequences of their ways."

"It was usual with the Persians, Grecians, and Romans, to signify in the night by signs of fire, and by burning torches, either the approach of an enemy, or succor from friends. The former was done by shaking and moving their torches; the latter by holding them still."—Burder.

[a] Comp. 2. Sa. xx. 15; Isa. xxxvii. 33; Je. xxxii. 24, xxxiii. 4; Eze. xvii. 17.

"Opportunities are the golden spots of time, like the pearl in the oyster-shell, of much more value than the shell that contains it. There is much time in a short opportunity."—Flavel.

If you commit one sin, it is like the melting of the lower glacier upon the Alps, the others must follow in time."—Spurgeon.

[a] Comp. Is. xvii. 6, xxiv. 13.

"How wretched a spectacle is a garden into which cloven-footed beasts have entered! That which yesterday was fragrant, and shone all over with crowded beauty, is to-day rooted, despoiled, trampled, and utterly devoured. Such to me is the Bible, when the pragmatic prophecy-monger and the swinish utilitarian have toothed its fruits and craunched its blossoms."—Beecher.

[a] Is. lvi. 11; Je. viii. 10.

[b] "They have used only lenitives, as if a surgeon should slightly skin over a sore that festers underneath."—Lowth.

[c] "Your country was once prosperous and bless-

ed. Try to learn what were the paths trodden in those days by your ancestors. Discover what the good path was wh. led them to happiness." — Spk. Com.

d Is. i. 11, lxvi. 3; Am. v. 21; Mi. vi. 6.

"Although every old way may not be good, the good way is certainly old; if, therefore, the traveler finds and follows the way that is both old and good, he is safe — he shall without fail reach his home at last, and "find rest for his soul." —Kitto.

e Ex. xxx. 23.

d "When God says He lays stumbling-blocks in men's way, we must remember that it is by the general action of His moral law, by which wilful sin in one point reacts upon the whole moral nature." — Spk. Com.

b Is. xlv. 13.

"When a person is hungry, or weary, or when he hears bad news, it is said, 'His hands have become weak,' c His hands have turned cold.'" —Roberts.

The old paths (vs. 16.—The figure: travelers and their guides. I. The denomination, "old paths." 1. Because ordained from eternity; 2. Because herein all the saints have walked; 3. Because tried. II. The description, "good way." A way is good—1. When safe; 2. When direct; 3. When frequented; 4. When pleasant; 5. When firm and passable. III. The directions, "stand, etc." 1. They who seek this path should be cautious in their observations; 2. They must be earnest in their inquiries; 3. They should be prompt in entering thereon. IV. The destination, "rest." 1. On the journey, contentment, satisfaction, etc.; 2. Afterwards eternal repose.—Stems and Twigs.

18—20. (18) **congregation,** or general assembly of mankind. (19) **O earth,** the appeal being even to nature to listen to God's charge against His people. (20) **To what purpose,**[d] or what is the value of any external ceremonies, when the heart is not in them? **Sheba,** a part of Arabia Felix, famous for its spices. **sweet cane,**[e] Is. xliii. 24. Necessary ingredients of the incense and anointing oil of the Temple. **burnt offerings,** which should testify to an entire devotion to My service.

Note on vs. 20.—The sweet-smelling reed grows in the deserts of Arabia. It is gathered near Jambo, a port town of Arabia Petræa, from whence it is brought into Egypt. Pliny says it is common to India and Syria. It is likely the sweet cane of Jeremiah, who calls it prime, or excellent, and associates it with incense from Sheba. "To what purpose cometh there to me incense from Sheba, and the sweet cane from a far country?" And, in allusion to the same plant, Isaiah complains in the name of Jehovah, "Thou hast bought Me no sweet cane with money." In the Book of Exodus it is called "sweet calamus," and is said to come "from a far country;" which agrees with the declaration of ancient writers, that the best is brought from India.—Paxton.

21—25. (21) **stumblingblocks,** in the way of the progress of this nation God shall place such an obstacle as shall cause it to fall.[d] Old and young—all shall be overthrown. (22) Here begins the fourth section in this chapter. **sides .. earth,** or remotest regions of the earth.[b] (23) **cruel,** inhuman, as they proved to be. **voice roareth,** Is. xvii. 12, 13. **horses,** ch. iv. 13. (24) **fame,** "the prophet identifies himself (comp., for the same phenomenon, ch. iv. 19—21; x. 19, 20) with his people, and expresses the general feeling of anxiety and pain. The phraseology of the closing lines reminds us of Isa. xiii. 7, 8."—Pul. Com. **hands .. feeble,** so that we cannot hold our weapons. (25) **every side,** there is danger all around.

Dufflas war prayer.—According to the Delhi Gazette, the Dufflas are in an uncomfortable state of mind about our approaching expedition into their country. A big-sounding war prayer has been drawn up by the local pope, who has enjoined all true Dufflas to repeat it twice a day. Among other things they are to pray: "Let their coasts be ruled by us! Let the demons of their forts be given to those of ours! Let the soul of him who is the chief cause of this quarrel be bound by that of our friend and chief, whom he has injured! Let the properties of their country be received by us! Let their warriors be seized by us; for which reason make strong all our warriors, that they may bind the spirits of all their able men for us to destroy them! Give us such help that they may not stand or hold, and that they be rendered insane and made to tremble! Come, our principal god, who art great, and powerful, and old, and whose words are always obeyed, destroy all our enemies, with all they possess, even that which is upon their backs! Let owls scream on their houses! Let all venomous reptiles scramble up the posts of their houses, and frighten them with terrific noises! Let fierce dogs, wild elephants, and ferocious tigers terrify them, so that they scratch each other's faces and tear their own hair! Let the rainbow drink up the water of their wells, and tanks, and rivers! Let a powerful tempest sweep them away! Come, spirits of our warriors, of our ancestors, seize the spirits of our enemies! Come, spirits of our great-grandmothers, with the demons of this powerful country, by whom we are governed, and whose eyes, and ears, and nostrils are ever open towards us!"

26—30. (26) **gird,** etc., as ch. iii. 25.[c] **wallow .. ashes,** the sign of wildness of grief. **only son,** Am. viii. 10; Zec. xii. 10. (27) **a fortress,** "compare i. 18. Jeremiah is promised that he shall receive protection while carrying out the duty which so exasperates the people against him." (28) **brass and iron,** i. e. base metal, "their impudence resembles brass, and their obstinacy may be cŏmpared to iron."—Lowth. (29) **burned,** R. V., "blow fiercely." But these metals will not be refined even in intense fires of chastisement.[d] (30) **Reprobate,** or refuse; only dross, with no basis of good metal.

Reprobate silver.—This then is the end: the Lord hath rejected them. The smelter is God's prophet, the bellows, the breath of inspiration; the flux, his earnestness in preaching; but in vain does the fervor of prophecy essay to melt the hearts of the people. They are so utterly corrupt, that no particle even of pure metal can be found in them. All the refiner's art is in vain. They have rejected all God's gifts and motives for their repentance and therefore Jehovah has rejected them, as an alloy too utterly adulterate, to repay the refiner's toil.—Speaker's Com. The Church.—Men seem to think, "Only let me get into the church that has apostolicity, and catholicity, and orthodoxy!" . . . An organized institution I believe in; but the New Testament idea of a Church was a moral society of those who had a common faith, hope and love. That Church which is most positive about its apostolicity, that thinks there is no other Church but itself in the world, is a mere crustaceous, not a Spiritual Church. And that Church which has the most altars, the most vestments, the most externalities, the most things that appeal to the lower nature of men, which has the most physical embodiment, and therefore occupies the largest space in men's sight, is farthest from the true Spiritual Church.—Beecher.

[c] Mi. i. 10.

[d] Pr. xvii. 3; Isa. i. 25; Zec. xiii. 9; Mal. iii. 2, 3; 1 Pe. i. 7.

"If slander be a snake, it is a winged one—it flies as well as creeps." —Douglas Jerrold.

"Where it concerns himself, who's angry at a slander makes it true."—Ben Jonson.

CHAPTER THE SEVENTH.

The four chapters vii.-x. are plainly a finished whole; the circumstances of the discourse are given in chap. xxvi. Date: early in the reign of Jehoiakim: 605 B. C. **1—4.** (1) **word,** a new prophecy. (2) **gate,** either the principal gate on the east side of the temple; or the gate of the court of Israel. (3) **Amend .. doings,** Zec. i. 6, ways or habits, doings or separate actions. (4) **lying words,** such as deceive. **temple**[a] **.. these,** the repetition emphasises their "fanatical confidence in the inviolability of the temple."—Exp. Bib. Perhaps the constant iteration of pagan worship was also in mind. As if the repetition had a worth of its own.

5—7. (5) **thoroughly,** sincerely, and heartily. "The true palladium of Judah would be the faithful performance of Jehovah's moral laws, especially those referring to the conduct of the rulers. Observe the stress which all the prophets lay on the virtues of civil life."—Pul Com. (6) **oppress not,** etc., comp. ch. v. 28; De. xiv. 29, xxiv, 19—21. (7) **dwell,** permanently and securely. **ever and ever,** from eternity to eternity: "the strongest formula by which perpetuity of duration is expressed in Hebrew."[a]

Thoroughness.—A proud Indian chief became deeply convicted of sin, and, trembling under a sense of guilt, sought the missionary, and proffered his belt of wampum to be freed from his anguish of fear. "No," said the missionary, "Christ cannot accept such a sacrifice." The Indian departed, but soon returned offering his rifle and the skins he had taken in hunting. "No," was the reply, "Christ cannot accept such a sacrifice." Again the Indian went away, but with a troubled conscience once more returned, and offered his wigwam, wife, child, everything, for peace and pardon. "No," was still the reply, "Christ cannot accept such a sacrifice." The chief seemed oppressed with surprise for a moment; then, lifting up tearful eyes to heaven, he feelingly cried out, "Here, Lord, take poor Indian too!"—Dictionary of Illustrations.

[a] The Jews supposed that bec. the temple was dedicated to Jehovah, He, as their tulelar God, would effectually protect it, and all who came to worship in it."—Henderson.

"It is much easier to give oneself to a church or a sect than to God."Toplady.

"Lais broke her looking-glass because it showed the wrinkles on her face. Many men are angry with them that tell them their faults, when they should be angry only with the faults that are told them." —Venning.

[a] Je. xxv. 5; Ne. ix. 5; Ps. xc. 2.

"With God there is no free man but his servant, though in the galleys; no slave but the sinner, though in a palace; none rich, but he that possesseth God, even in rags;

none happy but he whom the world pities. Let me be free, rich, happy, to God." -Bp. Hall.

b "The Prophet does not charge them with the transgression of the ritual ordinances of Moses, but with the breach of the weightier matter of the law." —Lowth.

c "At Silo, where once was the tabernacle and ark of the Lord, there can scarcely be pointed out the foundation of an altar."—S. Jerome.

d "When people are given up to judicial hardiness of heart, intercessory prayer for them is unavailing." —Fausset.

"Comfort, like the golden sun, dispels the sullen shade with her sweet influence, and cheers the melancholy house of care." —Rowe.

"God's promises are with a condition, which is as an oar in a boat or stern of a ship, and turns the promise another way."—Trapp.

a "Prob. very similar to those offered at Athens to Artemis in the middle of the month Munychion. These were round like the full moon, and covered with lights, and finally were burnt in her honor, forming with the added libation the symbol of a eucharist."—Spk. Com.

b Ro. viii. 20—22.

"Act! for in action are wisdom and glory; fame, immortality,—

8—11. (8) **lying words,** such were the assurances of the false prophets. (9) **steal,** etc., comp. these sins and vices with the signs of amendment God looks for, vss. 5, 6. (10) **delivered,** R. V., "We are delivered; that ye may do," etc. We are free to do all these things, because we have gone through the prescribed ceremonials of the temple.[b] (11) **den of robbers,** a place of retreat in the intervals between acts of violence. This verse is alluded to (in connexion with Is. lvi. 7) in Matt. xxi. 13, and the parallel passages (Mark xi. 17 and Luke xix. 46). "You make My house a place of sanctuary and protection to malefactors."

Sacrilege.—The Spirit of God will not have holy things profaned. Belshazzar converted the consecrated vessels of the temple into instruments of luxury and intemperance. Herod polluted the sepulchres of saints by a sacrilegious search for treasures presumed to be hidden there, and God made fire to rise out of the earth and consume the searchers. Antiochus ransacked the temples of the Lord. Heliodorus emptied the treasuries of their consecrated monies. Pompey defiled the Sabbath and the Sanctuary. Crassus robbed the house of God of 10,000 talents. But inquire unto the event of these insolences, and we shall find that true then of which later ages give many examples, that ruin is the child of sacrilege, that mischief setteth a period to the lives and designs of profane men.—Bp. Reynolds.

12—16. (12) **Shiloh,**[c] in the tribe of Ephraim, and north of Bethel. Jos. xviii. 1; 1 Ga. iv. 3; Ps. lxxviii. 60. **at the first,** before the tabernacle was removed to Zion, or the temple built. (13) **rising up early,** a fig. for doing a thing earnestly. "Speaking zealously and earnestly." **called,** etc., Pr. i. 24; Is. lxv. 12, lxvi. 4. (14) **as I have done,** i. e. I will utterly destroy it. "The reference is not to the tablernacle, the sacred Tent of the Wanderings, which was first set up at Nob (1 Sam. xxi. 22) and then removed to Gibeon (2 Chron. i. 3), but obviously to a building more or less like the temple, though less magnificent. The place and its sanctuary had doubtless been ruined in the great catastrophe, when the kingdom of Samaria fell before the power of Assyria (721 B. C.)."—Exp. Bib. (15) **your brethren,** the ten tribes, who had already come under Divine judgments. (16) **pray not,** spoken to Jeremiah.[d] **cry,** offering prayer aloud.

Intercessory Prayer.—Luther had boundless confidence in the power and prevalency of prayer. "At the time the Diet of Nuremburg was held," says Tholuck, "Luther was earnestly praying in his own dwelling; and at the very hour when the edict granting free toleration to all Protestants was issued, he ran out of his house, crying out, "We have gained the victory! Do you understand that?" On another occasion Melancthon was sinking into death through severe illness, and Luther entered his chamber. "We cannot spare you yet!" was Luther's exclamation to his dying friend; and then he threw himself upon his knees in wrestling prayer. Then, seizing Melancthon's hand, he said, "Be of good courage, Philip, thou shalt not die!" After his recovery, Melancthon wrote to Camerarieus, "If Luther had not come to me, I should certainly have died. He recalled me from the gates of the grave."

> More things are wrought by prayer
> Than this world dreams of. Wherefore, let thy voice
> Rise like a fountain for me, night and day.
>
> —Tennyson.

17—20. The reason why it is too late for prayer to avail. (17) **what they do,** in carrying out their worship of the most impure of all the heathen deities. (18) **children, etc.,** all taking some part in the degrading service. **cakes,**[a] made of honey, fine flour, etc., in a round flat shape, to resemble the disc of the moon, to whom they were offered. **queen of heaven,** the moon.[b] Ashtoreth, the wife of Baal, the sun-god. (19) **confusion .. faces?** Is it me they vex? Is it not themselves rather? And upon themselves they bring this shame. (20) **poured out,** ch. iv. 25, 26, ix. 10, xii. 4. As constantly in Isaiah, nature shares in man's redemption, so here in man's punishment.[b]

Suffering of backsliders.—I believe that if the mental sufferings of such backsliders could be written and faithfully published, they would astound you, and be a more horrible story to read than all the torments of the Inquisition. What racks a man is stretched upon who has been unfaithful to his covenant with God! What fires have burned within the souls of those men who have been untrue to Christ and his cause! What dungeons, what grim and dark prisons underground, have saints of God lain in who have gone aside into by-path meadows instead of keeping to the King's highway! He who sins must smart, especially if he be a child of God, for the Lord hath said of his people, "You only have I known of all the people of the earth, therefore I will punish you for your iniquities." Whoever may go unchastised, a child of God never shall.—Spurgeon.

21—24. (21) **burnt offerings,**[c] multiply your various sacrifices! what matters it. (22) **spake not**, etc., "If ye think to serve God by a multitude of sacrifices ye do greatly err. Jehovah did indeed allow your fathers to offer Him sacrifices, but He gave no special direction concerning them." —Cheyne.[d] (23) **Obey,** etc., De. vi. 3. (24) **imagination,** "stubbornness." **went backward,** like headstrong oxen.

Sacrifices.—Christ never despised sacrifice, but relatively He undervalued it. The idea of sacrifice among the Jews had taken precedence of humanity, justice and right. (Matt. v. 23, 24). What does it mean but this, Do not think that sacrifice to God is the highest religious duty. Sacrifice depends for its value, on preceding moral qualities. A principle is higher than the ordinance which you take to exhibit that principle. The life of religion in the soul is first in importance: the instruments by which you develop that life are of secondary consideration.—Beecher. Obedience.—Some persons would make religion to consist of little else than a self-denying course of the practise of virtue and obedience They make it a kind of house of correction work. But no! I love the service of my God; like the bird I fly on the wings of obedience to his holy will.—Chalmers.

25—28. (25) **sent unto you,** vs. 13. God had never failed to let them know His will through inspired messengers. (26) **hardened .. neck,** ch. xvi. 12. (28) **receiveth correction,** R. V. "instruction." **truth,** in the sense of fidelity. **from their mouth,** which only makes false professions.

God providing for the wants of his people.—It is no aimless, helpless anxiety that fills his breast. The most practical measures of help and direction are devised and carried into execution. Prophets, the plenipotentiaries of Divine grace, are sent in immediate response to the needs and demands of men. No age of the world or the Church but has its thick succession. Heaven is in continual activity on behalf of sinners. The choicest spiritual gifts are ceaselessly rained upon the earth. The most devoted servants of God are raised up and sent. Truth in quick evolution anticipates the spiritual necessities of those who would seek God. There is no flagging, no cessation, from Adam's fall to the uplifting of the second Adam. And onward from that Divine spectacle, in which was displayed the "fulness of the Godhead bodily," events hurry to the culminating glories of Pentecost and the marriage supper of the Lamb.—Pul. Com.

29—31. "The scene of their wickedness shall be also that of their punishment." (29—34.) (29) **Cut .. hair,** a sign of mourning.[a] It is commanded in anticipation of the desolation of Jerusalem. **generation .. wrath,** that is but the subject of His judgments. "This sinful generation, who have so highly provoked His anger." (30) **in the house,** etc., this must refer to the times of Manasseh.[b] (31) **high places,** here prob. meaning "altars." **Tophet,** 2 Ki. xxiii. 10. **burn,** etc., Le xx. 2—5.

Nature of repentance.—Repentance, as explained by John's ministry, is a conviction of the fact of sin, but a sharp and painful conviction. A conviction that never produced humility, never sighed, never wept, never "wept apart," and never sought solitude for the purpose of prayer and reflection, is not that which is an element of true repentance. It is a serious and painful apprehension of danger. Hence John asked the Pharisees and Sadducees that came to his baptism, "Who hath warned you to flee from the wrath to come?" Repentance is an humble confession of sin. The people confessed generally to John; for it was impossible for

these are its crown. Wouldst thou illumine the tablets of story? Build on achievements thy doom of renown."— Anon.

[c] "The Prophet tells the Jews that they may, if they please, eat the flesh of their burnt-offerings, as well as of their peace-offerings, for God will accept neither of them from their hands."—Lowth. Is. i. 11; Je. vi. 20; Am. v. 21.

[d] Ex. xix. 5, 6. Le. xi. 45.

"He that hides a dark soul and foul thoughts
Benighted walks under the midday sun;
Himself is his own dungeon."
—Milton.

"To be left alone, and face to face with my own crime, had been just retribution."— Longfellow.

[a] Je. xlvii. 5, xlviii. 37.

[b] 2 Ki. xxi. 3—5.

"The redeeming power of the blood of Christ is greater than the condemning power of sin. This excellency it hath from the dignity of His person (for it is called the blood of God, Acts xx. 28), which makes His obedience and sufferings give more glory to God than our suffering in hell would have done. Isaiah xlii. 21; Rom. v. 17."—Mather.

him to enter into the particulars of each case; but to God they confessed their sins in detail. Repentance is fruitful. Under its influence the churl becomes liberal; the unjust becomes righteous; and those who had formerly been careless of their spiritual interests wait upon God in the use of every means of grace. Repentance is despairing, but hopeful. The people who were awakened under John's ministry felt that in themselves there was no help; and he taught the whole of them to wait for Christ the Saviour.—R. Watson.

[a] Je. xvi. 9.

"Punishment is the recoil of crime; and the strength of the back-stroke is in proportion to the original blow."—French.

"Reference is made to the joyous processions in which the bride and bridegroom are led through the streets, accompanied by bands of singers and musicians." —Henderson.

"A sleep without dreams, after a rough day
Of toil, is what we covet most; and yet
How clay shrinks back from more quiescent clay!"
—Byron.

"Death! to the happy thou art terrible,
But how the wretched love to think of thee!
O thou true comforter, the friend of all
Who have no friend beside!"
—Southey.

"The Prophet, beginning with the heart, describes their worship in the various stages of its development, and then contrasts its fulness with the miserable reward that ensues." — Hitzig.

32—34. (32) **valley of slaughter,** bec. the enemies coming upon Jerusalem would make so great a slaughter of the people there. **till there be no place,** rather "for want of place" elsewhere. (33) **carcases,** dead bodies cast out, wh. none should bury. So many dead. So few survivors. Comp. Deut. xxviii. 26. (34) **cease,** etc., silence shall fall upon the utterly desolated and deserted city.[a]

Silence of sorrow.—It was the custom in the East, even in modern times, to conduct the bride and bridegroom through the streets, with the loudest demonstrations of joy. Rauwolf found this custom also prevalent in Aleppo. "When a Turkish woman is going to be married, and the bridegroom is conducted to her house, their relations and friends, who are invited to the wedding, as they go along through the streets cry with such a loud voice, which they gradually raise as they advance, that they can be heard from one street to the other." When the Prophet paints a period of public distress, he says among other things, "The voice of the bride and the bridegroom shall no longer be heard." Thus, in Persia, no marriages are celebrated during Lent (the month of Ramadan), and the solemnities of mourning in memory of Hossein; because everything must then be still and mournful.—Rosenmuller.

CHAPTER THE EIGHTH.

1—3. (1) **At that time,** when the city shall be taken. **bring .. bones,** ransacking even the very tombs, with contempt and malice, not for spoil, as the Jews did not so bury their dead. (2) **spread,** etc., or toss them out. **loved .. served .. walked .. worshipped,** "there is great force in the piled up verbs by wh. their worship of the heavenly bodies is described."—Spk. Com. The point is, that these gods prove utterly unable to prevent such desecration. "They are unconcerned spectators of the indignity offered to their former worshipers." (3) **residue,** or survivors of the great calamity. **evil family,** ch. i. 15.

Graves disturbed and dead molested.—It was "a hatred carried beyond the grave, a hatred which is a sort of impotent grasping at eternal vengeance, hatred which, having no power to work any real vengeance, has no object but to show its hatred."—Pusey. He (David) was buried by his son Solomon in Jerusalem, with great magnificence, and with all the other funeral pomp which kings used to be buried with; moreover he had great and immense wealth buried with him, the vastness of which may be easily conjectured by what I now say: for 1300 years afterwards, Hyrcanus, the high priest, when he was besieged by Antiochus, and was desirous of giving him money to get him to raise the siege, and draw off his army, and having no other method of compassing the money, opened one room of David's sepulchre and took out 3,000 talents, and gave part of that sum to Antiochus, and by this means caused the siege to be raised. Nay, after him, and that many years, Herod, the king, opened another room, and took away a great deal of money.—Josephus.

"In the second part of this great discourse (viii. 4—ix. 1) we have a fine development of thoughts which have already been advanced in the opening piece, after the usual manner of Jeremiah. The first half is mainly concerned with the sins of the nation (vss. 4-13), the second with a despairing lament over the punishment (14—ix. 1)."—Exp. Bib.

4—7. (4) **Shall they fall,** etc., R. V., "Shall men fall . . . shall one turn away," etc. **not arise,** or try to get up again. **turn away,** i. e. wander fr. his path. **return,** or try to find his path again. (5) **perpetual back-**

sliding, keeping on wandering further and further, with no attempts to return.[a] (6) **as the horse,** at full speed, that cannot be checked.[b] (7) **stork,** Is. i. 3. A migratory bird. **turtle,** a kind of dove, Cant. ii. 12. **crane .. swallow,** Is. xxxviii. 14. **judgment,** R. V., "ordinance," the birds obey their law—but man does not obey.

Human rejection of Divine love (vs. 6).—I. God's love. II. Man's rejection of it. 1. The wrong words; 2. The impenitence; 3. The recklessness; 4. Stupidity.—H. Bonar.

Here we are like birds of passage.—It is stated in the history of England that when the first missionary who arrived at Kent presented himself before the king, to solicit permission to preach the Gospel in his dominions, after long deliberation, when a negative was about to be put upon his application, an aged councillor, with his head silvered over with grey hairs, rose, and by the following speech obtained the permission which was requested. "Here we are," said the orator, "like birds of passage; we know not whence we come, or whither we are going; if this man can tell us, for God's sake let him speak." I say, if there are six hundred millions of our fellow-creatures who, like birds of passage, know not whence they came, nor whither they are going, for God's sake let us send them the Gospel, which will tell them whence they came, and which is able to make them wise unto salvation.—Philip.

8—12. (8) **law .. with us,** fr. this it appears that copies of the law multiplied. **Lo, certainly,** etc. R. V. "But behold the false pen of the scribes hath wrought falsely," in so explaining the Law as to assure men that they may sin with impunity.[c] **scribes,** or copyists, "we gather that the Law must have existed in writing before the class of scribes could have grown up, and therefore the modern view that the 'Books of Moses' were a late fabrication may be disproved even from this verse alone." —Camb. Bib. (9) **wise,** they who think themselves wise. **rejected .. Lord,** by persisting in false interpretations of the Word. (10—12) **wives,** etc., comp. ch. vi. 12—15.

Difficulties and dangers of infidelity (vs. 9).—The text includes three classes of men who do not believe the Scriptures. I. Sceptics, those who profess to be in uncertainty. 1. When sincere they must be miserable; 2. Wretched; 3. Continual mental conflict must be torment. II. Atheists. III. Deists.—Bennett.

13—17. (13) **surely,** R. V., "utterly." **consume them,** by the destructive power of the Chaldæans. **shall be,** better "there are," "it is the actual conditon of things which the prophet describes. Elsewhere Judah is compared to a vine with bad grapes (ch. ii. 21); here the vine does not even pretend to bear fruit. Another figure is that of a barren fig tree (comp. Matt. xxi. 19)."—Pul. Com. (14) **Why .. still?** this is the way the people will feel when the time comes. **water of gall,** poison, De. xxix. 18. (15) **health,** or rest. (16) **his horses,** those of the on-coming enemy. **Dan,** ch. iv. 15. **strong ones,** chargers. (17) **cockatrices,** R. V. "basilisks," types of dangerous enemies.

Despair may follow a Confident hope.—The Jews had looked for peace and for a time of health. Yet came none. Hope may be very bright and yet very delusive. The splendor of the sunrise contains little promise that the day will close without storms. Subjective confidence is no guarantee of objective truth. Things are not the more true because we believe them very firmly. We may feel safe and be in danger. A peaceful death is no security for a joyful resurrection. It is little that a man has overcome the fear of death; the important question is whether he has removed the ground for that fear. The faith that saves is not confidence in our own security, but submissive and obedient trust in Christ.—Pul. Com. Serpents.—Few animals excite more horror on their first appearance than these common enemies, both of man and beast. The possibility of some being made subject to certain incantations or charms is remarkable, and is often referred to in Scripture. The Hindoos, or at least the serpent-charmers, pretend to handle all sorts of snakes with impunity, to make them come and go at pleasure, and, in short, to have a cabalistic authority over the whole race. The cobra is the only serpent used for display by jugglers. When caught, it is held at arm's

[a] "An expostulation, implying that men are seldom so far gone in wickedness as not to be touched with some remorse for their evil doings, and make some general resolutions of amendment; whereas this people are guilty of one perpetual apostasy, as if they could deceive God by their hypocritical pretences, without making any steps towards a reformation." —Lowth.

Je. vii. 24.

[b] "A double metaphor: first, the determined persistence of the people in sin is compared to the blind fury which at the sound of the trumpet seizes upon the war-horse; and then its impetuous rush into the battle is likened to the overflowing of a torrent (the word rushing is lit. overflowing), wh. nothing can stop in its destructive course."—Spk. Com.

"Soon may this woe-worn spirit seek the bourne
Where, lulled to slumber, grief forgets to mourn."
—Campbell.

[c] Ezr. vii. 6; Ne. viii. 9, 13.

"So farewell, hope, and with hope farewell fear,
Farewell remorse; all good to me is lost
Evil be thou my good."
—Milton.

"No soul is desolate as long as there is a human being for whom it can feel trust and reverence."
—George Eliot.

"The vintage and harvest are frequently employed figuratively as images of complete destruction; but here the terms are to be taken in their literal application." —Henderson.

Je. ix. 15, xxiii. 15.

"Serpent charmers in the East entice serpents by music, and by a particular pressure on the neck render them incapable of darting."—Fausset.

a "Summer is the fruit-gathering, which follows the corn-harvest......Despair seized the people when they saw opportunities for their deliverance again and again pass by, till God seemed utterly to have forgotten them."—Spk. Com.

b "In an old version this word is translated treacle."—H. Macmillan.

c "Jeremiah implies that the fault lay wholly in the patients themselves, who refused to submit to the prescriptions." —Lowth.

Some one once asked a venerable minister of the Gospel this question:—"What is the hardest (meaning the most dreadful) text in the Bible?" The minister referred to a text, saying, "I know of no harder text than this, and yet there is nothing about damnation or hell in it." The words which he repeated were these:—"The harvest is past, the summer is ended, and we are not saved." —Jeremiah viii. 20. Certainly there are in the Bible no words more fearful

length by the tail, and as often as it attempts to strike, it is beaten off. It is then seized by the head, thrown on the ground, and its fangs knocked out with a hammer; after which its poison bag is squeezed dry. By these means the cobra is rendered harmless, though it may be easily excited, and made to raise itself in answer to the sounds of music (Ps. lviii. 4, 5). The basilisk is frequently mentioned in Scripture, but no description is given further than that it cannot be charmed. The Greek text calls it basilisc, and the Hebrew tsepha, while the English improperly renders it cockatrice, a fabulous animal that never existed. The eggs of the basilisk are referred to in Isa. lix. 5: hence it would appear to be a snake, and not a viper, as the latter brings forth its young alive.—Bib. Treas.

18—22. (18) **comfort myself,** R. V., "Oh that I could comfort myself," etc., find some ground of consolation. **faint in me,** it misgives me. (19) **Behold,** etc., "Hark! a cry of my people from distant lands: Is Jehovah not in Zion," etc."—Lange. Jer. anticipates the complaints of the captive Jews. (20) **summer,** vintage, ingathering of fruits. "As when the harvest was bad, there remained yet hopes from the yield of grapes, figs, olives, etc., and till these hopes had failed to be realized, men did not despair; so the people had lost one chance after another, and were now without any hope. It is the people who speak here, and use what is obviously a proverbial saying."—Camb. Bib.[a] (21) **black,** in mourning. (22) **balm,**[b] Ge. xxxvii. 25. **Gilead, ch.** xlvi. 11; this district was famous for balm, turpentine, and similar healing gums; therefore physicians and surgeons resorted thither.[c]

The day of grace (vs. 20).—I. A short time, and therefore requires diligence: the King's business requires haste. II. A limited time, as summer days are longer than winter days. III. A varying time: rainbow of mercy seen only in the day of grace.—G. S. Bowes.—The harvest past. —I. Every person who still remains in sin may, at the close of the year, usefully adopt this lamentation. II. A season in whch religion prevails is also eminently a time of harvest, and such as lose this season may well adopt the lamentation of the text. III. Another situation to which this melancholy reflection is peculiarly applicable is that of a dying sinner.—T. Dwight.

Opportunity lost.—One of the most ingenious tortures of the Hohenstaufen family, in the height of their despotic control, was that of a cell, which, at the prisoner's first entrance, presented an air of comfort and ease; so that it was not till he had been a few days confined that he observed the dimensions of his chamber beginning to contract. But the discovery once made, the fact became more appalling every day. Slowly but terribly, the sides drew closer and the unhappy victim was crushed to death. What an emblem does this suggest of the sinner's contracting day of grace! Oh, what would the poor victim in such a cell have given to see the door open, and hear a voice, "Escape for thy life!" Would that sinners would escape as eagerly by the door of grace!—Bowes.

The balm of life.—"Alexander the Great was dying of a wound, which did not seem very dangerous at first, but it baffled his physicians, and was rapidly becoming mortal. One night, however, it is said he dreamed that some one had brought him a peculiar-looking plant, which, when applied to the festering sore, had cleansed and closed it. In the morning, when he awoke, he described the plant; and the historian informs us that it was sought for and found, and when applied to the wound, the fiery pain subsided, and he was speedily healed. Now your soul has received a deadly hurt; it has been stung by the old serpent, the devil. The wound gets worse. There is a tender plant which is able to heal you; it is the Balm of Gilead. They used to wound the balsam tree, in order to obtain its healing essence; and so for our transgressions the Saviour was wounded, and 'by His stripes ye are healed.'"—J. Hamilton..—Poison and antidote.—There is a tree called the manchaneel, which grows in the West Indies; its appearance is very attractive, and the wood of it peculiarly beautiful; it bears a kind of apple, resembling the golden pippin. This fruit looks very tempting, and smells very fragrant; but to eat of it is instant death; and its sap or juice is so poisonous, that if a few drops of it fall on the skin it raises blisters, and occasions great pain. The Indians dip their arrows in the juice, that they may poison their enemies when they wound them. Providence hath so appointed it that one of these trees is never found, but near it there also grows a white wood, or a fig tree, the juice of either of which, if applied in time, is a remedy for the diseases produced by the manchaneel. Sin, like this poisonous apple, looks pleasant to the eye, and men desire it,—eat of it, and die. But there is a remedy at hand; it is the precious blood of the Son of God, which soothes the troubled conscience, and cleanses it from all sin.

> "Not balm, new bleeding from the wounded tree,
> Nor bless'd Arabia with his spicy grove,
> Such fragrance yields."

The balm of Gilead is a small evergreen; at five feet from the ground it branches out something like an old hawthorn; bark is smooth, shining, of a whitish grey color, with brown blotches; leaves are of a bright green, foliage is scanty and rugged. The greatest quantity of balsam flows from the wounded bark; but there are three kinds procured by art; best is the opobalsam, expressed from the green berry; second, from the ripe nut or berry; the last is obtained by bruising and boiling the young wood.—Scripture Herbal.

CHAPTER THE NINTH.

1—3. (1) In the Hebrew this verse closes chap. viii. **fountain,** or reservoir, fr. wh. tears might freely flow. **slain,** in the great coming calamity. (2) **lodging place,** or caravanserai,[a] a place offering only shelter for the traveler. No resident host, no food provided, no company. There he would escape the sights and sounds that now appall him. **assembly,** or gang. (3) **like their bow,** or just as soldiers before battle bend their bows, so they prepare to shoot out lying words, like arrows.[d] **not valiant,** etc. R. V., "and they are grown strong in the land, but not for truth."

Religious consolation (vs. 1).—I. Religon affords ample solace to the afflicted. 1. The poor; 2. The bereaved; 3. The sick. II. The Gospel bestows healing on the patient. III. Religion affords solid comfort to those mourning over their own corruptions. 1. The Word of God teaches them that the painful consciousness of their own imperfections has ever been a characteristic of the most eminent saints; 2. And assures every believer of a final triumph over his corruptions.—Pulpit Studies.

A lodge in the wilderness.—People in the East, on their journeys to other towns or countries, are obliged to travel through the most lonely wilds. On this account the native sovereigns, or opulent men, erect what are called "rest-houses," or choultries, where the travelers or pilgrims reside for the night. "In the wilderness," too, devotees and ascetics live retired from men: there, either for life, or for a short period, they perform their austerities, and live in cynical contempt of the rest of mankind. When a father is angry with his family, he often exclaims, "If I had but a shade in the wilderness, then should I be happy. I will become a pilgrim and leave you." Nor is this mere empty declamation to alarm his family; for numbers in every town and village thus leave their homes and are never heard of more. There are, however, many who remain absent for a few months or years, and then return. Under these circumstances, it is no wonder, when a father or husband threatens his family to retire to the katu, that is, "wilderness," that they become greatly alarmed. But men who have been reduced in their circumstances become so mortified, that they also retire from their homes, and all their future days wander about as pilgrims. "Alas! alas! I will retire to the jungle, and live with wild beasts!" says the broken-hearted widow. —Roberts.

than these. What can be more dreadful than the wail of a lost soul?

"Has a man lost a good situation, it is said, 'His harvest is past.' Is a person amassing much money, it is said, 'He is gathering in his harvest.'" — Roberts.

"Many do with opportunities as children do at the seashore; they fill their little hands with sand, and then let the grains fall through one by one till all are gone." — T. Jones.

"The balm of the soul is prayer, saith the Chaldee paraphrast; is repentance, saith Jerome; is Christ applied by faith, say we. Sanguis medici est curatio phrenetici." —Trapp.

[a] "This lodge generally consists of a large square building, enclosing a court open above, round the sides of which are small arches, and within each of these is a dark cell or dormitory, without furniture or accommodation of any kind." — Henderson.

[d] Is. xxii. 4; La. ii. 11, iii. 48.

"Need we wonder if the Infinite exceeds our weak, narrow minds? Would you measure God and His mysteries by your vision? Would He be infinite if you could measure Him and fathom His depths?"—Fénelon.

"Don't say, 'Lord, this is the way?' but 'Lord, is this the way?' Don't show Him the way you want

Oh for a lodge in some vast wilderness,
Some boundless contiguity of shade,
Where rumor of oppression and deceit,
Of unsuccessful or successful war,
Might never reach me more! My ear is pained,
My soul is sick with every day's report
Of wrong and outrage with which earth is filled.
There is no flesh in man's obdurate heart,
It does not feel for man; the natural bond
Of brotherhood is severed as the flax
That falls asunder at the touch of fire. —Cowper.

to take; stand still till He bids you go forward. Your work is coming to meet you just as truly as you are going to meet it."—J. M. D. Conklin.

4—8. (4) **Take ye heed,** "the mutual distrust, which had already in the time of Hezekiah broken up families and divided the nearest friends, and made a man's worst enemies those of his own household, had now reached the highest degree of intensity; 'Every man had to take heed of his neighbor and suspect his brother.'"—Camb. Bib. **supplant,** as Jacob did.[a] (5) **weary themselves,** through making such efforts. (6) **Thine habitation,** addressed to the people, continuation of the warning of vs. 4. **Through deceit,** etc., i. e. as a result of their unfaithfulness to one another they have come to deny Me. (7) **melt them,** in refining fires of national calamity. **how,** etc., i. e. how otherwise. (8) **an arrow shot out.** R. V. "a deadly arrow."[b] Vs. 3. **his wait,** R. V. "in his heart he layeth wait for him."[c]

[a] Ge. xxv. 26, xxvii. 36; Ho. xii. 3.

[b] "The arrow shot out" may be trans. "murderous arrow."

[c] "'Layeth his ambush.'"—Henderson.

Slander.—"Against slander there is no defence. Hell cannot boast so foul a fiend, nor men deplore so foul a foe. It stabs with a smile. It is a pestilence walking in darkness, spreading contagion far and wide, which the most wary traveler cannot avoid. It is the heart-searching dagger of the assassin. It is the poisoned arrow whose wound is incurable. It is as fatal as the sting of the most deadly asp; murder is its employment, innocence its prey, and ruin its sport."—Gray's "Topics."

"Each of the negroes took from his quiver a handful of arrows and putting two between his teeth, and one in his bow, waved to us with his hand to keep at a distance."—Mungo Park.

"The devil hath not, in all his quiver's choice,
An arrow for the heart like a sweet voice."
—Byron.

"Slander, the foulest whelp of sin! The man
In whom this spirit entered was undone;
His tongue was set on fire of hell; his heart
Was black as death; his legs were faint with haste
To propagate the lie his soul had framed;
His pillow was the peace of families
Destroyed, the sigh of innocence reproached,
Broken friendships, and the strife of brotherhoods."
—Pollok.

9—11. (9) **not visit,** ch. v. 9, 29. (10) "On the mountains let me raise a weeping and wailing and on the pastures of the desert a lamentation."—Lange. **habitations,** R. V. "pastures."[a] **burned up,** through lack of cultivation, marg. desolate. (11) **Jerusalem,** the city, as well as the country, was to be overwhelmed. **dragons,** R. V. "jackals."[b]

[a] "The wilderness sometimes signifies the plain or champaign country, and is opposed to the mountains."—Lowth.

[b] Ps. lxiv. 19; Is. xiii. 22, xxxiv. 13; Je. li. 37.

Cause of threatenings.—Love so yearns to rescue those it loves. The rope may cut and wound the hands of the drowning sailor to whom we have thrown it, but we do not mind that if thereby he be drawn safe to shore. The knife of the surgeon may cut deep and cause fearful pain, but if it saves the imperilled life we are thankful notwithstanding. So God sends forth these stern, rough, and terrible threatenings, that souls under the spell of sin may be awakened, alarmed, made to tremble, and to "seek the Lord while he may be found."—Pul. Com.

"Northern mythology tells of the Migdard serpent, whom Odin feared would bring much trouble to the gods. He caused it to be brought to him, when he hurled it into the deep ocean. But the monster grew to such enormous size, that it could hold its tail in its mouth, thus encircling the whole earth. So extensive is that depravity which follows the serpent's trail from Eden."

12—16. (12) **wise man,** able to trace the connection bet. suffering and sin. **for what the,** R. V. "wherefore is the land perished," etc., a new question. (13) **Lord saith,** speaking Himself bec. the wise men failed. **set before them,** made plainly and publicly known to them. (14) **imagination,** R. V. "stubbornness." **Baalim,** ch. ii. 8 23. **fathers taught,** this has been going on for generations. (15) **wormwood,** De. xxix. 18. **water of gall,** ch. viii. 14. (16) **scatter them,** Le. xxvi. 33.

An interpreter wanted (vs. 12).—When men are at a loss, or there is radical difference of opinion, it is evident that some authority is required to decide the question. The world and its canons are by the nature of the problem ruled out of court. And the apostate is too blinded with his own sin and too callous through repeated acts and prolonged habits of wrong-doing to be trusted in the matter. At this juncture the advantage of revelation and of the prophetic office appears. So far as God is concerned, the seer speaks with the authority of direct inspiration; so far as the culprit is concerned, he occupies a representative position, and as one of those implicated, yet himself innocent, acts as general conscience. This is God's way—to raise a testimony and extract a confession from the heart of the transgressor himself, or from the midst of those upon whom his judgments fall. And the same end is accomplished now through the Spirit and the Word. The saint becomes the mouthpiece of the Saviour, and the world is convinced of "sin, of righteousness, and of judgment."—Pul. Com.

17—22. (17) **mourning women,** who attended funerals to help the wailing.[c] **cunning,** or skilled in wailing. (18) **make haste,** the calamity is near at hand. **for us,** who mourn over Jerusalem as spiritually dead. (19) **cast us out,** R. V. "because they have cast down our dwellings." 2 Ki. xxv. 9. (20) **hear,** etc., even the younger women must join the wailing, for the number of dead would be so great. (21) "Death works in a twofold manner, viz.—within and without. In the shape of famine and sickness he steals in at the windows as a thief (compare Joel ii. 9) and the greatest houses are not exempted from his visit: he also cuts off the young and vigorous in the open (Compare Zech. viii. 5)." (22) **handful,** forgotten by the reaper. Neglect of the dead, who lie about in confusion, is the meaning.

Death (vs. 21.)—Death as an enemy is—I. Cruel. 1. Strikes at the dearest objects of our affections; 2. Robs us of our most useful men; 3. Drags us from the dearest things of the heart; 4. Reduces our bodies to the dust. II. He is unremitting. III. He is subtle. IV. He is resistless. V. He is ubiquitous. VI. He is conquerable. Christ has conquered death—1. In His own resurrection; 2. In His power upon the minds of His disciples.—Thomas.

Mourning at the grave.—I have noticed every morning since coming to Sidon, that women come forth very early to visit the graves. They move about under the trees and among the tombs in the grey dawn, wrapped up from head to foot in their white sheets, and looking for all the world like veritable ghosts. Sometimes I hear the voice of prayer; some weep and sob, while others sing or chant in a low, monotonous tone. In ninety-nine cases out of a hundred this public manifestation is the work of that arch-tyrant, custom, and nothing more. . . . Some of these mourners have tents pitched above the graves which require to be wept over. These, however, afford but slight protection against the pitiless storm and piercing wind. The great majority have no cover, and the mourners go home to nurse rheumatisms, burn in fevers, or go blind with ophthalmia. The real weeping is in the houses. And when you further know that many of these mourners and chanters are hired, and weep, howl, beat their breast, and tear their hair, according to contract, your compassion will fail fast, take another direction, and sigh for the victims of folly and fashion.—Thompson. Joy in death.—I congratulate you and myself that life is passing fast away. What a superlatively grand and consoling idea is that of death! Without this radiant idea, this delightful morning star, indicating that the luminary of eternity is going to rise, life would, to my view, darken into midnight melancholy. Oh, the expectation of living here and living thus always would be indeed a prospect of overwhelming despair. But thanks be to that fatal decree that dooms us to die! thanks to that Gospel which opens the vision of an endless life! and thanks, above all, to that Saviour Friend who has promised to conduct all the faithful through the Sacred trance of death into Scenes of Paradise and everlasting delight. —John Foster.

Death.—

"The glories of our blood and state
Are shadows, not substantial things;
There is no armor against fate;

"No large growth in holiness was ever gained by one who did not take time to be often and long alone with God."—Austin Phelps.

"A cruel Roman emperor wished that all Rome had but one neck, that he might kill it with one blow. God hath in his infinite grace gathered up all our humanity into one, even in Christ, so that, as sin had destroyed all by one stroke (Rom. v.), the grace of God in Christ might save all by the one righteousness of the One." — Pul. Com.

[c] "Those whose business it was to attend funerals, and by their skilled wailings aid the real mourners in giving vent to their grief. Hired mourners are still employed in Egypt." — Spk. Com.

2 Chr. xxxv. 25; Ec. xii. 5; Am. 7, 16; Mat. ix. 23; Mk. v. 38.

"What disarrays like death? It defaces the fascination of the beautiful. It breaks the lamp of the wise. It withers the strength of the mighty. It snatches the store of the rich. Kings are stripped of trapping, trophy, treasure: 'their glory shall not descend after them."—R. W. Hamilton.

"When God would educate a man He compels him to learn bitter lessons. He sends him to school to the necessities rather than to the graces, that by knowing all suffering, he may also know the eternal consolation." — Celia Burleigh.

"It has been well said that no man ever sank under the burden of the day. It is when tomorrow's burden is added to the burden of today that the weight is more than a man can bear. God begs you to leave the future to Him, and mind the present."— Geo. Macdonald.

"There are times when God asks nothing of his children except silence, patience, and tears." — Charles S. Robinson.

Death lays his icy hand on kings.
Sceptre and crown
Must tumble down,
And in the dust be equal made
With the poor crooked scythe and spade.

"Some men with swords may reap the field,
And plant fresh laurels where they kill;
But their strong nerves at last must yield;
They tame but one another still.
Early or late,
They stoop to fate,
And must give up their murmuring breath,
When they, pale captives, creep to death.

"The garlands wither on your brow:
Then boast no more your mighty deeds!
Upon Death's purple altar now
See where the victor-victim bleeds!
Your heads must come
To the cold tomb:
Only the actions of the just
Smell sweet and blossom in the dust." —Shirley.

[a] "Wisdom here is political sagacity. Might is military prowess."—Fausset.

[b] "Because the Jews valued themselves so much on their circumcision, God tells them. when He sends His judgments abroad in the world, they shall find no more favor than those who are not circumcised."—Lowth.

23—26. (23) **wise .. mighty .. rich,**[a] the three classes that might expect to defend and preserve themselves and their city in times of national distress. (24) **understandeth and knoweth,** "the former refers to the intellect, the latter to the emotions, the heart."—Camb. Bib. 1 Cor. i. 31; 2 Cor. x. 17. The true knowledge of God leads to obedience of His will. (25) **punish,** Heb. visit upon. **circumcised,** etc., R. V., "circumcised in their uncircumcision," i. e., consecrated outwardly while inwardly defiled.[b] (26) **Egypt,** etc., comp. list in ch. xxv. **corners,** R. V., "and all that have the corners of their hair polled." A peculiarity of certain Arabs (Le. xix. 27).

The glory of man (vs. 23).—I. The glory forbidden. 1. In wisdom; 2. In might; 3. In riches. II. The glory enjoined. 1. The knowledge that there is a God; 2. The knowledge of God as the moral Governor of the universe; 3. The knowledge of God as the God of redemption.—G. Brooks.

A man's three friends.—I read of a man who had a suit, and when his case was to be heard, he applied himself to three friends to see what they would do. One answered he would bring him as far on his journey as he could; the second promised to go with him to his journey's end; the third engaged to go with him before the judge and speak for him, nor leave him till his cause was determined. These three are a man's riches, his friends, and his graces. His riches may not very long stay with him; his friends can go with him to the grave, but there must leave him; but his graces will go with him before God, never forsake him, but accompany him to the grave and to glory.—Brooks.

[a] "The Heb., living, as they are supposed to do, in the midst of idolaters, were more or less exposed to their seductive influence. The Chaldæans specially employed their arts for the purpose of working on the superstitious fears of mankind."—Henderson.

[b] Is. xliv. 10, 11.

[c] "Like one of those stiff, inelegant pillars, something like a palm tree, which may be seen in Oriental architecture, and to wh., with their

CHAPTER THE TENTH.

1—5. (2) **signs of heaven,** eclipses, comets, etc., which heathen peoples greatly fear.[a] (3) **customs,** established institutions. **one cutteth,** R. V. marg., "it is but a tree which one cutteth." (4) **deck,** etc., covering the wooden body with platings of gold and silver.[b] **with nails,** to secure it from falling down. (5) **upright,** R. V., "they are like a palm tree, of turned work, and speak not." **as the palm tree,**[c] a pillar resembling a palm tree. These idols are stiff and lifeless as such. Others render "like pillars in a garden of cucumbers," in which sense the Hebrew word is found in Is. i. 8. That this was the sense in which the Jews themselves understood it at the time when the book of Baruch was written appears from the verse (Baruch vi. 70) evidently based on this, "as a scarecrow in a garden of cucumbers."—Camb. Bib. **do evil,** Is. xli. 23.

Hearing the Word of the Lord (vs. 1).—I. What is the Word of the Lord? His Law and Gospel. II. What is implied in hearing the Word of God? 1. That we attend His ordinances; 2. That we observe what we hear; 3. That we understand what we observe; 4. That we believe what we understand; 5. That we remember what we believe; 6. That we practise what we remember; 7. That we continue in what we practise. III. Why should we hear ? 1. Because God has commanded it; 2. Because it is for our great interest, it being the means of repentance, faith, light, comfort, and leads to eternal happiness. IV. How worthy of reproof are they—1. Who do not come to hear; 2. Who do not hear when they are come; 3. Who do not mind what they hear if they do come; 4. Who do not understand what they give attention to; 5. Who will not believe what they understand; 6. Who will not practise what they believe. V. Exhortation. 1. Hear God's Word with reverence; 2. Caution; 3. Attention; 4 Intention.—W. Stevens.

"Signs of heaven."—Heathenism in all ages has been a prolific system of doubt and dismay to its millions of votaries. It has laid prostrate, or warped aside, the finest intellects; and made created and lifeless objects the controllers of human hope and fear, rather than the great Creator. How lamentable that it was necessary for this holy patriot and prophet to warn the Jews from following the practices of the idolaters! and how vividly correct at this day are his descriptions of that soul-destroying system! Should a supposed malignant begin to rule in any given month, multitudes are in a state of terrible agitation, and, with the priests at their head, are devising a thousand plans to avert its direful potency. Though their astronomers can calculate with tolerable accuracy the time when an eclipse will occur, yet this will not serve in the least to pacify the vast tribes of the East. During its continuance they are all in a state of complete consternation; they abstain from their food and usual occupations, and yield themselves up to all the foolish impositions and absurd fantasies of their wily priests.—Roberts.

6—10. (6) **like .. thee,** Ps. lxxxvi. 8, 10. (7) **King of nations,** i. e. all nations.[a] (8) **brutish,**[b] "The original meaning of the idolatrous religions had begun, probably, to fade, and the worship of Bel and Nebo had become (as the worship of the Egyptian gods became at a later period) increasingly formal and ritualistic."—Pul. Com. **stock,** etc., R. V., "the instruction of idols, it is but a stock." The teaching is wooden like the teacher. (9) **Tarshish,**[c] port on Spanish coast. **Uphaz,** Da. x. 5.[d] **blue and purple,** expensive, as dyed with the valuable murex, or shell-fish. (10) **true God,** lit. a God who is truth; who is a real God, not a sham figure.

The true and living God (vs. 10).—I. The Lord is the true God. This is proved—1. By His Word; 2. His dealings; 3. His purposes; 4. His manifestations. II. The Lord is the living God, hence we should seek our spiritual life from Him. III. He is the everlasting King, hence we should inquire into and submit to His laws.—Pulpit Studies.

Folly of idolatry and power of the Gospel.—It was related at a public meeting that several missionaries once landed in India, who, anxious to lose no time in proclaiming the glad tidings of salvation, stopped at the first large village on their route, and, taking their stand under the shade of some large trees while the natives collected round them, they began to preach unto them Jesus. There was profound attention for more than an hour, when first one voice was raised and then another. "Jesus is the true God," "Jesus is the true God," they cried. "Come with us, and pull down our temples, and throw our gods down the hills." Then they led the way, and soon bore their wretched idol, which, though it had legs, could not walk, to the brow of a neighboring hill, where they contemptuously flung it over. But the words of the text may be applied to other idols besides those of heathen nations. It is a fact, and a sight to be met with any day in Madras and other large Eastern cities. A set of bearers are hired one day to bear on their shoulders a hideous idol, ornamented with gold and gems; and the next, the same set of men carry

arms and legs close to their sides, and their legs and feet mere unshaped blocks, they might well be compared." —Spk. Com.

Hab. ii. 19; 1 Cor. xii. 2.

"Superstition is the poesy of practical life. Hence, a poet is none the worse for being superstitious." —Goethe.

a Re. xy. 4.

b Is. xli. 29; Ha. ii. 18.; Zec. x. 2.

c Ge. x. 4.

d Poss. the Paz of Job xxviii. 17, "Jewels of Paz."

"All things in the natural world symbolize God yet none of them speak of Him but in broken and imperfect words. High above all he sits sublimer than mountains, grander than storms, sweeter than blossoms and tender fruits, nobler than Lords, truer than parents, more loving than lovers. His feet tread the lowest places of the earth, but his head is above all glory. and everywhere He is supreme."—Beecher.

"Wonderful alchemy of God's grace it is which transmutes tribulation into triumph, turns waters of Marah into a healthful fountain, enables one to gather grapes of thorns and figs of thistles, causes the rose to bloom through a whole winter of trials, and helps the soul to regard afflictions as promises, not threatenings."

"Liberal minds are open to conviction. Liberal doctrines are capable of improvement. There are proselytes from atheism, but none from superstition."—Junius.

[a] Job. xxviii. 25, 26.

"No man is born wise; but wisdom and virtue require a tutor, though we can easily learn to be vicious without a master"—Seneca.

"An Arab, when one day asked, 'How do you know there is a God?' turned indignantly upon the questioner, and replied, 'How do I know whether a man or a camel passed my tent last night?' His own footprints in creation and providence testify of Him."

[b] Comp. De. xxxii. 9; Ps. lxxiv. 2.

"Any opinion which tends to keep out of sight the living and loving God, whether it be to substitute for Him an idol, or any occult agency, or a formal creed, can be nothing better than the portentous shadow projected from the slavish darkness of an ignorant heart." — Hallam.

forth in state the Virgin Mary. One form of idolatry is perhaps a little more refined than another; but how truly may it be said of them all, "They that make them are like unto them; so is every one that trusteth in them!"—Bib. Treas. God's name.—A Jew entered a Persian temple, and saw there the sacred fire. He said to the priest, "How do you worship fire?" "Not the fire: it is to us an emblem of the sun and of his animating light," said the priest. The Israelite continued, "You dazzle the eye of the body, but darken that of the mind; in presenting the terrestrial light, you take away the celestial." The Persian asked, "How do you name the Supreme Being?" "We call him Jehovah Adonai; that is, the Lord who was, who is, and shall be." "Your word is great and glorious, but it is terrible," said the Persian. A Christian approaching said, "We call him Abba Father." Then the Persian and the Jew regarded each other with surprise and said, "Your word is the nearest and the highest; but who gives you courage to call the Eternal thus?" "The Father Himself," said the Christian, who then expounded to them the plan of redemption.—Krummacher. Christ, the true God.—Two gentlemen were once disputing on the divinity of Christ; one of them who argued against it said, "If it were true, certainly it would have been expressed in more clear and unequivocal terms." "Well," said the other, "admitting that you believed it, were you authorized to teach it, and allowed to use your own language, how would you express the doctrine to make it indubitable?" "I would say," replied he, "that Jesus Christ is the true God." "You are very happy," replied the other, "in the choice of your words, for you have happened to hit upon the very words of inspiration; for John, speaking of the Son, says 'This is the true God, and eternal life.'"—Wilson.

11—13. (11) The verse appears in Chaldee instead of Hebrew. The object is either (a) that the Jews might thus have put into their mouths the very words in which they should while in exile address their Chaldee conquerors, which is somewhat improbable; or (b) because it is a proverb and thus given in the language of the common people (Aramaic).—Camb. Bib. **made .. earth,** this is the exclusive claim of Jehovah. (12) **He hath made,** Ge. i. 6. (13) **multitude,** R. V., "tumult," etc., the forces of nature are under His guidance. **waters,** etc., comp. the account of the creation.[a]

Gods of the heathen.—An Indian chief, having sent for Hiacoomes, a converted native, with the view of receiving religious instruction from him, after some conversation, the chief asked him how many gods the English worshiped. Hiacoomes answered, "One and no more." On which the chief reckoned up about thirty-seven principal gods which he had. "And shall I," said he, "throw away all these thirty-seven for the sake of one only?" "What do you yourself think?" said Hiacoomes; "for my part, I have thrown away all these, and many more, some years ago, and yet I am preserved, as you see, to this day." "You speak true," said the chief, "and therefore I will throw away all my gods too, and serve that one God with you." Hiacoomes proceeded more fully to instruct him, and the rest of the company with him; and the chief having promised to worship the true God, and serve Him only, was as good as his word, for he carried himself as a true servant of God, all the days of his life after.—Whitecross.

14—16. (14) R. V., "Every man is become brutish and is without knowledge; every goldsmith is put to shame by his graven image." It is the object of his creation, how can it deliver him? (15) **work of errors,** or deluded notions. (16) **portion of Jacob,** a term for Jehovah. **rod .. inheritance,** "an expression taken from the first division of the land of Canaan, when the inheritance of each tribe and family was meted out with a line or a rod."—Lowth.

Idol-worship debasing.—The gods of Greece and Rome had at least human features, and were modelled after the likeness of men; but among the millions of the gods of India affecting the character of their worshipers, there is not one which represents a virtue, not one which is not a monster of iniquity. Brahma is acknowledged by the Hindoos themselves as too bad to be worshiped. Their God, Shiva, is distinguished for his revenge and malignity; Krishna bears a character of a notorious licentious profligate; Juggernaut is represented by an old idol without legs and arms, because the legs and arms of the god were cut off by a sentence of the gods for his incurable iniquity. What but impurity and cruelty can be the result of a religion which has such patterns in its gods?—Dict. of Illus.

17, 18. This passage (17—22) connects itself immediately with ch. ix., where the invasion of Judah and the dispersion of its inhabitants have been foretold. Here, after describing dramatically the departure of the latter into exile, the prophet reports a distinct revelation of the same fact. The Jewish people is then introduced, lamenting her sad fate, but expressing resignation.—Pul. Com. (17) **thy wares,** i. e. the few necessary things that time permits you to collect ere you are hurried into captivity. **O inhabitant,** etc., R. V., "O thou that abidest in the siege," i. e. in a besieged city. (18) **sling out,** indicating the suddenness and force of the desolation impending.[a] **at this once,** R. V., "at this time." **may find,** or feel intensely.

Shun delays.—

Shun delays, they breed remorse;
  Take thy time while time is lent thee:
Creeping snails have weakest force;
  Fly their fault, lest thou repent thee.
Good is best when sooner wrought,
Ling'ring labors come to naught.

Hoist up sail while gale doth last,—
  Tide and wind stay no man's pleasure!
Seek not time when time is past—
  Sober speed is wisdom's leisure;
After-wits are dearly bought:
Let thy fore-wit guide thy thought.

Time wears all his locks before—
  Take thou hold upon his forehead:
When he flees, he turns no more,
  And behind his scalp is naked.
Works adjourn'd have many stays;
Long demurs breed new delays. —Southwell.

19—22. (19) **Woe is me,** this is the cry of the Prophet, representing the stricken nation. **a grief,** R. V., "my grief"—my own burden. (20) **tabernacle,** poetical for dwellings. **none to stretch,** i. e. the men are all swept away. (21) **pastors,** the temporal rulers. (22) R. V., "the voice of a rumour, behold it cometh, and a great commotion," etc.[b] **dragons,** R. V., "jackals."

Jeremiah has been likened to several characters in profane history—to Cassandra, the Trojan prophetess, whose fate it was never to be believed, though prophesying nothing but the truth; to Phocion, the rival of Demosthenes in the last generation of Athenian greatness, who maintained the unpopular but sound doctrine that, if Athens were to escape worse evils, she must submit peaceably to the growing power of Macedon; to Dante, whose native state, Florence, was in relation to France and the Empire as Palestine was to Egypt and Babylon, while the poet like the prophet could only protest without effect against the thickening ills.—Camb. Bib. Jeremiah, in the age in which he lived, might be compared to a Puritan living in the age of the Stuarts, or a Huguenot living in the age of the Medici, or a Savonarola living in the age of Pope Alexander VI.

23—25. (23) **way .. himself,** Pr. xvi. 1, xx. 24. Jeremiah's prayer in prospect of the national calamity. **to direct his steps,** "to ensure success. The same word occurs Ps. xxxvii. 23 ("The steps of a good man are ordered by the Lord"), and its sense there seems to determine that in which it occurs here. All prosperity, as well as the converse, comes from God."—Camb. Bib. (24) **with judgment,** better, in measure; ch.

[a] Is. xxii. 18.

"Ignorance seldom vaults into knowledge, but passes into it through an intermediate state of obscurity, even as night into day through twilight." —Coleridge.

"To me to live is Christ." All other kinds of life will at last be found to have been only a living death.

"There is as much difference between the sufferings of the saints and those of the ungodly as between the bandages wherewith the tender surgeon binds his patients and the cords with which an executioner pinions a condemned malefactor."—Arrowsmith.

[b] Je. vi. 22, ix. 11.

"God is not a crutch coming in to help your lameness, unnecsary to you if you had all your strength. He is the breath in your lungs. The stronger you are, the more thoroughly you are yourself, the more you need of it, the more you need Him." —Phillips Brooks.

xlvi. 28. **bring .. nothing,** marg. diminish me. (25) **Pour,** etc., Ps. lxxix. 6, 7.[a]

The way of man not in himself (vs. 23).—I. Let us consider the conviction here expressed in its sources: "I know," says he. 1. The nature of our condition; 2. The limitation of our powers; 3. History; 4. Experience; 5. Scripture. II. Consider its uses. 1. It should produce gratitude; 2. Submission; 3. Check presumption; 4. Induce one to repair to God in earnest prayer. III. Let us glance at the encouragements of this conviction. God is—1. Able; 2. Willing; 3. Engaged to direct our steps.—W. Fay.

Verse 25.—A person of great quality was pleased to lodge a night in my house. I durst not invite him to my family prayer; and therefore, for that time, omitted it; thereby making a breach in a good custom, and giving Satan advantage to assault it. Yea, the loosening of such a link might have endangered the scattering of the chain. Bold bashfulness, which durst offend God whilst it did fear man. Hereafter, whosoever cometh within the doors shall be requested to come within the discipline of my house; if accepting my homely diet, he will not refuse my home devotion; and sitting by my table, will be entreated to kneel down by it.—T. Fuller.

a "'Since I (my nation) must be corrected, I do not deprecate all chastisement, but pray only for moderation in it, and that the full tide of Thy fury may be poured out on the heathen invaders for their cruelty towards Thy people.'"—Fausset.

"We must follow, not force Providence."—Shakespeare.

"Put thou thy trust in God,
In duty's path go on;
Fix on His Word thy steadfast eye,
So shall thy work be done."
—Luther.

CHAPTER THE ELEVENTH.

Chaps. xi., xii. form a connected prophecy, either as having been uttered at one definite time in the prophet's life, or as embodying the substance of his teaching during a particular epoch of his ministry.—Camb. Bib. **1—5.** (2) **covenant,** see 2 Ki. xxiii. 3.[b] This allusion to the law book discovered in Josiah's 18th year gives the date of the section, about that time.—Driver. (3) **Cursed,** etc., De. xxvii. 26; Ga. iii. 10. (4) **Obey,** etc., Le. xxvi. 3, 12. (5) **oath,** De. vii. 12, 13.

God, our rest. The soul whose God the Lord is, reposes on him. The storms of life may rage, its tempests beat, but "firm and unmoved are they who rest their souls on God." Everything may appear to be slipping away from a man, and he may seem to be like one gliding down a steep, smooth slope, ever faster and faster to the precipice over which he will be hurled into destruction, unable to grasp any friendly rock or branch, or to find foothold anywhere—and men's circumstances are like that sometimes; but they to whom this word, "I will be your God," is fulfilled, do find foothold in God and can stay themselves upon him. Hence, when heart and flesh fail, God is the Strength of their heart and their Portion forevermore.—Pul. Com. Result of disobedience.—Travelers along the Rhine or over the mountains of Switzerland know to their cost how often the most glorious scenery the world contains is completely hidden from their view by the uprising of some wretched mist, wrapping in cold, dark, impenetrable fog all that upon which their eyes would have so delightedly rested. They want to gaze upon all that loveliness; they have come for that very purpose; but they cannot for those thick clouds. And oh, what a beautiful vision is the face of God! How good it is to gaze upon Him, and to behold the shining of His countenance! And this we should do were it not for those mists with which disobedience to God's will ever blots out all that otherwise we should so delightedly see.—Pul. Com.

6—10. (6) **Proclaim,** "he was to take an itinerating mission in Judah to set forth the principles of Deuteronomy and exhort men to live accordingly."—Driver.[a] (7) **earnestly protested .. rising early,** the sign of earnestness of purpose. (8) **imagination,** R. V., "stubbornness." **will bring,** better, have brought: a fact constantly illustrated in their history that disobedience always brought calamity. (9, 10) **a conspiracy,**[b] possibly this may mean that there were actual measures taken in secret against Josiah on account of his reforms. At any rate the expression denotes a considerable amount of agreement in the pursuance of idolatry, and in all probability further points to a secrecy of combination.—Camb. B.

b "What they were specially to communicate was the contents of that portion of the book of the law, which had been found in the temple in Josiah's time."—Henderson.

"The Prophet puts the people in mind of the renewal of the covenant lately made in the time of Josiah."—Lightfoot.

"What was Christ doing in the carpenter's shop? Practising. Though perfect, we read that he learned obedience, and grew in wisdom and in favor with God."—Drummond.

a "2 Ki. xxiii. 15, 20. Prob. Jeremiah accompanied Josiah in his progress through the land, everywhere reading from the newly found book."—Nägelsbach.

b "They made some steps towards a reformation in the time of Josiah, but now they have agreed or con-

11—14. (11) **will bring,** better, am about to bring. **not hearken,** bec. the time for judgment has fully come.[a] (12) **cry .. gods,** ch. ii. 28; De. xxxii. 37, 38. (13) **shameful thing,** Heb. bôsheth, shame; the name of contempt for Baal. "The verse has been taken to imply that altars, such as are here mentioned, were actually set up in most if not all of the streets of Jerusalem, and hence it has been said that this portion of the prophecy cannot be as early as the reign of Josiah. The verse however need mean no more than that a strong though secret opposition existed to the reforming work of that king and that the worship of Baal was practised, though not openly, in all parts of the country and city.—Camb. Bib. (14) **pray not,** ch. vii. 16.[b]

Breaking covenant with Jehovah meant making a covenant with other gods; it was impossible to do the one thing without the other. And that is as true now, under totally different conditions, as it was in the land of Judah, twenty-four centuries ago. If you have broken faith with God in Christ, it is because you have entered into an agreement with another; it is because you have foolishly taken the tempter at his word, and accepted his conditions, and surrendered to his proposals, and preferred his promises to the promises of God. It is because, against all reason, against conscience, against the Holy Spirit, against the witness of God's Word, against the witness of His Saints and Confessors in all ages, you have believed that a Being less than the Eternal God could ensure your weal and make you happy. And now your heart is no longer at unity in itself, and your allegiance is no longer single and undivided.—Exp. Bib.

15—17. (15) **my beloved,** i. e. Judah. **lewdness,** better "hypocrisy." **holy flesh,** sacrifices, wh. were unacceptable bec. of their immorality and hypocrisy. The Sept. renders the whole vs., "How has my beloved wrought abomination in my house? Shall vows and holy flesh remove from thee thy wickedness, or by these shalt thou escape?" i. e. Shall promises or sacrifices profit thee? (16) **green olive,** comp. Ps. lii. 8.[c] **kindled,** etc., fig. of the desolation wrought by the Chaldæan army. (17) **planted thee,** and so hath all rights in thee. **against themselves,** the sinner's sin is always to his own hurt.

Sin within us.—The unforgiven sins are not away in keeping somewhere, to be let loose upon us when we die. They are here within us now. Today brings the resurrection of their past—tomorrow of today. And the powers of sin, to the exact strength that we have developed them, nearing their dreadful culmination with every breath we draw, are here, within us, now. The souls of some men are already honeycombed through and through with eternal consequences of neglect, so that taking the natural and rational view of their case just now, it is simply inconceivable that there is any escape just now. What a fearful thing it is to fall into the hands of the living God! A fearful thing even if, as the philosopher tells us, "The hands of the living God are the laws of nature."—Drummond.

18—20. (18) **given me knowledge,** i. e. of the evil designs that were being plotted against the Prophet himself.[d] (19) **like a lamb,** R. V., "a gentle lamb that is led to the slaughter." **tree .. fruit,** fig. for Jeremiah and his prophecies. (20) **triest the reins,** etc., 1 Sa. xvi. 7, etc. **thy vengeance,** in sense of righteous judgment.

Murderers in ambush.—Between the priesthood and the prophets there had hitherto been more or less of a conflict; but now that conflict was exchanged for a fatal union. "A wonderful and horrible thing was committed in the land: the prophets prophesied falsely, and the priests bore rule by their means;" and he (Jeremiah) who by each of his callings [Stanley regards Jeremiah as having been a priest before he was called to become a prophet] was naturally led to sympathise with both, was the doomed antagonist of both—victim of one of the strongest passions, the hatred of priests against a priest who attacks his own order,—the hatred of prophets against a prophet who ventures to have a voice and a will of his own. His own village of Anathoth, occupied by members of the sacred tribe, was for him a nest of conspirators against his life. Of

---

spired together to return back to their former idolatries." — Lowth.

[a] Ps. xviii. 41; Pr. i. 28; Is. i. 15; Mi. iii. 4.

"The erection of altars to Baal in every street of Jerusalem, betokens a public establishment of idolatry, such as actually took place in the reign of Manasseh." — Spk. Com.

[b] Je. xiv. 11, 12.

"The carnal mind, the mind which will not correspond with God, — this is not moral only, but spiritual death. And sin, that which separates from God, which disobeys God, which can not in that state correspond with God,—this is hell." — Drummond.

[c] Ro. xi. 17.

"He that offers in sacrifice a multitude of bulls and of goats, and imagines by this to conciliate the favor of God, is grossly mistaken, and has no solid understanding; for he that would sacrifice with success ought to be chaste and charitable. God, who is near thee, perpetually beholds thy actions." — From The Greek.

[d] "Jeremiah here digresses from his main subject, in order to take special notice of the attempt wh. had been plotted upon his life by his own townsmen. It would appear that he had not entertained the slightest suspicion of their intention, and that he must have remained ignorant of it, if it had not been immediately revealed to him by

him first in the Sacred history was the saying literally fulfilled, "A prophet hath no honor in his own birthplace."—Stanley.

21—23. (21) **Prophesy not,** trying thus to frighten God's Prophet with their threats.[a] (22) **young men,** "those of the legal age for military service." **famine,** in the time of the siege. (23) **no remnant,** this need not include the whole of Anathoth, but may refer only to the families of the actual conspirators against Jeremiah's life.[b] **even the year,** "in the year." "The time referred to is that of the siege and capture of Jerusalem. Anathoth, as lying in the neighborhood of the besieging armies, would be exposed to the horrors of war even to a greater extent than the capital city."—Camb. Bib.

Spiritual atavism; or, the sins of the fathers. There are punishments and consequences of ancestral sin which reach even to descendants of remote generations. In modern times the laws of heredity have been scientifically investigated, and startling results brought to light. Tendency can be traced from parent to child in gradually deepening lines and more confirmed manifestations. Spirit as well as body acknowledges this law, and, whether in health or disease, its operation is now placed beyond all dispute. But another law or modification of this law is perceived working alongside of it, namely, the law of atavism, in which not the general tendency towards improvement or degeneration is observed, but an apparently arbitrary and capricious recurrence of ancestral peculiarities that had long disappeared from the race. Of this nature seems to have been the present sin of Israel. It was not in the line of continuous succession, but a recurrent phase after intervals of normal and religious life. Thus it showed that the power of evil had only been "scotched," not killed; and that it was ready on the slightest provocation to assert itself in the rankest forms. How much that is mysterious in the conduct of individuals can be traced to the influence of such a principle! The two selves of every man represent influences that have been at work in his progenitors from remotest time.—Pul. Com.

the Omniscent Searcher of hearts." —Henderson.

[a] "This was the usage the Prophets commonly met with from those who became their enemies, because they told them those truths they had no mind to hear."—Lowth.

[b] Fr. Ezr. ii. 23, Ne. vii. 27, it appears that 128 men of Anathoth returned from exile.

"I venerate the man whose heart is warm,
Whose hands are pure, whose doctrines and whose life,
Coincident, exhibit lucid proof
That he is honest in the sacred cause."
—Cowper.

CHAPTER THE TWELFTH.

1—4. (1) **Righteous art thou,** the general acknowledgment of God's justice and holiness. **yet,** etc., R. V., "yet would I reason the cause with thee"[c] comp. Job ix. 2: xxi; xxiv. **Wherefore .. prosper?** the great question of the times of the later monarchy.[d] **happy,** R. V., "at ease." (2) **mouth,** i. e. in their professions. **reins,** regarded as the seat of the affections.[e] (3) **tried mine heart,** so as to prove my sinceriey. **pull .. out,** Heb. tear them out. (4) **see .. end,** his predictions are delusions; say the ungodly, we shall live longer than he.

Prosperity of the wicked. Satan with ease put fallacies upon us by his golden baits, and then he leads us and leaves us in a fool's paradise. The world hath by the glistering of her pomp and preferment slain millions; as the serpent Scytale, which, when she cannot overtake the fleeting passengers, doth with her beautiful colors astonish and amaze them, so that they have no power to pass away till she have stung them to death. Adversity hath slain her thousands, but prosperity her ten thousand.—Brooks.

[c] "However difficult Jeremiah found it to reconcile the apparent discrepancies of the Div. government, he still held fast his conviction of the rectitude of the character of Jehovah." —Henderson.

[d] Job xxi. 7—17; Ps. xxxvii. 1—35, lxxiii. 3, 5, 7, xcii. 7; Hab. i. 13.

[e] Ps. vii. 9.

5, 6. God replies to Jeremiah in these verses. He intimates to him by means of two proverbial expressions that he must brace himself to endure even worse things than any that he has as yet been called upon to face. The attacks of the men of Anathoth may have galled him, but the treachery set on foot against him includes men of his own family, and so is yet more wounding and bitter than he supposes. He must not therefore think of being impatient at anything that he may hitherto have been called upon to undergo, but feel that he has need of all his resolution to meet the trouble which shall presently be disclosed.—Camb. B. (5) **run,** etc., this is a proverbial saying, and intimates that further and higher indignities awaited the Prophet in Jerusalem.[a] **land of peace,** R. V., "and though in a land of peace thou art secure, yet how wilt

[a] "If he could not bear with the ill-usage of his acquaintance and neighbors at Anathoth, how would he be able to undergo the hardships he must expect to meet with from the great men at Jerusalem, who would unanimously set themselves against him?"—Lowth.

thou do in the pride of Jordan?" "The pride of Jordan means the thickets on its banks, which were notorious as the haunts of lions (ch. xlix. 19; l. 44; Zech. xi. 3). Lions' bones have been found by Dr. Roth in the gravel of the Jordan."—Pul. Com. (6) **brethren,** ch. ix. 4. **a multitude,** R. V., "cried aloud."

Gradations of trial (vs. 5).—Apply the text.—1. To those who are discouraged in the service of God by trifling difficulties; 2. To those who have succumbed to feeble temptations; 3. To such as have desponded at the presence of slight afflictions; 4. To the large class who have failed to gain spiritual profit under favorable providences.

Verse 5.—The strength which is barely sufficient for the cares and toils of a quiet home life will fail utterly if a man has to contend with lions in the wild thickets of the lonely Jordan valley. If health breaks down before the soft breezes of summer, how will it stand before the frost and fog of winter? If the young man falls into vicious habits while under the protection of his father's home, what will become of him when he goes out into the world? If the prospect of sickness and earthly sorrow fill one with hopeless distress, how will he pass through the valley of the shadow of death? how will he endure death itself? These questions should not make us despondent, but should drive us through self-diffidence to seek the help of God. Failure in small things will be good for us if it teaches us a wholesome lesson on our own weakness, and so inclines us to turn to a higher source of safety. Then we shall find that God's strength is made perfect in our weakness (2 Cor. xii. 9).—Pul. Com.

7—9. (7) **mine house,** i. e. the nation, not simply the temple.—Camb. Bib. Hos. viii. 1; Heb. iii. 6; 1 Tim. iii. 15. **dearly beloved,** ch. xi. 15. **hand,** Heb. the palm, here especially with its power to squeeze and crush. (8) **as a lion,** a savage beast of prey, roaring against Me.[b] **hated it,** treated it as if I hated it. comp. Mal. i. 3. (9) **speckled bird,** one differing in plumage from the others, which the other birds peck to death. **come to,** etc., R. V., "bring them to devour."

The speckled bird.—A great preacher relates the following incident.—He says, "I had during my early ministry to preach one evening at a neighboring village, to which I had to walk. After reading and meditating all day, I could not meet with the right text. Do what I would, no response came from the sacred oracle, no light flashed from the Urim and Thummim. I prayed, I meditated, I turned from one verse to another; but the mind would not take hold, or I was, as John Bunyan would say, 'much tumbled up and down in my thoughts.' Just then I walked to the window and looked out. On the other side of the narrow street in which I lived I saw a poor, solitary canary bird upon the slates, surrounded by a crowd of sparrows, who were all pecking at it as if they would tear it to pieces. At that moment the verse came into my mind, 'Mine heritage is unto me as a speckled bird; the birds round about are against her.' I walked off with the greatest possible composure, considered the passage during my long and lonely walk, and preached upon the peculiar people and the persecutions of their enemies, with freedom and ease to myself, and I believe with comfort to my rustic audience. The text was sent to me, and if the ravens did not bring it, certainly the sparrows did."

10—13. (10) **pastors,** as previously, rulers; here the reference is to the Chaldæan generals. **trodden .. foot,** comp. Is. v. 1, doing ruinous injury to the young shoots. **pleasant portion,** comp. ch. xi. 16. (11) **it mourneth,** waileth in its utter desolation; the very land seeeming to cry for inhabitants. (12) **no flesh,** etc., none of this sinful nation shall enjoy prosperity. (13) **shall reap,** R. V., "have reaped," etc., evidently a proverb, meaning, as the words that follow it shew. They have used their best endeavors to obtain pleasure, the object of their desire, and have been rewarded with the very opposite of that harvest which they sought.—Camb. Bib. **to pain,** the extreme labor of their idol service. **they .. ashamed,** R. V., "ye shall be ashamed of your fruits."

Note on vs. 10.—Besides successive invasions by foreign nations, and the systematic spoliation exercised by a despotic government, other causes have conspired to perpetuate the desolation of Judæa, and to ren-

"Great occasions do not make heroes or cowards; they simply unveil them to the eyes of men. Silently and imperceptibly, as we wake or sleep, we grow and wax strong, we grow and wax weak; and at last some crisis shows us what we have become."—Canon Westcott.

[b] "My people have blasphemed Me and My laws, just like a wild beast, that opens its mouth against every one that withstands it."—Lowth.

"There is a danger in the midst of ordinary human relations that Jehovah shall be considered simply as an addition to our obligations, instead of being the supreme and all-modifying influence of our life. In proportion to the severity of the experience will be the consolations to be received."—Pul. Com.

"Thorns, of course, could not be reaped unless thorns were planted, but no one would deliberately plant thorns. But the heart of man, rich, deep, inexhaustible ground as it is, has come under a curse of which Gen. iii. 18 is but a shadowy suggestion. Men shrink from the toil and suffering needful to uproot the false and the injurious, and still more difficult do they find the watchfulness and determination which would prevent thorns from getting hold at all; and yet it is perfectly certain that thorns, allowed to continue, will in time destroy anything like abiding fruit from the good seed."—Pul. Com.

"The heavier the the cannon, with the more difficulty are they drawn; but when arrived, they recompense the slowness of their march by the fierceness of their battery. The longer the stone is in falling, the more it will bruise and grind to powder. There is a great treasure of wrath laid laid up by the abuse of patience."—Charnock.

der abortive the substance that is in it. Among these has chiefly to be numbered its being literally trodden under foot by many "pastors." Volney devotes a chapter, fifty pages in length, to a description, as he entitles it, "Of the Pastoral, or Wandering Tribes of Syria," chiefly of the Bedouin Arabs, by whom especially Judæa is incessantly traversed. "The pachalics of Aleppo and Damascus may be computed to contain about thirty thousand wandering Turkmen (Turcomans). All their property consists in cattle." In the same pachalics, the number of the Kurds "exceed twenty thousand tents and huts," or an equal number of armed men. "The Kurds are almost everywhere looked upon as robbers. Like the Turkmen, these Kurds are pastors and wanderers. A third wandering people in Syria are the Bedouin Arabs." "It often happens that even individuals turn robbers, in order to withdraw themselves from the laws, or from tyranny, unite and form a little camp, which maintain themselves by arms, and, increasing, become new hordes and new tribes. It is evident that agriculture must be very precarious in such a country, and that, under a government like that of the Turks, it is safer to lead a wandering life than to choose a settled habitation, and rely for subsistence on agriculture." "The Turkmen, the Kurds, and the Bedouins, have no fixed habitations, but keep perpetually wandering with their tents and herds, in limited districts, of which they look upon themselves as the proprietors. The Arabs spread over the whole frontier of Syria, and even the plains of Palestine." Thus, contrary to their natural inclination, the peasants are often forced to abandon a settled life, and pastoral tribes in great numbers, and without fixed habitations, divide the country, as it were, by mutual consent, and apportion it in limited districts among themselves by an assumed right of property, and the Arabs, subdivided also into different tribes, spread over the plains of Palestine, "wandering perpetually," as if on very purpose to tread it down. What could be more unlikely or unnatural in such a land! yet what more strikingly and strictly true! or how else could the effect of the vision have been seen! "Many pastors have destroyed my vineyard; they have trodden my portion under foot."—Keith.

14—17. (14) **evil neighbours,** the nations in the vicinity of Judah, who doubtless took evil advantage of the times of her weakness and peril.[a] Syrians, Edomites, Moabites, Ammonites, and Philistines. **pluck .. Judah,** by its removal into captivity. (15) **return,** etc., or I will again have compassion. These neighbors shared, in measure, with Judah in the restoration. (16) **ways .. people,** who then shall have wholly given up their idolatry. **The Lord,** or Jehovah.[b] **as they taught,** R. V., "even as they taught." (17) **not obey,** Is. lx. 12.

Sinful companions to be abandoned by the Christian.—Sometimes great sinners must abandon their companions. For frequently there are sins which in their very nature are so wrapped up in companionship that no man can be safe who does not break with companions as well as with courses. It is not as a general rule. I do not say that a young man, violating no canons of morality, dwelling in a virtuous home, and only with his companions worldly and sinful by the higher sentiments misappropriated, ought, when he becomes a Christian, to abandon those companions. On the contrary, he ought to be a better companion than he ever was before. But if you have been in lust's companionship, if you have been in the fiery strifes and toils of the passions, then the fire burning in your companions will not easily be slaked in you. There must be something more than a simple and barren attempt to turn away from sin. You must break with your companions.—C. H. Spurgeon.

a "During the thirteen years that the Bab. besieged Tyre, Nebuchadnezzar, after subduing Cœla-Syria, brought Ammon, Moab, etc., and finally Egypt, into subjection."—Fausset.

b "The embracing of the true religion is represented as consisting in an avowal, with all the solemnity of an oath, that Jehovah alone was God."—Henderson.

CHAPTER THE THIRTEENTH.

We may subdivide this chapter as follows: (i) a symbolical action, or acted parable, with its moral and application (vss. 1-11); (ii) a parabolic saying and its interpretation, which leads up to a pathetic appeal for penitence (vss. 12-17); (iii) a message to the sovereigns (vss. 18, 19); and

(iv) a closing apostrophe to Jerusalem—the gay and guilty capital, so soon to be made desolate for her abounding sins (vss. 20—27).—Exp. Bib.

1—5. (1) **unto me,** in vision. Some think this symbolical act was literally done by Jeremiah.[c] **put .. water,** i. e. to wash it. Let it be in its dirty state,[d] representing the "deep-grained pollution of the people." (4) **Euphrates,** Heb. Phrath: corrupted form of name of a place near Anathoth, still known by the name Farah. It was not by the river Euphrates but in this rocky retreat, near Michmash, that Jeremiah hid the girdle.—Cheyne. **hole,** or cleft. Typical of the Jewish captivity.

Note on vs. 4.—The girdle of the Orientals is sometimes made of silver or gold, or embroidered silk, or highly dyed muslin. Its uses are, to keep the lower garments fast to the loins, to strengthen the body, and to command respect. Chiefs have numerous folds of muslin round that part, and they march along with great pomp, thus enlarged in their size. That, therefore, which was of so much use, and which indicated the dignity of the wearer, was to be marred, typifying the degradation of the Jews in their approaching captivity. The Hindoos have a custom of burying certain articles by the side of a tank or river, in order to inflict or prefigure evil in reference to certain obnoxious individuals who are thus placed under the ban. Thus eggs, human hair, thread, a ball of saffron, or a little of the earth on which the devoted person has had his feet, are buried in the situations alluded to.—Roberts.

6—11. (6) **after many days,** typical of the 70 yrs. of captivity. (7) **marred,** soiled, polluted as the people would become. (9) **the pride,** i. e. the temporal grandeur. The Jews returned fr. Bab. as a very feeble folk. (10) **evil people,** as being self-willed. The expression limits the application of this symbol. **imagination,** R. V., "stubbornness," chap. iii. 17. (11) **cleave unto me,**[b] the girdle is the closest cleaving part of a man's dress.

Contempt of God's mercies (vs. 11).—I. The honor which God has designed for His people; the primary use of the girdle is to bind up the garments around the loins, but a girdle is also of use for ornament. II. The way in which this honor is contemned by the Jews. What can be a more just description of ourselves? Address—1. In the way of appeal; 2. In a way of encouragement.—C. Simeon.

Reasons for humility.—Remember what thou wert before thy birth—nothing; what thou wert for many years after—weakness; what in all thy life—a great sinner; what in all thy excellencies—a mere debtor to God, to thy parents, to the earth, and to all creatures. Upon these or the like meditations, if we dwell, we shall see nothing more reasonable than to be humble, and nothing more foolish than to be proud.—Bp. Taylor.

12—14. (12) **bottle .. wine,** "under this figure is described the intoxication through which the people shall be rendered helpless to resist the foreign foe, while they quarrel one with onother. It was no doubt in part owing to factious strife as well as to national idolatry that the overthrow came. The figure of filling a person with wine in the sense of bringing upon him Divine punishment for perverseness and headstrong continuance in sin is found also chap. xxv. 15; Ps. lx. 3; Is. li. 17, while for Israel under the figure of a bottle or jar compare chap. xviii. 1—6.—Camb. Bib. **certainly know,** "we understand that," they say: failing utterly to perceive his meaning. (14) **dash them,** as drunken men tumble one against another.[c]

The drunkard's thraldom.—The writer of the pamphlet entitled "The Confessions of a Drunkard," says, "Of my condition there is no hope that I should ever change; the waters have gone over me; but out of the black depths, could I be heard, I would cry aloud to all those who have set a foot in that perilous flood. Could the youth to whom the flavor of his first wine is as delicious as the opening scenes of life, or the entering upon some newly-discovered paradise, look into my desolation, and be made to understand what a dreary thing it is when a man shall feel himself going down a precipice with open eyes and a passive will,—to see his destruction, and have no power to stop it, and yet to

[c] "The world the Proph. moved in was not the sensible, but the spiritual world. Inward acts were, however, when it was possible and proper, materialized by outward performance, but not always and necessarily so."—Fausset.

[d] "Jeremiah was to wear it constantly, though full of the effects of perspiration, and never to wash it."—Maurer.

[a] "To that condition the Jews had been reduced by the corrupting idolatries of the heathen. They had disqualified themselves for acting as witnesses for Jehovah as the only true God, and like a castaway girdle, they were to be humbled and rejected." — Henderson.

[b] Ex. xix. 5, 6; De. iv. 7; Ps. cxxxv. 4.

[c] "As wine intoxicates so God's wrath and judgments shall reduce them to that state of helpless distraction that they shall rush on their own ruin."—Fausset. Eze. v. 10; Mat. x. 21.

"Those boughs and branches of trees which are most richly laden with fruit bend downwards and hang lowest."—Gill.

"Lowliness is the base of every virtue:
And he who goes the lowest builds the safest.
May God keep all his pity for the proud!"
—Bailey.

feel it all the way emanating from himself; to perceive all goodness emptied out of him, and yet not able to forget a time when it was otherwise; to bear about the piteous spectacle of his own ruin;—could he see my fevered eye, feverish with the last night's drinking, and feverishly looking forward for this night's repetition of the folly; could he feel the body of death out of which I cry hourly, with feebler and feebler outcry, to be delivered, it were enough to make him dash the sparkling beverage to the earth in all the pride of its mantling temptation."

[d] "The metaphor is taken from the dangers to which travelers are exposed who, in a dark and stormy night, cross mountain regions, where they are liable at every step to stumble against some projecting angle of a rock, and so be precipitated into the abyss below."—Henderson.

15—18. (15) **not proud,** to reject the teaching, though given in humiliating forms. (16) **Give glory,** Hebrew idiom for "confess your sins." Jos. vii. 19. **darkness,** Is. viii. 22; ix. 2. **dark mountains,** where traveling is perilous.[d] **gross darkness,** De xxviii. 29. (17) **weep in secret,** indicating that he would, in sorrow, retire from pleading any longer with them. (18) "From this verse it is generally inferred that this prophecy belongs to the reign of Jehoiachin whose mother is also mentioned in xxii. 26; xxix. 3 and probably exercised unusual influence."—Driver. **king,** Jehoiachin, or Jeconiah. **queen,** R. V., "queen-mother."[e] **Principalities,** R. V., head-tires."

[e] 2 Ki. xxiv. 8—15.

"The Heb. kings generally married women who were not of royal race, but were subjects; they had also many wives. Hence the position of a Queen Consort was an inferior one, but that of a Queen Mother was one of considerable influence."—Wordsworth.

Pride (vs. 15).—I. Different kinds of pride. 1. Race pride—pride in ancestors; 2. Face pride—pride in outward appearance; 3. Place pride—pride in social position; 4. Grace pride—pride in godliness. II. The warning. Be not proud—1. Because we have nothing to be proud of; 2. Because it is abhorrent to God; 3. Because it is unlike Christ; 4. Because it is ruinous. Apply:—(1) Some are very proud; (2) Some occasionally; (3) Some are bravely struggling against pride.—J. Bolton.

Note on vs. 18.—The margin has instead of "principalities," "head tires." This again alludes to the threatened judgments which were to befall the people and their rulers. Of a proud man who treats another with contempt it is said, "Ah! his turban will soon fall." "Yes, imperious upstart! thy head-dress will soon come down." Jehoiakim and his queen-mother were to have their "head tires" brought down; they were to be humbled on account of their sins.—Roberts.

Humility.—

On bended knees, replete with godly grief,
See where the mourner kneels to seek relief,
No "God I thank Thee!" freezes on his tongue
For works of merit that to him belong;
Deep in his soul conviction's ploughshare rings,
And to the surface his corruption brings;
He loathes himself, in lowest dust he lies,
And, all-abased, "Unclean, unclean!" he cries.
From his full heart pours forth the gushing plea,
"God of the lost, be merciful to me!"
The light of life descends in heavenly rays,
And angels shout and sing, "Behold, he prays!"
—W. Holmes.

[a] "When Ahaz made himself tributary to the king of Assyria, he taught the Assyrs. how they might become masters and conquerors over his own country, whenever they pleased."
—Lowth.

19—22. (19) **cities . . south,** i. e. of the Negeb, or southern district of Judah. **shut up,** because ruins block all entrances and the land is deserted of any to clear the way. (20) **flock,** fig. for the cities grouped round Jerusalem. They are suddenly and wholly swept away by the enemy. (21) **he shall punish,** etc., R. V., "he shall set thy friends over thee as head, seeing thou thyself hast instructed them against thee;" i. e. the Egyptians and Babylonians.[a] (22) **Wherefore,** etc., ch. v. 19, xvi. 10. **made bare,** R. V., "suffer violence," from tramping into captivity over the rough roads.

"When at first from virtue's path we stray,
How shrinks the feeble heart with sad dismay!
More bold at length, by powerful habit led,
Careless and sear'd the dreary wild we tread;
Behold the gaping gulf of sin with scorn,
And plunging deep to endless death are borne."
—J. Scott.

God's retributive justice (vs. 21).—I. Let us endeavor to establish the doctrine that retributive justice belongs to God. II. This will lead us to assail your hope of impunity from it. 1. The first foundation of the sinner's hope is derivable from God's delay; 2. Prosperity; 3. The mercy of God. III. We proceed to answer the question. 1. Wilt thou say, I do not deserve the condemnation? 2. Or, I was not warned? 3. Or, There was no way of escape?—W. Jay.

23, 24. (23) **Ethopian,** the African negro, whose skin is nearly black.[a]

accustomed, practised, so that evil has become the settled habit. (24) **stubble,** left from the threshing. **wind .. wilderness, the east wind which** blew strong from the Arabian desert.

The alarming power of sin (vs. 23).—The **long-continued** impenitence of men augments the difficulties in the way of their **salvation.** I. The habits of men are strengthened and confirmed by **indulgence.** II. The influence of this world, as men advance in life, usually becomes more perplexing, and a greater hindrance to their conversion. III. As years increase, men become less interested in the subject of religion, and more obdurate and averse to any alteration in their moral **character.** IV. The thought of multiplied and long-continued transgression is **very** apt to discourage all attempts at repentance. V. There is awful **reason** to apprehend that God will leave men of this description to perish in their sins. Apply—(1) To the aged; (2) Those in middle life; (3) To the young.—G. Spring.

Washing the Ethiopian.—Then the shepherds led the pilgrims to a place where they saw one Fool, and one Want-wit washing an Ethiopian, with an intention to make him white; but the more they washed him the blacker he was. Then they asked the shepherds what this should mean. So they told them saying, "Thus it is with the vile person: all means used to get such an one a good name, shall in conclusion, tend but to make him more abominable. Thus it was with the Pharisees, and so shall it be with all hypocrites."—Bunyan.

The Christian sects in Syria appear to consider a true case of Druze conversion to Christianity as out of the question. "The wolf's whelps," they say, "are not tamed." The conversion of many sinners appears equally impossible, and yet how many such triumphs of grace are recorded as that which John Newton described in himself: "I was a wild beast on the coast of Africa once, but the Lord Jesus caught me, and tamed me, and now people come to see me as they would go to look at the lions in the tower."—Beecher.

Power of early habits.—In North America a tribe of Indians attacked a white settlement and murdered the few inhabitants. A woman of the tribe, however, carried away a very young infant and reared it as her own. The child grew up with the Indian children, different in complexion, but like them in everything else. To scalp the greatest possible number of enemies was, in his view, the most glorious and happy thing in the world. While he was still a youth, he was seen by some white traders, and by them conducted back to civilized life. He showed great relish for his new life, and especially a strong desire for knowledge, and a sense of reverence, which took the direction of religion, so that he desired to become a clergyman. He went through his college course with credit, and was ordained. He filled his functions well, and appeared happy and satisfied. After a few years he went to serve in a settlement somewhere near the seat of war which was then going on between Britain and the United States; and before long there was fighting not far off. I am not sure whether he was aware that there were Indians in the field (the British having some tribes of Indians for allies), but he went forth in his usual dress, black coat and neat white shirt and neckcloth. When he returned he was met by a gentleman of his acquaintance, who was immediately struck by an extraordinary change in the expression of his face, and the fire of his eye, and the flush on his cheek; and also by his unusually shy and hurried manner. After asking news of the battle, the gentleman observed, "But you are wounded!—No; not wounded? Why, there is blood upon the bosom of your shirt!" The young man crossed his hands firmly, though hurriedly, upon his breast; and his friend, supposing that he wished to conceal a wound which ought to be looked to, pulled open his shirt, and saw—what made the young man let fall his hands in despair. From between his shirt and his breast the gentleman took out—a bloody scalp! "I could not help it," said the poor victim of early habits, in an agonized voice. He turned and ran, too swiftly to be overtaken; betook himself to the Indians, and never more appeared among the whites."—Miss Martineau.

25—27. (25) **of thy measures,** R. V., "measured unto thee." (27)

Pr. xxvii. 22; Is. i. 5; Mat. xix. 24.

"Said Diogenes when he had reproved an ill man to no purpose, 'Æthiopem abluo ut casididum redham:' I do but wash a blackamoor. And the like said Nazianzen concerning Julian the Apostate. It is said that the negroes paint the devil white, as being a color contrary to their own, and which they less well affect."—Trapp.

"Bad habits are very easily formed, but when once formed they they are like the course of a mighty river. Some of the oldest rivers in the world have the same place in the map, and the same windings on the face of the earth which they first cut for themselves; and that way they have continued to follow through the succession of generations." —J. A. Wallace.

"If it were possible for those who have been for ages in hell to return to the earth (and not to be regenerated), I firmly believe that, notwithstanding all they have suffered for sin, they would still love it, and return to the practice of it." —**John Ryland.**

abominations, the shameless ceremonies and orgies of heathen and idolatrous religion.[a] **when .. be?** marg. "after when yet?" "Thou wilt not be made clean after how long a time yet?"

[a] Comp. Je. ii. 20, 23, 24, iii. 2, 6.

Power of habit.—"Habitual evils change not on a sudden. But many days must pass, and many sorrows; Conscious remorse and anguish must be felt, To curb desire, to break the stubborn will and work a second nature in the soul, ere virtue can resume the place she lost."—Rowe.

"Ill habits gather by unseen degrees,
As brooks make rivers, rivers run to seas."
—Dryden.

CHAPTER THE FOURTEENTH.

The immediate occasion of this chapter was a drought in which the prophet saw Jehovah's anger.—Driver.

1—6. (1) **dearth,** R. V., "drought," ch. xvii. 8. (2) **gates,** put for the people who congregate in the gates. **black .. ground,** R. V., they sit in black upon the ground." Comp. viii. 18; Ps. cxxxvii. 1, etc. (3) **sent,** R. V., "send"—present tense in all these verses. **little ones,** or common ones, servants. **pits,** cisterns for preserving the rainfall. **covered their heads,** the sign of uttermost distress.[b] (4) **chapt,** cracked with the dryness. (5) **forsook it,** bec. finding herself unable to feed it.[c] (6) **snuffed,**[d] R. V., "they pant for air like jackals," oppressed with heat and thirst.

[b] 2 Sa. xv. 30, xix. 4.

[c] "These creatures are very sharp - sighted; and travelers in the desert frequently avail themselves of their appearance, knowing that there must be herbage and water in the vicinity."—Henderson.

[d] "Asses, in defect of water, can continue long by drawing in the air; as Aristotle likewise testifieth of the goats of Cephalonia, that they drink not for divers days together, but instead thereof gape and suck in the fresh air."—Trapp.

Note on vs. 4.—The description that Sir J. Chardin gives us of the state of these countries, with respect to the cracking of the earth, before the autumnal rains fell, is so lively a comment on Jer. xiv. 4, that I beg leave to introduce it here as a distinct observation. The lands of the East, he says, which the great dryness there causes to crack, are the ground of this figure, which is certainly extremely beautiful; for these dry lands have chinks too deep for a person to see to the bottom of; this may be observed in the Indies more than anywhere, a little before the rains fall, and wherever the lands are rich and hard. The Prophet's speaking of ploughmen shows that he is speaking of the autumnal state of those countries; and if the cracks are so deep from the common dryness of their summers, what must they be when the rains are withheld beyond their usual time, which is the case Jeremiah is referring to? This refers to a drought which was to take place in Judah. At such times, in the East, the ground is "chapt;" large fissures meet your eye in every direction, and the husbandmen are then ashamed and put to confusion: they know not what to do; to plough the land under such circumstances is of no use, and therefore they are obliged to wait till it shall rain. Thus, should the rains be later than usual, the people are daily looking for them, and after one night's fall, the farmers may be seen in every direction working in their fields with the greatest glee, in the full hope of soon casting in the seed.

7—9. (7) **do thou,** R. V., work thou." **for thy name's sake,** "either (i) in accordance with the name, under which Thou hast revealed Thyself, The Lord God, merciful and gracious, etc. (Exod. xxxiv. 6); or (ii) for Thy honor, that the heathen may behold Thy might and faithfulness. This latter seems the more usual sense of the phrase, for which see Ps. lxxix. 9, cvi. 8; Is. xlviii. 9; Ezek. xx. 9, 14, 22; and for the thought Josh. vii. 7—9."—Camb. Bib. (8) **hope of Israel,** whose future rests on the Divine promise and covenant. **stranger,** R. V., sojourner, transient,[b] who concerns himself but little with the affairs of the land. **turneth aside,** or stretcheth out his tent. (9) **astonied,** astonished, and so losing presence of mind.

[a] 2 Chr. xxxiii. 8.

[b] ... man ever yet ...d to be, as ...lays pass by, ... and more ... and sweet ...ure and ...y-minded ... ever yet ...hat the ...its of ... pride ... and ...ness ... cast ...oul ...his ...ng ...d

A prayer for all seasons (vs. 9).—I. Here is a prayer for all seasons. 1. Times of joy; 2. of adversity; 3. of labor; 4. Of perplexity, etc. II. Here is a prayer for all saints. 1. All need to pray thus; 2. All must pray thus; 3. All will pray thus. III. Here is a prayer always answered. For it is according to His will; 2. For it honors His name.—Stems and Twigs.

God's withdrawal from his people.—"I know, as night and shadow ... good for flowers, and moonlight and dews are better than continual ... so is Christ's absence of special use, and it hath some nourishing virtue in it, and giveth sap to humility, and putteth an edge on hunger, and furnishes a fair occasion for faith to put forth her hand and lay hold on what she seeth not."—Rutherford.—"God sometimes hides Himself that we may cling the closer to Him and hang the faster upon Him. By withdrawing from His people, He prevents His people withdrawing from Him; and so by an affliction He prevents sin; for God to withdraw from me is but my affliction, but for me to withdraw from God, that is my sin; and, therefore, it were better for me that God should withdraw from me a thousand times than that I should once withdraw from God." (Heb. x. 38, 39).—Brooks.

10—12. God's reply to Jeremiah's prayer. (10) **loved to wander,** not merely, they do wander, but they love it; and persistently choose the evil way. (11) **Pray not,** ch. vii. 16. (12) **oblation,** Heb. minchah, a meat-offering.[c]

True fasting.—

Is this a fast—to keep
The larder lean, and clean
From fat of veals and sheep?
Is it to quit the dish
Of flesh, yet still to fill
The platter high with fish?
Is it to fast an hour,
Or ragged go, or show
A downcast look and sour?

No! 'tis a fast to dole
Thy sheaf of wheat, and meat
Unto the hungry soul.
It is to fast from strife,
From old debate, and hate—
To circumcise thy life
To show a heart grief-rent;
To starve thy sin—not bin—
And that's to keep thy Lent.

—Herrick.

13—16. (13) **Ah, Lord God,** ch. i. 6. **assured peace,** lasting, settled peace. (14) **lies,** their statements can only deceive. **divination,** De. xviii. 10. **thing of nought,** Heb. elil, a diminutive of el, (God), signifies a small idol made of the more precious metals.—Spk. Com. See ch. xxiii. 21. (15) **Therefore,** etc., ch. v. 12, 13. (16) **none to bury,** Ps. lxxix. 3. The people should not have let themselves be deceived by the prophets. Therefore the people shall be punished for their sin.

Faithless minister.—

Most guilty, villainous, dishonest man!
Wolf in the clothing of the gentle lamb!
Dark traitor in Messiah's holy camp!
Leper in saintly garb! assassin masked
In virtue's robe! vile hypocrite accursed!
I strive in vain to set his evil forth!
The words that should sufficiently accurse
And execrate such reprobate, had need
Come glowing from the lips of eldest hell.
Among the saddest in the den of woe,
Thou saw'st him saddest 'mong the damned now damned.

—Pollok.

17—22. (17) **Let,** etc., ch. xiii. 17; La. i. 16, ii. 18. **virgin daughter,** as never having been previously subdued by any foreign prince. (18) **go about into,** etc., R. V., "go about in the land and have no knowledge," i. e. know not what to do. (20) **have sinned,** Jeremiah makes himself one with the people and confesses the national sin. (21) **disgrace,** or show as if Thou didst lightly esteem. **throne .. glory,** fig. for the temple, as

c "It appears from this vs. that the people had again engaged in the external service of Jehovah, in the hope that this would avert His anger, but as they were not really weaned fr. idolatry, it is declared to be in vain."—Henderson.

Pr. i. 28, xxviii. 9; Is. i. 15, lviii. 3.

"We may be persuaded that nothing has power to separate us from the love of God which is in Christ Jesus our Lord. The mischief is that we reject the protections of that love and all other benefits flowing from it."
—Pul. Com.

"We judge ourselves by what we feel capable of doing, while others judge us by what we have already done."
—Longfellow.

"Our hope is not hung upon such an untwisted thread as 'I imagine so,' or, 'it is likely;' but the cable, the strong rope of our fastened anchor, is the oath and promise of Him who is eternal verity: our salvation is fastened with God's own hand and Christ's own strength to the strong stake of God's unchangeable nature. —Rutherford.

earthly dwelling of God. (22) **vanities,** or idols. **thou he,** who alone canst send the plentiful rain.

How to plead with God (vss. 20, 21).—We propose—I. To explain this prayer of the Prophet; his acknowledgments are plain and easy to be understood; his pleas require some explanation. II. To point out some important lessons contained in it. 1. The true nature of a sinner's humiliation; 2. The proper grounds of a sinner's encouragement. Apply:—(1) Have you ever pleaded with God in this manner? (2) Have you ever pleaded thus with God in vain?—C. Simeon.

Contrition necessary.—Take the cold iron and attempt to weld it, if you can, into a certain shape. How fruitless the effort! Lay it on the anvil, seize the blacksmith's hammer with all your might, let blow after blow fall on it, and you shall have done nothing; but put it in the fire, let it be softened and made malleable, then lay it on the anvil, and each stroke shall have a mighty effect, so that you may mold it into any shape you may desire. So take your heart, not cold as it is, but put it into the furnace; let it be molten, and after that it can be fashioned into the image of Jesus Christ.—Spurgeon.

CHAPTER THE FIFTEENTH.

[a] Ex. xxxii. 11—14; Nu. xiv. 13—20; 1 Sa. vii. 9, xii. 23; Ps. xcix. 6.

"If by prayer
Incessant I could hope to change the will
Of Him who all things can, I would not cease
To weary Him with my assiduous cries.
But prayer against His absolute decree
No more avails than breath against the wind,
Blows stifling back on him that breathes it forth:
Therefore to His great bidding I submit."
—Milton.

1—4. (1) **Moses and Samuel,** the most persuasive and successful of all the previous intercessors.[a] Comp. Eze. xiv. 14. **cast .. sight,** or send them away: it is too late for any answer of peace. (2) **Such .. death,** etc., i. e. each to the various form of Divine judgment under wh. they must come. (3) **kinds,** or classes of calamity. (4) **removed,** etc., R. V. "tossed to and fro among all the kingdoms," etc. De. xxviii. 25. **Manasseh,** 2 Ki. xxi. 3.

Note on vs. 3.—An Oriental enemy, as in former ages, cuts down the trees of the country which he invades, destroys the villages, and burns all the corn and provender which he cannot carry off: the surrounding plain, deprived of its verdure, is covered with putrid carcases and burning ashes; the hot wind wafting its fœtid odors, and dispersing the ashes among the tents, renders his encampment extremely disagreeable. During the night the hyenas, jackals, and wild beasts of various kinds, allured by the scent, prowl over the field with a horrid noise; and as soon as the morning dawns, a multitude of vultures, kites, and birds of prey, are seen asserting their claim to a share of the dead. Such was the scene which Forbes contemplated on the plains of Hindostan; "and it was to me," says that writer, "a scene replete with horrid novelty, realising the Prophet's denunciation: 'I will appoint over them four kinds, saith the Lord; the sword to slay, and the dogs to tear, and the fowls of the heaven, and the beasts of the earth, to devour and destroy.'"—Paxton.

[a] "Thy sins render thee unworthy of pity, and everybody that sees the calamities brought upon thee will own them to be just."—Lowth.

vs. 9. R. Hall, vs. 1.

"Be assured that life is best
Which finds us least afraid to die."
—Eliza Cook.

5—9. (5) **ask .. doest?** or make inquiry for thy welfare.[a] (6) **gone backward,** ch. vii. 24. **weary with repenting,** "In language adapted to the understanding of men God is spoken of as repenting, either as here, when punishment long delayed is at last to be inflicted (compare Gen. vi. 6); or when threatened evil has been averted by timely reformation, e.g: Jon. iii. 10."—Camp Bib. (7) **will fan,** R. V., "have fanned," denoting not mere defeat, but dispersion. **will bereave .. destroy,** R. V., "have bereaved .. destroyed." (8) **widows .. sea,** a strong poetical fig. .. **young men,** the word means, picked warriors. **caused .. city,** R. V., "caused anguish and terrors to fall upon her suddenly." (9) **sun .. day,** Am. viii. 9. "Fortune deserts her at the very height of her prosperity."—Fausset.

Early Death.—"What is this voice to us?" says Bonar of the early death of M'Cheyne. "Only this much we can clearly see, that nothing was more fitted to leave his character and example impressed on our remembrance for ever than his early death. There might be envy while he lived; there is none now. There might have been some of the youthful attractiveness of his graces lost had he lived many years; this cannot be impaired now. It seems as if the Lord had struck the flower from the stem ere any of the colors had lost their bright hues or any leaf its fragrance."

10—14. "The prophet vents his grief at the fate which (through the message he bears) obliges him to encounter the hatred of all men."—Driver.[b] (10) **strife .. contention,** called to reprove publicly the licentiousness of the times. **lent on usury,** fig. way of saying that he had no causes of personal quarrel. (11) **verily it shall,** etc., R. V. "Verily I will strengthen thee for good." (12) **iron,** R. V. "can one break iron, even iron from the north and brass?" The connection of thought in vss. 11-13 is, an evil time is approaching, a time in wh. the Jews will inevitably be vanquished by a superior foe and the land made a spoil. **northern iron,** fig. for Chaldæans. **steel,** should be brass. (13) **Thy substance,** not Jer.'s, but that of Judæa. **without price,** as if it were all of no value. (14) **fire,** etc., De. xxxii. 22.

Dr. Arnold (of Rugby).—We listened, as all boys in their better moods will listen (ay, and men too, for the matter of that), to a man who we felt to be, with all his heart and soul and strength, striving against whatever was mean and unmanly and unrighteous in our little world. It was not the cold clear voice of one giving advice and warning from serene heights to those who were struggling and sinning below, but the warm living voice of one who was fighting for us, and by our sides, and calling on us to help him and ourselves, and one another. And so, wearily, little by little, but surely and steadily on the whole, was brought home to the young boy, for the first time, the meaning of his life; that it was no fool's or sluggard's paradise into which he had wandered by chance, but a battle-field ordained from of old, where there are no spectators, but the youngest must take his side, and the stakes are the life and death. And he who roused this consciousness in them, showed them at the same time, by every word he spoke in the pulpit, and by his whole daily life, how that battle was to be fought; and stood there before them their fellow-soldier and the captain of their band. The true sort of captain, too, for a boy's army, one who had no misgivings and gave no uncertain word of command, and, let who would yield or make truce, would fight the fight out (so every boy felt) to the last gasp and the last drop of blood. Other sides of his character might take hold of and influence boys here and there, but it was this thoroughness and undaunted courage which more than anything else won his way to the hearts of the great mass of those on whom he left his mark, and made them believe first in him, and then in his Master.—Hughes.

Savonarola, the great Italian reformer (died 1498), while yet the ruling mind in Florence and in possession of full popularity, foresaw the troubles in which he, like the Old Testament prophet, would be involved by his fearless condemnation of vice, and in the midst of one of his striking sermons thus addressed the Almighty, "O Lord, whither hast thou led me? From my desire to save souls for Thee, I can no longer return to my rest. Why hast Thou made me 'a man of strife, and a man of contention to the whole earth?'"—W. R. Clark's Savonarola.

15—18. (15) **remember me,** "this verse is connected in sense with vs. 10. The Lord's reply to Jeremiah's lament in that verse fails to satisfy him, inasmuch as coupled with it have been mentioned again the coming afflictions of his countrymen, while at the same time his own present condition remains unaltered."—Camb. Bib. (16) **eat them,** Eze. iii. 3; Re. x. 9. (17) **Mockers,** i. e. "laughers," in their festivities. **because of thy hand,** i. e., because of his ordination to the sacred calling. (18) **pain perpetual,** figs. for his exceeding grief in his hopeless mission. **liar,** R. V. "as a deceitful brook," whose waters fail in time of need.

Soul-feeding (vs. 16.—I. The grandest discovery, "Thy words were found." 1. Explain the universe; 2. They reveal Himself; 3. They reveal His redemptive provisions. II. The richest repast. 1. They satisfy the cravings of hunger; 2. They invigorate the soul. III. The sublimest delights.—Thomas.

Henry Martyn.—"What do I not owe to the Lord," writes Henry Martyn, "for permitting me to take a part in the translation of His Word? Never did I see such wonders, and Wisdom, and love, in the

---

[b] Comp. Job iii. 1; Je. xx. 15. Je. xl. 4.

"This law is the magistrate of a man's life. It is not the pilot directing the vessel; it is the vessel abandoned to the force of the current, the influence of the tides, and the control of the winds."—Josepn Johnson.

"After you have been kind, after Love has stolen forth into the world and done its beautiful work, go back into the shade again and say nothing about it. Love hides even from itself. Love waives even self-satisfaction." —Drummond.

"I need not be missed if my life has been bearing
(As its summer and autumn moved silently on),
Its flower and its fruit, I shall still be remembered—
Yes, but remembered by what I have done."

"What is the limit of our prayer? This: 'Not my will but Thine be done!' Is that a limit? Why, that is glorious liberty! Not my will but Thine, — not a little will but a great will,—not my thought but Thine,—not my love but Thine. Is it a limit? It is the lark rising from its field-nest with the boundless liberty of the firmament. Truly we do not limit ourselves when we exchange the creature for the Creator." — Joseph Parker.

"Faithful ministers," says Henry, "are God's mouth to us, and we are to hear God speaking to us by them."

"God does not always frown, lest we should be cast into despair; He does not always smile, lest we should be careless and presume."—Owen.

"So thine own soul commend thee in thy ways,
Faint not, nor swerve from thine accepted aim,
Most diffident when men most loudly praise,
And unabashed beneath their harshest blame."

"The joy of the wicked is but for a moment; that of the righteous is everlasting. The wicked rejoice; but their joy is simply like letting off fire-works,—they blaze away, and seem to put the modest little stars to shame. But it is all for a little while: they are over in a moment, while the quiet stars are shining still."—T. Jones.

"A good man's prayers
Will from the deepest dungeon climb to heaven's height,
And bring a blessing down."
—Joanna Baillie.

blessed book, as since I have been obliged to study every expression; and it is a delightful reflection that death cannot deprive us of the pleasure of studying its mysteries." Appropriating God's Word. Have you an ear to hear Gospel truth as the voice of the Infinite God addressed to your own soul? The Dutch farmers at the Cape, at no very distant period, considered the Hottentots around them to be little better than beasts, quite incapable of anything beyond mere eating, drinking, stealing and lying. After our missionaries had labored among the natives for a time, one of them was found reading the Bible by the roadside. The Dutchman inquired of him, "What book are you reading?" "The Bible." "The Bible! Why, that book was never intended for you." "Indeed it was," said the black man, "for I see my name here." "Your name! where?" cried the farmer. "Show it to me." "There," said the Hottentot, putting his finger on the word 'sinners.' That's my name; I am a sinner, and Jesus Christ came to save me." It were well, indeed, if men would but read the Bible, saying, "In this volume the great God condescends to speak to me."—Spurgeon.

19—21. (19) **return,** God replies, that His happiness and success depend upon his giving up this mistaken tone of mistrust and despair.—Driver. **bring thee again,** "give thee a settled place," i. e. quiet and safety.—Cheyne. **precious .. vile,** "cause the precious metal to come forth from the dross."—Spk. Com. He is to cleanse his own heart from the unworthy suspicions as to God's faithfulness, which though mixed with better thoughts he had just shewn to be there entertained."—Camb. Bib. (20) **brasen wall,** ch. i. 18, vi. 27. (21) **the terrible,** those even who act towards thee with violence.

Waters that fail (vs. 18).—Heb. "Waters that are not to be trusted," i. e. such as are delusive, such as disappoint expectation. That which Mr. Harmer proposes simply as a query, may be stated as a very probable suggestion, viz. that in these words the Prophet alludes to the phenomenon of the mirage, so frequently mentioned by Eastern travelers. "There is," says Chardin, "a vapor or splendor, in the plains of the desert, formed by the repercussion of the rays from the sand, that appears like a vast lake. Travelers afflicted with thirst are drawn on by such appearances, but coming near find themselves mistaken; it seems to draw back as they advance, or quite vanishes." "To the south-east, at a distance of four or five miles, we noticed on the yellow sands two black masses, but whether they were the bodies of dead camels, the temporary hair-tents of wandering Bedouins, or any other objects, magnified by the refraction which is so strongly produced in the horizon of the desert, we had no means of ascertaining. With the exception of these masses, all the eastern range of vision presented only one unbroken waste of sand, till its visible horizon ended in the illusive appearance of a lake, thus formed by the heat of a midday sun on a nitrous soil, giving to the parched desert the semblance of water, and reflecting its scanty shrubs upon the view, like a line of extensive forests; but in no direction was either a natural hill, a mountain, or other interruption to the level line of the plain, to be seen."—Buckingham.

Evil shall not prevail.—In the dark ages the enemy thought he had destroyed the Church, but life came into the monk in his cell, and Luther shook the world. The Church in England fell into a deadly slumber in the day of Whitfield and Wesley; but she was not dead, and therefore a time of awakening came. The flame burned low, but the heavenly fire still lingered among the ashes, and only needed the Holy Spirit to blow upon it, and cause a hallowed conflagration. Six young men in Oxford were found guilty of meeting to pray: their offense was contagious, and soon there sprang up hundreds glorying in the same blessed crime. Earnest servants of the living God were forthcoming, and no man knew whence they came; like the buds and blossoms which come forth at the bidding of spring, a people made willing in the day of God's power came forward at once. Seeing that there is life in the Church of God, you can never calculate what will happen within its bounds to-morrow; for life is an unaccountable thing, and scorns the laws which bind the formal and inanimate.—Spurgeon.

CHAPTER THE SIXTEENTH.

1—4. (2) **not .. wife,** marriage was regarded as a duty by the Jews, and the blessings of the Mosaic law rested upon fruitfulness.[a] In commanding Jer. not to take a wife God intimated that during the impending calamities it would be impossible to bring up families: they would only increase the anxieties of siege and famine times. **this place,** the land of Judæa. (3) **mothers .. fathers,** who are so deeply affected when calamities come upon their children. (4) **grievous deaths,** "refers to the pestilence which always ensued upon the scarcity and vile quality of food, and the confinement of multitudes within the narrow bounds of a besieged city."—Exp. Bib. **lamented,** with the usual wailings for the dead.

The prophet forbidden to marry.—The reasons were probably that, by his abstaining from marriage, he might more powerfully confirm his words as to the coming calamities. It would show his own belief in what he had foretold when it was seen that he would not make for himself a home under such circumstances. It would leave him more free for the arduous duty which he had to discharge. It would save him great sorrow when the evil days should come. And so now there are special cases in which God's will seems to be that a man should not marry. The missionary exposed to daily peril of climate, pestilence, savage heathendom; or any to whom it is evident that by their marriage more evil than good will result;—then, just as we may be called upon to do without many other great earthly advantages, so we may be called upon to deny ourselves this. And there may be physical conditions forbidding marriage. No man has a right to transmit to others hereditary disease, whether of body or mind. And there are spiritual hindrances. A man ought to marry only "in the Lord." But all these exceptions are rare; God's general rule is that men should marry.—Pul. Com.

5—8. (5) **house of mourning,** forecasting the time when deaths would be so many that the usual customs would not be observed.[a] (6) **cut themselves,** etc., Le. xix. 28; De. xiv. 1. This was a heathen custom. wh. it seems the Jews had adopted with their idolatry.[b] **make .. bald,** shave a bare patch on the front of the head.[c] (7) **tear themselves,** R. V. "break bread for them," the reference is to the custom that the friends of those who were in mourning should urge them to eat. See 2 Sam. iii. 35, xii. 16, 17. Bread also was distributed to mourners and to the poor at funerals, "Pour out thy bread on the burial of the just," Tobit iv. 14. Compare Is. lviii. 7 (where the Heb. is the same "to deal thy bread" etc."—Camb. Bib. **cup of consolation,** it was the custom to provide food and drink for mourners. (8) **house of feasting,** vs. 5.

Verses 5-8.—Acting as prophet, that is, as one whose public actions were symbolical of a Divine intent, Jeremiah is henceforth to stand aloof, on occasions when natural feeling would suggest participation in the outward life of his friends and acquaintance. He is to quell the inward stirrings of affection and sympathy, and to abstain from playing his part in those demonstrative lamentations over the dead, which the immemorial custom and sentiment of his country regarded as obligatory; and this, in order to signify unmistakably that what thus appeared to be the state of his own feelings, was really the aspect under which God would shortly appear to a nation perishing in its guilt. "Enter not into the house of mourning . . . for I have taken away My friendship from this people, the lovingkindness and the compassion." In like manner, the prophet is forbidden to enter as guest "the house of feasting." He is not to be seen at the marriage-feast,—that occasion of highest rejoicing, the very type and example of innocent and holy mirth; to testify by his abstention that the day of judgment was swiftly approaching, which would desolate all homes, and silence for evermore all sounds of joy and gladness in the ruined city.—Expos. Bib.

9—13. (9) **voice,** etc., all private and public seasons of rejoicing.[d] **in**

[a] De. xxviii. 4.

"One who has known in storms to sail
I have on board;
Above the raging of the gale
I hear my Lord.
He holds me when the billows smite,
I shall not fall.
If sharp, 'tis short; if long, 'tis light;
He tempers all.
Safe to the land, safe to the land,—
The end is this;
And then with him go hand in hand
Far into bliss."
—Dean Alford.

[a] "God here anticipates the fulfilment of Jeremiah's prophecies, and tells him how to demean himself when they should have been accomplished."—Wordsworth.

[b] "Among the Greeks the custom of tearing, cutting off, or shaving the hair. was at least as common as among the Jews. Sometimes the hair was cast upon the funeral pile, and on other occasions it was laid upon the grave."—Kitto.

[c] Amos 8:10; Mi. 1:16.

[d] Je. vii. 34, xxv. 10; Eze. xxvi. 13.

your days, caution against assuming that the threatened penalty would be reserved for their posterity. (10) **Wherefore,** etc., ch. v. 19, xiii. 22.[d] (12) **worse,** etc., ch. vii. 26; 1 Ki. xiv. 9. **imagination,** R. V., "stubbornness." (13) **there,** in the captive land ye may do your own will. The sentence is ironical.[e] **not . . favor,** "since I will not grant you grace."—Exp. Bib.

Conscience is starved by neglect of that seeking of God's grace which is its nutriment and strength. And it is stunned by repeated acts of sin. Men can and do nibble, if we may so speak, at conscience, and gradually rid themselves of it. The clamor of sin drowns the still, small voice, and its protests, perpetually unheeded, are at last withdrawn. So that at length men find themselves able to do evil and think nothing of it; the little rift that sin first made has widened and widened until the whole torrent of waters bursts through, for the faithful dyke that held them back has been gradually destroyed, and so now the whole nature of the man is overwhelmed, submerged beneath the deluge of sin. And, what is most sad, the man feels, no more than do the sunken cities and towns that lie at the bottom of the Zuyder Zee, the rush of the waves that for centuries have rolled over them.—Pul. Com.

[d] De. xxix. 24; 1 Ki. ix. 8, 9.

[e] "There among idolaters you may indulge your evil propensities to the full; you may practise your idolatries without intermission." — Rosenmüller.

"A man to be a soul-winner must have holiness of character. The Eternal will never use dirty tools, the thrice-holy Jehovah will select only holy instruments of His work."—Spurgeon.

Salutariness of mourning.—

How wretched is the man who never mourn'd.
I dive for precious pearl in sorrow's stream:
Not so the thoughtless man that only grieves,
Takes all the torment, and rejects the gain
(Inestimable gain), and gives heaven leave
To make him but more wretched, not more wise.
—V. Young.

14, 15. (14) **Therefore,** or "yet surely." **days come,** ch. xxiii. 7, 8.[f] (15) **land of the north,** the usual appellation of Chaldæa wh. was north to Judæa.

Gratitude should be proportionate to favors. This is often not the case, because the best things are least appreciated. Their merits are not superficial nor discernible at first. The spiritual blessings are the highest; yet to unspiritual men they are the least valued. Thus the chief elements of the Messianic promises of restoration were spiritual, and therefore not so acceptable to the mass of the people as the material blessings promised to the Jews in the first possession of the "land flowing with milk and honey." We are too ready to complain of the present and regret the lost past, ungratefully selecting the troubles of our own time for notice and ignoring its bright features, while we forget the hardships of the past and remember only its last pleasant features, like the Jews, who forgot the rigors of the slavery from which they had escaped, but remembered with regret the flesh-pots of Egypt (Exod. xvi. 3). The Bible favors no sentimental regrets for "the good old times;" it teaches us that God's goodness is increasingly manifest.—Pul. Com.

God's guidance.—One of our poets, speaking of our birth, beautifully says, "Every soul leaves port under sealed orders. We cannot know whither we are going or what we are to do till the time comes for breaking the seal. But I can tell you something more beautiful than this. Every regenerated soul sets out on its voyage with an invisible Captain on board, who knows the nature of our sealed orders from the outset, and who will shape our entire voyage accordingly if we will only let him.—A. J. Gordon. Three epochs of confidence.—People have generally three epochs in their confidence in man. In the first they believe him to be everything that is good, and they are lavish with their friendship and confidence. In the next, they have had experience, which has smitten down their confidence, and they then have to be careful not to mistrust every one, and to put the worst construction upon everything. Later in life, they learn that the greater number of men have much more good in them than bad, and that, even when there is cause to blame, there is more reason to pity than condemn; and then a spirit of confidence again awakens within them.—Miss Bremer. Christian confidence.—A soldier lay dying in the hospital, in terrible agony. A visitor asked him, "What Church are you of?" "Of the Church of Christ," he replied. "I mean

[f] "The sufferings of Judah in the Babylonish captivity will be so great, that the deliverance from them will be more joyous than even their exodus from Egypt."—Wordsworth.

"A man who would have God's guidance must be willing to make spiritual things his main business." — H. C. Mabie.

"As the needle of the compass which points to it tells him which way he sails; thus the heart that is touched with the loadstone of Divine love tells the soul that its course is heavenward, towards the haven of eternal rest."—Leighton.

of what persuasion are you?" "Persuasion," said the dying man, as his eyes looked heavenward, beaming with love to the Savior, " I am persuaded that neither death, nor life, nor angels, nor principalities, nor powers, nor things present, nor things to come, nor height, nor depth, nor any other creature, shall be able to separate me from the love of God which is in Christ."

16—18. (16) **fishers .. hunters,**[a] reference in these figures is to the coming judgments, by the Chaldæans, who would hunt out the people from their hiding-places, and accomplish a general destruction.[b] (17) **eyes .. ways,** Job xxxiv. 21; Pr. v. 21. The judgment is one decided on after complete inquiry and perfect knowledge. (18) **first,** i. e. before accomplishing the return promised in vs. 15. **double,** i. e. in proportion to God's usual severity in punishing men's sins. "Because their sin was two-fold."—Camb. Bib. **carcases,** so in contempt the offering of animals in their idol sacrifices is called.[c] or "the idols themselves, which defiled those who worshipped them."—Pul. Com.

Divine comfort.—When a man walketh in the sun, if his face be towards it, he hath nothing before him but bright shining light and comfortable heat; but let him once turn his back to the sun, what hath he before him, but a shadow? And what is a shadow, but the privation of light, and heat of the sun? Yea, it is but to behold his own shadow, defrauding himself of the other. Thus there is no true wisdom, no true happiness, no real comfort but in beholding the countenance of God; look from that and we lose these blessings; and what shall we gain? a shadow, an empty image; instead of a substantial, to gain an empty image of ourselves, and lose the solid image of God. Yet this is the common folly of the world; men prefer this shadow before that substance, whereas there is not the least appearance of any true comfort but in God only.—Spencer.

[a] Am. iv. 2; Hab. i. 15.

[b] "Lit. understood, the fishers are the main armies who, in the towns and fortresses, capture the people in crowds as in a net, while the hunters are the light-armed troops, who pursue the fugitives over the whole country, and drive them out of their hiding-places with as eager pleasure as hunters track out their game."—Spk. Com.

[c] Some think the reference is to the offering of human beings, or of unclean animals.

19—21. (19) **fortress,** or place of defence. **Gentiles,** R. V. "Nations," i. e. a crowd of peoples, hitherto ignorant of the true God, shall hasten to the scene of Jehovah's great interposition; they have been convinced by Israel's unlooked-for restoration of the unique divinity of Jehovah."—Pul. Com.[a] (20) **make gods,** an inconceivable absurdity in the very statement.[b] (21) **this once,** i. e. in this overwhelming judgment.[c] **The Lord,** R. V., "Jehovah," the covenant name of God.

Worldly comforts.—The comforts of this world are but like the treasures of snow; do but take a handful of snow, and crush it in your hands, it will melt away presently; but if you let it lie on the ground, it will continue for some time; and so it is with the things of this world; if you take the comforts of this life in your hands, and lay them too near your hearts in affection and love to them, they will quickly melt and vanish away from you; but it you leave them in their proper place, and do not set an inordinate affection upon them, they will continue the longer with you; as if you should line a garment with linen, it would do very well, but if you line it with pitch or glue, that will stick fast to the body, and in all likelihood soil both garment and the man that wears it; so when the world is glued to our hearts, it spoils the comforts of all the mercies that we enjoy; and so it may be said that the otherwise lawful use of them is abused, when they are either used too affectionately in making gods of them, or being too eagerly bent in the gaining of them.—T. Brooks.

[a] "The result of God's judgments on the Jews will be that both the Jews when restored, and the Gentiles who have witnessed those judgments, shall renounce idolatry for the worship of Jehovah."—Fausset.

[b] Je. ii. 11.

[c] "The 'hand' and 'might' wh. they were to know and feel, were the severe afflictions to be suffered during the captivity, and which they required to experience only once more in order to be effectually weaned from idolatry." — Henderson.

CHAPTER THE SEVENTEETH.

1—4. (1) **pen of iron,** Job xix. 24. An iron chisel or stylus suitable for cutting inscriptions on stones; or engraving on metal. **point,** lit., "finger nail."[d] Such a pen made indelible marks, and so did the sin of Judah. **altars,** plural. God's altar was one, Baal's altars were many. Possibly the names of the idols to whose service the altar was devoted were put upon the horns. (2) **children,** whose lives might be sacrificed in the Moloch rites. Or indicating that the children are trained up in

[d] "On Assyrian contract - tablets witnesses who were too poor to possess a seal impressed a nail-mark. From these nail-marks the word translated point has been derived."—Bib. Things, etc.

e Is. xi. 9, lvi. 7, lvii. 13.

"Queen Mary when she died, told those about her that the loss of Calais had so impressed her, that its image would be found indelibly engraven on her heart."

"That was a beautiful tribute of Napoleon to the supremacy of mind over physical force in the long trial. 'Do you know, Fontanes,' he said, 'what I admire most in the world? It is the powerlessness of force to found anything. There are only two powers in the world—the sabre and the pen; and in the end the former is always conquered by the latter.'"—Anon.

the fathers' bad example. **groves,** R. V., "Asherim," the asherak was a wooden post, a kind of fetich, esteemed divine and worshipped with rites similar to those of Baal-worship. Earliest mention is Ex. xxxiv. 13. Comp. also Judges iii. 7. See Moore on Judges, Int. Com. (3) **mountain . . field,**[e] fig. for Zion. Field means "open country," the whole country of Judæa. **high places,** 1 Sa. ix. 12. **for sin,** or because of thy sin. (4) **even thyself,** the original probably means, "through thine own fault."—Camb. Bib. **discontinue,** cease to possess.

Indelible records of sin.—The great stone book of Nature reveals many records of the past. In the red sandstone there are found, in some places, marks which are clearly the impressions of showers of rain, and these so perfect that it can even be detected in which direction the shower inclined, and from what quarter it proceeded; and this, ages ago. Even so sin leaves its track behind it, and God keeps a faithful record of all our sins.—Bib. Treas. If you cut a gash in a man's head, you may heal it; but you can never rub out, nor wash out, nor cut out the scar. It may witness against you in his corpse; still it may be covered by the coffin or hidden in the grave; but then it is not till decomposition shall take place that it shall entirely disappear. But if you smite a soul, the scar remains; no coffin or grave shall hide it; no revolution, not even the upturning of the physical universe, shall obliterate it; no fire, not even the eternal fires shall burn it out.—Thomson. The record of sin.—It is written on the memory. Men who have forsaken the scenes of their evil deeds cannot shake off the clinging burden of the memory of them. The criminal is haunted by his crimes. They people his dreams with horrors; they overshadow his waking hours with gloom. Even when sin is put out of mind it is probably buried in the secret chamber of memory, to be ultimately brought to the light of consciousness. The experience of those who have been recovered from drowning and from delirium suggests the idea that forgotten memories can be revived, and that probably the whole of the soul's experience is indelibly written upon the memory. No other recording-angel may be wanted. The soul carries its own indictment in the record it bears of its own conduct.—Pul. Com. Inflictions—the effect of evil.—Great effects always have great and appropriate causes; and great causes, left to operate freely, will produce great and proper effects. Every human heart holds within it enough to make indescribable misery; and unless that greater cause which God offers to put in certain operation comes in with its counteracting force, we may be sure that indescribable misery will be produced. Wherefore let us pray that more and more we may have eyes to see and perceive, ears to hear and understand.—Pul. Com.

a De. xxix. 23; Ps. cvii. 34; Zep. ii. 9.

b "The pious man who makes God his confidence is truly happy, whatever may be the outward circumstances in which he may be placed." — Henderson.

"Trust in yourself, and you are doomed to disappointment; trust in your friends, and they will die and leave you; trust in money and you may have it taken from you; trust in reputation and some slanderous

5—8. "The beautiful strophes (5—13) are not obviously connected with the preceding text. They wear a look of self-completeness, which suggests that here and in many other places Jeremiah has left us, not whole discourses, written down substantially in the form in which they were delivered, but rather his more finished fragments; pieces which being more rhythmical in form, and more striking in thought, had imprinted themselves more deeply upon his memory."—Exp. Bib. (5) **trusteth in man,** as Judah was then trusting in Egypt and Assyria. **flesh,** contrasted with God. **arm,** of reliance. (6) **heath,** Heb. 'ar'ar, wh. is both a "juniper" and a "destitute man." Here a dry bush, or bare tree.—Ewald, Umbreit, etc. **salt land,** in Heb. saltness is a sign of barrenness.[a] (7) **Blessed,** etc., Ps. ii. 12, xxxiv. 8, cxxv. 1. (8) **tree,** etc., Ps. i. 3. **river,** or watercourse. **see,** R. V., "fear." **careful,** or anxious.[b]

The curse and the blessing (vss. 5—8).—I. The curse. 1. The person against whom it is denounced, the self-reliant, self-confident, etc.; 2. The language in which it is expressed implies that the person shall be unprosperous, useless, worthless, etc. II. The blessing. 1. The person to whom it is promised: he recognises God; 2. The language in which it is expressed. Apply:—On whom dost thou trust?—G. Brooks. Difference between trusting man and God (vss. 5—8).—Man not independent; must have a support; often selects a wrong one. I. The folly and evil of trusting in man. 1. Such trust is idolatrous in principle; 2. Grovelling in its aim; 3. Unreasonable in its foundation; 4. Destructive in its issue. II. The wisdom and benefit of trusting in the Lord. 1. It is pious in principle; 2. Elevated in its aim; 3. Rational in its foundation; 4. Glorious in its issue. Apply:—(1) A mistake to suppose the rich and gay happy, and the poor and pious miserable; (2) An unreserved confidence in God can alone secure our happiness and the Divine favor.—Delta in 400 Sks.

9—11. (9) **deceitful,** i. e. self-deluding. We may never trust it.[a] **wicked,** R. V., "sick." (10) **search,** etc., thoroughly, fr. God none of its secrets are hidden.[b] **give,** in righteous judgments. (11) **sitteth on eggs,** etc., R. V., "that gathereth young which she hath not brought forth;" the partridge calls the young of other birds under her wings, but they forsake her when they hear the cry of the true parent. The application is plain. Riches unlawfully gotten are as precarious and shortlived a possession as the young that have not been hatched by the bird that would pass for their parent.

The deceitfulness of the heart (vs. 9).—1. Men impose on themselves in respect of their own character; 2. In regard to their attachments; 3. In regard to their power in resisting temptation; 4. In regard to their promises of reformation and amendment. Apply:—(1) The danger of losing the soul; (2) You have a heart which is not to be trusted; (3) Wake from all delusions to the reality of your condition.—Albert Barnes. The human heart (vs. 9).—I. Its deceitfulness. 1. It misrepresents the nature of things; 2. It conceals the tendency of things; 3. It practices imposition on itself. II. Its wickedness. It is so—1. Universally; 2. Unsearchably; 3. Incurably. Learn—(1) Our need of regeneration; (2) The claims of the Saviour; (3) The duty of self-examination.—G. Brooks.

A New Year's petition.—

O that my eyes might closed be
To what becomes me not to see!
That deafness might possess my ear
To what concerns me not to hear!
That truth my tongue might always tie
From ever speaking foolishly!
That no vain thought might ever rest
Or be conceived in my breast!
That by each word, each deed, each thought,
Glory may to my God be brought!
But what are wishes? Lord, my eye
On Thee is fixed, to Thee I cry:
O purge out all my dross, my sin,
Make me more white than snow within.
Wash, Lord, and purify my heart,
And make it clean in every part;
And when 'tis clean, Lord, keep it so,
For that is more than I can do.

—Thomas Ellwood.

12—14. (12) Render, "Thou throne of glory, a height from the beginning, thou place of our sanctuary, thou hope of Israel, Jehovah." The temple is called "the throne of thy glory" in ch. xiv. 21; "height" is a common synonym for heaven (Ps. vii. 8, Hebrew; Isa. lvii. 15, Hebrew), but is also applied to Mount Zion (Ezek. xvii. 23; xx. 40), which is also in Isa. lx. 13 called, "the place of my sanctuary."—Pul. Com. **throne,**[c] the first reference is to the Temple as Jehovah's earthly dwelling-place, then the Prophet's thought rises to Jehovah Himself. (13) **hope of Israel,** on whose word alone Israel can safely hope. **forsake thee,** Ps. lxxiii. 27; Is. i. 28. **written .. earth,** or dust, where names are soon rubbed out. Contrasted with in the rock, where names may abide.[d] **fountain .. waters,** ch. ii. 13. (14) **thou .. praise,** i. e. Thou only. The expression of simple and entire trust in God.

A prayer for salvation (vs. 14).—1. These words express a deep concern about salvation, and an earnest desire to obtain it; 2. A firm persuasion that God alone can save; 3. A heartfelt application to God for

tongue may blast it; but trust in God, and you are never to be confounded in time or eternity."—D. L. Moody.

[a] "There is no sure reliance to be placed in the feelings of the heart, nor in the dictates of conscience, unless the conscience be informed and regulated by the will and Word of God."—Wordsworth.

[b] 1 Sa. xvi. 7; Ps. vii. 9, cxxxix. 1, 23.

"I am more afraid of my own heart than of the Pope and all his cardinals. I have within me the great pope—self."—Luther.

"All our actions take
Their hues from the complexion of the heart,
As landscapes their variety of light."
—Bacon

[c] The "throne of glory" is equivalent to Him who is enthroned in glory.

[d] "What is written in the earth may be easily effaced, as contrasted with what is written in a book, or engraven in the rock."—Henderson.

"The glory of God and the happiness of man are blended together by the Hand that united soul and body in one man, light and heat in one

salvation through the medium of prayer; 4. An unwavering confidence that the salvation which God bestows in answer to prayer will be a salvation suited to the wants of fallen man.—G. Brooks.

Salvation.—There is a natural principle in man, lowering him, deadening him, pulling him down by inches to the mere animal plane, blinding reason, searing conscience, paralyzing will. This is the active destroying principle, or Sin. Now, to counteract this, God has discovered to us another principle, which will stop this drifting process in the soul and make it drift the other way. This is the active saving principle, or Salvation. If a man finds the first of these powers furiously at work within him, dragging his whole life downward to destruction, there is only one way to escape his fate—to take resolute hold of the upward power, and be borne by it to the opposite pole.—Drummond.

The splendor of salvation.—Mark well the splendor of this idea of salvation. It is not merely final "safety," to be forgiven sin, to evade the curse. It is not, vaguely, "to get to heaven." It is to be conformed to the Image of the Son. It is for these poor elements to attain to the Supreme Beauty. The organizing Life being Eternal, so must this Beauty be immortal. Its progress toward the Immaculate is already guaranteed. And more than all, there is here fulfilled the sublimest of all prophecies; not Beauty alone, but Unity is secured by the type—Unity of man and man, God and man, God and Christ and man, till "all shall be one."—Drummond.

15—18. (15) "This verse shews that the time is before the capture of Jerusalem at the end of Jehoiakim's reign. If that event had occurred, the people would not, as here, challenge the prophet to point out a fulfilment of his prophecies of woe."—Camb. Bib. **Where,** etc., Is. v. 19. The questions of the sceptic and the scoffer. (16) **not hastened,** i. e. had not eagerly withdrawn from following the will of God, as a shepherd.[a] **desired .. day,** no wish to be a prophet of evil, bec. I had any vindictive feelings. **the woeful day,** i. e. the overthrow of Jerusalem. **was right before thee,** R. V., "was before thy face." The insertion of the word right is misleading. What Jeremiah really says is that his words were not his own, but were all spoken as in God's sight and in compliance with His will. (17) **terror,** or cause of dismay; i. e. by not fulfilling the threatenings Thou dost bid me deliver. **hope,** R. V., "refuge." (18) **confounded,** etc., Ps. xxxv. 4, xl. 14. **double,** twofold punishment for their twofold sin, in apostacy as a nation, and hostility to Jeremiah.—Camb. Bib. ch. xvi. 18.

Prophecies—attributed to God.—It is a natural course to hold a man responsible for all that comes from his lips. The prophet could not escape this responsibility. It was not his to complain that his auditors challenged him as the constructor of these unpalatable speeches. If they looked to him, he in turn did the wise thing, the only thing that could be done—he looked to God. He was able to do this because he had been faithful. He had not garbled or mutilated his message to make it more tolerable. He understood perfectly well what, nevertheless, many fail to understand, that truth depends, not on what men are able to understand, but on what God clearly reveals. The prophet was in no manner of doubt as to the authority by which he spoke. Looking back and reviewing his utterances, he was perfectly sure that he had not confused his own thoughts with the commanded words of Jehovah. If what God reveals for us to speak, we speak; and if what he reveals for us to believe and act upon, we do believe and act upon; then with the utmost confidence we can go to him for support and defence. What could Jeremiah have done in his extremity if he had not been conscious of his fidelity as a prophet of God?—Pul. Com.

19—23. A prophecy on the reward of obedience to the Law (vss. 19—27). (19) **gate,** wh. one is not certain. Evidently the one through which there was the most traffic. (20) **kings,** prob. including all the officials. (21) **Take heed,** on this point be very watchful. **burden .. day,** it appears that the inhabitants both of town and country habitually broke the fourth commandment by engaging in traffic on the Sabbath. The latter brought in their produce for sale in Jerusalem, while the former

---

sun, holiness and happiness in one heaven; and what God has joined together let not man put asunder."

"'What you demand is here, or at Ulubræ.' You traverse the world in search of happiness, which is within the reach of every man: a contented mind confers it on all."—Horace.

"When a teacher confines himself to the praise of the Cross, and lets all other matters of praise go which might adorn a theologian of these times, and adheres immovably to this: 'I am determined not to know anything among you save Jesus Christ and Him crucified'—amid all the shame of His Cross, he is victorious over the rest." — Zinzendorf.

[a] "I have not forced myself forward to follow thee as a shepherd."—Umbreit.

"It is not so much by the symmetry of what we attain in this life that we are to be made happy, as by the enlivening hope of what we shall reach in the world to come. while a man is stringing a harp, he tries the strings, not for music, but for construction. When it is finished it shall be played for melodies. God is fashioning the human heart for future joy. He only sounds a string here and there to see how far His work has progressed." —H. W. Beecher.

"With eyes turned upward, whence her help descends, Hope waits expecting till the tempest ends." —Holmes.

would bring from their houses commodities to be offered in exchange. Comp. Neh. xiii. 15—22.—Camb. Bib. (22) **hallow,** etc., Ex. xx. 8, etc. (23) **neck stiff,** the sign of rebellious opposition and wilfulness.[a]

Religious observance of the Sabbath.—The importance of the religious observance of the Sabbath is seldom sufficiently estimated. The violation of this duty by the young is one of the most decided marks of incipient moral degeneracy. Religious restraint is fast losing its hold upon that young man who, having been educated in the fear of God, begins to spend the Sabbath in idleness or in amusement. And so also of communities. The desecration of the Sabbath is one of those evident indications of that criminal recklessness, that insane love of pleasure, and that subjection to the government of appetite and passion, which forebodes that the "beginning of the end" of social happiness, and of true national prosperity, has arrived. Hence we see how imperative is the duty of parents, and of legislators, on this subject. The head of every family is obliged, by the command of God, not only to honor this day himself, but to use all the means in his power to secure the observance of it by all those committed to his charge. He is thus not only promoting his own, but his children's happiness; for nothing is a more sure antagonist force to all the allurements of vice, as nothing tends more strongly to fix in the minds of the young a conviction of the existence and attributes of God, than the solemn keeping of this day. And hence, also, legislators are false to their trust, who, either by the enactment of laws, or by their example, diminish, in the least degree, in the minds of a people, the reverence due to that day which God has set apart for Himself.—Wayland.

24—27. (24) **diligently,** with anxious carefulness and thought seeking fully to obey. (25) **kings,** etc., glory, fame, power, prosperity are promised. **remain for ever,** or permanently continue the centre of the covenant kingdom. (26) **shall come,** as at the great festivals. **sacrifices of praise,** i. e. sacrifices wh. should be sincere expressions of pious and grateful feeling. (27) **fire,** etc., La. iv. 11.[b] "The scene of their sin should be the scene of their punishment."

No work on Sunday.—The late William H. Smith began his business career by folding newspapers and addressing bundles. When he died he was the head of the house of W. H. Smith & Son, the largest "news" agents in Great Britain, and had been member of Parliament, Financial Secretary to the Treasury, First Lord of the Admiralty, and the Conservative leader of the House of Commons. He was a religious man, not only at church and in the family, but in his business. It was a rule in W. H. Smith & Son's business that no work should be done on Sunday. Only once is there recorded an exception to this rule. In September, 1854, shortly after the battle of Alma, the despatches containing the names of the killed and wounded arrived late on Saturday night. To put a speedy end to the doubts, fears and hopes of hundreds of distracted families, the employes were called upon to sacrifice their Sunday rest in order that the "extras" might be distributed in London and the provinces. Several years later W. H. Smith & Son received a "command" to supply a member of the royal family with newspapers. Among other journals on the list was the Observer, published on Sunday morning. The command was obeyed, but it was explained that as Sunday work was contrary to the rules of the firm, the Observer could not be supplied.

Types and uses of the Sabbath.—

Hail to the day which He, who made the heaven,
Earth, and their armies, sanctified and blest,
Perpetual memory of the Maker's rest!
Hail to the day when He, by whom was given
New life to man, the tomb asunder riven,
Arose! That day His Church doth still confess,
At once Creation's and Redemption's feast,
Sign of a world called forth, a world forgiven.
Welcome that day, the day of holy peace,
The Lord's own day! to man's Creator owed,

[a] "As the Sabbath was instituted as a sign or token of God's covenant with His people, the Jews profaning the Sabbath was in effect renouncing their share in the covenant."—Lowth.

"Bright Sabbath morning, on the moor, where all is still save praise."—Bailey.

"The Sundaies of man's life,
Thredded together on Time's string,
Make bracelets to adorn the wife
Of the eternal, glorious King.
On Sunday heaven's gates stand ope;
Blessings are plentifull and rife,
More plentifull than hope."
—Herbert.

[b] "In the siege the gates of Jerusalem and its palaces were actually burned with fire. Ne. ii. 13, 17."—Wordsworth.

"The green oasis where, after the week-days' journey, the pilgrim halts for refreshment and repose; where he rests beneath the shade of the lofty palm trees, and dips his vessel in the waters of the calm, clear stream, and recovers his strength to go forth again upon his pilgrimage in the desert with renewed vigor and cheerfulness."-Reade.

"He that would prepare for heaven, must honor the Sabbath on earth. He that would hope for the spiritual joys there, must acquire a taste and aptitude for them here."—Bp. D. Wilson.

And man's Redeemer; for the soul's increase
In sanctity, and sweet repose bestowed;
Type of the rest when sin and care shall cease,
The rest remaining for the loved of God!

—Bp. Mant.

CHAPTER THE EIGHTEENTH.

"This chapter is the introduction of a group of prophecies (extending to ch. xxv. of various dates; their sequence has evidently not been determined by chronological considerations. The prophet's first object is, perhaps, to refute the scoffing inquiry (ch. xvii. 15), "What has become of the [threatening] word of Jehovah?" and to justify the glorious promise given at the conclusion of the last chapter."—Cheyne. **1—4.** (2) **house,** or workshop. The clay-field lay south of Jerusalem, just beyond the valley of Hinnom.[a] (3) **wheels,** lit. the two wheels.[b] (4) **marred,** or spoiled: it was a failure. **made it again,** i. e. made up the clay again into a new vessel, and possibly one of another shape, and fitted for another purpose.

The parable of the potter (vss. 1—10).—Consider man in the hands of God—I. As morally defective: the clay marred, in moral judgment, moral affections, moral conduct. II. As morally improvable: God is mighty to save, emotionally, magisterially, reformatively. III. As morally free. It is here indicated that man is—1. Responsible for his destiny; 2. For his conduct.—Thomas.

The clay and the potter.—Every life has not the same purpose. The potter makes vessels of innumerable shapes. Yet each life is successful as its own particular purpose is fulfilled. The homely jug may be perfect, though it is very different from the graceful vase. A life is no failure because it is lowly and put only to lowly uses so long as it attains the end for which God designed it. It is important to note that God's first work with us is in forming our own souls aright. The first question is not as to what we do, but as to what we are. The potter is making vessels; God is making characters, souls, lives. After this we may be put to some further end—used for good after we have been made right, as the vessel is of service after the potter has done his work with it. . . The clay is refractory. It must be broken up and remodelled. Man is more than clay. He has free-will, mysterious as may be the connection of this with the almighty sovereignty of God. In a much more terrible way he too is refractory, wilfully and stubbornly. For this he must be broken. His life must be disturbed and shaken up, but only that God may begin again to fashion him for his destined end. Great disappointments, destructive events, the failure of a man's work, the disruption of a Church, the revolution of a nation, may seem simply disastrous. But we see how that by means of these things God, in his infinite patience and gracious perseverance, will finally effect his own great purposes, and so secure the true blessedness of his creatures.—Pul. Com.

5—10. (6) **cannot . . potter,** a strong assertion of God's absolute power and right over the creatures He makes and the nations He calls into being.[a] **ye in mine hand,** i. e. I can crush you down into a shapeless mass, out of which I may form a new nation. (7) **At what instant,** lit. "suddenly." **pluck up,** ch. i. 10. (8) **If that nation,** the action of God is not arbitrary, like that of the potter, but always in strict accordance with the manner in which they behave themselves towards Him.[b] (9) **build,** or establish it. (10) **of the good,** change My purpose of blessing it with prosperity.

Note on vss. 7—10.—"First of the prophets, Jeremiah proclaims distinctly what had been more or less implied throughout, that predictions were subject to no overruling necessity, but depended for their fulfilment on the moral state of those to whom they were addressed; that the most confident assurance of blessing could be frustrated by sin; that the most awful warnings of calamity could be averted by repentance."—Stanley's Jewish Church. The dignity of man.—When a piece of base metal is

[a] Zec. xi. 13; Matt. xxvii. 10.

[b] "By this is meant the horizontal lathe of the potter, consisting of two wheels or round plates, on the upper one of wh. was placed the clay, which he molded into vessels at his pleasure. These wheels were either of wood or stone, and were in use at an early period among the Egyptians." —Henderson.

"Repine not, nor reply;
View not what Heaven ordains with reason's eye;
Too bright the object is, the distance is too high.
The man who would resolve the work of fate,
May limit number and make crooked straight;
Stop thy enquiry, then, and curb thy sense,
Nor let dust argue with Omnipotence."
—Prior.

[a] Is. xlv. 9; Ro. ix. 20, 21.

[b] "God is said to repent of evil, when He changes His dealings with men and nations, on their turning to Him."—Augustine.

"When through the clay not being of a proper consistency, or otherwise not answering to the potter's will, the vessel is spoilt, he does not throw it away, but crushes it together, dashes it back upon the wheel, and begins his work afresh, till 'the

coined with the king's stamp, and made current by his edict, no man may henceforth presume either to refuse it, either in payment, or to abate the value of it; so God, having stamped His own image upon every man, and withal signified His blessed pleasure, how precious He would have him to be in our eyes and esteem, we must look to answer it as a high contempt of that sacred Majesty, if we set any man at nought, or make less account of him than God would have us.—Bp. Sanderson.

clay has taken the predetermined shape. So then, it was God's purpose that Judea should become the proper scene for the manifestation of the Messiah, and its sons be fit to receive the Saviour's teaching and carry the good tidings to all lands. If, therefore, at any stage of the preparation, the Jewish nation took, in its free will, such a course as would frustrate this purpose of Providence, it was crushed by affliction into an unresisting mass, in which the formative process forthwith began again."— Payne Smith.

Recessional.—

God of our fathers, known of old—
Lord of our far-flung battle-line—
Beneath Whose awful Hand we hold
Dominion over palm and pine—
Lord God of Hosts, be with us yet,
Lest we forget—lest we forget!

The tumult and the shouting dies—
The captains and the kings depart—
Still stands Thine ancient Sacrifice,
A humble and a contrite heart.
Lord God of Hosts, be with us yet,
Lest we forget—lest we forget!

Far-called our navies melt away—
On dune and headland sinks the fire—
Lo, all our pomp of yesterday
Is one with Nineveh and Tyre!
Judge of the Nations, spare us yet,
Lest we forget—lest we forget!

If, drunk with sight of power, we loose
Wild tongues that have not Thee in awe—
Such boasting as the Gentiles use
Or lesser breeds without the Law—
Lord God of Hosts, be with us yet,
Lest we forget—lest we forget!

For heathen heart that puts her trust
In reeking tube and iron shard—
All valiant dust that builds on dust,
And guarding calls not Thee to guard—
For frantic boast and foolish word,
Thy mercy on Thy people, Lord!
Amen.

—Rudyard Kipling.

11—14. (11) **go to,** Ge. xi. 3. **frame,** as a potter frames a work on his wheels. **devise,** etc., terms implying careful preparation. **return,** i. e. turn from the evil, and return to your God, and goodness.[c] (12) **"And they said,** rather, But they go on saying (comp. Ezek. xxxiii. 17, 20). **There is no hope,** the rendering may be easily misunderstood. "The speakers are not, as we might suppose, despondent about their state and prospects, but they seek to check the troublesome preacher by the warning that he has no chance of success (so ch. ii. 25)."—Pul. Com. (13) **Ask .. heathen,** see if you can find a parallel case.[d] **virgin,** a term intended to remind the people that they had been wholly separated unto God. (14) **will, etc.,** R. V., "shall the snow of Lebanon fail from the rock of the field? or shall the cold waters that flow down from afar be dried up?" The snow never leaves Lebanon, nor do the streams dry up—but Israel has forgotten her source, etc.

c 2 Ki. xvii. 13; Je. vii. 3.

"This language of the Jews involves the last stage of hardened wickedness."—Henderson.

d "Even among the heathen it was a thing unheard of, that a nation should lay aside its gods for foreign gods, though their gods are false gods." —Fausset.

Fallen man.—We saw at Hanover the unfinished palace of the deposed monarch; we were shown his state and private carriages and his stables of cream-colored horses. A saddening sight to see all the emblems of sovereignty and no king; the insignia of royalty and the monarch for ever exiled. How like to human nature, which has so much about it prepared for the service of the King of kings, so much of faculty for heavenly occupation; but the King has departed and the house is left desolate, and all the furnishing thereof perverted to alien uses. Thought, imagination, judgment, memory, all fit to be yoked to celestial chariots, become the very hacks of the devil, and the body once a palace now a haunt of thieves. Alas, alas! poor manhood!—Spurgeon.

15—17. (15) **Because,** better, "yet surely." **forgotten me,** the pure and living water; ch. ii. 13, xvii. 13. **vanity,** a word meaning falsehood. **and they,** i. e. the false gods; said to do what the false prophets and priests really did. **ancient paths,** the old beaten track, as set forth in the law of Moses. **paths,** R. V., "bypaths." **not cast up,** raised, and prepared, so as to be fit and safe to travel on.[a] (16) **hissing,** an expression of insult and contempt. **wag .. head,** in mockery and ridicule. (17) **east**

a "A road cast up means one raised sufficiently to keep it out of the reach of floods, etc. We still call our chief roads highways, bec. when the country was undrained it was necessary to raise them above the level of the adjoining fields." —Spk. Com.

Is. lvii. 14, lxii. 10.

[b] Job xxvii. 21, xxxviii. 24; Ps. xlviii. 7; Is. xxvii. 8.

[c] Is. i. 15, lix. 2.

[d] "They comforted themselves with the assurance that God had made these lasting institutions in His Church, and the Law declares they shall never perish. Le. vi. 18, x. 11; comp. Je. v. 11."—Grotius.

"If slander be a snake, it is a winged one—it flies as well as creeps."—Douglass Jerrold.

"Where it concerns himself,
Who's angry at a slander makes it true."
—Ben Jonson.

wind,[b] fig. for the calamities of war and wasting judgments. **the back,** R. V., "look upon their back," driving them before me in anger, ch. ii. 27.[c]

Man—perversion of his faculties.—According to the fable, the tail of the snake obtained precedence of the head and led the way in the creature's journeying. Being altogether blind the new guide dashed against a stone at one moment, and the next came violently against a tree, and at last drowned both itself and the head in the river of death. Here may be seen the unhappy condition of men in whom their baser nature is dominant, the animal controlling the intellectual. They invert the order of nature, they rebel against common sense; their course cannot but be unwise and dangerous, and their end must be fatal. God made man upright, and placed his thoughtful faculties aloft in the place of sovereignty, but man in his folly permits the appetites which he holds in common with the brute creation to reign supreme, while the mind, which ought to rule, is degraded to meanest servitude.—Spurgeon.

18—20. (18) **said they,** "the leaders among those whom Jeremiah had addressed." **devise devices,** or frame a plot to secure his ruin. **not perish,** etc., i. e. we need not fear if we put this troublesome Prophet away; we shall still have the Law, the priest, and the prophet among us.[d] **with the tongue,** by carrying malicious reports about him to the king, Jehoiakim. (19) **Give heed,** appeal to God from heedless man. (20) **digged .. soul,** Ps. xxxv. 7. **speak good,** to plead in their behalf. "Behold the glaring contrast between my innocence of all hurtful intent, and their clamorous injustice, between my truth and their falsehood, my prayers for their salvation and their outcry for my blood."—Exp. Bib.

Slander—poisonous.—This slander is compared to poison—"the tongue is an unruly evil, full of deadly poison." The deadliest poisons are those for which no test is known; there are poisons so destructive that a single drop insinuated into the veins produces death in three seconds, and yet no chemical science can separate that virus from the contaminated blood and show the metallic particles of poison glittering palpably, and say, "Behold, it is there."—F. W. Robertson.

'Tis slander
Whose edge is sharper than the sword, whose tongue
Outvenoms all the worms of Nile; whose breath
Rides on the posting winds, and doth belie
All corners of the world, kings, queens, and states,
Maids, matrons; nay, the secrets of the grave
This viprous slander enters.

—Shakespeare.

[a] "These words of malediction, regarded as utterances of personal feeling, are not exempt from the taint and stain of human infirmity and passion."—Wordsworth.

[b] "It redounds to the glory of God's justice that incorrigible sinners should meet with exemplary punishment."—Lowth.

"Suffering becomes beautiful when any one bears great calamities with cheerfulness, not through insensibility, but through greatness of mind."—Aristotle.

21—23. "This passage is lyrical in form and expression and something must be allowed for the fact in estimating its precise significance." —Exp. Bib. (21) **deliver,** etc., Ps. cix. 10.[a] "Let the calamities of war and famine, which Thou hast threatened, come upon them; I can intercede no more." **and pour,** etc., R. V., "and give them over to the power of the sword." **put to death,** R. V., "slain of death." (22) **cry,** such as arises in a city wh. is given over to be sacked. (23) **thou knowest,** in this the good man may ever find rest. **forgive not,** but execute Thy judgments on them.[b]

Jeremiah's supplication.—In reading this supplication, we vainly try to escape from feeling what a ferocious, savage tone the words have. The dreadful meaning of the words, taken in their natural signification, is only too plain. We must by no means try to defend the prayer; we can only do something to extenuate the language by remembering the provocation the prophet had received, and the spirit of the age in which he lived. It is at least important to remember that he is distinctly conscious of having had good motives towards these enemies. He knew that God meant their good, and he, in speaking, had meant the same. It must be noticed also that, whatever his feelings, he expresses them as a prayer to God. He does not take retaliation into his own hands. His rights and interests, whatever they are, he leaves in the hands of Jehovah. He has, indeed, his own estimate as to what his enemies deserve, but he seeks that they may get their deserts in the way of manifestly

Divine judgments. Then he evidently spoke in great excitement. The wrath even of a good man may boil over into language which he would not wish to be held by in cooler moments. We may be perfectly sure that if, in after years, Jeremiah had been reminded of this prayer, and asked if he really, seriously meant that the innocent connections of his enemies should be ruthlessly slaughtered, he would have been quick to plead that his words were those of excitement. Shall it be thought wonderful that he should utter such a wish when the disciples of the meek and lowly Jesus had drunk in so little of the spirit of their Master as to wish fire from heaven to come down upon the inhospitable Samaritans? The passage under consideration is just one of those which strongly shows the difference which has been made by the sermon on the mount. If Jeremiah had been a Christian apostle instead of a Jewish prophet, his prayer would have been a very lamentable utterance indeed. —Pul. Com.

"Most wretched men
Are cradled into poetry by wrong;
Then learn in suffering what they teach in song."
—Shelley.

"What nothing earthly gives, or can destroy, the soul's calm sunshine and the heartfelt joy."—Pope.

CHAPTER THE NINETEENTH.

1—5. (1) **earthen bottle,** Heb. bakbuk, a flask with a long neck, wh. took its name from the noise made by liquids in running out of it. **ancients,** R. V., "elders." **ancients .. priests,** i. e. the heads of the twenty-four courses.[a] These were to be witnesses of the symbolic action. (2) **Hinnom,** ch. vii. 31. **east gate,** R. V. "the gate Harsith," i.e. "the gate of the potsherds," the place where broken pottery was thrown away. (3) **ears .. tingle,** 1 Sa. iii. 11; 2 Ki. xxi. 12. (4) **estranged,** etc., alienating it from God by introducing the idol worship. **blood of innocents,** children offered to Moloch, as vs. 5. (5) **built also,** comp. ch. vii. 31, 32.[b]

The preliminaries of the breaking.—Spectators of the proper sort needed to be deliberately gathered together in the proper place. We may suppose that the elders of the people and of the priests were peculiarly responsible for all that concerned the safety of the city. This symbolic action was best performed before the select responsible few. As they went forth with the prophet they had time to ask themselves what the meaning of this unusual summons might be. It is, perhaps, a little to be wondered at that they should have gone with the prophet at all. And yet, although none might have quite the right motive for going, each would have his own motive, and so an acquiescent assembly be formed. God knows how to subdue and blend the motives of men for his own purposes. In some minds there would be a superstitious regard for the prophetic office; in others, curiosity would operate; and in a few there might be somewhat of the hearing ear and understanding mind. We are, then, to imagine this company going forth; and they do not go forth at random. It is not for mere seclusion they go out of the city. They are led to the very place which, because of the abominations practised in it, is to be one of the principal causes of future woe. Thus we see how carefully God arranges the circumstances in which his truth is to be proclaimed.—Pul. Com.

6—9. (6) **Tophet,** ch. vii. 32. (7) **I will make void,** the Heb. verb means literally, I will pour out. It has been thought that Jeremiah here suited the action to the word, and having previously filled with water the vessel which he bore, now poured out the contents on the ground.—Camb. Bib.[c] **carcases,** etc., ch. vii. 33, xvi. 4. (8) **hiss,** in contempt. (9) **eat,** etc., Le. xxvi. 29; De. xxviii. 53; La. iv. 10. "A ghastly reversal of natural affection, to which the severity of the siege will give rise."—Driver.

Fervency in preaching.—

Still thinking I had little time to live,
My fervent heart to win men's souls didst rive;
I preached as never sure to preach again,
And as a dying man to dying men! ..
Though God be free, He works by instruments,
And wisely fitteth them to His intents.

[a] 1 Chr. xxiv. 4.

[b] Baal and Moloch were names promiscuously given to the same idol. Prob. Baal was the general name, and Moloch distinctive of one form of his manifestation.

"George Herbert built a new church near Spaulding, and by his order the reading pew and pulpit were both of an equal height; for he would often say, 'They should neither have a priority of the other; but that prayer and preaching, being equally useful, might have an equal honor and estimation.'"—Life of Herbert.

[c] "Neumann supposes that Jer. carried the bottle to Tophet full of water, the symbol in the East of life, and at these words emptied it before the assembled elders." — Spk. Com.

"True eloquence consists in saying all that is necessary and nothing more."

A proud unhumbled preacher is unmeet
To lay proud sinners humbled at Christ's feet;
So are the blind to tell men what God saith,
And faithless men to propagate the faith:
The dead are unfit means to raise the dead,
And enemies to give the children's bread;
And utter strangers to the life to come,
Are not the best conductors to our home.
They that yet never learned to live and die,
Will scarcely teach it others feelingly. —R. Baxter.

10—13. (10) **break,** etc., as a sign of the entire and hopeless destruction of the city. "The people have the same custom of breaking a jar, when they wish to express their utmost detestation of any one. They come behind or near him, and smash the jar to atoms, thus imprecating upon him and his a like hopeless ruin."—Thomson, The Land and the Book. (11) **made whole,** or healed.[a] (12) **as Tophet,** ch. vii. 31, as it had been made unclean by idolatry so shall the houses of Jerusalem be defiled by corpses. (13) **because of,** better, even the very houses. **roofs,** flat, and often used as places for sacrifices.[b]

[a] "By these figures is set forth the distinction between chastisements and judgments."

[b] Zep. i. 5.

Purpose of the shattered vessel.—The thing was not done in mere wantonness and thoughtlessness, nor in passion, nor in carelessness. The prophet did not draw his lesson from a jar which some one else had happened to break. He got the vessel with the deliberate purpose, divinely put into his mind, of breaking it. This was far enough away from the purpose with which it was made, and the vessel, once shattered, could be of no further use for this first purpose; but in its destruction it served a far nobler end than if it had been carefully kept to carry water for many long years. Rightly considered, indeed, the vessel was not destroyed, but only its service divinely and wisely changed. So, looking from the symbol to the reality behind it, we must bear in mind that the capture of Jerusalem and the conquest of the land of Israel served certain purposes of God. He did not separate this people and give them this land that at last they might be scattered, even beyond the usual scattering of a conquered people. But when the scattering did come, he sought to make it evident that it was from his hand. It was not a mere chance of war, but something prepared for and prophesied—something to teach and warn the thoughtful among all nations. Israel's obstinacy.—It is hard to see how the religious instinct of men in this peculiar stage of belief and practice was to be enlightened and purified in any other way than the actual course of Providence. What arguments can be imagined that would have appealed to minds which found a fatal fascination, nay, we must suppose an intense satisfaction, in rites so hideous that one durst not even describe them; minds to which the lofty monotheism of Amos, the splendid eloquence of an Isaiah, the plaintive lyrical strain of a Jeremiah, appealed in vain? Appeals to the order of the world, to the wonders of organic life, were lost upon minds which made gods of the most obvious subjects of that order, the sun, moon, and stars; which even personified and adored the physical principle whereby the succession of life after life is perpetuated. —Exp. Bib.

"What a noble thing it is, the power of playing upon the souls and wills of men and rousing them to lofty purposes and holy deeds! Paul says, 'If I speak with the tongues of men and of angels and have not love, I am become as sounding brass, or a tinkling cymbal.' And we all know why. We have all felt the brazenness of words without emotion, the hollowness, the unaccountable unpersuasiveness, of eloquence behind which lies no love." —Drummond.

"Zeal for the public good is the characteristic of a man of honor and a gentleman, and must take place of pleasures, profits, and all other private gratifications. Whoever wants this motive is an open enemy, or an inglorious neuter to mankind, in proportion to the misapplied advantages with wh. nature and fortune have blessed him."—Steele.

14—15. "Here begins a fresh section of the narrative. Jeremiah has executed his commission, and now proceeds to the temple, where he repeats before the assembled people his announcement of the awful judgment."—Pul. Com. (14) **in the court,** indicating his fearless obedience, ch. xviii. 18. He chose the position in which he would be able to address the greatest crowd. (15) **all her towns,** or suburban villages.

Ministers of the Gospel.—An English merchant, who had occasion to visit Scotland on business about the year 1650, happened to hear three of the most eminent of the Scottish ministers of that age—Robert Blair, Samuel Rutherford, and David Dickson. Being asked, on his return, what news he had brought from Scotland, the gentleman, who had never shown any sense of religion before, replied, "Great and good news! I went to St. Andrew's, when I heard a sweet majestic-looking man (Blair),

"I find doing the will of God, leaves me no time for disputing about his plans."— George MacDonald.

and he showed me the majesty of God. After him, I heard a little fair man (Rutherford), and he showed me the loveliness of Christ. I then went to Irvine, where I heard a well-favored proper old man, with a long beard (Dickson), and that man showed me all my heart." "The whole general assembly," says Wodrow, "could not have given a better character of the three men."—Whitecross. Preaching without heart.—"Fine sermon, wasn't it?" asked one of Farmer Peters' boarders, referring to a scholarly discourse with which the Meadowville meeting-house congregation had been favored that morning by a city clergyman. "Mebbe," returned Farmer Peters. "Why," persisted the boarder, "that man knows more about the Bible, he has made a deeper study of Biblical history and geography, than almost any other minister in this country." "Has he, now?" inquired Farmer Peters, mildly. "Well, then, I reckon the trouble must've been with me. You see I'd cal'lated I sh'd hear somethin' about the way to heaven, an' I only learned the way from Jerusalem to Jericho."

"Every stone is a witness of God's revelation, and every ruin a monument of his wrath."—Pierotti.

"Alas! we were warned, but we recked not the warning,
Till our warriors grew weak in the day of despair;
And our glory was fled as the light cloud of morning,
That gleams for a moment, and melts into air."

CHAPTER THE TWENTIETH.

1, 2. The narrative begun in xix. 14 continues through vs. 6. (1) **Pashur,** prob. head of the 16th course of priests.[a] **chief governor,** better, deputy-governor.[b] Heb. Pakid Nagid, or high priest's deputy. (2) **smote,** "the utterance of these warnings and threats in the very Temple was too much for the authorities of that place. They proceeded to inflict punishment in its ordinary forms, viz., stripes (no doubt the forty save one which kept safely within the limits permitted in Deut. xxv. 3; comp. 2 Cor. xi. 24) followed by confinement in the stocks."—Camb. B. **the prophet,** so called here for the first time. **stocks,**[c] 2 Chr. xvi. 10; Ac. xvi. 24. **high gate,** or upper gate. Prob. the gate on the north of the Temple.

Huguenot persecutions.—The irreligious character of the Revolution which these and their fellow workmen and the Encyclopædists brought about, followed logically enough from the Revocation of the Edict of Nantes, and a century and a half of Satanic persecution directed against the Huguenots—persecutions in the time of Louis XV., not the work of fanatics, but proceeding from a vicious king and a sceptical Court. The injury permanently done to the nation by such insensate intolerance is incalculable. The most earnest and devotedly religious spirits of France were either driven into exile or extinguished. When the earnest spirit of Protestantism was driven out, the earnest spirit of Catholicism decayed likewise; a mocking hypocritical uniformity took its place; license and corruption flourished unreproved; and when deism and atheism arose, they found no antagonists worthy of respect. It were a melancholy thing to resign ourselves to the conclusion that so shameful a history as that of Louis XV., and the horrors of the French Revolution, were inflicted on a great people without any intelligible causes. One of the chief of these was the inhuman and odious persecution which the devoted adherents of an austere and sublime creed met with from the day of the Revocation of the Edict of Nantes.—Edinburgh Review.

3—6. (3) **Magor-missabib,** i. e. "terror on every side." Jeremiah means to say that Pashur would one day become an object of general horror. (4) **terror,** etc., interpretation of the name. We do not know the nature of his punishment. (5) **deliver,** etc., 2 Ki. xx. 17. **strength,** etc., R. V., "riches of this city, and all the gains thereof." **labours,** for produce of the labors. (6) **thy friends,** or partisans. **lies,** false assurances of peace and deliverance.

The wicked a terror.—Such terror befell Tullus Hostilius, King of Rome, who had for his gods Pavor and Pallor. Great pity but this should ever have had his gods at hand, since he was so fond of them. Richard III. and Charles IX. of France, a pair of bloody princes, were Magor-missabibs in their generations, as terrible at length to themselves as they had been formerly to others, and therefore could never endure

[a] 1 Chr. xxiv. 4.

[b] "Poss. he was set over the several watches or guards of the priests and Levites: for they kept watch and ward in the Temple both night and day."—Lowth.

[c] "An instrument of torture with five holes, in wh. the neck, two hands, and two feet were thrust, the body being kept in a crooked posture."—Fausset.

"And when religious sects ran mad,
He held, in spite of all his learning,
That if a man's belief is bad,
It will not be improved by burning."
—Praed.

"For modes of faith let graceless zealots fight; he can't be wrong whose life is in the right. In faith and hope the world will disagree, but all mankind's concern is charity."—Pope.

to be awakened in the night without music or some like diversion.—Trapp.

7—9. (7) **deceived,** better, persuaded.[a] **stronger than I,** this and vs. 9 show us that the prophets did not speak of their own will. It was an influence which they could not resist that urged them forward, in spite of the certain ills that should follow to themselves. Compare xxiii. 29; so Amos iii. 8 ("The Lord God hath spoken; who can but prophesy?"), and 1 Cor. ix. 16 ("Necessity is laid upon me").—Camb. B. **in derision,** R. V., "I am become a laughing-stock all the day." (8) **cried out,** R. V., "For as often as I speak, I cry out; I cry, Violence and spoil." **reproach,** bec. the people said of Jeremiah, "He does nothing but groan." (9) R. V., "And if I say, I will not make mention of him, nor speak any more in his name, then there is in mine heart," etc. **burning fire,** Ps. xxxix. 3. He found that he could not resist the impulses of God's spirit.

Testimony for God.—Have we not known seasons when the impulse was strong on us to say something for God? It has come when we have been preaching or teaching, and we have broken away from the calm, not to say cold, tone in which we have been going on, and have spoken to those before us words which have come up from the very depths of our soul, and we have seen in the countenances of our children or our congregation that they, too, were conscious that they were being spoken to in a manner other than usual, and that portion of the day's lesson or the sermon has been remembered when all the rest has been forgotten. And sometimes this impossibility of keeping silence for God has come to us on the railway journey, in the quiet walk with a friend or child, or in social converse, or in the casual talk with a stranger into whose society we may have been for a while thrown; and then we have felt we must say something for God, and it has been said feebly, weakly perhaps, but nevertheless the testimony has been borne, the endeavor has been made. God would not let us be silent; we could not stay from speaking; necessity was laid upon us. These are in their measure instances of the same Spirit as that which moved the prophets and apostles of old, though in a far less degree. But it is evident how well it would be for us all who bear Christ's name to possess in far larger measure than we do this holy and irresistible impulse. The spur is what we too often need; how rarely the bridle! not the holding back, but the urging on.—Pul. Com. A reproach unto me, and a derision.—Words applied to his own case by the great Florentine, Savonarola, in one of his many sermons from the Cathedral pulpit during the last years of the fifteenth century, when the fortunes of his State, owing to the misdeeds of rulers and people, were reduced to a very low ebb. "Thy sins, O Florence, are the cause of these stripes. And now repent, give alms, offer prayers, become united. O people, I have been a father to thee; I have wearied myself all the days of my life to make known to thee the truths of the faith and of holy living, and I have had nothing but tribulations, derision, and reproach."—Clark's Savonarola. I never thought the world had been so wicked, when the Gospel began, as now I see it is; I rather hoped that every one would have leaped for joy to have found himself freed from the filth of the Pope, from his lamentable molestations of poor troubled consciences, and that through Christ they would by faith obtain the celestial treasure they sought after before with such vast cost and labor, though in vain. And especially I thought the bishops and universities would with joy of heart have received the true doctrines; but I have been lamentably deceived. Moses and Jeremiah, too, complained they had been deceived.—Martin Luther.

10—13. (10) This explains the temptation to keep silence. **defaming,** or the people talking together, Ps. xxxi. 13. **report,** etc., R. V., "Denounce, and we will denounce him, say all my familiar friends, they that watch for my halting. Peradventure," etc. **my familiars,** Heb. men of my peace. Ps. xli. 9. men of my acquaintance. **enticed,** i. e. misled, so that some good ground of accusation against him might be found.[a] (11) **with me,** in this was assured safety, whosoever his enemies might be.[b] **for .. prosper,** etc., R. V., "because they have not dealt wisely, even with an everlasting dishonor which shall never be forgotten." (12)

[a] "The Prophet alludes to his reluctance to accept the prophetical office, wh. it required powerful inducements from Jehovah to overcome." — Henderson.

"I could have no temptation to run upon this errand without being sent, since it procures me nothing but ill-usage."—Lowth.

"Unnatural deeds
Do breed unnatural trouble; infected minds
To their deaf pillows will discharge their secrets."
—Shakespeare.

"This world," the liar to the laggard cried,
"Owes you a living. Snatch it if you can!"
"An earlier debt," the voice of Truth replied,
"Must first be paid. You owe the world a man!"

"This above all, to thine own self be true;
And it must follow, as the night the day,
Thou canst not then be false to any man."
—Shakespeare.

[a] "So the Jews often tried to persuade our Lord to say something that might form ground of accusation against Him: e. g. Mk. xii. 13—17."—Spk. Com.

[b] Ro. viii. 31.

"That thou art blamed shall not be thy defect; for slander's mark was ever yet the fair; so thou be good, slander doth not approve thy worth the greater." —Shakespeare.

triest, etc., ch. xi. 20, xvii. 10. **opened,** unfolded, and so committed. (13) **Sing,** in anticipation; bec. the Prophet was quite sure that God would work deliverance for him.

Thanksgiving for future blessings.—We may be thankful for blessings not yet received. Jeremiah closes his prayer with praise. No sooner has he asked for God's help than he feels so assured of receiving it that he anticipates it in imagination, and breaks forth into grateful song as though he were already enjoying it. This is a proof of genuine faith. Faith makes the absent seem near and the future appear present (Heb. xi. 1). It influences our whole being—the imgaination among other faculties—so that it enables us to conceive the good thing trusted for so vividly and so confidently that the thought of it affects the mind just as strongly as if we saw the object with our eyes and grasped it in our hands. Such an effect is a test of the earnestness and faith of prayer. Some people could not be more surprised than by receiving the exact answer to their prayers.—Pul. Com.

"A lie should be trampled on and extinguished wherever found. I am for fumigating the atmosphere when I suspect that falsehood, like pestilence, breathes around me."—Carlyle.

14—18. (14) **Cursed,** etc., comp. Job iii. 3, x. 18.[c] Wordsworth calls this "a passionate outbreak of human infirmity." (15) **very glad,** bec. of the possible future usefulness that seems to be in every new-born child. (16) **cities,** etc., Ge. xix. 25. **cry,** of alarm. **shouting,** of the warriors.[d] (17) **slew,** etc., a fig. for his wish that he had never known the miseries of life. (18) **Wherefore,** etc., Job x. 18, 19.

An outburst of passionate grief (vss. 17—18).—These words may be compared with those which Job (iii. 3; compare x. 18) first uttered after his seven days of silent grief, although those passages are even more violent than this. The words however are sufficiently intense in their tone to cause some difficulty, especially when we compare them with those which have gone immediately before. Hence it has been sought to explain them as (i) words put by Jeremiah in the mouth of Pashur, (ii) words misplaced by copyists, (iii) words placed here by Jeremiah, although really uttered by him at a different time, and only introduced now by way of contrast to the happier feelings to which he had just given expression, and to remind him of the passionate trouble from which he had been delivered. These explanations are all rather desperate remedies. We are probably nearer the true explanation, if we say that the words express in the intense language of Eastern emotions the bitterness of the pangs which ever and again seized upon the prophet's mind and heart, as he contemplated his position and that of his country. Compare David's imprecation on Gilboa, as the scene of the death of Saul and Jonathan (2 Sam. i. 21).—Camb. B.

"Mid pleasure plenty, and success,
Freely we take from Him who lends:
We boast the blessings we possess,
Yet scarcely thank the One who sends.

"But let affliction pour its smart,
How soon we quail beneath the rod!
With shattered pride, and prostrate heart,
We seek the long-forgotten God." —Eliza Cook.

[c] "Job's words are more violent and passionate, and more directly directed against God than Jeremiah's."—Keil.

"This lamentation is written in poetical figures, and it is not to be looked upon as expressing indignation and malice, but rather mourning and sorrow."—Lowth.

[d] "Let him be kept in alarm the whole day, not merely at night when terrors ordinarily prevail, but in daytime when it is something extraordinary."—Fausset.

CHAPTER THE TWENTY-FIRST.

Here begins a new division of the whole book, concerning the time of the last King of Judah. **1, 2.** (1) **son of Melchiah,** head of the fifth course. A different man from the Pashur of ch. xx. 1. (2) **Nebuchadrezzar,**[a] "This form predominates in Jeremiah and Daniel, and is the only form found in Ezekiel. It is, in fact, the correct way of spelling the name, which is in Babylonian Nabu-kudura-uçur, i. e. "Nebo, protect (or perhaps, 'has made') the crown."—Cheyne. **according . . works,** i. e. accomplishing our deliverance as in former days: comp. Is. xxxvii. 6. **go up,** withdraw his army from Jerusalem. Comp. the deliverance from **Sennacherib.**

[a] "This prophecy was given prob. when, after having repulsed the Egyptians who brought succor to the Jews, the Chaldees were a second time advancing against Jerusalem, but were not yet closely besieging it."—Fausset.

Note on chap. 21.—This commences a new division of the whole book. We here pass at once from the time of Jehoiakim to that of Zedekiah the last king of Judah, and the occasion on which (ver. 4) the city was attacked by the Chaldeans. Zedekiah under these circumstances follows the example set by Hezekiah towards Isaiah the great prophet of his time (2 Kings xix. 2) and sends Pashur and Zephaniah to Jeremiah to ask for a declaration of the future. The prophet replies in this and the three following chapters to the effect that the successive crimes of kings, prophets and priests, which he speaks of in detail, have secured for Judah the unenviable fate now visibly at hand, while there appear however from time to time gleams of brighter things.—Camb. B. God consulted in vain.—There is a moral necessity as well as a physical. No sane man would pray that two and two might make five. There are moral impossibilities equally impregnable. A just God cannot forgive the impenitent. All that God does must be for the best, and nothing can induce him to turn from what he knows is best. If men need chastisement God will give it them, though they may most earnestly desire to be delivered from it. It was good for the Jews as a discipline, as well as just as a punishment, that they should be carried captive to Babylon. Therefore, even if all thoughts of inflicting the penalties of justice were in abeyance, God's merciful intentions to his people would make their prayers for escape vain.—Pul. Com.

3—7. (3) **Then,** etc., a response was made that would be quite opposed to their wishes and hopes. (4) **in your hands,** i. e. the turning back will be on your part, not on the part of the Chaldæans. **then,** the weapons, i. e. the soldiers who had been outside the walls harassing the Chaldæans shall be driven back into the city. (5—6) **I myself,** and to this victory of the Chaldæans He would add His own vengeance, by pestilence.[b] (7) **not spare,** ch. lii. 10, 27.

Armies of God.—In heaven He hath armies: of fire to burn Sodom; of floods to drown a world; of hailstones to kill the Amorites; of stars to fight against Sisera; the sun which stood still in Gibeon, and the moon in the valley of Ajalon, whilst Israel slew their enemies. Yea, there are heavenly soldiers. "Suddenly there was with the angel a multitude of the heavenly host." One of those celestial soldiers slew in one night above a hundred thousand Assyrians. Below He hath seas to drown Pharaoh; the earth to devour Korah; with fierce lions, fell dragons, hissing serpents, crawling worms, He can subdue His rebels. In hell He hath an army of fiends, though bound in chains, that they should not hurt the faithful, yet let loose to terrify the wicked. There was an evil spirit to vex Saul; foul spirits in the Gospel made some deaf, others dumb, and cast many into fires and into waters.—T. Adams.

8—10. (8) **way .. death,** De. xxx. 19. Here life means securing their life by passing over to the Chaldæans. (9) **falleth to,** goes and makes his submission to. **life .. prey,** as of something not belonging to one but grasped hastily and insecurely for booty. (10) **against,** i. e. fully purposing its complete destruction.

Jeremiah.—It was not indifference to his country, but attachment to its permanent interests, with the yet larger consequences wrapt up in them, which induced him to counsel submission. It was his sense of the inestimable importance of that sacred spot, with its sacred institutions, which caused him to advise every sacrifice for the sake of retaining it. He had the courage, so rare in political leaders, to surrender a part for the sake of preserving the whole—to embrace in his view the complete relations of the great scheme of the world, rather than fix his attention exclusively on the one pressing question of the moment. As there are times when the constitution must be broken to save the commonwealth, when the interests of particular nations or doctrines must give way to the preponderating claims of mankind or of truth at large, so Jeremiah staked the eternal value of the truths which Jerusalem represented against the temporary evils of the Chaldæan dominion. It was a bitter pang, but the result seemed to him worth the cost.—Stanley.

11—14. (11) **house,** the royal house or family, who "appear, from this passage to have monopolized the judicial function."—Pul. Com.

"Let prayer be the key of the morning and the bolt of the evening."— Matthew Henry.

"Consult your friend on all things, especially on those which respect yourself. His counsel may then be useful, where your own self-love might impair your judgment."—Seneca.

"Good counsels observed are chains to grace."—Fuller.

b "Apparently this broke out at an early part of the siege, and was the result of the excessive crowding of men and animals in a confined space, with all sanitary regulations utterly neglected."—Spk. Com.

"A minister without boldness is like a smooth file, a knife without an edge, a sentinel that is afraid to let off his gun. If men will be bold in sin, ministers must be bold to reprove."— Gurnall.

Think of that Reformer, who, when some one said to him, "The whole world is against you," calmly replied, "Then I am against the world."

"Scriptures hard to be understood, must be explained by those that are plain."—Collins.

(12) **in the morning,** better "every morning," the ordinary time for such business, while it was still cool. (13) **inhabitant,** the population of Jerusalem. **rock,** Jerusalem is called both "valley" and "rock" (comp. xvii. 3) because, although it is lower than the surrounding mountains, yet the hills on which it is built rise high above the plain. (14) **forest,** the Jewish fig. for stateliness, and used here for the stately buildings of Jerusalem.[a]

Notions of God.—There are two notions of God that have more or less prevalence among men. One represents Him as a vast organ located in the very centre of heaven, and giving forth majestic sounds when touched, and silent when not. The other represents Him as a Being that is never silent, never still, never unheard; One that has such a nature that if there were not an angel in heaven, if there were not a man on earth, if there were nothing in all creation, from side to side, there is that in Himself that would make Him for ever overflow with taste, and feeling, and love. The one ascribes to Him a nature that is merely susceptible of being called out upon the application of the motive. The other ascribes to Him a nature that pours itself abroad in the earth by reason of its own fulness and richness. It is the latter of these two ideas that I hold, and suppose the Scriptures to teach.—Beecher.

CHAPTER THE TWENTY-SECOND.

Chaps. xxii—xxiv. were probably sent in writing to Zedekiah. They consist of prophecies uttered from time to time and now modified to suit present needs.—Camb. Bib. **1—5.** (1) **Go down,** the palace on Zion was actually higher than the Temple, but regarded as inferior.[b] (2) **servants,** or courtiers. **these gates,** the large space at the entry of the palace-courts, where the king would hold audience. (3) **Execute,** etc., ch. xxii. 12.[c] Comp. vs. 17. (4) **indeed,** truly and heartily. **enter,** etc., ch. xvii. 25. (5) **not hear,** ch. xvii. 27. **swear,** De. xxxii. 40—42. **this house,** the royal palace.

Reproving kings.—This is a message for the king and for such people as live in palaces. Remarkable to notice how God's messengers have been brought into contact with the kings and grandees of the earth. Divinely guided, they have been able to find their way where others, even with large worldly influence, have been excluded. So Moses comes to deal with Pharaoh; Jeremiah with this king here; John the Baptist with Herod; Jesus with Pontius Pilate; Paul with Felix, Festus, and Agrippa. As God can make a way for his servants out of prisons, so he can also make a way for them into palaces. And once entered into the palace, the prophet was to address himself first and chiefly to the king. Kings have many counsellors, and their temptation is to say what may be agreeable to the royal ears. This king, maybe, had not one honest, disinterested man about him; if so, all the more need for Jeremiah's counsels.—Pul. Com.

6—9. (6) **unto the king's house of Judah;** rather, concerning the house of the King of Judah; i. e. the royal palace, which, on account of its height and its being constructed so largely out of cedar-wood (comp. vss. 14, 23), is called, "Gilead, and the summit of Lebanon," just as Solomon's palace was called "the house of the forest of Lebanon."—Pul. Com. **art Gilead,** Gilead was famous for its aromatic plants, its grassy uplands, and its abundance of sheep and cattle: so it is fitly taken as the emblem of prosperity. **Lebanon,** the usual metaphor for everything magnificent.[a] **cities,** the judgment should include all the cities of Judah along with Jerusalem. (7) **prepare,** Heb. sanctify: appoint to execute My judgments. **choice cedars,** fig. for the princes and state officers: or perhaps for the chief dwellings. (8) **many,** etc.,[b] De. xxix. 24—26.

The basis of a kingdom's prosperity.—You might as well quench the sun, and suppose that the world can get on without light, as to think that men or that nations can do without God. I tell you on the

[a] "The metaphor of a forest is employed to convey the idea of a dense mass of buildings with which the city was filled."—Henderson.

"The unholy soul, like the mystical Babylon, makes itself a cage of unclean birds, and a habitation of filthy spirits: and if it continues to be such, it must, when it dislodges, take up its habitation with cursed spirits for ever in utter darkness." — Leighton.

[b] It was also necessary to descend from the Temple-mount in order to reach the palace on Mount Zion. Comp. 2 Chr. xxiii. 20.

[c] "There can be no doubt that the Prophet has in his eye the oppressive measures adopted by Jehoakim for raising the tribute wh. Necho, king of Egypt, had imposed upon him (2 Chr. xxxvi. 3); and defraying the cost of the expensive buildings which he caused to be erected in Jerusalem."—Henderson.

[a] "Though thou wert never so precious in my sight, wert as valuable for riches and plenty as the fat pastures of Gilead, and thy buildings as beautiful for their stateliness as the tall cedars of Lebanon, yet unless thy princes and people reform, thou shalt become nothing but ruin and desolation."—Lowth.

[b] "The Gentile nations, more intelligent than you, shall understand that which you do not, viz.,

evidence of all history that the streams of morals would dry up. It is turning from the best to the worst, deliberately loving darkness rather than light, because their deeds are evil. There is not a single historian of that period (the fifteenth century) who does not admit that a fearful moral retrogression followed on the overthrow of faith. Let the English working classes once adopt atheistic principles, and I would not give five years' purchase for England's happiness or England's fame.—Farrar. Heathen idolatry.—A singular phenomenon, known as the Spectre of the Brocken, is seen on a certain mountain in Germany. The traveler who at dawn stands on the topmost ridge, beholds a colossal shadowy spectre moving on the summits of the distant hills. But, in fact, it is only his own shadow projected upon the morning mists by the rising sun, and it imitates, of course, every movement of its creator. So heathen nations have mistaken their own image for Deity. Their gods display human frailties and passions and scanty virtues, projected and magnified upon the heavens, just as the small figures on the slide of a magic lantern are projected, magnified and illuminated, upon a white sheet.

that this city is a spectacle of God's vengeance."—Calvin.

10—12. (10) **the dead,** i. e. for Josiah. This is the first of the sections which treat consecutively of the three immediate predecessors of Zedekiah. The sense of the verse is that even the fate of Josiah, who was slain in battle at Megiddo (2 Kings xxiii. 29), was preferable to that of his son and successor, who was carried captive to Egypt only to die in that strange land (2 Kings xxiii. 34).—Camb. B. **goeth away,** into captivity. This was the fate of Jehoahaz: from the captivity he never returned.[c] (11) **Shallum,** most prob. a name of Jehoahaz: poss. given to him in irony by the Prophet bec. he only reigned three months.[d] (12) **die .. place,** i. e. in Egypt.[e] "He was the first king of Judah who died in banishment."

[c] 2 Ki. xxiii. 34.

[d] Comp. the Shallum of 2 Ki. xv. 13, who only reigned one month.

[e] "The people perhaps entertained hopes of Shallum's return fr. Egypt, in wh. case they would replace him on the throne, and thereby free themselves from the oppressive taxes imposed by Jehoiakim."—Fausset.

"A man may benefit the cause of God more by the faithful testimony of a Christian death than by fifty years of continued work."

Recollection of home.—

How dear to this heart are the scenes of my childhood,
When fond recollection recalls them to view;
The orchard, the meadow, the deep tangled wildwood,
And every loved spot which my infancy knew.
—Woodworth.

Thou spot of earth, where from my bosom
The first weak tones of nature rose,
Where first I cropp'd the stainless blossom
Of pleasure yet unmix'd with woes,
Where, with my new-born powers delighted,
I tripp'd beneath a mother's hand—
In thee the quenchless flame was lighted,
That sparkles for my native land. —Walker.

13—16. (13) **Woe unto him,** i. e. Jehoiakim, who seems to have been a heartless tyrant.[f] **chambers,** lit. upper chambers, wh. involved toilsome work in building.[a] **wrong,** R. V., "injustice." **service without wages,** in olden times kings were accustomed thus to exact forced labor on public works from their people.[b] (14) **wide house,** lit. "house of extensions." **windows,** lit. my windows, the language of boastfulness. Some think it should be "large or double windows." **ceiled,** roofed. **vermilion,**[c] Eze. xxiii. 14. Red sulphuret of mercury. (15) **reign,** permanently and securely. **closest,** etc., "strivest to excel in cedar," i. e. Solomon whom he would outdo. **eat and drink,** the sign of enjoying life and peace. (16) **know me?** in choosing what was righteous he shewed himself acquainted with the character of Him whose pleasure he was doing.

[f] For Jehoiakim's history see 2 Ki. xxiii. 34—37, xxiv. 1—6.

[a] "From the absence of machinery the raising of materials for the upper stories was a difficult task, especially when massive stones were used." — Spk. Com.

[b] Comp. De. xxiv. 14, 15.

[c] "A beautiful red paint, called sinopis, bec., according to Pliny, it was first discovered near the town of Sinope, in Pontus. It was composed of quicksilver and sulphur, and must not be mistaken for the preparation of red lead, known amongst us by the name of vermilion." — Henderson.

Buildeth by unrighteousness.—Such injurious and therefore accursed builders were the pyramid-makers in Egypt. Tarquinius Priscus, Caligula, Nero, Phocas, who is said to have heard this voice of heaven—"Though thou shouldst erect thine edifice as high as heaven, yet sin that lieth at the foundation will soon overturn all." Bernard inveigheth against some in his time who did with great care and cost (erigere muros, negligere moros) build high manors, but not amend their manners.—Trapp. What we read of here makes us regard very dubiously many of the monuments of architectural power belonging to ancient civilization. We may suspect that only too many of them were constructed by forced labor. How much of unrequited toil there must have been, not only in temples, palaces, Pyramids, but also in such plainly useful works as roads, bridges and aqueducts! The results have been pleasing enough to the eye and rich in giving resources to the lovers of art; but their beauty becomes only deformity, if we have reason to believe that force, fraud and cruelty had a considerable share in the production of them. Even Christian cathedrals and churches may have been built in this way to a greater extent than we should like to think possible.—Pul. Com.

17—19. (17) **covetousness**, including all kinds of getting for his own pleasure or aggrandisement.[d] **violence**, or crushing; applied to the liberties and rights of the people. Habakkuk (ii. 9—12) probably refers to this same king.—Cheyne. (18) **not lament**, the death of such a tyrant would only be felt as a national relief. **Ah sister**, a general expression, introduced here probably for the sake of the parallelism. (19) **burial .. ass**, the manner of Jehoiakim's death is not recorded,[e] the point of the prophecy is that his body would not be buried.

The doom of the defrauder (vs. 19).—This said of Jehoiakim; his life and death suggestive of the romance of crime. I. The romance of fraud-many think the poorest way to get money is to earn it. II. The romance of libertinism. III. The romance of assassination.—Talmage.

The safety of right-doing.—Truth has no revolution in it. Right has no change in it. Justice is always safe and sure. If you must crucify Christ because He will not join your party, your faction, your Church, your religion, then crucify Him; but remember the eighteen hundred years of darkness, and revolution, and turmoil that followed His first crucifixion. The great battle of God Almighty is not fought out yet, and you will have more of it in your day. If you want peace, do right. It you will not do right, remember that God is the incendiary of the universe, and that He will burn your plans, and will by-and-by burn you with unquenchable fire.—Beecher.

The Sinner's Burial.—

Wrapt in a Christless shroud,
He sleeps a Christless sleep;
Above him the eternal cloud,
Beneath, the fiery deep.

Laid in a Christless tomb,
There bound with felon-chain,
He waits the terrors of his doom,
The judgment and the pain.

O Christless shroud, how cold!
How dark, O Christless tomb!
O grief that never can grow old!
O endless, hopeless doom.

O Christless sleep, how sad!
What waking shalt thou know?
For thee no star, no dawning glad,
Only the lasting woe!

To rocks and hills in vain
Shall be the sinner's call;
O day of wrath, and death, and pain,
The lost soul's funeral!

O Christless soul, awake,
Ere thy last sleep begin!

d For Jehoiakim's character comp. Eze. xix. 6.

e "Prob. he was taken prisoner in some valley during the siege, then killed, and his dead body cast into the highway."—Lowth.

"Some men are so covetous, as if they were to live forever; and and others so profuse, as if they were to die the next moment."—Aristotle.

"The covetous man lives as if the world were made altogether for him, and not for the world, to take in everything and part with nothing."—South.

"The covetous man pines in plenty, like Tantalus up to the chin in water and yet thirsty."-Adams.

O Christ, the sleeper's slumbers break;
Burst Thou the bands of sin.

—Bonar.

20—23. (20) **Lebanon,** etc., the highest places in the surrounding country are mentioned as those from whence the people might see the victorious march of the Chaldæans and the failure of the Egyptian allies. **Bashan,** the northern part of the region beyond Jordan. **passages,** R. V., "Abarim," a range of mountains to the south of Gilead. **lovers,** Egypt and her allies. (21) **prosperity,** in thy prosperous days. **thy youth,** i. e. the time of the exodus. (22) **eat up,** strictly, shall pasture upon all thy pastors. The "wind" referred to is doubtless the parching east wind, the symbol of calamity, which is actually called a "sharp" wind in ch. iv. 11. (23) **inhabitant,** etc.,[a] a fig. of Jerus, in view of the palaces roofed with cedar fr. Lebanon. **gracious,** R. V., "how greatly to be pitied."

Man in material prosperity (vs. 21).—Here we have man in material prosperity—I. Addressed by Almighty God. 1. Be humble; 2. Be spiritual; 3. Be generous. II. Refusing an audience with his Maker. 1. Because I am happy as I am; 2. Because Thy voice will disturb me. Address the prosperous:—(1) Be wise in time; (2) Use the world as not abusing it, etc.—Thomas.

"Tom of Ten Thousand."—Among the thousand victims of that most disastrous adventure, the South Sea scheme, there was perhaps scarcely one more to be pitied than a native of Leeds, of the name of Thomas Hudson. In the early part of his life he filled a respectable situation as a Government clerk in London. While in this situation, he came into the possession of a large fortune by the death of an aunt; he then retired into the country, where he lived for some time very happily, until he unfortunately became an adventurer in the South Sea scheme; and so sanguine was he of its success, that he embarked the whole of his fortune in it. When the news reached him of the failure of his darling scheme, he left his residence in a state of distraction, and went to London. From this moment he became insane, and "Tom of Ten Thousand," as he called himself, wandered through the streets, wrapped in a rug, and leaning on a crutch, and without either shoes or stockings. In this state did the poor creature perambulate, even in the coldest weather, and crave assistance from the humane, until death released him from all his troubles at a very advanced age.—Percy Anec.

24—27. (24) **Coniah,** or Jehoiachin, son and successor of Jehoiakim. He surrendered to the Babylonians, and was carried captive to Chaldæa. **signet,** i. e. the royal ring used for sealing public documents.[b] (25) **give thee,** as a captive. (26) **mother,** i. e. the queen-mother,[c] who had great influence at the Jewish court. **there shall ye die,** "he was detained in prison at Babylon for thirty-six years, until released by Evil-Merodach, son and successor of Nebuchadnezzar, who nevertheless retained him in a sort of honorable captivity for the rest of his days (chap. lii. 31—34), which were probably not very many. At the end of two years Evil-Merodach himself was slain."—Camb. Bib. (27) **desire to return,** intimating that the bitterness of captivity shall partly be the "home-sickness" which they shall suffer.

Dr. Franklin.—It is recorded of Franklin that, when a young man expressed his surprise that a gentleman well known to them, of unbounded wealth, should appear more anxious after business than the most assiduous clerk in a counting-house, the doctor took an apple from the fruit basket, and presented it to a little child, who could just totter about the room. The child could scarcely grasp it in his hand; he then gave it another, which occupied the other hand. Then choosing a third, remarkable for its size and beauty. he presented that also. The child, after many ineffectual attempts to hold the three, dropped the last on the carpet, and burst into tears. "See there," said Franklin, "there is a little man with more riches than he can enjoy." The increase of painful care, anxiety, and trouble, generally bear at least an equal proportion to the increase of riches. The peace of the child was not broken until the

[a] "O Jerusalem, thou that art lifted up on high like Lebanon, and that makest thy nest in the stately cedars, that thinkest thyself secure, like an eagle which has built its nest in the loftiest trees of the highest mountain."—Wordsworth.

"A holy woman was wont to say of the rich—'They are hemmed round with no common misery; they go down to hell without thinking of it, because their staircase thither is of gold and porphyry.'"—Spurgeon.

"No sooner does the warm aspect of good fortune shine, than all the plans of virtue, raised like a beautiful frost-work in the winter of adversity, thaw and disappear."—Warburton.

[b] "The estimation in which signets were held is the point of the metaphor in the present instance."—Henderson.

[c] 2 Ki. xxiv. 15.

"Who feels no ills
Should therefore fear them; and when fortune smiles,
Be doubly cautious, lest destruction come
Remorseless on him, and he fall unpitied."
—Sophocles.

"It is a preposterous thing that men can venture their souls where they will not venture their money."—William Penn.

attempt was made to obtain the grasp of the third apple; had but two been thought of, its happiness would have been great.—R. T. S.

28—30. (28) **idol,** R. V., "vessel." The prophet's human feelings are stirred; he cannot withhold his sympathy from the sad fate of his king. What! he exclaims; is it possible that this Coniah is treated as a piece of ill-wrought pottery ware (comp. ch. xviii. 4), and "hurled" into a strange land?—Pul. Com. (29) **O earth,** etc., the repetition expresses deep feeling, as if Jeremiah thoroughly joined in the lamentation over Coniah. (30) **childless,**[a] he had children (1 Chron. iii. 17) but not to succeed him on the throne. "This is all the passage means;" and so in him the proper line of Davidic kings became extinct.[b]

A call to hear the Word of the Lord (vs. 29).—I. The subject of the address. 1. The Word of the Lord is unwritten as well as written; 2. It is threatening as well as promising. II. The duty inculcated in the address. 1. To hear and understand; 2. To hear and obey; 3. To hear and make known to others. III. The style of the address, apostrophe. 1. The universality of its range; 2. The earnestness and affection of its spirit.—G. Brooks.

Clement and Conradin.—We may find a mediæval analogy to the situation at Jerusalem in the relations of Clement IV. to Conradin, the last heir of the house of Hohenstaufen. When this youth of sixteen was in the full career of victory, the Pope predicted that his army would be scattered like smoke, and pointed out the prince and his allies as victims for the sacrifice. When Conradin was executed after his defeat at Tagliacozzo, Christendom was filled with abhorrence at the suspicion that Clement had countenanced the doing to death of the hereditary enemy of the Papal See. Jehoiachin's friends felt towards Jeremiah somewhat as these thirteenth-century Ghibellines towards Clement. Moreover the charge against Clement was probably unfounded; Milman says of him, "He was doubtless moved with inner remorse at the cruelties of 'his champion' Charles of Anjou." Jeremiah too would lament the doom he was constrained to utter. Nevertheless he could not permit Judah to be deluded to its ruin by empty dreams of glory.—Exp. Bib.

[a] No son of Jeconiah's is found in the list of Jewish kings.

[b] "Though Messiah, the heir of David's throne, was lineally descended from Jeconiah, it was only through Joseph, who, though his legal, was not his real father."—Fausset.

How many hearers of the Gospel are like Pharaoh's lean kine! They seem to devour everything, and digest nothing.

CHAPTER THE TWENTY-THIRD.

1—4. (1) **pastors,** here rulers.[c] **my pasture,** they used the sheep as if they had independent rights over them, whereas the sheep were the Lord's, and they only under-shepherds, not owners. (2) **scattered,** etc., i. e. the wrong-doing of the rulers first led the people away from God into idolatry, and then brought on them judgments and captivity. **driven,** eastern shepherds never drive the sheep; the sheep follow them. (3) **remnant,** left out of the coming calamities. **folds,** better, pastures. **fruitful,** ch. iii. 16. "The fertility of the Jewish race in modern times has been a frequent subject of observation, and supplies the best comment upon Jeremiah's prophecy." (4) **shepherds,** such as Ezra, Nehemiah, etc. **be lacking,** "none shall be missing."

The present God (vs. 4).—I. The text proves the folly and sin of every form of idolatry. 1. It is senseless; 2. Sinful. II. The truth of the text should stimulate us to the cultivation of an incessantly devotional spirit. III. See in the text a source of sure consolation to the Christian amidst the sorrows to which he is exposed. IV. What a safeguard against the seductions of sin may these noble words prove. 1. We are self-tempted; 2. We are socially tempted; 3. We are Satanically tempted. —Homilist.

The unfaithful minister.—

"But the unfaithful priest, what tongue
Enough shall execrate! . . . . .
By solemn, awful ceremony, he
Was set apart to speak the truth entire,

[c] Comp. Eze xxxiv. 2.

"Probably many who are called Gospel ministers are more chargeable with concealing truths than affirming direct error; with not properly building the house than wilfully pulling it down."—Witherspoon.

"Unfaithfulness is to undo our own souls as well as our people's."—Bridges.

"Preaching to some hearers is like throwing a ball against a wall; all that is said to them seems to rebound without producing any sensible effect. It is like playing upon a piano whose strings are all broken; there is no musical response. They are dead to the impressions which the truth is calculated to produce within them."— John Bate.

By action and by word; and round him stood
The people, from his lips expecting knowledge.

. . . .

They stood, for he had sworn, in face of God
And man, to deal sincerely with their souls;
To preach the Gospel for the Gospel's sake.

. . . .

Most guilty, villainous, dishonest man!
Wolf in the clothing of the gentle lamb!
Dark traitor in Messiah's holy camp!
Leper in saintly garb! assassin masked
In virtue's robe! Vile hypocrite, accursed!
I strive in vain to set his evil forth."—

—Pollok.

[a] Ps. lxxii. 2; Is. xi. 5, xxxii. 1.

[b] "He by whom Jehovah works righteousness."—Hengstenberg.

[c] "This view equally contains the doctrine of the Godhead of the Messiah, but not so directly. For it implies the existence of a vicegerent of God upon earth, by whom God will impart that perfect righteousness, to wh. no man can attain by himself."—Spk. Com.

5—9. (5) The mention of good shepherds serves as the introduction to one of the few clear Messianic prophecies of Jeremiah. Besides this we have xxxiii. 15—18, and less plainly xxx. 9.—Camb. B. **righteous Branch,** comp. Is. iv. 2, xi. 1, liii. 2; Zec. iii. 8, vi. 12. **and a King,** etc., R. V., "and he shall reign as king and deal wisely." **execute judgment,** the characteristic of the kingdom of Christ.[a] (6) **his days,** De. xxxiii. 28. **name,** Jehovah Tsidkenu, "the Lord our righteousness."[b] Righteousness here means "personal holiness," rather than "justification."[c] (7) Repeated from xvi. 14—15. (8) **north country,** the Prophet's description of Chaldæa. (9) R. V., "Concerning the prophets. Mine heart," etc. Here begins a new prophecy extending to vs. 40. **prophets,** i. e. the false prophets. **like a drunken man,** staggering under the words of Divine threatening which he had to utter. **his holiness,** R. V., "his holy words," on the unholy doing of the false prophets.

The Lord our righteousness (vs. 6).—I. Explain the title here given to the Redeemer. 1. The dignity of His nature; 2. The importance of His work; 3. The interest of His people in Him. II. Assign some reasons for the prominence of this title. Because it exhibits—1. A grand view of His character; 2. Views of His character which have been most virulently opposed; 3. But which must be cordially embraced by His people.—G. Brooks.

The Branch of David.—The glorious prophecy of the Messianic future which here bursts forth from Jeremiah, after his denunciation of his nation's sin and lamentation over its approaching calamities, is necessarily clothed in the language of the age, and viewed in an especial relation to contemporary wants. The people are suffering from bad rulers and an unrighteous government. A good king, administering his kingdom happily and justly, is promised for the golden age of the future.—Pul. Com.

[d] Je. xi. 3.

[e] "External circumstances assist in urging on to ruin those who choose the dangerous path of vice."—Spk. Com.

"To believe that happiness exists in a feverish ambition rather than in a tender and simple affection is to believe that the immensity of the sea will more readily quench thirst than the pure limpid water of a humble fountain."—Emilo Castelav.

"You know I say
Just what I think, and nothing more nor less,
And, when I pray, my heart is in my prayer,
I cannot say one thing and mean another,
If I can't pray, I will not make believe."
—Longfellow.

10—12. (10) **adulterers,** those living in immorality and sin. **swearing,** or "the curse," wh. iniquity has brought upon it.[d] **pleasant places,** R. V., "pastures." **course,** or mode of life. (11) **profane,** common and unholy by reason of iniquity. **in my house,** comp. 2 Ki. xxi. 5; xxiii. 12. (12) **slippery ways,** down which they must surely fall. **driven on,** pressed on by their very sins.[e] **visitation,** or the set time of Divine judgment.

Cure of profanity.—A merchant on fitting out a ship for India, told the captain, at the time of making the contract for the voyage, that he must engage not to swear, nor have any swearing among the crew. This must be the law of the ship. The captain said he was willing to reform. "But how can I suddenly break off an inveterate habit?" he inquired. "I will take care you are reminded of your duty," replied the owner. "Wear the ring that I will give you, and let the law of the vessel be explicitly known." The ring was provided, bearing this motto, "Swear not at all." The vessel performed the voyage, and returned to port. On inquiry, it was found that there had been no profaneness on board, excepting a little within the first twenty days after sailing; and the old habit was entirely destroyed.

13—16. (13) **folly,** the stupidity of prophesying by Baal. Heb. word means that which is unsavory, comp. Job i. 22; xxiv. 12. (14) **horrible thing,** even worse things than in Samaria. **strengthen,** by the influence of their bad example. **as Sodom,** Is. i. 9. (15) **wormwood,** ch. viii. 14, ix. 15. (16), **vain,** R. V., "they teach you vanity," i. e. they deceive you.[a] **vision .. heart,** i. e. one of their own invention, in wh. is no truth.

Strengthening the hands of the wicked (vs. 14).—I. All sin is horrible in its nature. II. To strengthen the hands and hinder the repentance of sinners is to oppose the great plan of God's government. III. It tends to the misery of mankind. IV. It is to operate with the spirit of evil who works in the children of disobedience. V. It is a horrible thing because we thus become partakers of their sins. VI. It is directly contrary to God's commands, and is marked with His peculiar abhorrence. Apply —1. To teachers of religion, to Christians in general, to heads of families, and the young; 2. It is also a horrible thing to be strengthened in evil-doing.—Lathrop.

[a] "They delude you with vain promises of security." — Maurer.

17—20. (17) **still,** R. V., "continually." **have peace,** ch. vi. 14. **imagination,** R. V., "stubbornness." (18) **who hath stood?** meaning, "manifestly they have not." (19) R. V., "Behold the tempest of the Lord, even his fury, is gone forth, yea a whirling tempest: it shall burst upon the head of the wicked," i. e. it will soon reach Jerusalem. (20) **not return,** not be restrained or withdrawn.[b] **latter days,** those following on the great calamities.

Governing of prophecy.—Unfortunately, when prophecy becomes professional in the lowest sense of the word, it is governed by commercial principles. A sufficiently imperious demand calls forth an abundant supply. A sovereign can "tune the pulpits;" and a ruling race can obtain from its clergy formal ecclesiastical sanction for such "domestic institutions" as slavery. When evildoers grow numerous and powerful, there will always be prophets to strengthen their hands and encourage them not to turn away from their sin.—Exp. Bib.

[b] "The expression is taken from a messenger that comes back without doing his business."—Lowth.

"Mystery such as is given of God, is beyond the power of human penetration, yet not in opposition to it."—Madame de Stäel.

21—24. In vss. 17—20 Jeremiah has shown that these cannot be true prophets, because their message is diametrically opposed to the true revelation. He now proves it from the absence of any moral effect from their preaching. (21) **ran,**[a] manifesting in the Prophet's work great eagerness. (22) **my counsel,** vs. 18. The sign of the true prophet is his influence in favor of morality. (23) **at hand,** then surely I see the wickedness of these false prophets. (24) **hide himself,** Ps. cxxxix. 7.[b]

The true pulpit (vs. 22).—The text enables us to sketch an ideal preacher. I. His mental position, "If they had stood in My counsel." This mental position is—1. Most necessary; 2. Most ennobling. II. His grand work caused My people to hear My words. 1. A most difficult work; 2. A most urgent work. III. His true test. 1. Conversion from evil is the great want of mankind; 2. The great tendency of God's Word. —Thomas.

Soul-converting preachers.—There are preachers, by myriads and majorities, and deeply pious ones too, that never once in all their lives distinctly concentrated their purposes to the single point of converting men. Their efforts are to finish an eloquent sermon, to develop theological or Biblical truth, to thrill æsthetically an audience, to pour forth general religious emotion, to spread a popular fame, to gather crowds, to build a large church. Verily these have often their reward, namely success in their objects. But here is a lonesome preacher, who does not object to all these; but with or without them, by study, by closet, by pulpit, by pastoral work, some or all, he means to convert souls, and just so many as he can. Where this is attained all the other success is well enough. Where this is not attained, all the other success does not comfort him a penny; he goes off crestfallen and disappointed, indignant at the devil and himself. He will not stay there where Satan has beaten him: but he will go where, please God, he can get some souls. Maffitt, in his golden days, did convert his thousands, for that was his unerring aim. Bascom aimed to be the pulpit orator; his purpose terminated in the elaborate harangue, the thrilled audience, and the gathering crowd. He did not entertain the downright purpose of conversion. Summerfield terminated his effort with pouring his own rich religious emotions upon his melting congregation; but his emotion did not go forth into the sharp

[a] Je. xiv. 14, xxvii. 15, xxix. 9.

[b] "Are ye so ignorant as to suppose that I can only see things near Me, viz., things in heaven, and not earthly things as being too remote?"—Fausset.

"Many a time when we stand in the pulpit some sinner may be present who will never hear the Gospel, or be exhorted to take care of his soul again. Should we not wish to pour upon such a one the whole force of our powers of persuasion; to speak to him emphatically, in the words of Baxter. 'as a dying man to dying men'?" —Christian Review.

"I believe it to be true that dreams are the true interpreters of our inclinations; but there is art required to sort and understand them." —Montaigne.

volition and the determined practical drudgery of action. And we think that this same analysis exercised upon every minister of strength and ability would, in nearly every case, bring out the answer to the question, What prevents this able minister from converting souls? He does not, in the full force of the word, try.—Wheedon.

25—28. (25) **dreamed,** De. xiii. 1. (26—27) **How long shall this be.** This and the following verse consist rather of two questions, the first being broken off short and the second undergoing in the middle a change of construction. "How long (shall this state of things continue)? Is it in the mind of the prophets that prophesy falsehood and the prophets of the deceit of their heart—do they think to make my people forget my name by their dreams which they declare every man to his neighbor, as their fathers forgot my name by (reason of) Baal?"—Camb. Bib. (28) **let him tell,** i. e. as a dream, not as inspiration. **chaff,** dreams out of men's mere imaginations. **wheat,** truth communicated by God.

A suggested contrast (vs. 28).—The contrast in this passage admits of a threefold application. 1. To true and false doctrines; 2. To true and false teachers; 3. To true and false professors.

29—32. (29) **like .. fire,** as in vss. 19, 20, so here, the prophet contrasts the message of the false prophets with that of the true. The former flatter their hearers with promises of peace; the latter speak a stern but potent word, which burns like a fire, and crushes like a hammer.—Pul. Com. (30) **steal .. neighbor,** i. e. try to catch up and imitate the true Prophets, bec. they have no message of their own. (31) **use,** their tongue as a tool to make prophecies with. He saith, this phrase, borrowed from the true prophets, will, they expect, help their sayings to pass as genuine. By the side of the Party of the Nobles "perhaps opposed to them, perhaps allied with them, in that strange combination which often brings together, for purposes of political or religious animosity, parties themselves most alien to each other, was the great body of the Sacerdotal, and even of the Prophetic order. There were those who directly lent themselves to magical rites .. who recited the old prophetic phrases, often careless of what they meant."—Stanley's F. Ch. (32) **lightness,** R. V., "vain boasting."

The Bible like a fire and a hammer (vs. 29).—I. Like a fire heaven kindled, all-penetrating, destructive, discriminating, refining, sanctifying. II. Like a hammer, heart hard and unimpressible, breaks down pride and self-righteousness. Apply:—1. Employ the Bible for our personal salvation; 2. Maintain its authority and power against all gainsayers; 3. Beware of immoderate expectations concerning effects.—G. Brooks.

Picture in Wyclif's Bible.—There is a picture frontispiece in Wyclif's Bible which was issued contrary to the commands of the church authorities. There is a fire burning and spreading rather rapidly, representing true Christianity. Around this spreading fire are congregated a number of significant individuals, all trying to devise methods whereby they can put the fire out. One with horns and tail represents Satan. Another is the Pope with his red-coated cardinals, who forbade the promulgating of the Bible among the common people. Another represents infidelity. At length one suggests that they all make a united effort to blow on the fire till they blow it out. The resolution is adopted and there they are with swollen cheeks and extended lips blowing upon the fire with all their might, but instead of blowing it out, they are blowing it up, and themselves out of breath. The fire is inextinguishable.

33—36. (33) **forsake you,** R. V., "I will cast you off," throw you as a burden away into captivity. (34) **say, The burden,** professing to be burdened with a Divine message. (35) **answered,** they were to speak in this form henceforth bec. the false prophets were making use of the word burden.[a] It had become cant and a new term was needed. (36) **word .. burden,** i. e. his derisive use of a prophetic phrase shall become a heavy burden to him.

Hints to preachers.—I. Preach Christ crucified, and dwell chiefly on the blessings resulting from His righteousness, atonement, and intercession. II. Avoid all needless controversies in the pulpit; except it be when your subject necessarily requires it; or when the truths of God are

We would fain have the ministry of the Word of God surrounded with all that can serve to win attention, command reverence, and excite interest; we should be alert to look out for such things, and to secure them so far as we may; but let us see to it that they be but subordinate, that they all are used as aids to what is far higher and more important than themselves—that within this husk the pure grain of God's Word is enshrined and preserved.—Pul. Com.

"A good theological definition of the nature and effects of the labors and mission of an atheist or infidel is 'The devil's whetstone to sharpen dull preachers on.'"—Driver.

"The truths of the Bible are like gold in the soil. Whole generations walk over it, and know not what treasures are hidden beneath. So centuries of men pass over the Scriptures, and know not what riches lie under the feet of their interpretation."—Beecher.

[a] This had been Jeremiah's characteristic word, and Isaiah's. Prob. the false prophets took it up and used it partly in ridicule.

"When God beckons you forward he is always responsible for the transport."—F. B. Meyer.

likely to suffer by your silence. III. When you ascend the pulpit, leave your learning behind you; endeavor to preach more to the hearts of your people than to their heads. IV. Do not affect too much oratory. Seek rather to profit, than to be admired.—Brewer.

Duty of the clergy.—The London Times delivered, some time since, an excellent homily to the English clergy, which applies equally well to ministers of all countries and denominations: "The clergy are ready to rely upon everything rather than on the substantial claims of their message. One party take to gay dresses, banners, and processions; another to penny readings, political lectures, and concerts. They change from one thing to another day by day, and the result is only a weary waste of their own time, and the creation of a certain amount of social feeling which might equally be produced without the supernatural aid of the Church and religion. Religious truths, if they are what they are believed to be, cannot need all this trivial machinery to recommend them; and the religious convictions, which are to be of any value, must be produced and sustained by more simple and permanent means. If we may judge by the history of the Church, both in early and modern times, a man of truly religious feeling needs nothing but a room and a Bible to bring about the greatest results. The one thing essential is not new plans and daily changes, but a belief in the power of the permanent truths of the Christian religion, and a devotion to these alone. The personal example and the public teaching of religion are the only necessary instruments of a clergyman, and, in our opinion, the less he is diverted from these to novel devices and elastic webs the better."

37—40. (38) **ye say,** wilfully refusing in this to yield to My commands. (39) **forget you,** the Heb. may also be rendered, will assuredly take you up (make you a burden). **forsake you,** R. V., "cast you off," by withdrawing My protection from you, leaving you to your calamities. (40) **everlasting reproach,** ch. xx. 11.

The office of the preacher.—If a man wants to indulge in levities, or fantasies, or imaginations, let him do it: I am not beset with superstitions. But still, if a child would play mumblety-peg, I would not advise him to go into the graveyard and play on his father's and mother's graves. There are proprieties and adaptations, and if a man is called merely to please, if he is to be a pleasure-monger, even of ideas, let him take the lecture-room or the theatre, let him go where pleasure is the normal end. But to take the Church, to take the crucified Saviour, to take the everlasting issues of human life, and in the midst of these tremendous verities, think of nothing but soft sentences, and sweet figures, and sentimental graces, and preaching these short sermons that please everybody, and particularly the closing passages of them—this I do not think is salutary. But if there is any case in which it is allowable, it is the case of men that preach for the sake of pleasing, and for that only. But they are said to be refined. Yes, they are refined. Oh! but they are said to be eloquent. Yes, they are eloquent. Oh! but they are said to be attractive. But when they stand on that awful, final day, between the living and the dead, before God Almighty's judgment, and all God's angels are gathered together, and there is nothing to stand between them and damnation, except elegancy, and refinement, and pleasant voices, and words, and gestures—in that hour, will it seem to them to have been worth their while to have bought their destruction at such a price.—Beecher.

The Church's power.—A factory is sometimes linked by a belt to a powerhouse. Christ is the centre and source of all power for his church. The Holy Ghost is the belt to the church, carrying up our needs and prayers, and bringing down Christ's answers and fullness. As I believe that wind power is the best for sail-boats, and steam power is the best for engines, so I believe that the Holy Ghost is the best power for churches. For a church to bring in an opera-singer or amusements and secular appliances to make the church go is as absurd as for an ocean steamer to uncouple its shaft from the engine and couple it on to the donkey-engine.—A. J. Gordon.

"Point to without trying to prop up the cross."—Theodore L. Cuyler.

"No condemnation can be too strong for the treachery and dishonesty of those persons who appropriate the consecrated phrases of Christianity as a subterfuge under which to attack its spiritual truths. Let us be careful in using the Bible, not to read our own thoughts into the text, but to search simply for the original meaning of it." —Pul. Com.

"A church is not of much account where the minister does all the preaching, and nearly all the praying, and all the visiting."—D. L. Moody.

"Winter brings blessings, so the chill
Of dark adversity;—from its cold grasp
The soul revives reanimate,—more strong,
And better armed."
—F. A. Mackay.

"I have read of a fountain that at noonday is cold, and at midnight it grows warm. So many a precious soul is cold Godward and Heavenward in prosperity, and grows warm in the midnight of adversity."—Brooks.

CHAPTER THE TWENTY-FOURTH.

"Again Jeremiah's ungrateful task is to take up an attitude of direct opposition to the king (comp. ch. xxii. 13—30), though, indeed, Zedekiah personally is so weak and dependent on others that he neither deserves nor receives a special rebuke. He and all the people that are left are likened to very bad figs, the good figs—the exiles—having been picked out and sent to Babylon, whence they will one day be restored."—Pul. Com. **1—3.** (1) **after,** etc., 2 Kings xxiv. 12; 2 Chr. xxxvi. 10. (2) **One basket,** of the two (vs. i.) put in the appointed place for offerings of firstfruits in the forecourt of the Temple. (2) **first ripe,** the fig bears three crops, of wh. the first is considered the best.[a]

Pictorial illustration.—Saints Cyril and Methodius, the earliest apostles of the Sclavonic tribes,—the Moravians, Bohemians, Hungarians, and Bulgarians,—were two Greeks monks of the order of St. Basil, and connected in a very interesting manner with the history of religious art. Cyril was learned and eloquent, a philosopher and a poet: Methodius was considered an excellent painter of that time, when his country produced the only painters known. These two monks departed together, by order of the patriarch of Constantinople, to preach to the savage nations along the shores of the Danube. Bogaris, the king or chief of Bulgaria, having heard of the art of Methodius, required of him that he should paint a picture in the hall of his palace; and that it should be "something terrible," to impress his subjects and vassals with awe. Methodius accordingly painted the Day of Judgment, representing at the summit our Lord seated in glory, and surrounded with angels: on His right, the resurrection of the blessed; and, on His left, the doom of sinners, swallowed up in flames, and tormented by the most hideous demons. When the king desired to have the interpretation of this "terrible" picture, Cyril, who was as eloquent in words as Methodius was in colors and forms, preached to the barbarian monarch and his attendants such a sermon as converted them all on the spot. Their mission was extended successfully through the surrounding nations. While Methodius painted the doctrines of the Christian faith, Cyril explained them in the language of the people.—Mrs. Jameson.

4—7. (5) **acknowledge,** R. V., "regard the captives of Judah," as one looks with pleasure on good fruit.[b] (6) **bring .. land,** fulfilled in the restoration under Zerubbabel, etc. (7) **return .. heart,** i. e. heartily give up their idolatry, and give themselves again sincerely to the worship of Jehovah. The return is to be both outward, to Jerusalem, and spiritual, to their allegiance.

Prosperity restored.—He sets his "eyes upon them for good." Men shrink from the eyes of God as from a keen and fatal scrutiny. But God is not always looking as the Judge. He beholds his children with love. There is a wonderful tenderness in this gaze, like that of a mother fondly watching over her suffering infant—a deep pity for sorrow, an earnest care to ward off harm, a kindly will to bestow all real good. It is blessed indeed to be so beheld by God. There are men possessed of such great power and influence that some consider a favorable look from them sufficient to make their fortune. What must be the effect of God setting eyes on a man for good?

8—10. (8) **evil figs,** by this term Zedekiah, and the remnant still in Judæa, are indicated. They were left in their corruptions. **of Egypt,** whither some had fled during the wars. (9) **removed,** R. V., "tossed to and fro," driven hither and thither, at home nowhere. **for their hurt,** these were to be scattered without hope of return.[a] (10) **be consumed,** so as never to be gathered together again.

Impenitence.—The reason why a wicked man doth not turn unto God is not because he cannot (though he cannot), but because he will not. He cannot say at the day of judgment, "Lord, thou knowest I did my best to be holy, but I could not." The man that had not on a wedding-garment could not say, "Lord, I was not able to get one." But he was

[a] "The bad figs may have been those of the sycamore tree, which, unless they are punctured as they ripen, contain an acrid juice which renders them uneatable. — Tristram.

"This prophecy was designed to encourage the despairing exiles, and to reprove the people at home who prided themselves as superior to those in Babylon, and abused the forbearance of God."—Fausset.

A bishop of the Church of England, who was tutor to a princess, said to her, "I find that my instructions have made you but little better." She replied, "Ah! but my lord, you do not know how much worse I should have been without them."

[b] "To have a kindly feeling towards the object regarded." — Henderson.

"Moral sympathy is the true key to knowledge of God. Reverence, humility, love, trust, submission, affections of the heart, are its conditions. Even right ideas of God depend very materially on the state of the heart towards him."—Pul. Com.

[a] Comp. De. xxviii. 25, 37.

"Here there is a well-beaten track under our feet. Let us keep it. It may not be quite the shortest way; it may not take us through all the grandeur and sublimity which

"speechless."—W. Fenner. A cure for a hard heart.—I was weary of a cold heart towards Christ, and his sacrifice, and the work of his Spirit —of a cold heart in the pulpit, in secret prayer, and in study. For fifteen years previously I had felt my heart burning within, as if going to Emmaus with Jesus. On a day ever to be remembered by me, as I was going from Dolgelly to Machynlleth, and climbing up towards Cadair Idris, I considered it to be incumbent upon me to pray, however hard I felt my heart, and however worldly the frame of my spirit was. Having begun in the name of Jesus, I soon felt as it were the fetters loosening, and the old hardness of heart softening, and, as I thought, mountains of frost and snow dissolving, and melting within me. This engendered confidence in my soul in the promise of the Holy Ghost. I felt my mind relieved from some great bondage: tears flowed copiously, and I was constrained to cry out for the gracious visits of God, by restoring to my soul the joy of his salvation.—Christmas Evans.

bolder pedestrians might see: we may miss a picturesque waterfall, a remarkable glacier, a charming view: but the track will bring us safe to our quarters for the night."—Dale.

"The door of heaven shuts from below, not from above."—Williams, of Wern.

"Judge not the preacher; for he is thy judge: if thou mislike him, thou conceiv'st him not. God calleth preaching folly. Do not grudge to pick out treasures from an earthen pot. The worst speak something good; if all want sense, God takes a text and preaches patience."—Herbert.

CHAPTER THE TWENTY-FIFTH.

1—3. (1) **fourth year,** comp. Da. i. 1. "The date assigned to this chapter is remarkable; it is the fatal year of the battle of Carchemish, which brought Syria and Palestine within the grasp of Babylon," 605 B. C. —Pul. Com. (3) **From .. year,** nineteen years in Josiah's reign, three months of Jehoahaz's, and four years of Jehoiakim's. **rising early,** the fig. for earnestly, ch. vii. 13.

Venn's account of Whitefield.—To give your ladyship any just description of what our eyes have witnessed and our hearts felt, within the last few days, exceeds my feeble powers. My inmost soul is penetrated with an overwhelming sense of the awful power and presence of Jehovah, who hath visited us with the blessed effusion of His Spirit, on this occasion, in a very eminent manner. Under Mr. Whitefield's first sermon, there was a visible appearance of much soul-concern among the immense crowd that filled every part of the burial-ground; so that many were overcome with fainting; others sobbed deeply; some wept silently; and a solemn concern appeared on the countenance of almost the whole assembly. When he came to press the injunction in the text (Isa. li. 1) upon the unconverted and the ungodly, his words seemed to cut like a sword upon several in the congregation; so that, whilst he was speaking, they could no longer contain, but burst out in the most piercing, bitter cries. At this juncture Mr. Whitefield made a pause of a few seconds, then burst into a flood of tears. During this short interval, Mr. Madan and myself stood up, and requested the people as much as possible to restrain from making any noise. Twice afterwards we had to repeat the same counsel, still advising the people to endeavor to moderate and bound their feelings, but not so as to resist or stifle their convictions. Oh, with what eloquence, what energy, what melting tenderness, did Mr. Whitefield beseech sinners to be reconciled to God—to come to Him for life everlasting, and rest their weary souls in Christ the Saviour! When the sermon was ended, the people seemed chained to the ground. Mr. Madan, Mr. Talbot, Mr. Downing, and myself, found ample employment in endeavoring to comfort those who seemed broken down under a sense of guilt. We separated in different directions among the crowd, and each was quickly surrounded by an attentive audience, still eager to hear all the words of this life. Of such a season as this it may well be said," I have heard thee in a time accepted, and in the day of salvation have I succoured thee: behold, now is the accepted time; behold, now is the day of salvation."

"A French officer whose ship had been taken by Nelson was brought on board Nelson's vessel and he walked up to the great admiral and gave him his hand. 'No,' said Nelson,' your sword first, please.' That is the gospel. Many people would take Christ's hand and say he is a noble character. Give up your rebellious will, first; admit your guilt; then Christ will take your hand and never let go."—John McNeil.

4—7. (4) **prophets,** "the people's wickedness was aggravated yet further by the fact that the call to repentance and amendment had come not from Jeremiah only, but from many other accredited messengers of God. Compare vii. 13, 25, xxxv. 15." Besides Jeremiah, Urijah, Zephaniah, and Habakkuk had prophesied during this period. (5) **Turn,** etc.,[a] 2 Ki. xvii. 13; Je. xviii. 11, xxxv. 15. (6) **works .. hands,** a severe and scornful description of the idols, and more widely of "the systematic en-

[a] "The great summons of God to mankind whether given by the Prophets of old, by John the Baptist, or by the Apostles and their successors." — Spk. Com.

During a flood, in St. Petersburg, the sentinel before the palace refused to leave his post (though ordered so to do by the empress, and death by drowning seemed imminent) till relieved by the proper officer.

gagement in idolatrous practices." (7) **not hearkened,** this was evident, for they had not obeyed.

The value of faithfulness.—It is the life of Paul, not his death that is of value to the world. The death-bed testimony impresses us only as it is the outgrowth of a life. Life is the test. Triumphant living is better than triumphant dying. Those who have fought the good fight are ready to be offered. Upon removing the ashes of Vesuvius from a buried city, there was found a Roman sentinel in armor, standing for eighteen hundred years in the place where his captain had placed him upon that fatal morning,—standing to his charge amid the terror and ruin of the perishing city. To do the present duty, to die doing it, is more important than to behold unutterable glories in the dying moment.—E. P. Tenney.

The call to repentance.—In the second century, Celsus, a celebrated adversary of Christianity, distorting our Lord's words, complained, "Jesus Christ came into the world to make the most horrible and dreadful society; for he calls sinners, and not the righteous; so that the body he came to assemble is a body of profligates, separated from good people, among whom they before were mixed. He has rejected all the good, and collected all the bad." "True," said Origen, in reply, "our Jesus came to call sinners—but to repentance. He assembled the wicked—but to convert them into new men, or rather to change them into angels. We come to him covetous, he makes us liberal; lascivious, he makes us chaste; violent, he makes us meek; impious, he makes us religious."—Exp. Bib.

A faithful clerk.—As a clerk in a country store in Illinois Abraham Lincoln quickly became known for his honesty. He was truthful in what he said about the goods, he gave good weight, and in particular, he lost no time and spared no pains in correcting mistakes.

He was closing the store one evening when a woman called for a half a pound of tea. In the morning he saw from the weight in the scale that he had given her only a quarter of a pound. Leaving everything else, he weighed out the other quarter and carried it to her.

Another customer paid him six and one-quarter cents more than was his due, and when the store was closed at night he hastened to correct the mistake, although she lived two miles away.—Anon.

a "The sound of the hand-mill is a familiar one in the East, and its cessation is aptly mentioned by the Prophets as one of the signs of utter desolation." —Van Lennep.

b "No night-light; so universal in the East, that the poorest house has it burning all night."—Fausset.

Job xxi. 17.

"There are some diseases that are called the reproaches of physicians; and there are some people that may be truly called the reproaches of ministers; and those are they who are great hearers, and talkers, and admirers of ministers, but never obey the doctrines delivered by them." —T. Brooks.

8—11. (9) **families .. north,** ch. i. 13, 14, races from the great region watered by the Tigris and Euphrates. **my servant,** we must take "servant" to be applied to Nebuchadrezzar in a lower sense than to the other bearers of the title. The Hebrew 'ebhed may be either "slave" in something approaching to the terrible modern sense, or in the sense in which Eliezer was one (i. e. little less than a son, and a possible heir, Gen. xxiv. 2; Gal. iv. 1), and which is still in full force in Arabia.—Pul. Com. **astonishment,** ch. ii. 12, v. 30. **hissing,** ch. xviii. 16, xix. 8. (10) **millstones,** "mention of the millstones[a] and of the candle (lamp)[b] is added, to increase the force of the warning. Not only all sign of mirth, but also of domestic labor and social cheer, should vanish. See the same description somewhat amplified in Rev. xviii. 22, 23.—Camb. Bib.

Delaying repentance.—"Now," thou resolvest, "I will hereafter look to it better than I have done before." Alas, this will for hereafter is no will! First: because it is only to shuffle off the willing of the present. The heart is unwilling to obey, and therefore it puts off the commandment to the future, not for any desire that it hath to do it hereafter, but only because it is unwilling to do it for the present; like a man that is unwilling to lend. "I'll lend you hereafter," says he, only because he would shuffle off lending at all. Secondly: this will for hereafter is no will, because it goes without God's will. God's will is now; thine is hereafter. "He that will not when he may, when he would he shall have 'Nay.'" Take heed lest when thou wouldst fain be pardoned, and criest, "Lord, open to me," thou dost find thyself too late.—William Fenner.

Hearing a voice from the unseen.—Lady Henry Somerset, whose philanthropies and eloquence in the cause of humanity have won for her world-wide fame, was during her earlier life a woman of the world, given up to fashion and pleasure. Inheriting immense wealth, she had the power to gratify every desire, but restless and unsatisfied, she began to question the meaning of life. Turning to the Bible and studying it earnestly, she soon felt the need of religious consecration and of greater motive power; but under the influence of the spirit of criticism about her, she found her faith weakening and her mind clouded by perplexity and doubt. One day while, alone in her garden, she was pondering the mysteries of life and questioning the very existence of God, she heard a voice say distinctly: "Act as if I were, and you shall know that I am." Though the voice was not audible to the material ear, Lady Henry declares that she heard the words with the ear of her soul as distinctly as though they had been spoken, and the sentiment they expressed made a powerful impression upon her mind. The more she thought of the mysterious utterance the more it seemed to her that only divine wisdom could have prompted the words, and she determined to live by their counsel. Soon her faith in God and Christ returned, and she entered into the life of active benevolence which is now universally recognized, and has been followed by such beneficent results. To every earnest yet perplexed and doubting soul, the voice which spoke to this devoted woman speaks today: "Act as if I were, and you shall know that I am."—Anon. Voices.—There is the voice of God, and the voice of Nature. I cannot be wrong if I listen to them. Sometimes, when uncertain of a voice from its very loudness, we catch the missing syllable in the echo. In God and Nature we have Voice and Echo. When I hear both, I am assured. My sense of hearing does not betray me twice. I recognize the Voice in the Echo; the Echo makes me certain of the Voice; I listen and I know.—Drummond.

"Those auditors who can find nothing to do but note elegant words and phrases, or perhaps an ill grace of gesture go away with little pleasure, and no profit."—Bp. Hall.

12—14. (12) **seventy years,** this number may be intended as a figure for the complete period ordered in the Divine Providence.[a] The number seven is in Scrip. the symbol of perfection or completion. **punish,** etc.,[b] comp. Isa. x. 5, 16. **perpetual desolations,** vs. 9,[c] true of its condition to the present day. (13) **And I will bring,** etc. "Clearly this verse cannot have formed part of the original prophecy, but must have been added whenever the collection of prophecies against foreign nations finally assumed its present form."—Pul. Com. (14) **serve themselves,** i. e. they shall reduce the Chaldæans to slavery. This was fulfilled in Cyrus and his confederates. **also,** R. V., "even of them." **deeds,** treatment of the Jews.

Fulfillment of prophecy.—Two rabbis, approaching Jerusalem, observed a fox running upon the hill Zion. And Rabbi Joshua wept; but Rabbi Eliezer laughed. "Wherefore dost thou laugh?" said he who wept. "Nay, wherefore dost thou weep?" demanded Eliezer. "I weep," replied the Rabbi Joshua, "because I see what is written in the Lamentations fulfilled: "Because of the Mount Zion, which is desolate, the foxes walk upon it." "And therefore," said Rabbi Eliezer, "do I laugh; for, when I see with mine own eyes that God has fulfilled His threatenings to the very letter, I have thereby a pledge that not one of His promises shall fail; for He is ever more ready to show mercy than judgment."

[a] Comp. Da. ix. 2, 24.

[b] "Though the Chaldæans and other nations were instruments in the hands of God in punishing the Jews, yet, as they had no knowledge of this fact, but merely gratified their cruel and ambitious passions, they, in their turn, thereby contracted guilt for which Jehovah threatens to punish them."—Henderson.

[c] Je. l. 40.

15—17. (15) **wine .. fury,** R. V., "the cup of the wine of this fury."[d] This figure expresses "stupifying judgments."[e] **to drink it,** this offering of the wine-cup took place in vision. (16) **moved,** R. V., "and reel to and fro," having all the symptoms of drunkenness. **sword,** the symbol of war. (17) **took I the cup,** not however in any literal sense, just as the cup was not a literal cup, but along with its contents a figurative expression for the wrath of God as manifested in a national subjugation. Hence the view, which has been maintained, that Jeremiah presented a cup of actual wine to the ambassadors of these various powers, assembled, according to this hypothesis, for counsel in Jerusalem, may be dismissed, as utterly improbable. The figure was sufficiently carried out by the proclamation of God's message in Jerusalem, whence it might be conveyed to the other nations united by a common danger.—Camb. B.

The wine-cup of fury.—Though "God is angry with the wicked every day," he is forbearing, and restrains his wrath till it cannot longer be justly withheld. Then we may suppose that the longer it has been accumulating the worse will be its outflow. Men have been treasuring

[d] Ps. lx. 3; Je. xiii, 12, 13.

[e] "God's judgments are metaphorically represented by a cup of intoxicating liquors, bec. they fill men with astonishment, and bereave them of their common judgment and discretion."—Lowth.

Ps. lxxv. 8; Is. li. 17; Je. xlviii. 26, xlix. 12, Ha. ii. 16; Re. xiv. 10, xvi. 19.

up wrath against the day of wrath. Such seasons of the outpouring of the cup of fury may be noted in history; e. g. in the invasions of Nebuchadrezzar, the destruction of Jerusalem by Titus, the sacking of Rome by Alaric. It is important to note that this happens in seasons. It is not always harvest. But the spring sowing prepares for the autumn reaping. We may be now preparing for an outburst of wrath. How foolish not to guard against it because it has not yet come! Delay of judgment is no excuse for doubt about it, for this is part of the Divine method of action.—Pul. Com.

"This is an allusion to those intoxicating draughts which used to be given to malefactors just before their execution, to take away their senses."—Lewis.

18—22. (18) "We may perceive a certain system (south to north) in the enumeration. After Jerusalem and Judah the prophet takes in order the furthest south (Egypt), (southeast (Uz), southwest (Philistines), east (Edom, etc.), west (Tyre, etc.), east and northwards (Dedan, etc. to the Medes), and finally the north far and near."—Camb. Bib. **kings,**[a] poss. to include Jeconiah and Zedekiah, the successors of Jehoiakim, as well as that monarch. **as .. day,** may have been a later insertion of Jeremiah —after the fulfillment of this prophecy (Camb. B.), or the addition of some later writer. (Cheyne.) (19) **Pharaoh,** the general title of the Egyptian kings, like Shah, or Czar. (20) **mingled people,** Heb. Ereb, prob. foreign mercenaries, serving in Egypt,[b] or the mixed races on the shores of the Red Sea. **Uz,** a district of Edom. **Philistines,** on the southern borders of the Mediterranean. **Azzah,** or Gaza. **remnant of Ashdod,** this town had been captured and destroyed by Psammeticus, after a siege of 29 years. (Heredotus.) (22) **Tyrus .. Zidon,** the great Phœnician seaports. **isles,** or coast-lands of the Mediterranean.[c]

a "Jerusalem must first drink of it, because judgment begins at the house of God." — Wordsworth.

"This clause may, however, have been inserted by Jer., at his final revision of his prophecies in Egypt."—Fausset.

b "Auxiliaries." —Gesenius.

c "The islands and maritime regions where the Phœnicians had planted colonies." —Henderson.

The growth of sin.—The thistle is the emblem of Scotland, and may be said to be worshiped by all patriotic Scotchmen. Well, it happened that a Scotch resident of Melbourne, while visiting the old country, took it in his head to carry a thistle with him on his return to Australia. So he placed the plant in a pot, and watered it carefully every day during the voyage from London to Melbourne. When he arrived, his performance was noticed in the newspapers, and a subscription-dinner was arranged in honor of the newly arrived plant. About 200 Scotchmen sat down to dinner at which the thistle was the centerpiece and the great object of attraction. The next day the thistle was planted with a great deal of ceremony in the public garden of Melbourne, and it was carefully watched and tended by the gardener who happened to be a Scotchman. The thistle blossomed and everybody rejoiced. The seeds of that thistle were borne on the breezes and all over the colony of Victoria, they found a lodging in the soil, grew, and prospered and sent out more seeds. That thistle has been the cause of ruin to many a sheep and cattle-run all over Australia. Thousands, yes millions of acres of grass have been destroyed by that pernicious weed. Anathemas without number and of the greatest severity have been showered on the Scotchman who brought the plant to Australia, and the other Scotchmen who placed it in the public garden.—Thomas W. Knox.

"Contempt is frequently regulated by fashion."— Zimmerman.

"I am no courtier, no fawning dog of State, to lick and kiss the hand that buffets me; nor can I smile upon my guest, and praise his stomach, when I know he feeds on poison, and death disguised sits grinning at my table."—Sewel.

23—26. (23) **Dedan,** Ge. xxv. 3, 4; Is. xxi. 13. **Tema .. Buz,** neighboring tribes of Arabia, Job xxxii. 2. **corners,** R. V., "and all that have the corners of their hair polled."[a] Comp. xlix. 28, 32. A description of the tribe of Kedar. (24) **mingled people,** "the intermingled people" (see on vs. 20); i. e. probably in this passage populations of a different race interspersed among the Aramaic tribes to which most of the inhabitants of the desert belonged."—Pul. Com.[b] (25) **Zimri,**[c] prob. a tribe on the east side of the desert, towards Persia; but not identified. **Elam,** at the head of the Persian Gulf, used for Persia. (26) **Sheshach,** or Babylon, ch. li. 41. **shall drink after them,** the turn of Babylon shall come to drink of the cup of divine wrath.

a Je. ix. 26.

b "A mixture of people in that part of Arabia, properly called the Desert, consisting of the nations called in Scrip. by the general name of the children of the East."—Lowth.

c Syr. renders Zamron, which may connect with Zimran, see Ge. xxv. 2.

Swiftness of destruction.—One bolt of lightning, and the whole goldhouse has gone down. One chill some damp night, and the healthhouse is ruined from attic to basement. One touch by the invisible hand, and the brain that had in it a thousand inventions trembles, and cannot remember. One keen disappointment, and pleasure is struck dead; its face is an annoyance, its rattle is an insult, its invitations are blasphemies, in face of a woe so terrible. There is but one abiding confidence—"Rock of Ages, cleft for me." There is but one refuge from the storm.—"Jesus, refuge of my soul."—Peop. Bib.

27—29. (27) **therefore,** R. V. "And thou." **be drunken,** etc., "metaphors denoting the utter helplessness to which the nations are reduced by drinking the wine-cup of fury."—Spk. Com. (28) **refuse to take,** endeavor to master the circumstances of difficulty and distress in which they will be placed.[d] (29) R. V. "For, lo, I begin to work evil at the city." **should .. unpunished?** if God did not spare His own people, there could be no hope for them.

Duty and danger.—The perils of good men in former days. Persecution; special trials and deliverances; Apostles the only preachers, hence, and for other reasons, God specially protected them. The common prison; strong, where common malefactors were kept. Subject, —Duty and Danger. I. Duty often involves danger. This the case with nearly every duty. Work, a duty, exposes to various risks. To save one from drowning or burning, a duty, yet there may be danger. A duty to live a Christian life, but it often entails danger: cross words, opposition, petty persecution. II. Danger does not absolve us from duty. When the doors were opened the angel did not tell the Apostles to go away from the city, but to proceed with their work and in the most public place. Other men would be in great danger, spiritual and eternal, if they did not hear "all the words of this life." III. God our trust and protection from danger, while we are in the way of duty. He saw His servants in prison: did not abandon them, sent an angel, etc. May not work a miracle in our behalf; but will not neglect us, sends inward supports if not outward deliverances. Learn:—Better to have external things against us, and our conscience at peace, than conscience disturbing us in the midst of surrounding prosperity.—Hive.

30—33. (30) **roar,** etc.[a] as a lion, filling with consternation both the shepherds and their sheep. **upon his habitation,** R. V. "against his fold," i. e. Judæa, his pasturage. **shout,** the vintage cry.[b] (31) **A noise,** that made by the trampling of the invaders. (32) **evil,** in the sense of calamity. **whirlwind,** ch. xxiii. 19. **coasts,** R. V. "the uttermost parts of" —the storm appears on the horizon and seems to come from the ends of the earth, as ch. vi. 22.[c] (33) **not lamented,** ch. viii. 2, xvi. 4.

"The Lord shall roar."—In highly poetic language the judgment of the Gentiles is described. Jehovah has risen like a lion from his covert, and at His roaring the whole world is filled with terror and confusion. Sheep and shepherds roll on the ground in consternation, but cannot escape; for, like a storm-wind, judgment stalks abroad, and the slain of the land cover the ground from one end of the earth unto the other, and lie unwept and without burial.—Payne Smith. The strict judgment of God sounds much stronger and clearer than we can bear. Hence the six hundred thousand men were so terrified when they heard the voice of God, that they said, "Let not God speak with us lest we die" (Exod. xx. 19). It is well that we do not refuse to hear, or stop our ears against the sweet sound of God's voice in the sacred office of the preacher, because we can have it (Ps. xcv. 8); or the time will come when we shall be obliged to hear its awful roaring, which God forbid. For when the lion roars, who shall not be afraid? (Amos iii. 8.)—Cramer.

34—38. (34) **shepherds,** fig. for kings and rulers. **wallow,** roll yourselves about in. **principal .. flock,** lit. "the strong ones of the flock," i. e. the leaders of society; the great and rich men. **of your slaughter,** etc., R. V. "of your slaughter are fully come, and I will break you in pieces, and ye shall fall," etc. **pleasant vessel,** precious vessel, "destroyed as a crystal glass."[a] (35) **to flee,** lit. flight shall fail the shepherds. (36) **hath spoiled,** or spoileth, ch. vi. 2, 3. (37) **peaceable habitations,** R. V. "and the peaceable folds are brought to silence because of the fierce anger of the Lord." (38) **forsaken his covert,** and come forth to judgment. **is desolate,** R V. "is become an astonishment." **oppressor,** R. V. "the oppressing sword." Heb. jonah, signifying also dove.[b]

Hypocrisy and sincerity.—Consider, hypocrisy lies close in the heart; if thou art not very careful thou mayest easily pass a false judgment on thyself. They who were sent to search the cellar under the Par-

[d] "If they either do not believe thy threatenings, or else disregard them, as thinking themselves sufficiently provided against any hostile invasion."—Lowth.

"It is vain to have a name to live if we are dead; the name will not galvanize us back into life."—Pul.Com.

"I am sometimes downright staggered at the exceeding riches of his grace. How Christ can go on pardoning day after day, and hour after hour; sometimes I feel almost afraid to ask, for shame."—A. L. Newton.

[a] Joel iii. 16; Am. i. 2.

[b] Comp. Is. xvi. 9, 10; Je. xlviii. 33.

[c] "The thunderstorm seen first on the edge of the horizon overspreads the heaven, and travels from nation to nation in its destructive course." — Spk. Com.

"Man-like is it to fall into sin,
Fiend-like is it to dwell therein,
Christ-like is it for sin to grieve,
God-like is it all sin to leave."
—Longfellow.

[a] "Your past excellency shall not render you safe now. I will turn to your ignominy whatever glory I conferred on you."—Calvin.

LXX. render, "Ye shall fall like chosen rams."

[b] "There may be a covert allusion to the Chaldæan standard bearing a dove on it, in honor of Semiramis, the first queen, said in popular supersti-

liament, at first saw nothing but coals and winter provisions; but upon a review, when they came to throw away that stuff, they found all but provision for the devil's kitchen: then the mystery of iniquity was uncased, and the barrels of powder appeared. How many are there that, from some duties of piety they perform, some seeming zeal they express in profession, presently cry, "Omnia bene," and are so kind to themselves as to vote themselves good Christians, who, did they but take the pains to throw those aside, they might find a foul hypocrite at the bottom of them all. Hypocrisy often takes up her lodging next door to sincerity, and so she passes unfound, the soul not suspecting hell can be so near heaven. And as hypocrisy, so sincerity is hard to be discovered. This grace often lies low in the heart, like the sweet violet in some valley or near some brook, hid with thorns and nettles—infirmities, I mean; so that there requires both care and wisdom, that we neither let the weed of hypocrisy stand, nor pluck up the herb of grace in its stead.—A Divine of the 17th Cent. God's withdrawment from man.—"Think of God sending a famine upon the soul, of minds pining and dying because Divine messages have been withdrawn! We know what the effect would be if God were to withdraw the dew, or to trouble the air with a plague, or to avert the beams of the sun; the garden would be a desert, the fruitful field a sandy plain, the wind a bearer of death, summer a stormy night, and life itself a cruel variation of death: so penetrating, so boundless is the influence of God in nature. Is it conceivable that the withdrawment of God's influence would be less disastrous upon the spirit of man?"—Joseph Parker.

tion to have been nourished by doves when exposed at birth, and at death to have been transformed into a dove."—Fausset.

"If you commit one sin, it is like the melting of the lower glacier upon the Alps, the others must follow in time. Set the coral insect at work, you cannot decree where it shall stay its work."—Spurgeon.

CHAPTER THE TWENTY-SIXTH.

"This chapter as a whole gives us a rapid sketch of the circumstances under which Jeremiah had delivered himself of the prophecies that went before. The more definite he had become in his warnings, the more he excited the wrath of the false prophets and of those who sided with them; and now that he had explicitly announced (xxv. 11) a seventy years' captivity, their indignation boiled over, and they sought to compass his death. From the contents of this chap. then we can realize better under what conditions and with what courage the prophet continued his forecastings of definite calamity in the chapters which follow. 'The beginning' will naturally denote some date earlier than the fourth year of Jehoiakim's reign, when the crisis came about, and Jeremiah was no longer listened to nor tolerated (chap. xxxvi.)"—Camb. Bib. **1—7.** (1) **beginning,** etc., "prob. soon before the critical battle of Carchemish, wh. established the supremacy of Nebuchadnezzar and Babylon."[c] (2) **in the court,** the largest court, where the males assembled for worship. (3) **repent me,** ch. xviii. 8. (6) **like Shiloh,** ch. vii. 12, 14. (7) **heard,** etc., Jer. spoke publicly, and at a time when the court was full of people.

Preaching the whole truth.—Somerfield, just before his death, speaking of his recovery, said, "Oh, if I might be raised again! How I could preach! I could preach as I never preached before. I have taken a look into eternity!"—Luther, of whom Richter has said that "his words were half battles," when he first began to preach, suffered unheard agony. "O Dr. Staupitz, Dr. Staupitz!" said he to the Vicar General of his order, "I cannot do it, I shall die in three months; indeed I cannot do it." Dr. Staupitz replied, "Well, Sir Martin, if you must die, you must; preach, man, preach; and then live or die as it happens." So Luther preached, and lived; and he became one great whirlwind of energy to work without resting in this world.—Spurgeon.

8—11. (8) **made an end of speaking,** "they allowed Jeremiah to finish his discourse (of which we have here only the briefest summary), either from a lingering reverence for his person and office, or to obtain fuller materials for an accusation (comp. the trial of Stephen, Acts vi. 12—14)." **priests and prophets,** these were more bitter against Jer. than the princes were. **Thou shalt surely die,** "that prophet, who spoke with-

[c] Je. xxv. 1, 11.

"God's ministers must have their hearts fired, not with passion, but with love. The thunderbolt may crash, but the sun melts. It is better to love as a pastor than speak as an angel." — Watson (1649).

"An iron key is better than one made of gold if it will better open the door, for that is all the use of a key." — Augustine.

"The words of a preacher ought purgere non palpare, to prick the heart, not smooth and coax."—Jerome.

out God's command, was according to the Mosaic Law (Deut. xviii. 20) to be put to death. The charge against Jeremiah then was of this nature, and the alleged proof, that it was impossible in the nature of things that such a calamity could be allowed to happen to the people of God. —Camb. Bib.[a] (9) **gathered against,** R. V. "gathered unto," i. e. in a judicial assembly. Comp. vs. 16. (10) **princes,** these were the true judges, without whose presence Jer. could not have had a true trial. **new gate,** or east gate. A judicial court was at once constituted. (11) **worthy to die,**[b] and they demand instant judgment and execution.

Heroic constancy.—A mother and her seven sons were brought before the tyrant Antiochus in the persecution of the Jews, and offered a discharge if they would but taste swine's flesh. They unanimously refused, were "tormented with scourges and whips," but still refused. "What wouldst thou ask of us? We are ready to die rather than transgress the laws of our fathers," they said. The enraged king ordered the speaker to be slain in the most excruciating manner. His mother and six brothers were compelled to witness his awful agony, yet, with unshaken constancy, exhorted one another to die manfully. The second son follows the first to martyrdom. The third stretched out his hands to the executioner to be cut off, saying, "These I had from heaven, and for his laws I despise them." The fourth, fifth, and sixth sons endured torture and death with the same dauntless fidelity. The mother and her youngest son remain. The mangled members of her six sons strew the ground. Antiochus now lays bribes before the youth. Wealth and station are proffered him, if he will but taste. The nobler than Spartan mother addresses him: "I beseech thee, my son, look upon the heaven and the earth, and all that is therein, and consider that God made them of things that were not; and so was mankind made likewise. Fear not this tormentor, but, being worthy of thy brethren, take thy death, that I may receive thee in mercy again with thy brethren." O wonderful woman! The record runs," "Last of all, after the sons, the mother died." These Jewish martyrs inherited the promise, being "faithful unto death."

a "They accused him of uttering falsehood in the name of Jehovah, a crime wh. was threatened in the law of Moses with death." — Henderson.

b Lit. "a sentence of death is to this man," i. e. is due to him.

"A Christian is the highest style of man."—Pope.

"Tender-handed stroke a nettle
And it stings you for your pains,
Grasp it like a man of mettle,
And it soft as silk remains."
—Aaron Hill.

"There's a brave fellow! there's a man of pluck!
A man who's not afraid to say his say,
Though a whole town's against him."
—Longfellow.

12—15. Jeremiah's defence—comp. Acts v. 39. (12) **The Lord sent me,** his message was from God, therefore not blasphemy nor treachery, but truth, which a wise people would hear. (13) **amend,** etc., ch. vii. 3. (14) **in your hand,** he was quite willing to submit to lawful government, but whatever the result, he must simply deliver the Divine message.[a] (15) **innocent blood,** i. e. the guilt of putting the innocent to death.

Fearlessness.—"What can I fear?" asked Chrysostom before the Pro-consul. "Will it be death? but you know that 'Christ is my life,' and that I shall gain by death. Will it be exile? but 'the earth with all its fulness is the Lord's.' Will it be the loss of wealth? but 'we brought nothing into this world, and we can carry nothing out.' Thus, all the terrors of the world are contemptible in my eyes, and I smile at all its good things. Poverty I do not fear; riches I do not sigh for; from death I do not shrink; and life I do not desire except for the progress of your souls." Courage.—I heard of a young man who went into the army. The first night in the barracks with about fifteen men playing cards and gambling around him, he fell on his knees and prayed, and they began to curse and throw boots at him. So it went on the next night and the next, and finally the young man told the chaplain what had taken place and asked him what he should do. "Well," the chaplain said, "those soldiers have just as much right in the barracks as you have. It makes them angry to have you pray and the Lord will hear you just as well in bed." Some weeks after that, the chaplain met the young man and asked, "By the way, did you take my advice?" "I did for two or three nights, but I felt like a whipped hound and the third night I knelt down and prayed." "Well," said the chaplain, "how did that work?" The young soldier answered, "We have a prayer-meeting there now every night. Three have been converted and we are praying for the rest."—D. L. Moody.

a See De. xviii. 20.

Comp. Jos. ix. 25; 2 Sa. xv. 26; Da. iii. 16.

"Base, grov'ling souls ne'er know true honor's worth, but weigh it out in mercenary scales: the secret pleasure of a generous act is the great mind's great bribe."—Dryden.

"'Tis much he dares;
And to that dauntless temper of his mind
He hath a wisdom that doth guide his valor
To act in safety."
—Shakespeare.

16—19. (16) **spoken .. name,** if Jer. was a true prophet, it was their duty to listen to his message.[a] (17) **elders,**[b] i. e. some of the elder

a "A prophet could not be put to death unless he prophesied in the name of other gods; or after his prophecy had failed in its accomplishment."—Fausset.

b Ac. v. 21.

ones among these princes. **the assembly,** "the word rendered 'assembly' is the traditional legal term for the 'congregation of Israel' (Deut. xxxi. 30). Thus, with all the faults of the government of Judah, which Jeremiah himself reveals to us, it was very far removed from the Oriental despotisms of our day. The 'elders' are still an important element in the social system, and form a link with that earlier period in which the family was the leading power in the social organization."—Pul. Com. (18) **Micah,** etc.,[c] comp. Mic. i. 1, iii. 12. This was a denunciation, and a prophecy of national calamities, like the prophecy of Jeremiah. (19) **fear the Lord,** so as to give heed to His message. **besought the Lord,** R. V., "entreat the favor of the Lord."[d] **Thus,** R. V., "thus should we commit great evil," etc., i. e. by doing any evil to Jer.

Zion a desolation.—Morning dawned; and with my kind host, to whom every spot in and around Jerusalem was familiar, I ascended to the terraced roof. Just behind Moriah, the Tyropean valley was distinctly marked by a deeply-shaded dell, running from north to south through the city. Beyond it rose Zion, higher and longer than Moriah. . . . As I looked, a moving object in one of the fields riveted my attention. "Haste, give me the glass," I said. I turned it upon the spot. Yes, I was right; a plough and a yoke of oxen were there at work. Jeremiah's prophecy was fulfilled before my eyes.—Porter.

20—24. (20) **Urijah,**[e] this narrative was probably introduced later by Jeremiah to shew the danger in which he stood at the time, and does not form a portion of that which was said on the occasion by any of the parties present. It would have been a dangerous attack to make upon Jehoiakim, the reigning king. It is hardly likely also that there would have been time between the accession of Jehoiakim and the somewhat vague date assigned to this attack on Jeremiah. (vs. 1) for all these events to have occurred in the case of Urijah.—Camb. Bib. (21) **mighty men,** captains of his army. (22) **Elnathan,** 2 Ki. xxiv. 8. **Achbor,** 2 Ki. xxii. 12. (23) **fetched,** etc., Jehoiakim was at the time a vassal of Egypt, so one accused of treason would be readily surrounded to him. **graves,** etc., 2 Ki. xxiii. 6. (24) **Nevertheless,** in spite of this attempt to urge the prince to put Jer. to death. **Ahikam,** 2 Ki. xxii. 12, 14.

Comparative peril.—Though at the present moment it is he who seems to be in danger, he well knows that his peril is but a surface trifle when compared with that attaching to the scowling enemies who are crowded around him. He can be rescued, if so it please God; but who is to rescue those who are striding onwards, ever more swiftly, to a righteous doom? God can deliver the prophet from his enemies, for the prophet himself interposes no obstacle to his deliverance; but these people of Judah and Jerusalem interpose insurmountable obstacles, in that they will not amend their ways and doings and obey the voice of God. More than that, it seems as if they were about to add a fresh obstacle by shedding the innocent blood of God's latest messenger. The persecutor is always in greater peril than the persecuted. Physical pain and physical death are transitory and unreturning ills, but the evildoer has to face the worm that dieth not. Compare with the words of the prophet here the words of Jesus as he was being led to crucifixion: "Daughters of Jerusalem, weep not for me, but weep for yourselves, and for your children" (Luke xxiii. 28).—Pul. Com.

[c] "He prophesied in the time of Jotham, Ahaz, and Hezekiah, and was contemporary with Hosea and Amos in Israel, and with Isaiah in Judah."—Wordsworth.

[d] 2 Chr. xxxii. 26.

"Seeing a Christian woman go cheerfully to prison, an observer said to her, "Oh, you have not yet tasted of the bitterness of death." She as cheerfully replied, "No, nor ever shall, for Christ hath promised that those who keep His sayings shall not see death."

[e] "The circumstances detailed in this and the three following verses appear to have been adduced in opposition to what had been related respecting Micah; and as they had taken place in the reign of the present monarch, they furnished an apt precedent for the condemnation of Jeremiah." — Henderson.

CHAPTER THE TWENTY-SEVENTH.

1—4. (1) **Jehoiakim,** this is prob. an error for Zedekiah. Spk. Com. etc. also the Syriac Ver. (2) **bonds and yokes,** R. V. "bands and bars." The yoke here is the carved piece of wood attached to the two yokes on the pair of oxen, and connecting them; but it stands for the entire instrument. The bonds are the straps or fastenings of these yokes. (3) **send them,** this was to be actually done. The nations referred to were those wh. God had given into the hand of the king of Babylon. The ambassadors of these kings had prob. come to Jerus., to make a league for resisting the king of Babylon.[f] (4) **their masters,** the great kings, vs. 3.

God and the earth (vss. 4, 5.)—I. God is the Creator of all earthly things; the earth is not eternal, not the production of chance, not the work of many gods. II. God is the Sovereign Disposer of all earthly things; might have built it and left it uninhabited; might have populated it with other creatures than those who tenant it now; He has given what He thinks fit of it to individuals, tribes, and nations.—Thomas.

5—8. (5) **given it,**[a] Da. iv. 17, 25, 32. "The terms of the message are these:—God, as Creator of the world and of all that is in it, has the right to give it to whomsoever He will. He has therefore placed Nebuchadnezzar in power for such time as it shall please Him, and none may resist His will."—Camb. Bib. (6) **my servant,** ch. xxv. 9, xliii. 10. **beasts,** etc., "the territories of these nations were to become mere hunting grounds for him."—Spk. Com. (7) **son .. son's son,** Evil-Merodach was his son, and Belshazzar his grandson.[b] **until, etc.,** R. V. "until the time of his own land come," i. e. the time of its destruction also. **serve .. him,** or bring him into servitude.

Parables.—The place of parable in teaching, and especially after the sanction of the greatest of Teachers, must always be recognized. The very necessities of language, indeed, demand this method of presenting truth. The temporal is the husk and frame-work of the eternal, and thoughts can be uttered only through things.—Drummond.

The creation.—

I saw when at His word the formless mass,
The world's material world, came to a heap;
Confusion heard His voice, and wild uproar
Stood ruled, stood vast infinitude confined;
Till at His second bidding darkness fled,
Light shone, and order from disorder sprung:
Swift to their several quarters hasted then
The cumbrous elements, earth, flood, air, fire;
And this ethereal quintessence of heaven
Flew upward, spirited with various forms,
That roll'd orbicular, and turned to stars
Numberless, as thou seest, and how they move;
Each had his place appointed, each his course;
The rest in circuit walk this universe. —Milton.

9—11. (9) **diviners,** etc., these arts were expressly forbidden to the Jews.[c] **enchanters,** R. V. "soothsayers." (10) **to remove you,** i. e. the certain effect of the delusion will be to remove you. (11) **bring .. neck under,** i. e. yield to the conqueror, and put themselves into subjection to him.

God's supreme control.—When the yoke is seen on the neck of the ox laboring at the plough or drawing the wagon, that yoke signifies, not only submission, but a submission that is inevitable. The ox is made for the service of man, and although when young it may rebel and defy for a while, it must submit at last. The superior intelligence and the ordained master cannot but conquer. And what the ox is in the hands of man, that every nation, even the strongest and bravest, is in the hands of God. Babylon, conqueror and spoiler as it was, was no more free from God's yoke than any of the nations it defeated. It is quite compatible with the carrying out of God's great purpose that there should be the most striking disparities in the temporal conditions of both individuals and nations. That Babylon should be the victor and these other nations the vanquished, was in His eyes a matter of very secondary moment.—Pul. Com.

12—15. (12) **Zedekiah,** who was restless under the Babylonian yoke. and, revolting, brought the final ruin on the land. Although Zedekiah is addressed, the plural is used throughout on account of his many sympathisers among all ranks. **Bring .. under,** fig. for quietly submitting. (13) **die, by stubborn and wilful resistance.** (14) **a lie,** ch. xiv. 14, xxiii.

---

[f] "The task assigned to Jer. required great faith, as it was sure to provoke alike his own countrymen, and the foreign ambassadors, and their kings, by a seeming insult, at the very time that all were full of confident hopes grounded on the confederacy."—Fausset.

[a] "God here, as elsewhere, connects with the symbol doctrine, which is as it were its soul, without which it would be not only cold and frivolous, but even dead." —Calvin.

[b] "The two kings mentioned in Ptolemy's Canon between Evil-Merodach and Belshazzar (or Nabonadus)—viz., Neriglissarus and Laborosoarchodus, had no right by lineal descent: for Neriglissarus was only husband to Evil-Merodach's daughter, and Laborosoarchodus was son to Neriglissarus."—Lowth.

[c] De. xviii. 11; Is. ii. 6.

"There is also an affected ignorance, such a one as is contracted by a wilful neglect of the means; and this is not excusing but condemning. . . . In the midst of light to be in darkness; for an Israel to have an Egypt in a Goshen; this is highly provoking, and may justly cause God to lay hold on vengeance."—South.

"To perceive truth by its proper evidence, is of the formal nature of the rational mind; as it is of the physical nature of the eye to see an object by the

21, xxix. 8, lyingly. (15) **not sent them,** so no kind of trust is to be put in their prophecies.

Detection of lying.—The folly of lying consists in its defeating its own purpose. A habit of lying is generally detected in the end; and after detection the liar, instead of deceiving, will not even be believed when he happens to speak the truth. Nay, every single lie is attended with such a variety of circumstances which lead to a detection, that it is often discovered. The use generally made of a lie is to cover a fault; but as this end is seldom answered, we only aggravate what we wish to conceal. In point even of prudence, an honest confession would serve us better.—Gilpin.

light that it reflects, or of the ear to hear the sounds which the air conveys to it."—Bp. Horsley.

16—18. (16) **vessels,** etc., these had been carried away in the reigns of Jeconiah, and also of Jehoiakim.[a] (18) **But if they be prophets,** etc. The "false prophets" have neglected one of the principal functions of a prophet, viz. intercessory prayer. Seeing that a part of the sacred vessels had been carried to Babylòn, all true prophets ought to intercede with Jehovah that those still left might be spared. The end was that the remaining vessels were carried off on the capture of Jerusalem (2 Kings xxv. 13)."—Pul. Com.[b]

[a] 2 Ki. xxiv. 13; 2 Chr. xxxvi. 5—7.

[b] 2 Ki. xxv. 13—17; 2 Chr. xxxvi. 18.

"Do not as some ungracious pastors do, show me the steep and thorny way to heaven, whilst like a puff'd and reckless libertine himself the primrose path of dalliance treads, and recks not his own road."—Shakespeare.

The prayer-test.—If it can be said of a person, "Behold, he prayeth!" we may know much of him. Prayer is the barometer that rises or falls with the changing tone of the spiritual atmosphere. When we "restrain prayer" this is a sad sign that our better life is failing. It is useless to boast of spiritual attainments such as those of the professional prophets; these are nothing but delusions if the prayer-test reveals a condition of spiritual deadness. The results of prayer are a further test. We cannot say that a particular prayer is not acceptable to God because its does not bring us the particular thing we seek, since we are always making foolish requests, and God mercifully deals with us according to his wise and good will rather than according to the letter of our language. Still, if no answer is ever received to prayer, something must be wrong.—Pul. Com.

19—22. (19) **pillars,** etc., 1 Ki. vii. 15, 23, 27.[c] (22) **then .. restore,** after the captivity, when God Himself shall arrange for the return of His people. This was fulfilled in the commission of Cyrus.[d]

[c] 2 Ki. xxv. 13; Je. lii. 17, 20, 21.

[d] Ezr. i. 7, v. 13, 14.

"He hath a heart as sound as a bell, and his tongue is the clapper; for what his heart thinks his tongue speaks."—Shakespeare.

Faith in God's promises.—If we can put our trust in God when we are in total darkness, when may we not trust Him? Sometimes we are called upon to trust in God when He seems to go right back against all His promises. That is trusting Him in the darkness. Weak faith will judge God's promises by one's feelings, by one's evidences, when we ought to judge the feelings and the evidences by the promises. As long as I have the promises, God give me grace to trust in Him whatever befall and bid my soul keep still, knowing that He will never fail. —Marcus Rainsford.

CHAPTER THE TWENTY-EIGHTH.

This chapter tells how the prophet opposed Hananiah who falsely encouraged the hopes of the people, promising the return of the sacred vessels within two years, and the restoration of the exiles. (Driver.)

1—4. (1) **beginning,** or earlier half. Zedekiah reigned eleven years.[e] **of Gibeon,** a priestly city, Jos. xxi. 17. (2) **the Lord of hosts, the God of Israel.** "Either this solemn form of introduction was a usual one with all who claimed the prophetic gift, or Hananiah assumed it as implying an equal claim to inspiration with Jeremiah, in whose mouth we so constantly find the formula, e. g. vii. 3, 21, xvi. 9, xix. 3, 15, xxv. 27, xxvii. 4, 21, vs. 14 of the present chapter and often subsequently (xxix. 4, 8, 21, 25, etc.)."—Camb. Bib. **broken .. king,**[f] by this declaration Hananiah assures the people that they will be relieved of Babylonian dependence and bondage. (3) **two full years,** lit. "two years of days."[g] (4) **Jeconiah,** whom the people regarded as their rightful king.

[e] "The Jews often divided any period into two halves, the beginning and the end. So the fourth year would be in the beginning of Zedekiah's reign; and during the first three years the country was in a very disturbed state."—Fausset.

[f] Better render, "I have determined to break."

[g] "Hananiah prob. fixed this date by the expectation that the confederacy then on foot would defeat Nebuchadnezzar."—Spk. Com.

The hallucination of patriotic prophets.—The popular doctrine of the inviolable sancity of the Temple had sustained a severe shock when

Nebuchadnezzar carried off the sacred vessels to Babylon. It was inconceivable that Jehovah would patiently submit to so gross an indignity. In ancient days the Ark had plagued its Philistine captors till they were only too thankful to be rid of it. Later on a graphic narrative in the Book of Daniel told with what swift vengeance God punished Belshazzar for his profane use of these very vessels. So now patriotic prophets were convinced that the golden candlestick, the bowls and chargers of gold and silver, would soon return in triumph, like the Ark of old; and their return would be the symbol of the final deliverance of Judah from Babylon. Naturally the priests above all others would welcome such a prophecy, and would industriously disseminate it.—Exp. Bib.

5—9. (5) **said,** in answer to this utterly false prophecy. (6) **Amen,** or even so I could heartily wish **it might be.** (7) **Nevertheless,** i. e. spite of all your prophecies and my wishes, I must give you God's message. (8) **prophets .. pestilence,** Jer. here intimates that he does not stand alone. He only carries on former Divine denunciations.[a] (9) **when .. pass,** Jer. is satisfied to wait the testing of events. Comp. Deut. xviii. 22 and xiii. 1—3.

The reply to Hananiah's challenge.—It was almost a mark of the true prophet that he should be the herald of disaster. The prophetical books of the Old Testament Canon fully confirm this startling and unwelcome statement. Their main burden is the ruin and misery that await Israel and its neighbors. The presumption therefore was in favor of the prophet of evil, and against the prophet of good. Jeremiah does not, of course, deny that there had been, and might yet be, prophets of good. Indeed every prophet, he himself included, announced some Divine promise, but:—"The prophet which prophesieth of peace shall be known as truly sent of Jehovah when his prophecy is fulfilled." It seemed a fair reply to Hananiah's challenge. His prophecy of the return of the sacred vessels and the exiles within two years was intended to encourage Judah and its allies to persist in their revolt. They would be at once victorious, and recover all and more than all which they had lost. Under such circumstances Jeremiah's criterion of "prophecies of peace" was eminently practical.—Exp. Bib.

10—14. (10) **took .. yoke,**[b] ch. xxvii. 2. This was done as a sign that Hananiah regarded Jer.'s predictions as wholly false. He matched Jer.'s symbolic act by an answering symbolical act. (11) **all nations,** ch. xxvii. 7. **went his way,** not deigning any reply. (13) **shalt make,** "rather, 'but thou hast made,' the sense in which Hananiah is said to have made 'a yoke of iron' (we should render in the singular) comes out in vs. 14. The point is that there was a certain justification for Hananiah's violent act, but not that which he supposed. Jeremiah's wooden yoke was really an inadequate symbol; the prophet was too tender to his people. Thus God made the truth appear in still fuller brightness from the very perverseness of its enemy."—Pul. Com. (14) **yoke of iron,** impossible to break, and heavy to bear.[a]

Ignorance of the future.—None, indeed, can open the "seven-sealed book," or look forward over the dim and shadowy field stretching out illimitably before him. The astronomer discourses on the rate at which a sunbeam travels, and explains how the flashing lightning may be dispersed, and its terrible swoop evaded. He even indicates those spheres where storms never gather, and thunders never roll; but he cannot solve the anxious problems of our future, nor help us by his great wisdom to avoid its manifold evils, because they come unforewarned. Nor will the lives of those gone before avail us, seeing no two lives are marked by the same vicissitudes, or chequered by the same light and shades, the same joy and sorrow. In the eloquent words of a foreign divine, "We can become familiar with a landscape; we know where to find the waterfall, and the shady ledge where the violets grow in spring, and the sassafras gives forth its odors; but we can never become familiar with our life-landscape; we can never tell where we shall come upon the shady dell, or where the fountains will gush, and the birds sing. That **is with God."** **And His name be praised that it is so! for a definite**

[a] "Hananiah had given no warning as the need of repentance and conversion, but had foretold prosperity unconditionally." —Fausset.

"Wolsey regretted that he had not 'served God with half the zeal he had served his king,' but none has ever bewailed the zeal with which he followed Christ!" —Hom. Com.

[b] "Hananiah resorts to violence, tears the yoke fr. the Prophet's neck, and breaks it, prob. to the great delight of the multitude, who saw in this spirited act a symbol of deliverance." —Spk. Com.

[a] Je. xxvii. 6, 7.

Christ's yoke easy.—Queen Elizabeth carried the crown in the procession of her sister Mary at the coronation, and she remarked that it was very heavy; but someone standing by told her it would not be heavy when she had to wear it herself. So the precepts which some men do but carry in their hands seem very heavy, but when a man comes to know Christ and to love Him, those very precepts become light and easy.—Spurgeon.

prescience thereof would, in most instances, cloud the whole course of life, poison every stream of enjoyment, and render existence a curse of no ordinary magnitude.—E. Davies.

15—17. (15) **not sent thee,** Jer. had courage to make this distinct charge when he had received the new message from God. (16) **this year,** Hananiah actually died two months after uttering his false prophecy. **taught rebellion,** "the prophet who misleads his countrymen is to be put to death, because he has been disloyal to Israel's divine Redeemer, and in order that the evil which he secretly meditates may be checked in the bud."—Driver on Deut. xiii. 5. (17) **seventh month,** comp. fifth month of vs. 1. This fulfilment of Jer.'s word must have greatly strengthened his authority as God's Prophet.

"Men should strive to live well, not to live long."—Earl of Stirling.

"Then let us fill
This little interval, this pause of life,
With all the virtues we can crowd into it."
—Addison.

The great possibility of the new year.—I. Life is the greatest uncertainty in the world. 1. Thousands have died since the last New-Year's day; 2. Thousands of others will die before the next; 3. Youth no preventive; 4. Health no safeguard; 5. You may have to leave your schemes unfinished; 6. Your education may be only begun; 7. You may be unprepared; 8. You may delay preparation; 9. You may be unwilling to think about it. II. You may have strong hopes of the contrary. Should you die this year.—1. You will be for ever cut off from all the pleasures of life; 2. All your hopes will be disappointed; 3. You will be deprived for ever of the means of salvation.—Pres. Davies.

CHAPTER THE TWENTY-NINTH.

"This chapter contains the letter sent by Jeremiah to the exiles (who had been disquieted by prophets announcing their speedy return to Judah exhorting them to settle down contendly where they were."—Driver. 1—7. (1) **residue of the elders,** those of them who were still alive. (2) **After that,** etc., 2 Ki. xxiv. 12, etc. **queen,** or queen-mother. (3) **Zedekiah .. sent,** the object of this embassy is not indicated. (4) **all .. captives,** the letter was written soon after they were carried away, and was intended to console them. (5) **Build,** etc., i. e. settle quietly down, for the captivity will certainly be prolonged. (6) **increased there,** in numbers and wealth. (7) **seek the peace,** or be peaceable citizens in the land of sojourn, duly obeying the laws.[a]

[a] "It would have degraded their whole moral nature to have lived as conspirators, banded together against the country that was for the time their home, and cherishing feelings of hatred towards those with whom they were every day brought into contact." — Spk. Com.

"When we have learned to offer up every duty connected with our situation in life as a sacrifice to God a settled employment becomes just a settled habit of prayer."—Thos. Erskine.

"All true opinions are living, and show their life by being capable of nourishment; therefore of change. But their change is that of a tree, not of a cloud."—Ruskin.

"What is truth?" was once asked of a deaf and dumb boy. He moved his finger in a straight line. "What is false-

Prayer for one's own country.—John Knox used to be in such agony for the deliverance of his country that he could not sleep. He had a place in his garden where he used to go to pray. One night, he and several friends were praying together, and as they prayed Knox spoke declaring that deliverance had come. He explained that he could not tell what had happened, but he felt sure that in some way their prayers had been answered. And the next news informed them that their enemy, Mary Queen of Scotland, was dead.—At one time during the Lutheran reformation, soon after the conference of Augsburg in 1530, when the Reformer's cause looked mournful, Melancthon, with Luther and other divines, met to consult about the situation; and, after spending some time in prayer to God, Melancthon was suddenly called out of the room, from which he retired heavily depressed. While absent he saw several elders of the reformed churches with their parishioners and families; and many, young and old, were in prayer for the triumph of their cause. He re-entered the room with a joyous countenance, which astonished Luther, who inquired, "What now has happened to you, Philip, that you are become so cheerful?" "Oh, sirs," replied Melancthon, "let us not be discouraged, for I have seen our noble protectors, and such as, I will venture to say, will prove invincible against every foe." "And pray," returned Luther, thrilling with surprise and pleasure, "who and where are these powerful heroes?" "Oh," said Melancthon, "they are the wives of our parishioners and their little children, whose prayers I have just witnessed—prayers which I am satisfied our God will hear; for as our Heavenly Father and the Father of our Lord Jesus Christ has never despised our supplications, we have reason to trust that He will not in the present alarming crisis." The event proved that Melancthon was not mistaken. God heard their prayers.—Cox's "Life of Melancthon."

8—11. (8) **Let not your prophets and your diviners,** etc. It seems as if the Babylonian "Jewry" were a copy of that at home. It had not only its "princes" and its "elders," but its "prophets" and its "diviners," who encouraged the same false hopes as those in Judah (comp. ch. xxvii. 9; xxviii. 2.)."—Pul. Com. (9) **falsely,** or in a lie. (10) **after seventy years,** ch. xxvi. 11, 12. (11) **peace,** or good will. **expected end,** R. V. "hope in your latter end," i.e. a good hope for the issue.

Divine purposes fulfilled in answer to prayer (vss. 8—13).—I. A certain danger declared. II. A blessed deliverance promised. 1. The grounds on which it rested; 2. The time of their return expressly declared; 3. In their restoration the Divine faithfulness would be strikingly manifested; 4. The procuring cause of their deliverance was the boundless compassion of God. III. An important duty enjoined. 1. It is Divinely ordained; 2. The greatest encouragement is afforded for its observance; 3. To be successful it must be attended to in no formal manner.

12—14. (12) **call upon me,** this explains the change that is to take place. The people themselves will be changed. They will unite in prayer to their God. Da. ix. 3. (13) **seek,** etc., Le. xxvi. 39, 40; De. xxx. 1; Ps. xxxii. 6. (14) **be found,** etc., comp. De. iv. 29, 30, xxx. 1—5.

"When ye shall search for Me with all your heart."—To help you in getting your whole soul united in seeking God, ponder these considerations. 1. The priceless value of the soul; 2. The shortness and uncertainty of life; 3. The sadness and bitterness of sin; 4. Your utter helplessness in saving yourself; 5. The full and sufficient salvation provided in Jesus Christ. If your heart is wholly set upon the search for God, it will be manifested by such things as these:—(1) The immediate and resolute giving up of all sin; (2) The earnestness of your own personal decision for Christ; (3) The importunity with which you carry your cry for mercy and salvation to the throne of the heavenly grace. Let then your whole heart seek.—Hive.

Fervency in prayer.—We must be earnest and fervent, or shall have but a cold answer. He that asks with a doubting mind and wavering lazy desire, begs for nothing but to be denied. God gives His people what they ask, or better. We beg for removal of present sadness—but He gives that which makes us able to bear twenty sadnesses, a cheerful spirit, peaceful conscience, joy in God, the antepast of eternal rejoicings in His kingdom. Remember how great a God you go to, how great a need you have, how great a thing you pray for.—S. Thodey.

15—19. (15) **ye have said,** these denunciations are addressed to the false prophets. (16) **king that sitteth,** Zedekiah, who was not the actual king while Jeconiah lived. (17) **vile figs,** ch. xxiv. 8. (18) **persecute them,** ch. xxiv. 9, also xix. 8, xxv. 18. **removed,** R. V. "tossed to and fro." (19) **Because,** etc., ch. xxv. 4, xxxii. 33.

Note on verses 15, 16.—The sense appears to be this. One of the difficulties raised by the exiles when the prospect of seventy years' captivity was held out to them would be, We have prophets here at Babylon who tell us just the reverse of all this. Which shall we believe? To this the reply of Jeremiah is twofold. (i) These prophets' teaching shall soon be disproved. The king and the remnants of the kingdom, upon whose continued existence at Jerusalem they lay such stress, will soon pass away. Ye shall not soon be restored to your brethren, but they shall be exiles and scattered like to you. (ii) The false prophets, who thus delude you, shall themselves miserably perish and become a proverb and by-word.—Camb. B.

20—23. (21) **Ahab .. Zedekiah,** false prophets, not otherwise known, (22) **a curse,** i. e. a formula of cursing (comp. Isa. lxv. 15). There is here a play upon words, such as the Biblical writers delighted in, partly with the view of assisting the memory. "A curse" is in Hebrew kelalah, and "to roast" is kalah. **roasted in the fire,** "casting into the midst of a burning fiery furnace" was a common punishment both among the Assyrians and the Babylonians, comp. Dan. iii.—Pul. Com. (23)

hood?" He made a zigzag motion with his finger. Truth is the straight line, falsehood is the crooked way.

"The truth is infinite as the firmament above you. In childhood both seem near and measurable; but with years they grow and grow; and seem further off, and further, and grander, and deeper, and vaster, as God Himself; till you smile to remember how you thought you could touch the sky, and blush to recollect the proud and self-sufficient way in which you used to talk of knowing or preaching 'The Truth.'"—F. W. Robertson.

"The undying love of the Jews for their Fatherland, and their ineradicable desire to return to it, are displayed in an affecting manner on the day of atonement. The services close with the beseeching shout, 'when next year comes, may we all be in Jerusalem!' We could almost make this prayer our own as we think of the 'Jerusalem above.'"

"It may be a sin to long for death, but I am sure it is no sin to long for heaven."—Matthew Henry.

"Blessed are the home-sick, for they shall come at last to the Father's house."—Heinrich Stillings.

a "Burning alive was a mode of punishment customary among the Chaldæans."—Henderson.

villainy, folly, or lewdness.[b] **even I know,** R. V., "and I am he that knoweth."

[b] Is. xxxii. 6.

Believers are God's workmanship; and the end or all His works is to form one vast mirror in which to reflect His own image.

Tortures.—The Assyrian king Assurbanipal says, in one of his inscriptions concerning a viceroy of Babylon who had revolted, that Assur and the other gods "in the fierce burning fire they threw him and destroyed his life"—possibly through the agency of Assurbanipal's servants. One of the seven brethren who were tortured to death in the persecutions of Antiochus Epiphanes is said to have been "fried in the pan." Christian hagiology commemorates St. Lawrence and many other martyrs, who suffered similar torments. Such punishments remained part of criminal procedure until a comparatively recent date; they are still sometimes inflicted by lynch law, and have been defended even by Christian ministers.—Exp. Bib.

24—29. (24) **Shemaiah** is only known through this passage.[a] (25) **letters,** prob. one to the people, and a separate and private one to the priest. (26) **officers,** Heb. pâkids; having the overcharge of the Temple. Overseers to keep order. **mad,** etc., intimating that Jeremiah was in such a state. (27) **reproved,** exerted your authority in silencing. (28) **is long,** this was the brunt of Jer.'s offending. The false prophets declared there would be a speedy return. Jer. said No, not for many long years. (29) **read this letter,** whether in a kindly spirit, or to annoy the Prophet, does not appear.

[a] "This was addressed to Shemaiah after the messengers who delivered the former message to the captives in Babylon were returned home, and they brought the letter of Shemaiah mentioned in the following verse."—Lowth.

Note on verses 24—29.—On the arrival at Babylon of Jeremiah's letter, which ends with vs. 23, there is much indignation on the part of the false prophets, and one of them, Shemaiah by name, writes to Zephaniah the acting high-priest, urging upon him that he should take severe measures to silence Jeremiah as a madman. This suggestion however Zephaniah is so far from following that he shews the letter to the prophet, who writes again to Babylon, this time for the purpose of condemning Shemaiah's conduct.—Camb. B.

30—32 (31) **trust .. lie,** in an utterly false representation. (32) **thus saith the Lord,** "these and the following words come at length as the part of the sentence answering to 'because thou hast sent,' etc. of vs. 25. The intervening break has resulted from the long explanation and detail which was necessary. The punishment to be inflicted on Shemaiah was twofold. First, he was to leave no children behind him, and secondly, he should see no good come upon his people, either in the way of the speedy return which he had been promising them, or in the way of peace and comparative prosperity in exile."—Camb. B.[b] **taught rebellion,** ch. xxviii. 16.

[b] "As he despised the lawful time, and wished to return before the time God had expressly announced, in just retribution he should not share in the restoration from Babylon at all."—Fausset.

You are sure to do all things spiritually, if you live in the spirit of sonship.

Deceiving the heart.—It is a lamentable fact that, without any hireling shepherd to cry "Peace," men will cry that for themselves. They need not the syren song to entice them to the rocks of presumption and rash confidence. There is a tendency in their own hearts to put sweet for bitter,—to think well of their evil estate and foster themselves in proud conceit. Let men alone, let no deluder seek to deceive them, hush for ever every false and tempting voice, they will themselves, impelled by their own pride, run to an evil conceit, and make themselves at ease, though God Himself is in arms against them. To be tormented on account of sin is the path to peace, and happy shall I be if I can hurl a firebrand into your hearts.—Spurgeon.

CHAPTER THE THIRTIETH.

This chapter and the next have been called "the triumphal hymn of Israel's salvation." **1—3.** (1) **word,** etc., different in tone to the preceding "words."[a] This prophecy chiefly concerns the restoration of the exiles. (2) **in a book,** "according to the present context the 'all,' in this case, refers merely to the following four chapters. These prophecies of restoration would be specially precious to the exiles; and now that the Jews were scattered through many distant lands, they could only be transmitted and preserved in writing."—Exp. Bib. (3) **Israel and Judah,** note that both sections of the people of Israel are included

[a] "The joyful transition is marked by a sudden change from grave and mournful accents in solemn prose, to a jubilant outburst of poetic ecstasy."—Wordsworth.

in the promises of restoration.[b] In ch. xxxi. distinct messages are given, first to the ten tribes, then to Judah.

The effect of mercy.—A soldier in the —th regiment, a fine, gallant fellow, heard of the severe sickness of his wife. He applied for leave of absence, but was refused. The officers of his regiment then made a new application in his behalf, which was again refused. He left the army; but before he got away, was retaken and brought in as a deserter. He was tried, found guilty, and summoned before the commanding officer to receive his sentence. He entered the tent—a fine, tall, soldierly-looking man—saluted, and stood perfectly unmoved, while the officer read his fearful doom—"To be shot to death with musketry on the next Friday." Not a muscle of his face twitched, not a limb quivered. "I deserve it, sir," he replied, respectfully; "I deserted from my flag. Is that all, sir?" "No," replied the officer; "I have something else for you;" and taking another paper, he read aloud the doomed man's pardon. The undaunted spirit, whom severity had failed to move, was completely broken down by clemency. He dropped to the ground shaking, sobbing, and overcome; and being restored to his regiment, proved himself grateful for the mercy shown him, and was soon promoted for good conduct. There are many who say, "We are not going to be frightened into religion," and who profess to be too brave to fear God's wrath. But will you withstand the proffers of His grace ? If you shrink not from the curse of the law, will you not hear the tender entreaty of the Cross? Ah! if, like the deserter, you really heard the sentence ringing in your ears; if, like him, you really felt that you deserved it; if you knew that the execution of it was near at hand, like him you would be broken down by the voice of Jesus saying, "Thy sins are forgiven thee;" gladly would you welcome the gracious pardon. Shut not your ears to that compassionate voice. Throw yourself at Jesus' feet, take the forgiveness He freely offers, and let your life henceforth show that His grace has not been bestowed in vain.—American Messenger.

[b] Je. iii. 18; Eze. xxxvii. 6, 21, 22; Ho. i. 11.

"Have we ever thought of those 'hands stretched forth' from heaven to this world, draining themselves of love, if it were possible, toward 'disobedient and gainsaying people?' Is not this wonderful—wonderful? Men have to run away from the love of God if they are ever without it. They must get somewhere—I know not where; some strange call of their own invention must be found by men who would escape the love of God; for God's hands are stretched out, and they drip with riches of mercy."—H. W. Webb-Peploe.

4—9. (5) **voice of trembling,** "rather, a sound of trembling, a sound causing men to tremble; doubtless it is "the sound of the trumpet, the alarm of war" (ch. iv. 19).—Cheyne. They feared the approach of Cyrus, who nevertheless was to be their deliverer. (6) **a man,** or "a male." The men seemed as full of trouble as women in the time of childbirth.[a] (7) **that day,** the day when Babylon is captured. (8) **break his yoke,** i. e. the yoke of Babylon. **serve themselves,** exact forced labor. (9) **David their king,** viz. the righteous Branch of ch. xxiii. 5, 6.

Trials.—It sometimes seems hard to find out any reason for God's dealings with his children. We may not be able to find out why we are afflicted and may think that perhaps it is because of some undiscovered sin; but I do not think that God often deals with us in that way. He generally likes to let His people know their faults when He chastises them. You remember how when Absalom could not get Joab to come and talk with him, he burned up his corn-fields and then Joab came. Now, the Lord often sends sore afflictions upon his children in order that they may come and talk with Him more. You remember that Christ took away Lazarus in order that the sisters might send for Him and that the people through all ages might get a wondrous discovery of Him as the resurrection and the life. And you remember too how John the Baptist was taken away from his disciples in order that they might rather go to Christ.—Andrew A. Bonar.

[a] Je. iv. 31, vi. 24; Nah. ii. 10.

"The fullest reference of this term must be to Messiah, in whom all the promises made to David were to be fulfilled."

Is. lv. 3, 4; Eze. xxxiv. 23, xxxvii. 24; Ho. iii. 5.

"People are always expecting to get peace in Heaven: but you know whatever peace they get there will be ready-made. Whatever, of making peace they can be blest for, must be on the earth here."—Ruskin.

10—13. (10) **fear .. not,** comp. Is. xli. 13, xliii. 5, xliv. 2. **my servant,** vss. 10, 11 are especially noticeable: the title of honor "my servant" here given to Israel for the first time (and applied to the actual nation), appears to have formed the basis upon which the second Isaiah constructs his great conception of Jehovah's ideal servant.—Driver. **from afar,** even "from the most distant provinces of the Chaldæan empire." (11) **full end,** ch. iv. 27, v. 18. **correct .. measure** ch. x. 23, 24. (12) **bruise,** etc., ch. xvii. 9. Only to be cured by such extreme afflictions and chastisements. **wound is grievous,** ch. x. 19, xiv. 17, xv. 18. (13)

bound up, or "for the pressing together of thy wound." None can help or heal.[a]

God's gracious designs towards His chosen people (vss. 10, 11.)—Observe then—I. That God has glorious things in reserve for His chosen people. 1. For the Jewish people; 2. For His people afar off among the nations. II. That even His darkest dispensations towards them are intended for their good. 1. This was, and still is, the case with respect to the Jews; 2. And may we not see the hand of God ordering and overruling everything for our good? III. That His presence with them is their never-failing security. Exhort—(1) Those who are afar off; (2) Those who are visited with any great affliction; (3) Those who are under discouragement of any kind.—C. Simeon.

14—17. (14) **lovers,** i. e. the nations which sought the alliance of Judah, esp. Assyria and Egypt. **seek thee not,** to show any concern for thy distress. **of a cruel one,** i. e. with a severity which looks like cruelty.[b] (15) **criest thou,** pleading as if I had dealt unjustly with thee. ch. xv. 18.[c] **sorrow,** or bodily pain. (16) **be devoured,** God would raise up Cyrus against them. (17) **restore health,** since even the incurable Gōd can cure. **Outcast,** or "one put away and rejected."

The Restorer of mankind (vs. 17).—How deep are the wants which our faith supplies, and how wide is the feeling of the beauty and the power of the remedy. 1. Faith in the Christian sacrifice and its attendant revelation of the Divine character alone answer the demands of the heart and reason of man for a higher state of moral perfection; 2. Christianity offers to maintain a communication between this world and that eternal world of holiness and truth; 3. Faith confirms and directs that principle of hope which even in our daily life we are perpetually forced to substitute for happiness; 4. But above all its recommendations to the wants and solicitudes of man, the Gospel commends itself by the adorable object which it presents to our affection.—Archer Butler.

18—22. (18) **Jacob's tents,** ch. iv. 20. The term "tent" is perhaps used to indicate the temporary character of their dwellings in Chaldæa. **own heap,** "meaning, not heap of ruins, but the hill on which she had previously stood, on her old site. A 'hill' was the usual position of the eastern cities (Matt. v. 14), as helping to protect them alike from sudden attack and from inundation. Hence the frequency with which the word Tel (which is the Heb. here translated heap) forms part of the name of a city; Telassar (Thelassar) (2 Kings xix. 12; Is. xxxvii. 12); Ten-Haresha=Tel-Harsa and Tel-Melah (Ezra ii. 59; Neh. vii. 61); Tel-Abib (Ezek. iii. 15)."—Camb. Bib.[a] **palace .. remain,** or "each palace shall be inhabited suitably. (19) **thanksgiving,** such would be becoming to the restored and redeemed people. **not small,** or not lightly esteemed. (20) **aforetime,** as in the prosperous days of David. (21) **of themselves,** the governors shall be natives, not foreigners. Reference is to Zerubbabel, a prince of the house of David. **draw near,** as a specially favored one.[b] **engaged his heart,** R. V. "hath had boldness." "None but the priests were permitted to enter the Lord's presence, and the Holy of Holies was open but once a year to the high-priest himself. To all others this was a profanity to be punished with death. For Messiah as being God the Son the approach to the Father was open. This is the thought concealed in the verse till Christian times should bring it to light. Even to Jewish ears however the expressions betokened the Messiah."—Camb. Bib. (22) **my people,** ch. xxiv. 7.

Encouragement to seek after God (vs. 21).—From this passage I shall call your attention to the following propositions:—1. That it is man's grand privilege that he can approach unto God; 2. That he has from Scripture a special warrant to draw near to God; 3. That God engages for the success of that man who thus seeks to approach unto Him.—R. Cecil.

A restoration to lost rights and possessions.—The city is to be built again "upon her own mound." The people not only find the vines they grow in Chaldæa fruitful; they are restored to their own land. The prodigal would not have been satisfied if his comrades had helped him to

[a] "So desperate were the circumstances of the Jews in Babylon, while enduring the punishment God had inflicted upon them for their crimes, that no human interposition which they could rationally expect, could avail for their deliverance."—Henderson.

[b] "God condescends to employ language adapted to human conceptions."—Fausset.

[c] "The fault is in thyself, not in Me; and the remedy is in thine own hands. Turn to Me by repentance, and thou shalt be healed."—Wordsworth.

"The sick body needs health, not wealth; and the sick soul needs healing before all external changes of condition." — Pul. Com.

[a] "Generally there was a castle or citadel in the middle of the ancient cities, upon a rising ground, for the greater strength and security of the place."—Lowth.

[b] "It is not only foretold that a native governor should be set over the house of Israel, but that he should be distinguished for his piety."—Rob. Hall.

One of my parishioners at East Hampton, converted after having lived through three or four revivals, to the age of fifty, and having given up hope, used to exclaim for several weeks after his change, "Is it I? Am I the same man who used to think it so hard to be converted, and my case so hopeless? Is it I?

affluence and pleasure again; he must return to the old home. There is something imperfect in the return of prosperity to Job in the fact that though he has greater riches and as many sons and daughters as before his calamities, his dead children are not raised from the grave, and the loss of them cannot be really compensated by the gift of a new family. So is it with earthly losses. The greatest are irretrievable. But the glory of God's ultimate salvation is that it restores old lost blessings as well as gives new blessings, both comforting memory and satisfying hope.—Pul. Com.

23, 24. "Vss. 23, 24, are apparently a gloss, added as a suitable illustration of this chapter, from xxiii. 19, 20, which are almost identical with these two verses."—Exp. Bib. (23) **whirlwind,** etc., 2 Ki. ii. 1; comp. Je. xxiii. 19, 20. **continuing,** R. V. "a sweeping tempest: it shall burst upon the head," etc. (24) **latter days,** first referring to the restoration times and then to the times of Messiah. **consider,** R. V. "understand."

Consideration.—There is much in a heart-searching retrospect, over the earliest and most innocent period of life, to awaken compunction and regret; but if the wholesome check, which the habit of considering the latter end imposes, be not found in good time, the blackening horror of the later and more advanced period makes that early time seem bright in the comparison, and gives birth to feelings which have found expression in such words as these—

"Lost days of youth! Oh, holy days,
When joy was blest with prayer and praise—
When this sad heart, now deeply dyed
With many a thought unsanctified,
Trembled at every venial stain,
And shrunk from sin as now from pain.

Oh, not that even in that hour
Of early reason's dawning power,
My soul was pure from thoughts of sin;
But now so dark the past has been,
That those first stains from young offence
Bear the bright hue of innocence." —Kitto.

The past.—Think of it! the past is not only focussed there, in a man's soul: it is there. All things that he has ever seen, known, felt, believed, of the surrounding world are now within him, have become part of him, in part are him; he has been changed into their image. He may deny it, he may resent it, but they are there. They do not adhere to him, they are transfused through him. He cannot alter or rub them out. They are not in his memory: they are in him. His soul is as they have filled it, made it, left it.—Drummond.

Is it I? Oh, wonderful!"—Lyman Beecher.

"The God of nature alone, can revive the flower the mind has withered."—Mme. De. Stael.

"We should echo in our thankfulness the first intimation that God gives in His providence of an approaching mercy. If you do but hear when the king is on his road towards your town, you raise your bells to ring him in, and stay not till he be entered the gates. Thus should we strike up our harps in praising God at the first appearance of a mercy."—Gurnall.

"Never yet were the feelings and instincts of our nature violated with impunity; never yet was the voice of conscience silenced without retribution." — Mrs. Jameson.

"The object of punishment is, prevention from evil; it never can be made impulsive to good."—Mann.

CHAPTER THE THIRTY-FIRST.

1—5. (1) **same time,** i. e. in the latter days mentioned **ch. xxx. 24. be the God,** be manifestly their God through My intervention on their behalf: ch. xxx. 22. **all the families of Israel,** the twelve tribes. Afterwards the Northern kingdom is dealt with (2—22), then the Southern (23—26), and then again both together (27—40). (2) **left of the sword,** referring either to the ancient deliverance from Egypt, or figuratively to the restoration from Babylon.[a] **went .. rest,** or planned to guide him to the rest of Canaan. (3) **of old,** marg. from afar.[b] The Church of the faithful Israel is the speaker. "From afar" (so we ought to render, rather than "of old") she sees Jehovah, with the eye of faith, approaching to redeem her; comp. Isa. xl. 10 and lix. 20 (only that in these passages it is to Jerusalem, and not to Babylon, that Jehovah "comes" as the Redeemer); also the promise in ch. xxx. 10, "I will save thee from afar," and ch. li. 50.—Pul. Com. **drawn thee,** better: "I have prolonged loving-kindness to thee." comp. Ps. xxxvi.

[a] "The Babylonish captivity may fitly be spoken of figuratively as a wilderness state." — Henderson.

[b] "Israel gratefully acknowledges in reply God's past grace; but at the same time tacitly implies by the expression of old, that God does not appear to her now."—Fausset.

"Bredren," said the old preacher, "whatever de good God tell me to do in dis blessed Book"—holding up an old and evidently much-read Bible—"dat I'se gwine to do. If I see in it dat I mus' jump troo a stone wall, I'm gwine to jump at it. Goin' troo it 'longs to God to 'tend to; but jumpin' at it 'longs to me, my bredren!"

"In Greenland, when a stranger knocks at the door, he asks, 'Is God in this house?' And if they answer 'Yes,' he enters."

10. (4) **tabrets,** alluding to Ex. xv. 20. (5) **and shall eat,** etc., R. V. "and shall enjoy the fruit thereof."

Everlasting Love.—A father, whose affluence was considerable, mourned over a reckless son, whose misconduct brought shame upon himself and family. From home the prodigal went into another country, and for years he was lost to his relatives. A chance occurring, he sent by a friend this message, should he meet his boy, "Your father loves you still." The bearer sought him long and in vain. At last he saw him enter a house of vice, and called him; and there, at a late hour of evening, he delivered this message. The dissolute gambler's heart was touched. The thought that his father still loved him, and wished to forgive him, broke the spell of Satan. He abandoned his profligacy and returned to his father. Oh! the power of such a message of inalienable love from God! Not as the world loves doth God love. They love today and hate tomorrow, wearing their friends like flowers, which we may behold in their bosoms whilst they are fresh and sweet, but soon they wither and then are laid aside. Whereas the love of God to His people is everlasting, and He wears them as a signet upon His right hand, which He will never part with.—White.

Could we with ink the ocean fill,
  Were the whole world of parchment made,
Were every single grass a quill,
  And every man a scribe by trade:
    To write the love
    Of God above
Would drain the ocean dry,
    Nor could the scroll
    Contain the whole,
Though stretched from earth to sky.

6—9. (6) **watchmen,** "these were placed on heights at the time of the new moon to give first notice of its appearance." **up to Zion,** both sections of the nation, Israel and Judah, uniting in the sacred festivals.[a] (7) **among,** or because of the restoration of Israel, regarded as the chief of the nations.[b] (8) **north country,** the Chaldæan districts to which Israel had been carried: ch. iii. 12, 18. **coasts,** R. V., "uttermost parts of," ch. xxv. 32. **thither,** to Palestine. (9) **weeping,** that of gladness, not of sorrow. **supplications,** indicating a right spirit of dependence on God. **walk .. rivers,** indicating full supply during their desert journey. **Ephraim .. firstborn,** these words may merely express the choice of Israel as against all other nations of the world. It is also, however, very possible that Ephraim may here mean the Northern kingdom (of which this was the principal tribe), and then the sense will be, Although its punishment came earlier than that of the Southern kingdom, yet if it repent, it shall be forgiven first.—Camb. Bib. 1 Chr. v. 1, 2.[c]

"Weeping and supplication." The return from Babylon was a season of joy and congratulation, yet productive of mixed feeling—they came with weeping and supplication. Great events in life often produce opposite emotions. The moment of transition is a critical one—calls up many recollections of the past, many anticipations of the future. The prisoner has been known to sigh at leaving his dungeon; the bride trembles at the altar; the prince receives the crown not without emotion; the Christian takes upon him the vows of God under mingled impressions. Tears and prayers do well together.

10—14. (10) **nations,** the pagan nations. **isles,** as before, the coast-lands of the Mediterranean.[d] (12) **flow,** "i. e. the Ephraimites, after praising God on the holy hill, shall spread themselves over their own territory like an overflowing stream, and enjoy the 'goodness' or good gifts of Jehovah—the corn, the wine, the oil, etc. (comp. Deut. viii. 8."—Pul. Com.[e] **watered garden,** fresh and growing, Is. lviii. 11. (13) **into joy,** at being settled in their own land and under God's blessings. (14) **satiate,** i. e. fully satisfy. **fatness,** through the great abundance of the thank-offerings.[f]

a "The schism of Jeroboam shall be healed in the captivity."—Wordsworth.

b De. xxvi. 19.

c "The house of Joseph is thus to be restored to its old pre-eminence."—Spk. Com.

Nature is true to itself, and so is grace; the ox is not better known by its lowing, nor a lion by its roar, than a Christian by his holy life.

"A saint's tears are better than a sinner's triumphs. Bernard saith, 'The tears of penitents are the wine of angels.'"—Secker.

d "The Jews call all countries islands wh. they go to by sea."—Lowth.

e "In Jerusalem they would be occupied with religious duties, but after these are rendered to God, they are to disperse each to his own fields."—Spk. Com.

f 1 Sa. ii. 28.

God's goodness satisfying (vs. 14).—I. The objects of His Divine complacency,—"My people." II. The measure of their joy.—"shall be satisfied." III. The source of their delight,—"My goodness."

15—17. (15) **voice .. Ramah,**[g] "this is a poetical figure, representing the miserable condition of the kingdom of Ephraim devastated by the sword of the Assyrians. Ramah is in Benjamin, two hours' journey from Jerusalem."[h] **Rachel,** as mother of Benjamin, Ephraim, and Manasseh, she stands as mother of the ten tribes.[i] (16) **rewarded,** the reward of mothers is for their children to grow up, and dwell in the land. (17) **in thine end,** ch. xxix. 11, R. V., "for thy latter end."

The captive Jews (vss. 15, 16).—Briefly allude to circumstances under which the words of text were spoken: while Ezekiel was prophesying to captive Israel in Chaldæa, Jeremiah was prophesying in Israel; the former preparing the captives for their return, the latter encouraging the remnant to expect that event. Consider—I. The place they had left. The promised land. For their sins God had permitted their captivity. You are now surrounded by good influences. If thoughtless, God may permit the loss to you of much that is good. Those who see this will grieve. II. The place they had gone to. Chaldæa, land of idolatry. Left home, friends, liberty; and worst of all, means of grace, comfort, instruction. You may wander to the far country (prodigal), and sigh for lost good. III. The hope of their return. By whom entertained. Old friends, teachers, etc. How brought about. Spirit of God awakening desire. Memory recalling the past. Providence preparing the way, Mercy calling.—Hive.

Historical types of future events.—It is worthy of note that in the New Testament some words are quoted from the Prophets which contain no prediction at all, and are yet spoken of as being fulfilled, because the event to which they allude was a type of that to which they are applied. Our Lord, and after Him the Apostles, laid down the principle that past history may represent that which is to happen hereafter. Thus the Saviour refers to the brazen serpent, and to Jonah as prefiguring His resurrection, and even the time of it on the third day. If Paul teaches that Hagar and Ishmael are typical of the covenants; the paschal lamb of Christ's atoning death; the passage of the Red Sea of baptism; the smitten rock of Christ; the author of the Epistle to the Hebrews, St. Peter in his allusion to the deluge, and St. John in his mystical application of the names Sodom, Egypt, and Babylon, confirm the principle which helps us to interpret passages of the Old Testament, such as those where the Messiah is called David, and to understand passages of the New Testament where what was spoken of David is applied to our Lord. The principle also solves the apparent difficulty of the two passages cited above,—a difficulty strongly insisted upon by the enemies of Christianity. In neither case does St. Matthew quote predictions, but Hosea's and Jeremiah's references to past history. When Hosea said, "Out of Egypt have I called My Son," or when Jeremiah spoke of Rachel weeping for her children, neither was uttering a prediction of the future, but alluding to facts long past. Hosea was alluding to the Exodus eight centuries before, and Jeremiah to the carrying away of the ten tribes one hundred years before he wrote. St. Matthew, therefore, speaks of them as being fulfilled in the only way in which facts can be fulfilled, in events the antitypes of those referred to.—A. McCaul.

18—21. (18) **bemoaning,** in a penitent and humble frame of mind. **bullock,** etc., lit. "like an untaught calf," Ho. x. 11.[a] (19) **turned,** by God's dispensations of chastisement. **instructed,** or brought to my senses by my suffering.[b] **smote .. thigh,** the natural expression of one who is suddenly struck with a thought or a conviction. **reproach .. youth,** burden of the memory of youthful sins.[c] (20) **since I spake,** R. V., "as often as I speak." God is represented as the speaker. He asks Himself whether Ephraim is still beloved by Him. The answer is contained in the words that follow. As often as He makes mention of him, His affection towards him is stirred. The picture is of course adapted to human modes of thought and feeling, and represents God as acting in the same way in which a man would, when thinking upon the ingratitude and rebellion of

[g] Mat. ii. 18.

[h] "By a beautiful figure, Rachel, the mother of the Ephraimites, who was buried at this place, is personified, and represented as risen from her grave, and bitterly lamenting the absence of her descendants, who had all been carried into exile."—Henderson.

[i] "The immediate reference of the allusion is to the assemblage at Ramah of Benjamin, by the captain of the Chaldæan guard, of the unfortunate captives whom he was carrying away from their country to Babylon."—W. H. Mill.

"A crowd is not company, and faces are but a gallery of pictures, where there is no love."—Bacon.

"When we would convince men of an error by the strength of truth, let us withal pour the sweet balm of love upon their heads. Truth and love are two of the most powerful things in the world; and when they both go together they cannot easily be withstood."—Cudworth.

[a] "Ephraim acknowledged that he had been chastised rightly, and for his good, bec., like an untrained steer, he had resisted Jehovah's will."—Spk. Com.

[b] "Chastisements are effects of displeasure, but not of a displeasure intended for the destruction of its object, but the amendment."—Rob. Hal.

[c] "The burden of punishment and shame due to the sins of my youth, my former

estate, ever since the exodus from Egypt."—Wordsworth.

"Much may be enjoyed now. Larger faith would open at once more abundant stores. God's hand is not shortened. It is we who limit our own enjoyment of his grace by unbelief and sinfulness. Still there can be no perfect satisfaction in this imperfect world." — Pul. Com.

Seeking satisfaction in this world is like trying to quench the thirst by drinking the salt waters of the sea. The more we drink, the thirstier we are. Alexander conquered the world, but it did not satisfy his soul; and if he could have conquered all the worlds that stud the heavens, he would still have wept for more. For God has not created a single human soul so small and poor that all the material universe can fill it. All literature is full of expressions of the failure of worldly things to satisfy the soul.—Peloubet's Notes.

"The Christian Fathers see a reference in this passage to the Virgin Mary."

"We look before
and after,
And pine for
what is not;
Our sincerest
laughter
With some pain
is fraught;
Our sweetest
songs are those
that tell of saddest thought."
—Shelley.

"There are three parts in truth: first, the inquiry, which is the wooing of it; secondly, the knowledge of it, which is the presence of it; and

a son, whom he nevertheless cannot but continue to love."—Camb. Bib. (21) **waymarks,** to mark the way back to Palestine.

The true penitent (vss. 18, 19).—We have here—I. The picture of a true penitent. 1. His position is solitary; 2. His language that of self-reproach; 3. He refers his state entirely to God; 4. He at length ventures on the filial relationship. II. The process of his restoration. 1. It was by affliction; 2. Instruction; 3. Conviction; 4. Humiliation. Apply:—(1) Consider afflictions as preparatives for conversion; (2) Consider them subsequently to conversion as preventives, restoratives, preparatives.

The yoke.—The simile is a most apt one. I had frequent opportunities of witnessing the conduct of oxen when, for the first time, put into the yoke to assist in dragging the wagons. On observing an ox that had been in the yoke for seven or eight hundred miles beginning to get weak, or his hoofs to be worn down to the quick, by treading on the sharp gravel, a fresh ox was put into the yoke in his place. When the selection fell on an ox I had received as a present from some African king, of course one completely unaccustomed to the yoke, such generally made a strenuous struggle for liberty,—repeatedly breaking the yoke, and attempting to make its escape. At other times such bullocks lay down upon their sides or backs, and remained so in defiance of the Hottentots, though two or three of them would be lashing them with their ponderous whips. Sometimes, from pity to the animal, I would interfere, and beg them to be less cruel. "Cruel!" they would say, "it is mercy, for if we do not conquer him now, he will require to be so beaten all his life." Some oxen would seem convinced of the folly of opposing the will of the Hottentots by the end of the first day; some about the middle of the second; while some would continue the struggle to the third; after which they would go on as willingly and quietly as any of their neighbor oxen. They seemed convinced that their resisting was fruitless as kicking against the pricks, or sharp-pointed iron, which they could not injure, but that every kick they gave only injured themselves.—Campbell. Yoke of Christ.—Did you ever stop to ask, what a yoke is really for? Is it to be a burden to the animal which wears it? It is just the opposite. It is to make its burden light. Attached to the oxen in any other way than by a yoke the plow would be intolerable. Worked by means of a yoke it is light. A yoke is not an instrument of torture; it is an instrument of mercy. It is not a malicious contrivance for making work hard: it is a gentle device to make hard labor light. It is not meant to give pain, but to save pain. And yet men speak of the yoke of Christ as if it were a slavery, and look upon those who wear it as objects of compassion.—Drummond.

22—26. (22) **daughter,** Israel. **compass,** there is no satisfactory interpretation of this verse. "The meaning of the concluding enigma is as profound a mystery as the fate of the lost tribes, and the solutions rather more unsatisfactory. An explanation often given is that, in the profound peace of the New Dispensation, the women will protect the men."—Exp. Bib.[a] (23) **As yet,** R. V., "Yet again." The old form of blessing shall be renewed. (24) **go forth with flocks,** i. e. the scattered peoples of the land, who live by shepherding. (25) **satiated,** fully satisfied. (26) **I awaked,** i. e. the Prophet, who had seen all this joy and prosperity of the restoration time in his dream or vision.

Waymarks in the East.—Dr. Bonar, writing of his journey through the Wilderness near the spot of Israel's first encampment, says, "We rode off about nine, through a fine large plain; but quite a plain of the desert, —no stream, no verdure; at first soft sand, then hard gravel, then stones, and all these generally of a white colour. Ras Atâkah towered upon our right, full in the morning sunshine. No trace of a road appeared, for though the camels do form a track, or rather a number of parallel tracks, yet the drifting sand obliterates them, or washes them out. Still the waymarks are visible everywhere.—consisting of small heaps of stones set up on each side, which are carefully preserved by the Bedouin; for even they might at times be at a loss as to the way so great is the sameness of the region for miles on every hand. Jeremiah's words came into mind, 'Set thee up waymarks; make thee high heaps, set thine heart toward the highway, even the way which thou wentest' (chap. xxxi. 21). The sand does not seem to obliterate these, or, if it does, they are renewed from time to time. They were always a welcome sight to us, assuring us that we were in the right track; for at times we began to ask whether even our Arabs were sure of their way; so waste did the desert appear, without a mark or foot-trace of any kind whatsoever."—Days and Nights in the East.

27—30. (27) **sow .. beast,** fig. to represent the swift and abundant increase of the population.[c] (28) **watched,** for the right opportunity for punishing them. **watch .. build,** using similar care and vigilance in restoring them. (29) **fathers,** etc.,[a] see Eze. xviii. 2. (30) **own iniquity,**[b] "with the fall of Jerusalem, a chapter in the history of Israel was concluded for ever; Jehovah blotted out the damning record of the past, and turned over a new leaf in the annals of His people. The account between Jehovah and the Israel of the monarchy was finally closed, and no penal balance was carried over to stand against the restored community." —Exp. Bib.

The bane of humanity is bad heredity. We cannot get rid of it. "The fathers have eaten sour grapes, and the children's teeth are set on edge," say the Scriptures. The fathers have drunk the cup of sinful pleasures and the children have drunk the dregs. The wondrous thing of the Gospel is that it gives us a new heredity. I count that the very highest and sublimest statement of the doctrine of regeneration. A man grafting trees saws off a limb to put in a scion. If the limb is rotten he has to saw it off nearer to the trunk. We were grafted in Adam, but it was discovered that the branch was rotten, and then God began at the very beginning and grafted us into Jesus Christ the Divine Son of God. Dr. Williams of Boston was asked, "How early do you think the training of a child ought to begin?" He replied instantly, "a hundred years before the birth of a child." When God would build up a child holy in all things, He goes back to the very beginning and gives us our birth in God, Himself. As from Adam we had this hereditary tendency to do wrong, so when we are grafted into Jesus Christ and given the eternal life, we have that influence impelling us to holiness.—A. J. Gordon.

31—34. (31) **new covenant,** He. viii. 8—12. (32) **an husband,** ever dealing with them compassionately and tenderly. (33) **inward parts,** giving them right principles, and a right disposition, so that obedience shall become easy to them. **their God,** ch. xxxii. 38. (34) **teach no more,** "the sense is not that there shall be no longer any need of instruction in religion, but that there shall be a directness of access to God, both for Jew and Gentile, which did not exist under the old covenant.—Camb. Bib.

Note on vss. 31—34.—We have here the announcement of a new covenant which should supersede that made at the time of the Exodus from Egypt, differing from it (i) in permanence, (ii) in the principle by which it should be maintained unbroken. The Mosaic Law consisted of duties imposed upon the people from without; the spring of action which should produce willing conformity to the new covenant was to be wholly within. Moses indeed (Deut. xxx. 6) speaks of the people's hearts being circumcized to love the Lord with all their heart and soul, but now the motive power that belongs to the new dispensation is for the first time made plain. The sense of forgiveness (vs. 34) through God's grace shall call out such a spirit of gratitude as shall ensure a willing service, depending on inward not outward motives, based on love, not fear. The new covenant therefore is at once to replace the old (see Heb. viii. 8—12), and yet, new in form, to be still the same in substance. "I will be their God, and they shall be my people," was the central object of the old (Exod. xxix. 45; Lev. xxvi. 12), even as it is now of the new.—Camb. B.

35—37. (35) **divideth,** R. V., "stirreth up," comp. ch. xxxiii. 20; Ps. lxxxix. 36, 37. (36) **those ordinances,** such as of the sun, moon, sea, etc. God's purpose concerning His people is as unchangeable as the laws of nature are. (37) **thus saith the Lord,** "it is not without meaning that the prophet so frequently repeats: 'Thus saith the Lord.' This formed the Alpha and Omega; his word was the sole ground of hope for Israel.

thirdly, the belief, which is the enjoyment of it."—Bacon.

[c] Eze. xxxvi. 8—11; Ho. ii. 23.

[a] "The proverb among the exiles' children born in Babylon, to express that they suffered the evil consequences of their fathers' sins, rather than of their own."—Fausset.

[b] Ga. vi. 5, 7.

"After all, the most natural beauty in the world is honesty and moral truth; for all beauty is truth. True features make the beauty of a face, and true proportions the beauty of architecture, as true measures that of harmony and music. In poetry, which is all fable, truth still is the perfection."—Shaftesbury.

"The difference between the regenerate and unregenerate man is that the unregenerate man lives in sin and he loves it; but the regenerate man lapses into sin, and he loathes it."—A. J. Gordon.

The Jewish rabbis repeat a tradition that David had a harp suspended at the head of his bed, and that, whenever the north wind blew upon it at night, it yielded the most agreeable music. The severest blasts which God sends upon the good man only awaken in his soul the harmony of sanctified emotions.

It is impossible to walk across so much as a rood of the natural earth, with mind unagitated and rightly poised, without receiving strength from some stone, flower, leaf, or sound, nor without a sense as of a dew falling on you out of the sky.—Samuel Johnson.

There is dew in one flower and not in another, bec. one opens itself and takes the moisture in, while the other closes itself and the drop runs off. So God rains goodness and mercy as wide as the dew, and if we lack them, it is because we will not open our hearts to receive them.

[a] Ne. iii. 1; Zec. xiv. 10; 2 Ki. xiv. 13.

"You needn't have such a reverence for truth as always to stand at an awful distance from it."

"Sir Walter Raleigh one day asking a favor from Queen Elizabeth, the latter said to him, 'Raleigh, when will you leave off begging?' To which he answered, 'When your Majesty leaves off giving.' Ask great things of God. Expect great things from God. Let his past goodness make us 'instant in prayer.' "—New Cyclopædia of Illustrative Anecdote.

[b] Je. xxxix. 1; 2 Ki. xxv. 1.

[c] Je. xxxvii. 5.

"The siege lasted from the tenth month of the ninth year of Zedekiah's reign to the fourth month of the eleventh year." —Lowth.

[d] "Zedekiah's was a harder fate than the words suggest; Je. xxxix. 6, 7, lii. 11."—Spk. Com.

Apart from it, despair was as reasonable as now it was unreasonable."—Hengstenberg.

The Church's security (vss. 35—37).—Let us contemplate—I. The promises here made to God's Church and people. Certainly they refer—1. To God's ancient people, the Jews; 2. To the Christian Church. II. The use which is to be made of them by individual believers. We should be careful—1. As to the persons to whom they belong; 2. As to the extent to which they are to be applied; 3. As to the use that is to be made of them when they are so applied. Lay down the following rules:—(1) Seek to gain Christ Himself as your portion; (2) Embrace His promises with humility; (3) Improve them will all care.—C. Simeon.

The uniformity of law.—This great doctrine has come to the forefront of modern science. By some it is thought to be a difficulty in the way of religious belief. But Jeremiah shows us how to regard it as an encouragement for faith. It proves us the unchangeableness of God. Events shift and vary, but laws remain. The seasons come and go, but the sun still shines and rules them. Though the sea rages and roars, its wild waves are curbed by invisible reins, linked to heavenly motions, obedient to unvarying laws. So we may learn that amid the changing circumstances of life and the varying actions of God in providence the same great principles are maintained and the promises of God work out their blessed results unceasingly. This is true of God's thoughts and will. It is true of our personal enjoyment of the privileges of his covenant. Israel is to endure. The Church is founded on a rock. The "final perseverance" of the Christian follows from his identification of his life with eternal laws of God. God will no more cast off his people than the sun cease to rule the seasons or the moon the tides; for in grace, as in nature, eternal laws and principles preserve eternal stability to the spiritual universe.—Pul. Com.

38—40. The connection is not very clear. The main point of these verses is that Jerusalem, when rebuilt, shall be altogether "the Lord's." Its circumference shall even be extended with the single object of including spots at present unclean, but then to become holy like the rest of the city. According to Hengstenberg and Keil, Jerusalem is here a figure of the kingdom of God in the latter days."—Pul. Com. (38) **tower .. corner,** the ancient limits of the city.[a] (39) **Gareb,** "the locality outside the city, where lepers were removed to." (40) **valley,** etc., ch. vii. 32. Tophet; S. of the city. **horse gate,** Ne. iii. 28. **not be plucked up,** the rebuilt city shall be established for long generations.

CHAPTER THE THIRTY-SECOND.

1—5. (1) **The word that came,** this is the introduction to a long section of the Book more continuously historical than any of the preceding portions. It gives the incidents of the two years preceding the capture of Jerusalem, the capture itself, and the events which immediately followed, with prophecies interspersed."—Camb. Bib. **tenth year,** the siege of Jerus. began in Zedekiah's ninth year.[b] It was temporarily raised upon the approach of an army fr. Egypt.[c] (2) **in the court,** etc., Jer. had been arrested on attempting to leave Jerusalem. At first he was only in custody, afterwards he was put into a dungeon. (3) **shut him up,** fearing the influence of his prophecies upon the people. (4) **not escape,** ch. xxxiv. 2, 3. (5) **visit him,** an expression that may either mean for restoration, or for punishment.[d]

Zedekiah's captivity, blindness, and death.—Some superficial or inattentive readers of the Bible have supposed this prophecy, which declares that Zedekiah should behold the king of Babylon, to be contradictory to Ezek. xii. 13, where it is said, he should be brought to Babylon, but should not see it; and, indeed, Josephus tells us that the seeming inconsistency of the two prophecies determined Zedekiah to believe neither of them. Both of them, however, were literally fulfilled. Zedekiah was taken in the plains of Jericho, and sent to the king of Babylon at Riblah (2 Kings xxv. 5, 6), where he then resided, whom he saw and spoke to, and who caused his eyes to be put out. He was then sent to Babylon, which he could not see, and was there imprisoned and died. —Carpenter. "Until I visit him."—Zedekiah does not seem to have been a bad man, though he did evil. Weak rather than wicked. One like Charles I. of England, or Louis XVI. of France. One of those men unhappily called to places of great responsibility and difficulty, without the moral strength requisite for so arduous a post. A sadder life than that of King Zedekiah, the last king of Judah and Jerusalem, cannot be conceived. It is a piteous tale. Bereaved, a captive, blinded, he was dragged to Babylon, and there died. And it is because the prophet of God recognizes that death to such an one could not but be a sweet messenger of relief, therefore he calls it "the Lord visiting him." True, the visit of the Lord often means the wrath of the Lord. He will "visit the sins of the fathers," etc. But it yet more often means the goodness of the Lord. "The Lord hath visited and redeemed his people." He visited Hannah. He visits his flock. And this gentler meaning it has here; for the sore punishment of his sins Zedekiah had already been visited. This visit, therefore, tells of God's merciful visitation.—Pul. Com.

If we work upon marble, it will perish, if we work upon brass, time will efface it; if we rear temples, they will crumble into dust; but if we work upon immortal souls, if we control them with principles, with the just fear of God and love of our fellow men, we engrave on these tablets something which will brighten to all eternity.—Daniel Webster.

6—12. (7) **Hanameel,** Jeremiah's first cousin. **field in Anathoth,**[e] a sacerdotal city, so having 2,000 cubits of suburban fields outside the walls attached to it. **right of redemption,** Le. xxv. 24, 25; Ru. iv. 3—6. (8) **right of inheritance,** since Hanameel had no children. **Then I knew,** i. e. the coming of Hanameel confirmed the directions I had received. (9) **weighed,** money does not seem to have been coined. **seventeen shekels,** or about 40 shillings. (10) **subscribed,** etc., did all that was necessary properly to secure the transfer of the property. (11) **evidence,** R. V. "the deed." **according to the law and custom,** rather, "the offer and the conditions," the two parts of which the deed consisted, as explained above, viz. the description of the property and the conditions under which it was sold. Camb. Bib. (12) **Baruch,** Jeremiah's agent.[a]

[e] This field was at the time in actual possession of the Chaldæan army.

"Blessed is that simplicity, which leaveth the difficult paths of dispute, and goeth on in the plain and sure path of God's commandments."—Thomas a Kempis.

[a] Je. xxxvi. 4.

A patriotic purchase.—When Hannibal was besieging Rome the ground on which his army was encamped was offered for sale in Rome and a Roman senator bought it at its full value.

13—15. (13) **charged Baruch,** gave him the following instructions. (14) **earthen vessel,** "the deed was made in two copies, so that if the open one were lost, or suspected of having been tampered with, an appeal might always be made to the sealed copy. The latter was to be placed in an earthen vessel, to preserve it from injury by damp."—Pul. Com. This would be hidden in the ground in some secure place, to be found when the land was again inhabited.[b] (15) **again,** i. e. subsequent to the captivity.

[b] "**Special care** was taken that the deed should sustain no injury from the length of time that would elapse before the Jews could recover their possessions in Palestine."—Henderson.

The contract and its terms.—The terms "that which is sealed" and "that which is open" may, however, be explained of either of one or two documents somewhat as follows: the record was written, signed, and witnessed; it was then folded up and sealed; part or the whole of the contents of this sealed-up record was then written again on the outside or on a separate parchment, so that the purport of the deed could easily be ascertained without exposing the original record. The Assyrian and Chaldean contract-tablets were constructed on this principle; the contract was first written on a clay tablet, which was further enclosed in an envelope of clay, and on the outside was engraved an exact copy of the writing within. If the outer writing became indistinct or was tampered with, the envelope could be broken and the exact terms of the contract ascertained from the first tablet. Numerous examples of this method can be seen in the British Museum. The Jews had been vassals of Assyria and Babylon for about a century, and thus must have had ample opportunity to become acquainted with their legal procedure; and, in this instance, Jeremiah and his friends may have imitated the Chaldeans. Such an imitation would be specially significant in what was intended to symbolize the transitoriness of the Chaldean conquest. The earthen vessel would preserve the record from being spoilt by the damp; similarly bottles are used nowadays to preserve the documents that

"I worship Thee,
sweet Will of God!
And all Thy ways adore;
And every day I live, I seem
To love Thee more and more.

"I have no cares,
O blessed will,
For all my cares are Thine;
I live in triumph, Lord, for Thou
Hast made Thy triumph mine."
—Faber.

"The trial of faith is by finding what we will do for God. To trust Him when we have securities in our own iron chest is easy, and not thankworthy. But to depend on Him for what we cannot see, as it is more hard for man to do, so it is more acceptable to God when done, for in that act we make confession of His deity."–Feltham.

are built up into the memorial stones of public buildings. In both cases the object is that "they may continue many days."—Exp. Bib.

16—20. (16) **prayed,** prob. to relieve his own anxiety, and to unburden his own fears. (17) **too hard,** marg. "too wonderful for Thee." (18) **shewest,** etc., Ex. xx. xxxiv. 7; Is. lxv. 6. (19) **eyes .. men,** Job. xxxiv. 21; Pr. v. 21. (20) **even unto this day,** "means that signs and wonders equal to those wrought in Egypt have continued to the present time."—Cheyne.

God's omniscience.—The Inquisition, or the record on high.—"Within those blood-stained walls, for whose atrocious cruelties Rome has a heavy account to render, a prisoner is under examination. He has been assured that nothing he reveals shall be recorded or used against him. While making frank and ingenuous confession, he suddenly stops. He is dumb—a mute. They ply him with questions, flatter him, threaten him; but he answers not a word. Danger makes the senses quick. His ear has caught a sound; he listens, and that sound ties his tongue. An arras hangs beside him, and behind it he hears a pen running along the pages. The truth flashes on him. Behind that screen there sits a scribe, committing to the fatal page every word he says, and he shall meet it all again on the day of trial. Ah! how solemn to think that there is such a pen going in heaven, and entering on the books of judgment whatever we say and wish, all we think and do. Would to God we heard it—heard it everywhere—always heard it! What a check it might prove!"—Guthrie.

[a] "Mounds of earth, raised as breastworks by the besieging army, behind which they employed their engines, and which they gradually pushed forward to the walls of the city." — Fausset.

"Faith and unfaith can ne'er be equal powers;
Unfaith in aught is want of faith in all."

"Rutherford has a quaint saying, that 'when he was cast into the cellars of affliction, he always remembered that the great King kept His wine there, and he at once searched for the wine-bottles and drank 'wines on the lees well refined.' "

"Christianity removes the attraction of the earth; and this one way in which it diminishes men's burden. It makes them citizens of another world." —Henry Drummond.

21—25. (21) **hast brought,** etc., De. xxvi. 8. **terror,** "for the terror caused to neighboring nations by the miracles attendant upon the Exodus compare Exod. xv. 14; Deut. iv. 34. (22) **flowing .. honey,** Ex. iii. 8. (23) **possessed it,** settled down in it. (24) **mounts,** siege-works, raised for the battering-rams.[a] (25) **Buy thee the field,** purchase of property when the State was just upon its ruin seemed very unreasonable. **for the city,** R. V. "whereas the city," etc., i. e. the command and the state of the city seem to be contradictory.

Trust in perplexity.—You are greatly troubled are you? It is a common lot with us all. And you have nothing on earth to trust to now, and are going to be cast on your God alone? Happy trouble that drives thee to thy Father! Blessed storm that wrecks thee on the Rock of ages! Glorious billow that washes thee upon this heavenly shore! And now thou hast nothing but thy God to trust to, what art thou going to do? To fret? Oh, do not thus dishonor thy Lord! Show the world that thy God is worth ten thousand worlds to thee. Show rich men how rich thou art in thy poverty when the Lord God is thy helper. Show the strong man how strong thou art in thy weakness when underneath thee are the everlasting arms. Now, now is thy time to glorify God. There was no room for courage before, but now there is space for feats of faith and valiant exploits. Be strong and very courageous, and the Lord thy God shall certainly, as surely as He built the heavens and the earth, glorify Himself in thy weakness, and magnify His might in the midst of thy distress. The Lord help us to lean wholly on Him, and never on ourselves, and let His name be had in remembrance while the earth endureth. Amen.—C. H. Spurgeon. The danger of the modern church.—The sin which Jeremiah denounced is by no means outside Christian experience; it is much nearer to us than conversion to Buddhism—it is possible to the Church in every stage of its history. The missionary finds that the lives of his converts continually threaten to revert to a nominal profession which cloaks the immorality and superstition of their old heathenism. The Church of the Roman Empire gave the sanction of Christ's name and authority to many of the most unchristian features of Judaism and Paganism; once more the rites of strange gods were associated with the worship of Jehovah, and a new Queen of Heaven was honored with unlimited incense. The Reformed churches in their turn, after the first "kindness of their youth," the first "love of their espousals," have often fallen into the very abuses against which their great leaders protested; they have given way to the ritualistic spirit, have put the Church in the place of Christ, and have claimed for human formulæ the authority that can only belong to the inspired Word of God. They have immolated their victims to the Baals and Molochs of creeds and confessions, and thought that they were doing honor to Jehovah thereby.—Exp. Bib.

26—30. (27) **God .. flesh,** Nu. xvi. 22. Difficulties are never hindrances to God. (28) **I will give,** or I am giving. That is My settled purpose. (29) **and burn it,** a still more significant prediction to Jewish hearers than to us, for it implies that Jerusalem had become utterly rebellious, and deserved the punishment of the old Canaanitish cities. It was to be made a chêrem. Deut. xiii: 12—16.—Pul. Com. **roofs,** etc., ch. xix. 13. (30) **only done,** so abundant were their idolatries and rebellions that nothing else could be seen in the review of their history. **youth,** or origin as a nation.[a]

God's revelation of Himself (vs. 27).—This is God's revelation of Himself, not the fancy of the speculator, dream of poet, etc. I. Here is a direct assertion of personality, not the voice of creation but of the Creator. II. Here is a direct assertion of dominion, not a Lord, but the Lord.—J. Parker.

31—35. (31) **as a provocation of,** literally upon. The preposition which Jeremiah uses is often employed by him in a vaguer sense than is usual elsewhere in the Bible. Here the meaning seems to be that the city constitutes a burden which rests on God's wrath, so to speak, and makes it incumbent upon Him to display it in the shape of punishment. —Camb. Bib. **remove .. face,** withdraw My protection from it. (32) **evil,** especially in the encouragement of idolatry, and its attendant immoralities. (33) **back,** Heb. neck: ch. ii. 27. (34) **set .. house,** ch. vii. 30, 31. (35) **cause,** etc., ch. vii. 31, xix. 5. **Molech,** here Baal and Molech are identified. "Molech the king and Baal the lord are simply different names of the sun god, but in altered relations."

God's power over the sinful heart.—Can God subdue sin in the heart of a man? When we see the outrages, the duration, the strength of hold, the universality, the attractiveness, the prestige, and the love of sin, it does seem as if the subjugation of this was too hard even for the Lord. To turn back the tides, to reverse the law of gravity, to alter any other law of the universe,—this were an easy task compared with the stupendous change which must be wrought in man before the love of sin can die out of him, and the love of God rule in its stead. What endeavors have been made! what schemes devised! what philosophies elaborated! but all in vain. Hence, despair for ourselves and for others too often predominates in our souls. Evil we are, and evil we must be. Who can bring a clean thing out of an unclean? Can a corrupt tree bring forth good fruit? But "there is nothing too hard for the Lord." The history of the Church of God proves that there is, in the regenerating, sanctifying Spirit of God, that power which is needed here.—Pul. Com.

36—38. (36) **now therefore,** this introduces the strange and lovely contrast to the gloomy picture which has gone before. It will be observed that there is no direct reference to Jerusalem, but the capital was only emphasized before as the heart of the nation, and it would, of course, be no comfort to say that Jerusalem's inhabitants (alone) would be restored.—Pul. Com. (37) **gather them,**[a] and so the seeming destruction shall only issue in a great restoration, when, through their afflictions, they are cured of their idolatry. (38) **my people,** ch. xxiv. 7.

God's thorough good will towards His people.—His will is ever to show favor and do good to mankind. That will is always in action, but it can only be in manifestation when men themselves, by their spirit of submission to God and obedience to his directions, make such a manifestation possible. As he is thorough in his anger against the rebellious and idolatrous, so he is thorough in his favor towards the repentant. It is well that we should ever remember this deep good will of God to men when things are going wrong with us. The fault of untoward experiences may be in us or it may be in others; it cannot be in God. We must not put down to arbitrariness in him the painful workings of that

[a] Je. ii. 7, 25, vii. 28, 28, xxii. 21.

"There is a contemptibly quiet path for all those who are afraid of the blows and clamor of opposing forces. There is honorable fighting for a man who is ready to forget that he has a head to be battered and a name to be bespattered. Truth wants no champion who is not as ready to be struck as to strike for her.—J. G. Holland.

"When God takes possession of a slow tongue, He can make it fast if he wants to, but you will get none of the credit."—H. W. Webb-Peploe.

"The goodness of a Christian lies in his holiness, as the goodness of the air lies in the clearness of it, and the worth of gold in its pureness."—T. Watson.

[a] Je. xxxi. 8, 9, 18—20, 33.

Truth will be uppermost one time or other, like cork, though kept down in the water.

"God's people have always in their worst conditions found out the best of their God."

Luther says: "Bene orare est bene studinsse.—To have prayed well is to have studied well."

law which manifests itself in sequence to human ignorance and folly. —Pul. Com.

39—41. (39) **one heart,**[b] Eze. xi. 19. Prob. referring to the reunion of Israel and Judah. (40) **everlasting covenant,** ch. xxxi. 31, 33.[c] (41) **assuredly,** i. e. in truth. Indicating God's fixed purpose.

Bible religion (vs. 40).—I. As having its seat in the heart. 1. Not merely in the intellect; 2. Not merely in the sentiments; 3. Not merely in occasional service. II. As imparted by God. 1. Not miraculously, not irrespective of man's activities; 2. By the ministry of His servants. III. As a safeguard against apostasy.—Thomas.

God rejoicing. We are to think of him as the "blessed" God, i. e. as essentially happy. The brightness and beauty of the world are reflections from the blessedness of God. Because he is glad, nature is glad, flowers bloom, birds sing, young creatures bound with delight. Nothing is more sad in perversions of religion than the representations of God as a gloomy tyrant. Less terrible, but scarcely less false, are those monkish ideas which deny the tyranny but cherish the gloom of a sombre divinity more suited to chill, dark cloisters than to that glorious temple of nature in which the eternal presence dwells and manifests himself symbolically. These fragrant meadows, broad rolling seas of moorland heather, rich green forest-cities of busy insect life, flashing ocean waves, and the pure blue sky above, and all that is sweet and lovely in creation, swell one symphony of gladness, because the mighty Spirit that haunts them is himself overflowing with joy. Our God is a Sun. And if divinity is sunny, so should religion be. The happy God will rejoice in the happiness of his children. Innocent mirth can be no offence to such a God. The typical citizens of his kingdom are little children; and what is so joyous as childhood?—Pul. Com.

b "In ch. iii. 13, the manifold paths of sins are described as the scattering of men's ways, but under the new covenant they will with one consent walk in the one narrow path of right doing." — Spk. Com.

c Ps. lxxxix. 34, 35; Is. lv. 3; He. viii. 10.

"Called an 'everlasting covenant,' not only bec. God will be for ever faithful to it, but bec. the consequences of it will be everlasting."— Mat. Henry.

42—44. (42) **Like as,** in similar faithfulness to My word. (43) **fields .. land,** "returning to the symbol of the purchased field, Jehovah declares that fields shall be bought, with all the legal formalities usual in settled and orderly societies, deeds shall be signed, sealed, and delivered in the presence of witnesses."—Exp. Bib.[d] (44) **subscribe evidences,** vs. 10. **in the land of Benjamin,** the several parts of the land are specified in order to make the promise more distinct that it should be possessed again in its entirety.

Variety in religious character.—We ought, if rightly minded, to rejoice in the exuberance and variety of the spiritual gifts possessed by Christians, just as we delight in the rich variety of nature, or in that of the Word of God. There are many lines of thought in religion, many forms which practical and personal piety takes, although, of course, they are all animated by the same essential principles. St. John and St. Paul were both equally devoted to the cause and person of our Lord, yet no two men ever existed who manifested this devotion in shapes more different. Both these members held of the Head by a living union, but they discharged for the Head functions altogether different. Let us not conceive of all genuine religion as moving in one groove of feeling and practice, and refuse to acknowledge any man as a Christian, because he does not run upon our particular groove. There are several points of view from which Christianity may be surveyed; and although it be one and the same object, from whatever point we look, yet eyes placed on different levels will see it grouped in different perspctives.—Goulburn.

d "Trade shall revive, for they shall have money enough to buy land with. Husbandry shall revive, for those that have money shall covet to lay it out upon lands." — Mat. Henry.

"As the dog in Æsop's fable lost the real flesh for the shadow of it, so the covetous man casts away the true riches for the love of the shadowy."—Adams.

"Whom God adopts, he anoints; whom he makes sons, he makes saints." —Watson.

CHAPTER THE THIRTY-THIRD.

"In this chap. the prophet looking out beyond the troubles of the present, depicts afresh the subsequent purification and restoration of the nation."—Driver. **1—3.** (1) **second time,** after the message about the field. **shut up,** ch. xxxii. 2, 3. (2) **maker,** R. V. "who doeth it," i. e. what he has purposed. Isa. xxxvii. 26. (3) **mighty things,** or things hidden, or shut up—in the mysterious counsels of God.[a]

Prayer (vs. 3).—I. The invitation to prayer. 1. Whose is it? 2. To whom is the invitation addressed? 3. What is the tenor of the invi-

a "This invitation betokens God's favor and loving-kindness; that He is ready to comply with the first intimations of His servant's desires."—Lowth.

tation? II. The promise. 1. It is general; 2. It is special. Apply:—(1) Reprove the prayerless; (2) Encourage the prayerful.—G. Brooks.

Prayer.—Thomas Brooks, alluding to the old classical myth of Daedalus, who, being imprisoned in the island of Crete, made wings for himself, by which he escaped to Italy, says, "Christians must do as Daedalus, who, when he could not escape by a way upon earth, went by a way of heaven." Holy prayers are the wings of the soul's deliverance. A Well of Consolation.—The dungeon of the Mamertine, where a probable tradition declares that Paul was for a while confined, is entered through a round hole in the floor of another dungeon above. The uppermost apartment is dark enough, but the lower one is darkness itself, so that the apostle's imprisonment was of the severest kind. We noticed, however, a strange fact:—in the hard floor there is a beautiful fountain of clear crystal water, which doubtless was as fresh in Paul's day as it is now; of course the Papists believe the fountain to be miraculous; we who are not so credulous of traditions rather see in it a symbol full of instruction:—there never was a dungeon for God's servants which was without its well of consolation.

"True, conscious honor is to feel no sin, He's armed without who's innocent within: Be this thy screen, and this thy wall of brass."—Pope's Horace.

4—8. (4) **thrown .. mounts,** R. V. "which are broken down to make a defence[b] against the mounts, and against the sword,"[c] i. e. they were thrown down to make room for defensive works. (5) **They come,** a poetical figure. These ramparts and inner defences are said to advance to fight the Chaldæans. (6) **health,** etc., first the cure of its moral evils, then gracious outward restoration. (7) **build them,** or establish them.[d] (8) **cleanse,** "this distinctive feature of the new covenant has been already brought out strongly in xxxi. 34. We shall have it again, l. 20."

[b] "In ancient sieges, as the works of the enemy approached the walls, it was usual to build inner fortifications, and for this purpose houses were pulled down, both to give the vacant space necessary, and to supply materials." — Spk. Com.

[c] Mattocks in 2 Chr. xxxiv. 6; axes in Eze. xxvi. 9.

[d] Je. xxiv. 6, xxxi. 4, 28, xlii. 10.

Peace is revealed in Jesus Christ. In him there is the secret of a composure and a steadfastness unaffected by all the common cause of discord and instability. He had an unusual number of enemies, and this because he was so persistent in declaring righteousness; and yet all the time he had that peace within which showed how outside forces only affected the mere shell of life. In this life there was ever the joint manifestation of peace and steadfastness, and the steadfastness was explained by the fact that he came from God, continued in God, did the will of God, and so, ever having this hold on the Eternal, and being held by the Eternal, the shaking influences of time did ever more and more both to reveal his strength and their own weakness. All the exhortations of Jesus with respect to faith are meant to reveal to us the abundance of peace and truth. With what pity Jesus must look on the abortive, melancholy attempts of men to trust in the untrustworthy! and yet the unveiled magnificence of peace and truth is unseen.—Pul. Com.

9—11. (9) **it shall be,** R. V. "this city shall be." **a praise,**[a] Is. lxii. 7. **fear and tremble,** with awe at the signs of the power and faithfulness of Israel's God.[b] (10) **shall be desolate,** better, "is desolate."[c] The Prophet seems to see the land as the people thought of it during the time of the captivity—uninhabited and silent. (11) **voice,** etc., ch. vii. 34, xvi. 9. **praise, etc.,** "these clauses seem to have been liturgical forms used in the Temple services. This we gather from such passages as 2 Chron. v. 13, vii. 3, 6; Ezra iii. 11; Ps. cvi. 1."—Camb. Bib. **cause to return,** or "reverse."[d]

[a] "That is, the subject of men's praise and admiration, the glory of which redounds to God, who is her protector."—Lowth.

[b] Comp. Ps. cxxxix. 14; Is. lx. 5.

[c] Je. xxxii. 43.

[d] "To 'reverse the captivity' does not here mean to restore the captives from their exile, but to restore the country from the circumstances of desolation to wh. it had been reduced, although this naturally presupposed the restoration of its inhabitants." — Henderson.

Jerusalem.—When, on one occasion, a crowd of crusaders approached the Holy City, and caught the first sight of its spires through the blue luminous tremors of the distance, some knelt in silent praise, some kissed the earth, some prayed, and laughed, and wept in wild emotion; and knight and palmer, old man and little child joined to raise the cry, "Jerusalem, Jerusalem!"—Stanford. The voices of the future.—The sounds of life are to flow back into the now desolate streets, but they are to be the sounds of a different kind of life. Sounds springing from righteousness within and from a principle of obedience to Jehovah. Sounds that come from a universally satisfied people. Not sounds of joy and gladness in palaces, and sounds of privation and despair in hovels; but sunshine falling everywhere, and everywhere the hearts of the people ready to break forth into song. In the eleventh

"Christianity has given to truth a dignity independent of time and numbers. It has required that truth should be believed and respected for itself."—Vinet.

verse there is first of all the general indication of gladness. Every one is full of healthy life, which, as a matter of course, breaks forth into joyful manifestation. Then, as a very significant illustration, there is the gladness of the bridegroom and the bride. This signifies a stable society, a hopeful prospect, the joys of home life. Probably there was no joy so demonstrative as that connected with wedding festivities. Then the joy of religion comes in to crown and conclude all. Praise to Jehovah for his goodness and his enduring mercy, and offerings of thanksgiving in his house. If joy of this kind had been absent, the other joy would not long have lasted. From what God sends down into our lives as causes of abiding joy, we must send back to him responses of intelligent and heart-felt praise.—Pul. Com.

12—14. (12) **habitation,** rather, a pasture (including the idea of an encampment).[a] (13) **telleth,** i. e. counteth.[b] There will be so many that they will have to be counted. A hint of the coming prosperity. (14) **good thing,** or good word: ch. xxix. 10, xxiii. 5, 6.[c]

Revival of prosperity.—It is remarkable how soon the battle-field with its hideous relics becomes a flowery meadow. The rapid revival of the French nation after the war of 1870 was an astonishment to Europe. This may be accounted for partly on natural principles, since war rarely touches the permanent resources of a country; if it drains the stream, it does not stanch the fountain-head. The capital of a country is always being consumed and remade in peaceful times, so that the destruction of it in war is not so great a calamity as might appear at first sight. But a true revival of prosperity depends on higher causes. A nation is only really prosperous when its people are advancing in moral tone, when there is a Divine root to their recovery. This is implied in the description of restored Israel.—Pul. Com.

15—18. (15) **Branch,** ch. xxiii. 5. (16) **our righteousness,** "the symbolic name which in xxiii. 6 is given to the Messianic king is here assigned to the restored, ideal city. The name is intended, of course, to symbolize the fact that Jehovah is the source of righteousness to the restored community."—Driver.[d] (17, 18) **never want a man,** Heb. "there shall not be cut off from David." "The permanence of the kingly and priestly line is here emphatically declared. But elsewhere Jeremiah no less plainly announces the cutting off of both, of the former in xxii. 30, xxx. 21, of the latter in iii. 16, xxxi. 33. We must therefore take the passage as one of the prophet's pictures of the Christian dispensation, clothed in a Jewish dress, the only form in which it could present any meaning to those to whom it was delivered."—Camb. Bib.

Hill and his gardener.—The Rev. Rowland Hill had great reason to rejoice in the consistent lives and zealous devotion to God of many of his people at Wotton. There was amongst them a person of the name of Rugg, of a piety so deep, and of a life so useful and unblemished, that even his enemies admired and were awed by his character. Mr. Hill's gardener at Wotton, who had always passed for an honest, quiet sort of man, was at length discovered to have been the perpetrator of several burglaries and other daring robberies in the neighborhood, though he had, till caught in the act, never been even suspected. He was tried at Gloucester, condemned, and executed. It need scarcely be said that his master visited him in jail. During his interview with him there, he confessed the many crimes of which he had been guilty. "How was it, William," he inquired, "that you never robbed me, when you had such abundant opportunity?" "Sir," replied he, "do you recollect the juniper bush on the border against the dining-room? I have many times hid under it at night, intending, which I could easily have done, to get into the house and plunder it; but, sir, I was afraid: something said to me, He is a man of God: it is a house of prayer; if I break in I shall surely be found out: so I never could pluck up courage to attempt it." In another conversation he told him, "Sir, I well knew that old Mr. Rugg was in the habit of carrying a deal of money in his pocket; times and times have I hid behind the hedge of the lane leading to his house—he has passed within a yard of me, when going home from the prayer-meeting, again and again; I could not stir; I durst not touch so holy

[a] Is. lxv. 10; Je. l. 19.

[b] "'Every shepherd tells his tale,' i. e. 'counts the number of his sheep.'"—Milton's L'Allegro.

[c] "'I will make to rise,' God's promise having for a time seemed to lie dead and abortive."—Calvin.

[d] "The name is here given to Jerus., i. e. to the Church, bec. it is her business immediately to work on earth that righteousness which Christ works absolutely."—Spk. Com.

The brightest Christian, in his graces is not unlike the sea, which never continues long at high water mark. "In the channel through which a running stream is directed upon a mill wheel, the same turning of a valve that shuts the water out of one course throws it into another. Thus the Jews, by rejecting the counsel of God, shut themselves out, and at the same moment opened a way whereby mercy might flow to us who were afar off."—William Arnot.

a man. I was afraid. I always began to tremble as soon as he came near me, and gave up the thought altogether, for I knew he was a holy man."—Cheever.

19—22. (20) **break .. day,**[a] "the constant, regular succession of day and night is an emblem of the equally regular supply of royal descendants of David and of Levitical priests, and the countless grains of sand are symbolic of the wonderful increase of their numbers."—Pul. Com. Ch. xxxi. 35, 36. (21) **covenant .. David,** 2 Sa. vii. 12—16. (22) **host,** etc., ch. xxxi. 37. Fulfilled spiritually in Christian believers.

Jerusalem discoveries.—Outside Jerusalem how much remains for us to learn! The field has been scarcely furrowed by the merest surface plough; and whole districts, with many a mountain nook, are virgin soil to the Western explorer. We have in the Book of Joshua the Domesday Book of the land of Israel. Who yet has taken that olden roll in hand, and verified by it the sites and caves, the living villages and the ruinous heaps which stud every corner of the land? Let us remember that what Rawlinson, and Layard, and Botta have done for the history of the later monarchy in the mounds of Assyria and Chaldæa, yet remains to be done for Numbers and Joshua, and for the golden period of the Israelitish monarchy. It is not for nothing, surely, that Providence has left it within our grasp, in a sceptical age—in an age devoted, beyond all others, to physical research and physical evidences to elucidate the details of the Word written by the numberless illustrations which every diligent exploration of the land, which is, as it were, the framework, the setting, of the Divine history, at once affords. It matters nothing to the truth of God's Word where stood the temple of Solomon, where are buried the ruins of Capernaum, where Israel pitched their tents in the wilderness, where John preached the baptism of repentance; but it does matter something to our understanding of that Word, that we should be able to show its minute and exact accordance with the existing facts of local topography.—Chr. Advoc. and Rev.

[a] "The perpetual succession of day and night, in virtue of the Divine ordinance to that effect, is appealed to as a pledge of the inviolability of the promise made by God both to David and the Levites." — Henderson.

Comp. Nu. xxv. 12, 13; Ps. lxxxix. 3, 28, 34; Mal. ii. 4, 5, 8.

"The richest promises are confirmed by the strongest assurances."—Cowles.

"God has hitherto kept promise with nights and days that one shall succeed the other; and will He not keep touch with His people?"—Trapp.

23—26. (24) **two families,** "the sense of this verse then is, that the people, seeing that both Israel and Judah ('the two families') are being apparently cast off, despise their own nation, despair of any better days, and consider their national existence to be a thing of the past."—Camb. Bib. **before them,** or in their judgment. Those who think thus of Israel and Judah are degenerate Jews who had lost faith. (25) **covenant,** vs. 20. (26) **Then,** but not till them.[a] **will cause,** etc., ch. xxxii. 44. "There shall yet be rulers and priests over Israel in its spiritual sense, viz. the Christian Church, the natural successor and development of Judaism. For this thought one step further advanced, and pointing faintly to the means by which the issue was to be brought about, compare Is. lxvi.. 19—21."—Camb. Bib.

Necessity of correct belief.—Go into New York, and in the Sixth Ward you shall find two representative men. One says, "I voted for the judge, and helped to put him where he is, and he will wink at my crimes. I can drink as much as I please, on Sundays and on weekdays, and he will not disturb me. He is easy and good natured, and he is not going to be hard with me if I do break the laws a little." And the man, because he believes that the judge does not care for his wickedness, and will not punish him, grows bold and corrupt in transgression. But at length he is brought before the court, and he finds there, instead of his bribed judge, a white-faced man—not red-faced; one of those men with a long head upward—not backward and downward; a man with a full sense of the value of justice and truth. The culprit begins his shuffling excuses. The judge listens to none of them; he reads the law, and says, "Your conduct is herein condemned, and sends him away to receive his just deserts. When the man has expiated his crime, he goes around in the same ward, and says, "You must walk straight hereafter. The judge that sits on the bench now is not the jolly old judge that used to sit there. If you go before him, he will make you smart." Does it not make a difference what a man believes **about a judge? If he believes that he is a lenient, conniving judge,**

[a] "Christ is that seed of David that is to be perpetual dictator to the seed of Ab., Is. and Jacob; and as this people shall never want such a King, so this King shall never want such a people. Christianity shall continue in the dominion of Christ, and the subjection of Christians to Him, till day and night come to an end."—Matthew Henry.

"Deep security commonly ends in deep despair; whereas those that keep up a holy fear at all times have a good hope to support them in the worst of times."—Henry.

"To every man who truly studies Nature there is a God. Call Him by whatever name—a Crea-

does it not make him careless? And if he believes that he is a straightforward judge, does it not make him afraid of transgression? Now lift up the judge's bench, and make it the judgment-seat; and take out the human judge, and put God Almighty there. If men believe Him to be an all-smiling God—a God that is all sunshine, an all-sympathizing God—a God that is nothing but kindness, and goodness, and gentleness, they say to themselves, "We will do as we have a mind to." Take away that miserable slander upon the revealed character of God, and lift up the august front of Justice, on whose brow love proudly sits, and let men see that there is a vast heart of love and gentleness indeed, but one that will by no means clear the guilty, and they will take more heed to their conduct. Does it, then, make no difference what a man believes about God's nature, and His manner of dealing with men? It makes all the difference between laxity and earnestness, between an endeavor to live truly and no endeavor at all in that direction; between right and wrong conduct.—H. W. Beecher.

tor, a Supreme Being, a Great First Cause, a Power that makes for Righteousness — Science has a God; and he who believes in this, in spite of all protest, possesses a theology."—Drummond.

CHAPTER THE THIRTY-FOURTH.

"Ch. xxxiv. 1—7 is virtually a postcript to ch. xxxii., xxxiii.; it apparently contains the prophecy referred to in ch. xxxii. 3—5 as the cause of Jeremiah's imprisonment. The same prophecy recurs in a shorter form in ch. xxxvii. 17, and, by comparing the context of this passage with ch. xxxii. 1, etc., we are enabled to infer that the original prophecy was uttered at the renewal of the siege of Jerusalem by the Chaldæans, who had withdrawn for a time on the news of the approach of Pharaoh's army."—Pul. Com. 1—3. (1) **of his dominion,** R. V. "that were under his dominion."[a] **people,** or peoples, tribes under his rule.[b] (2) **burn it,** a sign of the exasperated state of Nebuchadnezzar's mind.

The woe of weakness.—"Zedekiah, King of Judah." The life of this unhappy monarch is a piteous but powerful illustration of the misery of instability of character, the sorrows that dog the footsteps of the infirm will. What men need, in order to be happier and better than they are, is not more knowledge of what is right—they are amply supplied with that; or the presence of plentiful good purpose and desire to do the right—hell itself is paved with good intentions; but what is needed is strength of will, firmness and stability of character. It is for lack of that that men go so wrong and make such a miserable confusion of their own life and that of others. The history of Zedekiah illustrates all this.—Pul. Com. A common doom.—One of the mysteries of Providence is that those who are most responsible for national sins seem to suffer least by public misfortunes. Ambitious statesmen and bellicose journalists do not generally fall in battle and leave destitute widows and children. When the captains of commerce and manufacture err in their industrial policy, one great result is the pauperism of hundreds of families who had no voice in the matter. A spendthrift landlord may cripple the agriculture of half a county. And yet, when factories are closed and farmers ruined, the manufacturer and the landlord are the last to see want. In former invasions of Judah, the princes and priests had some share of suffering; but wealthy nobles might incur losses and yet weather the storm by which poorer men were overwhelmed. Fines and tribute levied by the invaders would, after the manner of the East, be wrung from the weak and helpless. But now ruin was to fall on all alike. The nobles had been flagrant in sin, they were now to be marked out for most condign punishment—"To whomsoever much is given, of him shall much be required."—Exp. Bib.

4—7. (4) **Thou .. sword,** this assurance, however, implies his captivity. (5) **burn odours,** R. V. "make a burning for thee."[c] (7) **Lachish,** 2 Ki. xviii. 13, xix. 8. These were outlying fortresses which, at the time of the prophecy, had not fallen into Nebuchadnezzar's hands.

Allegory of death.—Now I further saw, that betwixt them and the

[a] "This prediction belongs in point of time to ch. xxxii. 1—5, and is merely an amplification of what is contained in those vss. It was consequently delivered before Jeremiah was placed in custody."—Henderson.

[b] "The verbose description well suits the pomp of an Oriental army; and also describes the fact, that such an army consisted of a loose aggregate of tributary and half-conquered nations and tribes, held together by the personal influence of one man."—Spk. Com.

[c] "It was customary among the Jews, at the funeral of their kings, esp. of those whose memory they honored, to prepare a bed of spices (2 Chr. xvi. 14), which they made a perfume of by burning them, and therein to deposit the body of the deceased prince."—Lowth.

gate was a river; but there was no bridge to go over, and the river was very deep. At the sight, therefore, of this river, the pilgrims were much stunned; but the men that went with them said, "You must go through, or you cannot come at the gate." They then addressed themselves to the water; and, entering, Christian began to sink; and, crying out to his good friend Hopeful, he said, "I sink in deep waters; the billows go over my head; all his waves go over me." Then said the other, "Be of good cheer, my brother: I feel the bottom, and it is good." Then said Christian, "Ah! my friend, the sorrow of death hath compassed me about: I shall not see the land that flows with milk and honey." And with that a great darkness and horror fell upon Christian, so that he could not see before him. Hopeful, therefore, here had much ado to keep his brother's head above water; yea, sometimes he would be quite gone down, and then ere a while would rise up again half dead. Hopeful did also endeavour to comfort him, saying, "Brother, I see the gate, and men standing by to receive us;" but Christian would answer, "It is you they wait for: you have been hopeful ever since I knew you." "And so have you," said he to Christian. "Ah, brother!" said he, "surely, if I was right, He would now rise to help me; but for my sins He hath brought me into the snare, and hath left me." Then I saw in my dream that Christian was in a muse a while. To whom, also, Hopeful added these words, "Be of good cheer; Jesus Christ maketh thee whole." And with that Christian brake out with a loud voice, "Oh! I see Him again, and He tells me, 'When thou passest through the waters, I will be with thee; and through the rivers, they shall not overflow thee.'" Then they both took courage, and the enemy was after that as still as a stone until they were gone over.—Bunyan.

8—11. "The inhabitants of Jerusalem, under pressure of the siege, had solemnly engaged to emancipate their Hebrew slaves, but afterwards, when the siege was temporarily raised, had treacherously disregarded the engagement."—Driver. (8) **proclaim liberty,** Ex. xxi. 2. "By the law a Hebrew, after having been a bond-servant for six years, on the seventh was to be let go free."[a] (9) **serve himself of,** i. e. make the Hebrew serve him. (10) **obeyed,** carried out the wishes of the king. (11) **turned,** etc., this was during the time that the Chaldæans raised the siege, prob. in order to meet an Egyptian army.[b]

Futility of oaths.—Whatever influence oaths may have in causing a would-be liar to speak the truth, they are very poor guarantees for the performance of contracts. William the Conqueror profited little by Harold's oath to help him to the crown of England, though it was sworn over the relics of holy saints. The famous "blush of Sigismund" over the violation of his safe-conduct to Huss was rather a token of unusual sensitiveness than a confession of exceptional guilt. The Romish Church has exalted perfidy into a sacred obligation. As Milman says: "The fatal doctrine, confirmed by long usage, by the decrees of Pontiffs, by the assent of all ecclesiastics, and the acquiescence of the Christian world, that no promise, no oath, was binding to a heretic, had hardly been questioned, never repudiated."—Exp. Bib. Love of liberty.—John Milton, the chief of poets, held the post of Latin Secretary under Cromwell. At the restoration he was of course dismissed from his office. He was now poor and blind and to these afflictions Charles II. added political persecutions; he fined him, and doomed his writings on liberty to be publicly burned. Nothing daunted by these fierce and multiplied trials, the great poet retired into private life, evoked his mighty genius, and produced Paradise Lost. But after he had endured the ills of poverty several years, Charles, feeling the need of his matchless talents, invited him to resume his former post, with all its honors, emoluments, and court favors. But Milton knew that the price of this honor must be silence on the great question of human liberty. Therefore he did not hesitate a moment. It was a strong temptation —the bribe was splendid. By merely keeping silence, he could have honor, abundance, and high position, in exchange for poverty, persecution, and neglect! But this could not be. The poet loved truth too well. His soul was too noble, too sincere, too firm in its allegiance

"Dreadful is their doom, whom doubt has driven
To censure fate and pious hope forego;
Like yonder blasted boughs by lightning riven,
Perfection, beauty, life, they never know,
But frown on all that pass, a monument of woe."
—Beattie.

[a] De. xv. 12.

[b] Je. xxxvii. 7, also xxxiv. 21, 22.

"Hypocrisy, detest her as we may
(And no man's hatred ever wronged her yet),
May claim this merit still: that she admits
The worth of that she mimics with such care,
And thus gives virtue indirect applause."
—Cowper.

"No man's condition is so base as his,
None more accursed than he; for man esteems
Him hateful 'cause he seems not what he is;
God hates him 'cause he is not what he seems."
—Quarles.

"The love of liberty with life is given,
And life itself the inferior gift of heaven."
—Dryden.

"To refuse discussion is like sitting on the safety valve of a steam boiler. It will result in explosion and destruction. Powder burned loose on the rock in the open air makes a great blaze and smoke, but does little harm. That powder confined in a rock produces an earthquake. Whatever church or nation attempts to prevent free thought and free discussion is living on a volcano."—Peloubet's Notes.

to God and liberty, to barter away its right to condemn tyranny for place or gold. Hence he spurned the royal offer, and clung to his principles and his poverty, until death called his free soul to enter its congenial heaven. And so gentle was the summons, so sweetly calm was his unruffled spirit to the hour of dissolution, that his friends knew not the precise moment of his death.—W. Smith.

12—16. (12) **Therefore,** on account of this insulting act of disobedience (13, 14) **covenant,** etc., Ex. xxi. 2; De. xv. 12. It seems that the last year of Zedekiah was the Sabbatical year. Comp. 2 Chron. xxxvi. 21. The Sabbatical years had been neglected for 500 years previous to the captivity. (15) **ye .. turned,** i. e. at last a people were found who had obeyed. "Ye" is emphatic. **in the house,** or Temple. The matter had been public and solemn. The insult of the disobedience was the more marked. (16) **turned,** again to the old wilful ways. **polluted,** R. V., "profaned."

Christian liberty.—

Grace makes the slave a freeman. 'Tis a change
That turns to ridicule the turgid speech
And stately tone of moralists, who boast
As if, like him of fabulous renown,
They had indeed ability to smooth
The shag of savage nature, and were each
An Orpheus, and omnipotent in song:
But transformation of apostate man
From fool to wise, from earthly to divine,
Is work for Him that made him. He alone,
And He by means, in philosophic eyes
Trivial and worthy of disdain, achieves
The wonder; humanising what is brute
In the lost kind, extracting from the lips
Of asps their venom, overpowering strength
By weakness, and hostility by love . . .
He is the freeman whom the truth makes free,
And all are slaves besides. —Cowper.

[a] An ancient writer relates that Agamemnon, the leader of the Greeks, at the siege of Troy, "to confirm his faith sworn to Achilles, ordered victims to be brought. He took one, and with his sword divided it in the midst, placed the pieces opposite to each other, and holding his sword, reeking with the blood, passed between the separated pieces."

"Passing between the divided pieces implied the willingness of the parties to be so treated, if they failed in adhering to the stipulations." — Henderson.

17—22. That the institutions of Mosaic law fell out of use for centuries and were later re-introduced is in many passages. (Comp. 2. Chron. xxx. 26; xxxv. 18; xxxvi. 21; Neh. viii. 17, also 2 Ki. xxiii. 22.) These passages show, however, that there was no doubt of the antiquity of the enactments in question.—Oehler. (17) **liberty for you,** freedom fr. the Divine protection. **removed into,** R. V. "tossed to and fro among." (18) **cut the calf,** referring to the significant rite by which the covenant was sealed.[a] Ge. xv. 10. (19) **princes of Judah,** "territorial magnates." (20) **dead,** etc., ch. vii. 33, xvi. 4. (21) **gone up from you,** or have temporarily raised the siege. (22) **return,** and complete their work.

Liberty.—God is always on the side of liberty, for only to the free individual is full opportunity given of serving God. And yet this must be said with qualification. External liberty is only of use when it is accompanied with deliverance from inward bondage. Hence, in the New Testament, no great stress is laid upon civil liberty; that would come in due time, and, irresistibly, by the growth and conquering power of Christian principle. The stress in the New Testament is on the maintenance by the individual of liberty within himself. But in ancient Israel there was a God-governed nation as well as God-governed individuals, and civil liberty had to be sought as far as possible by Divine provisions and commands.—Pul. Com. Dividing victims for sacrifice. —It was a customary thing to cut the victim (which was to be offered as a sacrifice upon the occasion) into two parts, and so placing each half upon a different altar, to cause those who contracted the covenant to pass between them (Gen. xv. 9, 10, 17). This rite was practised both by believers and heathen at their solemn leagues. And the offering of these sacrifices, and passing between the parts of the divided victim, was symbolically staking their hopes of purification and salva-

The spiritually-minded Christian, when the Sun of Righteousness shines upon his path, looks upon all his sins as upon his shadow, viz., as "cast behind his back."

tion on their performance of the conditions on which it was offered. This remarkable practice may be clearly traced in the Greek and Latin writers. The following superstition is related by Pitts: "If the Algerine corsairs, at any time, happen to be in a very great strait or distress, as being chased, or in a storm, they will gather money, light up candles in remembrance of some dead marrabot (saint) or other, calling upon him with heavy sighs and groans. If they find no succor from their before-mentioned rites and superstitions, but that the danger rather increases, then they go to sacrificing a sheep, which is done after this manner: having cut off the head with a knife, they immediately take out the entrails, and throw them and the head overboard, and then, with all speed they can, they cut the body into two parts by the middle, and throw one part over the right side of the ship, and the other over the left, into the sea, as a kind of propitiation." In the case here referred to the ship passes between the parts thus thrown on each side of it.

CHAPTER THE THIRTY-FIFTH.

"This and the following chapter take us back into the reign of Jehoiakim. Ch. xxxv. is toward the close of that reign, when, the territory of Judah being overrun by marauding bands, (2 Ki. xxiv. 2,) the nomad tribe of Rechabites took refuge in Jerusalem."—Driver. **1—5.** (1) **Jehoiakim,** the predecessor of Zedekiah. (2) **Rechabites,** a tribe of Arabs, of the family of Jethro.[a] "A kind of nomadic ascetics belonging (1 Chron. ii. 55) to the Kenites, who from the time of Moses had enjoyed the rights of hospitality in Israel, and had been incorporated into the tribe of Judah."—Oehler. **wine to drink,** their allegiance to principle was to be tested. One of their rules was not to drink wine. (3) **Jaazaniah,** etc., chief men of the tribe. (4) **chamber .. princes,** these chambers were round the temple-courts. (5) **Drink,** "probably they were aware that the scene was intended to have symbolic religious significance."—Exp. Bib.

The Rechabites.—It is refreshing to meet these quiet, simple people after wearying ourselves with sickening sights of the vice and hypocrisy of the court and city life of Jerusalem. We are inclined to think too much of external civilization. Making allowance for exaggerations and eccentricities, we may find some much-needed lessons in the protest of Mr. Ruskin against the industrial ideal of the age. Inventions, commerce, wealth,—these are but means to an end. What is the use of the working of wonderful machinery if the outcome is poor and profitless? Many a man's business is a Frankenstein which becomes a tyrant to him. By others the science and resources of the age are only used as ministers to selfish pleasures. Thus the men and women may be none the better for all the advance that is made in the material appliances of the most complex civilization. Yet the personal condition of these men and women, and not that of the machinery of life, is the one matter of final importance. The quieter, simpler life of the Rechabites had many points which it would be instructive for us to consider. It was out of all the rush and worry of town-life. It was calm and comparatively free from care. With few wants, the Rechabites had few anxieties. Are we so much better off than they in this respect? Then, as a wandering life, it was a reminder of the truth, so often forgotten to our serious harm, that all men who live a life higher than the earthly must be pilgrims and strangers here, and must "seek a better country, that is, a heavenly."—Pul. Com. The Rechabites.—"On my arrival at Mesopotamia, some Jews that I saw there pointed out to me one of the ancient Rechabites. He stood before me, wild, like an Arab, holding the bridle of his horse in his hand. I showed him the Bible in Hebrew and Arabic, which he was much rejoiced to see, as he could read both languages, but had no knowledge of the New Testament. After having proclaimed to him the tidings of salvation, and made him a present of the Hebrew and Arabic Bibles and Testaments, I asked him, 'Whose descend-

[a] Ex. xviii. 9; Nu. x. 29, 32; Ju. i. 16; 1 Chr. ii. 55.

"This tribe came into Palestine with the Israelites, but, in order to maintain their independence, they led a nomadic life, without fixed settlements, and so were able without difficulty to remove on any attempt being made to subdue them."—Henderson.

"There are many traces of the Rechabites at present. They live entirely isolated, will not be recognized, and shun, or, rather, hate, all intercourse and every connection with the other Jews. They only sojourn in Arabia, and for the most part on the western shores of the Red Sea, and are engaged solely in the raising of cattle. They are called Arab Sebb, or Arabs who keep the seventh day."—Rabbi J. Schwartz.

"We read of a king of Poland who carried the picture of his father in a plate of gold about his neck; and when he was entering upon any great business he would kiss the picture and say, "God grant I may observe my father's charge, and do nothing unworthy of him."—Trapp.

"Thou sparkling bowl! thou sparkling bowl! Though lips of bards thy brim may press, And eyes of beauty o'er thee roll, And songs and dance thy power confess— I will not touch thee; for there clings A scorpion to thy side that stings." —Pierpoint.

ant are you?' 'Mousa,' said he, boisterously, 'is my name, and I will show you who were my ancestors;' on which he immediately began to read from the 5th to the 11th vss. of Jer. xxxv. 'Where do you reside?' said I. Turning to Gen. x. 27, he replied: 'At Hadoram, now called Simar by the Arabs; at Uzal, now called Sanan by the Arabs;' and again referring to the same chapter, verse 30th, he continued: 'At Mesha, now called Mecca, in the deserts around those places. We drink no wine, and plant no vineyard, and sow no seed; and live in tents, as Jonadab our father commanded us: Hobab was our father too. Come to us, and you will find us sixty thousand in number; and you see thus the prophecy has been fulfilled,—Therefore, thus saith the Lord of Hosts, the God of Israel; Jonadab, the son of Rechab, shall not want a man to stand before Me for ever;' and saying this, Mousa, the Rechabite, mounted his horse, and fled away, and left behind a host of evidence in favor of sacred writ." —Wolff.

6—11. (6) **Jonadab,** 2 Ki. x. 15. (7) **build house,** etc., "he probably desired to preserve their lives from the moral and religious corruption of town civilization."—Oehler. (10) **tents,** which can readily be removed from place to place. (11) **go to Jerusalem,** for the security of its walls and defences. **Syrians,** comp. 2 Ki. xxiv. 2. Syrians were allies of the Chaldæans at this time.

The power of strong drink.—If I were to tell you, says one, that there is in the British Isles a being into whose treasures are annually poured in unproductive consumption more than one hundred and forty millions of our national wealth; whose actions crush year by year more victims than have been crushed for centuries together by the car of Juggernaut; whose unchecked power causes year by year horrors incomparably more multitudinous than those which the carnage of any battlefields can present; if I were to say that the services wrought by this being were, if any at all, which is an open question, yet almost valueless in kind, infinitesimal in extent, while, on the other hand, the direct admitted indisputable miseries he inflicts were terrible in virulence and vast in ramification; if I were to say that at his right hand and at his left, as eager and ever active ministers, stood Idiocy and Pauperism, Degradation and Brutality; and at that point you were all to rise up at once and cry aloud, "Tell us the name of this being, that we may drive him with execration from the midst of us, and that every one of us may strive to extirpate his power and expel his polluting footsteps from our soil;" and if I were to say that, far from doing this, we all as a nation, and nearly all of us as individuals, crown him with garlands, honor him with social customs, introduce him into gladdest gatherings, sing songs in his glory, build myriads of temples to his service, familiarize our very children with his fame and praise;—were I to say this, then sentence by sentence, clause by clause, word by word, it would be literally true, not of a man, but of a thing, and that thing intoxicating drink.

12—15. (12) **Then came the word,** "Jeremiah is told to go and apply the lesson which the Rechabites taught. For this purpose he is to go forth from the chamber where his interview with them was held, and address the people we must suppose in the adjacent Temple court."—Camp. (13) **my words,** contrasted here with those of Jonathan. (14) **rising early,** the usual fig. for "earnestly." (15) **all my servants,** contrasting God's many messengers with this one lawgiver to the Rechabite. **Return ye** etc., ch. xviii. 11, xxv. 5.[a]

[a] "I enjoined nothing unreasonable, but simply to serve Me, and I attached to the command a gracious promise, but in vain. If Jonadab's commands, wh. were arbitrary, and not moral obligations in themselves, were obeyed, much more ought Mine, which are in themselves right." — Fausset.

Disobedience to God condemned (vss. 13, 14).—Let us consider this complaint—I. Simply. There is at this day—1. The same regard for the commands of men; 2. The same disregard for the commands of God. But let us consider the complaint more minutely—II. With its attendant aggravations. 1. The authority from which the different commands proceeded; 2. The commands themselves; 3. The manner in which they were enforced. Address—(1) Those who regard man, and not God; (2) Those who regard God, and not man; (3) Those who feel a united regard for both.—C. Simeon.

The simplest learner a true scholar.—The uncombed, ragged little wretch that has hardly got off from the briny sea—having come from the

Emerald Isle—and that goes into the mistress' school and begins to fumble the book, though he never saw the inside of a book before, and begins to learn, is a scholar just as much as the boy that is reaching out his hand to take his diploma and go to the next higher school. He is a scholar, though he has the bulk of his learning yet to acquire. And so it is with following Christ. Whoever will go to the Word of God, where four pictures open—Matthew, Mark, Luke, and John, whoever will read the life of Christ just as you would read the life of any other person, and follow that, he is a Christian.—H. W. Beecher. Obedience.—In nature we find great universal forces—light, heat, gravity, cohesion, magnetism, electricity, chemical affinity, life. We have only to understand the laws or conditions within which they act and we may command them; obey the law of the power, and the power obeys you. Thus we command light and it becomes our artist; heat and it becomes our refiner and purifier; gravity, and it becomes our giant mechanic; magnetism, our pilot; electricity our motor, messenger, illuminator. The Holy Spirit is the all subduing power of the Spiritual realm. Obey the laws of the Spirit, and all His power is at your disposal. In the work of God the believer may command Him.—Arthur T. Pierson.

"Some one asked Abraham Lincoln to appoint a day of fasting and prayer that God might be on their side. 'Don't bother about that,' said the man of common sense. God is now on the right side; you simply get with Him. The only way to command God is to obey Him, just as the only way to command electricity and steam is to obey the laws that govern them."—A. C. Dixon.

16—19. (17) **I will bring,** nothing shall remove the threatened penalty.[a] (18) **house,** or representatives of the family of. (19) **want a man,** i. e. the race should not be permitted to die out.[b]

Obedience to parents (vss. 18, 19).—I. Endeavor to impress on the attention of the young the necessity for a strict obedience to the commands of their parents. II. As also for a general obedience, under the limitation of altered circumstances and times, to the institutions and customs of our forefathers. III. Show that it is much more our duty implicity to respect and obey every command of God.—H. C. Cherry.

a Pr. i. 24; Is. lxv. 12.

b "Dr. Wolff and Sig. Pierotti bear witness to the existence of a large tribe who represent themselves as the descendants of the Rechabites."—Bib. Dict., Smith.

Many of the experiences of childhood are forgotten in after life, yet they all have had their influence; and this influence still exists secretly controlling our lives.

CHAPTER THE THIRTY-SIXTH.

"This chapter narrates the memorable incident of the 5th year of Jehoiakim, when the roll of Jeremiah's prophecies was burned by the king, leading to the writing of the second roll which was the basis of the prophecies as we have them."—Driver. **1—4.** (1) **Fourth year,** ch. xxv. 1. (2) **roll,** pieces of parchment joined together so as to make a roll, having a piece of wood at each end.[c] **write,** etc., i. e. he was to collect his prophecies, and make a permanent record of them.[d] Comp. Hab. ii. 2. ff. Is. viii. 1. "The purpose for which such records were made was to guarantee to coming generations the veracity of the Divine word. Isa. xxx. 8; xxxiv. 16; Jer. xxx. 2.—Oehler. (3) **may be,** comp. xxvi. 3.[e] (4) **Baruch,** ch. xxxii. 12, 13, 16.

c Is. viii. 1; Eze. ii. 9; Zec. v. 1.

d We may assume that many of these prophecies had been previously written.

e "In such places God is introduced, as speaking after the manner of men, and using such methods as in human probability may be most likely to prevail."—Lowth.

The names of writing materials and their origins.—Amongst the materials upon which the ancient Scriptures were written, were skins, tanned, or dyed red or yellow. These were not bound by the edge, but so fastened together as to form one continuous roll; hence the word volume, from Lat. volumen, a roll. Some were written on prepared skins called parchments, so called from Pergamos, the place where parchment was first made. "Sometimes tables of wood or stone, called caudices, or codices, were employed, hence the term codex (Lat. tablet) came to be applied to a manuscript on any material;" and hence also a system of laws was called a code, because the use of such tables was once frequent for legal purposes, where durability was important. "These tables were written on in their natural state (or, when used for temporary purposes, covered with wax) with an iron needle (Job xix. 24) called a stylus; hence we have the term style now applied to the style of the composition.

Exod. xxxii. 15; Deut. vi. 9; Isa. xxx. 8; Hab. ii. 2; Luke i. 63; 2 Cor. iii. 3.

The Bible.—

Within this ample volume lies
The mystery of mysteries:
Happiest they of human race

"Walls . . . will not hold out long without men, any more than men without walls; nor will both together stand people in any stead without God and his protection." — W. W. Dowling.

To whom their God has given grace
To read, to fear, to hope, to pray,
To lift the latch and force the way;
And better had they ne'er been born,
That read to doubt, or read to scorn.
—Scott.

[a] The great day of expiation, wh. was kept upon the tenth day of the seventh month. Le. xxiii. 27, 29.

[b] Keil supposes this fast to have been held in commemoration of the capture of Jerusalem by the Chaldæans in the previous year.

5—10. (5) **shut up,** "the same verb in the original is used chaps. xxxiii. 1, xxxix. 15, where it means imprisoned. Here, however, it cannot have that force, as we see by vs. 19, but simply means that he was hindered from addressing the people by some cause, probably danger to his life arising from the extreme unpopularity of his recent utterances."—Camb. Bib. (6) **fasting day,**[a] when the multitudes would be assembled in the temple-courts. (7) **supplication,** for pardon and mercy. (9) **proclaimed a fast,** i. e. a special one, perhaps on account of the national calamities.[b] (10) **higher court,** "there were two courts about the Temple," raised one above the other like terraces. The inner one was the higher court. The second court, or place of worship for the people, was separated from the first not by a wall but only by a railing, thus allowing the congregation to witness what was transacted in the court of the priests."—Oehler.

[a] "The honorable treatment which Baruch meets with shows that the princes were favorably inclined towards him and Jeremiah."—Spk. Com.

"Books are delightful when prosperity happily smiles; when adversity threatens, they are inseparable comforters. They give strength to human compacts, nor are grave opinions brought forward without books. Arts and sciences, the benefits of which no mind can calculate, depend upon books."—Richard Aungervyle.

11—15. (11) **son of Gemariah,** this Gemariah was the public scribe, or the secretary of state, but he had not been present at Baruch's reading. His son had no bad purpose in carrying the report to him. (12) **scribe's chamber,** or office of the secretary of state, prob. in the forecourt of the king's palace. **princes sat there,** holding a council of state. (13) **declared,** etc., i. e. recited the chief points. (14) **Jehudi,** his pedigree indicates that he was of good family. "He seems to have been a kind of court-usher."—Exp. Bib. (15) **read .. ears,** much of the substance of it was political, so if the utmost interest to them.[a]

The value of memorizing.—John Ruskin in his autobiography, tells of the foundation on which his character was reared. "After our chapters (from two to three a day according to their length) the first thing after breakfast (and no interruptions from servants allowed, none from visitors who either joined in the reading or had to stay upstairs and none from any visiting or excursions except real traveling) I had to learn a few verses by heart or repeat to make sure I had not lost something of what was already known; and with the chapters thus gradually possessed from first to last, I had to learn the whole body of the fine old Scotch paraphrases, which are good, melodious and forceful verses, and to which together with the Bible itself, I owe the first cultivation of my ear in sound. Though I have picked up the elements of a little further knowledge in mathematics, meteorology, and the like in after life—and owe not a little to the teaching of many people, this material installation of my mind in that property of chapters, I count very confidently the most precious and on the whole the one essential part of my education."

[b] "Jeremiah being prob. only under house-arrest, would find no difficulty in availing himself of the advice given by the princes."—Henderson.

18. Ink.—The Oriental ink is thicker than ours, and consists of lamp-black or charcoal mixed with gum and water. It is sold dry in grains.

16—19. (16) **afraid,** R. V., "they turned in fear one toward another." "Such an announcement as Jeremiah's at such a serious crisis startled them by its boldness. We may infer that the prophet had for some time, by Divine command, kept his sombre anticipations in the background."—Pul. Com. **tell the king,** bec. of the political importance of these writings. (17, 18) **Tell us,** etc., before speaking to the king the princes were anxious to be assured that they were the very words of the recognized Prophet, Jeremiah. (19) **hide thee,**[b] bec. the princes too truly guessed the effect of such denunciations on so jealous a tyrant as Jehoiakim.

Influence of books.—Benjamin Franklin tells us, in one of his lettters, that, when he was a boy, a little book fell into his hand, entitled Essays to do Good, by Cotton Mather. It was tattered and torn, and several leaves were missing. "But the remainder," he says, "gave me such a turn of thinking, as to have an influence on my conduct through life! for I have always set a greater value on the character of a doer of good than any other kind of reputation; and, if I have been a useful citizen, the public owes all the advantages of it to the little book." Jeremy Bentham mentions, that the current of his thoughts and studies was directed for life by a single phrase that caught his eye at the end of a pamphlet: "The greatest good of the greatest number." There are single sentences in the New Testament that have awakened to spiritual life hundreds of millions of dormant souls. In things of less moment, reading has a wondrous power. George Law, a boy on his father's farm, met an old, unknown book, which told the story of a farmer's son, who went away to seek his fortune, and came home, after many years' absence, a rich man. From that moment, George became uneasy, left home, lived over again the life he had read of, returned a millionaire, and paid all his father's debts. Robinson Crusoe has sent to sea more sailors than the pressgang. The story about little George Washington telling the truth about the hatchet and the plum tree, has made many a truth-teller. We owe all the Waverley novels to Scott's early reading of the old traditions and legends; and the whole body of pastoral fiction came from Addison's sketches of Sir Roger De Coverley in The Spectator. But illustrations are numberless. Tremble, ye who write, and ye who publish writing. A pamphlet has precipitated a revolution. A paragraph quenches or kindles the celestial spark in a human soul, in myriads of souls.—R. Donkersley.

"As companions and acquaintances, books are without rivals; and they are companions and acquaintances to be had at all times and under all circumstances. They are never out when you knock at the door; are never 'not at home when you call. In the lightest as well as in the deepest moods they may be applied to, and will never be found wanting." — Langford.

20—23. (20) **laid .. roll,** not venturing at first to show it to the king. (21) **fetch the roll,** being determined to see it for himself. **stood,** it seems that the king sat and the courtiers stood. (22) **winter house,** this is noticed to explain the presence of the fire.[a] **ninth month,** or December. **on the hearth,** R. V., "brazier."[b] (23) **he cut,** R. V., "the king cut it," treating the prophecy "with deliberate and ostentatious contempt."—Exp. Bib. **penknife,** lit. "the secretary's knife," used for trimming the reed-pen.[c]

Jehoiakim's penknife (vs. 23).—I. The use of the historical portions of Scripture is, that they represent to us embodied truth, and weave doctrine into the details of ordinary life. II. Christian parents should not let this and other instances of persons who have had godly parents dishearten them in their endeavor to train their children aright. III. Without literally mutilating the Word of God men may be practically guilty of the same act.—H. C. Milchenson. Efforts to destroy God's Word.—When Luther's books were publicly burned by order of the Papal Nuncio, the remark made to the Emperor Charles' ministers was, "Do you imagine that Luther's doctrines are found only in those books that you are throwing into the fire? They are written where you cannot reach them, in the hearts of the nation."—D'Aubigne. God's Word indestructible.—In the hand of a mummy, it is said, was found a seed three thousand years old, that given air and light and soil and water, grew and blossomed into a beautiful flower. True or not, it is a true illustration. God's Word might lie buried—hidden in dead hands or dead hearts—for centuries; but the life is in it, and when God's time comes it will bloom, and bless the place it grows in. Nothing can kill the life of it. I have heard of a Bible which was used (some leaves of it) to paste on the walls of a poor cabin, like wall paper. The people did not care for the words, perhaps could not even read them; I have forgotten about that. If they covered the rough, splintery boards, it was enough. But one day came a belated traveler, riding, and begging shelter from the storm. He was an unbeliever, who cared nothing for any of God's words, printed or spoken. Yet he could not help reading them as they stared him in the face all through that stormy day and evening. The writer who tells the story says that they at last led him to seek the Saviour and "keep his words" like a true disciple. You cannot hide or tear or burn or in any way destroy God's Word, any more than you could keep Christ in the grave. It is a living thing, and nothing can kill it.

a "The great men had distinct houses or apartments, fitted for the several seasons of the year Am. iii. 15."—Lowth.

b "In the East neither chimneys nor ovens are used, but, when the weather is cold, a pitcher of brass or iron, containing burning wood or charcoal, is used for the purpose of warming the chambers, and when the wood has burned to embers, a cover is placed over the pot to make it retain the heat." — Henderson.

c "As often as Jehudi read three or four columns, the king cut the piece he had read off, and threw it into the fire, until the entire roll was burnt." — Fausset.

24—26. (24) **not afraid,**[a] "contrast with this the conduct of the king's father when the newly found Book of the Law was read in his ears (and compare 1 Kings xxi. 27). Josiah on that occasion in sorrowful dismay rent his garments (2 Kings xxii. 11) but his son now rends not his garments, but tne Roll itself. And thus passed away "his last chance, his last offer of mercy: and as he threw the torn fragments of the roll on the fire he threw there in symbol his royal house, his doomed city, the temple,

a 2 Ki. xxii. 11.

"The drunken captain may cut in pieces the chart that tells of the rocks in the vessel's course, and put in irons the sailor who calls his attention to it, but neither will avert the

and all the people of the land.—Spk. Com. (25) **made intercession,** or entreaty. (26) **the son of Hammelech,** R. V., "the king's son," i. e. a royal prince, not necessarily son of Jehoiakim. **take,** i. e. arrest and put in prison. This the princes had expected, vs. 19.

Jeremiah's roll burnt (vs.2 4).—We learn hence.—I. The importance of the written Word. II. The value of Divine ordinances. III. The Lord's object in the Scriptures. IV. The rebellion of the carnal mind. V. The folly of destroying God's Word. Apply:—1. Make known this Word to others; 2. Study it for our own comfort.—C. Clayton.

Books and reading.—Of all the amusements which can possibly be imagined for a hard-working man, after his daily toil, or in its intervals, there is nothing like reading an entertaining book, supposing him to have a taste for it, and supposing him to have the book to read. It calls for no bodily exertion, of which he has had enough or too much. It relieves his home of its dulness and sameness, which in nine cases out of ten, is what drives him out to the alehouse, to his own ruin and his family's. It transports him into a livelier, and gayer, and more diversified and interesting scene; and while he enjoys himself there, he may forget the evils of the present moment, fully as much as if he were ever so drunk, with the great advantage of finding himself the next day with his money in his pocket, or at least laid out in real necessaries and comforts for himself and his family—and without a headache. Nay, it accompanies him to his next dav's work, and if the book he has been reading be anything above the idlest and lightest, gives him something to think of besides the mere mechanical drudgery of his every-day occupation,—something he can enjoy while absent, and look forward with pleasure to return to. But supposing him to have been fortunate in the choice of his book, and to have alighted upon one really good and of a good class. What a source of domestic enjoyment is laid open! What a bond of family union! He may read it aloud, or make his wife read it, or his eldest boy or girl, or pass it round from hand to hand. All have the benefit of it—all contribute to the gratification of the rest, and a feeling of common interest and pleasure is excited. Nothing unites people like companionship in intellectual enjoyment. It does more, it gives them mutual respect, and to each among them self-respect—that corner-stone of all virtue. It furnishes to each the master-key by which he may avail himself of his privilege as an intellectual being to

> Enter the sacred temple of his breast,
> And gaze and wander there a ravished guest,
> Wander through all the glories of his mind,
> Gaze upon all the treasures he shall find.

And while thus leading him to look within his own bosom for the ultimate sources of his happiness, warns him at the same time to be cautious how he defiles and desecrates that inward and most glorious of temples.—J. Herschel. Half of a Bible.—Perhaps you have seen a story in that wonderful life-story of "Uncle John Vassar" about a Bible that was cut in two. It belonged to a poor women who had never in all her married life owned a Bible. Her husband was a wicked man who never prayed, and she told Mr. Vassar that he had never allowed her to have one in the house. When the husband found out what had been given her, be snatched it up from the table and rushed out to the chopping block where he cut it through and through with the axe. Then he came back to the cabin and threw one of the pieces toward his wife, telling her that as she had a right to half of the property she might take her half of that. The other half he threw up into a cubbyhole where tools were sometimes kept, and it was forgotten. But one wet, dreary day in winter he was rummaging around in search of something to read, and came on this dark corner. There was nothing to reward his search, not even an old newspaper. But, yes!—what was this? Half of a Bible! He remembered how it came there. For want of something better to do, he picked it up and began to turn over the pages. He began to read the parable of the prodigal son, on the last page; but it was not all there. He did not like to ask his wife for the rest of the book. But he must have it to finish the

crash that must ensue unless the helm is turned." —F. B. Meyer.

"This is the bitterest of all,—to wear the yoke of our own wrong-doing."—George Eliot.

"Your non-searching of the Scriptures, your weariness under gospel preaching, your want of care to understand the mind of God, is prima facie evidence that there is some enmity in your heart against the Most High."— Charles H. Spurgeon.

"The same educations wall and press upon two lives. One rises on them into greatness, the other drags them down upon it and is crushed beneath them into ruin. . . . How is it that the Pharisee and the publican came down the same temple steps, one cold and proud and bitter, and the other with his heart full of tenderness and gratitude and humblest charity?" — Philips Brooks.

"God puts into our hands the Book of life, bright on every page with open secrets, and we suffer it to drop out of our hands unread."—F. W. Farrar.

"As long as one Bible remains, the empire of Satan is in danger." — Charles H. Spurgeon.

"It was a mercy to Jerusalem that when Bibles were scarce they had prophets, as that, afterward, when prophecy ceased, they had more Bibles: for

story. He hunted and prowled around in hope of finding it, but his poor wife had taken good care to hide that other half. He must finish that story. You know how hard it is to leave some stories unfinished. Finally he went to her and asked to see her piece of the Bible. She brought it and he read the story through and through and through again. By and by it became his story, for he was another "prodigal son" returned to his Father.

27—32. (27) **after that,** and in response to this act of public insult to God through His Prophet. (28) **another roll,** for man's wilfulness cannot be permitted to destroy God's Word.[a] (29) **Why,** etc., here is given the point which so greatly offended Jehoiakim. (30) **dead .. heat,** ch. xxii. 19. (31) **punish,** or visit his iniquity upon him. (32) **like words,** other prophecies of the same kind.[b] This is probably the basis of much of our book of Jeremiah and explains their form, i. e. not as originally uttered but as afterward recorded, with some explanatory additions, etc.

Jehoiakim burns the sacred roll (vss. 27, 28).—The folly of this act was great as the impiety, and take occasion to notice—I. The enmity of man's heart against the Word of God. The same disposition may be shown in a variety of ways. 1. By denying the Divine authority of Scripture; 2. By explaining away all its fundamental truths; 3. By entertaining doubts of its utility to the poor; 4. By setting its precepts at defiance; 5. By reviling and persecuting those who embrace it. II. The folly of indulging it. 1. We cannot change one declaration in all the Scriptures; 2. We cannot prevent the execution of one threatening; 3. We accumulate on our own heads the judgments we despise.—Simeon.

God's voice to the heedless.—There was a fisherman of the Bay of Fundy (so Frances Willard told the story in the Gospel Tabernacle, New York) who was one day watching his son out on the water fishing. He was not afraid to trust him, for the boy was well used to such work, and could take care of himself, so the father thought. But suddenly he did begin to grow anxious. Storm clouds were gathering. Far out at sea he saw them coming, and a low moaning wind gave its note of danger. It ruffled the water, and then even the boy saw it. Too late he understood. In the rough sea the boat went over—and under. Before long the father was carrying the dead boy home in his arms, and none of the friends and neighbors who went with him in a sad procession could give him any comfort. The old fisherman said a strange word, and he would say no other. This is what he said: "O God, I see that thou art bound to have my heart!" He and God knew what this trouble meant. It was God's sharp call to come to him. No doubt he had heard gentler ones, and never minded. Fathers and mothers make their voices sharp and stern when children will not hear the pleasant ones. So does our heavenly Father. Jehoiakim's conduct.—In opposing Jeremiah Jehoiakim was not defying clear and acknowledged truth. Like the Pharisees in their conflict with Christ, the persecuting king had popular religious sentiment on his side. According to that current theology which had been endorsed in some measure even by Isaiah and Jeremiah, the defeat at Megiddo proved that Jehovah repudiated the religious policy of Josiah and his advisers. The inspiration of the Holy Spirit enabled Jeremiah to resist this shallow conclusion, and to maintain through every crisis his unshaken faith in the profounder truth. Jehoiakim was too conservative to surrender at the prophet's bidding the long-accepted and fundamental doctrine of retribution, and to follow the forward leading of Revelation. He "stood by the old truth" as did Charles V. at the Reformation. "Let him that is without sin" in this matter "first cast a stone at" him. Though we extenuate Jehoiakim's conduct, we are still bound to condemn it; not, however, because he was exceptionally wicked, but because he failed to rise above a low spiritual average: yet in this judgment we also condemn ourselves for our own intolerance, and for the prejudice and self-will which have often blinded our eyes to the teachings of our Lord and Master.—Exp. Bib. The continuance of God's mercy.—Why should the roll be rewritten? The threats it contained could be executed without any reissue of them. If all fair warnings were disregarded, no more could be required. True, and no more were required. Yet out of His great,

God never leaves himself without witness." —Spurgeon.

[a] "Here is a sublime specimen of the triumph of God's Word, when repressed by the power, and burnt by the rage of this world, whether it be in the suppression of the Scriptures, or in preventing their circulation, or in casting copies of them into the fire, or in the imprisonment and martyrdom of God's preachers. That Word rises more gloriously out of all its persecutions." —Wordsworth.

[b] "To consume the material volume was not to defeat the design of Him who had inspired it."—F. Jacox.

"There was a king once who wanted to know what could best help his people, and so he left his palace to go and learn shipbuilding in a Dutch seaport. He put the workman's blouse on and made his own hands hard with tools and braved all weathers. No other workman seemed more humble or more hardy than he was. But all the time he was the king. He went back to his throne and that hard toil-marked hand held the king's scepter. So Christ was a king always. Though he stooped to be a man among men, he never lost his kingship."

long-suffering grace God issued His warnings afresh. This is the deeper truth that underlies the command to write out the prophecies once more. The same truth is illustrated in all the history of the Jews. God sent a succession of prophets, "rising up early and sending," to impress upon the people the same unheeded lessons. The continuance of revelation with us is a reminder of God's forbearing mercy.—Pul. Com.

CHAPTER THE THIRTY-SEVENTH.

Here we return to the narrative in chapter xxxiv., and are given an account of Jeremiah's personal history during the siege of Jerusalem by the Chaldæans. **1—5.** (1) **Zedekiah,** 2 Ki. xxiv. 17. (2) **did hearken,** more esp. to the advice to yield fully to the Chaldæans. (3) **sent,** etc., during the interval of hope excited by news of the approach of the Egyptian army. **Pray now,** "there seemed to be a hope that as in the time of Sennacherib's invasion, when Hezekiah was king (2 Kings xix. 35), there might now be given in answer to prayer a miraculous overthrow of the invading host." (4) **not .. prison,** i. e. not yet, see vs. 15. (5) **departed,** for a time raising the siege.[a]

Valueless Prayers.—Scarcely any ministers but can recall instances of their prayers being asked by persons who have been prayerless themselves. One will suffice. I went to see a woman in G——. She was dying but without a gleam of hope. "Oh, pray for me. I cannot, cannot pray for myself sir." "Indeed, but why not for yourself?" "My state is too hard; I have known all about religion since childhood, but have insulted my conscience, rejected God, resisted the Spirit, neglected Christ, and O, I dare not, I cannot speak to Heaven now!" All my pleading failed to awaken hope in her, or to induce her to an effort to pray. It seemed awful. No! She should be thankful if I would pray for her; but the could not even frame in her thoughts a petition; prayer in her was dead. Although I did kneel and earnestly plead for her, yet when I asked her is she had joined in any one of my direct and urgent prayers, she answered, "No, I have no power to bring my mind to any definite desire. I have killed prayer in my soul; I can't now speak a thought to God." The people did not wish when they asked these prayers to be severed from sin, only to be relieved of trouble. But such desire could not be granted; therefore God held them down to the consequences of their sin. Their request was an insult to God. Such men are well described in Mrs. H. W. B. Stowe's book, "Uncle Tom's Cabin," where one of them, Haley, is thus spoken to by a comrade: "After all, what's the odds between me and you? 'Tain't that you care one bit more or have a bit more feelin'; it's clean, sheer, dog meanness, wanting to cheat the devil and save your own skin. Don't I see through it? And your 'gettin' religion,' as you call it, arter all, is too p'isin mean for any crittur; run up a bill with the devil all your life, and then sneak out when pay-time comes! Boh!' Is there not a vast amount of this meanness?"—Pul- Com. Praying soldiers.—Nor are those the worst soldiers who are often upon their knees. Hume tells us that on the eve of the battle of Hastings the Saxons spent the night in drinking mead and metheglin; but that the Normans passed it in silence and religious devotions, and went into battle singing the hymn of Roland. The psalm-singers had the best of it in the bloody struggles around the standard; and the Cavaliers, in spite of their chivalry, went down before those terrible fellows who marked the "fighting verses" in their Bible with the blades of their swords. "Show me the men that pray," Gustavus Adolphus used to observe, "and I will show you those that you can't beat;" and we will be bound that the stout Highlander who grounded his arms at the door of Dum-Dum Church sooner than take part in a service which was against the grain of his conscience, never showed his back to an enemy, and never will.—Daily Paper.

6—10. (7) **Pharaoh's .. land,** i. e. their help will be of no practical value to you. (8) **come again,** comp. ch. xxi. 4—7.[a] (10) **wounded,** "our

[a] Pharaoh Hophra, the Apries of Herodotus, was an ally of Zedekiah, but his intervention availed nothing. Whether, however, he withdrew without giving Nebuc. battle, or whether he was defeated, we do not know." —Spk. Com.

"As that storm roars the loudest which has been the longest gathering, so God's reckoning day with sinners, by being long coming, will be the more terrible when it comes." —Guthrie.

"Dear as freedom is, and in my heart's
Just estimation, prized above all price,
I had much rather be myself the slave
And wear the bonds than fasten them on him."
—Cowper.

Those as much deceive themselves who think to escape God's judgments as those who think to brave them; the feet of him that flees from them will as surely fall as the hands of him that fights against them. —Matthew Henry.

[a] "God has the sovereign command of all the hosts of men, even of those that know Him not, that own Him not, and they are all made to serve his pur-

version fails to give the full force of the Hebrew, which is that even though but a few individuals remained, and those severely wounded (literally, transfixed), they would be more than a match for the Jews. So certainly was it God's purpose that Jerusalem should be overthrown."

The Great Advantage of Obeying God.—Connect with past history of Israel, and the day's lesson. I. Had the nation been obedient, instead of invasion and oppression, they had had increasing peace: instead of sin and idolatry, their moral and religious excellence had abounded. II. But it applies to us also. 1. We have a picture of what our peace may be if we serve the Lord. Picture a river; at first narrow, gets broader; at first shallow, gets deeper; at first a babbling brook, full of little eddies, turns, etc., by-and-by a majestic river, flowing on without a sound or a ripple. 2. Our righteousness is also illustrated by waves of sea; ocean an image of infinitude; waves wash round all coasts; how much they cover, how much they bear up. Learn:—(1) All this depends upon obedience and trust: then peace with God, conscience, etc.; (2) Some hearken to the advice of others rather than commands of God; and what the result?—Hive.

11—15. (11) **broken up,** the fig. intimates that they removed their siege-engines, and raised the siege. (12) **Then,** taking advantage of the openness of the country. **separate himself,** R. V., "to receive his portion there." "He saw too clearly the coming catastrophe, and was on the point of escaping from Jerusalem to end his days in his own loved village of Anathoth."—Stanley.[a] (13) **took Jer.,** "we may be sure that at this time the gates were in charge of trusty adherents of the princes of the Egyptian party." **fallest away,** their excuse for this false charge was that the prophet had advised such action, xxi. 9. (14) **false,** however he may have advised that as a national policy he did not intend to desert his countrymen in this crisis. (15) **prison . . house,** the place reserved for political offenders.[b]

Treatment of Prisoners.—The treatment of those that are shut up in the Eastern prisons differs from our usages, but serves to illustrate several passages of Scripture. Chardin relates several circumstances concerning their prisons, which are curious, and should not be omitted. In the first place, he tells us that the Eastern prisons are not public buildings erected for that purpose; but a part of the house in which their criminal judges dwell. As the governor and provost of a town, or the captain of the watch, imprisoned such as are accused in their own houses, they set apart a canton of it for that purpose, when they are put into these offices, and choose for the jailer the most proper person they can find of their domestics. Sir John supposes the prison in which Joseph, together with the chief butler and chief baker of Pharaoh, was put, was in Potiphar's own house. But I would apply this account to the illustration of another passage of Scripture: "Wherefore," it is said, Jer. xxxvii. 15, "the princes were wroth with Jeremiah, and smote him, and put him in prison in the house of Jonathan the scribe; for they had made that the prison." Here we see a dwelling-house was made a prison; and the house of an eminent person, for it was the house of a scribe, which title marks out a person of quality; it is certain it does so in some places of Jeremiah, particularly ch. xxxvi. 12, "Then he went down into the king's house into the scribe's chamber, and lo, all the prices sat there, even Elishama the scribe, and Delaiah," etc. The making the house of Jonathan the prison, would not now, in the East, be doing him any dishonor, or occasion the looking upon him in a mean light; it would rather mark out the placing him in an office of importance. It is probable it was so anciently, and that his house became a prison, when Jonathan was made the royal scribe, and became, like the chamber of Elishama, one of the prisons of the people.—Harmer.

16—21. (16) **dungeon,** lit. "house of the pit," undoubtedly implies an underground excavation. Ch. xxxviii. 6.[a] **cabins,** R. V. "cells." **many days,** prob. till the Chaldæans had returned again. (17) **secretly.** The poor, weak king had probably nothing to do with his imprisonment and seems to have had a superstitious veneration for the prophet.—Cheyne.

---

poses. He directs their marches, their counter - marches, their retreats, their returns, as it pleases Him; and furious armies, like stormy winds, in all their motions are fulfilling His Word." — Mat. Henry.

[a] Allusion, however, may be to Jer.'s going, as others did, to fetch a store of provisions from the neighboring country.

"When the siege was temporarily raised, the first object with everybody would be to obtain supplies of food, and accordingly Jeremiah in the midst of the people, i. e. accompanied by others, who, like himself, had a right to a share in the priests' produce at Anathoth, started thither to see whether any stores still remained which might be available for their common use."—Spk. Com.

[b] "Often in the E. part of the private house of a public officer serves as a prison."— Fausset.

[a] "That selected for Jer. appears to have been of a squalid description, consisting of a well, or pit, with vaults round the sides, in which the prisoners were lodged."— Henderson.

"The event hath now convinced you how much they have deceived you; for you see the siege renewed, and the city in imminent danger of being taken."—Lowth.

b "The streets in E. cities are generally distinguished fr. each other, not by the separate names which they bear, but by the sort of traffic or business carried on in them. The different branches of trade, instead of being intermixed, as with us, are usually assigned to a distinct locality."— Hackett.

"The essence of a lie is the intention to deceive."

The return of the Chaldæans had renewed the king's anxiety. **thou .. Babylon,** ch. xxxii. 3, 4, xxxiv. 2, 3. (18) **I offended,** R. V., "wherein have I sinned." He had been but God's agent. (19) **not come,** this the false prophets had constantly said. (21) **court,** a freer kind of custody. **A piece of bread** "is not sumptuous fare, but it is evidently mentioned as an improvement upon his prison diet: it is not difficult to understand why Jeremiah was afraid he would die in the house of Jonathan." **Bakers' street,** or quarter.[b]

Ovens.—In primitive times, an oven was designed only to serve a single family, and to bake for them no more than the bread of one day; a custom which still continues in some places of the East; but the increase of population in the cities, higher degrees of refinement, or other causes in the progress of time, suggested the establishment of public bakehouses. They seem to have been introduced into Judæa long before the captivity; for the Prophet Jeremiah speaks of "the bakers' street," in the most familiar manner, as a place well known. This, however, might be only a temporary establishment, to supply the wants of the soldiers assembled from other places to defend Jerusalem. If they received a daily allowance of bread, as is the practice still in some Eastern countries, from the royal bakehouses, the order of the king to give the Prophet daily a piece of bread, out of the street where they were erected, in the same manner as the defenders of the city, was perfectly natural. The custom alluded to still maintains its ground at Algiers, where the unmarried soldiers receive every day from the public bakehouses a certain number of loaves. Pitts indeed asserts, that the Algerines have public bakehouses for the accommodation of the whole city. The women prepare their dough at home, and the bakers send their boys about the streets, to give notice of their being ready to receive and carry it to the bakehouses. They bake their cakes every day, or every other day, and give the boy who brings the bread home, a piece or little cake for the baking, which is sold by the baker. Small as the Eastern loaves are, it appears from this account, that they give a piece of one only to the baker, as a reward for his trouble. This will perhaps illustrate Ezekiel's account of the false prophets receiving pieces of bread by way of gratuities: 'And will ye pollute me among my people, for handfuls of barley, and pieces of bread?" These are compensations still used in the East, but of the meanest kind, and for services of the lowest sort.—Paxton.

CHAPTER THE THIRTY-EIGHTH.

a "Jer. would not have so often repeated this unwelcome message, but that he could put them in a certain way, though not to save the city, yet to save themselves; so that every man might have his own life given him for a prey if he would be advised."—Mat Henry.

1—3. (1) **Shephatiah,** "the removal of Jeremiah from prison to the court of the guard was of course favorable to the publication of his message. Hence the princes take alarm and apply to the king for permission to put him to death. There was no doubt truth in their assertion that Jeremiah's words were 'weakening the hands of the men of war,' but the fact, that the words which he spoke were not his own but the Divine message with which he was charged, made all the difference in the case."—Camb. Bib. (2) **He that,** etc., ch. xxi. 9. (3) **surely,** so the defenders may cherish no hope of success.[a]

Life a River.—Pliny compares life to a river. The river, small and clear in its origin, gushes forth from rocks, falls into deep glens, and wantons and meanders through a wild and picturesque country; nourishing only the uncultivated tree or flower by its dew or spray. In this, in its state of infancy and youth, it may be compared to the human mind, in which fancy and strength of imagination are predominant: it is more beautiful than useful. When the different rills or torrents join, and descend into the plain, it becomes slow and stately in its motions, and able to bear upon its bosom the stately barge. In this mature state, it is deep, strong, and useful. As it flows on towards the sea, it loses its force and its motion, and at last, as it were, becomes lost and mingled with the mighty abyss of waters.—H. Davy.

4—6. (4) **Therefore,** i. e. bec. Jer.'s messages disheartened the soldiers: and he seemed to recommend their desertion to the enemy.[b] **that remain,** comp. vs. 19. Some had already gone over to the Chaldæans. (5) **in your hand,** Zedekiah felt powerless to resist his chief officers.[c] (6) **dungeon,** ch. xxxvii. 16: a pit, or cistern.[d] **son of Hammelech,** R. V., the king's son." **with cords,** this gives indication of the depth and unwholesomeness. The princes hoped Jer. would die in the pit. **the mire.** It is difficult not to connect this event with the 69th Psalm vss. 2, 14, 15, 20.—Stanley.

Prisons.—There were two prisons in Jerusalem; of which one was called the king's prison, which had a lofty tower that overlooked the royal palace, with a spacious court before it, where state prisoners were confined. The other was designed to secure debtors and other inferior offenders: and in both these the prisoners were supported by the public, on bread and water. Suspected persons were sometimes confined under the custody of state officers, in their own houses: or rather a part of the house which was occupied by the great officers of state, was occasionally converted into a prison. This seems to be a natural conclusion from the statement of the Prophet Jeremiah, in which he gives an account of his imprisonment: "Wherefore, the princes were wroth with Jeremiah, and smote him, and put him in prison, in the house of Jonathan the scribe; for they had made that the prison." The royal prison in Jerusalem, and especially the dungeon, into which the prisoner was let down naked, seems to have been a most dreadful place. The latter cannot be better described than in the words of Jeremiah himself (xxxviii. 6), who for his faithfulness to God and his country, in a most degenerate age, had to encounter all its horrors. A discretionary power was given to the keeper to treat his prisoners as he pleased; all that was expected of him being only to produce them when required. If he kept them in safe custody, he might treat them well or ill as he chose; he might put them in irons or not; shut them up close, or indulge them with greater liberty; admit their friends and acquaintances to visit them, or suffer no person to see them. The most worthless characters, the most atrocious criminals, if they can bribe the jailer and his servants with large fees, shall be lodged in his own apartment, and have the best accommodation it can afford; but if he be the enemy of those committed to his charge, or have received larger presents from their persecutors, he will treat them in the most barbarous manner.—Paxton.

7—9. (7) **Ebed-melech,** prob. keeper of the royal harem:[a] **Ethiopian,** Heb. Cushite. **sitting in the gate,** where causes were usually heard. It was the king's duty to sit there, as a magistrate, for a certain time every day. (9) **like to die,**[b] likely to die. **no more bread,** it would almost seem as if the little remaining bread had been brought together by command of the magistrates, and that it was given out in rations by them (comp. ch. xxxvii. 21). Nobody was likely to think of the poor prophet.

God's Care for His Own.—Mungo Park, faint and perishing, observes a single tuft of grass in the waste African desert, when he thought there was nothing left for him but to die, and his heart argued with the rapidity of lightning, that the Creator of that tuft of grass could not be unobservant of him, His child; and strengthened by the thought he persevered and was saved. And now Jehovah singled out an Ethiopian in the court of Zedekiah, and sent to him a message of His divine and fatherly love. To God the small and the great are alike (Isa. xl. 26, 29).—Hom. Com.

10—13. (10) **thirty men,** a sufficient number to prevent the princes from interfering. (11) **cast clouts,** rags of torn garments. **rotten rags,** pieces of worn-out garments.[c] (12) **under .. armholes,** to ease the strain of lifting Jer. up out of the well. (13) **in the court,** still in custody, but **not in peril of his life.**

[b] "Had Jer. not had a Divine commission he might justly have been accused of treason; but, having one, which made the result of the siege certain, he acted humanely as the interpreter of God's will under the theocracy, in advising surrender."—Fausset.

[c] "Zedekiah in his pusillanimity gives up Jeremiah to the princes, as Pilate gave up Christ to the chief priests."—Wordsworth.

[d] "Every house in Jerus. was supplied with a subterranean cistern, so well constructed that we never read of the city suffering in a siege from want of water."—Spk. Com.

"An old writer has said that we have two eyes and two ears, but only one tongue, that we may see and hear twice as much as we say; but unhappily men generally act the reverse; for, alas! they say far more than they see or hear."

[a] "Eunuchs of the present day, to whom the charge of harems is committed, are mostly from Nubia or Abyssinia." — Michaelis.

[b] Lit. "he is dead in his place;" the language of fear of the worst.

[c] "This thoughtful act of the negro shows his kindliness, the depth of the cistern, that force would be necessary in pulling out Jeremiah and therefore that the mire was deep, and

Divine Uses for Mean Things.—God, who made all things, can see a thousand adaptations and utilities for that which man supposes has been used up. Are there not weapons in the King's armory that have been allowed to rust when they might have done good service? talents that have been hid in a napkin when they should have been at usury? There need be no idle members in the King's household. He takes out of his treasury things new and old, and calls upon the blind, the halt, the maimed, the aged, the poor, the ignorant, to do him honor and service. "But I have no talents in that direction," etc. Yet God can use you if you will ask him. He will regenerate you by using you; purify you of all the moral dross and filth that adhere to you; and develop higher faculties and a diviner serviceableness, if you will but let him. There were kingly robes in Judah that day that had not a tithe of the honor of these "old rotten rags;" and there are great, wise, and noble who will have to give place in the day of judgment to the weak things, and things which have been despised (1 Cor. i. 26—31).

possibly that Jeremiah was enfeebled by his privations, and required gentle treatment."—Spk. Com.

"To refuse to hear the voice of God is a proof of idolatry."—W. W. Dowling.

14—16. (14) **third entry,** what this means exactly is not clear; probably the "entry" led from the palace to the temple. It must have been a private place, else it would not have been chosen for this interview. —Pul. Com. **a thing,** or a word, a prophetic revelation, as in xxxvii. 17. (15) **hearken,** R. V. "thou wilt not hearken." This is not a question in the Hebrew. The king was influenced momentarily by those in whose presence he happened to be. (16) **sware secretly,** being too weak to take a decided and open course.[a]

[a] "Zedekiah is an example of that moral cowardice which is the bane and destruction of many, especially in courts." — Wordsworth.

There is nothing in the universe that I fear, but that I shall not know all my duty, or shall fail to do it.—Mary Lyon.

"As flowers always wear their own colors and give forth their own fragrance every day alike, so should Christians maintain their character at all times and under all circumstances." — H. W. Beecher.

"Fear or guilt attends the deeds of darkness:
The virtuous breast ne'er knows it."
—Havard

"Cowards die many times before their deaths,
The valiant never taste of death but once."
—Shakespeare

"Fear is the tax that conscience pays to guilt."
—Sewell

A Prison.—

A prison is in all things like a grave,
Where we no better privileges have
Than dead men; nor so good. The soul, once fled,
Lives freer now than when she was cloister'd
In walls of flesh; and though the organs want
To act her swift designs, yet all will grant
Her faculties more clear, now separate,
Than if conjunction, which of late
Did marry her to earth, had stood in force,
Incapable of death or of divorce:
But an imprison'd mind, though living, dies,
And at one time feels two captivities:
A narrow dungeon, which her body holds,
But narrower body which herself enfolds.

—Bishop King.

17—19. (17) **go forth,** and give thyself up as prisoner. **the king of Babylon's princes,** "an intimation that Nebuchadnezzar was not himself at this time in command of the besieging forces. While the tedious blockade continued, he had no doubt taken up his position at Riblah, where we find him somewhat later (xxxix. 5)." **soul .. live,** or thy life shall be spared. (18) **given into,** as a conquered city. **thou .. hand,** ch. xxxix. 5. (19) **lest they,** i. e. the Chaldæans. **mock me,** for deserting at last, only when it was too late to save the city.

Zedekiah is a perfect monument of the miseries that wait upon weakness: he was everybody's friend in turn—now a docile pupil of Jeremiah and gratifying the Chaldæan party by his professions of loyalty to Nebuchadnezzar, and now a pliant tool in the hands of the Egyptian party persecuting his former friends. At the last he was afraid alike of the princes in the city, of the exiles in the enemy's camp, and of the Chaldeans. The mariner who had to pass between Scylla and Charybdis was fortunate compared to Zedekiah. To the end he clung with a pathetic blending of trust and fearfulness to Jeremiah. He believed him, and yet he seldom had courage to act according to his counsel. Zedekiah is a conspicuous example of the strange irony with which Providence entrusts incapable persons with the decision of most momentous issues; it sets

Laud and Charles I. to adjust the Tudor Monarchy to the sturdy self-assertion of Puritan England, and Louis XVI. to cope with the French Revolution. Such histories are after all calculated to increase the self-respect of those who are weak and timid. Moments come, even to the feeblest, when their action must have the most serious results for all connected with them. It is one of the crowning glories of Christianity that it preaches a strength that is made perfect in weakness.—Exp. Bib.

20—23. (20) **Obey,** all will then come right. (21) **this is the word,** viz., that both Zedekiah and the city would be taken. (22) **women,** of the court. These would be taken as prey by the Chaldæan officers, and they would reprove Zedekiah for following bad advice.[a] **Thy friends,** comp. Obad. 7. **they .. back,** i. e. the friends in whom Zedekiah trusted would forsake him in the hour of need. (23) **thou shalt cause,** i. e. the harder fate of the city shall be the consequence of thine obstinacy.[b]

How We are Linked Together.—You remember the touching story of the daughter of Sir Robert Peel. Her father gave her, as a birthday present, a gorgeous riding habit, and went out with her on the same day for an airing in the park, his heart swelling with parental pride as he rode by her side. Shortly afterwards, she sickened and died of typhus fever of the most malignant type; and when inquiry was made as to how she caught the infection, it was discovered that the habit, bought from one of the London West End tradesmen, had been made in a miserable attic, where the husband of the seamtress was lying ill of fever, and that it had been used by her to cover him in his shivering fits. Thus, whether we will believe it or not, the safety of the highest is bound up with the condition of the lowest.—W. N. Taylor.

The Mission of a True Prophet.—There is no greater peril than to turn away from any true messenger of God; and happily there is no need to do so, through uncertainty as to his credentials. Any one who points out a present wrong in our lives that needs to be put right immediately, is to that extent a prophet of God; and if, in addition, he ventures on certain predictions, then all we can do is to wait. Gamaliel's shrewd advice cannot be too constantly kept in mind. What we cannot be certain about while a thing is in the seed will be made clear when it comes to the fruit. The most important matters are ever those on which we have to decide at once; and God never fails to send forth his light and truth so as to make the decision right.—Pul. Com.

24—28. (24) **no man know,** throughout the interview Zed. shows himself to be utterly weak. (25) **the princes,** whom Zed. so greatly feared. (26) **Jonathan's house,** ch. xxxvii. 15. (27) **the matter,** i. e. the advice to desert to the Chaldæans, which Jer. had so earnestly given to the king. (28) **court,** ch. xxxix. 21. **and he was there,** etc., these words belong to chapter xxxix., and are to be translated "And it came to pass, when Jerusalem was taken (in the ninth year of Zedekiah . . . the city was broken up) then all the princes of the king of Babylon," etc.

Equivocation.—

Honesty, even by itself, though making many adversaries
Whom prudence might have set aside, or charity have softened,
Evermore will prosper at the last, and gain a man great honor.
Yet there are others that will truckle to a lie, selling honesty for interest.
And do they gain! They gain but loss; a little cash, with scorn.
Behold! sorrowful change wrought upon a fallen nature:
He hath lost his own esteem and other men's respect.
For the buoyancy of upright faith, he is clothed in the heaviness of cringing;
For plain truth, where none could err, he hath chosen tortuous paths;
In lieu of his majesty of countenance, the timorous glances of servility;
Instead of Freedom's honest pride, the spirit of a slave.

—Tupper.

[a] The Prophet now informs Zed. that if he refused to submit, he would become the object of more cutting derision on the part of his own mistresses, who, in order the more to gratify their new lords, would exult over his fallen condition."—Henderson.

[b] "It shall be thine own act, as completely as if done with thine own hand."—Spk. Com.

"His words are bonds, his oaths are oracles;
His love sincere, his thoughts immaculate;
His tears, pure mesengers sent from his heart;
His heart as far from fraud as heaven from earth."

"No matter how poor I am, no matter though the prosperous of my own time will not enter and take up their abode under my roof, if Milton will cross my threshold to sing to me of Paradise, and Shakespeare, to open to me the worlds of imagination and the workings of the human heart, and Franklin to enrich me with his practical wisdom, I shall not pine for want of intellectual companionship, and I may become a cultivated man though excluded from what is called the best society in the place where I live." — Channing.

CHAPTER THE THIRTY-NINTH.

1—3. (1) **ninth year,** 2 Ki. xxv. 1, 2; Je. lii. 4.[c] (2) **eleventh year,** the siege lasted just one year and six months. **broken up,** R. V., "a breach was made in the city." (3) **And all,** R. V., "that all," etc., continuing the last clause of chap. xxxviii. **middle gate,** that wh. separated the city of Zion from the lower town. **Rab-mag,** prob. the official title of the second Sharezer, meaning "Chief of the magicians," the sacerdotal caste of Chaldæa.[d]

The Retribution of God.—What an accumulation of woe do the eight verses with which this chapter opens present! Let thought dwell on the several statements made here, and let imagination seek to realize what they must have meant to those upon whom the calamities they speak of came; and it will be seen, in vivid lurid light, that the retribution of God upon sin and sinners has been in the past no mere empty threat, and it will lead to the salutary suggestion, so questioned now, that his like threatened retribution in the future is no empty threat either. How unreasonable, in the face of historic facts such as those told of here, and in the face of actual facts of today in which dread suffering and awful calamity are seen overtaking wicked doers, to doubt that God will do the like again should necessity arise!—Pul. Com.

4—7. (4) **fled,** "it was night and under cover of the darkness Zedekiah and his little army fled, by the rocky ravine of the Kedron; as far as the 'plains of Jericho,' doubtless hoping to cross the Jordan and elude their pursuers in the mountains of Moab."—Cheyne. 2 Ki. xxv. 4—12.[a] **plain,** or wilderness of Judæa. (5) **gave judgment,** pronounced his sentence. (6) **slew,** etc., Zedekiah's punishment was specially terrible bec. of the stubbornness of his resistance. (7) **put out . . eyes,** a cruel but not unusual punishment.[b]

Putting Out the Eyes.—By an inhuman custom, which is still retained in the East, the eyes of captives taken in war are not only put out but sometimes literally scooped or dug out of their sockets. This dreadful calamity Samson had to endure, from the unrelenting vengeance of his enemies. In a posterior age, Zedekiah, the last king of Judah and Benjamin, after being compelled to behold the violent death of his sons and nobility, had his eyes put out, and was carried in chains to Babylon. The barbarous custom long survived the decline and fall of the Babylonian empire, for by the testimony of Mr. Maurice, in his History of Hindostan, the captive princes of that country were often treated in this manner by their more fortunate rivals; a red-hot iron was passed over their eyes, which effectually deprived them of sight, and at the same time of their title and ability to reign.—Paxton. The blinding of captives was a common Assyrian practice. In the bas-reliefs representing the capture of Lachish by Sennacherib, the prisoners were represented. Some pegged down to the ground to be flayed alive and others having their eyes put out. In one of the sculptures at Khorsabad, Sargon represents himself in person holding a prisoner by a thong attached to a ring passed through his under lip. The victim kneels before him while with a spear he pierces his eyes. Others are held chained and with hooks through their lips are held awaiting their turn. In other cases, the king slays the prisoners with his own spear. In another, an executioner flays a captive fastened to the wall. It was especially in Persia that the cruel practice of blinding prisoners prevailed and it is mentioned by most of the Greek historians. In Turkey it was formerly the custom for a sultan on his accession either to slaughter or blind his half brothers that he might have no rivals or dangerous ones near his throne. In modern Persia the shahs have invariably, even up to the present century, put out the eyes of all their brothers who did not escape in time to distant provinces. The late shah

[c] "After his expedition to Jerusalem, Nebuchadnezzar himself seems to have retired to Riblah in the land of Hamath, to the north of Palestine, on the right bank of the river Orontes, about 35 miles N.E. of Baalbec, on the great road between Palestine and Babylonia."—Wordsworth.

[d] "It was customary among the Chaldæans to give the names of their idols, as an additional title, or mark of honor, to persons of distinction."—Lowth.

[a] "They took to flight by the double wall wh. ran along the south side of Zion, and reached the point whence two roads struck off, the one to Bethlehem, and the other across the south side of the Mount of Olives. They appear to have taken the latter route in order to reach the Jordan, having crossed wh. they might have escaped into Arabia Deserta."—Henderson.

[b] Comp. Je. xxxii. 4; Eze. xii. 13.

"Possibly he was deprived of sight by having a red-hot iron held before his eyes."—Michaelis.

"The Assyrian sculptures depict the delight with which the kings struck out, often with their own hands, the eyes of captive princes."—Fausset.

was the first Persian monarch who was prevailed upon to abandon the practice.—Tristram. Chains.—There is in the British Museum a pair of bronze fetters, brought from Nineveh, which weigh eight pounds eleven ounces, and measure sixteen and a half inches in length. These probably resemble the fetters put on Zedekiah. The rings which enclose the ankles are thinner than the other part so that they could be hammered smaller after the feet had passed through them.—Freeman.

8—10. "This section by way of introduction to the brief account of the treatment of Jeremiah, gives a sketch of the fate of the inhabitants generally. If we had only this summary, we might suppose that Nebuzar-adan was present at the time in person. We find from the two other forms of the account (chap. lii.; 2 Kings xxv.) that he did not arrive till a month after the taking of Jerusalem."—Camb. Bib. (8) **burned,** as Jer. had foretold.[a] (9) **captain .. guard,** or chief marshal. **remnant,** those left from the first deportation. **fell to him,** or deserted to him. (10) **gave them vineyards and fields,** "the parallel accounts (lii. 16; 2 Kings xxv. 12) say that they were left as vinedressers and husbandmen. Combining the accounts then we see precisely how the matter was. They were put in charge of this kind of property, which in a sense was given to them as their own, but might be resumed at any moment by the conqueror."

Burning the City of Jerusalem.—The temple, the palace, the houses of the nobles were deliberately set on fire. The very bones and framework of J. appeared to be wrapped in flames. The walls and gates seemed to lament and cry as they sank into the earth. Some of the princes were hung up by their hands on the temple walls; others were carried off to execution at Riblah. Age and youth, men and women, alike fell victims to the passion of cruelty of the emperor.—Farrar.

11—14. (11) **charge,** instructions how to treat the Prophet.[b] (12) **Take him,** secure his personal safety, and pay him every attention. (13) Compare the names with those in vs. 3. (14) **Gedaliah,** ch. xxvi. 24. He was the chief of the deserters to the Chaldæans. **home,** prob. to Gedaliah's home. **dwelt .. people,** as a freeman.

Trials of a Prisoner.—A prisoner is an impatient patient, lingring under the rough hands of a cruell phisitian; who having come to his disease, knowes his complainte, and hath power to cure him, but takes more pleasure to kill him. He is like Tantalus, who hath freedome running by his doore, yet cannot enjoy the least benefit thereof. His greatest griefe is that his credit was so good and now no better. His land is drawne within the compasse of a sheepe's skin, and his owne hand the fortification that barres him of entrance: hee is fortunes tossing-bal, an object that would make mirth melancholy: to his friends an abject, and a subject of nine dayes' wonder in euery barber's shop, and a mouthful of pitty (that he had no better fortune) to midwiues and talkatiue gossips; and all the content that this transitory life can giue him seems but to flout him in respect the restraint of liberty barres the true.—Sir T. Overbury.

15—18. A prophecy to Ebed-melech is here introduced, which, though uttered previously (see ch. xxxviii.), could not have been mentioned before without breaking the sequence of events. (15) **while .. prison,** but after Ebed-melech had rescued him from the pit. (16) **before thee,** the intimation that Ebed should see the evil, and live through it. (17) **deliver thee,** as a recognition of his services to God's Prophet. **afraid,** Ebed might well fear the wild slaughter and rioting that is usual when a city is sacked. (18) **for a prey,** or an unexpected and unlooked for gain.[c]

"In That Ye Ministered to the Saints."—How many instances there are!—the widow of Sarepta; the Shunamite woman; Dorcas; Paul's friends, Onesiphorus, etc.; Jonathan; Mary of Bethany; Cyrus and the Persian nation, for their goodness to Israel, the people of Malta (Acts xxviii.); our own country (England), for offering asylum to persecuted

[a] "The fate of the city was delayed for a month, probably until definite instructions had been received from Nebuchadnezzar.

"He that shuts
Love out, in
turn shall be
Shut out from
Love and on
her threshold
lie,
Howling in outer darkness."
—Tennyson.

[b] "No doubt he had been informed that the Prophet had exhorted both king and people to submit themselves to his authority." —Lowth.

"How often in the straits of God's people have they had to confess that He has raised up for them from most unlikely sources the helpers they have needed!"—Pul. Com.

[c] "The 'life' which he had risked in rescuing the Prophet was to be his reward, being spared beyond all hope when the lives of his enemies should me forfeited."—Fausset.

Je. xxi. 9, xxxviii. 2.

"This pious courtier had interceded for the prophet with the king; but the prophet had in turn interceded for him with God the Lord. Ebed-melech had drawn him out of the pit, but Jeremiah draws him by his prayer from the jaws of all Chaldean war-vortices." — Cramer.

Hollanders and Huguenots. And, besides such instances, there are repeated declarations to the same effect: "I will bless them that bless thee;" "They shall prosper that love thee." The cup of cold water given in the name of a disciple "shall in no wise lose its reward." "Whoso shall receive one such little child in my Name receiveth me." How comparatively slight was the ministry! how cup of cold water-like! yet how great the reward! How much this country owes, in her commerce, her character, her fame, to her ministry to God's saints! Many people denounce Cromwell for most things he did, but all applaud his interference with the bloody papists on behalf of the persecuted Waldenses. Milton's grand lines, "Avenge, O Lord, thy slaughtered saints," etc., have immortalized that deed as it deserved. No, indeed; "God is not unrighteous to forget," rather is he most gracious to remember all such ministries.—Pul. Com.

CHAPTER THE FORTIETH.

1—6. (1) **from** Ramah, ch. xxxi. 15.[a] He had **been carried,** with other prisoners, to Ramah, a short distance from Jerusalem. **chains,** or manacles. At first Jer. was mixed up with the other captives, who were bound together with chains on the hands. (2) **Lord,** etc., for the nonce, the prophet's mantle seems to have fallen upon the Chaldæan soldier. He speaks to his auditor just as Jeremiah himself had been wont to address his erring fellow-countrymen.—Exp. Bib. (3) **brought it,** to pass. (4) **loose thee,** so give thee thy personal liberty. **look well,** ch. xxxix. 12. (5) **while .. back,** or while he was hesitating.[b] **reward,** R. V., "present." (6) **Gedaliah,** ch. xxvi. 24, xxxix. 14. **Mizpah,** in Benjamin, 2 hours N. W. of Jerusalem, where Saul was named king, 1 Sam. x. 17. Comp. 1 Sam. vii. 5; 1 Ki. xv. 22. Identical with "Nob," Is. x.: 32.

Jeremiah's Choice.—Probably the motives that decided Jeremiah's course of action were, firstly, that devoted attachment to the sacred soil which was a passion with every earnest Jew; and, secondly, the inspired conviction that Palestine was to be the scene of the future development of revealed religion. This conviction was coupled with the hope that the scattered refugees who were rapidly gathering at Mizpah under Gedaliah might lay the foundations of a new community, which should become the instrument of the divine purpose. Jeremiah was no deluded visionary, who would suppose that the destruction of Jerusalem had exhausted God's judgments, and that the millennium would forthwith begin for the special and exclusive benefit of his surviving companions in Judah. Nevertheless, while there was an organized Jewish community left on native soil, it would be regarded as the heir of the national religious hopes and aspirations, and a prophet, with liberty of choice, would feel it his duty to remain.—Exp. Bib. Choice of a Residence.—Babylon was a heathen city. Jeremiah preferred to remain in the Holy Land. Surely the religious advantages of a neighborhood should be taken into account as of first importance. Yet many people seem to be strangely blind to all such considerations. The soil, the scenery, the society, the convenience of the house, are duly considered; but the Church accommodation is scarcely thought of. A gravel soil is most essential; healthy religious influences are regarded as of very secondary interest. A beautiful view must be got, though the enjoyment of it means banishment from all healthy Church life. How strange that heads of families professing to be Christian should act like pagans in this matter, and care so little for the spiritual atmosphere in which their children are to be brought up!—Pul. Com.

[a] "Prob. all the prisoners of note, who might be worth taking to Babylon, were collected at Ramah indiscriminately, and examined there."—Spk. Com.

[b] "From the signs of hesitation which Jer. manifested, the captain concluded that he would rather remain in the land than go to Babylon, and not only sent him to Gedaliah, but provided him with victuals for his journey, and dismissed him with a present."—Henderson.

"There is a power in real godliness which commands the reverence of those who hate it."— Robinson.

7—12. (7) **in the fields,** or scattered over the wilder parts of the country.[a] (8) **came to,** to offer their allegiance and service to him. **Netophathite,** fr. Netophah, a town in Judah.[b] **Maachathite,** from Maachath, at the foot of Mt. Hermon.[c] (9) **Fear not,** "the governor had

[a] "The leaders of the Jewish army had been scattered throughout the country on the capture of Zedekiah, in order to escape the notice of the Chaldæans."—Fausset.

[b] 2 Sa. xxiii. 28.

[c] De. iii. 14.

been carefully selected: his views were precisely those which Jeremiah had so long vainly inculcated in Jerusalem."—Cheyne. **serve .. Babylon,** comp. Jer.'s advice, ch. xxvii. 11, xxix. 7. (10) **to serve,** lit. "stand before." **come unto us,** i. e. whose officers will come with the king's commands and requirements. **gather,** etc., there would be fruit on the trees, though no corn in the fields. **taken,** "seized." There is implied in the verb what was no doubt the case, viz. that these captains had not scrupled to take possession of such walled towns or fortresses of any kind as best suited their purposes. (11) **in Moab,** etc., i. e. seeking shelter in neighboring lands. (12) **Mizpah,** vs. 6. There Gedaliah seems to have had his residence.

"Fire, and hammer, and file are necessary to give the metal form; and it must have many a grind and many a rub ere it will shine; so, in trial, character is shaped, and beautified, and brightened."—S. Coley.

Affliction Endears the Promises.—We never prize the precious words of promise till we are placed in conditions in which their suitability and sweetness are manifested. We all of us value those golden words, "When thou walkest through the fire thou shalt not be burned, neither shall the flame kindle upon thee," but few if any of us have read them with the delight of the martyr Bilney, to whom this passage was a stay, while he was in prison awaiting his execution at the stake. His Bible, still preserved in the library of Corpus Christi College, Cambridge, has the passage marked with a pen in the margin. Perhaps, if all were known, every promise in the Bible has borne a special message to some one saint, and so the whole volume might be scored in the margin with mementos of Christian experience, every one appropriate to the very letter.—C. H. Spurgeon.

13—16. (13) **Johanan,** vs. 8. (14) **Baalis,** perhaps the same king referred to as seeking alliance with Zedekiah.[d] He was naturally opposed to the Babylonian official, Gedaliah. **slay thee,** Heb. "strike thee in soul," i. e. a deadly stroke.[e] (15) **I will slay,** privately assassinate. (16) **falsely,** so Gedaliah, in his over-trustfulness, thought.

[d] Je. xxvii. 3.

[e] "This Ishmael, being of the seed royal of David, envied Gedaliah, who had the presidency to wh. he thought himself entitled. Therefore he leagued himself with the ancient enemy of Judah."

"Ingratitude is treason to mankind."—Thomson.

Trusting a Traitor.—Gedaliah was told that Ishmael meditated his death. Told, not by one man, but by all who had opportunity of knowing the traitor's designs. Was it, then, blameworthy in him to neglect the information? We cannot tell. It may have been that he knew of jealousies which made him think that the rest of the captains were slandering Ishmael. Slanderers, be it remembered, are quite as numerous as traitors. The fault of Gedaliah, if fault it was, was that of a generous heart. It is one of the weapons of a traitor to put on the semblance of a true man. Then probably Gedaliah was further influenced by the proposition to kill Ishmael. If the informers had merely urged him to guard himself, they might have been better attended to. But those were days when, if people wanted to get rid of a troublesome man, they had little scruple in taking the most effectual way.—Pul. Com.

CHAPTER THE FORTY-FIRST.

1—3. (1) **seventh month,** fr. this it appears that Gedaliah's presidency lasted only two months.[a] **and the princes,** R. V. "and one of the chief officers of the king, and ten men," he was a prince of the royal house and was doubtless jealous that Gedaliah should hold his place. **eat bread,** wh. is the Eastern sign of friendship. (2) **Then arose,** i. e. in the midst of the banquet. The day of this murder was kept as a fast day by the post-captivity Jews. Zech. vii. 5; viii. 19. (3) **slew,** etc., Gedaliah's death being the signal for a general massacre, but it was confined prob. to the men of war.

[a] 2 Ki. xxv. 8, 25.

"If there be a crime
Of deeper dye than all the guilty train
Of human vices, 'tis ingratitude."
—Brooke.

"It was said once of the whole world that it was nothing better than a prison for the man who had offended Cæsar; and I may say of the great universe, however wide it be, that it is but a narrow cell for the man who has offended God."—C. H. Spurgeon.

Gedaliah's Death.—Josephus suggests that Ishmael seized the opportunity of slaughter when Gedaliah and his guests were merry with wine, and his words are: "When Gedaliah had feasted Ishmael, and those that were with him, in a splendid manner at his table, and had given them presents, he became disordered in drink, while he endeavored to be very merry with them; and when Ishmael saw him in this case, and that he was drowned in his cups to the degree of insensibility and fallen asleep, he rose up on a sudden, with his ten friends, and slew Gedaliah and those that were with him at the feast.—Antiq. x. 9, 4. Hospitality.—Among the Greeks existed a custom of pledging lasting friendship in return for hospitality. It was in this wise: On a four-sided stone was written the name of each guest; the stone, called "Tessara hospitalis," was then broken, and each friend carried away the part of the stone bearing the other's name, and it entitled the holder of the part to ask protection and shelter from the other whenever necessity arose.—Hom. Com.

4—7. (4) **no man knew,** i. e. beyond the town of Mizpah. (5) **Shechem,** or Cychar, mod. Nablous.[b] **Shiloh, ch. vii. 12.**[c] **Samaria,** the chief town of the ten tribes. **beards shaven,** a sign of deep sorrow. **cut themselves,** Le. xix. 27, 28. De. xiv. 1.[d] These were pilgrims, descendants of the old ten tribes, on their way either to Jerusalem,—or to some place at Mizpah which Gedaliah had prepared as a centre of worship.—Pul. Com. (6) **weeping . . went,** as if in sympathy with the pilgrims. **Come to Gedaliah,** speaking as if he were a court-official. (7) **slew them,** the reason for this treacherous murder does not appear.

Ishmael's atrocities remind us of the Indian Mutiny, its leader, and the well at Cawnpore. Treachery, ingratitude, murder, massacre, greed, cowardice,—all are gathered in this detestable character. And such men are permitted to be. So clearly seen is this, that every drama has its villain; they are recognized as having definite place and function in this poor life of ours. History is full of them. But for them one might almost say there would be no history. Can we explain this permission? Wherefore are such men created and preserved? It is a part of the great question of moral evil, for the full solution of which we must wait. Like as was said to a lad of one of our public schools, who had heard his master say in a sermon in the school chapel that in mathematics there were lines in the same plane ever converging but which never met. The lad heard this, and as he knew something of mathematics himself, he believed and said to a senior in the school that the master was wrong. The senior defended the master, and told the lad of the lines that mathematicians call asymptotes. "But explain," said the astonished lad. "No, I can't," said the other. "You must wait till you get there." The lad had not read on so far in the science as that, and hence there was nothing for it but to believe that, though it was at present incomprehensible to him how such lines as those spoken of could be, nevertheless, when he had read on farther, he would see it clearly enough. And so we have to hear and see things which, to fully reconcile with the existence and superintendence of an all-loving and all-powerful God, is beyond our power, and there is nothing for it but that we must "wait till we get there"—there where the reading of these problems will be ready and clear.—Pul. Com.

8—10. (8) **we have treasures,**[a] these men knew that hidden stores of provisions would be important to Ishmael, and their secret would be lost with them if he put them to death. (9) **because of,** etc., R. V. "by the side of Gedaliah, (the same was that which Asa . . . . Israel)." "Nothing is said of this 'pit' in the historical books, but only (1 Kings xv. 22=2 Chron. xvi. 6) that Asa used the material with which Baasha had fortified Ramah to build Geba and Mizpah. It would seem that this 'pit' formed part of Asa's defensive works; probably it was a cistern to supply the town with water during the siege."—Camb. Bib. (10) **captive,** intending to set up a petty kingdom under the shelter of the Ammonites.

Granaries in the East.—In Palestine wells or cisterns are used for grain. In them the farmers store their crops of all kinds after the grain is threshed and winnowed. They are cool and perfectly dry. The top is hemetically sealed with plaster, and covered with a deep bed of earth; and thus

[b] Jno. iv. 5.

[c] "Some think should be Salem, close to Shechem."

[d] "The persons here spoken of belonged to the remainder of the ten tribes, who had retained their veneration for the God of their fathers, and prob. were in the habit of repairing at stated seasons to Jerus. The plight in which they now appeared was indicative of deep mourning on account of the destruction of that city." —Henderson.

"The man of pure and simple heart
Through life disdains a double part;
He never needs the screen of lies
His inward bosom to disguise."—Gay.

[a] "Subterranean storehouses for keeping grain safe from robbers."— Wordsworth.

vs. 8. "This refers to stores they had concealed, as is clear from the mentioning of 'the oil and honey.' During the time of the Kandian war many prisoners received lenient treatment, because of

they keep out rats, mice, an even ants—the latter by no means a contemptible enemy. The custom is doubtless an ancient one, and is extended from this country through the Carthaginians of North Africa into Spain. They seem to be alluded to in the passage cited above. These cisterns not only preserve the grain and other stores deposited in them from insects and mice, but they are admirably adapted to conceal them from robbers. These ten men had doubtless thus hid their treasures, to avoid being plundered in that time of utter lawlessness; and in a similar time I found people storing away grain in cisterns far out in the open country between Aleppo and Hamath; and they told me it was to hide it from the Government tax-gatherers. It is quite dangerous to come upon a deserted site full of these open cisterns and wells, especially at night, as I have often found. Frequently they are entirely concealed by the grass, and the path leads right among them. They must always be dug in dry places, generally on the side of a sloping hill. They would not answer in a wet country, but in these dry climates stores have been found quite fresh and sound many years after they were thus buried. —Thomson.

the assurance that they had treasures hid in the field, and that they should be the property of their keepers. In some cases there can be no doubt there were large sums thus acquired by certain individuals."—Roberts.

11—14. (11) **Johanan,** ch. xl. 13: the man who had warned Gedaliah. (12) **great waters,** a large open pool; doubtless the pool at which Abner and Joab met. (2 Sam. ii. 13) Gibeon was a city of the priests (Josh. xviii. 25; xxi. 17) in the tribe of Benjamin. (13) **glad,** at the prospect of deliverance. (14) **cast about,** turned round.

Liberty is quite as much a moral as a political growth—the result of free individual action, energy, and independence. It may be of comparatively little consequence how a man is governed from without, whilst everything depends upon how he governs himself from within. The greatest slave is not he who is ruled by a despot, great though that evil be, but he who is in the thrall of his own moral ignorance, selfishness and vice. There have been and perhaps there still are so-called patriots abroad who hold it to be the greatest stroke for liberty to kill a tyrant, forgetting that the tyrant usually represents only too faithfully the millions of people over whom he reigns. But nations who are enslaved at heart, cannot be freed by any mere change of masters or of institutions and so long as the fatal delusion prevails that liberty solely depends upon and consists in government, so long will such changes, no matter at what cost they be effected, have as little practical and lasting result as the shifting of the figures in a phantasmagoria.—Smiles. Triumph of Good.—John Huss once had a singular dream. He thought that the powers of evil thronged his chapel of Bethlehem to obliterate the pictures of Jesus upon the walls. But angels of light on the other side with swift hands repainted them in colors richer, and in more entrancing beauty. Such are the powers that contend in the place of our assemblies. But fairer, tenderer, stronger shall the influence of Jesus grow under angel hands. The saints witness its triumphs. The faithful ministry paints Emmanuel with impassioned force and many a loving repetition, till every stone and beam seem eloquent of His story, and the whole place a monument to His incomparable name.—Old Test. Anec.

"The wise and good wish well to liberty, throughout all lands; but aim to win her cause by some bold manly movement from the heart of all united nations; not by base assassin's craft, of hangman's well repaid. But how to gain this, how to inaugurate this grand blessing seems a knot time's wearied fingers work at till they bleed; and baffled races vainly pray for. Still the riddle must be read. The hour must come when retributive Mercy shall succeed her sterner sister Justice, and aye reign in parity divine with righteous love." —Bailey.

15—18. (15) **escaped,** fleeing at once, scarcely even showing fight, but losing two of his party. (16) **took Johanan,** he becoming the leader on the death of Gedaliah. (17) **Chimham,** Chimham was the son of the rich Gileadite Barzillai,[a] who probably founded this "habitation," or rather "hospice" ("khan," "caravanserai"), for the accommodation of travelers—a characteristic mark of public-spirited liberality. Josephus and Aquila, however, appear to have read "by the hurdles of Chimham" —a very possible name for a locality in such a pastoral country."—Pul. Com. (18) **Because of the Chaldæans,**[b] who would certainly take vengeance for the murder of the governor whom they had appointed.

Certainty of Judgment.—There was a man who committed a foul murder in a Scottish castle upon a young bridgegroom, at whose mar-

[a] 2 Sa. xix. 38, 40.

[b] "Lest the Chaldæans should suspect all the Jews of being implicated in Ishmael's treason, as though the Jews sought to have a prince of the house of David." — Fausset.

riage festivities he had hypocritically assisted. The assassin took horse in the dead of night, and fled for his life through wood and winding path. When the sun dawned, he slackened his pace, and behold! he was emerging from a thicket in front of the very castle whence he had fled, and to which, by tortuous paths, he had returned. Horror seized him; he was discovered, and condemned to death. So, however far and fast we may fly, we shall find ourselves, when light returns, ever in presence of our sin and of our Judge. Temptation.—Solitude hath its temptations as well as society. St. Anthony of Egypt before his conversion was a gay and fast young man of Alexandria, and when he was converted he found the temptations of the city so intolerable that he fled into the Egypt desert and became a hermit; but he afterward confessed that the temptations of a cell in the wilderness were worse than those of a city. It would not be safe to exchange our temptations for those of another. Every one has his own. The attraction of temptation is overcome by a counter attraction. The love of Christ in the heart destroys the love of sin and the new song of salvation enables us to despise the siren's song of temptation and pass it by.—James Stalker.

"God will put up with a great many things in the human heart, but there is one thing he will not put up with in it, a second place. He who offers God a second place offers him no place."—John Ruskin.

"The strength of the church lies not in the oratory of the pulpit, but in the oratory of the closet." — Spurgeon.

CHAPTER THE FORTY-SECOND.

1—3. (1) **came near,** "it was no slight matter for the choicest part of the remnant of Israel to return to the very land out of which their fathers had been divinely guided."—Cheyne. (2) **unto Jeremiah,** who poss. was one of the captives taken away by Ishmael. (3) **supplication,** etc., as ch. xxxvi. 7. **thy God,** intimating that he had prevailing power with Him. (4) **show us the way,**[a] "the desire to ascertain God's will expressed here, even when compared with their disobedience to that will when declared (chap. xliii. 4), need not imply hypocrisy. They may have made up their minds that it was necessary to flee into Egypt, and, assuming that this resolution would be confirmed by the divine response, desired only to know what particular course they should adopt in accordance with it."—Camb. Bib.

[a] "They profess great reverence for Jeremiah, as for God; but will not hearken to the one or the other, but prefer their own wilfulness to both."—Wordsworth.

"That which is called considering what is our duty in a particular case is very often nothing but endeavoring to explain it away."—Bishop Butler.

Importance of Prayer.—Many years ago, the late Duchess of Gordon called on good Harrington Evans, and said, "I have just five minutes, but I could not leave town without calling to say 'good-bye!'" "Five minutes," said Mr. Evans, with that solemn and impressive manner by which he was distinguished; "five minutes! Then pray! Pray! Pray! Good morning." "I felt so struck with these words," said the Duchess to a friend, "that I could not forget them; and, as I thought on them, I was led to study prayer, as a means of grace as well as an act of worship, and ever after my chief work in the Lord's service became the promotion of prayer-meetings."

4—6. (4) **heard,** ch. xxxiv. 10, xxxv. 17. (5) **Between** us, **or against** us,[b] i. e. to bear witness and punish us if we fail to do our part as we now promise.

[b] "It is the constant method of hypocrites to pretend a profound submission to the will of God till that comes to cross their inclinations or interest."—Lowth.

"Among all the graces that adorn a Christian soul, like so many jewels of various colors and lustres, against the day of her espousals to the Lamb of God, there is not one more brilliant than patience."— Bp. Horne.

Rewards of Obedience.—It is related how an aged couple in the vicinity of London, who in the early part of life were poor, but who by the blessing of God upon their industry enjoyed a comfortable independency in their old age, were called upon by a Christian minister, who solicited their contributions to a charity. The old lady was disposed to make out some excuse, and to answer in the negative, both for her husband and for herself, and therefore replied, "Why, sir, we have lost a deal by religion since we began; my husband knows that very well." And being wishful to obtain her husband's consent to the assertion, she said, "Have we not, Thomas?" Thomas, after a long and solemn pause, replied, "Yes, Mary, we have lost a deal by our religion! I have lost a deal by my religion. Before I got religion, Mary, I had got a water-pail in which I carried water; and that, you know, I lost many years ago. And then I had an old slouched hat, a patched old coat, and mended shoes and stockings; but I have lost them also long ago. And, Mary, you know that, poor as I was, I had a habit of getting drunk and quarrelling with you; and that, you know, I have lost. And then I had a burdened conscience and a wicked heart, and then I had ten thousand guilty feelings and fears; but all are lost, completely lost, and like a millstone cast into the deep sea. Before we got religion, Mary, you had a washing-tray, in which you washed for hire, and God Almighty blessed your industry; but since we got religion you have lost your washing-tray. And you had a gown and bonnet much the worse for wear, though they were all you had to wear; but you have lost them long ago. And you had many an aching heart concerning me at times; but those you happily have lost. And I could even wish that you had lost as much as I have lost, and even more; for what we lose by our religion will be our eternal gain."—Pul. Com.

7—12. (7) **ten days,** "nine days the prophet passed in meditation and prayer. Knowing him, as we do, we cannot doubt that he sustained a severe mental conflict. Common sense seemed to favor the policy of Johanan. And yet the prophetic spirit had distinctly assured him that in Babylon alone could the regeneration of Israel be effected."—Cheyne. (10) **still abide,** settling down quietly under the power of the Chaldæans. **repent,** ch. xviii. 11. (12) **I . . mercies,** by overruling the King of Babylon's plans concerning you.

The Great Work God is Disposed to Do.—It is indicated by these two not infrequent figures of building and planting. God was willing to make these people his husbandry, his building (1 Cor. iii. 9). He had been lately engaged in a great pulling down and rooting up; and why? Because his people had been putting up the wrong buildings, planting the wrong plant. Every plant not planted by God must be rooted up. God is the Builder, not a mere helper in building. We may be said to be fellow-workers with God, but it can never describe him rightly to call him fellow-worker with us. The work and the glory are his of building up the holy character, the perfect manhood, the everlasting home. He it is who makes his people fruitful in every good word and work. And the way for all this building and planting was now clear so far as God himself was concerned. All the pulling down and rooting up was done. Only let the people give the needed opportunity and all else would prosper.—Pul. Com. The Delayed Blessings Office.—In the charming little booklet, Expectation Corner, Adam Slowman was led into the Lord's treasure-houses, and among many other wonders there revealed to him was the "Delayed Blessings Office," where God kept certain things prayed for until the wise time came to send them. "It takes a long time for some pensioners to learn that delays are not denials. . . . Ah, there are secrets of love and wisdom in the 'Delayed Blessings Department,' which are little dreamt of. Men would pluck their mercies green when the Lord would have them ripe." (Isa. 30: 18.)—Peloubet.

13—16. (14) **Egypt,** seeking shelter there was the plan generally favored. **see no war,** if they thought they would escape the presence of war they were mistaken. Now that the barrier of Judæa had been swept away Egypt would be even more open to attack from the east. (15) **sojourn there,** seeking the protection of its king rather than the protection of God. (16) **which ye feared,** R. V., which ye fear. The calamities mentioned were precisely those of which the Jews were apprehensive in their own country. So afterwards, "whereof ye are afraid.—Pul. Com. **overtake you,** ch. xliv. 14. 18.[a]

The Desire to Go to Egypt.—Jeremiah knew too well what mingled hopes and fears drew his hearers towards the fertile valley and rich cities of the Nile. He sets before them the reverse of the picture: they might refuse to obey God's command to remain in Judah; they might say, "No, we will go into the land of Egypt, where we shall see no war, nor hear the sound of the trumpet, nor hunger for bread, and there will we dwell." As of old, they craved for the flesh-pots of Egypt; and with more excuse than their forefathers. They were worn out with suffering and toil,

"I worked with patience, which is almost power." —E. B. Browning.

"If a man is unsound in his faith the clergy take the ecclestical sword and cut him off at once. But he may be ever so unsound in charity, in patience, and nothing is said about that. We must be sound in faith, in love, and in patience if we are to be true to God." — D. L. Moody.

"What is the glory of a man who invented a useful art or founded a flourishing kingdom, what the glory of the greatest prince or potentate (and on such grounds did the heathen deify men), compared with the glory of the Creator of the world?"—Henry.

[a] "What our hearts are most set on often prove fatal to us. Those who think to escape troubles by changing their place will find them wherever they go."—Fausset.

Vigilance in watching opportunity, tact and daring in seizing upon opportunity, force and persistence in crowding opportunity to its utmost of possible achievement—these are the martial virtues which must command success.—Austin Phelps.

some of them had wives and children; the childless prophet was inviting them to make sacrifices and incur risks which he could neither share nor understand. Can we wonder if they fell short of his inspired heroism, and hesitated to forego the ease and plenty of Egypt in order to try social experiments in Judah?—Exp. Bib. "There is a machine employed at the Mint of such perfect accuracy and finish that, when a number of sovereigns are tested by it, it will automatically and instantly and infallibly reject every one that fails in the least degree to come up to the proper standard of weight. So if we thus bring into view the unseen and eternal, all the crowd of facts and events that come before us day by day will each one spontaneously, promptly, and infallibly be judged, and we shall neither under nor over estimate them but as we ought."—Pul. Com.

17—19. (17) **all the men,** for a limitation of this denunciation, comp. ch. xliv. 14, 28. (18) **execration,** etc., ch. xxiv. 9. (19) **admonished you,** R. V. "testified unto you."[b]

Foreseeing the Evil.—"No man can find himself over the abyss, the floor of which is paved with wrecks, and white with the bones of the shrieking myriads of human beings whom the waves have swallowed up, without some thought of the dread possibilities hanging over his fate. There is only one way to get rid of them; that which an old sea-captain mentioned to me, namely to keep one's self under opiates until he wakes up in the harbor where he is bound. I did not take this as serious advice, but the meaning is that one who has all his senses about him cannot help being anxious."—Oliver Wendell Holmes. It is equally true that on the voyage of life he who has his senses must be thoughtful about the dangers of the voyage, and only the opiates of folly, and pleasure, and worldliness can keep him from it.—Peloubet.

20—22. (20) **dissembled,** R. V. "for ye have dealt deceitfully against your own souls." See vss. 3, 5, 6. (21) **not obeyed,** as you so faithfully promised, and even swore to do.

Present Age Suitable to Hypocrisy.—There was an age of chivalry, when no craven courted knighthood, for it involved the hard blows, the dangerous wounds, the rough unhorsings, and the ungentle perils of the tournament; nay, these were but child's play: there were distant Eastern fields, where Paynim warriors must be slain by valiant hands, and blood must flow in rivers from the Red-cross knights. Then men who lacked valor preferred their hawks and their jesters, and left heroes to court death and glory on the battle-field. This genial time of peace breeds carpet knights, who flourish their untried weapons, and bear the insignia of valor, without incurring its inconvenient toils. Many are crowding to the seats of the heroes, since prowess and patience are no more required. The war is over, and every man is willing to enlist. When Rome commenced her long career of victory, it was no pleasant thing to be a soldier in the Roman legions. The power which smote the nations like a rod of iron abroad, was a yoke of iron at home. There were long forced marches, with hunger and cold and weariness; heavy armor was the usual load when the legionary marched at ease; but "ease" was a word he seldom used. Rivers were forded; mountains were scaled; barbarians were attacked; proud nations were assailed; kingdoms were subdued. No toil too stern for the scarred veteran, no odds too heavy, no onslaught too ferocious, no arms too terrible. Scarcely were his wounds healed, ere he was called to new fields; his life was battle; his home the tent; his repast was plunder; his bed the battle-field; while the eagle's bloody talons removed all need of sepulchre for his slaughtered body. But afterwards when Rome was mistress of the world, and the Prætorian cohorts could sell the imperial purple to the highest bidder, many would follow the legions to share their spoils. It is not otherwise to-day. Into the triumphs of martyrs and confessors few are unwilling to enter; in a national respect to religion, which is the result of their holiness, even ungodly men are will-

b "The Jews going into Egypt for protection, was in effect refusing to submit themselves to the king of Babylon, to whom God had decreed the government of Judæa, and all the neighboring countries."—Lowth.

"Ottocar, King of Bohemia, refused to do homage to Rodolphus I., till at last, chastised with war, he was content to do him homage privately in a tent; which tent was so contrived by the emperor's servants, that, by drawing a cord, all was taken away, and so Ottocar presented on his knees, doing his homage, to the view of three armies then in the field. Thus God at last shall uncase the closest dissembler to the sight of men, angels, and devils; having removed all veils and pretences of religion and piety."—Spencer.

"Thou mayest be sure that he that will in private tell thee of thy faults is thy friend, for he adventureth thy dislike and doth hazard thy hatred."—Sir W. Raleigh.

ing to share. They have gone before us with true hearts valiant for truth, and false traitors are willing to divide their spoils.—C. H. Spurgeon.

CHAPTER THE FORTY-THIRD.

1—4. (2) **Azariah,** comp. ch. xlii. 1. **proud,** or presumptuous.[a] (3) **setteth thee on,** "taking ch. xlv. 4, 5 in connection with ch. xlii. 10 I infer that Baruch believed that, even after its heavy losses, Israel as a nation would yet be 'built up' in its own land."—Cheyne. (4) **dwell .. Judah,** abide quietly under Chaldæan sway.

Refusing Unwelcome Demands.—Certain tacit conditions may always be considered attached to a profession of willingness to be guided by a friend's advice. Our newspapers frequently record breaches of engagements that should be as binding as that entered into by Johanan and his friends, and they do so without any special comment. For instance, the verdicts of arbitrators in trade disputes have been too often ignored by the unsuccessful parties; and—to take a very different illustration —the most unlimited professions of faith in the infallibility of the Bible have sometimes gone along with a denial of its plain teaching and a disregard of its imperative commands. While Shylock expected a favorable decision, Portia was "a Daniel come to judgment:" his subsequent opinion of her judicial qualities has not been recorded. Those who have never refused or evaded unwelcome demands made by an authority whom they have promised to obey may cast the first stone at Johanan. —Exp. Bib.

5—7. (5) **remnant,** ch. xl. 11, 12. (6) **men,** etc., comp. xli. 16. (7) **Tahpanhes,** ch. ii. 16, in the northern frontier of Egypt,[b] which was nearest to Palestine.

Discontent Cured.—All human situations have their inconveniences. We feel those that we find in the present: and we neither feel nor see those that exist in another. Hence we often make troublesome changes without amendment, and frequently for the worse. In my youth I was a passenger in a little sloop descending the river Delaware. There being no wind, we were obliged, when the tide was spent, to cast anchor and wait for the next. The heat of the sun on the vessel was excessive— the company strangers to me, and not very agreeable. Near the river side I saw what I took to be a pleasant green meadow, in the middle of which was a large shady tree, where, it struck my fancy, I could sit and read—having a book in my pocket—and pass the time agreeably until the tide turned. I therefore prevailed with the captain to put me ashore. Being landed I found the greatest part of my meadow was really a marsh; in crossing which, to come to my tree, I was up to my knees in mire; and I had not placed myself under its shade five minutes before mosquitoes in swarms found me out, attacked my legs, hands, and face, and made my reading and my rest impossible; so that I returned to the beach, and called for the boat to come and take me on board again, where I was obliged to bear the heat I had strove to quit, and also the laugh of the company. Similar cases in the affairs of life have since frequently fallen under my observation.—Franklin.

8—13. "Prophecy of the Fall of Egypt (8—14; xliv. 30) fulfilled in the 5th year after the destruction of Jerusalem (584) when Nebuchadnezzar invaded Egypt, slew its king and carried away a host of Jews to Babylon."—Oehler. (9) **great stones,** as large as he could carry. **hide .. clay,** R. V. "hide them in mortar in the brick work."[c] "he is directed to take great stones and imbed them in the mortar (not 'clay') in the brick pavement at the entry of the palace. When the events predicted came to pass, these stones would testify that Jeremiah had predicted them."—Pul. Com. (10) **my servant,** ch. xxv. 9. **set .. hid,** a symbolical declaration that he should surely conquer the country. (11) **and when,**

[a] Ps. xix. 13.

"Those that are resolved to contradict the great ends of the ministry, are industrious to bring a bad name upon it."—Henry.

"Observe the old diabolical trick; when preachers practice God's word and their office with zeal, the world understands how to conflict it with another name and call it personal interest." —Cramer.

[b] Je. xlvi. 14; Eze. xxx. 18.

"They that are not content with their present condition are like little children upon a hill; and they look a good way off, and see another hill, and think, if they were on the top of that, then they were able to touch the clouds with their fingers; but, when they are on top of that hill, alas, they are as far from the clouds as before."

[c] "Poss. the palace of Pharaoh was being built or repaired at this time; hence arose the mortar and brick at the entry."—Fausset.

R. V., "And he shall come," etc. **death to death,** ch. xv. 2; Zec. xi. 9. (12) **I will kindle,** etc., the king is but the instrument of Jehovah. **array himself,**[d] he shall carry off the spoil as easily as a shepherd wraps his garment about him. (13) **images,** R. V. "pillars," originally a natural boulder or block of stone, regarded as the abode of a deity. Then an obelisk. "The lofty obelisks in front of the Temple of the Sun (one of which is the Cleopatra's Needle) are here referred to. It was the distinguishing mark of a holy place."—Driver on Deut. xvi. 22. **Beth-shemesh,** i. e. "the house of the Sun," or Heliopolis, or On.

Dependence upon any earthly power is utterly vain. Egypt is dreamt of as a refuge from their woes. Its power, typified by the clay of the kiln or brick-field, only overlies the power of God, typified by the stones. They would be in his hands still, although they knew it not. Through the clay of worldly dependence they must needs fall upon the stones of Divine judgment. Man cannot flee from his Maker. There is no earthly security from the consequences of sin. If the remnant of Judah, pursuing its tendency towards worldly mindedness and idolatry to the bitter end, should persist in putting its trust in the Egyptian power, to whose religion and life it was in such imminent danger of assimilating itself, woe to it! Through Pharaoh even will they be confronted with Nebuchadnezzar yet again. God is the only true Helper and Saviour, and in the practice of holiness and the precepts of true religion is security alone to be found. What assurance company can shield the sinner from the consequences of his misdeeds? And if God be for any man, who can be against him?—Pul. Com. "Kindle a Fire in the Houses of the Gods of Egypt." Egypt was full of temples and idol-gods; those of wood the conquering army would commit to the flames; those of gold they would carry away as spoil to Babylon. This burning of temples and idols by Nebuchadnezzar, and afterwards by the Persian kings, was mercifully ordered by God to wean the exiles there from their idolatry into which they sank, and to revive their faith in the God of Israel.—Hom. Com. Recent Discoveries.—Mr. Flinders Petrie recently discovered at Tell Defenneh a large brickwork pavement, with great stones buried underneath, which he supposed might be those mentioned in our narrative. He also found there another possible relic of these Jewish émigrés in the shape of the ruins of a large brick building of the twenty-sixth dynasty—to which Pharaoh Hophra belonged—still known as the "Palace of the Jew's Daughter." It is a natural and attractive conjecture that this was the residence assigned to the Jewish princesses whom Johanan carried with him into Egypt.—Exp. Bib.

[d] "He shall invest the land of Egypt, and take entire possession of it, just as a shepherd's garment covers his body all over. So calamities, when they surround men on every side, are compared to a garment. Ps. cix. 19.—Lowth.

"With as great ease as a shepherd throws his cloak round him when going forth to watch his flock by night in the open field, so easily shall the King of Babylon take possession of all the wealth and glory of Egypt, and throw it round him, and depart without any one daring to resist his progress." — Spk. Com.

"There is no use of living if our lives do not help other lives." —**Phillips Brooks.**

CHAPTER THE FORTY-FOURTH.

1—6. (1) **The word that came,** "this is the last prophecy of Jeremiah in respect of time. The occasion we see to have been the unabated idolatry which characterized the people even in the midst of the punishment which they were undergoing in exile. It may have been uttered at any time between the arrival in Egypt (about 585 B. C.) and the fulfillment (not earlier than 572 B. C.)."—Camb. Bib. **dwell,** better, sojourn. These Jews expected soon to return to Judæa. **Migdol,** a city on the eastern frontier of Egypt, towards the Red Sea. This is not the Migdol of Ex. xiv. 2, but the Magdolon of Herodotus. Comp. xlvi. 14; Ezek. xxix. 10, etc.—Cheyne. **Tahpanhes,** ch. ii. 16. **Noph,** Memphis. **Pathros,**[a] or Upper Egypt. (2) **seen,** are eye-witnesses of the fulfilment of My threatened judgments. (3) **went to burn,** "implying perverse assiduity." **serve other gods, comp.** De. viii. 6, xxxii. 17. (4) **sent . . prophets,** ch. vii. 13, xxv. 4. (5) **inclined their ear,** to listen with a view to obedience. (6) **poured forth,** ch. xlii. 18.

The Abominable Thing (vs. 4).—I. Sin is an abominable thing, if we consider it—1. In reference to God; 2. In reference to the moral law;

[a] **Is. xi. 11; comp. Ge. x. 14.**

"Every religious life is woven of many diverse strands; if the web as a whole is rotten, the Great Taskmaster can take no account of a few threads that have a form and profession of soundness."–Exp. Bib.

"Why comes Temptation, but for man to meet
And master, and make crouch beneath his feet,
And so be pedestalled in triumph?"
—**Browning.**

3. In reference to its fatal influence on man. II. Sin is an abominable thing which God hates. 1. He has shown it in the expulsion of the rebel angels from heaven; 2. In the exile of our first parents from Eden; 3. In the prevalence of disease and death among men; 4. In a long series of recorded judgments; 5. In the cross of Christ. III. Sin is an abominable thing which God hates, and which He therefore exhorts and entreats us not to commit. 1. By the Bible; 2. By conscience; 3. By affliction.—G. Brooks.

7—10. (7) **to cut off,** i. e. to bring on yourselves the judgments of the God whom you offend.[a] (8) **be gone,** of your own accord. (9) **their wives,** it seems, from the history, that the Jewish queens were great promoters of idolatry.[b] (10) **humbled,** "literally, bruised, contrite and penitent for sin. The word is used of the vicarious bearing of the sins of the guilty by the innocent in Is. liii. 5, 'he was bruised for our iniquities.' The prophet changes to the third person, as including in his remark the previous generations also."—Camb. Bib.

Neglect of Past Warnings (vss. 9, 10).—"Have ye forgotten," etc. I. It was their duty to recollect the lessons taught by the past. II. They were not unwilling to recall the past glories of Israel. III. They ought to have remembered the connection between former sins and their punishment, in the light of God's unchanging justice. IV. Such remembering of the past, duly improved, had saved from present and future misery.

Memory: A Warning Voice.—A gracious soul remembers that Saul lost two kingdoms at once—his own kingdom and that of heaven—for sparing Agag and the fat of the cattle. He remembers how the unprofitable servant, for the non-improvement of his talent, was cast into outer darkness. He remembers how Ananias and Sapphira were struck dead suddenly for telling a lie. He remembers that Jacob smarted for his lying to his dying day. He remembers how God followed him with sorrow upon sorrow, and breach upon breach, filling up his days with grief and trouble. He remembers how Moses was shut out of the Holy Land, because he spake unadvisedly with his lips. He remembers how Zacharias was stricken dumb, because he believed not the report of the angel Gabriel; and the remembrance of these things stirs up his hatred and indignation against the least sins.—Brooks.

11—15. (11) **set .. evil,** Am. ix. 4. **all Judah,** i. e. "the Judah in Egypt, not that in Babylon. Notice the qualification of this too absolute statement in vss. 14, 28." (12) **remnant of Judah,** those are distinctly marked out who had sought shelter in Egypt in opposition to the commands of the Prophet. (13) **punish,** comp. ch. xlii. 15—18. (14) **none .. escape,** i. e. none but those mentioned in vs. 28. (15) **had burned,** better, "did burn."

The Frown of God (vs. 11).—I. The smile of God, the token of His favor, brightens all nature and life, "Thy favor is life," etc. II. The frown of God, the token of His displeasure, casts a shadow on the heart and life. Apply—1. To those who enjoy God's smile,—live in it, reflect it; 2. To those who have forfeited it,—seek reconciliation through Christ.

A Nullified Purpose.—This remnant, not finding in Egypt the expected safety, think there is nothing easier than to go back again to the land of Judah. Whereas they find too late that, while departure from their own proper place is easy enough, return to it may be impossible. Opening the door to get out was one thing; opening it to get in again quite another. Seventy years were to pass before they of the Captivity should return from Babylon—indeed, it would really be another generation altogether; and should those who sought Egypt in contumacy and rebellion expect to fare better? We must be wise in time. To be wise too late gives suffering its keenest edge. So Judas brought back in vain the thirty pieces of silver, and Esau found no place of repentance though he sought it carefully with tears. This is why God is so earnest in promising wisdom and light to those who seek for

[a] Comp. Nu. xvi. 38; Pr. viii. 36; Je. vii. 19.

"God designed that this remnant should have kept possession in Judæa, when the rest of their brethren were carried away captive. But by their going into Egypt, and defiling themselves with the idolatries of that nation, they have provoked God to make an utter destruction of them."—Lowth.

[b] 1 Ki. xi. 1—8, xv. 13, xvi. 31.

"Thus will you live until, with a seared conscience, you lie down on the bed of death, and there, perhaps, when it is too late, all your old fears will be awakened. You may send to your minister upon that bed of death, and he may come, but by your bedside he may be speechless; his very power to pray may depart from him, and in trying to ask mercy for you all his utterances may be choked; and you may go from that wretched dying bed to hell. And as you sink down into the pit, the millstone about your neck will be the abominable thing which God hates."—S. Martin.

them, that we may seek for them at the right time, at the beginning of the great opportunity of life, and at the beginning of every smaller opportunity.—Pul. Com.

16—19. (17) **goeth .. mouth,** "we should rather render 'all the thing,' (or, 'every word) that is gone forth,' i. e. the particular vow that we have avowed to the queen of heaven we will perform to the uttermost The people rely on the argument that this is no new worship of theirs, and that their experience shews that it was for their national advantage that it should be kept up. The queen of heaven has done more for them than the God whose prophet now addresses them."—Cam. Bib. **queen of heaven,** ch. vii. 18, xix. 13. "To the moon and the rest of the host of heaven." **had we plenty,** "fools attribute their seeming prosperity to God's connivance at their sin."[a] (18) **wanted all,** been starving and suffering. (19) **cakes,** ch. vii. 18. **without our men,** R. V. "husbands."[b] "A wife's vows were not valid without her husband's sanction, and the women avail themselves of this principle to shift the responsibility for their superstition on the men's shoulders.—Ex. Bib.

[a] "It is the curse of impiety not to perceive the hand of God in calamities."—Fausset.

"So perversely did they misconstrue providence, though God, by His prophets, had so often explained it to them, and the thing itself spoke the direct contrary."—Mat. Henry.

[b] Nu. xxx. 7, 8.

Worship of Venus.—St. Isaac the Great, of Antioch, who died about A. D. 460, tells us that the Christian ladies of Syria—whom he speaks of very ungallantly as "fools"—used to worship the planet Venus from the roofs of their houses, in the hope that she would bestow upon them some portion of her own brightness and beauty. This experience naturally led St. Isaac to interpret the Queen of Heaven as the luminary which his countrywomen venerated.—Exp. Bib.

20—23. (20) **the women,** notice that here, as in Isa. iii. 16—24, one of the most evident tokens of the nation's corruption is the condition of its women. (21) **remember them,** i. e. the various idolatrous acts. (22) **no longer bear,** even Divine patience being outworn by long-continued wilfulness and disobedience. (23) **sinned .. Lord,** not merely in idolatrous acts, but in the cherished spirit of disobedient wilfulness.[c]

[c] La. i. 8; Da. ix. 11, 12.

"We should regard as a divine part of virtue the clemency and longsuffering which God manifests, reforming few indeed by punishment, but, by the slowness of punishment, benefiting and admonishing many." — Plutarch.

Irreligion Tends to Immorality and Ruin.—Even a Machiavelli, cool and cynical and audacious as was his scepticism, could see and admit that faithfulness to religion is the secret of the happiness and prosperity of States. An irreligious society tends inevitably to become a dissolute society; and a "dissolute society is the most tragic spectacle which history has ever to present—a nest of disease, of jealousy, of dissensions, of ruin, and despair, whose last hope is to be washed off the world and disappear. Such societies must die sooner or later of their own gangrene, of their own corruption, because the infection of evil, spreading into unbounded selfishness, ever intensifying and reproducing passions which defeat their own aim, can never end in anything but moral dissolution."—Farrar.

24—28. (24) **Moreover Jeremiah said:** "the people in all likelihood obstinately pressed forward to carry out their idolatrous intentions. Jeremiah therefore declares the consequences of this persistence, and with the announcement that in their ruin shall be involved that of the Egyptian king Pharaoh-Hophra, closes, as far as we know, the whole series of his prophecies."—Camb. Bib. (25) **fulfilled .. hand,** "when Jer. said these words he pointed to their hands, in which they were carrying the crescent-shaped cakes wh. they had vowed to the goddess." **surely accomplish,** R. V. "establish then your vows, and perform your vows," read as an ironical phrase. (26) **I have sworn,**[a] comp. God's solemn vow with theirs. God refuses to recognize any longer His covenant relation to this remnant. (27) **watch,** etc., ch. i. 10; Eze. vii. 6. (28) **small number,** vs. 14. Isaiah's doctrine of the remnant. In the midst of judgment, God remembers mercy, and his ancient covenant. A remnant is saved as the nucleus of a regenerate people.—Pul. Com. **know,** by bitter and desolating experiences.

[a] "The Jews, heretofore, in the midst of all their idolatry, had retained the form of appeal to the name of God, and the law, the distinctive glory of their nation. God will allow this no more."—Fausset.

"It may be well for us to listen to Hesiod, who maintains not, with Plato, that punishment is a suffering that follows wrong doing, but that it is a twin birth with wrong doing, springing from the same soil and the same root."—Plutarch.

Man's Words and God's (vs. 28).—I. The words of man betray often the sin of the heart and the vanity of the mind. II. The words of God manifest His integrity, holiness, power and love. III. In regard to life and salvation, time and eternity, whose shall stand? IV. Whose word shall stand the test of the hour of repentance or death?

National Uprightness.—The character of a people decides its destiny. A would-be statesman said not long ago that purified politics were an "iridescent dream," and that the "decalogue and Golden Rule had no place in statesmanship." But the man or the nation that lives according to such principles will find their prosperity to be an "iridescent dream."—Peloubet. God's Judgment is Discriminating.—Even now it must be so; for "shall not the Judge of all the earth do right?" But we do not yet know its purposes and its methods, and therefore to us it looks as though it could not take note of individual deserts. Ultimately we shall see how God has overlooked no exceptional case. Noah is picked out of the drowning world. Lot is remembered in Sodom. Elijah is provided for in the general drought. We can look for no such evidences of an interfering Providence in earthly things now, perhaps, but the truth they illustrate holds good, and must work its blessed results in the day of final account. Natural selection does not always result in the survival of the morally fittest on earth. On the contrary, the good may become martyrs, the bad triumphant tyrants. But we see only the opening acts of the drama. The final catastrophe will reveal the justice that regulates.—Pul. Com.

"Vows are easily made, but more easily broken. A sea captain, while upon a single plank in the wide ocean, vowed to devote his life to God if he should be saved, but forgot his vow as soon as his feet were on the solid earth."

"The man who is confident in worldly wisdom is simply confident in the doctrine of chances. His chance success is equally good with that of others. But God would have us understand that success of this sort is only a deferred failure."—Pul.Com.

29, 30. (29) **sign,** a calamity wh. you shall witness shall be to you the assurance of calamities wh. you shall suffer. (30) **Pharaoh-hophra,** or Apries, who succeeded Psammis, the successor of Pharaoh-Necho, who was beaten by Nebuchadnezzar at Carchemish. The calamity of Hophra came about six or seven years after Jer.'s prophecy. He was kept prisoner in his palace at Saïs for more than ten years, and died B. C. 570. He was intensely hated by the Egyptians.

Historical Signs (vs. 29).—I. The sign mentioned in the text a reminder of the retributive justice of God. II. The events of history to be interpreted in the light of Divine justice and love. III. Some of them, as destruction of Armada, invention of printing, discovery of America, pre-eminently significant.

CHAPTER THE FORTY-FIFTH.

1—5. (1) **unto Baruch,** this address to an individual following upon words spoken to a nation has been compared to the Epistles addressed by St. Paul to individuals (Timothy, Titus, Philemon), which in like manner are placed after those which he indites to churches. Baruch was a man of high birth, grandson of Maaseiah (chap. xxxii. 12), who was governor of the city in the time of Josiah (2 Chron. xxxiv. 8). He seems to have expected to have either important office in the state or more probably the gift of prophecy bestowed upon him. His ambition is destined not to be gratified, and the prophet here warns him of the fact.—Camb. Bib. **when .. written,** see ch. xxxvi., which this should follow. (3) **grief .. sorrow,** R. V. "sorrow to my pain; I am weary with my groaning, and," etc. Baruch grieved for the nation's sins, and sorrowed for the punishments such sins must surely involve. Possibly also Baruch had to bear personal troubles in that anxious time. (4) **break down,** comp. ch. i. 10. (5) **great things,** matters of personal benefit. "Dost thou aspire to honor and dignity in a time of common calamity?"[a] **for a prey,** ch. xxxix. 18.

Ambition (vs. 5).—I. The evil denounced. It may be viewed under three aspects. 1. There are some who pursue worldly objects that are far above them; 2. There are some who pursue with undue eagerness worldly objects they might reasonably hope to attain; 3. There are some who pursue all classes of worldly objects in a selfish spirit. II. The reasons why it is denounced. 1. Because it attaches excessive value to worldly objects; 2. Because it misapprehends the comparative advan-

[a] "Baruch, who was of a noble house in Jerusalem, and whose brother Seraiah was advanced to high place in the court of Judah, felt, it seems, some disappointment in seeing that the avenues to the promotion and preferment of which he had a reasonable expectation, and to which he aspired, were closed by his call to the service of God."—Wordsworth.

"As the first step heavenward is humility, so the first step hellward is pride. Pride counts the Gospel foolish, but the Gospel always shows pride to be so." —Mason.

tages of the different ranks in the social scale; 3. Because it overlooks the duties which arise out of the relations we sustain to our race and our Maker; 4. Because it ignores all the facts, and objects, and interests, and blessings of the spiritual world.—G. Brooks.

Lowliness.—Men sigh for the wings of a dove, that they may fly away and be at rest. But flying away will not help us. "The Kingdom of God is within you." We aspire to the top to look for rest; it lies at the bottom. Water rests only when it gets to the lowest place. So do men. Hence be lowly.—Drummond. Ambition.—The deadness of John, Duke of Saxony, to the world was very remarkable. When he was informed of the rebellion of the ascetics, which led to so afflictive a war in Germany, he said, "If it be the will of God that I should continue a prince, as I have hitherto been, His will be done; but if otherwise, I can descend to a lower station; fewer horses and a humbler equipage will serve me as well."—Whitecross.

CHAPTER THE FORTY-SIXTH.

"Chaps. xlvi.—li. form the book of Jeremiah's prophecies concerning foreign nations, grouped together as in Isaiah and Ezekiel. The prophecies are closely connected with ch. xxv. and in the Sept. are inserted there."—Driver. **1—4.** (1) **Gentiles,** R. V. "concerning the nations." (2) **Pharaoh-necho,** "this monarch had defeated and slain Josiah at Megiddo, and set Jehoahaz on the throne. In three months he had deposed and imprisoned him at Riblah, and set up Jehoiakim. He was extending his conquests in the Asiatic direction when in the fourth year of Jehoiakim's reign he was overthrown at Carchemish.—Camb. Bib. **Carchemish,** not Circesium, but "discovered by Mr. George Smith to be at Jerâbis on the right bank of the Euphrates."—Pul. Com.: so Camb. Bib. (3) **Order,** or get in order. **buckler,** a small round shield, carried by light-armed troops. **shield,** a heavier defence, covering the whole body. (4) **Harness,** or mount. **furbish,** rub or scour to brightness. **brigandines,**[a] R. V. "coats of mail."

[a] "This term translates the Hebrew word siryon, a coat of mail. Brigandine is defined by Wedgwood and Richardson as a kind of scale armor, made of many-jointed plates, very pliant and, easy for the body, so called from being used by the light-armed foot soldiers known as brigands."—Venables.

"No man can do one thing well if he never does more than that one thing. Broadening the base of one's work is as essential as sharpening its point. — S. S. Times.

The Battle Cry (vs. 3).—I. There are wars of conquest, resulting from unrighteous ambition, pride, etc. II. There are wars of defence, as when men fight for home and liberty, etc.—as Switzerland, etc. III. There are wars of Divine retribution, as when God moves the hearts of men to punish sin and oppression. IV. In the midst of all war it is the believer's privilege to live at peace with God. V. Learn the folly of fighting against God. "Who hath fought against God and prospered?"

The Judgment of Egypt.—God is the God of the Gentile as well as the Jew, of a heathen as well as the Christian, of the godless as well as the godly. In Him all men live and move and have their being; from Him they receive every blessing of life; to Him they will have to give account of their deeds. Therefore God notes the conduct of heathen nations and chastises them when needful; so He does with individual men who renounce His authority over them or are brought up in ignorance of it. The heathen will be judged by their heathenish light and not by the high standards of Christian principles. But there is enough in that light to allow of a genuine judgment and a just sentence. The "Book of the Dead" contains a high and noble system of morality. With this in his possession, the Egyptian was without excuse in his vice and cruelty.—Pul. Com.

5—8. (5) **Wherefore,** etc., R. V. "Wherefore have I seen it? They are dismayed, etc., a sudden exclamation of astonishment.[b] So well equipped an army was nevertheless driven back in dismay. **look not back,** make no attempt to halt in their flight. (6) **Let not,** better, "the swift shall not." **north,** Euphrates was northward in relation to Judah. (7) **as a flood,** R. V. "Who is this that riseth up like the Nile." **waters .. rivers,** or "his waters toss to and fro as the rivers."[c] (8) R. V., "Egypt

[b] "The moment seized by the Prophet is that when the Eg. host first feels that the battle is lost, and, overborne by the enemy, loses heart, and in despair, yet not without a struggle, gives way." —Spk. Com.

[c] "The rise of the Nile is gentle, but at the mouth it, unlike most rivers, is much agitated, owing to the sand banks impeding its course, and so it rushes into the sea like a cataract."—Fausset.

riseth up like the Nile, and his waters toss themselves like the rivers." **the city,** better, cities in general, the expression of the world-conquering power.

Glorying in Self.—Have done with every glorying except glorying in the Lord. You cannot trust God too much, nor yourself too little. I read a book one day called "Self-made Men" and in its own sphere it was excellent; but spiritually I should not like to be a self-made man. I should think he would be an awful specimen of humanity. At any rate a self-made Christian is one of the sort the devil very soon takes. As I have seen a child so take a bran doll and shake it all out. He likes to shake out self-made Christians till there is nothing left of them. But God-made men,—these are they that do exploits; and God-made Christians who fall back upon the eternal strength at all times and confide there,—these are the men to hold on their way and to wax stronger and stronger.—Spurgeon.

For "day of the Lord" see Is. xiii. 6; Joel i. 15, ii. 1; Am. v. 18; Zep. i. 14, 15.

9—12. "A call to the two grand divisions of the army—the warriors in chariots, and the light and heavy armed infantry." (9) **Ethiopians,** Heb. Cush. **Libyans,** Heb. Put. **shield,** the heavy-armed detachments. **bow,** the light-armed troops. (10) **sacrifice,** this slaughter is looked upon as having a sacred meaning, as when a great sin offering is offered to Jehovah. (11) **virgin,** Egypt is so called bec. she had never been brought under the power of any foreign monarch. **not to be cured,**[a] R. V. "there is no healing for thee." (12) **the land,** i. e. the earth. **mighty .. mighty,** in the wild confusion the warriors trampled down each other.

The Balm of Gilead, or Balsam of Mecca.—The genuine balsam of Mecca (Amyris opobalsamum) is both scarce and expensive. The kings of Judah cultivated this shrub, but only to a very small extent. It will be interesting to learn that a bottle of this extraordinary balsam is kept at the botanical garden at Paris, as an object of the rarest and highest value. What is generally sold by the name of balsam of Mecca is merely the oil, obtained by boiling, from the seeds, stones, and branches of the tree. The balm itself is too rare to be purchased in the ordinary way. Josephus informs us that the queen of Sheba brought it first to Judæa, where balsam, myrrh, and incense, in the days of old, were to be seen used by the populace in abundance almost daily. This is one of the many things which we "mourn for" in "the days gone by." The reason of its excessive scarcity is supposed to be owing to the destruction of Jerusalem. The Jews, actuated by despair and hatred, destroyed all the balsam plants. There are none now to be found in Palestine. Only one plantation is now known to furnish it, and that is in Arabia Petræa. The whole plantation only yields about three pounds annually, and it is monopolized by the Grand Seignior.—Piesse's Art of Perfumery.

[a] Je. xxx. 13; Eze. xxx. 21.

"Physicians would be astonished at the numerous kinds of medicine wh. are administered to a patient. The people themselves are unwilling to take one kind for long together. Should a patient, when about to take his medicine, scatter or spill the least quantity, nothing will induce him to take the rest; it is a bad omen; he must have the nostrum changed."—Roberts.

13—17. (13) **The word,** this prophecy was probably delivered at the time of the prophet's residence in Egypt. (14) **Declare,** etc., ch. iv. 5. **Migdol,** etc., ch. xliv. 1. **Stand fast,** R. V. "Stand forth."[b] **sword shall devour,** R. V. "hath devoured;" alluding to the previous conquests of Nebuchadnezzar. (15) **thy valiant men,** or, "thy mighty one." The Sept. understands the reference to be to Apis, the Bull, the idol of Egypt.[c] (16) **one .. another,** as vs. 12. **to our own people,** this would be the cry of the hired troops in the Egyptian army, such as are mentioned in vs. 9. (17) **a noise,** or empty sound. **he hath passed,** R. V., "he hath let the time appointed pass by," i. e. he might have repented, but it is now too late.

The Real Cause of the Decline of empires.—A hardy, temperate, courageous people, driven by necessity or attracted by the hope of gain, fall upon some decrepit power, destroy it, and on its ruins build their own fortunes. For a while the same courage and virtue which enabled them to gain possession of their prize are manifested in consolidating their power and in building up their rule. But after the lapse of years, they have gained secure foothold and are able to live less on their

[b] "Some take this as an ironical address to Egypt, and a summons to them to stand upon their defence." — Henderson.

[c] "Apis, the bull-shaped Egyptian idol, worshipped at Noph, or Memphis. The contrast thus is between the palpable impotence of the idol, and the might attributed to it by its worshippers."—Fausset.

"If our religion means anything, it means composure, heroism, serenity, loyalty at all times and in all places."—Garrett Wyckoff.

"Nothing endures but personal qualities."—Walt Whitman.

guard against enemies. Wealth and luxury increase and exert their enervating power. In this soil the vices, whatever they may be, to which as a people they are predisposed, grow rapidly and affect the national habit and character. Then their decay has begun. It hastens rapidly on until, in their turn, this once victorious people are vanquished, overthrown by a nation more bold and righteous and therefore more powerful than themselves. This law can be readily traced in the histories of Egypt, Assyria, Babylon, Persia, Greece, Rome, and in more modern instances as well. Were there no moral causes at work in the overthrow of the French empire under Napoleon I.? In all cases it will be seen that, in one form or another, God's love of righteousness has been outraged, and vengeance has speedily, or surely if not speedily, come. What was the Reformation but the revolt of men's consciences against the abominable sins of the Catholic Church? But how came that Church —once so fair, so beautiful, so glorious—to have sunk so low as to become hateful in men's eyes? It was this same enervating influence of wealth, power, and other forms of earthly prosperity which sapped her spiritual strength until she became utterly unworthy of men's confidence, and she was punished, and is so to this day, by the loss of well-nigh all Northern Europe, the noblest half of her ancient domain."—Pul. Com.

18—21. (18) **as Tabor,** or "like a Tabor among the mountains."[a] So Nebuchadnezzar shall stand out conspicuous above all neighboring rulers. (19) **daughter .. Egypt,** fig. term for the people of Egypt.[b] **furnish .. captivity,** make preparations for captivity. (20) **destruction,** or "the destroyer." Lit. "a gadfly from the north has come upon her." The fly that destroys cattle. (21) **hired men,** mercenary troops. **fatted bullocks,** ready to be slaughtered. "We do not look for chronological sequence in such a poem, so that this picture of the flight and destruction of the mercenaries is not necessarily later in time than their overthrow and contemplated desertion in verse 15. The prophet is depicting a scene of bewildered confusion; the disasters that fell thick upon Egypt crowd into his vision without order or even coherence."—Exp. Bib.

The Oaths of Jehovah (vs. 18).—I. The Divine oaths recorded in Scripture exhibit and declare the glory of the Divine character. 1. As they show forth the infinite condescension of God; 2. As they furnish a sublime and awful manifestation of the sincere earnestness of the Divine mind in what He declares unto us in His Word, with such an attestation; 3. As they exhibit the benevolent solicitude of God for the welfare of the unworthy creatures whom He thus addresses; 4. As they intimate the unchangeableness of the Divine mind in relation to those arrangements in His moral and natural government which were in that manner established and confirmed. II. The Divine oaths also serve to illustrate the moral character of man, and to exercise a powerful influence on his moral and spiritual influence. 1. As they strongly corroborate the fact that the human heart is corrupt and alienated from God; 2. As they are fearful warnings of the perilous condition of the impenitent and unbelieving soul; 3. As they afford the strongest encouragment to believers in their onward progress to heaven.—W. Rees.

22—26. (22) **like a serpent,** R. V. marg. "Her sound is like that of a serpent as it goeth." Egypt (like Jersalem, in Isa. xxix. 4) is imagined as a maiden (comp. vs. 19) seated on the ground, and faintly sighing; and her feeble voice is likened to the rustling sound of a serpent in motion. (23) **though .. searched,** i. e. though it seems to be impenetrable. A fig. for the vast multitudes of the Egyptian army. **grasshoppers,** R. V. "locusts." (24) **daughter,** as vs. 19. (25) **multitude,** R. V., "Amon of No," i.e. the chief god worshiped in No (called also No Amon, margin of Nah. iii. 8). The name Amon signified invisible, and hence he was connected with the most spiritual form of Egyptian worship. The Greeks and Romans compared him to Zeus and Jupiter, and hence his name, familiar to us, of Jupiter Ammon."[c] Camb. Bib. **No,** the sacred city of Thebes. (26) **afterward,** after a time of Divine judgments, lasting some forty years.[d]

[a] "Tabor rises in the form of a truncated cone to the height of about 1,350 feet above the plain of Esdraelon, its total height above the sea level being 1,805 feet. Other mountains of equal elevation are in sight, but its shape and the wide extent of the plain around it, make it a far more conspicuous object. Carmel also is a most commanding mountain."—Robinson.

[b] Comp. Je. iv. 31.

"The most important thought I ever had was my responsibility to God."—Daniel Webster.

[c] "He was the first of the supreme triad of Thebes, and confessedly his form was the most elevated and spiritual under which the Egyptian priesthood represented the divinity to the adoration of the people. He was the deity invisible and unfathomable, whose name signifies the concealed, and was the mysterious mainspring, who created, preserves, and governs the world."—Lenormant.

[d] Eze. xxix. 13.

No-Amon (vs. 25).—No, or No-Amon, or Amon of No (marginal reading), was the metropolis of Upper Egypt, by the Greek geographers termed Thebes, a city eminently distinguished for the worship of Jupiter, who by the Egyptians was called Amon or Ammon; hence the city received the appellation of Diospolis, or the City of Jupiter. The grandeur of ancient Thebes must now be traced in the four small towns or hamlets of Luxor, Karnak, Medinet-Abou, and Gournou. Karnak is regarded by the most accurate modern travelers as the principal site of Diospolis; and the Egyptians seem to have called forth all the resources of wealth, and all the efforts of art, in order to render it worthy of their supreme divinity.—Horne.

27, 28. These vss. have probably been introduced here by the prophet as a quotation from the earlier passage (see ch. xxx. 10, 11), which is one prophetic of the return from exile, in order to shew that if Egypt's troubles were to be but temporary, much more should those of Judah and even of Israel also pass away.—Camb. B. (27) **fear not thou,** etc., Is. xli. 13, xliii. 5, xliv. 2; Je. xxx. 10. (28) **a full end,** ch. xxx. 11[e] in measure. R. V. "with judgment."

God's Promise Unchangeable.—Verse 28 is so clearly connected with vs. 27, that both must be read together. They resemble chap. xxx. 10, 11, and relate probably to the same subject. Towards the fall of the Jewish monarchy, Judæa became the battle-ground between the Egyptians, on one side, and the Babylonians on the other. It was subject now to one of these powers, now to the other, as they respectively conquered. At length Babylon became finally master of the territory from the river of Egypt to the Euphrates, 2 Kings xxiv. 7. In the days of Jehoiakim Jerusalem was held under vassalage to Nebuchadnezzar, who took Daniel and his companions, with probably others of its principal inhabitants, to Babylon. Subsequently Jerusalem was more thoroughly subdued by Nebuchadnezzar, and large numbers of its people were carried away to his distant empire. The Prophet, in the passage to be elucidated, comforts the Jews under the humiliation and sufferings thus inflicted on them. Their land should not be made "altogether desolate," Jer. xxx. 11. The nations which oppressed and enslaved Judæa should be destroyed, but God would not make a full end of her. She should be corrected with moderation, and her sons should afterwards be restored to their own land. This prediction was fulfilled when the Jews returned from Babylon under favor of Cyrus, the conqueror of all the East.

[e] "Nations have their periods; the Jewish nation itself has come to an end as a nation; but the Gospel Church, God's spiritual Israel, still continues, and will to the end of time; in that this promise is to have its full accomplishment, that, though God correct it, He will never make a full end of it."—Mat. Henry.

"They were, in truth, great rascals, and belonged to that class of people who find things before they are lost."—Grimm.

CHAPPTER THE FORTY-SEVENTH.

This chapter concerns the Philistines and indirectly also Tyre and Sidon. (vs. 4) **1—4.** (1) **against,** or, concerning. **before .. Gaza,** 'probably the allusion is to a capture of Gaza by the Egyptians not otherwise known to us, either on their retreat from Carchemish or in connection with movement noted in xxxvii. 5."—Driver.[a] (2) **waters rise,** Is. viii. 7. **overflowing flood,** or torrent, Is. xxx. 28. (3) **noise .. hoofs,** Nah. iii. 2. **fathers .. children,** each would care only to save himself; natural affections would be destroyed. **feebleness of hands,** by being made helpless with extreme fear. (4) **remnant .. Caphtor,** "the few of the Philistine nation that still survive after the wars with Egypt and Assyria, which they had long undergone. Caphtor is spoken of also in Deut. ii. 23; Amos ix. 7, as the origin of the Philistines. Its position is somewhat doubtful. Some identify it with Crete, but more probably it was the Delta of Egypt. 'The country' is literally the isle, or the sea-coast."[b] —Camb. Bib.

Ruins at Gaza.—The ruins of white marble sometimes found at Gaza prove that it was formerly the abode of luxury and opulence. It has shared in the general destruction; and, notwithstanding its proud

[a] 2 Chr. xxxv. 20, xxxvi. 8.

[b] "The Philistines, being the neighbors of the Phœnicians, would naturally make a common cause with them in case of foreign invasion."—Henderson.

"There can be no treaty of peace till we lay down these weapons of rebellion with which we fight against heaven; nor can we expect to have our distempers cured, if our daily food be poison."—Scougal.

title of the capital of Palestine, it is now no more than a defenceless village (baldness has come upon it), peopled by, at most, only two thousand inhabitants." It is forsaken and bereaved of its king." The seacoast, by which it was formerly washed, is every day removing farther from the deserted ruins of Ashkelon. "It shall be a desolation. Ashkelon shall not be inhabited." Amid the various successive ruins, those of Edzoud (Ashdod), so powerful under the Philistines, are now remarkable for their scorpions. "The inhabitants shall be cut off from Ashdod."—Keith.

5—7. (5) **Baldness,** the sign of mourning, ch. xvi. 6. **Ashkelon is cut off,** etc. R. V., "Ashkelon is brought to naught, the remnant of their valley." **valley,** or low-lying plain, known as Shephelah. **cut thyself,** i. e. will you never cease grieving? (6) **sword,** etc., the instrument of Divine judgment.[c] **how long,** "as Jeremiah contemplates this fresh array of victims of Chaldean cruelty, he is moved to protest against the weary monotony of ruin. (7) **given it a charge,** wh. it is bound to execute to the full. **sea shore?** the strip of shore-land held by the Philistines.

[c] Eze. xiv. 17, xxi. 3.

"The Word of the Lord is not bound. How men have sought to sheathe it in the scabbard, to hide and hold it there, so that they may go on unchecked in their own ways! But it has leapt forth in spite of them; and, in spite of pagan, Roman, and other persecutions, has asserted its supreme might."

"God smites, and not imperfectly; nor does He need to smite twice."

The Means of Terminating War.—(vss. 6, 7).—I. The evils of protracted war. 1. War is a tremendous evil; 2. Well might the Prophet desire its speedy termination. II. The reason of its continuance. 1. War is one of those judgments with which God punishes the sins of men; 2. Till He has effected His purposes by it, no human efforts can bring it to a close. III. Means of its termination. 1. The intention of God's chastisements is to bring us to repentance; 2. On the attainment of this end He will instantly remove His judgments from us. IV. Suggests some hints respecting those heavy judgments which God has denounced against sinners in another world, and respecting the best means of averting them from our souls.—C. Simeon.

An Appeal to God.—The prophet ceases to be the mouthpiece of God, and breaks out into the cry of human anguish. How often since, amid the barbarian inroads that overwhelmed the Roman Empire, amid the prolonged horrors of the Thirty Years' War, amid the carnage of the French Revolution, men have uttered a like appeal to an unanswering and relentless Providence! Indeed, not in war only, but even in peace, the tide of human misery and sin often seems to flow, century after century, with undiminished volume, and ever and again a vain "How long" is wrung from pallid and despairing lips. For the Divine purpose may not be hindered, and the sword of Jehovah must still strike home.—Exp. Bib.

CHAPPTER THE FORTY-EIGHTH.

1—3. (1) **Moab,** Ge. xix. 37.[a] "The prophets show a very keen interest in Moab. With the exception of the very short Book of Joel, all the prophets who deal in detail with foreign nations devote sections to Moab. The unusual length of such sections in Isaiah and Jeremiah is not the only resemblance between the utterances of these two prophets concerning Moab. There are many parallels of idea and expression, which probably indicate the influence of the elder prophet upon his successor; unless indeed both of them adapted some popular poem which was early current in Judah.—Exp. Bib.[b] **Nebo,** a town 8 Rom. miles S. of Heshbon.[c] **Kiriathaim,** prob. Et-teym, west of Medeba, and S. W. of Heshbon. **Misgab,** R. V. margin, "the high fort." Ref. is to the celebrated fortress, Kir-heres.[d] (2) **Heshbon,**[e] the capital city of the Moabites, Nu. xxi. 26. When the Chaldæans took this city, they there devised plans for subduing the whole country. Heshbon in Chaldee means "a device." **cut down,** R. V., "brought to silence." **Madmen,** the name of some unknown town used to make a play on words: "Thou shalt become still O House of stillness." (3) **Horonaim,** Is. xv. 5.

[a] "These districts were possessed by the Emim, a gigantic people, but the Moabites were successful in expelling them, and occupied at first a considerable region, the uplands east of the Dead Sea, and the Jordan as far as the mountains of Gilead, together with the lowlands between their own hills and the river, a region perhaps 50 miles in length, and 10 or 12 broad."—Ayre.

[b] 2 Ki. xxiv. 2.

[c] Nu. xxxii. 3, 38.

[d] Is. xv. 1, xvi. 7, 11.

[e] "An ancient and royal city, nearly midway between the rivers Jabbok and Arnon, the ruins of which cover the sides of an elevated hill, wh. commands an extensive view of the surrounding country."—Henderson.

The Departed Praise of Moab.—Those whose tongues had been full of the praises of Moab needed not to be silent. The very overthrow of Moab would be a signal for praise and congratulation among the good. When the unhallowed praises of men are silenced by destruction of the things they praised, then angels begin to sing. And they who praise low, earthly things may have their thoughts introduced to heavenly ones, and then they will discover what man was made to praise. How the words that are exaggerated and altogether disproportioned when applied to the works of men, have in them an exquisite fitness when we speak of the works of God or of Christ, or of men properly engaged in Christian service!—Pul. Com.

"War will never yield but to the principles of universal justice and love, and these have no sure root but in the religion of Jesus Christ." — Channing.

"So calm, the waters scarcely seem to stray, and yet they glide, like happiness, away."—Byron.

Moab.—It is easy to understand why the Jewish Scriptures should have much to say about Moab, just as the sole surviving fragment of Moabite literature is chiefly occupied with Israel. These two Terahite tribes—the children of Jacob and the children of Lot—had dwelt side by side for centuries, like the Scotch and English borderers before the accession of James I. They had experienced many alternations of enmity and friendship, and had shared complex interests, common and conflicting, after the manner of neighbors who are also kinsmen. Each in its turn had oppressed the other; and Moab had been the tributary of the Israelite monarchy till the victorious arms of Mesha had achieved independence for his people and firmly established their dominion over the debatable frontier lands. There are traces, too, of more kindly relations: the House of David reckoned Ruth the Moabitess amongst its ancestors, and Jesse, like Elimelech and Naomi, had taken refuge in Moab. Accordingly this prophecy concerning Moab frequently strikes a note of sympathetic lamentation and almost becomes a dirge.—Exp. Bib.

4—6. (4) **Moab,** prob. meaning here the city Ar-Moab, Nu. xxi. 15. **her little ones,** "her children augmenting the distressing scene by their pitiable shrieks." (5) **Luhith,** R. V. "For by the ascent of Luhith with continual weeping shall they go up;" it was a hill town. comp. Is. xv. 5. **going down,** descending into the valley towards Horonaim, highlands and lowlands suffer alike. (6) **like the heath,** literally, "and (your souls) shall be like destitute ones in the wilderness." Imagine the case of one who has been robbed of everything, and left alone in the desert; not less miserable is that of the Moabite fugitives.

Flee for Your Life (vs. 6).—I. Whence you are to flee. II. Where you are to flee. III. How you are to flee. IV. When you are to flee. V. Why you are to flee.—Hugh Macmillan.

The Cities of Moab.—In this inventory, as it were, of the ruin of Moab our attention is arrested by the constant and detailed references to the cities. This feature is partly borrowed from Isaiah. Ezekiel too speaks of the Moabite cities which are the glory of the country; but Jeremiah's prophecy is a veritable Domesday Book of Moab. With his epic fondness for lists of sonorous names—after the manner of Homer's catalogue of the ships—he enumerates Nebo, Kiriathaim, Heshbon, and Horonaim, city after city, till he completes a tale of no fewer than twenty-six, and then summarizes the rest as "all the cities of the land of Moab, far and near." Eight of these cities are mentioned in Joshua as part of the inheritance of Reuben and Gad. Another, Bozrah, is usually spoken of as a city of Edom. The Moabite Stone explains the occurrence of Reubenite cities in these lists. It tells us how Mesha took Nebo, Jahaz, and Horonaim from Israel. Possibly in this period of conquest Bozrah became tributary to Moab, without ceasing to be an Edomite city. This extension of territory and multiplication of towns points to an era of power and prosperity, of which there are other indications in this chapter.—Exp. Bib.

7—10. (7) **works,** or "idols," the works of their hands.—Cheyne. **Chemosh,** the object of Moab's national worship.[a] The oldest Heb. form of the word in this passage seems to be Chemish, and although it is not elsewhere found, yet probability is given to its existence by

[a] Nu. xxi. 29.

[b] "Solomon built a high place for Chemosh, near to Jerusalem (1 Ki. xi. 7, 33), which was defiled by Josiah (2 Ki. xxiii. 13). There are various conjectures concerning this false god; some identifying him with Mars, and some with Saturn."—Ayre.

"No greater grief! Is it then always grief
Remembering happier times in times of sorrow?
Does one day of delight ne'er bring relief
To the sick soul on a despairful morrow?
Past joys are a possession."
—Todhunter.

"According to Jewish tradition, Chemosh was worshipped under the symbol of a black star, wh. would seem to countenance the opinion that he corresponded to Saturn." — Henderson.

[a] Lit. tilters, who tip a vessel to drain the wine off from the dregs.

"There is a spirit of resistance implanted by the Deity in the breast of man, proportioned to the size of the wrongs he is destined to endure." — C. J. Fox.

"It always seems to me to be a very insane thing for a man to glory in his animal force, for there can be no merit in it. In the strength of those brawny limbs of theirs and those powerful muscles, some vaunt themselves abun-

such compounds as Car-chemish. If the god is powerless to prevent his own captivity, what chance is there for the people?—Camb. Bib.[b] **priests,** etc., ch. xlix. 3. (8) **valley,** or lowlands on the east bank of the Jordan. **plain,** comp. De. iv. 43, upland pasture districts. (9) **Give wings,** bec. only extreme haste can save any of them. (10) **deceitfully,** R. V. "negligently." Reference is to the agents sent by God to execute His judgments on Moab.

Lukewarmness and Zeal. vs. 10.—He serves God deceitfully—1. Who serves Him with the body without the soul; 2. He who serves Him with the soul without the body, when both may be conjoined in His service; 3. He who reserves one faculty for sin or one sin for themselves or one action to please himself and many for religion.—Bp. Taylor.

Moab.—Moab has often been a field of contest between the Arabs and Turks; and although the former have retained possession of it, both have mutually reduced it to desolation. The different tribes of Arabs who traverse it not only bear a permanent and habitual hostility to Christians and to Turks, but one tribe is often at variance and at war with another; and the regular cultivation of the soil, or the improvement of those natural advantages of which the country is so full, is a matter either never thought of, or that cannot be realized. Property is there the creature of power, and not of law; and possession forms no security when plunder is the preferable right. Hence the extensive plains, where they are not partially covered with wood, present a barren aspect, which is only relieved at intervals by a few clusters of wild fig trees, that show how the richest gifts of nature degenerate when unaided by the industry of man. And instead of the profusion which the plains must have exhibited in every quarter, nothing but "patches of the best soil in the territory are now cultivated by the Arabs;" and these only "whenever they have the prospect of being able to secure the harvest against the incursions of enemies." The Arab herds now roam at freedom over the valleys and the plains; and "the many vestiges of field enclosures" form not any obstruction; they wander undisturbed around the tents of their masters, over the face of the country; and while the valley is perished, and the plain destroyed, the cities also of Aroer are forsaken; they are for the flocks which lie down, and none make them afraid. The strong contrast between the ancient and the actual state of Moab is exemplified in the condition of the inhibitants as well as of the land; and the coincidence between the prediction and the fact is as striking in the one case as in the other.—Keith.

11—13. (11) **settled..lees,** as wine left, after fermentation. For similar figure comp. Zep. i. 12. **emptied..vessel,** by a refining process that removes the dregs. **taste,** his pride and luxury. (12) **wanderers,**[a] R. V. "them that pour off, and they shall pour him off." (13) **ashamed,** bec. her idol can give her no security. **of Beth-el,** ashamed of the golden calf that was set up there by Jeroboam I. 1 Ki. xii. 29.

Much Ease, Much Peril.—"There is a reference here to wine, or to the process by which it is prepared and finished. It is first expressed from the grape, when it is a thick discolored fluid or juice. It is then fermented, passing through a process that separates the impurities and settles them as lees at the bottom. Standing thus upon its lees or dregs in some large tun or vat, it is not further improved. A gross and coarse flavor remains, and the scent of the feculent matter stays by and becomes fastened, as it were, in the body of the wine itself. To separate this and so to soften or refine the quality, it is now decantered or drawn off into separate jars or skins. After a while this is done again and then again; and so, being emptied from vessel to vessel, the last remains of the lees or sediment are finally cleared, the crude flavors are reduced, the scent itself is refined by ventilation, and the perfect character is attained." Now, the prophet affirms here that Moab had been at ease from his youth. It is difficult in the face of the somewhat checkered history of Moab to see the exact meaning of this. Probably he refers to the long lapse of time since their great and awful defeat told of in 2 Kings iii. 21. Some two centuries and a half had rolled away since that dread day, and in that interval Moab regained all, and more than all, of its former prosperity. For the land was beautiful and rich in the extreme. Its pastures were covered over with sheep and its valleys with corn. The very name "Moab" is thought to mean the land of desire, that is, the desirable land. Now, during these long periods, the description here given is applicable. They had enjoyed much ease, and the natural evils engendered by their cruel idolatrous system had become more fixed and settled; "their scent had not changed." The truth, therefore, which is here taught is that prolonged and abundant ease, however coveted by men, is full of peril to their higher nature, and tends continually to the deterioration of character and the hardening of the habit of evil. Troubles Revive Us.—Staying for awhile in the valley of Aosta, in Northern Italy, we found the air to be heavy, close, and humid with pestilential exhalations. We were oppressed and feverish—one's life did not seem worth a pin. We could not breathe freely, our lungs had a sense of having a hundred atmospheres piled upon them. Presently, at midday, there came a thunder-clap, attended by big drops of rain and a stiff gale of wind, which grew into a perfect tornado, tearing down the trees; then followed what the poet calls "sonorous hail," and then again the lightning flash, and the thunder peal on peal echoing along the Alps. But how delightful was the effect! How we all went out upon the verandah to look at the lightning and enjoy the music of the thunder! How cool the air and bracing! How delightful to walk out in the cool evening after the storm! Then you could breathe and feel a joy in life. Full often it is thus with the Christian after trouble. He has grown to be careless, lethargic, feverish, heavy, and ready to die, and just then he has been assailed by trouble, thundering threatenings have rolled from God's mouth, flashes of lightning have darted from Providence: the property vanished, the wife died, the children were buried, trouble followed trouble, and then the man has turned to God, and though his face was wet with tears of repentance, yet he has felt his spirit to be remarkably restored. When he goes up to the house of God, it is far more sweet to hear the Word than aforetime. He could not pray before, but now he leans his head on Jesus' bosom and pours out his soul in fellowship. Eternity now exerts its heavenly attractions, and the man is saved from himself.—Spurgeon.

14—17. (14) **mighty,** and quite able to stand in the war. (15) **gone up,** R. V. "and they are gone up into her cities," i. e. the enemy. **chosen ..men,** the choice of them have only gone to battle to be slain. (16) **near to come,** Is. xiii. 22. About twenty-two years passed bet. this prophecy and the calamity. (17) **strong staff,** etc. for these expressions, as implying national glory and power over others, compare Ps. cx. 2; Is. xiv. 29; Ezek. xix. 11, 12, 14.

The Strong Staff and the Beautiful Rod (vs. 17.)—I. The purposes of our Heavenly Father in great bereavements. 1. To teach us that we should not misplace our trust; 2. To convince us of our sins and to sever us from them; 3. To teach us His own independence of the instruments He employs; 4. To remind us of the sovereignty of God; 5. To exhibit His wise and watchful providence. II. The duties to which we are, amid such scenes, specially called. 1. We are to exercise submission; 2. We should profit by the example of those who have died in the Lord; 3. We should cease from man and put our trust in God.—W. R. Williams.

18—20. (18) **Dibon,** Is. xv. 2. Dibon " now Dhiban (the "Moabite stone" was found there) stands on two hills. Hence the expression 'come down' in the text. The language here is intensified in both clauses from the corresponding passage relating to the daughter of Babylon in Is. xlvii. 1." **sit in thirst,** comp. "sit in the dust," Is. xlvii. 1.[a] "Sit in a

dantly. Though 'the Lord taketh not pleasure in the legs of a man,' yet some count it a very wonderful thing that they can outrun or outleap their fellows. O athlete, though thou be strong as Samson or swift as Asahel, what hast thou that thou hast not received? Hadst thou been born with a tendency to consumption, or with some other hereditary weakness, couldst thou have prevented it? And now that thou art strong, art thou to be praised for that, any more than a horse or a steam-engine?"—Spurgeon.

"A Roman custom was to bring in a bundle of rods tied hard with many knots to be laid before one who was about to be scourged. These knots must all be untied, slowly and in order. While this was going on, the judge watched the offender to see how he behaved. Sometimes his manner gained him mercy. The rods were so many warnings. Each told him silently of coming punishment. If he heard their voice, he might go free of it."

[a] "Jer. draws a picture of the conquered inhabitants, who formed a valuable part of the spoil of war, collected together outside the walls, waiting until the time comes for their captors to march them away to the slave - mart."—Spk. Com.

"Destruction o'ertakes as often those that fly as those that boldly meet it."—Denham.

"If we will not use our opportunities for God's purpose, God will secure in due time, that we should not use them for our own."—Pul. Com.

land where everything is parched." (19) **Aroer,** on the river Arnon, De. ii. 36. It lay in the way of the Moabites who fled to Arabia Deserta; and its inhabitants would learn from the fugitives the lot that surely awaited themselves. (20) **it is,** i. e. Dibon.

Dibon.—The ruins of Dhiban (Dibon) situated in the midst of a fine plain, are of considerable extent, but present nothing of interest. The neighboring hot wells, and the similarity of the name, identify the ruins of Myoun with Meon, or Beth Meon of Scripture. Of this ancient city, as well as of Araayr (Aroer), nothing is now remarkable but what is common to them with all the cities of Moab—their entire desolation. The extent of the ruins of Rabba (Rabbath Moab), formerly the residence of the kings of Moab, sufficiently proves its ancient importance, though no other object can be particularized among the ruins except the remains of a palace or temple, some of the walls of which are still standing; a gate belonging to another building; and an insulated altar. There are many remains of private buildings, but none entire. There being no springs on the spot, the town had two birkets, the largest of which is cut entirely out of the rocky ground, together with many cisterns. Mount Nebo was completely barren when Burckhardt passed over it, and the site of the ancient city had not been ascertained. Nebo is spoiled.—Keith. Ill-Effects of Prosperity.—History constantly illustrates how when Christians were disturbed and prosperous the wine of truth settled on the lees and came to taste of the cask; and—to change the figure—how affliction and persecution proved most effectual tonics for a debilitated Church. Continental critics of modern England speak severely of the ill-effects which our prolonged freedom from invasion and civil war, and the unbroken continuity of our social life have had on our national character and manners. In their eyes England is a perfect Moab, concerning which they are ever ready to prophesy after the manner of Jeremiah. The Hebrew Chronicler blamed Josiah because he would not listen to the advice and criticism of Pharaoh Necho. There may be warnings which we should do well to heed, even in the acrimony of foreign journalists.—Exp. Bib.

21—25. (21) **Holon,** Jos. xv. 51. **Jahazah,** Nu. xxi. 23; Is. xv. 4. **Mephaath,** Jos. xiii. 18, xxi. 37. (22) **Bethdiblathaim,** comp. Nu. xxxiii. 46, and Eze. vi. 14. (23) **Bethgamul,** the city of camels. The site is unknown. **Beth-meon,** comp. Jos. xiii. 17. Now Miun, a mere ruin. (24) **Kerioth,** Jos. xv. 25; Am. ii. 2. **Bozrah,** the capital of the Edomites at one time. Ge. xxxvi. 33; Is. lxiii. 1. (25) **horn,** the Eastern emblem of strength and sovereignty.[b]

[b] "Strength is often expressed by the horn, wherein the strength of bulls and such like creatures consists; and by the arm, wherein human strength doth chiefly discover itself."—Lowth.

Ps. lxxv. 5, 10; La. ii. 3.

"In God's own might
We gird us for the coming fight,—
And, strong in Him whose cause is ours
In conflict with unholy powers,
We grasp the weapons he has given—
The Light, and Truth, and Love of Heaven."
—Whittier.

Cities of Moab.—And the cities of Moab have all disappeared. Their place, together with the adjoining part of Idumæa, is characterized in the map of Volney's Travels, by the ruins of towns. His information respecting these ruins was derived from some of the wandering Arabs; and its accuracy has been fully corroborated by the testimony of different European travelers of high respectability and undoubted veracity, who have since visited this devastated region. The whole country abounds with ruins. And Burckhardt, who encountered many difficulties in so desolate and dangerous a land, thus records the brief history of a few of them: "The ruins of Eleale, Heshbon, Meon, Medaba, Dibon, Aroer, still subsist to illustrate the history of the Beni Israel." And it might with equal truth have been added, that they still subsist to confirm the inspiration of the Jewish Scripture, or to prove that the seers of Israel were the prophets of God, for the desolation of each of these very cities was the theme of a prediction. Everything worthy of observation respecting them has been detailed, not only in Burckhardt's Travels in Syria, but also by Seetzen, and, more recently, by Captains Irby and Mangles, who, along with Mr. Banks and Mr. Legh, visited this deserted district. The predicted judgment has fallen with such truth upon these cities, and upon all the cities of the land of Moab far and near, and they are so utterly broken down, that even the prying curiosity of such indefatigable travelers could discover among a multiplicity of ruins only a few remains so entire as to be worthy of particular notice. The subjoined description is drawn from their united testimony:—Among the ruins of El Aal (Eleale) are a number of large cisterns, fragments of buildings, and foundations of houses. At Heshban (Heshbon) are the ruins of a large ancient town, together with the remains of a temple, and some edifices. A few broken shafts of columns are still standing; and there are a number of deep wells cut in the rock. The ruins of Medaba are about two miles in circumference. There are many remains of the walls of private houses constructed with blocks of silex, but not a single edifice is standing. The chief object of interest is an immense tank or cistern of hewn stones, "which, as there is no stream at Medaba," Burckhardt remarks, "might still be of use to the Bedouins, were the surrounding ground cleared of the rubbish to allow the water to flow into it; but such an undertaking is far beyond the views of the wandering Arabs." There is also the foundation of a temple built with large stones, and apparently of great antiquity, with two columns near it.—Keith.

"His heart is black with pride.
He for himself hell's gate has opened wide,
For, weighed in God the All-Sufficient's scale,
Not claims nor righteousness or men avail:
But these are costly in His sight indeed,—
Repentance, contrite shame, and sense of need."
—Oriental, tr. by Trench.

26—30. (26) **Make..drunken,**[a] God's judgments are represented as a cup of intoxication: ch. xxv. 15. And what is Moab's crime? At an earlier point the prophet said that it was the callousness produced by long prosperity (vs. 11); but here another sin is mentioned—Moab's haughty contempt of Jehovah. For this it deserves that its contempt should be thrown back upon itself, by its being made, like a drunken man, the scorn of all.—Ewald. **wallow,** "Fall down as drunkards do."[b] (27) **Israel..thee,** Moab had made game of the calamities of the Jews. **among thieves,** what giveth thee the right to show such scorn and insolent triumph towards Israel, as if he were one who had been arrested in the very act of robbery (comp. ch. ii. 26)? **for since,** etc. R. V. "for as often as thou speaketh of him thou waggest the head." (28) **like the dove,** wh. often makes its nest in the sides and roofs of caverns: Is. xvi. 1, 2. (29) **pride of Moab,** Is. xvi. 6. (30) **but it shall not,** etc., R. V., "that it is naught; his boastings have wrought nothing."

[a] "The ministers of the Divine justice are to make Moab drink of the wine-cup of God's fury, till terror deprives him of his senses. His sin had been that of magnifying himself against Jehovah by depriving the Reubenites of the country which God had taken from the Amorites to give them." —Spk. Com.

[b] "Shall be so afflicted by God's wrath as to disgorge all his past pride, riches, and vainglory, and fall in his shameful abasement."—Fausset.

Pyrrhus and the Philosopher.—When Pyrrhus, king of Epirus, was making great preparations for his intended expedition into Italy, Cineas, the philosopher, took a favorable opportunity of addressing him thus: "The Romans, sir, are reported to be a warlike and victorious people; but if God permit us to overcome them, what use shall we make of the victory?" "Thou askest," said Pyrrhus, "a thing that is self-evident. The Romans once conquered, no city will resist us; we shall then be masters of all Italy." Cineas added, "And having subdued Italy, what shall we do next?" Pyrrhus, not yet aware of his intentions, replied, "Sicily next stretches out her arms to receive us." "That is very probable," said Cineas, "but will the possession of Sicily put an end to the war?" "God grant us success in that," answered Pyrrhus, "and we shall make these only the forerunners of greater things, for then Lybia and Carthage will soon be ours: and these things being completed, none of our enemies can offer any farther resistance." "Very true," added Cineas, "for then we may easily regain Macedon, and make an absolute conquest of Greece; and, when all these are in our possession, what shall we do then?" Pyrrhus, smiling, answered, "Why then, my dear friend, we will live at our ease, drink all day long, and amuse ourselves with cheerful conversation." "Well sir," said Cineas, "and why may we not do all this now, and without the labor and hazard of an enterprise so laborious and uncertain?" Pyrrhus, however, unwilling to take the advice of the philosopher, ardently engaged in these ambitious pursuits, and at last perished in them.—Cheever.

"No creature but is furnished with means of security and defence. The weakest creatures have often the strongest shelters. In religion the extremes of being meet. Human weakness and Divine strength; human folly and Divine wisdom; human insufficiency, Divine all-sufficiency."—Hom. Com.

"Crosses are of no use to us but inasmuch as we yield ourselves up to them, and forget ourselves." — Fenelon.

31—34. (31) **howl for Moab,** Is. xv. 5. **all Moab,** comp. "whole Palestina," Is. xiv. 31. **mine heart,** etc. R. V., "for the men of Kir-heres shall they mourn: Kir-heres was the chief stronghold of Moab. Is. xvi. 7, 11. (32) vine of Sibmah,** Is. xvi. 8. **thy plants,** R. V. "thy branches." **over**

[a] "Trans. 'Eglah Shelishiah;' 'fr. Zoar to Horonaim, even to the third Eglah;' several places seem to have borne the name of Eglah, and this is specified as the 'third Eglah.' "—Lightfoot.

"There are no crown wearers in heaven who were not cross-bearers here below." —Spurgeon.

"What we call the potency of life, its germ, may be conferred by a divine act; but if the life is to be more than a potency, more than a germ, we must live it."—R. W. Dale.

[b] Is. xvi. 12.

"'We find Arabs,'La Roque tells us, 'who have their arms scarred by the gashes of a knife, which they sometimes give themselves, to mark out to their mistresses what their rigor and the violence of love made them suffer.' From this extract we learn what particular part of the body received these cuttings. The Scripture frequently speaks of them in a more general manner."—Harmer.

[a] "Nebuchadnezzar's rise seemed to be like that of the mighty eagle, spreading out his wings, feathered with the innumerable colors of the variegated masses which composed the Chaldæan host, sweeping over different countries, and striking fear in his flight." — Stanley.

[b] De. xxviii. 49; Je. xlix. 22; Eze. xvii. 3.

the sea, i. e. the Dead Sea. **sea of Jazer,** the word "sea" was probably repeated by a scribe's error.—Cheyne. (33) **joy,** etc., Is. xvi. 10. (34) **Elealeh,** Is. xvi. 9. **Zoar,** Is. xv. 5. **as an heifer,** R. V. to Eglath.—Shelishiyah" or trans. "even to the third Eglah."[a] **Nimrim,** Is. xv. 6. at the S. E. end of the Dead Sea. The sense of vs. 34 is that the cry uttered from Heshbon is heard at Elealeh (about two miles distant) and is even carried on to Jahaz, a considerable distance southwest. Again, the wail uttered from Zoar is borne to Horonaim, both in the south of the land. Thus the lamentation shall be caught by one from another and be universal.—Camb. B.

The Cities of Moab.—When the towns of Moab existed in their prime, and were at ease, when arrogance, and haughtiness, and pride prevailed among them, the desolation and total desertion and abandonment of them all must have utterly surpassed all human conception. And that such numerous cities, which substituted for many ages, which were diversified in their sites, some of them being built on eminences, and naturally strong; others on plains, and surrounded by the richest soil; some situated in valleys by the side of a plentiful stream; and others where art supplied the deficiencies of nature, and where immense cisterns were excavated out of the rock, and which exhibit in their ruins many monuments of ancient prosperity, and many remains easily convertible into present utility, should have all fled away, all met the same indiscriminate fate, and be all desolate, without any to dwell therein, notwithstanding all these ancient assurances of their permanent durability, and their existing facilities and inducements for being the habitations of men, is a matter of just wonder in the present day, and had any other people been the possessors of Moab, the fact would either have been totally impossible or unaccountable. Trying as this test of the truth of prophecy is, that is the word of God, and not of erring man, which can so well and so triumphantly abide it. They shall cry of Moab, How is it broken down.—Keith.

35—39. (35) **in the high places,** this would be the last relic of the national religion. When the temples were destroyed, worship would be kept up on the "high places."[b] (36) **like pipes,** or like the flutes used at funerals. Comp. Is. xvi. 11. (37) **bald..clipped** the usual signs of mourning. Is. xv. 2 **cuttings,** ch. xvi. 6, xli. 5, xlvii. 5. (38) **generally,** better, "nothing but lamentation everywhere." (39) **They shall howl.. down,** R. V., "How is it broken down! how do they howl!" **turned the back,** to flee away.

Cuttings for the Dead (vs. 37).—The relations of the deceased often testify their sorrow in a more serious and affecting manner, by cutting and slashing their naked arms with daggers. To this absurd and barbarous custom the Prophet thus alludes: "For every head shall be bald, and every beard clipped; upon all hands shall be cuttings, and upon the loins sackcloth." And again, "Both the great and the small shall die in the land; they shall not be buried, neither shall men lament for them, nor cut themselves." It seems to have been very common in Egypt, and among the people of Israel, before the age of Moses, else he had not forbidden it by an express law: "Ye are the children of the Lord your God; ye shall not cut yourselves, nor make any baldness between your eyes for the dead." Mr. Harmer refers to this custom, the "wounds in the hands" of the Prophet, which he had given himself, in token of affection to a person.—Paxton.

40—43. (40) **he,** i. e. Nebuchadnezzar.[a] **as an eagle,** in the power and majesty and resistlessness of its flight toward its prey.[b] (41) **surprised,** taken by storm. (42) **destroyed..people,** its national existence shall be ended. (43) **Fear,** etc., Is. xxiv. 17, 18.

Cities of Moab.—While the ruins of all these cities still retain their ancient names, and are the most conspicuous amid the wide scene of general desolation, and while each of them was in like manner particularized in the visions of the Prophet, they yet formed but a small number of the cities of Moab: and the rest are also, in similar verification of the prophecies, desolate without any to dwell therein. None of the ancient cities of Moab now exist as tenanted by men. Kerek, which neither bears any resemblance in name to any of the cities of Moab which are mentioned as existing in the time of the Israelites, nor possesses any monuments which denote a very remote antiquity, is the only nominal town in the whole country, and in the words of Seetzen, who visited it, "in its present ruined state it can only be called a hamlet:" "and the houses have only one floor." But the most populous and fertile province in Europe (especially any situated in the interior of a country like Moab) is not covered so thickly with towns as Moab is plentiful in ruins, deserted and desolate though now it be. Burckhardt enumerates about fifty ruined sites within its boundaries, many of them extensive. In general they are a broken down and undistinguishable mass of ruins; and many of them have not been closely inspected. But, in some instances, there are the remains of temples, sepulchral monuments, the ruins of edifices constructed of very large stones, in one of which buildings "some of the stones are twenty feet in length, and so broad that one constitutes the thickness of the wall;" traces of hanging gardens; entire columns lying on the ground, three feet in diameter, and fragments of smaller columns; and many cisterns cut out of the rock.—Keith. Self-sufficiency.—In mid Atlantic, the other day, the "Etruria," in which I was sailing, suddenly stopped. Something had gone wrong with the engines. There were five hundred able-bodied men on board the ship. Do you think if we had gathered together and pushed against the mast we could have pushed it on? When one attempts to sanctify himself by effort, he is trying to make his boat go by pushing against the mast. He is like a drowning man trying to lift himself out of the water by pulling at the hair of his own head. Christ held up this method almost to ridicule when he said: "Which of you by taking thought can add one cubit to his stature?" The one redeeming feature of the self-sufficient method is this—that those who try it find out almost at once that it will not gain the goal.—Drummond.

"There is no passion which steals into the heart more imperceptibly and covers itself under more disguises than pride." — Addison.

"In pride, in reasoning pride, our error lies;
All quit their sphere, and rush into the skies.
Pride still is aiming at the blest abodes,
Men would be angels, angels would be gods."— Pope.

44—47. (44) **fleeth .. pit,** a forcible way of declaring that none shall escape. (45) R. V., "they that fled stand without strength under the shadow of Heshbon: for a fire is gone forth," etc., "the fugitives of Moab shall take refuge under the walls of the neighboring city of the Ammonites, but as they stand there in hopes of aid, there bursts forth from the city on which their only hopes rest a flame kindled by the Chaldæan foe." **a fire,** etc., comp. Nu. xxi. 28, 29. **crown,** etc., Nu. xxiv. 17.[c] (46) **Chemosh,** vs. 7. (47) **bring again,** "we gather that even this rough handling was disciplinary; at any rate, the former lack of such vicissitudes had been to the serious detriment of Moab. It is strange that Jeremiah did not apply this principle to Judah. For, indeed, the religion of Israel and of mankind owes an incalculable debt to the captivity of Judah, a debt which later writers are not slow to recognize."—Exp. Bib. Comp. ch xlvi. 26, xlix. 6, 39.

God's Judgment upon the Wicked.—Sometimes visitation is sudden, quick, and terrible, as in the case of Ananias and Sapphira. But oftener men go on sinning with no bad consequences to themselves, so far as appearance goes. They do not lose health; they do not seem to lose reputation; there are no checks in their success; and perhaps they even furnish an example whereby worldly wisdom hangs its maxim that it is not well to be too particular. The frequent prosperity of the wicked is indeed a fact not at all concealed or qualified in the Scriptures. A man of the world takes his own worldly way to keep peril at a distance, and he seems to fall into no pit, no snare. Let all this be allowed. Nothing is gained by trying to make out that the wicked have no advantages. It was an old-world legend that some men sold themselves to the devil, and that his protection secured to them their wonderful immunities and prosperity. All that is gained is in the way of postponement. Wicked

c "The meaning is that the fire of war consumes both far and near, both hair and beard, i. e. everything that the fire can singe or destroy."—Spk. Com.

"The devastation was to reach the most elevated, and the most remote, parts of the country."—Henderson.

"Open rebukes are for magistrates and courts of justice. Private rebukes are for friends; where all the witnesses of the offender's blushes are blind, and deaf and dumb."—Feltham.

men travel in a narrowing path, and at last are shut up to face the judgments of God. The moment of what seems to them complete success is quickly followed by the moment of complete ruin.—Pul. Com.

CHAPTER THE FORTY-NINTH.

[a] Ge. xix. 37, 38. "This prophecy seems to have been occasioned by their encroachments on the territory of Israel, E. of the Jordan, after the deportation of the ten tribes. The Ammonites were subdued by Nebuchadnezzar five years after the fall of Jerusalem."—Wordsworth.

[b] 1 Ki. xi. 5, 33; 2 Ki. xxiii. 13.

This chapter contains prophecies on the Ammonites (1—6); on Edom (7—22); on Damascus (23—27); on Kedar (28—33); and on Elam (34—39). "All of these except the last belong to the 4th year of Jehoiakim, and reflect the profound impression which Nebuchadnezzar's victory at Carchemish made on the prophet."—Driver. **1—3.** (1) **Ammonites,** the people settled north of the Moabites.[a] **no heir,** "in seizing Gilead the Ammonites acted as if the country had no rightful owner." or heir. **their king,** R. V., Malcam possess God," i. e. Moloch, the fire God, in whose worship children were destroyed in the fire.[b] (2) **Rabbah,** Am. i. 14; comp. 2 Sa. xii. 26—30. **daughters,** smaller towns and villages. **be heir,** R. V., "possess them that did possess him." This was partly fulfilled in the time of the Maccabees. (3) **Ai,** an unknown town, prob. near Heshbon. **hedges,** or vineyard walls. Running anywhere for shelter. **their king,** R. V., "Malcam."

Places of Burial (vs. 3).—The places of burial in the East are without their cities, as well as their gardens, and consequently their going to them must often be by their garden walls, not hedges. The ancient warriors of distinction who were slain in battle were carried to the sepulchres of their fathers; and the people often went to weep over the graves of those whom they would honor. These observations put together sufficiently account for this passage.—Harmer.

[c] "The abundance of thy valley."—Ewald.

"In the riches of thy fat and plentiful valleys, which overflow with abundance of all things."—Lowth.

"If thou art rich, thou art poor;
For like the ass whose back with ingots bows,
Thou bear'st thy heavy riches but a journey
And Death unloads thee."
—Shakespeare.

"Its inhabitants were among those children of the East, famed for wisdom, because of their skill in proverbs and dark sayings."-Spk. Com.

"Crœsus, whose name is a synonym for great wealth, was himself taken captive, stripped of all his treasures, and in old age was supported by the charity of Cyrus."

4—6. (4) **gloriest .. valleys,** the country was cut into valleys by the streams flowing towards the Jordan. **flowing,** i. e. "abounding."[c] (5) **right forth,** without even making effort at resistance. **gather up,** rally the fugitives. (6) **bring again,** ch. xlviii. 47.

Zeal for God.—Do not the "work of God negligently" and idly; let not thy heart be upon the world, when thy hand is lift up in prayer; and be sure to prefer an action of religion in its place and proper season before all worldly pleasure, letting secular things, that may be dispensed with in themselves, in these circumstances wait upon the other; not like the patriarch who ran from the altar in St. Sophia to his stable in all his pontificals, and in the midst of his office, to see a colt newly fallen from his beloved and much-valued mare Phorbante. More prudent and severe was that of Sir Thomas More, who being sent for by the king when he was at his prayers in public, returned answer, he would attend him when he had first performed his service to the King of kings. And it did honor to Rusticus, that when letters from Cæsar were given to him, he refused to open them till the philosopher had done his lecture. In honoring God and doing His work put forth all thy strength; for of that time only thou mayest be most confident that it is gained, which is prudently and zealously spent in God's service.—Jeremy Taylor.

7—11. (7) Much of vss. 7—16 is almost verbally the same as Obad. 1—8. **Edom,** "brought forward as an object of judgment as a type of those nations of heathendom whose origin and the course of whose history had placed them nearest to the kingdom of God, but who had only opposed that kingdom with the more deadly hatred."—Oehler. Comp. Is. xxxiv, 5; Am. i. 11; Obad. 3. Edom lay along the south of Judah, from the district of Moab to the Mediterranean. **wisdom .. Teman,** comp. Obad. 8. Noted for its wisdom (Eliphaz the Temanite, Job. ii. 11), "Has even Teman no advice or judgment?" (8) **dwell deep,** turn your caravans into the very depths of the desert, for there is danger in the well-known tracts. **Dedan,** this people was noted for conducting caravans. (9) **grape gatherers,** Obad. 5. (10) **secret places,** even the hiding-places of Mt. Seir. **his seed,**

i. e. the seed of Esau. (11) **Leave,** etc., the usual sign of mercy mingling with judgment.

Martin Luther's Will.—In the last will and testament of this eminent reformer, occurs the following remarkable passage:—"Lord God, I thank Thee that Thou hast been pleased to make me a poor and indigent man upon earth. I have neither house, nor land, nor money, to leave behind me. Thou hast given me wife and children, whom I now restore to Thee. Lord, nourish, teach, and preserve them, as Thou hast me." Comfort of religion.—We must always regard it as a grand peculiarity of the religion that comes from God that it brings relief and comfort under trials for which the world has no balm, and throws light upon dispensations which would be otherwise clouded with a hopeless and impenetrable gloom. The religion of Jesus comes as a comforter when other oracles are silent; comes as a star of promise and of hope when every other lamp is extinguished; comes to breathe upon our ear its still small voice of mercy, when we hear nothing besides but the earthquake, and the fire, and the great and strong wind; and clothes with a mantle of celestial light the darkest appearances of this lower world.—Hom. Com. Compassion.—The history of the Church tells out wonderful instances of compassion to parents and children. Look at the first mission of an angel to a world; was it not to deserted and widowed Hagar before the birth of her first child? And was not the second visit of an angel to Hagar and Ishmael when the Lord heard the voice of the lad? Did not the angel descend to wrestle with Jacob when involved in trouble for his family, lest Esau come and smite the mother with the children? Was it not to the widow of Zarephath Elisha was sent? Was not Elijah's greatest miracle employed on behalf of that pious mother mourning for her only son? Was not the Lord with Joseph when separated from his father? with Moses when left to the bulrushes? Look at our Lord's miracles.—Hom. Com.

"To steel his melting heart,
To act the martyr's sternest part;
To watch with firm, unshrinking eye
His darling visions as they die.
Too happy if, that dreadful day,
His life be given him for a prey.'
—Keble's "Christian Year."

12—16. (12) **they .. cup,** R. V., "they to whom it pertained was to drink" (see note on xiii. 12), the Jews, who might be expected to escape judgments, if any nation did. (13) **Bozrah,** ch. xlviii. 24. (14) **rumour,** etc., Obad. 1. (15) **heathen,** R. V., "nations." comp. Obad. 2. (16) **dwellest .. rock,** the cities of Edom were hewn in the sides of seemingly inaccessible rocks, and in this the people felt the utmost confidence and security.[a] **nest .. eagle,** Obad. 4.

Rock Dwellings.—In this beautiful passage the Prophet strictly adheres to the truth of history. Esau subdued the original inhabitants of Mount Hor, and seized on its savage and romantic precipices. His descendants covered the sides of their mountains "with an endless variety of excavated tombs and private dwellings, worked out in all the symmetry and regularity of art, with colonnades and pediments, and ranges of corridors, adhering to the perpendicular surface." On the inaccessible cliffs, which, in some places, rise to the height of seven hundred feet, and the barren and craggy precipices which enclose the ruins of Petra, the capital of the Nebatæi, a once powerful but now forgotten people, the eagle builds his nest, and screams for the safety of his young, when the unwelcome traveler approaches his lonely habitation.—Paxton.

[a] "The Idumæans proudly imagined that the terror with which the celebrity of their power had inspired those by whom they were surrounded, would secure them against any hostile attack."—Henderson.

"Ten thousand of the greatest faults in our neighbors are of less consequence to us than one of the smallest in ourselves."—Whately.

17—22. (17) **hiss,** in mockery at the utter abasement of its pride. **plagues,** or distresses. (18) **overthrow,** etc., Ge. xix. 25. **neighbour cities,** such as Admah and Zeboim.[b] (19) **he,** i. e. Nebuchadnezzar. **swelling,** or flood time.[c] But many with R. V. translate "pride of Jordan," i. e. the thickets on its banks. **make him run away,** a difficult clause. Means prob., make the Edomites flee from the habitation of the strong. **who is a chosen man,** etc., Camb. Bib. "I will appoint him who is (my) chosen." **appoint me the time,** "rightly explained in the Eng. margin, convent (i. e. convene) me in judgment, in other words, by naming, as the plaintiff in a suit had a right to do, the time of trial, claim the power of protesting against God's decision." (20) **least .. flock,** "the feeblest of the Israelites shall suffice for the rooting out of Edom." **draw,** or drag them about, as a lion would a sheep. (21) **is moved,** or quakes. (22) **as the eagle, ch. xlviii. 40.**

[b] "From A. D. 536 onwards, Petra suddenly vanishes from the pages of history. It was unknown to the Arabs, was confounded by the Crusaders with an entirely different place, and only in the present century was its real site discovered by Burckhardt, and full details given of its splendid but desolate remains by Laborde."—Spk. Com.

[c] "When the Jordan swells in the time of harvests, the lions that lie in the thickets on the river-side, are raised out of their coverts, and infest the country."—Lowth.

"'Tis to be happy that we run after pleasures. But we, alas! mistake our happiness, and foolishly seek it where it is not to be found. As silly children think to catch the sun, when they see it setting at so near a distance. They travel on, and tire themselves in vain; for the thing they seek is in another world."—Hickes.

Petra.—Petra, the ancient capital of Idumæa, hitherto wrapped up in the deep recesses of solitude, remained until lately unknown. Here was the cradle of commerce seventeen centuries ago; the emporium of northern Arabia, and the entrepôt between Palestine, and Syria, and Egypt. It was the birthplace of Balaam, and renowned for oracles and auguries; in it, as a stronghold, were deposited the treasures of the sultans of Egypt; and yet the name of Petra seemed to have become all but extinct with the declension of the Roman power in the East. Here is a town embosomed amid a fortress of mountains; utter desolation reigns over wonderful ruins, noble in decay, and sublime in their fall. Mount Hor, with Aaron's tomb, surmounts the city of desolations, the metropolis of moving sands, and a blighted desert. The entrance is from the east, through a deep gorge, or ravine, called El syk, and the river that supplied Edom flowed through this valley; the wall of rock is from four hundred to seven hundred feet high. The sides of this romantic chasm are clothed with tamarisk, wild fig, oleander, and the caper plant, the latter hanging in luxuriant festoons from cracks and crevices; the solitude is only disturbed by the screaming of eagles, hawks, owls, and ravens, which congregate here in vast multitudes. The ruins burst on the eye of the astonished and bewildered traveler in all their awful magnificence. This amphitheatre of mountains is tinged with extraordinary hues, and is at once romantic and picturesque. Sepulchres and tombs; sculptures, in all the majesty of art, decorate these "everlasting hills;" more than two hundred and fifty sepulchres are chiselled in the rock. And this is Edom, the metropolis of Idumæa! The stupendous ruins, the magnificent tombs, the amphitheatre, the columns, and capitals, obelisks, friezes—all attest the magnificence which once reigned in this mountain metropolis; a city of desolation, which even the bittern scarce disturbs, "lines of confusion, and stones of emptiness." The territory of the descendants of Esau is swept by "the besom of destruction," and remains a miracle of evidence, as palpable as any monument in the history of time. Its eighteen cities are moldered into dust, and the dwellers among the rocks that "made their nests among the stars," are brought low.—Murray.

23—27. (23) **Damascus,** in Syria, as it existed in the time of David, there were at least three cities of importance, Hamath, Zobah, and Damascus. The kingdom, of which the second of these was the capital, soon disappeared, and Damascus came to be held by a powerful dynasty of kings, who reduced the other cities under their own sway. It is not known, however, what was the political condition of Syria at the time that Jeremiah wrote, but it is clear that it was to be no more exempt than other countries, from the tread of the conqueror. The tidings of his approach reach one city after another, and fill them with dismay.—Camb. Bib. **Hamath .. Arpad,** 2 Ki. xvii. 24. **fainthearted,** R. V., "they are melted away." **sorrow .. sea,** i. e. as on the sea.[a] (25) **not left,** not spared in the time of general calamity. The prophet laments the destruction of the beautiful city.[b] **of my joy,** i. e. in which I delighted. (27) **fire,** Am. i. 4. **Ben-hadad,**[c] the name, prob., of a race or dynasty of kings of Syria.

Damascus.—As the traveler from the west climbs up and up the steep passes of the great Lebanon range, and at length nears their eastern side, there, on the summit of a cliff, high up above the plain beneath, he looks down on the city of Damascus. "At the foot of the cliff on which the beholder stands, a river bursts forth from the mountain in which it has had birth. That river, as if in a moment, scatters over the plain, through a circle of thirty miles, the verdure which had hitherto been confined to its single channel. It is like the bursting of a shell, the eruption of a volcano—but an eruption, not of death, but of life. Far and wide extends in front the level plain, its horizon bare, its lines of surrounding hills bare, all bare, far away on the road to Palmyra and Bagdad. In the midst of this plain lies at your feet the vast island of deep verdure, walnuts and apricots hanging above, corn and grass below." **The river is its life.**

[a] Comp. Is. lvii. 20.

[b] "This ancient city was celebrated for its felicitous position, the exquisite beauty of its environs, the magnitude of its temple, and the wealth of its inhabitants."—Henderson.

[c] 2 Ki. xiii. 3.

"Far sadder sight than eye can know,
Than proud bark lost, or seaman's woe,
Or battle-fire, or tempest cloud,
Or prey bird's shriek, or ocean shroud,
The shipwreck of a soul."

"There is no greater sign of a general decay of virtue in a nation, than a want of zeal in its inhabitants for the good of their country." — **Addison.**

It is drawn out in water-courses and spread in all directions. For miles around it is a wilderness of gardens—gardens with roses among the tangled shrubberies, and with fruit on the branches overhead. Everywhere among the trees the murmur of unseen rivulets is heard. Even in the city, which is in the midst of the garden, the clear rushing of the current is a perpetual refreshment. Every dwelling has its fountain; and at night, when the sun has set behind Mount Lebanon, the lights of the city are seen flashing on the water. Travelers in all ages have paused to feast their eyes on the loveliness of the city as they first behold it from the cliffs of Lebanon. Abana and Pharpar still flash and gleam as they flow along amid her fragrant gardens and by her dark olive groves. Snow-capped Hermon and the rugged range of Lebanon still keep over her their wonted watch and ward. Hence she may will be taken as the symbol of all that is lovely and fair in outward life, all that is bright and beautiful in the moral nature of man.—Pul. Com.

"He who reigns within himself, and rules passions, desires, and fears, is more than a king."—Milton.

"To do so no more is the truest repentance."—Luther.

28, 29. (28) **Kedar,** ch. ii. 10. **Hazor,** a district in Arabia Petræa, divided into districts, each presided over by a petty chief. **shall smite,** R. V. "smote." (29) **curtains,** or tent hangings. "All the possessions of the nomad are here mentioned, they are all to be seized by the Chaldæans." **Fear,** etc.,[a] a favorite expression of Jeremiah, from Ps. xxxi. 13. See Jer. vi. 25; xx. 3, 10; xlvi. 5.

"Fear on Every Side."—Jeremiah frequently exclaims, "Fear on every side!" We know not how many dangers surround us—political, social, domestic, personal; dangers to property, family, health, and life. The wonder is that they who have no refuge above themselves are so complacent. Such unwarrantable calmness must be traced to moral dullness rather than to true courage. For how truly terrible is the condition of the sinner! The laws of the universe are against him. If he flees from this life new horrors await him in the dread unknown land.—Pul. Com.

[a] "The very noise of the enemies shall fright them, and bring a panic fear upon them."—Lowth.

"The law of the Lord squares up the whole man, keeps him perpendicular, and puts him on good terms with himself, with the world, and with God."—Edward Beecher Mason.

30—33. (30) **get .. off,** or hurry hastily away. **dwell deep,** as vs. 8. (31) **Arise,** addressed to Nebuchadnezzar. "Rather, tranquil, dwelling at ease. Three grounds of encouragement are given to the invading army, (a) the people have felt hitherto secure against attack, (b) they have no walled towns, (c) they have no powerful neighbors, from whom to seek aid.—Camb. Bib. **neither .. bars,** comp. De. iii. 5; Eze. xxxviii. 11. (32) **utmost corners,** see ch. ix. 26. (33) **dragons,** R. V., "jackals;" (ch. x. 22).

Dragons.—Shaw represents the land of Edom, and the wilderness of which it now forms part, as abounding with a variety of lizards and vipers, which are very dangerous and troublesome. The Arabs, in general, avoid the ruins of the cities of Idumæa, "on account of the enormous scorpions with which they swarm." Its cities, thus deserted by man, and abandoned to their undisturbed and hereditary possession, Edom may justly be called the inheritance of dragons.—Keith.

"Winter brings blessings, so the chill
Of dark adversity;—from its cold grasp
The soul revives reanimate,—more strong,
And better armed."
—F. A. Mackay.

34—39. This prophecy is "about 7 yrs. later than the preceding prophecies of the group."—Camb. Bib. (34) **Elam,** the province of Elymais, part of Susiana, W. of Persia proper. (35) **bow of Elam,** this country was famed for its archers.[b] (36) **the four winds,** an emblem of the utter hopelessness of escape. The four winds (figuratively spoken of by Zechariah (vi. 5) as "presenting themselves" before God, to receive his commissions) shall combine their forces to scatter the doomed nation. (37) **dismayed,** etc., for confirmation of this prophecy, comp. Da. viii. 2, 27. (38) **destroy .. king,** i. e. Elam would lose its independent sovereignty. (39) **bring again,** comp. ch. xlviii. 47.[a] "The Elamites are chiefly mentioned as representatives of the distant and less civilized Gentile nations, and the fulfilment is granted whenever a similar people to the Elamites is brought to the knowledge of the true religion."—Pul. Com.

Restoration of Elamites.—The full restoration belongs to Gospel times: and "Elamites" were among the first who heard and accepted the Gospel. Their presence at the Pentecost shows that the Elamites were still preserved by the Divine Providence, and were there among the representatives of the Gentile world to whom the Evangel of Christ was proclaimed.—Hom. Com.

[b] Is. xxii. 6.

"The reason for the judgment on the Elamites does not appear. They do not seem, as a people, to have molested the Hebrews. It is possible that they may have been addicted to idolatry, and thus been distinguished from the Persians proper, whose religion in the main was monotheistic."—Henderson.

[a] Comp. Ac. ii. 9.

CHAPTER THE FIFTIETH.

"A long and impassioned prophecy against Babylon is given in chaps. l. and li."—Driver. This prophecy against Babylon forms an appropriate conclusion to the series. The nations immediately bordering upon Palestine have had their fate foretold, and then the more remote, but none the less is that Empire, which is to execute God's vengeance upon them, destined in its turn to fall. And this, the climax of the prophecies against foreign nations, is marked by the grandeur of the images employed by the prophet.—Camb. Bib. **1—3.** (1) **against,** as before, better rend. concerning. This prophecy was given in the fourth year of Zedekiah: see ch. li. 59, 60. (2) **set .. standard,** to call attention to the message. **Bel,** Is. xlvi. 1. **Merodach,** or Marduk, the tutelary God of Babylon, Is. xxxix. 1. **confounded,** R. V., "put to shame." (3) **north,** the district of Media.[b]

Sinners Returning to God (vss. 1—5).—I. In those days the children of Israel shall come, they and the children of Judah, together—so enmities are to be abolished. II. Going and weeping: going whither? weeping wherefore? going to Zion with tears of joy and gratitude. III. They seek the Lord their God. IV. They ask their way to Zion with their faces thitherward. V. Come and let us join ourselves to the Lord in a perpetual covenant.

Broken Images (vs. 2).—As it was generally believed that the divinity abandoned any figure or image which was mutilated or broken, this prophetic declaration may be considered as asserting the destruction of the idols. Such a sentiment still prevails among the heathen. Dr. Buchanan, who visited many Indian provinces at the commencement of the seventeenth century, mentions that a Polygar chief, about two hundred and fifty years before, had been directed by the god Ganesa to search for treasures under a certain image, and to erect temples and reservoirs with whatever money he should find. "The treasures were accordingly found, and applied as directed; the image from under which the treasures had been taken was shown to me, and I was surprised at finding it lying at one of the gates quite neglected. On asking the reason why the people allowed their benefactor to remain in such a plight, he informed me that the finger of the image having been broken, the divinity had deserted it; for no multilated image is considered as habitable by a god."—Burder.

4—8. (4) **come,** or return. **weeping,** partly with joy at so unexpected an opportunity; partly in penitence. (5) **perpetual covenant,** Ne. viii. 38, x. 29. "The new covenant is everlasting (Hos. ii. 19). It is possible by reason of the people's repentance. Hence it is that when the divine summons penetrates the lands of their captivity the rejected ones hasten with trembling, lest their deliverance should be delayed (Hos. xi. 10), and return with weeping and supplications (Jer. xxxi. 9). The divine forgiveness corresponds with the repentance."—Oehler. (6) **on the mountains,** where they sacrifice to their idols. **restingplace,** Jehovah, the only true source of good. (7) **devoured them,** as wild beasts would wandering sheep. **offend not,** excusing themselves as being agents of Jehovah, who was angry with His people.[a] **habitation of justice,** comp. ch. xxxi. 23. (8) **he goats,** which go first, and lead the flock.[b]

Faces Zionward.—Among the old Romans there prevailed the touching custom of holding the face of every new-born infant towards the heavens, signifying, by their presenting its forehead to the stars, that it was to look above the world into celestial glories. It was a vain superstition; but Christianity dispels the fable, and gives us a clear realization of the Pagan yearning. Young live should be turned with their faces heavenwards.—Hom. Com. A restingplace.—O ye children of God, ye have a Resting-place; how is it that ye can forget it? Touch upon the things of nature, how they chide you! Bring to your remembrance the birds of the air, the beasts of the forest, the dumb driven cattle accus-

[b] "The devastation of Babylon here foretold includes not only that by Cyrus, but also that more utter one by Darius, who took Babylon by artifice, when it had revolted from Persia, and mercilessly slaughtered the inhabitants, hanging 4,000 of the nobles; also the final desertion of Babylon owing to Seleucia having been built close by under Seleucus Nicator."—Fausset.

"Lowliness is the base of every virtue;
And he who goes the lowest builds the safest.
May God keep all His pity for the proud!"
—Bailey.

[a] "As long as the sheep are in the fold, it is a trespass to attack them, and is punished as such. But Israel having left the fold, has now no owner, and may therefore be maltreated with impunity." — Spk. Com.

[b] "Lead ye the way for the people, out of Babylon, as the he-goats press forward, and place themselves at the head of the flocks, and lead them to pasture." — Wordsworth.

tomed to the yoke, and let them chide you; for they forget not their restingplace. Carried away to the city the other day, the dove was taken from its cage, and they let it loose, fastening to it the message that was to be sent. It mounted aloft, it whirled around awhile, that it might see where it was. It was far, far away from the dove-cote; it was found hundreds of miles away; but whither did it fly? Swift as an arrow from the bow, it sought its restingplace with the infallibility of affection; it found its nearest way to the cote where it had been reared, and brought its message safely there. And even the dog which thou despisest, taken away from its master, carried many miles away, in darkness, too, so that it might not know its way, has been known to swim rivers, cross byways it could not have known, and then is found barking for admission at its master's door; oh, so happy when it hears its master's voice again. It could not rest elsewhere. O my heart, wilt thou let the pigeon outstrip thee in affection? art thou more doggish than a dog? Dost thou forget thy Lord, when dogs remember well their masters? Let us learn from them and forget our Resting-place nevermore.—Spurgeon.

"Take Him for what He is; oh, take Him all, And look above. Then shall thy tossing soul find anchorage And steadfast peace; Thy love shall rest on His, thy weary doubts For ever cease; Thy heart shall find in Him and in His grace Its rest and bliss." —W. M. Taylor.

9—13. (9) **assembly,** etc., the mixed armies of Medes, Persians, and their allies. **from thence,** i. e. by the great nations coming from the north. **none .. vain,** none of the warriors shall return without aiding in the conquest. (10) **satisfied,** with the abundance they bear away. (11) **heifer at grass,** who might eat her fill, indulge how she pleased.[c] **bellow,** etc., R. V., "neigh as strong horses." (12) **behold,** etc., R. V., "behold she shall be the hindermost of the nations, a wilderness," etc. (13) Comp. ch. xix. 8, xlix. 17.

[c] Some render, "as a heifer threshing," which being unmuzzled would eat abundantly an become frisky.

The spirit of the "destroyers."—Jehovah meant Babylon for the chastisement and the humiliation of his own people, that they might be enlightened and purified through the losses they thus sustained. They lost many things they loved, but at the same time they lost things which tempted and ensnared. The description here, "Destroyers of mine heritage," indicates sufficiently the spirit in which Babylon acted. What God wanted was the thorough purification of his heritage, not at all its destruction. Babylon cared nothing as to whether Israel was better or worse for its afflictions. It could only rejoice over another nation conquered, another territory acquired, and a fresh degree of brightness added to its military glory. It is surely a terrible thing when men do good work unconsciously and not meaning it to be good work at all. When we have to engage in any work that inflicts suffering, shame, and loss on others, it ought to be under the sternest pressure of necessity and as the sorrowing ministers of violated law. There are times when we cannot escape being the agents of suffering to wicked and foolish men; but if we only act in the right spirit, keeping our hearts free from all that is vengeful and exulting, we may even have some share in turning them from their wickedness. Everything that savors of our personal satisfaction and gain must be kept away when we have to make others suffer.—Pul. Com.

"Common happiness is sustained, not by great exertions, which are in the power of a few, and happen rarely even to them, but by great numbers doing every one a little, every one something in his particular province, to his particular neighborhood. This is the way in which Providence intended society to be carried on, and beneficence to be exercised." —Paley.

14—16. (14) **Put .. array,** post yourselves in good positions. (15) **Shout,** as conquerors do. **given her hand,** i. e. in submission, comp. Gen. xxiv. 2; 2 Ki. x. 15, etc. **foundations,** better, buttresses. Her walls are thrown down—this was not done by Cyrus, who entered the city beneath the walls by the river bed, after diverting the stream. It therefore points on to the later capture of Babylon by Darius, who "having become master of the place, destroyed the wall, and tore down all the gates; for Cyrus had done neither the one nor the other when he took Babylon." Herod. Bk. iii. (16) **sower,** so that even the fields shall not be tilled, referring probably to the larger district of Babylonia.

"The mighty monarchy of Chaldæa was under the control of the God of Israel, and He who made it flow like a stormy ocean, and overwhelm the nations with its flood, could say to its proud waves, Hitherto shalt thou go, and no farther." —Wordsworth.

Palace at Babylon.—The palace of the king of Babylon almost vied with the great temple of their god. And there is now some controversy, in which of the principal mountainous heaps the one or the other lies buried. But the utter desolation of both leaves no room for any debate on the question—which of the twain is bowed down and confounded, and which of them is broken in pieces. The two palaces, or castles, of Baby-

"It is the worst condition into which the Church of God can come when the enemies who desolate it maintain they are in the right in doing so. It is, however, a just Nemesis when those who will not hear the regular messengers of God must be told by the extraordinary messengers of God what they should have done." —Naegelsbach.

lon were strongly fortified. And the larger was surrounded by three walls of great extent. When the city was suddenly taken by Demetrius, he seized on one of the castles by surprise, and displaced its garrison by seven thousand of his own troops, whom he stationed within it. Of the other he could not make himself master. Their extent and strength, at a period of three hundred years after the delivery of the prophecy, are thus sufficiently demonstrated. The solidity of the structure of the greater as well as of the lesser palace, might have warranted the belief of its unbroken durability for ages. And never was there a building whose splendor and magnificence were in greater contrast to its present desolation. The vestiges of the walls which surrounded it are still to be seen, and serve with other circumstances to identify it with the Mujelibé, as the name Merodach is identified with the palace. It is broken in pieces, and hence its name Mujelibé, signifying overturned, or turned upside down. Its circumference is about half a mile; its height one hundred and forty feet. But it is "a mass of confusion, none of its members being distinguishable." The existence of chambers, passages, and cellars, of different forms and sizes, and built of different materials, has been fully ascertained. It is the receptacle of wild beasts, and full of doleful creatures; wild beasts cry in the desolate houses, and dragons in the pleasant palaces—"venomous reptiles being very numerous throughout the ruins." "All the sides are worn into furrows by the weather, and in some places where several channels of rain have united together, these furrows are of great depth, and penetrate a considerable way into the mound." "The sides of the ruin exhibit hollows worn partly by the weather." It is brought down to the grave to the sides of the pit.—Keith. The fate of Babylon.—When, because of iniquity, God determines the destruction of a city or empire, nothing can save it. If ever a city appeared impregnable, it was Babylon. Its walls, says one writer, "were above 300 feet high, 87 feet broad, and 48 miles in compass." In addition, the river Euphrates appeared an insuperable barrier to an enemy entering the city. Yet, notwithstanding its mighty wall with its hundred gates of solid brass, notwithstanding its wide and deep river, Babylon was taken, according to the word of the Lord.

17—20. (17) **scattered sheep,** "like a flock driven in all directions." **king of Assyria,** Shalmaneser. (18) **have punished,** in the destruction of Nineveh.[a] (19) **habitation,** R. V., "pasture." **Carmel,** etc., places noted for their rich pastures.[b] (20) **those days,** perhaps referring to the more distant times of the Messiah. **not . . found,** comp. Ps. x. 15, xxxviii. 36; Is. xli. 12. **I reserve,** R. V., "I leave as a remnant."

Treasures of Chaldæa.—And after the incessant spoliation of ages, now that the end is come of the treasures of Chaldæa, the earth itself fails not to disclose its hidden treasures, so as to testify that they once were abundant. In proof of this an instance may be given. At the ruins of Hoomania, near to those of Ctesiphon, pieces of silver having (on the 5th March, 1812) been accidentally discovered, edging out of the bank of the Tigris, "on examination there were found and brought away," by persons sent for that purpose by the pacha of Bagdad's officers "between six and seven hundred ingots of silver, each measuring from one to one and a half feet in length; and an earthen jar, containing upwards of two thousand Athenian coins, all of silver. Many were purchased at the time by the late Mr. Rich, formerly the East India Company's resident at Bagdad, and are now in his valuable collection, since bought by Government, and deposited in the British Museum." Amid the ruins of Ctesiphon "the natives often pick up coins of gold, silver and copper, for which they always find a ready sale in Bagdad. Indeed, some of the wealthy Turks and Armenians, who are collecting for several French and German consuls, hire people to go and search for coins, medals, and antique gems; and I am assured they never return to their employers empty-handed," as if all who spoil Chaldæa shall be satisfied, till even the ruins be spoiled unto the uttermost.—Keith.

[a] "At the taking of this city, the last king of Assyria was killed, and the seat and title of the empire removed to Babylon, wh. was no longer called the Assyrian, but the Babylonian monarchy." —Lowth.

[b] Is. lxv. 10; Eze. xxxiv. 13, 14.

Cicero said of Cæsar, "He forgiveth nothing but injuries only."

"These evils I deserve,
Yet despair not of His final pardon,
Whose ear is ever open, and His eye
Gracious to readmit the suppliant."
—Milton.

Restoration by itself will do nothing. If the man comes back to his possessions as he went away, then he can only misuse and squander as of old. The house swept and garnished only presented to the evil spirits a chance for greater riot and defilement than before. To the old land there comes back a new people. After tasting the bitterness of wanderings, they have tasted also the powers of the world to come—old carnal temptations no longer charm, new spiritual considerations stand full in view. Formerly, even on Carmel and Bashan, Mount Ephraim and Gilead, there had been discontent, because, with all the goodness in these places, there was not enough for the carnal heart. But now, when things are used spiritually, there is enough and more than enough. If only we follow where God leads there will be ample provision and ample blessedness.—Y.

21—24. (21) **Go up,** prob. addressed to Cyrus. **Merathaim .. Pekod,**[a] modern investigations have ascertained the existence of the latter name as that of a place in Babylonia; it is therefore at least possible that the former may also have existed. Whether, however, Jeremiah intended to play upon the names of actually existent places or not, he doubtless meant to emphasize the senses of these two names, viz., double rebellion . . . punishment.—Camb. Bib. (23) **hammer .. earth,** Is. xiv. 4—6, 16, 17. **desolation,** comp. Re. xviii. 19. (24) **snare.**

Destruction of Babylon by Fire.—On the summit of the hill are "immense fragments of brick-work of no determinate figures, tumbled together, and converted into solid vitrified masses." "Some of these huge fragments measured twelve feet in height, by twenty-four in circumference; and from the circumstance of the standing brick-work having remained in a perfect state, the change exhibited in these is only accountable from their having been exposed to the fiercest fire, or rather scathed by lighting." "They are completely molten—a strong presumption that fire was used in the destruction of the tower, which, in parts, resembles what the Scriptures prophesied it should become, 'a burnt mountain.' In the denunciation respecting Babylon, fire is particularly mentioned as an agent against it. To this Jeremiah evidently alludes, when he says that it should be 'as when God overthrew Sodom and Gomorrah,' on which cities, it is said, 'the Lord rained brimstone and fire.' 'Her high gates shall be burned with fire, and the people shall labor in vain, and the folk in the fire, and they shall be weary.'" "In many of these immense unshapen masses might be traced the gradual effects of the consuming power, which had produced so remarkable an appearance; exhibiting parts burnt to that variegated dark hue, seen in the vitrified matter lying about in glass manufactories; while, through the whole of these awful testimonies of the fire (whatever fire it was!) which, doubtless, hurled them from their original elevation" (I will roll thee down from the rocks), "the regular lines of the cement are visible, and so hardened in common with the bricks, that when the masses are struck they ring like glass.—Keith.

[a] "Because she is the land of Merathaim, or double rebellion, therefore she is the land of Pekod, or visitation; i. e. of punishment from God."—Wordsworth.

"God's Word, God's providence, God's Spirit, all unite to testify to the existence and by-and-by the exercise of that triumphant power by which all the might of evil shall be crushed, shattered, and broken for ever. On which side, then, are we taking our place?"—Pul. Com.

"Happiness is the rule, misery the exception. Were the order reversed, our attention would be called to examples of health and competency, instead of disease and want."—Paley.

25—28. (25) **armoury,** storehouse of weapons. "A truly grand figure. The north country is regarded by the prophet as a storehouse of young and "inexhaustible" nations, from which Jehovah can at any time "bring forth weapons of his indignation." The latter phrase occurs again in the parallel prophecy (Isa. xiii. 5), where it is evidently applied to the army of Medo-Persian invaders."—Pul. Com. God's weapons for the judgment of nations are war, famine, pestilence, disease and death. **for this is,** etc., R. V., "for the Lord, the Lord of Hosts hath a work to do in the land of the Chaldæans." (26) **as heaps,** of corn, to be burnt as a bonfire.[a] (27) **bullocks,** fig. for her strong youths, or princes, magnates. (28) **them that flee,** the liberated Jews. **of his temple,** wh. the Chaldæans had destroyed.

Destruction of Babylon by Fire.—The high gates of the temple of Belus, which were standing in the time of Herodotus, have been burnt with fire; the vitrified masses which fell when Bel bowed down rest on the top of its stupendous ruins. "The hand of the Lord has been

[a] "This metaphor describes the suddenness, ease, and completeness with which Babylon will be taken and spoiled; it will be like the conflagration of a barn of corn."—Wordsworth.

"Ariosto, in one of his romantic legends, tells us of a tree, many-branched, and covered with de-

stretched upon it; it has been rolled down from the rocks, and has been made a burnt mountain,"—of which it was further prophesied, "They shall not take of thee a stone for a corner, nor a stone for foundations, but thou shalt be desolate for ever, saith the Lord." The old wastes of Zion shall be built; its former desolations shall be raised up: and Jerusalem shall be inhabited again in her own place, even in Jerusalem. But it shall not be with Bel as with Zion, nor with Babylon as with Jerusalem. For as the "heaps of rubbish impregnated with nitre" which cover the site of Babylon "cannot be cultivated," so the vitrified masses on the summit of Birs Nimrood cannot be rebuilt. Though still they be of the hardest substance, and indestructible by the elements, and though once they formed the highest pinnacles of Belus, yet, incapable of being hewn into any regular form, they neither are nor can now be taken for a corner or for foundations. And the bricks on the solid fragments of wall, which rest on the summit, though neither scathed nor molten, are so firmly cemented, that, according to Mr. Rich, "it is nearly impossible to detach any of them whole," or, as Captain Mignan still more forcibly states, "they are so firmly cemented, that it is utterly impossible to detach any of them." "My most violent attempts," says Sir Robert Ker Porter, "could not separate them." And Mr. Buckingham, in assigning reasons for lessening the wonder at the total disappearance of the walls at this distant period, and speaking of the Birs Nimrood generally, observes, "that the burnt bricks (the only ones sought after) which are found in the Mujelibé, the Kasr, and the Birs Nimrood, the only three great monuments in which there are any traces of their having been used, are so difficult, in the two last indeed so impossible, to be extracted whole, from the tenacity of the cement in which they are laid, that they could never have been resorted to while any considerable portion of the walls existed to furnish an easier supply: even now, though some portion of the mounds on the eastern bank of the river" (the Birs is on the western side) "are occasionally dug into for bricks, they are not extracted without a comparatively great expense, and very few of them whole, in proportion to the great number of fragments that come up with them." Around the tower there is not a single whole brick to be seen.—Keith.

29—32. (29) **archers,**[a] vs. 14, "a dramatic way of indicating that the siege is about to begin."—Pul. Com. (30) **Therefore,** etc., ch. xlix. 26. (31) **most proud,** Heb. "O pride," "O man of pride." Bab. is the personification of pride. (32) **fire .. cities,** Cyrus seems to have ravaged the Babylonian district for twenty years before taking Babylon itself.

The Almighty Deliverer (vss. 31—34).—I. God's vengeance on His enemies. II. His merciful interposition on behalf of His people. 1. An interesting title to be considered; 2. An important qualification referred to; 3. A convincing proof adduced; 4. A gracious fact declared.

Retribution Though Slow, Yet Sure.—Slowly the hand had crawled along the dial plate, slowly as if the event would never come, and wrong was heaped on wrong, and oppression cried, and it seemed as if no ear had heard its voice, till the measure of the wickedness was at length fulfilled; the finger touched the hour, and as the strokes of the great hammer rang out above the nation, in an instant the mighty fabric of iniquity was shivered to ruins.

33, 34. (33) **refused .. go,** therefore the strong arm of Jehovah must deliver them by judgments on their enemies. (34) **Redeemer,** Heb. Goel, the title of the near kinsman, to whom according to Jewish law belonged the duty of revenging a murder, as well as that of advocate and general protector. In like manner the Lord is about to rescue His people and take vengeance upon their foe.[b]

The Strength of the Redeemer (vs. 34).—I. These words suggest a difficulty: why does Israel so often suffer? 1. God does not display His strength at once in order to glorify it; 2. In order to make His people lay hold of it; 3. Hereby He chastens His people; 4. And instructs them; 5. And that He may show mercy to their oppressors. II. These words

lectable bunches; but whoso shook that tree to win the fruit, found, too late, that not fruit, but stones of crushing weight, came down upon his head. The sensualities which fools call pleasure are such a tree: they who seek its fruit become its victims."—S. Coley.

"All men that have rambled after happiness have failed; neither learning, nor fame, nor wealth, nor pleasure, could ever give it, without a right set of principles for thought and practice; amongst which may be reckoned the love of justice, temperance, fortitude, and benevolence."—Antoninus.

"There is a temple in ruin stands,
Fashioned by long forgotten hands;
Two or three columns, and many a stone,
Marble and granite, with grass o'er grown."
—Byron.

[a] Comp. Job. xvi. 18.

"Unlamented pass the proud away,
The gaze of fools, the pageant of a day;
So perish all whose breast ne'er learned to glow
For others' good, or melt at others' woe."
—Pope.

[b] "Babylon has hitherto, by its ambition, kept the world in unrest: now by its fall men everywhere can dwell in security."—Spk. Com.

Is. xiv. 6—8.

convey a blessed truth; 1. Consider the might of the enemies from whom He delivers them; 2. Consider the completeness of the deliverance; 3. Consider that He upholds to the end all whom He has redeemed. III. These words imply a terrible warning—1. To all who oppress God's people; 2. To all who reject His help.—Stems and Twigs.

"What do we live for, if it is not to make life less difficult for each other?"—George Eliot.

35—40. (35) **wise men,** Magi, Da. i. 4. Partly the astronomers and astrologers at the various observatories in Babylonia, whose duty it was to send in monthly reports of the appearances in the sky, which were regarded as having an occult political significance (comp. Isa. xlvii. 13). In the next verse they are called liars, or praters.—Pul. Com. (36) **liars,** impostors. **dote,** talk foolishly. (37) **mingled people,** mixed races, many of whom had been brought to Babylon as captives, like the Jews. (38) **idols,** lit. terrors.[c] "Bugbears to frighten children with." (39) **wild beasts of the islands,** R. V., "wolves," Is. xiii. 21. **owls,** R. V., "ostriches." (40) **Sodom,** etc., Ge. xix. 25; Je. xlix. 18.

[c] "Many of their idols were huge and grotesque in appearance, and calculated to inspire beholders with terror."—Henderson.

Babylon and Prophecy (vs. 38).—Possibly refers to a circumstance attending the capture of the city by the Persians; but it more probably alludes to the physical condition of the country. The plain in which Babylon stands is exposed to long drought and intense heat in summer, so that the dry soil must have been at all times perfectly barren without artificial irrigation; but with such irrigation the ground is, even at this day, of unexampled fertility, except upon the wide-spread grit and debris of desolated cities. Therefore it was that the land exhibited one of the most extensive and complicated systems of irrigation that the world ever saw. It was overrun with innumerable canals in all directions—the largest of them navigable and feeding others, diminishing in importance with their distance from the trunk. These, as well as the parent river, were bordered with an infinity of hydraulic machines, by which the water was raised and distributed into the fields and gardens. The same plan is still pursued, to a limited extent, at some spots in the immediate vicinity of the rivers. But it is now literally true of Babylon that "a drought is upon her waters, and they are dried up." Yet still the lines and ridges of innumerable canals remain, which enable the spectator to trace the general system, and to verify the ancient historians as well as the prophecies of Scripture; the whole being strongly calculated to show the extent to which human skill and industry were once employed in giving to this now desolate region that fertility for which it was in old times celebrated. This explanation seems to us to give much force to the present prediction, since there can be no country the subsistence of which more entirely depended upon a complicated system of irrigation. Wherever water is applied in this region (with the exception already made), the productive powers of the soil and climate cannot be exceeded; but where that is wanting, it becomes a naked desert.

"Fully to understand this passage, a person must see the frenzy of the heathen when they get a sight of their idols. Thus, when the gods are taken out in procession, the multitudes shout, and the priests mutter and rave. The gestures are all distorted, and the devotees are affected with alternate sorrow or joy."—Roberts.

"This utter extinction of Babylon was not effected by one stroke, but gradually. Cyrus took away its supremacy. Darius Hystaspes deprived it, when it had rebelled again Persia, of its fortifications. Seleucus Nicanor removed its citizens and wealth to Seleucia, which he founded close by Babylon. The Parthians removed all that was left to Ctesiphon. Nothing but its walls were left under the Roman Emperor Adrian."

41—44. A repetition of vi. 22—24. See notes there. (41) **many kings,** in the allied army under Cyrus. **coasts,** or remote parts. (42) **cruel,** Is. xiii. 17, 18. **like a man,** in orderely array, so as to seem like one great man moving on. (43) **waxed feeble,** so that he attempted no resistance. Compare the panic of Belshazzar, Da. v. 6. This and following verses adapted from xlix. 19—21. See notes there.

The Destruction of Babylon.—The weapon which Babylon in its greed of conquest had used against Jerusalem is turned against itself. First of all, Babylon looks covetously on the land of Israel and spoils it of its people and their possessions. And then, enriched, Babylon becomes in turn an object of desire. God has only to leave covetousness and grasping alone, whether in nations or individuals. There will generally come in some human agency to dissipate ill-gotten gains. As Babylon became richer in external goods, it became weaker in manly resources. There was more to invite attack, more need of the best defences, and yet at the same time less ability to defend. Babylon took the sword and she in turn must perish by the sword; and that same sword successful against Babylon points to the destruction of those who wielded it.—Pul. Com.

"Every human soul has the germ of some flowers within; and they would open, if they could only find sunshine and free air to expand in. I always told you, that not having enough of sun-

45, 46. (45) **Therefore,** etc., comp. ch. xlix. 20. (46) **cry .. nations,** "who shall be astonished at the unexpected downfall of so great a city, and so potent an empire." Chs. l. and li. are apparently a mosaic, compiled from lost as well as extant sources; and dwell upon a few themes with a persistent iteration of ideas and phrases hardly to be paralleled elsewhere, even in the Book of Jeremiah. It has been reckoned that the imminence of the attack on Babylon is introduced afresh eleven times, and its conquest and destruction nine times. The advent of an enemy from the north is announced four times.—Exp. Bib.

shine was what ailed the world. Make people happy, and there will not be half the quarrelling, or a tenth part of the wickedness there is."—Mrs. Child.

The spoiling of Chaldæa.—When the Romans under Heraclius ravaged Chaldæa, "though much of the treasure had been removed from Destagered, and much had been expended, the remaining wealth appears to have exceeded their hopes, and even to have satiated their avarice." The deeds of Julian and the words of Gibbon show how Chaldæa was spoiled—how a sword continued to be on her treasures—and how, year after year and age after age, there was rumor on rumor and violence in her land.—Keith.

CHAPTER THE FIFTY-FIRST.

This chapter continues the prophecy against Babylon. **1—4.** (1) **in the midst .. against me,** R. V., "in Leb-kamai." "The Hebrew has leb-kamai, which is Kasdim, or Chaldea, written in the cypher called Athbash; just as Sheshach in vs. 41 is equivalent to Babel."—Pul. Com. **destroying wind,** ch. iv. 11. The metaphors used in this and succeeding verses are agricultural. (2) **fanners,** comp. ch. xv. 7.[a] (3) **brigandine,** R. V., "let not the archer bend his bow, and let him not lift himself up in his coat of mail," ch. xlvi, 4. (4) **in her streets,** or, more generally, in her land.

[a] The "vannus" of the Romans was a broad basket, into which the corn and chaff was received after thrashing, and then thrown towards the wind. The Jews used a shovel, and threw the corn and chaff against the wind.

"A time may come when it is well to separate one's self. There may come moments in the life of a Church when it will be a duty to leave the community. Such a moment is come when the community has become a Babylon."—Herzog.

What One Sin Will Do.—There was but one crack in the lanthorn, and the wind has found it out, and blown out the candle. How great a mischief one unguarded point of character may cause us! One spark blew up the magazine and shook the whole country for miles around. One leak sank the vessel and drowned all on board. One wound may kill the body. One sin destroy the soul. It little matters how carefully the rest of the lanthorn is protected, the one point which is damaged is quite sufficient to admit the wind; and so it little matters how zealous a man may be in a thousand things, if he tolerates one darling sin; Satan will find out the flaw, and destroy all his hopes. The strength of a chain is to be measured not by its strongest but by its weakest link, for if the weakest snaps, what is the use of the rest? Satan is a very close observer, and knows exactly where our weak points are; we have need of very much watchfulness, and we have great cause to bless our merciful Lord who prayed for us that our faith fail not. Either our pride, our sloth, our ignorance, our anger, or our lust, would prove our ruin unless grace interposed; any one of our senses or faculties might admit the foe, yea, our very virtues and graces might be gates of entrance to our enemies. O Jesus, if Thou hast indeed bought me with Thy blood, be pleased to keep me by Thy power even unto the end.—C. H. Spurgeon.

5—9. (5) **forsaken,** better, widowed. **filled with sin,** R. V., "is full of guilt." (6) **Flee,** etc., ch. l. 8.[a] (7) **golden cup,**[b] Babylon, as the instrument used by God for his judicial purposes, is likened to a wine-cup, which "made all the earth drunken" (comp. ch. xxv. 15, 16); and, more than this, to a golden cup, such was the impression made upon the Jewish prophets, by Babylon's unexampled splendor.—Pul. Com. (8) **howl for her,** this is addressed to her enemies, and means that her destruction shall be so terrible that even they will lament for her.[c] (9) **skies,** or clouds.

[a] Comp. Re. xviii. 4.

[b] "The cup in the hand of Babylon is a golden cup; she chooses such a cup, in order that men's eyes may be dazzled with the glitter of the gold, and may not inquire what it contains."—Origen.

[c] Re. xiv. 8, xviii. 2.

"Suffering, But Not Forsaken."—Israel is not forsaken because she is driven from her home. Babylon is not more favored because she flourishes for a season as a "golden cup in the Lord's hand." For the land of the Chaldæans is filled with sin against the Holy One of Israel.

I. When God chastises his people he must not be thought to have forsaken them. The chastisement is for their own good. It is, therefore, a proof that God has not neglected them.

II. Though God will chastise his people he will never forsake them. This is a further step. Not only is the chastisement no proof of God's having forsaken his people, but in no case will he forsake them; no such proof can ever be found. True, they may be separated from God and may become "castaways;" but this is only because they forsake him.

III. Outward circumstances are no indications of our relations with God.—Pul. Com.

"Man may lay out his plans, but God alone can give them effect in answer to the tongue of prayer."—Maurer.

10—13. (10) **Lord .. righteousness,** i. e. "their justification in their controversy with Babylon." (11) **Make bright,** or sharpen. **The Lord,** etc., the universality of the Divine kingdom is constantly taught in O. T. Jehovah uses the nations, heathen rulers for His purposes. Comp. Is. x. 5ff. xxxvii. 28; Is. xix.; Heb. i. 6; Jer. xxvii. 5; Ezek. xxx. 4; xxxi. 9; Dan. ii. 21; vii. 14. And the end of this government. Is. xlv. 22.—Oehler. **Medes,**[d] including the Persians. (12) **upon the walls,** R. V. "against the walls." A summons to the invaders. (13) **many waters,**[e] the turnings of the Euphrates, and the canals irrigating the land. **measure,** meted out as judgment on thy covetousness: the limit, to which it will be allowed to go.—Ewald.

Duty of Acknowledging God's Mercies.—Consider.—I. What is that word which we are now called to declare? 1. The agricultural; 2. The commercial; 3. The political; 4. The religious. II. In what manner should we declare them? 1. Let us acknowledge God in them; 2. We must adore Him for them; 3. By anticipation bless God for the yet richer mercies which he has in reserve for us.—C. Simeon.

Spoiling of Babylon (vs. 13).—On taking Babylon, Cyrus became immediately possessed of the treasures of darkness, and hidden riches of secret places. On his first publicly appearing in Babylon, all the officers of his army, both of the Persians and allies, according to his command, wore very splendid robes, those belonging to the superior officers being of various colors, all of the finest and brightest dye, and richly embroidered with gold and silver; and thus the hidden riches of secret places were openly displayed. And when the treasures of Babylon became the spoil of another great king, Alexander gave six minæ (about $75) to each Macedonian horseman, to each Macedonian soldier and foreign horseman two minæ ($25), and to every other man in his army a donation equal to two months' pay. Demetrius ordered his soldiers to plunder the land of Babylon for their own use. But it is not in these instances alone that Chaldæa has been a spoil, and that all who spoil her have been satisfied. It was the abundance of her treasures which brought successive spoilators. Many nations came from afar, and though they returned to their own country (as in formerly besieging Babylon, so in continuing to dispoil the land of Chaldæa), none returned in vain, From the richness of the country, new treasures were speedily stored up, till again the sword came upon them, and they were robbed. The prey of the Persians and of the Greeks for nearly two centuries after the death of Alexander, Chaldæa became afterwards the prey chiefly of the Parthians, from the north, for an equal period, till a greater nation, the Romans, came from the coasts of the earth to pillage it. Within the provinces of their empire, it was their practice, on the submission of the inhabitants, to protect and not to destroy. But Chaldæa, from its extreme distance, never having yielded permanently to their yoke, and the limits of their empire having been fixed by Hadrian on the western side of the Euphrates, or on the very borders of Chaldæa, that hapless country obtained not their protection, though repeatedly the scene of ruthless spoliation by the Romans. The authority of Gib-

[d] "The Medes, the Madai of Ge. x. 2, were a branch of the great Aryan family, who as conquerors had seized upon the vast regions extending from the Caspian Sea to the Eastern borders of Mesopotamia, but without being able to dispossess the Turanian tribes who had previously dwelt there. They were divided into numerous clans, each with its own local chief, the leaders of the larger sections being those who are called kings." — Spk. Com.

[e] Re. xvii. 1, 15.

"Cheerful tempers manufacture solace and joy out of very unpromising material. They are the magic alchemists which extract sweet essences out of bitter herbs, like the dear old colored saint in the smoky hut who was glad of anything to make a smoke with and though she had but two teeth thanked God that they were opposite each other." — Arthur T. Pierson.

"An extreme rigor is sure to arm everything against it, and at length to relax into a supine neglect."—Burke.

"Content's a kingdom, and I wear the crown."—Heywood.

"When the Master of the universe has points to carry in His government He impresses His will in the structure of minds." — Emerson.

"There are three kinds of praise: that which we yield, that which we lend, and that which we pay. We yield it to the powerful from fear, we lend it to the weak from interest, and we pay it to the deserving from gratitude." — Colton.

"When I am pressed with thoughts about worldly or home cares, I take a Psalm, or a saying of Paul, and go to sleep on it."—Luther.

bon, in elucidation of Scripture, cannot here be distrusted, any more than that of the heathen historians. To use his words, "a hundred thousand captives, and a rich booty, rewarded the fatigues of the Roman soldiers," when Ctesiphon was taken, in the second century, by the generals of Marcus. Even Julian, who, in the fourth century, was forced to raise the siege of Ctesiphon, came not in vain to Chaldæa, and failed not to take of it a spoil; nor, though an apostate, did he fail to verify by his acts the truth which he denied. After having given Perisador to flames, "the plentiful magazines of corn, of arms, and of splendid furniture, were partly distributed among the troops, and partly reserved for the public service; the useless stores were destroyed by fire, or thrown into the stream of the Euphrates." Outward Treasures.—We must not look too closely at the magnificent houses of a great city, with their contents, or else we shall be speedily undeceived as to their real glory. We shall see how much greed and unjust gain and the grinding of the poor had to do with such buildings. Grand buildings for some men to live in can have no charm to the Christian eye, if a necessary condition for their existence is that many others should live in ruinous hovels. The just and loving God must look on splendid cities with a very different eye from the human one. And doing so, he must of necessity fix a limit to covetousness. Covetousness goes on adding to its treasures, until at last it excites the covetousness of others. And even apart from this, outward treasures, unduly esteemed, must in time corrupt the inward man.—Pul. Com.

14—18. (14) **Lord .. himself,** Am. vi. 8. **I will fill,** etc., "it is better to render, with Ewald and Keil, 'Even though I have filled thee with men, as with locusts, they shall raise over thee the cheer of the vintage;' i. e. the millions of Babylon's population will not save her from the most utter ruin."—Pul. Com. **caterpillars,** R. V., "canker worms." (15, 16) **made,** etc., comp. ch. x. 12, 13. (17, 18) **every man,** etc., ch. x. 14, 15.

The resources of Jehovah.—Judged according to human standards, some men are powerful, some men wise, and some are men of understanding; but very seldom, even according to the human standard, are all three qualities united in one man; and it is not very often that even two of them are found. Man may have power, mere muscular strength, the power of the athlete, the power of the ox, without anything worthy the name of wisdom. So there may be wisdom without power; and there may be a very high degree of wisdom apart from large knowledge or a powerful understanding. Men are made so that what is defective in one may be supplied by another. The greatest human works are done when the power of one is joined with the wisdom of a second and the understanding of a third. But with Jehovah all these qualities, in their highest degree, are found united in One. The only account after all that man can give of the making of matter is that it has been made by a God. And then his wisdom has reduced everything to order, arranged the world in all its grades, organisms, and mutual connections. The natural man comes nearest to God when he can combine the power of one, the wisdom of another, and the understanding of yet a third, to make as it were one new man for the doing of special work; and the spiritual man comes nearest to God when, still preserving his individuality of action, he exchanges for his natural weakness the spiritual power of Christ, for his natural folly the spiritual wisdom of Christ, and for his often useless and deluding knowledge of the things of this world that knowledge which comes in the revelation of the glory of God in the face of Jesus Christ.—Pul. Com.

[a] "The mace, or mall, was among the weapons used by the soldiers, and by the Assyrian monarchs themselves." — Rawlinson.

19—24. (19) **portion,** etc., ch. x. 16. (20) **battle axe,**[a] the reference is to Cyrus. (21, 22) **break in pieces,** and so utterly ruin. (23) **captains,** Heb. Pakah, prob. the original of the title pasha. (24) **render unto,** bring upon Bab. retributive judgments.

The Church God's Battle-axe.—Notwithstanding the many accretions of error and superstition with which the pure faith of Christ so soon became encumbered, there yet remained inherent in it and inseparable from it such vital and mighty energy that it smote as with a "battle-axe" one falsehood after another, until they were well-nigh all slain. The forces against her in that ancient world were simply tremendous, but the Church went forth conquering and to conquer.

25—29. (25) **destroying mountain,** fig. for Babylon. "The description evidently points to a volcano. (1) Jehovah says that he will roll the mountain down from the rocks, which can only be understood of the stones and lava hurled down from the crater; (2) that he will make it a 'mountain of burning,' i. e. either to a burning, or, more forcibly, a burnt-out mountain; and (3) that, as a consequence of this, its stones shall be unsuitable for the purposes of the builder."—Pul. Com. **burnt mountain,** i. e. one burnt out, whose fires are quenched, and which is left a mere useless ruin. (26) **not .. stone,** bec. the stones of volcanoes are unfit for building purposes. (27) **Ararat,** in Armenia, 2 Ki. xix. 37. **Minni and Ashchenaz,** also in Armenia. Ge. x. 3. **captain,** or satrap. **caterpillars,** R. V. "canker-worm." (28) **Prepare,** lit. consecrate. (29) **tremble,** with its fear and confusion.

The Destroying Mountain Destroyed.—The mountain is a very fitting symbol of a people eminent among the nations and seeming easily to dominate over them. In such a symbol there is involved the undisputed assertion of superiority. The mountain looks down on the plains, and the plains accept the position. But whereas, in nature, the mountain looks down upon the plains with a mingling of benefits and injuries, of which even the injuries are seen to be benefits when looked at more closely, here we have a destroying mountain spoken of—a mountain that destroys the whole earth. God is against Babylon, not merely for the hurt it has inflicted on his own people, but because destruction is the very element in which it lives. Wheresoever Babylon came it brought spoliation, enslavement, and misery.—Pul. Com.

30—32. (30) **forborn,** etc., in utter hopelessness and despair. **bars are broken,** all her fortresses, and chief defences. (31) **One .. another,** intimating the simultaneous entry of the enemy at different points.[a] **at one end,** R. V., "on every quarter." (32) **passages,** prob. the ferries.

Effeminacy.—Woman has her natural limitations. Her usual place is not in the battle-field or on the walls of the attacked city. An army of women against an army of men would be an unnatural, a revolting spectacle. But this very difference between the proper place of women and the proper place of men intensifies the reproach against a man when it can truly be said of him that he has become as a woman. Those qualities which in a woman are womanly in a man are only effeminate.

33—35. (33) **threshingfloor,** such were in the open air, the ground being trodden down hard by cattle.[b] **time to thresh,** R. V. "at the time when it is trodden." (34) **devoured me,** i. e. the Jewish nation, wh. is here introduced, complaining of the injuries inflicted on them by the Chaldæans. **dragon,** or serpent which swallows its prey whole. A sea monster. **delicates,** delicacies, treasures; dainty meats, Ge. xlix. 20. **cast me out,** keeping up the fig. of the overgorged animal. (35) **my flesh,** wh. Nebuchadnezzar, as a wild beast, devoured.[a]

Babylon.—On the one side, near to the site of Opis, "the country all around appears to be one wide desert of sandy and barren soil, thinly scattered over with brushwood and tufts of reedy grass." On the other, between Bussorah and Bagdad, "immediately on either bank of the Tigris, is the untrodden desert. The absence of all cultivation,—the sterile, arid, and wild character of the whole scene, formed a contrast to the rich and delightful accounts delineated in Scripture. The natives, in traveling over these pathless deserts, are compelled to explore their way by the stars." "The face of the country is open and flat, presenting to the eye one vast level plain, where nothing is to be seen but here and there a herd of half-wild camels. This immense tract is very rarely diversified with any trees of moderate growth, but is an immense wild, bounded only by the horizon." In the intermediate region, "the whole

"A certain Austrian count, once climbing the Alps, was told by his guide that to go on to a cliff was dangerous. He disbelieved it, went, fell, and they found his body at the hotel at the foot of that cliff. The world is full today of disasters which are merely the consequences of unbelief."—A. F. Schauffler.

"The grand old book of God still stands, and this old earth, the more its leaves are turned over and pondered, the more it will sustain and illustrate the sacred word."—Professor Dana, the geologist.

[a] Herodotus says that the extreme parts of the city were taken before they who dwelt in the middle of it were sensible of their danger.

[b] "Near Jericho were no less than five such floors, all trodden by oxen, cows, and younger cattle, arranged in each case five abreast, and driven round in a circle, or rather in all directions, over the floor." — Robinson.

"Babylon is like a threshing-floor not trodden for a long time, but the time of harvest, when her citizens shall be trodden under foot, shall come." —Calvin.

[a] "Nebuchadnezzar had devoured Jerusalem, had treated her as ruthlessly as a crocodile does its prey, and for this cruelty he and Babylon are justly to be punished." — Spk. Com.

extent from the foot of the wall of Bagdad is a barren waste, without a blade of vegetation of any description; on leaving the gates, the traveler has before him the prospect of a bare desert, a flat and barren country." "The whole country between Bagdad and Hillah is a perfectly flat and (with the exception of a few spots as you approach the latter place) uncultivated waste. That it was at some former period in a far different state, is evident from the number of canals by which it is traversed, now dry and neglected; and the quantity of heaps of earth covered with fragments of brick and broken tiles, which are seen in every direction,—the indisputable traces of former population. At present the only inhabitants of the tract are the Sobeide Arabs. Around, as far as the eye can reach, is a trackless desert." "The abundance of the country has vanished as clean away as if the 'besom of desolation' had swept it from north to south; the whole land, from the outskirts of Babylon to the farthest stretch of sight, lying a melancholy waste. Not a habitable spot appears for countless miles." The land of Babylon is desolate, without an inhabitant. The Arabs traverse it; and every man met with in the desert is looked on as an enemy. Wild beasts have now their home in the land of Chaldæa; but the traveler is less afraid of them,—even of the lion,—than of "the wilder animal, the desert Arab." The country is frequently "totally impassable." "Those splendid accounts of the Babylonian lands yielding crops of grain two or three hundredfold, compared with the modern face of the country, afford a remarkable proof of the singular desolation to which it has been subjected. The canals at present can only be traced by their decayed banks."—Keith.

"Wealth is a weak anchor, and glory cannot support a man; this is the law of God, that virtue only is firm, and cannot be shaken by a tempest." — Pythagoras.

36—40. (36) **plead thy cause,** ch. l. 34. **dry .. sea,** poss. referring to the "great lake dug by Queen Nitocris to receive the waters of the Euphrates." **springs,** "the word is the same as that rendered 'fountain' in the Eng. Vers. of ii. 13. The literal sense is digging, and the noun is the singular. It refers to the network of canals dug throughout the country, which were necessary not only for commerce but also for irrigation. It is through the drying up of them that the country is barren to this day. See ver. 13, and l. 38."—Camb. Bib. (37) **heaps,** or ruins; ch. l. 26, 39. (38) **yell,** or growl; "the Heb. word is an imitation of the actual sound." (39) **heat,** i. e. when flushed with confidence and security. **drunken,** or a drinking-bout, a carousal. **a perpetual sleep,** the sleep of death at the hands of their conquering enemy.[b] (40) **lambs, etc.,** all classes of society are here indicated.[c]

[b] "The night in wh. the conquest of Babylon was effected, was during the great festival which had been instituted in honor of the idols, and at which revelry of every description was indulged in to such a pitch that most of the inhabitants were more or less in a state of inebriation." —Henderson.

[c] Is. xxxiv. 6.

Babylon.—"The soil of this desert," says Captain Mignan, who traversed it on foot, and who, in a single day, crossed forty water-courses, "consists of a hard clay, mixed with sand, which at noon became so heated with the sun's rays that I found it too hot to walk over it with any degree of comfort. Those who have crossed those desert wilds are already acquainted with their dreary tediousness even on horseback; what it is on foot they can easily imagine." Where astronomers first calculated eclipses, the natives, as in the deserts of Africa, or as the mariner without a compass on the pathless ocean, can now direct their course only by the stars over the pathless desert of Chaldæa. Where cultivation reached its utmost height, and where two hundredfold was stated as the common produce, there is now one wide and uncultivated waste; and the sower and reaper are cut off from the land of Babylon. Where abundant stores and treasures were laid up, and annually renewed and increased, fanners have fanned, and spoilers have spoiled them till they have emptied the land. Where laborers, shaded by palm trees a hundred feet high, irrigated the fields till all was plentifully watered from numerous canals, the wanderer, without an object on which to fix his eye but "stinted and shortlived shrubs," can scarcely set his foot without pain, after the noonday heat, on the "arid and parched ground," in plodding his weary way through a desert, a dry land, and a wilderness. Where there were crowded thoroughfares, from city to city, there is now "silence and solitude;" for the ancient cities of Chaldæa are desolations,

"Private credit is wealth, public honor is security; the feather that adorns the royal bird supports its flight; strip him of his plumage, and you pin him to the earth."—Junius.

"Much learning shows how little mortals know;
Much wealth, how little worldlings can enjoy."
—Young.

"When a man makes a fool of himself, he generally does the job well."

—where no man dwelleth, neither doth any son of man pass thereby.—Keith.

41—44. (41) **Sheshach,** ch. xxv. 26. **praise .. earth,** ch. xlix. 25.[a] (42) **The sea,** a fig. for the invading army.[b] (43) **cities,** related, or dependent cities. Poss. the reference may be to the inner and outer cities, the two parts into which Babylon was divided by the Euphrates. (44) **Bel,** Is. xlvi. 1. **swallowed up,** the treasures taken by the nation called after the name of this god.[c] **flow together,** in their pilgrimages to Bel's shrine. **wall,** vs. 58.

Cities of Chaldæa.—While the ancient cities of Chaldæa are thus desolate, the sites of others cannot be discovered, or have not been visited, as none pass thereby; the more modern cities, which flourished under the empire of caliphs, are "all in ruins." The second Bagdad has not indeed yet shared the fate of the first. And Hillah—a town of comparatively modern date, near to the site of Babylon, but in the gardens of which there is not the least vestige of ruins—yet exists. But the former, "ransacked by massacre, devastation and oppression, during several hundred years," has been "gradually reduced from being a rich and powerful city to a state of comparative poverty, and the feeblest means of defence." And of the inhabitants of the latter, about eight or ten thousand, it is said that "if anything could identify the modern inhabitants of Hillah as the descendants of the ancient Babylonians, it would be their extreme profligacy, for which they are notorious even among their immoral neighbors." They give no sign of repentance and reformation to warrant the hope that judgment, so long continued upon others, will cease from them: or that they are the people that shall escape. Indications of ruined cities, whether of a remote or more recent period, abound throughout the land. The process of destruction is still completing. Gardens which studded the banks of the Tigris have very recently disappeared, and mingled with the desert,—and concerning the cities also of Chaldæa the word is true that they are desolations. For "the whole country is strewed over with the debris of Grecian, Roman, and Arabian towns, confounded in the same mass of rubbish."—Keith.

45—49. (45) **deliver .. soul,** R. V. "save yourselves every man" preserve your lives from the perils of the time of judgment. (46) R. V. and let not your heart faint, neither fear ye for the rumor that shall be heard in the land; for a rumor shall come one year," etc., i. e. the air shall be full of all kinds of rumors.[a] **rumour,** of the approach of the Chaldæan army. (47) **Therefore,** the exiles should take warning from these events. (48) **sing for Babylon,** all nature shall rejoice at the downfall of the oppressor. Another illustration of the favorite idea that nature will participate with man in the redemption. (49) "The fact of Babylon's having caused the death of Israelites shall be visited upon many nations, which shall be mixed up in her overthrow."—Camb. Bib.

Characteristics of the Several Prophets.—Each of the prophets has his own characteristic place in the development of religion, and his own distinctive message. Amos, the Carlyle of Hebrew history, was the prophet of righteousness; Hosea, whom I have ventured to compare to John G. Whittier, was the prophet of God's tender compassion and deep, undying love; Micah, the prophet of the poor, himself a peasant, was the prophet of fraternity and equality, long before those words were coined or thought of in connection with communal life; Isaiah—the First Isaiah—was the prophet of the true method of return to God. He also laid stress on righteousness, as Amos did; he also laid stress on God's mercy, as Hosea did; he also laid stress on equality, as Micah did; but he pointed out more clearly than any of the others the way of return by repentance to God and the possibility of such return. But Amos, Hosea, Micah, and Isaiah all spoke to the nation as a nation. They did not deal to any considerable extent with individuals. They dealt with Israel as Israel, with Judah as Judah. Jeremiah foresaw the breaking up of the nation, and lived to see it overturned and the great majority of the people carried into captivity, and, before they were carried off into captivity,

[a] Is. xiii. 19.

"Babylon had been embellished with ornaments more than any city that we are acquainted with." —Herodotus.

[b] Comp. Is. viii. 7, xvii. 12, 13.

[c] "Reference may be to the holy vessels taken out of the temple of the Lord at Jerusalem, and placed in the temple of Bel." — Wordsworth.

vs. 42. "This metaphor is in common use to show the overwhelming power of an enemy. 'Tippoo Saib went down upon his foes; like the sea he swept them all away.' 'True, true, the British troops went like the sea upon Bhurtpore; the forts have been carried away.'" — Roberts.

[a] "The first rumor of war denounced against the head of that empire shall be the year before the siege, when Cyrus and Nabonnidus (or Belshazzar) shall engage in a battle, and the latter shall be overcome, upon which defeat the conqueror should in the following year lay siege to the city itself." —Lowth.

"Misfortune had conquered her, how true it is, that sooner or later the most rebellious must bow beneath the same yoke."—Mme. de Stael.

"Content can soothe, where'er by fortune placed; can rear a garden in the desert waste."—White.

carried away into paganism. He gave up his hope for the reformation of the nation, and turned from the nation to the individual. It is hardly too much to say that in Jeremiah moral individualism was born.—Lyman Abbott.

50—53. (50) **go away,** R. V. "go ye," i. e. be prepared to depart for Jerusalem. Keep that end in mind. (51) **confounded,** R. V. "ashamed." The exiles intimate their prostrate condition in Babylon, and the way in wh. they, and their God, were contemned.[a] (52) **do judgment,** "even on this account, says Jeremiah, skilfully repeating the opening words of the picture, shall the idols be visited and their land filled with the slain. The prophet speaks very appropriately of the visitation of the idols, for just this is the recompense for the disgrace inflicted on the house of Jehovah."—Lange. (53) **mount .. heaven,** a double allusion (1) to the tower of Babel Gen. xi. 4; (2) to the high walls by which Babylon was surrounded."—Lange. **height .. strength,** with allusion to her high and immense walls, 350 ft. high, according to Herodotus.[b]

[a] "We lead here a life of shame. Daily the reproach is cast in our teeth that Bel has proved more mighty than Jehovah; and, we are unable to answer the taunt, and shame covers our faces."— Spk. Com.

[b] "On the cylinder of Nebuchadnezzar, still extant, are these words: 'In Babylon is the tower of my abode. . . To make more difficult the attack of an enemy against Imgour-Bel, the indestructible wall of Babylon I constructed, a bulwark like a mountain. . . . I built my palace for the wonder of the people, . . it is proof against all attack.' "—Wordsworth.

Jeremiah.—Renan goes too far when he says, if there had been no Jeremiah there would have been no Christianity. Only a Frenchman will undertake to tell what would have been if something else had been otherwise than it was. And he goes, perhaps, too far in saying that two-thirds of the glory attributed to Moses belongs to Jeremiah. But it is certain that Jeremiah lays, in his prophecies, the foundations of Christianity, and marks more, perhaps, than any other of the preceding prophets the transition from the prophecy of righteousness and law to the revelation of grace, mercy, and truth, through Jesus Christ. To him what is vital is the change in the individual character. It is not enough that the nation, as a nation, reforms its constitution; that the king, as a king, executes the laws; that the priests administer the temple sacrifices as they should be administered. God, he says, trieth the hearts; circumcision, he says, must be of the heart. Paul borrowed that figure, as he did some others, from Jeremiah. Put hope into Jeremiah, and you get Paul. It is a great transformation; but then hope is a great transformer. It is Jeremiah, therefore, who is the prophet of the New Covenant. It is he who first used that term which has now become so familiar with us, New Testament, for "testament" means "covenant." He is the inventor of the phrase.—Lyman Abbott.

The Kingdom of God has its Broad Walls.—(Cf. Neh. iii. 8, where we read of the broad walls of Jerusalem.) Let us see to it that we maintain and preserve those walls. 1. For separation. Let us not seek to come close to the world, in its habits, maxims, spirit, behavior. Keep the wall broad, strong, high. We cannot serve God and mammon. Let there be no attempt at compromise. And these walls are also 2. For security. If we do not maintain them we run great risk for ourselves. Tampering with sin is perilous work. And let us not think that we are more likely to win the world by such breaking down of the broad walls. The result is all the other way. See how broad a wall Christ maintained between himself and the world. God has built these walls. His power, his wisdom, his love, his promise, are all portions of these walls by which his Church is guarded and against which the gates of hell shall not prevail. 3. For enjoyment. What comfort there is in the thought of them, of the sure defence, the wall of fire, which God will be to his people! And on these walls, as we "walk about Zion, and go round her, and tell the towers thereof," what rest, what communion one with another, and what bright prospects are ours! The broad walls of Babylon shall be "broken down;" but these are eternal. Are we within them?—C.

54—58. (54) **cry,** the war cry; ch. l. 22. (55) **waves,** the masses of her invading enemy pouring through her streets. (56) **mighty men,** vs. 30. **recompences,** R. V. "for the Lord is a God of recompences, he shall surely requite." Ch. l. 29. (57) **drunk,** so incapable of defence.[a] **wise men,** Da. ii. 2. (58) **broad walls,** Herodotus says, 85 Eng. feet wide: Strabo says, 32 feet.[b] **and the people,** etc., R. V. "and the peoples shall

[a] Comp. the proverb, "They whom the gods would destroy, they first dement."

[b] "The walls were from 41 to 60 miles in circumference, and from 75 to 335 feet in height, at different parts.

labor for vanity and the nations for the fire," etc. Quoted from Heb. ii. 13. In the end all these conquests of Chaldæa will bring nothing but suffering to the conquerors.

The Broad Walls.—According to Herodotus, the outer wall of Babylon was 200 royal cubits (about 373 English feet) high, while it was fifty cubits wide. This, however, both from the nature of the case, and from the conflicting testimony of other writers, seems exaggerated. Probably the height was about 60 or 70 English feet. The walls may have been 30 or 40 feet wide, as they allowed of a team of four horses being driven along them. See Herod., Bk. i. 179, and Rawlinson's notes on that passage.—Camb. Bib. They existed as walls for more than a thousand years after the prophecy was delivered; and long after the sentence of utter destruction had gone forth against them, they were numbered among "the seven wonders of the world." And what can be more wonderful now, or what could have been more inconceivable by man, when Babylon was in its strength and glory, that the broad walls of Babylon should be so utterly broken that it cannot be determined with certainty that even the slightest vestige of them exists. I have not been fortunate enough to discover the least trace of them in any part of the ruins at Hillah; which is rather an unaccountable circumstance considering that they survived the final ruin of the town, long after which they served as an enclosure for a park; in which comparatively perfect state St. Jerome informs us they remained in his time." In the sixteenth century they were seen for the last time by any European traveler (so far as the author has been able to trace), before they were finally so utterly broken as totally to disappear. And it is interesting to mark both the time and the manner in which the walls of Babylon, like the city of which they were the impregnable yet unavailing defence, were brought down to the grave, to be seen no more. "The meanwhile," as Rauwolf describes them, "when we were lodged there, I considered and viewed this ascent, and found that there were two behind one another" (Herodotus states that there was both an inner, or inferior, and outer wall), "distinguished by a ditch, and extending themselves like unto two parallel walls a great way about, and that they were open in some places, where one might go through like gates; wherefore I believe that they were the wall of the old town that went about them; and that the places where they were open have been anciently the gates (whereof there were one hundred) of that town. And this the rather because I saw in some places under the sand (wherewith the two ascents were almost covered) the old wall plainly appear."—Keith.

59—64. "When King Zedekiah, in the fourth year of his reign, made a journey to Babylon, Jeremiah gave to Seraiah, the brother of Baruch, the marshal, the prophecy against Babylon to take with him and read in Babylon, and then with prayer to the Lord to cast it into the Euphrates." —Lange. **Seraiah** was the brother of Baruch, ch. xxxii. 12. **Quiet prince,** R. V. "now Seraiah was chief chamberlain."[c] (60) **evil,** or calamity. (61) **and shalt see, and shalt read,** R. V., "then see that those read," not to the people of Babylon, nor even perhaps to a solemnly convoked assembly of Jews, as either course would have been at least attended with much danger, and the first of them probably impossible to carry out. The words are nevertheless to be pronounced in the presence of Jewish witnesses, who could in after days testify that thus, long before the overthrow of Babylon, these words had been read in the midst of the very city where they were to take effect, and then buried in the heart of the same.—Camb. B. (63) **cast .. Euphrates,** a symbolical act. (64) **Thus far,** intimating that the next ch. is an appendix.

God's Power of Utter Destruction.—The impossibility of discovering this stone has to be considered relatively. Strictly speaking, it might perhaps have been recovered if it had been worth while. But for all practical purposes it was finally lost. Here is the difference between human destructions and the Divine destruction. Babylon is a wilderness still. Where God has chosen to make special marks of his wrath

They formed a square, in each side of which were 25 gates leading into the city. Between these gates were 250 towers, so that it was considered to be impregnable." —Partly Henderson.

"There is a jewel which no
Indian mine can buy,
No chemic art can counterfeit;
It makes men rich in greatest poverty,
Makes water wine, turns wooden cups to gold,
The homely whistle to sweet music's strain;
Seldom it comes—to few from heaven sent—
That much in little—all in naught—content."
—Wilbye.

[c] "It was his business to ride forward each day, and select the place where the king would halt and pass the night." — Spk. Com.

"The utility of riches consists not in the welfare of the individual, but in the general good of society. Whatever tends to loss of health, or comfort, or deterioration of morals, in the main body of the nation, is not wealth but poverty, notwithstanding any superficial splendor of things wherewith it may be combined."—Quarterly Review.

with the unrighteousness of men there rests a blight which no human effort can overcome; and generally speaking there is no disposition to overcome it. But where destruction comes simply through human passion and power there may be comparatively speedy recovery. This is a side of war on which we do well to reflect. Wars, with all their terrible accompaniments, may do something to get rid of some evils, and may thus be the condition of great good. Man cannot destroy where God wills to preserve. But where God destroys he destroys finally, and it is just this dreadful possibility of final ruin that should make men cautious in their estimate of the future, and prompt to turn from all evil and selfish paths.—Pul. Com.

The Cities of Babylon.—The course of the Tigris through Babylonia, instead of being adorned, as of old, with cities and towns, is marked with the sites of "ancient ruins." Sitace, Sabata, Narisa, Fuchera, Sendia, "no longer exist." A succession of longitudinal mounds, crossed at right angles by others, mark the supposed site of Artemita, or Destagered. Its once luxuriant gardens are covered with grass; and a higher mound distinguishes "the royal residence" from the ancient streets. Extensive ridges and mounds (near to Houmania), varying in height and extent, are seen branching in every direction. A wall with sixteen bastions is the only memorial of Apollonia. The once magnificent Seleucia is now a scene of desolation. There is not a single entire building, but the country is strewed for miles with fragments of decayed buildings. "As far," says Major Keppet, "as the eye could reach, the horizon presented a broken line of mounds; the whole of this place was a desert flat." On the opposite bank of the Tigris, where Ctesiphon its rival stood, besides fragments of walls and broken masses of brickwork, and remains of vast structures encumbered with heaps of earth, there is one magnificent monument of antiquity, "in a remarkably perfect state of preservation," "a large and noble file of building, the front of which presents to view a wall three hundred feet in length, adorned with four rows of arched recesses, with a central arch, in span eighty-six feet, and above a hundred feet high, supported by walls sixteen feet thick, and leading to a hall which extends to the depth of one hundred and fifty-six feet," the width of the building. A great part of the back wall, and of the roof, is broken down; but that which remains "still appears much larger than Westminster Abbey." It is supposed to have been the lofty palace of Chosroes; but there desolation now reigns. "On the site of Ctesiphon; the smallest insect under heaven would not find a single blade of grass wherein to hide itself, nor one drop of water to allay its thirst." In the rear of the palace, and attached to it, are mounds two miles in circumference, indicating the utter desolation of buildings formed to minister to luxury. But, in the words of Captain Mignan, "such is the extent of the irregular mounds and hillocks that overspread the site of these renowned cities, that it would occupy some months to take the bearings and dimensions of each with accuracy."—Keith.

"We may kneel and cast our load,
E'en while we pray, upon our God,
Then rise with lightened cheer;
Sure that the Father, who is nigh
To hear the famished ravens cry,
Will hear in that we fear."

"The heathen mother takes her babe to the idol temple, and teaches it to clasp its little hands before its forehead, in the attitude of prayer, long before it can utter a word. As soon at it can walk, it is taught to gather a few flowers or fruits, or put a little rice upon a banana-leaf, and lay them upon the altar before the idol god. As soon as it can utter the names of its parents, so soon it is taught to offer up its petitions before the images. Whoever saw a heathen child that could speak, and not pray? Christian mothers, why is it that so many children grow up in this enlightened land without learning to pray?" — Vt. Chronicle.

CHALPTER THE FIFTY-SECOND.

This closing chapter was not written by Jeremiah. It gives an account of the capture of Jerusalem by the Chaldæans and the exile of the inhabitants. It corresponds closely to 2 Ki. xxiv. 18—xxv. 30, but is a better account.—Driver. **1—3.** (1) **Zedekiah,** etc. 2 Ki. xxiv. 18—20. (2) **Jehoiakim,** 2 Ki. xxiii. 34—37. (3) **anger .. Lord,** 2 Ki. xxiv. 3, 4. **it came to pass,** "this came to pass," i. e. the evil conduct of the king. **presence, that,** R. V., "presence: and Zedekiah," etc.

Advice to a Mother.—The first book read, and the last book laid aside by every child is the conduct of its mother. 1. First give yourself, then your child, to God. It is but giving Him His own. Not to do it is robbing God. 2. Always prefer virtue to wealth—the honor that comes from God to the honor that comes from men. Do this for yourself, do it for your child. 3. Let your whole course be to raise your child to a high standard. Do not sink into childishness yourself. 4. Give not heedless commands, but when you command require prompt obedience. 5. Never indulge a child in cruelty, even to an insect. 6. Cultivate sympathy with your child in all lawful joys and sorrows. 7. Be sure that you never correct a child until you know it deserves correction. Hear its story first and fully. 8. Never allow your child to whine or fret, or to bear grudges. 9. Early inculcate frankness, candor, generosity, magnanimity, patriotism, and self-denial. 10. The knowledge and fear of the Lord are the beginning of wisdom. 11. Never mortify the feelings of your child by upbraiding it with dullness; but do not inspire it with self-conceit. 12. Pray with and for your child, often and heartily. 13. Encourage all attempts at self-improvement. 14. Never deceive nor break a promise to a child. 15. Reprove not a child severely in the presence of strangers. 16. Remember that life is a vapor, and that you and your child may be called out of time into eternity any day.

4—11. (4) **forts,** moveable towers, sometimes with battering rams, such as Assyrian sculptures show.[a] (5) **besieged,** invested so closely that no provisions from outside could reach the inhabitants. (6) **famine was sure,** comp. Lam. i. 19, 20; ii. 11, 12, 20; iv. 9, 10. (7) **was broken up,** R. V. "then a breach was made in the city," i. e. the walls, probably on the north. **fled,** comp. 2 Ki. xxv. 4. (8) **pursued,** etc., 2 Ki. xxv. 5. (9) **land of Hamath,** omitted in 2 Kings: comp. Je. xxxix. 5. (10) **slew .. princes,** ch. xxxix. 6. (11) **put him in prison,** this information is additional to that given us in 2 Kings.

Zedekiah's army scattered.—Zedekiah's aim was to keep his army together, for as long as he could do that, there was a chance of averting the evil day, and perhaps in the end escaping it altogether. But without his army he was utterly helpless. He could not bring himself to heed Jeremiah's counsels, doing the right and putting his trust in Jehovah. And so when the army was gone everything was gone. Nothing remained but random, desperate attempts at flight, and the certainty of ultimate capture. We have to ask ourselves what we shall do when our army is scattered from us, when the resources of our own making are vanished. The chief battles of our life are not to be fought with external resources at all. In every warfare where the weapons are carnal the weapons must fail at last. Only when we are engaged in truly spiritual warfare, and have the hosts of heaven on our side, can we be sure that our army will not be scattered from us.—Pul. Com.

12—16. (12) **tenth,** comp. seventh of 2 Ki. xxv. 8.[b] **served the king,** or stood before him: implying that he was a personal attendant on the king. (13) **burned,** etc., 2 Ki. xxv. 9. Probably only the larger houses were burnt. (14) **all the walls,** to ensure that it could not again be made a centre of rebellion. (15, 16) Comp. 2 Ki. xxv. 11, 12. **multitude,** or of the workmen.[c]

Sparing the Poor.—Whilst the king, the nobles, the wealthy, and many others were carried into exile, certain of the poor were still left in the land. We are accustomed to speak of the hardships of poverty, but there are compensating advantages not a few. Many evils of the worst character only visit the rich. In times of public trouble the houses of the rich are attacked and the persons of the great are threatened, while the poor are left in happy neglect. Great men are beset with anxieties such as are unknown to the simpler lives of the poor. Who would be a king now that kings are all marks for the assassin? In those countries where the sovereign is compelled to take elaborate precautions for his safety, the poor citizen can move about the streets without fear. The one is a prisoner in his own palace, the other a free man with liberty to roam over the whole kingdom. Ambition aims at distinction, but that is a poor crown to win. Distinguished men have peculiar vexations and dangers of their own. There is more happiness in obscurity. The wise man will say, "Give me neither poverty nor riches;" and the Christian will add, "Not my will, but thine, be done," knowing well that for him that lot is best which his heavenly Father assigns to him.—Pul. Com.

a "Erected by the besieging party for the double purpose of observing what was done by those defending the city, and of annoying them by discharging missiles upon them from the elevation which was thus afforded." — Henderson.

"Do not think that you will have no battles if you follow the Nazarene; many battles are before you. Men do not object to a battle if they are confident that they will have victory, and, thank God, everyone of us may have the victory if we will."—D. L. Moody.

b In Heb. letters are used for numerals, and some of them are so much alike that confusion is easily made by copyists.

c "The object of Nebuchadnezzar was to people Babylon, not with paupers but with men of a better class, artisans and workmen, who would enrich it. The expense of taking them to Babylon must have been considerable." — Spk. Com.

"We must distinguish between what is essentially sacred and what is sacred only by association and to serve a purpose. When the purpose is accomplished the sacred sinks back into the common. God dwelleth not in temples made with hands. He was none the poorer for all this burning. Babylon learned hereafter that, though his house had been burned, his power was not at all diminished."

"The Jews fell as a nation because every man in it fell as an individual." —F. D. Burrell.

"The captivity of Judah was the fault of her religious men. . . . Men are more endangered by false uses of the religious nature than by the denial of it altogether." —A. E. Dunning.

"To give pain is the tyranny, to make happy the true empire, of beauty."—Steele.

"Satiety comes of riches, and contumaciousness of satiety." —Solon.

"If I were rich
and owned but pelf—
How poor in self I'd be;
If I were poor
and owned myself—
The wealth of worlds I'd see!"

17—23. "This description of the fate of the Temple furniture is much fuller than in the Kings' passage, and has no parallel whatever in chap. xxxix. For the vessels here mentioned see chap. xxvii. 19. They were too large to be conveniently carried as they were, and so were broken and taken to Babylon for the sake of the material. In Kings all is omitted before the brass."—Camb. Bib. (17) **pillars,** etc., 2 Ki. xv. 13—15. (20) **under the bases,** "the bases were under the ten lavers;" so this would better read, "The twelve brazen bulls which were instead of bases," to support the brazen sea. (21—23) **pillars,** etc., 2 Ki. xxv. 16, 17. (22) **five cubits,** 1 Ki. vii. 16.

The Finger as a Measure.—In the same way do the people of the East speak of anything which is less in measure than a span. "What height are your pepper vines?" "About two fingers." "When the rice becomes five fingers in height we shall want more rain." That which is less than a finger is spoken of as a grain of rice; the next gradation is an ellu, i. e. gingelly seed; the next is a mustard seed; and the last an anu, i. e. an atom.—Roberts.

24—27. (24) **Seraiah,** 2 Ki. xxv. 18. "Probably the son of Azariah and grandson of Hilkiah." (1 Chron. vi. 14.) (25) **seven men,** comp. "five men" of 2 Ki. xx . 19. **principal scribe,** R. V. " and the scribe of the captain of the host," i. e. the chief military scribe. (26, 27) **so .. land,** 2 Ki. xxv. 20, 21.

Pity for the Prisoner.—Mrs. Booth, who was the life and inspiration of the Salvation Army, and whose memory is likely to animate its work for many years, always placed herself on the side of misfortune and suffering, and the story of her first "open-air procession" is eminently characteristic of that spirit. When a little girl, running along the road with hoop and stick she saw a prisoner dragged along by the constable to the lockup. A mob was hooting the unfortunate culprit, and his utter loneliness appealed at once to the child; it seemed to her that he had not a friend in the world. Quick as the thought, she sprang to his side, and marched down the street with him, determined that he should know there was one heart that felt for him, whether he suffered from his own fault or that of another. One might call this the first procession ever held by the Salvation Army. Patience in Suffering.—More than a year ago a young girl, belonging to a prominent family in a Southern town, was stricken with a loathsome and incurable disease. For months she bore intense agony, the mere sight of which made strong men turn pale; but whenever a moment of relief came she was hopeful, loving and gay, as if in health, eagerly seeing the villagers in whom she was interested, and saying once to her father, who had been a soldier: "When your captain ordered you to march over a bad bit of ground, you knew he had a reason for it. You did it without complaining. So will I." When at last she was laid to rest, an intelligent working-man came up to her father as he turned from her grave, and said respectfully: "Sir, there's hardly a man or woman, black or white, in this village, who has not been helped by the sight of that child's courage and faith in the Master she loved. Perhaps you don't understand why such pain was sent to her, but we do. She suffered for us."

28—30. (28) **in the seventh year.** As Ewald and Keil agree, we should correct "seventh" into "seventeenth" (just as in 2 Chron. xxxvi. 9, for "eight" we should read "eighteen"). On the small number of Jews deported Ewald remarks, "Nothing so clearly shows the extent to which the best men from the upper classes had been already despatched by the Chaldæans across the Euphrates, as the fact that in all the years of the second, and, if it be insisted on, of the third revolt, put together, they found only 4,600 men more whom they thought worth the trouble of transporting."—Pul. Com. **three .. twenty,** comp. 2 Ki. xxiv. 14, 16. (29) **eighteenth year,** when Nebuc. raised the siege of Jerus., to march against the king of Egypt. He then sent all the captive Jews in his camp away to Babylon. (30) **three and twentieth year,** when Nebuc. laid siege to Tyre.

Count Ugolino and His Children.—Ugolino, a Florentine count, with his four children, was thrown into a dungeon by Archbishop Ruggieri. The horrors which he was here doomed to encounter have given a melancholy celebrity to his name. "The hour," says he, "approached, when we expected to have something brought us to eat; but instead of seeing any food appear, I heard the door of that horrible dungeon more closely barred. I beheld my little children in silence, and could not weep; my heart was petrified. The little wretches wept; and my dear Anselmo said, 'Father, you look on us! What ails you?' I could neither weep nor answer, and continued swallowed up in silent agony all that day, and the following night, even till the dawn of day. As soon as a glimmering ray darted through the doleful prison, that I could view again those four faces in which my own image was impressed, I gnawed both my hands with grief and rage. My children, believing I did this through eagerness to eat, raising themselves suddenly up, said to me, 'My father, our torments would be less if you would allay the rage of your hunger upon us.' I restrained myself, that I might not increase their misery. We were all mute that day, and the following. The fourth day being come, Gouldo, falling extended at my feet, cried, 'My father! why do you not help me?' and died. The other three expired one after another, between the fifth and sixth day, famished, as thou seest me now! and I, being seized with blindness, began to go grouping upon them with my hands and feet; and continued calling them by their names three days after they were dead; then hunger vanquished my grief."—Percy Anec.

31—34. Comp. 2 Kings xxv. 27—30. **Evil-merodach,** son and successor of Nebuchadnezzar; ascended the throne B. C. 561, ruled for two years and was murdered by Neriglissar, his brother-in-law. **lifted .. head,** fig. for cheered and encouraged him, by giving him liberty, and some kindly notice.[a] Comp. Gen. xl. 13, 20. (32) **kings,** i. e. the other captive kings kept to grace the court. (33) **eat bread,** i. e. take his place as an official of the palace. (Comp. 2 Sa. ix. 7, 11.) (34) **continual diet,** or daily provision for the maintenance of himself and his attendants.[d] **until the day of his death, all the days of his life,** the latter of these clauses as the text now stands, is probably either an addition to, or originally a substitution for, the former, in order to avoid the inauspicious ending with the word death. The general object too of the paragraph seems to have been somewhat similar, viz. to leave the reader with a parting ray of comfort and encouragement in the thought that even in exile the Lord remembered His people and softened the heart of the heathen tyrant towards David's seed.—Camb. Bib.

Jeremiah.—A strange, sad, self-contradictory, eloquent, brave man was this Jeremiah, who abhors that which is evil and cleaves to that which is good, a Puritan before the Puritans, a Protestant before the Protestants, a lover of God, a lover of righteousness, a long-lived martyr in an age that could not comprehend him; and yet he left God's message not wholly uttered. He saw that the reform of the nation had not been reform of the individual. He saw that it was in vain to write God's laws in a book and put them in a pulpit. He saw that the nation could be made righteous only as God is written in the heart of the individual. But he did not know that the righteous God, the just God, the good God, the God of Amos and Hosea and Isaiah and Micah, was yet to come, in the person of his Son, into human life. It was left for the Great Unknown, the Second Isaiah, to bring that message. Jeremiah understood that God is the secret of life, and that the individual citizens must be rightened or the nation is ruined; but it was left for the Second Isaiah, the Great Unknown, to bring the last great message of prophecy to the world—that the personality of God must come to dwell with the presence of men before mankind can know that God is just and loving and merciful, and become just and loving and merciful like him.—Lyman Abbott.

a "Evil-Merodack is said in Jewish tradition to have formed an acquaintance with Jehoiachin while they were companions in prison; Nebuchadnezzar having put his son in prison for a time."—Fausset.

d "This change of condition, vouchsafed at Babylon by God's mercy, after the terrible maledictions denounced against him, and after a long exile and captivity of 37 yrs., was like a presage of comfort and mercy from God Himself, and was a pledge of the liberation and exaltation of the Jewish nation, when it had been humbled and purified by the discipline of suffering, and of its return to its own land."—Wordsworth.

Introduction.

(For General Introduction see commencement of Prophecies of Jeremiah.)

This Book is a kind of appendix to the Prophecies of Jeremiah, of which, in the original Scriptures, it formed a part. It expresses with pathetic tenderness the Prophet's grief for the desolation of the city and temple of Jerusalem, the captivity of the people, the miseries of famine, the cessation of public worship, and the other calamities with which his countrymen had been visited for their sins. The leading object was to teach the suffering Jews neither to despise the chastening of the Lord, nor to faint when rebuked of Him, but to turn to God with deep repentance, to confess their sins, and humbly look to Him alone for pardon and deliverance. No Book in Scripture is more rich in expressions of patriotic feeling, or of the penitence and trust which become an afflicted Christian. The form of these poems is strictly regular, with the exception of the last. In the original Hebrew they are alphabetical acrostics, in which every stanza begins with a new letter. The third has this further peculiarity, that all the three lines in each stanza have the same letter at the commencement. As a composition this Book is remarkable for the great variety of pathetic images it contains expressive of the deepest sorrow, and worthy of the subject which they are designed to illustrate (Angus). The Book is almost universally accepted as the work of Jeremiah.

SYNOPSIS.—(According to Horne.) This Book, which in our Bible is divided into five chapters, consists of five distinct Elegies.

Elegy I.—A Lamentation of the sad reverse of fortune which the country had experienced, and a confession that the miseries were well deserved.

Elegy II.—A melancholy detail of the dire effects of the Divine anger in the subversion of the civil and religious constitution of the Jews.

Elegy III.—The inexhaustible mercies of God are set forth as the never-failing source of consolation, and an exhortation to patience.

Elegy IV.—A contrast between the present deplorable condition of the nation and their former flourishing affairs.

Elegy V.—An epilogue to the previous Elegies. This chapter is in some versions entitled "The Prayer of Jeremiah."

CHAPTER THE FIRST.

1—3. (1) **solitary,** alone; without her inhabitants.[a] **as a widow,** "cities are often described as the mothers of their inhabitants, and their kings and princes as their husbands;" in this instance Jehovah is the husband, for whose loss is the mourning. **nations . . provinces,** the surrounding kingdoms, e.g. Philistines, Edomites, etc. **tributary,** the word here means bond-servants. "Her only function now is to be a vassal unto others." (2) **weepeth sore,** picture of helplessness and hopelessness. Je. xiii. 17.[b] **lovers,** or allied states. **dealt treacherously,** utterly failing her in the hour of her need.[c] (3) **Judah,** etc., Je. lii. 27. **captivity,** R. V. marg. "exile," the long sufferings of the Jews at the hands of Egypt and Chaldæa had induced many of them to go voluntarily to dwell in other lands. **affliction . . servitude,** their breaking the Mosaic law in relation to setting at liberty the slaves, was one great sign and proof of their rebelliousness. **straits,** a metaphor taken from hunting: driven into a corner.[d]

Inactive Sorrow and Sympathy Worthless.—We are sorry (for the English are a kind-hearted people) for the victims of our luxury and neglect; sorry for the thousands whom we let die every year by preventible diseases, because we are either too busy or too comfortable to save their lives; sorry for the savages whom we exterminate by no deliberate intent, but by the mere weight of our heavy footstep; sorry for the thousands who are used up yearly in certain trades in ministering to our comfort, even to our very luxuries and frivolities; sorry for the Sheffield grinders, who go to work as to certain death; sorry for the people whose lower jaws decay away in lucifer-match factories; sorry for the diseases of artificial flower-makers; sorry for the boys working in glass-houses whole days and nights on end without rest, "laboring in the very fire, and wearying themselves with weary vanity." We are sorry for them all, as the giant is for the worm on which he treads. Alas! poor worm. But the giant must walk on. He is necessary to the universe, and the worm is not. So we are sorry, for half an hour, and glad too (for we are a kind-hearted people) to hear that charitable persons or the Government, are going to do something towards alleviating these miseries. And then we return, too many of us, each to his own ambition, comforting ourselves with the thought that we did not make the world, and we are not responsible for it.—C. Kingsley.

4—6. (4) **ways,** i.e. highways leading from the country districts to Jerusalem. **mourn,** bec. none journey on them to the solemn feasts.[e] Grass-grown roads and streets may, figuratively, be said to be in mourning. **her gates,** those of Zion, here were "the markets, al fresco tribunals, open spaces for public meetings." **virgins,** "who took a prominent part in all religious festivals."[f] (5) **chief,** R. V., "are become the head:" masters over her.[g] **prosper,** lit. "are at rest," so crushed is Zion, that they have no fear of her renewing her rebellion. **children . . enemy,** driven before them like a herd of cattle.[h] (6) **beauty,** R. V. "majesty," that of her temple, palaces, and walls. **harts,** or deer.

Illusions.—Viewed in the softened lights of memory the past is strangely simplified, its mixed character is forgotten, and many of its unpleasant features are smoothed out, so that an idyllic charm hovers over the dream, and lends it an unearthly beauty. This is why so many people foolishly damp the hopes of children, who, if they are healthily constituted, ought to be anticipating the future with eagerness, by solemnly exhorting them to make hay while the sun shines, with the gloomy warning that the sunny season must soon pass. Their application of the motto carpe diem is not only pagan in spirit; it is founded on an illusion. Happily there is some unreality about most of our yearning regrets for the days that have gone. That sweet, fair past was not so radiant as its effigy in the dreamland of memory now appears to be; nor is the hard present so free from mitigating circumstances as we suppose. And yet, when all is said, we cannot find the consolation we hunger after in hours of darkness among bare conclusions of common-sense. The melancholy that laments the lost past can only be perfectly mastered by that Chris-

a Jerusalem is described as a widow woman, sitting sad and pensive, on the ground, the position often taken by mourners.

"If these elegies are not quite contemporaneous with the scenes they describe so graphically they cannot have originated much later; for they are like the low wailings with which the storm sinks to rest, reminding us how recently the thunder was rolling and the besom of destruction sweeping over the land."—Exp. B.

b "The darkness or solitude of the night doth naturally promote melancholy reflections."—Lowth.

c Comp. 2 Ki. xxiv. 2.

d "Image from robbers, who, in the E., intercept travellers at the narrow passes in hily regions."—Fausset.

"It is the weeping cloud that blesses the earth."—Barlow.

e For the joy of these journeys comp. the Psalms of Degrees, cxx.—cxxxiii.

f Ex. xv. 20; Ps. lxviii. 25; Je. xxxi. 13.

g De. xxviii. 14.

h "In ancient sculptures such mournful processions of women and tender children are often engraved."—Spk. Com.

"The sorrows which the soul endures, not self-inflicted, are but hooded joys that when she touches the white strand of heaven, they cluster round her and slip off their robes, and laugh

tian grace, the hope which presses forward to a better future.—Adeney.

7—9. (7) **remembered,** better, remembers. In her afflicted state she thinks over the past, with the bitterness of regret.[a] **miseries,** Heb. "compulsory wanderings," "persecutions." **when,** better, "after which." **enemy,** R. V. "adversary." **sabbaths,** R. V. "desolations;" Heb. "ceasings." (8) **removed,** or she is as a thing which men remove from their sight. She is become an abomination. **sigheth,** "over the infamy of her deeds thus brought to open shame." **backward,** as if she would hide herself. (9) **skirts,** wh. were as if rolled in the mire.[b] **last end,** comp. De. xxxii. 29. **down wonderfully,** Is. xlvii. 1; Je. xlviii. 18.

The Terrible Havoc of Sin.—I. In its revolting defilement. II. In sinking the soul to a state of abject degradation. Sin dishonors the soul. 1. In the estimation of others; 2. In its own estimation. III. In rendering the soul reckless as to consequences. IV. In its desecration of sacred things. V. In reducing a people to want.—Hom. Com.

Love in Sorrow.—Always through the darkest part of every life there runs, though we may sometimes fail to see it, the golden thread of love, so that even the worst man on earth is not wholly cut off from God, since He will, by some means or other, eternally try to draw him out of death into life. We are astounded now and then to read that some cold-blooded murderer, some man guilty of a hideous crime, will ask in his last moments to see a child who loved him devotedly, and whom he also loved. We are astonished just because we do not understand the untiring heart of the Almighty Father, who in His goodness often gives to the vilest sinner the love of a pure-hearted woman or child. So true is the beautiful old Latin saying, Mergere nos patitur, sed non submergere Christus—Christ lets us sink, may be, but not drown.—Edna Lyall.

10, 11. (10) **pleasant things,** prob. with special reference to the sacred vessels of the temple.[c] **not enter,** De. xxiii. 3. (11) **All her people,** ref. to the sufferings of the survivors of the destruction of Jerusalem. **pleasant things,** here, their jewels and treasures. **relieve the soul,** or "cause the breath to return;" i.e. refresh a fainting person with food. **vile,** i.e. treated as vile.

The Horrors of Famine.—The besieged city of Leyden was at its last gasp. Bread, malt-cake, horse-flesh, had entirely disappeared; dogs, cats, rats, and other vermin were esteemed luxuries. A small number of cows, kept as long as possible for their milk, still remained; but a few were killed from day to day, and distributed in minute proportions, hardly sufficient to support life among the famishing population. Starving wretches swarmed daily around the shambles where these cattle were slaughtered, contending for any morsel which might fall, and eagerly lapping the blood as it ran along the pavement, while the hides, chopped and boiled, were greedily devoured. Women and children all day long were seen searching gutters and dunghills for morsels of food which they disputed fiercely with the famishing dogs. The green leaves were stripped from the trees, every living herb was converted into human food, but these expedients could not avert starvation. The daily mortality was frightful—infants starved to death on the maternal breasts which famine had parched and withered, mothers dropped dead in the streets with their dead children in their arms. A disorder called the plague, naturally engendered of hardship and famine, now came, as if in kindness, to abridge the agony of the people. The pestilence stalked at noonday through the city, and the doomed inhabitants fell like grass beneath its scythe. From six to eight thousand human beings sank before this scourge alone; yet the people resolutely held out, women and men mutually encouraging each other to resist the entrance of their foreign foe—an evil more horrible than pest or famine.—Motley's "Dutch Republic."

12—14. (12) **nothing . . by,**[a] as Zion sits in her desolateness and sorrow, she appeals to all who pass by to pity her woes. "As if the Prophet had said, Let any indifferent person judge, whether any calamity is like to mine."—Lowth. (13) **From above,** i.e. fr. heaven. When we come to the evolution of history we are introduced to a whole world of moral forces that are not at work in the material universe.—Exp. B. **fire,** or **inflammation. net,** image taken from hunting wild beasts. **turned me**

out angels in the world of light."—J. Stanyan Bigg.

a "The bitterest ingredient in the cup of adversity is the remembrance of lost possessions and enjoyments."—Henderson.

b "None could stain our glory if we did not stain it ourselves."—Mat. Henry.

"We are not worst at once. The course of evil begins so slowly and from such slight source, an infant's hand might stem its breach with clay; but let the stream get deeper, and philosophy shall strive in vain to turn the headlong current."

c 2 Chr. xxxvi. 10.

"What man should learn is, to reject all that is useless in remembrance, and to retain with cheerfulness all that can profit and amend. Forget not thy sins, that thou mayest sorrow and repent; remember death, that thou mayest sin no more; remember the judgment of God, that thou mayest justly fear; and never forget His mercy, that thou mayest never be led to despair."—Petrarch.

a "This sorrowful exclamation may, in a secondary and spiritual sense, be regarded as coming from the lips of Christ on the cross, bewailing the sins and miseries of the world wh. caused Him that bitter anguish, of which alone it could be properly said, that 'no sorrow was like unto His sorrow.'"
—Wordsworth.

back, to drive me into the nets. (14) **yoke,** an agricultural figure. **his hand,** as if He were the ploughman, who fastened firmly on the yoke. **wreathed,** i.e. the cords fastening the yoke are knotted together. **strength to fall,** R. V. "to fail." **from . . up,** R. V. "against whom . . . stand." This weakness is largely moral. "There is nothing so wretchedly depressing as the consciousness of guilt."

The Uses of Suffering.—

Though long days did Anguish,
And sad nights did Pain
Forge my shield, Endurance,
Bright and free from stain.

Doubt in misty caverns,
'Mid dark horrors sought,
Till my peerless jewel,
Faith, to me she brought.

Sorrow that I wearied
Should remain so long,
Wreathed my starry glory,
The bright crown of song.

Strife, that racked my spirit
Without hope or rest,
Left the blooming flower,
Patience, in my breast."—Proctor.

"There is a bondage which is worse to bear than his who breathes, by roof and floor and wall pent in, a tyrant's solitary thrall: 'Tis his who walks about in the open air, one of a nation who henceforth must wear their fetters in their souls."
—Wordsworth.

"Let never day nor night unhallow'd pass, but still remember what the Lord hath done."
—Shakespeare.

"Great abundance of riches cannot of any man be both gathered and kept without sin."—Erasmus.

15—17. (15) **trodden, etc.,**[a] R. V. "set at nought." **assembly,** of armies; of enemies. An ironical use of the term to signify that Jehovah summons the Chaldæans to destroy the Jews as if to a religious festival. **young men,** who are the strength and hope of a nation. **as . . winepress,** expressive of the indignation and judgment of God. Is. lxiii. 3. (16) **mine eye,** etc., Je. xiii. 17; xiv. 17; La. ii. 18. This is the plaintive lamentation of Zion, the widow, as she sits solitary. **relieve,** or revive. (17) **spreadeth . . hands,** in usual attitude of prayer, but of prayer under pressure of great distress.[b] **that . . him,** R. V. "that they that are round about him . . . adversaries." The last clause of the vs. represents Jerusalem as an object of contempt.

Discipline of Sorrow.—Sorrow is the noblest of all discipline. Our nature shrinks from it, but it is not the less for the greatness of our nature. It is a scourge, but there is healing in its stripes. It is a chalice, and the drink is bitter, but strength proceeds from the bitterness. It is a crown of thorns, but it becomes a wreath of light on the brow which it has lacerated. It is a cross on which the spirit groans, but every Calvary has an Olivet. To every place of crucifixion there is likewise a place of ascension. The sun that was shrouded is unveiled, and heaven opens with hopes eternal to the soul, which was nigh unto despair.—H. Giles.

[a] "They fell not on the battle-field but in the heart of the city."—Calvin.

[b] Ex. ix. 29, 33; Je. iv. 31.

"The most terrible trait in these pictures, one that is common to all of them, is the Divine origin of the troubles. 'It was God who sent fire into the bones, spread the net, made the sufferer desolate and faint.'" —Exp. B.

18—20. (18) **righteous,** Da. ix. 7, 14. **commandment,** lit. mouth, i.e. message by His prophets. This is the expression of penitence. **all people,** R. V. "all ye peoples." (19) **lovers,** vs. 2. **elders . . city,** i.e. died of famine, while vainly seeking for food. (20) **bowels,** etc., seat of the emotions. **troubled,** lit. "are red, inflamed" with sorrow. Is. xvi. 11; Je. xlviii. 36. **turned,** or violently agitated. **as death,** "pale pining forms, slowly wasting with hunger, and presenting the very image and appearance of death."—Spk. Com.

False Remedy for Sorrows.—You that in your sorrows give yourselves to mirth and pastime, and merry meetings, thinking thereby to drive them away, you do rather increase and augment them. Just like the pelican, of whom it is reported that, being naturally afraid of fire, the shepherds are wont to carry some coals and lay them by her nest, and the poor silly creature keeps fluttering with her wings, thinking thereby to extinguish and put them out, but does but inflame and kindle them; and by this means the fire burns both her nest and self too. So, for us to go to worldly joys and pastimes to quench the sorrows and

"The forms of expression used in this vs. are strongly indicative of that violently excited state of the intestines which is occasioned by excessive grief. The whole verse is the most affecting imaginable." — Henderson.

"In this widening outlook of the poet one sees a sign of the softening and enlarging effects of trouble."

troubles of our minds, is the ready way rather to increase than remove them.—Christopher Love.

21, 22. (21) **called,** or proclaimed. The day of judgments on the Babylonians;[c] the day of the capture of Babylon. (22) **do . . me,** I have had my punishment; do thou proceed to inflict upon the human agents of thy wrath their share. "The vengeance here sought for cannot be brought into line with Christian principles; but the poet had never heard the Sermon on the Mount. It would not have occurred to him that the spirit of revenge was not right, any more than it occurred to the writers of maledictory Psalms."—Exp. B.

The Day that will Right all Wrongs (vs. 21).—In that day—1. God shall no longer be shut out of His own world; 2. Christ shall no longer be denied and blasphemed; 3. Evil shall no longer prevail; 4. Error shall give place to truth; 5. The saints shall no longer be maligned.—H. Bonar.

Comfort in Sorrow.—I say there is comfort, real and deep, in thinking that the path of sorrow we tread has been beaten smooth and wide by the feet of the best that ever trod this world; that our blessed Saviour was a Man of Sorrows; and that the best of His Church have been suffered to journey by no other path than that their Master went. It is not alone that the mourner travels through this vale of tears: Apostles and Prophets are of the company; saints and martyrs go wtih him; and the sorrowful face of the Great Redeemer, though sorrowful now no more, remains for ever with the old look of brotherly sympathy to His servants' eyes and hearts. Nothing hath come to us, nothing will come to us, but has been shared by better men. Search out the human being suffering the sharpest sorrow, and we can match it in the best of the Church of God.—Boyd.

c Je. l. 1, 2, etc.

"For his was not that open, artless soul, that feels relief by bidding sorrow flow; nor sought he friend to counsel or condole, whate'er his grief mote be, which he could not control."—Byron.

"When God our Comforter hides the light of His countenance the night is most dark. Yet the darkness is not always perceived, or its cause recognised. Then to miss the consolations of God consciously, with pain, is the first step towards recovering them."—Adeney.

CHAPTER THE SECOND.

1—4. (1) **with a cloud,** a dark threatening thunder-cloud.[a] **in his anger,** "if God is tormenting His people it must be because He is their enemy—so the sad-hearted patriot reasons. The course of Providence does not shape itself to him as a merciful chastisement, as a veiled blessing; its motive seems to be distinctly unfriendly."—Adeney. **beauty of Israel,** Solomon's temple. The word "Israel" shows that the elegist recognizes the unity of the Jewish race, wh. civil war has not destroyed. **footstool,** i.e. the Mercy-Seat over the ark.[b] This was regarded as the very centre of the Divine presence. (2) **habitations,** homesteads, with pastures. If God does not spare the holiest by reason of its sacredness: neither does He spare the lowliest by reason of its obscurity. **strongholds,** fortified towns. **polluted,** R. V. "profaned;" made the sacred land common or unclean, free to the invader. (3) **horn,** the symbol of power. God took away all power of defence. **drawn . . enemy,** God no longer defends his people. **burned against,** R. V. "burned up." (4) **pleasant to the eye,** all the chiefest in worth and dignity. **tabernacle,** R. V. "tent," i.e. habitation, city.

The Lord as an Enemy.—The Lord may become to us as an enemy. We must not suppose the relations of God to those who forsake him to be purely negative. He cannot simply leave them to their own devices. He is a King who must needs maintain order and restrain and punish rebellion, a Judge who cannot permit law to be trampled underfoot with impunity, a Father who cannot abandon his children, but must chastise them in their wrong-doing just because he is so closely related to them. Let it be well understood, then, that, in opposing ourselves to God, we run counter to a power, a will, an active authority. We provoke the anger of God. We do not simply strike ourselves against the stone, we cause the stone to fall upon us and grind us to powder.—Pul. Com.

5—8. (5) **swallowed,** comp. Jer.'s likening Nebuchadnezzar to a lion. **increased,** or heaped it up. (6) **a garden,** i.e. as easily as a besieging army destroys a fruit orchard wh. lies unprotected beyond the city wall. **despised . . priest,** i.e. shown no regard for even the most honorable offices. He made all to share in His judgments.[c] (7) **cast off,** comp. Ps. lxxxix. 38, 39. This casting off of God's altar and abhorrence of the

a "The Lord hath poured out His fury upon Zion, as in a tempest, and has dashed down her beauty as with lightning, and has not spared the ark of His sanctuary."—Wordsworth.

b 1 Chr. xxviii. 2; Ps. lxxx. 1., xcix. 1, 5, cxxxii. 8.

"God keeps his thunder for his friends as certainly as for his enemies, if they be unfaithful to the covenant which unites them; nay, would it not be more correct to say that a more ter le thunder is reserved for those who, knowing the right, yet pursue the wrong."—Parker.

c "With the destruction of the city the royal authority fell; with the ruined temple and the cessation of the festivals the functions of the priest ceased."—Spk. Com.

Temple where mercy was to be expected showed plainly the hopelessness of the case. **made a noise,** their triumphant shouting on getting possession of the temple. (8) **stretched . . line,** the destruction is carried out with the same exactness as a builder exercises in constructing a building. Is. xxxiv. 11.

9—12. (9) **sunk,** covered up with ruins and rubbish. **bars,** or defences. **among the Gentiles,** carried away captive. **law is no more,** R. V. "where the law is not;" i.e. the exiles were enduring hardship in a land wh. did not observe the Torah of the Jews. **prophets . . vision,** with the destruction of the government, the voice of prophecy became silent. (10) **elders,** setting the example of extreme grief. **virgins,** "these young girls are the choristers whose clear, sweet voices used to ring out in strains of joy at every festival. Now both the grave utterances of magistrates and the blithe singing of maidens are hushed into one gloomy silence." (11) **liver . . earth,** the sight of the suffering among the little children aroused strong emotion. **swoon,** or faint.[a] (12) **to their mothers,** who could give them nothing. **as the wounded,** dying a lingering, miserable death.

Treatment of Sorrows and Pleasure.—That which the French proverb hath of sickness, is true of all evils, that they come on horseback, and go away on foot; we have often seen a sudden fall, or one meal's surfeit hath stuck by many to their graves; whereas pleasures come like oxen, slow and heavily, and go away like post-horses, upon the spur. Sorrows, because they are lingering guests, I will entertain but moderately; knowing that the more they are made of, the longer they will continue: and for pleasures, because they stay not, and do but call to drink at my door, I will use them as passengers with slight respect. He is his own best friend, that makes least of both of them.—Bishop Hall.

13—16. (13) **take to witness,**[b] or, What prophetic testimony can I give thee? The Prophet had no consoling or comforting message to deliver. **equal to thee,** what instance of national calamity can compare with thine? **breach . . sea,** measureless, like the sea. (14) **foolish things,** delusions, Jer. xxiii. 26.[c] **discovered,** or declared to thee; not sought to bring thee to a true sense of thy sins. **turn . . captivity,** R. V. "bring again, etc."; i.e. by producing in thee repentance. **false burdens,** or prophetic messages. **causes,** false reasons to account for your banishment.[d] (15) **clap their hands,** Job. xxvii. 23, xxxiv. 37. **wag . . head,** in token of joy or contempt. 2 Ki. xix. 21; Ps. xliv. 14. **perfection of beauty,** Ps. xlviii. 2. (16) **opened . . mouth,** as wild beasts.

Indelible Impressions.—The rapidity with which ideas grow old in our memories is in a direct ratio to the squares of their importance. Their apparent age runs up miraculously, like the value of diamonds, as they increase in magnitude. A great calamity, for instance, is as old as the trilobites an hour after it has happened. It stains backward through all the leaves we have turned over in the book of life before its blot of tears or of blood is dry on the page we are turning. Did you ever happen to see that most soft-spoken and velvet-handed steam-engine at the Mint? The smooth piston slides backwards and forwards as a lady might slip her delicate finger in and out of a ring. The engine lays one of its fingers calmly, but firmly, upon a bit of metal; it is a coin now, and will remember that touch, and tell a new race about it, when the date upon it is crusted over with twenty centuries. So it is that a great, silent-moving misery puts a new stamp on us in an hour or a moment—as sharp an impression as if it had taken half a lifetime to engrave it.—Holmes.

17—19. (17) **devised,** purposed, and previously intimated.[a] The elegist does not lose sight of the fact that behind the mockery and hatred of these enemies, is the real Power wh. has devised these miseries. (18) **wall,** appealing to the very wall, which was broken down, to join in weeping over the sorrows of the city.[b] **river,** or torrent. **apple,** i.e. the pupil, comp. Ps. xvii. 8. (19) **cry out,** in prayer. **beginning . . watches,** i.e. of each watch; cry all the night through. **young children,** nothing could be more pitiable than to see these dying of hunger. **top . . street,** at every street corner. Is. li. 20.

Ancient Wall.—Walls can not only be beautiful and even sublime, as Mr. Ruskin has shewn in his Stones of Venice; they may also wreathe

"Titus had the trees cleared from the Mount of Olives, so that one of the first incidents in the Roman siege of Jerusalem must have been the destruction of the Garden of Gethsemane." —Adeney.

a "The scene here depicted is presented in the most touching colors. The liver, denoting the bile, wh. is formed on the inferior surface of the liver, is copiously discharged when the passions are violently agitated." — Henderson.

In prosperity prepare for a change; in adversity hope for one.

"Law is to a nation what air is to the lungs, the unconscious source of life: without it the national life becomes anarchy and death."

b "What can I bring forward as a witness or instance, to prove that others have sustained as grievous ills as thou? I cannot console thee as mourners are often consoled by showing that thy lot is only what others too suffer." —Fausset.

c Comp. Je. ii. 8, v. 31, xiv. 14, xxiii. 16.

d "The false prophets, in their attempts to account for the captivity, invented any cause but the true one, the apostasy of the Jews." — Henderson.

a Lev. xxvi. 14—39; De. xxviii. 15—68.

b For the bold figure comp. Is. xiv. 31; Je. xxii. 29; Hab. ii. 11; Lu. xix. 40.

their severe outlines in a multitude of thrilling associations. This is especially so when, as in the present instance, it is the wall of a city that we are contemplating. Not a new piece of builder's work, neat and clean and bald, bare of all associations, as meaningless as in too many cases it is ugly, but an old wall, worn by the passing to and fro of generations that have turned to dust long years ago, bearing the bruises of war on its battered face, crumbling to powder, or perhaps half buried in weeds—such a wall is eloquent in its wealth of associations, and there is pathos in the thought of its mere age when this is considered in relation to the many men and women and children who have rested beneath its shadow at noon, or sheltered themselves behind its solid masonry amid the terrors of war. The walls that encircle the ancient English city of Chester and keep alive memories of mediæval life, the bits of the old London wall that are left standing among the warehouses and offices of the busy mart of modern commerce, suggest to us multitudinous reflections. But the walls of Jerusalem surpass them all in the pathos of the memories that cling to their old grey stones. It does not require a great stretch of imagination to picture these walls as once glowing and throbbing with an intense life, and now dreaming over the unfathomable depths of age-long memories.—Exp. B.

20—22. (20) **to whom,** even to Thine own chosen and covenant people.[c] **fruit,** i. e. their own children. **span long,** R. V., "that are dandled in the hands."[d] (21) **young . . old,** the slaughter was indiscriminate; a mere massacre of the population. (22) **solemn day,** or feast-day. Terrors come crowding round Zion, as people used to do at her festivals. The phrase, Magor-missabib, fear on every side, is found Je. vi. 25. **swaddled,** R. V., "dandled."

Light Beyond.—A traveler in Madeira set off one morning to climb the summit of a lofty mountain to gaze upon the distant scene and enjoy the balmy air. He had a guide, and they had with difficulty ascended some two thousand feet, when a thick mist was seen descending upon them, obscuring the heavens. The traveler thought there was no hope left but to retrace their steps or be lost. But as the cloud came nearer and darkness enveloped them, the guide stepped on before, penetrating the mist, calling out every now and then, "Press on, master, press on; there's light beyond!" They did press on, and in a few minutes, emerging from the thick mist, found themselves gazing upon a scene of transcendent beauty. Above, the sky was bright and cloudless; below, the almost level cloud through which they had passed was silvered with the rays of the sun, like a field of untrodden snow. In the darkest experiences, if we will but listen, we may hear the voice of our Divine Guide exclaiming, "Press on, press on; there is light ahead."—Barlow.

"Violent fires soon burn out themselves." —Shakespeare. "The misfortune is, that, when man has found honey, he enters upon the feast with an appetite so voracious, that he usually destroys his own delight by excess and satiety."—Knox. "Every inordinate cup is unblest, and the ingredient is a devil." —Shakespeare. "Too much is stark nought." Welsh. "One may be surfeited with eating tarts." "Gentleness does more than violence."—French. "Soon fire, soon ashes." —Dutch.

c "This is a continuation of the pathetic appeal from the wall which surrounded Jerusalem, and which now lay in ruins on the ground."—Wordsworth.

d Comp. Le. xxvi. 29; De. xxviii. 56, 57; Je. xix. 9.

"A mystery lies upon the whole scheme of life. Its best explanation I find is Christ. My hope is in His cross." —Parker. "A bow overbent will weaken." "Extremes meet." "Too far east is west." "A baited cat may grow as fierce as a lion." —English.

CHAPTER THE THIRD.

1—6. (1) **seen affliction,** in the sense of suffering or experiencing it Reference is rather to the suffering of the people, in the siege and destruction of Jerusalem, wh. he had personally shared. **rod,** etc., Babylon was God's instrument of chastisement; Pr. xxii. 8. (2) **brought,** etc., R. V., "caused me to walk in." **darkness,** the fig. for calamities.[a] (3) **turneth his hand,** in order to give a repetition of strokes; R. V., "turneth his hand again and again all the day." (4) **made old,** worn out as with constant rubbing and chafing. **broken my bones,** Is. xxxviii. 13.[b] (5) **builded,** as besiegers build mounds. **gall,** or bitterness. **travel,** "travail," "weariness." (6) **set me,** R. V., "made me to dwell." **dark places,** the victim of Divine wrath is a captive languishing in a dungeon, which is as dark as the abodes of the dead, as the dwellings of those who have been long dead. The horror of this metaphor is intensified by the idea of the antiquity of Hades."—Exp. B. **dead of old,** R. V., "have been long dead."

Unequalled Grief.—Every man feels, and not strangely, that there never were such experiences of life as his own. No joy was ever like our joy, no sorrow ever like our sorrow. Indeed, there is a kind of indignation excited in us when one likens our grief to his own. The soul is jealous of its experiences, and does not like pride to be humbled by

a Is. lix. 9; Je. xiii. 16; Am. v. 20.

b "The anguish I feel in my mind is as painful as if all my bones were broken."—Lowth.

"Very prob. the Prophet draws much of what he says from his own experience, but the whole that he sets forth is more than his own personality; it is the type and pattern of every individual." —Ewald.

"The excesses of our youth are drafts upon our old age, payable with interest, about thirty years after date."—Colton.

"The application of Ch. iii. to the Man of Sorrows is more than a case of literary illustration; for the idea of representative suffering which here emerges, and which becomes more definite in the picture of the servant of Jehovah in Isa. liii., only finds its full realization and perfection in Jesus Christ."

"Desperate tides of the whole world's anguish forced through the channel of a single heart."—Exp. B.

[a] "He conceives of himself as a traveller whose way is blocked up by a solid wall, and who, being compelled to turn aside into the devious pathways of the forest, is exposed to the rapacity of wild beasts."—Henderson.

"Small causes are sufficient to make a man uneasy, when great ones are not in the way; for want of a block, he will stumble at a straw.'—Swift.

[b] "Keeping up the metaphor of vs. 15, Jer. complains that his bread was so filled with grit that in eating it his teeth were broken."—Spk. Com.

"What would the nightingale care if the toad despised her singing? She would still sing on, and leave the cold toad to his dank shadows. And what care I for the sneers of men who grovel upon earth? I will still sing on

the thought that they are common. For though we know that the world groans and travails in pain, and has done so for ages, yet a groan heard by our ear is a very different thing from a groan uttered by our mouth. The sorrows of other men seem to us like clouds of rain that empty themselves in the distance, and whose long-traveling thunder comes to us mellowed and subdued; but our own troubles are like a storm bursting right overhead and sending down its bolts upon us with direct plunge.—Beecher.——Pitt Lying in Solitude.—Pitt died at a solitary house on Wimbledon Common. Not far off, by the roadside, stood a small country inn, where the various parties interested in the great statesman's life were accustomed to apply for information, and leave their horses and carriages. On the morning of the 23rd of January, 1806, an individual having called at the inn, and not being able to obtain a satisfactory reply to his inquiries, he proceeded to the house of Pitt. He knocked, but no servant appeared—he opened the door and entered—he found no one in attendance—he proceeded from rom to room, and at length entered the sick chamber, where, on a bed, in silence and in perfect solitude, he found to his unspeakable surprise, the dead body of that great statesman who had so lately wielded the power of England, and influenced, if he did not control, the destinies of the world. We doubt whether any much more awful example of the lot of mortality has even been witnessed.—Cheever.

7—12. (7) **hedged,** Job iii. 23, xix. 8; Ho. ii. 6. **chain,** lit. chain of brass. (8) **shutteth out,** as if the prisoner were shut down so deep in his dungeon that his prayers cannot reach his jailer; Job xxx. 20; Ps. xxii. 2. (9) **inclosed,** R. V., "fenced up." **paths crooked,** compelling me to turn aside from the ordinary road.[a] (10) **was,** R. V., "is." **bear . . lion,** the peril of those who take by-paths and forest-paths. (11) **turned,** etc., "caused me to go astray." **pulled . . pieces,** as by these wild beasts. **desolate,** i. e. stunned, stupefied. (12) **me as a mark,** Job vii. 20. Made me the mark or object of His indignation.

The Sinner's Hedges (vs. 7).—I. There is the hedge of moral sense. II. Of social life. 1. Of social relationship; 2. Of social sentiment. III. Of personal incapacity. 1. The lack of physical health; 2. The lack of intellectual ability; 3. The lack of secular means.—Dr. Thomas.

The Use of Trials.—A friend was asked concerning a beautiful horse feeding on the pasture with a clog on his foot, "Why do you clog such a noble animal?" The reply was, "I would a great deal sooner clog him than lose him; he is given to leap hedges." That is why God clogs his people. He would rather clog them than lose them, for if He did not, they would leap and be gone.—Spurgeon.

13—16. (13) **arrows . . quiver,** lit. "sons of his quiver;" "nay, arrow after arrow has already been let fly, and the dreadful Huntsman, too skilful ever to miss His mark, has been shooting 'the sons of His quiver' into the very vitals of the object of his pursuit."—Adeney. **veins,** seat of the affections, the vitals. (14) **derision,** Je. xx. 7. **their song,** a popular by-word, a butt of ridicule; Job xxx. 9. (15) **bitterness,** better pl., bitternesses. **wormwood,** De. xxix. 18. (16) **broken my teeth,** Pr. xx. 17.[b] **covered me,** better, "pressed me down into ashes;" fig. for extreme humiliation wh. the enemies forced upon Jerusalem.

Perfect Through Suffering.—The people of Verona, when they saw Dante in the streets, used to say, "See, there is the man that was in hell!" Ah, yes! he had been in hell—in hell enough, in long severe sorrow and struggle, as the like of him is pretty sure to have been. Commedias that come out divine are not accomplished otherwise. Thought, true labor of any kind, highest virtue itself, is it not the daughter of pain? Born as out of the black whirlwind; true effort, in fact, as of a captive struggling to free himself: that is thought. In all ways we are to become perfect through suffering.—Carlyle.

17—21. (17) **removed,** R. V. marg., "cast off." **peace,** prosperity. Ps. lxxxviii. 14. **prosperity,** or good. (18) **said,** or thought in my heart. **strength . . Lord,** the exceeding heaviness of the immediate misery keeps the hope of the light of a new day quite out of sight; Is. xl. 27. (19) **Remembering,** better rend., remember, an invocation to God. **misery,** or homelessness. (20) **humbled,** R. V., "bowed down;" sinks down as in a swoon. (21) **This,** the assurance of the faithfulness and mercy of God, wh. will not overlook or leave unrewarded true humility and contrition.

The Importance of Humility.—Dr. Franklin once received a very useful lesson from the excellent Dr. Cotton Mather, which he thus relates in a letter to his son:—"The last time I saw your father was in 1724. On taking my leave, he showed me a shorter way out of the house by a narrow passage, which was crossed by a beam overhead. We were still talking, as I withdrew, he accompanying me behind, and I turning towards him, when he said hastily, 'Stoop, stoop!' I did not understand him till I felt my head hit against the beam. He was a man who never missed an opportunity of giving instruction; and upon this he said to me, 'You are young, and have the world before you; learn to stoop as you go through it and you will miss many hard thumps.' This advice, thus beat into my head, has frequently been of use to me; and I often think upon it when I see pride mortified and misfortunes brought upon people by their carrying their heads too high."—Laconics.

22—25. (22) **we .. consumed,**[a] Adeney prefers the trans. of the Targum: "The Lord's mercies, verily they cease not." This restores balance to the triplet wh. designs to teach the amazing persistence of God's goodness. **compassions,** Ps. lxxxvi. 15. (24) **portion,** Ps. xvi. 5, lxxiii. 26, cxix. 57; Je. x. 16. (25) **wait for Him,** and so wait His time.

God's Unceasing Mercies.—I. God's mercies never cease. 1. We have no claim upon their continuance; 2. We have done much to provoke the cessation of them; (1) By ungratefully accepting them; (2) By complainingly ignoring them; (3) By sinfully abusing them; 3. They sometimes appear to cease; 4. They change their form. Even wrath is mercy in disguise. II. God's mercies are constantly renewed. III. The ceaselessness of God's mercy is a proof of his faithfulness.—Pul. Com.

Jeremiah and the Duke, a Contrast.—Imagine the Prophet in his solitariness. All around him is widespread desolation: the once gorgeous palace is in ruins; the temple, adorned with gold and silver, and the richest tapestry, no longer graces the heights of Moriah, but is reduced to ashes; the favored people are in exile; the Prophet is sorrowful and sad; yet, while the tear still glistens in his eye, and his bosom heaves with intense emotion, he exclaims, "The Lord is my portion, saith my soul; therefore will I hope." How different is it with the man whose portion is earthly! It is said of a certain duke that he has a passion for costly diamonds; and what is the consequence? His house resembles a castle rather than a mansion, and is surrounded with a lofty wall, over which no one can climb without giving alarm. His treasure is kept in a safe, let in the wall of his bedroom, so that it cannot be reached without first waking or murdering the owner; the safe is so constructed that it cannot be forced without discharging four guns, and setting an alarm-bell a-ringing in every room. His bedroom, like a prisoner's cell, has but one small window, and the bolt and lock of the massive door are of the stoutest iron. In addition to these precautions, a case, containing twelve loaded revolvers, stands by the side of his bed. Might we not inscribe over it, "Diamonds are my portion; therefore I do not fear?"—R. Gray.

26—30. (26) **good,** "the repetition of the word at the beginning of this and the connected verses heightens the effect." **quietly wait,** or wait in silence;[a] abstaining from all complaining. **salvation,** including all God's gracious ways of helping. (27) **yoke,** the yoke may stand for one of three things—for instruction, for labor, or for trouble. Divine disciplinary dealings. **youth,** early in life, when all lessons are more easily learned. (28) **keepeth silence,** comp. "quietly wait," of vs. 27; R. V., "Let him sit alone," etc.; vs. 29, "Let him put," etc.; vs. 30, "Let him give," etc. **borne it,** R. V., "laid it." (29) **mouth .. dust,** the attitude of deep humiliation.[b] (30) **cheek, etc.,** "the connection is, if suffering is really attended with benefit to the sufferer, then let him submit readily to it." —Cam. B. Is. i. 6; Mat. v. 39.

Wisdom Sought Early.—The human soul in youth is not a machine of which you can polish the cogs with any kelp or brick-dust near at hand, and, having got it into working order, and good, empty, and oiled serviceableness, start your immortal locomotive at twenty-five years old or thirty, express from the Strait Gate on the Narrow Road. The whole period of youth is one essentially of formation, edification, instruction

in the ear and bosom of God."—Beecher.

"No roses bloom upon my fading cheek, nor laughing graces wanton in my eyes; but haggard Grief, lean-looking, sallow Care, and pining Discontent—a rueful train—dwell on my brow, all hideous and forlorn."—Rowe.

"What a rich feast the canker grief has made; how has it suck'd the roses of thy cheeks! and drunk the liquid crystal of thy eyes!"—Sewell.

[a] Mal. iii. 6.

"Sometimes a light surprises the Christian while he sings: It is the Lord who rises with healing in His wings. When comforts are declining, He grants the soul, again, a season of clear shining, to cheer it after rain."

"In every distress, learn to wait with patience for the appointed time. Wait for it believing, wait for it praying, wait for it contending."

"Visiting a dying Christian woman, Dr. John Brown once said to her, 'What would you say, Janet, if, after God has done so much for you, He should let you drop into hell?' She calmly replied, 'E'en as He likes; but He'll lose more than I will.'"

[a] Ps. xxxvii. 7.

[b] Ps. cxix. 25.

The teacher is like the switchman, who holds the key to the switches on the railroad. If he does his duty faithfully, the train will reach its destination safely: if he neglects it, disaster and ruin

(I use the words with their weight in them), in taking of stores, establishment in vital habits, hopes, and faiths. There is not an hour of it but is trembling with destinies; not a moment of which, once past, the appointed work can ever be done again, or the neglected work struck on the cold iron.—Ruskin.

31—36. (31) **cast off,** He puts away in chastisement, but not in forsaking. Divine punishments are only temporary, hence the need of resignation. (32) **cause grief,** by His judgments. (33) **willingly,** lit. "from his heart."[c] (34) **crush,** etc., prob. referring to the excess of cruelty with which the Chaldæans had executed the Divine commisison. (35) **turn .. right,** so as to procure an unjust judgment. **most High,** here only a superior, a judge. The judges as representing God were called by His name; see Ex. xxi. 6.—Rev. Ver. (36) **approveth not,** or seeth not with approval.[d] The argument is: if God does not approve of these things in men, He cannot do them Himself, therefore mankind must wait patiently before the Lord.

Chastisement for a Season.—I. The fact that chastisement is only for a season. 1. Is no ground for reckless indifference. For (1) The wrath is terrible enough while it lasts; (2) It must endure as long as impenitent guilt is persisted in; (3) Sin that presumes on mercy is the most gross ingratitude. 2. Should be a consolation in trouble. 3. Is an encouragement to repentance. II. The reason why chastisement is only for a season. This is to be found in the character of God.—Pul. Com.

Suffering Preferred to Injustice.—While Athens was ruled by the thirty tyrants, Socrates was summoned to the senate-house and ordered to go with some other persons to seize one Leon, a man of rank and fortune, whom they determined to put out of the way that they might enjoy his estate. The commission Socrates flatly refused, and not satisfied therewith, added also his reason for such refusal. "I will never willingly," said he, "assist in an unjust act." Cherides sharply replied, "Dost thou think, Socrates, to talk always in this style and not to suffer?" "Far from it," answered he, "I expect to suffer a thousand ills, but none so great as to do unjustly."—Barlow.

37—41. Vss. 37—54. The order of thought in this group is, All events are absolutely in the hands of God. Thus evil comes from Him as well as good. But it is man's sin that procures for him the former; he therefore may not complain.—Cam. B. (37) **Who .. not?** Ps. xxxiii. 9. (38) **evil and good,** R. V., "cometh .. good?" not a statement of fact, but a question wh. must be ans. in the affirmative; Am. iii. 6. (39) **living,** the word is emphatic in the sentence. "As long as God spares a man's life, why does he murmur? The chastisement is really for his good; only let him use it aright, and he will be thankful for it in the end."—Spk. Com. (40) **try our ways,** our conduct, for in this we shall find the reason for our chastisement. **turn again,** or return.[a] (41) **heart .. hands,** the hands in the attitude of prayer; the heart with them, making the prayer both sincere and earnest.[b]

The Believer's Portion.—'Tis not a part and portion which can never be spent. You may live upon God: there is enough in Him for millions and millions and millions. God is better than heaven, better than grace, better than glory, better than things present, or things to come. The promises are like a rich ring of gold,—but this is the rare diamond in that ring; it is the crown, the top, excellency of all promises. His wisdom is the soul's for direction, His power for protection, His grace for its acceptation, His Spirit for its consolation, His creatures on earth to serve us, His angels to guard us, His ordinances to feed and strengthen us, His grace to adorn us, His riches to advance and crown us to eternity.—Benj. Keach.

42—45. (42) **We .. thou,** the pronouns are emphatic in the original. **not pardoned,** or overlooked our iniquity, but rather, has visited it upon us. (43) **covered .. anger,** i. e. covered Thy face in anger. **persecuted us,** R. V., "pursued us." (44) **covered .. cloud,** to hide Thy face from the observation of our distresses.[c] (45) **offscouring,** "the poet seems to be alluding to the exceptional severity with which the obstinate defenders of Jerusalem had been treated by their exasperated conquerors." 1 Cor. iv. 13.

A Delayed Answer to Prayer.—After Augustine had lost faith in

---

follow. A misplaced switch or a wrong signal may send hundreds into eternity unprepared.

c He. xii. 10.

d "As God takes no pleasure in oppressing the poor and helpless, so neither will He suffer any men to go unpunished that are guilty of such acts of injustice and cruelty, who never think that all the wrongs they do are committed in the sight of the supreme Judge of the world. —Lowth.

"O God! how thou breakest into families! Must not the disease be dangerous when a tender - hearted surgeon cuts deep into the flesh? How much more where God is the operator, who afflicteth not from His heart, nor grieveth the children of men.' —McCheyne.

a "The prep. in the Heb. is very forcible, implying, 'Let us go back, not halfway but the whole.'' — Nagelsbach.

b "The action of confession was not to be the mere outward extension of the hands towards God. Such outward expression, to be sincere, was to be accompanied with the inward feelings of the heart.''—Henderson.

"The greatest blessing to be sought for her was not liberty to return to the hills and cities of Palestine; it was permission and power to come back to God.''—Exp. B.

c "Our sins become the hiding cloud.''

"I have seen a father hold out at a distance from the child,

Manichæism, he found himself in the same situation as he was ten years before. There was the same longing after truth, but linked now with a feeling of desolation, a bitter sense of deception, and a large measure of scepticism. He was no longer at ease in Carthage, and resolved on a journey to Rome, where he ventured to hope for a more brilliant and profitable career as a rhetorician. His mother wished either to prevent his going, or to go with him. While she spent a night in the Church of the Martyr, praying and wrestling with God in tears to prevent the voyage, Augustine sailed for the coast of Italy, and his deceived mother found herself the next morning alone on the sea-shore. She had learned, however, the heavenly art of forgiving, and believing also where she could not see. In quiet resignation she returned to the city, and continued to pray for the salvation of her son. Though meaning well, she this time erred in her prayer, for the journey of Augustine was the means of his salvation. The denial of the prayer was, in fact, the answering of it. Instead of the husk, God granted rather the substance of her petition in the conversion of her son. "Therefore," says he, "hadst Thou, O God, regard to the aim and essence of her desires, and didst not do what she then prayed for, that Thou mightest do for me what she continually implored."—Schaff.

46—50. (46) **opened their mouths,** R. V., "their mouth wide;" **ch.** ii. 16. (47) **fear,** etc., cause or object of fear, Is. xxiv. 17; Je. xlviii. 43. **snare,** R. V., "pit." **desolation,** R. V., "devastation." (48) **Mine eye,** etc., Je. iv. 19. (49) **trickleth,** R. V., "poureth." **without .. intermission,** or because there is no intermission of my miseries. (50) **Till the Lord,** intimating that in his seeming hopelessness he yet held fast his hope in God.

The Treatment of Slanderers.—It is said that an eminent person of the present day has treasured up in a book all the fiercest attacks which have been made upon him, and without having answered one word either good or bad, keeps that book for the amusement of his friends. Better, perhaps, was the observation of another, "They cannot harm me by what they say of me. I am too near the Great White Throne for that." At any rate we can all imitate the forgiving spirit of good Archbishop Tillotson. Among his papers, at his death, was found a bundle of all the worst lampoons which had ever been written against him, with the pathetic memorandum, "May God forgive them; I am sure I do."—Farrar. ——The Power of Sympathy.—Happy is the man who has that in his soul which acts upon the dejected as April airs upon violet roots. Gifts from the hand are silver and gold; but the heart gives that which neither silver nor gold can buy. To be full of goodness, full of cheerfulness, full of sympathy, full of helpful hope, causes a man to carry blessings of which he is himself as unconscious as a lamp of its own shining. Such an one moves on human life as stars move on dark seas to bewildered mariners; as the sun wheels, bringing all the seasons with him from the south.—Beecher.

51—54. (51) **affecteth .. heart,** R. V., "soul," maketh my soul ache. **daughters,** the virgins of Jerusalem who had to suffer the horrors of Chaldæan lust and rapine. (52) **like a bird,** as hunters do a bird; tiring it down with long pursuit; ref. to the prophet himself, as persecuted by his countrymen. The other way of understanding it is of the Israelites generally in their hour of suffering, and specially of the godly, among whom the prophet in his sufferings would be a typical instance.—Cam. B. (53) **dungeon,** i. e. tried to destroy; Je. xxxvii. 16. **stone,** the princes did not cast stones at Jer. as he lay in the dungeon, but they placed a stone at its mouth to increase his suffering and secure him. (54) **Waters .. head,** a figurative expression of his great trouble. Comp. Ps. lxix. 2. **cut off,** Ps. lxxxviii. 5; Is. liii. 8. I am as good as dead.

An Etching of the Siege.—A graphic picture like this helps us to imagine the fearful accompaniments of the destruction of Jerusalem much better than any general summary. As we gaze at this one scene among the many miseries that followed the siege—the poet hunted out and run down, his capture and conveyance to the dungeon, apparently without a shadow of a trial, the danger of drowning and the misery of standing in the water that had gathered in a place so utterly unfit for human habitation—there rises before us a picture which cannot but impress our

a promised good. The child, as soon as he saw it, stretched out his hands to take it, but found that it was too far away for him to reach. He then came nearer, and stretched forth his hands with greater effort. Still the object was too far for his grasp. Again the child came nearer and made another mighty effort. The father seeing the child so much in earnest to seize the object, drew his hand toward the child, and smilingly allowed him to seize the promised blessing."—John Bate.

"Hide not thy tears; weep boldly, and be proud to give the flowing virtue manly way; 'tis nature's mark to know an honest heart by. Shame on those breasts of stone that can not melt in soft adoption of another's sorrow." — Aaron Hill.

"Remembrance is the only paradise out of which we cannot be driven away. Indeed, our first parents were not to be deprived of it."—Richter.

"Suffering is sweet when honor doth adorn it. Who slights revenge? not he that fears, but scorns it." — Buckingham.

"For sorrow is the messenger between the poet and men's bosoms. Genius can fill with unsympathizing gods the scene, but grief alone can teach us what is man."—Bulwer Lytton.

He who lays out most for Christ provides best for himself. He who serves not himself, but Christ, is most truly free.

He who belongs not to himself, but to Christ, possesses all things.

"Prayer is so mighty an instrument that no one ever thoroughly mastered all its keys. They sweep along the infinite scale of man's wants and God's goodness. —Hugh Miller.

As a wind musical instrument in the hands of the musician, so should Christians in prayer be in the hands of the Divine Spirit; they should present such prayers as He indites within them. The harmony, melody, sweetness, power, and effect of their prayers should be produced by the agency of the Spirit dwelling in them.

minds with the unutterable wretchedness of the sufferers from such a calamity as the siege of Jerusalem. Of course there must have been some special season for the exceptionally severe treatment of the poet. What this was we cannot tell. If the same patriotic spirit burned in his soul in the midst of the war as we now find at the time of later reflection, it would be most reasonable to conjecture that the ardent lover of his country had done or said something to irritate the enemy, and possibly that as he devoted his poetic gifts at a subsequent time to lamenting the overthrow of his city, he may have employed them with a more practical purpose among the battle scenes to write some inspiring martial ode in which we may be sure he would not have spared the ruthless invader.—Exp. B.

55—59. (55) **low dungeon,** R. V., "lowest dungeon." (56) **breathing,** or sighing. (57) **Thou drewest near,** in past time of trouble. (58) **hast pleaded,** as my Goël or avenger. (59) **judge .. cause,** at this present time also.

"Fear Not!"—I. We much need Divine encouragements to overcome fear. 1. In real danger; 2. In the threatening aspect of the future; 3. In the mystery of life; 4. In the fears of others; 5. In hours of weakness. II. We have many Divine encouragements to overcome fear. 1. In directly urging us not to fear; 2. In promises of help; 3. In the fatherly character of God; 4. In our personal relations with God. III. Divine assurances against fear should inspire our prayers for help in danger.—Pul. Com.

Prayer in Trouble.—Sinking times are praying times with the Lord's servants. Peter neglected prayer at starting upon his adventurous journey, but when he began to sink, his danger made him a suppliant, and his cry, though late, was not too late. In our hours of bodily pain and mental anguish we find ourselves as naturally driven to prayer as the wreck is driven upon the shore by the waves. The fox hies to his hole for protection, the bird flies to the wood for shelter, and even so the tried believer hastens to the mercy-seat for safety. Heaven's great harbor of refuge is All-prayer. Thousands of weather-beaten vessels have found a haven there, and the moment a storm comes on it is wise for us to make for it with all sail.—Spurgeon.

60—63. (60) **imaginations,** or devices.[a] The word carries the idea of plans formed by men in mere wilfulness. (62) **The lips,**[b] or the talk; the foolish and malicious speeches: supply, "thou hast heard." (63) **music,**[c] R. V., "song;" the subject of their merriment.

[a] Je. xi. 19, xviii. 18.

[b] Ps. xxii. 7.

[c] Ps. lxix. 12.

Treating Reproaches.—Pericles, as he was sitting before others in a meeting, a foul-mouthed fellow railed upon him all the day long; at night, when it was dark, and the meeting broke up, the fellow followed him and railed at him, even to his door, and he took no notice of what he said; but when he came home, this is all he said to him, "It is dark, I pray let my man light you home."—Jer. Burroughs.

64—66. (64) **Render,** etc., R. V., "Thou wilt render," etc. "Thou wilt give," etc. "Thou wilt persecute," etc. Comp. Ps. lxix. 22—28: the words are taken fr. Ps. xxviii. 4. (65) **sorrow of heart,** R. V., "hardness," or judicial blindness.[d] **curse,** we see here one of the worst effects of tyranny—the dark passion of revenge that it rouses in its victims. The fierce fires of Hebrew hatred for the oppressors of the much-suffering race here burst into a flame, and towards the end of this finest of elegies we read the dark imprecation, "Thy curse unto them!'" Exp. B. (66) **destroy,** etc., comp. Je. x. 11.. **heavens .. Lord,** Ps. viii. 3, cxv. 16.

[d] "Lit. a 'covering of the heart,' i. e. a mental disease, obstinacy, hardness, the worst calamity that can befall a human being."—Henderson.

When this patriotic poet thought of the desolated city and the authors of such atrocities, we cannot expect him to anticipate Christ's intercession for His enemies.

A Godly Life the Music of Society.—I. Like music, a godly life is—1. Harmonious. It is in harmony (1) With God; (2) With itself; (3) With the highest good of the race. 2. Cheerful. 3. Inspiring. 4. Calming. II. Are our lives morally musical?—The Lay Preacher.

Generosity Toward Enemies.—When Aristides, the Athenian general, sat to arbitrate a difference between two persons, one of them said, "This fellow accused thee at such a time." To whom Aristides answered, "I sit not to hear what he has done against me, but against thee." That was a noble reply of Philip the Good when urged by his courtiers to punish a prelate who had done him great injustice, he declined, saying, "It is a fine thing to have revenge in one's power; but it is a finer thing not to use it."—Barlow.

CHAPTER THE FOURTH.

1—4. (1) **gold .. dim,** gold is used metaphorically for the illustrious portion of the Jewish people.—Grotius. **stones .. sanctuary,** metaphorical, for the "noble sons of Zion;" ref. to the gems on the breastplate, or the stones of wh. the temple was built, is wide of the mark. **top .. street,** ch. ii. 19. (2) **earthen pitchers,** "they are regarded as of no more value than potter's work, though formerly they had been prized as the dainty art of a goldsmith." Je. xix. 10, 11. (3) **sea .. monsters,** R. V., "jackals." **ostriches,** Job xxxix. 13—17. (4) **cleaveth .. thirst,** bec. the mothers, in the famine time, have no milk.

Fine Gold Dimmed.—Fine gold is dimmed—I. When noble gifts of nature are put to base uses. II. When rare talents are wasted or abused. 1. When they are idly neglected; 2. When they are prostituted to base ends. III. When youth is ill spent. IV. When a Christian falls into sin. V. When the Church is corrupted.—Pul. Com.

5—8. (5) **delicately,** or daintily. "Faring sumptuously every day." **desolate,** i.e. there are none to wait on them, or provide for them. Such persons are the most helpless in famine times. **in scarlet,** prob. referring to the luxurious scarlet couches of the grand houses. **dunghills,** are content to lie on the dunghills to secure a little warmth.[a] (6) **For .. of,** R. V., "For the iniquity of .. than the sin of Sodom," i. e. the guilt rather than the punishment of Jerusalem is compared with that of Sodom. **is greater,**[b] bec. her knowledge and privilege were greater. **stayed upon,** R. V., "were laid upon;" i. e. no human hands were wearied in the work of destroying her. (7) **Nazarites,** R. V., "nobles," or separated ones; see Nu. vi. **purer .. milk,** ref. to the delicateness of their complexion in comp. with the bronzed appearance of the toilers. (8) **visage,** etc., these indicate the effects of prolonged famine.[c] **like a stick,** withered and dry.

God's Inexorable Law.—The punishment of Israel is greater than that of Sodom. But this is punishment; and the odious comparison would not be made unless the sin had been of the blackest dye. Thus in this elegy the calamities of Jerusalem are again traced back to the ill-doings of her people. The awful fate of the cities of the plain stands out in the ancient narrative as the exceptional punishment of exceptional wickedness. But now in the race for a first place in the history of doom Jerusalem has broken the record. Even Sodom has been eclipsed in the headlong course by the city once most favored by heaven. It seems well nigh impossible. What could be worse than total destruction by fire from heaven? The elegist considers that there are two points in the fate of Jerusalem that confer a gloomy pre-eminence in misery. The doom of Sodom was sudden, and man had no hand in it, but Jerusalem fell into the hands of man—a calamity which David judged to be worse than falling into the hands of God; and she had to endure a long, lingering agony.—Exp. B.

"With solid gold is contrasted the hollow pitcher, easily broken, and made of materials or no intrinsic value, but deriving its worth from mere human labor."—Spk. Com.

Dr. Shaw also says that, during the lonesome part of the night the ostriches often made a doleful and hideous noise, wh. would sometimes be like the roaring of a lion; at other times it would bear resemblance to the hoarser voices of other quadrupeds, particularly of the bull and the ox. I have often heard them groan, as if they were in the greatest agonies,—an action beautifully alluded to by the Prophet Micah (i 8), when it is said, 'I will make a . . mourning as the owls,' or rather, ostriches.

[a] Comp. Job xxiv. 8.

[b] "Sodom was not given up into the hands of an enemy that laid siege to it, nor condemned to the lingering destruction of famine."—Lowth

[c] Job xxx. 30.

9—12. (9) **better,** bec. at once put out of their misery. **pine away,** Heb. flow out; as if the famine struck them, and life slowly ebbed away.[a] (10) **hands .. children,** De. xxviii. 57; La. ii. 20. (11) **accomplished,** etc., by this expression we are recalled to the fact that this Divine visitation had been threatened. **devoured .. thereof,** a picture for complete destruction. (12) **not .. believed,** bec. the city seemed to be so well fortified.[b]

The Misery of the Conquered.

The wretched owner sees afar,
His all become the prey of war;
Bethinks him of his babes and wife,
Then smites his breast, and curses life!
Thy swains are famished on the rocks
Where once they fed their wanton flocks:
Thy ravished virgins shriek in vain;
Thy infants perish on the plain.
What boots it then, in every clime
Through the wide-spreading waste of time,
Thy martial glory, crown'd with praise,
Still shone with undiminished blaze?

[a] "Stricken through, or pierced through, is very expressive of the sharp pain occasioned by severe hunger." — Henderson.

[b] "Such was the natural strength of Jerusalem, and such the widespread belief that the God of the Jews was omnipotent, that the city was considered to be impregnable."
—Henderson.

"There is a sacredness in tears. They are not the mark of weakness, but of power. They speak more eloquently than ten thousand tongues. They are the messengers of overwhelming grief, of deep contrition, and of unspeakable love." — Washington Irving.

a Eze. xxii. 26, 28; Zep. iii. 4.

b Comp. Mat. xxiii. 31, 37; Ac. vii. 52.

"Sooner mayest thou trust thy pocket to a pickpocket than give loyal friendship to the man who boasts of eyes to which the heart never mounts in dew! Only when man weeps he should be alone; not because tears are weak, but they should be secret. Tears are akin to prayer—Pharisees parade prayers, impostors parade tears."—Bulwer.

"O may I join the choir invisible of those immortal dead who live again in minds made better by their presence." — George Eliot.

"Shed a tear of pity on their woes, which, as it drops, some soft-eyed angel bears, transformed to pearl, and in her bosom wears."—Sir W. Jones.

a Je. viii. 20, xxxvii. 4—10, xlvi. 17.

b "Towards the end of the siege the towers erected by the enemy would command the streets, and such spots would be avoided." — Spk. Com.

c Comp. Je. lii. 8, 9.

"Thales Milesius one of the wise men of Greece, being asked **what was the**

Thy towering spirit now is broke,
Thy neck is bended to the yoke.
. . . .
Yet, when the rage of battle ceased,
The victor's soul was not appeased.
The naked and forlorn must feel
Devouring flames, and murdering steel!
The pious mother, doomed to death,
Forsaken, wanders o'er the heath;
The bleak wind whistles round her head,
Her helpless orphans cry for bread;
Bereft of shelter, food and friend,
She views the shades of night descend,
And, stretched beneath the inclement skies,
Weeps o'er her tender babes and dies. —Smollett.

13—16. (13) **For the sins,** R. V., "It is because of the sins," the elegist ascribes the cause for this wonderful overthrow; Je. v. 31, xxiii. 21.[a] **shed .. just,** Je. xxvi. 7—24.[b] (14) **They,** these religious leaders. **wandered,** lit. "staggered," under the panic occasioned by the siege. **with blood,** their acts of violence have been continued to the very end of their term of power. Their garments are still stained with blood when the summons to depart into exile reaches them.—Pul. Com. **could not touch,** for fear of defilement. (15) **They cried,** i. e. men generally, even the heathen, cried against these "fugitives and vagabonds, with the mark of Cain upon them, driven out at the gates by the impatient mob," and would not let them settle amongst them. (16) **anger,** lit. the face. **divided them,** scattered them among the nations. **they respected,** men generally in the countries sought as asylums by the outlawed priests and elders.

The False Prophets Rewarded.—In the hour of their exposure these wretched prophets and priests lose all sense of dignity, even lose their self-possession, and stumble about like blind men, helpless and bewildered. Their behavior suggests the idea that they must be drunk with the blood they have shed, or overcome by the intoxication of their thirst for blood; but the explanation is that they cannot lift up their heads to look a neighbor in the face, because all their little devices have been torn to shreds, all their specious lies detected, all their empty promises falsified. This shame of dethroned popularity is the greatest humiliation. The unhappy man who has brought himself to live on the breath of fame cannot hide his fall in oblivion and obscurity as a private person may do. Standing in the full blaze of the world's observation which he has so eagerly focussed on himself, he has no alternative but to exchange the glory of popularity for the ignominy of notoriety.—Exp. B.——A Scoffer Nonplussed.—On a certain occasion, in the presence of a vast and brilliant assemblage, a person more noted for his self-esteem than for his learning was speaking against the Christian religion in terms of the severest scorn and derision. The celebrated Dr. Belknap, overhearing the orator, stepped up to him and asked, "Well, sir, have you found a religion that is better?" The scoffer, considerably abashed by this unlooked-for question, was forced to acknowledge that thus far he had not. "Well," responded the Doctor, "when you have, let me know, and I will join you in adopting it." The rebuke was as wise as it was just.—Hom. Com.

17—20. (17) **our eyes,** etc., "our eyes still waste away (as we look) for our help in vain." The expectation that Egypt or some other nation might come to the rescue, was cherished to the end of the year and a half of the siege, and here is set forth the heart-sickness caused by this hope deferred.[a]—Cam. B. (18) **They .. steps,** referring to the missiles of the besiegers, whose engines were now advanced close to the walls.[b] (19) **pursued,** any of the inhabitants who tried to escape, but the king and his followers in particular.[c] (20) **breath .. nostrils,** with this, as applied to a king, a sentence of Seneca has been well compared: "He (the Emperor) is the breath of life, which these many thousand (subjects) draw." Ge. ii. 7. **anointed,** the Jewish term for the king. **taken .. pits,** hunted like a wild beast.

Persecution.—One Palmer, of Reading, being condemned to die, in Queen Mary's time, was much persuaded to recant, and among other things a friend said to him, "Take pity on thy golden years and pleasant flowers of youth, before it be too late." His reply was as beautiful as it was conclusive, "Sir, I long for those springing flowers which shall never fade away." When he was in the midst of the flames he exhorted his companions to constancy, saying, "We shall not end our lives in the fire, but make a change for a better life; yea, for coals we shall receive pearls." Thus do we clearly see that, although "if in this life only we have hope in Christ, we are of all men most miserable," yet the prospect of a better and enduring substance enables us to meet all the trials and temptations of this present life with holy boldness and joy.

21, 22. (21) **Rejoice,** this call to an enemy of God's people appears to be ironical. "Rejoice while thou mayest." **cup,** of Divine judgment. (22) **accomplished,** carried through, and completed. **discover thy sins,** "when sins are forgiven they are said to be covered; therefore, when they are said to be discovered, it is as though we were told that God does the reverse of forgiving them—strips them of every rag of apology, lays them bare. That is their condemnation. Nothing is more ugly than a naked sin."[d]—Exp. B.

Injustice and Anger.—There is an anger that is damnable: it is the anger of selfishness. There is an anger that is majestic as the frown of Jehovah's brow: it is the anger of truth and love. If man meets with injustice, it is not required that he shall not be roused to meet it; but if he is angry after he has had time to think upon it, that is sinful. The flame is not wrong, but the coals are.—Beecher.

most difficult thing in life, answered, 'For a tyrant to live to old age.'"—Barlow.

"Whose hearts are ready at humanity's soft call to drop the tear."—W. Mason.

[d] "He will discover how great thine iniquities are, by the remarkable judgments wherewith He punisheth thee."—Lowth.

CHAPTER THE FIFTH.

1—5. (1) **O Lord,** this fifth elegy is addressed directly to God. It is a prayer; but not a string of petitions. It is a meditation in the presence of God. **reproach,** or national disgrace. (2) **Our inheritance,** Ps. lxxix. 1.[e] **aliens,** foreigners. (3) **fatherless .. widows,** bec. the war destroyed so many of the men. (4) **water for money,** the insult implied in paying a price for the common necessities of life fr. their own land and wells, signifies the abject servitude into wh. the Jews had been reduced. (5) **necks,** whereon yokes were laid.[f] R. V., "Our pursuers are upon our necks," i. e. gaining upon the fugitives.

God Answers Prayer.—I once saw a grand procession in which an Oriental monarch, surrounded by a thousand life-guards, moved to the sound of all kinds of music. Some unknown subject had a request to urge. He knew the utter impossibility of ever breaking through the guards that day and night surrounded his majesty. That humble person perhaps had some dear friend in prison, who, according to Oriental custom, could never be tried or freed while the prosecutor's malice or purse held out. They have no Habeas Corpus law among nations without the Bible. This poor creature took the only possible way known to one unable to bribe the officers, and flung his petition over the heads of the guards, and it fell at the feet of the sovereign. In a moment one of the life-guards pierced it with his bayonet, and flung it back into the crowd. Alas! the proud, pleasure-loving monarch, amid the luxuriant splendors of his court, palace, army, and plans of reaping renown, never so much as dreamed of noticing the prayer of that broken heart and crushed spirit. Not thus does the King of kings treat the humblest suppliant who seeks His help.—Van Doren.——I never was deeply interested in any object, I never prayed sincerely and earnestly for anything, but it came; at some time, no matter how distant a day, in some shape, probably the last I should have devised, it came.—Adoniram Judson.

6—10. (6) **given the hand,** as a pledge of fidelity; submitted **ourselves,** under stress of starvation. The exiles in the south submit to Egypt; those in the east to Babylon. **with bread,** i. e. to get mere food to keep us alive. (7) **Our .. not,** Je. xxxi. 29; Eze. xviii. 2. (8) **Servants have ruled,** better, "slaves;" the Satraps of the Chaldæan monarch were slaves promoted by favoritism to places of honor; Neh. v. 15. (9) **got,** "get." **sword .. wilderness,** fig. for the perils from the Arabs, who plunder those venturing outside the cities to reap the harvests. (10) **was black,** etc., Cam. B., "glows like an oven because of the burning blast of famine." The feverishness brought on by hunger is meant; ch. iv. 8.

Children Suffer for the Sins of Their Parents.—It is a fact that chil-

[e] Le. xx. 24.

[f] De. xxviii. 48.

"Every inward aspiration is God's angel undefiled, and for every 'O my Father!' slumbers deep a 'here, my child.'" —Royal Helps.

"Thy heart is big! Get thee apart and weep. Passion I see is catching; for mine eyes, seeing those beads of sorrow stand in thine, begin to water."—Shakespeare.

"Prayer is a key which, being turned by the hand of faith, unlocks all God's treasures." —Hannah More.

"Unvalued here such tears may fall; but know, each tear will prove a precious pearl in heaven above." — The Triumph of Time.

"The nunneries of silent nooks, the murmur'd longing of the wood."—Lowell.

"Look upon any duty or grace, and you will find it lie between Scylla and Charybdis, two extremes alike dan-

dren do suffer for the sins of their parents. It was apparent in the times of the Captivity; for owing to Josiah's reformation the moral condition of the nation then was better than it had been a generation or so before; yet the blow, which was caused by the greater guilt of the fathers, fell upon the children. It may often be observed in history that the greatest catastrophes do not fall on the most guilty, but on their successors, who are often better men. Thus James II. was a better man than Charles II., though the Stuart dynasty ended in the younger brother; and Louis XVI. was comparatively innocent, and yet he had to suffer for the vices of Louis XIV. and Louis XV. In private life, poverty, disease, and disgrace are inherited by children from their parents. Now, it is a sign of the robust truthfulness of the Bible that this dark fact is distinctly recognized. There is no attempt to shun it because it is mysterious. We have in the Bible an honest, brave confronting of the evils of life, and not a system which is only beautiful to contemplate in idea and which cannot be squared with facts.—Pul. Com.

gerous. Faith, the great work of God, cuts its way between the mountain of presumption and the gulf of despair. Patience (a grace so necessary that we cannot be without it a day, except we would be all that while beside ourselves) keeps us that we fall neither into the sleepy apoplexy of a blockish stupidity, nor into a raging fit of discontent."—Gurnall.

11—15. (12) **hanged,** prob. aft. their death they were impaled or crucified after the Babylonian custom, to expose them to public contumely.[a] **hand,** i. e. not a ref. to any mode of hanging, but to the enemy who insulted the dead. (13) **grind,** rather, "the young men have borne the mill." The lower millstone seems to have been specially heavy, and to carry it about must have required a more severe exertion even than the constant turning of the mill-handle. This was the work of female slaves. **under the wood,** i. e. under the heavy burdens of wood which they were compelled to fetch and carry. (14) **ceased .. gate,** from attending as magistrates. (15) **dance,** the sign of cheerfulness.

[a] "Comp. the boast of Sennacherib, who says of the people of Ekron, 'The chief priests and noblemen I put to death, on stakes all around the city I hung their bodies; the people of the city with their wives I gave to slavery." —Spk. Com.

Dishonored Old Age.—

"I have ventured,
Like little wanton boys that swim on bladders,
This many summers in a sea of glory,
But far beyond my depth; my high-blown pride
At length broke under me; and now has left me,
Weary and old with service, to the mercy
Of a rude stream, that must forever hide me.
Vain pomp and glory of this world, I hate ye!"
—Shakespeare.

16—18. (16) **crown,** fig. for the glory of the nation. **we have sinned,** not only does this generation suffer for the of the fathers, but also for their own sins is this woe come upon the nation. (18) **foxes,** or jackals, creatures that frequent desolated cities, and live among ruins.[a]

[a] "They were prob. first attracted thither by the bodies of the slain, of which they are particularly fond." — Henderson.

"When the fight begins inside himself a man's worth something." —Browning.

Yearning for God.—When my blood flows like wine, when all is ease and prosperity, when the sky is blue and birds sing and flowers blossom, and my life is an anthem moving in time and tune, then this world's joy and affection suffice. But when a change comes, when I am weary and disappointed, when the skies lower into a sombre night, when there is no song of bird, and the perfume of flowers is but their dying breath, when all is sunsetting and autumn, then I yearn for Him who sits with the summer of love in His soul, and feel that all earthly affection is but a glow-worm light compared to that which blazes with such effulgence in the heart of God.—Beecher.

"From these pearly eyes should there fall down more tears of penitence than the clouds drop to purchase a new spring, I could not be forgiven." — Old Play, Muleasses.

19—22. (19) **remainest,** etc., not even the destruction of Jerusalem, the death of the king or the subsequent horrors of exile can destroy the faith of the elegist in the steadfastness of Jehovah, Ps. ix. 7.[b] (20) **for ever,** if Jehovah's power is intact why does he permit Israel to feel herself forsaken? (21) **Turn .. us,** "bring us into a state of reconciliation with Thee," Je. xxxi. 18. (22) **thou hast,** R. V. marg., "unless thou .. and art, etc," an hypothesis not to be accepted as fact.

[b] Ps. xxix. 10, cii. 12, cxiv. 13.

Genuine Conversion (vs. 21).—The text teaches that—1. It is a turning of the soul to the Lord, not to creeds, not to churches; 2. It is a turning of the soul to the Lord, by the Lord; no one can turn the human soul to God but Himself.—Thomas.

"Our only hope is in the eternity and unchangeableness of Thy nature; and that Thou still governest the world, and orderest all the events of it; whereby Thou art always able to help us, and art never forgetful of the promises which Thou hast made to Thy people." —Lowth.

God's Faithfulness Inspires Hope.—So wide and deep is our Father's love, so firm is the adamantine strength of His eternal fidelity, we may be absolutely confident that, though the mountains be removed and cast into the sea, and though the solid earth melt away beneath our feet, He will still abide as the Eeternal Refuge of His children, and therefore that He will never fail to welcome all who seek His grace to help them return to Him in true penitence and filial trust. Thus we are led even by this most melancholy book in the Bible to see, as with eyes purged by tears, that the love of God is greater than the sorrow of man, and His redeeming power more mighty than the sin which lies at the root of the worst of that sorrow, the eternity of His throne, in spite of the present havoc of evil in the universe, assuring us that the end of all will be not a mournful elegy, but a pæan of victory.—Adeney.

"Talent is best nurtured in solitude; character is best formed in the stormy billows of the world."—Goethe.

"Happiness is not the end of life; character is." —Beecher.

Introduction.

I. Author. Ezekiel (God will strengthen) the son of Buzi, was, like Jeremiah, a priest as well as a prophet; "but with the priestly character more largely developed, and also one step farther removed from the ancient Prophets, inasmuch as he is the first in whom the author and the writer entirely preponderates over the seer, the poet, and the statesman" (Stanley).

"The period at which the prophet's youth was passed was rich in influences that must have powerfully affected him. Though too young to take part in the reform of Josiah (620), or perhaps to remember it, he grew up in the midst of the changes which it had introduced, and probably learned to estimate previous history from the point of view which it gave him. The tragic events which followed one another closely at this epoch, such as the death of Josiah (608), the exile of Jehoahaz to Egypt and of Jehoiachin to Babylon, made a lasting impression on his mind. The last event formed the chief landmark of his life, and that not solely because his own history was so closely connected with it. It was not, however, merely the silent teaching of events from which Ezekiel learned. He had a master interpreting events to him to whose influence every page of his prophecies bears witness. Jeremiah, indeed, may not have been Ezekiel's only master; there were other prophets of the time like-minded with him, such as that Urijah whom Jehoiakim dragged from his hiding-place in Egypt and slew with the sword (Jer. xxvi.), and perhaps others of whose names no record has been kept. Still the teaching and life of Jeremiah was probably the most powerful influence under which the young priest grew up. It could hardly have been otherwise. For 30 years before Ezekiel's captivity Jeremiah had been a prophet, speaking in the courts and chambers of the temple and in the streets of Jerusalem, and having such a history as made him the prominent figure of the day. In the year 597 B. C. Nebuchadnezzar took Jerusalem and carried into captivity the young king Jehoiachin, the flower of the population including many priests, Ezekiel among them, as well as a multitude of other citizens, particularly craftsmen. Ezekiel with a community of other exiles was settled at Tel-Abib by the river Chebar—not to be identified with the Chabor which falls into the Euphrates near Carchemish, but some stream or canal in Babylonia proper" (Cambridge Bible). Five years later, B. C. 592, Ezekiel began his ministry, and the latest date given in the book is the 27th year of the captivity, i. e., B. C. 570.

"The ascription of the book to Ezekiel is almost universally accepted, and there is no serious doubt as to the authorship of any considerable passage" (W. H. Bennett). "The picture, if it can be called so, which the prophet gives of the life of the exiles and their circumstances is singularly colorless. His interests were exclusively religious. His own mind was occupied with the largest conceptions, and the exiles were to his eye representatives of a larger subject. It is only on rare occasions that he draws any distinction between the exiles and those remaining in the land. When he does so he shares the feeling of Jeremiah (ch. xxiv, xxix. 16 seq.) that the flower of the people had been carried into captivity with Jehoiachin, and that the hope of the nation lay in them (xi. 14-21). But usually the exiles are regarded as the representatives of the house of Israel" (Cambridge Bible).

Synopsis.

(According to Hengstenberg.)

The First Cycle..........................i.—vii.
The Second Cycle.....................viii.—xix.
The Third Cycle.......................xx.—xxiii.
The Fourth Cycle..............................xxiv.
Foreign Nations ....xxv.—xxxii.
Words of Comfort.............xxxiii. 21—xxxix.
The Restoration ....xl.—xlviii.

(According to Litton.)

I.—Relating to the destruction of Jerusalem. Ezekiel's call (i.—iii.). Symbolical representations of siege and capture of Jerusalem (iv.—vii.). Vision of Jerusalem, exhibiting the idolatry of the people (viii.—xi.). Reproofs and warnings addressed to contemporaries (xii.—xix.). Another series, warning of the approaching calamity (xx.—xxiii.). Announcement of the commencement of the siege by the King of Babylon (xxiv.).

II.—Relating to heathen nations (xxv.—xxxii.).

III.—Relating to the restoration of the Jews (xxxiii.—xlviii.).

CHAPTER THE FIRST.

First Div. Ch. i.—xxiv., Proph. regarding the Downfall of Jerusalem.

1—3. (1) **Now it came,** better, "and it came." A discourse in Hebrew is usually begun with the particle vau or and. **thirtieth year,** it is impossible to determine from what era or event this 30th year is reckoned. It may be some unknown Babylonian era. **fourth month,** i. e. Tammuz, our June or July. **captives,** or people of the captivity. **Chebar,** the Chebar of Ezekiel is the Nahr-Malcha, or Royal Canal of Nebuchadnezzar, the greatest of that king's irrigation works, to which, therefore, the name Chebar (i. e. uniting) would be appropriate.—Pulp. Com. **visions of God,** sublime, mysterious, majestic visions, or better, actual theophanies of the divine being wh. would constitute a call to the prophetic office. These visions were prob. during his waking consciousness while he was in an ecstatic state, cf. 2 Cor. xii. 2, 3. (2) **Jehoiachin's captivity,** 2 Ki. xxiv. 12. 592 B. C. Ezekiel nowhere recognizes Zedekiah as king over Israel. (3) **Ezekiel,** nothing is known of Ezekiel or of his father. Buzi, except what may be gathered from the book. Heb. Jehezkel. **hand .. him,** indicating that he felt sensible impressions of God's power resting upon him.[b]

Visions of God.—I. The seer of the visions. 1. A priest; 2. A prophet. II. The time of the visions. 1. After years of preparation; 2. Before a life of work. III. The circumstances of the visions. 1. Ezekiel was among the captives. (1) He was an exile from his native land; (2) He was surrounded by sorrowful men; (3) He was himself a captive. IV. The source of the visions. 1. They were from heaven; 2. They were through the opening of heaven. V. The nature of the visions.—W. F. Adeney.

The River Chebar (vs. 1).—"The Khabour flows through the richest pastures and meadows. Its banks were now covered with flowers of every hue, and its windings through the green plain were like the coils of a mighty serpent. An uncontrollable emotion of joy seized all our party when they saw the end of their journey before them. The horsemen urged their horses to full speed; the Jebours danced in a circle, raised their colored kerchiefs on their spears, and shouted their war-cry; the Tizari sang their mountain songs and fired their muskets into the air. Trees in full leaf lined the water's edge. We rode through a mass of flowers, reaching high above the horses' knees, and such as I had never before seen, even in the most fertile parts of the Mesopotamian wilderness. We had passed several tels and the double banks of ancient canals, showing that we were still amidst the remains of ancient civilization. Flocks of sheep and herds of camels were spread over the meadows on both sides of the river. On the morning after our arrival we crossed the Khabour on a small raft, and pitched our tents on its northern bank, near the ruins of Arban, which consist of a large artificial mound of irregular shape, washed by the river. From the top of the mound the eye ranged over a level country bright with flowers, and spotted with black tents, and innumerable flocks of sheep and camels. During our stay at Arban the color of these great plains was undergoing a continual change. After being for some days of a golden yellow, a new family of flowers would spring up, and it would turn almost in a night to a bright scarlet, which would again as suddenly give way to the deepest blue. Then the meadows would be mottled with various hues, or would put on the emerald green of the most luxuriant of pastures. The glowing descriptions I had so frequently received from the Bedouins of the beauty and fertility of the banks of the Khabour were more than realized."——Experience of God.—Now and then a great experience comes unexpected and unsought. It touches the greater chords of the soul, and lifts it above the common level of emotion, outruns all former knowledge. . . . But what other experience is like that of the personal disclosure of God in the soul. . . . There comes an hour to some, to many, of transfiguration. It may be in grief; it may be in joy; it may be in the opening of the door of sickness; it may be in active duty; it may be under the roof or under the sky, where God draws near with such reality, glory,

b 1 Ki. xviii. 46.

"Be we where we may, we may be there with the unseen Christ and He will be its glory."

"While we view, amid the noontide walk, a limpid rill gush through the tickling herbage, to the thirst of summer yielding the delicious draught of cool refreshment; o'er the mossy brink shines not the surface clearer, and the waves with sweeter music murmur as they flow?" —Akenside.

"The one secret of life and development is not to devise and plan, but to fall in with the forces at work, to do every moment's duty aright, that being the part of the process allotted to us; and let come, not what will, for there is no such thing, but what the Eternal thought wills for each of us, has intended for each of us from the first." —G. Macdonald.

"Enemies may banish from home; they cannot banish from God." —Adeney.

"If poets learn in sorrow what they teach in song, may not the glory of the song justify the experience of the sorrow, and so explain some of the mystery of it?" —Adeney.

and power that the soul is filled, amazed, transported. All before was nothing; all afterwards will be but a souvenir. That single vision, that one hour, is worth the whole of life, and throws back a light on all that went before. It . . . gives to the soul some such certainty of invisible, spiritual truths as one has of his own personal identity. When one has had this hour of divine disclosure, of full and entrancing vision, it never can be retracted, or effaced, or reasoned against, or forgotten.—Beecher.

4—9. (4) **whirlwind,**[a] one of the mightiest of Fastern destructive agencies. **the north,** wh. was felt by the Jews to be the peculiar seat of the power of Jehovah, the vision granted to the exiled prophet on the plain of Babylonia embodied a truth opposed to the religious prejudices of his time, but reassuring to himself—that the fall of Israel leaves the essential sovereignty of Jehovah untouched; that He still lives and reigns, although His people are trodden underfoot by worshipers of other gods.—Exp. B. **infolding itself,** R. V. marg., "flashing continually." **brightness round about,** i. e. about the whole phenomenon of storm and cloud; though a great cloud it was illuminated all round by the continuous flashing of fire within it.—Cam. B. **colour,** or appearance. **amber,** comp. the sunset color just before the crimson flush.[b] As this great storm cloud advanced across the plain the first general splendor divided itself into the various features outlined. (5) **four .. creatures,** these were the cherubim, but Ezekiel did not at first recognize them, see Re. iv. 6. **of a man,** i. e. they were erect, and unlike the religious symbols sculptured upon the Assyrian temples. (6) **four faces,** vs. 10. (7) **straight feet,** i. e. like a man's leg, without the middle joint which four-footed beasts have. **sole .. feet,** the foot proper was shaped as a calf's, indicating solid, firm treading. (8) **hands .. wings,** i. e. hands under each of the wings. (9) **joined,** i. e. in flying, one wing of one creature touched the wing of the next.[c] **they turned not,** i. e. their faces; in whichever direction they went the man's face was presented first.

The Preparatory Vision for True Prophets (vs. 4).—Note—I. What is local and temporary in this vision. 1. The peculiar sources of impression and instruction of the prophet. II. The revelation of God's dealings with the Jews. Here we are taught—1. The Divine dealings would be marked by majesty of thought, by God's mode of manifesting Himself, by the agency of God's command. Note—II. What is universal and permanent in this vision. 1. That Divine providence possesses stupendous machinery; 2. That Divine providence has ever a moral aim in the use of its stupendous machinery; it teaches that all the mighty agencies of God are against evil, that with the Divine majesty of retribution there is also the majesty of mercy.—U. R. Thomas.

Clouds.—Those war-clouds that gather on the horizon, dragon-crested, tongued with fire;—how is their barbed strength bridled? What bits are these they are champing with their vaporous lips; flinging off flakes of black foam? Leagued leviathans of the sea of heaven, out of their nostrils goeth smoke, and their eyes are like the eyelids of the morning. . . . Where ride the captains of their armies? Where are set the measures of their march? Fierce murmurers, answering each other from morning until evening—what rebuke is this which has awed them into peace? What hand has reined them back by the way by which they came? "The wondrous works of Him which is perfect in knowledge?" We have too great veneration for cloudlessness.—Ruskin.

10—14. (10) **likeness,** or the things wh. their faces resembled. The human face was the prominent one, the lion face was on the right side, the ox face on the left, and at the back the eagle face. The man's face signifies that man is the highest symbol of the Eternal; the lion, for sovereignty; the ox for sacrifice; the eagle for kingly power. (11) **stretched upward,** this was the attitude when the figure was in flight. **two .. bodies,** although free from earthly imperfection they cover themselves with their wings before His majesty, in token of the reverence which is due from the creature in presence of the Creator. (12) **straight forward,** bec. they never needed to turn themselves round, seeing that, whichever way they went, they had a face looking that way. **spirit .. go,** whichever way the inward impulse constrained them. "One spirit of one conscious life guided all the motions in perfect harmony." (13)

[a] Ps. lviii. 9; comp. Is. xxi. 1; Je. xxiii. 19, xxv. 32.

[b] The word used may also be trans. "polished brass." LXX. and Vulg. render it by electrum, a compound of gold and silver.

[c] "Ezekiel was living in a country on the walls of whose temples and palaces were those strange mixed figures, human heads with the bodies of lions and the feet of calves, and the like, wh. we see in the Babylonian and Assyrian monuments. . . . The Prophet is not constructing his cherubim in imitation of these figures; the Spirit of God is revealing forms corresponding to the general rules of Eastern symbolism."
—Spk. Com.

"Incessant restless motion indicates the plenitude of life in these cherubim. Comp. Re. iv. 8."—Fausset.

"There has never been a weak deity worshiped, and it is safe to say there never will be one. Man is too strong himself not to admire strength, and looks with pity or contempt upon weakness. And no deity can be pitied or despised and hold his sovereignty over men's mind. The heavens must be braced beyond the possibility of fall, or they who live beneath the dome could

R. V., "and in the midst of the living creatures was an appearance like burning coals of fire, like the appearance of torches." **burning .. fire,** suggested by the altar fire in the temple. Here the vision of Ezekiel, in which the living creatures were thus incandescent, bathed, as it were, in the fire that played around them, yet not consumed, followed in the path of previous symbols—of the burning bush (Exod. iii. 2), of the pillar of fire by night (Exod. xiii. 22).—Pulp. Com. (14) This vs. not in the lxx. Davidson remarks: both in regard to the terminology and construction the verse is untranslateable. Prob. a gloss explaining vs. 13 wh. has crept into the text.

The Bright Fire.—I. Consider how good it is for the fire to be bright. There are men in whose breasts the fire of God burns dimly. The embers smoulder in a dull mass, threatening speedy extinction. Love is chilling, faith is fainting; as for the flame of hope, that is long since dead. On the other hand, the bright fire may stand for fresh warmth of soul, a burning zeal, a passion of devotion, a glow of heavenly love.

15—18. (15) **one wheel,** i. e. one wheel to each of the living creatures, arranged to fit exactly the motion of the creatures. **by,** R. V., "beside." **with .. faces,** R. V., "for each of the four faces thereof," i. e. "for each face of the individual living creature there was a wheel. The appearance would be so if the wheel really seemed two wheels cutting one another transversely." (16) **work,** or construction. **colour of a beryl,** the modern topaz, of fine golden color, suggesting to Ezek. the idea of fire. **wheel .. wheel,** "each wheel was composed of two circles, cutting one another at right angles, one only of wh. appeared to touch the ground, according to the direction the cherubim desired to move in."[a] (18) **rings,** or felloes, the circumferences of the wheels. **full of eyes,** symbolizing the divine omniscience.

The Wheels.—From all that we can gather of the form of these wheels, they appear to have been each composed of two of equal size, and inserted, the rim of the one into that of the other at right angles, and so consisting of four equal parts or half circles. They were accordingly adapted to run either forward or backward, to the right hand or the left, without any lateral turning; and by this means their motion corresponded with that of the four faces of the living creatures to which they were attached. . . . When it is said, "they turned not," it is not to be understood that they had not a revolving or rotary motion, but that they, like the faces, never forsook a straightforward course.—Bush.

19—25. (19) **went by them,** or along with them. (20) **spirit .. go,** vs. 12. (21) **in the wheels,** "One and the same spirit actuated the living creatures throughout, wheels and all."[b] (22) R. V., "And over the head of the living creature there was the likeness of a firmament, like the colour of the terrible," etc. **colour .. crystal,**[c] a perfectly, oppressively clear sky, in wh. the Divine glory appeared as upon the throne. (23) **straight,** i. e. level, cf. vs. 9, 11. **covered .. bodies,** the upper wings folding over their heads, the lower ones shading their limbs. (24) **noise,** rustling. **voice .. Almighty,** i. e. like thunder.[a] **voice of speech,** or tumult. (25) **from the firmament,** R. V., "above the firm." **let .. wings,** to take the attitude of waiting, listening for Divine commands.

Note on vs. 22.—Heb. "As for the likeness upon the heads of the living creatures, it was that of an expansion stretched over their heads above, like the aspect of the terrible crystal." This expansion was a splendid level pavement or flooring, of a crystal clearness, and resting upon the heads of the living creatures, as the temple lavers rested upon the four cornerstays, or "undersetters," of their bases. The resemblance to the crystal was not in color, but in transparency, for the color was like that of a sapphire stone, or the cerulean azure of the real firmament of heaven. This is evident from vs. 26, and also from Ex. xxiv. 9, 10, containing an evident allusion to this vision, and perhaps the germ of it. "Then went up Moses and Aaron, Nadab and Abihu, and seventy of the elders of Israel; and they saw the God of Israel: and there was under His feet, as it were, a paved work of a sapphire-stone, and, as it were, the body of heaven in its clearness." (Vs. 24).—Heb. "And there was a voice—in their standing they let down their wings." The design of the Prophet seems to be, to show the perfect obsequiousness of the living creatures to the word of command emanating from the throne above,

---

never gaze with awe into the overhanging spaces. . . . I do not expect that any of mortal kind have a correct idea of God. . . . How little do we know even yet of the qualities and uses of material and finite Nature!"

[a] "As it were one wheel put across within another, like two circles in a sphere, cutting one another at right angles, to signify the stability and uniformity of their motions, and the subserviency of one part of providence to another."
—Lowth.

"The holy power that clothes the senseless earth with woods, with fruits, with flowers, and verdant plains, whose bounteous hand feeds the whole brute creation, knows all our wants, and has enough to give us."
—Rowe.

[b] "All four creatures together with their wheels are here called the living creature, because they formed a whole, one in motion, and one in will, for one sprit was in them."
—Spk. Com.

[c] "Such as dazzles the eye with its lustre."
—Lowth.

[a] Job xxxvii. 4, 5; Ps. xxix. 3, 4, 5; Re. x. 3.

vs. 23. "The wings therefore of the whole four being in contact with each other, formed a kind of curtain beneath the incumbent pavement, and thus completed the resemblance to the temple

and directing their movements. When the word was given to move, their wings were at once expanded, the resounding din was heard, and the glorious vehicle, instinct with life, rolled on in amazing majesty. Again, when the counter mandate was heard, they in an instant stayed themselves in mid career, and relaxed their wings.—Bush.

26—28. (26) **throne,** comp. Ex. xxiv. 10. The throne appeared as if made of light, and resembling the colors and the brightness of sapphire. **appearance of a man,** "the prophet speaks with great reverence. What he saw was the "appearance" of a throne and of one sitting on it and of a rainbow; he does not venture to say that he saw these things themselves." (27) It may be assumed that in the prophet's mind each detail of the symbolism expressed some idea, though it may not be possible now to interpret the details with certainty. The firmament and throne represent Jehovah as God of heaven, God alone over all, the omnipotent.—Cam. B. (28) **of the bow,** i. e. spanning the scene with one splendid arch.[b]

Notes on ch. i.—The vision is intended to declare that the God of Israel was come in all His glory to dwell w. the exiles in Babylonia wh. was now, and till the restoration to Canaan was to be, the centre of the national life. Jehovah returns to the Temple in ch. 43, 2.—Polychrome Bib.——That which ch. i. presents is a theophany, a manifestation of God to the prophet. It is not a vision of the cherubim nor of anything else, but of God. The cherubim, wheels, firmament and throne are all subordinate, they have no meaning in themselves, they merely help to suggest what God is who thus manifests himself.—Cambridge Bib.

bases, and forming in fact a magnificent living chariot." —Bush.

b "This vision being an evident representation of the Word that was to be made flesh, whose incarnation is the foundation of God's covenant of mercy with mankind, a rainbow, the symbol and token of mercy, was a very fit attendant upon that glorious vision." —Lowth.

"Though you have no visions of God, unwavering fealty to His law will secure that He will guide you by His counsel, and afterwards receive you to glory." —Goulty.

CHAPTER THE SECOND.

1—5. (1) **Son of man,**[a] a term applied to Ezekiel 80 times: only applied otherwise to Daniel;[b] and our Lord. It may be used to put Ezekiel in mind of his frailty and personal insignificance, though he was honored with such sublime visions.[c] **stand,** in the attitude of one listening and ready to obey—"it is man erect, man in his manhood, with whom God will have fellowship and with whom he will speak." (2) **spirit entered into me,** i. e. the source of energy and vitality. This energy came from God. The Spirit which moved the "living creatures" and the "wheels" in the mysterious symbol was now in him. Ezekiel finds in that fact the ground of his prophetic inspiration.—Pulp. Com.——"Ecstasy was at first the ordinary condition of prophetic utterance (1 Sam. xix. 24; Mic. i. 8); it was gradually dispensed with, as prophecy became reflective and moral."—Polychr. Bib. **set .. feet,** Da. x. 11. Comp. Eze. i. 28. (3) **nation,** Heb. goyim, the word applied to heathen nations, and used to intimate that the Jews had outdone the wickedness of the heathen. R. V., "nations," i. e. the plural signifying the whole nation of Israel. He is a prophet to the whole house of Israel, including the lost kingdom of the ten tribes, as well as the two sections of the kingdom of Judah, those now in exile and those still remaining in their own land. This is his ideal audience; the sweep of his prophecy is to embrace the destinies of the nation as a whole, although but a small part be within the reach of his spoken words.—Exp. B. (4) **impudent,** Heb. hard of face. **stiffhearted,** unwilling to yield to counsel or chastisement. (5) **rebellious house,**[d] this stereotyped expression indicates that Ezek.'s clear insight into the spiritual condition of the "house of Israel," shows him conclusively that the people are not yet ready to be won back to Jehovah by assurances of His compassion and mercy. Is. xxx. 9.

Commission Given to Ministers (vs. 4).—1. To declare God's will; 2. To assert His authority; 3. To seek, notwithstanding all our discouragements, the salvation of their souls. Learn hence—1. The importance of the ministry; 2. The duty of those who are ministered unto.—C. Simeon.

a Heb. Ben Adam.

b Da. viii. 17.

c 2 Cor. xii. 7.

d "Whether they will regard what is said by thee or not, yet the event answering thy predictions shall render thy authority unquestionable, and them inexcusable for not hearkening to the warnings thou hast given them." —Lowth.

"He is good that does good to others. If he suffers for the good he does, he is better still; and if he suffers from them to whom he did good, he is arrived to that height of goodness that nothing but an increase of his sufferings can add to it." —Bruyere.

6—10. (6) **not afraid,** Je. i. 8, 18. **briers**[a] .. **scorpions,** figures for those who might annoy, resist and persecute the Prophet. (7) **speak my words,** i. e. God encourages Ezek. by promising him words to speak. **most rebellious,** or rebellion itself. (8) **Be not rebellious,** the work was

a Comp. 2 Sa. xxiii. 6; Sol. Song ii. 2; Is. ix. 18.

both arduous and painful: painful because it was against his own people that the prophet had to speak; and arduous because leading to opposition and persecution. There is no easy situation in God's service. Had the prophet refused the great commission he would have rebelled like Israel. **eat .. thee,**[b] fig. for receive the message, commit it to memory.[c] The meaning of this strange symbol appears to include two things. In the first place it denotes the removal of the inward hindrance of which every man must be conscious when he receives the call to be a prophet. Somthing similar occurs in the inaugural vision of Isaiah and Jeremiah. In the second place the eating of the book undoubtedly signifies the bestowal on the prophet of the gift of inspiration—that is, the power to speak the words of Jehovah.—Exp. B. (9) **sent,** or stretched forth. **roll,** ancient books were written on skins, rolled up, not folded. The message was definite. (10) **within and without,**[d] not as usually, on the one side only, but on both sides, because there was so much woe to record.

b Comp. Re. x. 9.

c "The idea is to possess himself fully of the message, and digest it in the mind: not literal eating, but such an appropriation of its unsavory contents, that they should become, as it were, part of himself, so as to impart them the more vividly to his hearers." —Fausset.

d "So as to be completely filled, as the sealed roll in the Apocalypse. Re. v. 1." —Wordsworth.

CHAPTER THE THIRD.

1—3. (1) **eat .. speak,** receive the truth thyself, then speak it to others. This iteration may denote some hesitation on Ezek.'s part. The message was too sorrowful and severe. But the true prophet must not expect to choose his own message. (2) **opened my mouth,** in the attitude of obedience. (3) **cause .. eat,** perhaps intimating that he should wait for a full impression of the message, and not act merely on a first impression of it. **mouth .. sweetness,**[a] any message given by God the good man feels to be precious, but he may afterwards be oppressed by finding it to be a message of woe.[b]

Eating a Book.—I. The food provided: 1. This is in the form of literature. God feeds our highest nature through literature. 2. This must be taken as it is provided. We do not create Divine truth. We find it in the Bible. 3. The Divine provision is full and ample. The Bible has far more in it than Ezekiel's roll. Its many words are rich and deep. No age will ever consume the whole of its vast and varied teachings. II. the meal consumed. We must feed on the Bible to profit by it. 1. There must be personal appropriation. 2. There must be internal consumption. We have much verbal knowledge of the Bible without ever making it our food. The meaning of texts, historical and geographical allusions, side-lights of manners and customs, may all be studied, and yet the Bible may lie outside us, and our souls starve for want of spiritual food, because we do not take its essential truths down into our inner being in comprehension, meditation and application. 3. There must be assimilation. III. The effects following: 1. There is a pleasant taste. He who only sympathizes with the spirit in which the Bible was written will never need to read it as a task. 2. Pain ensues (vs. 14). Conscience makes the pleasant reading of the Bible to be followed by painful reflections. Yet this bitterness is a wholesome tonic. 3. The final result is an increase of strength. Feeding on God's Word fits us to teach that Word and to exemplify it by our conduct.—Pul. Com.

a Re. x. 9.

b "The sweetness in the mouth denoted that it was good to be a messenger of the Lord, but the bitterness which accompanied it denoted that the commission brought with it much sorrow, for the tidings were sad and evil."—Spk. Com.

"I have seen angels by the sick one's pillow —theirs was the soft tone and the soundless tread; where smitten hearts were drooping like the willow, they stood between the living and the dead." — Elizabeth Wetheralt.

4—9. (5) **strange speech,** a people speaking an obscure and unintelligible language. The idea is that even they would more readily listen to the Prophet than Israel would. (6) **many people,** or peoples; the heathen nations. (7) **not .. me,** speaking through the law and prophets; by providences and judgments. (8) **face strong,**[c] with prob. reference to Ezekiel's name, wh. means "One whom God makes strong." (9) **adamant,** Heb. shamir, a diamond.[d] Zec. vii. 12; Je. xvii. 1. **flint,** De. viii. 15. The diamond was employed to cut flint.[e]

c "I have given thee courage and assurance proportionable to the hardiness and impudence of those thou hast to deal with." —Lowth.

d Formed from the Lat. adamas, it formed the point of the ancient pen, or stylus.

e Ezekiel's firmness being that of a diamond, he should cut a stroke home to the hardened

10—14. (10) Although the prophet for the whole house of Israel, Ezek's immediate work was with the captives at Tel-abib. Hence the command anew to obey God's message. **receive .. heart,** explanation of the fig. of eating the roll, ch. ii. 8. (11) **of thy people,** God does not say, "of My people." "They have disfranchised themselves by their sins." He is commanded to proclaim to the captives that his words are spoken with prophetic power. His message is a "Thus saith the Lord." (12)

took me up, to carry me to the place where the message was to be delivered. **rushing,** caused by the passing away of the wonderful theophany he had seen. **Blessed .. place,**[a] i. e. the place where God had given the revelation of His glory. (13) **wings,** etc., ch. i. 20. (14) **bitterness,** i. e. indignation or anger. "The prophet was lifted up into sympathy with God and shared his righteous indignation against Israel." **hand .. strong,** I could not resist the Divine impulses.

Ezekiel's Commission.—Never does the voice say, Ezekiel, excite thine imagination, call upon the fountain of thine eloquence, arouse thy noblest intellectual faculties, and consider what had better be said to people who are living in such moral neglect and corruption; on the contrary, Ezekiel is simply to listen, to receive, to hear, and then he is to go; and having gone, he is to open his commission and continue it, and conclude it with the words, "Thus saith the Lord God."—J. Parker.

15—17. (15) **Tel-abib,**[b] on the river Chebar (ch. i. 3), the chief seat of the Jewish exiles in Babylon. **and I sat where they sat,** R. V., "and to where they dwelt." **astonished,**[a] or astounded; having my spirit utterly cast down and overwhelmed. **seven days,** the usual period for mourning. At the end of that time the effects of the ecstasy seem to pass away, and more light breaks on him with regard to his mission. He realizes that it is to be largely a mission to individuals. He is appointed as a watchman to the house of Israel, to warn the wicked from his way; and as such he is held accountable for the fate of any soul that might miss the way of life through failure of duty on his part.—Exp. B. Job. ii. 13.[b] (17) **a watchman,** Is. lvi. 10; Je. vi. 17.[c] "One to look out from a city's walls, and see whether an enemy is coming, and give notice of his approach." Perhaps this passage, vs. 16—21, recounts the message wh. Ezek. uttered while he sought to "reprove" the exiles.

The Watchman (vs. 17).—I. His character and qualifications. 1. He must be a man of good repute; 2. He must produce proofs of past fidelity and good management; 3. He should have discernment, ingenuity, and courage; 4. He should be healthy and strong, able to bear exposure and fatigue; 5. He must be properly appointed; 6. He must have a proper dress and light. II. The watchman's duty. 1. One part is to tell the hour; 2. To protect the persons and property of the inhabitants from villains, accidents, and offences; 3. Go give alarm when danger is near; 4. To give account of the city to the magistrates.—Benson Bailey.

Waiting.—
Let tongue rest and quiet thy quill be!
Earth is earth and not heaven, and never will be.
Man's work is to labor and leaven—
As best he may—earth here with heaven.
'Tis work for work's sake that he is needing;
Let him work on and on as if speeding
Work's end, but not dream of succeeding;
Because if success were intended,
Why, heaven would begin ere earth ended.—Browning.

18—21. (18) **surely die,** i. e. surely, unless you repent. This condition is assumed in all the Divine messages. **speakest to warn,** implying that the Prophet ought to do this again and again. **die .. iniquity,** unforgiven, and therefore to meet the eternal penalties. **blood .. hand,** counting you guilty of his death, in his sins, if you failed to warn him.[d] (19) **delivered thy soul,** from the burden of the man's death in sin. The dread warning has for its complement a message of comfort. The judgment passed on the prophet does not depend on the results of his ministry. "Whether men will hear, or whether they will forbear," he has "delivered his soul," i. e. saved his life, when he has done his duty as a watchman.—Pulp. Com. (20) **lay a stumbling block,** or cause his iniquity to become his ruin. (21) **sin not,** and he manifestly ought not to sin if he be a righteous man. Ezek. has thrown the experiences of this period into a symbolical form; the thought of God, of the divine majesty and greatness, which filled his mind at first and constantly, is presented under the form of the Theophany (ch. i.) always present with him. The feeling that he was a true prophet of God, commissioned to declare his will, and

hearts of a rebellious people." —Spk. Com.

[a] "The idea seems to be that though God should forsake and destroy His temple, which is pre-eminently His place, yet His presence makes every place to be His temple, and He is attended there by multitudes of the heavenly host." —Wordsworth.

[b] Hill of Abib, meaning either hill of corn (Gesenius) or hill of grass land (Fuers) and so named on account of its fruitfulness.

[a] "The stunning of the faculties by fear or surprise conveys the ordinary idea of the word." —Woolrych.

[b] Ge. l. 10; 1 Sa. xxxi. 13.

[c] Hab. ii. 1.

"God has so arranged the chronometry of our spirits that there shall be thousands of silent moments between the striking hours." —Martineau.

"Vicarious atonement is a necessity. Personal guilt establishes a law that repentance is powerless to heal."

[d] "It shall be charged upon them in the day of account that it was owing to their unfaithfulness that such and such precious souls perished in sin; for who knows but if they had had fair warning given them, they might have fled in time from the wrath to come?" —Mat. Henry.

"The God who has placed his servants in responsible positions has designed to inform them what

that the divine presence was always with him is symbolized in the other actions which follow (ii. iii.).—Cam. B.

22—27. (22) **hand of the Lord,** i.e. a trance or ecstacy, in wh. his vision was transported to some lonely spot. (23) **glory,** etc., ch. i. 28. "Now he is to learn that there is a time to be silent, as well as a time to speak, and that both are appointed by God." (24) **shut . . house,** this signifies his almost entire withdrawal from public life. Instead of being like his great predecessors, a man living full in the public view, and thrusting himself on men's notice when they least desired him, he is to lead an isolated and a solitary life, a sign to the people rather than a living voice.—Exp. B. (25) **bands,** etc., this must be treated morally, for we have no account of Ezekiel's having been imprisoned. (26) **be dumb,** no judgment can be greater than that wh. comes by the silencing of God's prophets and ministers.[a] (27) **when I . . thee,** then thou shalt be free to speak. This silence broken only by prophetic utterance, characterized Ezek. until the fall of Jerus.

Ezekiel's Preparation.—Ezekiel went forth from Tel-abib into the plain, that there he might have further talk with the Most High God. Again he fell on his face, and again the spirit set him upon his feet, and talked with him as a man might talk with his friend. Not yet was the preparation complete. Ezekiel was commanded in these words, "Go, shut thyself within thine house." There he might either pray in secret, or begin his mission in a small degree, speaking to one and another, but not yet publicly declaring himself as the prophet and the reformer of Israel. Thus we begin by being overthrown and filled with a sense of humiliation; then we are invigorated by the Spirit of God; then we are driven away that we may see somewhat of the field wherein we are to work; then we have imposed upon us a discipline of silence; then we go forth into the plain to hear, as it were, the whispers, the last trembling cadences, of the divine instruction and exhortation; then we begin within the small limits of our house to speak the word with which we have been entrusted: all the while God will be with us, to watch us, chasten us, help us; and inasmuch as we are identified with him we have the assurance that, troublous as our ministry may be, it will end in victory and in immortal joy.—J. Parker.

CHAPTER THE FOURTH.

1—4. (1) Ezek. preaches to the exiles by means of various symbols. 1st, the symbol of the siege of Jerus. This prophecy occurred some four years before the actual siege, and put an end to the delusive hopes of a speedy return fr. captivity. **a tile,** or brick. "Such are found in Babylon, covered with cuneiform inscriptions, often two feet long, one broad." **pourtray,** i.e. draw the picture of. (2) **lay siege,** i.e. represent the laying of a siege. **fort,** or watch-tower. **mount,** for the engines. **battering rams,** the engine used for thrusting down walls.[b] (3) **iron pan,** or plate: as a kind of shield. This was to be Ezekiel's defence as he conducted (in symbol) the siege of the city. "The fate of Jerusalem represented the disappearance of everything that had constituted the glory and excellence of Israel's national existence." This message would fill the captives with horror and dismay. (4) vss. 4—8, 2nd symbol: the people fearing the hardship of the exile as punishment for the national sins. In the first symbol Ezek. besieges Jerus., in this symbol he represents the besieged. **bear their iniquity,** i.e. the punishment due to iniquity. **lie . . side,** to represent the prostrate and bound condition of Jerusalem in the time of siege.

5—8. (5) **three . . ninety,**[a] the text of the Greek translation helps us past this difficulty. The Hebrew manuscript from which this version was made had the reading a "hundred and ninety" instead of "three hundred and ninety" in vs. 5. This alone yields a satisfactory sense, and the reading of the Septuagint is now generally accepted as representing what Ezekiel actually wrote.—Exp. B. See Nu. xiv. 34. (6) **forty days,** representing the forty years of the Judean exile. (7) **set thy face.** This

---

shall be the effects of neglect and cowardice. The wicked might have died, though warned; but he might have repented and lived. For every position of influence, or honor, or usefulness we hold, 'we must give account of ourselves before God.'" —Davies.

[a] 'The silence of prophets is God's punishment of a people." — S. Chrysostom.

The memory of good actions is the starlight of the soul.

"Our memories, corrupted by the fall, are often like those ponds where frogs live and the fish die." — Cripplegate Lectures.

"The Word of God counts the years and months and days of our distress to make us understand that it is not unknown to God how long we have borne the yoke of the cross and the oppression of tyrants." —Starck.

[b] "Those used by the Assyrians appear to have consisted of a strong framework on wheels, so covered as to protect the soldiers working it, and armed with one, sometimes two, pointed weapons. It differed considerably from the more familiarly known ram employed by the Romans." —Ayre.

[a] "Prob. dating from Jeroboam's first setting up the idolatrous worship of the golden calves, to the last captivity of the Jews, in the twenty-

vs. resumes the symbol of vss. 1—3; i.e. direct thy mind. **arm . . uncovered,** so as to wield a weapon.[b] (8) **bands.** This vs. resumes the symbol of vss. 4—6; to keep you from moving; a symbol of the straitness of the siege.

9—12. (9) vs. 9—17, 3rd symbol: the rigors of famine in Jerus. during the prolonged siege. **wheat,** etc., needful food for the time of his lying down. **fitches,** or spelt. **three . . days,** cf. vs. 5. (10) **meat,** i.e. food, although so poor the people could have only scant rations. **by weight,** carefully doled out. **shekels,** eight or nine ounces, as compared with 2 lbs., an ordinary allowance, indicates great scarcity. Ge. xxiii. 15. (11) **hin,** Ex. xxix. 40. About a quarter of a pint. (12) **bake . . man,** indicating the lack of ordinary firing materials. The dried dung of cattle is constantly used for firing in the East.[c]

Millet.—This word (millet) occurs more than once in the sacred volume. It is made into bread, with camel's milk, oil, butter, and other unctuous substances, and is almost the only food eaten by the common people of Arabia Felix. Niebuhr found it so disagreeable, that he would willingly have preferred plain barley bread. This is certainly the reason that it was appointed to the Prophet Ezekiel as a part of his hard fare. —Paxton.

13—17. (13) **defiled bread,** i.e. unclean according to Levitical rules. "This typifies the unclean relig. condition of the people when in exile." The idea is that all food which has not been consecrated by being presented to Jehovah in the sanctuary is necessarily unclean, and those who eat of it contract ceremonial defilement. In the very act of satisfying his natural appetite a man forfeits his religious standing. This was the peculiar hardship of the state of exile, that a man must become unclean. —Exp. B. (14) **polluted,** by infringement of the laws concerning the clean and the unclean.[a] **abominable flesh,** i.e. meat left over till the 3rd day, Lev. vii. 18; xix. 7. (15) **cow's dung,** which was commonly used: camel's dung makes the clearest fires. (16) **break the staff,** Le. xxvi. 26. (17) **astonied,** comp. ch. iii. 15.[b] Ezek. sought to teach his fellow exiles that this sad religious condition was to continue for a generation.

Fuel.—In consequence of the want of wood, camel's dung is used in the East for fuel. Shaw, in the preface to his Travels, where he gives a detailed description of the mode of traveling in the East, says that in consequence of the scarcity of wood, when they wanted to bake or boil anything, the camel's dung which had been left by a preceding caravan was their usual fuel, which, after having been exposed to the sun during three days, easily catches fire, and burns like charcoal. We will also add what Niebuhr says in his description of Arabia. "The Arabs of the desert make use of an iron plate to bake their bread-cakes; or they lay a round lump of dough in hot coals of wood or camel's dung, and cover them entirely with it, till the bread in their opinion is quite done, when they take the ashes from it, and eat it warm."—Rosenmüller.

CHAPTER THE FIFTH.

1—4. (1) **vss. 1—4,** 4th symbol: fate of the population of Jerus. when the city is taken. **knife,** or sword, symbol of the destruction of the inhab. of Jerus. by the sword of the Chaldæans. **barber's razor,** R. V., "as a barber's razor shalt thou take it unto thee." **balances,** to signify the exactness of Divine justice. (2) **burn,** to indicate the destruction of this proportion of the inhab. by famine and pestilence. **smite . . knife,** as a symbol of this proportion killed by the sword. **scatter . . wind,** to represent the captivity of the last third. (3) **few,** to represent those left in the land, Je. xl. 5, 6. (4) **cast . . fire,** to signify the calamity of even the few that were spared for a time.[c] **for thereof,** etc., omit "for," R. V., "therefrom," i. e. the afflicted remnant.

The Scriptures a Record of Human Sorrow.—The Bible, from the third of Genesis, is the history of a sorrowful race. This fact should teach us—I. That sorrow is mightily present in our world. Here is a book—1. The product of many lands and ages, expressing their sorrows; **2. Intended for all lands and times.** This reflection should—(1) Stir our

---

third year of Nebuc.'s reign." —Lowth.

[b] Is. lii. 10.

[c] "To use human dung for such a purpose implies the most cruel necessity. It was in violation of the law. De. xiv. 3, xxiii. 12—14." —Fausset.

Those periods of tribulation and chastisement, which the prophet here represents, have they not a voice for other times? . . . The lukewarm and fruitless professor is in bondage to the elements of the world, and therefore can have no part in that good land which floweth with milk and honey." —Fairbairn.

[a] Comp. Ac. x. 14.

[b] "Look one upon another as persons under astonishment for the greatness of your calamities, and pining away or dying a lingering death through famine and other hardships." —Lowth.

"Let it teach us not to be rigid and stick to our wills, and think it disparagement to abate of our wills and right, and yield to others, when God, who is infinitely above us, can yield to us, and doth so daily, bearing our infirmities." —Greenhill.

[c] Je. xlii. 18, xliv. 11—15.

Some judgments crush, others cut.

"Look, who comes here; a grave unto a soul, holding the eternal spirit, against her will, in the vile prison of afflicted breath. —Shakespeare.

thought; (2) Cultivate our soberness; (3) Quicken our sympathies. II. Sorrow is present in this world because of sin. The Scriptures, as the record of human sorrow, teach—1. That sorrow is here bceause of sin; 2. As the penalty of sin; 3. As one means of purification from sin.—Thomas.

"Memory, the bane of the wicked, the home of the past, the mind's magnetic telegraph." — Family Friend.

5—9. (5) vss. 5—17. Ezek. explains these four symbols (a) 5—10, reasons for these judgments, (b) 11—17, the nature of the judgment. **in the midst,** with the intention that she should hold forth My truth and claims before the nations. Notice the locally central position of Palestine: esp. as between Egypt, Phœnicia, and Assyria. (6) **changed my judgments,** R. V., "she hath rebelled against my judgments in doing wickedness . . . and against my statutes." Jerus. "had proved herself unworthy of her distinction and privileges, and tried to live as the nations around." Therefore her chastisement shall be unexampled in its severity. (7) **multiplied,** better, "raged tumultuously," in your self-will and rebellion. **neither . . you,** the words find their explanation in Jer. ii. 10, 11. In doing as the nations (ch. xi. 12; xvi. 47), Jerusalem had not done as they did, for they were at least true to the gods whom they worshiped, and she had rebelled against her God.—Pulp. Com. (8) **execute judgments,** those who beheld Israel's wickedness were to behold God's righteousness. (9) **not done,** comp. Mat. xxiv. 21.[a]

[a] La. iv. 6; Da. ix. 12; see also Zec. xiii. 8, 9, xiv. 2.

"As God connected Himself peculiarly with Israel, so there was to be a peculiar manifestation of God's wrath against sin in their case." — Fairbairn.

The opposition of God is unspeakably dreadful. It is dangerous for a man to run counter to the will of God. The very fact that He loves us, instead of mitigating the honor of the opposition, must heighten it, for no plea can soften the blow, when love itself acquiesces in it.—Pulpit Com.

10—13. (10) **eat . . thee,** Le. xxvi. 29; De. xxviii. 53; La. ii. 20, iv. 10. **remnant . . scatter,** fulfilled in the present condition of the remnant of the Jews; they are found in every land. (11) **defiled,** etc., 2 Chr. xxvi. 14; Jer. viii. This pollution of the sanctuary through false worship was the taproot fr. wh. sprung all the other evils. **detestable things,** i.e. idols. **diminish thee,** R. V. marg., "withdraw mine eye that it shall not spare." (12) **third part,** as in the symbol, vs. 2. (13) **fury to rest,** or cease, when its purpose of punishment is completed. **comforted,** appeased, either bec. his vengeance is satisfied, or the punishment has led men to repentance. **my zeal,** or just regard for My honor and authority.[b]

[b] "This is only a partial and imperfect mode of representing God's dealings with men." —Spk. Com.

"The completely human clothing of ideas in this passage is a sensible representation of the personality of God, in His being and in His actions." —Schroeder.

14—17. (14) **waste,** etc., De. xxviii. 37. **sight . . by,** the scorn and contempt of the heathen was one of the most humiliating punishments Israel could receive. Lamentations 11, 15, 16. (15) **it shall be,** rather, "she shall be," i. e. Jerusalem. **instruction,** they shall learn of God and His claims from such an example of judgment. (16) **arrows,** De. xxxii. 23. **staff of bread,** ch. iv. 16. (17) **evil beasts,** wh. soon multiply in a desolate and uninhabited country.[a]

[a] Ex. xxiii. 29; De. xxxii. 24; 2 Ki. xvii. 25.

Punishment of Pre-eminent Severity.—Notice—1. The great Agent in this punishment; 2. The nature of this punishment; 3. The retributary character of this punishment; 4. The exemplary aspect of this punishment; 5. The awful certainty of the punishment.—Pul. Com.

Figurative Use of the Word "Arrow."—The arrow in this passage, means the pestilence. The Arabs thus denote it: "I desired to remove to a less contagious air. I received from Solyman, the emperor, this message: that the emperor wondered what I meant, in desiring to remove my habitation. Is not the pestilence God's arrow, which will always hit His mark. If God would visit me herewith, how could I avoid it? 'Is not the plague,' said he 'in my own palace; and yet I do not think of removing.' "—Busbequies.

Tokens of Doom on Created Things.—Judgments were executed upon them, not because they could be held guilty, but because they had been the scenes of human wrong-doing. We are taught the needed lesson that sin is to be abhorred, not only because it defiles the sinner, but also because it draws the trail of the serpent over all he uses in his sin.—Preacher's Com.

CHAPTER THE SIXTH.

1—4. (2) **set thy face,** as if directing thy message. Cf. Dan. vi. 10. Vss. 2—10 are an apostrophe to the mountain land of Israel, which seems to stand out before the exile's mind with its mountains and hills, its ravines, and valleys, in contrast to the monotonous plain of Babylonia which stretched around him. But these mountains were familiar to the prophet as the seats of the rural idolatry in Israel. Exp. B. (3) **mountains,** etc., Palestine was a hilly, though it can hardly be called a mountainous country. **rivers,** "ravines."[a] **high places,** Canaanitish sanctuaries wh. had been adopted by Israel and sanctified to the worship of God. (4) **images,** or sun images, Le. xxvi. 30.[b] **slain .. idols,** to show the manifest connection between idolatry and calamity, and to put the idol-trusting to shame. The figure is a very graphic one. The idols were no longer to have a living congregation of worshipers, but were to be surrounded by a cordon of dead men, so that the gods and their worshipers should resemble one another.—Pul. Com.

Preachers to be Acquainted with Human Nature.—Michael Angelo, when painting an altar-piece in the conventual church, in Florence, in order that the figures might be as death-like as possible, obtained permission of the prior to have the coffins of the newly-buried opened and placed beside him during the night; an appalling expedient, but successful in enabling him to reproduce with terrible effect, not the mortal pallor only, but the very anatomy of death. If we would preach well to the souls of men, we must acquaint ourselves with their ruined state, must have their case always on our hearts both by night and day, must know the terrors of the Lord and the value of the soul, and feel a sacred sympathy with perishing sinners. There is no masterly, prevailing preaching without this.—Spurgeon.

5—7. (5) **dead carcases,** of those killed by famine and the sword. **bones,** to intimate that no decent burial should be given to the dead bodies.[c] (6) **works,** i. e. your idols, which are not gods, but the mere work of men's hands. (7) **I .. Lord,** by the display of My glory as the "All-powerful punisher of sin." The term Jehovah is used in the later prophets to mean the true and only God. In this prophet the purpose and the effect of all the judgments on Israel is that they may know that He who inflicts them is Jehovah—God alone. The same is the purpose and effect of His judgments on the heathen—these learn also the same truth.—Cam. B.

A Ruined Civilization.—Palestine is now a land of ruins, and the prophecy before us predicted that condition. But there is more behind. Houses broken down, altars overthrown, streets grass-grown, inhabited places made desolate,—these are the outward and visible signs of a decayed and broken civilization. The destruction of the civilization is the real disaster. This happened in Israel when wild beasts came out from the forests and prowled over the once safe and populous country; and it happened in another form in Europe when the hardy barbarians poured over the plains of Italy, and destroyed, not only buildings, but also the whole fabric of ancient society, and so ushered in the gloom and disorder which took possession of the early part of the Middle Ages. Christian civilization has been lost on the north coast of Africa, where Tertullian, Cyprian, and Augustine were once shining lights; it has almost vanished from the site of the seven Churches of Asia. Modern Egypt is far below the Egypt of the Pharaohs in civilization: the fellaheen of to-day build mud hovels; their ancestors forty centuries ago constructed the great Hall of Columns at Karnak—one of the wonders of the world. The ancient civilization of Mexico had entirely vanished before the discovery of South America by the importers of a new Roman Catholic civilization. The Christian civilization that has grown out of the experience of ages and slowly ripened through generations of culture is the most precious heritage we have received from our forefathers. Let us guard and treasure it as a sacred trust.—Pul. Com.

8—10. (8) **a remnant,** Is. iv. 2; Je. xliv. 14. These would comprehend the purposes of Jehovah and would become connected to true monotheism. (9) **remember me,** when under the pressure of calamity, they would, in penitence, turn thought and heart to God. **broken,** better, "when I have broken their whorish heart," etc. **with their eyes,** omit "with." **lothe themselves,** lit. "loathe themselves in their own sight;" R. V., "eyes and heart were alike involved in the sin (ch. xx. 7, 8, 24; Numb. xv. 39), and both came under the same chastisement that was to

[a] Mentioned as the favorite seat of idol rites, just as hill-tops were.

[b] 2 Chr. xxxiv. 4; Is. xvii. 8.

We get life, as we lost it; both the one and the other independently of ourselves. "As in Adam all die, even so in Christ shall all be made alive."

"God does not fulminate merely for the sake of showing his greatness; when he makes us afraid it is that he may bring us to final peace."

[c] Comp. 2 Ki. xxiii. 14, 16.

With love, the heart becomes a fair and fertile garden, with sunshine and warm hues, and exhaling sweet odors: but without it, it is a bleak desert covered with ashes."

"The spell shall at last be broken in the new knowledge of Jehovah which is produced by calamity; and the heart of the people, purified from its delusions, shall turn to Him who has smitten them, as the only true God." — John Skinner.

lead them to repentance."—Pul. Com. (10) **said in vain,** i. e. without adequate cause, or full intention and power to execute.

11—14. (11) **Smite .. foot,**[a] gestures indicating deep concern at the wickedness of the people.[b] "Call attention by acts of grief and consternation." **Alas,** etc., Woe! because of all the abominations of the house of Israel.—Polychr. Bib. (12) **far off,** i. e. out of reach of the perils of the siege. **remaineth,** in the city. **besieged,** R. V., "preserved," i. e. for the worst evil of all. (13) **slain .. altars,** vss. 4, 5. **hill,** etc., noted places for idolatrous worship.[c] **sweet savour,** the smoke of the sacrifice was regarded as a sweet savor or fragrance to the idol. (14) **Diblath,**[d] a wilderness of Diblath is unknown; Diblathaim besides being in Moab could not be called desert. The construction is difficult, but probably the reading should be: from the wilderness to Riblah, i. e. from south to north. Riblah was situated on the northern border of the country.—Cam. B.

Stages of the Soul's Progress from Sin unto Salvation.—1. Sin leading to punishment. Sooner or later, penalty follows trangsgression. 2. Punishment leading to recollection. Trials should lead us to review our life and consider our ways. 3. Recollection leading to repentance. The true penitent never seeks to excuse himself on account of his sins, or to explain them away, or to extenuate the guilt of them. 4. Repentance leading to devout recognition of God. "They shall know that I am the Lord." "The Lord would have spoken in vain or to no purpose if the event had not corresponded with the utterance. By the correspondence of utterance and event it appears that He who was spoken of by the Son of Man is Jehovah" (Hengstenberg). Pain and trial are blessed when by Divine grace they lead to earnest reflection and sincere repentance and saving knowledge of God.—Pul. Com.

[a] Nu. xxiv. 10; Eze. xxi. 17.

[b] "In indignation at the abominations of Israel, extend thine hand towards Judea, as if about to 'strike' and 'stamp,' shaking off the dust with thy foot, in token of how God shall 'stretch out His hand upon them,' and tread them down." —Fausset.

[c] Je. ii. 20; Ho. iv. 13.

[d] Nu. xxxiii. 46; Je. xlviii. 22.

"The name, in the modified form Diblathan, is found on the Moabite stone." —Spk. Com.

CHAPTER THE SEVENTH.

"Ch. vii. is one of those singled out by Ewald as preserving most faithfully the spirit and language of Ezekiel's earlier utterances. Both in thought and expression it exhibits a freedom and animation seldom attained in Ezekiel's writings, and it is evident that it must have been composed under keen emotion." **1—4.** (1) **Moreover,** etc., the ch. beginning thus is a dirge rather than a prophecy. Only three or four years were to intervene before the final overthrow of Jerusalem by the Chaldæans. (2) **land of Israel,** this is the term for the whole land that is used after the captivity of the northern nation.[a] **four corners,** or wings;[b] fig. to include the whole land; the inevitableness and finality of doom (3) **recompense,** etc., God speaks of the people's sin as if it had been a personal injury to Him. (4) **not spare,** or set limits to the calamities that are coming. Punishment and bitter suffering are necessary to reveal the hateful character of sin. **know .. Lord,** i. e. that He who is able to inflict such punishments is Jehovah; and what the nature of their Jehovah is by the righteousness of his vengeance.

The Hand of the Clock on the Hour of doom.—1. Retribution, though apparently tardy, has its own set time. 2. Retribution is not a haphazard accident. 3. Retribution from God is most equitable. 4. Retribution, when it comes, is most complete. 5. This retribution is the natural fruitage of sin.—Pulpit Com.

5—9. (5) **an only evil,** lit. "one evil," an evil wh. is one and final. Hag. ii. 6, "Yet once, it is a little while, and I will shake," etc. **is come,** R. V., "it cometh;" the nearness of the punishment fills the prophet's vision. (6) **the end,** the final manifestation of the Divine judgment on the land. **watcheth,** "wakes up for thee," slumbering vengeance is about to fall upon Israel. (7) **morning,** R. V., "doom." **sounding,** R. V., "a day of tumult, and not of joyful shouting upon the mountains." no vintage shouting, but the sullen tumult of invasion. (8) **shortly,** in a very few years; at most three or four. (9) **not spare,** vs. 4.

Sin in Blossom (vs. 5).—The teaching of the figure before us is—I. That beauty may be associated with evil, as beauty of countenance, Absalom, poetry, eloquence, art, magnificent mansions and picturesque

[a] Mal. i. 1, ii. 11.

"Possibly Manasseh and his successors in the kingdom of Judah had the dominion of the whole land of Canaan, formerly divided into the two kingdoms of Judah and Israel, as tributaries under the kings of Assyria." —Prideaux.

[b] Nu. xxiv. 17.

"What stronger breastplate than a heart untainted? Thrice is he armed who hath his quarrel just; and he but naked, though locked up in steel, whose conscience with injustice is corrupted." —Shakespeare.

"Justice looks at us straight and treats us accordingly."

"Obligation to do right is a blessed tyranny."

acres. II. That success is no test of moral right or wrong. III. That the forces of retribution are ever at work.—W. R. Thomas.

10—15. (10) **morning,** i. e. doom springs out of the earth; the rod of Divine vengeance flowers, the pride of Israel's stiffheartedness bears fruit. **rod .. blossomed,** a fig. to represent the fact that the iniquity of Judah was now full, and demanded immediate Divine interference.[a] (11) **rod of wickedness,** or a rod that must punish wickedness.[b] **multitude .. theirs,** R. V., "of their multitude nor of their wealth neither shall there be eminency among them." Israel was to be entirely swept away. (12) **day,** i. e. the day of doom.[c] **buyer .. mourn.** We have to read, between the lines, the story of Ezekiel's companions in exile. They belonged, it will be remembered, to the nobler and wealthier class (2 Ki. xxv. 19). They, it would seem, had been compelled to sell their estates at a price which made the "buyer rejoice and the seller mourn." In each case the joy and the sorrow would be but transient. Wrath had gone out against the whole multitude.—Pulp. Com. (13) **not return,** to occupy his land, the lease of which he sells. The coming calamity is about to obliterate all titles, and prevent their reoccupation by the exiles of Tel-abib. **although .. alive,** i. e. during their lifetime. **for the vision .. return,** i. e. "for wrath is upon all," and shall go straight onward to do its work. **neither .. life,** better, "Neither shall any strengthen for himself his life by his iniquity." (14) **none .. battle,** bec. of failing hearts. (15) **sword,** etc., v. 2, vi. 12, etc.

Destiny is the Summing up of Previous Actions.—1. Punishment for sin comes slowly. 2. Punishment for sin comes surely.—Preachers' Com.

16—19. (16) **escape .. mountains,** even if any escape the immediate doom, it will be only to the mountains where they will mourn for the ruined city. **doves,** noted for the mournfulness of their note, and their fond attachment to their homes and mates.[d] (17) refers to the besieged. **hands .. feeble,** for the fig. see Job iv. 3, 4; Is. xxxv. 3. (18) **gird,** etc., Is. xv. 3; Je. xlviii. 37. **baldness,** Is. xxii. 12; comp. De. xiv. 1. (19) **cast,** etc., this would be done in the misery of famine, when they found gold and silver could feed nobody.[e] **stumbling block,** curse was on the gold and silver because they had made idol gods, and ornaments for idol gods with it.[f]

20—22. (20) **beauty .. ornament,** better, "and the beauty of their ornament they turned into pride, and they made images .. thereof." The thing spoken of is still their silver and gold; this they not only turned into pride, but made also images of it.—Cam. B. **images,** of their idol gods. **set .. them,** "made it as an unclean thing;" given it into the hands of the Gentiles. (21) **strangers,** barbarous and savage nations. (22) **face .. them,** so as not to interfere and defend the temple from their outrages.

Strangers.—Instead of abiding under a settled and enlightened government, Judæa has been the scene of frequent invasions which have introduced a succession of foreign nations. When the Ottomans took Syria from the Mamelouks, they considered it as the spoil of a vanquished enemy. According to this law, the life and property of the vanquished belong to the conqueror. The Government is far from disapproving of a system of robbery and plunder which it finds so profitable.—Volney.

23—27. (23) **Make a chain,** comp. Je. xxvii. 2. A chain is the symbol of captivity.[g] **bloody crimes,** lit. judgment of blood, i. e. "murder committed with hypocritical formalities of justice." (24) **worst,** the most cruel and terrible.[a] **pomp .. strong,** or the pride of power, Le. xxvi. 19. **their holy places,** God no longer owns them as His. (26) **mischief,** Is. xlvii. 11. **seek a vision,** comp. Je. xxxvii. 17, xxxviii. 14. "A powerful description of the dismay and despair that will seize all classes in the state as the day of wrath draws near. Calamity after calamity comes, rumor follows hard on rumor, and the heads of the nation are distracted and cease to exercise the functions of leadership." (27) **king .. troubled,** general consternation making all the leaders and counsellors of the land helpless; "prince," i. e. chief civil ruler. **deserts,** "In the correspondence bet. desert and retribution men shall be made to acknowledge the operation of the divine righteousness."

---

a "Wickedness daily spreads and increases, till it becomes ripe for judgment." —Lowth.

b "The violence and fury of the enemy have risen up so as to become a rod to punish the wickedness of the people." —Spk. Com.

"From the body of one guilty deed
A thousand ghostly fears and haunting thoughts proceed."
—Wordsworth.

c Joel ii. 2; Zep. i. 14.

d "As doves, whose natural abode is the valleys, when driven by fear into the mountains mourn lamentably, so shall the remnant, who have escaped actual death, moan in the land of their exile." —Spk. Com.

e "Their wealth will not procure them the necessaries of life under the straits of famine, or miseries of bondage." —Lowth.

f Eze. xiv. 3, xvi. 17, xliv. 12.

g "It was customary to lead away captives in a row with a chain passed from the neck of one to the other." —Fausset.

a De. xxviii. 49, 50.

"This expression appears to indicate that at this time the Bab. empire contained in it an element of rude, rough, and uncultivated warriors, while at the same time there must have been a highly civilized population long settled in Nineveh or Babylon."—Ewald.

No Help or Hope.—Pitiable is the figure which is brought before our vision—men seeking the spiritual, men inquiring for the prophet, men crying out for Samuel, men praying that they may be enabled to pray; yet every cry returning to the suppliant without an answer, and every expectation falling back upon its author only to increase his sense of mortification and loss.—People's Bible.

b Comp. 2; Ki. xvi. 10—15, xxi. 7.

c "Ezekiel has this repeated vision of the glory of God to aggravate the sin of Israel, in changing their own God, the God of Israel (who is a God of so much glory as here He appears to be), for dunghill gods, scandalous gods, false gods, and indeed no gods." Mat. Henry.

"Surely if sin attacks the sovereignty of God, self-righteousness is equally guilty of treason: for as sin boasts, 'I will not keep God's law,' self-righteousness exclaims, 'I will not be saved in God's way; I will make a new road to heaven.'"

CHAPTER THE EIGHTH.

1—4. (1) one year and two months after the first vision. **elders,** those carried away with Jehoiachin, and now at the Chebar. These had come to inquire of the Lord, through His Prophet, concerning the affairs in Jerus. They were aware, whether the information was recent or not, that they were absolutely disowned by the new authorities in Jerusalem, and that it was impossible that they should ever come back peaceably to their old place in the state. This created a problem which they could not solve.—Exp. B. **hand .. me,** i. e. the trance-state, ch. i. 3. (2) **likeness,** etc., lxx. "the appearance of a man," comp. ch. i. 26, 27. **loins .. fire,** to intimate the vengeance of God kindled against the wicked Jews. **amber,** ch. i. 4. (3) **form of a hand,** comp. Da. v. 5. **in the visions,** i. e. he seemed to have all these things done to him in the vision. In all probability we have here the actual picture of the terrible state of affairs due to the degenerating influences of irreligion, wh. existed in Jerus, when Ezek. fell into this trance. **door .. gate,** R. V., "door of the gate of the inner court," i. e. the entrance to the court of the priests. **image of jealousy.** some idol figure that provoked Jehovah to jealousy.[b] (4) **glory .. there,** showing plainly that it was the residence of Jehovah alone. Ref. is to the Shekinah cloud,[c] wh. appeared to Ezek. in his first vision.

An Idol Provokes the Jealousy of God.—1. Pleasure. "Love not pleasure, love God: for the supreme love of the one excludes the supreme love of other."—Carlyle. 2. Money—a hard, helpless idol. 3. Earthly love. When a human affection will not yield in submission to the will of God, the object of it becomes an "image of jealousy." 4. Self-will. We may think we serve God, yet are only working according to our own will. This also is idolatry. 5. All these images of jealousy are just so many embodiments of self, the monster idol of the soul and rival of God.—Pulpit Com.

a "The locality of the idol enhance the heinousness of the sin before God's own altar."—Fausset.

b Comp. Eze. vii. 21, 22, x. 18.

"What is there so ponderous in evil, that a thumb's bigness of it should outweigh the mass of things not evil which were heaped into the other scale.—Hawthorne.

"Many prayers which seem earnest are not answered because they supplicate for gratification to some lust of the flesh or mind. Many a religious meeting dissolves as a vapour wherein no appearance of God is traceable, because they have

5, 6. (5) **toward the north,** comp. 2 Ki. xvi. 14[a] **the altar,** i. e. the great altar of burnt-offering. (6) **great abominations,** by thus in the most insulting way setting up an idol image right in front of Jehovah's shrine. The first effect of the sense that "Jehovah hath forsaken his land," was the multiplication of false objects of worship. "Syncretism in religion and fatalism in politics—these were the twin symptoms of the decay of faith among the upper classes in Jerusalem." **go .. sanctuary,** being compelled to forsake it, and deliver it up to its pollution.[b] **turn .. abominations,** R. V., "but thou shalt again see yet other great abom." "Bad begins but worse remains behind."

7—11. (7) vss. 7—12, the Elders practising idolatry in secret. **hole in the wall,** through which he could see into one of the very side chambers of the sanctuary itself. (8) **dig,** etc., the secrecy of these rites is thus forcibly indicated: the ordinary entrance had been covered up, and some secret entrance made, poss. through the other rooms. Or the very chamber itself may have been secretly made in the foundations. (9) **Go in,** so as to get demonstration of the evil. (10) **pourtrayed,** etc., these pictures were objects of worship. "The words obviously paint the theriomorphic worship of Egypt, the scarabæus probably being prominent. The alliance between Jehoiakim and Pharaoh (2 Kings xxiv. 33—35), and which Zedekiah was endeavoring to renew, would naturally bring about a revival of that cultus." (11) **seventy,** etc., a company of the elders or leaders of the nation. Poss. members of the great council, or Sanhedrim. That the very highest and most influential citizens of Jerus should embrace this heathenish abomination, indicated the utter collapse of Jehovah worship.

The Chamber of Imagery (vss. 7—12).—From this vision we learn the following truths. I. That the degenerating tendency in the most advanced people has ever been strong. II. That the greatest sins of humanity are generally the hidden ones. 1. Man has power to conceal his sins; 2. As a sinner he has the strongest reasons for concealment. III. That an insight of the hidden iniquity of a population is a necessary qualification for a true reformer. 1. It serves to impress him with the justice of human suffering; 2. Also with the greatness of God's love in redemption; 3. With the sublime mission of Christianity. IV. That the most hidden sins are destined to be exposed. Of this exposure of sin there are two kinds. 1. Unconscious; 2. Conscious. V. That a practical disregard of the constant presence and inspection of God is an explanation of all sin.—Thomas.

Secret Wickedness.—All that was done by rebellious Israel was done "in the dark." By the "dark" we are to understand that the idolatry was performed in secret. There was an open and public idolatry in Jerusalem at this very time, but such is the downward tendency of all evil that it was not sufficient to have a public and an almost established idolatry, but something further should be done in darkness and concealment. Stolen waters are sweet. Man cannot have enough of evil. He always invents another sweetness, another luxury, another delight in the service of his evil master. When wickedness can be enjoyed in public it ceases to be an enjoyment. It would appear as if the darkness were necessary to bring out the full savor of a bad man's delight.—Peop. Bib. ——In reading Dr. Madden's account of the way in which he got access to the chamber of imagery of the temple of Edfu, we were strongly reminded of the similar chamber which the prophet saw. Hassan, an old man, disclosed to Dr. Madden a secret passage, "a chink in an old wall, which I should creep through on my hands and feet. This passage, not two feet and a half high, that my mouth and nose were sometimes buried in the dust. After proceeding about ten yards in utter darkness, I had the inexpressible satisfaction of standing once more on my feet. We found ourselves in an apartment of great magnitude, and adorned with sacred paintings and hieroglyphics."—Kitto.

12—14. (12) **ancients,** i. e. elders. **in the dark,** or in secret.[a] **chambers .. imagery,** or his chambers painted with images.[b] **Lord .. earth,** R. V. marg., "land." The wish was father to the thought; men who so readily yielded to the belief in Jehovah's absence were very willing to be persuaded of its truth. The religion of Jehovah had always imposed a check on social and civic wrong, and men whose power rested on violence and oppression could not but rejoice to be rid of it.—Exp. B. (14) **weeping for Tammuz,** or Adonis, poss. the same as Osiris, a symbol of the sun.[c] "The sun-god mourned by his lover Astarte, the personification of vegetable and animal life, at his departure in the decline of the year to dwell in the region of gloom with Persephone."

the love-tale
Infected Sion's daughters with like heat;
Whose wanton passions in the sacred porch
Ezekiel saw, when, by the vision led,
His eyes surveyed the dark idolatries
Of alienated Judah.—Par. Lost.

15—18. (16) **inner court,** that of the priests. **between .. altar,** positions which even the priests only took on the most solemn occasions, and then they turned to the west of the temple.[d] "During all this time the glory of Jehovah has stood in the court, and there is something very impressive in the picture of these infatuated men and women preoccupied with their unholy devotions and all unconscious of the presence of Him whom they deemed to have forsaken the land." **faces .. east,** offering thus the insult of their backs to Jehovah, and the worship of their faces to the sun.[e] (17) **branch .. nose,** "as the Persians, who, when worshiping the rising sun, held a tamarisk branch in their hands. Polychrome Bib. reads, "behold they are sending a stench to my nostrils." (18) **not spare,** ch. v. 11.

Ezekiel's Vision.—It is not easy to say how far the representation that the idolatrous usages were practiced in the temple is to be taken

not come to the Father only by Christ. Get a single eye, purify hearts by faith, search out all doublemindedness in private or public means of worship, lest God go far off, refusing to accept and hear. 'Beside Him there is no God,' and a divided worship is worthless."

"Conscience is harder than our enemies; knows more, accuses with more nicety." — George Eliot.

"It is not the loud voice but upright heart, that God will regard."
—Pul. Com.

a As vss. 7, 8.

b "Every one of the 70 elders had his own imagery, his favorite object of idolatrous worship portrayed upon the wall of the chamber; and to it he did homage with his censer, according to the device of his own heart."
—Wordsworth.

c "This was a form of Nature-worship. It was a festival held when Nature in the E. seems to wither and die under the scorching heat of the sun, to burst forth again into life in due season. The death of Adonis symbolised the suspension of the productive powers of Nature, wh. were in due time revived. The excitement of the festival led to unbridled license and excess." — Biblical Things.

d Joel ii. 17.

e "To understand this clearly it should be observed that, as if purposely to prevent the

abomination referred to, the entrance of the temple was on the E. side of the building, so that, in looking towards it in worship, the worshipers necessarily turned their backs upon the sun at its rising in the E., at wh. time the luminary was most usually worshiped."
—Kitto.

literally. Such practices are not referred to by Jeremiah nor other prophets of the time. It is possible that the chambers and cells about the gateways, which appear in some cases to have belonged to private persons, may have been used for illegitimate purposes, but that sun-worship was actually practiced between the temple and the altar has little probability. And the scene in the chamber of imagery is obviously ideal. The prophet certainly desires to shew that idolatry both public and in private was practised by all classes, the elders representing the nation, the women, and perhaps also the priests; and that these idolatries were not only the old native ones of Israel, but new imports at this period from all the nations around.—Camb. B.

CHAPTER THE NINTH.

[a] Comp. 2 Ki. x. 24.

[b] Re. vii. 1.

"A noble yet most solemn thought is it that every man has near him the angel of the Lord, bringing blessing or inflicting judgment, or training the life in all the mystery of progress." —People's Bible.

1—4. (1) **loud voice,** as giving a command requiring immediate attention. **have charge,** i. e. the angels charged to execute God's judgments on the city.[a] **draw near,** quickly; ready to act at once. (2) **slaughter weapon,** such as Levites used for preparing the sacrifices. **one man,** the leader of them. **linen,** the dress of the priests, and symbol of purity. **inkhorn .. side,** it was quite usual for scribes to carry the receptacle for ink and pen stuck in their girdle. (3) **gone up,** departed from the inner sanctuary to the threshold, to direct the work of his supernatural agencies of execution. (4) **mark,**[b] to indicate that such should be spared. **sigh,** etc., in their grief at the iniquity around them, but had still remained faithful to true Jehovah worship.

Christians a Living Protest Against Sin (vs. 4).—I. God's people described. 1. They are sighing ones, sorrowing; 2. They are crying ones, protesting. II. Their peculiar mark, a mark of—1. Separation; 2. Service; 3. A visible mark; 4. A mark of safety.—Whythe.

[a] 2 Chr. xxxvi. 17.

"Judgment often begins at the house of God, bec. such persons sin against greater light and clearer convictions."
—Lowth.

[b] Nu. xix. 11.

"Where much is given, much shall be required. There are never privileges to enjoy without corresponding duties to fulfil in return." —Phillips Brooks.

"Every great and original writer, in proportion as he is great or original, must himself create the taste by which he is to be relished." —Wordsworth.

Dr. Thompson, spaking of one of these scribes or letter-writers, says:—"This is a sort of Moslem confessional, and that fellow's head must be crammed with the secrets and the scandal of half

5—7. (5) **smite,** all that have not the mark of vs. 4. (6) **begin .. sanctuary,** where idolatry was most shamefully developed. "There he was most present, there most fully known, there if possible most forgotten and provoked, and there his holiness and godhead will assert themselves with most terribleness against the sins of men." This work of destruction was in fact done by the Chaldæans.[a] **ancient men,** ch. viii. 11, 12, 16. (7) **Defile the house,** this was done by shedding human blood in it, and leaving in it dead bodies.[b]

Beginning at the Sanctuary.—1. There is no protection in the sanctuary. 2. The greatest guilt is found in the sanctuary. 3. The doom of the sanctuary is a warning to the world. Let us flee from the sanctuary to the Saviour.—Pulpit Com.

Preaching: its Force the Main Consideration.—I had tried to drive certain long brass-headed nails into a wall, but had never succeeded except in turning up their points, and rendering them useless. When a tradesman came who understood his work, I noticed that he filed off all the points of the nails, the very points upon whose sharpness I had relied; and when he had quite blunted them, he drove them in as far as he pleased. With some consciences our fine points in preaching are worse than useless. Our keen distinctions and nice discriminations are thrown away on many; they need to be encountered with sheer force and blunt honesty. The truth must be hammered into them by main strength, and we know from whom to seek the needed power.—Spurgeon.

8—11. (8) **left,** bec. the avengers were gone forth from the temple to slay in the city. Then the Prophet intercedes. **residue,** etc., Ezek., like Moses and St. Paul, inquires of God whether he will utterly destroy the Jewish nation, or in his graciousness only chastise. (9) **full of blood,** the sign of violence. **perverseness,** or wresting of judgment, ch. viii. 23. He is reassured by the declaration that the guilt of Judah and Israel demands no less a punishment than this, because the notion that Jehovah had forsaken the land had opened the floodgates of iniquity, and filled the land with bloodshed and the city with oppression.—Exp. B. (10) **not spare,** ch. v. 11. (11) **reported,** his report concerned his safe preservation of God's elect by affixing on them the required mark.

The Work of Justice Proceeds Side by Side with that of Mercy.—

Along with the six officers appointed to destroy was one differently clad, whose work was to save. His clothing was the attire of peace—white linen—i. e. the dress of a true priest. Against six destroyers there was one protector, which denoted how few was the number of the faithful. They were to have a distinguishing mark in the most conspicuous place—in their foreheads. The owner of the flock will take care to put his own sign-manual on his sheep. "The Lord knoweth them that are his." In every time of trouble "he has hidden them in his pavilion—in the secret of his tabernacle will he hide them." Noah and his family in the ark; Lot and his daughters in Zoar; the early Christians safe in Pella when Jerusalem was destroyed.—Pul. Com.

CHAPTER THE TENTH.

1—4. (1) **in the firmament,** better, "above the firmament;" **the** glory of the Lord had returned fr. the threshold to the throne above the cherubim. **cherubims,** R. V., "cherubim," comp. ch. i. 26. **sapphire stone,** Ex. xxiv. 10. (2) **he spake,** i. e. the being seated on the throne. **cherub,** i. e. the fourfold fig. described in ch. i. **coals,** with which to burn up, or destroy the city.[a] (3) **right side,** or south side. **cloud .. court,** i. e. the Shekinah cloud was moved from the entrance of the sanctuary, and filled the priest's court.[b] (4) **went up,** as if ascending and passing away.

5—7. (5) **sound .. wings,** ch. i. 24. The cherubic figure appears to move, as if in close attendance on the Divine glory. **voice .. God,** the use of "God Almighty" (El Shaddai; comp. Exod. vi. 3), the name of God as ruling over nature, while "Jehovah" expressed his covenant relationship to Israel, is characteristic of the early stage of the religion of Israel (Gen. xvii. 1; xxviii. 3).—Pulp. Com. (6) **Take fire,** vs. 2. (7) **clothed with linen,** symbol of his priestly office; but now he has to become a minister of Divine vengeance. **took .. went out,** to put the command at once into execution.

8—12. The whole passage (vss. 8—17) is certainly superfluous, and might be omitted but for the difficulty of imagining any motive that would have tempted a scribe to insert it. We must keep in mind the possibility that this part of the book had been committed to writing before the final redaction of Ezekiel's prophecies, and the description may have served a purpose than which is superseded by the fuller narrative which we now possess in ch. 1.—Exp. B. (8) **man's hand,** ch. i. 8. (9) **beryl stone,** ch. i. 16. (10) **appearances,** etc., ch. i. 13, 15, 17. (11) **head looked,** either the "principal" wheel wh. for the time determined the course of the whole cherubic chariot; or "the front of the chariot." (12) **eyes,** ch. i. 18.

The Hand and the Wing (vs. 8).—There are two proofs of our religious life—our great thoughts of God; our great deeds for God. In religion, as in life, there are two ideas—the sense of farness, the sense of nearness. I. See what a Divine work creation is. II. Then you see what Divine providence is. III. See in the human hand, beneath the wing of the angel, the relation of a life of action to a life of contemplation. IV. In a word, you see what religion is; it is the human hand beneath the angel's wing—E. P. Hood.

13—17. (13) **O wheel,** Polychr. B. "And in my hearing the wheels were called 'chariot.'" Heb. the galgal, or the whirling. These wheels were most rapid in their revolutions. (14) **of a cherub,** why we have "cherub" here instead of "ox" it is difficult to see. (15) **lifted up,** to attend the Divine Glory on this its removal from the Temple. (16) **cherubims went,** ch. i. 19. (17) **spirit .. them,** ch. i. 20, 21.

Note on vs. 14.—It seems possible to explain the verse only by making some suppositions which may appear rather artificial, viz. first that the prophet looking at the phenomenon of the chariot and four creatures as a whole saw four faces presented to him, one (and a different one) by each of the creatures, and that he named the faces which were thus presented to him. We should then translate "the face of the first," "the face of the second," etc., though this seems opposed to the meaning of the first words of the verse. And secondly, that he assumes the side of

the city. No matter; I suppose, like other confessors, he keeps dark and may be trusted. Still, this letter writing would not be a very thriving business in our own country."

God is infallible, and His commands make right. Obedience to them must characterize His people.

[a] For coals of fire as denoting the Divine vengeance, see Ps. cxl. 10; Re. viii. 5.

[b] "The Shekinah, or Divine glory, is represented as a bright flame breaking out of a thick cloud." —Lowth.

"The Most High, if he pleases, can turn our greatest comforts into our direst curses; and he may do so if we misuse them. 'They had abused fire,' says Greenhill, 'to maintain their gluttony, for fulness of bread was one of their sins; they burned incense to idols, and abused the altar fire, which had been the greatest refreshing to their souls; . . . and now even this fire kindled upon them.' And as a matter of fact, fire was used in destroying the temple and other places in Jerusalem. Josephus tells how Nebuzaradan, by command of the King of Babylon, having despoiled the temple of its precious and sacred treasures, set fire to it. 'When he had carried these off, he set fire to the temple in the fifth month, the first

the chariot presented to him not to be the front, but regards the side looking in another direction as the front or head.—Cam. Bib.

18—22. (18) **departed,**[a] moved again, as if ascending. "It now quite leaves the house itself, and settles upon the cherubim which stood in the court adjoining it, vs. 3." Ezek. considered the temple deserted of God fr. that moment. It was like Shiloh. (19) **wheels .. them,** ch. i. 19, 26. (20) **knew .. cherubims,** i. e. now I recognized that this strange living creature represented the cherubim that guarded the glory, in the holy of holies. (21) **hands,** ch. i. 8. (22) **saw .. Chebar,** as narrated in ch. i. Now, as it were, he understands why the first vision was seen as coming from the north. He does not tell us whether the journey of which he saw the beginning was to end. For the present there was a halt, as we learn from ch. xi. 23, "over the midst of the city." Even when the vision ended, it had not gone further than the Mount of Olives. It was, at any rate, no longer in the temple. The banks of Chebar or any other place might become, as Bethel had been to Jacob (Gen. **xxviii. 17**), as "the house of God" and "the gate of heaven."—Pul. Com.

day of the month, in the eleventh year of the reign of Zedekiah, and in the 'eighteenth year of Nebuchadnezzar; he also burnt the palace and overthrew the city.'"—W. F. Adeney.

[a] "The cherubim (or chariot) had stood first on the threshold of the temple door, and there received the glory of the Lord. They then lifted their wings, rose and left the temple by the east gate of the outer court, at the entrance of which they now for a time stood. It was by the east gate of the outer court that the glory of the Lord returned to the new temple. Ch. xliii. 4."—Spk. Com.

CHAPTER THE ELEVENTH.

1—4. (1) **lifted me up,** ch. iii. 12, 14, viii. 3. **east gate,** where the glory tarried awhile in its departing. **five .. men,** "princes of the people," who were plotting rebellion against the king of Babylon in opposition to the teachings of Jeremiah. The priests forsake God's laws, the rulers spurn his counsel. **Jaazaniah,** comp. ch. viii. 11; but the names cannot be identified with any known persons. (2) **wicked counsel,** esp. in bidding the people not to believe the Divine threatenings by the Prophets. (3) **not near,** i. e. the threatened day of calamity. R. V., "the time is not near to build houses." I incline, while adopting the Revised Version rendering, to interpret the words, as Smend takes them, as the defiant utterance of despair: "It is no time for building houses, here or elsewhere. We are doomed. Well, let us meet it as we best may."—Pul. Com. **caldron,**[a] likening their safety within the impregnable walls of Jerusalem, to the safety of flesh in a caldron, wh. the fire cannot reach."[b] (4) **prophesy,** declare the denunciations of God against them.

Note on chs. 9—11.—Davidson concisely points out the relation existing betw. chs. ix, x; and ch. xi. in these words: "The city was thought impregnably strong, and Jehovah's presence would protect it. The prophet symbolizes the departure of Jehovah from it, and warns those who trust to its strength that their trust is vain. Yet the fall of the city is not the last act in Israel's hisory; the 'house of Israel' is wider than the population of Jerusalem, and towards the larger Israel Jehovah has purposes of mercy. He will restore them to their ancient heritage, where they shall serve him in a land purified from all its uncleanness."

5—12. (5) **fell upon me,** comp. ch. iii. 24. **I know the things,** i. e. their plottings. Ezek. read their thoughts before they issued in deeds. (6) **multiplied your slain,** ch. xxii. 3, 4. The conspirators put to death all who opposed their evil policies. (8) **the sword,** or judgment by war. (9) **hands of strangers,** who shall carry you into captivity: the Babylonian army under Nebuchadnezzar. (10) **border of Israel,** at Riblah in the land of Hamath,[c] where the king of Babylon judged and condemned Zechariah.[d] (11) **not .. caldron,** i. e. it shall be no defence from the fire of the Divine indignation. (12) **not walked,** etc., De. xii. 30, 31.

13—16. (13) **Pelatiah,** vs. 1. This stroke of God indicated the destruction of the idolaters, of whom Pelatiah was a leader. **full end,** or a complete, irremediable destruction.[a] (15) **thy brethren,** i. e. those of thy kindred and acquaintance who are carried captive with thee. **men .. kindred,** Polychr. B. and Sept. "thy fellow-exiles." As in Jeremiah's vision (xxiv. 1), they were the "good figs;" those in the city, the vile and worthless. They were the remnant, the residue, for whom there was a hope of better things. They were despised as far off from the Lord. They were really nearer to his presence than those who worshiped in the temple from which Jehovah had departed.—Pulp. Com. **us .. possession,** i. e. those left in Jerusalem regarded their captive brethren as

[a] Je. i. 13; Eze. xxiv. 3, 4.

[b] "These infidels purpose to deride the Prophet; as if they had said —If this city be a caldron, we had rather take our chances of being consumed in it, than leave our fine houses and run the risk of war or captivity."—Lowth.

[c] 1 Ki. viii. 65; 2 Ki. xiv. 25.

[d] Je. lii. 9, 10.

"There would be peculiarities in the woes which should befall Israel that would be marked as unique throughout all time. If acts as shocking are observed in the distressed periods of other nations, we must remember that when a wife or child is expelled from the home, the calamity, though similar, is far worse than when a guest or servant is expelled." —D. G. Watt.

[a] Comp. Je. iv. 27, v. 10, 18.

coming under Divine judgments, and themselves as in the Divine favor. The idea which lay under their religious attitude was that the exiles had gone into captivity because their sins had incurred Jehovah's anger, and that now His wrath was exhausted and the blessing of His favor would rest on those who had been left in the land.—Exp. B. (16) **little sanctuary,**[b] R. V., "a sanctuary for a little while." Religiou perhaps perishes sooner from the overgrowth of ritual than fr. its deficiency."

The Sanctuary of the Exile.—I. God is the best sanctuary. 1. God vouchsafes His presence to His people. He does not only give a house of worship; He comes Himself. 2. God's presence sanctifies. Wherever God visits us He makes a sanctuary. The workshop is a holy place when God is in it. 3. God's presence saves; for He is "a Sun and a Shield." II. This sanctuary is to be found in exile. 1. In exile from the native land. 2. In exile from the old delights. 3. In exile from heaven. 4. For a short season.—W. F. Adeney.

Spiritual Religion.—It is a historical fact that the very meagreness of the religion which could be practised in exile was the means of strengthening the more spiritual and permanent elements which constitute the essence of religion. The observances which could be maintained apart from the Temple acquired an importance which they never afterwards lost; and although some of these, such as circumcision, the Passover, the abstinence from forbidden food, were purely ceremonial, others, such as prayer, reading of the Scriptures, and the common worship of the synagogue, represent the purest and most indispensable forms in which communion with God can find expression. That Jehovah Himself became even in small measure what the word "sanctuary" denotes indicates an enrichment of the religious consciousness of which perhaps Ezekiel did not perceive the full import.—Exp. Bib.

[b] "They have been carried far away from the literal and material sanctuary at Jerusalem, but I myself will be their sanctuary." —Wordsworth. Is. viii. 14; Ps. xci. 9.

"My shrine is the humble heart—a preparation for Gospel catholicity when the local and material temple should give place to the spiritual."—Fausset.

"God and all that He has made is not more than God without anything that He has made. It is therefore better to enjoy Him without anything else than to enjoy everything else without Him."—Secker.

17—21. (17) **gather you,** etc., the point seems to be that the earlier captives should return, but the proud remnant then in Jerusalem should be destroyed, or, if taken into capitivity, never return from it to their own land. (18) **they,** i. e. the people of the earlier captivities. **detestable things,** or things associated with idolatry. (19) **one heart,** a united feeling of devotion to the sole service of God (Is. xxxii. 39).[c] **new spirit,** comp. the stiff-neckedness and rebelliousness which they had formerly shown.[d] **stony .. flesh,** the old stony heart, unimpressible and obstinate, shall be taken away, and a heart of "flesh," sensitive and responsive to the touch of Jehovah, shall be given them.[e] (20) **my people,** as serving Me heartily and sincerely, keeping faithfully their covenant with God. (21) **heart .. heart,** we should prob. read, "whose heart goeth after their detestable things," etc.

A New Heart—An Indian Chief.—The efforts of some Christian missionaries had been the means of diffusing much Scriptural knowledge among the Delaware Indians of North America, and their doctrines were frequently the subject of conversation among them. One evening, Tedynscung, a native chief, was sitting by the fireside of his friend, who mentioned the golden rule to him as very excellent,—"For one man to do to another as he would the other should do to him." "It is impossible!—It cannot be done!" said the Indian chief. After musing for about a quarter of an hour, Tedynscung again gave his opinion, and said, "Brother, I have been thoughtful on what you told me. If the Great Spirit that made man would give him a new heart, he could do as you say, but not else."

[d] Zec. xii. 10.

[c] Ac. iv. 32.

[e] "The contrast is not, as usual, between the spirit anu the flesh, but, between the heart unnaturally hardened, and tue heart reawakened to feeling proper to man." —Spk. Com.

"A heart unspotted is not easily daunted." —Shakespeare.

22—25. (22) **lift up,** as in attitude for flying. (23) **upon the mountain,** i. e. the Mount of Olives. The Shekinah thus left altogether the temple and city: yet, in great grace, it lingered near.[a] (24) **brought .. Chaldaea,** i. e. back again to the banks of the Chebar.[b] (25) **them .. captivity,** see ch. viii. 1.

Departure of God from His temple (vs. 23).—I. How averse God is to forsake His people. Look we to His declarations; look we to examples. II. What are the different steps by which His departure may be discovered? He withholds—1. The manifestations of His love; 2. The influences of His grace; 3. The warnings of His spirit. III. The dreadful state of those who are forsaken by Him. 1. They are delivered up into the hands of their spiritual enemies; 2. They live only to

[a] The Rabbis say that the glory lingered for three years over the Mount of Olives, but of this Scripture says nothing.

[b] "Not in actual fact, but in ecstatic vision. He had been as to the outward world all the time before the elders in Chaldaea; he now reports what he had witnessed with the inner eye."—Fausset.

"The form of the vision changes, but the God of the vision abides the same."—Parker.

increase their guilt and misery. Apply:—(1) How are we to reconcile this doctrine with other parts of Scripture? (2) How are we to avert this awful calamity? C. Simeon.

CHAPTER THE TWELFTH.

1—7. (1, 2) **dwellest,** i.e. even now, in the captivity, such is the character of the people around you.[a] They will not heed the prophet's instructions. They will not read the moral meaning of history. (3) **stuff,** or household goods, symbolic of the movements of people in a besieged city who look for its speedy overthrow. (4) **by day,** so that all may see, take notice, and be warned by it. (5) **Dig,** etc., to illus. the escape of Zedekiah from Jerusalem.[b] **wall,** the city wall. (6) **cover thy face,** prob. symbolic of the king's blindness. **twilight,** R. V., "dark;" so vss. 7, 12.

The Divine Expectation (vs. 3).—I. The subject to which this expectation refers. 1. Men do not consider that they are sinful creatures; 2. Nor that they are dying creatures; 3. Nor that they are immortal creatures. II. The means employed for bringing about the expectation which is here expressed. 1. The Divine forbearance; 2. The afflictive dispensations of Divine Providence; 3. The ministry of the Gospel.

The Necessity of Israel's Destruction.—The preceding symbols, such as those in ch. iv.—xii. and ch. viii.—xi., had foreshewn the certainty of the nation's fall, a new series of discourses demonstrate the necessity of it. Many thoughts and considerations occurred to men's minds which invalidated the force of the prophet's threats and disinclined them to receive them, or at least left them in hesitation. They had been for long familiar with threats of judgment, but the threatened storm had passed over. There were also men who saw into the future as well as Ezekiel, who, however, discerned no signs of approaching calamity, but foretold peace and security. And further, was not Israel the people of Jehovah, whom he could not cast away? In a new series of discourses (ch. xii.—xix) the prophet disposes of such considerations, adding also positive reasons which demonstrate the moral necessity of the nation's removal.—Camb. Bib.

8—12. vss. 8—16. The symbol explained. (9) **house of Israel,** those among whom Ezekiel dwelt. (10) **burden,** or prediction of woe.[a] **prince,** or King Zedekiah.[b] Possibly Ezekiel avoided the title "king," as seeing in him one who was a ruler de facto, but not a king de jure. (11) **your sign,** i.e. a warning to you of what shall surely come to pass. (12) **bear,** etc., trans. "shall carry forth on his shoulder; in the darkness shall he go forth." just as the Prophet had represented. Comp. the historical account.

Ezekiel's Symbolic Acts.—Ezekiel's collecting together his goods, does not look like a person's flying in a hurry, and by stealth; and consequently his going forth in the evening, in consequence of this preparation, cannot be construed as designed to signify a stealing away. These managements rather mark out the distance of the way they were going—going into captivity in a very far country. The going into captivity had not privacy attending it; and accordingly, the sending their goods to a common rendezvous beforehand, and setting out in an evening, are known to be Eastern usages.—Harmer.

13—16. (13) **My net,** Zedekiah was caught in escaping by the Chaldæans, but the net was really God's. **not see it,** bec. his eyes were put out. (14) **scatter,** etc., 2 Ki. xxv. 4, 5. (15) **know,** by the fulfilment of the threatened Divine judgments. Jerusalem and Israel is set in the midst of the nations round about (ch. v. 5), its history is a drama enacted before the eyes of mankind, and the drama when finished will reveal, not only to Israel but the nations of the world, Jehovah in his fulness.—Cam. B. (16) **a few men,** ch. vi. 8—10.[c]

Unbelief.—Josephus reports that an account of this prophetic action and its explanation was sent to Zedekiah, but that he, on comparing it with the danger which Jeremiah had warned him of, found that the latter

[a] De. xxix. 4.

[b] 2 Ki. xxv. 4; Je. xxxix. 4.

"Leaning upon God, upheld by Him, but not mixed up with Him in our affairs. — Of ourselves we cannot stand a single moment." — Lange.

"The earnest men are so few in the world that their very earnestness becomes at once the badge of their nobility; and as men in a crowd instinctively make room for one who seems eager to force his way through it, so mankind everywhere open their ranks to one who rushes zealously toward some object lying beyond them."—Dwight.

[a] "Ezekiel, bearing his stuff on his shoulder, was a sign of the weight of calamity coming upon king and people." — Spk. Com.

[b] Eze. vii. 27.

"Some troubles can be endured and lived down by fortitude, by patient submission, or by the comforting resources of the inner life. But this is not possible with the judgments of Heaven. They are too terrific to be calmly endured. The inner sources of consolation are withheld. The soul is punished as well as the body."

[c] 2 Ki. xxiv. 14, xxv. 12.

"Constitutional bravery will exclude the possibility of fear.

said that he should be carried to Babylon, while Ezekiel said that he should not see it. The discrepancy was so glaring in the king's view that he concluded, not that one was right and the other wrong, but that both were false! "In this he but showed the captious disposition of superficial inquirers and shallow unbelievers of all ages, who no sooner discover some obvious difficulties on the surface of Revelation than they conclude the whole to be a cunningly devised fable, or treat it as unworthy of their serious consideration. Would they but search a little deeper, and survey, in a spirit of impartiality, the entire field of Revelation, they would find that the things which at first stagger their belief disappear on closer inspection, or remain only as difficulties inseparable from communications which bear respect to the character and purposes of Godhead."—Fairbairn.

17—20. (17, 18) **with quaking,** i.e. with such signs of alarm as persons would feel in a time of siege; and with anxiety to limit the quantity of food to that barely necessary to sustain life.[a] (19) **people of the land,** i.e. the captives. They were to feel that the lot of their brethren in Jerusalem was far worse than their own. **desolate . . therein,** i.e. desolated of her people and her treasures. (20) **cities,** dependent on the fall of the chief city, Jerusalem.

Fear.—I. Fear arises from evil causes. The sound and innocent soul in healthy circumstances should not know fear. Observe some of the causes of fear. 1. Ignorance; 2. Weakness; 3. Guilt. II. Fear is hurtful. 1. It is one of the most painful elements of punishment; 2. Fear is a cause of disaster; 3. Worse than all, fear is often morally degrading. III. Fear may be conquered by faith.—Pul. Com.

21—25. vss. 21-28, Warning against those who cry down the truthfulness of prophecy. (22) **days..faileth,** the point of the prov. is that the threatened judgment was so long in coming that the people need not fear its ever coming at all.[b] The reference is specially to prophecies of judgment, and there was room for misapprehension in regard to these, because being drawn forth by moral evils existing when they were uttered, they were of the nature of threats, the object of which was to bring the people to repentance, and thus prevent their own fulfilment. For the same reason they were often of a general character, and thus when their fulfilment was postponed or when they were not literally fulfilled, men judged that they were merely uttered in the air.—Cam. B. **vision,** i. e. prophetic vision. (23) **at hand,** close at hand. Very close when Ezekiel wrote. The immediate reference is to the destruction of Jerusalem which the prophet saw to be one of those events which were unconditionally decreed, and an event which must bulk more and more largely in the vision of the true prophet until it was accomplished.—Exp. B. **effect,** lit. the word or contents. (24) **vain vision,** one that will not be fulfilled. One of the great hindrances to the effectiveness of prophecy was the division in the ranks of the prophets. They contradicted one another in the name of Jehovah, and the people were tempted to give the preference to those who prophesied smooth things. **flattering divination,** one that encourages the people to think they will yet be spared. Very soon the national calamities will silence the false diviners.[c] (25) **in your days,** before you die: in your time.

Trouble Exposes Delusions.—So long as Jerusalem prospered the vain visions continued, and the flattering divination was practised without intermission. It was the touch of real trouble that broke the bubble. Many a comfortable soul is living in a fool's paradise or direful error without fear or pain until some real adversity comes. Then the utter delusiveness of the admired notions is suddenly revealed with appalling amazement. If we are able to hold to fatal notions till the end of life, we shall find at last that they are but rotten planks, which will break up when we try to float on them over the chill waters of death.—W. F. Adeney.

26—28. (27) **many days,** i. e. it belongs only to the far off future.[a] (28) **prolonged,** even Divine long-suffering now shall fail, and judgment come speedily.

'Fear!' exclaimed the hero Nelson, when only a boy, to his grand mother, who had asked if he had not met fear when he had lost his way, 'what is it like? I have never seen it.' "

"The direst foe of courage," says George Macdonald, "is the fear itself, not the object of it; and the man who can overcome his own terror is a hero and more."

[a] "A symbolical representation of the famine and fear with which they should eat their scanty morsel at the siege."—Fausset.

"Even sin demands patience—we cannot spell out misery in a moment."

[b] Je. xvii. 15, xx. 7; Zep. i. 12; Is. v. 19; 2 Pe. iii. 3, 4.

[c] "The false prophets who foretold peace and safety, shall see their prophecies so confuted by the events quite contrary to what they foretold, that they will never pretend any more to publish new prophecies."
—Lowth.

Notice in the seed the germ of the tree. Cut it open; study it under the microscope. Root, trunk, branches, leaves, are all there. So in the Christian's heart is planted the germ of all that makes a son of God.

[a] "Not a mere repetition of the scoff (vs. 22). There the scoffers asserted that the evil was so often threatened and postponed, it must have no reality; here formalists do not go so far as to deny

that a day of evil is coming, but assert it as far off yet. The transition is easy from this carnal security to the gross infidelity of the former class."—Fausset.

b Je. vi. 14, xxiii. 11, etc. xxvii. 14, xxix. 8, 22, 23; Mic. iii. 5.

c Comp. Is. i. 1, ii. 1.

d "In deserts the foxes become so ravenous and crafty in their devices to get food. So the prophets wander in Israel, a moral desert, unrestrained, greedy of gains which they get by craft.—Fausset.

e "It was the office and duty of prophets, if they were truly what they pretended, by their prayers and intercessions to put a stop to God's vengeance when it was just ready to be poured out upon a sinful people." —Lowth.

"Reference is to jackals, which in desolate ruins are more hungry and rapacious than others." —Wordsworth.

a "They come to believe their own lies. 'The Lord hath not sent them that they should hope,' i. e. so that they should have grounds to hope that the words will be confirmed." — Spk. Com.

b "They shall die in their captivity and shall die childless, and so their names shall not be found among those who either themselves or their posterity returned out of Babylon, of whom a particular account was kept in a public register."— Mat. Henry.

CHAPTER THE THIRTEENTH.

1—5. Ch. xiii: Ezek. continues his denunciation against the false prophets. (2) **prophesy .. hearts,** i. e. of their own will, and not as delivering a Divine message.[b] "Whatever there might be in their prophetic experiences that resembled those of a true prophet, there was nothing in the oracles that did not belong to the sphere of worldly interests and human speculation." To one who knew that his vision was fr. God, this false prophecy seemed peculiarly heinous and revolting. (3) **foolish prophets,** i. e. those lacking the moral qualities necessary in a prophet. "True prophets had a stringent personal and state morality In their view the true cause of the destruction of the state was its immoralities. But the false prophets had no such deep moral convictions, and seeing nothing unwonted or alarming in the condition of things prophesied of 'peace.' They were not necessarily irreligious men; but their religion had no truer insight into the nature of the God of Israel than that of the common people."—Davidson. **seen nothing,** had no Divine vision given them.[c] "Seers of what they have not seen." (4) **like the foxes,** these creatures find their homes in desolate and ruined countries and cities.[d] (5) **gaps,** or breaches. The fig. is taken from stopping the way of an enemy when a breach in the walls has been made.[e] **made .. hedge,** or thrown up any works of defence. These prophets knew neither what measures to adopt to stop the way of the invading dangers, nor what protective methods to recommend that the state might be successfully defended.

The Condemnation of the False Prophets.—"Woe unto the foolish prophets, saith the Lord God:" "I am against you." This condemnation is apparent from several facts. 1. Their predictions are falsified, and their counsels brought to nought. 2. They mislead the people to destruction. 3. They bring confusion upon themselves. This sentence is pronounced in language very plain and very smiting. The hypocritical pretenders to a Divine commission are excluded from the register of the house of Israel, and are denied entrance into the land of Israel. All their plotting and lies are not only unmasked; they issue in confusion and destruction to themselves.—Thomson.

The False Prophets.—The prophets are like foxes; ruins are congenial to them; a condition of decay is their proper sphere; there they can burrow as their instincts prompt them. The main idea, however, is that their operations only increase the devastation and undermine and bring down anything that may yet be standing. In a declining and disastrous time the minds of men are excited and fed on the wildest schemes, and feeling themselves helpless they readily turn to those who pretend to speak to them in God's name. And it only adds to their ruin when those to whom they turn have no higher wisdom than themselves.—Camb. B.

6—9. (6) **made to hope,** R. V. marg., "they have hoped for the confirmation of the word;" reference is rather to their own delusive hope that the event might confirm their word.[a] (7) **vain vision,** one that was a mere mental deception; an imagination of one's own mind. (8) **am against you,** or I come against you to punish your wickedness. (9) **assembly,** etc., here referring to the roll of the sacred people, as recognized by God. The Heb. word used means a privy council; and the Prophets may be spoken of as constituting God's privy council. **written .. Israel,** the city of Jerusalem, perhaps every city of Judah, had its register of citizens. In such a register were inscribed also the names of proselytes of other races (Ps. lxxxvii. 6), and so men came to think of a like register as kept by the King of kings, containing the names of those who were heirs of the "life" of the true Israel (Exod. xxxii. 32; Isa. iv. 3; Dan. xii. 1).—Pul. Com. **enter,** etc., on the return of the people to their land.[b]

Self-assumption is Sure to Collapse.—Vaulting ambition overleaps itself. The frog that would swell its dimensions to the size of a bull destroyed itself. 1. False teachers make God their direct enemy. "I am against you, saith the Lord God." The God of truth hates hypocrisy.

All falseness shall be like empty thistle-down, which the wind scatters. 2. They shall be excluded from the circle of honor. They had assumed to be heads and leaders in the councils of the nation; they shall be dishonored, and cast out of the deliberative assembly. The false shall be, sooner or later, excommunicated—blackballed. 3. Their posterity shall become extinct. There shall be none to perpetuate their name. New honor often comes to the memory of a righteous man from children of renown. Such honor and satisfaction shall be denied to them. They shall perish root and branch. 4. They shall not participate in the coming restoration. "Neither shall they enter into the land of Israel." The distinctive possession which God gives shall be for the true Israel, "even for those who have no guile." In the time of Israel's real prosperity there "shall not come into them the uncircumcised or the unclean." He is a Jew who is one inwardly.—Davies.

10—13. (10) **saying, Peace,** Je. vi. 14. **a wall,** very slightly: as we would say, "run up a wall." The people build a wall and the prophets cover it with plaster (vs. 10)—that is to say, when any project or scheme of policy is being promoted they stand by glozing it over with fine words, flattering its promoters, and uttering profuse assurances of its success. The uselessness of the whole activity of these prophets could not be more vividly described.—Exp. B. **untempered mortar,** or slight coating of lime to make it look sound. Walls in the E. are often made of unbaked bricks, or rather masses of clay, smeared over with cement. This will not stand heavy rains.[a] (11) **overflowing shower,** i. e. one so heavy as to make an overflow. God's judgments are often compared to storms.[b] (12) **be said,** your folly shall even pass into a popular proverb. (13) **rend it,** force it asunder so that it shall come down with an utter destruction.

Delusive Confidence Reproved (vss. 10—12).—I. Who are obnoxious to this reproof? 1. Unfaithful ministers; 2. Unbelieving people. II. The warning here given to them. Their labor will end—1. In certain and bitter disappointment; 2. In irremediable and endless ruin. Address—(1) Careless sinners; (2) Self-complacent formalists; (3) Inconsistent professors.—Simeon.

14—16. (14) **discovered,** uncovered, laid bare. **ye .. consumed,** fr. this expression it appears that the city of Jerusalem is figured by this wall which is about to be destroyed. (15) **they .. daubed,** i. e. the false prophets, who helped it to cherish a false security by proposing first an Assyrian and then an Egyptian alliance, ignoring the while that God was the covenanted ruler of Israel. (16) **visions of peace,** Je. vi. 10, viii. 11.

"Untempered Mortar."—I. A false hope is like a wall built with untempered mortar. 1. It offers protection. A false hope is planted between men and their danger, like a city wall, and it encourages them to despise the danger. 2. It presents a fair appearance. It has a certain mortar holding the stones together, which may appear to be of the very best quality. So false hopes charm with an appearance of solidity. 3. It contains solid materials. It is not a mere mound of earth. There are good hewn stones in the structure. We may have certain solid truths of the Christian religion. Yet if these are not united by personal faith they hang loosely together, and will not save us. 4. It lacks an essential element. The mortar is rotten. Then all the rest goes for nothing. Our system of religion, like the teaching of the false prophets, may have every commendable element, beauty, symmetry, fulness, etc., except one—truth. II. The tempest of trial will shatter a false hope. 1. The tempest of trial will come. If our bark is only made for fair weather, it is doomed to shipwreck, because the storm will break at last on every life. 2. The false hope will then crumble away. Hail and hurricane dash down the feeble, pretentious wall. Trouble overthrows false hopes. Then the refuge of lies tumbles into a hopeless ruin. 3. The builder of the false hope will suffer in its overthrow. "Ye shall be consumed in the midst thereof." The greater the hope, the more fearful will be its fall, and the more dreadfully will they be bruised and crushed who take up their abode in it. 4. The false hope is overthrown that we may turn to the true Hope. "Christ our Hope."—Pul. Com.

17—19. Vss. 17—23: the false prophetesses denounced. These were **private fortune-tellers who made a living off the credulous and sim-**

a "In a Median village the men were building a wall of beaten earth rammed into molds or boxes, to give the parts the requisite shape and consistence, and so deposited, by the withdrawal of the mold, layer by layer, upon the wall, each layer drying in its place as the work proceeds. The blocks are usually of considerable size, and are of various quality and strength, as well as cost, according to the materials employed, and the time expended upon them. Unless the climate be very dry, such a wall requires to be faced or coated with a tempered mortar of lime or sand, as a fence against the weather."—Kitto.

b Job xxvii. 20; Ps. xi. 6, xviii. 13, 14; Eze. xxxviii. 22.

"Some men, says Dr. Bushnell, are like flagstaffs — they grew; other men are like trees,—they grow. If we stop growing, our work is done." — S. S. Times.

"As a thistle, if stroked upward, will not molest a man, but, if stroked downward, will prick him: so many hearers of the word, so long as the minister preaches pleasant things, are pleased with him; but so soon as he rubs them a little on the gall, and touches them home to the quick, then they kick and storm at the same." — Cawdray.

ple. (17) **daughters,** some women prophets are noticed in Scripture:[a] this encouraged others of the same sex to pretend to the same gift. (18) **sew .. armholes,** Polychr. Bib., "sew amulets on all wrists." **kerchiefs .. stature,** magical veils put on the heads of those who consulted these false prophetesses. **to hunt souls,** "they hunted lives in that they based their predictions not on moral grounds but on pay, ignored the relation bet. chance and life, and fostered the immoral popular craving for fortune-telling."—Polychr. Bib. **will ye save,** nay rather, how surely you will deceive and destroy all you gain. (19) **will ye pollute,** R. V., "ye have profaned," i. e. brought God down into the region of the impure. **for handfuls, etc.,** i. e. for mere gain putting the name of God to dishonor. For even the meanest and most trifling rewards. **slay .. live** "promising life to the ungodly and prophesying disaster to those who were righteous."

Female prophets were not unknown in Israel whether in earlier or later times, as Deborah (Judg. iv. 3) and Huldah (2 Kings xxii. 14). The prophetesses referred to here were like the prophets, prophesying out of their own heart (vs. 17). Their prophesying was by some species of divination, which they used in order to obtain oracles. The methods of divination practiced are somewhat obscure: they bound fillets upon the joints and threw cloths or veils over the heads of those who consulted them. By these means they "hunted" souls; they saved souls alive that should not live and slew souls that should not die (vs. 19), or as expressed otherwise, they made the heart of the righteous sad and strengthened the hands of the wicked.—Camb. B.

20—23. (20) **make them fly,** R. V. marg., "hunt as birds." That is to say, while Ezekiel and all true prophets were exhorting men to live resolutely in the light of clear ethical conceptions of providence, the votaries of occult superstitions seduced the ignorant into making private compacts with the powers of darkness in order to secure their personal safety. **tear .. arms,** and expose your deceptions. (21) **kerchiefs,** vs. 18. (22) **lies,** false representations, leading the righteous to mistrust the Word of God.[b] and deluding the sinners with vain hopes. **hands .. wicked,** by wh. his evil works were wrought. **by promising him life,** R. V., "and be saved alive." (23) **see no more vanity,** bec. the fulfillment of Divine threatenings, and your own destruction, are close at hand.

Prophetesses.—It is evident—(1) That their inspiration came from their own heart; and (2) That the substance of their so-called prophecies was false. They were animated by a desire to please those who resorted to them; and this they did to gratify their own prejudices or to display their own worldly wisdom.—Pul. Com.

[a] Ex. xv. 20; Ju. iv. 4; 2 Ki. xxii. 14; comp. Joel ii. 28.

"There is nothing so sacred which men of mercenary spirits will not profane if they can but get money by the bargain. But they did it for poor gain; if they could get no more for it, they would sell you a false prophecy that should please you to a nicety for a piece of bread or a handful of barley; and yet that was more than it was worth." — M. Henry.

[b] "Disheartened the righteous with groundless fears."—Lowth.

"Our life is a trust, not a gift; let us use it accordingly." —R. E. Speer.

CHAPTER THE FOURTEENTH.

1—5. (1) **elders,** comp. ch. viii. 1. These were fellow-exiles with Ezekiel, who was at this time fully recognized as a prophet of Jehovah.[a] (3) **idols .. heart,** hankering after the old false worship, the elders' mind and affections were busied with idols.[b] **stumblingblock,** etc., comp. ch. vii. 19. **inquired of,** i. e. God is under no obligation to answer such inquiries. (4) **will answer him,** or as we say in sarcasm, "He shall have his answer." **that cometh,** better, "by myself," i. e. by "involving them in the consequences of their own idolatries and destroying them." **according .. idols,** i. e. the chastisement will be proportionable to the idolatry. A reply adjusted not to his inquiry but to his evil practices.[c] (5) **take,** as in a snare; their own evil heart being the snare and pitfall in which they are caught. It seems clear that one part of the threat here uttered is that the very withholding of the answer. will unmask the hypocrisy of men who pretend to be worshipers of Jehovah, but in heart are unfaithful to Him and servants of false gods.

The Idols in the Heart a Barrier to the Truth (vss. 2, 3).—I. The idols that are in the heart, and the stumbling-blocks that are before the face, are the sins with which God's people are sometimes chargeable. II. Men professing to inquire after God while their idols are in their hearts,

[a] "They look for encouragement and comfort. But Ezekiel, with the genuine prophetic spirit, sees deep into their hearts, and finds them at variance with devotion to the true God. The idols of self-will and unsubmissiveness are set up therein. The Prophet warns them that God will not be inquired of in such a spirit as this." Spk. Com.

[b] "Lit. 'They have made their idols to go up upon their hearts, as if their hearts were an altar and throne for idols." — Wordsworth.

[c] "Turn thee fr. these, or dare not to inquire of Him whose name is Jealous, lest in wrath He hear and answer thine unblest desire: far better we should cross His lightning's path than be according to our idols

and their stumbling-blocks before their faces; or the gross inconsistency of seeking to mingle the service of God with the pursuit of sin. 1. Men may pray from the influence of custom; 2. From the promptings of conscience; 3. From the desire to stand well with their fellow-men; 4. From a vain desire to set themselves right with God. III. God taking notice of the idols that are in men's hearts, and the stumbling-blocks that are before their faces, or the faithful warnings which God addresses to those who follow sin while they profess to serve Him. 1. He intimates that He is perfectly acquainted with us; 2. He tells us that He cannot answer the requests of those who indulge in sin; 3. He shows us how unreasonable it is to expect that He will be inquired of by us.

6—8. (6) **Repent and turn,** the word repent deals with the right feeling; the word turn deals with the corresponding action in ordering life and conduct. (7) **stranger,** comp. Le. xvii. 10, xx. 2. **by myself,** not by the agency of a prophet, but by a direct visitation of judgment.[d] (8) **will make him a sign,** etc., De. xxviii. 37; R. V., "will make him an astonishment for a sign," etc. His punishment will strike terror into others.

"Repent."—When did the Lord ever conclude a discourse without some evangelical tone in it? We have seen him step from his chariot of thunder that he might put his arms around some poor sinner and say, Come home ere the sun set, for we will wait for thee in night's darkest hour, and receive thee when they who would be ashamed of thee are lost in slumber. The Bible is terrific in denunciation, awful beyond all other books in its denunciation of sin and its threatening of perdition; yet through it, and through it again, and ruling it, is a spirit of clemency and pity and mercy and hope, yea, across hell's burning mouth there lies the shadow of the cross.—Parker.

9—11. (9) **I .. deceived,** i. e. suffered him to be deceived,[a] but both he and those who are deceived by his false prophecies will alike come into the Divine judgment. (10) **bear .. iniquity,** both for their idolatry, and their hypocrisy in seeking Jehovah when they loved their idols. "The man who wittingly commits sin had better keep clear of religious ordinances and performances. And the "prophet" (even the modern one) had better keep clear of wicked men, lest he should be used as the instrument of their punishment and perish with them." (11) **go no more astray,** this was the Divine purpose in inflicting the punishments. For the Divine love works through the Divine judgments.[b]

"I, the Lord, have Deceived" (vs. 9).—The meaning appears to be: if the prophet, entering into the "heart" of the idolaters, the circle and direction of their thoughts, and the general spirit which animates them, gives them a prophetic oracle which coincides with the line of their thoughts, and thus helps to foster their delusions, that prophet himself has been seduced or enticed; and it is the Lord who has enticed him. The passage has a resemblance to 1 Kings xxii. 20. There a lying spirit came forth from the Lord and entered into the prophets of Ahab and deceived them, so that they entered into the designs of the wicked king and gave an answer favorable to him. Here it is the Lord Himself who entices the prophet. In both cases this enticement or deception was in punishment for previous sin. Ezekiel does not appear to reflect upon the point whether the prophet before being deceived was true or false. The "prophet" became false when deceived, when he entered into the spirit and purposes of the idolaters, and spoke a word to them in the line of their sinful conduct and hopes.—Camb. B.

12—14. (13) **the land,** better, a land, any land. **grievously,** in a way that compels Divine interference. **staff,** etc., ch. iv. 16, v. 16. (14) **three men,** comp. Ge. xv. 1. **Noah, Daniel, and Job,** three men eminent in righteousness and holiness, who lived in evil days. Obs. the indication that in Ezekiel's time Daniel was known and honored among the exiles.

Noah, Daniel, and Job.—Some make great inquiry why these three men should be mentioned rather than others, and they give in their answer:—1. It is thought that they are named, for that they could not divert God's wrath by their holiness and prayers from the people of their times. Noah could not keep off the flood, nor Job the sad things which befel him and his, nor Daniel the captivity. 2. Others think they are named because they freed others in imminent danger in their times. Noah

heard, and God should take us at our own vain word."—Keble.

[d] "I will punish him immediately by My own hands." See vs. 8.—Lowth.

"Much need, indeed, had Peter to weep bitterly; and if there are no bitter tears betimes in our religious life, it is not because we have less of Peter's sin, but little of Peter's grace." —Drummond.

[a] "Not merely permissively, but by overruling their evil to serve the purposes of His righteous judgment, to be a touchstone to separate the precious from the vile, and to 'prove His people.' "—Fausset.

De. xiii. 1—3; 1 Ki. xxii. 23; Je. iv. 10; 2 Th. ii. 11, 12.

[b] "God punishes sins by means of sins."

"To believe in Him is to be like Him. All other faith is a mere mist of words, dissolving into empty air. To live our human lives as He lived His—purely, lovingly, righteously — is to share His eternity."—Lucy Larcom.

"They signally prevailed in saving others. Noah, in saving the human family; Daniel, in saving the Chaldaean astrologers from destruction (Da. ii. 24); Job, in interceding for his friends (Job xlii. 8—10)."—Wordsworth.

b "There may be times when the very Divine love must refuse to hear intercessors."

"Were there in it the most perfect of all men that have been, or are still living, they should avail nothing towards interceding for a land already doomed to destruction." —Calvin.

a "This will compose your minds, and make you give glory to God and acknowledge His judgments to be righteous, though they touch you very nearly in the destruction of your friends and country." —Lowth.

"The great qualification for work for Christ in the hearts of others is love to Christ in the worker's heart."— Principal Moule.

saved his family from the flood; Job prayed for his friends, and they were spared; Daniel preserved the magicians and wise men. But rather they are named, because they were men of great holiness, exercised with great trials, and so the more fervent in prayer. And what if these men, who were so acceptable to me, had so much interest in me and often prevailed with me, should pray for you, yet they should do nothing for your deliverance by their prayers. These were men in great afflictions, and affliction is the whetstone of prayer, the bellows to blow up that fire.—Greenhill.

15—18. (15) **noisome beasts,** hurtful, comp. Le. xxvi. 6. (16) **deliver .. daughters,** i. e. their intercessions should be unavailing, bec. the inquiry would be such as necessitated Divine visitation.[b] (17) **sword, ch.** xxi. 4, xxxviii. 21. (18) **Though,** etc., comp. vs. 16.

19—23. (19) **pour .. blood,** i. e. with great destruction of men's lives, by the pestilence. In Heb. blood expresses any premature kind of death. (20) **own souls,** or own lives. (21) **upon Jerusalem,** the former references had been general, now the principle of Divine healing is applied to the city of privilege, Jerusalem, whose iniquity was more hateful by reason of its superior position and privilege. (22) **remnant,**[a] if some of the wicked in Jerusalem escape it is with a special design, viz., that those spared should reveal their great wickedness to the earlier exiles among whom they shall come, and thus shew how inevitable the destruction of the city was.—Cam. B. (23) **without cause,** i. e. without sufficient cause; or without a definite and gracious purpose.

Blessings of Unanswered Prayer.—Some time ago the beautiful daughter of wealthy parents failed to appear one morning at breakfast. The parents, alarmed, forced the door of her room and found her apparently dying with a bottle labeled "Poison" in her hand. Almost frantic with grief, the father hastened to the druggist's and demanded information as to what the bottle had contained. The druggist bade the father fear nothing. The young lady had asked him for some poison, but he had feared to give it to her or to let her go to another druggist, and so had substituted an innocent mixture. After several hours of sleep the young lady awoke, to the unutterable joy of her family, and with them thanked God that her request had been denied. A wife once prayed for the recovery of her husband from illness and stamped her feet, saying, with frightful emphasis, "I will not have him die; God shall not take him!" Her prayer was answered; but a few years afterward the community was shocked by the fact that he, in a moment of anger, had killed her.—E. S. Lewis.

CHAPTER THE FIFTEENTH.

b Is. v. 1; Ps. lxxx. 8.

c "The branches of the vine are pruned every spring, being cut close to the stem and, when not needed to thatch the top of the earth-wall, are burned to put them out of the way, as they are too porous and light to serve any purpose."—Van Lennep.

"In this passage the Prophet gives us a fig. representation of man, considered especially as the object of Divine care and culture. He is naturally capable of yielding a precious fruit; in this consists his sole excellency; this is the sole end of his existence, and if he fails in this he is of no use but to be destroyed." —Robert Hall.

1—5. (2) **vine .. tree,** the vine is a symbol of the Jewish Church.[b] The reference here is to the wood of the tree, wh. is useless to the carpenter.[c] "Men might dwell, perhaps were actually dwelling, on the thought that they were branches of the true vine, and therefore could not perish. He exposes the groundlessness of that hope in tones of scornful sarcasm. If the vine did not bear fruit, or if it only brought forth wild grapes, then its special excellence was gone, and it challenged comparison with other trees only as a timber tree, and what was its worth as such? If Israel was not true to its vocation, it was poorer and weaker than the heathen nations round it."—Pul. Com. **branch,** an ordinary branch of any tree. (3) **pin,** or peg. These were driven into walls of houses for domestic uses. (4) **for fuel,** sometimes the vine branches are burned for charcoal, but they do not give out heat enough for cooking purposes, and vine-wood charcoal is chiefly used in the houses of the wealthy to heat the tandoor, or warming apparatus. (5) **is burned,** as Jerusalem was in the prophetic vision.

Most Trees Serve Many Uses.—From root to topmost twig, every part of some trees is serviceable to man. The bark is used for cordage or for tanning. The root is often a valuable medicine. The juice which exudes is a precious gum. The fruit is wholesome food. And when cut down, the wood is devoted to house-building or forms implements of husbandry. Which fact is a parable. A nation may produce a superior literature which shall serve for the education of other lands. It may be famous for legislation, for commerce, for manufactures. Egypt and Greece and Rome were justly celebrated for many of these things.

6—8. (6) **will I give,** as useless, and only fit for the burning. "Naturally the supposition is made that the vinewood flung into the fire has been plucked out after having been burnt and charred, and the question is asked, Is it good for anything now? This is the condition of Jerusalem: it has been given into the fire for fuel, plucked out of it, as it were, half-burnt; is it good for anything?"—Cam. B. (7) **one fire,** R. V., "shall go forth from the fire, but the fire." (8) **trespass,** or "they have perversely fallen into perverse rebellion."

The vine tree has but one use—its fruit. Of all the trees it is the most prolific in bearing fruit. Under proper culture, its fruitfulness is certain, regular, copious. All the life and vigor of the tree are poured into its clusters. But failing this, it renders no other service to man. Its cells are not stored with any known medicinal qualities. Its wood is too brittle to bear any strain or burden. Hence, unless fruitful, it is worthless. In this respect the vine is an apt figure of the Hebrew nation. It was raised up by God for a single purpose, viz., to exhibit to the world righteousness, loyalty to the will of the invisible God. Israel was designed to be a lighthouse, to diffuse on every side the rays of moral and spiritual truth.—Davies.

"The fallen Christian is lower than the 'man of the world,' and of less use to society, as the fruitless vine is of less account than the forest tree. A fruitless Church stands in the place of a useful one, and therefore it is positively injurious. There is but one good that come of it. The very destruction of it may be a warning to others."—Adeney.

CHAPTER THE SIXTEENTH.

1—5. (2) **abominations,** to understand and feel the grievous sin of her idolatries, and the necessity for Divine punishment. (3) **of .. Canaan,** i. e. it would seem, by your manners, as if you had been born in Canaan, as if your "father had been an Amorite and your mother a Hittite."[a] (4) **salted .. swaddled,** references to the E. mode of treating new-born infants.[b] The vs. describes an utterly neglected infant.[c] (5) **lothing .. person,** or the contempt of thy life.

Without God.—The verses illustrate man's spiritual condition apart from the grace of God and the provisions of that grace. Man is morally unclean as an unwashed infant, morally neglected as an uncared-for infant, left to live or die, no one taking an interest in its condition, and being completely incapable of self-help. Is not that a picture of man's spiritual state apart from the grace of God? We inherit a sinful nature. We cannot convert or sanctify ourselves, or even do anything with a view to such results without Divine influence. We cannot repent except as we are summoned and strengthened to do so from heaven. And man cannot save us if he would; for every man is a sinner, and needs salvation himself. Neither can angels save us. Their utmost wisdom, love, and might are inadequate to the difficult task. God alone has pity enough and power enough for this work. If he leaves us we must perish. If we are to be saved He must begin and carry on the gracious work. And we rejoice to know that He does not leave any people to perish without witness of Himself, or without some gracious influences from him (cf. Acts xiv. 17; Rom. i. 19, 20; 1 Tim. ii. 4).—W. Jones.

6—9. (6) **polluted,** etc., R. V., "weltering," still regarding Israel as an untended infant. **Live,** i. e. when so utterly uncared for, I took thee up, and saved thy life. (7) **come .. ornaments,** fig. for "thou becamest most beautiful." **whereas,** R. V., "yet," i. e. when puberty would have demanded clothing. **naked .. bare,** i. e. nakedness and bareness itself. God presided over all the growth of the naked infant into the beautiful woman. (8) **time of love,** marriageable age. **spread .. thee,**[d] symbol of taking a woman under a man's protection. (9) **oil,** the symbol of health and rejoicing. "There is no passage in the book of Ezekiel at once so powerful and so full of religious significance as the picture of Jerusalem, the foundling child, the unfaithful spouse, and the abandoned prostitute, which is here presented."

The Life of Souls the Ordinance of God (vs. 6).—I. Servants of God, **what then is our office? II. There are souls dead. 1. Men are ignorant**

a "Those are said to be our parents in the Scrip. dialect, whose manners we resemble. Mat. iii. 7; Jno. viii. 44." —Lowth.

b "In the East at the present day, as soon as a babe is born it is washed in salted water, clothed, and swathed in a long bandage or swaddling cloth, three or four inches wide, and about ten feet long, which is firmly wound around it from the neck downward, including the arms, which are thus pinioned to its sides, so that it can stir neither hand or foot."—Van Lennep.

c Ho. ii. 3.

d "I have been delighted at the marriage ceremonies of the Hindoos, to see amongst them the same interesting custom." —Roberts.

"Each day, each week, each month, each year is a new chance given you by God. A new chance, a new leaf, a new life, —this is the golden, the unspeakable gift which each new day offers to you." — Canon Farrar.

of the nature of their souls; 2. The souls of men are not fulfilling the end of their being; 3. The souls of men are strangers to the peculiar joys of their being. III. Therefore, as the servants of God, the cry of our ministry is, Live.—J. Pulsford.

Love.—In the French Revolution a young man was condemned to the guillotine and shut up in one of the prisons. He was greatly loved by many, but there was one who loved him more than all put together. How know we this? It was his own father, and the love he bore his son was proved in this way: when the lists were called, the father, whose name was exactly the same as the son's, answered to the name, and the father rode in the gloomy tumbril to the place of execution, and his head rolled beneath the axe instead of the son's, a victim to mighty love. See here an image of the love of Christ to sinners; for thus Jesus died for the ungodly.—Spurgeon.

10—14. (10) **broidered work,** i. e. embroidered work of variegated colors, gold, silver, etc. **badger's skins,** R. V., "sealskin." **fine linen,** byssus of Egyptian manufacture; Ex. xxv. 5. **silk,** "silk was used for clothing first in the North of China, thence it came to Syria and Egypt by way of India."[a] (11) **ornaments,** wh. were highly prized by brides. (12) **jewel .. forehead,** R. V., "ring upon thy nose."[a] (13) **fine flour,** etc., signs of delicate provision and treatment. **into a kingdom,** R. V., "royal estate," as in the reigns of David and Solomon. (14) **perfect,** comp. ch. xxvii. 3, 4. **comeliness,** R. V., "majesty." These verses allegorically set forth the second period of Israel's history: her redemption by Jehovah from Egypt, his covenant with her to be her God, his leading her into the promised land, and making her the paramount power there, and loading her with all the riches of that good land. But all her grace must be traced to the provision and the care of God.

15—19. (15) **trust,** etc., didst think too much of thyself, and so fell into temptation. **harlot,** idolatry if often described by the prophets as adultery. **fornications,** R. V., "whoredoms," i. e. the abandonment of an ethical religion for one in which the powers of nature were regarded as the highest revelation of the divine.—Exp. B. (16) **deckedst,** etc., with reference to the efforts of the lewd woman to make herself attractive. **like things,** etc., i. e. there shall never anything happen again so revolting and so dreadful. (17) **images,** i. e. idol-images. (18) **garments,** wh. I had given thee as my bride. "The very gifts of God, designed for His worship, were prostituted to that of his rivals." (19) **sweet savour,** or incense offered to idols of the good things I gave thee.

Israel's Apostacy: an Example of Monstrous Iniquity.—I. It was the prostitution of God's best gifts. II. It took the worst possible forms. 1. They devoted all God's gifts to idols; (1) The common gifts of Providence; (2) Luxuries; (3) Even their own children; 2. They took special pains to spread idolatry; 3. Their lust of idolatry was insatiable; 4. They loved the sin of idolatry for its own sake; 5. They sinned thus grievously after due chastisement.—T. H. Leale.

20—24. (21) **pass .. fire,** to Moloch, Je. xxxii. 35. (22) **remembered,** or thought on. **naked,** etc. (vs. 7, etc.). (23) **wickedness,** was of two stages: (1) the heathenism wh. crept in fr. contact with the Canaanites, vs. 15—23; (2) The deliberate intro. of the idolatrous practices of the great world-powers.—Exp. B. (24) **eminent place,** meaning a house in which to carry on thy wicked idolatries; a heathen temple.

Moloch Sacrifice.—The immolation of children to Baal or Moloch was a common practice amongst the nations surrounding Israel, and when introduced there seems to have been regarded as part of the worship of Jehovah. What Ezekiel here asserts is that the practice came through Israel's illicit commerce with the gods of Canaan, and there is no question that this is historically true. The allegory exhibits the sin in its unnatural heinousness. The idealized city is the mother of her citizens, the children are Jehovah's children and her own, yet she has taken them and offered them up to the false lovers she so madly pursued. Such was her feverish passion for idolatry that the dearest and most sacred ties of nature were ruthlessly severed at the bidding of a perverted religious sense.—Exp. Bib.

25—29. (25) **built, etc.,** allusion is made in this vs. to the rude man-

Bessus, a Grecian, gave as a reason for pulling down the birds' nests about his house, that the birds never ceased to accuse him of the murder of his father.

"It is interesting to notice that we have in all these descriptions, not the view which Ezekiel took of the condition of Israel,—we have the condition of Israel as it revealed itself to the Divine eyes." — People's Bible.

[a] Oriental women are notoriously fond of decking with jewelry not only their heads, but other parts of their body as well.

Comp. Ge. xxiv. 22, 47.

"A just and reasonable modesty does not only recommend eloquence, but sets off every great talent which a man can be possessed of. It heightens all the virtues which it accompanies. Like the shades in paintings, it raises and rounds every figure, and makes the colors more beautiful, though not so glaring as they would be without."—Addison.

"Oh! there are no tears in heaven; but when angels come down to earth, it may be they can fall into companionship with human sadness, and even learn to weep; and where is the spectacle which shall wring tears from eyes which they were never meant to stain, if it be not that of the obstinate rejection of the Gospel of reconciliation, and of

ners of such lewd women. (26) **Egyptians,** by depending on them rather than on God, thy true Husband. **great of flesh,** "in an obscene sense." (27) **stretched,** etc, in severe dealings; abridging thee of necessaries and conveniences. **daughters,** or cities. Reference may be intended to the calamitous times of the Judges. **ashamed,** etc., other nations had at least been faithful to their inherited religion, while Judah had forsaken hers. (28) **Assyrians,** in depending, as a nation, on their help; 2 Kings xvi. 7. (29) **land of Canaan,** R. V., "unto the land of traffic, unto Chaldæa."

Time Serving.—The treacherous and wanton dealing was all on Israel's part, she conceded everything to them, they yielded back nothing in return to her—her wickedness was gratuitous and unrequited folly. A solemn and pregnant truth, which the Church of God should never forget. She loses all, and the world gains all, when she foolishly stoops to impair the testimony of God, or adjust the claims and services of religion to the tastes and practices of the carnal mind. A nominal advance or apparent reconciliation may possibly be made by the manœuver; but it can be no more than nominal or apparent; the interests that really profit by such a policy are those of the flesh and the world. It is only when the Church is faithful to her testimony—when she stands in the truth of Christ, and in that truth shines forth "bright as the sun, clear as the moon," that she is found also, in her conflict with evil, " terrible as an army with banners."—Fairbairn.

30—39. (30) **weak,** or wasted with passion and grown weak to resist desire. Sin ever weakens both intellect and heart. **imperious,** subject to no outward restraint. (31) **eminent place,** vs. 24. **scornest hire,** which the harlot seeks. (32) **wife,** adultery being a much deeper sin than fornication, because it involves unfaithfulness. (33) **hirest,** or bribest. (34) **contrary,** manifesting stronger wilfulness, and more shameless wickedness. (37) **lovers,** heathen nations, whose religion Israel had adopted. **against thee,** fig. of the invasion of the Assyrians, etc. (38) **break wedlock,** are unfaithful to marriage vows.[a] **shed blood,** ref. to child murder. **blood in fury,** R. V., "will bring upon thee the blood of fury," i. e. "bring on thee the bloody death wh. fury and jealousy execute.",

40—43. (40) **stone thee,** Jno. viii. 5—7. (41) **burn .. fire,** comp. Ge. xxxviii. 24; De. xiii. 16. **sight .. women,** i. e. of other nations, as Syrians, Philistines, etc.[a] There may be reference to a custom of making women witness the fate of the adulteress, that they might take warning. (42) **to rest,** when the fitting punishment has been brought on thee.[b] (43) **fretted me,** a word suitable to a grieved and injured husband. Is. lxiii. 10. **lewdness,** better, "and thus hast thou committed lewdness in (amidst) all thine abominations." Comp. Le. xix. 29.

It is Wise to Remember the Days of Youth.—1. In thankfulness. It was the sin and shame of Israel that she forsook her Deliverer, not remembering those days of her youth when he had found her forlorn and destitute, and had saved her from destruction. We have had many mercies from our youth up. It is right to remember them with thankfulness. 2. In warning. Remembering Egypt should have kept Israel from the danger of Babylon. It is well to remember the sad scenes of youth. Some of these may be burnt into the memory beyond hope of forgetfulness. "If cutting off this hand," said a great speaker, holding out his right hand, "would blot out all memories of my misspent youth, I would gladly lose it." But he who orders our lives knows that even these terrible memories may be converted into helpful warnings for the future. 3. In humility. Israel's recollection of her old abject condition should humble her. People who have risen in society do not like to be reminded of their lowly youth. Yet the humility that comes from knowing how feeble we once were is wholesome. 4. In encouragement. When in the most abject wretchedness Israel was saved by God. That was a glorious fact to be ever treasured up in the memories of youth. The recollection of such a deliverance should cheer with hope of similar mercy in future times of need.—W. T. Adeney.

44—47. (44) **the mother,** with reference to the Hittite mother (vs. 3). (45) **lothed her husband,** in the sense of the allegory "lothing her husband" should mean changing her god for another; and in the case of Jerusalem and Samaria the charge is intelligible, Jehovah being the husband (ch. xxiii.). But such a charge could hardly be made against the

careless trifling with a thing so inestimably precious as the soul?"—H. Melvill.

[a] Le. xx. 10; De. xxii. 22.

All the wickedness you have done in your life, was first done in your heart.

"Never for one hour do I expect the Christian to reach a stage at which he can say, 'I have no self to deny.' His fellowship with the cross of Christ will be an unceasing denial of self every hour and every moment." — Andrew Murray.

[a] "The judgment I will execute upon thee shall be for an instruction to other nations, how they follow thine ill-practices."—Lowth.

[b] "It is not a mitigation of the penalty that is here foretold, but such an utter destruction of all the guilty that there shall be no need of further punishment." — Calvin.

"The soul of man is a splendid menagerie and museum of curiosities, as each can ascertain for himself when he ventures to pull down the blinds and expose his private collection to the public."

Canaanites, the Hittite mother and Sodom (Jer. ii. 11). The prophet appears to desert the allegory, introducing real features into his description, and referring to actual adultery and unfaithness, which were characteristic of the Canaanite nations.—Cam. B. **sister..sisters,** i. e. of Sodom and Samaria. (46) **elder sister,** lit. "greater": bec. the capital of the more important kingdom of Israel, and as setting the example of idolatry. **left hand,** i. e. of one looking eastward. Samaria lay to the north. **her daughters,** her neighboring and dependent towns.[a] (47) **very little thing,** or loathed as a small thing. Judah had even gone to extreme lengths in idolatrous wickedness.

The Way of Good and of Evil.—"This must be the right way, see how smooth it is! How many feet have trodden it!" Alas, that is precisely the mark of the broad road which leadeth to destruction. "But see how it winds about, and what a variety of directions it takes! It is no bigot's unbending line." Just so; therein it proves itself to be the wrong road; for truth is one and unchanging. "But I like it so much." This also is suspicious; for what an unrenewed man is so fond of is probably an evil thing. Hearts go after that which is like themselves, and graceless men love graceless ways. "Would you have me go that narrow and rough road?" Yes, we would; for it leadeth unto life; and though few there be that find it, yet those who do so declare that it is a way of pleasantness. It is better to follow a rough road to heaven than a smooth road to hell.—Spurgeon.

48—52. (48) **not done..as thou,** yet Sodom's sins brought an awful Divine judgment. Matt. x. 15, xi. 24. (49) **idleness,** the secret of immorality, and the service of formal religions.[b] R. V., "prosperous ease." The fruitful land of Sodom[c] made her people proud, wealthy, idle, and voluptuous. **hand of the poor,** neglect of the poor and suffering is a high moral offence in the sight of God. (50) **took them away,** Ge. xix. 24. (51) **justified,** i. e. made them appear almost good, when set in contrast with thee. (52) **bear shame,** i. e. the disgrace which an overwhelming punishment will bring upon thee. "The point of the sentence is that Judah condemned those who were less guilty than herself."—Pul. Com.

53—57. (53) **When I bring,**[a] R. V., "And I will turn again, etc." All that follows in the chapter shows that what is meant is a promise of restoration, not for Judah only, but also for her less-guilty sisters. Ezekiel sees a far-off hope for his own nation, and he cannot limit the mercy of God in bringing them also, as she was to be brought, to repentance.—Pulp. Com. (54) **That shame,** better, "that thou mayest bear thy shame, and be ashamed because of all that thou hast done in comforting them." Jerusalem "comforted" Samaria and Sodom in surpassing them in wickedness, and causing them to feel less their own guilt, as also in causing their restoration.—Cam. B. (55) **When,** etc., comp. note on vs. 53. (56) **not mentioned,** bec. it was utterly despised, and thought to be an awfully wicked place. It was held in utter contempt. (57) **discovered,** manifested by calamity; Sam. i. 8, 9. **at .. Syria,** R. V., "as at the time of the reproach of the daughters of S.," i. e. wh. they cast upon Jerusalem. **despise thee,** in turn when thou hast become the object of Divine indignation.

Sodom.—Ezekiel's estimate of Sodom is noteworthy. He appears not to have in mind the story of Genesis xix. His picture was perhaps drawn from the tradition of his time. Sodom appears to have vanished from the scene before the Israelites entered Canaan.—Polychrome Bible.

Restoration of Sodom.—Another question of great interest and difficulty is the attitude towards the heathen world assumed by Ezekiel. The prophecy of the restoration of Sodom is certainly one of the most remarkable things in the book. It is true that Ezekiel as a rule concerns himself very little with the religious state of the outlying world under the Messianic dispensation. Where he speaks of foreign nations it is only to announce the manifestation of Jehovah's glory in the judgments He executes upon them. The effect of these judgments is that "they shall know that I am Jehovah;" but how much is included in the expression as applied to the heathen it is impossible to say. This, however, may be due to the peculiar limitation of view which leads him to concentrate his attention on the Holy Land in his visions of the perfect kingdom of God. We can hardly suppose that he conceived all the rest of

a "The worship of Moloch was generally practiced by the ten tribes, whose metropolis was Samaria; as it was by the Amorites, who derived their original from Lot, an inhabitant of Sodom."—Lowth.

"He who would enter the realm of penitence must be girded with meekness, and his face must be washed in the pure dew of heaven, gathered in the shady places of godly sorrow."—Dean Farrar.

A little religion makes us afraid.

b "Satan finds some mischief still for idle hands to do."—Watts.

c Ge. xiii. 10.

a "This is not a promise of restoration, but a denunciation of hopeless ruin. When Sodom shall be rebuilt and shall flourish, when Samaria shall be again a mighty people, then, but not till then, shall Jerusalem be restored."—Spk. Com.

"Perhaps you think, 'If I could have the garden over the way, the trees on the other side of the road, if my estate could take in that morsel of plantation, I would never ask for more.' God will give you as much garden and as many trees as you can bear."—Joseph Parker.

"Thou judgest us; Thy purity
Doth all our lusts condemn;
The love that draws us nearer Thee
Is hot with wrath to them."
—Whittier.

the world as a blank or filled with a seething mass of humanity outside the government of the true God. It is rather to be supposed that Canaan itself appeared to his mind as an epitome of the world such as it must be when the latter-day glory was ushered in. And in Canaan he finds room for Sodom, but Sodom turned to the knowledge of the true God and sharing in the blessings bestowed on Jerusalem. It is surely allowable to see in this the symptom of a more hopeful view of the future of the world at large than we should gather from the rest of the prophecy. If Ezekiel could think of Sodom as raised from the dead and sharing the glories of the people of God, the idea of the conversion of heathen nations could not have been altogether foreign to his mind. It is at all events significant that when he meditates most profoundly on the nature of sin and God's method of dealing with it, he is led to the thought of a Divine mercy which embraces in its sweep those communities which had reached the lowest depths of moral corruption.—Exp. Bib.

58—60. (58) **borne,** the consequences of. (59) **deal .. done,** God would withdraw from His covenant of protection as they had withdrawn from their covenant of service.[a] (60) **remember .. covenant,** i. e. by-and-by call it to mind, and return to thee with restoring mercies. The mind of Jehovah and the mind of Jerusalem both go back on the past; but while Jehovah thinks only of the purpose of love which he had entertained towards Jerusalem in the days of her youth and the indissoluble bond between them, Jerusalem retains the memory of her own sinful history, and finds in the remembrance the source of abiding contrition and shame.—Exp: B. **everlasting covenant,** the spiritual one of the Gospel.

61—63. (61) **for daughters,** Gal. iv. 26.[b] **thy covenant,** not by any covenant of thy making, but by sovereign grace alone. (62) **establish,** etc., Ho. ii. 19, 20. **know .. Lord,** not then in judgments, but in wondrous restoring grace. (63) **never .. mouth,** in any attempted self-vindication. **when I am pacified,** R. V., "when I have forgiven thee." It is through the grace of forgiveness that she is overwhelmed with shame and sorrow for sin, and learns the humility which is the germ of a new hope towards God. **all .. done,** as detailed in this chap.[c]

The Effect of God's Mercy on the Renewed Soul (vss. 62, 63).—I. The extent of man's wickedness. 1. Give a brief summary of the chapter; mark how this image was applicable to Judah and Jerusalem; to us also it may be applied. II. The exceeding riches of God's grace; vile as the Jews had been He promised to restore them to favor; this promise is no doubt to be extended to us. III. The effect of this grace upon every soul of man; it is thought by some calculated to puff up pride and conceit in all who receive it. But this is—1. Contrary to reason; 2. Contrary to fact. Remember—(1) Your covenant mercies; (2) Your covenant engagements.—Simeon.

"Not Patched, but Whole."—The preacher at a rescue mission was pressing home the question of Jesus at Bethesda, "Wilt thou be made whole?" Suddenly he leaned forward, paused an instant, then shot these words out: "Remember, men, it's not patched, but made whole." "That's it, that's just it, and all of it," responded a man, who, when the meeting was open, rose and said: "I patched for years, but the patches fell off or made bigger holes. I had become a hard drinker. I lost my situation. I sobered up, got another situation, failed again and again. Still I patched, and still I fell. At last my wife and children had to go away to her father's, and decency and clothes were gone. One wet, cold, November night, as I sat, half asleep, in the doorway of an empty house, a Bible-woman asked me to come into the misison. There Jesus found me. He didn't patch; he just made me whole. And now we're all together and happy again."—J. S. MacIntosh.

CHAPTER THE SEVENTEENTH.

1—6. (2) **riddle,** Ju. xiv. 12. Here meaning a figurative speech, or continued metaphor. One requiring serious thought to discern its meaning.[a] (3) **great eagle,** representing Nebuchadnezzar. The eagle was an Assyrian emblem.[b] **feathers,** symbols of the many nations of wh. the

[a] De. xxix. 12, 14.

Parricide was by the Roman law punished in a much severer manner than any other kind of homicide. Solon, in his laws, made none against parricide, conceiving it impossible that any one should be guilty of so unnatural a barbarity.

It is through the grace of forgiveness that she is overwhelmed with shame and sorrow for sin, and learns the humility which is the germ of a new hope towards God.

[b] "In the times of the Apostles there was a particular deference paid to the Church at Jerusalem as the mother Church of the Christian world."—Lowth.

[c] "Enhancing the grace of God, which has pardoned so many and so great sins. Nothing so melts into love and humility as the sense of the riches of God's pardoning grace." — Fausset.

It argues a tender heart to feel you have a hard one.

"We can only give the precious products of personality — love, friendship, esteem, reverence, worship. Bargain and sale are not so much a profanation as an impossibility."

[a] "The Heb. is derived from a root meaning 'sharp,' i.e. calculated to stimulate attention and whet the intellect." —Fausset.

[b] For the figure see De. xxviii. 49; Je. iv. 13; Ho. viii. 1.

Bab. kingdom was composed. **divers colors,** intimating the variety of language, habits, and costumes of the peoples subject to Babylon. **came unto Lebanon,** "the kingdom of Judah is represented as a cedar in Lebanon—a comparison which shows how exalted were Ezekiel's conceptions of the dignity of the old regime which had now passed away." **highest branch,** or top shoot; i. e. king Jeconiah. (4) **top,** or head. **young twigs,** princes of the royal family. **traffic,** or commerce, i. e. Babylon, the great merchant city of that age; Is. xliii. 14. (5) **seed,** i. e. the king's seed: ref. is to Zedekiah. **great waters,** R. V., "many waters," fig. for the wealth with wh. Nebuc. supplied Zedekiah. (6) **spreading vine,**[c] one not trained to a pole, but lying on the ground. Kept low so as to secure its dependence on the Bab. king. **branches .. under him,** better, might turn .. be under him, that the new principality should derive all its strength from Babylon and yield all its produce to the power which nourished it.

[c] The kingdom of Judah is no longer likened to an independent cedar: in its depressed state it is only like a dependent vine.

"When people have lost all enjoyment in the word of God, this is no reason why they should relinquish its study. They may lose all enjoyment in their morning ablutions, but that is no reason why they should not bathe. A man should go on reading because of the almost unconscious effect the Bible may have upon the inner life, and because he may thereby learn to love it."
—F. B. Meyer.

"A City of Merchants."—An apt designation this of Babylon the great, the very center and emporium of commerce in the East. The description of Babylon is applicable to the great centers of population in our own and other lands, which serve both to concentrate and to diffuse the products which constitute so large a part of the wealth of the world, and which minister to human convenience and luxury. I. Commercial cities are an expression of a deep-seated tendency of human nature. There are, indeed, impulses which estrange and isolate men; but there are others which draw them together. II. Commercial cities are the scene of very varied experiences and of remarkable friction of mind with mind. As compared with those engaged in rural pursuits, the dwellers in cities are quick and enterprising. III. Commercial cities abound with temptations to sin. There is in great cities a possibility of concealment, by which many are encouraged to form habits of self-indulgence and dissipation from which they might in more favorable circumstances have been restrained by the gentle pressure of home influence and wholesome public opinion. IV. Commercial cities are the center and source of great influence for both good and evil. Intelligence and wealth, luxury and vice, patriotism and public spirit, law and religion, spread from the great centers of population, and affect the remotest regions. V. Commercial cities afford especial opportunities for works of benevolence and evangelization.—Thomson.

7—10. (7) **another .. eagle,** this represents Pharaoh Hophra, king of Egypt. **bend .. him,** Zedekiah, inclined to favor the Egyptian alliance. **that he might .. plantation,** etc., R. V., "from the beds of its plantation, that he might water it."[a] (8) "Ezekiel repeats, as justifying Nebuchadnezzar's action, that his first intention had been to leave Zedekiah under conditions which would have given his kingdom a fair measure of prosperity. The vine might have borne fruit." (9) **Shall it prosper?** in such manifestly unfaithful ways. **he,** i. e. the insulted Nebuchadnezzar. **wither .. spring,** R. V., "that all the fresh springing leaves may wither." Zedekiah is to be severely punished. (10) **east wind,** in the E., so injurious to vegetation.[b]

[a] "Zedekiah was courting the favor of Egypt while he owed his very position to the bounty of Assyria."— Spk. Com.

[b] "The Prophet compares the Chaldaean army to a parching wind that blasts the fruits of the earth, withers the leaves of the trees, and makes everything look naked and bare."
—Lowth.

"All the fresh leaves of her sprouting shall wither."
—Wordsworth.

Vss. 11—21: Interpretation of the riddle. **11—15.** (12) **king of Babylon,** i. e. the great eagle. (13) **king's seed,** R. V., "seed royal," i. e. Zedekiah. **oath,** of allegiance, on condition of wh. oath Zedekiah was given the throne. (14) **base,** as a dependent kingdom: tributary to Babylon. **lift itself up,** in rebellion. (15) **sending .. Egypt,** comp. 2 Ki. xxiv. 20; 2 Chr. xxxvi. 13; Je. xxxvii. 5—7. **prosper,** in violating his oath to Nebuc. and sinning against God's commands, De. xvii. 16. "In all this Nebuchadnezzar is conceived as acting within his rights; and here lay the difference between the clear vision of the prophet and the infatuated policy of his contemporaries."

Justice of Ezekiel.—Throughout this passage Ezekiel shows that he possessed in full measure that penetration and detachment from local prejudices which all the prophets exhibit when dealing with political affairs. The interpretation of the riddle contains a statement of Nebuchadnezzar's policy in his dealings with Judah, whose impartial accuracy could not be improved on by the most disinterested historian. The carrying away of the Judæan king and aristocracy was a heavy blow to religious susceptibilities which Ezekiel fully shared, and its severity was not mitigated by the arrogant assumptions by which it was explained in Jerusalem.

Yet here he shows himself capable of contemplating it as a measure of Babylonian statesmanship and of doing absolute justice to the motives by which it was dictated.—Exp. Bib.

16—18. (16) **shall die,** comp. ch. xii. 13. (17) **Neither,** etc., the aid of Pharaoh shall be in vain, Je. xxxvii. 7; Sam. iv. 17. **by casting up,** R. V., "when trey (the Chaldæan besiegers) cast up." (18) **despised the oath,** vs. 13. **given his hand,**[a] and so pledging his troth and fealty.

The Sacredness of Treaties.—The Old Testament abounds in illustrations of the bearings of religion upon national and corporate life. In this passage of prophecy Ezekiel rebukes his countrymen for their discontent under the Assyrian rule, and for their treacherous intrigues with Egypt. Speaking in the name of the King of kings, he upbraids them for deliberate infraction of a covenant which they were bound to observe. He shows them that political action may be sinful, and that, when such is the case, the Divine Ruler will not suffer it to go unpunished.—Thomson.

19—21. (20) **spread my net,** comp. ch. xii. 13, xxxii. 3. **plead with him,** i. e. there subject him to the consequences of his treachery, bringing it thereby to his knowledge that he is suffering the penalty of it, cf. xx. 35, 36, xxxviii. 22; Jer. ii. 35. (21) **fugitives,** those belonging to him who would try to escape: ch. xii. 14.

The Broken Covenant.—I. Unfaithfulness to man is unfaithfulness to God. II. Those who are pledged to the service of God are especially unfaithful to Him when they are unfaithful to their fellow-men. III. Unfaithfulness to a covenant with God is a heinous sin. Christians now stand in the ancient position of the Jews. 1. Christians are peculiarly privileged; 2. Christians are especially pledged.—Adeney.

Broken Covenants.—Princes and politicians are apt to trifle with solemn oaths and treaties, and to devise specious pretences for violating them; but the Lord will not hold them guiltless who thus take His name in vain; and few of them will be able to plead more plausibly for perfidy and prying than Zedekiah might have done, against whom these awful threatenings were denounced for breaking his covenant with the King of Babylon, and despising the oath sworn to him.—Scott.

22—24. Vss. 22—24: The ideal monarchy of the future. (22) **highest branch,** this shoot is taken from the "top of the cedar"—that is, the section of the royal house which had been carried away to Babylon—indicating that the hope of the future lay not with the king de facto Zedekiah, but with Jehoiachin and those who shared his banishment.—Exp. B. **high mountain,** this indicates the conspicuousness to the eyes of the nations of this great cedar; Is. ii. 2. (23) **mountain of the height,** cf. ch. xx. 40, xl. 2. **fowl of every wing,** as fowls flock to a great tree so all peoples will put their trust in the shadow of this great monarchy in the land of Israel; ch. xxxi. 6; Dan. iv. 12; Matt. xiii. 32. (24) as this kingdom is compared to a cedar other kingdoms are, likewise, called trees; cf. ch. xxxi. 5, 8, 14, 16, 18.—Cam. B.

Fowl of Every Wing (vs. 24).—The cedar a royal tree. Christ the true cedar, and all people are the birds that lodge in its branches. 1. The young may come; 2. The aged may come; 3. The very bad, the outrageously sinful, may come; 4. All the dying may find their nest in this goodly cedar.—Talmage.

[a] "This ceremony was especially used when an inferior made profession of his subjection to his superior." —Lowth.

"As the interests of a nation are greater than those of a private person, so the violation of a national compact is a sin of blackest hue."—Davies.

"Think not to whom, but remember by whom thou hast sworn an oath."

"Christ's kingdom shall by degrees exalt itself above all the kingdoms of the world; and shall at length put an end to them, and itself continue unto all eternity."—Lowth.

Da. iv. 25, 34, vii. 27; Lu. i. 33; 1 Co. xv. 24.

Every nation has its own heroes; every religion its saints, confessors and martyrs. Some of these will live in history while the world endures, and receive the homage and veneration of mankind. But the name of Jesus is above every name. At that name every knee shall bow. —The Interior.

CHAPTER THE EIGHTEENTH.

Vss. 1—20, the individual is not implicated in the sins of his forebears. **1—4.** (2) **concerning .. Israel,** i. e. in reference to its desolations. **fathers .. edge,** the present generation suffers for the sins committed by previous generations.[a] The proverb expresses the fatalism and despair which settled down on the minds of that generation when they realized the full extent of the calamity that had overtaken them. In whatever spirit this saying may have been first coined, there is no doubt that it had come to be used as a witticism at the expense of Providence. It indicates that influences were at work beside the word of prophecy which tended to undermine men's faith in the current conception of the divine

[a] "It is nowhere said in O. T. or N. T. that God visits the iniquities of the fathers upon the children, except where the children obstinately persist in imitating the iniquity of the fathers." —Wordsworth.

government.—Exp. B. In opposition to this teaching, Ezek. insists upon the personal responsibility of each individual. (3) **not .. use,** bec. God will plainly punish this generation for their own sins; and they will not be able to shift the blame on to their fathers. (4) **all .. mine,** implying direct and individual dealing with each. No sin is entailed.

An Old Proverb Discarded. I. The truths behind the proverb. 1. Children share in the sufferings produced by the sins of their parents. 2. Children inherit the appetites and habits of their parents. II. The falsity of the proverb. 1. God does not inflict real punishment on innocent children; 2. Actual sin is not hereditary. III. The exposure and rejection of the proverb. 1. A familiar saying may be false; 2. It is the duty of the teacher of religion to correct popular notions; 3. There is an advance in revelation.—Pul. Com.

The Influence of Heredity upon Character.—Physically, the power of heredity is vast. A man's birth, breeding, and training count for very much; they determine the locality of his early days, the climate, the political and social circumstances, the religious education, the associations, of childhood and of youth. The bodily constitution, including the nervous organization, the temperament and the inclinations springing from it, are to a very large extent hereditary. The environment is largely the effect of birth, and the early influences involved in it. Even those who advocate spiritual ethics, and who believe in human liberty, are quite willing to admit that all men owe to hereditary causes and influences very much which makes them what they are.—Thomson.

"God draweth straight lines, but we think and call them crooked. Ezek. xviii. 25." —Rutherford.

"Heathen systems will not be conquered in a generation. They survive many severe wounds and rally even after they appear to be conquered. That they can be conquered, however, and that they will be, is as true as Christianity itself. When they yield, then will be the golden age of missions." —The Independent.

5—9. (5) **just,** comprehensive term for all moral rightness. (6) **eaten .. mountains,** sharing in the sacrificial feasts on the high places, where are the idol-shrines.[b] **lifted .. eyes,** in supplication and adoration. (7) **oppressed,** etc., Ex. xxii. 25, 26; De. xxiv. 12. **restored .. pledge,** De. xxiv. 6, 13. **given .. hungry,** De. xv. 7. (8) **usury,** Ex. xxii. 25; Le. xxv. 36, 37; De. xxiii. 19; Ps. xv. 5. **executed .. man,** free from judicial corruption so prevalent in the East. (9) **truly,** obediently, faithfully, and kindly. **live,** or preserve his life. Such a man comes into no Divine judgment.

[b] De. xii. 2; Eze. vi. 13, xvi. 16, 24, xx. 28; 1 Co. x. 21.

"The humblest trade has in it elbow-room for all the virtues. That huckster can be true and honest and honorable: what more can Rothschild be? The excellence of a circle lies in its roundness, not its bigness." —S. Coley.

Ezekiel's Individualism.—This emancipation of the individual soul, whether from a doom inherited from a former generation or from one entailed on it by its own evil past, was perhaps the greatest contribution made by Ezekiel to the religious life and thought of his time. He probably reached his individualism by reflection on such events as the downfall of the state, leaving now no place for religion except in the individual mind, and on the sentiments which he heard expressed by men around him. His contemporary Jeremiah reached the same truth from another direction, from his own experience of the inwardness of the relation of God to men. The very nature of this relation required that the religious subject should be the individual mind.—Camb. B.

10—13. (10) **robber,** or "breaker up of a house." (11) **that doeth .. duties,** a very difficult clause which seems so meaningless that many consider it a copyist's error. (12) **lifted .. eyes,** in adoration or supplication. (13) **blood,** "his destruction is owing wholly to himself."[a]

[a] "Upon his own head, but not on the heads of his children, if they do not imitate him." — Wordsworth.

"We must dig through the hardpan of evil before we strike the living springs of good."

"A man's own heart must ever be given to gain that of another."—Goldsmith.

God's Remonstrance with Man's Reason.—I. We are reminded of man's responsibility. II. Idolatry is a root of various immorality. III. Parental influence is potent yet not fatal. IV. Repentance, at any stage of human probation, is possible. V. Repentance leads to complete and perfect righteousness. VI. Righteousness is incipient life.—Davies.

The Only Foe.—

Remember this—not all the wild,
  Huge, untamed elements have force
To reach thee, though the seas were piled
  In weltering mountains in thy course.

Only thyself, thyself can harm.
  Forget it not! and full of peace,
As if the south wind whispered warm,
  Wait then till storm and tumult cease.—Celia Thaxter.

14—18. (14) **if he,** i. e. the utterly bad man, who brings destruction down upon his own head. **considereth,** R. V., "feareth." **not such like,** not any of the evil things. (15—17) comp. vss. 5—9. **withholden the pledge,** R. V., "hath not taken aught to pledge." **taken .. poor,** i. e. hath not oppressed. **not.. father,** but judgment shall spend itself on the sinful father.[b] (18) **his brother,** i. e. his brother-man, or neighbor.

Heredity.—The very same difficulties which Ezekiel had to encounter in his time confront us still in a somewhat altered form, and are often keenly felt as obstacles to faith in God. The scentific doctrine of heredity, for example, seems to be but a more precise modern rendering of the old proverb about the eating of sour grapes. The biological controversy over the possibility of the transmission of acquired characteristics scarcely touches the moral problem. In whatever way that controversy may be ultimately settled, it is certain that in all cases a man's life is affected both for good and evil by influences which descend upon him from his ancestry. Hardly anything is better established by experience than that the consequences of past actions persist through all changes of spiritual condition, and, further, that children do suffer from the consequences of their parents' sin. Do not these facts, it may be asked, amount practically to a vindication of the theory of retribution against which the prophet's argument is directed? How can we reconcile them with the great principles enunciated in this chapter? The solution of the contradiction referred to lies in the separation between the natural and the penal consequences of sin. There is a sphere within which natural laws have their course, modified, it may be, but not wholly suspended by the law of the spirit of life in Christ. The physical effects of vicious indulgences are not turned aside by repentance. But there is also a sphere into which natural law does not enter. In his immediate personal relations to God a believer is raised above the evil consequences of the past. Tribulations no longer bear the aspect of penalty and are no longer a token of the wrath of God.—Exp. Bib.

19—23. (19) **Why?** R. V., "Yet say ye, wherefore doth not, etc.," i. e. is it not a well-known fact that the son bears the father's iniquity? The Jews appeal to their own experience. **When,** etc., implying that if the Jews of that generation had done right, they would not have been punished for their fathers' sins of the previous generations. (20) **son,** etc., comp. De. xxiv. 16.[a] (21) vss. 21—32. The individual is not dominated by his own past life. **turn .. sins,** then he shall not be dealt with on the ground of the forsaken sins, but on the ground of the new obedience. (22) **not be mentioned,** R. V., "remembered against;" being forgiven they shall be forgotten.[b] (23) **any pleasure,** the frequency of prophetic denunciation might produce such an impression.[c] The death of the wicked, the loss, i, e, of true life, for a time, or even for ever, might be the necessary consequence of laws that were righteous in themselves, and were working out the well-being of the universe; but that death was not to be thought of as the result of a Divine decree, or contemplated by the Divine mind with any satisfaction.—Pulp. Com.

24—26. (24) **righteous,** etc., this is the answering side of the truth of God's dealings declared in vss. 21, 22.[d] **turneth away,** in utter apostasy. Reference is not to the temporary failures and fallings of the godly. **mentioned,** taken into account as a mitigation of sentence. (25) **not equal,** or weighed out, balanced; properly adjusted to the several cases.[e] (26) **his iniquity,** i. e. you need go no further for explanation than the fact of his own sin.

Sin, not God, Changes Us.—There is something picturesque and awful in the instant change which a sudden crime makes in the whole relation which a man holds to the state he lives in. He has grown up protected by his nation's law. It cared for him even before his birth, and there has never been a moment in his boyhood, youth, or manhood when its shield has not been over him and its sword drawn to strike down any one who dared to do him harm. Some day he does a sudden crime, he disobeys the law, he takes a brother's life, and instantly, as his dagger pierces and the life-blood flows, everything alters. The law which has protected him becomes his enemy. Her sword is pointed at his heart. Her shield is spread before him only lest any one should snatch him from her certain punishment. Instead of trusting in her quiet smile, he quails

[b] It is nevertheless true that hereditary disabilities do follow on parental wrong - doings; but rather on parental vices and immoralities than on such acts of unkindnes, injustice, and idolatry as are dealt with by Ezekiel.

On an Alaskan steamer the passengers were proving that an Indian could not be civilized. So Dr. Hill, of Portland, called up a graduate of Marietta and Lane, a native Alaskan with bronze skin and black hair, who told the story of what the gospel had done for his people. Scepticism was impossible on deck after that demonstration.—North and West.

[a] 2 Ki. xiv. 6; 2 Chr. xxv. 4; Je. xxxi. 29.

[b] Je. xxxi. 34; Am. viii. 7.

[c] 1 Ti. ii. 4; 2 Pe. iii. 9.

It must be a strange sensation for a painter to see an image of beauty, out of nothing, so to speak, gradually developing itself on the canvas and living there. But what is this compared with seeing a soul emerging from death unto life, its wings freeing themselves from the hard, ugly chrysalis of its natural condition, to flutter forth into the sunshine of eternity? — James Stalker, D. D.

[d] Comp. 2 Pe. ii. 21.

[e] "It was really their way that was unequal, since living in sin they expected to be dealt with as if they were righteous. God's way was invariably to

deal with different men according to their deserts."—Fausset.

under her pitiless eye. She is transformed the moment that he disobeys.—Phillips Brooks.

27—32. (27) **turneth,** in penitence of heart that makes him alter his conduct. The essential truth which he inculcates is the emancipation of the individual, through repentance, from his own past. In virtue of his immediate personal relation to God each man has the power to accept the offer of salvation, to break away from his sinful lie and escape the doom which hangs over the impenitent.—Exp. B. (28) **considereth,** see vs. 14. (29) **not equal,** vs. 25. (30) **every one .. ways,** and surely no principle of judgment can be better than this. **Repent,** the inward feeling of penitence. **turn yourselves,** the corresponding outward act. This call intimates that, if thus strictly judged, the whole nation would be found guilty. **ruin,** R. V., "stumbling-block." (31) **make .. heart,** set yourselves on the endeavor to cherish other feelings and wishes. The "new heart" indicates a religion that is spiritual, not ceremonial. The effort to renew our own heart will surely drive us to seek the new heart from God, who alone can give it by His Spirit.[a] Comp. Ps. li. 1—5, 10, 11. (32) **no pleasure,** ref. to the eternal character of Jehovah as the God of salvation.

[a] Je. xxxii. 39; Eze. xi. 19, xxxvi. 26.

Each sin I cast away shall make my soul more strong to soar.—T. H. Gill.

"Repentance is sorrow converted into action, into a movement to a new and better life."—M. R. Vincent.

The Repentant.—What man among you can stand against his children's tears? When King Henry II., in the ages gone by, was provoked to take up arms against his ungrateful and rebellious son, he besieged him in one of the French towns, and the son being near to death, desired to see his father, and confess his wrong-doing; but the stern old sire refused to look the rebel in the face. The young man being sorely troubled in his conscience, said to those about him, "I am dying, take me from my bed, and let me lie in sackcloth and ashes, in token of my sorrow for my ingratitude to my father." Thus he died, and when the tidings came to the old man outside the walls, that his boy had died in ashes, repentant for his rebellion, he threw himself on the earth, like another David, and said, "Would God I had died for him." The thought of his boy's broken heart touched the heart of the father. If ye, being evil, are overcome by your children's tears, how much more shall your Father who is in heaven find in your bemoanings and confessions an argument for the display of His pardoning love through Christ Jesus our Lord? This is the eloquence which God delights in, the broken heart and the contrite spirit.—Spurgeon.

CHAPTER THE NINETEENTH.

1—4 (1) **lamentation,** a dirge over the princes of Judah. **princes of Israel,** those of the house of Judah. Two princes are lamented, one captured and carried to Egypt, viz. Jehoahaz, son and successor of Josiah (vss. 1—4); and another carried to Babylon, who must be Jehoiachin (vss. 5—9). The elegy does not appear to extend further. Verses 10—14 refer to Zedekiah, and are prophetic.—Cam. B. (2) **thy mother,** the land or people of Judah, as the native country of the princes addressed. **lioness,**[a] bec. fierce at catching prey. (3) **one .. whelps,** viz. Jehoahaz.[b] **learned .. prey,** alluding to this king following the evil and idolatrous practices of his predecessors. (4) **nations,** esp. Egypt.[c] **pit, hunter's pit,** arranged for securing wild animals,[d] 2 Ki. xxiii. 33; Je. xxii. 11.

[a] Ge. xlix. 9; Nu. xxiii. 24.

[b] 2 Ki. xxiii. 33.

[c] "There is an allusion to the custom, when the news arrives that a lion or other savage savage beast is committing mischief, of assembling on all sides to seize and slay it." —Michaelis.

[d] Ps. xxxv. 7, xciv. 13.

"God would have us sensitive, responsive, easily impressible, so that we can be moved by divine appeals and instantly respond to every call to the enjoyment of divine fellowship."

Ezekiel's Dirge.—The whole passage is highly poetical, and represents a side of Ezekiel's nature which we have not hitherto been led to study. But it is too much to expect of even the most logical of prophets that he should experience no personal emotion but what fitted into his system, or that his poetic gift should be chained to the wheels of his theological convictions. The dirge expresses no moral judgment on the character or deserts of the two kings to which it refers: it has but one theme—the sorrow and disappointment of the "mother" who nurtured and lost them, that is, the nation of Israel personified according to a usual Hebrew figure of speech. All attempts to go beyond this and to find in the poem an allegorical portrait of Jehoahaz and Jehoiachin are irrelevant. The mother is a lioness, the princes are young lions and behave as stalwart young lions do, but whether their exploits are praiseworthy or the reverse is a question that was not present to the writer's mind.—Exp. Bib.

5—9. (5) **waited,** i. e. when Judah saw that her hope of the return of Jehoahoz delayed and was finally lost. **another,** viz. Jehoiachin, 2 Ki. xxiv. 6. He was put on the throne by the consent of the people. Jehoiakim, who intervened, is not mentioned bec. he died in peace. The dirge is for princes that were captured by foreign nations. (6) **catch .. prey,** followed the same idolatrous course as his predecessors.[e] (7) **knew .. palaces,** Polychr. B. "their dwelling-places he ravaged." (8) **nations,** here the Chaldæans. For the fate of Jehoiachin see 2 Ki. xxiv. 10—12. (9) **voice .. mountains,** as a lion seeking her prey. "The poetry here is simple and sincere. The mournful cadence of the elegiac measure, which is maintained throughout, is adapted to the tone of melancholy which pervades the passage and culminates in the last beautiful line."

e "Or, he learned and practiced all the methods of tyranny and oppression."—Lowth.

10—14. (10) **Thy mother,** the land of Judah. The ruling prince is here addressed as such; not as any particular person. **is like,** R. V., was like; contrast with vs. 13. **vine .. blood,** "vine in her height."—Davidson. **full of branches,** the people multiplied under God's blessing.[a] (11) **sceptres,** Ge. xlix. 10. **appeared,** etc., "was beheld from afar." (12) **east .. fruit,** Ho. xiii. 15. (13) **wilderness,** that of Babylon. (14) **fire .. out,** comp. Ju. ix. 15. Allusion is to Zedekiah's rebellion against Babylon wh. involved the whole nation in ruin.

a "The country of Judea, from whence the royal family have their original, was like a fruitful vine in a flourishing condition."—Lowth.

"The metaphor of the blood is less harsh in the Heb. because the juice of a vine is called in Scripture its blood. Ge. xlix. 11." — Wordsworth.

Sceptres.—The allusion here is evidently to the sceptres of the ancients, which were no other than walking-sticks, cut from the stems or branches of trees, and decorated with gold, or studded with golden nails. Thus Achilles is introduced as swearing by a sceptre, which being cut from the trunk of a tree on the mountains, and stripped of its bark and leaves, should never more produce leaves and branches, or sprout again. Such a one the Grecian judges carried in their hands. See Homer, Il. i. 234.—Burder.

CHAPTER THE TWENTIETH.

A review of Israel's history designed to show Jehovah's respect for his own name. **1—4.** (1) **seventh .. month,** Aug. 590 B. C. **elders,** as ch. viii. 1, xiv. 1. (3) **not be inquired,** i. e. not pay any heed to your inquiries.[b] (4) **judge,** i. e. act in the capacity of a judge; pass sentence upon Israel by a rehearsal of the past history. Addressed to Ezekiel.

b "Because ye inquire with an evil temper, a cavilling spirit, and a murmuring tone, and not with penitential meekness, and self - abasement for your sin, and with humble submission to the will of God." —Wordsworth.

God will Give no Answer to the New Questions of Those Who Refuse to Give Heed to His Word Already Received.—We cannot be surprised that Ezekiel's oracle was silenced. Such insolence as that of the elders of Israel could meet with no more gracious reception. 1. If we refuse to hear God's Word, we must expect to be left in darkness. Before we cry for more light, let us use the light we have. We may indeed pray for God's Spirit to help our interpretation of the Bible, and having read the written Word we may crave more light still. But first to reject the Divine revelation and then to seek for new light is not the way to receive more truth. 2. God will not give light to those who harden themselves in impenitence. The Jews had been charged with sin and called to repentance. They had refused to admit the charge and had declined to repent. Thus they had shut the door against further Divine communications. The spiritual vision is best purged by the tears of penitence. A hard heart is deaf to God's Word. 3. It is useless to be informed about the future unless we listen to the spiritual teachings of God. Men resorted to oracles to satisfy idle curiosity or to seek mere worldly guidance. God does not speak for such comparatively worthless ends. We most need spiritual instruction for the guidance of our souls into the way of life. Till we have received and obeyed that instruction any other form of revelation must be irrelevant, distracting, and therefore positively injurious.—Adeney.

There is but one way in which man can ever help God—that is, by letting God help him; and there is no way in which His name is more guiltily taken in vain than by calling the abandonment of our own work the performance of His.

5—9. (5) **lifted .. hand,** the sign of swearing. **known,** by My judgments and deliverances.[c] **I .. God,** i. e. I am the God you should serve, and I alone. (6) **espied,** observed and chose, as specially suitable for them. **glory,** or the fairest flower of all lands. (7) **Cast,** etc., though

c Ex. iii. 8, iv. 31.

Moses gives no positive record of the Israelites having taken up with Egyptian idolatries, inclination towards such is implied in the readiness of the people to worship the golden calf. (8) **then I said,** i. e. even while they were in Egypt I thought of destroying them. (9) **my name's sake,**[a] the honor of wh. was pledged in the covenant with the patriarchs. This thought is the key to the meaning and significance of the whole chapter. Not Israel's deserts but God's char. accounts for past events. **polluted,** R. V., "profaned."

Israel in Egypt.—The question how far Jehovah was known and worshiped in Egypt is an obscure one. The name could not have been altogether unknown or the people could not have been rallied by Moses to his service nor induced to put themselves under his protection. That his worship, however, was mixed with impurities may be assumed. How far the people partook in the worship of Egyptian deities cannot be ascertained.—Cambridge Bible.

10—13. (10) **caused .. Egypt,** Ex. xiii. 18. (11) **statutes,** as on Mt. Sinai, Ex. xx. **man do,** Le. xviii. 5; Ro. x. 5; Ga. iii. 12. (12) **sabbaths,** Ex. xx. 8, xxxi. 13, xxxv. 2; De. v. 12. (13) **polluted,** failed to dedicate them to Jehovah, Nu. xv. 32; Ex. xvi. 27. **I said,** etc., comp. Nu. xiv. 29, xxvi. 65.

The Sabbath God's Institution and Gift to Man (vs. 12).—We observe—I. That the Sabbath is God's institution. II. That the Sabbath is God's gift, man not made of iron, the body needs it, the mind needs it, above all the soul needs it. III. The ends for which the Sabbath was given. 1. To be a sign between a nation and Him; 2. To be the means of sanctifying a nation.—J. D. Hull.

14—17. (14) **name's sake,** as vs. 9. Hence Jehovah did not make an end of the people. (15) **not bring them,** i. e. the very people who came out of Egypt: only their descendants entered Canaan. (16) **heart went,** they hankered after the idolatries of Egypt, which seemed to them connected with plenty of food. (17) **make an end,**[b] even in the judgments I brought upon them I remembered mercy, I pitied the sinners.

The Christian Sabbath.—It is a memorial of a completed creation work and of Christ's resurrection. In an ironmonger's shop in a country town in Scotland, the shopkeeper sat at his desk at the window. A young apprentice in the cellar below had stuck the candle which he carried in a barrel of gunpowder; the gunpowder exploded, the shop window was blown out, and the good man who sat in it was carried in the current of air to the top of the street, and there landed safely on his feet, while the apprentice was blown to pieces. It was such a wonderful deliverance that the ironmonger observed the day as a day of prayer and thanksgiving to the end of his life. Is it difficult to understand how he should have done so? And shall we not gladly commemorate our deliverance—our emancipation—the announcement that the sinner's salvation was complete, by the rising of Jesus from the dead? Shall we ever suffer ourselves to be deprived of a day that has such happy and hallowed associations?—F. S. Schenck.

18—22. (18) **their children,** when the fathers had fallen by the judgments in the wilderness. The Bk. of Deuteronomy contains these gracious Divine pleadings. (20) **hallow,** or separate, keep holy.[a] (21) **the children rebelled,** trying in each fresh generation the patience of God. **polluted,** profaned. (22) **withdrew my** hand, from inflicting the meditated judgment.

The Sabbath (vs. 20).—I. The design of the Sabbath. 1. An emblem of creation; 2. A memorial of redemption; 3. A covenant sign; 4. A foretaste of heaven. II. Its necessity. 1. Physical need; 2. Moral influence. III. Its duties. 1. To God; 2. To ourselves; 3. To our families; 4. To others.—W. W. Wythe.

23—26. (23) **lifted up,** i. e. made a solemn asseveration. **scatter them,** Le. xxvi. 33; De. iv. 27, xxviii. 64. No time stated; prob. the condition of affairs during the period of the judges saw this judgment partially fulfilled; the present exile was the culmination. (24) **eyes .. idols,** comp. vs. 16. (25) **statutes .. good,** "the reference is to the law which required the consecration of the firstborn of all animals to Jehovah. This was interpreted in the most rigorous sense as dedication in sacrifice; and

a "God's name means the sum total of His perfections; to manifest these, His gratuitous mercy abounding above their sins, yet without wrong to His justice, and so to set forth His glory, was and is the ultimate end of His dealings."—Fausset.

vs. 12. Though a few passages might be cited where the word "Sabbath" is perhaps used in a general sense, yet there is here a particular reference to the seventh-day Sabbath, which stood in a different position from all the other celebrations.

"The sabbaths of eternity,
One sabbath, deep and wide."
—Tennyson.

b Ps. lxxviii. 38.

"The Sundaies of man's life,
Thredded together on time's string,
Make bracelets to adorn the wife
Of the eternal, glorious King.
On Sunday heaven's gates stand ope;
Blessings are plentiful and rife,
More plentiful than hope."
—Geo. Herbert.

a "The pollution of the Sabbath consisted in failing to make the day holy in deed as well as in name by earnest worship and true heart service."—Spk. Com.

"Only tranquil souls reflect. Stormy natures, like ruffled streams, reveal no beautiful images upon their surfaces or within their depths."

then the principle was extended to the case of human beings. The divine purpose in appearing to sanction this atrocious practice was to 'horrify' the people—that is to say, the punishment of their idolatry consisted in the shock to their natural instincts and affections caused by the worst development of the idolatrous spirit to which they were delivered."—Exp. B. (26) **polluted .. gifts,**[b] i. e. by leaving them unrestrained to all the evil practices of their idolatry.

"To Be Obeyed, Not Answered."—When Leonard Woods, president of Bowdoin College, was in France, he was invited to dine with the king. He presented himself at the palace, and was met with his accustomed courtesy by the king, who said: "We did not know that we were to have the pleasure of your company to-day. You did not answer our invitation." Leonard Woods replied: "I thought the invitation of a king was to be obeyed, not answered." When the Spirit says, "Come," it is equal to a command, and we would better put off all other engagements and come. No matter how gently and winsomely the invitation comes, let us never forget that there is a voice of royal, imperial, imperious urgency and authority behind it.—John McNeill.

27—32. (27) **in this,** which the Prophet proceeds to state, viz., the defiling of the sacred land of covenant and promise with such self-willed idolatries. **blasphemed,** or grieviously insulted. (28) **lifted .. hand,** made an oath. **every high hill,** "to Ezekiel the unity of Jehovah and the unity of the sanctuary were inseparable ideas." In the oldest prophets, Amos and Hosea, it is the kind of worship at the high-places that is condemned, the revelry and heathenish merrymaking (Hos. ix. 1), the sensuousness (Hos. viii. 13; Am. v. 21), and the false conception of deity implied in it (Hos. vi. 6). The mere localities or multitude of altars do not seem assailed, except that the more there were of them the more sin was committed, because the whole worship was sinful.—Cam. B. **provocation,** etc., reference is to the meat-offering; see **ch. xvi. 19.** "Being offered to idols, it became abominable, and was turned into a provocation." **drink offerings,** Le. xxiii. 18. **(29) Bamah,** or high place.[a] (30) **Are ye,** this appeal is addressed to the exiles. Notwithstanding all the warnings of men, they persisted in following the evil example of their fathers." (31) **offer .. gifts,** vs. 26. **Enquired of,** vs. 3. (32) cometh mind, if the temple were destroyed, they thought, then the one restraint on the idolatries they loved would be removed. They would be no longer a separate people, and would be free to adopt the cultus of the heathen among whom they lived.—Pul. Com. **as the heathen,**[b] such a resolve indicated a repudiation of their rights and privileges as Jehovah's people.

The Paganism of the Heart (vs. 32).—Look at it—I. As an evil to which the godly are liable. 1. The force of early habits; 2. Of social influence; 3. Of Satanic agency. II. As an evil against which the godly should struggle—1. By the growth of heavenly senstiments; 2. By closer fellowship with the Divine; 3. By a moral conquest over spiritual foes.—Thomas.

Formalism.—Never was more truth packed in a nutshell than in Dr. G. F. Pentecost's retort to an educated Buddhist who was swinging his prayer-wheel and repeating meaningless words. "What are you praying for?" asked the doctor. "O, nothing." "Whom are you praying to?" "O, nobody." "And that," said the doctor, "is Buddhism. Praying for nothing—to nobody."——The memory of the past makes our whole life one. We cannot part from our former selves. However Israel might have sunk into idolatry, the fact of their glorious privileges in the past still remained. None of those who dwell in a land visited by the light of God's Revelation can become, in all respects, like the heathen. We may choose the sins of heathenism, but we must be judged as those who have had opportunity for the knowledge of God.—T. H. Leale.

33—38. (33) **mighty,** etc., signs of ujdgment and severe dealing; in store for the exiles. God will shatter their resolution to be like the heathen.[c] (34) **the people,** better, the peoples; the various nations. (35) **wilderness,** R. V., "wilderness of the peoples," **i.** e. the wilderness betw. Babylonia and Canaan, adjoining the peoples among whom they were dispersed. **plead with you,** a legal expression, to implead, to contend against one in a court of justice, which should be to them what the wilder-

[b] "I judicially gave them up to pollute themselves. Their own sin I made their punishment." —Fausset.

"God sometimes makes sin to be its own punishment and there needs no more to make men miserable than to give them up to their own vile appetites and passions. Let them be put into the hand of their own counsels, and they will ruin themselves and make themselves desolate." —Mat. Henry.

[a] There is here a play upon the words, Ba, signifying "go," and mah, "what." Bamah, or, What go they to? Comp. Ex. xvi. 15.

"Instead of the word Misbeach, the name which God appropriated to His own altar, the place is usually called Bamah, a name taken from an idolatrous custom."—Lowth.

[b] "Such was Israel's infatuated resolve. But God mercifully interposed to prevent its execution, by dispersing them, as He had mercifully delivered them from Egyptian idolatry, by bringing them into the wilderness." —Wordsworth.

[c] "I will no longer try to reclaim you by the gentle methods of patience and forbearance, but will govern you as masters do ill servants, by stripes and corrections, and by this means cure you of your hankering after the heathen customs and idolatries." —Lowth.

ness time had been to the people on their coming out of Egypt. (37) **under the rod,**[d] a metaphor from the shepherd, and meaning, to be gathered into the flock. Le. xxvii. 32.[a] The shepherd takes account of the condition of each sheep as the flock passes, one by one, under his rod. **bond,** or obligations and responsibilities. (38) **purge you,** etc., "the election of the good involves the rejection of the bad."[b]

Passing Under the Rod.—It was the custom among the Jews to select the tenth of their sheep (see Le. xxvii. 32) after this manner. The lambs were separated from the dams, and enclosed in a sheep-cote with only one narrow way out. The dams were left immediately without. On opening the gate their young instantly hastened to join their mother, when a man, placed at the entrance, with a rod dipped in ochre, touched every tenth lamb, and so marked it with his rod, and said, "Let this be holy in the name of the tenth." The passage in Ezekiel, divested of its figurative form, appears to have this signification, that God would deliver a remnant of His people who were then in captivity in Babylon; that He would take particular notice of them, and count them one by one, as a shepherd does his sheep; and, marking them for His own peculiar service, bring them into the privileges of the covenant which He had made with them.—Visitor.

d "Lord wave again Thy chastening rod, till every idol throne crumble to dust, and Thou, O God, reign in our hearts alone."." —Keble.

a Je. xxxiii. 13.

b Ro. xi. 7—11.

39—44. (39) **Go ye, serve,** this is evidently spoken in irony; indicating that God prefers the open idolater to the secret hypocrite. Be not half and half, naming My name, and serving your idols at the same time. The present text must read: "Go, serve ye every one his idols; but hereafter ye shall hearken unto me, and no more profane my holy name with your gifts."—Cam. B. (40) **holy mountain,** where God's temple was. "There we have the thought which is expanded in the vision of the purified theocracy which occupies the closing chapters of the book." **all of them,** both those of Judah and of Israel. **first fruits,** or chief. (41) **be sanctified,** or honored, by shewing Himself holy in Israel's restoration in the sight of the heathen, Je. xxxiii. 9. (42) **know,** or fully experience and realize. (43) **remember,** call to mind, and on account of past doings humble yourselves in the dust. (44) **my name's sake,**[c] the supreme reason for the Divine action is the necessity for upholding, in the view of men, the Divine hour.

c "His reasons were all fetched from Himself. Had He dealt with them 'according to their wicked ways and corrupt doings,' He would have left them to be scattered and lost, but He recovered and restored them for the sake of His own name, not only that it might not be polluted, but that He might be sanctified in them before the heathen." —Mat. Henry.

45—49. (45) **Moreover,** this is properly the beginning of a new prophecy, and so should have commenced ch. xxi. (46) **south,** so Judæa is situated in relation to the place where Ezekiel was in the north of Babylonia. **drop thy word,** De. xxxii. 2; Is. lv. 10.[d] **forest .. field,** fig. for land of Israel;[e] perhaps the prophet is reminded of the stately cedars of Lebanon. (47) **fire,** fig. for the destruction wrought by the Chaldæans. **green tree,** a man relatively righteous. **dry tree,** a sinner whose life is withered. (48) **not .. quenched,** until its full mission of destruction is wrought out. (49) **parables,** or in metaphors wh. we cannot understand, and behind wh. there lies no reality.[a]

Ezekiel's Preaching.—It was a fact that Ezekiel had been speaking in parables. No other prophet indulged so freely in symbolical language. His writings are a garden of luxuriant metaphors, which often blossom into elaborate allegories. This style is characteristic of Oriental literature, and it is a feature of the Bible teaching generally, though in Ezekiel it is carried out more fully than elsewhere. There is an analogy between the seen and the unseen. Unattentive hearers may be arrested by what strikes them on the plain of their own earthly living. It is not enough that we receive a bold abstract statement of truth into our understandings, for this may never fructify. An imaginative grasp of truth, even when it is less clearly defined, may be more vital and fruitful.—Pul. Com.

d "The gift of prophecy is compared to rain, or the dew of heaven, which makes everything fruitful.

e "Judah and Jerusalem are called forests, not only bec. they had been full of people, as a wood of trees, but bec. they had been empty of fruit, for fruit trees grow not in a forest. Those that should have been as the garden of the Lord had become like a forest " —Mat. Henry.

a Mat. xiii. 14, 15.

CHAPTER THE TWENTY-FIRST.

1—5. With far other feelings than his fellows, but with as keen an interest as theirs, Ezekiel follows the development of what he knows to be the last act in the long controversy between Jehovah and Israel. It is his duty to repeat once more the irrevocable decree—the divine "delenda est" against the guilty Jerusalem.—Exp. B. (2) **Jerusalem,** comp. south, ch. xx. 46. **holy places,** i. e. the temple and its surrounding buildings. (3) **my sword,** wh. is the king of Babylon. **righteous,** etc., in a general calamity wh. would affect all classes. Comp. ch. xx. 47[b] (4) **south .. north,** i. e. from the one end of the land to the other.[c] (5) **not return,** i. e. into its sheath until its mission is accomplished.

The Common Fate of Righteous and Wicked.—I. It is a fact that the righteous suffer with the wicked. II. The common life of mankind necessitates this common fate. III. It is an aggravation of a calamity that the righteous share the fate of the wicked. IV. The righteous who suffer with the wicked are not ultimately injured. V. The common fate of the righteous and wicked may be a means of saving both.—Pul. Com.

The Future.—What we know not now we shall know hereafter. The anomalies of the present state of being are such as to suggest that this is only a probationary state, that we do not now and here see the unfolding of the complete purposes of the Lord and Judge of all. The Scriptures reveal a state in which retribution and compensation shall be complete, as we know they are not here. The righteous and the wicked shall not always be confused in one common category, and consigned to one common doom. The discrimination which is not exercised now shall be exercised hereafter. Prosperous sinners shall not for ever elude the righteous judgment of God. The suffering and patience of the virtuous and pious shall one day be rewarded, not only by the approbation of the Judge, but by an everlasting recompense.—Thomson.

6, 7. (6) **Sigh,** i. e. give public indication of your intense grief and concern. **breaking .. lions,** as if utterly bowed down by the weight of troubles. "The loins are the seat of strength."[d] The breaking of the loins is a fig. for the utter prostration of the strength. (7) **tidings,** of the peril and woe of Jerusalem. **melt,** etc., ch. vii. 17.

8—13. (9) **a sword,** vs. 2.[a] **furbished,** or brightened, made every way ready for immediate war. (10) **glitter,** and to excite alarm. **should .. mirth,** etc., R. V., "shall we then make mirth? the rod of my son it contemneth every tree;" i. e. the rod (sword of Babylon) with which Jehovah now chastises his son contemneth (exceeds in severity) every tree, or all wood (all rods of chastisement wh. are mere wood, for this is glittering steel). But the passage is very difficult and the text may be corrupt. (11) **handled,** and put at once to its use. (12) **Cry and howl,** addressed to the prophet. **terrors .. people,** R. V., "they (the princes of Judah (are delivered over to the sword with my people.." **smite .. thigh,** one of the natural expressions of exceeding distress. (13) **trial,** or time of trial. the rod, or sceptre, R. V., "and what if even the rod (i. e. sceptre) that contemneth shall be no more?" reference being to the royal house of Judah wh. shall perish, vss. 25—27.[b]

14—17. (14) **third time,** to express the violence of the threatening judgment. Let its stroke be repeated again and again. "Doubled" means "repeated." **great men,** R. V., "great one," ref. being to Zedekiah. **privy chambers,** better, with R. V. marg., "which compasseth them about." "Whirling around them" with ref. to the triple intensity of the sword. (15) **ruins,** "stumbling-blocks." **wrapped,** "sharpened." (16) **Go .. hand,** R. V., "gather thee together, go to the right; set thyself in array, go to the left!" The sword is addressed by the Lord and bidden concentrate its force to smite on the right, and set itself on to slaughter on the left. **face,** i. e. edge. (17) **smite .. hands,** as an expression of indignation. **fury to rest,** R. V., "satisfy my fury."

"Smite Thy Hands Together."—To smite the hands together, in the East, amounts to an oath! In the seventeenth verse, the Lord says, in reference to Jerusalem, "I will also smite My hands together, and I will cause My fury to rest: I the Lord have said." By the solemn smiting of hands it was shown the word had gone forth, and would not be recalled. When a priest delivers a message to the people, when he relates anything which he professes to have received from the gods, he smites his hands together, and says, "True."—Roberts.

18—20. (19) **two ways,** these were to be marked, as on a map—one leading to Jerusalem, the other to Ammon. **choose . . place,** "grave a

---

b "The Prophet is not now touching the question as to the extent to which the righteous suffer with the wicked. That, as a matter of fact, national judgment involves the innocent in the temporal ruin of the guilty, there is no doubt. The equity of God is vindicated by the ruin being only temporal." —Spk. Com.

c Eze. xx. 47.

"The eternal work of laboring with God for our own sanctification, that is the progress of the Christian life." — Phillips Brooks.

d Job xl. 16; Ps. lxvi. 11; Is. xxi. 3.

"A man's mind may be aroused by another, but he must mold his own character. What if a man fails in one thing? Let him try again—he must quarry his own nature. Let him try hard, and try again, for he does not know what he can do till he tries."

a De. xxxii. 41. "The faithful servant of God saw God arming Himself as a mighty man for the war, and the glittering sword of vengeance in His hand, and he calls aloud to his countrymen all at ease, with awakening thunder, 'A sword,' etc." —McCheyne.

b "What horrors will not arise when the sword shall cut down, without regard, the ruling sceptre of Judah?" — Karlsruhe Trans. of Bible.

"If you always live with those who are lame, you will yourself learn to limp." — From the Latin.

hand" as a pointer or sign-post. The hope was cherished in Jerusalem. and probably also among the Jews in Babylon, that the first assault of the Chaldæans would be directed against the Ammonites, and that time would thus be gained to complete the defences of Jerusalem.—Exp. B. (20) **to Rabbath,** etc., it seems that Zedekiah invited the Ammonites to an alliance in opposition to the Chaldæans:[a] this, however, would only draw down destruction on both.

Note on vss. 18—27.—The prophet is commanded to represent a way which parts into two ways. At the parting of the ways he is to set up two guide-posts, the one pointing to Rabbath Ammon, the other to Jerusalem. The king of Babylon, coming to the parting of the ways, hesitates which he shall take. He consults the oracle, draws lots by means of the arrows, and the arrow that he draws out in his right hand is the one inscribed "Jerusalem."—Camb. B.

21—24. (21) **stood,** better, "standeth." All the verbs should be in the present. **parting . . way,** i.e. where the roads divided, one leading to Ammon, and one to Jerusalem. He was uncertain which to attack first. **divination,** "the common word for any kind of superstitious omen."[b] **arrows bright,** or he shook his arrows.[c] **images,** or teraphim.[d] **looked . . liver,** or entrails of animals offered for sacrifice. Particular appearances, wh. were really due to the animal's freedom fr. disease, were regarded as hopeful. (22) **for Jerusalem,** "into his right hand comes the lot marked 'Jerusalem.'"—Polyc. Bib. **appoint captains,** etc., "to set battering rams, to open the mouth with a cry, etc.—Cam. B. **appoint . . rams,** ch. iv. 2. (23) "It (what Nebuchadnezzar has done) shall be as a vain divination in their sight (in that of the men of Jerusalem), which have sworn unto them (have taken oaths of fealty to the Chaldæans, and are ready to take them again), but he (Nebuchadnezzar) brings iniquity to remembrance." The fact represented is that when the people of Jerusalem heard of the divination at the parting of the ways, they still lulled themselves in a false security. Prob. Nebuc.'s anger at their unfaithfulness decided his going first to Jerus. (24) **taken . . hand,** or fall into the hands of the Bab. king. The truth conveyed is that the Babylonian army is moving under the immediate guidance of Jehovah, and that not only the political projects of the king, but his secret thoughts and even his superstitious reliance on signs and omens, are all overruled for the furtherance of the one purpose for which Jehovah has raised him up.—Exp. B.

Divination by Arrows.—"He made his arrows bright." This was for the purpose of divination. Jerome on this passage says that "the manner of divining by arrows was thus: They wrote on several arrows the names of the cities they intended to make war against, and then putting them promiscuously all together into a quiver, they caused them to be drawn out in the manner of lots, and that city whose name was on the arrow first drawn out, was the first they assaulted." The method of divination practiced by some of the idolatrous Arabs, but which is prohibited by the Koran, is too singular to be unnoticed. "The arrows used by them for this purpose were like those with which they cast lots, being without heads or feathers, and were kept in the temple of some idol, in whose presence they were consulted. Seven such arrows were kept at the temple of Mecca; but generally in divination they make use of three only, on one of which was written, My Lord hath commanded me; on another, My Lord hath forbidden me; and the third was blank. If the first was drawn, they looked on it as an approbation of the enterprise in question; of the second, they made a contrary conclusion; but if the third happened to be drawn, they mixed them, and draw over again till a decisive answer was given by one of the others. These divining arrows were generally consulted before anything of moment was undertaken, as when a man was about to marry, or about to go a journey, or the like."—Burder.

25—27. (25) **profane, wicked,** R. V., "and thou, O deadly wounded, wicked one, the prince of Israel."[a] **when iniquity,** etc., R. V., "in the time of the iniquity of the end," i.e. in the doom of Jerusalem and the captivity of the king. (26) **diadem,** for he shall no longer be king. **this**

---

a Je. xxvii. 2, 3. For Rabbah or Rabbath, see 2 Sa. xii. 26; Je. xlix. 2; Eze. xxv. 5.

"To do some thing, anything, to cause the sun to shine more brightly on the clouded lives of despondent fellow-creatures, is the one thing worth being in this world for."—Macdonald.

b Nu. xxiii. 23.

c "The Chaldaeans marked upon the arrows the names of the places they had in view, or the alternatives they submitted to this determination. They then drew the arrows from the quiver at a venture, and the one that first came forth with one of the marks upon it, was regarded not only as supplying the response required but as manifesting the will of the gods, and as conveying an assurance of success in the enterprise in view." —Kitto.

d Ge. xxxi. 19.

"At the best, we see but a tiny fragment of God's method of rule; if we could comprehend the whole, we should admire the skill and power and beneficence of his vast administration." —Davies.

a "To Ezekiel's idealizing view Zedekiah was the grand victim 'pierced through' by God's sword of judgments.—**Fausset.**

. . **same,** i.e. the present royal house in Jerusalem shall not remain; the hope of Israel is centered in Jehoiachin, the legitimate heir of David, now in exile. (27) **overturn,** etc., repeated to increase the solemnity. **whose right it is,** comp. Ge. xlix. 10. Many regard vss. 26, 27 as referring to the Messiah.

Crowns (vs. 26).—I. Some of the crowns that will at death be taken off,—of wealth, of nobility, etc. II. Some of the crowns that will not be taken off,—of character, of life, etc.

28—32. It is probably in mockery that the prophet uses such language regarding the puny pretensions of Ammon. (28) **Ammonites,** vs. 20. **reproach,** or scorning of Judah. **consume . . glittering,** R. V. marg., "it is furbished to the uttermost that it may be as lightning." (29) **see vanity,** or indulge false confidences of their victory bec. of false divinations. **upon the necks,** by reason of such lying divination the Ammonites would meet a common fate with the princes of Judah, upon whose dead bodies their own would be flung. **have an end,** or reach its doom. (30) **shall . . sheath?** R. V., "cause it to return into its sheath!" not a question addressed by Jehovah, but an imperative addressed to the Ammonites. **in the place,** i.e. thou shalt be destroyed in thy land; all ideas of conquest abroad are vain. (31) **blow . . wrath,**[a] see ch. xxii. 20—22. **brutish,** wild and savage men. So in xxv. 4 it is the men of the East, the children of the desert, who are to execute judgment on Ammon. (32) **no more remembered,** ch. xxv. 10. They should, as a nation, be consigned to oblivion.[b]

[a] An image taken from the smelting of metals.

[b] "Justly is their name blotted out who would have Israel's name for ever lost." —Mat. Henry.

"No cheating nor bargaining will ever get a single thing out of nature's 'establishment' at half-price. Do we want to be strong? — we must work. To be hungry?—we must starve. To be happy? — we must be kind. To be wise?—we must look and think."

CHAPTER THE TWENTY-SECOND.

1—4. (2) **judge,** or pronounce judgment on. Comp. ch. xx. 4, xxiii. 36. **bloody city,** lit. "city of bloods."[c] **shew her,** or make her to know. (3) **time may come,** of her chastisement, ch. vii. 7.[d] (4) **thy blood,** i.e. child sacrifice and judicial murders. **unto thy years,** i.e. thy years of visitation and judgments. "Thou hast filled up the measure of thine iniquities, and brought the time of vengeance upon thyself." **reproach,** etc., De. xxviii. 37.

Guilt Cannot be Hidden.—In the reign of Louis XIV. a brilliant abbé was one of a large party who had assembled round the royal supper-table. There were clever talkers, sharp dealers in epigram, skilful bandiers of compliment and repartee. The abbé added to the mirth of the evening by telling the adventures of a memorable career. "I remember," he said, "very well the first penitent who came to my confessional. I was young then, and little accustomed to hear the secrets of court life. It was a murderer, who told me the story of his crime." The abbé was pressed to tell the tale, or to give a clew to the culprit; but he kept a guarded and wary silence. Presently in came one of the most trusted of the king's favorites. "Ah, M. l'Abbé," he said, recognizing an old friend. "Gentlemen, I was the first penitent whom the abbé ever shrived, and I promise you when I told him my story he heard what astonished him." That night the nobleman was carried to the Bastile, and the evidence of a crime committed thirty years before was complete, and the culprit detected.

[c] 2 Ki. xxi. 16; Eze. xxiii. 37, 45, xxiv. 6, 9.

[d] "Instead of deriving advantage from her bloody sacrifice to idols, she only thereby brought on herself the time of her punishment." —Fausset.

"We often do more good by our sympathy than by our labors, and render to the world a more lasting service by absence of jealousy, and recognition of merit, than we could ever render by the straining efforts of personal ambition." — Archdeacon Farrar.

5—8. (5) **Those,** i.e. those countries.[a] **infamous,** or defiled in name. **much vexed,** R. V., "and full of tumult," i.e. great moral disorder. (6) **princes,** including the king's family, and the chief officers. **to their power,** or up to the measure of their ability, each was guilty of violence and bloodshed.[b] (7) **they,** said generally, not confined to the princes. **light . . mother,** so transgressing the foundation-law of social morality.[c] **stranger,** who should have been the object of kindly hospitality and charity. (8) **holy things,** those connected with sacred worship; whole range of Divine ordinances.

Corporate Guilt.—Such a conception of corporate guilt undoubtedly appeals more directly to our ordinary conscience of public morality than the more poetic representations where Jerusalem is compared to a faithless and treacherous woman. We have no difficulty in judging of any

[a] Eze. xvi. 57.

[b] Eze. ix. 9, xvi. 38, xxiii. 37, 45.

[c] De. xxvii. 16.

"He who comes from the kitchen smells of its smoke; the college air pursues the student."—Lavater.

modern city in the very same way as Ezekiel here judges Jerusalem; and in this respect it is interesting to notice the social evils which he regards as marking out that city as ripe for destruction.—Exp. Bib.

9—12. (9) **carry tales,** bear false witness so as to bring others into judgment.[d] (10) **In thee,** etc., an execrable form of incest against which even the heathen protested. Comp. ch. xviii. 6. (11) **committed abomination,** reference is to sins related to the social and moral relationships, which are carefully defined in the laws of Moses. (12) **taken gifts,** bribes, Ex. xxiii. 8; De. xvi. 19. **extortion,** R. V., "oppression."

The Reproach of Jerusalem.—It certainly seems strange, all but incredible, that the highly favored Jerusalem should be famed among the very heathen for degradation in iniquity and moral debasement. But the language of Ezekiel is explicit; and he would be more likely to soften than to exaggerate the charge. Jerusalem a reproach, a mocking, infamous, defiled, full of tumult! How are the mighty fallen! The city of the great King, the seat of the temple of Jehovah, the home of the consecrated priesthood,—infamous among the surrounding idolaters for flagitious violation of those very moral laws which the city was consecrated to conserve!—Thomson.

13—16. (13) **smitten my hand,** as an expression of my indignation.[a] (14) **Can,** etc., ch. xxi. 7. (15) **consume,** by the fires of national calamity, but Israel is not to be destroyed by this chastisement. Only the filthiness is to be consumed. (16) **shalt take,** better, "Thou shalt be profaned by thyself in the sight of the heathen."[b] "No longer enjoy the privileges of a city called by My name."

The Fruit of Sin.—Many are the lessons deducible from our subject. We mention three. 1. The fearful growth of sin. Forgetfulness of God may develop into idolatry, adultery, murder. 2. The essential ruinousness of sin. It is of its very nature to blight and destroy everything that is true and beautiful, wise and good, right and strong, both in individuals and communities. "Sin, when it is full-grown, bringeth forth death." 3. The righteous judgment of God against sin. (Rom. ii. 2—11.)—W. Jones.

"Can thine heart endure?"—The question of the text is not answered; but the doleful silence with which it is received suggests the misery that is to follow. If heart and hand fail, the ruin and wretchedness must be complete. While a good man fighting against adversity is said to be a sight for the admiration of gods as well as men, a bad man crushed by misery is only an object of horror. The stout heart of honest intentions can bear up against unmerited woes and find in its own fortitude a certain solace. But this solace will be wanting in the collapse of the false hope of the sinner. Then will follow the deepest misery, the sense of being confounded, the helpfulness of being swept away in a flood of destruction. Pain is not the worst evil. The depth of hell is reached when heart and strength fail, and the sinner loses all power to withstand his fate. Hence the supreme need of a Saviour (Rom. viii. 1).—W. F. Adeney.

17—22. (18) **dross,** comp. Is. i. 25; Mal. iii. 3.[c] (20) **midst of the furnace,** the terrible trials imminent upon Jerusalem would be like the furnace for the purifying away of the national dross. (21) **I will gather,** "the city is compared to the crucible in which all the refuse of Israel's national life is to undergo its final trial by fire. The prophet sees in imagination the terror-stricken provincial population swept into the capital before the approach of the Chaldæans." **blow upon you,** to raise high the heat. (22) **my fury,** or Divine vengeance, which is like a purifying fire.

23—26. (24) **rained upon,** Is. v. 6; Am. iv. 7. Temporal and spiritual blessings are withheld from the rebellious land. (25) **prophets,** etc., Cam. B., "whose princes in the midst of her are like," etc. **devoured souls,** by their deceits. **taken the treasure,** making gain by violence. (26) **violated,** offered violence to, by misrepresenting it.[a] **profane,** R. V., "common." **hid .. Sabbaths,** i. e. were blind to the essential need and value of holiness of the Sabbath.

Hypocrisy Easy, but Dangerous.—The counterfeit will always have some admirers, from its cheapness in the market. One must dig deep

[d] Le. xix. 16.

"Alas, for the misery which is caused by a long tongue! The quantity of the gossip could not be kept up if it were restricted to truth, and so evil inventions are added thereto. These at first are a sort of spice and flavoring; but in time they become the principal ingredient. —Spurgeon.

[a] Eze. xxi. 14, 17.

[b] "Thou shalt by thine own fault forfeit the privileges of a holy nation." —Spk. Com.

"I warn every aspirant for wealth against the infernal canker of selfishness. The heart of avaricious old age stands like a bare rock in a bleak wilderness, and there is no rod of authority, nor incantation of pleasure, which can draw from it one crystal drop to quench the raging thirst for satisfaction." —Beecher.

[c] Also Isa. iv. 4; Je. vi. 29; Zec. xiii. 9.

"Great vices are the proper objects of our detestation, smaller faults of our pity; but affectation appears to be the only true source of the ridiculous." —Fielding.

[a] Le. x. 10.

"The kite is a bird which delights in the free air, and soars aloft, as if it would fain approach to heaven. All the while, however, it keeps its sharp eye continually directed to the earth, if haply it may

in dark mines for gold and silver; the precious treasure must be brought from far across the seas; it must be melted down; it must pass through many assays, and the dies must be worked with ponderous engines before the coin can be produced: all this to the sluggish many is a heavy disadvantage. Hush! hearken! steal silently upstairs; the spirit of Deceit invites you to her chamber; a little plaster of Paris, a fire, a crucible, molten lead, the mould, and there is your money, sir, without troubling Peru, Potosi, California, or the Mint. Slink out and change your fine new shillings, and your fortune's made without the ignoble waste of sweat and labor. But be quiet, for a detective may be near, a coarse-minded minion of unpoetic law, who may cruelly block up your road, or even lead you into prison. Short cuts to wealth have brought many to the hulks; and, let me add, there are short cuts to godliness which have brought many to perdition.—Spurgeon.

27—31. (27) **princes,** etc., Mic. iii. 11; Zep. iii. 3. (28) **daubed,** R. V., "daubed for," i. e. have seconded the princes in their cruelty, etc. Polychr. B. reads "daub walls with whitewash." **untempered mortar,** ch. xiii. 10. (29) oppression, even the masses are filled with greed—like rulers like people. The moral energies of the nation as a whole were completely spent. (30) **hedge,** or wall. **gap,** or breach, Ps. cvi. 23. "This was a proof of the general corruption, that there was among them no faithful servant to stand in the gap, and build up the hedge."

The Influence of One Man May be Enormous.—Had one real man been found to reprove the people, restore religious worship, and plead with God, Israel might have been spared its overthrow. One man may save a nation or plunge it into perdition. Paul, on board ship, obtained the lives of all the crew. The intercession of Moses brought a deed of pardon for the Hebrew host. For David's sake God conferred large favors on the nation. Luther's firm faith brought deliverance both spiritual and temporal to all Europe. What one man can do no language can portray, imagination can scarce conceive. A man of wisdom, piety, and faith may quietly revolutionize the world.—Davies.

there spy some prey to seize. And like it are hypocrites; they love to speak of heavenly and spiritual things; they go to church and take the holy supper; they read, and pray, and sing; but, nevertheless, their heart retains its earthly inclination, and they seek that which is temporal more than that which is eternal." —Gotthold.

"The Sabbath is profaned, not only when the shops are open and when crowds throng the public resorts of amusement, but when the congregations at church play the part of ostentatious Pharisees, and mock God with pretentious prayers while their hearts and thoughts are far from him." —Pul. Com.

CHAPTER THE TWENTY-THIRD.

1—4. (2) **two women,** viz. Samaria and Jerusalem.[b] Israel and Judah were branches of the same stock. (3) **in Egypt,** the 2 kingdoms are represented ideally as already existing in Egypt. In fact, the great tribes of Judah and Ephraim from the first stood apart; ch. xvi. 7, xx. 8. (4) **Aholah,** R. V., "Oholah, Oholibah," meaning, "Her tent or tabernacle," and applied to Samaria, which had a temple and worship, but not Jehovah's. **Aholibah,** denotes, "My tabernacle is in her." It is applied to Jerusalem, magnifies her privilege, aggravates her guilt. **they were mine,** became my wives.

Aholah and Aholibah.—These names stand respectively for Israel and Judah, and suggest certain traits of national character. I. Independence. Israel is named Aholah. This national independence has its counterpart in indivdiual independence. There are special opportunities, duties, and dangers in having one's own tent. II. Divine fellowship. Judah is named Aholibah. This represents high privileges, with corresponding guilt when God is forsaken. No sinners are so guilty as apostatized Christians. Mark:—It is possible to be Aholibah and to enjoy God's presence, and yet to turn against Him, fall, and be ruined.—Pul. Com.

5—8. (5) **when .. mine,** while she was mine; before the days when the separate worship was set up. **doted .. lovers,** i. e. her foreign alliances. **her neighbours,** Polychr. B., "high dignitaries." The Assyrians could hardly be called neighbors. (6) **blue,** or purple. Garments dyed with the expensive purple dye. **horses,** these were scarce in Judæa. The first intimate contact of North Israel with Assyria was in the reign of Menahem (2 Kings xv. 19), and the explanation of it given in these words of Ezekiel must be historically true. It was the magnificent equipment of the Assyrian armies, the imposing display of military power which

[b] Je. iii. 7, 8, 10.

"Paltry affectation, strained allusions, and disgusting finery, are easily attained by those who choose to wear them; they are but too frequently the badges of ignorance or of stupidity, whenever it would endeavour to please." —Goldsmith.

"A Christian's conscience and character are his white garments. The conscience is the inner, hidden garment. The character is the outer, visible garments. Sin is what defiles them both." —Bolton.

their appearance suggested, that impressed the politicians of Samaria with a sense of the value of their alliance.—Exp. B. (7) **defiled herself,** her idolatry being figured as spiritual immorality. (8) **left she,** but added new idolatries to those brought from Egypt. Samaria intrigued with Egypt and Assyria alternately, all the while increasing her idolatry.

Idolatry.—1. When people embrace false worship they are violent and strong in their affections towards it. 2. What evil persons have practiced in their youth that they affect in their age. 3. Idolatry may continue long in a nation, but shall at last be severely punished by the Lord. 4. God makes places and persons remarkable by the judgments He executeth upon them.—Greenhill.

Blue.—Blue was a sky color in great esteem among the Jews, and other Oriental nations. The robe of the ephod, in the gorgeous dress of the high priest, was made all of blue; it was a prominent color in the sumptuous hangings of the tabernacle; and the whole people of Israël were required to put a fringe of blue upon the border of their garments, and on the fringe a riband of the same color. The palace of Ahasuerus, the king of Persia, was furnished with curtains of this color, on a pavement of red, and blue, and white marble; a proof it was not less esteemed in Persia than on the Jordan. And from Ezekiel we learn that the Assyrian nobles were habited in robes of this color. It does not appear, however, that the Jews ever wore garments wholly of this color; and perhaps they abstained from it as sacred and mysterious, than which none was more used about the tabernacle and the temple, in the curtains, veils, and vestments, belonging to these sacred edifices."—Paxton.

9—12 (9) R. V. **"I .. delivered,"** etc., ref. to overthrow of Samaria by Assyria 722 B. C. **hand .. Assyrians,** 2 Ki. xvii. 23.[a] (10) **nakedness,** those carried into captivity were usually stripped bare. **famous,** R. V., "a by-word." Spoken of as a striking example of the judgments that came upon the idolatrous.[b] (11) **sister Aholibah,** vs. 4. **inordinate love,** passionate and wilful service of the idols. (12) **doted .. neighbours,** Ahaz began the alliance with Assyria, and encouraged the adoption of the Assyrian idolatries.[c] **horsemen,** vs. 6.

Doting on the Assyrians.—I. God's people are required to separate themselves from the world. II. The world endeavors to ensnare the people of God. Its fascinating influence comes through various means. 1. Proximity; 2. Earthly attractiveness; 3. Natural inclination. III. The snares of the world are fatal to those who are entangled in them. 1. Religious ruin; 2. Moral ruin; 3. Life ruin.—Pul. Com.

The Tempter a Scourge.—The neighboring nations, whose idolatries she had conformed to and whose friendship she had confided in, and in both had affronted God, are now made use of as the instruments of her destruction. The Assyrians, on whom she doted, soon spied out the nakedness of the land, discovered her blind side, on which to attack her, stripped her of all her ornaments and all her defences, and so uncovered her, and made her naked and bare, carried her sons and daughters into captivity, slew her with the sword, and quite destroyed that kingdom and put an end to it. . . . And that the Assyrians, whom they had been so fond of, should be employed in executing judgments upon them, was very remarkable, and shows how God, in a way of righteous judgment, often makes that a scourge to sinners which they have inordinately set their hearts upon. The devil will for ever be a tormentor to those impenitent sinners who now hearken to him and comply with him as a tempter.—Matthew Henry.

13—17. (13) **defiled,** in heart and purpose. **one way,** and that a bad way. "Both alike forsaking God for heathen confidences." (14) **men pourtrayed,** pictures, or bas-reliefs, representing deified heroes. The mere recital of Babylonian greatness was sufficient to inflame Oholibah to seek an alliance. In later times (604 B. C.) the rivalry of Babylon and Egypt brought Israel under the dominion of Babylon. **vermilion,** or red ochre.[d] Vermilion seems to have been the peculiar color of the Chaldæans, as purple was of the Assyrians. (15) **girdles,** these were the mark of dignity, and to this part of the dress much care was given. **dyed attire,** or "in ample dyed turbans:" lofty and richly adorned head-dresses. **princes,** "heroes." **manner of,** R. V., "likeness of." (16) **doted,** this word

a "God made these very Assyrians the executioners of His judgments upon the ten tribes: many of them being carried away by Pul, 1 Chr. v. 25, 26; afterward by Tiglath-Pileser, 2 Ki. xv. 29; and at length the whole country was subdued and depopulated by Shalmaneser, 2 Ki. xvii. 6."—Lowth.

b "'The report of her infamy went abroad to all women,' i.e. to all provinces." —Kimchi.

c 2 Ki. xvi. 7, 11; 2 Chr. xxviii. 16—23; Isa. vii. 20, lvii. 9.

d 'In striking agreement with this vs. is the fact that the Assyrian sculptures lately discovered have painted and colored bas-reliefs, red, blue, and black." —Fausset.

indicates a kind of love that is passionate and foolish; trans. "she doted upon them after the sight of her eyes;" i. e. with delight and desire. (17) **alienated,** i. e. she soon grew weary of the alliance, and turned from Babylon to Egypt.[e]

Vermilion.—The nature of those images, and the practices, may be seen from the context, and the portraying was of the color of vermilion. In the Hindoo temples and vestibules, figures of the most revolting descriptions are portrayed on the walls.—Roberts.

18—21. (18) **discovered,** i. e. uncovered, revealed. **my mind,** i. e. (God's. (19) **calling to remembrance,** Judah being situated between the two great empires of Babylon and Egypt and coveted by both, was naturally a hotbed of intrigue by partisans on both sides. The influence of the Egyptian party was great even in the Assyrian age (Is. xxx.—xxxi.), and the imposing and pretentious power of the Nile valley continued to delude the politicians of Judah throughout the period of Chaldæan supremacy (ch. xxix.—xxxii.; Jer. ii. 18, xxxvii. 5 seq.; Lam. iv. 17).—Cam. B. (20) **paramours,**[a] or lovers of either sex. **horses,** "The horse was made by the Egyptians the hieroglyphic for a lustful person." (21) **callest to remembrance,** Cam. B., "didst recall," i. e. renew.

22—27. (22) **raise .. lovers,** i. e. the Babylonians, whose alliance had been given up for the sake of Egypt. These would become the agents for the destruction of Jerusalem. (23) **Pekod, and Shoa, and Koa,** names of peoples lying East of the Tigris. (24) **chariots,** R. V., "weapons." **set judgment before,** R. V., "commit judgment unto." **their judgments,** with their accustomed fury and cruelty. (25) **jealousy,** God here speaks as a grieved husband concerning an unfaithful wife. **nose .. ears,** this was an Egyptian form of punishment for an adulteress. (27) **Thus,** i. e. by severe and terrible judgments. **remember Egypt,** i. e. in exile Israel would not think of Egypt or cultivate the worship of Egyptian idols.

28—31. (28) **alienated,** vs. 18. (29) **hatefully,** R. V., "in hatred." **take .. labour,** i. e. the fruits of thy labor. **naked,** as female captives were served. (31) **thy sister,** Oholah, or Samaria. **her cup,** that which she drank. Is. li. 22, 23; Jer. xxv. 15, 16.

A Bad Example.—I. The evil influence of a bad example. Consider how this fell power is exerted. 1. By the fascination of suggestion; 2. By the attraction of sympathy; 3. By the delusion of a false excuse. II. The sin of following a bad example. Inexcusable. 1. Because the evil of the way is known; 2. Because of the freedom of the will; 3 Because of one's own advantages. III. The fatal consequences of following a bad example.—Pul. Com.

An Old Author on Sin.—God needs no other light to discern our sins by but the light of his own face. It peereth through the darkest places; the brightness thereof enlighteneth all things, discovers all things; so that the sins that are committed in deepest darkness are all one to Him, as if they were done in the face of the sun. For they are done in His face, that shines more, and from which proceeds more light, than from the face of the sun. So that this, it ought to make us the more fearful to offend; He sees us when we see not Him, and the light of His countenance shines about when we think ourselves hidden in darkness.—W. Bradshaw (1621).

32—35. (32) **deep and large,** R. V., "which is deep." Is. li. 17; Re. xiv. 9, 10. **it containeth much,** i. e. the cup of judgment. (33) **filled with drunkenness,** God's judgments are often compared to a cup of intoxicating liquors.[a] (34) **suck it out,** so as to drain every drop. **sherds,** or pieces.[b] R. V., "gnaw the sherds." (35) **cast back,**[c] as if determined not to see me: a sign of contempt and aversion. **bear,** i. e. endure the punishment of.

Forgetting God.—I. Forgetting God implies that He has formerly been known. 1. Men have a natural knowledge of God; 2. They who have seen the Jewish and Christian revelations have a larger knowledge of God; 3. The people of God have the fullest knowledge of God. II. There are many inducements to forget God. 1. He is invisible; 2. Earthly interests distract our thoughts; 3. Sinful inclinations rouse an aversion to the thought of God. III. Forgetting God is itself a great sin. 1. God

[e] 2 Ki. xxiv. 7; Je. xxxvii. 5, 7.

"God commonly employs tempters to punish those who listen to them." —Scott.

"God excites those against us for punishment to please whom we sinned."

"The exact historic reference is uncertain. It cannot be to the compact between Merodachbaladan and Hezekiah, since at that time the initiative seems to have been taken by the rebel prince, whose sovereignty over Babylon proved to be of short duration. It may rather be some transaction about the time of the battle of Carchemish (604) that Ezekiel is thinking of; but we have not as yet sufficient knowledge of the circumstances to clear up the allusion. —Exp. Bib.

"Smend thinks that the illustration is explained by the secluded life of females in the East which makes it quite intelligible that a woman might be captivated by the picture of a man she had never seen, and try to induce him to visit her."

[a] Je. xxv. 15, xlviii. 26; Hab. ii. 16.

[b] "Thou shalt behave thyself as drunken people do, who first throw away, or break in pieces, the cup, and then are angry with themselves as the cause of their own misfortunes." —Lowth.

[c] 1 Ki. xiv. 9; Ne. ix. 26.

has never forgotten us; 2. God claims our attention and obedience. IV. Forgetting God is hurtful to man. 1. This is the loss of the best blessings of heaven; 2. This incurs a fatal doom. V. God mercifully interferes to save us from forgetting Him. 1. He reveals Himself in His Word; 2. God comes to us in His Son; 3. God rouses us by His providence.—Adeney.

36—39. (36) **judge,** comp. ch. xx. 4, xxii. 2. **yea, declare,** R. V., "then declare," i. e. what follows is the prophet's judgment. (37) **That,** "For." **pass .. fire,** this Moloch worship was regarded as the very height of their idolatrous iniquity. (38) **same day,** i. e. at the very time of making their offerings to Moloch, they immediately entered the temple of Jehovah and offered him other sacrifices, see vs. 39.[a] (39) **profane it,** by the hypocritical show of worshiping Me, when their hearts were gone after their idols.

40—49. (40) **ye have sent,** embassies to Egypt, Assyria, and Babylon courting alliances. **wash thyself,** etc., these were the usual preparations made by an Eastern bride for her husband's coming. **paintedst thine eyes,** with Kohl.[b] "Orientals admire eyebrows that meet over the nose, presenting the appearance of a bow; and when nature has denied them this ornament, they imitate it by artificial paint." (41) **bed,** "divan." **table,** fig. for the idol altar. (42) **voice of a multitude,** etc., Polychr. Bib., "and there was the sound of music; they sent for men of the common sort, drunkards from the Wilderness, on whose hands they put," etc. (43) **now commit,** or still keep on in these wicked ways, even with so old an adulteress; yet the sin is of too long standing to be cured even if the heathen nations shun her. (44) **Aholah,** etc., ch. xxiii. 4. (45) righteous men, the Chaldæans as instruments of God's righteous judgments. Ref. may, however, be to the Prophets, who are sometimes said to execute the judgments which they foretell. (46) **removed,** into captivity. (47) **stone them,** this was the Mosaic punishment of the adulteress.[a] (48) **Thus,** by great judgments. **women .. taught,** after such an exhibition of Divine chastisement idolatry would be eradicated. (49) **bear the sins,** i. e. the proper punishment of the sinful. "God is known by the judgment which He executeth."

Madness of Sinners.—A recent traveler, relating the incidents of his voyage to India, writes:—"Flocks of greedy albatrosses, petrels, and Cape pigeons, crowded round the ship's stern. A hook was baited with fat, when upwards of a dozen albatrosses instantly rushed at it, and as one after another was being hauled on deck, the remainder, regardless of the struggles of the captured, and the vociferations of the crew, kept swimming about the stern. Not even did those birds which were indifferently hooked and made their escape, desist from seizing the bait a second time." Thus to the letter do ungodly men rush at the baits of Satan; they see others perish, but remain careless, and even when they are all but destroyed themselves they persist in their infatuation.—Spurgeon.

CHAPTER THE TWENTY-FOURTH.

1—5. (1) **ninth year,** of Jehoiachim's captivity, Jan., 587 B. C. The prophet's last oracle against Judah. (2) **this same day,** i. e though Ezekiel is far away fr. Jerus., he is to tell his fellow-exiles that on the very day when he spoke to them, Nebuc. had commenced the siege.[b] (3) **parable,** or illustrative teaching. **pot,** or caldron for boiling flesh. "The caldron is Jerusalem; the pieces of flesh the inhabitants; the fire and boiling the siege with its terrible severities. The pieces of flesh shall be pulled out of the caldron indiscriminately, symbol of the universal dispersion when the siege is over." Ironically reminding them of their boast that they were the choice members of the community. (5) **bones,** better, "wood."

The Boiling Caldron (vs. 1).—From the vision and its first fulfilment we gather—I. That the sins of any city are an offence to God. They are—1. Seen by Him; 2. With anger. II. That the sins of any city will

[a] "On the very day that they had burned their children to Moloch in the valley of Gehenna, they shamelessly and hypocritically presented themselves as worshipers in Jehovah's temple."—Fausset.

[b] "This Kohl consists of a collyrium of antimony, or other substance, considered beneficial to the eye as will as ornamental, which is kept in a small bottle, and applied with a probe of silver, ivory, or wood to the edges of the eyelids, for the purpose of blackening them, and thus enhancing the brightness of the eye, which is usually large, shaded by long lashes, and decidedly the finest feature of Oriental women."
—Van Lennep.

[a] Le. xx. 10; De. xxii. 22; Jno. viii. 5.

"We are not practical unless good. Nothing so visionary, impolitic and absurd as vice."

[b] 2 Ki. xxv. 1; Je. lii. 4.

"That Ezekiel on the banks of the Chedar knew what was taking place at Jerus, on the very day of its occurrence, may be a difficulty to those expositors who deny that God can make any prophetical communication, but need not incline us to discover, with them, in this passage a prediction after the event."
—Kliefoth.

ensure its doom. 1. History illustrates this; 2. Prophecy predicts this; 3. The law of causation involves this. III. That the sins of any city concern every individual inhabitant. 1. They bring sorrow on all; 2. They give a misison to all. Learn:—(1) Seek to evangelize the entire city, so as to save it; (2) Seek to convert individuals, that at least they may be saved.—U. R. Thomas.

6—9. (6) **scum,** R. V., "rust," not what floats on the top in process of boiling, but the "deeply-grained verdigris and rust in the pot itself." **piece by piece,** i. e. bring out the contents piece by piece. Ref. is to the chief men of the city. **no lot,** taken usually to decide which should go into captivity, and which remain. All would go forth to captivity or death. (7) **top .. rock,** R. V., "bare rock," i. e. the sin of Jerusalem is open and cries unto heaven for vengeance. (8) **fury .. vengeance,** the blood crying as Abel's did.[a] (9) **pile,** fig. for the preparations for the city's destruction.

Arab Camel-feast.—The following account of a royal Arab camel-feast will afford some illustration of the parable contained in this chapter: "Before midday, a carpet being spread in the middle of the tent, our dinner was brought in, being served up in large wooden bowls between two men, and truly, to my apprehension, load enough for them. Of these great platters there were about fifty or sixty in number, perhaps more, with a great many little ones; I mean, such as one man was able to bring in, strewed here and there among them, and placed for a border or garnish round about the table. In the middle was one of a larger size than all the rest, in which were the camel's bones, and a thin broth in which they were boiled. The other greater ones seemed all filled with one and the same sort of provision, a kind of plum-broth, made of rice and the fleshy part of the camel, with currants and spices, being of a somewhat darker color than what is made in our country."—Philosophical Transactions Abridged.

10—14. (10) **spice it well,** R. V., "make thick the broth. (11) **set it,** i. e. the very pot itself. **scum,** "rust," a fig. of the burning of Jerusalem, and the purifying judgments which were to be continued. (12) As the words stand they seem to read: "she hath wearied my labors, and her great rust goeth not out from her; let her rust be in the fire!" Previous efforts to purify Jerusalem have been in vain, her uncleanliness will go out only by fire (vs. 13).—Cam. B. **not forth,** by the previous admonitions of the Prophets, or providential dealings.[a] (13) **caused .. rest,** R. V., "satisfied my fury upon thee." (14) **according .. doings,** ch. xxiii. 24.

Punishment of Sin.—What a diabolical invention was the "Virgin's kiss," once used by the fathers of the Inquisition! The victim was pushed forward to kiss the image, when, lo, its arms enclosed him in a deadly embrace, piercing his body with a hundred hidden knives. The tempting pleasures of sin offer to the unwary just such a virgin's kiss. The sinful joys of the flesh lead, even in this world, to results most terrible, while, in the world to come, the daggers of remorse and despair will cut and wound beyond all remedy.—Spurgeon.——Sin: the Toil of It.—There was a man in the town where I was born who used to steal all his fire-wood. He would get up on cold nights, and go and take it from his neighbors' wood-piles. A computation was made, and it was ascertained that he spent more time and worked harder to get his fuel, than he would have been obliged to if he had earned it in an honest way, and at ordinary wages. And this thief is a type of thousands of men who work a great deal harder to please the devil than they would have to work to please God.—Beecher.

15—18. Vss. 15—27: "A symbol of the stupefaction of the people at the news of the fall of the city." (16) **desire .. eyes,** i. e. Ezekiel's wife. She is to represent the sanctuary in which the Jews so much gloried; vs. 21. **mourn,** etc., to indicate that there would be no time for the ordinary lamentations over the dead.[b] (17) **Forbear to cry,** R. V., "Sigh, but not aloud." **tire,** ref. to the high priest's mitre, wh. he might not put off.[c] In times of mourning the head was often shaved, or dust was cast on it. **cover .. lips,** a usual sign of mourning.[d] **bread of men,** or of mourners. Food was usually supplied for the comfort of mourners. (18) **wife died,**

[a] Ge. iv. 10.

"By retaining any branch of our own wills or desires unrenounced, as not resigned up into God's hand, we give him hold of us, who will never let hold go, unless we cut off the member which offendeth us. For, as one very well observes, so the snare be strong and hold sure, a bird, though caught but by one claw,, shall as certainly be the fowler's portion, as if she had been taken by both wings." —Jackson.

[a] "I did what was requisite on my part towards thy conversion, but thou refusedst to comply with those frequent calls and exhortations I gave thee." —Lowth.

"In plain terms, the Lord was no longer going to deal with them by half-measures; their condition called for the greatest degree of severity compatible with their preservation as a distinct and separate people, and so the indignation of the Lord was to rest on them till a separation was effected between them and sin." —Fairbairn.

[b] "The times that were coming were so extraordinary as to leave no room for the quiet lamentation for the dead according to the usual forms of mourning." —Spk. Com.

[c] Le. xxi. 10.

[d] Le. xiii. 45; 2 Sa. xv. 30; Je. xiv. 4; Mic. iii. 7.

"The path of sorrow, and that path alone, leads to the land where sorrow is unknown; no traveler ever reached that blest abode, who found not thorns and briers on his road."
—Cowper.

"There are occasions when a good man can do little in the way of directly benefiting or influencing the ungodly by whom he may be surrounded. But even in such circumstances he may be a witness to God, and he may render service to his fellow-men, by his own life, and especially by his demeanor in times of affliction and trial."
—Thomson.

How do you know whether you are pure gold, or base metal? Gold, if pure, must bear the royal stamp to give it currency. If you lack the impress of Christ, you cannot pass current in the kingdom of heaven.

"He praiseth God best that serveth and obeyeth Him most: the life of thankfulness consists in the thankfulness of the life." — W. Burkitt.

note the submissive obedience of the Prophet. The death of the Prophet's wife was no doubt an actual occurrence. And there is nothing improbable in his demeanor after it, with the view of attracting the attention of his fellow-captives. At the same time his tendency to idealize occurrences precludes absolute certainty.—Cam. B.

"The Desire of Thine Eyes."—I. A picture of domestic love. 1. The blessedness of wedded love is a solace in trouble; 2. Wedded love is a type of Divine love; 3. Such a great blessing should be tenderly guarded. II. A stroke of fearful trouble. 1. "The desire of his eyes" is taken from Ezekiel; 2. This trouble comes by a sudden stroke; 3. The trouble comes from God. III. A requirement of unnatural reticence. 1. Public men must repress private emotion; 2. Private sorrow is buried in public calamity; 3. Divine judgments are not to be gainsaid; 4. God has consolations for patient sorrow.—W. F. Adeney.

19—23. (19) **people,** i. e. the fellow-exiles. (21) **excellency .. strength,** or object of your boasting; the temple of which you were so proud. **soul pitieth,** or "spareth," i. e. holds dear. (22) **cover .. men,** comp. vs. 17. (23) **pine away,** bec. forbidden to find the usual relieving expressions of grief; left to a secret, inward, heart-consuming sorrow. "While their sorrow will be too deep for words, it will not yet be the godly sorrow that worketh repentance. It will be the sullen despair and apathy of men disenchanted of the illusions on which their national life was based, of men left without hope and without God in the world."—Exp. B.

Sin the Worst Sorrow (vss. 15—24).—It is so because—I. Other sorrows may have no evil, but even good in them; this is essentially and eternally evil. II. Other sorrows are remediable; this leads to destruction. III. Other sorrows may come direct from God; this is ever in direct antagonism to Him. IV. Other sorrows have to do with men in their relation to others; this with his own inner being and his relation to God. Learn:—1. Rightly weigh your own sorrows; 2. Rightly deal with the world's sorrows; 3. Rightly value the Saviour's mission.—U. R. Thomas.

24—27. (24) **a sign,** typical representation of what would befall them. **this cometh,** the destruction of the temple. (25) **strength,** stronghold, vs. 21. (26) **in that day,** this phrase is used with some latitude, to indicate the period marked by any great event and following it. **escapeth,** as a fugitive, to carry the terrible tidings. (27) **mends,** R. V., "heart." **mouth .. him,** R. V. marg., "together with him." The messenger does not come till nearly three years afterwards (ch. xxxiii. 21); and we must infer that there was no spoken message during the interval, but that from ch. xxv. 1 onward we have the written words of the Lord that came to Him from time to time, not as messages to Israel, but as bearing on the fate of the surrounding nations. We have, i. e., what is, strictly speaking, a parenthesis in the prophet's work.—Pul. Com. **sign,** portent, or wonder. When the event has happened, they shall be convinced that your action and experience had been a prophetical sign for them.

The Preacher.—

The pulpit
Must stand acknowledged, while the world shall stand,
The most important and effectual guard,
Support and ornament of virtue's cause.
There stands the messenger of truth: there stands
The legate of the skies. His theme divine,
His office sacred, His credentials clear.
By Him the violated law speaks out
Its thunders; and by Him, in strains as sweet
As angels use, the Gospel whispers peace.
He 'stablishes the strong, restores the weak,
Reclaims the wanderer, binds the broken heart,
And, armed Himself in panoply complete
Of heavenly temper, furnishes with arms

Bright as His own, and trains, by every rule
Of holy discipline, to glorious war,
The sacramental host of God's elect!—Cowper.

CHAPTER THE TWENTY-FIFTH.

In ch. xxv.—xxxii. Ezekiel prophecies against the Nations. These were not uttered, they unfold the significance of the prophetic activity during the years of Ezekiel's silence. They form the proper intro. to the positive oracles of Israel's return. But this restoration of Israel cannot be without great judgments on the nations who have hitherto harassed or seduced her. These judgments will awaken the nations to the knowledge who the God of Israel is—they shall know that He **is** Jehovah; and they will ensure that in the future his people shall not be troubled or led astray.—Cam. B.

1—4. (2) **Ammonites,**[a] ch. xxi. 28. "In the fifth year after the destruction of Jerusalem, Nebuchadnezzar subdued the Ammonites and Moabites." (3) **Aha,** the expression of contempt. They insolently exulted over the fall of the temple, regarding it as the triumph of heathenism over the claims of Jehovah. This is the first of the two sins for wh. God chastises the heathen. **desolate,** "made desolate." (4) **men of the east,** the wild Eastern tribes who should distress the Ammonite country after it had been conquered by the Chaldæans. **palaces,** better, "encampments." **thy milk,** Ammon was a pastoral country.

5—7. (5) **Rabbah,** De. iii. 11. **couching-place,** place for resting and feeding the sheep. "It is a proverbial expression for utter destruction to say that grass grows where a town has stood."[b] **know,** etc., object of all this chastisement. Jehovah is to be recognized everywhere as the one, only God. The scorn of the heathen was not directed against a mere tribal god. Does not mean that Ammon is to be converted to the worship of Jehovah. (6) **clapped,** etc., signs of gladness at the destruction of Jerusalem, but in God's sight proofs of envy and malice; a savage kind of joy. (7) **spoil,** or portion to be devoured. **heathen,** R. V., "nations." **people,** R. V., "peoples."

The Dirge Over the Nations (chapters xxv.—xxxiii.).—The universal and permanent lessons of all this are clearly—1. The interest of a true man in other nations beside his own; 2. The universality of God's dominion; 3. The similarity in the laws of moral history in all lands and times; 4. The degress in retribution according to the degrees of sin.—U. R. Thomas.

8—11. (8) **Moab,** the neighbor country of Ammon. Kindred people of Israel, Gen. xix. 30; bet. Reuben and Moab there was continual rivalry for the fertile district of the former. The Moabite Stone is evidence of a fair degree of civilization. **Seir,** the Septuagint omits "and Seir." If retained it must refer to the inhabitants of Mount Seir. Elsewhere Ezekiel uses the term to designate Edom. **house .. heathen,** signifies the proud and boastful spirit of Moab. (9) **open the side,** or shoulder: expose them to the attacks of the invaders. **frontiers,** defence-cities, in which the people placed the utmost confidence. **Beth-jeshimoth,** etc., Nu. xxxii. 38; Jos. xiii. 20; Je. xlviii. 25; situated in Israel's territory. (10) Put a period after Kinathaim and read vs. 10, "Unto the children of the East will I give it for possession together with the children of Ammon;" i. e. both Moab and Ammon were to be inundated by Arabs.[c] (11) **judgments,** deserved and long called for, now to be executed.

The Revengeful Nation.—I. The wicked revenge. 1. Vengeance is presumptuous; 2. Vengeance is cruel; 3. Vengeance is unchristian; 4. Vengeance is mean-spirited. II. The natural punishment. 1. Revenge does not end a quarrel; 2. Revenge provokes the most bitter punishment.—Adeney.

12—14. (12) **Edom,** Nu. xxiv. 18, 19. The descendants of Esau kept up their grudge against the descendants of Jacob. **taking vengeance,** manifesting a most implacable resentment.[d] They joined the Chaldæans in the capture of Jerusalem; they cut off the fugitives; they occupied portions of Israel during the exile. John Hyrcanus finally defeated them

a Ammon, descended from Lot, held the region E of Jordan, separated fr. the Amorites on the N. by the river Jabbok, and from Moab on the S. by the river Arnon.

"Your few things may be very few, and small things; but he expects you to be faithful over them."—Havergal.

b Is. xvii. 2, xxxii. 14; Zep. ii. 14, 15.

"'The meteor, if it once fall, cannot be rekindled.' When those who once flashed before the eyes of the religious public with the blaze of a vain profession, fall into open and scandalous sin, it is impossible to renew their glory. Once break the egg of hypocrisy, and who can repair the damage?" —Spurgeon.

c "Upon the children of Ammon, i.e. I will open Moab to the men of the East, who, having overrun the children of Ammon, shall then fall upon Moab."—Fairbairn.

"The happiness of life is made up of minute fractions, — the little, soon-forgotten charities of a kiss, a smile, a kind look, — and the countless other infinitesimals of pleasant thought and feeling."—Coleridge.

d The subduing of Edom by David further deepened the ill-feeling, 2 Sa. viii. 14.

and restored their land to Israel, 126 B. C. (13) **Teman,** Ge. xxxvi. 11—15. **Dedan .. they of Dedan,** R. V., "even unto D. shall they;" Ge. x. 7.[b] (14) **know my vengeance,** that it is I who take v. upon them.

The Judgment of Edom.—Not in one event alone may we trace the fulfillment of this prediction, but in several. In the time of the Maccabees, Judas the Maccabee slew more than forty thousand Edomites (1 Macc. v. 3; 2 Macc. x. 15—23). About thirty years afterwards, John Hyrcanus turned his forces against Edom, completely subdued the country, and compelled the people to submit to circumcision and to conform to the Jewish religion, or to suffer expatriation. And they were so desirous of remaining in the country of their forefathers, that they yielded to his conditions, and, as Josephus says, "they were hereafter no other than Jews" (Josephus, 'Ant.,' xiii. 9. 1). So complete was their incorporation with the Jews "that the name of Idumæa appears no more in history as a separate kingdom." As Schröder remarks, "The vengeance of God could not in a more marked retribution manifest itself upon Edom than by the extirpation of his nationality, and that precisely in the form of an absorption by Israel." The desolation of the land was at length accomplished by the Mohammedans. "In the seventh century," says Dr. J. L. Porter, "the Mohammedan conquest gave a death-blow to the commerce and prosperity of Edom. Under the withering influence of Mohammedan rule, the great cities fell to ruin, and the country became a desert. The followers of the false prophet were here, as elsewhere, the instruments, in God's hands, for the execution of His judgments." And so "the Edom of prophecy—Edom considered as the enemy of God and the rival of Israel—has perished for ever: all, in that respect, is an untrodden wilderness, a hopeless ruin; and therein the veracity of God's Word finds its verification."—Pul. Com.

b "Teman and Dedan were districts, the former in the S., the latter in the N. Hence from Teman to Dedan means 'over the whole country.'" —Spk. Com.

"How great a mischief one unguarded point of character may cause us! One spark blew up the magazine and shook the whole country for miles around. One leak sunk the vessel and drowned all on board. One wound may kill the body; one sin destroy the soul." —Spurgeon.

15—17. (15) **Philistines,**[a] ancient foes of Israel, dwelling in the plains towards the coast, S. W. of Judah. **old hatred,** carrying on into later times the early hatred of the races. **for .. hatred,** R. V., "with perpetual enmity." (16) **Cherethims,** R. V., "Cherethites," another name for the Philistines, representing prob. one of the immigrations which formed the nation.[b] **remnant,** etc., they were at this time a mere "remnant," having been exhausted by the Assyrian and Egyptian wars. Their fate is not precisely indicated in the prophecy. They were in point of fact gradually extinguished by the revival of Jewish domination under the Asmonean dynasty.—Exp. B. Am. i. 8. (17) **furious rebukes,** or heavy judgments.

National Character.—1. There is such a thing as national morality. Apart from the character and conduct of individuals, a nation by its collective action proves itself to possess a certain moral unity. 2. There is such a thing as national responsibility. The people sin, and the people suffer; the people repent and call upon God, and the people are saved. 3. There is especial scope for the display of national virtues, and for the right use of national opportunity and probation, in the relations which subsist between different and sometimes rival communities. 4. National pride, power, and prosperity are of no avail in God's sight, if injustice and malevolence are exhibited by nations in their intercourse and transactions with each other. "The righteous Lord loveth righteousness."—Thomson.

a Comp. Is. xi. 14, xiv. 29—32, etc.

b 1 Sa. xxx. 14; Je. xlvii. 4; Zep. ii. 5.

"The growing good of the world is partly dependent on unhistoric acts; and that things are not so ill with you and me as they might have been is half owing to the number who have lived faithfully a hidden life, and rest in unvisited tombs." —George Eliot.

"Let us be content to do little, if God sets us at little tasks. It is but pride and self-will which says, 'Give me something huge to fight, and I should enjoy that; but why make me sweep the dust?'" —Charles Kingsley.

CHAPTER THE TWENTY-SIXTH.

1—6. (1) **eleventh year,** that in which Jerusalem fell, on the 10th day of the fifth month. Tyre had already heard of this catastrophe before Ezekiel utters this prophecy. **first .. month,** wh. precise month is not stated; prob. the eleventh or twelfth. (2) **Tyrus,** the Latin form of the word Tyre,[c] Jos. xix. 29; 2 Sa. xxiv. 7. **gates,** etc., trans. "the gate (door) of the peoples is broken, it is turned unto me." "The satisfaction with which the fall of Jerusalem was regarded in Tyre showed how completely she was debased by her selfish commercial policy, how oblivious she was to the spiritual interests bound up with the future of Israel." Jerusalem

c Nebuch.'s siege of Tyre lasted thirteen years.

had long been a center-place on the highway of commerce, and Tyre was jealous of its prosperity.[d] (3) **many nations,** alluding to the composite character of the Bab. army. **as the sea,** in its storm-time. A suitable fig. in a message to a sea-port town. (4) **scrape her dust,** i. e. sweep away her soil. **top .. rock,** R. V., "make her a bare rock." Tyre was situated on a rock-island. (5) **spreading of nets,** travelers say that this is literally fulfilled. (6) **daughters,** or dependent towns and cities on the mainland.

Destruction of Tyre.—One of the most singular events in history was the manner in which the siege of Tyre was conducted by Alexander the Great. Irritated that a single city should alone oppose his victorious march, enraged at the murder of some of his soldiers, and fearful for his fame—even his army's despairing of success could not deter him from the siege. And Tyre was taken in a manner, the success of which was more wonderful than the design was daring; for it was surrounded by a wall one hundred and fifty feet in height, and situated on an island half a mile distant from the shore. A mound was formed from the continent to the island; and the ruins of old Tyre, two hundred and forty years after its demolition, afforded ready materials for the purpose. Such was the work, that the attempts at first defeated the power of an Alexander. The enemy consumed and the storm destroyed it. But its remains, buried beneath the water, formed a barrier which rendered successful his renewed efforts. A vast mass of additional matter was requisite. The soil and the very rubbish were gathered and heaped. And the mighty conqueror, who afterwards failed in raising again any of the ruins of Babylon, cast those of Tyre into the sea, and took her very dust from off her.—Keith.——Mockery.—That "Aha" cost Tyrus her life. No mockery, no taunting of man against man on religious or solemn subjects! Controversy if you will; sneering none. We were not made to sneer. Sneer at no man's prayers. They may be very imperfect as compared with ours, but they are not to be sneered at. Do not sneer at the idolater in the jungle. He is worshiping a fetich, some poor stone or branch of wood; or mayhap he is a little higher, and is worshiping the dawn and paying homage to the evening star. Do not laugh at him; any man who can fall down on his knees worshipfully before any object is not far from the kingdom of God. Your business is not to sneer at him, but to show him a more excellent way, and to show that way by walking it.—Parker.

7—10. (7) **king of kings,** one who has subdued other kings, and holds them in subjection. (8) **fort,** etc., movable tower fr. which the archers shot. **mount,** "embankment," in this instance a huge mole bet. the mainland and the island. **buckler,** the "testudo or roof of shields under cover of which the besiegers operated." (9) **engines,** battering rams. **axes,** i. e. grappling irons, with which to pull down the city walls. (10) **dust,** etc., when they rush in through the breaches to sack the city.

National Selfishness.—Tyre should have sympathized with her old ally in the time of adversity. But her commercial greed bears down all thoughts of friendship and all feelings of commiseration. She only looks at the direful event as an opportunity for enlarging her trade. The same miserable mercantile selfishness is even witnessed in ecclesiastical regions, when one Church takes pleasure in the misfortunes of a neighboring Church. In this case there is far less excuse, for Christians profess brotherhood, and a true Church exists for the glory of God, not for the pomp and aggrandizement of its members. God is not glorified when one Church fattens on the wreck of another Church.—Adeney.——History of Tyre.—This history of the city is most affecting. It was probably a colony of the Sidonians, as it is called "the daughter of Sidon." From its present name appears to have been taken the general name of Syria. Its first mention is in Joshua, where it is called "the strong city Tyre." At an early period it became the mistress of the seas; traded even to Britain, and planted colonies in different parts of the Mediterranean, among which Carthage became the most celebrated. It was also referred to by our Saviour, when He pronounced woe upon the inhabitants of Chorazin and Bethsaida, because they had seen His mighty works and repented not.

[d] "In the true spirit of mercantile competition, Tyre exulted on the thought that the trade of Je.us. would now be diverted into her markets."
—Spk. Com.

"The disappointments of worldly confidence drive us to Christ. When earthly friends 'fail or leave us,' we need the true Friend who 'sticketh closer than a brother.' If Christian ministers have been unworthy, Christ abides faithful. Perhaps too much confidence was given to the human instruments; then the shock of discovering this to be misplaced may not be wholly hurtful; it may help the Church to look away from men and trust only in Christ."
—Pul. Com.

Tyre, as is well known, suffered two memorable sieges: one from Nebuchadnezzar, the other from Alexander the Great. "Alexander the Great was much offended with those who refused the presents that he offered them. So with Christ to His children. He is not pleased with us when we do not expect large things from Him, and accept the large things that He offers us."

"All the glory and beauty of Christ are manifeted within, and there He delights to dwell; His visits there are frequent, His condescension amazing, His conversation sweet, His comforts refreshing; and the peace that He brings passeth all understanding." —Thos. a Kempis.

11—14. (11) **tread down,** the people in the streets. **strong garrisons,** lit. pillars of strength. "The multitude and strength of the pillars of Tyre are attested by its ruins." (12) **pleasant houses,** the homes of the merchant princes were palatial. **in .. water,** where they can even to this day be seen.[a] (13) **noise .. cease,** Tyre was the operatic city of the ancient world. Culture and commerce go hand in hand. Is. xxiv. 8; Je. vii. 34, xvi. 9. (14) **like the top of a rock,**[b] R. V., "make thee a bare rock."

Tyre.—No great city which has played so important a part for centuries has left fewer traces than Tyre. Ezekiel was a true prophet when he said of Tyre, "They shall seek for thee, and thou shalt be no more" (ch. xxvi. 21). A traveler who was not informed of its existence might pass along the whole coast, from La Kasmie to Ras-el-Ain, without being aware that he was close to an ancient city. . . . Tyre is now the ruin of a town built with ruins.—Rénan.

15—18. (15) **isles,** the coast-lands. **shake,** by a strong hyperbole the prophet appears to represent the crash of the city's fall and the cries of the wounded as being heard in the neighboring coasts, ch. xxvii. 28, xxxi. 16; cf. Jer. xlix. 21. (16) **princes of the sea,** the merchant rulers of Carthage, and other colonies founded by Tyre. These would be in extreme distress on account of the fall of Tyre. (17) **lamentation,** comp. Re. xviii. 9. **of seafaring men,** or of the seas. "Tyre was an inhabited city rising out of the sea that surrounded her." **haunt it,** R. V. marg., "inhabited her." (18) **isles,** or colonies on the Mediterranean islands and shores.

19—21. (19) **bring .. deep,** the sea did actually come to cover the ruins. (20) **When,** R. V., "then." The prophet regards Tyre's sinking beneath the waters as her entrance upon the descent into the pit, the place of the dead, just as frequently elsewhere (ch. xxxii.) he makes the grave the entrance into the underworld of the dead. Cf. Is. xiv. 11, 19. **down,** etc., comp. Is. xiv. 9. **and I shall set thy glory,** R. V. marg., "nor set thy glory." (21) **terror,** will utterly destroy thee. The Bible is silent concerning the fulfillment of this prophecy. Ch. xxix. 17—21 suggests that Nebuc. was not fully successful. **be no more,** as a great commercial city. "As to old Tyre the prophecy was literally fulfilled, not a vestige of it being left."

The Ruins of Tyre.—Relentless desolation seems to brood over this devoted region. Fragments of clustered columns and broken walls, at the south-east extremity of the town—the only visible remains of the structures even of the Middle Ages—perhaps mark the site of the magnificent metropolitan church, once the conspicuous ornament of Christian Tyre. In that splendid edifice of rich Gothic architecture, distinguished by three spacious naves and two lofty towers, where councils were held and princes and prelates assembled, the bones of the Emperor Frederick Barbarossa were deposited in a sumptuous sepulchre. Every trace of the mausoleum of Origen, raised in the third century, and still existing in the twelfth, has now disappeared. Broken shafts thrown into a narrow creek awkwardly serve the purpose of a bridge; others piled in the sea, form a barrier against hostile approach. A few columns of marble, of granite, and of porphyry lie unheeded round a small cove, now the only landing-place, while mounds of sand, thinly strewn with architectural fragments, alone point out the ancient circuit of the town.—Hogg.

CHAPTER THE TWENTY-SEVENTH.

Apart from its poetic or prophetic interest this chapter is for us almost the locus classicus as to the geography and commerce of that old world of which Tyre was in some sense the centre. We may compare it, from that point of view, with the ethnological statements in Gen. x.—Pulp. Com.——He compares her to a stately vessel riding at anchor near the shore, taking on board her cargo of precious merchandise, and ready

[a] "The number of granite columns that lie in the sea, particularly in the north of the island, is surprising. The east wall of the inner harbor is entirely founded upon them, and they are thickly spread over the bottom of the sea on every side." —Thomson.

[b] "Alexander, as Arrian relates, scraped off the very dust of old Tyre to build his causeway and now you can find none of the remains except by digging below the surface."—Ibid.

"I know of a surety that the diligent Christian is the only happy Christian. True religion is above all other things a business which is not only worth doing but is worth doing well. High farming in the fields of the soul is the only farming which pays." —Spurgeon.

"If you can laugh over your trial, it is half conquered; if you can pray over it, it is wholly conquered."

"Trade and intercourse cease where God sends His judgments. The Lord destroys nations that delight in war."—Lange.

"Late repentance should be carefully distinguished from delayed repentance. True repentance is never too late, but late repentance is seldom true. The penitent thief's was late repentance, but we have no evidence that it was deferred repentance." —Anon.

to start on the perilous voyage from which she is destined never to return.—Exp. B.

1—6. (2) **lamentation,** or funeral dirge.[a] (3) **entry,** lit. entries. Ancient Tyre had two ports. It was a harbor to and from which ships went from all parts of the Mediterranean, and connected seas. **perfect beauty,** completely fitted, and grandly adorned. (4) **midst .. seas,** lit. "in the heart of the sea."[b] **builders,** ship-builders. (5) **ship boards,** R. V., "planks." **Senir,** the Amorite name for Mt. Hermon.[c] (6) **Bashan,** a district celebrated for its oaks. **company .. ivory,** Polychr. Bib., "thy deck they made of ivory inlaid in cedar-wood from the isles of Chittim." **isles of Chittim,**[d] or Cyprus.

A State of Sin is a State of Death (vs. 3).—1. We are all destitute of spiritual life; 2. The Word of God is the appointed means of communicating spiritual life; 3. The influence of the Holy Spirit is indispensable to the production of spiritual life. 4. The influence of the Holy Spirit is to be obtained through prayer; 5. We have every encouragement to pray for the influence of the Holy Spirit; 6. The consequences of the outpouring of the influence of the Holy Spirit will be beneficial and glorious.—G. Brooks.

Ancient Tyre.—The Saracens and Turks were the unconscious instruments who carried these prophecies into their fulfilment: they utterly destroyed Sidon and Tyre, that they might not afford further refuge to the crusaders. There were two harbors, formed by the island—one towards the north, and the other towards the south; and there was a passage between the island and the shore from the one to the other. The island is represented by Pliny as having been four miles in circumference, but the peninsula upon which the present town is situated is of much less extent. It would therefore appear that it is built, for the most part, upon the mole thrown up by Alexander, including a small portion of the original island.

a "This alludes to the mournful ditties used at funerals, wherein the mourning women recounted everything that was valuable or praiseworthy belonging to the deceased, and then lamentd his loss." — Lowth.

b "Tyre, in consequence of her sea-girt position, separated by a strait of half a mile from the mainland, is described as a ship built of the best materials, and manned with the best mariners and skilful pilots, but at last in tempestuous seas wrecked." —Fausset.

c De. iii. 9.

Virgil mentions the fir tree as especially useful for ships, the cedar and cypress for houses.

d Je. ii. 10.

7—11. (7) **Fine linen,**[a] Ge. xli. 42. **blue and purple,** i. e. material dyed with costly murez-dyes.[b] **isles of Elishah,** "Ionia or Grecian Asia," Ge. x. 4. **that which covered thee,** R. V., "thine awning." The whole picture signifies the great architectural beauty of Tyre. (8) **Arvad,** Ge. x. 18. **mariners,** rowers. (9) **Gebal,** a province of Phœnicia, near Tyre.[c] **calkers,** stoppers of chinks; it was their business to make the vessels water-tight. **occupy,** R. V. marg., "exchange." (10) **Lud and Phut,** prob. in Africa, Nah. iii. 9. **hanged .. thee,** it was customary to ornament the walls with weapons. (11) **Gammadims,** an unknown nation.

12—16. (12) **Tarshish,** prob. Tartessus in Spain, Ge. x. 4. Spain was rich in metals. Ezekiel in speaking of the vast area of territory subject to the commercial spirit of Tyre begins farthest west. **traded in thy fairs,** R. V., "traded for thy wares." (13) **Javan,** Greece. **Tubal, and Meshech,** "the Moschi and Tibareni, whose habitation was near the Euxine Sea. **persons of men,** i. e. slaves. **in thy market,** R. V., "for thy merchandise." (14) **Togarmah,** Armenia, Ge. x. 2. (15) **Dedan,** Lxx., "the Rhodians," i. e. the coasts of the Mediterranean sea. **for a present,** i. e. rendered as thy tribute. The representation is not that Tyre is traded with by the nations, though this is the fact lying under the figures employed. The nations are not customers of Tyre. Tyre neither buys nor sells, nor does she exchange one article for another. The nations are her merchants, who bring to her wares from every land; or they are her dependents, and the merchandise which they bring is a tribute which they render her.—Cam. B. (16) **Syria,** lxx., "Edom." Ge. x. 7. **emeralds,** or carbuncle. **coral,** poss. precious stones, are meant by the word. **agate,** R. V., "rubies."

a Caligula, the extravagant Roman emperor, furnished his pleasure-boats with costly sails and other expensive ornaments. —Suetonius.

b This was used for awnings over the deck.

c Ps. lxxxiii. 7.

"The domestic utensils of the Orientals are nearly always brass: and to these they often refer as a sign of property. 'He is a rich man; his house is full of brass vessels.' 'Begone! fellow, I have more brass in my house than would purchase all thy property.' 'The miserable man has not a brass dish in his house.' " —Roberts.

17—21. (17) **wheat of Minnith,** 1 Ki. v. 9—11. Minnith is in the country of the Ammonites, wh. was famous for its cornlands.[a] **Pannag,** R. V., "pannag," perhaps some kind of gum. **balm,** for wh. Gilead was famous.[b] (18) **Damascus,** the chief city of Syria. **wares .. making,** R. V., "thy handy works," not Tyre's own making, but the wares which the nations brought to her, all of which are hers. **multitude .. riches,** Cam. B., "because of every kind of riches." **Helbon,** or Chalybon,[c] a district in Syria famous for its wine. (19) **Dan,** poss. should be Vedan, the modern Aden. **Javan,** poss. a Greek settlement in Arabia. **Dan .. Javan,**

a 2 Chr. xxvii. 2.

b Je. viii. 25.

c Now Aleppo.

Camb. B., "Wedan and Javan of Uzal furnished thy wares; bright iron, cassia and calamus were among thy goods." **bright iron,** i. e. wrought iron. **cassia,** Ex. xxx. 24. **calamus,** "sweet cane," which supplied one of the ingredients for the anointing oil of the priests, Ex. xxx. 23. (20) **precious clothes,** perhaps "saddle-cloths for riding." (21) **Kedar,** Ge. xxv. 13.

Business.—This account of the trade of Tyre intimates to us that God's eye is upon men, and that he takes cognizance of what they do when they are employed in their worldly business, not only when they are at church, praying and hearing, but when they are in their markets and fairs, and upon the exchange, buying and selling, which is a good reason why we should in all our dealings keep a conscience void of offence, and have our eye always upon him whose eye is always upon us.—M. Henry.

22—25. (22) **Sheba,** in Arabia, Felix. **Raamah,** on the Persian Gulf. (23) **Haran,** Carrhœ, in N. W. Mesopotamia. **Canneh,** prob. a town on the Tigris. **Eden,** in Mesopotamia.[a] **Asshur,** here prob. the town Sura or Essurieh on the Euphrates. **Chilmad,** prob. Kalwada, near Bagdad. (24) **all sorts,** or in excellent wares. **bound with cords,** Cam. B., "with cords twined and durable," i. e. the cords were articles of merchandise. **made of cedar,** to give the clothes a fine scent.[b] (25) **did sing of thee,** R. V., "were thy caravans." The ships of Tarshish, i. e. deep-sea ships, those trading with the distant ports. "Beneath all her opulence and refinement the prophet's eye detected that which was opposed to the mind of Jehovah—the irreligious spirit which is the temptation of a mercantile community, manifesting itself in overweening pride and self-exaltation, and in sordid devotion to gain as the highest end of a nation's existence."

Lessons from Old Tyre.—There is no security out of heaven. He builds too low who builds beneath the skies. All other security is partial, relative, good as far as it goes; but so long as old Tyre lies in ruins, a rock on which fishermen dry their nets, let us believe that the proudest gold store may be a barren place and the very city of poverty and chagrin in the working out of the evolution of providence. We should learn from ruins. O vain man, poor boaster, you shall beg to-morrow! You that steep your arms to the elbows in gold shall write a begging letter ere the year closes. Riches make to themselves wings and fly away, and the great Babylon which you have builded is but a bubble in the air. Lay not up for yourselves riches where moth and dust doth corrupt, and where thieves break through and steal: have riches in heaven; have riches in the word of God. Then you can never be poor; yea, though there be not one penny-piece in all your fortune, you may be richer than you ever were. There is a poverty that is unconscious of need; there is a poverty that can pray and hope.—J Parker.

26—30. The vessel steered by her pilots into dangerous waters, is shipwrecked and her cargo and crew cast into the sea. Dismay and lamentation of all seafaring men. (26) **great waters,** scenes of peril. **east wind,** Tyre's fall was due to a force and a wisdom above men, Ps. xlviii. 7. (27) **riches,** etc., "All who have been enumerated as sharing in and constituting the glory of Tyre are now recounted as partakers in her wreck."—Spk. Com. **fairs,** R. V., "wares." **occupies,** "exchangers." (28) **suburbs,** perhaps "waves." (29) **stand .. land,** "being cast out of the ships wherein they prided themselves," or in fear of the sea in view of the wreck of the gallant ship of Tyre. (30) **against thee,** better, over thee: on account of thy wreck and ruin. **cast .. ashes,** the signs of intense and hopeless mourning.

31—36. (31) **utterly bald,** ch. vii. 18. (33) **wares,** or merchandise. (34) R. V. marg., "Now thou art broken .. are fallen." (35) **isles,**[a] including cities on the neighboring coasts. (36) **people,** "peoples." **hiss,** with astonishment. **terror,** i. e. utterly destroyed. In the new world inaugurated by Israel's Restoration, the prophet sees no place for this arrogant, proud commercial city. Tyre is irrevocably doomed.

A Celebration of Remarkable Prosperity.—I. A celebration of remarkable prosperity. 1. Her advantageous situation; 2. The grandeur of her buildings; 3. Her great riches, important handicrafts, and extensive commerce; 4. Her strong fortifications. II. A celebration of re-

---

"If you stand half a mile off from a man and throw the gospel at him, you will miss him; but if you go close to him and lay hold upon him, giving him a hearty grip of the hand, and show that you have an affection for him, you will, by God's blessing, lead him in the right way."
—Spurgeon.

a 2 Ki. xix. 12.

b "Still fine clothes are kept in large chests of cypress-wood, whose odor preserves them from the ravages of moths. Ezekiel speaks of such made of cypress."
—Van Lennep.

"Our business must be the main drain of our intellectual activities day by day. It is the channel we have chosen for them: they must flow in it with a diffusive energy, filling every nook and corner."—Tulloch.

"There is no such wholesome air—there is no such kindly physic—there is no such sovereign cordial—as the fear of the Lord. That makes the days of the godly as long as the years of the wicked.—Jermin.

"Let your light shine. Revolving flash-lights are all right on the sea coast, but all wrong in the Christian life. Shine, keep shining!" — Carlos Martyn.

a Eze. xxvi 15, 16.

"There is both folly and weakness in those who love and seek after pleasure, for it cannot satisfy the soul nor give the heart repose."—Thomas a Kempis.

markable prosperity inordinately gloried in. III. A celebration of remarkable prosperity with a significant omission. IV. A celebration of remarkable prosperity disastrously terminated. V. The disastrous termination of remarkable prosperity variously regarded. 1. With lamentation; 2. With affright; 3. With scoffing.—W. Jones.

CHAPTER THE TWENTY-EIGHTH.

1—5. (2) **prince,** or king; prob. Ithobal II. But he is regarded here as the impersonation of the spirit of a prosperous commercial system. Tyre is the representative of commercial greatness, and the truth which Ezek. here seeks to illustrate is, that the abnormal development of the mercantile spirit had in her case destroyed the capacity of faith in that which is truly divine.—Exp. B. **lifted up,** in self-confidence and pride. This ungodly pride and self-deification is the second sin for which the heathen nations were chastised, cf. xxv. 12, 15; xxvi. 2. They must know that Jehovah is God. **a God,** comp. Da. iv. 30,[a] better, "I am God," the prophet speaks fr. his own point of view, wh. makes such a statement, blasphemy. **seat,** i. e. Tyre, bec. of its great wealth and renown. **midst .. seas,** ch. xxvii. 4. **man,** and only a man. **heart .. God,** self-apotheosis; comp. the action of the Roman Emperors (3) **than Daniel,**[b] spoken in irony, ch. xiv. 14. (4) **thy wisdom,** etc., this represents the prince's boasting and self-esteem, not the actual facts. (5) **because .. riches,** the usual consequence of riches swiftly gathered is inordinate pride, and carnal reliance on mere temporal wealth.

Worldly Religion.—We have, indeed, a nominal religion, to which we pay tithes of property and sevenths of time; but we have also a practical and earnest religion, to which we devote nine-tenths of our property, and six-sevenths of our time. And we dispute a great deal about the nominal religion: but we are all unanimous about this practical one; of which I think you will admit that the ruling goddess may be best generally described as the "Goddess of Getting-on," or "Britannia of the Market." The Athenians had an "Athena Agoraia," or Athena of the Market; but she was a subordinate type of their goddess, while our Britannia Agoraia is the principal type of ours. And all your great architectural works are, of course, built to her. It is long since you built a great cathedral; and how you would laugh at me if I proposed building a cathedral on the top of one of these hills of yours, to make it an Acropolis! But your railroad mounds, vaster than the walls of Babylon; your railroad stations, vaster than the temple of Ephesus, and innumerable; your chimneys, how much more mighty and costly than cathedral spires! your harbor-piers; your warehouses; your exchanges! —all these are built to your great Goddess of "Getting-on;" and she has formed, and will continue to form, your architecture, as long as you worship her; and it is quite vain to ask me to tell you how to build to her; you know far better than I.—Ruskin, "The Crown of Wild Olive."

6—10. (6) **Lord God,** note that, in the use of this full name is given the assertion that Jehovah is the only God. (7) **strangers,** even the Babylonian army, made up of people from unknown regions. **beauty .. wisdom,** i. e. all the magnificence wh. the commercial spirit has produced **defile,** R. V. marg., "profane," bec. the prince has assumed divinity for the city and himself. (8) **the pit,** or bottom of the sea. The fig. of this vs. is taken from a sea-fight, where the dead are cast overboard without burial. (9) **a man,** R. V., "thou art man, and not God," and so entirely in the power of the foe. You shall show no Divine powers in the time of trouble, so as to be able to deliver yourself. (10) **uncircumcised,** heathen idolaters as opposed to the covenant people.[a] This ignominious death was one of the severest punishments of wh. a Jew was cognizant. Deprivation of burial did not hinder the dead persons from descending into Sheol, the place of the dead, but the dishonor done them here followed them there, and they were subject to reproach.—Cam. B.

The Prince of Tyre.—The proud boast of the Tyrian prince is partly **accounted for by the situation of the island-city, full of luxury and beauty,**

---

[a] Also Ac. xii. 21—23; 2 Th. ii. 4.

"The words are put in the mouth of the speaker to denote his arrogant pride; but the situation of the island city, full of luxury and beauty, in the midst of the blue water of the Mediterranean, gives force to the expression."
—Spk. Com.

[b] Da. i. 17, vi. 3.

"My father bought for me, in childhood, a golden seal-ring. A pedler, in exchange for a date, carried off the ring from my hand. For a little child cannot estimate the value of a ring, and will easily part with it for anything sweet. And thou, too, dost not estimate the value of a life, who throwest it away in luxurious indulgences."
—Saadi.

[a] "Thou shalt die by such a remarkable judgment as God usually inflicts upon notorious offenders."
—Lowth.

"In ways of greatness think on this — that slippery all ambition is."
—Herrick.

Towns turned to ashes, fanes involved in fire! These deeds the guilt of rash ambition tell.
—Fawkes.

"The knowing of God, that we may serve Him, and the serving Him, that we may enjoy Him, take up the whole duty of man's obedience." — Herle.

b "Thou art the consummation of the model of perfection. The king of Tyre, who was the head of the Tyrian community, and completed and crowned its organization, was like a seal which gave perfection to it."—Wordsworth.

"As the union of the branch with the vine is one of growth, never-ceasing growth and increase, so our abiding in Christ is a life process in which the divine life ever takes fuller and more complete possession of us." — Andrew Murray.

in the midst of the blue water of the Mediterranean. Moreover, Tyre was regarded by many as a sacred island. Fairbairn says that "Sanchoniathon expressly calls it 'the holy island;' and it is known that the Tyrian colonies all reverenced it as the mother-city of their religion, not less than the original source of their political existence. It was only in the spirit of ancient heathenism to conclude that a state which was not only strong by natural position, and by immense maritime resources, but also stood in such close connection with the Divine, might be warranted in claiming, through its head, something like supernatural strength and absolute perpetuity of being."—W. Jones.

11—15. Vss. 11—19 are very difficult to explain bec. of obscure expressions and unintelligible allusions. The simple thought is that there was sin enough in Tyre to hurl the most radiant celestial fr. heaven to hell. (12) **sealest .. sum,** or completest the perfect pattern.[b] "Thou settest the seal to thy perfection. Thou deemest that thou hast attained the consummation of all beauty and wisdom."—Pulp. Com. (13) **in Eden,** no doubt the prophet has in mind the story of Paradise (Gen. ii., iii). Not unlikely he was in possession of traditions more ample than those in Genesis.—Cam. B. **tabrets,** or drums. (14) **anointed cherub,** trans. "with the cherub with spreading wings overshadowing I set thee." **covereth,** as the cherub in the holy of holies overshadoweth the mercy-seat. The cherub was a symbol of perfection. **stones of fire,** i. e. bright jewels, such as named vs. 13. (15) **perfect,** to all appearance, and in thine own estimation.

Note on vss. 12-16.—The passage presents certain obvious affinities with the account of the Fall in the second and third chapters of Genesis; but it also contains reminiscences of a mythology the key to which is now lost. It can hardly be supposed that the vivid details of the imagery, such as the "mountain of God," the "stones of fire," "the precious gems," are altogether due to the prophet's imagination. The mountain of the gods is now known to have been a prominent idea of the Babylonian religion; and there appears to have been a widespread notion that in the abode of the gods were treasures of gold and precious stones, jealously guarded by griffins, of which small quantities found their way into the possession of men. It is possible that fragments of these mythical notions may have reached the knowledge of Ezekiel during his sojourn in Babylon and been used by him to fill up his picture of the glories which surrounded the first estate of the king of Tyre.—Exp. Bib.

a Comp. Re. xvii. 10, xviii. 9.

"It is bad for an age to die rusting in its error, or even rusting in its truth." —Fairbairn.

16—19. (16) **filled .. violence,** swift prosperity often leads to violence, cheating, and extortion. In haste to be rich, virtue and charity are often put aside. This is the only allusion in the three chapters to the wrong and oppression and the outrages on humanity which were the inevitable accompaniments of that greed of gain which had taken possession of the Tyrian community. **will I cast,** R. V., "have I cast." **as profane,** no longer to be regarded as sacred. **I .. cherub,** prob. "the cherub with spreading wings hath destroyed thee, driving thee from," etc.—Cam. B. The meaning seems to be that the prince of Tyre had his place in the abode of God until he defiled by the lust of riches the perfection in which he was created, then the cherub destroyed him, driving him from the mount of God. (17) **brightness,** or splendor, alluding to the luxuries wh. wealth encourages. **lay .. kings,** R. V., "have laid," as an example of the end of presumptuous pride. (18) **iniquity .. traffic,** wh. had become dishonest and overreaching. (19) **astonished,** at thy ruin.[a]

b Joel iii. 4.

c Ge. x. 19.

"Accurate and careful detail, the minding of the common occasions and small things combined with general scope and vigor, is the secret of all the efficiency and success in the world. It is only thus that any disciple will become efficient in the service of his Master." — Horace Bushnell.

Note on vs. 18.—By a sudden change of metaphor the destruction of the city is also represented as a fire breaking out in the vitals of the prince and reducing his body to ashes—a conception which has not unnaturally suggested to some commentators the fable of the phœnix which was supposed periodically to immolate herself in a fire of her own kindling.—Exp. Bib.

20—23. (21) **Zidon,**[b] the neighboring, but older[c] Phœnician city. It was famous for its fishery, and increased in wealth after Tyre was humbled. (22) **against thee,** bec. of the idolatries wherewith the Zidonians had corrupted Israel. **glorified,** i. e. get me glory in the light of the peoples by the righteousness executed. (23) **pestilence,** another agent used in executing the Divine vengeance on nations. **wounded .. judged,** R. V., "wounded shall fall."

Pestilence and Blood.—This judgment by pestilence and sword can hardly be said to have been executed in the invasion by Nebuchadnezzar, seeing that Zidon submitted to him apparently without offering any serious resistance. But this threatening of pestilence and sword may point to the sufferings of the Zidonians at a later period of their history, in consequence of their revolt against the Persians, to whom they were then subject. Zidon was at that time a wealthy and flourishing city; and the revolt would probably have been successful but for the treachery of Tennes, their king, who, in fulfilment of a compact with Artaxerxes Ochus, the Persian monarch, betrayed into his "power one hundred of the most distinguished citizens of Zidon, who were all shot to death with javelins. Five hundred other citizens, who went out to the king with ensigns of supplication, shared the same fate; and by concert between Tennes and Mentor, the Persian troops were admitted within the gates, and occupied the city walls. The Zidonians, before the arrival of Ochus, had burnt their vessels to prevent any one leaving the town; and when they saw themselves surrounded by the Persian troops, they adopted the desperate resolution of shutting themselves up with their families, and setting fire each man to his own house (B. C. 351). Forty thousand persons are said to have perished in the flames."—Smith.

24—26. (24) **pricking brier,** "first ensnaring the Israelites to sin, and then being made the instrument of punishing them." See Nu. xxxiii. 55. The hostile nations are all to be removed for the benefit of Israel after the Restoration. (25) **gathered .. scattered,** here the Lord's mercy to Israel is set in contrast with His dealings with the surrounding nations.[a] **sanctified in them,** i. e. in their return to Palestine. (26) **build houses,** Is. lxv. 21. **know .. God,** this oft-repeated phrase is not a mere formula. The prophet's idea is that Jehovah does all, brings all calamities, causes all catastrophes and revolutions in states, and guides the fortunes of Israel in the sight of the nations, with one great design in view—to make himself, the true and only God, known to all mankind.—Cam. B.

"He preaches Christ best, who lifts Him up most." Christianity is itself a living breathing presence, not a mere dull, dead thing; a life, not a book; a Person, and that Person our Friend and Saviour, our Reconciliation and our Rest, our hope and our Victory.
—Hom. Com.

[a] "This transition from the enemies to the people of God is made to close the portion of the prophecies against the heathen, which concerns the nations in the immediate vicinity of the Israelites, 'them that despise them round about them, before passing to the more distant Egypt."
—Spk. Com.

CHAPTER THE TWENTY-NINTH.

1—7. (1) **tenth year,** i. e. of the captivity. Jerusalem had, at this time, been besieged, but not taken, seven months were yet to elapse. (2) **Pharaoh,** the common name of the Eg. kings. This Pharaoh was Hophra, or Apries, in the Greek.[b] (3) **great dragon,** Heb. tannim, prob. the crocodile,[c] the chief creature of the Nile made a symbol of the king, suggests sluggish and unwieldy strength. **midst .. rivers,** the royal city, Sais, was situated in the Delta, among the many branches or streams of the Nile. **river .. myself,** the expression of Hophra's boastful pride.[d] The Nile is the life and wealth of Egypt. The arrogance of Pharaoh, wh. is but the impersonation of the consciousness of the people, is blasphemy against Jehovah the one only true God. cf. xxviii. 2. (4) **hooks,** Job. xli. 2. **fish .. rivers,** a fig. for the people of the land. (5) **thrown,** etc., this was the fate of Hophra's army. **gathered,** i. e. buried. (6) **staff of reed,** a staff wh. proved but a reed when leaned upon. The two sins for which Egypt, represented by Pharaoh, is chastised are, first, pride of heart which recognizes no God above it, which says, My River is mine, I have made it (xxix. 3); and second, the deceptive fascination which the imposing and pretentious power of the Nile valley exerted on the people of God, seducing them away from trust in Jehovah alone (cf. Is. xxx. 1—5, xxxi. 1—3), and proving always a delusive support (xxix. 6, 7)—Cam. B. (7) **break,** and so utterly fail the Jews in the hour of their need. **be at a stand,** better, "to shake."

Egypt.—Egypt was famous for her learning and her science. Long before the Babylonian and Persian astronomical science arose by the Euphrates, there were schools of literature, philosophy, and physical science on the banks of the Nile. It was a help in the training of Israel's great deliverer that he was educated in the greatest centre of light of

[b] "The most powerful king of Egypt next to Psammeticus, whose great grandson he was. He besieged and captured Gaza (Jer. xlvii. 1), and attacked Sidon, and encountered the king of Tyre in an engagement by sea, and recovered much of the influence wh. Eg. had lost since its defeat at Carchemish by Nebuchadnezzar, in the fourth year of Jehoiakim (2 Ki. xxiv. 7; Je. xlvi. 2."
—Wordsworth.

[c] On Roman coins the crocodile is the emblem of Egypt.

[d] Herodotus says that this king persuaded himself that even the gods could not dispossess him of his kingdom.

his age (Acts vii. 22). Yet the great intelligence of ancient Egypt did not preserve its sons from gross moral corruption, and no worldly wisdom was able to provide against the descending arm of judgment. Culture will not dispense with the need of conscience. University honors are not passports to heaven. Knowledge and thought will not shield the sinful against the wrath of future judgment.—Pul. Com.

8—11. (8) **a sword,** fig. for invasion of Chaldæan army.[a] (9) **because,** etc., i. e. it must be distinctly understood that the judgment will come upon him for his impiety and his insolence. (10) **tower of Syene,** or modern Assouan, near to which are the First Cataracts. (11) **forty years,** an ideal number, signifying that the time was to be short. (12) **scatter,** etc., "the scattering was to be mainly the dissipation of their power."

Egypt's Desolation.—Egypt could still be a country, though shorn of the glory and power which had made her a snare to the people of God. The geographical isolation of the land made it impossible that she should lose her individuality amongst the nations of the world. Accordingly the prophet does not contemplate an utter annihilation of Egypt, but only a temporary chatisement succeeded by her permanent degradation to the lowest rank among the kingdoms.—Exp. Bib.

13—16. (13) **gather,** etc., comp. Je. xlvi. 26. (14) **land of Pathros,** the Thebaid, or Upper Egypt.[b] **habitation,** R. V., "birth." **base kingdom,** in a depressed or low state: poss. meaning a tributary kingdom. (15) **basest of kingdoms,** travelers still attest the "deplorable and debased state of this country."[c] (16) **confidence,** etc., referring to the disposition to trust Egypt in the conflict with Nebuchadnezzar. **look after,** or seek aid from. **they shall know,** i. e. the house of Israel.

The Meager Restoration of Egypt.—I. God has mercy on the heathen. II. There are irreparable losses which are brought about by sin. 1. The temporal consequences of sin are unavoidable; 2. Without a return to God the worst consequences of sin must continue. III. It is well that false grounds of confidence should be exposed. 1. When the nature of false hopes is exposed we are driven to the truth for refuge; 2. The ruin of false hopes is a perpetual warning.—Adeney.

Egyptian Splendors.—The great temple of Karnak has twelve principal entrances, each of which is composed of several propyla and colossal gateways, besides other buildings attached to them, in themselves larger than most other temples. One of the propyla is entirely of granite, adorned with the most finished hieroglyphics. On each side of many of them there have been colossal statues of basalt and granite, from twenty to thirty feet in height, some of which are in the attitude of sitting, while others are standing erect. A double range of colossal sphinxes extends across the plain from the temple at Luxor (a distance of nearly two miles), which terminates at Karnak in a most magnificent gateway, fifty feet in height which still remains unimpaired. From this gateway the great temple was approached by an avenue of fifty lofty columns, one of which only now remains, leading to a vast propylon in front of the portico. The interior of this portico presents a coup d'œil, which surpasses any other that is to be found among the remains of Egyptian architecture. Twelve columns, sixty feet high, and of a beautiful order, form an avenue through the centre of the building, like the nave of a Gothic cathedral, and they are flanked on each side by sixty smaller ones, ranged in six rows, which are seen through the intervals in endless perspective.—Horner.

17—21. (17) **seven and twentieth,** see vs. 1. This is a later prophecy, 570 B. C., sixteen years after the destruction of Jerusalem, inserted here to show that Nebuchadnezzar would fulfil the previous threatenings on Egypt. (18) **serve,** etc., not merely to carry out a great undertaking, but to fulfil a Divine commission against Tyre. It was a long and exhausting siege of thirteen years. **head .. peeled,** figs. to express the hard service of the soldiers, who carried on their heads and shoulders rock and rubbish to build a causeway to the city. **no wages,** bec. the inhabitants succeeded in removing their treasures. (19) **give .. Egypt,** compensating Nebuc. with the spoils of Egypt. **take,** etc., i. e. deport, carry away. (20) **his labour,** R. V., "recompence," i. e. as the hire for his labor in the siege

[a] "Prob. Nebuc. was encouraged by the revolt of Amasis against Pharaoh and Hophra, to invade Egypt, and was thus enabled to subdue it with greater ease." —Wilkinson.

[b] Ge. x. 14; Is. xi. 11.

[c] "Upon its revolting from the Persians it was finally subdued by Ochus, the Persian emperor, and has been governed by strangers ever since." —Lowth.

"On the failure of the Persian empire, it became subject to the Macedonians, after them to the Romans, then to the Saracens, then to the Mamelukes, and it is now a province of the Turkish empire." —Prideaux.

"Accurst ambition, how dearly have I bought you!"—Dryden.

'Liberty is not the right to do what one wills but freedom to do what one ought. —Fairbairn.

"A little religion makes us afraid."—J. H. Newman.

of Tyre. **for me,** as agents in fulfilling My purposes. (21) **that day,** of Egypt's overthrow. **horn,** Ps. cxxxii. 17,[a] R. V., "an horn to bud forth unto the house of Israel;" "horn" a symbol of power. **bud forth,** i. e. to increase, to show itself. **opening,** etc., i. e. freedom to speak.[b] The prophet was ready now to resume his labors after a silence of many years.

Service Done for God Rewarded (vss. 17—20).—These words furnish us with three reflections. I. The disposal of states and nations is the work of Divine providence. II. That men may serve God really, when they do not serve Him by design. III. We shall never be losers by anything we do for God.—W. Jay.

a 1 Sa. ii. 1; Job xvi. 15.

b "When thy predictions shall have come to pass, thy words shall be more heeded." —Fausset.

"The eagle-winged pride of sky-aspiring and ambitious thoughts." —Shakespeare.

CHAPTER THE THIRTIETH.

1—5. This prophecy was uttered with ch. xxix. 1—16, about seven months before the fall of Jerusalem. (2) **Howl ye,** i. e. ye Egyptians. **woe worth,**[a] or alas! (3) **near,** a time for the manifestation of the divine judgments, Joel ii. 2, 3. **cloudy day,** darkened with calamities. **time .. heathen,** or for judging the nations. (4) **pain,** R. V., "anguish." (5) **Ethiopia,** etc., Heb. Cush, Phut, and Lud.[b] **mingled people,**[c] the mercenary forces of Egypt from various nations. **Chub,** the site is unknown.[d] **men .. league,** i. e. all allied lands in league with Egypt.

A Cloudy Day.—I. Prognostications of a cloudy day. 1. The laws of God are changeless and eternal; 2. Clouds do not come without causes. II. The experience of a cloudy day. 1. A cloudy day is dark; 2. A cloudy day obscures the heavens; 3. A cloudy day blots out the beauty of the earth. III. The consequences of a cloudy day. 1. The cloudy day may usher in a storm; 2. The cloudy day may break in refreshing showers; 3. The cloudy day may be followed by a bright day.—Adeney.

Egypt.—Egypt was one of the most ancient and one of the mightiest of kingdoms, and the researches of the traveler are still directed to explore the unparalleled memorials of its power. While the vestiges of other ancient monarchies can hardly be found amid the moldering ruins of their cities, those artificial mountains, visible at the distance of thirty miles, the pyramids of Egypt, without a record of their date, have withstood, unimpaired, all the ravages of time. No country ever produced so long a catalogue of kings. The learning of the Egyptians was proverbial. The number of their cities, and the population of their country, as recorded by ancient historians, almost surpass credibility. Nature and art united in rendering it a most fertile region. It was called the granary of the world. Yet the knowledge of all its greatness and glory deterred not the Jewish Prophets from declaring that Egypt would become "a base kingdom, and never exalt itself any more among the nations."—Keith.

a Comp. Sir W. Scott's 'Woe worth the chase; woe worth the day, that cost thy life, my gallant grey."

b Je. xlvi. 9.

c Je. xxv. 20.

d The Cubii are mentioned by Ptolemy as a people of Mareotis, a province of Egypt.

"He only is advancing in life whose heart is getting softer, whose blood warmer, whose brain quicker, whose spirit is entering into living peace. And the men who have this life in them are the true lords or kings of the earth—they, and they only." —John Ruskin.

"The pleasure that we cannot enjoy to the glory of the Lord will leave the ashes of bitterness behind it." — W. T. Ellis.

6—9. (6) **They .. uphold,** perhaps a ref. to the idols of Egypt. **pride .. down,** travelers tell how impressive are the ruins of Egypt.[e] **tower,** etc., see ch. xxix. 10. (7) **desolate,** etc., ch. xxix. 12. (8) **set a fire,** a fig. of Divine judgment.[f] (9) **messengers,** etc., Is. xviii. 1, 2. Egypt being the chief embodiment of secular power on the basis of pagan religion, the sudden collapse of her might is equivalent to a judgment on heathenism in general, and the moral effect of it conveys to the world a demonstration of the omnipotence of the one true God whom she had ignored and defied.—Exp. B. **careless Ethiopians,** they were dwelling in fancied security.[g]

Egypt.—Egypt became entirely subject to the Persians about three hundred and fifty years previous to the Christian era. It was afterwards subdued by the Macedonians, and was governed by the Ptolemies for the space of two hundred and ninety-four years; until about thirty years before Christ, it became a province of the Roman empire. It continued long in subjection to the Romans—tributary first to Rome, and afterwards to Constantinople. It was transferred, A. D. 641, to the dominion of the Saracens. In 1250 the Mamelukes deposed their rulers, and usurped the command of Egypt. A mode of government the most singular and surprising that ever existed on earth was established and maintained. Each successive ruler was raised to supreme authority, from being a stranger

e "Thebes appeared to me like entering a city of giants, who, after a long conflict, were all destroyed, leaving the ruins as the only proofs of their former existence." —Belzoni.

f Ps. lxxviii. 63; Je. vii. 20; Am. i. 4.

g "The cataracts interposing between them and Egypt should not save them."—Fausset.

Ju. viii. 11; Zep. ii. 15.

and a slave. No son of the former ruler—no native of Egypt succeeded to the sovereignty; but a chief was chosen from among a new race of imported slaves. When Egypt became tributary to the Turks in 1517, the Mamelukes retained much of their power, and every pacha was an oppressor and a stranger.—Keith.

10—12. (10) **multitude,** or large population. Egypt was noted for the swift increase of her people. (11) **terrible .. nations,** ch. xxviii. 7. (12) **rivers dry,** i. e. the artificial canals constructed for purposes of irrigation, and threading the whole land. This indicates a time of drought which would prepare the way for the invaders.[a]

A Divine Instrument.—The power that was to crush Egypt was already hovering over the fated nation. The vast populations of the Nile were to be opposed by a multitude of strangers whose warlike exploits had made them "the terrible of the nations;" the military genius of Pharaoh-Hophra was to come into conflict with Nebuchadnezzar, a still more able and victorious warrior. It was not the first time the great Babylonish monarch had come in contact with the arms of Egypt. Before his accession, while Crown Prince, he had fought the great battle of Carchemish, which expelled Pharaoh-Necho from Western Asia. During the siege of Jerusalem he had been disturbed by the attempt of Pharaoh-Necho to relieve that city, and during the siege of Troy, Egypt again interfered to help the Phœnicians. Nebuchadnezzar chafed under these annoyances; the proud prestige and pretensions of Egypt roused his envy and wrath, and he vowed to be revenged. All the time Jehovah was preparing him to be the agent to punish Egypt, and a rebellion against Pharoah-Hophra by Amasis, one of his officers, presented a favorable opportunity. Gathering his army of veterans, inured to warfare and flushed with recent victories, Nebuchadnezzar invaded Egypt and utterly subdued it from Migdol to Syene, the extreme frontiers of the kingdom, creating a horrible devastation, from which it did not recover for forty years. The Babylonish king knew not that he was simply the instrument of Jehovah in inflicting well-merited punishment, and thus fulfilling the words of the Divinely-inspired prophet. Whenever a nation reaches the crisis of its infamy, Divine justice fails not to provide the means of adequate retribution.—Hom. Com.

13—19. (13) **destroy their idols,**[a] idolatry is the great sin wh. calls for Divine vengeance on nations. **Noph,** or Memphis.[b] **a prince,** i. e. one of a native dynasty. (14) **Pathros,** Upper Egypt; ch. xxix. 14. **Zoan,** or Tanis.[c] **No,** or Thebes.[d] (16) **Sin,** or Pelusium.[e] (17) **Aven,** or Heliopolis.[f] **Pi-beseth,** the Bubastis of Herodotus, the seat of one of the annual festivals. Egyptian "Pa Bast," house of Bast or Pasht, the goddess to whom the cat was sacred, and who herself was represented under the aspect of the cat. The cat mummies were here preserved. The place lay on the Pelusiac arm of the Nile; the ruins, bearing the name Tell Basta, are not far from the modern Zagazig.—Cam. B. (18) **Tehaphnehes,** or Tahpanhes, about 30 miles S. W. of the ancient Pelusium, Je. ii. 16. **break .. yokes,** i. e. those imposed by Egypt. **cloud,** vs. 3. **daughters,** literally, or said figuratively of her towns. (19) **Thus,** in this thorough and complete manner.

Pharaoh-Hophra, the king of Egypt referred to in this paragraph, was a man of considerable capacity and enterprise. During the first years of his reign he subdued the island of Cyprus, besieged the city of Sidon by land and sea, and took it and made himself master of Phœnicia and Palestine. Elated with success, his pride knew no bounds, and he insanely boasted that it was not in the power of the gods to dethrone him. Libya, harassed by the Greeks, appealed for assistance. He despatched an army for their deliverance, but the Egyptians were disastrously defeated. It was whispered he had sent the Egyptian army into Libya to destroy it, and by surrounding himself with Greek mercenaries he was seeking to rule Egypt as a tyrant. His subjects rose in rebellion. Hophra sent Amasis, one of his officers, to quell the revolt; but the soldiers crowned him with a helmet and made him king. Hophra was compelled to retire into Upper Egypt, where he defended himself for some years, and Amasis made himself master of the rest of his dominions. The army of Nebuchadnezzar, taking advantage of these intestine troubles, swept down

"He who would avoid sin must not stand at the door of temptation."—Anon.

a "I will destroy the strength of Egypt; the metaphor is taken from the decrease or failing of the Nile, upon whose overflowing all the plenty and prosperity of Egypt depended." —Lowth.

"Did you ever feel the joy of winning a soul for Christ? I tell you there is no joy out of heaven which excels it — the grasp of the hand of one who says, 'By your means I was turned from darkness." — C. H. Spurgeon.

a Zec. xiii. 2.

b "Famous for the temple of Ptah (the god of fire), and for the worship of Osiris and Apis (from the conjunction of which came Osiri-apis, or Serapis), and the centre of Egyptian idolatry."—Wordsworth.

Comp. Is. xix. 3; Je. ii. 16; Ho. ix. 6.

c Ps. lxxviii. 12.

d Je. xlvi. 25.

e Ex. xvi. 1.

f Ge. xli. 45; Je. xliii. 13; Ho. iv. 15.

"What is meant by our neighbor we cannot doubt; it is every one with whom we are brought into contact, he or she, whosoever it be, whom we have any means of helping." — Dean Stanley.

upon Egypt and wrecked it from end to end. Egypt was made tributary to Babylon, and Nebuchadnezzar, having appointed Amasis as his viceroy, returned to his capital laden with the spoils of victory. As soon as the great king had departed Hophra emerged from his obscurity, and gathering an army of 30,000 mercenaries, made war against Amasis. The royal army was routed, Hophra taken prisoner, and was strangled by the populace.—Hom. Com.

20—23. (20) **eleventh year,** four months before fall of Jerusalem, comp. ch. xxix. 1, xxx. 1. (21) **broken the arm,** by a defeat in war, a ref. perchance to the defeat of Pharoah by the Chaldeans when he undertook to aid the Jews during this last siege. **Pharaoh,** i. e. Hophra, as in ch. xxix. **roller,** or bandage. (22) **arms,** both of them,[g] **to render him utterly helpless.** (23) **scatter, ch.** xxix. 12.

Self-destruction.—As Noah was drunk with his own wine, Goliath beheaded with his own sword, the rose destroyed by the canker bred in itself, the apple by the worm, Agrippina killed by Nero to whom she gave breath, so we are undone by ourselves, our destruction is of ourselves. The bitter waters of Marah and Meribah that we drink so deep of are of our own mingling and embittering; the rods that scourge us are of our own making. Sin, like a friar, whips itself; punishment is connate, innate to sin. We may thank our own folly for our own bane.—Spencer.

24—26. (24) **strengthen,** so that he may fully execute My mission. **groan,** as one dying of his wounds. (25) **know . . Lord,** bec. God has a high spiritual purpose, **even in His judgments of heathen nations. scatter,** ch. xxix. 12.

g The king of Babylon had previously dispossessed the king of Egypt of all his new conquests. This was the breaking of one arm. The attack on Egypt itself was the breaking of the other.

"Infallibility is the inability to confess error." —Fairbairn.

Two things are enough: 1. Never to set a bad example, and thereby never to be ashamed of Jesus Christ and His gospel. 2. To do whatever a real love of God requires without affectation or display." —Fenelon.

"Ambition is the mind's immodesty." —Davenant.

CHAPTER THE THIRTY-FIRST.

1—9. (1) **third month,** rather more than a month before Jerus. was taken.[a] (2) **multitude,** or people over whom he reigns. Like king like people. (3) **Assyrian,** the word "asshur" here is the name of a tree. We should therefore read, "Behold a T'asshur, a cedar in Lebanon," etc.; and the answer to the question of vs. 2 is that the position of Egypt is as unrivalled among the kingdoms of the world as this stately tree among the trees of the forest.—Exp. B. **cedar,** the kingly among trees. **shadowing shroud,** or garment of leaves casting a wide shadow. **thick boughs,** better as LXX., "the clouds." (4) **waters,** the Nile and its canals. **deep,** i. e. deep river, with its shallower streams and canals. With Egypt the river was the source of fertility. (5) **therefore,** bec. so well nourished.[b] **shot forth,** "shot them forth." (6) **fowls,** etc., comp. Da. iv. 12. The figs. of this vs. intimate that other nations sought the protection of Egypt. (7) **fair,** or beautiful, as a tree, and as a nation. (8) **garden of God,** paradise.[c] **hide him,** i. e. or "equal him." **chestnut,** or plane tree. (9) **envied him,** reference is to the feeling of surrounding nations towards Egypt. "All the kings of the East envied him and his greatness."

The Mighty Cedar in Lebanon.—Pharaoh, the impersonation of the spirit and might of Egypt, was a lofty cedar, with spreading branches, and its stop in the clouds. The allegory is easily read. The mighty cedar burying its head in the clouds, is the proud king and his powerful state, aspiring to a greatness that belongs to heaven. The fowls and beasts lodging under the shadow of the tree are the nations of the earth seeking his protection and subject to him (Dan. iv. 12). The trees in the garden of God are other mighty states impersonated in their rulers. The universal meaning which was given to the judgment on Egypt by representing it as the day of the Lord in ch. xxx. is suggested here in other ways, by the imposing height of the cedar, unapproachable by other trees in the garden of God; by the fowls and beasts of the field lodging in the tree—all nations seeking the protection of the Pharaoh; and by the shock which all nature receives when the great tree is cut down and flung upon the ground; and finally by the commotion occasioned in Sheol when Pharaoh descends among the dead (ch. xxxii.; Is. xiv.).—Cam. Bib.

10—14. (10) **thou. .he,** observe the blending of reference to the tree and the king. **thick boughs,** "clouds." **heart is lifted up,** herein lay **the sin that brought the judgment.** God did not visit for the prosperity,

a Je. xxxix. 2.

b Comp. Ps. i. 3.

c Ge. ii. 8; Ps. lxxx. 10.

"Beneficence, justice, protection, encouragements that subjects need and good princes disperse among them. So the deep filled this king, and he sent out his streams to all his subjects in his kingdom."—Pool.

"We should ask to be free from temptations of pleasure and comfort, no less than those of pain and sorrow." — Mary Lyon.

but for the pride which the prosperity engendered.[a] **I have delivered,** R. V., "I will even deliv." (11) **mighty one,** here referring to Nebuchadnezzar, king of Babylon.[b] **heathen,** "nations." (12) **strangers,** the Chaldean invaders. **his shadow,** vss. 3, 6. (13) **ruin,** i. e. fallen trunk and branches. **remain,** R. V., "dwell." (14) **to the end,** i. e. this is the design of the Divine judgments.[c] **stand .. height,** rely on themselves, on their own height.

Conceits of Pride.—When a proud man thinks best of himself, then God and man think worst of him; all his glory is but like a vapor, which climbeth as though it would go up to heaven, but when it comes to a little height, it falls down again, and never ascends more. So Adam thought that the fair apple should make him like his Maker, but God resisted his pride, and that apple made him like the serpent that tempted him with it. Absalom thought that rebellion would make him a king, but God resisted his pride, and his rebellion hanged him on a tree.—H. Smith.

15—18. (15) **went down, ch. xxvi. 15.** .**covered the deep,** as a mourner covers himself with sackcloth.[d] **great waters,** or flood-waters. **Lebanon to mourn,** (16) **shake,** with fear. **to hell,** "to Sheol;" note the sense in wh. a nation can be said to go down to Sheol; it is a fig. of shameful and hopeless desolation. **comforted,** ref. is to tributary peoples, or other great nations already overthrown in measure comforted bec. this great nation shares their fate. (17) **into hell,** vs. 16. **his arm,** auxiliaries, used for his purposes. (18) **thou like,** comp. vs. 2. The application is now made to Egypt. **uncircumcised,**[e] the term is applied to those slain w. the sword and buried indiscriminately w. no funeral rites. ch. xxviii. 10, xxxii. 19, 20.

"Caused Lebanon to Mourn."—The prophet's representation naturally is not quite consistent. The home of Pharaoh, as a cedar, is Lebanon, but it is the waters of Egypt, magnified here into the "deep" absolutely, that nourish him. Hence both the deep and Lebanon, with all the trees thereon, mourn and faint (Is. li. 20) over his fall. What the language primarily expresses is the idea of the world-wide importance of the Egyptian power, so that, as the greatest forces of nature minister to its growth, all creation is affected by its fall. Cf. xxxii. 9, 10.—Camb. Bible.

a Pr. viii. 13, xi. 2, xvi. 18.

b "Called the 'mighty one' (El, a name of God), bec. he was God's representative and instrument of judgment." —Fausset.

c "Thy destruction shall be a warning to other kings and potentates, to deter them from priding themselves in the time of their prosperity." —Lowth.

d "The deep, the source of Egypt's prosperity (vs. 4) was made to mourn, being dried up, instead of giving forth its waters, its glad abundance." —Spk. Com.

e "As circumcision was an object of mocking to thee, thou shalt lie in the midst of the uncircumcised, slain by the sword." —Grotius.

CHAPTER THE THIRTY-SECOND.

1—5. (1) **twelfth year,** etc., prob. one year and seven months after the destruction of Jerusalem.[a] (2) **lamentation,** or dirge. **Thou art,** etc., R. V., "Thou wast likened unto" i.e. flatterers, and courtiers made Pharaoh think himself to be the king of beasts, whereas he was in reality only a crocodile in his own river.[b] **camest forth,** etc., R. V., brakest forth." Ewald translates, "thou didst spout with thy nostrils." The thought suggested is Egypt's activity in war. **troubledst .. feet,** as a crocodile on landing and going forth. (3) **spread .. net,** ch. xii. 13. **with a company,** i.e. the Chaldæans. Their invasion was God's net, i.e. God's judgment. (4) **leave, etc.,** comp. ch. xxix. 5. (5) **thy height,** fig. taken from the high cedar, wh. when prostrate, shall seem to fill up the valleys.

Princes Compared to Lions (vs. 2).—Nothing is more common, in the East, than the comparing princes to lions; but the comparing them to crocodiles, if possessed of naval power, or strong by a watery situation, has hardly ever been mentioned. D'Herbelot, however, cites an Eastern poet, who, celebrating the prowess of Gelaleddin, surnamed Mankberni, and Khovarezme Shah, a most valiant Persian prince, said, "He was dreadful as a lion in the field, and not less terrible in the water than a crocodile." The power of the ancient kings of Egypt seems to be represented after the same manner, by the Prophet Ezekiel, ch. xxix. 3, "Behold I am against thee, Pharaoh, king of Egypt, the great dragon (the great crocodile) that lieth in the midst of his rivers, which hath said, My river is mine own, and I have made it myself."—Harmer.

6—10. (6) **water..blood,** indicating the abundance of the slain. **land ..swimmest,** or the land of thy swimming.[d] The land watered by the Nile. (7) **put thee out,** R. V., "extinguish," as a candle is put out. Phar-

a "Jerusalem was by this time overthrown, and Amasis was beginning his revolt against Pharaoh Hophra." —Fausset.

b "Pharoah should have been like the king of beasts, but he is a mere sea-monster. There is strong irony here, bec. the Eg. king was proud of the comparison between himself and the mighty crocodile." —Spk. Com.

"The first step in the art of painting is to learn the value of shadow; the first step in the art of living is to learn the value of misfortune." —Ivan Panin.

d Carrying on the figure of the crocodile.

aoh is figured here as a star. comp. Isa. xiv. 12, "How art thou fallen from heaven, O shining one, morning star!" (8) **set darkness,** so that everything shall look dark and dismal.[a] (9) **vex,** etc., trouble terrify by the story wh. the exiles shall carry of Egypt's utter desolation. (10) **amazed at thee,** ch. xxvi. 16, xxvii. 35, xxx. 9. **brandish,** or flourish.

Darkness. 1. A symbol of destruction and mourning. 2. A proof of the awfulness and completeness of the destruction. 3. Suggests how all the forces of nature are subservient to the purpose of an avenging Deity.—Hom. Com.

11—16. (11) **sword,** emblem of the destructive power. (12) pomp, the splendid temples, palaces, etc., for which Egypt was famous. (13) **destroy .. beasts,** comp. ch. xxix. 11.[b] "Henceforth Pharaoh was no longer to flood other peoples with his overwhelming forces." (14) **deep,** R. V., "make their waters clear" **like oil,** i.e. smoothly, peacefully.[c] "The waters of Egypt, no more troubled by the foot of man or beast, shall run smooth like oil." (15) **then .. Lord,** i.e. this shall be the gracious issue of My judgments. (16) **lamentation,** vs. 2.

Unhappiness of Ambition.—Look at the tender climbing plant of summer: it takes hold of some object, and creeps along upward till its tendrils shoot high and beautifully into the air; but the prop is taken away, and there it stands, reaching out its fingers for something to fasten upon: full of life and vigor still, but sinking because its support is taken away, and falling like a worthless weed to the ground. Such, even at the very moment of its greatest vigor, is often the state of those who seek worldly greatness. Look at all history: when were its great men so wretched, as when they had attained the highest point of exaltation! "He has gained everything," said a companion of Napoleon, when he was in the zenith of prosperity, "and yet he is unhappy."—Lewis.

17—21. vss. 17—32, Dirge of the Vision of Hades, which is the most weird in all literature. (17) **the month,** prob. the twelfth month.[d] a fortnight later than vss. 1—16. (18) **wail comp.** vss. 2, 16; **cast .. down, i.e.** foretell its destruction. **nether parts .. pit.** fig. for utter and hopeless destruction.[e] (19) **pass,** or surpass. Other nations have perished, so shalt thou.[f] **uncircumcised,** i.e. those dishonored and profaned in death, slain by the sword and deprived of proper burial. (20) **delivered .. sword,** better, "the sword is put forth." **draw her,** like carcasses to the grave addressed to the warders of Sheòl.. (21) **The strong,** etc.: this vs. represents the great tyrants in Sheol coming to meet and welcome the king of Egypt and his auxiliaries.[g]

Sympathetic Sorrow.—I. Sympathetic sorrow is called for by the troubles of our fellow-men. II. It is especially required by the world's sin. 1. We should grieve more over sin than over external calamity. 2. We should grieve over sin rather than coldly condemn it. III. Sympathetic sorrow is a ministering angel of mercy. 1. It is a source of consolation. 2. It is an inspiration of deliverance.—Pul. Com.

Dirge Over Egypt and Its Multitude (vss. 17—32).—It is a funeral dirge primarily over the multitude or nation of Egypt; and so in the case of the other nations referred to, Asshur, Elam, and the rest. These peoples are all gone down to Sheol, uncircumcised, slain with the sword. There in the world of the dead each people has an abode to itself. Around one chief grave the graves of the general mass are gathered. The chief grave is probably that of the prince, though the prince is considered the genius, the embodiment of the spirit and being of the nation. The prophet regards the nations, even when no more existing on earth, as still having a subsistence in the world of the dead (cf. on Sodom, ch. xvi.). They are beings, who, having once lived, continue throughout all time. Though passed from the stage of history they still subsist in Sheol.—Camb. Bib.

22—25. (22) **Asshur,** i.e. the king of Assyria. his graves, the masc. or fem. gender is used as the king or country is thought of. (23) **sides .. pit,**[a] R. V., "uttermost parts," i. e. the depths of the pit. **terror,** which Asshur caused among the nations by his might. (24) **Elam,**[b] in Persia; an auxiliary of Assyria, conquered by Nebuchadnezzar.[c] **borne their shame,** "the just retribution of their lawless pride." (25) **bed,** a final bed, or a grave.

[a] So brilliant is the shining of the stars in the East that a great horror of darkness is represented by their being covered.

[b] "The picture is ideally true, not to be interpreted by the letter; the political ascendency of Egypt was to cease with the Chaldaean conquest." —Fairbairn.

[c] "No longer shall they descend violently, as the overflowing Nile, on other countries, but shall be still and sluggish in political action." —Fausset.

[d] vs. 1. The LXX. say the first month.

[e] Eze. xxxi. 14; Is. xiv. 15.

[f] "What reason hast thou now to prefer thyself before others? Since thou shalt undergo the same fate with the worst of them." —Lowth.

[g] Is. xiv. 9.

"Vaulting ambition which o'erleaps itself."—Shakespeare.

"Genuine humility brings to elevation its only corrective. It fixes the eye on the lowliness which in all human greatness is present with the greatness." — Hengstenberg.

[a] Is. xiv. 15.

[b] Ge. xiv. 1; Is. xxii. 6.

[c] Je. xlix. 34—38.

"The Elamites were a fierce and warlike people. In the records of Assurbanipal we have a detailed account of five campaigns

against Elam, and his final triumph over Elam seems to have been one of his proudest boasts."
—Spk. Com.

d "Northern nations; the Moschi and Tibareni, between the Black and Caspian Seas."
—Fausset.

To live in the presence of great truths and eternal laws, to be led by permanent ideals — that is what keeps a man patient when the world ignores him, and calm and unspoiled when the world praises him.—Balzac.

a Is. lviii. 1; 1 Cor. xiv. 8.

"It is the duty of each to be ever in a wakeful, listening attitude. The look-out on board the ocean steamer and the advanced night-picket of a slumbering army has each a responsible post. The safety of both vessel and army depends upon their keenness of vision and delicacy of hearing. The duties of the civil and spiritual watchman are alike in demanding a highly sensitive alertness and heroic fidelity." Hom. Com.

b "Think not that bec. the walls and gates of Jerus. may be destroyed, thy duty as a watchman to the house of Israel will cease. No; from that very time it will have new obligations, and thou wilt have new admonitions, consolations, and promises to give. The fall of Jerusalem will be a renewal of thy commission." —Wordsworth.

c Je. ii. 25.

Companionship in Woe.—I. Duty ofttimes is exceedingly painful. II. Sin always leads to terrible degradation. III. Self-esteem is no safeguard against just retribution. IV. Association with others will be determined by moral affinities. V. The ruin of others is impotent to deter from sin. VI. Self-inflation is the prelude to eternal shame. VII. God's terror is supreme over man's.—Davies.

26—29. (26) **Meshech,** ch. xxvii. 13. **Tubal,** ch. xxvii. 13.[d] (27) **hell,** Sheol, the Underworld. . **iniquities . . bones,** comp. expression "with their sins upon their heads." (28) **thou,** i.e. Pharaoh himself must prepare himself **broken,** by a violent death. **(29) Edom, ch. xxv. 12. with their might,** R. V., "in their might."

The Burial of Warriors (vs. 27.)—The ancients, in every part of the world, were accustomed to inter their warriors in complete armor. We are informed by Chardin that the Mingrelian soldier sleeps with his sword under his head, and his arms by his side; and he is buried in the same manner, his arms being placed in the same position. The allusion of Ezekiel to this ancient custom is extremely clear.—Paxton.

30—32. (30) **princes . . north,** i.e. of Syria. **Zidonians,** who shared the fate of Tyre. **their terror,** R. V., "in the terror wh. they caused by their might they are ashamed." (31) **comforted,** with the miserable comfort that others have to suffer even as he. (32) **my terror,** God making these nations marked examples of His vengeance on iniquity. Cam. B. "for he caused his terror."

A Vision of the Unseen World.—I. The prophet's vision itself. II. Its historical parallel. III. Its personal application. 1. A common impending fate. 2. A poetical consolation. 3. The real redeeming thought, viz. that the future to which we look forward, as the disciples and followers of Christ, is neither the dark grave in the cemetery nor the little less inviting Sheol of Hebrew thought, but the home of the blessed in the near presence of God, where life is free and full and pure, the mansions of the Father's house.—Clarkson.

CHAPTER THE THIRTY-THIRD.

Ch. xxxiii—xxxix. form a section of the Prophecy which deals with Israel's Restoration and Eternal Security. The greatness of the blow had stunned them, and, as the prophet had foreshewn (xxiv. 23), a stupor had fallen on them. Yet the Lord had not made a full end of Israel. The old era was closed, but a new era was about to open, and a new Israel about to arise. It is of this new era that the prophet has now to speak, and of the hopes of the new Israel and of the conditions of being embraced in it.—Cam. B.

1—6. (2) **the sword,** God's judgment by a hostile army. **coasts,** or borders; put generally for "their country." R. V., "from among them." **watchman,** to warn of the enemy's approach. Watchmen were placed in turrets on the city walls, or in outposts. (3) **blow,** etc.,[a] this was the appointed signal. (4) **blood . . head,** i.e. he must bear the responsibility himself, and cannot accuse the watchman. (5) **deliver his soul,** i.e. preserve his life, by adequate defence, or by timely flight. (6) **taken . . iniquity,** so comes under judgment. **blood . . require,** i.e. the watchman must answer to me for his unfaithfulness and its consequences.

The True Watchman (vs. 6).—I. The true watchman's vision of his work. He sees—1. It entails great responsibility on himself; 2. Involves the greatest results to his hearers; 3. Utters the emotions of God; 4. Proclaims both the hope and the method of man's improvement. II. The true watchman's vision of the conduct of others. He sees—1. The gross sins of many of them; 2. The hypocrisy of many more.—W. R. Thomas.

7—11. (7) **thee a watchman,** ch. iii. 17.[b] (8) **surely die,** i.e. by a violent death. "The qualification, if thou dost not repent, is supposed." (9) **delivered thy soul,** from the responsibility of his doom. (10) **If our,** etc. R. V., "Our transgressions are upon us." **pine . . them,** ch. xxiv. 23. These are the words of persons despairing of God's mercy, and thence taking encouragement to go on in sin,[c] while they harden their heart against the prophet's instructions. The chief task for Ezek. was to change this attitude of sullen impenitence into hopefulness and submission as they learn the possibility and conditions of Divine forgiveness. (11) **no pleasure,** etc., 2 Sa. xiv. 15; Eze. xviii. 32. God desires men to live; the past is not irrevocable.

A Solemn Question.—"Why will ye die?" The death to which this question relates is not temporal death, which is unavoidable; it is death eternal. 1. Do you think that it is imaginary? 2. Do you think that it is a trivial evil? 3. Do you think that it is uncertain in its occurrence? 4. Do you think that it is imposed upon you by an unalterable decree? 5. Do you think that the Divinely-appointed method of escape from it is not satisfactory? 6. Do you think that on a view of the whole circumstances it is to be preferred?—G. Brooks.

Mercy Divine and Human.—I have seen the life-buoy spun out to a drowning man, and, amid the crowd on the pier that gazed in horror, there was none, as they watched its course over the roaring waves, but wished in his heart that it might reach its mark. Nor is it only that God is "willing that all should come to Him, and live." What mother but would open her door who heard the knocking, and recognized the well-known voice of some poor, fallen child, that had sunk down there amid the winter drift, and cried, with failing breath, O mother, mother dear, open and let me in. And who thinks so ill of God as to believe that when He hears such a cry at the door of mercy, He will not rise to let us and to welcome us in!—T. Guthrie.

12—16. (12) **righteousness,** etc., ch. xviii. 24, 26, 27. The past life does not of necessity determine the future either in itself or in the judgment of God. Man is free to repent and live; to this end God punishes sin. (13) **live,** i.e. "enjoy the favor of God and have this favor reflected in outward felicity." This principle of individual responsibility is not to prevail in the old order, but in the new epoch wh. is just about to be inaugurated. **trust to,** or lean upon, think the good will outweigh his evil. (14) **lawful and right,** or judgment and justice. (15) **restore the pledge,** ch. xviii. 7. **give .. robbed,**[a] make the full restitution which is the sign of a true penitence. **walk .. life,** ch. xx. 11. (16) **mentioned,** R. V., "remembered against" ch. xviii. 22.

Past Righteousness will not Excuse Present Sin.—We are judged chiefly, at all events, by what we are, rather than by what we were. Moreover, there is no possibility of our having acquired an extra stock of merit in the past which we can set off against our present failings. We never have a balance on the credit side of our account with Heaven. An employer cares little for old testimonials. He must see a certificate of character up to date. If a man has borne an excellent reputation for years, and at last breaks down and disgraces himself, he is said to have "lost his character." His good name in the past now counts for nothing. It is utterly gone. Now, the practical warning that issues from these considerations is that we must take good heed to our present life. We need to be on our guard against falling, even to the last.—Pul. Com.

17—20. (17) **not equal,** or fair. (18, 19) **when,** etc., comp. vss. 13—16. (20) **way .. equal,** ch. xviii. 25. **Every one,** etc., "the time was come to call for personal decisions, to appeal to each man to embrace for himself the offer of pardon and salvation." This is the supreme aim of the prophet in this chapter—to create a consciousness of the worth and responsibility of the individual: to point out that the new Israel must be composed of individuals who enter it on the condition of repentance. Character not birth is to count in the new epoch.

21—24. (21) **captivity,** i.e. Jehoiachin's. **one .. escaped.** There is something suspicious, in the date of the arrival of the fugitives, a year and a half after the fall of the city. The Syr. read or suggested "eleventh year," which would leave about six months for the news of the city's fall to be carried by messengers to the exiles in Babylon, and this date is now very generally accepted.—Cam. B. **city is smitten,** comp. 2 Ki. xxv. 4. (22) **hand,** etc., the expression prob. indicates a state of trance. **opened,** to speak to the people, who were stricken dumb. with the sad tidings This was the turning point of Ezekiel's prophecy, no longer silent he enters upon his ministry of consolation and hope. (24) **wastes,** so recently

[a] Le. vi. 5.

"God's seed will come to God's harvest." —Rutherford.

"Even when the preacher's conscience is free from guilt in regard to the ungodly who perish in their sins, what a sorrow does it occasion in the life of the preacher when he has to see the impenitent die in their sins! 'I would not willingly be saved,' said Augustine, 'without you.' "

"We may talk of the best means of doing good, but, after all, the greatest difficulty lies in doing it in a proper spirit; 'speaking the truth in love,' 'in meekness instructing those that oppose themselves,' with the meekness and gentleness of Christ. I have known anxious sinners drop the subject of religion in consequence of a preacher addressing them in an angry tone."—Nettleton.

"Ignorance is always obstinately one-sided. Reminds one of the Irish juryman who had never met eleven such obstinate men as his fellow-jurors; and of

desolated by the conqueror. **one,** a single person; yet he found God faithful to His promise; much more shall we, who are many. The words of the infatuated men who exulted in the havoc they were making on the mountains of Judæa may sound to us like a blasphemous travesty of this argument; but they were no doubt seriously meant. They afford one more instance of the boundless capacity of the Jewish race for religious self-delusion, and their no less remarkable insensibility to that in which the essence of religion lay.—Exp. B.

The Fallacy. 1. The descendants of Abraham may not be his true children. They are Abraham's children who inherit Abraham's faith. 2. Where no right exists, the number of claimants will not create it. 3. Each individual must seek individual grace. We cannot be made citizens of the kingdom of heaven en masse. We must go single file through the strait gate. 4. There is room in the grace of God for the greatest number. The multitude of applicants can never be too great for infinite bounty. Christ came to give his life a ransom "for many."—W. F. Adeney.

25—29. (25) **eat .. blood,** i.e. flesh slaughtered in such a way that the blood remains in it. This was prohibited by the Levitical law.[a] (26) **stand .. sword,** i.e. rely on your own power. Might is your right. (27) **they .. wastes,** prob. referring to Gedaliah's party, wh. hoped to settle in Jerusalem, and re-establish the kingdom. The hope of Israel was not this lawless remnant, God will surely destroy it. (28) **most desolate,** by the destruction of the remaining remnant. **pomp, etc., ch. xxiv. 21.** (29) **Then,** i.e. when the judgments are complete.

Fear of Judgment.—Jerome used to say that it seemed to him as if the trumpet of the last day was always sounding in his ear, saying: "Arise, ye dead, and come to judgment." The generality, however, think but little of this awful and important period. A Christian king of Hungary being very sad and pensive, his brother, who was a gay courtier, was desirous of knowing the cause of his sadness. "O brother!" said the king, "I have been a great sinner against God, and know not how to die, or how to appear before Him in judgment." His brother, making a jest of it, said: "These are but melancholy thoughts." The king made no reply; but it was the custom of the country that if the executioner was to sound a trumpet before any man's door, he was presently led to execution. The king, in the dead hour of the night, sent the executioner to sound the trumpet before his brother's door, who, hearing it, and seeing the message of death, sprang into the king's presence, beseeching to know in what he had offended. "Alas! brother," said the king, "you have never offended me. And is the sign of execution so dreadful, and shall not I, who have greatly offended, fear to be brought before the judgment-seat of Christ?"—Biblical Treasury.

30—33. (30) **against thee,** R. V., "of thee." The character of his last utterance, vindicating, as it might seem, the claim of the exiles to "possess the land," as against that of the remnant "in the wastes," may even have made him popular.—Pulp. Com. Yet while they listened self-interest hindered the reception of God's word, their conduct was not altered. **in the doors, where** the people often sit.[a] (31) **as the people,** as if they meant to listen and obey, but with no real intention of doing what you enjoin. (32) **lovely song,** of wh. they like the sound, not the words.[b] (33) **this .. pass,** esp. what Ezekiel had been saying about the remnant left amid the desolations of Jerusalem.

On Hearing Sermons.—I. The Gospel may be heard with pleasure but without profit. 1. When the mind only is gratified; 2. When the affections are merely excited. II. The converse is true. 1. Does the Word make you watchful?. 2. Prayerful? 3. Lead you to obedience? III. It is desirable that the Gospel should be heard both with pleasure and profit. 1. The pleasure should arise from the message, not from the rhetoric.; 2. From our felt sense of participation in the benefits of which the message speaks; 3. From our determination to obey the message.—Stems and Twigs.

Careless Hearers.—We crossed and recrossed the river several times by the ferry-boat at Basle. We had no object in the world, but merely amusement and curiosity, to watch the simple machinery by which

---

the recruit who maintained he was the only man of his company who was keeping step. The sinner is ready to blame any one but himself, and even dares to impugn the equity of the great Judge of all the earth. The reckless audacity of such a charge reveals his own condemnation."
—Hom. Com.

[a] See Ge. ix. 4; Le. iii. 17, vii. 26, xvii. 10—14; De. xii. 16; Ac. xv. 29.

"Perhaps the phrase should be trans. 'near the blood,' in allusion to the idolatrous rite of pouring the blood of the slain beast into a vessel or pit, and then eating part of the sacrifice just by it."—Spencer.

"We are the basket of the sower—that is, of Christ. He has deigned to put the seed in us, which we must scatter among our ignorant brethren." — St. Augustine.

[a] "The ruling race take great pride in their fine and lofty gates, whose double doors stand open all day long, revealing the refreshing shade within of the peacock tree, etc. . . On the carved benches, each side of the gate, lounge the gaily-clad retainers of the great man. And he himself often takes his seat there."—Van Lennep.

[b] "They praise thy eloquence, but care not for the subject of it as a real and personal thing; just as many do in the modern Church."
—S. Jerome.

the same current is made to drift the boat in opposite directions from side to side. To other passengers it was a business, to us a sport. Our hearers use our ministry in much the same manner when they come to it out of the idlest curiosity, and listen to us as a means of spending a pleasant hour. That which should ferry them across to a better state of soul they use as a mere pleasure-boat, to sail up and down in, making no progress after years of hearing. Alas! it may be sport to them, but it is death to us because we know it will ere long be death to them.—Spurgeon.

"A true prophet will always leave behind him the impression of a true prophet."

CHAPTER THE THIRTY-FOURTH.

1—6. (2) **shepherds,** or unfaithful rulers and princes.[a] **feed themselves,**[b] comp. 2 Cor. xii. 14; Ph. ii. 21. (3) **fat,** the Sept. has "the milk." These figures imply the levying of exorbitant taxes. (4) **diseased,** or convalescent: those, weak while recovering from disease. **broken,** as by wolves. **driven away,** by force, **lost,** i.e. wandered away. **sought .. lost,** contrast Lu. xv. 4. **force,** etc., comp. Ex. i. 13, 14[c] (5) **meat,** or a prey; bec. not defended. (6) **mountains,** etc., i.e. the nation weakened by misrule loses its power of defence, its national spirit, and falls an easy victim to foreign powers.

The Divine Shepherd (chapter xxxiv.)—I. All rulers have great responsibilities, they are shepherds. II. The failure of rulers is ever a great misfortune to subjects. III. All misrule will only come to an end in the proportion that God Himself reigns over a people. 1. What is the method by which God will become consciously the ruler of man? 2. What will be the results of such rule?—W. R. Thomas.

Rulers.—The ruler is raised to a lofty dignity and endowed with special resources in order to watch over and protect the interests of his people. The wants and even the luxuries of life are secured to him that he may be free to devote his powers to the general good. He is keenly alive to any act of treachery on the part of his people; but he is none the less treacherous when he abuses his high trust in seeking only his own advantage. He has basely abdicated the highest functions of his kinghood. The king should be a father to his people, providing for, watching over, and protecting them. It is a severe strain on the loyalty of a people when their sufferings win no pity from their selfish ruler. It is a blot on the brilliant reign of Queen Elizabeth that the brave seamen who defeated the Spanish Armada were left to rot in their ships or die in the streets of the naval ports because there were no hospitals to receive the wounded. "It would grieve any man's heart," wrote Lord Howard, the High Admiral of that day, "to see men that have served so valiantly die so miserably." Modern hospitals and infirmaries are the practical outcome of an enlightened Christian philanthropy.—Geo. Barlow.

[a] Je. xxiii. 1.

[b] "It was characteristic of the last kings of Judah that while the distress and misery of the people daily increased the kings exacted more and more of their subjects, and lavished more and more on personal luxury and show."
—Spk. Com.

[c] Le xxv. 43, 46.

"A magistrate should look upon himself as sustaining the office of a shepherd, that makes it his chief business to take care of his flock, not as if he were going to a feast to fill himself and satiate his appetite, or to a market to make what gain he can to himself."
—Plato.

7—10. (8) **became meat,** vs. 5. **search for,** so as to be sure that none were missing, and so as quickly to bring back the wandering. (10) **require my flock,** or demand an account of My flock from them, and punish them if there are any missing.[a] **cease,** or remove fr. the office in wh. they have proved unfaithful.

Tyranny and Wrong cannot last for ever: the reckoning-day comes on apace. In all wickedness there is weakness that will soon or later be fatal to its reign. It is related of Lord Ampthill, British Ambassador to the Court of Berlin, that during his mission in Rome he possessed a huge boa-constrictor, and interested himself in watching its habits. One day the monster escaped from the box where he supposed it was asleep, quietly wound itself around his body, and began gradually to tighten its folds. His position became extremely perilous; but the consummate coolness and self-possession which had enabled him to win many a diplomatic triumph befriended him in this dangerous emergency. He remembered there was a bone in the throat of the serpent which, if he could find and break, he would save himself. He was aware that either he or the snake must perish. Not a moment must be lost in hesitation. He deliberately seized the head of the serpent, thrust his hand down its throat and snapped the vital bone. The coils were relaxed, the victim fell at his feet, and he was free. So one day the weak place in wrong-doing is sure

[a] Comp. Je. lii. 9—11.

"Rather than the work shall be undone, I will do it myself, and then it is sure to be well done. Aristotle tells of a certain Persian who, being asked, 'What did most of all feed the horse?' answered, 'The master's eye;' and of a certain African who, when it was demanded, 'What was the best manure or soil for a field?' answered 'The owner's footsteps'—that is, his presence.

Shepherds should reside with their flocks; the Arch-shepherd will not fail to do so."—Trapp.

b "Of sin, error, and unbelief."—S. Augustine.

c Is. lxv. 9, 10; Je. xxiii. 3; Eze. xxviii. 25, xxxvi. 24, xxxvii. 21, 22.

d "The pastures of the mountains of Israel on which the sheep feed, and the rivers of which they drink, may be interpreted to mean the spiritual pastures and stream of Holy Scripture, which have flowed into all lands."—S. Augustine.

"When things are at the worst God himself will set in: He reserveth His holy hand for a dead lift."—Trapp.

a Lit. "Between the small cattle and the cattle of rams and he-goats." A fig. for "between the poor and the rich."

b "The flock was obliged to eat what they had trodden into the dirt, and drink that which they had muddied. . . The great men were so vexatious to the poor that what little coarse food they had was submitted to them."—Mat. Henry.

"It is a consolation to the suffering that deliverance from the highest source will come, and will come at the best possible moment. Men will not be judged (as they are often now) in classes, but as individuals. A rich man may be saved in spite of the encumbrance of riches; some poor men will be outcasts eternally

to be smitten and it must succumb. Over the head of every tyrant there hangs the sword of retributive justice.—Geo. Barlow.

11—14. (11) **search .. out,** God Himself will do what the shepherds neglected. He is the proper Owner of the fleck, they were only under-shepherds. The repetition of the pronoun I makes it emphatic. (12) **cloudy .. day,**[b] of national calamity and humiliation. (13) **people,** "peoples." . . **gather them,** this would be the first sign of returning favor.[c] (14) **good pasture,** Ps. xxiii. 2. **high mountains,** R. V. "upon the mountains of the height of Israel," ch. vi. 2, 3.[d] **good fold,** secure and pleasant under the just and beneficient rule of God.

"I will seek out my Sheep and Deliver Them."—1. The restoration of the exiled Jews may be one part of the fufilment of this promise. 2. The coming of the Son of man "to seek and to save that which was lost" was a later and better fulfilment. And we find a further, a perpetual Divine redemption of this ancient word of promise in: 3. The putting forth by the Church of Christ of all its redeeming energies. Whenever and however any one that, filled with the spirit of his Saviour, seeks to raise the fallen, to bring back to truth and piety those that have gone away in the darkness, to heal the stricken and suffering spirit and to enrobe it with "the garment of praise," there God is himself "searching out his sheep," and "delivering them from the places whither they have wandered." How excellent is the portion of those who are his agents in this gracious work!—Clarkson.

15—19. (15) **lie down,** the sign of their being satisfied and secure, Ps. xxiiil. 2. (16) **I will seek,** etc., marks the individualizing pity of the good Shepherd over each particular sheep. **destroy the fat,** i.e. those who have made themselves fat at the expense of the sheep. **judgment,** or discretion; treating each one according to his deserts: see vs. 17. (17) **between .. cattle,** i.e. bet. weak and strong cattle[a] even among the people the strong shall no more crush the weak. (18) **tread down,** etc., spoiling so that others cannot use, what they do not want themselves.[b] **deep** R. V., "clear" (19) **my flock,** wh. for My sake ought to be so carefully tended.

A Poor but Good Preacher.—

A good man ther was of religioun,
That was a poure persone of a toun:
But riche he was of holy thought and werk.
He was also a lerned man, a clerk,
That Cristes gospel trewely wolde preche.
His parishens devoutly wolde he teche.
Benigne he was, and wonder diligent,
And in adversite ful patient:
And swiche he was ypreved often sithes.
Ful loth wer him to cursen for his tithes,
But rather wolde he yeven out of doute,
Unto his poure parishens aboute,
Of his offring, and eke of his substance.
He coude in litel thing have suffisance.
Wide was his parish, and houses fer asonder,
But he ne left nought for no rain ne thonder,
In sickenesse and in mischief to visite
The ferrest in his parish, moche and lite,
Upon his fete, and in his hand a staf.
This noble ensample to his shepe he yaf,
That first he wrought, and afterward he taught.
Out of the Gospel he the wordes caught,
And this figure he added yet thereto,
That if gold ruste, what shuld iren do!
For if a preest be foule, on whom we trust,
No wonder is a lewed man to rust:
Wel ought a preest ensample for to yeve,
By his clenenesse, how his shepe shulde live.
He sette not his benefice to hire,
And lette his shepe acombred in the mire,
And ran unto London unto Seint Poules,

To seken him a chantere for soules,
Or with a brotherhede to be with old:
But dwelt at home, and kepte wel his fold,
So that the wolfe ne made it not miscarie.—Chaucer.

20—23. (20) **judge between,** so as to relieve the sufferers and punish the oppressors. The fat stands for the rich and arrogant rulers; the lean for the humble poor of the people. (21) **thrust,** etc., fig. taken from the rough ways of rams and he-goats.[a] (22) **save,** out of the hand of such self-seeking oppressors. (23) **one shepherd,** the full and final reference must be to Messiah.[b] **servant David,** a second and a greater **David.**[c] "All that the word means is that the Messiah will be one who comes in the spirit and power of David, a representative of the ancient family who carries to completion the work so nobly begun by his great ancestor."—Exp. B.

24—27. (24) **their God,** i.e. I will be in manifest and gracious relations with them as their God. **a prince,** or living representative and agent of God. God manifest. (25) **covenant of peace,** one that shall ensure peace for them. **evil beasts,** fig. expression for heathen foes. **sleep .. woods,** a sure sign of security. The peopling of a country results in driving the wild beasts from the woods and forests. (26) **showers,** periodical rains, on which the fruitfulness of the land depended.[d] **a blessing,** i.e. altogether blessed. So the last words of the vs. imply. **showers of blessing,** i.e. bringing blessing. (27) **safe,** ref. prob. is to the harvest of land and tree, wh. should be secured to the people, not stolen by marauders.[e] **bands,** R. V., "bars."

Showers of Blessing (vs. 26.)—I. We are to observe that this communication is needed by the world. 1. The condition of the heathen world; 2. The slow progress of religion among men. II. That this communication is promised by God. 1. Its nature is defined by His promise; 2. Its extent is also defined; 3. His purpose defines the result of this communication. III. It must be sought by the Church. 1. By removal from the world; 2. By the cultivation of union and love; 3. By the employment of zealous and vigorous exertions; 4. By the offering of fervent and importunate prayer.—J. Parsons.

28—31. (28) **prey,** reference to the perils of foreign invasions. **dwell safely,** Je. xxiii. 6. (29) **plant of renown,** R. V.. "plantation for renown;" i. e. in the Messianic days the earth will yield abundant crops, no more danger fr. scarcity at home. Comp. Is. lx. 21, lxi. 3. **shame .. heathen,** refers to the reproaches of the heathen on account of the national humiliation. (30) **I the Lord,** vs. 24. (31) **my flock,** Jno. x. 11. **men,** only **men,** so remember the contrast, "ye are men, I am God."

The Plant of Renown (vs. 29).—1. Some plants are renowned for their rareness; 2. For their beauty; 3. For their fragrance; 4. For their healing virtue; 5. For their shelter from the sun; 6. For their excellent fruits. The person, work, blessings, and promises of the Lord Jesus considered under each of these representations.—J. Laird.

Ezekiel's Gospel.—God's condescensions are never any abdications of his majesty. When He stoops it is with the stoop of a King; He is never less than King, never less than God. He knoweth our frame, He remembereth that we are dust; He knoweth that we are of yesterday and know nothing; He describes us as "a wind that cometh for a little time, and then passeth away," but He pledges His Godhead that manhood is precious and shall not be lost if love can save it. Here is the gospel before the incoming of the historical Christ. But Christ was always in the world. Christ is the God of the Old Testament, according to Christian interpretation. He was in the world, and the world knew Him not. Abraham, He says, rejoiced to see His day; He said, "Abraham saw My day, and was glad," and beginning at Moses and all the prophets He expounded to two auditors in all the Scriptures the things concerning Himself. When therefore we preach an Old Testament gospel, we are in reality preaching a New Testament gospel. There is only one Testamen—old as God, new as the present day.—J. Parker.

because destitute of faith and love. The balance of God is an even balance, and in his presenec the smallest deception is impossible."
—Davies.

[a] Da. viii. 3, 5.

[b] Is. xl. 11; Jno. x. 11.

[c] Is. lv. 3, 4; Je. xxx. 9; Ho. iii. 5.

[d] Mal. iii. 10.

[e] "The literal fulfilment is the primary one, though the spiritual also is designed. In correspondence with the settled reign of righteousness internally, all is to be prosperity externally, fertilising showers, and productive trees and lands."
—Fausset.

"'He shall guide you into all the truth.' That is not a promise of omniscience, but the assurance of gradual and growing acquaintanec with the spiritual truth revealed in Jesus. Not today, nor to-morrow, will it all be known, but step by step we shall be led."—Alexander McLaren.

"A wall of crystal is a safe defence against the force of fire, yet it is no obstruction to the beams and cherishing light of the sun. Such a crystal wall is Christ; He keeps off God's fiery indignation from us, but yet conveys to us the cherishing and reviving influences of His love." — Bishop Hopkins.

"Only by the way do the pilgrims of God doubt; not at the beginning, and at the end not at all. At first they proceed in faith, at last they shall see face to face."—Lange.

CHAPTER THE THIRTY-FIFTH.

1—6. (2) **Mount Seir,** the country of Edom, inhabited by the descendants of Esau.[a] (3) **stretch .. hand,** the usual fig. of Divine judgments. (4) **waste,** as cities overrun by hostile armies. (5) **perpetual hatred,** hast kept up thy hatred from of old. This effort of Edom to help destroy the Israelites is one of the causes of the nation's downfall. **iniquity .. end,** or received its just doom, ch. xxi. 29. (6) **prepare thee,** i. e. give thee over to universal slaughter. Edom showed experience the great law of Divine retribution, blood for blood. There seems to be a play on the name, "I will change thee from Edom into Dam (blood). **sith,** or since. **not hated,** but rather taken delight in.

a De. ii. 5; Eze. xxv. 12—14.

"It is only in their national character of foes to God's people that the Edomites are to be utterly destroyed."—Fausset.

"This is the law of benefits between men — the one ought to forget at once what he has given, and the other ought never to forget what he has received." —Seneca.

Not Far from the Kingdom.—There was one reason why Edom should receive exceptional treatment. She was not only a near neighbor to Israel, she was a blood-relation. Her people were the descendants of Esau, the brother of Jacob. Though a foreign nation, her cousinly relationship with Israel was like that of America with England. She could reckon two—the two best—of the patriarchs as her ancestors. Like Israel, she was descended from Abraham and Isaac. Might not she, then, expect the blessings of the patriarchs? Esau had begged for a blessing with bitter tears, and he had received one, but not the best blessing (Gen. xxvii. 38—40). The young man whom Christ loved was "not far from the kingdom of God" (Mark xii. 34). Yet for all we know, he did not enter it. The members of Christian families are favored with great religious privileges. It is much to be able to claim godly ancestors. But these advantages will not serve as substitutes for personal piety. Nay, they will make the guilt of the godlessness greater. We may be like Edom, very near to Israel, yet like Edom we may be cast aside and lost, if we have not really entered ourselves into the Divine covenant.—W. F. Adeney.

7—11. (7) **most desolate,** vs. 3. Heb. "desolation and desolation." **passeth .. returneth,** i. e. such shall be the peril of the country that no traveler will go through it. (8) **mountains,** Edom is characteristically a mountain district, ch. xxxii. 4, 5. (9) **cities .. return,** R. V., "shall not be inhabited."[a] (10) **two nations,** Israel and Judah.[b] **whereas,** or "although Jehovah dwelt there." "The invasion of Israel did not cease to be an act of aggression because there were no human defenders to bar the way. It was still Jehovah's land, although it was unoccupied; and to intrude upon it was a conscious defiance of His power." This sacrilege was the second cause of Edom's destruction. When once the relation existing bet. a Deity and His territory as conceived by the ancients is understood, then the heinousness of Edom's sin appears. (11) **known .. them,** i. e. among My people, whom I will surely defend against thee.

a Comp. Is. xxxiv. 1—15.

"From Mount Hor, a part of Mount Seir, nothing is to be seen but ruggedness and desolation."—Gadsby.

b Ps. lxxxiii. 12.

"One thing wh. contributed to make Caesar's soldiers invincible was their seeing him always take his share in danger, and never desire any exemption from labor or fatigue. We have a far higher incentive in the war for truth and goodness when we consider Him who endured such contradiction of sinners against Himself." —Spurgeon.

The Presence of God.—1. A reality though unrecognized. 2. A comfort in the midst of desolation and suffering. 3. The hope and guarantee of deliverance and future prosperity. 4. A startling revelation to His enemies.—Geo. Barlow.

12—15. (12) **blasphemies,** evil things said against Israel are regarded as blasphemies against Israel's God. (3) **against me,** not against the nation merely. "You boast as if I could not assert My right in Judæa." (14) **rejoiceth,**[a] prob. we should read, "to the rejoicing of the whole earth will I make thee desolate." This gives the requisite antithesis to vs. 15: as Edom rejoiced over the destruction of Judah, the whole earth will be overjoyed at her desolation. **desolate,** the Edomites never recovered their country. (15) **didst rejoice,** this malicious exultation over the downfall of the chosen nation was the third sin for wh. Edom must be punished. **all Idumaea,** i. e. all the several tribes and divisions of it.

a "When all the land of the living rejoices, and when the land of the saints and all other lands are converted to the service of God, then thou, O Mount Seir, and all Idumaea, that is, all ye powers of this world which delight in blood, shall be desolate, and shall know that I am the Lord."—S. Jerome.

Edom's Condemnation.—As Edom had been active in the destruction of Judah, their own desolation must follow. The great empires which brought destruction upon Jerusalem were acting under commission from Jehovah and the work was according to His will. But in the first place there is a difference between the work itself and the spirit in which it is done. Jehu received commendation for his act in cutting off the seed of Ahab, but later his house was extirpated for the guilt of this same "blood of Jezreel" (Hos. i. 4). The Assyrian was entrusted with a commission against the ungodly nation; but he meant not so, it was in his heart to cut off nations not a few (Is. x. 7), and the decree that he should be broken upon the mountains of Israel went out against him (Is. xiv. 25). Nebuchadnezzar was the "servant" of the Lord, but because Babylon laid her yoke heavily on the aged of the people, not considering the issue of such things, bereavement and widowhood shall come upon her in one day (Is. xlvii. 6—8). Here the prophet reprobates both the actions and the spirit of Edom, and threatens that Jehovah will recompense it into their bosom. In truth they knew Jehovah only as the God of Israel, but it was he whom they knew, though they might not have such knowledge of Him as Ezek. had attained to. But it was possible to be guilty of great sins against God, even though they are done unwittingly and without full knowledge of that which He is.—Camb. Bib.

"The profane swearer is compared to a fish who bites at the naked hook."

"We are ourselves the children of foreign missions. Foreign missionaries from Rome brought Christianity to England, and England sent it across the sea in Huguenot and Pilgrim to America."—The Outlook.

"There is no dispute managed without a passion, and yet there is not a dispute worth a passion."—Shelley.

CHAPTER THE THIRTY-SIXTH.

1—4. (1) **mountains,** ch. vi. 2. (2) **the enemy,** Edom, as in the previous chapter. **Aha,** a scornful and exulting expression. **ancient high places,** comp. "everlasting hills," Ge. xlix. 26. Not used here in the ordinary religious sense referring to rural sanctuaries. **in possession,** ch. xxxv. 10. (3) **Because they,** R. V., "because, even because, showing the intense emotion of the prophet as the beloved mountains rise before his vision. Five times Ezek. tries to speak to the mountains of Israel, but stops to breathe out prophecies against the heathen. **residue,** i. e. those of the surrounding nations that had survived the fall of Jerusalem. **infamy,** or treated as infamous. (4) **rivers,** lit. wadies or watercourses.

Premature Triumph.—We have not yet reached the end of the story. The battle is still raging; it is too early for the foe to sing his pæans of victory. All along the dark recitals of victories of evil there has been the alternative picture of Divine deliverance. We make a mistake when we dwell only on the gloomy side of history. God has been revealing Himself in history. Not only did He save the eight in the ark. He delivered all Israel from Egypt. He gave Canaan, and He gave restoration from the Captivity. He sent His Son to save the world. In the darkest hour when Christ hung dying on the cross while evil seemed to be most triumphant, victory was really being won by that very death of the world's Saviour. We have not seen the end yet. Perhaps we are on the fringe of a great contest between the servants of Christ and His foes. By the grace of God we may trust that, though the battle is still fierce, we are moving on to victory under the Captain of our salvation.—Pul. Com.

5—7. (5) **fire .. jealousy,** or fervent zeal for the honor of My name. **Idumaea,** ch. xxxv. 12, 15. **despiteful minds,** the bad feeling of Edom towards Israel is the thing specially noticed. **to cast it out,** Polychr. Bib., "that they might possess it." (6) **my fury,** active indignation. **borne the shame,** cast upon them by the heathen; ch. xxxiv. 29, xxxv. 12, 13. (7) **lifted .. hand,** the sign of taking an oath. **bear their shame,**[a] wh. would be the disgrace of perpetual irremediable desolation.

The righteous God, to whom vengeance belongs, will render shame for shame. Those that put contempt and reproach on God's people will sooner or later have it turned upon themselves; perhaps in this world, either their follies or their calamities, their miscarriages or their mischances, shall be their reproach; at farthest, in that day when all the impenitent shall rise to shame and everlasting contempt."—M. Henry. ——The Better Future.—I. The better future of the world. There is a natural tendency among men to say, "The former times were better." Nations cherish legends of an ancient golden age. People talk about "the good old times." But when we search history we cannot find these happy days. Waiving the point, however, as to whether the past history of our race has been characterized by progress or by a process of degeneration, we have still to ask whether the future may not be better than anything that has been experienced in the past. Now, it is the distinct teaching of the Bible that it will be so. "The earth shall be full of the knowledge of the Lord, as the waters cover the sea." The New Testa-

[a] The shame which they cast on you shall recoil on themselves."—Wordsworth.

"A most interesting relic of Cromwell has just come to light — a Bible given by Oliver Cromwell to his son-in-law Fleetwood. On the first page is a Latin motto, signed 'O. C.,' which runs as follows, 'Qui cessat esse melior, cessat esse bonus,'—He who ceases to be better ceases to be good."

"The happiness of life depends very much on little things; and one can be brave and great and good while making small sacrifices and doing small duties faithfully and cheerfully."—L. M. Alcott.

"It is a blessing to the earth to be made serviceable to men, especially to good men that will serve God with cheerfulness in the use of those good things which the earth serves up to them."—M. Henry.

ment points to a redemption and more than a restoration, to a perfection of humanity never attained in the past. II. The better future of the Church. The Church, which has the seed of Divine life in her, should be continually growing in grace. We think we can see progress in our own day—a wiser thought, a larger charity, a more practical activity in the service of man. But we are far indeed from realizing Christ's great ideal. That ideal, however, is the picture of the future, and the pattern after which we are to toil with the utmost hopefulness. The New Testament promises a glorious future to the people of God (Eph. ii. 21). III. The better future of the soul.—In our melancholy moods we yearn after the old sweet days of childhood—their innocence, their simplicity, their joyousness. We forget their limitations, their fears, their infantine distresses. The victorious Christian, with all his scars, and even with his memory of shameful unfaithfulness, stands higher than the unfallen because untried child.—W. F. Adeney.

8—11. (8) **shoot forth,** in the time of your restoration. **they .. hand,**[a] these restored days were really near, though no signs of them then appeared. God's promise is ever near, it does not really tarry. (9) **for you,** acting on your behalf. **tilled and sown,** after the time of captivity, during which the land shall keep her Sabbaths. (10) **multiply men,** contrast ch. xiv. 17. (11) **old estates,** "former condition." **better .. beginnings,** i. e. give you more secure and lasting possession of the land, and prosperity in it.

a Will soon come under Zerubbabel.

"To see Jesus clearly with the eye of faith is to see the deep opening away from Egypt's shore—is to see the water gush sparkling from the desert rock—is to see the serpent gleaming on its pole over a dying camp—is to see the lifeboat coming when our bark reels among foaming breakers—is to see a pardon when the noose is on our neck and our foot is on the drop."—Guthrie.

The Land of Canaan was an Important Factor in Israel's Past Renown.—This land has been specially selected by God as the most fitting scene for the training of the Hebrew nation. It was the glory of all lands, the envy of surrounding nations. Compared with the territory north, or east, or south, it was splendidly fertile, while its mountains made it a secure fortress. According to the known law, that the physical features of a country mold unconsciously the character of the inhabitants, Canaan had been a benefit to the Jewish tribes. The relaxing climate of Lower Egypt, together with the wondrous facility of obtaining large crops, made the people indolent and effeminate—impatient of arduous exertion. In Palestine a totally different condition of things prevailed. The sides of the hills required to be built in terraces in order to retain the soil. It was a territory in which it was scarcely possible for one to grow rich; it was a territory eminently suitable for the development of hardy and industrious peasants. Especially the land was singularly dependent upon the periodic rainfall. For, devoid of rain and dew, the olives dropped withered and unripe, the vines were blighted, the young corn was shriveled. Hence, in an eminent degree, the people hung in constant dependence on the good will of God.—Davies.

12—15. (12) **upon you,** i. e. upon the mountains of Israel, vs. 1. **bereave,** R. V., "bereave them of children," i. e. destroy the citizens. (13) **devourest up men,** it was represented as a land exposed to famine and pestilence.[b] **Comp.** Nu. xiii. 32. **nations,** R. V., "nations," i. e. the population. (15) **shame,** or contemptuous speeches, vs. 6. **cause .. fall,** better, "bereave thy nation."[c]

b "The neighboring people raised this ill character upon the land of Judea, because of the severe judgments of the sword, famine, and pestilence, which had destroyed the greater part of its inhabitants."—Lowth.

c "The land of Israel will receive an outpouring of grace. Its idolatry will be removed from its high places. This was fulfilled at the return from Babylon, and how much more by the restoration in Christ!"—Wordsworth.

"Painted deceit, tyrannical ambition. Chase these far from you."—Bowring.

Human Works.—In the age succeeding the flood, they piled old Babel's tower, and said, "This shall last for ever." But God confounded their language: they finished it not. Old Pharaoh and the Egyptian monarchs heaped up their pyramids, and they said, "They shall stand for ever:" and so, indeed, they do stand, but the time is approaching when age shall devour even these. The most stable things have been evanescent as shadows and the bubbles of an hour, speedily destroyed at God's bidding. Where is Nineveh? and where is Babylon? Where the cities of Persia? Where are the high places of Edom? Where are Moab and the princes of Ammon? Where are the temples of the heroes of Greece? Where are the millions that passed from the gates of Thebes? Where are the hosts of Xerxes? or where the vast armies of the Roman emperors? Have they not passed away? And though in their pride they said, "This monarchy is an everlasting one, this queen of the seven hills shall be called the eternal city," its pride is dimmed; and she who sat alone, and said, "I shall be no widow, but a queen for ever," she hath fallen; and in a little while she shall sink like a millstone in the flood, her name being a curse and a byword, and her site the habitation of dragons and of owls. Man calls his works eternal; God calls them fleeting: man conceives they are built of rock; God says, "Nay, sand; or, worse than that, they are air." Man says he erects them for eternity; God blows out for a moment, and where are they? Like baseless fabrics of a vision, they are passed and gone for ever.—Spurgeon.

16—20. (17) **defiled it,** making it unclean, and unfit to be regarded as God's holy land. **removed woman,** R. V., "a woman in her separation," Le. xv. 19. (18) **blood .. shed,** esp. in idolatrous sacrifices, such as the worship of Moloch.[a] (19) **according to,** or with judgments proportioned and fitted to their wickedness. (20) **profaned,** i. e. dishonored, disgraced. Give a false and unworthy impression of Jehovah, the God of their land. **when they said,** R. V., "in that men said of them;" **i.** e. the heathen had an idea that the exile revealed the weakness of Jehovah, who was acknowledged by all to be the god of Palestine. The heathen argued from the exile th. Jehovah was not able to protect His people.

The Messenger (vss. 16—28).—I. This portion of Scripture, from vs. 16, presents an epitome of the Gospel; vs. 17, man sinning; vs. 18, suffering; vs. 21, an object of pity; vs. 24, his salvation resolved upon; vss. 26, 27, renewed and sanctified; vs. 28, restored. II. Who is commissioned to deliver God's message? not an angel, but a man. Observe —The kindness of God to man; the honor conferred by God on man; the wisdom of God.—Guthrie.

Grief.—
Weep not for broad lands lost;
Weep not for fair hopes crossed;
Weep not when limbs wax old;
Weep not when friends grow cold;
Weep not that death must part
Thine and the best loved heart:
Yet weep—weep all thou can—
Weep, weep, because thou art
A sin-defiled man.

21—24. (21) **had pity,** or a pitiful regard to;[b] ch. xx. 9. (22) **not .. sakes,**[c] i. e. not for what Israel has been or deserved. The ref. is to Israel's past history; such a meaning as that it is not for any interest which he has in Israel or in order to benefit them that Jehovah delivers them, but only to magnify His own name, is entirely extraneous to the passage and a distortion of its sense. Cf. Is. xliii. 22—28, xlviii. 9—11.—Cam. B. (23) **sanctify my great name,** to sanctify is the opposite of to profane. As the latter term means to detract from the power, majesty, or purity of Jehovah, or from any of those attributes which belong to His godhead, to sanctify is to manifest or make these attributes conspicuous. **be sanctified,** have My name cleared and honored by My operations in Israel, which can be appreciated by all the nations. (24) **take you,**[d] after enduring the judgments and chastisements.

Man an Act of Divine Mercy.—I. The doctrine that God is not moved to save man by any merit or worth in him, is a truth of the highest importance to sinners. II. It is important for the saint also. III. While it keeps the saint humble, this doctrine will help to make the saint holy.—Guthrie.

25—28. (25) **sprinkle,** etc., the sign of the recovered remnant being separated as priests unto the Lord.[a] **filthiness,** the moral evils always associated with idolatry. (26) **new heart,** the sign of changed feelings and views; ch. xi. 19; Je. xxxii. 39. **stony heart,** so long unimpressible by teachings and by judgments. **heart of flesh,** impressible and docile. (27) **my spirit,**[b] as a spirit of obedience. **to walk in my statutes,** being endowed with the spirit of God they will walk in His statutes, for these are expresisons of His spirit. The spirit of God will appear both as an inward impulse to fulfill God's will, and as a power to do it. In the Old Testament the spirit of God, even the prophetic spirit, is usually a dynamic influence, an elevation of the natural human faculties.—Cam. B. (28) **dwell,** permanently and securely, and in the full covenant relations.

The New Heart (vs. 26).—I. The heart of man is by nature a heart of stone; it is impervious to religious impressions. Try it—1. By the beauties of nature; 2. By the wonders of Providence; 3. By the joys and sorrows of common life; 4. By the solemnities of the future world; 5. By the disclosures of the Bible; 6. By the attractions of the cross. II. It is the prerogative of God alone to change the heart. 1. This may be argued from the explicit testimony of Scripture; 2. From the nature and extent of human depravity; 3. From the figures which are employed by

[a] Eze. xvi. 36, 38, xxiii. 37.

"God His own justification in this world. God sanctifies His name among men by benefits as well as by his judgments and punishments."—Lange

"No one will know how much he ought to give unless he has a strong desire to know."

[b] "And a thousand pities it was that that should be trampled on and abused. He looked with compassion on His own honor, wh. lay bleeding among the heathen on that jewel which was trodden into the dirt."—Matt. Henry.

[c] De. ix. 6.

[d] Eze. xxxiv. 13 xxxvii. 21, xxxix. 25.

[a] Nu. viii. 5-22; Is. lxi. 6; He. x. 22.

"The rite thus prescribed by the Law and explained by the Prophets, gave occasion to the use of water at the admission of proselytes in later days, and to its adoption by John in his baptism unto repentance."—Spk. Com.

[b] Is. xxxii. 15, xliv. 3; Joel ii. 28; Zec. xii. 10; Jno. vii. 38; Ac. ii. 17, 18.

the sacred writers to represent the change; 4. From the frequent inefficiency of the most abundant and best-assorted means. III. The new heart is a heart of flesh. Try it—1. By the law of God; 2. By the Gospel; 3. By affliction; 4. By the sins of others; 5. By the glories of heaven.—G. Brooks.

29—32. (29) **save .. uncleannesses,** Cam. B., "save you out of," i. e. save you by purifying you from. **corn,** type of both material and spiritual prosperity and increase. Material prosperity was part of the Divine pledge given in the Mosaic covenant. (30) **reproach of famine,** see vss. 13—15. (31) **remember,** with due penitence and humility.[c] **lothe yourselves,** omit "in your own sight," ch. vi. 9. (32) **your sakes,**[d] vs. 22.

Ezekiel's Prophecies.—The present and the future of Ezekiel's prophecies are illustrated by two works of art in Rome. Israel was then like the Laocoon in the famous statue of the Vatican, after the description of Virgil. He and his sons are being crushed in the folds of the serpent, writhing in agony, unable to escape. But Ezekiel saw in his vision a time represented by the picture of St. Michael and the dragon—the dragon beneath the saint and being slain by his victorious sword.—Peloubet.

[c] Eze. xvi. 61.

[d] "The Prophet repeats this sentence on purpose to check all vain presumption in the Jews, and confidence of their own intrinsic worth or merit, a fault they have been very prone to in all ages."—Lowth.

33—38. Vss. 33—36: The lessons wh. Israel's restoration will teach the surrounding nations. (33) **cleansed,** this was the gracious issue of the chastisement of the captivity. The Jews have never since then relapsed into idolatry. (35) **garden of Eden,** a fig. of rich and perfect beauty.[a] (36) **I the Lord,** the signs of My power and grace will be so manifest, that in your blessing and prosperity My name will be glorified. **build .. plant,** R. V., "have builded" .. "planted." (37) **for this,** as usual "this refers to what follows. **inquired of,** i. e. sought in prayer.[b] It will be characteristic of the restored conditions that God will then be ready to answer prayer. **flock,** the multiplication of the people is dwelt upon with great joy. The remembrance of the sacrificial flocks that used to throng the streets leading to the Temple at the time of the great festivals, supplies Ezekiel with an image of the teeming population that shall be in all the cities of Canaan when this prophecy is fulfilled; ch. xxxiv. 23, 31. (38) **holy flock,** the great flock of choice animals for sacrifice.

Note on Verses 16—38.—The passage is remarkable and deserves to be studied almost more than any other part of Ezek. when one is seeking to understand his general conceptions. It exhibits his philosophy of history (cf. ch. xx.), and also describes with great beauty the principles of Jehovah's redemption of his people, and how step by step this shall be accomplished. The prophet reviews the history of the people from the beginning, running it out till it is lost in its eternal issues, and shewing how it will read to all the nations of the earth the true lesson of that which Jehovah, the God of Israel, is, and leave ineffaceable impressions on the mind of His own people. Probably no passage in the Old Testament of the same extent offers so complete a parallel to New Testament doctrine, particularly to that of St. Paul. It is doubtful if the Apostle quotes Ezek. anywhere, but his line of thought entirely coincides with his. The same conceptions and in the same order belong to both—forgiveness (vs. 25); regeneration, a new heart and spirit (vs. 26); the spirit of God as the ruling power in the new life (vs. 27); the issue of this, the keeping of the requirements of God's law (vs. 27; Rom. viii. 4); the effect of being "under grace" in softening the human heart and leading to obedience (vs. 31; Rom. vi., vii); and the organic connection of Israel's history with Jehovah's revelation of Himself to the nations (vss. 33—36; Rom. xi.). The prophet's idea of the Divine pedagogic is not precisely the same as that of the Apostle, and the present passage has in some particulars to be supplemented from ch. xvi. As put here it is Israel's historical experiences, their dispersion and restoration, with the thoughts which these suggest, that impress the nations and teach them what Jehovah is.—Camb. Bible.

[a] Is. li, 3.

[b] "What is the matter of God's promises must be the matter of our prayers. By asking for the mercy promised we must give glory to the donor, express a value for the gift, own our dependence, and put honor upon prayer which God has put honor upon."—Mat. Henry.

"Grace works shame, and so much the more as it makes the wilderness a paradise, the beggar a king, and the sinner a priest. We boast of nothing in Christ and we boast of all things."—Lange.

CHAPTER THE THIRTY-SEVENTH.

The last step in the reconstruction of the new Israel is the resurrection of the people. The nation is dead, and its bones scattered and dry. But it shall rise from the dead; the bones shall come together and the spirit of life from Jehovah shall enter into them and they shall live.

1—4. (1) **hand,** etc., prophetic ecstasy; ch. i. 3. **in the spirit,** meaning, in a vision. This was one mode of Divine communication with Ezekiel. **valley,** prob. the valley mentioned ch. iii. 22. (2) **very dry,** representing the Israelites dispersed abroad, destitute of life, national and spiritual." (3) **thou knowest,** the words imply, "it seems impossible to me."[c] (4) **Prophesy,** in sense of "preach," "proclaim." **O .. bones,** etc., the whole house of Israel, as individuals alive, as a nation dead, and hopeless of revival; comp. Jno. v. 28, 29.

Can These Bones Live? (vs. 3).—I. All men are spiritually dead. 1. Destitute of the principle of spiritual life; 2. Insensible to the beauty and attractions of the spiritual world; 3. Incompetent to discharge the functions of holy beings; 4. Under the dominion of sinful propensities. II. No created power can communicate spiritual life to man. 1. Not the diffusion of knowledge; 2. Not external reformation; 3. Not civil government; 4. Not ecclesiastical rites; 5. Not moral suasion. III. It is the prerogative of the Holy Spirit to quicken the spiritually dead. 1. His influence is obtained in answer to prayer; 2. It operates through the instrumentality of the Word; 3. It produces faith in Christ; 4. The mode of His working is inscrutable. Apply:—(1) Prophesy unto the bones; (2) Prophesy unto the winds.—G. Brooks.

The Vision of the Dry Bones.—The vision seems suggested by the saying current among the people, "our bones are dried, our hope is lost; we are wholly cut off." This idea and feeling of the people takes form in the vision which the prophet saw in the valley. The language of the people is figurative: they speak of the nationality, which is no more,—it is dead and its bones scattered and dry. And this idea regarding the nationality, figuratively expressed by the people, is embodied to the prophet in a vision. Hence the passage is not a literal prophecy of the resurrection of individual persons of the nation, dead or slain; it is a prophecy of the resurrection of the nation, whose condition is figuratively expressed by the people when they represent its bones as long scattered and dry. Perfect consistency is not maintained by the prophet; in vss. 1, 2 the dry bones are represented as lying on the face of the valley, very many and very dry; in vs. 12 they are represented as buried and brought up out of their graves. Hosea had already used the figure of resurrection for the resuscitation of the nation (vi. 2, xiii. 14); but, though the language used both here and by Hosea shews familiarity with the idea of the raising again of individuals, this is not what is prophesied. In Is. xxvi. 19; Dan. xii. the actual resurrection of individual members of Israel is predicted, cf. Job xiv. 13 seq.—Camb. B.

5—8. (5) **cause breath,** the sign of returning life, Ge. ii. 7. God Himself the real Agent in this resurrection of the nation. (6) **sinews,** etc., the parts which corruption speedily and completely destroys. A fig. for the reviving and restoring of a nation. (7) **noise,** of movement; symbol of the gathering of Israelites from different parts. **shaking,** R. V., "earthquake. **bone to his bone,** each fitting into the proper place and relation. (8) **no breath,** so only as yet the forms of life.[a]

No Breath, No Life (vs. 8).—I. Our creed may be sound and yet we may not be Christians. II. Our religion may be externally complete and yet we may not be Christians. III. Our good works may be numerous and praiseworthy, yet we may not be Christians. IV. Our life may be exemplary, and yet we may not be Christians. A life with no breath must be—1. A very imperfect life; 2. A very unhappy life; 3. A very unsuccessful life.—H. Bonar.

9, 10. (9) **wind,** or breath, symbol of the spirit of life. **four winds,** "the universal life-giving spirit of God." (10) **lived,** showed signs of movement and expression. **great army,** to indicate the large numbers who will gather for the return and restoration.

Life is the Breath of God.—Still, under Divine direction, the prophet invokes the help of the life-giving Spirit. A mysterious breath passes over the prostrate forms; they move and leap to their feet, "an exceeding great army." The Spirit that renews the face of the earth, robing it with velvet verdure and decorating it with nodding flowers, can alone raise the dead to life and adorn the soul with spiritual beauty. A lady

c "Faith leaves the question of possibility to rest with God, with whom nothing is impossible."—Fausset.

"Resurrections of communities have been seen more than once in history. But while this material form of national resurrection is not infrequent, a moral resurrection is more rare. A true national restoration is only possible as a work of God. Degenerate nations need more than liberation from external tyranny — they need national regeneration."
—Pul. Com.

"First the inward and then the outward change is God's order, while we men always proceed in the reverse order. What good a man does is not his, but God's work in him."—Starke.

a "This was fulfilled when, upon Cyrus' proclamation of liberty, those whose spirits God had stirred up began to think of making use of their liberty, and getting ready to be gone." — Mat. Henry.

A man without Chrit is a world without a sun.

"Divine grace even in the heart of weak and sinful man is an invincible thing."— Leighton.

"God's gifts are seldom in man's currency. "Happiness is not perfected until it is shared."—Jane Porter.

who recently visited the Fijian Archipelago writes:—"As I lived for two years in the midst of this kindly, courteous people, and marked the reverent devoutness of their lives and the simple earnestness of their bearing at the never-failing morning and evening family worship and frequent church services, I found it hard to believe the facts related to me by reliable eye-witnesses of the appalling scenes of carnage, fighting, human sacrifices, debasing idolatry, and loathsome cannibal feasts which five, ten, or fifteen years previously formed the incidents of daily life in districts where now English ladies and their children may travel or settle in perfect security." What had wrought this change? The breath of the Divine Spirit had blown through those lovely islands and transformed the moral wastes.—Hom. Com.

11—14. (11) **are,** i. e. they represent the deplorable and forlorn condition of the house of Judah and Ephraim. **cut off,** hopelessly. We shall never be a nation again. **our parts,** or for our lot; as far as we are concerned. Indicating a condition of extreme despair. (12) **open your graves,** the opening of Israel's graves could only signify the reawakening of the politically and religiously dead people to national and spiritual life. This was the first step in the restoration of the future held up before the minds of the despairing people.—Pul. Com. (13) **know,** by a great and impressive proof and persuasion. The process has three stages: (a) the political awakening; (b) the higher spiritual consciousness; (c) the return to and occupation of Canaan. "The passage teaches with striking clearness the continuity of God's redeeming work in the world, in spite of hindrances which to human eyes seem insurmountable."

Despair is called by the Catholics one of the six sins against the Holy Ghost, and certainly any Protestant will be equally emphatic in banishing it from the neighborhood of the spiritual graces.—H. C. Trumbull.

15—17. (16) **one stick,** comp. Nu. xvii. 2. One rood, or rod, equivalent to sceptre, Num. xvii. 2; so vss. 17, 19, 20. **Judah,** with Benjamin[b] (17) **join them,** as a symbol that in the restoration they should alike share, and from that time only one nation occupy the Holy Land.

[b] Add, however, Levi, and part of Simeon, and the Jehovah - worshipers from the northern nation, who settled in Judea.

Joining the Sticks (vss. 15—17).—I. The sad condition of the people of Israel at the time the prophet wrote. It was—1. Contrary to nature; 2. Displeasing to God; 3. Disastrous to themselves. II. The happy condition to which the people were about to be restored. 1. It is of great importance to the Church itself; 2. It is an immense advantage to the surrounding community; 3. It is well-pleasing and highly honoring to God. III. The agency by which this delightful change has to be effected. 1. He breathed into them the principle of spiritual life; 2. He sent them wise advisers and earnest intercessors; 3. He visited them with a sore trial; 4. He appointed them a common work; 5. He makes His residence in their midst.—F. Morgan.

18—23. (18) **shew us,** this would seem to be unnecessary, but the question may be asked in a contemptuous spirit. (19) **hand of Ephraim,** regarded as the ruling tribe.[a] **fellows,** allies. **put them,** perhaps the meaning is they miraculously grew into one. (20) **before their eyes,** "as a visible token or pledge of the truth of what I enjoin thee to speak to them." (23) **idols,**[b] as we have already seen, this has been fulfilled to the present day. No people witness more simply and purely to the Divine unity than do the Jews. **dwelling places,** their backslidings.

[a] Je. iii. 18, l. 4; Zec. x. 6.

[b] 2 Co. vi. 16.

"Politically speaking, they never had a king from that day to this, and the grand junction and government spoken of here must refer to another time—to that in which they shall be brought into the Christian Church with the fulness of the Gentiles, when Jesus, the King of kings and Lord of lords, shall rule over them."—A. Clarke.

A Common Religion.—Religion, which should be the great bond of union, has become the great divider of men. People who could agree to live together peaceably on all other accounts fall out about their religion and stand apart in hopeless divisions on this one ground. Thus Israel and Judah were divided by their religion. Israel was jealous of the temple privileges of Jerusalem, and Judah was indignant at the calf-worship of Israel. But now the idolatry is over, and a new temple is to be built at which all parties can work. Christ is our Peace (Eph. ii. 14). He breaks down distinctions of race and party. It is the Christlessness of religion that makes religious differences. If we all had more of Christ we should all be more united; for he is the one center of union in the Christian Church.—Pul. Com.

24—28. (24) **David,** etc., Is. xl. 11; Je. xxiii. 5, xxx. 9; Eze. xxxiv.

23. (25) **dwell,** securely and permanently.[a] **servant David,** the type of the Messiah's kingdom. (26) **covenant of peace,** ch. xxxiv. 24.[b] **my sanctuary,** fulfilled in the spiritual sense. The Church is God's earthly temple. (27) **tabernacle,** or earthly dwelling-place.[c] Zerubbabel's temple was a partial fulfillment. (28) **santify,** in sense of setting apart, and consecrating.

Confessing Christ.—It cost something to acknowledge Christ in those early days of His Church. When Symphorianus, a young Roman, acknowledged himself a believer in Jesus, he was seized and scourged nearly to death, and then dragged away to a place of execution. His heroic Christian mother walked by his side, not shrieking and bewailing his terrible fate, as her mother's heart prompted, but encouraging and cheering him with such words as these: "Son, my son, remember life eternal! Look up to heaven! Lift up thine eye to Him that reigneth there! Life is not taken from thee, but exchanged for a better." At these words, the young man's heart was wondrously cheered, as if God had sent an angel to strengthen him. He went to the block with a face all glowing with holy joy. What power but that of a "living God" could sustain a mother and son in such an hour? What a glorious exchange was such a belief for the dead system of heathen worship in which they had been born!

[a] Is. lx. 21; Joel iii. 20; Am. ix. 15.

[b] Ps. lxxxix. 3, 4; Is. lv. 3; Je. xxxii. 40.

[c] Am. ix. 11; Jno. i. 14; Re. xxi. 3.

"The truest dignity and sacredness of this earthly life consists in the opportunity it offers of communion with the unseen but ever-present God and Saviour. The strongest attraction of the life to come lies in the prospect of a closer approach to God, a more uninterrupted fellowship with God, and a nearer assimilation to his perfect and glorious character. — Thomson.

CHAPTER THE THIRTY-EIGHTH.

1—7. (2) **Gog,** a symbolical name,[a] the impersonation of the powers of the north. **the land,** R. V., "of the land." **Magog,** Ge. x. 2. **Meshech and Tubal,** R. V., "prince of Rosh, Meshech and Tubal;" ch.. xxvii. 13, xxxii. 26. (4) **hooks** etc., ch. xxxix. 2. The fig. is taken from the mode of securing the Nile crocodiles. (5) **Persia,** etc., ch. xxvii. 10, xxx. 5. (6) **Gomer,** the Cimmerians of Crim-Tartary, Ge. x. 2. **Togarmah,** Armenians. The northern parts of Asia Minor, ch. xxvii. 14. (7) **Be thou prepared,** this is God's challenge to a contest. "In it there is a strain of irony, as if it were foolish indeed to measure strength with Jehovah." **guard,** etc., R. V. marg., "commander." Lxx trans. "unto me" for "unto them," i. e. Gog is summoned to hold himself in reserve against the day when God shall reveal to him the purpose for wh. he was raised up.

The nations lying in the outskirts of the earth, as another prophet expresses it, "have not heard Jehovah's fame, neither have seen His glory" (Is. lxvi. 19), and He who is God alone must reveal Himself to all flesh, for He has sworn by Himself that to Him every knee shall bow (Is. xlv. 23). Such is the meaning of this last act in the drama of the world's history. As it is Jehovah's final revelation of Himself to all the nations of the earth, it is accompanied by all those terrors and convulsions in nature which in earlier prophets usually signalize the day of the Lord (xxxviii. 19—23).—Cam. B.

[a] Standing for the world regarded as antagonistic to God.

"Thus God is a heart - searcher: He knows the evil purpose in the man himself." — Starck.

"He loves not Christ at all who does not love Christ above all."—**Austin.**

8—17. (8) **visited,** Polychr. Bib., "mustered for service." **latter years,** beyond the historical events with which Ezekiel has been dealing. Comp. the conflict in the Bk. of Rev. **always waste,** i. e. for a long time. (9) **storm,** suddenly, and with a great show of terror. (10) **think an evil thought,** better, "conceive an evil purpose. (11) **unwalled villages,** unmolested bec. of the moral effect of Jehovah's name upon all the nations wh. know Israel's history; but Gog is ignorant and greedy. Comp Zec. ii. 4, 5. **safely,** securely, without thought of approaching danger. (12) **take a spoil,** easily, without any conflict. **midst,** etc., R. V., "navel of the earth," i. e. Israel is regarded as the center of the world, ch. v. 5. (13) **Sheba,** etc., merchant nations aroused to cupidity by this vast expedition against so prosperous a country.[b] **young lions,** i. e. smaller tradesmen who were rapacious for gain. (14) **know it,** and try to take advantage of such prosperity and security.[c] (16) **sanctified in thee,** i. e. honored in thy overwhelming destruction. Gog is, by his defeat, to procure honor to the God of Israel. (17) **thou he,** etc., the final opposer of God, represented by the Pharaohs and Sennacheribs of former times. "Gog is the person in whom the substance of previous oracles is to be accomplished."

[b] Merchants from these nations are represented as coming to Gog's camp to see if they can buy the spoil.

[c] Comp. Re. xvi. 13, 14.

Love Christ not for what He has, or gives simply, but love Him for His own sake.

"When we find ourselves ready to give up even lawful pleasures and possessions, how happy is our life!"

"Everything has been told before: they who hold to the Word have to fear no surprises."

The Final Uprising of Evil.—The invasion and overthrow of the Chaldæans, the conflict of the Maccabees with Antiochus Epiphanes, the temporary successes and defeat of the Turks—to each of which historical events some interpreters would limit the application of the prophecy—were but feeble prototypes of a coming struggle with a powerful embodied Antichrist.—Geo. Barlow.

18—23. (19) **jealousy,** etc., ch. xxxvi. 5, xxxix. 25. **shaking,** the terrible overthrow of Gog would produce within the heathen mind a great tremor as if the fabric of the earth were being ruined. (20) **fishes,** etc., the figs. of the verse are taken from the effects of a terrible earthquake.[1] **steep places,** or Polyc. Bib., "cliffs shall topple over." (21) **sword,** comp. ch. xiv. 17. **against his brother,** the sign of intestine quarrels, which are fatal to any enterprise. (22) **plead,** urge my cause by the agency of pestilence and fighting. **hailstones, ch. xiii. 11. (23) magnify myself, ch.** xxxvi. 23, xxxvii. 28.

The Invasion of Gog.—The prophet is not the author of the idea of this invasion. It has been predicted of old by the prophets of Israel, prophesying over long periods (xxxviii. 17, xxxix. 8). Neither is it probable that the idea was one read out of certain prophecies merely by Ezekiel. More likely it was an idea widely entertained. The former prophecies on which the belief was founded are not to be supposed to have contained the name of Gog, any more than the prophecies applied by the author of Is. xl. seq. to the career of Cyrus need have referred to him by name. The conception is rather shadowy and vague. The time is indefinite, it is far into the years to come; the nations who cluster around the standard of Gog, himself a somewhat nebulous personage, are those lying in the uttermost regions of the world, which had been heard of but never seen.—Camb. Bib.

[a] "The Prophets often describe God's judgments upon particular countries or persons, as if it were a dissolution of the whole world, because His particular judgments are an earnest of the general judgment."—Lowth.

"Thus undeniably prove that I am the mighty, just, faithful, wise, holy and merciful God toward My people; and that I am the great, just, and terrible One against Mine and My church's enemies."—Pool.

"I will disarm thee. As Herodotus reports of Sennacherib and his Assyrians in Egypt, that their quivers, bow-strings and targets were gnawed to pieces by mice and rats in one night, so that they were forced to fly for their lives. And as our chroniclers tell us that in the battle between Edward III. of England and Philip of France there fell such a piercing shower of rain as dissolved their strings and made their bows useless."
—Trapp.

[b] Joel ii. 11, 31; Zep. i. 14; Re. vi. 17, xvi. 17, xxi. 6.

[c] "The features of the prophecy show clearly that it is not to be understood literally but spiritually."
—Wordsworth.

[d] "The burning of the foe's weapons implies that nothing belonging to them should be left to pollute the land. The seven years spent on this work implies the completeness of

CHAPTER THE THIRTY-NINTH.

Chapters xxxviii., xxxix. give the impression of having been intended to stand at the close of the book of Ezekiel. Their present position is best explained on the supposition that the original collection of Ezekiel's prophecies actually ended here, and that the remaining chapters (xl.—xlviii.) form an appendix, added at a later period without disturbing the plan on which the book had been arranged. In chronological order, at all events, the oracle on Gog comes after the vision of the last nine chapters. It marks the utmost limit of Ezekiel's vision of the future of the kingdom of God.—Exp. B.

1—7. (1) **Gog,** ch. xxxviii. 1. (2) **chief prince,** "prince of Rosh." **leave .. thee,** R. V., "turn thee about and will lead thee on and will cause," etc. (3) **thy bow,** chief of the war weapons. (4) **fall,** smitten and defeated. **ravenous birds,** that crowd battle fields. (5) **open field,** where shall be no shelter from the ravenous creatures. It was a great indignity to leave dead bodies exposed. (6) **fire, comp.** Re. xx. 9. **carelessly,** R. V., "securely." **isles,** including coast lands. (7) **So,** i. e. by this manifestation of power in the discomfiture of My people's enemies. **pollute,** profane.

Note on vs. 7.—Israel's sins constrained Jehovah to cast them out of His land, and thus to profane His holy name. Now they are another people, a new heart has been given them, and His signal protection of them in their defenceless condition (xxxviii. 11) from so extreme a danger (xxxviii. 4—6) will reveal both to Israel and the nations what Jehovah is, and what are the principles on which He rules His people (vs. 23). Thus shall His name be sanctified—He shall be known to be God alone, all powerful and righteous.—Cam. B.

8—10. (8) **it is come,** i. e. the time of the great threatened destruction.[b] The Prophet declares it to be so certain that it is "as good as done." (9) **dwell .. cities,** the people of the land would find a supply of fuel for seven years in the multitude of weapons left on the battle-field. This is to be regarded as a poetical figure.[c] **handstaves,** or javelins. **burn .. fire,** R. V., "make fires of them." **seven years,**[d] the number seven is here used as the ideal or perfect number. (10) **spoil,** etc., Is. xiv. 2, xxxiii. 1.

The Signal of Defeat of God's Enemies.—In this chapter we have a prophetic description of the ultimate fate of Gog, the ideal impersonation of the power of evil, and the utter destruction of his vast armies. The embattled hosts march to the conflict with proud ostentation and confident of victory. Their swords shall soon provide a banquet for the birds of prey that hover over them, and for the wild beasts whose hungry growls are heard around them, little dreaming that the stricken bodies of the invaders must furnish the feast. An unseen and irresistible power lures them on to their ruin; they are smitten with paralysis, their weapons drop from their hands and cover the ground like corn newly cut with the reaper; they perish in myriads on the mountains and the open fields, the birds and beasts are summoned to gorge themselves on the human carrion, and the only remnants of the once formidable warriors of Gog are found in innumerable graves. In this boldly conceived vision we have a realistic picture of the final and utter destruction of all the enemies of God's people.—Hom. Com.

11—16. (11) **place .. graves,** where he expected a triumph he shall **find a grave. Valley,** etc., this may be an imaginary valley, seen in the Prophet's vision, or a place on the high road, E. of the Dead Sea,[a] the highway between Syria and Petra, and Egypt, **passengers,** Cornill, "valley of Abarine," E. of the Dead Sea, **stop the noses,**[b] R. V., and it shall stop them that pass through i. e. the valley shall be so filled with the graves, that the way of passers through shall be barred. **Hamon-gog,** or "the multitude of Gog." (12) **seven months,** during all this time they would be finding scattered corpses.[c] (13) **to them,** i. e. to Israel. A day of joy and triumph. (14) **sever out,** set apart to this work. **Men .. employment,** dedicated entirely to this work until it was completed.[d] **With the passengers,** i. e. with the help of the passers by, as next vs. (15) **set .. sign,** to direct the attention of the buriers to it. (16) **Hamonah,** or "the multitude."

The Rival Armies.—I. The enemies of the Lord. 1. Their character. (1) The idolater; (2) The forgetful; (3) The indifferent; (4) The undecided; (5) The reckless. 2. Their doom. They perish—(1) Without God, and so cut off from the only source of true life; (2) Without hope; (3) Fighting against God. II. The friends of the Lord. The course of the sun is—1. Very quiet; 2. Gladdening; 3. Regular and sure; 4. One of increasing brightness.—H. G. Parrish.

Continual Employment (vs. 14).—Men of continual employment! and women also. These are the persons everywhere needed to originate and sustain Christian enterprise throughout the world. From those who come forward to offer themselves for the work it is not easy to discriminate at first, but on making a farther selection from those who have undergone a measure of testing or probation, it is on those who have shown themselves to be "men of continual employment" that we would rely.

17—22. (17) **feathered fowl,** all carrion birds. **sacrifice,** the heaps of slain are regarded as a sacrificial feast provided by God for them. (18) **rams,** etc., prob. here figures of the various classes of people in the slain armies. **fatlings of Bashan,**[a] De. xxxii. 14. (19) **drunken,** or satiated. (20) **my table,** poetical carrying out of the figure of the sacrificial feasts. **chariots,** i. e. charioteers.[b] (21) **set .. heathen,** ch. xxxviii. 16, 23. (22) **know,** or fully apprehend and realise. . Israel shall no more recall their former rejection with fear of its repetition.

Heathenism Doomed.—Some of the most interesting pages in history are those which describe the siege of cities. The walls of the beleaguered city are surrounded on all sides by men trying to force an entrance. Some make sudden onsets on the gates. Some batter the walls with rams and engines. Some plant ladders against the walls and fight hand to hand with the defenders. Everywhere there is noise, and tumult, and capture, and death, the shouts of the fighters and the moans of the dying, yet still the city is not taken. But all the while there is, unknown to the defenders, a body of men digging and mining under the very wall of the city. They are undermining the foundations of the city ramparts —the city is doomed. I sometimes think that this is the work which our

the cleansing, and the people's zeal for purity."—Fausset.

[a] "A place frightful in its physical character, and admonitory of past judgments." — Spk. Com.

[b] Comp. the same Heb. word, trans. muzzle, in De. xxv. 4.

[c] "Usually the survivors of an army bury their own dead; but here the rout is so complete that the house of Israel bury the corpses of their foes." — Wordsworth.

[d] Is. lxvi. 24.

"The conclusion is, that the result of everything is to magnify and sanctify God. We ought, therefore, to begin all our affairs with God."—Lange.

[a] "The cattle of Palestine are generally small, and decidedly inferior to those of more northern climes. The cause is doubtless to be found in the scanty pastures of a land laid waste for many centuries by ever-returning foes, and many of whose springs of water have been drying up; but there are districts in which the cattle are finer, and in a far better condition. There are probably as fine 'bulls of Bashan' now grazing on the plains of the Hauran as there were in king David's time." — Van Lennep.

[b] Comp. Ps. lxxvi. 6.

Christian schools and colleges in heathen lands are doing. We are sapping the foundations of heathenism. The city is strong and ancient; its walls are thick and ugly and deep. But it is doomed. In our hands God has put an ax, and we are digging, digging; and in the end, through the darkness we shall reach the light.—John Lendrum.

c "They were not carried away by their enemies bec. I wanted power to rescue them, but as a just punishment of their sins."—Lowth.

"After they have become sensible of their guilt, and ashamed of it."—Fausset.

23—26. (23) **hid I my face,**[c] the character of Israel's captivity, as Divine chastisement for sin will be made plain when God has restored and sanctified them. (24) **uncleanness,** by reason of their idolatry. (25) **bring again,** ch. xxxiv. 13, etc. **whole house,** the entire covenant people. (26) **after .. borne** R. V., "and they shall bear," i. e. be conscious of their unworthiness. **dwelt safely,** R. V., "shall dwell securely." **made,** "shall make."

Note on vss. 23, 24.—Jehovah's dealing with his people Israel is the great lesson which he reads to the heathen; it is the history of Israel in the hand of Jehovah their God that reveals to the nations what Jehovah is. For the nations knew Jehovah only as God of Israel, and it was thus only through Israel that he could reveal himself to them. This last great event in the history of Israel, Jehovah's signal defence of them now that they are his people in truth, casts light on his former hiding of his face from them. Deeper elements than mere power enter into his rule of his people; a conception of God is suggested to the nations unlike any they had hitherto entertained—there is a God who is omnipotent and who rules the nations in righteousness, the God of Israel.—Cam. B.

e "The pouring out of His spirit is a pledge that He will hide His face no more."—Fausset. "St. Peter distinctly appropriates these prophecies to the outpouring of the Holy Spirit on the day of Pentecost, and the inauguration of the Church of Christ by that miraculous event."—Spk. Com.

27—29. (27) **am sanctified,** ch. xxxvi. 23. (28) **read,** "and they shall know..in that I caused them..and will gather..and will leave." (29) **poured .. spirit,**[e] Joel ii. 28.

The promise of the Spirit.—1. The constant theme of Old Testament prophets. 2. Blessedly realised in the history of the Church in all ages. 3. Fulfilled in the remarkable advances of the Gospel in the present day. 4. The guarantee of future universal victory.—Hom. Com.

In this and the remaining chapters of Ezekiel, is given an ideal picture of the restored Jewish temple.

CHAPTER THE FORTIETH.

Ch. xl.—xlviii.—"It remains to sketch the outline of a perfect theocracy—in other words, to describe the permanent forms and institutions which shall express the ideal relation between God and men. To this task the prophet addresses himself in the chapters now before us. That great New Year's Vision may be regarded as the ripe fruit of all God's training of His prophet, as it is also the part of Ezekiel's work which most directly influenced the subsequent development of religion in Israel."—Exp. B.

a Zec. ii. 1.

b Re. xxi. 15.

"The words describe the situation of the temple on the south side of Mount Zion, wh., with all its courts, buildings and walls encompassing the courts and the whole area, or holy mountain, resembled a city for bigness." Lowth.

1—5. (1) **In .. captivity,** B. C. 572, **beginning of the year,** of the ecclesiastical year i. e. in the month Abib (Mch.—Apr.) **hand .. me,** ch. i. 3. **thither,** i. e. to Jerusalem. (2) **visions of God,** or Divinely-sent visions. **high mountain,** fr. which a broad and general view could be obtained. Reference may be to Mount Zion, from wh. a good view of Mt. Moriah could be obtained. **frame,** Com. B., "upon wh. was as it were a building of a city," i. e. a city—like building. The pre-exile temple occupied the south slope. (3) **man,** not Jehovah, but a living symbol of Jehovah. **brass,** i. e. brightly shining. **line of flax,**[a] for measuring the ground. **measuring reed,**[b] for the walls. (4) No one can study the detailed measurements of the buildings without being convinced that the prophet is working from a ground plan which he has himself prepared; indeed his own words leave no doubt that this was the case.—Exp. B. (5) **wall,** i. e. boundary wall. **and an handbreadth,** or the cubit used by the man in measuring was one handbreadth over the cubit used in Chaldæa.

Reverence for the House of God.—
"When once thy foot enters the church, beware!
God is more there than thou; for thou art there
Only by His permission. Then, beware;
And make thyself all reverence and fear.
Kneeling ne'er spoil'd silk stocking: quit thy state;
All equal are within the church's gate.

"Let vain or busy thought have there no part;
Bring not thy plots, thy plough, thy pleasure thither;
Christ purged His temple—so must thou thy heart.
All worldly thoughts are but thieves met together
To cozen thee: look to thy actions well,
For churches either are our heaven or hell."
—G. Herbert.

6—10. (6) **gate .. east,** the east-gate building is described as a model for all the buildings at the other gates. **stairs,** for their number see vs. 22. **threshold,** the whole structure was in the form of a triple terrace, each rising above the others inward, the outer court, the inner court and the temple proper. The threshold refers to the space bet. the step and the guardrooms. **the other threshold,** R. V. marg., "even one threshold," i. e. the first as distinguished fr. the second (vs. 7). (7) **little chamber,** or "guard room" prepared for the Levitical guard, who attended to and kept the gate.[a] **within,** R. V., "toward the house." Beyond the three lodges on each side there was a second space like the first threshold of equal size. (9) **inward,** i. e. towards the court of the temple. (10) **posts,** prob. the wall-fronts or spaces bet. the guardrooms.

"The Jews called the east the fore part of heaven; the west the back-part: by the first they denote spiritual things; by the second temporal and earthly things. Those that come into this Temple must mind spiritual things; they must not let out their hearts to the world and worldly delights—they are western things, and there was no door in the west. They must go upwards, not downwards; keep within, not go out."—Greenhill.

The Gate which Looketh toward the East.—I. An Oriental outlook. II. An outlook towards the light. III. An outlook towards the new day. IV. An outlook towards Christ.—Pul. Com.

11—15. (11) **length of the gate thirteen cubits,** it seems impossible to explain this. (12) **space,** a limit, or barrier, to protect the guard-rooms projecting into the passageway one cubit each side in front of the guard-room thus contracting passage fr. 10 to 8 cubits there. (13) **from the roof,** etc., i. e. across the gate-building from north to south. From the roof of one chamber to the roof of the corresponding opposite one. (14) **He made also posts,** etc., Polyc. Bib., "He measured the vestibule (porch) 20 cubits and adjoining the vestibule of the gateway was the court round about." (15) **face,** or outside front.

Entrance to the Kingdom.—I. There is one way into the kingdom. II. There are many approaches to the kingdom. III. Men come from all quarters to the kingdom. IV. The gate is too narrow for some. V. It is broad enough for all earnest seekers.—Clarkson.

16—19. (16) **narrow,** Heb. closed[b] **posts,** i. e. the 5 cubit wall fronts bet. the guard-rooms. **arches,** Cam. B. suggests, "and to the porch thereof," i. e. of the gate. (17) outward court, R. V., "outer" answering to the Court of the Women in Herod's temple. The first on passing the gate. **pavement,** of mosaic work. (18) **lower pavement,** on the outer court, wh. was lower than the inner court. R. V., "and the pavement was by the side of the gates, answerable unto the length of the gates, even the lower pavement." (19) **without,** marg. "from without."

The outer and inner courts of the Temple.—"In the outward court the people stood; and it represented the nations outside the Church. The inward court represented the Church, where the Word of God enlightens and nourishes us, and Christ is our altar of perfumes. The Holy of Holies represented heaven; into it the high priest only entered—typifying our High Priest, the Lord Jesus, His entrance in there alone by His own power, to bring us thither. So that the first signified the state of nature; the second the state of grace; the third the state of glory. Hereby the greatness of the Church in the time of the Gospel, and especially in the time of the New Jerusalem, is pointed out. These courts were of great compass, and had gates looking to the several parts of the world."—Greenhill.

20—23. (20) **that looked,** Heb. "whose face was." (21) **arches,** vs. 16. (22) **seven steps,** vs. 6. "There was the same number of steps, no doubt,

a "Along the wall of the porch were chambers, three on each side; vs. 10. —Lowth.

These chambers were about 10ft. 6in. square.

"The porch reminds us of the peace and repose connected with the consciousness of the grace of God."—Oecolampadius.

"If we know ourselves, we shall love others."

"We literally lay down our lives for our worthless and ungrateful selves."

"Cruelty is universal — more from lack of imagination than love."

b "Closed windows, with shut lattices, the bars of which, being let into the wall, could not be opened or shut at pleasure." —Gesenius.

"In the Church of God darkness has no place, but the light of truth and faith shines everywhere; yea, believers themselves are a light in the Lord, whose works shine before men."
—Lange.

"May not taste be compared to that exquisite sense of the bee, which instantly discovers and extracts the quintessence of every flower, and disregards all the rest?—Greville.

"Why should not the strong be beautiful as well as helpful? Why should they not add grace to power? It is a serious mistake men make when

to each of the gates from the precincts to the outer court." (23) **over against,** better, proportionable with.

His share.—Standing in front of the noble cathedral of Cologne, a lady overheard some one behind her say, "Didn't we do a fine piece of work here?" Turning quickly, she saw that the speaker was a man in the plainest of working clothes, and on a sudden impulse she said to him, "Pray, what did you do about it?" "O, I mixed the mortar for two years across the street," was his reply.—The Well Spring.

24—31. (24) **according measures,** i. e. to those previously given. (25) **windows,** vs. 16. (26) **seven steps,** vs. 22. (27) **gate to gate,** or the distance between the gates.

(28) **by .. gate,** or through the south gate. (29) **little chambers,** guard-rooms. (30) this vs. is not easily explained—It is omitted in the Sept. (31) read: "and the porch thereof was toward the outer court," etc.

Old Cathedrals.—When we enter one of those antique piles in southern Germany, or in Spain—for there only can a Catholic Gothic cathedral be seen in all its glory,—I know not that it is possible for the heart of man to desire any addition to the magnetic solemnity of the whole scheme. The tall, narrow windows, quite dark with the long purple garments of pictured martyrs, apostles, and kings, tinge every ray that passes through them with the colors and the memory of a thousand years of devotion.—Washington Irving.

32—34. (32) **into,** before, they were looking at the inner court, now they actually entered it. (33, 34) **the arches thereof,** etc. "the porch thereof was toward the outer court." **eight steps,** comp. the seven steps of the other gates: vss. 22, 26.

Wonders of the Bible.—If you ever tried it, you must have been struck with the few solid thoughts, the few suggestive ideas which survive the perusal of the most brilliant of human books. Few of them can stand three readings; and of the memorabilia which you have marked in your first reading, on reverting to them, you find many of those were not so striking or weighty or original as you thought. But the Word of God is solid: it will stand a thousand readings; and the man who has gone over it the most frequently and carefully is the surest of finding new wonders there.—James Hamilton.

35—38. (35) **north gate,** similar in all respects to the others. (36, 37) **chambers,** etc., see vss. 7, 16. (38) **chambers,** etc. R. V., "and a chamber with the door thereof..there they washed." **washed** offering, Le. i. 11—13.

39—43. (39) **porch,** "not under the covered portico, wh. was only ten cubits broad, but in the angles formed by the porch and gate-front. These tables were blocks for killing and preparing the sacrifices.[a] (40) **at the side,** R. V., "on the one side without, at the stairs of the entry." **was at the porch,** "belonged to the porch." (41) **eight tables,** these were prob. of wood. (42) **four tables,** Cam. B., "and there were four," etc., i. e. four others. (43) **within,** in the porch. **hooks,** to wh. the beasts might be fastened: or perhaps on which the carcasses might be hung, **the tables,** prob. the stone tables.

Sacrifices in the new Temple.—As we read the dry details of the city that is to be rebuilt and its new temple, we are suddenly pulled up by a startling item. Among the various arrangements of the ancient temple that are to be revived, provision is made for the sacrificial rites. Then sacrifices will be needed after the restoration. It might have been supposed that these would now be dispensed with, since sin was put away and the people were re-dedicated to God. I. We need repeated re-dedication of our lives to God. The sacrament of baptism, which signifies the first dedication, is taken but once; but it is followed by that of the Lord's Supper, which suggests renewal of dedication in deliberate intention, as when the Roman soldier took the oath of allegiance to his general. This sacrament we repeat many times. II. We need repeated cleansing from sin. There were to be sin and trespass offerings in the new temple. Even while the people are returning, penitent and restored, provision has to be made for future falls and sins. 1. Christian people sin. We know that this is only too true of all Christian people. 2. God has provided for the recovery of Christians when they sin. It is a shame

they think that they may dispense with the finer excellences of Christian character and life because they contribute an efficiency which others cannot render. The uncultivated rudeness of many a pillar in the Christian "temple" detracts most seriously from its worth; on the other hand, the palm trees upon the posts constitute a very appreciable addition. Be beautiful as well as strong. "Whatsoever things are lovely and of good report" should be "considered well, and should be secured as well as 'whatsoever things are true, honest, just and pure.' Strive after, pray for, carefully cultivate, all that is beautiful in the sight of man, in temper, in bearing, in spirit, in word and deed; so shall the value of your strength be greatly enhanced in the estimate of Christ."

—Clarkson.

"A thing of beauty is a joy for ever. Its loveliness increases; it will never pass into nothingness." —Keats.

[a] "If the gate-building projected with its porch forward on to the pavement of the inner court, the tables were fitly placed for carrying out the directions of the law."—Spk. Com.

"Taste and elegance, though they are reckoned only among the smaller and secondary morals, yet are of no mean importance in the regulation of life. A moral taste is not of

that they who have once washed their robes and made them white in the blood of the Lamb should again stain them with the ruin of sin. Yet as this is done, God provides even again for cleansing—not now by repeated sacrifices, but by the eternal efficacy of the one perfect Sacrifice.—Pul. Com.

44—49. (44) "And without the inner gate were two chambers in the inner court, one at the side of the N. gate, and its prospect was toward the S.; and one at the side of the S. gate, having its prospect towards the N." (45) **prospect** or outlook. **charge of the house,**[b] Nu. iii. 25, etc. (46) **charge of the altar,** Le. vi. 12, 13. **Zadok,** 1 Ki. ii. 27, 35. (47) **court,** i.e. the inner court. (48) **porch .. house,** i.e. of the sanctuary, or temple itself. Comp. Sol.'s porch, 1 Ki. vi. 3[c]. **post,** "jamb of the advancing wall on each side of the entrance." **breadth .. gate,** "and the side pieces of the entrance of the porch." (49) **Eleven cubits,** "twelve cubits." **pillars .. posts,**[d] "meaning that upon the bases (posts) stood shafts (pillars). These shafts were prob. in the form of palm trees."

Note on chs. 40—48.—This section gives a picture of the people in their final condition of redemption and felicity. It does not describe how salvation is to be attained, for the salvation is realized and enjoyed; it describes the people and their condition and their life now that their redemption has come. This accounts for the strange mixture of elements in the picture—for the fact that there is "so much of earth, so much of heaven" in it. To us who have clearer light the natural and the supernatural seem oddly commingled. But this confusion is common to all the prophetic pictures of the final condition of Israel redeemed, and must not be allowed to lead us astray. Ezekiel of course expects a restoration in the true sense, but it is a restoration which is complete, embracing all the scattered members of Israel, and final, being the entrance of Israel upon its eternal felicity and perfection, and the enjoyment of the full presence of Jehovah in the midst of it. The restoration expected and described by the prophet is no more the restoration that historically took place than the restoration in Is. lx. is the historical one. Both are religious ideals and constructions of the final state of the people and the world.—Cambridge Bible.

force to turn vice into virtue; but it recommends virtue, with something like the blandishments of pleasure."—Burke.

b "The priests who keep watch as guards of the temple." — Vulgate.

c The breadth does not agree with that of Sol.'s porch, the length does.

d Comp. 1 Ki. vii. 21; 2 Chr. iii. 17.

"Beauty was lent to nature as the type of heaven's unspeakable and holy joy, where all perfection makes the sum of bliss." —Mrs. Hale.

CHAPTER THE FORTY-FIRST.

1—6. (1) **temple,** the actual sanctuary, the holy place:[a] 1 Ki. vi. 17. **posts,** i. e. the piers, or door-cases on each side of the entrance. **tabernacle,** Com. B., "posts." (2) **sides** etc. i. e. the side pieces of the entrance. (3) **inward,** or inside. **post,** etc., R. V., "each post of the entrance." (4) **before,** in front of. **measured,** etc., comp. the holy of holies of Sol.'s temple.[b] **most holy,** the Oracle as distinguished fr. the temple or holy place. (5) **wall,** or outer wall, wh. was of immense thickness. **side chamber,** comp. 1 Ki. vi. 5—10. (6) **three,** i. e. there were 3 stories of 10 chambers in each. **hold .. house,** i. e. the beams were made to rest, not on the actual wall, but on rests projecting from the wall.

The Spiritual Temple.—If we diligently attend to the instructions given us in the plainer parts of religion, and profit by them, we shall be led further into an acquaintance with the mysteries of the Kingdom of God. They that are willing to dwell in God's courts shall at length be brought into His Temple. Ezekiel was himself a priest, but by the iniquity and calamity of the times was cut short of his birthright privilege of ministering in the Temple; but God made up the loss to him by introducing him into this prophetical, evangelical, celestial Temple, and employing him to transmit a description of it to the Church, in which he was dignified above all the rest of his order.—M. Henry.

7—12. (7) **enlarging,** what the verse means to say is that the side-chambers widened in the second and third stories through the retreating of the wall of the house. **increased .. midst,** R. V., "so one went up fr. the lowest chamber to the highest by the middle chamber."[a] (8) **saw .. about,** R. V., "the house had a raised basement round about." **six great cubits,**[b] ch. xl. 5. (9) **that .. left,**[c] i. e. that wh. was left of the raised platform unoccupied by the temple buildings. (10) **between,** etc., from the

a "The holy place, to which we have come from the fore-court. The measurement begins from the east wall, where the entrance was. this wall had pillars six cubits broad, and bet. the pillars a door ten cubits broad, with doorposts five cubits broad on each side; so that the whole breadth of the wall was thirty-two cubits." — Keil.

b 1 Ki. vi. 20.

a "Winding stairs, which enlarged as the rooms did, went up between each two chambers from the bottom to the top; and there were two doors at the top of each pair of stairs, one door opening into one room, the other into that over against it." — Lowth.

b Lit. "Six cubits to the arm-pit."

c "Rather, 'and so also was what was left free to the side chambers of the house.' " —Wordsworth.

outer wall to the wall of the court.[d] (12) **building,** behind the sanctuary, in the vacant space, and prob. used for receiving the offal, etc., of the sacrifices.

The Spiritual Temple.—Ezekiel never intended that a structure should be reared precisely according to the plan and measurements he furnishes, otherwise he would have been still more minute in his delineations. He has given enough, however, for his great object, which was chiefly to show that in the Divine purpose respecting the future there was to be a full and every way complete reconstruction of the House of God, if not in the outward and material sense, yet in the higher things, which that represented and symbolised, and with the effect of securing a far purer and more elevated condition for the covenant-people. It is this last point which throughout he seeks to render prominent by the nature of his descriptions.—Fairbairn.

13—17. (13) **house,** or sanctuary proper, the holy place. **separate place,** "the court of 20 cubits broad wh. ran round the house" **building,** that mentioned in vs. 12. (14) **face,** or front. (15) **which was behind it,** rather "behind which it was." **galleries,** terraces-buildings; poss. the word means the side-chambers, vss. 6, 7. (16) **cieled with wood,** or overlaid with woodwork.[e] **covered** or hidden from view from below. Or the meaning may be, covered with lattice-work. (17) **by measure,** i.e. even this woodwork was done by careful measurement.

The Spiritual Temple.—"The spiritual lesson to be learned by us from the description here is, that the Church of God, the Temple of the Holy Ghost, as it shall hereafter be manifested on earth, shall be on a scale of grandeur such as has never yet been witnessed, and its worship shall be on a corresponding scale of glory, beauty, and blessedness. Not till then shall the Lord be worshiped visibly in the beauty of holiness by the whole congregation of earth, led on by Israel as the leader of the mighty choir. None of the defects which attend our present liturgical worship shall alloy the perfection of the public services of God which shall then be rendered to Him through Christ. There shall be no divisions. Now the catholicity of the Church is but partially seen, though it is a blessed reality, and its unity is hardly to be recognised at all, split up as it is into a hundred denominations with varying confessions of faith and different forms of worship; then all shall be one in outward worship, as well as in inward unity of the spirit, and the world will in consequence be attracted to believe the Divine mission of Messiah (John xvii. 21)."—Fausset.

18—22. (18) **made,** or ornamented with carved work, in the wood, wh. took shape of cherubim, palm trees, etc. **two faces,** comp. ch. i. 10. As carved on the flat they could not show four faces. (19) **made through,** or the design was repeated all through the house. (20) **unto .. door,** comp. up to the windows, vs. 16. (21) **posts,** or side pilasters. **squared,** not round, nor arched. **face of the sanctuary,** the clause is to be connected with vs. 22. Perhaps: "and in front of the sanctuary (the holiest) was the appearance as the appearance 22 of an altar of wood, three cubits the height thereof," etc. So the Sept. In the holy place in front of the holiest there stood an object having the appearance of an altar of wood. —Cam. B. (22) **altar,** of incense, Ex. xxx. 1, etc.[a] **table,** another word for an altar.[b] The only article mentioned in the holy place **before the Lord,** in front of the holy of holies.[c]

The Magic of the Inner Life.—The Arabs have a saying about the palm-tree, that it stands with its feet in salt water and its head in the sun. They often cannot drink of the brackish water found in the oasis where the palm grows; but they tap the tree and drink the sweet palm wine. The palm-tree, by the magic of its inner life, can so change the elements found in the unkindly soil around it that they minister to its growth and strength and fruit-bearing.—J. B. Johnston.

23—26. (23) **two doors,** 1 Ki. vi. 31. The holy place and the holy of holies "each had one door composed of two turning (or, folding) leaves, ornamented, like the walls of the house, with carvings of cherubim and palms." (24) **turning leaves,** the leaves in turn had two leaves, each door therefore had four small leaves like a screen. (25) **made,** or carved. **thick planks,** made to form a kind of landing of wood in front of the porch on the outside. (26) **narrow windows,** ch. xl. 16. **thick planks.**

The Ideal Sanctuary.—What are the chief impressions suggested **by**

---

[d] "As the rows of chambers ran E. and W., one set of chambers opened to the south, another set to the north." — Spk. Com.

[e] 1 Ki. vi. 15, 16.

"The higher we build up ourselves in our most holy faith, the more should our hearts, those living temples, be enlarged."—M. Henry.

"The Lord Christ will measure Christians of what height, breadth and depth they are; their actions, affections, and graces will be measured (Rev. xi. 1)."—Greenhill.

[a] "The altar here is a cubit higher, and double the breadth to that of Moses, which is supposed to be agreeable to the dimensions of the altar made by Solomon who did not exactly observe the proportions prescribed to Moses, in making the cherubim and other furniture of the temple." —Lowth.

[b] Mal. i. 7.

[c] The altar of incense was before the veil of the holy of holies, where was the Divine presence over the ark." — Wordsworth.

"Let every man examine himself by this measuring-rod how far he has advanced."—Gregory.

"Friendship may be to us merely a cut flower that graces our ban-

this description of the ideal sanctuary. The prophet has no care for the element of ecclesiastical architecture; aesthetics do not appeal to his idea of worship. His conceptions of true worship are conveyed to us by the mathematical precision with wh. he outlines the ground plan. It is obvious enough that the design is influenced by certain ruling principles, of which the most conspicuous are these three: separation, gradation, and symmetry. And these again symbolise three aspects of the one great idea of holiness, which the prophet desired to see embodied in the whole constitution of the Hebrew state as the guarantee of lasting fellowship between Jehovah and Israel. What Ezekiel did was to carry out the idea of separateness with a thoroughness never before attempted, and in such a way as to make the whole arrangements of the sanctuary an impressive object lesson on the holiness of Jehovah.—Exp. B.

quet for a day and then dies a natural death; or it may be a live plant, daily unfolding its blossoms with sweetness and beauty that all may share." —Lucy Larcom.

CHAPTER THE FORTY-SECOND.

1—4. (1) **utter,** or outer. This would be the priests' court; some prefer to regard these chambers as connected with the separate building, ch. xli. 12, and so in the outer court of the people. **chamber,** better, block of chambers.[a] (2) **Before,** etc., better, "unto the place whose length was," etc. (3) **gallery,** or row of chambers. (4) vss. **4—6** may be read: "And before the chambers was a walk of **10** cubits breadth inward, with a length of 100 cubits; and their doors were toward the north. (5) Now the upper chambers were shorter; for the galleries took away from them compared with the lower and middle (chambers) in room. (6) For they were in three stories, and they had not pillars like the pillars of those in the outer court; therefore" etc.—Cam. B. [For an adequate description of these buildings of the inner court compare the Pulp. Com. or the Cam. B. where diagrams of the temple may be found.] **walk,** or cloister, dividing the building into two sets of rooms, one half of wh. looked into the outer court, the other into the inner. **one cubit,** no doubt should be "100 cubits."

[a] "There were two equal clusters of chambers on the north and south of the Gizrah, or separate place. These two clusters of chambers were one hundred cubits from east to west, and fifty cubits fr. north to south, and they had three stories." —Wordsworth.

Note on vss. 1—4.—These chambers were intended for shelter, rest, and refreshment for those who waited on God in worship; every necessary comfort and convenience was provided. The priests were wholly devoted to their sacred calling; they renounced the world and all its most tempting prizes, and gave themselves up body and soul to a life-long consecration to the work of the Temple. The law of worship demanded this complete self-renunciation; and at the same time it secured to the servant of God everything that was essential to his well-being and to help him in his hallowed work. The minister of the Divine Word must be relieved from the fret and care of worldly things, that he may be free to apply himself with a whole-hearted abandon to the study and interpretation of spiritual things (1 Tim. iv. 15).—Geo. Barlow.

5—9. (5) **shorter,** or shortened.[b] **were higher,** R. V., "took away from these, more than from the lower," etc. (6) **not pillars,** "the two upper stories had balconies standing out of them, the breadth of which was taken out of the rooms themselves, and made them so much narrower, bec. the weight of the balconies was not supported by pillars, as the rooms over the cloisters of the outward court were, but only by the wall." (7) **wall, or fence...** (8) **length,** from N. to S. (9) **entry,** or passage into the court.

The Chambers, though near the Temple, were separate from it, were strictly private, placed in the midst of stillness and retirement favorable to meditation and prayer. The power of the worker for God in public is acquired by diligent devotion in private. God is known in the greatness and glory of His character and the wisdom and righteousness of His ways; not in the midst of noise and uproar, but in quietness and solitude. The thinker must isolate himself for the time being from all distraction, and quietly and prayerfully wait on God. "Be still, and know that I am God" (Ps. xlvi. 10). Not in the wild commotion and brazen clangor of the battlefield, not in the whizzing hurricane of national strife and uproar, not in the rush and worry of excessive worldly care, are the holy secrets **of Divine things divulged to the soul, but in the solitude of retirement, in**

[b] "The building rose in terraces, as was usual in Bab. architecture, and so each of the two upper stories receded from the one below it."—Spk. Com.

"The Bible, without a spiritual life to interpret it, is like a trellis on which no vine grows—bare, angular, and in the way. The Bible, with a spiritual life, is like a trellis covered with a luxuriant vine—beautiful, odorous, and heavy with purple clusters shining through the leaves."—Beecher.

"Dependable people!—their price is above rubies. The world would be a dreary place, if there were not some Christians who need no prodding nor watching, who can be told and then trusted. A wise old Roman once said, 'I do not like a soldier who moves his hands in marching and his feet in battle.' "—S. S. Times.

"Hold fast to the Bible as the sheet-anchor of our liberties; write its precepts on your hearts and practice them in your lives. To the influence of this book we are indebted for the progress made in true civilization, and to this we must look as our guide in the future." — U. S. Grant.

[a] Le. xvi. 23.

"What a pin is when the diamond has dropped from its setting, that is the Bible when its emotive truths have been taken away."—Beecher.

[a] Here meaning, devoted to only common uses.

[b] "The lowness of the wall renders it unfit for the purpose of defence. But its square form is the emblem of the kingdom that cannot be shaken, resting on Prophets and Apostles, Jesus Christ being the chief cornerstone."

—Fausset.

"Thus every way it exhibits to the eye of faith the true ideal of that pure and

the hush and stillness of some meditative retreat, where the tocsin of war is never heard and the peal of cannon and crash of arms never penetrate. Not that we are to indulge in a life of useless quietism and inactivity. We must silence our meaningless clamor and pause in our demonstrative activities in order that God may speak and may work His purpose in us: then we receive our commission and are inspired to speak and work for Him.—Geo. Barlow.

10—12. (10) **building** i.e. "the wall of the outer court with its stories of cells." (11) **way before them,** appearance to one looking at them from the front. **appearance,** lxx. "measure." The thought is that the chambers on the N. and S. side of the temple were just alike.

The Bible.—As in Beethoven's matchless music there runs one idea, worked out through all the changes of measure and of key, now almost hidden, now breaking out in rich, natural melody, whispered in the treble, murmured in the bass, dimly suggested in the prelude, but growing clearer and clearer as the work proceeds, winding gradually back until it ends in the key in which it began, and closes in triumphant harmony; so throughout the whole Bible there runs one great idea: man's ruin by sin, and his redemption by grace; in a word, Jesus Christ, the Saviour. This runs through the Old Testament, that prelude to the New, dimly promised at the fall, and more clearly to Abraham; typified in the ceremonies of the law; all the events of sacred history paving the way for His coming; His descent proved in the genealogies of Ruth and Chronicles; spoken of as Shiloh by Jacob, as the Star by Balaam, as the Prophet by Moses; the David of the Psalms; the Redeemer looked for by Job; the Beloved of the Song of Songs. We find Him in the sublime strains of the lofty Isaiah; in the writings of the tender Jeremiah; in the mysteries of the contemplative Ezekiel; in the visions of the beloved Daniel; the great idea growing clearer and clearer as the time drew on. Then the full harmony broke out in the song of the angels, "Glory to God in the highest; on earth peace, goodwill towards men." And Evangelists and Apostles taking up the theme, the strain closes in the same key in which it began; the devil, who troubled the first paradise, for ever excluded from the second; man restored to the favor of God; and Jesus Christ the key-note of the whole.—H. W. Beecher.

13—16 (13) **eat,** etc., Le. iii. 3, 10, vii. 9—11, x. 12, vi. 30, vii. 6. (14) **there,** i.e. in these appointed places, within the specially holy precincts of the inner court.[a] **those things which are for,** R. V., "that wh. pertaineth to" i.e. the outer court. (15) **gate .. east,** i.e. the eastern gate of the outer court. (16) **measuring reed,** whose length is given in ch. xli. 8.

Sacerdotal Sanctity.—I. Ceremonial holiness. This is described as affecting. 1. The priests. 2. Their residences. 3. Their food. 4. Their garments. 5. Their offerings. II. The spiritual significance of ceremonial holiness. A complete explanation is perhaps not possible. But it is evident that it was intended to convey to Israel and to mankind: 1. A conception of the holiness of God. 2. A conception of the holy character of acceptable worship. 3. A conception of the holy services of obedience and praise.—Thomson.

17—20. (17) **round about,** i.e. including the precincts (20) **profane place,**[a] i.e. Jerusalem itself only called profane, as not being specially consecrated.[b]

The Grandeur of the Divine Temple.—1. It is of vast extent. He measured the east, north, south, and west sides, each side being 500 reeds, —in all a square of 1 1-7 of a mile—exceeding the limits of all ancient Jerusalem. This signifies the great enlargement of the Church of God in future times. 2. It is immovably secure. "He measured by the four sides." Its square form betokened the strength and solidity of the whole —an emblem of the kingdom that cannot be moved. 3. It marks off an unmistakable distinction between the holy and profane.—Hom. Com.

The Bible to be Learned by the Heart.—Bring down from the dusty garret an old file of papers, and while the venerable old dame sits near the fire, almost unconscious of passing things, read there the simple names of two that long years ago were married. They are nothing at all to the antiquarian reader, a stranger, seeking more lore; but how much they are to the aged one, who feels as if resurrection had dawned upon her mind, and before whom all the long past rises up, brighter and clearer the further it goes back towards childhood! For a moment she sees all this in the reading of those words, and but for a moment; then they sing again under the ashes, and go out. Even thus it is with the passages of God's Word. On the surface they are smooth and simple; but if your heart knows how to plumb them, great depths, and often unsearchable, there are in them. But as the Bible is but a record of life, and as it addresses itself to life again, so, for its comprehension, there must have been life-experience. Dictionaries and grammars are like keys to a house. A key can unlock the outward door, but cannot introduce you to the people that live there, nor tell you what they are. And so, though dictionaries and grammars, and exegetical and hermeneutical helps can introduce you into the books of the Bible, your own heart must be your teacher after that, or you will have none. If you have no depths, no wants, no joys, no sorrows, with which to read, and through which to understand, then you cannot interpret this world-book. For the Bible is the heart-book of the world. Only the heart can ever tell its secret meanings; for "with the heart man believeth unto righteousness."—Beecher.

glorious Temple which, resting on the foundation of the eternal Son and girt round with all the perfections of Godhead, shall shine forth the best and noblest workmanship of Heaven."
—Fairbairn.

"It is in the desert and on the mount that God speaks to man face to face. The desert is the weaned heart, the mount is the lowly spirit."

CHAPTER THE FORTY-THIRD.

1—6. (1) **gate .. east,** the eastern gate of the priests' court. (2) **glory,** etc., the visible token of God's coming to dwell in this new temple. See for His forsaking the temple, ch. x. 19, xi. 23. **voice .. waters,** see Re. i. 15.[c] (3) **vision,** ch. i. 3, iii. 23. **to destroy,** i.e. to prophesy the destruction of. (4) **came .. house,** returning to His place in the holy of holies. (5) **filled the house,** comp. Ex. xl. 34, 35; 1 Ki. viii. 10, 11. (6) **heard him speaking,** R. V., "heard one speaking. . . . and a man," etc. The man is merely the divine voice and word personified and interposed between the Lord and the prophet, hence though Ezekiel appears to hear one speaking from the house, the voice immediately takes the shape of a man beside him.—Com. B.

The Revelation of the Glory of Jehovah.—I. It was a revelation of the Divine Word. 2. It was a revelation of visible splendor. 3. It was a revelation of overwhelming majesty. II. It was a revelation of the glory of Jehovah consecrating His temple. III. It was a revelation requiring spiritual help to see and understand. 1. The help of the spirit is necessary to see the visions of God. 2. The help of the spirit is necessary to interpret the Word of God.—Geo. Barlow.

7—9. (7) **he said,** this was the voice the Prophet heard from the Glory. **the place,** better, "this is the place." **throne .. feet,** comp. Is. lxvi. 1, 2. **defile,** by yielding to idolatries, and bringing into it idolatrous rites. **in .. places,** R. V., Marg. "in their death" i.e. the sepulchres of the Kings had been placed so near the temple that defilement had taken place. Contact with a dead body produced under all circumstances the highest degree of ceremonial uncleanness, and nothing could have been more abhorrent to Ezekiel's priestly sense of propriety than the close proximity of dead men's bones to the house in which Jehovah was to dwell. In order to guard against the recurrence of these abuses in the future it was necessary that all secular buildings should be removed to a safe distance from the Temple precincts.—Exp. B. (8) **their thresholds,** ref. to the fact that the royal palace and Solomon's temple virtually occupied the same enclosure.

Seeing God.—A wise answer was that given by a humble young Hindoo convert when met by one of those enemies of truth that are found in heathen and Christian lands alike, and whose objections are much the same wherever met. "My god can be seen by every one," said a Hindoo who wanted to confuse and deride him; "for he is there at the end of the street. What is the use of a god you can't see?" Then the boy asked a question in turn. "Have you ever seen the tax-collector?" "Yes, often," said the Hindoo. "The governor?" "Well, rarely." "Have you ever seen the great queen empress?" "No; how should a poor villager like me ever see her?" "Ah,!" rejoined Vadivelu triumphantly, "the little people

c "The noise of purling streams is grateful, of a roaring sea dreadful."
—Mat. Henry.

"The glory of the God of Israel must take possession of the new Sanctuary, as in time past of the Tabernacle and of Solomon's Temple. But it is in a different form. The glory was of old veiled in a cloud resting on the mercy-seat, as though the mercy and the power of God were in some sort restricted to the material building and the people to whom it belonged. Now a personal and living God enters the Sanctuary, condescending to occupy it, not merely as a fixed dwelling-place, but as a centre from whence His power and mercy radiate freely to the utmost ends of the earth. Hence amidst the detailed preparations of the house no mention is made of mercy-seat, so important a part in the former Sanctuary."
—Spk. Com.

you can see any day, but the great people seldom or never. We can see your gods in street-corners, because they are such little ones, but Christ, our God, the great and true, is in the heavens. We cannot see him now, but those who love him here shall see him hereafter."—C. E. World.

10—12. (10) **measure the pattern,** so as to prove their returning obedience by exactly carrying out the directions given. (11) **write it,** so that they may carefully study it. (12) **whole limit,** all embraced within the enclosing walls, and even the mountain itself.[a]

The Temple of the Future (vs. 10).—This vision illustrates for us—I. The characteristics of the kingdom of God; it is sacred, it is conspicuous, it is vast, it is complete, it is sacrificial, it is beautiful, it is God-inhabited. II. The qualification for having to do with this kingdom.—U. R. Thomas.

13—17. (13) **cubit,** the bottom was the basement in wh. sat the altar; it was a cubit in height and extended a cubit beyond the altar itself, see ch. xl. 5. **higher place,** or back. The edge was arranged to keep the blood from running on to the pavement. It formed a kind of shooting and led into a drain. (14) **settle,** or stage. "The narrowings, or inbenchings, of the altar are here called settles." (15) four **horns,** Ex. xxvii. 2.[b] (16) **squares,** sides, see Ex. xxvii. 1; Re. xxi. 16. (17) **settle,** the higher one, vs. 14. **stairs,** or steps.

18—22. (19) **young bullock,** Le. viii. 14. The statement in vss. 19, 20 is somewhat elliptical, the writer's object being to advert specially to the difference between the sin-offering on the first day and that on the following days. Hence he describes the ritual of the sin-offering on the first day fully, omitting to refer to the burnt-offering, which he mentions only in connexion with the second and following days.—Cam. B. (20) **four horns,** vs. 15. **cleanse,** purify fr. sin. **purge,** to make atonement for. (21) **appointed place,** comp. Ex. xxix. 14[a] (22) **kid .. goats,** R. V., "he-goat" **cleanse,** by sprinkling the blood.[b]

Consecration.—The consecration of the altar corresponds to the consecration of the people to Jehovah, their entire surrender and presentation of themselves to Him. The burnt-offerings usher in the class of offerings which obtain in the state of grace. The justified man lives henceforth not to himself; the service of the Lord which is ministered in the Church is symbolized by this purpose of the altar of burnt-offering; hence there is no act of worship without burnt-offering. The self-surrendering reliance on grace continues to be taken into account, as in the past so for the future, and so the burnt-offering may be called the perpetual offering of the Church of God.—Lange.

23—27. (23) **ram,** comp. Ex. xxix. 31; Le. viii. 22. (24) **cast salt,** Le. ii. 13; Mk. ix. 49.[c] (25) **Seven days,** the same sacrifices were to be offered on each of these days, except that a bullock was offered on the first day. (26) **consecrate themselves,** R. V., "consecrate it," i.e. the altar. The above passage deals entirely with the consecration of the altar, according to Mosaic regulations. (27) **peace offerings,** or thank offerings.[d] Mal. i. 11. **accept you,** ch. xx. 40, 41: Ro. xii. 1; 1 Pe. ii. 5.

Acceptance.—The purpose of the temple is the establishment and maintenance of harmonious relations between God and the sons of men. By sin those relations have been interrupted; by religion they are restored. What was symbolized by the material temple at Jerusalem—its priesthood and services and sacrifices.—is realized in the spiritual temple of the new covenant, in which Christ is the Sacrifice and the Priest, and in which the Holy Spirit sheds the Shechinah-glory through the holiest of all. Acceptance thus takes the place of estrangement. I. Acceptance is of God's grace, and is undeserved. II. Acceptance is in virtue of the high priest's mediation and intercession. III. Acceptance is for the obedient, the compliant, the submissive. IV. Acceptance is alike of the person and of the service. V. Acceptance involves the enjoyment of all the manifestations and consequences of the Divine favor. Application.—1. One aim of a spiritual ministry to men is to convince them that in their sinful state they are without acceptance with God. 2. Another aim of such a ministry is to exhibit the divinely appointed method of obtaining and enjoying acceptance with God. 3. Yet another aim is to expose false and delusive representations of the way of acceptance.—Thomson.

---

[a] Is. ii. 2, 3; Mi. iv. 1, 2.

"Conscience is not free from hallucinations — we aim at personal righteousness, for instance, and hit the target of bigotry, hypocrisy and pharisaical conceit."

[b] "The altar regarded as to its height is called Har-El, the Mount of God; and in its area, or upper surface, is called Arie, the lion of God, or as some render it, the hearth of God, as consuming the sacrifices." —Wordsworth.

[a] Le. iv. 12; He. xiii. 11.

[b] Le. iv. 27, 28, 30.

"He who has given us our work to do, can easily commit it to other hands."

[c] "In the second temple no sacrifice was complete without the use of salt, and the Rabbis tell us that there was a great heap of salt close to the altar, always ready for use, and that the inclined plane to the altar was kept covered with salt." — Edersheim.

[d] "Under the guidance of the Epistle to the Hebrews we cannot fail to recognise in this vision the symbol of the purification of the Church of God by the cleansing blood of Christ, Victim and Priest, Heb. viii. ix., x." — Spk. Com.

CHAPTER THE FORTY-FOURTH.

Ch. xliv.—xlvi. The Priesthood, Revenues, Ritual of this New Sanctuary. Temple and priesthood are so related that a reform of the one implies of necessity a reform of the other. It is therefore not in itself surprising that Ezekiel's legislation should include a scheme for the reorganization of the Temple priesthood. But these general considerations hardly prepare us for the sweeping and drastic changes contemplated in the forty-fourth chapter of the book.—Exp. B.

1—3. (1) **outward sanctuary,** R. V., "outer," or court of the priests. "Only a prince of the house of David might sit down in the priests' court." (2) **shall be shut,** i.e. usually shut, and only opened for one person, and on special occasions for him. **Lord .. entered,** by the smybol of His presence passing in that way.[a] (3) **the prince,** ch. xxxiv. 24. The head of the nation regarded as the vicegerent and earthly representative of God. **eat bread,** a custom connected with sacrifices.[b] "A religious feast made of the remainder of a sacrifice."

Shutting the Gate Through which the King has Entered.—Caron, in his Account of Japan, tells us that whenever any of the chief nobles builds a new palace, he causes an entrance to be made for common use, and also one which is more elegant, adorned with carvings from top to bottom, varnished and gilt. This is covered over with planks, in order that it may not be damaged either by the sun or by the rain; and it remains thus covered till the emperor goes to feast in the new-built palace. As soon as he has passed in and out of it, it is again shut and covered up, nor is it either opened or uncovered again, except upon a like occasion, because no one may enjoy the honor of treading on the same threshold with the emperor; whilst at the same time it would be considered as derogatory to his majesty to pass over one that had been worn. In the words of the text "This gate shall be shut. It is for the prince."

4—8. (4) **north gate,** ch. xl. 20. **glory,** etc., comp. 1 Ki. viii. 10, 11. (5) **entering .. going forth,** these were carefully arranged so as to secure that nothing profane or idolatrous should be admitted within the temple precincts. (6) **let it suffice,**[a] let the past suffice; don't repeat it any more. (7) **strangers** R. V., "aliens." 2 Ki. xi. 7; 1 Ki. xiv. 27, 28. Here we have historical evidence of the admission to the sanctuary of a class of foreigners answering in all respects to the uncircumcised aliens of Ezekiel's legislation. That the practice of enlisting foreign mercenaries for the guard continued till the reign of Josiah seems to be indicated by an allusion in the book of Zephaniah, where the prophet denounces a body of men in the service of the king who observed the Philistine custom of "leaping over the threshold."—Exp. B. **my bread,** the fat and the blood were regarded as peculiarly appropriated to God.[b] **because of,** R. V., "to add unto." (8) **set keepers,** i.e. set them, the aliens, as keepers without solicitude for the holiness of God's house. **charge,** Le. viii. 35. **for yourselves,** i.e. at your own pleasure, not according to the revealed will and law.[c]

The Attempt to Satisfy the Claims of Religion by Proxy.—There are now many Jews in Jerusalem kept in idleness by their more wealthy brethren in Europe, who hope by this expedient to secure for themselves the merit of living and dying in the Holy City, without undergoing the irksome experience of actual residence. In Roman Catholic countries it is common to devote a sum of money to the payment of the priest who is to say so many Masses on behalf of a person. Among ourselves there is an unconfessed but common notion that the minister in some way perform the offices of religion on behalf of the people, who stand by as idle spectators, and yet enjoy the religion on behalf of the people, who stand by as idle spectators, and yet enjoy the fruits of his vicarious service. There is a common feeling that the mere attendance at church when a service is being conducted is of some religious efficacy, the officiating minister carrying on the real worship on behalf of the congregation, which may be listless and indifferent, so long as he discharges his duty faithfully. **Or perhaps the religion by proxy is attempted in the way of**

---

a Eze. xliii. 2.

b Ge. xxxi. 54; Ex. xviii. 12, xxiv. 11; 1 Co. x. 18.

"A difference is to be put between common and sacred things, between God's name and other names, between His day and other days, His Book and other books, His institutions and other observances; and a distance to be put between our worldly and religious actions, so as still to go about the worship of God with a solemn pause." —M. Henry.

a 1 Pe. iv. 3.

b Le. iii. 16, xvii. 11.

c "Or, 'Ye have not yourselves kept the charge of My holy things, but have set others as keepers of My charge in My sanctuary for yourselves." —Maurer.

"The more diligently I pursue my search into these oracles of eternal truth, the Scriptures, I perceive a wider, a deeper, an ever-increasing fund of spiritual treasures." — Hervey.

"My practice, since I was thirty years old, has been to read in the Bible the first thing I do every morning. This practice I have followed, with but few interruptions, for fifty years." — John Quincy Adams.

"That Book is the rock on which our republic rests."—Andrew Jackson.

"The Bible furnishes the only fitting vehicle to express the thoughts that overwhelm us when contemplating the stellar universe." — O. M. Mitchel, the astronomer.

[d] 2 Chr. xxxv. 11.

[e] Very few Levites returned from the captivity. See Ezra ii. 40—42; Neh. vii. 43-45; comp. Ezr. ii. 36—39, and viii. 15, 18, 19.

"The gap in the number of Levites was filled up by 220 Nethinim (given ones), prob. original strange and captives, who were held by the Jews in lowest repute." —Edersheim.

[f] "To perform the servile offices belonging to My temple and worship." —Lowth.

[a] "The material of wh. the four vestments of the ordinary priests were made was 'linen,' or more accurately, 'byssus,' the white shining cotton stuff of Egypt. These two qualities of the byssus are especially marked as characteristic, and on them part of the symbolic meaning depended." —Spk. Com.

[b] "Wool soon induces perspiration in the sultry east, and so becomes uncleanly." —Fausset.

[c] "Jerome supposes that the Jewish priests were forbidden to shave their heads, thereby to distinguish them fr. several of the heathen priests, particularly the Eg. priests of Isis and Serapis."—Lowth.

[d] "Long hair was a sign of effeminacy. 1 Cor. xi. 14."—Wordsworth.

[e] 2 Sa. xiv. 26.

money payments. Lastly, living in a Christian land, belonging to a Christian home, and having Christian associates are regarded as matters of some religious value by people who possess no real religion of their own. Thus they too would be religious by proxy.—W. F. Adeney.

9—14. (9) **shall enter,** to perform service. (10) **gone .. me.** R. V., "But the Levites that went." The exclusion of the Levites is founded on the unquestioned moral ground that their unfaithfulness to the basic principles of the national religion deserved this permanent degradation. By yielding themselves to the popular clamor for impure and idolatrous worship the Levites had caused Israel to stumble and profane Jehovah. 2 Chr. xxxvi. 14. **bear their iniquity,** i.e. the due consequence of their iniquity. (11) **ministers,** or attendants at the gates; porters. **slay,** etc., this was the work of Levites.[d] The Levites mentioned were to minister to the priests.[e] (12) **caused,** better, were an occasion to; they led the people by their bad example. (13) **near,** so as to be in actual contact with the holy things. (14) **keepers,** i.e. doorkeepers and attendants.[f]

Gone astray.—You cannot stop one inch away from God; one inch means two, and two inches mean a foot, and the foot soon grows into furlongs and miles. When some men do not pray it is as if there were silence in the whole universe; their voices seem necessary to the completeness of things; a great awful breach or rupture has been made in the music of creation when such voices cease their adoration and the utterance of their desires. Here, then, is a wonderful difference in men. Sometimes one man is as a thousand. If that one man be found true he will bring the thousand right, if they can be brought right; but if that one man be gone astray and far away from God, who can set the thousand in their places? It is as if a section of the stars had been shattered.—Parker.

15—19. (15) **sons of Zadok,** ch. xl. 46, xliii. 19. **fat and the blood,** vs. 7. (16) **sanctuary,** the first chamber, known as the holy place. **table,** or altar of burnt offering. (17) **linen garments,**[a] including the linen breeches, the coat, the girdle, and the bonnet. **no wool,** regarded as unclean,[b] vs. 18. (18) **bonnets,** or caps. **sweat,** regarded as unclean. (19) **utter court,** or outer court of the people. **with their garments,** i. e. while having on their special priestly garments.

The Use of a Bible.—It was customary in Cromwell's time for his soldiers to carry each a Bible in his pocket. Among others, a profligate young man was ordered to attack some fortress. During the engagement a bullet had perforated his Bible, and gone so far as to rest opposite these words in Ecclesiastes: "Rejoice, O young man, in thy youth, and let thy heart cheer thee in the days of thy youth, and walk in the ways of thy heart, and in the sight of thine eyes; but know thou, that for all these things God will bring thee into judgment." The words, so appropriate to his case, powerfully affected his mind, and proved by the blessing of God the means of his conversion. He used to observe that the Bible had been the happy means of saving both his soul and body.—J. Evans.

20—35. (20) **shave,** etc.,[c] Le. xxi. 5. **grow long,**[d] wh. was an ordinary sign of mourning. **poll,**[e] cut and trim. (21) **drink wine,** Le. x. 9. The prohibition refers to times when the priests were actually engaged in holy service. (22) **widow,** Le. xxi. 13. Te Levitical law for the high priest is extended to all priests. **her .. away,** i.e. a divorced woman. (23) **teach,** etc., Le. x. 10, xi.—xvi.; Mal. ii. 7. (24) **controversy,** i. e. when controversies or disputes arise among the people. **in judgment,** R. V., "to judge." (25) **dead person,** Le. xxi. 1, 11. (26) **cleansed,** fr. the defilement ensuing in relation to a dead body, Nu. xix. 11. The relations of these requirements to the corresponding parts of the Levitical law are somewhat complicated. The great point of difference is that Ezekiel knows nothing of the unique privileges and sanctity of the high priest.—Exp. B. (27) **his sin offering,** Le. iv. 3. (28) **it shall be, etc.,** Cam. B., "they shall have no inheritance;" while the remaining tribes had portions of the promised land, the priests received none. (29) **eat,** etc., for their necessary support. **dedicated,** or devoted thing, Le. xxvii. 21, 28. (30) **first,** chief, or best. **oblation,** or offering; gift from the produce of the ground.

dough, made from the new corn. Nu. xv. 20. (31) **dead of itself,**[f] Ex. xxii. 31; Le. xxii. 8.

Infidels and the Bible.—No matter how infidel philosophers may regard the Bible; they may say that Genesis is awry, and that the Psalms are more than half-bitter imprecations, and the prophecies only the fantasies of brain-bewildered men, and the Gospels weak laudations of an impostor, and the Epistles only letters of a mad Jew, and that the whole book has had its day; I shall cling to it until they show me a better revelation. The Bible emptied, effete, worn-out! If all the wisest men of the world were placed man to man, they could not sound the shallowest depths of the Gospel of John. O philosophers! break the shell, and fly out and let me hear how you can sing. Not of passion, I know that already; not of worldly power, I hear that everywhere; but teach me, through your song, how to find joy in sorrow, strength in weakness, and light in darkest days; how to bear buffeting and scorn, how to welcome death, and to pass through its ministration into the sphere of life; and this not for me only, but for the whole world that groans and travails in pain; and until you can do this, speak not to me of a better revelation. —H. W. Beecher.

f "The Mohammedans are forbidden to eat that wh. dieth of itself or killed by the horns of another beast; and that which hath been torn by a wild beast, and that which hath been sacrificed unto idols." —Gadsby.

"In God' service there is no filthy lucre. The Lord purifies everything for them who eat with Him." — Diedrich.

CHAPTER THE FORTY-FIFTH.

1—5. (1) **by lot,** or allotment, apportionment. Reference here is to the portion assigned to Jehovah, and used for His sanctuary, priests and Levites. **oblation,** Heb., heave-offering.[a] **reeds,** this word is supplied by the translators, prob, incorrectly; "cubits" is much better. **ten thousand,** R. V. marg., "twenty thousand." (2) **sanctuary,** including the entire temple-area. **suburbs,** void places; ground immediately about the temple-walls, wh. might not be built on. (3) **this measure,** vs. 1. (4) **for the priests,** for their work, dwellings, and maintenance. (5) **twenty chambers,** LXX. trans. better, "for cities to dwell in."[b]

Devotement and Consecration.—In the ideal kingdom there was to be a certain portion of the land devoted to sacred objects—to the sanctuary of Jehovah and to the residence of his ministers. This was called "a holy portion;" it was "an oblation unto the Lord." Thus in the very heart of the metropolis, in the most commanding situation, on the very best possible site, there was an abiding witness of the presence and the claims of God, and a continual recognition of and response to those claims on the part of the nation. In a country as Christian as ours the towers and spires of our sanctuaries, rising heavenward under every sky, standing strong and even thick among the homes and the shops and counting-houses of town and city, bear their testimony that God is remembered, that Jesus Christ is honored and worshiped by the people of the land. But better than this devotement of land and this building of sanctuaries, good as that is, is the consecration of heart and life to the Person and the service of the Redeemer.—Clarkson.

a "So called bec. when anything was offered to God, the offerer raised the hand."

Ex. xxv. 2, xxix 24, 27.

b Nu. xxxv. 2.

"Forgiveness that waits for repentance is a thing to be repented of."

6—8. (6) **possession..city,** or the portion to be occupied by the city. **for the whole house,** i. e. it was to be regarded as belonging to the nation, and free for the use of the entire people. (7) **for the prince,** for his palace and private estate.[c] His portion is thus carefully defined to prevent future encroachments such as there had been in the past.[d] **length .. portions,** R. V., "in length answerable to one of the portions." (8) **oppress,** by seizing on private property.

Supposed Loss of the Bible.—[The late Henry Rogers, in his Eclipse of Faith, records a dream which he entitles "The Blank Bible," in which it appeared that every copy of the Bible had in a single night become blank paper. The following is an extract from his description.] It was very early suggested that the whole Bible had again and again been quoted piecemeal in one book or other—that it had impressed its own image on the surface of human literature, and had been reflected on its course as the stars on a stream. But alas! when lost, on investigation it was found as vain to expect that the gleam of starlight would still remain mirrored in the water when the clouds had veiled the stars themselves, as that the bright characters of the Bible would remain reflected in the books of men when they had been erased from the book of God.

c "On either side of the 25,000 reeds a strip of land, running westwards to the sea, eastwards to the Jordan, formed the possession of the prince."—Spk. Com.

d 1 Sa. viii. 14, etc.; 2 Ki. xxiii. 35; Je. xxii.

A proud Indian nabob going along the streets one day, was attracted by the sounds proceeding from a mission school, and he drew near to listen. The boys were reading the fifth chapter of Matthew. The eyes of the prince flashed with unwonted fire; and when they had finish-

On inspection, it was found that every text, every phrase which had been quoted, not only in books of devotion and theology, but in those of poetry and fiction, had been remorselessly expunged. Never before had I had any adequate idea of the extent to which the Bible had molded the intellectual and moral life of the last eighteen centuries, nor how intimately it had interfused itself with habits of thought and modes of expression; nor how naturally and extensively its comprehensive imagery and language had been introduced into human writings, and most of all where there had been most of genius. A vast portion of literature became instantly worthless, and was transformed into so much waste-paper. It was almost impossible to look into any book of merit, and read ten pages together, without coming to some provoking erasures and mutilations, some "hiatus valde deflendi," which made whole passages perfectly unintelligible. Many of the sweet passages of Shakespeare were converted into unmeaning nonsense, from the absence of those words which his own all but divine genius had appropriated from a still diviner source. As to Milton, he was nearly ruined, as might naturally be supposed. Walter Scott's novels were filled with perpetual lacunæ. I hoped it might be otherwise with the philosophers, and so it was: but even here it was curious to see what strange ravages the visitation had wrought. Some of the most beautiful and comprehensive of Bacon's aphorisms were reduced to enigmatical nonsense.

ed their lesson, he exclaimed, "Well, if you only live that chapter as well as you read it, I will never say another word against Christianity."

During the persecution of the Nonconformists, in the reign of James II., one of them copied out the whole Bible in shorthand for his own use, fearing the re-establishment of popery, and the suppression of the Holy Scriptures.

9—12. (9) **suffice,** ch. xliv. 8. **exactions,**[a] lit. ejections, such as Ahab's, 1 Ki. xxi. 19. These minute details regarding the crown lands, etc., show the prophet's concern for the rights and welfare of the common people. **(10) just .. bath,** Le. xix. 35, 36; Pr. xi. 1. Just as later sovereigns were wont to meet their deficits by debasing the currency, so the kings of Judah had learned to augment their revenue by a systematic falsification of weights and measures. The taxes were surreptitiously increased by the use of a large shekel (for weighing out money payments) and a large bath and ephah (for measuring tribute paid in kind).—Exp. Bib. (11) **bath,** a measure for fluids.[b] **homer,** distinguish from omer, Ex. xvi. 36. (12) **gerahs,** Ex. xxx. 13. **maneh,** or pound.[c] The Sept. reads: "And the shekel shall be twenty gerahs; five (shekels) shall be five, and ten shekels ten, and fifty shekels shall be your maneh (mina)." The statement that "five shekels shall be five," etc., does not imply that there were five and ten shekel pieces but means that just weighing of money shall prevail, and five go for five, no more and no less.—Cam. B.

a "Your evictions of My people." —Wordsworth.

b 1 Ki. vii. 26, 38; 2 Chr. ii. 10, iv. 5; Is. v. 10.

c 1 Ki. x. 17; Ezr. ii. 69; Ne. vii. 71.

The following lines are said to have been found in Lord Byron's Bible.

"Within this awful volume lies the mystery of mysteries; O, happiest they of human race to whom our God has given grace to hear, to read, to fear, to pray, to lift the latch and force the way! But better had they ne'er been born who read to doubt or read to scorn."

Insincere Reform.—I happened to reach Paris the day after the Czar of all the Russias left the city, and the whole gay metropolis was several degrees gayer than usual by reason of the wonderfully elaborate decorations in his honor. Walking along the Champs Elysées, the most magnificent avenue, which leads from the Tuilleries to the Arc de Triomphe, I was almost startled to see that many of the trees by the roadside were putting forth buds and blossoms in those bleak October days as if it were genial springtime. But upon looking a little more closely, I saw that the cherry blossoms and peach blows and apple buds were all made of tissue paper, and were skilfully wired to the trees in countless thousands, evidently to give the Czar the impression that in his honor the seasons had been reversed, and spring for once had come in October. But even while I looked at these unnatural glories of the autumn, an army of workmen came along and began to strip the streets of their decorations; and I suppose that after a day or two scarcely a paper blossom could be found on one of the wind-swept trees.—F. E. Clark.

13—17. (13) **oblation,** the tribute to be given to the prince. (14) **cor,** prob. a synonym for homer;[d] the due in oil was one hundredth part. (15) **lamb,** or kid. **peace offerings,** or thank-offerings. (17) **prince's part,** his special duty as the prince. **prepare,** i. e. provide. **reconciliation,** R. V., "atonement." **solemnities,** R. V., "stated feasts."

d 1 Ki. v. 11; 2 Chr. ii. 10, xxvii. 5.

"The surest way to reveal your weakness is to hide your motives." — Ivan Panin.

"To find Christ is to lose selfishness and find yourself."

System in Benevolent Giving.—Systematic giving is less difficult than irregular giving. II. Systematic giving is generous giving. People who give without method or consideration rarely know how little they give. III Systematic giving should be wise giving. Spasmodic charity may be very generous, but it is likely to be foolish and misdirected. A more thoughtful method would lead to a more just apportioning of the funds that are contributed. It is not right that the cause of Christ should depend on irregular gushes of liberality.—Pul. Com.

xlv. 18—xlvi. 24. The offerings appointed for the stated seasons.

18—21. (18) **first month,**[a] see Le. xvi. 16. **cleanse,** Polychr. B. "Make atonement for." (19) **upon the posts,** etc., comp. ch. xliii. 20. (20) **seventh .. month,** Polychr. B. "in the seventh month on the first day of the month." Not for any one person in particular, but for the people bec. there may be among them one that erred through ignorance and thus caused Israel to profane God. (21) **passover,** Ex. xii., etc.

The Bible.—You find the Bible the patriot's charter-book, the child's delight, the old man's comfort, and the young man's guide. In its pages the sick and weary find the solace which they need, and the tempted meet with timely succor. Its words whisper hope and peace to the dying, and minister daily food to the healthy and vigorous household. With the pious music of its sublime or plaintive songs echo the roofs of ten thousand times ten thousand Christian temples, and the child's prayer, night and morn, is lisped forth in the simple and comprehensive words which were dictated by Him who is its central light.—Beard.

22—25. (22) **prepare, or provide.** (23) **seven,** etc., comp. Nu. xxviii. 19—24. **kid of the goats,** "he-goat." (24) **meat offering,** etc., vss. 11, 15. **hin,** sixth part of an ephah or bath. (25) **feast .. days,** Nu. xxix. 12. **shall .. days,** R. V., "in the feast, shall he do the like the seven days." This has ref. to the feast of the tabernacles, "the feast par excellence of the year."

The Feasts.—This order of solemn services does not follow exactly the order of Moses, of Solomon, or of Ezra, who, on the return from captivity, rearranged the festivals on the Mosaic pattern. Familiar as Ezekiel was with every detail of the Levitical law, this deviation can scarcely have been accidental, and we may herein recognise fresh indications that the whole vision is symbolical, representative of the times when, after the oblation of the one Sacrifice, reconciliation and sanctification were effected for man through the presence of God dwelling in the midst of the people.—Spk. Com.

[a] "The offerings here, and the manner of offering as to the sprinkling of the blood, etc., differ in many respects from the injunctions of the Levitical law." — Wordsworth.

"Do I cast away the Bible? No. But the Bible is like a telescope. If a man looks through his telescope, then he sees worlds beyond; but if he looks at his telescope, then he does not see anything but that. The Bible is a thing to be looked through to see that which is beyond; but most people only look at it; and so they only see the dead letter." Beecher.

CHAPTER THE FORTY-SIXTH.

1—4. (1) **gate,** etc., ch. xliv. 2, 3. "The system of external observances which he foreshadows in his vision was not meant to be the life of religion, but it was, so to speak, the trellis-work which was necessary to support the delicate tendrils of spiritual piety until the time when the spirit of filial worship should be the possession of every true member of the Church of God."—Exp. B. (2) **worship .. gate,**[b] comp. Sol.'s position at the dedication, 2 Chr. vi. 12, 13.[c] (3) **people .. land,** standing behind their prince, and represented by him. (4) **burnt offering,** comp. Nu. xxviii. 9.

Worship.—I. The object of worship is God only. II. The worshipers are the Church of the living God. III. The seat of acceptable worshipers is the heart. IV. The character of true worship corresponds with the nature and need of the worshipers. 1. There must be acknowledgment of the Divine attributes, contemplated with reverence. 2, There must be humiliation and confession of sin. 3. There must be the presentation of the due offering of gratitude to him from whom all blessings proceed. 4. There must be petitions and intercessions for needed good. V. The expression and form of worship must vary with the individual worshiper and his circumstances. VI. The seasons for worship are both occasional and continuous.—Thomson.

5—8. (5) **able to give,** i.e. the amount is to be settled by his own ability and willingness. (6) **new moon,** Nu. xxviii. 11, 15, (7) **meat offering,** vs. 5. **as his hand .. unto,** R. V., "as he is able." (8) **that gate,** vs. 1.

Choose Your God.—I. What will you live for if not for God? 1. Pleasure. And what does this promise you? Live as you like, it says; but will it last? 2. Wealth. But will your wealth make you happy? Is a miser happy? 3. Praise. Fame says, I will blow my trumpet loud over

[b] "This worship was offered by bowing his head, and bowing down his face to the earth, or falling down upon the ground, as the posture of Dios worship is elsewhere described." —Lowth.

[c] "The prince occupies an analogous position, standing in front of the porch of the eastern gate of the inner court, while the priests are sacrificing before him." — Spk. Com.

"Pleasant is it to entertain the picture of our selves in some future scene, planning wisely, feeling nobly, and executing with the holy triumph of the will; but it is a different thing—not in the green avenues of the future, but in the hot dust of the present moment—to do the duty that waits and wants me." —Anon.

your grave. Over your grave! Will you hear it then? Will you sleep the sweeter for it? At God's bar it may be a heavy curse. 4. Affection: friendship. Now, this in itself is beautiful. But earthly friends must die; and then they are not perfect. No, you want something better than this. II. Why you should live for God. In Him—1. You have what nothing else can give. 2 You may have all the other portions, too, as far as they are worth having.—J. Edmonds.

"We do not know when we have given enough—let us give a little more. We can only give what is given us if we give all we have."

"The Bible will not be less, but rather more, prized by our occasionally turning from it to open another and equally divine volume, to read some pages of the Book of Nature."—Guthrie.

9—15. (9) **over against it,** i.e. by the gate on the opposite side. (10) **in the midst,** as their representative. **go forth,** R. V., "they shall go forth together." (11) **solemnities,** appointed seasons. **able to give,** vs. 5. (12) **voluntary,** etc., as an act and expression of personal piety. (13) **daily,** etc., Ex. xxix. 38. (14) **continually,** a daily solemn recognition that all things they had were the Lord's. **temper,** R. V., "moisten," i.e. mix with. (15) **prepare,** or provide.

Proportionate Giving.—The offerings mentioned here are on a scale of liberality exceeding anything known under the Mosaic regimen. The prince set an example in generous giving, which the people cheerfully imitated. Our gifts to God's cause should not be more nor less than our circumstances justify. A missionary was staying with a wealthy Christian philanthropist, whose house was richly ornamented with paintings and sculpture, and was eulogising an exquisite marble statue of Silence—the figure of a boy with his finger to his lips. They had known each other from boyhood, and were free and confidential in conversation. "Do you admire that statue?" asked the friend of the missionary. "I never saw anything in my life equal to it for grace," replied he. "What do you think I gave for it?" "I cannot imagine." "I gave ninety guineas." "And what did you give at the collection to-night?" asked the missionary. "Oh, I gave five pounds." "Five pounds!" said the missionary. "Shame on you! Here you give ninety guineas for a marble statue of Silence and five pounds towards sounding the Gospel all over the earth. That is badly laid out money."—Geo. Barlow.

[a] Sons may have freehold rights, but servants only leasehold rights.

"The Jubilee year was restored after the captivity." — Josephus.

"There is a pleasure in accumulating, but there is a nobler pleasure in giving. Gonsalvo, the great Spanish captain, used to say, 'Never stint your hand. There is no way of enjoying one's property like giving it away;' and he acted up to his own precept." — Geo. Barlow.

16—24. (16) **give a gift,** it could only be from his allotted portion; and to his sons, not to his servants. He must not alienate any portion from his family. (17) **year of liberty,** jubilee year, when property was restored.[a] The object of this regulation apparently is to prevent the formation of a new hereditary aristocracy between the royal family and the peasantry. A life peerage, so to speak, or something less, is deemed a sufficient reward for the most devoted service to the king or the state. —Exp. B. (18) **take .. oppression,** ch. xlv. 8. (19) **a place,** for cooking the priests' food. **on .. westward,** R. V., "the hinder part." (20) **boil,** 2 Chr. xxxv. 13. **bake,** Le. ii. 4, 5, 7. (21) **every corner .. a court,** for cooking the flesh of the peace-offerings, of wh. the people partook along with the priests. (22) **courts joined,** Polyc. B. "small courts." (23) **row of buildings.** The "row" is probably not a series of separate buildings running round the court, but a continuous course of building, in which at the bottom ("under" the row) were recesses in which were the hearths where the pots were set in which the sacrifices were cooked. (24) **ministers,** the Levites.

Ezekiel's System succeeded in the important object of infusing a new spirit into the celebration of the feasts, and impressing on them a different character. The ancient Hebrew festivals were all associated with joyous incidents of the agricultural year. The tendency of the post-exilic ritual was to detach the sacred seasons more and more from the secular associations which had once been their chief significance.—Exp. B.

CHAPPTER THE FORTY-SEVENTH.

[a] "The Prophet Joel, taking occasion of the fact in nature, that there was a fountain under the temple at Jerusalem, wh. carried off the blood of the sacrifices, speaks of a fountain flowing forth from the house of the Lord, and watering the valley of Shittim, whither by nature its waters could not flow."—Pusey.

1—5. (1) **waters,** there was a fountain under the temple of **Jerusalem,** and this suggests the fig. here used.[a] **toward the east,** looking eastward. The inner sanctuary was placed toward the west. (2) **on the right side,** the prophet is conducted round to the E. gate via the N. gate and there beholds the stream emerge at the south side of the gate. (3) **waters .. ancles,** stated as indicating their depth. (4) **knees,** gradually increasing in depth. (5) **river,** symbolical of the full gifts of the Spirit in the later days.

The Vision of the Holy Waters (vss. 1—12).—I. This river in the place and character of its origin, in the gradual increase of it, and also in the healing, vitalizing properties of its waters, may be regarded as a type of the gradual development of the plan of salvation. II. They may be regarded as a figure of the rise and progress of religious Christianity in its origin, diffusion, and general results.

6—8. (6) **seen this,** taken full and careful observation of this. (7) **many trees,** the natural accompaniment of a fresh flowing stream. (8) **desert,** or plain of the Jordan. **sea,** the Dead Sea, R. V., "into the sea shall the waters go wh. were made to issue forth; and the waters shall be healed" i.e. the putrid waters of the Dead Sea shall be rendered salubrious. **healed,**[b] typical of the gracious work of God's Spirit.[c]

The Trees of Life.—On the cover of one of his books Ingersoll placed three crosses and under them the legend, "For the glory of God;" and three telegraph poles with their cross-bars which bore a resemblance to crosses, and under them the legend, "For the good of man." But without the crosses there would have been no telegraph poles. All the blessings of civilization are from the trees that grow upon the banks of the river of life.—Peloubet.

Living Waters.—There is an Oriental legend of a fountain into whose waters a good angel infused a mysterious power, such that a new fountain rose and gushed wherever some drops fell on the barren plain, so that a traveler, carrying a portion of this water, could safely traverse any desert, because he took with him the secret of unfailing springs; and he could impart their water to others.

Beneath the cross those waters rise, and he who finds them there
All through the wilderness of life the living stream may bear;
And blessings follow in his steps, until wher'er he goes
The moral wastes begin to bud and blossom as the rose.
—Peloubet's Notes.

9—12. (9) **rivers,** R. V., Marg. "two rivers," a Heb. dual of intensification sig. the greatness and power of this life-giving current. **shall live,** or, there shall be abundance of life. (10) **fishers,** the sign of its being known as a river full of life. **En-gedi,**[a] Ge. xiv. 7. **En-eglaim,** on the E. side of Dead Sea, where the Jordan falls into it. **great sea,** or Mediterranean. (11) **marishes,** or marshy places; from these salt was obtained for commerce. These will not be healed because the living stream will not reach them. (12) **fruit,** etc., comp. Re. xxii. 2. **waters,** etc., R. V., "waters thereof issue." Jehovah himself is the giver of all blessings to men, and from his presence all blessings flow. He was now present in his fulness and for ever in his temple. Hence the prophet sees the life-giving stream issue from the sanctuary. Another current idea was that in the regeneration of men, when the tabernacle of God was with them, external nature would also be transfigured. Then every good would be enjoyed and there would be no more evil nor curse. The desert would blossom like the rose, and the field that aforetime was thought fruitful should be accounted no better than bush.—Com. B.

13—17. (13) **border,** or, arrangement. A new allotment of the land was necessary on the return from captivity. **two portions,** Ge. xlviii. 5; Jos. xiv. 4, this made good the loss of Levi's portion and maintained the twelve tribes. (14) **one as .. another,** each receiving an equal portion. **lifted,** etc., ch. xx. 5, 6. **fall unto you,** by Divine arrangement, so that about it you need have no disputings. (15) **Hethlon,** a place near Damascus; ch. xlviii. 1.[b] **Zedad,** Nu. xxxiv. 7, 8. R. V., "unto the entering in of Zedad." (16) **Hamath,** at the foot of Mt. Hermon.[c]. **Berothah,** 2 Sam. viii. 8. **Sibraim,** unknown. **Hazar-hatticon,** or the middle Hazar, to distinguish it from Hazar-enan. **Hauran,**[d] the district S. of Damascus. (17) **Hazar-enan,** or village of fountains.

Additional note on vss. 1—12.—But "good" to the Israelite was not exclusively spiritual, it was also material. It would be an error to regard this fertilizing, healing stream in the light of a mere symbol for blessings which we call "spiritual." It is well fitted in other connexions to be such as symbol; but to take it so here would be to overstep the limits of the

[b] "The waters of the sea will be sweetened by the stream flowing into them." —Mosheh Ben Shesheth.

"In its bituminous waters no vegetable or animal life is said to be found. But now death is to give place to life in Judea, and throughout the world, as symbolised by the healing of those death - pervaded waters covering the doomed cities." — Fausset.

[c] "We find in it only a spiritual allegory, which foreshadows miracles of mercy in store for the whole world far more stupendous." — Thomson.

[a] "South of Engedi the sea is contracted, by a peninsula jutting into the sea northwards, so as to give to the whole southern part of the sea the appearance, not of a broad sheet of water, but rather of a long winding bay, or the estuary of a large river when the tide is out and the shoals are left dry."—Robinson.

An Irish boy being commanded by a priest to burn his Bible, reluctantly complied; but at the same time said, "I thank God that you can't take from me the twenty chapters that I have in my mind."

[b] "Prob. the defile between the ranges of Libanus and anti-Libanus, from the sea to Hamath." —Spk. Com.

[c] 1 Ki. viii. 65; Am. vi. 2, 14.

[d] Auranitis.

"The Christian graces are like perfumes, the

Old Testament and anticipate a later revelation. As yet the Israelite had no conception of a transcendent sphere of existence for men in the fellowship of God, such as we name heaven. Man's final abode even in his perfect state was considered to be still on the earth. God came down and dwelt with men; men were not translated to abide with God. But God's presence with men on earth gave to earth the attributes of heaven. —Camb. Bible.

more they are pressed by affliction the sweeter they smell; or, like the stars, they appear best in the darkness of trouble."—J. Beaumont.

The Division of the Land.—I. The division was into separate allotments. The land of Israel was not held in common by the whole people. Certain dues were attached to it, and certain regulations governed the treatment of it by its owners. Thus it was forbidden for any one to make an absolute sale of his estate. God divides our lives out severally. Each must live his own separate life and discharge his individual duty while he receives his personal grace. II. The division was clear and definite. We ought to have no doubt as to our portion in life. In the region of personal religion each should see what is his portion and mission for the world. III. The division included a portion for every Israelite. It was so carefully made that the most insignificant family should not be overlooked. There should be a share for every one in the produce of our great fruitful earth. This holds good also in the spiritual world. There is room in the kingdom of heaven for all. There is a portion in Christ's redemption for every soul of man.—Adeney.

[a] Nu. xxxiv. 5.

"No one ever found Christ that was merely willing that Christ should find him."

18—21. (18) **east sea,** i.e. the Dead Sea. (19) **Tamar,** or **Engedi. strife,** or Meribah. De. xxii. 52. **river of Egypt,** Wady-el-Arish.[a] R. V. "to the brook of Egypt, unto the great sea" i.e. the line follows this Wady fr. Kadesh to the Mediterranean. (20) **from .. Hamath,** Cam. B., "fr. the (south) border as far as over against where one goeth . . . ." (21) **So,** according to this outline.

22, 23. (22) **strangers,** foreigners dwelling with them as proselytes.[b] (23) **sojourneth,** or settles down.

[b] "Foreigners never before had the privilege of purchasing or possessing any inheritance among the Jews."—Lowth.

Le. xxv. 10; Nu. xxxvi. 7; De. xxiii. 3.

The Stranger's Portion.—I. Strangers should receive a brotherly welcome from Christian people. Hospitaity is an Eastern habit; it should be a Christian grace. 1. In the church. 2. In the home. 3. In the world. II. Strangers are welcomed by Christ into the kingdom of heaven. 1. Gentiles. 2. Heathen. 3. Sinners. III. Strangers must become true citizens in order to enjoy the privileges of the kingdom of heaven.—Pul. Com.

CHAPTER THE FORTY-EIGHTH.

1—7. (1) **Dan,** taking the first allotment, with border to Damascus. (2) **border of Dan,** i.e. on his south side. (3—7) These tribes are all to be on the northern side of the holy portion.

The Arrangement of the Tribes.—All the tribes are now settled on the West of the Jordan. The land is divided into zones running from E. to W. of the country, one of which falls to the lot of each tribe. The dimensions of the zone are not mentioned, neither is there any indication whether the greater or less breadth of the country from the Jordan to the sea was taken into account. The oblation of land given to the priests and Levites lay not strictly in the middle of the country, but in the neighborhood of Jerusalem, and therefore more toward the south; hence seven tribes are located to the north of the oblation and five to the south of it. Of the tribes beyond Jordan, the half of Manasseh is now united with the other half, forming one tribe, and receiving one portion; while Gad and Reuben are provided with new settlements, the former in the extreme south, and the latter in the northern half of the country. Judah and Benjamin change places, the former lying to the north of the oblation and the city, and the latter to the south. In other respects the position of the tribes remains nearly what it was, except that Issachar and Zebulun have to be provided for in the south. It is perhaps accidental that the children of Leah and Rachel occupy the centre, while the sons of the handmaids are placed at the extremities.—Camb. Bible.

"When we feel ourselves defective in the glow and operative driving power of love to God, what is the right thing to do? When a man is cold he will not warm himself by putting a clinical thermometer into his mouth and taking his temperature, will he? Let him go into the sunshine and he will be warmed up. So do not think about yourselves and your own loveless hearts so much, but think about God, and the infinite welling up of love in his heart to you, a great deal more. 'We love Him because He first loved us.' Therefore, to love Him more, we must feel more that he does love us."—McLaren.

8—14. (8) **offering,** or portion devoted to God. **reeds, better,** "cubits." (9) **oblation,** ch. xlv. 1. **of ten thousand,** Sept. "of twenty thousand." (10) **for them,** for their maintenance. (11) **sons of Zadok,** the lawful line of priests...**charge,** ward or ordinance. (12) **and this oblation,** etc. R. V., "and it shall be unto them an oblation from the oblation of the land, a thing most holy," etc. (13) **over against,** i.e. along side of on the north. **Levites,** as previously narrated, ch. xlv. 7. (14) **alienate,** devoting any of it to common purposes.

Religion the Nucleus of Human Life. I. Religion fills a central place in a renovated world. As the light of truth permeates men's minds, they shall discover the supreme excellence of piety. II., Religion provides a graduated scale of excellence. God leads us step by step from a lower to a loftier life, from one stage of holiness to another. III. Religion promotes unity amid diversity. The several tribes of Israel were allotted their territory (in Ezekiel's ideal sketch) in relation to the holy place. IV. Religion brings God equally near to all. V. Religion has ample reward for faithful services. VI. Religion is supremely valuable. God's friendship is treasure which no arithmetic can express. All comparisons fail.—Davies.

15—20. (15) **profane,** common, unsanctified; ch. xlii. 20. (16) **the measures,** or measurements. (17) **suburbs,** or outskirts of the communal land.[a] (18) **the increase,** or produce. **unto them that serve the city,** Polychr. B. "of the inhabitants of the city." (19) Polyc. B. "the inhabitants of the city shall come from all the tribes of Israel." (20) **foursquare,** a square fig. is the emblem of perpetuity, strength, and solidity.[b]

The Holy City.—"The description of the Temple does not correspond with the plan of the Tabernacle, or that of the first Temple. These were real buildings, and were erected according to the patterns shown by God Himself to Moses and to David; but this is an ideal communicated, not to a leader or king in order to be actually carried out, but to a seer, who wrote down his vision for the consolation of the captives of Babylon. It cannot even have been meant that this ideal structure should have been built by the Jews after the return from captivity, or at any subsequent period. Plainly the Temple is ideal, and so is the city. The vision was given to keep before the minds of the exiles the duty of rebuilding Jerusalem and the Temple on their restoration to their own land. The stupendous scale of the vision was, we presume, intended to project the thoughts of devout readers into far-distant times—not the times of the present Church of God, but those of the future glory and blessing on the earth, centering at Zion and Jerusalem, when the Lord shall be King over all the earth, and the Holy City shall be named Jehovah-Shammah, "The Lord is there."—Donald Fraser.

21—24. (21) **for the prince,** ch. xlv. 7. (22) **from the possession,** i.e. measuring from.[c] (23, 24) **a portion,** better, "one portion." Comp. Joseph's double portion.

Company of the Bible.—By opening this voloume we may at any time walk in the garden of Eden with Adam; sit in the ark with Noah; share the hospitality or witness the faith of Abraham; ascend the mount of God with Moses; unite in the secret devotions of David, or listen to the eloquent and impassioned address of Paul. Nay, more, we may here converse with Him who spake as never man spake; participate, with the spirits of the just made perfect, in the employment and happiness of heaven; and enjoy sweet communion with the Father of our spirits through His Son Jesus Christ. Such is the society to which the Scriptures introduce us; such the examples which they present to our imitation.—Payson.

25—29. And by, etc., these tribes were located on the further or southern side of the Holy Portion. Ezekiel's arrangement is manifestly an ideal rather than a practical one...**river** .. **sea,** R. V., "to the brook of Egypt, unto the great sea."

The City of God.—"It is a great thought which presents itself unadorned to our view in the prophetico-symbolic Temple: God henceforth dwells in perfect peace, revealing Himself in the unbounded fulness of His glory, making Himself known in the living Word of progressive, saving, and sanctifying redemption. Everything is placed upon the ample circuit of the Temple, whose extended court receives all people, and through whose high and open gates the King of Glory is to enter in (Ps.

a "The city being 4,500 cubits square, leaves 250 north, 250 south, for suburbs; the like are marked off on the east and west fr. the city land." — Spk. Com.

b Re. xxi. 16.

"No one can ask honestly or hopefully to be delivered from temptation unless he has himself honestly and firmly determined to do the best he can to keep out of it."

"Whoever finds Christ seeks to help others to find Him."

c "The prince's portion shall extend from the boundary of Judah, on the north of the Holy Portion, to the border of Benjamin on the south, so as to flank the Holy Portion on the E. and W., and to fill up what lies between it and the Jordan on the E., and bet. it and the Medit. on the W." — Wordsworth.

"Kind listening leads to kind speaking. . . . The occasions for kind actions are manifold. No one passes a day without meeting with these fortunate opportunities. They grow around us even while we lie on a bed of sickness, and the helpless are rich in a power of kindness toward the helpful." — F. W. Faber.

xxiv. 7—9), and then upon the order and harmony of the Divine habitations, the well-proportioned building (chap. xlii. 10); and the revelations of the holiest are stored up in the pure deep water of His Word, which in life-giving streams issues from the Temple. The stone tables of the Law are consumed, and the fresh and free fountain of eternal truth streams forth from the Temple of the Spirit, quickening and vivifying in land and sea, awakening by its creative and fructifying power a new and mighty race on earth. And thus hast thou, much-misjudged yet lofty seer, in the unconscious depth of thy mysteriously flowing language, set up upon the great undistinguishing, well-proportioned, and beautifully compacted building a type of the simple yet lofty Temple of Christ, from which flows the spiritual fountain of life."—Umbreit.

a Re. xxi. 12.

b "Not that the city will be called so in mere name, but that the reality will be best expressed by this descriptive title." —Fausset.

Je. iii. 17, xxxiii. 16; Zec. ii. 10; Re. xxi. 3, xxii. 3.

"I have found in my own life that there is a very close proportion between the time I spend in communion with God and the amount of power that I have in dealing with men." —R. A. Torrey.

30—35. (30) **goings out,** not the gates but the boundary lines of the city. **Measures,** Cam. B. "cubits." (31) **after the names,** called after the names of the several tribes.[a] (32—34) **Joseph,** the name covers the tribes of Ephraim and Manasseh. (35) **the Lord is there,** Heb. Jehovah-Shammah.[b] The prophet beheld the Lord forsake his temple (xi.), and he beheld him again enter it (xliii.); now he abides in it among his people for ever. The covenant ran that he should be their God and they his people; this is perfectly fulfilled in his presence among them. The end in view from the beginning has been reached.—Cam. B.

The Apex of Glory.—"The name of the city from that day shall be, The Lord is there." The final words of the prophet are golden, and deserve to be written in largest capitals. The architecture of the holy city is ideally complete; its finial shines out with immortal lustre. The city is baptized with a new name. Instead of "Jerusalem," it shall be "Jehovah-Shammah." Names are often labels which falsify the reality. A worthless mine may be named "El Dorado." A rotten ship may still bear the name Impregnable. But this name shall express the distinctive feature of the renovated city. Its glory shall not appear in chiselled marble and in burnished gold. In the new kingdom Christ shall set up, all the materials shall be spiritual, therefore impervious to decay. The charm and enchantment of the place will be this.—"The Lord is there." It shall be nothing less than heaven in miniature.—Davies.

Introduction.

I. **Author.** Daniel, whose name sig. "Judge of God," was of the tribe of Judah, and prob. of the royal house (i. 3). In the fourth year of Jehoiakim (B.C. 606) he was carried to Babylon; i.e. eight years before Ezekiel, and probably about the twelfth (Ignatius) or the eighteenth year (Chrysostom) of his age (i. 4). There he was placed in the court of Nebuchadnezzar, and became acquainted with the science of the Chaldees, compared with whom, however, God gave him, as he records, superior wisdom. By this king he was raised to high rank and great power, and, with some interruptions, he retained his position both under the Babylonish and Persian dynasties. He died at an advanced age, having prophesied during the whole of the captivity (i. 21), and his last prophecy being delivered two years later, in the third year of the reign of Cyrus (Angus). II. **Language.** From ii. 4. to end of vii. was written in Chaldee, the remainder in Hebrew. III. **Contents.** The book has commonly been divided into two parts, consisting of six chapters each. The first six are regarded as historical, and the remaining six as prophetical; or the first part is called the "Book of History," the second the "Book of Visions." IV. **General Character.** Quite apart from the significancy of these predictions are many of the moral and spiritual lessons of this book. It was written in the darkness of the most terrible captivity which the people of God had ever known, and yet it contains some of the grandest revelations of the future glories of the Church. Everywhere, moreover, the providence of God is seen working or overruling all for her good. The predictions of the book extend from the establishment of the Medo-Persian monarchy to the general resurrection, the faith of believers being confirmed by the fulfilment of intermediate predictions foretelling the speedy punishment of two proud and impious kings. The history of the temptation of Daniel and his companions, their constancy and deliverance, is highly instructive, illustrating at once the mystery of the Divine dispensations and the spirit of fidelity and patience with which good men submit to them (Angus).

Synopsis.

(According to Keil.)

CHAPTER THE FIRST.

1, 2. (1) **third year,** comp. 2 Ki. xxiv. 1; 2 Chr. xxxvi. 5, 6; Je. xxv. 1.[a] **Jehoiakim,** i.e. "Jehovah raises up." **Nebuchadnezzar,** "prince of the god Nebo." **besieged it,** this actually took place in the fourth year; but Nebuc. had taken away some of the nobles, prob. as hostages, in the end of the third year, and before the battle of Carchemish. (2) **part .. God,** as the temple had been previously spoiled, only part of its treasures could be taken by Nebuc. **land of Shinar,** Ge. x. 10, xi. 2. The older name of Babylonia, which was preserved in the district. **his god,** Bel-Merodach, as a thank offering for his successful campaign.

Punishment for Desecration.—The Church that shed the blood of the Huguenots like water saw its communion vessels seized and melted down to be coined into money for the payment of revolutionary armies, its bells converted into cannon, and the ancient cathedral of Notre Dame at Paris desecrated by the ownership of the Goddess of Reason in the person of a prostitute. Such desecration was often the chastisement of abused privileges and rejected truth. The warning addressed to Oriental Churches is still applicable to those of the West, "Repent, or else I will come to thee quickly, and will remove thy candlestick out of its place, except thou repent" (Rev. ii. 5). Matthew Henry remarks: "See the righteousness of God; His people had brought the images of other gods into His Temple, and now He suffers the vessels of the Temple to be carried into the treasuries of those other gods.—Hom. Com.

3—5 (3) **master .. eunuchs,** comp. the Kislar-aga of the Turkish sultans.[b] **bring, away from** Jerusalem. **king's seed,** Josephus says that Daniel was of the family of Zedekiah. **princes,** parthemim, not a Semitic word, poss. Persian.[c] (4) **blemish,** of body. **wisdom,** learning. **cunning,** or showing signs of quickness and intelligence. They were to be youths, not mere children. **understanding,** i.e. power to discern properties and relations. **learning .. Chaldaeans,** "The Chaldees were the depositories of the philosophy and learning of the East at that time."[d] (5) **daily provision,** wh. all the members of the court shared. **meat,** R. V. marg. "dainties."

The Janissaries were originally Christian youths who had been taken captive by the Turks and brought to the Ottoman court, after which they were placed under the care of the chief of the white eunuchs, under whom they were trained and educated, taught some trade, and brought up in the religion of their masters. Those most gifted were employed about the ruler's person, and in due time advanced to high and suitable offices in the state, to military commands, and to the government of provinces. Their Christian names were changed for such as their Moslem masters delighted in.—Kitto. Comeliness. Curtius says, that in all barbarous or uncivilised countries, the stateliness of the body is held in great veneraiton; nor do they think any capable of great services or actions to whom nature has not vouchsafed to give a beautiful form and aspect. It has always been the custom of the Eastern nations to choose such for their principal officers, or to wait on princes and great personages. Sir Paul Ricaut observes, "that the youths that are designed for the great offices of the Turkish empire must be of admirable features and looks, well shaped in their bodies, and without any defects of nature; for it is conceived that a corrupt and sordid soul can scarce inhabit in a serene and ingenuous aspect; and I have observed not only in the seraglio, but also in the courts of great men, their personal attendants have been of comely, lusty youths, well habited, deporting themselves with singular modesty and respect in the presence of their masters; so that when a pacha aga spahi travels, he is always attended with a comely equipage, followed by flourishing youths, well clothed and mounted, in great numbers."—Burder.

6, 7 (6) **Daniel,** meaning, "God is my judge."[a] **Hananiah,** "God is gracious." **Mishael,** "Who is as God." **Azariah,** "God is a helper." (7) **names,** wh. were adaptations of the names of the Bab. gods, as their previous names had been adaptations of the names of Jehovah. Nebo, and Beltis, the goddess wife of Bel, were objects of Bab. worship. Sac also

---

a "Nebuc. started fr. Bab. in Jehoiakim's third year and arrived at Jerus. in his fourth."
—Wordsworth.

"Nebuc. is called king by anticipation. He was for two years associated with his father in the government, before he became sole king."—Josephus.

b "There are 3,000 goolans (slaves) who live in the palace and attend the person of the Shah wherever he goes. At Constantinople this class is called "ishoglan," they are promising boys, stolen or forcibly taken from their Christian parents and brought up as Muslims. They are kept in the seraglio, under strict discipline, receive a good education, and then have appointments in the civil and military service."
—Van Lennep.

c "The plural of a Persian word."
—Max Muller.

Est. i. 3 vi. 9.

d "Besides the study of politics and the art of war, the learning chiefly valued among them was astrology, or the knowledge of the heavenly motions, the interpretation of dreams and architecture." —Lowth.

a One that kept his station in the greatest of revolutions, reconciling policy and religion, business and devotion, magnanimity and humility,

was a Chaldæan idol. **Belteshazzar,** or Bel's prince. **Shadrach,** "Inspired by the sun-god." **Meshach,** "who is as Shak," the Venus of Bab. mythology. **Abed-nego,** "Servant of the shining fire."

The new Name of Favoritism.—"When any Indian subject stands so fair in the eye of his prince as to be raised to some advanced degree of trust or honor, he acquires at the same time a new name according to the prince's fancy. Thus the preceding governor of Surat was named Muckteu-chan (Lord after my own heart); the present is styled Anamat-chan (Conscientious lord) because of his fidelity and integrity."—Ovington.——The Change of Names.—Still in modern times this is continued in the head of Roman Catholic Christendom, who has for the last twelve centuries always assumed another than his original name on ascending the papal throne. With members of a monarch's court this is easily intelligible. The desire was to have names of good omen; a foreign name might either be meaningless or suggest anything but thoughts full of good omen.—Pulp. Com.

8—10. (8) **defile himself,** by partaking of food which had been offered to idols[b] and also killed with the blood.[c] **wine,** offered in libation to idols; and doubtless having also intoxicating properties. (9) **tender love,** R. V., "compassion," intimating that the officer had a personal affection for him. Comp. case of Joseph, Ge. xxxix. 11. (10) **worse liking,** Heb. "sad," "troubled," i.e. looking less healthy and comely, so indicating that you have been underfed. **sort,** of the same age among the rest of your party. **endanger my head,** Eastern kings at once order the execution of servants who they think are proving unfaithful.

Jewish Adherence to Principle.—In the days of Antiochus Epiphanes the ordinary feeling on this subject was very different, for the religion and nationality of the Jews were at stake. Hence we read: "Howbeit many in Israel were fully resolved and confirmed in themselves not to eat any unclean thing. Wherefore they chose rather to die, that they might not be defiled with meats, that they might not profane the holy covenant; so then they died." And in the Second Book of Maccabees we are told that on the king's birthday Jews "were constrained by bitter constraint to eat of the sacrifices," and that Eleazar, one of the principal scribes, an aged and noble-looking man, preferred rather to be tortured to death, "leaving his death for an example of noble courage, and a memorial of value, not only unto young men, but unto all his nation." . . . . The brave Judas Maccabæus, with some nine companions, withdrew himself into the wilderness, and "lived in the mountains after the manner of beasts with his company, who fed on herbs continually, lest they should be partakers of the pollution."—Exp. B.

11—13. (11) **Melzar,** R. V., "the steward," an officer under Ashpenaz, who had the special care of these four young men, whose food was to differ from that of the others. (12) **Prove,** test us: experiment for a short time and watch the result. **pulse,** a general term for a vegetable diet. (13) **as thou seest,** these words were spoken with quiet confidence in the righteousness of Jehovah.

Resolution—Gives a man moral strength, energy, backbone, constitutes force of character, makes a man strong, forms the hero, the scholar, the statesman, the artist, makes the successful merchants, the man of science, the philanthropist, and the benefactor of his kind. "I will be a hero," was the turning-point in Nelson's history. Reynolds resolves at Rome to study the works of the old masters till he has understood their excellence, and becomes a master himself. Paley at college resolves to shake off his habitual indolence and rise at four o'clock to his studies, and produces works that cannot die. Daniel's resolution in regard to his diet is one of the means of strengthening his character and fitting him for future greatness. Each resolution carried out in spite of difficulty or natural reluctance makes a man stronger.—Hom. Com.

14—16. (14) **consented,** bec. the test was a very fair one. (15) **fairer,** complexion healthier and clearer. (16) **Melzar,** vs. 11. **pulse,** vegetable diet, including fruits,[a] De. viii. 3.

Youthful Piety.—This is one great lesson which dominates the historic section of this Book: "Them that honour Me I will honour, and they that despise Me shall be lightly esteemed." It is the lesson of Joseph's superiority to the glamor of temptation in the house of Potiphar; of the

---

authority and affability, conversation and retirement, interest and integrity, heaven and the court, the favor of God, and the favor of the king."— Bishop Ken.

[b] Comp. Ex. xxxiv. 15; 1 Co. x. 20; Ho. ix. 3.

[c] Le. iii. 17, vi. 26, xvii. 10—14, xix. 26.

One result of communion with God is to make us tender of all that respects God's honor. Moses forgot himself; he had no room for thought of self, hence God was able to clothe him with a halo of glory. An earthly king likes to clothe his servants in fine robes, and God is pleased when we enable him to bless us. —Andrew A. Bonar.

"Hold fast the belief that Daniel made not this request rashly, or as if it originated with himself, but because he was moved so to do by the Holy Spirit."—Calvin.

"O madness! to think use of strongest wines and strongest drinks our chief support of health, when God, with these forbidden, made choice to rear His mighty champion, strong above compare, whose drink was only from the liquid brook!"—Milton.

[a] "Dried dates pressed into cakes, gourds, melons and cucumbers formed the ordinary diet and goat's milk the ordinary drink, among the Babylonians of Daniel's day."—Rawlinson.

choice of Moses, preferring to suffer affliction with the people of God rather than all the treasures of Egypt and "to be called the son of Pharaoh's daughter;" of Samuel's stainless innocence beside the corrupting example of Eli's sons; of David's strong, pure, ruddy boyhood as a shepherd-lad on Bethlehem's hills. It is the anticipated story of that yet holier childhood of Him who—subject to His parents in the sweet vale of Nazareth—blossomed 'like the flower of roses in the spring of the year, and as lilies by the water-courses." The young human being who grows up in innocence and self-control grows up also in grace and beauty, in wisdom and "in favor with God and man." The Jews specially delighted in these pictures of boyish continence and piety, and they lay at the basis of all that was greatest in their national character.—Exp. B.

17. learning and wisdom, prob. in those things which appertain to politics and government, wh. would fit them to become able diplomatists and wise counsellors. **understanding,** i.e. "ability to discern the significance of: "God thus rewarded the pious resolve of these 4 Hebrews. **visions and dreams,** by which in ancient times God was pleased sometimes to reveal His will.

Youthful piety (vss. 17—19).—In the example of Daniel we have—I. Youthful piety possessed. II. We have youthful piety tried. III. We have to observe youthful piety honored. IV. We have also to contemplate youthful piety useful.—J. Parsons.

Genius of Youth.—Almost everything that is great has been done by youth. For life in general there is but one decree. Youth is a blunder; manhood a struggle; old age a regret. Do not suppose that I hold that youth is genius; all that is genius, when young, is divine. Why, the greatest captains of ancient and modern times both conquered Italy at five-and-twenty! Youth, extreme youth, overthrew the Persian empire. Don John of Austria won Lepanto at twenty-five—the greatest battle of modern times. Gaston de Foix was only twenty-two when he stood a victor on the plain of Ravenna. Every one remembers Condé and Rocroy at the same age. Gustavus Adolphus died at thirty-eight. Cortes was little more than thirty when he gazed upon the golden cupolas of Mexico. When Maurice of Saxony died at thirty-two, all Europe acknowledged the loss of the greatest captain and the profoundest statesman of the age. Then there is Nelson, Clive;—but these are warriors, and perhaps you may think there are greater things than war. I do not; I worship the Lord of hosts. But take the most illustrious achievements of civil prudence. Innocent III., the greatest of the popes, was the despot of Christendom at thirty-seven. John de Medici was pope as Leo X. at thirty-seven. Luther robbed even him of his richest province at thirty-five. Take Ignatius Loyola and John Wesley; they worked with young brains. Ignatius was only thirty when he made his pilgrimage and wrote the Spiritual Exercises. Pascal wrote a great work at sixteen, and died at thirty-seven. Was it experience that guided the pencil of Raphael when he painted the palaces of Rome? He died at thirty-seven. And Acquaviva—Acquaviva was general of the Jesuits, ruled every cabinet in Europe, and colonised America, before he was thirty-seven. What a career! It is needless to multiply instances. The history of heroes is the history of youth.—J. D'Israeli.

18—21. (18) **end .. days,** vs. 5, three years. (19) **communed,** talked with them, to find out which of them might be best suited for his purposes. **stood .. king,** were appointed to offices in direct relation to the royal person. As they had been admitted to the class of magicians and astrologers, it would seem they were admitted to the number of those who were royal magicians and astrologers—those whom the king consulted.—Pul. Com. (20) **wisdom,** practical skill and judgment.[a] **better,** the Jews are still remarkable for their business gifts. (21) **continued,** "held his post through all changes, bec. found both skilful and faithful.[b] The earliest in exile, he still lived to see the end of it."—Stuart.

Recompense for Fidelity.—Dr. Cox remarks that the king's preference of the four young Jews was all the more remarkable from the fact that the Chaldeans boasted of their literature and science, and deemed all other nations to be barbarians; their superiority, which thus so greatly attracted the royal favor, being certainly from the Lord, who exalts and depresses according to His own good pleasure, and to subserve the pur-

"Amid innumerable false, unmoved, unshaken, unseduced, unterrified, their loyalty they kept, their faith, their love." —Milton.

"The retrospect on youth is too often like looking back on what was a fair and promising country; but is now desolated by an overwhelming torrent, from which we have just escaped. Or it is like visiting the grave of a friend whom we had injured, and are precluded by his death from the possibility of making him an atonement."—J. Foster.

[a] "Daniel's reputation for wisdom and sanctity became proverbial in the East." —Wordsworth.

[b] "Simple words, but what a volume of faithfulness is unrolled by them! Amid all the intrigues; amid all the envy towards a foreign captive in high office as a king's councillor; amid all the trouble incidental to the insanity of the king, or the murder of two of his successors; in that whole critical period for his people, Daniel continued." —Pusey.

Wisdom does not show itself so much in precept as in life—in a firmness of mind and mastery of appetite. It teaches us to do, as well as to talk; and to make our actions and words all of a color.—Seneca.

pose of His universal government. Keil observes that Daniel needed to be deeply versed in the Chaldean wisdom, as formerly Moses was in the wisdom of Egypt (Acts vii. 22), so as to be able to put to shame the wisdom of this world by the "hidden wisdom" of God. Gaussen notices that four benefits were bestowed by God on these faithful youths as a recompense for their fidelity: knowledge, skill in all learning, wisdom in the conduct of themselves, and, in the case of Daniel at least, something supernatural, prophetic gifts, a miraculous knowledge of the secrets of the Lord. Matthew Henry quaintly remarks that the king was soon aware that a little of their divinity was preferable to a great deal of the divinations he had been used to—Hom. Com.——God's Gifts.—A Scotchwoman who received kind letters from her son found bank-bills inside them, but having never seen such money, thought they were only pretty pictures and put them aside. Many people think the promises found in the Bible are very pretty pictures, and perhaps some of you have put them away in an old tea-pot. Is it not time to understand that they are drafts on the bank of heaven that will be honored night and day? God make us ashamed that we have such a poverty-stricken spiritual life, when all the resources of the Holy Ghost are ready to supply our need.—A. J. Gordon.

CHAPTER THE SECOND.

a The second year of Nebuc.'s sole sovereignty. About the sixth year of Jehoiakim." — Spk. Com.

b For word "dream," as used in a prophetic sense, see 1 Sa. xxviii. 6; Nu. xii. 6.

c "The absence of his sleep was heavy upon him." —Pusey.

d "Prob. a certain order of priest-magicians, who wore a peculiar dress, like that seen on the gods and deified men in Assyrian sculptures." —Fausset.

e the use of this dialect continues to the end of the seventh chapter.

f What Nebuc. did was this—he tried the wise men of Babylon by two tests: 1. Whether they could tell him his dream; 2. Whether they could tell him the meaning of it. See v. 9." —Wordsworth.

a "There is prob. a reference to the notion of the Chaldees, as among the Persians, that some days were more

1—3. (1) **second year,** perhaps by Bab. computation, fourth year by the Scripture computation; but there are many hist. events fr. wh. reckonings were made of wh. we have now no record. Hence seeming contradictions.[a] **dreams,**[b] or a continued dream. "The plural form marks the vastness of the subject of these dreams." **brake,** or "was gone away from him."[c] (2) **magicians,** etc., there seem to have been three distinct classes of Chaldæan doctors, the Chartummim, or conjurers, "sacred scribes," Stuart; the Chakamim, or physicians; R. V., "enchanters;" and the Asaphim, or theosophists. These were distinct from the Kasdim[d] and Gazrim, the astrologers and divines. (3) **spirit .. troubled,** R. V., "is troubled." **know the dream,** i. e. to remember it, and to have it interpreted.

Astrology.—A supposed art of foretelling future events from the positions and aspects of the heavenly bodies, originating in the notion that the stars have an influence for good or evil on the affairs of men; which influence may be discovered. This art originated in Chaldæa, and was from thence transmitted to the Egyptians, Greeks, and Romans. Astrologers were in high esteem among the Babylonians, Dan. i. 20, ii. 2, iv. 7, v. 7, 11, 15, and other nations, Dan. ii. 10, and also with the ungodly Jews, Isa. xlvii. 13—15. The Scripture styles them star-gazers, monthly prognosticators, magicians, sorcerers, Chaldæans, soothsayers, and wise men. Astrology was intimately connected with Sabaism, or the worship of the stars; it, in effect, denies God and His providence, and is therefore ranked in Scripture with practices most offensive to Him.—Green's Dict.

4—6. (4) **Syriack,** R. V., "in the Syrian language," or Aramaic, the popular language of Babylon.[e] **O king,** etc., ch. iii. 9; Ne. ii. 3. (5) **gone from me,** passed from my memory.[f] **dunghill,** or heaps of rubbish. The houses being made of only sun-burnt bricks, were easily destroyed. (6) **rewards,** fee, largess; comp. vs. 48.

Oriental Cruelty.—The language was that of brutal despotism such as had been customary for centuries among the ferocious tyrants of Assyria. The punishment of dismemberment, dichotomy, or death by mutilation was common among them, and had constantly been depicted on their monuments. It was doubtless known to the Babylonians also, being familiar to the apathetic cruelty of the East.—Exp. B.

7—9. (7) **again,** R. V., "a second time." **tell .. dream,** they could do the easy part of making up an interpretation; but they would readily be found out if they attempted to make up the dream. (8) **gain the time,** or buy the time;[a] i. e. make longer delay and thus postpone the fulfillment of the **king's decree, or find some way to extricate themselves fr.**

a very difficult situation. (9) **one decree.** R. V., "law;" that given in vs. 5. **corrupt,** or deceitful. **time be changed,** i. e. till there be a change in the relations of the heavenly bodies.

Coleridge's Dream.—An interesting incident in Coleridge's life refers to the composition of his metrical fragment, entitled "Kubla Kahn," which, he says, came to him during sleep, into which he fell while reading in "Purchas's Pilgrims." He continued for about three hours, apparently in sleep, during which he had the most vivid impression that he had composed between two and three hundred lines. "The images," he says, "rose up before me as things with a parallel production of the correspondent expresions, without any sensation or consciousness of effort." On awaking, he had so distinct a remembrance of the whole, that he seized his pen and wrote down the fragment, which is still preserved. Unfortunately, however, he was called away to attend some business. The interruption lasted more than an hour, and, on his return to his study, he found, to his intense surprise and mortification, that though he still retained some vague and dim recollection of the general purport of the vision, yet, with the exception of some eight or ten scattered lines and images, all the rest had passed away, like the images on the surface of a stream into which a stone has been cast. Thus the thing had gone from him as in the case before us.—Taylor.

10—13. (10) **not a man,** quite true; but there might be a Divinely-inspired man.[b] **king, lord, ruler,** R. V. marg., "no king be he never so great and powerful hath," etc. These wise men claim that the king's test is unfair, he is asking for an impossibility. (11) **rare,** unusual; never-before-heard-of. Or, a heavy, hard, unreasonable thing. **whose .. flesh,** ref. to the dii majores, and indicating their immortal nature, in opposition to the frailty of humanity: it is not likely that these Magi had correct notions of pure spirit, such as are now common with us.—Stuart. (12) **furious,** overborne with passion, he instantly commanded the execution of his tyrannous decree. **wise .. Babylon,** i. e. the city rather than the province of B. (13) **wise men,** it seems that, being under the instruction of these wise men, Daniel and his companions were in danger of being classed with them.

The Helplessness of Heathenism.—Babylon's wise men, with all their learning and science, unable either to find direction in their difficulty or deliverance from their danger. Like the mariners in the storm, they are "at their wit's end." They believed the gods could tell the king his dream, but they had no access to them. Their "dwelling is not with flesh." Their gods do not dwell with them, and they confess that they have no converse with them. Thus heathenism, by its own confession, is powerless. Sorry gods, indeed, that cannot approach men, nor be approached by them! Even the great Bel of Babylon is unable to help his royal and devoted worshiper. Contrast with this the God of the Bible, "a very present help in trouble," and "near to all who call upon Him in truth." Blessed are the people who know the "mystery of godliness, God manifest in the flesh;" and that, having been "made flesh" Himself, He can and does dwell with men on the earth. Matthew Henry notices the righteousness of God in causing men who imposed on others by pretending to do what they could not, to be threatened with death for not doing what they did not even pretend to do.—Hom. Com.

Lessons in Dreams.—
Some dreams were useless—moved by turbid course
Of animal disorder; not so all:
Deep moral lessons some impressed, that naught
Could afterwards deface. And oft in dreams
The master passion of the soul displayed
The huge deformity, concealed by day,
Warning the sleeper to beware, awake.
And oft in dreams, the reprobate and vile,
Unpardonable sinner—as he seemed
Toppling upon the perilous edge of Hell—
In dreadful apparition, saw before
His vision pass the shadows of the damned.
And sometimes, too, before his fancy passed

lucky than others. The day then present was an ill-omened one and they would gain one more propitious to their own destiny."—Wordsworth.

Is. xli. 22—24, 28, 29; Zec. x. 2.

"The days are made on a loom, whereof the warp and woof are past and future time." —Emerson.

"To the true teacher, time's hourglass should still run gold-dust."—Douglas Jerrold.

b "God makes the heathen, out of their own mouth, condemn their impotent pretensions to supernatural knowledge, in order to bring out in brighter contrast His power to reveal secrets to His servants." — Fausset.

"A man that is young in years may be old in hours, if he have lost no time. Generally, youth is like the first cogitations, not so wise as the second; for there is a youth in thought as well as in ages, and yet the invention of young men is more lively than that of old and imaginations stream into their minds better, and as it were more divinely."
—Bacon.

"Glory is due to those only who dare to associate with pain, and have trampled pleasure under their feet." —Fenelon.

The Worm that never dies, writhing its folds
In hideous sort and with eternal Death
Held horrid colloquy; giving the wretch
Unwelcome earnest of the woe to come.—Robert Pollok.

14—16. (14) **answered .. wisdom,** R. V., "prudence," Vulg. trans. "Daniel inquired concerning the law and decree."[a] **captain .. guard,** or chief of the executioners. Comp. Potiphar.[b] This indicates that these Hebrews were not with the Magi when they had an interview with the king. (15) **hasty,** R. V., "so urgent," comp. Ha. i. 6. (16) **time,** comp. vs. 8; R. V., "appoint him a time." Daniel while asking for time, promised to provide both the dream and the interpretation. Daniel wanted the time that he might engage, with his companions, in earnest prayer. **would shew,** R. V. marg., "that he might;" the language of confident faith.

17, 18. (17) **his house,** not necessarily his own, but that in wh. he lived. (18) **That .. desire,** an example of united prayer.[a] **God of heaven,** who dwells or reigns in heaven, is exalted over all; a decided assertion that this God is the only God,[b] Ge. xxiv. 7. **secret,** De. xxix. 29. **fellows,** R. V., "companions."

Prayer of Friends for Divine Help.—We are reminded of an interesting episode, in the history of the Westminster Assembly of Divines: When that learned company was engaged in the composition of the shorter catechism, and had come to the question "What is God?" no one would attempt to furnish an answer. At length, as a way out of the difficulty, and without knowing who the person was that might be appointed, they agreed that the youngest man present should be required to write the answer. When they discovered who he was, there was still the same shrinking in his heart, but at length he agreed to do as his brethren wished, provided they would permit him to retire, and would promise that all the time he was away, they would pray for the Divine assistance to be accorded to him. They did so, and in a short while he returned with that answer with which we are all familiar and the comprehensive brevity and clearness of which have awakened the admiration of every thoughtful mind.—W. M. Taylor.

19—23. (19) **night vision,**[c] in wh. he saw just what Nebuc. had seen, and had given to him the key of the meaning of the dream. **blessed,** offered worship and thanksgiving for this gracious answer to prayer. (20) **said,** etc.,[d] comp. Ps. cxiii. 2, cxv. 18. **name of God,** this expression due to man's consciousness that he could not comprehend what God in Himself is, and so "name" is designed to comprehend all that is known and unknown of Him.—Stuart. (21) **changeth,** etc., suitable to the vision he had seen, wh. concerned the changes of kingdoms.—Jerome. (22) **in the darkness,** i. e. things whose causes are yet quite hidden from human sight. **light .. him,** God is the source of all progress and advancement. (23) **thank thee,** heartily ascribing all the honor to god.

Joseph and Daniel.—Joseph and Daniel were alike in that they were both men of incorruptible fidelity and devout humility; and they stand out in Jewish history—one at its beginning and the other near its close—as men in whom few, if any, defects of character or blemishes of conduct appear. As Auberlen has beautifully said, "They were both representatives of the true God and His people at heathen courts; both were exemplary in their pure walk before the Lord; both were endowed with the gift of bringing into clear light the dim presentiments of truth which express themselves among the heathen in God-sent dreams; both were gifted with marvelous wisdom and insight, and, for this reason, highly honored by the powers of this world.—W. M. Taylor.

24—26. (24) **Destroy not,** the execution of the king's decree had been delayed; now, Daniel says, it may be abandoned. **bring,** etc., none could enter the royal presence without distinct permission. (25) **I have found,** etc., this may be the only formal language of the courtier.[e] (26) **Art thou able,** this question enabled Daniel to turn the king's thoughts from himself to his God.

The Mission of a Captive.—That interpreter was found in unexpected places, as all interpreters are found. Said Arioch, "I have found a man of the captives of Judah." That is God's inscrutable way. It was not

a "The word trans. 'wisdom' is very frequent in the Assyrian inscriptions, in the sense of judgment, advice, and also in the sense of command, will, decree."
—Spk. Com.

b Ge. xxxvii. 36, marg.

a Mat. xviii. 19; Ac. xii. 5—12.

b "It involves the recognition of the supreme sovereignty of Him whose handiwork — the moon, the sun, the planets—were the principal objects of Bab. worship." —Spk. Com.

"Thy will be done" is the key-note to which every prayer must be tuned. — A. J. Gordon.

c Job xxxiii. 15, 16.

d "Of the four vss. of this thanksgiving, two are, for cadence and language, as remarkable as any in Hebrew. . . . The simplicity of the narrative, the pathos of the prayer, the simple stateliness of the prophetic style, and the vivid condensation of this historical prophecy, combined in one, are no slight evidence of the grasp which the writer had of the language wherein he wrote in styles so varied."—Pusey.

e "This officer, according to the manner of courtiers, takes this opportunity of ingratiating himself with the king, as if the discovery of Dan.'s abilities in this kind were owing purely to his diligence."
—Lowth.

a brother-king that told Nebuchadnezzar what had troubled him; nor was it some man that drove to the king's house in a chariot of gold, with steeds of fire, whose scarlet nostrils were distended as if in pride that they were called upon to enter such lofty service: it was a man among the captives of Judah. How wondrously events touch and interrelate in life! Thus captivity is made true freedom, and thus men far from home established a second nativity, and thus persons who suppose themselves to be instances of humiliation find that those circumstances are but a stairway up to primacy, to sovereignty.—Peop. B.

27—30. (27) **The secret,** of the dream and interpretation. (28) **God in heaven,** vs. 18, who dwells in heaven, as distinguished fr. the idols of Babylon. **latter days,** the after-times. Nebuc., as great founder of a nation, would be deeply interested in its future history.[a] (29) **thoughts,** meditations during his wakefulness: dropping asleep this meditation becomes a dream. (30) **revealed to me,** the language of piety as well as modesty. **their sakes,** better intransitive; R. V., "but to this intent that the interpretation may be made known to the king."

[a] "Nebuc. had but lately become the sole and undisputed monarch of the empire he was destined to raise to such greatness. The past was to him full of glory, of success, of triumph, . . . what would the future be?" —Spk. Com.

Ac. iii. 12.

God as a Revealer of Secrets (vs. 28).—Looking at the Great One as the Revealer of secrets we observe—1. That He makes no omissions; 2. That He commits no mistakes; 3. That He has no unkindness. God is constantly revealing the secrets of men now. 1. Through the dictates of human conscience; 2. And through the unguarded actions of human life.—Thomas.

"Happy season of virtuous youth, when shame is still an impassabl. barrier, and the sacred air-cities of hope have not shrunk into the mean clay hamlets of reality; and man, by his nature, is yet infinite and free." —Carlyle.

Humility.—There is always a modesty about true greatness, and you may know whether or not piety is genuine by inquiring if it be characterized by humility. The good man will never seek to hide God from the view of his fellow-men. He will endeavor to make his light shine, but he will not make it shine so as to draw attention to himself. He will arrange it so that its rays will all converge in God, and men shall glorify the Father in heaven. See how beautifully John the Baptist was clothed with that humility. When the Jews came to him, asking, "Who art thou?" he would not yield to their desire, but said, "I am not the Messiah, but I am sent before Him to prepare His way;" and when afterwards men sought to provoke his envy of Jesus by telling him how the prophet of Nazareth was attracting more followers than he, his only answer was, "He must increase but I must decrease!"—W. M. Taylor.

"What God wants is men great enough to be small enough to be used."—H. W. Webb-Peploe.

31—33. (31) **great image,** one great image, made up of four parts.[a] "The dream was evidently such as might be born of the waking thoughts of one accustomed to Bab. magnificence, God using the mental associations as the vehicle of Divine predictions."—Robjohns. **brightness,** fr. the burnished gold and silver. **form,** R. V., "aspect." (32) **fine gold,** lit. "good," i. e. pure. **thighs,** or sides. (33) **iron,** iron and brass are the emblems of strength in the prophetical writings. **iron and clay,** rep. a kingdom of very heterogenous peoples, very weak and brittle, and so of most unstable dynastic power.

[a] "The world-power in its totality appears as a colossal human form. Bab., the head, of gold; Medo,-Persia, the breast and two arms, of silver; Graeco-Macedonia the belly and two thighs, of brass; and Rome the legs, of iron, and feet of iron and clay; the fourth still existing." —Fausset.

The Prophecy of Daniel (vs. 31).—Regarding the four great dynasties fulfilled in the successive rise and overthrow of the Babylonian, Persian, Macedonian, and Roman monarchies. I. Notice the objects which Nebuchadnezzar saw. 1. A colossal image, its head of gold—Babylon called by Isaiah "the golden city,"—breast and arms of silver (Persia), belly and thighs of brass (Greece), legs of iron (Rome); 2. The wondrous stone. II. The collision between these two objects which the Prophet witnessed. III. The result which the Prophet predicted.—J. Blackburn.

A Picture of Evil.—The image is a picture of all evil—"gold," "silver," "brass," "iron," "clay." That is the difficulty of the case. If evil were only evil we could easily get rid of it; it is when evil has a head of gold that we are bewitched or bewildered by it. It is true personally. Men are not always instances of black evil, all over, from head to foot, in and out, through and through. Some evil men have heads of gold, tongues of silver, looks that are fascinations, tones that importune the soul with the solicitude of music. If you look more clearly and closely at them you see that they are not all gold.—Peop. B.

"Proprietors rear strong fences round young trees. Permit not the immortal to be twisted, at the very starting of its growth, for the want of such protection as it is in your power to afford." —Arnot.

34—36. (34) **stone .. hands,** the Jews agree that this is a figure of the Messiah and His kingdom. The fig. declares the stone to have been prepared without human agency, i. e. by Divine power. **smote .. feet,** "the blow is struck during the existence of the fourth empire."[a] **brake,** i. e. crushed the feet to powder. The four monarchies are not rep. as coexisting. They follow one another successively so that the last became the rep. of the whole. Note in particular that an end of all is made when the fifth kingdom begins to be set up.—Stuart. (35) **chaff,** Ps. i. 4; Is. xli. 15. Ancient threshing floors were on the tops of hills.[b] **great mountain,** R. V. marg., "rock," fig. for the way in which the Messiah's kingdom would grow. (36) **we will tell,** speaking in the name of the companions who had shared in the prayer.

Small Beginnings.—The language of the vision indicates that the stone grew from a small size until it became a huge mountain. Frequently earthly kingdoms have had very insignificant beginnings; but usually that which has given them the last accession of greatness has been some mighty movement of its armies or some grand achievement of its statesmen. Thus, to take an instance, every one is familiar with the almost contemptible sovereignty of the first of the Hohenzollern dynasty; but when, a few years ago, while yet he was laying siege to the first city on the continent of Europe, the king of Prussia caused himself, in the palace of a conquered monarch, to be proclaimed Emperor of Germany, the pomp and ceremonies of the occasion were so great that the correspondent of the leading English journal finished his description of the event with these high-sounding words: "This will live in history." That is how empires are founded among men.—Taylor.

a "The kingdom of Christ, a kingdom of God's own creating, shall break to pieces the fourth and last monarchy, in which the remainders of the other three were comprehended."—Lowth.

b "Grain was winnowed in the E. on an elevated space in the open air, by throwing the grain into the air with a shovel, so that the wind might clear away the chaff." —Fausset.

37, 38. (37) **king of kings,**[c] the high-flown style in wh. the Persian king is still addressed. It was true of Nebuc., who ruled over subject kings. **God .. thee,** Daniel wished to impress upon Nebuc. that all his greatness was the gift of Jehovah, who was supreme above the Bab. monarch. (38) **men .. beasts .. fowls,** comp. the dominion originally given to man, Ge. i. 28, ii. 19, 20. **he given,** i. e. the God in heaven. **Thou .. gold,** not Nebuc. personally, but as rep. of the Babylonian dynasty. There is no attempt here to flatter the king, but the fig. required that the Bab. dynasty should rep. the beginning of the prophecy.

The King's Dream.—In the dream of the king and its interpretation by Daniel, we see how God prepared the world for the coming of Christ. 1. These successive monarchies, by aiming at universal dominion, did much to destroy the mutual estrangement and antagonisms of nations. The "walls of partition" between the nations were thrown down. "To that resolute king of Babylon, Nebuchadnezzar, may this proud and magnificent notion" of a universal empire be first ascribed (Luthardt). It was taken up by Alexander and the Romans. When our Lord appeared the nations were so far united that old jealousies were far too weak to arrest the progress of Christianity. 2. By these successive empires the vitality of the ancient religions was greatly weakened, if not destroyed, and with it faith in their truth. These were the religions of nations, of races; their deities could only be worshiped in particular places. The old religions languished, lost their hold upon the minds of men, until in the age of Augustus scepticism prevailed. 3. In the wide diffusion of the Greek language we see another effect of the rise of these empires, and a preparation for the advent of our Lord. Alexander's conquests spread it in the East, Rome's victories in the West; this contributed marvelously to the spread of Christianity. 4. These are a few of the ways in which God brought about "the fulness of time" when the world was ripe for the work of our Lord.

Nebuchadnezzar's Kingdom.—Dr. Rule observes that "this great king could not have forgotten that his father was only a satrap at first, a successful rebel, who perfidiously allied himself with his master's enemies, and by that means overthrew Nineveh and set up as king at Babylon. By a suddenly acquired sovereignty over all the servant-kings, he became king of kings; and thus Nebuchadnezzar, as son of Nabopolassar, was the first Babylonian king of kings by inheritance."—Hom. Com.

c Eze. xxvi. 7.

"Let fools and cowards start at fancy's visions; thy well-taught spirit knows these dreams are bred from fumes and indigestions that oppress the mind, which thus o'erloaded, still throws off these crudities, these ordures of the soul: as such despise them."—Madden.

"Count nothing small. The smallest thing may be a link in the golden chain which binds a man to the Divine Master himself. — A. F. Schauffler.

"On fickle wings the minutes haste, and fortune's favors never last."—Seneca.

39, 40. (39) **inferior,** in duration, in antiquity, in power, and in wealth. Prob. this represents the Medo-Persian kingdom.[a] **third kingdom, the** Greek monarchy. (40) **fourth, the Roman.**[b] **and as iron, etc., Stuart,**

a "Not united, organized, compacted, and consolidated within like thine; and not so capable of resisting and repelling attacks from without; as was proved by its sudden fall beneath the arms of Alex, the Great." — Wordsworth.

b "'The Rom. empire to be the fourth kingdom of Daniel, was

"even as iron which dashes in pieces—all these will it crush and dash in pieces."

Divulgements of Dreams.—

"In thy faint slumbers, I by thee have watch'd,
And heard thee murmur tales of iron war;
Speak terms of manage to thy bounding steed;
Cry, Courage!—to the field! And thou hast talk'd
Of sallies, and retires; of trenches, tents,
Of pallisadoes, fortins, parapets;
Of basilisks, of cannon, culverin;
Of prisoners' ransom, and of soldiers slain,
And all the currents of a heady fight.
Thy spirit within thee hath been so at war,
And thus hath so bestirr'd thee in thy sleep,
That beads of sweat have stood upon thy brow,
Like bubbles in a late-disturbed stream:
And in thy face strange motions have appear'd,
Such as we see when men restrain their breath
On some great sudden haste."—Shakespeare.

41—43. (41) **toes,** ten, representing ten sub-kingdoms, or kings.[a] **clay .. iron,** things wh. will not properly blend. In the very constitution of this kingdom should be the certainty of its ultimate failure and ruin. (42) **broken,** or brittle.[b] (43) **mingle,** etc., this would seem to refer to mixed marriages, wh. were doomed to meet with disappointment, comp. xi. 6, 7, 17.

The Rise and Dominion of Roman Empire.—Asia had been for ages the seat of power, the mightiest and most populous region of the globe. Europe was buried in darkness, and its western tribes were like outcasts from the family of nations. Greece itself had scarce risen into notice, and presented only a confused multitude of feeble and jarring tribes. That an empire was thus born among the barbarians of Latium which would extend its power over Judæa, Syria, and Babylon itself, was an event which no human wisdom could possibly divine. That this empire, like iron, should be endued with a political firmness beyong the mightiest monarchies of the East, was a prediction no less surprising, and would nowhere seem less credible than amidst the proud courtiers of Babylon. Two centuries later, in his various accounts of every region of the earth and of innumerable towns and rivers, Herodotus never once mentions the Tiber or the city of Rome. Yet here, amidst the splendor of Babylon, the prophet announces the rise and dominion of this fourth and greater empire.—Birks.

44, 45. (44) **these kings,** the ten represented by the toes. **break .. kingdoms,** not by the force of arms, but by the permeation of Christ's principles. **never .. destroyed,** Christ's kingdom is called an everlasting kingdom, bec. as a spiritual kingdom it is not subject to change and dissolution. **not .. left,** or pass from hand to hand in the generations. (45) **stone .. hands,** fig. of Divinely-founded spiritual kingdom.[a] **known .. king,** thus assuring the publicity of these great truths. **certain .. sure,** the correctness of the account of the dream proved the fidelity of the interpretation.

The Glorious Consummation of Christ's Kingdom.—

"The time of rest, the promised Sabbath, comes.
Six thousand years of sorrow have well nigh
Fulfilled their tardy and disastrous course
Over a sinful world; and what remains
Of this tempestuous state of human things,
Is merely as the working of the sea
Before a calm, that rocks itself to rest.
For He whose ear the winds are, and the clouds
The dust that waits upon His sultry march,
When sin hath moved Him and His wrath is hot,
Shall visit earth in mercy; shall descend
Propitious in His chariot, paved with love;
And what His storms have blasted and defaced
For man's revolt, shall with a smile repair."

believed by the Church of Israel before our Saviour's time; and this belief was received by the disciples of the Apostles, and the whole Christian Church for 300 years.' "—Jos. Mede.

[a] Comp. Da. vii. 2; Re. xvii. 12.

[b] "Some explain thus. 'The chief power in these ten kingdoms shall be partly secular, and partly ecclesiastical, and the encroaching of the one upon the other shall endanger their existence.' " —Lowth.

"Fellowship does not mean uniformity of work, it means uniformity of purpose. It takes many different workmen to build a house, but it is the same house they are building."

[a] "A stone from the holiest of mounts — the heavenly Zion—looses itself and falls. If it destroys the earthly material that it strikes, it brings also with it that new, pure heavenly spirit and material wh. shall fill again the earth with a stronger mount, and found a new and better city, Zion."— Ewald.

Lu. xx. 17, 18; Mat. xxi. 44.

We are workers together with God; do not let us forget God. —Francis Murphy.

b Comp. Ac. xxviii. 6.

The senses are the cinque-ports by which sin is let out and taken in.—Manton.

46—49. (46) **worshipped,** offered reverent homage to, as to a superior being. **oblation,** etc., we may be sure that Daniel would only allow these offerings to be made to his God.[b] "He was the medium of worship rather than the object of it." (47) **Of a truth,** the excited expression of the king's wonder and delight. (48) **ruler,** or prince-president. **chief, etc.,** ch. iv. 9. (49) **over the affairs,** i. e. he gave them important political offices. **in the gate,** where the court business was done.

The Prophet's Self-forgetful Spirit.—He has but one request to make of the king, and this request was not for himself, but for others. Having been highly exalted, he seeks gifts for men. Nowhere does the nobility and magnanimity of the man come more into view than here. His sudden elevation to rank and riches and rule have not spoilt him. In him lurks no ambitious pride. He has no thought of invidious rivalry. He is unwilling to enjoy his honors alone. In that hour of unexpected triumph he does not forget his fellow-captives who had joined their prayers to his in the hour of exigency. It may seem a bold petition: it may imperil his reputation with the king. To ask that the native Chaldæans—the officers who had gained illustrious honor by the conquest of Jerusalem—should be displaced to make room for three obscure and captive Jews: truly, this was a large request. Does not Daniel jeopardize all his gain by this daring proposal? Come what will, he will serve his nation, he will serve his God. And if, by sagacious foresight, he can diminish the oppressions of his countrymen, or pave the path for their return to Palestine, he will do it. The sacred fire aglow in his heart is revealed. Self is obliterated. To do good to Jew and Gentile alike—this is his sweet ambition! O man, "beloved of God," thy name shall be embalmed in fragrant remembrance.—Pul. Com.

CHAPTER THE THIRD.

a "Prob. a bust upon a pedestal, and not solid, but of some material covered with plates of gold."
—Arch. Rose.

b "Nebuc. had just returned fr. finishing the Jewish and Syrian wars, the spoils of which would furnish the means of rearing such a colossal statute."
—Prideaux.

c "Oppert has identified the spot, and found a large square pedestal of brick, which may be the remains of the pedestal."
—Wordsworth.

d "Whatsoever part of the empire ye come from, and whatever language you speak."
—Lowth.

e "Such harps are found in Egyptian and Assyrian monuments."
—Layard.

f "The division of the day into twelve hours was received by the Babylonians, and passed fr. them into Greece."
—Herodotus.

g Je. xxix. 22.

1—3. (1) **image of gold,**[a] either representing Bel, the Bab. god; or, perhaps, Nebuc. himself. If the latter the king's purpose was political. **threescore cubits,** prob. the fig. was thirty-six and the pedestal twenty-four cubits.[b] **Dura,** prob. only a little distance from Bab., and convenient for assembling a great multitude.[c] (2) **princes,** satraps. **judges,** R. V. marg., "chief soothsayers." **sheriffs,** Arab. mufti; men learned in the law.—Gesenius. (3) **stood before,** in front of; ready for the act of devotion required.

Nebuchadnezzar's God.—"We commonly observe, as peculiar to Nebuchadnezzar, a disposition to rest his fame on his great works rather than in his military achievements; and a strong religious spirit, manifesting itself especially in a direction which is almost exclusive to one particular god, though his own tutelary deity and that of his father was Nebo (Mercury), yet his worship, his ascriptions of praise, his thankgivings, have in almost every case for their object the god Merodach. Under his protection he placed his son Evil-Merodach. Merodach is his 'lord,' his 'great lord,' the 'joy of his heart,' the 'great lord who has appointed him to the empire of the world, and has confided to his care the far-spread people of the earth.' He was to him 'the supreme chief of the gods.'"—Rawlinson.

4—7. (4) **nations and languages,** intended to intimate the vast and varied extent of the Bab. empire;[d] including both Semitic and Aryan people. (5) **cornet,** or horn. **flute,** or pipe. **harp,** cithara, or guitar. **sackbut,** Lat. sambuca, a four-stringed instrument with a shrill tone. **psaltery,** kind of harp with strings below the sounding board.[e] **dulcimer,** Chaldee sumponya, a kind of bagpipe. **fall down,** prostrate themselves in the attitude of adoration. (6) **same hour,**[f] or at once. **furnace,** or oven; a kind of punishment peculiar to the Babs.[g] (7) **fell down,** yielding prompt obedience.

Religious Persecution.—In the matter of religion, the State has no authority, and it ought, therefore, to leave every man to his own conscience. The kingdoms and communities of the world have been long in learning these principles; and there is hardly a nation or even a religious denomination now existing which has not at some point in its past history been guilty of practicing, or of advocating, persecution for the holding of some peculiar religious opinions. The Protestants may not imagine that Roman Catholics alone have indulged in it; nor are the hands of the Puritans themselves clean in this matter.—W. M. Taylor. ——The Fiery Furnace.—This mode of putting to death was not unusual in the East in more modern times. Chardin, in his Travels, after speaking of the most common modes of punishing with death, says, "But there is still a particular way of putting to death such as have transgressed in civil affairs, either by causing a dearth, or by selling above the tax by a false weight, or who have committed themselves in any other manner. The cooks are put upon a spit and roasted over a slow fire (see Jer. xxix. 22), bakers are thrown into a hot oven. During the dearth in 1668, I saw such ovens heated on the royal square in Ispahan, to terrify the bakers, and to deter them from deriving advantage from the general distress."

8—12. (8) **certain Chaldaeans,** prob. court officers, who were jealous of the Jews, who had been advanced to places of trust. **the Jews,**[a] those three Jews who had refused to render the required worship. Daniel does not seem to have been present. (9) **O king,** ch. ii. 4. (10) **a decree,** an expression of the king's will. (11) **whoso,** without any exceptions. (12) **not regarded,** note how skillfully the accusation is framed so as to excite Nebuc.'s anger. It is made out that the Jews offered personal insult to Nebuc., as well as to his gods.[b]

Pliny's Letter to Trajan.—Soon after the emperor Trajan's great persecution, beginning A. D. 100, Pliny, the author, wrote a letter to the emperor, concerning the Christians who were brought before him, and he was perplexed to know what to do on account of the great number of persons, "who are in danger of suffering; for many of all ages and every rank, of both sexes likewise are accused. They refused to worship the image of the emperor. They affirmed that the whole of their fault or error lay in this, that they were wont to meet together on a stated day, before it was light, and sing among themselves, alternating, a hymn to Christ as God, to bind themselves by sacramentation, not to the commission of any wickedness, but not to be guilty of theft, or robbery, or adultery, never to falsify their word, nor to deny a pledge committed to them."—Peloubet.

13—15. (13) **rage,** etc., this indication of Nebuc.'s character, shows his lack of self-control. (14) **true,** R. V., "of purpose;" is it designed? His rage does not prevent his seeking to be just, by making careful inquiries. (15) **Now,** etc., Nebuc. would give them the opportunity of correcting their mistake. **that God,** R. V., "god," a distinct challenging of the power of Jehovah, whom the three Jews served.[c] In his rage Nebuc. forgot what Jehovah had done through Daniel.

Nero's Persecutions.—There were no persecutions of Christians by the Romans till a year after Paul was released, when, "on the night of the 18th of July 64, a fire broke out in the city and raged six days and seven nights before it could be extinguished." It broke out again in another quarter and raged three days more. Two-thirds of the city, its homes and its temples were laid in ashes. The people accused Nero of setting the fire and to ward off the accusation he charged it upon the Christians and began a terrible persecution. They were crucified. They were sewed up in skins to resemble wild animals and hunting dogs tore them to pieces. They were covered with tow, smeared with pitch, chained to posts, and set on fire to illuminate Nero's gardens. It was a very carnival of hell.—Peloubet.

16—18. (16) **not careful,** R. V., "we have no need to"[a] i.e. we need not take any time for deliberation: our mind is fully made up: we commend the matter to our God, whom you challenge. (17) **will deliver,** the language of firm faith, that gives calmness and courage. (18) **if not,** this shows that they had no knowledge of what God would do for them, only their faith in Jehovah as sure to stand by the right.

Active Religious Principles (vs. 18).—I. The principles for which we contend should be true. II. True principles should be maintained against all opposition. 1. They had to contend against the authority of the king; 2. They were under great obligations to the king; 3. Universal example was against them; 4. Disobedience was to be followed by tremendous punishment. III. Truth should be maintained in the spirit of

a "The word trans. 'accused' is a singular one, lit. meaning, 'ate the pieces of the Jews,' i. e. they calumniated, they slandered, they informed against them."—Spk. Com.

b "The Bab. and Assyr. exacted from the nations, which they conquered, submission to their own gods."—Wordsworth.

c Ex. v. 2; 2 Ki. xviii. 35.

The fires of persecution begin to kindle when the fires of the Spirit begin to burn. — A. T. Pierson.

"The fairest flower in the garden of creation is a young mind, offering and unfolding itself to the influence of Divine wisdom, as the heliotrope turns its sweet blossoms to the sun."—Sir J. E. Smith.

a "They keep their temper admirably well, do not call the king a tyrant or an idolator, but, with an exemplary calmness, and sedateness of mind, they deliberately give in their answer, which they resolve to abide by."— Matthew Henry.

love. If we fail in this—1. We injure our cause before men; 2. We deprive ourselves of Almighty help. IV. There are abundant encouragements for us thus to maintain true principles. V. Glorious results will follow the consistent maintenance of right principles.—E. Thompson.

19—21. (19) **visage,** face; the expression of his countenance. **seven times,** seven is here used as the ideal number. The furnace was to be heated as hot as it could be heated.[b] (20) **most mighty,** R. V., "certain mighty," it required brave men to venture near enough to cast them in. The flames, driven by the wind, would put in peril those who ventured near. (21) **coats,** or mantles. **hosen,** not stockings, wh. are seldom worn in the East: but inner tunics. **hats,** or turbans,[c] i.e. they were taken just as they stood before Nebuc.

Palissy and Henry III.—Bernard de Palissy, a native of Agen in France, was a maker of earthenware at Saintes, and distinguished himself by his knowledge and talents. He was a Calvinist; and the French king, Henry III., said to him one day, that he should be compelled to give him up to his enemies unless he changed his religion. "You have often said to me, sire," was the undaunted reply of De Palissy, "that you pitied me; but as for me, I pity you, who have given utterance to such words as 'I shall be compelled.' These are unkingly words; and I say to you, in royal phrase, that neither the Guises, nor all your people, nor yourself, are able to compel a humble manufacturer of earthenware to bend his knee before statues."

Martyrs.—

Who lived unknown till persecution
  Dragged them into fame, and chased them
Up to heaven; whose blood was shed
  In confirmation of the noblest claim—
Our claim to feed upon immortal truth,
  To soar, and to anticipate the skies.

22, 23. (22) **urgent,** requiring instant obedience. **flame,** roaring from the furnace, and driven against them. (23) **fell down,** they had been hurriedly flung in, so they fell right into the very midst of the flames. **bound,** and so helpless to deliver themselves, or each other. Every point makes the miraculous deliverance more wonderful.

24, 25. (24) **astonied,** see Ezr. ix. 3. **three men,** Nebuc.'s surprise seems chiefly to have concerned the presence of the guardian angel. (25) **no hurt,** from the fire. **Son of God,** R. V., "a son of the gods,"[a] comp. vs. 28.

True Souls (vs. 25).—Here we have true souls.—I. Immensely tried. II. Morally unconquerable. III. Essentially uninjurable. IV. Divinely accompanied.—Thomas.

The Martyr not Alone.—In the ecclesiastical history of Socrates, there is mention made of one Theodorus, a martyr put to extreme torments by Julian the Apostate, and dismissed again by him when he saw him unconquerable. Ruffinus, in his history, saith, that he met with this martyr a long time after his trial, and asked him whether the pains he felt were not insufferable. He answered, that at first it was somewhat grievous, but after a while there seemed to stand by him a young man in white, who, with a soft and comfortable handkerchief, wiped off the sweat from his body (which, through extreme anguish, was little less than blood) and bade him be of good cheer, insomuch as then it was rather a punishment than a pleasure to him to be taken off the rack, sith when the tormentors had done the angel was gone.—Spencer.

Christ's Presence.—

Dying with Jesus, his death reckoned mine;
Living with Jesus a new life divine;
Looking to Jesus till glory doth shine
Moment by moment, O Lord, I am thine.

Never a trial that He is not there;
Never a burden that He doth not bear;
Never a sorrow that He doth not share
Moment by moment, I'm under his care.

2 Ti. iv. 17.

b "Passion overdoes and defeats its own end, for the hotter the fire, the sooner were they likely to be put out of pain."—Fausset.

c Some render, "Their shirts, their tunics, and their mantles."

According to Herodotus the dress worn in Babylon consisted of an under linen garment reaching to the feet, a woolen garment over it, and a woolen mantle.

"Zinzendorf, when a boy, used to write little notes to the Savior, and throw them out of the window, hoping that He would find them; such were his thoughts of Jesus and his love to Him."—Phelps.

a "The Chaldaeans believed in families of gods: Bel, the supreme god, accompanied by the goddess Mylitta, being the father of the gods; thus by the expression Nebuc. meant one sprung from and sent by the gods."—Fausset.

"The king saw in that flame fed by human sacrifice the greatest and most active of the gods with whom the priest had direct communication by sacred rites, and magic incantations; and he recognized the intervention in favor of his victims."—Spk. Com.

"The more your religion costs you, the richer returns it will bring you."—T. Cuyler.

"The blood of the martyrs is the seed of the church." — Tertullian.

Never a heart-ache and never a groan,
Never a tear-drop and never a moan
Never a danger, but there on the throne
Moment by moment, He thinks of His own.

Never a weakness that He doth not feel;
Never a sickness that He cannot heal;
Moment by moment, in woe or in weal,
Jesus my Savior abides with me still.

—D. W. Whittle.

"A broken fortune is like a falling column; the lower it sinks, the greater weight it has to sustain." —Ovid.

26—27. (26) **mouth,** or door. **servants,** etc., acknowledging thus that their God had proved Himself mightier than all the gods of Babylon. **come forth,** he recognizes that it was reality, not a vision, which he had seen in the furnace. (27) **saw,** etc., so the miracle became a witness for Jehovah to all the vast nation. Jehovah manifested himself as Master of one of the gods high in the Babylonian pantheon—Iz-bar, fine,—consequently the Jews in exile could maintain their faith unchallenged.—Pul. Com.

Polycarp's Martyrdom.—When Polycarp was brought to the tribunal before whom he was tried, the pro-consul asked him if he was Polycarp; to which he assented. The pro-consul then began to exhort him, saying, "Have pity on thine own great age: swear by the fortune of Cæsar; repent; say, Take away the Atheists" (meaning the Christians). Polycarp, casting his eye solemnly over the multitude, said, "Eighty and six years have I served Him, and He hath never wronged me, and how can I blaspheme my King, who hath saved me?" "I have wild beasts," said the proconsul, "and will expose you to them unless you repent." "Call them!" said the martyr. "I will tame your spirit by fire," said the Roman. "You threaten me," said Polycarp, "with the fire which burns only for a moment, but are yourself ignorant of the fire of eternal punishment, reserve for the ungodly." Soon after, being bound on the burning stake, he exclaimed, "O Father of Thy beloved and blessed Son, Jesus Christ! O God of all principalities and of all creation! I bless Thee that Thou hast counted me worthy of this day, and of this hour, to receive my portion in the number of the martyrs, in the cup of Christ. I praise Thee for all these things; I bless Thee, I glorify Thee, by the eternal High Priest, Jesus Christ, Thy well-beloved Son, through whom, and with whom, in the Holy Spirit, be glory to Thee, both now and for ever. Amen."

28—30. (28) **Blessed,** etc., comp. ch. vi. 26. **changed . . word,** "transgressed the commandment of the king and gave up their bodies." —Stuart. (29) **amiss,** etc., Jehovah was to be reverently acknowledged, not, however, to be worshiped;[a] Nebuc. does not intend to change the national religions. **cut in pieces,**[b] ch. ii. 5. (30) **promoted,** to higher and more responsible state offices.[c]

God's Miracles.—"On the one side was the world-monarchy, irresistible, conquering, as the heathen thought, the God of the vanquished. On the other, a handful of the worshipers of the one only God, captives, scattered, with no visible centre or unity, without organization or power to resist save their indomitable faith, inwardly upheld by God, outwardly strengthened by the very calamities which almost ended their national existence; for they were the fulfilment of His Word in whom they believed Thrice during the seventy years human power put itself forth against the faith; twice in edicts which, if obeyed, would have extinguished the true faith on earth; once in direct insult to God. Faith, as we know, 'quenched the violence of fire, stopped the mouth of lions.' In all cases the assault was signally rolled back; the faith was triumphant in the face of all the representatives of the power and intelligence of the empire; in all, the truth of the one God was proclaimed by those who had assailed it. Unbelief, while it remains such, must deny all true miracles and all superhuman prophecy. But, if honest, it dare not designate as objectless miracles which decided the cause of truth in such battlefields." —Hom. Com.——Following Christ.—When Garibaldi was raising his army he said, "I have no money, no food, nor clothing, no stores, no resources: let every man that is willing to suffer poverty, shame, hunger,

a Ps. lxxxix. 8, xcv. 3, cxiii. 5.

b "This decree promulgated throughout the vast empire of Nebuc. must have tended much to keep the Jews from idolatry in the captivity and henceforth." —Fausset.

c "It is the wisdom of princes to prefer and employ men of steadfastness in religion; for those are most likely to be faithful to them who are faithful to God and it is likely to be well with them when God's favorites are made theirs." —Mat. Henry.

disease and death, and who loves Italy, follow me." It is the measure of our suffering that will enable us to be like the Master. It has been said that when he died he left his purse to Judas, his clothes to the soldiers, his mother to John, his pardon to the dying thief and his peace to the disciples. Someone has said, "I look for the world and I find it in the church and I look for the church and find it in the world." You may try all you please for the Baptism of the Holy Ghost, and unless you are willing to present your bodies a living sacrifice to God you cannot be filled with the Spirit.—D. W. Whittle.

CHAPTER THE FOURTH.

1—3. (1) **Peace,** etc., the usual form of E. salutation. This is an abbreviated copy of the royal decree, or proclamation.[a] (2) **thought it good,** or "it was seemly before me." **signs,** "tokens significant of God's omnipotent agency." (3) **everlasting,**[b] as comp. with the perishing nature of a reign like his own; see ch. ii. 44.

[a] "This royal decree was doubtless preserved in the archives of Bab. It was a State paper; and the accuracy of this transcript could therefore easily be tested." —Wordsworth.

[b] Ps. x. 16, ciii. 19.

The Use of Dreams.—"Dreams become significant when they are the concentrated essence of the main stream of the waking thoughts, and picturesquely exhibit the tendency of the character. This is precisely the use of dreams: our tendencies unbridled by reason and fact run on to results; and we see the character unimpeded by social checks, and as it would be were it unmodified by the restraints, and efforts, and external considerations of our concious hours. Our vanity, our pride, our malice, our deceit, our every evil passion has free play, and shows us its finished result, and in so vivid and true, though caricatured, a form, that we are startled and withdrawn from our purpose."—Marcus Dods.

4—7. (4) **at rest,** having finished his wars, and holding undisputed possession of the world. Ewald suggests by comp. with the lxx., that this was the 28th yr. of Nebuc.'s reign. **flourishing,** like a tree. At full ease and prosperity. (5) **afraid,** though he did not understand it, he felt that there was something ominous about it. **thoughts . . bed,** i.e. "the reflections of his mind upon the dream after he had awaked."—Stuart. (6) **made. . . .decree,** or issued a command. **wise men,** a part of whose profession it was to interpret dreams.[a] (7) **magicians,** ch. ii. 2. . . **Chaldeans,** in much later ages the name was used, as it was among the Roman writers, for wandering astrologers and quacks.—Exp. B.

[a] "The king's request was a fair one when addressed to men whose elaborate system of augury contained tables of omens from dreams, as well as the interpretation of every possible dream." —Spk. Com.

"I shall see the winged vengeance overtake such children." —Shakespeare.

Tartini's Devil's Sonata.—"Tartini a distinguished violin player, is said to have composed his 'Devil's Sonata' under the inspiration of a dream, in which the devil appeared to him and invited him to a trial of skill upon his own instrument, which he accepted, and awoke with the music of the Sonata so vividly impressed upon his mind that he had no difficulty in committing it to paper."—Amer. Cycl.

8, 9. (8) **came in,** or was called in. Prob. as president of the province he was no longer classed with the magicians, and so had to be specially called in the emergency. **name . . god,** Bel, or Beltis. **holy gods,** this is Nebuc.'s view. Daniel would say, "the spirit of the one and only God."[a] (9) **master,** not in office, but in the sense of being able to do what they could not do.

[a] "The language of the king constantly vacillates bet. polytheism and monotheism, but he never admits one God to the exclusion of all others; his monotheism only implies that one God is supreme among many." —Arch. Rose.

Youthful Piety.—You will make a terrible mistake if you suppose that piety unfits you for life, or imagine that its existence in youth is an abnormal thing that indicates the presence of disease. Believe me, there is nothing so healthy, or so wholesome, as to give yourselves early to the Lord. It will lay in you the foundation of a vigorous and energetic character. It will bring the highest of all motives to bear alike upon education, recreation, and business, and enable you to make the very best of yourselves for God and for your fellowmen. It will secure for you all that is best worth having in the world, while along with that, you will have the enjoyment of God's favor, and the prospect of heaven's happiness. For the case of Daniel is not exceptional. You have the same things illustrated in the lives of Joseph and Moses and Samuel, and in some degree also, in that of Timothy; while, if you care to look around you and inquire into the histories of many of those among ourselves who

According to a tradition current among the natives of Puerto Rico, there was an island of the Bahama group which had upon it a marvellous fountain, whose waters produced perpetual youth. For this marvel of nature, Juan Ponce de Leon, the Spanish navigator, sought long and earnestly, yet in vain.

are most loved and trusted by their fellow-citizens, you will discover that they also have "feared God from their youth."

10—12. (10) **a tree,** for the fig. comp. Ezek. xxxi. 3. The reference here may be to the sacred tree of the Assyrians, the symbol of life, which is so perpetually introduced into the sculptures of Nineveh, and seen also in some Babylonian cylinders, especially in connection with royal acts of worship.—Pul. Com. **midst,** middle, or centre; perh. Babylon was considered as the middle point of the earth. (11) **grew,** etc., symbol of the rise of Nebuc.'s own power. **unto heaven,** a strong fig. for a great height. (12) **meat,** or food, a general term. **beasts,** etc., symbol of the subjects of Nebuc.'s kingdom.

Trees.—Trees of the pine and fir tribes, when cut down, do not send up fresh stems, like broad-leaved trees in general; but their roots immediately begin to decay. . . . The magnificent cedar of Lebanon might have been looked upon by Nebuchadnezzar as a suitable emblem of his own glory and power, but it cannot have been this tree that he saw in his dream,—a tree that grew "and was strong, and the height thereof reached unto heaven, and the sight thereof to the end of all the earth." Had it been a resinous tree, a cedar, pine, or fir, it would have been in vain to have left the "stump of his roots in the earth," until "seven times" would "pass over him," expecting that vitality would again show itself. It must, therefore, have been a broad-leaved tree, having the power, which trees of the fir tribe do not possess, of forming fresh buds, and putting forth fresh branches at any part of the stem, and at any time when the flow of sap has been accidentally stopped. This idea is confirmed by the statement that it was a fruit-producing tree, affording "meat for all." Bearing fruit, and growing afresh when cut down, are properties that apply conjointly to some trees, and there are other trees to which neither of them can properly apply.—Gorrie.

13—15. (13) **watcher,** etc., i.e. a holy watcher, an angel. (14) **aloud,** or "with might." (15) **stump,** so that he may yet sprout again. **with a band,** to be put round the trunk to prevent it fr. cracking open in the sun. A symbol of the care with wh. the germ of the tree would be preserved until the time for sprouting.—Stuart. **in . . grass,** in the midst of. **portion . . beasts,** of whom, in his lunacy, Nebuc. would fancy himself one.

Prosperity and Reverses.—It was a common method in olden time to represent a prosperous man under the image of a flourishing tree. "The righteous shall prosper as a palm tree: he shall grow as a cedar in Lebanon." The greatness and splendor of Nebuchadnezzar resembled such a tree. He reigned in Babylon—well-nigh the centre of the then known world. His power among earthly kings was supreme. Neighboring monarchs were his vassals. In all his wars he had been successful. Israel and Syria, Egypt and Arabia, lay at his feet. His throne was strong, and his fame reached, as it seemed, to heaven. Nor did his rule appear, on the whole, injurious. The peoples found protection under his sceptre. He encouraged the growth of art and science. But this military glory fed and pampered his pride. He deemed himself something more than man. He imagined himself a demi-god. The prosperity was outward, material, plausible. . . . He who had "set his heart as the heart of God," who had aspired to a place among the stars, was to fall below the level of a man—was to have the heart of a beast, abject weakness instead of imperial might, imbecility in place of boasted wisdom. This disaster is said to be proclaimed by a holy watcher. This language was an accommodation to prevalent beliefs. The unfallen angels watch our course, grieve over our declensions, and correct us for our follies. So did an angel scatter the hosts of Sennacherib. So did an angel smite Herod with a fatal disease. "Are they not all ministering spirits?" "Excelling in strength, they do his commands, hearkening to the voice of his word."—Pul. Com.

Angels.—

The good one, after every action, closes
His volume, and ascends with it to God.
The other keeps his dreadful day-book open
Till sunset, that we may repent, which doing,

"Pleasure has been the business of my life, and every change of fortune easy to me, because I still was easy to myself." —Dryden.

"It is with youth as with plants; from the first fruits they bear, we learn what may be expected in future." — Demophilus.

"Angels for the good man's sin, weep to record, and blush to give it in." — Campbell.

"Intemperate youth, by sad experience found, ends in an age imperfect and unsound. — Denham.

Youth scatters its affections with a liberal hand, like a young heir, ignorant as yet of the value of his possessions.

"The youth . . yielding like wax, th' impressive folly bears; rough to reproof, and slow to future cares." — Horace.

"Youth is not like a new garment, which we can keep fresh and fair by wearing sparingly. Youth, while we have it, we must wear daily and it will fast wear away." —Foster.

The record of the action fades away.
Now, if my act be good, as I believe,
It cannot be recalled. It is already
Sealed up in heaven as a good deed accomplished.
The rest is yours. —Longfellow.

16—18. (16) **heart,** thoughts or ideas. **beast's heart,** the notions, and feelings, and tastes of a brute beast.[a] **seven times,** not a definite period, but the complete time Divinely allotted to him. Most commentators give the word "time" the meaning of "year." (17) **decree,** or sentence. The view seems to be that the Almighty had a council of angels, and before them was every question discussed ere it was decreed. In short, that there was a heavenly sanhedrin, corresponding to that on earth.—Pul. Com. **basest,** or lowest in condition.[b] (18) **thou .. able,** the king's confidence is based on Daniel's former success.

Nebuchadnezzar's Insanity.—"My opinion is that of all mental powers or conditions the idea of personal identity is but rarely enfeebled, and that it is never extinguished. The ego (self) and non ego (not self) may be confused. The ego, however, continues to preserve the personality. I have seen a man declaring himself the Savior, St. Paul, yet sign his own name James Thomson, and attend worship as regularly as if the notion of Divinity had never entered into his head. I think it probable, therefore, because consistent with experience in similar forms of mental affection, that Nebuchadnezzar retained a perfect consciousness that he was Nebuchadnezzar during the whole course of his degradation."—Browne. If Dr. Browne's idea that the king kept all thro' the consciousness that he was Nebuchadnezzar be correct, his agony must at times have been most acute. What an anguish it was now and then to Robert Hall, with that noble intellect of his, to awake to the fact, as he sometimes did after a paroxysm of madness, that he had become so irrational! And similar shocks must have gone thro' the heart of Nebuchadnezzar during his time of affliction.—Taylor.

a "It is now conceded that the madness of Nebuc. agrees with the description of a rare sort of disease called Lycanthropy, of which our earliest notice is in a Greek medical writer of the 4th century after our Lord, in which the sufferer retains his consciousness in other respects, but imagines himself to be changed into some animal and acts, up to a certain point, in conformity with that persuasion." — Pusey.

b 1 Sa. ii. 8; Lu. i. 52.

19—22. (19) **astonied,** as one rapt, or entranced. He seems to have feared to tell the interpretation.[c] **one hour,** R. V., "for a while." **hate thee,** such only as they will be pleased to hear; or Daniel wishes that what this dream indicates might fall upon the king's enemies. (20) **tree,** vs. 10. (21) **leaves,** etc., vs. 12. (22) **thou,** the tree was the symbol of the king himself.

Personal Reproof.—God's prophet is bold as well as skilful; fearless as well as affectionate. Being God's messenger, he is bound to represent God; and, with all God's might for his defence, nothing can really harm him. Beside, his very eagerness to promote men's welfare inspires him with courage. He is conscious that he has no other end in view, except to please his Master and to benefit men; hence he proceeds straightway to put his finger upon the plague-spot of men's disease, and to prescribe the remedy. In dealing with those who desire their guidance, God's prophets cannot be too plain, too pointed, or too faithful. If a wanderer seeks guidance through a perilous wilderness, his guide cannot be too plain in his instructions, nor too persistent in requiring a faithful following of his words. Fearless vindication of the truth is a mark of a genuine prophet.—Pul. Com.

23—25. (23) **watcher,** etc., vss. 13, 14. (24) **most High,** Daniel does not call it a decree of the "watcher" or of the gods of Nebuc., but the One God of Daniel, who was Nebuc.'s God also, though unacknowledged. (25) **drive,** etc., indicating force, used against the king's will. **dwelling.. beasts,** this was prob. done to humor his mania. **eat grass,** man cannot live on grass, so that other food must have been provided for him.

Failure of Worldly Things to Satisfy.—Solomon tried all that the world can give, and under the most favorable circumstances, yet found all to be vanity and vexation of spirit. Byron, with rank, and wealth, and all manner of pleasure, failed of content and happiness. Alexander conquered the world, but it did not satisfy his soul; and if he could have conquered all worlds that stud the heavens, he would still have wept for more. For God has not created a single human soul so small and poor that all the material universe can fill it. All literature is full of expressions of the failure of worldly things to satisfy the soul.—Peloubet.

c "Being amazed and distressed by the dreadful calamity wh. he saw was portended by the vision, he felt tender compassion for his king and benefactor." —Wordsworth.

"Youth is ever apt to judge in haste, and lose the medium in the wild extreme."— Aaron Hill.

"It requires greater virtues to support good than bad fortune." — La Rochefoucauld.

The young should be spared from sorrow as much as possible. Never dim the sunshine of hope and joy, so as to leave them without even the memory of its glory.

"O, I have ta'en too little care of this! Take physic, pomp; expose thyself to feel what wretches feel; that thou mayst shake the superflux to them, and show the heavens more just." — Shakespeare.

26, 27. (26) **sure,** i.e. kept for thee, when the great lesson shall be learned, pride is broken down, and the living God acknowledged. **heavens,** mentioned for God, bec. His dwelling place. (27) **acceptable,** so that you at once give practical heed to it. **break,** etc., make an end of thy sins by a change of life. **mercy . . poor,** these Nebuc. may have crushed by exactions of forced labor. **lengthening,** bec. God may, if He will, delay judgment when there are signs of repentance.[a]

Necessity of Contrition.—Take the cold iron, and attempt to weld it, if you can, into a certain shape. How fruitless the effort! Lay it on the anvil, seize the blacksmith's hammer with all your might, let blow after blow fall upon it, and you shall have done nothing; but put it in the fire, let it be softened and made malleable, then lay it on the anvil, and each stroke shall have a mighty effect, so that you may fashion it into any form you may desire: so take your heart, not cold as it is, not stony as it is by nature, but put it into the furnace; there let it be molten, and after that it can be turned like wax to the seal, and fashioned into the image of Jesus Christ.—Spurgeon.

28—30. (28) **came,** not at once, but when, having forgotten the warning, his heart was lifted up in pride.[b] (29) **twelve months,** prob. a time of peace during wh. Nebuc. was concerned with the adornment of the capital. **palace,** R. V., "royal palace of," to this the king's special attention had been given.[c] (30) **spake,** giving actual expression to the proud thoughts he cherished. **built,**[d] here not meaning "founded," but "restored and enlarged." In this vs. the words "I, my," are emphatic.

The Pride of Nebuchadnezzar (vs. 30).—Three things I note in this saying. I. What a glorious opinion Nebuchadnezzar had of his vain building. 1. Out of these words, "Is not this great Babel?" 2. Out of these words, "Which I have built by the might of my power:" wherein he termeth himself the founder of it, as if he had done it all without a helper; 3. That in all his work he sought nothing but vainglory. Out of these words, "For the honor of my majesty." These three sins Nebuchadnezzar doth bewray in one brag; and in all these three we are so like, that the beasts were not so like him when he became a beast.—H. Smith.

Walking on the Roof.—The custom of walking upon the roof in the cool of the day, to inhale the refreshing breeze, and to survey the surrounding scenery, may serve to explain a Scripture incident of considerable interest. If Nebuchadnezzar walked upon the roof of his palace, which proudly rose above the surrounding habitations, and surveyed the vast extent, the magnificence, and the splendor of that great city, the mistress of the world—its walls of prodigious height and thickness—its hanging gardens, reputed one of the most astonishing efforts of art and power—its glittering palaces; the Euphrates rolling his majestic flood through the middle of the place, shut in on both sides by strong bulwarks and doors of brass; it was quite natural for such a man to feel elated with the sight, and indulge his pride and arrogance in the manner described by the Prophet.—Paxton. Pride and its Fall.—The Bible always represents to us that pride and arrogant self-confidence are an offence against God. And something like this we see again and again in what the late Bishop Thirlwall called the "irony of history"—the very cases in which men seem to have been elevated to the very summit of power only to heighten the dreadful precipice over which they immediately fall. He mentions the cases of Persia, which was on the verge of ruin, when with lordly arrogance she dictated the Peace of Antalcidas; of Boniface VIII., in the Jubilee of 1300, immediately preceding his deadly overthrow; of Spain, under Philip II., struck down by the ruin of the Armada at the zenith of her wealth and pride. He might have added the instances of Ahab, Sennacherib, Nebuchadnezzar, and Herod Antipas; of Alexander the Great, dying as the fool dieth, drunken and miserable, in the supreme hour of his conquests; of Napoleon, hurled into the dust, first by the retreat from Moscow, then by the overthrow at Waterloo.—Exp. B.

31—33. (31) **While . . mouth,** the moment of pride becoming the moment of judgment.[a] **fell a voice,** of the watcher; this must have been heard by others. It did but recall the judgment of wh. Daniel had given warning. (33) **body was wet,** he persisted in going naked like the beasts.

[a] 1 Ki. xxi. 29.

How near we are to each other when we are all united to God!— Fenelon.

[b] "The influence upon Nebuc. of the dream, as interpreted by Daniel is not indicated in Scripture. Very poss. Nebuc was offended and annoyed."

[c] "The 'Stand. Inscription' contains the following: 'I have adorned no part of Babylon—that city wh. is the pupil of my eye—as I have the palace. That is the house which commands the admiration of men; it is the central spot of the country, high and elevated; it is the house of royalty in the country of Babylonia." — Spk. Com.

[d] "The words 'I have built' occur again and again in the inscription which is preserved in the British Museum." — Wordsworth.

[a] Comp. Ac. xii. 23.

b "The nails, so long as they are cut, grow unremittingly: when this is omitted, their growth is confined. In this case, as may be observed in the sick when long bedridden, the nails become 1 or 2 inches long and curve round the fingers and ends of the toes."—Kolliker.

hairs, etc., a natural growth of hair covering his body. **nails,** etc.,[b] they had a tendency to curve round.

Antiochus and Nebuchadnezzar.—The madness of Antiochus was recognized in the popular change of his name from Epiphanes to Epimanes. But there were obvious points of resemblance between these potentates. Both of them conquered Jerusalem. Both of them robbed the Temple of its holy vessels. Both of them tried to dictate the religion of their subjects. What happened to the kingdom of Babylon during the interim is a point with which the writer does not trouble himself. It formed no part of his story or of his moral. There is, however, no difficulty in supposing that the chief mages and courtiers may have continued to rule in the king's name—a course rendered all the more easy by the extreme seclusion in which most Eastern monarchs pass their lives, often unseen by their subjects from one year's end to the other. Alike in ancient days as in modern—witness the cases of Charles VI. of France, Christian VII. of Denmark, George III. of England, and Otho of Bavaria—a king's madness is not allowed to interfere with the normal administration of the kingdom.—Exp. B. Standard Inscription.—The monarch himself seems to have recorded an event to which profane historians make no allusion. In an inscription known as the 'Standard Inscription' of the great Babylonian sovereign, occurs a remarkable passage, which is thus translated by Sir H. Rawlinson: "Four years (?).... the seat of my kingdom in the city . . . which . . . did not rejoice my heart. In all my dominions I did not build a high place of power; the precious treasures of my kingdom I did not lay up. In Babylon, buildings for myself, and for the honor of my kingdom, I did not lay out. In the worship of Merodach, my god, the joy of my heart(?) in Babylon, the city of his sovereignty, and the seat of my empire, I did not sing his praises(?) and I did not furnish his altars (with victims), nor did I clear out the canals."

a "I recovered the use of my reason, and became sensible of my dependence upon God, and lifted up mine eyes to heaven in a devout acknowledgment of His sovereign majesty, whose dominion alone is unchangeable, and endures for ever."—Lowth.

b "It is a mark of true contrition to condemn oneself, and justify God."—Fausset.

34—37. (34) **end .. days,** the "seven times" of the judgment. **lifted .. eyes,** the uplook is a sign of returning reason. Designates the posture of prayer. **understanding,**[a] or power of mental control; relation of will to the ordering of the mental associations. **everlasting,** etc., ch. vii. 14. (35) **all .. nothing,** Is. xl. 15, 17. **what doest thou?** no human power able to stand against the irresistible dominion of Jehovah. Job ix. 12; Is. xlv. 9. (36) **brightness,** prob. alluding to the proper feeling and sentiment of a man. **sought,** to receive directions for the government of the kingdom. (37) **King of heaven,** the characteristic name for Jehovah in this book. **pride .. abase,** this was the lesson wh. his humiliation was designed to teach.[b]

There is a Spiritual Insanity in which Men Renounce the Privileges and Duties of Their Higher Nature, and Live as if They Had Nothing above the Animal in Them.—The degradation of Nebuchadnezzar finds its spiritual counterpart in the voluntary behavior of multitudes. They have human souls, yet they live as though they should perish like mere animals. They are made in the image of God, yet they act after the manner of brutes. They have spiritual faculties which they blind and deaden with animal passions. If we were not so familiar with such people, and did not all of us, more or less, share their faults, it would be difficult not to regard them as the worst of madmen. While we shudder at the calamity of Nebuchadnezzar, should we not be far more appalled at the awful depravity of so large a part of the human world which calmly accepts a fate in all moral respects its equivalent?—Pul. Com. Light at Eventide.—It is a perilous thing to abuse any of God's gifts. Thereby we interfere with the order of the government, and justly provoke his anger. The darkening of intellect with prejudice is no mean offence. Bribing reason with sensual delights not to recognize God—this is a serious injury to one's self, and daring rebellion against God. Such was the aggravated sin of Nebuchadnezzar; yet the judgment of God was tempered with mercy. The abuse of reason resulted in its loss, yet the loss was temporary. The deplorable darkness was designed as a prelude to clearer light.

CHAPTER THE FIFTH.

1—4. (1) **Belshazzar,**[a] prob. joint king with his father. **great feast,** kept an annual festival season, and regardless of the presence of an active enemy outside the walls. **drank wine,** this was usually after the feasting. **before,** prob. the king's seat was a separate one, at the head of the table, so that his guests might have a full view of him.—Stuart. (2) **whiles .. wine,** or when excited with wine. **bring,** etc., ch. i. 2. **drink therein,** not only putting sacred things to secular use, but intentionally insulting the God whose vessels they were. (4) **praised,** etc., in their drunken insolence offering public insult to the King of heaven.

The Fiery Inscription.—In this chapter again we have another magnificent fresco-picture, intended, as was the last—but under circumstances of aggravated guilt and more terrible menace—to teach the lesson that "verily there is a God that judgeth the earth." The truest way to enjoy the chapter, and to grasp the lessons which it is meant to inculcate in their proper force and vividness, is to consider it wholly apart from the difficulties as to its literal truth. To read it aright, and duly to estimate its grandeur, we must relegate to the conclusion of the story all worrying questions, impossible of final solution, as to whom the writer intended by Belshazzar, or whom by Darius the Mede. All such discussions are extraneous to edification, and in no way affect either the consummate skill of the picture or the eternal truths of which it is the symbolic expression. To those who, with the present writer, are convinced, by evidence from every quarter—from philology, history, the testimony of the inscriptions, and the manifold results obtained by the Higher Criticism—that the Book of Daniel is the work of some holy and highly gifted Chasid in the days of Antiochus Epiphanes, it becomes clear that the story of Belshazzar, whatever dim fragments of Babylonian tradition it may enshrine, is really suggested by the profanity of Antiochus Epiphanes in carrying off, and doubtless subjecting to profane usage, many of the sacred vessels of the Temple of Jerusalem.—F. W. Farrar.

5, 6. (5) **fingers,** perhaps the semblance of a hand. **over .. candlestick,** i.e. just where the light shone fully on the wall. **the plaister,** the word means "plain stucco."[b] (6) **countenance,** Chal. brightness, his excited look.[c] **joints,** etc., "prob. his hip-joints, or the joints in the lower part of the spine. The meaning seems to be that he was unable to keep his standing by reason of these natural supports being rendered tremulous."—Stuart.

The Awakening Hour of Conscience (vss. 5, 6).—I. It is an hour that must dawn on the most obdurate natures. II. It is an hour introduced by a Divine manifestation. III. It is an hour associated with great mental distress. IV. It is an hour which is sometimes the harbinger of eternal retribution.—Thomas.

Conscience.—Everyone knows Victor Hugo's beautiful poem, "La Conscience," the story of Cain, fleeing away before the eye of God. He walks thirty days and thirty nights, until he reaches the shores of the ocean. "Let us stop here," says he. But as he sits down his face turns pale; he has seen in the mournful skies the Eye in the same place." His sons, full of awe, try to erect barriers between him and the Eye; a tent, then a wall of iron, then a tower and a city; but all is vain. "I see the Eye still," cries the unhappy man. At last they dig a tomb. The father is put into it. But,—

> Tho' overhead they closed the awful vault,
> The Eye was in the tomb and looked on Cain.
>
> —Reuben Saillens.

7—9. (7) **aloud,** or with impatient instancy. **read,** so as to understand. **scarlet,** the color of honor and high rank. **chain of gold,**[a] emblem of high office. **third ruler,** or "one of a board of three."[b]—Exp. B. (8) **king's wise men,** those belonging to the court. **not read,** not decipher. (9) **lords .. astonied,** R. V., "perplexed;" there was a "panic of the assembled spectators as they find themselves in the presence of an enigma which they cannot decipher."—Stanley.

---

a "Bil-shar-uzar, on the monuments, the son and colleague of Nabunahid. The Chaldaean list of kings is Nebuc., Evil - Merodach, Neriglissar, Laboroscarchod, and Nabunahid. In Herodotus the interval is filled up by the one name of Labynetus."—Stanley.

"Rationalists must now retract the assertion that the last king of Babylon has a false name in Daniel, since it is now an admitted fact that the name of Belshazzar occurs on Bab. cylinders, as the eldest son of Nabunahid, the Nabonidus of Berosus, the Labynetus of Herodotus." —Pusey.

b "The great candlestick wh. lighted up the pale stucco on the wall of the palace to which the banqueting hall was attached."—Stanley.

c "His color and the flush of wine left his cheek, and a deadly paleness came over him." —Arch. Rose.

a Ge. xli. 42.

b Xenophon narrates that the Babylonians thought themselves secure and laughed at the measures of the besiegers; therefore we need not be surprised that Belshazzar made this promise."—Wordsworth.

Conscience.—Upon the coast of France, the sailors say there is a buried city; and on quiet nights, as they are rocked upon the deep, they think they can hear the tones of the buried bells, coming up from the steeples far down in the ocean depths, with muffled sound. So in the hearts of men of the world who have lived lives of self-indulgence and evil, there are muffled tones from the depths of their nature, ringing in the steeples of conscience, that tell them to choose what is right, and to shun what is wrong.—F. B. Meyer.

c "The Sultana Valide; very possibly the great Nitocris, the daughter of Nebuc., herself the architect of some of the great art works of the city."

d Da. iv. 8, 9, 18.

e "As Daniel was prob., according to Oriental custom, deprived of the office to wh. Nebuc. had promoted him, at the king's death, Belshazzar might easily be ignorant of his services." —Fausset.

10—12. (10) **queen,** prop. queen-mother.[c] **reason .. words,** this may mean, a message from the king, or a report of the excitement in the banqueting house. **O king,** the established mode of publicly addressing the royal person. (11) **a man,** etc., one within thy reach. **holy gods,** this represents the common idea about Daniel.[d] He was possibly at this time in retirement, bec. out of favor at court.[e] **father,** forefather. **master,** etc., ch. iv. 9. (12) **doubts,** or knots; intricate and difficult things.

Doubts (note on vs. 12).—The margin (Chald.) has, instead of "doubts," "knots." A very difficult subject is called a mudiche, a knot! Thus the explaining of a riddle is called "untying the knot." Of a talented man it is said, "Ah! he is very clever, he can tie or untie any knot." Of a dream, it is asked, "Who can loose this knot?" Of any mysteries, or of deep plans, it is asked, "Ah! who can untie these knots?" "How difficult that passage was, but he soon unravelled the knot."—Roberts. True Wisdom Gains her Ends at last.—She has often to hide her head for a time, while Folly is jingling her bells and is making a blustering noise; but her occasion is sure to come. Her voice will prevail at last, and men will chide themselves bitterly that they had not followed her counsels at an earlier day. Wisdom is always patient, because she knows that, sooner or later, her presence will be sought and her guidance followed. Belshazzar had "sown the wind;" now he was "reaping the whirlwind;" and, dismayed with the menacing storm, he became a docile pupil of Wisdom. Without hesitation or delay, he sent for the counsellor whom he had long neglected, and confesesd his need of the prophet's service. Even the king is dependent on his subjects for a thousand things. Supercilious pride is the sure forerunner of disaster. —Pul. Com.

"In the wildest anarchy of man's insurgent appetites and sins, there is still a reclaiming voice; a voice which, even when in practice disregarded, it is impossible not to own; and to wh., at the very moment that we refuse our obedience, we find that we cannot refuse the homage of what ourselves do feel and acknowledge to be the best, the highest principles of our nature." — Chalmers.

13—16. (13) **that Daniel,** the man to whom the queen-mother referred. It is curious that the king should address him by his Jewish name. (14) **heard of thee,** the words plainly prove that Daniel was not an acting official in the court or kingdom of Belshazzar. **light, intelligence.** (15) **read,** decipher. (16) **dissolve doubts,** see note on vs. 12.

God and a Guilty Conscience.—Alcibiades thus expresses himself in speaking of Socrates:—"I stop my ears, therefore, as from the syrens, and flee away as fast as possible, that I may not sit down beside him and grow old in listening to his talk; for this man has reduced me to feel the sentiment of blame which I imagine no one could readily believe was in me; he alone inspires me with remorse and awe, for I feel in his presence my incapacity of refuting what he says, or of refusing to do that which he directs; but when I depart from him, the glory which the multitude confers overwhelms me. I escape, therefore, and hide myself from him, and when I see him I am overwhelmed with humiliation, because I have neglected to do what I have confessed ought to be done; and often have I wished that he were no longer to be seen among men." If such were the feelings excited by a near view of the character of Socrates, how much more overwhelming must be the feelings created by a view of the infinite purity of God by a guilty conscience? Hence the conduct of sinners who have any sense of Him. They will not abide in His presence. They escape away from Him in the forgetfulness of this world; but when, alas, they do get a view of Him through the eye of a guilty conscience, how do they wish there was no such a Being! And some of them, prevailed upon by their wishes, really say in their hearts, "There is no God."—McCook.

"Trust that man in nothing who has not a conscience in everything."—Sterne.

The King's Despair.—Washington Allston spent more than twelve years attempting to paint the scene of Belshazzar's feast, and then left his work unfinished. It is said that the chief difficulty which the artist's genius could not overcome, was that of depicting the despair of the doomed king. Well it might be so; for it was the despair of a lost soul brought suddenly face to face with the retributive judgment of God, written by a mysterious hand from another world.—Phelps.

17—19. (17) **Let .. another,** as one who had openly insulted Jehovah Daniel would have nothing whatever to do with him or his gifts.[a] "There is more of respectful than of indignant pity in the words of his protest." (18) **O thou king,** a solemn direct address. **most high God,** whom Daniel proclaimed as the only God. Nebuc. had to learn in bitter humiliation whence his power really came.[b] (19) **whom he would,** the description of irresponsible authority.

Tyranny not Essential to Kingly Power.—At the court of France, whilst Louis XIV. was yet in his youth, some abject courtiers were entertaining the prince in public with the policy of the Turkish government. They observed, that the Sultan had nothing to do but to say the word, whatever it was, whether to take off a great man's head, or strip him of his employment or estate, and that there was a train of servants they called mutes, who executed it without reply. "See," said the prince, "what it is to be a king!" The old Count de Grammont, who heard the corrupters of the youth with indignation, immediately interposed: "But, Sire; of these same sultans I have known three strangled by their own mutes within my memory." This silenced the flatterers; and the Duke de Montausier, the French Cato, who was lolling in a chair behind the circle that surrounded the prince, forced his way through the crowd, and publicly thanked the Count de Grammont for his noble and seasonable liberty.—Whitecross. Nebuchadnezzar and Babylon.—Nebuchadnezzar is the great monarch of the Babylonian empire, which, lasting only eighty-eight years, from B.C. 625 to B.C. 538, was for nearly half the time under his sway. The chief works ascribed to him by the ancient writers are the following: He built the great wall of Babylon, which, according to the lowest estimate, must have contained more than 500,000,000 square feet of solid masonry, and must have required three or four times that number of bricks. He constructed a new and magnificent palace in the neighborhood of the ancient residence of the kings. He made the celebrated "hanging garden," for the gratification of his wife, Amyitis. He repaired and beautified the great temple of Belus, at Babylon. He dug the huge reservoir near Sippara, said to have been 140 miles in circumference and 180 feet deep, furnishing it with floodgates, through which its waters could be drawn off for purposes of irrigation. There are said to be at least a hundred sites in the tract immediately about Babylon which give evidence, by inscribed bricks bearing his legend, of the marvelous activity and energy of this king.—Rawlinson.

20, 21. (20) **hardened in pride,** R. V. "spirit was hardened that he dealt proudly," ch. iv. 30. **deposed,** made to come down. This occurred not by the rebellion of his people, but by the direct visitation of God. (21) **driven,** etc., ch. iv. 32. **appointeth,** R. V. "setteth up."

Loss—Sometimes a Means of Salvation.—An artist was once frescoing the lofty ceiling of a church and gradually stepping back on the scaffolding to watch the effect of his work; he was so absorbed in his picture that he did not notice that he was about to step off the edge, and fall upon the pavement far below. A brother artist, seeing his danger, and knowing that a word would but hasten his fall, threw his brush at the picture. The painter, indignant, rushed forward and was saved. Sometimes our pictured hopes, and visions of happiness, must be destroyed in order that we may be able to realize the evil of sin and be turned away from our own ruin.—Peloubet.

22—24. (22) **not humbled,** but instead hast only changed Nebuc.'s haughty pride for an insolent and utterly offensive form of pride. (23) **praised .. gods,** this was the insult which could not be passed over.[a] **in whose hand,** etc., "at whose disposal thy life is." **whose .. ways,** Je. x. 23. (24) **Then,** i.e. just then; in the very moment when your insolent pride reached its climax.

The God of Our Life (vs. 23).—I. Our dependence on God—1. For our existence; 28. For our well-being. II. The duty we owe to God in consequence of this dependence. 1. We ought to believe in Him and to love Him; 2. We ought to worship Him; 3. We ought to obey Him; 4. We ought to consult for His glory. III. Our neglect of this duty.

[a] "Daniel's address to Belshazzar is in a very different tone fr. that of his language to Nebuc. Belshazzar was at this time guilty of profane sacrilege against God and the Prophet, as His minister, pronounced sentence upon him."—Wordsworth.

[b] Da. iv. 35—37.

Cynanthropy, Lycanthropy, and similar names, are given to the various hallucinations of this form of disease. The patient howls like a wolf, or attempts to bark like a dog, and to imitate the gestures and habits of the animal he believes himself transformed into. In such a condition of mind the natural food of that animal would be preferred.

[a] "The language of Daniel here evidently implies that Belshazzar's use of these holy vessels in unholy revels was in the highest degree sacrilegious." —Arch. Rose.

1. In some it is total; 2. In some it is partial; 3. In all it is heinous.—Brooks.

25—28. (25) **Mene,** etc., lit. "numbered, numbered, weighed, broken." (26) **finished,** R. V. "brought it to an end." (28) **Peres** is singular, Pharsin is plural. "U" in Upharsin is "and." **divided,** "broken" is the better meaning here, for "divided," etc., would convey the idea that the Medes and Persians were each a separate and independent power; which was not the fact when Babylon was captured.—Stuart.

Weighed in the Balance.—Roberts remarks that this striking form of speech is much used in the East at this day. Thus, should two men be disputing respecting the moral character of a third person, one will say, "I know the fellow well; I have weighed him, and he is found wanting." "He found wanting! you are much lighter than he." "What, miscreant; do you wish to weigh against me." "Thou art but as one part in a thousand." "Begone, fellow, or I will soon weigh thee." "Yes, yes, there is no doubt about it; you have weighed me; I am much lighter than you." "What kind of times are these? the slaves are weighing their masters." "The judge has been weighing the prisoners, and they are all wanting."

29. clothed, etc., prob. Daniel submitted bec. he knew what would happen before the night was over.[b] **scarlet,** i.e. with a robe of scarlet color.

Rewards of Virtue.—We are to be careful not to confound outward rewards with the real reward of virtue. As "Love in loving finds its joy;" as the Savoyard singer, neglected and forgotten, declares that

"The song itself shall yet reward
The labors of the Savoyard,"

so virtue contains in itself, in the approval of God, in peace of conscience, in spiritual life and character, in helpfulness and service, its best reward. And yet the reward is not perfect without outward conditions to match the inward grace. So shall it be in heaven.—Peloubet.

30, 31. (30) **In that night,** etc., the reading of the Sept. is here very different: "and the interpretation came upon Belshazzar, the king, and the kingdom was taken from the Chaldæans, and given to the Medes and the Persians." **slain,** in his palace.[a] (31) **and Darius the Median,** etc., the Sept. reads: "And Artaxerxes of the Medes received the kingdom, and Darius was full of days and reverenced in old age." Some think Darius was "a viceroy set up by Cyrus. **took,** R. V. "received."

Belshazzar's Death (vs. 30).—Consider—I. The time of Belshazzar's death. It was the night—1. Of his feasting; 2. Of his impiety; 3. Of his warning. II. The instruction to be gathered from it. Learn—(1) Not to provoke the Lord to jealousy; (2) Not to despise the warnings you receive; (3) Not to delay the great work you have to do.—C. Simeon.

The Conquest of Babylon.—In October of the year 538 B.C. Cyrus at last turned his victorious armies towards the tottering capital of southwestern Asia. Persian intrigue, favored by the resentment and suspicion aroused among the Babylonians by the strange conduct of their king, Nabonidus, had prepared the way for an easy conquest. On the northern borders of Babylonia, a battle was fought between the Persians and Babylonians. The army of the latter was defeated and Nabonidus fled. A few days later, the north Babylonian town of Sippar surrendered to Gobryas, the commander of the forces of Cyrus. Within two days more the Persian general was in possession of Babylon. As the recently discovered Nabonidus-Cyrus chronicle distinctly states, the gates of the city were opened to the Persians without a battle (Nab.-Cyr. Chr. ii. 8—16). In the clear light of the inscriptions it is evident that the elaborate tale of Herodotus to the effect that Cyrus turned the waters of the Euphrates into the great basin made by Nebuchadnezzar and entered the city while its inhabitants were so engaged in a feast that they neglected to close the water gates, has been given a wrong setting. It must refer rather to the second capture of Babylon by Darius about twenty years later.—Kent, Hist. of the Jewish People, 1899.

a "The whole passage is an instance of the early mode of exegesis. The explainer took each word, and added to it his comment." —Ewald.

"Mene, the days of the kingdom were numbered and ended; Tekel, it was weighed and found light; Peres, it was divided, and given to the Persians." — Stanley.

b "Belshazzar desired to conciliate Daniel, and Daniel's God."— Wordsworth.

"As the capture of the city by Cyrus was not till near daylight, there is no want of time in that eventful night for accomplishing all that is here recorded."— Fausset.

a "Two deserters, Gadata and Gobryas, having assisted some of the Persian army to kill the guards and seize upon the palace, they entered into the room where the king was, whom they found standing up in a posture of defence; but they soon despatched him, and those that were with him." — Xenophon.

Je. li. 39, 57.

CHAPTER THE SIXTH.

1—3. (1) **set . . princes,** or satraps; rulers who were like petty kings in their respective districts.[a] "Their duties—both civil and military—consisted, broadly speaking, in the supervision of the whole kingdom." (2) **presidents,** Chal. sarac., prob. head-man.[b] **first,** R. V. "was one." The three presidents would constitute a kind of privy council. **damage,** fr. loss of revenues either withheld or pilfered. (3) **preferred,** R. V. "distinguished," much to the disgust of the ruling classes. **excellent spirit,**[c] ch. v. 12. **thought . . realm,** i.e. the province of Babylon of wh. this so-called Darius was ruler under Cyrus; some indication of this purpose excited the jealousy against Daniel.

Success Due to Work.—All primacy has to be paid for. Do not understand that men go forward to any possessions they please up banks of glory, slopes of flowers, fancy work written in imaginary paradises. A Burmese student has lately been contesting with European claimants and candidates, and he has taken everything before him. He said the other day, "Everything is possible here to a man who works." That is an old English word. What a rebuke to those who do not toil! If the Burmese student so successful had used a long word, how many thousands of English youths would have found that long word a grand opening for a thousand excuses! But he explained his position by a very simple term, that term being none other than the good old English term "works." His primacy was paid for. Some men pay for it by work, and others pay for it by work and suffering too.—Peopl. B.

4, 5. (4) **occasion,** something of wh. they might take advantage so as to secure Daniel's destruction.[a] **faithful,** the first political virtue of government officials. (5) **concerning . . God,** in relation to his religion.[b]

The Character of Daniel (vs. 5).—Let me—I. Open to you the constituent parts of this character. Here we behold, in combined and unintermittent exercise—1. Piety; 2. Wisdom; 3. Consistency; 4. Firmness. II. Urge you all to the attainment of it. Let me invite you to consider—1. How it honors God; 2. How it disarms prejudice; 3. How it tends to the welfare of your own soul.—C. Simeon.

Envy.—Eschylus, in "Agamemnon," says:

"Envy at others' good is evermore
Malignant poison sitting on the soul;
A double woe to him infected with it.
Of inward pain the heavy load he bears,
At sight of joy without, he ever mourns."
—Tayler Lewis.

Envy is the daughter of Pride, the author of Murder and Revenge, the perpetual tormentor of virtue. Envy is the filthy slime of the soul; a venom, a poison, a quicksilver, which consumeth the flesh and drieth up the bones.—Socrates.

6—9. (6) **assembled,** marg. "came tumultuously;" as if the matter was one of instant and pressing importance.[c] Daniel knew nothing of their plot, and prob. he could not interfere as the matter did not belong to his department. (7) **establish,** i.e. get the king to establish. **decree,** or interdict. **save of thee,** this shows that they represented the necessity for thus securing a universal acknowledgment of Darius's authority and rights.[d] **den of lions,** a kind of punishment not previously mentioned in the Bible. (8) **altereth not,** Esth. i. 19. (9) **signed,** etc., Stuart, "Because of this King Darius wrote down a writing even a prohibition."

Evils of Flattery.—

A man I knew who lived upon a smile,
And well it fed him; he look'd plump and fair,
While rankest venom foamed through every vein;
Living, he fawn'd on every fool alive;
And, dying, cursed the friend on whom he lived.—Young.

Religious Homage.—The Persian kings were regarded as incarna-

a "When Cyrus was at Bab. it pleased him to send satraps to rule the conquered nations. Darius acted as the representative of Cyrus."—Xenophon.

b "Prob. descriptive of an office peculiar to the Medo - Persian government." —Wordsworth.

c "Daniel had gained great experience in the public affairs, it being now 65 years ago since he was first advanced by Nebuc." — Lowth.

a Comp. the efforts of the Pharisees to find occasion against our Lord.

b "We shall find 'occasion' against him concerning the law (Thorah) of his God if we can obtain from the king a decree which will make him transgress that law; he will not obey the king's command; and that will be our occasion."—Rashi.

c "Had they come more deliberately the king might have refused their grant; but they gave him no time for reflection, representing that their test decree was necessary for the safety of the king." — Fausset.

d In Persia the king is regarded as the image of the good god, Ormuzd

"Flatterers are as inseparable from prosperous princes, as flies are from fruit in the summer; whom adversity, like cold weather, drives away." — Eikon Bas.

tions of the deity. Gaussen observes that Nebuchadnezzar claimed divine honors. Alexander the Great pretended to be a god, and the son of a god. The Roman emperors required themselves and their images to be worshiped. And in our own day the Pope lays claim to religious homage, being at his consecration fumed with incense and placed on the altar of God, while the people kiss his feet, and all the cardinals cry, Venite adoremus, "Come let us adore him!"—Hom. Com.

10—12. (10) **knew,** was informed. His enemies would be ready enough to give him such information. **windows,** etc., this is stated to indicate that he made no change whatever in his habits.[a] **towards Jerus.,** 1 Ki. viii. 48. **three times,** Ps. lv. 17.[b] **as .. aforetime,** showing that when in full work, he had been a man of prayer. (11) **assembled,** see note on vs. 6. "The spy-system was well organized among the Medo-Persians." (12) **Hast,** etc., these men sought a confirmation of the decree before they mentioned Daniel's name.

Persistent, Fearless Prayer.—Some time ago, a law was passed in the House of Assembly at Kingston, which contained several clauses highly injurious to the missionary cause in Jamaica. No time was lost in carrying its oppressive enactments into effect. A Wesleyan missionary was thrown into prison for the alleged "crime" of preaching till after eight o'clock in the evening. Two persons connected with the congregation at Montego Bay, had their houses levelled with the ground—their feet made fast in the stocks—and were sent in chains to the workhouse, charged with the heinous offence of praying to the God of heaven. One of these, however, proved so incorrigible, that they were obliged to give him up in despair. Having nothing to do besides in the jail, he spent his time—morning, noon, and night—in singing, and in calling upon God; which so annoyed the jailor, that he repeatedly went into his cell and beat him, till at length the jailor brought him again before the court for this sin. The man, however, resolutely declared his purpose to pray. "If you let me go," said he, "me will pray—if you keep me in prison, me will pray—if you flog me, me will pray; pray me must, and pray me will!" The jailor was fairly confounded; and, rather than be annoyed any longer by this "praying fellow," he gave up his fees, and a part of the fine was remitted; and so the man was dismissed, to go and pray elsewhere.—Whitecross. Touching God in Prayer.—There is an old story of mythology about a giant, named Antæus, who was born by the earth. In order to keep alive, this giant was obliged to touch the earth as often as once in five minutes, and every time he thus came in contact with the earth he became twice as strong as before. The Christian resembles Antæus. In order to be a living Christian, he must often approach his heavenly Father in prayer; and every time he thus approaches, he becomes stronger and more able to resist the wiles and assaults of the adversary.—Old Test. Anec.

13, 14. (13) **That Daniel,** this expression seems to let out their spite. **children .. Judah,** some time ago a mere captive. **regardeth not,** simply bec. he regarded God, and he could not both obey God's law and the king's, and there could be no question which of the two he must choose. (14) **sore displeased,**[c] vexed at thus being overreached, for he saw that it was enmity towards Daniel, and not anxiety for the maintenance of his authority which had led to the plot. **laboured, etc.,** to find some pretext for not executing the decree.[a]

Protection of Prayer.—Communion with God kept Daniel pure in Babylon. Nothing else can keep us safe in London. In the "secret of God's presence" you might tread these giddy streets, and your eyes never view the vanity. You might pass theatres and taverns, and never dream of entering in. You might get invitations to noisy routs and God-forgetting assemblies, and have no heart to go. Golden images, public opinion, with its lion's den; and fashion, with its fiery furnace, would never disturb you. A man of prayer in this mart of nations, you could pass upon your way unseduced and undistracted, a Christian in Vanity Fair, a pilgrim in a paradise of fools, a worshiper amidst idolaters, a Daniel in Babylon.—Hamilton. Mr. Moody and Gen. O. O. Howard, with many others, were passengers on the steamer Spree, in the autumn of 1892, when the great shaft broke, and the whole company were in momentary danger of sinking. There was a great prayer meeting on

a "On the roof of his house there was a chamber, with windows whose cross-bars or lattices could be shut or opened at pleasure." —Spk. Com.

b "Daniel did not court persecution; he did not run recklessly into danger, and tempt his enemies to the sin of accusing him. He retired to his upper chamber, his private oratory; and his accusers pressed in upon his privacy violently and tumultuously." —Wordsworth.

"A man is running as if for life, looking fearfully behind him. He has let his sword drop in his haste to escape; the scabbard only remains in his hand. Nothing but a harmless rabbit follows in pursuit. sinister bird, the owl, sits in a tree above, screeching and adding to the terror of the poltroon. This is Cowardice."

c "Having too late discovered that the princes, in procuring him to sign this decree, had no other aim but to take advantage of it to the prejudice of Daniel."—Lowth.

a "We often do that, through inconsideration, which afterwards we see cause a thousand times to wish undone again, which is a good reason why we should ponder the path of our feet." —Mat. Henry.

"Yet show some pity.—I show it most of all when I show justice; for then I pity those I do not know, which a

board, led by Mr. Moody, and while they were praying, help came. General Howard thus speaks of the relation of prayer to their rescue: "Did the people of the Spree receive help miraculously from the Heavenly Father? In these things, that is in extreme dangers, it has been my good fortune to have had abundant experience. But I cannot tell where the natural and ordinary helps of Providence end or where the supernatural begins. The finite will never be allowed to know this dividing line. I only know this, at this time, on this ship, as on other times in my life, the demonstration is as clear as daylight that the Lord is a hearer and is an answerer of the prayers of his children. He evidently loves so to arrange his blessings as he does our daily bread so as to make them come as much as possible through common-sense ways and human instrumentality. There was one blessing on the wrecked steamer that was beyond human procuring. It was the almost universal lifting up of human souls into the very sunlight of God's presence."

15—17. (15) **assembled,** vss. 6, 11. **Know, O king,** their tone was masterful now, for they felt able to compel the king to work their will. (16) **he will,** the king means, "I hope he will." (17) **den,** lit. "pit." **sealed it,** to secure that none opened it without due authority. **signet, a ring** wh. contained the engraving of the king's name.

Benevolence Impotent Before Law.—A similar conflict between justice and mercy occurred when Major André, the British spy, was condemned to death by the American court-martial. Probably Washington never set his hand to a document which cost him a more severe struggle than that caused by the death warrant of André. But the safety of our young republic would not permit the deed of mercy. Its very life hung in a trembling scale. Twenty Arnolds might have been the fruit of pardoning one André. "Therefore," said the commander-in-chief, "he is a spy. By the laws of war, his life is forfeit. He must die." And die he did.—Phelps.

18—20. (18) **instruments,** etc., Gesenius trans. the word "concubines;" R. V. marg. "dancing girls." "Nothing could divert the king's thoughts from the prisoner in the den."[a] (19) **very early,** lit. in the glimmer of morning. (20) **lamentable voice,** full of fear and sorrow. **living God,** in comp. with the lifelessness of heathen idols.

Religion a Thing for Every Day.—Henry Ward Beecher, speaking of taking religion into the week, says, "The tides come twice a day in New York harbor, but they come only once in seven days in God's harbor of the sanctuary. They rise on Sunday, but ebb on Monday, and are down and out all the week. Men write over their store-door, 'Business is business,' and over the church door, 'Religion is religion,' and they say to religion, 'Never come in here,' and to business 'Never go in there.' Let us never have secular things in the pulpit. Here we want repose, and sedatives and healing balm. We have enough of knives and probes and lancets in the week. Here let us have poetry; we want to sing hymns and to hear about heaven. God's law is not allowed to go into the week. If the merchant spies it in the store, he throws it over the counter. If it is found in the street, the multitudes pursue it, pelting it with stones, as if it were a wolf, escaped from a menagerie, and shouting, 'Back with you; you have got out of Sunday.' There is no religion in all this. It is mere sentimentalism. Religion belongs to every day."

21—23. (21) **said Daniel,** the sound of his voice was the all-sufficing assurance. (22) **innocency,** purity, straightforwardness. **no hurt,** no wrong; nothing that could damage the king's authority. Daniel had only disobeyed to preserve a good conscience. (23) **glad,** his regard for Daniel was sincere. **believed .. God,** showing faith by the act of allegiance.

Daniel in the Lion's Den (vs. 22).—I would take these words—I. Literally, as regards Daniel, and as it regards the king. 1. As regards the king, look at the positivity of his conduct, unhappiness; 2. As regards Daniel, captivity, beauty, learning, piety, devotion, persecution, age, society, name. II. I come now to take it spiritually, his portion, my God, the messenger, the lion's mouth shut, the law, the world. III. Taking the text mediatorially. 1. Daniel a type of Christ; 2. The lion, like the world, rough: like sin, sudden in attack.—Andrews.

The Agency of God.—The story of the lions in the den recalls inci-

dismissed offence would after gall; and do him right that, answering one foul wrong, lives not to act another."
—Shakespeare.

"Accuse not Heaven's delay; if loth to strike, —its judgments, like the thunder-gather'd storm, are but the greater."—Webster.

a "For Darius it was a wretched night. He was sad and horror-stricken. He was a prey to remorse. Perhaps he was beginning to see how he had been the dupe of his lords, and furious indignation was rising like a storm in his soul." —Robjohns.

"Reputation oft got without merit, and lost without deserving." — Shakespeare.

"Many as the waves, but one as the sea," is the motto of the true Church of Christ. But equally true is it of the works of God and the Word of God."—Peloubet.

dents very like it in the experience of African travelers. Mungo Park once found himself confronted by a raging lion, against which he had no other available weapon than the look of his eye. Yet the beast which had, a moment before, come bounding and roaring towards him, stopped suddenly, looked abashed upon the ground, and then turned and slunk away. Another traveler in African wilds was once actually seized by a hungry lion, thrown to the ground, and had begun to feel the mysterious anæsthesia which the magnetism of wild beasts is said to produce in their victims, when suddenly opening his eyes and fixing them steadily on the eye of the beast, he saw that its bloodshot look wavered. The soul of the beast recognized the soul of its natual lord. He let go his hold on the prostrate man, turned with tail between his legs, and fled. Marvel or miracle, it matters little what we call it, the agency of God in such events is beyond question.—Phelps.

[a] "It was in accordance with Oriental notions of justice, and was in keeping with Persian precedent, that all their kindred should perish with the guilty." —Robjohns.

Ps. ix. 16; Pr. xxvi. 27.

"Conscience as a faculty includes a moral sense, or the power of discerning the distinction between right and wrong; which, combining with the understanding, or faculty of comparing and judging, judges of the right or wrong of our own moral dispositions and voluntary actions and of the dispositions and voluntary actions of other free agents." —A. A. Hodge.

24. accused Daniel, prob. the leaders of the malicious party; the death of these plotters is a remarkable instance of retribution. **children,** etc.,[a] comp. Est. ix. 13, 14. **broke .. den,** this sudden attack by the lions proved that Daniel's escape was due to divine power.

Retribution.—Rev. H. G. Keene states, in his Persian Stories, that the following narrative was related by a person of authority and reputation, who was one of the party. A vessel set sail from Bassorah to Bagdad, with several passengers on board. In the course of the voyage, the sailors, by way of a joke, put a man in irons as he lay asleep, and he became a subject of diversion to the whole party till they drew near to the capital. But when the sailors wanted to let him loose, the key was nowhere to be found, and after a long and fruitless search, they were compelled to send for a blacksmith to knock off the fetters. When, however, the blacksmith came, he refused to do what they wanted, till he had the authority of the magistrate; for he thought the man might be some criminal whom the officers of justice had laid hold of, and that his friends wished to favor his escape. To the magistrate they accordingly went, who sent down one of his attendants to see into it. But the officer, when he had heard the story, and had taken the evidence of some of the most respectable among the passengers, shook his head, and with a look of solemnity, said it was much too serious a case for him to decide. So they repaired in a body to the magistrate, and carried the poor captive with them. So strange a procession was sure to attract notice; and a crowd soon collected about them, each curious to know the prisoner's offence, and to catch a sight of him: till at length one man, springing forward, seized the captive by the throat, and exclaimed: Here is the villain I have been looking for these two years; ever since he robbed and murdered my poor brother." Nor would he quit his hold till they came before the magistrate; and the murder being clearly proved, the man, who had been confined in joke only, was given up to death, as a punishment for the blood that he had shed.

[b] Comp. Da. iii. 29, iv. 3, 34.

"In Rome no temple was so low as that of honor built to show how humble honor ought to be, though there 'twas all authority." —Butler.

"Honor's a fine imaginary notion, that draws in raw and unexperienced men to real mischiefs, while they hunt a shadow." —Addison.

"Heaven's gate is shut to him who comes alone; save thou a soul, and it shall save thy own!"

25—28. (25) **wrote,** etc., this may have been necessary bec. the previous edict had been widely circulated, and this new decree practically acted as a reversal, or withdrawal, of the former one. (26) **fear,** etc., this is simply a warning, like unto that of Nebuc.'s, against showing any disrespect to Jehovah, who had so signally proven his power; it does not involve any worship of Him.—Pul. Com. **God of Daniel,** i.e. the God whose claim to universal recognition has been proved by His deliverance of Daniel.[b] (28) **prospered,** was restored to his rank and honor, and held his position securely.

Dangers of Prosperity.—The ancient Greeks fancied that on a certain shore dwelt the beautiful sirens who sang so charmingly that the seamen sailing by were attracted almost irresistibly to the shore, where their vessels were wrecked on the hidden reefs. Even the wise Ulysses did not dare to sail past these islands without binding himself to the mast, altho' he could see that the shores were lined with wrecks and the bleaching bones of those who had yielded to the sirens' seductions. But Orpheus took the wiser plan. With his own lyre he made sweeter music than the sirens' songs, a music that saved both himself and the sailors from the deadly attraction of the charmed song, to which—

"Everyone that listens, presently
Forgetteth home, and wife, and children dear
All noble enterprise and purpose high,
And turns his pinnace here."

The safe-guard against temptations of wealth and prosperity is found in the greater attractions of righteousness, and love, and duty, and God, which fill the soul with heavenly music.—Peloubet.

CHAPTER THE SEVENTH.

"This ch. begins the second and peculiarly prophetic part of the book of Daniel."—Stuart.

1—3. (1) **first year,** when the Bab. kingdom was apparently stable.[a] **the sum,** i.e. the summary, or general outline. **matters,** better, words. (2) **four winds,** emblems of commotions of nations. **strove,** R. V. "broke forth upon." **great sea,** the sea is to be regarded as the great mass of Gentile nations, and the winds are, therefore, the spiritual agencies by which God carries on the history of the world.[b]—Pul. Com. (3) **beasts,** symbols of nations. "The symbolization of kings and kingdoms under the form of 'beasts' was a most ancient practice; and in Egypt and Assyria the practice was prevalent."—Ewald.

Daniel Seventh.—The present chapter, in its matter as well as its position, the central portion of the book. It is in both respects to the Book of Daniel what the eighth chapter of the Epistle to the Romans is to that epistle. Next to the fifty-third chapter of Isaiah, and perhaps the ninth chapter of this same book, we have here the most precious and prominent portion of the sure word of Messianic prophecy. The chapter is worthy of the most careful prayer and study. Referred to directly or indirectly by Christ and His apostles perhaps more than other portions of the Old Testament of similar extent. Appears to have been regarded by the Old Testament Church, in the centuries preceding the Messiah's first advent, as pre-eminently the "word of prophecy."—Hom. Com. "The Great Sea."—The mind, in its infantile state, is most impressed with visible and tangible things. "The great sea" is a significant picture of the mobility and restlessness of the multitude. The masses of men, having no settled beliefs, no fixed principles of action, are as fickle, and as easily wrought upon, as the unstable sea. As the briny waters are promptly driven hither and thither by every wind that blows, so the multitudes are moved and tossed by every passing passion—by the faintest prospect of self-advantage—or by the fevered ambition of a stronger will than their own. The Jews, having relinquished their safe anchorage, viz. faith in God, were driven helplessly north and south, east and west, by the wild passions of unscrupulous conquerors. It seemed as if the four winds of heaven strive at one and the same time upon this Hebrew sea. "The wicked are like the troubled sea."—Pulp. Com.

a "The time is 17 years before the incidents narrated in ch. vi.

b "The earth itself is a sea, the sea is an emblem of the world, swelling with human pride and passion, and troubled with political agitations and popular revolutions."
—Wordsworth.

"As the mother bird shrieks when the hawk is in the sky, that her young ones may hide themselves under her wings, so God, the Father of men, utters His voice of warning against sinners, that they may rush to His mercy's protection, before the devouring lion of Hell overtake them in destruction."
—John Bate.

4—6. (4) **like a lion,** comp. the colossal figures of winged lions, with human heads, and eagle's wings, in Assyrian sculptures. This beast stands for the Bab. monarchy.[a] **wings,** "additional image of swiftness and strength." **plucked,** reference may poss. be to Nebuc.'s illness. **man's heart,** or understanding. The animal character of the kingdom was changed, and the higher powers of intellect ruled; represents "the greater moderation and humanity wh. the Babylonish dominion exhibited after Nebuc.'s malady and restoration."—Stuart. (5) **bear,** prob. standing for the Medo-Persian empire. **raised,** etc., the fig. may symbolize how one race was stronger than the other. This done by putting one of its forelegs into an erect posture. **three ribs,** signifying the conquest by Medo-Persia of those countries, poss. Lydia, Babylon, and Egypt. These were its prey, or booty. **Arise .. flesh,** i.e. make extensive conquests. (6) **leopard,**[b] the Græco-Macedonian kingdom. **four wings,** denoting the swiftness of its victories. **four heads,** not four kings, but fig. for universal dominion in the four corners of the earth.

Cruelty of Oriental Princes.—Bishop Newton says: Cambyses, Ochus, and others of their princes, were indeed more like bears than

a "The king of Bab. was a lion in strength and an eagle in swiftness; and in his variegated feathers, we may recognize an emblematical symbol of the plumage of many tributary nations in his armies, with which he flew to victory in all lands."—Wordsworth.

b "A leopard is a creature of extraordinary swiftness and jumps upon its prey."— Lowth.

men. Instances of their cruelty abound in almost all the historians who have written of their affairs, from Herodotus down to Ammianus Marcellinus, who describes them as proud, cruel, exercising the power of life and death over slaves and obscure plebeians. "They pull off the skin (says he) from men alive, in pieces or altogether." The cruelty of their modes of punishment indicative of the cruelty of their character. Rollin relates that one of the royal judges, condemned to death for receiving a bribe, was to have his skin taken off and fastened on the seat where he used to sit and give judgment, to be a warning to his son, who was to occupy it after him. Witness also the lions' den.—Hom. Com.

c "To an Oriental mind there is nothing unnatural or improbable in the Prophet Daniel's beast." — Van Lennep.

The world will never believe that Jesus is the Lord till it sees its end; nor will it ever pray, till it is forced to utter the cry of despair, saying "to the mountains and rocks, Fall on us and hide us from the face of Him that sitteth on the throne, and from the wrath of the Lamb."

7, 8. (7) **fourth beast,** the Roman empire, comp. ch. ii. 40. **great iron teeth,** i.e. it had great destructive power: it was not marked by swiftness but by its ability to crush and destroy. **ten horns,**[c] or was divided into ten principalities, or sub-kingdoms. (8) **among them,** Stuart says that this little horn is "the symbol of Antiochus Epiphanes, on his first accession to the throne." After he became strong and secure he persecuted the Jews beyond measure, comp. vs. 20. **three .. roots,** ref. to the overthrow of three kings by this little horn. **eyes of man,** denoting great cunning and foresight. **speaking .. things,** words of boasting, haughtiness and rebelliousness.

The Four Great Monarchies.—It has been satisfactorily proved by the best writers on the subject that the vision refers to the four great monarchies—the Babylonian, the Medo-Persian, the Macedonian or Grecian, and the Roman; and that the second beast, which was like to a bear, symbolizes the empire of the Medes and Persians. All the four monarchies are represented by beasts of prey, to intimate their agreement in the general character of fierceness and rapacity; and by beasts of different species, to intimate the existence of important differences in their character and mode of operation. The Babylonish empire is symbolized by a lion with eagle's wings, because it was strong and fierce as a lion; it was swift and rapid in its movements, as a lion with eagle's wings; rising in a few years, under the conduct of Nebuchadnezzar, to the highest pinnacle of power and greatness. The third kingdom is represented by another beast, "like a leopard, which had upon the back of it four wings of a fowl; the beast had also four heads; and dominion was given unto it." This is the Grecian monarchy; the distinguishing characters of which are great variety of disposition and manners, undaunted boldness, and rapidity of conquest, never before or since exemplified in the history of nations. The fourth beast was so great and horrible that no adequate name could be found for it; this nondescript was the symbol of the Roman empire, which differed from all others in the form of its government, in strength, in power, in greatness, in length of duration, and in extent of dominion. The Persian monarchy, symbolized by the bear, has also certain specific differences, which are to be learned from the natural history of that animal. Such was the empire of the Medes and Persians: weaker and less warlike than the Babylonian, and less rapid in its conquests than the Macedonian. But the bear surpasses them in ferocious cruelty and insatiable voracity; and such was the empire of the Medes and Persians. They are stigmatized by ancient historians as the greatest robbers and spoilers that ever oppressed the nations.

a "Lit. 'They (the attendant ministers) set the seats.' The Prophet here describes the last great assize as a regular proceeding, like the preparations made for holding a judicial assembly or royal court." —Wordsworth.

b "This title appears to have a Bab. origin. It is one of the titles of the God Anu, who during the earliest period of the religion of the Euphrates, represented the idea of a cosmic (earthly) durance (heavenly) god, one who was at once heaven, earth and time."—Biblical Things.

9, 10. (9) **cast down,** R. V. "placed." The thrones were set for the heavenly assessors at the great judgment.[a] **Ancient of days,**[b] the Divine Being, who can only be apprehended by man under some form. Comp. John's vision, Re. i. **garment .. snow,** "indication both of dignity and purity." **hair .. wool,** prob. an exceeding splendor, "like the white heat of a metal in the fire."—Stuart. **throne .. fire,** sym. either of splendor, or of a destroying power. (10) **fiery stream,** Ps. 1, 3, xcvii. 3. **thousand,** etc., De. xxxiii. 2; Ps. lxviii. 17; He. xii. 22; Re. v. 11. **judgment .. set,** better, "the assize began." The court was now open. "We find that this description of the judgment in the first Apocalypse reappears, modified and made yet more solemn, in the last Apocalypse. We are, however, not to regard this as the final judgment. Daniel is rather admitted into the presence of God in the heavens, and sees his judgment continually being prepared against the wicked."—Pul. Com. **books,** Re. xx. 12. "The books both of God's laws and men's actions."

Christ Unveiled.—A Spanish artist was once employed to paint "The Last Supper." It was his object to throw all the sublimity of his art into the figure and countenance of the Lord Jesus; but he put on the table in the foreground some chased cups, the workmanship of which was exceedingly beautiful. When his friends came to see the picture on the easel, every one said, "What beautiful cups." "Ah!" said he, "I have made a mistake; these cups divert the eyes of the spectator from the Lord, to whom I wished to direct the attention of the observer." And he forthwith took up his brush and blotted them from the canvas, that the strength and vigor of the chief object might be prominently seen and observed.

"It is quite clear that if I am to enter heaven no outward reform will ever do it, for if I wash my face, that does not change my heart." — C. H. Spurgeon.

Opening of the Book of Life.—

Almighty Judge! how shall poor wretches brook
Thy dreadful look,
Able a heart of iron to appall,
When thou shalt call
For every man's peculiar book?

But I resolve, when thou shalt call for mine,
That to decline;
And thrust a Testament into thy hand;
Let that be scanned;
There shalt thou find my faults are thine.—George Herbert.

11, 12. (11) **great words,** vs. 8.[c] (12) **dominion,** their characteristic world-wide authority. **lives,** national lives, or existence. **season .. time,** not any definite period.

"The Little Horn."—When the three horns had thus fallen before him, the little horn—Antiochus Epiphanes—sprang into prominence. The mention of his "eyes" seems to be a reference to his shrewdness, cunning, and vigilance. The "mouth that spoke very great things" alludes to the boastful arrogance which led him to assume the title of Epiphanes, or "the illustrious"—which his scornful subjects changed into Epimanes, "the mad"—and to his assumption even of the title Theos, "the god," on some of his coins.—Exp. B.

c Proud and blasphemous language.

"Oh, the wasted hours of life that have drifted by; oh, the good we might have done, lost without a sigh."

"The owner ought to be more honorable than his estate." — Xenophon.

Pride.—

He that is proud, eats up himself. Pride is
His own glass, his own trumpet, his own chronicle;
And whatever praises itself but in
The deed, devours the deed in the praise. —Shakespeare.

13, 14. (13) **like the Son of man,** R. V., "a son of man." The sequel plainly points to the king Messiah. Why is he then called "a son of man"? I reply, prophecy had declared that the Messiah would be a son of David, Isa. xi. 1; Mic. v. 1, etc. The new kingdom is on earth; Christ is to appear and act as the head of it; and to do this he must assume a human form.—Stuart. **clouds, etc.,** Mat. xxvi. 64; Re. i. 7. **brought him near,** etc., with the destruction of the four great empires, the new kingdom of God is now ushered in, not in the form of a beast but of a man. (14) **given him,** etc., ch. iii. 4, iv. 3, 34, vi. 27.[a] **Everlasting dominion, i.e.** as comp. with the perishing earthly dynasties.

a Eph. i. 20, 23; He. i. 3, 4.

"Be patient with every one, but above all with yourself. I mean do not be disturbed because of your imperfections, and always rise up bravely from a fall. There is no better means of progress in the spiritual life than to be continually beginning afresh, and never to think that we have done enough."— Francis de Sales.

The Son of Man.—As to the question of the reference of the title, it has been doubted whether it is to be held as applying to the Messiah, the Messianic kingdom, or to the people of Israel. From 1 Pet. i. 10 we see that prophets did not necessarily know the meaning of their own prophecies. It might well be, then, that to Daniel the distinction between the Messianic King and the Messianic kingdom was not one clearly apprehended. We see in the prophecies of the second Isaiah that the "servant of the Lord" is first the holy people, then the prophetic order. If latterly a person. There probably was a similar uncertainty here. If we grant this indefiniteness, the next question that rises is—What is the special aspect of the Messianic kingdom that is intended to be portrayed when this title is given to its King? If we are guided by what is incomparably the oldest interpretation, that of the second Book of Enoch, this title implies an incalculable dignity. When we come to our Lord's use

"The glory of Christ shone as the lightning, brighter in the depths of night than in the glory of day."— Guthrie.

"Just as the Church cannot have two heads, so the one Head cannot have two bodies; for as that body were a monster which had two heads, so the head which had two separate bodies." —Guthrie.

of it in the Gospels, there is nothing to oppose this. Thus John v. 22, "And hath committed all judgment unto him, because he is the Son of man;" so Matt. ix. 6, "The Son of man hath power on earth to forgive sins."—Pulp. Com.——But who is the "one even as a son of man," who "comes with the clouds of heaven," and who is brought before the Ancient of Days," to whom is given the imperishable dominion? We should naturally answer, in accordance with the multitude of ancient and modern commentators both Jewish and Christian, that the Messiah is intended; and, indeed, our Lord alludes to the prophecy in Matt. xxvi. 64. That the vision is meant to indicate the establishment of the Messianic theocracy cannot be doubted. But if we follow the interpretation given by the angel himself in answer to Daniel's entreaty, the personality of the Messiah seems to be at least somewhat subordinate or indistinct. For the interpretation, without mentioning any person, seems to point only to the saints of Israel who are to inherit and maintain that Divine kingdom which has been already thrice asserted and prophesied. It is the "holy ones," "the holy ones of the Most High," upon whom the never-ending sovereignty is conferred (Dan. iv. 3, 34; vi. 26); and who these are cannot be misunderstood, for they are the very same as those against whom the little horn has been engaged in war (Dan. vii. 16, 22, 23, 27). The Messianic kingdom is here predominantly represented as the spiritual supermacy of the chosen people. Neither here, nor in ii. 44, nor in xii. 3, does the writer separately indicate any Davidic king, or priest upon his throne, as had been already done by so many previous prophets. This vision does not seem to have brought into prominence the rule of any Divinely Incarnate Christ over the kingdom of the Highest. At any rate, it seems that, if truth is to guide us rather than theological prepossession, we must take the significance of the writer, not from the emblems of the vision, but from the divinely imparted interpretation of it; and there the figure of "one as a son of man" is persistently (vss. 18, 22, 27) explained to stand, not for the Christ Himself, but for "the holy ones of the Most High," whose dominion Christ's coming should inaugurate and secure.—F. W. Farrar.

b "Each of the four kings represents a dynasty. Nebuchadnezzar, Alexander, Antiochus, and Antichrist." —Fausset.

15—18. (15) **body,** lit. sheath; the spirit is thought of as being like a sword in its sheath. (16) **the truth,** or the explanation. (17) **kings,** or kingdoms: or perhaps dynasties.[b] (18) **the saints,** under Messiah. **take,** R. V. "receive."

Our instinct tells us that we are not to live simply to acquire; society does not want mere effigies, whether stuffed with bran or brains; but the world wants men, living, working, serving others, who acquire in order to impart, who have at heart the good of the race."—A. T. Pierson.

Not Hercules himself could resist such odds.—Latin. Three helping each other are as good as six.—Spanish.

The Reign of the Saints (vs. 18).—I. The event predicted. 1. How they will take possession of the kingdom; 2. How they will administer it. II. The advantages that will accrue from it. 1. Those of a temporal nature; 2. Those of a spiritual nature. Address:—(1) Let none be ashamed of being accounted saints; (2) Let all endeavor to help forward the expected day.—C. Simeon.

Grief for God's Cause.—Daniel was grieved in spirit, not because of personal ill, nor from fear of the lions' den, but because of the obscurity of the vision; in other words, because of the uncertain fortune of God's kingdom. The symbol of the fourth beast seemed to betoken disaster, suffering, yea, even destruction, for the people of God. That under the violence of this unnatural monster the saints of the Most High should be worn out with oppression, and that rude wickedness should prevail; this distressed and overwhelmed the heart of Daniel. He lived for one object. His life, from the early days of youth, had been directed towards one end—viz. the reversal of Israel's overthrow—the restoration of the Hebrews to Canaan. If this end seemed nearer, he was content; if this event was shrouded in doubt, he grieved. In his case self was repressed—kept down. He was consumed with pious zeal for others' good—for God's honor. Never once do we find him plotting for his own elevation or for his own interests. He did not live for fame. Yet he had it. He thought mainly of God, and God set his thought and care upon him. He had so completely identified himself with God's cause on earth, that all his interest and happiness were indissolubly bound up with it. Herein God observed his promise, "Them that honor me I will honor." To him heaven was open. He moved in the society of angels. And, when his mind was enveloped with difficulty, he gladly sought counsel and instruction from one of the heavenly host. A wise man will ever seek to increase his wisdom. He welcomes light from every quarter.—Pul. Com.

19—22. (19) **fourth beast,** vs. 7. (20) **look .. more stout,** or his appearance was more excellent than his fellows. He ultimately claimed superiority over them all. Stuart and Farrar apply this symbol to Antiochus Epiphanes: Pul. Com. to the Roman emperors; in particular Titus, 70 A.D. (21) **war .. saints,** comp. Re. xi. 7, 9, xiii. 7, xvii. 14.[a] (22) **came,** manifested himself for judgment. **saints .. kingdom,** 2 Ti. ii. 11.

The Fourth Empire.—The fourth empire is symbolized by "a dreadful and terrible beast," for which the Prophet found no name in the kingdom of nature. It resembled the fabulous monsters which poetic imagination sometimes delights to portray; for in the Book of Revelation John describes it as compounded of the three which preceded it: "The beast which I saw was like unto a leopard, and his feet were as the feet of a bear, and his mouth as the mouth of a lion." It possessed all the qualities which render beasts of prey a terror to man and other animals; the swiftness and cunning of the leopard, the ferocity of the bear, and the boldness and strength of the lion. The Roman empire, which it symbolized, resembled no state of society known among men; it displayed, in its character and proceedings, the vigor and courage of the Babylonians, the various policy and alacrity of the Greeks, and the unchanging firmness of the Medes and Persians: qualities which have been equally conspicuous in the papal state of that empire.—Paxton.

23—25. (23) **diverse,** perh. in its system of gov't. The Roman Law was infinitely superior to the absolutism of Babylon, Persia and Greece. **the whole earth,** Stuart claims that this has reference to Palestine. "For the history of the whole world is not intended to be given, but only of that part of it which had to do with the people of God." (24) **rise afer them,** ref. to line of succession. The precise historical references depend upon the school of prophecy to which the commentator belongs. (25) **speak,** etc., blasphemy, Re. xiii. 5, 6. **wear out,** by persecutions. **change times,** etc., by interfering with existing and established governments. **time .. time,** i.e. three times and a half, or three years and a half of prophetical time. No explanation of the period can be more than conjectural.

Wearing Out the Saints.—Josephus is authority for the statement that Antiochus Epiphanes "made war against the saints," with the aid of "Jason and Menelaus, those ungodly wretches," and "prevailed against them." He "wore out the saints of the Most High," for he took Jerusalem by storm, plundered it, slew eighty thousand men, women, and children, took forty thousand prisoners, and sold as many into slavery, B.C. 170. "As he entered the sancutary to plunder it, under the guidance of the apostate high priest Menelaus, he uttered words of blasphemy, and he carried off all the gold and silver he could find, including the golden table, altar of incense, candlesticks, and vessels, and even rifled the subterraneous vaults, so that he seized no less than eighteen hundred talents of gold." He then sacrificed swine upon the altar, and sprinkled the whole Temple with the broth. He made also a determined attempt to put down the Jewish feasts, the Sabbath, circumcision, and all the most distinctive Jewish ordinances.—Exp. B.

26—28. (26) **judgment,** etc., the assize shall convene, vs. 9. (27) **kingdom,** Lu. i. 27. **whose kingdom,** etc., Stuart, "their k. shall be an ev. k. and all dominions shall serve and obey them." **all dominions,** or rulers. (28) **Hitherto,** R. V., "here." **cogitations,** R. V., "thoughts." **countenance changed,** "was sicklied o'er with the pale cast of thought." **kept .. heart,** often pondering over it.[a] but communicating it to no one.

The Reign of the Saints (vs. 27).—I. The doctrine of the text does not require us to believe that the Lord Jesus Christ is at some future time to return in person to our world, and set up a visible and theocratic empire upon these continents. II. The Scriptures do not require us to teach or to believe this doctrine even in any absolute, extreme, and unexceptionable sense. III. As to the way in which this great conquest is to be achieved. IV. According to all Scriptural allusions it will be a very gradual conquest. V. It is to be, and in a twofold sense, complete and universal.—W. Clarke.

Prevalence of Christ's Kingdom Against Opposition.—The bush burns, but is not consumed, because the Lord Himself is in it. The

[a] Da. viii. 10, 24, xi. 32, 33, 35.

"The pleasures of the world are not like the waters of the Nile, which leave when they are gone, the germs of beauty and fertility, to bud and blossom and cheer the heart of man; on the contrary, they are like those streams polluted by the washings of poisonous minerals, depositing the seeds of death and disease to all who drink them." —Anon.

"What art thou? Have not I an arm as big as thine? A heart as big? Thy words, I grant, are bigger, for I wear not my dagger in my mouth."
—Shakespeare.

"An old English author says that there are four parts to repentance, which makes a ladder whereby we may climb from the pit of perdition up into the castle of endless salvation. The rounds of this ladder are contrition, confession, faith and amendment. If a single round is missed, we fall through."—A. R. Wells.

"Waldus, a rich merchant in Lyons, seeing one drop down dead in the streets, went home, and repented, changed his life, and became a preacher, and was the father and the founder of the people called Waldenses. 'Tis good to take warning by others' harms, and by the sight of their death, to look after our own life."—Venning.

[a] Lu. ii. 19, 50, 51.

gates and power of hell are unable to prevail against the Church of Christ, because founded on the Rock of Ages. "If this counsel or work be of men, it will come to nought; but if it be of God, ye cannot overthrow it." "Although," says Sismondi, himself a Roman Catholic, "for two hundred years the fires were never quenched, still every day saw Catholics abjuring the faith of their fathers, and embracing the religion which often guided them to the stake. In vain Gregory IX., in 1231, put to death every heretic whom he found concealed in Rome."—Pul. Com.

CHAPTER THE EIGHTH.

1—4. (1) **third year,** two years after the vision of the preceding chapter. The last year of Belshazzar's reign, wh. he exercised in conjunction with his father. **vision,** etc., esp. referring to the rise of Antiochus, king of Syria.[a] (2) **was at Shushan,** or seemed in my trance to be at S. Susa, "the city of lilies," now Shuster.[b] **Elam,** western portion of Persia, wh. was either at this time subject to Babylonia, or a province of Media. **Ulai,** now the Kerah, or Karasu.[c] (3) **ram,** fig. for the Medo-Persian monarchy.[d] **two horns,** representing the Medes and the Persians. **higher .. last,** the Persian power came to overtop the Median. (4) **pushing,** fig. for extending its conquests. **became great,** R. V. "magnified himself," i.e. became proud.

The Light Side of the Triumph of Evil.—1. It is foreseen and predicted. Therefore it should not surprise us. It was foreknown by God from the Creation. It was known when the promises of Divine blessing were given. All the plans of Providence were made in view of it. Yet they are bright and hopeful (Rom. viii. 19—23). 2. It is converted into a chastisement for sin and a means of purifying those who suffer by it. Though wicked men may only intend harm to God's people, the wrong they do may be the means of the highest good. 3. Its duration is limited. A period is named for the termination of its sway (vss. 13, 14). Evil is but for a time, and this is short compared with eternity. God holds power over it and fixes its limitations. 4. Ultimately evil shall be entirely cast out. Then the triumph of goodness will be the greater by its contrast with the sway of evil. The glory of Christ in redeeming from sin and restoring the world to God is only possible after evil has had an opportunity of asserting its power (2 Thess. ii. 7, 8).—Pul. Com.

5—7. (5) **he goat,** fig. of Alexander the Great.[e] **touched .. ground,** indicating the swiftness with which he marched.[f] Comp. ch. vii. 6. **notable horn,** Heb. "horn of sight," i.e. conspicuous, subject of remark. **between his eyes,** a formidable position for thrusting. (6) **ram .. power,** by one sudden thrust overturning the Medo-Persian kingdom. **unto,** R. V. "upon." **power,** Stuart, "rage, indignation." (7) **moved with choler,** concentrated wrath. **smote,** etc., Arrian tells that, at the river Granicus, Alex. plunged into the stream, swam across it, rushed on the Persians in the fury of his power, and overwhelmed them.

Alexander's Conquests.—The he-goat is Greece. Its one great horn represents "the great Emathian conqueror." So swift was the career of Alexander's conquests, that the goat seems to speed along without so much as touching the ground. With irresistible fury, in the great battles of the Granicus, B.C. 334, Issus, B.C. 333, and Arbela B.C. 331, he stamps to pieces the power of Persia and of its king, Darius Codomannus. In this short space of time Alexander conquers Syria, Phœnicia, Cyprus, Tyre, Gaza, Egypt, Babylonia, Persia, Media, Hyrcania, Aria, and Arachosia. In B.C. 330 Darius was murdered by Bessus, and Alexander became lord of his kingdom. In B.C. 329 the Greek king conquered Bactria, crossed the Oxus and Jaxartes, and defeated the Scythians. In B.C. 328 he conquered Sogdiana. In B.C. 327 and 326 he crossed the Indus, Hydaspes, and Akesines, subdued Northern and Western India, and—compelled by the discontent of his troops to pause in his career of victory—sailed down the Hydaspes and Indus to the Ocean. He then returned by land through Gedrosia, Karmania, Persia, and Susiana to Babylon.—Exp. B.

8—10. (8) **broken,** Alex. died at the early age of thirty-two, B.C. 323.

a "This vision is writ in Heb. bec. that part of it wh. relates to the time of Antiochus Epiphanes did chiefly concern the Jews."—Lowth.

b "Susa was a royal residence of Persian kings in the days of Cyrus. The ruins of Susa, 300 miles E. of Babylon, are still visible, between the left branch of the Kerkhah and the right branch of the Dizful, wh. flows into the Kuran river."—Wordsworth.

c Called in Kings, Euloeus, by the Greeks, Choaspes.

d "The ram was the royal ensign of Persia." —Marcellinus.

e "The goat was the acknowledged symbol of Macedonia. Figures of a goat with a single horn are found on ancient Macedonian monuments." — Biblical Things.

f Alexander over-ran the world in less than twelve years.

"Alexander in his rages, and his wraths, and his furies, and his cholers, and his moods." —Shakespeare.

As soon may you draw all the rays of light out of the sun, or all the water out of the ocean, as to exhaust all the fulness of blessing there is in Christ.

four notable ones, the four divisions into which the Macedonian kingdom was divided. (9) **little horn,** Antiochus Epiphanes,[a] who sprang fr. one of the four dynasties and became a great conqueror. **pleasant land,** Palestine.[b] (10) **to,** better, against. **host of heaven,** prob. referring to the Jewish priests and high officials; the imagery is taken from the Bab. conception of the gods and their satellites forming the heavenly host. **cast,** etc., prophesying this king's shameful treatment of the Jewish priests, etc. **stars,** i.e. leaders among the priesthood.

a "'There came out of them (i.e. the successors of Alexander) a wicked root, Antiochus, surnamed Epiphanes, son of Antiochus the king, who had been a hostage at Rome.' "—Bk. of Maccabees, i. 10.

b Ps. xlviii. 2; Eze. xx. 6.

The Conqueror, Conquered.—The strength of one evil habit may overcome even the mightiest conqueror. Very suggestive in this regard is the history of Alexander the Great, and it is not without a sigh of regret that we read of the pupil of the famous Aristotle dying as the victim of his own excesses at the early age of thirty-three. He could conquer the world by his armies, yet intemperance was his master and destroyer. He was filled with rage and disappointment because he was foiled in his efforts to reach the Eastern ocean, yet was he never fired with the nobler ambition of overmastering the world within himself. He had the greatness of taking not cities only, but empires; yet he knew nothing of ruling his own spirit; and the contrast between his life and that of another which lasted only three-and-thirty years cannot but strike every thoughtful reader of ancient history.—Taylor.

11, 12. (11) **prince,** etc., or against God Himself.[a] Some think the reference may be to Onias, the high priest. **daily sacrifice,** see Nu. xxviii. 3. **place .. down,** by Antiochus both the altar and the temple were profaned. (12) **an host,** etc., Stuart: "an host was placed over the daily sacrifice by wickedness (i.e. the wicked one, Antiochus) and it cast down faithfulness (the faithful ones) to the ground, and it accomplished (its desire) and was prosperous."

a In the Bk. of Maccabees this Antiochus is described as the man "who thought that he could reach to the stars of heaven."

The Bk. of Maccabees traces all the calamities suffered under Antiochus to the transgression of certain Jews who introduced heathen customs into Jerusalem just before.

Antiochus.—Antiochus Epiphanes is described as a king "bold of visage, and skilled in enigmas," vs. 23. His boldness is sufficiently illustrated by his many campaigns and battles, and his braggart insolence has been already alluded to in vii. 8. His skill in enigmas is illustrated by his dark and tortuous diplomacy, which was exhibited in all his proceedings, and especially in the whole of his dealing with Egypt, in which country he desired to usurp the throne from his young nephew, Ptolemy Philometor. The statement that "he will have mighty strength, but not by his own strength," vs. 24, may either mean that his transient prosperity was due only to the permission of God, or that his successes were won rather by cunning than by prowess. After an allusion to his cruel persecution of the holy people, Gabriel adds that "without a hand shall he be broken in pieces," vs. 25; in other words, his retribution and destruction shall be due to no human intervention, but will come from God Himself.—Exp. Bib.

13, 14. (13) **saint,** holy one, or angel; ch. iv. 13. **How long,** for what length of time should such awful profanation last? **of desolation,** R. V. "that maketh desolate."[b] Stuart suggests, "the wicked one wh. ought to be destroyed," Mat. xxiv. 15. (14) **Unto .. days,** these prophetical times are very difficult, and all explanations are conjectural. Poss. 6 yrs., 4 months, and 20 days.[c] **cleansed,** or justified and vindicated from the transgression wh. brought the calamity. This was done by Judas Maccabæus, 165 B.C. Just 6 yrs. before this Menelaus, the priest, appointed by Antiochus, had profaned the Temple.—Stuart.

b "There is prob. a special reference to the idol which Antiochus caused to be set up on God's altar, and there to be worshiped." —Lowth.

c "Though God hath revealed to His Church the hope of better days, so that no doubt should be entertained of the fact, yet hath He seen fit to keep in His own power the actual times or seasons when those better days shall begin to end no more." —Spk. Com.

Angels in the Household.—In one of Murillo's pictures in the Louvre he shows us the interior of a convent kitchen; but doing the work there are not mortals, in old dresses, but beautiful, white-winged angels. One serenely puts the kettle on the fire to boil, and one is lifting up a pail of water with heavenly grace, and one is at the kitchen dresser reaching up for plates; and I believe there is a little cherub running about and getting in the way, trying to help. . . . All are so busy, and working with such a will, and so refining the work as they do it that somehow you forget that pans are pans, and pots are pots, and only think of the angels, and how very natural and beautiful kitchen work is,—just what the angels would do, of course.—Wm. C. Gannett. The Ministry of Angels.—I believe that angels wait on us as truly as ever they waited on Abraham, or Jacob, or Moses, or Elijah, or Mary, or Jesus himself. The medieval painters were fond of filling the background of the Infancy with countless angels; the representation tho' literally false was morally true. —Geo. D. Boardman.

15—18. (15) **sought .. meaning,** by earnest studying and thought. **a man,** the angel for the moment assumed the likeness of a man. (16) **Gabriel,** ch. ix. 21. This was the name of the man who stood before him. The first instance of naming an angel in the Bible. (17) **afraid,** struck with fear and astonishment.[a] **son of man,** intended to remind Daniel that he was only man, though to him were thus given great prophetic visions. **at the time,** R. V. "for the vision belongeth to the time of the end," i.e. "the vision reaches only to the end of those special afflictions that are to come on the Jews before the Messianic period."—Stuart. (18) **deep sleep,** or **trance.**[b]

Angels.—

"God will deign
To visit oft the dwelling of just men,
Delighted, and with frequent intercourse,
Thither will send his winged messengers
On errands of supernatural grace." —Milton.

19—21. (19) **last end,** or "I will explain to thee the whole series of God's judgments upon His people to the end and conclusion of them." **time .. end,** R. V. "for it belongeth to the appointed time of the end," i.e. when Antiochus is punished and the Temple cleansed. (20) **ram,** vs. 3. (21) **rough,** or hairy. **first king,** not first in order, but first in importance. Philip was the first king of Macedon.[c] **Grecia,** in this vs., is literally Javan,[d] Ge. x. 2.

The Future.—When a heavy morning mist veils the beautiful valley and mountain, the landscape is shut out from our vision. But suddenly there comes a breath, or the sun's rays; the mist parts, and the magnificent scenery stands unveiled. So God often parts the mist that hides the future, and shows what a man may be. Young people, especially, seek from God the vision of what your life may be, and then follow out that revelation, because when you catch God's vision, you will always find him responsible for the outworking of it.—F. B. Meyer.

Futurity.—

"Happy he whose inward ear
Angel comfortings can hear,
O'er the rabble's laughter;
And, while Hatred's fagots burn
Glimpses through the smoke discern
Of the good hereafter." —Whittier.

22—24. (22) **four kingdoms,** see on vs. 8. **not .. power,** not so mighty as he. (23) **come to the full,** Stuart: "completed the full measure of their iniquity." **fierce countenance,** indicating an untractable temper. **dark sentences,**[a] practiced in craft and policy. Description suitable to Antiochus. (24) **not .. power,** that wh. belonged properly to him, or his kingdom; but by craftily gaining over others to his side.[b] **practise,** R. V. "do his pleasure." **holy people,** Heb. people of the holy ones.[c]

Moslem Oppression.—The Caliph Omar, in the seventh century, obtained possession of Jerusalem, and immediately caused a magnificent mosque to be erected on the site of the ancient Temple. In place of the worship of the Triune Jehovah through the one Mediator Jesus Christ and His atoning sacrifice, was substituted the worship of a Being of whom Mahomet taught that it was unbecoming to say that He could have a son, and who was to be approached through no Mediator unless it might be himself, and through no offering except a man's own meritorious actions. The daily sacrifice was taken away in its true sense, as it had been by Antiochus in its typical one. The religion of Jesus, with its one sacrifice for sin, was banished from the precincts of the Temple area. Everywhere Christian churches were either demolished or converted into mosques, and were permitted to remain as such only on the payment of a tribute, the memorials of this profane desolation meeting you everywhere in the East at the present day, as well as in Constantinople itself, where the most splendid mosques, as that of St. Sophia,

a Rev. i. 17.

b Eze. i. 28, ii. 1, 2; Lu. ix. 22; Re. i. 17.

As the sun is as ready to pour its radiance upon the daisy on a village common as upon the oaks in Windsor Park, so is Christ as willing to visit the home of the poorest and feeblest as that of the richest and noblest of earth.

c "Alexander was the first who as generalissimo of Greece, subdued the Persian empire." — Fausset.

d "Cuneiform discovery has made it evident that Ionia was well known to the Assyrians under the name of Yaranu, or Yaonai, long before the Bab. captivity." —Spk. Com.

The glories of the Possible are ours. — Bayard Taylor.

a Artifices. — Gesenius.

b Re. xiii. 5—8.

c Re. xiv. 12.

The majority of church-members give nothing to missions, in money, prayer, or thought. Many give in small sums, as they can. There are also large givers, who first give themselves to the Lord, and then consecrate all theirs to him. On a wealthy man's desk was seen over one drawer the letters "M. P.," which he said stood for "My Partner;" and God's portion was never lacking. — Bishop Ninde.

were originally employed for Christian worship before the Crescent supplanted the Cross. The well-known option to the Christian was between renouncing Christianity, tribute, and death. How Mahomet magnified himself against the Prince of princes, and cast down the truth to the ground, was made only too obvious by the well-known watchword, "There is no God but one, and Mahomet is His prophet;" and by the law, rescinded only a few years ago under British influence, that made it death for a Moslem to become a Christian.—Hom. Com.

25—27. (25) **by peace,** i.e. by pretending peace and friendship. **Prince of princes,** Jehovah Himself. **broken without hand.**[d] i.e. without any human invention, by an immediate judgment of God. (26) **shut .. vision,** "presupposes that Daniel will write the vision, so he is warned to guard it from interpolation, to preserve its integrity."—Stuart. Comp. ch. xii. 4. **many days,** R. V. "belongeth to many days to come." (27) **sick,** with grief at the calamities thus revealed as coming on his nation. **did .. business,** intimating that he was in some public office during Belshazzar's reign.[e]

The Future Peace.—The day is coming, I think, when the Quaker idea shall have a new interpretation, a larger sphere: when men shall love their enemies, bless those that curse them, do good to those that hate them, and pray for those that despitefully use them and persecute them; when they shall receive injury and not resent it; when they shall requite wrong with love. To one who sees the revengeful, vindictive feelings of men; the volcano heavings which are so common in the most harmonious families; how business is carried on regardless of rectitude; how governments in their course will hardly stop for justice; how in all departments of life the law of might is made the law of right—to such a one it seems almost absurd to hear a minister say that a day is coming when, the world over, the law of love shall be the reigning law. But that day is coming, or else prophecies are false, and Christ came in vain. —Beecher.

d 2 Mac. ix. 9.

e "Though Daniel was neglected by Belshazzar, yet (such was his faithfulness and loyalty) he did not neglect the king's business." —Wordsworth.

"As long as we live in this world we must have something to do in it; and even those whom God has most dignified with His favors must not think themselves above their business." — Mat. Henry.

CHAPTER THE NINTH.

1—6. (1) **Darius,** ch. v. 31, vi. 28. 538 B.C.; the 68th yr. of Daniel's captivity. **Ahasuerus,** the Jewish name given to Astyages. **made king,** or appointed ruler of Babylon by Cyrus the conqueror. (2) **by books,** those written by such Prophets as Isaiah, Jeremiah, etc. **word .. prophet, Je.** xxv. 12, xxix. 10. **seventy years,** R. V., "for the accomplishing of the desolations of Jerus., even seventy years;" these are to be dated from the end of the third or beginning of the fourth year of Jehoiakim. (3) **set my face,** fig. for earnestness of purpose. Perhaps also alluding to the custom of praying with the face looking towards Jerusalem. **fasting, etc.,**[a] signs of penitence. (4) **dreadful,** worthy of dread, or holy fear.[b] (5) **We have sinned,** Daniel pleads as standing for and representing the Jewish people. (6) **hearkened,** so as to heed and obey.

Religious Fasting (vs. 3).—I. The duty of religious fasting. 1. The light of nature seems to recognize this duty; 3. We have decisive examples in the Bible; 3. The precepts of the Bible show that it is a Divine institution. II. The benefits that may be expected to result from the proper performance of this duty. 1. An expression of penitence; 2. To keep the body under; 3. Clears the mind; 4. Ministers to bodily health; 5. Aids charity. III. Consider the method of observing a religious fast which will render it profitable. Learn:—1. In vain without the heart is in it; 2. It should be thorough; 3. Retirement is needful; 4. Set times should be observed; 5. There should be no ostentation; 6. Should be associated with benevolence to the poor.—S. Miller.

Faith in Prayer.—When I receive a check from a fellow man, I am not deterred from presenting it at the bank because I know that the money is sure to be forthcoming. Nay, I am only thereby the more encouraged to take it and turn it into money. But the same thing holds good when we take God's promises and present them at the throne of grace. It is not because we do not believe in them or in him that we ask for their fulfilment, but rather because we do put implicit trust in

a "The soul and body are so nearly related, that the humiliation of both is necessary to make our repentance complete." —Lowth.

"The knowledge of God's merciful intentions to Jerusalem did not supersede Daniel's prayers, but quickened them." —Wordsworth.

b Comp. prayers of Ezra. Ez. ix. 6—15; Nehemiah, Ne. i. 5—11, ix. 6—38.

After teaching theology for forty years, the elder Alexander said: "The longer I live, the more I incline to sum up my theology in the single sentence, 'Christ Jesus came into the world to save sinners, of whom I am chief.'"

them both; and the firmer our faith is, the more earnest will be our supplication.—W. M. Taylor.

7—10. (7) **righteousness,** this is the solemn acknowledgment that the national calamities had been deserved and needed. **confusion,** such as those feel who are convicted of sin. **far off,** some being found in the most distant countries.[c] **trespass,** the word means, "covert dealing, deception, and faithlessness." (8) **fathers,** elders, who are responsible for showing good example. (9) **mercies.**[d] **laws,** i.e. instructions. (10) **walk,** the usual Bible fig. for ordering life and conduct.

Prayer in Emergencies.—In our own civil war, on one occasion, the general in command of certain forces broke out with the exclamation, on the eve of battle, "We have got them now, and they know it. God Almighty cannot save them." So he had "got them" by all human reckoning of the chances. His staff responded, "Yes, we are sure of them." But it happened,—how much it had to do with the fortunes of the day, we will not presume to say, but it happened,—that the commander-in-chief on the other side was a praying man. He had that morning spent an hour in his tent, invoking Divine interposition in the coming conflict. The close of the day found him again in his tent, offering thanksgiving for a victory, while the presumptuous general who thought that "God Almighty could not defeat him" was in ignominious flight down the valley of the Shenandoah.—Phelps.

11—15. (11) **curse,** etc., that threatened in the law.[e] **oath,** or imprecation. (12) **confirmed,** lit. made to stand: comp. Is. xliv. 26. **judges,** Heb. Shofetim. Here used generally of the princes and rulers. (13) **understand,** R. V. "have discernment in." **thy truth,** or revealed word, in wh. God conveyed the knowledge of His will. (14) **watched upon,**[f] observing carefully, and waiting the opportunity for corrective judgments. (15) **gotten .. renown,** or made Thee a name.

The Omnipotence of Prayer.—The man of prayer exerts a greater influence over national affairs than even crowned heads. "Prayer moves the hand that moves the world." Daniel on his knees was a mightier man than Darius on his throne. Daniel was in the service of the King of kings; was admitted to the audience-chamber of the Most High; and received the announcements of the Divine will. Darius now mainly serves as a landmark on the course of time to indicate a date; Daniel is still the teacher and molder of men.—Pul. Com.

16—19. (16) **righteousness,** wh. ensures the fulfilment of Divine promises, as well as of Divine threatenings. **thy city,** chosen as Thine in the election of grace which changes not. Daniel is solicitous for the honor of God and religion wh. the sins of the Jews have reproached. (17) **prayer .. servant,** who pleads as an intercessor. **Lord's sake,** the Sept. reads: "for thy servant's sake lift up thy countenance upon thy holy mountain which is desolate, O Lord." (18) **our righteousness,** on the ground of personal merit.[a] (19) **defer not,** tarry not.[b] "Observe the fervor of the prayer in the triple repetition of the holy name Adonai." **for thine own sake,** i.e. in order to vindicate thine own power and truthfulness.

A Humble Cry.—Fishermen of Brittany utter this simple prayer when they launch their boats upon the deep: "Keep me, my God; my boat is small and the ocean is wide." How very beautiful the words, the thought. Might not the same petition be uttered night and morning by God's children journeying on the sea of life? My boat is small, I am so weak, so helpless, so forgetful of thy loving kindness. Tossed to and fro at the mercy of the world, except thou dost help me, I perish. Keep me, my God, for "thy ocean is so wide."

Greatness of Mercy.—

Had not the milder hand of mercy broke
The furious violence of that fatal stroke
Offended justice struck, we had been quite
Lost in the shadows of eternal night.
Thy mercy, Lord, is like the morning sun,
Whose beams undo what sable night had done;
Or, like a stream, the current of whose course,

c "Some Jews were not cast off so far from Jerusalem as others, but all alike were sharers in the guilt." —Fausset.

d Ne. ix. 16, 17; Ps. cxxx. 4, 7.

Today
Slips quickly by,
— to-morrow's but a link,
And while we idly dally, dream, or think,
Our golden opportunity goes by. — Mrs. E. V. Hill.

e Le. xxvi. 14, De. xxviii. 15, xxix. 18.

f Jer. xxxi. 28, xliv. 27.

Jesus never taught his disciples how to preach, but he did teach them how to pray. I would rather be able to pray like Daniel than to preach like Gabriel. If men know how to pray they know how to work for God. — D. L. Moody.

a "In the word trans. "present" the Heb. "cause to fall" better preserves the idea. There is an allusion intended to the practice of kneeling or falling prostrate in prayer." — Spk. Com.

b "Defer not the accomplishment of the promise Thou hast made to restore us to our own country, and the free exercise of our religion. So remarkable a turn of providence will very much redound to the honor of Thy name." —Lowth.

"'Twas thus upon his fasting day, the 'Man of Loves' was

Restrained awhile, runs with a swifter force.
Oh! let me glow beneath those sacred beams,
After bathe me in those silver streams;
To Thee alone my sorrows shall appeal;
Hath earth a wound too hard for heaven to heal?
—Quarles.

20—23. (20) **whiles,** etc., at the very time. Even before the prayer was actually complete. (21) **Gabriel,** ch. viii. 16. **being caused .. swiftly,** Stuart: "having been hastened in a swift course." **touched,** Stuart: "approached." **evening oblation,** three o'clock in the afternoon. (22) **skill,** etc., or ability to understand. (23) **greatly beloved,** Heb. a man of desires. "The object of God's delight."

God's Mysterious Answers to Prayer.—A few years ago there appeared in our skies the most brilliant comet of the century. It was six millions of miles distant from our globe. Such was the speed of its movement, that, if it had been aimed hither in its march, it would have come crashing upon us in less than two days, with the momentum of a 150,000 miles an hour. Yet God held that blazing meteor in its appointed groove, worn by millions of years of travel, so that it glided gently across our world's orbit with motion imperceptible. It had the stillness of a painting. Our infant children looked out upon it, and bade it good-night as a beautiful plaything in the sky, without so much as the closing of an eyelid, at the eternal rush of its progress. So calm, so facile, so beautifully silent are God's wonder-workings in answer to prayer. Mysteries so vast and so anomalous that astonished angels desire to look into them, occur with the ease of a summer twilight.—Phelps.

fain to pray, his lattice open toward his darling west, mourning the ruin'd home he still must love the best." — Keble.

"Hezekiah prays, and an angel destroys the host of the Assyrians. Cornelius prays, and an angel directs him to send for Peter. The Church at Jerusalem prays, and an angel opens the doors of Peter's prison. At Elisha's prayer his servant's eyes were opened."
—Hom. Com.

24—27. (24) **Seventy weeks,** for a discussion of this expression comp. Stuart, p. 264; Exp. B., p. 268; Pulp. Com., p. 266. The clearest view is that 70 times 7 yrs. are to pass by before the coming of the Messiah consummates the hopes of the Jews. **holy city,** still so called, though in ruins and desolate.[a] **finish,** R. V. marg. "restrain." **make .. sin,** or seal up the sins. **everlasting,** or abiding; perhaps with the full meaning of spiritual, and so referring to Messianic times. **seal .. prophecy,** i.e. confirm, authenticate by fulfilment. **most Holy,** lit. "holy of holies," i.e. a sanctuary such as is appropriate to the new state of things. Comp. Heb. ix. 11, 12.—Stuart. (25) **the Messiah, the Prince,** R. V. "the anointed one, the prince." Stuart confesses himself unable to say to whom reference is here made. **troublous times,** Ne. ix. 36, 37. (26) **Messiah,** Stuart: "an anointed one." R. V. "the anointed one." Many commentators, including Stuart and Farrar, suppose Onias III. to be referred to here. **cut off,** by a violent death. **not for himself,** R. V. "shall have nothing." Stuart, "shall be none for it," i.e. no anointed one for the people." **prince that shall come,** Stuart and Farrar understand Antiochus. (27) **he, i.e.** Antiochus. **for the overspreading of abominations,** R. V. "upon the wing of abominations shall come one that maketh desolate;" few modern commentators doubt that the allusion is to the smaller heathen altar built by Antiochus above the "Most Holy," i.e. the great altar of burnt sacrifice, overshadowing it like a wing.[b]—Farrar.

Prayer Opens Wider Horizons of God's Kingdom (vss. 20—27).—We have here a signal instance of the fact that God not only answers human prayer, but gives "more than we ask" or conceive. The thing which Daniel asked was small compared with what God bestowed. I. Prayer is the best preparation for receiving larger revelation. The exercise of real prayer develops humility, dependence, self-forgetfulness; and these states of mind are favorable to ingress of light. "The meek will God show his way;" "To that man will he look, who is of humble and contrite heart." Prayer brings the soul near to God; it lifts us up to heavenly elevations; it clears the eye from mist and darkness. The Apostle John was engaged in lonely worship, when the final revelation of Scripture was made to him. Our Lord was in the act of prayer when heaven came down to earth, and his whole Person was enwrapt in glory. The response to Daniel's prayer was immediate. He had not ceased to pray when the answer came. Swifter than the electric current came the oracle's response. II. Larger revelation comes by a pure and personal

a "The common Oriental name of Jerusalem at the present day, given to no other city even by Muslims, is El-Kuds—the Holy. The Heb. shekel bore the inscription, 'Jerusalem Kadusha, or Jerusalem the Holy.'" — Van Lennep.

b "Prophecies are of the nature of the Author, with whom a thousand years are as one day; and therefore are not fulfilled punctually at once, but have a springing and germinant accomplishment through many years, though the height and fulness of them may refer to one age." — Lord Bacon.

"If I can put one touch of a rosy sunset into the life of any man or woman, I shall feel that I have worked with god." — George Macdonald.

"Where there is little practical outcome in the life, there has been but little incoming of the Spirit into the heart. Outflow and inflow will always correspond." —James M. Campbell.

spirit. We may fairly conclude that angels have larger knowledge of God's will than have we, because they are free from the darkness and the doubt which sin generates. If they are not counsellors in the heavenly court, they are heralds, ambassadors, couriers. What God wills should happen they know is wise and right and good. In their estimation it is an incomparable honor to be engaged on Divine errands. Swift as their natures will allow, they fly to convey instruction or help to men. It is consonant, no less with reason than with Scripture, that there are ranks and orders of intelligent beings with natures more ethereal than ours, and that communication between us and them is possible. Every form of service is attributed to the angels. An angel ministered to our Saviour's bodily hunger. An angel strengthened him in the garden. An angel rolled the stone from his sepulchre. An angel released Peter from prison. Gabriel interpreted the vision to Daniel. Gabriel announced to Zacharias and to Mary the approaching advent of a Saviour. III. Larger revelation is an evidence of God's special love. The despatch of a special messenger from the court of heaven was in itself a signal token of God's favor. Not often in the history of our race had such a favor been shown. Further, Gabriel was well pleased to assure the man of prayer that, in heaven, he was "greatly beloved." Every act of devotion to God's cause had been graven on the memory of God. His character was an object of God's complacency. On account of God's great love for Daniel he gave him larger understanding, and disclosed to him the purposes and plans for man's redemption. God's intention was that Daniel should enlarge the area of his vision, and look with solicitude, not on Israel after the flesh, but on the true Israel of God. Yet all revelation is a mark of God's love to men. Because men are "greatly beloved" of God, therefore he has given them this complete canon of Scripture, therefore he gives them understanding to discern the meaning, therefore he leads them further into the truth.—Pul. Com.

CHAPTER THE TENTH.

1—3. (1) **third .. Cyrus,** B.C. 535. Daniel must at this time have been ninety years old. **was long,** R. V. "and the thing was true, even a great warfare," i.e. the message discloses very severe trials and great sufferings for the Jews. (2) **mourning,** with the grief induced by the visions.[c] (3) **pleasant bread,** Heb. bread of desire, the food of the wealthy. He lived on the coarse bread the fare of the poor. **anoint,** the body after bathing with highly perfumed oils; a great luxury.[d]

4—6. (4) **Hiddekel,** i.e. Tigris, Ge. ii. 14. (5) **clothed in linen,** the usual dress of priests, as the symbol of sanctity. **girded,** etc., Re. i. 13. **fine,** R. V. "pure." **Uphaz,** a place unknown, Je. x. 9. (6) **beryl,** topaz, yellowish hue.[a]

c "The reason of Daniel's fasting and mourning seems to be, because the adversaries of the Jews began to obstruct the building of the temple. Ezr. iv. 4, 5."—Lowth.

d Mat. vi. 17.

Nothing has ever shown the real state of the world like the cross of Christ.

"Christ is willing to save us from our sins, but He will not save us in our sins."

a Eze. i. 26—28, ii. 1, 2; Re. xix. 11—16; i. 13—15.

Visions.—Our brightest visions often come in our hardest trials. The valley of the shadow of death is often the way to the land of Beulah and Delectable Mountains. Often from a pillow of stones come, as to Jacob at Bethel, the brightest visions of the soul. From weariness and pain and trouble arise the steps that lead to heaven. Life's Pisgahs and Mounts of Transfiguration are built of the hardest rocks of affliction and trial.—Peloubet.

Voice of God.—

There is a voice, a mighty voice, that everywhere doth come,
Or in the hum of multitudes or the solitude of home;
A voice that whispereth to the soul of a viewless presence nigh
As the murmurings of the leaflets tell that a breeze is passing by.

It cometh in the breath of morn, and in the noon-tide glow,
Where the torrent stream in its rock-bed swells, where the babbling
brooklets flow;
Upborne upon the parting sigh of the evening from the hill
It whispereth, and in the black-browed night, when the tongue of man
is still.

"His voice attention still as midnight draws; his voice more gentle than the summer's breeze, that mildly whispers through the waving trees, soft as the nightingale's complaining song, or mur-m'ring currents as they roll along." — Dryden.

Amid the war of the tempest rage that thrilling voice we hear,
Summoning many a silent sigh, and many a thought of fear;
And in the thunder-peal it comes, like a warning from the sky,
Telling to trembling man of death and desolation nigh.

In the turbulent tumult of the waves, woke by the whirlwind's sweep,
When the giant might of the winter storm doth revel on the deep;
And in the breath of the soft south wind it comes—that varying voice—
Now bearing doubt and terror, now making all things rejoice.

In visible characters is it writ upon the heaven-vault high,
In the daystar, and the morn, and all the travelers of the sky,
In the sunbeam and the lightning flash that fadeless form I see,
That in the noon-day or the night cometh unceasingly.

Oh! know ye not what is that voice that wandereth everywhere,
That tongue whose soothing melody or fearful wrath you hear
Oh! know ye whence it cometh, where it maketh its abode?
Its dwelling-place is in all space, it is—the Voice of God!—Edw. W. Coxe.

7—9. (7) **quaking,** the sign of fear of some unknown thing or presence.[b] (8) **no strength in me,** comp. Re. i. 17.[c] **comeliness,** the bright color of the skin of a healthy person. **corruption,** the yellow pallor of death. (9) **deep sleep,** or trance. He saw nothing with his bodily eyes, but much with his awakened spiritual vision.

Human Loneliness (vs. 7).—Though men are gregarious, they have an individuality. A man feels himself to be alone—I. In his profoundest thoughts. II. In his moral convictions. III. In his greatest sorrows. IV. In his dying moments.—Thomas.

Man in His Loneliness.—
Thou must go forth, alone, my soul, thou must go forth alone,
To other scenes, to other worlds, that mortal hath not known.
Thou must go forth alone, my soul, to tread the narrow vale;
But He whose word is sure hath said His comforts shall not fail,
His rod and staff shall comfort thee across the dreary road,
Till thou shalt join the blessed ones in heaven's serene abode.

10, 11. **hand,** etc., comp. Re. i. 17. **set me,** "placed me in a tottering state upon," etc. (11) **greatly beloved,** ch. ix. 23. "The angel calls him Daniel, not Belteshazzar: he gives him the name by which he was known to the saints of God."—Spk. Com.

Angels are Employed to Increase Our Strength.—It is noteworthy that as Daniel's needs arose one after the other, the angel was prepared to meet each one. Daniel was prostrate; the angel set him upright. Daniel was so stunned with the intelligence, that he was dumb; the angel opened his mouth, and gave him speech. Daniel fainted under a sense of awe and wonder; the angel imparted new strength with his touch. We are impressed with the considerateness, the tenderness, the thoughtful sympathy, of this angelic visitor. There was strength imparted to his physical nature by a touch; there was strength imparted to his soul by the angel's words. According to the constitution of man's nature is the agency employed by God. The angel who strengthened Christ Jesus in the garden of suffering can also strengthen us.—Pul. Com.

12—14. (12) **from .. day,** showing that if there had seemed to be any delay in the answer to prayer, there had not been one moment's inattention or neglect. **chasten,** R. V. "humble." (13) **prince,** etc., poss. here meaning the guardian angel of Persia; figurative of the hindrance to the Div. purposes offered by national and political movements. **Michael,** see Jude 9; Re. xii. 7. **remained,** to resist political movements that might be prejudicial to the interests of the Jews.[a] R. V. marg. "was not needed." lxx, "I left him (Michael) there to continue the contention with the guardian angel of Persia." "We can have little idea what is meant by this conflict in the heavens between angelic beings."—Pul. Com. (14) **many days,** covers a long stretch of time.

Conflict of Good with Evil.—It is difficult to know whether this is meant to be ideal or real—whether it represents a struggle of angels

You go to Christ for justification, that the condemning power of sin may be taken away; but do you go to Christ for sanctification, that the reigning power of sin may be taken away?

"Hope nothing from luck, and the probability is that you will be so prepared, forewarned, and forearmed, that all shallow observers will call you lucky." —Bulwer.

Christianity removes the attraction of the earth; and this is one way, in which it diminishes men's burden. It makes them citizens of another world.—Drummond.

b Comp. Ac. ix. 7.

c Comp. Job xlii. 5, 6; Is. vi. 5.

"We love Him because He first loved us." No one of the Apostles loved Christ more than he who is called the "beloved" disciple.

To obey instant orders of the living God, is the highest qualification for command. This is the meaning of that great saying of Cromwell's "One never mounts so high as when one knows not whither one is going"—a saying which the wise and prudent scorned as a confession of blindness, but which reveals to simpler minds the deepest truth. — Martineau.

a "I gained my point against the adverse angel of Persia, so as to influence the Persian authorities to favor Israel's restoration." — Fausset.

"Divine power in man is like the electric current in a piece of steel." — Peloubet.

"In one of England's great cathedrals rests one whose gravestone, according to his own direction, bears but the single word Miserrimus 'most miserable.' He was a man of wealth and position, or his sepulchre could not have been there." "A spiritual giant buried under a mountain of gold." Peloubet.

against demons, or is merely meant for a sort of parable which represents the to-and-fro conflicting impulses which sway the destinies of earthly kingdoms. In any case the representation is too unique and too remote from earth to enable us to understand its spiritual meaning, beyond the bare indication that God sitteth above the water-floods and God remaineth a king for ever. It is another way of showing us that the heathen rage, and the people imagine a vain thing; that the kings of the earth set themselves and the rulers take counsel together; but that they can only accomplish what God's hand and God's counsel have predetermined to be done; and that when they attempt to overthrow the destinies which God has foreordained, "He that sitteth in the heavens shall laugh them to scorn, the Lord shall have them in derision."—Exp. B.

God's Promises.—

As the deep blue of heaven brightens into stars,
So God's great love shines through in promises
Which, falling softly through our prison bars,
Daze not our eyes, but with their soft light bless.

Ladders of light God sets against the skies,
Upon whose golden rungs we step by step arise,
Until we tread the halls of Paradise. —A. E. Hamilton.

15—17. (15) **face .. ground,** in humble reverence. **dumb,** as one overawed. (16) **touched my lips,** so restoring the power of speech.[b] **my sorrows,** comp. for the words 1 Sa. iv. 19. "It expresses the overpowering grief which masters mind as well as body."—Spk. Com. (17) **how .. lord?** meaning "How can I who am so feeble talk with one who is so majestic?"[c]

[b] Comp. Re. i. 17, 18.

[c] "How can thy servant, a poor mortal man, maintain a discourse with a person of your rank and dignity?" —Lowth.

The Ministry of Angels.—

"O the exceeding grace
Of highest God, that loves his creatures so,
And all his works with mercy doth embrace,
That blessed angels he sends to and fro
To serve to wicked men, to serve his wicked foe!
How oft do they their silken bowers leave
To come to succor us that succor want!
How oft do they with golden pinions cleave
The flitting skies like flying pursuivant,
Against the foul fiends to aid us militant!
They for us fight, they watch and duly ward,
And their bright squadrons round about us plant;
And all for love, and nothing for reward.
Oh, why should Heavenly God to man have such regard!"
—Spencer.

18—21. (18) **again,** see vss. 10, 16. (19) **peace,** etc., this is the assurance that no evil would result from the vision of angels, wh. seems always to have awakened fear in men.[a] (20) **Knowest,** etc., vs. 14. **fight .. Persia,** intimating that new difficulties in the way of the restoration of the Jews had arisen, and would have to be overcome. **prince of Grecia,** R. V. "Greece," another subsequent world-power, whose evil influence would have to be resisted.[b] **prince,** i.e. the guardian angel of Persia and Greece. The angel of the Greek nation began to stir up his people. Then came the Ionian revolt, and the successive invasions of Greece, which compelled the Persians to leave the "holy people" alone.—Pul. Com. (21) **noted,** R. V. "inscribed." **scripture of truth,**[c] i.e. in the book of God's designs. Comp. Ps. cxxxix. 16. **holdeth,** Stuart, "putteth forth his strength with me against, etc." **in these things,** better, "against these princes."

[a] Ju. xiii. 21, 22.

[b] "The hostility towards God's people which 'the prince of Persia and the prince of Grecia' showed, is illustrated historically in the opposition and hindrances endured by the Jews at Jerusalem, not only during the reigns of Darius Hystaspes, Xerxes, and Artaxerxes, but also, if in a less degree, in that of Alexander and his successors." —Spk. Com.

[c] "In the secret book of God's decrees, which are truth." —Fausset.

Confidence in Strong Leadership.—"You remember the story of Henry of Navarre. It was just before a battle. Riding in front of his troops he thus addressed them: 'You are Frenchmen; yonder is the enemy; I am your king.' Then, pointing to a white plume that he had fixed in his helmet, he said to them: 'My children, look well to your ranks; if your standard falls, rally around this white plume; it shall lead you to victory.' His soldiers fought like heroes, and the enemy was routed."—Anon. The True Majority.—Suppose a young composer of music should say, The world has rejected my compositions; there is no sale for my books; there is only one man who has uttered a word of promise or comfort to me; there is none that stands by me in all these endeavors but Beethoven! What a noble "but"! The very singularity of the exception creates a majority in the young man's favor. Where Beethoven has contributed his signature it is of but little consequence what the rest of the world may have done as to the merit of the music which has been submitted for criticism.—Peop. B.

CHAPTER THE ELEVENTH.

1—4. (1) This vs. should have concluded ch. x. "It seems to furnish the reason why Gabriel could rely on the help of Michael, and therefore may delay for a few moments his return to the scene of conflict with the Prince of Persia and the coming King of Javan. Michael will for that brief period undertake the sole responsibility of maintaining the struggle, because Gabriel has put him under a direct obligation by special assistance which he rendered to him only a little while previously in the first year of the Median Darius."—Exp. B. **first year,** when it would be uncertain what position Darius would take with regard to the people of Israel. **I stood,** i.e. Gabriel stood. **him,** prob. Michael is intended.[a] (2) **yet,** i.e. after Cyrus. **three kings,** Cambyses, son of Cyrus, B.C. 529; Pseudo-Smerdis, B.C. 522; Darius Hystaspes, B.C. 521. **fourth,** Xerxes, whose riches were proverbial. **against .. Grecia,**[b] wh. Xerxes invaded, B.C. 480. He was defeated at Salamis, and from that time Persia is viewed as politically dead. (3) **mighty king,** Alexander the Great. (4) **broken,** comp. ch. viii. 8, 23. **posterity,** Alex.'s sons did not live to succeed him.[c]

His Kingdom shall be Broken.—Soon after the death of Alexander the Great, his kingdom was divided, but not to his posterity: four of his captains, Ptolemy, Antigonus, Lysimachus, and Cassander reigned over Egypt, Syria, Thrace, and Greece. The kingdoms of Egypt and of Syria became afterwards the most powerful; they subsisted as independent monarchies for a longer period than the other two; and as they were more immediately connected with the land of Judæa, which was often reduced to their dominion, they form the subject of the succeeding predictions.

[a] Da. x. 21.

[b] "These wars, carried on by Xerxes successors, ended at last in the conquest of the Persian monarchy by Alexander the Great." —Lowth.

[c] "Alex.'s son, Alexander Aegus, was slain, by Cassander; his other son, Hercules, was soon after murdered by instigation of Cassander." —Wordsworth.

"A lonely man is insulated from the eternal — inaccessible to the subtle currents which ought to be flowing hourly into his soul." —Drummond.

5—9. (5) **south,** or Egypt.[a] **strong, and one,** etc., R. V. marg. "strong; but one of his princes," etc. The king of the south is Ptolemy Soter, the first Grecian king of Egypt and one of Alexander's generals. "One of his princes" is Seleucus Nicator. (6) **end of years,** i.e. some half century later, about 250 B.C. **join .. together,** fulfilled in the union of Ptolemy Philadelphus and Antiochus Theus, the grandson of Seleucus Nicator. **daughter,** etc., Berenice, daughter of Ptolemy, married Antiochus Theus. **agreement,** R. V. marg. "equitable conditions," i.e. by marriage the two nations hoped for peace. **retain the power,** Antiochus subsequently divorced her. **he stand,** i.e. Antiochus. "The agreement was that Antiochus Theos should divorce his wife and half-sister Laodice, and disinherit her children, and bequeath the throne to any future child of Berenice, who would thus unite the empires of the Ptolemies and the Seleucidæ. But there was overwhelming disaster. Berenice's escort, her father, her husband, all perished, and she herself and her infant child were murdered by her rival, Laodice, B.C. 246, in the sanctuary of Daphne, whither she had fled for refuge."—Exp. B. (7) **out of,** etc., ref. is to Ptolemy Euergetes.[b] **king of the north,** i.e. of Syria. (8) **gods,** etc., for the spoil he brought back, the Egyptians called him Euergetes, or Benefactor. **princes,** R. V. "molten images." **continue,** R. V. "refrain some years fr." after this success. (9) **so the king of the south,** etc., R. V. "and he (Seleucus Kallinikos, king of Syria) shall come into the realm of the king of the south, but he shall return," etc.

Power in Union.—Dr. Wood, the naturalist, tells us that there is a race of very small ants in Africa, who travel in great armies, covering

[a] Egypt was conquered by Alexander in B.C. 332, and placed under the lieutenancy of Ptolemy who assumed the title of king about B.C. 304.

"It is not the design of the Scripture to give us an historical narrative of the actions of heathen princes any further than the affairs of the Jewish nation were concerned in them." S. Jerome.

[b] "He avenged the death of Berenice by overrunning Syria, even to the Euphrates." —Fausset.

several miles, and that, as they go, every living creature flies before them. The elephant rushes off into the wilderness. The lion, who flies from nothing else, plunges into the forest with a cry of terror. He well knows that if he once got into that crowd, he would never get out. Millions and millions of little teeth would fasten upon him, and millions more would surround him on every side, and devour every fragment of his flesh. The most powerful wild beast of Africa—the king of the great forest—is a little ant. The secret of his power lies in one little word, —union,—the union of a great multitude of little beings, all moving together.—Gospel for all Lands.

"A great commentator on the Psalms says that it is not unity with one another (Ps. 133:1) that is meant, but unity with the great Head which makes unity with one another." — A. J. Gordon.

10—13. (10) **his sons,** those of Seleucus. **stirred up,** R. V. "shall war." **one shall .. come,** Antiochus the Great. **overflow,** representing the passing of a mighty army as a devastating flood. (11) **king of the south,** a weak and profligate prince, Ptolemy Philopater. **his hand,** that of Ptolemy,[c] **at** the battle of Raphia. (12) **lifted up,** so that he tried to force his way into the holiest part of the Jewish temple. He did not follow up his victory, but made a hasty peace, that he might return to his licentious pleasures. (13) **after .. years,** 12 yrs. later, upon the death of Philopater; in the interval Antiochus was otherwise engaged in the East.

Christian Warfare.—As long as the soldier slinks outside the battle he carries a whole skin; but let him plunge in and follow the captain, and he will soon have the bullets flying about him. Some have had a good time because there was no use in the devil wasting powder and shot upon you; you haven't been doing him any harm; but directly you begin to wake up and set to work for God, the devil will set a thousand evils to worrying you, or he may come himself to see you.—F. B. Meyer.

c "The author of the Third Book of Maccabees ascribes this victory to the passionate importunity of Arsinoe, Ptolemy's sister, who ran about the army with her hair about her shoulders, and by promises and entreaties engaged the soldiers to fight with more than ordinary resolution."—Lowth.

14—16. (14) **many .. south,** Philip of Macedon being one. **robbers .. people,** or law-breakers.[a] "Sons of violent ones of thy people." Factious and seditious adventurers among the Jews, who broke the treaty between Egypt and the Jews by aiding Antiochus. They destroyed the Egyptian garrison placed in Jerusalem. **shall exalt themselves,** etc., Stuart: "will lift themselves up, so as to establish prophetic vision." In thus rising up they do but establish the prophecies respecting the troubles of the Jews under the fourth dynasty, ch. vii. 19—25; viii. 9—11. (15) **king .. north,** Antiochus. **fenced cities,** such as Zidon, Gaza, Abila, Samaria, Gadara, etc. **chosen people,** or choicest troops. (16) **glorious land,** i.e. Judæa.[b] **consumed,** lit. perfected, i.e. perfectly brought under his sway.[c]

Reward of Apostasy.—However much any of the Jews may have helped Antiochus under the hope of ultimately regaining their independence, their hopes were frustrated. The Syrian king came, besieged, and took a well-fenced city—perhaps an allusion to the fact that he wrested Sidon from the Egyptians. After his great victory over the Egyptian general Scopas at Mount Panium, B.C. 198, the routed Egyptian forces, to the number of ten thousand, flung themselves into that city. This campaign ruined the interests of Egypt in Palestine, "the glorious land." Palestine now passed to Antiochus, who took possession "with destruction in his hand."—Exp. B.

a "The phrase is usually taken to describe those who set law and right at defiance when these come in conflict with their own supposed interests." —Spk. Com.

b Ez. xx. 6, 15; Da. viii. 9.

c "Josephus shows that the meaning is not that the Jews should be utterly consumed; for Antiochus favored them for taking his part against Ptolemy, but that their land should be subjected to him.

17—19. (17) **set his face,** the sign of a formed purpose on the part of Antiochus to have predominance in Egypt and thus check and resist the power of Rome. **upright ones,** better, "he shall make agreements with him."[d] **daughter of women,** Cleopatra is so called on account of her great beauty. **corrupting her,** or with the intent to corrupt her, by making her use her influence against her husband's interests. **neither .. him,** Cleopatra took her husband's, not her father's side. (18) **isles,** or the maritime cities of Lesser Asia.[a] **a prince,** R. V. omits "for his own behalf;" the ref. is to Lucius Scipio, the Rom. consul, who utterly routed Antiochus at Magnesia, 190 B.C., forcing him to make ignominious terms. **without,** etc., R. V. "yea, moreover." (19) **not be found,** ref. to his sudden and violent death.[b]

Failure.—Did you ever notice that when some of the strongest men in the Bible failed, they almost always failed on the strongest point of their character? Moses was renowned for his meekness, humility and gentleness; yet he became angry and killed the Egyptian; he was angry and said, "Must I bring water out of this rock, ye rebels?" God kept

d Prob. referring to his proposals for a contract of marriage between his own daughter Cleopatra and king Ptolemy.

a All countries lying upon the sea coasts are called islands in the Heb. dialect.

b "When attempting to rob the temple at Elymais, to raise money to pay the Romans, as

him out of the Promised Land because he lost his temper. If you think you are meek, it is a good sign you are not. Peter was one of the boldest of all the disciples, but when one little maid looked at him and said, "You are one of his disciples," he began to curse and to swear and to say that he was not, and down he fell. John and James were noted for their meekness and gentleness, and yet they wanted to call fire down from heaven to consume a town in Samaria. Do you not see that man is a complete failure away from God? But he that is in you is greater than he that is in the world. When Jesus Christ on the cross said, "It is finished," it was the shout of a conqueror. He had fought and overcome the world. Now if I have Christ in me, I will overcome the world, and if I have not, it is the height of madness for me to undertake to overcome the world.—D. L. Moody.

20—22. (20) **raiser of taxes,** Seleucus Philopater is so called bec. he seized the treasures of the temple at Jerusalem. **glory kingdom,** i.e. in the temple at Jerusalem. **few days,** his reign was comparatively short, reaching only to twelve years. **neither .. battle,** he was poisoned by Heliodorus, his treasurer, who designed to usurp the kingdom.[c] (21) **vile person,** R. V. "contemptible," Antiochus Epiphanes.[d] **to .. kingdom,** i.e. he had no rightful claim to the royal dignity of succession. **peaceably,** R. V. "in time of security." He gained the kingdom by craft and flattery. (22) **flood,** fig. for an overflowing army. **prince,** prob. Ptolemy Philometor.

Successful Dissimulation.—I. Dissimulation is often more successful than violence. The successful usurper grasps the honors of royalty for himself; he perpetrates no violence to obtain them. He wins power by dissimulation. 1. Dissimulation is most common in an age of advanced civilization. As life becomes more complex, evil becomes more subtle. 2. It has most power at a time of moral corruption. 3. It is most successful under circumstances of material prosperity. Then we are off our guard. II. The success of dissimulation is more injurious to the world than the success of violence. The greatest enemies to a state are its traitors. III. Though dissimulation may succeed for a time, truth will ultimately triumph. There is "an end" at "the time appointed." 1. By its own nature evil ultimately declares its true character. By dissimulation power is won, which in being used casts off the mask. 2. When evil is declared, it is seen to be hateful and weak. Once fairly known, it loses its attraction and becomes a despicable thing. 3. God will finally interfere to destroy all false appearances, and judge the world in truth according to real character and conduct.—Pul. Com.

23—26. (23) **league .. him,** i.e. with Ptolemy Philometor. **small people,** his forces were but small in this first expedition. (24) **peaceably,** R. V. "in time of security," i.e. by deceit and chicanery. **fattest,** etc., the rich tracts of Cœle-Syria and Palestine. **scatter,** etc., by this unusual generosity he sought to win favor, and secure his throne. **forecast,** etc., or think his thoughts: plan for the future by keeping his hold on the chief places of strength, esp. Pelusium, the key of Egypt. (25) **south,** Egypt. **not stand,** history records that at this battle Ptolemy was deserted and his power treacherously undermined by his own generals, so that his army was destroyed. (26) **feed,** etc., his own trusted courtiers, Eulacus and Lennæus. **overflow,** Stuart: "rush on like a flood," to its own ruin.

Result of Wrong.—It is recorded of Marius, that after his overthrow by Sylla, he was always in consternation, as if he heard the sound of the trumpets, and the noise of the victorious army pursuing him. His fears were no longer quiet than whilst charmed with wine or sleep: he therefore was continually drunk, that he might forget himself, his enemy, and his danger. Thus men make a pitiful shift to forget their latter end, and, whilst they are following their secular affairs or sensual pleasures, are unconcerned for what is to be hereafter.—Bates.

27—29. (27) **one table,** they met at Memphis. Antiochus pretended to take care of the interests of his nephew Philometor, and he seemed to confide in his uncle's protection. Both were trying to deceive. **shall not prosper,** the Romans interrupted the progress of Antiochus in Egypt. (28) **Then,** when he had taken the spoils of Egypt. **heart,** or purpose.

agreed, he was slain by the inhabitants."
—Lowth.

Christian faith is a grand cathedral, with divinely pictured windows. Standing without, you see no glory, nor can possibly imagine any; standing within, every ray of light reveals a harmony of unspeakable splendors.
—Hawthorne.

c So Appian relates.

d "The younger son of Antiochus the Great. He was a hostage at Rome, from whence he escaped. He was brother and successor of Seleucus, and a usurper, for he supplanted his nephew Demetrius, the son of Seleucus and lawful heir to the throne."
—Wordsworth.

"'Tis wrong to sleep in church; 'tis wrong to borrow what you can never pay; 'tis wrong to touch with unkind word the heart that pines in sorrow; 'tis wrong to scold too loud; to eat too much; 'tis wrong to put off acting til to-morrow." —J.T. Watson.

"No adulation; 'tis the death of virtues;
Who flatters is of all mankind the lowest
Save he who courts the flattery." — Hannah More.

"Do you find it hard to work with others? Remember how hard God must find it to work with you!"

against .. covenant, or covenant people, who, he understood, showed signs of revolting.[a] **exploits,** R. V. "his pleasure," esp. the massacre of the Jewish people, and despoiling the temple. (29) **return,** for a third expedition, wh. did not result so gloriously as the former one. Rome interfered on behalf of Ptolemy, 168 B.C.

The Self-Seeking Spirit leads to Satan's kingdom, not to Christ's. It is the spirit of hell, not of heaven. It begets evils innumerable and sorrow unspeakable. "Fling away ambition; by that sin angels fell. "Aut Cæsar aut nullus," "to be first or nothing," leads to crimes and wars. It was Milton's Satan who said, "Better to reign in hell than to serve in heaven." "How like a mounting devil in the heart rules the unreined ambition!" But distinguish between the strong desire to improve, to have large usefulness, to grow in holiness and love, and the desire to have more honor and power, or even to be better than others. To do the very best we can in everything is our duty.—Peloubet.

30—32. (30) **Chittim,** Ge. x. 4; Rev. xxiv. 24. Ships of Macedonia,[b] the Roman fleet. **intelligence with,** R. V. "regard unto," i.e. an understanding with. **forsake,** etc., i.e. renegade Jews, who joined Antiochus. The king used these deserters to work out his schemes. (31) **arms,** "he shall set physical forces in motion."—Pul. Com. **pollute,** etc., profaning the temple, and stopping the sacrifices. **of strength,** R. V. "even the fortress." **abomination,** idol, wh. was set on God's altar. Prob. an image of Jupiter, to whom the temple was dedicated. (32) **corrupt,** or corrupted. Ref. is to such apostates as Jason and Menelaus. **know their God,** and keep faithful to Him. **do exploits,** as illus. in the career of the Maccabees.

Christian Seamen, Strong in Valor.—"I have had the honor," said Capt. Parry, at a public meeting in 1826, "and I may truly say the happiness, of commanding British seamen under circumstances requiring the utmost activity, implicit and immediate obedience, and the most rigid attention to discipline and good order; and I am sure, that the maintenance of all these was, in a great measure, owing to the blessing of God upon our humble endeavors to improve the religious and moral character of our men. In the schools established on board our ships during the winter, religion was made the primary object, and the result was every way gratifying and satisfactory. It has convinced me, that true religion is so far from being a hindrance to the arduous duties of that station in which it has pleased Providence to cast the seaman's lot, that, on the contrary, it will always incite him to their performance, from the highest and most powerful of motives; and I will venture to predict, that in proportion as this spring of action is more and more introduced among our seamen, they would become such as every Englishman would wish to see them. The very best seamen on board the "Hecla" were, without exception, those who had thought the most seriously on religious subjects; and if a still more scrupulous selection were to be made out of that number, the choice would fall, without hesitation, on two or three individuals possessing dispositions and sentiments eminently Christian."—Whitecross.

33—35. (33) **understand,** R. V. marg. "the teachers of the people," comp. ch. xii. 10. **instruct,** so as to keep them from being corrupted by the flatterers. **fall,** etc., in time of persecution, and of patriotic warfare. (34) **little help,** ref. to the Chasidim,—"the Pious,"—a sect wh. rallied round the Maccabees, most of them were sincere but some were waverers. **cleave .. flatteries,** i.e. not sincerely.[a] (35) **them of understanding,** i.e. some of the patriot party. **try them,** R. V. "refine," test and prove them,[b] and call out more energy and effort. **time of the end,** i.e. end of Antiochus' reign. **time appointed,** the evils will not go beyond the set time of God's appointment.

Every Christian a Teacher (vs. 33).—Taking these words as applicable to every Christian man and woman, let us see what they teach us. 1. A Christian is one among the people; 2. He is one that has understanding; 3. He is one who does not keep his knowledge to himself; 4. A Christian is an instructor; 5. He is an instructor of many.—Bonar.

Flatteries and Persecutions.—"The Roman magistrates and officers, it is well known, made use of the most alluring promises, as well as the most terrible threatenings, to prevail upon the primitive Christians to

---

a "The bent of Antiochus was towards Hellenism; and the surest way to his favor was to decry the laws and ceremonies of Moses, and to encourage the gymnasium and other foreign introductions. The patriotic Jews were compelled to witness what they had no power to prevent." —Spk. Com.

"Hateful to me, as are the gates of hell, Is he who, hiding one thing in his heart, Utters another." —Bryant.

b "The Roman Senate sent an envoy who met Antiochus near Alexandria, and demanded that he should retire fr. Egypt, which was an ally of Rome. Antiochus said he would consider the mandate, whereupon the envoy drew a circle round him with his staff on the sand of the shore, and commanded him not to go forth of it till he had given an answer to the message. Antiochus was confounded, and after a little hesitation, obeyed, and evacuated Egypt." —Wordsworth.

"Self-sacrifice is at the root of all the blossoms of goodness that have survived the wreck of Paradise." —Geikie.

a "Some were found, after their death, with idols consecrated under their clothes." —Lowth.

b 1 Pe. i. 7.

"Peace for the past, grace for the present, and glory for the future; nothing before the true believer that isn't glory." —D. L. Moody.

renounce their religion, and offer incense to the statues of the emperors and images of the gods." He quotes an old commentator, who says: "There are some who think that the prophet here had respect to the Christians whom the wicked idolaters endeavored, from the beginning of the rising Church, to seduce by flatteries; but the persecution of tyrants raged chiefly against the apostles and holy teachers." Times of persecution will doubtless have much in common; and Christians, suffering as they did, and so long and often so severely under the Roman emperors and magistrates, would naturally find much in the description of the times of Antiochus applicable to their own. The word of prophecy was intended to be a "light shining in a dark place," in the New as it had been in the Old Testament dispensation. "These things happened unto them (the Old Testament Church) for ensamples; and they are written for our admonition, upon whom the ends of the world are come" (1 Cor. x. 11). The bishop adds: "It may, too, with the strictest truth and propriety be said of the primitive Christians that, being dispersed everywhere, and preaching the Gospel in all the parts of the Roman empire, they 'instructed many,' and gained a great number of proselytes to their religion: yet they fell by the sword, etc., 'many days;' for they were exposed to the malice and fury of ten general persecutions, and suffered all manner of injuries, afflictions, and tortures, with little intermission, for the space of three hundred years."—Pul. Com.

36—39. (36) **the king,** Antiochus. **indignation,** i.e. till God's anger should be turned away from Israel. **that that,** R. V. "that which." (37) **god,** better, gods. Antiochus desired to Hellenise everything. **desire of women,** poss. referring to the Syrian Venus, who was esp. worshiped by women. (38) **estate,** R. V. marg. "office." **God of forces,** or fortresses. "Prob. a general and purposely indefinite title." Indicating that he would only honor war, brute force. **pleasant things,** or jewels. (39) **strange god,** new even to his own people. R. V. "And he shall deal with the strongest fortresses by the help of a strange god"—namely, the Capitoline Jupiter—and shall crowd the strongholds of Judæa with heathen colonists who worship the Tyrian Hercules.—Exp. B. **cause them,** i.e. those who join him in worshiping this god of his own.

Self.—In looking at the stars thro' a great telescope, it is necessary first to put out every light until you are left in total darkness. Every light sets the air in motion, and disturbs the focus, and blurs the vision of the stars. How often our vision of God is blurred, and dimmed by the flames of self-consciousness that float about us! How many times we have to put out the light of self-seeking, earthly ambition and false pride of position in order to look upward, and in the clear, still air know whither God's lights are leading us and what God will have us do.—W. H. P. Faunce.

40—42. (40) **push at him,** this may refer to Antiochus's third expedition; we have no record of a fourth; but the historical explanation of this vs. cannot be assured. (41) **glorious land,** i.e. Palestine. **chief,** lit. firstlings.[a] (42) **stretch,** etc., fig. for putting forth power.

The Last Expedition.—"Antiochus in the course of his march shall pass through Palestine, 'the glorious land,' with disastrous injury; but Edom, Moab, and the bloom of the kingdom of Ammon shall escape his hand. Egypt, however, shall not escape. By the aid of the Libyans and Ethiopians who are in his train he shall plunder Egypt of its treasures." How far these events correspond to historic realities is uncertain. Jerome says that Antiochus invaded Egypt a third time in B.C. 165, the eleventh year of his reign; but there are no historic traces of such an invasion, and most certainly Antiochus towards the close of his reign, instead of being enriched with vast Egyptian spoils, was struggling with chronic lack of means. Some therefore suppose that the writer composed and published his enigmatic sketch of these events before the close of the reign of Antiochus, and that he is here passing from contemporary fact into a region of ideal anticipations which were never actually fulfilled.—Exp. B.

43—45. (43) **Libyans,** etc., allies of Egypt. **at his steps,** i.e. among his followers. (44) **tidings,** etc., concerning Artaxias, king of Armenia, who revolted in the N., and Arsaces, leader of the Parthians in the E. **Stuart: "to lay waste many."** (45) **plant,** etc., sign of entire conquest.[a]

"Oh blindness to the future! kindly given, That each may fill the circle marked by heaven." — Pope.

"Learning without thought is labor lost; thought without learning is perilous." — Confucius.

"Knowledge is proud that he learned so much; Wisdom is humble that he knows no more." — Comper.

"Learning maketh young men temperate, is the comfort of old age, standing for wealth with poverty, and serving as an ornament to riches." —Cicero.

"He that is proud, eats up himself; pride is his own glass, his own trumpet, his own chronicle; and whatever praises itself but in the deed, devours the deed in the praise." —Shakespeare.

[a] "Any invader on his way to Egypt through Palestine would leave untouched the tribes to the E. of the Jordan, esp. if rapid progress were his object." — Spk. Com.

"We let go the present, which we have in our power, and look forward to that which depends upon chance — and so quit a certainty for an uncertainty." — Seneca.

[a] His palace-like military tents.

between the seas, R. V. "betw. the sea and the glorious holy mountain," i.e. betw. the Mediterranean and Jerusalem. **come to his end,**[b] on his return from the expedition indicated in vs. 44.

Napoleon's Conquests and End.—Notwithstanding the expressed presentiment of the first Napoleon that his nephew should be the ultimate representative of the Napoleonic dynasty, and the profound conviction of that nephew, even from early life, that he had a great mission and destiny to fulfil in relation to France; notwithstanding that, singularly, after becoming president of the French Republic in 1851, he became emperor of France in 1852, being crowned on the anniversary of the battle of Austerlitz and the coronation of Napoleon I., thus restoring the Napoleonic dynasty, when the French people inscribed on an arch erected in his honor the remarkable words, "The uncle that was, the nephew that is," as if in literal fulfilment of Rev. xvii. 8, 11; notwithstanding that from 1849 to 1870 he maintained military occupation of Rome, and declared that the temporal power of the pope was incompatible with the advance of civilization and must be put down, being termed the "modern Augustus, nephew and heir of Cæsar;" and finally, notwithstanding that he succeeded in acquiring an almost paramount influence over Spain and Italy, while he extended his power in Algeria, and the northern coast of Africa, and appeared determined to possess himself of Palestine, and that, as in the case of the first Napoleon, Great Britain appeared to be the only impediment to his attainment of uncontrolled dominion over the Roman world; yet he passed away, broken apparently in the zenith of his prosperity and power, and left the prophecy still unfulfilled.—Hom. Com. Retribution for Sin.—A royal tyrant may as well knock his head against a granite wall—and better—than to work against God, or to fling himself on the bosses of the Almighty's shield. In the midst of apparent success, such a man feels ofttimes that fate (as he calls it) is against him. Strangely are his ends defeated, as were Napoleon's, by a snowstorm. The mightiest warrior is working, with his blustering noise, within a very tiny circle; and all imperial and martial events are embraced within the supreme purpose and administration of God. Let appearances be as they may, "God has prepared his throne in the heavens;" "His kingdom ruleth over all." At last, reward and retribution shall be distributed by royal and impartial hands. Every one shall "receive the due reward of his deeds." God's end may be far off, humanly speaking, yet it shall "surely come." Though it tarry, childlike faith will wait for it.—Pulp. Com.

Gold.—

"Commerce has set the mark of selfishness;
The signet of its all enslaving power
Upon a shining ore and called it gold:
Before whose image bow the vulgar great,
The vainly rich, the miserable proud,
The mob of peasants, nobles, priests and kings,
And with blind feelings reverence the power
That grinds them to the dust of misery.
But in the temple of their hireling hearts
Gold is a living god, and rules in scorn
All earthly things but virtue." —Shelley.

CHAPTER THE TWELFTH.

1—4. (1) **that time,** about 163 B.C., ch. xi. 40—45. **Michael,** regarded as the protector of the Jewish nation, ch. x. 13, 21. **time of trouble,** prob. refer. to the last struggle against Antiochus[a]. **in the book,** the book of the living; God's book, in which thou who are to outlive the Antiochean persecutions stand recorded as survivors.[b]—Stuart. (2) **many,** i.e. "multitudes," not a contrast with "few" who do not rise. **sleep,** in death. **awake,** in the general resurrection. While vs. 1 seems to refer to the time of Antiochus, vs. 2 passes on to the scenes of the last day. **life,** etc., Matt. xxv. 46. (3) **wise,** or teachers: ch. xi. 33, 35. These had been great lights in the world, so their reward is to shine for

[b] "The most brilliant of the Syro-Macedonian kings died in the mountain-town of Tabal, consumed in body by a loathsome ulcer, afflicted in mind by horrible apparitions and remorse of conscience." —Milman.

2 Th. ii. 8.

"Midas longed for gold, and insulted the Olympians. He got gold, so that whatever he touched became gold, and he, with his long ears, was little the better for it. Midas had insulted Apollo and the gods; the gods gave him his wish, and a pair of long ears, which also were a good appendage to it. What a truth in these old fables!"—Carlyle.

"At a revival meeting, a little lad who was used to Methodist ways, went home to his mother and said, 'Mother, John So-and-so is under conviction an seeking for peace, but he will not find it tonight, mother.' 'Why, William,' said she. 'Because he is only down on one knee, mother, and he will never get peace until he is down on both knees.' Until we are completely humbled, we cannot find the Saviour."

[a] Comp. Joel ii. 2; Je. xxx. 7; Mat. xxiv. 21.

[b] "The phrase alludes to the registers that used to be kept of the members of any city or corporation; the privileges of wh. society none can lay a claim to but those whose names are found in such registers."—Lowth.

ever in more glorious spheres. (4) **shut . . words,** ch. viii. 26. "The charge is one of caution, not of absolute reservation: they only should see the words who were fit to see them."—Spk. Com. **run to and fro,** Stuart: "many shall make diligent search," etc.

The Good in the Future (vs. 3).—I. Their present character and conduct. 1. They are wise; 2. They turn many to righteousness; 3. The means they use for this end; 4. The ends accomplished are valuable; 5. This work is not confined to ministers. II. Their future reward. 1. They shall shine as the firmament; 2. Glory of the stars that of reflected light; 3. Stars of different magnitudes; 4. The glory of heaven will endure; 5. The obvious sense of the text is that the good will be exalted to high honor in the future. Learn:—(1) Study wisdom; (2) Study usefulness; (3) Be encouraged by the prospect of a vast reward.—Sigma in 400 Sks.

The Light of Eternity.—Michelangelo once went into the studio of a young artist who had just executed a statue to stand in the public square. Angelo saw its grave defects, and pointed them out to his young friend. The exultant artist did not appreciate the criticism of his work, and supposed the greater man to be moved with envy. So he told him, in the dim obscurity of his workshop he could not see the defects which were so apparent to the aged critic, and in passion sneered at the opinion given. "Well," said Angelo, not the least disturbed, "the light of the public square will test it. "The light of the public square will test it." Ah, yes! The light of the public square is to test every human life. Eternal blaze shall pour upon it, and defects unseen by the poorer light of earth will grow to ghastly deformities. The light of the public square will test it! Some to Everlasting Life.—There is an Eastern story of the "Amreeta water of Immortality," which, when drunk by the impure, ran through their veins in the liquid fire of unspeakable agony; but, when drunk by the pure, this water spread through their whole being the glow of eternal life and peace.—Old Test. Anec.

5—7. (5) **other two,** i. e. two other angel forms. **river,** the Hiddekel. (6) **clothed in linen,** ch. x. 5. **upon the waters,** R. V., "above the waters," who had made the communication. An angel asks the question for Daniel. (7) **held,** etc., comp. Re. x. 5. **time . . half,** comp. ch. vii. 25. **scatter,** R. V., "when they have made an end of breaking in pieces the power," etc.; i. e. when Israel is, as it were, crushed, then the death of Antiochus shall take place, and the fulfillment of the preceding prophecy shall begin to be accomplished.—Stuart.

The Signs of the End (vs. 6).—I. Signs of the end in the world. 1. Progress of false religion; 2. A rampant infidelity; 3. Persecution of the good; 4. Unbelief of the world. II. Signs in the Church. 1. Increased activities—missions; 2. Quickened zeal—personal effort; 3. New appliances—education, art, inventions.—W. W. Whythe.

Working for Eternity.—It is told of Zeuxis, the famous painter, that he was remarkable for the pains which he bestowed upon his works, and that on one occasion, when he was accused of being long in drawing his lines and slow in the use of his pencil, he replied, "I am long in doing what I take in hand, because I want to do it with care; for what I paint, I paint for eternity."—Wm. Taylor.

Destiny —
"The tissue of the life to be, we weave with colors all our own,
And in the field of destiny we reap as we have sown;
Still shall the soul around it call, the shadows which it gathered here,
And, painted on the eternal wall, the past shall reappear."

8—9. (8) **understood not,** i. e. the time was only told him in prophetical form, he could not translate it into actual years. (9) **Go thy way,** i. e. do not press this question; let all be until God shall please to unfold it. **till the time,** or nearer the time.

Premonition of the End.—"My next undertaking," said Hogarth to a company of friends around his table, "shall be the 'End of all Things.'" "If that is the case," replied one of his friends, "your business will be finished; for there will be an end to the painter." "There will be so," answered Hogarth, sighing heavily; "and therefore the sooner my work is done the better." He began the next day, by grouping everything

"Gain may be temporary and uncertain; but ever while you live expense is constant and certain; and it is easier to build two chimneys than to keep one in fuel."—Franklin.

"'Tis the divinity that stirs within us, 'tis heaven itself that points out an hereafter, and intimates eternity to man."—Addison.

"The end of learning is to know God, and out of that knowledge to love Him, and to imitate Him, as we may the nearest, by possessing our souls of true virtue."—Milton.

"God is the author, men are only the players. These grand pieces which are played upon earth, have been composed in heaven." — Balzac.

"Sooner or later that which is now life shall be poetry, and every fair and manly trait shall add a richer strain to the song." — Emerson.

"The contented mind wants nothing that he hath not; the covetous mind wants not only what he hath not, but likewise what he hath."—J. Beaumont.

which denotes the end of all things,—a broken bottle; an old broom worn to the stump; the butt-end of an old fire-lock; a cracked bell; a bow unstrung; a crown tumbling into pieces; towers in ruins; the sign-post of a tavern called the "World's End," tumbling; the moon in her wane; the map of the globe burning; a gibbet falling, the body gone, and chains which held it falling down; Phœbus and his horse dead in the clouds; a vessel wrecked; Time, with his hour-glass and scythe broken, a tobacco pipe in his mouth, the last whiff of smoke going out; a play-book open, with exeunt omnes stamped in the corner; an empty purse; and a statute of bankruptcy taken out against Nature. "So far so good," cried Hogarth: "nothing remains but this," taking his pencil in a sort of prophetic fury, and dashing off the similitude of a painter's palette broken. "Finis!" exclaimed Hogarth, "the deed is done, all is over." He never again took the palette in hand; and he died in about a year after he had finished this extraordinary tail-piece.

10, 11. (10) **made white,** the sign of purity. This is the design of persecution and trial. **wise .. understand,** "an honest and good heart is a necessary qualification for the receiving and understanding of Divine truths." (11) **daily sacrifice,** etc., ch. xi. 31.[a]

The Blessedness of Sanctified Trouble.—Trouble is sanctified and blessed in two different ways, and to two different classes. It is sanctified to the ungodly, and to those still out of Christ; and it is so when, accompanied by God's quickening and convicting Spirit, it leads the troubled one to a consideration of sin and its baneful effects, and to an earnest desire to be saved from it, and to be reconciled to God. Such a case was that of Manasseh, who in his captivity and affliction sought the Lord and found Him. Of such santcified trouble the prodigal son is a standing and divinely given picture. The conversion of Israel in the great tribulation probably to be a distinguished example of the same thing. But trouble is also and especially sanctified to the godly, who are already in Christ.—Hom. Com.——Everlasting Life.—Archbishop Ussher, in his declining years, had a room built with windows facing the east, south, and west, so that he could warm himself by the rays of the sun. In the morning he stationed himself at the east window, at noon at the south window, and in the evening at the west window, where he could watch the setting of the sun. The west window as at that time symbolical of the setting of his sun of life. But sunrise follows the setting of the sun, and the sunset of life is the sunrise of immortality.—A. T. Pierson.

12, 13. (12) **waiteth,** watchingly, expectantly. **thousand .. days,** i. e. to the death of Antiochus Epiphanes 45 days after the cleansing of the Temple. Profane hist. does not tell us when Antiochus died, but it was after the reconsecration of the Temple by Judas Maccabæus. (13) **rest,** in the grave. **in thy lot,** as one of the glorified saints by-and-by.[b] The image is taken from the allotment of the earthly Canaan. The Prophet Daniel was at this time at least ninety years of age.

The Way and the End (vs. 13).—I. Describe the way Daniel was exhorted to walk in. 1. Self-denial and mortification; 2. Humility and prayer; 3. Faith; 4. Holiness. II. Point out the necessity of walking in that way. 1. God commands it; 2. Our salvation depends on our obedience; 3. It will redound to the glory of God. III. The advantages of obedience. 1. Thou shalt rest from a war with Nature, with Satan, with the world, from toil; 2. And stand in thy lot, among the holiest of the ransomed, a conqueror of the first order, near the throne of God.—W. Stevens.

The Torn Bible Leaf.—In Providence, R. I., there lived two young men, who were intimately acquainted. The one was godly; and the other, a fellow-clerk, paid no attention to Divine things. On one occasion the latter took up a leaf of the Bible, and was about to tear it in pieces, and use it for packing some small parcel in the shop, when the other said, "Do not tear that: it contains the word of eternal life." The young man did not relish the reproof, and put it in his pocket. Shortly after this, he said to himself, "Now I will see what kind of life it is of which this leaf speaks." On unfolding the leaf, the first words that caught his eye were the last in the book of Daniel: "But go thou thy way till

a "The time is from the profanation of the temple by Antiochus in the month Ijar of the year 168 B. C. to the restoration of the worship by Judas Maccabeus on the 25th of Chisleu, 165, and was, according to the Seleucid era, 1,290 days; 45 days more elapsed before Antiochus' death in the month Shebat, so ending the Jews' calamity." —Maurer.

"It is through the deeper sense of the holy love of God that repentance grows deeper also."—S. S. Times.

b "That the words contain a reference to and a belief in the resurrection is self-evident; his lot would fall to him in the heavenly Canaan." — Spk. Com.

"When I see the heavenly sun buried under earth in the evening of the day and in the morning find a resurrection of his glory, why (think I) may not the sons of heaven, buried in the earth in the evening of their days, expect the morning of their glorious resurrection? Each night is but the past days funeral, and the morning his resurrection; why then should our

the end be: for thou shalt rest, and stand in thy lot at the end of the days." He began immediately to inquire what his lot would be at the end of the days, and the train of thought thus awakened led to the formation of a religious character. By means so various are the purposes of Divine grace accomplished.——Contrast in the Death of the Righteous and Ungodly.—Dying beds often bear witness to a contrast; and dying beds do not generally tell lies. Dying circumstances, when the approach of eternity opens men's eyes, usually discover the wise man and the fool. "My principles," said Altamont when in those circumstances, "have poisoned my friend; my extravagance has beggared my boy; my wickedness has murdered my wife: and is there another hell? Oh thou blasphemed, yet most indulgent Lord God, hell itself is a refuge if it hide me from Thy frown." "Give me more laudanum," said Mirabeau, "that I may not think of eternity and of what is to come." "I would give worlds," said Thomas Paine, "that the Age of Reason had never been written." Let us hear from the other side. "I have pain," said Richard Baxter—"there is no arguing against sense—but I have peace; I have peace." "The battle is fought," said Dr. Payson, "and the victory is won for ever: I am going to bathe in an ocean of purity, and benevolence, and happiness, to all eternity." "My soul," said John Brown of Haddington, "hath found inexpressibly more sweetness and satisfaction in a single line of the Bible, nay, in two such words as these, Thy God and My God, than all the pleasures found in the things of the world since the creation could equal."—Hom. Com.

funeral sleep be otherwise than our sleep at night? Why should not we as well wake to our resurrection as in the morning? I see night is rather an intermission of day than a deprivation, and death rather borrows our life of us than robs us of it. Since, then, the glory of the sun finds a resurrection, why should not the sons of glory?" —Warwick.

Introduction.

Hosea was no doubt a native of the Northern kingdom. The moral condition of that kingdom was exceedingly corrupt. This moral degradation the prophet visits with unsparing rebuke and denunciation. "As Stanley has said, he was the Jeremiah of Israel; no wonder, therefore, that he met Jeremiah's fate of opposition and contempt (ix. 7, 8, comp. Jer. xxix. 26, 27)." The time covered by his prophecies was probably about 750 to 725 B.C. "Amid all his threats and denunciations his tender love for Israel beams forth. He rejoices when he has a message of mercy to deliver; and his style loses its stern abruptness, and he dwells with placid delight on the prospect before him; his impetuous boldness sobers down into the gentle flow of calm confidence. But this happier aspect of his prophecy is rarely seen. His message is generally full of mourning and woe. The prophets of Judah could look forward to a restored people and a repaired polity. The ten tribes had no separate future. Their temporal punishment was irreversible. It was only as associated with, and absorbed in, Judah that they could hope for restored vitality. This feeling colors all the prophet's language and darkens his mental view. His love is disquieted and saddened by the prospect; yet his trust in Jehovah triumphs over all. His confidence in the spiritual mercies which are in store for Israel is unshaken, and abides with him as a living certainty. To this confidence he is guided by his unalterable conviction of the Lord's love for his people; he has learned that 'God is love.' Hosea's wedded life is the outward symbolizing of this truth, and taught that man should in like manner love his fellow. Those who were embraced in the arms of one Father should love as brethren; they should have that filial affection to Jehovah which none could feel for a heathen deity, and that affection for one another which can reign only in a united family. These ideas will be found to run through the whole book, and to underlie each rebuke, prophecy, and expostulation."—Pulpit Com.

Synopsis.

(According to Angus.)

This Book may be divided into Two Parts:

I. A Symbolical Narrative....chaps. i.—iii.

II. Prophetic Discourses......chaps. iv.—xiv.

(According to Horne.)

Into Five Sections or Discourses:

Discourse I. ....i.—iii.
Discourse II. ....iv.—vi. 3.
Discourse III. ....vi. 4—viii.
Discourse IV. ....ix.—xiii. 8.
Discourse V. ....xiii. 9—xiv.

CHAPTER THE FIRST.

1. word, etc., the common formula for prophetic inspiration.[a] **Hosea,** the name means deliverance, safety. He was prob. an Israelite.[b] "His rough Aramaising diction indicates the north as his residence."[c] **Beeri,** an unknown name, not the same as Beerah in 1 Chr. v. 6. **Uzziah,** etc., "the kings here mentioned are the same as those in Isaiah i. 1, with the addition of Jeroboam, the son of Joash (comp. 2 Ki. xiv. 23—28), a very prosperous but wicked king who greatly promoted idolatry in Israel."—Barrows. **Jeroboam,** the second, in whose reign the kingdom of the Ten Tribes rose to the highest pitch of prosperity. After Jeroboam a period of anarchy ensued.

Scripture, Kings, and Truth (vs. 1).—This verse leads us to consider them. I. The essence of Scripture. 1. It is a word; 2. A Divine word; 3. Concerning men; 4. A Divine word concerning man coming through man. II. The mortality of kings, kings die. 1. This fact is a blessing; 2. A lesson. III. The perpetuity of truth. 1. Adapted to all generations; 2. Is necessary for all generations.—Thomas.

The Prophecies of Hosea.—The prophecies of Hosea were addressed immediately to the kingdom of the Ten Tribes, yet so that he did not overlook Judah; for he considered the two kingdoms of Judah and Israel as constituting together the covenant people of God. As it is generally agreed that Isaiah began to prophesy in the last year of Uzziah's reign, or but a few years before his death, while Hosea prophesied in the reign of Jeroboam II., the great-grandson of Jehu, who died about twenty-six years before Uzziah, it follows that Hosea, though partly contemporary with Isaiah, was called to the prophetic work at an earlier period. If we suppose him to have commenced prophesying two years before the death of Jeroboam, and then add the remaining twenty-six years of Uzziah's reign, the sixteen of Jotham, the sixteen of Ahaz, and two of the first years of Hezekiah, we shall have a period of sixty-two years. To Israel this was a calamitous period, embracing four usurpations and murders of the reigning sovereigns, and three invasions of the Assyrians. In the last of those Hosea, king of Israel, became tributary to Shalmaneser, king of Assyria; but he proved unfaithful to his master, and sought the alliance of So, king of Egypt. For this the Assyrian king besieged him in Samaria, and after a siege of three years took him with the city, and put an end to the kingdom of Israel in the fifth year of Hezekiah, king of Judah. Hosea seems to have closed his writings when Hoshea was seeking the help of Egypt, while he had, at the same time, a covenant with Assyria, consequently somewhere early in Hezekiah's reign.—Burrows.——Condition of Israel.—This is the darkest period in the history of Israel. The obligations of the law were relaxed and the claims of religion disregarded. Baal was a rival to Jehovah, and in the dark recesses of groves were practiced the cruel rites of idolatry. The land was distracted by domestic broils and foreign invasion. Might was marshalled against right. Princes and priests were accused of bribery and impiety. Murder and bloodshed were steps to the throne; stream met stream and deluged the land like a flood. Remonstrance was useless; the knowledge of God was wilfully rejected; the people hated rebuke; the more they were called the more they refused; they forbade their prophets to prophesy; and their false prophets hated God greatly. All attempts to heal this disease only showed its incurableness.—Pusey.

2, 3. (2) **beginning .. Hosea,** better, "the beginning of the Lord's talking with Hosea." **wife .. whoredoms,** i. e. one who will be faithless to thee, and so represent the Israelitish nation as unfaithful to God.[d] "His wife is brought before us throughout as a type of Israel; she must at first have been innocent in act to symbolize what Jehovah elsewhere calls 'the kindness of thy (Israel's) youth, the love of thine espousals' (Jer. ii. 2). Upon this view it follows that the language employed is dictated by Hosea's subsequent experience. He could not, of course, know that Gomer had an inclination to infidelity, until it had been exhibited in act." **children of whoredoms,** i. e. either children inheriting

a Comp. Joel i. 1; Mic. i. 1; Zep. i. 1.

b "He prophesied before the captivity of the ten tribes, to whom he chiefly directs his prophecy, and threatens them with a sudden destruction for their great and crying sins, wh. he, in all probability, lived to see brought upon them."
—Lowth.

c "The phrase 'spake with Hosea' in the Heb. is somewhat peculiar; it seems to denote the internal converse which the Divine Spirit held with one who was intended to impart the communications he received to others."
—Spk. Com.

"There is no teacher of divine truth to be compared for one moment for excellence so deep and great as trouble. You can learn but little in the schools. Information, except for temporary purposes, is worthless. A well-informed man may be a nuisance; his information may tend to the increase of his vanity; but when information is followed by a sanctified moral excellence it becomes valuable and helpful for educational and religious purposes."—Peop. Bib.

d Poss. not externally acted, but internally, and in vision, as a pictorial illus. of Israel's unfaithfulness."
—Hengstenberg.

their mother's evil tendencies, or the offspring of an adulterous union. (Comp. ii. 4.)—Camb. B.

Gomer's Unfaithfulness.—

"Now I sit
All lonely, homeless, weary of my life,
Thick darkness round me, and the stars all dumb,
That erst had sung their wondrous tale of joy.
And thou hadst done it all, O faithless one!
O Gomer! whom I loved as never wife
Was loved in Israel, all the wrong is thine!
Thy hand hath spoiled all my tender vines,
Thy foot hath trampled all my pleasant fruits,
Thy sin hath laid my honor in the dust."—Dean Plumptre.

4, 5. (4) **Jezreel,**[a] after the place where Ahab and Jezebel had committed their crimes. The word means, "God will scatter." **avenge,** visit in judgment.[b] **house,** or dynasty, see 2 Ki. xv. 12. **cease the kingdom,** it lasted only some forty or fifty years after the overthrow of Jehu's house. (5) **that day,** or season.[c] **bow,** the chief weapon of the warrior in those days, and the symbol of power.[d] **valley of Jezreel,** "it seemed fitting that this 'battlefield of Palestine' (as the valley of Jezreel had already become) should be the scene of so momentous an event, fitting also that where Jehu had sinned, Jehu's house should be punished. There would have been a 'poetical justice' in such an arrangement, had such been the will of Providence. But there can be no doubt that Hosea had an accurate knowledge of the Assyrians as the destined instruments of Israel's overthrow."—Camb. Bib.

a "No child in the E. receives more than one name at its birth, and this name is generally given in accordance with some particular circumstance existing at the time."—Gadsby.

b 2 Ki. x. 11.

c "The express. day in the Prophets signifies a season marked out by Providence for some extraordinary act of God's justice or mercy."—Lowth.

d Ge. xlix. 24; Job xxix. 20. Comp. 1 Sa. ii. 4; Ps. xviii. 34; Je. xlix. 35.

"If your crossness makes some one else bear a cross, you will not be the one to wear the crown."

Retribution (vs. 5).—I. God's retribution takes away the power of its victim. II. God's retribution despises the prestige of its victim. III. God's retribution defies the opposition of its victim.—Thomas.

Responsibility of the Care of Children.—It is a very solemn and serious matter for you to be entrusted with the care of God's little children. One would think, to see the mating that goes on in society—and it is a beautiful thing in its way—that butterflies were let loose, so light and gay and happy are the hearts that sail together and play around each other. One would think, to hear the cheerful congratulations that accompany the putting out of a young life in the family state, that there was no responsibility connected with the event. And when there begin to be "angels unawares" coming into the household, one after another, how joyous it is! And the silver cups and little congratulatory notes are plenty. But how few there are who feel that, from the time the door of life opens, and a child is born, God has drawn His hand out from near to His own heart and lent something of Himself to the parent, and said, "Keep it till I come; take this, My own child, and educate it for Me, and bring it to heaven, and let its improving and profiting appear when ye and it stand together in the last day."—Beecher.

6, 7. (6) "And she conceived again, and bare a daughter; and He said to him, Call her name Un-Loved, or That-never-knew-a-Father's-Pity; for I will not again have pity—such pity as a Father hath—on the house of Israel, that I should fully forgive them."—G. A. Smith. **Lo-ruhamah,**[e] meaning, "Not pitied." **utterly . . away,** R. V., "that I should in any wise pardon them." (7) **mercy,** in prolonging her day of grace, and restoring her as a nation. **by the Lord,** by special Divine intervention, not by mere human instrumentalities. **not . . by bow,** "Judah, then, was in danger of trusting in warlike equipments, as Isaiah afterwards describes it as doing (Isa. ii. 7). And yet, if Israel, with all his natural strength, could not resist the Assyrian attack, it was clear that the weaker kingdom could only do so by supernatural aid. Comp. Isa. xxxi. 8, xxxvii. 33. 'Battle' should be equipment of war."—Camb. Bib.

e "The birth and naming of this child mark a further phase of the northern kingdom: it is now presented in the character of a daughter who by her own shameless profligacy has utterly lost her father's affection."
—Spk. Com.

Help in God Alone (vs. 7).—Here we learn—1. That all human and material succors are alone and by themselves inadequate; 2. That Divine succors are alone and by themselves adequate; 3. That in all cases such Divine succors are therefore to be solely trusted.—Clark.

8, 9. (8) **weaned,** in the E. children are usually nursed by the mother for nearly three years.[a] (9) **Lo-ammi, i. e. not my people.** Observe the

a "'I am a missionary in my nursery,' once observed a Christian mother. 'Six pair of little eyes are daily watching mamma's looks, and listening to her words, and I wish my children never to see in me that which they may not imitate.' 'The mother lives again,' says Smiles, 'in her children. They

climax in the names. 'Jezreel' announces the judgment; Lo-ruhamah, the withdrawal of Jehovah's affection; Lo-ammi, the treatment of Israel as a foreign people."

10, 11. "The correct arrangement combines vss. 10 and 11 of ch. i. with vs. 1 of ch. ii., and concludes the first chapter with these three verses. which are so closely joined together in sense."—Pul. Com. (10) **Yet .. sea,** the threatenings apply to their national life. Their actual numbers would be preserved. Some think the assurance refers to the ingathering from all nations to the Church of Christ.[a] **in the place,** Israel would return with Judah from captivity, but would not exist as a separate people. The return was the Divine recognition of penitence and conversion. (11) **gathered together,** thus the schism of north and south shall be healed. **one head,** or prince.[b] **out of the land,** i. e. the captive land.

The Destiny of the Race (vss. 10, 11).—I. The race is destined to an indefinite increase in the number of good men. II. The race is destined to a transcendent privilege. 1. To a general conversion to God; 2. To a general adoption into the family of God. III. The race is destined to a common leadership—1. Which shall unite the most hostile; 2. Be by common appointment; 3. And be glorious.—Thomas.

The Future.—
For I dipt into the future, far as human eye could see,
Saw the vision of the world, and all the wonders that would be:
Saw the heavens fill with commerce, argosies of mighty sails,
Pilots of the purple twilight drooping down with costly bales,
Heard the heavens fill with shouting, and there rained a ghastly dew
From the nation's airy navies grappling in the center blue:
Far along the world-wide whisper of the south wind rushing warm,
Were the standards of the peoples plunging through the thunder-storm,
Till the war-drum throbbed no longer, and the battle-flags were furled,
In the Parliament of man, the federation of the world.
There the common sense of most shall hold a fretful realm in awe,
And the kindly earth shall slumber, lapt in universal law.
—Tennyson.

CHAPTER THE SECOND.

"In this second chapter the same cycle of events recurs as in the first, with this difference, that what is expressed by symbol in the one is simply narrated in the other."—Pul. Com. 1—5. (1) **Ammi .. Ruhamah,** the names of the children without the Heb. negative lo. The not would be removed from their names in the day of restoration: ch. i. 11. (2) **mother,** i. e. the nation collectively.[a] **not my wife,** Is. l. 1. **breasts,** Eze. xxiii. 3. (3) **Lest I strip her naked,** "so far the punishment of the adulteress agrees with that customary among the Germans. But the punishment of the Hebrew adulteress is not intended to stop here; death was the penalty she had to fear—death by strangling, according to the Rabbinical explanation of Lev. xx. 10, Deut. xxii. 22, death by stoning, according to Ezekiel in a passage which alludes to the present (Ezek. xvi. 39, 40, comp. John viii. 5). But the prophet speaks here of neither form of punishment, but of death by thirst in the desert. The meaning of the allegory is, that the people of N. Israel shall be put to open shame, and deprived of the rich temporal blessings vouchsafed to them."—Camb. Bib. **born,** Eze. xvi. 4. **wilderness,** comp. Is. lviii. 11; Je. xxxi. 12.[b] **thirst,** as one in a parched desert: Je. ii. 6. (4) **children,** who were devoted to the service of idols. (5) **after my lovers,**[c] away from God, her true and only husband. **bread,** etc., i. e. my food, clothing, and luxuries.

Lot of Woman.—Woman's is comparatively a fixed, a secluded, and a meditative life. She is more the companion of her own thoughts and feelings; and if they are turned to ministers of sorrows, where shall she look for consolation? Her lot is to be wooed and won; and if unhappy in her love, her heart is like some fortress that has been captured, and sacked, and abandoned, and left desolate. How many bright eyes grow dim—how many soft cheeks grow pale—how many lovely forms fade

unconsciously mold themselves after her manner, her speech, her conduct, and her method of life. Her habits become theirs, and her character is visibly repeated in them.' "
—Hom. Com.

a Ro. ix. 25, 29; 1 Pe. ii. 10.

b Most perfectly fulfilled in Messiah, the Christ. "A Jewish rabbi regards the good as the sand, not only in relation to number, but to usefulness. As the sand keeps the sea from breaking in and drowning the world, so the saints keep the world from being drowned by the waves of eternal retribution."
—Pulp. Com.

"O, if this were seen, the happiest youth,—viewing his progress through what perils past, what crosses to ensue, — would shut the book and sit him down and die."
—Shakespeare.

"All that time is lost which might be better employed."
—Rousseau.

a "The Prophet urgently calls upon all who in the northern kingdom still remained firm in their allegiance to Jehovah to come promptly forward, and make an earnest and public protest against the idolatry and wickedness which so widely prevailed."
—Spk. Com.

b Je. vi. 8; Zep. ii. 13.

c "The idols with whom the Israelites committed spiritual fornication; and the idolatrous nations, whose alliance the Israelites court-

away into the tomb, and none can tell the cause that blighted their loveliness? As the dove will clasp its wings to its side, and cover and conceal the arrow that is preying on its vitals, so it is the nature of woman to hide from the world the pangs of wounded affection. The love of a delicate female is always shy and silent. Even when fortunate, she scarcely breathes it to herself; but when otherwise, she buries it in the recesses of her bosom, and there lets it cower and brood among the ruins of her peace. With her, the desire of her heart has failed—the great charm of her existence is at an end. She neglects all the cheerful exercises which gladden the spirits, quicken the pulse, and send the tide of life in healthful currents through the veins. Her rest is broken, the sweet refreshment of sleep is poisoned by melancholy dreams; "dry sorrow drinks her blood," until her enfeebled frame sinks under the slightest external injury. Look for her, after a little while, and you will find friendship weeping over her untimely grave, and wondering that one, who but lately glowed with all the radiance of health and beauty, should so speedily be brought down to "darkness and the worm." You will be told of some casual indisposition that laid her low; but no one knows the mental malady that sapped her strength and made her so easy a prey to the spoiler.—Washington Irving.

ed, and in order to it practised their idolatries."—Lowth.

Je. xxii. 20, 22; Eze. xvi. 33, 36, 37, xxiii. 5, 9.

"During seventeen years I kept an accurate record concerning those who united with the church under my ministry leaving out eleven whose record is unknown, of the remaining 374 one or both parents of 327 were religious, and forty-seven had neither parents pious; seven to one."—Peloubet.

6—8. (6) **hedge,** etc., reference is to "the hindrances which the captivity interposed bet. Israel and her idols."[a] **find her paths,** by which she had been wont to go to her lovers, or idols. (7) **follow,** eagerly. **I will go,** or let me now go. "Her language at present is hardly that of penitence; she is only casting about to be rid of her misery."[b] (8) **I,** Jehovah, the true and the only source of all good. **prepared,** R. V., "used;" bestowed, as offerings, on Baal; the grossest insult to Jehovah. They gave Jehovah's gifts to Baal.

Divine Restraints (vs. 6).—God puts restraints on the sinner here. I. These restraints are manifold. 1. Affliction; 2. Public sentiment; 3. Conscience. II. These restraints are necessary. 1. For the sinner himself; 2. For the world; 3. For the Church.—Thomas.

A Return to God.—A popular and successful young minister in America became entangled in the meshes of infidelity, left the pulpit, joined an infidel club, and derided the name he had preached to others as the Saviour of the world. But he sickened, and came to his death-bed. His friends gathered round him, and tried to comfort him with their cold and icy theories, but in vain. The old thought came back to him—the old experience came before him. He said, "Wife, bring me my Greek Testament." Upon his bed he turned to the fifteenth chapter of the First Epistle to the Corinthians. When he had finished the chapter, great tears of joy rolled down his cheeks. He closed the book, and said, "Wife, back again at last upon the old rock to die."—Spurgeon.

a "I will obstruct the roving vagrancy after thy idols; I will stop it up by afflictions and banishment into a far-off land; and thus I will show the vanity of thy idols, who cannot save thee in thy distress."—Wordsworth.

Job xix. 8; Le. iii. 7, 9.

b "Her afflictions will bring her to a sense of her duty, and the happiness she enjoyed as long as she cleaved steadfastly unto God."—Lowth.

9—11. (9) **return,** R. V., "Therefore will I take back my corn," etc. **recover,** or take back. (10) **lewdness,** R. V. marg., "shame." The figure of a faithless female being continued, the calamities of Israel are pictured in the extreme deplorableness of her condition. **sight..lovers,** the idols who will be wholly helpless to deliver her. (11) **mirth,** etc., the characteristic of her festal times.[c]

Royal Continency.—Antiochus, the third king of Macedon, perceiving a growing passion for the priestess of Diana, a young lady of incomparable beauty, left his palace and retired for some time into Ephesus; lest the sight of such an alluring object might tempt him to transgress against the piety due to her order.—L. M. Stretch.

c These had been arranged by Jeroboam I.—1 Ki. xii. 32.

"When men will not know God as the giver of all their temporal blessings, they shall be compelled to know him as the withholder of them."—Fausset.

12, 13. (12) **destroy,** marg. make desolate. **my rewards,** vs. 5. **forest,** "a frequent feature in descriptions of desolation (comp. Isa. v. 6, vii. 23, xxxii. 13; Mic. iii. 12). 'A forest,' however, is misleading; the word often means low, tangled brushwood. The idea in the prophet's mind is inaccessibility, not stateliness (like that of forest-trees)." **beasts,** i. e. wild beasts. (13) **visit upon,** the usual term for bringing judgments upon: I will punish her. **days of Baalim,** time of her wilful service to the various forms of Baal.[a] **burned incense,** intended to stand for, and include, all offerings and worship, the entire heathen cult. **earrings, or** nose-rings, Ge. xxiv. 47.

Forgetfulness of God.—Such is the character of all engrossing pas-

a Baal, in the plural Baalim, denotes Baal as worshiped under different characters.

"The tinsel glare upon a sinner is too apt to offend the weak eyes of a saint. Alas! why should he envy him, a little light who is

sion, such is the source of sin to which the soul gives way, in avarice, ambition, worldliness, sensual sin, godless science. The soul at last does not rebel against God; it forgets him. It is taken up with other things, with itself, with the subjects of its thoughts, the objects of its affections, and it has no time for God, because it has no love for him.—Pusey.

14—17. (14) **Therefore,** because without Jehovah's help, Israel will never come to herself and reform. **allure,** Keil thinks that Israel is to be led into the wilderness, not for punishment, but for deliverance from bondage.[a] **comfortably,** lit. to her heart; i. e. tenderly, persuasively.[b] (15) **vineyards, etc.,** i. e. make the land that had become a wilderness again fruitful for her. **valley of Achor,** a rich pasture ground near Jericho; classed with Sharon.[c] **sing,** in the joy of deliverance and restoration.[d] (16) **Ishi,** my husband; the term of endearment, and of pleasant relations. **Baali,** my lord; the term of fear and slavery. (17) **Baalim,** see vs. 13. **remembered,** R. V., "mentioned."

The Valley of Trouble a Door of Hope (vs. 15).—I. The soul was at first betrothed and espoused of God; each several soul ought to be so. II. Here you have the case of a soul that has strayed from God and its rest. III. It has deserted God and gone after its lovers—and what are the results? 1. There is the discipline of disappointment; 2. There is the discipline of deprivation; 3. There is the discipline of desolation.

The Allurement of Love.—Some years ago an affecting incident was reported in reference to the ex-Empress Charlotte, an Austrian princess, whose husband was for a short time Emperor of Mexico. In the year 1867 he was shot by the revolutionists, and his unhappy widow became the victim of melancholy madness, which her physicians gave up all hope of curing. As in similar cases, she returned to the tastes and habits of childhood, one of which was a passion for flowers, and she spent most of her time over them. Their attractiveness for her was touchingly manifested on the occasion in question, when, having eluded the watch of her attendants, she had fled from the castle. When overtaken it was found impossible to induce her to return, except by the use of means which would certainly have proved hurtful. One of her physicians happily bethought himself of her intense affection for flowers; and by showing them from time to time before her, she was gradually lured on her way back to her home. May not this story be taken as an illustration of the way in which God allures wandering souls back to himself by the invitations and promises of the gospel?—Spurgeon.

18—20. (18) **covenant,** etc., Job v. 23. "The language reminds us of Zech. xi. 10, where Jehovah 'breaks his covenant which he has made with all the peoples,' restraining them from injuring the Israelites, and still more of Ezek. xxxiv. 25 (evidently based on this passage). The 'covenant' (Heb. b'rith) is in fact an ordinance imposed by Jehovah; it is not correct to say that it is a 'treaty' between Israel and the wild beasts. Probably 'ordinance' is the original meaning, which was afterwards widened into 'covenant.' Comp. vi. 7; Deut. xxxiii. 9; 2 Kings xi. 4; Jer. xi. 6; Job xxxi. 1; Ps. cv. 10."—Camb. Bible. **break the bow,** indicating security from surrounding enemies. **lie down safely,** Eze. xxxiv. 25. (19) **betroth,** the formality that was preliminary to marriage, and regarded as quite as binding. The new covenant is likened to a marriage covenant bec. there would be so much love and grace in it.[a] **righteousness,** etc., terms assuring the sincerity of the bond, and the deep feeling expressed in it. (20) **faithfulness,** or fidelity.

God's Loving Forgiveness.—A young girl who had run away from home was living a life of sin, and her mother wanted a friend to find her daughter. This friend took a number of photographs of the mother and wrote beneath the sweet face these words: "Come back." Then he took those pictures down into the haunts of sin, and the mission stations, and left them there. Not long after, this daughter was going into a place of sin, and there she saw the face of her mother. The tears ran down her face. so that at first she could not see the words beneath; but she brushed away the tears and looked, and there they were: "Come back." She went out to her old home, and when she put her hand on the latch, the door was opened, and when she stepped in, her mother, with her arms about her, said, "Why, dear child, the door has never been fastened since you went away." The door of God's great heart of love has never

to be shrouded in everlasting darkness?
—Pulp Com.

a "As used here the verb strikingly illus. the difficulty which the Almighty has in persuading the guilty conscience to believe in His love."
—Spk. Com.

b Is. xl. 1, 2.

c Is. lxv. 10.

"The valley of Achor runs up fr. Gilgal towards Bethel. There Achan was stoned, and the Divine indignation removed. The word Achor means trouble, affliction, and it is just possible that from it we get our word ache. The Lord promises to lead Israel to peace and rest through the valley of trouble."
—Bib. Things.

d Ex. xv. 1, 20.

a "A marriage covenant wherein I will display My attributes of righteousness, and equity, of loving-kindness, mercy, and faithfulness."
—Lowth.

"So binding is the betrothal engagement that any improprieties committed by the girl are visited with the severities due to unfaithfulness after marriage."
—Bib. Things.

"It is better to be nobly remembered than nobly born."
—Ruskin.

"Hope is a heavenly bird of passage, with faith and love as its wings."—Munhall.

been closed against his sinning and erring children; it is wide open.—J. Wilbur Chapman.

21—23. (21) **will hear,** R. V., "will answer," and so throughout. This and the following vs. indicate the union of the whole people and land in supplication.[b] (22) **Jezreel,** here used not in its meaning, "God will scatter," but in its meaning, "God will plant." (23) **sow,** the idea in the word Jezreel, sow or plant. **have mercy,** etc., "and I will have a father's pity upon Un-Pitied; and to Not-My-People I will say, My people thou art! and he shall say, My God!" The circle is thus completed on the terms from which we started. The three names which Hosea gave to the children, evil omens of Israel's fate, are reversed, and the people restored to the favor and love of their God.—G. A. Smith. **will say,** etc., Rom. ix. 26; 1 Pe. ii. 10.

God and His Universe (vss. 21—28).—I. That the operations of the universe are under the intelligent direction of the great God. This will —1. Account for the unbroken order of nature; 2. Should impress us with the sanctity of nature. II. That the operations of the universe are generally conducted upon the mediatorial principle. III. That they are mercifully subordinated to the interests of the good.—Thomas.

b "God would hearken to the skies, as it were supplicating Him to fill them with rain to pour on the earth; and the skies again would hearken to the earth begging for a supply of the rain it requires; and again, the earth would hearken to the corn, wine, and oil, begging it to bring them forth; and these again would hear Jezreel, i.e would fulfil Israel's prayers for a supply of them." —Fausset.

CHAPTER THE THIRD.

1—3. (1) **Go yet,** or again. **woman,** prob. the same Gomer, who had been removed from the Prophet. **friend,** the Heb. term means husband. **flagons of wine,** R. V., "cakes of raisins," comp. Isa. xvi. 7; 2 Sam. vi. 19; a superior kind of cake used in royal and sacrificial feasts;[c] a special offering made to idols. (2) **bought her,** why Hosea had to buy his wife back, does not appear; had he lost his rights over by her flight and adultery? (3) **abide,** etc., "rather, 'shalt sit still' (as Isa. xxx. 7; Jer. viii. 14 in A. V.). Gomer is to lead a quiet secluded life; her licentious course is cut short, and her conjugal intercourse may not yet be resumed. This is to last for 'many days,' i. e. as long as is necessary to assure Hosea of Gomer's moral amendment."—Camb. Bib.

c "They seem to symbolize the voluptuous and self-indulgent character of idolatrous rites in general." —Spk. Com.

"Nonsense! there needs no satire on men's rage for gold, their nature is the best one, and excuse." —Bailey.

The Wife's Return.

"Weeping blinding tears,
I took her to myself, and paid the price
(Strange contrast to the dowry of her youth
When first I wooed her); and she came again
To dwell beneath my roof. Yet not for me
The tender hopes of those departed years,
And not for her the freedom and the love
I then bestowed so freely. Sterner rule
Is needed now. In silence and alone,
In shame and sorrow, wailing, fast, and prayer,
She must blot out the stains that made her life
One long pollution."—Plumptre.

4, 5. (4) **children of Israel,** the ten tribes. **without . . teraphim,**[a] even as Hosea's wife was separated for a while from her wifely privileges. "The teraphim were the household gods and the domestic oracles, like the Roman penates. The first mention of them is in Gen. xxxi. 19, and the name occurs fifteen times in the Old Testament. They appear to have been of Syrian or Chaldæan origin."—Pul. Com. (5) **David,** comp. Je. xxx. 9; Eze. xxxiv. 23. **latter days,** Is. ii. 2. The times of Messiah.—S. Kimchi.

God's Grace.—A sinner, telling of his conversion, may at one time say, "If it had not been for that sermon, I should have been a sinner still." Another time, "If it had not been for that person." Another time, "If I had not turned." But when he looks solemnly into the whole case, he says, "Unless He who is exalted a Prince and a Saviour had called me, and the Holy Spirit had brought home the Word, I should have been a lost sinner still."—Bonar.

a "Tutelary household gods, in the shape of human busts cut off at the waist." —Maurer.

"For gold the hireling judge distorts the laws; wealth heap'd on wealth, nor truth nor safety buys, the dangers gather as the treasures rise." —Johnson.

CHAPTER THE FOURTH.

1—5. This chapter "states God's general charge against the people." —G. A. Smith. (1) "Hear the word of Jehovah, sons of Israel! Jehovah hath a quarrel with the inhabitants of the land, for there is no troth nor leal love nor knowledge of God in the land. (2) Perjury and murder and theft and adultery! They break out and blood strikes upon blood." —G. A. Smith. **controversy,** Mic. vi. 2. A judicial ground of complaint, an accusation to make.[b] **no truth,** etc., Pr. iii. 3;[c] Mic. vi. 8. (2) **swearing,** i. e. false swearing. **break out,** or through. Scorning all reasonable bonds and limitations. **blood,** etc., one violent deed follows close on the heels of another. (3) **languish,** Is. xix. 8, xxiv. 4; Joel i. 10, 12. **sea,** used in the Bible of all bodies of water. (4) **strive,** against the prevailing evil. **strive .. priest,** the guilt is not that of the whole people, but of their religious guides. "Let none find fault and none upbraid, for My people are but as their priestlings. O Priest, thou hast stumbled to-day: and stumble to-night shall the prophet with thee." One order of the nation's ministers goes staggering after the other! "And I will destroy thy Mother," presumably the nation herself.—G. A. Smith.

The Fruit of Sin.—"The fruit of sin in time," says Chalmers, "when arrived at full and finished maturity, is just the fruit of sin through eternity. It is merely the sinner reaping what he has sown. It makes no violent or desultory step, from sin in time to hell in eternity. The one emerges from the other, as does the fruit from the flower."—Hom. Com.

6—8. (6) **lack of knowledge,** of the true principles of religion,[a] due to the ignorance of the priests. **no priest,** though God regarded them before as a nation of priests.[b] **forget,** or purposely ignore. (7) **increased,** or Divinely blessed.[c] **sinned,** etc., employing their influence in accelerating the religious degeneracy of the nation." (8) **eat,** etc., fig. for seeking their own advantage from the idolatries of the people. **set .. iniquity,** they encourage the people in their idolatry.

Knowledge.—Some years ago a vessel sailing on the northern coast of South America was seen to make signals of distress. When hailed by another vessel, they reported themselves as "dying for water!" "Dip it up, then," was the response; "you are in the mouth of the Amazon river." There was fresh water all around them, they had nothing to do but to dip it up, and yet they were dying of thirst. How often are men ignorant of their mercies! How sad that they should perish for lack of knowledge! Jesus is near the seeker even when he is tossed upon the oceans of doubt. The sinner has but to stoop down and drink and live; and yet he is ready to perish, as if salvation were hard to find.—Spurgeon.

9—11. (9) **like .. priest,** Is. xxiv. 2. **punish them,** i. e. both of them, those that go astray and those that lead astray. (10) **eat,** vs. 8. **not increase,** licentiousness places limits on the natural increase of a population. (11) **new wine,** or drunkenness.[d] Such vicious self-indulgences always deprive men of their judgment, and darken their understanding.[e]

The Reciprocal Influence of Priesthood and People (vs. 9).—"Like priest, like people." I. There is sometimes a disgraceful reciprocal influence. 1. When the true priest becomes like the people; 2. When the people become like a bad priest. II. There is sometimes an honorable reciprocal influence. 1. When people become like a true priest; 2. When the true priest has succeeded in making the people like him.—Thomas.

12—14. (12) **stocks,** Je. ii. 27; Ha. ii. 19. By the "stocks" is meant an idol carved out of wood; while the staff may likewise have an image carved at the top for idolatrous purposes, or it may denote a mode of divination by a staff which by the way it fell determined their course.—Pul. Com.[f] (13) **sacrifice,** etc., Is. i. 29, etc.[g] (14) **I will not,** this is an emphatic statement that it is to be expected that the daughters of such people would sin. **themselves,** i. e. the fathers of Israel, or perhaps even the priests.

Divination by Rods.—During our stay in Constantinople we were fortunate in meeting with one specimen of great antiquity and of con-

[b] "The expression is taken from the actions or pleas wh. one man hath against another for injuries or damages received."—Lowth.

[c] "Integrity and mercy or compassionate sympathy make up the sum of man's duty to man."—Spk. Com.

"Christ never gave any one the command to march until he had first shouldered arms—the cross."

[a] See 2 Chr. xi. 14.

[b] Ex. xix. 6.

[c] "The greater were the favors I heaped upon them, the more presumptuously they sinned against Me."—Lowth.

[d] Is. xxviii. 1, 7, 8.

[e] "A moral truth applicable to all times. The special ref. here is to the licentious orgies connected with the Syrian worship, wh. lured Israel away from the pure worship of God."—Fausset. Am. iv. 1.

[f] "The false prophets of old often pretended to divine and even perform miracles with their staves, ... just as our sleight of hand men with their wands pretend to do so many wonderful things, though it is the quickness of their hands and not their wands at all."—Gadsby.

[g] Is. lvii. 5, 7; Eze. vi. 13, xx. 28.

"Think what it would be if all our men had the earnestness

of Wesley and the faith of Gordon, if all our women had the saintliness of Hilda and the self-devotion of Elizabeth Fry."—Arch-deacon Sinclair.

siderable Biblical interest. This was a beautiful alabaster bas-relief, in excellent preservation, representing the ancient practice of shabdomancy, or divination by rods. There is one allusion to this form of superstition in Hosea iv. 12, from which it appears that the revolted Israelites had adopted it, in common with so many other heathen practices: "My people ask counsel at their stocks, and their staff declareth unto them." One mode of divining by this means was to set up a number of rods in the earth, and when they fell, during the muttering of certain verses and incantations, to derive the wished-for passages from the direction of the fall. But another method was for a person to take a rod and measure its length by spans, saying each time alternately, "I will go: I will not go;" or, "I will do: I will forbear;" and then he decided, according to the alternative which was associated with the last span. It is this second method that is represented in the bas-relief we are describing. A woman is the diviner, and two persons are consulting her, and waiting her decision with an interest evidently not unmixed with fear. This alabaster was drawn up a few years since by some fishermen from the Bosphorus, near its entrance to the Black Sea, opposite the sacred promontory of Jupiter Oarios, on which was a temple to which mariners used to resort and pray for favorable winds. It is supposed to date five hundred years before Christ.—A. Thomas.

a "Despairing of Israel, the Prophet has still some hope of Judah, whom, therefore, he will fain save from becoming involved in Israel's sin."—Spk. Com.

b Comp. Ho. ix. 15, xii. 11; Am. iv. 5, v. 5.

c "Leave him to his fate."

"Fellowship does not mean every fellow in his own little sectarian rowboat. It means fellows, comrades, on the old ship of Zion." — J. F. Cowan.

15—19. (15) G. A. Smith says "this obvious parenthesis may be either by Hosea or a later writer; the latter is more probable." **Judah offend,** this is a gracious warning for the kingdom of Judah, wh. was in danger of being led away into the idolatries of the sister-kingdom.[a] **Gilgal,** noted for the worship of idol-gods.[b] **Beth-aven,** same as Bethel, where Jeroboam's calf-worship was established. **The Lord liveth,** comp. Am. v. 5. There seems to be a ref. to going to Beersheba, the well of the oath. (16) **heifer,** "Yea, like a wild heifer Israel has gone wild. How now can Jehovah feed them like a lamb in a broad meadow?"—G. A. Smith. (17) **joined to idols,** wholly devoted to idols. **let him alone,** cease attempting to restrain or to change him.[c] (18) **Their drink .. continually,** "When their carousal is over they indulge in lewdness." When tired of one sin they plunge into another.—Camb. B. **her rulers,** etc., R. V. "her rulers dearly love shame." (19) **wind,** etc., "the Assyrian tempest," the storm-wind of Divine judgment.

Retributive Justice.—

Nature has her laws,
That will not brook infringement, in all time,
All circumstances, all states, in every clime,
She holds aloft the same avenging sword;
And, sitting on her boundless throne sublime,
The vials of her wrath, with justice stored,
Shall, in her own good hour, on all that's ill be poured.
—Percival.

CHAPTER THE FIFTH.

1, 2. (1) **Hear,** etc., see Joel i. 2; Mic. i. 2; Is. i. 2. **house of Israel,** the northern nation. **house .. king,** the royal court, including the court officers. **judgment,** or sentence. **snare,** or such a snare as may be found on Mizpah, spread to catch birds, etc.[d] **Mizpah,** prob. a hill in Gilead. **Tabor,** Jer. iv. 6, 12, 14. (2) **profound,** "are gone deep in corrupting."—Camb. B. **a rebuker,** "but I am bent upon chastisement for them all."—Pul. Com.

d "Ye have laid snares for others, just as hunters spread their nets upon mountains and hills to catch their prey." — Lowth.

National Depravity (vss. 1—3).—1. Priests and people are involved in it; 2. Unfaithfulness to God is a proof of it; 3. The Judge of the world is cognisant of it.—Thomas.

3—5. (3) **know Ephraim,** have full understanding of all his wilfulness and sin. **not hid,** Ps. lxix. 5. (4) R. V. "Their doings will not suffer them to turn." (5) **pride,** self-will, and self-conceit, which are the secret force of idolatry. This pride should be openly humbled.[e]

e "Trans. 'Therefore shall be humbled the pride of Israel in his own sight.'"—Spk. Com.

Necessary Preliminaries to a Godly Life (vs. 4).—How are men to frame their doings as to turn to God? I. By thinking on certain subjects. II. By thinking of those subjects in a certain way. 1. With concentration; 2. With persistency; 3. With devotion. III. By thinking on certain subjects with a practical intent. Apply:—Thoughtlessness is the curse of humanity; think on the right subjects; think in the right way.—F. W. Robertson.

"Bearing crosses daily might be a play-spell, but bearing the same old cross day in and day out is heroism."

6, 7. (6) **with their flocks,** i.e. prepared to offer large and valuable sacrifices. **not find,** bec. the day of grace will be past, and the day of judgment will be come. **withdrawn,** 1 Sa. xxviii. 15. (7) **treacherously,** as a wife false to her husband. **month,** R. V. "Now shall the new moon devour them with their fields."[a] "The time for punishment has arrived. Instead of watching gladly for the new moon to fix the various hallowed festivals (comp. i.. 11), they should have a 'fearful looking for of judgment' increasing as each new moon arose. If not this, then perhaps the next would bring with it a slaughtering, plundering horde of invaders."—Camb. Bib. **portions,** i. e. portions of land they inherited.[b]

Judgments of God.—Mercy, in this the day of her reign, sovereignly seizes judgment before its time, and works that mighty lever to move mankind. The terrors of the Lord are not permitted to sleep unnoticed and unknown, till the day when they shall overwhelm and overflow all his enemies; they are summoned forth in the interval, and numbered among the all things that work together for good.—Arnot.

a "By a month's devouring is meant a speedy and sudden destruction." —Lowth.

b "The ancient tenures should be brought to an end by the general captivity of the people, and the desolation of the country."—Keil.

8—12. (8) **Gibeah,** four miles N. of Jerus. **Ramah,** two miles further N. The trumpet was to be blown to summon the tribes to repel the Assyrian invader. **after thee,** etc., probably the ancient war-cry of the clan." (9) **day of rebuke,** "time when the sinner's doings are laid bare." (10) **remove the bound,**[c] De. xxvii. 17. **like water,** in full flood. (11) "Ephraim is oppressed, crushed is his right, for he wilfully went after vanity."—G. A. Smith. (12) **moth,** to garments. **rottenness,** to wood.

The Moth, or God's Quiet Method of Destroying (vs. 12).—I. He works decay thus sometimes in the bodies of men. II. And in the enterprises of men. III. And in the kingdoms of men.—Thomas.

c "In various parts we saw stakes driven into the ground, and in others large stones placed to divide the fields, instead of hedgerows, of which there were none."—Gadsby.

13—15. (13) **sickness,** political adversity. **went .. Assyrian,** seeking alliances.[d] **Jareb,** "King Combative, King Pick-Quarrel,—a nick-name for the Assyrian monarch. The verse probably refers to the tribute which Menahun sent to Assyria in 738."—G. A. Smith. **not heal,** bec. no political aid could touch the national moral evils, which were the real cause of calamity. (14) **lion,** roaring and devouring. **young lion,** or strong lion. (15) **go,** etc., waiting until judgment shall effectually humble.[e] **early,** the fig. for earnestly.

d 2 Ki. xv. 19.

e "I will withdraw My presence from them, and will retire from their earthly temple into My heavenly sanctuary; and by making them feel the need of My help in their distress, I will bring them to repentance." —Targum.

God's End and Design in Affliction (vs. 15).—I. The procuring cause of God's afflicting His people. 1. We see how unwilling God is to afflict His people; 2. Whence the many sufferings of the Church arise. II. God's way of afflicting His people: the withdrawing of His gracious presence is the source of greatest suffering to the Church. III. The end of God in thus afflicting His people, "till they acknowledge," etc. 1. God's intention to bring them to sorrow for sin; 2. The power of these means for accomplishing it; affliction concentrates the thoughts of a man upon himself; drives a man off from worldly comforts, and brings him back to God.—Leighton.

A Personal God.—A leader of thought in Germany, famous as a poet, famous as a man of letters, who had through his long literary career fought against the idea of a personal God, when poor in purse, paralytic in body, and in his last week of life, wrote thus to one of his old class-mates, and under its style of banter there is a pathetic minor tone of earnest feeling: "A religious reaction has set in upon me for some time. God knows whether the morphine or the poultices have anything to do with it. It is so. I believe in a personal God. To this we come when we are sick to death and broken down. Do not make a crime of it. If the German people accept the personal king of Prussia in their need, why should not I accept a personal God? My friend, here is a great truth. When health is used up, money used up, and sound senses used up, Christianity begins."—Old Test. Anec.

Punishment of Vice.—Vice is sometimes punished instantly and sometimes gradually. This seems to be the method of Divine procedure.

We have slow and rapid consumption in the bodies of men. We have the gradual decay and the sudden overthrow of empires, the seed-time of evil and the harvest of judgment. The changes of circumstances are so various and frequent, so great and sudden, that the same person, the same people, afford an example of the greatest prosperity and the greatest misery. Henry the Fourth of France was despatched by a sacrilegious hand in his carriage, in the midst of popular applause and the triumphs of peace. Like Herod, the grandson of Herod the Great, he found but one step between adoration and oblivion. The ruin which God inflicts upon the impenitent and presumptuous sinners is often beyond precedent most sudden and most fearful. What folly, then, to trust in man, when God can easily destroy him!—Hom. Com.

"Certain animals have a mysterious sense by which they discern the coming-on of an earthquake, or the presence of death, before the dull eyes and ears of human kind detect them. So there seems to be in man a spiritual sense which under certain conditions feels the presence of God as it cannot at other times."—Phelps.

CHAPTER THE SIXTH.

1—3. (1) **Come,** etc., the language of the humble and penitent. The Prophet indicates what they will say, by-and-by. **he hath torn,** acknowledging judgment to be chastisement from God, and not mere calamity. (2) **two days,** a fig. for a little while. **revive,**[a] quicken from the death of calamity. (3) R. V. "and let us know, let us follow[b] on to know the Lord; his going forth is sure as the morning; and he shall come unto us as the rain, as the latter rain that watereth the earth." **latter .. former,**[c] rain falls in Palestine at two special periods—March and November. "The Israelites count upon the return of God's favor with the same confidence with which, at the autumnal and vernal equinoxes, a farmer counts upon the former and latter rain. Their confidence is excessive; they presume on God's forgiveness without complying with His conditions."—Camb. Bib.

[a] Ps. lxxi. 20, lxxxv. 6, cxxxviii. 7; Is. lvii. 15.

[b] De. xvi. 20; Ps. xxxiv. 14.

[c] Comp. Ps. lxxii. 6; Pr. xvi. 15; Is. lv. 10.

"The climate of Palestine differs from our own. There are 'early' rains at sowing-time. Rain continues from autumn until spring. That which swells the corn and prepares for harvest is the 'latter' rain. Deficiency of rain is fatal to the hopes of the husbandman; regular and abundant rains ensure his crops. Accordingly these rains serve as figures of the spiritual influences of God in producing and perfecting spiritual life and fruitfulness." —Pulp. Com.

Perseverance.—Arago says, in his Autobiography, that his master in mathematics was a word or two of advice which he found in the binding of one of his text-books. Puzzled and discouraged by the difficulties he met with in his early studies, he was almost ready to give over the pursuit. Some words which he found on the waste leaf used to stiffen the cover of his paper-bound text-book caught his eye and interested him. "Impelled," he says, "by an indefinable curiosity, I dampened the cover of the book and carefully unrolled the leaf to see what was on the other side. It proved to be a short letter from D'Alembert to a young person disheartened like myself by the difficulties of mathematical study, and who had written to him for counsel. 'Go on, sir, go on,' was the counsel which D'Alembert gave him. 'The difficulties you meet will resolve themselves as you advance. Proceed, and light will dawn and shine with increasing clearness on your path.' That maxim," says Arago, "was my greatest master in mathematics. Following out those simple words, "Go on, sir, go on," made him the first astronomical mathematician of his age. What Christians it would make of us! what heroes of faith! what sages in holy wisdom should we become, just by acting out that maxim, Go on, sir, go on!—Old Test. Anec.

4—7. (4) **morning cloud,** quickly dispelled by the sunshine. **early dew,** wh. evaporates with the warmth of the day.[b] (5) **hewed,** or cut down. **thy judgments,** "and My judgment goeth forth like the lightning. For leal love have I desired, and not sacrifice; and the knowledge of God more than burnt-offerings."—G. A. Smith. (6) **desired mercy,** 1 Sa. xv. 22; Mic. vi. 6—8. (7) **like men,** R. V. "like Adam." **there,** in the holy Canaan country.

[b] "Bright was the promise of innocent dawn, but the promise was unfulfilled." —F. Jacox.

"The Eden stamped upon our hearts in childhood 'chafes and rubs' in our rough struggles with the world, and soon wears away; too often to leave nothing but a mournful blank remaining."—C. Dickens.

Inconstancy in Religion (vs. 4).—I. Consider the causes of this wretched inconstancy. 1. Men do not consider as they ought the nature of the great change; 2. Are not sufficiently enlightened on the reasons on which they should act; 3. Do not consider the pains they must take and the time they must spend; 4. Are but half resolved; 5. Do not watch against temptation; 6. Neglect the means of grace and duties of religion. II. The certainty that ineffective purposes of amendment will not be accepted instead of true repentance and holiness of life. 1. The Gospel requires these; 2. Transient goodness is not Gospel repentance; 3. No mercy except on Gospel terms. III. What methods we should take if we would not only begin in the ways of religion, but continue to the end. 1. Avoid the errors before mentioned; 2. Meditate on the great truths of religion; 3. Often renew holy resolutions; 4. Bend our chief force against besetting sins; 5. Reflect on the shortness and uncertainty of life. IV. Consider instances of inconstancy in good men. 1. They are apt to change as to diligence and activity in the Christian life; 2. Relax vigilance and circumspection; 3. Decline of sensibility of conscience; 4. Stronger worldly affections; 5. A spirit of devotion not maintained.—H. Grore (1740).

Transitoriness.—When Daguerre was working at his sun-pictures, his great difficulty was to fix them. The light came and imprinted the image; but when the tablet was drawn from the camera, the image had vanished. Our lamentation is like his, our want the same, a fixing solution that shall arrest and detain the fugitive impressions. He discovered the chemical power which turned the evanescent into the durable. There is a Divine agency at hand that can fix the truth upon the heart of man, —God's Holy Spirit.—J. Stoughton.

"What is this prosperity? What this pleasure? Ah! what are my riches, and what my glory? Alas! 'tis like the dew, which flies off at the sight of the morning sun." —Roberts.

"No action, whether foul or fair, is ever done, but it leaves somewhere a record, written by fingers ghostly, as a blessing or a curse, and mostly in the greater weakness or greater strength of the acts which follow it." — Longfellow.

8—11. (8) **Gilead,** prob. ref. to Ramoth-Gilead, chief town of the hilly country beyond Jordan, see ch. xii. 11. It seems to have been peculiarly licentious, and so taken as a representative. **blood,** lit. filled with bloody foot tracks, comp. the striking expression used of Joab in 1 Kings ii. 5. The Gileadites, half-civilized mountaineers, seem to have been distinguished for their ferocity (comp. 2 Kings xv. 25). From the next verse we may perhaps infer that at Gilead too the priests were foremost in lawlessness. (9) **by consent,** R. V. "in the way toward Shechem," "long notorious for the highway robberies committed by its inhabitants." **lewdness,** or enormity. (10) **horrible thing,** "such an apostasy from God as cannot be mentioned without horror." (11) **set an harvest,** R. V. "there is an harvest appointed for thee when I bring again the captivity of my people." "It is as though God said, 'Let not Judah claim superiority over Israel, nor expect to escape Divine judgment more than Israel.'"

Best and Worst.—The best things when abused become the worst: there is no devil like a fallen angel; no enemy to the gospel like an apostate Christian; no hate like the "theological hate;" no war like a religious war; and no corruption like religious corruption. The reasons are not far to seek. The best things are the strongest: they can do most always, most evil when used in an evil way. Bad men know this: Simon the magician was not the only one that has cast a covetous look at Christianity and said, "Give me also this power."—A. J. Morris.

CHAPTER THE SEVENTH.

1—7. The moral degradation of Israel, especially of its ruling class, which, so far from stemming the tide of corruption, applauds and encourages its progress. (1) "When I turn the fortunes of my people, when I heal Israel, then will be manifest Ephraim's guilt and Samaria's wickedness, how they practice falsehood, and the thief cometh in, and bandits roam abroad without."—Ewald. **healed Israel,** i.e. restored the prosperity of the nation. **Ephraim,** the chief of the ten tribes composing the northern nation. **Samaria,** the capital and royal city.[a] **falsehood,** comp. ch. iv. 2.[b] **thief .. robbers,** indicating the prevalence of sins of violence. **spoileth,** or strippeth, alluding to highway robbers. Neither the roads nor the towns were safe. (2) **remember,** observe and keep count, so as in due time to punish. **beset them,** gathering round them like so many witnesses against them, or "entangled them." (3) **king glad,** instead of sorry, as he should be. (4) **as an oven,** a fig. of heated passion.[c] **ceaseth,** etc., when he knows that it is well heated, he ceases from stirring it till the dough is leavened. (5) **day,** "on the day of our king"—some coronation or king's birthday—"the princes were sick with fever from wine. He stretched forth his hand with loose fellows," presumably made them his associates. "Like an oven have they made their hearts with their intriguing. All night their anger sleepeth: in the morning it blazes like a flame of fire. All of them glow like an oven, and devour their rulers:

[a] "The gleam of prosperity wh. Jehovah had accorded His people had only been attended by growing corruption, which, under the princes and usurpers that succeeded (Jeroboam II.) burst forth into the most frightful disorders."—Spk. Com.

[b] Is. lix. 3, 13.

"The transgressions which we see and confess are but like the farmer's small sample which he brings to market, when he has left his granary full at home."—Spurgeon.

[c] "The expression may be metaphorical, implying that they were apostates from God, to whose service they were engaged by the most solemn bond and covenant."—Lowth.

Comp. Je. ix. 2; Mat. xiv. 4; Ja. iv. 4.

"An unclean heart is like an oven heated; and the unclean lusts and affections of it are as the fuel that makes it hot."—Mat. Henry.

a "The simplest form of the oven is that of a hole dug in the earth; the sides being coated with clay, and the bottom laid with pebbles. The bread is placed against the sides and is soon prepared. A rougher way still was to kindle a fire and let it burn fiercely, then to clear away the embers and lay the cakes on the heated spot, covering them up again with the hot ashes which had just been removed." — Bib. Things.

b Compare Arab prov., "Thy grey hairs are the publishers of thy death."

"It is every Christian's duty not only to do his own work, but to help other Christians do their work. Often this last is more important than the first. Think of those that helped Paul!"

all their kings have fallen, without one of them calling on Me."—G. A. Smith. (6) **lie in wait,** as the baker waits when his oven is hot and ready, so these bad men wait to destroy the king when their plans are fully made. **burneth,** stirred up, it then flames forth into action. (7) **kings are fallen,** comp. 2 Ki. xv.

Poison in the Cup.—Cyrus, when a youth, being at the court of his grandfather Cambyses, undertook one day to be a cup-bearer at table. It was the duty of this officer to taste the liquor before it was presented to the King. Cyrus, without performing this ceremony, delivered the cup in a very graceful manner to his grandfather. The king observed the omission, which he imputed to forgetfulness. "No," replied Cyrus, "I was afraid to taste, because I apprehended there was poison in the liquor; for not long since, at an entertainment which you gave, I observed that the lords of your court, after drinking of it, became noisy, quarrelsome, and frantic. Even you, sir, seemed to have forgotten that you were a king."—Whitecross.

8—10. (8) **not turned,** and therefore burned to ashes on one side, and useless.[a] (9) **Strangers,** etc., "by heavy tribute and desolating invasions," for historical truth of this statement see 2 Ki. xiii. 7, xv. 19, 20, 29. **gray hairs,** etc.,[b] "expressive of a reckless people's unconscious decline, whose lapses were taken account of on high." (10) **pride,** etc., ch. v. 5.

Spiritual Declension (vs. 9).—I. The condition here deplored. II. The causes in which it originated. III. The prevention and cure.—Forgetfulness of God (vs. 10).—I. The duty. It is to seek God. 1. Because with Him we have principally to do; 2. We are to seek to enjoy Him; 3. To obey Him; 4. To resemble Him. II. The neglect of this duty. Of neglecters there are—1. Infidels; 2. The careless; 3. The profligate; 4. The moralist; 5. Backsliders and apostates. III. The aggravation of all this neglect. 1. God's benefits to draw; 2. The Bible to instruct; 3. The preaching of the Gospel; 4. The power of conscience; 5. The various associations in life; 6. Public judgments. Appeal—(1) On the ground of gratitude; (2) Danger.—W. Jay.

The Cake not Turned.—The Book of Hosea contains strains of poetry of surpassing splendor; yet here is an illustration from the cottager's kitchen. Let us look at this cake. It is burnt to a cinder on one side, and remains damp and doughy on the other. It is partly underdone, partly overdone; and thus, being neither dough nor bread, it is quite spoiled, and fit only to be thrown away. The metaphor reminds us of the English legend of good King Alfred, when a wanderer in the forest of Selwood: the royal fugitive kept mending his bow and arrows, and forgot to turn the cakes which the neat-herd's wife had committed to his care.—Pulp. Com.

The Natural State of Mankind.—

Low, but majestic, though most strangely formed
Of contradictions and antitheses,
With head of gold and feet of miry clay,
One-half of dust, one-half of deity;
Touching the angel here, and there the brute.
Here, thoughts that wander through eternity;
There, passions sounding all the sties of time;
His rooted selfishness and lofty love,
His little life, his princely intellect,
His pure desires, his hateful selfishness,
His deeds of darkness, and his thoughts of light.—Gilfillan.

c "No doubt it was a policy constantly in the minds of Hebrew statesmen in both kingdoms, how they might secure themselves against either one of these two empires by calling in the assistance of the other."—Spk. Com.

d Le. xxvi. 14—39; De. xxviii. 15—68.

e 2 Ki. xvii. 13, 14.

11, 12. (11) **silly dove,** an Arab prov. says, "There is nothing more simple than a dove." "The prophet compares Ephraim to a dove which gets caught in a net owing to its simplicity, because it has no sense to perceive that, when it goes to gather grains of corn, a net is spread there to catch it. So Ephraim, when they went and asked help from Assyria or from Egypt, (did not perceive) that they went to their hurt, when they sought help from the foreign nations and not from God, in whose hand all is."—Kimchi. **without heart,** or understanding. **Egypt, etc.,** by turns Israel sought the aid of these rival nations, and so secured its own ruin.[c] (12) **net,** the symbol of ruin. **as the fowls,** as the fowler does the birds. **hath heard,** in the Pentateuch,[d] and from the **Prophets.**[e]

The Silliness of Sin (vs. 11).—I. It is too silly to defend its own. **II.** It is too silly to feel its loss. III. It is too silly to escape danger. Apply:—Sin is a folly. The fool and sinner are, in God's vocabulary, convertible terms.—Thomas.

13—16. (13) **Woe,** etc., as Is. iii. 9; Je. xiii. 27. **redeemed them,** "While I would have redeemed them, they spoke lies about Me. And they have never cried unto Me with their heart, but they keep howling on their beds for corn and new wine." No real repentance theirs, but some fear of drought and miscarriage of the harvests, a sensual and servile sorrow in which they wallow. They seek God with no heart, no true appreciation of what He is, but use the senseless means by which the heathen invoke their gods: "they cut themselves, and so apostatize from Me! And yet it was I who disciplined them, I strengthened their arm, but with regard to Me they kept thinking only evil!"—G. A. Smith. **lies,** see Ro. i. 25.[f] (14) **cried,** comp. Jer. iii. 9, 15, vi. 6, 7. **howled,**[g] **assemble,** should be "cut themselves."—Camb. Bib. **for corn,** i.e. to cry and pray for it in famine time. (15) **bound,** the fig. is that of a surgeon's binding to strengthen the sinews. (16) **deceitful bow,** or a slack bow; see Ps. lxxviii. 57. "An ill-contrived bow, which never directs the arrow to the mark." **rage,** etc., Ps. lxxiii. 9.

Ingratitude.—At the battle of the Alma, in September, 1854, a wounded Russian was piteously calling for water. Captain Eddington, whose heart was kind and charitable, ran up to him, and stooping, gave him the much-desired beverage. The wounded man revived. The captain ran forward to join his regiment, when the wretch who had just been restored by his kindness fired and shot him who had been his friend in time of need. So many seek to injure God by returning him evil for good.—Bib. Treasury. Bowstrings (vs. 16).—The strings of African bows are all made of the entrails of animals, a kind of catgut. Moist weather renders it so soft that they cannot shoot with it; should they try it, the string would either instantly break, or it would stretch to such a length that it could not impel the arrow. In consequence of this being the case, I have heard the remark made in Africa that the safest time to travel among the wild bushmen is in wet weather, for then they cannot shoot you.—Campbell. Apostasy of Bricconet.—When those who stand in a commanding position at a time when society is agitated by a great moral struggle, fail to do and suffer what duty requires, their influence, even after death, is often signally mischievous. A noted and pertinent example is that of Bricconet, Bishop of Meaux in France, in the sixteenth century. Catching the spirit of reform at that time pervading Germany and Switzerland, he zealously opposed some grosser errors and views of the Romish Church. Having been twice ambassador to Rome—a bishop, a noble—an intimate friend of the reigning and preceding monarch, he was looked upon as one of the great pillars of the Reformation. A change of government comes, the Inquisition is set up, and Bricconet becomes the first object of their vengeance. "The poor bishop," says D'Aubigné, "who had been so sanguine in the hope to see the Reformation gradually and silently winning its way in men's minds, trembled in dismay when he found at the eleventh hour that it must be purchased by life itself. No alternatives were presented him but death or recantation, and to the latter the minions of the Pope urged him by the most plausible pretexts. Bricconet heard, considered, his resolution was shaken; he staggered under the cross—he stumbled—he fell! The day of his recantation was a dark day for France. What might not have been the consequence if Bricconet had possessed the courage of Luther? If one of the most eminent of the French bishops had ascended the scaffold, and there, like the poor of this world, sealed by martyrdom the truth of the Gospel, would not France herself have been put upon reflection? Would not the blood of the Bishop of Meaux have served, like the blood of Polycarp and Cyprian, as the seed of the Church? And should we not have seen these provinces emancipating themselves in the sixteenth century from the darkness in which they are still enveloped?—Cheever.

f "Pretending to be My worshipers when they all the while worshiped idols; also defrauding Me of the glory of their deliverance, and ascribing it and their other blessings to idols."—Calvin.

g "When they were bemoaning their calamities, as sick men bewail themselves upon a bed of sickness."—Lowth.

"As some eagle pierced with a shaft feathered from its own wing, so many a sufferer, even in this present time, sees and cannot deny that it was his own sin that fledged the arrow of God's judgment, which has pierced him and brought him down."—Trench.

"Whether I chastised them, or strengthened their arms, they imagined mischief against Me."—Grotius.

"Not power I blame, but power obtained by crime. Amidst the glare of courts will not the apostate feel the pangs of guilt, and wish too late for innocence and peace? curst as the tyrant of the infernal realms with gloomy state, and agonizing pomp."—Johnson.

"The canon law denes apostasy to be a wilful departure from that state of faith which any person has professed himself to hold in the Christian Church." — J. Farrar.

a Heb. nesher, the griffon vulture.

b Ps. cxix. 68.

c "Jeroboam, during his sojourn in Egypt, saw Apis worshiped at Memphis, and Mnevis at Heliopolis, in the form of an ox; this, and the temple-cherubim, suggested the idea of the calves set up at Dan and Bethel."—Fausset.

"When children get high notions and despise home, when they throw off parental authority and restraint, they become wayward and self-willed; make the path of life difficult, which their parents had pioneered and made easy. So one who casts off the fear of God and sets up his own, or the authority of others, insults his Maker and injures himself, makes his future miserable, and may be cast off himself at last." — Hom. Com.

CHAPTER THE EIGHTH.

1—7. (1) **thy mouth,** to give notice of the approaching judgment. **as an eagle,**[a] swiftly and fiercely. (2) **cry,** etc., their language right enough, their hearts and their actions far from right. (3) **good,** i.e. the service of God, which alone is true good.[b] (4) **made .. idols,** abusing their wealth to idolatry. **cut off,** rushing thus upon their own destruction. (5) **Thy calf,** R. V. "He hath cast off thy calf, O Samaria," refers to the golden bull, symbol of Jehovah, set up in Samaria and other places."[c] **innocency,** "How long will they be incapable of innocence?" i.e. be unable to clear themselves of guilt.—G. A. Smith. (6) **from Israel,** i.e. he himself made the idol which he calls his God. **workman made it,** a frequent scornful expression of the Prophets. **broken in pieces,** lit. "for chips for firing." (7) **sown,** etc., a proverbial expression to signify that as men's works are, so must their reward be. **it .. stalk,** i.e. no standing corn; **the** harvest fails. **bud,** or flower. **strangers,** foreign enemies, who shall **reap Israel's** harvests.

Idolatry (vss. 5—7).—These verses present to us idolatry in five aspects. 1. As abhorrent to Jehovah; 2. As antagonistic to moral purity; 3. As an outrage on reason; 4. As doomed to destruction; 5. As productive of great evil.—Thomas.

Growth of Sin.—An Eastern apologue tells us of Abdallah, to whom an evil spirit came at first as a fly, sipping an atom of syrup. He did not drive away the creature, and to his surprise it increased to the size of a locust. Being further indulged, the creature went on growing, and made such rapid increase that it became an enormous monster, devoured his substance, and in the end murdered him, leaving in the garden, where it slew its victim, a foot-print six cubits long. Thus does sin grow upon men, till it becomes a giant habit, and slays them.—Beecher. Reaping the Whirlwind.—The history of the Rev. Caleb Colton, M. A., the author of "Lacon," may serve as a striking illustration of the truth of our text. He was a clergyman at Tiverton, popular and clever, but very fond of field-sports. One day, however, a friend suddenly expired while uttering most impious language. The awe-struck minister abjured dogs and guns, and vowed to live henceforth for his sacred calling. For months his preaching was earnest, but at the end of that time he resumed the sporting life. He had, moreover, acquired a love for gambling. A presentation to the vicarage of Kew and Petersham brought him to London, and while numbers were reading with delight his "Lacon; or, Many Things in Few Words; addressed to those who think," the wretched author was sitting far into the night among swindlers. His passion for play involving him in pecuniary difficulties, he was forced to abscond, and his living was declared void. After leading a vagabond life, he perished by his own hand at Fontainebleau, in 1832.—Spurgeon.

d Ps. cxxiv. 3; Pr. i. 12; Je. li. 34.

e Job. xxxix. 5; Je. ii. 24.

8—14. (8) **swallowed up,**[d] it was Israel's fate to be so absorbed by other nations as never again to have a separate national existence. **vessel .. pleasure,** which is of no use, Je. xlviii. 38. (9) **wild ass,**[e] "like a runaway wild ass."—G. A. Smith. Lonely and wilful, forcing its own way, and swayed only by passion. (10) **hired,** i.e. paid for foreign allies and helpers. **gather them,** i.e. now will I restrain their roving propensities. **sorrow a little,** "and then shall they have to cease a little from the anointing of a king and princes."—G. A. Smith. (11) **unto him to sin,** i.e. to him as a ground of punishment. The many altars were the plain and open proof of his idolatry. (12) **written,** R. V. "Though I write for him my law in ten thousand precepts they are counted," etc. De. iv. 6, 8. (13) **flesh,** mere flesh. They do not put their hearts into their sacrifices. **to Egypt,** not literally. Going into Egypt was a proverbial speech for extreme misery. (14) **fire,** "referring to both Israel and Judah.[a] Remarkably enough, we find these words repeated seven times in Amos as a refrain to as many denunciations (Am. i. 4—ii. 5). It seems hardly likely that so original a prophet should have quoted these words; perhaps they were a well-known prophetic commonplace." —Camb. Bib.

a "Judah, though less idolatrous than Israel betrayed want of faith in Jehovah by trusting more to its fenced cities than to Him." — Fausset.

The Divine Letter Neglected by Man (vs. 12).—I. God has written to man. II. The great things in the law are the things which God has written to man. They are great—1. In the matters to which they refer; 2. In the manner in which they are addressed to us; 3. In the influence which they are fitted to exert over us; 4. In the results with which they are followed both here and hereafter. III. Men often count the great things of His law, which God has written to them, as a strange thing. They think them unauthoritative, unintelligible, unsuitable, or uninfluential.

"There are many books which are good, but, like half-pence, there goes a great quantity to a little amount. There are a few silver books, and a very few golden books; but I have one book worth more than all, called the Bible, and that is a book of bank notes." — J. Newton.

CHAPTER THE NINTH.

"Hosea now turns to describe the effects of exile upon the social and religious habits of the people. It must break up at once the joy and the sacredness of their lives. Every pleasure will be removed, every taste offended. Indeed, even now, with their conscience of having deserted Jehovah, they cannot pretend to enjoy the feasts of the Baalim in the same hearty way as the heathen with whom they mix. But, whether or no, the time is near when nature-feasts and all other religious ceremonies—all that makes life glad and regular and solemn—shall be impossible."—G. A. Smith. **1—4.** (1) **Rejoice not,** addressed to the people prob. at harvest thanksgiving-time. **loved a reward,** lit. harlot's hire.[a] **every cornfloor,** alluding to the various local festivals. (2) **winepress,** or vat into wh. the juice of the grape was pressed. **fail in her,** i.e. disappoint her expectations. (3) **dwell,** or permanently abide. **to Egypt,** comp. ch. viii. 13. **unclean things,** "ceremonially unclean, as it would be impossible to conform to the requirements of the Law, according to which the eating of certain animals was prohibited." (4) **not offer, etc.,** lit. pour as a libation.[b] **bread of mourners,** wh. was regarded as unclean.[c] **bread .. soul,** R. V. "for their bread shall be for their appetite," i.e. to satisfy their hunger, they will not be able to pay tithes of their harvest, etc.

[a] Je. xliv. 17.

[b] Ex. xxx. 9; Le. xxiii. 13.

[c] De. xxvi. 14; Je. xvi. 7.

"Or, their bread is for their own soul, for their own self-indulgence, not for God's glory."—Wordsworth.

Bitterness of Sin.—"Life, they say, is sweet; I have found it bitter," said a young artist in the closing scenes of death. Lord Chesterfield echoed the sentiment, when he said, "I have run the silly rounds of business and of pleasure, and have done with them all. I have enjoyed all the pleasures of the world and know their futility, and do not regret their loss. I appraise them at their real value, which is very low; whereas those who have not experienced them always overrate them. They only see the gay outside, and are dazzled with their glare; but I have been behind the scenes. I look back on all that is passed as one of those romantic dreams which opium commonly produces, and I have no wish to repeat the nauseous dose." "Everything that I love, everything that belongs to me, is stricken," cried Napoleon. "Heaven and mankind unite to afflict me." Lord Byron declared that his days were "in the yellow leaf"—"the flowers" and the fruits were gone, and "the worm, the canker, and the grief are mine alone." The poet Burns said in dying hours, "I close my eyes in misery, and open them without hope."

"Man first makes his God like his own corrupt self, or to some corruption in himself; and then, worshiping this ideal of his own, he becomes the more corrupt through copying that corruption. He makes his god in his own image and likeness, the essence and concentration of his own bad passions, and then conforms himself to the likeness, not of God, but of what was most evil in himself."

5—7. (5) **will ye do,** in your captivity, when the times of the solemn and joyous festivals come round, and you find that you cannot keep them in the stranger's land. (6) **destruction,** "from the devastation." **Memphis,** Heb. Moph; the capital of lower Egypt.[a] **pleasant .. silver,** R. V. "their pleasant things of silver," silver ornaments. **nettles,** or thistles, the sign of desolation. (7) **days,** etc., the times of Divine judgment. **a fool,** this is one of the signs of judgment, a judicial blindness is on the national leaders. **great hatred,** R. V. "and because the enmity is great."

The Solemn Days of Life (vs. 5).—I. The day of personal affliction is a solemn day. II. The day of social bereavement. III. The day of death. IV. The day of judgment. Apply:—What will ye do in that day?

8—10. (8) R. V. "Ephraim was a watchman with my God: as for the prophet, a fowler's snare is in all his ways, and enmity in the house of his God." **watchman,** or true prophet. **prophet,** or false prophet. (9) **Gibeah,** Ju. xix. 16—22. (10) **like grapes,** wh. the traveler in a wilderness is delighted to find and quench his thirst with. **firstripe .. fig,** esteemed

[a] "It is curious that this city should be spoken of by Hosea as a burying - place; but travelers tell us that throughout the whole district, monuments and ruins of a great city have been, and still are being, constantly found buried in the sand; whilst the rear forms one unbroken cemetery pyramids, tombs, and mummy pits; so that this vast receptacle for the dead separated the desert from the great city and the cultivated lands." — Bib. Things.

"In the day of prosperity there is a forgetfulness of affliction; and in the day of affliction there is no more remembrance of prosperity. (Ecclus. xi. 25)."—Hom. Com.

a great delicacy in the E. **Baal-peor,** Nu. xxv. 3. **and separated,** etc., R. V. "and consecrated themselves unto the shameful thing and became abominable like that which they loved." **shame,** Besheth, a nickname for Baal.

Grapes in the Wilderness.—The Lord is telling of His gladness in finding these lost sheep, His delight in taking them up when they were wayward, sinful, wandering souls. It gave Him great joy to save them. It was as refreshing to Him as is a cluster of grapes to a traveler in the weary wilderness, whose lips are parched, and whose eyes have long rested on barrenness, and who hails with satisfaction and delight the sight of a vine and its juicy grapes. Dr. Livingstone gives an instance of this feeling: "In latitude 18° we were rewarded with a sight which we had not enjoyed for a year before—large patches of grape-bearing vines. There they stood before my eyes." The traveler thus gives utterance to his delight: "The sight was so entirely unexpected, that I stood for some time gazing at the clusters of grapes with which they were loaded, with no more thought of plucking, than if I had been beholding them in a dream."

b "This terrible threat, or rather, perhaps, prediction, of extermination, addressed to the Ten Tribes in general, but applying most esp. to Ephraim, the most populous of them all, serves to explain the fact that there are so few traces left in the world of their continued existence."—Spk. Com.

c 2 Ki. xv. 29; 1 Chr. v. 26.

11—16. (11) **from the birth,** R. V. "there shall be no birth, and none with child, and no conception." "Such is the retribution for sins against chastity."—Camb. Bib. (12) **bereave them,** comp. De. xxxii. 25. **man left,** better, "that mankind shall not be." An entire riddance shall be made of them and their posterity. **depart from them,** withdrawing My protection and favor.[b] (13) **Tyrus,** or Tyre, Ez. xxvii. 3. (14) **Give them,** in severe Divine judgment. (15) **Gilgal,** the principal focus of idolatrous worship. **mine house,** i.e. the Holy Land. **princes .. revolters,** in Heb. a play on words: their Sarim are Sorerim. (16) **smitten,** with blight. (17) **wanderers,** having no more a settled and permanent home.[c]

Value of Home-training.—The destiny of the rising generation and the fate of the nation is in the "Home School." The great German teacher Fröbel declared that the great motto of the people should be, "Let us live for our children." If Simon had thought of what Judas might have been, would not this have affected his treatment of the boy? What if the mother of Napoleon, and of his brother kings and sister queens, had foreseen what became of those around her humble fireside in Corsica? We do not know what part our children may play in life, what joy or sorrow they may cause to millions yet unborn. Think how much depends upon early training!—Hom. Com.

CHAPTER THE TENTH.

a 1 Ki. xviii. 21; Mat. vi. 24; Ja. iv. 8.

b "Instead of justice and fair dealing injustice increases everywhere, as bitter and poisonous weeds grow up in a field, where there is no care taken to destroy them."—Lowth.

1—4. (1) R. V. "Israel is a luxuriant vine, which putteth forth his fruit," alluding to the years of prosperity—perhaps the reign of Jeroboam II. **goodness .. images,** ch. ii. 8, viii. 4. But the prosperity of Israel only served to increase its idolatry. (2) **divided,** between Jehovah and idols.[a] **now,** or speedily. (3) **no king,** i.e. none worthy of the name, for a king should be judge, counseller, general; hence, they continue, "and the king [whom we have], what can he do for us?" (4) **hemlock,** De. xxix. 18.[b]

The Abuse of Worldly Prosperity (vs. 1).—I. A fruitlessness that makes life worthless. II. A fruitfulness that makes life wicked. 1. When prosperity is used with an exclusive regard to our own selfish ends; 2. For self-indulgence; 3. For self-aggrandizement. III. When it is used without a supreme regard to the claims of God. 1. For the amelioration of human woes; 2. For the dispersion of human ignorance; 3. For the elevation of the human soul. Apply:—(1) How are we, as a nation, using our enormous prosperity? (2) How as individuals?—Thomas.

5—8. (5) **Beth-aven,** i.e. Beth-el, the house of God, wh. has become Beth-aven, the house of vanity, or idols. "The statement is keenly ironical. So far from being able to help their worshipers, the 'calves of Beth-aven' shall occasion the greatest anxiety to their worshipers. **mourn over it,** the idol, Jereboam's calf, the chief of the "calves" just referred to.

priests, Heb. chemarim, prob. idolatrous priests.[c] (6) "Yea, himself shall they pack to Assyria; he shall be offered as tribute to King Pick-Quarrel. Ephraim shall take disgrace, and Israel be ashamed because of his counsel. Undone Samaria! Her king like a chip on the face of the waters! This may refer to one of the revolutions in which the king was murdered. But it seems more appropriate to the final catastrophe of 724-1."—G. A. Smith. **king Jareb,** ch. v. 13. (8) **Aven,** vanity, iniquity, here for the calf idol. **Cover us,** seeking death as a relief from their misery and shame.[d]

Impatient of Life.—A lady once said to Fred. Robertson: "I thought you of all people were like St. Paul, and that you would wish for a heavenlier life as much as he did." He replied in words as true of others as of himself: "First of all, you thought wrong; next, if I do wish to die, it is when I am in pain or out of conceit with life, which happens pretty often, but which I do not consider spirituality. It is only an ungracious way of saying, 'I am dissatisfied with what thou hast given me, and do not like the duties that are mine at all. I am in pain, and want to be out of pain; and I suppose a great many people could say the same piece of sublime discontent."

9—15. (9) **days of Gibeah,** comp. ch. ix. 9. (10) R. V. "when it is my desire I will chastise them." **bind .. furrows,** "when I chastise them for their two iniquities," viz. their revolt from Jehovah, their God, and David, their king. (11) **And Ephraim,** etc., rather, "Ephraim indeed is a heifer broken in and loving to thresh, and I have spared the beauty of her neck; (but now) will I make Ephraim to draw." Israel's punishment is enhanced by contrast with her former prosperity.—Camb. B. **plow,** hard, toilsome work. (12) **Sow to yourselves,** etc., rather, "Sow to yourselves according to righteousness, and ye shall reap in proportion to love;" employ yourselves in works wh. will bring good fruitage. **break .. ground,** i.e. remove your superstitions and your vices.[e] **rain righteousness,** Ps. lxxii. 6; Is. xlv. 8. (13) **plowed wickedness,** Job iv. 8. (14) **Shalman,** etc., 2 Ki. xviii. 34, xix. 13.[f] (15) **great wickedness,** "the phrase seems to come fresh from the mint of Hosea's own indignant feeling."

The Culture of the Heart (vs. 12).—I. The figure employed. 1. Naturally unproductive; 2. Obdurate; 3. Fruitful in weeds. II. The means to be used. 1. Consideration; 2. Repentance. III. The reason assigned. 1. Indecision is inconsistent; 2. It is presumptuous to defer; 3. It is dangerous; 4. Now is God's time.—Whythe.

Reaping.—In the natural world a man expects to reap if he sows; he expects to reap the same kind of seed; he expects to reap more than he sows; and ignorance of the kind of seed sown makes no difference in the reaping. The man who sows "wild oats" will find that the same is true in his experience.—D. L. Moody. Showers of Blessing (vs. 12).—It is said of a good king, "What a blessing is he to the land; he is always raining justice upon us." "You talk to me about the merit of remaining with such a master: he is always raining blessings upon him." A son after the decease of his father, asks, "Where is now the rain of love? alas! I am withered and dry." The figure is also used sarcastically, "Yes, indeed, you are a very good friend, you are always raining favors upon me."—Roberts.

[c] Comp. 2 Ki. xxiii 5; Zeph. i. 4.

"The word is taken fr. a root meaning either the black garment in wh. they were attired; or to resound, referring to their howling cries in their sacred rites."—Calvin.

[d] Lu. xxiii. 30; Re. vi. ix. 6.

"Any act is noble that responds to a law of God. Nothing is cheap that an immortal can do, and no sphere common where an immortal toils."—W. K. Davis.

[e] "Be not content with what ye have cultivated, but bring new ground into cultivation. Grow in grace; forget what is behind; reach forward to what is before; add to your faith virtue, and every Christian grace; and do you, who have been brought to God, bring others to Him."— Wordsworth.

[f] "As Arbela was chiefly noted for its great temple of the goddess Istar, or Ashtoreth, it is possible that the expression used by the Prophet—Beth-Arbel, or Temple of Arbel has special reference to the destruction of the temple in question." — Lenormant.

CHAPTER THE ELEVENTH.

From the thick jungle of Hosea's travail, the eleventh chapter breaks like a high and open mound. The prophet enjoys the first of his two clear visions—that of the Past.—G. A. Smith. **1—4.** (1) **child,** or but a nation in its infant beginnings. Referring to patriarchal times. **called .. Egypt,**[a] "called" him, locally, into the land of Canaan, and morally, to set an example of true religion. Like the portraiture of the Servant of Jehovah in the second part of Isaiah, the description of Israel as Jehovah's Son was held to be at least in part applicable to the one perfect Israelite. The national ideal never realized in the nation was realized in the Christ. The divine purpose so often baffled in the one was completed

[a] "Or, From the time that he (Israel) was in Egypt, I called him My son."—Bengel.

Ex. iv. 22, 23; Mat. ii. 15. "St. Mat. apparently quotes these words, not to prove anything, but in order to point out the

in the other.—Camb. Bib. (2) **As they called, i.e. prophets, etc.,** sent by God. **went from them,** turned away, avoiding these advisers. **Baalim,** a plural word.[b] (3) **to go,** i.e. to walk, to go alone; to use his feet.[c] De. i. 31. **I healed them,** or purposed correction and training by My dealings with them. (4) **drew them,** Song Sol. i. 4.[d] **cords .. man,** with the persuasions a man might use with his fellow man. **yoke,** etc., rather, "that lift up the yoke over their cheeks." Jehovah compares himself to a considerate master, who raises the yoke from the neck and cheeks of the animal, that it may eat its food more conveniently. **I laid meat,** etc., rather, "(dealing) gently with him I gave him food."

Graven Images (vs. 2).—We read frequently of graven images and of molten images, and the words are become so familiar, as names of idolatrous images, that although they are not well chosen to express the Hebrew names, it seems not advisable to change them for others, that might more exactly correspond with the original. The graven image was not a thing wrought in metal by the tool of the workman we should now call an engraver; nor was the molten image an image made of metal, or any other substance melted and shaped in a mold. In fact, the graven image and the molten image are the same thing, under different names. The images of the ancient idolaters were first cut out of wood by the carpenter, as is very evident from the Prophet Isaiah. This figure of wood was overlaid with plates either of gold or silver, or sometimes perhaps of an inferior metal; and in this finished state it was called a graven image (i.e. a carved image) in reference to the inner solid figure of wood, and a molten (i.e. an overlaid, or covered) image in reference to the outer metallic case or covering. Sometimes both epithets are applied to it at once. "I will cut off the graven and molten image" (Nahum i. 14). Again, "What profiteth the graven and molten image?" (Hab. ii. 18). It is on account of this metallic case that we find a founder employed to make a graven image (Judges xvii. 3); and that we read in Is. xl. 19, of a workman that melteth a graven image; and in another place (chap. xliv.) we find the question, "Who hath molten a graven image?" In these two passages the words should be overlayeth, and overlaid.—Horsley.

5—7. (5) **not return,** literally.[a] Previously the Prophet had spoken of such return mystically (ch. viii. 13, ix. 3). **refused to return,** in penitence to Jehovah. (6) **branches,** lit. bars, or defenders.[b] **own counsels,** seeking idols, and thinking to rely on Egypt. (7) **bent,** fully purposed.[c]

Shall Consume.—Guilt and punishment are bound together. One should act as a warning to the other. The threat of punishment is a merciful declaration to some, though a terror to others. If there are rocks and shoals in the ocean of life, it is not cruelty to chart them down; it is eminent and great mercy.—Beecher.

8, 9. (8) **How, etc.,**[d] the expression of strong reluctance and deep pain. **deliver thee,** up to thine enemies. **Admah? .. Zeboim?** Ge. xix. 24; De. xxix. 23. **heart,** etc., comp. Is. lxiii. 15; Je. xxxi. 20. **my repentings are kindled,** even this inaccurate rendering cannot quite conceal the fine intuition of the prophet. By partly humanizing God's nature, he as it were divinizes man's. Human sympathy is but a rill from the mighty stream of God's tender mercy. A closer rendering would be, "I am wholly overcome with sympathy."—Camb. Bib. (9) **fierceness,** etc., God will not act as a man in uncontrolled rage, but with Divine wisdom and goodness order penalty so that it may prove corrective. **enter .. city,**[e] better. "I will not come to exterminate."

God's Feeling in the Face of Man's Obstinacy (vss. 8, 9).—Three things suggested. I. That man is able to resist God in the dispensation of His mercy. The idea that we are governed by some Divine fate arises—1. From unacquaintance with the nature of the human will; 2. Unacquaintance with God's moral government; 3. Misinterpretation of some particular portions of God's Word. II. That man's resistance renders it necessary on God's part to give him up. 1. The most applicable means is insufficient for recovering him; 2. The only means is insufficient for recovering him. III. That there is an infinite, compassionate reluctance on God's part to give up man. 1. The relation that exists between God and man renders Him reluctant to give him up; 2. God's

relation of God's former dealings with the latter, the beginning and the close, what relates to the body, and what relates to the head."—Pusey.

b "Or, images of Baal set up in different places."—Fausset.

Ho. ii. 13, xiii. 1.

c "As a mother doth teach her child to go, leading it by the arms, protecting him, and providing for him in the wilderness."—Lowth.

d Jno. xii. 32.

"One backslider will do more harm than twenty Christian men can do good."—W. E. Blackstone.

"Many Christians get cold warming themselves by this world's fires."—A. J. Gordon.

a The inclination of the people was to seek shelter in Egypt. This God would not permit.

b "His villages, which are the branches or dependencies of cities."—Calvin.

c "Are hung and fastened to apostasy from Me, instead of allegiance to Me."—Wordsworth.

d "This is one of the most pathetic passages in all Scripture, and is accordingly marked with the parallelism wh. is so characteristic of poetry in Hebrew in a much higher degree than is usual with Hosea."—Spk. Com.

e "I am not one such as human dwellers in a city, who take cruel vengeance; I save those whom I correct."—S. Jerome.

knowledge of man renders Him reluctant to give him up; 3. God's dealings with man prove that He is infinite in mercy, reluctant to give him up.—J. A. Morris.

10—12. (10) **shall walk,** by-and-by, in the days of restoration after chastisement. **They shall walk,** etc., rather, "They shall go after Jehovah as after a lion that roareth; for he himself shall roar and sons shall come hurrying from the west." (11) **tremble as a bird,** or "fly hastily as a flock of birds." **place .. houses,** comp. habits of migratory birds, wh. return year by year to the same spot. (12) **Ephraim,** here standing for the northern nation. **Judah,** the kingdom of the two tribes. **yet ruleth .. saints,** "is yet wayward towards God, and towards the faithful Holy One."

"I will not come in wrath." —Maurer.

"If you've tried and have not won, never stop for crying; all that's great and good is done just by patient trying."

The Hypocrite.—

His virtues being o'erdone, his face
Too grave, his prayers too long, his charities
Too pompously attended, and his speech
Larded too frequently, and out of time,
With serious phraseology—were rents
That in his garments ope'd in spite of him,
Through which the well-accustomed eye could see
The rottenness of his heart.—Pollok.

CHAPTER THE TWELFTH.

"In chaps. xii. and xiii. Hosea turns upon the now familiar trail of his argument, full of the Divine jealousy, determined to give the people one other chance to turn; but if they will not, he at least will justify God's relinquishment of them."—G. A. Smith. **1, 2.** (1) **feedeth on wind,** a prov. expression, signifying labor in vain. **east wind,** blighting and desolating: a fig. of the idol helps, and national alliances, wh. Israel sought. **lies,** by wh. they deceive themselves. **desolation,** better, "violence." **oil .. Egypt,** as a present or tribute, to win favor and protection.[a] (2) **controversy,** or charges to urge against. **Jacob,** here used for Judah.

Worthless Soul-food (vs. 1).—"Wind." I. Sensual indulgences are worthless soul-food. II. So are worldly distinctions. III. And also religious formalities.—Thomas.

Oil (vs. 1).—Syria is a land in which olives abound, and particularly that part of it which the people of Israel inhabited. The Israelites, in the decline of their national glory, carried the produce of their olive plantations into Egypt, as a tribute to their ancient oppressors, or as a present to conciliate their favor, and obtain their assistance, in the sanguinary wars which they were often compelled to wage with the neighboring states. Oil is now presented in the East, to be burnt in honor of the dead, whom they reverence with a religious kind of homage. Mr. Harmer thinks it most natural to suppose that the Prophet Hosea refers to a similar practice, when he upbraids the Israelites with carrying oil into Egypt. They did not carry it thither in the way of lawful commerce; for they carried it to Tyre without reproof, to barter it for other goods. But if they burnt oil in those early times in honor of their idols, and their departed friends, and the Jews sent it into Egypt with that intention, it is no wonder the Prophet so severely reproaches them for their conduct. Oil is in modern times very often presented to the objects of religious veneration in Barbary and Egypt. The Algerines, according to Pitts, when they are in the mouth of the straits, throw a bundle of wax candles, together with a pot of oil, overboard, as a present to the marabot or saint who lies entombed there, on the Barbary shore, near the sea.—Paxton.

3—6. "Two episodes in the history of Jacob are applied to the spiritual wants of his descendants. Jacob in the very womb seemed ambitious of the blessing, and when a grown man, he wrestled with the angel for a still higher blessing than before. But, as we interpret the Prophet's thought, the Israelites, instead of justifying their name, and 'waiting upon their God,' have denied Jehovah, and sought for weak human help."—Camb. Bib. (3) **took .. heel, Ge. xxv. 26.** A symbol of his spirit

[a] "Oil was an important article of commerce with Egypt, as the oil-olive does not thrive in that country. Along the Nile the avenues are of mulberry, sycamore and acacia trees. In Palestine the olives were abundant enough to make olive oil an article of export." —Biblical Things.

"No one is strong enough and wise enough to be safe in constant intercourse with persons of wrong principle and false religion, any more than one is healthy enough to be safe physically in a malarial or fever-laden atmosphere. Indeed, one who goes by choice into bad company and loves to remain there is already more than half fallen. The only time when one is safe in bad company is when he is laboring to do them good." —Peloubet.

as the supplanter. **by his strength,** R. V., "in his manhood," when he wrestled with the angel. **power with God,** Ge. xxxii. 24. (4) angel, who was the manifested Jehovah; God in human form for a man's apprehension. **wept,** this is not stated in Genesis.[a] **found him,** or met with him, Ge. xxxv. 9. **spake with us,** better, "with him." (5) **his memorial,** Ex. iii. 15. "A name wh. is also a remembrancer of the great characteristic of the Being spoken of." (6) **turn thou,** from wilfulness and idolatry back to God. **keep mercy,** etc., Mi. vi. 8.

Beth-el (vs. 4).—1. The most household name of all the villages or towns of the Bible; 2. The home of the patriarchs; 3. Jacob came here; 4. It has come to be one of the most pathetic names in the Bible; 5. Its after-history; 6. What is it now?—Hood.

7—11. (7) **He . . merchant,** "Canaan! in his hand are deceitful balances; he loveth to extort."[b] **balances of deceit,** Am. viii. 5; Mi. vi. 11. (8) **become rich,** Ephraim in this verse boasts of his riches, though procured by fraud and violence, while he maintains at the same time that he has not sinned thereby so as to expose himself to punishment or deserve severe reprehension."—Pul. Com. (9) **will yet make thee,** etc., "will again make thee to dwell in tents, as in the days of the festal season." A contrast: you have dwelt in booths for festivity, soon you shall do so by compulsion. **feast,** Le. xxiii. 42, 43. (10) **similitudes,** comparisons, parables, types, etc.[c] (11) R. V., "Is Gilead iniquity? they are altogether vanity." **Gilead,** E. of Jordan. **Gilgal,** W. of Jordan; together representing the whole country. **heaps,** i.e. no better than heaps. The verse points to the ruin of those two famous centers of idolatry.

God's Method of Teaching the Great Teachers of the World (vs. 10).—I. By visions which serve to show—1. The distinguishing glory of the human mind; 2. The accessibility of the human mind to God. II. By similitude. 1. It makes the spiritual more attractive; 2. It makes the material appear more divine.

12—14. (12) **fled,** Ge. xxviii. 5. **served, etc.,** Ge. xxix. 20, 28. (13) **prophet,** Ex. xii. 50, 51, xiii. 3. Hosea contrasts the helplessness and the hardships of Jacob-Israel with the wonderful deliverance and preservation of his descendants. (14) **leave his blood,**[d] or his blood-guiltiness to bring down on him the merited punishment. **his reproach,** or blasphemy.

a "From bodily wrestling Jacob betook him to spiritual weapons; he poured forth tears with earnest supplications and prayers, and strove not so much for victory as for a blessing."—Lowth.

"The heavenly ladder is changed into steps to hell; and devils are dancing for joy where angels came down from heaven to earth."—T. Fuller.

b "A play on the double sense of the Heb. word Canaan, i.e. a Canaanite and a merchant."—Fausset.

c "It was an ancient custom in the E. parts of the world to convey instructions under symbols and sacred hieroglyphics."—Lowth.

d "Not take away the guilt and penalty of the innocent blood shed by Ephraim in general, and to Moloch in particular." — Fausset.

"Being cross as a bear because you are crossed, is the opposite of bearing the cross."

CHAPTER THE THIRTEENTH.

1—5. (1) **trembling, R. V., "there was trembling," such was the fear** inspired, and the deference paid to the authority of that powerful tribe.[a] —Pul. Com. **died, i. e.** "sealed their doom as a nation," ceased to be a factor in the progress of the world. (2) **kiss the calves,** comp. 1 Ki. xix. 18. An act of adoration to the golden calves. (3) **morning dew,** these, in the E., suddenly and utterly vanish when the sun rises.[b] **chaff,** comp. Ps. i. 4, xxxv. 5; Is. xvii. 13. **chimney,** or "lattice-work placed under the wall-plate of the roof." (4) **Yet,** etc., Is. xliii. 11. (5) **I did know,** an expressive sentence, meaning, "it was indeed I who did it." I took special care of thee in the long wilderness-time.

The Life of the Wicked (vs. 3)—I. It is deceptive. II. It is worthless. III. It is evanescent. IV. It is offensive.—Thomas.

The Vanity of Human Life.—

Like to the falling of a star,
Or as the flight of eagles are;
Or like the fresh spring's gaudy hue,
Or silver drops of morning dew;
Or like a wind that chafes the flood,
Or bubbles which on water stood—
E'en such is man, whose borrowed light
Is straight called in, and paid to-night,
The wind blows out, the bubble dies,
The spring entombed in autumn lies,
The dew dries up, the star is shot,
The flight is past,—and man forgot.—H. King.

a "His words were listened to with deference, through the power with wh. he could back them. For the pre-eminency of the tribe of Ephraim see Ge. xlix. 26; De. xxxiii. 17; Ju. viii. 1, xii. 1.

b Da. ii. 35; Ho. vi. 4.

We might be like Bartholomew, who is said to have had a hundred prayers for the morning, and as many for the evening, and all be of no avail. "Fervency of spirit" is that which avails much.—Bp. Hall.

6—8. (6) **According,** etc., Camb. B., "when they fed they waxed full," i. e. the more I took care of them, the more perversely they acted towards me. (7) **as a leopard,** "leopards lurk in thickets, and thence spring on their victims." (8) **bear,** she-bear, in the time of her most dangerous irritation. **caul,** or chamber; the pericardium; the membrane enclosing the heart.

Prosperity Injurious (vs. 6).—I. The evils of unsanctified prosperity. 1. Selfish indulgence; 2. Pride; 3. Unmindfulness of God. II. The instruction derived from this example. 1. A very humbling view of human nature; 2. The necessity of caution and circumspection; 3. The perils of prosperity should check our eagerness after worldly ease and affluence; 4. Learn resignation under afflictive dispensations.—W. Jay.

Salvation from God without the Intervention of Saints.—A Protestant who rented a small farm under Alexander, second Duke of Gordon, having fallen behind in his payments, a vigilant steward, in his Grace's absence, seized the farmer's stock, and advertised it to be sold by auction on a fixed day. The duke happily returned home in the interval, and the tenant went to him to supplicate for indulgence. "What is the matter, Donald?" said the duke, as he saw him enter with sad, downcast looks. Donald told him his sorrowful tale in a concise, natural manner: it touched the duke's heart, and produced a formal acquittance of the debt. Donald, as he cheerfully withdrew, was staring at the pictures and images which he saw in the ducal hall, and expressed to the duke, in a homely way, a wish to know what they were. "These," said the duke, "are the saints who intercede with God for me." "My lord duke," said Donald, "would it not be better to apply yourself directly to God? I went to muckle Sawney Gordon, and to little Sawney Gordon, but if I had not come to your grace's self, both I and my bairns had been turned out from house and home."

"Dew falls insensibly and invisibly. You may be in the field all night, and not perceive the dew falling, and yet find great dew upon the grass. So the operations and blessings of God's Word, and graces thereof, are invisible; we feel the work, but the manner of the working is unknown to us. No man can see the conversion of another, nor can well discern his own. The Word works by little as the dew falls."
—B. Keach.

9—11. (9) **O Israel,** etc., R. V., "It is thy destruction, O Israel, that thou art against me, against thy help." (10) **I will,** etc., R. V., "Where now is thy king, that he may save thee in all thy cities? and thy judges," etc.; the now being emphatic. (11) **king .. anger,** 1 Sa. viii. 5, xv. 23, xvi. 1.

Man His Own Destroyer: God Alone His Saviour (vs. 9).—I. Destruction is possible to us men, even that of the highest, noblest, and divinest part of our nature. II. The only power by which we can destroy ourselves is the power of sinning. III. Every finally destroyed man is self-destroyed. IV. The self-destroyer who is in this perilous position may be saved from self-destruction. 1. A man cannot save himself; 2. No fellow-man can save a sinner; 3. God the only Saviour—what an encouragement to return to him.—S. Martin.

Theocracy.—God is the ultimate foundation of all human society; without Him you can neither cement nor govern society. The mad attempt, if you remember, was made in France. The governing council decreed that there was no God. What was the result? Anarchy, confusion, license, bloodshed, terror. Robespierre, one of the leading spirits of the Revolution, had to declare to his comrades in conclave assembled, "If there be no God, we must make one—we cannot govern France without Him.—J. Cynddylan Jones.

"The mark of a man of probity is in his keeping reason at the head of practice; in being easy in his condition; to live in a crowd of objects, without suffering either in his sense, his virtue, or his quiet; to have a good understanding at home, and to be governed by that Divine principle that is within him; to be all truth in his words; and justice in his actions."—Antoninus.

12—14. (12) **bound up,** laid by in store, and will surely be remembered and punished. (13) The Prophet declares that the troubles which are already closing around Israel, are in reality a last opportunity graciously vouchsafed of repentance. But he in his unwisdom neglects to embrace it, though every moment of delay increases his danger. Notice the two-fold application of the figure of childbirth. Israel is first of all the travailing woman, and then the child whose birth is imperilled by its weak will.—Camb. Bib. **sorrows,** etc., great calamities are often likened to the pains of childbirth. **for he should not,** rather, "for now he standeth not in the place where children break forth. The passage is akin to Isa. xxxvii. 2, where Judah's utter incapacity to emerge out of its troubles is compared to the inability of a woman to perform the act of bringing forth. Here, however, to suggest a moral lesson to Israel, the weak will of the child is represented as the cause of the failure. It is a new birth which Israel needs; and if calamity only had its right effect on the conscience, the language ascribed to Israel in vi. 2

"In this world, he that is today conqueror may tomorrow himself be defeated. Pompey is eclipsed by Caesar, who then falls by the hands of conspirators; Napoleon conquered nearly all Europe, and was then himself conquered. But the Christian's conquest of death is absolute. The result is final. He has vanquished the last enemy, and has no more battles to fight."—Foster.

would be verified, 'on the third day .. we shall live in his sight.'"—Camb. Bib. (14) G. A. Smith translates, "From the hand of Sheol shall I deliver them?" etc., implying the negative, and he adds: "This great verse has been very variously rendered. Some have taken it as a promise: "I will deliver ... I will redeem." So the Septuagint translated, and St. Paul borrowed, not the whole Greek verse, but its spirit and one or two of its terms, for his triumphant challenge to death in the power of the Resurrection of Christ. As it stands in Hosea, however, the verse must be a threat. The last clause unambiguously abjures mercy, and the statement that His people will not be saved, for God cannot save them, is one in thorough harmony with all Hosea's teaching." **O death,** etc., R. V., "O death, where are thy plagues? O grave, where is thy destruction?" Comp. 1 Co. xv. 55.[a] **repentance,** here change of mind and purpose respecting thy recovery and restoration.

Death Conquered.—Death, which sin brought into the world, is now become the only means to destroy and kill sin. Death, which is contrary unto life, is now turned into a port and passage into life. Death, that before was an armed enemy, is now made a reconciled and firm friend, a physician to cure all diseases, and an harbinger to make way for glory. The grave, also, by Christ's lying in it, is become a bed of rest, in which His saints fetch a short slumber until He awaken them to a glorious resurrection. It is the chamber into which He invites His beloved ones, to hide themselves until His indignation be past; the ark into which He shuts his Noahs while he destroys the world with an overflowing deluge of wrath and displeasure.—W. Spurstowe, 1659.——The Chaff and the Corn.—There is an old rabbinical legend which runs thus: "When Joseph was prime minister to Pharaoh, during the famine, he emptied the chaff of his granaries into the Nile. It floated far away on the current, and the people on the banks at a great distance below saw it. It was only chaff, but it meant that there was corn in plenty somewhere. Chaff always means corn; and yet the chaff is worthless. You could not persuade these people that they were mistaken. They were suffering the pangs of hunger, and had supposed that the famine extended throughout the entire country, and that everybody was as hungry as themselves. They were sure that if their strength would hold out they would reach the point at wh. the chaff had been thrown into the river. . . . Adown the stream of time there come floating to our hearts certain dreams of bliss; reunion with those we have loved, and lost; the longing for rest; and the desire for a future life and holiness. The race has enjoyed these hopes since it first began to struggle. They are the chaff; but the corn, which is higher up the stream in the granaries of God, will be ours by-and-by.—Hepworth.

15, 16. (15) **east wind,** i. e. the Assyrian conqueror, Eze. xix. 12. **spring,** or cistern. **pleasant vessels,** He—not the Assyrian, but Menahem, who had to send gold to the Assyrian—"shall strip the treasury of all its precious jewels. Samaria must bear her guilt: for she hath rebelled against her God." To this simple issue has the impenitence of the people finally reduced the many possibilities of those momentous years; and their last prophet leaves them looking forward to the crash which came some dozen years later in the invasion and captivity of the land.—G. A. Smith. (16) **become desolate,** R. V., "shall bear her guilt."[a] Samaria is here introduced as representing the whole kingdom.

Reverses of Fortune in Human Life (vs. 15).—I. Reverses in human fortune are sometimes very striking. II. They are generally brought about by secondary instrumentality. III. They are under the direction of God. Learn—1. To acquiesce in His dispensations; 2. To look to Him for all that is good.—Thomas.

CHAPTER THE FOURTEENTH.

1—3. (1) **return,** or "return quite home to the Lord."[b] **fallen,** into all your troubles as a direct consequence of your sins (ch. xiii. 9). (2) **words,** "it is one of the most undoubtedly ancient of the religious laws of the Pentateuch that 'none shall appear before Jehovah empty' (Ex.

a "Applied to Ephraim these strong figures signify, that though they be in never so hopeless and desperate a condition, God will, in due time, deliver them out of it." —Lowth.

"Christ came to grapple with Death on the cross, and that horrid monarch was armed with all his terrors: he had his full force upon him, and darted his sting with such violence and vengeance into His whole frame, that he struck that sting through His body and soul into the cross, and could never draw it out any more."—Ryland.

"He went down into death's dark dominions, fought him upon his own ground, tore his crown from off his head, broke his sceptre to shivers, and with the triumph of a conquering God He said, 'O death! I will be thy plague. O grave! I will be thy destruction.'" —F. Ryland, 1786.

"Patient, hopeful waiting is hard work, when it is the only work possible to us in an emergency. But patient waiting is in its time the highest duty of a faithful soul." —Trumbull.

a 2 Ki. xvii. 6.

"Shalmaneser began the siege of Samaria in 723 B. C. Its close was in 721 B. C., the first year of Sargon, who seems to have usurped the throne of Assyria whilst Shalmaneser was at the siege of Samaria."—Fausset.

b "Our Rabbins say, 'Great is repentance, which maketh (men) reach even the

xxiii. 15, xxxiv. 20). What gift then will be most acceptable from the Israelites to their heavenly King? The answer that will naturally rise to the lips of a half-converted Israelite will be 'sacrifice and burnt-offering;' but the Prophet in his present mood cherishes the belief that Israel's repentance will after all not be as superficial as he once feared (contrast v. 6). He therefore urges his people, after the bitter lessons of experience, to take as their offering, not cattle, but penitent words spoken out of the abundance of the heart."—Camb. Bib. **receive us graciously,** lit. give good.[c] **calves .. lips,** i. e. instead of formal and heartless sacrifices we will render the penitent confessions of our lips; He. xiii. 15, praises of our lips. (3) **Asshur, or** Assyria. With this nation Israel had been in alliance. **horses,** the type of Egypt, from whence the horses had first been brought. **in thee,** "for in thee the fatherless findeth a father's pity."—G. A. Smith. Comp. Ps. x. 14, lxviii. 5.

Horses.—It comes to this, that a man must at some point say good-bye to his old ruined self. There were cleansing days in the moral life—days when Assyria must be warned away as a helper that is helpless, as only a name of pride without being an arm of power. Asshur must go. "We will not ride upon horses:" the stables must be cleansed. The horse has always in ancient history, as given in the Old Testament, been regarded as an emblem of pride. Israel at one period bought horses; Solomon committed the folly of having a boundless stable, he would have horses like the Egyptians. The Lord will not have anything to do with such horses in such relations. Men must ride upon His almightiness, and not upon the bared back of some steed of the wilderness; though he fly with the wind, and tear up the desert in the passion of his urgency, it is running itself to death.—Peop. Bib.——Gods.—At the introduction of Christianity into England, a general council was summoned to consider the new doctrines of Paulinus. All present were unanimous as to the utter inefficiency of the gods whom they worshiped. Coifi, the pagan high-priest, in an eloquent harangue, proposed their overthrow, and casting aside his priestly garments, called for arms, which Saxon priests were forbidden to wield, and for a horse, which they were not permitted to mount; and thus accoutred, galloped to the shrine at Godmundham, where the chief idol stood, hurled his lance into the enclosure, and profaned the consecrated shrine. The people, encouraged by the example of their priest, destroyed the sacred temple.—Hom. Com.

4—7. (4) **backsliding,** i. e. the damage which their backsliding has brought upon them. **freely,** "with spontaneous, overflowing generosity." (5) **dew,** comp. Job xxix. 19; Pr. xix. 12; Mi. v. 7. **lily,**[a] prob. the scarlet lily, growing as freely as our poppy in the E. fields, **as Lebanon,** i. e. as the cedars of Lebanon. The slender roots of the lily supply no fit image for stability; for this Hosea turns to the "cedars of God" (Ps. lxxx. 10, A. V. "goodly cedars").—Camb. Bib. (6) **olive tree,** wh. never loses its leaves.[b] **smell,** the fragrance of the cedars has been noticed by travelers.[c] (7) "They shall return and dwell in His shadow. They shall live well-watered as a garden, till they flourish like the vine, and be fragrant like the wine of Lebanon."—G. A. Smith.

The Dew an Emblem of the Holy Spirit (vs. 5).—I. The influences of the Spirit are like dew, early in their descent. II. They are copious. III. Silent. IV. Fertilizing and refreshing. V. Temporary, they need to be renewed.—T. Lee.

The Smell of Lebanon.—The approach to Lebanon is adorned with olive plantations, vineyards, and luxuriant fields; and its lower regions, besides the olive and the vine, are beautified with the myrtle, the styrax, and other odoriferous shrubs; and the perfume which exhales from these plants is increased by the fragrance of the cedars which crown its summits, or garnish its declivities. The great rupture which runs a long way up into the mountain, and is on both sides exceedingly steep and high, is clothed from the top to the bottom with fragrant evergreens, and everywhere refreshed with streams, descending from the rocks in beautiful cascades, the work of Divine wisdom and goodness. These cool and limpid streams uniting at the bottom, form a large and rapid torrent, whose agreeable murmur is heard over all the place, and adds greatly to the pleasure of that romantic scene. The fragrant odors wafted from the aromatic plants of this noble mountain have not been over-

very throne of Glory.' " —Kimchi.

c "Whensoever we do any good, God works in us and by us; and whenever He rewards our acts He crowns His own gifts."— S. Augustine.

"Consumption, when it once comes to be really consumption, is beyond all doubt utterly incurable by ordinary medicine; and though many remedies may assist the sufferer and prolong his life, yet as a rule, consumption is the herald of death; and so backsliding is incurable by any human means, and would be the forerunner of total apostasy were it not for Divine grace." — Spurgeon.

"In the last moment, even at the eleventh hour, for the remnant of your wasted life, there is an opportunity for escape."—Beecher.

a "No plant is more productive than the lily, one root often producing fifty bulbs."—Pliny.

b Ju. ix. 9; Ps. lii. 8, cxxviii. 3; Je. xi. 16.

c "The fresh mountain breezes, filled in early summer with the fragrance of the budding vines, and throughout the year with the rich odors of numerous aromatic shrubs, call to mind the words of Sol., 'The smell of thy garments is like the smell of Lebanon.' " —Porter.

"Writing in view of an olive grove, Thomson says: 'To me this noble grove, spreading like a silver sea along the base of the hills, and climbing the ascending terraces, is perfectly charming; and it speaks of peace and plenty, food and gladness.' " —Land and Book. In the course of his travels in the East, Dr. Bonar informs us that he came to immense beds of lilies and hyacinths of various kinds. They grew thickly together and covered miles of sand. "They grow," he tells us, "in almost incredible numbers and luxuriance, often where nothing else flourishes, corroborating the Prophet's allusion, 'He shall grow as the lily.' It grows on hill and valley all over this region. Nor is it of one species only, but of several, as we could easily see, though only one species was in flower."

a "Ephraim gratefully acknowledges that he is in a flourishing and thriving condition, and then God puts him in mind that his fruitfulness is wholly owing to the Divine blessing."—Lowth.

"God does not say, I will heal thy backsliding for any certain term of years, but I will heal thy backslidings in general. If you have been a backslider these fifty years—nay, were it possible for you to have been a backslider a thousand years, yet if with hearty repentance and true faith you turn unto Him, He will abundantly pardon you. Oh, dear sir, if any one had need to despair of mercy, I had: but Jesus had washed me in His blood, and I know that my Redeemer liveth." — Whitefield.

looked by the sacred writers. The eulogium which Christ pronounces on the graces of the Church contains the following direct reference: "The smell of thy garments is like the smell of Lebanon." The richness and flavor of the wines produced in its vineyards have been celebrated by travelers in all ages. Rauwolf declares that the wine which he drank at Canobin, a Greek monastery on Mount Libanus, far surpassed any he had ever tasted. His testimony is corroborated by Le Bruyn, who pronounces the wines of Canobin better and more delicate than are to be found anywhere else in the world. In striking allusion to the scenery and productions of that mountain, it is promised in the sixth verse: "His branch shall spread, and his beauty shall be as the olive tree, and his small (or his memorial, as the original term signifies) as Lebanon." His branches shall spread like the mighty arms of the cedar, every one of which is equal in size to a tree; his beauty shall be as the olive tree, which is generally admitted to be one of the most beautiful productions of nature; and his smell, his very memorial, shall be as the wine of Lebanon, which delights the taste, and the very recollection of which excites the commendation of those that have drank it, long after the banquet is over. The meaning of these glowing figures undoubtedly is, that the righteous man shall prosper by the distinguishing favor of heaven; shall become excellent, and useful, and highly respected while he lives; and after his death his memory shall be blessed and embalmed in the affectionate recollection of the Church, for the benefit of many who had not the opportunity of profiting by his example. —Paxton.——Forgiveness.—A dear old woman lay dying, and an infidel came in to scoff at her, and said, "They tell me you are not afraid to die, and are very happy." "Yes, thank God." "Do you believe in a God?" "Yes, I do." "Do you believe God punishes sin?" "Yes, I do." Then the infidel said, "I should like to know how you are happy, for if there ever was a bad old woman, you are one. If what you say could be believed, it would be a great deal too good to be true." She looked him in the face, and said, "It is—it is a good deal too good to be true. But, bless the Lord, it is true for all that!"—H. W. Webb-Peploe.

8, 9. (8) **What .. idols?** G. A. Smith understands this verse to be the utterance of God, and translates: "Ephraim, what has he to do any more with idols! I have spoken" for him, "and I will look after him. I am like an ever-green fir; from Me is thy fruit found." **I .. tree,** this is the satisfied expression of Israel, rejoicing in God's restoring mercies, and heartily acknowledging that all grace and good has come from God.[a] (9) "An epilogue or conclusion to the prophecy, unspecializing it, as it were, and extracting, cf. Ps. cvii. 43, the moral which underlies it all. The tone and language of it remind us of the Book of Proverbs (Prov. xi. 5, xv. 19)."—Camb. Bib. **wise,** Da. xii. 3. Comp. "He that hath ears to hear, let him hear."

Destruction of Idols.—On the 8th of September last, the Chief Secretary of State, with others high in rank, were sent to the village where the royal idols were kept, with orders to burn them. They started at about half-past three in the afternoon well armed, and hasted to Ambohimanambolu, a distance of seven miles, to execute the queen's commands. On arriving at the village, the first thing to do was to read the Prime Minister's letter, and secure possession of the idol's house. This done, a fire was kindled with the materials of the fence which surrounded the house, and had been pulled down by the queen's orders on the day she laid the corner-stone of the Chapel Royal. Then first the long cane, called Tsoutsonaraka, which usually preceded the idol in processions or journeyings, was cast into the fire; then twelve bullock's horns, from which the sacred sprinklings were made; three scarlet umbrellas followed; and the silk lamba or loose-flowing garment which concealed the idol when suspended on the person of its keeper when it traveled. The idol's case succeeded; this case was made of a small tree hollowed, having a lid or cover fitted to it; and lastly the idol itself. This idol consisted altogether of two thicknesses of scarlet silk, about three feet long and three inches wide, having a small piece of wood, about the length and size of a finger to the second joint, inserted in the middle between the silks, in such a manner that, by turning the silks a little way, the point of the wood could be made to touch water, or anything else that was to be sanctified: at either extremity of the silk a silver chain was sewed or fastened, equal in length to the width of the silk. On seeing the idol the people said, "You cannot burn him, he is a god!" to which the Christian officer replied, "If he be a god he will not burn, we are going to try;" and when enveloped in flames one of them held it up on a stick to show it was burning. On the day following, four others were burned, and on the 10th of September two more. One of those burnt was the sovereign's private idol, which was found to consist of a small quantity of sand, tied in a cloth.—W. Pool.

"When two join in the same adventure, one perceives before the other how they ought to act; while one alone, however prompt, resolves more tardily, and with a weaker will." —Bryant's Iliad.

Introduction.

I. **Author.** Joel, = Jehovah is his God. Nothing known of him save that he was the son of Pethuel (i. 1). II. **Time,** and **Place.** His prophecies give no specifications of time or place; but all the internal indications of the book point to Judæa—probably to Jerusalem, with its temple, altar, priesthood, and solemn assemblies, as the sphere of his labors. Widely diverging opinions have been held as to the date of the book; but most recent scholars would assign it to the fifth or sixth century before Christ. III. **Style,** and **Theme.** The writings of Joel bear the full impress of culture in a prophetic school. His Hebrew is of the purest kind; his style is easy, flowing, elegant, and adorned with magnificent imagery; and for vividness and power of description he is not surpassed by any of the Prophets. The immediate occasion of his prophecies is a double plague of drought and locusts, which has already invaded the land, and whose desolating progress he describes in poetic strains of matchless elegance and power. He summons the people of all classes to repentance, and promises upon this condition not only the restoration of the land to its former fruitfulness, but also the outpouring of God's Spirit upon all flesh, the triumph of the covenant people over all their foes, and an era of universal holiness and peace. In this respect he is at one with all the Prophets. They all with one accord look forward beyond the calamities of the present time, and the heavier impending calamities which they are commissioned to foretell in the near future, to the glory of the latter days, when Zion shall be made triumphant over all her foes, and the whole earth shall be given her for her inheritance. The Apostle Peter, in his address on the day of Pentecost, quotes a remarkable prophecy of Joel. (Acts ii. 16—21; comp. with Joel ii. 28—32.)

Synopsis.

(According to Horne.)

This Book consists of three chapters, which may be divided into three discourses or parts.

PART I. Is an exhortation, both to the priests and to the people, to repent, by reason of the famine brought upon them by the palmer-worm, etc., in consequence of their sins (i. 1—20); and is followed by a denunciation of still greater calamities if they continue impenitent....................ii. 1—11

PART II. An exhortation to keep a public and solemn fast (ii. 12—17); with a promise of removing the calamities of the Jews on their repentance ....ii. 18—26

PART III. Predicts the general conversion and return of the Jews, and the destruction of their opponents, together with the glorious state of the Church that is to follow....iii.

CHAPTER THE FIRST.

1—4. (1) **Joel,** the name means, "Whose God is Jehovah." **Pethuel,** not known. In the E. men were thus distinguished by giving their father's name. (2) **this .. days,** had they any experience of such a calamity as he recounts? (3) **Tell,** etc., i.e. not only former generations have known nothing so terrible, but the marvel of it will outlast three more generations. (4) **palmerworm,** etc.,[a] by these terms four species or stages of locusts, rather than four different kinds of insects, are probably intended.

The Life-work of an Obscure Prophet.—The literary style of this book deserves the consideration of every student of Scripture. With the exception of Isaiah and (as some think) of Habakkuk, Joel surpasses all his brethren in sublimity. His pictures of the disasters following upon sin are marvelously vivid, and his promise of the coming of the Holy Spirit was still living in the memory of the Jews when Peter, on the day of Pentecost, declared that its fulfillment had come. The first half of the book describes the Divine judgments, and the second half (beginning with the eighteenth verse of ch. ii.) unfolds the promise of Divine favor. Its readers pass from darkness to light, from grief to joy, from estrangement to reconciliation; and in this book, as in experience, the transition hinges on the penitential prayer to which it was the prophet's mission to summon the people. We know scarcely more of Joel than the fact that he was the son of Petruel.—Pul. Com.——Locusts.—"We know," says Burke, "that a swarm of locusts, however individually despicable, can render a country more desolate than Genghis Khan or Tamerlane. When God Almighty chose to humble the pride and presumption of Pharaoh and bring him to shame, he did not effect his purpose with tigers and lions. He sent lice, mice, frogs, and everything loathsome and contemptible, to pollute and destroy the country."

5—7. (5) **drunkards,** these would be specially affected bec. the locusts would ruin the vineyards. (6) **a nation,** the locusts are so called because their progress is as orderly as a national army. **my land,** the prophet speaks in the name of the people. **teeth,** comp. Re. ix. 8.[b] **cheek teeth,** R. V., "jaw teeth," grinders. (7) **barked .. fig,** the locust "strips the vines of every leaf, and every cluster of grapes, and of every green twig." **white,** by the stripping off of the bark.

The Fig Tree.—So valuable is the fig tree in the land of Canaan, and so high is the estimation in which it is held, that to bark and kill it is reckoned among the severest judgments which God inflicted upon His offending people. The Prophet alludes in these words to the destructive progress of the locust, which, with insatiable greediness, devours the leaves and bark of every tree on which it lights, till not the smallest portion of rind is left, even on the slenderest twig, to convey the sap from the root, and leaves it white and withering in the sun, for ever incapable of answering the hopes of the husbandman. Such were the people of Israel, delivered by Jehovah, for their numerous and inveterate transgressions, into the hands of their cruel and implacable enemies.—Paxton. ——The Eternal Foundation.—Said the Bishop of Calcutta, on the platform of a native society for the improvement of Hindoo morals, "If you wish to make anything eternal, you must build it on the Christian religion. That is the only thing in this world that is eternal." He was right. No reform is worth its cost, which is not important enough to rise to the level of a religious duty.—Phelps.——Locusts.—The quantity of these insects is a thing incredible to any who has not seen it himself; the ground is covered by them for several leagues. The whole face of the mountain (Lebanon) was black with them. On they came like a living deluge. We dug trenches and kindled fires, and beat and burnt to death heaps upon heaps, but the effort was utterly useless. They rolled up the mountain-side, and poured over rocks, walls, ditches, and hedges, those behind covering up and passing over the masses already killed. For some days they continued to pass. The noise made by them in marching and foraging was like that of a heavy shower falling upon a

[a] "The Prophet crowds together a number of locust-names to show that nothing shall remain undevastated by one or the other. The form of the vs. shows it to be poetical."— Spk. Com.

"The marvel is that they all come in one year." — S. Jerome.

[b] "A large vineyard and garden aujoining mine was green as a meadow in the morning; but long before night it was naked and bare as a newly-ploughed field or dusty road." — Thomson.

"The jaws of the locusts are excessively hard and strong, capable of devouring not only the leaves, but when these fail, the bark, and even the solid wood of the trees."
—Newman.

"These lessons are fit for England, where ancient sobriety hath given place to superfluity, where many such men are as fare daintily day by day. God grant their end be not like his, who riotously wasting here the creatures of God, wanted afterwards a drop of water when he would gladly have had it."—Sandys.

"The judgments of God are often linked together like a chain, each one drawing on the other. Yet, says one, 'at each link of the lengthening chain, allowing

distant forest.—Thompson.——The roads were covered with them, all marching and in regular lines, like armies of soldiers, with their leaders in front; and all the opposition of man to resist their progress was in vain. Having consumed the plantations in the country, they entered the towns and villages. When they approached our garden all the farm servants were employed to keep them off, but to no avail; though our men broke their ranks for a moment, no sooner had they passed the men, than they closed again, and marched forward through hedges and ditches as before. Our garden finished, they continued their march toward the town, devastating one garden after another.—Jour. Sac. Lit.

8—10. (8) **Lament,**[a] words addressed poetically to the land. **like a virgin,** "the interruption of the fellowship between the land and Jehovah through the failure of the sacrifices the Prophet throws into the figure of a young wife bereaved and in mourning. The land is the virgin; the dreary bleak aspect of it is the mourning which she wears. The bereavement lies in this: that through the cutting off of the meal-offering, and the drink-offering, the tokens of Jehovah's presence and favor, manifested in His acceptance of the offerings, have been removed; communications between the land and its God have been removed, and the land is bereaved." —A. B. Davidson. **sackcloth,** the usual accompaniment of mourning. **husband,** or betrothed, snatched away before marriage. (9) **meat offering,** mincha, Le. ii. 1; Ex. xxiv. 40, 42. "The unbloody offering made of flour, oil, and frankincense." **the priests mourn,** etc., in this passage the same feeling is attributed to men and to the fruits of the land: "the priests mourn," "the land mourneth."—G. A. Smith. (10) **wasted,** or fallow: or the crop on it is destroyed.

The Fig Tree Peeled.—The Prophet Joel, in describing the ravages of a swarm of locusts, speaks of them as alighting on the fig trees, peeling off the bark with their teeth, and then leaving them entirely white, after completing this work of devastation. From the Prophet singling out the fig tree as exhibiting this appearance, one would suppose the wood of this tree to have a peculiar whiteness, which other trees do not possess in the same degree. On meeting with the fig tree for the first time, I was curious to ascertain whether this expectation was well founded or not. I broke off some of the tender twigs, removed the bark, and was pleased to find that the result confirmed my conjecture. Though I examined several other trees with reference to the same point, I satisfied myself that no one of them would present to the eye so remarkable an object as the fig tree, with its bark stripped off from top to bottom. To look over a landscape and see a multitude of these trees leafless, newly peeled, exposing to view the white wood, so peculiar to them as compared with other trees, would impress the spectator strongly with the idea of the desolating power of the locust; it was a master-stroke of the poet to fix on that circumstance for the purpose of conveying such an idea.—Hackett.——Famine.—When we bear in mind that, in spite of the help given them from this country, one-fourth part of the people of Ireland died in one year (1847) through the failure of a single article of food, we may have some idea of the distress of successive years. Not all the vast wealth of England would restore the withered joy that would result from the failure of the harvest and the destruction of herds for a single year. The blight of a fly might consume cereal crops and prove more terrible than destructive war—Hom. Com——Temporal Prosperity. —What reason we have to praise God for bountiful seasons, and for His goodness in filling our hearts with food and gladness! But cleave not too closely to temporal blessings, which may be cut off by judgment, and taken suddenly away. God takes from an ungodly people the means of gratifying their lusts, and will bring them to repentance by deep afflictions. The prosperity of the Church depends not on a grand ceremonial, or crowds of admiring devotees, or the countenance of the State, however desirable these things may be, but only on the favor of God, whose blessings and whose Spirit will be withdrawn, if we defile his sanctuary with superstitious rites.—Robinson.

11—13. (11) **ashamed,** etc., "Be ye abashed, O ploughman."—G. A. Smith. Comp. Je. xiv. 3. (12) **pomegranate,** Ex. xxviii 34. **palm,** wh. long resists drought, because of its deep rooting. **the apple tree,** Cant.

space and time for repentance to break it through.'" —Hom. Com.

[a] Is. xxii. 12.

"On rolls the stream with a perpetual sigh; the rocks moan wildly as it passes by; Hyssop and wormwood border all the strand, and not a flower adorns the weary land." —Bryant.

Two are more than twice one. There is not only double experience, but the wisdom of each reacts on the wisdom of the other, vivifying it and brightening it.

"If we are to live after death, why don't we have some certain knowledge of it?" said an old sceptic of a clergyman. "Why don't you have some knowledge of this world before you come into it?" was the caustic reply.

"Some years ago, when preaching at Bristol, amongst other notes I received to pray for individuals, one was this: 'A person earnestly desires the prayers of the congregation, who is prospering in trade.' 'Ah,' said I to myself,' 'Ah,' 'here is a man who knows something of his own heart, and who has read the Scriptures to some purpose.'" —W. Jay.

ii. 3, viii. 5; cf. apples Cant. ii. 5, vii. 8; Prov. xxv. 11. "It has been doubted whether tappuah is really the apple; and Tristram adduces grounds tending to shew that it was more probably the apricot. But the corresponding Arabic word (tuffah) certainly means the apple; and though it is true that the Syrian apple is much inferior in flavor to the European apple, it has nevertheless been long esteemed in the East as a grateful and refreshing fruit, and valued in sickness on account of its restorative properties."—Camb. Bib. (13) **Gird yourselves,** R. V. adds, "with sackcloth." **come,** or lead the way; show the example to the nation of bitter grief, distress, and humiliation.[a]

The Advantages of a Bad Harvest (vs. 11).—What do we mean by a bad harvest? Bad as compared with expectation; as compared with former years; as compared with the harvest of other lands. Let us mark some of the advantages. I. It recalls us to a sense of our dependence on God. II. It awakens us to a deeper feeling of the evil of sin. III. It serves as a tie of discipline for the improvement of character and the promotion of the general good. IV. It impresses the soul with a sense of its higher needs and duties. V. It invites us to draw nearer to God, and to regard Him as the only true and supreme God.—W. Forsyth.

14—17. (14) **fast,** comp. 2 Chr. xx. 3, 4. **cry,** in penitential pleadings. (15) **the day,** "the usual designation of the final theocratic judgment is, from Joel i. 15 and ii. 1 onward; 'the day of Jehovah,' comp. Zeph. i. 7, ii. 3; Mal. iv. 5; Amos v. 18. It is the day on which the Lord will humble all the loftiness of man, and will alone be exalted."—Oehler. (16) **joy,** such as usually prevailed at the vintage feasts. (17) **rotten,** dried up in the ground.[b]

Granaries.—Dr. Shaw informs us that "in Barbary, after the grain is winnowed, they lodge it in mattamores, or subterraneous magazines, two or three hundred of which are sometimes together, the smallest holding four hundred bushels." And Dr. Russell says, "that about Aleppo, in Syria, their granaries are even at this day, subterraneous grottoes, the entry to which is by a small hole or opening like a well, often in the highway; and as they are commonly left open when empty, they make it not a little dangerous riding near the villages in the night."—Burder.——The Day of the Lord.—It is the day, when Jehovah is conceived as manifesting Himself in His fulness, striking down wrong-doing and illusion, and giving the final victory to righteousness and truth. The origin of the conception as applied by the prophets, is to be found in Amos' transformation of a popular idea (see on Am. v. 18). The presentiment of the approach of Jehovah's Day was often awakened in the minds of the prophets by the prospect of some great political movement among the nations of the earth. In the case of Joel the Day of Jehovah is invested, more distinctly than is the case in the earlier prophets, with an eschatological significance; see esp. ii. 31, iii. 1, 2, 9—17.—Camb. B.——The Practice of Self-Restraint.—"Fasting" is a word which ought to have given to it the widest signification. Generally used to denote abstinence from food, it may be as fairly applied to any refusal of indulgence to animal appetite, however innocent such indulgence, under other circumstances, may be. The keeping of a fast in mere deference to a social custom or to ecclesiastical ordinance is of no great value. But true fasting is inculcated by our Lord Himself, though he personally refused to keep the ecclesiastical fasts of His own day. The restraint of appetite, the curbing of the animal nature, is essential to the doing of great works for Him. Of the lunatic boy Jesus said to His disciples, "This kind goeth not out but by prayer and fasting." This has its application to indulgence in strong drink. Total abstinence has a part to play as well as a prayer in driving out the demon of drunkenness. Such fasting would do much to remove a curse which is as terrible as was the devastation of the land of Judah by locusts.—Pul. Com.

18—20. (18) **beasts groan,** bec. there is no green food left for them.[a] **perplexed,** "huddle together," lit. "press themselves."—G. A. Smith. "There is a tacit contrast between the sense of the brute creation, and the insensibility of the people."—Fausset. (19) **wilderness,** or plains. (20) **cry,** R. V., "put unto thee."

The Influence of National Calamities on the Minds of the Good (vs. 19).—The effect on Joel was to excite him to prayer. I. This was right.

[a] "Reference is to those priests whose turn it is to keep the night - watches in the temple." —Lowth.

"The French revolution was not as Wendell Phillips said, 'the greatest blessing of modern times,' but some such terrible upheaval was necessary for the nation. The leaders would not be induced to right the wrongs of the nation in any other way." —Peloubet.

[b] "The seed is sure to rot if they sow too long before the rains come."—Thomson.

"But, to us, probability is the very guide of life."—Butler.

Seneca says. "The good man God accustoms to hardships, and prepares him for himself. But the luxurious, whom he seems to indulge and to spare, he reserves for evils to come. For you are mistaken if you think any one excepted. The man who has been long spared will at last have his portion of misery; and though he seems to have escaped it, it is only delayed for a time." "Thus ought we always to believe," says Plato, "those ancient and sacred words, which declare to us that the soul is immortal, that judges are appointed, and that they pass the highest sentences of condemnation when the spirit is separate from the body."

[a] "This is poetic but true. A field over which this flood of desolation has rolled

1. God requires it; 2. Christ engaged in it. II. This was wise. III. This was natural. Apply:—1. It is well when trial leads to prayer; 2. Trials prayerfully endured become blessings.—Thomas.

Prayer for the Church.—During the troublous times of Scotland, when the Popish court and aristocracy were arming themselves to suppress the Reformation in that land, and the cause of Protestant Christianity was in imminent peril, late on a certain night John Knox was seen to leave his study, and to pass from the house down into an enclosure to the rear of it. He was followed by a friend, when, after a few moments of silence, his voice was heard as if in prayer. In another moment the accents deepened into intelligible words, and the earnest petition went up from his struggling soul to heaven, "O Lord, give me Scotland, or I die!" Then a pause of hushed stillness, when again the petition broke forth, "O Lord, give me Scotland, or I die!" Once more all was voiceless and noiseless, when, with a yet intenser pathos the thrice-repeated intercession struggled forth, "O Lord, give me Scotland, or I die!" And God gave him Scotland, in spite of Mary and her Cardinal Beatoun; a land and a church of noble loyalty to Christ and His crown.—Spurgeon.——God's Humanity.—Let us here recall the fact, that it is the Spirit of God who speaks by the mouth of His prophet; for it is to be feared that we do not make enough of the humanity of God, of His intense delight in trees and flowers, in herds and flocks; of His humane care for them, of His tender sympathy with them. The Psalms and Prophecies are full of this Divine humanity, no Prophecy fuller, perhaps, than that of Joel; and in no passage of Joel's is that tender, intense humanity more beautifully and pathetically expressed than in these verses. —Cox.

Prayer.—

More things are wrought by prayer
Than this world dreams of. Wherefore, let thy voice
Rise like a fountain for me night and day;
For what are men better than sheep or goats,
That nourish a blind life within the brain,
If, knowing God, they lift not hands of prayer
Both for themselves and those who call them friends,
For so the whole round world is every way
Bound by gold chains about the feet of God.—Tennyson.

CHAPTER THE SECOND.

1, 2. (1) **trumpet,** cornet. The horn which is to be blown is an alarm horn, to warn the people of the approach of the Day of the Lord, and not the Shophar which called the people to a general assembly, as in vs. 15.—G. A. Smith. **holy mountain,** i. e. Mount Zion. **day .. Lord,** see on i. 15. (2) **darkness,** "so Zeph. i. 15. Four synonyms are combined, for the purpose of emphasizing the darkness, which the prophet has in view. Darkness is, in Hebrew poetry, a common figure for calamity (comp. on Am. v. 18); but here, no doubt, the image is suggested by the fact that a flight of locusts, as it approaches, presents the appearance of a black cloud, which, as it passes, obscures the sun, and even sometimes darkens the whole sky."—Camb. Bib. **great people,** poetical figure, ch. i. 6.

The Need of Revival (vs. 1).—I. From the state of the Church. 1. Ignorance; 2. Conformity to the world; 3. Want of activity; 4. Neglect of prayer. II. From the state of the general community. 1. Indifference; 2. Infidelity; 3. Intemperance; 4. The race for riches; 5. The love of pleasure.—G. Brooks.

Dangers Besetting Reformers.—Lycurgus was the noblest of Spartans; he was a rigorous disciplinarian; in some aspects he was the admired and all but idolized of his country; but when he denounced the misuse of its wealth, when he levelled his guns against the corruption of his day, he was stoned in the city that was proud of him, and had to seek refuge from common ruffianism behind the altar of the temple; his flesh was cut by the ruffians' cane, and whilst the blood ran down his noble face no word of reproach escaped him.—Peop. Bib.——Aim for

shows not a blade for even a goat to nip."—Thomson.

"When the fruit is yet green, the stem holds tightly to the bough; but when it is ripe it falls with the first wind. So hold on tightly to your plans in life until God shows you that they are ripe, that they have accomplished their purpose; and then let them go —let them go without a murmur."—Beecher.

"At the time the Diet of Nuremburg was held," says Tholuck, "Luther was earnestly praying in his own dwelling; and at the very hour when the edict, granting full toleration to all Protestants, was issued, he ran out of his house, crying out 'We have gained the victory.' " —Spurgeon.

"There's a power which man can wield,
When mortal aid is vain,
That eye, that arm, that love, to reach,
That listening ear to gain:
That power is prayer, which soars on high,
And feeds on bliss beyond the sky."
—Anon.

"Anything is favorable to advancement in Christian manhood which tends to countervail that flow of sympathetic action by which the mind is carried away from intercourse with Christ and God." —Spurgeon.

Dr. Chalmers at Kilmeny preached the law with all the force of his eloquent nature. And he in his farewell address bears this witness: "I never heard of any

Revivals.—There are preachers by myriads and majorities, and deeply pious ones too, that never once in all their lives distinctly concentrated their purposes to the single point of converting men. Their efforts are to finish an eloquent sermon, to develop theological or Biblical truth, to thrill aesthetically an audience, to pour forth general religious emotion, to spread a popular fame, to gather crowds, to build a large church, etc. Verily these have often their reward, namely, success in their objects. But here is a lonesome preacher who does not object to all these; but with or without them, by study, by closet, by pulpit, by pastoral work, some or all, he means to convert souls, and just so many as he can. Where this is attained, all the other success is well enough. Where **this is not attained,** all the other success does not comfort him a penny; he goes off crestfallen and disappointed, indignant at the devil and himself. He will not stay there where Satan has beaten him; but he will go where, please God, he can get some souls.——The Power of a Revival Atmosphere.—Many years ago an eminent officer in the government of Mass. returned from Europe to his home in an inland town in which a powerful work of divine grace was in progress. He had not heard of it. As he passed thro' the streets, the look of things seemed strange to him. The countenances of those whom he met impressed him with a sense of something unusual. The church-bell was tolling at an unusual hour. "What has happened here?" was his inquiry. "Something is in the air. Things seem like the day of judgment." There was no mystery in this. It was like the day of judgment. God was there, deciding the eternal destiny of hundreds of souls. It proved so to that awe-struck man, for he was soon one of the rejoicing converts.—Phelps.

3—5. (3) **fire,** or like a fire, the effects of a fire on everything before them and behind. Their work is likened to that of spreading fire.[a] **as the garden of Eden,** "like a park, richly watered, and well stocked with majestic trees (Gen. ii. 8—10): the comparison, as Ezek. xxxvi. 35 (of the restored land of Israel) 'this land that was desolate is become like the garden of Eden': similarly the garden of Jehovah, Gen. xiii. 10, Is. li. 3 (in the parallel clause, Eden); cp. also the trees of Eden, Ez. xxxi. 9, 16, 18."—Camb. Bib. **shall escape,** from the ravages of the devouring insect. (4) "The allegory now becomes special and minute in its features, which are selected from the operations of an invading army."—Barrows. **horses,** the locust's head somewhat resembles that of the horse.[b] (5) **noise,** "the noise made in marching and foraging was like that of a heavy shower on a distant forest."[c]

Locusts.—I never saw such an exhibition of the helplessness of man, as I have seen to-day. While we were sitting at dinner, a person came into the house, quite pale, and told us that the locusts were coming. Every face gathered darkness. I went to the door—I looked above, and all round, and saw nothing. "Look to the ground," was the reply, when I asked where they were. I looked to the ground, and there I saw a stream of young locusts without wings, covering the ground at the entrance of the village. The stream was about five hundred feet broad, and covering the ground, and moving at the rate of two miles an hour. In a few minutes they covered the garden wall some inches deep, and the water was immediately let into the channel, into which it flows to water the garden. They swim with the greatest ease over standing water, but the stream carried them away, and after floating in it about a hundred paces, they were drowned. All hands were now at work to keep them from the gardens, and to keep them from crossing the streams. To examine the phenomenon more nearly, I walked about a mile and a half from the village, following the course of the stream. Here I found the stream extending a mile in breadth, and, like a thousand rivulets, all flowing into one common channel. It appeared as if the dust under my feet was forming into life, and as if God, when He has a controversy with a people, could raise the very dust of the earth on which they tread in arms against them.—Campbell.

6—8. (6) R. V., "at their presence the peoples are in anguish; all faces are waxed pale." **blackness,** or paleness. (7) **run,** etc., this is literally true.[a] (8) **thrust another,** out of rank; each shall preserve its place. **and when,** etc., R. V., "and they burst through the weapons, and break not off their course."

such reformation being effected among them in this way. I am not sensible that all the vehemence with which I urged the virtues and proprieties of social life had the weight of a feather on the moral habits of my parishioners." Dr. Chalmers while at Kilmeny, was truly converted to Christ; and then when he preached the love and atonement of Christ, he again bears witness that by this he found that men obeyed the moral law, and he declares, "You have at least taught me that to preach Christ is the only effective way of preaching morality in all its branches."—Wayland.

a "Every blade of grass and every leaf is gnawed off as tho' it had been scorched by fire."—Ludolf.

b Re. ix. 7.

Locusts. The head is exceedingly like that of a horse.—Theodoret. Their noise is like the rushing of a wind. — Forbes. "They overshadow the sun, the nations looking up with anxiety, lest they should cover their lands."—Pliny.

Nothing in their habits is more striking than the pertinacity with which they all pursue the same line of march, like a disciplined army. —Thompson.

a "When the head of the mighty column came in contact with the palace of the Emeer Asaad in Abeih, they did not take the trouble to wheel round the corners, but climbed the wall like men of war, and marched over the top of it."—Thomson.

Locusts Producing Famine.—The "panic terror" produced by an invasion of locusts on a large scale, can be readily imagined, if we remember not only the immense loss of property, of which they are the cause, but also the terrible destitution, which often follows in their train. In Algiers, after an invasion of locusts in 1866, 200,000 persons are said to have perished from famine. The destruction wrought frequently by the Rocky Mountain locust, over a large area of the United States, is almost incalculable.—Riley, The Rocky Mountain Locust.

a "As they approached, the density of the host obscured the solar rays, cast an awful gloom like that of an eclipse on the garden, and caused a noise like the rushing of a torrent."—Forbes.

b Ho. xii. 6, xiv. 1.

c Ps. xxxiv. 18, li. 17, cxlvii. 3.

9—14. (9) "They course about in the city; they run upon the wall," no sooner have they gained an entrance than they make the city their own, and take possession of the walls. The exact force of the word rendered course about is not certain: it is used of locusts in Is. xxxiii. 4 ("like the attack of locusts, shall they attack it"), of a bear in Prov. xxviii. 15 ("A growling lion, and a ranging bear"), and (in a reflexive form) of chariots charging the suburbs of a city in Nah. ii. 4 ("they justle one another in the broad places").—Camb. Bib. **enter .. windows,** "if not carefully watched, they would have devoured the flowers wh. were carried into the inner rooms in pots."—Thomson. (10) **earth,** etc., Is. xiii. 10; Mat. xxiv. 29.[a] (11) **utter his voice,** Je. xxv. 30. (12) **turn,** etc., Je. iv. 1.[b] (13) **rend your heart,** fig. for be sincere. Be anxious to secure inward contrition.[c] **gracious,** etc., Ex. xxxiv. 6. **slow to anger,** etc., "long suffering and plenteous in love."—G. A. Smith. (14) **Who knoweth,** etc., Jno. iii. 9. **blessing,** viz., by permitting the earth again to mature its fruits and yield materials for the offerings in the sanctuary (i. 9). The fruits of the earth are a blessing bestowed by God upon man (Deut. vii. 13, xvi. 10, 15, 17).—Camb. Bib.

They teach us the necessity of unity, steadfastness, and order. Many prefer an individual course instead of going by bands. They belong to no cohort, and are under no discipline. The strength of the Church lies in united, concentrated action. Every soldier well-disciplined and in his ranks; every officer at his post, and ready for the contest; each under rule, helpful to each other and to the common cause. — Hom. Com.

Repentance Recommended (vs. 13).—I. The important direction given presupposes—1. A state of heedless inattention; 2. Of careless and criminal negligence; 3. Of obstinate disobedience. "Rend your hearts." this implies—(1) Excessive grief; (2) Great loathing and abhorrence; (3) Deep humility and earnest deprecation. II. The cheering assurance afforded, "For He is gracious," etc. 1. This revelation warrants our approach; 2. Requires our return; 3. Encourage our address.—400 Sks.

Inward Piety.—An old Hebrew story tells how a poor creature came one day to the Temple, from a sick bed, on tottering limbs. He was ashamed to come, for he was very poor, and he had no sacrifice to offer; but as he drew near he heard the choir chanting, "Thou desirest not sacrifice; else would I give it: thou delightest not in burnt offerings. The sacrifices of God are a broken spirit: a broken and a contrite heart, O God, thou wilt not despise." Other worshipers came, pressed before him, and offered their sacrifices; but he had none. At length he prostrated himself before the priest, who said, "What wilt thou, my son? Hast thou no offering?" And he replied, "No, my father, for last night a poor widow and her children came to me, and I had nothing to offer them but the two pigeons which were ready for the sacrifice." "Bring, then," said the priest, "an ephah of fine flour." "Nay, but, my father," said the old man, "this day my sickness and poverty have left only enough for my own starving children; I have not even an ephah of flour." "Why, then, art thou come to me?" said the priest. "Because I heard them singing, 'The sacrifices of God are a broken spirit.' Will not God accept my sacrifice if I say, 'Lord, be merciful to me, a sinner?'" Then the priest lifted the old man from the ground, and he said, "Yes, thou art blessed, my son; it is the offering which is better than thousands of rivers of oil."—World of Prov. and Par., E. P. Hood.

d De. xxiv. 5.

"We are apt to think our duty done if we are faithful here at home. But our responsibility in carrying out the great commission is not fulfilled as long as we are withholding in the smallest degree of our ability the gospel message from the last man at the 'uttermost part of the earth' to whom the gospel has never been preached." — G. F. Pentecost.

15—17. (15) **Blow,** etc., vs. 1. **sanctify,** set apart, or appoint. (16) **elders,** R. V., "old men," all classes, old and young, none are exempt from the humiliation. **bridegroom,** who was legally exempt from the necessity of attending the feasts.[d] (17) **weep,** as leading the penitence of the people. **porch .. altar,** the place where the priests usually stood. **heathen,** R. V., "the nations."

Repentance.—The Roman Catholic definition of penitence is not a bad one, though they draw bad conclusions from it—"Confessio oris, contritio cordis, satisfactio vitæ"—that is, for true repentance there should be confession with the mouth, grieving in the heart, and amendment made for our faults as far as possible in our life.—Richard Glover.——Repentance. —Cowper, the poet, in his own memoirs of his early life, describes the time when he reflected on the necessity of repentance. "I knew that many persons had spoken of shedding tears for sin; but when I asked myself whether the time would ever come when I should weep for mine, it seemed to me that a stone might sooner do it. Not knowing that Christ was exalted to give repentance, I despaired of ever attaining it." A friend came to his bed-side, and declared to him the gospel. He insisted on the all-atoning efficacy of the blood of Jesus, and his righteousness for our justification. "Then," says Cowper, "while I heard this part of his discourse, and the Scriptures on which he founded it, my heart began to burn within me; my soul was pierced with a sense of my bitter ingratitude to so merciful a Saviour; and these tears, which I thought impossible, burst forth freely."—Spurgeon.

"Repentance—the tear dropped from the eye of faith."
—Spurgeon.

18—20. "Probably an interval has elapsed between vss. 17 and 18, but in any case, the people having repented, nothing more is said of their need of doing so, and instead we have from God Himself a series of promises, vss. 19—27, in answer to their cry for mercy. These promises relate to the physical calamity which has been suffered. God will destroy **the locusts**, still impending on the land, and restore the years which His great army has eaten. There follows in vss. 28—32 the promise of a great outpouring of the Spirit on all Israel, amid terrible manifestations in heaven and earth."—G. A. Smith. (18) **jealous,** word applied to Jehovah's anxiety to preserve His covenant name from insults. "Jehovah is jealous not for Himself alone but also for His holy people. The idea is found in Deut. xxxii. 36 ff. But the expression is here used for the first time, and afterward Lech. i. 14; viii. 2."—Oehler. (19) **send you corn,**[a] restoring thus the blessings wh., in judgment, had been destroyed. (20) **northern army,** these locusts probably came from the north, but there may be a further reference to the enemies from the north wh. other Prophets had threatened. **east sea,** i. e. the Dead Sea. **utmost sea,** the Mediterranean. "The description of the removal of the locusts is naturally not to be understood with prosaic literalness: it is intended rather as an imaginative representation of their rapid and complete destruction, though a wind rising first in the N. W., and afterwards gradually veering round to the N. E., would produce approximately the effects indicated." **stink,** from decaying mass of locusts.[b]

[a] Ho. ii. 22.

[b] "Locusts perish when blown by a storm into the sea, or the desert, and emit from their putrefying bodies such a stench as often breeds a pestilence."
—Fausset.

"The south and east winds drive the clouds of locusts with violence into the Mediterranean, and drown them in such quantities that when their dead are cast on to the shore, they infect the air to a great distance.—Volney. Wonderful image of the instantaneousness, ease, completeness, of the destruction of God's enemies; a mass of active life exchanged, in a moment, into a mass of death."
—Pusey.

Interaction of the Divine and the Human (vs. 13).—We learn—I. That the material condition of a people depends upon the Divine operations. 1. The withdrawal of calamities; 2. The bestowment of blessings. II. That the Divine operations are influenced by the moral condition of the people. III. That the right moral conduct of a people will ensure them Divine benedictions.—Thomas.

God's Mercy.—He is a skilful physician indeed who, finding a man sorely afflicted, not only succeeds in restoring him to health, but actually causes him to be better than he was before, dealing with his medicine, not only with the disease which caused pain, but with some other which lay deeper, but had scarcely been perceived by the patient. Such is the medicine of mercy. Thus graciously doth God deal with repenting sinners. He must be worse than a brute beast who would turn this into an argument for sinning. A true child of God feels the water standing in his eyes when he thinks of such superabounding love.——Free as the sun that shineth, and gilds the mountain's brow, and makes glad the valleys, without fee or reward, so free is the mercy of God to every needy sinner. Free as the air which belts the earth, and penetrates the peasant's cottage, as well as the royal palace, without purchase or premium, so free is the mercy of God in Christ. It tarrieth not for thee; it cometh to thee as thou art. It waylayeth thee in love: it meeteth thee in tenderness.—Spurgeon.——God's Love and Pity.—It will give a kind of exaltation to the saint's happiness to look down upon that moral depth from which he was taken. A man on the edge of a precipice, at night, cannot clearly see it; but when the morning dawns, he will be able to see the danger he has been in. So the saint cannot, while on earth, conceive the depth of sin from which he has been raised; but he will be able to measure it by the light of heaven, and he may go down ages before he comes to the place where he once was: and then to think what he is—how deep once, but how high now—it will augment the sense of happiness and glory:—and then to recollect who has been the cause—

"What are all the forms of moral beauty in the Pharisee of religion, compared with the true and holy life of the heart of the devoted Christian?"—Bishop Thompson.

"A few days ago, the heaviest snow storm of the year, came the evening of a special meeting for the good of the church, and spoiled all the plans we had earnestly and hopefully made. Within a week, everyone of the committee 'was full of gratitude for the storm for a far better plan was inaugurated."
—Peloubet.

and every time he looks down at what he was, it will give greater emphasis to the ascription, "Unto him that loved us, and washed us from our sins in his own blood, and hath made us kings and priests unto God and his Father: to him be glory and dominion for ever and ever."—John Foster.——Pray.—The gracious God is pleased to esteem it his glory to have many beggars thronging at the beautiful gate of his temple, for spiritual and corporal alms. What an honor it is to our Great Landlord that multitudes of tenants flock together to his house to pay their rent of thanks and worship for all which they hold of him! How loud and lovely is the noise of many golden trumpets! Good Lord, what an echo do they make in heaven's ears! When many skilful musicians play in concert with well-tuned and prepared instruments, the music cannot but be ravishing to God himself.—George Swinnock.

21, 22. (21) **O land,** or O earth. Reference is to the fields, etc., wh. had borne the weight of Divine judgment.[a] **great things,** in the way of deliverance and restoration. (22) **do spring,** "are springing with new grass."—G. A. Smith. Start growing again after the time of desolation; see ch. i. 19. **their strength,** in rich and abundant fruitage.[b]

A Change of Moral Character.—It is too clear for either argument or illustration, that if you change the moral character of any country from ignorance to intelligence, from indolence to industry, from intemperance to self-discipline, from sensualness to spirituality, from enmity to love, that the whole material region in which they live may abound with plentifulness and beauty. Such a change throughout the whole human population to-day will give to all a new heaven and earth.—Thomas.

Golden Harvest of Autumn.—
Autumn! and the red sun through mottled clouds,
Like fire-bark through blue waves, his passage cleaves;
In ripening raiment all the orchard shrouds,
And gilds with glory all the saffron sheaves.
The wind, swift handmaid of the harvest field,
Curling the yellow tresses of the corn,
Brings, on the breaking silence of the morn,
The reapers' song. Lo! where they wildly wield
Their glittering sickles, brandish'd high in air,
Ere they begin their merry toil! and now
The shout is hushed into a murmur low:
The sun advancing from his cloud-girt lair,
Chases from sorest hearts sad dreams of night,
For darkest waters will reflect his light.—Campbell.

23—25. (23) **children of Zion,** or of Judah; for Joel was a prophet of the southern kingdom. **moderately,** Heb. "according to righteousness;"[c] R. V., "in just measure." **former rain .. latter rain,** "the rains which marked respectively the beginning and the close of the wet season, coming in Oct.—Nov. and March—April respectively. The 'former rain' moistens the earth and fits it to receive the seeds which are sown shortly afterwards: the 'latter rain' is important for giving fulness and strength to the ripening crops: if either rain fails, the ensuing harvest is seriously damaged. Comp. Deut. xi. 14; Jer. v. 24. The refreshing and invigorating effects of the 'latter rain' are alluded to in Hos. vi. 3; Prov. xvi. 15; Job xxix. 23: in Jer. iii. 3 it is spoken of as having been 'withheld.'"—Camb. Bib. (24) **floors,** i. e. the threshing-floors. **fats,** i. e. vats into wh. the wine and oil were pressed.[d] (25) **locust,** etc., ch. i. 4.

Repentance Necessary to Regain Lost Blessings.—A man upon the way, having accidentally lost his purse, is questioned by his fellow-traveler where he had it last. "Oh!" says he, "I am confident that I drew it out of my pocket when I was in such a town, at such an inn." "Why, then!" says the other, "there is no better way to have it again than by going back to the place where you last had it." This is the case of many a man in these loose, unsettled times; they have lost their love to Christ, and his truth, since their corn and wine and oil have increased; since outward things are in abundance added unto them they have slighted the light of God's countenance. When they were poor and naked of all worldly comfort, then they sought God's face both early and late, and

"I never was deeply interested in any object. I never prayed sincerely and earnestly for anything, but it came, at some time, no matter at how distant a day; somehow, in some shape, probably the last I should have devised, it came." —Adoniram Judson.

a "The Prophet had declared that the earth and the animal and the vegetable kingdoms are involved in suffering for man's sin; and he now reveals the joyful truth that they will be renewed in God's mercy, on man's repentance and faith. Comp. Ho. ii. 21—23; Ro. viii. 19—22." — Wordsworth.

b Ps. lxvii. 6; Zec. viii. 12.

"The Holy Spirit is the all-subduing power of the spiritual realm. Obey the laws of the Spirit, and all His power is at your disposal." — A. T. Pierson.

c Comp. Je. x. 23, xxx. 11.

d "The effect of the seasonable rains shall be abundance of all articles of food."
—Fausset.

"If we desired more, we should receive more. It is because our prayers are too narrow, because we only want to fill the cup up within an inch of the top that we are poor; when we are willing that the cup shall run over there comes a springing out from heaven, a pouring down from above of that wh. fills the cup from the great wealth and mercy of our God." — Alexander McKenzie.

nothing was more dear and precious unto them than the truth of Christ. What, then, is to be done to recover this lost love to Christ? Back again, back again directly where you last had it! Back to the sign of the broken and contrite heart! There it was that you drew it out into good words and better works; and though it be since lost in the crowd of worldly employments, there and nowhere else, you shall be sure to find it again.—Spencer's "Things New and Old."

26, 27. "The future prosperity is characterized in terms which obviously mark the period which succeeded that of the Babylonish captivity."—Barrows. (26) **be satisfied,** comp. Le. xxvi. 5, 26. **be ashamed,** by reason of disappointed hopes of harvest. This caused shame because it was a sure sign of their Lord's displeasure. (27) **I am the Lord your God,** Cf. iii. 17. "The phrase is a stereotyped one, which occurs (with or without 'your God') often in certain parts of the O. T., usually to denote the conviction produced by some great act of judgment or deliverance upon those who witness it. In Ezekiel (who uses it—with ye, they, or thou, as the case may be—more than 50 times) it is a standing refrain, coming often at the end of a paragraph, or a prophecy."—Camb. Bib. **none else,** i. e. no other supposed god has any claim to your allegiance.[a]

The Courage and Confidence of God's People (vs. 26).—I. The nature and grounds of that confidence under which they shall never be moved. 1. They rest on the strong arm of Omnipotence; 2. They build on a firm foundation; 3. They have the promises; 4. The anchor of hope. II. The effect of this godly boldness and confidence. 1. Note the effect of the opposite quality; 2. The godly have a state of peace; 3. They stand up for the cause of God.—W. Stone.

Courage in Lowly Places.—Go ask God's angels where they see the most courage. Not at the cannon's mouth; not at the hilted sword. Go see the saintly Christian mother that, for the space of twenty years, has suffered days and nights of pain, in order to give, literally, her life for her children. Left, when her husband died, a widow, in extreme poverty, she determines, by the love she bore him, as well as by the love she bears them, that they shall grow up to intelligence and education; and through toiling pain, as much as martyrs feel at the stake, by day and by night, willingly, in long months—Oh! how long the year is to misery! —she has given herself to these children. And now, one by one, as they have come upon the stage, in answer to her heroic efforts, they are prospered. But the sands are running out. She has used herself up. And at that time when woman should become matron, and, after all her suffering and shattering, should begin to be serene and happy, her forces are failing; and in poverty she is dying. She looks back upon her whole life, and there has never been a day that has not been bitter. There has never been a day in which she could have lived if she had not believed in God; and now she is dying. Ask God's angels if there is any hero on the battle-field that is so heroic as this poor spent Christian, that is dying, and glad to die, that has literally poured her life out like a cup of bitterness and pain for other people.——Bravery in Reproving Sin.—A merchant and shipowner of New York was standing at the entrance of his warehouses, conversing with a gentleman on business. A pious sailor belonging to one of his vessels came to the warehouse to enter it, but observing that the door was occupied, modestly stepped aside, not willing to interrupt the conversation. While waiting there, he heard the name of Jesus profanely used. "Sir, will you excuse me if I speak a word to you?" "Certainly," replied the merchant. "Well, then, sir," said the sailor, with much feeling, "will you be so kind as not to take the name of my blessed Jesus in vain? He took my feet out of 'the horrible pit and miry clay, and established my goings.' He is your Creator as well as mine; and He has made you, and preserves you, and is always doing you good." This was said with so much earnestness and feeling, that the gentleman was quite touched. His eyes filled with tears, and he said, "My good fellow, God helping me, I will never again take the name of the Lord Jesus Christ, the Saviour, in vain." "Thank you, sir," said the honest tar; and, putting on his hat, he went away to his work.

28, 29. (28) **afterward,** in the last days;[a] in the Messianic times. The immediate temporal blessings were to be the sign of the future spiritual blessings. **pour .. spirit,** the gift of the Spirit is presented under the fig-

---

[a] Eze. xxxvii. 26, 27, xxxix. 22; Zep. iii. 15, 17.

"He's truly valiant that can wisely suffer the worst that man can breathe, and make his wrongs his outsides, to wear them like his raiment, carelessly; and ne'er prefer his injuries to his heart, to bring it into danger." —Shakespeare.

"To stand with a smile upon your face against a stake from which you cannot get away—that, no doubt is heroic. But the true glory is resignation to the inevitable. To stand unchained, with perfect liberty to go away, held only by the higher claims of duty, and let the fire creep up to the heart,—this is heroism." —F. W. Robertson.

When the assembled senate of Rome, begged Regulus not to return to Carthage to fulfill an illegal promise, he calmly replied, "Have you resolved to dishonor me? Torture and death are awaiting me, but what are these to the shame of an infamous act, or the wounds of a guilty mind? Slave as I am to Carthage, I still have the spirit of a Roman. I have sworn to return. It is my duty. Let the gods take care of the rest." — O. S. Marden.

[a] Ac. ii. 17.

b Is. xliv. 3; Eze. xxxix. 29.

c "Prophecy, visions, dreams, are naturally selected by Joel as being the recognised forms of the manifestation of the Spirit under the old Testament." Spk. Com.

d Ga. iii. 28; Co. iii. 11.

Such a string of pearls, I think, were never put around the neck of any favorite, as Christ put around the neck of His disciples, when He pronounced the Beatitudes.

"Some one asked an Indian how he became converted. He built a fire in a circle round a worm, and then after the worm had crawled round every way and then lay down to die, he reached over and took him out. That is the way in which God saves us." — D. L. Moody.

ure of refreshing rains,[b] wh. is used in the previous verses. "In the O. T. theocracy the guidance of the Holy Spirit was given (Is. lxiii. 11), but it was the prerogative especially of the prophets, effected by an influence, not an indwelling. The church of the future, on the contrary, is founded upon an outpouring of the Spirit upon all flesh."—Oehler. **prophecy,** "i. e. will have insight into Divine truth, and will be moved to express it, in the manner which is at present confined to such as specially bear the name of prophets. The term is of course not to be misunderstood, as if it referred merely to predictions relating to the future: the reference is in general to inspired instruction in moral and religious truth. Two special modes of consciousness in which Divine truths frequently presented themselves to the prophet (Num. xii. 6) are then particularized, the dream and the vision: in illustration of the former, see Deut. xiii. 2, Jer. xxiii. 25, 32, xxvii. 9, xxix. 8 (in these passages the dream is spoken of in terms of disparagement, on account of its liability to become a source of self-deception); for the latter, see on Am. i. 1 and vii. 1."—Camb. Bib. **dreams,** etc., the various modes of Divine communication previously given.[c] (29) **servants,** etc., the new grace would be set under no class restrictions. To the poor the Gospel was preached; and upon the slaves the Divine Spirit came.[d]

The Gospel Dispensation (vs. 28).—The Gospel dispensation was to be characterized—I. By spirituality. 1. Formerly the Spirit dwelt with men; 2. Now He dwells in them. II. By liberty. 1. The Gospel finds us in chains; 2. It bursts our bonds asunder. III. Power. 1. Marvellous spiritual signs; 2. Stupendous physical wonders. IV. Expansiveness. 1. Its salvation is universally free; 2. Its conditions are level to all capacities; 3. It triumphs over all conventionalities.—J. A. Macdonald.

Unclaimed Blessings.—The Scottish bankers have published the fact that they have lying in their vaults, a sum of £40,000,000 in unclaimed deposits. Some of those who owned a share of this money may have died in the workhouse. Some of them may be living to this moment in direst need, and they might have their money for the claiming, but they do not know it is theirs. What vast unclaimed deposits are lying in God's Treasury! Some of his people have died spiritually poor; some are living today in spiritual penury, a hand-to-mouth existence with such unclaimed riches lying at call, at deposit in their name. What have we done with our deposit?—John McNeil.——Endless Supply of the Holy Spirit.—In driving between Melbourne and my home, I often stop at a wayside trough to give my horse a drink. I notice that the trough is quite full of water, and that there is a box at one end of it. As the horse drinks, the water is lowering, and presently I hear a sound as of a running tap. Yes, the sound is coming from the box. That box is covering a mechanism that needs explanation. Within it, there is a tap, connected by pipes with the Yan Yean reservoir up in the Plenty Ranges. Attached by the lever to the tap is a metal ball which rests on the surface of the water. As the horse drinks, the water on which the ball is floating is lowered, and thus the ball is lowered. The lowering of the ball opens the tap and the Yan Yean begins to pour in; so that although the water is being withdrawn by the thirsty animal, a fresh supply is being poured in. The trough is being filled so that it is always full. Thus may it be with the soul of the believer .. there is the continual inflow so that there may be the constant "fulness."—McNeil.

a "We have two kinds of sirocco, one accompanied with vehement wind, which fills the air with dust and fine sand. I have often seen the whole heavens veiled in gloom with this sort of sand-cloud, through which the sun, shorn of his beams, looked like a globe of dull smoldering fire. It may have been this phenomenon wh. suggested that strong prophetic fig. of Joel. The pillars of smoke are probably those columns of sand and dust raised high in the air by local whirlwinds, wh. often accompany the sirocco."—Thomson.

b Mat. xxiv. 29; Mk. xiii. 24; Lu. xxi. 25; Re. vi. 12.

30—32. "The signs of approaching judgments which will then appear." (30) **wonders,** etc., these "features of natural phenomena are not to be regarded as poetic coloring but rest upon the scriptural view of the inalienable connection between the course of nature and the progress of the Divine kingdom. Comp. Is. xiii. 9 ff; Zeph. i. 15 ff."—Oehler.[a] (31) **sun .. blood,**[b] these figures may denote the melancholy condition of public affairs previous to the destruction of Jerusalem. There may also be intended a reference to the time of general judgment. (32) **whosoever,** etc., Ro. x. 13. **and in Jerusalem,** comp. Lu. xxiv. 47. **deliverance,** etc., R. V., "there shall be those that escape .. and among the remnant those whom the Lord doth call." **remnant,** "among the fugitives," G. A. Smith, also Camb. Bib., which refers to those scattered in exile summoned to enjoy Jehovah's salvation.

Note on vss. 28—32.—These words are quoted in Acts ii. 17—21 by St. Peter, with reference to the outpouring of the Spirit upon the Apostles on the day of Pentecost. It would be incorrect, however, to regard a particular occasion as exhausting the fulfilment of the prophecy. Joel's words—like Jer. xxxi. 33 f., for instance,—look rather to that fuller illumination to be enjoyed in general by God's people in the future, which is to be a characteristic of the Christian Church throughout the ages; they are "not a prediction of the event of Pentecost, but of the new order of things of which Pentecost was the first great example."—Camb. B. ——Two Ways of Deliverance.—There are two ways of deliverance. The Christian is not always delivered from sickness and pain and death, as is witnessed by a long train of saints and martyrs. They are delivered like Peter, or delivered like Stephen with his vision of the Son of God. But they are always delivered, delivered from falling, from the power of temptation, from the powers of evil, which can no more touch them than the flames could touch the three men in Nebuchadnezzar's furnace; they were delivered into the roll of heroes and martyrs, into the company who sing the new song. Many a seeming defeat is a victory. So in the seeming victory of Satan and the world when Christ was crucified there was real defeat. The mightiest blow against the kingdom of evil was struck by that apparent victory. Yet often, very often, there is an earthly deliverance too. "Everyone is immortal and invulnerable till his work is done." Till then "thou shalt tread upon the lion and adder; the young lion and the dragon shalt thou trample under foot." "They shall take up serpents in their hands; and if they drink any deadly thing, it shall not hurt them."—F. N. Peloubet.

"The soil is full of seeds. Darwin found 500 in a single cup of mud. If a forest covers the ground and shades it from the sun, many seeds will never spring up. But cut down the forest, give light and air, and many otherwise unknown plants will come into being, and cover the ground with their luxuriance. So with our souls; if we cut down the prejudices and worldliness, and let the Holy Spirit shine upon our souls, many talents and powers will develop that otherwise would have been unknown." — Peloubet.

Hallowing Effects of Daybreak.—

What soul was his when from the naked top
Of some bold headland he beheld the sun
Rise up and bathe the world in light! He look'd—
Ocean and earth, the solid frame of earth
And ocean's liquid mass, beneath him lay
In gladness and deep joy. The clouds were touched,
And in their silent faces did he read
Unutterable love. Sound needed none,
Nor any voice of joy; his spirit drank
The spectacle; sensation, soul, and form
All melted into him; they swallowed up
His animal being; in them did he live,
And by them did he live; they were his life.

In such access of mind, in such high hour
Of visitation from the Living God,
Thought was not; in enjoyment it expired;
No thanks he breathed, he proffer'd no request
Rapt into still communion that transcends
The imperfect offices of prayer and praise,
His mind was a thanksgiving to the Power
That made him; it was blessedness and love!—Wordsworth.

CHAPTER THE THIRD.

Hitherto Joel has spoken no syllable of the heathen, except to pray that God by His plagues will not give Israel to be mocked by them. But in the last chapter of the Book we have Israel's captivity to the heathen taken for granted, a promise made that it will be removed and their land set free from the foreigner. Certain nations are singled out for judgment, which is described in the terms of Apocalypse; and the Book closes with the vision, already familiar in prophecy, of a supernatural fertility for the land.—G. A. Smith. 1—3. (1) **those days,** "the outpouring of the Holy Spirit is here conceived of as a single act amid tremendous natural phenomena. In the fulfilment, however (as in the judgment of the world), that which is momentary in the prophetic intuition is accomplished by a process of long and natural development."—Oehler. **bring again,** this is usually referred to a restoration of the Jews wh. is yet to be accomplished.[a] (2) **all nations,** hostile nations, enemies of God's Church. **val-**

[a] "The Prophet comprises the whole redemption, beginning from the return out of Babylon, then continued from the first advent of Christ down to the last day (His second advent) when God will restore His Church to perfect felicity."—Calvin.

Je. xxx. 3.

ley of Jehoshaphat, or the valley of Divine judgment, such as was revealed in the days of Jehoshaphat.[b] **plead,** see Is. lxvi. 16; Eze. xxxviii. 22. **parted my land,** this was done by the Chaldæans and Romans. (3) **cast lots,** Na. iii. 10. **boy,** etc., "during the Jewish war Titus took 97,000 prisoners, of whom he publicly sold all that were under 17 years of age."[c]

Valley.—In the days of Joel valleys were the usual fields of battle, mountainous and wooded country being unfavorable to the movements, tactics, and strategical combinations of ancient military art. Naturally, therefore, the Prophet would select some valley as the arena of the final conflict. But this conflict was also to be a judgment. Was it possible to select a valley whose very name should convey the idea of judgment and of Divine judgment? Yes; close outside the eastern wall of Jerusalem lay a valley, known as the valley of Jehoshaphat. Jehoshaphat means. "Jehovah judges." Here ready to his hand were the very symbols the Prophet required. The scene of the final conflict and the final judgment would be the valley in which Jehovah judgeth and will judge.—S. Cox.

4—6. (4) **what .. Palestine?**[d] R. V., "Yea, and what are ye to me .. and all the regions of Philistia?" i. e. "Why do ye too, even now, harass my people?" **will ye render,** etc., "will ye repay a deed of mine, or will ye do aught unto me?" (R. V. marg.) i. e. is there any injustice that I have done to you (through Israel) which you would avenge, or would you even assail me gratuitously? The question is a rhetorical one, to which of course a negative answer is expected: their treatment of Israel has been unprovoked; it is they, and not Israel, who merit vengeance; accordingly the retort follows, "Swiftly and speedily will I return your deed (R. V. marg.) upon your own head."—Camb. B. (5) **my silver,** Mine because belonging to My people. (6) **the Grecians,** or people of Javan;[e] Ionians, a Greek colony on the coast of Asia Minor, who were the first Greeks known to the Jews. "It is said particularly of Javan (i. e. Greece), that they dealt in that sort of traffic, the buying and selling of slaves."[f]

Persecution.—Oh, if when we oppress and goad our fellow-creatures, we bestowed but one thought upon the dark evidences of human error, which, like dense and heavy clouds, are rising slowly, it is true, but not less surely, to heaven, to pour their after-vengeance on our heads—if we heard but one instant, in imagination, the deep testimony of dead men's voices, which no power can stifle, and no pride can shut out, where would be the injury and injustice, the suffering, misery, cruelty, and wrong, that each day's life brings with it.—Dickens.——Slavery (vs. 3).—Morgan, in his History of Algiers, gives us such an account of the unfortunate expedition of the Emperor Charles V. against that city, so far resembling a passage of the Prophet Joel as to induce me to transcribe it into these papers. That author tells us, that besides vast multitudes that were butchered by the Moors and the Arabs, a great number were made captives, mostly by the Turks and citizens of Algiers; and some of them, in order to turn this misfortune into a most bitter, taunting, and contemptuous jest, parted with their new-made slaves for an onion apiece. "Often have I heard," says he, "Turks and Africans upbraiding Europeans with this disaster, saying, scornfully, to such as have seemed to hold their heads somewhat loftily, 'What! have you forgot the time when a Christian at Algiers was scarce worth an onion?' The treatment of the Jewish people by the heathen nations, which the Prophet Joel has described, was, in like manner, contemptuous and bitterly sarcastic. They that know the large sums that are wont to be paid, in the East, for young slaves of either sex, must be sensible that the Prophet designs, in these words, to point out the extreme contempt in which these heathen nations held the Jewish people."—Harmer.

7, 8. (7) **raise them,** by restoring either them or their posterity. (8) **sell your sons,** "you sold the children of Judah into slavery to a nation far off in the North West; I will sell your children into the hand of the Judahites, that they may sell them into slavery to a nation far off in the South East," this was fulfilled when, at the taking of Tyre, Alexander sold 30,000 of the inhabitants for slaves; at the same time Gaza, a town on the coast of Palestine, was sacked, and the women and children sold

b 2 Chr. xx.

"There is no reference to the valley close beside Jerusalem which has been thus named. At what period the name was first applied to that spot is not known; there is no trace of it in the Bible or Josephus."—Grove.

c "After Hadrian's Jewish war four Jews were sold for a measure of barley at Hebron."—Spk. Com.

d "These were some of the Jews' evil neighbors, who took all occasions to distress them."—Lowth.

e Gen. x. 2, 4.

f Eze. xxvii. 13.

"So hideous were the cruelties practised by Oriental victors upon their captives, that, were it not for the most convincing evidence in sculpture and inscription, where the perpetrators glory in their deeds, we should hardly believe it possible for men to treat their fellow-creatures with such barbarity."—Wm. Ewing.

"Corrupted freed-men are the worst of slaves."—Garrick.

for slaves. **Sabeans,** people of Sheba, at the remote extremity of Arabia Felix.[a]

True Liberty.—Liberty is the fullest opportunity for man to be and do the very best that is possible for him. .. You see a man coming forward and offering himself as one of the defenders of his country in his country's need. You see him standing at the door where men are being received as recruits into the army of the country. He wants liberty. He wants to be able to do that which he cannot do in his poor, personal isolation here at home. He wants the badge which will give him the right to go forth and meet the enemies of his country and he enrolls himself among these men. He makes himself subject to obligations, duties, drill. They are a part of his enfranchisement. They are really the breaking of the fetters upon his slavery, the sending him forth into freedom. .. This, then, is freedom; everything is part of the enfranchisement of a man which helps to put him in the place where he can live his best. Therefore every duty, every will of God, every commandment of Christ, every self-surrender that a man is called upon to obey or to make—do not think of it as if it were simply a restraint to liberty, but think of it as the very means of freedom by which we realize the very purpose of God, and the fulfilment of our life.—Phillips Brooks.—— Abraham Lincoln and Slavery.—If ever the face of a man writing solemn words, glowed with a solemn joy, it must have been the face of Abraham Lincoln as he bent over the page where the Emancipation Proclamation of 1863 was growing into shape, and giving manhood and freedom as he wrote it to hundreds of thousands of his fellowmen. .. And as the swarthy multitudes came in, ragged and tired, and hungry, and ignorant, but free forever from anything but the memorial scars of the fetters and the whip, singing rude songs in which the new triumph of freedom struggled and heaved below the sad melody that had been shaped for bondage; as in their camps and hovels, there grew up to their half-superstitious eyes the image of a great Father, almost more than man, to whom they owed their freedom—were they not half right?—P. Brooks.

9, 10. "After the digression on the Phoenicians and Philistines (vss. 4—8), the thought of vss. 1—3 is resumed; and the description of the judgment on the nations, announced in vs. 2 is continued. The heathen are invited to arm themselves, and advance for the great contest with Israel in the valley of Jehoshaphat, vss. 9—12; but once arrived there, they are annihilated, amid celestial portents, by the agents of Jehovah's will, whom He commissions to engage with them, while His own people look on securely."—Camb. Bib.[a] (9) **Proclaim,**[b] etc., "the words are addressed to those whose duty it would be to make such a proclamation, i. e. the heralds, whom the prophet pictures as ready to carry Jehovah's command to the nations." (10) **Beat,** etc., comp. Is. ii. 4. **pruninghooks,** the sickles; not, as marg., the scythe, an instrument quite unknown in the East. **am strong,** the general rage against God's people would lead even the weak and the aged to join the army.

The Syrian Plough (vs. 10).—The Syrian plough, which was probably used in all the regions around, is a very simple frame, and commonly so light, that a man of moderate strength might carry it in one hand. Volney states that in Syria it is often nothing else than the branch of a tree, cut below a bifurcation, and used without wheels. It is drawn by asses and cows, seldom by oxen. And Dr. Russell informs us, the ploughing of Syria is performed often by a little cow, at most with two, and sometimes only by an ass. In Persia it is, for the most part, drawn by one ox only, and not unfrequently even by an ass, although it is more ponderous than in Palestine. With such an imperfect instrument the Syrian husbandman can do little more than scratch the surface of his field, or clear away the stones or weeds that encumber it, and prevent the seed from reaching the soil. The ploughshare is a "piece of iron, broad, but not large, which tips the end of the shaft." So much does it resemble the short sword used by the ancient warriors, that it may, with very little trouble, be converted into that deadly weapon; and when the work of destruction is over, reduced again to its former shape. —Paxton.

[a] Je. vi. 20; Eze. xxiii. 42.

"When liberty is gone, life grows insipid, and has lost its relish." — Addison.

The following sentence forms the striking inscription to be found in an inn at Savoy: "Understand well the force of the words, a God, a moment, an eternity; — God who sees thee, a moment which flees from thee, an eternity which awaits thee; a God, whom you serve so ill; a moment, of which you so little profit, an eternity which you hazard so rashly."

[b] Zec. xiv. 2, 3.

"The word prepare war, is lit. sanctify war, bec. the heathen always began war with religious ceremonies."—Fausset.

"Here, as in other respects, the predictions and promises are but partially fulfilled in the literal Israel. Their real accomplishment, their awful completion, will be when Zion's King comes in glory and majesty, with a rod of iron, to dash in pieces the great antichristian confederacy of kings and peoples, and to take possession of his long-promised and dearly-bought inheritance. The signs of the times seem to indicate that the coming of the Lord draws nigh."

—Hom. Com.

11, 12. (11) **Assemble,** R. V., "Haste ye and come." **thy mighty ones,** "the prophet suddenly turns aside to address Jehovah: he has bidden the nations assemble, for the contest against Israel, in the valley of Jehoshaphat: he now prays Jehovah to cause His warriors also to descend thither to meet them. The mighty ones are, no doubt, the angelic hosts (Ps. lxviii. 17; Zech. xiv. 5), whom Joel pictures as the agents of Jehovah's will, and who are called in Ps. ciii. 20 the 'mighty in strength.'"—Camb. Bib. (12) **be wakened,** R. V., "bestir themselves." **there,** not in the valley near Jerusalem, but in the ideal spot named in vs. 2 the valley of Jehoshaphat, i. e. of God's judgment.

Valley of Jehoshaphat.—This valley, running from north to south, between Jerusalem and the Mount of Olives, is a little more than a mile long. Its greatest breadth is supposed to be from 150 to 200 yards, but in other places it is only a deep, narrow ravine. The bottom is ordinarily dry, excepting after heavy rains. The valley is rocky on both sides, and abounds in sepulchres of various shapes and sizes, with only a few scattered olives to relieve the eye. For nearly three thousand years it has been used as a place of burial by Jews, Mohammedans, and Christians. In addition to the tombs of kings and patriarchs, there are tens of thousands of stones, the only memorials of the mighty dead. Thither persons repair from all parts of the world, to seek from the Turks a last resting-place for their bodies, even though it be at great cost, believing that Christ will there appear in judgment. "The valley is divided into three parts, of which the northern is called the Valley of Kedron; the middle the Valley of Jehoshaphat; and the southern the Valley of Siloam, from the fountain of that name on the one side, and the village on the other. These three names are also applied, respectively, to the whole extent of the valley, but that of the Valley of Siloam less frequently than the other two." It is also called the King's Dale (2 Sam. xviii. 18), and the Vale of Shaveh (Gen. xiv. 17).—Meen.

13, 14. (13) **Put .. sickle,** Re. xiv. 15.[a] "The sickles of the East, as represented on Egyptian monuments, resembled ours, only were smaller."—Barrows. **harvest is ripe,** i.e. the wickedness of the wicked is come to a head, and demands Divine interference. (14) **valley of decision,** "this and the following verses, instead of expressly narrating the execution of the Divine command, present a picture of it. In one part the prophet sees in vision and shows us pictorially the multitudes of the nations pouring on in one continuous stream into the fatal valley." "Philip, king of Macedon, as he was wrestling at the Olympic games, fell down in the sand; and, when he rose again, observing the print of his body in the sand, cried out, 'O how little a parcel of earth will hold us, when we are dead, who are ambitiously seeking after the whole world whilst we are living!'"—Whitecross.

Valley of Jehoshaphat.—Wilson, in the Lands of the Bible, says: "One of the most picturesque, and, at the same time, deeply interesting scenes, is the Valley of Jehoshaphat viewed from the brow of the hill descending from the high places of Tophet. There is a magnificence in its outlining which lives in the memory. It cannot be forgotten. The bed of the brook Kedron lies along the lowest part of it; and on either side, fig, olive, and pomegranate trees cast a lovely shade; while gardens of melons and cucumbers give an idea of fresh luxuriance. On either side of the valley the heights are terraced, and in some places slightly cultivated, and the breadth of the valley is very bold and striking. Independent of all the heart-stirring associations which Scripture narrative gives rise to, the Valley of Jehoshaphat, viewed from south to north, on the east side of the city, is a scene in which a gifted painter would luxuriate. On the right slope, north of En-rogel, and formed by the meeting of the valleys of Hinnom and Jehoshaphat, are the best cultivated gardens near Jerusalem, and undoubtedly those mentioned in Scripture by the name of King's Garden. The present gardens are watered by channels and streamlets from the Pool of Siloam. Their trees and kitchen vegetables are of the finest quality. Close upon the gardens there is an aged mulberry tree, surrounded by a stone terrace which, it is said, marks the spot where the Prophet Isaiah was sawn asunder."

15—17. (15) **sun .. darkened,** ch. ii. 31. (16) **roar,** as a lion.[c] **hope**

---

[a] "The Mohammedans have borrowed from the Jews a tradition, which locates the judgment in the Kidron, or valley of Jehoshaphat." —Porter.

"Enslave a man, and you destroy his ambition, his enterprise, his capacity. In the constitution of human nature, the desires of bettering one's condition is the mainspring of effort. The first touch of slavery snaps this spring." —Mann.

"Timorous obeyed Christ through fear, and Christ rewarded him; Faithful with delight, and Christ loved him."

"Without reverence there is no obedience; without obedience there is no reverence."

[a] Mat. xiii. 30—39.

[b] "Like sheaves crushed on the threshing-floor by the sharp toothed instrument which was formed with revolving cylinders, and by which they were threshed." —Wordsworth.

"Nature shall make me careful of myself, but hateful to none: reason shall make me wise for myself, but harmless to all; religion shall make me loving to all, but not careless of myself. I may hear the former, I will hearken only to the latter. I subscribe to some things in all, to all things in religion." —Warwick.

[c] Je. xxv. 30; Am. i. 2, iii.

.. **people,** R. V. "but the Lord will be a refuge unto his people and a stronghold to the children of Israel." (17) **holy,** consecrated entirely to God. **strangers .. more,** comp. Is. xxxv. 8; Je. xxx. 8; Ob. 17; Re. xxi. 27; this refers to the reign of peace, the new city of God is no more to be desecrated by enemies.

Note on vss. 15, 16.—The densely packed masses are already in the valley of decision, awaiting the judgment about to be executed upon them. But before the judgment actually bursts upon them, and in preparation for it, the sky is overcast; darkness, as a portent of the approaching storm, envelops them; the lights of heaven are put out. The pitchy darkness of a night in which neither moon nor stars appear is sufficiently dismal and awful; still more terrible, if possible, is darkness in the daytime, when the light of the sun is turned into blackness. The first accompaniment of the storm is addressed to the eye, and consists in the extinguishing of the greater light which rules the day, and the lesser lights which rule the night. The next accompaniment of the coming tempest is addressed to the ear, and consists in the voice of the Lord rolling in terrific peals along the heavens—the voice of the Lord like the roaring of a lion ready to pounce upon its prey; the utterance of the Divine voice when the God of glory thundereth. The third accompaniment is yet more awe-inspiring, consisting in a convulsion that pervades both earth and sky; the whole frame of nature shakes; the earthquake's shock, so frightful to bird and beast and man, has a corresponding agitation in the heavens.—Pulp. Com. God, the only Judge.—Elizabeth said she felt the blood of a hundred kings in her veins, burning in anger, or rising in pride; we who are not in the line of kings nominally may be in a mysterious line nevertheless. The drunken ancestor; the diseased mind; the relative that died two hundred years ago a raving maniac; the saintly mother and the saintly grandmother, Eunice and Lois; the man that prayed all day, and thought the day too short because he had more to say to God; all these are in a man. What wonder if in the morning he blaspheme, and at night he pray, if this moment he rave like one in whose disordered brain "reason has lost her way," and the next moment be giving himself out in acts of love, in alms of tender pity and all-including charity? Who can judge him? Only the Lord. The Lord knows every drop of blood that is in the fountain of the heart; the Lord, the mighty Judge, presides over that fountain, and says concerning each drop, This tells of five centuries ago: this drop tells of the praying soul that importuned my throne, and took many blessings by gracious violence; this drop has in it bodily disease, poison generated a century since. He knows our frame, he remembereth that we are but dust; let him judge; let no man ascend the judgment seat.—Peop. Bib.

"God's sieve drives away the chaff, and saves the wheat.
Satan's sieve saves the chaff, and drives away the wheat."
—Van Doren.

Safety in God.—The only place of safety in this world is the one in which we are sure to meet God, and to be "under the shadow of his wing." The Bible sets forth, in grand metaphor, this idea, by speaking of a "fortress into which the righteous runneth, and is safe;" and of "a strong tower," and of "the shadow of a great rock." When we were in the Yosemite Valley, lately, our driver told us of a series of terrific earthquakes, which visited the valley several years ago. The few inhabitants who dwelt there were thrown out of their beds in the night. Frail cottages were overturned. Loose rocks were hurled down from the precipices into the valley. These shocks were repeated for several days until the people were panic-stricken and ready to despair. "What did you do?" we inquired. The driver (pointing to the mighty and immovable rock, El Capitan, which rises for three thousand feet on the south side of the valley, and has a base of three solid miles) replied: "We determined to go and camp under old Capitan; for if that ever moved we knew the world would be coming to an end."—Cuyler.

18—21. (18) **drop,** etc., comp. Am. ix. 13. Figurative for abundance of vines grown on the terraced hill-sides. **fountain,**[a] "peace is also to pervade nature. The harmony between it and man, which, according to Gen. iii. was disturbed by sin, is to be restored: the Holy Land is to be glorified, and a fountain of life to flow from the Temple (Ezek. xlvii. 6

Awakening the heathen or minds like sieves. "Have you ever heard the gospel before?" asked an Englishman, at Ningpo, of a respectable Chinaman, whom he had not seen in his mission-room before. "No," he replied, "but I have seen it. I know a man who used to be the terror of his neighborhood. If you gave him a hard word, he would shout at you, and curse you for two days and nights without ceasing. He was as dangerous as a wild beast, and a bad opium-smoker; but when the religion of Jesus took hold of him, he became wholly changed. He is gentle, moral, not soon angry, and has left off opium. Truly, the teaching is good!"—Word and Work.

a Zec. xiv. 8; Re. xxii.1.

If I had the choice of preaching like Gabriel, swaying men at my will, without winning them to Christ, or taking them one by one in private and leading them to the truth, how gladly would I choose the latter!
—D. L. Moody.

If you are beginning to despair of ever emerging from the clouds that overshadow you, search your life for the sin that is devouring that immortal assurance of victory given to every soul that will serve God by obedience to his law; look for the causes of your defeat, not in your inheritance nor in your surroundings, but in yourself. Victory lies within reach of every true life; at all costs set yourself to win it.—Christian Union.

seq.)."—Oehler. (19) **Egypt .. and Edom,** types of the enemies of Israel. (20) **Judah .. ever,** this is true if regarded spiritually, and Judah be put for the Church of God in the world. (21) **cleanse,** R. V. marg. "And I will hold as innocent their blood which I have not held as innocent." "By the desolation of Egypt and Edom, Jehovah will shew openly that the murdered Judahites (vs. 19) had suffered innocently. So long, namely, as He permitted their blood to remain unavenged, it might be supposed that they had not been slain unjustly: but by the punishment of the murderers, Jehovah declares (implicitly), what He had not declared before, that their blood was innocent and had been unjustly shed."—Camb. Bib.

God and the Church (vs. 21).—I. The Church is the greatest witness for God. 1. As decidedly opposed to the principles and practices of the great mass of mankind; 2. A great proportion of mankind have in every age opposed the Church; 3. Still the Church has not only existed but increased. II. The Church is the brightest revelation of God. 1. By publishing God's own revelations; 2. By imitating His moral perfections. III. The Church is the highest instrument of God. 1. It ameliorates the outward sufferings of the world; 2. It converts the moral heart of the world.—Caleb Morris.

Safe in God's Hands.—Possibly ye may be hid from punishment, probably ye shall escape sorrow: but pardon of sin ye shall be sure of; mitigation also of sorrow, if not prevention of it. Saved ye shall be, or more gently handled, or so inwardly calmed, that ye shall be able to call your souls to rest when others are at their wits' ends. You shall be safe under the cover of God's wings, and in the hollow of his hand; when others, that are without God in the world, shall be as a naked man in a storm, as an unarmed man in the field of battle, or as a ship at sea without an anchor, subject to dash and split against rocks and quicksands.—Trapp. God's Marvelous Love to Man.—If it would be marvelous to see one river leap up from the earth full-grown, what would it be to gaze upon a vast spring from which all the rivers of the earth should at once come bubbling up, a thousand of them born at a birth? What a vision would it be! Who can conceive it? And yet the love of God is that fountain, from which all the rivers of mercy, which have ever gladdened our race—all the rivers of grace in time, and of glory hereafter—take their rise. My soul, stand thou at that sacred fountain-head, and adore and magnify for ever and ever God, even our Father, who hath loved us.—C. H. Spurgeon.

Introduction.

I. **Author.** Amos, a native of Tekoah, a small town of Judah, ab. 12 ms. S. of Jerusalem; at least, this was his ordinary dwelling-place. He was not trained in the prophetic schools, and is said to have been among the shepherds of Tekoah (i. 1); he also describes himself as a gatherer of sycomore fruit, and says that he was taken from the flock (vii. 14, 15); but though this seems to indicate a mean condition, and none but the poorest (we are told by travelers) now gather or use sycomore fruit in Palestine, yet it does not follow that Amos was uneducated—a mere working man. David was taken from the sheepfolds; and the word used in Am. i. 1 is the same that is applied to Mesha, the tributary king of Moab (2 Kings iii. 4). II. **Time.** (B.C. 860-850.) We only know that Amos must have prophesied somewhere during the last part of the reign of Jeroboam II., when he was contemporary with Uzziah. The very specific date, "two years before the earthquake," indicates that his whole mission to Israel was executed within a single year, perhaps within a few months. It seems to have been after his return to Judah, when at least two years had elapsed, that he collected his prophecies and put them into their present form. III. **Style.** It has not the flowing fulness of Joel, but charms the reader by its freshness and simplicity. His writings abound in images taken from rural scenes and employments, some of which are very unique and striking in their character. The composition would seem to show that Amos was not a coarse rustic, but a person of considerable attainments. His book is cited twice in the New Testament (Acts vii. 42, 43, xv. 15, 17). "Amos is the earliest of the prophets whose writings we possess, and his book is a short one; nevertheless it is surprisingly full of acute observation of men and manner, and of teaching, at once profound and lofty, on the things of God. He is not more conspicuous on account of his literary power than for the breadth of human interest, embracing both acute observation, and wide historical knowledge, which his writings display. 'As a wool-grower, he must have had his yearly journeys among the markets of the land; and to such were probably due his opportunities of familiarity with Northern Israel, the originals of his vivid pictures of her town-life, her commerce, and the worship at her great sanctuaries.' The breadth of Amos' thought is apparent at once in the fundamental element in his theology, his conception of Jehovah. He is Jehovah of Hosts, i.e. the God who has untold forces and powers at His command; in other words, the All-Sovereign or the Omnipotent. There is a note of austerity in the terms in which Amos speaks. With him God is the God of righteousness; he himself is the apostle of righteousness; he is the preacher, whose moral nature is moved by the spectacle of outraged right, but who does not unbend in affection or sympathy: on the contrary, he announces Israel's doom with the austere severity of the judge."—Cambridge Bible.

Synopsis.

(According to the Pulpit Commentary.)

PART I. Approaching judgment: a prelude.i, ii.

Sec. 1. Summons of the nations bordering on the Holy Land..............i.—ii. 3.
Sec. 2. Summons of Judah...........ii. 4, 5.
Sec. 3. Summons and general denunciation of Israel ....ii. 6—16.

PART II. Three addresses particularizing the sins of Israel and announcing imminent punishment ....iii.—vi.

Sec. 1. First address ....iii.
Sec. 2. Second address ....iv.
Sec. 3. Third address ....v. vi.

PART III. Five visions, with explanations, vii.—ix. 10.

Sec. 1. First vision: locusts.......vii. 1—3.
Sec. 2. Second vision: fire.........vii. 4—6.
Sec. 3. Third vision: plumb-line....vii. 7—9.
Sec. 4. Historical parenthesis....vii. 10—17.
Sec. 5. Fourth vision: basket of fruits, viii. 1—14.
Sec. 6. Fifth vision: the Lord at the altar, ix. 1—10.

PART IV. Epilogue: establishment of the new kingdom ....ix. 11—15.

CHAPTER THE FIRST.

1, 2. (1) **words of,** comp. Je. i. 1. **Amos,** = "borne up, or a burden;" perhaps in allusion to the grievous message he had to deliver. Probably the earliest of the written Prophets. Though a native of Judah, his prophecies chiefly bear reference to the northern kingdom. **among,** i.e. one of. **herdmen,** or shepherds; the term used appears to indicate his care of a particular breed of sheep.[a] **Tekoa,** six miles S. from Bethlehem. **concerning Israel,** the Northern kingdom. **days of Jereboam,** i.e. Jereboam II., whose great military prowess advanced Israel to the acme of its national greatness (775-745 B.C.) **earthquake,** Zec. xiv. 5.[b] (2) **The Lord,** the prophet uses the word Yohiveh, i.e. Jehovah, the personal name by wh. God was known to the Hebrews. **roar,** like a lion about to pounce upon his prey. Joel iii:16. **utter,** etc., like the rolling thunder. **habitations,** R. V. "pastures," i.e. the south country, the chief part for flocks. **top,** or headland. The Prophet intimates thus that the whole land from south to north shall suffer under the judgments.

A Sketch of Amos (vs. 1).—I. The sphere of life in which he moved. 1. Worldly pride Divinely rebuked; 2. Human nature Divinely honored. II. The age in which he lived. 1. The political event of this period; 2. The physical event of this period. III. The mission to which he was called,—he announced a judgment as coming. 1. According to his vision; 2. In a terrible form; 3. An issuing from a scene of mercy; 4. As fraught with calamitous results.—Thomas.

Station in Life.—Low station is no obstacle to God's favor. Men great in science, literature, and art, apostles of great thoughts and lords of the great heart,—have sprung indiscriminately from the English farm and the Scotch hill-side, from the workshop and the mines, from the blacksmith's stithy, and the cobbler's stool. The illustrations which present themselves are indeed numerous. Take, for instance, the remarkable fact that from the barber's shop rose Sir Richard Arkwright, the inventor of the spinning-jenny, and the founder of the cotton manufacture of Great Britain; Lord Tenterden, one of the most distinguished of English Lord Chief Justices; and Turner, the very greatest among landscape-painters.—Cardinal Wolsey.

3—5. (3) **Damascus,** the capital of Syria. The first denunciation lights upon the Syrian kingdom of Damascus, the best-organized and most formidable of Israel's neighbors, with whom, shortly before, during the 80 years of the "Syrian wars" (c. 880—800 B.C.), the dynasties of Omri and Jehu had had many a severe struggle.—Cam. B. **for four,** in this poetical form Amos declares that the sin punished has been continued and aggravated after warning.[c] **turn away,** so as to prevent it from falling. God "turns away" judgments upon men's repentance, but a time comes when they can be turned away no longer. **threshed,** etc.,[d] typical example of Syrian transgression; ref. to the cruelties of Hazael during his invasions against Gilead. See 2 Ki. x. 32, 33. (4) **fire,**[e] used as a symbol of destructive warfare. **house,** dynasty. Ben-hadad, either Hazael's son, who continued the paternal cruelties; or the monarch then reigning in Syria. (5) **bar,** wh. fastens the city-gate, and so lay the city at the command of its enemy. **inhabitant,** R. V. marg. "him that sitteth on the throne," cf. vs. 8. **plain of Aven,** Cœele Syria, the country between Libanus and Anti-Libanus.[f] **house of Eden,** this is prob. a proper name; Beth-eden, some town in the N., perhaps the modern Ehden, 20 m. N.W. of Baalbek. **Kir,** Is. xxii. 6.[g]

Ideal Cruelty is Utterly Indiscriminate.—Elisha's prophecy to Hazael (2 Kings viii. 12), of which this horrid butchery was the fulfilment, mentions women and children as the chief victims of the outrage. There is a bloodhound instinct in wicked men which is aroused to fury by the taste of blood. The horrors of the French Revolution and of the Spanish Inquisition reveal it in the infidel and the fanatic respectively. It knows no distinction of age, or condition, or sex. It simply wants to "slay, and slay, and slay." It is a humiliating thought about our species, but it is a fact that must be faced by all who would humanize the race. The tie of

a "The word is from an Arab root, to mark with pricks, or, as some say, a species of sheep and goats ill-shapen and short-footed, but distinguished by their wool." —Fausset.

b Josephus relates it as a tradition among the Jews that this earthquake was sent as a punishment for Uzziah's presumption in invading the priest's office. 2 Chr. xxvi. 18, 19."—Lowth.

c It is a common way of speaking, to use a certain number for an uncertain, e.g. Job v. 19; Pr. xxx. 15, 18, 21, 29.

d "The thresher was a sort of wain, that moves on iron wheels set with teeth, so that it threshes out the corn, and breaks the straw in pieces." —S. Jerome.

e Nu. xxi. 28; De. xxxii. 22.

f "Eden is prob. Beit-el-janne (House of Paradise) situated 8½ hours from Damascus on the way from Banias."—Porter.

g 2 Ki. xvi. 9.

Defoe, Akenside and Kirke White were the sons of butchers; Bunyan was a tinker, and Joseph Lancaster a basket-maker. Michel Faraday, the son of a poor blacksmith was in early life apprenticed to a

blood is perhaps a natural one, and respected more or less by even heathen peoples, as it is by the very beasts that perish. But even this scarcely operates beyond the filial relation and the period of childhood. And then, as for friendship and philanthropy, they have no place in the sphere of mere nature.—Pulp. Com.

book-binder and . . . . he now occupies the very first rank as a philosopher, excelling even his master, Sir Humphrey Davy. —Smiles.

6—8. (6) **Gaza,** Ge. x. 19; Jos. xiii. 3. **carried,** etc., the Philistines seem, without excuse of war, to have descended upon certain districts and swept the whole of the population before them, for purely commercial purposes. It was professional slave-catching. The Philistines were exactly like the Arabs of to-day in Africa—not warriors who win their captives in honorable fight, but slave-traders, pure and simple.—Exp. B. Comp. 2 Chr. xxi. 16, 17; Joel iii. 6. (7) **fire,** figure of speech as in v. 4. (8) **Ashdod,**[a] Jos. xv. 46, 47. Celebrated for its worship of Dagon. **holdeth the sceptre,** i.e. the prince, or lord, of the place.[b] **Ashkelon,** Ju. i. 18. In later times famous for the worship of Derceto, the Syrian Venus. **turn mine hand,** i.e. bring my hand again upon. **Ekron,** Jos. xiii. 3. In the plain country, on the N.W. border of Judah. **remnant,** the last of the people; comp. Eze. xxv. 16; Je. xlvii. 4.

a "Ashdod stood about 3 miles from the Mediterranean, midway between Joppa and Gaza, on the great high road from Egypt into Palestine. It was hence a place of importance, and was frequently besieged." —Ayre.

Persecution a Most Cruel Crime.—What ruthless inhumanities are in these verses charged against the various peoples mentioned—those of Damascus, Gaza, Tyrus, etc.! It has often been observed that no anger is so savage as the anger which springs up between relations of blood. A brotherly hate is the chief of hates; and it may be truly said that there is no animosity that burns with a more hellish heat than that connected with religion.—Pulp. Com. Cruelty to the helpless, and persecution of God's people, ripen nations and individuals for destruction with great rapidity.—Hom. Com.

"Levity will operate with greater force, in some instances than rigor. It is therefore my first wish, to have my whole conduct distinguished by it." —Geo. Washington.

9, 10. (9) **Tyrus,** represents the kingdom of Phœnicia, Jos. xix. 29.[b] **delivered,** etc., not slave-catchers, but slave-merchants, middlemen. **brotherly covenant,** see 1 Ki. v. 1, 12, ix. 13. (10) **fire,** etc., fulfilled when it was taken by Nebuc. after a thirteen years' siege.

b Is. xxiii. 1, etc.; Je. xlvii. 4; Eze. xxvi. 2—21, xxvii. 2—36, xxviii. 1—26.

The Brotherly Covenant.—The allusion is commonly supposed to be to the league, or "covenant," concluded between Hiram and Solomon, 1 Ki. v. 12 (for "brother" used figuratively of one joined in amity to another, see 1 Ki. ix. 13, xx. 32); but it is scarcely likely that the crowning offence of Tyre should be forgetfulness of a treaty entered into nearly 300 years previously; more probably the reference is to the way in which, repudiating some alliance formed with other Phœnician towns, the Tyrians were the means of procuring slaves from them for Edom. As ii. 1 shews, Amos does not restrict his censure to wrongs perpetrated against Israel: it is the rights common to humanity at large, which he vindicates and defends.—Camb. B.

"Cruelty to the helpless, and persecution of God's people, ripen nations and individuals for destruction with great rapidity." —Hom. Com.

11, 12. (11) Edom, S. of the Dead Sea, the S. part of the Arabah, Ge. xxv. 30. **his brother,** see Nu. xx. 14.[c] **cast .. pity,** Heb. "corrupted his compassions." **kept,** nursed in a spirit of revenge. (12) **Teman .. Bozrah,** two principal cities of Edom.[d] See Ge. xxxvi. 11, 33.

c For the enmity of Edom to Israel comp. 2 Chr. xxviii. 17; Je. xlix. 7; Eze. xxv. 12, xxxv. 2; Joel iii. 19; Ob. 1—11.

d "Edom was a kingdom 500 yrs. before there reigned any king in Israel. Now it is a field of waste desolations. The sand from the Red Sea has absorbed nearly all its springs and streams, and made it one sheet of desert, from Mount Sinai to Moab. The sand is so deep that it is utterly out of the power of man ever again to cultivate the land." (Mal. i. 4).—Gadsby.

Advantage of Pity.—When the Grecians had won Troy, before they fell to plunder it, they gave every man leave to bear his burden out of what he would. And, first of all, Æneas marched out, carrying his household gods; which when they saw, and that he did them no great damage thereby, they bade him take another burthen; which he did, and returned with his old father, Anchises, on his back, and his young son, Ascanius, in hand. Which the Grecians seeing, passed by his house, as Joshua did by the house of Rahab, saying, that no man should hurt him that was so religious. And thus that man that hath his mind set on his God shall receive no hurt by his enemy; for, when a man's ways please the Lord, he maketh even his enemies to be at peace with him. Nay, he shall be "in league with the stones of the field, and the beasts of the field shall be at peace with him." And, which is yet more, God will break the bow and the sword, and snap the spear asunder: he will make all those terrible instruments of war so unserviceable, that they shall lie down quietly by him, not offering the least hurt that may be.

Casting Off Pity.—"Bonaparte," says Robert Wilson, "having carried the town of Jaffa by assault, many of the garrison were put to the sword, but the greater part flying to the mosques, and inploring mercy from their pursuers, were granted their lives. Three days afterwards, Bonaparte, who had expressed much resentment at the compassion manifested by his troops, and determined to relieve himself from the maintenance and care of 3,800 prisoners, ordered them to be marched to a rising ground near Jaffa, where a division of French infantry formed against them. When the Turks had entered into their fatal alignment, and the mournful preparations were completed, the signal gun fired. Volleys of musketry and grape instantly played against them, and Bonaparte, who had been regarding the scene through a telescope, when he saw the smoke ascending, could not contain his joy."

Radiance of Pity.—

No radiant pearl which crested fortune wears,
No gem that, twinkling, hangs from beauty's ears,
Not the bright stars which night's blue arch adorn,
Nor rising suns that gild the vernal morn,
Shine with such lustre as the tear that treaks
For others' woe down virtue's manly cheeks. —Darwin.

"There is no Christian so feeble that the strongest Christian cannot learn something from him. There is no Christian so strong that the feeblest Christian should shrink from seeking his fellowship and offering aid to him."

13—15. (13) **Ammon,** descended fr. Ammon, son of Lot, Ge. xix. 38. Dwelling in the mountainous country round the sources of the Arnon and the Jabbok, Nu. xxi. 24; De. ii. 20. **because,** etc., "As the Ammonites had been in league with the Syrians in David's time,[a] it is not improbable that they may have joined Hazael in his atrocious cruelty towards the Gileadites."—Spk. Com. (14) **Rabbah,** De. iii. 11. **tempest,** etc., figs. of an irresistible destruction.[c] (15) **king,** Je. xlix. 3.

Persecution a Most Arrogant Crime.—The religious persecutor acts upon the assumption that his ideas of religion are absolutely true, that his theological knowledge is the test by which all other opinions are to be tried. Such a man is represented by the apostle as one that "sitteth in the temple of God, showing himself that he is God" (2 Thess. ii. 4). Presumptuous mortal! The proud tyrant who has won his way through seas of blood to the throne, and claims authority over men's bodily movements, shows an arrogance before which servile spirits bow, but from which all thoughtful and noble men recoil with disgust and indignation. But his arrogance is shadowy and harmless compared with the arrogance of him who enters the temple of human conscience, and claims dominion over the moral workings of the soul.—Pul. Com.

a 2 Sa. x. 6.

2 Ki. viii. 12, x. 32.

c Is. v. 26; Je. xxv. 32; Da. xi. 40; Zec. ix. 14.

"Envy is a littleness of soul, which cannot see beyond a certain point, and if it does not occupy the whole space, feels itself excluded."
—Hazlitt.

Man's inhumanity to man
Makes countless thousands mourn."
—Burns.

CHAPTER THE SECOND.

1—3. (1) **Moab,** descended fr. Lot: inhabited the land E. of the Dead Sea, S. of the Arnon, Ge. xix. 37. **burned .. lime,**[d] a vindictive spirit wh. was ready to do sacrilege to one of the most sacred religious beliefs of antiquity. (2) **Kirioth,** Je. xlviii. 24, 41. (3) **judge,** comp. the office of judge in Israel: chief magistrate; the king regarded under the aspect of his most important office.

Divine Cognizance of Human Sins (vss. 1—8).—This fact—I. Should lead men to great circumspection of life. 1. They should sedulously avoid evil; 2. They should devoutly pursue good. II. It should impress men with the wonderful patience of God. 1. Which implies the greatest power; 2. Implies the greatest compassion. III. It should impress men with the certainty of retribution.—Thomas.

Divine Knowledge of Sin.—

The book is opened and the seal removed,—
The adamantine book, where every thought,
Though dawning on the heart, then sunk again
In the corrupted mass, each act obscure,
In characters indelible remain.
How vain the boast, vile caitiff, to have 'scaped
An earthly forum; now, thy crimson stains
Glare on a congregated world; thy judge
Omniscience, and omnipotence thy scourge!
Thy mask, hypocrisy, how useless here,
When, by a beam shot from the fount of light,
The varnished saint starts up a ghastly fiend. —Bailey.

d "The historical connection of this expression is doubtful. Some think ref. is to the revenge wh. prob. the king of Moab took on the king of Edom, when the forces of Isreal and Judah had retired after their successful campaign against Moab, leaving Edom without allies. The Heb. tradition is, that Moab in revenge tore from their grave and burned the bones of the king of Edom, the ally of Jehoram and Jehoshaphat, who was already buried."
—Fausset.

4—8. (4) **Judah,** the nation having higher privileges, and consequently higher responsibilities. **despised the law,** R. V. "rejected." **Commandments,** R. V. "statutes." "The Jews are not accused of violating, in some particular, the unwritten law of God, but of ignoring a distinct and comprehensive revelation of the will of Jehovah."—Mitchell. **lies,** idols, Ho. vii. 3. (5) **fire,** in this case the prophecy was literally fulfilled. (6) **sold,** etc., ch. viii. 6. Prob. referring to the custom of taking bribes in judgment, and betraying the innocent. The indictment (vss. 6—8) consists of four counts: 1. maladministration of justice; 2. oppression of the poor; 3. immorality; 4. inordinate self-indulgence, practiced in the name of religion—all, in view of the signal favors conferred by Jehovah upon Israel in the past, aggravated by ingratitude (vss. 9—12).—Cam. B. **poor .. shoes,** or sandals. Ref. not to the judge but to the hard-hearted creditor who for a mere trifle would enslave his debtor.[b] (7) **pant .. poor,** or "tread down the heads of the poor into the dust of the earth." Utterly and shamefully oppress the poor. **turn aside,** etc., by these legal and commercial hindrances the humble are hindered in the pursuit of their modest aims. **profane,** etc., this indicates that the reference is to the immorality connected with idolatrous rites. (8) **laid to pledge,** explained by De. xxiv. 12, 13, R. V. "taken in pledge." **condemned,** or those wickedly fined or mulcted.[c]

"Clothes Taken in Pledge."—To be understood in connection with the previous clause: the carnally-minded Israelites visit the heathen sanctuaries for the purposes indicated in vs. 7; they lay themeslves down there, with their partners in sin (Hos. iv. 14), beside the altars; and to aggravate their offence they repose, not on their own garments, but on garments which they have taken in pledge from men poorer than themselves, and which, in contravention of the Law, Ex. xxii. 26f., they have neglected to return before nightfall. The large square outer garment, or cloak, called the salmah, thrown round the person by day, was used as a covering at night; and hence the provision that, if a poor man (whose sole covering it probably would be) were obliged to pawn it, it should be restored to him for the night.—Camb. B.——Oppression.—To rob and oppress the rich is a great sin; but to rob and oppress the poor is a greater; but to rob and oppress the poor, because he is poor and wants money to buy justice, is the top of all inhumanity and impiety. To oppress any one is a sin, but to oppress the oppressed is the height of sin. Poverty and want should be motives to pity; but oppressors make them whetstones of their cruelty and severity, and therefore the Lord will plead the cause of his poor oppressed against their oppressors without fee or fear.—Brooks.

9—12. (9) **Amorite,**[a] Amos contrasts the goodness of Jehovah with this ingratitude of Israel, Nu. xxi. 24; De. ii. 31; Jos. xxiv. 8. **height, etc.,** Nu. xiii. 32, 33. **fruit .. beneath,** i.e. root and branch, completely. (10) **brought .. Egypt,** Ex. xii. 51, xx. 2. (11) **Nazarites,** R. V. "Nazirites," one set apart or consecrated to God. Luxury, then, and a very sensual conception of religion, with all their vicious offspring in the abuse of justice, the oppression of the poor, the corrupting of the innocent, and the intolerance of spiritual forces—these are the sins of an enlightened and civilized people, which Amos describes as worse than all the atrocities of barbarism, and as certain of Divine vengeance.—G. A. Smith. Nu. vi. 2—21; Ju. xiii. 5; La. iv. 7. (12) **gave .. wine,**[b] forcing them thus to break their vows. **Prophesy not,** for illus. of their so doing, comp. 1 Ki. xxii. 26, 27; 2 Chr. xvi. 9; Is. xxx. 10; Am. vii. 10—13.

God and Nations (vs. 9).—I. He reminds nations of the greatness of His kindness to them. 1. He often sacrifices one people in order to advance the interests of another; 2. The mightiest human powers cannot obstruct Him in His procedure; 3. He fulfils His great purposes with nations by the agency of man. II. He reminds the nations of the abuse of the mercies He has conferred on them. 1. A spiritual ministry; 2. Virtuous young men.—Thomas.

Nazirites.—The Nazirites were men who, when the sensual and self-indulgent habits of the Canaanites threatened to make their way into Israel, endeavored by a vow of abstinence to set an example of moderation and self-denial, which might help to preserve the old simplicity of

a 2 Ki. xxv. 9; Je. xvii. 27.

b "They sell the precious souls of the poor for the meanest thing, with which they trample on the dust, or in the mire."
—S. Jerome.

c "Extortion, self-indulgence, and hard-heartedness were combined under a show of religion."
—Spk. Com.

The gospel is for the poor: they can worship in the most expensive buildings. Printing has made Bibles so cheap that the poorest can read, and learn to read them in free schools which are better than most private schools of the rich. Colleges are endowed, so that the poor can have the highest education.

"Public libraries and galleries of art are open to all. The poor can ride as fast in railroad cars as the rich, can have their daily papers, can enjoy music and home comforts such as only kings and princes could have had a few hundred years ago."
—Peloubet.

a "The most powerful of all the Canaanite nations, and therefore put for them." —Fausset.

b "For Amos's reference to the drinking habits of his day, see ch. ii. 8, iv. 1, vi. 6

"And earthly power doth then show likest God's;
When mercy seasons justice."
—Shakespeare.

"The mighty hosts of Persia were no defense at the battle of Arbela. Napoleon

Israelitish life. The chief obligations of the Nazirite were to abstain from all intoxicating drinks, to eat no "unclean" thing, and (according to Num. vi. 6 f.) to avoid the ceremonial "uncleanness" occasioned by contact with a corpse: as a sign of his "separation" (cf. Num. vi. 7 end), also, his hair was not shaved, but suffered to grow in its natural state. The only certain historical example of a Nazirite, mentioned in the O. T., is Samson (cf. Jud. xiii. 5, 7, 14, xvi. 17). But from the present passage it may be inferred that they formed a numerous class. The law regulating the vow of the Nazirite is codified in Num. vi. 1—21: but this, in its present form, springs probably from a later age than that of Amos, and represents the form which the regulations on the subject finally assumed. Samson was dedicated to the life of a Nazirite before his birth; but this, no doubt, was exceptional; it is implied by Amos that "young men," when they felt the inner call, spontaneously dedicated themselves to the ascetic life. The Rechabites (Jer. xxxv.), whose founder was a contemporary of Jehu's (2 Ki. x. 15 ff.), were a sect or guild, established with the same object of maintaining a simple habit of life, in contrast to the laxity and effeminacy too often prevalent in these cities. Amos regards the Nazirites as a living protest against the luxury and sensuality to which Israel was now too much addicted (cf. iv. 1, vi. 3—7); and sees in their appearance, as in that of the prophets, a mark of God's care for the higher welfare of His people.—Camb. B.

led more than half a million of men into Russia, but could not escape the danger by retreat. His valiant guards could neither uphold his Empire nor protect his person at Waterloo, when he cried out — "It is all over; save yourselves who can." — Hom. Com.

13—16. (13) **as a cart,**[c] R. V. "I will press you in your place, as a cart presseth," i.e. I will press you with the full force of war, as a loaded wain presses the earth over which it passes. (14) **flight,** or place of flight; where refuge is sought. **strengthen his force,** i.e. collect his powers. (15) **swift of foot,** as Asahel. 2 Sa. ii. 18. (16) **naked,** in the sense of having thrown away his weapons and looser garments in his hurried flight. "The word naked is used of those who lay aside their upper garments, or the habit proper to their quality or profession."

God's Complaint Against Us (vs. 13).—Let us consider—I. What reason God has for this complaint against us. 1. Our disregard of His laws; 2. Our unmindfulness of His mercies; 3. Our contempt of His blessed Gospel. II. What reason we have to be deeply concerned about our state. 1. God is able to vindicate the honor of His injured majesty; 2. He is determined to avenge Himself; 3. The time of retribution is fast approaching. Infer—(1) What a burden ought sin to be to us; (2) What obligations do we owe to Jesus Christ.—Simeon.

c "In many portions of the country the sheaves are piled into a rude cart, upon wh. they are kept from falling by a wicker work about four feet high. These carts, or arabas, are prob. similar to those used by the Heb., and drawn by a pair of oxen." — Van Lennep.

CHAPTER THE THIRD.

1, 2. (1) **whole family,** including both Israel and Judah, though the context shows that the prophet is thinking chiefly of Israel. (2) **known,** in the sense of watched over and cared for; they were the people of special Divine privilege.[a] Ex. xix. 5; De. iv. 20. **punish you,** or "visit upon you."[b] "However severe the punishment, God visited His people in love."

God's Chastisements a Covenant (vss. 1, 2).—I. The grounds for chastisement. 1. Peculiar relationships abused; 2. Distinguishing privileges neglected; 3. Special obligations denied. II. The design of this chastisement. 1. Punishment to purify moral character; 2. Punishment to fit for greater service; 3. Punishment to warn others of danger.—Wolfendale.

Note on vs. 2.—In Eastern language, to say you know a person, means you approve of him. Thus, should a man be well acquainted with two brothers, and should he not approve of one of them, he will say, "I do not know him." But of him he loves, he says, "Ah! I know him well. Jehovah had known, i.e. approved of, Israel, but because of their abominations he had determined to punish them.—Roberts.

3—6. (3) **walk together,** in the companionship of life. Implying that God cannot walk with man, unless man maintains the fellowship of obedience. The figure is drawn from the wilderness in which two men will hardly meet except they have arranged to do so; but the truth, he would illustrate by the figure, is that two sets of phenomena which co-

a "Their being the elect people of God only heightened their sin." — Calvin.

b "When God's people do not glorify Him, He glorifies Himself by punishing them." — Fausset.

Comp. Mat. x. 15, xi, 21, 22.

"Men are not to be envied simply because they are endowed with special favors. Those very endowments, unless they are faithfully used, only augment responsibility, deepen guilt, and ensure a more terrible retribution. Where much has been given much

incide must have sprung from a common purpose. Their conjunction forbids mere chance.—Exp. B. Consequently his strange and unexpected prophecy must be the consequent of evil deeds wh. he proceeds to enumerate. **agreed,** R. V. marg. "made appointment." (4) **lion, etc.,** as the roar is the assurance that he has, or will soon have, his prey, so God's warning by His Prophets is the assurance that He is coming to judge you. (5) **gin,** better, "bait." **shall .. earth,** R. V. "shall a snare spring up fr. the ground;" the construction of the snare was such that the flaps would not start up from the ground unless a bird had entered the snare. (6) **evil,** in the sense of calamity, not of sin. Over all calamities Divine providence presided; the Hebrews took no acct. of secondary causes.[c]

Requisites for Friendship with God (vs. 3).—I. Inquire what it is for men to walk with God. 1. When they have a constant sense of His presence; 2. When they have habitual communion; 3. When they have cordial friendship with God. II. Inquire why there cannot be this walking with God without agreement. 1. There must be a process of reconciliation; 2. There must be correspondence of taste and sentiment.—Brooks.

A Wise Decision.—Eliza Ambert, a young Parisian lady, resolutely discarded a gentleman to whom she was to have been married, because he ridiculed religion. Having given him a gentle reproof, he replied, "that a man of the world could not be so old-fashioned as to regard God and religion." Eliza started, but, on recovering herself, said, "From this moment, sir, when I discover that you do not regard religion, I cease to be yours. He who does not love and honor God, can never love his wife constantly and sincerely."—Cheever.

7, 8. (7) **Lord God,** or Jehovah God. **the prophets,** who were called out in each generation.[d] (8) **lion hath roared,** figure of speech, meaning God has announced His judgment. **who .. prophesy?** a perfectly clear claim by Amos that his message has divine sanction. His prophecy is the result of God's command. Comp. Je. xx. 9.

Monitions.—I saw a cannon discharged. The men at whom it was leveled fell flat on the ground, and so escaped the bullet. Against such blows, falling is all the fencing, and prostration all the armor of proof. But that which gave them notice to fall down was their perceiving of the fire before the ordnance was discharged. Oh! the mercy of that fire, which, as it were, repenting of the mischief it had done, and the murder it might make, ran a race, and outstripped the bullet, that men (at the sight thereof) might be provided, when they could not resist to prevent it! Thus every murdering-piece is also a warning-piece against itself. God, in like manner, warns before he wounds; frights before he fights. "Yet forty days, and Nineveh shall be overthrown." Oh, let us fall down before the Lord our Maker! Then shall his anger be pleased to make in us a daily pass-over, and his bullets leveled at us must fly above us.—Thomas Fuller.

9—11. (9) **Ashdod,** Am. i. 8. **Assemble,** etc., "the Philistines and Egyptians are summoned to witness the enormities of wh. God's people had been guilty." **mountains of Samaria,** i.e. those round about the city.[a] **tumults,** or disorders. **oppressed,** R. V. "oppressions;" i.e. the civic condition of a state where might rules at the expense of right. (10) **know not,** the wealthy and powerful are so corrupted as to have lost all sense of the right, and all care for the right.[b] **store up,** implying that they think they store up wealth and security, but they really store up injustice and oppression, and such stores surely become curses to those who store them.[c] (11) **strength,** etc., i.e. the city of Samaria, the strong "crown," shall be razed to the earth.

National Calamities (vss. 9—12).—I. National guilt. 1. Moral sensibility impaired; 2. Public justice perverted; 3. Shameless fraud committed. II. National disorder. III. National disgrace. IV. National invasion. 1. Power which they abused shall be taken away; 2. Palaces which they stored shall be destroyed.—J. Wolfendale.

12—15. (12) **shepherd .. ear,** when a lion is forced to leave his prey the shepherd is seldom able to save more than scraps of the torn. So when God's judgment is wrought on Samaria, there will be only scraps and remnants of it left.[d] **corner .. bed,** the robbers, vs. 10, that live

---

will be required. It will be more tolerable for Sodom and Gomorrah in the day of judgment, &c. —Thomas.

c Ps. xciv. 7, 9, 10.

Two men once took the lease of a hotel. One was a professing Christian, the other not. The enterprise threatened to bankrupt them both. Nothing could save them but the secret and illegal sale of intoxicating drinks. The Christian partner's faith was not strong enough to withstand the resolute selfishness of the other. —Phelps.

d "There was a succession of prophets among the Jews from Samuel's time till the captivity; the people commonly consulted them upon extraordinary occasions, and they gave them counsel and direction as to what was proper to be done." —Lowth.

a "The site of Samaria is very remarkable. 'The fine round swelling hill, or almost mountain, of Samaria stands alone in the midst of a great basin of some two hours in diameter, surrounded by higher mountains on every side." — Robinson.

b Je. iv. 22.

c Hab. ii. 8—10.

d "When a flock was entrusted to the care of a shepherd, or other person, he was expected to make good to the owner the loss of any sheep or goat 'torn of beasts,' unless he could produce the carcass, or some portion of it, to assure the

luxuriously. The bed is the divan, or raised part of the room, covered with cushions. **in Damascus in a couch,** R. V. "on the silken cushions of a couch," i.e. damask cloth manufactured in Damascus. The fig. is a sign of ease and security. (13) **in,** R. V. "against." (14) **altars of Bethel,**[e] the one raised by Jeroboam, and others raised since his day. **cut off,** destroyed by the enemy. (15) **winter .. house,** separate buildings, such as the wealthy might be able to indulge in, appear to be intended. Both terms are to be understood collectively, and not confined to the royal palaces alone. Je. xxxvi. 22. **great houses,** R. V. marg. "many houses." **ivory,** inlaid with ivory, 1 Ki. xxii. 39.[f]

The Destroyer and the Rescuer (vs. 12).—I. There is a destroying power at work in the world. 1. Variously represented; 2. His doings described; 3. He possesses mighty power; 4. Supreme subtlety. II. There is a rescuing power at work in the world. 1. Possessed of all power; 2. Possessed of all wisdom. III. God is ready to receive even the fragments. 1. Destruction was very near; 2. None need despair; 3. None may presume.—R. Berry.

Samaria.—They might seem to be secure and at ease in Samaria, but vain would every such remedy against fear and sorrow prove. From the strong city, from the soft couch, they would be dragged to misery and destruction. In about 40 years after the time of this prophecy we read (2 Kings xvii. 3) of a siege of Samaria which lasted three years, at the end of which the city was taken; and after the horrors of war, the spoiling of their palaces and their wealth, the remnant was dragged into a distant land, to endure the miseries of captivity and exile.—Ryan. Punishment Returning on Sinner's Head.—When sin is done it is not done with. Like the dead bird around the Ancient Mariner's neck, an avenging Providence ties the memory of it to our soul. Like the crime of Eugene Aram, it becomes an evil-haunting memory, to dog our steps for ever.—Pulp. Com. The Duke of Wellington once said that he could have saved the lives of a thousand men a year, had he had chaplains, or any religious ministers. The uneasiness of their minds reacted on their bodies, and kept up continual fever, once it seized upon their frames. It is our blessed office to tell of One who can "minister to a mind diseased," whose grace can deliver from "an evil conscience," and through whom all inward fear and trouble are removed.—Spurgeon. National Judgments.—Judgments do not come on men as a matter of necessity; they do not roll on man like the billows of ocean on the shore, by blind force; nor do they come because the Governor of the universe is malevolent, and has pleasure in the sufferings of his creatures. No; he is love. He "desireth not the death of a sinner." They come because of sin. The sins of a nation draw judgment after them as the moon draws after it the billows that beat upon the shore. Let no nation hope to escape judgments until it gets rid of sin. Judgments are but sins ripened into a harvest, subterranean fires breaking into volcanoes. Eternal love requires for the order and happiness of the universe that sins and sorrows, transgressions and troubles, should be inseparably linked together.—Pulp. Com.

master that his servant had not improperly disposed of it for his own benefit."—Kitto.

e Ho. x. 15.

f "Houses whose internal decorations consisted chiefly of ivory—panels of ivory on their walls—couches of ivory on which the inmates reclined, and, if palaces, a throne of ivory for the king."—Bib. Things.

"As the ant-hill, when stirred, sets in motion its living insects in every direction, so the conscience of the sinner, disturbed by the Spirit, or judgments of God, calls up before its vision thousands of deeds which fill the soul with agony and woe."—McCosh.

"It strikes me that our sins arise partly from disdain of others, but mainly from contempt of self, both working the despite of God."—R. D. Blackmore.

CHAPTER THE FOURTH.

1—3. (1) **kine of Bashan,** a district famous for its fat cattle.[a] These **kine** represent voluptuous, effeminate women. Thoughtlessness and ease are able to brutalize women of gentle nurture. It was the women who urged on the men to cruelty. **masters,** "lords," i.e. husbands. (2) **by his holiness,** wh. ensures His keeping His word of threatening. **hooks,** etc.,[b] they shall be dragged violently by the foe out of the luxury of their palaces, like fishes out of the water; invaders and spoilers are elsewhere compared to fishers.[c] **posterity,** R. V. "residue;" none to be left. (3) **every cow,** etc., R. V. "every one straight before her;" no turning back to save anything. **cast .. palace,** prob. corrupt text: R. V. "cast yourself into Harmon," i.e. the place of exile. But H. is not located.

Sad Pictures of Human Life (vss. 1—3).—I. Indolent abuse of prosperity. II. Might ruling over right—1. In oppressing the poor; 2. In

a "The luxury and insolence of oppressors is often compared to the wantonness of full-fed cattle. Ps. xxii. 12, lxviii. 30."—Lowth.

b "The modes of catching fish were the same as are still in use in all parts of Western Asia. They were taken with the hook, or with a scoop-net fastened round a hoop and suspended from a pole. And on a larger scale fishing is done by means of a long net."—Van Lennep.

c Je. xvi. 16; Ha. i. 15.

crushing the needy. III. Confederacy in wickedness. IV. Debauchery in social conduct. V. Life terminating in great calamities. 1. Calamities fixed in time; 2. With great sacrifice; 3. From which none can escape; 4. Entailed upon posterity.—Wolfendale.

Evil Influences.—We cannot but notice the insignificance to which Jezebel reduced her husband. She presents the spectacle, so often reproduced in history and reflected in literature, of a strong, fierce woman —a Clytemnestra, a Brunhault, a Lady Macbeth, an Isabella of France, a Margaret of Anjou, a Joan of Naples, a Catherine de Medicis,—completely dominating a feebler consort.—Farrar. Influence of Woman.—"At one time, I was sorely vexed and tried by my own sinfulness, by the wickedness of the world and by the dangers that beset the church. One morning I saw my wife dressed in mourning. Surprised, I asked her who had died. 'Do you not know?' she replied. 'God in heaven is dead.' 'How can you talk such nonsense, Katie?' I said. 'How can God die? Why he is immortal and will live through all eternity.' 'Is that really true?' she asked. 'Of course,' I said, still not perceiving what she was aiming at. 'How can you doubt it? As surely as there is a God in heaven, so sure is it that he can never die.' 'And yet,' she said, 'though you do not doubt that, yet you are so hopeless and discouraged.' Then I observed what a wise woman my wife was and mastered my sadness."—Luther.

Luxury and dissipation, soft and gentle as their approaches are, and silently as they throw their silken charms about the heart, enslave it more than the most active and turbulent vices." —Hannah More.

"When a finely constituted nature wishes to go into baseness it has first to bribe itself. Evil is never embraced, undisguised as evil, but under some fiction which the mind accepts, and with which it has singular power of blinding itself in the face of daylight." —Harriet Beecher Stowe.

"He who runs from God in the morning will scarcely find Him the rest of the day."—John Bunyan.

4, 5. (4) **Beth-el,** one centre of idol worship. Amos now addresses the people at large, prob. on some great feast day. **transgress,** the words of course are ironical. The very worship is offensive to Jehovah, the worshiper a transgressor against the Law. The more altars the more multiplied such transgression. **Gilgal,** another such centre. **after three years,** R. V. "every three days," an ironical exaggeration. (5) **offer,** lit. by burning; comp. Le. ii. 11, vii. 12. **with leaven,** of that wh. is leavened. The mistaken zeal of Israel offered leavened bread. **liketh you,** or this you like. "They thought highly of themselves, and of their gifts."

Worship and Sin (vss. 4, 5).—The subject of the text is abounding worship with abounding sin. I. Abounding worship often implies abounding sin. This is the case when worship is—1. Selfish; 2. Formal. II. Abounding worship often springs from abounding sin. From—1. A desire to conceal sin; 2. A desire to appear good; 3. A desire to compensate for evils.—Thomas.

Amos's Irony.—What a sting is there—"this liketh you!" how it should pierce the conscience of every sinner—"for this liketh you, O ye children of Israel!" Far indeed was everything like levity from the prophet's mind in treating such a subject as the sinfulness of the people; far enough was he from making a mock of sin as fools do. It was holy sorrow that prompted the irony; it was with deep solemnity of soul that he wielded that cutting weapon, and withal he could be tender and touching in expostulation.—Stoughton.

6—8. (6) **And I also,** on my part, in answer to such lawless zeal. **cleanness of teeth,** by reason of having little or no food to eat. **not returned,** under the persuasion of former and partial judgments. (7) **rain,** so essential to the harvest.[a] In this case, God sought to give warnings by making the fall of rain partial. (8) **wandered,** lit. staggered: seeking wherever they could hear that there was water.[b]

Unavailing Chastisements (vss. 6—12).—I. The design of God is in all His dispensations to bring men from their wanderings back again to Himself. II. These dispensations often fail to answer the end for which they were intended. III. When such dispensations are disregarded the most disastrous consequences are likely to ensue.

Effect of National Chastisement.—As in the case of Pharaoh, king of Egypt, afflictions may increase insensibility and rebelliousness. There are cases in which chastisements of the kind here described produce national humiliation and repentance. Such was the case with Nineveh, even when Jonah preached and foretold the city's doom; the people repented even before the calamity came, and so averted it. And there were instances in the history of stiff-necked Israel where chastisement led to general abasement and repentance. There are cases in which

a "Want of rain at this critical season is utterly ruinous to the hopes of the farmer; a little earlier, or a little later, would not be so fatal; but drouth three months before harvest is entirely destructive." —Thomson.

b "The Israelites were obliged to leave their cities and homes to seek water at a distance." —Calvin.

"One glance of God, a touch of His love, will free and enlarge the heart, so that it can deny all and part with all and make an entire renouncing of all to follow him." —Archbishop Leighton.

calamity fails to produce a general reformation, but is nevertheless the means of effecting in individuals a genuine repentance and a sincere conversion unto God.—Pulp. Com. Chastisements.—It cost Him much (oh, how much!) trouble, sorrow, beating, grinding, before He became bread for us. There may be a scarcity of other Bread; there is none of this to those who rightly seek it. It is dear in regard of the preciousness, not dear in regard of the price; we pay nothing for it but faith and love. Though thousands pray at once with the disciples, "Lord, evermore give us this bread," Jesus's storehouse can never be emptied. He only grows not rich with receiving, neither grows poor with giving. Rejoice, then, beloved, the Lord is the giver, the Lord is the gift. Let not your souls be starved with these inferior things, which are few in number, small in measure, bad in nature, "while there is bread enough, and to spare, in your Father's house."—Thos. Adams (1623).

9—11. (9) **blasting,** etc., injuries affecting the ripe grain and the vineyards. By blasting is meant the "scorching of the poisonous east wind." **when your gardens,** R. V. "the multitude of your gardens." **palmerworm,** a species of locust.[a] (10) **pestilence,** affecting the people. Is. x. 26. There is here no reference to the plague of Exod. ix. 3, etc., or xii. 29. The allusion is to the plague which was reckoned to be epidemic in Egypt, and to other loathsome diseases for which that country was notorious.—Pul. Com. **your horses,** 2 Ki. xiii. 7. (11) **overthrown,** etc., prob. referring to some local destructions by earthquake. **Sodom,** ref. to the deadly effects rather than the agency of destruction. **firebrand,**[b] Zec. iii. 2. "What concerns us in this passage is the very effective contrast between men's treatment of God and God's treatment of men. They lavish upon Him gifts and sacrifices. He sends them cleanness of teeth, drought, blasting of their fruits, pestilence, war and earthquake. They regard Him as a being only to be flattered and fed. He regards them as creatures with characters to discipline, even at the expense of their material welfare."—Exp. B.

Pestilence.—There are those who will not hear of great pestilences being God's scourges of man's sins, who fain would find out natural causes for them, and account for them by the help of these. They may do so, or imagine that they do so; yet every time they use the word "plague" they implicitly own the fact which they are endeavoring to deny; for "plague" means properly and according to its derivation, "blow" or "stroke," and was a title given to those terrible diseases, because the great universal conscience of men, which is never at fault, believed and confessed that these were "strokes" or "blows" inflicted by God on a guilty and rebellious world.—French.

12, 13. (12) **thus,** i.e. with severer judgments threatened but unannounced; hence all the more fearful bec. mysterious. **meet thy God,** in His most terrible aspects, as the just punisher of overwhelming transgressions. (13) **formeth,** etc.,[c] this, and the other similar words in this vs. indicate the ease with wh. God fashions and controls all things. So it is a "fearful thing to fall into the hands of the living God." **declareth,** etc., by the prophet, or by conscience. **morning darkness,** i.e. suddenly darkens the sky with storm-clouds. **treadeth,** figure of the storm-cloud sweeping along over the hills.

Mountains.—Loveliness of color, perfectness of form, endlessness of change, wonderfulness of structure, are precious to all undiseased human minds; and the superiority of the mountains in all these things to the lowlands is as measurable as the riches of a painted window matched with a white one, or the wealth of a museum compared with that of a simply furnished chamber. They seem to have been built for the human race, as at once their schools and cathedrals; full of treasures of illuminated manuscript for the scholar, kindly in simple lessons to the worker, quiet in pale cloisters for the thinker, glorious in holiness for the worshiper. These great cathedrals of the earth, with their gates of rock, pavement of cloud, choirs of stream and stone, altars of snow, and vaults of purple, traversed by the continual stars!—Ruskin.

God.—
Oh, import deep as life is, deep as time!

[a] Joel i. 4.

[b] "Those who had escaped had escaped as narrowly as a half-consumed stick snatched from the fire." —Spk. Com.

"The acts of God's providence are as certainly a part of His administration, now, as in former ages, and as directly affect each individual of the race as they did the children of Abraham. It is to those who are subdued under his rebukes that he sends his word to heal them. They who watch the ruling hand of God shall become wiser in leading his purposes and their own necessities." — Duncan.

[c] Both God's knowledge and power are infinite, then who can resist His will?

"They say that the truth is not to be spoken at all times; which is the equivalent of saying that truth is an invalid, who can only take the air in a close carriage with a gentleman in a black coat on the box." — Holmes.

"Many live in constant fear of death, quite forgetting Christ's promise and proof of eternal life. They are like the ignorant soldier who lived for years in poverty carrying around with him an unused certificate, which would have given him a pension."

There is a Something sacred and sublime
Moving behind the worlds, beyond our ken,
Weighing the stars, weighing the deeds of men.

Take heart, O soul of sorrow, and be strong!
There is One greater than the whole world's wrong.
Be hushed before the high Benignant Power
That moves wool-shod through sepulcher and tower!
No truth so low but He will give it crown;
No wrong so high but He will hurl it down.
O men that forge the fetter, it is vain;
There is a Still Hand stronger than your chain.
'Tis no avail to bargain, sneer, and nod,
And shrug the shoulder for reply to God.
—Edwin Markham, 1899.

"I never had a sight of my soul," said the Emperor Aurelius, "and yet I have a great value for it, because it is discoverable by its operations; and by my constant experience of the power of God, I have a proof of His being, and a reason for my veneration." —Whitecross.

Let us incessantly bear in mind, that the only thing we have really to be afraid of, is fearing anything more than God. —Book of the Fathers.

CHAPTER THE FIFTH.

1—3. (1) **lamentation,** or funeral dirge, "bemoaning the state of the kingdom of Israel, as dead and irrecoverably lost."[a] (2) **virgin,** Is. xxiii. 12, xxxvii. 22. The term usually stands for a city or kingdom which has not been conquered.[b] **fallen,** as one wounded in battle; not literally, but to the prophet's vision. **forsaken,** better, "flung, or dashed on the ground:" prostrated upon. Such an announcement during the prosperous times of Jeroboam II. was very startling. (3) **went out,** etc., or from wh. there used to go forth a thousand armed men. **leave an hundred,** "have a hundred left."[c]

A Prosperous People.—Palestine, their national inheritance, was the very garden of the earth; unique in the combination of the highest agricultural capacities, with the finest commercial situation. The prosperity of an industrious, peaceful nation in it was, so far as favorable circumstances went, a foregone conclusion. But war had devastated, and mildew blighted, and drought laid bare its fertile fields. God saw his gifts abused and made the ministers of sin, and he was driven to destroy these in their hands. When temporal good begins to be made the occasion of moral evil, our tenure of it will soon end.—Pulp. Com.

a Je vii. 29; Eze. xix. 1.

b "Or, the term 'virgin' may apply to a state on account of its beauty, and the delights on which it prides itself, its luxuries, power, and wealth." — Calvin.

c De. xxviii. 62; Is. xxx. 17.

4—6. (4) **Seek ye me,** in penitence, prayer, and obedience. Let the people turn to Jehovah Himself—and that means let them turn from the ritual, and instead of it purge their civic life, restore justice in their courts and help the poor. For God and moral good are one.—Exp. B. **live,** in the sense of being secure and prosperous as a nation. (5) **Beth-el,** ch. iv. 4. **Beer-sheba,**[d] on the S. frontier of Judah. At this time a great centre of idolatry. **Gilgal .. captivity,** lit. a play on words, "Gilgal (the place of rolling) shall rolling be rolled away." **Beth-el .. nought,** i.e. Beth-el, "House of God" shall become Beth-aven, "House of nothingness." The thought is, Bethel shall be a ruin and will bring Israel to ruin. (6) **the Lord,** the covenant God, Jehovah. **house of Joseph,** the father of Ephraim, rep. the whole Northern kingdom. Ob. 18; Zech. x. 6.[e]

Note on vss. 4—6.—Jeroboam pretended that it was too much for Israel to go up to Jerusalem. Yet Israel thought it not too much to go to the extremest point of Judah towards Idumea, perhaps four times as far south of Jerusalem as Jerusalem lay from Bethel. For Beersheba is thought to have lain some 30 miles south of Hebron, wh. is 22 miles south of Jerusalem; while Bethel is but 12 to the north. So much pains will men take in self-willed service, and yet not see that it takes away the excuse for neglecting the true.—Pusey. Bethel.—During the still evening, when the shadows were deepening in the glens, and the last rays of the declining sun gilding the top of rock and cliff, I explored the site of this the most ancient of Israel's holy places. I looked all round, in the hope of identifying the spot where Jacob slept, and which he consecrated and called the "house of God." I explored the rock sepulchres, too, which dot the sides of "the mount" (2 Ki. xxiii. 16), thinking that

d Ge. xxi. 33, xxii. 19.

e Eze. xxxvii. 19.

"The visible is the ladder up to the invisible; the temporal is but the scaffolding of the eternal. Then when the last immaterial souls have climbed through this material to God, the scaffolding shall be taken down, and the earth dissolved with fervent heat, not because it was base, but because its work was done." — H. Drummond.

"The Father gives the Holy Spirit to them that askfl Him, not least, but most, when they ask for others." —Andrew Murray.

one or other of them might be that of "the man of God from Judah," whose bones Josiah respected (vss. 17, 18). Clambering to the top of a shattered tower which crowns the hill of Bethel, I looked long, and in sadness, over that dreary field of ruin, only inhabited by a few shepherds.—Porter.

7—9. (7) **wormwood,** De. xxix. 18, "Ye that pervert the law wh. was designed to protect innocence, and under color of it exercise the greatest oppression." **leave .. earth,** better, "cast righteousness down to the ground;" righteousness here means civil justice. (8) **seven stars,** the Pleiades; see Job ix. 9, xxxviii. 31. **shadow of death,** fig. for the night.[f] **the waters,** or floods; ref. either to inundations of the lowlands, or long continued rains. (9) **spoiled,** better, "that causeth devastation to flash forth upon the strong so that devastation cometh upon the fortress."[g]

Science the Handmaid to Religion (vs. 8).—I. Science exalts our conceptions of our Lord Jesus Christ by enlarging our views of the vastness of the universe. II. Confirms our persuasion of the supremacy of moral and spiritual law by establishing the supremcay of natural law. III. Illustrates the power of love to God and to the Redeemer by revealing the power of the principle of attraction. IV. Points out a guarantee for the safety of the believer by demonstrating the stability of the heavenly bodies. V. Suggests an analogy of the preparation of heaven for the saints in the preparation of the earth for man. VI. Furnishes a parallel to the devising of a plan of salvation before the fall, in the prospective arrangements of the natural world.—Brooks.

Need of Strength from God.—Sir Walter Scott relates in his autobiography that, when he was a child, one of his legs was paralyzed, and when medical skill failed, a kind uncle induced him to exert the muscles of the powerless limb by drawing a gold watch before him on the floor, tempting him to creep after it, and thus keeping up and gradually increasing vital action and muscular force. So God deals with us in our spiritual childhood, and the weakness of our faith. How weak our efforts; how slow our movements! But spiritual vitality is elicited, developed, strengthened by those efforts and movements, slow and weak as they are. Brethren, a Christian's strength can come only by his being strengthened. There is not within the man, as a man, nor within him as a Christian, any stock or store of strength given him at the commencement of his life. Day by day, stage after stage, first as a babe, then as a young man, and then as a father in Christ, does the man need strengthening. And what a glorious thing it is that, instead of our resources being given to us at the beginning of our Christian life, they are supplied to us as we need them. Does not this arrangement keep us in close communion with the Father of our spirits, and with the Source of all energy and wisdom? So that the very application to God, apart from the things which application always secures, tends to strengthen you.—S. Martin.

10—13. (10) **gate,** chief place of concourse.[a] Ref. is to the magistrate who is faithful enough to rebuke the oppressors. (11) **take .. wheat,** exact presents of wheat.[b] **built,** etc., Zep. i. 13. Comp. the prophecy of Moses, De. xxviii. 30, 38, 39. Hewn stone would be a sign of wealth and luxury. (12) **manifold transgressions,** R. V. "how manifold . . . how mighty." **turn aside,** refusing to give due heed to their pleadings. (13) **prudent,** or judicious, sensible man. He will refuse to take part in magistracy or politics.[c] **evil time,** when one fears for his personal security.

God Knows Our Sins (vs. 12).—Let us consider—I. The information here given to us: He knows our sins—1. In all their extent and variety; 2. In all their heinousness and aggravation. II. The use we should make of it. 1. We should beg of God to discover to us the real state of our souls; 2. We should entreat Him to humble us in the dust before Him; 3. We should look to our Lord Jesus Christ as our hope; 4. We should walk with all possible circumspection before God.—C. Simeon.

Keep Silence.—Euler lived at Petersburg during the administration of Biron, one of the most tyrannical ministers that ever breathed. On the philosopher's coming to Berlin, after the tyrant's death, the late queen of Prussia, who could hardly get a word out of him, asked him

f "God can create the light, and make it spring from darkest night: and when He covers o'er the day, the darkness chases light away." — Pindar.

g "Maketh devastation (or destruction) suddenly to arise, lit. maketh it to gleam forth like the dawn." — Maurer.

"The Christian life is a going to the Father. Some travel swiftly, some are long upon the road, some meet many pleasant adventures by the way, others pass through fire and peril: but though the path be short or winding, and though the pace be quick or slow, it is a going to the Father." — Drummond.

"The habit of looking at the bright side of things is worth more than a thousand a year." — Samuel Johnson.

a De. xxv. 7, 1 Ki. xxii. 10.

b "Burdensome taxes levied in kind from the wheat of the needy, to pamper the lusts of the great." — Henderson.

c "He will live as much as may be in retirement, taking no part where he can do no good, and may be grievously wronged." —Spk. Com.

the reason of his silence. "Because," said he, "I come from a place where if a man says a word he is hanged."—Whitecross.

Results of Dishonest Gains.—"The rogue cozened not me, but his own conscience," said Bishop Latimer of a cutler who made him pay two pence for a knife not worth a penny. Money, earned by screwing, cheating and over-reaching, may for a time dazzle the eyes of the unthinking; but the bubbles blown by unscrupulous rogues, when full blown, usually glitter only to burst. The Sadleers, Dean Pauls and Redpaths, for the most part come to a sad end even in this world; and tho' the successful swindles of others may not be found out, and the gains of their roguery may remain with them, it will be as a curse and not as a blessing.—Smiles.

Matthew Hale in Disguise.—The younger of two brothers had endeavored to deprive the elder of an estate of £500 a year, by suborning witnesses to declare that he died in a foreign land. Coming into the court in the guise of a miller, Sir Matthew Hale was chosen the twelfth juryman, to sit on this cause. As soon as the clerk of the court had sworn in the jurymen, a little dexterous fellow came into their apartment and slipped ten gold pieces into the hands of eleven of the jury, and gave the miller five, while the judge was known to be bribed with a great sum. The judge summed up the evidence in favor of the younger brother, and the jury were about to give their assent, when the supposed miller stood up and addressed the court with such energetic and manly eloquence, as astonished the judge and all present; unravelled the sophistry to the very bottom, proved the fact of bribery, evinced the elder brother's title to the estate from the contradictory evidence of the witnesses, and gained a complete victory in favor of truth and justice.—Cheever.

d Mi. iii. 11.

e Eccl. xii. 5.

"All funeral processions, except those of the very poorest, are attended by wailing women. There are many women who let themselves out as wailers, at so much for the day, just as charwomen are hired in our own country. Of course those who can utter the most horrid shrieks are the most approved."—Gadsby.

Men do not love to be brought into contact with realities, or be reminded of coming "days of darkness." There is an unwelcome message to the conscience. Art thou ready to meet this solemn — this hastening season? If you regard death as a friend, prepare to entertain it; if an enemy, prepare to overcome it. —Hom. Com.

14—17. (14) **ye have spoken,** R. V. "as ye say."[d] (15) **Hate,** etc., Is. i. 16, 17; Ro. xii. 9. **love .. good,** instead of mere ceremonial. **judgment,** upright, honorable magistracy. **remnant of Joseph,** not a "remnant" at this time, but in the prophet's vision of the future. The passage contains in germ the doctrine of the preservation, through judgment, of a faithful remnant, which became shortly afterwards a distinctive feature in the teachings of Isaiah.—Cam. B. Comp. "house of Joseph," vs. 6. (16) **Therefore,** bec., that is, of the sins of wh. they were guilty, and of wh. they refused to repent. **Wailing,** "the orig. word means, smiting on the breast as a sign of sorrow, and esp. in mourning for the dead."—Spk. Com. **streets,** R. V. "broad ways," i.e. open spaces near the city gates. **highways,** R. V. "streets." **skilful,** etc., wailing for the dead was a business for wh. some were trained;[e] these were usually females. (17) **vineyards,** places where songs were generally heard. **pass .. thee,** R. V. "pass through the midst of thee." "It is the solemn formula of the Great Passover, when Egypt was filled with wailing and there were dead in every house."

"Establish Judgment in the Gate."—Unjust judgment was a prevalent and crying evil. The Jewish character was prone to it, and the experience of it at the hands of strangers only strengthened the tendency. Perversion of justice is one of the most constant elements in natural corruption everywhere. A corrupt man makes a dishonest trader, an unjust judge, and an oppressive master. Fair and upright dealing between man and man has no natural basis, unless in the fear of God. The fear of God, on the other hand, will naturally co-ordinate itself with regard for man. The man who "does justly and loves mercy" is one who "walks humbly with God."—Pulp. Com.

18—20. (18) **Woe unto you,** Cam. B., "Ah! they that desire;" commiseration rather than denunciation. **desire,** etc., reference is to the hypocritical desires and hopes of Israel. **what end,** or how can it meet your wishes, seeing it must come as national calamity. Jehovah's day meant to the people the day of His judgment, or of His triumph: His triumph in war over their enemies, His judgment upon the heathen. But Amos, whose keynote has been that judgment begins at home, cries woe upon such hopes, and tells his people that for them the day of Jehovah is not victory, but rather insidious, importunate, inevitable death.—Exp. B. (19) **lion,** etc., representing calamities in such a succession that a man may not hope to escape them. **leaned .. wall,** to support himself from falling.[a] (20) **very dark,** comp. Ex. x. 22.

Serpents in Eastern Houses.—Serpents sometimes conceal themselves in the holes and chinks of the walls of Eastern houses. This is confirmed by a remarkable story related by D'Herbelot: "Arnadeddulat, who reigned in Persia in the tenth century, found himself reduced to great difficulties arising from want of attention to this treasury. Walking one day in one of the rooms of his palace, which had been before that time the residence of Jacout, his antagonist, he perceived a serpent, which put its head out of a chink in the wall; he immediately ordered that the place should be searched, and the serpent killed. In opening the wall there, they found a secret place in which they could not discover the serpent, but a treasure which was lodged in several coffers, in which Jacout had deposited his most precious effects."

21—24. (21) **I hate,** etc., the folly and vanity of relying upon their elaborate ritualism. Is. i. 11; Je. vi .20. **smell,** fig. applied to the rising incense, and signifying accept.[b] (22) **meat offerings,** R. V. "meal offerings," and so throughout the O. T. **peace-offerings,** or thank-offerings. (23) **viols,** or harps. (24) **judgment,** with special ref. to righteous administration of the laws. **run down,** lit. roll, flow abundantly. This is the only condition on wh. sacrifice can be acceptable to God.

The Formalist.—There are some, if you would see their goodness, and be acquainted with their godliness, you must hit the right time, or else you will find none, like some flowers that are seen but some months in the year. This may be in the morning: you may take the hypocrite on his knees in a saint's posture; but when that fit is over, you shall see little of God in all its course, till night brings him again, of course, to the like duty. The watch is nought that goes only at first winding up, and stands all the day after; and so is that heart, sure, that desires not always to keep in spiritual motion.—A Divine of the 17th Century. "Shall Not?"—He appeals to their own consciences, "Is it not so, as I have said?" Men's consciences are truer than their intellects. However they may employ the subtlety of their intellect to dull their conscience, they feel, in their heart of hearts, that there is a Judge, that guilt is punished, that they are guilty. The soul is a witness to its own deathlessness, its own accountableness, and its own punishableness.—Pusey.

25—27. (25) **Have ye,** etc., R. V., "did ye bring," etc.; the prophet argues, "put not your trust in ritual. It, without righteouosness, is vain. Have ye not heard how it was neglected while your fathers wandered in the desert?"—Mitchell. Ac. vii. 42. (26) **But ye have borne,** etc., Cam. B., "But ye shall take up Sakkuth your king, and Kaiwan your images, the star of your god, which ye made to yourselves; and I will cause you to go into exile beyond Damascus." You and your idols (cf. Jer. xlviii. 7 b, xlix. 3 b; Is. xlvi. 1—2) will go into exile together; this will be the end of your self-chosen course. But though the general sense of the verse is clear, some of the details are obscure. (27) **beyond Damascus,** into wild and unknown regions. Comp. Ac. vii. 43.

Forms of Idolatry.—Asia worships the true God, but has false conceptions of Him. This is the land of dreamy intellect, of morbid sensibilities, of stationary civilizations. We see the conception of God variously modified in different nations, and we mark, as we pass over them, a ripening of the human mind in proportion to the approach to a right and perfect conception of the Almighty. Lowest in the scale, perhaps, we may place the Brahmins. They acknowledge a supreme God, Brahm, but they put him afar off, and ascribe creation, preservation, and destruction to inferior divinities. As might be expected, they overthrow his altars, neglect his temple, and leave him nothing but the name, while they give their chief adoration to the god Vishnu and his nine incarnations, of which Juggernaut is one. What is their intellectual state? Next comes Buddhism, which overspreads farther India, the Chinese empire, and Japan. This is a reformation of Brahminism. While it recognizes an eternal First Cause, it represents Him as reposing in profound slumber, from which He only now and then awakes to send down some perfected spirits, that they may make certain necessary alterations in the universe.—Bp. Thomson.

[a] "Serpents often lurk concealed in the walls of Eastern houses." —Lane.

"One ought to talk only as loud as he lives — a rule wh. would deprive some people of the privilege of shouting." — Wilbur Chapman.

[b] Ge. viii. 21.

"In one of the heathen temples of Canton are seen plaster representatives of the transmigration of souls. A boy is changing into a dog; a man has horns growing from his forehead, his feet and hands are changing to hoofs, a tail is sprouting from his back; another is changing into an ass, etc." —B. B. Atterbury.

The Venetian ambassador wrote of Cardinal Wolsey: — "I do perceive that every year he groweth more and more in power." When I first came to Engalnd, he used to say, "His Majesty will do so and so;" subsequently, he said, "We shall do so and so;" but now he says, "I shall do so and so." But history records how Wolsey's pride went before destruction, and his haughty spirit before a fall. — Spurgeon.

"As to the evil of being neither one thing nor the other, one finds an illustration in the waterways of Southern China, which in winter-time are quite useless for purposes of commerce. The temperature is most tantalizing, for it is neither cold enough to freeze the canals, so that the

CHAPTER THE SIXTH.

ice would be able to tear traffic; nor warm enough to thaw them, so that they could be navigable by boats." — Spurgeon.

As God hath two dwelling - places, heaven and a contrite heart, so hath the devil —hell and a proud heart.—T. Watson.

Poverty of spirit is the bag into which Christ puts the riches of his grace.—Rowland Hill.

"A holy woman was wont to say of the rich: 'They are hemmed round with no common misery; they go down to hell without thinking of it, because their staircase thither is of gold and porphyry.' " —C. H. Spurgeon.

1, 2. (1) **at ease,** in their self-security, and false political confidence, engendered by such ritualism. **trust,** etc., better, "and to the self-confident ones in the mountain of Samaria." So both the self-indulgent of Judah and Israel are here addressed. **chief,** R. V., "the notable men of," i. e. spoken in irony of the exalted opinion of the Jews as a whole. **came,** R. V., "come," i. e. for judgment. (2) **Calneh,** Ge. x. 10. **Hamath,** Nu. xxxiv. 8. **Gath,** Jos. xiii. 3. **border,** or territory, continuing the argument of vs. 1, the cities named in it being referred to as examples of prosperity: Can you find, from Calneh and Hamath in the North of Syria to the Philistine border on the South, a single kingdom "better" (i. e. more flourishing) than your own? Thus has Jehovah favored you; and ye requite Him with indifference and neglect (vss. 3—6). Therefore (vs. 7) the sentence is, Ye shall be amongst the first to go into exile.—Cam. B. But Wellhausen conjectures that the places named are examples of fallen greatness, and if God could destroy such cities why should Samaria hope to escape?

Uncomfortableness in Church.—Archbishop Whately related the following anecdote. During his ministry at Halesworth, one of his parishioners told him that he thought a person should not go to church to be made uncomfortable. Whately replied that he thought so too, but whether it should be the sermon or the man's life that should be altered, so as to avoid the discomfort, must depend on whether the doctrine was right or wrong.

3—6. (3) **put far away,** or have a habit of putting far away. **seat of violence** i. e. turning the seat of judgment into the seat of oppression, taking advantage of the seeming delay of God's threatenings. (4) **beds of ivory,** ch. iii. 15. **stretch,** etc., in listless self-indulgence. **lambs,** etc., or the very best of everything. (5) **chant,** marg. quaver, "improvise idly," "babble." **like David,** who invented or improved the nebel and the kinnor, kinds of harps, the former played with the hand, the latter with the plectrum. (6) **bowls,** intimating there was no limit to the quantity. **ointments,** used as scents are with us. **affliction of Joseph,** the rich are indifferent to it; they have wealth, art, patriotism, religion, but neither heart for the poverty nor conscience for the sin of their people. For the real woes and sores of the people, the poverty, the overwork, the drunkenness, the dissoluteness, which more affect a nation's life than anything else, they have no pity and no care.—Exp. B.

Man's Evil Day (vs. 3).—I. All men have an evil day in their future. II. Some men adjourn in thought this evil day—1. Not because they have any doubt as to its advent; 2. Nor because they lack reminders of its approach. But because of—1. The strength of our material attachments; 2. Our dread of the mysterious; 3. Lack of interest in the spiritual; 4. A conscious unpreparation for the scenes of retribution. III. None who adjourn this evil day in thought can delay it in fact.—Thomas.

7—11. (7) **with the first,** better, "at the head of them;" leading the procession. **banquet,** R. V., "revelry;" luxurious opportunities of self-indulgence. (8) **excellency,** "pride." (9) **ten .. die,** though so many survive the siege, they shall all die in the following pestilence. (10) "A grim episode imagined by the propohet (cf. Is. iii. 6 f.) for the purpose of illustrating vividly the terrors of the time: the relative of the deceased man enters his house to perform the last duties to the corpse: he finds no living person in it except one, secreted in a far corner, who tells him he is the solitary survivor of the household, all the others having perished (cf. vs. 9): so desperate is the outlook that men dread even to mention Jehovah's name, for fear lest it should call down a fresh judgment upon them."—Camb. B. **uncle,** he will have to act as near relative, bec. the father and the brothers will be dead. **he that burneth him,** lit. "his burner," perhaps, not of the body, but of spices in his honor. **bones,** i. e. corpse. **sides,** R. V., "innermost parts." **any with thee,** i. e. alive.

(11) **commandeth,** i. e. the human agents who are to carry out his will, vs. 4. **with breaches,** R. V., "into fragments."

Pestilence.—"In 1813," says one, "such was the violence with which the plague raged at Malta, such the certain destruction wh. attended the slightest contact with the infected, that at last every better feeling of the heart was extinguished in a desire of self-preservation, and nobody could be found to perform the melancholy offices which make up the funeral train of sickness and death."—Hom. Com.

12—14. (12) **upon the rock,**[a] or cliffs, crags; a very unreasonable thing; so unreasonable is the conduct of Israel towards God, ch. v. 7, and esp. of the corrupt judges. **gall,** i. e. "poison." **hemlock,** R. V., "wormwood." (13) **thing of nought,** their material prosperity. **horns,** De. xxxiii. 17; Ps. lxxxix. 17. "These boasters attributed all their success to themselves." "By our own strength have we taken to ourselves Karnaim." So Gratz reads the verse. The Hebrew text and all the versions take these names as if they were common nouns—Lo-Debar, "a thing of nought;" Karnaim, "a pair of horns." These two fortresses, with many others, Israel had lately taken from Syria; but not, as they boasted, by their own strength. It was only Syria's pre-occupation with Assyria now surgent on the northern flank, which allowed Israel these easy victories.—Exp. B. (14) **river .. wilderness,** prob. Wady el Ahsa, on the southern border of Moab.

Pride, the Destroyer.—When a proud man thinks best of himself, then God and man think worst of him; all his glory is but like a vapor, which climbeth as though it would go up to heaven, but when it comes to a little height, it falls down again, and never ascends more. So Adam thought that the fair apple should make him like his Maker, but God resisted his pride, and that apple made him like the serpent that tempted him with it. Absalom thought that rebellion would make him a king, but God resisted his pride, and his rebellion hanged him on a tree.—Henry Smith.——Need of Humility.—A heart full of pride is but a vessel full of air, this self-opinion must be blown out of us before saving knowledge be poured into us. Humility is the knees of the soul, and to that posture the Lamb will open the book; but pride stands upon tip-toes, as if she would snatch the book, and unclasp it herself. The first lesson of a Christian is humility; and he that hath not learned the first lesson is not fit to take out a new.—Thomas Adams.

[a] "As horses and oxen are useless on a rock, so ye are incapable of fulfilling justice." Grotius.

There is something intensely amusing, according to our notions, in the name which the Eskimo bestow upon themselves. It appears they call themselves the "Innuit,"—that is, "the people" par excellence. If a man is a perfectionist, and thinks he is sinless, it is a proof not that he is better, but only that he is blinder, than his neighbors.—Richard Glover.

"Australian papers state that in the Riverina district the grasshoppers, or locusts, have been very troublesome recently, not only destroying crops, but filling up wells and waterholes, and even consuming textile fabrics, such as blinds and window-curtains, in the houses."—Pulp. Com.

CHAPTER THE SEVENTH.

The visions recounted in this chapter form the substance of Amos's address at Bethel. The religion of his time—religion as mere ritual and sacrifice—was what God sent him to beat down, and he faced it at its headquarters, and upon one of its high days, in the royal and popular sanctuary where it enjoyed at once the patronage of the crown, the lavish gifts of the rich, and the thronged devotion of the multitude. As Savonarola at the Duomo in Florence, as Luther at the Diet of Worms, as our Lord Himself at the feast in Jerusalem, so was Amos at the feast in Bethel.—Exp. B. **1—3.** (1) **grasshoppers,** or young locusts. **latter growth,** or the aftermath. **king's mowings,** so the first crop of grass was called, poss. bec. a proportion of it went for the king's use. (2) **I beseech,** the true prophet prays for the people to whom he reveals the message of God. **by .. arise?** R. V., "how shall Jacob stand?" How can he stand and endure, if thus visited? **small,** bec. of continued judgments and calamities. (3) **repented,** or granted a respite at the Prophet's entreaty. **It,** i. e. the final execution of doom upon Israel.

Vision was a frequent mode of prophetic intuition (comp. Hos. xii. 10). The vision is a projection or creation of the mind, analogous to the dream: the subject falls into a state of trance, or ecstasy, in which the channels connecting the brain with external objects are closed; the conscious operation of the senses is consequently in abeyance; the power of the will to guide thought is relaxed: on the other hand, the imagination, or faculty of combining images and ideas, which have been previously apprehended, into new forms, is abnormally active; and the pic-

"Eager clutching at the delights of natural life, and making it one's chief aim, is the sure way to lose all its sweetness and to miss the higher life; while the subordination, and, if needful, the sacrifice, of 'life in this world,' leads straight to the possession of 'life eternal.'"—Alexander McLaren.

"Whitefield often affirmed that he would rather have a church with ten men in it right with God, than one with five hundred at whom the world would laugh in its sleeve." — Joseph Cook.

"Livingstone, as a missionary, was anxious to avoid a large church of nominal adherents. 'Nothing,' he wrote, 'will induce me to form an impure church. "Fifty added to the church" sounds well at home, but if only five of these are genuine, what will it profit in the Great Day?' "—Blaikie.

Set thine heart upright, if thou wouldst rejoice, And please thyself in thine heart's pleasing choice: But then be sure thy plumb and level be Rightly applied to that which pleaseth me.—Christopher Harvey.

tures created by it stand out the more vividly, not being contrasted with the sharper impressions produced in a waking state by the senses. In other words, the vision may be described as a combination into new forms, under the influence of a determining impulse, of the images and impressions with which the mind, through its waking experience, is stored. In a prophetic vision, the determining impulse will have been due to the operation of the revealing Spirit; in the case of Amos, as we may suppose, the thought of an impending judgment, which, borne in upon him at the time when Jehovah's "hand" seized him, determined the direction taken by his imagination, and took shape accordingly in the concrete forms presented in these visions. It is in agreement with the character of the vision, as thus explained, that its imagery is generally supplied by the surroundings, amid which the prophet who experiences it lived himself; the basis of Isaiah's vision (ch. vi.) is thus the Temple of Jerusalem (though what he sees is not, of course, an exact copy of it); the forms described by Ezekiel (ch. i.) are modelled upon the sculptured figures of Babylonia; and the material imagery in Amos' visions is suggested similarly by objects, or scenes, with which the prophet would himself be familiar. The vision is thus the forcible symbolic presentation of a prophetic truth.—S. R. Driver in Camb. Bib.

4—6. (4) **called,** etc., G. A. Smith, "was calling fire into the quarrel." Jehovah already had a contention with Israel. **fire,** "the imagery may be suggested by the conflagrations which in the East break out in field and forest in the dry season, and spread with alarming rapidity." **great deep,** "the vast subterranean reservoirs whence the Hebrews believed the springs of the earth to be fed" (Gen. i. 7; Ex. xx. 4; Ps. xxiv. 2). **did .. part,** R. V., "would have eaten up the land;" threatened to destroy the solid earth. (5) **by whom,** vs. 2. (6) **repented,** vs. 3.

Human Prayer Leading to a Divine Revelation.—Though we are far enough from holding that human prayer affects any alteration in the ordinances of nature or the purposes of the Almighty, we nevertheless hold with a tenacious faith the doctrine that a man gets from God by prayer that which he would not get without it. Indeed, in every department of life man gets from the Almighty, by a certain kind of activity, that which he would never obtain without the effort. A man has a field which he has never tilled, and on which Providence has bestowed no crop for many a long year. He tills it this year, and in autumn God crowns it with His goodness. Another man has no health; for many years he has neglected the conditions of physical vigor, and he is infirm and afflicted. This year he attends rigorously to the laws of his physical well-being. He takes the proper exercise, the right food, the pure air, and he feels his infirmities and his pains decrease, and new vigor pulsating through his veins. Another man has never enjoyed the light of Divine knowledge; his soul has been living in the region of indolence; he has neglected all the means of intelligence. He alters his course and sets to work; he reads and thinks, studies God's holy book, and prays; he feels his nature gradually brightening under the genial rays of truth. Thus everywhere God reveals to man his goodness in connection with his activity, which never comes without human effort. It is so in prayer. "The effectual fervent prayer of a righteous man availeth much." It puts the soul in that angle on which the Divine light falls, in that soil in which its intellectual and moral powers will grow. "Ask, and ye shall receive."—Pul. Com.

7—9. (7) **upon,** R. V., "beside." **plumbline,** string with a weight attached, used in securing the straightness of an erection. (8) **set a plumbline,** i. e. apply a strict moral test, and destroy what does not conform to the standard.[a] **pass by,** pardon, spare; justice must take its course. (9) **high places,** like Bethel, Gilgal, etc. **Isaac,** poetic synonym of Israel. **rise .. sword,** an army of invasion as the agent of punishment.[b]

The Folly of Sin.—To them who believe another life after this, an eternal state of happiness or misery in another world (which is but a reasonable postulatum or demand among Christians), there is nothing in mathematics more demonstrable than the folly of wicked men; for it is not a clearer and more evident principle that the whole is greater than a part, than that eternity and the concernments of it are to be preferred

a 2 Ki. xxi. 13; Is. xxviii. 17.

b See 2 Ki. xv. 10.

"One danger of secret sin is that a man cannot commit it without being by-and-by betrayed into a public sin. If a man commit one sin, it is like the melting of the lower glacier upon the Alps, the other must follow in time.—Spurgeon.

It is said of the Areopagites, in Athens, that their sentence was so upright that none could ever say he was unjustly condemned of them. How much more true is this of the righteous judgment of God, who must needs therefore be justified, and every mouth stopped. —Trapp.

before time. . . . Is that man wise, as to his body and his health, who only clothes his hands, but leaves his whole body naked? who provides only against the toothache, and neglects whole troops of mortal diseases that are ready to rush in upon him? Just thus does he who takes care only for this vile body, but neglects his precious and immortal soul, who is very solicitous to prevent small and temporal inconveniences, but takes no care to escape the damnation of hell. Is he a prudent man, as to his temporal estate, that lays designs only for a day, without any prospect to, or provision for, the remaining part of his life? —Tillotson.

10—13. (10) **priest of Beth-el,** so the idolatrous priest. **conspired,** etc., he considered that Amos's preachings stirred up rebellion, esp. against the established national religion. In Amaziah's eyes he was guilty of "constructive treason." (11) **Jeroboam,** but Amos's words applied to the house of Jeroboam, not to Jeroboam himself.[a] (12) **O thou seer,** "spoken in a tone of supercilious contempt," "thou visionary." **into .. Judah,** from whence Amos came. **eat bread,** i. e. earn thy living as do the soothsayers. (13) **king's chapel,** or sanctuary. Bethel means God's house; it had become only the king's house.[b] It is a chief shrine of the recognized and authoritative national worship. Amaziah speaks as a thorough Erastian; as if the human authority were everything, and the Lord, of Himself, had no claims on the land.—Pul. Com.

A Faithful Minister.—Bishop Latimer, in preaching before King Henry the Eighth, spoke his mind very plainly; which some of his enemies thought to make their advantage of, by complaining of him to the king, that they might thus get him out of the way. Soon after his sermon, he and several others being called before the king to speak their minds on certain matters, one of them kneeled before his majesty, and accused Latimer of having preached seditious doctrines. The king turned to Latimer, and said, "What say you to that, sir?" Latimer kneeled down, and turning first to his accuser, said, "What form of preaching would you appoint me to preach before a king? Would you have me to preach nothing concerning a king, in a king's sermon? Have you any commission to appoint me what I shall preach?" He asked him several other questions, but he would answer none at all; nor had he anything to say. Then he turned to the king, and said, "I never thought myself worthy, nor ever sued, to be a preacher before your Grace. But I was called to it, and would be willing, if you mislike me, to give place to my betters. But if your Grace allow me for a preacher, I would desire your Grace to discharge my conscience, give me leave to frame my discourse according to mine audience. I had been a very dolt to have preached so at the borders of your realm, as I preach before your Grace." These words were well received by the king, as Latimer concluded, because the king presently turned to another subject. Some of his friends came to him with tears in their eyes, and told him, they looked for nothing but that he should have been sent to the Tower the same night. —Whitecross.

14, 15. (14) **no prophet,**[a] in the sense of properly belonging to the order of the prophets. **herdman,** ch. i. 1.[b] **gatherer .. fruit,** a dresser, or cultivator of sycamores.[c] The fruit is infested with an insect (the Sycophaga crassipes), and till the "eye" or top has been punctured, so that the insects may escape, it is not eatable. This operation, it is probable, is what is here alluded to.—Cam. B. Only the poor gather and use these sycamore figs. (15) **took me,** separating him from his common avocation by a special Divine call.

Great Men of Humble Origin.—The common class of day-laborers has given us Brindley the engineer, Cook the navigator, and Burns the poet. Masons and bricklayers can boast of Ben Jonson, who worked at the building of Lincoln's Inn, with a trowel in his hand and a book in his pocket; Edwards and Telford the engineers, Hugh Miller the geologist, and Allan Cunningham the writer and sculptor; whilst among the distinguished carpenters we find the names of Inigo Jones the architect, Harrison the chronometer-maker, John Hunter the physiologist, Romney and Opie the painters, Prof. Lee the orientalist, and John Gibson the sculptor. From the weaver class have sprung Simpson the mathematician, Bacon the sculptor, the two Milners, Adam Walker, John Foster,

"When a building is noticed to bulge a little, our builders hasten to shore it up with timbers; and before long the surveyor bids them take it down. Should we not see great changes in our churches if all the bowing walls were removed? Yet this would be no real loss, but in the Lord's sight an actual gain to the city of God." —Spurgeon.

a "Had he really predicted the king's violent death, a jealous ruler might have suspected him of treason, of taking measures to make his words good. Hence this perversion of his prophecy by Amaziah."—Spk. Com.

b "Bethel is the place where the king performs his religious worship in person, and often resides there with his court, that he may the better attend upon the service performed at this place." —Lowth.

a "Not a prophet by profession, nor bred up in the schools of the prophets, as those usually were who took that office upon them." —Lowth

b Comp. Zec. xiii. 5.

"It is an arduous life, and those alone among the people pursue it who can find no easier mode of support." —Van Lennep.

c "The sycamore is a large tree, with a leaf like that of the mulberry tree, and fruit like a fig. The fruit is naturally bitter, and to remove this the bark is

Wilson the ornithologist, Dr. Livingston the missionary traveler, etc. Shoemakers have given us Sturgeon the electrician, Sam'l Drew the essayist, Gifford the editor of the "Quarterly Review," Bloomfield the poet, and Wm. Carey the missionary.—Smiles.

wounded at the time of budding, and the fruit is slightly scarified with an iron comb as it approaches to ripeness." —Kitto.

16, 17. (16) **hear thou,** addressed to Amaziah, vs. 12. **drop .. word,** comp. De. xxxii. 2; Job xxix. 22. The expression probably has ref. to the flow of words wh. streamed fr. the prophet's lips.[a] **house of Isaac,** i. e. Israel. (17) **Therefore,** as a judgment for trying to silence God's Prophet. **wife,** etc., reference is to the license and cruelty of the Assyrian conquerors. **divided by line,** among the Assyrians. **polluted land,** R. V., "unclean;" foreign country defiled by the service of idols.

Recalling Personal History—Amos always kept good hold of his history. Because we let our personal history slip from the memory we lose a great deal of power. Remember your poverty; remember early hardships; remember through what difficulty you had to fight for every inch of foothold you have secured; remember how you were sustained in weakness; recall the time when men were so savage against you that you were not certain whether you would end your days in the workhouse or in the madhouse; recall your history, have it as a daily companion, because keeping fellowship with your memories you can take the next step with the greater ease and grace, and it shall be by the goodness of God a step upward and a step heavenward.—Peop. Bib.

a "Possibly Amaziah had used this word in ridicule of the prophetic utterances of Amos." —Wordsworth.

"Some people," says Philip Henry, "do not wish to hear much of repentance, but I think it so necessary that, if I should die in the pulpit, I wish to die preaching repentance; and if out of the pulpit, practising it."

"No sin is ever alone. Dr. Macdonald says, "There is no fault that does not bring its brothers and sisters and cousins to live with it." —Spurgeon.

"Nothing warrants unlawful fear in the performance of duty or neglect of it. Providence must never be construed to sanction flight or withdraw us from our work." —Hom. Com.

Re. xiv. 18.

CHAPTER THE EIGHTH.

1—3. (1) **basket .. fruit,** i. e. of ripe fruit. "Partly the thought of Israel's ripeness for judgment, but chiefly the Heb. word kêtz, 'end,' brings up before the prophet's mental eye in his vision, agreeably with the principles explained on vii. 1, the basket of kaitz, 'summer fruit.' Similarly, in Jeremiah's inaugural vision (Jer. i. 11, 12), the thought of Jehovah's watching (shoked) over His word to perform it, produces by association of sounds the image of the almond tree (shaked), the symbolism of which is afterwards explained, as that of the 'summer fruit' is explained here."—Camb. B. (2) **my people,** even in judgment God acknowledges His relationship. **pass by,** ch. vii. 8. (3) **temple,** i. e. the idol palace, or temple, at Bethel. **howlings,** of pain and despair. **with silence,** Camb. Bib., "many the corpses! in all places have they cast them forth: hush!" By the use of the perfect tenses the prophet represents the future vividly as already accomplished. The figures intimate a very great slaughter.

Fruitfulness (vs. 1).—I. Notice the figure of the text as applied to the harvest. 1. Fruit from the earth, God's bounty, not man's production; 2. Summer fruit, seasonable, in due time, ripened; 3. A basket, at man's disposal; 4. The Lord showed, etc., a reminder that thanks are due to the Giver. II. Notice the figure of the text as to its personal lessons. 1. Fruit is the result of cultivation; 2. The ripening fruit points to the coming of the end; 3. Suggestive of inquiries as to our own fruitfulness. —Analyst.

4—7. (4) **swallow .. needy,**[a] better, "pant after them to devour them, like a dog or wild beast panting and yelping after his prey."[b] (5) **new .. corn?**[c] the new moon, the first of the month was observed as a holiday and marked by relig. services (Isa. i. 13, 14; Hos. ii. 11). On the holy days trade was suspended. **sabbath,** the Sabbath is threatened by the same worldliness and love of money which tramples on the helpless. The interests of the Sabbath are the interests of the poor: the enemies of the Sabbath are the enemies of the poor. And all this illustrates our Saviour's saying, that the Sabbath was made for man. Ne. xiii. 15, 16. **ephah,** by wh. the merchants sold their goods. **shekel,** by wh. the money of the purchaser was weighed. **falsifying,** etc., comp. Le. xix. 35—37. (6) **silver,** the final issue of the rapacious conduct described in vs. 5 is that the poor are more and more impoverished, and, falling into debt, have in the end to sell themselves—or their children—as slaves (Lev. xxv. 39) to their rich oppressors, who were only too ready to buy the poor for the silver which they owed them, and the needy for the sake of a

a "The Prophet again addresses the proud, grasping nobles, and rebukes them for their avarice, their dishonesty, and their meanness." —Spk. Com.

b Isa. v. 8.

c Nu. xxviii. 11.

pair of sandals, i. e. for a trifle (cf. ii. 6), the price of which they were unable to pay.—Camb. B. **refuse,** making the poor buy what was not fit for human food. (7) **excellency of Jacob,** ch. vi. 8. Jehovah swears—ironically—by that which, however deeply He disapproves of it, He knows to be unalterable." **never forget,** God is said to remember when He punishes.

Avarice (vss. 4—10).—I. It is execrable in spirit. 1. It is sacrilegious; 2. Dishonest; 3. Cruel. II. It is abhorrent to Jehovah. 1. Repugnant to His nature; 2. Hostile to universal happiness. III. It is a curse to society.

Honoring the Sabbath.—In 1633 the town of Taunton had a good Puritan pastor in Mr. George Newton. He was the great light of its Puritanism, and was Vicar of St. Mary Magdalene. Though naturally timid, "strength was made perfect in weakness," and he was not timid in the assertion of his principles, and soon became a noted "gospeller." When the "Book of Sports" came out by order of Council, and was commanded to be read in all the churches, Mr. Newton read it, but said immediately to his congregation, "These are the commandments of men." He then read the twentieth chapter of the book of Exodus, saying, "These are the commandments of God; but whereas in this case the laws of God and the laws of men are at variance, choose ye which ye will obey." Thus he took the side of the Sabbath against the profane decrees of the king.—Old Test. Anec.

8—10. (8) **for this,** i. e. for all this wickedness of the nobles and avaricious wealthy. **it shall rise,** trans. "and it shall rise up, all of it, as the Nile, and it shall be tossed about and sink (again), as the Nile of Egypt." As the Nile, at the time of its annual inundation, rises, overflows, and sinks again, so will the land of Israel, in all its length and breadth, heave, and be convulsed, as by an earthquake, as it labors to rid itself of its guilty inhabitants.—Cam. B. (9) **sun .. noon,** the figure of an eclipse is taken to represent public calamity.[e] (10) **sackcloth,** etc., all these terms indicate a time of terrible national trouble.[f] **baldness,** artificial, caused by shaving. **only son,** the greatest of family sorrows.

Some Can Only Do Their Work by Dying.—The errand of Bath-sheba's first child into the world was by its death to bring David to his knees and a right mind (2 Sam. xii. 13—23). And how many an early death in a careless family has been that family's salvation! Even the minister cut down in his early prime, with a life of usefulness opening out, as it seems, before him, may preach a sermon by his death more potent for good than all he could have said alive. Untimely death may even in certain cases anticipate the loss of influence for good. We know men of influence in the Church who in their erratic age are undoing the good they were honored to do in their earlier years. Such men have only lived too long. If their sun had set at noon their life-work would have been far greater, humanly speaking, than it will now be. Looking as we do at the surface of things, and blind to their deeper relations and far-reaching issues, we are not in a position to criticise the providential arrangements of God. To believe that there is order in the seeming tangle, and ultimate and wider good behind the present partial evil, is the attitude of that enlightened faith which argues that Infinite Wisdom, omnipotent on the one hand and benevolent on the other, being at the helm of things, will steer in character.—Pul. Com.

11—14. (11) **famine,** etc., this was a just retribution on those who would not hear the word of the Lord as spoken by Amos.[g] (12) **wander,** etc., from the Dead Sea to the Mediterranean, i. e. all through the land. Nowhere should any prophet of the Lord be found. (13) **fair virgins,** from the general suffering not even the loveliest, the strongest, and the best should be exempted. (14) **sin of Samaria,**[a] wh. was its idol calf. **Thy god,** better put in swearing form, "By the life of thy god, O Dan."[b] **the manner,** etc., better, "By the life of the way of Beersheba." Strange as it may appear to us to speak of the life of the lifeless, this often happens among the Semites. To-day Arabs "swear wa hyât, 'by the life of,' even of things inanimate; 'By the life of this fire, or of this coffee.'" And as Amos here tells us that the Israelite pilgrims swore

Ho. viii. 13, ix. 9; Is. xlii. 25; Je. xxxi. 34.

"After poor Sabat, an Arabian, who had professed faith in Christ by the means of the labors of the Rev. H. Martyn, had apostatized from Christianity, and written in favor of Mohammedanism, he was met at Malacca by the late Rev. Dr. Milne, who proposed to him some very pointed questions, in reply to which, he said, 'I am unhappy! I have a mountain of burning sand on my head. When I go about, I know not what I am doing!' It is indeed an evil thing and bitter to forsake the Lord our God."—Bate's Cyclopoedia.

e "There were two great eclipses of the sun about eleven years after the time that Amos prophesied. . . . Calamitous times are expressed by the failing of the light of the sun, and the day's being overspread with darkness." —Lowth.

Is. xiii. 10; Mi. iii. 6.

f Is. xv. 2; Je. xlviii. 37; Eze. vii. 18.

"To think we are able is almost to be so; to determine upon attainment is frequently attainment itself. Thus earnest resolution has often seemed to have about it almost a savor of omnipotence." —Samuel Smiles.

g Pr. xxix. 18; Ps. lxxiv. 9; Eze. vii. 26.

a Ho. viii. 5, 6.

b "The god of Dan was the golden calf set up there by Jeroboam. 1 Ki. xii. 29."—Spk. Com.

by the way to Beersheba, so do the Moslems affirm their oaths by the sacred way to Mecca.—Exp. B.

Vss. 11—14.—When Divine judgments come upon a race which has forgotten and forsaken God, the once despised and hated word is appreciated again. Men "hunger and thirst" for it, but often at first not in the right way. They desire as speedily as possible to hear of promises and consolations, and to these every ear is open. But it is in vain. We now need expect no new revelation from God. We have "His word" in the Scripture. But when this is a long time despised, it follows at last that there is no one to preach it, and without a living preacher it is finally lost. Or if it is preached it has no power to console, and men fail to find what they seek. Thus ensues a longing which is not satisfied.—Lange.

CHAPTER THE NINTH.

1—4. (1) **upon,** R. V., "beside." **altar,** prob. that at Bethel.[c] The Lord doubtless appeared as a fire, or a cloud. **he said,** to the avenging angel, commissioned to carry out His judgments. Some think that the command was given to the Prophet. **Smite the lintel,** etc., R. V., "smite the chapiters that the thresholds may shake; and break them in pieces on the head of all of them."[d] (2) **dig into hell,** fig. for hiding themselves in the deepest holes and caves. **climb .. heaven,** fig. for the most inaccessible heights. (3) **Carmel,** famous for its thick forests. **serpent,** a monster supposed to inhabit the deep; fig. for calamity, and punishment. (4) **go into captivity,** or voluntarily surrender themselves. **before,** driven like sheep.

Great Sins, Great Calamities, Great Efforts.—I. Under the righteous government of God, great sin exposes to great calamity. II. The consciousness of great calamities will stimulate to great efforts for escape. III. The greatest efforts to escape must prove utterly futile when God has given the sinner up.—Thomas.

Carmel.—Carmel was one of the barriers of the promised land, which Sennacherib boasted he would scale with the multitude of his horses and his chariots: "I will enter into the lodgings of his borders, and into the forest of his Carmel." Ungrateful as the soil of this mountain is, the wild vines and olive trees that are still found among the brambles which encumber its declivities prove that the hand of industry has not labored among the rocks of Carmel in vain. So well adapted were the sides of this mountain to the cultivation of the vine, that the kings of Judah covered every improvable spot with vineyards and plantations of olives. Its deep and entangled forests, its savage rocks and lofty summit, have been in all ages the favorite retreat of the guilty or oppressed. The fastnesses of this rugged mountain are so difficult of access that the Prophet Amos classes them with the deeps of hell, the height of heaven, and the bottom of the sea. The Church, in her most affluent state, is compared to a fugitive lurking in the deep recesses of this mountain: "Feed thy people with thy rod, the flock of thy heritage which dwell solitarily in the midst of Carmel." Lebanon raises to heaven a summit of naked and barren rocks, covered for the greater part of the year with snow; but the top of Carmel, how naked and sterile so ever its present condition, seems to have been clothed with verdure in the days of Amos, which seldom was known to fade: "And he said, The Lord will roar from Zion, and utter His voice from Jerusalem, and the habitation of the shepherds shall mourn, and the top of Carmel shall wither."—Paxton.——Sin Brought to Remembrance.—Not many years since a large steam vessel, crossing the Atlantic Ocean, was caught in a fearful storm, and wrecked. All on board perished except a few, who, clinging to portions of the wreck, were rescued by a passing vessel and brought safely to land. One of the survivors relates that, during the time he was thus floating on the water, lashed to a spar, now engulphed in the roaring waters, then violently cast to the surface, expecting every moment to be his last, there seemed continually ringing in his ears the inquiry, "Tom, did you steal

[c] Am. iii. 14.

[d] The people are conceived as fleeing from the Assyrians, and seeking protection in the temple at Bethel. There, however, they would perish in the overthrow of the temple.

"God is everywhere, not as the air is everywhere. The air is part in one place and part in another; God is all in every place. God is wholly in the height of heaven, and wholly in the depth of hell; wholly in the length of the earth, and wholly in the breadth of the sea. All God is in all things, and all God is without all things; He is without all things, and not shut out of anything. He is in all things, and not included in anything. So the ancients speak of this wonderful mystery of God's omnipresence."—Caryl.

"The mountains are nature's monuments."
—J. Hamilton.

"Depend upon it it is not the want of greater miracles, but of the soul to perceive such as are allowed us still, that makes us push all the sanctities into the far spaces we cannot reach. The devout feel that wherever God's hand is there is miracle; and it is simply an undevoutness which imagines that only where miracle is, there can be the real hand of God."

sister's grapes?" The hurricane raged round him, the wind howling in fearful blasts, which blended with crashing peals of thunder; but, loud and clear above the tumult of the storm, again he heard a well-known voice inquire, "Tom, did you steal sister's grapes?" Whilst yet a lad, his sister was dangerously ill, and a neighbor kindly sent some grapes. These his mother put aside for use during the weary watches of the night; but the boy, though well acquainted with the purpose for which they were sent, stole and ate them. They were not missed until required late in the evening; and then, his mother coming to his bedside, gently shook him, and in tones of tender rebuke, asked, "Tom, did you steal sister's grapes?" As he opened his eyes, the light of the candle shining on her face, he saw the tears trickling down her cheeks, and, muttering some partial confession of his fault, lay expecting further reproach, if not punishment; but, without another word, she sorrowfully retired: and now, with nothing in the circumstances by which he was surrounded to recall it—alone—buffeted hither and thither on the waves of the Atlantic, this sin of his boyhood was rising up in judgment against him.

5, 6. (5) **toucheth,** by cyclone, earthquake, or pestilence. **melt,** even the stoutest hearts being filled with fear. **rise,** etc., ch. viii. 8.[a] (6) **stories,** better, R. V., "chambers," i. e. his dwelling. **troop in,** R. V., "vault upon," i. e. "the starry dome by wh. the earth is overhung," Is. lxvi. 1. **calleth,** etc., vs. 8, long continued rains.

Note on vs. 6.—The Hebrews pictured the sky as a solid vault (firmamentum), resting at its extremities upon the earth (Job xxvi. 11): in this vault the heavenly bodies were imagined to revolve: "in front of it" (i. e. in the open air below its lower surface) the birds flew (Gen. i. 20): above it were reservoirs in which rain was stored (as also snow and hail); and above these "waters above the firmament" Jehovah sat enthroned. The words of vs. 6 are thus intended to illustrate Jehovah's power by pointing to the palace which He has constructed for Himself on high, and firmly secured, by resting its foundations upon the solid earth. —Camb. Bib.——Amos's Spiritual Discernment.—The poor little telescope has raked up more than a hundred thousand worlds, and when the telescope is tired with looking, it says, I have not yet begun to see; beyond is the real life of the worlds; improve me, rub these lenses, burnish them, enlarge them, throw them away and replace them with others, for I have not yet begun to see the stories in God's palace. A few of the under-stories I have seen, and they are entrancingly and inexpressibly lovely and glorious; I cannot get inside them, but their windows are ablaze with light; yet I am sure I have only begun, or hardly begun; the stories are miles, millions at once, higher and higher. He was a singular herdman who saw that thousands of years ago. He had no telescope; he had only the natural vision as an outward instrument, but he had a soul that used that vision to advantage.—Peop. Bib.

7—10. (7) **as .. Ethiopians,** i. e. degenerate Israel is no more to God than these despised Kushites. **Have not I,** the pronoun I is here emphatic. Amos proclaims the universal providence of God. Bec. He is exalted in righteousness He guides all nations. (8) **eyes,** etc., vs. 4. **sinful kingdom,** i. e. the separate kingdom of the ten tribes, founded by Jeroboam. **saving,** etc., i. e. God's chastisement is not doom but discipline. (9) **sift,** "a beautiful image, representing clearly God's beneficent design in the captivity and dispersion of Israel." (10) **sinners,** only the sinners, not one grain of the good. **overtake us,** press on us from behind. **prevent,** impede us by getting in the way before us.

Judgment and Mercy (vs. 9).—I. The determination avowed. 1. The comparison employed points to the only distinction of character recognized in Scripture—the righteous and the wicked; 2. The character of the individual Christian is not one of unmingled purity; 3. The mixture of character which exists in the Church of God; 4. Consider the process—sifting. II. The security promised. 1. The process has exclusive reference to the wheat; 2. The security arises from God's care over His people in affliction—this care arises out of God's love for them —this love and care extends to all, even the least. III. Inferences. 1. The safety of true believers amidst surrounding troubles; 2. Learn to recognize the hand of God in all events.

Much of the glory of God in creation is hid by a train of second causes, through which few look to the first."—Howe.

The first article in the commission of General Booth and his wageless "army" is renunciation. Their reward is rescued immortal lives.—Anon.

"In every quarter of the world, and in well-nigh every nation in every quarter, Jews have been found. The whole earth is, as it were, one vast sieve in the hands of God, in which Israel is shaken from one end to the other. . . . The chaff and dust would be blown away by the air; . . . but no solid corn, not one grain, should fall to the earth."

—Pusey.

"Gold in the ore is a treasure; but it is when it has passed through the refiner's hands, and has received the stamp of currency, that it becomes of acknowledged value, and fit for adaptation to all the circumstances and conveniences of life."—W. S. M.

"Fiery trials make golden Christians; sanctified afflictions are spiritual promotion."

—Dyer.

a Comp. Nu. xxiv. 18.

Conscience is the unbiased head and heart approving or condemning the will."

"Carlyle, speaking of the changes made by time, says, 'How tragic to me is the sight of old friends; a thing I always really shrunk from!' Sin has made still more painful changes in some once numbered amongst the friends of God."

Le. xxvi. 5.

b "The kingdom of the Messiah shall take such deep rooting in the world as never to be rooted out of it."—Mat. Henry.

Is. lx. 21; Je. xxxii. 41; Eze. xxxiv. 28; Joel iii. 20, 21.

"Souls are made sweet not by taking the acid fluids out, but by putting something in — a great Love, a new Spirit, the Spirit of Christ."—Henry Drummond.

"Nothing good bursts forth all at once. The lightning may dart out of a black cloud; but the day sends his bright heralds before him, to prepare the world for his coming." —Hare.

11, 12. (11) **that day, i. e.** after the chastisement of discipline. **tabernacle, or house and family of David.** The word tent, or booth, indicates the low condition into which Dav.'s house had fallen. **breaches,** with prob. allusion to the separation of the kingdom of David into two parts, and the evil condition of country under Amaziah. **days of old, i. e.** of David and Solmon. (12) **Edom,** ch. i. 12.[a] **all .. name,** Cam. B., "all the nations, over whom thy name has been called," as owner or **conqueror.** Ref. to David's conquests.

The Epilogue.—Amos closes, as the prophets are wont to close their discourses, with the promise of a brighter future. The dynasty of David, though for the time humbled, will be reinstated in its former splendor and power (vss. 11—12); and the blessings of peace will be shared in perpetuity by the entire nation (vss. 13—15).

Divine Discernment.—Everybody can find a bird's nest in winter when the trees are bare, but in summer the green leaves hide them; so are believers discovered by adversity. One thing, however, should never be forgotten: whether we know believers or not, God knows them. He does not include one hypocrite in the number, nor exclude one sincere truster, even though he be of little faith. He knows infallibly and universally. Does He know me, even me, as one of those who trust in Him? The Lord knoweth them that are His, and they know Him as their stronghold. Have I such knowledge?—Spurgeon.

13—15. (13) **plowman,** etc., "There is to be no interval between ploughing and harvest, and the vintage is to last till next year's sowing." **hills .. melt,** lit. "dissolve themselves:" so abundant will be the produce of the vineyards, that it will be "as though the hills dissolved themselves in the rich streams which they poured down." Comp. Joel iii. 18.—Cam. B. (14) **bring again,** De. xxx. 3. (15) **plant them,** etc., it is generally assumed that these promises refer to a yet unfulfilled restoration of Israel.[b]

The Golden Age.—Nothing short of inspiration can account for such a close to such a book. Throughout his prophecies Amos has been exposing national sinfulness, threatening Divine chastisement, picturing the degradation, the desolation, the captivity of the kingdoms of Israel and of Judah. How comes it that he is able to transcend this distressing representation? to look beyond these gloomy clouds? to discern, whether far or near, the vision of a smiling earth, a happy people, a splendid prosperity, an eternal joy? It is not the force of human reasoning; it is not the impulse of delusive hope. No; it is the presence of the Divine Spirit that has purged the prophet's spiritual vision, so that he sees the glory yet to be; it is this that touches the prophet's tongue, so that the wail of sorrow and distress is changed into the shout of triumph and the song of joy.—Pul. Com.

Amos—the Prophet of Social Justice.—

No prophet, neither prophet's son, but called
From following the flock to be a voice
For God, a seer of truth for people walled
About with insincerity, a choice
And gifted workman, trained in field, not in school.
Beneath the silent stars he thought by night,
And wrought the livelong day with busy tool.
So measured he to manhood's fullest height.

No golden glamour hides from eyes made keen
By desert air the nation's sure decay.
His plumb-line makes the social structure lean
So far from truth that naught its fall can stay.
He sees the Lord above the altar stand
To smite the temple and to scourge the land.—C. S. Hoyt.

Introduction.

I. Author. **Obadiah...**"Of the personal history of Obadiah nothing is known. The contents of his prophecy show that he belonged to the Kingdom of Judah. The name which he bears, 'servant of Yah,' or 'worshipper of Yah,' is a common one in the Old Testament. We are specially familiar with it as borne by the godly chamberlain of Ahab in the time of Elijah (1 Kings xviii. 3—16). But neither with him, nor with any other of the persons who are called by it in the sacred history, can the author of this Book be identified." II. **Time.** B. C. 588-583. Expositors are not agreed concerning the date. "The probability would certainly seem to be, that Obadiah is commissioned to fortell the punishment of Edom for the recent wrongdoing which he so vividly depicts. His prophecy would thus have been delivered shortly after the destruction of the city, or between its first capture and final destruction, by the Chaldeans." III. **Theme.** He first denounces judgment against Edom (1—9), then (10—16) dwells upon the special sin committed, the malicious joy with which the Edomites had abetted Judah's enemies, reiterating the threatening; and afterwards (17—21), he describes the restoration of Jewish prosperity, their dominion being largely extended. The accomplishment of the earlier part of the prophecy took place about five years after the taking of Jerusalem, that of the latter in the victories of the Maccabean princes; this has, however, no doubt its fullest completion in the establishment of Messiah's kingdom. IV. **Comparison with other Old Testament passages.** "It is impossible to lay side by side the denunciation of Edom by Obadiah (vv. 1—9) and the prophecy of Jeremiah on the same subject (xlix. 7—22) without being convinced that they are either derived from the common source or that one of them is a reproduction of the other. The most probable conclusion is, that Obadiah, stirred by the recent wrongs inflicted by the Edomites upon his people, wrongs which perhaps he had himself witnessed, was commissioned to pour forth this brief denunciation against them; while Jeremiah, his contemporary, took up and repeated shortly after in his own more elaborate parable of reproach much of what his brother prophet had uttered. Two other Old Testament denunciations against Edom belong to the same period of Jewish history and serve to throw light upon the prophecy of Obadiah. Compare: Ezekiel xxv. 12—14; xxxv. 2—15; and Psalm cxxxvii."—(Cambridge Bible.) On the Psalm, see selection under verses 20 and 21, of this Book.

Synopsis.

(According to the Pulpit Commentary.)

PART I. (Vers. 1—16.) The destruction of Edom, and the cause thereof.

Sec. 1. (Vers. 1—9.) The heathen nations are summoned to take vengeance on Edom. In spite of her impregnable position, they shall bring her low and strip her of her wealth, being aided and encouraged by her allies.

Sec. 2. (Vers. 10—14.) This punishment falls upon her as the result of the malice and unfriendliness which she has displayed towards Israel in the time of her calamity, in that she rejoiced at her sister's disaster, and took part with her enemies.

Sec. 3. (Vers. 15, 16.) For this cause Edom shall be remembered in the day of the Lord; she shall suffer at the hands of the heathen what she inflicted on others.

PART II. (Vers. 17—21.) The restoration of Israel.

Sec. 1. (Vers. 17—20.) The house of Jacob shall be delivered, and shall add to its possessions, and spread far and wide.

Sec. 2. (Vers. 21.) Salvation shall come to Zion, and "the kingdom shall be the Lord's."

CHAPTER THE FIRST.

The Book of Obadiah.. About 1030 B. C. David, about 130 the Hasmoneans, were equally at war with Edom; and few are the prophets between those distant dates who do not cry for vengeance against him or exult in his overthrow. The Book of Obadiah is singular in this, that it contains nothing else than such feelings and such cries. It brings no spiritual message. It speaks no word of sin, or of righteousness, or of mercy, but only doom upon Edom in bitter resentment at his cruelties, and in exultation that, as he has helped to disinherit Israel, Israel shall disinherit him. . . . Justice, mercy and truth; the education of humanity in the law of God, the establishment of His will upon earth — these things, it is true, are not mentioned in the Book of Obadiah, but it is for the sake of some dim instinct of them that its wrath is poured upon foes whose treachery and malice seek to make them impossible by destroying the one people on earth who then believed and lived for them.—Geo. Adam Smith.

1, 2. (1) **Obadiah,** "Servant of Jehovah." **Lord God,** Heb. Adonai Jehovah. "This is the formula claiming Divine authority for the whole prophecy." **We, rumour,**[a] R. V., "tidings." I and my people. **is sent,** i.e. already sent, to call the nations to execute God's judgments. (2) **Arise ye,** etc. This is the message of the ambassador. **I have made thee small,**[b] Jehovah is the speaker. Edom is made small and despised in Jehovah's purpose.

3—6. (3) **The pride,** etc., i.e. in her seemingly impregnable position. **dwellest .. rock,** the great Edomite capital Selah, or Petra, is here referred to; one of the most curious and wonderful cities on the earth; consisting exclusively of houses and temples cut in the solid rock[c]. (4) **exalt,** R. V., "mount on high," etc., Je. xlix. 16. **among the stars,** fig. for seemingly inaccessible height. (5) **thieves,** etc., so in your case; whatever they wanted your enemies have taken. There are not even any gleanings left behind. Robbers and vine-croppers could not have used you worse. Je. xlix. 9. (6) **How .. searched out!** the Prophet sees the hostile soldiers seeking booty.[b]

7—9. (7) **men .. confederacy,** i.e. thy allies. Probably those Arabian tribes who surrounded Edom and were its frequent confederates, comp. Gen. xxv. 13: xxxvi. 3, 12, etc. Exp. Bib. **laid a wound,** R. V. "a snare," i.e. dealt treacherously. (8) **wise men,** Edom seems to have been proverbial for its wisdom.[d] "Eliphaz, the chief of Job's friends, the representative of human wisdom, was a Temanite." **mount of Esau,** Mount Seir. (9) **Teman,** a district in southern part of Edom, perhaps used here as synonymous with Edom. **dismayed,** so as to be unable to offer effective resistance. **everyone,** etc., R. V. "everyone may cut off from the mount of Esau," etc.

Edom's Security.—The purple mountains, into which the wild sons of Esau clambered, run out from Syria upon the desert, some hundred miles by twenty of porphyry and red sandstone. They are said to be the finest rock scenery in the world. "Salvator Rosa never conceived so savage and so suitable a haunt for banditti." From Mount Hor, which is their summit, you look down upon a maze of mountains, cliffs, chasms, rocky shelves and strips of valley. On the east the range is but the crested edge of a high, cold plateau, covered for the most part by stones, but with stretches of corn land and scattered woods. The western walls, on the contrary, spring steep and bare, black and red, from the yellow of the desert Arabah. The interior is reached by defiles, so narrow that two horsemen may scarcely ride abreast, and the sun is shut out by the overhanging rocks. Eagles, hawks and other mountain birds fly screaming round the traveler. Little else than wild-fowls' nests are the villages; human eyries perched on high shelves or hidden away in caves at the ends of the deep gorges. There is abundance of water. The gorges are filled with tamarisks, oleanders and wild figs. Besides the wheat lands on the eastern plateau, the wider defiles hold fertile fields and terraces

---

a Je. xlix. 14.

b "Thy reduction to insignificance is as sure as if it were already accomplished. Therefore the past tense is used."—Maurer.

c "Selah was situated on either side of a deep ravine, wh. runs winding like a stream through precipitous and overhanging cliffs, for a distance of not less than a mile and a half. The cliffs are honeycombed with caverns and in these caverns, reached by artificial means of access, the Edomites dwelt."—Spk. Com.

b Je. xlix. 10.

"Paulius, when he was told that the Goths had sacked Nola and plundered him of all he had, lifted up his eyes to heaven, and said, 'Lord, thou knowest where I have laid up my treasure.'"—Bib. Museum.

d "The wanderers in that region are now sunk in the grossest folly, regarding the ruins around them as the work of evil spirits. Travelers assert that the minds of the Bedouins are as bare and uncultivated as the deserts they traverse."—Biblical Things.

"It is in vain to depend upon mighty men for our protection, if we have not an Almighty God for us, much less if we have an Almighty God against us."—Lange.

"Edom is a type of worldly wisdom and secular policy, as well as of unbrotherly enmity to God's people. In both respects the punishment of Edom is a warning to all Machiavellian politicians in these latter days."—Wordsworth.

"He that is not wise will not be taught; but there is a wisdom which multiplieth bitterness." — Ecclus. xxi. 12.

"The circumstances of Obadiah's country and family are designedly passed over, that we may not rest and depend upon the outward respectability of men, but derive the authority of such prophecy, and the certainty of its issues, from God alone. Preachers must be, not in name alone, but also in fact, Obadiahs, i. e. servants of God (1 Cor. iv. 1). — Starke.

[a] "The words are addressed to Edomites by way of apostrophe on what he sees them doing before his face, not as a warning against their so-doing in future." —Spk. Com.

"Be more glad to see a man's amendment than his punishment. He that is not concerned that his brother should perish, is in danger of perishing himself."—Bp. Wilson.

"For a Turk to oppress a Christian, an infidel a believer, is but a trespass against humanity; for Hebrews to strive, and one Christian to afflict another, woundeth. relig-

for the vine. Mount Esau is, therefore, no mere citadel with supplies for a limited siege, but a well-stocked, well-watered country, full of food and lusty men, yet lifted so high, and locked so fast by precipice and slippery mountain, that it calls for little trouble of defence.

The Edomites.—Esau is a profane person, with no conscience of a birthright, no faith in the future, no capacity for visions; dead to the unseen, and clamoring only for the satisfaction of his appetites. The same was probably the character of his descendants; who had, of course, their own gods, like every other people in that Semitic world, but were essentially irreligious, living for food, spoil and vengeance, with no national conscience or ideals—a kind of people who deserved even more than the Philistine to have their name descend to our times as a symbol of hardness and obscurantism. It is no contradiction to all this that the one intellectual quality imputed to the Edomites should be that of shrewdness and a wisdom which was obviously worldly. The wise men of Edom, the cleverness of Mount Esau were notorious. It is the race which has given to history only the Herods—clever, scheming, ruthless statesmen, as able as they were false and bitter, as shrewd in policy as they were destitute of ideals. That fox, cried Christ, and crying stamped the race.—Exp. Bib. The wisdom of Edom.—If the question now be asked, Is understanding perished out of Edom? the answer, like every response of the prophetic word, may be briefly given: It is. The minds of the Bedouins are as uncultivated as the deserts they traverse. Practical wisdom is, in general, the first that man learns, and the last that he retains. And the simple but significant fact, that the clearing away of a little rubbish, merely "to allow the water to flow" into an ancient cistern, in order to render it useful to themselves, "is an undertaking far beyond the views of the wandering Arabs," shows that understanding is indeed perished from among them. They view the indestructible works of former ages not only with wonder, but with superstitious regard, and consider them the work of genii. They look upon a European traveler as a magician, and believe that, having seen any spot where they imagine that treasures are deposited, he can afterward command the guardian of the treasure to set the whole before him. In Teman, which yet maintains a precarious existence, the inhabitants possess the desire without the means of knowledge. The Koran is their only study, and contains the sum of their wisdom. And, although he was but a "miserable comforter," and was overmastered in argument by a kinsman stricken with affliction, yet no Temanite can now discourse with either the wisdom or the pathos of Eliphaz of old. Wisdom is no more in Teman, and understanding has perished out of the Mount of Esau.

10—12. vss. 10, 11, "give the ground of the preceding denunciation, viz. the violence and outrage of which Edom had been guilty in the day of Jerusalem's calamity." (10) **violence,** Ge. xxvii. 41; Eze. xxxv. 5; Am. i. 11. **brother Jacob,** comp. Deut. xxiii. 7 for God's command to the Hebrews. **cut off for ever,** the Nabathæans drove the Edomites out of their ancient possessions, and these they have never since regained. (11) **on the other side,** meaning, in a position of hostility, **his forces** R. V. "his substance." **cast lots,** "over the population whom they thus distributed to be sold into slavery." Lange. (12) **But,** etc., better and more forcibly read ... "Do not look ... do not rejoice ... do not enter .. do not deliver."[a] **became a stranger,** R. V. "in the day of his disaster." **to look on,** indifferently, then was a sin worthy of some punishment.

God superintending human history.—In all Bible history we find God upon the circle. There is no page dedicated to atheism. God is always there, in shining person, or guiding eye, or directing voice, or celestial effluence; this book is, so far as one world is concerned, the very biography of God! Aye, God himself is the central character, and as he sweeps in majesty across our tiny globe, age by age, we see kings and thrones, and empires and nations attached to his flaming chariot. This sublimest of all historical books is not a mere registry of facts or dates; it is not a mere accumulation of meteorological tables, showing the variations of political or moral climate, or representing the tide-marks of national advancement or recession—it is a chronicle of the one heart of God, and the one heart of humanity; it is the blended story of the heavens and the earth.—Peop. Bib.

13, 14. (13) **the gate,** i.e. Jerusalem. implying that they not only looked on, but helped themselves to booty in the hour of Judah's calamity. (14) **crossway,** narrow mountain passes: by wh. the fleeing Israelites hoped to escape. These the Edomites closed, securing and delivering up the fugitives.

Brethren, we are members one of another. Why, then, do we hurt and annoy one another? There ought to be no discord in the home or in the church, because we are called to be one body, and if I wound a brother Christian I am blighting my own life; I am spoiling the body which is one.—H. W. Webb-Peploe.

My neighbor.—

Thy neighbor? 'Tis that toiling slave,
Fetter'd in thought and limb,
Whose hopes are all beyond the grave:
Go thou and ransom him.

Thy neighbor? 'Tis that weary man
Whose years are at the brim,
Bent down by sickness, care, and pain:
Go thou and comfort him.

Thy neighbor? 'Tis the fainting poor,
Whose eyes with want are dim,
Whom hunger drives from door to door:
Go thou and cherish him.—Montgomery.

15, 16. (15) **heathen,** nations surrounding Israel, and at enmity with God's people. **as .. thee,** Eze. xxxv. 15; Ha. ii. 8. **reward,** R. V. "dealing." (16) **drunk,** some understand that the prophet here addresses his own countrymen, "As ye have drunk (who are) on my holy mountain," as ye have tasted the cup of my wrath, "so," etc. But it is better to take the clause as still addressed to the Edomites who had profaned the holy mountain with their idolatrous festival. The drinking in the first clause is literal, in the second, figurative. **all the heathen,** including Edom. Edom is taken as a type of all nations hostile to God's people. **swallow down,** "a full draught, and that not because they desire it, because they must." —Lange.

Retribution.—In society men reap as they sow. Kindness begets love, and cruelty begets hatred. The suspicious are suspected, the dishonest robbed, and the tyrants in turn led into captivity. "There is an important element," says a writer, "of the judicial action of God in the retributive instincts of men. It is one of his ways of bringing the self-conceited and the censorious to his bar. He whose hand or tongue is against every man, need not wonder that Divine providence should so balance the scales of justice, that every man's hand or tongue will be ultimately against him. He reaps what he sows."—Hom. Com. To the revengeful God will be robed in vengeance, and to the merciful he will be a God of love. Thus our own characters, whether good or bad, will be thrown back upon ourselves, with the conscious force of Divinity. What is hell but sin's reflections of the Divine character—the rays of the Eternal falling upon the soul through the combustible medium of the moral corruption, and thus setting all on fire? Let us remember, then, that there is to be a Divine reflection of ourselves, and that exactly with what measure we mete, it will be measured to us again.—Thomas.

17—19. (17) R. V. "But in Mount Zion there shall be those that escape, and it shall be holy." A remnant shall be there, and the place, now polluted shall be made clean—holy. **their possessions,** i.e. their own. "The perpetual possession of the Holy Land is declared as a feature of the times of Redemption from Joel iii. 20 and Amos ix. 15 onward," with increase even, (as in Obad.) of their territory."—Oehler. (18) **Jacob .. Joseph,** implying that the restoration would include exiles from both the

ion. Brethren by nation, brethren by religion, should live as brethren by nature; live as brethren, and our Father will be angry if we do not, and the God of peace wil fight against us." — Adapted from Marbury.

"Heaven is above all, yet there sits a Judge that no king can corrupt." — Shakespeare.

"There is a debt of mercy and pity, of charity and compassion, of relief and succor, due to human nature, and payable from one man to another, and such as deny to pay it the distressed in the time of their abundance may justly expect it will be denied themselves in time of want."—Burkitt.

" Faith saves, and grace saves; faith as the instrument, and grace as the Divine efficacy; faith the channel, and grace the heavenly stream; faith the finger that touches the garment's fringe, and grace the virtue that pours from the Saviour's heart. Faith cannot scale the dreadful precipice from which Nature has fallen; but it can lay hold on the rope which grace has let down even into his hands from the top.and which will draw up again with all the burden faith can bind to it. And this is all the mystery of faith's saving. Christ reaches down from heaven and faith reaches up from earth; and each hand grasps the other—one in weakness, the other in power."—Hoge.

"Many souls are being exercised about holiness, but not equally about righteousness. Holiness is the hidden thing we cannot see; righteousness is the manifestation of holiness in act and life." — Andrew A. Bonar.

"Unless our faith is manifested in righteousness, we must beware lest we think it is genuine when it is not; there must be in it the seed of all holy life."—Teunis S. Hamlin.

"The devil never tempts us with more success than when he tempts us with a sight of our own good actions."—Bishop Wilson.

kingdoms of Judah and Israel. **stubble,** etc., this prophecy was fulfilled in the time of the Maccabees. (19) **of the south,** the Negeb, or southern district of Judah. **plain,** low country along the shores of the Mediterranean. **Gilead,** the region E. of Jordan. Judah and Benjamin are to obtain possession of the ancient inheritance.

Blessed effects of the Gospel in the latter days (vs. 17).—I. The deliverance here spoken of. 1. It has already come to Zion; 2. It is also experienced yet daily; 3. But it will be yet more largely experienced in the latter days. II. Its never-failing attendant—holiness. 1. Found only in Zion; 2. Found there from the time of deliverance. III. Its ultimate effect—rest. 1. Believers do now enter into rest; 2. But the full possession of it is reserved for another world. Address—1. Those who oppose the Church of God; 2. Those who are looking for redemption in Jerusalem.—C. Simeon.

The beauty of holiness.—What a lustre from the life of one "beautified with salvation"! His outward conduct is attractive in every part, and his inward dispositions of love and humility are well-pleasing to God himself. Man transformed into God's image is more attractive and more durable than natural beauty. "God in the redemption of the soul," says Emerson, "has solved the problem of restoring to the most original internal beauty."—Hom. Com. Holiness.—In order to be the disciples of Christ, there is much that we must instantly renounce. It is a profession of holiness; it therefore demands the immediate renunciation of criminal and forbidden pleasures. The moment we become Christ's disciples, we commence a warfare with the flesh, engaging for its crucifixion, with all its sinful lusts and appetites. "They that are Christ's have crucified the flesh, with its affections and lusts." To the severities of monastic discipline, in which the body is torn in scourges, and emaciated by abstaining from the nourishment required to sustain it in health and vigor, the religion of Christ is a stranger: "For every creature of God is good, if it be received with thanksgiving." But a soft, voluptuous, and sensual life is repugnant, not only to the example of Christ, but to the whole genius and spirit of His institutes. By His Gospel, and by His Son, God has "called us, not to uncleanness, but to holiness;" so that he that despiseth the precepts of purity, despiseth not man but God. However painful the sacrifice of forbidden gratifications may be, however deep and inveterate the habit of indulgence; though it may seem as necessary to us, and as much a part of ourselves, as the right hand, or the right eye, relinquished it must be, or we cannot be Christ's disciples. Some men talk of holiness as if it meant that it was wrong to laugh, be bright, engage in manly sports, play the piano, read any book but the Bible, or follow certain pursuits for which we have natural aptitudes. I believe that God in his word will not contradict the nature which he has given, and that which is wrong in us is not our natural aptitudes, but the self-life around which those aptitudes revolve. The life which God desires his children to live is not a life of denial of anything which God has imparted, but the transference of these from the pivot of self to the pivot of not self—which is Jesus Christ, incarnate love. The man who enters this life is still a bright companion, a manly athlete, still enters into all that home and friendship and life may mean; but everything is hallowed, elevated, ennobled, because revolving evermore round the will of Jesus Christ.—F. B. Meyer.

20, 21. (20) **captivity,** i.e. those restored from the captivity. **shall possess that,** etc., R. V. "which are among the Canaanites, shall possess even unto," etc. **Zarephath,** the Sarepta of the N. T. (Luke iv. 26) and in Elijah's history (1 Ki. xvii. 9—24) a considerable town on the coast road between Tyre and Sidon.—Camb. Bib. **Sepharad,** a district unknown. "Whatever uncertainty attaches to the word Sepharad, the drift of the prophecy is perfectly clear, viz. that not only the exiles from Babylon, but Jewish captives from other and distant regions shall be brought back to live prosperously within the enlarged borders of their own land.—Camb. Bib. (21) **saviours,** deliverers, "heroes, who should gain for the people their rights."—Lange.[a] "Like the Maccabees."—Camb. Bib. **kingdom .. Lord's,** Re. xi. 15—17.

[a] "Or we may understand the word in a spiritual sense, for the preachers of salvation, whose office it is to convert unbelievers and aliens to the commonwealth of Israel." — Lowth.

"The world is an old woman, that mistakes any gilt farthing for a gold coin; whereby, being often cheated, she will henceforth trust nothing but the common copper."—Carlyle.

Execration of Edom.—There remains a yet later reference to the crowning injury inflicted by Edom upon Israel which it is interesting to notice in this connection. It occurs in the 137th Psalm. Probably the writer was a Levite who had been carried away by the armies of Nebuchadnezzar and who after the edict of Cyrus returns to Jerusalem. He sees again the old familiar scenes, but the change and desolation are terrible. The House of his God is a heap of ruins. His heart is bitter with the memory of wrong and insult from which he has but lately escaped. "He takes his harp, the companion of his exile, the cherished relic of happier days,—the harp which he could not string at the bidding of his conquerors by the waters of Babylon; and now with faltering hand he sweeps the strings, first in low, plaintive, melancholy cadence pouring out his griefs, and then with a loud crash of wild and stormy numbers of his verse, he raises the pæan of vengeance over his foes. .. As he broods over his wrongs, as he looks upon the desolation of his country, as he remembers with peculiar bitterness how they who ought to have been allies took part with the enemies of Jerusalem in the fatal day of her overthrow, there bursts forth the terrible cry for vengeance; vengeance first on the false kindred, and next on the proud conquerors of his race. Deepest of all was the indignation roused by the sight of the nearest of kin, the race of Esau, often allied to Judah, often independent, now bound by the closest union with the power that was truly the common enemy of both. There was an intoxication of delight in the wild Edomite chiefs, as at each successive stroke against the venerable walls they shouted, 'Down with it! down with it! even to the ground.' They stood in the passes to intercept the escape of those who would have fled down to the Jordan valley; they betrayed the fugitives; they indulged their barbarous revels on the Temple hill. Long and loud has been the wail of execration which has gone up from the Jewish nation against Edom. It is the one imprecation which breaks forth from the Lamentations of Jeremiah: it is the culmination of the fierce threats of Ezekiel: it is the sole purpose of the short, sharp cry of Obadiah; it is the bitterest drop in the sad recollections of the Israelite captives by the waters of Babylon: and the one warlike strain of the Evangelical Prophet is inspired by the hope that the Divine Conqueror should come knee-deep in Idumæan blood (Lam. iv. 21, 22; Ezek. xxv. 8, 12—14; Obad. 1—21; Jer. xlix. 7—22; Is. lxiii. 1—4)."—Camb. Bib. quoting Perowne and Stanley.

The Kingdom Shall be the Lord's.—The grand climax is here certainly, however indistinctly, before the prophet's mind. It is this that stamps the writings of the Hebrew prophets with a character which is all their own, and proves them to be inspired with an inspiration of God, other and higher far than that of the most gifted seers and poets of other lands and ages. With them the national and the human reach forth ever to the Divine and the universal. The kingdom of Israel gives place to and is lost in the kingdom of God. Never in any adequate realization even of Jewish idea and conception, could it be said of any period of the history of Israel after the return from Babylon, "The kingdom is the Lord's." Never of any country or any church, much less of the world at large, has so great a word been true, since in the person and the religion of Christ the kingdom of God has come among us. Still the Church prays as for a thing still future, "Thy kingdom come." Still Obadiah's last note of prophecy, "the kingdom shall be the Lord's," vibrates on, till at last it shall be taken up into the great chorus of accomplished hope and satisfied expectation, "Hallelujah! for the Lord God Omnipotent reigneth."—Cambridge Bible.

"God never meant that man should scale the heavens by strides of human wisdom. In His works, though wondrous, he commends us in His word to seek Him rather where His mercy shines."—Cowper.

"The true disciples of Jesus are not those who are not satisfied with admiring Him, with praising Him, wth celebrating Him, who, externally, or to a certain point, follow Him. His true disciples are those who listen to Him internally and everywhere; who observe His precepts, who deny themselves, who take His cross on them, and follow Him everywhere."
—Bossuet.

"The brightest day has not yet dawned, the widest conquests have not yet been achieved. Is not the Church challenged to nerve herself for greater effort, and to array herself in a more imposing habit? 'Put on thy strength, O Zion; put on thy beautiful garments, O Jerusalem!" —Hom. Com.

"O! scene surpassing fable, and yet true, scene of accomplished bliss, which who can see, Though but in distant prospect, and not feel his soul refreshed with foretaste of the joy?"

Introduction.

The Prophet Jonah is referred to in the second book of Kings xiv. 25. He lived probably about 780 B. C., a generation earlier than Amos. He was evidently a prophet of the Northern Kingdom.

The following views have been held as to the object of the book: (1) To set forth the readiness of God to forgive the penitent. (2) To show why Divine warnings and predictions of punishment are not always fulfilled. (3) To correct Jewish exclusiveness and to show God's equal regard for the Gentiles.

Jonah, though a sincere servant of the Most High, is a representation of the narrow bigotry and jealousy of the Jewish people. He fears that God will forgive the Ninevites, believing that such clemency will be dishonorable to God and unjust to his chosen people, who as such, have suffered terribly under the persecution of the heathen, and who have come to regard themselves as the only objects of the Divine favor.

CHAPTER THE FIRST.

1—3. (1) **Jonah,** (see introduction). **Amittai,** Heb. truth, or truth-telling. (2) **Nineveh,** Ge. x. 11. **great city,** "480 stadia (about 60 miles) in circuit, 150 in length, and 90 in breadth."—Diodorus Siculus. **wickedness .. me,** Ge. vi. 11, 12, xviii. 20, 21. (3) **flee,** etc., to get beyond the bounds of the holy land, and so out of God's reach. The reason for this flight is given iv. 2. Not fear of Nineveh, but the instinct that God intended something else than Nineveh's destruction. .. To the natural man in Israel (whom Jonah represents) the idea of the heathen's repentance and forgiveness was abhorrent.—G. A. Smith. **Tarshish,** Tartessus in Spain, the direction opposite to that of Nineveh. **Joppa,** 2 Chr. ii. 16; Ac. ix. 43; "now Jaffa, the well-known port of Palestine, one of the oldest cities in the world. It has a very inconvenient and insecure harbor."—Camb. Bib.

Jonah's Flight (vs. 3).—We have here—I. A man collapsing before the great occasions of life. II. A man rebelling against God, and yet strangely favored by circumstances. III. A man dishonest with God, yet prompt and conscientious in observing the laws of social justice and equity. Apply:—1. The word of the Lord still comes to men; 2. When God calls a man to go to Nineveh, there is success or safety nowhere else; 3. To flee to Tarshish is a most terrible mistake, and must end in sorrow and disappointment, no matter how many ships may be waiting for us at Joppa.—T. Kelly.

Wrong-Doing and its Punishment.—We are tied to our duty like horses with a very long tether. So long as we are content with the allotted area, we are not troubled with the rope; but when we try to escape into the surrounding thicket, we are vexed with all kinds of entanglements. Mr. Beecher, in his Life Thoughts, says that "some troubles are God dragging us; and they would cease if we were to stand up and walk where God wishes us."——Flight From Duty.—Many are of Jonah's temper, try his experiment, and feel the presence of God too painful for them. A scholar leaves the Sabbath school to avoid the contact of truth with conscience. A young man brought up under religious influence quits home and native country. An ungodly man feels miserable, shuns godly company, and stifles impressions by fleeing into business, worldly society, and amusements. The believer knows his duty, but will not do it. Such efforts often succeed in spite of the restraints of providence and the voice of conscience. But fear gets hold of men at length, God meets them in the way, and it is impossible to escape. "Lo, they that be far from thee shall perish."—Hom. Com.

4—6. (4) **sent out,** Heb. cast forth, implying God's absolute disposal of the wind. "Josephus speaks of a violent wind called 'the black North wind,' which he says sometimes visited the sea off the coast of Joppa. And we read of 'a tempestuous wind called Euraquilo' in another part of the same sea, which rushing down the highlands of Crete suddenly caught the ship in which St. Paul was sailing, and brought on a tempest scarcely less severe than that to which Jonah was exposed (Acts xxvii. 14). The modern name Levanter is a witness to the prevalence of such winds in those seas."—Camb. Bib. **ship .. broken,** Heb. "the ship thought to be broken," or was in great peril of being wrecked.[a] (5) **mariners,** they seem to have been of mixed nationalities, as they worshiped different gods.[b] **wares,** or cargo which they were carrying. **into the sides,** R. V., "into the innermost parts." **fast asleep,**[c] being tired out with his hurried journey from Gathhepher. (6) **What meanest thou,** an exclamation of indignant surprise at the unreasonableness of Jonah's conduct. The word for sleep here and in vs. 5 means heavy or deep sleep, such as Adam's (Gen. ii. 21), or Sisera's (Judg. iv. 21).—Camb. Bib. **God,** lit. "the God," seeming to imply a faith in a supreme Being over all the gods.

A Call to Sleepers (vs. 6).—I. Persons to whom this appeal may be addressed in a spiritual sense. 1. The indifferent; 2. The hardened; 3. The procrastinating. II. The considerations by which this appeal may be

"The phrase with which this vs. begins seems to represent 'the word of the Lord' as an atmosphere of kindling holy thought, a sphere of spiritual truth encompassing the Prophet, illuminating and moving his whole soul, and finally taking shape in language of exhortation, or prediction, or teaching, or resolve, as the case might be."—Liddon.

a "The living consciousness and apprehension of the ship, fearing to be wrecked in the tempestuous sea, is set in striking contrast to the lethargic stupor of the Prophet, whose conscience was, as it were, entranced in a swoon."
—Wordsworth.

b "Never was the conduct of a heathen crew during a storm more naturally and graphically described than it is in this passage. No sooner does danger appear, than one begins to beat his head, and cry aloud. 'Siva, Siva!' another beats his breast, and piteously shrieks forth 'Vishnoo!' and a third strikes his thigh and shouts out with all his might, 'Varuna!' Thus do they cry to their gods, instead of doing their duty."—Roberts.

c "Sleep is no necessary proof of innocence; it may be the fruit of carnal security and a seared conscience." —Fausset.

"Sometimes it is necessary to lighten the ship; for our wealth, our cares, our treasures may become burdens, and sink us, as men in the wreck of the Central America tied their belts of gold around them, and sank instead of floating till help could come." — Peloubet.

enforced. 1. Consider the value of the soul; 2. Consider the imminent hazard to which the soul is exposed; 3. Consider the price which has been paid for the soul. Appeal:—(1) Arise or be for ever fallen; (2) Call upon thy God; (3) Thou shalt be saved.—G. Brooks.

Chinese Superstition.—The amazing velocity with which the Yellow River runs at the place where the yacht and barges of the embassy were to cross it, rendered, according to the notions of the Chinese crews, a sacrifice necessary to the spirit of the river, in order to ensure a safe passage over it. For this purpose the master, surrounded by the crew of the yacht, assembled upon the forecastle, and holding as a victim in his hand a cock, wrung off his head, which committing to the stream, he consecrated the vessel with the blood spouting from the body by sprinkling it upon the deck, the masts, the anchors, and the doors of the apartments; and stuck upon them a few of the feathers of the bird. Several bowls of meat were then brought forward, and ranged in a line across the deck. Before these were placed a cup of oil, one filled with salt, one with tea, and a fourth with some ardent spirit; the captain making, at the same time, three profound inclinations of his body, with hands uplifted, and muttering a few words, as if of solicitation to the deity. The loo, or brazen drum, was beaten, in the meantime, forcibly; lighted matches were held towards heaven; papers, covered with tin or silver leaf, were burnt; and crackers fired off in great abundance by the crew. The captain afterwards made libations to the river, by emptying into it, from the vessel's prow, the several cups of liquids; and concluded with throwing in also that which held the salt. All the ceremonies being over, and the bowls of meat removed, the people feasted on it in the steerage, and launched afterwards, with confidence, the yacht into the current. As soon as she had reached the opposite shore, the captain returned thanks to heaven, with three inclinations of the body.—Sir J. Staunton.

d 1 Sa. xiv. 42; Pr. xvi. 33.

e "The mariners sailing with Diagoris, an atheist, attributed a storm that overtook them to his presence in the ship."—Cicero.

a "The word occurs in O. T. 33 times, whether in the mouth of heathen or Israelite, it always stands opposed to the notion, expressed or implied, of Gentiles."
—Spk. Com.

7—10. (7) **cast lots,** a usual method of referring things to the appointment or discovery of Providence.[d] **whose cause,** "Primitive tradition and natural conscience led even the heathen to believe that one guilty man involves all his associates, though innocent, in punishment."[e] (8) **What . . thou?** note the hurried accumulation of questions. (9) **Hebrew,** the name by wh. the Israelites were known to foreigners.[a] **Lord,** better rend. Jehovah. (10) **afraid,** bec. it was now plain that they were under Divine judgment. **Why hast,** etc., R. V., "What is this that thou hast done?" Why have you enraged the god who made the sea and then involved us by coming into this ship?

"Leave out the fact that Jonah was sinful, and he becomes an eminent type of Christ. Substitution saved the mariners; substitution saves sinners. Jesus dies, and there is a calm. Conscience accuses no longer. Judgment decides for and not against the sinner. Memory looks back with sorrow for sin, but with no dread of penalty to come. Let us enjoy the peace 'that passeth all understanding.' Then go to work for God, not to win life and heaven, for they are ours already; but loved by him, let us love and serve him with perfect heart." — Spurgeon.

Lots.—Religion even in its rudest forms, has always been faithful to its general principle thus far, that when the anger of the Divinity has been apprehended, it has been understood to be against sins and crimes; and also that the Divinity was believed to know who was the criminal. The mariners, therefore, referred it to the avenging Power to point out the criminal by a common ancient practice. A reference not to chance, but to a superior intelligence. Could our prophet have any doubt where the lot would fall? No; his conscience must have been a prophet to him.—John Foster.

The Storm and Its Effects.—As men have sometimes seen upon a mass of wreckage or on an ice-floe a number of wild animals, by nature foes to each other, reduced to peace through their common danger, so we descry the prophet and his natural enemies upon the strained and breaking ship. In the midst of the storm they are equally helpless, and they cast for all the lot which has no respect of persons. But from this the story passes quickly, to show how Jonah feels not only the human kinship of these heathen with himself, but their susceptibility to the knowledge of his God. They pray to Jehovah as the God of the sea and the dry land; while we may be sure that the prophet's confession, and the story of his own relation to that God, forms as powerful an exhortation to repentance as any he could have preached in Niniveh. At least it produces the effects which he has dreaded. In these sailors he sees heathen turned to the fear of the Lord. All that he has fled to avoid happens there before his eyes and through his own mediation.—Exp. Bib.

11—13. (11) **What . . thee,** since it was the God of Jehovah who had brought on this storm Jonah would know how to appease Him. **wrought,**

R. V., "grew more and more tempestuous." (12) **cast .. sea,** a glimpse of the fine nature of Jonah not to be overlooked. He prefers to die rather than that these others should perish. (13) **rowed,** they tried prob. to get the ship back to Joppa.

Hard Rowing (vss. 13, 14).—This unavailing effort of these oarsmen has a counterpart—I. In the efforts we are making to bring souls to the shore of safety, and set their feet on the Rock of Ages. II. To bring this world back to God, His pardon and safety. III. In every man that is trying to row his own soul into safetv.—Talmage.

"He who is false to present duty breaks a thread in the loom, and will find the flaw when he may have forgotten its cause."—H. W. Beecher.

Chinese Superstition.—The following advertisement is copied from a Chinese newspaper: "Achen Tea Chinchin, sculptor, respectfully acquaints masters of ships, trading from Canton to India, that they may be furnished with figure-heads of any size, according to order, at one-fourth of the price charged in Europe. He also recommends, for private venture, the following idols, brass, gold, and silver: the hawk of Vishnoo, which has reliefs of his incarnation in a fish, boar, lion, and turtle. An Egyptian apis, a golden calf and bull, as worshiped by the pious followers of Zoroaster. Two silver mammosits, with golden ear-rings: an aprimanes for Persian worship; a ram, an alligator, a crab, a laughing hyæna, with a variety of household gods, on a small scale, calculated for family worship. Eighteen months' credit will be given, or a discount of 15 per cent. for prompt payment of the sum affixed to each article. Direct China-street, Canton, under the Marble Rhinoceros and Gilt Hydra."

14—16. (14) **the Lord,** i. e. to Jonah's God. **innocent blood,**[a] "they shrank from being the instruments of his punishment. What a striking contrast is this spirit of the heathen with the impatience and resentment later shown by Jonah because the Divine menace against Nineveh was not fulfilled."—Dale. **done .. thee,** in sending the great storm. (15) **ceased .. raging,** Heb. stood. Comp. Lu. viii. 24[b] (16) **offered,** etc., according to their usual custom, but acknowledging Jehovah as a true God. They also vowed to offer sacrifice to Jehovah when they should land.

[a] De. xxi. 8.

[b] "God spares the prayerful penitent, a truth illustrated now in the case of the ailors, presently in that of Jonah, and thirdly in that of Nineveh." —Fausset.

"From how many unthought-of, unimaginable situations the Sovereign of the world has drawn devotional aspirations! but never, except once, from a situation like this." — John Foster.

Prayer Opposed to Sin.—A sanctified soul never goeth to pray, but it desires sin may have some wound, and points by prayer to the place where it is most pained. How doth it bemoan itself with Ephraim, and pour forth grief for sin at the eyes! It never heareth a sermon, but it labors to set its strongest corruption in the fore-front of the battle, that when Christ shoots His arrows, and draws His sword in the preaching of the word, sin may be hit. If God send any affliction, the sanctified soul concludes that some corruption must go to the lions. If there arise any storms, presently it inquires for Jonah, and labors to cast him overboard. A sanctified soul will bear every chastisement cheerfully, even death itself, that sin may die too.—Wm. Jenkin, 1656.

17. prepared, rather: "assigned," or "appointed." The same word and tense are used of the gourd, the worm, and the East wind, ch. iv. 6, 7, 8. They do not necessarily imply any previous or special preparation, much less the creation of these various agents for the purpose to which they were put; but merely that they were appointed to it by Him, whom "all things serve." He sent the fish there to do His bidding.—Camb. Bib. **great fish,**[a] the precise kind is nowhere indicated. "It was prob. a large shark, wh. is common in the Mediterranean, and has so large a throat that it can swallow a man whole." The allegorical interpretation is that Jonah represents Israel, which for its apostasy was swallowed up by the world-pawn Babylon (Jer. li. 34), in exile it sought Jehovah, and was afterwards disgorged uninjured.—Cheyne, Dale, et al. **three .. nights,**[b] the Heb. count the first and third parts of days as whole twenty-four hour days. Comp. Christ's time in the grave.

[a] "The word ketos, in Mat. xii. 40, is not restricted in its meaning to a whale or a cetecean; it may denote any sea monster, either a whale or a shark, a seal or a tunny of enormous size." — Biblical Things.

[b] Mat. xii. 39, 40, xvi. 4; Lu. xi. 30.

The Great Fish.—It has been satisfactorily proved that the common or white shark (Carcharias vulgaris) is found in the Mediterranean, and well-authenticated instances have been given of its having swallowed men and other large animals entire. "A natural historian of repute relates, 'In 1758, in stormy weather, a sailor fell overboard from a frigate in the Mediterranean. A shark was close by, which, as he was swimming and crying for help, took him in his wide throat, so that he forthwith disappeared. Other sailors had leaped into the sloop, to help their comrade, while yet swimming; the captain had a gun which stood on the

"It is faith's work to claim and challenge loving kindness out of all the roughest strokes of God." — S. Rutherford.

"Every duty we omit, obscures some truth we should have known." —John Ruskin.

deck discharged at the fish, which struck it so, that it cast out the sailor which it had in its throat, who was taken up, alive and little injured, by the sloop which had now come up. The fish was harpooned, taken up on the frigate and dried. The captain made a present of the fish to the sailor who, by God's Providence, had been so wonderfully preserved. The sailor went round Europe exhibiting it. He came to Franconia, and it was publicly exhibited here in Erlangen, as also at Nurnberg and other places. The dried fish was delineated. It was 20 feet long, and, with expanded fins, nine feet wide, and weighed 3924 pounds. From all this, it is probable that this was the fish of Jonah.'"—Camb. Bib.

CHAPTER THE SECOND.

1—3. (1) **prayed,** not so much in the sense of "offered supplications," as "expressed his trust and thankfulness."[a] (2) **cried .. affliction,** comp. Ps. xviii. 2. **belly of hell,** or the grave,[b] to wh. he likens his strange resting-place inside the fish. (3) **thou,** not the sailors. Jonah does not stop with the mere agents; but fully recognizes the hand of God. **thy billows,** etc., comp. Ps. xlii. 7. He recognizes that the sea in which he is engulfed is God's.

The Cry From the Depths.—You want nothing more than this cry. If you cry to God out of the depths, you will cry yourself out of them. Here is a man at the foot of a cliff that rises beetling like a black wall behind him, the sea in front, the clear upright rock at his back, not a foothold for a mouse between the tide at the foot and the grass at the top there. There is only one thing he can do. Shout! Perchance somebody will hear him, and a rope may come dangling down in front, and, if he has nerve, he may shut his eyes and make a jump and catch it. There is no way for you up out of the depths but to cry; and that will bring the rope down.—Old Test. Anec.

4—7. (4) **cast .. sight,** comp. Ps. xxxi. 22. **yet,** or, if nothing else is left me. **temple,** "one thing is left me still, one resource is still open to me, I will still pray, I will look (mentally) yet again towards Thy holy temple." The phrase "to look towards the temple," denoting prayer, has its origin in the prayer of Solomon at the dedication of the Temple. See 1 Kings viii. 29, 30, 48, and comp. Dan. vi. 10. The fact that Jonah was a prophet of the Northern Kingdom is no valid objection to this view. The Temple on Mount Sion was the only centre of the true worship of Jehovah, and was recognized as such by all faithful Israelites.[c]—Camb. Bib. (5) **waters,** etc., Ps. lxix. 1. **weeds,** i. e. sea-weeds. Jonah sank to the bottom before he was swallowed by the fish."—Pulpit Com. (6) **The earth with her bars;** as for the earth, her bars were about me; "return to it was shut out for me; the gate by which I might return was locked behind me." **for ever,** so far as his own power of deliverance was concerned. **corruption,**[d] R. V., "from the pit," i. e. from the place of the dead. He is still alive. (7) **came in,** reached to Thy heaven.

The Resolve of Faith (vs. 4).—Jonah a type of Christ, disciplined but not destroyed. Learn—I. That the darkest day has its particular duty. II. That no true believer ever looked to God's holy temple in vain.—R. Cecil.

Prayer Heard in Heaven.—A man of God, when speaking to a poor sufferer in the Blackrock Convalescent Home, at Brighton, who was bowed down by despairing remorse, inquired, "Have you asked to-day for the pardon of your sins?" "That I have." "And do you think God has written down your prayers in His book?" "I did not know that He kept one for my prayers." "He tells us He has a book of remembrance for our thoughts, when we think upon His name; and elsewhere, that our words are kept account of; and, between the two, do you not think that your prayers are included? And do you think the loving God has written in that book to-day, 'On the 25th of February, 1868, William T—— asked Me for the forgiveness of all his sins, for My dear Son's sake, and I refused him?'" "No, sir; I cannot believe that." "What then has He written beside your prayer? It is not with Him, as with you or me to say, 'I think I may.' There is no uncertainty in His mind." **The man**

a "The sentiments of his ode are those wh. he had then felt; the form, into which they here appear cast, and which present a highly finished specimen of Hebrew poetry, we must suppose to have been the production of a later and more tranquil hour."—Spk. Com.

b Is. xiv. 9.

c "Upon recollecting myself, I thought it my duty not to despair of Thy mercy, but direct my prayer towards Thy heavenly habitation."—Lowth.

d Ps. xvi. 10; Isa. xxxviii. 17.

"As God doth plant and actuate grace in the soul, so he is pleased to come in with seasonable supplies and reinforcements to the weak and decayed graces of his people. Thus he feeds the believer's lamp with fresh oil; gives in more faith, more love, more hope and more desires; and hereby he gives power to the faint, and strengthens the things which remain and are ready to die."—John Willison.

"Night brings out stars, as sorrow teaches truth."

"That a sorrow's crown of sorrow is remembering happier things."—Tennyson.

thought deeply for a time, and at length replied, "Then it is more likely He has written, 'Granted,' by its side." From that moment the fetters of his fears were broken; and the man was set free to trample on his sins, and to serve his Saviour.—Shining Light.

8—10. (8) **lying vanities,**[a] i. e. idols, the purposes of self-will. **their .. mercy,** i. e. God, who is the only source of mercy and loving-kindness to all His creatures. The sentiment is similar to that which is figuratively expressed by the prophet Jeremiah: "They have forsaken Me, the fountain of living waters, and hewed them out cisterns, broken cisterns, that can hold no water." (ii. 13). So God is called, "my mercy," Ps. cxliv. 2 (margin), the same word being used as here.—Camb. Bib. (9) **sacrifice,** evidently the voice of hope, expecting deliverance, etc., Ps. l. 14, 23, cxvi. 17; Ho. xiv. 2. **Salvation .. Lord,** Ps. iii. 8. (10) **spake .. fish,** when the punishment had done its work the Lord ordered release from captivity.[b]

Salvation of the Lord (vs. 9).—I. Let us expound the doctrine. 1. The plan of salvation is entirely of God; 2. So it was of the Lord in execution; 3. In the application; 4. As to the sustaining of the Word in any man's heart. II. How God has hedged this doctrine about. III. What is and what should be the influence of this doctrine upon men? 1. It is a great battering-ram against their pride; 2. It is the key-stone of all divinity. IV. The obverse of this truth is that damnation is of men.—C. Spurgeon.

[a] Ps. xxxi. 6.

"All who hug a lie, lose God, who is truth and love."—Wordsworth.

[b] Ps. viii. 6—9.

"As well try to fill the yawning chasm with a few grains of sand as satisfy the gulf of the soul's desires with the pleasure of an empty world." — Macduff.

"He must have been the subject of strange and conflicting emotions when he entered the gates of that proud capital. . There was enough to shake his faith, and to cowardise his bold, haughty, and scornful spirit; yet he dared not a second time abandon his mission."—J. Blackburn.

Open the door: let in the sun! He hath a smile for every one. He hath made of the raindrops gold and gems; He may change our tears to diadems. Open the door!

CHAPTER THE THIRD.

1—4. (1) **second time,** renewing the Divine commission. Jonah would not venture to go to Nineveh without such a new charge. (2) **preach,** proclaim, as a herald: vs. 4. (3) **exceeding great city,** lit. "a great city to God," i. e. "great" not only in man's thought but even in the thought of God, comp. iv. 11, Gen. x. 9. **three days' journey,** in circumference, i. e. some 60 miles around. (4) **day's journey,** this indicates rather the length of time wh. he spent in preaching, than the distance he traversed. **forty days,** the usual Scripture time of probation. **overthrown,** Ge. xix. 21, 25.

Zeal in Preaching.—Dr. Payson being taken suddenly ill, and, as every one thought, about to die, he remarks: "What gave me most concern was, that notice had been given of my being about to preach! Whilst the doctor was preparing my medicine, feeling my pains abated, I on a sudden cried out, 'Doctor, my pains are suspended; by the help of God, I will go and preach, and then come home and die.' In my own apprehension, and in appearance to others, I was a dying man; the people heard me as such. The invisible realities of another world lay open to my view. Expecting to stretch into eternity, and to be with my Master before the morning, I spoke with peculiar energy. Such effects followed the word, that I thought it was worth dying for a thousand times."—R. T. S.

Verses 1—3.—This is substantially the same commission, and yet different. The "second" call to a man is never exactly the same as the first. The third is never a repetition of the second. Another tone is in the voice of the speaker, firmer or milder. Other shades of meaning are in the message. If it is the "second time," still more if it is the message corresponding with changes which time has wrought in circumstances and in character. It may seem a refinement, but properly understood, it is but a simple truth, that a man never receives exactly the same command or invitation from God more than once. "If slighted once, the season fair can never be renewed."—Raleigh.

5—8. (5) **believed God,** Ge. xv. 6. "The most amazing thing in this book is, not the story of the fish, but the story of the impression which was at once produced by Jonah's warning on men of all ranks in Nineveh, from the king to the humblest of his subjects."—Dale.[a] **fast,** usual national mode of expressing penitential feeling. **sackcloth,** the sign of humiliation. (6) **For word came,** etc., R. V., "and the tidings reached the king." The king did not begin the fast, but yielded to, and directed the

[a] "The expression betokens admiration for the simplicity of their faith, not without oblique reference to Israel's unbelief." —Spk. Com.

national feeling.[b] **sackcloth and .. ashes,** see Est. iv. 1, 3; Is. lviii. 5, etc.[c] (7) **nobles,** lit. great men. **beast,** heathen nations thus made their cattle share in their mournings. (8) **turn,** etc., obs. that they recognize the necessity for signs of sincerity, "fruits meet for repentance." **the violence,** "this was their chief sin, as all we learn of the Assyrians, both from sacred and secular history, shows. Comp. Nahum ii. 11, 12, iii. 1, and Isaiah x. 13, 14. The form of expression, in their hands, the hand being the instrument of violence, is the same as in Ps. vii. 3 (Heb. 4), and elsewhere."—Camb. Bib.

A Great City.—Nineveh covered a great extent of ground. Historians say that its walls were 480 stadia, or 60 miles, in circumference. It was great in population. Jonah mentions 120,000 who could not discern between their right hand and their left. It was great in splendor and power. "The researches in the mounds have astonished Europe with the barbaric grandeur of the statuary, and the full details of life and history sculptured on marble, or stamped in arrow-headed characters upon the bricks. But it was morally great to God on account of the human souls and their spiritual condition. In God's sight, grandeur, territory and architectural beauty are nothing to immortal souls and the influence which they exert. The material worlds, the sun with its satellites are not so great as a man. Try to realize how great you are in the sight of God.—Hom. Com.

b "The king seems to have resided in the royal palace at Khorsabad, in the N. E. corner of the Tetrapolis of Nineveh."— Wordsworth.

c "Mourners take off their outer clothing, and cover themselves from head to foot with a piece of brown, coarse sackcloth, such as is worn by slaves while offered for sale; and occasionally they throw dust or ashes upon their heads when thus covered, as a token of grief and humiliation." — Van Lennep.

9, 10. (9) **Who .. repent,** Joel ii. 14. The only ground they had for their hope in God's mercy, lay in the fact that He had so graciously sent them warning. (10) **works,** proving the sincerity of their words. **repented,** Ex. xxxii. 14. **did it not,** "Here is shown the main lesson of the whole book of Jonah (in opposition to the narrow exclusive view, popular with the Jews), that God's purposes of grace are not limited to Israel alone but are open to the heathen as well, if only they abandon their sinful courses and turn to Him in true penitence."—Driver.[a]

God Repented.—When we regard the relations of Almighty God to men and His dealings with them from the divine side, so far as it is revealed to us and we are able to comprehend it, then they are all foreseen and planned and executed in accordance with His perfect foreknowledge. Then there is no place for repentance, no room for change. "Known unto God are all His works from the beginning of the world." But when we alter our stand-point, and regard them from the human side, free scope is given in the aspect in which God then presents Himself to us for human effort and prayer and feeling, then His purpose waits upon our will. Both of these sides are freely and fearlessly set forth in Holy Scripture. On the one side, "God is not a man that He should lie, neither the son of man that He should repent" (Num. xxiii. 19). With Him "is no variableness, neither shadow of turning" (James i. 17). On the other side we read, "It repented the Lord that He had made man on the earth, and it grieved Him at His heart" (Gen. vi. 6); "God repented of the evil that He had said that He would do unto them, and He did it not." Both views are equally true, and they are in perfect harmony with each other, but Holy Scripture never attempts to harmonize them, nor is it wise for us to attempt to do so; we cannot look upon both sides of the shield at once.—Camb. Bib.

a "God's sparing Nineveh when in the jaws of destruction, on the first dawn of repentance encourages the timid penitent, and shows beforehand that Israel's doom, soon after accomplished, is to be ascribed, not to unwillingness to forgive on God's part, but to their own obstinate impenitence." — Fausset.

Je. xviii. 7, 8.

CHAPTER THE FOURTH.

1—3. (1) **displeased Jonah,** "it is clear that the immediate cause of Jonah's anger and vexation was the preservation of Nineveh and the non-fulfillment of the threat which he had been sent to pronounce. It was the anticipation of this result, founded on the revealed character of God, that made him decline the errand at first."—Camb. Bib.[a] (2) **prayed .. Lord,** he did not keep away from God, but took his vexed feeling to Him. **fled before,** R. V., "hasted to flee." **gracious,** etc., Ex. xxxiv. 6; Joel ii. 13. **evil,** i, e. threatened evil.[b] (3) **take .. life,**[c] as if he thought it no longer of value, bec. he was made to appear a deceiver. It is the language of morbid feeling.

Anger.—A lady who was somewhat quick-tempered but was very

a "Jonah had a character, no doubt, solidly good, and open to conviction, but habitually irascible and morose, and apt, under exciting circumstances, to view things in their worst and most gloomy aspects."— Kitto.

b "I anticipated by fleeing the disappointment of my design through Thy long suffering mercy."— Fausset.

c 1 Ki. xix. 4.

desirous of becoming a Christian, once said to me: "Mr. Peploe, I assure you there is no fault in my case, because I never lose my temper unless I am provoked!" No, and I do not think the devil does! To lose your temper shows that you are out of communion with your blessed Lord. If the peace of Christ ruled in our hearts, we could never again be provoked. Think of that! Moses was so provoked that he spoke unadvisedly, and yet he was the meekest man that ever lived. But Moses had not the risen Christ to dwell in his heart. Be not discouraged, or fear lest you may fall to-morrow. You need only live one moment at a time. Can Christ keep you this minute in good temper? Then he can keep you the next moment, and the next and so on forever. He can keep you in peace amid the severest trials, even such as he had to bear—in loss of friends, in persecution, in death.—H. W. Webb-Peploe.——Temper is significant. It is not in what it is alone, but in what it reveals. It is a test for love, a symptom, a revelation of an unloving nature at bottom. It is the intermittent fever which bespeaks unintermittent disease within; the occasional bubble escaping to the surface which betrays some rottenness underneath; a sample of the most hidden products of the soul dropped involuntarily when off one's guard; in a word, the lightning form of a hundred hideous and un-Christian sins. For a want of patience, a want of kindness, a want of generosity, a want of courtesy, a want of unselfishness, are all instantaneously symbolized in one flash of temper.—Drummond.

"Our dispositions wil be suitable to that which we most frequently think on; for the soul is, as it were, tinged with the color and complexion of its own thoughts."—Marcus Antoninus.

4—6. (4) **Doest .. angry?** God calls him to self-consideration. (5) **booth,** temporary hut of branches and leaves. **become .. city,** either the forty days were not expired, or he had some hope that God would yet show some signs of His power, if not actually destroying the city. (6) **gourd,** "it is an old controversy dating back as far as the times of Jerome and Augustine, whether Jonah's plant was a gourd or not. It is now generally admitted that it was not, but that the plant intended is the ricinus communis or castor-oil plant."[a]—Camb. Bib. **his grief,** R. V., "his evil case."

[a] "No gourd actually grows up in a single night and the expression, 'wh. was the son of a night,' must be regarded as giving in strong poetic figure the fact of swift growth. The gourd is a climbing vine of rapid growth, always trained to run up trees, trellis and temporary booths, the size of its leaves affording a pleasant shade." — Bib. Things.

God Refreshing Physical Nature.—The gourd was prepared "to be a shadow over his head." The first lesson and cure of despondency is to remove fatigue and bodily weariness from over-work. Elijah's despondency was partly physical, and the angel brought him refreshment. Food and rest are required, and God seeks to quiet the mind by cooling the body. There is an intimate connection between both, and we often get at one through the other. Regard for the body is urged from the lofty nature and the important use of the soul. They are helpmates in God's service now, and will be in his kingdom above. Fretfulness, petulance, and irritability oftener spring from physical weakness than moral unloveliness. If God in providence deals mercifully we should not be harsh with such feelings.—Hom. Com.

"The ricinus grows from 8 to 10ft. high. Only one leaf grows on a branch, but that leaf being often more than a foot large, the collective leaves give good shelter from the heat." — Fausset.

7—9. (7) **worm,** may be a singular or a collective name, in the latter case refering to a species of black caterpillar which is a familiar pest in the region. (8) **vehement .. wind,** R. V., "sultry east wind." E. hot winds are more suffocating and oppressive than even the sun's rays. **wished,** R. V., "requested for himself." Comp. 1 Ki. xix. 4. Elijah thought he had failed. Jonah was grieved because he had succeeded. (9) **even unto death,** i. e. "my anger is so great that it well-nigh kills me, and even in that excess it is justified by the circumstances."

"Anger begins with folly and ends with repentance." —Maunder.

"Anger and haste hinder good counsel"—Fielding.

The Gourd.—The gourd which defended the Prophet is said to have been prepared by the Lord. We have no reason to conclude from this expression that the Almighty created it for the special purpose; He only appointed and promoted its growth in that particular spot, raising its stem and expanding its branches and leaves according to the ordinary laws of nature, till it formed a most refreshing shade over the place where the angry seer waited the fulfilment of his prediction. "We may conceive of it," says Calmet, "as an extraordinary one of its kind, remarkably rapid in growth, remarkably hard in its stem, remarkably vigorous in its branches, and remarkable for the extensive spread of its leaves, and the deep gloom of their shadow; and after a certain duration, remarkable for a sudden withering and uselessness to the impatient Prophet."—Paxton.

"Passions," saith Fuller, "like heavy bodies down steep hills, once in motion, move themselves, and know no ground but the bottom."

"More helpful than all wisdom is one draught of simple human pity that will not forsake us." —George Eliot.

a Ge. xviii. 23—33.

b De. i. 39; Is. vii. 15, 16.

"The teachings of Nature may prepare for the Word, and be used to convey it, illustrate it, and fix it in the memory. God schooling Jonah in patient, tender love, and through him preparing instruction for Israel and for us, uses Nature to prepare the way for the lessons of the Word. He will make his pity for the plant explain God's pity for Nineveh, and condemn Jonah's want of pity for that multitude of souls." —Mitchel.

"A merchant that keeps a book of debit and credit, writes both what is owing him, and what he oweth himself, and then casteth up the whole; but God does not so, His mercy is triumphant over his justice, and therefore he wipes out what we owe him, and writes down what he owes us by promise; much like the clouds that receive ill vapors from us, yet returning them to us again in sweet, refreshing showers." — Nath. Shute, 1626.

"Therefore, Jew, Though justice be thy plea, consider this,— That in the course of justice none of us should see salvation: we do pray for mercy, and that same prayer doth teach us all to render the deeds of mercy."

10, 11. (10) **pity .. gourd,** wh. was not Jonah's own, and was naturally so shortlived and comparatively worthless. The gourd and Nineveh are to be contrasted: the one in its relation to Jonah, the other in its relation to God. **came up in a night,** etc., "lit. was the son of a night, and perished the son of a night, i. e. it came into existence and reached maturity in a single night, and no less rapidly (not literally in a single night, for it was when the morning arose) withered away."—Camb. Bib. (11) **should not I,**[a] "suggesting that the great city had been the object of the Divine thought and care—had not grown up of itself or under the protection of the false gods, but under the guidance and defence of the living God. A startling truth to affirm in an ancient Jewish book."—Dale. **discern .. hand,**[b] children: these, with the cattle, must have shared in any general destruction of the city. "God has vindicated His love to the jealousy of those who thought that it was theirs alone. And we are left with this grand vague vision of the immeasurable city, with its multitude of innocent children and cattle, and God's compassion brooding over all." —G. A. Smith.

Does God Care for Oxen? (vs. 11).—I. God's care for cattle. 1. He made and preserves the lower creatures; 2. He made them to be happy; 3. Sin has made them a sharer in man's sufferings; 4. God is sorry to see them suffering. II. The lessons for us. 1. If God cares for them, so should we. 2. If God cares for oxen, how much more for us!—Edmond.

Teachings From Jonah.—This wonderful book of Jonah has given us a picture of the human heart, not in its lowest degradation, but taught by revelation, restrained by conscience, influenced more or less by piety, but stripped of its disguises and company dress. God takes us behind the scenes to show us how in Nature his hand and purpose are working by storm and sunshine, fish and worm, and so puts a window for us in the heart of man. Jonah speaks out to God, and acts out before us, and writes down for us to read, without suppression, palliation, or extenuation, the sinful thoughts which often men have, but do not make known. We have at once a picture of God's character, and a mirror in which to behold our own.—Hom. Com.

Nineveh.—The vast area assigned to Nineveh in this book as well as by secular writers, was not, however, completely covered as in the case of our own cities, with streets and squares and buildings. That was a feature unusual, and almost unknown, in the ancient cities of the East. It was perhaps the feature which, belonging to Jerusalem by virtue of the deep ravines by which it was surrounded, and which "determined its natural boundaries," and prevented its spreading abroad after the fashion of other oriental cities, called forth the surprise and admiration of the Jews after their return from Babylon. "Jerusalem," they exclaim, "(unlike Babylon where we so long have dwelt) is built as a city which is compact together." Like Babylon, Nineveh included not only parks and paradises, but fields under tillage and pastures for "much cattle" (iv. 11) in its wide embrace. The probable site of the city has been identified by recent explorers. It lies on the eastern bank of the Tigris in the fork formed by that river and the Ghazr Su and Great Zab, just above their confluence. The whole of this district abounds in heaps of ruins. Indeed, "they are found," it is said, "in vast numbers throughout the whole region watered by the Tigris and Euphrates and their confluents, from the Taurus to the Persian Gulf." "Such mounds," it is added, "are especially numerous in the region to the east of the Tigris, in which Nineveh stood, and some of them must mark the ruins of the Assyrian capital." (Dict. of the Bible.) Four of these great masses of ruins, Kouyunjik, Nimrud, Karamless, Khorsabad, form together an irregular parallelogram of very similar dimensions to those mentioned in the text. From Kouyunjik (lying opposite Mosul) on the Eastern bank of the Tigris, a line drawn in a S. E. direction, parallel to the course of the river, to Nimrud is about eighteen miles. From Nimrud, in a northerly direction, to Karamless is about twelve. The opposite sides of the parallelogram, from Karamless to the most northerly point Khorsabad, and from Khorsabad to Kouyunjik again, are about the same. These four vast piles of buildings, are now generally identified with the site of the Nineveh which Jonah visited.—Camb. Bib.

Introduction.

I. **Author.** Micah, = "Who like Jehovah?" Of his personal history little is known. His designation as "the Morasthite" probably indicates his home as Moresheth-gath (i. 14). Moresheth was a place in the Shephelah or low range of hills which lie between the hill-country of Judea and the Philistine plain. It was some twenty-five miles southeast from Jerusalem. Micah was thus a representative of the common people and of the country life of Judea, while Isaiah, with whom he was contemporary, stands nearer to the life of the city and the court. "To Micah, the villager, the unjust treatment of the helpless poor by men of wealth and power is the sin that cries aloud to heaven. He has but little to say about idolatry or display or immorality." II. **Time.** About B.C. 725-700. III. **Style.** The style in some degree resembles that of Isaiah. It is forcible, pointed, and concise, frequently animated and sublime. "The abrupt transitions with which the book abounds prove that the Book of Micah, like most of the other prophetic writings, was mainly founded on discourses or notes of discourses, composed on various occasions."

CHAPTER THE FIRST.

1, 2. (1) **Micah,** same as Micaiah. The word means, "Who is as Jah?" **Morasthite,** from the town of Moresheth-gath. **saw,** "the meaning is that the prophet had an inward perception of certain facts through the influence of the Divine Spirit."—Camb. B. **Samaria and Jerusalem,** mentioned as capitals, and standing for the respective kingdoms of Israel and Judah. (2) **all . . is,**[a] lit. "the fulness thereof." **against you, i. e.** against all peoples. The judgment upon Judah is a warning to other nations. **holy temple, i. e.** heaven.

Hearing the Word.—An innkeeper, addicted to intemperance, on hearing of the particularly pleasing singing at a church some miles distant, went to gratify his curiosity, but with a resolution not to hear a word of the sermon. Having with difficulty found admission into a narrow open pew, as soon as the hymn before sermon was sung, which he heard with great attention, he secured both his ears against the sermon with his forefingers. He had not been in this position many minutes, before the prayer finished, and the sermon commenced with an awful appeal to the consciences of the hearers, of the necessity of attending to the things which belonged to their everlasting peace; and the minister, addressing them solemnly said, "He that hath ears to hear, let him hear." Just the moment before these words were pronounced, a fly had fastened on the face of the innkeeper, and, stinging him sharply, he drew one of his fingers from his ears, and struck off the painful visitant. At that very moment the words, "He that hath ears to hear, let him hear," pronounced with great solemnity, entered the ear that was opened, as a clap of thunder. It struck him with irresistible force: he kept his hand from returning to his ear, and, feeling an impression he had never known before, he presently withdrew the other finger, and hearkened with deep attention to the discourse which followed. A salutary change was produced on him. He abandoned his former wicked practices, became truly serious, and for many years went, during all weathers, six miles to the church where he first received the knowledge of divine things. After about eighteen years' faithful and close walk with God, he died rejoicing in the hope of that glory which he now enjoys.—Whitecross.

3—5. (3) **cometh forth,** anthropomorphic, comp. Is. xxvi. 21. **his place,** Ps. cxv. 3. **tread . . places,** comp. De. xxxii. 13, xxxiii. 29. (4) **mountains, etc.,** Ps. xcvii. 5. "The figure is that of a storm, but no ordinary storm. Lightning descends, and dissolves the very mountains, and torrents of rain scoop out channels in the valleys. Similar symbolic descriptions occur in Judg. v. 5, Isai. lxiv. 1, Hab. iii. 6; comp. Ex. xix. 18."—Camb. B. (5) **what . . Jerusalem?** "The sin of each kingdom is here identified with the capital city as the place in which it assumed its most aggravated and concentrated form. Jerusalem is regarded as a great idol temple."—Spk. Com. Jacob is a poetical synonym for Israel.

Hearing the Word.—There is a form of deafness known to physicians in which the person affected is able to hear everything except words. In such a case the ear, as an apparatus for mere hearing, may be so perfect that the tick of a watch or the song of a bird is readily appreciated, but owing to a local injury deeper than the ear, for it is in the brain itself, all spoken words of his mother tongue are as unintelligible to the sufferer as those of a foreign language. Give him a book, and he may read as understandingly as ever, but every word addressed to him through the ear reaches his consciousness only as a sound, not as a word. There is a moral deafness which corresponds to this physical infirmity, but which, instead of being rare, is as common as it is harmful and disabling. To all men there is given an inner ear, which has been fashioned to hear wisdom's words, but that ear often seems so dull of hearing, that there appears no sign of response to her utterances. Now it was just such an unreceptive state of soul and of feeling in the people which we are told led Jesus to speak to them in parables.—W. H. Thomson.

6—9. (6) **will make,** "this prophecy therefore was delivered before

a "The Prophets sometimes address their speech to inanimate things, to upbraid the stupidity of men." —Lowth.

"The Word of God is the bodying forth of his mind, the incarnation of his thought, the vehicle of his will; by which he would bring himself near to us, to woo us and save us, to attract us by his love or terrify us by his judgments. It is the sum of all that the world knows of him. It is the expression of his character, the history of his procedure." —Legge.

"I have an ear for other preachers," Sir John Cheke used to say, 'but I have a heart for Latimer.' Here is a very clear and main distinction. Too often men hear the Word sounding its drums and trumpets outside their walls, and they are filled with admiration of the martial music, but their city gates are fast closed and vigilantly guarded, so that the truth has no admittance, but only the sound of it. Would to God we knew how to reach men's affections, for the heart is the target we aim at, and unless we hit it we miss altogether."— Spurgeon.

the destruction of Samaria in the 4th year of Hezekiah."—Pulpit Com. **heap .. field, i. e.** the ruins would be gathered into heaps, as farmers gather up the stones when they clean a field.[a] **as plantings,** better, "into the plantings;" i. e. vineyards should be planted upon the site of Samaria. **valley,** below Samaria, wh. stood on a hill. **discover, i. e.** lay bare the very foundations. (7) **hires,**[b] riches of the idol-shrines, afterwards called "the hire of a harlot" with reference to the shameful practices of heathenish religion (Deut. xxiii. 14). **shall return,** etc., the material of the costly images acquired through the offerings of devotees shall again be used for votive offerings in other no less shameful religions, based, like those of heathen Syria, on the worship of the powers and processes of nature.—Camb. B. (8) **wail, etc., i. e.** in anticipation of the desolation I will at once assume the garb, etc., of the mourner. **dragons .. owls,** R. V., "jackals," "ostriches;" with reference to the nocturnal howls and screeches of these creatures. (9) **incurable,** nothing can now heal it, or stay the threatened corruption.

Samaria.—On the morning of the third day after our departure from Jerusalem we left Shechem—the Shechem of the Old Testament, but bearing in the New Testament the name of Sychar. We started early in the morning on our way to another city of still greater celebrity, the ancient city of Samaria. Our tents had been pitched on a beautiful plain at the foot of Mount Gerizim. Before the light of the morning sun had reached them they were once more struck, our Syrian horses were saddled, and we went down at once into a deep valley. Through this valley there flows a bright and musical stream. The trees and shrubs which spring up around it are pomegranates, almonds, olives, mulberries, the fig tree, the vine, the orange, the oleander.—Upham.

10—12. (10) **Declare ye it not,** "may we at last be spared the sight of the malicious joy of our envious neighbors!" Here begins a series of paronomasias, which, however, are far from indicating a playful mood in the prophet. Most of them refer to Judæan towns in the prophet's own neighborhood. He sees a pre-ordained correspondence between names and fortunes.—Camb. B. **Gath,** see 2 Sa. i. 20.[c] **Aphrah,** i.e. dust. **roll .. dust,** the sign of deepest sorrow. (11) **Saphir,** a village among the hills of Judah. **the inhabitant of Zaanan,** etc., R. V. "the inhabitant of Z. is not come forth; the wailing of Beth-ezel shall take from you the stay thereof." **Zaanan,** poss. the Zenan of Jos. xv. 37. (12) **but evil came down,** R. V. "because evil is come down."

Samaria was once the residence of the kings of Israel, after the revolt of the ten tribes against the kings of the house of David. It is said in the Book of Kings that Ahab built a palace of ivory in Samaria; and prophetic denunciations, called forth by the luxury and oppressions of the Samaritans, are found in the Book of the Prophet Amos. "I will smite the winter house with the summer house; and the houses of ivory shall perish; and the great houses shall have an end, saith the Lord." These expressions indicate with some distinctness the magnificence of the city of Samaria at an early period. It had its vicissitudes; but its wealth and splendor remained for many years. After the conquest of Palestine by the Romans, and during their authority here, Samaria was selected as a place of viceregal residence, and was enriched and beautified by works of art. Herod the Great once resided here; and expending upon it all the vast resources of his genius and tyrannical power, he gave it the proud name of Sebaste, in honor of Augustus Cæsar. Christianity also, at a later period, left the impress of its piety and genius. Ascending the eastern brow of the Samaritan mount, one of the objects that first met our view was the lofty remains of a Christian church, said to have been built over the body of John the Baptist. Standing afterwards upon the western brow, at a mile's distance from this church, around us the dust was literally sown with columns; some prostrate at full length on the ground; some partially buried and projecting from the side of the hill; some standing erect in rows and at stated intervals, but without capitals, like wounded and mutilated soldiers on the field of battle; some leaning towards the ground, as if they were borne down with hearts of sorrow, and were mourning the loss of their former greatness.—Prof. Upham.

a "The stones wh. yet lie on its surface, bereft of the glory that might seem to hover round a ruin, however defaced, have been gathered singly, and cast into heaps, as it were, the heaps of a field, and not the remains of a capital."—Keith.

b "Here again we have unalloyed and rampant heathenism: the 'sacred' courtesans of the temple give a part of their hire towards the repairing and beautifying of the building; and also to purchase idols, or carry on the festivals. At the annual festival of Scandan, which continues twenty-four days, the females alluded to defray the expenses of the last day from the proceeds of their own wickedness." — Roberts.

c "The Prophet here refers in sad irony to the shame which the Israelite should feel in exposing his woes and his fears to the gaze of enemies." — Spk. Com.

"This passage of Micah (vss. 10—16) is to be compared with that noble one in Isaiah (x. 28—32), where the Prophet describes the panic which spreads from one town to another near Jerusalem, when the Assyrian army under Sennacherib invaded Judah, and took all its fenced cities (xxxvi. 1). Micah continues the prophetic description of Isaiah. Isaiah

13—16. (13) **Lachish,** 2 Ki. xviii. 13, 14. **bind .. to the swift beast,** in order to flee. **beginning,** etc., or "the first place in the kingdom of Judah to adopt idolatry of the northern kingdom." (14) **give presents,** or farewell presents, meaning that Judah will have to give up Moresheth-Gath. **Moresheth-gath,** a place belonging to, or near, the Philistine Gath. **Achzib,** Jos. xv. 44. **lie,** lit. a deceptive brook that dries up and disappoints the thirsty wayfarer. The meaning is that Judah shall lose Achzib. **kings of Israel,** after the fall of the northern kingdom predicted in vss. 6, 7, "Israel" is applied to Judah. (15) R. V. "I will yet bring unto thee; O inhab. of M., him that shall possess thee: the glory of Isr. shall come even unto Adullam." The nobility of Jsr. shall fly for refuge to such places as the cave of Adullam, David's asylum (1 Sam. xxii. 1, 2). **Mareshah,** Jos. xv. 44. (16) **bald,** addressed to Judah. **poll thee,** or shave thy hair, in token of mourning. **eagle,** better, "vulture," wh. is distinguished for its bald head.

With Samaria we associate the denunciations of Elijah and Elisha, and the peace, forgiveness, and purity of the New with its early and humble teachers. The weary foot of the Son of God, the Teacher from another world, the man unknown, trod these hills and valleys. He came from the Jordan to Jerusalem, and from Jerusalem to Galilee; and He "must needs go through Samaria." The moral change is greater—the name of Mahomet is substituted for that of Christ; and the precepts of the Koran; in this part of Palestine, as well as in other parts, have taken the place of the doctrines and precepts of the Gospel. But it cannot be so always.—Upham.

represents the panic, alarm, and havoc produced in the days of Hezekiah by the Assyrian army under Sennacherib invading Jerusalem from the north-east. Micah represents his career to the south-west, even to Lachish, mentioned by both the prophets (See vs. 13)."—Wordsworth.

"To be indifferent to the honor of God, and to have no sorrow at reproach being brought on the cause of religion through the fall of its professors, is the mark of the carnal, unregenerate mind." —Fausset.

CHAPTER THE SECOND.

1—3. (1) **devise,** intimating deliberate design in the outworking of evil. **power .. hand,** Ge. xxxi. 29.[a] (2) **covet fields,** etc., Is. v. 8. **oppress,** etc., i.e. defraud him both of his liberty and his property. (3) **family,** or race, Am. iii. 1. **remove .. necks,** the coming evil is likened to a yoke fixed on a beast's neck. **time is evil,** being characterized by moral evil it must be visited with evil consequences.

[a] "Might, not right, is what regulates their conduct." —Fausset.

The Besetting Sin.—We all have what the negro called our "upsetting sin," but we don't always know what it is. I will tell you what is the besetting sin of every one of us. When man fell from God, originally, he fell into himself. There is your besetting sin—self. Self is the house devil, after all, that every one of us has to fight; smooth-tongued, suave, hoodwinking us all. "O, how much good I am doing." Are you? Self whispered that. When they told a noted preacher at the foot of the stairs that he had preached a good sermon, he said, "The devil told me that before I left the pulpit." I tell you self in some form, my brother, will be an enemy all the time to be fought. We must get rid of self, or we can never be filled with the Spirit. Charles G. Finney said that when he went into the cities to begin his evangelistic work, he would sometimes preach a day or two without one atom of power. What did he do? He just let himself down before God, and prayed God to empty him of Charles G. Finney,—as it were, to take the bump of self-reliance, and self-trust, and self-seeking out of him. "Seekest thou great things for thyself?"—even in Christian work—"seek them not." Let them be for Christ. Pray that you may be so filled with Christ, that there shall not be room for the house devil of self.—T. L. Cuyler.

4—9. (4) **shall one take,** i.e. one of your enemies. In a mocking and derisive spirit they would take up your own lamentations. **lament,** etc., Heb. naha, nehi, nihyah, a repetion representing the continuous and monotonous wail.—Fausset. "Shall wail a wail of woe."—Pusey. **changed the portion,** or removed His people from their inheritance. **turning,** etc., R. V. "to the rebellious (i.e. the king of Assyria) he divideth our fields." (5) **none that shall cast,** etc., there shall be no restoration at time of Jubilee of the lands taken away.[a]—Expos. Bib. (6) vss. 6 and 7 seem to be the words of the rich oppressors. Expos. Bib. translates:—"Prate not, they prate, let none prate of such things! revilings

[a] Jos. xiv. 1, 2; see also De. xxxii. 8, 9.

vs. 4. He hath divided our fields. The land was but the outward symbol of the inward heritage. Unjust gain kept back is restored with usury; it taketh away the life of the owners thereof (Prov. i. 19). The vineyard whereof the Jews said, the inheritance shall be ours, was taken from them and given to others. So now is that aw-

will never cease! O thou that speakest (thus) to the house of Jacob, is the spirit of Jehovah cut short? or are such His doings? Shall not His words mean well with him that walketh uprightly?" They claim that they are God's people and no harm can come to them. (8) Here God speaks (vss. 8—10), reproving the oppressors. Exp. Bib. translates:—"But ye are the foes of my people, rising against those that are peaceful," etc. (9) **my glory,** the privileges which every Israelite possessed as a member of God's people.

ful change begun when Christians, leaving God, their only unchanging good, turn to earthly vanities, and for the grace of God which he withdraws have these only for their fleeting portion, until it shall be finally exchanged in the day of judgment.—Pusey.

A Parable.—The stones from the wall said, we come from the mountains far away, from the sides of the craggy hills. Fire and water worked on us for ages, but only made us crags. Human hands have made us into a dwelling where the children of your immortal race are born, and suffer, and rejoice, and find rest and the view of infinite wisdom; the small things may be as important in their place, as necessary for instrumentally accomplishing God's pleasure, as the great. It is a small thing in itself that Lord Mounteagle is visited by some stirrings of conscience and affection; but is the instrument in God's hand of frustrating the Gunpowder Plot—of saving the British King, Lords, and Commons from destruction—of preserving the British empire for its lofty part in Providence as the bulwark of Protestant Christendom. What thing is in itself more small and (to our apprehension) accidental than the cackling of a goose? And yet that is the instrument in God's hand of rousing Titus Manlius at midnight to discover that the Gauls are stealing into the citadel, and so of saving Rome from perishing in her infancy, and preserving her for those mighty destinies, in reference to the whole world and Church, which God's purpose had assigned to her—which His Word has prescribed for her—as the empress city, the queen of the nations.—Macgregor's "Christian Doctrine."

10, 11. (10) **arise .. depart,** as a just retribution for the expulsion of others, the oppressors shall be expelled themselves. **not your rest,** it can be no secure resting-place for you in your wilfulness and wickedness. As a sin-stricken land it is under Divine judgments.[a] **because it is polluted,** etc., Camb. B. "because of uncleanness ye shall be destroyed with," etc. (11) **spirit and falsehood,** or, in a lying spirit. **prophesy .. drink,** promising you abundance of self-indulgent things. These are the Prophets whom the people would approve and accept.

a "Since such are your doings, my sentence on you is irrevocable, however distasteful to you: ye who have cast out others from their homes and possessions, must arise, depart, and be cast out of your own, for this is not your rest."—Fausset.

A Call to Depart (vs. 10).—I. The unhappiness that belongs to human life lessened—1. By ignorance; 2. By insensibility; 3. By prosperity; 4. By employment; 5. By friendship; 6. By religion. II. What are the causes of the unhappiness of life. 1. The infinite disproportion between our desires and our power; 2. The weakness of our judgment continually making mistakes; 3. One evil destroys the pleasure of almost all the good for a time; 4. Almost every good has its peculiar kindred evil; 5. Whatever good is given only excites the infinite wish for more; 6. The hazardous uncertainty of everything future; 7. Sin is the mighty evil that destroys and transforms everything; 8. The soul is not at home here. III. What is to be done? IV. Arise ye, and depart.—J. Foster.

"This is the scene of combat, not of rest;
Man's is laborious happiness at best;
On this side death his dangers never cease,
His joys are joys of conquest, not of peace."

As the needle in a compass trembles till it settles in the north point, so the heart of a sinner can get no rest but in Christ.

No Rest on Earth—The Prairie on Fire.—One night, ages ago, a fire broke out in an American wilderness. A spark dropped on dry leaves, the lighted leaves flew before the wind, the flames raced along the grass, and glanced from tree to tree, till all the forest was ablaze, and night was turned into a terrible day. Certain Indians, driven out of their hunting-grounds by the red storm, fled for their lives: hour after hour they ran, until, half dead with fatigue, they reached a noble river; they forded it, and after scaling the opposite bank, their chief struck his tent-pole into the ground, threw himself on the cool turf, and cried, "Alabama!"—"Here we may rest!" But that chief was no prophet. The land was claimed by hostile tribes. The fugitives reached no resting-place there; they were soon beset by foes more relentless than the elements: having escaped the fury of the fire, they perished from the cruelty of man, and where they looked for the still delight of a home, found but the quiet of a grave. Let this tradition serve as a parable. Earth has no Alabama for the soul. "Arise, depart; for this is not your rest."—Stanford.

"Oh, some seek bread—no more—life's mere subsistence,
And some seek wealth and ease—the common quest;
And some seek fame, that hovers in the distance;
But all are seeking rest."
—Langbridge.

12, 13. (12) **assemble,** again, after the objects of the captivity have been accomplished in you; a promise of restoration from Babylon. **as the sheep of Bozrah,**[a] etc., i.e. in great numbers. **great noise,** comp. the bleating of a large flock.[b] (13) **breaker,** the leader who shall break down every obstacle in the way of their return. Henderson understands Jehovah himself as the mighty Leader of His people. **Lord .. them,** Is. lii. 12.

The Breaker is Come up Before (vs. 13).—I. Since Christ has gone before us things are not as they would have been had He not passed that way. II. Every foe is conquered. III. The power of hurtful things is destroyed. IV. We have but to march on and take the prey.—C. H. Spurgeon.

a 2 Ki. iii. 4.

b "He says men, in order that the comparison of Israel to a flock may be better understood." —Wordsworth.

CHAPTER THE THIRD.

1—4. (1) **heads .. princes,** official rulers, magistrates. Those who should be examples to the people. (2) **pluck .. bones,** robbing those who come to the judgment-seat, instead of doing them justice.[c] (3) **eat,** etc., the Prophet likens their cruel outrages to cannibal feasting.[d] (4) **then,** i.e. in the time of God's judgment, see ch. ii. 3. **not hear,** the cruel oppressors of the poor shall receive no money.

Why Some Prayers not Answered.—"Certainly all the 'pretence' prayers must go among the eternal strays. Like many letters which never reach their destination, many prayers have to be marked 'missent,' or with some other fatal brand, and consigned to oblivion. Sometimes prayers remain unanswered because they are not directed right—not addressed to God, but to the audience. Other prayers never 'go through' because the address is illegible. They are too full of pomp and rhetorical flourish—mere 'monologues of flowery prose.' Other prayers get lost because they are 'unavailable matter'—prayers whose answers might gratify us, but would fall like showers of daggers on our neighbors—and so are denied passage through the divine channels, as sharp-edged tools, corroding acids, explosives, and the like, are not allowed in the mails. No legally 'stamped,' sincerely directed, and well-meaning prayer is ever lost. The answer may be delayed. but the prayer is 'on file.'"—Anon.

The Old French Régime.—One of the greatest abuses of the French Government, previous to the Revolution, was to be found in the administration of justice, which, from the reign of Louis XII., was really bought and sold. When the sale of an office took place, the purchaser petitioned the crown for a grant of it; and when that grant was signed, he paid, besides the price which the vendor was to receive for it, a sum of money into the royal treasury. The amount of that sum varied from one thousand to two thousand French crowns. A worse feature in the French administration of justice was the épices, or presents made by the parties in a cause to the judges before whom it was tried. To secure the judges the proportion which the suitors were to contribute towards the expense of justice, it was provided, by an ordinance of St. Louis, that, at the commencement of a suit, each party should deposit in court of the amount of one-tenth part of the property in dispute; that the tenth deposited by the unsuccessful party should be paid over to the judges on their passing sentence; and that the tenth of the successful party should then be returned to him. This was varied by subsequent ordinances; insensibly it became a custom for the successful party to wait on the judges, after sentence was passed, and, as an acknowledgment of their attention to the cause, to present them with a box of sweetmeats, which were then called épices, or spices. By degrees this custom became a legal perquisite of the judges; and it was converted into a present of money, and required by the judges before the cause came to a hearing: "Non deliberetur donec solventur species," say some of the ancient registers of the Parliaments of France.—Percy Anec.

5—7. (5) **bite .. teeth,** ch. ii. 11. "The Heb. word is always used to denote biting venomously, like a serpent, or to perform a malicious act."—Spk. Com. **cry peace,** their words and their works in no way agree. **putteth not,** by neglecting, or refusing, to give these prophets bribes.[a] (6) **night,** etc., the fig. of calamities. The prophet is address-

c "Who exercise all manner of cruelty upon their inferiors, as if they were so many butchers cutting meat for the shambles." —Lowth.

d Comp. Eze. xxiv. 3—5.

The Princess Elizabeth, daughter of Charles I., was found dead one day, with her head leaning on the Bible, and the Bible open at the words, "Come unto Me all ye that labor and are heavy laden, and I will give you rest." Her monument in Newport church consists of a female figure reclining her head on a marble book, with the above text engraved on the book.

Judgment. It is neither the great man's power, nor the poor man's meanness, that a judge is to mind in judgment. A judge, a justice, must never cry out, "Oh, he is a poor man!" nor yet out of base fear they cry out, "Oh, he is a great man!" The judges in Egypt were portrayed without hands and without eyes, to signify that they were not to take bribes, nor to accept men's persons. —Brooks.

a 1 Sam. 2—16.

ing the rulers. Because of their rapacity, and their league with false prophets, their land shall be overshadowed by adversity, and there shall be no prophecy, whether false or true, to guide them. The false prophets will be ashamed, because of the non-fulfilment of their oracles; and the true will have no fresh revelation till the old cycle of prophecies has been fulfilled. Comp. Lam. ii. 9.—Camb. B. (7) **cover their lips,** a usual token of shame and sorrow.[b]

Preachers and Preaching.—The injustice of the vulgar tone of preaching is not less flagrant to Jesus than it is to the souls which it profanes. The preachers do not see that they make His Gospel not glad, and shear Him of the locks of beauty and the attributes of heaven. When I see a majestic Epaminondas or Washington—when I see among my contemporaries a true orator, an upright judge, a dear friend—when I vibrate to the melody and fancy of a poem, I see beauty that is to be desired. And so lovely, and with yet more entire consent of my human being, sounds in my ear the severe music of the bards that have sung of the true God in all ages. Now, do not degrade the life and dialogues of Christ out of the circle of this charm—by insulation and peculiarity let them lie, as they befall, alive and warm, part of human life, and of the landscape, and of the cheerful day. Another defect of the traditionary and limited way of using the mind of Christ is that the moral nature—that law of laws, whose revelations introduce greatness, yea, God Himself, into the open soul—is not explored as the fountain of the established teaching in society. Men have come to speak of the revelation as somewhat long ago given and done, as if God were dead. The injury to faith throttles the preacher, and the goodliest of institutions becomes an uncertain and inarticulate voice. It is very certain that it is the effect of conversation with the beauty of the soul to beget a desire and need to impart to others the same knowledge and love. If utterance is denied, the thought lies like a burden on the man. Always the seer is a sayer. Somehow his dream is told. Somehow he publishes it with solemn joy. Sometimes with pencil on canvas; sometimes with chisel on stone; sometimes in towers and aisles of granite, his soul's worship is builded; sometimes in anthems of indefinite music; but clearest and most permanent in words. The man enamored of this excellency becomes its priest or poet. The office is coeval with the world. But observe the condition, the spiritual limitation of the office. The Spirit only can teach. Not any profane man, not any sensual, not any liar, not any slave can teach; but only He can give who has; He only can create who is. The man on whom the soul descends, through whom the soul speaks, alone can teach. Courage, piety, love, wisdom, can teach; and every man can open his door to these angels, and they shall bring him the gift of tongues. But the man who aims to speak as books enable, as synods use, as the fashion guides, and as interest commands, babbles. Let him hush.—Emerson.

8—12. (8) **I am,** i.e. I, Micah, as God's true and faithful Prophet. (9) **pervert all equity,** judgment is right according to law, equity is right between man and man. With both the magistrate has to deal. (10) **blood,** a figure for oppression and violence, Eze. xxii. 27; Zep. iii. 3. (11) **reward,** etc., in all cases money, not right, nor the fear of God, ruled the rulers. **lean,** in their self-deception, or their hypocrisy. (12) **plowed as a field,** Is. xxvi. 18.[a] **mountain of the house,** i.e. Mt. Moriah.

Plowed as a Field.—This striking prophecy was quoted at a critical point in the history of Jeremiah when "the priests and the prophets and all the people" had pronounced sentence of death upon the prophet by acclamation. "Certain of the elders of the land," we are told, invoked the respectful treatment of Micah by king Hezekiah as a precedent for granting Jeremiah a similar immunity. So far from putting Micah to death, Hezekiah, they declare, had been moved by his sombre prediction to "fear the Lord and beseech the Lord," "and the Lord repented him of the evil which he had pronounced upon them" (Jer. xxvi. 17—19). This implies a belief that prophecy is conditional. The prophets declare the principles of God's rule, and apply them to individual cases. But if the moral conditions of the cases to which these principles are applied be altered, the threatening or the promise is postponed, modified, or recalled.—Camb. B.

[b] Le. xiii. 45; Eze. xxiv. 17, 22.

"They shall be so ashamed of themselves as not to dare to open their mouths or boast of the name of prophet." — Calvin.

"Misery assails riches as lightning does the highest towers; or as a tree that is heavy laden with fruit breaks its own boughs. So do riches destroy the virtue of their possessor." —Burton.

"My aim in every sermon is a stout and lusty call to sinners, to quicken the saints, and to be made a universal blessing to all."— Rowland Hill.

"The waters of happiness are not for a luxurious bath where a man may lie till, like flax steeped too long, the very fibre be rooted out of him; a quick bath will brace him, and he will come out refreshed for work." — Alexander Maclaren.

[a] "It has been remarked that when this prophecy was delivered it must have seemed a most daring utterance. This hill appears to have been densely crowded with the best and strongest edifices in Jerusalem. But luxuriant crops of grain may now be found growing on all the south-eastern face of the mount." — Bib. Things.

Zion Ploughed.—At the time I visited this sacred ground, one part of it supported a crop of barley, another was undergoing the labor of the plough, and the soil turned up consisted of stone and lime, filled with earth, such as is usually met with in the foundations of ruined cities. It is nearly a mile in circumference.—Richardson's Travels.—On the south-east Zion slopes down, in a series of cultivated terraces, sharply, though not abruptly, to the sites of the king's gardens. Here and round to the S. the whole declivities are sprinkled with olive trees, which grow luxuriantly among the narrow slips of corn.—Porter.

CHAPTER THE FOURTH.

1, 2. (1) **last days,** etc., comp. Is. ii. 2, etc. The usual prophetic expression for the times of Messiah. **mountain .. Lord,** Mt. Moriah, but apparently including Jerusalem as a whole. **people .. flow,** "heathen shall resort thither to be instructed in the way of salvation." (2) **law,** or teaching, instruction. **word of the Lord,** or the Gospel message.[b]

A Missionary Discourse (vss. 1—3).—I. The Church rendered conspicuous to all. 1. She shall be exalted above the hills; 2. She shall be established. II. A disposition in all towards the Church. 1. Friendly co-operation; 2. A definite and sacred object; 3. Proper intentions and correct views; 4. Right dispositions; 5. Confidence in the excellency of the Divine instructions. III. The blessings resulting from these great events.—Gamma in 400 Sks.

3, 4. (3) **among,** R. V., "between many peoples." God shall be the arbiter of all disputes. **rebuke,** R. V. marg. "decide concerning," as an umpire. **beat .. hooks,** comp. Is. ii. 4; Joel iii. 10.[a] (4) **sit .. tree,** a poetical figure of perfect security and quietness.[b] **mouth .. spoken,** therefore we may be quite sure that it will come to pass.

The Vine and the Fig Tree.—When we had proceeded some distance, the sounds of the somtora coming upon our ears indicated that the scene of rejoicing was close at hand. My companion stopped at a house with a mean little door, through which, having entered, she led the way into a large open patio, or courtyard, shaded on one side by a trellis of cane work, supporting heavy bunches of luscious grapes. In the midst of the court grew, in full vigor, a verdant fig tree, spreading abroad its expansive branches, and affording an agreeable shelter from the oppressive rays of the noon-day sun. The vine and the fig tree are invariably found in the Moorish patio. The family grow up under this shade; the little ones sport, with the thoughtless glee of childhood, among the foliage, and the grave elders pass the greater part of their time in more serious conversation, and sometimes, doubtless, mere trifling gossip. They dwell under their own vine and fig tree, none daring to make them afraid.—Murray. "This expression most probably alludes to the delightful Eastern arbors, which were partly composed of vines; and the agreeable retreat which was enjoyed under them might also be found under their fig trees. Norden expressly speaks of vine arbors as common in the Egyptian gardens, and the Prænestine pavement, in Dr. Shaw, gives us the figure of an ancient one."—Burder.

5—7. (5) **all people will walk,** R. V. "all the peoples walk." The nations all worship gods of their own; let us therefore all the more steadily walk in the name of Jehovah. To walk in the name of any one, means to frame one's conduct acc. to his will, to act by his authority and in accordance with his character. (6) **assemble,** the people in their own land again. (7) **a remnant,** i.e. I will treat Israel as the "remnant" to which the promises belong. Zep. iii. 19. **reign,** etc., Da. vii. 14.

Fulfilment of the Ancient Vision.—Such is the ideal world, seen and promised two thousand five hundred years ago, out of as real an experience of human sin and failure as ever mankind awoke to. Are we nearer the Vision to-day, or does it still hang upon time's horizon, that line which seems so stable from every seer's point of view, but which moves from the generations as fast as they travel to it? So far from this being so, there is much in the Vision that is not only nearer us than it was to the Hebrew prophets, and not only abreast of us, but actually

[b] Lu. xxiv. 47.

Last days. God's promises are dated, but with a mysterious character; and for want of skill in God's chronology, we are prone to think God forgets us, when, indeed, we forget ourselves in being so bold to set God a time of our own, and in being angry that He comes not just then to us. —Gurnall.

[a] "This prophecy began to be fulfilled in the peaceful days of the first appearance of the Gospel. The world was in a quiet condition when Christ came to visit it. That universal peace was an earnest of the peace in earth and heaven which is the fruit of the Gospel of Christ." —Wordsworth.

[b] "The fig tree affords a thick shade and is, on this account, a favorite resort of the family, where they may often be seen seated on mats, partaking of a meal, or entertaining friends. So the expression denotes at once security, domestic enjoyment, and competence." —Van Lennep.

"As the pleasures of the future will be spiritual and pure, the object of a good and wise man in this transitory state of existence should be to fit himself for a

achieved and behind us, as we live and strive still onward. Yes, brothers, actually behind us! History has in part fulfilled the promised influence of religion upon the nations. The Unity of God has been owned, and the civilized peoples bow to the standards of justice and of mercy first revealed from Mount Zion. Many nations and powerful nations acknowledge the arbitrament of the God of the Bible. We have had revealed that High Fatherhood of which every family in heaven and earth is named; and wherever that is believed the brotherhood of men is confessed. We have seen Sin, that profound discord in man and estrangement from God, of which all human hatreds and malices are the fruit, atoned for and reconciled by a Sacrifice in face of which human pride and passion stand abashed. The first part of the Vision is fulfilled. The nations stream to the God of Jerusalem and His Christ.—G. Adam Smith.

8—13. (8) **tower of the flock,**[e] allusion is to the high wooden tower, erected in large pastures, from which the scattered flocks might be watched. Jerusalem is so regarded in this poetical figure. **the first dominion,** the empire as in the days of David and Solomon. (9) **cry aloud,** at the sorrow so soon to come on thee; the prospect of future restoration should prevent such despair. **"no king,"** referring to the captivity of Jehoiachin and Zedekiah. (10) **Be in pain,** etc., the anguish is not to be escaped, but shall end in deliverance. **dwell in the field,** the inhabitants of Jerusalem are encamped in the open country, in preparation for the journey to Babylon. (11) **defiled,** i.e. profaned, despoiled of her boasted holiness and inviolability. **look upon Zion,** R. V. "see its desire upon Z." (12) **shall gather,** "hath gathered." The fate they have prepared for Z. will come upon themselves. (13) **horn,** symbol of destructive power.[a] **hoofs brass,** threshing was done by the treading of the feet. **I will consecrate,** R. V. "thou shalt devote."

Horn Iron and Hoofs Brass.—"When God," says an old writer, "has conquering work for his people to do, he will furnish them with strength and ability for it—will make the horn iron and the hoofs brass; and when he does so, they must exert the power he gives them, and execute the commission: even the daughter of Zion may arise and thresh." The nations thought to ruin Christianity in its infancy, but it was victorious over them. Those who persisted in their enmity were broken to pieces (Matt. xxi. 44), particularly the Jewish nation; but multitudes by Divine grace were joined to the Church, and they and their substance were consecrated to the Lord Jesus, the Lord of the whole earth.—Pulp. Com.

better, by controlling the unworthy propensities of his nature and improving all his better aspirations; to do his duty, first to God, then to his neighbor; to promote the happiness and welfare of those whom he has the means of assisting; never wantonly to injure the meanest thing that lives; and to encourage, as far as he can, whatever is useful and tends to refine and exalt humanity."
—Southey.

e "The tower of the flock is the Church of Christ, wh. had its origin in Jerusalem and to which all nations are gathered, so as to make one flock and one shepherd."—A. Lapide.

Constant revival, no autumn, no winter, but perpetual summer, is what the Church needs, and which must precede the coming millennium.

a "Zion being compared to an ox treading corn, and an ox's strength lying in the horns, her strength is implied by giving her a horn of iron." — Fausset.

CHAPTER THE FIFTH.

1—3. (1) **Now gather,** R. V. "Now shalt thou gather." Assyria may marshal her hosts, may lay siege against the holy city, may violate the person of the king, but from insignificant Bethlehem a royal Deliverer shall arise. **daughter of troops,** or city having many troops. **he hath laid,** i.e. the enemy. **against us,** i.e. the people shut up in the city. **smite .. cheek,** an act of insult.[b] (2) **Beth-lehem Ephratah,**[c] Mat. ii. 6. To be distinguished from Bethlehem in Zebulun. **out of thee,** a little and humble village. **goings .. old,** prob. the best translation is, "whose comings forth have been of old, from the ancient days." The clause then may express either the descent of the Messiah from the ancient Davidic family, or, as some understand it,—his pre-existence.[d] (3) **Therefore will he,** etc. Because the deliverance of Israel is to proceed from the insignificant Bethlehem, God will deliver Israel into the hands of her enemies. **she,** the virgin mother. **his brethren shall return,** the Messiah's brethren according to the flesh who are in foreign lands shall return to Judea.

The Essential Existence and Divine Manifestations of the Son of God (vs. 2).—I. Consider that essential perfection of the Deity which is attributed to Him. II. Those special manifestations of His glory which are recorded—1. In the creation of all things; 2. In His covenant with His Father; 3. In His communion with men. Application:—(1) These considerations may prove to you that the Saviour is worthy of your love;

b 1 Ki. xxii. 24; Job xvi. 10, etc.

c Bethlehem means house of bread, and Ephratah means fruitful.

d "This is an illustrious testimony to the Divine generation, before all time, of Christ the Eternal Son of God." — Wordsworth.

Bethlehem, thou art not worthy to be counted among the Gileads of Judah, but out of thy little thousand there shall stand

(2) Worthy of your confidence; (3) Worthy of your service.—J. Blackburn.

Bethlehem.—By a remarkable interposition of Providence, interwoven, however, with the course of events in the world, was it brought about that the promised King should be born in Bethlehem (as Micah the prophet had foretold), the very place where the house of David had its origin; while, at the same time, the lowly circumstancses of his birth were in striking contrast with the inherent dignity and glory that were veiled in the new-born child.—Mander. The Humble Origin of the Messiah.—The value of such a prophecy of Christ lies in the correctives which it supplies to the Christian apocalypse and theology. Both of these have raised Christ to a throne too far above the actual circumstances of His earthly ministry and the theatre of His eternal sympathies. Whether enthroned in the praises of heaven, or by scholasticism relegated to an ideal and abstract humanity, Christ is lifted away from touch with the common people. But His lowly origin was a fact. He sprang from the most democratic of peoples. His ancestor was a shepherd, and His mother a peasant girl. He Himself was a carpenter: at home, as His parables show, in the fields and the folds and the barns of His country; with the servants of the great houses, with the unemployed in the market; with the woman in the hovel seeking one piece of silver, with the shepherd on the moors seeking the lost sheep. The poor had the gospel preached to them; and the common people heard Him gladly. As the peasants of Judæa must have listened to Micah's promise of His origin among themselves with new hope and patience, so in the Roman empire the religion of Jesus Christ was welcomed chiefly, as the Apostles and the Fathers bear witness, by the lowly and the laboring of every nation. In the great persecution which bears his name, the Emperor Domitian heard that there were two relatives alive of this Jesus whom so many acknowledged as their King, and he sent for them that he might put them to death. But when they came, he asked them to hold up their hands, and seeing these brown and chapped with toil, he dismissed the men, saying, "From such slaves we have nothing to fear." Ah but, Emperor! it is just the horny hands of this religion that thou and thy gods have to fear!—G. Adam Smith.

Both names were derived from "fruitfulness," "House of Bread" and "fruitfulness;" and despite the centuries of Mohammedan oppression, it is fertile still. It had been rich in the fruitfulness of this world; rich, thrice rich, should it be in spiritual fruitfulness.—Pusey.

4—7. (4) **feed,** i.e. feed, or rule, the flock.[a] "Over this restored people the Messiah shall preside in the plenitude of Divine power." **abide,** remain undisturbed in their land. **be great,** Lu. i. 32. (5) **peace,** comp. Is. ix. 6.[b] It is better to read: "And this man shall be Peace." with a full stop after Peace. **Assyrian,** prob. put here as the representative of all Israel's foes. **seven .. eight,** an idiom for a full and sufficient number. **principal men,** lit. anointed men, such as the Apostles. (6) **waste,** or eat up, as with their flocks the shepherds do. **land of Nimrod,** another name for Assyria. **entrances,** gates, or passes. (7) **dew from the Lord,** "the mysterious origin of the dew and the rain seems to be the point of comparison." Job xxxviii. 28. **that tarrieth not for man,** "man can neither help nor hinder the works of God in nature; friendship and hostility will be equally unimportant to the destiny of Israel."

The Celestial Flora.—I. "Though thou be little, etc." You can buy complete sets of all the flowers of the Alpine district at the hotel near the foot of the Rosenlani glacier, very neatly pressed and enclosed in cases. Some of the flowers are very common, but they must be included, or the flora would not be completely represented. The botanist is as careful to see that the common ones are there, as he is to note that the rarer specimens are not excluded. Our blessed Lord will be sure to make a perfect collection of all the flowers of his field, and even the ordinary believer, the every-day worker, the common convert, will not be forgotten. To Jesus' eye, there is beauty in all his plants, and each one is needed to perfect the flora of paradise. May I be found among his flowers, if only as one out of myriad daisies, who in sweet simplicity shall look up and wonder at his love for ever.—Spurgeon.

a man who shall rule all men. There is a wonderful spirit of compensation in providence. God is saying to each of us, Though thou art poor, thou mayest be wise; though thou art slow, thou mayest be painstaking and persevering; thou art—though misunderstood by men — thou art fully comprehended by thy Father. Look for the "though" in every history; look for th compensation in every life." — Parker.

Sin—a fruit of unbelief. "I tell you that that bottle contains arsenic, and it will kill you if you take it, that is true. If you disbelieve the truth, and take it, your unbelief will cost you your life. A certain Austrian count, once climbing the Alps, was told by his guide that to go out onto a cliff was dangerous. He disbelieved it, went, fell—and they found his body at the hotel, at the foot of that cliff. The world is full today of disasters which are merely the consequences of unbelief." — A. F. Schauffler.

a Is. xl. 9—11.

b Comp. Eph. ii. 14.

"It belongs, in truth, to the Church of God to suffer blows, not to strike them. But at the same time let it be remembered that the Church is an anvil which has worn out many a hammer." — Beza.

8—12. (8) **as a lion,** the type of irresistible strength.[c] (9) **thine hand,** the emblem of power. (10) **horses .. chariots,**[d] cf. i. 13. So Isaiah regards war-horses and war-chariots as equally hateful to God with idolatry, ii. 7. (11) **cities strongholds,** signs of man's self-confidence. (12) **witchcrafts,** Ex. xxii. 18. **soothsayers,** Is. ii. 6.

Dew comes down from heaven, is of heavenly, not earthly, origin, transparent, glistening with light, reflecting the hues of heaven; gentle, slight, weak in itself, refreshing, cooling the strong heats of the day; consumed itself, yet thereby preserving life; falling on the dry and withered grass, wherein all nature droops, and recalling it to freshness of life. And still more in those lands, where from the beginning of April to the end of October, the close of the latter and the beginning of the early rain, during all the hot months of summer, the life of all herbage depends upon the dew alone.—Pusey.

13—15. (13) **graven images,** ch. i. 7.[e] **standing images,** R. V. "pillars." (14) **groves,**[f] R. V. "Asherahs." "The Asherah was prob. a post or pole fixed in the ground besides an altar of Baal or Jehovah, and regarded as sacred."—Camb. B. **cities,** marg. enemies. (15) **heathen, such as,** etc., R. V. "nations which hearkened not," i.e. were disobedient.

Heathenism in Africa.—Africa is the home of superstition. It does not take the form of a regular mythology, or embody itself in the grotesque images of Hindostan. Any trifle which awakens fear, or to which mystery may attach, is an object of reverence or worship. Spirits, both bad and good, are imagined to exist everywhere. The rocks, trees, mountains, rivers, caverns, and groves, may all or each be the home of a spiritual being. Such spots are sacred. Every passer-by will deposit an offering, however small, to show his respect or to deprecate the anger of the spiritual inhabitant. The bodies of living creatures are thought to be the favorite abode of the spirits. At one place the monkeys that live in the wood around the graveyard are thought to be animated with departed spirits. Those monkeys, therefore, are sacred animals. Nobody would dare to touch them; and the creatures seem to know this, for they are quite tame, and not a little impudent. At another place there are many crocodiles, in which, as the people think, departed spirits live. These, too, are sacred, and the natives treat them so kindly, that the scaly monsters will come out of their holes when called, and allow themselves to be handled, and will follow any one who carries a fowl in his hand, for half a mile from his den. At Calabar and Bonny the shark is sacred, for the same reason; and at Benin it is so tame, that it will come up every day to the river bank for food. And what is still more strange is the fact, that at St. Catherine, a species of tiger burrows near the town, and walks through its streets at night, without disturbing the people, who believe these fierce creatures to be sacred. Experience shows that the African is peculiarly receptive of religious impressions. His intellectual powers are wholly uncultivated. He has not worked out for himself a system of religious belief. What he believes is the result of feeling, and not of conviction.

c "What characteristics the Messiah, as well as His works, is the perfect union of force with gentleness. He was the lion of the tribe of Judah, yet the lamb of God."—Spk. Com.

d "The war chariot and the convenient carriage, once so common in these lands, have totally disappeared."—Van Lennep.

e Ex. xx. 4.

f Le. xxvi. 1.

g "The Circassians celebrate their religious ceremonies exclusively in sacred groves, where an emblem, shaped like a cross, is carefully preserved. When a warrior returns home victorious, or has escaped some impending calamity, he repairs to the grove, and presents a thank offering to the god."—Van Lennep.

"As the several nations that the king of Assyria placed in Samaria made idols of their own, and set them up for worship; so we may see the different classes of men in these days, with their idols of worship—the ambitious, the covetous, the pleasure-taker, the miser, the scientific."
—John Bate.

CHAPTER THE SIXTH.

1—5. (1) **before the mountains,** regarded as the witnesses of God's dealings all through the ages.[a] (2) **controversy,** a ground for complaint against them. **strong,** R. V. "enduring." (3) **wearied thee,** by too hard exactions,[b] Is. xliii. 22; Mal. i. 13. (4) **house of servants,** Ex. xiii. 3. (5) **Balak,** etc., Nu. xxii. 5, xxiii. 7. **from Shittim,** etc., R. V., "remember from Shittim to Gilgal."

A Great Controversy (vs. 2).—I. The appeal. 1. Common in its form, Is. i. 3; Jer. viii. 7; Pro. vi. 6; Lu. xii. 24, etc.; 2. Sublime in conception; 3. Humiliating in substance. II. The parties. 1. God as the moral Governor of the universe, and men as His subjects. III. The case: the question is whether God has done us any injury—1. By the strictness of His laws; 2. By the harshness of His providential dispensations; 3. By the severity of the punishments He has threatened in a

a Comp. Is. i. 2.

b "'Tis then we hear the voice of God within, pleading with care and sin: Child of My love how have I wearied thee? Why wilt thou err from Me? Have I not brought thee from the house of slaves, parting the drowning waves, and set

future world. Apply:—(1) We have no just complaints against God; (2) God has many just complaints against us.

Hear.—If Adam needed to hear his Father's voice, sounding amid the fair bowers and the unshaded glory of Paradise, surely much more does this prodigal world, that has gone astray from him, need to hear a Father's voice asking after us, and the first intimations of a Father's desire that the lost may be found, and the dead at length become alive.—Cumming.

6—9. (6) **wherewith,** etc., the question supposed to be asked of the Prophet by the people with whom he pleads. They would know what will appease Jehovah. **calves,** etc., Le. ix. 2, 3. (7) **rivers of oil,** this was used with the meat-offerings.[c] **my firstborn,** as was required in the Moloch rites[d] (see preceding pages). (8) "the prophet denies that any external forms will make up for the want of spiritual qualities. The sacrifice of the heart is what God requires." **showed thee,** De. x. 12. **do justly,** etc., these being moral, not ceremonial, duties. **walk . . God,** implying habitual converse. (9) **the city,** i.e. Jerusalem. **man of wisdom,** i.e. the man who is wise will easily see God's authority in this demand for moral obedience. **rod,** or threatened judgment; prob. the Assyrian invasion.

Is it not True? (vs. 8).—I. The revelation. 1. What He has revealed; 2. How He has revealed these things—by nature, by history, by Jesus Christ, by our own experience. II. The requisition. 1. He requires us to demonstrate our knowledge; 2. To display this in a particular way, to do justly, to love mercy, to walk humbly with God.—Stems and Twigs.

A Condition of Receiving Mercy.—Being sent for by a slave-holder who was seriously unwell, to pray with him, Father Craven approached his bedside and inquired if he had in his will bequeathed liberty to his slaves? "No," said the slave-holder, "I have bequeathed them to my children." "Then," said Father Craven, "prayer will be of no avail—God will not show mercy to those who show none to their fellow-men." So he bade him farewell. Soon after a second message was sent for Father Craven to visit the slave-holder and pray with him. He went and asked the slave-holder if he had emancipated his slaves? "Yes," said the slave-holder, "I have now emancipated them by my will. Will you pray for me?" "Certainly," said the good man, and he knelt down and commended to God the soul of the sufferer, who seemed near his end.

10—12. (10) **yet,** although such constant and earnest warnings have been given. **scant measure,** lit. a lean ephah, Am. viii. 5. (11) **shall I count them pure,** R. V. "shall I be pure?" Cheyne would read: "Canst thou (Jerusalem) be pure?" **bag . . weights,** Pr. xvi. 11. (12) **thereof,** of her, i.e. the city of Jerusalem.

Treasures of Wickedness (vss. 10, 11).—I. Resulting from short weights and defective measures. II. Adulterations of food, and manufacturing articles. III. Results of vulgar theft, fraud, etc. IV. Results of marriage for money without love. V. Results of conquests, national and personal loot, slave trade, etc. VI. The numerous ways in which riches are got, but not by right.

The Sin of the Scant Measure.—This section of the Book of Micah is one of the most poignant criticisms of a commercial community which have ever appeared in literature. In equal relief we see the meanest instruments and the most prominent agents of covetousness and cruelty—the scant measure, the false weights, the unscrupulous prince and the venal judge. And although there are some sins denounced which are impossible in our civilization, yet falsehood, squalid fraud, pitilessness of the everlasting struggle for life are exposed exactly as we see them about us to-day. Through the prophet's ancient and often obscure eloquence we feel just those shocks and sharp edges which still break everywhere through our Christian civilization. Let us remember, too, that the community addressed by the prophet was, like our own, professedly religious.—Expos. Bible.

13—16. (13) **sick,** with a wasting, consuming sickness. (14) **casting down,** R. V. "humiliation." **take hold,** etc., R. V. "remove, but shalt not

My saints before thee in the way, lest thou shouldst faint or stray?"—Keble.

c Le. ii. 1, 4, 15.

d There is every reason to believe that the Jews actually offered human sacrifices in the Valey of Hinnom.

"Vss. 6 and 7 are an exact description of the temper of hypocrites and habitual sinners, who hope to obtain God's favor by performing the external duties of religion; and are willing to purchase their own pardon upon any terms but that of reforming their lives." —Lowth.

"Oft, beneath the saintly veil, the votary of sin may lurk unseen, and to that eye alone which penetrates the inmost heart revealed."

—Bally.

Antonio Guevasa used to say, "That heaven would be filled with such as had done good works, and hell with such as intended to do them."

"The ermine rather chooseth to die than defile her beautiful skin. There is more evil in a drop of sin than in a sea of affliction; affliction is but like a rent in a coat, sin a prick at the heart. In affliction there is some good; in this lion there is some honey to be found. 'It is good for me that I was afflicted' (Ps. cxix. 71). St. Augustine saith, 'Affliction is God's flail to thresh off our husks; not to consume but to refine.' There

carry away safe; and that which thou carriest away," etc. The enemy will fall so suddenly upon the Jews th. they will not be able to save their property. (15) **sow,** etc., comp. De. xxviii. 38, 40. **sweet wine,** R. V. "the vintage." (16) **statutes of Omri,** 1 Ki. xvi. 25, 26. **reproach of my people,** the reproach wh. attaches to the people of Jehovah when cast out of "Jehovah's land."

Sharp Dealing is Destructive to Society.—The speed of modern life tends to shorten the time expended on every piece of work, and to turn it out untempered and incomplete. The struggle for life in commerce, the organized rivalry between labor and capital, not only puts every man on his guard against giving any other more than his due, but tempts him to use every opportunity to scamp and curtail his own service and output. Who is responsible for the enmity of classes, and the distrust which exists between capital and labor? It is the workman whose one aim is to secure the largest amount of wages for the smallest amount of work, and who will, in his blind pursuit of that, wreck the whole trade of a town or a district; it is the employer who believes he has no duties to his men beyond paying them for their work the least that he can induce them to take; it is the customer who only and ever looks to the cheapness of an article—procurer in that prostitution of talent to the work of scamping which is fast killing art, and joy and all pity for the bodies and souls of our brothers. These are the true anarchists and breakers-up of society.—Expos. Bible.

is no good in sin; it is the spirit and quintessence of evil. Sin is worse than hell; for the pains of hell only are a burden to the creature; but sin is a burden to God. 'I am pressed under your iniquities, as a cart is pressed under the sheaves' (Amos ii. 13)." — T. Watson.

"Public reformers had need first practice on their own hearts that which they purpose to try on others."—Charles I.

CHAPTER THE SEVENTH.

1, 2. (1) The speaker **here is the true Israel personified. grape-gleanings,** a complaint of the fewness of the Church's numbers.[a] **my soul desired,** etc., better as R. V. marg., "nor firstripe fig which my soul desired." **firstripe,** these were especially valued, and regarded as being of superior quality. (2) This vs. explains the figure of vs. **1. good .. earth,** comp. Ps. xii. 1, xiv. 2; Is. lvii. 1.

3, 4. (3) **both hands,** indicating thorough earnestness and activity in their evil schemes. Lit. "Both hands are upon evil to make it good."[b] **the prince asketh,** etc., the prince asketh (an illegal favor), and the judge is ready for a reward (i. e. a bribe). **wrap it up,** R. V. "weave it together," twist their wicked schemes together. (4) **brier .. thorn,** to such sinners are often compared, on account of their barrenness, and hurtful qualities. **watchmen,** i. e. the day foreseen by thy prophets.

Sin Wrappings (vs. 3).—The endeavor of people to wrap up sin is worthy of attention, because—I. It is general. The sinner seeks to wrap up sin—1. From society; 2. From his own conscience. II. Because it is wicked. Concealing sin is—1. A sin against society; 2. Against our constitution; 3. Against God. III. Because it is unwise. 1. The endeavor must pove inevitably fruitless; 2. It is eternally inimical to happiness; 3. If persisted in, will involve in unutterable ruin.—Thomas.

Skilfulness in Sin.—There are men who make a study of doing things that are wrong, skilfully, cunningly, well. There are thieves who are discovered, and there are thieves who are not discovered, because they thieve so well, so skilfully; they shake hands with the man they have robbed, and say Good-night to the soul they have plundered. Men may become experts in the devil's academy. The cleverness does not excuse the iniquity; the ability does not restore the character. If that ability had been devoted otherwise, what fortunes lay within its grasp, what influence belonged of right to its mastery! But men love to work in the dark, they seem to be more at home there than in the sunlight; they have a gift of sight which enables them to see all their spectral comrades in the black darkness of night.—Peop. Bib.

5—10. (5) **trust .. guide,** bec. such is the prevailing selfishness and corruption that none can be trusted. (6) **son,** etc., comp. Mat. x. 21, 35, 36. (7) "here the thread of thought is broken; the following verses appear to have been attached later. The speaker is, indeed, still the **true** Israel; but here she appears already overpowered by her enemies, whereas in vss. 1—6 the day of chastisement is still far off."—Camb. B. **There-**

a "It is with me as with one seeking fruits after the harvest, grapes after the vintage. There is not a cluster to be found, no first-ripe fruit."—Fausset.

b "The meaning is either, to do evil thoroughly, or to do evil in such a way as to appear good, or in the very spirit of Satan, to make evil their good." — Spk. Com.

"We'll mock the time with fairest show; fair face must hide what the false heart does know."— Shakespeare.

fore, R. V., "But as for me." **unto the Lord,** away from frail and untrustworthy man. (8) **mine enemy,** i. e. the instrument of God's "visitation," the heathen oppressor of Israel. **darkness,** etc.,[a] oftentimes the darkest part of the night is that wh. is just before the dawn. (9) **bear,** patiently and submissively. **plead,** etc., Ps. xxxv. 1, xliii. 1. **righteousness,** here His gracious faithfulness to His promises. (10) **she that is mine enemy,** the worldly power is personified. **shame .. her,** "in seeing how utterly mistaken she was in supposing that I was utterly ruined." **where .. God?** Ps. xlii. 3—10. **as the mire,** into the Eastern streets the refuse of the houses is swept, and there trodden down.

Our Mother of Sorrows.—From these fragments, it may be of many centuries, there rises clear the One Essential Figure: Israel, all her secular woes upon her; our Mother of Sorrows, at whose knees we learned our first prayers of confession and penitence. Other nations have been our teachers in art and wisdom and government. But she is our mistress in pain and in patience, teaching men with what conscience they should bear the chastening of the Almighty, with what hope and humility they should wait for their God. Surely not less lovable, but only more human, that her pale cheeks flush for a moment with the hate of the enemy and the assurance of revenge. Her passion is soon gone, for she feels her guilt to be greater; and, seeking forgiveness, her last word is what man's must ever be, praise to the grace and mercy of God.—Expos. Bib.

The 9th verse contains a beautiful specimen of submissiveness and patient endurance of suffering, from a humbling conviction of the demerit of sin; accompanied by the firm persuasion that when the chastisement had answered its end, Jehovah would graciously afford deliverance.—Henderson.

"Where is Your God?"—A Nonconformist minister, Mr. Norman, had been condemned to lie in Ilchester gaol for preaching. On his way thither the officers stopped to rest at the sheriff's house. Lady Warre, the sheriff's wife, came to look at the prisoner, and to insult him with cruel words, saying, "Where is your God now, Mr. Norman?" "Madam," he replied, "have you a Bible in the house?" "Yes; we are not so heathenish as to be without a Bible." On getting it into his hands, he turned to Micah and read the words, "Rejoice not against me, O mine enemy: when I fall, I shall arise; when I sit in darkness, the Lord shall be a light unto me. I will bear the indignation of the Lord, because I have sinned against Him, until He plead my cause, and execute judgment for me: He will bring me forth to the light, and I shall behold His righteousness. Then she that is mine enemy shall see it, and shame shall cover her which said unto me, Where is the Lord thy God? mine eyes shall behold her: now shall she be trodden down as the mire of the streets." The lady retired silenced, and the dealings of God with her family soon made this warning to be noted and remembered.—Old Test. Anec.

11—13. (11) **In the day,** etc., Spk. Com., "a day for building thy walls is at hand." Zion is represented as a vineyard whose walls have been broken down. **shall the decree,** etc., Camb. B., "shall the bound be afar off;" i. e. the boundaries of Isr. shall be widely extended.[b] Isa. xxxiii. 17 R. V. (12) **he shall come,** or they shall come; prob. meaning that from all districts the dispersed of Israel should come to Zion. **from the fortified cities,** etc., R. V., "the cities of Egypt, and from Egypt even to the River" (i. e. the Euphrates. **from sea to sea,** from the Mediterranean to the Persian Gulf, Joel ii. 20. **from mountain to mountain,** from Sinai to Lebanon. (13) **land,** or earth, as opposed to the kingdom of heaven, the Church of God. Some think the ref. is to the intervening period of desolation for Palestine before the restoration from the captivity.

Earnestness of a Convinced Sinner.—If a man knew that the ship in which he and his family were sailing, and which contained all his property, was leaking day and night, do you suppose he would be careless about it? Would he not be constantly baling out the water lest it should sink the vessel with its precious freight? If a man understood that a spark from the flue of the furnace had set fire to the timber of his dwelling, and that, smothered, it was creeping along and charring the wains-

[a] Ps. xxxvii. 24; Pr. xxiv. 16.

"Lean not on earth; 'twill pierce thee to the heart; a broken reed at best, but oft a spear; On its sharp point peace bleeds, and hope expires."
—Young.

"Dost thou know what friendship is? 'Tis not the fawning cringe, the studied smile, the oil-smooth speech, big word or solemn vow; it is a sacred ray of heav'nly love; like that, rejoicing in the good of others, it scorns the narrow bounds of selfishness, and knows no bliss sincere but social joy; simple and plain, it shines in naked truth, and opens all the sluices of the heart." —Hawkins.

Mr. Finney tells of a blacksmith whose agony became so great at thought of the condition of the Church and of sinners, that he could not work; so locked up his shop, and spent the afternoon in prayer. This was followed by a powerful revival.

[b] "In a spiritual sense this began to be fulfilled on the day of Pentecost, when multitudes from Assyria and Egypt were received by the Apostles into the Church of Christ."
—Wordsworth.

"There are two sorts of hypocrites; one that are deceived with their outward morality and external religion; and the other are those that are deceived with false discoveries and elevations; which often cry down works, and men's own righteousness, and talk much of

coting and partition, do you suppose he would content himself merely with saying, "I have no doubt that this house is on fire, and that it is dangerous?" Would he not do something? Many men read the Bible and say, "My dear children, we are all sinful; we are sold in sin; may God lead us out of our sinfulness, and draw us toward Him!" and yet they put forth no effort to reform their lives. And when a man is touched by the Spirit of God, and he is made conscious that the fires of hell are in him, with what earnestness does he enter upon a course of repentance! How does he say, "God have mercy on me! Help me; teach me; lead me!"—H. W. Beecher.

14, 15. (14) **feed,** as before, in the sense of a shepherd's ordering, providing, and ruling. **rod,** the shepherd's staff or crook. **solitarily,** or apart from the enemies, Num. xxiii. 9. **in the wood,** with the idea of safety and cool repose. **Bashan and Gilead,**[b] districts noted for their rich pastures. (15) **days .. Egypt,** this Divine deliverance is constantly referred to as altogether a model deliverance.[c]

Wonder.—Coleridge says that "in wonder all philosophy began, in wonder it ends, and admiration fills up the interspace; but the first wonder is the offspring of ignorance, and the last is the parent of devotion." There is great inconsistency in man's wonder. He will sometimes wonder at the works of man, but not at the works of God. How often does an archway of more than the ordinary span and beauty excite his "wonder;" while the arch of the heavens with a span measureless and a beauty Divine is looked upon with cold indifference. A piece of human mechanism calls forth his "wonder," while the marvelous structure of his own body is seldom or ever contemplated with interest.—John Bate.

16, 17. (16) **see,** God's deliverance. **their might,** wh. they shall feel bears no comparison with God's.[a] **hand upon their mouth,** etc., in astonishment and consternation. (17) this vs. describes the terror and humiliation of the enemies. **shall be afraid,** etc., R. V., "shall come with fear unto the Lord our God."

Hearers.—1. The inattentive hearer that taketh very little heed to what he heareth; 2. The inconsiderate hearer, that never ponders what he hears, nor compares one thing with another; 3. The injudicious hearer, that never makes any judgment, whether it be true or false; 4. The unapprehensive hearer, who hears all his days, but is never the wiser; 5. The stupid unaffected hearer, that is as a rock and stone under the Word; 6. There are your prejudiced, disaffected hearers, who hear with dislike, especially those things which relate to practice; 7. Your fantastical, voluptuous hearers, that hear only to please their fancy or imaginations: they come on purpose to try if they can hear a pretty sentence, any fine jingle, any flashes of wit; 8. Your notional hearers, that are of somewhat a higher form and sect than the others: they always come to learn some kind of novelty; 9. Those talkative persons, who only come to hear, that they may furnish themselves with notions for the sake of discourse; 10. The censorious and critical hearers, who come on purpose not as doers of the law, but as judges; 11. Malicious hearers, that come on purpose to seek an advantage against those they come to hear, particularly from what they preach. Thus you see the characters of those who are "hearers only," which are various and manifold.—Howe.

The Glory of Christianity.—We cannot keep ourselves; our lamps are only of a certain little size, and our oil is but a spoonful, and there is no independence in man; we live and move, and have our being in God. No man can go to the fountain once for all and take out water enough to keep his life going evermore. He may take his vessel full of water, and may quench his thirst for the moment, but he must keep the way to the fountain always open; never shut up the road: you are full and you abound for the present, but the time of necessity and of pain will inevitably recur. Here is the glory of Christianity: it provides for all time and for all need; it is the salt of the earth, it is the light of the world, it is the disinfector of all pestilential atmosphere.—Peop. Bib.

18—20. (18) **who,** etc., Ex. xv. 11. **pardoneth,** etc., Ex. xxxiv. 6, 7. (19) **subdue our iniquities,** sins are personified as enemies as in Gen. iv. 7; Ps. lxv. 3. **cast .. sea,** Ps. ciii. 12. "Buried out of sight in eternal oblivion." (20) **perform,** carry into full effect.[b] **truth,** or sure promise. **mercy,** or gracious promise.[c]

free grace; but at the same time make a righteousness of their discoveries, and of their humiliation, and exalt themselves to heaven with them."—Edwards.

b "The expressions denote that the Jews shall enjoy full and free possession of their land after their return to it, with the same security and happiness with which they possessed it in their most flourishing state under the reigns of David and Solomon."—Lowth.

c Ps. lxxviii. 12, 13; Je. xvi. 14, 15.

a "Once they had eagerly drunk in all rumors as so many messages of victories, but then they shall be afraid of hearing them, because they continually fear new disasters, when they see the God of Israel to be so powerful."—Calvin.

"This is what society comes to without God. Lose the religious element, and society falls to pieces. Society thinks not; for a time society thinks it can keep itself very well together but experience shows that when the morale of society goes down, its money securities are waste paper." — People's Bible.

b Comp. Ge. xii. 2, xxvi. 24, xxviii. 13.

"The unchangeable promise implied an engagement that the seed of the patriarchs should never perish, and should be restored to their inheritance as often as they turned wholly to God."—Fausset.

c Lu. i. 70—74.

Divine Mercy (vs. 18).—I. The greatness of God's mercy as it is manifested in the Gospel. 1. He pardons; 2. He passes over; 3. He retaineth not His anger; 4. He delights. II. The exercise of God's mercy toward penitent believers. 1. He turns again; 2. He will have compassion; 3. He will subdue; 4. He will cast into the sea. III. The confirmation of God's mercy derived from the covenant of grace. 1. The relation between the Abrahamic covenant and the covenant of grace; 2. The harmony of mercy with truth in the covenant of grace.

God's Abundant Pardon.—There are two ways of covering sin, man's way and God's way. You cover your sins and they will have a resurrection some time; let God cover them, and neither devil nor man can find them. There are four expressions in the Bible with regard to where God puts sins. He puts them behind His back. If God has forgiven me, who shall bring a charge against me? He has blotted them out as a thick cloud. You see a cloud to-night, and tomorrow there isn't a cloud to be seen. He casts them into the depths of the sea. Some one has said, "Thank God that it is a sea and not a river; a river might dry up, but the sea cannot." The greatest blessing that ever comes to me this side of heaven, is when God forgives me. Have you been forgiven? The fourth expression is that he removes them "as far as the east is from the west." Do you know how far that is? Perhaps some good mathematician will figure that up. "If we confess our sins, He is faithful and just to forgive us our sins and to cleanse us from all unrighteousness." Then make sure that you are forgiven.—D. L. Moody.

Abundant Pardon.—It is His promise not only to pardon ordinary sins, but those also which be as scarlet, and red like crimson. It is His free compassion to cast all our sins into the depths of the sea. Now, the sea, by reason of his vastness, can drown as well mountains as molehills: the boundless ocean of God's mercies can swallow up our mightiest sins much more. It is His merciful power to blot out our sins as a cloud. Now, the strength of the summer's sun is able to scatter the thickest fog, as well as the thinnest mist—nay, to drive away the darkest midnight; the irresistible heat of God's free love shining through the Sun of Righteousness upon a penitent soul, to dissolve to nothing the desperatest work of darkness and most horrible sin, far more easily. But this mystery of mercy and miracle of God's free love is a jewel only for truly humbled souls. Let no stranger to the life of godliness meddle with it. Let no swine trample it under his feet.—Bolton.

Verse 20.—The return from captivity, while it furnished a striking specimen of the covenanted fidelity and kindness of Jehovah, was only preliminary to the infinitely greater display of those attributes in the mission of the Messiah, the Seed of Abraham, in whom all the families of the earth were to be blessed. The words of this verse are quoted with scarcely any variation, in the inspired song of Zacharias, with direct application to Him of whom His Son had just been born to be the forerunner, Luke i. 72, 73.—Henderson.

Pardon of Sin.—

Darkness, the world, the flesh, spiritual sin,
With such infectious stains thy soul defile,
No earthly spring can wash thy conscience clean,
The streams of Ganges, or the floods of Nile.
The secret source of what in thee is vile
Heaven's grace alone can fitly purge away;
Turn to thy Saviour then, in lowly style,
Ask for forgiveness, all thy sins display,
Cling to the Cross in faith, weep, tremble, praise, and pray.

Forgiveness.—

Why, all the souls that were, were forfeit once;
And He that might the vantage best have took,
Found out the remedy. How would you be,
If He which is the top of judgment, should
But judge you as you are? O think on that!
And mercy then will breathe within your life,
Like man new made.—Shakespeare.

"Go to the prisoner in his cell under sentence of death; show him the royal mandate proclaiming his pardon, properly signed and sealed; knock off his galling fetters; open his prison doors and introduce him once more to the forfeited sunshine of heaven. What transports of rapture would thrill through his heart, when, in the consciousness of pardon, he rejoiced in the light of liberty! But how much greater cause of joy has the pardoned sinner, called out of darkness into marvelous light, renovated by the Holy Spirit, and fitted for the joys of heaven!"—W. J. Brock.

Tell me the distance from the east to the west and I will tell you the distance which the pardoned sinner is from sin. It is a casting them into the "depths of the sea." Not on the shore. to be washed back by the incoming waves, but into the "depths." Into the abysses of some mighty Atlantic, where no storms shall stir them up, no trump shall wake them from their graves. "In those days, saith the Lord, the iniquity of Israel shall be sought for, and shall not be found." — Pulpit Com.

Introduction.

I. **Author.** Nahum, = "the consoler." When he is called the Elkoshite, no doubt the place of his nativity is referred to. Three positions have been suggested for this place: (1) The modern Al-Kush, a town 24 miles north of the site of Nineveh; (2) Jerome claims Eleese, a small village in Galilee, as the birthplace; (3) A third tradition places Elkosh in the south of Judah. "These conflicting traditions leave the prophet's birthplace quite uncertain," though some things in the book itself seem to favor the location in Judah. II. **Time.** "There are two fixed points between which the date of the prophecy must lie: the capture of No Amon or Thebes by the armies of Assurbanipal, cir. 664—2, and the destruction of Nineveh by the Medes, cir. 608—6. Some event or some combination of powers menacing to Nineveh, falling within these fifty or sixty years, must have given occasion to the oracle, for the catastrophe to No Amon referred to can hardly be any other than its capture by the Assyrians. A date 610—8 for the prophecy, is well within the range of possibility." (Cambridge Bible). III. **Style.** "The prophet's language is forcible and graphic, and his descriptions condensed and brilliant. He is animated by the intensest hatred of Assyria. In ch. i. there are elements of patriotism in this feeling; in ch. ii. iii., it is purer and simply human. The prophecy is the voice of the human mind expressing its revolt against the spirit and deeds of the brutal foe of the human race, and might almost have come from the heart of any of the oppressed nationalities trodden under the foot of Assyria. It is the blood, the wiles and demonic witchcrafts (iii. 1—4), and the spirit of the wild beast (ii. 11—13) that in the name of mankind the prophet appeals against; and if he adds the traffic and riches and luxury of Nineveh, it is only to complete the picture of the immoral spirit of the people. This universal voice of humanity is no new thing in Hebrew prophecy; it is heard in Am. i., ii.; even more distinctly in a contemporary of Nahum, Hab. i. 12—17, and all down history, as in Is. xiv. 5—8, xlvii. 7—15, and many psalms. And the prophet is assured that the voice of mankind is also the voice of God: 'Behold, I am against thee, saith the Lord of Hosts, and I will cut off thy prey from the earth, and the voice of thine emissaries shall no more be heard' (ii. 13)" (Camb. Bib.)

Synopsis.

(From the Pulpit Commentary.)

PART I—The judgment upon Nineveh decreed by God .... i. 1—15

Sec. 1. The heading of the book....... i. 1

Sec. 2. The Divine justice is described, and the irresistible power of God illustrated by his control of the material world .... i. 2—6

Sec. 3. But the wrath of God falls not on those who trust in him; it is reserved for his enemies generally...... i. 7—11

Sec. 4. And especially for Nineveh, which shall be utterly destroyed, while Zion shall rejoice at the joyful news of its ruin, and keep her feasts in safety .... i. 12—15

PART II—The execution of the decree; the destruction of Nineveh........ ii. 1—13

Sec. 1. Nineveh shall be besieged, because God is about to exalt his people by taking vengeance on the enemy, whose defence is of no avail.......... ii. 1—8

Sec. 2. The city is plundered, and lies waste in terrible contrast with its former excellency .... ii. 9—13

PART III—The cause of the judgment—the sins of the city, which bring inevitable punishment .... iii. 1—19

Sec. 1. The crimes that have brought this fate upon Nineveh............ iii. 1—7

Sec. 2. The ruin can be no more averted than was that of No-Amon.... iii. 8—13

Sec. 3. In spite of all its efforts and all its resources, it will meet with a terrible end .... iii. 14—19

CHAPTER THE FIRST.

1—3. (1) **burden,** R. V. marg., "oracle concerning. **Nineveh,** see the earlier mission of Jonah to this city.[a] **Nahum,** meaning consolation. A Prophet not otherwise known. **Elkoshite,** poss. a village in Judah.[b] (2) **jealous,** Ex. xx. 5. **revengeth,** better, avengeth. **furious,** R. V., "full of wrath."[c] **reserveth .. enemies,** holdeth it till His own appointed times. (3) **slow to anger,** Ex. xxxiv. 6, 7. **way .. feet,** comp. Ps. xviii. 7, xcvii. 2. "Large as the clouds are He treads on them, as a man would on the small dust."

God's Forbearance (vs. 3).—It seems as if the Prophet meant, God is slow to anger because He is great in power. This leads us to think of—I. His exquisite sensibility. II. His abhorrence of sin. III. His provocation by the world. IV. His right to do whatever He pleases.—Thomas.

The Prophet Nahum arose probably in Judah, if not about the same time as Zephaniah and Jeremiah, then a few years later. Whether he prophesied before or after the great Reform of 621 we have no means of deciding. His book does not reflect the inner history, character or merits of his generation. His sole interest is the fate of Nineveh. Zephaniah had also doomed the Assyrian capital, yet he was much more concerned with Israel's unworthiness of the opportunity presented to them. The yoke of Asshur, he saw, was to be broken, but the same cloud which was bursting from the north upon Nineveh must overwhelm the incorrigible people of Jehovah. For this Nahum has no thought. His heart, for all its bigness, holds room only for the bitter memories, the baffled hopes, the unappeased hatreds of a hundred years. And that is why we need not be anxious to fix his date upon one or other of the shifting phases of Israel's history during that last quarter of the seventh century. For he represents no single movement of his fickle people's progress, but the passion of the whole epoch then drawing to a close. Nahum's book is one great At Last! And, therefore, while Nahum is a worse prophet than Zephaniah, with less conscience and less insight, he is a greater poet, pouring forth the exultation of a people long enslaved, who see their tyrant ready for destruction. His language is strong and brilliant; his rhythm rumbles and rolls, leaps and flashes, like the horsemen and chariots he describes.—Expos. Bible.——The Burden.—There is a sense in which every prophet must make a burden of his work. If he himself had to do it all it would be nothing but burden. Instead of idealizing the word, making it poetical, bringing up before the eye of the mind some stalwart pilgrim carrying his easy load upon his shoulder, think of it as a man whose heart is sore because of the wickedness of the people, whose sleep is taken away from him because night is turned into a day of wickedness and wrath. Think of a man who has more to say than he can utter, whose tongue cannot keep pace with his heart because his heart is full of the thunder and lightning of judgment, and full of the music and pathos of gospel, and would utter itself incoherently, paradoxically, so that men not versed in this species of eloquence would say, What doth this babbler exclaim? for now he thunders, and now he whispers, and now he storms like a whirlwind, and now he cries like a broken-hearted mother. What would he be at? Yet through all this whirl and tumult and conflict must men come before they can understand what the old prophets had to do in the name and strength of God. —Peop. Bib.

4—6. (4) **rebuketh the sea,** Ex. xiv. 21; Ps. civ. 7—9. **maketh it dry,** Ps. xviii. 15. **Bashan,** etc., the hot wind which withers wooded Bashan and Carmel and Lebanon is the fiery breath of Jehovah. **Lebanon,** see Is. xxxiii. 9.[a] (5) **is burned,** R. V., "is upheaved;" lifts itself up, as with earthquake. (6) **poured .. fire,** as in a volcanic eruption. **rocks .. down,**[b] or burst asunder. Referring to the great convulsions of nature.

The Anger and the Goodness (vss. 6, 7).—I. Jehovah's anger—1. Righteous; 2. Terrible; 3. Real; 4. Inexorable. II. Jehovah's goodness —1. Sincere; 2. Powerful; 3. Watchful; 4. Unchanging. Improvement:

a Dr. Prideaux places the taking of Nineveh in the twenty-ninth year of king Josiah.

b "According to S. Jerome, El-Kosh was a village in Galilee, and his tomb was shown at Bethogabra near Emmaus. But as his prophecies were written after the captivity of the ten tribes, the tradition which points to his death in an Assyrian village may have some probability. Layard visited a village called Alkosh, which contains a so-called tomb of Nahum."—Bib. Things.

c "One who, if He pleases, can most readily give effect to His fury."—Grotius.

"There never was a saint yet that grew proud of his fine feathers, but what the Lord plucked them out by and by; there never yet was an angel that had pride in his heart, but he lost his wings, and fell into Gehenna, as Satan and those fallen angels did; and there shall never be a saint who indulges self-conceit and pride and self-confidence, but the Lord will spoil his glories, and trample his honors in the mire. —Spurgeon.

a "There is nothing in the world so blooming that God cannot change it when He is wroth."—Fausset.

b "As Hannibal burst asunder the Alpine rocks by fire to make a passage for his army."—Grotius.

—(1) In the great day of His wrath who shall be able to stand? (2) He is longsuffering to usward, not willing that any should perish, but that all should come to repentance.—H. Bonar.

God—a God of Nature.—History is the root out of which God grows flowers and wheat, great trees and flowerets that little children may gather with their tiny hands. We protest against the division of the God of nature and the God of grace, the God of nature and the God of revelation, as if only atheists or agnostics had to do with the God of nature, whilst Christians were worshiping some totally distinct being. Christians claim both. Nature and revelation are God in two volumes. Is he a wise reader who, having been entranced in the first volume of the drama, simply declines to read the second? What shall we say of his entrancement when he flushes with the purple of wonder, and expands under the enthusiasm of delighted gratitude, because he has read the first volume, but says he will have nothing to do with the volume that succeeds it? Such indifference to the succeeding volume throws suspicion upon the reality of his admiration when he offers that mockery to volume one. In Nahum you find the God of the book and the God of nature, the God of moral attributes and the God of majestic revelation, in the forms, the palpitations, and the changing colors of this dissolving scene.—Peop. Bib.

A Dearth of Good Men.—The prophet, speaking in the name of the godly remnant of the land, laments their terrible isolation. We are thus reminded of the sad condition of a land in which there is a dearth of good men. For: 1. They are the choice fruit of the land—wholesome, fragrant, delicious. The ideal Israel is compared to "grapes" and "the first ripe in the fig tree" (Hos. ix. 10). The Lord "taketh pleasure" in such; they satisfy the hunger of the Divine heart for godliness in the creature (Ps. cxlvii. 11; cxlix. 4; Prov. xi. 20). So far as they share the spirit of Christ, they are, like Him, "beloved of God," and should be attractive to men. 2. They are the salt of the earth—the one element that preserves from universal corruption.—Pulp. Com.——The Fall of Nineveh.—When Nahum prophesied, Assyria was at the height of its prosperity. No enemy in its neighborhood was left unsubdued; the distant Egypt had submitted to its arms; Phœnicia and Cyprus owned its sway; Judæa paid annual tribute; commercial enterprise had drawn unto it the riches of all nations. No one at this epoch could have foreseen the speedy end of this prosperity. Nahum needed a single-hearted courage and a full persuasion of the truth of his misison to denounce the crimes of this flourishing kingdom, and to proclaim its coming downfall. In fifty years the end came. A combination of enemies overthrew this mighty empire. On the death of Assurbanipal matters began to assume a dangerous attitude. Egypt rose against its former conqueror; Babylon revolted, the Medes, now become a powerful monarchy, prepared to attack Nineveh. The reigning monarch (whose name is uncertain), the successor of Assurbanipal, himself marched against the latter, sending Nabopolassar to recover Babylon. The Medes were defeated, and for a time driven back. Nabopolassar also was successful, and received as a reward for his services the title of King of Babylon. Here he managed affairs so skilfully, and strengthened himself so effectually, that, after fifteen years, he found himself able to throw off the Assyrian yoke, and to establish his own independence. The Medes. meantime, under Cyaxares, had recovered from their late defeat, and were only deterred from attacking Nineveh by an inroad of the Scythians into their own country. In order to strengthen his position, Nabopolassar made alliance with all the enemies of Assyria, and became the ruling spirit of a strong confederacy, which comprised Medes and Persians, Egyptians, Armenians, and other nations, all animated with the fierce desire of revenging themselves on Assyria. Josiah of Judah, as a tributary prince, was drawn into the contest, and fell at Megiddo, while endeavoring to arrest the advance of the Egyptian army. About B. C. 612 the allied forces attacked Nineveh, but were repulsed with loss. Victory for some time hovered over the Assyrians; but the enemy, reinforced from Bactria, proved irresistible. The Ninevites, fearing for their final safety, attempted to escape from the city. They were, however,

"The developments of pride are numerous and often unsuspected as to their real character. The love of dress and display; the undue deference to the opinions of others, which leads us to adopt forms of speech and modes of action foreign to our usages; the man-fearing spirit which imposes silence in reference to our religion in social circles, and particularly the sentiment which ignores all physical manifestations in connection with religious experience—these are all the offshoots of the one great principle— pride of heart." — S. H. Platt.

Vers. 3 4. This passage is so sublime, says one, that it would be difficult to find its equal. May the reader's heart adore the God before whom the unconscious earth and sky act as if they recognized their Maker, and were moved with a tremor of reverence. "Vain are the attempts of men to conceal anything from Him whose word unbars the deep, and lifts the doors of earth from their hinges! Vain are all hopes of resistance, for a whisper of his voice makes the whole earth quail in abject terror."— Spurgeon.

"What if a body might have all the pleasures in the world for asking? Who would so unman himself, as by accepting them, to desert his soul, and become a perpetual slave to his senses?"— Seneca.

overtaken, and again shut up within their walls. Here they valiantly defended themselves for more than two years, when a circumstance, against which no remedy availed, laid them at the mercy of the besiegers. An unusually heavy and long-continued flood of the river Tigris carried away a large section of the huge rampart that surrounded the city. Through the gap thus formed the enemy forced their way within the walls and captured the place. The king, rather than fall into the hands of his implacable foes, gathered his wives and his treasure into the palace, and burned himself with them there; the town was sacked, and a great number of the inhabitants were massacred.—Pulpit Com.

"Though sages may pour out their wisdom's treasure, there is no sterner moralist than pleasure."— Byron.

7—10. (7) **good,** in the sense of being gracious and long-suffering. **stronghold,** Pr. xviii. 10. **knoweth,** so as to care for.[a] (8) **flood,** the frequent fig. for Divine judgments. **the place thereof,** or "her place," i. e. Nineveh's.[b] (9) **affliction,** or the stroke. It should be so complete as to need no renewal. Once should suffice. (10) **folden .. thorns,** wh. tangled together may seem to make an impregnable hedge. **while they be drunken,** etc., R. V., "and be drenched as it were in their drink." **devoured,** by fire.[c]

a. Ps. i. 6; 2 Ti. ii. 19.

b "The populous imperial city should become a perpetual desolation, according to the vivid prediction of another prophet, Zeph. ii. 13, 14, 15."—Spk. Com.

c "These thorns, esp. the kind called bellan, wh. covers the whole country, and is that wh. is thus burned, to clear the ground, are so folden together as to be utterly inseparable, and being united by thousands of small intertwining branches, when the torch is applied they flash and flame instantly like stubble full dry."—Thomson.

The Vengeance of the Lord.—The Proem to the Book of Nahum is thoroughly Oriental in its sense of God's method and resources of destruction; very Jewish and very natural to that age of Jewish history, in the bursting of its long-pent hopes of revenge. We of the West might express these hopes differently. We should not attribute so much personal passion to the Avenger. With our keener sense of law, we should emphasize the slowness of the process, and select for its illustration the forces of decay rather than those of sudden ruin. But we must remember the crashing times in which the Jews lived. The world was breaking up. The elements were loose, and all that God's own people could hope for was the bursting of their yoke, with a little shelter in the day of trouble. The elements were loose, but amidst the blind crash the people little knew that Jehovah knew them.—Expos. B.——Man Powerless before God.—When God shakes men as dust from under the summer thrashing-floor, the right hand of a man's strength is as powerless as the left hand of a man's weakness, and his wisdom is as folly. What avails the wisdom of the apple to make it cling to the bough when it is ripe in autumn time? or the wisdom of the leaf to hold it fast to the stem when the tempest calls? or the wisdom of the tree to make it stand secure when a rock from the cliff comes crashing down through its puny branches? When God sends storms upon men, they must imitate the humble grass, which saves itself by lying down. Therefore it is said, "Humble yourselves before the mighty hand of God, that in due season he may raise you up."—H. W. Beecher.——Dasher in Pieces.—Demetrius was surnamed Poliorcestes, the destroyer of cities; Attilas called himself Orbis flagellum, the scourge of the world. Julius Cæsar was Fulmen belli, the thunderbolt of war; he had taken in his time a thousand towns, conquered three hundred nations, took prisoners one million of men, and slain as many. These were dissipatores indeed, and dashers in pieces, rods of God's wrath; and this they took to be a main piece of their glory.—Trapp.——The Lord a Stronghold.—From whence does this trouble arise? From danger? He is our strength for protection. "The Lord is the strength of my life, of whom shall I be afraid?" "We are more than conquerors." From duty? He is the strength to assist. If oppressed with a sense of our inability, "our sufficiency is of God." From affliction? He is our strength to support and deliver. If he does not release, he sustains and comforts. "My grace is sufficient for thee." Whatever the nature and degree of affliction, in God we find a "very present help in the day of trouble."—Jay.

Vs. 7. J. Milner, ii. 47; E. Cooper, v. 50.

"He who begins by halving his heart between God and mammon will end by being wholehearted for the world and faint-hearted for Christ." — A. J. Gordon.

11—15. (11) **one .. thee,** Sennacherib out of Nineveh.[a] **wicked counsellor,** Heb. "a counsellor of Belial." (12) **quiet,** etc., R. V., "Though they be in full strength and likewise many, even so shall they be cut down and he shall pass away." The Assyrian army shall be destroyed and Sennacherib shall flee. **cut down,** Is. xvii. 12—14. **no more,** by the hand of the Assyrian. (13) **break .. sunder,** comp. Is. x. 27. (14) **concerning thee,** the address seems to be to the Assyrian people; they shall become extinct. (15) **mountains,** etc., comp. Is. lii. 7. Here the language expresses the general rejoicing, and sense of safety, after the overthrow

a Is. xxxvi. 14—20.

"The roses of pleasure seldom last long enough to adorn the brow of him who plucks them, and they are the only roses which do not retain their sweetness after they have lost their beauty."—Blair.

of Sennacherib's army. **keep .. feasts,** this they could not do while the enemy was in the land.

The Song of Peace is a strange one to be heard amid the wars and contentions of earth, and the discordant tumults of the human heart, restless as the sea. Yet Jesus has brought peace to the earth,—peace between man and God, resulting in peace between man and man, and the soul's peace with itself and with its surroundings, and with the law of God,—peace such as the world cannot give and the world cannot take away. This peace is the fruit of the gospel in each soul that receives it, and the ultimate result of the gospel in all the world. And even now the rays of this peace are illuminating the mountain-tops of human experience.—Peloubet's Notes.——Peace, newly granted by the grace of God, was to be celebrated by a new consecration of the people. This has special reference to the king of Nineveh and Assyria, and the promise must have been very precious to contemporaries oppressed by Assyria. But to us the fundamental truth is far more important, that to the people of God a perfect deliverance is near at hand, and has already appeared in Christ, by which the Belial, from whom every wicked spirit proceeds, is forever cast out.—Lange.

"Come, and begin Thy reign
Of everlasting peace;
Come, take the kingdom to Thyself,
Great King of Righteousness."—Bonar.

"It was related of an atheist who was dying that he appeared very uncomfortable, unhappy and frightened. Another atheist who stood at his bedside said to him, 'Don't be afraid. Hold on, man; hold on to the last.' The dying man said, 'That is what I want to do, but tell me what to hold on to.' "—D. L. Moody.

CHAPTER THE SECOND.

1, 2. (1) dasheth in pieces, or the scatterer; a poetical name for the besieger, who should destroy the kingdom of Assyria, whose capital was Nineveh.[a] **keep,** etc., do all you can, in your self-confidence: you will need it all, and yet all will be in vain. The advice is ironical. (2) **turned away,** R. V., "bringeth again." The destruction of Nineveh is deliverance and prosperity to Jacob, i. e. Judah. **emptiers,** or Assyrian spoilers. **vine branches,** Ps. lxxx. 8—16.[b]

Example of the Watchcare of God.—David Zeisberger was traveling with several Christian Indians. They went to sleep, one night, in a room where several barrels of gunpowder were stored, grains of which were scattered about the floor. The host urged them not to take a candle in the room, but yielded, on a promise of the utmost caution. The missionaries went to sleep. A traveler who had the candle in special charge forgot to extinguish it. In the morning Zeisberger called out one of his brethren, and said, "Had we not had the eye of Him upon us who never slumbereth or sleepeth, we should all have been this night precipitated into eternity. I slept soundly, being extremely fatigued, and was in my first sleep, when I felt as if some one roused me. I sat up, and saw the wick of the candle hanging down on one side, in a flame, and on the point of falling into the straw, which I was just in time to prevent. I could not fall asleep again, but lay awake silently thanking the Lord for the extraordinary preservation we had experienced."

Cause of the War.—The Assyrians had oppressed God's people. They had abused their power in the chastisement of Israel, plundered the people, and outrageously destroyed their vines. Now the emptiers must be emptied, and those who chastised others must be chastised themselves. "Power abused brings a curse upon its possessors. Power gives temptation, which in turn sets aside honor, social duty, law, and right; creates abuse; and abuse, strife, confusion, retribution, bloodshed, sin."—Bailey.

[a] Lit. "The hammer is come up against thee. See Je. i. 23.

[b] Reference is to the evils inflicted on Sennacherib's first invasion of Palestine.

"Pleasure must first have the warrant that it is without sin; and then the measure that it is without excess."—Adams.

"Thou mayest choose whether thou wilt be remembered to thy praise or to thy shame."—Bishop Pilkington.

"He left a name, at which the world grew pale, to point a moral, or adorn a tale."—Samuel Johnson.

"Pleasure soon exhausts us and itself also; but endeavor never does."—Richter.

3—5. (3) description of the hostile army "in the day of its preparation, i. e. before engaging the Ninevites. The pronoun, "his" mighty men, refers to the destroyer of Nineveh mentioned in vs. 1. From vs. 3 to vs. 7 all the tenses should be in the present, as R. V. **made red,** in the Nineveh monuments, the shields and dresses of the warriors are generally painted red.[a] **in scarlet,** the Oriental military cloak. **flaming torches,** R. V., "the chariots flash with steel." **fir trees,** or spears made

[a] "The ancients dyed their bull's hide shields red, partly to strike terror into the enemy, chiefly lest the blood from wounds wh. they might receive should be perceived and give confidence to him." — Calvin.

of fir wood. (4) **rage,** or are driven furiously. **streets,** this might be translated "fields," as in Job v. 10. (5) **He shall recount his worthies,** Camb. B., "He bethinketh himself of his worthies (or valiant men)." This 5th vs. seems to describe the defensive action of the Ninevites. **they .. well,** the Ninevites, hurrying to the wall, see the towers for the rams, and other preparations for the siege.[b]

The siege was no easy task. History declares that the king, at the approach of the enemy, collected all his active forces—that the besieging army was three times severely defeated, and that the Medes could only be held with great difficulty to the work. The Assyrians abandoned themselves to negligent rejoicing in the camps before the gates on account of victory, but were attacked in the night and driven back to the walls. Salæmenes, brother-in-law to the king, who had resigned the command to him, was driven into the Tigris (cf. ch. iii. 3); but the city was still uninjured, and the enemy encamped in vain before the gates. In the spring of the third year other powers interfered. The river became "an enemy to the city" (cf. ii. 7; i. 8—10). The inundation occurred suddenly, and violently broke down in one night the walls on the river. The king despaired of his life, and having sent his family to the north, shut himself up with all his treasures, and burned himself in the royal citadel. Immense booty was carried away. The city was plundered, sacked, and set on fire.—Lange, Introd. to Nahum.

6, 7. (6) **rivers** the streams and canals fed by the Tigris. As these led into the city, their seizure was of the utmost advantage to the enemy. The "gates of the rivers" are probably not city gates situated on the rivers, but rather the points in the wall where the rivers or canals enter the city.—Camb. B. **dissolved,** with fear and terror. (7) **Huzzab,** etc., Expos. B., "Huzzab is stripped, is brought forth, with her maids sobbing like doves, beating their breasts." Huzzab prob. refers to the queen. Isa. xlvii. 2, 3. **maids .. doves,** or "with dove-like plaints."[a] **tabering,** beating on their breasts, as sign of distress and grief.

The city of Nineveh lay on the left or E. side of the Tigris. The city proper was of the form of an irregular parallelogram, stretching from N. W. to S. E., the broader end being on the N. This city proper was enclosed by walls protected by moats. It was only at the N. W. point that the city touched the Tigris, from which it gradually retreated to the S. E., leaving between it and the river a considerable space of territory, though an arm of the river again approached the city at the S. W. corner of the parallelogram. Billerbeck computes the length of the north wall at 2,000 mètres (6,561 feet), that of the south wall at 800 m., and the length of the east wall N. to S. at 5,000 m., and conjectures that there was room in the city for 300,000 inhabitants. Through the city ran a mountain stream, the Choser, cutting the city into two parts and falling into the Tigris, and from this stream and other streams and canals from the hills on the N. E. was drawn the water that filled the moats as well as the water supply of the city, the Tigris being unsuited for drinking. Besides the walls of the city proper with their moats there were extensive outer defenses. A wall ran along the east bank of the Tigris, and an immense rampart protected the city on the east side, between which and the city walls rose various kinds of fortifications. These outer walls were also protected by moats. The moats did not wash the walls, but were trenches at some distance from them, and the walls could only be approached by drying the moats or throwing dams across them. The "gates of the rivers" are not city gates situated on the rivers, but rather the points in the wall where the rivers or canals enter the city. Such "gates" would be structures provided with sluices regulating the supply of water, and if these were opened the walls would be undermined or the city inundated.—Camb. Bib.

8—10. (8) **like a pool,** or as a city well watered. The river and streams formed a part of her defence and confidence. Or, the city may be compared to a pool on account of the multitude of her inhabitants.[a] **flee away,** their numbers not availing to preserve them. **stand,** the unheeded voice of those who would rally the fugitives. (9) **take ye,** addressed to the victors. **glory out of,** etc., R. V., "glory of all pleasant furniture." **pleasant furniture,** costly and luxurious things.[b] (10) **heart,**

[b] Some apply this vs. to the anxious efforts made by the defenders of the city.

"If thou art rich, thou art poor; for like an ass whose back with ingots bows, thou bearest thy heavy riches but a journey, and death unloads thee." — Shakespeare.

[a] Is. xxxviii. 14, lix. 11.

"In the depraved nature of man, pride is the radical reigning sin that first lives and last dies. . . A man may visibly despise the pomp and vanities of the world, and this may raise his esteem in the minds of real saints; and the outward practice of goodness will be productive of the praise of goodness in others; this will afford a strong temptation of pride. All the operations of virtues, even the exercise of humility, that are the matter and argument of praise, may be incentives of pride; and those diseases are extremely dangerous which are nourished by that food that is necessary to support life."—Dr. Bates.

"Conquerors proud, to seal her doom, swept her to ruin's all-engulfing tomb. Long ages past, and turf o'ergrew the walls, and silence reigned in Ninus' buried halls."

[a] Re. xvii. 1, 15.

[b] "The enemy may easily plunder the city of all its riches and costly furniture, for there is none to make any resistance."—Lowth.

The Roman soldiers at the sacking of Jerusalem entered the temple, and went into the sanctum sanctorum; but seeing no images tnere, as they used to have in their own idolatrous temples, gave out, in a jeer, that the Jews worshiped the clouds. So the worldling can see no pleasure in religion.

etc., Is. xiii. 7, 8. **gather blackness,** R. V., "are waxed pale." Joel ii. 6 R. V.

The Destruction of Nineveh.—The Medes and Persians were conquering Assyria (B. C. 625), and within twenty years Nineveh, its capital, was destroyed. It was slowly "bleeding to death in consequence of its many wars." Zephaniah's prophecy was fulfilled. Nineveh shall become so complete a desolation that "pelicans and hedge-hogs shall bivouac upon her chapiters, the owl shall hoot in her windows, and the crow croak upon the threshold. Crushed! desolate! and all that pass by shall hiss and wag their heads" (Zeph. ii. 12—15). She was so "swept with the besom of destruction that she vanished suddenly, like a dream when one awaketh; and those who passed over its ruins, like Xenophon and his ten thousand in B. C. 401, knew not what they were (Anab. iii., iv. 7)." Her very name had become forgotten in two centuries.—Farrar. ——And Napoleon encamped near its site and was not aware of it. It was not "till 1842 that the relics of her former splendor began to be revealed to the world," and confirm the mighty kingdom of God which twenty-five centuries before she had tried to destroy.—Peloubet's Notes.

11—13. (11) **where,** etc., the exclamation of surprise at the desolation of this famous city. **lions,** here used as emblems of majesty and strength. (12) **lion .. ravin,** fig. description of the way in wh. Nineveh had plundered the nations she subdued. (13) **against thee,** to bring upon thee the overwhelming judgments wh. their iniquity had so long called down. **messengers,** perhaps with allusion to such mockers as Rabshakeh.

Desolation of Nineveh.—"Where is the dwelling of the lions," etc. Great must be the desolation to call forth such an expression. Where indeed is the proud city? Its place was unknown for ages, and is only just discovered by the ruins which have been dug up. It was secure, the dwelling of the lions; spacious walked; and wealthy, the feeding-place of the young lions; but its battlements were destroyed and its glory departed. The dust of Nineveh is a witness for the truth of God, and a warning to the nations of the earth. "Assyria lies buried there with all its people; round about are their graves, all of them are slain and fallen by the sword; they have made their graves deep there below."—Hom. Com.

CHAPTER THE THIRD.

1—6. (1) **bloody city,** comp. 2 Sa. xvi. 7, xxi. 1. In the great Eastern cities life was little valued, and crimes of violence abounded.[a] **prey departeth not,** she ceases not to plunder. (2) **noise .. chariots,** this is what the Prophet sees in his vision. The figures describe the vigor of the enemies' attack. (3) **horseman,** or horse-soldier.[b] (4) **because,** etc.,[c] Nineveh was treacherous in dealing with other nations, and skilful in seducing them into idolatry. (5) **against thee,** ch. ii. 13. **discover,** etc., Is. xlvii. 2, 3; Je. xiii. 22, 26. (6) **cast,** etc., as on one put up to public dishonor. "Nineveh shall be like a vile woman, exposed to the insults and ill treatment of the rabble."

Geo. Adam Smith gives a spirited, though somewhat free, translation of the first vss. of chap. 3:—

Woe to the City of Blood,
All of her guile, robbery-full, ceaseless rapine!

Hark the whip,
And the rumbling of wheels!
Horses at the gallop,
And the rattling dance of the chariot!
Cavalry at the charge,
Flash of sabres, and lightning of lances!

The Besieger Besieged.—It is siege, irresistible and full of cruelty, which Assyria records as her own glory. Miles of sculpture are covered with masses of troops marching upon some Syrian or Median fortress.

[a] "Nineveh not only practiced cruelties, but handed the record of them down to posterity by representing them in all their horrors on the palace walls."—Rawlinson.

Jno. iii. 8.

[b] "Horsemen are seen in the most ancient sculptures of Nimrod. Disciplined bodies of cavalry were represented in the bas-reliefs of Kouyunjik. The horsemen were armed with swords and bows, or with swords and long spears; they wore short tunics, and their legs and feet were bare. When riding without pads or saddles they sat with their knees almost on a level with the horse's back."—Layard.

[c] 2 Ki. ix. 22.

"Great cities are often called harlots upon the account of those vices wh. prevail in them, and infect others by their example."—Lowth.

Scaling ladders and enormous engines are pushed forward to the walls under cover of a shower of arrows. There are assaults and breaches, panic-stricken and suppliant defenders. Streets and places are strewn with corpses, men are impaled, women led away weeping, children dashed against the stones. The Jews had seen, had felt these horrors for a hundred years, and it is out of their experience of them that Nahum weaves his exultant predictions. The Besieger of the world is at last besieged; every cruelty he has inflicted upon men is now to be turned upon himself. Again and again does Nahum return to the vivid details, —he hears the very whips crack beneath the walls, and the rattle of the leaping chariots; the end is slaughter, dispersion and a dead waste.—Exp. Bib.

7—12. (7) **flee,** in fear and loathing. **bemoan,** express sorrow for thy richly deserved calamities. (8) **No,** marg. No Amon, or Thebes in Upper Egypt.[a] **rivers,** i. e. arms, or canals, of the Nile. **sea,** usual term for considerable bodies of water. (9) **Ethiopia,** Heb. Cush. poss. at the time master of Upper Egypt. **strength,** as allies. **Put .. Lubim,** Ge. x. 6, 13. Put or Punt was a part of the coast of Egypt opposite Arabia. Lubim or the Lybians dwelt west of the Canopic mouth of the Nile. **helpers,** or auxiliaries. (10) **yet,** nevertheless; in spite of all the help she had. **young,** etc., comp. 2 Ki. viii. 12; Is. xiii. 16. **cast lots,** as if they were mere slaves. (11) **drunken,** a fig. for the stupefaction caused by calamity. **be hid,** Camb. B., "shalt faint." **strength,** Camb. B., "a place of refuge." Je. xxv. 17. (12) **first ripe figs,** Is. xxviii. 4. Figs readily drop off when ripe.

Pride and progress can never go together. Pride and education are sworn enemies. Self-trust and reality of character can never cohere. We live our greatest life in our humility, in our reverence, in our aspiration. Why fight against this God? If the cities have outwitted him, where are they? You should be able to find them. Where is old Babylon? Where the mocking, mighty, pompous, overbearing Rome? Where are those cities that have threatened God and lived? You ought to be able to find them if they have been victorious. Now we are called upon to acquaint ourselves, and be at peace with him; we are called into harmony, and the way by which this harmony is attained is one way and only one, and unchangeable and complete, and that is the way we call the Gospel of Christ, the doctrine of the Cross, the doctrine of atonement, the doctrine of something being done for man that man could never do for himself, and which he lays hold of by the energy called faith.—Peop. Bib.

Thebes, the No of Prophecy.—The identity of No, mention of which occurs several times in the Prophets, with Thebes, is now scarcely disputed. This city was the most ancient capital, and renowned city of Egypt. It was also the chief seat of the worship of Jupiter Ammon, one of the gods of the Egyptians. It could furnish 20,000 armed chariots for warfare, and when captured by the Persians under Cambyses (B. C. 525), the spoil, in gold and silver talents, which fell into the hands of the conquerors, amounted to nearly two million pounds sterling. The ancient city was twenty-three miles in circumference. The valley of the Nile was not large enough to contain it, and its extremities rested upon the bases of the mountains of Arabia and Africa. The whole of this great extent is more or less strewed with ruins, broken columns, and avenues of sphinxes, colossal figures, obelisks, pyramidal gateways, porticoes, blocks of polished granite, and stones of extraordinary magnitude, while above them, "in all the nakedness of desolation," the colossal skeletons of giant temples are standing "in the unwatered sands, in solitude and silence. They are neither grey, nor blackened; there is no lichen, no moss, no rank grass or mantling ivy, to robe them, and conceal their deformities. Like the bones of man, they seem to whiten under the sun of the desert." The sand of Africa has been their most fearful enemy; blown upon them for more than three thousand years, it has buried the largest monuments, and, in some instances, almost entire temples. On the Arabian side of the Nile are the great temples of Luxor and Carnac. The temple of Luxor stands near the bank of the river, built there, as is supposed, for the convenience of the Egyptian boatmen. Before the magnificent gateway of this temple, until within a few years,

[a] "The deity Ammon appears to have been first worshiped by the Ethiopians, or Libyans, and afterwards by the Egyptians, who called him Amun. Herodotus tells us that there was an oracle sacred to Ammon at Meroe, and also at Thebes, the capital of upper Egypt." — Bib. Things.

vs. 7. J. Randall, 71.

"As the angel stood in the path of Balaam while going on in his stubborn determination to disobey, so God puts warnings, and entreaties, and mercies, and the love of Christ, and trials and punishments, in the path of the sinner, as his good angels to withstand his downward course and to cry out to him, 'Go back, go back.' "

"Pride and choler are like the fox offering to go out when his belly was full, which enlarging him bigger than the passage, made him stay, and be taken with shame. They that would come to preferment by pride are like those who would ascend stairs on horseback."

"Remember what thou wert before thy birth —nothing; what thou wert for many years after — weakness; what in all thy life—a great sinner; what in all thy excellences—a mere debtor to God, to thy parents, to the earth, to all the creatures. Upon these or the like meditations, if we dwell, and frequently retire to them, we shall see nothing more reasonable than to be humble, and nothing more foolish than to be proud."—Bp. Taylor.

"Love not this world, because if you love it you cannot love Him. Love not this world, because if you love it you love something that by and by will be ashes, and, while you thought you were grasping the honors of the world that now is and is to come, you will find you have grasped only the hot, dusty ashes of the world that is to come." — Robert E. Speer.

stood two lofty obelisks, each a single block of red granite more than eighty feet high, covered with sculptures and hieroglyphics, fresh as if but yesterday from the hands of the sculptor. But great and magnificent as was the temple of Luxor, it served but as a portal to the greater Carnac. Standing nearly two miles from Luxor, the whole road to it was lined with rows of sphinxes, each of a solid block of granite. At this end they are broken, and, for the most part, buried under the sand and heaps of rubbish. But approaching Carnac they stand entire, still and solemn as when the ancient Egyptian passed between them to worship in the great temple of Ammon. Four grand propylons terminate this avenue of sphinxes, and, passing through the last, the scene which presents itself defies description. The field of ruins is about a mile in diameter; the temple itself 1,200 feet long and 420 broad. It has twelve principal entrances, each of which is approached through rows of sphinxes, as across the plain from Luxor, and each is composed of propylons, gateways, and other buildings, in themselves larger than most other temples; the sides of some of them are equal to the bases of most of the pyramids, and on each side of many are colossal statues, some sitting, others erect, from twenty to thirty feet in height.

No-Ammon fell; the sacred name of the capital of Upper Egypt was rubbed out as the merest speck upon the page of Time. We know the city referred to by the more modern name of Thebes—a city of a hundred gates and twenty thousand chariots—and the Pharaohs of this great capital warred and conquered riotously from the Soudan to Mesopotamia; trampling down everything, and showing their pride and pomp and power in all manner of ridiculousness of ostentation and wickedness and infamy of royal display. But God blotted out the city.—Peop. Bib. ——Thebes was renowned for its numerous gates and vast extent. Its remaining ruins describe a circuit of twenty-seven miles [Henderson]. There is no definite historical account of its capture by Assyrians. But from brief notices in Scripture, we have hints of a struggle for supremacy between Assyria and Egypt (cf. 2 Kings xvii. 4). See Smith's Dict. of the Bible, article Thebes; and Keil on vss. 8—10.

"A couple of men, in a crazy craft, being caught in a squall, betook themselves, one to praying, and the other to poling toward the shore. Soon the latter touched bottom, and turning to his devout comrade, said: 'What's the use of praying when you can touch the bottom with the pole?' So say multitudes by their conduct, who would not, for the world, say anything so ludicrous by word. The only difference is, that they are not half so truthful in expressing themselves as bold unbelievers are, but their piety is of no higher type."—Old Test. Anec.

[a] Is. xix. 16; Je. l. 37, li. 30.

[b] "Nineveh's doom is fixed, yet is she bidden ironically to make every preparation for a long siege." — Spk. Com.

"No wise man ever lost anything by cession; but he receives the hostility of violent persons into his embraces, like a stone into a lap of wool, it rests and sits down softly and innocently; but a stone falling upon a stone makes a collision, and extracts fire, and finds no rest; and just so are two proud persons, despised by each other, contemned by all, living in perpetual dissonances, always fighting against affronts, jealous of every person, disturbed by every accident, a perpetual storm within, and daily hissing from without."—Taylor.

13—15. (13) **women,** i. e. as women for helplessness.[a] **gates,** or passes by wh. access is gained into thy country. (14) **draw,** etc., i. e. make every possible provision for the siege, but all shall not avail.[b] **go into clay, etc.,** i. e. prepare bricks to strengthen the walls. **brickkiln,** both baked and sun-dried bricks seem to have been used. (15) **fire,** the remains of Nineveh show that the city was destroyed by fire. **cankerworm,** Joel i. 4.

Human Efforts as Directed Against the Divine Purpose.—We have furnished us in these verses an illustration of human effort as directed against the accomplishment of the purpose of God. Sometimes this course is taken by men unconsciously, but it was scarcely so in this instance. We know that the Assyrian power in the time of Sennacherib boldly defied the God of heaven, and it seems with the lapse of time to have gone from bad to worse. It was the Divine will that at length the arm of Assyria should be broken, and that its haughty and oppressive rule should cease; and the prophet here set forth how that, in the day of trial, human strength should do its best in order to avert the destruction divinely intended to be wrought. Some regard vs. 14 as simply indicating the fact that the Assyrian power would maintain a prolonged defence; whilst others view the prophet as speaking ironically, and as mocking the vain endeavours of the defenders of Nineveh, just as Isaiah ridiculed the makers of idols (xliv. 9—20).—Pulpit Com.

16, 17. (16) **spoileth,** marg. spreadeth himself. (17) **crowned,** "the high officers of state were adorned with diadems, closely resembling the lower band of the royal mitre, separated from the cap itself."—Spk. Com. **camp .. day,** settling in clusters on walls of loose stone or earth.[b] Locusts become torpid in cold weather; under the warmth of the sun they revive and take flight. So the captains and princes of Nineveh are paralyzed and useless in the day of calamity.

Nineveh's Desolation.—Nahum's prophecy of the future destruction of Nineveh was fulfilled by the Medes and Babylonians (cf. ch. ii. 1); and according to his prediction, the vast power of Nineveh completely vanished, and its glory was utterly eclipsed, so that in the year B. C. 401, Xenophon passed by the site without learning its name (Xen. Anab. iii. 4—7). Four hundred years afterwards a small fortress was standing on the site, to guard the passage of the river Tigris (Tacitus, Ann. xii. 13), and opposite to it, on the west bank of the Tigris, has arisen the city of Mosul. In the year 1776, Niebuhr visited the spot, and supposed that what were the heaps of ruins of Nineveh, were natural undulations in the soil (See Rawlinson, i. 326). In more modern times it has been explored by Botta, the French Consul (in 1842), and more recently by Layard and others, who have brought to light those gigantic remains of palaces, statues, and other monuments which testify to the ancient grandeur of Nineveh, and those annalistic inscriptions which confirm the veracity of the prophecies of Nahum and of Isaiah, and of the historical narrative of Holy Scripture: and bear witness to the Divine foreknowledge of the Holy Ghost who speaks in it; to whom with the Father and the Son, Three Persons and one God, be honor and glory now and for evermore. Amen.—Wordsworth.

b "In the evenings, as soon as the air became cool, at Abeih, they literally camped in the hedges and loose stone walls, covering them over like a swarm of bees settled on a bush. There they remained until the next day's sun waxed warm, when they again commenced their march. —Thomson.

18, 19. (18) **shepherds,** or chief rulers. **slumber,** in death. **nobles,** marg. valiant ones. (19) **bruise,** better, breaking. **bruit,** sound, report.[a] **clap .. hands,** in exulting triumph and joy. **wickedness passed,** Assyria has been the foe and scourge of the human race.

The Danger of Foreign Population.—The swift decay of these ancient empires from the climax of their commercial glory is often employed as a warning to ourselves. But the parallel, as the previous paragraphs suggest, is very far from exact. If we can lay aside for the moment the greatest difference of all, in religion and morals, there remain others almost of cardinal importance. Assyria and Babylonia were not filled, like Great Britain, with reproductive races, able to colonize distant lands, and carry everywhere the spirit which had made them strong at home. Still more, they did not continue at home to be homogeneous. Their native forces were exhausted by long and unceasing wars. Their populations, especially in their capitals, were very largely alien and distraught, with nothing to hold them together save their commercial interests. They were bound to break up at the first disaster. It is true that we are not without some risks of their peril. No patriot among us can observe without misgiving the large and growing proportion of foreigners in that department of our life from which the strength of our defence is largely drawn—our merchant navy. But such a fact is very far from bringing our empire and its chief cities into the fatal condition of Nineveh and Babylon. Our capitals, our commerce, our life as a whole are still British to the core. If we only be true to our ideals of righteousness and religion, if our patriotism continue moral and sincere, we shall have the power to absorb the foreign elements that throng to us in commerce, and stamp them with our own spirit.—Exp. Bib.——Hopelessness.—"There is no healing of thy bruise; thy wound is grievous." Nothing can be more distressing than the consciousness of powerlessness in the presence of the deepest human need; to witness from the seashore the wreck, and to be utterly unable to save the shipwrecked mariners; to be sure that some one is in the burning edifice, and yet for it to be impossible to reach him and to bring him out; to stand before an audience alarmed by some needless cry, and to see the rush towards the doors, and to be unequal to checking it; or even to be by the bedside of one in life's youth or manhood's prime, and to hear that disease has, humanly speaking, prematurely seized its victim, and that medical help cannot cure, but only, and that for a time, alleviate. This position is occupied by many an earnest-hearted worker for God and the good of souls, in relation to the moral salvation of men. Nahum sustained it in reference to the Ninevites. He saw in them a people wrecked through

a **Fr. bruit Lat. brugire to rustle, roar, rattle.**

"Antisthenes, on a time, walked in the common place at Athens, with a cloak all torn and tattered, that every one beholding it might judge that he did it through humility; but Socrates, having discovered the hypocrisy, said that he saw his ambition through the holes of his cloak. Diogenes, once entering Plato's chamber, discovered his bed neatly made and jumping upon it, trampled it down, saying that he trampled down Plato's pride. Plato answered that it was done with greater pride.

"In for a penny, in for a pound. He that takes the devil into his boat must ferry him over the sound." — English.

"It is the first shower that wets."—Italian.

"It is all the same whether a man has both legs in the stocks, or one." —German.

"There is nothing like being bespattered for making one defy the slough." —French.

"Make yourself an honest man, and then you may be sure that there is one rascal less in the world."—Carlyle.

"It was said of Vespasian, that he was even a better man for being an emperor. So the prosperity of some, instead of destroying them, displays and increases their excellency; they are rich, not only in temporal things, but in faith and good works."—Jay.

the adverse winds and tempests of evil, consumed by the fires of unholy passion, on the mad rush to ruin and death, diseased through and through so that recovery was impossible; and hence, unable to heal, he cried in the sadness of his heart, "There is no healing of thy bruise; thy wound is grievous."—Pulpit Com.——"Monuments and inscriptions prove the pitiless cruelty of Assyria. In sculptures are rows of impaled prisoners, whose eyes were put out, and whose lips were fastened by rings. God had long borne this oppression, but now guilt must be punished. Judgment must fall, and there is not the least hope of recovery. Cruelty and oppression will be rewarded in their own coin."—Hom. Com.——The Overthrow of Evil-doers a Source of Thankful Joy.—"All that hear the bruit of thee shall clap the hands over thee: for upon whom hath not thy wickedness passed continually?" These last words in the Book of Nahum are truly impressive. The messenger closes his brief prophecy in the same tone in which he commenced it, the vengeance of God being still his theme. At the outset he declared the solemn fact; at the end he applies the truth thus announced to the particular case in hand. The magnificent dirge forming this third chapter is one sustained shout of wild exultation that the oppressor has fallen at last. The naked discrowned corpse of the glorious city is cast out to the scorn and disgust of the world. No spark of pity mingles with the prophet's delight. In this storm of indignation and vengeance the spirit of prophecy in the northern kingdom breathes its last. Under this doom Nineveh vanishes from view, to be no more seen till in our day the discovery of her buried remains has given new life to the whole of this portion of sacred history.—Stanley's "Jewish Church."

Redeeming the Time.—

Lose this day, loitering, 'twill be the same story
To-morrow, and the next more dilatory.
The indecision brings its own delays,
And days are lost lamenting o'er lost days.
Are you in earnest? seize this very minute!
What you can do, or think you can, begin it!
Boldness has genius, power and magic in it!
Only engage, and then the mind grows heated;
Begin it, and the work will be completed!

Introduction.

I. **Author.** Habakkuk, = "embrace." Of his history nothing whatever is known. II. **Time.** B.C. 630—598. III. **Design,** etc. The design of the book is to portray the coming destruction of Judah by the Chaldæans, and the retribution which should befall the latter. It concludes with an ode, which presents one of the most perfect specimens of Hebrew lyrical poetry. References to this book occur in Heb. x. 37, 38; Rom. i. 17; Gal. iii. 11; Acts xiii. 41. IV. **Style.** Habakkuk holds a distinguished place among the sacred poets; whoever reads his prophecy must be struck with the grandeur of his imagery and the sublimity of its style, especially of the hymn in the third chapter, which Bp. Lowth considers one of the most perfect specimens of the Hebrew ode.

"Habakkuk is the earliest who is known to us of a new school of religion in Israel. He is called 'prophet,' but at first he does not adopt the attitude which is characteristic of the prophets. His face is set in an opposite direction to theirs. They address the nation Israel, on behalf of God: he rather speaks to God on behalf of Israel. Their task was Israel's sin, the proclamation of God's doom and the offer of His grace to their penitence. Habakkuk's task is God Himself, the effort to find out what He means by permitting tyranny and wrong. They attack the sins, he is the first to state the problems, of life. To him the prophetic revelation, the Torah, is complete: it has been codified in Deuteronomy and enforced by Josiah. Habakkuk's business is not to add to it but to ask why it does not work. Why does God suffer wrong to triumph, so that the Torah is paralyzed, and Mishpat, the prophetic justice or judgment, comes to nought? The prophets travailed for Israel's character—to get the people to love justice till justice prevailed among them: Habakkuk feels justice cannot prevail in Israel, because of the great disorder which God permits to fill the world. It is true that he arrives at a prophetic attitude, and before the end authoritatively declares God's will; but he begins by searching for the latter, with an appreciation of the great obscurity cast over it by the facts of life."—Geo. Adam Smith.

CHAPTER THE FIRST.

1—4. (1) **burden,** G. A. Smith translates: "The oracle which H. the prophet received by vision." **Habakkuk,** meaning "embrace." The word should be pronounced Habák-kuk. (2) **cry,** for help against the violent, who seem to prosper.[a] When the prophet says "I," he probably speaks not so much for himself personally, as for the godly in Israel. (3) **shew me,** or let me see iniquity appearing to triumph. **there are that raise,** etc., R. V., "there is strife and contention riseth up." (4) **slacked,** seems to hesitate to touch these successful wicked men. **wicked,** etc., Job xxi. 7; Je. xii. 1.

The Importunate Prayer (vs. 2).—How long will He suffer His people to pray, and still neglect to hear? 1. Till they see the plague of their own hearts; 2. Till the Church feels that she stands in the gap between God and a sin-destroyed world, and that He will be inquired of to do all that He has promised; 3. Till they are willing to do whatever of duty He requires, in addition to praying; 4. Till they have removed the stumbling-blocks out of the way of a revival of His work; 5. Till He sees in them a disposition to give Him the glory of the work He does.—A. Clark.

Habakkuk conducts a kind of dialogue, and if the paradox may be allowed it seems to be a dialogue mainly on his own side. To call it a monologue would be hardly correct. He talks to God; he has it out with God; he plies God with sharp questions. He will have practical matters attended to; he says, Lord, this is evil; how did it come to be in thy universe, thou fair One, whose face is beauty, whose voice is music? He could not write a long prophecy in that strain. Jesus Christ could not be a minister more than three years; Habakkuk can only write his three chapters. He was no magician in the elaboration of sentences; every sentence in Habakkuk was itself a Bible. There is no such book in all the canon as Habakkuk. The very word means strong embrace. He gets hold of God, and throws him in the gracious wrestle. He will not let God go. On the one side he represents pessimism or despair as it never was represented before, and on the other he rises to heights of faith which even David did not attain with all his music. We shall find sentences in Habakkuk that leave all the prophets and minstrels of the Old Testament far away down in the clouds, whilst Habakkuk himself is up beyond the cloud-line, revelling in morning light.—Parker.

5—8. Vss. 5—11 seem to be the answers of God to the prophet's complaint. "The wrongs complained of will bring their punishment." (5) **behold ye, etc.,**[b] observe what is happening among the Gentiles. God will use a heathen nation to chastise the sinners in Judæa. **wonder,** or be astounded. (6) **Chaldaeans,** Ge. xi. 28. **bitter,** i. e. cruel.[c] **hasty,** sudden and overwhelming inroads were characteristic features of their warfare. **which shall march,** R. V., "which march through the breadth of the earth." (7) **judgment,** etc., i. e. they act entirely on their own will, without any consideration for others.[d] (8) **horses,** Nah. iii. 2. **leopards,** noted for swift, gliding running.[e] **evening wolves,** sharp set with hunger.

Evening Wolves (vs. 8).—May not the furious creature represent—I. Our doubts and fears, after a day of distraction of mind losses in business, and perhaps ungenerous tauntings from our fellow men? II. False teachers who craftily and industriously hunt for the precious life, devouring men by their falsehoods? III. What a wonder of grace it is when fierce persecutors are converted, for then the wolf dwells with the lamb, and men of cruel ungovernable dispositions become gentle and teachable.—Spurgeon.

The Chaldeans (Heb. Kasdim), in the Assyrian inscriptions Kaldu, were properly neither Assyrians nor Babylonians, though no doubt like them a Shemitic people. Their seats were in the southmost parts of the Babylonian plain, towards and on the Persian Gulf. Here they formed a number of small states, one of which was Bit Yakin, the kingdom of

"The prophecy of Habakkuk is an organic whole divided into two parts, the first of which is a colloquy between God and the prophet, in which is announced the judgment coming upon Judah through the instrumentality of the Chaldeans; the second is a magnificent ode celebrating the punishment of God's enemies and the salvation of the pious."

a "The Prophet proposes the common objections against Providence taken from the prosperity of the wicked and the oppression of the righteous, which have been a stumbling block to good men."—Lowth.

b Acts xiii. 41; Paul quotes from the Sept. version.

c Comp. Je. l. 42.

d "The Chaldee will be a law unto himself. . . Self-asserting and irresponsible judgment will be the fit instrument of punishment on the authors of wrong judgment.
—Spk. Com.

e "Agile, swift, and when irritated the most terrible and cruel of beasts."
—Tristram.

"Others only look and wonder, the Christian only looks and loves."
—Hurrion.

That God cannot be indifferent to sin, to the wickedness of nations or to the

Merodach Baladan, which lay on the coast and is called in inscriptions "the land of the sea." If the Shemites penetrated into the plains of the two rivers from the north, the Chaldeans must have formed the vanguard of the immigration and been thrown into the furthest south by the successive waves of population that followed them; if they entered from the south or south-west the Chaldeans would be the latest to arrive. This is most probable, for the movement appears always to have been northward, and the steady aim of the Chaldeans was to gain possession of the country lying to the north of their abode and seat themselves upon the throne of Babylon. This their princes succeeded in doing more than once. Merodach Baladan, who gave trouble to three Assyrian monarchs, Tiglath-Pileser, Sargon and Sennacherib, appears to have occupied the throne of Babylon from B. C. 721 to 709, when after a war with Sargon he was dispossessed. The indefatigable veteran renewed the struggle for the crown of Babylon in the time of Sennacherib, but without success, and disappears from history, though his descendants are spoken of in the annals of the succeeding Assyrian kings. The Chaldean states allied themselves with Shamash-shumukin, the Babylonian viceroy, in his revolt against his brother Assurbanipal, but were severely chastised by the Assyrian king and overrun by his armies. Finally, on the death of Assurbanipal (cir. 626), the Chaldean Nabopolassar, taking advantage of the weakness of Assyria, succeeded, by what steps is unknown, in placing the crown of Babylon on his head, and transmitting it to his descendants. The Chaldean empire of Babylon dates from the usurpation of Nabopolassar (B. C. 625), though it was his son Nebuchadnezzar (605), the greatest ruler of the East, to whom its splendor was due. Nebuchadnezzar was succeeded by several princes of feeble character, the last of whom was Nabonidus (Nabuna'id), in whose reign the empire fell before the attack of the Medes and Persians under Cyrus (B. C. 538), having lasted less than a century, and with its fall the empire of the East passed from the Shemites to a people of the Aryan race.—A. B. Davidson.

9—11. (9) **They shall come,** R. V., "They come all of them." **for violence,** with violent intentions. **their faces,** etc., R. V., "their faces are set eagerly as the east wind," i. e. their movement is impetuous and rapid. **they shall gather,** etc., R. V., "they gather captives as the sand," i. e. "as the wind drives the sand before it in confused heaps," or perhaps, "innumerable, like the sand." (10) R. V., "Yea, he scoffeth at kings and princes are a derision unto him: he derideth .. he heapeth up dust," making thus an embankment, from whence to attack the city.[a] (11) R. V., "Then he sweepeth onward as the wind and passeth through and becometh guilty: thus his might becometh his god." His success intoxicates him and he deifies his own might.

The Agger or Mount (vs. 10).—Another contrivance which the besiegers employed was the Agger or Mount, which they raised so high as to equal, if not exceed, the top of the besieged walls: the sides were supported with bricks or stones, or secured with strong rafters to hinder it from falling; the forepart only remained bare, because it was to be advanced by degrees nearer the city. The pile itself consisted of all sorts of materials, as earth, timber, boughs, stones; into the middle were cast also wickers, and twigs of trees to fasten, and, as it were, cement the other parts. The prophet Habakkuk manifestly refers to the mount, in that prediction where he describes the desolating march of the Chaldæans, and the success of their arms.—Paxton.

12, 13. Vss. 12—17 seem to be a remonstrance of the prophet with God over the cruelties of the Chaldeans. (12) **art,** etc.,[a] these are the words of Habakkuk, as representing believing Israel. They are spoken in "opposition to the impious deifying of the Chaldæans' power as their god." **not die,** or be destroyed under Thy judgments. **for correction,** of Israel, not for his destruction. To His people all Divine dealings are chastisements. (13) **purer eyes,** etc., Ps. v. 4, 5; Je. xii. 1, 2. **wherefore,** etc., reference is to the strangeness of God's using so bad a nation as the Chaldæans for His purposes.[b]

14—17. (14) **makest men,** etc., i. e. sufferest the Chaldæans to commit these cruelties. **as the fishes,** men under the cruel rapacity of these tyrants ceased to be men, the very humanity in them was disregarded,

transgressions of individuals, is self-evident; otherwise he could not be God. But that, loving righteousness and hating iniquity, he should seem to make no effort to protect, vindicate, strengthen, and diffuse the one, or to punish, restrain, and overthrow the other,—this is what occasions trouble to religious souls reflecting on the course of providence. The solution of the problem can only be that, on the one hand, he deems it better that righteousness should be purified, tested, and established by contact with evil, while, on the other hand, it seems preferable to his wisdom and love that wickedness should have free scope to reveal its true character, and ample opportunity either to change its mind or to justify its final overthrow.
—Pulp. Com.

[a] "No fortress could withstand the Babylonian conqueror. Not even, Tyre whose very name (Rock) betokened its strength. The most impregnable garrison seemed only to require that he should heap up a little dust against it, and it was taken."

[a] Ps. xc. 2, xciii. 2, cii. 27.
[b] The prophet's reasoning admits of a more extended range of application, and has an important bearing upon the immortality of man. Jehovah is "from everlasting." He is "the eternal

and the brutal conqueror in his pride treated them like the lower creatures. **creeping things,** Ps. civ. 25. **no ruler over them,** "this hardly means that the creeping things have no king to protect them, but rather that, as the lowest creatures that have life, they have no higher instincts, no organization, they are a mere swarming disorder, and to this condition do the conquerors reduce mankind. Prov. vi. 7, xxx. 27."—Camb. B. (15) **angle,** or hook. **drag,** or long net, wh. is dragged through the water.[b] **rejoice,** glorying in their crimes because they are successful. (16) **sacrifice .. net,** i. e. they put their trust in, and as it were deify and worship their arms, power, and military skill. (17) **empty,** etc., i. e. carry away the spoil of the nations successfully. "Shall they, without interruption, be permitted to enjoy the fruits of their violence?"

Self-Sufficiency.—"They say in their heart, My power and the might of mine hand hath gotten me this wealth" (Deut. viii. 17). So Pharaoh said, "My river is mine own, and I have made it for myself" (Ezek. xxix. 3). So Nebuchadnezzar said, "Is not this great Babylon, that I have built," etc. (Dan. iv. 30). Pusey refers in illustration of this to certain North American Indians, "who designate their bow and arrow as the only beneficent deities whom they know;" to the Romans sacrificing to their military standards; and to the French referred to in the Times during the Franco-German War as "almost worshiping the mitrailleuse as a goddess." And this is still our peril. Because our possibilities are so great, we think that we can win all blessings for ourselves. Everywhere we see the worship of our human powers and means—the workman worshiping the strength of his arm and the deftness of his fingers, the man of business worshiping his skill and acuteness, and the man of science, human knowledge. Nor is the Church of God free from this spirit: for there is far too much of trusting to forms and ceremonies, to worldly alliances, to machinery and organization, as though these were the great essentials, and far too little of "looking up unto the hills whence cometh her help."—S. D. Hillman.

God;" hence our immortal destiny: "We shall not die." Surely the Divine Father will not allow his children to fade away and be no more. Certainly, he whose tender love to his children the love of human parents so faintly images, will not dwell through the eternal ages and "leave himself childless when time shall end." — Pulp. Com.

[b] "Fishing on a larger scale is done by means of a long net, some three or four feet in width, with pieces of lead attached one side to sink it, and of cork on the other to keep it afloat. The operation is performed by men occupying two boats." — Van Lennep.

CHAPTER THE SECOND.

1—4. (1) **stand .. watch,** Is. xxi. 8. As a watchman looks out from his watch-tower into the distance, the prophet will watch for the answer from heaven.[a] **What I shall answer,** etc., Camb. B. "what answer I shall bring to my plea." (2) **make it plain,** De. xxvii. 8. **table,** or tablets, suitable for public inscriptions. **run,** etc., so plain that he that reads may run on in his reading, i. e. read rapidly. (3) **appointed time,** but there will be some delay before it is fulfilled. **but at the end,** etc., R. V., "and it hasteth toward the end, and shall not lie." **not tarry,** not really, though to human view the period may seem to be prolonged: God's time is always kept. (4) **lifted up,** or haughty. **just .. faith,**[b] R. V. margin, and Camb. B., "the just shall live in his faithfulness." Let the righteous, however baffled his faith be by experience, hold on in loyalty to God and duty, and he shall live.

The Watch-Tower of Prayer (vs. 1).—I. Watch for things to pray about. II. Watch for times to pray. III. Watch for answers to prayer.—Edmond.

Habakkuk, the Prophet of a Tried but Triumphant Faith.—

O Thou of ear so keen that it must hear
The prayer of faith for healing of our shame,
O Thou of eyes so pure that they must flame
In vivid lightnings on our darkness drear,
And clarify our murky atmosphere,
When wilt Thou come to manifest Thy name,
To vindicate the right, Thy cause reclaim?
Bold watchman on thy tower of hope, what cheer?

Swift comes the answering vision; make it plain:
The Lord is on His throne,—keep silence, earth,—
Shall punish wrong, and crown the just with life;

[a] "The Prophets often compare themselves, awaiting the revelations of Jehovah with earnest patience, to watchmen on an eminence watching with intent eye all that comes within their view." — Fausset.

Is. xxi. 11; Je. vi. 17; Eze. iii. 17, xxxiii. 2, 3;

[b] Jno. iii. 36; Ro. i. 17; Ga. iii. 11; He. x. 38.

"But the righteous shall live by his faithfulness." This word, wrongly translated faith by the Greek and other versions, is concentrated by Paul in his repeated quotation from the Greek upon that single act of faith by which the sinner secures forgiveness and

Revive His ancient work; by second birth
Flood all the world with glory, quenching strife,
Till men their heritage of joy regain.—C. S. Hoyt.

justification. Of course it has faith in God as its secret—the —the verb from which it is derived is the regular Hebrew term to believe —but it is rather the temper which faith produces of endurance, steadfastness, integrity. — G. Adam Smith.

a "The acquisitions of the Chaldaeans are represented as so many pledges extorted from the conquered, and reclaimable by them; the greater the amount the heavier the debt and the retribution." —Spk. Com.

5—8. (5) **transgresseth by wine,** R. V., "Yea, moreover, wine is a treacherous dealer, a haughty man," etc., the description of the Chaldæan as one "intoxicated with his successes, and not knowing how to set any bounds to his ambition."—Lowth. **hell,** here the emblem of an insatiable temper. **as death,** the foe with whom no man can make reconciliation. (6) **all these**, the nations crushed by the Chaldæans. **parable,** or figurative speech. **against him,** in the day of his calamity. **thick clay,** R. V., "pledges;" i. e. contracts a heavy burden of debt.[a] (7) **they,** etc., the Medo-Persian conquerors. (8) **remnant .. thee,** the conquerors of Babylon were a mixed people made up of the nations crushed by Babylon. **violence of the land,** R. V., "violence done to the land."

The True Life.—God will not have these high nests. You know it. When you were young, what you were going to be! What adornment and finery and vanity and presumption! Now that you are a wrinkled old woman tell us what life really is; tell us what you would be and do if you had the chance to begin again. And when you came from school to college, you remember, you were going to trample down everybody and set everything right, and now that you are a disappointed old greybeard, tell us what is life: how would you do if you had to start once more? Where is the girl that was simple, frank, self-distrustful, industrious, almost silent, and absolutely without pretence? She is crowned among the mothers of Israel. Where is the young man that began at the bottom, and went up and said, I am afraid I am getting almost too high now: what am I in my father's house that I should have this elevation? Where will he end? In heaven. Here is your choice then: the life of the just, or the life of the clay-gatherer; the life of holiness, or the life of covetousness; the life that will have nothing that reason cannot explain and conscience justify and merit claim, or the life that will have a high nest without working for it and without climbing to it. It need be no Habakkuk who can forecast the future of men now. The Bible has, if we have inhaled its true spirit, made us all prophets.—Parker.

a Pr. viii. 36, xx. 2.

They who wrong their neighb rs do much greater wrong to their own souls.

b "The special witness made is that the money and materials wherewith he built the house were unjustly gotten." — Mat. Henry.

9—11. (9) **coveteth,** etc., Je. xxii. 13. "A covetousness so surpassingly evil as to be fatal to himself." R. V., "getteth an evil gain." **nest,** perhaps referring to the royal citadel, wh, was built high, like the Babel-tower, or the figure may be taken from birds that build in inaccessible places. (10) **shame,** or ruin. Brought disgrace upon yourself.[a] (11) **stone,** this, and the tie-beam, are supposed to be witnesses of the wickedness.[b]

Note on vs. 11.—The margin of the A. V. has, instead of "answer it," "witness against it." When a man denies what he has solemnly promised, the person who complains of his perfidy says, "The place where you stood shall witness against you." "A beautiful princess was once enjoying herself in a fragrant grove, when a noble prince passed that way; she became enamored of his person, and he solemnly promised to return and marry her. When he left her, she wept bitterly, and said, 'Ah! should he not return, this tali-tree shall witness against him. Yes, the birds shall be my witnesses.'"—Roberts.

"Sweet are the thoughts that savor of content—the quiet mind is richer than a crown; sweet are the nights in careless slumber spent—the poor estate scorns fortune's angry frown. Such sweet content, such minds, such sleep, such bliss, beggars enjoy when princes oft do miss. The homely house that harbors quiet rest, the cottage that affords no pride nor care, the man, that 'grees with country music best, the sweet consort of Mirth's and Music's fare. Obscured life sits

No Satisfaction in Self-Indulgence.—A reporter was talking with the distinguished lawyer, the Hon. Joseph H. Choate, our ambassador to Great Britain, and the conversation is given in Ainslee's Magazine. Here is a fine passage: "Are not," I said, "a few hours of toil, a luxuriously furnished home, hosts of friends, the applause of the people, sumptuous repasts, and content in idleness, knowing that enough has been done, the conditions of happiness?" "We never know that enough has been done," he said meditatively. "All that you speak of sounds pleasant; but the truth is, that minds whose great exertions have made such things possible for themselves are the very last to crave or rejoice in their possession. You have described what appeals to the idler, the energyless dreamer, the fashionable dawdler, and the listless voluptuary. Enjoyment of such things would sap the strength and deaden the ambition of a Lincoln. The man who has attained to the position where such things are possible is one whose life has been a constant refutation of their need. He is one who has abstained, who has conserved his mental and physical strength by living a simple and frugal life. His enjoyment has been in working, and I guarantee that you will always find successful men plain-mannered persons of simple tastes, to whom sumptuous repasts are a bore, and luxury a thing apart. They may live surrounded by these things, but personally take little interest in them, counting them mere trappings which neither add to nor detract from greatness."

12—14. (12) **blood,** or violence and blood-shedding.[a] (13) **is it not of the Lord,** hath not God ordained that these blood stained splendors shall come to naught? **in the very fire,** R. V., "for the fire," they are erecting structures which are to be burned up. **very vanity,** see Je. li. 58. (14) **earth .. sea,** Is. xi. 9,[b] "the verse explains the preceding. The Lord of Hosts, God Omnipotent, whose purposes overrule all, shall bring in His kingdom, and in the judgments that precede its coming the great fabrics reared by heathenism for its idolatries and its oppressions shall become fuel for the fire (Is. ix. 5)."—Camb. B.

15—17. (15) **neighbour drink,** "not only do the Chaldæans oppress and pillage the peoples, but they expose them to the vilest derision and contumely. They behave to the conquered nations like one who gives his neighbor intoxicating drink to stupefy his faculties and expose him to shame."—Pulp. Com. **look,** etc., a fig. for shameful defeat. (16) **shame for glory,** i. e. instead of glory. "Thou hast feasted thyself on that which is shameful rather than on that which is decorous and honorable." **drink thou also,** etc., let the same ignominy come to thee which thou hast visited on others. **the cup,** etc., God shall bring round the cup of suffering and vengeance to thee in thy turn, so that foul shame shall be on thy glory. (17) **Lebanon,** R. V., "the violence done to Lebanon," the reckless devastation of the forests. **spoil of beasts,** R. V., "destruction of the beasts."[c] "The earth, the woods and the beasts no less than man have rights; there is nothing that exists which is not moral; wanton excess on anything recoils on the head of the perpetrator. The ravage and terror carried into the world of creatures shall come back in terror and destruction on the Chaldean." **violence of the land,** R. V., "violence done to the land, to the city, and to all," etc.

Degrading Effects of Drink.—A minister of the gospel told me in 1847 one of the most thrilling incidents I ever heard in my life. A member of his congregation came home for the first time in his life intoxicated, and his boy met him on the doorstep, clapping his hands and exclaiming, "Papa has come home!" He seized that boy by the shoulder, swung him around, staggered, and fell with him in the hall. The minister said to me, "I spent that night in that house. I went to the door, and bared my brow that the night air might fall upon it and cool it; I walked up and down the hall. There was his child dead; there was his wife in strong convulsions, and he asleep. A man but thirty-five years of age asleep with a dead child in the house, having a blue mark upon the temple where the corner of the marble steps had come in contact with the head as he swung him round, and a wife upon the very brink of the grave! I felt I must remain until he awoke, and I did. When he awoke he passed his hand over his face, and exclaimed, 'What is the matter? Where am I? Where is my boy?' 'You cannot see him.' 'Where is my boy?' he inquired. 'You cannot see him.' 'Stand out of my way. I will see my boy!' To prevent confusion, I took him to that child's bedside, and, as I turned down the sheet and showed him the corpse, he uttered the shriek, 'Ah, my child!' One year afterwards that man was brought from a lunatic asylum to lie side by side with his wife in one grave, and I attended his funeral." The minister of the gospel who told me that fact is to-day a drunken hostler in a stable in Boston! Now tell me what drink will do. It will debase, degrade and imbrute everything that is noble, bright, glorious and godlike in a human being.—J. B. Gough.——Conscientious Charity.—If you give sixpence to a poor creature, when you know, or may know, if you think or inquire, that the sixpence will be turned at once into intoxicating drink, you are putting a stumbling-block or occasion of falling in the way of a brother or sister

down a type of bliss; a mind content both crown and kingdom is."
—Greene.

[a] Mi. iii. 10.

"Who hath raised the greatness of his capital city Babylon upon the ruins of many other cities, and the destruction of their inhabitants." — Lowth.

"Shall not God have His turn, when cruel rapacious men have triumphed so long, though He seems now to be still?"—Calvin.

[b] "The earth will not only be filled with the glory of the Lord, but with the knowledge of it. Men will recognize it. It will be filled with that knowledge, as the sea is covered with waters, which lie deep, spread far, and will never be dried up." — Wordsworth.

[c] "As thou didst hunt men as wild beasts, so shalt thou be hunted thyself as a wild beast, which thou resemblest in cruelty." — Fausset.

"I drank; I liked it not; 'twas rage, 'twas noise, an airy scene of transitory joys. In vain I trusted that the flowing bowl would banish sorrow, and enlarge the soul; to the late revel, and protracted feast, wild dreams succeeded and disorder'd rest." — Prior.

for whom Christ died. What is it that forbids you to do this? Is it political economy? Perhaps, but it is certainly also Christian duty, Christian love. I once heard an excellent clergyman say, "Warn as you will. if I were to refuse help to the apparently hungry woman who begs me to give her money to buy food, I could not eat my own dinner in comfort." My answer to such a remark would be, "What does it matter whether you eat your own dinner in comfort or not? This is a very secondary consideration, compared with the question of doing good or harm to the brother or sister for whom Christ died."—Davies.

18—20. (18) **what profiteth,** Isa. xliv. 10; Jer. ii. 8, 11, xvi. 17, 20. **dumb idols,** Ps. cxv. 5. (19) **wood .. stone,** of wh. the idol figures were made. **it shall teach,** R. V., "Shall this teach?" **no breath,** as sign of life. (20) The prophet contrasts the majesty of Jehovah with these dumb and lifeless idols. **Lord,** Jehovah: the One and living God. **temple,** not the shrine at Jerusalem, but heaven itself, Ps. xi. 4. **silence,**[a] so that they may hear what He may say unto them: or in token of reverent and submissive attention to His judgments.

[a] LXX. rend. "Stand in awe of Him."

"Comp. the silence in a court of justice when a judge pronounces the sentence."—Lowth.

"An outsider is very useful to an insider. As the engineer cannot steer, being down below among the machinery, he is very much helped by the man who is on the look-out: and men that are buried in the hull of their affairs ought to be thankful if there is anybody on deck that can keep a look-out, and tell which way the ship is going."—Spurgeon.

Seeking the True God.—Twenty years ago, when Christian missions scarcely existed in Japan, a young Japanese of good family met with a book on geography in the Chinese language, which had been compiled by an American missionary in China. It began with these words: "In the beginning God created the heaven and the earth." What could this mean? Who was that God? Certainly He was not known in Japan; perhaps He might live in America, whence the author of the book came. The young man determined to go to America and seek for God. He left Japan secretly, at the peril of his life; for the old law was then still in force, under which death was the penalty incurred by any Japanese who quitted his country. He made his way to China, and thence to the United States. There, after some perplexing experiences, he did find the God he had been seeking, and with his whole heart embraced the faith of Christ. That young man, Joseph Nisima, became principal of a Native Christian College at Kioto, the ancient sacred capital of Japan.—E. Stock.

CHAPTER THE THIRD.

1—4. (1) **a prayer,** including praise and meditation, as well as petition. **upon Shigionoth,**[a] R. V., "set to Shigionoth." The word is plur. of Shiggaion in the title of Ps. vii. and may mean a wild, tumultuous and ecstatic poem. The word "upon" in such superscriptions appears to mean "after the mode of," "to the music of" Shigionoth. (2) **thy speech,** R. V., "the report of thee;" perhaps an allusion to the divine manifestation at the Exodus. **revive thy work,** accomplish once again the rescue and deliverance of Thy people. "Though we seem, as it were, dead nationally, revive us." **midst .. years,** i. e. during our very captivity. (3) "The Theophany is pictured as a great tempest in the heavens in the midst of which God is present. It comes from the south, the region of Paran and Sinai (vs. 3 a); there is a terrible splendor around the advancing God, which lightens the heavens and the earth (vss. 3 b, 4); pestilence and fever-glow follow in His wake (vs. 5); all nature shudders, the eternal hills sink down (vs. 6); the nations and tribes in the desert are dismayed (vs. 7)."—Camb. B. **Teman .. Paran,** the region of God's manifestation at the giving of the law.[b] (4) **horns .. hand,** R. V. marg., "rays coming forth at his side." **there was the hiding,** in that ineffable light was the hiding-place of his majesty.

[a] "The term appears to mean a composition characterized by vehement emotions and sudden transitions."—Wordsworth.

[b] "He adopts the imagery of Moses (De. xxxiii. 2), of Deborah (Jud. v. 4, 5), and of David (Ps. lxviii. 7).

"In His hand He took the golden compasses prepar'd, in God's eternal store, to circumscribe this universe and all created things; one foot he centred, and the other turn'd round through the vast profundity obscure, and said, thus far extend, thus far thy bounds, this be thy just circumference, O world." — Milton.

Teman and Paran.—Teman is the name given to the region extending from the south of Palestine to Mount Sinai; Paran is the name of a mountain in the wilderness of Paran, also south of Palestine. Dr. Henderson (on the Minor Prophets at this place) remarks: "From Sinai occurring along with Seir and Paran (Deuteronomy xxxiii. 2), and with Seir and the country of Edom (Judges v. 4, 5), it is probable that Habakkuk here alludes to the regions to the south of Palestine generally, as the theatre of the Divine manifestations to Israel, only, specifying the two points nearer to that country." Teman in the one clause is parallel to Paran in the other, as God is to Holy One, according to the style of

Hebrew poetry. God came down on the top of Sinai, and thence displayed His glory before His people, and marched with them through the wilderness towards the Holy Land. The Prophet refers, in the highest style of poetry, to the Lord's former favors bestowed on the Israelites, as encouraging the hope that He will bless His people still.—S. S. Times.

5, 6. (5) **pestilence,** as His agent in His judgments. **burning coals,** or burning heat, a poetical figure for fever-disease, or perhaps lightning-strokes. (6) **measured,** etc., as a general first estimates his work, and forms his plans. **drove asunder,** or convulsed, with the first signs of His wrath. **mountains,** etc., figures of the most stable things.[a] **His ways are everlasting,** R. V., "His goings were as of old."

The Pestilence (vs. 5).—The place of the pestilence under the Divine administration, as connected with the moral government of God. I. Examine some prevalent opinions in regard to the matter which seem to be erroneous. 1. Some do not recognize the hand of God in such visitations; 2. Some do, but not on Bible principles. II. What are we to regard as the true doctrine on the subject, and as the true principles of judging in the case? 1. There is a class of sins that bring their own punishment; 2. All things, even storms, etc., are under the control of God. III. The lessons of the visitation. 1. God rules in the nations of the earth; 2. God has hidden resources for effecting His purposes; 3. This may be regarded as an extraordinary means of arresting the attention of mankind; 4. Such a visitation is of the nature of a proclamation in favor of virtue and piety.—Barnes.

7—12. (7) **I saw,** in prophetic vision. **Cushan,** poetical allusion to the Egyptian overthrow, when Israel was delivered. **in affliction,** panic-stricken. **curtains,** tent curtains. (8) **rivers,** the Red Sea, and the Jordan. By this sudden question the Prophet sets us on considering the gracious purpose of the Divine dealings. **salvation,** for Thy people: though they seemed to be only for destruction. (9) **quite naked,** drawn out from its sheath, and set quite ready for use. **oaths,** etc., a very obscure passage; meaning uncertain. R. V. translates: "the oaths to the tribes were a sure word." **cleave the earth,** etc., Camb. B.: "cleave the rivers into dry land." (10) **lifted up his hands,** fig. of the great storm-driven waves. (11) **stood still,** i.e. remained in their habitation, behind the storm-cloud. **at the light of thine arrows,** etc., the sun and moon are hidden and outshone by the terrible brightness of the lightnings of Jehovah.[b]

Oriental Bows (vs. 9).—The Oriental bows, according to Chardin, were usually carried in a case hung to their girdles; it was sometimes of cloth, but more commonly of leather.—Harmer.

13—16. (13) **woundedst,** etc., R. V. marg. "thou didst smite off the head from the house," etc. **discovering the foundation,**[a] overturning the house or city, so that the very foundations are disclosed. (14) **strike through,** etc., R. V. "Thou didst pierce with his own staves the head of his warriors;" the enemies of Israel were made to destroy each other. **devour,** as wild beasts carry their prey to their dens to enjoy it secretly. (15) **heap,** etc., Ex. xv. 8. (16) This vs. returns to vs. 2, taking up the words "I have heard thy speech and was afraid." **belly,** heart or inward parts.[b] **rottenness,** fig. for utter failure of strength. **that I might rest,** etc., Pulp. Com.: "I who shall rest in the day of tribulation." **when he cometh,** etc., R. V. marg. "when he that shall invade them in troops cometh up against the people."[c]

God's Work.—A story is told of an Eastern king, which illustrates God's work in giving growth. He was seated in a garden, and one of his counsellors was speaking of the wonderful works of God. "Show me a sign," said the king, "and I shall believe." "Here are four acorns," said the counsellor; "will your majesty plant them in the ground, and then stoop down for a moment, and look into this clear pool of water?" The king did so. "Now," said the other, "look up." The king looked up, and saw four oak-trees where he had planted the acorns. "Wonderful!" he exclaimed; "this is indeed the work of God." "How long were you looking into the water?" asked the counsellor. "Only a second," **said the king.** "Eighty years have passed as a second," said the other.

[a] Na. i. 5.

"The mountains and hills are spoken of as emblems of eternity, because time seems to make no change or alteration in them." —Lowth.

"Pleasures of the mind are more at command than those of the body. A man may think of a handsome performance, or of a notion that pleases him, at his leisure. This entertainment is ready, with little warning or expense; a short recollection brings it upon the stage, brightens the idea, and makes it shine as much as when it was first stamped upon the memory." — Jeremy Collier.

[b] "His brazen arms like flames of lightning shone, which the great Thunderer launches from his arm."—Homer.

"As alchemists spend that small modicum they have to get gold, and never find it, so we lose and neglect eternity for a little momentary pleasure which we cannot enjoy, nor shall we ever attain to in this life."— Burton.

[a] The neck is the emblem of dignity and power, and sometimes of stubbornness and pride.

[b] In the Heb. idea, the belly is the seat of physical emotion; the bones are the seat of intensest pain.

[c] "The allusion is evidently to the bands of Chaldaeans, Syrians, etc., sent against Jehoiakim after his rebellion. (2 Ki. xxiv. 2.)" —Spk. Com.

The king looked at his garments; they were threadbare. He looked at his reflection in the water; he had become an old man. "There is no miracle here, then," he said angrily "Yea," said the other, "it is God's work, whether He do it in eighty years or in one second."

Activity of God.—The most intensely thoughtful, and the most intensely active, of any being in the universe, is God; and all the power and all the majesty of His administration are for the production of good everywhere; and every violation of His wishes is a violation of a tendency towards the production of good. He is never tired, He is never weary, of His work. Such is our God, that sits in the heavens for ever and for ever, legislating by His thoughts and by His will—for He has no framework of government such as we imagine when we speak of legislation. By the whole personal influence of His being, by all His breathings, by His wishes, by His thoughts and feelings, He is perpetually studying how to raise about Him in this world, and in other worlds—if there be any that are populated—those intelligences that shall approach to Him in power of thought, and moral excellence, and perfectness of joy. This is God's avocation.—Beecher.

17—19. (17) **although,** etc., the expression of a simple but assured confidence, which could endure through all calamity. **fig .. vines .. olive,** the three principal and most important fruit trees of Canaan. All those were carefully cultivated.[a] **no meat,** i.e. food, corn and vegetables. (18) **rejoice,** in the quiet assurance that Jehovah will both deliver and provide. (19) **hinds' feet,** implying swiftness and security. Ps. xviii. 32, 33. **stringed instruments,** Heb. neginoth.[b] See titles of Ps. iv., vi.

Conscious and Unconscious Testimony.—Daniel Webster was a firm believer in Divine revelation, and a close student of its sacred pages. On one occasion, a small company of select friends spent an evening at his house. Tea over, the Bible, and the relative beauties of its several parts, became the topic of conversation. Each one of the guests had a preference. When the turn came to Webster, he said: "The masterpiece of the New Testament, of course, is the Sermon on the Mount. That has no rival, no equal. As to the Old-Testament writings, my favorite book is that of Habakkuk, and my favorite verses, chapter iii. 17, 18: 'Although the fig tree shall not blossom, neither shall fruit be in the vines—the labor of the olive shall fail, and the fields shall yield no meat—the flock shall be cut off, and there shall be no herds in the stall—yet will I rejoice in the Lord, and joy in the God of my salvation.' This," continued Webster, "I regard as one of the sublimest passages of inspired literature. And often have I wondered that some artist, equal to the task, has not selected the Prophet and his scene of desolation as the subject of a painting. When in Paris, some years ago," continued Webster, "I received an account of a French infidel, who happened to find in a drawer of his library some stray leaves of an unknown volume. Although in the constant habit of denouncing the Bible, like most infidel writers, he had never read any part of it. These fugitive leaves contained the above prayer of Habakkuk. Being a man of fine literary taste, he was captivated with its poetic beauty, and hastened to the club-house, to announce the discovery to his associates. Of course they were anxious to know the name of the gifted author, to which inquiries the elated infidel replied: 'A writer by the name of Hab-ba-kook, of course, a Frenchman!' Judge of the infidel's surprise, when informed that the passage he was so enthusiastically admiring was not produced by one of his own countrymen, nor even by one of his own class of so-called Freethinkers, but was penned by one of God's ancient Prophets, and was contained in that much despised book—the Bible."—Lutheran Observer.

Although the fig tree blossom not, O Lord,
  And henceforth fruit be found not on the vine,
The labor of the olive fail, the gourd
  Be dried and lend no shelter, and the kine
Be taken from the stalls: though at Thy word
  The fleeced flocks be cut from off the fold,

a "Of the olive it is said, 'The fruit of this tree is indispensable for the comfort, and even the existence of the mass of the community. Almost every kind of dish is cooked in oil, and without it the good wife is utterly confounded; and when the oil fails the lamp in the dwelling of the poor expires.'"—Bib. Things.

b The word "my" strongly confirms the inference drawn from other notices, that Habakkuk was a member of the Levitical choir."—Spk. Com.

"As for a little more money and a little more time, why it's ten to one if either one or the other would make you a whit happier. If you had more time, it would be sure to hang heavily. It is the working man is the happy man. Man was made to be active and he is never so happy as when he is so. It is the idle man is the miserable man. Money never made a man happy yet, nor will it. There is nothing in its nature to produce happiness. That was a true proverb of the wise man, rely upon it: "Better is little with the fear of the Lord, than great treasure, and trouble therewith."
—Franklin.

And all our enemies when waxen bold
Should decimate our cities with the sword;
Though the fair fields of happy Israel
Be wither'd in Thy glance, and yield no meat;
Though in Thy temples rude unholy feet
Tread down the altars we have loved so well:
Though powers and kingdoms fall beneath Thy rod,
Yet shall I safely dwell with Thee, my God! —G. Smith.

"Grant, Almighty God, as the dulness and hardness of our flesh is so great that it is needful for us to be in various ways afflicted—oh grant that we patiently bear Thy chastisement, and under a deep feeling of sorrow flee to Thy mercy displayed to us in Christ, so that we depend not on the earthly blessings of this perishable life, but relying on Thy word go forward in the course of our calling, until at length we be gathered to that blessed rest which is laid up for us in heaven, through Christ our Lord. Amen."—From the prayer with which Calvin concludes his exposition of Habakkuk.

We overstate the ills of life. . . We sigh so loud, the nightingale within refuses to sing loud, as else she would. O brothers! let us leave the shame and sin of taking vainly, in a plaintive mood, the holy name of Grief,—holy herein, that, by the grief of one, came all our good. — Mrs. Browning.

Introduction.

Nothing is known of Zephaniah beyond what may be gathered from his book. The opening verse makes him a descendant in the fifth generation from Hizkiah (R. V., Hezekiah). It is unusual to carry the genealogy of a prophet beyond his father. The exception in this case favors the supposition that our prophet was a descendant of King Hezekiah. Chap. i. 4, ("this place") shows that the prophet lived in Jerusalem. "He is familiar with the different localities in the capital, as the Fish gate, the Second Quarter, and the Maktesh, apparently the quarter of the merchants (i. 10, 11), and with the various classes inhabiting the city; and his picture of the social and religious practices prevailing among the people is drawn from observation (i. 4—8, 12)."

The date of the prophecy is between the years 639 and 621 B.C., probably toward the latter part of that period.

The book has been called the Dies irae of the Old Testament. Its burden is "the day of the Lord," a day of darkness and terrors and wrath, against Judah and the surrounding nations. The instrument of the divine visitation has been by many supposed to be the Chaldæans. Later scholars, however, are inclined to find this instrument in the Scythians, who ravaged Western Asia in the latter part of the seventh century. "But the judgment has not its end in itself, it is but the means of making Jehovah known to the world, and this knowledge of Him is salvation. The lips of the nations are purified that they may call upon the name of the Lord, and Israel comes forth from the judgment a chastened and humble people, trusting in Jehovah their God alone (iii. 9—13)."

CHAPTER THE FIRST.

1—3. (1) **Zephaniah,** meaning "Whom the Lord covers," in times of storm and distress.[a] **Hizkiah,** the same as Hezekiah, and probably the good king of that name. **king of Judah,** these words refer to Josiah, not to Amon. (2) **utterly consume,** marg. "by taking away I will make an end."[b] **the land,** R. V. "the face of the ground," not the land of Judah alone. (3) **man and beast,** etc., the creatures, esp. the domestic creatures, sharing the judgments brought on man.[c] **stumbling blocks,** or idols.[d]

The Book has two great divisions: First, ch. i. 2—iii. 8, a threat of judgment on the world: on Judah and the nations; and secondly, a promise of salvation equally universal, ch. iii. 9—20. The judgment is that of the great day of the Lord. The prophet represents it as universal, but concentrating itself on Judah, ch. i. 2—ii. 3; then as involving the nations, ch. ii. 4—15; and finally he speaks of Judah and the nations together, ch. iii. 1—8.——Camb. B.

4—6. (4) **Judah,** previously to this, the ten tribes had been carried away captive. "As in Am. i., ii. the cloud laden with judgment trails round the horizon, discharging itself on one nation after another, and finally settles over Israel, so here Jehovah's wrath against all created things concentrates itself on Judah and Jerusalem." **remnant of Baal,** this may refer to the altars wh. have been spared in the time of Josiah's reformation,[e] or it may mean simply "the last vestige," i.e. "the whole." Isa. xiv. 22. **Chemarims,** idol-priests.[f] **with the priests,** i.e. the unfaithful priests of Jehovah. (5) **housetops,** chosen for worship-places, bec. in full view of the heavenly bodies.[g] **by the Lord,** better, to Jehovah, and yet, with strange inconsistency, swear also to Malcham, or Moloch, or the word may be trans. "your king," and then it may be referred to Baal. (6) **turned back,** in apostacy.[h] **not sought,** etc., the indifferent who do not trouble themselves about religion.

Vs. 7.—The Soul's Silence before the Presence of the Lord.—I. A silence of adoration. As becomes a creature in the presence of his Creator (Zech. ii. 13; Hab. ii. 20), and a sinner in the presence of the Holy One (Job. xl. 4). II. A silence of contemplation. As befits the soul in those moments in which God reveals himself in nature (Job xxxvii. 14) or in grace (Gen. xvii. 3; Exod. xiv. 13). III. A silence of expectation. As a praying soul maintains when looking out for a response to his supplications (Ps. lxii. 1, 5, margin), or a perplexed spirit when waiting for God to clear up the mystery of his providence (Ps. xxxvii. 7, margin). IV. A silence of submission. As they preserve who recognize the ills of life to proceed from the hand of God (Ps. xxxix. 2; Lam. iii. 28, 29). V. A silence of approbation. As God's judgments will enforce upon all who behold them (Ps. xlvi. 10).—T. Whitelaw.

7—10. (7) **hold thy peace,** Heb. Hush![i] **day, etc.,** the expression usually signifies God's time of judgment. **sacrifice,** the wicked Jewish people, who are now to be offered up. **bid,** R. V. "sanctified." **guests,** fig. for the foes who shall devour Judah.[j] (8) **punish,** lit. visit upon. **strange apparel,** R. V. "foreign apparel," such as imitate foreign manners and customs. (9) **leap,** etc.,[k] prob. referring to deeds of violence and robbery, as the following clause indicates. Am. iii. 10; Je. v. 27. (10) **fish gate,** 2 Chr. xxxiii. 14; Ne. iii. 3, xii. 39. Situated in the northern wall of Jerusalem. **second,** R. V. "second quarters." **hills,** of Jerusalem. The vs. describes the noise and terror of an enemy breaking into the city on the north.

That Leap on the Threshold.—A great number of attendants is a modern piece of Oriental magnificence; it appears to have been so anciently, Eccles. v. 11; these servants, now, it is most certain, frequently attend their master on horseback, richly attired, sometimes to the number of twenty-five or thirty: if they did so anciently, with a number of servants attending great men, who are represented by this very Prophet as at that time in common terrible oppressors, ch. iii. 3, they may be naturally supposed to ride into people's houses, and having gained ad-

[a] Gesenius.
[b] Je. viii. 13.
[c] Ro. viii. 22.
[d] Eze. vii. 19, xiv. 3, 4.

"To know the pains of power, we must go to those who have it; to know its pleasures, we must go to those who are seeking it; the pains of power are real, its pleasures imaginary."— C. Colton.

[e] "The remains of Baal worship, which as yet Josiah was unable utterly to eradicate in remoter places. Baal was the Phoenician tutelary god." —Fausset.
[f] 2 Ki. xxiii. 5.
[g] 2 Ki. xxiii. 5, 12; Je. xix. 13, xxxii. 29.
[h] Je. ii. 13, 17.

[i] Ha. ii. 20; Zec. ii. 13.
[j] "The illus. is drawn from those sacrifices in wh. the offerer invited his friends to share the flesh of the victim, see 1 Sa. ix. 12, 13."—Spk. Com.
[k] "'Leap over the threshold:' in imitation of the Philistine custom of not treading on the threshold. 1 Sa. v. 5." — Rosenmuller.

Submission is the most becoming attitude. The praise of silence has its pre-eminent advocate

mission by deceit, to force from them by violence considerable contributions: for this riding into houses is not now only practiced by the Arabs; it consequently might be practiced by others, too, anciently. It is not now peculiar to the Arabs, for Le Bruyn, after describing the magnificent furniture of several of the Armenian merchants at Julfa, that suburb of Ispahan in which they live, tells us, that the front door of the greatest part of these houses is very small, partly to hinder the Persians from entering into them on horseback, and partly that they may less observe the magnificence within. If this text refers to a violence of this sort, they are the thresholds of the oppressed over which they leaped, not the thresholds of the oppressive masters, which some have supposed, when they returned laden with spoil.—Harmer.

in Carlyle, who writes: "Nay, in thy own perplexities, do thou thyself but hold thy tongue for one day: on the morrow, how much clearer are thy purposes and duties; what wreck and rubbish have those mute workmen within thee swept away, when intrusive noises were shut out."

11—13. (11) **Maktesh,** probably a part, or street, of Jerusalem. **merchant people,** or people of Canaan.[a] **bear silver,** those who have gotten wealth by trade and usury. (12) **search .. candles,** the darkest places shall be penetrated and those hiding in them discovered. In the pictures of Zephaniah as a saint he is represented carrying a lantern. **settled .. lees,** marg. curded, crusted, thickened.[b] **good .. evil,** i.e. He does not concern Himself about us. The vs. describes a prosperous, self-indulgent, semi-sceptical class. (13) **therefore,** etc., comp. De. xxviii. 39; Am. v. 11.

[a] Ho. xii. 7.

"Those whose souls were engrossed in buying and selling, and getting money, had forfeited the honored name of Israel, and deserved to be called by the name of the original inhabitants, whom they closely resembled." — Spk. Com.

[b] "Image from the crust formed at the bottom of wines long left undisturbed." —Fausset.

The Diligent Search and the Certain Discovery (vs. 12).—I. The nature of the search. 1. Determined; 2. Universal. (a) No bribe can avert it; (b) No strength can resist it. II. The design of the search. 1. To rouse the spiritually hardened; 2. To reprove the practically indifferent; 3. To punish the worldly-minded.—Hom. Com.

Settled on Their Lees (vs. 12).—The margin has, in place of "settled," "curdled or thickened." The Tamul translation has this, "dregs stirred up," i.e. sediment shaken together well thickened. Of people who are in great straits, of those who are a strange compound of good and evil, of things which are difficult to understand, it is said, "Ah! this is all kullumbinvandal," i.e. stirred up dregs. This appears to have been the state of the Jews, and they wanted to show that the Lord would neither do good nor evil; that in Him was not any distinct character; and that He would not regard them in their thickened and mixed condition; that though they were joined to the heathen, it was not of any consequence. "I will search Jerusalem with candles;" thus were they mistaken in their false hopes. Does a man declare his innocence of any crime, the accusers say, "We will search thee with lamps." "Yes, yes, I will look into that affair with lamps!" "What! have your lamps gone out? You see I am not guilty."—Roberts.

"There is no keeping back the power we have. He hath no power who hath not power to use."—Bailey.

"Let him that would be at quiet take heed not to provoke men in power." —Seneca.

14—16. (14) **day of the Lord,** sometimes in the Scriptures the terrors of the day of the Lord are represented as due to His manifestation of Himself and the convulsions of nature that accompany His appearing, "when he arises to shake terribly the earth" (Is. ii. 10—22); at other times, as in the present passage and in Is. xiii., besides the supernatural gloom and terrors that surround Him when He appears, He is represented as using some terrible distant nation as the instrument by which He executes His judgment.—Camb. B. **hasteth,** seems, to the Prophet, to be hurrying swiftly.[a] **voice,** it is near, so that the sound of it is heard. **cry,** or shriek, comp. Is. xiii. 7, 8. (15) **wrath,** Je. xxx. 7; Joel ii. 11. The first words of the Vulgate translation of this verse, Dies iræ dies illa, were adopted by Thomas of Celano as the opening words of his splendid hymn on the Last Judgment. (16) **trumpet,** or signal of war. **alarm,** or war-shout.

[a] Joel ii. 1, 11; Ro. xiii. 12; He. x. 37; Re. xxii. 20.

"Let not sinners be laid asleep by the patience of God, for when the measure of their iniquity is full, His justice will both overtake and overcome, wil make quick work and thorough work." —Mat. Henry.

Zephaniah, the Prophet of the Day of the Lord.—
A day of wrath, of darkness and distress,
When God will search with candles, and will seize
The careless doubters, settled on their lees,
Who live in luxury and selfishness.
The enemy, resentful, pitiless,
With banners waving in the morning breeze,
The city gates shall enter at their ease,
And all its treasures spoil beyond redress.

"Power! 'tis the favorite attribute of gods, who look with smiles on men, who can aspire to copy them." —Martyn.

But sing, O Zion! There's another day
Of God, when He, thy King, who 's in the midst
Of thee, shall joy o'er thee, and rest in love;
Thy foe cast out, thy judgments take away;
Let thee no more see evil, since thou didst
Not doubt, but patiently His goodness prove.—C. S. Hoyt.

17, 18. (17) **bring distress,** comp. De. xxviii. 52. **like blind,** in utter and hopeless bewilderment. **dust .. dung,** refuse and worthless things. (18) **neither,** etc., Pr. xi. 4; Eze. vii. 19. **speedy riddance,** R. V. "an end, yea, a terrible end."

"Thou, whosoever hast been wont to speak against God, as if he had no care about earthly affairs, cease thy murmurs and self-justifications: submit thyself to God, and repent in time." —Calvin.

"As the vintner goes through his cellars, torch in hand; or as the head of the household, taper in hand, searches every nook and corner of his house before the Passover, lest any morsel of leaven should be hidden in it, so Jehovah will 'search Jerusalem with candles,' hunting the evil out of every dark nook in which they have concealed themselves, suffering none to escape."

The Greatness of God.—

A million torches, lighted by Thy hand,
Wander unwearied through the blue abyss;
They own Thy power, accomplish Thy command,
All gay with life, all eloquent with bliss;
What shall we call them? Piles of crystal light?
A glorious company of golden streams?
Lamps of celestial ether, burning bright?
Suns, lighting systems with their joyous beams?
But Thou to these art as the noon to night!

Yes! as a drop of water in the sea,
All this magnificence in Thee is lost.
What are ten thousand worlds compared to Thee?
And what am I, then? Heaven's unnumber'd host,
Though multiplied by myriads, and array'd
In all the glory of sublimest thought,
Is but an atom, in the balance weigh'd
Against Thy greatness,—is a cypher brought
Against infinity! What am I? Nought!

CHAPTER THE SECOND.

1—3. (1) **Gather yourselves together,** to make confession and supplication to God. **not desired,** R. V. "that hath no shame."[a] (2) **before the decree,** etc., before the Divine purpose bring forth its effects. **before the day,** etc., Camb. B.: "before ye become like the chaff that passeth by." (3) **meek,** or pious, humble souls.[b] **hid,**[c] so as to be preserved in the time of judgment and calamity, Is. xxvi. 20. Such preservation, however, cannot be absolutely assured. Oftentimes the righteous have to share national troubles with the wicked.

Now.—When a course is felt by us to be right, we ought at once to pursue it. "What is 'now'? 'A bright presence.' Wrestle with it, and say, 'I will not let thee go except thou bless me'! 'A sweet garden.' Go, gather in it the fruits of life! 'A true temple.' Bow down in it, and consecrate yourself to him who has placed you within its shrine! 'A living rescue.' Use it, that you may run into the ark of safety! 'A rich banquet.' Now the feast is spread: 'Come, eat, O friends, drink, O beloved! yea, eat and live for ever'!"—M. F. Tupper.

4—7. (4) The nations on whom the impending judgment shall fall are: (1) the Philistines (vss. 4—7); (2) Moab and Ammon (vss. 8—11); (3) Cush or the Ethiopians (vs. 12); and (4) Assyria (vss. 13—15). In relation to Judah the four nations named lay respectively west, east, south, and north. **Gaza,** etc., the principal cities of the Philistine plain.[a] **at the noon day,** perhaps the meaning is "in the half of the day."—Camb. B. appendix. (5) **Cherethites,** 1 Sa. xxx. 14. **Canaan,** wh. included Philistia. (6) **dwellings and cottages,** etc., R. V. marg. "pastures with caves for shepherds," etc., the sign of a desolate and uninhabited district. (7) **remnant,**[b] those restored fr. captivity. They did pasture their flocks in this seacoast region. **turn away,** etc., R. V. "bring again their captivity."

Ascalon.—The site of Ascalon is in form like an old Roman theatre, —the sea in front, and the ground once occupied by the city rising grad-

[a] "Or, 'O nation not ashamed,' lost to all sense of shame, and therefore unwilling to receive correction, and incapable of amendment." —Wordsworth.

[b] Mat. v. 5.

[c] Ps. xxvii. 5.

"Lord," says Augustine, "I have viewed the world over, in which thou hast set me; I have tried how this and that thing will fit my spirit and the design of my creation; and can find nothing in which to rest, for nothing here doth itself rest. Lo, I come to thee, the eternal Being, the Spring of Life, the Centre of rest, the Fulness of all things!"

[a] This prophecy has been literally fulfilled; scarcely a trace of these once flourishing cities is now left.

[b] Hag. i. 12, ii. 2.

ually and uniformly to the wall, which runs in a semicircle from shore to shore. Not a house, not a fragment of a house, remains standing. Not a foundation of temple or palace can be traced entire. One half of it is occupied by miniature fields, and vineyards, and fig orchards; rubbish-mounds here and there among them, and great heaps of hewn stones, and broken shafts, and sculptured slabs of granite and marble. The rude fences exhibit similar painful evidences of ancient wealth and magnificence. The other half of the site was still more fearfully desolate. It is so thickly covered with drift sand, that not a heap of rubbish, not a vestige of ruin, remains visible, save here and there where the top of a column rises like a tombstone above the smooth surface. The sand is fast advancing; it has already covered some of the highest fragments of the southern and western wall, and ere a quarter of a century has passed, the site of Ascalon will have been blotted out for ever.—Porter.

G. Adam Smith translates vss. 4, 5 as follows: For Gaza forsaken shall be, Ashk'lon a desert. Ashdod—by noon shall they rout her, and Ekron be torn up! Ah! woe, dwellers of the sea-shore, folk of Kerethim. The word of Jehovah against thee, Kena'an, land of the Philistines!

8—11. **reproach .. Ammon,**[a] the neighboring nations, wh. had long manifested bitter enmity against the Jews. **magnified .. border,** Am. i. 13. (9) **as Sodom,** the type of utter and overwhelming destruction. **nettles,**[b] the growth of waste places. (10) **this,** overwhelming judgment, comp. Is. xv. 6; Je. xlvii. 29. (11) **famish,** etc., by depriving them of their worship, offerings, and worshipers. **worship him,** i.e. Jehovah. **every one from his place,** this seems to mean that without making pilgrimages to Jerusalem (Is. ii. 3; Zech. viii. 22, xiv. 16) the peoples shall worship Jehovah, every man in his own land (Mat. i. 11).

a For prophecies against Moab, see Nu. xxiv. 17; Is. xv., xvi.; Am. ii. 1—3; Je. xlviii.

For prophecies against Ammon see Am. i. 13—15; Je. xlix.; Eze. xxv. 1—7.

b Poss. it designates the prickly acanthus, a very common and troublesome weed . abounding among ruins."—Tristram.

12—15. (12) **Ethiopians,** Ge. x. 6; allies of the Egyptians. These were conquered by Nebuchadnezzar. "Ethiopia or Cush was the country lying south of Egypt. Stretching from Syene (Assouan) southward, it corresponded to Nubia and the modern Soudan." (13) **Assyria,** the earlier kingdom, whose capital was Nineveh, and which Babylon conquered and absorbed. (14) **beasts of the nations,** "beasts" is in apposition with "flocks." The flocks and herds of all nations shall make Assyria their pasture ground. **cormorant,** or pelican, Ps. cii. 6. **bittern,** Tristram says: "the bittern is very abundant in these swamps of the Tigris.[c] **upper lintels,** or capitals of her columns. **uncover .. work,** laying bare the interior decorations as the palaces dropped into ruins. (15) **carelessly,** heedless of all warnings, Is. xlvii. 8. **I am,** etc., this is the expression of the pride and self-satisfaction of Nineveh. **hiss,** etc., Na. iii. 19.

Pride. That wh. first overcame man, is the last thing he overcomes.—Augustine.

"It is a dangerous indiscretion for a man not to know the bounds of his own calling."—Bp. Hall.

c "A bird somewhat smaller than a heron, of solitary habits, and frequenting marshy lands. It is a bird of the wilds, almost a bird of desolation, avoiding alike the neighborhood of man and the progress of man's improvements."—Bib. Things.

Nineveh.—This doom on Nineveh was carried out to the very letter. It was not simply the largest city of the ancient world. In the mouth of the Hebrew prophets it was the name of a district, 25 miles long, by 15 broad, which included four large cities, besides villages and forts, within its protecting walls. About six centuries B.C., this vast populous district was conquered and destroyed by the Medes (under Cyaxares), and the Chaldæans (under Nabopolasser, father of Nebuchadnezzar). So complete was the destruction, that with startling abruptness the great city vanished from the face of the earth, and its very ruins were hidden from the eyes of men. In A.D. 1766, Niebuhr, the great historian, stood on the eastern bank, which he took to be acclivities wrought by the hand of nature. It was not till A.D. 1842 that Layard, Rawlinson, and Botta dug into these mounds, exhumed and interpreted the remains which tell the story of the city's greatness, luxury, and culture with a power beyond that of words.—S. Cox.

CHAPTER THE THIRD.

1—4. (1) **her,** i.e. Jerusalem, wh. at the time was filled with the sins of luxury and cruelty. **filthy,** R. V. "rebellious." (2) **the voice,** of gracious warning. (3) **roaring lions,** resembling such in their violent dealings with the people. **evening wolves,** fiercely ravening for their prey.[d] **gnaw .. morrow,** R. V. "they leave nothing till the morrow." (4) **light,** reckless, unprincipled.[e] **violence .. law,** Eze. xxii. 26.

d Ha. i. 8.

e "They were so given to bantering, that it was hard to say when they were serious."—Mat. Henry.

Special Need of Watchfulness.—When cast by Providence among sinful persons who respect us, we ought to be peculiarly watchful. The

"Sins of commission are usual punishments for sins of omission. He that

hatred of the ungodly, when poured upon Christians in the form of persecution, is seldom harmful to their spiritual nature, but the friendship of the world is always to be suspected. When the servants of the high priest allowed Peter to warm his hands at the fire, had Peter been a wise man, he would have been afraid that evil would come to it. We are disarmed by kindness, but it is never safe to be disarmed in an enemy's country. "Who," says the old proverb, "could live in Rome and yet be at war with the pope?" Who can have much to do with sinners and not have something to do with their sins? The smiling daughters of Moab did more mischief to Israel than all Balak's frowning warriors. All Philistia could not have blinded Samson if Delilah's charms had not deluded him. Our worst foes will be found among our ungodly friends. Those who are false to God, are not likely to be true to us. Walk carefully, believer, if thy way lie by the sinner's door, and especially if that sinner hath acted a friendly part to thee.—Spurgeon.

5—7. (5) all these wrongs they practice undeterred by the presence and operations of the righteous Lord in the midst of them. **just Lord,** etc., R. V. "The Lord in the midst of her is righteous." **every morning,** or "morning by morning."[a] His moral rule is as constant and as visible as the material law that brings in the dawn. Cf. Hos. vi. 5. The fact that God was in the midst of them, witnessing against their wrongdoings, aggravated their iniquity...**no shame,** on account of his sin. Jer. vi. 15; viii. 12. (6) Jehovah's righteous rule is exercised not only in the midst of Israel itself, but also among the nations without. **cut off the nations,** R. V. "cut off nations." "No particular nations are named; history is full of God's judgments on the peoples for their unrighteousness, the Flood, the overthrow of Sodom, the destruction of Samaria, and the like." (7) God's purpose in these judgments on the nations was that Israel should take warning from them and receive instruction. **so their dwelling, etc.,** R. V. "so her dwelling should not be cut off, according to all that I have appointed concerning her." **rose early,** the usual sign of doing things earnestly.[b]

Effect of Neglecting God (vss. 7, 8).—I. What God has been expecting of us. 1. There have been judgments of God on surrounding nations; 2. God has been speaking to us by these events. II. How we have disappointed His expectations. 1. Hear the accusation of God against us; 2. The accusation is applicable to all. III. What we may expect from Him—1. In a way of judgment; 2. In a way of mercy.—Simeon.

God's Watchful Care.—A little boy was running about in an apartment, amusing himself, as children are accustomed to do. His money was potsherds, his house bits of wood, his horse, a stick, and his child a doll. In the same apartment sat his father, at a table, occupied with important matters of business, which he noted and arranged for the future benefit of his young companion. The child frequently ran to him, asked many foolish questions, and begged one thing after another as necessary for his diversion. The father answered briefly, did not intermit his work, but, all the time, kept a watchful eye over the child, to save him from any serious fall or injury. Gotthold was a spectator of the scene, and thought with himself: "How beautiful an adumbration of the fatherly care of God! We, too, who are old children, course about in the world, and often play at games which are much more foolish than those of our little ones: we collect and scatter, build and demolish, plant and pluck up, ride and drive, eat and drink, sing and play, and fancy that we are performing great exploits, well worthy of God's special attention. Meanwhile, however, the Omniscient is sitting by, and writing our days in His book. He orders and executes all that is to befall us, overruling it for our best interests in time and eternity: and yet His eye never ceases to watch over us and the childish sports in which we are engaged, that we may meet with no deadly mischief."

8—10. (8) **wait ye upon me,** R. V. "for me." The exhortation is addressed to the pious among the Jews, as in ch. ii. 3, and is used in a good sense (Ps. xxxiii. 20), urging them not to despair, but to be patient under the affliction, in the assured hope of salvation.—Pulp. Com. **fire ..jealousy,** ch. i. 18. (9) **pure language,** or lip. They shall sincerely take upon their lips the name of Jehovah. **one consent,** lit. one shoulder:

leaves a duty may fear to be left to commit a crime."—Gurnall. "We may lose heaven by neutrality as well as by hostility, by wanting oil as well as by drinking poison. An unprofitable servant shall as much be punished as a prodigal son. Undone duty will undo our souls."—Bowes. The last words of the industrious Archbishop Usher were, "Lord, in special, forgive me my sins of omission."

[a] "The morning is the usual time in the sultry East for dispensing justice." —Fausset.

[b] "God rose up early, to send them His Prophets, to reduce and reclaim them, but they were up before Him, to shut and bolt the door against Him." —Mat. Henry.

"Never put much confidence in such as put no confidence in others. A man prone to suspect evil is mostly looking in his neighbor for what he sees in himself. As to the pure all things are pure, even so to the impure all things are impure." — J. C. Hare.

[c] Is. lx. 4, 9, lxvi. 20.

"The confidence we have in ourselves creates a great part of that trust which we have in others. The greatest part of our confidence proceeds from a desire either to be pitied or admired."— Beaumont.

"as of men helping one another to support a heavy load." (10) **my suppliants,**[a] "looking to the thought in Isa. lxvi. 20 (where it is said that the Gentiles shall bring the Israelites out of all nations as a meat offering unto the Lord), we had better render the passage as the R. V. margin, "They shall bring my suppliants, even the daughter of my dispersed, for an offering unto me." The remote Gentiles shall show their faith in God by aiding the Hebrews among them to turn to the Lord; this shall be their offering to the true God, whom they have learned to adore."—Pulp. Com.

With One Shoulder.—Only when all men serve God with one shoulder the sense of strain and distress will pass from us. To love God is to love man. Till they share our freedom, it cannot be a happy freedom. Till they love him and do his will, they will put many hindrances and temptations in our way which make obedience hard and painful. If they do not take their full share in bearing the burden, it will press unduly upon our shoulders. If some are morally taller and others morally shorter, men do not keep step. Only when the whole world stands under the Divine burden with one shoulder, and moves with one step, will our freedom be a happy freedom, and God's statutes become our songs. Seeing how men suffer from the sins of men, and nations from the sins of nations, we may well long and pray for the time when all men shall speak with a pure lip and serve with a single shoulder.—Preacher's Lantern.

11—13. (11) **not be ashamed,** God addresses Israel repentant, and assures her that she shall not have cause to blush for her iniquities, because she has become humble and obedient. **them that rejoice in thy pride,** R. V. "thy proudly exulting ones." (12) **I will also leave,** R. V. "But I will leave." **an afflicted and poor people,** "afflicted in its modern sense is too strong. The idea is "lowly," not "haughty." (13) **The remnant,** the idea that only a remnant shall be saved, is common to all the prophets. Isa. x. 21, 22; Joel ii. 32.

The Restored Remnant—I. Their spiritual charcter. 1. They are few in number; 2. They are humble in spirit; 3. They are dependent upon God; 4. They are upright in conduct. II. Their blessed condition. 1. They are cleansed from shame for sin; 2. They are delivered from spiritual pride; 3. They are redeemed from proud oppressors; 4. They are specially protected by God.—Hom. Com.

14, 15. (14) **daughter of Zion,** Is. xii. 6, liv. 1. "Such hymns of joy properly belong to the times of the Gospel." (15) **taken away,** removed them, bec. their end was sufficiently accomplished. **the king,** the only true King. "The prophecy of the perpetual Divine presence is fulfilled in God the Son, Emmanuel, God with us."

Shalt Not See Evil Any More.—Tell the mariner that no more shall the sea be lashed into a storm; tell the wayfaring man that no more shall the lion rise up suddenly in his path; tell the toiler that no more shall blight devastate his harvest; and he will have some idea of the joy that must have filled the heart of Jerusalem when the Lord predicted that evil should not be seen any more within the lines of her beauty, within the security of her defences. What great feasts the Lord provides his people! How rapturous is the music of reconciliation!—Parker.

16, 17. (16) **slack,** or faint.[a] This is gracious comforting for the feeble-minded and timid. (17) **rejoice over thee,** in having now the opportunity of doing thee good. **rest,** literally "be silent in his love," the words seem to mean that God's love will be so deep as to hush motion or speech; it will be a silent ecstasy.—Camb. B.

God and His People.—I. God's relation to his people. 1. Their covenant God; 2. Their rightful King; 2. Their mighty Saviour. II. God's presence with his people. He is in their midst. 1. In the Spirit of his Son; 2. In the Word of his truth; 3. In the ordinances of his Church. III. God's work for his people. Salvation: 1. From the guilt and power of sin; 2. From the danger of ignorance and error; 3. From the temptations and corruptions of the world; 4. From the fear of death and the dominion of the grave. IV. God's delight in his people. 1. True and tender; 2. Full and deep; 3. Perfect and abiding.—T. Whitelaw.

Vs. 13— "We little expected this when Zephaniah opened his judgment. We expected the fire to devour every root, and that nothing would be left behind but white ashes; and lo! such has been the effect of the threatened judgment of God, that truth takes the place of lies, vice is displaced by virtue, and the mouth that was befouled with deceit is now found to be the instrument of purity and music. Do not despair of the worst. The worst should not despair of themselves." —J. Parker.

"What is public history but a register of the successes and disappointments, the vices, the follies, and the quarrels of those who engage in contention for power?"—Paley.

"Prayer sancties all our actions. When the mind in the morning opens to God, as the eye to the sun's clear light, by the radiance of the Divine beams we become enlightened inwardly all the day."—Feltham.

a He. xii. 12; Is. xxxv. 3, 4.

Through love to light! Oh, wonderful the way,
That leads from darkness to the perfect day!
From darkness and from sorrow of the night,
To morning that comes singing o'er the sea.
Through love to light! Through light, O God! to thee,
Who art the love of love, the eternal light of light.
—Richard W. Gilder.

18—20. (18) **them that are sorrowful,** etc., the reference is to the Jews dispersed among the nations, far from the sanctuary and the feasts.[b] **of thee,** i.e. of thy true citizens. **the reproach,** of being under Divine judgments, and in bitter captivity. (19) **undo all,** R. V. "deal with all." **halteth,** the afflicted of Israel are compared to a lame and footsore flock of sheep. Hence the feminine gender. Mic. iv. 6, 7; Ezek. xxxiv. 16. (20) **even in the time,** R. V. "and at that time will I gather you!" **before your eyes,** the deliverance shall not be delayed till their eyes are closed and be seen only by their children. Their own eyes shall see it.

The Wonderful Restoration.—I. A restoration glorious in its character. 1. It will be divinely performed; 2. It will be completely performed; 3. It will be visibly performed. II. A restoration certain in its accomplishment. 1. Unimpeded by outward enemies; 2. Unimpeded by internal weakness.—Pul. Com.

Divine Restoration.—The Lord did not build the universe that he might destroy it; wherever there are marks of destruction they are footprints of an enemy; the purpose of the Lord is to obliterate such footprints, to rebuild all shattered strength, to restore all marred beauty; and when the Lord has set himself to work out a purpose, who can withstand the pressure and the progress of his omnipotence? Let all evangelical thinkers and workers, yea, all evangelical men, know that they are moving in the line of the divine intent. Let them nourish themselves with the fatness of the divine promises, and be assured that, come what may, the Lord will ultimately prevail.—J. Parker.

b La. ii. 6.

"The immediate judgment with which Zephaniah threatened Jerusalem was averted. But his prophecy began to be fulfilled in the disasters which befell neighboring nations. It was fulfilled yet further in those great convulsions of the nations of the East which followed shortly. It was fulfilled for Judah in the captivity and destruction of the guilty nation. For these were all steps of progress advancing towards the great end, elements contributing to the fulness of the times, preludes to the establishment of the universal divine kingdom."
—Kirkpatrick.

Introduction.

I. **Author.** Haggai. He was the first of the three prophets, who belong to that final stage of Jewish history which began with the return from the captivity in Babylon. Two of them, he and Zechariah, prophesied at its commencement. Malachi followed about a hundred years later. After that, the voice of prophecy was silent for four centuries till the days of John the Baptist. Of the personal history of Haggai scarcely anything is known. His tribe and parentage are not told us. It would seem most probable that he was among the captives who returned from Babylon, and there is a tradition that he was born during the exile in that city. The Book of Ezra, which contains the history of the return from Babylon, and of the events which followed immediately upon it, mentions both Haggai and Zechariah by name, and describes the effect upon the people of their prophecies, of which the written records are preserved to us in their Books (Ezra v. 1; vi. 14).—Cambridge Bible. II. **Time.** B.C. 520, September to December. III. **Style.** Prosaic, but parallelisms occasionally appear (see i. 6, 9, 10, ii. 6, 8, 22). He frequently introduces interrogatories (as in i. 4, 9, ii. 3, 12, 13, 19). It may be added that "the desire of all nations" (ii. 7) cannot directly apply to Christ; it should rather be rendered "the choice of all nations." All shall be shaken, or fear; but the choicest, the best, shall come to give honor to God. It is not denied that this has its full accomplishment in Messianic times. IV. **Theme.** Haggai was commissioned to stir up the flagging zeal of the people, informing them that the unproductive seasons which they had experienced were the punishment of their negligence, and assuring them that the second temple, far from being inferior to that of Solomon, should exceed it in glory.—Litton.

Synopsis.

(According to Horne.)

DISCOURSE I. The people reproved for delay in building the temple; and told that their neglect has resulted in bad seasons..i. 1—12

They are encouraged to undertake the work, and promised Divine assistance......13—15

DISCOURSE II. The builders are promised that the glory of the second temple should surpass that of the first—this prophecy was fulfilled by Jesus Christ honoring the second temple with His presence, and there publishing His saving doctrine to the world (see Luke xix. 47, xx. 1, xxi. 38; John xviii. 20); and that the harvest of the following year should be good........ii. 1—19

DISCOURSE III. The setting up of Messiah's kingdom under the name of Zerubbabel foretold ....ii. 20—23

CHAPTER THE FIRST.

The first prophecy, chap. 1. 1, 2. (1) **Darius,** Darius Hystaspes.[a] **sixth month,** "i.e. of the Jewish year. While they had kings of their own the Jewish historians were wont, as we see throughout the Books of Kings and Chronicles, to date events by the years of their reigns. Now that their own monarchy was at an end, they use instead the year of the foreign Sovereign to whom they were tributary. The transition is observable in vs. 8 of 2 Kings xxv. as compared with vs. 1. But the months are still those of their own calendar. The sixth month was called Elul after the return from Babylon. (Neh. vi. 15; 1 Macc. xiv. 27.)" —Camb. Bib. **Haggai,** meaning, as some suppose, festive; but this is uncertain. **Zerubbabel,** comp. Ezr. i. 8, iii. 8. (2) **this people,** bec. of their sinful state of mind God does not address them as My people. **not come,** R. V., "It is not the time for us to come." An idle excuse with no special reason. "By and by. It is not time yet."[b]

The House of God.—You have all got into the habit of calling the church the "house of God." I have seen over the doors of many churches the legend actually carved, "This is the house of God, and this is the gate of heaven." Now, note where that legend comes from, and of what place it was first spoken. A boy leaves his father's house to go on a long journey on foot, to visit his uncle; he has to cross a wild hill desert; just as if one of your own boys had to cross the wilds of Westmoreland, to visit an uncle at Carlisle. The second or third day your boy finds himself somewhere between Hawes and Brough, in the midst of the moors, at sunset. It is stony ground, and boggy; he cannot go one foot further that night. Down he lies to sleep on Wharnside where best he may, gathering a few of the stones together to put under his head—so wild the place is he cannot get anything but stones. And there, lying under the broad light, he has a dream; and he sees a ladder set up on the earth, and the top of it reaches to heaven, and the angels of God are ascending and descending upon it. And when he wakes out of his sleep, he says, "How dreadful is this place: surely, this is none other than the house of God, and this is the gate of heaven." This place, observe; not this church; not this city; not this stone even, which he puts up for a memorial—the piece of flint on which his head has lain. But this place; this windy slope of Wharnside; this moorland hollow, torrent-bitten, snow-blighted; this any place where God lets down the ladder. And how are you to know where that will be? or how are you to determine where it may be, but by being ready for it always? Do you know where the lightning is to fall next? You do know that, partly: you can guide the lightning; but you cannot guide the going forth of the Spirit, which is as the lightning when it shines from the east to the west. But the perpetual and insolent warping of that strong verse to serve a merely ecclesiastical purpose, is only one of the thousand instances in which we sink back into gross Judaism.

Haggai, the Prophet of Reconstruction.—
'Mid blended shouts of joy and grief were laid
The stones whereon the exile's hopes were based.
Then foes conspired. The king his course retraced,
His throne against the enterprise arrayed.
And now self-seeking, apathy, invade
All hearts. The pulse grows faint, the will unbraced.
They rear their houses, let God's house lie waste.
So heaven from dew and earth from fruit are stayed.

There comes swift messenger from higher court,
With rugged message, of divine import:—
"Your ways consider; be ye strong and build;
With greater glory shall this house be filled."
He touched their conscience, and their spirit stirred
To nerve their hands for work, their loins regird.

a Ezr. iv. 5, 24.

"Darius was a common name of the Persian kings, as Pharaoh of those of Egypt, and Caesar of those of Rome."—Fausset.

b "The temple began to be rebuilt in the year B. C. 535. But in consequence of opposition from without, and the failure of faith and courage within, the work of building the temple was intermitted for fifteen years." —Wordsworth.

Christians in Greenland very seldom, if ever, absent themselves from public worship on account of the weather. When it is so cold that their breath freezes and forms icicles on their faces, they yet go long distances—men, women, and children — through snow and ice, storm etc., to the house of prayer. Through much greater sacrifice than the Christians of more favored lands do the poor Greenlanders obey the injunction not to forsake the assembling of themselves together.

3—6. (3) **then,** in special application to this sinful negligence. (4) **you, O ye,** "the repetition of the pronoun is emphatic." "Is it a time for you—you—to be dwelling in houses ceiled with planks, while this House is waste?"—G. A. Smith. **ceiled,** or wainscoted, a favorite form of ornamentation.[c] **this house,** the temple of Jehovah. (5) **consider,** set your heart on; wisely estimate your past and present conduct. (6) **sown,** etc., Le. xxvi. 16; De. xxviii. 38. **he that earneth wages,** "The judgment is not confined to the fruits of the earth, but extends to all branches of human industry. Disappointment and loss mar all alike. 'The labor pictured is not only fruitless, but wearisome and vexing. There is a seeming result of all the labor, something to allure hopes; but forthwith it is gone. The heathen assigned a like baffling of hope as one of the punishments of hell."—Pusey, in Camb. B. **bag .. holes,** a proverbial expression for labor spent to no profit, or permanent advantage.

Idleness.—It was the speech of Mr. Greenham (some time a painful preacher of this nation), that, when the devil tempted a poor soul, she came to him for advice, how she might resist the temptation; and he gave her this answer: "Never be idle, but be always well employed; for in my own experience I have found it, when the devil came to tempt me, I told him that I was not at leisure to hearken to his temptation, and by this means I resisted all his assaults."—Cawdray.

7—9. (7, 8) **mountain,** R. V. margin, "the hill country." Neh. ii. 8, viii. 15. "The wood-work, wainscoting and panelling, was the chief point now demanding attention." **will be glorified,** or, as the Chaldee expounds it, "I will place My glory there." (9) **blow,** so scattering it as chaff before the wind." **run,** "you are indifferent to the miserable condition of the house of God, while you haste with all diligence to your own houses for business or pleasure, being entirely absorbed in worldly interests, or eager only to adorn and beautify your own habitations."—Pul. Com.

A Dying Request.—"I have one request to make to you," said a dying Christian to his son; "will you grant it me?" The son promised compliance. "That you will, for six months after my death, retire alone to your room for half an hour every day, and think." "On what subject?" inquired the boy. "That," replied the father, "I leave entirely to yourself." He had been a disobedient son, but in this solemn hour he felt that no sacrifice was too great if he could only make amends for the past. The father died. The promise was fulfilled. At first his thoughts wandered to all sorts of subjects, till at length conscience began to work in him. He was alarmed, and was at length led to the Saviour; lived from thenceforth a useful life.—Bib. Treasury.

10, 11. (10) **heaven,** etc., R. V. "Therefore for your sake the heaven is stayed," etc., i.e. on your account, because of your sin. De. xxviii. 23. **dew,** one of the most important agents in the sultry East, where rain only falls at fixed periods. "The dews generally are remarkably heavy, and in the summer months take the place of rain. Dr. Thomson speaks of the dew rolling in the morning off his tent like rain."—Pul. Com. (11) **drought,** Heb. choreb, sounding like chareeb, waste: wh. was the condition in wh. they allowed God's house to be. The terms used indicate a correspondence bet. the sin and the punishment, and so a special appropriateness in the punishment.[a]

God in Nature.—To those who believe in God, and try to see God in all things, the most minute natural phenomenon cannot be secular. It must be divine—deliberately divine; and I can use no more lofty word. The grain of dust can no more go from God's presence, or flee from God's Spirit, than you or I can. If it go up to the physical heaven, and float—as it actually often does—far above the clouds, in those higher strata of the atmosphere which the æronaut has never visited, even there it will be obeying physical laws, which we term hastily laws of nature, but which are really laws of God; and if it go down into the abyss, if it be buried fathoms, miles, below the surface, and become an atom of some rock in the process of consolidation, has it escaped from God, even in the bowels of the earth? Is it not there obeying the will and mind of God?—Kingsley.

12—15. (12) **remnant,** or rest, Ne. vii. 72. **fear,** in the sense of hum-

c "It argues a great contempt of God and religion, when men think no cost or finery too much to bestow upon themselves, and the meanest accommodation good enough for the service of God."—Lowth.

In the East at the present day "the chief ornament of a room on which the chief expense is laid out, is the ceiling. The favorite ceiling is made of wood, carved in intricate and graceful arabesque figures painted in brilliant, gorgeous colors, and sometimes extremely beautiful. A favorite color for ceilings in Asia Minor, and one of the most enduring, is vermilion."—Van Lennep.

"Get the work done, then the blessing will come. There are some of us who want the blessing without the work, and we cannot have it. You cannot have the harvest without having first the seedtime, and that seedtime may be very cold and harsh, and you may have to face many a morning that is all keenness and coldness."—Parker.

a "If God cross us in our temporal affairs, and we meet with trouble and disappointment, we shall find this is the cause of it; the work we have to do for God and our own souls is left undone, and we seek our own things more than the things of Jesus Christ." —Mat. Henry.

bly receiving the Divine reproof, and proceeding, at once and earnestly, to mend their ways. (13) **messenger,** "The word is that commonly used for an angel in the O.T., but its first and proper meaning is messenger. In the same way in the N.T., the same word is used generally in its restricted sense for an angel, and occasionally in its wider sense for a messenger (Luke vii. 27, ix. 52; James ii. 25). Haggai is the only prophet who uses this title of himself. It is, to say the least, doubtful whether Moses as a prophet is intended by it in Num. xx. 16. Malachi ("my angel or messenger") has it for the only name by which we know him, and he uses it of the Jewish priest (ii. 7), and of John Baptist the forerunner of our Lord, and of our Lord Himself, "the messenger of the Covenant (iii. 1)."—Camb. Bib. **with you,** graciously recognizing your penitential spirit, and active efforts to do the right. (14) **the spirit of,** etc., "Note how the narrative emphasizes that the new energy was, as it could not but be from Haggai's unflattering words, a purely spiritual result. It was the spirit of Zerubbabel, and the spirit of Jehoshua, and the spirit of all the rest of the people, which was stirred—their conscience and radical force of character. Not in vain had the people suffered their great disillusion under Cyrus, if now their history was to start again from sources so inward and so pure."—G. A. Smith. (15) **four and twentieth,** etc.,[a] the time is noted to show that, once aroused, the people set at once about the work.

[a] "The 24th day of the sixth month of the second year of Darius would fall in Sept. B. C. 520.

"The longer the soul hath neglected duty, the more ado there is to get it taken up; partly through shame, the soul having played the truant, knows not how to look God in the face, and partly from the difficulty of the work. It requires more time for him to tune his instrument than for another to play the lesson." — An Old Divine.

"It was now about 66 years since the destruction of the first temple by the Chaldeans." —Wordsworth.

CHAPTER THE SECOND.

The second prophecy, chap. ii. 1—9. 1—3. (1) **seventh month,** Tisri, or Ethanim. **one and twentieth day of the month,** "It has been pointed out that this was the seventh and last day of the Feast of Tabernacles (Lev. xxiii. 33—36, 39—43); and it has been suggested that the depressing contrast between the former Temple and the present would be heightened and brought home to the people by the rites and services of the festive season. "The return of this festal celebration, especially after a harvest which had turned out very miserably, and showed no signs of the blessing of God, could not fail to call up vividly before the mind the difference between the former times, when Israel was able to assemble in the courts of the Lord's house, and so to rejoice in the blessings of His Grace in the midst of abundant sacrificial meals, and the present time, when the altar of burnt sacrifice might indeed be restored again, and the building of the temple be resumed, but in which there was no prospect of erecting a building that would in any degree answer to the glory of the former temple.'"—Keil's Minor Prophets. (2, 3) **first glory,** as built by Solomon, and as seen before the Babylonish invasion. There might well have been some old men living who could remember it.[a] **as nothing,**[b] R. V. omits "in comparison of it."

[b] The Jews note the foll. 5 points of inferiority. The absence from the second temple of (1) the sacred fire; (2) the Shekinah; (3) the ark and cherubim; (4) the Urim and Thummim; (5) the spirit of prophecy."— Fausset.

[a] Ezr. iii. 12.

The Desire of All Nations (vss. 3—9).—I. The inquiry which is here made. II. The exhortation which is here addressed. III. The assurance which is here given. 1. The character under which Christ is here set forth; 2. The time of His manifestation; 3. The precursors of His coming; 4. The results with which it would be attended.

Memory.—The man who has been since boyhood a stranger from his home and country, and long a wanderer in many lands, will assure you that the past is to him like a dim and confused dream, and that there are few things which he can vividly recall. But let him only return to the home of his childhood, to the rural village, or the old house in which he was nurtured, how touching is it to watch in him the opening up of page after page filled with memories which he cannot choose but read, though each page in the old life-book may be blotted by his tears. As he journeys to the place from which, long ago, he took his departure as a boy, and sees the old hills, the fields, the streams, the rocks, the trees, the church and churchyard, the school, the scattered homesteads,—there is not an object that does not summon up persons who have passed away, and incidents of joy and sorrow, which, up to that moment, he had forgotten!—Macleod.

"Too often a mischievous gloom enters the mind of God's people Their hands slacken, their energies are paralyzed for the work of God, and they sink into desponding apathy and indolence. Did we realize our present privileges and future prospects, the gleam of sunshine would be to us the earnest of what it will be, when —as Rutherford beautifully observes—'we shall be on the sunny side of the Brae.'"

—Bridge.

4—7. (4) **be strong,**[c] "This is repeated three times for emphasis' sake. The same exhortation was given by David to Solomon before the building of the first temple (1 Chron. xxviii. 10; comp. Josh. i. 6, 7, 9). Haggai seems to suggest comfort in the thought that such admonition was needed at that time as well as now when they are so depressed (comp. Zech. viii. 9)."—Pul. Com. (5) **covenanted,** God's mercies are ever set before us in this light, they are faithfulness to His covenant and His promise. **my spirit,** R. V. "and my spirit abode among you." "It is remarkable that the presence of the Spirit should be used as an equivalent to a fulfilment of the covenant on God's part: the idea which pervades the N.T. (comp. Is. lxiii. 10, 11, 14; Neh. ix. 20.)"—M. Dods. Ne. ix. 20. (6) **a little while,** "The true explanation would seem to be that it is not the actual birth of Christ, but the preparation for that event in the 'shaking of all nations,' to which the 'little while' refers. The whole grand future, embracing not only the first but the second coming of Christ and the final consummation of all things, is indeed included in the prophecy. But it was the beginning of the great drama, not its last act, that was then closely at hand. That beginning was the then immediate object of the Church's hope; in that she was to welcome the promise and the presage of all that should follow. Time alone would unfold the plot. In prophetic prospect coming events were confused and blended, just as in our Lord's great prophecy were the circumstances of the destruction of Jerusalem and of the end of the world. But the beginning was near at hand. This shaking commenced immediately. The axe was already laid at the root of the Persian empire, whose subsequent and visible fall was but the manifestation of a far earlier one, which had been hidden from view." (Hengstenberg.)—Camb. Bib. **shake the heavens,** etc., this apparently refers to prophetical convulsions; see vss. 21, 22. (7) **desire,** etc.,[a] R. V., "and the desirable things of all nations," etc. "We may understand what he says," writes Calvin, "of Christ; we indeed know that Christ was the expectation of the whole world; . . . but as it immediately follows, Mine is the silver and Mine is the gold, the more simple meaning is that which I first stated: that the nations would come, bringing with them all their riches, that they might offer themselves and all their possessions a sacrifice to God."—G. A. Smith; so Camb. Bible, M. Dods and most modern comm.

The Glory of the Latter House (vs. 7).—I. The fulfillment of this prediction in reference to the second temple. 1. By the presentation of Jesus; 2. By His teaching; 3. By His expulsion of the traders; 4. By His miracles. II. The fulfillment of this prediction in reference to the Christian Church. 1. By the spiritual presence of the Redeemer; 2. By the observance of His ordinances; 3. By the perpetuation of His doctrine; 4. By the display of His saving power; 5. By the character of His worshipers.—G. Brooks.

Offices of the Holy Spirit.—He is represented as undertaking and sustaining a great variety of offices in behalf of men; as endowing men with a great variety and abundance of gifts, of which He is the source and author, and in reference to all these offices and gifts they are said to partake of Him, and to have, in proportion to their faith, and according to their faith, a common participation in Him, a right in Him, enduring so long as there is a Church to sustain in the world, till faith is swallowed up in sight. These offices are, perhaps, most compendiously described by the word "Comforter" in the text, which seems to convey the idea of all the help which men stand in need of, and which they may call upon Him to exercise in their behalf. One of our old divines says: "In the sense in which the term Advocate is here employed, we may apply it to a great variety of persons. If we are sick we call to us a physician; if we are perplexed we call to us a lawyer; if we are going to build, we call to us an architect; if we are in trouble, we call to us some kind and affectionate friend; and so as we want it we get advice, and instruction, and comfort from day to day." And so all these persons may be called advocates, or persons called to us, as our necessities or circumstances dictate. But with far greater propriety may we say this of the Holy Ghost. If we are ignorant we call to Him, and He is the Spirit of wisdom and revelation; if we are sorrowful we call to Him, and

c "The Jews hesitated about going forward with the work, through dread of the world-power, Medo-Persia, influenced by the craft of Samaria. The Prophet assures them that these and all other world-powers are to fall before Messiah, who is to be associated with this temple; therefore they need fear nought."—Fausset.

a "If the Messias was to come while the second temple stood and if that temple many ages hath ceased to be, then is that Messias already come." — Bp. Pearson.

Be strong, all ye people of the land, saith the Lord, and work (vs. 4). This verse is an admirable prescription for all workers. First, "be strong," have genuine and settled determination. Second, "work." Do not merely determine, but actualize your determination in work. Your doing will react on your determination to do. Third, be sure of God's presence and truth to you as these were for four forefathers. He helped them; He will help you. — Wayland Hoyt.

"To unconverted persons, a great part of the Bible resembles a letter written in cipher. The blessed Spirit's office is to act as God's decipherer, by letting His people into the secret of ce-

He is the Holy Ghost the Comforter; if we are oppressed with unbelief, we call to Him and He gives us power to believe; if we are unholy and under the influence of strong passion, we call to Him and He allays the tumult in our breasts; sanctifies us in body, soul, and spirit. And so, in whatever thing we call upon Him for, suited to our spiritual nature the Lord our God, blessed be His name, is nigh unto us. And that is the peculiar and crowning glory of the Christian dispensation. We may say far more truly than it was said by Israel of old, even with the tabernacle and pillar of cloud in the midst of them, "What people is there that hath the Lord their God so nigh unto them in all things that they call upon Him for?"—Osborn.

8, 9. (8) **silver is mine,** the wealth of the nations is in my hand and under my control and it shall be brought for the glory of my house. (9) **latter house,** R. V., "the latter glory of this house," etc. "The glory here promised is first and most obviously material glory, the desirable things, the precious gifts of all nations. But it includes the spiritual glory, without which in the sight of God material splendor is worthless and unacceptable. Christ Himself, present bodily in the temple on Mount Sion during His life on earth, present spiritually in His Church now, present in the holy city, the heavenly Jerusalem, of which He is the Temple (Rev. xxi. 22), calling forth the spiritual worship and devotion, and as the legitimate and necessary expression of that, the wealth and treasure of all nations, is the glory here predicted. But all this is rather implied, to be discerned by the Church in the growing light of its fulfillment, than expressed, to be understood by those to whom the prophecy was first delivered."—Camb. Bib. **peace,** Eze. xxxiv. 25, 26; Mi. iv. 3, 4.

The third prophecy, vss. 10—19. **10—14.** (10) **ninth month,** or Chisleu. (12, 13) the force of these vss. is that the evil reaches farther than the good. If one is unclean by a corpse his touch conveys uncleanliness; but if he is holy by bearing holy flesh, his touch does not convey holiness. (14) **so is this people,**[a] etc., that is to say, while the Jews had expected their restored ritual to make them holy to the Lord, this had not been effective, while, on the contrary, their contact with sources of pollution had thoroughly polluted both themselves and their labor and their sacrifices." (14) **there,** on the "work of their hands," **i. e.** on the altar built on their return from Babylon. Ezra iii. 3.

The Abiding Influence of Evil.—These poor colonists, in the hope deferred, were learning the old lesson, which humanity finds so hard to understand, that repentance and new-born zeal do not immediately work a change upon our material condition; but the natural consequences of sin often outweigh the influence of conversion, and though devoted to God and very industrious we may still be punished for a sinful past. Evil has an infectious power greater than that of holiness. Its effects are most extensive and lasting. It was no bit of casuistry which Haggai sought to illustrate by his appeal to the priests on the ceremonial law, but an ethical truth deeply embedded in human experience.—Exp. Bib.

15—17. (15) The vs. may be rendered more clearly thus: "And now consider, I pray you, from this day (the 24th day of the 9th month) and upward (that is backward), from (the time when) not yet stone was laid," etc. This covers the time during which, after laying the foundation of the temple, they had ceased to labor upon it. (16) **since those days,** R. V., "through all that time," etc., **i. e.** the fourteen years referred to in vs. 15. **heap,** that should have been, in a good season, twenty measures. God sent bad seasons, as a sign of His displeasure. **pressfat,** R. V., "winefat." (17) **blasting and with mildew,** "two diseases of the corn which Moses had foretold (Deut. xxviii. 22) as chastisements on disobedience, and God's infliction of which Amos had spoken of in these selfsame words (Amos iv. 9). Haggai adds the hail as destructive of the vines (Psalm lxxviii. 47)."—Pusey. **turned not,** not recognizing in My judgments the designs of correcting love.[a]

Contemplation.—Some there may be that say, "It is not worth so much time and trouble, to think of the greatness of the joys above: so that we can make sure they are ours, we know they are great." But as these men obey not the command of God, which requires them to have "their conversation in heaven," and to "set their affections on things above;" so they wilfully make their own lives miserable, by refusing the

lestial experience, as the key and clue to those sweet mysteries of grace which were before as a garden shut up, or as a fountain sealed, or as a book written in an unknown character."
—Toplady.

The later Jewish age shows at least a partial fulfilment of the prophecy (vss. 7—9) in its spiritual significance. "Rites and ceremonies retired more into the background; and prayer began to assume its true place in public worship. The religious knowledge of the people was kept up through the regular public reading and distribution of the Scriptures. Synagogues were established, the people having learnt at Babylon that God's presence might be enjoyed in their assemblies in any place or circumstances. Thus there was kept alive throughout the nation a higher and purer type of religion than it had known before."
—McCundy.

a "Though this people live in a holy land, it does not communicate any holiness to the people by any intrinsic virtue of its own, but it entails upon them all an obligation to personal holiness."
—Wordsworth.

a "This people either saw not the hand of God in it (imputing it to chance), or saw not their own sin as the provoking cause of it, and so turned not to Him." — Mat. Henry.

delights which God hath set before them. . . . As for you whose heart God hath weaned from all things here below, I hope you will value this heavenly life, and take one walk every day in the New Jerusalem. God is your love and your desire; you would fain be more acquainted with your Saviour; and I know it is your grief that your hearts are not nearer to Him, and that they do not more feelingly love and delight in Him. Oh, try this life of meditation on your heavenly rest. Let the world see by your heavenly lives, that religion is something more than opinions and disputes, or a talk of outward duties. If ever a Christian is like himself, and answerable to his principles and profession, it is when he is most serious and lively in this duty.—Baxter.

18, 19. (18) **upward,** i. e. "backward." (19) **yet in the barn,** i. e. is it any longer in the barn? Is it not all exhausted and used up? The meager yield of the blighted corn was soon consumed and the granary left empty. Some have thought that by "the seed" is here meant what would be required to sow the land for another year, and that the dearth and distress are heightened by the fact that there is not even corn enough left to sow. But as the word is frequently used, not of seed corn, but of produce (e. g. 1 Sam. viii. 15; Isaiah xxiii. 3; Job xxxix. 12), and as the remainder of the verse refers to produce, it is better taken in that sense here."—Camb. Bib.

Verses 10—19.—This then is the substance of the whole message. On the 24th day of the 9th month, the Jews had been discouraged that their attempts to build the temple, begun three months before, had not turned the tide of their misfortunes and produced prosperity in their agriculture. Haggai tells them, there is not yet time for the change to work. If contact with a holy thing has only a slight effect, but contact with an unclean thing has a much greater effect (verses 11—13), then their attempts to build the temple must have less good influence upon their condition than the bad influence of all their past devotion to themselves and their secular labors. That is why adversity still continues, but courage! from this day on God will bless. The whole message is, therefore, opportune to the date at which it was delivered, and comes naturally on the back of Haggai's previous oracles.—G. A. Smith.

The fourth prophecy, vss. 20—23. **20—23.** (20) "Temporal blessings had been promised to the people generally; now spiritual blessings are announced to Zerubbabel as the head of the nation and the representative of the house of David." **and again,** this revelation took place on the same day as the preceding one. (21) **Zerubbabel,** as the head of the civil government. **shake,** etc., the usual fig. for violent political convulsions.[a] (22) **overthrow,** etc., the terms here employed are too wide to be satisfied by any event in the life of Zerubbabel: "There was in Zerubbabel's time no shaking of the heaven or of nations. Darius had indeed to put down an unusual number of rebellions in the first few years after his accession; but, although he magnified himself on occasion of their suppression, they were only so many distinct and unconcerted revolts, each under its own head. All were far away in the distant East. The Persian empire, spread "probably over 2,000,000 square miles, or more than half of modern Europe, was not threatened."—Pusey. The prophecy reaches forth to the more distant future, and still awaits its full accomplishment. "All other world-kingdoms are to be overthrown to make way for Christ's universal kingdom."[b] **come down,** or, brought down, and laid low. (23) **Lord of hosts,** lit. "Jehovah Tsevaoth," a title used 14 times in Haggai, in Zech. 48 times, in Malachi 25 times, while in the Pentateuch it does not occur once. The first use was in 1 Sam. i. 3. It refers to Jehovah as ruler of the highest material objects and spiritual agencies.—M. Dods. **O Zerubbabel,** here treated as the representative of Messiah. **as a signet,** or as one who bears the king's signet, as the sign of his authority.[c] **I have chosen thee,** "with these words the Messianic promise made to David was transferred to Zerubbabel and his family among David's descendants, and would be fulfilled in his person in just the same way as the promise given to David, that God would make him the highest among the kings of the earth (Ps. lxxxix. 27). The fulfillment culminates in Jesus Christ, the son of David, and descendant of Zerubbabel (Matt. i. 12; Luke iii. 27), in whom Zerubbabel was made the signet-ring of Jehovah. Jesus Christ

"Modern science has shown that blasting and mildew are produced by plants—they are the diseases occasioned by the growth of minute fungi, . . . the functions of vegetable nature are reversed in them, their pores inhale oxygen, and exhale carbonic gas, like animals."—Hugh Macmillan.

"The prophet's strong faithful speech indicates that there had been amongst these returned captives much of indifference, in reference to the work of God, and it was only right that they should be reminded of this, and that by the painful memory of past failure they should be stimulated to more thorough consecration in the future. The past is irrevocable and irretrievable. No tears, no regrets, can win it back to us. The future, however, is available, and hence, leaving the past, with all our shortcomings in relation to it, and rejoicing in God's mercy, let us 'go and sin no more.'"

b Mat. xxiv. 29.
c Da. ii. 44; Rev. xi. 15.

"Zerubbabel was a man of indomitable courage. Had he been a craven, he never would have done so outwardly foolish a thing as join himself with a handful of pilgrims who proposed to quit their comfortable homes and prosperous estates in Babylon, and undertake a long and perilous journey to a promised land on the other side of the Syrian desert.

has raised up the kingdom of His father David again, and of His kingdom there will be no end (Luke i. 32, 33). Even though it may appear oppressed and deeply humiliated for the time by the power of the kingdoms of the heathen, it will never be crushed and destroyed, but will break in pieces all these kingdoms, and destroy them, and will itself endure for ever (Dan. ii. 44; Heb. xii. 28; 1 Cor. xv. 24)."—Keil.

The Signet Ring.—In the eyes of Orientals the finger-ring or signet, was regarded as a valuable possession, to lose which was esteemed a dire calamity. To speak of one as a signet-ring was to assure him of tender regard and watchful preservation. Reversing the threat pronounced against Jeconiah, the last king of Judah, and the grandfather of Zerubbabel (Jer. xxii. 24), Jehovah promises that Zerubbabel shall be as a signet-ring upon his own finger, i. e. shall be indissolubly associated with himself and regarded with sincere affection; and this promise may be said to have been fulfilled, so far as Zerubbabel was concerned, in that he was henceforth inseparably linked with the history of God's people, and in fact constituted an ancestor of Messiah, who afterwards sprang from his line. But as the day when the promised distinction should be conferred on Zerubbabel was expressly specified as the day when the process begun by Jehovah of shaking the heavens and the earth should have been brought to a completion, at which time Zerubbabel should have been long dead, it becomes obvious that the promise must be understood as having reached its highest fulfillment in Zerubbabel's distinguished descendant, who should then be made Jehovah's signet-ring, in reward for a greater work of emancipation and temple-building than had been performed by Zerubbabel. And in this reward all share who, whether before his coming or since, have been fellow-workers with him by serving the will of God in their day and generation.—Pul. Com.

Nor, had he been a weakling, would he have succeeded in carrying these pilgrims in safety to their destination. But with the help of God and his own stout heart he did it. It was a feat only second to that of Moses, who brought their fathers out of Egypt, led them through the scorching wilderness, and set them down at the gate of Canaan. Nor again, unless Zerubbabel had been a hero, could he have brought the temple to completion, working, as he did, with a company of builders who became alarmed at every menace uttered against them by the people of the land, and who threw down their tools on encountering the smallest resistance." — Pulpit Com.

Introduction.

I. **"Of the Prophet Zechariah,** as of his colleague and contemporary Haggai, very little is known. He tells us himself that he was the son of Berechiah and the grandson of Iddo (i. 1). If the Iddo thus spoken of is to be identified, as with much probability he may be, with the person of that name mentioned in the Book of Nehemiah, we have this explanation confirmed by the fact, that while Iddo is among the 'priests' who returned with Zerubbabel and Joshua (xii. 4), 'Zechariah of Iddo' takes his place amongst 'the priests, the chief of the fathers,' under Joiakim, the son of Joshua, in the next generation (vss. 12, 16). If this view be adopted, it follows that Zechariah was a priest as well as a prophet, and that, since his grandfather was still living when the first caravan returned under Zerubbabel, he must have been a comparatively young man when sixteen years later he entered upon his prophetical office. That he was born and spent his early years in Babylon is highly probable. This would account for his frequent use of visions and allegories; the divine Spirit adapting Himself as ever, to the capacity and training of the human instrument, in imparting His revelations."—Cambridge Bible. II. **Unity of the Book.** The manifest difference of style and diction between the first eight and the last six chapters with other considerations, has led many scholars to believe that chapters ix. to xiv. are not the work of Zechariah, but of an unknown author. III. **Time.** The text itself clearly fixes the date of the earlier portion of the Book as in the second and fourth years of Darius, i.e. B.C. 520 and 518. If Zechariah wrote the closing chapters, it was probably many years later, when the prophet was becoming an old man. Those who do not accept Zechariah's authorship of the latter part of the book are divided in opinion as to the date, some favoring a time before the captivity, others naming the early part of the fourth century before Christ. IV. **Theme.** "The prophecies of Zechariah containing as they do a portraiture of the destiny of God's people to the end of time, and comprehending so many mighty events which yet await their fulfilment, present to the interpreter many difficulties, some of which have hitherto been found insoluble, and will probably remain unsolved till the mystery of God contained in them shall have been fulfilled. One thing, however, they clearly reveal to us—that the future triumph of God's kingdom is certain, and that all the great movements in the history of the nations, however unpropitious they seem at the time, are parts of the mighty plan of Divine providence, which shall end in making the kingdoms of this world 'the kingdoms of our Lord and of His Christ.'"—Dr. Barrows.

Synopsis.

PART I.—......................chaps. i.—viii.

1. Introduction ....i. 1—6
2. Vision of the angelic horsemen....i. 7—17
3. Vision of the horns and smiths...i. 18—21
4. Vision of the man with a measuring line ....ii. 1—13
5. Vision of the high priest accused by Satan ....iii. 1—10
6. Vision of the golden candlestick......... ....iv. 1—14
7. Vision of the flying roll ....v. 1—4
8. Vision of the woman in the ephah....... ....v. 5—11
9. Vision of the four chariots ....vi. 1—8
10. Crowning of the high priest......vi. 9—15
11. Concerning fasts ....vii., viii.

PART II...............................ix.—xiv.

The First Burden.............chs. ix.—xi.

1. The coming of the King............ix., x.
2. The rejection of the Shepherd..........xi.

The Second Burden ....chs. xii.—xiv.

1. Deliverance and repentance of Jerusalem.. ....xii. 1—xiii. 6
2. The Shepherd smitten for the flock........ ....xiii. 7—9
3. Judgment of the nations and sanctification of Jerusalem ....xiv.

CHAPTER THE FIRST.

1—3. (1) **eighth month,** "coincides with our November and with the rainy season in Palestine. Haggai's first prophecy had been delivered in the sixth month, and his second prophecy in the seventh month of this same year. (Hag. i. 1, ii. 1.)" **second year of Darius,** B. C. 520. **the prophet,** the designation of Zechariah, not of Iddo. (2) **sore displeased, Heb.** "displeased with displeasure," i. e. vehemently displeased.[a] (3) **them,** the Jews of that day. **turn ye,**[b] R. V., "return unto me." **The Lord of Hosts,** "this phrase is of unusually frequent occurrence in the first eight chapters of this book and in that of Haggai. Its use appears designed to inspire the mind with unshaken confidence in the irresistible power of God."—Barrows.

God's Call to Repentance.—I. The call is founded on God's absolute right to obedience. II. Urged by God's judgments on transgressors. III. Encouraged by God's promises. IV. Enforced by the experiences of life.—Forsyth.

Rebuilding the Temple.—From the book of Ezra it appears that the rebuilding of the temple was brought about largely through the influence of the prophets, Haggai and Zechariah. The zeal with which the returned exiles had begun the work 16 years before, building the altar and laying the foundations of the temple, had been checked by the jealousy and intrigues of the Samaritans. But now the accession of Darius to the throne of Persia gives promise of security to the little colony at Jerusalem, and Haggai and Zechariah are commissioned to arouse and encourage the people to resume the work. Ezra v. 1, vi. 14.

The Message and the Messenger.—The Lord chooseth both old men and young; his message will fit any age: sometimes he has a word to us that a boy could not utter; sometimes he has a message to deliver that only a young heart can properly announce, because it alone has the requisite freshness of sympathy and music. The Lord has a word which only men of business can speak; and they will not speak it. There are some sermons that ought never to be preached in the pulpit; they ought to be preached in the market-place, or over the counter, or on high 'Change; and men of business only can speak them with clearness and precision, and moral, because personal, authority. There are some texts that preachers have no business with; they cannot pronounce the words aright; they can utter the individual syllables, but they cannot run them into that persuasive music which belongs only to the tongue of honest commerce.—J. Parker.

4—6. (4) **former prophets,** those before the captivity, as Nathan, Gad, Shemaiah, Hanani, Elijah, Elisha, Hosea, Joel, Isaiah, Jeremiah, and Ezekiel.[a] Those who listened to these prophets, but neither heeded nor obeyed, had set a bad example. (5, 6) "The lesson conveyed by these two verses, which must be taken together, is the same as that contained in the words of Isaiah (xl. 6, 8), 'All flesh is grass, and all the godliness thereof is as the flower of the field The grass withereth, the flower fadeth, but the word of our God shall stand for ever.' There, however, the lesson has reference to God's word of promise, for comfort (comp. 1 Peter i. 24, 25). Here it has reference to His word of threatening, for warning."—Camb. Bib. **where are they?** i. e. recall the Divine judgments under wh. they have fallen. **live for ever,** or abide from generation to generation.[b] **words, etc.,** i. e. denunciations and judgments. **statutes,** or "decrees," the root of the Heb. word means to hack or cut—as letters in stone or other hard substance, therefore decrees, enduring permanently. **take hold,** R. V., "overtake," the idea is of punishment dogging a person until it overtakes him. **and said,** comp. La. i. 18, ii. 17.

Be Not as Your Fathers.—This is an inversion of a common exhortation. We are often counselled to keep in our father's way, and attend to our father's word, and reflect our father's example; but in this case we are to turn away from our fathers as from our enemies. The fact that such a command is given shows that obedience to it is possible: if that is the case, here is a most remarkable instance of men separating them-

a "The Heb. root conveys that idea of breaking forth into anger or displeasure wh. we have in the word ebullition."
—Spk. Com.

b "Though God hath brought you back from captivity, yet this state will not long last unless ye are really converted. God has heavier scourges ready, and has begun to give symptoms of displeasure."
—Calvin.

"In a revival of religion in Jackson county, Ga., in the summer of 1846, out of eighty hopeful conversions, sixty-three of whom united with the church, not more than three or four were past the age of twenty-five. In the great work in Athens, which followed, there was a similar proportion of youth. In other revivals in the same state, in 1845 and 1846, including in all not far from five hundred additions to the churches, at least as large a proportion were from twelve to twenty-five years of age, and these facts are, perhaps, a fair average throughout the country.
—Dr. Haven.

a Comp. Is. xxxi. 6; Je. iii. 12, xviii. 11; Eze. xviii. 30; Ho. xiv. 1.

b "The thought appears to be this: 'Your fathers have perished, as was foretold, and their fate ought to warn you. But you may

say, The prophets too are dead. I grant it, but still, My words do not die; though dead, their prophetical words from Me, fulfilled against your fathers, are not dead with them. Beware, then, lest ye share their fate!'"
—Fausset.

"'Tis law as steadfast as the throne of Zeus,
Our days are heritors of days gone by."
—Aeschylus.

"We need no reed, no pole, no measuring line, wherewith to take the dimensions of our days, nor any skill in arithmetic, wherewith to compute the number of them. No; we have the standard of them at our fingers' ends; and there is no multiplication of it; it is but one handbreadth in all."
—Mat. Henry.

a "By myrtles I do not mean the dwarf myrtles which grow in greenhouses in England, but such as Zechariah spoke of, eight or ten feet high. They grow nearest to perfection in shaded valleys, and therefore at once associate themselves with everything serene and peaceful."—Gadsby.

selves from their antecedents. Science teaches us that no man can get away from his antecedents; but Scripture insists that such a detachment is possible, and indeed is requisite for entrance into the kingdom of heaven. Nature allowed to go on in its uninterrupted course would possibly prove the scientific position; but we are not only in an economy of nature, we are also in an economy of grace or of distinct spiritual action; the God who created nature has also committed himself to certain spiritual ministries, the end of which is new creatureship. Let some who have had bad fathers be encouraged by this exhortation; let those who have had good fathers follow in good ways; but let no man's heart be cast down simply because he started from a bad human origin. History is full of instances in which the children of bad parents have become conspicuous Christians. Do not quote the authority of bad men simply because they happen to be your fathers. It is possible for a youth to say that by following an evil course he is only doing what his father did; that is no excuse; certainly it is no reason, and he knows in his own heart that it is a vain and hollow plea.—J. Parker.

7, 8. Here begins "a series of eight visions, with accompanying interpretations, seen by the prophet on the same night, which, like dissolving views, melt into one another, and so gradually open up the whole prospect, i. 7—vi. 8."—Camb. Bib. "In the FIRST VISION (vss. 7—17) it is revealed to Zechariah that the Gentile nations should be overthrown, and that whatever might be the present condition of the Jewish people, God's purpose of mercy toward them was unshaken and would be fulfilled."—Pul. Com. (7) **Sebat,** the name for the eleventh month in use subsequent to the captivity, corresponding to our January or February. (8) **by night,** may intimate that it was a mental vision. **myrtle trees,** "it was one of the myrtle-covered glens in the neighborhood of Jerusalem:[a] Zechariah calls it the Glen or Valley-Bottom, either because it was known under that name to the Jews, or because he was himself wont to frequent it for prayer. He discovers in it what seems to be a rendezvous of Persian cavalry-scouts, the leader of the troop in front, and the rest behind him, having just come in with their reports. Soon, however, he is made aware that they are angels. They are scouts of God come in from their survey of the whole earth."—G. A. Smith. **behind him,** etc., R. V., "and behind him there were horses, red, sorrel, and white." These colors may have been only to distinguish the horses as coming from different countries.

Angels.—Angels are men of a superior kind.—Young. They bear his will about to every part of the universe. This is their delight. They bless God, who vouchsafes thus to employ them. But when they have fulfilled God's message, then they return back to him by whom they were sent forth, and stand before him, drinking in fresh streams of life and strength and purity and joy from his presence.—Hare.

"They fight for us, they watch and duly ward,
And their bright squadrons round about us plant;
And all for love, and nothing for reward,
Oh! why should heavenly God to man have such regard."
—Spenser.

9—11. (9) two angels appear in this vision, first: he who is spoken of as "a man riding upon a red horse," and afterwards as "the angel of the Lord," and second: the interpreting angel, who is near to the prophet through all the eight visions (excepting perhaps the fourth) to explain to him their meaning. (10) **walk .. earth,** ch. vi. 7. (11) **at rest,** none of that "shaking of the nations" which had been promised. Peace and prosperity everywhere except among God's people.

Verses 9—11.—Calvin's view is, that the obscurity in which the vision is shrouded, the dark night, the low valley, the sombre myrtles, is intended to remind the prophet that God's judgments are unsearchable and His ways past finding out, while the angel riders are a help to his human weakness to understand how, like a king whose couriers are continually passing to and fro throughout his dominions, the Almighty is intimately acquainted with all that is done upon earth, and the different colored horses picture to his mind the truth, that all human events, whatever be their complexion, are alike under the cognizance and control of the never-failing Providence, which ordereth all things both in heaven and earth; and we may add, however diverse they appear, are all working harmoniously to accomplish His will.—Camb. Bib.

12—15. (12) **threescore and ten years,** the predicted seventy years of captivity (Jer. xxv. 11; xxix. 10) were past; it was time that the punishment should cease. There are two computations of this period. The first dates from the first capture of Jerusalem by Nebuchadnezzar, B. C. 606, when Judæa was made tributary to Babylon (2 Kings xxiv. 1; 2 Chron. xxxvi. 6; Dan. i. 1, etc.), unto the return of the company of exiles under Zerubbabel, B. C. 536; the second dates from the final destruction of Jerusalem, B. C. 588, unto the second year of Darius, B. C. 519, when Zechariah saw these visions. However reckoned, the dark period was now over; might they not now expect the commotion among the nations which was to precede their own restitution?—Pul. Com. (13) **comfortable,** such as brought comfort and assurance. (14) **jealous,** ch. viii. 2. Full of anxious concern for the well-being of His people. (15) **heathen,** R. V., "nations;" here esp. the Chaldæans, who had exceeded their commission in their severe dealings with God's people.[a] **at ease,** means, in a bad sense, to be carnally secure. They had treated the Jews wantonly and were "at ease."—Barrows.

The Wrath of God and the Wrath of Man.—I. God's wrath is the highest reason. It is not a mood or passion; not the outburst of arbitrary power; but the calm expression of the Eternal Mind. He who does wrong identifies himself with the wrong, and so far must be an object of indignation. II. God's wrath is the purest justice. Law must stand. Government and order must be maintained. Else anarchy. But nothing will be done beyond what is necessary for the ends of justice. How different with the wrath of man! Often carried beyond the bounds of right, and becomes oppression. Often continued beyond the limits of justice, and becomes revenge (Isa. xlvii. 6). III. God's wrath is the holiest love. It is consistent with pity for the sufferer, mercy for the penitent, and deliverance for the oppressed. In his hand pains are disciplinary, trials are remedial, chastisements are benedictions in disguise. "The end of the Lord is merciful." But with men how often is wrath pitiless and cruel, working evil instead of good, rejoicing in destruction instead of deliverance!—Forsyth.

16, 17. (16) **line,** measuring it out for rebuilding. (17) R. V., "cry yet again." **my cities,** not Jerusalem only. **spread abroad,** overflow, as a vessel or fountain.[a] **choose,** or show, by gracious signs, His choice. "The scope, then, of the first vision is clear. It conveys a distinct promise and prophecy of three future events. 'My house shall be built,' vs. 16. This was accomplished four years later in the sixth year of Darius (Ezra vi. 15). 'A line shall be stretched forth upon Jerusalem,' vs. 16. This was done some seventy years later, when the city was rebuilt by Nehemiah (Neh. vi. 15). 'My cities through prosperity shall yet be spread abroad,' vs. 17. The fulfillment of this is to be found in the history of the Jews under the Asmonean princes. Beyond this the first prophecy does not expressly go; though its concluding words, 'The Lord shall yet comfort Zion, and shall yet choose Jerusalem,' are at least an implied promise of better things, than any which befell the Jews before the coming of Christ."—Camb. Bib.

Two things are to be noted in this oracle. No political movement is indicated as the means of Jerusalem's restoration: this is to be the effect of God's free grace in returning to dwell in Jerusalem, which is the reward of the building of the temple. And there is an interesting explanation of the motive for God's new grace: in executing His sentence upon Israel, the heathen had far exceeded their commission, and now themselves deserved punishment. That is to say, the restoration of Jerusalem and the resumption of the worship are not enough for the future of Israel. The heathen must be chastised. But Zechariah does not predict any overthrow of the world's power, either by earthly or by heavenly forces. This is entirely in harmony with the insistence upon peace which distinguishes him from other prophets.—Exp. Bib.

SECOND VISION, vss. 18—21. **18—21.** (18) **four horns,** the horns[b]

---

[a] "Reference may be to the new troubles brought by their enemies upon the Jews after their return to Jerus, and especially in hindering them from rebuilding the temple."—Lowth.

Is xlvii. 6; Am. i. 9, 11.

Most wonderfully did God prepare political events, in the restoration from Babylon and in the coming of Christ, for the special condition of his Church. Quietness may reign in all quarters except in the Church. Divine justice may seem to sleep; but it is only the calm before the storm.

[a] "A prediction of the coming occupation of the land by Jews returning from Babylon, and of the increase of population under the Asmonaean princes." —Spk. Com.

Da. ix. 25; Na. vi. 15, 16.

[b] Poss. the Samaritans, Arabians, Ammonites, and Philistines; or, these as representing all earthly powers so far as they are hostile to the Church of God.

Je. i. 8, 9; Eze. xxv. 1.

"So just and wonderful are the overruling councils of God's Providence, that the arrow which strikes through the heart of the transgressor is oftentimes directed from the very bow which he had vainly trusted would be his strength. The companion of his sin is the first to cast reproach and shame on him for the evil which he has done." — J. S. M. Anderson.

which have tossed and gored Israel are to be prevented from doing further injury. (20) **carpenters,** R. V., "smiths," the various human agencies by which the foes of Israel would be defeated. **fray them,** strike terror into them. **to cast out,** etc., R. V., "to cast down the horns of the nations, which lifted up their horn against the land of Judah to scatter it."

The Castle of Banias.—Two hours later we reached the foot of a tall isolated mountain, which is crowned by the crumbling castle of Banias, the stateliest ruin of that kind on earth, no doubt. It is a thousand feet long and two hundred wide, all of the most symmetrical and at the same time the most ponderous masonry. The massive towers and bastions are more than thirty feet high, and have been sixty. From the mountain's peak its broken turrets rise above the groves of ancient oaks and olives, and look wonderfully picturesque. It is of such high antiquity that no man knows who built it or when it was built. It is utterly inaccessible except in one place, where a bridle-path winds upward among the solid rocks to the old portcullis. The horses' hoofs have bored holes in these rocks to the depth of six inches during the hundreds and hundreds of years that the castle was garrisoned. We wandered for three hours here among the chambers and crypts and dungeons of the fortress, and trod where the mailed heels of many a knightly crusader had rung, and where Phœnician heroes had walked ages before them. We wondered how such a solid mass of masonry could be affected even by an earthquake, and could not understand what agency had made Banias a ruin; but we found the destroyer after a while, and then our wonder was increased tenfold. Seeds had fallen in crevices in the vast walls; the seeds had sprouted; the tender, insignificant sprouts had hardened; they grew larger and larger, and by a steady, imperceptible pressure forced the great stones apart, and now are bringing sure destruction upon a giant work that has even mocked the earthquakes to scorn! Gnarled and twisted trees spring from the old walls everywhere, and beautify and overshadow the grey battlements with a wild luxuriance of foliage.—Mark Twain.

CHAPTER THE SECOND.

a Eze. xl. 3; Re. xi. 1, xxi. 15, 16.

"Oh, there are no tears in heaven; but, when Angels come down to earth, it may be they can fall into companionship with human sadness, and even learn to weep: and where is the spectacle which shall wring tears from eyes which they were never meant to stain, if it be not that of the obstinate rejection of the gospel of reconciliation, and of careless trifling with a thing so inestimably precious as the soul? Old men, buried with your gold, angels weep over you! Young men, frittering away your days in vanities and pleasures, angels weep over you!"—H. Melvill.

THIRD VISION, vss. 1—3. "The way being thus cleared by the destruction of the enemies of Judah, the next vision reveals the rebuilding of Jerusalem. A man with a measuring line comes upon the stage. But, as he is about to mark out the ground-plan of the city, he is stopped by an intimation that the Jerusalem of the future shall neither admit of walls, because of its overflowing population, nor require them, inasmuch as Jehovah Himself will be a wall of fire about her."—Camb. Bib. **1, 2.** (1) **a man,** "the prophet beholds a young man—by this term he probably means a servant or apprentice—who is attempting to define the limits of the new city. In the light of what this attempt encounters, there can be little doubt that the prophet means to symbolize by it the intention of building the walls upon the old lines, so as to make Jerusalem again the mountain fortress she had previously been."—G. A. Smith. (2) **measure,** preparatory to rebuilding.[a]

Ministering Angels.—That there is an order of beings superior to man, who feel a deep interest in his welfare, is a doctrine which appears quite evident in various parts of Divine Revelation. These beings are called angels; a word in the Hebrew and Greek languages (from which it is derived) signifying a messenger. That they are of different gradations in rank and intelligence appears to be set forth by terms applied to the angelic hosts: such as thrones, dominions, principalities, and powers (Col. i. 16). The ancient Jews reckoned four orders or companies of angels, each headed by an archangel; the first order being that of Michael, the second of Gabriel, the third of Uriel, and the fourth of Raphael. Of the creation of man it is stated in Heb. ii. 7, that he was made but a little lower than the angels; and the idea has prevailed in most nations that he has in some manner been connected with them. Their principal employment, however, was to wait upon the Almighty and execute His commands. It has also been a generally prevalent and very ancient opinion that certain classes of angels were appointed to watch over the welfare of the human race; and that every individual had some spirit or angel, either good or bad, who had control over his mind to a greater or less degree. It is well known that something like the above belief universally prevailed among the Jews, Greeks, Romans, and Persians; and indeed among many of the barbarous nations of antiquity. Hesiod, one of the most ancient of the Greek poets, tells us in some of his writings that "the men of the golden age are the good angels of the present degenerate race; they watch near us, protect us from harm, and strive to the utmost of their power to purify our hearts, and save us from misery." Socrates, called the wisest of the heathen philosophers, publicly avowed himself under the guidance of a good genius or spirit, very much in accordance with the Christian idea of a guardian angel. Angels are first spoken of in the Book of Genesis, where two of them appeared for the deliverance of righteous Lot, who dwelt in Sodom, from the fate which overwhelmed the Cities of the Plain for their wickedness. There are also many other accounts in the Old Testament of the appearance of angels among men—sometimes for the deliverance of His chosen people, and at other times for the destruction of their enemies. In the New Testament an angel announced the advent of the Saviour; and a multitude of the heavenly host were heard praising God for the glad tidings of salvation for fallen men. Having assumed the nature of man, the Redeemer became subject to his trials and temptations. After successfully resisting the temptation of the devil, angels came and ministered unto him. In His agony and bloody sweat in the Garden of Gethsemane there appeared an angel from heaven strengthening Him. At His ascension angels were in attendance, and at the day of judgment all the holy angels will be with Him.

"We are not able to measure, and far less, as we suppose, to overrate the amount of benefit which results to Christians from these spiritual ministrations. But if, as it was with the Prophet's servant, the eyes were opened to discern the chariot of fire and the horses of fire marshalled to our protection—who will not allow that we should have a greater sense of security than is ordinarily conveyed through an infusion of fresh vigor into the principle of faith?" —H. Melvill.

3—5. (3) **talked .. me,** ch. i. 9. **anothei,** apparently the "angel of the Lord" who in vs. 4 sends the interpreting with the message to the young man, and who is the "me" of vss. 8, 9, and 11. (4) **towns,** R. V., "villages," open and unwalled. Comp. Ezek. xxxviii. 11. **without walls,** i. e. the population will so extend that no walls can contain it; nor will they be needed.[a] (5) **wall of fire,** "she will not need walls. God will be her protection, not only defending her from attack,[b] but consuming the enemy who may presume to assault her (comp. Deut. iv. 24; Ps. lxviii. 2). **glory,** God will make His glory conspicuous by the mighty deeds He will do in Jerusalem and the providential care He will take of her. He shall be known to be dwelling there, as He revealed His presence by the pillar of fire and the Shechinah (comp. Isa. lx. 1, 2, 19)."—Pul. Com.

a "This imagery represents extent and peace. The prophecy was not accomplished in the literal Jerusalem, but is fulfilled in the spiritual Jerusalem, the City of Peace, the universal Church of Christ, diffused throughout the world, and defended by the Divine protection as with a wall of fire."—Wordsworth.

Speak to Young Men (vs. 4).—I. Why should young men be an object of special solicitude? II. Who should speak to young men? III. How should we speak to them? IV. What shall we say to them?

God's Care of His People.—This is an encouraging promise, made to the Jews when in captivity in Babylon, assuring them that they should yet again return to their favorite city, Jerusalem; where God was used to show the tokens of His favor to them, above all people on the face of the earth, and from which they were driven on account of their grievous sins. That city, indeed, now looked desolate, and its walls were broken down, but God yet promised to restore His people, and to protect them; for He was unwilling to give them up to total ruin, if they would repent and turn sincerely to Him. Then they would not have to fear any enemy that might come against them, even if they had no walls to defend the city: "For I, saith the Lord, will be unto her," meaning the city of Jerusalem, "a wall of fire round about, and will be the glory in the midst of her." "A wall of fire" seems a singular expression to us; for whoever built a wall of fire? But it will be easily understood, by referring to a practice of the Eastern shepherds, who, in order to protect their flocks and tents from the attacks of wild beasts, were accustomed, at night, to make fires all around them, over which the most furious animals always dreaded to pass. Indeed, this custom is still adopted in various parts of the world, where there are many wild beasts. How many promises of protection God has graciously given to them that love Him! He is their shield, their buckler, their tower, their "wall of fire." There shall

"A fire's a good companionable friend, a comfortable friend, who meets your face with welcome glad, and makes the poorest shed as pleasant as a palace. Are you cold? he warms you; weary? he refreshes you; hungry? he doth prepare your food for you. Are you in darkness? he gives light to you; in a strange land? he wears a face that is familiar from your childhood. Are you poor? what matters it to him; he knows no difference between an emperor and the poorest beggar! Where is the friend, that bears the name of man, will do as much for you?" — Mary Howitt.

a "God is very sensible of every injury offered to His people; it is like hurting the eye, which is the most tender and sensible part of the body." —Lowth.

Ps. xvii. 8; 2 Th. i. 6.

b Zep. i. 7; Hab. ii. 20.

"Dear child of the Father, oh! never forget, That the love of thy Father on thee hath been set, That out of the heavens it floweth to thee Forever and ever, a great tidal sea." — M. E. Sangster.

"Of joys departed, never to return, how painful the remembrance. . . . In that dread moment, how the frantic soul raves round the walls of her clay tenement, runs to each avenue, and shrieks for help —but shrieks in vain!"—Blair.

"Satan suggested to the Jews that so consciously polluted a priesthood and people could offer no acceptable sacrifice to God, and therefore they might as well desist from the building of the temple." —Fausset.

A minister of the Gospel one day saw a piece of ivy entwined round a brand in the fire. He took it out, planted it in front of his house. It took root, grew,

no real evil come nigh them, and He will preserve them to His kingdom and glory through Jesus Christ.

6—9. (6) **Ho,** Is. lv. 1. **flee .. north,** "the north country, although its capital and center was Babylon, was the whole Babylonian empire, called 'the north' because its invasions always came upon Israel from the north. But the Book of Esther shows that sixty years after this the Jews were dispersed over the 127 provinces of the Persian empire, from India (the Punjaub) to Ethiopia (Esther i. 1; iii. 8, 12—14; viii. 5, 9); whether they were purposely placed by the policy of the conquerors in detached groups, as the ten tribes were in the cities of the Medes, or whether, when more trusted, they migrated of their own accord."—Pusey in Camb. Bib. **spread,** etc., or scattered you. (7) **deliver thyself,** R. V., "Ho Zion, escape, thou that dwellest with," etc. **daughter of Babylon,** Ps. cxxxvii. 8. **after the glory,** R. V., "after glory," i. e. in pursuit of glory; to manifest His glory in the punishment of the nations. **hath he sent me,** i. e. "hath the Lord sent me (the angel of the Lord)." **toucheth .. eye,** De. xxxii. 10.[a] (9) **shake,** in threatening; Isa. xix. 16.

Verse 9.—In the fourth or fifth year of Darius, the Babylonians, after long and cautious plotting, revolted and shut themselves up in their city, prepared for a long siege. Zophyrus, Darius's friend and general, cut off his own ears and nose, and by pretending that he had been thus mutilated by Darius, gained entrance into the city and the confidence of the besieged. By his craft the gates were opened to the Persians, and when the city was mastered three thousand Babylonians were crucified.—M. Dods.

10—13. (10) **sing,** etc., Is. xii. 6, liv. 1. **dwell in the midst of thee,** this prophecy had a fulfillment, when the temple was rebuilt and the worship of God was resumed on Mount Zion. But it had a higher fulfillment when "the Word was made flesh and dwelt among us" (John i. 14, Malachi iii. 1), and the promise of the Gentiles being joined to the Lord, vs. 11, was also accomplished. It awaits its highest fulfillment in both particulars in the times that are yet future. Rev. vii. 15; xxi. 3, 22—26.—Camb. Bib. (11) **many nations,** Gentiles who will unite to form the new kingdom of Messiah. **know,** by personal experiences. (12) **inherit,** or take actual possesison of. (13) **silent,**[b] "in the expectation of these mighty events, men are called upon to wait in awe and wonder." **raised up,** R. V., "waked up."

Joy an Attribute of Heaven.—Some people are afraid of anything like joy in religion. They have none themselves, and they do not love to see it in others. Their religion is something like the stars, very high and very clear, but very cold. When they see tears of anxiety, or tears of joy, they cry out, Enthusiasm, enthusiasm! "I sat down under His shadow with great delight." Is this enthusiasm? "May the God of hope fill you with all joy and peace in believing." If it be really in sitting under the shadow of Christ, let there be no bounds to our joy. Oh, if God would but open our eyes and give us simple childish faith to look to Jesus, to sit under His shadow, then would songs of joy arise from all our dwellings. "Rejoice in the Lord alway, and again I say, Rejoice."—Cheyne.

"Be Silent, O All Flesh, before the Lord."—The profoundest emotions of the soul are always mute. Superficial feelings are noisy and chattering. The shallow stream babbles amongst the hills. The deep river rolls by unheard. There are emotions of a pleasurable kind, that go off in the boisterous laugh, or the jocund song, or the sentimental hymn. But deep joy is silent as the stars. The real lover of art has joy in gazing at a magnificent piece of art, but his joy is inarticulate. The real lover of nature has deep joy in surveying some landscape of unparalleled grandeur. It is a joy that cannot go out in laughter, or speech, or song; it is silent. It is so with the godly soul. In the presence of the supremely beautiful it is filled with a joy that cannot speak, "a joy unspeakable, but full of glory."

CHAPTER THE THIRD.

FOURTH VISION, vss. 1—10. "Joshua the High Priest accepted and blessed as the people representative; a vision intended to restore the people's confidence in the priesthood and their ministry."—M. Dods. **1, 2.** (1) **Joshua,** Hag. i. 1. **standing,** etc., his proper attitude in the discharge of high-priestly duties. **right hand,** the position taken by the accuser in a court of justice. **to resist him,** R. V., "to be his adversary," Rev. xii. 10. (2) **the Lord said,** apparently the same as "the angel of the Lord" in vss. 1, 5, 6. **brand .. fire,** a proverbial expression, comp. Am. iv. 11. "Charred and unsightly as the bit of wood may be, the fact of its being plucked out of the fire proves its value to the owner, and that he sees a farther purpose it can serve."—M. Dods.

A Scripture Object Lesson.—Objects: A charred stick, a napkin, a pocket knife. Subject: The plucked brand. I. The sinner's danger. The noble house which God builded to be a temple for the spirit is ruined. The soul consumed by sinful lusts; separate from God; under the curse of the law; sentenced, etc. (see Is. xxxiii. 14; Mk. ix. 44). This is the doom of guilty men. II. The sinner's safety. Jesus Christ bears in His own body the curse; plucks the soul from the fire by His loving hand; quenches the smoking embers of sin by His grace. [Take up the brand, as if to represent the sinner plucked from the burning.] III. The sinner saved. 1. He still bears the marks of sin, you can see he has been in the fire; he has no comeliness of outer life; his influence still is bad, just as this brand blackens my hand and mars this napkin. [Proof by experiment.] Can this state of things be improved? Let us see. [Cut off the charred surface until the white wood appears.] What do we see? Yes, the black disappears, and the pure, clean wood come out. Christ not only saves us from death, but He, at the same time, takes away our sin. He is "the Lord our righteousness." We shall never be wholly perfect here; but it is our duty, by the help of God, to cut off every possible mark and trace of sin from our characters. Cut off your sins, children. [The napkin may now be applied to the brand without being soiled.] 2. One thing more: the future state of the changed sinner. I have seen in houses, as I passed, charred boards and blackened bricks nailed and built into the walls again. They have been saved from the fire, and now were once more filling their place in the homes of men. So Jesus takes the sinner, the brand plucked out of the fire, and builds him into His glorious spiritual temple. May we all have a part and place there.—H. C. McCook.

A Countryman's Conversion.—A plain countryman, who was effectually called by Divine grace under a sermon from Ze. iii. 2, was some time afterwards accosted by a quondam companion of his drunken fits, and strongly solicited to accompany him to the alehouse. But the good man strongly resisted all his arguments, saying, "I am a brand plucked out of the fire." His old companion not understanding this, he explained it thus:—"Look ye," said he, "there is a great difference between a brand and a green stick; if a spark flies upon a brand that has been partly burned, it will soon catch fire again; but it is not so with a green stick. I tell you, I am that brand plucked out of the fire, and I dare not venture into the way of temptation, for fear of being set on fire."—Whitecross.

3—5. (3) "Yet something remains: Israel is rescued, but not sanctified. The nation's troubles are over: their uncleanness has still to be removed. Zechariah sees that the High Priest is clothed in filthy garments, while he stands before the Angel of Judgment. The Angel orders his servants, those that stand before him, to give him clean festal robes." —G. A. Smith. **filthy garments,** as representative of a sinful people. (4) **he answered,** i. e. the angel of the Lord. **take .. him,** as the sign of his justification and acceptance.[a] **change of raiment,** R. V. "rich apparel." (5) **and I said,** i. e. Zechariah. "So Isaiah in the midst of a solemn vision gives vent to his feelings (Isa. vi. 5) and St. John mingles his own sentiments and actions with what he beholds." (Rev. v. 4; x. 9; xi. 1.) **fair mitre,** "a clean turban," this brings the headdress, in Ezekiel of the Prince of Israel, and in the Priestly code of the High Priest."—G. A. Smith. See Ex. xxviii. 36 and note there.

Fifthy Garments (vs. 3).—It was usual, especially among the Romans, when a man was charged with a capital crime, and during his arraignment, to let down his hair, suffer his beard to grow long, to wear filthy ragged garments, and appear in a very dirty and sordid habit; on account of which they were called sordidati. When the person accused

grew higher, and spread wider, until it covered the front most luxuriantly, forming a beautiful ornament, and admired by the passers-by. To all inquiries he gives the history of its planting and growth, and then asks the question, "Is not this a brand plucked from the burning?"

The promise is that Zerubbabel, notwithstanding all the difficulties he had to contend with in rebuilding the temple, should see it completed, should see the crowning stone laid on the building, amid the hosannahs of the people. "Grace, grace unto it!" So it will be with every genuine work to which a true man puts his hand in the name of God. It will be finished; there will be no failure, success is inevitable. "As I live, saith the Lord, the whole earth shall be filled with My glory." (Numb. xiv. 21.)

[a] "When the people in the E. are in deep distress, or when they have been charged with some capital crime, it is customary for them not to wash themselves, but to allow the dirt to accumulate both on their person and dress. The angel of the Lord ordered the officers of justice to take his filthy garments off, as a mark of his acquittal, and to clothe him with a change of raiment, as an emblem of his justification."
—Gadsby.

was brought into court to be tried, even his near relations, friends, and acquaintances, before the court voted, appeared with dishevelled hair, and clothed with garments foul and out of fashion, weeping, crying, and deprecating punishment. The accused sometimes appeared before the judges clothed in black, and his head covered with dust. In allusion to this ancient custom, the Prophet Zechariah represents Joshua, the high priest, when he appeared before the Lord, and Satan stood at his right hand to accuse him, as clothed with filthy garments. After the cause was carefully examined, and all parties impartially heard, the public crier, by command of the presiding magistrate, ordered the judges to bring in their verdict."—Paxton.

6—10. (6) **protested,** or declared in a very solemn manner. (7) **charge,** or ordinance.[b] **judge my house,** rule my temple. **places to walk,** R. V. "a place of access." "Instead of being an outcast he will have a place among those who are most familiarly known in the heavenly court." —M. Dods. **these that stand by,** the company of angels "that stood before him," vs. 4. (8) **that sit before thee,** Joshua's fellow-priests who were accustomed to sit with him in council. **men wondered at,**[a] R. V. "men which are a sign." "Men who in their persons (and office) shadow forth future events. Ezek. xii. 6, 11; xxiv. 24, 27." This clause is a quasi-parenthesis. The direct address is interrupted, and a reason, as it were, given for making it: "To Joshua and his fellows I foretell the coming of 'my servant, Branch,' because they, the priesthood, in all their office and ministry, as well as in what has just happened to them in the vision in the person of their chief, are types of Him."—Camb. Bib. **my servant,** a frequent name of the Messiah in Isaiah, e. g. xlii. 1; xlix 6; lii. 13; liii. 11. **the branch,**[b] as there is no article in the Hebrew, this seems to be used as a proper name, "My Servant, Branch." This is first found as a designation of the Messiah in Isa. ix. 2. "Other passages point to the idea that out of the stem of Jesse now so marred, there would one day spring a branch in which the whole family should be glorified."—M. Dods. (9) **the stone** "the primary and immediate reference is to the Temple, in re-building which Joshua was then engaged. The "stone," which was perhaps seen lying before him in the vision, is most probably not the foundation-stone, which had been laid years before, but the head-stone (iv. 7, 9), which would complete the building, and which He, with whom to purpose is to accomplish, here announces that He has already laid; so certainly shall it be set in its place in due time. The ultimate reference is to Him, who as "the Branch" should hereafter "build the temple of the Lord" (vi. 12).—Camb. B. **seven eyes,** we may "understand the words to be a promise that the seven eyes (i. e. the perfect watchfulness and care—seven being the number of perfection) of God shall be fixed upon this stone; that He will never, so to speak, take His eyes off either type or anti-type, till His purpose respecting them is accomplished." **I will engrave,** i. e. I will have a hand in every detail of this building.—Dods. **in one day,** in a short time, either "soon," or "suddenly." (10) **under the vine,** 1 Ki. iv. 25. "In this cleansed and purified kingdom shall be found peace, happiness, and plenty, recalling the prosperous days of Solomon (1 Kings iv. 25). (For a similar picture of prosperity, see Micah iv. 4). —Pul. Com.

[b] Used in the Bk. of Num. to denote the offices and duties of priests and Levites.

[a] "They are men to be gazed at with wonder, because they typify a great mystery, which was no other than the incarnation and everlasting priesthood of Jesus the Son of God."—Wordsworth.

[b] The Alex. Jews trans. this word the sunrise, the dayspring from on high.

"My own experience is that the Bible is dull when I am dull. When I am really alive, and set in upon the text with a tidal pressure of living affinities, it opens, it multiplies discoveries, and reveals depths even faster than I can note them. The worldly spirit shuts the Bible; the Spirit of God makes it a fire, flaming out all meanings and glorious truths." —Horace Bushnell.

The Golden Age.—Mankind have always clung to the hope of better times to come. We give a passage from the famous fourth Eclogue of Virgil:—

The last great age, foretold by sacred rhyme,
Renews its finished course; Saturnian times
Roll round again; and mighty years, begun
From their first orb, in radiant circles run.
The base, degenerate, iron offspring ends,
A golden progeny from heaven descends. . . .
See, labouring nature calls thee to sustain
The nodding frame of heaven and earth and main!
See, to their base restored earth, seas, and air,
And joyful ages from behind in crowding ranks appear.

CHAPTER THE FOURTH.

1—4. FIFTH VISION: vss. 1—14. "This is intended to give Zerubbabel, the civil head, the assurance that he is also God's anointed, endowed with power from God to do God's work."—M. Dods. (1) **waked me,** from trance. (2) **looked,** R. V. "seen."..**candlestick,**[c] the same word that is used of the lamp-stand in the Tabernacle, which this resembles. **bowl,** comp. Ex. xxvii. 20, 21. **seven pipes,** to convey new oil from the olive trees. (3) **olive trees,** living sources of fresh oil.[d] In a secret manner these supplied the bowls. (4) **spake,** better, said.

Shining Lamps (vs. 2).—There are four things necessary to lamps giving light properly. 1. They must be lighted; 2. They must be set; 3. They must be fed; 4. They must be trimmed. Apply:—(1) Have you lamps? (2) Are you lamps?—Edmond.

5—7. (5) **knowest,** etc., as if the Prophet should have discovered the meaning. (6) **This is the word of the Lord,** i. e. this is God's way of saying to Zerubbabel. **not by might,** or mere human force. **by my spirit,**[e] a sure, lasting but secret strengthening and replenishing, like that of the olive trees. (7) **great mountain,** of difficulty. The mountain-like obstacles that had risen up before Z. shall be overcome. **headstone,** or topstone, the sign of the completion of the building.[f] **Grace, grace unto it,** with shouts of festive joy he shall set in its place the crowning stone of the edifice.

8—10. (8, 9) **his hands.** The Temple was finished in Darius's sixth year. (Ezra. vi. 15.) (10) "For whoever hath despised the day of small things, they shall rejoice when they see the plummet in the hand of Zerubbabel."—G. A. Smith. **small things,**[g] or beginnings. The unfinished temple, and the feeble and depressed condition of the people. **plummet,** used in building operations, and here as a final testing of the completed work. **those seven,** R. V. "Even these seven." The meaning of the verse is: "For who hath despised the day of small things? (comp. Hag. ii. 3) For these seven eyes of Jehovah, which run to and fro throughout all the earth, shall rejoice to see the plummet in the hand of Zerubbabel." Since, then, God beholds the progress of the work with joy and favor, who will venture to despise it?—Camb. B. **run .. earth,** ch. iii. 9.

The Day of Small Things (vs. 10).—1. Little errors not to be overlooked; 2. Small sins not to be indulged; 3. The beginnings of grace not to be contemned; 4. Slight means not to be neglected; 5. Weak Christians not to be despised; 6. A rising cause not to be despaired of.

Small Things.—It is a curious fact that the sun which shines seven times in the course of the week is spoken of as the "seven eyes" of the Deity, because there is an eye for each day. Thus, the Sunday, the "first eye" of God shines, and so on through the rest of the days. In the 9th verse mention is made of laying the foundation stone of a temple for Jehovah, and again in the 10th verse it is asked, "Who hath despised the day of small things?" saying it is only the foundation, this is a small beginning: fear not, for the "seven eyes" of the Lord are over the work. His good providence shall accomplish the whole, because He has an eye for each day of the week. Has a man suffered a great evil, has an antagonist triumphed over another, either in a court of justice or any other way, he says, in talking about his misfortunes, "God has lost His eyes, or I should not have fallen into this trouble." "Well, friend, how is this? I hear you have gained the day." "True, true, the eyes of God were upon me." Should there not have been rain for some time, the people say, "God has no eyes in these days," i. e. He does not take care of us. In the book Neethe-veanpa it is said, "To all there are two eyes: to the learned there are three; to the giver of alms there are seven eyes (alluding to each day); but to those who through penance have received gracious gifts there are innumerable eyes."—Roberts.

"They've Forgotten the Rope."—A tall chimney had been completed, and the scaffolding was being removed. One man remained on the top to superintend the process. A rope should have been left for him to

c Ex. xxv. 31—39.

"It is interesting to note, that throughout the Scriptures oil is used to represent the Holy Spirit, and that in their union to the Holy Spirit, formed by their faith in Christ, and maintained by their constant study of His word, their habitual dependence on Him in prayer, and their continuous obedience to his commands, believers are represented as having that unfailing supply of strength by wh. they are sustained in every duty and prepared for every emergency. As in Zechariah's vision the two olive trees stood, one on each side of the golden lamp, emptying into its bowls the oil out of themselves, and thus sustaining its never-failing light; so the Holy Spirit in the believer's heart gives him grace sufficient for him in every hour of need."

d "The oil is supplied by God Himself through the olive trees, which represent the functions of Christ, who is the great High Priest and King.'—Wordsworth.

e "The secret assistance of My providence." —Lowth.

f Ezr. iii. 11, vi. 15.

g Comp. Mat. xiii. 31, 32.

"The little coral insects that build up the beautiful islands which stud the face of the Southern sea work, we are told, for ages in

descend by. His wife was at home washing, when her little boy burst in with "Mother, mother, they've forgotten the rope, and he's going to throw himself down!" She paused—her lips moved in the agony of prayer—and she rushed forth. A crowd were looking up to the poor man, who was moving round and round the narrow cornice, terrified and bewildered! He seemed as if at any moment he might fall, or throw himself down in despair. His wife from below cried out—"Wait a bit, John!" The man became calm. "Take off your stocking—unravel the yarn." And he did so. "Now tie the end to a bit of mortar and lower gently." Down came the thread and the bit of mortar, swinging backwards and forwards. Lower and lower it descended, eagerly watched by many eyes; it was now within reach, and was gently seized by one of the crowd. They fastened some twine to the thread. "Now pull up." The man got hold of the twine. The rope was now fastened on. "Pull away again." He at length seized the rope and made it secure. There were a few moments of suspense, and then, amidst the shouts of the people, he threw himself into the arms of his wife, sobbing—"Thou'st saved me, Mary." The worsted thread was not despised—it drew after it the twine, the rope, the rescue! Ah, my friend, thou mayest be sunk very low down in sin and woe, but there is a thread of Divine love, that comes from the throne of heaven, and touches even thee. Seize that thread. It may be small, but it is golden. Improve what you have, however little, and more shall be given. That thin thread of love, if you will not neglect it, shall lift even you up to God and glory. "What hath despised the day of small things?"

11—14. (11) **what .. trees,** "To this question no answer is immediately forthcoming, the answer being delayed in order to augment the prophet's desire of understanding the vision, and to induce him to make the question more definite.—Pul. Com. (12) **pipes, etc.** The Prophet noticed the peculiarity that the trees fed the bowls without any pressing of the hand of man. (13) **knowest,** etc., see note on vs. 5. (14) **anointed ones,** R. V. "These are the two sons of oil," "the reference here is generally supposed to be to Zerubbabel and Joshua, as representing the kingly and priestly offices, the channels through which God supplies His Church. It may be doubted, however, whether the angel does not purposely avoid giving a definite, and especially a human meaning to these symbols. The tenor of the whole vision is, 'by My Spirit, saith the Lord of hosts.' These 'sons of oil,' then, are agents or agencies, near to God and beyond our ken, 'that stand by the Lord of the whole earth.' With this view would seem to accord the fact, that the two mysterious 'Witnesses,' in the Book of Revelation (xi. 4), are spoken of as being 'the two olive trees...standing before the God of the earth;' with an obvious reference to Zechariah's vision."—Camb. B.

The Two Sons of Oil.—I think the best interpretation is that these stand for and represent all those high and hidden agencies, beyond our human sight, which God is steadily using for and applying to the furtherance of his benignant purposes in the world. Behind every builder for God, though he may not see them much, or understand about them clearly, stand, set there by God, these "sons of oil," assisting him. Let the builder for God in any sphere keep up good heart. He cannot fail. God is on his side. The temple shall go on to the turret-stone.—Wayland Hoyt.

CHAPTER THE FIFTH.

SIXTH VISION, vss. 1—4. The flying roll, sent for the cleansing of the people by the punishment of individual sinners. **1—2.** (1) **flying roll,** "Its flight signified the swift coming of punishment; its flying from heaven that the sentence proceeded from the judgment-seat above." (2) **twenty cubits,** etc., an immense roll of parchment, large enough to be inscribed with a vast number of offences.

The Flying Roll seen by Zechariah.—The roll indicates the form in which books were formerly written—not in separate leaves, and bound in pasteboard and leather backs, as ours are at the present day, but the

the dark caves of the ocean, regardless of their perishing in obscurity long before their graceful architecture even begins to peep above the surface of the waters. So it is with those who labor under the guidance of Providence for the accomplishment of some remote good. They may work on for generations in obscurity and contempt, conscious only that they are working in harmony with the plans of God."—Peace Society's Report 1859.

"We see this illustrated in the world of nature, and in the world of grace. The little humming-bird, the little gnat, the little violet, the little minnow, the little mite, the little atom, He makes use of in a wise and beautiful manner in creation, for the manifestation of His glory. So He does in grace. The little promise, the little faith, the little talent, all have their place, and are used by Him for His glory." —John Bate.

"The appointed means and channels by wh. the favor and grace of God were conveyed and bestowed on the Heb. people." —Wordsworth.

"The dimensions of the roll seem to have no special meaning beyond implying that it was a roll of great magnitude." —Spk. Com.

Eze. ii. 9, 10.

"Books are a part of man's prerogative; in formal ink they thoughts and voices hold, that

skins of goats, or some other animal, having been dried and cut into square pieces, were attached together, and made to extend to a length of several yards. Then one end was fastened to a roller, and the whole was rolled up just as we roll up a map. Indeed, our word volume comes from this ancient usage of forming a book by rolling it up; for the word volume means a something rolled up. The roll which Zechariah saw was such a volume, and it was a very large one, being twenty cubits, or thirty feet, in length, and ten cubits, or fifteen feet, in breadth. All this space was written on, full of the curses or threatenings of God against sinful men. Now God has recorded His threatenings as well as His promises, for He is alike faithful in the fulfilment of both. But the passage speaks of the roll flying, and what is meant by this? It seems simply that when the Prophet saw the roll it seemed to be moving swiftly across the heavens—thereby indicating that, as the roll was not stationary, so God's judgments against wicked men are not for one place only, but for all places where sin reigns; and as the roll moved swiftly, so God's judgments were not to be long delayed, but to be speedily poured forth on the guilty nations."—W. Cooke.

3—4. (3) **curse,** or rather, the document on wh. the curse is inscribed. For judgments denounced against the Jews see De. xxvii. 15—26, xxviii. 15—68. **earth,** R. V., "land." **As on this side,** etc., R. V. "on the one side"..."on the other side." i. e. there was writing on both sides of the roll. **sweareth,** i. e. falsely, vs. 4. (4) **remain.** R. V. "abide," take up its lodging there until it has wrought out its purpose.[a]

The Curse (vs. 4).—It abides in the house to curse everything, even the timber and the stones. Guilt, not only, like a ravenous beast, crouches at the door of the sinner, but rather, like a blasting mildew, spreads its baneful influence over the whole dwelling. The sin of one member of a family brings its curse on the others. The sins of the parents bring a curse upon the children. "Between parents and children," says Jeremy Taylor, "there is so great a society of nature and of manners, of blessing and of cursing, that an evil parent cannot perish in a single death; and holy parents never eat their meal of blessing alone; but they make the room shine like the fire of a holy sacrifice; and a father's or a mother's piety makes all the house festival, and full of joy from generation to generation."—Pul. Com.

5—7. SEVENTH VISION. vss. 5—11. "A woman, in whom the wickedness of the land is personified, is pressed down into a great ephah, or measure, and carried, fast shut up in it, by swift ministers, into the land of Babylon, the proper home of all iniquity."—Camb. Bib. (5, 6) **ephah,** "the largest vessel in use among the Jews, of more than seven gallons in capacity, and round like a barrel."—G. A. Smith.[a] **their resemblance,** or the thing that their iniquity is like. **the earth,** R. V. "the land." (7) **talent of lead,** R. V., marg. "a round piece of lead;" a leaden cover so heavy that the woman inside, who is the personification of the national wickedness, cannot escape. The cross is lifted, to show to the prophet the contents of the ephah.

Angels: objects of their Ministry.—Their ministry relates especially to believers; (Heb. i. 14) "are they not all ministering spirits, sent forth to minister for them who shall be heirs of salvation?" (Ps. xxxiv. 7) "The angel of Jehovah encampeth round about them that fear Him." (Ps. xci. 11) "He shall give His angels charge over thee." (Isa. lxiii. 9) "The angel of His presence saved them." (Matt. xviii. 10) "Their angels do always behold the face of My Father." (Matt. xiii. 41) "The Son of Man shall send forth His angels, and they shall gather out of His kingdom all things that offend." (xxiv.) "They shall gather together His elect from the four winds." (Acts xii. 15) "It is his angel."—Milton.

8—11. (8) **this is,** etc. R. V. "This is Wickedness;[b] and he cast her down into the midst of the ephah." (9) **two women,** poss. symbolising the two agents in the captivities, Assyria and Babylon. **wings,** comp. De. xxviii. 49. (10, 11) **to build it,** R. V., "to build here an house." **land of Shinar,**[a] "The counter part of the Holy Land."—Ewald. "The land in which men first conspired against God." (Gen. xi. 2). **and it shall be,** etc., R. V. "and when it is prepared she shall be set there in her own place."

Verses 5—11.—In this striking hieroglyphic we are taught how idol-

we to them our solitude may give, and make time present travelled that of old. Our life, fame pierceth longer at the end, and books it farther backward do extend.' —Overbury.

[a] Comp. the oracle at Delphi against the perjurer: "The curse shall swiftly enter, and shall bring the man himself and all his house to ruin." Pr. iii. 33; Is. xxiv. 5, 6.

"It is said that a prisoner standing at the bar, indicted for felony, was asked by the judge what he could say for himself. 'Truly, my lord,' says he, 'I did mean no hurt when I stole; it is an evil custom that I have gotten; I have been used to it ever since I knew anything."—'Why, then,' says the judge, 'if it be thy custom to steal, it is my custom to hang up thieves."—Spencer.

[a] "An ephah being the measure of dry things, denotes the Jews' unjust dealings in buying and selling."—Lowth.

[b] "The article is emphatic, implying the lawlessness and wantonness which had prevailed in Judah, and wh. is to be borne away into the land of Shinar, the home of lawless and licentious men."—Spk. Com.

[a] "The capital of the God-opposed world kingdoms, and so representing in general the seat of irreligion."—Fausset.

atry, with all its accompanying atrocities, was removed from the land of the Hebrews which it had desecrated, to a country devoted to it and where it was to commingle with its native elements, never to be re-imported into Canaan. How exactly has the prediction been fulfilled! From the time of the captivity to the present, a period of more than two thousand years, the Hebrew people have never once lapsed into idolatry. The whole vision was intended to convince them of the greatness of the evil.—Henderson.

CHAPTER THE SIXTH.

EIGHTH VISION. vss. 1—8. This vision gives assurance that the peace of Israel would not again be disturbed by her enemies. Babylonia and Egypt especially would be visited with such divine judgments as should appease the spirit of God, aroused to anger by the sufferings of Israel.—Dods. **1—4.** (1) **four chariots,** these according to vs. 5, represent the winds, which again represent the invisible mighty agencies sent forth by God to accomplish his purpose. Ps. civ. 3; cxlviii. 8; Dan. vii. 2. They are four because God's agents are sent to every quarter.—Dods. **between two mountains,** perhaps Zion and Moriah are intended, "thus representing Jerusalem as the point of departure of God's judgments."—Dods. Or the allusion may be more general, to valleys between mountains as the highways of invaders. **brass,** the symbol of might.[b] (2) **red,** etc., comp. ch. i. 8, color for bloodshed; black may represent famine and mourning; white, victory; grisled, mixed fortunes. But it is by no means certain that these colors have special significance.

Angels:—

They are God's ministering spirits, and sent,
His messengers of mercy, to fulfil
Good for salvation's heirs. For us they still
Grieve when we sin, rejoice when we repent:
And on the last dread day they shall present
The severed righteous at His holy hill,
With them God's face to see, to do His will,
And bear with them His likeness.

—Bp. Mant.

5—8. (5) **spirits,** better, winds, as Divine agents,[a] **standing,** etc., as servants waiting their Lord's bidding. (6) **north country,** usual term for Babylon. **after them,** to complete their work...**south country,** i. e. Egypt.[b] (7)..**and he said,** i. e. the Lord. (8) upon me, "me" may refer to the prophet... **quieted,** or satisfied, by the full execution of the Divine judgment. It is striking that none are sent eastward. This appears to mean that, in Zechariah's day, no power oppressed or threatened Israel from that direction; but in the north there was the centre of the Persian Empire, to the south Egypt, still a possible master of the world, and to the west the new forces of Europe that in less than a generation were to prove themselves a match for Persia. The horses of the fourth chariot are therefore given the charge to exercise supervision upon the whole earth. The centre of the world's power is in the north, and therefore the black horses, which are dispatched in that direction, are explicitly described as charged to bring God's spirit, that is His anger, or His power, to bear on that quarter of the world."—G. A. Smith.

"Symbolical action. Crowning of the high-priest, vss. 9—15. Zechariah is directed to go to the house of Josiah in Jerusalem, and to take from certain Jews who were lodging there gold and silver, a portion of the offerings to the House of God, which they had brought from their brethren still in exile, vss. 9, 10. Of this gold and silver he is to make a crown, and put it on the head of Joshua the High-priest, vs. 11. The significant action is to be accompanied by a prediction in the name of Jehovah, that in due time there shall 'grow up the Branch,' who shall be the true builder of the temple of the Lord, who shall be both King and Priest, and in the exercise of those two offices the author and dispenser of peace, vss. 12, 13." **9—13.** (10) **of them,** i. e. from them. **Take**

"Wickedness or lawlessness is carried to Babylon, and is settled there because at Babylon is its proper place."—S. Jerome.

A thousand liveried angels lackey her, driving far off each thing of sin and guilt, and in clear dream and solemn vision, tell her of things that no gross ear can hear; till oft converse with heavenly habitants begins to cast a beam on the outward shape.

[b] "The metal among the ancients representing hard solidity; so the immovable and resistless firmness of God's people."—Fausset.

"The secret purpose of God from eternity does not come forth to view before the execution, but is hidden and kept back irresistibly till the fit time, as it were, between lofty mountains; the chariots are the various changes wrought in nations, which, as swift heralds, announce to us what before we knew not."—Calvin.

[a] Comp. Je. xlix. 36. Rev. vii. 1.

[b] Da. xi. 6.

"How absolute and omnipotent is the silence of night! And yet the stillness seems almost audible! From all the measureless depths of air around us comes a half-sound, a half-whisper, as if we could hear the crumbling and falling away of earth and all created things, in the great miracle of nature, decay and reproduction, ever beginning, never ending—the gradual lapse

silver and gold from them. (11) **then take,** etc., R. V., "yea, take of them silver and gold." **crowns,**[a] i. e. two crowns, or the double crown of the king and the priest. (12) **The Branch,** ch. iii. 8, the Messiah, whom Joshua was to represent. **out .. place,** lit. "from under him." Comp. for the expresion Ex. x. 23; and for the meaning Is. xi. 1; liii. 2. Other less satisfactory renderings are, it shall grow up under Him, i. e. all things fair and good shall spring up and flourish under Him."—Camb. Bib. **he shall build,** in the full and higher sense, Messiah.[b] (13) **the glory,** i. e. the full glory of both the regal and the priestly offices. Messiah would be both King and Priest. **counsel of peace,** i. e. there would be no clashing of jurisdictions, bec. both offices would be united in one person.[c]

The Matchless Man.—The prophet is commanded to go to certain of the more distinguished men who had returned from Babylonian captivity, representative men and envoys it may be. He was to take these men, whose names are here given, who were entertained in the house of another distinguished man, here called Josiah the son of Zephaniah. From that house the silver and gold which they had brought from Babylon were to be taken, with which crowns were to be made and placed upon the head of Joshua the son of Josedech, the high priest. By the general consent of expositors, this was a mere symbolical transaction—a transaction pointing to some great Man whom Heaven will require all men to crown with the highest dignity. Here is a character symbolized by the name of Joshua, to whom the people are called upon by God Himself to render honor. Who is this Man? Can you find him anywhere amongst the millions of your contemporaries in any land, or on the page of the history of the people of any time? anywhere but in the records of the four evangelists—the Man Christ Jesus? "When He bringeth in the First Begotten into the world, he saith, Let all the angels of God worship Him."—D. Thomas.

14, 15. (14) **the crowns shall be to Helem,** etc., the crowns are to be for a memorial to H. and his companions of the symbolical act that had taken place, and for this purpose are to be placed in the temple.—Henderson. **Helem,** or Heldai. **Hen,** "the Authorized version considers this a proper name. In that case it would be another name for Josiah. But it is really an appellative, and the rendering should be, as in R. V. margin, 'for the kindness of the son of Zephaniah.' The crowns would be also a memorial of his kindness in receiving and entertaining these exiles (comp. Matt. x. 41)."—Pul. Com. **memorial,** of the promise of Messiah wh. had been given in connection with them. (15) **far off,** distant nations, symbolized by these emissaries from Babylon.[d] A first reference may be to the fact that other Jews shall return from Babylon bringing aid to the present work of rebuilding the temple.

A Lost Crown.—A lady in a dream wandered around heaven, beholding its glories, and came at last to the crown-room. Among the crowns, she saw one exceedingly beautiful. "Whom is this for?" "It was intended for you," said the angel; **"but you did not labor for it, and now another will wear it."**

CHAPTER THE SEVENTH.

The Deputation from Bethel. Chaps. vii., viii. After the lapse of nearly two years, Zechariah is again called to prophesy, the occasion of his doing so being the arrival at Jerusalem of a deputation, sent from Bethel to enquire whether they ought still to observe a national fast, which had been instituted in the time of the captivity, vii. 1—3. The answer of Almighty God by the prophet falls into four sections (marked by separate paragraphs in R. V.), each of which is introduced by the same formula, vii. 4, 8; viii. 1, 18. The return in the last of these sections (viii. 19) to the question out of which the whole arose, shews that the prophecy is really one.—Camb. B. **1—7.** (1) **fourth year,** B. C. 518.[a] **Chisleu,** or Kisleu, the name in use after the captivity. (2) **when they had sent unto the house of God, Sharezer,** etc., R. V., "Now they of

and running of the sand in the great hour glass of time."—Longfellow.

[a] "No time was to be lost to mark the significancy of their coming from afar to offer gifts to the temple, typifying in the double crown made of their gifts, and set on Joshua's head, the gathering in of Israel's outcasts to Messiah hereafter, who shall then be recognized as the true King and Priest."—Fausset.

[b] "The building of God's spiritual temple, the Church, was a work reserved for the Messiah."—Lowth.

[c] "Neither will the regal office overshadow the sacerdotal nor the sacerdotal the regal."—Spk. Com.

[d] Is. lx. 10.

"It is not enough to begin in the spirit and end in the flesh; it is not for him that runneth, but for him that runneth to the end, that persevereth, that the crown is reserved; it is he that shall eat of the hidden manna,—he that shall have the white stone and in the stone a new name written, which no man knoweth, saving he that receiveth it."—Spencer.

[a] "With returning prosperity and power, it was only natural that a question should arise as to the propriety of retaining these services of humiliation which had been instituted as memorials of the destruction of the city and temple." —Spk. Com.

Bethel had sent Sharezer," etc. To inquire God's will in the matter of the fastings. (3) **priests .. prophets,** through whom they might expect the Divine will to be communicated. **weep,** as in a time of humiliation. **fifth month,**[b] "the deputation limited their inquiry to the fast of the fifth month, which commemorated the burning of the temple and the city, now practically restored. But with a breadth of view which reveals the prophet rather than the priest, Zechariah replies, in the following chapter, upon all the facts by which Israel for seventy years had bewailed her ruin and exile. He instances two, that of the fifth month, and that of the seventh month, the date of the murder of Gedaliah,[c] when the last poor remnant of a Jewish state was swept away."—G. A. Smith. **separating myself,** from food, etc. (4, 5) The people are reminded that their fasting and feasting had alike been observances terminating upon themselves and devoid of religious motive and spiritual aim, and consequently unacceptable to God; in accordance with the teaching of the earlier prophets, in the times of Jerusalem's prosperity.—Camb. B. **fasted,** etc., comp. Is. lviii. 5. **seventh month,** probably on account of Gedaliah.[c] **to me,** Hag. i. 4. Was it really religious fasting, the sign of a true heart-penitence? (6) **when ye did eat,** etc., R. V., "when ye eat and when ye drink, do not ye." **for yourselves,** for your own self-pleasing.. You neither honored Me in your feeding or in your fasting. (7) **should ye not, etc.,** or "is it not the words which the Lord hath cried by the former prophets;" i. e. "is not this what the prophets said would happen?" —Dods. **south,** the Negeb. **the plain,** Heb. Shephelah, the maritime district.[d] Perhaps the third division of the territory of Judah, "the hill country," Luke i. 39, is pointed at in the words, "Jerusalem and the cities thereof round about her." Judg. i. 9; Obad. 19.

b The tenth day of the fifth month was kept as the day on which the temple was destroyed by the Babylonians.

"These are heart - wrung tears. At these words, sympathetic tears swam o'er for the first time, from each celestial eye, as trees autumnal shed their leafy tears in golden showers, shaken by sudden gust; tears not to be forbid." — Bailey.

c 2 Ki. xxv. 25; Je. xli. 1—3.

National Fasts.—In 1853, when cholera prevailed, the Presbytery of Edinburgh (Church of Scotland) suggested to Lord Palmerston, then Home Secretary, the propriety of ordering a national fast. His lordship, in his reply, recommended observance of natural laws rather than fasting. If this were attended to, all would be well. Otherwise pestilence would come, "in spite of all the prayers and fastings of a united but inactive nation." He does not seem to have understood that the two things were quite compatible. Prayer and inaction is folly; but prayer and action is the highest wisdom. Surely there is something grand and beautiful in a whole nation bowed in humility and supplication before the Most High.—Pul. Com.

"In the next section, vss. 8—14, the substance of the teaching of the earlier prophets, as insisting on moral reformation and not on outward observances, is given; and to the neglect of it are traced the rejection by God of His people, and the calamities that had come upon them in their captivity and dispersion."—Camb. B. **8—10.** (8, 9) **execute,** etc., expression of God's demand for moral not merely ceremonial goodness.[a] (10) **oppress not,** Je. v. 28. **imagine evil,** plot or plan evil schemes.

a Comp. Ex. xxii. 21; Is. i. 23, lviii. 6, 7; Mi. vi. 6—8.

"Compassion is an emotion of which we ought never to be ashamed. Graceful, particularly in youth, is the tear of sympathy and the heart that melts at the tale of woe. We should not permit ease and indulgence to contract our affections and wrap us up in a selfish enjoyment; but we should accustom ourselves to think of the distresses of human life, of the solitary cottage, the dying parent, and the weeping orphan. Nor ought we ever to sport with pain and distress in any of our amusements, or treat even the meanest insect with wanton cruelty." — Dr. Blair.

Compassion and Its Reward—The Cup of Cold Water.—A young Englishwoman was sent to France to be educated in a Huguenot school in Paris. A few evenings before the fatal massacre of St. Bartholomew's day, she and some of her young companions were taking a walk in some part of the town where there were sentinels placed—perhaps on the walls; and you know that when a soldier is on guard he must not leave his post until he is relieved, that is, till another soldier comes to take his place. One of the soldiers, as the young ladies passed him, besought them to have the charity to bring a little water, adding that he was very ill, and that it would be as much as his life was worth to go and fetch it himself. The ladies walked on, much offended at the man for presuming to speak to them,—all but the young Englishwoman, whose compassion was moved, and who, leaving her party, procured some water and brought it to the soldier. He begged her to tell him her name and place of abode, and this she did. When she rejoined her companions, some blamed and others ridiculed her attention to a common soldier; but they soon had reason to lament that they had not been equally compassionate, for the grateful soldier contrived, on the night of the massacre, to save this young Englishwoman, while all the other inhabitants of the house she dwelt in were killed.—Paxton Hood.——A Soldier Overcome by Kindness.—There was in a barrack an incorrigible soldier, who had been fined, imprisoned, flogged, and put on extra drill, but all to no purpose. His colonel, seeing him one day in the guardhouse for some misdemeanor, said to him, "What! you here again?" "Yes, sir," he replied, with a dogged hardihood that showed he cared for no punishment. The colonel turned round to the sergeant and said, "I don't know what to do with this fellow. We've flogged him, fined him, imprisoned him, put him on extra drill; in fact, we've tried everything." "No, sir," answered the sergeant, touching his cap with the military salute, "there's one thing you've not tried; you've never forgiven him." The colonel held down his head, somewhat ashamed, and after consultation with his brother officers, returned to the soldier, and said to him, "There, sir, you may go; you're forgiven; you will not be punished for this." A new light seemed to break upon the mind of that man, and from that time, two years past, said the chaplain, there has not been a better behaved or more easily managed man in the regiment.

11—14. (11) **pulled .. shoulder,** as a stubborn beast wh. will not be yoked. (12) **adamant stone,** Eze. iii. 9, poss. diamond. (13) **so they cried,** R. V., "so they shall cry and I will not hear .. but I will scatter," etc. (14) **desolate after them,** or behind them, when they had gone into captivity.[b] **pleasant land,** Je. iii. 19. Lit. "land of desire."

Tastes in Hearers.—One is like an Athenian, and he hearkeneth after news: if the preacher say anything of our armies beyond the sea, or council at home, or matters of court, that is his lure: another is like the Pharisee, and he watcheth if anything be said that may be wrested to be spoken against persons in high place, that he may play the devil in accusing of his brethren; let him write that in his tables too: another smacks of eloquence, and he gaps for a phrase, that when he cometh to his ordinary, he may have one figure more to grace and worship his tale: another is malcontent, and he never pricketh up his ears till the preacher come to gird against some whom he spiteth, and when the sermon is done, he remembereth nothing which was said to him, but that which was spoken against another: another cometh to gaze about the church; he hath an evil eye, which is still looking upon that from which Job did avert his eye: another cometh to muse; so soon as he is set, he falleth into a brown study; sometimes his mind runs upon his market, sometimes of his journey, sometimes of his suit, sometimes of his dinner, sometimes of his sport after dinner; and the sermon is done before the man thinks where he is: another cometh to hear, but so soon as the preacher hath said his prayer, he falls fast asleep, as though he had been brought in for a corpse, and the preacher should preach at his funeral.—Henry Smith.

b "It was ordered remarkably by God's providence that no occupants took possession of it, but that during the Jews' absence it was reserved for them against their return, after seventy years." —Fausset.

"They might thank themselves (for the desolations of their land); it was they that by their own wickedness laid the pleasant land desolate. It was not so much the Chaldeans that did it. No, they did it themselves. The desolations of a land are owing to the wickedness of its inhabitants."— M. Henry.

CHAPTER THE EIGHTH.

"Passing now to a happier strain of hope and promise (vss. 1—17), the prophetic word tells of the bright days of holiness and prosperity in store for Jerusalem, in contrast with her earlier condition of distress and discord, and urges the people, on the strength of these promises, to holy obedience."—Camb. B. **1—3.** (1, 2) **was jealous,** R. V., "are jealous;" the Hebrew word is derived from the redness of the face which betrays strong emotion."—Dods. **fury,** here, in a good sense, warmth, or zeal. (3) **city of truth,** no longer full of lies and treachery and infidelity. God dwelling therein, it shall be "the faithful city" (Isa. i. 26), in which all that is true and real shall flourish (comp. vs. 16; Zeph. iii. 13).—Pul. Com. **mountain,**[a] with special reference to Moriah.

a Comp. Is. ii. 2; Mi. iv. 1; Eze. xl. 2.

A Safe Resting Place.—These are solid doctrines to rest upon—God calling for judgment; God approving the moral, the righteous, and the true; God connecting His heaven with His earth, and God's heaven shrouding itself in frowns when God's earth rushes into sin and selfishness. This is the economy in which we live. We can pull out the shoulder, chafe against the bars of the cage, but the cage is there, and we cannot escape. Much better surrender, obey; seek the appointed way to peace, which is the way of the Cross, the way of Calvary, the way of that wonder which is called by this name—none nobler—the Atonement. Do not define it, but receive it in its largeness of reconciliation and hospitality of love. Oh, fall down before it, and say, "Lord, I believe, help thou mine unbelief."—J. Parker.

4—6. (4) **old men,** a sign of settled times, when men are not cut off in their prime by war or pestilence. **dwell,** better, "sit," which gives a more graphic picture of the peaceful state indicated. Comp. 1 Macc. xiv. 9. Long life and abundance of children were reckoned among the blessings of the O. T.—Dods. (5) **streets,** etc., the sign of peace and security.[b] Mt. xi. 16, 17. (6) **marvelous,** Heb. "signifies to be impossible to human power, something miraculous."—Barrows. **should it also be marvellous,** i. e. the things that are impossible with men are possible with God.

Old Men and Children.—Like many another emigration, for religion's sake, from the heart of civilization to a barren coast, the poor colony of Jerusalem consisted chiefly of men, young and in middle life. The barren years gave no encouragement to marriage. The constant warfare with neighboring tribes allowed few to reach grey hairs. It was a rough and a hard society, unblessed by the two great benedictions of life, childhood and old age. But this should all be changed, and Jerusalem filled with placid old men and women, and with joyous boys and girls. The oracle, we say, had its motive in Zechariah's day. But what an oracle for these times of ours! Whether in the large cities of the old world, where so few of the workers may hope for a quiet old age, sitting in the sun, and the children's days of play are shortened by premature toil and knowledge of evil; or in the newest fringes of the new world, where men's hardness and coarseness are, in the struggle for gold, unawed by reverence for age and unsoftened by the fellowship of childhood,—Zechariah's great promise is equally needed. Even there it shall be fulfilled if men will remember his conditions—that the first regard of a community, however straitened in means, be the provision of religion, that truth and whole-hearted justice abound in the gates, with love and loyalty in every heart towards every other.—Exp. Bib.

Playing Together.—Yes, it is a happy sight, the sports of children! What life! what joy! what consequential airs! Bring out the baby, Bridget. Let the trumpet and the drum do their best, only let it be at a proper time, and in a proper place, and not to disturb the sick and nervous. We never know what children really are while we keep apart from them, or watch them as a sentinel does a prisoner. Let us get hold of your hands and your hearts, little ones, and we will try to enter into your joys.

7—12. (7) **east country,** lit. "land of the sun-rising;" "from the rising to the going down of the sun;" i. e. from all parts of the world. (8) **in truth, etc.,** Ho. ii. 19, 20. (9) vss. 9—13 form one continuous exhortation to persevere in rebuilding the temple. The exhortation is grounded upon a comparison of their condition, before and after the time when they began in earnest to build the house of the Lord. The improvement which had already taken place since that time should encourage them to go on building, cheered by fresh prophecies and promises from the mouth of the same prophets who had urged them to begin the work. and of Him whose messengers of good they were.—Camb. B. **prophets,** esp. Haggai and Zechariah. **foundation,** etc., see Ezr. v. 1, 2. (10) **these days,** R. V., "those days." **no hire,** Hag. i. 6, i. e. "the fruits of the earth would not pay the labor of those who cultured it, bec. the Divine judgments lay on a negligent people. **peace,** etc., in the time of neglect.[a] **the affliction,** R. V., "the adversary;" the Samaritans and Amorites who plundered the caravans. Comp. Ezra viii. 22. (11) **residue,** R. V., "remnant;" the returned captives. Hag. i. 12. (12) **seed,** etc., general signs of returning prosperity.

Value of Religion.—Let me tell business men that they cannot have any real success unless they are profoundly religious. Appearances are often to the contrary. Appearances amount to nothing. We cannot take in the case within the limits of three years or thirty years; we must look upon the whole field-space and upon the whole time-space, and this is written at the root of all things: A man cannot neglect God and be really rich. He may have heaps of money, but he has not wealth; he is

[b] "This imagery, which represents a time when there is no alarm of war, or plague, or famine, but everything is peaceful and joyous, describes, in a spiritual sense, the condition of the Church, as defended by Christ, and enriched with blessings by Him." — S. Jerome.

"Now, roughly, not with vain subtilty of definition, but for plain use of the words, 'Play' is an exertion of body or mind made to please ourselves, and with no determined end; and work is a thing done because it ought to be done and with a determined end. You play, as you call it, at cricket, for instance. That is as hard work as anything else, but it amuses you, and it has no result but the amusement. If it were done as an ordered form of exercise, for health's sake, it would become work directly." —Ruskin.

[a] Ezra iv. 1, 4.

"The illustrious officer of day first worship'd in the east, 'gins to display the glory of his beams; then buds unfold their chary leaves, each dew - drown'd marigold insensibly doth stir itself and spread; each violet lifts up his pensive head."—Poole.

not the owner of the wealth, the wealth is his owner; he is not proprietor, he is slave. He has locked himself up in his own gold-chest, and there he famishes as if he were a beggar. His soul is fat who makes the lives of others pleasant; he is strong who shares his strength with the weak.—J. Parker.

13—15. (13) **curse, or byword and reproach.**[b] "Either the object of cursing and blessing, as men cursed you before so now they shall bless you (Jer. xxii. 9); or a formula of imprecation or benediction, God make thee like them (Jer. xxix. 22; Gen. xlviii. 20; Ruth iv. 11, 12)." (14) **repented not,** found no occasion for changing My purpose. (15) **well,** or graciously; granting restoring mercies.

The Sinner a Curse; the Saint a Blessing.—By their declension in religion the Jews had become a curse to the heathen instead of a blessing—"blind leaders of the blind." Hence it is suggested—I. That ungodly persons are a curse in the world; i. e. in the measure of their sinfulness. Illustrate this by showing how the indolent, dishonest, intemperate, etc., tempt others—make their homes unhappy, are a curse to themselves. Show that any one may fall into evil habits and become a great injury to others. II. That godly persons are a blessing. By word, deed, and example, others are encouraged to become like them. World improved. Good laws passed. Sabbath kept. Sin rebuked. Peace maintained, etc. III. That the ungodly are made godly by the salvation of God. God saves from sin and its consequences. Salvation through faith in Christ. Faith works by love. Obedience of faith and love.—Hive.

16, 17. "The prophet has promised them a prosperous and happy condition in which fasting would be out of place. This condition they are to prolong by righteousness, truthfulness, and loving-kindness."—Marcus Dods. (16) **speak .. neighbour,** Eph. iv. 25. **truth and peace,** Jerusalem would indeed "be called a city of truth" (vs. 3), when alike in the private intercourse of her citizens (speak ye every one the truth to his neighbor), and in the public administration of justice (in your gates, Deut. xxv. 7; Job v. 4), truth reigned supreme. The judgment of peace is righteous judgment, which alone secures peace.—Camb. B. **in your gates,** the usual place of judgment,[a] and of concourse. But the term often stands for the city itself. Here it means, wheresoever you come into social relationships. (17) **imagine evil,** ch. vii. 10.

Kings as Judges (vs. 16).—It appears from the above, and other passages of Scripture, that the kings of Israel distributed justice, or sat in judgment to decide causes that might be brought before them, at the gate; that the gate of the city was the place where these causes came before them, and whence they pronounced their decision; that the king held his councils at the gate, or where the elders or chiefs met the king, to consider the affairs of the nation; and that, in fact, all their principal assemblies were held at the gates of the city. This Jewish custom still exists in the interior of South Africa. While in Kurreechane, a city about twelve or thirteen hundred miles up from the Cape of Good Hope, I was told that a cause was going to be brought before the king. Being anxious to witness it, I was led in haste to the gate, where I saw the king sit down at the right side of it, with his secretary on his right hand, and the prosecutor, or complainer, on his left, who stated his case across to the secretary. During his narrating his case, the king was looking about, as if not attending to what was said, but I saw from his eye that he was attending to what, for form's sake, was addressed to the secretary. When the party had finished what he had to say, the secretary repeated the whole to the king, as if he had been entirely ignorant of the matter. The king immediately gave judgment.—Campbell.

The question of the deputation from Bethel (vii. 1—3) is now definitely answered. The fasts of the captivity are to be transformed into joyful feasts, to which willing multitudes shall throng from all parts of the land; heathen nations joining also in their celebration, and counting it an honor and protection to be associated with a Jew. **18—23.** (18, 19) **cheerful feasts,** i. e. they shall still be duly kept, but their character shall be changed; bec. they need be no longer memorials of the desolation of their city and temple, seeing that these had been rebuilt. "In the tenth month the siege of Jerusalem had begun (2 Kings xxv. 1); on the ninth of the fourth month Jerusalem was taken (Jer. xxxix. 2); on the

b "A standing monument of the Divine vengeance, so that the heathen used this as a common form of imprecation, 'God do so to me as He did to the Jews.'"— Lowth.

Is. lxv. 15; Je. xxix. 32.

a "The administration of justice tends to promote peace and concord." — Spk. Com.

"A Chinese, justly irritated at the oppressions of the Government, gained access to the emperor with his complaints. "I come," said he, "to present myself to the punishment to wh. similar remonstrances have brought six hundred of my fellow creatures; and I give you notice to prepare for new executions, since China possesses ten thousand patriots, who, for the same cause, will follow each other, to ask the same reward." The emperor was not proof against such intrepid virtue; he granted the Chinese the reward that pleased him best — the punishment of the guilty, and the suppression of the obnoxious impost.

There is a fable of a princess who must make her escape from a castle, or starve. The gate is open; the bright sun invites her forth. Only a spider's web hangs across the passage. This she brushes

seventh of the fifth, city and temple were burnt down (2 Kings xxv. 8); in the seventh month Gedaliah was assassinated and the poor relics of a Jewish state swept from the land (Jer. xli.)."—G. A. Smith. (20) **people,** R. V., "peoples," prob. the tribes of Israel. (21) **to pray,** R. V., "to intreat the favor of the Lord." Is. ii. 3; Mi. iv. 1, 2. A prophecy also of the Gentiles flocking into the Gospel Church. (22) **many people,** R. V., "many peoples," Is. lxvi. 19—23. **ten men,** i. e. an indefinite number. "Ten expresses totality, and signifies a large number. Comp. Gen. xxxi. 7; Neh. iv. 12; Lev. xxvi. 26."—Dods. **take hold,** the gesture of entreating friendly assistance. **skirt,** this with its fringe and blue riband was a distinguishing badge of the Jew.[a]

aside, when, lo! another, and so on, till she sits down and weeps, feeling that though there is only a spider's web between her and liberty, she cannot escape. Habit is like these spiders' webs. To meet each act is an herculean task, but grace can uproot and conquer it.

a Nu. xv. 38; De. xxii. 12.

CHAPTER THE NINTH.

Part II., chaps. ix.—xiv. After a lapse, it may be, of many years (for there is no date to this second division of the Book), when, perhaps, the active work of a long life was done, Zechariah is again called to prophesy. The event, which was the immediate subject of his earlier prophecies, had now become an accomplished fact. The temple was restored and its worship resumed. "Moved by the Holy Ghost," he soars now into loftier regions of prophetic inspiration, and in two "burdens of the word of the Lord," depicts in glowing language and vivid imagery the nearer and more distant future as they expand before him. —Camb. B.

[But many scholars are convinced that chaps. ix.—xiv. were written after the exile and not by Zechariah. The marked difference, in many respects, of these chaps. from the earlier portion of the book gives much probability to this view.—G. M. A.]

1—4. (1) **Hadrach,** prob. a region of Syria, near Damascus. **the net,** R. V., "its resting place," i. e. the place on which the "burden" or heavy judgment of the Lord shall light. **eyes, etc.,** "for Jehovah hath an eye upon the heathen and all the tribes of Israel—and on Hamath," etc.—G. A. Smith.[b] (2) **Hamath,** Nu. xxxiv. 8; Jos. xiii. 5. The principal city of Upper Syria, bordering on the land of Hadrach. **shall border thereby,** R. V., "which bordereth thereon." **wise** R. V., "because she is very wise." This no doubt refers to Tyre. The prophets generally refer the fall of Tyre to her over-confidence in her own wisdom. Ezek. xxviii. 1—4. (3) **stronghold,** on an island half a mile from the shore, wh. seemed impregnable. (4) **cast her out,** many of her wealthy inhabitants fled over the Mediterranean. **power .. sea,** i. e. her sea defences.[c]

b "Another rend. is, 'The eyes of men in general and of all Israel in particular, through consternation at the victorious progress of Alexander, shall be directed to Jehovah.'"— Fausset.

c Comp. Eze. xxviii. 12—19.

Tyrus, a Stronghold.—Proudly confident in the strength of their island fortress, the Tyrians mocked the attempts of Alexander to reduce their city. Every engine of war for defence had been stored up in their bulwarks, and every device which their skilful engineers could suggest was had recourse to, and for a time with marked success. "Ye despise this land army through confidence in the place that ye dwell in as an island, but I will show you that ye dwell on a continent," was the language of Alexander. The shallow channel between the mainland and the island was at last bridged over by a huge dam of earth erected after repeated failures, and the city which had stood a five years' siege from the Assyrians, a thirteen years' siege from the Chaldæans, was taken after a short siege of seven months by Alexander. Ten thousand of its brave defenders were either massacred or crucified, the rest were sold into slavery; none escaped save those who were concealed by the Sidonians in the ships. Q. Curtius adds distinctly that "Alexander having slain all, save those who fled to the temples, ordered the houses to be set on fire."—C. H. H. Wright.

Vss. 1—8. The foreground of this prophecy is the course of the victories of Alexander, wh. circled round the Holy Land without hurting it, and ended in the overthrow of the Persian empire. The surrender of Damascus followed first, immediately on his great victory at the Issus; then Sidon yielded itself and received its ruler from the conqueror. Tyre he utterly destroyed; Gaza, we know, perished; he passed harmless by Jerusalem. Samaria, on his return from Egypt, he chastized. History gives no other explanation of Zechariah's prophecy than his conquest by Alexander: that conquest agrees minutely with the prophecy.

5—8. (5) **Ashkelon,** etc., cities of the Philistine plain and shore. **very sorrowful,** "and Gaza writhe in anguish, and Ekron, for her confidence is abashed."—G. A. Smith. (6) **bastard,** "half-breeds,"—G. A. Smith. A term of contempt. (7) **blood .. abominations,** the foul and idolatrous sacrifices of Phil. idolatry. **remaineth,** R. V., "and he also shall be a remnant for our God." "The Philistine also shall become a choice remnant unto the God of Israel, no longer to be regarded as alien and impure."—Pul. Com. **as .. Judah,** the meaning is that the Philistine, the nation personified as before, shall take his place, ruler and people, as one of the divisions of the Jewish nation. **Ekron as a Jebusite,** the Jebusites had held their own in the midst of the chosen people, possessors of the stronghold of Zion up to the time of David (Josh. xv. 63); but at last had been merged and lost in Israel. So should it be with the Philistines, who are here intended by Ekron. They too shall be absorbed into the Jewish church and nation, when the ultimate goal of the prophecy is reached.—Camb. B. (8) **encamp,** for their defence.[a] **because of the army,** etc., R. V., "against the army, that none pass through or return;" i. e. to defend it against the incursions of enemies.

The Security of Jerusalem.—The prophecy of vs. 8 was remarkably fulfilled in the unexpected sparing of Jerusalem by Alexander. Furious as he was at the refusal of the high-priest Iuddua to furnish him supplies while besieging Tyre, and resolved as he was to make an example of Jerusalem, he yet no sooner saw the high-priest in his official robes than he recognized him as the same person who had appeared to him in a dream and promised him victory over the Persians. Accordingly he honored Iuddua, exempted the Jews from tribute each Sabbatical year, and allowed them to live according to their own laws. The story no doubt has been embellished, but the nucleus of fact is remarkable.—Dods.

The coming of the King, vss. 9—17. **9. rejoice,** etc., Is. lxii. 11; Mat. xxi. 15; Jno. xii. 15. The joy is to be on account of the coming of Messiah. **shout,** Zep. iii. 14. **King,** i.e. Messiah. **riding .. ass,**[b] "which in the East does not convey an idea of poverty, but only of peace. Had he been a warrior he would have come in his war-chariot, or on his war-horse."—Dods.

The Ideal King.—I. Beautiful vision. Poets in rapt moments have had glimpses of the highest (Ps. xlv. 72). "Find me the true king or able man, and he has a Divine right over me" (Carlyle). II. Passionate longing. The heart yearns for what is best. The need presses. Circumstances now and again arise that intensify the feeling and the cry. There is much to be done—evils to remove, wrongs to be redressed, rights and liberties to be secured. Oh for the coming of the true King! III. Immortal hope. The true King "not yet." Still hope. Faith in the possibilities of human nature; above all, faith in the promise of God.

"Ring out false pride in place and blood,
The civic slander and the spite;
Ring in the love of truth and right,
Ring in the common love of good. . . .

"Ring in the valiant man and free,
The larger heart, the kindlier hand;
Ring out the darkness of the land.
Ring in the Christ that is to be."

10—17. (10) **cut off,** destroy all war weapons, bec. Messiah brings the reign of peace. **Ephraim,** i. e. the ten tribes. **Jerusalem,** the two tribes. **sea to sea,** Ps. lxxii. 8. (11) **thee,** the daughter of Zion, in vs. 9. **by the,** R. V., "because of the." **blood .. covenant,** or in fulfillment of the covenant that was ratified with blood.[a] "It was this that had sealed God's promise to be their helper in every such emergency as the present."—Marcus Dods. **sent forth,** i. e. liberated. **prisoners,** etc., Is. lxi. 1. **pit,** or prison.[b] (12) **stronghold,** wh. God offers to be to you. **render double,** Is. xl. 2. "The prophecy now moves forward (vss. 13—17) and takes for its ground work a later epoch in the future history of the Jews. As their deliverance from their enemies without fighting, in the times of Alexander (vss. 1—8), was foretold as the pledge and type of Mesiah's kingdom of peace (vss. 9—12), so their victories over the Selucidæ, in the times of the Maccabees, are in these verses foretold as the pledge and type of Messiah's victories over all His enemies."—Camb. Bib. (13) **bent Judah,** R. V., "For I have bent Judah for me, I have filled the bow with Ephraim; and I will stir up thy sons, . . . and will make thee," using these as Divine instruments. **O Greece,**[c] reference may be to the valiant efforts of the Maccabees to free the country from the Syrian op-

a "Reassuring the Jews while engaged in the rebuilding, who might otherwise have feared that their work would be undone by the conqueror."—Maurer.

b "This prophecy does not produce on the mind of an Oriental that idea of abject poverty and humility wh. would be suggested to an Occidental. Had He come riding in a chariot, it would have been an emblem of earthly grandeur; had He rode upon a horse. He would have seemed a conqueror; His riding upon an ass only showed that He was gentle, and that the weapons of His warfare were persuasion and the diffusion of truth."—Van Lennep.

a Ex. xxiv. 8; He. ix. 18—20.

b "An image of the misery of the Jewish exiles in Egypt, Greece, etc., under the successors of Alexander."—Fausset.

"Would you taste the tranquil scene? Be sure your bosoms are serene: devoid of hate, devoid of strife, devoid of all that poisons life; and much it 'vails you, in their place, to graft the love of human race."—Shenstone.

c Is. lxvi. 19.

pressions. (14) **Lord shall be seen,** present to give His special aid and defence. (15) **subdue .. stones,** R. V., "shall tread down the sling stones."[d] **make a noise,** the joyous noise of feasting after victory. **filled,** with blood; "to be wet with blood is an image of victory."[e] **like bowls,** i. e. the bowls of the altar, in wh. the blood of the sacrifices was received. (16) **stones of a crown,** "the people shall be in God's sight as precious as these are in the eyes of men, and shall be highly exalted."—Pul. Com. **ensign .. lifted up as an ensign,** etc., R. V., "lifted on high over his land." The land is the crown in which the precious jewels are set."—Pul. Com. (17) **goodness,** "How great is the prosperity and beauty of God's people when thus favored by Jehovah."—Marcus Dods. **corn,** etc., signs of plenty.[f] **cheerful,** R. V., "flourish."

[d] Comp. Job xli. 28.

[e] Is. lxiii. 1—3.

[f] "The spiritual blessings of the Gospel, esp. in God's Holy word and sacraments, are the corn and new wine which strengthen and refresh chaste and holy souls, who are here compared to men and maidens."—S. Cyril.

The Coming of the King (vss. 9—17).—The great event for which all that had been foretold in the preceding verses of the chapter, and indeed all the preceding history of Israel and of the world, had been a preparation, and in which as purposed and promised by God was the pledge of Israel's preservation for its accomplishment, is now announced and its consequences are unfolded. Sion is called upon to welcome with exultation her just and lowly King, who comes to her in humble state (vs. 9), whose kingdom of peace shall cover all the land and embrace all nations (vs. 10), and who, mindful of His covenant with her, shall give deliverance to the captives of Israel (vss. 11, 12). Using them, now once more an united nation, as the instruments of His warfare (vs. 13), Himself fighting for them and manifesting Himself as their Protector (vs. 14), He will make them victorious over all their enemies (vs. 15), and will promote them to safety and honor (vs. 16), magnifying His "goodness" and His "beauty" in the prosperity with which He crowns them (vs. 17).—Camb. B.

CHAPTER THE TENTH.

1—4. (1) **latter rain,** this was early spring, March or April. It came in time to swell the grain now ripening to maturity. **bright clouds,** R. V., "even of the Lord that maketh lightnings; and he shall give them showers," etc.[a] Great rains are usually associated with thunder and lightning.[b] **grass,** a general term for cultured vegetation. (2) **idols,** R. V., "teraphim,"[c] household gods of human form, sometimes of life size. Comp. Judges xvii. 5; xviii. 5, 24. **diviners,** De. xviii. 10—14. **went their way,** "the Israelites, bec. they have had recourse to idols and diviners, wander and stray about to their hurt like sheep without a shepherd." (3) **shepherds,** fig. for the princes and leaders. **goats,**[d] referring still to the unfaithful rulers. **goodly horse,** comp. Song Sol. i. 9. "From being timid and helpless sheep, the people were to become like the war-charger of Jehovah."—Dods. (4) **out of him,** i. e. Judah. **corner,** R. V., "corner-stone." **nail,** or peg, by wh. the shepherd's tent is fastened. **battle .. bow,** ch. ix. 13. **oppressor,** or, ruler, as in R. V. margin, a sense which the word will bear in Is. iii. 12; lx. 17. Every ruler, civil and military, "the corner-stone," "the nail," "the battle-bow," shall proceed from Judah, blessed by God, or from God, as His gift to Judah, as the need of the state requires.

[a] Job xxviii. 25.

[b] Je. x. 13.

[c] Gen. xxxi. 19.

[d] "The term he goats describes what these rulers were, the emblem of headstrong wantonness and offensive lust."—Fausset.

"Then with uplifted hands, and eyes devout, grateful to heaven, over his head beholds a dewy cloud, and in the cloud a bow conspicuous, with three listed colors gay, betokening peace from God, and covenant new."— Milton.

"For, faithful to its sacred page, heaven still rebuilds thy span; nor lets the type grow pale with age that first spoke peace to man."—Campbell.

Parable of the Rain.—I. Man's great need. Without rain the ground is impoverished and dead. So is the soul without God. II. Man's great resource. Not idols or enchantments, not human devices or philosophies, but appeal to God. He will withhold no good from them that walk uprightly. III. Man's great consolation. 1. Sweet (cf. Deut. xxxii. 2); 2. Timely. God does not give in an arbitrary way, but according to His own wise and holy laws. When rain is most needed it is most appreciated. So in spiritual things (cf. Ps. xliv. 3); 3. Abundant "showers." Rain sometimes slight, partial or temporary. Here promise of "abundance of rain," meeting the needs of all, reaching to the farthest limits of the parched land; 4. Invigorating and fertilizing. "To every one grass in the field," call for thankfulness and joy.—Forsyth.

Eastern Dreamers.—The Hindoos may be called a nation of dreamers; they are often elevated or depressed by the gay or sorrowful scenes of their sleeping hours. The morning is the time for the young and the old to tell their wondrous stories, and many a sage prognostication is then delivered to the attentive hearers. Men and women often take long journeys, perform arduous penances, and go through expensive ceremonies, from no other cause than that of a dream. The crafty Brahmin finds this to be a powerful medium of access to the superstition and purses of the people. How many splendid temples have been built or repaired, how many rest-houses erected, how many costly presents have been made, as the result of a real or pretended dream! Mendicants, pandarams, priests, and devotees have all had their profitable revelations from the gods. Does a needy impostor wish to have a good berth and a settled place of abode? He buries an idol in some lonely place, and, at the expiration of about twelve months, he has a dream, and a vision into the bargain, for the god actually appears to him when he is not asleep, and says, "Go to such a place, and you will find my image; there long, long has it been in disgrace, but now you must build a temple to my glory."—Roberts.

5—10. (5) **they,** etc., God's people, when God manifests His power in them, and through them. **mire .. streets,** the house refuse is freely swept into the narrow streets of Eastern cities. **riders,** etc., in this respect the Hebrews were especially weak, and their enemies strong. Victory over the horsemen therefore equals complete victory.—Marcus Dods. (6) **house of Joseph,** survivors of the ten tribes.[a] **bring them,** comp. vs. 10. **to place them,** omitted in R. V. (7) **they of Ephraim,** i. e. as well as Judah, shall be heroes. Not many members of the northern kingdom returned at first from the captivity; but the prophet gives the assurance that they shall come and prove themselves mighty warriors."—Pul. Com. **rejoice .. wine,** ch. ix. 15. (8) **hiss for them,** fig. fr. attraction of bees into a hive.[b] **increase,** Is. xlix. 19. "Josephus informs us that 200 years after the time here referred to, Galilee was peopled to an amazing extent, studded with cities, towns, and villages, some of the latter containing as many as 15,000 inhabitants."—Barrows. (9) **sow them,** "their dispersion among the nations of the earth shall not be for their destruction, but like the sowing of corn, which is scattered broad-cast, not that it may be lost and perish, but that it may bring forth much fruit. Comp. Hos. ii. 23." "As Merivale says (Hist. of the Romans, xxix.), the Jews made themselves homes in every country from the Tiber to the Euphrates, from the pines of the Caucasus to the spice-groves of Happy Arabia." —Dods. **live with their children,** i.e. permanently, generation after generation, in security. **turn again,** return to their own land. (10) **Assyria,** etc., comp. 2 Ki. xv. 29; Is. xi. 11—16; Ho. xi. 11.

The Nature of Prophetic Utterance.—The truth is that such descriptions suit many different events, and have various applications. Though their complete fulfilment may be expected only in Messianic times and circumstances, yet we may see many anticipatory and preparative transactions, which are meant to introduce the final accomplishment. The Jewish prophet is not always foretelling certain definite events. Oftentimes he is teaching, warning, and exhorting; and generally he is enunciating great principles, the truth of which shall be clear in the future, rather than predicting facts. Not unfrequently commentators have neglected this consideration, and sought too curiously to restrict the prophet's words to some one issue. It may be noted, further, that where the prophetic language concerning the destiny of the restored people seems to be exaggerated, and not borne out by subsequent facts, the promises are always conditioned by the moral state of the recipients. If they answered fully and consistently to God's call, the result would be such as was predicted. That the event in all respects did not correspond with the high ideal previously announced must be attributed, not to the prophet's mistake, but to the people's waywardness and disobedience.

11, 12. (11) **he,** i. e. Jehovah. Imagery taken from the first deliverance through the Read Sea. **with affliction,** i. e. to His enemies. Comp Exod. xiv. 24, 25, 27, xv. 3—7. This is perhaps the best rendering of this difficult and much disputed clause.—Camb. B. G. A. Smith translates: **"And they shall pass through the sea of Egypt, and He shall smite the**

a "They who were served by Jeroboam's schism, will dwell together in Christ; and there will be one flock and One Shepherd." — S. Jerome

Eze. xxxvii. 19—22.

"As one who in some frightful dream would shun his pressing foe, labors in vain to run, and his own slowness in his sleep bemoans, in thick short sighs, weak cries, and tender groans." —Dryden.

b "As bees are gathered by hissing, or whistling, into a swarm and into a hive."
—Wordsworth.

Is. v. 26, vii. 18.

"Summon them fr. distant countries, by a certain signal, as a shepherd calls his flock together with his whistle."
—Lowth.

"The slight hold the Jews have on every soil where they now live, as also the commercial, and therefore cosmopolitan character of their pursuits, making a change of residence easy to them, fit them peculiarly for missionary work."— Moore.

sea of breakers, and all the deeps of the Nile shall be dried, and the pride of Assyria brought down, and the sceptre of Egypt swept aside. And their strength shall be in Jehovah, and in His Name shall they boast themselves—oracle of Jehovah." **smite,** i. e. God shall smite the sea for them. **river,** R. V., "the Nile,"[c] i. e. "the fertilizing inundations of the Nile shall be dried up, the source of Egypt's wealth shall fail."—Dods. (12) **walk up and down,** i. e. pursue the course of their lives. Mic. iv. 5, Col. iii. 7.

Verses 10—12.—These verses seem to point not so much to any specific restoration of Israelites at that time in exile, as to a general re-assembling and reorganization of the people of God. This is rendered more apparent by the highly poetical language of vs. 11, in which the prophet borrows his imagery of the future deliverance and organization of God's people from the normal emancipation, the Exodus, the birth-day of the nation.—Dods.

c "This is equivalent to an assurance that all obstacles will be surmounted that now restrain the Jews in spiritual bondage, and that they will be delivered by a glorious exodus from their present spiritual Egypt of darkness and thraldom into the glorious light and liberty of the Gospel in the Church of Christ."
—Wordsworth.

CHAPTER THE ELEVENTH.

1, 2. (1) **doors,** i. e. passes, or mountain defiles. "The passage is highly poetical and dramatic, but in its first reference literal and physical. In the path of the invading army stands Lebanon, at once the pride and bulwark of the land. As the priestly herald of the approaching host the prophet summons it to open wide an access, and to surrender to the reckless torch of the fierce foe its goodly pines and noble cedars. Comp. 2 Kings xix. 23; Is. xxxvii. 24, xiv. 8." **fire,** typical of invading enemies. Poss. this is prophetic of the Rom. invasion under Vespasian and Titus. (2) **fir tree,** or cypress. **mighty,** R. V., "the goodly ones," if the cedars, the mighty trees are destroyed what hope is there for the little cypresses! **forest .. down,** R. V., "the strong forest is come down," hitherto untrodden by the foot of men. The inaccessible forest.

Fallen Greatness (vs. 2).—I. The differences there are among men, physical, social, moral, intellectual, religious, spiritual. II. Their fall, however, distinguished. 1. There is a moral fall to which all are exposed; 2. There is a mortal fall which to all is inevitable. III. The sorrow caused by their removal. 1. Sympathetic; 2. Rational; 3. Moral and pious; the death of a good man is a public loss; such is a benefactor, an intercessor, etc.—W. Jay, funeral sermon for Rowland Hill.

Cedars of Lebanon.—These far-famed trees are situated on a small eminence in a valley at the foot of the highest part of the mountain: the land on the mountain's side has a sterile aspect, and the trees are remarkable by being altogether in one clump. There are, in fact, two generations of trees; the oldest are large and massy, four, five, or even seven trunks springing from one base; they rear their heads to an enormous height, spreading their branches afar; and they are not found in any other part of Lebanon, though young trees are occasionally met with. The ancient cedars—those which superstition has consecrated as holy, and which are the chief object of the traveller's curiosity—have been gradually diminishing in number for the last three centuries. In 1550, Belloni found them to be twenty-eight in number; Rauwolf, in 1575, counted twenty-four; Dandini, in 1600, and Thevenot, about fifty years after enumerated twenty-three, which Maundrell, in 1697, states were reduced to sixteen. Dr. Pococke, in 1738, found fifteen standing, and one which had been recently blown down. Burckhardt, in 1810, counted eleven or twelve; twenty-five others were very large ones, about fifty of middling size, and more than three hundred smaller and young ones. Lastly, in 1818, Dr. Richardson found that the old cedars, "the glory of Lebanon," were no more than seven in number. In the course of another century, it is probable that not a vestige of them will remain, and the predictions of the Prophets will then be most literally fulfilled: "Lebanon is ashamed and hewn down. The high ones of stature shall be hewn down: Lebanon shall fall mightily" (Isa. xxxiii. 9, x, 33, 34). The trunks of the old trees are covered with the names of travellers and other persons who have visited them, some of which go as far back as 1640. Maundrell, in 1697, measured one, which he found to be twelve yards and six

"The groves were God's first temples. Ere man learn'd to hew the shaft, and lay the architrave, and spread the roof above them: ere he framed the lofty vault, to gather and roll back the sound of anthems; in the darkling wood, amid the cool and silence, he knelt down and offer'd to the Mightiest solemn thanks and supplication. For his simple heart might not resist the sacred influences which, from the stilly twilight of the place, and from the grey old trunks, that high in heaven mingled their mossy boughs, and from the sound of the invisible breath, that sway'd at once all their green tops, stole over him, and bow'd his spirit with the thought of boundless power and inaccessible majesty. Ah, why should we, in the world's riper years, neglect God's ancient sanctuaries, and adore only among the crowd and under roofs that our frail hands have raised?"—Bryant.

"And there is another beauty produced by a number of differently formed

inches in girth, and thirty-seven yards in the spread of its boughs; at above five or six yards from the ground it was divided into five limbs, each of which was equal to a great tree. They send forth a fragrant odor, which seems to be intended by "the smell of Lebanon" (Hos. xiv. 6; Sol. Song iv. 11). Its timber was used in the erection of the first and second temple at Jerusalem, as well as of the palace of Solomon; and in the last-mentioned edifice, so much cedar-wood appears to have been used, that it was called "the house of the forest of Lebanon" (1 Kings vii. 2, x. 19). The Tyrians used it in shipbuilding (Ezek. xxvii. 5, 6).

3—9. (3) "Hark to the wailing of the shepherds! for their glory is destroyed. Hark how the lions roar! for blasted is the pride of Jordan." —G. A. Smith. **shepherds,** who keep their flocks on the slopes of Lebanon; not only the forests but the pastures are destroyed. **their glory,** i. e. the rich pasture land. **pride of Jordan,** the thick woods on the banks, in wh. the lions found covert. These also were ruthlessly cut down by the invader. (4) **feed,** "The person addressed is Zechariah. The passage is dramatic. The prophet is represented as personating, inclusively perhaps, as is so generally the case in O. T. prophecy, the long line of Jehovah's true shepherds, but chiefly and ultimately the Good Shepherd of whom they all were types."—Camb. B. **flock .. slaughter,** i. e. destined for the slaughter. (5) **slay them,** instead of tending them.[a] God's people were bought and sold. The governors of Judah and Israel abused their position for their own ends, and their blindness in doing so is exhibited in their saying, "Blessed be Jehovah." The prophet sets forth the pious complacency with which these men contemplate their ill-gotten gains. (6) **no more pity,** "show no more pity for the main body of the people than their rulers do."[b] **king,** perhaps Vespasian or Titus. "They shall have a chance to test whether human government is less oppressive than divine government. This verse may well have been remembered and produced in the days of Herod and the Romans."—Dods. (7) R. V., "so I fed the flock of slaughter, verily the poor," etc. Vss. 7—14 are a description of what the prophet did in compliance with the injunction of vs. 4.—Dods. **staves,** or shepherds' rods. **beauty,** or God's favor towards His people. **bands,** implying bond of brotherhood bet. Israel and Judah. (8) **three shepherds,** "This has been understood to refer either to three historical persons, e. g. Zachariah, Shallum (2 Kings xv. 8, 13) and some third usurper, not mentioned in the history, of the same time, or Antiochus Epiphanes, Antiochus Eupator and Demetrius I., in the time of the Maccabees (though it is difficult to believe that these could have been called shepherds of Israel); or else to the three offices of king, priest and prophet. But all these references break down, and it is better to take the words generally, as describing the prompt and vigorous action of Jehovah's shepherd in dealing with the evil shepherds (x. 3), as well as in feeding the flock."—Camb. B.[a] **in one month,** i.e. in a short time. **lothed them,** referring to the people, the flock. (9) **dieth,** etc., Je. xv. 2.

10—14. (10) **break my covenant,**[b] declare it to be no longer binding. **the people,** R. V., "the peoples." This may mean the nations of the earth, in which case the sense will be that the prosperity which the shepherd on assuming office had guaranteed to the flock, and of which his staff "Beauty" was the symbol, was assured to them by a covenant, so to speak, into which he had entered with all nations not to molest them (comp. Hos. ii. 18; Job. v. 23). (11) **waited upon me,** R. V., "gave heed unto me." "Though the bulk of the nation took no heed, learned no lesson, yet the humble and the suffering among them, who paid respect to his words, recognized that what happened was according to God's Word, and knew that all the rest would be fulfilled."—Pulpit Com. (12) **my price,** R. V., "my hire." It is as much as to say, "I will be no more your shepherd: give me therefore my wages, that I may go my way." It is further designed to bring out in bold relief the mutual aversion and contempt, that had sprung up between the shepherd and the flock (vs. 8). He asks as one who cares not whether his request be granted: "Give, or forbear." They reply by a gift more insulting than refusal. **thirty pieces,** the value of a slave that had been killed.[c] (13) **cast .. potter,**[a] "implies contemptuous rejection of the sum, and at the same time intimates the ultimate destination to which, in the sight of Omniscience, it was directed. The potter is named as the workman who makes the meanest utensils out

trees standing on the same lawn, and each showing its separate mould and features. For as one star differeth from another in glory, and as one saint in heaven differeth from another in glory, so one tree differeth from another in glory. There is one glory of the oak, which looks as if it had faced a hundred storms, and, having stood them all, were ready to face as many more; another glory of the sycamore, that 'spreads in gentle pomp its honeyed shade.' "—Dr. McCosh.

a Am. ii. 6, 7, viii. 4—6.

b "Jehovah, in vengeance for their rejection of Messiah, gave them over to intestine feuds and Rom. rule. The Zealots and other factious Jews expelled and slew one another by turns at the last invasion by Rome." — Fausset.

a "Possibly representing the civil power, the priesthood, and prophecy. These have been removed from the Jews since their rejection of Messiah."— Wordsworth. Some think a more definite reference to John, Simon, and Eleazar, three leaders of factions in the Jewish war.

b "Thus the covenant which I had made with the whole nation of the Jews was broken, and I excluded them from having any benefit in the second covenant, that of the Gospel."—Lowth.

c Ex. xxi. 32 Ho. iii. 2; Mat. xxvii. 9.

a "Thrown to the potter with

of the vilest material. That this was ordered and executed in vision is plain; how much the prophet understood we cannot tell. The ambiguous and highly typical order was explained and fulfilled to the letter by the action of Judas Iscariot, as the evangelist testifies (Matt. xxvii. 5—10)."—Pul. Com. **in the house of the Lord,** both because He it was who, whether in the person of His servants or of His Son, was the real subject of the insulting valuation, and also because what was done in the house of God was done that He might see and take action about it. **goodly price,** ironical. (14) **I cut asunder mine other staff,** "to signify both the completion of the rupture between the shepherd and the flock, with which he had now nothing more whatever to do, and also the second evil consequence of that rupture, which would befall the flock. Its beauty was gone already: its unity would now be gone also."—Camb. B.

Agony of Christ.—Is it possible for us to understand that expression which dropped from His lips on that memorable night of His agony—"My soul is exceeding sorrowful, even unto death"? Not only sorrowful, but exceeding sorrowful; so exceeding sorrowful that it approached the state of death. It was not possible for His eyes to give full relief to His pent-up sorrow in tears, or His lips in wailing lamentation; but the pores of His body came to His help. These, infinite in number, became so many outlets to the profound anguish of His smitten soul. What was it that occasioned this exceeding sorrowfulness of His soul in the agony of the garden? If we bear in mind that on Him were laid the iniquities of us all—that He knew each and all the sins of which the world was and would be guilty—that His pure and Divine nature was so susceptible of abhorrence of sin—that He was despised of the world for whom He was so benevolently suffering—that there were yet, not far away, the scenes of His trial, Peter's unfaithfulness, Judas's treachery, the cowardice of all the Apostles, and the tragic doings of Calvary—that the Father who had delighted in Him from eternity, who smiled on angels, and whose countenance of love gave radiancy to creation, was soon to lay His hand upon Him in chastisement and affliction, which would have annihilated the whole universe of finite life; when we consider these things, do we not perceive the reasons why His soul was exceeding sorrowful, even unto death?—John Bate.

15—17. (15) **foolish shepherd.** Folly is in Scrip. often a synonym for wickedness. (16) **visit,** etc., just the things wh. the good shepherd and ruler ought to do. **seek .. young one,** R. V., "seek those that be scattered." **that standeth still,** R. V., "which is sound," i. e. the healthy ones. **eat .. fat,** enriching and satisfying himself, and heedless of the people's needs and sufferings.[b] Reference is to the Antichrist of the N. T.[c] **claws,** R. V., "hoofs. (17) **idol,** R. V., "worthless." **his arm,** "the arm that ought to have defended the flock shall be withered; the eye that should have watched for their safety shall be blinded."

Evil Shepherds.—

Blind mouths! that scarce themselves know how to hold
A sheep-hook, or have learned aught else the least
That to the faithful herdsman's art belongs!

The hungry sheep look up and are not fed,
But swollen with wind, and the rank mist they drew,
Rob inwardly, and foul contagion spread;
Besides what the grim wolf with furry paw
Daily devours apace, and nothing said.—Milton.

CHAPTER THE TWELFTH.

1—5. (1) **for Israel,** R. V., "concerning Israel. Thus saith," etc. **stretched,** etc., Is. xlii. 5, etc. (2) **cup of trembling,** "a bowl of reeling[a]—a bowl whose contents cause staggering and reeling. Jerusalem is the capital and type of the Messianic theocracy; the hostile powers of the world crowd around her, like thirsting men round a bowl of wine; but

disdain. 'Let him take it to buy clay with, or for any use that a little money will serve to, for it is not worth hoarding; it may be enough for a potter's stock, but not for the pay of such a shepherd, much less for his purchase.' "— Mat. Henry.

"It seems too costly for Him who is the Prince of life and glory to let His fair limbs be tortured in agony; that the hands which carried mercies should be pierced with accursed nails; that the temples that were always clothed with love should have cruel thorns driven through them! It appears too much. Oh! weep, Christian, and let our sorrow rise. Is not the price all but too great, that your Beloved should for you resign Himself?" — Spurgeon.

b Eze. xxxiv. 3.

c "If taken as pointing to an individual king, there is none to whom it will more aptly apply than to Herod, who was totally regardless of the real interests of the Jews, and whose reign was marked by the perpetration of the most shameful and barbarous cruelties."
—Henderson.

"I venerate the man whose heart is warm, whose hands are pure, whose doctrines, and whose life coincident, exhibit lucid proof that he is honest in the sacred cause." — Cowper.

a Is. li. 17, 22; Je. xiii. 13.

they find the draught is fatal to them; they stagger back discomfited and destroyed. The figure of the cup and drunkenness is often employed to denote the judgment of God upon transgressors, which makes them incapable of defence or escape (comp. Jer. xxv. 15, etc.; li. 39, 57; Hab. ii. 16)."—Pul. Com. **when .. Jerusalem,** R. V., "and upon Judah also shall it be in the siege against Jerusalem," i. e. the burden which was upon, or concerned Israel, should also be upon Judah. (3) **burdensome stone,** one difficult and dangerous to lift or to carry. "Since Jerome, commentators have thought of a stone by throwing or lifting which men try their strength, what we call a 'putting stone.' But is not the idea rather of one of the large stones half-buried in the earth which it is the effort of the husbandman to tear from its bed and carry out of his field before he ploughs it? Keil and Wright think of a heavy stone for building. This is not so likely."—G. A. Smith. **cut in pieces,** R. V., "sore wounded." **Though all the people,** etc., R. V., "and all the nations of the earth shall be gathered together against it." (4) **that day,** of Divine deliverance.[b] Different days seem referred to in this prophecy. **open .. upon,** in kindly regard. **the people,** R. V., "the peoples," who fight against Jerusalem. (5) **governors of Judah,** the tribe leaders would join with Jerusalem in resisting the invader.

Jerusalem, a Burdensome Stone.—God's Church is founded on the rock, and persecutors dash against it in vain. It is a rock of offence by virtue of its charter and power, a stone of stumbling to many. In times of persecution kings and rulers have tried to upset or remove this stone, but it has torn, lacerated, or ground to powder those upon whom it has fallen. Israel escaped, but Pharaoh was drowned in the sea. The Philistines captured the ark, but Dagon was broken to pieces. Diocletian built a monument to commemorate the extinction of Christianity, but he perished, and it survives. In a conference with Andrew Rivet, the King of France threatened severe measures against the cause of truth, but the Reformer answered, "May it please your Majesty, the Church of God is an anvil which hath broken a great many hammers."

6—8. (6) **hearth,** R. V., "pan," i. e. a chafing-dish full of fire.[a] (7) **tents,** fig. for the open towns and villages. "God will first appear in behalf of those Jews that live in the open country." **magnify .. Judah,** there was danger of this, as inhab. of towns are disposed still to overestimate themselves. (8) **he that is feeble,** etc., in the day of need the weaklings of the future shall equal the heroes of the past; and the strong shall resemble the angel that led the hosts of Israel. Ex. xxiii. 20; Josh. v. 13.

Yearning for Redemption.—The elect yearned, and knew what they yearned for; the nations yearned, and knew not for what. But still they yearned; for as the earth in its long polar night seeks to supply the absence of the day by the generation of the Northern Lights; so does each people in the long night of its heathen darkness bring forth, in its yearning after the life of Christ, a faint and glimmering substitute for the same. From these dreamy longings after the break of day have proceeded oracles, priests, sacrifices, lawgivers, and the like. Men have nowhere given up hoping, nor acquiesced in the world's evil as the world's law. Everywhere they have had a tradition of a time when they were nearer to God than now, a confident hope of a time when they should be brought nearer again.—Abp. French.

9—14. (9) **seek to destroy,** or exert myself to destroy.[b] (10) **spirit .. supplication,** i. e. the spirit which conveys grace and calls forth supplications; an extraordinary outpouring of divine influence. **look upon me whom they have pierced,** R. V., "unto me." "The speaker is Almighty God. The Jews had pierced Him metaphorically by their rebellion and ingratitude throughout their history. They pierced Him, literally and as the crowning act of their contumacy, in the person of His Son upon the cross, John xix. 37. Comp. Rev. i. 7."—Camb B. **for his only son,** "among the Hebrews the preservation of the family was deemed of vast importance, and its extinction regarded as a punishment and a curse, so that the death of an only son would be the heaviest blow that could happen (see Isa. xlvii. 9; Jer. vi. 26; Amos viii. 10)."—Pul. Com. (11) **Hadadrimmon,** 2 Chr. xxxv. 24. "This is one of the few ethical strains which run through these apocalyptic chapters. It

"What profusion is there in His work! What unnumbered cathedrals has He reared in the forest shades, vast and grand, full of curious carvings, and haunted evermore by tremulous music, and in the heavens above, how do stars seem to have flown out of His hand faster than sparks out of a mighty forge!"—H. W. Beecher.

[b] Eze. xxxviii. 3, 4.

"It is said that an unhelped cross is the heaviest thing a man ever carried; but a Christ - touched cross is about the lightest thing a man ever carried."—Beecher.

"How exquisite is pleasure after pain! Why throbs my heart so turbulently strong, pain'd at thy presence, this redundant joy, like a poor miser, beggar'd by his store?"—Young.

[a] "The leaders of Judah are to be a fire bursting out on every side, the enemies that beleaguer Jerusalem being the fuel by wh. it is fed." — Spk. Com.

[b] "This cannot be applied in all its fulness to the literal Jerusalem; no suhc combination of all nations against Jerus. has ever been formed."—Wordsworth.

"True repentance arises from the sight by faith of the crucified Saviour. It is the tear that drops fr. the eye of faith looking on Him."—Fausset.

forms their highest interest for us. Jerusalem's mourning is compared to that for Hadad-Rimmon in the valley or plain of Megiddo. This is the classic battle-field of the land, and the theatre upon which Apocalypse has placed the last contest between the hosts of God and the hosts of evil. In Isael's history it had been the ground not only of triumph but of tears. The greatest tragedy of that history, the defeat and death of the righteous Josiah, took place there; and since the earliest Jewish interpreters the mourning of Hadad-Rimmon has been referred to the mourning for Josiah."[a]—G. A. Smith. (12, 13) **David .. Nathan .. Levi .. Shimei,** "two families are singled out as examples, and in each case the family or tribe is first described by its general name, and then one branch of it is mentioned, to indicate that to every part and division the wide-spread mourning shall extend." (14) **every family apart,** indicating individual grief and mourning of the most solemn character.

Flowers of Memory.—"As one mourneth for his only son." An investigator of pedigrees was searching in a midland county of England for any traces that might still be found of an old family of the district. He went to the records of the church, but their name was not there, it had perished. He repaired to the supposed site of their ancient hall. Not a stone remained to tell its place. Disappointed in these attempts, he accosted an aged peasant: "Do you know anything of the Findernes?" "Findernes?" was the reply. "We have no Findernes here, but we have Findernes' flowers." Here was a clue. The old man led the way to a field where there were traces of an ancient terrace. "There," said he, pointing to a bank of garden-flowers grown wild, "there are Findernes' flowers, brought by Sir Geoffrey from the Holy Land, and, do what we will, they will never die."

Inconsolable Grief.—

I pray thee, cease thy counsel,
Which falls into mine ears as profitless
As water in a sieve: give not me counsel,
Nor let no comforter delight mine ear,
But such a one, whose wrongs do suit with mine.
Bring me a father, that so loved his child,
Whose joy of her is overwhelmed like mine;
And bid him speak of patience,
Measure his woe the length and breadth of mine,
And let it answer every strain for strain
As thus for thus, and such a grief for such
In every lineament, branch, shape, and form.
If such a one will smile, and stroke his beard,
Cry—sorrow, wag! and hem when he should groan;
Patch grief with proverbs; make misfortune drunk
With caudle-water; bring him yet to me,
And I of him will gather patience:
But there is no such man.—Shakespeare.

a 2 Ki. xxiii. 29.

"The prophet uses the strongest metaphors known to human experience. No pang which death can inflict is so severe as that which wrings the heart of parents following to the tomb the remains of a first-born or an only son. It seems as all hope and glory were interred in the same grave. When President Lincoln was assassinated in 1865, a shuddering horror seized every heart throughout the land, and multitudes who had never seen the kindly leader were as deeply moved as if the blow had fallen on their own kindred. A gloomy pall settled down over all hearts and all households."—Lange.

CHAPTER THE THIRTEENTH.

1—6. (1) **that day,** "the mourning for sin of ch. xii. 10—14 shall be the precursor of cleansing from sin, for which ample and lasting provision shall be made." **fountain,** the form of the promise is Jewish, the substance Christian. For the lustral waters of the Law, the "water of sin" (Num. viii. 7) and the "water of uncleanness" (Num. xix. 9), which were contained and renewed in bowl or laver, and which did but "sanctify to the purifying of the flesh," shall be substituted the living fountain of the Gospel.—Camb. B. **sin .. uncleanness,**[b] personal guilt, and the corruption which sin produces. (2) **cut .. land,** Eze. xxx. 13. **unclean spirit,** or lying spirit, or false pretence to prophetic inspiration.[c] (3) **when,** etc., comp. De. xiii. 1—11; Eze. xiii. 1—9.[d] (4) **rough garment,** R. V., "a hairy mantle," the customary garb of a prophet; comp. Elijah's, 2 Ki. i. 8; also John Baptist's, Mat. iii. 4. (5) **taught me,** etc., R. V., "for

b "Provision made for the cleansing of all those from the pollutions of sin who truly repent, and are sorry for them."—Mat. Henry.

c "The Jews were always very much addicted to sorcery, charms, and other sorts of divination."—Lowth.

d "It is the triumph of Christian faith and charity to love the erring without loving their errors, and to hate the errors without hating the erring."—Wordsworth.

I have been made a bondman from my youth," so "if I had the will I could never have had the chance of setting up as a prophet."—Dods. (6) **wounds .. hands,** R. V., "wounds between thine arms," i. e. probably, on thy breast. Comp. "between his arms," i. e. in his back, 2 Kings ix. 24; "between your eyes," i. e. on your foreheads, Deut. xi. 18. The interrogator, in his zeal against false prophets, is still unsatisfied, and detecting wounds, or scars, on the breast of the quondam false prophet, charges them upon him as proofs of his guilt, because he regards them either as self-inflicted in the service of idols (1 Kings xviii. 28), or as given him by his parents, from whose righteous indignation he had escaped wounded, when they went about to kill him (vs. 3).—Camb. B. **wounded .. friends,** i. e. in token of grief for deceased relatives.[a]

The Smile of God.—I have seen in an African desert a beautiful patch of green, a luxurious blending of graceful palm, waving grass, rippling spring, pendent fruits, and tropic flowers—an island of verdure, refreshment, and comfort, in the midst of a sea of sand, of dreary brushwood, and of stunted thorn. Hither came both man and beast, hot with travel, scorched with heat, oppressed with hunger, faint with thirst, and found food and drink, shelter and repose. The negroes who dwelt in the surrounding region called the weary tract around "The Torment," because it was hard, dry, difficult, inhospitable. The patch of natural garden-ground in the centre they called by an African word which means a god or a spirit in a good temper, or rather, the smile of God. The smile of God! Verily a good name and a beautiful; a smile that lightens the heart and cheers the lot of every drooping traveller that passes that way. As he gazes with hand-shaded eyes through the haze of the desert heat, and catches a glimpse of the green isle upon the border line, that smile of God begets a smile on his own tired and weary face, and with quickened step and hopeful eye he presses thitherward and rejoices in its cool and grateful shade!—J. J. Wray.

7—9. G. A. Smith supposes these three verses to belong directly after chap. xi, "developing the tragedy of the nation to its climax in the murder of the Good Shepherd. (7) **my shepherd,** the ruler of the Jews; here it must be referred to Messiah. **my fellow,** lit. "the man of my union."[b] **smite,** etc., Mat. xxvi. 31; Mk. xiv. 27. **turn .. ones,** Is. i. 25. "I will show mercy to My little flock, dispirited by the death of their Master, and will quickly show Him to them alive again, to their joy and comfort."—Lowth. (8) **two parts,** this should come to pass in the Rom. siege of Jerus. (9) **refine them,** "this third part, like its Master, passes through much tribulation, and is thereby refined and purified (comp. Ps. lxvi. 10; Isa. xlviii. 10; Jer. ix. 7; Dan. xii. 10; Mal. iii. 3; 1 Pet. i. 6, 7)."—Pul. Com.

The Day of the Lord (xiii. 7—xiv. 21).—This closing prophecy seems less a chronological continuation of the preceding than a closer, more penetrating and far-reaching view of the results of those ruling principles whose operation was to some extent described in the former. The highly figurative representation here given cannot be taken as if it were a realistic picture of some one event. It is intended to show the working of certain principles, and to convey the impression that God's people will triumph, but only by their passing through most critical times, and by His miraculous and personal interposition. It shows us the day of the Lord opening in gloom, but light at evening, when it promised to be darkest; great calamities falling on the city of God, but resulting in her being lifted up as the conspicuous, life-giving metropolis of the race. —M. Dods.

CHAPTER THE FOURTEENTH.

"Judgment of the heathen and sanctification of Jerusalem." 1—3. (1) **day .. cometh,** "lit. a day to (or, of) Jehovah, i. e. which is in a special manner His. The previous prophecy (xiii. 7—9) is now expanded, attention being concentrated, however, on the city rather than on the land (xiii. 8), and on the final act rather than on the long previous process of purifying discipline. It is impossible satisfactorily to adapt the terms of

---

[a] "The worshipers of Bacchus had an ivy leaf imprinted upon their bodies."—Maccabees, bk. iii.

"The detection of one of the false prophets is here dramatically represented."—Fausset.

[b] "My equal."—De Wette. "My nearest kinsman." — Hengstenberg.

"Reference may also be to the preservation of the Christians at the siege of Jerus., they having retired to Pella when Cestuis Gallus so unaccountably withdrew from Jerusalem."—Fausset.

"A man's purpose of life should be like a river, which was born of a thousand little rills in the mountains; and when at last it has reached its manhood in the plain, though, if you watch it, you shall see little eddies that seem as if they had changed their minds and were going back again to the mountains, yet all its mighty current flows changeless to the sea. If you build a dam across it, in a few hours it will go over it with a voice of victory. If tides check it at its mouth, it is only that when they ebb it can sweep on again to the ocean. So goes the Amazon or the Orinoco across a continent—never

this prophecy, either to the taking of Jerusalem under the Maccabees, or to its destruction by the Romans. As Pusey well remarks, 'those who explain it solely of this, are obliged to mingle explanations partly literal, as that Jerusalem should be the earthly Jerusalem which was destroyed, partly metaphorical, as to the mount of Olives, its division into two parts, &c.' It should moreover be observed that there is no word here of the city being destroyed."—Camb. B. (2) **all nations,** comp. Joel iii. 2, 9—11; Ezek. xxxviii. ff; Rev. xx. 7—9. **taken,** Heb. "Be encompassed as in a net."[a] (3) **in the day of battle,** Ex. xiv. 14, 25.

"The city shall be taken, and the houses rifled."—In the account given by Josephus of the destruction of Jerusalem by the Romans, we have a record of enormities at which we might well stand aghast. Christ said, concerning this event, "There shall be great tribulation, such as was not from the beginning of the world until this time, no, nor ever shall be." "The particulars," says Dr. Wardlaw, "here noted, are such as usually, it might be said invariably, attend the besieging, the capture and the sacking of cities; especially when, as in this case, the assailing army has been exasperated by a long, harassing, and wasting defence. The entrance of the unpitying soldiery, the rifling of houses, the deeds of violence, the indiscriminate massacre, and the division of the spoil, are just what all expect, and what require no comment. And never were such scenes more frightfully realized than at the destruction of Jerusalem, when God in his providence, in judicial retribution, gathered all nations against the devoted city to battle."

4, 5. (4) **shall cleave,** "as the enemy are supposed to beset Jerusalem, so as to make escape by any ordinary road impossible, the Lord will open a way through the very centre of the mountain (as he opened a path through the Red Sea), by cleaving the hill in sunder, the two parts moving north and south, and leaving a great valley running east and west, and leading to the Arabah."—Pul. Com. (5) R. V., "And ye shall flee by the valley of my mountains." **Azal,** prob. a name by wh. a part of Olivet was called. **earthquake,** Am. i. 1. "There is no mention of this in the historical books. The references to it here and in Amos i. 1 show that it made a deep impression on the people and was long remembered. The story of Josephus (see Stanley, Jewish Church, 11, 439) connecting it with Uzziah's attempt to burn incense (2 Chron. xxvi. 19) is probably only an embellishment of this passage of Zechariah. Ewald puts the earthquake in 'one of the first years of Uzziah.'"—Camb. Bib. **saints,** "holy ones," or angels. **with thee,** i. e. with the Lord.

6—8. (6) **clear, nor dark,** R. V. margin, "there shall not be light, the bright ones shall contract themselves," i. e. the heavenly bodies shall be darkened. It shall be a dark day. Comp. Joel iii. 5. (7) **one day, a** unique day, none like it. Jer. xxx. 7. **shall be known,** R. V., "is known." Mi. xiii. 32. **evening time,** Is. lx. 19, 20. The day that opened in gloom shall close, unexpectedly, with light. (8) **living waters,** etc., Eze. xlvii. 1; Joel iii. 18; Re. xxii. 1. **former sea,** the Dead Sea, R. V., "the eastern sea the western sea." **hinder sea,** the Mediterranean. **summer and winter,** indicating that the streams should be perennial.

At Evening Time Light.—In "life's evening" light is desired. "Nothing is more common than the craving and demand for light a little before death," says an author. "Open the windows," cried M. de Lescure, on his dying bed. Rousseau wished to have "a parting look at the glorious orb of day." Goethe's request was for "more light, more light." Dark indeed has been the evening time to many. But as the sun often struggles through the clouds of day and sinks in brilliant light, so the chamber of death has been filled with light and glory from the Sun of righteousness. To Bunyan's Mr. Fearing "all was well at last." The gloom of the poet Cowper endured long, but passed away at length. Dr. Johnson dreaded death through life, but met it with hope and unusual patience. Happy those to whom the valley of the shadow of death is lit up with God's presence! Unhappy those whose darkness is eternal night! "Unto the upright there ariseth light in the darkness."—Hom. Com.

I will not faint, but trust in God,
Who this my lot hath given;
He leads me by the thorny road,

losing its way or changing its direction for the thousand streams that fall into it on the right hand and on the left, but only using them to increase its force, and bearing them onward in its resistless channel." — H. W. Beecher.

a "The expression imports that the whole land shall have a plentiful share of these blessings."— Lowth.

"Nature is but a name for an effect whose cause is God."— Cowper.

"In nature things move violently to their place, and calmly in their place."
—Bacon.

"Since a few minutes can turn the healthiest bodies into breathless carcases, and put those very things which we had principally relied on into the hands of our enemies, it were little less than madness to repose a distrustless trust in these transitory possessions, or treacherous advantages, which we enjoy but by so fickle a tenure. No; we must never venture to wander far from God, upon the presumption that death is far enough from us; but rather, in the very height of our jollity, we should endeavor to remember, that they who feast themselves today, may, themselves prove feasts for the worms to-morrow."—Boyle.

Which is the road to heaven.
Tho' sad my day that lasts so long,
At evening I shall have a song;
Tho' dim my day until the night,
At evening-time there shall be light.—Rossetti.

9—11. (9) **one Lord,** R. V., "In that day shall the Lord be one, and his name one." All men shall recognize the one Lord. (10) **as a plain,** R. V., "as the Arabah," a tract of level country wh. stretches along the lower Jordan to the Dead Sea. **Geba to Rimmon,** meaning, from north to south.[a] **lifted up,** R. V., "and she shall be lifted up and shall dwell in her place." The "plain" which the prophet here pictures to himself, may be a table-mountain or elevated platform, all other hills and mountains sinking down to the present level of the "valleys and plains" of Palestine, and leaving Jerusalem standing aloft on this elevated base, the queen-like city and mistress of the world.—Camb. B. **Benjamin's gate,** 2 Ki. xiv. 13. **first gate,** W. of the city. **corner gate,** E. of the city. **tower of Hananeel,** N. of the city.[b] **king's winepress,** Song Sol. viii. 11; in the southern portion of the city. **utter destruction,** R. V., "curse." **safely,** or securely.

Christ's Reign on Earth (vs. 9).—I. The incalculable importance of this prophecy—1. To the world at large; 2. To the Church in particular; 3. To every individual of mankind. II. The blessedness of the period to which it refers. 1. Surely it will be a period of great temporal prosperity; 2. Spiritual blessings will most richly abound; 3. God will manifest Himself on earth.

12—15. The deliverance and prosperity of Jerusalem shall be accomplished by a terrible plague sent upon those who fought against her, vs. 12; and by a panic which shall cause them to slay one another, vs. 13, and also by the courage and prowess of Judah. The wealth of their enemies shall be the spoil of the Jews, vs. 14; while the consuming pestilence shall extend to all the cattle in the hostile camp, vs. 15.—Camb. B. (12) **plague,** some contagious disease. Comp. Ex. ix. 14; Nu. xiv. 37. (13) **tumult,** or panic.[a] (14) **Judah,** i. e. the people of the towns and villages of Judah.[b] (15) **plague of the horse,** as was the plague that came on men (vs. 12), so shall be the plague that falls on their beasts and cattle.

Preparation for the Judgment.—The Gospel of Jesus Christ alone will prepare men aright for the last things wherewith they will have to do. Philosophy and science may teach things useful as to this life. History may bring the experience of the past to bear on the duties of the present in the conduct of states. One system of education may instruct the young how to acquire wealth; another how to spend it with gentility; a third, how to glitter in society; and a fourth, how to make the stores of classical learning all one's own. But Christianity has a higher aim; its object is more extensive. While it overlooks not the things present, it looks onward to things future. While it neglects not the concerns of time, it subordinates them to those of eternity. It brings indeed, and rejoices to hold out. the promise of the life that now is; but, on the other hand, it also brings, and smiles with a brighter and a sweeter look in holding out, the promise of the life which is to come. The last things of man are the most important things.—John Hambleton.

16—19. (16) **left,** etc., intimating that the relics of the nations shall come into the converting power of the Gospel.[c] **go up,** or share in Christian acts of worship, wh. are here represented by the old Jewish solemnities. (17) **no rain,** Am. iv. 7, 8. "The Feast of Booths was specially one of thanksgiving for the harvest; that is why the neglect of it is punished by the withholding of the rain which brings the harvest."—G. A. Smith. (18) **family of Egypt,** specially mentioned bec. the threat of no rain would not affect a country wh. does not depend on the rains. **that have no rain,** R. V., "neither shall it be upon them." (19) **punishment,** lit. "sin;" here, sin as manifested in its consequences.

"The Withholding of the Rain," says Dr, Dods, "was not only one of the ways by which idolatry and apostasy were punished under the theocracy, but it was the appropriate punishment of those who refused to acknowledge Jehovah as the Giver of the harvest. This suiting of punishment to offence is a marked characteristic of God's government, and

---

a 2 Ki. xxiii. 8.

b Ne. iii. 1, xii. 39; Je. xxxi. 38.

"The world is preparing day by day for the millennium; but you do not see it. Every season forms itself a year in advance. The coming summer lays out her work during the autumn, and buds and roots are forespoken. And so 'the kingdom of God cometh not with observation.'" —Beecher.

a Ju. vii. 22.

b Zec. xii. 7.

"Traverse the earth,—enter the gorgeous cities of idolatry, or accept the hospitality of its wandering tribes,—go where will-worship is most fantastic, and superstition most gross,—and you will find in man 'a fearful looking for of judgment.' The mythology of their Nemesis may vary,—their Elysium and Tartarus may be differently depicted, — the Metempsychosis may be the passage of bliss and woe,—still the fact is only confirmed by the diversity of the forms in which it is presented." —R. W. Hamilton.

c "This vs. declares that even the judgment upon the enemies of Israel was not to be universal in its operation. The renewed prosperity of Jerusalem would attract many heathen as proselytes." —Spk. Com.

should probably be more used in education than it is (e. g. by secluding for a time, from all intercourse with his companions, the boy who has told a lie, and so on). Dante has largely utilized the principle in his great poem. In his vision of the realms of punishment he saw tyrants immersed in blood; gluttons exposed in all their pampered softness to a sleety tempest of cold, discolored, stinking hail; the proud bending for ever under heavy burdens; schismatics, who have rent the Church, themselves cleft asunder; those who had pried into the future, and professed prophetic foresight, with faces reversed, unable to see their own way."

20, 21. (20) **upon the bells,** i. e. even upon the smallest and the commonest things. Everything shall be consecrated and holy.[a] **Holiness,** R. V., "Holy;" so in vs. 21. **pots .. bowls,** the pots for boiling the meat had been held less sacred than the bowls which held the blood of the victims; but now all shall be alike holy. (21) **Canaanite, i. e.** any heathen, or unclean person.[b]

[a] Is. xxiii. 18; Ob. 17; Joel iii. 17.

[b] Re. xxii. 15.

"No hypocrite or unclean person shall have any share in the society of the faithful." —Lowth.

"If a man would have the beginnings of heaven, it must be by absolute consecration of everything to God on earth. Let his life be a liturgy, a holy service of acted worship." —Moore.

The Bells of the Horses (vs. 20).—I. Let us hear the horse's bells, they speak of power, holiness, pleasure, journeying, merchandise, toil, such are the uses of horses. II. Let us commend their music, for loudness, clearness, constancy, universality, divinely long. III. Let us go home and tune our bells, the chamber-bell, the shop-bell, the kitchen-bell, the visiting-bell.—Spurgeon.

The Jerusalem That is To Be.—How fitting a close of the whole is this thought! How rightly does this chief prophet of the post-Captivity Jerusalem tell us thus, in conclusion, of that far more glorious Jerusalem which is some day to shine forth! It is much the same that the Prophet Daniel does at the end of his prophecy. It is the same also that "St. John the divine" does at the end of his song. They bring their message to an end when they have given us a glimpse of the end which God has in store. It is for us to take care that we are truly numbered with those for whom that "end" is prepared.—Pul. Com.

Zechariah, the Prophet of Restored Jerusalem.—

Despise not things so small. Thou'rt not alone,
But God is with thee and will bless thy toil.
Mid shouts of "Grace!" thou'lt lay the topmost stone,
And feed the temple lamps with golden oil.
The city shall o'erleap its ancient bounds,
And God shall be its glory and defence.
The boys and girls shall fill its streets with sounds
Of laughter, till old age its care relents.
Men call the city "truth," therein find peace.
Its fasts are turned to feasts. Its sacred shrine
Is altar for the nations. Never cease
The living streams to flow, the light to shine.

Wouldst know the secret of this vision's flower?
By Spirit of the Lord, and not by power.—Chris. End. World.

Introduction.

I. Author. Nothing is known of the author of the book of Malachi beyond what may be gathered from the book itself. The word "Malachi" means "messenger" or "angel," and is used in that sense in ch. ii. 7 and iii. 1 of this book; and it is not unlikely that we have here the message of an unnamed prophet whom we know only as the messenger of the Lord. II. **Time.** The contents of the book point to a date near the time of Ezra and Nehemiah, somewhere between 464 and 424 B.C. III. **Style.** "The prophecy is eminently practical in its character. It is almost throughout minatory in tone. The dark page of the prophet's roll, though illumined at its close by a gleam of the coming glory, is for the most part inscribed with denunciation and threatening and rebuke. And with these its contents the style of the Book accords. It is not wanting, however, in literary merit. It has elements both of grace and power. If he soars not to the sublime heights of Isaiah, nor unfolds the mystic visions of Ezekiel and Zechariah, the writer moves with firm and dignified tread along his humbler and more trodden path. He is concise and yet lucid; energetic and yet collected. There is peculiar force in his manner of making the object of his rebuke turn upon him with a sharp, short question, which he uses as a point of vantage to repeat and expand his charges."—Cambridge Bible. We must not fail to appreciate "the genuine prophetic spirit of our book. Far more fully than, for instance, that of Haggai, to the style of which its practical simplicity is so akin, it enumerates the prophetic principles: the everlasting Love of Jehovah for Israel, the Fatherhood of Jehovah and His Holiness, His ancient Ideals for Priesthood and People, the need of a Repentance proved by deeds, the consequent Promise of Prosperity, the Day of the Lord, and Judgment between the evil and the righteous."—Geo. Adam Smith.

Synopsis.

(According to Cambridge Bible.)

Title and introductory appeal............i. 1—5
Rebuke of the priests....................i. 6—14
Threatened punishment of the priests...ii. 1—9
Rebuke of the people for heathen marriages and divorce ....ii. 10—16
Rebuke of the people for profane impiety, ii. 17—iii. 6
Rebuke in the matter of tithes and offerings ....iii. 7—12
The righteous judgment of God.....iii. 13—iv. 3
Conclusion ....iv. 4—6

CHAPTER THE FIRST.

1—3. (1) **to Israel,** i. e. the whole covenanted nation. **Malachi,** meaning, "Messenger of Jehovah." (2) **loved you,** Deut. vii. 8, x. 15.[a] "This is the keynote of all that follows. On this rests Jehovah's claim to the filial honor and reverential fear which had been withheld from Him (i. 6); on this the patient forbearance of the present (iii. 6), and the bright promise of the future (iv. 2). This is the light that casts the dark shadow of the people's ingratitude across the prophet's page, and that shines through and beyond the darkness, unquenched and unquenchable." —Camb. Bible. **Was not Esau,** etc., "The argument of these vss. is this: If you would see the difference between hatred and love, look at the different conditions and prospects of Edom and Israel."—Marcus Dods. **Jacob's brother,** comp. Ho. xii. 3—5, 12, 13. (3) **hated Esau,** in Scrip. hating often stands for a less degree of love, Lu. xiv. 26. **laid his mountains,** etc. R. V. "made his mountains a desolation, and gave his heritage to the jackals of the wilderness." God dealt much more severely with Edom than with Israel. "The desolation of Edom here referred to was in all probability caused by Nebuchadnezzar, in fulfilment of the prophecy of Jeremiah (xlix. 17—22. Comp. xxvii. 3—6)."

Ingratitude.—"Yet ye say, Wherein hast thou loved us?" Here is ingratitude. Here, however, is our own experience. This is the law of the family. You have been supporting some one a long time, and because you do not attend to the very last appeal, all you did in the years that are gone is simply forgotten, and the inquiry is, Wherein have you been so kind? Treacherous is the memory when it has charge of recollections of good and favor and help rendered under circumstances which ought to have made the offering of such assistance an imperishable remembrance. Have we not had familiarity and experience in this matter? All you have done for your friends, let me assure you, is forgotten. They never speak well of you, except it may be in some general sense. Favors are soon forgotten. Yet whoso forgets a favor is no true man; he is a bad man, whatever his doctrinal professions may be. We should keep all our friends' kindnesses as so many evergreens, every kind action kept in the heart like a precious plant and not allowed to die. But God's favors are forgotten principally because they are so numerous. The very circumstance that ought to have made their memory indelible is a circumstance which causes the record to be soon obliterated. We become familiar with God's blessings, and we seem to have established some right in their succession. We expect the sun to rise; we complain to one another if there be anything like disappointment attending the circumstances of his rising; we say, Do you call this April? Why, in April we ought not to have such fog and darkness: where is the sun? What right have you to the sun? Why not rather say, God be praised, here is the sun: God might have kept back the light from a world that has forfeited every claim upon his complacency, yet here is the shining sun. Keep your gratitude green. Never let your thankfulness fall into decay. You might thus by keeping a perfect remembrance of favors received multiply those favors tenfold; the assistance that was rendered to you in childhood should be with you as a stimulating memory to old age.—J. Parker.

4—5. "Should the people of Edom say, 'We are destroyed, but we will rebuild the waste places,' thus saith Jehovah of Hosts, They may build, but I will pull down: men shall call them 'The Border of Wickedness' and 'The People with whom Jehovah is wroth for ever.' And your eyes shall see it, and yourselves shall say, 'Great is Jehovah beyond Israel's border.'"—G. A. Smith. (4) **impoverished,** R. V. "beaten down," **will return,** both Edom and Israel desired to return to their own lands, but God had not permitted Edom to succeed in its attempt. "Edom never recovered its power; it became the prey of the Persians, the Nabatheans, the Jews under the Maccabees, the Macedonians, the Romans; and finally the Mohammedan conquest effected its utter ruin."—Pul. Com. **the border,** so named because Edom lay close on the border of the Holy

[a] "I have chosen you for My peculiar people, out of pure love and kindness, without any antecedent merits on your side."—Lowth.

"The Jews at this time were in an ungrateful temper. They were disappointed and impatient, and murmured against God, and charged Him with unfaithfulness fickleness, and inconstancy. The Prophet replies to these allegations."
—Wordsworth.

"We are as water, weak, and of no consistence, always descending, abiding in no certain place, unless where we are detained with violence; and every little breath of wind makes us rough and tempestuous, and troubles our faces; every trifling accident discomposes us; and as the face of the waters wafting in a storm, so wrinkles itself, that it makes upon its forehead furrows deep and hollow like a grave: so do our great and little cares and trifles first make the wrinkles of old age, and then they dig a grave for us."—Bishop Taylor.

"Edom is a perpetual waste. It is a desolate monument of Divine wrath. —Gadsby.

Land. (5) **will be,** etc., R. V., "The Lord be magnified beyond the border of Israel,"[b] i. e. by the overthrow of Edom.

The City of Petra (vs. 4).—Astonishment, for which language can scarcely find utterance, is the sentiment expressed by every traveler who has been able to explore the magnificent ruins of the once proud metropolis of Idumæa or Edom. A narrow and circuitous defile, surrounded on each side by lofty and precipitous or perpendicular rocks, forms the approach to the desolate yet magnificent scene. The ruins of the city here burst upon the view in their full grandeur, shut in on the opposite side by barren, craggy precipices, from which numerous ravines and valleys branch out in all directions; the sides of the mountains, covered with an endless variety of excavated tombs and private dwellings, present altogether the most singular scene that can well be conceived. The theatre is the first object which presents itself to the traveler on entering Petra from the eastward. Captains Irby and Mangles state that it was entirely hewn out of the live rock. Fragments of columns are strewed on the ground in front. This theatre is surrounded by sepulchres. Every avenue leading to it is full of them; and it may be safely affirmed, that one hundred of the largest dimensions are visible from it. Indeed, throughout almost every quarter of this metropolis, the depositories of the dead must have presented themselves constantly to the eyes of the inhabitants, and have almost outnumbered the inhabitants of the living. Of all the ruins of Petra, the mausoleums and sepulchres are among the most remarkable; and they give the clearest indication of ancient and long-continued royalty, and of courtly grandeur. Their immense number corroborates the accounts given of their successive kings and princes by Moses and by Strabo. The structure of the sepulchres also shows that many of them are of a more recent date. Great must have been the opulence of a city which could dedicate such monuments to the memory of its rulers. —Horne.

6—8. (6) **honoureth,** is bound to honor. **If then I be a father.** "We are so accustomed to associate with the Divine Fatherhood only ideas of love and pity that the use of the relation to illustrate not love but Majesty, and the setting of it in parallel to the Divine Kingship, may seem to us strange. Yet this was very natural to Israel. In the old Semitic world, even to the human parent, honor was due before love. Honor thy father and thy mother, said the Fifth Commandment; and when, after long shyness to do so, Israel at last ventured to claim Jehovah as the Father of His people, it was at first rather with the view of increasing their sense of His authority and their duty of reverencing Him, than with the view of bringing Him near to their hearts and assuring them of His tenderness."—G. A. Smith. **O priests,** these are esp. addressed, bec. they ought to be the leaders and examples of the nation...**wherein,** etc., comp. vs. 2. "Asked in a spirit of self-satisfied insensibility." "Impudently persisting in justifying themselves." (7) **bread,** here used generally of the sacrificial offerings. **ye say,** in conduct if not in words. **table,** same as the altar.[a] (8) R. V. "And when ye offer the blind for sacrifice, it is no evil! and when ye offer the lame and sick, it is no evil!"—Spoken ironically. **blind,** see Le. xxii. 22.[b]

Jehovah lightly esteemed (vss. 6—11).—I. An indignant expostulation. II. A solemn accusation. III. An important prediction. 1. It has been already fulfilled in a large measure; 2. The time is coming when it will be completely accomplished.

9—11. (9) **beseech God,** as the national intercessors. **this,** i. e. the peril the nation was in of Divine judgment. **your means,** through your unconcern about the character of the offerings and the worship.[c] **regard your persons,** R. V. "Will he accept any of your persons?" (10) R. V. "Oh that there were one among you that would shut the doors, that ye might not kindle fire on mine altar in vain!"—Better no sacrifices at all than such sacrifices as these. Better a temple closed than a temple profaned.—Isa. i. 12, 13. (11) **shall be great,** R. V. "is great," with "shall be" in the margin; so through the verse. G. A. Smith and others believe that this teaches the acceptable nature of many heathen sacrifices in contrast to Hebrew worship. "Never have we had in prophecy a statement so generous and so catholic as this."—G. A. Smith.——But the Cambridge

b "Just across the narrow Jordan valley Edom always lay threateningly upon the skirts of Palestine. It was the country where Israel's most inveterate enemies lived. No other nation pressed on them so constantly or gave them such continual trouble as the Edomites." — Phillips Brooks.

"We talk of human life as a journey, but how variously is that journey performed! There are those who come forth girt, and shod, and mantled, to walk on velvet lawns and smooth terraces, where every gale is arrested and every beam is tempered. There are others who walk on the Alpine paths of life, against driving misery, and through stormy sorrows, over sharp afflictions; walk with bare feet and naked breast, jaded, mangled, and chilled." — Sidney Smith.

a "By your actions you declare how little value you have for the worship of God, since you care not in how slight and contemptuous a manner it is performed."—Lowth.

b "Whatever is given as a present in the East, whether of great or small value, a diamond or an orange, a pistol or a knife, a turban or a garment, it should not be in any way damaged or imperfect. If you give a sheep or a lamb, it must not be lame or sick; and if you give a piece of gold, it should be full weight." —Gadsby.

c "The priests were specially

Bible presents the opposite view and says: The view that Almighty God is here recognising the worship of the heathen world as in reality offered to Him is quite inadmissible. The whole tenor of the Old Testament emphatically contradicts it, and the teaching of the New Testament is accordant and explicit. "The things which the Gentiles sacrifice, they sacrifice to devils and not to God" (1 Cor. x. 20, cited from Deut. xxxii. 17.) **Gentiles,** who shall be taken into Divine favor, when you are cast off for your sins.[c] **incense,** of praise. **offering,** of the broken and contrite heart.

The Universal Spread of the Gospel (vs. 11).—I. The Scripture testimony to the ultimate universal spread of the Gospel. II. The same truth is evident from the nature of the case. 1. The need of redemption is universal; 2. The Gospel alone can satisfy this craving of mankind; 3. The Gospel is fitted for universal diffusion. III. The voice of history confirms the conclusions. 1. The importance of the conquests already won by the Gospel; 2. The proved weakness of the only weapons with which it can be assailed.

12—14. (12) **have profaned,** R. V., "profane," by making it seem no matter what is the character of the offerings made to Me. **ye say,** by your actions. (13) **weariness,** finding no joy in My worship, counting it only a painful drudgery.[a] **snuffed,** or sniffed, as an animal would who rejects food. **torn,** R. V. "And ye have brought that which was taken by violence." (14) **deceiver,** who brings the imperfect, and makes out that it is the best he has. "The cheat," "the man who seeks to stand well with God and yet to be at no expense in the matter."—Dods. **corrupt thing,** R. V. "a blemished thing," **is dreadful,** "is reverenced," G. A. Smith, "is to be feared."—Dods.

The Times of Malachi.—After Nehemiah had been working for some twelve years at the moral reformation of the people of Jerusalem and Judæa, he was recalled to Persia; and immediately on his departure the old evils which he had stoutly resisted came back like a flood. In spite of the presence of Ezra in Jerusalem, it was seen that a reformation enforced by the civil power, rather than as the fruit of individual conviction, had no permanent vitality. When Nehemiah's back was turned, "the tithes due to the temple, the Levites, and the priests were not delivered, and the greatest distress was thus caused to all those who depended on them for maintenance. The choristers, the guards of the gates, and the ordinary Levites alike, were compelled to go back to their homes, and cultivate their fields for a living. Public worship was thus interrupted, and the temple, forsaken by its ministers, was neglected by the people. Nor was the refusal to pay tithes the only sign of an altered spirit. The sabbath was profaned, both in town and country, winepresses were busy in its sacred hours, and the roads and fields were dotted with the workers taking sheaves to the barn on their heavily laden asses. Jerusalem itself was disturbed by a sabbath fair, to which loads of wine, grapes, figs, and much else were carried in during sacred hours. After all the professed zeal to put an end to mixed marriages, things were rapidly drifting to almost a worse condition than of old. The very priests had rapidly lost their high tone. Their irreverence, indifference, and worldliness shocked the thoughtful. Everything that Ezra and Nehemiah had effected was well-nigh undone." The Prophet Malachi had the "burden" laid upon him of recalling both priests and people to their duties. And this he did partly by vigorous denunciations of surrounding evils, and partly by anticipations of the times of Messiah. The "Coming One" would surely prove to be a stern Rebuker of national sin.—Pulpit Com.

CHAPTER THE SECOND.

1—3. (1) "In this third section of his book "Malachi" addresses himself to the priests. He charges them not only with irreverence and slovenliness in their discharge of the Temple service—for this he appears to intend by the phrase filth of your feasts—but with the neglect of their intellectual duties to the people."—G. A. Smith. (2) **a curse,** De. xxvii.

guilty, because it was their duty to reject improper offerings."
—Spk. Com.

c Mat. xxi. 43.

a "Ye regard God's service as irksome, and therefore try to get it over by presenting the most worthless offerings."
—Fausset.

Anaxagoras being asked what he thought he was born for? answered, "That I may meditate upon heaven." O my soul! what dost thou think thou wast reborn for? Is it not that thou mayest live in heaven God hath made thee to enjoy communion with Himself; thou need'st not stay one hour on earth, but, with Enoch, spend thy days with God, walk and converse with Jesus Christ in the galleries of His love, with Moses live on the mount of glory.

"Malachi is like a late evening which closes a long day, but he is at the same time the morning twilight which bears in its bosom a glorious day."
—Pusey.

"Scriptures, sacraments, sermons, Sundays, all have a double edge; if used well, they lead men on to heaven; but if despised or misused, they aggravate men's sin, and increase their condemnation."
—Wordsworth.

15—26; xxviii. 15—68. **curse your blessings,** or turn your blessings into curses. (3) **corrupt your seed,** R. V. "Behold I will rebuke the seed for your sake" so as to prevent due harvest. **feasts,**[b] R. V. "sacrifices." "The figure is very forcible. It is as though Jehovah sees nothing in the droves of diseased and blemished animals that are brought to His altar on some great Festival, but the mass of filth and offal that necessarily accompanies the sacrifice. It is all one vast abomination! Flinging back in holy indignation the polluted offerings into the faces of the unworthy priests, He overwhelms them beneath the fœtid heap, and thus they are swept forth with it from the sacred precincts. Comp. Exod, xxix. 14, 1 Kings xiv. 10."—Camb. Bib. **take you away,** R. V. "and ye shall be taken away," cast away as if you were dung.

[b] "The worshippers of the Hindoo god Siva have to this day a spot on their foreheads made of the ashes of cow's dung."—Gadsby.

Curses.—The late Rev. John Brown, of Haddington, once passing the Firth of Forth, between Leith and Kinghorn, had for a fellow-passenger, one who appeared to be a Highland nobleman. Mr. Brown observed, with grief, that he frequently took the name of God in vain; but suspecting that to reprove him in the presence of the other passengers might tend only to irritate him, he forebore saying anything, till he reached the opposite shore. After landing, Mr. Brown, observing the nobleman walking alone, stepped up to him, and said, "Sir, I was sorry to hear you swearing while on our passage. You know it is written, 'Thou shalt not take the name of the Lord thy God in vain.'" On this the nobleman, lifting his hat, and bowing to Mr. Brown, made the following reply: "Sir, I return you thanks for the reproof you have now given me, and shall endeavor to attend to it in future; but," added he, "had you said this to me while in the boat, I believe I should have run you through with my sword."—Whitecross.

[a] Nu. iii. 6, etc.

[b] Nu. xxv. 12, 13.

"All the blessings that make up human welfare, were summed up for the Hebrew in one word—peace." Cox.

4—7. (4) **might be,** or, might stand fast.[a] For the breach of the covenant they must be held responsible. (5) **was,** implying that you, his descendants, have changed it into a covenant of woe. **life,** or prosperity. **peace,** or security.[b] **fear,** R. V. "and I gave them to him that he might fear, and he feared me," etc., reverential, godly fear, expressed in earnest and careful keeping of My ordinances.

(6) **The law of truth,** "teaching, as a function of the priesthood, entered into the original idea and constitution of the office (Deut. xxxiii. 10; Lev. x. 11), and was revived in connection with it after the return from Babylon (Ezra vii. 10, 25; Nehem. viii. 1—8). To be without "a teaching priest" was a national calamity (2 Chron. xv. 3)."—Camb. Bib. **iniquity,** R. V. "unrighteousness." **walked with me,** conducted all his relationships and duties. **equity,** R. V. "uprightness." "He directed all his actions by the rule of My laws." **turn,**[c] etc., "What a history of zeal for the glory of God and the conversion of sinners in those, of whom the world knows nothing; of whose working, but for the three words (many he-turned-away from-iniquity) in the closing book of the Old Testament, we should have known nothing."—Pusey. (7) "The lips of a priest guard knowledge, and men seek instruction from his mouth, for he is the Angel —the revealing Angel—of Jehovah of Hosts. Once more, what a remarkable saying to come from the legal age of Israel's religion, and from a writer who so emphasises the ceremonial law!"—G. A. Smith. **seek the law,** i. e. to know its applications to particular cases.[d] **messenger,** or interpreter. "The priest is here called, as elsewhere the prophet, the angel, or messenger, through whom and by whom Jehovah speaks to and acts upon men."—Marcus Dods.

[c] Ja. v. 19, 20.

[d] De. xvii. 9—11, xxiv. 8. See also Ezr. vii. 10.

"Man's uncertain life is like a rain-drop hanging on the bough, amongst ten thousand of its sparkling kindred, the remnants of some passing thunder shower, which have their moments, dropping one by one, and which shall soonest lose its perilous hold we cannot guess."—Joanna Baillie.

Did Turn Many Away from Iniquity.—By influence, by example, by tender words, many are turned away from iniquity, from selfishness, from drunkenness, from baseness, from evil pursuits of ever kind; not by the thunder of eloquence, not by the lightning of logic or high reasoning, not by the mystery of metaphysics, but by calm, quiet, loving, tutorial interest in private life,—who knows what triumphs have been wrought within the sanctuary of the house? God is not unrighteous to forget our work of faith and labor of love; God knows how many lambs we have tended; how many straying sheep we have brought back to the fold; how many hopeless hearts we have reinspired; to how many we have given of the oil of grace. Let no man, therefore, fail of heart and courage because he does not speak from a public pedestal. His name may not be known far away from his own fireside; there are private priests, there are household evangelists, there are ordained missionaries whose names are not published; there are women-shepherds who are seeking the very worst sheep—the sheep that the shepherds would not look after, the shepherdesses are following still; all the service is written down, and attached to it is the commendation of God.—Joseph Parker.

8—10. (8) **ye,** the priests of Malachi's days. **departed,** R. V. "turned aside." De. xvii. 10. **stumble .. law,** R. V. "in the law," the law being the way in which men should walk, they are made to stumble while in the way, by misrepresenting it, and making it appear to be hard and unreasonable. **covenant of Levi,** vs. 4. (9) **therefore,** because they are unfaithful. **contemptible,** etc., for while men use the liberty wh. unfaithful priests allow, they despise them in their hearts, bec. of their unfaithfulness. **partial,**[a] R. V. "had respect of persons." (10) Here begins a new section (10—17) on the cruelty of divorce as practiced by the Hebrews in order to marry in influential heathen families. **against his brother,** for a man's wrong-doing is never merely an injury to himself; it is an aggravation of the sin that it hurts others. Out of the common Fatherhood springs a common brotherhood.

[a] 1 Ti. v. 21.

"The nature of the profession exercises a great influence on longevity; thus out of 100 of each of the following professions the number of those who attain their seventieth year is—among clergymen, 42; agriculturists, 40; traders and manufacturers, 33; soldiers and clerks 32; lawyers, 29; artists, 28; professors, 27; physicians, 24; so those who study the art of prolonging the lives of others are most liable to die early, probably on account of the effluvia to which they are constantly exposed."—Abeille Medicale.

Spirituality of Malachi.—It really is fine to observe with what native ease Malachi rises into the higher region of thought. While dwelling on the sins of the priests he moves in the lower, the ceremonial elements; he insists on the maimed rites and blemished sacrifices, on the perfunctory and the contemptuous spirit with which they lounged through the service of the Temple. But no sooner does he attempt to frame a conception of what the true priest should be, than all that is forgotten; we hear no more of altar and sacrifice: his thoughts are riveted on the moral aspects of the priestly vocation—how holy a man, how wise a teacher, how careful and friendly a guide, the priest should be. When we are thinking only to hear that the sons of Levi are to offer clean and perfect, instead of blemished and polluted, sacrifices, to delight in the ministrations of the sanctuary instead of despising them, as much to our surprise as pleasure, he places before us a lofty spiritual ideal of character and service, well-nigh, if not altogether beyond the reach of mortal powers: he pronounces a eulogium on Levi which we should hardly dare to inscribe, as an epitaph, on the tomb of the holiest saint, or even on that of an inspired apostle.—S. Cox.

11—13. (11) **abomination,** a thing regarded as such by the holy law of God. **loved,**[a] i. e. which God loved. **the daughter of a strange god,** "as those who worship and serve the true God are called His sons and daughters, so they that worshiped any strange god are, by like reason, here called the daughters of that god." (12) R. V., "The Lord will cut off to the man that doeth this, him that waketh and him that answereth, out of the tents of Jacob." **master and scholar,** (him that waketh and him that answereth), a prov. expression for every living member of the transgressor's family. "It is taken from sentries or watchmen who as they go their rounds give their challenge and receive the watch-word in reply. In the same sense the Arabs say, 'no one crying out, and no one answering, i. e. no one alive.'" **him that offereth,** comp. Ne. xiii. 28, 29. (13) **have ye done,** R. V., "ye do," referring to a habit. For a second thing, they not only marry heathen women, but they are in the habit of treating cruelly and divorcing their lawful wives. **with tears,** etc., these were shed by the repudiated Jewish wives.

[a] "This is the reproof of those who contracted marriages with foreigners, and repudiated their Jewish wives. To intermarry with the heathen would defeat the purpose of Jehovah, who was the common Father of the Israelites in a peculiar sense in wh. He was not Father of the heathen." —Fausset.

"The Master and the Scholar" (vs. 12).—This should rather be rendered, "the watchman and the answerer." The true explanation is probably to be brought from the temple service, in which there was appointed a constant watch, day and night, by the Levites; and among them this seems to have belonged particularly to the singers (1 Chron. ix. 33). Now the watches in the East are, to this day, performed by a loud cry from time to time, by the watchmen, one after another, to mark the hour, and that very frequently, in order to show that they are constantly attentive to their duty. Tavernier remarks that the watchmen in the camps go their rounds, crying one after another, "God is one. He is merciful;" and often add, "Take heed to yourselves." The hundred and thirty-fourth Psalm gives us an example of the temple-watch. The whole

Psalm is nothing more than the alternate cry of the two different divisions of the watch. The allusion is similar in the passage before us.—Bush.

b Or, Why does God thus refuse to accept our offerings?

14—16. (14) **wherefore?**[b] as if you did not know well the reason. **wife of thy youth,** thy proper and honorable Jewish wife. **dealt treacherously,** etc., "with whom thou hast broken faith, though she is thy mate, and thy wife by covenant."—G. A. Smith. **covenant,** comp. Pr. ii. 17. (15) R. V., "and did he not make one although he had the residue of the spirit? and wherefore one? He sought a godly seed." The meaning of this much controverted passage seems to be this: Did not God make us (the Jewish people) one, separating us from other nations? But He had the residue of the spirit and might have extended the same favor to other nations. Why then did he choose one? That He might make a godly seed, a people to be the stock of His Messiah. But if you ally yourselves with these idolaters you defeat the Divine plan. **to your spirit,** see that your conscience is clear in what you do. (16) **putting away,**[a] or divorce. **For one covereth,** etc., R. V., "and him that covereth his garment with violence," probably referring to cruel treatment of the lawful wives. "The Fatherhood of God is not merely a relation of power and authority, requiring reverence from the nation. It constitutes the members of the nation one close brotherhood, and against this divorce is a crime and unnatural cruelty. Jehovah makes the wife of a man's youth his mate for life and his wife by covenant. He hates divorce, and His altar is so wetted by the tears of the wronged women of Israel that the gifts upon it are no more acceptable in His sight. No higher word on marriage was spoken except by Christ Himself."—G. A. Smith.

a "Can anything justify your violent and treacherous conduct towards your wives, wh. is contrary to moral sense, and a violation of the moral laws?" —Spk. Com.

False views of God are fatal to consistent conduct towards our fellow-men. We must recognize such truths as these: that we are creatures of the one God; that we are pensioners on his bounty; that we are sinners dependent on his mercy; and that, nevertheless, we are children entitled to claim our place in his family. We shall then recognize that we are bound to treat all our fellow-creatures as members of the same family.

Marriage (vs. 14).—I. Marriage is represented in its claims as a social compact. 1. She is thy wife; here is the peculiarity of the relation; 2. Thy companion; here is the propriety and solace of the relation; 3. Of thy youth; here is the tenderness of the relation. II. As a religious institution. 1. In its formation; 2. In its design; 3. In its connection with the altar; 4. In its responsibilities; 5. In its duties; 6. In the typical use made of it.

17. Here begins a new section (ii. 17—iii. 6), in which the prophet passes to a new subject. "The abuses in connection with Divine worship and the social evils which he has already rebuked culminate in avowed unbelief (with your words), as to the justice of Almighty God and His moral government of the world. Though the righteous Judge be strong and patient, yet is He 'wearied,' His longsuffering worn out, by blasphemous charges of favoring and delighted in the wicked, or by the profane challenge to shew Himself, if He be indeed 'the God of judgment.'" —Camb. Bib. **evil is good,** comp. Is. v. 19, 20. "God answers the murmurs of the godless sceptics by an announcement of judgment to come."

Wearying God (vs. 17).—I. This may be done in many ways. 1. By our carelessness; 2. Opposition; 3. Unteachableness; 4. Unbelief; 5. Want of zeal; 6. Inconsistency.—Bonar.

CHAPTER THE THIRD.

a Is. xl. 2; Mat. xi. 10; Mk. i. 2; Lu. vii. 27.

b "A herb the fullers used to take spots out of clothes." —S. Jerome.

1—3. (1) **messenger,** Jno. Baptist.[a] This and the following verses are the reply to the sceptical question, Where is the God of judgment? The delay was occasioned not by indifference on His part—but on theirs." —Marcus Dods. **the Lord,** or Messiah. "Malachi gives to Christ the name wh. belongs to God only. **seek, .. delight in,** prob. spoken in irony. (2) **abide,** stand the testing wh. His coming must prove to be. **fuller's soap,** Je. ii. 22.[b] "For He is like the fire of the smelter and the acid of the fullers. He takes his seat to smelt and to purge; and He will purge the sons of Levi, and wash them out like gold or silver, and they shall be to Jehovah bringers of an offering in righteousness."—G. A. Smith. (3) **purge,** "the orig. notion of the root is cleansing or purifying by filtering or straining, but it also admits the notion of melting by fire."

How wonderfully colored is the Bible! What a mystery of light and shade, mercy and judgment, goodness and severity! We have found this all the way through the rec-

Sit as a Refiner.—There were a few ladies in Dublin who met together to read the Scriptures and converse upon them. When reading the third chapter of Malachi, one of the ladies gave it as her opinion that the fuller's soap and the refiner of silver were only the same image, intended to convey the same view of the sanctifying influences of the grace of Christ. "No," said another, "they are not just the same image: there is something remarkable in the expression in the third verse, 'He shall sit as a refiner and purifier of silver.' They all said that possibly it might be so. This lady was to call upon a silversmith, and promised to report to them what he said on the subject. She went, without telling him the object of her errand, and begged to know the process of refining silver, which he fully described to her. "But do you sit, Sir," said she, "while you are refining?" "O yes, Madam, I must sit with my eyes steadily fixed on the furnace, since if the silver remain too long it is sure to be injured." "And how do you know when it is sufficiently refined, Sir?" "Whenever I see my own image reflected in it, I know the process is completed." She at once saw the beauty and the comfort too of the expression, "He shall sit as a refiner and purifier of silver." Christ sees it needful to put His children into the furnace, but He is seated by the side of it. His eye is steadily intent on the work of purifying, and His wisdom and love are engaged to do all in the best manner for them. Their trials do not come at random; the very hairs of their head are all numbered.

The Great Refiner.—

'Tis sweet to feel that He who tries
  The silver, takes His seat
Beside the fire that purifies,
  Lest too intense a heat—
Raised to consume the base alloy,
The precious metal, too, destroy.

'Tis blessedness to know that He
  The piece He has begun,
Will not forsake till He can see
  To prove the work well done
An image by its brightness known,
The perfect likeness of His own.

But, ah! how much of earthly mold,
  Dark relics of the mine,
Lost from the ore, must He behold
  How long must He refine,
Ere in the silver He can trace
The first faint semblance of His face.

Thou great Refiner sit Thou by
  Thy promise to fulfill;
Moved by Thy hand, beneath Thine eye,
  And melted at Thy will;
O may Thy work forever shine,
Reflecting beauty pure as Thine.

4—7. (4) **pleasant,** acceptable, Je. vi. 20. **former,** R. V., "ancient." (5) **witness,** bringing to light all iniquity in practical living and relationship, so that it may be judged and punished. **sorcerers,** 2 Chr. xxxiii. 6. **false swearers,** Zec. viii. 17. (6) **change not,** R. V., "For I, the Lord, change not: therefore ye, sons of Jacob, are not consumed. The unchangeableness of Jehovah is appealed to as the ground of His dealings with Israel. He changes not in His promises and purposes of grace (Rom. xi. 29); therefore, in spite of their rebellions and provocations, the sons of Jacob are still preserved. It is the same argument that is expanded in Psalm lxxxix. 28—37."—Camb. Bib. (7) **return,** Zec. i. 3. "I am ready to be reconciled to you upon your repentance."

Messiah's Relation to Society Sins.—It is important to see that God both considers and deals with society sins as well as individual sins. Not sufficiently is it pressed on attention, that he deals with the evils which are characteristic of aggregates of men—with sins of classes and of na-

ord, and now we find it on the last page of the revelation. God is the same God, and he changes not. All the change has been in form, in outward relation, in merely trivial circumstance; there has been no change in God; the standard of righteousness has never been lowered; hell has always been hot and bottomless. Make of the testimony what we will, there it is; many men wrote the Book—many men who never saw one another, and who never read what the other had written, and yet when all the parts of the Book are brought together they are one. The unity of the Bible is one of the strongest arguments in expression and defence of its inspiration. — Joseph Parker.

Am. ix. 9.

"One of the deaf and dumb pupils in the institution of Paris, being desired to express his idea of the eternity of the Deity, replied, 'It is duration, without beginning or end; existence, without bound or dimension; present, without past or future. His eternity is youth, without infancy or old age; life, without birth or death; to-day, without yesterday or to-morrow.' "

tions. It is in the necessary judgment of classes and nations as such that the innocent are wont to suffer with the guilty; and then the interest of the class must be seen to override the interests of the single individual. Society sins are much the same in every age. They are classed in this verse. They run riot when the religious restraint is weakened. 1. Religious deceptions. 2. Immoralities specially bearing on family life. 3. Untrustfulness in everyday relations. "False swearers." 4. Sweating the workman, and forcing down the wage of the laborer. 5. Taking advantage of the distressed to secure selfish advantage; the "widow, fatherless, and stranger." How these sins corrupt society to-day may be unfolded according to the skill of the preacher. The prophets teach that whenever God manifests Himself, He puts forth His power against society sins, and Malachi declares this to be one of the most marked characteristics of Messiah.—Pul. Com.

8, 9. (8) **rob God,** or defraud Him of His just rights. **tithes,** "by the Law of Moses (1) 'the tenth of all produce, as well as of flocks and cattle, belongs to Jehovah and must be offered to Him" (Lev. xxvii. 30, 32); and (2) this tenth is 'assigned to the Levites as the reward of their services" (Num. xviii. 21, 24). Nehemiah in his day had to deal once and again with the evil here rebuked. Notwithstanding the 'sure covenant' into which they had entered (Neh. ix. 38 with x. 32—39), he had occasion, on his return to Jerusalem after an absence of a few years, to reform them again in this very particular (xiii. 10—14)."—Camb. Bib. (9) **cursed,**[a] with scarcity in your fields, bec. you have withheld the Lord's dues. "In trying to defraud God we only defraud ourselves."

God's Rights (vs. 8).—I. How can a man rob God? 1. By not loving Him; 2. By not obeying Him; 3. By not using our influence for Him; 4. By not giving our all to Him. II. The awful nature of the sin. 1. Audacious; 2. Reckless; 3. Desperate; 4. Ungrateful.—W. Whythe.

Robbing God—The Benefactor and the Robber.—One Sunday a gentleman was going to church. On his way he saw a number of boys playing on the common. He wanted very much to show them how wrong it was for them to be so doing; but he knew that if he began to reprove them they would not listen to him. So he walked leisurely up to them, and sat down on the grass. Presently, in a pleasant, familiar tone, he said, "Boys, I want to tell you a story." Directly they all gathered unsuspectingly around him, and he began as follows: "There was once a good man who was noted for his kindness and liberality. At the time of which I speak he was on a journey. As he was pursuing his way along a lonely road, he met a man who represented himself as having suffered a great loss, in consequence of which he was in deep distress. With his usual kindness the good man instantly drew out his purse, and after examining it, he said, 'I have only seven pounds with me, but I think that with one pound I can get to the end of my journey, and you shall have the rest.' With this he handed the man six pounds. Was not that generous? Would not you have thought that the beggar must have gone off, feeling very grateful and contented? Certainly, we should have expected this. But he did no such thing. He was not a beggar at all, but a robber; and seeing that the good man had still one pound in his purse, he knocked him down with a club, and stole his last pound from him." The boys were very indignant on hearing this. They all cried out against the shameful conduct of the robber. One of them went so far as to say he didn't think anybody could be found quite so wicked as that. "Now, stop," said the gentleman; "let me tell you, boys, this is just what you are doing. God has given you freely six days out of seven for your own use. He has kept only one for Himself, to be kept holy, and spent in worshiping Him; and yet you are so mean as to rob Him even of that!" The boys hung down their heads. They had not a word to say, but broke up their play and went off.

10—12. (10) **all the tithes,** R. V., "the whole tithe," wh. you have so sinfully withheld. **storehouse,** comp. Neh. xiii. 5. **meat,** or provision for My priests, etc. (11) **devourer,** the locust. **cast her fruit,** as not being nourished enough to mature it. (12) **delightsome land,** Da. xi. 16; Zech. vii. 14.

The Luxury of Doing Good.—The language of Malachi iii. 10 is often used in prayer by those who are not aware that it is rather a chal-

[a] Ne. xiii. 10—12.

"So long as we stand in need of a benefit, there is nothing dearer to us; nor anything cheaper when we have received it. And yet a man may as well refuse to deliver up a sum of money that's left him in trust, without a suit, as not to return a good office without asking; and when we have no value any further for the benefit, we do commonly care as little for the author. People follow their interest; one man is grateful for his convenience, and another man is ungrateful for the same reason." — L'Estrange.

"The being of grace must go before the increase of it; for there is no growth without life, no building without a foundation. Put a dry stick into the ground, and dress and water it as much as you will, it will continue the same till it rot; but set a living plant by the side of it, and though much less at first, yet it soon begins to shoot, and in time becomes a wide-spreading tree."
—Lavington.

lenge than a promise—"Prove me now herewith, saith the Lord of hosts." We naturally ask whether God does "open the windows of heaven and pour down blesing" upon the faithful givers of tithes. Instances are not wanting among ourselves to supply the answer. No workers in our day have enjoyed larger blessing than George Müller and Charles Spurgeon, both of whom have, from the beginning of their work, put the sacred rule into practice with believing and humble hearts. Years ago Mr. Spurgeon said: "I knew a lad in Christ once who adopted the principle of giving a tenth to God. When he won a money prize for an essay on a religious subject, he felt that he could not give less than one-fifth of it. He has never since been able to deny himself the pleasure of having a fifth to give. God has wonderfully blessed that lad, and increased his means and his enjoyment of that luxury of luxuries—the luxury of doing good."

13—15. (13) **stout,** Job xxi. 14. **what have we,** etc., R. V., "wherein have we spoken against thee?" (14) **vain,** there is no real advantage to be gained from it.[a] **mournfully,** R. V. margin, "in mournful apparel." (15) **proud,** Pr. xxi. 24; Is. xiii. 11; Ps. cxix. 21, 51, 69, 78. **set up,** etc., R. V., "built up; yea, they tempt God and are delivered."

Stout Words Against God.—I was talking with a young business man, and he said essentially: "That man around the corner there, he is in the same sort of business as myself; he is prospering far more than I am, but he is doing it by all sorts of mean shifts and dishonest practices; why does he prosper so, while I, who keep my hands clean from such things, do not get on so well and swiftly? Isn't it better, after all, just to throw conscience and right-doing to the winds, and seize the main chance, anyhow?" You see this young business man was almost, if not quite, saying these "stout words" against God which the prophet charges some of the men of his time with saying. Never let the seeming prosperity of those saying and doing evil tempt you to words or ways against God and His righteousness.—Wayland Hoyt.

16—18. (16) **feared,** sincerely. **book of remembrance,** the figure of a Book of record or remembrance, as kept or directed to be kept by Almighty God, is of early as well as of very general occurrence in Holy Scripture. Moreover there was a 'Recorder' in the court of the Hebrew kings. See Exod. xvii. 14, xxxii. 32; Psalm lxix. 28; Dan. vii. 10; Luke x. 20; Revelation xx. 12."—Camb. Bib. **thought upon,** or highly esteemed. (17) **in that day,** etc., R. V., "in the day that I do make, even a peculiar treasure."[b] (18) **discern,** see clearly that God makes and keeps distinctions.

Precious Jewels.—Describe regalia of England. Speak of jewels. Show one or two; as rings, brooches, etc. The text introduces to us the crown jewels of the King of kings. Some Roman ladies were once talking about and showing their jewels. One went out to fetch hers, and presently returned, leading her children, and saying, "Here are my jewels." The great King places His children before us, and says, "These are My jewels." What do God's children as jewels remind us of? 1. Like jewels, they are rare. "Little flock;" many common stones and pebbles, few pearls and diamonds. 2. Like jewels, they are beautiful, brilliant, ornamental; shine, "lights in the world." 3. Like jewels, they are found in strange and unlikely places. Pearl diving. Mine. 4. Like jewels, they are obtained only with much risk and trouble. 5. Like jewels, they have to be cut and polished, to bring out their beauty and value. "Furnace of affliction." Interior of jeweler's shop. Wheels, files, etc. God superintends the process. "Refiner of silver." When the Koh-i-noor was recut, the Duke of Wellington superintended the process. 6. Like jewels, they are very valuable; hence they cost a great deal. "Bought with a price." "Elect, precious." Wars have been occasioned by desire to possess jewels of great value. 7. Like some jewels, some Christians have a great historical interest (name some famous gems, as the Pitt diamond, etc.). Thus Luther, Knox, Calvin, Wesley, etc. 8. Like jewels, they are carefully preserved. Casket. Safe. "Kept by the power of God," etc. Regalia of England in Tower of London. 9. Like jewels, they are sometimes collected and exhibited. Grand occasions when jewels are worn. Queen's drawing room. Court festivals. So Christians

[a] "A rebuke of persons who were impatient under temporal trials, and murmured against God, bec. they did not at once reap the fruit of their service in temporal prosperity." —Spk. Com.

"Holiness in the heart will be holiness in the life too; not some good actions, but a good conversation; a uniform even tract of life, the whole revolution of it regular." —Leighton.

[b] Tit. ii. 14; 1 Pe. ii. 9.

"Incredible as it may appear to ignorance, on whose admiring eyes it flashes rays of light, science proves that the diamond is formed of the very same matter as common, dull, black coal. It boasts no native light; and dark in the darkness as the mud or rock where it lies imbedded, it shines, if with a beautiful, yet with a borrowed splendor. How meet an emblem of the priceless jewels that adorn the Saviour's crown!" —Guthrie.

"Be such a man, live such a life, that if every man were such as you, and every life a life like yours, this earth would be a paradise." —Phillips Brooks.

in meetings of the Church here, and in the great gathering of the Church triumphant. May we all be found in that day as gems in the Redeemer's crown.—Hive.

"They shall be mine, saith the Lord of hosts, in the day that I do make, even a peculiar treasure" (vs. 17). Those described in the previous verses are the Lord's "peculiar treasure;" He cherishes them as one guards jewels; and a day is coming when this shall be evidently seen to be the fact. Better than jewels, God loves, treats, cares for such as His sons. In God's day of disclosure nothing shall be plainer than that there is a vast and vital distinction between those who serve God, and those who do not.—Wayland Hoyt.

CHAPTER THE FOURTH.

1—3. (1) R. V., "For behold, the day cometh, it burneth as a furnace." **burn,** see Joel ii. 31; Ho. vii. 4.[a] **neither .. branch,** Eze. xvii. 8, 9; Am. ii. 9. (2) **sun,**[b] etc., Lu. i. 78. **healing in his wings,**[c] comp. "the wings of the morning," Ps. cxxxix. 9. In both cases the rising of the sun is compared, not to the use of the wings in flight, but to lifting them up, or spreading them out. In the Psalm the suddenness and rapidity with which this is done, when the sun "flares up from behind the mountain wall of Moab," is the point of comparison (comp. "the morning spread upon the mountains," Joel ii. 2; and the swift traveling of the light across the landscape in our own country, when the sun emerges from a cloud on a windy day). Here the healing virtue of the outstretched wings is in view. "A pleasant," and a wholesome, "thing it is for the eyes to behold the sun." Eccles. xi. 7."—Camb. Bib. **grow up,** R. V., "gambol," as stall-fed animals leap about, when loosed from the stall. (3) concluding section, vss. 3—6. "With his last word the prophet significantly calls upon the people to remember the Law. This is their one hope before the coming of the great and terrible day of the Lord. But, in order that the Law may have full effect, Prophecy will be sent to bring it home to the hearts of the people—Prophecy in the person of her founder and most drastic representative."—G. A. Smith. **tread down,** as oxen tread the wheat on the threshing-floors. **I shall do this,** R. V., "that I do make," comp. iii. 17. **ashes,** to which the stubble (vs. 1) has been reduced.

Christ the Light of the World (vs. 2).—1. Christ is the source of light; 2. Of heat; 3. The center of the spiritual world; 4. The center of attraction.—Whythe.——Dies Iræ (vss. 1—6).—Here we have—I. A great warning, vs. 1. II. The consolation of the faithful, vs. 2. III. The mighty victory, vs. 3. IV. The unchangeable standard of holiness, vs. 4. V. The world's last sermon.—Bonar.

The Sun of Righteousness.—There is a manifest Messianic reference here. The personal Messiah shall come to bring in a reign of righteousness. The winged disk is a frequent and most ancient Oriental symbol. You have often seen pictures of it. When the "sun flares up from behind the mountain wall of Moab," there is a spreading forth of his light like wings. This light is healing. It cures and scatters the glooms and distortions of the night. Such shall be the coming of the Messiah. Those who have waited for, trusted in, served Him, shall be blessed beneath His spreading wings of light; those who have done evil and served themselves shall be scattered, disgraced, condemned, as the spreading wings of light of the rising sun annihilate the fleeing night's glooms and shadows.—Wayland Hoyt.——"To you that fear my name shall the Sun of Righteousness arise with healing in His wings." It is true He speaks more especially of His incarnation, or visible appearance in the world; but, by this manner of speaking, He intimates withal that this Sun of Righteousness is always shining upon His faithful people, more or less, in all ages, from the beginning to the end of the world. For in that it is said, "He shall arise," it is plainly supposed that He was the Sun of Righteousness before, and gave light unto the world, though not so clearly as when He was actually risen. As we see and enjoy the light

[a] Comp. Mat. iii. 12.

[b] Is. lx. 1, 2.

[c] "So called to signify that his light consists in clearing up men's understandings, and chasing away the darkness of their minds; whose rays and kindly warmth will heal all the diseases of the soul." —Lowth.

"'If we say we have no sin, we deceive ourselves, and the truth is not in us.' But although we have sin still abiding in us, and, like the bias in a bowl, warping us to the world, yet that vital seminal principle of the grace of God in Christ always keeps its ground, its life and tendency towards heaven, and wears out, wastes, and gradually subdues the contrary tendency of sin and corruption." —Sir M. Hale.

of the sun long before he riseth, from the first dawning of the day, though it grows clearer and clearer all along, as he comes nearer and nearer to his rising; so the Sun of Righteousness began to enlighten the world, as soon as it was darkened by sin; the day then began to break, and it grew lighter and lighter in every age. Adam himself saw something of this light, Abraham more; "Abraham rejoiced to see My day," saith this glorious Sun: "He saw it and was glad" (John vii. 56). David and the Prophets after him saw it more clearly, especially this, the last of the Prophets: he saw this Sun in a manner rising so that he could tell the people that it would suddenly get above the horizon. "The Lord whom you seek;" saith he, "shall suddenly come to His temple." Mal. iv. 2.—R. T. S.——Beholding the Sun.—I have read that near the North Pole, the night lasting for months and months, when the people expect the day is about to dawn, some messengers go up on the highest point to watch; and when they see the first streak of day they put on their brightest possible apparel, and embrace each other and cry, "Behold the sun!" and the cry goes through all the land, "Behold the sun!" Some of you have been trudging on in the darkness of sin. It has been a long and wearisome night for your soul; but now I cry, "Behold the Sun of Righteousness rising with healing in His wings!"—Talmage.

4—6. (4) **law,** Ex. xx. 3. **with the,** R. V., "even." (5) **Elijah,** i. e. one in the spirit and power of Elijah.[a] **great .. day,** the manifestation of Messiah, regarded on its testing, judging, condemning side. (6) **turn,** by the persuasions of his preaching. "He shall produce a general reformation in the minds and manners of all sorts of persons." **the heart of the fathers,** the "fathers" here are the patriarchs, whom the prophet regards as estranged from their degenerate "children," or descendants, and ceasing to acknowledge them on account of their unworthy character and conduct. (Comp. Isaiah lxiii. 16; Matthew iii. 9.) **curse,** this has fallen upon the land of Canaan bec. the Messiah, so graciously sent, was rejected and crucified. "The passage which seems to hrow most light on the phraseology of vs. 6 is Isa. xxix. 22—24, comp. Luke i. 17."—Dods.

The Reappearance of Elijah.—Elijah was the Prophet for whose return in later years his countrymen have looked with most eager hope. . . . It was a fixed belief of the Jews that he had appeared again and again, as an Arabian merchant, to wise and good rabbis at their prayers or on journeys. A seat is still placed for him to superintend the circumcision of the Jewish children. Passover after passover, the Jews of our own day place the paschal cup on the table, and set the door wide open, believing that that is the moment when Elijah will reappear. When goods are found and no owner comes, when difficulties arise and no solution appears, the answer is, "Put them by till Elijah comes."—Stanley's Jewish Church.

Malachi, the Prophet of a Violated Fatherhood.—

If I'm a Father, where's the honor due
From loving children? Why do ye profane
My name with hollow service? Why in vain
Burn fire upon Mine altar, and, in lieu
Of perfect gifts, with refuse think to sue
For favor? Weariness ye ill contain;
Ye rob both God and man; your one refrain,
"Wherein?" to all your empty life the clew.

Behold! the Lord shall suddenly appear
To purge His temple, a refiner's fire,
To purify the silver and the gold.
Then they that serve the Lord, His name do fear,
Shall be My jewels and My heart's desire,
Of lustre rare, of beauty manifold.
—Christian Endeavor World.

[a] Mat. xi. 14; Mk. ix. 11—13; Lu. i. 17.

"We cannot understand how utterly, how ineffably sublime these predictions are until we get into a certain spiritual mood, until we feel the wickedness of wickedness, and see all evil in some degree as God sees it. God has a great fire, and he is going to bring it that it may burn up all the lies of hypocrisy, all the insincerity and selfishness of the world, cleansing it, — heaven's great fire: a glorious prophecy! If we could see things as they really are from his point of view, we should know that the day had already come. All wickedness is being burned down. The wicked man has a terrible time of it today. Do not believe him when he laughs; his life is a lie; his last stroke of merriment is his last forgery. He cannot be happy —or God cannot; I must leave it between them." —Joseph Parker.

"Both prophesied in a time of great unbelief and apostasy from the law; both sought to bring back the people to the piety of their fathers; both prophesied before great and terrible judgments. The historical circumstances in which they lived were remarkably parallel. Ahab appears in Herod, Jezebel in Herodias. The words of Mark vi. 20, where he speaks of Herod fearing John, may apply without any alteration to Ahab.—Lange.

INDEX I.

VOL. III.

[*First Index of subjects, illustrations etc. in the main body of the page, according to the heads which appear at the beginning of the paragraph.*]

INDEX II.

VOL. III.

[*Index for Marginal References of Quotations, Notes, Etc. The small figure indicates the number of paragraph.*]

PAGE.

Printed in U.S.A.